Richard Strauss, Smithsonian Institution, Collection of the Supreme Court of the United States.

CONSTITUTIONAL LAW

CASES, COMMENTS, AND QUESTIONS

Twelfth Edition

■ ■ ■

by

Jesse H. Choper

Earl Warren Professor of Public Law,
University of California, Berkeley

Richard H. Fallon, Jr.

Ralph S. Tyler, Jr. Professor of Constitutional Law,
Harvard University

Yale Kamisar

Distinguished Professor of Law, University of San Diego
Clarence Darrow Distinguished University Professor Emeritus of Law,
University of Michigan

Steven H. Shiffrin

Charles Frank Reavis, Sr., Professor of Law,
Cornell University

Michael C. Dorf

Professor of Law
Cornell University

Frederick Schauer

David and Mary Harrison Distinguished Professor of Law
University of Virginia

AMERICAN CASEBOOK SERIES®

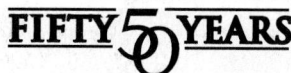 

FIFTY 50 YEARS   WEST ACADEMIC PUBLISHING

American Casebook Series is a trademark registered in the U.S. Patent and Trademark Office.

COPYRIGHT © 1964, 1967, 1970 WEST PUBLISHING CO.
COPYRIGHT © 1975, 1981, LOCKHART, KAMISAR & CHOPER
COPYRIGHT © 1986 LOCKHART, KAMISAR, CHOPER & SHIFFRIN
COPYRIGHT © 1991, 1996 WEST PUBLISHING CO.
© West, a Thomson business, 2001, 2006
© 2011 Thomson Reuters
© 2015 LEG, Inc. d/b/a West Academic
     444 Cedar Street, Suite 700
     St. Paul, MN 55101
     1-877-888-1330

West, West Academic Publishing, and West Academic are trademarks of West Publishing Corporation, used under license.

Printed in the United States of America

ISBN: 978-1-62810-013-6

PREFACE

Casebooks are teaching tools, and this is no exception. The hallmark of this book since it first appeared—and we believe that this twelfth edition is the best yet—is its commitment to the proposition that a student's understanding of constitutional law is greatly enriched by exposure to diverse perspectives drawn from the best of legal scholarship. To that end, we have reproduced many selections from the literature or woven them into notes and questions that follow almost every main case. Overall, the book furnishes the resources to teach a broadly intellectual (as well as doctrinal) Constitutional Law course, but seeks to do so without imposing a comprehensive framework that teachers must either adopt or "teach against."

In the four years since the last edition of this book was published, many significant decisions have been handed down and a wealth of scholarly commentary has been generated. Accordingly, this new edition represents a complete revision and a fresh re-evaluation, for purposes of re-editing and re-organizing, of all existing materials. It also constitutes the product of an extensive examination of the recent literature—in an effort to further enrich the notes, comments and questions. Although this edition is 58 pages longer than its predecessor, nearly all of the increment is traceable to the use of a larger print face that should make the book easier to read. We hope that users of past editions will applaud the change.

In addition to full updating, the restructuring that has been undertaken in each new edition where called for by recent developments is reflected in the reorganization of the Affirmative Action section of Chapter 9. Finally, this edition continues to be one of the very few that contains a substantial section on the death penalty (Chapter 6, Section 4), important most recently not only because of the connection to substantive due process but also because, like the sodomy cases, of the opinions' use of foreign and international law.

Significant cases handed down during the 2014–15 Supreme Court Term will appear in a supplement to be published in August 2015. Important developments thereafter will appear in annual supplements.

Case and statute citations as well as footnotes of the Court and commentators have been omitted without so specifying; other omissions are indicated by asterisks or by brackets. Footnotes in each chapter proceed in numerical order, except footnotes of the Court or in statutes and scholarly writings, which are so indicated. The three editions of Laurence H. Tribe, American Constitutional Law are cited simply as "Tribe." The composition of the Court on any date may be obtained by consulting the

Table of Justices in Appendix A, which also includes a compilation of basic biographical data on all individuals who have ever served on the Court.

As the list of authors below indicates, this edition shows the passage of responsibility from Yale Kamisar, one of the original participants for over 50 years, and Steven Shiffrin, who has been with us for nearly 30 years. Their contributions have been immeasurable. To them, we dedicate this edition. The two of us remaining are extremely fortunate to have Michael Dorf and Frederick Schauer, two outstanding scholars, take their places. The two newcomers are, in turn, honored to build on the foundation built by our predecessors and co-authors.

Special thanks to Catharine M. Schultz for exceptionally skillful and helpful administrative assistance far beyond the call of duty, and to Niko Bowie, Gabriel Daly, Kaitlin Halpern, Justin Mungai Ndichu, Max Rosen, and Joshua Tannen for their help as research assistants.

JESSE H. CHOPER
RICHARD H. FALLON, JR.
MICHAEL C. DORF
FREDERICK SCHAUER

May 2015

ACKNOWLEDGMENTS

Bickel, Alexander M., The Least Dangerous Branch (1962). Copyright © 1962 by the Bobbs-Merrill Co. Reprinted by permission.

Fallon, Richard H., Jr., Marbury and the Constitutional Mind: A Bicentennial Essay on the Wages of Doctrinal Tension, 91 Calif.L.Rev. 1 (2003). Copyright © 2003 by the California Law Review. Reprinted by permission.

Friedman, Barry, The Will of the People (2009). Copyright © 2009 by Farrar, Straus & Giroux, LLC. Reprinted by permission.

McConnell, Michael W., The Right to Die and the Jurisprudence of Tradition, 1997 Utah L.Rev. 665 (1997). Copyright © 1997 by the Utah Law Review. Reprinted by permission.

Tribe, Laurence H., American Constitutional Law (2d ed. 1988). Copyright © 1988 by Foundation Press. Reprinted by permission.

_____, American Constitutional law (3d ed. 2000). Copyright © 2000 by Foundation Press. Reprinted by permission.

Van Alstyne, William W., A Critical Guide to Marbury v. Madison, 1969 Duke L.J. 1. Copyright © 1959 by the Duke Law Journal. Reprinted by permission.

SUMMARY OF CONTENTS

TABLE OF CONTENTS

TABLE OF CASES

The principal cases are in bold type.

TABLE OF AUTHORITIES

CONSTITUTIONAL LAW

CASES, COMMENTS, AND QUESTIONS

Twelfth Edition

CHAPTER 1

NATURE AND SCOPE OF JUDICIAL REVIEW

■ ■ ■

1. ORIGINS, EARLY CHALLENGES, AND CONTINUING CONTROVERSY

"Whoever hath an absolute authority to interpret any written or spoken laws, it is he who is truly the lawgiver, to all intents and purposes, and not the person who first spoke or wrote them."

> —Bishop Hoadly's Sermon, preached before the King, 1717.

MARBURY V. MADISON
5 U.S. (1 Cranch) 137, 2 L.Ed. 60 (1803).

[The framers of the Constitution expected the federal government to function without political parties, but by the end of President George Washington's second term, the country divided into Federalists and Democratic-Republicans (sometimes simply called Republicans, although not related to the modern Republican Party, which originated in the 1850s). In the election of 1800, the Republican candidate (and sitting Vice President) Thomas Jefferson defeated the Federalist candidate (and sitting President) John Adams. Jefferson was to take office in March 1801, but in January Adams nominated John Marshall, then Secretary of State, as fourth Chief Justice of the United States. Marshall assumed office in February but continued to serve as Secretary of State until the end of the Adams administration. During February, the lame-duck Federalist Congress passed (1) the Circuit Court Act, which, inter alia, doubled the number of federal judges and (2) the Organic Act, which authorized appointment of 42 justices-of-the-peace in the District of Columbia. Senate confirmation of Adams' "midnight" appointees, virtually all Federalists, was completed one day before Jefferson's inauguration. Their commissions were signed by Adams and sealed by Acting Secretary of State Marshall, but due to time pressures, several for the justices-of-the-peace (including that of William Marbury) remained undelivered when Jefferson assumed the presidency the next day. Jefferson instructed the new Secretary of State, James Madison, to withhold delivery.

[Late in 1801, Marbury and several others sought a writ of mandamus in the Supreme Court to compel Madison to deliver the commissions. The

Court ordered Madison "to show cause why a mandamus should not issue" and the case was set for argument in the 1802 Term.

[While the case was pending, the new Republican Congress—incensed at Adams' efforts to entrench a Federalist judiciary and at the "Federalist" Court's order against a Republican cabinet officer—moved to repeal the Circuit Court Act. Federalist congressmen argued that repeal would violate Art. III's assurance of judicial tenure "during good behavior" and of the Constitution's plan for separation of powers assuring the independence of the Judiciary. It "was in this debate that for the first time since the initiation of the new Government under the Constitution there occurred a serious challenge of the power of the Judiciary to pass upon the constitutionality of Acts of Congress. Hitherto, [it had been the Republicans] who had sustained this power as a desirable curb on Congressional aggression and encroachment on the rights of the States, and they had been loud in their complaints at the failure of the Court to hold the Alien and Sedition laws unconstitutional. Now, however, in 1802, in order to counteract the Federalist argument that the Repeal Bill was unconstitutional and would be so held by the Court, [Republicans] advanced the proposition that the Court did not possess the power."[1]

[The Repeal Law passed early in 1802. To forestall its constitutional challenge in the Supreme Court until the political power of the new administration had been strengthened, Congress also eliminated the 1802 Supreme Court Term. Thus, the Court did not meet between December, 1801 and February, 1803.]

[On] 24th February, the following opinion of the court was delivered by CHIEF JUSTICE MARSHALL: * * *

No cause has been shown, and the present motion is for a mandamus. The peculiar delicacy of this case, the novelty of some of its circumstances, and the real difficulty attending the points which occur in it require a complete exposition of the principles on which the opinion to be given by the court is founded. * * *

1st. Has the applicant a right to the commission he demands? * * *

Mr. Marbury, [since] his commission was signed by the President and sealed by the Secretary of State, was appointed; and as the law creating the office gave the officer a right to hold for five years, independent of the executive, the appointment was not revocable, but vested in the officer legal rights, which are protected by the laws of his country.

To withhold his commission, therefore, is an act deemed by the court not warranted by law, but violative of a vested legal right.[2] * * *

---

[1]   1 Charles Warren, *The Supreme Court in United States History* 215 (1922).

[2]   Consider William Van Alstyne, *A Critical Guide to Marbury v. Madison,* 1969 Duke L.J. 1: "[T]here is clearly an 'issue' of sorts which preceded any of those touched upon in the opinion.

2dly. If he has a right, and that right has been violated, do the laws of his country afford him a remedy?

The very essence of civil liberty certainly consists in the right of every individual to claim the protection of the laws, whenever he receives an injury. One of the first duties of government is to afford that protection.

[The] government of the United States has been emphatically termed a government of laws, and not of men. It will certainly cease to deserve this high appellation, if the laws furnish no remedy for the violation of a vested legal right.

[W]here the heads of departments are the political or confidential agents of the executive, merely to execute the will of the president, or rather to act in cases in which the executive possesses a constitutional or legal discretion, nothing can be more perfectly clear than that their acts are only politically examinable. But where a specific duty is assigned by law, and individual rights depend upon the performance of that duty, it seems equally clear that the individual who considers himself injured, has a right to resort to the laws of his country for a remedy. * * *

It remains to be inquired whether,

3dly. He is entitled to the remedy for which he applies? This depends on,

1st. The nature of the writ applied for; and,

2dly. The power of this court.

1st. The nature of the writ. * * *

This writ, if awarded, would be directed to an officer of government, and its mandate to him would be, to use the words of Blackstone, "to do a particular thing therein specified, which appertains to his office and duty, and which the court has previously determined, or at least supposes, to be consonant to right and justice." Or, in the words of Lord Mansfield, the applicant, in this case, has a right to execute an office of public concern, and is kept out of possession of that right.

These circumstances certainly concur in this case.

Still, to render the mandamus a proper remedy, the officer to whom it is to be directed, must be one to whom, on legal principles, such writ may be directed; and the person applying for it must be without any other specific and legal remedy.

Specifically, it would appear that Marshall should have recused himself in view of his substantial involvement in the background of this controversy. * * * Proof of the status of Marbury's commission not only involved circumstances within the Chief Justice's personal knowledge, it was furnished in the Supreme Court by Marshall's own younger brother who had been with him in his office when, as Secretary of State, he had made out the commissions."

1st. With respect to the officer to whom it would be directed. The intimate political relation subsisting between the President of the United States and the heads of departments, necessarily renders any legal investigation of the acts of one of those high officers peculiarly irksome, as well as delicate; and excites some hesitation with respect to the propriety of entering into such investigation. Impressions are often received without much reflection or examination, and it is not wonderful that in such a case as this the assertion, by an individual, of his legal claims in a court of justice, to which claims it is the duty of that court to attend, should at first view be considered by some, as an attempt to intrude into the cabinet, and to intermeddle with the prerogatives of the executive.

It is scarcely necessary for the court to disclaim all pretensions to such a jurisdiction. An extravagance, so absurd and excessive, could not have been entertained for a moment. The province of the court is, solely, to decide on the rights of individuals, not to inquire how the executive, or executive officers, perform duties in which they have a discretion. Questions in their nature political, or which are, by the constitution and laws, submitted to the executive, can never be made in this court.

But [what] is there in the exalted station of the officer, which shall bar a citizen from asserting, in a court of justice, his legal rights, or shall forbid a court to listen to the claim, or to issue a mandamus, directing the performance of a duty, not depending on executive discretion, but on particular acts of congress, and the general principles of law?

[This], then, is a plain case for a mandamus, either to deliver the commission, or a copy of it from the record; and it only remains to be inquired,

Whether it can issue from this court.

The act to establish the judicial courts of the United States authorizes the supreme court "to issue writs of mandamus, in cases warranted by the principles and usages of law, to any courts appointed, or persons holding office, under the authority of the United States."[3]

---

[3] § 13 of the Judiciary Act of 1789 provided: "That the Supreme Court shall have exclusive jurisdiction of all controversies of a civil nature, where a state is a party, except between a state and its citizens; and except also between a state and citizens of other states, or aliens, in which latter case it shall have original but not exclusive jurisdiction. And shall have exclusively all such jurisdiction of suits or proceedings against ambassadors or other public ministers, or their domestics, or domestic servants, as a court of law can have or exercise consistently with the law of nations; and original, but not exclusive jurisdiction of all suits brought by ambassadors or other public ministers, or in which a consul, or vice consul, shall be a party. And the trial of issues of fact in the Supreme Court in all actions at law against citizens of the United States shall be by jury. The Supreme Court shall also have appellate jurisdiction from the circuit courts and courts of the several states, in the cases hereinafter specially provided for; and shall have power to issue writs of prohibition to the district courts, when proceeding as courts of admiralty and maritime jurisdiction, and writs of mandamus, in cases warranted by the principles and usages of law, to any courts appointed, or persons holding office under the authority of the United States."

The secretary of state, being a person holding an office under the authority of the United States, is precisely within the letter of the description; and if this court is not authorized to issue a writ of mandamus to such an officer, it must be because the law is unconstitutional, and therefore absolutely incapable of conferring the authority, and assigning the duties which its words purport to confer and assign.

[In] the distribution of [the judicial power of the United States] it is declared that "the supreme court shall have original jurisdiction in all cases affecting ambassadors, other public ministers and consuls, and those in which a state shall be a party. In all other cases, the supreme court shall have appellate jurisdiction."

It has been insisted, at the bar, that as the original grant of jurisdiction, to the supreme and inferior courts, is general, and the clause, assigning original jurisdiction to the supreme court, contains no negative or restrictive words, the power remains to the legislature, to assign original jurisdiction to that court in other cases than those specified in the article which has been recited; provided those cases belong to the judicial power of the United States.

If it had been intended to leave it in the discretion of the legislature to apportion the judicial power between the supreme and inferior courts according to the will of that body, it would certainly have been useless to have proceeded further than to have defined the judicial power, and the tribunals in which it should be vested. The subsequent part of the section is mere surplusage, is entirely without meaning, if such is to be the construction. If congress remains at liberty to give this court appellate jurisdiction, where the constitution has declared their jurisdiction shall be original; and original jurisdiction where the constitution has declared it shall be appellate; the distribution of jurisdiction, made in the constitution, is form without substance.

Affirmative words are often, in their operation, negative of other objects than those affirmed; and in this case, a negative or exclusive sense must be given to them, or they have no operation at all.

It cannot be presumed that any clause in the constitution is intended to be without effect; and, therefore, such a construction is inadmissible, unless the words require it.

[The] authority, therefore, given to the Supreme Court, by the Act establishing the judicial courts of the United States, to issue writs of mandamus to public officers, appears not to be warranted by the Constitution;[4] and it becomes necessary to inquire whether a jurisdiction so conferred can be exercised.

---

[4]   Consider Van Alstyne, supra: "It can be plausibly argued, however, that the Article III division of judicial power between appellate and original jurisdiction served a useful purpose other

The question whether an Act repugnant to the Constitution can become the law of the land, is a question deeply interesting to the United States; but, happily, not of an intricacy proportioned to its interest. It seems only necessary to recognize certain principles, supposed to have been long and well established, to decide it.

That the people have an original right to establish, for their future government, such principles as, in their opinion, shall most conduce to their own happiness, is the basis on which the whole American fabric has been erected. The exercise of this original right is a very great exertion; nor can it nor ought it to be frequently repeated. The principles, therefore, so established, are deemed fundamental. And as the authority from which they proceed is supreme, and can seldom act, they are designed to be permanent.

This original and supreme will organizes the government, and assigns to different departments their respective powers. It may either stop here, or establish certain limits not to be transcended by those departments.

The government of the United States is of the latter description. The powers of the legislature are defined and limited; and that those limits may not be mistaken, or forgotten, the constitution is written. To what purpose are powers limited, and to what purpose is that limitation committed to writing, if these limits may, at any time, be passed by those intended to be restrained? The distinction between a government with limited and unlimited powers is abolished, if those limits do not confine the persons on whom they are imposed, and if acts prohibited and acts allowed, are of equal obligation. It is a proposition too plain to be contested, that the constitution controls any legislative act repugnant to it; or, that the legislature may alter the constitution by an ordinary act.

Between these alternatives there is no middle ground. The constitution is either a superior paramount law, unchangeable by ordinary means, or it is on a level with ordinary legislative acts, and, like other acts, is alterable when the legislature shall please to alter it.

If the former part of the alternative be true, then a legislative act contrary to the constitution is not law: if the latter part be true, then

---

than that insisted upon by Marshall. Had Congress *not* adopted the Judiciary Act of 1789 or taken any other action describing Supreme Court jurisdiction, the division itself would have provided a guideline for the Court to follow until Congress was inclined to act." See also Steven G. Calabresi & Gary Lawson, *The Unitary Executive, Jurisdiction Stripping, and the* Hamdan *Opinions: A Textualist Response to Justice Scalia*, 107 Colum. L. Rev. 1002 (2007) (arguing that the Necessary and Proper Clause of Art. I, § 8 "and Article III permit Congress to move cases back and forth between the Supreme Court's original and appellate jurisdiction but not to remove cases from that jurisdiction altogether.").

By Marshall's interpretation of Art. III, may Congress authorize the Court to exercise appellate jurisdiction in cases involving foreign consuls? See *Bors v. Preston,* 111 U.S. 252 (1884).

written constitutions are absurd attempts, on the part of the people, to limit a power in its own nature illimitable.

Certainly all those who have framed written constitutions contemplate them as forming the fundamental and paramount law of the nation, and consequently, the theory of every such government must be, that an act of the legislature, repugnant to the constitution, is void.

This theory is essentially attached to a written constitution, and is, consequently, to be considered, by this court, as one of the fundamental principles of our society. It is not therefore to be lost sight of in the further consideration of this subject.

If an act of the legislature, repugnant to the Constitution, is void, does it, notwithstanding its invalidity, bind the courts, and oblige them to give it effect? Or, in other words, though it be not law, does it constitute a rule as operative as if it was a law? This would be to overthrow in fact what was established in theory; and would seem, at first view, an absurdity too gross to be insisted on. It shall, however, receive a more attentive consideration.

It is emphatically the province and duty of the judicial department to say what the law is. Those who apply the rule to particular cases, must of necessity expound and interpret that rule. If two laws conflict with each other, the courts must decide on the operation of each.

So if a law be in opposition to the constitution; if both the law and the constitution apply to a particular case, so that the court must either decide that case conformably to the law, disregarding the constitution; or conformably to the constitution, disregarding the law; the court must determine which of these conflicting rules governs the case. This is of the very essence of judicial duty.

If, then, the courts are to regard the constitution, and the constitution is superior to any ordinary act of the legislature, the constitution, and not such ordinary act, must govern the case to which they both apply.

Those then who controvert the principle that the constitution is to be considered in court, as a paramount law, are reduced to the necessity of maintaining that courts must close their eyes on the constitution, and see only the law.

This doctrine would subvert the very foundation of all written constitutions. It would declare that an Act which, according to the principles and theory of our government, is entirely void, is yet, in practice, completely obligatory. It would declare that if the legislature shall do what is expressly forbidden, such Act, notwithstanding the express prohibition, is in reality effectual. It would be giving to the legislature a practical and real omnipotence, with the same breath which professes to restrict their powers within narrow limits. It is prescribing limits, and declaring that those limits may be passed at pleasure.

That it thus reduces to nothing what we have deemed the greatest improvement on political institutions, a written constitution, would of itself be sufficient, in America, where written constitutions have been viewed with so much reverence, for rejecting the construction. But the peculiar expressions of the Constitution of the United States furnish additional arguments in favor of its rejection.

The judicial power of the United States is extended to all cases arising under the Constitution.

Could it be the intention of those who gave this power, to say that in using it the Constitution should not be looked into? That a case arising under the Constitution should be decided without examining the instrument under which it arises?

This is too extravagant to be maintained.

In some cases, then, the Constitution must be looked into by the judges. And if they can open it at all, what part of it are they forbidden to read or to obey?

There are many other parts of the Constitution which serve to illustrate this subject.

It is declared that "no tax or duty shall be laid on articles exported from any State." Suppose a duty on the export of cotton, of tobacco, or of flour; and a suit instituted to recover it. Ought judgment to be rendered in such a case? Ought the judges to close their eyes on the Constitution, and only see the law?

The Constitution declares "that no bill of attainder or ex post facto law shall be passed."

If, however, such a bill should be passed, and a person should be prosecuted under it, must the court condemn to death those victims whom the Constitution endeavors to preserve?

"No person," says the Constitution, "shall be convicted of treason unless on the testimony of two witnesses to the same overt act, or on confession in open court."

Here the language of the Constitution is addressed especially to the courts. It prescribes, directly for them, a rule of evidence not to be departed from. If the legislature should change that rule, and declare one witness, or a confession out of court, sufficient for conviction, must the constitutional principle yield to the legislative act?

From these, and many other selections which might be made, it is apparent, that the framers of the constitution contemplated that instrument as a rule for the government of courts, as well as of the legislature.

Why otherwise does it direct the judges to take an oath to support it? This oath certainly applies in an especial manner, to their conduct in their official character. How immoral to impose it on them, if they were to be used as the instruments, and the knowing instruments, for violating what they swear to support!

The oath of office, too, imposed by the legislature, is completely demonstrative of the legislative opinion on this subject. It is in these words: "I do solemnly swear that I will administer justice without respect to persons, and do equal right to the poor and to the rich; and that I will faithfully and impartially discharge all the duties incumbent on me as _____, according to the best of my abilities and understanding agreeably to the constitution and laws of the United States."

Why does a judge swear to discharge his duties agreeably to the constitution of the United States, if that constitution forms no rule for his government? If it is closed upon him, and cannot be inspected by him?

If such be the real state of things, this is worse than solemn mockery. To prescribe, or to take this oath, becomes equally a crime.

It is also not entirely unworthy of observation, that in declaring what shall be the supreme law of the land, the constitution itself is first mentioned; and not the laws of the United States generally, but those only which shall be made in pursuance of the constitution, have that rank.

Thus, the particular phraseology of the Constitution of the United States confirms and strengthens the principle, supposed to be essential to all written constitutions, that a law repugnant to the constitution is void; and that courts, as well as other departments, are bound by that instrument.

The rule must be discharged.[5]

———

"We are under a Constitution, but the Constitution is what the judges say it is."

—Charles Evans Hughes, Speech, 1907.

COMMENTARY ON MARBURY

Further Historical Context

Marbury is most frequently cited as the case establishing the Supreme Court's power of judicial review, but the assumption that courts would decline

---

[5]   Six days later, the Supreme Court refused to consider whether the Circuit Court Act Repeal Law was constitutional, thus tacitly upholding it. *Stuart v. Laird,* 5 U.S. (1 Cranch) 299, 2 L.Ed. 115 (1803). After *Marbury,* the Court did not hold an act of Congress unconstitutional until *Dred Scott v. Sandford,* 60 U.S. (19 How.) 393, 15 L.Ed. 691 (1857).

to enforce unconstitutional laws appears to have been relatively widespread and uncontroversial in the early Republic.

WILLIAM MICHAEL TREANOR, *Judicial Review Before Marbury*, 58 Stan.L.R. 455 (2005): "[T]he sheer number of" pre-*Marbury* colonial, state, and federal cases in which one or more judges voted to find a law unconstitutional "not only belies the notion that the institution of judicial review was created by Chief Justice Marshall in *Marbury*, it also reflects widespread acceptance and application of the doctrine." *See also* Mary Sarah Bilder, *The Corporate Origins of Judicial Review*, 116 Yale L.J. 502 (2006) (tracing American judicial review to the English judicial practice of rejecting corporate acts that were "repugnant" to the law of nations, and thence to the practice of invalidating American colonial laws that were repugnant to the laws of England); Philip Hamburger, *Law and Judicial Duty* (2008) (classifying judicial review as one aspect of the broader duty of common law judges to decide cases according to the law of the land); Michael J. Klarman, *How Great Were the "Great" Marshall Court Decisions?*, 87 Va.L.Rev. 1111 n.14 (2001) (collecting sources demonstrating the widespread acceptance of judicial review before *Marbury*).

———

In what sense, then, was *Marbury* controversial? In its day, controversy centered on the particular remedy that Marbury sought.

RANDY E. BARNETT, *Restoring the Lost Constitution* 144 (2004): "While historical evidence strongly supports the conclusion that the original meaning of 'judicial power'[6] included the power to nullify [unconstitutional legislation], there is little if any evidence to support a claim that the original meaning of 'judicial power' also included a power to command other branches. Nor was such a power exercised by the Supreme Court in *Marbury*.[7]

———

CHARLES WARREN, 1 *The Supreme Court in United States History*, 232, 242–43 (1922): "Contemporary writings make it very clear that the republicans attacked the [*Marbury*] decision, not so much because it sustained the power of the court to determine the validity of congressional legislation, as because it enounced the doctrine that the court might issue mandamus to a cabinet official who was acting by direction of the president. In other words, Jefferson's antagonism to Marshall and the court at that time was due more to his resentment at the alleged invasion of his

---

[6]   This is a reference to Art. III, § 2, cl.1, providing that "[t]he judicial power of the United States shall extend to all cases * * * arising under this Constitution [and] the Laws of the United States * * * ."

[7]   See also Robert G. McCloskey, *The American Supreme Court* 25 (2d ed. Levinson, 1994); Richard H. Fallon, Jr., Marbury *and the Constitutional Mind: A Bicentennial Essay on the Wages of Doctrinal Tension*, 91 Calif.L.Rev. 1 (2003); Daniel A. Farber, *Judicial Review and Its Alternatives; An American Tale*, 38 Wake Forest L.Rev. 415 (2003) (part of a large symposium in commemoration of the bicentennial of *Marbury*).

executive prerogative than to any so-called 'judicial usurpation' of the field of congressional authority. [It] seems plain [that Marshall might] have construed the language of the section of the judiciary act [to escape the necessity] to pass upon its constitutionality. Marshall naturally felt that in view of the recent attacks on judicial power it was important to have the great principle firmly established, and undoubtedly he welcomed the opportunity of fixing the precedent in a case in which his action would necessitate a decision in favor of his political opponents."

———

MORRIS COHEN, *The Faith of a Liberal* 178–80 (1946) (written in 1938): "The section of [the] act of 1789 which Marshall declared unconstitutional had been drawn up by Ellsworth, his predecessor as chief justice, and by others who a short time before had been the very members of the constitutional convention that had drafted its judicial provisions. It was signed by George Washington who had presided over the deliberations of that convention. Fourteen years later, John Marshall by implication accused his predecessor on the bench, the members of congress such as James Madison, the father of the constitution, and President Washington, of either not understanding the constitution (which some of them had drawn up), or else wilfully disregarding it. [To] a secular historian, it is obvious that John Marshall was motivated by the fear of impeachment if he granted the mandamus or dared to declare the republican judiciary repeal act of 1802 unconstitutional. Having thus refused aid to his fellow federalists ousted from offices created for them by a 'lame duck' congress, he resorted to a line of sophistical dicta to get even with his political enemy, as indeed he did also in the *Aaron Burr* case. In his letter to his colleague Chase, Marshall offered to abandon judicial supremacy in the interpretation of the constitution in return for security against impeachment."[8]

The Three Faces of Marbury

RICHARD H. FALLON, Jr., *Marbury and the Constitutional Mind: A Bicentennial Essay on the Wages of Doctrinal Tension*, 91 Calif.L.Rev. 1 (2003): "John Marshall's canonical opinion includes at least three facets or faces. It could plausibly be claimed that any of these reflects an essential element of Marshall's reasoning and expresses the foundational insights that subsequent judicial practice must follow in order to be true to *Marbury*. * * *

---

[8] In 1804, the House impeached Justice Chase due, inter alia, to what the Republicans believed to be Chase's partisan Federalist activities and statements both on and off the Bench. After a lengthy trial in the Senate, the constitutional majority to convict was not obtained. It was generally assumed that, if the effort had been successful, Marshall and other Federalist judges would suffer the same fate. See generally 1 Warren, supra, ch. 6. For a further account of *Marbury*, see 3 Albert Beveridge, *The Life of John Marshall* 105–156 (1919).

"1. *The Private-Rights Face.* Judicial review gives federal judges, who are not directly accountable to the electorate, a power that is potentially threatening to more representative branches of the government and to political democracy. *Marbury*'s private-rights face responds directly to this threat and attempts to disarm it. This face represents *Marbury* as a species of traditional private litigation. It casts the Justices of the Supreme Court as ordinary judges humbly doing their best to apply the law to disputes between individuals. In *Marbury*, the Justices claimed no general authority to resolve constitutional issues that might arise in American politics. Rather, Marshall's reasoning grounds the Court's exercise of judicial review in its need to decide the case before it, which involved Marbury's claimed right to judicial relief under the law of the United States. [*Marbury*'s] private-rights face suffuses and inspires what has been called 'the private rights model' of constitutional adjudication. Within the model, courts have no warrant to decide constitutional issues except as necessary to adjudicate a concrete dispute.

"[2.] *The Special-Functions Face.* In justifying the Court's exercise of judicial review, *Marbury* asserted that 'it is emphatically the province and duty of the judicial department to say what the law is.' The force of this proposition can be seen as conditioned by the case's facts, involving a concrete and traditional claim of individual right, but acceptance of this limit is not strictly necessary. The grounds for a broader view lie in *Marbury*'s expressly functional argument: If other branches of government, especially Congress, could exceed constitutional bounds without being subject to judicial check, then the restraining function of a written constitution would be obliterated. * * * According to what has been called a 'special functions' or 'public rights' model, the courts should provide safeguards against constitutional violations by other branches, even in cases that do not involve the kinds of private rights and material injuries that typically underlie suits at common law. This model holds that there is a public interest, appropriately enforced through public-rights litigation, in ensuring official conformity to legal and especially constitutional norms. * * *

"3. *The Political or Prudential Face.* *Marbury*'s third face becomes visible when one looks beneath the Court's rhetoric and considers the decision in its political context. This is a political face of judicial prudence tinctured with guile. Its central prescription is that the Court must sometimes recede from the conflict with the political branches or with aroused public opinion in order to maintain its prestige and thus its power. [To] sustain and legitimatize its place in a constitutional democracy, the Court must define for itself a democratically acceptable role. The sources of the Court's vulnerability are several. First, the Court's orders are not self-executing. Thomas Jefferson and James Madison seemed poised to ignore the Supreme Court's writ of mandamus if one had issued in

Marbury. [Second,] Article III vests Congress with express power to control and limit the appellate jurisdiction of the Supreme Court. [Third,] the political branches possess constitutional authority not only to determine the membership of the Supreme Court through appointment and confirmation processes, but also to adjust its size. In conjunction, these powers make 'Court packing' at least a potential response to judicial decisions that aroused political majorities adjudge intolerable. In *Marbury* the Court reached the only prudent conclusion: It could not, indeed must not, issue a quixotic order to Madison to deliver Marbury's commission. But never before or since has the Court, in prudent retreat, displayed more guile to emerge in glory from the spectre of defeat.

"[The] core insight [of *Marbury*] is that the Court must sometimes avoid conflicts that might subject it to rebuff or retaliation. [In] *Marbury* itself, for example, the Court arguably invented a nonexistent statutory jurisdiction in order to be able to hold, at least debatably, that Congress had overstepped constitutional bounds. [*Marbury's*] political and prudential face [is] perhaps the best possible face to represent the school of constitutional thought that emphasizes the need for judicial prudence. Vivid illustration comes from a recent article by Laurence Tribe, in which he imagines how disastrous the result might have been had *Marbury* been decided by a Court displaying the brazen arrogance that he ascribes to the current Court.[79] Tribe's imagined scenario ends with the Court's conclusions that '[h]ence the writ shall issue'—at which point all hell breaks loose, Jefferson tells Madison to defy the Court, Marshall and several colleagues are impeached and convicted, and the next 200 years look entirely different."

Text of the Constitution

Is the doctrine of "judicial review," which gives the Court power to declare an act of a coordinate branch of the government unconstitutional, compelled because a contrary rule "would subvert the very foundation of all written constitutions"?

WILLIAM VAN ALSTYNE, *A Critical Guide to Marbury v. Madison,* 1969 Duke L.J. 1: "[E]ven in Marshall's time (and to a great extent today), a number of nations maintained written constitutions and yet gave national legislative acts the full force of positive law without providing any constitutional check to guarantee the compatibility of those acts with their constitutions [e.g.,] France, Switzerland, and Belgium (and to some extent Great Britain where magna carta and other written instruments are

---

[79] **[Orig. Note]** See Laurence H. Tribe, *eroG v. hsuB and Its Disguises: Freeing Bush v. Gore from Its Hall of Mirrors,* 115 Harv.L.Rev. 170 (2001).

roughly described as the constitution but where acts of parliament are not reviewable)."[9]

———

Does the "judges' oath" provision (Art. VI, cl. 3) furnish the necessary textual support for the doctrine of judicial review?

JUSTICE GIBSON, dissenting in *Eakin v. Raub,* 12 S. & R. 330 (Pa.1825):[10] "The oath to support the Constitution is not peculiar to the judges, but is taken indiscriminately by every officer of the government, and is designed rather as a test of the political principles of the man, than to bind the officer in the discharge of his duty: otherwise, it were difficult to determine, what operation it is to have in the case of a recorder of deeds, for instance, who, in execution of his office, has nothing to do with the Constitution. But granting it to relate to the official conduct of the judge, as well as every other officer, and not to his political principles, still, it must be understood in reference to supporting the Constitution, only as far as that may be involved in his official duty; and consequently, if his official duty does not comprehend an inquiry into the authority of the legislature, neither does his oath.

"[But] do not the judges do a positive act in violation of the Constitution, when they give effect to an unconstitutional law? Not if the law has been passed according to the forms established in the Constitution. The fallacy of the question is, in supposing that the judiciary adopts the acts of the legislature as its own; whereas, the enactment of a law and the interpretation of it are not concurrent acts, and as the judiciary is not required to concur in the enactment, neither is it in the breach of the constitution which may be the consequence of the enactment; the fault is imputable to the legislature, and on it the responsibility exclusively rests."

———

What of Art. III, § 2, cl. 1, extending "the judicial Power" "to all Cases * * * arising under this Constitution [and] the Laws of the United States"?

ALEXANDER M. BICKEL, *The Least Dangerous Branch* 5–6 (1962), asks: "Is the Court empowered, when it decides a case, to declare that a duly enacted statute violates the Constitution, and to invalidate the statute? Article III does not purport to describe the function of the Court;

———

[9] Since 1998, courts in the United Kingdom have been authorized by the Human Rights Act to declare legislation "incompatible" with the rights set forth in the European Convention on Human Rights. Such a declaration does not render the legislation void or otherwise unenforceable absent further action by parliament. For discussion of the modern growth of various forms of judicial review in other countries, see Mauro Cappelletti, *Judicial Review in Comparative Perspective,* 58 Calif.L.Rev. 1017 (1970). See also Mark Tushnet, *New Forms of Judicial Review and the Persistence of Rights—And Democracy-Based Worries,* 38 Wake Forest L.Rev. 813 (2003).

[10] This opinion is widely regarded as the most effective answer of the era to Marshall's reasoning supporting judicial review.

it subsumes whatever questions may exist as to that in the phrase 'the judicial power.' It does not purport to tell the Court how to decide cases; it only specifies which kinds of case the Court shall have jurisdiction to deal with at all."

Compare MATHEW D. ADLER & MICHAEL C. DORF, *Constitutional Existence Conditions and Judicial Review*, 89 Va.L.Rev. 1105 (2003): "Ingredient in most forms of judicial review skepticism is the implicit claim that it would be possible for courts to accept the word of Congress as final on matters of constitutional interpretation. Once one acknowledges that courts have the duty to apply statutes and other nonconstitutional sources of law, however, it becomes difficult to understand how they could not exercise at least some version of the *Marbury* power, [as] a schematic example illustrates. Suppose plaintiff Smith appears before federal judge Jones waving a piece of paper that appears to be a federal statute entitling Smith to a judgment against defendant Acme Manufacturing for Acme's alleged violation of Smith's rights as set forth in the purported federal statute. Before the judge can apply the statute she must be sure that the piece of paper in fact is a statute.

"Suppose that, contra *Marbury*, the judge accepts the authoritative utterances of Congress as binding on matters of constitutional interpretation. Accordingly, Smith claims that the piece of paper granting him rights against Acme is an authoritative utterance of Congress. The judge cannot simply take Smith's word for it; she must ask whether Congress actually enacted the purported statute.

"Identifying authoritative utterances of Congress involves a two-step process. First, the judge must identify Congress. Second, she must identify its authoritative utterances. The Constitution speaks to both steps. Congress is the body chosen by the process set forth in Article I, Sections 2 through 4 and the Seventeenth Amendment, rather than, say, a group of self-styled patriots meeting on a Washington, D.C. tennis court. And Congress's authoritative utterances are those that (at a minimum) satisfy the criteria for lawmaking set forth in Section 7 of Article I. With respect to the piece of paper that purports to grant Smith rights against Acme, the judge must ask whether the body designated as Congress by the Constitution enacted it in accordance with the procedures set forth in the Constitution. In other words, even in a world in which judicial review were formally abolished, the courts would still be guided by their own, independent interpretation of the Constitution in identifying the authoritative utterances of Congress."

————

What of the supremacy clause (Art. VI, cl. 2)?

HERBERT WECHSLER, *Toward Neutral Principles of Constitutional Law*, 73 Harv.L.Rev. 1 (1959): "Judge [Learned] Hand [*The Bill of Rights* 28 (1958)] concedes that under this clause 'state courts would at times have to decide whether state laws and constitutions, or even a federal statute, were in conflict with the federal constitution' but he adds that 'the fact that this jurisdiction was confined to such occasions, and that it was thought necessary specifically to provide such a limited jurisdiction, looks rather against than in favor of a general jurisdiction.'

"Are you satisfied, however, to view the supremacy clause in this way, as a grant of jurisdiction to state courts, implying a denial of the power and the duty to all others? This certainly is not its necessary meaning; it may be construed as a mandate to all of officialdom including courts, with a special and emphatic admonition that it binds the judges of the previously independent states. That the latter is the proper reading seems to me persuasive when the other relevant provisions of the Constitution are brought into view.

"Article III, section 1 [represented] one of the major compromises of the Constitutional Convention and relegated the establishment vel non of lower federal courts to the discretion of the Congress. None might have been established, with the consequence that, as in other federalisms, judicial work of first instance would all have been remitted to state courts. Article III, section 2 goes on, however, to delineate the scope of the federal judicial power, providing that it 'shall extend [inter alia] to all Cases, in Law and Equity, arising under this Constitution [and] further, that the Supreme Court 'shall have appellate jurisdiction' in such cases 'with such Exceptions, and under such Regulations as the Congress shall make.' Surely this means, as section 25 of the Judiciary Act of 1789 took it to mean, that if a court passes on a constitutional issue, as the supremacy clause provides that it should, its judgment is reviewable, subject to congressional exceptions, by the Supreme Court, in which event that Court must have no less authority and duty to accord priority to constitutional provisions than the court that it reviews. And such state cases might have encompassed every case in which a constitutional issue could possibly arise, since, as I have said, Congress need not and might not have exerted its authority to establish 'inferior' federal courts.

"If you abide with me thus far, I doubt that you will hesitate upon the final step. Is it a possible construction of the Constitution, measured strictly as Judge Hand admonishes by the test of 'general purpose,' that if Congress opts, as it has opted, to create a set of lower courts, those courts in cases falling within their respective jurisdictions and the Supreme Court when it passes on their judgments are less or differently constrained by the supremacy clause than are the state courts, and the Supreme Court when it reviews their judgments? Yet I cannot escape, what is for me the most astonishing conclusion, that this is the precise result of Judge Hand's reading of the text."

Did Judge Hand concede too much in reading the text of the supremacy clause to empower state courts to decide the constitutionality of *federal* statutes? If so, is Chief Justice Marshall's reference to Art. VI persuasive?[11]

––––––––

WILLIAM VAN ALSTYNE, supra: "The phrase 'in pursuance thereof' might as easily mean *'in the manner prescribed by this constitution,'* in which case acts of congress might be judicially reviewable as to their procedural integrity, but not as to their substance. An example of this more limited, procedural, judicial review is found in *Field v. Clark* [143 U.S. 649 (1892)]; it is, moreover, far more common in other countries than is substantive constitutional review. * * *

"The phrase might also mean merely that only those statutes adopted by Congress *after* the re-establishment and reconstitution of Congress pursuant to the Constitution itself shall be the supreme law of the land, whereas acts of the earlier Continental Congress, constituted merely under the Articles of Confederation, would not necessarily be supreme and binding upon the several states. Under this view, acts of Congress, like acts of Parliament, *are* the supreme law and not to be second-guessed by any

––––––––

[11] Consider Charles L. Black, Jr., *The People and The Court* 23–25 (1960): "[T]he most impressive thing in firming the claims of judicial review is the operation of our history since its beginning. And the most striking thing about this history is that the other departments of government, preeminently Congress, have operated under the assumption (and not through mere oversight, for the assumption has in several epochs been passionately challenged) that judicial review is an authentic part of our system of government. One of the most decisive Congressional expressions of this assumption, of special interest because it was passed by the First Congress, is the 25th Section of the first federal Judiciary Act [which] explicitly recognizes and provides for review of state court decisions by the Supreme Court, and lays it down with certainty that the Supreme Court may, by reversing a state judgment that has upheld a state law as against constitutional attack, hold state laws unconstitutional. But it says more than that. It clearly recognizes, first, that the validity of a 'treaty or statute of [the] United States' may be drawn in question in a state court and that the decision of the state court may be 'against their validity.' It then goes on to say, not only that the Supreme Court may review such a judgment, but that it may be 'reversed or affirmed' in that Court. If the Supreme Court may 'affirm' a state judgment holding a federal law invalid, then the Supreme Court obviously may, in such a case at least, hold a federal law invalid. [But] does it not seem likely that it was also assumed that the federal courts were empowered to pass and would pass, in all cases within their jurisdiction, on the validity of the state laws? Actually, the absurdity of the contrary assumption, in the context of the Judiciary Act of 1789, is even greater than this bare statement makes it appear. For that Act provided (as the law still provides) that parties from different states could sue and be sued in the federal courts. So the hypothesis that the state courts might, while the federal courts might not, pass on the validity of federal statutes, would necessarily imply that parties who were citizens of the same state could appeal to the federal Constitution in court, while those who were citizens of different states could not. This is sheer lunacy—but to clear the members of the First Congress (as they deserve to be cleared) of this charge of lunacy, we have to assume that they took it for granted that the federal constitutional validity of state and federal laws could be passed on by all courts, state and federal."

court, state or federal, so long as they postdate ratification of the Constitution.[12]

" * * * *Assuming that an act repugnant to the Constitution is not a law 'in pursuance thereof' and thus must not be given effect as the supreme law of the land, who, according to the Constitution, is to make the determination as to whether any given law is in fact repugnant to the Constitution itself?* [T]he supremacy clause itself cannot be the clear textual basis for a claim by the judiciary that this prerogative to determine repugnancy belongs to it.

"[The phrase] could mean merely that the people should regard the Constitution with deep concern and that *they* should act to prevent Congress from overstepping the Constitution. It might even imply, moreover, a right of civil disobedience or serve as a written reminder to government of the natural right of revolution against tyrannical government which oversteps the terms of the social compact. Such a construction would be consistent with philosophical writings of the period, consistent with the Declaration of Independence, and consistent also with the view of some antifederalists of the period."[13]

The Court as "Final" Arbiter

THOMAS JEFFERSON, writing in 1804, 8 *The Writings of Thomas Jefferson* 310 (1897): "The judges, believing the [sedition law] constitutional, had a right to pass a sentence of fine and imprisonment; because that power was placed in their hands by the constitution. But the

---

[12] For a careful elaboration of this point, see 2 William Crosskey, *Politics and the Constitution* 990–1007 (1953).

As distinguished from acts of Congress, treaties were binding upon the several states according to this view merely by having been entered into "under the Authority of the United States," and irrespective of whether they were approved by the Senate as it was proposed to be established pursuant to the new Constitution.

[13] Contemporary scholars and judges who consider themselves originalists typically aim to unearth the original meaning of the words of the Constitution, rather than the subjective intentions and expectations of the framers or ratifiers. See Michael C. Dorf, *The Undead Constitution*, 125 Harv.L.Rev. 2011 (2012) (reviewing Jack M. Balkin, *Living Originalism* (2011) and David A. Strauss, *The Living Constitution* (2010)). However, earlier scholarship focused on those intentions and expectations. With respect to judicial review, that older work generally examined pre-Convention judicial precedents in England and the colonies, statements of the framers both within and outside the Constitutional Convention (see especially Alexander Hamilton in Nos. 78 and 80 of *The Federalist* (1788)), and debate during the ratification period, arriving at conflicting conclusions. See, e.g., Louis Boudin, *Government by Judiciary* (1932); Edward Corwin, *The Doctrine of Judicial Review* (1914); William Crosskey, *Politics and the Constitution in the History of the United States* (1953); William Nelson, *Changing Conceptions of Judicial Review: The Evolution of Constitutional Theory in the States, 1790–1860*, 120 U.Pa.L.Rev. 1166 (1972); Charles Warren, *Congress, the Constitution, and the Supreme Court* (1925). For brief discussion see Leonard W. Levy, *Judicial Review, History, and Democracy: An Introduction,* in Judicial Review and the Supreme Court 1–12 (1967). For the view that this method of "strict intentionalism" is not a "tenable approach to constitutional decision making," see Paul Brest, *The Misconceived Quest for the Original Understanding*, 60 B.U.L.Rev. 204 (1980).

For review of the broader historical setting, see Bernard Bailyn, *The Ideological Origins of the American Revolution* (1967); Gordon Wood, *The Creation of the American Republic, 1776–1787* (1969).

executive, believing the law to be unconstitutional, was bound to remit the
execution of it; because that power has been confided to him by the
constitution. The instrument meant that its co-ordinate branches should
be checks on each other. But the opinion which gives to the judges the right
to decide what laws are constitutional, and what not, not only for
themselves in their own sphere of action, but for the legislative and
executive also in their spheres, would make the judiciary a despotic
branch."

––––––

ANDREW JACKSON, veto message in 1832 on Act to Recharter Bank
of United States (the constitutionality of which had earlier been upheld by
the Court), 2 Richardson, *Messages and Papers of the Presidents* 576, 581–
82 (1900): "It is as much the duty of the house of representatives, of the
senate, and of the president to decide upon the constitutionality of any bill
or resolution which may be presented to them for passage or approval as it
is of the supreme judges when it may be brought before them for judicial
decision. The opinion of the judges has no more authority over congress
than the opinion of congress has over the judges, and on that point the
president is independent of both. The authority of the supreme court must
not, therefore, be permitted to control the congress or the executive when
acting in their legislative capacities, but to have only such influence as the
force of their reasoning may deserve."

––––––

ABRAHAM LINCOLN, inaugural address in 1861, 2 Richardson,
supra, at 5, 9–10: "I do not forget the position assumed by some that
constitutional questions are to be decided by the Supreme Court, nor do I
deny that such decisions must be binding in any case upon the parties to a
suit as to the object of that suit, while they are also entitled to very high
respect and consideration in all parallel cases by all other departments of
the government. And while it is obviously possible that such decision may
be erroneous in any given case, still the evil effect following it, being limited
to that particular case, with the chance that it may be overruled and never
become a precedent for other cases, can better be borne than could the evils
of a different practice. At the same time, the candid citizen must confess
that if the policy of the government upon vital questions affecting the whole
people is to be irrevocably fixed by decisions of the Supreme Court, the
instant they are made in ordinary litigation between parties in personal
actions the people will have ceased to be their own rulers, having to that
extent practically resigned their government into the hands of that
eminent tribunal. Nor is there in this view any assault upon the court or
the judges. It is a duty from which they may not shrink to decide cases

properly brought before them, and it is no fault of theirs if others seek to turn their decisions to political purposes."

Are these views inconsistent with *Marbury*? Does *Marbury* decide anything more than that *"the Court may refuse to give effect to an act of Congress where the act pertains to the judicial power itself"*? Van Alstyne, supra. Than that the Court claimed the power of judicial review "only in the defensive sense of safeguarding the Court's original jurisdiction from congressional enlargement"? Frank Strong, *Judicial Review: A Tri-Dimensional Concept of Administrative-Constitutional Law*, 69 W.Va.L.Rev. 111 (1967). *See also* David P. Currie, *The Constitution in Congress: The Federalist Period, 1789–1801*, at 296 (1997) (noting the primacy of legislative and executive constitutional interpretation in the early Republic); Larry D. Kramer, *The People Themselves: Popular Constitutionalism and Judicial Review* (2004) (expounding a limited, "departmentalist" conception of judicial review, in which primary authority for interpreting and enforcing the Constitution rests with the People).

If the Court upholds the constitutionality of a federal statute, may the President refuse to enforce it because he believes it to be unconstitutional? May he refuse to enforce it on this ground after Congress has enacted it but before it comes before the Court? May he refuse to enforce it on this ground if Congress overrides his veto? May the President continue to enforce a statute (e.g., by pressing charges for its violation) after the Court has held it unconstitutional? May he refuse to return property that the Court has held was unconstitutionally seized? If Congress forbids the President from taking certain action, may he do so on the ground that Congress' restriction is unconstitutional? Even after the Court has upheld its constitutionality?

———

COOPER v. AARON, 358 U.S. 1 (1958) (also in Ch. 9, Sec. 2, III) arose several years after the landmark ruling in *Brown v. Board of Education* (1954) (Ch. 9, Sec. 2, II) that segregation of public school children on the basis of race violated the Fourteenth Amendment. A plan approved by the lower federal courts to desegregate Little Rock public schools was blocked by the Governor of Arkansas and other state officials. In the face of a federal court injunction, the Governor backed off, and National Guard soldiers, called out to keep the public schools desegregated, were withdrawn. For a short time, black students were able to attend previously all-white public schools under the protection of federally-commanded troops. However, in early 1958, citing deep tension and concern about violence, the school board sought, and a federal court granted, a long postponement of the desegregation plan. The Court of Appeals reversed, and the Supreme Court affirmed—in an opinion delivered not by any one justice, as is ordinarily the case, but signed by all nine. Arkansas contended that because it was not a party to the litigation that culminated in the

Brown ruling, it was not bound by that decision. This claim stirred the Supreme Court to make a broad and forceful statement about its supremacy in constitutional matters—as Laurence H. Tribe, *American Constitutional Law* 255 (3d ed. 2000) (hereafter Tribe, 3d ed.) described it, "a statement uniquely punctuated by the Justices' individual signatures of the opinion":

"Article VI of the Constitution makes the Constitution the 'supreme law of the land.' In 1803, Chief Justice Marshall, speaking for a unanimous Court, referring to the Constitution as 'the fundamental and paramount law of the nation,' declared [in] *Marbury* [the] basic principle that the federal judiciary is supreme in the exposition of the law of the Constitution, and that principle has ever since been respected by this Court and the Country as a permanent and indispensable feature of our constitutional system. It follows that the interpretation of the Fourteenth Amendment enunciated by this Court in the *Brown* case is the supreme law of the land. [Every] state legislator and executive and judicial officer is solemnly committed by oath taken pursuant to art. VI, cl. 3 'to support this Constitution.' * * * No state legislature or executive or judicial officer can war against the Constitution without violating his undertaking to support it. Chief Justice Marshall spoke for a unanimous court in saying that: 'If the legislatures of the several states may, at will, annul the judgments of the courts of the United States, and destroy the rights acquired under those judgments, the constitution itself becomes a solemn mockery * * * .' *United States v. Peters,* 5 Cranch 115. A Governor who asserts a power to nullify a federal court order is similarly restrained."[14]

———

TRIBE, 3d ed., at 255–58: "The Meaning of *Cooper v. Aaron.* [A] broad reading of Cooper would seem to embody two central assumptions. The first is that the Court, in rendering a constitutional decision, announces a general norm of wide applicability. This viewpoint ignores the competing conception that the Court, in making constitutional determinations pursuant to its responsibility under *Marbury*, simply resolves the claims of the parties before it. But an expansive view of the judicial function was clearly warranted in *Brown*; the Court's unanimous opinion was couched in the most general terms and was perceived at the time as applying to all public schools.

"[The] second possible assumption—that the Court's interpretation is *itself* the 'supreme law of the land' and that state officials are directly bound by oath to support that interpretation—is more troubling. This view has been criticized as wrongly equating the Constitution with the Court's interpretation of it—as saying that *Marbury* means that the Constitution

---

[14] For a strong defense of this "judicial supremacy" analysis, see Larry Alexander & Frederick Schauer, *On Extrajudicial Constitutional Interpretation,* 110 Harv.L.Rev. 1359 (1997).

is what the Court says it is, no less and no more. So construed, *Cooper* ignores the reality that, at least so long as the manner in which our nation's fundamental document is to be interpreted remains open to question, the 'meaning,' of the Constitution is subject to legitimate dispute, and the Court is not alone in its responsibility to address that meaning. Rather, a variety of actors must make their own constitutional judgments, and possess the power to develop interpretations of the Constitution which do not necessarily conform to the judicially enforced interpretation articulated by the Supreme Court: the president, legislators, state courts and the public at large.

"The *Cooper* opinion as a whole, however, does not require so literal a reading of its invocation of absolute judicial supremacy; conceived with sufficient subtlety, it is readily compatible with American democracy. Plainly, in *Cooper* the Court does say that its *Brown* decision is binding law under the Supremacy Clause. But the Court need not be understood to say anything more than that *Brown* and its progeny, including the case at hand, are binding in the same way that any other judicial decision is binding, so that state officials who interfere with enforcement of a judgment, or act to undermine its goals, are acting unlawfully. On this view, *Brown* need not be seen as itself 'part' of the Constitution, but as a constitutional judgment, an exercise of judicial power entitled to respect under the Supremacy Clause not because it *is* the Constitution but because it is an exercise of power *under* the Constitution—just as the [Court's] interpretation of a federal statute, is binding. On this view, to declare that the 'federal judiciary is *supreme* in the exposition of the law of the Constitution' is to make a statement more about the role of the federal judiciary than about the content of the Constitution's commands."

———

UNITED STATES v. WINDSOR (Ch. 9, Sec. 4, I) invalidated § 3 of the Defense of Marriage Act (DOMA), which defined marriage for purposes of over one thousand federal statutes as "a legal union between one man and one woman." It was challenged by a woman who was treated as never having been married for purposes of federal estate tax law after the death of the woman to whom she was married under New York law. While the lawsuit was pending, the Attorney General concluded that DOMA § 3 was unconstitutional and declined to defend its validity in court. However, to facilitate judicial review, the Department of Justice continued to enforce the law. En route to the merits decision, the Court found that the case was appropriate for judicial resolution:

"The Executive's failure to defend the constitutionality of an Act of Congress based on a constitutional theory not yet established in judicial decisions has created a procedural dilemma. On the one hand [the] Government's agreement with Windsor raises questions about the propriety of entertaining a suit in which it seeks affirmance of an order invalidating a federal law and ordering the United States to pay money. On the other hand, if the Executive's agreement with a plaintiff that a law is unconstitutional is enough to preclude judicial review, then the Supreme Court's primary role in determining the constitutionality of a law that has inflicted real injury on a plaintiff who has brought a justiciable legal claim would become only secondary to the President's. This would undermine the clear dictate of the separation-of-powers principle that 'when an Act of Congress is alleged to conflict with the Constitution, '[i]t is emphatically the province and duty of the judicial department to say what the law is.' Similarly, with respect to the legislative power, when Congress has passed a statute and a President has signed it, it poses grave challenges to the separation of powers for the Executive at a particular moment to be able to nullify Congress' enactment solely on its own initiative and without any determination from the Court."

SCALIA, J., joined by Thomas, J., and Roberts, C.J., dissented, calling the majority's jurisdictional holding a "jaw-dropping [assertion] of judicial supremacy over the people's Representatives in Congress and the Executive. It envisions a Supreme Court standing (or rather enthroned) at the apex of government, empowered to decide all constitutional questions, always and everywhere 'primary' in its role.

"This image of the Court would have been unrecognizable to those who wrote and ratified our national charter. [The] judicial power as Americans have understood it (and their English ancestors before them) is the power to adjudicate, with conclusive effect, disputed government claims (civil or criminal) against private persons, and disputed claims by private persons against the government or other private persons. Sometimes (though not always) the parties before the court disagree not with regard to the facts of their case (or not only with regard to the facts) but with regard to the applicable law—in which event (and only in which event) it becomes the 'province and duty of the judicial department to say what the law is.' "

Judicial Review and Democracy:
The Countermajoritarian Difficulty

ALEXANDER BICKEL, supra, at 16–20: "The root difficulty is that judicial review is a counter-majoritarian force in our system. [W]hen the Supreme Court declares unconstitutional a legislative act or the action of an elected executive, it thwarts the will of representatives of the actual people of the here and now; it exercises control, not in behalf of the prevailing majority, but against it. That [is] the reason the charge can be made that judicial review is undemocratic.

"Most assuredly, no democracy operates by taking continuous nose counts on the broad range of daily governmental activities. [Nevertheless], although democracy does not mean constant reconsideration of decisions once made, it does mean that a representative majority has the power to accomplish a reversal. This power is of the essence, and no less so because it is often merely held in reserve.

"It is true, of course, that the process of reflecting the will of a popular majority in the legislature is deflected by various inequalities of representation and by all sorts of institutional habits and characteristics, which perhaps tend most often in favor of inertia. Yet, impurities and imperfections, if such they be, in one part of the system are no argument for total departure from the desired norm in another part.

"[It] does not follow from the complex nature of a democratic system that, because admirals and generals and the members, say, of the Federal Reserve Board or of this or that administrative agency are not electorally responsible, judges who exercise the power of judicial review need not be responsible either, and in neither case is there a serious conflict with democratic theory. For admirals and generals and the like are most often responsible to officials who are themselves elected and through whom the line runs directly to a majority. What is more significant, the policies they make are or should be interstitial or technical only and are reversible by legislative majorities * * *—a fact of great consequence. Nor will it do to liken judicial review to the general lawmaking function of judges. In the latter aspect, judges are indeed something like administrative officials, for their decisions are also reversible by any legislative majority—and not infrequently they are reversed. Judicial review, however, is the power to apply and construe the Constitution in matters of the greatest moment, against the wishes of a legislative majority, which is, in turn, powerless to affect the judicial decision."

––––––––––

JESSE CHOPER, *The Supreme Court and the Political Branches: Democratic Theory and Practice,* 122 U.Pa.L.Rev. 810 (1974): "In the main, the effect of judicial review in ruling legislation unconstitutional is to nullify the finished product of the lawmaking process. It is the very rare supreme court decision on constitutionality that affirmatively mandates the undertaking of government action. To make the point in another way, when the Supreme Court finds legislative acts unconstitutional it holds invalid only those enactments that have survived the many hurdles fixed between incipient proposals and standing law.

"The significance of this [is] that most of the antimajoritarian elements that have been found in the American legislative process [are] negative ones. They work to *prevent* the translation of popular wishes into governing rules rather than to *produce* laws that are contrary to majority sentiment. [S]enators representing only fifteen percent of the population may hold sway in the upper house; but their real impact (as is obviously the case with the filibuster as well) is to halt ultimate action rather than facilitate it. For the enactment of law also requires the concurrence of the lower [house]. Furthermore, within each legislative chamber, the ability of the committees and their chairmen and minority members—and frequently of the lobbies and other interest groups as well—to circumvent the majority will of the assembly is most saliently manifested in obstructing the process rather than in making laws. The more formidable task usually is not to stall or defeat a proposal but to organize the requisite support among the dispersed powers so as to form a coalition for its passage.

"[Thus], although exceptions exist, '[a] distinguishing feature of our system, perhaps impelled by heritage of sectional division and heterogeneity, is that our governmental structure, institutional habits, and political parties with their internal factional divisions, have combined to produce a system in which major programs and major new directions cannot be undertaken unless supported by a fairly broad popular consensus. This normally has been far broader than 51 percent and often bipartisan as well.'[15] [Consequently,] when the Supreme Court, itself without conventional political responsibility, says 'thou shalt not' to acts of Congress, it usually cuts sharply against the grain of majority rule. The relatively few laws that finally overcome the congressional obstacle course generally illustrate the national political branches operating at their majoritarian best while the process of judicial review depicts that element of the Court's work and that exertion of federal authority with the most brittle democratic roots.[59]"

––––––

RONALD DWORKIN, *Freedom's Law*, 17 (1996): "Democracy means government subject to conditions—we might call these the 'democratic' conditions—of equal status for all citizens. When majoritarian institutions provide and respect the democratic conditions, then the verdicts of these institutions should be accepted by everyone for that reason. But when they do not, or when their provision or respect is defective, there can be no objection, in the name of democracy, to other procedures that protect and respect them better. The democratic conditions plainly include, for example, a requirement that public offices must in principle be open to members of all races and groups on equal terms. If some law provided that only members of one race were eligible for public office, then there would be no moral cost—no matter for moral regret at all—if a court that enjoyed the power to do so under a valid constitution struck down that law as unconstitutional."

––––––––––––

[15] Here Professor Choper is quoting Robert G. Dixon, Jr., *Democratic Representation: Reapportionment in Law and Politics* 10 (1968).

[59] **[Orig. Note]** Although no detailed examination of the legislative systems in the states and their political subdivisions has been ventured here, the same conclusion appears to have substantially similar merit in respect to the Court's overturning the laws they produce.

———

BARRY FRIEDMAN, *The Will of the People*, 370, 372, 380–81, 384–85 (2009): "The people and their elected representatives have had the ability all along to assert pressure on the judges, and they have done so on numerous occasions. The accountability of the justices (and thus the Constitution) to the popular will has been established time and time again. To the extent that the judges have had freedom to act, it has been because the American people have given it to them.

"[If] any worry seems legitimate, it is that the 'hope' of judicial review too often proves effervescent, that the justices kowtow to public opinion and pay insufficient heed to the traditional role of judicial review in protecting minority rights. [Take], for example, what might be the Court's greatest single failure (at least from this perspective) in all its history, the decisions in the Japanese internment cases. During World War II, more than one hundred thousand American citizens of Japanese descent (along with many other noncitizen Japanese) were herded from their homes on the West Coast and locked in detention camps in the middle of the country. There was virtually no evidence of a security risk; the stark racism behind the internment later became clear. [It] is difficult to understand *Korematsu* (Ch. 9, Sec. 2, II), the most prominent of the internment cases, as anything but stark capitulation to the decisions made by military and political authorities.

"[In] theory, [the] desire to separate law and politics is an admirable one. [Yet] the instinct to keep politics entirely separate from decisions about constitutional law is plainly impossible with regard to the Supreme Court. It simply is the case that the judiciary's capacity to give the Constitution meaning to protect minority rights always has been limited by popular support for those decisions. The *Dred Scott* justices believed they were protecting constitutional rights (Ch. 9, Sec. 2, I); ultimately that judgment fell to popular contrary opinion and American's bloodiest war. [The] justices in *Brown v. Board of Education* (Ch. 9, Sec. 2, II) argued they were protecting constitutional rights, but once again it was evolving national views that supported the Court's judgment and enabled its enforcement.

"[Perhaps] the central function of judicial review today is to serve as the catalyst for the people to take their Constitution seriously, to develop their constitutional sensibilities, in the hope that they will adhere to those sensibilities when the chips are down. [Ultimately], we have nothing but ourselves to fall back upon. But it is wrong to claim, as many have, that the judges have stolen the Constitution from us. Judicial review is our invention; we created it and have chosen to retain it. Judicial review has served as a means of forcing us to think about, and interpret, our

Constitution ourselves. In the final analysis, when it comes to the Constitution, we are the highest court in the land."

MARTIN V. HUNTER'S LESSEE
14 U.S. (1 Wheat.) 304, 4 L.Ed. 97 (1816).

[Lord Fairfax, a Virginia citizen, willed his Virginia land known as the Northern Neck of Virginia to his nephew, Martin, a British subject resident in England. In 1789, Virginia, acting pursuant to state laws confiscating lands owned by British subjects, granted land in the Northern Neck to Hunter. The latter brought an action of ejectment against Martin. The Virginia district court ruled for Martin, whose claim was fortified by the anti-confiscation clauses of the treaties of 1783 and 1794 with Great Britain. But the Virginia Court of Appeals reversed, holding that (1) the state's title to the Northern Neck had been perfected before any treaty and (2) in any event, a 1796 Act of Compromise between the Fairfax claimants and the state claimants, formally adopted by the Virginia legislature, had settled the matter against Martin.

[Acting for the purchasers of the Fairfax estate, John Marshall, then a member of the Virginia legislature, had negotiated the compromise. Since he and his brother had organized a syndicate which purchased 160,000 acres of Northern Neck from Martin in 1793, Marshall had a great interest in the case's outcome.

[In *Fairfax's Devisee v. Hunter's Lessee,* 11 U.S. (7 Cranch) 603, 3 L.Ed. 453 (1813), the Supreme Court (Marshall, C.J., not participating) reversed the Virginia Court of Appeals, ruling that Virginia had not perfected title to the Northern Neck prior to the grant to Hunter and that therefore the Treaty of 1794 confirmed the title remaining in Martin. Neither Story, J.'s majority opinion nor Johnson, J.'s dissent mentioned the Act of Compromise.

[The cause was remanded to the Virginia Court of Appeals with instructions to enter judgment for appellant, but that court refused to obey the Supreme Court's mandate. All four judges then sitting maintained that insofar as it extended the appellate jurisdiction of the Supreme Court to "this court," § 25 of the Judiciary Act was unconstitutional. Judge Roane— Marshall's arch political enemy—and Judge Fleming (the two judges sitting when the court had decided the case against Martin on the merits) contended further that even if the Judiciary Act were valid the case had not properly been before the Supreme Court because the Virginia decision turned not upon a treaty, but on a matter of state law, the Act of Compromise.

[The case again came to the Supreme Court, Marshall again not sitting.[16]]

STORY, J., delivered the opinion of the court. * * *

The third article of the constitution is that which must principally attract our attention. [A]ppellate jurisdiction is given by the constitution to the supreme court, in all cases [within "the judicial power of the United States"] where it has not original jurisdiction; subject, however, to such exceptions and regulations as congress may prescribe. [W]hat is there to restrain its exercise over state tribunals, in the enumerated cases? [If] the judicial power extends to the case, it will be in vain to search in the letter of the constitution for any qualification as to the tribunal where it depends. It [is] plain, that the framers of the constitution did contemplate that cases within the judicial cognisance of the United States, not only might, but would, arise in the state courts, in the exercise of their ordinary jurisdiction [pointing to the supremacy clause]. Suppose, an indictment for a crime, in a state court, and the defendant should allege in his defence, that the crime was created by an ex post facto act of the state, must not the state court [have] a right to pronounce on the validity and sufficiency of the defence? [It] was foreseen, that in the exercise of their ordinary jurisdiction, state courts would incidentally take cognisance of cases arising under the constitution, the laws and treaties of the United States. Yet, to all these cases, the judicial power, by the very terms of the constitution, is to extend. It cannot extend, by original jurisdiction, if that was already rightfully and exclusively attached in the state courts, which (as has been already shown) may occur; it must, therefore, extend by appellate jurisdiction, or not at all. It would seem to follow, that the appellate power of the United States must, in such cases, extend to state tribunals.

[It] has been argued, that such an appellate jurisdiction over state courts is inconsistent with the genius of our governments, and the spirit of the constitution. That the latter was never designed to act upon state sovereignties, but only upon the people, and that if the power exists it will materially impair the sovereignty of the states, and the independence of their courts. [But the Constitution] is crowded with provisions which restrain or annul the sovereignty of the states, in some of the highest branches of their prerogatives. The tenth section of the first article contains a long list of disabilities and prohibitions imposed upon the states. [The] language of the constitution is also imperative upon the states, as to the performance of many duties. It is imperative upon the state legislatures, to make laws prescribing the time, places and manner of holding elections for senators and representatives, and for electors of president and vice-president. And in these, as well as some other cases, congress have a right

---

[16] For further exploration of the historical background, see 4 Albert Beveridge, *The Life of John Marshall* 144–61 (1919); 2 William Crosskey, *Politics and the Constitution* 785–817 (1953); 1 Charles Warren, *The Supreme Court in United States History* 442–53 (1922).

to revise, amend or supersede the laws which may be passed by state legislatures. When, therefore, the states are stripped of some of the highest attributes of sovereignty, and the same are given to the United States; when the legislatures of the states are, in some respects, under the control of congress, and in every case are, under the constitution, bound by the paramount authority of the United States; it is certainly difficult to support the argument, that the appellate power over the decisions of state courts is contrary to the genius of our institutions. The courts of the United States can, without question, revise the proceedings of the executive and legislative authorities of the states, and if they are found to be contrary to the constitution, may declare them to be of no legal validity. Surely, the exercise of the same right over judicial tribunals is not a higher or more dangerous act of sovereign power.

Nor can such a right be deemed to impair the independence of state judges. It is assuming the very ground in controversy, to assert that they possess an absolute independence of the United States. In respect to the powers granted to the United States, they are not independent; they are expressly bound to obedience, by the letter of the constitution.

[The] argument urged from the possibility of the abuse of the revising power, is equally unsatisfactory. [From] the very nature of things, the absolute right of decision, in the last resort, must rest somewhere— wherever it may be vested, it is susceptible of abuse. [A]dmitting that the judges of the state courts are, and always will be, of as much learning, integrity and wisdom, as those of the courts of the United States (which we very cheerfully admit), it does not aid the argument. It is manifest, that the constitution has proceeded upon a theory of its own, and given or withheld powers according to the judgment of the American people, by whom it was adopted. We can only construe its powers, and cannot inquire into the policy or principles which induced the grant of them. The constitution has presumed (whether rightly or wrongly, we do not inquire), that state attachments, state prejudices, state jealousies, and state interests, might sometimes obstruct, or control, or be supposed to obstruct or control, the regular administration of justice.

[This] is not all. A motive of another kind, perfectly compatible with the most sincere respect for state tribunals, might induce the grant of appellate power over their decisions. That motive is the importance, and even necessity of *uniformity* of decisions throughout the whole United States, upon all subjects within the purview of the constitution. Judges of equal learning and integrity, in different states, might differently interpret the statute, or a treaty of the United States, or even the constitution itself: if there were no revising authority to control these jarring and discordant judgments, and harmonize them into uniformity, the laws, the treaties and the constitution of the United States would be different, in different states, and might, perhaps, never have precisely the same construction, obligation or efficiency, in any two states. The public mischiefs that would attend such a state of things would be truly deplorable.

[On] the whole, the court are of opinion, that the appellate power of the United States does extend to cases pending in the state courts; and that the 25th section of the judiciary act, which authorizes the exercise of this jurisdiction in the specified cases, by a writ of error, is supported by the letter and spirit of the constitution. [It] is an historical fact, that this exposition of the constitution, extending its appellate power to state courts, was, previous to its adoption, uniformly and publicly avowed by its friends, and admitted by its enemies, as the basis of their respective reasonings, both in and out of the state conventions. It is an historical fact, that at the time when the judiciary act was submitted to the deliberations of the first congress, composed, as it was not only of men of great learning and ability, but of men who acted a principal part in framing, supporting or opposing that constitution, the same exposition was explicitly declared and admitted by the friends and by the opponents of that system. It is an historical fact, that the supreme court of the United States have, from time to time, sustained this appellate jurisdiction, in a great variety of cases, brought from the tribunals of many of the most important states in the Union,[17] and that no state tribunal has ever breathed a judicial doubt on the subject or declined to obey the mandate of the supreme court, until the present occasion.

[The Court next rejected the contention that the case was not properly before it because the Virginia decision turned on the Act of Compromise.]

We have not thought it incumbent on us to give any opinion upon the question, whether this court have authority to issue a writ of mandamus to the court of appeals, to enforce the former judgments, as we did not think it necessarily involved in the decision of this cause.

It is the opinion of the whole court, that the judgment of the court of appeals of Virginia, rendered on the mandate in this cause, be reversed, and the judgment of the district court [be] affirmed.

JOHNSON, J. It will be observed, in this case, that the court disavows all intention to decide on the right to issue compulsory process to the state courts; thus leaving us, in my opinion, where the constitution and laws place us—supreme over persons and cases, so far as our judicial powers extend, but not asserting any compulsory control over the state tribunals. In this view, I acquiesce in their opinion, but not altogether in the reasoning or opinion of my brother who delivered it. * * *

---

[17] See, e.g., *Clerke v. Harwood,* 3 U.S. (3 Dall.) 342 (1797) (state law in conflict with treaty). The first Supreme Court decision holding a state law unconstitutional was *Fletcher v. Peck,* Ch. 5, 1, I, (1810) but the case arose in a lower federal court.

NOTES AND QUESTIONS

1. *Uniformity.* Consider Oliver Wendell Holmes, Jr., Law and the Court, *Collected Legal Papers* 291, 295–96 (1920): "I do not think the United States would come to an end if we lost our power to declare an Act of Congress void. I do think the Union would be imperiled if we could not make that declaration as to the laws of the several states." If understood to mean that courts in a federal system need the power of judicial review of state legislation in order to maintain the uniformity of federal law, Holmes was wrong. "The Swiss constitution is a perfect example of a federal system without the judiciary having such power." Cohen, supra, at 185. But Holmes was not talking about constitutions in general. Although the U.S. Constitution might have granted Congress a general power to void state laws on constitutional or other grounds, the 1787 Convention rejected just such a proposal, instead granting Congress power to legislate on specific subjects. To be sure, some constitutional limits on the states—such as those contained in the Thirteenth, Fourteenth, and Fifteenth Amendments—expressly authorize congressional enforcement, but might these provisions carry the negative implication that that Congress lacks the power to enforce other provisions of the Constitution against the states? If the Court had held that it lacked the general power to declare state laws invalid, would Congress have been justified in assuming such a power for itself?

2. COHENS v. VIRGINIA, 19 U.S. (6 Wheat.) 264 (1821)—which sustained the Court's appellate jurisdiction under § 25 of the Judiciary Act to review state criminal proceedings, and is generally viewed as reaffirming and "supplementing" *Martin,* see 2 Warren, supra, at 10—has stronger historical links with *McCulloch v. Maryland* (Ch. 2, Sec. 1), see 4 Beveridge, *The Life of John Marshall* 343 (1919).

Appellants were found guilty in a Virginia court of selling lottery tickets in violation of state law. Their defense was that the lottery was organized by the City of Washington, under a congressional statute authorizing the lottery. On appeal to the Supreme Court, they were met with the contentions that the Court had no jurisdiction to review a state criminal case and, in any event, Congress had no power to permit the sale of lottery tickets in a state which prohibited such sale. On the jurisdictional point, Virginia argued that: (1) if when the state is a party the Supreme Court has original jurisdiction, this grant excludes appellate jurisdiction; (2) federal courts cannot take original jurisdiction over criminal cases, because that rightfully belongs to the courts of the state whose laws have been violated; and (3) consequently, the Supreme Court has no jurisdiction at all. As in *Marbury,* MARSHALL, C.J., used the occasion to express a broad view of the Court's powers, but decided the case on a narrow ground in favor of the Jeffersonians—the federal statute authorizing a lottery had no effect outside the City of Washington.

2. POLITICAL QUESTIONS

Does the principle of judicial review comprehend the Court's acting as "final arbiter" on *all* constitutional questions presented by a case properly within its jurisdiction? Or are some constitutional issues inappropriate for judicial resolution and thus nonjusticiable "political questions"? The Supreme Court has answered the former question in the negative and the latter in the affirmative, but its decisions have left a good deal of uncertainty and debate about when the political question doctrine does, and should, apply.

NIXON V. UNITED STATES
506 U.S. 224, 113 S.Ct. 732, 122 L.Ed.2d 1 (1993).

CHIEF JUSTICE REHNQUIST delivered the opinion of the Court.

Petitioner Walter L. Nixon, Jr., [a] former Chief Judge of the United States District Court for the Southern District of Mississippi, was convicted by a jury of two counts of making false statements before a federal grand jury and sentenced to prison. The grand jury investigation stemmed from reports that Nixon had accepted a gratuity from a Mississippi businessman in exchange for asking a local district attorney to halt the prosecution of the businessman's son. Because Nixon refused to resign from his office as a United States District Judge, he continued to collect his judicial salary while serving out his prison sentence.

On May 10, 1989, the House of Representatives adopted three articles of impeachment for high crimes and misdemeanors. The first two articles charged Nixon with giving false testimony before the grand jury and the third article charged him with bringing disrepute on the Federal Judiciary.

After the House presented the articles to the Senate, the Senate voted to invoke its own Impeachment Rule XI, under which the presiding officer appoints a committee of Senators to "receive evidence and take testimony." The Senate committee held four days of hearings, during which 10 witnesses, including Nixon, testified. Pursuant to Rule XI, the committee presented the full Senate with a complete transcript of the proceeding and a report stating the uncontested facts and summarizing the evidence on the contested facts. Nixon and the House impeachment managers submitted extensive final briefs to the full Senate and delivered arguments from the Senate floor during the three hours set aside for oral argument in front of that body. Nixon himself gave a personal appeal, and several Senators posed questions directly to both parties. The Senate voted by more than the constitutionally required two-thirds majority to convict Nixon on the first two articles. The presiding officer then entered judgment removing Nixon from his office as United States District Judge.

Nixon thereafter commenced the present suit, arguing that Senate Rule XI violates the constitutional grant of authority to the Senate to "try" all impeachments because it prohibits the whole Senate from taking part in the evidentiary hearings. [The] District Court held that his claim was nonjusticiable and the Court of Appeals for the District of Columbia Circuit agreed.

A controversy is nonjusticiable—i.e., involves a political question—where there is "a textually demonstrable constitutional commitment of the issue to a coordinate political department; or a lack of judicially discoverable and manageable standards for resolving it." *Baker v. Carr,* 369 U.S. 186, 217 (1962). [The] lack of judicially manageable standards may strengthen the conclusion that there is a textually demonstrable commitment to a coordinate branch.

In this case, we must examine Art. I, § 3, cl. 6, to determine the scope of authority conferred upon the Senate by the Framers regarding impeachment. It provides: "The Senate shall have the sole Power to try all Impeachments. When sitting for that Purpose, they shall be on Oath or Affirmation. When the President of the United States is tried, the Chief Justice shall preside: And no Person shall be convicted without the Concurrence of two thirds of the Members present." * * *

Petitioner argues that the word "try" in the first sentence imposes by implication an additional requirement on the Senate in that the proceedings must be in the nature of a judicial trial. From there petitioner goes on to argue that this limitation precludes the Senate from delegating to a select committee the task of hearing the testimony of witnesses * * * .

There are several difficulties with this position which lead us ultimately to reject it. The word "try," both in 1787 and later, has considerably broader meanings than those to which petitioner would limit it. [Thus], we cannot say that the Framers used the word "try" as an implied limitation on the method by which the Senate might proceed in trying impeachments. * * *

The conclusion that the use of the word "try" in the first sentence of the Impeachment Trial Clause lacks sufficient precision to afford any judicially manageable standard of review of the Senate's actions is fortified by the existence of the three very specific requirements that the Constitution does impose on the Senate when trying impeachments: the members must be under oath, a two-thirds vote is required to convict, and the Chief Justice presides when the President is tried. These limitations are quite precise, and their nature suggests that the Framers did not intend to impose additional limitations on the form of the Senate proceedings by the use of the word "try" in the first sentence.

Petitioner devotes only two pages in his brief to negating the significance of the word "sole" in the first sentence of Clause 6. [We] think that the word "sole" is of considerable significance. Indeed, the word "sole" appears only one other time in the Constitution—with respect to the House of Representatives' "*sole* Power of Impeachment." Art. I, § 2, cl. 5 (emphasis added). The common sense meaning of the word "sole" is that the Senate alone shall have authority to determine whether an individual should be acquitted or convicted. The dictionary definition bears this out. "Sole" is defined as "having no companion," "solitary," "being the only one," and "functioning . . . independently and without assistance or interference." If the courts may review the actions of the Senate in order to determine whether that body "tried" an impeached official, it is difficult to see how the Senate would be "functioning . . . independently and without assistance or interference."

Nixon [argues] that even if significance be attributed to the word "sole" in the first sentence of the clause, the authority granted is to the Senate, and this means that "the Senate—not the courts, not a lay jury, not a Senate Committee—shall try impeachments." Brief for Petitioner 42. It would be possible to read the first sentence of the Clause this way, but it is not a natural reading. Petitioner's interpretation would bring into judicial purview not merely the sort of claim made by petitioner, but other similar claims based on the conclusion that the word "Senate" has imposed by implication limitations on procedures which the Senate might adopt. Such limitations would be inconsistent with the construction of the Clause as a whole, which, as we have noted, sets out three express limitations in separate sentences.

The history and contemporary understanding of the impeachment provisions support our reading of the constitutional language. The parties do not offer evidence of a single word in the history of the Constitutional Convention or in contemporary commentary that even alludes to the possibility of judicial review in the context of the impeachment powers. This silence is quite meaningful in light of the several explicit references to the availability of judicial review as a check on the Legislature's power with respect to bills of attainder, ex post facto laws, and statutes. See *The Federalist* No. 78.

The Framers labored over the question of where the impeachment power should lie. Significantly, in at least two considered scenarios the power was placed with the Federal Judiciary. [See] *The Federalist* No. 65. The Supreme Court was not the proper body because the Framers "doubted whether [it] would possess the degree of credit and authority" to carry out its judgment if it conflicted with the accusation brought by the Legislature—the people's representative. In addition, the Framers believed the Court was too small in number: "The awful discretion, which a court of impeachments must necessarily have, to doom to honor or to infamy the most confidential and the most distinguished characters of the community, forbids the commitment of the trust to a small number of persons." Id.

There are two additional reasons why the Judiciary, and the Supreme Court in particular, were not chosen to have any role in impeachments. First, the Framers recognized that most likely there would be two sets of proceedings for individuals who commit impeachable offenses—the impeachment trial and a separate criminal trial. In fact, the Constitution explicitly provides for two separate proceedings. See Art. I, § 3, cl. 7. The Framers deliberately separated the two forums to avoid raising the specter of bias and to ensure independent judgments. [Certainly] judicial review of the Senate's "trial" would introduce the same risk of bias as would participation in the trial itself.

Second, judicial review would be inconsistent with the Framers' insistence that our system be one of checks and balances. In our constitutional system, impeachment was designed to be the *only* check on the Judicial Branch by the Legislature. * * * Judicial involvement in impeachment proceedings, even if only for purposes of judicial review, is counterintuitive because it would eviscerate the "important constitutional check" placed on the Judiciary by the Framers. * * *

Nevertheless, Nixon argues [that] if the Senate is given unreviewable authority to interpret the Impeachment Trial Clause, there is a grave risk that the Senate will usurp judicial power. The Framers anticipated this objection and created two constitutional safeguards to keep the Senate in check. The first safeguard is that the whole of the impeachment power is divided between the two legislative bodies [which] "avoids the inconvenience of making the same persons both accusers and judges; and guards against the danger of persecution from the prevalency of a factious spirit in either of those branches." The second safeguard is the two-thirds supermajority vote requirement. * * *

In addition to the textual commitment argument, we are persuaded that the lack of finality and the difficulty of fashioning relief counsel against justiciability. See *Baker*. We agree with the Court of Appeals that opening the door of judicial review to the procedures used by the Senate in trying impeachments would "expose the political life of the country to months, or perhaps years, of chaos." This lack of finality would manifest itself most dramatically if the President were impeached. The legitimacy of any successor, and hence his effectiveness, would be impaired severely, not merely while the judicial process was running its course, but during any retrial that a differently constituted Senate might conduct if its first judgment of conviction were invalidated. Equally uncertain is the question of what relief a court may give other than simply setting aside the judgment of conviction. Could it order the reinstatement of a convicted federal judge, or order Congress to create an additional judgeship if the seat had been filled in the interim?

Petitioner finally contends that a holding of nonjusticiability cannot be reconciled with our opinion in *Powell v. McCormack,* 395 U.S. 486 (1969). The relevant issue in *Powell* was whether courts could review the House of Representatives' conclusion that Powell was "unqualified" to sit as a Member because he had been accused of misappropriating public funds and abusing the process of the New York courts. We stated that the question of justiciability turned on whether the Constitution committed authority to the House to judge its members' qualifications, and if so, the extent of that commitment. Article I, § 5 provides that "Each House shall be the Judge of the Elections, Returns and Qualifications of its own Members." In turn, Art. I, § 2 specifies three requirements for membership in the House: The candidate must be at least 25 years of age, a citizen of the United States for no less than seven years, and an inhabitant of the State he is chosen to represent. We held that, in light of the three requirements specified in the Constitution, the word "qualifications"—of which the House was to be the Judge—was of a precise, limited nature. [The] claim by the House that its power to "be the Judge of the Elections, Returns and Qualifications of its own Members" was a textual commitment of unreviewable authority was defeated by the existence of this separate provision specifying the only qualifications which might be imposed for House membership. The decision as to whether a member satisfied these qualifications was placed with the House, but the decision as to what these qualifications consisted of was not.

In the case before us, there is no separate provision of the Constitution which could be defeated by allowing the Senate final authority to determine the meaning of the word "try" in the Impeachment Trial Clause. We agree with Nixon that courts possess power to review either legislative or executive action that transgresses identifiable textual limits. [But] we conclude, after exercising that delicate responsibility, that the word "try" in the Impeachment Clause does not provide an identifiable textual limit on the authority which is committed to the Senate.

Affirmed.

JUSTICE STEVENS, concurring.

[Respect] for a coordinate Branch of the Government forecloses any assumption that improbable hypotheticals like those mentioned by Justice White and Justice Souter will ever occur. * * *

JUSTICE WHITE, with whom JUSTICE BLACKMUN joins, concurring in the judgment.

[The] Court is of the view that the Constitution forbids us even to consider [petitioner's constitutional] contention. I find no such prohibition and would therefore reach the merits of the claim. I concur in the judgment because the Senate fulfilled its constitutional obligation to "try" petitioner.

I.   It should be said at the outset that, as a practical matter, it will likely make little difference whether the Court's or my view controls this case. This is so because the Senate has very wide discretion in specifying impeachment trial procedures and because it is extremely unlikely that the Senate would abuse its discretion and insist on a procedure that could not be deemed a trial by reasonable judges. Even taking a wholly practical approach, I would prefer not to announce an unreviewable discretion in the Senate to ignore completely the constitutional direction to "try" impeachment cases. When asked at oral argument whether that direction would be satisfied if, after a House vote to impeach, the Senate, without any procedure whatsoever, unanimously found the accused guilty of being "a bad guy," counsel for the United States answered that the Government's theory "leads me to answer that question yes." Especially in light of this advice from the Solicitor General, I would not issue an invitation to the Senate to find an excuse, in the name of other pressing business, to be dismissive of its critical role in the impeachment process.

Practicalities aside, however, since the meaning of a constitutional provision is at issue, my disagreement with the Court should be stated.

II.   [T]he issue in the political question doctrine is not whether the Constitutional text commits exclusive responsibility for a particular governmental function to one of the political branches. There are numerous instances of this sort of textual commitment, e.g., Art. I, § 8 [enumerating congressional powers], and it is not thought that disputes implicating these provisions are nonjusticiable. Rather, the issue is whether the Constitution has given one of the political branches final responsibility for interpreting the scope and nature of such a power.

[T]here are few, if any, explicit and unequivocal instances in the Constitution of this sort of textual commitment. [In] drawing the inference that the Constitution has committed final interpretive authority to one of the political branches, courts are sometimes aided by textual evidence that the judiciary was not meant to exercise judicial review—a coordinate inquiry expressed in *Baker's* "lack of judicially discoverable and manageable standards" criterion. See, e.g., *Coleman v. Miller,* 307 U.S. 433, 452–454 (1939), where the Court refused to determine the life span of a proposed constitutional amendment given Art. V's placement of the amendment process with Congress and the lack of any judicial standard for resolving the question.

A.   [That] the word "sole" is found only in the House and Senate Impeachment Clauses demonstrates that its purpose is to emphasize the distinct role of each in the impeachment process. As the majority notes, the Framers, following English practice, were very much concerned to separate the prosecutorial from the adjudicative aspects of impeachment. Giving each House "sole" power with respect to its role in impeachments effected this division of labor. While the majority is thus right to interpret the term "sole" to indicate that the Senate ought to " 'function independently and without assistance or interference,' " it wrongly identifies the judiciary, rather than the House, as the source of potential interference with which the Framers were concerned when they employed the term "sole."

Even if the Impeachment Trial Clause is read without regard to its companion clause, the Court's willingness to abandon its obligation to review the constitutionality of legislative acts merely on the strength of the word "sole" is perplexing. Consider, by comparison, the treatment of Art. I, § 1, which grants "All legislative powers" to the House and Senate. As used in that context "all" is nearly synonymous with "sole"—both connote entire and exclusive authority. Yet the Court has never thought it would unduly interfere with the operation of the Legislative Branch to entertain difficult and important questions as to the extent of the legislative power. * * *

The historical evidence reveals above all else that the Framers were deeply concerned about placing in any branch the "awful discretion, which a court of impeachments must necessarily have." *The Federalist* No. 65. Viewed against this history, the discord between the majority's position and the basic principles of checks and balances underlying the Constitution's separation of powers is clear. In essence, the majority suggests that the Framers conferred upon Congress a potential tool of legislative dominance yet at the same time rendered Congress' exercise of that power one of the very few areas of legislative authority immune from any judicial review. [In] a truly balanced system, impeachments tried by the Senate would serve as a means of controlling the largely unaccountable judiciary, even as judicial review would ensure that the Senate adhered to a minimal set of procedural standards in conducting impeachment trials.

B.   [The] majority finds this case different from *Powell* only on the grounds that, whereas the qualifications of Art. I, § 2 are readily susceptible to judicial interpretation, the term "try" does not provide an "identifiable textual limit on the authority which is committed to the Senate." [Yet the] term "try" is hardly so elusive as the majority would have it. Were the Senate, for example, to adopt the practice of automatically entering a judgment of conviction whenever articles of impeachment were delivered from the House, it is quite clear that the Senate will have failed to "try" impeachments. Indeed in this respect, "try" presents no greater, and perhaps fewer, interpretive difficulties than some other constitutional standards that have been found amenable to familiar techniques of judicial construction, including, for example, "Commerce . . . among the several States," Art. I, § 8, cl. 3, and "due process of law." Amdt. 5.[3]

---

[3]   **[Ct's Note]** The majority's in terrorem argument against justiciability—that judicial review of impeachments might cause national disruption and that the courts would be unable to fashion effective relief—merits only brief attention. In the typical instance, court review of impeachments would no more render the political system dysfunctional than has this litigation.

III. [T]extual and historical evidence reveals that the Impeachment Trial Clause was not meant to bind the hands of the Senate beyond establishing a set of minimal procedures. Without identifying the exact contours of these procedures, it is sufficient to say that the Senate's use of a factfinding committee under Rule XI is entirely compatible with the Constitution's command that the Senate "try all impeachments." * * *

JUSTICE SOUTER, concurring in the judgment.

[As] we cautioned in *Baker,* "the 'political question' label" tends "to obscure the need for case-by-case inquiry." The need for such close examination is nevertheless clear from our precedents, which demonstrate that the functional nature of the political question doctrine requires analysis of "the precise facts and posture of the particular case," and precludes "resolution by any semantic cataloguing."

[Whatever] considerations feature most prominently in a particular case, the political question doctrine is "essentially a function of the separation of powers," ibid., existing to restrain courts "from inappropriate interference in the business of the other branches of [the Federal] Government," and deriving in large part from prudential concerns about the respect we owe the political departments. Not all interference is inappropriate or disrespectful, however, and application of the doctrine ultimately turns, as Learned Hand put it, on "how importunately the occasion demands an answer." Learned Hand, *The Bill of Rights* 15 (1958).

This occasion does not demand an answer. The Impeachment Trial Clause [contemplates] that the Senate may determine, within broad boundaries, such subsidiary issues as the procedures for receipt and consideration of evidence necessary to satisfy its duty to "try" impeachments. Other significant considerations confirm a conclusion that this case presents a nonjusticiable political question: the "unusual need for unquestioning adherence to a political decision already made," as well as "the potentiality of embarrassment from multifarious pronouncements by various departments on one question." * * *

One can, nevertheless, envision different and unusual circumstances that might justify a more searching review of impeachment proceedings. If the Senate were to act in a manner seriously threatening the integrity of its results, convicting, say, upon a coin-toss, or upon a summary determination that an officer of the United States was simply "a bad guy,"

Moreover, the same capacity for disruption was noted and rejected as a basis for not hearing *Powell.* The relief granted for unconstitutional impeachment trials would presumably be similar to the relief granted to other unfairly tried public employee-litigants. Finally, as applied to the special case of the President, the majority's argument merely points out that, were the Senate to convict the President without any kind of a trial, a constitutional crisis might well result. It hardly follows that the Court ought to refrain from upholding the Constitution in all impeachment cases. Nor does it follow that, in cases of Presidential impeachment, the Justices ought to abandon their constitutional responsibilities because the Senate has precipitated a crisis.

judicial interference might well be appropriate. In such circumstances, the Senate's action might be so far beyond the scope of its constitutional authority, and the consequent impact on the Republic so great, as to merit a judicial response despite the prudential concerns that would ordinarily counsel silence. "The political question doctrine, a tool for maintenance of governmental order, will not be so applied as to promote only disorder." *Baker.*

NOTES AND QUESTIONS

1.   *Political questions and the judicial function.* Is the Court's decision in *Nixon*—that the constitutional lawfulness of the procedures used in an impeachment trial is a nonjusticiable political question—consistent with *Marbury v. Madison* and its central holding that "[i]t is emphatically the province and duty of the judicial department to say what the law is"? Distinguished commentators have given a broad range of answers to this and related questions about the political question doctrine. (Recall that Marshall, C.J., contemplated that "in cases in which the executive possesses a constitutional or legal discretion," the lawfulness of implementing acts would be "only politically examinable.")

(a)   Consider Herbert Wechsler, *Principles, Politics, and Fundamental Law* 11–14 (1961): "[All the political question] doctrine can defensibly imply is that the courts are called upon to judge whether the Constitution has committed to another agency of government the autonomous determination of the issue raised, a finding that itself requires an interpretation. [T]he only proper judgment that may lead to an abstention from decision is that the Constitution has committed the determination of the issue to another agency of government than the courts. Difficult as it may be to make that judgment wisely, [what] is involved is in itself an act of constitutional interpretation, to be made and judged by standards that should govern the interpretive process generally. [That is totally] different from a broad discretion to abstain or intervene."

(b)   Martin H. Redish, *Judicial Review and the "Political Question,"* 79 Nw.U.L.Rev. 1031 (1984), argues that the political question doctrine is irreconcilable with the judicial function as understood since *Marbury* and should therefore be abandoned: "By its nature, the Constitution imposes supermajoritarian limitations on the federal government [primarily] to insure, through a complex system of checks and balances, the maintenance of liberty and the avoidance of tyranny. If the federal government or one of its branches is permitted to breach these boundaries, immune from judicial review, we are effectively left with a lawless government, a result harmful to society, both in itself and for the message it communicates to its citizens."

(c)   Louis Henkin, *Is There a Political Question Doctrine?*, 85 Yale L.J. 597 (1976), maintains that the political question doctrine is "an unnecessary, deceptive packaging of several established doctrines," each of which would better be identified separately and none of which excuses the Court from the obligation of interpreting the Constitution. According to Henkin, one of these doctrines requires the courts to "accept decisions by the political branches within their constitutional authority" (as Marshall, C.J., recognized in *Marbury*), and another recognizes the ability of the courts to "refuse some (or all) remedies for want of equity" under doctrines investing courts with equitable discretion. The Court does a disservice, Henkin argues, by misleadingly implying that there is an additional, extraordinary doctrine calling for it to turn a blind eye to constitutional violations that would otherwise be judicially remediable.

(d) Compare Michael J. Gerhardt, *Rediscovering Nonjusticiability: Judicial Review of Impeachments After* Nixon, 44 Duke L.J. 231 (1994): "[A] finding of nonjusticiability [is] different from a court's deciding that a wide realm of governmental behavior is constitutional in that a determination of nonjusticiability forecloses a range of potential litigation and signals once and for all that there is no judicial remedy available for any official misconduct within a certain area."

2. *"Textually demonstrable constitutional commitment."* (a) **Impeachment.** Is the *Nixon* Court persuasive in maintaining that the constitutional text gives the Senate exclusive power to determine the requisites of impeachment trials? Would (should) the Court decline review if an impeached federal judge credibly claimed that the Senate's conviction was by less than a ⅔ vote? If a federal judge sought judicial review of an impeachment and conviction alleging denial of the right to counsel or discrimination based on race or political affiliation? Consider Redish, supra: "I fail to understand a logic that suggests that an appeal to the Due Process Clause of either the Fifth or Fourteenth Amendments can be precluded by a constitutional provision's vesting of power in one of the political branches of government. If the particular exercise of power violates the Due Process Clause, then the fact that a provision in the body of the Constitution authorizes the practice is wholly irrelevant. [It] may well be subject to control through protections contained in the constitutional amendments."[18]

Consider also Raoul Berger, *Impeachment: The Constitutional Problems* 117–20 (1973): "Although impeachment was chiefly designed to check Executive abuses and oppressions, there was no thought of delivering either the President or the Judiciary to the unbounded discretion of Congress. This is attested by the Framers' rejection of the unfettered removal by Address [formal request of Congress], by their rejection of 'maladministration' because that was 'so vague' as to [amount to] tenure 'at the pleasure' of the Senate, and by the substitution of 'high crimes and misdemeanors' with knowledge that it had a 'limited' and 'technical meaning.'"

---

[18] Compare Rebecca L. Brown, *When Political Questions Affect Individual Rights: The Other* Nixon v. United States, 1993 Sup.Ct.Rev. 125 (arguing that, despite broader formulations, the Court "persists in applying the [political question] doctrine in such a way as, most of the time, to do the least violence to [constitutional] rights").

Compare Charles L. Black, Jr., *Impeachment: A Handbook* 61–62 (1974): "If the Supreme Court [were] to order reinstatement of an impeached and convicted president, there would be [a] very grave and quite legitimate doubt whether that decree had any title to being obeyed, or whether it was [as] widely outside judicial jurisdiction as would be a judicial order to Congress to increase the penalty for counterfeiting. To cite the most frightening consequence, our military commanders would have to decide for themselves which president they were bound to obey. [It] would be most unfortunate if the notion got about that the Senate's verdict was somewhat tentative."

(b) ***Amending process.*** COLEMAN v. MILLER, supra, held that the questions whether a state could ratify a constitutional amendment that it had previously rejected and whether a proposed amendment lapses if not ratified within a reasonable time were nonjusticiable political questions. But there was no majority opinion. Concurring, Black, J., joined by Roberts, Frankfurter, and Douglas, JJ., stated that Art. V grants Congress "exclusive power over the amending process" and that Congress "is under no duty to accept the pronouncements upon that exclusive power by this Court." Does the language of Art. V support Black, J.? What if Congress submitted a proposed constitutional amendment to the states and provided that no African-American could participate in the state ratification process? Is it relevant to the question of justiciability that constitutional amendment, like impeachment, is a constitutionally mandated check on judicial power? See Laurence H. Tribe, *A Constitution We Are Amending: In Defense of a Restrained Judicial Role,* 97 Harv.L.Rev. 433 (1983).

(c) ***Regulating the militia.*** In GILLIGAN v. MORGAN, 413 U.S. 1 (1973), students at Kent State University sought relief against government officials to prevent the repetition of events that had included the shooting of a number of students by National Guard members on that campus in May 1970. The court of appeals instructed the federal district court to evaluate the "pattern of training, weaponry and orders in the Ohio National Guard" so as to determine whether it made "inevitable the use of fatal force in suppressing civilian disorders." The Court, per BURGER, C.J., reversed, relying heavily on Art. I, § 8, cl. 16—which grants to Congress "the responsibility for organizing, arming and disciplining the Militia (now the National Guard), with certain responsibilities being reserved to the respective States"—and on federal legislation enacted pursuant thereto: "[T]he nature of the questions to be resolved on remand are subjects committed expressly to the political branches of government. [It] would be difficult to think of a clearer example of the type of governmental action that was intended by the Constitution to be left to the political branches [or] of an area of governmental activity in which the courts have less competence. The complex, subtle, and professional decisions as to the composition, training, equipping, and control of a military force are essentially professional military judgments, subject *always* to civilian control of the Legislative and Executive Branches [which] are periodically subject to electoral accountability."

BLACKMUN, J., joined by Powell, J., concurred: "This case relates to prospective relief in the form of judicial surveillance of highly subjective and technical matters involving military training and command. As such, it presents an '[inappropriate] subject matter for judicial consideration,' for respondents are asking the District Court, in fashioning that prospective relief, 'to enter upon policy determinations for which judicially manageable standards are lacking.' *Baker.* [On] the understanding that this is what the Court's opinion holds, I join that opinion."

Absent the difficulty in crafting and enforcing an injunction, would a suit alleging misconduct by the militia necessarily present a nonjusticiable political question? Cf. *Scheuer v. Rhodes*, 416 U.S. 232 (1974) (holding that *Gilligan* did not bar a damages action by estates of students killed at Kent State).[19]

3. *"Judicially manageable standards."* In VIETH v. JUBELIRER, 541 U.S. 267 (2004), SCALIA, J., concluded for a four-Justice plurality that no judicially manageable standards exist to determine when partisan political gerrymanders of voting districts violate the Constitution. The plurality opinion appeared to accept that partisan gerrymanders would violate the Constitution if they went "too far" in deliberately advantaging the candidates of one party and disadvantaging those of another, but maintained that the courts lack sufficiently clear standards, rooted in the Constitution, for determining when partisan scheming exceeds constitutional bounds: "The issue we have discussed is not whether severe partisan gerrymanders violate the Constitution, but whether it is for the courts to say when a violation has occurred, and to design a remedy."

KENNEDY, J., concurred in the judgment dismissing the plaintiffs' complaint. He agreed with the plurality that no constitutionally adequate and judicially manageable standard for identifying forbidden partisan gerrymanders "has emerged in this case," but he declined to pronounce partisan gerrymandering claims categorically non-justiciable, based on the possibility that an administrable standard might emerge in the future. In separate dissenting opinions, Stevens, J., Souter, J. (joined by Ginsburg, J.), and Breyer, J., all disagreed about the absence of judicially manageable standards and indeed identified the (diverse) standards that they would apply.[20]

Consider Richard H. Fallon, Jr., *Judicially Manageable Standards and Constitutional Meaning*, 119 Harv.L.Rev. 1274 (2006): "[A]ll of the Justices [in

---

[19] Curtis A. Bradley & Trevor W. Morrison, *Historical Gloss and the Separation of Powers*, 126 Harv.L.Rev. 411 (2012), argue judicial findings of "a textually demonstrable constitutional commitment of [an] issue to a coordinate political department" often reflect an assessment of historical practice.

[20] The Court again divided about whether there are manageable standards that would permit courts to adjudicate when political gerrymanders violate the Equal Protection Clause, and if so about whether any such standard has yet been identified, in *League of United Latin American Citizens v. Perry*, 548 U.S. 399 (2006). In an opinion in which he sometimes spoke for shifting majorities and sometimes only for himself, Kennedy, J., declined to "revisit the justiciability holding" of *Vieth* and determined that the plaintiffs had failed to identify any judicially manageable standard under which their claim could succeed.

Vieth] recognized at least a potential distinction between constitutional norms and the judicial tests through which constitutional norms are enforced. With respect to the former, the Justices unanimously assumed that the Equal Protection Clause forbids partisan gerrymanders that excessively disadvantage a political party, but they also agreed that the existence of a prohibitory norm did not suffice to make partisan gerrymandering claims justiciable. [The] need for judicially manageable standards that are distinct from an underlying constitutional norm arises when the norm itself fails the requirement of judicial manageability. [In] cases in which constitutional norms are not themselves judicially manageable standards, courts properly seek to devise such standards. [Strikingly,] Justice Scalia's plurality opinion mounted no criticism of the dissenting Justices' assumption that it was the role of judges, when possible, to devise workable standards to implement constitutional norms. Instead, Justice Scalia argued that the dissenters had [not] succeeded in fashioning standards that deserved to count as judicially manageable."

When the Justices cannot identify a judicially manageable standard to implement a constitutional norm, should the failure be ascribed to the Constitution or to the Court? Consider Redish, supra: "Ultimately, *any* constitutional provision can be supplied with working standards of interpretation. To be sure, those standards often will not clearly flow from either the language or history of the provision, but that fact does not distinguish them from many judicial standards invoked every day." If Professor Redish is correct, the principal division in *Vieth* was not just about judicially manageable standards, but about whether standards existed that were *both* judicially manageable and otherwise constitutionally appropriate. As Scalia, J., put it: "This Court may not willy-nilly apply standards—even manageable standards—having no relation to constitutional harms."

But how determinate does a standard need to be to count as judicially manageable, and how close does the fit need to be between a manageable standard and the Constitution's meaning? Consider Fallon, supra: "[T]hese questions have no transsubstantive answer. [Scalia, J.] hinted as much [when] he said that although 'courts might be justified in accepting a modest degree of unmanageability to enforce a constitutional command which (like the Fourteenth Amendment obligation to refrain from race discrimination) is clear,' comparable degrees of 'unmanageability' would not be acceptable in enforcing other constitutional norms. [The requisite inquiry] seems perhaps no better defined than the question whether, all things considered, the costs of permitting adjudication under a particular proposed standard outweigh the benefits." Do you agree? In support of this conclusion, Professor Fallon quotes the following language from Scalia, J.'s, opinion in *Vieth*: "Is the regular insertion of the judiciary into districting, with the delay and uncertainty that it brings to the political process and the partisan [enmity] that it brings upon the courts, worth the benefit to be achieved—an accelerated (by some unknown degree) effectuation of the majority will? We think not."

Compare Jesse H. Choper, *The Political Questions Doctrine: Suggested Criteria*, 54 Duke L.J. 1457 (2005): "[T]he task of developing manageable standards to address political gerrymandering is by no means impossible. The Court could adopt either a principle of proportional representation, or a rule that all consideration of politics in districting violates equal protection, or, most comprehensively a requirement that some form of 'neutral' apportionment system (such as a computer program or bipartisan commission) be used." Even so, Professor Choper tentatively concludes that partisan gerrymandering claims should be deemed to present political questions, apparently because such mandates would diverge too far from "the nation's longstanding tradition and practice" and have too little grounding in the constitutional text to count as being "judicially discoverable."

Ernest A. Young, *Popular Constitutionalism and the Underenforcement Problem: The Case of the National Healthcare Law*, 75 Law & Contemp.Probs. 157 (2012), argues that courts often respond to constitutional indeterminacy not by finding a claim nonjusticiable, but by invoking principles that call for deference to the judgments of the political branches. In light of what you have read, consider carefully grounds of overlap and distinction between "ordinary" principles of judicial deference and the political question doctrine. If Professor Young is correct, why does the Court rest its conclusion on the political question doctrine in some cases and principles of deference in others?

4. ***Prudence.*** Consider Maurice Finkelstein, *Judicial Self-Limitation*, 37 Harv.L.Rev. 338 (1924): The term "political question" applies "to all those matters of which the court, at a given time, will be of the opinion that it is impolitic or inexpedient to take jurisdiction. Sometimes this idea of inexpediency will result from the fear of the vastness of the consequences that a decision on the merits might entail." The most famous formulation of this view was offered by Alexander M. Bickel, *The Least Dangerous Branch* 125–26, 183–84 (1962). Professor Bickel maintained that the political question doctrine—though functionally necessary—was "something that cannot exist within the four corners of *Marbury*" and its assumption that the courts have an unyielding duty to apply the law in every case properly before them: "[O]nly by [a] play on words can the broad discretion that the courts have [exercised] be turned into an act of constitutional interpretation governed by the general standards of the interpretive process. The political question doctrine simply resists being domesticated in this fashion. There is [something] different about it, in kind, not in degree; something greatly more flexible, something of prudence, not construction and not principle.

"[Such] is the foundation, in both intellect and instinct, of the political-question doctrine: the Court's sense of lack of capacity, compounded in unequal parts of (a) the strangeness of the issue and its intractability to principled resolution; (b) the sheer momentousness of it, which tends to unbalance judicial judgment; (c) the anxiety, not so much that the judicial judgment will be ignored, as that perhaps it should but will not be; (d) finally ('in a mature democracy'), the inner vulnerability, the self-doubt of an institution which is electorally irresponsible and has no earth to draw strength from."

In his concurring opinion in *Nixon*, Souter, J., described the political question doctrine as "deriving in large part from prudential concerns" and expressly cited to Bickel, supra.

5. *Guarantee Clause: republican form of government.* (a) *Initiative process.* In PACIFIC STATES TEL. & T. CO. v. OREGON, 223 U.S. 118 (1912), four years after Oregon amended its constitution to allow the people to enact laws through an initiative process, petitioner challenged a tax enacted by an initiative on the ground that the process violated Art. IV, § 4, which provides that "[t]he United States shall guarantee to every State in this Union a Republican Form of Government." In essence, the company argued that the initiative process is democratic, not republican. The Court, per WHITE, J., held that the case presented a political question, quoting from *Luther v. Borden,* 48 U.S. (7 How.) 1 (1849), an action arising out of the Dorr Rebellion in Rhode Island, in which the question of whether the defendant's arrest of the plaintiff was a trespass turned on which of two groups was the lawful government of the state: "[Under Art. IV, § 4], it rests with Congress to decide what government is the established one in a State. For, as the United States guarantee to each State a republican government, Congress must necessarily decide what government is established in the State before it can determine whether it is republican or not. And when the senators and representatives of a State are admitted into the councils of the Union, the authority of the government under which they are appointed, as well as its republican character, is recognized by the proper constitutional authority. And its decision is binding on every other department of the government, and could not be questioned in a judicial tribunal. It is true that the contest in this case did not last long enough to bring the matter to this issue; and as no senators or representatives were elected under the authority of the government of which Mr. Dorr was the head, Congress was not called upon to decide the controversy. Yet the right to decide is placed there, and not in the courts."

Turning from *Luther,* the Court noted that the telephone company's argument proceeds "upon the theory that the adoption of the initiative and referendum destroyed all government republican in form in Oregon. This being so, the contention, if held to be sound, would necessarily affect the validity, not only of the particular statute which is before us, but of every other statute passed in Oregon since the adoption of the initiative and referendum. And indeed the propositions go further than this, since in their essence they assert that there is no governmental function, legislative or judicial, in Oregon, because it cannot be assumed, if the proposition be well founded, that there is at one and the same time one and the same government which is republican in form and not of that character.[21] * * *

"Do the provisions of § 4, Art. IV, bring about these strange, far-reaching and injurious results? [D]o they authorize the judiciary to substitute its

---

[21] Consider Tribe 3d ed., at 369: "[I]f a court found that a particular feature of state government rendered the government unrepublican, why could not the court simply declare that feature invalid?" See also Erwin Chemerinsky, *Cases Under the Guarantee Clause Should Be Justiciable,* 65 U.Colo.L.Rev. 849 (1994).

judgment as to a matter purely political for the judgment of Congress on a subject committed to it and thus overthrow the Constitution upon the ground that thereby the guarantee to the States of a government republican in form may be secured, a conception which after all rests upon the assumption that the States are to be guaranteed a government republican in form by destroying the very existence of a government republican in form in the Nation?

"[The] defendant company does not contend here that it could not have been required to pay a license tax. It does not assert that it was denied an opportunity to be heard as to the amount for which it was taxed, or that there was anything inhering in the tax or involved intrinsically in the law which violated any of its constitutional rights. If such questions had been raised they would have been justiciable, and therefore would have required the calling into operation of judicial power. Instead, however, of doing any of these things, the attack on the statute here made is of a wholly different character. Its essentially political nature is at once made manifest by understanding that the assault which the contention here advanced makes is not on the tax as a tax, but on the State as a State. It is addressed to the framework and political character of the government by which the statute levying the tax was passed. It is the government, the political entity, which (reducing the case to its essence) is called to the bar of this court, not for the purpose of testing judicially some exercise of power assailed, on the ground that its exertion has injuriously affected the rights of an individual because of repugnancy to some constitutional limitation, but to demand of the State that it establish its right to exist as a State, republican in form."

(b) *Malapportionment.* BAKER v. CARR, per BRENNAN, J., held that a suit challenging Tennessee's legislative apportionment scheme, under which some districts had vastly larger populations than others, presented a justiciable question under the Equal Protection Clause: "Judicial standards under the Equal Protection Clause are well developed. [This] case does, in one sense, involve the allocation of political power within a State, and the appellants might conceivably have added a claim under the Guarantee Clause. [Although such a claim] could not have succeeded it does not follow that appellants may not be heard on the equal protection claim which in fact they tender."

FRANKFURTER, J., joined by Harlan, J., dissented: "The present case [is], in effect, a Guarantee Clause claim masquerading under a different label. But it cannot make the case more fit for judicial action that appellants invoke the Fourteenth Amendment rather than Art. IV, § 4, where, in fact, the gist of their complaint is the same."

(c) *Meaning of the Guarantee Clause.* Consider the *substantive* issues that would arise if the Court were to deem Guarantee Clause issues justiciable. Should the Court hold that the initiative process violates the Guarantee Clause? Suppose that a city provided all citizens with a technology that made legislative debates on all issues fully available and then allowed citizens to enact legislation on certain issues by popular vote from their own homes. Would legislation through this form be consistent with the structure and history of the Constitution? With its spirit? Consider Chemerinsky, supra: "Madison was particularly concerned that states might be controlled by stable majority coalitions that would systematically impede minority rights.[78] He saw that an integral part of solving the dangers of democracy is having a republican government where people elect representatives and representatives make laws that must comply with state and federal constitutional provisions. [Recently,] historians such as Bernard Bailyn and Gordon Wood, and law professors such as Cass Sunstein and Frank Michelman have argued that the core of a republican government is citizen participation in important public deliberations.[80] Perspectives from both the republican revival and the founders' debates indicate that the Guarantee Clause is not primarily about guaranteeing a particular structure of government in states or even about protecting state governments from federal encroachments. Instead, it is meant to protect the basic individual right of political participation, most notably the right to vote and the right to choose public officeholders."[22]

6. *Foreign relations.* (a) BAKER v. CARR, noted: "[I]t is error to suppose that every case or controversy which touches foreign relations lies beyond judicial cognizance. Our cases in this field seem invariably to show a discriminating analysis of the particular question posed, in terms of the history of its management by the political branches, of its susceptibility to judicial handling in the light of its nature and posture in the specific case, and of the possible consequences of judicial action. For example, [w]hile recognition of foreign governments so strongly defies judicial treatment that without executive recognition a foreign state has been called 'a republic of whose existence we know nothing,' and the judiciary ordinarily follows the executive as to which nation has sovereignty over disputed territory, once sovereignty over an area is politically determined and declared, courts may examine the resulting status and decide independently whether a statute applies to that area. [Also, in respect to dates of duration of hostilities,] analysis reveals isolable reasons for the presence of political questions, underlying this Court's refusal to review the political departments' determination of when or whether a war has ended. Dominant is the need for finality in the political

---

[78] **[Orig. Note]** *The Federalist* No. 10.

[80] **[Orig. Note]** See, e.g., Cass R. Sunstein, *Beyond the Republican Revival*, 97 Yale L.J. 1539 (1988); Frank I. Michelman, *Foreword: Traces of Self-Government*, 100 Harv.L.Rev. 4 (1986). But see Richard H. Fallon, Jr., *What is Republicanism, and Is It Worth Reviving?*, 102 Harv.L.Rev. 1695 (1989).

[22] In *New York v. United States*, 505 U.S. 144 (1992), Ch. 2, Sec. 5, II, infra, the Court ruled that a federal statute effectively mandating state legislative action (to deal with nuclear waste within the states' borders) exceeded congressional authority under the Commerce Clause. Turning to an argument that federal statutory provisions creating incentives for the states to legislate violated the Guarantee Clause, the Court, per O'Connor, J., noted that the Court had ruled on the merits of Guarantee Clause claims in the late nineteenth and early twentieth centuries, "before the holding of *Luther* was elevated into a general principle of nonjusticiability," but found no need to pronounce on the circumstances under which Guarantee Clause challenges might be justiciable: "[E]ven indulging the assumption that the Guarantee Clause provides a basis upon which a State or its subdivisions may sue to enjoin the enforcement of a federal statute, petitioners have not made out such a claim in this case," since the challenged provisions did "not pose any realistic threat of altering the form or the method of the functioning of New York's government."

determination, for emergency's nature demands 'a prompt and unhesitating obedience,' *Martin v. Mott*, 25 U.S. (12 Wheat.) 19 (1827) (calling up of militia). [But] deference rests on reason, not habit."

(b) If a soldier seeks a federal declaratory judgment that American participation in a particular armed conflict is "unconstitutional in that it was not initially authorized or subsequently ratified by Congressional declaration," is the question "justiciable"? See the opinions of Marshall and Douglas, JJ., in *Holtzman v. Schlesinger,* 414 U.S. 1304, 1316 (1973). Virtually without exception, the federal courts have declined to adjudicate such issues—if not on political question grounds, then on grounds of ripeness or mootness. See, e.g., *Campbell v. Clinton*, 203 F.3d 19 (D.C. Cir. 2000), Ch. 3, Sec. 1, II infra.[23]

Should it make any difference to the justiciability issue if a soldier were court-martialed for refusing to engage in combat and sought federal habeas corpus relief? Consider Michael E. Tigar, *Judicial Power, The "Political Question Doctrine," and Foreign Relations,* 17 UCLA L.Rev. 1135 (1970): "[It is] the duty of the Court to consider the legality of a detention by consideration of all the legal rules which are conceded to be operative under the Constitution, laws and treaties of the United States. This determination does not necessarily involve the Executive in litigating the validity of its claim to possess lawfully the power it exercises in conducting a war: it says only that [when] the Executive [comes] into court it must be bound by the rules fashioned by the judiciary and the Congress for the protection of litigants' rights." See also John H. Ely, *War and Responsibility: Constitutional Lessons of Vietnam and Its Aftermath* 55–58 (1993).

(c) ZIVOTOFSKY v. CLINTON, 132 S.Ct. 1421 (2012), per Roberts, C.J., rejected political question objections and held that the federal courts could determine the constitutionality of a statute requiring the State Department to list "Israel" as the place of birth on the passports of Americans born in Jerusalem who requested that listing. The State Department refused to comply with the law on the ground that, by purporting to recognize Jerusalem's status as part of Israel, it unconstitutionally interfered with the president's foreign affairs powers. It further argued that a suit seeking to compel compliance with the statute presented a political question. Without reference to additional factors considered in previous political question cases, the Court found that (1) there was no "textually demonstrable constitutional commitment of the issue" of the constitutionality of a federal statute to any branch other than the judiciary, and (2) "the textual, structural, and historical evidence put forward by the parties" revealed no lack of "judicially discoverable and manageable standards."

SOTOMAYOR, J., joined in relevant part by Breyer, J., concurred, emphasizing that in "rare case[s]" the Court should find questions nonjusticiable based principally on prudential considerations, but that this

---

[23] See also *Dellums v. Bush*, 752 F.Supp. 1141 (D.D.C.1990) (asserting, in dictum that the issue of whether the Persian Gulf War required congressional authorization was justiciable in principle, but dismissing a challenge for lack of ripeness).

was not such a case. Alito, J., also concurred separately. BREYER, J., dissented, relying on a conjunction of "prudential considerations" that included the potential foreign policy ramifications of having U.S. passports denominate Jerusalem as part of Israel when Jerusalem's status is a subject of international contention.

7. *Cases with political implications.* In two decisions arising from the 2000 presidential election in the state of Florida, *Bush v. Palm Beach County Canvassing Board*, 531 U.S. 70 (2000) (per curiam), and *Bush v. Gore*, 531 U.S. 98 (2000) (per curiam), there were colorable arguments, raised in amicus curiae briefs, that at least some of the issues involved political questions in the technical sense. In particular, amici argued that the Twelfth Amendment commits to Congress the question whether a state's electors have been chosen in accord with Art. II's requirements. Yet the Court did not refer to the political question doctrine in either decision. Nor did Rehnquist, C.J.'s concurring opinion in *Bush v. Gore*, joined by Scalia and Thomas, JJ., even though it rested on Art. II grounds. Should the Court, possibly for prudential reasons, have taken the political question argument more seriously?

Consider Jesse H. Choper, *Why the Supreme Court Should Not Have Decided the Presidential Election of 2000,* 18 Const.Comm. 335 (2001): "[T]he Court's adjudication was both unnecessary and unwise, creating a widely based popular perception of partisanship by the Judicial Branch." Did the Justices' failure to grapple with political question arguments in these cases signal their growing sense of the Court's irreducibly central role in the constitutional scheme? Consider Rachel E. Barkow, *More Supreme Than Court? The Fall of the Political Question Doctrine and the Rise of Judicial Supremacy*, 102 Colum.L.Rev. 237 (2002): "[T]he fall of the political question doctrine is part of a larger trend in which the Supreme Court has embraced the view that it alone among the three branches of government has the power and competency to provide the full substantive meaning of constitutional provisions."

3. CONGRESSIONAL REGULATION OF JUDICIAL POWER

Under the Constitution, Congress possesses undisputed power to regulate the jurisdiction of the federal courts. Article III contemplates that the Supreme Court's appellate jurisdiction shall be subject to "such Exceptions * * * as the Congress shall make." And Congress, if it chose, would not need to create any lower federal courts at all. As a result of the so-called "Madisonian Compromise" at the Constitutional Convention between those who favored and those who opposed the establishment of lower federal courts, Article III provides that the judicial power "shall be vested in one supreme Court, and in such inferior Courts as the Congress may from time to time ordain and establish." Beginning with the first Judiciary Act, Congress has *never* vested the lower federal courts with the maximum jurisdiction that the Constitution would allow, and it has always imposed limitations on the appellate jurisdiction of the Supreme Court. For example, it was not until 1914 that the Court was authorized to review state court decisions holding that state laws violate the Constitution. (The Court did previously have jurisdiction to review state court decisions that state laws did *not* violate the Constitution.)

Although Congress has always limited the jurisdiction of the federal courts (largely to protect them against being swamped by too many cases), difficult questions would be presented if Congress should attempt to use its power over jurisdiction to stop the federal courts from deciding cases that they would likely resolve in ways that Congress dislikes. Proposals to restrict federal jurisdiction in response to politically unpopular doctrines and decisions have been common in American history.[24] Since the late 1970s, for example, critics of the Supreme Court's school prayer and abortion decisions have regularly attempted to pass legislation stripping the Supreme Court, the lower federal courts, or both of jurisdiction in such cases. Although opponents of the Court's decisions would prefer to overturn its rulings by constitutional amendment, amendments are exceedingly difficult to enact. Jurisdiction-stripping bills are thus viewed as substitutes. Their characteristic aim is to achieve, by less onerous means, a de facto change in the substantive law through the procedural device of a limitation on federal jurisdiction.

Yet jurisdiction-stripping legislation has itself proven very difficult to enact.[25] As a result, despite much discussion and debate about jurisdiction-stripping proposals, the most difficult issues remain unresolved. Indeed, the case that is usually viewed as the "leading case" on the stripping of Supreme Court jurisdiction, *Ex parte McCardle* (which appears immediately below), can be read in ways that limit its holding almost entirely to its facts. Moreover, different jurisdiction-stripping proposals may raise different constitutional issues in view of the language, history, and structure of the Constitution. More specifically, it may be relevant whether Congress attempts just to limit Supreme Court jurisdiction (while leaving the lower federal courts alone), just to limit the jurisdiction of the lower federal courts (while retaining Supreme Court jurisdiction to review the decisions of state courts), or to eliminate *both* Supreme Court and lower federal court jurisdiction over a class of cases. (In this last scenario, state courts would still be required to entertain federal claims under the

---

[24] See Max Baucus & Kenneth R. Kay, *The Court Stripping Bills: Their Impact on the Constitution, the Courts, and Congress,* 27 Vill.L.Rev. 988 (1982); Gerald Gunther, *Congressional Power to Curtail Federal Court Jurisdiction: An Opinionated Guide to the Ongoing Debate,* 36 Stan.L.Rev. 895 (1984).

[25] In seeking to explain this phenomenon, Professor Grove has emphasized that nearly every political constituency has long-term incentives to want to maintain an independent judiciary to protect its interests when it is out of power. See Tara Leigh Grove, *The Structural Safeguards of Federal Jurisdiction,* 124 Harv.L.Rev. 869 (2011). See also Tara Leigh Grove, *The Article II Safeguards of Federal Jurisdiction,* 112 Colum.L.Rev. 250 (2012) (citing reasons for the President and Department of Justice to oppose jurisdiction-stripping bills).

Supremacy Clause, but query whether they could be relied on to do so in every case.)[26] Try to keep these distinctions in mind as you read the material that follows.

EX PARTE MCCARDLE

74 U.S. (7 Wall.) 506, 19 L.Ed. 264 (1869).

[On February 5, 1867, Congress empowered federal courts to grant writs of habeas corpus (and thus to order the release of prisoners who were unlawfully held in custody) "in all cases where any person may be restrained of his or her liberty in violation of" federal law. Enacted by a Reconstruction Congress, the 1867 Act was intended primarily to establish federal authority to review detentions by state and local authorities; federal courts already possessed jurisdiction to review federal detentions. Among its incidental provisions, the Act authorized appeals to the Supreme Court in cases in which circuit courts denied applications for the writ of habeas corpus.

[Following the passage of the 1867 Act, McCardle, the virulently racist editor of the Vicksburg Times, was imprisoned by the military government of Mississippi pursuant to the Reconstruction Acts for publishing "incendiary and libelous" articles tending to incite violence and impede Reconstruction. Alleging "unlawful restraint by military force," he sought habeas corpus, but his petition was denied by the Circuit Court. He thereupon appealed to the Supreme Court under the 1867 Act.

[McCardle's case presented the Supreme Court with the opportunity to rule on the constitutionality of the Military Reconstruction Act, which had placed ten former Confederate states under military jurisdiction. The constitutional arguments were clearly substantial, and the Court, in *Ex parte Milligan*, 71 U.S. (4 Wall.) 2 (1867), had hinted that it might be ready to hold military Reconstruction unconstitutional. Fearing this result, Congress, in 1868, after argument in the *McCardle* case but before the Supreme Court had rendered a decision, passed the following repealing act (over President Johnson's veto):] "That so much of the act approved February 5, 1867 [as] authorized an appeal from the judgment of the Circuit Court to the Supreme Court of the United States, or the exercise of any such jurisdiction by said Supreme Court, on appeals which have been, or may hereafter be taken, [is] hereby repealed." [The purpose and effect of this legislation was to strip the Court of jurisdiction over McCardle's pending appeal.]

---

[26] For an in-depth discussion, see Richard H. Fallon, Jr., John F. Manning, Daniel J. Meltzer, & David L. Shapiro, *Hart & Wechsler's The Federal Courts and the Federal System* 270–324 (6th ed. 2009).

The CHIEF JUSTICE [CHASE] delivered the opinion of the Court.

[T]he appellate jurisdiction of this Court is not derived from acts of Congress. It is, strictly speaking, conferred by the Constitution. But it is conferred "with such exceptions and under such regulations as Congress shall make." * * *

We are not at liberty to inquire into the motives of the legislature. We can only examine into its power under the Constitution * * * .

What, then, is the effect of the repealing act upon the case before [us?] Jurisdiction is power to declare the law, and when it ceases to exist the only function remaining to the court is that of announcing the fact and dismissing the cause. And this is not less clear upon authority than upon principle. [J]udicial duty is not less fitly performed by declining ungranted jurisdiction than in exercising firmly that which the Constitution and the laws confer.

Counsel seem to have supposed, if effect be given to the repealing act in question, that the whole appellate power of the court, in cases of habeas corpus, is denied. But this is an error. The act of 1868 does not except from that jurisdiction any cases but appeals from Circuit Courts under the act of 1867. It does not affect the jurisdiction which was previously exercised.

The appeal [must] be dismissed for want of jurisdiction.

NOTES AND QUESTIONS

1. **Court's holding.** Although *McCardle* is capable of being read as recognizing a broad congressional power to make "exceptions" to the Supreme Court's appellate jurisdiction, it did not, on its facts, involve a limitation of great significance, as hinted by the sentence stating that the Act before the Court did "not affect" the jurisdiction that the Court had previously possessed and continued to possess pursuant to statutes other than the 1867 legislation. Subsequently, in *Ex parte Yerger,* 75 U.S. (8 Wall.) 85 (1869), also challenging the Reconstruction Acts, the Court upheld its jurisdiction in a habeas corpus proceeding in which the petitioner sought review based on pre-1867 legislation that provided for discretionary review by writ of certiorari.[27] Consider Leonard G. Ratner, *Congressional Power over the Appellate Jurisdiction of the Supreme Court,* 109 U.Pa.L.Rev. 157 (1960): "The statute [involved in *McCardle* did] not deprive the Court of jurisdiction to decide McCardle's case; he could still

---

[27] The Court has subsequently treated *Yerger* as having established the principle that implied repeals of Supreme Court appellate jurisdiction should be disfavored. Thus *Felker v. Turpin,* 518 U.S. 651 (1996), per Rehnquist, C.J., held unanimously that a statute withdrawing the Court's certiorari jurisdiction in certain habeas cases had not affected its authority to review the case before it upon a petition for an original writ of habeas corpus under 28 U.S.C. §§ 2241 and 2254. As in *McCardle*, the availability of an alternative mechanism for the Court to exercise jurisdiction "obviate[d]" any constitutional challenge to the jurisdiction-limiting legislation under Art. III, § 2. In a concurring opinion, Souter, J., joined by Stevens and Breyer, JJ., reserved the question whether the statute might be held unconstitutional as applied to subsequent cases if, in practice, it stopped the Court from reviewing "divergent interpretations" of a federal statute.

petition the Supreme Court for [an original] writ of habeas corpus. [The] legislation did no more than eliminate one procedure for Supreme Court review of decisions denying habeas corpus while leaving another equally efficacious one available."

2. ***Essential functions thesis.*** Commentators are divided about the scope of Congress's power, if any, to eliminate the Supreme Court's appellate jurisdiction to resolve particular constitutional issues. In a celebrated and broad-ranging commentary on Congress' power over federal jurisdiction, Professor Henry M. Hart, Jr., argued that in order for "exceptions" to the Court's jurisdiction to be constitutionally permissible under Article III, the exceptions "must not be such as will destroy the essential role of the Supreme Court in the constitutional plan." *The Power of Congress to Limit the Jurisdiction of Federal Courts: An Exercise in Dialectic*, 66 Harv.L.Rev. 1362 (1953). Hart acknowledged the indeterminacy of this test, but pointedly queried whether "the difficulties of the test" were not "less [than] the difficulties of reading the Constitution as authorizing its own destruction."

Would elimination of Supreme Court appellate jurisdiction over school prayer cases, for example, deprive the Court of its "essential role [in] the constitutional plan"? Consider Leonard G. Ratner, *Majoritarian Constraints on Judicial Review: Congressional Control of Supreme Court Jurisdiction,* 27 Vill.L.Rev. 929 (1982): "The Supremacy Clause of Article VI mandates one supreme federal law throughout the land, and Article III establishes the Supreme Court as the constitutional instrument for implementing that clause. [As] such, its essential functions under the Constitution are: 1) ultimately to resolve inconsistent or conflicting interpretations of federal law, and particularly of the Constitution, by state and federal courts; 2) to maintain the supremacy of federal law, and particularly the Constitution, when it conflicts with state law or is challenged by state authority." Compare Martin H. Redish, *Congressional Power to Regulate Supreme Court Appellate Jurisdiction Under the Exceptions Clause: An Internal and External Examination,* 27 Vill.L.Rev. 900 (1982): "[I] might well agree, as a policy matter, that Congress should not possess the power to tamper with performance of the Supreme Court's role, [but] I can find no constitutional basis for erecting such a [limitation]." Steven G. Calabresi & Gary Lawson, *The Unitary Executive, Jurisdiction Stripping, and the Hamdan Opinions: A Textualist Response to Justice Scalia,* 107 Colum.L.Rev. 1002 (2007), argue that under a proper interpretation of the Exceptions and Necessary and Proper Clauses, Congress can shift cases from the Supreme Court's appellate to its original jurisdiction, but that it cannot deprive the Court of both original and appellate jurisdiction over the same cases. Whatever other attractions this theory may hold, note that it calls for rejection of the holding of *Marbury v. Madison* that Congress cannot expand the constitutionally mandated original jurisdiction of the Supreme Court.

According to Charles L. Black, Jr., *The Presidency and Congress*, 32 Wash. & Lee L.Rev. 841 (1975), Congress' power to restrict federal court jurisdiction is "the rock on which rests the legitimacy of the judicial work in a democracy." Crudely summarized, his view is that the vast power exercised today by courts, and especially the Supreme Court, is legitimate only insofar as it rests on popular consent—and any claim that the people have consented would be empty unless it were recognized that the people, through their elected representatives, could limit the federal judiciary's exercise of judicial review. Black offers his argument as a friend, not a critic, of federal judicial power. Should other friends of judicial review be persuaded?

3. *Restraints from constitutional provisions other than Article III.* Congress clearly could not eliminate either Supreme Court or lower federal court jurisdiction solely over cases brought by litigants of a certain race or gender. Even if hypothetical restrictions of this kind did not violate Article III, they would indisputably violate *other* constitutional provisions, such as the equal protection component of the Due Process Clause. Are proposals to restrict jurisdiction of suits involving challenges to school prayer or restrictions on abortion constitutionally objectionable in the same way? According to Gerald Gunther, *Congressional Power to Curtail Federal Court Jurisdiction: An Opinionated Guide to the Ongoing Debate,* 36 Stan.L.Rev. 895 (1984), arguments to that effect "too readily extend[ ] the analysis of the obvious flaw in laws that distinguish among *litigants* on the basis of race or other forbidden criteria to jurisdictional statutes that differentiate on the basis of *subject matter.*" Do you agree?

For a discussion of restrictions on Congress's power to withdraw jurisdiction arising from the Suspension Clause of Art. I, § 9, cl. 2, see Note 9, infra.

4. *Jurisdictional limitations vs. substantive directions.* In UNITED STATES v. KLEIN, 80 U.S. (13 Wall.) 128 (1872), the Court held unconstitutional a statute directing the federal courts to dismiss for want of jurisdiction any suit in which the plaintiff relied on a presidential pardon to prove loyalty during the Civil War and, thus, entitlement to recover for property seized by the government. An earlier decision had found that a presidential pardon, apparently as a constitutional matter, must be treated as conclusive proof of loyalty. The Court reasoned:

"The substance of this enactment is that an acceptance of a pardon [shall] be conclusive evidence of the acts pardoned, but shall be null and void as evidence of the rights conferred by it, both in the Court of Claims and in this court on appeal.

"[Undoubtedly] the legislature has complete control over the organization and existence of [the Court of Claims] and may confer or withhold the right of appeal from its decisions. And if this act did nothing more, it would be our duty to give it effect. If it simply denied the right of appeal in a particular class of cases, there could be no doubt that it must be regarded as an exercise of the power of Congress to make 'such exceptions from the appellate jurisdiction' as should seem to it expedient.

"But the language of the proviso shows plainly that it does not intend to withhold appellate jurisdiction except as a means to an end. Its great and controlling purpose is to deny to pardons granted by the President the effect which this court had adjudged them to have. The proviso declares that pardons shall not be considered by this court on appeal. We had already decided that it was our duty to consider them and give them effect, in cases like the present, as equivalent to proof of loyalty.

"[It] is evident from this statement that the denial of jurisdiction to this court, as well as to the Court of Claims, is founded solely on the application of a rule of decision, in causes pending, prescribed by Congress. The court has jurisdiction of the cause to a given point; but when it ascertains that a certain state of things exists, its jurisdiction is to cease and it is required to dismiss the cause for want of jurisdiction.

"It seems to us that this is not an exercise of the acknowledged power of Congress to make exceptions and prescribe regulations to the appellate power.

"The court is required to ascertain the existence of certain facts and thereupon to declare that its jurisdiction on appeal has ceased, by dismissing the bill. What is this but to prescribe a rule for the decision of a cause in a particular way? In the case before us, the Court of Claims has rendered judgment for the claimant and an appeal has been taken to this court. We are directed to dismiss the appeal, if we find that the judgment must be affirmed, because of a pardon granted to the intestate of the claimants. Can we do so without allowing one party to the controversy to decide it in its own favor?

"[We] think not.

"[The] rule prescribed is also liable to just exception as impairing the effect of a pardon, and thus infringing the constitutional power of the Executive.

"[The] legislature cannot change the effect of such a pardon any more than the executive can change a law. Yet this is attempted by the provision under consideration. The court is required to receive special pardons as evidence of guilt and to treat them as null and void. It is required to disregard pardons granted by proclamation on condition, though the condition has been fulfilled, and to deny them their legal effect. This certainly impairs the executive authority and directs the court to be instrumental to that end."

Amanda L. Tyler, *The Story of Klein: The Scope of Congress's Authority to Shape the Jurisdiction of the Federal Courts,* in *Federal Courts Stories* 87 (V. Jackson & J. Resnik, eds., 2010), cautions that *Klein* "may be read to stand for a number of things, many of which have not held up over time."[28] In particular, it is normally permissible for Congress to prescribe substantive rules of decision to the courts, including rules applicable to pending cases, as long as it does so through otherwise valid statutes that change the substantive law. See, e.g., *Robertson v. Seattle Audubon Soc'y,* 503 U.S. 429 (1992). Given this

---

[28] For discussion of *Klein* and the principle on which it should be held to rest, see, e.g., Gordon G. Young, United States v. Klein, *Then and Now,* 44 Loy.U.Chi.L.J. 265 (2012); Martin H. Redish & Christopher R. Pudelski, *Legislative Deception, Separation of Powers, and Democratic Process: Harnessing the Political Theory of* United States v. Klein, 100 Nw.U.L.Rev. 437 (2006); Lawrence G. Sager, Klein's *First Principle: A Proposed Solution,* 86 Geo.L.J. 2525 (1998); Daniel J. Meltzer, *Congress, Courts, and Constitutional Remedies,* 86 Geo.L.J. 2537 (1998).

qualification, most commentators agree that the most solid part of the *Klein* decision is its holding that Congress cannot use its power over jurisdiction in such a way as to require a court to reach a decision that violates some part of the Constitution other than Article III—as, in *Klein,* by impairing the effect of a presidential pardon and thus infringing on the Article I powers of the President.

5. ***Congressional motive.*** In *McCardle*, in which Congress had deprived the Court of jurisdiction in order to forestall a feared ruling on the merits of a particular case, the Court observed that it was "not at liberty to inquire into the motives of the legislature." Does *Klein* contradict this dictum when it asserts that Congress may not use its power "to withhold appellate jurisdiction [as] a means to [a constitutionally forbidden] end"?

Consider Caleb Nelson, *Judicial Review of Legislative Purpose*, 83 N.Y.U. L.Rev. 1784 (2008): "Modern scholars have puzzled over the alleged tension [between *McCardle* and *Klein,* but] the tension dissolves once we appreciate the [prevailing] norms of judicial review" in the nineteenth century, which did in fact make congressional motive relevant to judicial review under some circumstances. "Under the doctrine of the day, courts could impute impermissible purpose to a statute when 'the language of the proviso' made them clear (as in *Klein*), but not when the imputation required reference to things beyond the face of the statute (as in *McCardle*)."

If Congress were to strip the Supreme Court's appellate jurisdiction today—for example, in a case involving challenges to the constitutionality of school prayer—would and should Congress's motives bear on the constitutionality of the jurisdiction-stripping legislation? How pertinent is it that, since *McCardle*, the Court has established that legislative motive is relevant to whether the government has exercised its power lawfully under, for example, the Establishment Clause of the First Amendment (see e.g., *Wallace v. Jaffree,* Ch. 8, Sec. I, III infra) and the Equal Protection Clause (see, e.g., *Washington v. Davis,* Ch. 9, Sec. 2, III infra)? By vesting power to limit jurisdiction in Congress, does the Constitution implicitly leave a broad scope for politically motivated decisionmaking? Compare Paul M. Bator, *Congressional Power over the Jurisdiction of the Federal Courts*, 27 Vill.L.Rev. 1030 (1982) (yes), with Richard H. Fallon, Jr., *Jurisdiction-Stripping Reconsidered,* 96 Va.L.Rev. 1043 (2010), and Laurence H. Tribe, *Jurisdictional Gerrymandering: Zoning Disfavored Rights Out of the Federal Courts*, 16 Harv. C.R.-C.L. L.Rev. 129 (1981) (no).

6. ***Limitation of lower federal court jurisdiction.*** It is settled that Congress, which under Article III does not need to establish any lower federal courts at all, also has broad, discretionary power to prescribe and limit the lower federal courts' jurisdiction. See *Sheldon v. Sill,* 49 U.S. (8 How.) 441 (1850). It was not until 1875, for example, that Congress gave the lower federal courts general jurisdiction to decide questions "arising under" the Constitution, laws, and treaties of the United States. Due to jurisdictional limitations based on the amount in controversy, among others, the lower

federal courts have never enjoyed the full jurisdiction that would be permitted by Article III.

Statutes curbing the jurisdiction of lower federal courts in response to federal decisions on the merits are not wholly unprecedented. Perhaps the most prominent example is the Norris-LaGuardia Act, which greatly restricted federal courts from issuing injunctions in "labor disputes" and expressly framed its prohibitions as restrictions on federal "jurisdiction." Rejecting a constitutional challenge, *Lauf v. E.G. Shinner & Co.,* 303 U.S. 323 (1938), said "[t]here can be no question of the power of Congress thus to define and limit the jurisdiction of the inferior courts of the United States."

Commentators continue to debate whether *Lauf* necessarily contemplated that Congress could purposefully and discriminatorily close the doors of the lower federal courts to cases involving congressionally disfavored *constitutional* rights. For a discussion, see Gordon G. Young, *A Critical Reassessment of the Case Law Bearing on Congress's Power to Restrict the Jurisdiction of the Lower Federal Courts,* 54 Md.L.Rev. 132 (1995).

7.   ***Simultaneous curbs of both Supreme Court and lower federal court jurisdiction.*** (a) If—as many people think—Congress could eliminate Supreme Court jurisdiction (as long as the lower federal courts were open), and could eliminate Supreme Court jurisdiction to review decisions of the lower federal courts, would it follow that Congress could eliminate all federal jurisdiction and force the litigation of federal issues entirely into state courts? In considering whether simultaneous stripping of both Supreme Court and lower federal court jurisdiction (for example, over cases involving challenges to school prayer), it is important to remember that state courts not only can entertain claims under the Constitution of the United States, but are affirmatively required to do so under the Supremacy Clause. Most commentators also think that state courts would be constitutionally bound to follow Supreme Court precedents. See, *e.g.,* Fallon, supra. It is a separate question, however, whether all state courts could realistically be expected to do so.

(b)   Beginning with Story, J., in *Martin v. Hunter's Lessee,* Sec. 1, supra, a line of jurists and scholars has maintained that the Constitution's language and structure require the availability of *some* federal court to rule on claims by litigants that they have suffered violations of their federal rights. The basic idea is that the Constitution requires that the judicial branch be co-equal to the legislature and the executive, but that either the Supreme Court or the lower federal courts can play the constitutionally contemplated checking and balancing role. On this view, Congress could thus eliminate Supreme Court jurisdiction over school prayer cases, for example, but only if it retained jurisdiction in a lower federal court; and it could curb lower federal court jurisdiction in such cases, but only if the Supreme Court retained appellate jurisdiction of suits brought in state court. The most prominent defense of a theory of this kind comes from Akhil R. Amar, *A Neo-Federalist View of Article III: Separating the Two Tiers of Federal Jurisdiction,* 65 B.U. L.Rev. 205

(1985).[29] For criticisms, see William Fletcher, *Congressional Power Over the Jurisdiction of Federal Courts: The Meaning of the Work "All" in Article III,* 59 Duke L.J. 929 (2010); Daniel J. Meltzer, *The History and Structure of Article III,* 138 U.Pa.L.Rev. 1569 (1990).[30]

(c)   Consider the argument of Brian T. Fitzpatrick, *The Constitutionality of Federal Jurisdiction-Stripping Legislation and the History of State Judicial Selection and Tenure,* 99 Va.L.Rev. 839 (2012), that although the text of Article III would originally have permitted Congress to remit federal constitutional claims entirely to state courts, state judges in the Founding Era possessed a degree of independence comparable to that of federal judges. Today, when most state judges serve limited terms and many are subject to popular election, Professor Fitzpatrick argues that "translating" the original meaning and purposes of Article III to apply to modern circumstances yields the conclusion that a total stripping of all Article III jurisdiction over a selected class of cases would today be impermissible: "[T]he state judges who would hear cases when federal judges did not were the background against which Article III's requirements were written and interpreted. [W]hen constitutional backgrounds change, what the Constitution requires can change as [sometimes] the way to be most faithful to the original meaning of the Constitution is to change how the Constitution applies to particular questions."

8.   ***Stripping of all courts' jurisdiction.*** Suppose that Congress were to enact a statute denying jurisdiction to *any* court—state or federal—to rule on a claim of constitutional right (such as a right not to be subjected to school-sponsored prayer). Would the prohibition be constitutional? (Note that this is a different question from the constitutionality of proposals to curtail federal jurisdiction, while leaving state courts open to hear federal claims.) The Court has often suggested that the preclusion of all judicial review of constitutional issues would raise a "serious" constitutional question under the Due Process Clause and, accordingly, has frequently construed statutes that could easily be read to preclude all judicial review to permit review of constitutional questions in some court. See, e.g., *Webster v. Doe,* 486 U.S. 592, 603 (1988); *Bowen v. Michigan Academy of Family Physicians,* 476 U.S. 667, 681 n.12 (1986); *Johnson v. Robison,* 415 U.S. 361 (1974). See also *Battaglia v. General Motors Corp.,* 169 F.2d 254 (2d Cir. 1948).

Consider Fallon, supra: "Simultaneous stripping of state and federal jurisdiction would violate the Constitution when it precludes the award of constitutionally necessary remedies. [Issues] involving substantive constitutional rights, rights to judicial remedies, and congressional power over jurisdiction are complexly interrelated. The emergence of new constitutional rights in the twentieth and twenty-first centuries may entail new constitutionally necessary remedies to make those rights meaningful. And

---

[29]   See also Calabresi & Lawson, supra; Robert Pushaw, *Congressional Power Over Federal Court Jurisdiction: A Defense of the Neo-Federalist Interpretation of Article III,* 1997 BYU L.Rev. 847.

[30]   For a rebuttal, see Akhil R. Amar, *The Two-Tiered Structure of the Judiciary Act of 1789,* 138 U.Pa.L.Rev. 1499 (1990).

constitutional rights to remedies may, in turn, limit congressional power to curb jurisdiction."

9. *Habeas corpus jurisdiction.* BOUMEDIENE v. BUSH, 553 U.S. 723 (2008), Ch. 3, Sec. 1, III infra, held that Congress's powers to limit the federal courts' jurisdiction are limited by the Suspension Clause of Art. I, § 9, cl. 2, which provides that "[t]he Privilege of the Writ of Habeas Corpus"—a judicial writ used to inquire into the lawfulness of detentions—"shall not be suspended, unless when in Cases of Rebellion or Invasion the public Safety may require it." Rejecting the Government's arguments that the Suspension Clause confers no protections on aliens held outside the sovereign jurisdiction of the United States, the Court, per KENNEDY, J., invalidated a provision of the Military Commissions Act ("MCA") that withdrew habeas jurisdiction for aliens held by the United States as enemy combatants at Guantanamo Bay, Cuba: "[The Suspension Clause] ensures that, except during periods of formal suspension, the Judiciary will have a time-tested device, the writ, to maintain the delicate balance of governance that is itself the surest safeguard of liberty. [The] Court has been careful not to foreclose the possibility that the protections of the Suspension Clause have expanded along with post-1789 developments that define the present scope of the writ. See *INS v. St. Cyr*, 533 U.S. 289 (2001). But the analysis may begin with precedents as of 1789, for the Court has said that 'at the absolute minimum,' the Clause protects the writ as it existed when the Constitution was drafted and ratified."

Examining the historical record, Kennedy, J., concluded that "[in] none of the cases cited do we find that a common-law court would or would not have granted, or refused to hear for lack of jurisdiction, a petition for a writ of habeas corpus brought by a prisoner deemed an enemy combatant, under a standard like the one the Department of Defense has used in these cases, and when held in a territory, like Guantanamo, over which the Government has total military and civil control. [Declining] to infer too much, one way or the other, from the lack of historical evidence on point," Kennedy, J., next reviewed both Suspension Clause and non-Suspension Clause cases addressing "the Constitution's extraterritorial application." From those cases—all decided in the twentieth century—he extracted the principle that constitutional guarantees sometimes extend outside the United States and that "questions of extraterritoriality turn on objective factors and practical concerns, not formalism." Based on those factors and concerns, including the Government's complete and apparently permanent control of Guantamano Bay, he held that the *Boumediene* petitioners had a constitutional right of access to the writ (or a constitutionally adequate substitute, which the applicable statutes had failed to provide them).

SCALIA, J., joined by Roberts, C.J., and Thomas and Alito, JJ., dissented on the ground that the Suspension Clause confers no rights on aliens, such as the petitioner Guantanamo detainees, who are held outside the United States. But Scalia, J., did not appear to dispute—as he had in *St. Cyr*, supra—that the Suspension Clause affirmatively guarantees the availability of the writ of habeas corpus, at least to citizens detained within the United States, absent a formal suspension.

Consider Fallon, supra: "By employing a multi-factored interpretive approach that reads constitutional language in light of precedent, the separation of powers, and functional concerns, *Boumediene* furnishes a possible model for a broader reframing of jurisdiction-stripping debates. [First, although] Justice Kennedy's majority opinion described the original understanding [of the Constitution] as the appropriate starting point for the Court's inquiry into the constitutionality of the MCA, he also suggested, over the dissenting protest of Justice Scalia, that founding-era understandings and expectations may not control how the Constitution applies to circumstances that the founding generation could not have anticipated. Justice Kennedy also reserved the possibility, which Justice Scalia again thought foreclosed, that the necessary role of the federal courts in habeas cases might have expanded over time. [Second, the] *Boumediene* majority [thus] implicitly rejected the methodological position, [which has often been taken for granted in debates about Congress's power to strip judicial jurisdiction,] that courts in principle could, and in practice should, resolve every constitutional dispute based on the best evidence of the original understanding, typically as evidenced by prevailing expectations concerning how constitutional language would be applied. [Third, *Boumediene*] rested its invalidation of a jurisdiction-stripping statute partly on the premise, which Justice Kennedy traced to *Marbury v. Madison* and described as fundamental to the separation of powers, that it is the necessary and proper function of the Judicial Branch to 'say [authoritatively] what the law is.' [After] *Boumediene*, [it] is an open question whether, and if so how, analysis of jurisdiction-stripping statutes would and should be affected by the idea that the separation of powers and the rule of law require authoritative exposition of the Constitution by the federal judiciary as a whole or the Supreme Court in particular." Do you agree with this assessment? If so, do you regard the developments identified by Professor Fallon as salutary?

For insightful commentary on *Boumediene*, see Daniel J. Meltzer, *Habeas Corpus, Suspension, and Guantanamo: The Boumediene Decision*, 2008 Sup.Ct.Rev. 1.

10. ***Other levers of political control.*** Control of federal jurisdiction is by no means the only, and perhaps not even the most important, means by which the political branches may register their disagreement with Supreme Court decisionmaking or seek to influence its future course.

(a) Article III leaves it to Congress to determine the number of justices who sit on the Supreme Court. The first Judiciary Act provided for a chief justice and five associate justices. The number of justices briefly grew as high as ten before settling at the current nine in 1869. When a conservative Court threatened to wreck the New Deal, President Franklin Roosevelt notoriously sought authority to "pack" the Supreme Court by appointing one additional justice for each justice over the age of 70. Although the proposal failed, Roberts,

J., nearly contemporaneously altered his voting pattern to create a 5–4 majority upholding key New Deal legislation. Historians continue to debate whether this celebrated "switch in time that saved nine" was in fact motivated by Roosevelt's Court-packing effort.[31] Others debate whether the Court-packing plan, which would not appear to violate any judicially enforceable constitutional norm, was in accord with the Constitution's spirit.

(b)   Consider Richard H. Fallon, Jr., *Legitimacy and the Constitution,* 118 Harv.L.Rev. 1789 (2005): "In recent decades, presidential candidates have repeatedly campaigned against unpopular claims of judicial authority and promised to appoint Justices whom their constituencies would regard as more right-thinking. Justices who defy aroused public opinion risk, and know that they risk, provoking a political backlash that ultimately could cause their doctrinal handiwork to collapse [following the appointment of Justices hostile to their decisions]. Possibly as a result of the Court's concern for its own sociological legitimacy, it has seldom remained at odds with aroused public opinion for extended periods." For a sustained historical argument that public opinion and fear of public backlash exert a strong influence on the Court, see Barry Friedman, *The Will of the People: How Public Opinion Has Influenced the Supreme Court and Shaped the Meaning of the Constitution* (2009).

4. DISCRETIONARY REVIEW

The Supreme Court's original jurisdiction, which typically comprises at most a handful of cases each year (mainly concerning "controversies between two or more states"), is presently governed by 28 U.S.C.A. § 1251. The most important current provisions respecting the Court's appellate jurisdiction are 28 U.S.C.A. §§ 1254 (federal courts of appeals) and 1257 (state courts), both of which provide for review of lower court decisions only by "writ of certiorari"—a discretionary writ that permits the Court to decide for itself which cases most deserve its attention.[32]

In the exercise of its certiorari jurisdiction, the Court, in the words of Vinson, C.J., Address to the American Bar Association: The Work of the Federal Courts, *in* 69 S.Ct. v, vi (1949), is not "primarily concerned with the correction of errors in lower court decisions": "In almost all cases within the Court's appellate jurisdiction, the petitioner has already received one appellate review. [If] we took every case in which an interesting legal question is raised, or our prima facie impression is that the decision below is erroneous, we could not fulfill the Constitutional and statutory responsibilities placed upon the Court. To remain effective, the Supreme Court must continue to decide only those cases which present questions

---

[31]   For an insightful review of the scholarly debate and the evidence on which it is based, see Laura Kalman, *The Constitution, the Supreme Court, and the New Deal,* 110 Am.Hist.Rev. 1052 (2005).

[32]   Until 1988, Sections 1254 and 1257 both provided for appeal as of right in some cases, although they gave the Court discretion with respect to others.

whose resolution will have immediate importance far beyond the particular facts and parties involved."

United States Supreme Court Rules

Rule 10.   Considerations Governing Review on Writ of Certiorari

1.   A review on writ of certiorari is not a matter of right, but of judicial discretion. A petition for a writ of certiorari will be granted only when there are special and important reasons therefor. The following, while neither controlling nor fully measuring the Court's discretion, indicate the character of reasons that will be considered: (a) When a United States court of appeals has rendered a decision in conflict with the decision of another United States court of appeals on the same matter; or has decided a federal question in a way in conflict with a state court of last resort; or has so far departed from the accepted and usual course of judicial proceedings, or sanctioned such a departure by a lower court, as to call for an exercise of this Court's power of supervision. (b) When a state court of last resort has decided a federal question in a way that conflicts with the decision of another state court of last resort or of a United States court of appeals. (c) When a state court or a United States court of appeals has decided an important question of federal law which has not been, but should be, settled by this Court, or has decided a federal question in a way that conflicts with applicable decisions of this Court. * * *

MARYLAND V. BALTIMORE RADIO SHOW, INC.
338 U.S. 912, 70 S.Ct. 252, 94 L.Ed. 562 (1950).

Opinion of JUSTICE FRANKFURTER respecting the denial of the petition for writ of certiorari. * * *

A variety of considerations underlie denials of the writ, and as to the same petition different reasons may lead different Justices to the same result. This is especially true of petitions for review on writ of certiorari to a State court. Narrowly technical reasons may lead to denials. [For detail, see Sec. 5 infra.] A decision may satisfy all these technical requirements and yet may commend itself for review to fewer than four members of the Court. Pertinent considerations of judicial policy here come into play. A case may raise an important question but the record may be cloudy. It may be desirable to have different aspects of an issue further illumined by the lower courts. Wise adjudication has its own time for ripening.

Since there are these conflicting and, to the uninformed, even confusing reasons for denying petitions for certiorari, it has been suggested from time to time that the Court indicate its reasons for denial. Practical considerations preclude. [The] time that would be required is prohibitive, apart from the fact as already indicated that different reasons not infrequently move different members of the Court. [It] becomes relevant here to note that failure to record a dissent from a denial of a petition for writ of certiorari in nowise implies that only the member of the Court who notes his dissent thought the petition should be granted. * * *

NOTES AND QUESTIONS

1. ***Volume of business.*** In recent years, over 8,000 cases have been filed annually in the Supreme Court. For the Court's 2013–14 Term, the total was 8,580. Only a few come within the Court's original jurisdiction or its now nearly non-existent mandatory appellate jurisdiction; virtually all are petitions for certiorari, which the Court may, but need not, choose to hear. The Court decided only 72 cases with written opinions in the 2013–14 Term, down from an average of 172 cases each year for the five Terms spanning 1984–88 and an average of 113 for the five Terms spanning 1990–97. See the annual November issue of the Harv.L.Rev. for each Term's statistics. Thomas W. Merrill, *The Making of the Second Rehnquist Court: A Preliminary Analysis*, 47 St.L.U.L.J. 569 (2003), attributes the origins of the decline to a deliberate policy choice by the Rehnquist Court.

2. ***The screening process.*** To assist them in selecting the cases in which to grant certiorari, the justices rely heavily on law clerks to summarize the petitions and recommend dispositions. Most of the justices now reportedly share "pool memos," which are prepared by law clerks and distributed to all justices participating in the "cert. pool." See H. W. Perry, Jr., *Deciding to Decide: Agenda Setting in the United States Supreme Court* 51–64 (1991); John P. Stevens, *The Life Span of a Judge-Made Rule*, 58 N.Y.U.L.Rev. 1 (1983); Adam Liptak, *A Second Justice [Alito] Opts out of a Longtime Custom: The "Cert. Pool,"* N.Y. Times, Sept. 26, 2008, at A21. The justices then meet in conference to decide which cases to accept. The Chief Justice prepares a list of cases potentially worthy of consideration, and any other justice may add a case to the "discuss" list. Cases not put on the list are automatically denied review. At conference, there reportedly is relatively little discussion of which cases to grant and which to deny.

Despite the "cert. pool" and a streamlined process of consideration, the screening process makes heavy demands on the justices' time and energy. From time to time, proposals have surfaced to transfer responsibility for management of the Court's docket to some other tribunal.[33] Among the objections to such proposals is that deciding which cases to review is crucial to the Supreme Court's function of overseeing the coherent development and evolution of a uniform body of federal law.

3. ***The "rule of four."*** (a) By long tradition, it takes the votes of four justices to put a case on the Court's plenary docket.

---

[33] The most prominent was advanced by a committee chaired by Professor Paul Freund, *Report of the Study Group on the Caseload of the Supreme Court* (Federal Judicial Center 1972); see Paul A. Freund, *Why We Need the National Court of Appeals*, 59 A.B.A.J. 247 (1973).

(b)   When, after oral argument, upon further study, or due to intervening factors, the Court feels that the basis upon which certiorari was granted no longer exists, the Court may "dismiss the writ as improvidently granted." See Stephen M. Shapiro, Kenneth S. Geller, Timothy S. Bishop, Edward A. Hartnett, & Dan Himmelfarb, *Supreme Court Practice* § 5.15 (10th ed. 2013). Suppose, however, that the four justices who voted to grant certiorari continue to want the case to be heard. Is a vote to dismiss at that point inconsistent with the "rule of four"? Compare *Triangle Improvement Council v. Ritchie,* 402 U.S. 497 (1971) (dismissing certiorari as improvidently granted over the dissent of four Justices) with *Burrell v. McCray,* 426 U.S. 471 (1976) (dismissing certiorari with the support of one of the original four). Consider Stevens, J., concurring in *New York v. Uplinger,* 467 U.S. 246, 251 (1984): "[T]he Rule of Four is [a] device for deciding when a case must be argued, but its force is largely spent once the case has been heard. At that point, a more fully informed majority of the Court must decide whether some countervailing principle outweighs the interest in judicial economy in deciding the case."

(c)   Suppose that four justices vote to grant certiorari in a capital case, and the successful petitioner then applies to the Court for a stay of execution, which would ordinarily require the votes of five justices. Are the five justices who would have denied certiorari obliged by the "rule of four" to grant the stay in order to forestall execution of the prisoner so that the case can be decided? See, e.g., *Herrera v. Collins,* 502 U.S. 1085 (1992) (denying stay by vote of 5–4); Mark Tushnet, *"The King of France with Forty Thousand Men":* Felker v. Turpin *and the Supreme Court's Deliberative Process,* 1996 Sup.Ct.Rev. 163. Shapiro et al., supra, § 18.8, report the observation of a knowledgeable observer that "the practice in the Roberts Court is to provide a courtesy fifth vote for a stay whenever there are four votes to grant certiorari," but stop short of saying so on their own authority, and add that "no statute or Supreme Court Rule requires such a practice."

4.   ***Criteria for granting the writ.*** Although each of the subparagraphs of Rule 10 refers to a "conflict" of authorities as a basis for certiorari, studies indicate that the Court does not invariably grant certiorari in such cases,[34] and commentators are divided both about how to identify "conflicts" and about the importance of resolving conflicts at an early stage before issues have been fully explored in the lower courts.[35]

---

[34]   See, e.g., Arthur D. Hellman, *By Precedent Unbound: The Nature and Extent of Unresolved Intercircuit Conflicts,* 56 U.Pitt.L.Rev. 693 (1995); Arthur D. Hellman, *Light on a Darkling Plain: Intercircuit Conflicts in the Perspective of Time and Experience,* 1998 Sup.Ct.Rev. 247; see also Wayne A. Logan, *Constitutional Cacophony: Federal Circuit Splits and the Fourth Amendment,* 65 Vand. L. Rev. 1137 (2012) (presenting evidence that the Court has left open numerous conflicts of authority in Fourth Amendment cases).

[35]   Compare Richard A. Posner, *The Federal Courts: Challenge and Reform* 195 (2d ed. 1996) (observing that the Court's diminishing case load indicates that it does not regard unresolved conflicts as a major problem at this time) with Thomas E. Baker & Douglas D. McFarland, *The Need for a New National Court,* 100 Harv.L.Rev. 1400 (1987) (asserting the importance of uniform national law).

5. *Significance of denials of certiorari.* The Court has often asserted that the denial of certiorari carries no precedential significance; the Court does not approve the judgment of the lower court, but merely—for unexplained reasons—allows it to stand. Consider Peter Linzer, *The Meaning of Certiorari Denials*, 79 Colum.L.Rev. 1227 (1979): "[A] certiorari denial is often not based on the merits and never should bind anyone. [Yet] it seems time to stop pretending that denial of certiorari means nothing. Many times it gives us a glimpse, imperfect to be sure, into the Justices' preliminary attitudes on a given issue."

6. *Summary reversals.* On relatively rare occasions, the Court will reverse a decision below on the certiorari papers without further briefing or argument; when it does so, the Court usually issues a brief, per curiam opinion explaining its decision. Is it troubling that the Court would render decision based on so cursory a review?

5. PREREQUISITES TO FEDERAL JURISDICTION AND JUDICIAL REVIEW: AN INTRODUCTION

Under Article III, federal judicial power extends only to "cases" and "controversies." Thus, federal courts are precluded from giving "advisory opinions" or deciding "moot" cases. Parties asserting constitutional challenges must have "standing." Further, claims must be asserted at a time when they are "ripe" for adjudication: "[a] hypothetical threat is not enough";[36] "[d]etermination of [the] constitutionality of legislation in advance of its immediate adverse effect in the context of a concrete case involves too remote and abstract an inquiry for the proper exercise of the judicial function."[37]

Because matters such as standing, mootness, and ripeness all must be resolved before a federal court may consider the merits of a constitutional contention, they could profitably be explored in detail here. But their consideration is often intertwined with and requires understanding of the substantive constitutional provision in issue. Thus, the presentation of these topics is deferred to Ch. 12, for study when students will be better equipped to comprehend and evaluate them.

A number of additional requirements must also be satisfied for the Supreme Court to be able to review *state court* decisions (as opposed to the decisions of the *federal* courts of appeals, which—for reasons that will become clear—seldom if ever present the same obstacles). While these requirements are considered at length in courses on Federal Courts, the most important are briefly described below.

1. *Final judgments or decrees.* The Court will ordinarily review only the final judgment or decree of the highest state court in which review

---

[36] *United Public Workers v. Mitchell*, Ch. 12, Sec. 3, II, infra.

[37] *International Longshoremen's and Warehousemen's Union v. Boyd*, 347 U.S. 222 (1954).

of a decision could be had—typically, though not invariably, the state's supreme court. The "final judgment" rule reflects intertwined policies aimed at avoiding (i) unnecessary constitutional decisions; (ii) inefficient, piecemeal review; and (iii) unnecessary interference with state court processes. In its traditional formulation, the "final judgment" rule barred Supreme Court review until the completion of all lower court proceedings in a case. Since the 1970s, however, the rule has been relaxed somewhat. In the leading case of *Cox Broadcasting Corp. v. Cohn*, 420 U.S. 469 (1975), the Court acknowledged that there were "at least four categories" of cases in which it had treated and would continue to treat "the decision on the federal issue as [final] without awaiting the completion of the additional proceedings anticipated in the lower state courts."[38] Although important, the exceptions appear not to have swallowed the rule, and review in the Supreme Court is generally not available until a case has come to final judgment in the state system.[39]

2. ***Review limited to issues of federal law.*** Under *Murdock v. Memphis*, 87 U.S. (20 Wall.) 590 (1875)—a precursor of sorts to the later decision in *Erie Railroad Co. v. Tompkins*, 304 U.S. 64 (1938)—the Court will generally not review state court decisions of state law issues. Nor, for the most part, will it review determinations of fact. Review, in other words, is ordinarily limited to questions of federal law.[40]

3. ***Issues duly raised in state court.*** To be litigable in the Supreme Court, a federal issue generally must have been duly raised in state court. This requirement helps to ensure that the facts bearing on federal issues will have been adequately explored and the competing arguments ventilated. Sensible exceptions to this requirement exist for cases in which state procedural rules unduly impede the effort to raise a federal issue or

---

[38] The Court defined the four categories as follows: (i) those in which, although further state proceedings remain to be completed, the federal issue has been authoritatively decided and is effectively "conclusive" so that the outcome is "preordained"; (ii) cases "in which the federal issue, finally decided by the highest court in the State, will survive and require decision regardless of the outcome of future state-court proceedings"; (iii) "those situations where the federal claim has been finally decided, with further proceedings on the merits in the state courts to come, but in which later review of the federal issue cannot be had"—for example, because a state, having lost on the appeal of a constitutional issue in a criminal case, would not subsequently be able to appeal if the accused were acquitted at trial; and (iv) "those situations where the federal issue has been finally decided in the state courts with further proceedings pending in which the party seeking review here might prevail on the merits on nonfederal grounds, thus rendering unnecessary review of the federal issue by this Court, and where reversal of the state court on the federal issue would be preclusive of any further litigation on the relevant cause of action rather than merely controlling the nature and character of, or determining the admissibility of evidence in, the state proceedings still to come." Concerning the fourth exception, the Court explained that review would be appropriate only "if a refusal immediately to review the state-court decision might seriously erode federal policy."

[39] For lucid discussion of the final judgment rule, see Erwin Chemerinsky, *Federal Jurisdiction* 712–34 (6th ed. 2012).

[40] For a discussion of complications that trigger exceptions to the general rules, see Richard H. Fallon, Jr., John F. Manning, Daniel J. Meltzer, & David L. Shapiro, *Hart & Wechsler's The Federal Courts and the Federal System* 462–96 (6th ed. 2009).

the highest state court actually decides a federal question, even if the question was not raised in compliance with state procedural rules.

4. ***Adequate and independent state grounds.*** Perhaps the most complex limitation on the Court's appellate jurisdiction is the doctrine barring review of decisions that rest on "adequate and independent state grounds." In a nutshell, the rationale of the doctrine is that the Court's "only power over state judgments is to correct them to the extent that they incorrectly adjudge federal rights. [If] the same judgment would be rendered by the state court after we corrected its views of federal laws, our review could amount to nothing more than an advisory opinion." *Herb v. Pitcairn*, 324 U.S. 117 (1945).

For the most part, a state law ground of decision will be "adequate" to support a judgment if it dictates that a case would come out the same way, regardless of how the Supreme Court might decide a federal issue also presented in the case. Suppose, for example, that a state court were to rule against the plaintiff in a libel case on the alternative grounds that (i) liability was barred by the First Amendment to the United States Constitution and (ii) the defendant's allegedly libelous comments were also privileged as a matter of state law. Even if the Supreme Court were to grant review and reverse on the federal constitutional issue, the plaintiff would still not be able to recover on a state law libel claim, due to the state law privilege. The ruling on the state law privilege issue thus would be "adequate" to support the judgment.

The ruling on the state law privilege issue would also be "independent" of the federal First Amendment issue, since the rulings on the two issues do not appear to be connected in any way: the state law privilege would apply even if the First Amendment should be construed not to preclude liability.

The issue of independence becomes trickier, however, in cases in which it appears that a state court may have decided an issue in a particular way *because of* its arguable misunderstanding of federal law. For example, many states have interpreted provisions of their state constitutions to confer protections identical to those conferred by the parallel provisions of the federal Constitution. Thus, a state court might hold, for example, that liability for a defamatory publication is barred by the state constitution *because* it is barred by the federal Constitution; in other words, the ruling with respect to state constitutional law might be dictated by the ruling with respect to federal law. In such a case, a state court's determination that speech is not actionable under the state constitution would not be "independent" of its decision of the federal issue. If the Supreme Court were to grant review and reverse on the federal constitutional issue, the state court, on remand, would presumably reverse its ruling on the state constitutional issue, and the outcome of the case could change.

The concept of "independence," which is complicated even in theory, frequently becomes even more complicated in practice, since state courts do not always make clear whether their rulings with respect to state issues are independent of their decisions of federal issues—that is, whether they would decide the state law issue the same way, even if they thought the federal issue should be decided differently. After experimenting with various approaches to cases in which it was unclear whether a state law ground of decision was independent of the federal ground, the Court has now decided to presume, in *ambiguous* cases, that state grounds of decision are *not* independent and thus do not bar Supreme Court review of the federal issues in a case. According to *Michigan v. Long*, 463 U.S. 1032 (1983), "when [a] state court decision fairly appears to rest primarily on federal law, or to be interwoven with the federal law, and when the adequacy and independence of any possible state law ground is not clear from the face of the opinion, we will accept as the most reasonable explanation that the state court decided the case the way it did because it believed that federal law required it to do so."[41]

---

[41] For further discussion and critical assessment of the "independent and adequate state ground doctrine," see Chemerinsky, supra, at 735–62.

CHAPTER 2

NATIONAL LEGISLATIVE POWER

■ ■ ■

1. SOURCES AND NATURE

Introduction

By 1787, the minimal power of the national government under the Articles of Confederation—including its inability to directly raise armies, collect taxes, regulate foreign commerce (in particular to establish tariffs to protect new domestic industries), enforce domestic laws, and require the states to conform to the Peace Treaty with Great Britain[1]—produced what many considered to be a political crisis. Among the major defects in the Articles that led to the Constitutional Convention was the lack of authority to eliminate trade barriers erected by the individual states that treated other states like foreign nations and threatened to result in interstate commercial warfare.[2]

With these concerns in mind, the framers set out to construct a new central government that would have sufficient authority to address national problems, but whose powers would be limited to those designated in the Constitution. The framers recognized the conflict between generalized grants of federal power (which might threaten the liberty of the people) and in overly specific listing of powers (which might leave the new government as ineffective as its predecessor). At one point, the Convention tentatively approved Virginia's proposal that the national legislature should have power "to legislate in all cases for the general interests of the Union, and also in those to which the States are separately incompetent."[3] But the Committee on Detail's final report chose instead to enumerate a series of powers—mainly in Art. I, § 8—and to add at the end the power to "make all laws that shall be necessary and proper for carrying

---

[1] See *The Federalist* No. 15 (Alexander Hamilton). The Federalist was a series of essays published in New York newspapers in late 1787 and early 1788 to defend the proposed Constitution against attacks aimed at defeating its ratification in New York. The essays were republished in book form as "The Federalist" in the Spring of 1788. The principal authors, anonymous at time of publication, were Alexander Hamilton, James Madison, and John Jay.

[2] Indeed, it was not until more than 100 years later that the Court held that Congress' power in Art. I, § 8, cl.3 "to regulate Commerce . . . among the several States" (Sec. 2 infra) was not limited to protecting interstate commerce "from acts of interference by state legislation," but also included the regulation of "private contracts between citizens" if they obstruct interstate commerce. *Addyston Pipe & Steel Co. v. United States*, 175 U.S. 211 (1899).

[3] 2 Max Farrand, *Records of the Federal Convention* 26–27 (1911).

into execution the foregoing powers, and all other powers vested, by this Constitution." This change may be interpreted in different ways. It might indicate that the Committee intended to reject any generalized grant of power in favor of the more limited enumeration.[4] On the other hand, it has been interpreted to mean that the Committee's report simply confirmed "that the enumeration conformed to the standard previously approved, and that the powers enumerated comprehended those matters as to which the states were separately incompetent and in which national legislation was essential."[5]

Although the Necessary and Proper Clause was adopted by the Convention with little discussion, it was hardly understood uniformly. In 1791, shortly after the Constitution's ratification, before signing a bill chartering a national bank, President Washington sought opinions on its constitutionality. Secretary of the Treasury Alexander Hamilton argued that the Necessary and Proper Clause had to be interpreted broadly, and that the bank legislation was clearly constitutional. To him, laws "necessary" to carry out Congress' powers meant laws "needful, requisite, incidental, useful" to such powers. Limiting Congress' authority to strict necessity would unreasonably curtail the government's ability to act. Although Hamilton acknowledged limits on the federal legislative power,[6] he took the Necessary and Proper Clause to mean that Congress had implied powers: it was given broad means to achieve its relatively circumscribed ends.

Secretary of State Thomas Jefferson argued that the bank would be flatly unconstitutional, strictly reading the Necessary and Proper Clause: a national bank was in no sense *essential* to carry out the duties of the federal government. If the clause were read so broadly as to make the bank "necessary," then Congress would effectively be authorized to enact any legislation that would be "convenient" in carrying out its goals, thus rendering the Convention's careful enumeration irrelevant.[7]

Hamilton's co-Federalist, James Madison, appeared to believe that the substance of the Necessary and Proper Clause was such an integral part of

---

[4] Support for this position comes from the Tenth Amendment, which ensures that "powers not delegated to the United States . . . are reserved to the States respectively, or to the people."

[5] Robert L. Stern, *That Commerce Which Concerns More States than One*, 47 Harv.L.Rev. 1335 (1934) (arguing that the Convention's accepting the replacement in the "absence of objection or comment upon the change" argues for this interpretation). Accord, Donald H. Regan *How to Think About the Federal Commerce Power and Incidentally Rewrite United States v. Lopez*, 94 Mich.L.Rev. 554 (1995).

[6] Hamilton had argued *against* the need for a Bill of Rights on the ground that such documents normally enumerate rights a monarch's subjects do *not* surrender, whereas the people under the proposed Constitution "surrender nothing, and as they retain every thing, they have no need of particular reservations." *The Federalist* No. 84. Indeed, he had contended that explicitly preventing the federal government from legislating in some areas might give weight to arguments that the power to do so existed in the first place. Id.

[7] See John C. Yoo, *McCulloch v. Maryland*, in Constitutional Stupidities, Constitutional Tragedies 241 (1998).

the Constitution that its explicit presence in the text was unnecessary: "No axiom is more clearly established in law, or in reason, than that wherever the end is required, the means are authorized; wherever a general power to do a thing is given, every particular power necessary for doing it, is included."[8] To him, "had the Constitution been silent on this head, there can be no doubt that all the particular powers, requisite as means of executing the general powers, would have resulted to the government, by unavoidable implication."[9] Nevertheless, by the time of the bank controversy, Madison had moved to Jefferson's camp, believing that Hamilton's interpretation threatened the delicate balance of federalism. The matter was addressed by the Court in *McCulloch v. Maryland*, infra, involving a second law, chartering another national bank, passed in 1816 and not vetoed by President Madison.

The early controversy over the contours of America's system of federalism has continued unabated. On the one hand, it is generally agreed that the framers feared that a too powerful federal government might trample the liberties of its citizens. They hoped to check potential tyranny both by limits upon national legislative powers, and also by maintaining viable state governments that would tend to counter efforts by the national government to aggrandize its powers.[10] To this day, the Court adheres to this understanding of a balanced strength, reiterating that state and federal governments "will act as mutual restraints only if both are credible. In the tension between federal and state power lies the promise of liberty."[11] As also underlined regularly by the Court, the framers recognized further benefits to the federalist structure: "It assures a decentralized government that will be more sensitive to the diverse needs of a heterogenous society; it increases opportunity for citizen involvement in democratic processes; it allows for more innovation and experimentation in government; and it makes government more responsive by putting the States in competition for a mobile citizenry."[12] For a compact but thorough evaluation of the historic and contemporary values of federalism, see David L. Shapiro, *Federalism: A Dialogue* (1995).

---

[8]   *The Federalist* No. 44.

[9]   Id. Madison added: "Had the Convention attempted a positive enumeration of the powers necessary and proper for carrying their other powers into effect; the attempt would have involved a complete digest of laws on every subject to which the Constitution relates." Id.

[10]   See, e.g., *The Federalist* No. 28 (Alexander Hamilton), No. 51 (James Madison).

[11]   *Gregory v. Ashcroft*, 501 U.S. 452 (1991).

[12]   Id. For the view that "federalism in America achieves none of the beneficial goals that the Court claims for it," and that these goals "call for a decentralized regime, not a federal one," see Edward L. Rubin & Malcolm Feeley, *Federalism: Some Notes on a National Neurosis*, 41 UCLA L.Rev. 903 (1994). For the view that the judiciary and academic commentators have largely ignored (1) the widely discussed "justifications for regulating at the central or national level, rather than retaining regulatory authority in the states," and (2) "any serious study" of "the supposed values of federalism" or "any sustained attempt to measure their true worth," see Barry Friedman, *Valuing Federalism*, 82 Minn.L.Rev. 317 (1997).

Background of McCulloch v. Maryland. The first Bank of the United States engaged in a private banking business, but also acted as a depository for United States funds wherever it established branches. The preamble of the Act incorporating the Bank stated that its establishment "will be very conducive to the successful conducting of the national finances; will tend to give facility to the obtaining of loans, for the use of the government, in sudden emergencies; and will be productive of considerable advantages to trade and industry in general." The second Bank was incorporated over strenuous political opposition, and made itself extremely unpopular, particularly in the West and South, when it over-expanded credits and later drastically curtailed them, contributing to the failure of many state-incorporated banks. As a result, a number of states sought to exclude the Bank, either by state constitutional prohibitions against operating within the state any bank not chartered by the state, or by imposing heavy discriminatory taxes on such banks. The tax in *McCulloch* was one of the milder taxes.

McCULLOCH v. MARYLAND

17 U.S. (4 Wheat.) 316, 4 L.Ed. 579 (1819).

CHIEF JUSTICE MARSHALL delivered the opinion of the Court.

[Maryland taxed any bank operating in the state without state authority 2% of the face value of all banknotes issued unless it paid a $15,000 tax. The Maryland Court of Appeals upheld judgment for the statutory penalty against the cashier of the Baltimore branch of the Bank of United States for issuing bank notes without payment of the tax. The Supreme Court reversed only three days after completion of nine days of oral argument.[13]]

The first question [is], has Congress power to incorporate a bank? * * *

This government is acknowledged by all to be one of enumerated powers.[14] [Among] the enumerated powers, we do not find that of establishing a bank or creating a corporation. But there is no phrase in the

---

[13] See G. Edward White, *The Working Life of the Marshall Court, 1815–1835*, 70 Va.L.Rev. 1 (1984), commenting on the frequent short intervals between arguments and decisions during the Marshall period of unlimited oral arguments, unanimous opinions, light appellate calendars, short sojourns in Washington, and heavy circuit-riding duties.

[14] The Court rejected Maryland's argument that the Constitution was "the Act of sovereign and independent states," who "delegated" the "powers of the federal government," which must be exercised in subordination to the states: "The convention which framed the Constitution was, indeed, elected by the state legislatures. But the instrument, when it came from their hands, was a mere proposal [to] the then existing Congress of the United States, with a request that it might 'be submitted to a convention of delegates, chosen in each state, by the people thereof, under the recommendation of its legislature, for their assent and ratification.' This mode of proceeding was adopted; and by the convention, by Congress, and by the state legislatures, the instrument was submitted to the people. They acted upon it, in the only manner in which they can act safely, effectively, and wisely, on such a subject, by assembling in convention [in] their several states * * * .

instrument which, like the Articles of Confederation [Article II: "Each state retains [every] power [not] expressly delegated."] excludes incidental or implied powers; and which requires that everything granted shall be expressly and minutely described. Even the tenth amendment, which was framed for the purpose of quieting the excessive jealousies which had been excited, omits the word "expressly," and declares only that the powers "not delegated to the United States, nor prohibited to the states, are reserved to the states or to the people"; thus leaving the question, whether the particular power which may become the subject of contest has been delegated to the one government, or prohibited to the other, to depend on a fair construction of the whole instrument. The men who drew and adopted this amendment had experienced the embarrassments resulting from the insertion of this word ["expressly"] in the Articles of Confederation, and probably omitted it to avoid those embarrassments.[15] A constitution, to contain an accurate detail of all the subdivisions of which its great powers will admit, and of all the means by which they may be carried into execution, would partake of the prolixity of a legal code, and could scarcely be embraced by the human mind. It would probably never be understood by the public. Its nature, therefore, requires, that only its great outlines should be marked, its important objects designated, and the minor ingredients which composed those objects be deduced from the nature of the objects themselves. [In] considering this question, then, we must never forget, that it is *a constitution* we are expounding.

Although, among the enumerated powers of government, we do not find the word "bank," or "incorporation," we find the great powers to lay and collect taxes; to borrow money; to regulate commerce; to declare and conduct a war; and to raise and support armies and navies. The sword and the purse, all the external relations, and no inconsiderable portion of the industry of the nation, are intrusted to its government. It can never be pretended that these vast powers draw after them others of inferior importance, merely because they are inferior. [But] it may, with great reason be contended that a government, intrusted with such ample powers, on the due execution of which the happiness and prosperity of the nation so vitally depends, must also be intrusted with ample means for their execution. The power being given, it is the interest of the nation to facilitate its execution. It can never be their interest, and cannot be presumed to have been their intention, to clog and embarrass its execution by withholding the most appropriate means. [The] exigencies of the nation may require, that the treasure raised in the North should be transported to the South, that raised in the East conveyed to the West, or that this

---

[15] For the view that "both in terms of the Constitution's text and historical understanding," Marshall, C. J., was "almost certainly wrong" in relying on "the omitted word 'expressly' in support of broad interpretations of federal power," see Kurt T. Lash, *The Original Meaning of the Omission: The Tenth Amendment, Popular Sovereignty, and "Expressly" Delegated Power,* 83 Notre D. L. Rev. 1889 (2008).

order should be reversed. Is that construction of the Constitution to be preferred which would render these operations difficult, hazardous, and expensive? Can we adopt that construction (unless the words imperiously require it) which would impute to the framers of that instrument, when granting these powers for the public good, the intention of impeding their exercise by withholding a choice of means? * * *

The creation of a corporation, it is said, appertains to sovereignty. This is admitted. But to what portion of sovereignty does it appertain? [In] America, the powers of sovereignty are divided between the government of the Union, and those of the states. They are each sovereign, with respect to the objects committed to it, and neither sovereign with respect to the objects committed to the other. [We] cannot well comprehend the process of reasoning which maintains, that a power appertaining to sovereignty cannot be connected with that vast portion of it which is granted to the general government, so far as it is calculated to subserve the legitimate objects of that government. The power of creating a corporation, though appertaining to sovereignty, is not, like the power of making war, or levying taxes, or of regulating commerce, a great substantive and independent power, which cannot be implied as incidental to other powers, or used as a means of executing them. It is never the end for which other powers are exercised, but a means by which other objects are accomplished. * * *

But the Constitution of the United States has not left the right of Congress to employ the necessary means, for the execution of the powers conferred on the government, to general reasoning. To its enumeration of powers is added that of [the Necessary and Proper Clause].

The counsel for the state of Maryland have urged [that] this clause, though in terms a grant of power, is not so in effect; but is really restrictive of the general right, which might otherwise be implied, of selecting means for executing the enumerated powers. [T]he argument on which most reliance is placed, is drawn from the peculiar language of this clause. Congress is not empowered by it to make all laws, which may have relation to the powers conferred on the government, but such only as may be *"necessary and proper"* for carrying them into execution. The word *"necessary"* is considered as controlling the whole sentence, and as limiting the right to pass laws for the execution of the granted powers, to such as are indispensable, and without which the power would be nugatory. That it excludes the choice of means, and leaves to Congress in each case, that only which is most direct and simple.

Is it true, that this is the sense in which the word "necessary" is always used? [If] reference be had to its use, in the common affairs of the world, or in approved authors, we find that it frequently imports no more than that one thing is convenient, or useful, or essential to another. To employ the means necessary to an end, is generally understood as employing any means calculated to produce the end, and not as being confined to those single means, without which the end would be entirely unattainable. [A] thing may be necessary, very necessary, absolutely or indispensably necessary. To no mind would the same idea be conveyed, by these several phrases. This comment on the word is well illustrated [by] the tenth section of the first article of the Constitution. It is, we think, impossible to compare the sentence which prohibits a state from laying "imposts, or duties on imports or exports, except what may be *absolutely* necessary for executing its inspection laws," with that which authorizes Congress "to make all laws which shall be necessary and proper for carrying into execution" the powers of the general government, without feeling a conviction that the convention understood itself to change materially the meaning of the word "necessary" by prefixing the word "absolutely." This word, then like others, is used in various senses; and in its construction, the subject, the context, the intention of the person using them, are all to be taken into view.

Let this be done in the case under consideration. The subject is the execution of those great powers on which the welfare of a nation essentially depends. It must have been the intention of those who gave these powers, to insure, as far as human prudence could insure, their beneficial execution. [This] provision is made in a constitution intended to endure for ages to come, and, consequently, to be adapted to the various crises of human affairs. To have prescribed the means by which government should, in all future time, execute its powers, would have been to change, entirely, the character of the instrument, and give it the properties of a legal code. It would have been an unwise attempt to provide, by immutable rules, for exigencies which, if foreseen at all must have been seen dimly, and which can be best provided for as they occur. To have declared that the best means shall not be used, but those alone without which the power given would be nugatory, would have been to deprive the legislature of the capacity to avail itself of experience, to exercise its reason, and to accommodate its legislation to circumstances. If we apply this principle of construction to any of the powers of the government, we shall find it so pernicious in its operation that we shall be compelled to discard [it.]

But the argument which most conclusively demonstrates the error of the construction contended for by the counsel for the state of Maryland, is founded on the intention of the convention, as manifested in the whole clause: * * *

1st. The clause is placed among the powers of Congress, not among the limitations on those powers.

2nd. Its terms purport to enlarge, not to diminish the powers vested in the government. It purports to be an additional power, not a restriction on those already granted. [If] no other motive for its insertion can be suggested, a sufficient one is found in the desire to remove all doubts respecting the right to legislate on that vast mass of incidental powers which must be involved in the Constitution, if that instrument be not a splendid bauble.

We admit, as all must admit, that the powers of the government are limited, and that its limits are not to be transcended. But we think the sound construction of the Constitution must allow to the national legislature that discretion, with respect to the means by which the powers it confers are to be carried into [execution]. Let the end be legitimate, let it be within the scope of the Constitution, and all means which are appropriate, which are plainly adapted to that end, which are not prohibited, but consist with the letter and spirit of the Constitution, are constitutional. * * *

If a corporation may be employed indiscriminately with other means to carry into execution the powers of the government, no particular reason can be assigned for excluding the use of a bank, if required for its fiscal operations. [That] it is a convenient, a useful, and essential instrument in the prosecution of its fiscal operations, is not now a subject of controversy. * * *

But were its necessity less apparent, none can deny its being an appropriate measure; and if it is, the degree of its necessity, as has been very justly observed, is to be discussed in another place. [S]hould Congress, under the pretext of executing its powers, pass laws for the accomplishment of objects not entrusted to the government; it would become the painful duty of this tribunal, should a case requiring such a decision come before it, to say that such an act was not the law of the land. But where the law is not prohibited, and is really calculated to effect any of the objects entrusted to the government, to undertake here to inquire into the degree of its necessity, would be to pass the line which circumscribes the judicial department, and to tread on legislative ground. * * *

[The Court invalidated Maryland's tax on the United States Bank, invoking the Supremacy Clause (Art. VI, cl. 2). This ruling and its progeny are considered in Sec. 5 infra.]

NOTES AND QUESTIONS

1.   *Court's reasoning.* Does *McCulloch* leave room for effective judicial review over congressional action not expressly authorized by the Constitution but arguably designed to effectuate one or more of the expressly granted powers? What standard of review does the Court indicate it will apply in deciding such cases? What ought the standard to be? As for a "substantive" limit, is there "a vast difference between those powers reasonably *ancillary* to an enumerated power—in the sense that the powers thus implied are at least useful in effectuating the power expressly enumerated—and the far larger set

of powers that merely *relate*, in some loose sense, to the power expressly enumerated"? Tribe 3d ed., at 801. For a "procedural" limit, consider David E. Engdahl, *Casebooks and Constitutional Competency*, 21 Seattle U.L.Rev. 741 (1998): "From the beginning it has been deemed '*the right of the legislature* to exercise *its* best judgment in the selection of measures to carry into execution the constitutional powers of the government,' [*McCulloch*,] and therefore that *judgment by Congress* is the indispensable requisite of this power. [T]he Constitution entitles the people to have their electorally answerable *political* organs *actually and openly* inquire, debate, compromise, and resolve whether and how far it is necessary to reach matters otherwise beyond the national government's scope, *in order to* effectuate enumerated federal powers."[16] To what extent would this help determine whether laws are "really calculated" to accomplish permissible objectives, rather than being a "pretext" for Congress to go beyond its delegated powers? *Should* the Court make this determination? (The problem of judicial inquiry into legislative or executive motivation arises for many constitutional provisions—e.g., Sec. 2 infra (commerce power); Sec. 3 infra (taxing power); Ch. 4 (state power to regulate commerce); Ch. 7, Sec. 2 (freedom of speech); Ch. 8 (freedom of religion); Ch. 9, Secs. 2, III and 5, I, B (equal protection).)

2. ***Contemporary judicial analysis of McCulloch.*** (a) The most recent extensive consideration, UNITED STATES v. COMSTOCK, 130 S.Ct. 1949 (2010), per BREYER, J., basing its "conclusion on five considerations, taken together," upheld "a federal civil-commitment statute [that] authorizes the Department of Justice to detain a mentally ill, sexually dangerous federal prisoner beyond the date the prisoner would otherwise be released. 18 U.S.C. § 4248. [1. The government] must first 'make all reasonable efforts to cause' the State where that person was tried, or the State where he is domiciled, to 'assume responsibility for his custody, care and treatment.'

"[I]n determining whether the Necessary and Proper Clause grants Congress the legislative authority to enact a particular federal statute, we look to see whether the statute constitutes a means that is rationally related to the implementation of a constitutionally enumerated power. *Sabri v. United*

---

[16] For the view "that legal actors during the founding era understood the words 'necessary' and 'proper' to have distinct meanings in many contexts, [and that the] meaning of 'proper' would require executory laws to be laws that are peculiarly within the jurisdiction or competence of Congress—that is, to be laws that do not tread on the retained rights of individuals or states, or the prerogatives of federal executive or judicial departments," see Gary Lawson & Patricia B. Granger, *The "Proper" Scope of Federal Power: A Jurisdictional Interpretation of the Sweeping Clause*, 43 Duke L.J. 267 (1993). For another historically based view, narrower than that in *McCulloch*, see Randy E. Barnett, *The Original Meaning of the Necessary and Proper Clause*, 6 U.Pa.J.Con.L. 183 (2003). For the view that "Chief Justice Marshall understood his *McCulloch* opinion to [require] a relatively close proximity between a legislative measure and the enumerated powers of Congress," see J. Randy Beck, *The New Jurisprudence of the Necessary and Proper Clause*, 2002 U.Ill.L.Rev. 581. Compare Calvin H. Johnson, *The Dubious Enumerated Power Doctrine*, 22 Const. Comm. 25 (2005): "The enumerated powers [are] best read as desirable activities that are *illustrative* of the appropriate national sphere, but not exhaustive. [The] enduring principle intended by the founders was that the new federal government would undertake only things for the common or general interest. [Thus,] the common defense and general welfare standard [of] Art. I, § 8, cl. 1 (see Sec. III infra)] tells us when implied powers are appropriate."

States, [Sec. 3, II infra]; *Gonzales v. Raich,* [Sec. 2, IV infra]. Congress routinely exercises its authority to enact criminal laws in furtherance of, for example, its enumerated powers to regulate interstate and foreign commerce, to enforce civil rights, to spend funds for the general welfare, [and] so forth. [2. Here,] Congress has long been involved in the delivery of mental health care to federal prisoners, and has long provided for their civil commitment [including] insane criminals [who are sexually dangerous] upon the expiration of their terms of confinement * * * .

[3] "[Section] 4248 is 'reasonably adapted,' *United States v. Darby,* [Sec. 2, II, B infra], to Congress' power to act as a responsible federal custodian (a power that rests, in turn, upon federal criminal statutes that legitimately seek to implement constitutionally enumerated authority,) [and] Congress could have reasonably concluded [that] § 4248 satisfies 'review for means-end rationality,' i.e., that it satisfies the Constitution's insistence that a federal statute represent a rational means for implementing a constitutional grant of legislative authority.

[4. "Nor] does this statute invade state sovereignty or otherwise improperly limit the scope of 'powers that remain with the States.' To the contrary, it requires *accommodation* of state interests. [5. The dissent's argument] that Congress' authority can be no more than one step removed from a specifically enumerated power [is] irreconcilable with our precedents. [A]s Chief Justice Marshall recognized in *McCulloch,* [from] the power to "to establish post offices and post roads" [has] been inferred the power and duty of *carrying* the mail along the post road, from one post office to another. And, from this *implied* power, has *again* been inferred the right to *punish* those who steal letters from the post office, or rob the mail.' "

KENNEDY, J., concurred in the judgment because § 4248 "is a discrete and narrow exercise of authority over a small class of persons already subject to the federal power," but "when the inquiry is whether a federal law has sufficient links to an enumerated power to be within the scope of federal authority, the analysis depends not on the number of links in the congressional-power chain but on the strength of the chain. * * *

"The terms 'rationally related' and 'rational basis' must be employed with care, particularly if either is to be used as a stand-alone test. The phrase 'rational basis' [as used in connection with the Due Process Clause is] one of the most deferential formulations of the standard for reviewing legislation in all the Court's precedents, [and] should not be extended uncritically to the issue before us. [The] Court's discussion of the Tenth Amendment invites the inference that restrictions flowing from the federal system are of no import when defining the limits of the National Government's power, as it proceeds by first asking whether the power is within the National Government's reach, and if so it discards federalism concerns entirely. [But it] is of fundamental importance to consider whether essential attributes of state sovereignty are compromised by the assertion of federal power under the Necessary and Proper

Clause; if so, that is a factor suggesting that the power is not one properly within the reach of federal power."

ALITO, J., also concurred only in the judgment: "The Necessary and Proper Clause [requires] an 'appropriate' link between a power conferred by the Constitution and the law enacted by Congress. And it is an obligation of this Court to enforce compliance with that limitation.

"The law in question here satisfies that requirement. This is not a case in which it is merely possible for a court to think of a rational basis on which Congress might have perceived an attenuated link between the powers underlying the federal criminal statutes and the challenged civil commitment provision. Here, there is a substantial link to Congress' constitutional powers."

THOMAS, J., joined by Scalia, J., dissented: Under *McCulloch*, "unless the end itself is 'legitimate,' the fit between means and end is irrelevant. In other words, no matter how 'necessary' or 'proper' an Act of Congress may be to its objective, Congress lacks authority to legislate if the objective is anything other than 'carrying into Execution' one or more of the Federal Government's enumerated powers. [But the] Government identifies no specific enumerated power or powers as a constitutional predicate for § 4248, and none are readily discernable. [It] is clear [that] § 4248 is aimed at protecting society from acts of sexual violence, not [to] execute *any* enumerated power. Section 4248 is therefore unconstitutional.

"[The] Necessary and Proper Clause does not provide Congress with authority to enact any law simply because it furthers *other laws* Congress has enacted in the exercise of its incidental [authority]. Federal laws that criminalize conduct that interferes with enumerated powers, establish prisons for those who engage in that conduct, and set rules for the care and treatment of prisoners awaiting trial or serving a criminal sentence satisfy this test. [Civil] detention under § 4248, on the other hand, lacks any such connection to an enumerated power.[17] § 4248 permits the term of federal civil commitment to continue beyond the date on which a convicted prisoner's sentence expires. [Thus, it] authorizes federal detention of a person even *after* the Government loses the authority to prosecute him for a federal crime.

" * * * States plainly have the constitutional authority to 'take charge' of a federal prisoner released within their jurisdiction. In addition, the assumption that a State knowingly would fail to exercise that authority is, in my view, implausible. [E]ven in the event a State made such a decision, the Constitution assigns the responsibility for that decision, and its consequences, to the state government alone. * * *

"Nevertheless, 29 States appear as amici and argue that § 4248 is constitutional. * * * Congress' power, however, is fixed by the Constitution; it does not expand merely to suit the States' policy preferences, or to allow State officials to avoid difficult choices regarding the allocation of state funds. [T]he duty to protect citizens from violent crime, including acts of sexual violence,

---

[17]   Scalia, J., did not join the analysis of this paragraph.

belongs solely to the States. [The] Constitution gives States [no] power to decline this responsibility."

(b) In UNITED STATES v. KEBODEAUX, 133 S.Ct. 2496 (2013), respondent was convicted by court-martial of a federal sex offense. After he had completed his sentence, Congress enacted a statute (SORNA) that required federal sex offenders to register in the state where they lived. SORNA was retroactively applied to persons like respondent who had failed to reregister when he moved within Texas. The Court, per BREYER, J., noting that an earlier federal statute—predating respondent's "offense, conviction, and release from federal [custody, that] imposed upon him registration requirements very similar to those that SORNA later mandated"—fell "within the scope of Congress' authority under the Necessary and Proper Clause": "Congress could reasonably conclude that registration requirements applied to federal sex offenders after their [release]. SORNA, like the earlier statute, [conditioned] Spending Clause grants to encourage States to adopt its uniform definitions and requirements."

ROBERTS, C.J., concurred only in the judgment: "[All] that matters [is] that Congress could have rationally determined that 'mak[ing] the civil registration requirement at issue here a consequence of Kebodeaux's offense' would give force to the Uniform Code of Military Justice adopted pursuant to Congress's power to regulate the Armed Forces."

ALITO, J., concurred in the judgment "solely on the ground that the registration requirement at issue is necessary and proper to execute Congress' power '[t]o make Rules for the Government and Regulation of the land and naval forces.'"

THOMAS, J., joined by Scalia, J., dissented,[18] relying on his analysis in *Comstock*: SORNA "is not directed at carrying into execution any of the federal powers enumerated in the Constitution [including] the Regulation of the Land and Naval Forces power (because "Congress does not retain a general police power over every person who has ever served in the military)."

3.   *McCulloch's* interpretation of the Necessary and Proper Clause has been held to apply to other grants of congressional power, most notably the "enforcement" provisions of the Civil War amendments. (Ch. 11, Sec. 2.) For the view that recent qualifications on the scope of that congressional enforcement power applies as well to the Necessary and Proper Clause, see Engdahl, supra.

4.   ***Specified powers as only sources of federal legislative power.*** The general rule has been[19] that federal legislation must be based on powers granted to the federal government in the Constitution.

Kansas v. Colorado, 206 U.S. 46 (1907) (Congress had no legislative power to irrigate non-federal lands). Several constitutional provisions other than Art.

---

[18]   Scalia, J., did not join that part of this opinion that repeated the paragraphs in *Comstock* referred to in fn. 17.

[19]   One exception has been for foreign affairs, see Sec. 4 infra.

I, § 8, also expressly authorize lawmaking by Congress, e.g., Art. I, § 4 (alter state regulations for election of Senators and Representatives); Art. III, § 1 (establish a system of "inferior" federal courts and make "exceptions and regulations" concerning the appellate jurisdiction of the Supreme Court); and Art. IV, § 3 ("make all needful Rules and Regulations respecting the Territory or other Property belonging to the United States.") Amendments 13, 14, 15, 19, 23, 24 and 26 also authorize Congress to enforce the amendment by "appropriate legislation."

In addition, sources of congressional legislative power have been found in express assignments in the Constitution to the federal courts or the President. For example, Art. III, § 2 extends the federal judicial power "to all Cases of admiralty and maritime Jurisdiction."[20] Art. III, § 1 declares that "the judicial power of the United States shall be vested in one Supreme Court 'and in such inferior courts as the Congress may from time to time ordain and establish." In contrast, *Erie R.R. v. Tompkins*, 304 U.S. 64 (1938), ruled that in diversity cases neither Congress nor the federal courts could disregard the applicable state common law to apply "federal common law."[21]

2. THE NATIONAL COMMERCE POWER

I. DEVELOPMENT OF BASIC CONCEPTS

GIBBONS V. OGDEN
22 U.S. (9 Wheat.) 1, 6 L.Ed. 23 (1824).

CHIEF JUSTICE MARSHALL delivered the opinion of the Court.

[A New York statute granted Livingston and Fulton the exclusive right to navigate steamboats in state waters; they assigned to Ogden the right to navigate between New York City and New Jersey. Ogden secured an injunction in the state courts against Gibbons, who was navigating two steamboats licensed under an act of Congress between New York and New Jersey.]

The appellant contends that [the] laws which purport to give the exclusive privilege it sustains, are repugnant [to] that clause in the constitution which authorizes Congress to [regulate] "commerce with foreign nations, and among the several states, and with the Indian tribes."

The subject to be regulated is commerce [and to] ascertain the extent of the power, it becomes necessary to settle the meaning of the word. The counsel for the appellee would limit it to traffic, to buying and selling, or the interchange of commodities, and do not admit that it comprehends

---

[20] In 1789, Congress gave the federal courts exclusive jurisdiction of all admiralty and maritime cases. This is still the law. See 28 U.S.C.A. § 1333.

[21] May a treaty obligating the United States to adopt laws not otherwise authorized be the source of congressional legislative power? See Sec. 4, I infra.

navigation. This would restrict a general term, applicable to many objects, to one of its significations. Commerce, undoubtedly, is traffic, but it [also] describes the commercial intercourse between nations, and parts of nations in all its branches, and is regulated by prescribing rules for carrying on that intercourse.[22] [All] America understands, and has uniformly understood the word "commerce" to comprehend navigation, [and it] must have been so understood, when the Constitution was framed. The power over commerce, including navigation, was one of the primary objects for which the people of America adopted their government, and must have been contemplated in forming [it].

To what commerce does this power extend? [It] has, we believe, been universally admitted that these words comprehend every species of commercial intercourse between the United States and foreign nations. * * *

The subject to which the power is next applied is to commerce "among the several States." The word "among" means intermingled [with.] Commerce among the states cannot stop at the external boundary-line of each state, but may be introduced into the interior. * * * Comprehensive as the word "among" is, it may very properly be restricted to that commerce which concerns more states than one. [The] enumeration of the particular classes of commerce to which the power was to be extended [presupposes] something not enumerated; and that something, if we regard the language or the subject of the sentence, must be the exclusively internal commerce of a state. The genius and character of the whole government seem to be, that its action is to be applied to all the external concerns of the nation, and to those internal concerns which affect the states generally; but not to those which are completely within a particular state, which do not affect other states, and with which it is not necessary to interfere for the purpose of executing some of the general powers of the government. The completely internal commerce of a state, then, may be considered as reserved for the state itself.[23]

But, in regulating commerce[,] the power of Congress does not stop at the jurisdictional lines of the several states. [What] is commerce "among" them; and how is it to be conducted? Can a trading expedition between two adjoining states commence and terminate outside of each? And if the

---

[22] See Jack M. Balkin, *Commerce*, 109 Mich. L. Rev. 1 (2010): "[A]t the time of the founding, 'commerce' included far more than purely commercial activity. It meant 'intercourse'—that is, interactions, exchanges, interrelated activities, and movements back and forth, including, for example, travel, social connection or conversation." Contra, Robert J.Pushaw, Jr., *Obamacare and the Original Meaning of the Commerce Clause: Identifying Historical Limits on Congress's Powers*, 2012 U. Ill. L. Rev. 1703 (2012).

[23] See Robert D. Cooter & Neil S. Siegel, *Collective Action Federalism: A General Theory of Article I, Section 8,* 63 Stan L. Rev. 115 (2010): The theory "interprets Article I, Section 8 [as] a coherent response to collective action problems, not a heterogeneous collection of unrelated powers. * * * Governmental activities that do not pose collective action problems for the states are 'internal to a state' or 'local' ".

trading intercourse be between two states remote from each other, must it not commence in one, terminate in the other, and probably pass through a third? Commerce among the states must, of necessity, be commerce with the states. [The] power of Congress, then, whatever it may be, must be exercised within the territorial jurisdiction of the several states.

[What] is this power? It is the power to regulate; that is, to prescribe the rule by which commerce is to be governed. This power, like all others vested in Congress, is complete in itself, may be exercised to its utmost extent, and acknowledges no limitations other than are prescribed in the Constitution. These are expressed in plain terms, and do not affect the questions which arise in this case. [A]s has always been understood, the sovereignty of Congress, though limited to specified objects, is plenary as to those objects, the power over commerce with foreign nations, and among the several States, is vested in Congress as absolutely as it would be in a single government, having in its constitution the same restrictions on the exercise of the power as are found in the constitution of the United States. [The] wisdom and the discretion of Congress, their identity with the people, and the influence which their constituents possess at elections, are, in this, as in many other instances, as that, for example, of declaring war, the sole restraints on which they have relied, to secure them from its abuse. They are the restraints on which the people must often rely solely, in all representative governments. * * *

[Ch. 4, Sec. 1 considers Marshall, C.J.'s discussion of Gibbons' claim that Congress' power to regulate commerce was exclusive. The Court left that issue unresolved when it ruled that Ogden's claim of a steamboat monopoly under New York's law must yield to the federal law under which Gibbons held a license.]

The boats of the appellant were, we are told, employed in the transportation of passengers, and this is no part of that commerce which Congress may regulate. [But no] clear distinction is perceived between the power to regulate vessels employed in transporting men for hire, and property for hire. The subject is transferred to Congress, and no exception to the grant can be admitted which is not proved by the words or the nature of the thing. * * *[24]

NOTES AND QUESTIONS

1. *Meaning of "commerce."* (a) The Court's Commerce Clause concepts were first developed largely in cases challenging state regulatory laws and taxes as regulations of "commerce," which were claimed to be exclusively within the power of Congress. Congress had left most business regulation to

---

[24] Johnson, J., concurred on the ground that the power of Congress to regulate commerce was exclusive. 2 Charles Warren, *The Supreme Court in United States History,* 75 (1922), pointed out the dramatic effect of *Gibbons* in opening up greater freedom in interstate transportation: "Marshall's opinion was the emancipation proclamation of American commerce."

the states,[25] and had made little use of its power to regulate commerce until the Interstate Commerce Act in 1887 and the Sherman Act in 1890.

(b) PAUL v. VIRGINIA, 75 U.S. (8 Wall.) 168, 19 L.Ed. 357 (1869), upheld state regulation of interstate insurance business on the ground that "issuing a policy of insurance is not a transaction of commerce" and insurance contracts "are not articles of commerce." Would *Paul* be a persuasive precedent for insurance companies contending that the Sherman Act's bar on restraints of trade in interstate commerce may not apply to an interstate insurance rate-fixing arrangement? See *United States v. South-Eastern Underwriters Ass'n*, 322 U.S. 533 (1944) (prosecution upheld under broader approach to Congress' commerce power).

(c) KIDD v. PEARSON, 128 U.S. 1 (1888), upheld Iowa's ban on manufacture of liquor as applied to an Iowa distillery that sold its entire output in other states. It rejected the contention that manufacture for exclusively out-of-state sales was interstate commerce subject only to congressional regulation: "No distinction is more popular to the common mind, or more clearly expressed in economic and political literature, than that between manufacturing and commerce. [The] buying and selling and the transportation incident thereto constitute commerce. [If] it be held that the term includes the regulation of all such manufactures as are intended to be the subject of commercial transactions in the future, [the] result would be that Congress would be invested, to the exclusion of the States, with the power to regulate, not only manufactures, but also agriculture, horticulture, stock raising, domestic fisheries, mining—in short, every branch of human industry. For is there one of them that does not contemplate, more or less clearly, an interstate or foreign market? [It] would follow as an inevitable result that the duty would devolve on Congress to regulate all these delicate, multiform and vital interests—interests which in their nature are and must be, local in all details of their successful management." The Court continued to adhere to this ruling in *United States v. E.C. Knight Co.*, 156 U.S. 1 (1895) (Sherman Act could not be applied to monopoly of sugar refiners: "commerce succeeds to manufacture, and is not part of it").

2. *Meaning of "among the several states."* THE DANIEL BALL, 77 U.S. (10 Wall.) 557 (1871) sustained, a federal safety regulation as applied to a small ship navigating in shallow water on a river exclusively within Michigan: "So far as she was employed in transporting goods destined for other States, or goods brought from without the limits of Michigan and destined to places within that State, she was engaged in commerce between the States. [She] was employed as an instrumentality of that commerce. [The] fact that several different and independent agencies are employed in transporting the commodity, some acting entirely in one State, and some acting through two or more States does in no respect affect the character of the transaction. [If Congress'] authority does not extend to an agency in such commerce, when that

---

[25] Ch. 4 concerns the Court's protecting interstate commerce from what it perceives as harmful state regulation and taxes, but permitting state efforts to protect other interests.

agency is confined within the limits of a State, its entire authority over interstate commerce may be defeated."

3. ***Business purpose.*** Is a business or "commercial" purpose needed for Congress to exercise its commerce power over interstate movement or transportation? See *Caminetti v. United States,* 242 U.S. 470 (1917) (transportation of mistress for non-commercial but immoral purposes). May Congress forbid a fundamentalist Mormon from driving his wives from Utah to Nevada to set up housekeeping? See *Cleveland v. United States,* 329 U.S. 14 (1946). Forbid carrying liquor for one's own use across state lines? See *United States v. Hill,* 248 U.S. 420 (1919). Forbid fleeing from one state to another to avoid state criminal prosecution? See *Hemans v. United States,* 163 F.2d 228 (6th Cir.), cert. denied, 332 U.S. 801 (1947). Forbid a parent from "kidnapping" a child from the other parent's custody in another state? See *Gooch v. United States,* 297 U.S. 124 (1936). Are there good reasons for making the commerce power applicable to such non-commercial actions?

Foundations for Extending the Reach of Congressional Power

Significant problems concerning Congress' commerce power have related to its use over (1) national economic problems by regulating local aspects that may be seen as neither "commerce" nor "among the several states," such as labor relations or wages in a local factory, or crops produced and used on a farm; (2) disfavored local activities, such as gambling, prostitution, distribution of harmful or improperly labeled foods and drugs, and local loan shark enterprises; and (3) other socially undesirable conduct, such as discrimination based on race, sex, or age, and activities harmful to the environment.

The next two cases develop two different methods of using the Commerce Clause to deal with such problems, followed by the evolution of these two "approaches."

THE LOTTERY CASE (CHAMPION V. AMES)
188 U.S. 321, 23 S.Ct. 321, 47 L.Ed. 492 (1903).

JUSTICE HARLAN delivered the opinion of the Court.

[The Federal Lottery Act, prohibiting interstate carriage of lottery tickets, was applied to shipping a box of tickets from Texas to California. Are] we prepared to say that [a] *prohibition* of the carriage of such articles from state to state is not a fit or appropriate mode for the *regulation* of that particular kind of commerce?[26] * * *

---

[26] For the view that a law enacted "to effectuate the commerce power [that] purports to regulate, but is really intended as a prohibition" violates the Necessary and Proper Clause, see Randy E. Barnett, *Necessary and Proper*, 44 UCLA L.Rev. 745 (1997).

If a state, when considering legislation for the suppression of lotteries within its own limits, may properly take into view the evils, that inhere in the raising of money, in that mode, why may not Congress, invested with the power to regulate commerce among the several states, provide that such commerce shall not be polluted by the carrying of lottery tickets from one state to another? [I]t must not be forgotten that the power of Congress to regulate commerce among the states is plenary, is complete in itself, and is subject to no limitations except such as may be found in the Constitution. [What] clause can be cited which, in any degree, countenances the suggestion that one may, of right, carry or cause to be carried from one state to another that which will harm the public morals? * * *

Congress [does] not assume to interfere with traffic or commerce in lottery tickets carried on exclusively within the limits of any state, but has in view only commerce of that kind among the several [states]. Congress, for the purpose of guarding the people of the United States against the "widespread pestilence of lotteries" and to protect the commerce which concerns all the states, may [supplement] the action of those states— perhaps all of them— [for] the protection of the public morals. [It] said, in effect, that it would not permit the declared policy of the states [to] be overthrown or disregarded by the agency of interstate commerce. We should hesitate long before adjudging that an evil of such appalling character, carried on through interstate commerce, cannot be met and crushed by the only power competent to that end. * * *

It is said, however, [that] principle leads necessarily to the conclusion that Congress may arbitrarily exclude from commerce among the states any article, commodity, or thing, of whatever kind or nature, or however useful or valuable, which it may choose, no matter with what motive. [It] will be time enough to consider the constitutionality of such legislation when we must do so. [T]he possible abuse of a power is not an argument against its existence. * * *

CHIEF JUSTICE FULLER, with whom concur JUSTICE BREWER, JUSTICE SHIRAS, and JUSTICE PECKHAM, dissenting.

[The power] prohibiting the carriage of lottery matter [belongs] to the states and not to Congress. To hold that Congress has general police power would be to hold that it may accomplish objects not intrusted to the general government, and to defeat the operation of the 10th Amendment.[27] * * *

Is the carriage of lottery tickets from one state to another commercial intercourse? The lottery ticket purports to create contractual relations, and to furnish the means of enforcing a contract right. This is true of insurance policies, and both are contingent in their nature. Yet this court has held

---

[27] The dissent later quoted the sentence in *McCulloch* about Congress, "under the pretext of executing its powers, pass[ing] laws for the accomplishment of objects not entrusted to the government."

that the issuing of fire, marine, and life insurance policies, in one state, and sending them to another, to be there delivered to the insured on payment of premium, is not interstate commerce. *Paul v. Virginia.* * * *

If a lottery ticket is not an article of commerce, how can it become so [when] transported by an express company? [This] would be to say that everything is an article of commerce the moment it is taken to be transported from place to place, and of interstate commerce if from state to state. [The] necessary consequence is to take from the states all jurisdiction over the subject so far as interstate communication is concerned. It is a long step in the direction of wiping out all traces of state lines, and the creation of a centralized government.[28] * * *

The power to prohibit the transportation of diseased animals and infected goods over railroads or on steamboats is an entirely different thing, for they would be in themselves injurious to the transaction of interstate commerce, [and] are essentially commercial in their nature. And the exclusion of diseased persons rests on different ground, for nobody would pretend that persons could be kept off the trains because they were going from one state to another to engage in the lottery business. * * *

NOTES AND QUESTIONS

Commerce Clause as source of national police power. In the next 15 years, Congress excluded from interstate commerce commodities and activities "injurious, not to that commerce or to any of the agencies or facilities thereof, but to the health, morals, safety, and general welfare of the nation." Robert E. Cushman, *The National Police Power Under the Commerce Clause of the Constitution,* 3 Minn.L.Rev. 289 (1919) (cases involving obscene materials, prostitution, misbranded products, and unwholesome or adulterated food or drugs).

In HOKE v. UNITED STATES, 227 U.S. 308 (1913), a unanimous Court explained: "The principle established by the cases is the simple one, [that] Congress has power over transportation among the several States; that the power is complete in itself, and that Congress, as an incident to it, may adopt not only means necessary but convenient to its exercise, and the means may have the quality of police regulations."[29]

---

[28] Consider Deborah J. Merritt, *The Third Translation of the Commerce Clause: Congressional Power to Regulate Social Problems,* 66 Geo.Wash.L.Rev. 1206 (1998): "Compared to the constitutional firestorm over Congress's authority to regulate the national economy, a power the Framers clearly intended to confer, barely a candle has flickered over Congress's power to regulate a variety of social issues. Yet it is in the latter cases that the Court has wandered farthest from the apparent meaning of the Commerce Clause and has engaged in the most extreme forms of one type of textualism. The Court has taken the phrase 'Commerce . . . among the several States' out of its documentary, historical, and cultural context and has used that phrase to uphold regulation of any activity that has some link to interstate commerce—even if the nexus is purely incidental to the law's purpose."

[29] Consider Jesse H. Choper, *On the Warren Court and Judicial Review,* 17 Cath. U. L. Rev. 20 (1967): "The great purpose of the Commerce Clause was to enable Congress to *facilitate*

HOUSTON, EAST & WEST TEXAS RY. v. UNITED STATES (SHREVEPORT CASE)

234 U.S. 342, 34 S.Ct. 833, 58 L.Ed. 1341 (1914).

JUSTICE HUGHES delivered the opinion of the Court.

[The Interstate Commerce Commission fixed interstate railroad rates westward from Shreveport, La., to Texas markets. The ICC also ordered the affected railroads to raise their rates for intrastate shipments to the same Texas markets. These rates had been prescribed by the Texas Railroad Commission and discriminated against interstate commerce.[30]

[Where the power of Congress to regulate commerce] exists, it dominates. Interstate trade was not left to be destroyed or impeded by the rivalries of local government. The purpose was to make impossible the recurrence of the evils which had overwhelmed the Confederation, and to provide the necessary basis of national unity by insuring "uniformity of regulation against conflicting and discriminating state legislation." [Congress'] authority, extending to these interstate carriers as instruments of interstate commerce, necessarily embraces the right to control their operations in all matters having such a close and substantial relation to interstate traffic that the control is essential or appropriate to the security of that traffic, to the efficiency of the interstate service, and to the maintenance of conditions under which interstate commerce may be conducted upon fair terms and without molestation or hindrance.

[While *Baltimore & O.R. Co. v. ICC*, 221 U.S. 612 (1911),[31] and *Southern R. Co. v. United States,* 222 U.S. 20 (1911)[32]] relate to measures adopted in the interest of the safety of persons and property, they illustrate the principle that Congress [may] prevent the common instrumentalities of interstate and intrastate commercial intercourse from being used in their intrastate operations to the injury of interstate commerce. This is not to say that Congress possesses the authority to regulate the internal commerce of a state, as such, but that it does possess the power to foster and protect interstate commerce, and to take all measures necessary or

---

interstate trade [and] to *encourage* economic growth. [But] the Fuller Court upheld Congressional power to *hinder* interstate trade and, effectively to *destroy* those national industries that it wished." For a fuller discussion, see Barry Friedman & Genevieve Lakier, *"To Regulate," Not to "Prohibit": Limiting the Commerce Power*, 2012 Sup. Ct. Rev. 255.

   [30] For example "a rate of 60 cents carried first-class traffic [160 miles] from Dallas, while the same rate [carried] the same class of traffic only 55 miles into Texas from Shreveport. [The] rate on wagons from Dallas to Marshall, Texas, 147.7 miles, was 36.8 cents, and from Shreveport to Marshall, 42 miles, 56 [cents]."

   [31] *Baltimore & O.R.* upheld federal regulation of hours of service of employees working on interstate railroads, even though the effect was to control their hours on intrastate service as well, because of the impracticality of limiting their work to one or the other.

   [32] *Southern R.* upheld the federal safety appliance act's application to vehicles used by an interstate railroad only in intrastate traffic, as well as those used interstate, in order to assure the safety of interstate traffic moving over the same railroad as the intrastate.

appropriate to that end, although intrastate transactions of interstate carriers may thereby be controlled.

This principle is applicable here. [In] removing the injurious discriminations against interstate traffic arising from the relation of intrastate to interstate rates, Congress is not bound to reduce the latter below what it may deem to be a proper standard, fair to the carrier and to the public. Otherwise, it could prevent the injury to interstate commerce only by the sacrifice of its judgment as to interstate rates. * * *

JUSTICE LURTON and JUSTICE PITNEY dissent.

NOTES AND QUESTIONS

1. *Local activities "burdening" interstate commerce.* Does *Shreveport's* rationale apply to rates for passengers? WISCONSIN R.R. COMM'N v. CHICAGO, B. & Q. R.R., 257 U.S. 563 (1922), per TAFT, C.J., upheld an ICC order raising Wisconsin-prescribed intrastate railroad passenger fares to equal those in interstate commerce: "Congress [can] impose any reasonable conditions on a State's use of interstate carriers for intrastate commerce it deems necessary or desirable." What result in *Shreveport* and *Wisconsin R.R.* if the unduly low, state-prescribed intrastate rates were charged by railroads that operated entirely within Texas and Wisconsin?

2. *"Current of commerce" concept.* STAFFORD v. WALLACE, 258 U.S. 495 (1922), per TAFT, C.J., upheld federal regulation of rates and practices of persons engaged in local buying and selling in stockyards. Relying on *Swift & Co. v. United States,* 196 U.S. 375 (1905) (upholding application of Sherman Act to local sales in stockyards by viewing the sales as part of a "current of commerce" between states), the Court reasoned that the regulated activities, while "usually lawful and affecting only intrastate commerce," were subject to federal control when Congress "reasonably fear[s] that such [acts] will probably [constitute] a direct and undue burden on [interstate commerce. It] is primarily for Congress to consider and decide the fact of the danger and meet it." McReynolds, J., dissented without opinion.

II. REGULATION OF NATIONAL ECONOMIC PROBLEMS

A. Limitations on Commerce Power Through 1936

HAMMER V. DAGENHART
247 U.S. 251, 38 S.Ct. 529, 62 L.Ed. 1101 (1918).

JUSTICE DAY delivered the opinion of the Court.

[Ruling that Congress exceeded its commerce power by prohibiting interstate transportation of products from factories that used child labor, the Court distinguished the *Lottery* line of cases:] In each of these instances the use of interstate transportation was necessary to the accomplishment of harmful results. * * *

This element is wanting in the present case. [The] act in its effect does not regulate transportation among the states, but aims to standardize the ages at which children may be employed in mining and manufacturing within the states. The goods shipped are of themselves harmless. [B]efore transportation begins, the labor of their production is over, and the mere fact that they were intended for interstate commerce transportation does not make their production subject to federal control. [T]he production of articles, intended for interstate commerce, is a matter of local regulation. [If] it were otherwise, all manufacture intended for interstate shipment would be brought under federal control to the practical exclusion of the authority of the states, a result certainly not contemplated by the framers of the Constitution * * * .

It is further contended that the authority of Congress may be exerted [because] of the effect of the circulation of such goods in other states where the evil of this class of labor has been recognized by local legislation, and the right to thus employ child labor has been more rigorously restrained than in the state of production. [I.e.,] that the unfair competition, thus engendered, may be controlled by closing the channels of interstate commerce to manufacturers in those states where the local laws do not meet what Congress deems to be the more just standard of other states.

There is no power vested in Congress to require the states to exercise their police power so as to prevent possible unfair competition. Many causes may cooperate to give one state, by reason of local laws or conditions, an economic advantage over others. The commerce clause was not intended to give to Congress a general authority to equalize such conditions. In some of the states laws have been passed fixing minimum wages for women, in others the local law regulates the hours of labor of women in various employments. Business done in such states may be at an economic disadvantage when compared with states which have no such regulations; surely, this fact does not give Congress the power to deny transportation in interstate commerce to those who carry on business where the hours of labor and the rate of compensation for women have not been fixed by a standard in use in other states and approved by Congress. [The] grant of power to Congress over the subject of interstate commerce [was] not to give it authority to control the states in their exercise of the police power over local trade and manufacture. [To] sustain this statute [would] sanction an invasion by the federal power of the control of a matter purely local in its character * * * .

JUSTICE HOLMES, [joined by McKenna, Brandeis, and Clarke, JJ.,] dissenting.

* * * Regulation means the prohibition of something, and when interstate commerce is the matter to be regulated I cannot doubt that the regulation may prohibit any part of such commerce that Congress sees fit to forbid[, despite] its possible reaction upon the conduct of the States in a matter upon which [they] are free from direct control. I [should] have thought that the most conspicuous decisions of this Court had made it clear that the power to regulate commerce and other constitutional powers could not be cut down or qualified by the fact that it might interfere with the carrying out of the domestic policy of any State. [They] may regulate their internal affairs and their domestic commerce as they like. But when they seek to send their products across the State line they are no longer within their rights. If there were no Constitution and no Congress their power to cross the line would depend upon their neighbors. Under the Constitution such commerce belongs not to the States but to Congress to regulate. It may carry out its views of public policy whatever indirect effect they may have upon the activities of the States. Instead of being encountered by a prohibitive tariff at her boundaries the State encounters the public policy of the United States which it is for Congress to express. [The] national welfare as understood by Congress may require a different attitude within its sphere from that of some self-seeking State. * * *

NOTES AND QUESTIONS

1.   *Harmful effects.* Which "harmful results" were more of a threat to the interests the Commerce Clause was intended to protect—those guarded against by the laws sustained in the *Lottery, Hoke* and similar cases or those guarded against by the law held invalid in *Dagenhart?*

2.   *The need for national power.* (a) *Dagenhart* sought to preserve "the authority of the states over matters purely local." Did *Dagenhart's* invalidation of federal control advance or impede the states' ability to make effective their own child labor laws? Cf. *Baldwin v. Seelig* (1935), Ch.4, Sec. 2, I (state cannot forbid sale within state of milk bought outside of state at price lower than minimum price established by state for its own milk producers).

(b)   Nine months after *Dagenhart,* Congress enacted a law seeking to control child labor through use of the taxing power. See *Child Labor Tax Case,* Sec. 3 infra.

Constitutional Struggle: The New Deal vs. The Great Depression

The Great Depression of the 1930s gave rise to unprecedented unemployment, drastic cutbacks in production, 60% declines in farm and labor income, widespread business and bank failures, devastating home and farm mortgage foreclosures, all reacting on each other in an extraordinary downward spiral. For a classic analysis of the constitutional litigation in the successful struggle to find bases for national regulatory power, see Robert L. Stern, *The Commerce Clause and the National Economy,* 1933–1946, 59 Harv.L.Rev. 645 (1946): "[Because] the products of the national economy were distributed throughout a national market. The channels of interstate commerce were the arteries through which the impact of these forces affected the nation. Because of the nation-wide market, and the constitutional impediment placed by the Commerce Clause itself in the way of regulation by the states, the state governments were unable to cope with economic problems affecting the nation as a whole. The depressed state of business activity obviously affected interstate commerce in the most elementary sense, since it greatly reduced the quantity of products to be transported across state lines. Nevertheless there could be no assurance that federal legislation directed at the economic causes of the depression would be constitutional. For that depended on what the Supreme Court thought. And there was ample authority in the Supreme Court opinions looking both ways."

Early in the litigation over New Deal legislation, SCHECHTER POULTRY CORP. v. UNITED STATES, 295 U.S. 495 (1935), per HUGHES, C.J., struck down a Code, adopted under the National Industrial Recovery Act, to regulate trade practices, wages, hours, and collective bargaining in the New York poultry wholesale slaughtering market where 96% of the poultry came from other states. Schechter bought poultry only on the local market and, after slaughtering, sold it only to local retailers. The Court ruled that the regulation fell outside the commerce power because the regulated conduct had no "direct" effect upon interstate commerce, but said little to clarify this, possibly because the major basis for invalidity was that the Act unconstitutionally delegated legislative power to the Act's Administrator, see Ch. 3, Sec. 2, I.

One year later, CARTER v. CARTER COAL CO., 298 U.S. 238 (1936), per SUTHERLAND, J., expanded on *Schechter's* "direct effect" test ruling that the Commerce Clause did not give Congress power to require Bituminous Coal Code members to observe the hours and wages agreed to by producers of two-thirds of the bituminous coal volume and one-half of the employed bituminous mine workers: "[T]he effect of the labor provisions of the [act] primarily falls upon production and not upon commerce; [p]roduction is a purely local activity. It follows that none of these essential antecedents of production constitutes a transaction in or forms any part of interstate commerce. [T]he local character of mining, of manufacturing, and of crop growing is a fact, and remains a fact, whatever may be done with the products. * * *

"That the production of every commodity intended for interstate sale and transportation has some effect upon interstate commerce may [be] freely granted; and we are brought to the final and decisive inquiry, whether here that effect is direct [or] indirect. The distinction is not formal, but substantial in the highest degree, as we pointed out in *Schechter*. 'If the commerce clause were construed [to] reach all enterprises and transactions which could be said to have an indirect effect upon interstate commerce, the federal authority would embrace practically all the activities of the people, and the authority of the state over its domestic concerns would exist only by sufferance of the federal government.' * * *

"Whether the effect of a given activity or condition is direct or indirect is not always easy to determine. The word 'direct' implies that the activity or condition invoked or blamed shall operate proximately—not mediately, remotely, or collaterally—to produce the effect. It connotes the absence of an efficient intervening agency or condition. And the extent of the effect bears no logical relation to its character. The distinction between a direct and an indirect effect turns, not upon the magnitude of either the cause or the effect, but entirely upon the manner in which the effect has been brought about. If the production by one man of a single ton of coal intended for interstate sale and shipment, and actually so sold and shipped, affects interstate commerce indirectly, the effect does not become direct by multiplying the tonnage, or increasing the number of men employed, or adding to the expense or complexities of the business, or by all combined. It is quite true that rules of law are sometimes qualified by considerations of degree, as the government argues. But the matter of degree has no bearing upon the question here, since that question is not—What is the *extent* of the local activity or condition, or the *extent* of the effect produced upon interstate commerce? but—What is the *relation* between the activity or condition and the effect?

"Much stress is put upon the evils which come from the struggle between employers and employees over the matter of wages, working conditions, the right of collective bargaining, etc., and the resulting strikes, curtailment, and irregularity of production and effect on prices; and it is insisted that interstate commerce is *greatly* affected thereby. But [the] conclusive answer is that the evils are all local evils over which the federal government has no legislative control. [Such] effect as they may have upon commerce, however extensive it may be, is secondary and indirect. An increase in the greatness of the effect adds to its importance. It does not alter its character.

"[The] only perceptible difference between [*Schechter*] and this is that in the *Schechter Case* the federal power was asserted with respect to commodities which had come to rest after their interstate transportation; while here, the case deals with commodities at rest before interstate commerce has begun. That difference is without significance. The federal regulatory power ceases when interstate commercial intercourse ends; and, correlatively, the power does not attach until interstate commercial intercourse begins."[33]

B. Expansion of Commerce Power After 1936

By the 1936 Presidential election the Court had invalidated six federal laws designed to advance President Franklin D. Roosevelt's New Deal program for economic recovery, four of major importance: the National Industrial Recovery Act and the Bituminous Coal Act, both supra, the Agricultural Adjustment Act, *United States v. Butler* (1936) (6–3), Sec. 3, II infra, and the Railway Pension Act, *Railroad Retirement Bd. v. Alton R.R.,* 295 U.S. 330 (1935) (5–4).[34]

Only one New Deal measure had been sustained, the Gold Clause legislation. *Norman v. Baltimore & O.R. Co.,* 294 U.S. 240 (1935) (5–4). More vital Acts of the New Deal program still awaited the Court's scrutiny. These included the National Labor Relations Act, the Social Security Act (both old age pensions and unemployment compensation), and the Public Utility Holding Company Act. In addition, new legislation was needed to replace the minimum labor standards lost in *Schechter* and *Carter Coal* and the control over agricultural surpluses lost in *Butler.*

Viewing his overwhelming victory in the 1936 elections as "an endorsement of his legislative program [despite] the recent Supreme Court opinions which seemingly blocked his path," President Roosevelt "determined not to permit the Court to flout the popular will by what he, as well as Justices Brandeis, Stone and Cardozo, felt to be a reactionary interpretation of the Constitution." Stern, supra. The president sought congressional approval of what became known popularly as the "Court Packing" plan, which would have authorized appointment of as many as six new justices, one to sit in addition to each justice over seventy years of age. For the story of the battle over the plan, see Joseph Alsop & Turner Catledge, *168 Days* (1938); Robert H. Jackson, *The Struggle for Judicial Supremacy* (1941); Alpheus T. Mason, *Harlan Fiske Stone and FDR's Court Plan,* 61 Yale L.J. 791 (1952); William E. Leuchtenburg, *The Origins of Franklin D. Roosevelt's "Court Packing" Plan,* 1966 Sup.Ct.Rev. 347.

The first major Commerce Clause decision after *Carter,* several months before Congress rejected the court-packing plan,[35] NLRB v. JONES & LAUGHLIN STEEL CORP., 301 U.S. 1 (1937), per HUGHES, C.J., upheld application of the National Labor Relations Act to the nation's fourth

---

[33] For the rationale articulated in later cases for the Court's additional ruling on unconstitutional delegation, see Ch. 3, Sec. 2, I.

[34] The other two were the Farm Mortgage Act and the Municipal Bankruptcy Act. *Louisville Joint Stock Land Bank v. Radford,* 295 U.S. 555 (1935) (9–0); *Ashton v. Cameron County Water Imp. Dist.,* 298 U.S. 513 (1936) (5–4).

[35] Two weeks earlier, *West Coast Hotel Co. v. Parrish* (1937), Ch. 5, Sec. 3, held that a state minimum wage law did not violate the Fourteenth Amendment Due Process Clause, overruling several earlier decisions.

largest steel producer, most of whose production was shipped and sold in interstate commerce. The NLRB found that J & L had engaged in unfair labor practices by discharging employees at one of its plants: "[J&L's] argument rests upon the proposition that manufacturing in itself is not commerce. [Although] activities may be intrastate in character when separately considered, if they have such a close and substantial relation to interstate commerce that their control is essential or appropriate to protect that commerce from burdens and obstructions, Congress cannot be denied the power to exercise that control. Undoubtedly the scope of this power must be considered in the light of our dual system of government and may not be extended so as to embrace effects upon interstate commerce so indirect and remote that to embrace them, in view of our complex society, would effectually obliterate the distinction between what is national and what is local and create a completely centralized government. The question is necessarily one of degree.

"[In] *Schechter,* we found that the effect there was so remote as to be beyond the federal power. To find 'immediacy or directness' there was to find it 'almost everywhere,' a result inconsistent with the maintenance of our federal system. In *Carter Coal,* the Court was of the opinion that the provisions of the statute relating to production were invalid upon several grounds,—that there was improper delegation of legislative power, and that the requirements not only went beyond any sustainable measure of protection of interstate commerce but were also inconsistent with due process. These cases are not controlling here.

"[T]he stoppage of [J&L's] operations by industrial strife would have a most serious effect upon interstate commerce. In view of respondent's far-flung activities, it is idle to say that the effect would be indirect or remote. It is obvious that it would be immediate and might be catastrophic. We are asked to shut our eyes to the plainest facts of our national life and to deal with the question of direct and indirect effects in an intellectual vacuum. Because there may be but indirect and remote effects upon interstate commerce in connection with a host of local enterprises throughout the country, it does not follow that other industrial activities do not have such a close and intimate relation to interstate commerce as to make the presence of industrial strife a matter of the most urgent national concern."

McREYNOLDS J., joined by Van Devanter, Sutherland and Butler, JJ., dissented: "[At one plant,] ten men out of ten thousand were discharged; in the other cases only a few. The immediate effect in the factory may be to create discontent among all those employed and a strike may follow, which, in turn, may result in reducing production, which ultimately may reduce the volume of goods moving in interstate commerce. By this chain of indirect and progressively remote events we finally reach the evil with which it is said the legislation under consideration undertakes to deal. A more remote and indirect interference with interstate commerce or a more definite invasion of the powers reserved to the states is difficult, if not impossible, to imagine. [Almost] anything—marriage, birth, death—may in some fashion affect commerce."

UNITED STATES V. DARBY
312 U.S. 100, 61 S.Ct. 451, 85 L.Ed. 609 (1941).

JUSTICE STONE delivered the opinion of the Court. * * *

The Fair Labor Standards [Act's] purpose [is] to exclude from interstate commerce goods produced [under] conditions detrimental to the maintenance of the minimum standards of living necessary for health and general well-being; and to prevent the use of interstate commerce [as] the means of spreading and perpetuating such substandard labor conditions among the workers of the several [states].

The indictment charges that appellee is engaged, in the state of Georgia, in the business of acquiring raw materials, which he manufactures into finished lumber with the intent when manufactured, to ship it in interstate commerce * * * .

The prohibition of shipment of the proscribed goods in interstate commerce. Section 15(a)(1) prohibits, and the indictment charges, the shipment in interstate commerce, of goods produced for interstate commerce by employees whose wages and hours of employment do not conform to the requirements of the Act. * * *

While manufacture is not of itself interstate commerce the shipment of manufactured goods interstate is such commerce and the prohibition of such shipment by Congress is indubitably a regulation of the commerce. The power to regulate [extends] not only to those regulations which aid, foster and protect the commerce, but embraces those which prohibit it. It is conceded that the power of Congress to prohibit transportation in interstate commerce includes noxious articles, stolen articles, [and] articles such as intoxicating liquor or convict made goods, traffic in which is forbidden or restricted by the laws of the state of destination.

But it is said that the present prohibition falls within the scope of none of these categories; that while the prohibition is nominally a regulation of the commerce its motive or purpose is regulation of wages and hours of persons engaged in manufacture, the control of which has been reserved to the states and upon which Georgia and some of the states of destination have placed no restriction. [But] Congress, following its own conception of public policy concerning the restrictions which may appropriately be imposed on interstate commerce, is free to exclude from the commerce articles whose use in the states for which they are destined it may conceive to be injurious to the public health, morals or welfare even though the state has not sought to regulate their use. * * *

The motive and purpose of the present regulation are plainly to make effective the Congressional conception of public policy that interstate commerce should not be made the instrument of competition in the distribution of goods produced under substandard labor conditions. [The] motive and purpose of a regulation of interstate commerce are matters for the legislative judgment upon the exercise of which the Constitution places no restriction and over, which the courts are given no control [citing cases on Congress' taxing power, Sec. 3, I infra]. Whatever their motive and purpose, regulations of commerce which do not infringe some constitutional prohibition are within the plenary power conferred on Congress by the Commerce Clause. [We] conclude that the prohibition of the shipment interstate of goods produced under the forbidden substandard labor conditions is within the constitutional authority of Congress.

[T]hese principles of constitutional interpretation have been so long and repeatedly recognized by this Court as applicable to the Commerce Clause, that there would be little occasion for repeating them now were it not for the decision of this Court twenty-two years ago in *Dagenhart* [by] a bare majority of the Court over the powerful and now classic dissent of Mr. Justice Holmes [*Dagenhart*] has not been followed. The distinction on which the decision was rested that Congressional power to prohibit interstate commerce is limited to articles which in themselves have some harmful or deleterious property—a distinction which was novel when made and unsupported by any provision of the Constitution—has long since been abandoned. The thesis of the opinion that the motive of the prohibition or its effect to control in some measure the use or production within the states of the article thus excluded from the commerce can operate to deprive the regulation of its constitutional authority has long since ceased to have force. [It] should be and now is overruled.

Validity of the wage and hour requirements. Section 15(a)(2) and §§ 6 and 7 require employers to conform to the wage and hour provisions with respect to all employees engaged in the production of goods for interstate commerce. [T]he validity of the prohibition turns on the question whether [their employment] in the production of goods for interstate commerce is so related to the commerce and so affects it as to be within the reach of the power of Congress to regulate it.

[The] power of Congress to regulate interstate commerce extends to the regulation [of] activities intrastate which have a substantial effect on the commerce or the exercise of the Congressional power over it. [H]aving by the present Act adopted the policy of excluding from interstate commerce all goods produced for the commerce which do not conform to the specified labor standards, [Congress] may choose the means reasonably adapted to the attainment of the permitted end, even though they involve control of intrastate activities. Such legislation has often been sustained with respect to powers, other than the commerce power granted to the national government, when the means chosen, although not themselves within the granted power, were nevertheless deemed appropriate aids to the accomplishment of some purpose within an admitted power of the national government. [A] familiar like exercise of power is the regulation of intrastate transactions which are so commingled with or related to interstate commerce that all must be regulated if the interstate commerce is to be effectively controlled. *Shreveport*; *Wisconsin Railroad Comm.* [Similarly], Congress may require inspection and preventive treatment of all cattle in a disease infected area in order to prevent shipment in interstate commerce of some of the cattle without the treatment. [And] we have recently held that Congress in the exercise of its power to require inspection and grading of tobacco shipped in interstate commerce may compel such inspection and grading [at] local auction rooms from which a substantial part but not all of the tobacco sold is shipped in interstate commerce. *Currin v. Wallace,* 306 U.S. 1 (1939). * * *

We think also that § 15(a)(2), now under consideration, is sustainable independently of § 15(a)(1), which prohibits shipment or transportation of the proscribed goods. As we have said the evils aimed at by the Act are the spread of substandard labor conditions through the use of the facilities of interstate commerce for competition by the goods so produced with those produced under the prescribed or better labor conditions; and the consequent dislocation of the commerce itself caused by the impairment or destruction of local businesses by competition made effective through interstate commerce. The Act is thus directed at the suppression of a method or kind of competition [which] it has in effect condemned as "unfair", as the Clayton Act, has condemned other "unfair methods of competition" made effective through interstate commerce. * * *

The means adopted by § 15(a)(2) for the protection of interstate commerce by the suppression of the production of the condemned goods [is] so related to the commerce and so affects it as to be within the reach of the commerce power. Congress, to attain its objective in the suppression of nationwide competition in interstate commerce by goods produced under substandard labor conditions, has made no distinction as to the volume or amount of shipments in the commerce or of production for commerce by any particular shipper or producer. * * *

So far as *Carter* is inconsistent with this conclusion, its doctrine is limited in principle by the decisions under the Sherman Act and the National Labor Relations Act, which we have cited and which we follow.

Our conclusion is unaffected by the Tenth Amendment [which] states but a truism that all is retained which has not been surrendered. There is nothing in the history of its adoption to suggest that it was more than declaratory of the relationship between the national and state governments as it had been established by the Constitution before the amendment or that its purpose was other than to allay fears that the new national government might seek to exercise powers not granted, and that the states might not be able to exercise fully their reserved powers.[36]

Reversed.

NOTES AND QUESTIONS

1. ***Unanimity.*** The unanimity in *Darby* can be attributed to the departure of the four Justices who dissented in *Jones & Laughlin,* Butler, J., by death in 1938, and the other three by retirement: Van Devanter, J., in 1937, Sutherland, J., in 1938 and McReynolds, J., in 1940, just two days before the announcement of *Darby.* Of the five who joined the majority opinion in *Carter Coal,* only Roberts, J., remained, and his views appeared to have undergone much change since 1936.

2. ***Power to exclude from interstate commerce.*** (a) *Darby's* revival of *Lottery* and its progeny encouraged widespread use by Congress of its "police" power to exclude from interstate commerce commodities and activities thought harmful to the nation, though the harm itself often occurred only at a local level. (See note 3 after *Gibbons* supra and note 1 after *Lottery* supra.) Additional uses of this power include prohibitions on interstate transportation of stolen vehicles or other stolen goods, and of persons in furtherance of a scheme to defraud; interstate shipment of gambling devices and wagering materials, and of firearms to or by persons indicted or convicted of a serious crime; and interstate travel to incite, encourage or participate in a riot, or in aid of "racketeering enterprises."

(b) ***"Jurisdictional nexus."*** What are the limits on Congress' "police" power through this use of the Commerce Clause? Consider Robert F. Nagel, *The Future of Federalism*, 46 Case W. Res. L.Rev. 643 (1996): "[A]ny conceivable object of regulation will necessarily involve *something* that has traveled in interstate commerce. Everyone knows that schools, police departments, and families all purchase goods that have been a part of commerce. [T]he asserted tie to commerce would potentially allow national regulation of any imaginable activity." May Congress use this "jurisdictional nexus" with interstate commerce to regulate the curricula of schools that buy goods from out of state? To regulate child care providers that deal with parents who make purchases in interstate commerce? To regulate any tortfeasor who wears clothing that was shipped interstate? Of what relevance is the relationship between the movement of goods across state lines and the policy that Congress is seeking to achieve? See Thomas W. Merrill, *Toward a Principled Interpretation of the Commerce Clause*, 22 Harv. J.L. & Pub.Pol. 31 (1998) ("we must ask whether the intent of Congress is to regulate commerce insofar as it affects the movement of matter and energy across state lines (a permissible objective) or whether it is to regulate commercial activity without

---

[36] The Court also held that the minimum wage and maximum hours provisions did not violate the Due Process Clause of the Fifth Amendment, citing *West Coast Hotel Co. v. Parrish*, Ch. 5, Sec. 3.

regard to whether there is any effect on interstate movements (an impermissible usurpation of the states' police powers"); Diane McGimsey, Note, *The Commerce Clause and Federalism after Lopez and Morrison: The Case for Closing the Jurisdictional-Element Loophole*, 90 Calif.L.Rev. 1675 (2002) ("the inclusion of the jurisdictional element (the line crossing requirement) must support Congress's purposes in enacting the statute" and "the regulated activity must be linked to commerce" as defined in *Lopez & Morrison*, Sec. 2, IV infra); Harry Litman & Mark D. Greenberg, *Federal Power and Federalism: A Theory of Commerce-Clause Based Regulation on Traditionally State Crimes*, 47 Case W.Res.L.Rev. 921 (1997) ("an analogy to common law principles of liability is useful," for the jurisdictional nexus, i.e., proximate cause); Thomas R. Powell, *Vagaries and Varieties in Constitutional Interpretation* 63 (1956). See also fn. 47.

(c) *After interstate commerce ends.* May Congress use the Commerce Clause to pass a law requiring that anyone traveling in interstate commerce for the purpose of getting a divorce must obtain a divorce that meets federal standards? May Congress require compliance with federal divorce standards for anyone who has traveled in interstate commerce in the past or does so in the future? Of what relevance is the amount of time that has passed between the use of interstate commerce and the policy that Congress wishes to implement? What results under the following decisions:

UNITED STATES v. SULLIVAN, 332 U.S. 689 (1948), per BLACK, J. upheld the conviction of a retail druggist under the federal Food, Drug and Cosmetic Act for selling two pill boxes, in which he had placed 12 tablets, and failing to affix the required warning label that was printed on the large bottle of pills bought from an in-state wholesaler, who had secured them through interstate commerce: "[The Act] was designed [to] safeguard the consumer by applying the Act to articles from the moment of their introduction into interstate commerce all the way to the moment of their delivery to the ultimate consumer."[37]

SCARBOROUGH v. UNITED STATES, 431 U.S. 563 (1977), per MARSHALL, J., interpreted a federal statute as making it a crime for a convicted felon to possess a firearm as long as there existed "the minimal nexus that the firearm have been, at some time, in interstate commerce, [with] little concern for when the nexus with commerce occurred"—even before the accused was convicted. Although the Court did not resolve any constitutional issue, it indicated that "Congress [asserted] its full Commerce Clause power so as to cover all activity substantially affecting interstate commerce."

Of what relevance is it that "at the time of *Lottery*, most if not all of the states had decided that lotteries were immoral and had legislated against them"? Regan, fn. 5. Consider id.: "Lottery tickets are small, portable, concealable, and in some views dangerous—like guns. Stamping out lotteries may have been something the states were individually incompetent to do,

---

[37] Rutledge, J., concurred. Frankfurter, J., joined by Reed and Jackson, JJ., dissented. All were concerned only with statutory construction.

practically speaking. [But] there is all the difference in the world between Congress's legislating against lotteries just because it disapproves of them and Congress's legislating against lotteries to help the states give effect to their own judgments of disapproval. The former is not something we need the national government for."

3.   ***Power over local activities affecting commerce.*** (a) WICKARD v. FILBURN, 317 U.S. 111 (1942), per JACKSON, J., upheld a penalty imposed under the Agricultural Adjustment Act of 1938 on Filburn for raising 239 bushels of wheat in excess of his marketing allotment. Filburn's practice was to plant a small acreage of wheat, to sell some, feed some to livestock, and use some for home-consumed flour and for seed: "[The Commerce Clause] question would merit little consideration since our decision in [*Darby*], except for the fact that this Act extends federal regulation to production not intended in any part for commerce but wholly for consumption on the farm. [A] few dicta and decisions of this Court [might] be understood to lay it down that activities such as 'production,' 'manufacturing,' and 'mining' are strictly 'local' and, except in special circumstances which are not present here, cannot be regulated under the commerce power because their effects upon interstate commerce are, as matter of law, only 'indirect.' [But] questions of the power of Congress are not to be decided by reference to any formula which would give controlling force to nomenclature such as 'production' and 'indirect.' [Even] if appellee's activity be local and though it may not be regarded as commerce, it may still, whatever its nature, be reached by Congress if it exerts a substantial economic effect on interstate commerce * * * .

"The wheat industry has been a problem industry for some years. [D]ecline in the export trade has left a large surplus in production which in connection with an abnormally large supply of wheat and other grains in recent years caused congestion in a number of markets; tied up railroad cars; and caused elevators in some instances to turn away grains, and railroads to institute embargoes to prevent further congestion. * * *

"[During] 1941 producers who cooperated with the Agricultural Adjustment program received an average price on the farm of about $1.16 a bushel as compared with the world market price of 40 cents a bushel. [The] effect of consumption of home-grown wheat on interstate commerce is due to the fact that it constitutes the most variable factor in the disappearance of the wheat crop. Consumption on the farm where grown appears to vary in an amount greater than 20 per cent of average production. [The] effect of the statute before us is to restrict the amount which may be produced for market and the extent as well to which one may forestall resort to the market by producing to meet his own needs. That appellee's own contribution to the demand for wheat may be trivial by itself is not enough to remove him from the scope of federal regulation where, as here, his contribution, taken together with that of many others similarly situated, is far from trivial. [*NLRB v. Fainblatt*, 306 U.S. 601 (1939),[38] *Darby*].

"It is well established by decisions of this Court that the power to regulate commerce includes the power to regulate the prices at which commodities in that commerce are dealt in and practices affecting such prices. One of the primary purposes of the Act in question was to increase the market price of wheat and to that end to limit the volume thereof that could affect the market. It can hardly be denied that a factor of such volume and variability as home-consumed wheat would have a substantial influence on price and market conditions. [Such wheat] overhangs the market and if induced by rising prices tends to flow into the market and check price increases. But if we assume that it is never marketed, it supplies a need of the man who grew it which would otherwise be reflected by purchases in the open market. Home-grown wheat in this sense competes with wheat in commerce. The stimulation of commerce is a use of the regulatory function quite as definitely as prohibitions or restrictions thereon. This record leaves us in no doubt that Congress may properly have considered that wheat consumed on the farm where grown if wholly outside the scheme of regulation would have a substantial effect in defeating and obstructing its purpose to stimulate trade therein at increased prices."

(b) MARYLAND v. WIRTZ, 392 U.S. 183 (1968), per HARLAN, J., upheld expanded congressional coverage of the Fair Labor Standards Act to include hospitals, nursing homes, and educational institutions—elementary, secondary or higher education—whether private or public.[39] This was justified on two grounds: (1) the competitive position of an interstate enterprise is affected by *all* its labor costs, not simply the costs of employees producing goods for commerce; and (2) schools and hospitals are major users of goods imported from other states, and work stoppages involving their employees would interrupt this flow of goods across state lines.

(c) As indicated in *Wickard* and *Wirtz*, in addition to regulating interstate *movement* of persons or commodities to achieve police-type objectives, Congress has increasingly resorted to direct regulation of the undesired local activity when it "in any way or degree obstructs, delays or adversely affects [interstate] commerce."[40] In some cases, Congress has simply concluded that the controlled local activity adversely affects interstate commerce.[41] For example, Title VIII of the Organized Crime Control Act of

---

[38] *Fainblatt* upheld application of the National Labor Relations Act to a New Jersey shop where 60 employees did piece work for a New York company: "[C]ommerce may be affected in the same manner and to the same extent in proportion to its volume, whether it be great or small. [There] are not a few industries in the United States which, though conducted in relatively small units, contribute in the aggregate a vast volume of interstate commerce."

[39] For application of the Act to state government activities, see Sec. 5 infra.

[40] See, e.g., 18 U.S.C.A. § 231 (teaching another to use a firearm or explosive for use in a civil disorder, or interference with fireman or police carrying out duties during civil disorder, where commerce is adversely affected).

[41] For a comprehensive summary and discussion of these developments, see Boris I. Bittker, *Regulation of Interstate and Foreign Commerce* (1999).

1970, the widely used RICO ("Racketeer Influenced and Corrupt Organizations") statute, makes it a federal offense for "any person employed by or associated with any enterprise engaged in, or the activities of which affect, interstate or foreign commerce, [to] participate in the conduct" of its affairs through a "pattern of racketeering activity," defined to embrace two or more of a wide range of acts made criminal by state or federal law.

(d)   May a federal statute regulate local gambling or local racketeering not shown to be related to organized crime or to have any discernable impact on interstate commerce?

PEREZ v. UNITED STATES, 402 U.S. 146 (1971), per DOUGLAS, J., upheld the federal Consumer Credit Protection Act's ban on "extortionate credit transactions, though purely intrastate, [because they] may in the judgment of Congress affect interstate commerce. [R]eports and hearings [supplied] Congress with the knowledge that the loan shark racket provides organized crime with its second most lucrative source of revenue, [coerces] its victims into the commission of crimes against property, and causes the takeover by racketeers of legitimate businesses.

" * * * Congress need [not] make particularized findings in order to legislate. [But petitioner's claim] that all that is involved in loan sharking is a traditionally local activity. [It] appears, instead, that loan sharking in its national setting is one way organized interstate crime holds its guns to the heads of the poor and the rich alike and syphons funds from numerous localities to finance its national operations."

The Court rejected the contention that the extortionate activities of Perez were not shown to have any effect on commerce: "Where the *class of activities* is regulated and that *class* is within the reach of federal power, the courts have no power 'to excise, as trivial, individual instances' of the class. *Wirtz.*"

STEWART, J., dissented: "[I]t is not enough to say that loan sharking is a national problem, for all crime is a national problem. It is not enough to say that some loan sharking has interstate characteristics, for any crime may have an interstate setting. [F]or interstate business suffers from almost all criminal activity, be it shoplifting or violence in the streets. [The] definition and prosecution of local, intrastate crime are reserved to the States under the Ninth and Tenth Amendments."

4.   ***"Aggregation" principle (or "cumulative impact" doctrine).*** (a) Does *Wickard's* "trivial by itself [but] taken together with that of many others similarly situated" approach give Congress effectively unlimited power? Would this be ameliorated by limiting it to products and services that have a unified national market and thus produce interstate competition? See Regan, supra at 588–90; notes following *Gonzales v. Raich*, Sec. IV infra.

5.   ***Analogous rationale for war powers.*** WOODS v. CLOYD W. MILLER CO., 333 U.S. 138 (1948), per DOUGLAS, J., upheld continuation of federal rent control long after hostilities had ceased, using effect-type reasoning analogous to the Commerce Clause opinions: "The legislative history

of the present Act makes abundantly clear that there has not yet been eliminated the deficit in housing which in considerable measure was caused [by] the cessation or reduction in residential construction during the period of hostilities due to the allocation of building materials to military projects. Since the war effort contributed heavily to that deficit, Congress has the power even after the cessation of hostilities to act to control the forces that a short supply of the needed article created. If that were not true, the Necessary and Proper Clause would be drastically limited in its application to the several war powers. * * *

"We recognize the force of the argument that [if] the war power can be used in days of peace to treat all the wounds which war inflicts on our society, it may not only swallow up all other powers of Congress but largely obliterate the Ninth and the Tenth Amendments as well. [But we] cannot assume that Congress is not alert to its constitutional responsibilities. And the question whether the war power has been properly employed in cases such as this is open to judicial inquiry."[42]

III. PROTECTION OF OTHER INTERESTS THROUGH THE COMMERCE CLAUSE

HEART OF ATLANTA MOTEL, INC. V. UNITED STATES
379 U.S. 241, 85 S.Ct. 348, 13 L.Ed.2d 258 (1964).

JUSTICE CLARK delivered the opinion of the Court. * * *

[Heart of Atlanta, near interstate highways with 75% of its guests from other states and 216 rooms, refused to rent to African Americans. The issue presented was] the constitutionality of the Civil Rights Act of 1964[43] as applied to these facts. [The Court held that "Congress possessed ample power" under the Commerce Clause.]

The Senate Commerce Committee made it quite clear that the fundamental object of Title II was to vindicate [pursuant to the Equal Protection Clause of the Fourteenth Amendment] "the deprivation of personal dignity that surely accompanies denials of equal access to public establishments." At the same time, however, it noted that such an objective has been and could be readily achieved "by congressional action based on the commerce power of the Constitution." Our study of the legislative

---

[42] For other economic regulations based on the war powers, see *Yakus v. United States,* Ch. 3, Sec. 2, I; *Bowles v. Willingham,* 321 U.S. 503 (1944).

[43] Sec. 201(a) provided: "All persons shall be entitled to the full and equal enjoyment of the goods, services, facilities, [and] accommodations of any place of public accommodation * * * without discrimination or segregation on the ground of race, color, religion, or national origin." Sec. 201(b) defined of several types of establishments as "a place of public accommodation [if] its operations affect [interstate or foreign commerce], or if discrimination or segregation by it is supported by State action." Sec. 201(c) provided that "any inn, hotel, motel or other establishment which provides lodging to transient guests" is a place of public accommodation whose "operations * * * affect commerce," except when a live-in owner rents five or less rooms.

record [has] brought us to the conclusion that Congress possessed ample power [under the Commerce Clause], and we have therefore not considered the other grounds relied upon. * * *

While the Act [carried] no congressional findings the [legislative record is] replete with evidence of the burdens that discrimination by race or color places upon interstate commerce. This testimony included the fact that our people have become increasingly mobile with millions of all races traveling from State to State; that Negroes in particular have been the subject of discrimination in transient accommodations, having to travel great distances to secure the same; that often they have been unable to obtain accommodations and have had to call upon friends to put them up overnight; and that these conditions had become so acute as to require the listing of available lodging for Negroes in a special guidebook. [These] exclusionary practices were found to be nationwide [and] there is "no question that this discrimination in the North still exists to a large degree" and in the West and Midwest as well. This testimony indicated a qualitative as well as quantitative effect on interstate travel by Negroes. [As] for the latter, there was evidence that this uncertainty stemming from racial discrimination had the effect of discouraging travel on the part of a substantial portion of the Negro community. [T]he voluminous testimony presents overwhelming evidence that discrimination by hotels and motels impedes interstate travel.

[The] same interest in protecting interstate commerce [led Congress to] extend the exercise of its power to gambling, to criminal enterprises, to deceptive practices in the sale of products, to fraudulent security transactions, to misbranding of drugs, [to] discrimination against shippers, to the protection of small business from injurious price cutting, [and] to racial discrimination by owners and managers of terminal restaurants.

That Congress was legislating against moral wrongs in many of these areas [does] not detract from the overwhelming evidence of the disruptive effect that racial discrimination has had on commercial intercourse.

[T]he power of Congress to promote interstate commerce also includes the power to [regulate] local activities in both the States of origin and destination, which might have a substantial and harmful effect upon that commerce. [Thus,] Congress may—as it has—prohibit racial discrimination by motels serving travelers, however "local" their operations may appear. * * *

[The concurring opinions of Douglas and Goldberg, JJ., appear after *Katzenbach v. McClung, infra.*]

———

KATZENBACH v. McCLUNG, 379 U.S. 294 (1964), per CLARK, J., upheld application of Sec. 201 to Ollie's Barbecue, a Birmingham restaurant eleven blocks from an interstate highway. It catered to a family and white collar trade with only a take-out service for African Americans: "There is no claim that interstate travelers frequented the restaurant, receiving about $70,000 worth of food which has moved in commerce [out of a total of $150,000].[44]

"[A] comparison of per capita spending by Negroes in restaurants, theaters, and like establishments indicated less spending, after discounting income differences, in areas where discrimination is widely practiced. This condition, which was especially aggravated in the South, was attributed in the testimony of the Under Secretary of Commerce to racial segregation. This diminutive spending [has,] regardless of the absence of direct evidence, a close connection to interstate commerce. The fewer customers a restaurant enjoys the less food it sells and consequently the less it buys. [In] addition, there were many references to discriminatory situations causing wide unrest and having a depressant effect on general business conditions in the respective communities.

"Moreover there was an impressive array of testimony that discrimination in restaurants * * * obviously discourages travel and obstructs interstate commerce for one can hardly travel without eating. Likewise, it was said, that discrimination deterred professional, as well as skilled, people from moving into areas where such practices occurred and thereby caused industry to be reluctant to establish there.

"[As] said in *Wickard:* 'That appellee's own contribution to the demand for wheat may be trivial by itself is not enough to remove him from the scope of federal regulation where, as here, his contribution, taken together with that of many others similarly situated, is far from trivial.'

"[Here, as *in Darby*], Congress has determined for itself that refusals of service to Negroes have imposed burdens both upon the interstate flow of food and upon the movement of products generally. [This] does not preclude further examination by this Court. But where we find that the legislators, in light of the facts and testimony before them, have a rational basis for finding a chosen regulatory scheme necessary to the protection of commerce, our investigation is at an end. [The] absence of direct evidence connecting discriminatory restaurant service with the flow of interstate food, a factor on which the appellees place much reliance, is not, given the evidence as to the effect of such practices on other aspects of commerce, a crucial matter."[45]

---

[44] Sec. 201(b)(2) classified as a public accommodation, "any restaurant [or] other facility principally engaged in selling food for consumption on the premises." Sec. 201(c)(2) stated that the operations of such an establishment "affect commerce [if] it serves or offers to serve interstate travelers or a substantial portion of the food it serves [has] moved in commerce."

[45] Black, J., joined the Court's opinion and also concurred in both *Heart of Atlanta* and *McClung*, noting that "every remote, possible speculative effect on commerce" is not "an adequate

DOUGLAS, J., concurred: "Though I join the Court's opinion, I am somewhat reluctant [to] rest solely on the Commerce Clause. My reluctance is not due to any conviction that Congress lacks power to regulate commerce in the interests of human rights. It is rather my belief that [there] is a right of people to be free of state action that discriminates against them because of race. [Hence] I would prefer to rest on the assertion of legislative power contained in § 5 of the Fourteenth Amendment." [46]

NOTES AND QUESTIONS

1. *The Court's reasoning.* (a) *Congress' "motive."* Do you agree that the fact "that Congress was legislating against moral wrongs" should not affect its ruling? Consider Gil Seinfeld, *The Possibility of Pretext Analysis in Commerce Clause Adjudication*, 78 Notre D. L.Rev. 1251 (2003): "[E]xercises of the commerce power—at least when predicated on the substantial effects rationale—ought to have a *commercial* purpose. [Otherwise we are left] with the non-sequitur of an argument that because an activity substantially affects interstate commerce, Congress may regulate that activity so as to achieve whatever goal it pleases, commercial or otherwise. [Courts could either] reject Congress's invocation of a commercial purpose as pretextual [under] an aggressive form of judicial scrutiny into legislative purpose, [or under] a less intrusive method [e.g., only] where the legislature completely fails to identify a rational relationship between a regulation and some legitimate government objective would that regulation be subject to invalidation."

(b) *Standard of review.* Do you agree that if Congress, "in light of the facts and testimony before [it, has] a rational basis for finding a chosen regulatory scheme necessary to the protection of commerce," then the Court's "investigation is at an end"? Consider Richard A. Epstein, *Constitutional Faith and the Commerce Clause*, 71 Not.D.L.Rev. 167 (1996): "The basic design of the Constitution sought to achieve some balance between the powers ceded [to the union] and the powers retained by the states. [This] delicate balance requires that both forms of error have about the same weight, so that the right standard of review under the Commerce Clause [should provide for] a rough parity between the two kinds of error costs."

2. *Employment.* (a) Title VII of the Civil Rights Act of 1964 prohibits discrimination in employment practices based on "race, color, religion, sex, or national origin" when an employer with 25 or more employees is "engaged in an industry affecting commerce," defined as one "in commerce or in which a labor dispute would hinder or obstruct commerce or the free flow of commerce." The Age Discrimination in Employment Act of 1967 also prohibits discrimination in employment because of an individual's age in "industries

---

constitutional ground to uproot [all] traditional distinctions between what is purely local [and] what affects the national interest."

[46] Goldberg, J., also joined the opinion of the Court but in a separate opinion stated his view that the Fourteenth Amendment also authorized enactment of the Civil Rights Act, stressing that its "primary purpose" was "vindication of human dignity."

affecting commerce" as defined above for the Civil Rights Act. On what Commerce Clause reasoning can such national regulation best be sustained?

3.   ***Problem.*** Prior to enactment of Sec. 201, peaceful "sit ins" at Ollie's Barbecue by protestors of discrimination resulted in their arrests for trespass. After enactment of the Civil Rights Act, Congress passes a statute immunizing prior state prosecutions of this kind that had not become final. Constitutional? *See Hamm v. Rock Hill*, 379 U.S. 306 (1964) (even though the statute might not affect interstate commerce, Congress "clearly intended to eradicate an unhappy chapter in our history") (dicta). Would allowing the convictions to stand affect interstate commerce?

4.   ***Land regulation.*** HODEL v. VIRGINIA SURFACE MINING AND RECLAMATION ASS'N, 452 U.S. 264 (1981), per MARSHALL, J., unanimously upheld the Surface Mining Control and Reclamation Act of 1977: "In light of the evidence available to Congress[47] and the detailed consideration that the legislation received, we cannot say that Congress did not have a rational basis for concluding that surface coal mining has substantial effects on interstate commerce." REHNQUIST, J., concurred in the judgment, emphasizing that "there *are* constitutional limits on the power of Congress to regulate pursuant to the Commerce Clause. [I]t has long been established that the commerce power does not reach activity which merely 'affects' interstate commerce. There must instead be [a] *substantial effect* on that commerce. [Moreover,] simply because Congress may conclude that a particular activity substantially affects interstate commerce does not necessarily make it so. Congress' findings must be supported by a 'rational basis' and are reviewable by the courts."

IV. NEW LIMITATIONS IN THE 21st CENTURY

UNITED STATES v. MORRISON
529 U.S. 598, 120 S.Ct. 1740, 146 L.Ed.2d 658 (2000).

CHIEF JUSTICE REHNQUIST delivered the opinion of the Court.

[Petitioner Brzonkala, alleging that respondent, a fellow college student repeatedly raped her, sued him under 42 U.S.C. § 13981 (part of the Violence Against Women Act of 1984) which provides a federal civil remedy for the victims of gender-motivated violence. The United States intervened to defend § 13981's constitutionality.]

As we discussed at length in *United States v. Lopez*, 514 U.S. 549 (1995), our interpretation of the Commerce Clause has changed as our

---

[47] The opinion recited these findings of Congress: "[M]any surface mining operations result in disturbances of surface areas that burden and adversely affect commerce and the public welfare by destroying or diminishing the utility of land for commercial, industrial, residential, recreational, agricultural, and forestry purposes, by causing erosion and landslides, by contributing to floods, by polluting the water, by destroying fish and wildlife habitats, by impairing natural beauty, by damaging the property of citizens, by creating hazards dangerous to life and property by degrading the quality of life in local communities, and by counteracting governmental programs and efforts to conserve soil, water, and other natural resources."

Nation has developed. [I]n the years since *Jones & Laughlin,* Congress has had considerably greater latitude in regulating conduct and transactions under the Commerce Clause than our previous case law permitted.

Lopez emphasized, however, [that] Congress' regulatory authority is not without effective bounds. [In] *Jones & Laughlin,* the Court warned that the scope of the interstate commerce power "must be considered in the light of our dual system of government and may not be extended so as to embrace effects upon interstate commerce so indirect and remote that to embrace them, in view of our complex society, would effectually obliterate the distinction between what is national and what is local and create a completely centralized government."

As we observed in *Lopez,* modern Commerce Clause jurisprudence has "identified three broad categories of activity that Congress may regulate under its commerce power." "First, Congress may regulate the use of the channels of interstate commerce" (citing *Heart of Atlanta; Darby*). "Second, Congress is empowered to regulate and protect the instrumentalities of interstate commerce, or persons or things in interstate commerce, even though the threat may come only from intrastate activities" (citing *Shreveport*). "Finally, Congress' commerce authority includes the power to regulate those activities having a substantial relation to interstate commerce, i.e., those activities that substantially affect interstate commerce" (citing *Jones & Laughlin*).

Petitioners [seek] to sustain § 13981 as a regulation of activity that substantially affects interstate commerce. Given § 13981's focus on gender-motivated violence wherever it occurs (rather than violence directed at the instrumentalities of interstate commerce, interstate markets, or things or persons in interstate commerce), we agree that this is the proper inquiry.

[In] *Lopez,* [per REHNQUIST, C.J.], we held that the Gun-Free School Zones Act of 1990, 18 U.S.C. § 922(q)(1)(A), which made it a federal crime to knowingly possess a firearm in a school zone, exceeded Congress' authority under the Commerce Clause. Several significant considerations contributed to our decision.

First, we observed that § 922(q) was "a criminal statute that by its terms has nothing to do with 'commerce' or any sort of economic enterprise, however broadly one might define those terms." [A] fair reading of *Lopez* shows that the noneconomic, criminal nature of the conduct at issue was central to our decision in that case. See, e.g., ("Even *Wickard,* which is perhaps the most far reaching example of Commerce Clause authority over intrastate activity, involved economic activity in a way that the possession of a gun in a school zone does not"), ("Admittedly, a determination whether an intrastate activity is commercial or noncommercial may in some cases result in legal uncertainty. But, so long as Congress' authority is limited to those powers enumerated in the Constitution, and so long as those enumerated powers are interpreted as having judicially enforceable outer limits, congressional legislation under the Commerce Clause always will engender 'legal uncertainty' "), ("The possession of a gun in a local school zone is in no sense an economic activity that might, through repetition elsewhere, substantially affect any sort of interstate commerce"); see also id. (Kennedy, J., concurring) (stating that *Lopez* did not alter our "practical conception of commercial regulation" and that Congress may "regulate in the commercial sphere on the assumption that we have a single market and a unified purpose to build a stable national economy"), ("Were the Federal Government to take over the regulation of entire areas of traditional state concern, areas having nothing to do with the regulation of commercial activities, the boundaries between the spheres of federal and state authority would blur"), ("[In] a sense any conduct in this interdependent world of ours has an ultimate commercial origin or consequence, but we have not yet said the commerce power may reach so far"). * * *

The second consideration that we found important [was] that the statute contained "no express jurisdictional element which might limit its reach to a discrete set of firearm possessions that additionally have an explicit connection with or effect on interstate commerce." * * * [48]

Third, we noted that neither § 922(q) "nor its legislative history contains express congressional findings regarding the effects upon interstate commerce of gun possession in a school zone." While "Congress normally is not required to make formal findings as to the substantial burdens that an activity has on interstate commerce," (citing *McClung*, *Perez*), the existence of such findings may "enable us to evaluate the legislative judgment that the activity in question substantially affects interstate commerce, even though no such substantial effect [is] visible to the naked eye."

Finally, our decision in *Lopez* rested in part on the fact that the link between gun possession and a substantial effect on interstate commerce was attenuated. The United States argued that the possession of guns may lead to violent crime, and that violent crime "can be expected to affect the functioning of the national economy in two ways. First, the costs of violent crime are substantial, and, through the mechanism of insurance, those costs are spread throughout the population. Second, violent crime reduces the willingness of individuals to travel to areas within the country that are perceived to be unsafe." The Government also argued [that] guns at schools poses a threat to the educational process, which in turn threatens to produce a less efficient and productive workforce, which will negatively affect national productivity and thus interstate commerce.

---

[48] After *Lopez*, Congress amended the Gun-Free School Zones Act to add that the prosecution must demonstrate that the gun "has moved in or otherwise affects interstate or foreign commerce."

We rejected these "costs of crime" and "national productivity" arguments because they would permit Congress to "regulate not only all violent crime, but all activities that might lead to violent crime, regardless of how tenuously they relate to interstate commerce." We noted that, under this but-for reasoning: "Congress could regulate any activity that it found was related to the economic productivity of individual citizens: family law (including marriage, divorce, and child custody), for example.[49] Under these theories, [it] is difficult to perceive any limitation on federal power, even in areas such as criminal law enforcement or education where States historically have been sovereign.[50] Thus, if we were to accept the Government's arguments, we are hard pressed to posit any activity by an individual that Congress is without power to regulate."

With these principles underlying our Commerce Clause jurisprudence as reference points, the proper resolution of the present cases is clear. Gender-motivated crimes of violence are not, in any sense of the phrase, economic activity. While we need not adopt a categorical rule against aggregating the effects of any noneconomic activity in order to decide these cases, thus far in our Nation's history our cases have upheld Commerce Clause regulation of intrastate activity only where that activity is economic in nature.

Like the Gun-Free School Zones Act at issue in *Lopez*, § 13981 contains no jurisdictional element establishing that the federal cause of action is in pursuance of Congress' power to regulate interstate commerce. * * * Congress elected to cast § 13981's remedy over a wider, and more purely intrastate, body of violent crime.[51]

In contrast with the lack of congressional findings that we faced in *Lopez*, § 13981 *is* supported by numerous findings regarding the serious impact that gender-motivated violence has on victims and their families. But [as] we stated in *Lopez*, "Simply because Congress may conclude that

---

[49] See also Holmes, J., dissenting in *Northern Securities Co. v. United States*, 193 U.S. 197 (1904): "Commerce depends upon population, but Congress could not, on that ground, undertake to regulate marriage and divorce. [Otherwise,] I can see no part of the conduct of life with which on similar principles Congress might not interfere."

[50] See also Douglas, J., joined by Whittaker, J., dissenting in *United States v. Oregon*, 366 U.S. 643 (1961) (upholding federal escheat to United States of property of veteran who dies in veterans hospital without will or heirs): "[W]hen the Federal Government enters a field as historically local as the administration of decedents' estates, some clear relation of the asserted power to one of the delegated powers should be shown. [Today's] decision does not square with our conception of federalism."

[51] Title 42 U.S.C. § 13981 is not the sole provision of the Violence Against Women Act of 1994 to provide a federal remedy for gender-motivated crime. Section 40221(a) of the Act creates a federal criminal remedy to punish "interstate crimes of abuse including crimes committed against spouses or intimate partners during interstate travel and crimes committed by spouses or intimate partners who cross State lines to continue the abuse." [The] Courts of Appeals have uniformly upheld this criminal sanction as an appropriate exercise of Congress' Commerce Clause authority, reasoning that the provision properly falls within the first of *Lopez's* categories as it regulates the use of channels of interstate commerce—i.e., the use of the interstate transportation routes through which persons and goods move.

a particular activity substantially affects interstate commerce does not necessarily make it so." (quoting *Hodel* (Rehnquist, J., concurring in judgment)). Rather, " 'whether particular operations affect interstate commerce sufficiently to come under the constitutional power of Congress to regulate them is ultimately a judicial rather than a legislative question, and can be settled finally only by this Court.' " (quoting *Heart of Atlanta* (Black, J., concurring).

In these cases, Congress [found] that gender-motivated violence affects interstate commerce "by deterring potential victims from traveling interstate, from engaging in employment in interstate business, and from transacting with business, and in places involved in interstate commerce; [by] diminishing national productivity, increasing medical and other costs, and decreasing the supply of and the demand for interstate products." Given these findings and petitioners' arguments, the concern that we expressed in *Lopez* that Congress might use the Commerce Clause to completely obliterate the Constitution's distinction between national and local authority seems well founded. The reasoning that petitioners advance seeks to follow the but-for causal chain from the initial occurrence of violent crime (the suppression of which has always been the prime object of the States' police power) to every attenuated effect upon interstate commerce. If accepted, petitioners' reasoning would allow Congress to regulate any crime as long as the nationwide, aggregated impact of that crime has substantial effects on employment, production, transit, or consumption. Indeed, if Congress may regulate gender-motivated violence, it would be able to regulate murder or any other type of violence since gender-motivated violence, as a subset of all violent crime, is certain to have lesser economic impacts than the larger class of which it is a part.[52]

[The] regulation and punishment of intrastate violence that is not directed at the instrumentalities, channels, or goods involved in interstate commerce has always been the province of the States. See, e.g., *Cohens v. Virginia,* (Marshall, C. J.) (stating that Congress "has no general right to punish murder committed within any of the States," and that it is "clear [that] congress cannot punish felonies generally").[53] Indeed, we can think

---

[52] Justice Souter's dissent theory [is] remarkable because it undermines this central principle of our constitutional system. As we have repeatedly noted, the Framers crafted the federal system of government so that the people's rights would be secured by the division of power. [No] doubt the political branches have a role in interpreting and applying the Constitution, but ever since *Marbury* this Court has remained the ultimate expositor of the constitutional text. Contrary to Justice Souter's suggestion, [that] from *Gibbons* on, public opinion has been the only restraint on the congressional exercise of the commerce power is true only insofar as it contends that political accountability is and has been the only limit on Congress' exercise of the commerce power within that power's outer bounds. As the language surrounding that relied upon by Justice Souter makes clear, *Gibbons* did not remove from this Court the authority to define that boundary.

[53] For the view that "the Domestic Violence Clause [Art. IV, § 4] plays the role of a Tenth Amendment for crime, [providing] a guarantee to the states that the federal government will not interfere with a state's administration over crime [and creating] a presumption demanding that Congress justify an overlap of federal and state action against crime," see Jay S. Bybee, *Insuring*

of no better example of the police power, which the Founders denied the National Government and reposed in the States, than the suppression of violent crime and vindication of its victims. * * *

[The issue of Congress' power to enact § 13981 under § 5 of the Fourteenth Amendment is discussed in Ch. 11, Sec. 2.]

JUSTICE THOMAS, concurring.

The majority opinion correctly applies our decision in *Lopez,* and I join it in full. I write separately only to express my view that the very notion of a "substantial effects" test under the Commerce Clause is inconsistent with the original understanding of Congress' powers and with this Court's early Commerce Clause cases. [Thomas, J.'s concurring opinion in *Lopez* contended:

["At the time the original Constitution was ratified, 'commerce' consisted of selling, buying, and bartering, as well as transporting for these purposes [in] contradistinction to productive activities such as manufacturing and agriculture.[54] Alexander Hamilton, for example, repeatedly treated commerce, agriculture, and manufacturing as three separate endeavors. * * *

["The Constitution [does] not support the proposition that Congress has authority over all activities that 'substantially affect' interstate commerce. [After] all, if Congress may regulate all matters that substantially affect commerce, there is no need for the Constitution to specify that Congress may enact bankruptcy laws, cl. 4, or coin money and fix the standard of weights and measures, cl. 5, or punish counterfeiters of United States coin and securities, cl. 6. Likewise, Congress would not need the separate authority to establish post offices and post roads, cl. 7, or to grant patents and copyrights, cl. 8, or to 'punish Piracies and Felonies committed on the high Seas,' cl. 10. It might not even need the power to raise and support an Army and Navy, cls. 12 and 13, for fewer people would engage in commercial shipping if they thought that a foreign power could expropriate their property with ease. [An] interpretation of cl. 3 that makes the rest of § 8 superfluous simply cannot be correct."]

[Until] this Court replaces its existing Commerce Clause jurisprudence with a standard more consistent with the original

---

Domestic Tranquility: Lopez, Federalization of Crime, and the Forgotten Role of the Domestic Violence Clause, 66 Geo.Wash.L.Rev. 1 (1997).

[54] For support, see Raoul Berger, *Judicial Manipulation of the Commerce Clause,* 74 Tex.L.Rev. 695 (1996); Richard A. Epstein, *The Proper Scope of the Commerce Power,* 73 Va.L.Rev. 1387 (1987); Randy E. Barnett, *The Original Meaning of the Commerce Clause,* 68 U.Chi.L.Rev. 101 (2001). For the view that Justice Thomas's list of sources illustrating contemporary usage hardly reflects the range of *Judicial Restraint and Constitutional Federalism: The Supreme Court's Lopez and Seminole Tribe Decisions,* 96 Colum.L.Rev. 2213 (1996).

understanding, we will continue to see Congress appropriating state police powers under the guise of regulating commerce.

JUSTICE SOUTER, with whom JUSTICE STEVENS, JUSTICE GINSBURG, and JUSTICE BREYER join, dissenting. * * *

One obvious difference from *Lopez* is the mountain of data assembled by Congress, here showing the effects of violence against women on interstate commerce. Passage of the Act in 1994 was preceded by four years of hearings [and] includes reports on gender bias from task forces in 21 [States]. Congress received evidence for the following findings:

"Three out of four American women will be victims of violent crimes sometime during their life." "[A]s many as 50 percent of homeless women and children are fleeing domestic violence." "[B]attering 'is the single largest cause of injury to women in the United States.' " "An estimated 4 million American women are battered each year by their husbands or partners." * * * "Between 2,000 and 4,000 women die every year from [domestic] abuse." "[A]rrest rates may be as low as 1 for every 100 domestic assaults." "[E]stimates suggest that we spend $5 to $10 billion a year on health care, criminal justice, and other social costs of domestic violence."

The evidence as to rape was similarly extensive, supporting these conclusions: "[The incidence of] rape rose four times as fast as the total national crime rate over the past 10 years." "According to one study, close to half a million girls now in high school will be raped before they graduate." "[T]hree-quarters of women never go to the movies alone after dark because of the fear of rape and nearly 50 percent do not use public transit alone after dark for the same reason." "[Forty-one] percent of judges surveyed believed that juries give sexual assault victims less credibility than other crime victims." "Less than 1 percent of all [rape] victims have collected damages." " '[A]n individual who commits rape has only about 4 chances in 100 of being arrested, prosecuted, and found guilty of any offense.' " "Almost one-quarter of convicted rapists never go to prison and another quarter received sentences in local jails where the average sentence is 11 months." "[A]lmost 50 percent of rape victims lose their jobs or are forced to quit because of the crime's severity." * * *

Congress thereby explicitly stated the predicate [quoted in the Court's opinion at p. 113 supra] for the exercise of its Commerce Clause power. [T]he sufficiency of the evidence before Congress to provide a rational basis for the finding cannot seriously be questioned. * * *

The Act would have passed muster at any time between *Wickard* in 1942 and *Lopez* in 1995, a period in which the law enjoyed a stable understanding that congressional power under the Commerce Clause, complemented by the authority of the Necessary and Proper Clause, extended to all activity that, when aggregated, has a substantial effect on interstate commerce. [T]his understanding was secure even against the turmoil at the passage of the Civil Rights Act of 1964, in the aftermath of which the Court not only reaffirmed the cumulative effects and rational basis features of the substantial effects test, but declined to limit the commerce power through a formal distinction between legislation focused on "commerce" and statutes addressing "moral and social wrongs," *Heart of Atlanta.*

[I]t is clear that some congressional conclusions about obviously substantial, cumulative effects on commerce are being assigned lesser values than the once-stable doctrine would assign them. These devaluations are accomplished [by] supplanting rational basis scrutiny with a new criterion of review.

* * * From the fact that Art. I, § 8, cl. 3 grants an authority limited to regulating commerce, [it] does not at all follow that an activity affecting commerce nonetheless falls outside the commerce power, depending on the specific character of the activity, or the authority of a State to regulate it along with Congress. [H]istory has shown that categorical exclusions have proven as unworkable in practice as they are unsupportable in theory.

[T]o declare "noncommercial" primary activity beyond or presumptively beyond the scope of the commerce power. That variant of categorical approach is not, however, the sole textually permissible way of defining the scope of the Commerce Clause, and any such neat limitation would at least be suspect in the light of the [Necessary and Proper Clause]. Accordingly, for significant periods of our history, the Court has defined the commerce power as plenary, unsusceptible to categorical exclusions. [In] the half century following the modern activation of the commerce power with passage of the Interstate Commerce Act in 1887, this Court from time to time created categorical enclaves beyond congressional reach by declaring such activities as "mining," "production," "manufacturing," and union membership to be outside the definition of "commerce" and by limiting application of the effects test to "direct" rather than "indirect" commercial consequences.

Since adherence to these formalistically contrived confines of commerce power in large measure provoked the judicial crisis of 1937, one might reasonably have doubted that Members of this Court would ever again toy with [it]. And yet [today's] enquiry into commercial purpose, first intimated by the *Lopez* concurrence (opinion of Kennedy, J.), is cousin to the intent-based analysis employed in *Hammer*, but rejected for Commerce Clause purposes in *Heart of Atlanta* and *Darby.*

Why is the majority tempted to reject the lesson so painfully learned in 1937? An answer emerges from contrasting *Wickard* with one of the predecessor cases it superseded. It was obvious in *Wickard* that growing wheat for consumption right on the farm was not "commerce" in the common vocabulary.[13] [Just] a few years before *Wickard*, however, it had certainly been no less obvious that "mining" practices could substantially affect commerce, even though *Carter Coal* had held mining regulation beyond the national commerce power. [T]he Court in *Carter Coal* had a reason for trying to maintain its categorical, formalistic distinction. [It] was still trying to create a laissez-faire world out of the 20th-century economy, and formalistic commercial distinctions were thought to be useful instruments in achieving that object. * * *

The Court finds it relevant that the statute addresses conduct traditionally subject to state prohibition under domestic criminal law. [Again,] history seems to be recycling, for the theory of traditional state concern as grounding a limiting principle has [been repudiated in *Garcia v. San Antonio Met. Trans. Auth.* (1985) [Sec. 5 infra], which held that the concept of "traditional governmental function" [was] incoherent * * * .[14]

The objection to reviving traditional state spheres of action as a consideration in commerce analysis [is] compounded by a further defect[:] the majority's rejection of the Founders' considered judgment that politics, not judicial review, should mediate between state and national interests as the strength and legislative jurisdiction of the National Government inevitably increased through the expected growth of the national economy. [quoting Madison (in *Federalist* No. 46), James Wilson, and Marshall, C.J., in *Gibbons*]. * * *

The *Garcia* Court's rejection of "judicially created limitations" in favor of the intended reliance on national politics was all the more powerful owing to the Court's explicit recognition that in the centuries since the framing the relative powers of the two sovereign systems have markedly changed. Nationwide economic integration is the norm, the national political power has been augmented by its vast revenues, and the power of the States has been drawn down by the Seventeenth Amendment,

---

[13] **[Ct's Note]** [The] *Wickard* Court admitted that Filburn's activity "may not be regarded as commerce" but insisted that "it may still, whatever its nature, be reached by Congress if it exerts a substantial economic effect on interstate commerce." [If] substantial effects on commerce are proper subjects of concern under the Commerce Clause, what difference should it make whether the causes of those effects are themselves commercial? The Court's answer is that it makes a difference to federalism, and the legitimacy of the Court's new judicially derived federalism is the crux of our disagreement.

[14] **[Ct's Note]** The Constitution of 1787 did, in fact, forbid some exercises of the commerce power. Article I, § 9, cl. 6, barred Congress from giving preference to the ports of one State over those of another. More strikingly, the Framers protected the slave trade from federal interference, see Art. I, § 9, cl. 1. [These] reservations demonstrate the plenary nature of the federal power; the exceptions prove the rule. [T]o suppose that enumerated powers must have limits is sensible; to maintain that there exist judicially identifiable areas of state regulation immune to the plenary congressional commerce power even though falling within the limits defined by the substantial effects test is to deny our constitutional history.

eliminating selection of senators by state legislature in favor of direct election. * * * 19

Amendments that alter the balance of power between the National and State Governments, like the Fourteenth, or that change the way the States are represented within the Federal Government, like the Seventeenth, are not rips in the fabric of the Framers' Constitution, inviting judicial repairs. The Seventeenth Amendment may indeed have lessened the enthusiasm of the Senate to represent the States as discrete sovereignties, but the Amendment did not convert the judiciary into an alternate shield against the commerce power.

The Court [finds] no significance whatever in the state support for the Act based upon the States' acknowledged failure to deal adequately with gender-based violence in state courts, and the belief of their own law enforcement agencies that national action is essential. The National Association of Attorneys General supported the Act unanimously, and [as] the 1993 Senate Report put it, "The Violence Against Women Act is intended to respond both to the underlying attitude that this violence is somehow less serious than other crime and to the resulting failure of our criminal justice system to address such violence. Its goals are both symbolic and practical." [It] is, then, not the least irony of these cases that the States will be forced to enjoy the new federalism whether they want it or not. * * *

JUSTICE BREYER, with whom JUSTICE STEVENS joins, and with whom JUSTICE SOUTER and JUSTICE GINSBURG join as to Part I–A, dissenting.

No one denies the importance of the Constitution's federalist principles. [The] question is how the judiciary can [best] impose some meaningful limit, but not too great a limit, upon the scope of the legislative authority that the Commerce Clause delegates to Congress.

A.   Consider the problems. The "economic/noneconomic" distinction is not easy to apply. Does the local street corner mugger engage in "economic" activity or "noneconomic" activity when he mugs for money? Would evidence that desire for economic domination underlies many brutal crimes against women save the present statute?

The line becomes yet harder to draw given the need for exceptions. The Court itself would permit Congress to aggregate, hence regulate, "noneconomic" activity taking place at economic establishments. See *Heart of Atlanta.* And it would permit Congress to regulate where that regulation is "an essential part of a larger regulation of economic activity, in which the regulatory scheme could be undercut unless the intrastate activity

---

19   **[Ct's Note]** [Neither] Madison nor Wilson nor Marshall, nor the *Jones & Laughlin, Darby, Wickard,* or *Garcia* Courts, suggested that politics defines the commerce power. Nor do we, even though we recognize that the conditions of the contemporary world result in a vastly greater sphere of influence for politics than the Framers would have envisioned. * * *

were regulated." *Lopez*.[55] Given the former exception, can Congress simply rewrite the present law and limit its application to restaurants, hotels, perhaps universities, and other places of public accommodation? Given the latter exception, can Congress save the present law by including it, or much of it, in a broader "Safe Transport" or "Workplace Safety" act?

More important, why should we give critical constitutional importance to the economic, or noneconomic, nature of an interstate-commerce-affecting cause? If chemical emanations through indirect environmental change cause identical, severe commercial harm outside a State, why should it matter whether local factories or home fireplaces release them? * * *

Most important, the Court's complex rules seem unlikely to help secure the very object that they seek, namely, the protection of "areas of traditional state regulation" from federal intrusion. The Court's rules, even if broadly interpreted, are underinclusive. The local pickpocket is no less a traditional subject of state regulation than is the local gender-motivated assault. Regardless, the Court reaffirms, as it should, Congress' well-established and frequently exercised power to enact laws that satisfy a commerce-related jurisdictional prerequisite—for example, that some item relevant to the federally regulated activity has at some time crossed a state line. *Heart of Atlanta*; see also *Scarborough*.

And in a world where most everyday products or their component parts cross interstate boundaries, Congress will frequently find it possible to redraft a statute using language that ties the regulation to the interstate movement of some relevant object, thereby regulating local criminal activity or, for that matter, family affairs. See, e.g., Child Support Recovery Act of 1992. [How] much would be gained, for example, were Congress to reenact the present law in the form of "An Act Forbidding Violence Against Women Perpetrated at Public Accommodations or by Those Who Have Moved in, or through the Use of Items that Have Moved in, Interstate Commerce"? Complex Commerce Clause rules creating fine distinctions that achieve only random results do little to further the important federalist interests that called them into being. That is why modern (pre-*Lopez*) case law rejected them.[56] * * *

---

[55] In *Lopez*, Breyer, J., joined by Stevens, Souter and Ginsburg, JJ., dissenting, noted that "although the majority today attempts to categorize *Perez, McClung,* and *Wickard,* as involving intrastate 'economic activity,' the Courts that decided each of those cases did *not* focus upon the economic nature of the activity regulated. Rather, they focused upon whether that activity *affected* interstate or foreign commerce."

[56] See Thomas, J., joined by Scalia, J., dissenting from denial of certiorari in *Alderman v. United States*, 131 S.Ct. 700 (2011): "*Scarborough* cannot be reconciled with *Lopez* because it reduces the constitutional analysis to the mere identification of a jurisdictional hook [and] could very well remove any limit on the commerce power [and] permit Congress to regulate or ban possession of any item that has ever been offered for sale or crossed state lines."

Since judges cannot change the [world,] Congress, not the courts, must remain primarily responsible for striking the appropriate state/federal balance. Congress is institutionally motivated to do so. Its Members represent state and local district interests. They consider the views of state and local officials when they legislate, and they have even developed formal procedures to ensure that such consideration takes place. See, e.g., Unfunded Mandates Reform Act of 1995. Moreover, Congress often can better reflect state concerns for autonomy in the details of sophisticated statutory schemes than can the judiciary, which cannot easily gather the relevant facts and which must apply more general legal rules and categories.

* * * Congress focused the federal law upon documented deficiencies in state legal systems. And it tailored the law to prevent its use in certain areas of traditional state concern, such as divorce, alimony, or child custody. Consequently, the law before us seems to represent an instance, not of state/federal conflict, but of state/federal efforts to cooperate in order to help solve a mutually acknowledged national problem.

[This] Court on occasion has pointed to the importance of procedural limitations in keeping the power of Congress in check. See *Garcia* ("Any substantive [limitations] must be tailored to compensate for possible failings in the national political process rather than to dictate a 'sacred province of state autonomy.' ") [Of] course, any judicial insistence that Congress follow particular procedures might itself intrude upon congressional prerogatives and embody difficult definitional problems. But the intrusion, problems, and consequences all would seem less serious than those embodied in the majority's approach.

I continue to agree with Justice Souter that the Court's traditional "rational basis" approach is sufficient. But I recognize that the law in this area is unstable and that time and experience may demonstrate both the unworkability of the majority's rules and the superiority of Congress' own procedural approach—in which case the law may evolve towards a rule that, in certain difficult Commerce Clause cases, takes account of the thoroughness with which Congress has considered the federalism issue. [57]
* * *

NOTES AND QUESTIONS

"Substantial effects." How are, or should these be, defined? Does this criterion help articulate a coherent (principled) limit on the commerce power? Consider Deborah J. Merritt, *Commerce!*, 94 Mich.L.Rev. 674 (1995): "The majority's use of 'substantial effect' is more akin to the notion of proximate cause in tort law [—] that the relationship between the regulated activity and

---

[57] The question of whether the national political process or judicial review is more desirable and effective in "safeguarding" federalism is considered further in Sec. 5, IV infra.

interstate commerce must be strong enough or close enough to justify federal intervention. [T]hese judgments are qualitative ones, resting on a host of contextual factors,[58] rather than simple quantitative calculations." See also H. Jefferson Powell, *Enumerated Means and Unlimited Ends,* 94 Mich.L.Rev. 651 (1995): "*Lopez* suggests that it [is] necessary to make the essentially negative demonstration that one can with logical consistency prove some other, hypothetical statute unconstitutional. This [confirms that] the Court is not inadvertently 'conclud[ing] that the Constitution's enumeration of powers does not presuppose something not enumerated' [*Lopez*] contrary to the principle of enumerated and therefore limited federal power."

GONZALES V. RAICH
545 U.S. 1, 125 S. Ct. 2195, 162 L. Ed. 2d 1 (2005).

JUSTICE STEVENS delivered the opinion of the Court.

[The Controlled Substances Act, part of "a comprehensive regime to combat the international and interstate traffic in illicit drugs"—"prohibited the local cultivation and use of marijuana" even when in compliance with state law authorizing its use for medical purposes.]

Wickard establishes that Congress can regulate purely intrastate activity that is not itself "commercial," in that it is not produced for sale [if] Congress had a rational basis for believing that, when viewed in the aggregate, leaving home-consumed wheat outside the regulatory scheme would have a substantial influence on price and market conditions. Here too, Congress had a rational basis for concluding that leaving home-consumed marijuana outside federal control would similarly affect price and market conditions [given] the likelihood that the high demand in the interstate market will draw such marijuana into that market [and given] the enforcement difficulties that attend distinguishing between marijuana cultivated locally and marijuana grown elsewhere, and concerns about diversion into illicit channels [which] would leave a gaping hole in the CSA.

[Respondents] nonetheless insist that the CSA cannot be constitutionally applied to their activities because Congress did not make a specific finding that the intrastate cultivation and possession of marijuana for medical purposes based on the recommendation of a physician would substantially affect the larger interstate marijuana market. [But] we have never required ["that legislation must contain detailed findings proving that each activity regulated within a comprehensive statute is essential to the statutory scheme"], absent a special concern such as the protection of free speech.

---

[58] "One of those factors is whether the government's argument is so all-encompassing that it sweeps all conduct within congressional control." Deborah J. Merritt, *The Fuzzy Logic of Federalism*, 46 Case W.Res.L.Rev. 685 (1996).

[I]n both *Lopez* and *Morrison,* the parties asserted that a particular statute or provision fell outside Congress' commerce power in its entirety. This distinction is pivotal for we have often reiterated that "[w]here the class of activities is regulated and that class is within the reach of federal power, the courts have no power 'to excise, as trivial, individual instances' of the class." *Perez.* [Unlike] *Lopez* and *Morrison,* the activities regulated by the CSA are quintessentially economic [—] production, distribution, and consumption of commodities for which there is an established, and lucrative, interstate market.

[I]f, as the principal dissent contends, the personal cultivation, possession, and use of marijuana for medicinal purposes is beyond the " 'outer limits' of Congress' Commerce Clause authority," (O'Connor, J., dissenting), it must also be true that such personal use of marijuana (or any other homegrown drug) for recreational purposes is also beyond those "outer limits," whether or not a State elects to authorize or even regulate such use. Justice Thomas' separate dissent suffers from the same sweeping implications. [One] need not have a degree in economics to understand why a nationwide exemption for the vast quantity of marijuana (or other drugs) locally cultivated for personal use (which presumably would include use by friends, neighbors, and family members) may have a substantial impact on the interstate market for this extraordinarily popular substance. The congressional judgment that an exemption for such a significant segment of the total market would undermine the orderly enforcement of the entire regulatory scheme is entitled to a strong presumption of validity. Indeed, that judgment is not only rational, but "visible to the naked eye," *Lopez,* under any commonsense appraisal of the probable consequences of such an open-ended exemption.

[The dissents' limiting] the activity to marijuana possession and cultivation "in accordance with state law" cannot serve to place respondents' activities beyond congressional reach. The Supremacy Clause unambiguously provides that if there is any conflict between federal and state law, federal law shall prevail. * * * [38] [The] notion that California law has surgically excised a discrete activity that is hermetically sealed off from

---

[38] **[Ct's Note]** California's decision (made 34 years after the CSA was enacted) to impose "stric[t] controls" on the "cultivation and possession of marijuana for medical purposes," (Thomas, J., dissenting), cannot retroactively divest Congress of its authority under the Commerce Clause.

[Thomas, J.'s dissent responded: "The majority apparently believes that even if States prevented any medical marijuana from entering the illicit drug market, and thus even if there were no need for the CSA to govern medical marijuana users, we should uphold the CSA under the *Commerce* Clause and the *Necessary* and Proper Clause. [T]o invoke the Supremacy Clause, as the majority does, is to beg the question. The CSA displaces California's Compassionate Use Act if the CSA is constitutional as applied to respondents' conduct, but that is the very question at issue."]

the larger interstate marijuana market is a dubious proposition,[59] and, more importantly, one that Congress could have rationally rejected. * * *

JUSTICE SCALIA, concurring in the judgment [to describe a "more nuanced doctrinal foundation" and to respond to O'Connor, J.'s dissent].

[Although *Lopez* and *Morrison*] rejected the argument that Congress may regulate *noneconomic* activity based solely on the effect that it may have on interstate commerce through a remote chain of inferences, [under the Necessary and Proper Clause, Congress has] regulatory authority over intrastate activities that are not themselves part of interstate commerce [even when they] do not themselves substantially affect interstate commerce [if they are] "an essential part of a larger regulation of economic activity, in which the regulatory scheme could be undercut unless the intrastate activity were regulated." [*Lopez*.] Unlike the power to regulate activities that have a substantial effect on interstate commerce, the power to enact laws enabling effective regulation of interstate commerce can only be exercised in conjunction with congressional regulation of an interstate market. [Therefore, that] simple possession [of drugs] is a noneconomic activity is immaterial to whether it can be prohibited as a necessary part of a larger regulation. Rather, Congress's authority to enact all of these prohibitions of intrastate controlled-substance activities depends only upon whether they are appropriate means of achieving the legitimate end of eradicating [illegal] substances from interstate commerce. [T]hat the CSA regulates an area typically left to state regulation [is] not enough to render federal regulation an inappropriate means. * * *

JUSTICE O'CONNOR, with whom THE CHIEF JUSTICE and JUSTICE THOMAS join, dissenting.

This case exemplifies the role of States as laboratories. The States' core police powers have always included authority to define criminal law and to protect the health, safety, and welfare of their citizens. [Today's] decision suggests that the federal regulation of local activity is immune to Commerce Clause challenge because Congress chose to act with an ambitious, all-encompassing statute, rather than piecemeal. [If so], then *Lopez* stands for nothing more than a drafting guide: Congress should have described the relevant crime as "transfer or possession of a firearm anywhere in the nation"—thus including commercial and noncommercial activity, and clearly encompassing some activity with assuredly substantial effect on interstate commerce. [This is] a signal to Congress to enact legislation that is more extensive and more intrusive into the domain

---

[59] The Court refers here to O'Connor, J's argument "that California's Compassionate Use Act and similar state legislation may well isolate activities relating to medicinal marijuana from the illicit market," through controls such as the requirement of a "recommendation by a physician" and "an identification card system for qualified patients."

of state power. If the Court always defers to Congress as it does today, little may be left to the notion of enumerated powers. * * *

A number of objective markers are available to confine the scope of constitutional review here. Both federal and state legislation [recognize] that medical and nonmedical (i.e., recreational) uses of drugs are realistically distinct and can be segregated, and regulate them differently. [Moreover] it is relevant that this case involves the interplay of federal and state regulation in areas of criminal law and social policy, where "States lay claim by right of history and expertise." *Lopez* (Kennedy, J., concurring); see also *Morrison*. [To] ascertain whether Congress' encroachment is constitutionally justified in this case, then, I would focus here on the personal cultivation, possession, and use of marijuana for medicinal purposes.

[It] will not do to say that Congress may regulate noncommercial activity simply because it may have an effect on the demand for commercial goods, or because the noncommercial endeavor can, in some sense, substitute for commercial activity. Most commercial goods or services have some sort of privately producible analogue. Home care substitutes for daycare. Charades games substitute for movie tickets. Backyard or windowsill gardening substitutes for going to the supermarket. To draw the line wherever private activity affects the demand for market goods is to draw no line at all, and to declare everything economic. [As for *Wickard*, in] contrast to the CSA's limitless assertion of power, Congress provided an exemption within the AAA for small producers. [Thus] *Wickard* did not hold or imply that small-scale production of commodities is always economic, and automatically within Congress' reach.

[S]omething more than mere assertion is required when Congress purports to have power over local activity whose connection to an interstate market is not self-evident. Otherwise, the Necessary and Proper Clause will always be a back door for unconstitutional federal regulation. [And] here, in part because common sense suggests that medical marijuana users may be limited in number, [the] effect of those activities on interstate drug traffic is not self-evidently substantial.

In this regard, again, this case is readily distinguishable from *Wickard* [because] the parties had "stipulated a summary of the economics of the wheat industry" [which showed] that consumption of homegrown wheat was the most variable factor in the size of the national wheat crop, and that on-site consumption could have the effect of varying the amount of wheat sent to market by as much as 20 percent. [The] Court recognizes that "the record in the *Wickard* case itself established the causal connection between the production for local use and the national market" and argues that "we have before us findings by Congress *to the same effect*." The Court refers to a series of declarations in the introduction to the CSA saying that (1) local distribution and possession of controlled substances causes "swelling" in interstate traffic; (2) local production and distribution cannot be distinguished from interstate production and distribution; (3) federal control over intrastate incidents "is essential to effective control" over interstate drug trafficking. These bare declarations cannot be compared to the record before the Court in *Wickard.* [If] as the Court claims, today's decision does not break with precedent, how can it be that voluminous findings, documenting extensive hearings about the specific topic of violence against women, did not pass constitutional muster in *Morrison,* while the CSA's abstract, unsubstantiated, generalized findings about controlled substances do? * * *

JUSTICE THOMAS, dissenting.

[The] Government contends that banning ["a distinct and separable subclass (local growers and users of state-authorized, medical marijuana)"] is "necessary and proper for carrying into Execution" its regulation of interstate drug trafficking. However, in order to be "necessary," the intrastate ban [must] be an "obvious, simple, and direct relation" between the intrastate ban and the regulation of interstate commerce. *Sabri v. United States,* [Sec. 3, II infra] (Thomas, J., concurring in judgment).[60] * * *

[E]ven assuming Congress has "obvious" and "plain" reasons why regulating intrastate cultivation and possession is necessary to regulating the interstate drug trade, none of those reasons applies to medical marijuana. [E]ven assuming that States' controls[61] allow some seepage of medical marijuana into the illicit drug market, [i]t is difficult to see how this vast market could be affected by diverted medical cannabis, let alone in a way that makes regulating intrastate medical marijuana obviously essential to controlling the interstate drug market. [I]t is implausible that this Court could set aside entire portions of the United States Code as outside Congress' power in *Lopez* and *Morrison,* but it cannot engage in the more restrained practice of invalidating particular applications of the CSA that are beyond Congress' power. This Court has regularly entertained as-applied challenges under constitutional provisions, including the

---

[60] Consider Bradford R. Clark, *Translating Federalism: A Structural Approach,* 66 Geo.Wash.L.Rev. 1161 (1998): "Because Congress's commerce power has become so pervasive, the constitutional structure arguably no longer counsels in favor of a broad interpretation of the Necessary and Proper Clause to augment this power. [That would] permit Congress to regulate any activity that affects interstate commerce [or] 'practically every activity of social life' [citing Lawrence Lessig, *Translating Federalism: United States v. Lopez,* 1995 Sup.Ct.Rev. 125.]. Thus, even if a plausible interpretation of the clause allowed Congress to regulate *intra*state commerce as a means of regulating *inter*state commerce in 1819, changed circumstances arguably have rendered this reading of the text obsolete today."

Should the Court hold that an otherwise seemingly proper exercise of the commerce power is invalid because used as a pretext (see fn. 27) to accomplish a goal prohibited through exercise of a different power? See Michael Paisner, Note, *Boerne Supremacy: Congressional Responses to City of Boerne v. Flores and the Scope of Congress's Article I Powers,* 105 Colum.L.Rev. 537 (2005). How would this affect the decision in *Heart of Atlanta?*

[61] See fn. 38 to the Court's opinion.

Commerce Clause, see *McClung*; *Heart of Atlanta*; *Wickard*. There is no reason why, when Congress exceeds the scope of its commerce power, courts may not invalidate Congress' overreaching on a case-by-case basis. * * *

The majority's rewriting of the Commerce Clause seems to be rooted in the belief that, unless the Commerce Clause covers the entire web of human activity, Congress will be left powerless to regulate the national economy effectively. The interconnectedness of economic activity is not a modern phenomenon unfamiliar to the Framers. *Lopez* (Thomas, J., concurring). Moreover, the Framers understood what the majority does not appear to fully appreciate: There is a danger to concentrating too much, as well as too little, power in the Federal Government. This Court [has] casually allowed the Federal Government to strip States of their ability to regulate *intra* state commerce—not to mention a host of local activities, like mere drug possession, that are not commercial. * * *

NOTES AND QUESTIONS

1.   (a) **Relevance of "interstate market."** Consider Grant S. Nelson & Robert J. Pushaw, Jr., *Rethinking the Commerce Clause: Applying First Principles to Uphold Federal Commercial Regulations but Preserve State Control Over Social Issues*, 85 Ia.L.Rev. 1 n. 518 (1999): "This argument [in the article's title] is appealing because it limits the Wickard 'aggregating' principle to its factual context—a fungible commodity with an interstate market (e.g., wheat) where transactions in one state influence those in another. Aggregation becomes progressively more attenuated as it is extended to more unique goods, to small service providers, and to businesses lacking a multistate organization. Thus, for example, the price charged by an independent, family-run laundry in Los Angeles to press a shirt does not seem to bear any obvious relation to the price of the identical service in Peoria, Illinois. [But] in our integrated national economy almost any commercial activity might reasonably be viewed as affecting interstate commerce. [M]any restaurants and laundries are part of huge franchises, and those that are not compete against these national chains. Hence, it would make little sense to require McDonald's to pay a minimum wage, but not a local burger joint that competes with McDonald's."[62]

Does the interstate market factor sustain the lower courts that have upheld Congress's bar on possession of a machine gun? "Although the conduct at issue is neither economic nor commercial, prohibiting it may be fairly characterized as 'integral to a larger federal scheme for the regulation of trafficking in firearms.'[63] Similarly, since Oregon's permissive assisted suicide

---

[62]   Consider further Robert J. Pushaw, Jr. & Grant S. Nelson, *The Likely Impact of National Federation on Commerce Clause Jurisprudence*, 40 Pepperdine L. Rev. 975 (2013): "Market transactions [cannot] plausibly be stretched to cover actions taken merely to fulfill personal or household needs, such as growing wheat or marijuana for home consumption (contrary to the holdings in *Wickard* and *Raich*)."

[63]   United States v. Franklyn, 157 F.3d 90, 94 (2d Cir. 1998).

law has been used only [a limited number of times], *Lopez* and *Morrison* might well make it difficult to find a substantial effect on interstate commerce when an Oregon physician prescribes lethal drugs for a terminally ill patient. But the 'comprehensive-scheme' approach, relying on a national drug policy, might provide the solution.[64] Jesse H. Choper, *Taming Congress's Commerce Power: What Does the Near Future Portend?* 55 Ark.L.Rev. 731 (2003). How about a federal ban on gay marriage?

(b) ***Products "similarly situated."*** The law in *Wickard* regulated corn, cotton, rice, peanuts and tobacco, as well as wheat. Could production for home consumption of all these be regulated by "aggregating" them with wheat, even though, unlike wheat, home consumption of none of them had any significant impact on interstate prices? For the view that "that kind of aggregation would justify any federal legislation," see John C. Nagle, *The Commerce Clause Meets the Delhi Sands Flower-Loving Fly,* 97 Mich.L.Rev. 174 (1998) (discussing the Endangered Species Act). Compare Bradford C. Mark, *After Gonzales v. Raich: Is the Endangered Species Act Constitutional Under the Commerce Clause?*, 78 U. Colo. L. Rev. 375 (2007): "Congress may protect all endangered species, including intrastate species or those with no direct commercial value in interstate commerce, because [there] is reasonable evidence [that] the ESA's comprehensive scheme is necessary to preserve interdependent species and ecosystems that do have significant impacts on interstate commerce." For further possibilities, dealing with such matters as gun control and endangered species, see Adrian Vermeule, *Does Commerce Clause Review Have Perverse Effects?* 46 Vill.L.Rev. 1325 (2001) ("congressional coalitions [will have] incentives to legislate more broadly, and to create national programs that are more comprehensive, than they would otherwise choose").

2. ***The "commercial/economic" criterion.*** (a) Should "we give critical constitutional importance to the economic, or noneconomic, nature of an interstate-commerce-affecting cause" (Breyer, J.)? Consider Jesse H. Choper & John C. Yoo, *The Scope of the Commerce Clause After Morrison*, 25 Okla.City U.L.Rev. 843 (2000): "Given the success that the law and economics movement has encountered in revealing the underlying economic motivations that might underlay many actions, Congress may have little difficulty in persuasively characterizing many activities as economic in nature. [Thus,] while Congress might not be able to enact criminal penalties for all violence, it may still be able to ban any violence that has an economic motive or purpose. Not only would crimes that are fundamentally financial in nature, such as fraud or theft, fall wholly within federal power, but large subsets of other offenses also could come within national jurisdiction. Congress probably cannot, for example, enact a law that prohibits all physical assaults, but it could prohibit all muggings—which are, by definition, physical assaults undertaken to get the victim's money. It probably could not prohibit all breaking-and-entering, [but] could enact a nationwide law that prohibited all robbery. Congress may not be able to prohibit all possession of a certain product, but it could ban any

---

[64] See Susan R. Klein, *Independent-Norm Federalism in Criminal Law*, 90 Calif.L.Rev. 1541 (2002).

transaction or exchange that involved that product. To push the commercial distinction even further, neither *Lopez* nor *Morrison* prevent Congress from [making] a federal offense of any crime that involved the use of the federal currency." Compare Nelson & Pushaw, supra: "[M]ost criminal behavior does not constitute 'commerce' [which] at its core is a consensual transaction. [For] instance, crimes against the person, such as battery and rape, can hardly be classified as commercial. The addition of a financial purpose does not alter this conclusion, [even when it is the impetus for murder, armed robbery or burglary.] Even kidnapping for ransom is not a true commercial transaction. Although there is an 'agreement' to pay money in exchange for the release of the victim, it is made under duress." Contrast Allan Ides, *Economic Activity as a Proxy for Federalism: Intuition and Reason in United States v. Morrison*, 18 Const.Comm. 563 (2001): "Judge Posner [defines] crime, including violent crime, as representing an economic transaction in which there is a 'coercive transfer either of wealth or utility from victim to wrongdoer.' [In] short rape is an economic crime, and the act of rape constitutes economic activity. [Lopez] was exercising [a] property interest in the gun he brought to school. He possessed and asserted dominion over it. Indeed, he brought it to school to sell [it]. All this talk about economic or commercial activity (or any of the other doctrinal elements mentioned in these two opinions) was simply a proxy for this much more significant theme[:] Congress was attempting to regulate matters that in the Court's view were traditionally and perhaps exclusively left to the states." Consider Robert J.

Pushaw, Jr., *The Medical Marijuana Case: A Commerce Clause Counter-Revolution*, 9 Lewis & Clark L.Rev. 879 (2005): "All of the Justices mistakenly used 'commerce' and 'economics' interchangeably, instead of recognizing that the former is a subset of the latter. [Any] attempt to impose serious limits under the Commerce Clause, therefore, will be doomed if 'commerce' is equated with 'economics,' which sweeps in virtually all human activity." Compare Robert A. Schapiro & William W. Buzbee, *Unidimensional Federalism: Power and Perspective in Commerce Clause Adjudication*, 88 Corn.L.Rev. 1199 (2003): "[T]he Rehnquist Court's five-Justice majority has revived a categorical approach [where] the economic versus noneconomic activity distinction is crucial, [as is] whether an area of regulation is one traditionally dealt with by state governments. [But] laws typically reflect a multiplicity of goals and cannot be reduced to being 'about' a particular purpose or activity." Contrast Cooter & Siegel, fn. 23. "Economic activity does not generally cause collective action problems among the states, and noneconomic activity is not generally free from collective action problems. Consequently, Congress is not generally better at regulating economic activity, and the states are not generally better at regulating noneconomic activity."

(b) JONES v. UNITED STATES, 529 U.S. 848 (2000), per GINSBURG, J., unanimously held that the federal arson statute (covering buildings "used [in] any activity affecting interstate or foreign commerce") did not apply to an owner-occupied residence not used for commercial purposes, thus avoiding the constitutional question under the Commerce Clause.

(c) *"Instrumentalities of interstate commerce."* May Congress use the Commerce Clause to regulate the labor relations of a nonprofit organization? See *Polish Nat'l Alliance v. NLRB*, 322 U.S. 643 (1944). To make it a crime to obstruct access to abortion clinics? See Note, *Abortion as Commerce: The Impact of United States v. Lopez on the Freedom of Access to Clinic Entrances Act of 1994*, 50 Vand.L.Rev. 239 (1997). To prohibit partial-birth abortions? See David B. Kopel & Glenn H. Reynolds, *Taking Federalism Seriously: Lopez and the Partial-Birth Abortion Ban Act*, 30 Conn.L.Rev. 59 (1997). Are nonprofit organizations and abortion clinics *themselves* "enterprises engaged in interstate commerce" because they purchase materials and have clients and employees that come from other states? Cf. *United States v. Robertson*, 514 U.S. 669 (1995) (gold mine was such an "enterprise" within federal RICO law). If so, do they fall within *Lopez*'s second "broad category of activity that Congress may regulate under its commerce power"?

Consider Choper & Yoo, supra "While as yet not fully used by Congress, the instrumentalities aspect of the Commerce Clause could sweep a great deal of intrastate, non-economic activity within the ambit of national authority. Mail and wire fraud require only one use of the mails or the phones to trigger federal jurisdiction. Congress could add other common-law crimes in addition to fraud to the mail and wire statutes: conspiracy to commit murder, robbery, assault, and so on. Seemingly, all it would take is one phone call in the course of planning to rob or attack a victim to make something a federal crime. Further, Congress could make it a federal crime to use the interstate highways, or any road connected to a federal road, in the commission of any crime. Congress could make a federal crime out of using the internet or a computer network attached to the internet to commit any crime." See also Joshua A. Klein, Note, *Commerce Clause Questions After Morrison: Some Observations on the New Formalism and the New Realism*, 55 Stan.L.Rev. 571 (2002).

PIERCE COUNTY v. GUILLEN, 537 U.S. 129 (2003), per THOMAS, J., upheld Congress' power to grant a privilege from pretrial discovery in state and federal courts, for information (e.g., data regarding "potential accident sites, hazardous roadway conditions"), "compiled or collected" in connection with a federal program funding highway improvement: the law was "aimed at improving safety in the channels of commerce and increasing protection for the instrumentalities of interstate commerce." See also *Reno v. Condon*, Sec. 5, IV infra; Mitchell N. Berman, *Guillen and Gullibility: Piercing the Surface of Commerce Clause Doctrine*, 89 Ia.L.Rev. 1487 (2004). Does the Commerce Clause authorize "regulation of intrastate activity only where that activity is economic in nature" (*Morrison*)?

(d) If the Court intends to impose serious restraints on Congress' commerce power, must its recent efforts be supplemented by refining its "commercial/economic" criterion and by redefining its "jurisdictional nexus" and "instrumentalities" categories? What of the statute in fn. 50? Consider Dan T. Coenen, *Constitutional Law: The Commerce Clause* 118 (2004): "*Lopez* [noted] that the defendant had not '*recently* moved in interstate commerce' and that the challenged statute imposed 'no requirement [that] possession of the firearm have any *concrete* ties to interstate commerce.' These passages provide tools for building a variety of limiting principles—for example, a requirement that the *defendant* (and not just the gun) must have crossed a state line; that the defendant must have crossed a state line *with the gun*; or that the defendant (or both the defendant and the gun, or at least the gun) must have *recently* crossed a state line."

(e) **Avoiding the constitutional question.** In addition to *Jones*, note b supra, see SOLID WASTE AGENCY OF NORTHERN COOK COUNTY v. UNITED STATES ARMY CORPS OF ENGINEERS, 531 U.S. 159 (2001), per REHNQUIST, C.J., interpreting the Clean Water Act as not covering "nonnavigable, isolated intrastate waters" used as a habitat for migratory birds, thus avoiding "significant constitutional and federalism questions." STEVENS, J., joined by Souter, Ginsburg and Breyer, JJ., dissenting, disagreed with "the Court's miserly construction of the statute" and thus "comment[ed] briefly" on the Commerce Clause: First, [the] discharge of fill material into the Nation's waters is almost always undertaken for economic reasons." Second, "millions of people regularly participate in birdwatching and hunting [and] those activities generate a host of commercial activities of great value." Finally, "waters that serve as habitat for birds that migrate over state lines also satisfies this Court's expressed desire for some 'jurisdictional element' that limits federal activity to its proper scope. *Morrison*."

3. **Other proposed approaches.** (a) **"Commerce."** Consider Nelson & Pushaw, supra: "[Under] the original meaning of the Commerce Clause ['commerce'] includes buying and selling goods; [their] production through activities [as] manufacturing, farming, and mining; and byproducts of that production, like environmental and safety effects[, the] provision of services for money (e.g., labor, insurance, and banking), which many eighteenth-century commentators deemed 'commercial,' and which form a critical component of our modern economy. [If] a statute meets our 'commerce' requirement, the Court should then determine whether the activity or enterprise at issue has a commercial impact in more than one state [u]nder a 'rational basis' test, which means that virtually all such statutes will be upheld. [The] Court should halt the increasing reliance by Congress on the Commerce Clause to impose a specific cultural or moral viewpoint simply because it disagrees with that taken by certain states."

(b) **"Separate states' incompetence."** Consider Regan, fn. 5: "[We should ask]: 'Is there some reason the federal government must be able to do this, some reason why we cannot leave the matter to the states?' Federal power exists where and only where there is special justification for it." See also Balkin, fn a in *Gibbons*: "Congress's powers were designed [to deal with] interactions that create spillover effects or collective action problems." See, too, note 2(c) after *Darby*. Must "commercial activity also be implicated"? Douglas W. Kmiec, *Rediscovering a Principled Commerce Power*, 28 Pepp.L.Rev. 547 (2001). See further Choper, note 1(a) supra, at 773: In *Wickard*, "the legislative goal was to raise agricultural prices by setting production quotas. [N]o state would benefit its farmers by reducing their acreage unless enough other states did likewise. If they did not do so, [the] optimal benefit would redound to those few states who maintained production if most others diminished it. *Only* a uniform rule would accomplish the desired result and treat all market participants fairly." See also Ann Althouse, *Enforcing Federalism After United States v. Lopez*, 38 Ariz.L.Rev. 793 (1996): "[T]he kind of activity involved in *Lopez* was not only susceptible to local regulation, states had traditionally assumed responsibility in this area and were in all likelihood better suited to handle [it.] [M]any matters that absorb Congress today do not represent any sort of considered analysis about whether a national *solution* is needed. [M]embers of Congress, inclined to pursue their personal political goals, commonly resort to legislative gestures designed to appeal to the passions of the electorate. The expansive federalization of criminal law shows this force in action."

(c) ***Substantive and procedural judicial review.*** Consider Stephen Gardbaum, *Rethinking Constitutional Federalism*, 74 Tex.L.Rev. 795 (1996): "[The Court should] prevent Congress from preempting the states or regulating local activities that affect interstate commerce [unless Congress balances] the advantages and disadvantages of its proposed course of action from a federalism perspective [by] deliberating seriously about the need and merits of so doing, [and] having reasonable grounds for its decision. [65] [Under] such an enhanced rational basis test, [even] if there is an extremely tight fit between means and legitimate end, consideration of the interests and capabilities of the states may still render it inappropriate [for Congress to act]." Compare H. Geoffrey Moulton, Jr., *The Quixotic Search for a Judicially Enforceable Federalism*, 83 Minn.L.Rev. 849 (1999): "As to choosing between state-and national-level lawmaking, the framers did not claim to have worked out the political science and economics of federalism, and did not contemplate that later courts would do that work for them. As a consequence, the Constitution grants no license to courts to second-guess congressional resolution of questions of institutional choice. Moreover, as a practical matter courts are simply ill-suited for the enormously complex (and contestable) task of determining the optimal allocation of power in a federal system."

NATIONAL FEDERATION OF INDEPENDENT BUSINESS V. SEBELIUS
___ U.S. ___, 132 S.Ct. 2566, 183 L.Ed.2d 450 (2012).

CHIEF JUSTICE ROBERTS announced the judgment of the Court and delivered the opinion of the Court with respect to Parts I, II, and III–C, an opinion with respect to Part IV, in which JUSTICE BREYER and JUSTICE KAGAN join, and an opinion with respect to Parts III–A, III–B, and III–D. * * *

---

[65] See also Vicki C. Jackson, *Federalism and the Uses and Limits of Law: Printz and Principle?*, 111 Harv. L. Rev. 2180 (1998).

I.   In 2010, Congress enacted the Patient Protection and Affordable Care Act [ACA], to increase the number of Americans covered by health insurance and decrease the cost of health care. [It does so mainly by prohibiting insurance companies from (a) denying coverage for preexisting conditions, and (b) charging unhealthy persons higher premiums than healthy ones.] [This] case concerns constitutional challenges to two key provisions [:] the individual mandate and the Medicaid expansion.[66]

The individual mandate requires most Americans to maintain "minimum essential" health insurance coverage [and] those who do not comply with the mandate must make a [payment] to the Federal Government [which] the Act describes as a "penalty," calculated as a percentage of household income, subject to a floor based on a specified dollar amount and a ceiling based on the average annual premium the individual would have to pay for qualifying private health insurance.[67] [The Eleventh Circuit held that the individual mandate exceeds Congress's power under the Commerce Clause. The Sixth and D.C. Circuits reached the opposite conclusion.]

[III. A.1.]   Congress has never attempted to rely on the [commerce power] to compel individuals not engaged in commerce to purchase an unwanted product.[68] [The] power to *regulate* commerce presupposes the existence of commercial activity to be regulated. If the power to "regulate" something included the power to create it, many of the provisions in the Constitution would be superfluous. For example, [the] power to regulate the armed forces or the value of money. [As] expansive as our cases construing the scope of the commerce power have been, [they] uniformly describe the power as reaching "activity" [citing, *Lopez, Perez, Jones & Laughlin*].[69]

Wickard has long been regarded as "perhaps the most far reaching example of Commerce Clause authority over intrastate activity," but the Government's theory in this case would go much further. Under *Wickard* it is within Congress's power to regulate the market for wheat by supporting its price. But price can be supported by increasing demand as

---

[66]   The Medicaid expansion is discussed at p. 157.

[67]   Part II of the opinion held that the Anti-Injunction Act—which provides that "no suit for the purpose of restraining the assessment or collection of any tax shall be maintained in any court"—did not intend the payment to be treated as a "tax" for its purposes. Ginsburg, J.'s dissent, infra, agreed.

[68]   The examples of other congressional mandates cited by Justice Ginsburg, are not to the contrary. Each of those mandates—to report for jury duty, to register for the draft, to purchase firearms in anticipation of militia service, to exchange gold currency for paper currency, and to file a tax return—are based on constitutional provisions other than the Commerce Clause.

[69]   In reply, see Michael C. Dorf, *Commerce, Death Panels, and Broccoli: Or Why the Activity/Inactivity Distinction in the Health Care Case Was Really About the Right to Bodily Integrity,* 29 Ga. L. Rev. 897 (2013): "[F]ederal labor law and federal antitrust law have been construed to forbid secondary boycotts. A boycott is economic inactivity—a refusal to engage in business with the targets—in more or less the same way that the non-purchase of health insurance is economic inactivity."

well as by decreasing supply. The aggregated decisions of some consumers not to purchase wheat have a substantial effect on the price of wheat, just as decisions not to purchase health insurance have on the price of insurance. Congress can therefore command that those not buying wheat do so. [The] farmer in *Wickard* was at least actively engaged in the production of wheat, and the Government could regulate that activity because of its effect on commerce. The Government's theory here would effectively override that limitation, by establishing that individuals may be regulated under the Commerce Clause whenever enough of them are not doing something the Government would have them do.

[To] consider a different example in the health care market, many Americans do not eat a balanced diet, [a] larger percentage of the total population than those without health insurance. The failure of that group to have a healthy diet increases health care costs, to a greater extent than the failure of the uninsured to purchase insurance. [Under] the Government's theory, Congress could address the diet problem by ordering everyone to buy vegetables. * * *

To an economist, perhaps, there is no difference between activity and inactivity; both have measurable economic effects on commerce. But the distinction between doing something and doing nothing would not have been lost on the Framers, who were "practical statesmen," not metaphysical philosophers, ["]dealing with the facts of political life as they understood them, putting into form the government they were creating, and prescribing in language clear and intelligible the powers that government was to take." *South Carolina v. United States*, 199 U.S. 437 (1905).

[The Government argues] that because sickness and injury are unpredictable but unavoidable, "the uninsured as a class are active in the market for health care, which they regularly seek and obtain." The individual mandate "merely regulates how individuals finance and pay for that active participation—requiring that they do so through insurance, rather than through attempted self-insurance with the back-stop of shifting costs to others." [But t]he phrase "active in the market" cannot obscure the fact that most of those regulated by the individual mandate are not currently engaged in any commercial activity involving health care. [The] proposition that Congress may dictate the conduct of an individual today because of prophesied future activity finds no support in our precedent. * * *

2.   The Government next contends that Congress has the power under the Necessary and Proper Clause to enact the individual mandate because it is an "integral part of a comprehensive scheme of economic regulation" [that requires insurance companies to provide coverage even to those with preexisting medical conditions—a requirement that would be

financially unsustainable if currently healthy individuals were not required to purchase coverage.] Under this argument, it is not necessary to consider the effect that an individual's inactivity may have on interstate commerce; it is enough that Congress regulated commercial activity in a way that requires the regulation of inactivity to be effective. [W]e have been very deferential to Congress's determination that a regulation is "necessary." [But] we have also carried out our responsibility to declare unconstitutional those laws that undermine the structure of government established by the Constitution [on the ground that they] are not "proper [means] for carrying into Execution" Congress's enumerated powers.

[Each] of our prior cases upholding laws under that Clause involved exercises of authority derivative of, and in service to, a granted power. For example, we have upheld provisions permitting continued confinement of those already in federal custody when they could not be safely released, [*Comstock*]. The individual mandate, by contrast, vests Congress with the extraordinary ability to create the necessary predicate to the exercise of an enumerated power. This is in no way an authority that is "narrow in scope," *Comstock*, or "incidental" to the exercise of the commerce power, *McCulloch*. Rather, such a conception of the Necessary and Proper Clause would work a substantial expansion of federal authority. No longer would Congress be limited to regulating under the Commerce Clause those who by some preexisting activity bring themselves within the sphere of federal regulation. Instead, Congress could reach beyond the natural limit of its authority and draw within its regulatory scope those who otherwise would be outside of it. Even if the individual mandate is "necessary" to the Act's insurance reforms, such an expansion of federal power is not a "proper" means for making those reforms effective. * * *[70]

[SCALIA, KENNEDY, THOMAS and ALITO, JJ., who filed a long separate dissent, other parts of which are at p. 145. Although they agreed with the conclusions of and made similar arguments to Roberts, C.J. regarding the Commerce and Necessary and Proper Clauses, they did not join any part of his opinion. With regard to the Commerce Clause issue, they took special pains to distinguish *Raich* as "no precedent for what Congress has done here. That case's prohibition of growing (cf. *Wickard*), and of possession (cf. innumerable federal statutes) did not represent the expansion of the federal power to direct into a broad new field. The mandating of economic activity does.

["Moreover, *Raich* is far different from the Individual Mandate in another respect[: the] growing and possession prohibitions were the only practicable way of enabling the prohibition of interstate traffic in marijuana to be effectively enforced. Intrastate marijuana could no more be distinguished from interstate marijuana than, for example, endangered-

---

[70] Roberts, C.J.'s opinion of the Court in Part III–C, upholding the individual mandate under the taxing power, is in Sec. 3 infra.

species trophies obtained before the species was federally protected can be distinguished from trophies obtained afterwards—which made it necessary and proper to prohibit the sale of all such trophies, see *Andrus v. Allard*, 444 U.S. 51 (1979).

["With the present statute, by contrast, there are many [ways]. For instance, those who did not purchase insurance could be subjected to a surcharge when they do enter the health insurance system. Or they could be denied a full income tax credit given to those who do purchase the insurance."][71]

JUSTICE GINSBURG, with whom JUSTICE SOTOMAYOR joins, and with whom JUSTICE BREYER and JUSTICE KAGAN join as to Parts I, II, III, and IV, concurring in part, concurring in the judgment in part, and dissenting in part.

* * * I [would hold] that the Commerce Clause authorizes Congress to enact the minimum coverage provision. * * *

[I.] The large number of individuals without health insurance, Congress found, heavily burdens the national health-care market. [Unlike] markets for most products, however, the inability to pay for care does not mean that an uninsured individual will receive no care. Federal and state law, as well as professional obligations and embedded social norms, require hospitals and physicians to provide care when it is most needed, regardless of the patient's ability to pay. * * *

Health-care providers do not absorb these bad debts. Instead, they raise their prices, passing along the cost of uncompensated care to those who do pay reliably: the government and private insurance companies. In response, private insurers increase their premiums. [The] net result: Those with health insurance subsidize the medical care of those without it. As economists would describe what happens, the uninsured "free ride" on those who pay for health insurance. The size of this subsidy is considerable. Congress found that the cost-shifting just described "increases family [insurance] premiums by on average over $1,000 a year." [Moreover, since] those without insurance generally lack access to preventative care, they do not receive treatment for conditions—like hypertension and diabetes—that can be successfully and affordably treated if diagnosed early on. When sickness finally drives the uninsured to seek care, once treatable conditions have escalated into grave health problems, requiring more costly and extensive intervention. * * *

States cannot resolve the problem of the uninsured on their own. [A] universal health-care system, if adopted by an individual State, would be

---

[71] Compare Abbe R. Gluck, *Federalism from Federal Statutes: Health Reform, Medicaid, and the Old-Fashioned Federalists' Gamble*, 81 Ford. L. Rev. 1749 (2013): "[The ACA] is state empowering in many respects [ ] precisely the kinds of state partnerships that maintain the states' relevance in the modern [federal] statutory era."

"bait to the needy and dependent elsewhere, encouraging them to migrate and seek a haven of repose." [To] cover the increased costs, a State would have to raise taxes, and private health-insurance companies would have to increase premiums [which] would, in turn, encourage businesses and healthy individuals to leave the State. [Facing] that risk, individual States are unlikely to take the initiative in addressing the problem of the uninsured, even though solving that problem is in all States' best interests. Congress' intervention was needed to overcome this collective action impasse.

Aware that a national solution was required, Congress could have taken over the health-insurance market by establishing a tax-and-spend federal program like Social Security. Such a program, commonly referred to as a single-payer system (where the sole payer is the Federal Government), would have left little, if any, room for private enterprise or the States. [Instead] the ACA, [is] a solution that retains a robust role for private insurers and state governments. * * *

In the 1990's, several States—including New York, New Jersey, Washington, Kentucky, Maine, New Hampshire, and Vermont—enacted [ACA] laws without requiring universal acquisition of insurance coverage. The results were disastrous. "All seven states suffered from skyrocketing insurance premium costs, reductions in individuals with coverage, and reductions in insurance products and providers." * * * Massachusetts, Congress was told, cracked the adverse selection problem. By requiring most residents to obtain insurance, the Commonwealth ensured that insurers would not be left with only the sick as customers.[72]

II.   The Commerce Clause, it is widely acknowledged, "was the Framers' response to the central problem that gave rise to the Constitution itself." The Framers' solution[,] as they perceived it, granted Congress the authority to enact economic legislation "in all Cases for the general Interests of the Union, and also in those Cases to which the States are separately incompetent." 2 Records of the Federal Convention of 1787. * * *73

Consistent with the Framers' intent, we have repeatedly emphasized that Congress' authority under the Commerce Clause is dependent upon "practical" considerations, including "actual experience." *Jones & Laughlin;* see *Wickard; Lopez* (Kennedy, J., concurring). When appraising such legislation, we ask only (1) whether Congress had a "rational basis" for concluding that the regulated activity substantially affects interstate commerce, and (2) whether there is a "reasonable connection between the regulatory means selected and the asserted ends." [W]e presume the

---

[72] Despite its success, Massachusetts' medical-care providers still administer substantial amounts of uncompensated care, much of that to uninsured patients from out-of-state.

[73] In their separate dissent, Scalia, Kennedy, Thomas and Alito, JJ., responded that "Article I contains no whatever-it-takes-to-solve-a-national problem power."

statute under review is constitutional and may strike it down only on a "plain showing" that Congress acted irrationally. *Morrison*.

[Beyond] dispute, Congress had a rational basis for concluding that the uninsured, as a class, substantially affect interstate commerce. Those without insurance consume billions of dollars of health-care products and services each year. Those goods are produced, sold, and delivered largely by national and regional companies who routinely transact business across state lines. The uninsured also cross state lines to receive care. [Their] inability to pay for a significant portion of that consumption drives up market prices, foists costs on other consumers, and reduces market efficiency and stability. [T]he decision to forgo insurance is hardly inconsequential or equivalent to "doing nothing." [By giving] individuals a strong incentive to [insure,] Congress had good reason to believe, would reduce the number of uninsured and, correspondingly, mitigate the adverse impact the uninsured have on the national health-care market.

[Even] assuming, for the moment, that Congress lacks authority under the Commerce Clause to "compel individuals not engaged in commerce to purchase an unwanted product," such a limitation would be inapplicable here. Everyone will, at some point, consume health-care products and services. [But,] The Chief Justice insists, the uninsured cannot be considered active in the market for health care, because "[t]he proximity and degree of connection between the [uninsured today] and [their] subsequent commercial activity is too lacking."

This argument has multiple flaws. First, more than 60% of those without insurance visit a hospital or doctor's office each year. Nearly 90% will within five [years.] Equally evident, Congress has no way of separating those uninsured individuals who will need emergency medical care today (surely their consumption of medical care is sufficiently imminent) from those who will not need medical services for years to come. [See] *Perez* ("[W]hen it is necessary in order to prevent an evil to make the law embrace more than the precise thing to be prevented it may do so.") [It] is Congress' role, not the Court's, to delineate the boundaries of the market the Legislature seeks to regulate. * * *

Third, contrary to The Chief Justice's contention, our precedent does [indeed] acknowledge Congress' authority, under the Commerce Clause, to direct the conduct of an individual today (the farmer in *Wickard*, stopped from growing excess wheat; the plaintiff in *Raich*, ordered to cease cultivating marijuana) because of a prophesied future transaction (the eventual sale of that wheat or marijuana in the interstate market). Congress' actions are even more rational in this case, where the future activity (the consumption of medical care) is certain to occur, the sole uncertainty being the time the activity will take place. [Thus, it is not] accurate to say that the minimum coverage provision "compel[s] individuals . . . to purchase an unwanted product." * * *

At bottom, The Chief Justice's and the joint dissenters' "view that an individual cannot be subject to Commerce Clause regulation absent voluntary, affirmative acts that enter him or her into, or affect, the interstate market expresses a concern for individual liberty that [is] more redolent of Due Process Clause arguments." Plaintiffs have abandoned any argument pinned to substantive due process, however, and now concede that the provisions here at issue do not offend the Due Process Clause.

Underlying The Chief Justice's view [is] a fear that the commerce power would otherwise know no limits. [But] the unique attributes of the health-care market render everyone active in that market and give rise to a significant free-riding problem that does not occur in other markets. * * *

Supplementing these legal restraints is a formidable check on congressional power: the democratic process. As the controversy surrounding the passage of the Affordable Care Act attests, purchase mandates are likely to engender political resistance. [Additionally, the Chief Justice] emphasizes the provision's novelty. [But as] our national economy grows and changes, we have recognized, Congress must adapt to the changing "economic and financial realities." * * *

[III.]   Asserting that the Necessary and Proper Clause does not authorize the minimum coverage provision, The Chief Justice focuses on the word "proper." A mandate to purchase health insurance is not "proper" [because] it is less "narrow in scope" than other laws this Court has upheld under the Necessary and Proper Clause (citing *Comstock*). [But how] is a judge to decide [whether] Congress employed an "independent power," or merely a "derivative" one? Whether the power used is "substantive," or just "incidental"? The instruction The Chief Justice, in effect, provides lower courts: You will know it when you see it. * * * [74]

3.   THE NATIONAL TAXING AND SPENDING POWERS

Art. I, § 8, cl. 1, grants Congress power "to lay and collect taxes, duties, imposts and excises, to pay the debts and provide for the common defense and general welfare of the United States." Its language includes both power to tax and to spend.[75] This section is concerned primarily with use of these two related powers to achieve regulatory ends.

---

[74] For support of the Court's result by the use of game theory, see Leslie M. Henry & Maxwell L. Stearns, *Commerce Games and the Individual Mandate*, 100 Geo. L. J. 1117 (2012).

[75] For the view that cl. 1 does *not* clearly authorize *general* federal "spending" (and is "utterly inadequate to authorize routine *deficit* spending)," and that "a careful parsing of the records of the Constitutional Convention indicates that [the] Article IV Property Clause was specifically designed for the purpose, among several others, of authorizing Congress to spend—even for objects

The Court has long recognized that Congress may use its taxing power as both a "necessary and proper" way to enforce its regulatory powers, and as a way to raise revenue which may produce "incidental" regulatory effects. The issues raised by the latter use of the taxing power, and analogous use of the spending power, declined in importance as the expanded view of Congress' regulatory powers between 1936 and 1995 left few occasions for Congress to resort to taxing or spending for regulatory purposes. But the limitations imposed on the commerce power by *Lopez* and *Morrison* (as well as on Congress' ability to enforce the Civil War Amendments, see Ch. 11, Sec. 2) have given the national taxing and spending powers a potentially renewed importance.

I. REGULATION THROUGH TAXING

BAILEY v. DREXEL FURNITURE CO. (CHILD LABOR TAX CASE), 259 U.S. 20 (1922), per TAFT, C.J., held invalid the Child Labor Tax Law which, nine months after *Dagenhart,* imposed a 10% excise tax on the net profits of employers of child labor, defined identically as in the law in *Dagenhart:* "The law is attacked on the ground that it is a regulation of the employment of child labor in the states—an exclusively state function. [Does] this law impose a tax with only that incidental restraint and regulation which a tax must inevitably involve? Or does it regulate by the use of the so-called tax as a penalty? [This act] provides a heavy exaction for a departure from a detailed and specified course of conduct in business. [The] amount is not [proportioned] to the extent or frequency of the departures, but is to be paid by the employer in full measure whether he employs 500 children for a year, [or] one for a day. Moreover, if he does not know the child is within the named age limit, he is not to [pay]. Scienters are associated with penalties, not with taxes. The employer's factory is to be subject to inspection at any time not only by the taxing officers of the Treasury, [but] also by the Secretary of Labor and his subordinates, whose normal function is the advancement and protection of the welfare of the workers. In the light of these features of the act, a court must be blind not to see that the so-called tax is imposed to stop the employment of children within the age limits prescribed. [Grant] the validity of this law, and all that Congress would need to do, hereafter, in seeking to control any one of the great number of subjects reserved to [the states], would be to enact a detailed measure of complete regulation of the subject and enforce it by a so-called tax upon departures from it. To give such magic to the word "tax" would be to break down all constitutional limitation of the powers of Congress and completely wipe out the sovereignty of the states.

" * * * Taxes are occasionally imposed in the discretion of the Legislature on proper subjects with the primary motive of obtaining

---

that would not be within any enumerated power," see David E. Engdahl, *The Spending Power*, 44 Duke L.J. 1 (1994).

revenue from them and with the incidental motive of discouraging them by making their continuance onerous. They do not lose their character as taxes because of the incidental motive. But there comes a time in the extension of the penalizing features of the so-called tax when it loses its character as such and becomes a mere penalty, with the characteristics of regulation and punishment. Such is the case in the law before us.

" * * * *Veazie Bank v. Fenno,* 8 Wall. 533, 19 L.Ed. 482, [involved] a law which increased a tax on the circulating notes of persons and state banks from one per centum to 10 per centum. [To the objection that the tax was so excessive as to indicate a purpose to destroy state banks, *Veazie*] answered: [T]he sole objection to the [*Veazie* tax] was its excessive character. Nothing else appeared on the face of the act. It was an increase of a tax admittedly legal to a higher rate and that was all. But more than this, what was charged to be the object of the excessive tax was within the congressional authority [to] secure a national currency.

" * * * *McCray v. United States,* 195 U.S. 27 (1904), [upheld a federal excise tax of 10 cents per pound on yellow oleomargarine when the tax on white oleo was ¼ cent per pound and when the price of butter was 28 cents per pound.] This court held that the discretion of Congress [in] selecting its subjects for taxation, might impose the burden where and as it would and that a motive disclosed in its selection to discourage sale or manufacture of an article by a higher tax than on some other did not invalidate the tax. In neither of these cases did the law objected to show on its face as does the law before us the detailed specifications of a regulation of a state concern and business with a heavy exaction to promote the efficacy of such regulation.

" * * * *United States v. Doremus,* 249 U.S. 86 (1919) [upheld the Narcotic Drug Act, which imposed a $1 annual tax on the manufacture, importation and sale of named narcotics. It required all subject to the tax to register with the Commissioner of Internal Revenue and to sell the narcotics only on a written order of the buyer or a physician's prescription. Copies were required to be kept, subject to official inspection, for two years.] The provisions for subjecting the sale and distribution of the drugs to official supervision and inspection were held to have a reasonable relation to the enforcement of the tax and were therefore held valid.[76] The court said that the act could not be declared invalid just because another motive than taxation, not shown on the face of the act, might have contributed to its passage. This case does not militate against the conclusion we have reached in respect of the law now before us. The court, there, made manifest its view that the provisions of the so-called taxing act

---

[76] *Doremus* explained: "The provisions [tend] to keep the traffic aboveboard and subject to inspection by those authorized to collect the revenue. They tend to diminish the opportunity of unauthorized persons to obtain the drugs and sell them clandestinely without paying the tax imposed by the federal law."

must be naturally and reasonably adapted to the collection of the tax and not solely to the achievement of some other purpose plainly within state power."[77]

NOTES AND QUESTIONS

1. *Legislative motives.* Did the *McCray* tax impose a "heavy penalty for departure from a specified course of conduct"—selling only white margarine? Did the *Doremus* detailed record-keeping regulations establish a congressional motive to control the dispensing of narcotics, rather than to produce revenue?[78] Would (should) the amount of revenue produced by the Child Labor Tax Law influence its constitutionality? Does the amount of revenue produced by a tax reveal (indicate) the motive(s) of its enactors? May the Court's treatment of legislative motive in *Dagenhart, Lottery, Child Labor Tax Case, McCray,* and *Doremus* be reconciled? Consider Robert D. Cooter & Neil S. Siegel, *Not the Power to Destroy: An Effects Theory of the Tax Power,* 98 Va.L.Rev. 1195 (2012): A tax is "an exaction that is less than the usual gain from the taxed conduct. [It] dampens conduct but not prevent it, thereby raising revenues." A penalty requires payment of "more than the usual gain from the forbidden conduct. [It] prevents behavior, thereby raising little revenue." For criticism, see Stewart Jay, *On Slippery Constitutional Slopes,* 44 Conn.L.Rev. 1133 (2012).

2. *Subsequent developments.* While never repudiated, and occasionally cited, the *Child Labor Tax Case* has been applied by the Court to invalidate a federal tax only once since 1922, and that was during the *Schechter-Carter* era of restrictive commerce power interpretation.

UNITED STATES v. CONSTANTINE, 296 U.S. 287 (1935), per ROBERTS, J., found a "purpose to usurp the police power of the State" in a tax 10 to 40 times heavier on a liquor business operating "contrary to state law" than on other liquor businesses. Cardozo, J., joined by Brandeis and Stone, JJ., dissented, protesting disregard of the "wise and ancient doctrine that a court will not inquire into the motives of a legislative body or assume them to be wrongful."

Due to the broad expansion of the commerce power after 1936, Congress has had few occasions to use the taxing power for regulatory purposes. Since *Constantine,* no federal tax has been held invalid because of a regulatory motive outside federal power. See *Sonzinsky v. United States,* 300 U.S. 506 (1937) ($200 tax on each transfer of concealable firearms; "inquiry into hidden motive is beyond competence of the courts"); *United States v. Sanchez,* 340 U.S. 42 (1950) (Congress expressed two objectives: raising revenue and making "extremely difficult the acquisition of marihuana"); *United States v. Kahriger,*

---

[77] Clarke, J., dissented without opinion.

[78] Nine years after *Doremus, Nigro v. United States,* 276 U.S. 332 (1928), noted that the Narcotic Drug Act rates had been increased to provide substantial revenue, and added: "If there was doubt as to the character of this Act—that it is not as alleged a subterfuge—it has been removed by the change whereby what was a nominal tax before was made a substantial one."

345 U.S. 22 (1953) (ten percent tax on all wagers coupled with registration of all wager takers, whose names must be given to state prosecutors, if requested.)[79]

———

In NATIONAL FEDERATION OF INDEPENDENT BUSINESS v. SEBELIUS, Sec. 2, IV, ROBERTS, C.J.'s opinion for the Court (Part III–C) held that the "exaction the Affordable Care Act imposes on those without health insurance looks like a tax in many respects. The [individual mandate payment] is paid to the Treasury by 'taxpayer[s]' when they file their tax returns. It does not apply to individuals who do not pay federal income taxes because their household income is less the threshold in the Internal Revenue Code. For taxpayers who do owe the payment, its amount is determined by such familiar factors as taxable income, number of dependents, and joint filing status. The requirement to pay is found in the Internal Revenue Code and enforced by the IRS, [which] must assess and collect it 'in the same manner as taxes.' This process yields the essential feature of any tax: it produces at least some revenue for the Government. *Kahriger.* Indeed, the payment is expected to raise about $4 billion per year by 2017.

"It is of course true that the Act describes the payment as a 'penalty,' not a 'tax.' But that label [does] not determine whether the payment may be viewed as an exercise of Congress's taxing power. [See] *Nelson v. Sears, Roebuck & Co.*, 312 U.S. 359 (1941) ("In passing on the constitutionality of a tax law, we are concerned only with its practical operation, not its definition or the precise form of descriptive words which may be applied to it"); *United States v. Sotelo*, 436 U.S. 268 (1978) ("That the funds due are referred to as a 'penalty' does not alter their essential character as taxes"). * * *[80]

"The same analysis here suggests that the [individual mandate] payment may for constitutional purposes be considered a tax, not a penalty: First, for most Americans the amount due will be far less than the price of insurance, and, by statute, it can never be more.[81] It may often be a reasonable financial decision to make the payment rather than purchase insurance, unlike the 'prohibitory' financial punishment in the *Child Labor Tax Case.* Second, the individual mandate contains no scienter requirement. Third, the payment is collected solely by the IRS through the

---

[79] The registration requirement was later held to violate the Fifth Amendment Privilege Against Self-Incrimination. *Marchetti v. United States,* 390 U.S. 39 (1968).

[80] *Sotelo,* in particular, would seem to refute the joint dissent's contention that we have "never" treated an exaction as a tax if it was denominated a penalty. * * *

[81] In 2016, for example, individuals making $35,000 a year are expected to owe the IRS about $60 for any month in which they do not have health insurance. Someone with an annual income of $100,000 a year would likely owe about $200. The price of a qualifying insurance policy is projected to be around $400 per month.

normal means of taxation—except that the Service is not allowed to use those means most suggestive of a punitive sanction, such as criminal prosecution. * * *

"None of this is to say that the payment is not intended to affect individual conduct. [I]t is plainly designed to expand health insurance coverage. But taxes that seek to influence conduct are nothing new. [Today,] federal and state taxes can compose more than half the retail price of cigarettes, not just to raise more money, but to encourage people to quit smoking. And we have upheld such obviously regulatory measures as taxes on selling marijuana and sawed-off shotguns. See *Sanchez; Sonzinsky.* * * *

"Indeed, it is estimated that four million people each year will choose to pay the IRS rather than buy insurance. [That] suggests that Congress did not think it was creating four million outlaws. * * *[82]

"There may, however, be a more fundamental objection to a tax on those who lack health insurance. [The] Court today holds that our Constitution protects us from federal regulation under the Commerce Clause so long as we abstain from the regulated activity. [But] Congress's use of the Taxing Clause to encourage buying something is, by contrast, not new. Tax incentives already promote, for example, purchasing homes and professional educations. * * *

"Second, Congress's ability to use its taxing power to influence conduct is not without limits. [See *Child Labor Tax Case.* More] recently we have declined to closely examine the regulatory motive or effect of revenue-raising measures. See *Kahriger,* (collecting cases). We have nonetheless maintained that 'there comes a time in the extension of the penalizing features of the so-called tax when it loses its character as such and becomes a mere penalty with the characteristics of regulation and punishment.' *Department of Revenue of Mont. v. Kurth Ranch,* 511 U.S., at 779 (1994).

"We have already explained that the [individual mandate] payment's practical characteristics pass muster as a tax under our narrowest interpretations of the taxing power. [W]e need not here decide the precise point at which an exaction becomes so punitive that the taxing power does not authorize it. * * *

"Third, although the breadth of Congress's power to tax is greater than its power to regulate commerce, the taxing power does not give Congress the same degree of control over individual behavior. [It] is limited to requiring an individual to pay money into the Federal Treasury, no more. If a tax is properly paid, the Government has no power to compel or punish individuals subject to it. We do not make light of the severe burden that taxation—especially taxation motivated by a regulatory purpose—can

---

[82] The Court also rejected the argument that the individual mandate violates the Direct Tax Clause, Art. 1, § 9, ch. 4.

impose. But imposition of a tax nonetheless leaves an individual with a lawful choice to do or not do a certain act, so long as he is willing to pay a tax levied on that choice."

SCALIA, KENNEDY, THOMAS and ALITO JJ., dissented: The individual mandate "is either a penalty or else a tax. [But] we know of no case [in] which the imposition was, for constitutional purposes, both. [The] issue is not whether Congress had the *power* to frame the minimum-coverage provision as a tax, but whether it *did* so.

"[In] this case, there is simply no way, 'without doing violence to the fair meaning of the words used' to escape what Congress enacted: a mandate that individuals maintain minimum essential coverage, enforced by a penalty. [We] have never held that any exaction imposed for violation of the law is an exercise of Congress' taxing power—even when the statute calls it a tax, much less when (as here) the statute repeatedly *calls* it a penalty. * * *

"So the question is, quite simply, whether the exaction here is imposed for violation of the law. It unquestionably is. [T]hat Congress (in its own words) 'imposed . . . a penalty' for failure to buy insurance is alone sufficient to render that failure unlawful. [W]e have never—*never*—treated as a tax an exaction which faces up to the critical difference between a tax and a penalty, and explicitly denominates the exaction a 'penalty.' Eighteen [times], Congress called the exaction in § 5000A(b) a 'penalty.' [T]he nail in the coffin is that the mandate and penalty are located in Title I of the Act, its operative core, rather than where a tax would be found—in Title IX, containing the Act's 'Revenue Provisions.'"

NOTES AND QUESTIONS

1. ***Court's reasoning.*** What happens to individuals who neither buy insurance nor pay the tax as provided in the ACA? Although this may not be the "lawful choice" granted by the ACA, in what way will the "severe burden" that will result be different in any meaningful way? May the IRS seek a "punitive sanction, such as criminal prosecution"? In what way does this bear on the Court's decision?

2. ***Future potential.*** After the ACA decision, what will cause the Court to find a tax unauthorized by the federal tax power? What if the subject of the tax is not "commercial" activity? Consider Choper & Yoo, Sec. 2, IV supra: "Although much of the income tax code certainly can find justification as the regulation of commercial activity, other provisions that do not might be brought into question on the ground that their purpose and effect is not to raise revenue, but rather to achieve regulatory ends. Moreover, while gift and estates taxes involve the transfer of wealth, large portions do not seem to involve commercial or economic activity of the sort contemplated by *Lopez* and *Morrison*. Building on the tax code, Congress could deny anyone who possessed a handgun near a school zone or who committed gender-motivated violence any

deductions or exemptions, or could impose a very high tax on any gifts or inheritances they receive."

II. REGULATION THROUGH SPENDING

UNITED STATES v. BUTLER, 297 U.S. 1 (1936), per ROBERTS, J., held invalid the Agricultural Adjustment Act of 1933. To raise farm prices by reducing supply, the Act authorized the government to contract with farmers to reduce acreage for particular commodities in exchange for benefit payments paid for from a tax on processors of that commodity: "The government concedes that the phrase 'to provide for the general welfare' [in cl.1] qualifies the power 'to lay and collect taxes.' The view that the clause grants power to provide for the general welfare, independently of the taxing power, has never been authoritatively accepted. Mr. Justice Story points out that, if it were adopted, ['the] government of the United States [would be], in reality, a government of general and unlimited powers, notwithstanding the subsequent enumeration of specific powers.' * * *

"Since the foundation of the nation, sharp differences of opinion have persisted as to the true interpretation of the phrase. Madison asserted [that], as the United States is a government of limited and enumerated powers, the grant of power to tax and spend for the general national welfare must be confined to the enumerated legislative fields committed to the Congress. * * * Hamilton, on the other hand, maintained the clause confers a power separate and distinct from those later enumerated, is not restricted in meaning by the grant of them, and Congress consequently has a substantive power to tax and to appropriate, limited only by the requirement that it shall be exercised to provide for the general welfare of the United States. * * * Mr. Justice Story, in his *Commentaries,* espouses the Hamiltonian position. [The] writings of public men and commentators [and] legislative practice [lead] us to conclude that the reading advocated by Mr. Justice Story is the correct one. * * *

"We are not now required to ascertain the scope of the phrase 'general welfare of the United States' or to determine whether an appropriation in aid of agriculture falls within it. Wholly apart from that question, another principle embedded in our Constitution prohibits the enforcement of the Agricultural Adjustment Act. [May] the taxing power [be] employed to raise the money necessary to purchase a compliance which the Congress is powerless to command? The government asserts that whatever might be said against the validity of the plan, if compulsory, it is constitutionally sound because the end is accomplished by voluntary co-operation. [The] farmer, of course, may refuse to comply, but the price of such refusal is the loss of benefits. The amount offered is intended to be sufficient to exert pressure on him to agree to the proposed regulation. The power to confer or withhold unlimited benefits is the power to coerce or destroy. If the cotton grower elects not to accept the benefits, he will receive less for his crops; those who receive payments will be able to undersell him. The result may well be financial ruin. [This] is coercion by economic pressure. * * *

"But if the plan were one for purely voluntary co-operation it would stand no better so far as federal power is concerned. At best, it is a scheme for purchasing with federal funds submission to federal regulation of a subject reserved to the states. [C]ontracts for the reduction of acreage and the control of production are outside the range of [federal power]. * * *

"We are not here concerned with a conditional appropriation of money, nor with a provision that if certain conditions are not complied with the appropriation shall no longer be available. [Instead this Act is] effective only upon assumption of a contractual obligation to submit to a regulation which otherwise could not be enforced. [N]o one has doubted the power of Congress to stipulate the sort of education for which money shall be expended. But an appropriation to an educational institution which by its terms is to become available only if the beneficiary enters into a contract to teach doctrines subversive of the Constitution is clearly bad. An affirmance of the authority of Congress so to condition the expenditure of an appropriation would tend to nullify all constitutional limitations upon legislative power."

STONE, J., joined by Brandeis and Cardozo, JJ., dissented: "As the present depressed state of agriculture is nation wide in its extent and effects, there is no basis for saying that the expenditure of public money in aid of farmers is not within the specifically granted power of Congress to levy taxes to 'provide for [the] general welfare.' [The] suggestion of coercion finds no support in the record or in any data showing the actual operation of the act. Threat of loss, not hope of gain, is the essence of economic coercion. Members of a long-depressed industry have undoubtedly been tempted to curtail acreage by the hope of resulting better prices and by the proffered opportunity to obtain needed ready money. But there is nothing to indicate that those who accepted benefits were impelled by fear of lower prices if they did not accept, or that at any stage in the operation of the plan a farmer could say whether, apart from the certainty of cash payments at specified times, the advantage would lie with curtailment of production plus compensation, rather than with the same or increased acreage plus the expected rise in prices which actually occurred. [Of] the total number of farms growing cotton, estimated at 1,500,000, 33% in 1934 and 13% in 1935 did not participate. * * *

"The Constitution requires that public funds shall be spent for a defined purpose, the promotion of the general welfare. Their expenditure usually involves payment on terms which will insure use by the selected recipients within the limits of the constitutional purpose. [The] power of Congress to spend is inseparable from persuasion to action over which

Congress has no legislative control. Congress may not command that the science of agriculture be taught in state universities. But if it would aid the teaching of that science by grants to state institutions, it is appropriate, if not necessary, that the grant be on the condition [that] it be used for the intended purpose. Similarly it would seem to be compliance with the Constitution [for] government [to] contract that the grant would be so [used]. Condition and promise are alike valid since both are in furtherance of the national purpose for which the money is appropriated.

"[The] spending power of Congress is in addition to the legislative power and not subordinate to it. [It] is a contradiction in terms to say that there is power to spend for the national welfare, while rejecting any power to impose conditions reasonably adapted to the attainment of the ends which alone would justify the expenditure. [If] appropriation in aid of a program of curtailment of agricultural production is constitutional, and it is not denied that it is, payment to farmers on condition that they reduce their crop acreage is constitutional. It is not any the less so because the farmer at his own option promises to fulfill the condition."

NOTES AND QUESTIONS

Butler's reasoning. Did the majority *really* adopt Hamilton's position? Is there a difference of constitutional dimension between educational grants conditioned on the education meeting federal standards beyond the federal power to command and financial grants to farmers conditioned on their reduction of planted acreage?

STEWARD MACHINE CO. V. DAVIS
301 U.S. 548, 57 S.Ct. 883, 81 L.Ed. 1279 (1937).

JUSTICE CARDOZO delivered the opinion of the Court.

[Under the Social Security Act program for unemployment compensation, proceeds of a federal tax on employers went into the general federal treasury. But these employers received 90% credit on this tax for payments to a state unemployment compensation fund under a state law that met federal requirements.]

The excise is not void as involving the coercion of the states in contravention of the Tenth Amendment. [To] draw the line intelligently between duress and inducement, there is need to remind ourselves of facts as to the problem of unemployment. [During] the years 1929 to 1936, when the country was passing through a cyclical depression, the number of the unemployed mounted to unprecedented heights. [T]he states were unable to give the requisite relief. [It] is too late today for the argument to be heard with tolerance that in a crisis so extreme the use of the moneys of the nation to relieve the unemployed and their dependents is a use for any purpose narrower than the promotion of the general welfare. Cf. *Butler*; *Helvering v. Davis* [infra], decided herewith.

[The] assailants of the statute say that its dominant end and aim is to drive the state Legislatures under the whip of economic pressure into the enactment of unemployment compensation laws at the bidding of the central government. Supporters of the statute say that its operation is not constraint, but the creation of a larger freedom, the states and the nation joining in a co-operative endeavor to avert a common evil. [I]f states had been holding back before the passage of the federal law, inaction was not owing, for the most part, to the lack of sympathetic interest. Many held back through alarm lest in laying such a toll upon their industries, they would place themselves in a position of economic disadvantage as compared with neighbors or competitors. [I]n so far as there was failure by the states to contribute relief according to the measure of their capacity, a disproportionate burden, and a mountainous one, was laid upon the resources of the government of the nation.

The Social Security Act is an attempt to find a method by which all these public agencies may work together to a common end. Every dollar of the new taxes will continue in all likelihood to be used and needed by the nation as long as states are unwilling. [On] the other hand, fulfillment of the home duty will be lightened and encouraged by crediting the taxpayer upon his account with the Treasury of the nation to the extent that his contributions under the laws of the locality have simplified or diminished the problem of relief and the probable demand upon the resources of the fisc. [Who] then is coerced[?] Not the taxpayer. He pays in fulfillment of the mandate of the local legislature. Not the state. Even now she does not offer a suggestion that in passing the unemployment law she was affected by duress. For all that appears, she is satisfied with her choice, and would be sorely disappointed if it were now to be annulled. * * *

[E]very rebate from a tax when conditioned upon conduct is in some measure a temptation. But to hold that motive or temptation is equivalent to coercion is to plunge the law in endless difficulties. The outcome of such a doctrine is the acceptance of a philosophical determinism by which choice becomes impossible. Till now the law has been guided by a robust common sense which assumes the freedom of the will as a working hypothesis in the solution of its problems. The wisdom of the hypothesis has illustration in this case. [We] cannot say that [Alabama] was acting, not of her unfettered will, but under the strain of a persuasion equivalent to undue influence, when she chose to have relief administered under laws of her own making, by agents of her own selection, instead of under federal laws, administered by federal officers, with all the ensuing evils, at least to many minds, of federal patronage and power. * * *

[We] do not say that a tax is valid, when imposed by act of Congress, if it is laid upon the condition that a state may escape its operation through the adoption of a statute unrelated in subject-matter to activities fairly within the scope of national policy and power. [In] the tender of this credit Congress does not intrude upon fields foreign to its function. The purpose of its intervention, as we have shown, is to safeguard its own treasury [its "fiscal need"] and as an incident to that protection to place the states upon a footing of equal opportunity. [In] such circumstances, if in no others, inducement or persuasion does not go beyond the bounds of power.

[*Butler*] was by a divided court, a minority taking the view that the objections were untenable. None of them is applicable [here]. (a) The proceeds of the tax in controversy are not earmarked for a special group. (b) The unemployment compensation law which is a condition of the credit has had the approval of the state and could not be a law without it. (c) The condition is not linked to an irrevocable agreement, for the state at its pleasure may repeal its unemployment [law], terminate the credit, and place itself where it was before the credit was accepted. (d) The condition is not directed to the attainment of an unlawful end, but to an end, the relief of unemployment, for which nation and state may lawfully cooperate.

[The] statute does not call for a surrender by the states of powers essential to their quasi sovereign existence. [A] credit to taxpayers for payments made to a state under a state unemployment law will be manifestly futile in the absence of some assurance that the law leading to the credit is in truth what it professes to be. [What] is basic and essential may be assured by suitable conditions. The terms embodied in these sections are directed to that end. A wide range of judgment is given to the several states as to the particular type of statute to be spread upon their books. [What] they may not do, if they would earn the credit, is to depart from those standards which in the judgment of Congress are to be ranked as fundamental. * * *[83]

NOTES AND QUESTIONS

1. ***Coercion or inducement?*** Were the farmers in *Butler* or the states in *Steward* more free to resist the federal "inducement" or "coercion" or "temptation"? More subject to "persuasion equivalent to undue influence"? Consider Jesse H. Choper, *The Supreme Court and Unconstitutional Conditions: Federalism and Individual Rights*, 4 Corn.J.L. & Pub.Pol. 460 (1995): "[T]he Court [has] refused to recognize 'coercion,' when it has 'stared the Court in the face.' [T]here is no clearer example [than *Steward*]. The national government took the states' money. The states received nothing in

---

[83] McReynolds and Butler, JJ., dissented in separate opinions. Sutherland, J., joined by Van Devanter, J., agreed that the act did not coerce the states, but contended that the administrative provisions of the act unconstitutionally encroached on state powers (an issue considered in Sec. 5 infra).

return if they did not comply with the federal government's demands. However, the states did regain 90% of the funds if they established a proper unemployment compensation system." Or do "offers of conditioned benefits expand rather than contract the options of the beneficiary class, and so present beneficiaries with a free choice"? Kathleen M. Sullivan, *Unconstitutional Conditions*, 102 Harv.L.Rev. 1415 (1989) If Congress offers a state university funds to enhance science education (or build a new athletic stadium), is this "coercive" or does it simply "expand its options"? Consider Tribe 3d ed.: "[T]he Court has provided little guidance on the question, and it implicates the deeper philosophical question whether—assuming that choice and free will can sometimes be meaningful—there is any form or level of inducement that can truly render someone unable to choose, as well as the question of what choice and compulsion mean when we are talking about *states* rather than persons." See also Michael T. Gibson, *Congressional Authority to Induce Waivers of State Sovereign Immunity: The Conditional Spending Power (and Beyond)*, 29 Hast.Con.L.Q. 439 (2002) ("coercion simply does not make sense in the context of federal grants").[84]

2. ***Federal "fiscal need."*** Can the spending in *Butler* (to "purchase" compliance by the farmers with a reduced acreage program in order to provide relief for a depressed national agriculture) be fairly distinguished from the tax and credit device in *Steward* (to induce states to adopt unemployment compensation) on the ground that, in *Steward*, Congress did not "intrude upon fields foreign to its function" in view of the national fiscal responsibility for relief of the unemployed? Can most conditions on federal funding to induce state regulation (or private conduct) that Congress feels are needed to advance the general welfare be justified on the basis of Congress' "fiscal need [to] safeguard its own treasury"?

3. ***Definition of "general welfare."*** (a) HELVERING v. DAVIS, 301 U.S. 619 (1937), per CARDOZO, J., upheld the Social Security Act's old age pension program, supported exclusively by federal taxes: "The line must still be drawn between one welfare and another, between the particular and the general. [The] discretion [belongs] to Congress, unless the choice is clearly wrong, a display of arbitrary power, not an exercise of judgment. [Nor] is the concept of the general welfare static. Needs that were narrow or parochial a century ago may be interwoven in our day with the well-being of the nation. * * *

"The problem is plainly national in area and dimensions. Moreover, laws of the separate states cannot deal with it effectively. Congress, at least, had a basis for that belief. States and local governments are often lacking in the resources that are necessary to finance an adequate program of security for the aged. [Apart] from the failure of resources, states and local governments are at times reluctant to increase so heavily the burden of taxation to be borne by

---

[84] For the view that spending is "coercive" if intended to "penalize or discourage" certain state conduct rather than to "serve the national interest" independent of regulating that conduct, see Mitchell N. Berman, *Coercion Without Baselines: Unconstitutional Conditions in Three Dimensions*, 90 Geo.L.J. 1 (2001).

their residents for fear of placing themselves in a position of economic disadvantage as compared with neighbors or competitors. [A] system of old age pensions has special dangers of its own, if put in force in one state and rejected in another. The existence of such a system is a bait to the needy and dependent elsewhere, encouraging them to migrate and seek a haven of repose. Only a power that is national can serve the interests of all." Butler and McReynolds, JJ., dissented.

(b) *United States v. Gerlach Live Stock Co.*, 339 U.S. 725 (1950), upheld federal spending for large scale federal land reclamation projects: "Congress has substantive power to tax and appropriate for the general welfare, limited only by the requirement that it shall be exercised for the common benefit as distinguished from some mere local purpose." Is some nationwide need or some common benefit, widely shared, a requisite for federal spending? Is an appropriation for an irrigation project that only benefits land within a 50 mile radius valid? An appropriation to prevent the bankruptcy of a major city? See John C. Eastman, *Restoring the "General" to the General Welfare Clause*, 4 Chap. L. Rev. 63 (2001) (Congress may not spend "for the special welfare of particular regions or states, even if the spending was undertaken in all regions or all states and therefore might be said to enhance 'general' welfare in the aggregate").

(c) *Judicial review.* Assuming standing to challenge a federal expenditure,[85] should courts make independent judgments on "general welfare"? Should the Court rule such issues nonjusticiable, thus leaving them for congressional judgment without abdicating its "duty [to] say what the law is" (*Marbury*) on constitutional issues?

SOUTH DAKOTA V. DOLE
483 U.S. 203, 107 S.Ct. 2793, 97 L.Ed.2d 171 (1987).

CHIEF JUSTICE REHNQUIST delivered the opinion of the Court.

[In] 1984 Congress enacted 23 U.S.C. § 158 [withholding 5%] of federal highway funds otherwise allocable from States "in which the purchase or public possession [of] any alcoholic beverage by a person who is less than twenty-one years of age is lawful." * * *

The spending power is of course not unlimited, *Pennhurst State School and Hospital v. Halderman*, 451 U.S. 1 (1981). [The] first of these limitations is derived from the language of the Constitution itself: the exercise of the spending power must be in pursuit of "the general welfare." In considering whether a particular expenditure is intended to serve general public purposes, courts should defer substantially to the judgment of Congress. *Helvering*.[86] Second, we have required that if Congress desires

---

[85] Standing to challenge federal spending is considered in Ch. 12, Sec. 2, II.

[86] The level of deference to the congressional decision is such that the Court has questioned whether "general welfare" is a judicially enforceable restriction at all. See *Buckley v. Valeo*, 424 U.S. 1 (1976) (per curiam).

to condition the States' receipt of federal funds, it "must do so unambiguously, [enabling] the States to [be] cognizant of the consequences of their participation." *Pennhurst*.[87] Third, our cases have suggested (without significant elaboration) that conditions on federal grants might be illegitimate if they are unrelated "to the federal interest in particular national projects or programs." *Massachusetts v. United States*, 435 U.S. 444 (1978) (plurality opinion). Finally, we have noted that other constitutional provisions may provide an independent bar to the conditional grant of federal funds.

South Dakota does not seriously claim that § 158 is inconsistent with any of the first three restrictions mentioned [above.] Indeed, the condition imposed by Congress is directly related to one of the main purposes for which highway funds are expended—safe interstate travel. [A] Presidential commission appointed to study alcohol-related accidents and fatalities on the Nation's highways concluded that the lack of uniformity in the States' drinking ages created "an incentive to drink and drive" because "young persons commut[e] to border States where the drinking age is lower." * * *

The remaining question about the validity of § 158—and the basic point of disagreement between the parties—is whether the Twenty-first Amendment constitutes an "independent constitutional bar." [Petitioner] asserts that "Congress may not use the spending power to regulate that which it is prohibited from regulating directly under the Twenty-first Amendment." But our cases [have] established that the constitutional limitations on Congress when exercising its spending power are less exacting than those on its authority to regulate directly.

[In] *Oklahoma v. Civil Service Comm'n*, 330 U.S. 127 (1947), the Court considered the validity of the Hatch Act insofar as it was applied to political activities of state officials whose employment was financed in whole or in part with federal funds. The State contended that an order under this provision to withhold certain federal funds unless a state official was removed invaded its sovereignty in violation of the Tenth Amendment. [See Sec. 5 infra.] Though finding that "the United States is not concerned with, and has no power to regulate, local political activities as such of state officials," the Court nevertheless held that the Federal Government "does have power to fix the terms upon which its money allotments to states shall be disbursed." The Court found no violation of the State's sovereignty because the State could, and did, adopt "the 'simple expedient' of not yielding to what she urges is federal coercion. The offer of benefits to a state

---

[87] For a careful review of the cases and literature on the spending power, see Samuel R. Bagenstos, *Spending Clause Litigation in the Roberts Court*, 58 Duke L. J. 345 (2008), concluding that "the Court will likely apply [a] super-strong clear-statement rule [to] a greater extent in the near future."

by the United States dependent upon cooperation by the state with federal plans, assumedly for the general welfare, is not unusual."

[T]he language in our earlier opinions stands for the unexceptionable proposition that the [spending] power may not be used to induce the States to engage in activities that would themselves be unconstitutional. Thus, [a] grant of federal funds conditioned on invidiously discriminatory state action or the infliction of cruel and unusual punishment would be an illegitimate exercise of the Congress' broad spending power. But no such claim can be or is made here. Were South Dakota to succumb to the blandishments offered by Congress and raise its drinking age to 21, [it] would not violate the constitutional rights of anyone.

Our decisions have recognized that in some circumstances the financial inducement offered by Congress might be so coercive as to pass the point at which "pressure turns into compulsion." *Steward*. Here, however, Congress has directed only that a State desiring to establish a minimum drinking age lower than 21 lose a relatively small percentage of certain federal highway funds. [A] conditional grant of federal money of this sort is [not] unconstitutional simply by reason of its success in achieving the congressional objective.[88] [T]he enactment of [drinking age] laws remains the prerogative of the States not merely in theory but in fact. Even if Congress might lack the power to impose a national minimum drinking age directly, we conclude that encouragement to state action found in § 158 is a valid use of the spending power. * * *

JUSTICE O'CONNOR, dissenting.

[T]he Court's application of the requirement that the condition imposed be reasonably related to the purpose for which the funds are expended is cursory and unconvincing. [When] Congress appropriates money to build a highway, it is entitled to insist that the highway be a safe one. But it is not entitled to insist as a [that] the State impose or change regulations in other areas of the State's social and economic life because of an attenuated or tangential relationship to highway use or safety. Indeed, if the rule were otherwise, the Congress could effectively regulate almost any area of a State's social, political, or economic life on the theory that use of the interstate transportation system is somehow enhanced. If, for example, the United States were to condition highway moneys upon moving the state capital, I suppose it might argue that interstate transportation is facilitated by locating local governments in places easily accessible to interstate highways—or, conversely, that highways might become overburdened if they had to carry traffic to and from the state

---

[88] *Pennhurst*, per Rehnquist, J., observed that "legislation enacted pursuant to the spending power is much in the nature of a contract: in return for federal funds, the States agree to comply with federally imposed conditions. The legitimacy of Congress' power to legislate under the spending power thus rests on whether the State voluntarily and knowingly accepts the terms of the 'contract.'"

capital. In my mind, such a relationship is hardly more attenuated than the one which the Court finds supports § 158.

There is a clear place at which the Court can draw the line between permissible and impermissible conditions on federal grants. [It] turns on whether the requirement specifies in some way how the money should be spent, so that Congress' intent in making the grant will be effectuated. [A] requirement that is not such a specification is not a condition, but a regulation, which is valid only if it falls within one of Congress' delegated regulatory powers. [The] error in *Butler* was not the Court's conclusion that the Act was essentially regulatory, but rather its crabbed view of the extent of Congress' regulatory power under the Commerce Clause. * * *

[If] the spending power is to be limited only by Congress' notion of the general welfare, the reality, given the vast financial resources of the Federal Government, is that the Spending Clause gives "power to the Congress to tear down the barriers, to invade the states' jurisdiction, and to become a parliament of the whole people, subject to no restrictions save such as are self-imposed." This, of course, as *Butler* held, was not the Framers' plan and it is not the meaning of the Spending Clause. Our later cases are consistent with the notion that, under the spending power, the Congress may only condition grants in ways that can fairly be said to be related to the expenditure of federal funds [discussing *Oklahoma v. CSC.* But] a condition that a State will raise its drinking age to 21 [has] nothing to do with how the funds Congress has appropriated are expended. Rather [it] is a regulation determining who shall be able to drink liquor. As such it is not justified by the spending power. * * *

NOTES AND QUESTIONS

1.   ***Reach of spending power.*** (a) (i) SABRI v. UNITED STATES, 541 U.S. 600 (2004), per SOUTER, J., held that Congress had power to make it a crime to bribe state or local officials whose government agency received federal funds in excess of $10,000 in any year: "Congress has authority under the Spending Clause [to] see to it that taxpayer dollars appropriated under that power are in fact spent for the general welfare, and not frittered away in graft or on projects undermined when funds are siphoned off or corrupt public officers are derelict about demanding value for dollars. See generally *McCulloch* (establishing review for means-ends rationality under the Necessary and Proper Clause)."

Sabri claimed that, even though his alleged actions may have been related to the federal funds, the statute itself must require proof that the bribe will be "traceably skimmed from specific federal payments." The Court responded: "Money is fungible, bribed officials are untrustworthy stewards of federal funds, and corrupt contractors do not deliver dollar-for-dollar value. [M]oney can be drained off here because a federal grant is pouring in there."

THOMAS, J. observed that "the Court appears to hold that the Necessary and Proper Clause authorizes the exercise of any power that is no more than a 'rational means' to effectuate one of Congress' enumerated powers. [The Court] does not explain how there could be any federal interest in 'prosecut[ing] a bribe paid to a city's meat inspector in connection with a substantial transaction just because the city's parks department had received a federal grant of $10,000,' *United States v. Santopietro,* 166 F.3d 88, 93 (C.A.2 1999). It would be difficult to describe the chain of inferences and assumptions in which the Court would have to indulge to connect such a bribe to a federal interest in any federal funds or programs as being 'plainly adapted' to their protection."

(ii)   *Sabri* distinguished *Dole* because the bribery statute "is authority to bring federal power to bear directly on individuals who convert public spending into unearned private gain, not a means for bringing federal economic might to bear on a State's own choices of public policy." Which way does this cut in respect to the scope of congressional power? Consider Richard W. Garnett, *The New Federalism, the Spending Power, and Federal Criminal Law,* 89 Corn.L.Rev. 1 (2003): "In [*Sabri*], there simply is no federal-spending 'contract' to which those whose conduct is being regulated and punished are parties. [I]t is one thing for Congress to condition States' receipt of federal highway funds on their adoption of a particular drinking age; it is quite another for this receipt of funds to [authorize] federal prosecutions for underage drinking. * * * Congress can buy the States' cooperation in furthering its policy objectives, but it cannot buy a national police power, or spend its way to criminal jurisdiction that is not otherwise tethered to its few, enumerated, and defined powers." See also George D. Brown, *Stealth Statute—Corruption, The Spending Power, and the Rise of 18 U.S.C. § 666,* 73 Notre D.L.Rev. 247 (1998). May Congress provide that an emergency room doctor, in any hospital that receives federal funds, who withholds emergency room services from persons because of their inability to pay, is guilty of a federal crime? Cf. Emergency Medical Treatment and Active Labor Act, 42 U.S.C. § 1395dd. Does *Sabri* permit Congress to make it a crime for underage drinkers to drive on highways that have been federally subsidized? Do you agree that under *Dole,* "Congress may effectively regulate almost any area of a State's social, political, or economic life" (O'Connor, J.)? Might Congress use the spending power to achieve the results invalidated in *Lopez* and *Morrison?*

(b)   Does O'Connor, J.'s approach provide an effective limit on the spending power? Consider Kimberley Sayers-Fay, *Conditional Federal Spending: A Back Door to Enhanced Free Exercise Protection,* 88 Calif.L.Rev. 1281 (2000): "The requirement that conditions 'specify in some way how the money should be spent' is exceedingly porous. [In *Dole,* what] if Congress dictated that the funds be expended in order to build 'safe roads' or even 'safe roads where a twenty-one-year-old drinking age obtains'? Would that not be specifying in some way how the money should be spent?" Could Congress allocate funds for new state judges, including those needed to adjudicate civil damages actions against perpetrators by victims of gender-motivated violence?

Could Congress allocate "Safe School Funds" to those states that make it a crime to possess guns in a school zone?

2.   ***Other approaches.*** (a) Lynn A. Baker, *Conditional Spending After Lopez*, 95 Colum.L.Rev. 1911 (1995): "[T]hose offers of federal funds to the states which, if accepted, would regulate the states in ways that Congress could not directly mandate, will be presumed invalid. This presumption will be rebutted upon a determination that the offer of funds constitutes 'reimbursement spending' rather than 'regulatory spending.' 'Reimbursement spending' legislation specifies the *purpose* for which the states are to spend the offered federal funds and simply reimburses the states, in whole or in part, ["an amount of money no greater than that necessary"] for their expenditures for that purpose."

(b)   Choper, note 1 after *Steward Machine*: "There is a feeling that if the spending power is an independent power, then Congress must be able to engage in conditioned spending. However, [t]he Court could hold that Congress [does] not have authority to condition its spending on conduct it could not directly require using one of its regulatory powers. For example, suppose Congress has no power to require tiny lakes throughout the nation be free of pollution. Nonetheless, if Congress wishes to spend federal money to accomplish this goal, it may accomplish it through the independent use of the spending power."

3.   ***Coercion with "some" bite.*** In NATIONAL FEDERATION OF INDEPENDENT BUSINESS v. SEBELIUS, Sec. 2, IV, ROBERTS, C.J.'s opinion (Part IV), joined by Breyer and Kagan, JJ., addressed the ACA's "Medicaid expansion": "The States also contend that the Medicaid expansion exceeds Congress's authority under the Spending Clause. They claim that Congress is coercing the States to adopt the changes it wants by threatening to withhold all of a State's Medicaid grants, unless the State accepts the new expanded funding and complies with the conditions that come with it.

"[The] current Medicaid program requires States to cover only certain discrete categories of needy individuals—pregnant women, children, needy families, the blind, the elderly, and the disabled. [On] average States cover only those unemployed parents who make less than 37 percent of the federal poverty level, and only those employed parents who make less than 63 percent of the poverty line.

"The Medicaid provisions of the Affordable Care Act, in contrast, require States to expand their Medicaid programs by 2014 to cover all individuals under the age of 65 with incomes below 133 percent of the federal poverty line. The Act [also] provides that the Federal Government will pay 100 percent of the costs of covering these newly eligible individuals through 2016. In the following years, the federal payment level gradually decreases, to a minimum of 90 percent. In light of the expansion in coverage mandated by the Act, the Federal Government estimates that its Medicaid spending will increase by approximately $100 billion per year, nearly 40 percent above current levels.

"[O]ur cases have recognized [that] Congress may use its spending power to create incentives for States to act in accordance with federal policies. But when 'pressure turns into compulsion,' *Steward Machine*, the legislation [would] threaten the political accountability key to our federal system. '[W]here the Federal Government directs the States to regulate, it may be state officials who will bear the brunt of public disapproval, while the federal officials who devised the regulatory program may remain insulated from the electoral ramifications of their decision.' *New York v. United States.* [T]his danger is heightened when Congress acts under the Spending Clause, because Congress can use that power to implement federal policy it could not impose directly under its enumerated powers. * * *

"The States [argue] that the Medicaid expansion is far from the typical case [in] the way it has structured the funding: Instead of simply refusing to grant the new funds to States that will not accept the new conditions, Congress has also threatened to withhold those States' existing Medicaid funds. [In *Dole*,] we found that the inducement was not impermissibly coercive, because Congress was offering only 'relatively mild encouragement to the States.' We observed that 'all South Dakota would lose if she adheres to her chosen course as to a suitable minimum drinking age is 5%' of her highway funds. In fact, the federal funds at stake constituted less than half of one percent of South Dakota's budget at the time. * * *

"In this case, the financial 'inducement' Congress has chosen is much more than 'relatively mild encouragement'—it is a gun to the head. [A] State that opts out of the Affordable Care Act's expansion in health care coverage thus stands to lose not merely 'a relatively small percentage' of its existing Medicaid funding, but *all* of it. Medicaid spending accounts for over 20 percent of the average State's total budget, with federal funds covering 50 to 83 percent of those costs.

"[T]he Government claims that the Medicaid expansion is properly viewed merely as a modification of the existing program because [the] original Medicaid provisions contain a clause expressly reserving '[t]he right to alter, amend, or repeal any provision' of that statute. So it does. But [a] State confronted with statutory language reserving the right to 'alter' or 'amend' [might] reasonably assume that Congress was entitled to make adjustments to the Medicaid program as it developed. [The] Medicaid expansion, however, accomplishes a shift in kind, not merely degree. [It] is no longer a program to care for the neediest among us, but rather an element of a comprehensive national plan to provide universal health insurance coverage.[89] * * *

---

[89] Justice Ginsburg suggests that the States can have no objection to the Medicaid expansion, because "Congress could have repealed Medicaid [and,] [t]hereafter, could have enacted Medicaid II, a new program combining the pre-2010 coverage with the expanded coverage required by the ACA." But it would certainly not be that easy. Practical constraints would plainly inhibit, if not preclude, [putting] every feature of Medicaid on the table for political reconsideration. * * *

"The Court in *Steward Machine* did not attempt to 'fix the outermost line' where persuasion gives way to coercion. [We] have no need to fix a line either.[90] It is enough for today that wherever that line may be, this statute is surely beyond it."[91]

GINSBURG, J., joined by Sotomayor, J., dissented: The Chief Justice *"for the first time ever*—finds an exercise of Congress' spending power unconstitutionally coercive.

"Medicaid, as amended by the ACA, however, is not two spending programs; it is a single [program]. Given past expansions, plus express statutory warning that Congress may change the requirements participating States must meet, there can be no tenable claim that the ACA fails for lack of [notice.] Congress is simply requiring States to do what States have long been required to do to receive Medicaid funding: comply with the conditions Congress prescribes for participation. [Even] if courts were inclined to second-guess Congress' conception of the character of its legislation, how would reviewing judges divine whether an Act of Congress, purporting to amend a law, is in reality not an amendment, but a new creation? At what point does an extension become so large that it 'transforms' the basic law? * * *

"Since 1965, Congress has amended the Medicaid program on more than 50 occasions, sometimes quite sizably. Most relevant here, between 1988 and 1990, Congress [added] millions to the Medicaid-eligible population. Between 1966 and 1990, annual federal Medicaid spending grew from \$631.6 million to \$42.6 billion; state spending rose to \$31 billion over the same period. * * *

"Compared to past alterations, the ACA is notable for the extent to which the Federal Government will pick up the tab. [The] Congressional Budget Office (CBO) projects that States will spend 0.8% more than they would have, absent the [ACA.] Whatever the increase in state obligations after the ACA, it will pale in comparison to the increase in federal funding.

"Finally, any fair appraisal of Medicaid would require acknowledgment of the considerable autonomy States enjoy under the [Act.] States, as first-line administrators, will continue to guide the distribution of substantial resources among their needy populations. [U]ndoubtedly the interests of federalism are

---

[90] The joint opinion of Scalia, Kennedy, Thomas, and Alito, JJ., dissenting, concurred in the result of the Part of Roberts, C.J.'s opinion, adding that "whether federal spending legislation crosses the line from enticement to coercion is often difficult to determine, and courts should not conclude that legislation is unconstitutional on this ground unless the coercive nature of an offer is unmistakably clear. In this case, however, there can be no doubt."

[91] Roberts, C.J., held that under the ACA's severability clause, Congress intended that, if the Medicaid expansion were found unconstitutional, it would be fully remedied by permitting the states that wished to do so to decline the federal funding for the expansion without having *all* federal funding for Medicaid withdrawn. Ginsburg, J., joined by Sotomayor, J., who dissented on the merits (see below), agreed with Roberts, C.J.'s view that "the Medicaid's severability clause determines the appropriate remedy." The joint dissent of Scalia, Kennedy, Thomas and Alito, JJ., would invalidate the expansion in full, and since they would find that both the individual mandate and the expansion are invalid, "all other provisions of the Act must fail as well."

better served when States retain a meaningful role in the implementation of a program of such importance.[92]

"The Chief Justice appears to find [a] requirement that, when spending legislation is first passed, or when States first enlist in the federal program, Congress must provide clear notice of conditions it might later impose. If I understand his point correctly, it was incumbent on Congress, in 1965, to warn the States clearly of the size and shape potential changes to Medicaid might take. And absent such notice, sizable changes could not be made mandatory. Our decisions do not support such a requirement.

"[In] *Bowen v. Public Agencies Opposed to Social Security Entrapment*, 477 U.S. 41 (1986), [Congress] changed Social Security from a program voluntary for the States [to cover their employees] to one from which they could not escape. [By] including in the Act 'a clause expressly reserving to it "[t]he right to alter, amend, or repeal any provision" of the Act,' we [unanimously] held, Congress put States on notice that the Act 'created no contractual rights.' As *Bowen* indicates, no State could reasonably have read § 1304 [of the Medicaid Act] as reserving to Congress authority to make adjustments only if modestly sized. [In] short, given § 1304, this Court's construction of § 1304's language in *Bowen*, and the enlargement of Medicaid in the years since 1965, a State would be hard put to complain that it lacked fair notice when, in 2010, Congress altered Medicaid to embrace a larger portion of the Nation's poor. * * *

"When future Spending Clause challenges arrive, as they likely will in the wake of today's decision, how will litigants and judges assess whether 'a State has a legitimate choice whether to accept the federal conditions in exchange for federal funds'? Are courts to measure the number of dollars the Federal Government might withhold for noncompliance? The portion of the State's budget at stake? And which State's—or States'—budget is determinative: the lead plaintiff, all challenging States (26 in this case, many with quite different fiscal situations), or some national median? Does it matter [that] the coercion state officials in fact fear is punishment at the ballot box for turning down a politically popular federal grant? [The] coercion inquiry, therefore, appears to involve political judgments that defy judicial calculation."

See generally Ruth Mason, *Federalism and the Taxing Power*, 99 Calif.L.Rev. 975 (2011) (taxes and spending raise both similar and different federalism concerns).

4. FOREIGN AFFAIRS POWER

The preceding materials on the commerce, taxing, and spending powers should provide adequate background for consideration of issues relating to the many other congressional powers. See, e.g., note 5 after

---

92 The Chief Justice and the joint dissenters perceive in cooperative federalism a "threa[t]" to "political accountability." [But] Medicaid's status as a federally funded, state-administered program is hardly hidden from view.

Darby (war powers). This section, however, involves a significant, atypical congressional power.

I.   TREATIES AS A SOURCE OF LEGISLATIVE POWER

MISSOURI v. HOLLAND, 252 U.S. 416 (1920), per HOLMES, J., upheld a federal statute implementing a treaty with Canada that obligated both countries to seek legislation[93] protecting birds that traversed both countries, and were valued for food and as destroyers of insects harmful to vegetation: "[It] is not enough to refer to the Tenth Amendment [because] by Article 2, Section 2, the power to make treaties is delegated expressly, and by Article 6 treaties [are] declared the supreme law of the land.[94] If the treaty is valid there can be no dispute about the validity of the statute [as] a necessary and proper means to execute the powers of the Government. * * *[95]

"It is said [that] there are [constitutional limits] to the treaty-making power, and that one such limit is that what an act of Congress could not do unaided, in derogation of the powers reserved to the States,[96] a treaty cannot do. [Acts] of Congress are the supreme law of the land only when made in pursuance of the Constitution, while treaties are declared to be so when made under the authority of the United States. It is open to question whether the authority of the United States means more than the formal acts prescribed to make the convention. We do not mean to imply that there are no qualifications to the treaty-making power; but they must be ascertained in a different way. It is obvious that there may be matters of the sharpest exigency for the national well being that an act of Congress could not deal with but that a treaty followed by such an act could, and it is not lightly to be assumed that, in matters requiring national action, 'a power which must belong to and somewhere reside in every civilized government' is not to be found.[97] [W]hen we are dealing with words [in] the

---

[93] Thus, the treaty was not, by its terms, "self-executing" (see Ch. 3, fn. 93), but rather required congressional implementation.

[94] "[A] treaty is placed on the same footing [with] an act of legislation. [When] the two relate to the same subject, the courts will always endeavor to construe them so as to give effect to both, [but] if the two are inconsistent, the one last in date will control the other." *Whitney v. Robertson*, 124 U.S. 190 (1888).

[95] See Nicholas Q. Rosenkranz, *Executing the Treaty Power*, 118 Harv.L.Rev. 1867 (2005), for the view that this "crucial sentence [runs] counter to the textual and structural logic of the Constitution." Although the President may "make treaties that reach beyond the enumerated powers of Congress," Congress has no "power to enact implementing legislation pursuant to a non-self-executing treaty [if] it would not have power to pass the same legislation absent the treaty."

[96] At the time of *Holland*, "the Commerce Clause had not been read in a sufficiently sweeping fashion to permit birds flying across state lines to be treated as articles in interstate commerce, especially since there was very little evidence that birds were actually transported across state lines, as distinguished from flying across them of their own volition." G. Edward White, *The Transformation of the Constitutional Regime of Foreign Relations*, 85 Va.L.Rev. 1 (1999).

[97] Compare Carlos M. Vazquez, *Missouri v. Holland's Second Holding*, 73 Mo. L. Rev. 939 (2008): Congress's "power to implement treaties [only includes] the power to require compliance with treaty *obligations*," in contrast to "aspirational provisions [which] commit the parties merely

Constitution of the United States, we must realize that they have called into life a being the development of which could not have been foreseen completely by the most gifted of its begetters. It was enough for them to realize or to hope that they had created an organism; it has taken a century and has cost their successors much sweat and blood to prove that they created a nation. The case before us must be considered in the light of our whole experience and not merely in that of what was said a hundred years ago. The treaty in question does not contravene any prohibitory words to be found in the Constitution. The only question is whether it is forbidden by some invisible radiation from the general terms of the Tenth Amendment. We must consider what this country has become in deciding what that amendment has reserved. * * *

"Here a national interest of very nearly the first magnitude is involved. It can be protected only by national action in concert with that of another power. The subject matter is only transitorily within the State and has no permanent habitat therein. But for the treaty and the statute there soon might be no birds for any powers to deal with. We see nothing in the Constitution that compels the Government to sit by while a food supply is cut off and the protectors of our forests and our crops are destroyed. It is not sufficient to rely upon the States. The reliance is vain, and were it otherwise, the question is whether the United States is forbidden to act. We are of opinion that the treaty and statute must be upheld." Van Devanter and Pitney, JJ., dissented without opinion.

NOTES AND QUESTIONS

1. *Scope of treaty power.* Are there judicially manageable limits on the federal government's power to expand its regulatory power through treaties? *Geofroy v. Riggs*, 133 U.S. 258 (1890), stated that the power "extends to all proper subjects of negotiation between our government and the government of other nations." In 1965, *Restatement (Second) of the Foreign Relations Law of the United States* provided that the treaty power is limited to matters "of international concern," i.e., it "must relate to the external concerns of the nation as distinguished from matters of a purely internal nature." But in 1987, *Restatement (Third)* declared that "contrary to what was once suggested, the Constitution does not require that an international agreement deal only with 'matters of international concern.' "[98] Does this approach make it "difficult to perceive any limitation on federal power" (*Lopez/Morrison*)? Consider Curtis A. Bradley, *The Treaty Power and American Federalism*, 97

---

to attempt to achieve certain ends"; because these often "vaguer" aspirations "might easily gain the consent of two-thirds of the Senate because they do not seem to require very much from the nation," if they "address matters beyond Article I, implementation would be left to the States."

[98] The Chief Reporter for *Restatement (Third)* had earlier written: "What is of international concern, what affects American foreign relations and is relevant to American foreign policy, what matters the United States wishes to negotiate about, differ from generation to generation, perhaps from year to year, with the ever-changing character of relations between nations." Louis Henkin, *The Constitution, Treaties, and International Human Rights*, 116 U.Pa.L.Rev. 1012, 1025 (1968).

Mich.L.Rev. 390 (1998): "This dichotomy [between internal and external concerns] might have been accurate at one time in American history, when treaties were generally bilateral and regulated matters such as diplomatic immunity, military neutrality, and removal of trade barriers. [During] the latter [20th] century, however, there has been a proliferation of treaties [that] take the form of detailed multilateral instruments [designed] to operate as international 'legislation' binding on much of the world. [Many] concern matters that in the past countries would have addressed wholly domestically. This change in treaty-making is most evident in the area of international human rights law, [on] issues such as racial and gender equality, criminal procedure and punishment, and religious freedom [where] conflict is likely to occur at the state level." For the view that the Founders understood "that the treaty power was limited either by subject matter, by the reserved powers of the states, or both" and that, therefore, "the treaty power should be subject to the same federalism limitations that apply to Congress's legislative powers," see Bradley, supra at 417, 450.[99] Accord, Gary Lawson & Guy Seidman, *The Jeffersonian Treaty Clause*, 2006 U. Ill. L. Rev. 1.

2.   ***"Prohibitory words."*** REID v. COVERT, 354 U.S. 1 (1957), per BLACK, J. (plurality), reversed murder convictions of U.S. military dependents for denial of jury trials by U.S. military courts in Great Britain, pursuant to jurisdiction under a treaty: "No agreement with a foreign nation can confer power on Congress, or any other branch of Government, which is free from the restraints of the Constitution. [The] reason treaties were not limited [in the Supremacy Clause] to those made in 'pursuance' of the Constitution was so that agreements made by the United States under the Articles of Confederation [would] remain in effect. [*Holland*] carefully noted that the treaty involved was not inconsistent with any specific provision of the Constitution."[100]

II. OTHER BASES FOR LEGISLATIVE POWER OVER FOREIGN AFFAIRS

Is congressional power to legislate on foreign affairs limited to laws implementing treaties and to such sources as are found in Art. I, § 8, the Civil War Amendments, and similar grants of legislative power? *Should* it be?

PEREZ v. BROWNELL, 356 U.S. 44 (1958), per FRANKFURTER, J., upheld a federal statute mandating loss of U.S. citizenship for "voting in a

---

[99] Suppose that a treaty serves "as a pretext for the federal government to pass a law that it would otherwise be unable to pass"? Oona A. Hathaway, Spencer Amdur, Celia Choy, Samir Deger-Sen, John Paredes, Sally Pei & Haley Nix Proctor, *The Treaty Power: Its History, Scope and Limits*, 98 Cornell L.R. 239 (2013), suggests that the Court should find it unconstitutional, using "a rational basis test ["with bite" (see Ch. 9, Sec.1)] in which the court asks whether there is some valid ["objectively discernable"] international purpose fo the treaty."

[100] Warren, C.J., Douglas and Brennan, JJ., joined in Black, J.'s plurality opinion. Frankfurter and Harlan, JJ., concurred as to capital cases. Clark, and Burton, JJ., dissented. Whittaker, J., took no part.

political election in a foreign state." The Court viewed this effort, to prevent the international tensions risked by a citizen's "participat[ing] in the political or governmental affairs of another country," as based upon Congress' "power to regulate foreign affairs": "Although there is in the Constitution no specific grant to Congress of power to enact legislation for the effective regulation of foreign affairs, there can be no doubt of the existence of this power in the law-making organ of the nation. See *United States v. Curtiss-Wright Export Corp.*, 299 U.S. 304, 318 (1936).[101] The states that joined together to form [a] federal government to conduct the affairs of that nation must be held to have granted that government the powers indispensable to its functioning effectively in the company of sovereign nations. The government must be able not only to deal affirmatively with foreign nations, as it does through the maintenance of diplomatic relations with them and the protection of American citizens sojourning within their territories. It must also be able to reduce to a minimum the frictions that are unavoidable in a world of sovereigns sensitive in matters touching their dignity and interests."[102]

NOTES AND QUESTIONS

Scope of power. Are there judicially manageable standards by which to limit Congress' power over foreign affairs? *Perez* reasoned that "a rational nexus must exist between the content of a specific power in Congress and the action of Congress. [In this case,] withdrawal of citizenship [must] be reasonably related to the end—here, regulation of foreign affairs." For a comprehensive view of Congress' "foreign affairs power" under the *Curtiss-Wright* and *Perez* rationale, coupled with a recognition of the breadth of Congress' power over foreign affairs derived from the specified powers of Congress, see Henkin, Ch. 3, fn. 17.

5. APPLYING NATIONAL POWERS TO STATE GOVERNMENTS: INTERGOVERNMENTAL IMMUNITIES

I.   ORIGINS OF IMMUNITIES

Intergovernmental immunity as a constitutional limit on state and federal power started with McCULLOCH v. MARYLAND, Sec. 1 supra, which held invalid Maryland's taxes on the Bank of United States: "[The] great principle [that sustains the bank's] claim to be exempted from the power of the state to tax its operations [is] that the Constitution and the

---

[101] *Curtiss-Wright* appears in Ch. 3, Sec. 3.

[102] In three opinions Warren, C.J., and Black, Douglas and Whittaker, JJ., dissented from the ruling that Congress could impose involuntary expatriation, but did not question the *Perez* comments on Congress' power to legislate on foreign affairs. Nor did *Afroyim v. Rusk*, 387 U.S. 253 (1967), which overruled the *Perez* expatriation ruling as inconsistent with § 1 of the Fourteenth Amendment.

laws made in pursuance thereof are supreme. [From this, other] propositions are deduced as corollaries[:] 1st. That a power to create implies a power to preserve. 2d. That a power to destroy, if wielded by a different hand, is hostile to, and incompatible with, these powers to create and to preserve. 3d. That where this repugnancy exists, that authority which is supreme must control. [That] the power of taxing [the bank] by the states may be exercised so as to destroy it, is too obvious to be denied. * * *

"The argument [of] Maryland, is, not that the states may directly resist a law of Congress, but that they may exercise their acknowledged powers upon it, and that the Constitution leaves them this right in the confidence that they will not abuse it. [But if] the states may tax one instrument, employed by the government in the execution of its powers, they may tax any and every other instrument. They may tax the mail; they may tax the mint; they may tax patent rights; they may tax the papers of the customhouse; they may tax judicial process; they may tax all the means employed by the government, to an excess which would defeat all the ends of government. [If state] supremacy as to taxation be acknowledged; what is to restrain their exercising this control in any shape they may please to give it? Their sovereignty is not confined to taxation. That is not the only mode in which it might be displayed. The question is, in truth, a question of supremacy * * * .

"This opinion does not deprive the states of any resources which they originally possessed. It does not extend to a tax paid by the real property of the bank, in common with the other real property within the state, nor to a tax imposed on the interest which the citizens of Maryland may hold in this institution, in common with other property of the same description throughout the state. But this is [a] tax on the operation of an instrument employed by the government of the Union to carry its powers into execution. Such a tax must be unconstitutional."

NOTES AND QUESTIONS

1. **State immunity from federal taxes.** Just as *Dobbins v. Commissioners,* 41 U.S. (16 Pet.) 435 (1842), invoked *McCulloch* to strike down a state tax on the salary of a federal officer, COLLECTOR v. DAY, 78 U.S. (11 Wall.) 113 (1871), per NELSON, J., invalidated a federal income tax on the salary of a state judge as an "instrumentality" of state government. It viewed the "sovereign powers" reserved to the states by the Tenth Amendment as the foundation for state immunity from federal taxes, analogous to the Supremacy Clause as the foundation for federal immunity from state taxes: "In both cases the exemption rests upon necessary implication, and is upheld by the great law of self-preservation; as any government, whose means employed in conducting its operations, if subject to the control of another and distinct government, can exist only at the mercy of that government."

2. *Expansion and contraction.* *Dobbins* and *Collector* led to broad expansion of intergovernmental immunities to relieve private taxpayers from state or federal taxes arising from transactions with the other government, even to application of a state income tax to royalties from a federal patent.[103] But beginning in 1938, this line of cases was abandoned,[104] and the Court has not invoked immunity for private taxpayers, even when their tax burden was passed on to the other government,[105] except for discrimination against state employees.[106]

The focus, then, in the following materials is on (1) the remaining immunity from federal taxes for state and local governments and vice versa, and (2) the impact of these tax immunity policies upon state immunity from federal regulation.

II. STATE IMMUNITY FROM FEDERAL TAXES

Since 1938, although the Court has invalidated no federal tax on a state, its activities, agencies or property, both cases to reach the Court have not questioned a state's right to immunity in appropriate situations. But in neither did a majority agree on a statement of the controlling considerations.

NEW YORK v. UNITED STATES, 326 U.S. 572 (1946), upheld application of a federal excise tax to New York's sale of mineral waters bottled and sold by the state to provide funds for a state health resort. FRANKFURTER, J., joined by Rutledge, J., would have accorded state immunity from nondiscriminatory federal taxes only when imposed on "state activities and state-owned property that partake of uniqueness from the point of view of intergovernmental relations. [Only]a state can get income by taxing. These could not be included for purposes of federal taxation in any abstract category of taxpayers without taxing the state as a state." STONE, C.J. joined by Reed, Murphy and Burton, JJ., would grant a broader state immunity: "It is plain that there may be non-discriminatory taxes which, when laid on a State, would nevertheless impair the sovereign status of the State quite as much as a like tax imposed by a State on property or activities of the national government. [T]he tax, even though non-discriminatory, may be regarded [as] unduly interfer[ing] with the

---

[103] *Long v. Rockwood,* 277 U.S. 142 (1928).

[104] See, e.g., *Helvering v. Gerhardt,* 304 U.S. 405 (1938) (federal income tax on state employee salaries); *Alabama v. King & Boozer,* 314 U.S. 1 (1941) (state sales tax on cost-plus federal contractor for material purchased to build army camp). Cf. *United States v. Fresno,* 429 U.S. 452 (1977) (state property tax on U.S. Forest Service employees for value of U.S.-owned houses provided as mandatory living quarters).

[105] See, e.g., *United States v. New Mexico,* 455 U.S. 720 (1982). The latest decision, *South Carolina v. Baker,* 485 U.S. 505 (1988) (only O'Connor, J., dissenting), upheld a federal tax on private income from a class of state and municipal bonds, overruling *Pollock v. Farmers' Loan and Trust Co.,* 157 U.S. 429 (1895). *Pollock* had not been challenged earlier because Congress had made no earlier effort to tax income from state bonds.

[106] *Davis v. Michigan Dept. of Treas.,* 489 U.S. 803 (1989) (exemption from state income tax of pensions of state, but not federal, employees).

performance of the State's functions of government." DOUGLAS, J., joined by Black, J., dissented: "Many state activities are in marginal enterprises where private capital refuses to venture. Add to the cost of these projects a federal tax and the social program may be destroyed before it can be launched."

———

MASSACHUSETTS v. UNITED STATES, 435 U.S. 444 (1978), upheld, as applied to state police planes, a federal registration tax on all civil aircraft, imposed to pay part of the cost of federal air navigation services. BRENNAN, J., joined by White, Marshall and Stevens, JJ., observed that "when the scope of the States' constitutional immunity is enlarged beyond that necessary to protect the continued ability of the States to deliver traditional governmental services, the burden of the immunity is thrown upon the National Government without any corresponding promotion of the constitutionally protected values. [T]he National Government may tax revenue-generating activities of the States that are of the same nature as those traditionally engaged in by private persons. See, e.g., *New York v. United States* (1946); *Allen v. Regents,* 304 U.S. 439 (1938) (tax on admissions to state athletic events approved notwithstanding use of proceeds for essential state functions); *Helvering v. Powers,* 293 U.S. 214 (1934) (tax on operations of railroad by State); *Ohio v. Helvering,* 292 U.S. 360 (1934) (tax on state liquor operation). [A] nondiscriminatory taxing measure that operates to defray the cost of a federal program by recovering a fair approximation of each beneficiary's share of the cost is surely no more offensive to the constitutional scheme than is either a tax on the income earned by state employees or a tax on a State's sale of bottled water. [A] revenue provision that forces a State to pay its own way when performing an essential function will increase the cost of the state activity. But [an] economic burden on traditional state functions without more is not a sufficient basis for sustaining a claim of immunity."[107]

NOTES AND QUESTIONS

Major issues. What are "traditional state functions"? "Essential state activities"? Can they almost always (always) be "of the same nature as those traditionally engaged in by private persons"? When does a federal tax "infringe a state's sovereignty"? "Unduly interfere with the performance of the State's functions of government"? These issues are extensively considered in Part IV infra.

---

[107] Stewart and Powell, JJ., saw "no need to discuss the general contours of state immunity from federal taxation," but concurred in the ruling that the registration tax was valid as a "user fee." Rehnquist, J., joined by Burger, C.J., dissented on the user fee issue. Blackmun, J., did not participate.

III. FEDERAL IMMUNITY FROM STATE TAXES

Federal immunity from state taxes has not undergone the same attrition as state immunity from federal taxes. Indeed, since *McCulloch* "the Court has never questioned the propriety of absolute federal immunity from state taxation," nor has it upheld a single state tax laid "directly upon the United States" without the consent of Congress, despite its elimination of immunity for private taxpayers, starting in 1938.[108] But the Court has restricted such immunity to state taxes imposed "on the United States itself, or an agency or instrumentality so closely connected to the Government that the two cannot realistically be viewed as separate entities, at least insofar as the activity being taxed is concerned."[109]

Is such broad federal immunity justified in view of the much more limited state immunity from federal taxes? What makes the difference? A view that all federal activities are "governmental"? The Supremacy Clause? Judicial deference due to Congress, as compared to that due a single state legislature whose action has adverse impact on a national interest?

Federal immunity from state regulation. For consideration of analogous federal immunity from state *regulatory* power, and the extent of immunity for individuals acting on behalf of the government, see Tribe 3d ed.

IV. STATE IMMUNITY FROM FEDERAL REGULATION

MARYLAND v. WIRTZ (1968), Sec. 2, II, B, per HARLAN, J., upheld application of the Fair Labor Standards Act to state schools and hospitals, stressing that "Congress has 'interfered with' these state functions only to the extent of providing that when the state employs people in performing such functions it is subject to the same restrictions as a wide range of other employers whose activities affect commerce * * * ." Douglas, J., joined by Stewart, J., dissented.

———

NATIONAL LEAGUE OF CITIES v. USERY, 426 U.S. 833 (1976), per REHNQUIST, J., overruled *Wirtz* on this issue: Federal regulation of the wages, hours, and overtime compensation for those whom states employ "to carry out their governmental functions" would increase costs and "substantially restructure" ways by which "state and local governments [discharge] their dual function of administering the public law and furnishing public services." It is not within Congress' commerce power "to directly displace the States' freedom to structure integral operations in

---

[108] See note 2, Part II supra.

[109] See *United States v. New Mexico,* 455 U.S. 720 (1982) (government contractors whose tax costs are passed on to the federal government are not to that extent "government instrumentalities" immune from state taxation). For detail, see Tribe 3d ed.

areas of traditional governmental functions." Though "not untroubled by [possible] implications of the Court's opinion," BLACKMUN, J., joined it "with the understanding" that it "adopts a balancing approach, and does not outlaw federal power where the federal interest is demonstrably greater and [state compliance] would be essential." Brennan, J., joined by White, Marshall and Stevens, JJ., dissented.

During the next seven years, the *National League of Cities* principle was unsuccessfully urged upon the Court five times. The first two decisions were unanimous.[110] In the next two, Blackmun, J., joined the *National League of Cities* dissenters to rule 5 to 4 that the principle was not applicable.[111] The fifth follows:

GARCIA V. SAN ANTONIO METROPOLITAN TRANSIT AUTHORITY

469 U.S. 528, 105 S.Ct. 1005, 83 L.Ed.2d 1016 (1985).

JUSTICE BLACKMUN delivered the opinion of the Court.

[The Court upheld application of the Fair Labor Standards Act wage and hour provisions to a municipally-owned and operated mass transit system.]

The prerequisites for governmental immunity under *National League of Cities* were summarized by this Court in *Hodel*[:] First, it is said that the federal statute at issue must regulate "the 'States as States.' " Second, the statute must "address matters that are indisputably 'attribute[s] of state sovereignty.' " Third, state compliance with the federal obligation must "directly impair [the States'] ability 'to structure integral operations in areas of traditional governmental functions.' " Finally, the relation of state and federal interests must not be such that "the nature of the federal [interest] justifies state submission."

The controversy in the present cases has focused on the [third] requirement. * * *

The distinction [between governmental and proprietary functions that] the Court discarded as unworkable in the field of tax immunity has proved no more fruitful in the field of regulatory immunity under the Commerce Clause. Neither do any of the alternative standards that might be employed to distinguish between protected and unprotected

----

[110] *Hodel v. Virginia Surface Mining* (1981), note 4 after *Heart of Atlanta* (upholding federal regulation of surface mining); *United Transp. Union v. Long Island R. R.,* 455 U.S. 678 (1982) (Long Island R.R. ruled not a "traditional government function").

[111] *Federal Energy Regulatory Comm'n v. Mississippi* (1982), fn. 121. *Equal Employment Opportunity Comm'n v. Wyoming,* 460 U.S. 226 (1983) (upholding federal ban on mandatory age retirement for state game wardens as not involving a "serious federal intrusion").

governmental functions appear manageable. We rejected the possibility of making immunity turn on a purely historical standard of "tradition" in *Long Island* [because] it prevents a court from accommodating changes in the historical functions of States [that] have resulted in a number of once-private functions like education being assumed by the States and their subdivisions. * * *

We believe, however, that there is a more fundamental problem at work [here]. The essence of our federal system is that within the realm of authority left open to them under the Constitution, the States must be equally free to engage in any activity that their citizens choose for the common weal. [Any] rule of state immunity that looks to the "traditional," "integral," or "necessary" nature of governmental functions inevitably invites an unelected federal judiciary to make decisions about which state policies it favors and which ones it dislikes.[112] [If] there are to be limits on the Federal Government's power to interfere with state functions—as undoubtedly there are—we must look elsewhere to find them. * * *

We doubt that courts ultimately can identify principled constitutional limitations on the scope of Congress' Commerce Clause powers over the States merely by relying on a priori definitions of state sovereignty. In part, this is because of the elusiveness of objective criteria for "fundamental" elements of state sovereignty, a problem we have witnessed in the search for "traditional governmental functions." There is, however, a more fundamental reason: [the] States unquestionably do "retai[n] a significant measure of sovereign authority." [But the] fact that the States remain sovereign as to all powers not vested in Congress or denied them by the Constitution offers no guidance about where the frontier between state and federal power lies. In short, we have no license to employ freestanding conceptions of state sovereignty when measuring congressional authority under the Commerce Clause. [In] *The Federalist* No. 39 (J. Madison), [a] different measure of state sovereignty emerges. [T]he principal means chosen by the Framers to ensure the role of the States in the federal system lies in the structure of the Federal Government itself. It is no novelty to observe that the composition of the Federal Government was designed in

---

[112] Consider Jesse H. Choper, *Judicial Review and the National Political Process* 202 (1980): "Whatever the judiciary's [special] competence in articulating the values and defining the scope of those constitutional clauses that declare individual rights, when the fundamental issue turns in large measure on the relative competence of different levels of government to deal with societal problems, the Court is no more inherently capable of correct judgment than its companion federal branches. Indeed, the judiciary may well be less capable, given both the highly pragmatic nature of federal-state questions and the forceful representation of the states (which are most directly affected by their resolution) in the national process of political decisionmaking." "The President and Congress are in a trustworthy position to view the issues involved in federalism disputes. In contrast, beneficiaries of individual rights, such as members of minority groups, are often not adequately represented in the deliberations of the political branches. A more active judicial role in personal rights cases is thus necessitated." Jesse H. Choper, *The Scope of National Power Vis-à-Vis the States; The Dispensability of Judicial Review*, 86 Yale L.J. 1552 (1977).

large part to protect the States from overreaching by Congress.[11] [The] States were vested with indirect influence over the House of Representatives and the Presidency by their control of electoral qualifications and their role in presidential elections. They were given more direct influence in the Senate, where each State received equal representation and each Senator was to be selected by the legislature of his State. The significance attached to the [former] is underscored by the prohibition of any constitutional amendment divesting a State of equal representation without the State's consent. Art. V.

---

[11] **[Ct's Note]** See, e.g., Jesse H. Choper, *Judicial Review and the National Political Process* 175 (1980); Herbert Wechsler, *The Political Safeguards of Federalism: The Role of the States in the Composition and Selection of the National Government,* 54 Colum.L.Rev. 543 (1954); D. Bruce La Pierre, *The Political Safeguards of Federalism, Redux: Intergovernmental Immunity and the States as Agents of the Nation,* 60 Wash.U.L.Q. 779 (1982).

[For the view that "the Wechsler-Choper thesis is wrong, at least in today's political world, insofar as it assumes that national elected officials safely can be made the exclusive enforcers of constitutional federalism guarantees," see Steven G. Calabresi, *"A Government of Limited and Enumerated Powers": In Defense of United States v. Lopez,* 94 Mich.L.Rev. 752 (1995). See also John O. McGinnis & Ilya Somin, *Federalism vs. States' Rights: A Defense of Judicial Review in a Federal System,* 99 Nw.U.L.Rev. 89 (2004) ("state officials may disregard the appropriate federalist distribution of power because of their own personal interests [or] the parochial interests of their states [while] federal officials who depend on parochial constituencies and interest groups for reelection support may often be unwilling to take the initiative to protect the free flow of interstate commerce against state-level protectionist interests").

[For the view that American political parties have "protected the states by making national officials politically dependent upon state and local party organizations," see Larry D. Kramer, *Putting the Politics Back into the Political Safeguards of Federalism,* 100 Colum.L.Rev. 215 (2000). Contra, Paul Frymer & Albert Yoon, *Political Parties, Representation, and Federal Safeguards,* 96 Nw.U.L.Rev. 977 (2002): "Today, national party leaders bear far less of a relationship to local or state party organizations, and instead shape the nomination process and raise the money to mount national campaigns that are in many ways divorced from local concerns and political pressures." Also, Saikrishna B. Prakash & John C. Yoo, *The Puzzling Persistence of Process-Based Federalism Theories,* 79 Tex.L.Rev. 1459 (2001): "Efforts to salvage the political-safeguards theory by relying on the national political parties prove equally unconvincing." But see Jessica Bulman-Pozen, *Partisan Federalism,* 127 Harv.L.Rev. 1077 (2014): "[A]t the turn of the twenty-first century, [that] states oppose federal policy because they are governed by individuals who affiliate with a different political party than do those in charge at the National [level] reveals that our contemporary federal system generates a check on the federal government"; Franita Tolson, *Benign Partisanship,* 88 Notre D.L.Rev. 395 (2012) ("the process of congressional districting [by state legislatures] is a political safeguard"). See generally Heather K. Gerken, *Federalism as the New Nationalism: An Overview, Symposium,* 123 Yale L. J. 1889 (2014), contending that modern federalism "can be a tool for improving" and entrenching national politics and national policymaking.

[Is there a difference between the "structure of the Federal Government" being "responsive to state and local interests" and being responsive to "state governmental institutions"? See Lynn A. Baker, *Putting the Safeguards Back into the Political Safeguards of Federalism,* 46 Vill.L.Rev. 951 (2001). See also Lynn A. Baker & Ernest A. Young, *Federalism and the Double Standard of Judicial Review,* 51 Duke L.J. 75 (2001). For responses to these points, see Choper, *supra* ("Identifying the 'Viewpoint' of a 'State' "), ("Defeat of Regional Interests in the National Political Process"). See also David J. Barron, *A Localist Critique of the New Federalism,* 51 Duke L.J. 377 (2001) ("central governments can protect local power [by encouraging] their role as components of a larger coordinated system that benefits from cooperative interlocal behavior"). Compare Bradford R. Clark, *Separation of Powers as a Safeguard of Federalism,* 79 Tex. L. Rev. 1321 (2001): The role of courts should be limited to assuring "strict adherence to federal lawmaking procedures" for enacting laws (Art. I, § 7), and treaties (Art. II, § 2), and amending the Constitution (Art. V). Cf. Carlos M. Vazquez, *The Separation of Powers as a Safeguard of Federalism,* 83 Notre D. L. Rev. 1601 (2008).]

The extent to which the structure of the Federal Government itself was relied on to insulate the interests of the States is evident in the views of the Framers. James Madison explained that the Federal Government "will partake sufficiently of the spirit [of the States], to be disinclined to invade the rights of the individual States, or the prerogatives of their governments." *The Federalist* No. 46.[113] * * *

The effectiveness of the federal political process in preserving the States' interests is apparent even today. [T]he States have been able to direct a substantial proportion of federal revenues into their own treasuries in the form of general and program-specific grants in aid.[114] [At] the same time [they] have been able to exempt themselves from a wide variety of obligations imposed by Congress under the Commerce Clause. For example, the Federal Power Act, the National Labor Relations Act, the Labor-Management Reporting and Disclosure Act, the Occupational Safety and Health Act, the Employee Retirement Insurance Security Act, and the Sherman Act all contain express or implied exemptions for States and their subdivisions. The fact that some federal statutes such as the FLSA extend general obligations to the States cannot obscure the extent to which the political position of the States in the federal system has served to minimize the burdens that the States bear under the Commerce Clause.[115]

[A]gainst this background, we are convinced that [a]ny substantive restraint on the exercise of Commerce Clause powers must find its justification in the procedural nature of this basic limitation, and it [must] be tailored to compensate for possible failings in the national political process. [W]e perceive nothing in the overtime and minimum-wage requirements of the FLSA, as applied to SAMTA, that is destructive of state [sovereignty]. SAMTA faces nothing more than the same minimum-wage and overtime obligations that hundreds of thousands of other employers, public as well as private, have to meet.[116] [The] political process

---

[113] For conflicting views on the "original understanding", compare John C. Yoo, *The Judicial Safeguards of Federalism,* 70 So.Cal.L.Rev. 1311 (1997): "The Framers believed judicial review would work in conjunction with the political process to maintain the proper balance between federal and state powers"; with Kramer, fn. 11 supra: "The Founding generation had a widely shared understanding of how Congress would be restrained [that] assigned no meaningful role to courts"; and responding, Prakash & Yoo, fn. 11 supra.

[114] Compare Mark Tushnet, *Judicial Enforcement of Federalist-Based Constitutional Limitations: Some Skeptical Comparative Observations,* 57 Emory L. J. 135 (2007): "It is not obvious that flows of money from the federal government to the states are a good measure; perhaps the states are being bribed to forgo assertions of authority that are more important according to a decent normative theory of federalism."

[115] See also Jesse H. Choper, *Federalism and Judicial Review: An Update,* 21 Hast.Con.L.Q. 577 (1994): "Perhaps the most dramatic confirmation came within eight months after *Garcia* when Congress amended the Fair Labor Standards Act to substantially reduce its financial impact on state and local governments."

[116] The Court noted that when FLSA changes subjected state mass-transit systems to higher costs the federal government simultaneously provided "substantial countervailing financial assistance."

ensures that laws that unduly burden the States will not be promulgated. * * * *National League of Cities* is overruled. * * *

JUSTICE POWELL, with whom THE CHIEF JUSTICE, JUSTICE REHNQUIST, and JUSTICE O'CONNOR join, dissenting.

[T]oday's decision effectively reduces the Tenth Amendment to meaningless rhetoric when Congress acts pursuant to the Commerce Clause. * * * *National League of Cities* [adopted] a familiar type of balancing test [which] explicitly weighed the seriousness of the problem addressed by the federal legislation [against] the effects of compliance on State sovereignty.[5]

* * * Members of Congress are elected from the various States, but once in office they are members of the federal government. Although the States participate in the Electoral College, this is hardly a reason to view the President as a representative of the States' interest against federal encroachment. We noted recently "the hydraulic pressure inherent within each of the separate Branches to exceed the outer limits of its [power]." *INS v. Chadha,* [Ch. 3, Sec. 2, II]. The Court offers no reason to think that this pressure will not operate when Congress seeks to invoke its powers under the Commerce Clause.[9]

[The] fact that Congress generally does not transgress constitutional limits on its power to reach State activities does not make judicial review any less necessary to rectify the cases in which it does do so.[117] [J]udicial

---

5   [Ct's Note] In undertaking such balancing, we have considered [the] strength of the federal interest in the challenged legislation and the impact of exempting the States from its reach. Central to our inquiry into the federal interest is how closely the challenged action implicates the central concerns of the Commerce Clause, viz., the promotion of a national economy and free trade among the states. [On] the other hand, we have also assessed the injury done to the States if forced to comply with federal Commerce Clause enactments.

9   [Ct's Note] * * * Professor Wechsler, whose seminal article in 1954 proposed the view adopted by the Court today, [wrote]: "National action [has] always been regarded as exceptional in our polity, an intrusion to be justified by some necessity, the special rather than the ordinary case." Not only is the premise of this view clearly at odds with the proliferation of national legislation over the past 30 years, but "a variety of structural and political changes in this century have combined to make Congress particularly *insensitive* to state and local values." Advisory Comm'n on Intergovernmental Relations, *Regulatory Federalism: Policy, Process, Impact and Reform* 50 (1984). The adoption of the Seventeenth Amendment (providing for direct election of senators), the weakening of political parties on the local level, and the rise of national media, among other things, have made Congress increasingly less representative of State and local interests, and more likely to be responsive to the demands of various national constituencies. [See] also Lewis B. Kaden, *Politics, Money, and State Sovereignty: The Judicial Role,* 79 Colum.L.Rev. 847 (1979). [Compare Robert A. Mikos, *The Populist Safeguards of Federalism,* 68 Ohio St. L. J. 1669 (2007): "[P]reviously neglected political science and legal research [suggest] that the political process is not so prone to aggrandize federal power."]

117 Consider Kennedy, J., joined by O'Connor, J., concurring in *Lopez,* Sec. 2, IV supra: "[T]he federal balance is too essential a part of our constitutional structure and plays too vital a role in securing freedom for us to admit [the Court's] inability to intervene when one or the other level of Government has tipped the scales too far. [T]he substantial element of political judgment in Commerce Clause matters leaves our institutional capacity to intervene more in doubt than when we decide cases, for instance, under the Bill of Rights even though clear and bright lines are often

enforcement of the Tenth Amendment is essential to maintaining the federal system. [Indeed,] the Court's view of federalism appears to relegate the States to precisely the trivial role that opponents of the Constitution feared they would occupy.

[Under] the balancing test [the] state interest [in this case] is compelling. The financial impact on States and localities of displacing their control over wages, hours, overtime regulations, pensions, and labor relations with their employees could have serious, as well as unanticipated, effects on state and local planning, budgeting, and the levying of taxes. [I]ntracity mass transit system [is] a classic example of the type of service traditionally provided by local government. It [is] indistinguishable in principle from the traditional services of providing and maintaining streets, public lighting, traffic control, water, and sewerage systems. Services of this kind are precisely those "with which citizens are more 'familiarly and minutely conversant.' " The *Federalist*, No. 46. State and local officials [know] that their constituents and the press respond to the adequacy, fair distribution, and cost of these services. It is this kind of state and local control and accountability that the Framers understood would insure the vitality and preservation of the federal system that the Constitution explicitly requires. * * *[118]

NOTES AND QUESTIONS

1. *"Failings in national political process."* SOUTH CAROLINA v. BAKER, fn. 105, per BRENNAN, J., ruled that the "national political process did not operate in a defective manner" when Congress banned certain types of state bonds by relying on anecdotal, not "concrete" evidence that such bonds were being used to conceal taxable income. For discussion of judicial remedies under a "process-oriented approach to federalism," see Andrzej Rapaczynski, *From Sovereignty to Process: The Jurisprudence of Federalism after Garcia,* 1985 Sup.Ct.Rev. 341.

2. *State "sovereignty."* What is the precise nature of the "state sovereignty" or "state interests" that federalism seeks to safeguard? Is it "the institutional interests of state governments," Deborah J. Merritt, *Three Faces of Federalism: Finding a Formula for the Future,* 47 Vand.L.Rev. 1563 (1994),

---

absent in the latter class of disputes. But our cases do not teach that we have no role at all in determining the meaning of the Commerce Clause."

[118] While joining the Powell and and separate O'Connor dissents, Rehnquist, J., withheld full acceptance of their "balancing" approaches and concluded: "[U]nder any one of these approaches the judgment in this case should be affirmed, and [the] principle that will, I am confident, in time again command the support of a majority of this Court."

For helpful commentaries on *Garcia* and *National League of Cities,* see Martha A. Field, *Garcia v. San Antonio Metropolitan Transit Authority, The Demise of a Misguided Doctrine,* 99 Harv.L.Rev. 84 (1985); William W. Van Alstyne, *The Second Death of Federalism,* 83 Mich.L.Rev. (1985); Robert F. Nagel, *Federalism as a Fundamental Value: National League of Cities in Perspective,* 1981 Sup.Ct.Rev. 81; Sotirios A. Barber, *National League of Cities v. Usery, New Meaning for the Tenth Amendment?* 1976 Sup.Ct.Rev. 161.

or the "viewpoint of the people of the state" Choper, fn. 11 in *Garcia*. To what extent does the answer to this question affect the issue in *Garcia*?

3. ***Alternative approach.*** GREGORY v. ASHCROFT, 501 U.S. 452 (1991), per O'CONNOR, J., advanced many of the considerations in the *Garcia* dissent in refusing to apply the federal Age Discrimination in Employment Act to a state judge required by state law to retire at 70, by importing a "plain statement" rule from Eleventh Amendment cases: "If Congress intends to alter the 'usual constitutional balance between the States and the Federal Government' it must make its intention to do so unmistakably clear in the language of the statute. *Atascadero State Hospital v. Scanlon,* 473 U.S. 234(1985)." Of the five justices in the *Garcia* majority, the four remaining on the Court dissented from this reasoning because it "directly contravenes our decision in *Garcia*." For a critique of the plain statement rule, see Laurence H. Tribe, *Clear Statement Rules, Federalism and Congressional Regulation of States,* 107 Harv.L.Rev. 1941 (1994).

PRINTZ V. UNITED STATES
521 U.S. 898, 117 S.Ct. 2365, 138 L.Ed.2d 914 (1997).

JUSTICE SCALIA delivered the opinion of the Court.

[Under the] Brady Handgun Violence Prevention Act[, r]egulated firearms dealers are required to forward Brady Forms not to a federal officer or employee, but to the CLEOs ["chief law enforcement officers"], whose obligation [is] to make "reasonable efforts" within five days to determine whether the sales reflected in the forms are lawful. While the CLEOs are subjected to no federal requirement that they prevent the sales determined to be unlawful (it is perhaps assumed that their state-law duties will require prevention or apprehension), they are empowered to grant, in effect, waivers of the federally prescribed 5-day waiting period for handgun purchases by notifying the gun dealers that they have no reason to believe the transactions would be illegal.

The petitioners here object to being pressed into federal service * * * . Because there is no constitutional text speaking to this precise question, the answer to the CLEOs' challenge must be sought in historical understanding and practice, in the structure of the Constitution, and in the jurisprudence of this Court.

[The Court concluded that the relevant historical practice "tends to negate" Congress' power to impose federal responsibilities on state officers without the States' consent. "[E]nactments of the early Congresses [contain] no evidence of an assumption that the Federal Government may command the States' executive power in the absence of a particularized constitutional authorization," such as the Extradition Clause of Art IV, Sec. 2."][119]

* * * We turn next to consideration of the structure of the Constitution * * * .[120] We have set forth the historical record in more detail elsewhere, see *New York v. United States,* [505 U.S. 144 (1992), per O'Connor, J. (discussed below)], and need not repeat it here. It suffices to repeat the conclusion: "The Framers explicitly chose a Constitution that confers upon Congress the power to regulate individuals, not States." [This] separation of the two spheres is one of the Constitution's structural protections of liberty. [The] power of the Federal Government would be augmented immeasurably if it were able to impress into its service—and at no cost to itself—the police officers of the 50 States. [F]ederal control of state officers would [also] have an effect upon [the] separation and equilibration of powers between the three branches of the Federal Government itself. The Constitution [says] the President "shall take Care that the Laws be faithfully executed," personally and through officers whom he appoints. [The] Brady Act effectively transfers this responsibility to thousands of CLEOs in the 50 States, who are left to implement the program without meaningful Presidential control. [T]he power of the President would be subject to reduction, if Congress could act as effectively without the President as with him, by simply requiring state officers to execute its laws.[12] * * *

[Recent] opinions of ours have made clear that the Federal Government may not compel the States to implement, by legislation or executive action, federal regulatory programs. [*Hodel*, note 4 after *Katzenbach v. McClung*] concluded that the Surface Mining Control and Reclamation Act of 1977 [merely] made compliance with federal standards a precondition to continued state regulation in an otherwise pre-empted field. In *FERC* [*v. Mississippi*, 456 U.S. 742 (1982),] we construed the most troubling provisions of the Public Utility Regulatory Policies Act of 1978 to

---

[119] The dissents argued: "Absent even a modicum of textual foundation for its judicially crafted constitutional rule, there should be a presumption that if the Framers had actually intended such a rule, at least one of them would have mentioned it."

[120] For the view that *Printz* "embraces [a] formalist approach to interpreting [the] Constitution [and] eschewed a more 'functionalist' approach [in] that it pointedly avoided a sensitive assessment of whether such commandeering undermines any of the diverse values or purposes thought to underlie our various divisions of governmental authority, either at its founding or today," see Evan H. Caminker, *Printz, State Sovereignty, and the Limits of Formalism,* 1997 Sup.Ct.Rev. 199, 201. See also Erwin Chemerinsky, *Formalism and Functionalism in Federalism Analysis,* 19 Ga. St. U.L.Rev. 959 (1997).

[12] **[Ct's Note]** There is not, as the dissent believes, "tension" between the proposition that impressing state police officers into federal service will massively augment federal power, and the proposition that it will also sap the power of the Federal Presidency. It is quite possible to have a more powerful Federal Government that is, by reason of the destruction of its Executive unity, a less efficient one. The dissent is correct that control by the unitary Federal Executive is also sacrificed when States voluntarily administer federal programs, but the condition of voluntary state participation significantly reduces the ability of Congress to use this device as a means of reducing the power of the Presidency.

contain only the "command" that state agencies "consider" federal standards.[121] * * *

When we were at last confronted squarely with a federal statute that unambiguously required the States to enact or administer a federal regulatory program, our decision should have come as no surprise. At issue in *New York* [were] the so-called "take title" provisions of the Low-Level Radioactive Waste Policy Amendments Act of 1985, which required States either to enact legislation providing for the disposal of radioactive waste generated within their borders, or to take title to, and possession of, the waste—effectively requiring the States either to legislate pursuant to Congress's directions, or to implement an administrative solution. We concluded that Congress could constitutionally require the states to do neither. [122] * * *

The Government contends that *New York* is distinguishable on the following ground: unlike the "take title" provisions invalidated there, [the] Brady Act does not require state legislative or executive officials to make policy. [But is] it really true that there is no policymaking involved in deciding, for example, what "reasonable efforts" shall be expended to conduct a background check? It may well satisfy the Act for a CLEO to direct that (a) no background checks will be conducted that divert personnel time from pending felony investigations, and (b) no background check will be permitted to consume more than one-half hour of an officer's time.[123] [Even assuming,] that the Brady Act leaves no "policymaking" discretion with the States, we fail to see how that improves rather than worsens the intrusion upon state sovereignty. Preservation of the States as independent and autonomous political entities is arguably less undermined

---

[121] *FERC*, per Blackmun, J., emphasized that since "Congress could have preempted the field of utility regulation, at least insofar as private rather than state activity is concerned, [the Act] should not be invalid simply because, out of deference to state authority, Congress adopted a less intrusive scheme and allowed the States to continue regulating in the area on the condition that they *consider* the suggested federal standards."

[122] For the view that the original understanding supports this "anti-commandeering" conclusion, see Saikrishna B. Prakash, *Field Office Federalism*, 79 Va.L.Rev. 1957 (1993). Contra, H. Jefferson Powell, *The Oldest Question of Constitutional Law*, 79 Va.L.Rev. 633 (1993); Evan H. Caminker, *State Sovereignty and Subordinacy: May Congress Commandeer State Officers to Implement Federal Law?*, 95 Colum.L.Rev. 1001 (1995); Wesley J. Campbell, *Commandeering and Constitutional Change,* 122 Yale L.J. 1104 (2013) ("historical evidence suggests" that as a concession "to the opponents of centralization, [the] federal government would generally rely on state officers rather than create new federal positions"); Erik M. Jensen & Jonathan L. Entin, *Commandeering, The Tenth Amendment, and the Federal Requisition Power: New York v. United States Revisited*, 15 Const. Comm. 355 (1998).

[123] Dissenting in *FERC*, O'Connor, J., joined by Burger, C.J. and Rehnquist, J., argued that: "the power to make decisions and set [policy] embraces more than the ultimate authority to enact laws; it also includes the power to decide which proposals are most worthy of consideration, the order in which they should be taken up, and the precise form in which they should be debated. [The Act] intrudes upon all of these functions. It chooses twelve proposals, forcing their consideration even if the state agency deems other ideas more worthy of immediate attention. [By] taxing the limited resources of these commissions, and decreasing their ability to address local regulatory ills, [the Act] directly impairs the power of state utility commissions to discharge their traditional functions efficiently and effectively."

by requiring them to make policy in certain fields than [by] "reduc[ing] [them] to puppets of a ventriloquist Congress." * * *

The Government purports to find support for its proffered distinction of *New York* [in] *Testa v. Katt,* 330 U.S. 386 (1947), [which] stands for the proposition that state courts cannot refuse to apply federal law—a conclusion mandated by the terms of the Supremacy Clause. [T]hat says nothing about whether state executive officers must administer federal law. * * *

The Government also maintains that requiring state officers to perform discrete, ministerial tasks specified by Congress does not violate the principle of *New York* because it does not diminish the accountability of state or federal officials.[124] [But by] forcing state governments to absorb the financial burden of implementing a federal regulatory program, Members of Congress can take credit for "solving" problems without having to ask their constituents to pay for the solutions with higher federal taxes. And even when the States are not forced to absorb the [costs,] they are still put in the position of taking the blame for its burdensomeness and for its defects. Under the present law, for example, it will be the CLEO [not] some federal official, who will be blamed for any error (even one in the designated federal database) that causes a purchaser to be mistakenly rejected.

[The] Brady Act, the dissent asserts, is different [from] *New York* because the former is addressed to individuals—namely CLEOs—while the latter were directed to the State itself. [But while] the Brady Act is directed to "individuals," it is directed to them in their official capacities * * * .

Finally, the Government puts forward a cluster of arguments [under] the heading: "The Brady Act serves very important purposes, is most efficiently administered by CLEOs during the interim period, and places a minimal and only temporary burden upon state officers." [Assuming] the mentioned factors were true, they might be relevant if we were evaluating whether the incidental application to the States of a federal law of general applicability excessively interfered with the functioning of state

---

124 *New York* reasoned that "where the Federal Government compels States to regulate, the accountability of both state and federal officials is diminished. If the citizens of New York, for example, do not consider that making provision for the disposal of radioactive waste is in their best interest, they may elect state officials who share their view. That view can always be preempted under the Supremacy Clause if is contrary to the national view, but in such a case it is the Federal Government that makes the decision in full view of the public, and it will be federal officials that suffer the consequences if the decision turns out to be detrimental or unpopular. But where the Federal Government directs the States to regulate, it may be state officials who will bear the brunt of public disapproval, while the federal officials who devised the regulatory program may remain insulated from the electoral ramifications of their decision. [See] D. Bruce La Pierre, *Political Accountability in the National Political Process—The Alternative to Judicial Review of Federalism Issues,* 80 Nw.U.L.Rev. 577, 639–665 (1985)." Compare Thomas O. Sargentich, *The Rehnquist Court and State Sovereignty: Limitations of the New Federalism,* 12 Widener L.J. 459 (2003): "If a state official follows federal law because of preemption, an affected citizen would be likely to blame the state official for any resulting harm to him or her. There is no difference, with respect to laying blame, between this situation and that of a 'commandeering' federal statute."

governments. See, e.g., *Fry; National League of Cities*. But where, as here, it is the whole object of the law to direct the functioning of the state executive, and hence to compromise the structural framework of dual sovereignty, such a "balancing" analysis is inappropriate.[17] * * *

JUSTICE O'CONNOR, concurring.

[T]he Court appropriately refrains from deciding [whether] purely ministerial reporting requirements imposed by Congress on state and local authorities pursuant to its Commerce Clause powers are similarly invalid. See, e.g., 42 U.S.C. § 5779(a) (requiring state and local law enforcement agencies to report cases of missing children to the Department of Justice).[125]

JUSTICE STEVENS, with whom JUSTICE SOUTER, JUSTICE GINSBURG, and JUSTICE BREYER join, dissenting. * * *

[S]ince the ultimate issue is one of power, we must consider its implications in times of national emergency. Matters such as the enlistment of air raid wardens, the administration of a military draft, the mass inoculation of children to forestall an epidemic, or perhaps the threat of an international terrorist, may require a national response before federal personnel can be made available to respond. If the Constitution empowers Congress and the President to make an appropriate response, is there anything in the Tenth Amendment [that] forbids the enlistment of state officers to make that response effective? * * *

Unlike the First Amendment, which prohibits the enactment of a category of laws that would otherwise be authorized by Article I, the Tenth Amendment [does] not purport to limit the scope or the effectiveness of the exercise of powers that are delegated to Congress.[126] Thus, the Amendment

---

[17] **[Ct's Note]** The dissent observes that "Congress could require private persons, such as hospital executives or school administrators, to provide arms merchants with relevant information about a prospective purchaser's fitness to own a weapon," and that "the burden on police officers [imposed by the Brady Act] would be permissible if a similar burden were also imposed on private parties with access to relevant data." That is undoubtedly true, but [t]he Brady Act does not merely require CLEOs to report information in their private possession. It requires them to provide information that belongs to the State and is available to them only in their official capacity; and to conduct investigations in their official capacity, by examining databases and records that only state officials have access to. In other words, the suggestion that extension of this statute to private citizens would eliminate the constitutional problem posits the impossible.

[125] The Court commented that "federal statutes [which] require only the provision of information to the Federal Government, do not involve the precise issue before us [here]." Thomas, J., who joined the Court's opinion, also concurred.

[126] *New York*, however, explained that "the Tenth Amendment confirms that the power of the Federal Government is subject to limits that may, in a given instance, reserve power to the States. [It] thus directs us to determine [whether] an incident of state sovereignty is protected by a limitation on an Article I power."

The debate concerning the relationship between the Tenth Amendment and the "essential postulates" (*Printz* majority) of state sovereignty is helpfully explored in Tribe 3d ed. For the view that the Guarantee Clause (Art. IV, § 4) "might plausibly be invoked [for] the proposition that the Constitution recognizes in the National Government a duty, running directly 'to every State in this Union' rather than to individuals, to respect the state's most fundamental structural choices

provides no support for a rule that immunizes local officials from obligations that might be imposed on ordinary citizens.[2] [The] majority expresses special concern that were its rule not adopted the Federal Government would be able to avail itself of the services of state government officials "at no cost to itself." But this [problem] of imposing so-called "unfunded mandates" on the States has been identified and meaningfully addressed by Congress in recent legislation.[18] * * *

Perversely, [by] limiting the ability of the Federal Government to enlist state officials in the implementation of its programs, the Court creates incentives for the National Government to aggrandize itself. In the name of State's rights, the majority would have the Federal Government create vast national bureaucracies to implement its policies.[127]

Finally, the majority provides an incomplete explanation of our decision in *Testa* [which] unanimously held that state courts of appropriate jurisdiction must occupy themselves adjudicating claims brought by private litigants under the federal Emergency Price Control Act of 1942,

---

as to how its people are to participate in and shape the processes of their own governance," see id. See also Merritt, note 2 after *Garcia*.

    [2]   **[Ct's Note]** Recognizing the force of the argument, the Court suggests that this reasoning is in error because—even if it is responsive to the submission that the Tenth Amendment roots the principle set forth by the majority today—it does not answer the possibility that the Court's holding can be rooted in a "principle of state sovereignty" mentioned nowhere in the constitutional text. As a ground for invalidating important federal legislation, this argument is remarkably weak. The majority's further claim that, while the Brady Act may be legislation "necessary" to Congress' execution of its undisputed Commerce Clause authority to regulate firearms sales, it is nevertheless not "proper" because it violates state sovereignty, is wholly circular. [Our] ruling in *New York* that the Commerce Clause does not provide Congress the authority to require States to enact legislation—a power that affects States far closer to the core of their sovereign authority— does nothing to support the majority's unwarranted extension of that reasoning today.

    [18]   **[Ct' Note]** The majority also makes the more general claim that requiring state officials to carry out federal policy causes states to "tak[e] the blame" for failed programs. The Court cites no empirical authority to support the proposition. [Unlike] state legislators, local government executive officials routinely take action in response to a variety of sources of authority: local ordinance, state law, and federal law. It doubtless may therefore require some sophistication to discern under which authority an executive official is acting. [But] the majority's rule neither creates nor alters this basic truth. The problem is of little real consequence in any event, because to the extent that a particular action proves politically unpopular, we may be confident that elected officials charged with implementing it will be quite clear to their constituents where the source of the misfortune lies. These cases demonstrate the point. Sheriffs Printz and Mack have made public statements, including their decisions to serve as plaintiffs in these actions, denouncing the Brady Act. [See also Mark Tushnet, *Globalization and Federalism in a Post-Printz World*, 36 Tulsa L.J. 11 (2000): "Preemption is an exercise of a power of negative commandeering. If affirmative commandeering is constitutionally impermissible, why is negative commandeering constitutional?"]

    [127] White, J., joined by Blackmun and Stevens, JJ., dissenting in *New York*, made a similar argument: "The ultimate irony of the decision today is that in its formalistically rigid obeisance to 'federalism,' the Court gives Congress fewer incentives to defer to the wishes of state officials in achieving local solutions to local problems. This legislation was a classic example of Congress acting as arbiter among the States in their attempts to accept responsibility for managing a problem of grave import. The States urged the National Legislature not to impose [a] solution to the country's low-level radioactive waste management problems. [By] invalidating the measure designed to ensure compliance for recalcitrant States, such as New York, the Court upsets the delicate compromise achieved among the States." See generally Neil S. Siegel, *Commandeering and Its Alternatives: A Federalism Perspective*, 59 Vand. L. Rev. 1629 (2006).

regardless of how otherwise crowded their dockets might be with state-law matters. That is a much greater imposition on state sovereignty than the Court's characterization of the [case]. Even if the Court were correct in its suggestion that it was the reference to judges in the Supremacy Clause [that] dictated the result in *Testa*, the Court's implied expressio unius argument that the Framers therefore did not intend to permit the enlistment of other state officials is implausible. [The] notion that the Framers would have had no reluctance to "press state judges into federal service" against their will but would have regarded the imposition of a similar—indeed, far lesser—burden on town constables as an intolerable affront to principles of state sovereignty can only be considered perverse. * * *

JUSTICE BREYER, with whom JUSTICE STEVENS joins, dissenting.

[T]he fact that there is not more precedent—that direct federal assignment of duties to state officers is not common—likely reflects, not a widely shared belief that any such assignment is incompatible with basic principles of federalism, but rather a widely shared practice of assigning such duties in other ways. See, e.g., *Dole* (spending power); *New York* (general statutory duty); *FERC* (pre-emption). Thus, there is neither need nor reason to find in the Constitution an absolute principle, the inflexibility of which poses a surprising and technical obstacle to the enactment of a law that Congress believed necessary to solve an important national problem.* * *[128]

NOTES AND QUESTIONS

1.   *Generally applicable laws.* (a) How persuasive is the *Printz* (and *New York*) distinction of *Garcia* on the ground that it involves a "federal law of general applicability"? Consider La Pierre, fn. 11 in *Garcia*: "When a regulation applies both to state and private activity, the political checks on Congress' power to regulate private activity provide vicarious protection for state interests and make Congress politically accountable." See also Vicki C. Jackson, *Narratives of Federalism: Of Continuities and Comparative Constitutional Experience*, 51 Duke L.J. 223 (2001) (applicability to private entities *and* to *federal government*). For the view that "*New York* and *Printz* do not establish a narrow anti-commandeering rule, but instead prohibit laws that target state and local governments for unique burdens," see Thomas H. Odom & Marc R. Baluda, *The Development of Process-Oriented Federalism: Harmonizing the Supreme Court's Tenth Amendment Jurisprudence from Garcia Through Printz*, 31 Urb.Law. 993 (1999). For the view that *New York* "provides no explanation for why such generally applicable laws burden political accountability less than laws that apply only to governmental

---

[128] Souter, J., dissented, noting that "I do not read any of *The Federalist* material as requiring the conclusion that Congress could require administrative support without an obligation to pay fair value for it."

entities," see Roderick M. Hills, Jr., *The Political Economy of Cooperative Federalism: Why State Autonomy Makes Sense and "Dual Sovereignty" Doesn't*, 96 Mich.L.Rev. 813 (1998).

(b) ***Definitional problems.*** Do you agree that Congress "could not impose a minimum wage on the state governor, state legislators, or state judges, because these state workers have no private counterparts"? Ronald D. Rotunda, *The Powers of Congress Under Section 5 of the Fourteenth Amendment After City of Boerne v. Flores*, 32 Ind.L.Rev. 163 (1998). If the minimum wage applied to corporate presidents and boards of directors, might they be "private counterparts"? See further *Reno v. Condon* (last ¶), below.

2.   ***Purely ministerial reporting.*** What result after *Printz* in respect to such requirements? Consider Tribe 3d ed.: "Perhaps requiring state officials to *gather* information would be tantamount to requiring them to play a role in administering a federal program, whereas merely requiring the *reporting* of pre-existing information would not be." Compare Jackson, fn. 65: "Given the 'separate sphere' of 'state autonomy' model of sovereignty on which *Printz* is based, the model's logic—that Congress had no power (outside of constitutionally specified exigencies) to compel state or local governments to act—would argue against the constitutionality of many such laws." Contrast Tribe 3d ed.: "Consider [the] provision of the Brady Act requiring CLEOs to destroy Brady forms if they find no reason to deem the would-be-purchaser ineligible to receive a handgun—a provision whose constitutionality the Court [did not] decide. If expressed as a command that local officials exert their sovereign power to destroy certain forms, this requirement would violate the anticommandeering principle; but if expressed as a prohibition against retention of certain forms by anyone, including private citizens, the requirement would seem constitutionally unobjectionable. It is difficult to see, then, why the strict, exceptionless rule of *Printz* is superior to a judicial approach that would permit realistic appraisal of the operation of federal requirements on states and of the extent to which objectionable commandeering has gratuitously taken place."

3.   ***Scope of "anti-commandeering" principle.*** (a) Can Congress make it a crime for state and local officials to *engage* in certain conduct (assuming a substantial effect on interstate commerce), such as engaging in corrupt government practices? See George D. Brown, *Should Federalism Shield Corruption?—Mail Fraud, State Law and Post-Lopez Analysis*, 82 Corn.L.Rev. 225 (1997). Can Congress make it a crime to *fail* to take certain action, such as investigating government corruption? See generally Matthew D. Adler & Seth F. Kreimer, *The New Etiquette of Federalism: New York, Printz, and Yeskey*, 1999 Sup.Ct.Rev. 71.

(b)   RENO v. CONDON, 528 U.S. 141 (2000), per REHNQUIST, C.J., unanimously upheld Congress' power under the Commerce Clause to pass the Driver's Privacy Protection Act, which bars state motor vehicle departments from disclosing (or selling) personal information (such as name, address, telephone number, vehicle description, Social Security number, medical information, and photograph) required for a driver's license or car registration: "[T]he vehicle information [is] used by insurers, manufacturers, direct marketers, and others engaged in interstate commerce [and] by various public and private entities for matters related to interstate motoring. * * *

"We agree [that] the DPPA's provisions will require time and effort on the part of state employees ["to learn and apply its complex provisions"], but reject the State's argument that the DPPA violates the principles laid down in either *New York* or *Printz*. [Such] 'commandeering' [is] an inevitable consequence of regulating ["States acting purely as commercial sellers."] That a State wishing to engage in certain activity must take administrative and sometimes legislative action to comply with federal standards regulating that activity is a commonplace that presents no constitutional defect.[129]

"Like the statute [in *South Carolina v. Baker*, note 1 after *Garcia*, which "prohibited States from issuing unregistered bonds"], the DPPA does not require the States in their sovereign capacity to regulate their own citizens. The DPPA regulates the States as the owners of databases. It does not require the South Carolina Legislature to enact any laws or regulations, and it does not require state officials to assist in the enforcement of federal statutes regulating private individuals. We accordingly conclude that the DPPA is consistent with the constitutional principles enunciated in *New York* and *Printz*."[130]

Nor does the DPPA "regulate the States exclusively. [It] regulates [the] States as initial suppliers of the information in interstate commerce and private resellers or rediscloseres of that information in commerce."

Can *Condon* be squared with fn. 17 in *Printz*? Can it be squared with *Printz's* rejection of any "balancing analysis"? See Odom & Baluda, note 1 supra (DPPA invalid under *Printz* analysis). Reconsider note 2 supra.

(c) JINKS v. RICHLAND COUNTY, 538 U.S. 456 (2003), per SCALIA, J., unanimously upheld a federal statute—enacted pursuant to Congress' Art I, §§ 8, cl. 9 power to "constitute" lower federal courts—providing that the state statute of limitations will be tolled on state law claims, that are joined to federal causes of action filed in federal court, if the federal court declines to exercise jurisdiction over those claims which then must be refiled in state

---

[129] Is this an effort to resurrect the *National League of Cities* "traditional government functions" approach, also evidenced in *Lopez* and *Morrison* ("areas of traditional state concern")? See Choper note 3(b) after *Morrison*.

[130] Compare Sargentich, fn. 124: "[T]he statute in *Printz* [could] readily be described as prohibiting the issuance of permits for handguns without background checks. The line between regulation that impermissibly 'commandeers' states and regulation that acceptably prohibits state action is thus fundamentally manipulable." See also Michael C. Dorf & Barry Friedman, *Shared Constitutional Interpretation*, 2000 S.Ct.Rev. 61: "Both the background check requirement in *Printz* and the prohibition on the release of driver information in *Condon* take the form of commands to state actors, and both laws have a substantial regulatory impact on private parties: In *Printz* the effect is to delay or deny permission for a seller and purchaser of a handgun to complete their transaction; in *Condon* the effect is to prevent commercial advertisers and others from obtaining drivers' private information." May the decisions be reconciled "in terms of acts and omissions"? Id.

court: Although "we need not (and do not) hold that Congress has unlimited power to regulate practice and procedure in state courts," state statutes of limitations do not "fall into the category of 'procedure' immune from congressional regulation."

4. *State "consent."* The *New York* dissenters described the extended negotiations among the states that led to the 1985 Act and viewed New York's participation and its actions under the Act as "approval of the interstate agreement process embodied in [the] Act" within the meaning of the Interstate Compact Clause. The majority responded: "The Constitution does not protect the sovereignty of States for the benefit of the States or state governments as abstract political entities, or even for the benefit of the public officials governing the [States. 'Rather,] federalism secures to citizens the liberties that derive from the diffusion of sovereign power.' [State] officials thus cannot consent to the enlargement of the powers of Congress beyond those enumerated in the Constitution." How does the issue in note 2 after *Garcia* bear on this dispute?

5. *Alternative sources of national power.* (a) *Spending.* New York made clear that there are "a variety of methods, short of outright coercion, by which Congress may urge a State to adopt a legislative program consistent with federal interests. [First,] under Congress' spending power, 'Congress may attach conditions on the receipt of federal funds.' *Dole.*" Could Congress condition receipt of some portion of *existing* federal law enforcement assistance funds on CLEOs performing background checks? For the view that, as in *New York*, "conditional spending [programs] undermine the accountability of state officeholders [and should be subject to challenge under the Guarantee Clause]," see Dennis Murashko, *Accountability and Constitutional Federalism: Reconsidering Federal Conditional Spending Programs in Light of Democratic Political Theory,* 101 Nw. U. L. Rev. 931 (2007).

(b) *Treaty.* Do the "essential postulates of state sovereignty" impose *New York* and *Printz*-like limits on the treaty power as well as on Art. I powers— for example, as to the Vienna Convention's requirement that state police notify accused foreign nationals of their right to contact their consulates?[131] Are there reasons for distinguishing the treaty power from domestic lawmaking powers? See Janet R. Carter, Note, *Commandeering Under the Treaty Power,* 76 N.Y.U.L.Rev. 598 (2001) (yes). Consider Carlos M. Vasquez, *Breard, Printz, and the Treaty Power,* 70 U.Colo.L.Rev. 1317 (1999): "As a general matter, treaties address the rights and obligations of governments vis-à-vis each other. [Even] when a treaty's ultimate object is the protection or regulation of individuals, it typically accomplishes that goal by placing obligations, whether of an affirmative or negative character, on the states-parties. [Thus,] an anticommandeering rule that bars the imposition of obligations on states that are not also imposed on private individuals would invalidate the typical rather than the odd treaty [and could not] plausibly apply to the treaty power."

---

[131] This provision was before the Court in *Medellin v. Dretke,* 544 U.S. 660 (2005), but not addressed on the merits.

Accord, Martin S. Flaherty, *Are We to be a Nation? Federal Power vs. "States' Rights" in Foreign Affairs*, 70 U.Colo.L.Rev. 1277 (1999). Contra, Tribe 3d ed.

CHAPTER 3

DISTRIBUTION OF FEDERAL POWERS: SEPARATION OF POWERS

■ ■ ■

This chapter addresses the distribution of powers *within* the federal government. Its principal concern is how the Constitution's text and structure, and the separation-of-powers and checks-and-balances concepts they embody, define the powers of Congress and the Executive. A related issue is the extent to which a power expressly granted to one branch must be exercised to avoid interference with the power of another branch. These matters are considered in this chapter's four sections: (1) presidential action affecting "congressional powers"; (2) congressional action affecting "presidential powers"; (3) executive privilege and immunity; and (4) impeachment of the president.

1. PRESIDENTIAL ACTION AFFECTING "CONGRESSIONAL" POWERS

I. INTERNAL MATTERS: DOMESTIC LAWMAKING

YOUNGSTOWN SHEET & TUBE CO. V. SAWYER
[THE STEEL SEIZURE CASE]
343 U.S. 579, 72 S.Ct. 863, 96 L.Ed. 1153 (1952).

JUSTICE BLACK delivered the opinion of the Court. * * *

We are asked to decide whether [President Truman] was acting within his constitutional power when he issued an order directing the Secretary of Commerce [Sawyer] to take possession of and operate most of the Nation's steel mills. The mill owners argue that the President's order amounts to lawmaking, a legislative function which the Constitution has expressly confided to the Congress and not to the President. The Government's position is that the order was made on findings of the President and that his action was necessary to avert a national catastrophe which would inevitably result from a stoppage of steel production [during the Korean War].

[When efforts to settle a labor dispute—including reference to the Federal Wage Stabilization Board—failed, the union called a nationwide strike to begin April 9, 1952. Finding that the strike would jeopardize national defense, a few hours before the strike deadline the President issued Executive Order 10340, directing the Secretary of Commerce to take possession of most of the country's steel mills and keep them operating. The President sent a message to Congress reporting his actions on the next day. On May 3, the Court granted direct review of a U.S. District Court order that enjoined the Secretary's possession of the steel mills, and set argument for May 12. On June 2, the Court upheld the injunction, ruling the seizure unconstitutional.]

The President's power, if any, to issue the order must stem either from an act of Congress or from the Constitution itself.

[T]he use of the seizure [to] prevent work stoppage was not only unauthorized by any congressional enactment; prior to this controversy, Congress had refused to adopt that method of settling labor disputes. When the [Labor Management Relations Act of 1947] was under [consideration], Congress rejected an amendment which would have authorized such governmental seizures in cases of emergency. [Instead], the plan sought to bring about settlements by use of the customary devices of mediation, conciliation, investigation by boards of inquiry, and public reports. In some instances temporary injunctions were authorized to provide cooling-off periods. All this failing, unions were left free to strike after a secret vote by employees * * * .[1]

It is clear that if the President had authority to issue the order he did, it must be found in some provision of the Constitution. [The] contention is that presidential power should be implied from the aggregate of his powers under the Constitution. Particular reliance is placed on provisions in Article II which say that "The executive Power shall be vested in a President"; that "he shall take Care that the Laws be faithfully executed"; and that he "shall be Commander in Chief of the Army and Navy of the United States."

* * * We cannot with faithfulness to our constitutional system hold that the Commander in Chief of the Armed Forces has the ultimate power as such to take possession of private property in order to keep labor disputes from stopping production. This is a job for the Nation's lawmakers, not for its military authorities. [In] the framework of our Constitution, the President's power to see that the laws are faithfully executed refutes the idea that he is to be a lawmaker. The Constitution limits his functions in the lawmaking process to the recommending of laws he thinks wise and the vetoing of laws he thinks bad. And the Constitution is neither silent nor equivocal about who shall make laws which the

---

[1] Sections 206–210 of the Act provided that "[w]henever in the opinion of the President [a] threatened or actual strike [will], if permitted to occur or to continue, imperil the national health or safety," on the President's initiative, the strike could be enjoined while a board of inquiry studied the dispute, but that the strike could continue after 80 days if the employees reject the employer's last offer of settlement. The President was then obligated under the Act to report on the emergency to Congress.

President is to execute. The first section of the first article says that "All legislative Powers herein granted shall be vested in a Congress of the United States." * * *

The President's order does not direct that a congressional policy be executed in a manner prescribed by Congress—it directs that a presidential policy be executed in a manner prescribed by the President. The preamble of the order itself, like that of many statutes, sets out reasons why the President believes certain policies should be adopted, proclaims these policies as rules of conduct to be followed, and again, like a statute, authorizes a government official to promulgate additional rules and regulations. [The] power of Congress to adopt such public policies as those proclaimed by the order is beyond question. It can authorize the taking of private property for public use. It can make laws regulating the relationships between employers and employees, prescribing rules designed to settle labor disputes, and fixing wages and working conditions in certain fields of our economy. The Constitution did not subject this lawmaking power of Congress to presidential or military supervision or control.

It is said that other Presidents without congressional authority have taken possession of private business enterprises in order to settle labor disputes. But even if this be true, Congress has not thereby lost its exclusive constitutional authority to make [laws].

Affirmed.

JUSTICE FRANKFURTER, concurring in the judgment and opinion of the Court.

Although the considerations relevant to the legal enforcement of the principle of separation of powers seem to me more complicated and flexible than may appear from what Mr. Justice Black has written, I join his opinion because I thoroughly agree with the application of the principle to this case. * * *

[We] must [put] to one side consideration of what powers the President would have had if there had been no legislation whatever bearing on the authority asserted by the seizure, or if the seizure had been only for a short, explicitly temporary period, to be terminated automatically unless Congressional approval were given. These and other questions, like or unlike, are not now here. [It] cannot be contended that the President would have had power to issue this order had Congress explicitly negated such authority in formal legislation. [And Congress's decision reflected in the Labor Management Relations Act of 1947 should be given the same effect, since] Congress has expressed its will to withhold this power from the President as though it had said so in so many words. [It has] said to the President, "You may not seize. Please report to us and ask for seizure power if you think it is needed in a specific [situation]."

[The] content of the three authorities of government is not to be derived from an abstract analysis. The areas are partly interacting, not wholly disjointed. The Constitution is a framework for government. Therefore the way the framework has consistently operated fairly establishes that it has operated according to its true nature. Deeply embedded traditional ways of conducting government cannot supplant the Constitution or legislation, but they give meaning to the words of a text. [But the] list of executive assertions of the power of seizure in circumstances comparable to the present reduces to three in the six-month period from June to December of 1941. [T]hese three isolated instances do not add up [to] the kind of executive construction of the Constitution [necessary to justify the action here]. Nor do they come to us sanctioned by the long-continued acquiescence of Congress* * *.

JUSTICE JACKSON, concurring in the judgment and opinion of the Court.

The actual art of governing under our Constitution does not and cannot conform to judicial definitions of the power of any of its branches based on isolated clauses or even single Articles torn from context. While the Constitution diffuses power the better to secure liberty, it also contemplates that practice will integrate the dispersed powers into a workable government. It enjoins upon its branches separateness but interdependence, autonomy but reciprocity. Presidential powers are not fixed but fluctuate, depending upon their disjunction or conjunction with those of Congress. We may well begin by a somewhat over-simplified grouping of practical situations in which a President may doubt, or others may challenge, his powers * * *.

1. When the President acts pursuant to an express or implied authorization of Congress, his authority is at its maximum, for it includes all that he possesses in his own right plus all that Congress can delegate. * * *

2. When the President acts in absence of either a congressional grant or denial of authority, he can only rely upon his own independent powers, but there is a zone of twilight in which he and Congress may have concurrent authority, or in which its distribution is uncertain. Therefore, congressional inertia, indifference or quiescence may sometimes, at least as a practical matter, enable, if not invite, measures on independent presidential responsibility. In this area, any actual test of power is likely to depend on the imperatives of events and contemporary imponderables rather than on abstract theories of law.

3. When the President takes measures incompatible with the expressed or implied will of Congress, his power is at its lowest ebb, for then he can rely only upon his own constitutional powers minus any constitutional powers of Congress over the matter. Courts can sustain

exclusive Presidential control in such a case only by disabling the Congress from acting upon the subject. Presidential claim to a power at once so conclusive and preclusive must be scrutinized with caution, for what is at stake is the equilibrium established by our constitutional system.

Into which of these classifications does this executive seizure of the steel industry fit? It is eliminated from the first by admission, for it is conceded that no congressional authorization exists for this seizure. [It] seems clearly eliminated from [the "second category"] because Congress has not left seizure of private property an open field but has covered it by three statutory policies inconsistent with this seizure [e.g., fn. 1, none of which] were invoked. In choosing a different and inconsistent way of his own, the President cannot claim that it is necessitated or invited by failure of Congress to legislate upon the occasions, grounds and methods for seizure of industrial properties.

This leaves the current seizure to be justified only by the severe tests under the third grouping, [where] we can sustain the President only by holding that seizure of such strike-bound industries is within his domain and beyond control by Congress. * * * I cannot accept the view that [Art. II, § 1, cl. 1, vesting "the executive power" in the President] is a grant in bulk of all conceivable executive power but regard it as an allocation to the presidential office of the generic powers thereafter stated.

The [Commander in Chief] appellation is sometimes advanced as support for any presidential action, internal or external, involving use of force, the idea being that it vests power to do anything, anywhere, that can be done with an army or navy. [But the] Constitution expressly places in Congress power "to raise and *support* Armies" and "to *provide* and *maintain* a Navy." (Emphasis supplied.) * * * Congress alone controls the raising of revenues and their appropriation and may determine in what manner and by what means they shall be spent for military and naval procurement. I suppose no one would doubt that Congress can take over war supply as a Government enterprise. * * *

The third clause in which the Solicitor General finds seizure powers is that "he shall take Care that the Laws be faithfully executed." That authority must be matched against [the Due Process Clause of the Fifth Amendment]. One [clause] gives a governmental authority that reaches so far as there is law, the other gives a private right that authority shall go no farther. * * *

The Solicitor General lastly grounds support of the seizure upon nebulous, inherent powers never expressly granted but said to have accrued to the office from the customs and claims of preceding administrations. The plea is for a resulting power to deal with a crisis or an emergency according to the necessities of the case, the unarticulated assumption being that necessity knows no law. Loose and irresponsible use of adjectives colors all non-legal and much legal discussion of presidential powers. "Inherent" powers, "implied" powers, "incidental" powers, "plenary" powers, "war" powers and "emergency" powers are used, often interchangeably and without fixed or ascertainable meanings. * * *

In view of the ease, expedition and safety with which Congress can grant and has granted large emergency powers, certainly ample to embrace this crisis, I am quite unimpressed with the argument that we should affirm possession of them without statute. Such power either has no beginning or it has no end. If it exists, it need submit to no legal restraint. I am not alarmed that it would plunge us straightway into dictatorship, but it is at least a step in that wrong direction.

[The] Executive, except for recommendation and veto, has no legislative power. The executive action we have here originates in the individual will of the President and represents an exercise of authority without law. [With] all its defects, delays, and inconveniences, men have discovered no technique for long preserving free government except that the Executive be under the law, and that the law be made by parliamentary deliberations. * * * * [2]

CHIEF JUSTICE VINSON, with whom JUSTICE REED and JUSTICE MINTON join, dissenting.

[The dissent emphasized the country's international commitments for economic and military aid to preserve the free world and congressional action directing the President to strengthen the armed forces. It called attention to the legislation directly related to supporting the Korean War. It quoted affidavits showing the enormous demand for steel in vital defense programs and attesting that a work stoppage would imperil the national defense.] Accordingly, if the President has any power under the Constitution to meet a critical situation in the absence of express statutory authorization, there is no basis whatever for criticizing the exercise of such power in this case.

[Our] Presidents have on many occasions exhibited the leadership contemplated by the Framers when they made the President Commander in Chief, and imposed upon him the trust to "take Care that the Laws be faithfully executed." With or without explicit statutory authorization, Presidents have [dealt] with national emergencies by acting promptly [to] enforce legislative programs, at least to save those programs until

---

[2]   Burton, J., concurred in Black, J.'s opinion but also wrote a separate concurrence, similar in thrust to those of Frankfurter and Jackson, JJ., stressing that "the President's [order] invaded the jurisdiction of Congress," which "reserved to itself" the remedy of seizure. Douglas, J., concurred in Black, J.'s opinion, noting that "the branch of government that has the power to pay compensation for a seizure [Congress] is the only one able to authorize a seizure [under] the condemnation provision in the Fifth Amendment." Clark, J., concurred in the judgment because "Congress had prescribed methods to be followed by the President in meeting the emergency at hand, [but] in the absence of such action by Congress, the President's independent power to act depends upon the gravity of the situation confronting the nation."

Congress could act. Congress and the courts have responded to such executive initiative with consistent approval. [Historic episodes from George Washington to Franklin D. Roosevelt were summarized in 17 pages. A brief excerpt follows:]

Some six months before Pearl Harbor, a dispute at a single aviation [plant] interrupted a segment of the production of military aircraft. [President] Roosevelt ordered the seizure of the plant "pursuant to the powers vested in [him as] Commander in Chief of the Army and Navy of the United States." The Attorney General (Jackson) vigorously proclaimed that the President had the moral duty to keep this Nation's defense effort a "going concern." [A]lso prior to Pearl Harbor, the President ordered the seizure of a ship-building company and an aircraft parts plant. Following the declaration of war, [five] additional industrial concerns were seized to avert interruption of needed production. During the same period, the President directed seizure of the Nation's coal mines to remove an obstruction to the effective prosecution of the war.

[This] is but a cursory summary of executive leadership. But it amply demonstrates that Presidents have taken prompt action to enforce the laws and protect the country whether or not Congress happened to provide in advance for the particular method of execution. [T]he fact that Congress and the courts have consistently recognized and given their support to such executive action indicates that such a power of seizure has been accepted throughout our history.

Flexibility as to mode of execution [of the laws] to meet critical situations is a matter of practical necessity. [The] broad executive power granted by Article II [cannot], it is said, be invoked to avert disaster. Instead, the President must confine himself to sending a message to Congress recommending action. Under this messenger-boy concept of the Office, the President cannot even act to preserve legislative programs from destruction so that Congress will have something left to act upon.

[T]here [is no] question of unlimited executive power in this case. The President himself closed the door to any such claim when he sent his Message to Congress stating his purpose to abide by any action of Congress, whether approving or disapproving his seizure action [or] regulating the manner in which the mills were to be administered and returned to the owners. [J]udicial, legislative and executive precedents throughout our history demonstrate that in this case the President acted in full conformity with his duties under the Constitution. * * *

NOTES AND QUESTIONS

1. *Emergency powers.* Do the opinions of Black and Jackson, JJ., imply that the President has no "emergency" or "implied" powers whatsoever? Does a majority of the Court agree? Should it matter to separation-of-powers

analysis that a particular branch of government has exercised the challenged power in the past? Should practical necessities matter? It seems clear, in retrospect, that the government in *Youngstown* overestimated the practical emergency. And the President had further, statutorily authorized options. Would (should) the result have been the same if the success of the Korean War effort or the safety of troops in combat were genuinely at risk?

Does the President possess inherent authority, in the absence of congressional authorization, to deploy American troops to repel sudden attacks, to safeguard American property, or to protect or rescue governmental personnel or American citizens abroad? If so, what are the limits of this power? A dictum in *Home Bldg & Loan Ass'n v. Blaisdell*, Ch. 5, Sec. 4, stated that "while emergency does not create power, emergency may furnish the occasion for the exercise of power." See also Souter, J., concurring and dissenting in *Hamdi v. Rumsfeld*, Part III infra: "[I]n a moment of genuine emergency, when the Government must act with no time for deliberation, the Executive may be able to [do so] if there is reason to fear [an] imminent threat to the safety of the Nation, [but] an emergency power of necessity must at least be limited by the emergency."

What role should the Court play? Consider Eric A. Posner & Adrian Vermeule, *Emergencies and Democratic Failure*, 92 Va. L. Rev. 1091 (2006): "In times of emergency, judges' information is especially poor, their ability to sort justified from unjustified policies especially limited, and the cost of erroneously blocking necessary security measures may be disastrous. Included among those costs is the cost of delay, which amounts to a temporary blockage of new policies, and which is especially serious during emergencies, where time is critical." Compare Oren Gross, *Chaos and Rules: Should Responses to Violent Crises Always Be Constitutional?*, 112 Yale L.J. 1011 (2003): In responding to "*violent* emergencies and crises," public officials "may act extralegally [if] they openly and publicly acknowledge the nature of their actions [so as to] put the burden squarely on society to decide [on] ratification (or rejection)." See generally Henry P. Monaghan, *The Protective Power of the Presidency*, 93 Colum.L.Rev. 1 (1993). See further Sec. II infra.

2. *Executive "lawmaking."* (a) *Delegation.* As considered more fully in Sec. 2 infra, executive branch agencies, typically pursuant to authority delegated by Congress, routinely engage in rulemaking, and the President alone has developed and implemented tariff schedules.[3] Is the exercise of delegated rulemaking authority "legislative" action that is forbidden to executive officials?

(b) *Executive orders.* Presidents have long asserted a power to issue "Executive Orders" relating to organization of the executive branch, use of federal property, and the terms on which the federal government will enter contracts. The most prominent include President Lincoln's Emancipation Proclamation and President Truman's racial integration of the armed forces.

---

[3]   See, e.g., *J.W. Hampton, Jr. & Co. v. United States*, 276 U.S. 394 (1928); *Field v. Clark*, 143 U.S. 649 (1892); *The Aurora*, 11 U.S. (7 Cranch) 382 (1813).

Presidents have also issued executive orders forbidding race discrimination by private firms receiving federal contracts, and later mandating "affirmative action" by federal contractors. Does the Constitution permit or authorize such action by the President? See Michael Brody, *Congress, The President, and Federal Equal Employment Policymaking: A Problem in Separation of Powers*, 60 B.U.L.Rev. 239 (1980). When President Nixon withheld expenditures authorized and appropriated by Congress without its authorization, Congress responded with the Congressional Budget and Impoundment Control Act of 1974, 2 U.S.C.A. 681. It required that an appropriation be "available for obligation" unless Congress rescinds it within 45 days after a required notice to Congress that the President "has determined" that the appropriation should be rescinded.[4] Later Presidents have set policies on how executive and administrative agencies should enforce certain laws against private citizens. Most recently, President Obama has used "prosecutorial discretion" to stop enforcing federal drug and immigration laws. For criticism, see Robert J. Delahunty & John C. Yoo, *Dream On: The Obama Administration's Nonenforcement of the Immigration Laws, the DREAM Act, and the Take Care Clause*, 91 Tex. L.Rev. 781 (2013). For the proposal, pursuant to "strong textual, structural, and normative considerations [as well as] early historical practice," that without explicit statutory authorization, "executive officials should presume [that] they lack discretion to categorically suspend enforcement or prospectively exclude defendants from the scope of statutory prohibitions," but may "make case—specific exceptions [and recognize] resource limitations," see Zachary S. Price, *Enforcement Discretion and Executive Duty*, 67 Vand.L. Rev. 1045 (2014).

(c) DAMES & MOORE v. REGAN, 453 U.S. 654 (1981), per REHNQUIST, J., unanimously upheld presidential executive orders to implement an executive agreement between Iran and the United States securing release of American hostages held in Iran for 15 months in 1979–81. The executive agreement called for termination of "all litigation between the government of each party and the nationals of the other" and for settlement of pending claims through binding arbitration before a tribunal established under the agreement. The executive orders (1) suspended all claims in American courts that were within the jurisdiction of the claims tribunal, (2) nullified all prejudgment attachments against Iran's assets in actions against Iran in American courts, and (3) ordered transfer to Iran of all its assets in U.S. banks, except for one billion dollars to cover awards against Iran by the claims tribunal.

---

[4] Conflicts over presidential impoundment of appropriated funds reached their peak in the Nixon administration. Its constitutionality has been considered in non-judicial studies and in a few federal court cases, but it has not been addressed by the Supreme Court. See Abner J. Mikva & Michael F. Hertz, *Impoundment of Funds—The Courts, The Congress and The President: A Constitutional Triangle*, 69 Nw.U.L.Rev. 335 (1974); Timothy R. Harner, *Presidential Power to Impound Appropriations for Defense and Foreign Relations*, 5 Harv.J.L. & Pub. Pol. 131 (1982); Roy E. Brownell II, *The Constitutional Status of the President's Impoundment of National Security Funds*, 12 Seton Hall L.J. 1 (2001).

Dames & Moore's prejudgment attachment of Iranian bank assets, to secure its large claim for services rendered to Iran, was vacated pursuant to the executive orders. The Court rejected Dames & Moore's challenge: "Because the President's action in nullifying the attachments [was] taken pursuant to specific congressional authorization [under the International Emergency Economic Powers Act (IEEPA)][5] it is 'supported by the strongest of presumptions and the widest latitude of judicial interpretation, and the burden of persuasion would rest heavily upon any who might attack it.' [*Youngstown*] (Jackson, J., concurring). [We] cannot say that petitioner has sustained that heavy burden. A contrary ruling would mean that the Federal Government as a whole lacked the power exercised by the President, and that we are not prepared to say."

By contrast, "neither the IEEPA nor the Hostage Act constitutes specific authorization of the President's action suspending claims. [But this is] not to say that these statutory provisions are entirely irrelevant to the question of the validity of the President's [action.] Congress cannot anticipate and legislate with regard to every possible action the President may find it necessary to take. [E]nactment of legislation closely related to the question of the President's authority in a particular case which evinces legislative intent to accord the President broad discretion may be considered to 'invite' 'measures on independent presidential responsibility.' *Youngstown* (Jackson, J., concurring). At least this is so where there is no contrary indication of legislative intent and when, as here, there is a history of congressional acquiescence in conduct of the sort engaged in by the President. * * *

"Crucial to our decision today is the conclusion that Congress has implicitly approved the practice of claim settlement by executive agreement. This is best demonstrated by Congress' enactment of the International Claims Settlement Act of 1949. The Act had two purposes: (1) to allocate to United States nationals funds received in the course of an executive claims settlement with Yugoslavia, and (2) to provide a procedure whereby funds resulting from future settlements could be distributed. To achieve these ends Congress created the International Claims Commission, now the Foreign Claims Settlement Commission, [and] gave it jurisdiction to make final and binding decisions with respect to claims by United States nationals against settlement funds. By creating a procedure to implement future settlement agreements, Congress placed its stamp of approval on such agreements. Indeed, the legislative history of the Act observed that the United States was seeking settlements with countries other than Yugoslavia and [stated] that the bill contemplates settlements of a similar nature in the future.

"[As] Justice Frankfurter pointed out in *Youngstown*, 'a systematic, unbroken executive practice, long pursued to the knowledge of the Congress and never before questioned [may] be treated as a gloss on "Executive Power" vested in the President by § 1 of Art. II.' [Our] conclusion is buttressed by the

---

[5]   Section 1702(a)(1)(B) of IEEPA empowered the President to "compel," "nullify," or "prohibit" any "transfer" with respect to, or transactions involving, any property subject to the jurisdiction of the United States in which any foreign country has any interest.

fact that the means chosen by the President to settle the claims of American nationals provided an alternative forum, the Claims Tribunal, which is capable of providing meaningful relief. [Just] as importantly, [we are] clearly not confronted with a situation in which Congress has in some way resisted the exercise of Presidential authority.

" * * * We do not decide that the President possesses plenary power to settle claims, even as against foreign governmental entities. [But] where, as here, the settlement of claims has been determined to be a necessary incident to the resolution of a major foreign policy dispute between our country and another, and where, as here, we can conclude that Congress acquiesced in the President's action, we are not prepared to say that the President lacks the power to settle such claims."

(d) MEDELLIN v. TEXAS, 552 U.S. 491 (2008), per ROBERTS, C.J., invalidated President G.W. Bush's "Memorandum" that state courts must adhere to the International Court of Justice's decision that the Vienna Convention on Consular Relations required (1) that law enforcement authorities inform arrested foreign nationals of their right to notify their consulate of their detention, and if this was not done, (2) that the United States provide reconsideration of convictions without regard to state procedural default rules:[6] While the treaty "constitutes an *international* law obligation on the part of the United States," it is "not domestic law unless Congress has either enacted implementing statutes or the treaty itself conveys an intention that it be 'self-executing' and is ratified on these terms. [Because] none of [the] treaty sources creates binding federal law in the absence of implementing legislation, and because it is uncontested that no such legislation exists, we conclude that the [ICJ's decision] is not automatically binding domestic law."

As for the President's independent constitutional power under Art.II, "given the absence of congressional legislation, [the] non-self-executing treaties at issue here did not 'express[ly] or implied[ly]' vest the President with the unilateral authority to make them self-executing. Accordingly, the President's Memorandum does not fall within the first category of the *Youngstown* framework. [When] the President asserts the power to 'enforce' a non-self-executing treaty by unilaterally creating domestic law, he acts in conflict with the implicit understanding of the ratifying Senate [and] is therefore within Justice Jackson's third category, not the first or even the second."[7]

---

[6] Petitioner, a Mexican national, was convicted of gang rape and murder and sentenced to death. Although he had been given the *Miranda* warnings prior to his confession, he was not informed of his Vienna Convention right. The Texas courts refused to consider this claim because he had not raised it in timely fashion.

[7] Therefore, even if there were "congressional acquiescence" in respect to the President's action—"which does not exist here"—it would be of no consequence: "Under the *Youngstown* tripartite framework, congressional acquiescence is pertinent when the President's action falls within the second category—that is, when he 'acts in absence of either a congressional grant or denial of authority.' "

Dames & Moore is "based on the view that 'a systematic, unbroken, executive practice, long pursued to the knowledge of the Congress and never before questioned,' can 'raise a presumption that the [action] had been [taken] in pursuance of its consent.' *Dames & Moore*. [The] President's Memorandum is not supported by a 'particularly longstanding practice' of congressional acquiescence. [Indeed,] the Government has not identified a single instance in which the President has attempted (or Congress has acquiesced in) a Presidential directive issued to state courts, much less one that reaches deep into the heart of the State's police powers and compels state courts to reopen final criminal judgments and set aside neutrally applicable state laws. [The] Executive's narrow and strictly limited authority to settle international claims disputes pursuant to an executive agreement cannot stretch so far as to support the current Presidential Memorandum."

BREYER, J., joined by Souter and Ginsburg, JJ. dissented, concluding that "a strong line of precedent, likely reflecting the views of the Founders, indicates that the treaty provisions [and the ICJ judgment] address themselves to the Judicial Branch and consequently are self-executing." STEVENS, J., concurred in the Court's judgment, although agreeing largely with Breyer, J., because "the text and history of the Supremacy Clause, as well as this Court's treaty-related cases, do not support a presumption against self-execution. I also endorse the proposition that the [treaty] is itself self-executing and judicially enforceable." But its unclear language leaves the manner of compliance "to the political, not the judicial department."[8]

(e) ***Congressional "acquiescence."*** In neither *Dames & Moore* nor *Youngstown* nor *Medellin* had Congress either expressly prohibited or authorized the President's action. To what extent should congressional "silence" amount to "implicit approval"? Consider Tribe 3d ed.: "[J]udicial reasoning that allows Congress to legislate by silence is constitutionally dubious: The internal system of checks and balances is thwarted because legislative silences are not subject to presidential veto, and external political accountability is diminished because Congress cannot realistically be held accountable by the electorate for laws it 'enacts' by silence." Compare Jack Goldsmith & John F. Manning, *The President's Completion Power,* 115 Yale L. J. 2280 (2006), who suggest that *Dames & Moore* illustrates the "completion power," effectively following Vinson, C.J.'s analysis in *Youngstown*: "Where Congress has failed to specify in full the manner of enforcement, the executive necessarily exercises some discretion in specifying incidental details necessary to carry into execution a legislative program [even] in the absence of an express or implied authorization to do so. [The] President's power greatly resembles the one used to analyze Congress's authority under the Necessary and Proper Clause." Whether *Dames & Moore* may be grounded in the President's special authority over foreign affairs is considered in Sec. II infra.

---

[8] For a "narrow" reading of *Medellin*, see Michael D. Ramsey, *The Supremacy Clause, Original Meaning, and Modern Law,* 74 Ohio St. L.J. 559 (2013).

3.   **The Fifth Amendment.** How important was it (or should it be) that the President in *Youngstown* was claiming power to act in violation of the constitutional right against the taking of property without just compensation? Does the Constitution *ever* authorize the President to violate constitutional rights? See Monaghan, note 1 supra at 10, asserting this limit on the President's "protective" powers.[9]

4.   **Justice Jackson's categories.** As indicated in *Dames & Moore*, and *Medellin,* the opinion in *Youngstown* that has had the greatest subsequent influence is that of Jackson, J. Is his analysis consistent with Black, J.'s, in whose opinion Jackson, J., joins? Are Jackson, J.'s categories analytically helpful?[10] Within Jackson, J.'s "zone of twilight," where both Congress and the President may reasonably claim independent authority, which should be recognized as paramount? According to Edward S. Corwin, *The Steel Seizure Case: A Judicial Brick Without Straw*, 53 Colum.L.Rev. 53 (1953), *Youngstown* "would unquestionably have assented to the proposition that in all emergency situations the last word lies with Congress when it chooses to speak such last word." Is congressional predominance always appropriate? See note 1 (b) after *Campbell v. Clinton* infra.

5.   **Accretion of presidential power.** Consider Charles L. Black, Jr., *The Working Balance of the American Political Departments*, 1 Hast. Con.L.Q. 13, 20 (1974): "On paper, and as a matter of irreducible minimum, the presidency is an office of very little uncontrollable power. [The five powers specifically enumerated in Art. II that seem most important either (i) do not amount to much, such as the powers to receive ambassadors and to grant pardons, or (ii) are hemmed in by congressional powers, such as the commander-in-chief power, which is limited by Congress' powers to declare war and vote military appropriations, and the power to enforce the law, which depends on the laws that Congress enacts and the enforcement resources that it provides.] Congress, on the other hand, holds virtually all the national

---

[9]   *Dames & Moore* did not "think it appropriate at the present time to address petitioner's contention that the suspension of claims, if authorized, would constitute a taking of property in violation of the Fifth Amendment." For consideration of this issue, see Phillip R. Trimble, *Foreign Policy Frustrated—Dames & Moore, Claims Court Jurisdiction and a New Raid on the Treasury,* 84 Colum.L.Rev. 317 (1984).

[10]   For criticism, see Martin H. Redish & Elizabeth J. Cisar, *"If Angels Were to Govern": The Need for Pragmatic Formalism in Separation of Powers Theory,* 41 Duke L.J. 449 (1991), questioning the suggestion that the President's powers are at a "maximum" when acting pursuant to congressional authorization, since the powers of Congress and the President are substantially distinct, and Congress can neither delegate congressional powers to the President nor nullify presidential power arising from the Constitution. For the suggestion that more categories must be recognized, see Abner S. Greene, *Checks and Balances in an Era of Presidential Lawmaking,* 61 U.Chi.L.Rev. 123 (1994); Mark D. Rosen, *Revisiting Youngstown: Against the View that Jackson's Concurrence Resolves the Relation Between Congress and the Commander-In-Chief,* 54 UCLA L. Rev. 1703 (2007), contending that Jackson, J.'s assumption—that "wherever congressional power overlaps with antecedent presidential powers, congressional action categorically trumps"—was not adequately justified, and that "the Constitution itself does not identify" how to resolve "conflicts between Congress's powers and the president's commander-in-chief powers." For a review and appraisal of Youngstown's (especially Jackson, J.'s concurrence) doctrinal importance in cases involving separation of powers (foreign affairs particularly), see Patricia L. Belles, *Executive Power in Youngstown's Shadows,* 19 Const. Comm. 87 (2002).

power, if only it wants to keep or to resume [it]. But Congress is very poorly structured for initiative and leadership; the presidency is very well structured for these things. The result has been a flow of power from Congress to the presidency. [The] one fundamental error is that of supposing that the modern expansion of presidential power is based on the Constitution by itself, and hence is inaccessible as a matter of law to congressional correction." Should this mean that since the presidency "is now the most powerful office in the nation," our system of checks-and-balances requires "congressional regulation of the executive [to be] presumptively valid"? See Martin S. Flaherty, *The Most Dangerous Branch*, 105 Yale L.J. 1725 (1996). Or does the fact that Art. II grants the President an undefined "executive Power," while Art. I only vests Congress with "the legislative Powers herein granted," suggest that the framers intended a more unbounded presidential authority? See Steven G. Calabresi & Saikrishna B. Prakash, *The President's Power to Execute the Law*, 104 Yale L.J. 541 (1994).

6. *Formalism and functionalism.* (a) *Description.* Commentators have frequently distinguished between "formal" and "functional" approaches to separation-of-powers issues.[11] Although there is no canonical definition of these terms, formalist approaches, such as Black, J.'s in *Youngstown*, generally assume that the Constitution recognizes three functions—legislative, executive, and judicial—that must be assigned to the corresponding branch of government. Within this framework, separation-of-powers issues turn largely on classification of functions (as either legislative, executive, or judicial). There can be no inter-branch interference not expressly authorized by the Constitution.

Functionalists acknowledge that each branch may have certain "core" functions that cannot be curbed or usurped, but beyond the core accept that the constitutionality of challenged institutional arrangements should be measured by reference to such characteristic *functions* of the separation of powers as (i) maintaining a system of checks and balances,[12] (ii) preventing the concentration of excessive power in a single branch, (iii) protecting individual liberty, and (iv) allowing—subject to check—a cooperative ebb and flow of power among the branches to promote effective government.

Roughly speaking, formalists tend to criticize functionalism as inconsistent with constitutional structure and the framers' intent, and as requiring judgments that are too ad hoc and political to be consistent with the rule of law. Functionalists, by contrast, often claim that a formalist

---

[11] For an early, influential development of the distinction, see Peter L. Strauss, *The Place of Agencies in Government: Separation of Powers and the Fourth Branch*, 84 Colum.L.Rev. 573 (1984). For discussion of this and related distinctions that have become prominent in the literature, see Rebecca L. Brown, *Separated Powers and Ordered Liberty*, 139 U.Pa.L.Rev. 1513 (1991); Flaherty, supra.

[12] See generally Lawrence Lessig & Cass R. Sunstein, *The President and the Administration*, 94 Colum.L.Rev. 1 (1994); Peter L. Strauss, *The Place of Agencies in Government: Separation of Powers and the Fourth Branch*, 84 Colum. L.Rev. 573 (1984).

methodology is unhistoric and unworkable,[13] since it would require the dismantling of much of the modern administrative state. Functionalists also claim that formalism is too aridly conceptual to reflect the most basic structural presuppositions of a Constitution designed to be adaptable to unforeseen exigencies.

(b) *Different perspectives.* "[Instead of focusing on] the words 'executive,' 'judicial,' and 'legislative,' [the] question should be whether the proposed structural innovation yields substantial increased risks to majorities and minorities. This view finds support not only in historical, but also modern understandings of politics. [For Congress, the] Constitution demands the agreement of two different forms of constituency, one reflected in the Senate and the other in the House [because] they satisfy the majoritarian preferences of *both* larger and smaller aggregations of voters. [The] President has a more national focus and members of Congress a more local one." V.F. Nourse, *Toward a New Constitutional Anatomy*, 56 Stan.L.Rev. 835 (2004). See also M. Elizabeth Magill, *Beyond Powers and Branches in Separation of Powers Law*, 150 U.Pa.L.Rev. 603 (2001): "[We] have no satisfactory definitions of [the] three essential powers exercised by three undifferentiated branches [, and] the commitment [to] preservation of three roughly 'balanced' branches [is] both conceptually underdeveloped and flawed. [Instead], government authority is diffused among a large and diverse set of government decisionmakers [and an] effort to match particular state powers with particular government decisionmakers must start with an understanding of how those decisionmakers might exercise that authority." Compare Daryl J. Levinson & Richard H. Pildes, *Separation of Parties, Not Powers,* 119 Harv. L. Rev. 2312 (2006): "[T]he Madisonian assumption [that] vigorous, self-sustaining political competition between the legislative and executive branches [would] check and balance each other [is] not how American democracy turned out. Instead, political competition and cooperation [quickly] came to be channeled [through] an institution the Framers could imagine only dimly but nonetheless despised: parties. [T]he way formally separated political institutions actually work is whether the same political party controls the House, the Senate, and the presidency—that is, whether government is unified or divided. [Under] unified government and cohesive [parties,] interbranch checks and balances are at a minimum and standard separation-of-powers analyses and constitutional rules will tend to point and push in exactly the wrong directions."

---

[13] Functionalists rely especially on *The Federalist* No. 47 (Madison): "No political truth is certainly of greater intrinsic value [than the separation of governmental powers. But Montesquieu, the theorist whose authority is most often invoked,] did not mean that these departments have no partial agency in, or no control over, the acts of each other. His meaning, [can] amount to no more than this, that where the whole power of the department is exercised by the same hands which possess the whole power of another department, the fundamental principles of a free constitution are subverted."

II. EXTERNAL MATTERS: FOREIGN AFFAIRS AND WAR

UNITED STATES V. CURTISS-WRIGHT EXPORT CORP.
299 U.S. 304, 57 S.Ct. 216, 81 L.Ed. 255 (1936).

JUSTICE SUTHERLAND delivered the opinion of the Court.

[A joint resolution of Congress authorized the President to prohibit the sale of arms to Bolivia and Paraguay, which were engaged in armed conflict, if the President found that such prohibition would "contribute to the reestablishment of peace between those countries." The President proclaimed an embargo, and Curtiss-Wright was indicted for violating its terms. The lower court found the joint resolution an unconstitutional delegation of legislative power.]

The powers of the federal government in respect of foreign or external affairs and those in respect of domestic or internal affairs [are] different, both in respect of their origin and their nature. The broad statement that the federal government can exercise no powers except those specifically enumerated in the Constitution, and such implied powers as are necessary and proper to carry into effect the enumerated powers, is categorically true only in respect of our internal affairs.

As a result of the separation from Great Britain by the colonies acting as a unit, the powers of external sovereignty passed from the Crown not to the colonies severally, but to the colonies in their collective and corporate capacity as the United States of America. [The] powers to declare and wage war, to conclude peace, to make treaties, to maintain diplomatic relations with other sovereignties, if they had never been mentioned in the Constitution, would have vested in the federal government as necessary concomitants of nationality.

[Another difference is that] participation in the exercise of power [over external affairs] is significantly limited. In this vast external realm, [the] President alone has the power to speak or listen as a representative of the nation. He *makes* treaties with the advice and consent of the Senate; but he alone negotiates [and] the Senate cannot intrude. [As] Marshall said [in] the House of Representatives, "The President is the sole organ of the nation in its external relations, and its sole representative with foreign nations."

It is important [that] we are here dealing not alone with an authority vested in the President by an exertion of legislative power, but with such an authority plus the very delicate, plenary and exclusive power of the President as the sole organ of the federal government in the field of international relations. [If] embarrassment—perhaps serious embarrassment—is to be avoided and success for our aims achieved, congressional legislation [must] often accord to the President a degree of discretion and freedom from statutory restriction which would not be admissible were domestic affairs alone involved. Moreover, he, not Congress, has the better opportunity of knowing the conditions which prevail in foreign countries, and especially is this true in time of war. He has his confidential sources of information. * * * Secrecy in respect of information gathered by them may be highly necessary. [In] the light of the foregoing observations, it is evident that this court should not be in haste to apply a general rule which will have the effect of condemning legislation like that under review as constituting an unlawful delegation of legislative power. * * *

Reversed.[14]

NOTES AND QUESTIONS

1. **Nonenumerated presidential powers.** (a) Is the federal government's possession of unenumerated foreign affairs powers consistent with basic tenets of American constitutionalism?[15] Is the capacity to respond effectively to foreign emergencies a necessary predicate for maintenance of constitutional democracy? Does the constitutional text support the conclusion that the President is "the sole organ of the federal government in the field of international relations"? Compare Joel R. Paul, *The Geopolitical Constitution: Executive Expediency and Executive Agreements*, 86 Calif.L.Rev. 671 (1998): "The history from the Framers' time to the present reveals a clear, consistent understanding of a more limited role for the President in foreign affairs up until the Cold War." Is it significant that the President can make treaties only with the advice and consent of the Senate and that Congress is vested with authority to regulate foreign commerce, to declare war, and to provide for the funding and regulation of the armed forces? For comprehensive and conflicting views, on both textual and historical grounds, as to whether the President has *all* power over foreign affairs not *specifically* allocated to Congress, compare John Yoo, *The Powers of War and Peace* 30 (2005) and Saikrishna B. Prakash & Michael D. Ramsey, *The Executive Power Over Foreign Affairs*, 111 Yale L.J. 231 (2001) (yes) with Curtis A. Bradley & Martin S. Flaherty, *Executive Power Essentialism and Foreign Affairs*, 102 Mich.L.Rev. 545 (2004).

---

[14] McReynolds, J., dissented without opinion. Stone, J., did not participate.

[15] For a critique of both the historical and constitutional analysis of *Curtiss-Wright*, see Charles A. Lofgren, *"Government From Reflection and Choice": Constitutional Essays on War, Foreign Relations, and Federalism* 167 (1986). For support of Sutherland, J.'s view, see Jack N. Rakove, *Original Meanings: Politics and Ideas in the Making of the Constitution* 163 (1996). For a detailed account of the evolution of the view "that there was an essential difference between foreign relations policymaking and domestic policymaking, and that difference reflected the consummate importance of human flexibility and discretion in the delicate realm of international relations," see G. Edward White, *The Transformation of the Constitutional Regime of Foreign Relations*, 85 Va.L.Rev. 1 (1999). On the constitutionality of delegations to *international* institutions, see Curtis A. Bradley, *International Delegations, the Structural Constitution, and Non-Self-Execution*, 55 Stan.L.Rev. 1557 (2003); David Golove, *The New Confederalism: Treaty Delegations of Legislative, Executive, and Judicial Authority*, 55 Stan.L.Rev. 1697 (2003).

(b) Is *Curtiss-Wright* inconsistent with *Youngstown*? See Harold H. Koh, *The National Security Constitution: Sharing Power After the Iran-Contra Affair* 134 (1990): While "the *Youngstown* theory [generally requiring the President to seek congressional concurrence] took hold powerfully" under the Warren Court, the Burger and Rehnquist Courts—as in *Dames & Moore*—have followed the *Curtiss-Wright* approach of recognizing broad presidential discretion. Which of the two approaches is more sound?

2. ***Executive agreements.*** (a) Executive agreements with foreign nations originally played a minor role as compared to treaties, but since World War II, they have overwhelmed the process.[16] These agreements often have been authorized or approved by congressional action or entered into pursuant to treaties.[17] But from early days Presidents have entered into significant

---

[16] Between 1939–1999, the nation entered into 15,733 executive agreements but only 951 treaties. See Committee on Foreign Relations, United States Senate, *Treaties and Other International Agreements: The Role of the United States Senate*, S. Prt. 106 106th Cong. 2d Sess. 39 (2001). See generally Michael D. Ramsey, *Executive Agreements and the (Non) Treaty Power*, 77 N.C.L.Rev. 133 (1998). For the view that "compared to congressional-executive agreements, treaties have weaker democratic legitimacy, are more cumbersome and politically vulnerable, and create less reliable legal commitments," and that "nearly everything that is done through the Treaty Clause can and should be done through congressional-executive agreements approved by both houses of Congress," see Oona A. Hathaway, *Treaties' End: The Past, Present, and Future of International Lawmaking in the United States*, 117 Yale L. J. 1236 (2008).

[17] See Louis Henkin, *Foreign Affairs and the U.S. Constitution* 215–18 (2d ed. 1996). See also *Medellin v. Texas*, Sec. I supra (President has no power independent of Congress to implement a *non-self-executing* treaty).

May a statute or joint resolution, passed by majority vote in both houses of Congress, be a constitutionally adequate substitute for the process of Senatorial advice and consent to treaties, which requires a two-thirds majority (Art. II, § 2, cl. 2)? Compare Bruce Ackerman & David Golove, *Is NAFTA Constitutional?*, 108 Harv.L.Rev. 799 (1995) (a de facto constitutional amendment has allowed use of congressionally approved executive agreements in circumstances once requiring senatorial consent to a "treaty") with Laurence H. Tribe, *Taking Text and Structure Seriously: Reflections on Free-Form Method in Constitutional Interpretation*, 108 Harv.L.Rev. 1221 (1995) (although the President can bind the nation by executive agreement on matters that do not "seriously affect state or national sovereignty," other international agreements are necessarily "treaties" in the constitutional sense, and are not constitutionally valid without Senate confirmation). See David Golove, *Against Free-Form Formalism*, 73 N.Y.U.L.Rev. 1791 (1998) (responding to Tribe). For an intermediate view, see Peter J. Spiro, *Treaties, Executive Agreements, and Constitutional Method*, 79 Tex.L.Rev. 961 (2001) (an "increments model takes the familiar method of precedential case analysis and expands it to historical sources beyond the court reports"—using "criteria of acceptance, contestedness, age, and pedigree"). For the position that "congressional-executive agreements [*must*] be used to approve international agreements that regulate matters within Congress's Article I powers," and that "treaties [*must*] be used if the nation seeks to make agreements outside of Congress's competence or bind itself in areas where both President and Congress exercise competing, overlapping powers," see John C. Yoo, *Laws as Treaties?: The Constitutionality of Congressional-Executive Agreements*, 99 Mich.L.Rev. 757 (2001).

A similar tension regarding action that may be taken either by (a) the executive and the Senate (treaty), or (b) by Congress and the President (statute) arises in respect to the legitimacy of a *self-executing* treaty. The issue is considered extensively in John C. Yoo, *Globalism and the Constitution: Treaties, Non-Self-Execution, and the Original Understanding*, 99 Colum.L.Rev. 1955 (1999) (since "self-execution invites a conflict between the textual grants of the executive and legislative powers and resolves the clash by allowing the treatymaking authority to trump Congress's Article I powers," the original understanding (as well as the Constitution's text and structure) require that treaties "should not generally be judicially enforceable unless Congress passes implementing legislation"). Contra, Martin S. Flaherty, *History Right? Historical Scholarship, Original, Understanding, and Treaties as "Supreme Law of the Land,"* 99 Colum.L.Rev. 2095 (1999) ("the Framers crafted a Constitution that made treaties self-executing

international executive agreements strictly on their own authority.[18] *United States v. Belmont*, 301 U.S. 324 (1937), *United States v. Pink*, 315 U.S. 203 (1942), and *Dames & Moore* upheld the President's authority to enter into such executive agreements without Senate or congressional approval.[19] Are these decisions consistent with the assertion of Black, J.'s opinion in *Youngstown* that the President is categorically excluded from the exercise of lawmaking authority? Should the President be so excluded?

(b)   In 1996, Professor Henkin noted that "[o]ne is compelled to conclude that there are agreements which the President can make on his sole authority and others which he can make only with the consent of the Senate (or of both houses), but neither Justice Sutherland [who wrote *Belmont*] nor any one else has told us which are which."[20] Do *Dames & Moore, Pink,* and *Belmont* provide any guidance to the extent or source of the President's power to enter into such "sole executive agreements?"[21]

CAMPBELL V. CLINTON
203 F.3d 19 (D.C.Cir.2000).

SILBERMAN, CIRCUIT JUDGE.

A number of congressmen [filed] suit claiming that the President violated the War Powers Resolution [WPR] and the War Powers Clause of the Constitution by directing U.S. forces' participation in the recent NATO campaign [when Yugoslavia sent armed forces into Kosovo]. The district court dismissed for lack of standing. * * *

---

upon ratification"); Carlos Vasquez, *Laughing at Treaties*, 99 Colum.L.Rev. 2154 (1999). For a middle ground, see Vasan Kesavan, *The Three Tiers of Federal Law*, 100 Nw.U.L.Rev. 1479 (2006) (treaties that conflict with federal statutes must be non-self-executing).

[18]   Henkin, supra.

[19]   *Belmont* and *Pink* involved the Soviet Union's assignment to the United States of amounts owed to it by American nationals so that outstanding claims of other American nationals could be paid. The Court ruled that the executive agreement became the "supreme Law of the Land," overriding New York's court-made policy not to recognize government appropriation of property. *Pink* explained: "The powers of the President in the conduct of foreign relations included the power, without consent of the Senate, to determine the public policy of the United States with respect to the Russian nationalization [decrees]. Power to remove such obstacles to full recognition as [claims settlement] certainly is a modest implied power of the President who is the 'sole organ of the federal government in the field of international relations.' *Curtiss-Wright.* Effectiveness in handling the delicate problems of foreign relations requires no [less]." See also *American Ins. Ass'n v. Garamendi*, 539 U.S. 396 (2003) (executive agreement with Germany preempted a state law, enacted to help Holocaust victims, requiring insurance companies to disclose information on policies issued during the Nazi era). For criticism of this approach on the ground that, as a matter of the original understanding of the Supremacy Clause, the President can "adopt foreign policy" but has no "lawmaking power" to preempt state laws, see generally Michael D. Ramsey, *The Constitution's Text in Foreign Affairs* (2007) and Bradford R. Clark, *Domesticating Sole Executive Agreements*, 93 Va. L. Rev. 1573 (2007). Contra, Henry P. Monaghan, *Supreme Clause Textualism*, 110 Colum. L. Rev. 731 (2010).

[20]   Henkin, supra at 222.

[21]   For exploration of such issues see Henkin, supra. See also Ackerman & Golove, supra; Tribe, supra.

On March 24, 1999, President Clinton announced the commencement of NATO air and cruise missile attacks on Yugoslav targets. Two days later he submitted to Congress a report, "consistent with the War Powers Resolution," detailing the circumstances necessitating the use of armed forces, the deployment's scope and expected duration, and asserting that he had "taken these actions pursuant to [his] authority [as] Commander in Chief and Chief Executive." On April 28, Congress voted [down] a declaration of war 427 to 2 and an "authorization" of the air strikes 213 to 213, but it also voted against requiring the President to immediately end U.S. participation in the NATO operation and voted to fund that involvement. The conflict between NATO and Yugoslavia continued for 79 days. [The] WPR requires the President to submit a report within 48 hours "in any case in which United States Armed Forces are introduced [into] hostilities or into situations where imminent involvement in hostilities is clearly indicated by the circumstances," and to "terminate any use of United States Armed Forces with respect to which a report was submitted (or required to be submitted), unless the Congress [has] declared war or has enacted a specific authorization" [within] 60 days * * * .[22]

[W]e agree with the district court that the congressmen lack standing * * * .

SILBERMAN, CIRCUIT JUDGE, concurring.

[I]n my view, no one is able to bring this challenge because the two claims are not justiciable. We lack "judicially discoverable and manageable standards" for addressing them, and the War Powers Clause claim implicates the political question doctrine. See *Baker v. Carr* [Ch. 1, Sec. 2].

Appellants contend this case is governed by *Mitchell v. Laird*, 488 F.2d 611 (D.C.Cir.1973), where we said that "[t]here would be no insuperable difficulty in a court determining whether" the Vietnam conflict constituted a war in the Constitutional sense. See also *Dellums v. Bush*, 752 F.Supp. 1141 (D.D.C.1990) ("[T]he Court has no hesitation in concluding that an offensive entry into Iraq by several hundred thousand United States servicemen [could] be described as a 'war' within the meaning [of] the

---

[22] The War Powers Resolution was passed in 1973, in response to the Vietnam War, over presidential veto on the ground, inter alia, that it unconstitutionally constrained the President's war powers. Nearly all commentators agree that the Resolution has failed to fulfill its intended aims. First, it does not deal at all with military operations that can be completed in less than 60 days. Second, Presidents have ignored the Resolution in cases—such as President Reagan's dispatch of troops to Lebanon, President G.H.W. Bush's initial introduction of forces in the Persian Gulf, and President Clinton's sending troops to Haiti—in which it would seem relevant. See John H. Ely, *War and Responsibility: Constitutional Lessons of Vietnam and Its Aftermath* 49 (1993); Koh, note 1(b) after *Curtiss-Wright*; John C. Yoo, *Kosovo, War Powers, and the Multilateral Future*, 148 U.Pa.L.Rev. 1673 (2000). For a range of views on legal issues raised by the War Powers Resolution, see Stephen L. Carter, *The Constitutionality of the War Powers Resolution*, 70 Va.L.Rev. 101 (1984); Robert F. Turner, *The War Powers Resolution: Unconstitutional, Unnecessary, and Unhelpful*, 17 Loy.L.A.L.Rev. 683 (1984).

Constitution."). But a careful reading of both cases reveals that the language upon which appellants rely is only dicta. * * *

Appellants cannot point to any constitutional test for what is war. See, e.g., *Holtzman v. Schlesinger*, 414 U.S. 1316 (1973) (Justice Douglas, in chambers, vacating order of Court of Appeals granting stay of district court's injunction against bombing of Cambodia), 414 U.S. at 1321 (Justice Marshall, in chambers, granting stay the same day with the concurrence of the other Justices); *Holtzman v. Schlesinger*, 484 F.2d 1307 (2d Cir.1973) (holding legality of Cambodia bombing nonjusticiable because courts lack expertise to determine import of various military actions). Instead, appellants offer a rough definition of war provided in 1994 by an Assistant Attorney General to four Senators with respect to a planned intervention in Haiti, as well as a number of law review articles each containing its own definition of war. I do not think any of these sources, however, offers a coherent test for judges to apply to the question what constitutes war, a point only accentuated by the variances, for instance, between the numerous law review articles. [Even] if this court knows all there is to know about the Kosovo conflict, we still do not know what standards to apply to those facts.

Judge Tatel points to numerous cases in which a court has determined that our nation was at war, but none of these cases involved the question whether the President had "declared war" in violation of the Constitution. For instance, in *Bas v. Tingy*, 4 U.S. (4 Dall.) (1800), the question whether there was a "war" was only relevant to determining whether France was an "enemy" within the meaning of a prize statute. * * *

Even assuming a court could determine what "war" is, it is important to remember that the Constitution grants Congress the power to declare war, which is not necessarily the same as the power to determine whether U.S. forces will fight in a war. This distinction was drawn in the *Prize Cases*, 67 U.S. (2 Black) 635 (1862). There, petitioners challenged the authority of the President to impose a blockade on the secessionist States, an act of war, where Congress had not declared war against the Confederacy. The Court, while recognizing that the President "has no power to initiate or declare a war," observed that "war may exist without a declaration on either side." In instances where war is declared against the United States by the actions of another country, the President "does not initiate the war, but is bound to accept the challenge without waiting for any special legislative authority." Importantly, the Court made clear that it would not dispute the President on measures necessary to repel foreign aggression. * * *

I read the *Prize Cases* to stand for the proposition that the President has independent authority to repel aggressive acts by third parties even without specific congressional authorization, and courts may not review the level of force selected. [If] the President may direct U.S. forces in response to third-party initiated war, then the question any plaintiff who challenges the constitutionality of a war must answer is, who started it? The question of who is responsible for a conflict is, as history reveals, rather difficult to answer, and we lack judicial standards for resolving it. Then there is the problem of actually discovering the necessary information to answer the question, when such information may be unavailable to the U.S. or its allies, or unavailable to courts due to its sensitivity. Perhaps Yugoslavia did pose a threat to a much wider region of Europe and to U.S. civilian and military interests and personnel there.

Judge Tatel does not take into account the *Prize Cases* when he concludes that the President was not exercising his independent authority to respond to foreign aggression because "in fact, the Kosovo issue had been festering for years." [T]he President alone "must determine what degree of force the crisis demands." See 67 U.S. at 670. Judge Tatel would substitute our judgment for the President's as to the point at which an intervention for reasons of national security is justified, after which point—when the crisis is no longer acute—the President must obtain a declaration of war.[23] One should bear in mind that Kosovo's tensions antedate the creation of this republic.

In most cases this will also be an issue of the greatest sensitivity for our foreign relations. Here, the President claimed on national television that our country needed to respond to Yugoslav aggression to protect our trading interests in Europe, and to prevent a replay of World War I. A pronouncement by another branch of the U.S. government that U.S. participation in Kosovo was "unjustified" would no doubt cause strains within NATO. * * *[24]

TATEL, CIRCUIT JUDGE, concurring.

* * * I do not agree that courts lack judicially discoverable and manageable standards for "determining the existence of a 'war.'" Whether the military activity in Yugoslavia amounted to "war" within the meaning of the Declare War Clause, is no more standardless than any other question regarding the constitutionality of government action. Precisely what police conduct violates the Fourth Amendment guarantee "against unreasonable searches and seizures"? When does government action amount to "an establishment of religion" prohibited by the First Amendment? [I]n *The Prize Cases,* the Court had to determine whether a state of war, though undeclared, existed "de facto" between the United States and the confederacy, and if so, whether it justified the U.S. naval blockade of confederate ports. [There] was no formal declaration of war, the Court

---

[23] Compare Souter, J.'s view, note 1 after *Youngstown* supra.

[24] Randolph, J.'s concurrence in the judgment, on grounds of standing and mootness, is omitted.

explained, because the Constitution does not permit Congress to "declare war against a State, or any number of States." Yet the Court, guided by the definition of war as "[t]hat state in which a nation prosecutes its right by force," determined that a state of war actually existed. [In] making this determination, the Court looked to the facts of the conflict, to the acts of foreign governments recognizing the war and declaring their neutrality, and to congressional action authorizing the President's use of force. Given these facts, the Court refused "to affect a technical ignorance of the existence of a war, which all the world acknowledges to be the greatest civil war known in the history of the human race."

[If] in 1799 the Supreme Court could recognize that sporadic battles between American and French vessels amounted to a state of war, and if in 1862 it could examine the record of hostilities and conclude that a state of war existed with the confederacy, then surely we, looking to similar evidence, could determine whether months of daily airstrikes involving 800 U.S. aircraft flying more than 20,000 sorties and causing thousands of enemy casualties amounted to "war" within the meaning of Article I, section 8, clause 11. * * *

The government also claims that this case is nonjusticiable because it "requires a political, not a judicial, judgment." The government has it backwards. Resolving the issue in this case would require us to decide not whether the air campaign was wise—a "policy choice[ ] and value determination [ ] constitutionally committed for resolution to the halls of Congress or the confines of the Executive Branch"—but whether the President possessed legal authority to conduct the military operation. Did the President exceed his constitutional authority as Commander in Chief? Did he intrude on Congress's power to declare war? Did he violate the War Powers Resolution? Presenting purely legal issues, these questions call on us to perform one of the most important functions of Article III courts: determining the proper constitutional allocation of power among the branches of government. Although our answer could well have political implications, "the presence of constitutional issues with significant political overtones does not automatically invoke the political question doctrine. Resolution of litigation challenging the constitutional authority of one of the three branches cannot be evaded by courts because the issues have political implications." This is so even where, as here (and as in the other cases discussed above), the issue relates to foreign policy. See *Baker v. Carr* ("[I]t is error to suppose that every case or controversy which touches foreign relations lies beyond judicial cognizance"). * * *

The Government's final argument—that entertaining a war powers challenge risks the government speaking with "multifarious voices" on a delicate issue of foreign policy—fails for similar reasons. Because courts are the final arbiters of the constitutionality of the President's actions, "there is no possibility of 'multifarious pronouncements' on this question." Any short-term confusion that judicial action might instill in the mind of an authoritarian enemy, or even an ally, is but a small price to pay for preserving the constitutional separation of powers * * * .[25]

NOTES AND QUESTIONS

1. ***Constitutional sources of power to wage war.*** (a) The phrase "war powers" does not appear in the Constitution, but rather "describes a cluster of powers exercised by the President or Congress, together or separately, to combat both domestic insurgency and foreign military enemies." Charles A. Lofgren, *War Powers*, in Encyc. Amer. Const. 2013 (1986). Art. I, § 8 authorizes Congress to "lay and collect Taxes, [to] provide for the common Defence" (cl. 1); to "declare War (cl. 11);" to "grant Letters of Marque and Reprisal (cl. 11);" to "raise and support Armies" (cl. 12); to "provide and maintain a Navy" (cl. 13); to "make Rules for the Government and Regulation of the land and naval Forces" (cl. 14); to "provide for calling forth the Militia to execute the Laws of the Union, suppress Insurrections and repel Invasions" (cl. 15); to "provide for organizing, arming, and disciplining, the Militia" (cl. 16); and (in § 9, cl. 2) to suspend the "privilege of the Writ of Habeas Corpus [in] Cases of Rebellion or Invasion." As for the President, Art. II, § 1, cl. 1 vests him with the "executive Power,"[26] § 2, cl. 1 declares that he "shall be Commander in Chief of the Army and Navy of the United States, and of the Militia of the several States, when called into the actual Service of the United States," and § 3 charges the President to "take Care that the Laws be faithfully executed."

(b) *Commander in Chief.* What is the scope of this power? Consider Michael Stokes Paulsen, *The Emancipation Proclamation and the Commander in Chief Power*, 40 Ga. L. Rev. 807 (2006): "[T]he President, [by] virtue of [this] Clause, possesses the full military and executive power of the nation with respect to the conduct of legally authorized war against an enemy power, nation, or force [in] matters of military strategy and tactics [and] prevails over any legislative enactment that violates that assignment of power." Contra, Louis Fisher, *Domestic Commander in Chief: Early Checks by Other Branches*, 29 Card. L. Rev. 961 (2008). For the view that "the Constitution creates a powerful Commander in Chief who may direct military operations in a host of ways [but] text, structure, and history [grant] Congress complete control over all war and military matters," including the "ability to micromanage military

---

[25] For the view that *all* separation of powers issues, including the war power, should be nonjusticiable, see Jesse H. Choper, *Judicial Review and the National Political Process* ch. 5 (1980) (arguing that the line between legislative and executive authority is ambiguous and shifting, and that the Court's involvement is unnecessary to police constitutional violations because both branches have enormous incentives and impressive weapons to protect their prerogatives). Contra, Barron & Lederman, note 1 (b) *infra*; Jonathan Turley, *Recess Appointments in the Age of Regulation*, 93 B.U.L.Rev. 1523 (2013). See also Jessica Bulman-Pozen, *Federalism As a Safeguard of the Separation of Powers*, 112 Colum.L.Rev. 459 (2012) ("states often resist executive power [and act] as champions of Congress," discussing immigration policy and implementation of the Clean Air Act).

[26] For discussion of a range of views on the scope of authority granted under this clause, see Gary Lawson, *What Lurks Beneath: NSA Surveillance and Executive Power*, 88 B. U. L. Rev. 375 (2008).

operations," even though "Congress's inability to gather information and act quickly" poses a practical constraint; and in areas of "concurrent powers," where "congressional statutes conflict with executive orders, the former always trumps the latter," see Saikrishna B. Prakash, *The Separation and Overlap of War and Military Powers,* 87 Texas L. Rev. 299 (2008). Compare David J. Barron & Martin S. Lederman, *The Commander in Chief at the Lowest Ebb— Framing the Problem, Doctrine, and Original Understanding,* 121 Harv. L. Rev. 689 (2008): "[T]he text and evidence of original understanding provide [that] the President must to some considerable extent retain control over the vast reservoirs of military discretion that exist in every armed conflict, even when bounded by important statutory limitations." But as a matter of "longstanding practice * * * Congress has been an active participant in setting the terms of battle and the conduct and composition of the armed forces and militia more generally, while the Executive (at least until recently) generally has accepted such legislative constraints as legitimate. [This] prevailed without substantial challenge through World War II[, and the time thereafter] did not establish anything like a consistent political branch practice akin to that concerning the unilateral executive power to deploy troops and to use force abroad." David J. Barron & Martin S. Lederman, *The Commander in Chief at the Lowest Ebb—A Constitutional History,* 121 Harv. L. Rev. 941 (2008).

2. ***Range of issues and relevance of original understanding.*** Especially because relatively few Supreme Court opinions address foreign affairs or war powers, much modern debate involving a host of controversial issues has concerned the original understanding and historical practice.[27]

First, and foremost, who has the power to *"commence* war," the President or Congress? Moreover, may Congress "authorize" a war by mechanisms other than a formal declaration—e.g., a joint resolution of Congress, which also requires majority votes of both Houses? A widely shared view—generally stated, and with various detailed qualifications—is that "Congress exclusively possesses the constitutional power to initiate war, whether declared or undeclared, public or private, perfect or imperfect, de jure or de facto," the only exception being the President's power to repel sudden attacks.[28] These scholars reason that the Founders "determin[ed] not to let such decisions be taken easily. [Their] assumption was not that Congress was any more expert on the

---

[27] For discussion of the criteria for faithful and persuasive use of historical sources respecting original understanding, see Martin S. Flaherty, *History "Lite" in Modern American Constitutionalism,* 95 Colum.L.Rev. 523 (1995); John C. Yoo, *Clio at War: The Misuse of History in the War Powers Debate,* 70 U. of Colo.L.Rev. 1169 (1999). For discussion of the view "that if the constitutional text clearly and straightforwardly answers a particular question, the burden of proof required to credit any argument for departing from that answer will [be] very heavy. [And] a practice by one branch of government that implicates the prerogatives of another branch gains constitutional legitimacy only if the other branch can be deemed to have 'acquiesced' in the practice over time." Curtis A. Bradley & Trevor W. Morrison, *Historical Gloss and the Separation of Powers,* 126 Harv.L.Rev. 411 (2012).

[28] Francis D. Wormuth & Edwin B. Firmage, *To Chain the Dog of War* 299 (2d ed. 1989). Similarly, see Michael J. Glennon, *Constitutional Diplomacy* 80 (1990); Koh, note 1(b) after *Curtiss-Wright* supra; William M. Treanor, *Fame, The Founding, and the Power to Declare War,* 82 Corn.L.Rev. 695 (1997) (nor did Founders intend to give the President a veto power over a congressional declaration of war).

subject of war than the executive—if anything they assumed the contrary—but rather that requiring its assent would reduce the number of occasions on which we would become thus involved. [A]uthorization by the entire Congress was foreseeably calculated, [to] slow the process down [before] the nation was plunged into anything as momentous as war. [Given] the way the burdens of war get distributed, it was felt that the people's representatives should have a say [and the Houses's voting] would increase the participation of the people themselves in the debate."[29] A contrary view interprets Congress' power to "declare War" narrowly, merely "trigger[ing] the international laws of war, which would clothe in legitimacy certain actions taken against one's own and enemy citizens"[30]—thus placing in the executive the power to initiate and escalate hostilities leading to a formal congressional declaration. Advocates of this position contend that "while the bulk of the foreign affairs power was vested in the executive, the legislature retained control over the domestic effects of these decisions through its control over legislation and funding. [T]he political branches could opt to cooperate or compete. The Constitution did not intend to institute a fixed, legalistic process for the making of war."[31]

The *Campbell* decision discusses a second question: What is meant by the word "war" in the phrase "commence *war*"? What about small-scale offensive military operations?[32] Or those that do not clearly involve initiating war or

---

[29] Ely, fn. 22. For detailed disagreement with the view "that congressional participation leads to better decisions on making war by slowing down a rush to war," especially in light of "WMD proliferation, the rise of international terrorism, and the persistence of rogue states," see John Yoo, *War, Responsibility, and the Age of Terrorism*, 57 Stan.L.Rev. 793 (2004). See also Jide Nzelibe, *Are Congressionally Authorized Wars Perverse?*, 59 Stan. L. Rev. 907 (2007), for the theory that "rather than create a drag effect that minimizes the impulse to rush into imprudent wars, congressional authorization might actually do the opposite: because such authorization allows the President to spread the potential political costs of military failure or stalemate to other elected officials, it will lead the President to select into more high-risk wars than he would otherwise choose if he were acting unilaterally."

[30] John C. Yoo, *The Continuation of Politics by Other Means: The Original Understanding of War Powers*, 84 Calif. L. Rev. 167 (1996) (Congress would use its sole control over funding to check the President in foreign affairs). Similarly, see H. Jefferson Powell, *The President's Authority Over Foreign Affairs: An Essay in Constitutional Interpretation* (2002); Philip Bobbit, *War Powers: An Essay on John Hart Ely's War and Responsibility: Constitutional Lessons of Vietnam and Its Aftermath*, 92 Mich. L. Rev. 1364 (1994); Robert Bork, *Erosion of the President's Power in Foreign Affairs*, 68 Wash.U.L.Q. 693 (1990); Henry P. Monaghan, *Presidential War-making*, 50 B.U.L.Rev. 19 (special issue) (Spring, 1970); W. Michael Reisman, *Some Lessons from Iraq: International Law and Democratic Politics*, 16 Yale J.Int'l L. 203 (1991).

[31] John Yoo, *The Powers of War and Peace* 8 (2005). But see Tom Campbell, *Responsibility and War: Constitutional Separation of Powers Concerns*, 57 Stan.L.Rev. 779 (2004) (from experience as four-term member of Congress and petitioner in *Campbell*: "alternatives to an explicit authorization for a specific war are unavailing").

[32] Many "exclusively Congress" scholars invoke the Marque and Reprisal Clause as intended "to ensure that lesser forms of hostilities came within congressional power." Jules Lobel, *Covert War and Congressional Authority: Hidden War and Forgotten Power,* 134 U. Pa. L. Rev. 1035 (1986). Indeed, some deny *any* "emergency" war power for the President, arguing, for example, that Lincoln's Civil War blockade (undertaken "in a genuine emergency" when Congress was not in session) lacked "legal or constitutional authority," but was "ventured upon under what appeared to be a popular demand and a public necessity, trusting then, as now, that Congress would readily ratify" it. Louis Fisher, *Presidential War Power* 48 (2004) (quoting Lincoln). See Richard H. Fallon, Jr., *Interpreting Presidential Powers,* 63 Duke L.J. 347 (2013), invoking "moral and political philosophy" for the view that although "the president can do some things that would be flatly illegal or unconstitutional under the ordinarily applicable rules," such "extraordinary claims

commencing offensive action—such as the U.S. deployment of forces in Somalia to secure humanitarian relief operations, and the U.S. military involvement in Bosnia to implement the Dayton Peace Agreement (in which American forces arrived "not to impose peace, but rather to monitor a negotiated settlement accepted by the parties on the ground."[33]) A somewhat related issue concerns the President's universally acknowledged power to "repel sudden attacks." What is the extent of this authority? Does it supercede the need for a formal declaration of war by Congress?[34] Did the Founders contemplate imminent as well as actual attacks against the United States? What about attacks against U.S. citizens and vessels beyond the nation's borders? Or attacks that threaten American interests, but against or within other countries, (e.g., use of drones in Pakistan against Al Qaeda leaders)?

Further, to what extent can the Founders' basic purposes be effectively "transposed" into the modern world? For example, a highly significant contemporary issue concerns Presidential action taken pursuant to a treaty, such as sending American troops to Iraq by President G.W. Bush and to Haiti and Kosovo by President Clinton under auspices of the U.N. Does the fact that the U.S. is a treaty signatory to the U.N. Charter authorize the President to "execute" it in this way without specific approval of Congress? Compare Thomas M. Franck & Faiza Patel, *Agora: The Gulf Crisis in International and Foreign Relations Law, UN Police Action in Lieu of War: "The Old Order Changeth,"* 85 Am.J.Int'l L. 63 (1991) with Michael J. Glennon & Allison R. Hayward, *Collective Security and the Constitution: Can the Commander in Chief Power Be Delegated to the United Nations?*, 82 Geo.L.J. 1573 (1994). Under international law, if the treaty obligation of the U.S. authorizes the President to do so, may he send American troops to serve under foreign commanders who have not been designated under the Appointments Clause? See generally Yoo, fn. 22.

Finally, while war powers scholars agree that the historical practices of Presidents and Congress matter for the constitutional division of war powers today, there is considerable disagreement in respect to how those practices should be characterized. The "exclusively Congress" commentators concede that a number of post World War II practices—President Truman's sending troops into the Korean War without congressional permission, President G.H.W. Bush's similar conduct in the Gulf War, and President Clinton's military intervention in Kosovo, and in Haiti (in the context of a unanimous Senate Resolution that he had no authorization to do so)—conflict with their

---

[should be limited] to truly extraordinary cases," and we should "accord strong precedential authority only to past presidential practices that emerge as adequately justified"; and that we should apply similar reasoning to "congressional legislation [that] might be interpreted to restrict presidential authority, even with respect to the Commander-in-Chief power."

[33] Jane E. Stromseth, *Understanding Constitutional War Powers Today: Why Methodology Matters*, 106 Yale L.J. 845 (1996). See generally Walter Dellinger, *After the Cold War: Presidential Power and the Use of Military Force*, 50 U. Miami L. Rev. 107 (1995).

[34] For the view that historical materials show that "the President is limited to a lethal but calibrated defensive response, reserving to Congress the decision whether to wage an offensive war," see Saikrishna Prakash, *Unleashing the Dogs of War: What the Constitution Means by "Declare War,"* 93 Cornell L. Rev. 45 (2007).

position.[35] But they contend that "the original constitutional understanding was quite consistently honored from the framing until 1950"[36] distinguishing the more than two hundred situations in which the "presidential power" advocates allege unilateral executive uses of force: "Almost seventy of the cases, for instance, involved small, relatively low-risk, and self-contained naval landings to protect or rescue American nationals overseas, which are a far cry from committing U.S. forces to a major and sustained combat operation. At least eight of the cases involved limited military actions against pirates. Many of the cases on the lists, moreover, were in fact authorized by Congress by statute [or] regulations authorized by statute. The lists do not include cases in which presidents refrained from using force because they knew Congress would oppose it or because they were unsuccessful in obtaining congressional authorization. Nor do the lists generally examine whether Congress was presented with a fait accompli that made it practically impossible for it to object or whether Congress protested the action after the fact."[37]

III. INDIVIDUAL RIGHTS AND THE WAR ON TERRORISM

HAMDI v. RUMSFELD, 542 U.S. 507 (2004): In the immediate aftermath of the al Qaeda terrorist attacks on September 11, 2001, Congress authorized the President to "use all necessary and appropriate force" against "nations, organizations, or persons" that he determines "planned, authorized, committed, or aided" in the attacks. Authorization for Use of Military Force (AUMF). Late in 2001, when American forces were engaged in active combat, petitioner Hamdi, an American citizen residing in Afghanistan at the time, was seized by a military group opposed to the Taliban and turned over to the U.S. military as a Taliban fighter captured on the battlefield. When the U.S. military learned that Hamdi was an American citizen he was transferred to a naval brig in the U.S. The Government maintained that he was an "enemy combatant" who had fought against the U.S. and its allies and that his enemy combatant status justified the U.S. in holding him indefinitely without bringing any charges against him.

---

[35] Consider Michael D. Ramsey, *Presidential Declarations of War*, 37 U.C. Davis L.Rev. 321 (2003): "[T]he essence of a formal declaration of war has long been simply the public announcement that the nation is entering into sustained military hostilities, together with a statement of the reasons for, and the goals of, the conflict. In modern practice, the President routinely makes such a formal public statement, as can be seen from events surrounding the 1991 Gulf War, the 1999 campaign to protect Kosovo, the response to the 2001 terrorist attacks, and the 2003 conflict in Iraq. [W]e should describe congressional authorizations of the use of force [as] delegations to the President of the power to declare war." For the view that Congress's "modern authorization for the use of military force," "shields legislators from personal responsibility for the decision to go to war, and gives Presidents a free hand to choose war," and is contrary to the "original understanding" of the Framers, see Alfred W. Blumrosen & Steven M. Blumrosen, *Restoring the Congressional Duty to Declare War*, 63 Rutgers L.Rev. 407 (2011).

[36] Ely at 10.

[37] Stromseth, supra at 877. For detail, see Ely at 147–150; Fisher, fn. 32.

Hamdi's father filed this habeas petition, alleging that the Government was holding his son in violation of (a) the Fifth Amendment and (b) the Non-Detention Act, 18 U.S.C. § 4001(a), which forbids any imprisonment or detention of an American citizen "except pursuant to an Act of Congress." Hamdi's father contended that his son had not engaged in any combat against the U.S. or its allies and that he had not received any military training.

There was no opinion of the Court. Doctrinally, the Justices disagreed over how to read cases from earlier military conflicts, especially *Ex parte Milligan*, 71 U.S. (4 Wall.) 2 (1867)—in which the Court, per Davis, J., held that military jurisdiction "can never be applied to citizens in states which have upheld the authority of the government, and where the courts are open and their process unobstructed"—and *Ex parte Quirin,* 317 U.S. 1 (1942)—in which the Court, per Stone, C.J., upheld the trial and conviction on war crimes charges before a military commission of German combatants, including one U.S. citizen. The principal opinion was written by O'CONNOR, J., joined by Rehnquist, C.J., and Kennedy and Breyer, JJ. Although she concluded that the initial detention of Hamdi was authorized by the AUMF, and that the Non-Detention Act was satisfied because Hamdi's detention was "pursuant to an Act of Congress" (the AUMF), O'Connor, J., rejected the government's argument that Hamdi could be held indefinitely, without formal charges or proceedings.

O'Connor, J., recalled that "the ordinary mechanism that we use for balancing such serious competing interests, and for determining the procedures that are necessary to ensure that a citizen is not 'deprived of the life, liberty, or property, without due process of law,' is the test that was articulated in *Mathews v. Eldridge* (1976) [Ch. 6, Sec. 6, II]. *Mathews* dictates that the process due in any given instance is determined by weighing 'the private interest that will be affected by the official action' against the Government's asserted interest. [Hamdi's] 'private interest' [is] the most elemental of liberty interests—the interest in being free from physical detention by one's own government. [We hold] that a citizen-detainee seeking to challenge his classification as an enemy combatant must receive notice of the factual basis for his classification, and a fair opportunity to rebut the Government's factual assertions before a neutral decisionmaker. [These] essential constitutional promises may not be eroded.

"At the same time, the exigencies of the circumstances may demand that, aside from the core elements, enemy combatant proceedings may be tailored to alleviate their uncommon potential to burden the Executive at a time of ongoing military conflict. Hearsay, for example, may need to be accepted as the most reliable available evidence from the Government in such a proceeding. Likewise, the Constitution would not be offended by a presumption in favor of the Government's evidence, so long as that presumption remained a rebuttable one and fair opportunity for rebuttal were provided. [There] remains the possibility that the standards we have articulated could be met by an appropriately authorized and properly constituted military tribunal. [In] the absence of such process, however, a court that reviews a petition for habeas corpus from an alleged enemy combatant must itself ensure that the minimum requirements of due process are achieved.

"[Hence,] we necessarily reject the Government's assertion that separation of powers principles mandate a heavily circumscribed role for the courts in such circumstances. [We] have long since made clear that a state of war is not a blank check for the President when it comes to the rights of the Nation's citizens [*Steel Seizure* Case]."

SOUTER, J., joined by Ginsburg, J., concurring and dissenting in part, disagreed with the plurality that if Hamdi's designation as an enemy combatant were correct, his detention, at least for some period, was authorized by the AUMF. He maintained that not only was detention of a citizen like Hamdi unauthorized by the AUMF, but it was forbidden by the Non-Detention Act, a statute meant to prevent a repetition of the World War II internment of citizens of Japanese ancestry: "Since this disposition does not command a majority of the Court, however, the need to give practical effect to the conclusions of eight members of the Court rejecting the Government's position calls for me to join with the plurality in ordering remand on terms closest to those I would impose. Although I think litigation of Hamdi's status as an enemy combatant is unnecessary, the terms of the plurality's remand will allow Hamdi to offer evidence that he is not an enemy combatant, and he should at least have the benefit of that opportunity."

SCALIA, J., joined by Stevens, J., dissented, emphasizing that absent suspension of the writ of habeas corpus by Congress—and nobody claimed it was suspended—"the Executive's assertion of military exigency has not been thought sufficient to permit detention without charge" of an *American citizen*. He contended that, "having discarded the categorical procedural protection of the Suspension Clause, the plurality then proceeds under the guise of the Due Process Clause, to prescribe what procedural protection *it* thinks appropriate."

THOMAS, J., dissented, maintaining that Hamdi's "detention falls squarely within the Federal Government's war powers, and we lack the expertise and capacity to second-guess that decision. As such, [the] habeas challenge should fail, and there is no reason to remand the case." He deemed it "crucial to recognize" that "*judicial* interference" in foreign affairs and national security "destroys the purpose of vesting primary responsibility in a unitary Executive."

———

Another war-on-terrorism case decided the same day as *Hamdi* settled some questions involving the jurisdiction of the federal courts to review the detentions of suspected terrorists, but did not resolve any substantive constitutional issues.

RASUL v. BUSH, 542 U.S. 466 (2004), per STEVENS, J., ruled that federal courts have jurisdiction under the same habeas corpus statute involved in *Hamdi* to consider challenges to the legality of the detention of foreign nationals captured abroad and imprisoned at an American naval base at Guantanamo Bay, Cuba. Significantly, however, the Court left open the question of what substantive rights the detainees might assert. Nor did the Court make it wholly clear whether its opinion would apply to prisoners detained by the U.S. in foreign locations other than Guantanamo (where the U.S. had a permanent lease).

SCALIA, J., joined by Rehnquist, C.J., and Thomas, J., dissented, maintaining that the federal courts lacked statutory jurisdiction to review the Guantanamo detentions at all.

NOTES AND QUESTIONS

1. ***British and Israeli experiences fighting terrorism.*** After examining the experience of two other nations, Britain and Israel, that confronted grave terrorist threats for extended periods before September 11, 2001, Stephen Schulhofer, *Checks and Balances in Wartime: American, British and Israeli Experiences*, 102 Mich.L.Rev. 1906 (2004) concludes: "Confronted by acute contemporary threats of terrorism, both Britain and Israel [granted] executive and military authorities some extraordinary powers but preserved a system of effective checks on the executive and the assurance of *prompt, fully independent* judicial review. In the current 'war on terrorism,' however, the U.S. government has claimed emergency powers that exceed by very large margins—indeed, by light years—the executive powers accepted as necessary and legitimate in Britain and Israel."

2. ***Congressional authorization.*** Before the *Hamdi* plurality found congressional authorization for military jurisdiction in the AUMF, some commentators thought that President Bush had largely acted alone. Consider Neal K. Katyal & Laurence H. Tribe, *Waging War, Deciding Guilt: Trying the Military Tribunals*, 111 Yale.L.J. 1259 (2002): "[T]he Constitution at least requires, at a bare minimum, that offenses be defined in advance by positive legislation, that the judicial branch be open to test whether any given individual is properly subject to the jurisdiction of the tribunals at issue and whether the system of tribunals as a whole comports with constitutional commands, and that appeal to some body independent of the President as the convening and prosecuting authority be available to test whether any conviction and sentence handed down by one of the President's tribunals is supportable in law on the evidence presented." Similarly, Samuel Issacharoff & Richard H. Pildes, *Between Civil Libertarianism and Executive*

Unilateralism: An Institutional Process Approach, 5 Theoretical Inquiries L. 1 (2004), described prior case law as endorsing the view that "the judicial role in reviewing assertions of power during exigent circumstances should focus on ensuring whether there has been bilateral institutional endorsement [by the President and Congress] for the exercise of such powers—rather than a view that the judicial role should be to determine on its own the substantive content and application of 'rights' during wartime." For a view closer to the one expressed by the *Hamdi* plurality, consider Curtis A. Bradley & Jack L. Goldsmith, *Congressional Authorization and the War on Terrorism*, 118 Harv.L.Rev. 2047 (2005). They argue "that the President's congressionally authorized powers in the war on terrorism are broad, but not unlimited. [For example,] because the AUMF's scope is informed by the international laws of war, it does not, at least as a general matter, authorize military actions that are not permitted under the laws of war."

HAMDAN v. RUMSFELD, 548 U.S. 557 (2006): In November 2001, while the United States was engaged in active combat with the Taliban, the President issued the November 13 Order, which gave the Secretary of Defense the authority to appoint military commissions. Shortly after American forces invaded Afghanistan, allied militia captured Hamdan, a Yemeni national, and turned him over to the Americans. Hamdan was then transported to Guantanamo. In July 2003, the President announced his determination that Hamdan was subject to the November 13 Order and thus triable by military commission. A year later, he was charged with having conspired with al Quaeda to commit offenses "triable by military commission," including "attacking civilians," "murder by an unprivileged belligerent," and "terrorism."

A 5–3 majority, per STEVENS, J., emphasized that the military commission at issue was not authorized by any congressional act: "Together, the Uniform Code of Military Justice (UCMJ), the Authorization for Use of Military Force (AUMF) and the Detainee Treatment Act of 2005 (DTA) at most acknowledge a general Presidential authority to convene military commissions where justified under the 'Constitution and Laws,' including the law of war."

Moreover, concluded the Court, "the UCMJ conditions the President's use of military commissions on compliance [with] the rest of the UCMJ itself [and] with the 'rules and precepts of the law of nations, including, *inter alia*, the four Geneva conventions signed in 1949.' The procedures that the Government has decreed will govern Hamdan's trial by commission violate these laws. [At] a minimum, a military commission [can] be 'regularly constituted' by the standards of our military justice system only if some practical need explains deviation from court-martial practice [and] no such need has been demonstrated here."

The Court underscored the fact "that Hamdan does not challenge, and we do not today address, the Government's power to detain him for the duration of active hostilities in order to prevent [great] harm. But in undertaking to try Hamdan and subject him to criminal punishment, the Executive is bound to comply with the rule of law that prevails in this jurisdiction."

BREYER, J., joined by Kennedy, Souter and Ginsburg, JJ., all of whom joined the Court's opinion, concurred: "Nothing prevents the President from returning to Congress to seek the authority he believes necessary. Where, as here, no emergency prevents consultation with Congress, judicial insistence upon that consultation does not weaken our Nation's ability to deal with danger. To the contrary, that insistence strengthens the Nation's ability to determine—through democratic means—how best to do so."[38]

BOUMEDIENE V. BUSH
553 U.S. 723, 128 S.Ct. 2229, 171 L.Ed.2d 41 (2008).

JUSTICE KENNEDY delivered the opinion of the Court.

[In response to *Rasul* and *Hamdan*, Congress enacted the Military Commissions Act of 2006 (MCA), which purported to strip all United States courts of habeas corpus jurisdiction over the Guantanamo detainees. As a substitute for habeas corpus—the traditional mechanism by which courts have ruled on the lawfulness of executive detentions of persons not convicted of crimes by civilian courts—Congress provided a limited form of review by the D.C. Circuit over decisions of Combatant Status Review Tribunals (CSRTs) that had been set up by the Department of Defense under the Detainee Treatment Act of 2005 (DTA). The D.C. Circuit could exercise review only after the CSRTs had found detention to be warranted on the ground that the detainees were enemy combatants, with review limited to whether the CSRTs had acted in accordance with applicable law and procedures specified by the Secretary of Defense.

[Petitioners argued that the MCA's withdrawal of habeas corpus jurisdiction violated the Suspension Clause, Art. I, § 9, cl. 2, which provides that "The Privilege of the Writ of Habeas Corpus shall not be suspended, unless when in Cases of Rebellion or Invasion, the public Safety may require it," and thereby implicitly guarantees that the writ must be available unless Congress validly suspends it. In response, the Government did not argue that Congress had invoked its Art. I, § 9, cl. 2 power to

---

[38] Scalia, J., Thomas, J., and Alito, J., each wrote a dissent that was joined in whole or in part by the other two. Scalia, J., disagreed with the majority's conclusion that the DTA's restrictions on jurisdiction over habeas corpus petitions by Guantanamo detainees did not apply retroactively. The other two dissents addressed the merits. Roberts, C.J., did not participate, having ruled on the matter as a judge on the Court of Appeals before his elevation to the Supreme Court.

suspend the writ on grounds of "Rebellion or Invasion," but contended instead that the Suspension Clause did not guarantee the availability of the writ to noncitizens held outside the United States, and thus conferred no rights on petitioners. Even if the Clause did apply, the Government argued, withdrawal of habeas jurisdiction did not violate it, because the DTA provided a constitutionally adequate substitute.]

[The Suspension Clause] ensures that, except during periods of formal suspension, the Judiciary will have a time-tested device, the writ, to maintain the 'delicate balance of governance' that is itself the surest safeguard of liberty. [In] none of the cases cited [by the parties] do we find that a common-law court would or would not have granted, or refused to hear for lack of jurisdiction, a petition for a writ of habeas corpus brought by a prisoner deemed an enemy combatant, under a standard like the one the Department of Defense has used in these cases, and when held in a territory, like Guantanamo, over which the Government has total military and civil control.

We know that at common law a petitioner's status as an alien was not a categorical bar to habeas corpus relief. [T]he Government says the Suspension Clause affords petitioners no rights because the United States does not claim sovereignty over the place of detention. Guantanamo Bay is not formally part of the United States. And under the terms of the lease between the United States and Cuba, Cuba retains 'ultimate sovereignty' over the territory while the United States exercises 'complete jurisdiction and control.' [But] the history of common-law habeas corpus provides scant support for [the proposition that de jure sovereignty is the touchstone of habeas corpus jurisdiction, and] that position would be inconsistent with our precedents and contrary to fundamental separation-of-powers principles.

[Fundamental] questions regarding the Constitution's geographic scope first arose at the dawn of the 20th century when the Nation [acquired] Puerto Rico, Guam, and the Philippines [at] the conclusion of the Spanish-American War. [In] a series of opinions later known as the *Insular Cases*, the [Court] held that the Constitution has independent force in these territories. [Yet the Court was wary of applying the Anglo-American legal tradition (for example, the use of grand and petit juries) to territories that followed the civil law system, especially when, as with the Philippines, the United States intended to grant independence to the territory.] These considerations resulted in the doctrine of territorial incorporation, under which the Constitution applies in full in incorporated Territories surely destined for statehood but only in part [and mostly in cases involving fundamental rights] in unincorporated Territories.

[Practical] considerations weighed heavily [in] *Johnson* v. *Eisentrager*, 339 U.S. 763 (1950), where the Court addressed whether habeas corpus jurisdiction extended to enemy aliens who had been convicted of violating the laws of war. The prisoners were detained at Landsberg Prison in Germany during the Allied Powers' post-war occupation. The Court stressed the difficulties of ordering the Government to produce the prisoners in a habeas corpus proceeding. It "would require allocation of shipping space, guarding personnel, billeting and rations" and would damage the prestige of military commanders at a sensitive time.

[True,] the Court in *Eisentrager* denied access to the writ, and it noted the prisoners "at no relevant time were within any territory over which the United States is sovereign, and [that] the scenes of their offense, their capture, their trial and their punishment were all beyond the territorial jurisdiction of any court of the United States." The Government seizes upon this language as proof positive that the *Eisentrager* Court adopted a formalistic, sovereignty-based test for determining the reach of the Suspension Clause. We reject this reading.

[Because] the United States lacked both de jure sovereignty and plenary control over Landsberg Prison, it is far from clear that the *Eisentrager* Court used the term sovereignty only in the narrow technical sense. [Moreover, the Government's reading] of *Eisentrager* overlooks [a] common thread uniting the *Insular Cases* [and] *Eisentrager*, [namely] the idea that questions of extraterritoriality turn on objective factors and practical concerns, not formalism.

The Government's formal sovereignty-based test raises troubling separation-of-powers concerns as well. [The] necessary implication of the [government's] argument is that by surrendering formal sovereignty over any unincorporated territory to a third party, while at the same time entering into a lease that grants total control over the territory back to the United States, it would be possible for the political branches to govern without legal constraint. Our basic charter cannot be contracted away like this.

Based on [language] from *Eisentrager*, and the reasoning in our other extraterritoriality opinions, we conclude that at least three factors are relevant in determining the reach of the Suspension Clause: (1) the citizenship and status of the detainee and the adequacy of the process through which that status determination was made; (2) the nature of the sites where apprehension and then detention took place; and (3) the practical obstacles inherent in resolving the prisoner's entitlement to the writ.

Applying this framework, we note [that the detainees here, unlike those in *Eisentrager*, deny they are enemy combatants. Moreover, whereas the *Eisentrager* petitioners were represented by counsel and could introduce evidence on their own behalf and could cross-examine the prosecution's witnesses,] the procedural protections afforded to the detainees in the CSRT hearings are far more limited, and [fall] well short of the procedures and adversarial mechanisms that would eliminate the need for habeas corpus review. Although the detainee is assigned a "Personal Representative" to assist him during CSRT proceedings, [that] person is not the detainee's lawyer or even his "advocate." The Government's evidence is accorded a presumption of validity.

[With respect to the sites of the petitioners' apprehension and detention], Guantanamo Bay [is] no transient possession. In every practical sense Guantanamo is not abroad; it is within the constant jurisdiction of the United States.

As to the third factor, we recognize, as the Court did in *Eisentrager*, that there are costs to holding the Suspension Clause applicable in a case of military detention abroad, [but] we do not find them dispositive. [The] Government presents no credible arguments that the military mission at Guantanamo would be compromised if habeas corpus courts had jurisdiction to hear the detainees' claims.

[It] is true that before today the Court has never held that noncitizens detained by our Government in territory over which another country maintains de jure sovereignty have any rights under our Constitution. But the cases before us lack any precise historical parallel.

[Because we] hold that Art. I, § 9, cl. 2, of the Constitution has full effect at Guantanamo Bay [and that this] Court may not impose a de facto suspension by abstaining from these controversies, the question becomes whether [Congress] has provided adequate substitute procedures for habeas corpus. [We] do not endeavor to offer a comprehensive summary of the requisites for an adequate substitute for habeas corpus. We do consider it uncontroversial, however, that the privilege of habeas corpus entitles the prisoner to a meaningful opportunity to demonstrate that he is being held pursuant to "the erroneous application or interpretation" of relevant law. And the habeas court must have the power to order the conditional release of an individual unlawfully detained—though release need not be the exclusive remedy and is not the appropriate one in every case in which the writ is granted.

[To] determine the necessary scope of habeas corpus review, therefore, we must assess the CSRT process. [The] Government [argues that the CSRT scheme under which determinations of enemy combatants status are initially made by military tribunals] was designed to conform to the procedures suggested by the plurality in *Hamdi*. Setting aside the fact that the relevant language in *Hamdi* did not garner a majority of the Court, it does not control the matter at hand. [Even] if we were to assume that the CSRTs satisfy due process standards, it would not end our inquiry. Habeas corpus is a collateral process that exists, in Justice Holmes' words, to "cu[t] through all forms and g[o] to the very tissue of the structure. It comes in from the outside, not in subordination to the proceedings, and although every form may have been preserved opens the inquiry whether they have been more than an empty shell." *Frank* v. *Mangum*, 237 U. S. 309 (1915) (dissenting opinion). Even when the procedures authorizing detention are structurally sound, the Suspension Clause remains applicable and the writ relevant.

[We can assume that the DTA may be read to authorize the Court of Appeals to order the release of an applicant, even though the statute does not explicitly so provide. And the DTA might be read to permit judicial review of] most, if not all, of the legal claims [the petitioners] seek to advance, including their most basic claim: that the President has no authority under the AUMF to detain them indefinitely.

[More] difficult [is] whether the DTA permits the Court of Appeals to make requisite findings of fact. [But a]ssuming the DTA can be construed to allow the Court of Appeals to review or correct the CSRT's factual determinations, as opposed to merely certifying that the tribunal applied the correct standard of proof, we see no way to construe the statute to allow what is also constitutionally required in this context: an opportunity for the detainee to present relevant exculpatory evidence that was not made part of the record in the earlier proceedings. [N]ewly discovered evidence [may] be critical to the detainee's argument that he is not an enemy combatant and there is no cause to detain him. This is not a remote hypothetical. One of the petitioners, Mohamed Nechla, requested at his CSRT hearing that the Government contact his employer. Petitioner claimed the employer would corroborate Nechla's contention he had no affiliation with al Qaeda. Although the CSRT determined this testimony would be relevant, it also found the witness was not reasonably available to testify at the time of the hearing. Petitioner's counsel, however, now represents the witness is available to be heard.

[We] do not imply DTA review would be a constitutionally sufficient replacement for habeas corpus but for these limitations on the detainee's ability to present exculpatory evidence. For even if it were possible [to] read into the statute each of the necessary procedures we have identified, [the] cumulative effect of [holding] that the detainees at Guantanamo may, under the DTA, challenge the President's legal authority to detain them, contest the CSRT's findings of fact, supplement the record on review with exculpatory evidence, and request an order of release would come close to reinstating the § 2241 habeas corpus process Congress sought to deny them. The language of the statute, read in light of Congress' reasons for enacting it, cannot bear this interpretation.

[T]he question remains whether there are prudential barriers to habeas corpus review under these circumstances. [It likely would be an impractical and unprecedented extension of judicial power to make habeas corpus available at the moment a foreign citizen is detained abroad by the Executive. Proper] deference can be accorded to reasonable procedures for screening and initial detention under lawful and proper conditions of confinement and treatment for a reasonable period of time. [The] cases before us, however, do not involve detainees who have been held for a short period of time while awaiting their CSRT determinations. [And] there has been no showing that the Executive faces such onerous burdens that it cannot respond to habeas corpus actions. To require these detainees to complete DTA review before proceeding with their habeas corpus actions would be to require additional months, if not years, of delay.

[The] only law we identify as unconstitutional is [the provision of the MCA barring habeas review.] Accordingly, both the DTA and the CSRT process remain intact. [Moreover, except] in cases of undue delay, federal courts should refrain from entertaining an enemy combatant's habeas corpus petition at least until after the Department, acting via the CSRT, has had a chance to review his status.

[W]e make no attempt to anticipate all of the evidentiary and access-to-counsel issues that will arise during the course of the detainees habeas corpus proceedings. We recognize, however, that the Government has a legitimate interest in protecting sources and methods of intelligence gathering; and we expect that the District Court will use its discretion to accommodate this interest to the greatest extent possible. These and the other remaining questions are within the expertise and competence of the District Court to address in the first instance.

[Security] depends upon a sophisticated intelligence apparatus and the ability of our Armed Forces to act and to interdict. There are further considerations, however. Security subsists, too, in fidelity to freedom's first principles. Chief among these are freedom from arbitrary and unlawful restraint and the personal liberty that is secured by adherence to the separation of powers. [The] laws and Constitution are designed to survive, and remain in force, in extraordinary times. Liberty and security can be reconciled; and in our system they are reconciled within the framework of the law. The Framers decided that habeas corpus, a right of first importance, must be a part of that framework, a part of that law. * * *

CHIEF JUSTICE ROBERTS, with whom JUSTICE SCALIA, JUSTICE THOMAS, and JUSTICE ALITO join, dissenting.

[The] critical threshold question in these cases, prior to any inquiry about the writ's scope, is whether the system the political branches designed protects whatever rights the detainees may possess. [If] the CSRT procedures meet the minimal due process requirements outlined in *Hamdi*, and if an Article III court is available to ensure that these procedures are followed in future cases, there is no need to reach the Suspension Clause question. [*Hamdi*] concluded that American citizens detained as enemy combatants are entitled to only limited process, and that much of that process could be supplied by a military tribunal, with review to follow in an Article III court. That is precisely the system we have here. It is adequate to vindicate whatever due process rights petitioners may have. [The] DTA provides more opportunity and more process, in fact, than that afforded prisoners of war or any other alleged enemy combatants in history.

Despite these guarantees, the Court finds the DTA system an inadequate habeas substitute, for one central reason: Detainees are unable to introduce at the appeal stage exculpatory evidence discovered after the conclusion of their CSRT proceedings. The Court hints darkly that the DTA may suffer from other infirmities, [but] it does not bother to name them. [The] Court objects to the detainees' limited access to witnesses and classified material, but proposes no alternatives of its own. Indeed, it simply ignores the many difficult questions its holding presents. What, for example, will become of the CSRT process? The majority says federal courts should *generally* refrain from entertaining detainee challenges until after the petitioner's CSRT proceeding has finished. But to what deference, if any, is that CSRT determination entitled?

There are other problems. Take witness availability. What makes the majority think witnesses will become magically available when the review procedure is labeled "habeas"? Will the location of most of these witnesses change?—will they suddenly become easily susceptible to service of process? [Speaking] of witnesses, will detainees be able to call active-duty military officers as witnesses? If not, why not?

The majority has no answers for these difficulties. What it does say leaves open the distinct possibility that its "habeas" remedy will, when all is said and done, end up looking a great deal like the DTA review it rejects.

[So] who has won? Not the detainees. The Court's analysis leaves them with only the prospect of further litigation to determine the content of their new habeas right, followed by further litigation to resolve their particular cases, followed by further litigation before the D. C. Circuit—where they could have started had they invoked the DTA procedure. Not Congress, whose attempt to "determine—through democratic means—how best" to balance the security of the American people with the detainees' liberty interests has been unceremoniously brushed aside. Not the Great Writ, whose majesty is hardly enhanced by its extension to a jurisdictionally quirky outpost, with no tangible benefit to anyone. Not the rule of law, unless by that is meant the rule of lawyers, who will now arguably have a greater role than military and intelligence officials in shaping policy for alien enemy combatants. And certainly not the American people, who today lose a bit more control over the conduct of this Nation's foreign policy to unelected, politically unaccountable judges. * * *

JUSTICE SCALIA, with whom THE CHIEF JUSTICE, JUSTICE THOMAS, and JUSTICE ALITO join, dissenting.

[The] writ of habeas corpus does not, and never has, run in favor of aliens abroad; the Suspension Clause thus has no application, and the Court's intervention in this military matter is entirely ultra vires.

[The] game of bait-and-switch that today's opinion plays upon the Nation's Commander in Chief will make the war harder on us. It will almost certainly cause more Americans to be killed. [At] least [30] prisoners hitherto released from Guantanamo Bay have returned to the battlefield. Some have been captured or killed. But others have succeeded in carrying on their atrocities against innocent civilians. [These], mind you, were detainees whom *the military* had concluded were not enemy combatants. Their return to the kill illustrates the incredible difficulty of assessing who is and who is not an enemy combatant in a foreign theater of operations where the environment does not lend itself to rigorous evidence collection. Astoundingly, the Court today raises the bar, requiring military officials to appear before civilian courts and defend their decisions under procedural and evidentiary rules that go beyond what Congress has specified.

[But] even when the military has evidence that it can bring forward, it is often foolhardy to release that evidence to the attorneys representing our enemies. [During] the 1995 prosecution of Omar Abdel Rahman, federal prosecutors gave the names of 200 unindicted co-conspirators to the "Blind Sheik's" defense lawyers; that information was in the hands of Osama Bin Laden within two weeks. In another case, trial testimony revealed to the enemy that the United States had been monitoring their cellular network, whereupon they promptly stopped using it, enabling more of them to evade capture and continue their atrocities.

[What] competence does the Court have to second-guess the judgment of Congress and the [President]? None whatever.

What drives today's decision is neither the meaning of the Suspension Clause, nor the principles of our precedents, but rather an inflated notion of judicial supremacy. The Court says that if the extraterritorial applicability of the Suspension Clause turned on formal notions of sovereignty, "it would be possible for the political branches to govern without legal constraint" in areas beyond the sovereign territory of the United States. That cannot be, the Court says, because it is the duty of this Court to say what the law is. It would be difficult to imagine a more question-begging analysis. [Our] power "to say what the law is" is circumscribed by the limits of our statutorily and constitutionally conferred jurisdiction. And that is precisely the question in these cases: whether the Constitution confers habeas jurisdiction on federal courts to decide petitioners' claims. It is both irrational and arrogant to say that the answer must be yes, because otherwise we would not be supreme.

[Today] the Court [breaks] a chain of precedent as old as the common law that prohibits judicial inquiry into detentions of aliens abroad absent statutory authorization. And, most tragically, it sets our military commanders the impossible task of proving to a civilian court, under whatever standards the Court devises in the future, that evidence supports the confinement of each and every enemy prisoner.

The Nation will live to regret what the Court has done today. I dissent.

NOTES AND QUESTIONS

1. *Justice Breyer's reflections on the leading cases growing out of the "War on Terror."* In his book, Stephen Breyer, *Making Our Democracy Work* 194–212 (2010), the Justice discusses four Supreme Court cases that grew out of the "War on Terror": *Rasul*; *Hamdi*; *Hamdan*; and *Boumediene*: "I have focused [on] the way the Court tried to protect the individual rights of highly unpopular individuals in circumstances where the president's and Congress's constitutional powers to detain those individuals were particularly strong. And I have emphasized the Court's efforts to understand, and to respect, the role that other governmental institutions must play in wartime or where there is a special risk to national security.

"[The] strongest criticism of the Court's holdings, and one that the dissenters emphasized, is that the Court has not set forth clear criteria that would bind lower and future courts. It has created constitutional uncertainty about where the line is that presidents acting with congressional support may not cross. But what is the alternative? Although constitutional interpretations that did not restrain the president would have created more certainty, they would have come at the price of eliminating protections on which the Constitution insists. At the same time, a set of clear legal rules—a matrix of what and how and when and where and whom the Constitution protects—runs the risk of doing just what the critics seek to avoid, namely, interfering significantly with the powers of Congress and the president to protect the nation.

"[Widespread] public acceptance of the Court's Guantanamo decisions may reflect in part political or other circumstances over which the Court had no control. But the way in which the Court decided the cases may have helped as well. The Court independently wrote decisions designed to safeguard constitutional protection of individual rights while also interpreting the Constitution in a workable way. The Court sought to respect the roles of other government branches. It sought to recognize the practical security needs that underlie enemy combatant detention. It proceeded cautiously, step-by-step. It decided the ultimate constitutional issue presented in *Boumediene* only after the Court had engaged in a dialogue with the other government branches through other case decisions over a period of several years. Regardless, the other government branches thought it natural and appropriate to abide by the Court's decisions. That fact reflects two hundred years of American history."

2. ***Boumediene beyond Guantanamo.*** "Perhaps the most anticipated case to interpret *Boumediene* was *Al Maqaleh v. Gates*, 605 F.3d 84 (D.C.Cir.2010), which addressed habeas petitions filed by detainees at Bagram Airfield in Afghanistan. In deciding whether to apply *Boumediene*'s extension of habeas rights to a military base other than Guantanamo, the D.C. Circuit adopted a narrow interpretation of *Boumediene*'s extraterritorial reach. The result was a decision that strongly suggested that Guananamo's peculiar 'not abroad' position would circumscribe any further extension of the writ." Developments, *Extraterritoriality and the War on Terror*, 124 Harv.L.Rev. 1258 (2011).

3. ***Has the D.C. Circuit tried to undermine Boumediene?*** Consider Stephen I. Vladeck, *The D.C. Circuit After Boumediene*, 41 Seton Hall L.Rev. 1451 (2011): "[W]hile it smacks of hyperbole to refer to the D.C. Circuit as being engaged in a collective effort to subvert *Boumediene*, it is equally unconvincing to assert that the entire court of appeals has faithfully administered the Supreme Court's commands. [T]he most troubling aspects of the court's post-*Boumediene* jurisprudence can all be traced to some combination of four [Republican appointees who] are effectively fighting a rear-guard action while their colleagues coalesce around substantive and procedural rules that are materially consistent with what little guidance the Supreme Court has provided in these cases—and, as importantly, that have the general endorsement of virtually all of the district judges and the executive branch."

4. ***Did President Obama change course?*** According to Joseph Margulies, *What Changed When Everything Changed* 261–273 (2013), as a presidential candidate in 2008, Barack "Obama had promised to correct the abuses of the Bush administration's war on terror. He vowed to end torture, [restore] the dominant role of civilian courts as the preferred venue for terrorism prosecutions, and close the prison at Guantanamo. [Yet] by 2010 [the] apparently broad national consensus [that supported Obama's plans] had all but disappeared. [In] polls taken since early 2010, respondents have consistently opposed closing Guantanamo, sometimes by large margins. Similar numbers have voiced support for trying alleged terrorists in a military commission rather than a civilian court. [How] do we account for the paradox of the Obama era? [Partisanship] no doubt partly explains the paradox, [but] it cannot be the whole answer. [T]he essence of the punitive turn is the shared determination to *jointly* create a monster and *collectively* respond to the construction by dramatically expanding the executive branch's power to track, seize, and imprison the new demon in order to protect 'us' from 'them.' It is a communal exercise. The Bush administration outran the limits of this sentiment by claiming an inherent power to ignore Congress, bypass the courts, and exclude the public. [But] the Obama administration has disavowed this claim to inherent power and relies instead on the power granted to it by Congress. [The] Obama administration is doing precisely what presidents have done for decades, working in partnership with the other branches of

government and the organs of civil society to denounce and pursue the monster in our midst by expanding the power of the executive branch."

2. CONGRESSIONAL ACTION AFFECTING "PRESIDENTIAL" POWERS

I. DELEGATION OF RULEMAKING POWER

YAKUS v. UNITED STATES, 321 U.S. 414 (1944): The World War II emergency price control act authorized the president-appointed administrator to issue regulations establishing maximum prices and rents [w]hen in the administrator's judgment prices "have risen or threaten to rise in a manner inconsistent with the purposes of this act." The administrator was to "make adjustments for such relevant factors as he may determine and deem to be of general applicability." The Court, per STONE, C.J., upheld this delegation: "The Act [is] an exercise by Congress of its legislative power. In it Congress has stated the legislative objective, has prescribed the method of achieving that objective—maximum price fixing—, and has laid down standards to guide the administrative determination of both the occasions for the exercise of the price-fixing power, and the particular prices to be established.

"The Act is unlike the National Industrial Recovery Act [in] *Schechter Poultry Corp.*, [Ch. 2, Sec. 2, III, A], which proclaimed in the broadest terms its purpose 'to rehabilitate industry and to conserve natural resources.' It prescribed no method of attaining that end save by the establishment of codes of fair competition, the nature of whose permissible provisions was left undefined. It provided no standards to which those codes were to conform.

"[The] Constitution [does] not require that Congress find for itself every fact upon which it desires to base legislative action. [The] essentials of the legislative function [are] preserved when Congress has specified the basic conditions of fact upon whose existence or occurrence, ascertained from relevant data by a designated administrative agency, it directs that its statutory command shall be effective. It is no objection that [this calls] for the exercise of judgment, and for the formulation of subsidiary administrative policy within the prescribed statutory framework."[39]

NOTES AND QUESTIONS

1. *Nondelegation doctrine.* (a) *Law.* The Court has continued to give voice to a "nondelegation doctrine," under which "Congress [cannot] delegate its legislative powers to another branch," *Mistretta v. United States*, Sec. III

---

[39] Only Roberts, J., dissented on the delegation issue.

infra, but has not invalidated legislation under it since 1935.[40] Although some justices have occasionally sought to enforce this principle,[41] the decisions establish that delegations will be upheld if Congress furnishes an "intelligible principle" that rulemakers are bound to follow, and leave little reason to believe that the requisites stated in *Yakus* are effective limits on the delegation of legislative power. See 1 Kenneth C. Davis & Richard J. Pierce, Jr., *Administrative Law Treatise* 98–123 (5th ed. 2010); *Mistretta*, Sec. III infra.

WHITMAN v. AMERICAN TRUCKING ASSN'S, INC., 531 U.S. 457 (2001), per SCALIA, J. held that the Clean Air Act's delegation to the EPA to set air quality standards—"the attainment and maintenance of which [are] requisite to protect the public health" with "an adequate margin of safety"— stated an "intelligible principle." THOMAS, J., agreed, but was "not convinced that the intelligible principle doctrine serves to prevent all cessions of legislative power. [On a future day], I would be willing to address the question whether our delegation jurisprudence has strayed too far from our Founders' understanding of separation of powers."

The broad scope of Congress' power to delegate in the modern administrative state is further emphasized by

UNITED STATES v. MEAD, 533 U.S. 218 (2001), which concerns a federal agency's interpretation of a statutory authorization when "Congress has not directly addressed the precise question at issue." The Court held that "if Congress has explicitly left a gap for the agency to fill," the agency's interpretations of its governing statute are valid "unless they are procedurally arbitrary, capricious, or manifestly contrary to the statute"; if the delegation is "implicit rather than explicit," the agency's interpretation is valid if "reasonable." If the authorization is neither explicit nor implicit, "considerable weight should be accorded to an executive department's construction of a statutory scheme it is entrusted to administer," with the outcome ultimately based on multiple factors. In addition to this judicial "deference" to the agency's interpretations, "an agency to which Congress has delegated policymaking responsibilities may, within the limits of that delegation, properly rely upon the incumbent administration's views of wise policy to inform its judgments. While agencies are not directly accountable to the people, the Chief Executive is [and may appropriately resolve] the competing interests which Congress itself either inadvertently did not resolve, or intentionally left to be resolved by the agency charged with the administration of the statute in light of everyday realities."

---

[40] In only two cases, both involving New Deal legislation, has the Court invalidated congressional delegation of legislative power to a federal officer or agency. *Schechter*, supra; *Panama Refining Co. v. Ryan*, 293 U.S. 388 (1935). See also *Carter v. Carter Coal Co.*, Ch. 2, Sec. 2, III, A, invalidating a congressional delegation to a private industry association with a potentially adverse interest to the objects of the regulation. See generally Tribe 3d ed., supra.

[41] See, e.g., *American Textile Mfg. Institute, Inc. v. Donovan*, 452 U.S. 490 (1981) (Rehnquist, J., joined by Burger, C.J., dissenting). Cf. the opinions of Breyer and Scalia, JJ., dissenting in *Clinton v. New York*, Sec. II infra.

(b) **Policy.** Consider Cass R. Sunstein, *Is the Clean Air Act Unconstitutional?*, 98 Mich.L.Rev. 303 (1999): "The vesting of lawmaking power in Congress is designed to ensure the combination of deliberation and accountability that comes from saying that government power cannot be brought to bear on individuals unless diverse representatives, from diverse places, have managed to agree on the details. Consider, as an extreme example, the early decision by the German legislature to confer on Adolf Hitler the power to rule by 'decree'; this delegation made possible lawmaking exercises that would otherwise have been extremely cumbersome, and hence removed an important check on arbitrary rule." See generally John H. Ely, *Democracy and Distrust: A Theory of Judicial Review* (1980); Martin Redish, *The Constitution as Political Structure* ch. 5 (1995).

In contrast, it has been argued that "broad delegation to administrators" *enhances* "accountability." Presidents, who "are heads of administrations," are unlike Congress because they have "no particular constituency [with] special responsibility to deliver benefits." Rather, they are concerned with "the responsiveness of government to the desires of the general electorate." Jerry L. Mashaw, *Greed, Chaos, and Governance* 152 (1997). See also Peter H. Schuck, *Delegation and Democracy*, 20 Cardozo L. Rev. 775 (1999): "[T]he agency is often the site in which public participation is most effective. This is not only because [the] policy stakes for individuals and interest groups are most immediate, transparent, and well-defined at the agency level. [It] is also because the agency is where the public can best educate the government about the true nature of the problem that Congress has tried to address." See also Cass R. Sunstein, *Beyond Marbury: The Executive's Power to Say What the Law Is*, 115 Yale L. J. 2580 (2006): "[A]n allocation of policymaking authority to the executive seems to reduce the nondelegation concern, precisely because the executive, far more than courts, has a measure of accountability." Compare Vikram D. Amar, *Indirect Effects of Direct Election: A Structural Examination of the Seventeenth Amendment*, 49 Vand.L.Rev. 1347 (1996): "[T]he inability to retrieve delegated authority accounts for much of the nondelegation principle. [Broad] delegations to the President are thus the most structurally problematic; the President's dual role as recipient of delegated authority and participant in decisions about its retrieval [through the veto] creates the very real potential that lawmaking power is ceded in such a way that Congress's ultimate power to make laws is diminished." But see Eric A. Posner & Adrian Vermeule, *Interring the Nondelegation Doctrine*, 69 U.Chi.L.Rev. 1721 (2002): "[A]ny such delegation would be revocable by a subsequent statute: Congress may not bind the legislative authority of its successors. The president could, of course, veto the subsequent statute, so that two-thirds of both houses of Congress would be necessary to revoke the delegation, but that is true whether or not the statute contains an intelligible principle."

(c) **Reasons for delegation.** Why does Congress, which might be expected to be jealous of its authority, so frequently delegate rulemaking power to the executive branch? Consider Redish, supra at 35: "[D]ramatic relaxation of the so-called nondelegation doctrine [was] dictated by the social goals and political philosophy of the New Deal, which focused on the need for efficiency and expertise in the administration of governmental programs and which therefore called for substantial administrative discretion in substantive policymaking." See also Richard B. Stewart, *The Reformation of American Administrative Law*, 88 Harv.L.Rev. 1667 (1975): "Administration is an exercise in experiment. [T]here appear to be serious institutional constraints on Congress' ability to specify regulatory policy in meaningful detail. Legislative majorities typically represent coalitions of interests that must not only compromise among themselves but also with opponents. Individual politicians often find far more to be lost than gained in taking a readily identifiable stand on a controversial issue. [Furthermore,] detailed legislative specification [of] specialized and complex issues [requires] resources that Congress has, in most instances, been unable or unwilling to muster. [Finally,] one may question whether a legislature is likely in many instances to generate more responsible decisions on questions of policy than agencies."[42]

(d) ***Rejection of doctrine.*** Consider Posner & Vermeule, supra: "Neither Congress nor its members may delegate to anyone else the authority to vote on federal statutes. [But a] statutory grant of authority to the executive isn't a *transfer* of legislative power, but an *exercise* of legislative power.[43] [The] nondelegation position lacks any foundation in constitutional text and structure, in standard originalist sources, or in sound economic and political theory."[44] For the view that the nondelegation doctrine should be replaced with an "exclusive delegation" doctrine, which "enjoys at least as much support in terms of the structure, original understanding, and evolved interpretation of the Constitution as the traditional nondelegation doctrine does," see Thomas W. Merrill, *Rethinking Article I, Section 1: From Nondelegation to Exclusive Delegation*, 104 Colum.L.Rev. 2097 (2004). Compare David Schoenbrod, *Politics and the Principle That Elected Legislators Should Make the Laws*, 26 Harv.J.L. & Pub.Pol. 239 (2003): Reliance on the *INS v. Chadha's*, infra, definition of "lawmaking," as action with "the purpose and effect of altering the legal rights, duties, and relations of persons," and on Black, J.'s opinion in

---

[42] For an argument that virtually the entire administrative state is unconstitutional and thoughts about what to do about it, see Gary Lawson, *The Rise and Rise of the Administrative State*, 107 Harv.L.Rev. 1231 (1994). For strong criticism of the Court's "failure to enforce" the nondelegation principle and thus undermining an effective separation of powers, see Douglas H. Ginsburg & Steven Menashi, *Nondelegation and the Unitary Executive*, 12 U. Pa. J. Con. L. 251 (2010).

[43] Compare Larry Alexander & Saikrishna Prakash, *Reports of the Nondelegation Doctrine's Death Are Greatly Exaggerated*, 70 U.Chi.L.Rev. 1297 (2003): Posner & Vermeule argue that " Congress may statutorily delegate all of its authority over commercial affairs to the Secretary of Commerce. [This] would be functionally equivalent to giving the Secretary of Commerce 218 (of 435) votes in the House and 51 (of 100) votes in the Senate." For general response, see Eric A. Posner & Adrian Vermeule, *Nondelegation: A Post-Mortem*, 70 U.Chi.L.Rev. 1331 (2003).

[44] Compare Gary Lawson, *Discretion as Delegation: The "Proper" Understanding of the Nondelegation Doctrine*, 73 Geo.Wash.L.Rev. 235 (2005) "[Under Marshall, C.J.'s] formulation of the 'traditional nondelegation doctrine,' * * * 'Congress must make the central, fundamental decisions, but Congress can leave ancillary matters to the President or the courts.' [The] essence of the executive power is 'the execution of validly enacted law,' but a law that exceeds Congress's [is] not 'validly enacted' and therefore does not count as 'law' that the President may permissibly execute."

Youngstown would be "a major improvement on the 'intelligible principle' test. The [proposed] test rides on the qualitative question of whether Congress is doing the work of a legislature, not the quantitative question of whether Congress has said enough about the goals that lawmakers in an agency should pursue. [Then, legislators] could not confine their accountability to those rare occasions when political capital is to be made by putting a regulation to a vote."

2. ***Military and foreign affairs.*** Did the functional imperative of averting a crippling wartime inflation justify the result in *Yakus*? See also *Loving v. United States,* 517 U.S. 748 (1996), per KENNEDY, J., holding unanimously, on the assumption that its death penalty jurisprudence applied to courts-martial, that Congress could delegate to the President responsibility for prescribing aggravating factors warranting capital sentences. Because the assigned duties were "interlinked" with the President's constitutional powers as Commander in Chief, Congress, which had already defined the underlying capital offense, was not required to supply the President with "further guidance" concerning aggravating factors.[45] For further consideration of the foreign affairs context, see Sec. 1, II supra. Is the judicial branch competent to assess claims of necessity and importance in ruling on congressional delegations in other contexts?

3. ***Proposals for revitalization.*** (a) "[L]imitations on executive discretion [are] best promoted not by invalidating legislation, but by statutory construction[46] and by clear statement principles[47]—the real place where contemporary American law recognizes a nondelegation doctrine, and where that doctrine now flourishes—and also by judicial invalidation in the extremely rare cases where even aggressive statutory construction is able to identify neither floors nor ceilings." Sunstein, supra. Compare John Manning, *The Nondelegation Doctrine as a Canon of Avoidance,* 2000 Sup.Ct.Rev. 223: "If the nondelegation doctrine seeks to promote legislative responsibility for policy choices and to safeguard the process of bicameralism and presentment, it is odd for the judiciary to implement it through a technique that asserts the prerogative to alter a statute's conventional meaning and, in so doing, to disturb the apparent lines of compromise produced by the legislative process. [This] strategy defeats, at least as much as it promotes * * * legislative responsibility."

(b) "The new delegation doctrine [accepts] Congress's assignment of power and consequent relinquishment of policy control, [but] also ensures that agencies implement their delegated authority in [a manner] necessary for democratic lawmaking [by supplying] a limiting standard, rationally related to the goals of the Act [citing *AT & T Corp. v. Iowa Utilities Bd.,* 525 U.S. 366

---

[45] Scalia, J., joined by O'Connor, J., concurred, but declined to join the majority's treating English history as a source of relevant separation-of-powers principles in this case. Thomas, J., concurred in the judgment only.

[46] "As between an open-ended and less open-ended understanding of agency authority, the less open-ended interpretation should be preferred."

[47] "Often courts say that statutes will not be interpreted to allow agencies to engage in certain conduct unless there has been a clear statement of authorization from Congress."

(1999), a decision yet to be regularly applied]." Lisa S. Bressman, *Schechter Poultry at the Millennium: A Delegation Doctrine for the Administrative State*, 109 Yale L.J. 1399 (2000).[48]

II. LEGISLATIVE AND LINE ITEM VETOES

INS v. CHADHA
462 U.S. 919, 103 S.Ct. 2764, 77 L.Ed.2d 317 (1983).

CHIEF JUSTICE BURGER delivered the opinion of the Court.

[The Immigration and Nationality Act authorized the Attorney General to suspend deportation of a deportable alien if he met specified conditions and would suffer "extreme hardship" if deported. It required a report to Congress on each suspension. Sec. 244(c)(2) provided that if, within a specified period thereafter, either house of Congress "passes a resolution stating [that] it does not favor the suspension [the] Attorney General shall thereupon deport such alien." The Attorney General suspended the deportation of Chadha. Accepting a House Committee's conclusion that Chadha did not satisfy the hardship requirements, the House of Representatives passed a resolution that the "deportation should not be suspended." It was not submitted to the Senate, nor "presented to the President" under Art. I, § 7.]

Although not "hermetically" sealed from one another, the powers delegated to the three Branches are functionally identifiable. [Whether] actions taken by either House are, in law and fact, an exercise of legislative power depends not on their form but upon "whether they contain matter which is properly to be regarded as legislative in its character and effect."

[In] purporting to exercise power defined in Art. I, § 8, cl. 4, to "establish an uniform Rule of Naturalization," the House took action that had the purpose and effect of altering the legal rights, duties, and relations of persons, including the Attorney General, Executive Branch officials and Chadha, all outside the legislative branch. [The] one-House veto operated in [this case] to overrule the Attorney General and mandate Chadha's deportation; absent the House action, Chadha would remain in the United States. Congress has *acted* and its action has altered Chadha's status.

The legislative character of the one-House veto in [this case] is confirmed by the character of the congressional action it supplants. Neither the House of Representatives nor the Senate contends that, absent the veto provision in § 244(c)(2), either of them, or both of them acting together,

---

[48] Should Congress *ever* be able to delegate governmental power *outside* the federal government? See Harold J. Krent, *Fragmenting the Unitary Executive: Congressional Delegations of Administrative Authority Outside the Federal Government*, 85 Nw.U.L.Rev. 62 (1990); John C. Yoo, *New Sovereignty and the Old Constitution: The Chemical Weapons Convention and the Appointments Clause*, 15 Const. Comment. 87 (1998) (delegation to foreign officials).

could effectively require the Attorney General to deport an alien once the Attorney General, in the exercise of legislatively delegated authority,[16] had determined the alien should remain in the United States. Without the challenged provision in § 244(c)(2), this could have been achieved, if at all, only by legislation requiring deportation. * * *

The nature of the decision implemented by the one-House veto in [this case] further manifests its legislative character. After long experience with the clumsy, time-consuming private bill procedure, Congress made a deliberate choice to delegate to [the] Attorney General, the authority to allow deportable aliens to remain in this country in certain specified circumstances. [Disagreement] with the Attorney General's decision on Chadha's deportation—that is, Congress' decision to deport Chadha—no less than Congress' original choice to delegate to the Attorney General the authority to make that decision, involves determinations of policy that Congress can implement in only one way; bicameral passage followed by presentment to the President. Congress must abide by its delegation of authority until that delegation is legislatively altered or revoked.[19]

Finally, we see that when the Framers intended to authorize either House of Congress to act alone and outside of its prescribed bicameral legislative role, they narrowly and precisely defined the procedure for such action [in] only[: the House of Representatives' power to initiate impeachments, and the Senate's powers to try impeachments, to approve presidential appointments, and to ratify treaties.]

The bicameral requirement, the Presentment Clauses, the President's veto, and Congress' power to override a veto were intended to erect enduring checks on each Branch and to protect the people from the improvident exercise of power by mandating certain prescribed steps. [In]

---

[16] **[Ct's Note]** Congress protests that affirming the Court of Appeals in [favor of Chadha] will sanction "lawmaking by the Attorney General." * * * Executive action under legislatively delegated authority that might resemble "legislative" action in some respects is not subject to the approval of both Houses of Congress and the President for the reason that the Constitution does not so require. That kind of Executive action is always subject to check by the terms of the legislation that authorized it; and if that authority is exceeded it is open to judicial review as well as the power of Congress to modify or revoke the authority entirely. A one-House veto is clearly legislative in both character and effect and is not so checked; the need for the check provided by Art. I, §§ 1, 7, is therefore clear. Congress' authority to delegate portions of its power to administrative agencies provides no support for the argument that Congress can constitutionally control administration of the laws by way of a Congressional veto.

[19] **[Ct's Note]** This does not mean that Congress is required to capitulate to "the accretion of policy control by forces outside its chambers." [Beyond] the obvious fact that Congress ultimately controls administrative agencies in the legislation that creates them, other means of control, such as durational limits on authorizations and formal reporting requirements, lie well within Congress' constitutional power. See also n.9, supra.

[Fn. 9 stated: "Without the one-House veto, § 244 resembles the 'report and wait' provision approved by the Court in *Sibbach v. Wilson & Co.,* 312 U.S. 1 (1941). [The statute in] *Sibbach* did *not* provide that Congress could unilaterally veto the Federal Rules. Rather, it gave Congress the opportunity to review the Rules before they became effective and to pass legislation barring their effectiveness if the Rules were found objectionable. This technique was used by Congress when it acted in 1973 to stay, and ultimately to revise, the proposed Rules of Evidence."]

purely practical terms, it is obviously easier for action to be taken by one House without submission to the President; but it is crystal clear from the records of the Convention, contemporaneous writings and debates, that the Framers ranked other values higher than efficiency. [The] choices we discern as having been made in the Constitutional Convention [were] consciously made by men who had lived under a form of government that permitted arbitrary governmental acts to go unchecked. There is no support in the Constitution or decisions of this Court for the proposition that the cumbersomeness and delays often encountered in complying with explicit constitutional standards may be avoided, either by the Congress or by the President. * * *

JUSTICE POWELL concurring in the judgment.

[In] my view, the case [may] be decided on a narrower ground. When Congress finds that a particular person does not satisfy the statutory criteria for permanent residence in this country it has assumed a judicial function in violation of the principle of separation of powers. [The Framers'] concern that a legislature should not be able unilaterally to impose a substantial deprivation on one person was expressed not only in [the] general allocation of power, but also in more specific provisions, such as the Bill of Attainder Clause, Art. I, § 9, cl. 3 [,both of which] reflect the Framers' concern that trial by a legislature lacks the safeguards necessary to prevent the abuse of power. * * *

JUSTICE WHITE dissenting. * * *

The prominence of the legislative veto mechanism in our contemporary political system [has] become a central means by which Congress secures the accountability of executive and independent agencies. Without the legislative veto, Congress is faced with a Hobson's choice: either to refrain from delegating the necessary authority, leaving itself with a hopeless task of writing laws with the requisite specificity to cover endless special circumstances across the entire policy landscape, or in the alternative, to abdicate its lawmaking function to the Executive Branch and independent agencies. To choose the former leaves major national problems unresolved; to opt for the latter risks unaccountable policymaking by those not elected to fill that role. Accordingly, over the past five decades, the legislative veto has been placed in nearly 200 statutes [:] reorganization, budgets, foreign affairs, war powers, and regulation of trade, safety, energy, the environment, and the economy. [T]he increasing reliance of Congress upon the legislative veto suggests that the alternatives to which Congress must now turn are not entirely satisfactory.[10]

---

[10] [Ct's Note] While Congress could write certain statutes with greater specificity, it is unlikely that this is a realistic or even desirable substitute for the legislative veto. [Political volatility] and [t]he controversial nature of many issues would prevent Congress from reaching agreement on many major problems if specificity were required in their enactments.

The history of the legislative veto also makes clear that it has not been a sword with which Congress has struck out to aggrandize itself at the expense of the other branches—the concerns of Madison and Hamilton. Rather, the veto has been a means of defense, a reservation of ultimate authority necessary if Congress is to fulfill its designated role under Art. I as the Nation's lawmaker. While the President has often objected to particular legislative vetoes, generally those left in the hands of congressional Committees, the Executive has more often agreed to legislative review as the price for a broad delegation of authority. * * *

[The] power to exercise a legislative veto is not the power to write new law without bicameral approval or Presidential consideration. The veto must be authorized by statute and may only negative what an Executive department or independent agency has proposed. On its face, the legislative veto no more allows one House of Congress to make law than does the Presidential veto confer such power upon the President. * * *

If Congress may delegate lawmaking power to independent and Executive agencies, it is most difficult to understand Art. I as prohibiting Congress from also reserving a check on legislative power for itself. Absent the veto, the agencies receiving delegations of legislative or quasi-legislative power may issue regulations having the force of law without bicameral approval and without the President's signature. It is thus not apparent why the reservation of a veto over the exercise of that legislative power must be subject to a more exacting test. In both cases, it is enough that the initial statutory authorizations comply with the Art. I requirements. * * *

The central concern of the presentation and bicameralism requirements of Art. I is that when a departure from the legal status quo is undertaken, it is done with the approval of the President and both Houses of Congress—or, in the event of a Presidential veto, a two-thirds majority in both Houses. This interest is fully satisfied by the operation of § 244(c)(2). The President's approval is found in the Attorney General's action in recommending to Congress that the deportation order for a given alien be suspended. The House and the Senate indicate their approval of the Executive's action by not passing a resolution of disapproval within the statutory period. Thus, a change in the legal status quo—the deportability of the alien—is consummated only with the approval of each of the three relevant actors. The disagreement of any one of the three maintains the alien's pre-existing status* * * .[49]

---

[49] For commentaries on *Chadha*, see, e.g., Stephen Breyer, *The Legislative Veto After Chadha*, 72 Geo.L.J. 785 (1984); E. Donald Elliott, *INS v. Chadha: The Administrative Constitution, the Constitution, and the Legislative Veto*, 1983 Sup.Ct.Rev. 125; Peter L. Strauss, *Was There A Baby in the Bathwater? A Comment on the Supreme Court's Legislative Veto Decision*, 1983 Duke L.J. 789 (1983).

NOTES AND QUESTIONS

1. ***Independent regulatory agencies.*** Two weeks after *Chadha,* PROCESS GAS CONSUMERS GROUP v. CONSUMER ENERGY COUNCIL OF AMERICA, 463 U.S. 1216 (1983), summarily affirmed decisions invalidating a one-house legislative veto of regulatory rulemaking by the Federal Energy Regulatory Commission and a two-house veto of such rulemaking by the Federal Trade Commission. Rehnquist, J., would have noted probable jurisdiction and set the cases for oral argument. Powell, J., took no part. WHITE, J., dissented: "Where the veto is placed as a check upon the actions of the independent regulatory agencies, the Art. I analysis relied upon in *Chadha* has a particularly hollow ring. [These] regulations have the force of law without the President's concurrence; nor can he veto. [To] invalidate the [legislative veto,] which allows Congress to maintain some control over the lawmaking process, merely guarantees that the independent agencies, once created, for all practical purposes are a fourth branch of the Government not subject to the direct control of either Congress or the Executive Branch."[50]

2. ***Formalism and functionalism.*** (a) In upholding delegation of rulemaking to regulatory agencies, the Court stressed the practical governmental necessity for such delegations. See, e.g., *Yakus.* Should the Court also have considered the practical governmental needs for legislative vetoes? Since Congress may authorize a regulatory agency to engage in rulemaking without the formalities of bicameral approval and presentment, already satisfied when the law was enacted, why can't the same Act of Congress also authorize one or both houses to review, disapprove, and revoke the resulting rules without repeating those formalities? If the executive branch can make rules with the force of law, why can't Congress exercise quasi-executive authority (analogous to the "quasi-legislative" power recognized in *Yakus*)? Consider Tribe 3d ed., at 146: "The Framers regarded the legislature as the most dangerous branch, and even two centuries later it remains a plausible proposition to many that there is more to fear when Congress—which is the source of all statutorily delegated authority—delegates not to the other branches, but to itself." Compare the *Line Item Veto* case, infra. Is it relevant whether the legislature or executive is the "most dangerous"? If so, which branch is it?

(b) Consider Greene, fn. 10: "The framers of the Constitution were centrally concerned with avoiding the concentration of executive and legislative powers in the same hands [because] of the harm that concentrated power can bring and the good that can result from diffused power. [I]f we accept sweeping delegations of lawmaking power to the President, then to capture

---

[50] Should *Chadha* have limited its reach to legislative vetoes of individual deportation decisions, perhaps recognized as representative of a potentially broader class of decisions on "highly individual matters" involving the application of law to fact? Cf. Rebecca L. Brown, *Separation of Powers and Ordered Liberty*, 139 U.Pa.L.Rev. 1513 (1991) (arguing that "the Court [should] examine governmental acts in light of the degree to which they tend to detract from [individual] fairness [in] the process of government"). For discussion and classification of the various types of legislative veto provisions employed since 1932, when Congress authorized the President to reorganize the executive departments subject to a one-House veto, see Strauss, supra.

accurately the framers' principles [we] must also accept some (though not all) congressional efforts at regulating presidential lawmaking. [The legislative veto] might be far from the specific structure that the framers envisioned, but it is far closer to their underlying principles than the present system, which allows the President to make policy while effectively preventing Congress from doing anything about it."

(c) Compare arguments that, measured against the purposes of the framers' checks and balances, the legislative veto was *dys*functional. See Harold H. Bruff & Ernest Gellhorn, *Congressional Control of Administrative Regulation: A Study of Legislative Vetoes*, 90 Harv.L.Rev. 1369 (1977), A "primary purpose of the legislative veto [was] to increase the political accountability of administrative rulemaking" by ensuring that [it] is consistent with the intent of Congress. But "political accountability is likely to be attenuated in practice, [because much] settlement of policy occurred in behind-the-scenes negotiations between the staffs of the committees and the agencies." See also Jonathan R. Macey, *Separated Powers and Positive Political Theory: The Tug of War Over Administrative Agencies*, 80 Geo.L.J. 671 (1992): "[T]he subject of a particular legislative veto is extremely narrow. It will commonly be a particular administrative act that has reached the attention of Congress, but rarely will be of such moment that it catches the attention of the popular press or the public. Consequently, the congressional veto inevitably will be the focus of interest group struggle, rather than public-spirited political debate."

3. ***Alternatives to legislative veto.*** After *Chadha*, what options are available to Congress to ensure that administrative rulemaking, in particular, conforms to statutory policy? See, e.g., *Chadha*, n. 19 and n. 9; Breyer, supra; Elliott H. Levitas & Stanley M. Brand, *Congressional Review of Executive and Agency Actions After Chadha: "The Son of Legislative Veto" Lives On*, 72 Geo.L.J. 801 (1984). Consider Tribe 3d ed.: "[C]areful post-*Chadha* case studies of the actual operation of legislative veto provisions indicate [that] the elimination of this short-cut has invigorated the performance by Congress of its traditional role in democratic self-government: bereft of the unilateral power [for legislative vetoes as in *Chadha*], Members of Congress have instead resorted to raising the public visibility of their policy views, to taking responsibility for the programs that they enact, and to sharpening use of existing mechanisms for ensuring that the regulatory process is responsive to their constituents." Compare Louis Fisher, *The Unitary Executive and Inherent Executive Power*, 12 U. Pa. J. Con. L. 569 (2010): "Hundreds of committee vetoes appeared in statutes after *Chadha* [and] Presidents used their signing statements to object that these provisions are unconstitutional, [but] agencies [regularly] comply with [the] provisions."

CLINTON V. NEW YORK

524 U.S. 417, 118 S.Ct. 2091, 141 L.Ed.2d 393 (1998).

JUSTICE STEVENS delivered the opinion of the Court.

[The Line Item Veto Act gave the President the power to "cancel in whole" three types of provisions that have been enacted by Congress and signed into law: "(1) any dollar amount of discretionary budget authority; (2) any item of new direct spending; or (3) any limited tax benefit." The President exercised his "line item veto" to nullify the two provisions involved in this case: a section of the Balanced Budget Act of 1997 that waived the federal government's statutory authority to seek recoupment of as much as $2.6 billion in taxes that New York had levied against Medicare providers, and a section of the Taxpayers Relief Act of 1997, which authorized favorable tax treatment of certain parties selling food processing facilities to farmers' cooperatives.]

The Act requires the President [to] determine, with respect to each cancellation, that it will "(i) reduce the Federal budget deficit; (ii) not impair any essential Government functions; and (iii) not harm the national interest." Moreover, he must transmit a special message to Congress notifying it of each cancellation within five calendar days.

[If] a "disapproval bill" pertaining to a special message is enacted into law, the cancellations set forth in that message become "null and void." The Act sets forth a detailed expedited procedure for the consideration of a "disapproval bill," but no such bill was passed for [the] cancellations involved in these cases. A majority vote of both Houses is sufficient to enact a disapproval bill. The Act does not grant the President the authority to cancel a disapproval bill, but he does, of course, retain his constitutional authority to veto such a bill.

[There] are important differences between the President's "return" of a bill pursuant to Article I, § 7, and the exercise of the President's cancellation authority pursuant to the Line Item Veto Act. The constitutional return takes place before the bill becomes law; the statutory cancellation occurs after the bill becomes law. The constitutional return is of the entire bill; the statutory cancellation is of only a part. Although the Constitution expressly authorizes the President to play a role in the process of enacting statutes, it is silent on the subject of unilateral Presidential action that either repeals or amends parts of duly enacted statutes.

There are powerful reasons for construing constitutional silence on this profoundly important issue as equivalent to an express prohibition. The procedures governing the enactment of statutes set forth [in] Article I were the product of the great debates and compromises that produced the Constitution itself. [Our] first President understood the text of the Presentment Clause as requiring that he either "approve all the parts of a

Bill, or reject it in toto." What has emerged in these cases from the President's exercise of his statutory cancellation powers, however, are truncated versions of two bills that passed both Houses of Congress. They are not the product of the "finely wrought" procedure that the Framers designed.

[R]elying primarily on *Field v. Clark* [fn. 3], the Government contends that the cancellations were [not repeals or vetoes in the constitutional sense, but] merely exercises of discretionary authority granted to the President by the Balanced Budget Act and the Taxpayer Relief Act read in light of the previously enacted Line Item Veto Act. [In] *Field*, the Court upheld the constitutionality of the Tariff Act of 1890. That statute contained a "free list" of almost 300 specific articles that were exempted from import duties[, but] directed the President to suspend [the] exemption for sugar, molasses, coffee, tea, and hides "whenever, and so often" as he [determined] that any country producing and exporting those products imposed duties on the agricultural products of the United States that he deemed to be "reciprocally unequal and unreasonable."

[But there are] critical differences between the power to suspend the exemption from import duties and the power to cancel portions of a duly enacted statute. First, the exercise of the suspension power was contingent upon a condition that did not exist when the Tariff Act was passed: the imposition of "reciprocally unequal and unreasonable" import duties by other countries. In contrast, the exercise of the cancellation power within five days after the enactment of the Balanced Budget and Tax Reform Acts necessarily was based on the same conditions that Congress evaluated when it passed those statutes. Second, under the Tariff Act, when the President determined that the contingency had arisen, he had a duty to suspend; in contrast, [the Line Item Veto Act] did not qualify his discretion to cancel or not to cancel. * * *

The Government's reliance upon other tariff and import statutes [that] contain provisions similar to the one challenged in *Field* is unavailing [for] all relate to foreign trade, and this Court has recognized that in the foreign affairs arena, the President has "a degree of discretion and freedom from statutory restriction which would not be admissible were domestic affairs alone involved." *Curtiss-Wright*. Although Congress presumably anticipated that the President might cancel some of the items in the Balanced Budget Act and in the Taxpayer Relief Act, Congress cannot alter the procedures set out in Article I, § 7, without amending the Constitution.[40]

---

[40] **[Ct's Note]** The Government argues that the Rules Enabling Act, 28 U.S.C. § 2072(b), [provides] that this Court may promulgate rules of procedure for the lower federal courts and that "all laws in conflict with such rules shall be of no further force or effect after such rules have taken effect." In enacting § 2072(b), however, Congress expressly provided that laws inconsistent with the procedural rules promulgated by this Court would automatically be repealed upon the

Neither are we persuaded by the Government's contention that the President's authority to cancel new direct spending and tax benefit items is no greater than his traditional authority to decline to spend appropriated funds. [The] critical difference between this statute and all of its predecessors [is] that unlike any of them, this Act gives the President the unilateral power to change the text of duly enacted statutes.

[Because] we conclude that the Act's cancellation provisions violate Article I, § 7, [we] find it unnecessary to consider [whether] the Act [impermissibly delegates lawmaking authority to the President].

JUSTICE KENNEDY, concurring.

[To] say the political branches have a somewhat free hand to reallocate their own authority would seem to require acceptance of two premises: first, that the public good demands it, and second, that liberty is not at risk. The former premise is inadmissible. The Constitution's structure requires a stability which transcends the convenience of the moment. The latter premise, too, is flawed. Liberty is always at stake when one or more of the branches seek to transgress the separation of powers. Separation of powers was designed to implement a fundamental insight: concentration of power in the hands of a single branch is a threat to liberty. [If] a citizen who is taxed has the measure of the tax or the decision to spend determined by the Executive alone, without adequate control by the citizen's Representatives in Congress, liberty is threatened.

JUSTICE BREYER, with whom JUSTICE O'CONNOR and JUSTICE SCALIA join as to Part III, dissenting.* * *

III. * * * Imagine that the canceled New York health care tax provision at issue here [said] *"that the President may prevent the just-mentioned provision from having legal force or effect if he determines x, y and z.* (Assume x, y and z to be the same determinations required by the Line Item Veto Act)." [One] could not say that a President who "prevents" the deeming language from "having legal force or effect" has either repealed or amended this particular hypothetical statute. Rather, the President has exercised the power it explicitly delegates to him. He has executed the law, not repealed it.

It could make no significant difference to this linguistic point were the italicized proviso to appear, not as part of [the statute's text] but, instead, at the bottom of the statute page, say referenced by an asterisk, with a statement that it applies to every spending provision in the act next to

---

enactment of new rules.[As] in the tariff statutes, Congress itself made the decision to repeal prior rules upon the occurrence of a particular event—here, the promulgation of procedural rules by this Court. [See also Leslie M. Kelleher, *Separation of Powers and Delegations of Authority to Cancel Statutes in the Line Item Veto Act and the Rules Enabling Act*, 68 Geo.Wash.L.Rev. 395 (2000): "REA delegated to the judicial branch prospective rulemaking authority in an area in which the judicial branch has inherent authority under Article III, [and these] valid procedural rules [will] not conflict with substantive policies of Congress."]

which a similar asterisk appears. And that being so, it could make no difference if that proviso appeared, instead, in a different, earlier-enacted law, along with legal language that makes it applicable to every future spending provision picked out according to a specified formula.

But, of course, this last-mentioned possibility is this very case. [T]hat the Act's procedures differ from the Constitution's exclusive procedures for enacting (or repealing) legislation is beside the point. The Act itself was enacted in accordance with these procedures, and its failure to require the President to satisfy those procedures does not make the Act unconstitutional.

IV. Because I disagree with the Court's holding of literal violation, I must consider whether the Act nonetheless violates Separation of Powers principles. [O]ne cannot say that the Act "encroaches" upon Congress' power, when Congress retained the power to insert, by simple majority, into any future appropriations bill, into any section of any such bill, or into any phrase of any section, a provision that says the Act will not apply. [Nor] can one say the Act's grant of power "aggrandizes" the Presidential office. The grant is limited to the context of the budget. It is limited to the power to spend, or not to spend, particular appropriated items, and the power to permit, or not to permit, specific limited exemptions from generally applicable tax law from taking effect.* * *

The "nondelegation" doctrine [raises] a more serious constitutional obstacle here. [The] Constitution permits only those delegations where Congress "shall lay down by legislative act an intelligible principle to which the person or body authorized to [act] is directed to conform." [The standards in the Act] are broad. But this Court has upheld standards that are equally broad, or broader. See, e.g., *National Broadcasting Co. v. United States*, 319 U.S. 190 (1943) (upholding delegation to Federal Communications Commission to regulate broadcast licensing as "public interest, convenience, or necessity"). [L]ike statutes delegating power to award broadcast television licenses, [the] Act is aimed at a discrete problem: namely, a particular set of expenditures within the federal budget. [Second], like the award of television licenses, the particular problem involved—determining whether or not a particular amount of money should be spent or whether a particular dispensation from tax law should be granted a few individuals—does not readily lend itself to a significantly more specific standard. [Third], insofar as monetary expenditure (but not "tax expenditure") is at issue, the President acts in an area where [Congress] has frequently delegated the President the authority to spend, or not to spend, particular sums of money.

[The] "limited tax benefit" question [is] more difficult. [But this] Court has upheld tax statutes [involving tariffs] that delegate to the President the power to change taxes under very broad standards. [These] statutory delegations [have often involved] a duty on imports, which is a tax [that] in the last century was as important then as the income tax is now, for it provided most of the Federal Government's revenues.[51]

[I] recognize that the Act before us is novel. [But the] Constitution, in my view, authorizes Congress and the President to try novel methods in this way. * * *

JUSTICE SCALIA, with whom JUSTICE O'CONNOR joins, and with whom JUSTICE BREYER joins as to Part III, concurring in part and dissenting in part. * * *

III. [Article I, § 7] of the Constitution obviously prevents the President from canceling a law that Congress has not authorized him to cancel. [But] that is not this case. [Article I, § 7] no more categorically prohibits the Executive reduction of congressional dispositions in the course of implementing statutes that authorize such reduction, than it categorically prohibits the Executive augmentation of congressional dispositions in the course of implementing statutes that authorize such augmentation— generally known as substantive rulemaking. * * *[52]

I turn, then, [to] whether Congress's authorizing the President to cancel an item of spending [violates the non-delegation doctrine by giving] him a power that our history and traditions show must reside exclusively in the Legislative Branch. [Insofar] as the degree of political, "law-making" power conferred upon the Executive is concerned, there is not a dime's worth of difference between Congress's authorizing the President to cancel a spending item, and Congress's authorizing money to be spent on a particular item at the President's discretion. And the latter has been done since the Founding of the Nation. From 1789–1791, the First Congress made lump-sum appropriations for the entire Government—"sums not exceeding" specified amounts for broad purposes. From a very early date Congress also made permissive individual appropriations, leaving the

---

[51] For the view that there are two types of "lawmaking delegation": "positive" ("creating rules or standards that are binding with the force of law") and "negative" ("allowing the discretionary executive negation of statutory text"); and that negative ones "are more problematic than positive ones because they allow the override of specific legislative compromises, often undermining legislative success achieved by political minorities," see R. Craig Kitchen, *Negative Lawmaking Delegations: Constitutional Structure and Delegations to the Executive of Discretionary Authority to Amend, Waive, and Cancel Statutory Text*, 40 Hast.Con.Law Q. 525 (2013). Which of these two types was involved in *Clinton*?

[52] For detailed description of "numerous statutes authorizing cancellation or modification of statutory provisions of law" and of congressional sanctioning of "regulatory modification of statutes," see Saikrishna B. Prakash, *Deviant Executive Lawmaking*, 67 Geo.Wash.L.Rev. 1 (1998). For the view that "the central problem with the Court's opinion is its failure to justify applying a stricter standard to the delegation of cancellation authority than to other delegations [of regulatory authority] to the executive," see Michael B. Rappaport, *The Selective Nondelegation Doctrine and the Line Item Veto: A New Approach to the Nondelegation Doctrine and Its Implications for Clinton v. City of New York*, 76 Tul.L.Rev. 265 (2001), who argues that the nondelegation doctrine does not apply to appropriation laws, but does apply to authorization laws that make the basic policy decisions about how the program is to operate.

decision whether to spend the money to the President's unfettered discretion. * * *[53]

NOTES AND QUESTIONS

1. **Clinton's reasoning.** "Because the Constitution does not permit the President to veto particular provisions in a bill," does it necessarily follow "that Congress may not convey additional authority"? Prakash, fn. 52. Consider Elizabeth Garrett, *Accountability and Restraint: The Federal Budget Process and the Line Item Veto Act*, 20 Cardozo L.Rev. 871 (1999): "[In the Line Item Veto Act], Congress seeks to give away power; its instincts for self-preservation should provide some safeguard against decisions resulting in excessive concentrations of governmental power in other branches."

2. **Delegation and accountability.** Consider Tribe 3d ed., supra: "[T]he Act attempted to hand off to the President the tough decisions about federal spending that Congress was unwilling or unable to make on its own—or that Congress did not want to take the political heat for making. It is hard to imagine a statute much more subversive [of] democratic accountability itself." Do the criteria for the exercise of FCC regulatory authority in *National Broadcasting* ("public interest, convenience, or necessity") assure congressional accountability more so than the criteria for the exercise of presidential cancellation authority in *Clinton*? For the view that the "nondelegation" issue is more difficult than the *Clinton* dissenters acknowledge, see Garrett, supra.

3. **Alternatives to line item veto.** Consider Garrett, supra: "Congress could adopt a separate enrollment procedure to give the President the same kind of power. Using this process, Congress would disaggregate the provisions usually contained in omnibus spending and revenue bills and pass each provision as a separately enrolled bill. [In] this age of computers, the enrolling clerks have, or could develop, the capacity to follow the directions of separate enrollment." For a more detailed alternative procedure, see Prakash, supra.

III. APPOINTMENT AND REMOVAL OF OFFICERS

Art. II, Sec. 2, cl.2 states the President's power to "appoint * * * Officers of the United States," but nowhere does the Constitution address the power to remove officers, an issue disputed in the First Congress concerning President Washington's authority to unilaterally remove the Secretary of the Department of Foreign Affairs.

MYERS v. UNITED STATES, 272 U.S. 52 (1926), going well beyond the issues raised, ruled that the President's authority included the power to remove executive officers of the United States, even when their

---

[53] Which of the opinions in *Clinton* was "formalist" or "functionalist"? See Tribe 3d ed., supra.

appointment was subject to the advice and consent of the Senate.[54] TAFT, C.J., reasoned that, as the President's "selection of administrative officers is essential to the execution of the laws by him, so must be his power of removing those for whom he can not continue to be responsible." This point soon became increasingly important as to which branch of government would have "control" over the greatly enlarged administrative state.

———

HUMPHREY'S EXECUTOR v. UNITED STATES, 295 U.S. 602 (1935), per SUTHERLAND, J., held that Congress could limit the grounds for removal of a Commissioner of the Federal Trade Commission: "[*Myers*] cannot be accepted as controlling our decision here. A postmaster is an executive officer restricted to the performance of executive functions. He is charged with no duty at all related to either the legislative or judicial power. [*Myers*] finds support in the theory that such an officer is merely one of the units in the executive department [and] the decision goes far enough to include all purely executive officers. It goes no farther * * * .

"[The] authority of Congress, in creating quasi-legislative or quasi-judicial agencies, to require them to act in discharge of their duties independently of executive control, cannot well be doubted; and that authority includes, as an appropriate incident, power to fix the period during which they shall continue in office, and to forbid their removal except for cause in the meantime. For it is quite evident that one who holds his office only during the pleasure of another, cannot be depended upon to maintain an attitude of independence against the latter's will.

"The fundamental necessity of maintaining each of the three general departments of government entirely free from the control or coercive influence, direct or indirect, of either of the others, has often been stressed and is hardly open to serious question. [The] power of removal here claimed for the President falls within this principle, since its coercive influence threatens the independence of a commission, which is not only wholly disconnected from the executive department, but [which] was created by Congress [as] an agency of the legislative and judicial departments."[55]

NOTES AND QUESTIONS

1. *A headless fourth branch?* Does the "independence" of the FTC imply that it falls within none of the three branches of government created by

---

[54] *Myers* held unconstitutional a statute establishing a four year term for first class postmasters, subject to removal for cause "by the President [with] the advice and consent of the Senate."

[55] McReynolds, J., concurred in the result, noting that his views on the President's removal power were stated in his separate opinion in *Myers*.

the Constitution? Within both the legislative and judicial branches? How may either of these arrangements be justified under the Constitution?[56]

2. *Delegation of judicial power to non-Article III tribunals.* Although reliance on non-Art. III tribunals traces to the early years of the republic, the justification for the practice has always been uncertain, and the permissible bounds of adjudication by so-called "legislative courts" and "administrative agencies" have occasioned recurrent litigation. See generally Erwin Chemerinsky, *Federal Jurisdiction* (6th ed. 2012); Richard H. Fallon, Jr., *Of Legislative Courts, Administrative Agencies, and Article III*, 101 Harv.L.Rev. 915 (1988). On the relationship between separation-of-powers issues involving the judiciary and those involving the executive, see Steven G. Calabresi & Kevin H. Rhodes, *The Structural Constitution: Unitary Executive, Plural Judiciary*, 105 Harv.L.Rev. 1153 (1992).

3. *Executive agencies vs. independent commissions.* Could Congress have located the FTC within the executive branch? The FTC performs the characteristically executive functions of conducting investigations and initiating prosecutions. Moreover, Congress frequently does delegates "quasi-legislative" (rulemaking) and "quasi-judicial" functions to executive officials. See, e.g., Strauss, supra, ("regulatory and policymaking responsibilities are scattered among independent and executive-branch agencies in ways that belie explanation in terms of the work agencies do" and characterization of agencies as "executive" or "independent" is typically a function of ad hoc political considerations). Is it a matter of congressional choice whether an agency with rulemaking and adjudicatory functions is designated as independent or assigned to the executive branch?

4. *The "unitary" executive?* *Humphrey's Executor* appears to have been animated largely by the view that the President must have untrammeled authority over officials performing properly "executive" functions in the executive branch. See Strauss, supra. Might it be "necessary and proper" for Congress, under Art. I, to establish limits on the removal of *some* executive officials? Is recognizing such a congressional power *less* consistent with the Constitution's structure than the proposition that it allows creation of agencies lying wholly outside the constitutionally established departments of government?

Whether the Constitution requires a "unitary executive," i.e., a direct "chain of command" running from the President to all federal officials performing functions not clearly located within the legislative or judicial branch—or whether, on the contrary, Congress has power under the Necessary and Proper Clause to structure the government including the executive branch—is vigorously debated. Among the controverted questions: (i) does the

---

[56] For a range of views on the status of the "independent" agencies, and whether they should generally be conceptualized as located within the executive branch, see Lawrence Lessig & Cass R. Sunstein, *The President and the Administration*, 94 Colum.L.Rev. 1 (1994); Cass R. Sunstein, *Constitutionalism After the New Deal*, 101 Harv.L.Rev. 421 (1987); Symposium, *The Independence of Independent Agencies*, 1988 Duke L. J. 215–99; Peter L. Strauss, *The Place of Agencies in Government: Separation of Powers and the Fourth Branch*, 84 Colum.L.Rev. 573 (1984).

"vesting" clause of Art. II dictate that all executive power necessarily resides *exclusively* in the President;[57] (ii) are the powers specifically vested in the President by Art. II the *only* executive powers that must be assigned to the President (if Congress creates offices or enacts laws that call for exercise of further executive powers);[58] (iii) do early practice and the framers' intent distinguish between offices and functions that must, and those that need not, be subject to direct presidential control;[59] and (iv) what is the relevance of later historical practice and functional and policy concerns?[60]

———

BUCKLEY v. VALEO, 424 U.S. 1 (1976), per curiam, invalidated the Federal Election Campaign Act's provision for the Federal Election Commission because it assigned appointment of two commissioners to the President pro tem of the Senate and two to the Speaker of the House of Representatives, leaving two for Presidential appointment: "[A]ny appointee exercising significant authority pursuant to the laws of the United States is an 'Officer of the United States,' and must, therefore, be appointed in the manner prescribed by [the Appointments Clause]. While the second part of the Clause authorizes Congress to vest the appointment of the officers described in that part in 'the Courts of Law, or in the Heads of Departments,' neither the Speaker of the House nor the President pro tempore of the Senate comes within this language.

"[The] position that because Congress has been given explicit and plenary authority to regulate a field of activity, it must therefore have the power to appoint those who are to administer the regulatory statute is both novel and contrary to the language of the Appointments Clause [which] controls the appointment of the members of a typical administrative

---

[57] Compare Steven G. Calabresi & Christopher S. Yoo, *The Unitary Executive: Presidential Power from Washington to Bush* (2008) (upholding unitary executive thesis) with A. Michael Froomkin, *The Imperial Presidency's New Vestments*, 88 Nw.U.L.Rev. 1346 (1994) (asserting that the Constitution contemplates broad congressional power to structure the executive branch). See also David M. Driesen, *Toward a Duty-Based Theory of Executive Power*, 78 Ford. L. Rev. 71 (2009): The "original intent" of the Constitution "explicitly creates duties applicable to both the President and all other executive branch officials to obey the law [and] requires lower executive branch officials to disobey illegal presidential orders in order to allow them to check presidential abuse."

[58] Compare Froomkin, supra (yes) with Steven G. Calabresi, *The Vesting Clauses as Power Grants*, 88 Nw.U.L.Rev. 1377 (1994) (no).

[59] Compare Lessig & Sunstein, supra (yes) with Steven G. Calabresi & Saikrishna B. Prakash, *The President's Power to Execute the Laws*, 104 Yale L.J 541 (1994) (no).

[60] See, e.g., Steven G. Calabresi, *Some Normative Arguments for the Unitary Executive*, 48 Ark.L.Rev. 23 (1995); Greene, fn. 10 (arguing that current doctrine must allow compensating adjustments to check and balance earlier departures from original intent that unduly aggrandized the executive branch); Martin H. Redish & Elizabeth J. Cisar, *"If Angels Were to Govern": The Need for Pragmatic Formalism in Separation of Powers Theory*, 41 Duke L.J. 449 (1991) ("functional" considerations support endorsement of a "formalist" conception of the separation of powers, including presidential power); Strauss, supra (defending a "functional" approach under which a unitary presidency is not required, but the President must retain opportunities to influence policy and policymaking officials). See generally Symposium: *Presidential Power in Historical Perspective*, 12 U. Pa. J. Con. L. 241 (2010).

agency even though its functions, as this Court recognized in *Humphrey's Executor*, may be 'predominantly quasi-judicial and quasi-legislative' rather than executive. The Court in that case carefully emphasized that although the members of such agencies were to be independent of the Executive in their day-to-day operations, the Executive was not excluded from selecting them. * * *

"All aspects of the Act are brought within the Commission's broad administrative powers: rulemaking, advisory opinions, and determinations of eligibility for funds and even for federal elective office itself. These functions [are] of kinds usually performed by independent regulatory agencies or by some department in the Executive Branch under the direction of an Act of Congress. [Yet] each of these functions also represents the performance of a significant governmental duty exercised pursuant to a public law. While the President may not insist that such functions be delegated to an appointee of his removable at will, *Humphrey's Executor*, none of them operates merely in aid of congressional authority to legislate or is sufficiently removed from the administration and enforcement of public law to allow it to be performed by the present Commission."

NOTES AND QUESTIONS

Court's rationale. Is the method of analysis in *Buckley* consistent with *Humphrey's Executor*? Is the result? Can Congress, in creating an independent agency, provide that no more than a certain number of its members shall come from of any one political party? (Congress in fact had done so in a section of the Federal Election Campaign Act that was not challenged in *Buckley*.) How "tightly" may Congress define the criteria for appointment? May it submit a list of eight candidates from which the President must appoint four? See Note, *Congressional Restrictions on the President's Appointment Power and the Role of Longstanding Practice in Constitutional Interpretation*, 120 Harv. L. Rev. 1914 (2007). For the view that "to the extent that the President's ability to control policy making by 'independent agencies' is unduly impaired, the root of that problem lies in unconstitutional statutory limits on the President's appointment power rather than in the innocuous statutory limits on his removal power," see Richard J. Pierce, Jr., *Saving the Unitary Executive Theory From Those Who Would Distort and Abuse It*, 12 U. of Pa. J. Con. L. 593 (2010).

———

BOWSHER v. SYNAR, 478 U.S. 714 (1986): The Balanced Budget and Emergency Deficit Act of 1985 set maximum yearly permissible deficits with the goal of reducing the federal deficit to zero by 1991. If needed to keep the deficit within the maximum, the Act required across-the-board cuts, half in defense programs and half elsewhere. Sec. 251 set out the procedure: (1) For each year the directors of the Office of Management and Budget and of the Congressional Budget Office were to estimate the deficit and calculate, program by program, the cuts required to meet the goal, and to report their estimates and calculations to the Comptroller General. (2) After reviewing the directors' figures, the Comptroller was to report to the President on the estimates and required budget reductions. (3) The President was then to issue an order placing in effect reductions specified by the Comptroller, unless within a specified period Congress met the deficit goal in other ways. The Court, per BURGER, C.J., held this procedure unconstitutional: "Congress cannot reserve for itself the power of removal of an officer charged with the execution of the laws except by impeachment. [To] permit an officer controlled by Congress to execute the laws would be, in essence, to permit a congressional veto. Congress could simply remove, or threaten to remove, an officer for executing the laws in any fashion found to be unsatisfactory to Congress. [*Chadha*.] With these principles in mind, we turn to consideration of whether the Comptroller General is controlled by Congress.

"[Although] the Comptroller General is nominated by the President from a list of three individuals recommended by the Speaker of the House of Representatives and the President pro tempore of the Senate, and confirmed by the Senate,[61] he is removable only at the initiative of Congress [not] only by impeachment but also by joint resolution of Congress 'at any [time'].[7] [T]he removal powers over the Comptroller General's office dictate that he will be subservient to Congress.

"[The] Comptroller General heads the General Accounting Office, 'an instrumentality of the United States Government independent of the executive departments,' which was created by Congress [in] 1921 [because] it believed that it 'needed an officer, responsible to it alone, to check upon the application of public funds in accordance with appropriations.' Harvey C. Mansfield, *The Comptroller General* 65 (1939).

"It is clear that Congress has consistently viewed the Comptroller General as an officer of the Legislative Branch. [T]he Comptrollers General have also viewed themselves as part of the Legislative Branch. [The] remaining question is whether the Comptroller General has been assigned [executive powers under the Act].

"The primary responsibility of the Comptroller General under the instant Act is [outlined in (2) of the first paragraph above. Under] § 251, the Comptroller General must exercise judgment concerning facts that affect the application of the Act. He must also interpret the provisions of the Act to determine precisely what budgetary calculations are required.

---

[61] The Comptroller General was limited to a single 15-year term.

[7] **[Ct's Note]** Although the President could veto such a joint resolution, the veto could be overridden by a two-thirds vote of both Houses of Congress. Thus, the Comptroller General could be removed in the face of Presidential opposition. [We] therefore read the removal provision as authorizing removal by Congress alone.

Decisions of that kind are typically made by officers charged with executing a statute.

"The executive nature of the Comptroller General's functions under the Act is revealed in § 252(a)(3) which gives the Comptroller General the ultimate authority to determine the budget cuts to be made. Indeed, the Comptroller General commands the President himself to carry out, without the slightest variation (with exceptions not relevant to the constitutional issues presented), the directive of the Comptroller General as to the budget reductions. [A]s *Chadha* makes clear, once Congress makes its choice in enacting legislation, its participation ends. Congress can thereafter control the execution of its enactment only indirectly—by passing new legislation."

In deciding the remedy, the Court invalidated the procedure that gave "executive" authority to the Comptroller General, resorting to the Act's "fallback" provisions[62] that were to take effect "[i]n the event [*any*] of the reporting procedures described in section 251 are invalidated."[63]

WHITE, J., dissented: "[The] Court's decision rests on a feature of the legislative scheme that is of minimal practical significance and that presents no substantial threat to the basic scheme of separation of powers. [Thus], the Court neglects what has in the past been recognized as a fundamental principle governing consideration of disputes over separation of powers: 'The actual art of governing under our Constitution does not and cannot conform to judicial definitions of the power of any of its branches based on isolated clauses or even single Articles torn from context. While the Constitution diffuses power the better to secure liberty, it also contemplates that practice will integrate the dispersed powers into a workable government.' *Youngstown* (Jackson, J., concurring). * * *

"Determining the level of spending by the Federal Government is [a] peculiarly legislative function, and one expressly committed to Congress by Art. I, § 9. [Delegating] the execution of this legislation—that is, the power to apply the Act's criteria and make the required calculations—to an officer independent of the President's will does not deprive the President of any power that he would otherwise have or that is essential to the performance of the duties of his office. Rather, the result of such a delegation, from the standpoint of the President, is no different from the result of more

---

[62] Under the fallback provisions, Congress makes the ultimate budget decision by joint resolution, which is subject to Presidential veto unless overridden by two-thirds votes in both houses of Congress.

[63] Stevens, J., joined by Marshall, J., concurred in the judgment but dissented from "labeling the function assigned to the Comptroller General as 'executive powers.'"

"I am convinced that the Comptroller General must be characterized as an agent of Congress because of his longstanding statutory responsibilities; that the powers assigned to him under the [Act] require him to make policy that will bind the Nation; and that, when Congress, or a component or an agent of Congress, seeks to make policy that will bind the Nation, it must follow the procedures mandated by Article I of the Constitution—through passage by both Houses and presentment to the President."

traditional forms of appropriation: under either system, the level of funds available to the Executive Branch to carry out its duties is not within the President's discretionary control.

" * * * Congress may remove the Comptroller only through a joint resolution, which by definition must be passed by both Houses and signed by the President. [In] other words, a removal of the Comptroller under the statute *satisfies the requirements of bicameralism and presentment laid down in Chadha.* [The] requirement of Presidential approval obviates the possibility that the Comptroller will perceive himself as so completely at the mercy of Congress that he will function as its tool. If the Comptroller's conduct in office is not so unsatisfactory to the President as to convince the latter that removal is required under the statutory standard, Congress will have no independent power to coerce the Comptroller unless it can muster a two-thirds majority in both Houses—a feat of bipartisanship more difficult than that required to impeach and convict.

"[Those] who have studied the office agree that the procedural and substantive limits on the power of Congress and the President to remove the Comptroller make dislodging him against his will practically impossible. [The] majority's contrary conclusion rests on the rigid dogma that, outside of the impeachment process, any 'direct congressional role in the removal of officers charged with the execution of the laws [is] inconsistent with separation of powers.' Reliance on such an unyielding principle to strike down a statute posing no real danger of aggrandizement of congressional power is extremely misguided and insensitive to our constitutional role."[64]

NOTES AND QUESTIONS

1.   *The Comptroller's function.* (a) Was the comptroller's function necessarily "executive"? Could Congress have provided for the required calculations to be made by an independent "Balanced Budget Commission" appointed by the President, with Senate confirmation, and removable by the President only for "inefficiency, neglect of duty, or malfeasance"?

(b) *Bowsher vs. Clinton.* Is *Bowsher's* holding that the Comptroller's "ultimate authority to determine the budget cuts to be made" is an exercise of *executive* power inconsistent with *Clinton's* conclusion that the President's "cancellation authority pursuant to the Line Item Veto Act" was an exercise of

---

[64] Blackmun, J., separately dissenting, agreed with White, J., that it was "unrealistic" to claim that the removal power makes the Comptroller General "subservient to Congress." But to the extent removal power was found incompatible with the constitutional separation of powers, he would "cure" it by refusing to allow congressional removal "—if it ever is attempted—and not by striking down the central provisions of the Deficit Control Act."

For the view that "text, structure, and history" show that contrary to *Bowsher*, while "the Executive can remove all Executive officers [however] appointed, [the] Constitution does not grant him the authority to remove quasi-judicial and quasi-legislative officers," see Saikrishna Prakash, *Removal and Tenure in Office*, 92 Va. L. Rev. 1779 (2006).

legislative power to "effect the repeal of laws"? See H. Jefferson Powell & Jed Rubenfeld, *Laying It on the Line: A Dialogue on Line Item Vetoes and Separation of Powers*, 47 Duke L.J. 1171 (1998); Garrett, note 1 after *Clinton*.

2. ***Formalism and functionalism.*** Did *Bowsher* adopt a "formal" style of separation-of-powers analysis requiring a rigid assignment of "executive," "legislative," and "judicial" functions to the corresponding branch of government, with no cross-branch interference. See Peter L. Strauss, *Formal and Functional Approaches to Separation-of-Powers Questions—A Foolish Inconsistency?*, 72 Corn.L.Rev. 488 (1987). Did *Bowsher* threaten the underlying premises of *Humphrey's Executor?* Or the notion in *Yakus* and many other decisions that Congress can assign rulemaking and adjudicative functions to executive branch agencies?

MORRISON V. OLSON
487 U.S. 654, 108 S.Ct. 2597, 101 L.Ed.2d 569 (1988).

CHIEF JUSTICE REHNQUIST delivered the opinion of the Court.

[The Ethics in Government Act of 1978 called for appointment of an "independent counsel" to investigate, and, if appropriate, to prosecute certain high-ranking government officials[65] for violating any federal criminal law.[66] Upon receipt of information that the Attorney General considers "sufficient grounds," the Attorney General conducts a preliminary investigation and then reports to a special division of the Court of Appeals for the District of Columbia Circuit whether there are "reasonable grounds to believe that further investigation or prosecution is warranted." If so, the Attorney General must request the Special Division to appoint, and provide it with sufficient information to enable it to appoint, "an appropriate independent counsel and define that independent counsel's prosecutorial jurisdiction."[67] The Act grants the independent counsel the "full power and independent authority" of the Department of Justice to investigate and prosecute. The department must suspend all its investigations and proceedings regarding any matter referred to independent counsel.[68] The Special Division appointed Morrison to

---

[65] These include the President, Vice-President, cabinet officers, high ranking officers in the Executive Office of the President and the Justice Department, and the like.

[66] Except Class B or C misdemeanors.

[67] The Act created the Special Division of three Circuit Court Judges appointed by the Chief Justice of the United States for two-year terms. The Court upheld the Special Division's authority to appoint the independent counsel and specify her jurisdiction. It invoked the Appointments Clause reference to courts of law appointing "inferior officers," the congruity of "a court having the power to appoint prosecutorial officers" with a "court's normal functions," and the Act's ban on Special Division judges' participation in other matters relating to the independent counsel.

[68] After having been allowed to lapse during the G.H.W. Bush Administration, the statute involved in *Morrison* was re-enacted, with amendments, in the Independent Counsel Reauthorization Act of 1994. Among its more significant changes, the new statute applied to members of Congress. Its most famous use was in the Whitewater/Lewinsky investigation under Kenneth W. Starr, lasting more than six years, costing in excess of $55 million and leading to the impeachment of President Clinton. This new law expired in 1999 and has not been reauthorized.

investigate a charge of perjury before the House Judiciary Committee by Olson, an Assistant Attorney General. The first issue] is whether the provision of the Act restricting the Attorney General's power to remove the independent counsel to only those instances in which he can show "good cause," taken by itself, impermissibly interferes with the President's exercise of his constitutionally appointed functions. * * *

Unlike both *Bowsher* and *Myers,* this case does not involve an attempt by Congress itself to gain a role in the removal of executive officials. [The] Act instead puts the removal power squarely in the hands of the Executive Branch. [There] is no requirement of congressional approval of the Attorney General's removal decision, though the decision is subject to judicial review. * * *

Appellees contend that *Humphrey's Executor* and *Wiener* [*v. United States,* 357 U.S. 349 (1958),] are distinguishable from this case because they did not involve officials who performed a "core executive function." They argue [that] when a "purely executive" official is involved, the governing precedent is *Myers,* not *Humphrey's Executor.* And, under *Myers,* the President must have absolute discretion to discharge "purely" executive officials at will.

We undoubtedly did rely on the terms "quasi-legislative" and "quasi-judicial" to distinguish the officials involved in *Humphrey's Executor* and *Wiener* from those in *Myers,* but our present considered view is that the determination of whether the Constitution allows Congress to impose a "good cause"-type restriction on the President's power to remove an official cannot be made to turn on whether or not that official is classified as "purely executive." The analysis contained in our removal cases is designed not to define rigid categories of those officials who may or may not be removed at will by the President, but to ensure that Congress does not interfere with the President's exercise of the "executive power" [under] Article II. *Myers* was undoubtedly correct in its holding, and in its broader suggestion that there are some "purely executive" officials who must be removable by the President at will if he is to be able to accomplish his constitutional role.[29] [At] the other end of the spectrum from *Myers,* the characterization of the agencies in *Humphrey's Executor* and *Wiener* as "quasi-legislative" or "quasi-judicial" in large part reflected our judgment that it was not essential to the President's proper execution of his Article II powers that these agencies be headed up by individuals who were

---

[29] [Ct's Note] The dissent says that the language of Article II vesting the executive power of the United States in the President requires that every officer of the United States exercising any part of that power must serve at the pleasure of the President and be removable by him at will. This rigid demarcation—a demarcation incapable of being altered by law in the slightest degree, and applicable to tens of thousands of holders of offices neither known nor foreseen by the Framers—depends upon an extrapolation from general constitutional language which we think is more than the text will bear. * * *

removable at will.[30] [There] is no real dispute that the functions performed by the independent counsel are "executive" in the sense that they are law enforcement functions that typically have been undertaken by officials within the Executive Branch.[69] As we noted above, however, the independent counsel is an inferior officer under the Appointments Clause, with limited jurisdiction and tenure and lacking policymaking or significant administrative authority. Although the counsel exercises no small amount of discretion and judgment in deciding how to carry out his or her duties under the Act, we simply do not see how the President's need to control the exercise of that discretion is so central to the functioning of the Executive Branch as to require as a matter of constitutional law that the counsel be terminable at will by the President.

[This] is not a case in which the power to remove an executive official has been completely stripped from the President. [Although] we need not decide in this case exactly what is encompassed within the term "good cause" under the Act, the legislative history of the removal provision also makes clear that the Attorney General may remove an independent counsel for "misconduct." Here, as with the provision of the Act conferring the appointment authority of the independent counsel on the special court, the congressional determination to limit the removal power of the Attorney General was essential, in the view of Congress, to establish the necessary independence of the office. We do not think that this limitation as it presently stands sufficiently deprives the President of control over the independent counsel to interfere impermissibly with his constitutional obligation to ensure the faithful execution of the laws.

The final question to be addressed is whether the Act, taken as a whole, violates the principle of separation of powers. [We] observe first that this case does not involve an attempt by Congress to increase its own powers at the expense of the Executive Branch. [The] Act does empower certain Members of Congress to request the Attorney General to apply for the appointment of an independent counsel, but the Attorney General has

---

[30] **[Ct's Note]** The terms also may be used to describe the circumstances in which Congress might be more inclined to find that a degree of independence from the Executive, such as that afforded by a "good cause" removal standard, is necessary to the proper functioning of the agency or official. It is not difficult to imagine situations in which Congress might desire that an official performing "quasi-judicial" functions, for example, would be free of executive or political control.

[69] Compare Tribe 3d ed., supra: "[C]riminal prosecution historically was *not* a core executive function. [In] eighteenth-century England, for example, private individuals could instigate criminal prosecutions, and 'although the Attorney General brought some cases and could defeat a private prosecution by filing a writ of nolle prosequi, the system was essentially private.' In most of the colonies, a dual system of public and private prosecution was the norm." Contrast Saikrishna Prakash, *The Chief Prosecutor*, 73 Geo. Wash. L. Rev. 521 (2005): "The Constitution, as originally understood, made the president the constitutional prosecutor of all offenses against the United States. [Although] early history sheds little light on whether Congress can abridge the president's control over prosecution, the better view is that the Constitution does not authorize the Congress to create independent prosecutors, of whatever sort."

no duty to comply with the request, although he must respond within a certain time limit. * * *

Similarly, we do not think that the Act works any *judicial* usurpation of properly executive functions. [T]he Special Division has no power to appoint an independent counsel sua sponte; it may only do so upon the specific request of the Attorney General, and the courts are specifically prevented from reviewing the Attorney General's decision not to seek appointment. In addition, [the court] has no power to supervise or control the activities of the counsel. [The] Act does give a federal court the power to review the Attorney General's decision to remove an independent counsel, but in our view this is a function that is well within the traditional power of the Judiciary.

Finally, we do not think that the Act "impermissibly undermine[s]" the powers of the Executive Branch. [It] is undeniable that the Act reduces the amount of control or supervision that the Attorney General and, through him, the President exercises over the investigation and prosecution of a certain class of alleged criminal activity. The Attorney General is not allowed to appoint the individual of his choice; he does not determine the counsel's jurisdiction; and his power to remove a counsel is limited. Nonetheless, [the] Attorney General retains the power to remove the counsel for "good cause," [and] the Attorney General's decision not to request appointment if he finds "no reasonable grounds to believe that further investigation is warranted" is committed to his unreviewable discretion. The Act thus gives the Executive a degree of control over the power to initiate an investigation by the independent counsel. In addition, the jurisdiction of the independent counsel is defined with reference to the facts submitted by the Attorney General, and once a counsel is appointed, the Act requires that the counsel abide by Justice Department policy unless it is not "possible" to do so. Notwithstanding the fact that the counsel is to some degree "independent" and free from executive supervision to a greater extent than other federal prosecutors, in our view these features of the Act give the Executive Branch sufficient control over the independent counsel to ensure that the President is able to perform his constitutionally assigned duties.[70] * * *

JUSTICE SCALIA, dissenting.

[It] effects a revolution in our constitutional jurisprudence for the Court, once it has determined that (1) purely executive functions are at issue here, and (2) those functions have been given to a person whose

---

[70] For the view that "the 'good cause' provision, while surely expected to give the independent counsel *some* insulation from outside executive control, nonetheless might be construed to avoid a serious constitutional question" by "authoriz[ing] the independent counsel's removal for disobeying the President's legal directives, at least on matters of reasonably contestable legal judgment," see John F. Manning, *The Independent Counsel Statute: Reading "Good Cause" in Light of Article II*, 83 Minn.L.Rev. 1285 (1999).

actions are not fully within the supervision and control of the President, nonetheless to proceed further to sit in judgment of whether "the President's need to control the exercise of [the independent counsel's] discretion is *so central* to the functioning of the Executive Branch" as to require complete control (emphasis added), whether the conferral of his powers upon someone else "*sufficiently* deprives the President of control over the independent counsel [and] whether "the Act give[s] the Executive Branch *sufficient* control over the independent counsel to ensure that the President is able to perform his constitutionally assigned duties" (emphasis added). It is not for us to determine [how] much of the purely executive powers of government must be within the full control of the President. The Constitution prescribes that they *all* are.

[Before] this statute was passed, the President, in taking action disagreeable to the Congress, or an executive officer giving advice to the President or testifying before Congress concerning one of those many matters on which the two branches are from time to time at odds, could be assured that his acts and motives would be adjudged—insofar as the decision whether to conduct a criminal investigation and to prosecute is concerned—in the Executive Branch, that is, in a forum attuned to the interests and the policies of the Presidency. That was one of the natural advantages the Constitution gave to the Presidency, just as it gave Members of Congress (and their staffs) the advantage of not being prosecutable for anything said or done in their legislative capacities. [It] deeply wounds the President, by substantially reducing the President's ability to protect himself and his staff. That is the whole object of the law, of course, and I cannot imagine why the Court believes it does not succeed.

[Worse] than what [the Court] has done, however, is the manner in which it has done it. A government of laws means a government of rules. Today's decision on the basic issue of fragmentation of executive power is ungoverned by rule, and hence ungoverned by law. It extends into the very heart of our most significant constitutional function the "totality of the circumstances" mode of analysis that this Court has in recent years become fond of. Taking all things into account, we conclude that the power taken away from the President here is not really *too* much. The next time executive power is assigned to someone other than the President we may conclude, taking all things into account, that it *is* too much. That opinion, like this one, will not be confined by any rule[;] it is ad hoc judgment. And it fails to explain why it is not true that—as the text of the Constitution seems to require, as the Founders seemed to expect, and as our past cases have uniformly assumed—all purely executive power must be under the control of the President. * * *[71]

---

[71] Kennedy, J., took no part.

NOTES AND QUESTIONS

1. ***Morrison's reasoning.*** Consider Tribe 3d ed., supra: "The Appointments Clause embodies a concern for political accountability in the exercise of executive power. [If] an inferior officer is appointed by persons who are themselves not politically accountable—such as the special panel of judges charged with appointing independent counsels—ongoing supervision by a politically accountable official, whether by the President or by someone serving at the President's pleasure, seems particularly important. [W]here there is little or no political accountability at the front end for the choice of that officer, a 'for cause' limitation on removal that renders political supervision impossible appears troubling from an accountability perspective." Compare Akhil R. Amar, *Intratextualism*, 112 Harv.L.Rev. 747 (1999): "If the President truly disagrees with the Independent Counsel, the President can make the Counsel vanish with one stroke of the presidential pardon pen: no underlying targets of prosecution, no prosecutor. [A] truly skillful chief executive can wield this mighty broadsword as a surgical scalpel by explaining the facts of life to an Independent Counsel (publicly or privately): unless she does *X* and *Y* and refrains from *Z*, the President will be obliged to pardon." Contrast Tribe 3d. ed., supra: "When the President is the target of an independent counsel's investigation, however, no supervision is possible [because] the President may not pardon himself. [Arguably,] the pardon power is too blunt a tool to constitute a means of supervision adequate to render an independent counsel an inferior officer; a Chief Executive [should] not be required to take the extreme step of pardoning the target of investigation in order to rein the independent counsel in."

2. ***Alternative plans.*** (a) "[O]nce a preliminary investigation by the Attorney General shows reasonable grounds to believe that further investigation of high executive officials is warranted, just as it was under the recently lapsed Independent Counsel law, [then] *the President* (not a panel of judges) would have the statutory duty to nominate, subject to Senate advice and consent, a three-member panel—the Special Litigation Committee—who would be principal officers within the Executive Branch, serving at the pleasure of the President." Michael S. Paulsen, *A Constitutional Independent Counsel Statute*, 5 Widener L.Symp.J. 111 (2000). (b) A congressionally designated "Independent Investigator," who could make a full investigation and recommendation to the Attorney General, but with no authority to initiate.

3. ***Formalism and functionalism.*** Is the only alternative to a "formal" conception of the separation of powers, which requires that all "executive" functions be vested in officials subject to the direct supervision of the President, a mode of analysis that Scalia, J., criticized in *Morrison* as involving "not analysis" but "ad hoc judgment?"[72] Is a "functional" approach to the separation of powers sufficiently rigorous to satisfy basic requirements of

---

[72] For critical analysis of the *Morrison* opinion, see Lee S. Liberman, *Morrison v. Olson: A Formalistic Perspective on Why the Court Was Wrong*, 38 Am.U.L.Rev. 313 (1989); Stephen L. Carter, *The Independent Counsel Mess*, 102 Harv.L.Rev. 105 (1988).

the rule of law? Is it an answer to Scalia, J.'s objection that many constitutional tests—including those for issues of individual rights and federalism—involve multi-factor balancing inquiries? Do structural questions, involving legitimacy of the basic design of government and responsibility and accountability of various governmental actors, require clearer, more historically and textually grounded answers?[73] Or should Congress have greater flexibility to structure what it believes to be a workable government?

4. *After Morrison.* (a) MISTRETTA v. UNITED STATES, 488 U.S. 361 (1989), per BLACKMUN, J., upheld the Sentence Reform Act of 1984, which created the U.S. Sentencing Commission charged with devising guidelines for federal sentencing that would establish, within the limits of existing law, ranges of determinate sentences for categories of offenses and defendants according to specified factors, "among others." The Commission was established as an independent commission in the Judicial Branch, consisting of seven voting members appointed by the President, of whom three must be federal judges:

"[Jackson, J.'s *Youngstown* opinion] summarized the pragmatic, flexible view of differentiated governmental power to which we are heir. [As a general principle], 'executive or administrative duties of a nonjudicial nature may not be imposed on [Art. III judges].' *Morrison.* Nonetheless, we have recognized significant exceptions [as in] *Sibbach* [fn. 19 in *Chadha*, in which] we upheld a challenge to certain rules promulgated under the Rules Enabling Act of 1934, which conferred upon the Judiciary the power to promulgate federal rules of civil procedure." Thus, the constitutionality of conferring rulemaking authority on federal judges lay within the "twilight area" recognized by Jackson, J. In light of the judiciary's traditional role in sentencing, there was nothing "incongruous" about the judicial role on the Commission and no "vesting within the Judiciary [of] responsibilities that more appropriately belong to another Branch." Whatever "constitutional problems might arise if the powers of the Commission were vested in a court, the Commission is not a court, does not exercise judicial power, and is not controlled by or accountable to members of the Judicial Branch. The Commission [is] an independent agency in every relevant sense." Moreover, "placement of the Sentencing Commission in the Judicial Branch has not increased the Branch's authority. Prior to the passage of the Act, the Judicial Branch, as an aggregate, decided precisely the questions assigned to the Commission: what sentence is appropriate to what criminal conduct under what circumstances." Nor did this "extrajudicial assignment" undermine the integrity or independence of the Judicial Branch, nor "threaten, either in fact or in appearance, [its] impartiality."[74]

---

[73] See Stephen L. Carter, *From Sick Chicken to Synar: The Evolution and Subsequent De-Evolution of the Separation of Powers,* 1987 B.Y.U.L.Rev. 719.

[74] Only Scalia, J., dissented. He would uphold "delegation of legislative authority" under "congressionally prescribed standards" only "in conjunction with the lawful exercise of executive or judicial power. [The] whole theory of *lawful* congressional 'delegation' is [that] a certain degree of discretion, and thus of lawmaking, *inheres* in most executive or judicial action, and it is up to Congress, by the relative specificity or generality of its statutory commands, to determine—up to a point—how small or how large that degree shall be. [But] the lawmaking function of the

(b) METROPOLITAN WASHINGTON AIRPORTS AUTH. v. CITIZENS FOR ABATEMENT OF AIRPORT NOISE, 501 U.S. 252 (1991), per STEVENS, J., invalidated a compact between the District of Columbia and Virginia, approved by Congress, leasing Reagan and Dulles airports from the federal government. The compact conditioned the lease on the vesting of veto power over the management of the airports in a Review Board comprised of nine members of Congress, selected from designated congressional committees but serving in their "individual" capacities. If the powers of the Review Board were "executive," congressional involvement in their exercise was impermissible under *Bowsher*. If the functions of the Review Board were instead classified as legislative, the arrangement ran afoul of principles laid down in *Chadha*: This statute is "a blueprint for extensive expansion of the legislative power beyond its constitutionally defined role. [Congress] could [use] similar expedients to enable its Members or its agents to retain control, outside the ordinary legislative process, of the activities of state grant recipients charged with executing virtually every aspect of national policy."[75]

(c) FREE ENTERPRISE FUND v. PUBLIC COMPANY ACCOUNTING OVERSIGHT BOARD, 561 U.S. 477 (2010): Respondent (Board), which has "expansive powers" over the accounting industry, was created by the Sarbanes-Oxley Act of 2002 as part of a set of reforms in response to a "series of celebrated accounting debacles." Its five members are appointed by the SEC, which has oversight of the Board but cannot remove Board members except "for good cause." SEC Commissioners "cannot themselves be removed by the President except [for] inefficiency, neglect of duty, or malfeasance in office." The Court, per ROBERTS, C.J., held this to "contravene the Constitution's separation of powers" because it was "contrary to Article II's vesting of the executive power in the President":

"[In *Humphrey's Executor* and *Morrison*], "only one level of protected tenure separated the President from an officer exercising executive power. [The] Act before us [not] only protects Board members from removal except [under a "rigorous good-cause standard"], but withdraws from the President any decision on whether that good cause exists. That decision is vested instead in other tenured officers—the Commissioners—none of whom is subject to the President's direct control. [The] President therefore cannot hold the Commission fully accountable for the Board's conduct to the same extent that he may hold the Commission accountable for everything else that it does. * * *[4]

Sentencing Commission is completely divorced from any responsibility for execution of the law or adjudication of private rights under the law. [The] only governmental power the Commission possesses is the power to make law; and it is not the Congress."

[75] White, J., joined by Rehnquist, C.J., and Marshall, J., dissented.

[4] **[Ct's Note]** [Without] a second layer of protection, the Commission has no excuse for retaining an officer who is not faithfully executing the law. With the second layer in place, the Commission can shield its decision from Presidential review by finding that good cause is absent— a finding that, given the Commission's own protected tenure, the President cannot easily overturn. * * *

[For the view that "the Act does not insert Congress directly into the appointment or removal process for board members or in any other way insert Congress directly into the administration of the Act [and] the Constitution requires" no more, see Richard H. Pildes, *Separation of Powers,*

[Moreover, neither] respondents nor the dissent explain why the Board's task, unlike so many others, requires *more* than one layer of insulation from the President. [The] parties have identified only a handful of isolated positions [in the government] in which inferior officers might be protected by two levels of good-cause tenure. [But none, such as "civil service tenure-protected employees in independent agencies or administrative law judges,"] are similarly situated to the Board."[76]

BREYER, J., joined by Stevens, Ginsburg and Sotomayor, JJ., dissented: Our governmental system involves "vast numbers of subjects, concerned with vast numbers of different problems [within] many different kinds of administrative structures, exercising different kinds of administrative authority. [Compared] to Congress and the President, the Judiciary possesses an inferior understanding of the realities of administration, and the manner in which power, including and most especially political power, operates in context."

The dissent emphasized that since "the Commission's control over the Board's investigatory and legal functions is virtually absolute [then], as a practical matter, the President's control over the Board should prove sufficient as well. [Moreover, the] Accounting Board members supervise, and are themselves, technical professional experts [and] the justification for insulating the 'technical experts' on the Board from fear of losing their jobs due to political influence is particularly strong. [H]istorically, this regulatory subject matter— financial regulation—has been thought to exhibit a particular need for independence."

5. ***Emerging framework?*** Consider Froomkin, fn. 57: "[T]he Court's decisions fit a pattern in which Congress's power to check the other branches by determining their structure is very great, but Congress is checked by the requirements that it act through persons outside the legislature (which usually means persons in the executive or the judiciary) and that Congress not aggrandize its own powers. Thus, in *Myers, Buckley, Chadha, Bowsher,* and *Metropolitan Airports,* separation of powers was violated by Congress seeking to reserve an executive power for itself. *Humphrey's Executor, Wiener, Morrison,* [and] *Mistretta* all concerned cases in which Congress had lessened the President's power (or increased the judiciary's) without reserving a corresponding power for itself. Indeed, when the issue is an unenumerated presidential power, such as the power to remove executive branch officials, the Supreme Court [has] consistently focused on whether Congress has

---

Independent Agencies, and Financial Regulation: The Case of the Sarbanes-Oxley Act, 5 N.Y.U.J. of L. & Bus. 485 (2009).]

[76] Without dissent, the Court also held that "the Board members have been validly appointed": The Commission, whose members are "Officers of the United States," "constitutes a 'Departmen[t]' for purposes of the Appointments Clause," "the Board members are inferior officers whose appointment Congress may permissibly vest in a 'Hea[d] of Departmen[t].'"

impermissibly aggrandized itself, not on whether the President's 'nebulous' executive power is being undermined."[77]

Does this framework reflect an analytically sound and practicable approach? Does it account for *Clinton v. New York*? (See note 2 after *Clinton*.)

3. EXECUTIVE PRIVILEGE AND IMMUNITY

UNITED STATES v. NIXON, 418 U.S. 683 (1974), grew out of the burglary of Democratic national headquarters in the Watergate hotel, during the 1972 presidential campaign, by employees of the president's re-election committee. After investigations by the press and a Senate committee revealed involvement by high officials in the Nixon administration, the President authorized appointment of a special prosecutor,[78] who subpoenaed presidential tapes and documents based on an indictment, naming Nixon an unindicted "co-conspirator," and charging seven of his staff and political associates with obstructing justice and other Watergate-related offenses. The Court, per BURGER, C.J., rejected Nixon's claim of executive privilege against the subpoena: "The President's counsel [reads] the Constitution as providing an absolute privilege of confidentiality for all presidential communications. Many decisions of this Court, however, have unequivocally reaffirmed the holding of *Marbury v. Madison* that '[i]t is emphatically the province and duty of the judicial department to say what the law is.' [Notwithstanding] the deference each branch must accord the others, the 'judicial power of the United States' [can] no more be shared with the Executive Branch than the Chief Executive, for example, can share with the judiciary the veto power.

"[T]he President's counsel urges [the] valid need for protection of communications between high government officials and those who advise and assist them in the performance of their manifold duties; the importance of this confidentiality is too plain to require further discussion. Human experience teaches that those who expect public dissemination of their remarks may well temper candor with a concern for appearances and for their own interests to the detriment of the decisionmaking process. Whatever the nature of the privilege of confidentiality of presidential communications in the exercise of Art. II powers, the privilege can be said to derive from the supremacy of each branch within its own assigned area of constitutional duties.[79] Certain powers and privileges flow from the

---

[77] See also Dean Alfange, Jr., *The Supreme Court and the Separation of Powers: A Welcome Return to Normalcy?*, 58 Geo.Wash.L.Rev. 668 (1990).

[78] Footnote 8 of the opinion provides details concerning the Special Prosecutor's independence.

[79] On the constitutional, political and historical basis for executive privilege, compare Saikrishna B. Prakash, *A Critical Comment on the Constitutionality of Executive Privilege*, 83 Minn.L.Rev. 1143 (1999) (casting doubt "that an executive privilege necessarily emanates from the

nature of enumerated powers; the protection of the confidentiality of presidential communications has similar constitutional underpinnings. * * *

"However, neither the doctrine of separation of powers, nor the need for confidentiality of high level communications, without more, can sustain an absolute, unqualified presidential privilege of immunity from judicial process under all circumstances. [When] the privilege depends solely on the broad, undifferentiated claim of public interest in the confidentiality of such conversations, a confrontation with other values arises. Absent a claim of need to protect military, diplomatic, or sensitive national security secrets, we find it difficult to accept the argument that even the very important interest in confidentiality of presidential communications is significantly diminished by production of such material for in camera inspection with all the protection that a district court will be obliged to provide.

"The impediment that an absolute, unqualified privilege would place in the way of the primary constitutional duty of the Judicial Branch to do justice in criminal prosecutions would plainly conflict with the function of the courts under Art. III. In designing the structure of our Government [the] Framers [sought] to provide a comprehensive system, but the separate powers were not intended to operate with absolute independence.

"[The need for confidentiality justifies] a presumptive privilege for presidential communications. [But] this presumptive privilege must be considered in light of our historic commitment to the rule of law. [To] ensure that justice is done, it is imperative to the function of courts that compulsory process be available for the production of evidence needed either by the prosecution or by the defense. * * *

"In this case the President [does] not place his claim of privilege on the ground [of] military or diplomatic secrets [where courts] have traditionally shown the utmost deference to presidential [responsibilities]. No case of the Court [has] extended this high degree of deference to a President's generalized interest in confidentiality. * * *

"The right to the production of all evidence at a criminal trial similarly has constitutional dimensions. The Sixth Amendment explicitly confers upon every defendant in a criminal trial the right 'to be confronted with the witnesses against him' and 'to have compulsory process for obtaining witnesses in his favor.' Moreover, the Fifth Amendment also guarantees that no person shall be deprived of liberty without due process of law. It is the manifest duty of the courts to vindicate those guarantees and to

Constitution itself") and Raoul Berger, *Executive Privilege: A Constitutional Myth* (1974) with Mark J. Rozell, *Executive Privilege: The Dilemma of Secrecy and Democratic Accountability* (1994).

accomplish that it is essential that all relevant and admissible evidence be produced.

"In this case we must weigh the importance of the general privilege of confidentiality of presidential communications in performance of [the President's] responsibilities against the inroads of such a privilege on the fair administration of criminal justice.[19] The interest in preserving confidentiality is weighty indeed and entitled to great respect. However, we cannot conclude that advisers will be moved to temper the candor of their remarks by the infrequent occasions of disclosure because of the possibility that such conversations will be called for in the context of a criminal prosecution.

"On the other hand, [the] constitutional need for production of relevant evidence in a criminal proceeding is specific and central to the fair adjudication of a particular criminal case in the administration of justice. Without access to specific facts a criminal prosecution may be totally frustrated. [The] generalized assertion of privilege must yield to the demonstrated, specific need for evidence in a pending criminal trial."[80]

NOTES AND QUESTIONS

1. **Types of privilege.** "[P]residential refusals to furnish information may be actuated by any of at least three distinct kinds of considerations. [1.] Presidents of the United States beginning with George Washington have invoked executive privilege on the ground that disclosure of the desired information would subvert crucial military or diplomatic objectives. [In] *Chicago & Southern Air Lines v. Waterman Steamship Corp.*, 333 U.S. 103 (1948), [The Court] proclaimed that '[t]he President has available intelligence services whose reports are not and ought not to be published to the world.' [T]he Court has [also noted] that the 'privilege against revealing military secrets [is] well established in the law of evidence.' More generally, a President can successfully claim that a measure of secrecy, and thus a qualified executive privilege from required disclosure, is a necessary condition for the successful conduct of foreign affairs.

"[2.] The law of evidence has also long recognized an informer's privilege—that is, 'the Government's privilege to withhold from disclosure the identity of persons who furnish information of violations of law to officers charged with enforcement of that law.' [3.] Finally, a generic privilege for internal deliberations has been said to attach to 'intragovernmental documents reflecting advisory opinions, recommendations and deliberations comprising

---

[19] **[Ct's Note]** We are not here concerned with the balance between the President's generalized interest in confidentiality and the need for relevant evidence in civil litigation, nor with that between the confidentiality interest and congressional demands for information, nor with the President's interest in preserving state secrets.

[80] The Court stressed the obligation of the District Court to examine the tapes and documents in camera and to excise and keep confidential all material not admissible and relevant.

Rehnquist, J., did not participate.

part of a process by which governmental decisions and policies are formulated.' "

Tribe 3d ed., supra.

2. ***Marbury and judicial resolution of privilege claims.*** Does the Court's reliance on *Marbury* for the proposition that it must determine the merits of the President's claim of privilege "convey a misleadingly broad view of judicial competence, exclusivity and supremacy"? See Gerald Gunther, *Judicial Hegemony and Legislative Autonomy: The Nixon Case and the Impeachment Process,* 22 U.C.L.A.Rev. 30 (1974). Did *Marbury* prevent the Court from "declar[ing] 'the law' to be that the President is the sole determiner of the need for protecting the confidentiality of particular communications, just as 'the law' grants him sole authority over recognition of the legal government of a foreign state"? See Paul A. Freund, *On Presidential Privilege,* 88 Harv.L.Rev. 13 (1974).

3. ***Executive privilege in judicial proceedings.*** (a) Does *Nixon* mean that executive privilege must *always* yield when the communications are relevant to criminal cases? Should the constitutionally based executive privilege receive less protection than traditional husband-wife, doctor-patient, lawyer-client privileges that exclude relevant, otherwise admissible evidence? Consider Tribe 3d ed., supra: "Since relevance, admissibility, and necessity must in any event be shown in order to require production of evidence prior to trial, the Court's [statement] that the trial judge should demand a showing that the materials are 'essential to the justice of the [pending criminal] case,' [may] indicate that an even greater showing must be made to overcome the claim of privilege. [*Nixon*] may eventually be construed as dealing only with the scope of presidential privilege when the President appears to have a conflict of interest, hence posing no threat to privileges in a more traditional setting."

Of what relevance are the "constitutional dimensions" of criminal trials—such as the Confrontation Clause and the Due Process Clause? Consider Akhil R. Amar, *Nixon's Shadow,* 83 Minn. L.Rev. 1405 (1999): "[In the famous *Aaron Burr Case,* relied on in *Nixon*], a criminal defendant sought to subpoena evidence to prove his innocence. [*Nixon*] turned *Burr* upside down, insisting that due process demanded that all possible evidence of the criminal defendant's guilt *must* be produced, even if both the defendants and the President preferred otherwise. [But due process] says nothing about any government right or duty to prosecute every possible defendant using every possible scrap of evidence." What about "the primary constitutional duty of the Judicial Branch to do justice in criminal prosecutions [under Art III]"? Consider Neil Kinkopf, *Executive Privilege: The Clinton Administration in the Courts,* 8 Wm. & Mary Bill Rts. J. 631 (2000): "Article III does not create a criminal justice system [or] define criminal law. Nothing in Article III required prosecution of the Watergate defendants." May the lesser protection for the executive privilege in *Nixon* have resulted from the high public interest in making evidence available in a case involving serious criminal charges against high government officials, in which the indictment named the President himself as an unindicted co-conspirator?

(b) Should the need for relevant evidence in a civil proceeding outweigh the interests underlying the "presumptive executive privilege"? Should the answer depend on whether the government is plaintiff or defendant in the civil case?

4. **After Nixon.** "Presidents either have avoided uttering the words 'executive privilege' and have protected secrecy through other sources of authority (Ford, Carter, Bush), or they have tried to restore executive privilege and failed (Reagan, Clinton)." Mark J. Rozell, *Restoring Balance to the Debate Over Executive Privilege*, 8 Wm. & Mary Bill Rts. J. 541 (2000).

5. **Executive privilege in Congress.** (a) Despite frequent assertion of executive privilege to deny information to Congress, beginning with President Washington's refusal to turn over treaty negotiating records to the House of Representatives, the Court has never adjudicated the issue. Though some commentators have advocated that the Court undertake to resolve such issues,[81] others have counseled restraint. See, e.g. Archibald Cox, *Executive Privilege*, 122 U.Pa.L.Rev. 1383 (1974): "Courts are accustomed to weighing the need for specific pieces of evidence in a judicial proceeding against the public interest in preserving the confidentiality of particular relationships, but they have no experience in weighing the legislative needs of Congress against other public interests." See also Josh Chafetz, *Executive Branch Contempt of Congress*, 76 U. Chi. L. Rev. 1083 (2009): History demonstrates that "when an executive branch official raises executive privilege as a defense justifying her defiance of a congressional subpoena, the house of Congress is the proper tribunal to determine whether [to] hold executive branch officials in contempt and [to] enforce compliance with [the] powers of arrest, impeachment, and obstruction of the president's agenda. [This] means that legislative-executive disputes over the contempt power should be understood to be nonjusticiable." Contra, David A. O'Neil, *The Political Safeguards of Executive Privilege*, 60 Vand. L. Rev. 1079 (2007).

(b) Should the President's privilege also shield communications among lower executive branch officials? See *In re Sealed Case*, 121 F.3d 729 (D.C.Cir.1997) (yes).

6. **A former President's papers.** NIXON v. ADMINISTRATOR OF GENERAL SERVICES, 433 U.S. 425 (1977), per BRENNAN, J., rejected a claim of executive privilege against an act of Congress, passed after President Nixon's resignation and pardon by President Ford, required the Administrator to take "possession" of Nixon's presidential materials, screen them and return those that were private and not of "general historical interest": "[A]dequate justifications [for] this limited intrusion into executive confidentiality [were]

---

[81] See Norman Dorsen & John H.F. Shattuck, *Executive Privilege, The Congress and the Courts*, 35 Ohio St.L.J. 1 (1974); Berger, fn. 79.

comparable to those held to justify the in camera inspection [in *Nixon I*]."[82] BURGER, C.J., dissented, noting that all prior Presidents were allowed "to provide unilaterally for disposition of [their] workpapers."[83]

———

After his departure from office, President Nixon was sued by Fitzgerald, who claimed that Nixon and White House aides caused him to be fired from his federal job (for "whistle-blowing") in violation of his statutory and constitutional rights.

NIXON v. FITZGERALD, 457 U.S. 731 (1982), per POWELL, J., affirmed summary dismissal of the action against Nixon: A President is entitled to *absolute immunity* from "damages liability predicated on his official acts."[27] This immunity is "a functionally mandated incident of the President's unique office, rooted in the constitutional tradition of the separation of powers and supported by our history. [As] is the case with prosecutors and judges—for whom absolute immunity now is established—a President must concern himself with matters likely to 'arouse the most intense feelings.' Yet [it] is in precisely such cases that there exists the greatest public interest in providing an official 'the maximum ability to deal fearlessly and impartially with' the duties of his office [where he] must make the most sensitive and far-reaching decisions entrusted to any official under our constitutional system. [In] view of the special nature of the President's constitutional office and functions, we think it appropriate to recognize absolute Presidential immunity from damages liability for acts within the 'outer perimeter' of his official responsibility. * * *

"A rule of absolute immunity for the President will not leave the Nation without sufficient protection against misconduct on the part of the chief executive. There remains the constitutional remedy of impeachment. In addition, there are formal and informal checks on Presidential action that do not apply with equal force to other executive officials. The President is subjected to constant scrutiny by the press. Vigilant oversight by Congress also may serve to deter Presidential abuses of office, as well as [a] desire to earn re-election, the need to maintain prestige as an element of Presidential influence, and a President's traditional concern for his historical stature."

---

[82] White, Blackmun, Powell, and Stevens, JJ., each concurred separately.

[83] Rehnquist, J., also dissented. For a contrary view, see Laurent Sacharoff, *Former Presidents and Executive Privilege,* 88 Texas L. Rev. 301 (2009): " [T]he text and historical context of the Constitution reflect [a] strong antimonarchical norm [and] Congress has none of its usual tools to check any abuse or overuse of executive privilege by a former President," such as withholding appropriations or impeachment.

[27] **[Ct's Note]** [Our] holding today need only be that the President is absolutely immune from civil damages liability for his official acts in the absence of explicit affirmative action by Congress. * * *

WHITE, J., joined by Brennan, Marshall and Blackmun, JJ., dissented: "Attaching absolute immunity to the office of the President, rather than to particular activities that the President might perform, places the President above the law. [The] wholesale claim that the President is entitled to absolute immunity in all of his actions stands on no firmer ground than did the claim that all presidential communications are entitled to an absolute privilege [Nixon I]. Therefore, whatever may be true of the necessity of such a broad immunity in certain areas of executive responsibility,[30] the only question that must be answered here is whether the dismissal of employees falls within a constitutionally assigned executive function, the performance of which would be substantially impaired by the possibility of a private action for damages. I believe it does not."[84]

NOTES AND QUESTIONS

1. **Constitutional foundation.** Art. I, § 6, cl. 1, expressly confers a limited immunity on members of Congress by providing that "for any Speech or Debate in either House, they shall not be questioned in any other Place."[85] Should the absence of any comparable immunity in Art. II imply a deliberate denial?

2. **Types of immunity.** (a) There are generally two types of immunity from suits for damages: (i) absolute immunity, protecting an official even for egregious or intentional constitutional violations, and (ii) "qualified" or "good faith" immunity, permitting liability only for violations of "clearly established" rights of which a reasonable person would have known. See *Harlow v. Fitzgerald*, 457 U.S. 800 (1982). Qualified immunity is the norm; absolute immunity is the exception. *Harlow* made clear that high presidential aides are not entitled to absolute presidential immunity. *Butz v. Economou*, 438 U.S. 478 (1978) had held that "members of the Cabinet ordinarily enjoy only qualified immunity from suit," and it would be "untenable" to hold that all White House aides enjoy absolute immunity when cabinet members do not.[86]

(b) Aside from the President, the prevailing doctrine generally establishes that the type of immunity to which an official is entitled depends on the *function* performed when the allegedly unlawful conduct occurred. Within this framework, the judicial, legislative, and prosecutorial functions have been held protected by absolute immunity. But a judge, for example,

---

[30] [Ct's Note] [A] clear example would be instances in which the President participates in prosecutorial decisions.

[84] Blackmun, J., joined by Brennan and Marshall, JJ., also dissented. For commentary, see Stephen L. Carter, *The Political Aspects of Judicial Power: Some Notes on the Presidential Immunity Decision,* 131 U.Pa.L.Rev. 1341 (1983).

[85] Decisions have limited the immunity to suits for damages predicated on the performance of expressly *legislative* functions. See, e.g., *Hutchinson v. Proxmire*, 443 U.S. 111 (1979). For critical commentary, see Senator Sam J. Ervin, Jr., *The Gravel and Brewster Cases: An Assault on Congressional Independence,* 59 Va.L.Rev. 175 (1973); Note, 93 Harv.L.Rev. 161 (1979).

[86] Burger, C.J., dissenting, was "at a loss" to reconcile the Court's decision with the derivative extension of absolute congressional immunity under the Speech and Debate Clause to congressional aides in *Gravel v. United States*, 408 U.S. 606 (1972).

enjoys only qualified immunity in a suit predicated on the performance of a non-judicial function such as hiring or firing a court employee.[87] Correspondingly, an executive branch employee may claim absolute immunity from suits based on quasi-judicial acts (such as imposing administrative sanctions for violations of a federal regulation).[88]

3. *Immunity and the rule of law.* Has the Court elevated the President "above the law"? What of the famous dictum of *Marbury v. Madison* that for every right the laws of the United States must supply a remedy? See Richard H. Fallon, Jr. & Daniel J. Meltzer, *New Law, Non-Retroactivity, and Constitutional Remedies*, 104 Harv.L.Rev. 1731 (1991)(effective remediation in every case is an aspiration, not a promise, which must sometimes yield to other values, but the Constitution minimally requires an adequate structure of remedies—including injunctions and habeas corpus—to keep the government "generally within the bounds of law").

4. *Injunctions.* The immunity doctrines for damages generally do not apply in suits for injunctions or other specific relief. Under what circumstances could a court enjoin the President? *Mississippi v. Johnson*, 71 U.S. 475 (1867), held that it could not enjoin the President from enforcing a law—an act that it classified as "purely executive and political."[89] Compare *Youngstown*, upholding an injunction technically directed at the Secretary of Commerce but when he was implementing a presidential order.[90]

5. *Congress and presidential immunity.* Could Congress eliminate the presidential immunity recognized in *Fitzgerald*? See fn. 27 of the Court's opinion. If the immunity is constitutionally based, could it be overcome by a mere statute? Is this a case contemplated by Jackson, J.'s opinion in *Youngstown*, in which presidential power may ebb and flow with congressional action?

6. *President's "private" acts.* (a) CLINTON v. JONES, 520 U.S. 681 (1997): An Arkansas state employee, filed a federal civil suit against President Clinton, seeking damages for " 'abhorrent' sexual advances that she vehemently rejected," allegedly made while he was governor of Arkansas. The Court, per STEVENS, J., rejected Clinton's effort to have the suit dismissed without prejudice, and the statute of limitations tolled, until expiration of his term: "Petitioner's strongest argument [relies] on separation of powers. [He] contends that this particular case—as well as the potential additional litigation that [it] may spawn—may impose an unacceptable burden on the President's time and energy, and thereby impair the effective performance of his office. [But this] predictive judgment finds little support in either history or the relatively narrow compass of the issues raised in this particular case. [In] the more than 200 year history of the Republic, only three sitting

---

[87] See *Forrester v. White*, 484 U.S. 219 (1988).

[88] See *Butz v. Economou.*

[89] See also *Franklin v. Massachusetts*, 505 U.S. 788 (1992).

[90] See also Laura K. Ray, *From Prerogative to Accountability: The Amenability of the President to Suit*, 80 Ky.L.Rev. 739 (1992).

Presidents have been subjected to suits for their private actions. [It therefore] seems unlikely that a deluge of such litigation will ever engulf the Presidency. As for the case at hand, if properly managed by the District Court, it appears to us highly unlikely to occupy any substantial amount of petitioner's time.

"[We] have long held that when the President takes official action, the Court has the authority to determine whether he has acted within the law. [E.g., *Youngstown*. If] the Judiciary may severely burden the Executive Branch by reviewing the legality of the President's official conduct, and if it may direct appropriate process to the President himself [e.g., *Nixon I*], it must follow that the federal courts have power to determine the legality of his unofficial conduct [including that occurring before he became President.]

"The District Court has broad discretion to stay proceedings as an incident to its power to control its own docket [and] potential burdens on the President [are] appropriate matters for the District Court to evaluate in its management of the case. The high respect that is owed to the Office of the Chief Executive [is] a matter that should inform the conduct of the entire proceeding, including the timing and scope of discovery." Nonetheless, "the proponent of a stay bears the burden of establishing its need." And so far there was "nothing in the record to enable a judge to assess the potential harm that may ensue from scheduling the trial promptly after discovery is concluded."

BREYER, J., concurred in the judgment only, noting that "once the President sets forth and explains a conflict between judicial proceeding and public duties, [the] Constitution permits a judge to schedule a trial in an ordinary civil damages action [only] within the constraints of a constitutional principle [that] forbids a federal judge in such a case to interfere with the President's discharge of his public duties." Breyer, J., was less "sanguine" than the majority that permitting suits against sitting Presidents would not lead to a proliferation of such actions. He would make clear that the Constitution does "not grant a single judge more than a very limited power to second guess a President's reasonable determination (announced in open court) of his scheduling needs."

(b) *Court's reasoning.* Is *Clinton* consistent with *Fitzgerald*? See Akhil R. Amar & Neal K. Katyal, *Executive Privileges and Immunities: the Nixon and Clinton Cases*, 108 Harv.L.Rev. 701 (1994) (constitutional history and structure more strongly support a suspension of damages actions against the incumbent President than the absolute immunity established in *Fitzgerald*). Does *Clinton* apply to a *state* civil damages suit? Are such suits more vulnerable to constitutional challenge?

Does *Clinton* also cover a federal *criminal* prosecution against the President? At least for "unofficial conduct"? Consider Michael S. Paulsen, *Nixon Now: The Courts and the Presidency After Twenty-five Years*, 83 Minn.L.Rev. 1337 (1999): "[T]hat the President may be impeached for commission of criminal offenses does not mean he might not first be tried in the courts for such offenses (as has happened with some federal judges Congress has impeached). And if the President *were* immune from prosecution on this score, that would be in tension with *Clinton* [since] a serious civil wrong could, in the judgment of Congress, constitute an impeachable offense—imagine for example a President who engaged in twelve proven instances of non-criminal quid pro quo sexual harassment with executive branch employees. [If] anything, the judicial system's interest in enforcement of the criminal law would appear to be higher." Compare Tribe 3d ed., supra: "Although the text of the Constitution provides no unambiguous guidance, [b]ecause the Constitution charges one unique official—the President—with the duty to 'take Care that the Laws be faithfully executed,' neither the federal judicial branch nor a state court should be permitted to imprison a sitting President and thereby to threaten the effective execution of the laws."

    7.   *Civil litigation and the Vice President.* CHENEY v. U.S. DIST. CT., 542 U.S. 367 (2004), involved a discovery order against Vice President Cheney seeking information about the members and activities of a task force established to develop a national energy policy for the President. After noting that "the need for information for use in civil cases, while far from negligible, does not share the urgency or significance of the criminal subpoena requests in *[Nixon I]* where a court's ability to fulfill its constitutional responsibility to resolve [cases] within its jurisdiction hinges on the availability of certain indispensable information," the Court, per KENNEDY, J., remanded to the D.C. Circuit because that court had "labored under the mistaken assumption that the assertion of executive privilege is a necessary precondition to the Government's separation-of-powers objections. [T]here is sound precedent in the District of Columbia itself for district courts to explore other avenues, short of forcing the Executive to invoke privilege, when they are asked to enforce against the Executive Branch unnecessarily broad subpoenas."[91]

4. IMPEACHMENT OF THE PRESIDENT

    In 1998, for the second time in our history, the House of Representatives impeached the President who was then tried by the Senate. (In both cases—Andrew Johnson in 1868 and William Clinton in 1999—the Senate voted to acquit.) Because of the Courts' ruling in 1993 (Ch. 1, Sec. 2) that matters respecting congressional impeachments present nonjusticiable political questions, there are no Supreme Court opinions that address any of the important constitutional questions that may arise. The following notes consider some of these:

    1.   *Definition of impeachable offense.* Art. II, § 4 provides that "all Civil Officers" may be impeached for "Treason, Bribery, or other high Crimes and Misdemeanors."

    (a)   *Crimes only?* It is generally agreed that an impeachable offense need not be a statutory crime. President Johnson was impeached for the noncriminal act of removing the Secretary of War without the Senate consent that was required by statute. The Articles of Impeachment against

---

[91] Scalia, Souter, Thomas, and Ginsburg, JJ., dissented on procedural issues.

President Richard Nixon included misusing federal agencies to discredit his political opponents and for refusing to comply with congressional demands for information; neither alleged misconduct was criminal. (Nixon resigned before the full House voted on the charges.) Consider Frank O. Bowman III & Stephen L. Sepinuck, *"High Crimes & Misdemeanors": Defining the Constitutional Limits on Presidential Impeachment*, 72 So.Calif.L.Rev. 1517 (1999): "[A] President would certainly be subject to impeachment for refusing to organize the defense of the country against foreign invasion, or refusing to cooperate with military officers charged with command and control of the nuclear arsenal, or firing all cabinet officers and refusing to name replacements. Likewise, it is inconceivable that Congress could not remove a President who drank himself into insensibility by lunchtime on a daily basis." For discussion of "two centuries of practice" involving presidential impeachments, see Cass R. Sunstein, *Impeaching the President*, 147 U.Pa.L.Rev. 279 (1998).

(b) ***All crimes?*** Should *every* criminal offense be impeachable? Consider Jonathan Turley, *Congress as Grand Jury: The Role of the House of Representatives in the Impeachment of an American President*, 67 Geo.Wash.L.Rev. 735 (1999): "Labeling some criminal acts as 'private' [creates] an obvious anomaly in retaining a President under his oath to fully and faithfully enforce federal laws. [C]riminal conduct by a President [should] create a presumption of submission to the Senate." Compare Michael J. Gerhardt, *The Lessons of Impeachment History*, 67 Geo.Wash.L.Rev. 603 (1999): "[The words 'other high Crimes and Misdemeanors'] constitute technical terms of art that refer to political crimes [which] the Framers considered [to] consist of 'great' and 'dangerous' offenses committed by certain federal officials. Oftentimes, these offenses were characterized further as serious abuses of official power or serious breaches of the public trust." Accord, Jack Rakove, *Statement on the Background and History of Impeachment*, 67 Geo.Wash.L.Rev. 682 (1999) ("an expansive reading of 'other high Crimes and Misdemeanors' simply cannot be squared with the Framers' desire to insulate the presidency as much as possible from the danger of domination by the legislature"). See also Charles L. Black, Jr., *Impeachment: A Handbook* (1974); Michael J. Gerhardt, *The Federal Impeachment Process* (1996). Should this exclude "an extremely heinous 'private' crime, such as murder or rape"? See Cass R. Sunstein, *Impeachment and Stability*, 67 Geo.Wash.L.Rev. 699 (1999). Or other "monstrous crimes" such as "child molestation"? See Arthur M. Schlesinger, *Reflections on Impeachment*, 67 Geo.Wash.L.Rev. 693 (1999). Perjury in a criminal prosecution? In a civil case? Of what significance is it that "the false statement involves conduct that by itself raises serious questions about abuse of office"? Sunstein, note (a) supra. May *bribery* occur in a context that does not "raise serious questions about abuse of office"? For the view that perjury is *not* impeachable, see Monroe H. Freedman, *Perjury as a Ground for*

Impeachment—A Textual and Contextual Analysis, 28 Hofstra L. Rev. 343 (1999). Contra, see Gary L. McDowell, *"High Crimes and Misdemeanors": Recovering the Intentions of the Founders*, 67 Geo.Wash.L.Rev. 626 (1999) (based on "review of the historical record"). See also John O. McGinnis, *Impeachment: The Structural Understanding*, 67 Geo.Wash.L.Rev. 650 (1999): "[L]abeling murder 'heinous' and describing perjury or obstruction of justice as 'not heinous' [is] simply a matter of personal judgment. Moreover, it would cause lasting damage to our system of republican government for the House of Representatives to accept a *legal* definition of 'high Crimes and Misdemeanors' [that] tolerates any and all 'private' tax evasion, 'private' perjury, and 'private' obstruction of justice from officials who then would continue to have the power to throw their own citizens into prison for the very same offenses." Accord, Stephen B. Presser, *Would George Washington Have Wanted Bill Clinton Impeached?* 67 Geo.Wash.L.Rev. 666 (1999).

Compare Jonathan Turley, *Reflections on Murder, Misdemeanors, and Madison*, 28 Hofstra L. Rev. 439 (1999): "[T]he most fundamental question of any impeachment is not an abuse of power but the lack of capacity of a President to lead. This is why certain crimes seem to invite impeachment. [It] is not that murder is unique as a crime, but that it is the most obvious example of an act that robs a President of legitimacy to govern." Contrast Tribe 3d ed., supra: Given "the Framers familiarity with [the] long history in English impeachments [of the phrase 'high Crimes and Misdemeanors,' the discussions] of the Constitutional Convention and the ratification debates therefore strongly reinforce what the Constitution's text suggests—namely, that a civil officer may be impeached only for serious subversions of the government or for grave abuses of power. [A]ddressing generalized concerns of presidential 'legitimacy' [may] topple a prime minister in a parliamentary government, but they do not constitute 'high Crimes and Misdemeanors' under our Constitution, where the legislature is merely a coordinate, not a superior, branch of government."

(c) ***Differing standards.*** Should the definition of an impeachable offense be the same for presidents as for judges? Consider Tribe 3d ed., supra: "There [are] categories of misconduct that one might plausibly argue are *functionally* and *operationally* incompatible with carrying out a *particular* official role. [For] example, it would seem that a person guilty of perjury—on *any* subject, however personal—cannot credibly function for life as a judge, administering oaths to trial witnesses and deciding [who] is telling the truth and who is lying. But it is far from clear that a president who is thought to have committed perjury on income tax returns filed with the IRS, or in the judicial investigation of his sexual conduct, is similarly disabled [to] 'take Care that the Laws be faithfully executed.' [T]he same standard for impeachable offenses [may] well make a judge—whose potential for harming the nation in the future is virtually unlimited due to

his life tenure—removable for conduct that would not warrant removal of
a president, particularly since Senate removal of a judge entails reversing
the Senate's own action in confirming the judge whereas Senate removal of
a president entails reversing an action of the entire national electorate."
See also Akhil R. Amar, *On Impeaching Presidents*, 28 Hofstra L. Rev. 291
(1999).

2.   ***Roles of House and Senate.*** Should the House vote to impeach
if it doubts that the Senate will convict? Consider Turley, 67
Geo.Wash.L.Rev. supra: "Academics have stated that such an
impeachment would be as improper as a prosecutor indicting with the
expectation that he could never secure a conviction. [But if] deterrence is
achieved primarily through detection of presidential crimes, [when]
credible allegations of impeachable offenses exist, the House performs a
vital role in articulating and presenting those allegations for resolution in
the Senate." Should the House exercise something akin to "prosecutor's
discretion" in determining whether to impeach? Consider Turley, id.: "To
argue in the House for nullification of an incumbent President's crimes is
much like arguing for nullification of criminal acts before a grand jury. It
would be outrageous for a grand jury to nullify any indictment of an
individual for alleged crimes due to his popularity or the unpopularity of
his accuser. It is the function of a trial jury to weigh the evidence." If the
House votes to impeach, does Art. I, § 3, cl.6 require the Senate to conduct
a full trial. Or may it grant a motion to dismiss? See Michael J. Klarman,
Constitutional Fetishism and the Clinton Impeachment Debate, 85
Va.L.Rev. 631 (1999).

3.   ***Sanctions.*** Do Art. II, § 4 and Art. I, § 3, cl.7 require that the
President be removed from office if convicted by the Senate? See
Christopher L. Eisgruber & Lawrence G. Sager, *Impeachment and
Constitutional Structure*, 5 Widener L. Symp. J. 249 (2000). Or may a lesser
sanction—such as censure, or a finding of fact—be employed? Does this
affect the question of how an impeachable offense should be defined? See
generally Akhil R. Amar & Stuart Taylor, Jr., *On Impeaching Presidents:
A Constitutional Conversation*, 28 Hofstra L.Rev. 317 (1999). May both (or
either) Houses of Congress censure the President even if he is not
impeached or convicted? See Michael J. Gerhardt, *The Historical and
Constitutional Significance of the Impeachment and Trial of President
Clinton*, 28 Hofstra L.Rev. 349 (1999).

CHAPTER 4

STATE POWER TO REGULATE

■ ■ ■

Introduction

As discussed in Ch. 2, the Commerce Clause is principally a grant of legislative power to Congress. From the beginning, however, it has been assumed that the grant of authority to Congress necessarily implies a withdrawal of at least some regulatory power from the states, even though the Commerce Clause does not expressly negate state power.[1] This chapter explores the impact of national legislative authority on the states' power to regulate. The focus is on the "dormant Commerce Clause," the term commonly used to refer to the Commerce Clause in cases in which Congress possesses regulatory power but has not exercised it. Since the early nineteenth century, the Supreme Court has invoked the dormant Commerce Clause to invalidate various types of state legislation affecting interstate commerce on the ground that such legislation is incompatible with national interests.

When Congress enacts valid legislation under the Commerce Clause (and thus asserts its power, rather than leaving it "dormant"), there is no doubt that Congress can preclude, displace, or "preempt" state law.

CROSBY v. NATIONAL FOREIGN TRADE COUNCIL, 530 U.S. 363, 372–73 (2000), summarized the relevant principles as follows: "A fundamental principle of the Constitution is that Congress has the power to preempt state law. Art. VI, cl. 2; *Gibbons v. Ogden* [Sec. 1 infra]. Even without an express provision for preemption, we have found that state law must yield to a congressional Act in at least two circumstances. When Congress intends federal law to 'occupy the field,' [all] state law in that area is preempted. And even if Congress has not occupied the field, state law is naturally preempted to the extent of any conflict with a federal statute. We will find preemption where it is impossible for a private party to comply with both state and federal law, and where 'under the circumstances of [a] particular case, [the challenged state law] stands as an obstacle to the accomplishment and execution of the full purposes and objectives of Congress.' " The basic concept of preemption is taken for

---

[1]   Except for the special, express limits on tonnage duties and duties on imports and exports. Art. I, § 10.

granted, rather than studied, in the materials that follow.[2] Once the principle is accepted, preemption questions essentially involve the interpretation of federal statutes, not the Constitution, and are better addressed in a course on statutory interpretation.

Accepting that valid federal legislation will "preempt" any incompatible state law, this chapter considers issues that arise in contexts in which Congress has the power to legislate but has not done so.

1. STATE REGULATION WHEN CONGRESS' POWER IS "DORMANT": HISTORY AND FUNDAMENTAL ISSUES

In GIBBONS v. OGDEN (1824), Ch. 2, Sec. 2, MARSHALL, C.J., in the course of upholding federal regulatory power over interstate navigation and recognizing its preemptive force when exercised, discussed but did not decide whether the grant of commerce power to Congress impliedly excluded all state regulation of interstate and foreign commerce: "In support of [the argument for concurrent or joint federal and state regulatory power] it is said, that [the states] possessed it as an inseparable attribute of sovereignty, before the formation of the constitution, and still retain it, except so far as they have surrendered it by that instrument; that this principle results from the nature of the government, and is secured by the tenth amendment; that an affirmative grant of power is not exclusive, unless in its own nature it be such that the continued exercise of it by the former possessor is inconsistent with the grant, and that this is not of that description.

"The appellant [contends, however], that full power to regulate a particular subject, implies the whole power, and leaves no residuum; that a grant of the whole is incompatible with the existence of a right in another to any part of it.

"[The] grant of the power to lay and collect taxes is, like the power to regulate commerce, made in general terms, [but it] is capable of residing in, and being exercised by, different authorities at the same time. [When], then, each government exercises the power of taxation, neither is exercising the power of the other. But, when a State proceeds to regulate commerce with foreign nations, or among the several States, it is exercising the very power that is granted to Congress, and is doing the very thing which Congress is authorized to do. There is no analogy, then, between the power of taxation and the power of regulating commerce.

"[The] inspection laws are said to be regulations of commerce, and are certainly recognized in the constitution, as being passed in the exercise of a power remaining with the States. That inspection laws may have a

---

[2]   For a more extensive introduction, see Tribe 3d ed., at 1172–1220.

remote and considerable influence on commerce, will not be denied; but that a power to regulate commerce is the source from which the right to pass them is derived, cannot be admitted. The object of inspection laws, is to improve the quality of articles produced by the labor of a [country]. They act upon the subject before it becomes an article of foreign commerce, or of commerce among the States, and prepare it for that purpose. They form a portion of that immense mass of legislation, which embraces every thing within the territory of a State, not surrendered to the general government: all which can be most advantageously exercised by the States themselves. Inspection laws, quarantine laws, health laws of every description, as well as laws for regulating the internal commerce of a State, and those which respect turnpike roads, ferries, &c., are component parts of this mass.

"No direct general power over these objects is granted to Congress; and, consequently, they remain subject to State legislation. [It] is obvious, that the government of the Union, in the exercise of its express powers, that, for example, of regulating commerce with foreign nations and among the States, may use means that may also be employed by a State, in the exercise of its acknowledged powers; that, for example, of regulating commerce within the State. [If] a State, in passing laws on subjects acknowledged to be within its control, and with a view to those subjects, shall adopt a measure of the same character with one which Congress may adopt, it does not derive its authority from the particular power which has been granted, but from some other, which remains with the State, and may be executed by the same means. All experience shows, that the same measures, or measures scarcely distinguishable from each other, may flow from distinct powers; but this does not prove that the powers themselves are [identical. The] acknowledged power of a State to regulate its police, its domestic trade, and to govern its own citizens, may enable it to legislate on this subject to a considerable [extent].

"It has been contended by the counsel for the appellant, that, as the word to 'regulate' implies in its nature, full power over the thing to be regulated, it excludes, necessarily, the action of all others that would perform the same operation on the same thing. That regulation is designed for the entire result, applying to those parts which remain as they were, as well as to those which are altered. It produces a uniform whole, which is as much disturbed and deranged by changing what the regulating power designs to leave untouched, as that on which it has operated. There is great force in this argument, and the Court is not satisfied that it has been refuted."

NOTES AND QUESTIONS

1. **Basic questions.** A few powers of Congress are exclusive because the Constitution expressly withholds the power from states. For example, Article I, § 8 authorizes Congress to "coin money," and Article I, § 10 expressly denies

such power to the states. The Commerce Clause, by contrast, includes no explicit preclusion of state regulatory authority. What inferences, if any, should be drawn from the absence of an express preclusion of state authority? Is it workable for the states to retain a concurrent regulatory authority? Would it be workable for the states *not* to retain a concurrent regulatory authority?

According to Norman R. Williams, *Gibbons*, 79 N.Y.U.L.Rev. 1398 (2004), Marshall, C.J., chose to avoid questions such as these in *Gibbons* because he preferred to put Congress, rather than the courts, at "the forefront of the [politically charged] battle against state protectionist legislation."

2. ***States' "police" power.*** An early judicial response to the question of exclusive vs. concurrent power involved an appeal to the states' "police" power—a power not to regulate "commerce" but to protect citizens in ways that might sometimes affect commerce. Invocation of the idea of state police power permitted the Court to uphold state legislation that aimed to achieve permissible goals, even when the legislation had effects on interstate commerce.

(a) WILLSON v. BLACK-BIRD CREEK MARSH CO., 27 U.S. (2 Pet.) 245 (1829), per MARSHALL, C.J., upheld a Delaware statute authorizing a dam that obstructed a small navigable stream, impeding the passage of a boat licensed by the federal navigation laws: "The act of assembly by which the plaintiffs were authorized to construct their dam, shows plainly that this is one of those many creeks, passing through a deep level marsh adjoining the Delaware [River], up which the tide flows for some distance. The value of the property on its banks must be enhanced by excluding the water from the marsh, and the health of the inhabitants probably improved. Measures calculated to produce these objects, provided they do not come into collision with the powers of the general government, are undoubtedly within those [police powers] which are reserved to the states. But the measure authorized by this act stops a navigable creek, and must be supposed to abridge the rights of those who have been accustomed to use it.

"[If] Congress had passed any act which bore upon the case; any act in execution of the power to regulate commerce, the object of which was to control state legislation over those small navigable creeks into which the tide flows, and which abound throughout the lower country of the middle and southern states; we should feel not much difficulty in saying that a state law coming in conflict with such act would be void. But Congress has passed no such act. The repugnancy of the law of Delaware to the constitution is placed entirely on its repugnancy to the power to regulate commerce with foreign nations and among the several states; a power which has not been so exercised as to affect the question.

"We do not think that the act empowering the [company] to place a dam across the creek, can, under all the circumstances of the case, be considered as repugnant to the power to regulate commerce in its dormant state, or as being in conflict with any law passed on the subject."

(b)   Shortly after Marshall, C.J.'s death, CITY OF NEW YORK v. MILN, 36 U.S. (11 Pet.) 102 (1837), again avoided the exclusive-concurrent power issue by upholding a New York requirement that ships report details on incoming passengers as "not a regulation of commerce, but of police." Thompson, J., separately concurring, would have upheld the law under both the Marshall police power theory and the concurrent commerce power theory. Story, J., dissenting, contended for exclusive power in Congress, claiming this was Marshall, C.J.'s, view after an earlier argument of the same case.

Would a state health law banning entry of unpasteurized milk be any less a regulation of interstate commerce than an act of Congress excluding unpasteurized milk from interstate commerce? Did the term "regulation of police," as used in *Miln*, serve a useful function?

COOLEY v. BOARD OF WARDENS
53 U.S. (12 How.) 299, 13 L.Ed. 996 (1852).

JUSTICE CURTIS delivered the opinion of the Court.

[The Court upheld Pennsylvania's 1803 law that required ships using the Philadelphia port to hire a local pilot,[3] considered in the light of a 1789 act of Congress providing that harbors and ports of the United States shall "continue to be regulated in conformity with the existing laws of the States [or] with such laws as the States [may] hereafter enact."]

If the Constitution excluded the States from making any law regulating commerce, certainly Congress cannot regrant, or in any manner reconvey to the States that power. And yet this act of 1789 gives its sanction only to laws enacted by the [States]. Entertaining these views we are brought [to the] question, whether the grant of the commercial power to Congress, did *per se* deprive the States of all power to regulate [pilots].

[When] it is said that the nature of the power requires that it should be exercised exclusively by Congress, it must be intended to refer to the subjects of that power, and to say they are of such a nature as to require exclusive legislation by Congress. Now the power to regulate commerce, embraces a vast field, containing not only many, but exceedingly various subjects, quite unlike in their nature; some imperatively demanding a single uniform rule, operating equally on the commerce of the United States in every port; and some, like the subject now in question, as imperatively demanding that diversity, which alone can meet the local necessities of navigation.

Either absolutely to affirm, or deny that the nature of this power requires exclusive legislation by Congress, is to lose sight of the nature of the subjects of this power, and to assert concerning all of them, what is

---

[3]   Ships not doing so were required to pay a fee for "the use of the society for the relief of distressed and decayed pilots" and their families.

really applicable but to a part. Whatever subjects of this power are in their nature national, or admit only of one uniform system, or plan of regulation, may justly be said to be of such a nature as to require exclusive legislation by Congress. That this cannot be affirmed of laws for the regulation of pilots and pilotage is plain. The act of 1789 contains a clear and authoritative declaration by the first Congress, that the nature of this subject is such, that until Congress should find it necessary to exert its power, it should be left to the legislation of the States; that it is local and not national; that it is likely to be the best provided for, not by one system, or plan of regulations, but by as many as the legislative discretion of the several States should deem applicable to the local peculiarities of the ports within their limits.

[The] practice of the States, and of the national government, has been in conformity with this declaration, from the origin of the national government to this time; and the nature of the subject, when examined, is such as to leave no doubt of the superior fitness and propriety, not to say the absolute necessity, of different systems of regulation, drawn from local knowledge and experience, and conformed to local wants. How then can we say, that by the mere grant of power to regulate commerce, the States are deprived of all the power to legislate on this subject, because from the nature of the power the legislation of Congress must be exclusive? * * *[4]

NOTES AND QUESTIONS

1.   *Constitutional basis.* Although *Cooley* affirms that the Commerce Clause will tolerate some state police power regulation of matters that Congress could regulate if it so chose, it also recognizes that the Commerce Clause, which is framed as a conferral of regulatory authority on Congress, of its own force invalidates state regulation of matters of "such a nature as to require exclusive legislation by Congress." In recent years, Scalia, J., and Thomas, J., have sometimes denied that fundamental proposition and maintained that the Clause "contains no 'negative' component." *Itel Containers Int'l Corp. v. Huddleston*, 507 U.S. 60, 79 (1993) (Scalia, J., concurring in part and concurring in the judgment). Scalia, J., has said, however, that he will enforce dormant Commerce Clause doctrine "on *stare decisis* [grounds in] two situations: (1) against a state law that facially discriminates against interstate commerce, and (2) against a state law that is indistinguishable from a type of law previously held unconstitutional by the Court." *United Haulers Ass'n v. Oneida-Herkimer Solid Waste Management Authority*, 550 U.S. 330, 348 (2007) (Scalia, J., concurring in part).

Compare Barry Friedman & Daniel T. Deacon, *A Course Unbroken: The Constitutional Legitimacy of the Dormant Commerce Clause*, 97 Va.L.Rev. 1877 (2011): "[T]here is plain textualist and originalist support for the dormant Commerce Clause. The doctrine has firm roots in an understanding of the

---

[4]   Daniel, J., concurred on other grounds. McLean and Wayne, JJ., dissented.

Constitution and its enumerated powers in which the commerce power belonged exclusively to Congress. Even [s]keptics concede that if the commerce power is exclusive, the dormant Commerce Clause doctrine is legitimate. It is only because they are looking through presentist eyes that they neither understand nor accept the argument for exclusivity."

Either echoing or anticipating arguments made by Justices Scalia and Thomas, some commentators, too, have called for an abandonment of judicial scrutiny of state legislation under the Commerce Clause. In doing so, they have usually relied on an assumption that some other constitutional provision, such as the Privileges and Immunities Clause of Article IV, § 2, cl. 1, which provides that "The Citizens of each State shall be entitled to all Privileges and Immunities of Citizens in the several States," would authorize adequate judicial review to protect national interests. See, e.g., Julian N. Eule, *Laying the Dormant Commerce Clause to Rest*, 91 Yale L.J. 425 (1982). The Privileges and Immunities Clause is discussed in Sec. 4 infra.

Thomas, J., joined by Scalia, J., similarly suggested in *Camps Newfound/Owatonna, Inc. v. Harrison,* 520 U.S. 564 (1997), that some state regulation now subject to dormant Commerce Clause review should instead be scrutinized under the Import-Export Clause of Art. I, § 10, cl. 2, which provides that "[n]o state shall, without the Consent of Congress, lay any Imposts or Duties on Imports or Exports." See also Brannon P. Denning, *Justice Thomas, The Import-Export Clause, and* Camps Newfound/Owatonna v. Harrison, 70 U.Colo.L.Rev. 155 (1998), arguing that historical evidence supports Thomas, J.'s interpretation of the Import-Export Clause as barring discriminatory taxes on imports and exports from other states, but concluding that the Import-Export Clause does not prohibit other discriminatory state taxes.

Compare Friedman & Deacon, supra: "[E]ven those who question the legitimacy of the dormant Commerce Clause would relocate much of the judicial power to strike down state laws in other parts of the Constitution or struggle to find a congressional law that supposedly preempts offending state measures. Thus, there is reason to doubt on policy grounds whether anyone believes this judicial power is dispensable."

2. *Functional considerations.* Regardless of whether judicial scrutiny is based on the Commerce Clause or other constitutional provisions, the historically prevailing view appears to have been that political pressures on, and possibly the responsibility of, state legislators to protect and advance local concerns indicate the desirability if not the necessity of review by a body charged to protect truly national interests.[5] Does this view overlook the

---

[5]   See, e.g., Tribe, 3d. ed. at 1024–29; Norman R. Williams & Brannon P. Denning, *The "New Protectionism" and the American Common Market,* 85 Notre Dame L.Rev. 247 (2009). But see, e.g., Edmund W. Kitch, *Regulation and the American Common Market,* in *Regulation, Federalism, and Interstate Commerce* 9 (A. Dan Tarlock ed., 1981) (arguing that the costs of judicial oversight exceed the benefits); Patrick C. McGinley, *Trashing the Constitution: Judicial Activism, the Dormant Commerce Clause, and the Federalism Mantra,* 71 Or.L.Rev. 409 (1992) (arguing that dormant Commerce Clause review reflects a structurally unjustified intrusion on state political autonomy).

possibility that Congress could legislate to preempt state legislation whenever it thought the national interest required? Or is a judicial role in reviewing state legislation functionally necessary because Congress has "too little time and too few resources to give attention to 'low visibility' state programs that have protectionist purposes or effects"?[6]

2. BASIC DOCTRINAL PRINCIPLES AND THEIR APPLICATION

Although the Court, since *Cooley*, has regularly reviewed state legislation for possible conflict with the negative implications of the Commerce Clause, uncertainty and controversy have persisted concerning the standard against which legislation should be tested. Through the nineteenth and into the twentieth century, the *Cooley* distinction between subjects that did and did not require national uniformity was consistently applied to invalidate purposefully discriminatory regulations that favored local interests. However, other applications were less certain. After the turn of the twentieth century, the Court frequently distinguished between "direct" burdens on commerce, which were impermissible, and "indirect" burdens that could be sustained.[7] But observers complained that these labels were conclusory and, what is more, that it had become "difficult, if not impossible" to tell "whether these expressions merely constituted different methods of stating the *Cooley* doctrine, or whether the Court was applying different tests."[8]

In *Di Santo v. Pennsylvania,* 273 U.S. 34, 44 (1927), Stone, J., dissenting, mounted a forceful attack on the direct-indirect "formula." In its place, he suggested a balancing test, under which the validity of a state regulation would depend upon whether "a consideration of all the facts and circumstances, such as the nature of the regulation, its function, the character of the business involved and the actual effect on the flow of commerce, leads to the conclusion that the regulation concerns interests peculiarly local and does not infringe the national interest in maintaining the freedom of commerce across state lines."[9]

---

[6]   Dan T. Coenen, *Untangling the Market-Participant Exception to the Dormant Commerce Clause,* 88 Mich.L.Rev. 395 (1989).

[7]   In contrast to "direct" burdens such as taxes or licensing requirements, "indirect" burdens included traditionally local matters (e.g. labeling requirements, inspection statutes, and quarantine laws) as well as regulations of matters that were not considered part of commerce (e.g. production, manufacture, and insurance). Brandon P. Denning, *Reconstructing the Dormant Commerce Clause Doctrine,* 50 Wm. & Mary L.Rev. 417 (2008). The Court also "used many other expressions—such as whether the state law was a 'burden,' or a 'substantial' or 'undue' burden, on commerce, [and] whether the regulation was or was not imposed 'on' interstate commerce itself." Robert L. Stern, *The Problems of Yesteryear—Commerce and Due Process,* 4 Vand.L.Rev. 446 (1951).

[8]   Stern, supra note 7.

[9]   Holmes and Brandeis, JJ., joined Stone, J.'s dissent.

Two decades later, the Court adopted a balancing approach in *Southern Pacific Co. v. Arizona* (1945), involving a challenge to a state law prohibiting railroad trains of more than 14 passenger or 70 freight cars. In an opinion by Stone, C.J., the Court framed the judicial inquiry as turning on "the nature and extent of the burden which the state regulation of interstate trains, adopted as a safety measure, imposes on interstate commerce, and whether the relative weights of the state and national interests" justify the prohibition.

In the modern era that *Di Santo* and *Southern Pacific* inaugurated, judicial review under the dormant Commerce Clause has occurred within a sharply two-tiered framework. Under it, state regulations that *purposely* or *facially* discriminate against interstate commerce—such as restrictions on the sale of goods imported from other states—are invalid unless supported by an extraordinary justification.

WYOMING v. OKLAHOMA, 502 U.S. 437, 454–55 (1992), formulated this aspect of the doctrine as follows: "[The] 'negative' aspect of the Commerce Clause prohibits economic protectionism—that is, regulatory measures designed to benefit in-state economic interests by burdening out-of-state competitors. When a state statute clearly discriminates against interstate commerce, it will be struck down unless the discrimination is demonstrably justified by a valid factor unrelated to economic protectionism. Indeed, when the state statute amounts to simple economic protectionism, a 'virtually per se rule of invalidity' has applied."

By contrast, when state regulations only "incidentally" (rather than facially or purposefully) restrict the flow of interstate commerce—for example, by regulating containers in which an item of commerce can be marketed, regardless of where it was produced—the Court will balance the national and local interests at stake. The most frequently invoked formulation of the balancing formula was first articulated in PIKE v. BRUCE CHURCH, INC., 397 U.S. 137, 142 (1970): "Where [a state statute] regulates evenhandedly to effectuate a legitimate local public interest, and its effects on interstate commerce are only incidental, it will be upheld unless the burden imposed on such commerce is clearly excessive in relation to the putative local benefits. If a legitimate local purpose is found, then the question becomes one of degree. And the extent of the burden that will be tolerated [will] depend on the nature of the local interest involved, and on whether it could be promoted as well with a lesser impact on interstate activities."

As you read the cases that follow, consider whether the Court's two-tiered analytical framework, including the balancing test articulated in *Pike*, (i) is constitutionally defensible and (ii) actually describes the Court's processes of decision.

I. STATUTES THAT DISCRIMINATE ON THEIR FACES AGAINST INTERSTATE COMMERCE

BALDWIN V. G.A.F. SEELIG, INC.
294 U.S. 511, 55 S.Ct. 497, 79 L.Ed. 1032 (1935).

JUSTICE CARDOZO delivered the opinion of the Court.

[New York regulated the minimum prices at which producers could sell milk to dealers. It also prohibited the sale in New York of milk bought outside the state at lower prices. The Court held the prohibitions invalid.]

New York has no power to project its legislation into Vermont by regulating the price to be paid in that state for milk acquired there. [It] is equally without power to prohibit the introduction within her territory of milk of wholesome quality acquired in Vermont, whether at high prices or [low]. Accepting those postulates, New York asserts her power to outlaw milk so introduced by prohibiting its sale thereafter if the price that has been paid for it to the farmers of Vermont is less than would be owing in like circumstances to farmers in New York. The importer in that view may keep his milk or drink it, but sell it he may not.

Such a power, if exerted, will set a barrier to traffic between one state and another as effective as if customs duties, equal to the price differential, had been laid upon the thing transported.

[Nice] distinctions [between] direct and indirect burdens [are] irrelevant when the avowed purpose of the obstruction, as well as its necessary tendency, is to suppress or mitigate the consequences of competition between the states. [If] New York, in order to promote the economic welfare of her farmers, may guard them against competition with the cheaper prices of Vermont, the door has been opened to rivalries and reprisals that were meant to be averted by subjecting commerce between the states to the power of the nation.

The argument is pressed upon us, however, that the end to be served by the Milk Control Act is something more than the economic welfare of the farmers. [The] end to be served is the maintenance of a regular and adequate supply of pure and wholesome milk; the supply being put in jeopardy when the farmers of the state are unable to earn a living income. [On] that assumption we are asked to say that intervention will be upheld as a valid exercise by the state of its internal police power, though there is an incidental obstruction to commerce between one state and another. [Let] such an exception be admitted, and all that a state will have to do in times of stress and strain is to say that its farmers and merchants and workmen must be protected against competition from without, lest they go upon the poor relief lists or perish altogether. To give entrance to that excuse would be to invite a speedy end of our national solidarity. The Constitution was framed under the dominion of a political philosophy less parochial in range. It was framed upon the theory that the peoples of the several states must sink or swim together, and that in the long run prosperity and salvation are in union and not division.

[Another argument] seeks to establish [that] farmers who are underpaid will be tempted to save the expense of sanitary precautions. [But] the evils springing from uncared for cattle must be remedied by measures of repression more direct and certain than the creation of a parity of prices between New York and other states. Appropriate certificates may be exacted from farmers in Vermont and elsewhere (*Mintz v. Baldwin*, 289 U.S. 346; *Reid v. Colorado*, 187 U.S. 137); milk may be excluded if necessary safeguards have been omitted; but commerce between the states is burdened unduly when one state regulates by indirection the prices to be paid to producers in another, in the faith that augmentation of prices will lift up the level of economic welfare, and that this will stimulate the observance of sanitary requirements in the preparation of the [product.] Whatever relation there may be between earnings and sanitation is too remote and indirect to justify obstructions to the normal flow of commerce in its movement between states.

[What] is ultimate is the principle that one state in its dealings with another may not place itself in a position of economic isolation. Formulas and catch-words are subordinate to this over-mastering requirement. Neither the power to tax nor the police power may be used by the state of destination with the aim and effect of establishing an economic barrier against competition with the products of another state or the labor of its residents. Restrictions so contrived are an unreasonable clog upon the mobility of commerce. They set up what is equivalent to a rampart of customs duties designed to neutralize advantages belonging to the place of origin. They are thus hostile in conception as well as burdensome in result. The form of the packages in such circumstances is immaterial, whether they are original or broken. The importer must be free from imposts framed for the very purpose of suppressing competition from without and leading inescapably to the suppression so intended. * * *

NOTES AND QUESTIONS

1. ***Analogy to tariffs.*** The Court analogizes the New York law to a tariff on competing milk from out of state. How close is the analogy? If allowed to stand, would the New York regulation open the door "to rivalries and reprisals that were meant to be averted by subjecting commerce between the states to the power of the nation"?

Consider Donald H. Regan, *The Supreme Court and State Protectionism: Making Sense of the Dormant Commerce Clause*, 84 Mich.L.Rev. 1091 (1986): "We all have an intuitive idea of the [core 'protectionist' behavior that the Commerce Clause should be construed to prevent.] It is the imposition of tariffs, embargoes, quotas, and the like, [all of which were well known to the Constitution's Framers,] for the purpose of protecting local producers (farmers, manufacturers, laborers) against foreign competition. [There] are three objections to state [protectionism.] [1.] The concept-of-union objection is [that state] protectionism [is] inconsistent with the very idea of political union[.] Protectionist legislation is the economic equivalent of war. [2.] Protectionist impositions cause resentment and invite protectionist retaliation. [3. Protectionism] is inefficient. [T]ariffs, embargoes, quotas, and the like [divert] business from low-cost (foreign) to high-cost (local) producers." See also Brannon P. Denning, *Reconstructing the Dormant Commerce Clause Doctrine*, 50 Wm. & Mary L.Rev. 417 (2008), arguing that the Commerce Clause "restricts states' abilities to tax or otherwise regulate interstate commerce in ways that tend to undermine the political union established by the Constitution by adopting measures likely to provoke retaliation by other states."

2.   ***Other elements of the rationale.*** (a) The Court reasons in *Baldwin* that New York has attempted to "project its legislation into Vermont by regulating the price to be paid in that state for milk acquired there." Is this analysis sound? Would New York be projecting its legislation into Vermont if, to protect the health of its citizens, it forbade the sale in New York of milk produced by cattle (whether in New York, Vermont, or any other state) that had been fed a chemical that New York adjudged dangerous?[10]

Consider Regan, supra: "If we consider [our] three objections to protectionism—the concept of union objection, the resentment/retaliation objection, and the efficiency objection—we shall see that in connection with each [the] centrally relevant feature of classical protectionist legislation is protectionist purpose"—that is, a purpose of protecting in-staters against fair economic competition *at the expense of* out-of-staters. Because state legislation that is legitimately intended to protect the health of its citizens and does not favor local products over out-of-state products is not protectionist in this sense, Professor Regan thinks it can and should be distinguished from legislation such as that in *Baldwin*. More generally, he thinks that the touchstone of judicial inquiry in dormant Commerce Clause cases should be whether state legislation reflects a protectionist purpose. Do you agree? Is Regan's position consistent with the Court's analysis in *Baldwin* rejecting New York's attempt to justify its regulation as a health measure?

Note that the Court says in *Baldwin* that commerce is "burdened unduly" by a state regulation that ostensibly aims to ensure the observance of sanitary requirements, but does so in a way that is "remote and indirect." Is this possibly another way of saying that the "health" justification for the law was a pretext for protecting in-state farmers from fair economic competition with out-of-state farmers?

(b)   When the Court says that "New York, in order to promote the economic welfare of her farmers, may [not] guard them against competition

---

[10]   On extraterritorial legislation, see Sec. 2, IV infra.

with the cheaper prices of Vermont," does it mean to imply that New York could not try to help its farmers by offering them free advice on best agricultural practices? That it could not provide cash subsidies to its dairy industry? For discussion, see Sec. 2, VI infra.

3. *Reasonable alternatives.* The Court in *Baldwin* noted that New York could achieve its legitimate objectives—maintaining a regular supply of milk produced in compliance with its sanitation standards—through other means. A subsequent case also involving milk regulation reached a similar result: In *Dean Milk Co. v. Madison*, 340 U.S. 349 (1951), the Court addressed a Madison, Wisconsin, ordinance that prohibited the sale of milk not processed at approved pasteurization plants within five miles of Madison's central square. Writing for the Court, Clark, J., found that "reasonable and adequate alternatives are available. If Madison prefers to rely upon its own officials for inspection of distant milk sources, such inspection is readily open to it without hardship for it could charge the actual and reasonable cost of such inspection to the importing producers and processors. [Alternatively, Madison could exclude] milk not produced and pasteurized conformably to standards as high as those enforced by the receiving city." Quoting *Baldwin*, the Court therefore concluded that "the regulation must yield to the principle that 'one state in its dealings with another may not place itself in a position of economic isolation.' "

The Court added in a footnote: "It is immaterial that Wisconsin milk from outside the Madison area is subjected to the same proscription as that moving in interstate commerce."

Black, J., joined by Douglas and Minton, J.J., dissented. The dissent argued that "[n]either of the alternatives suggested by the Court would assure the people of Madison as pure a supply of milk as they receive under their own ordinance." Further, the dissent critiqued the "reasonable alternatives" approach: "[W]hile the "reasonable alternative" concept has been invoked to protect First Amendment rights, [it] has not heretofore been considered an appropriate weapon for striking down local health laws. [In] my view, to use this ground now elevates the right to traffic in commerce for profit above the power of the people to guard the purity of their daily diet of [milk]."

What is the relationship between the existence of a reasonable alternative and a law's legitimacy under dormant Commerce Clause doctrine? Does the availability of a less restrictive alternative suggest that a legislature's actual purpose may be protectionist rather than health-related?

Since the decision was based on "discrimination," why was it "immaterial" that the regulation also excluded Wisconsin milk not pasteurized in Madison? Is it an adequate response that discrimination against interstate commerce is constitutionally suspect, even if some intrastate commerce is also discriminated against? In considering these questions, note that in *Fort Gratiot Sanitary Landfill, Inc. v. Michigan Dept. of Natural Resources,* 504 U.S. 353 (1992), the Court reaffirmed the holding of *Dean Milk* that limited intrastate discrimination will not excuse otherwise impermissible discrimination against interstate commerce.

PHILADELPHIA V. NEW JERSEY
437 U.S. 617, 98 S.Ct. 2531, 57 L.Ed.2d 475 (1978).

JUSTICE STEWART delivered the opinion of the Court.

[Operators of New Jersey landfills, and out-of-state cities that had agreements with them for waste disposal, brought a Commerce Clause challenge against Ch. 363, N.J.Laws, 1973, which provided: "No person shall bring into this State any solid or liquid waste which originated or was collected outside [the] State." The New Jersey Supreme Court upheld the statute, ruling that it advanced vital health and environmental objectives with no economic discrimination against interstate commerce and that its substantial benefits outweighed its "slight" burden on interstate commerce. The Supreme Court reversed.]

[The] New Jersey Supreme Court questioned whether the interstate movement of [wastes] is "commerce" at all within the meaning of the Commerce Clause. [All] objects of interstate trade merit Commerce Clause protection; none is excluded by definition at the outset. [Just] as Congress has power to regulate the interstate movement of these wastes, States are not free from constitutional scrutiny when they restrict that movement.

[The] opinions of the Court through the years have reflected an alertness to the evils of "economic isolation" and protectionism, while at the same time recognizing that incidental burdens on interstate commerce may be unavoidable when a State legislates to safeguard the health and safety of its people. Thus, where simple economic protectionism is effected by state legislation, a virtually per se rule of invalidity has been erected. See, e.g., *Baldwin*. [But] where other legislative objectives are credibly advanced and there is no patent discrimination against interstate trade, the Court has adopted a much more flexible approach, the general contours of which were outlined in [*Pike*]. [The] crucial inquiry, therefore, must be directed to determining whether ch. 363 is basically a protectionist measure, or whether it can fairly be viewed as a law directed to legitimate local concerns, with effects upon interstate commerce that are only incidental.

The purpose of ch. 363 is set out in the [statute]: "The Legislature finds and determines that [the] volume of solid and liquid waste continues to rapidly increase, that the treatment and disposal of these wastes continues to pose an even greater threat to the quality of the environment of New Jersey, that the available and appropriate landfill sites within the State are being diminished, that the environment continues to be threatened by the treatment and disposal of waste which originated or was collected outside the State." [The] state court additionally found that New Jersey's existing landfill sites will be exhausted within a few years; that to go on using these sites or to develop new ones will take a heavy environmental [toll;] that new techniques to divert waste from landfills to other methods of disposal and resource recovery processes are under development, but that these changes will require time; and finally, that "the extension of the lifespan of existing landfills, resulting from the exclusion of out-of-state waste, may be of crucial importance in preventing further virgin wetlands or other undeveloped lands from being devoted to landfill purposes."

[The] dispute about ultimate legislative purpose need not be resolved, because [the] evil of protectionism can reside in legislative means as well as legislative ends. Thus, it does not matter whether the ultimate aim of ch. 363 is to reduce the waste disposal costs of New Jersey residents or to save remaining open lands from pollution, for we assume New Jersey has every right to protect its residents' pocketbooks as well as their environment. And it may be assumed as well that New Jersey may pursue those ends by slowing the flow of *all* waste into the State's remaining landfills, even though interstate commerce may incidentally be affected. But whatever New Jersey's ultimate purpose, it may not be accomplished by discriminating against articles of commerce coming from outside the State unless there is some reason, apart from their origin, to treat them differently. Both on its face and in its plain effect, ch. 363 violates this principle of nondiscrimination.

[Also] relevant here are the Court's decisions holding that a State may not accord its own inhabitants a preferred right of access over consumers in other States to natural resources located within its borders. [E.g.,] *West v. Kansas Natural Gas Co.*, 221 U.S. 229 (1911). [On] its face, [the New Jersey law] imposes on out-of-state commercial interests the full burden of conserving the State's remaining landfill space. It is true that in our previous cases the scarce natural resource was itself the article of commerce, whereas here the scarce resource and the article of commerce are distinct. But that difference is without consequence. In both instances, the State has overtly moved to slow or freeze the flow of commerce for protectionist reasons. It does not matter that the State has shut the article of commerce inside the State in one case and outside the State in the other. What is crucial is the attempt by one State to isolate itself from a problem common to many by erecting a barrier against the movement of interstate trade.

[It] is true that certain quarantine laws have not been considered forbidden protectionist measures, even though they were directed against out-of-state commerce. But those quarantine laws banned the importation of articles such as diseased livestock that required destruction as soon as possible because their very movement risked contagion and other evils. Those laws thus did not discriminate against interstate commerce as such, but simply prevented traffic in noxious articles, whatever their origin.

The New Jersey statute is not such a quarantine law. There has been no claim here that the very movement of waste into or through New Jersey endangers health, or that waste must be disposed of as soon and as close to its point of generation as possible. The harms caused by waste are said to arise after its disposal in landfill sites, and at that point, as New Jersey concedes, there is no basis to distinguish out-of-state waste from domestic waste. If one is inherently harmful, so is the other. Yet New Jersey has banned the former while leaving its landfill sites open to the latter. The New Jersey law blocks the importation of waste in an obvious effort to saddle those outside the State with the entire burden of slowing the flow of refuse into New Jersey's remaining landfill sites. That legislative effort is clearly impermissible under the Commerce Clause of the Constitution.

Today, cities in Pennsylvania and New York find it expedient or necessary to send their waste into New Jersey for disposal, and New Jersey claims the right to close its borders to such traffic. Tomorrow, cities in New Jersey may find it expedient or necessary to send their waste into Pennsylvania or New York for disposal, and those States might then claim the right to close their borders. The Commerce Clause will protect New Jersey in the future, just as it protects her neighbors now, from efforts by one State to isolate itself in the stream of interstate commerce from a problem shared by all.

JUSTICE REHNQUIST, with whom CHIEF JUSTICE BURGER joins, dissenting.

[New] Jersey should be free under our past precedents to prohibit the importation of solid waste because of the health and safety problems that such waste poses to its citizens. The fact that New Jersey continues to, and indeed must continue to, dispose of its own solid waste does not mean that New Jersey may not prohibit the importation of even more solid waste into the State.

[I] do not see why a State may ban the importation of items whose movement risks contagion, but cannot ban the importation of items which, although they may be transported into the State without undue hazard, will then simply pile up in an ever increasing danger to the public's health and safety. The Commerce Clause was not drawn with a view to having the validity of state laws turn on such pointless distinctions.

[T]hat New Jersey has left its landfill sites open for domestic waste does not, of course, mean that solid waste is not innately harmful. Nor does it mean that New Jersey prohibits importation of solid waste for reasons other than the health and safety of its population. New Jersey must out of sheer necessity treat and dispose of its solid waste in some fashion, just as it must treat New Jersey cattle suffering from hoof-and-mouth disease. It does not follow that New Jersey must, under the Commerce Clause, accept solid waste or diseased cattle from outside its borders and thereby exacerbate its problems. * * *

NOTES AND QUESTIONS

1. *"Protectionism" and "non-economic" problems.* Are the Commerce Clause considerations underlying the "principle of nondiscrimination" soundly applicable to the conflict between New Jersey's interest in prolonging the life of its limited landfills and other states' interest in using New Jersey's landfills? Is the policy against "protectionism" soundly applicable to a state's efforts to isolate itself from environmental, rather than economic, problems generated by interstate commerce?

2. *Governmental "out-of-state commercial interests."* The only out-of-state litigants in *Philadelphia* were cities claiming the right to continue to "send their waste into New Jersey for disposal"—a governmental function. Was it appropriate to invoke Commerce Clause concerns to protect such interests? Were they "out-of-state commercial interests"?

MAINE v. TAYLOR, 477 U.S. 131 (1986), per BLACKMUN, J., upheld a Maine law that prohibited importation into Maine of live baitfish that competed with Maine's native baitfish industry. The Court relied on two district court findings: (1) "Maine 'clearly has a legitimate and substantial purpose in prohibiting the importation of live bait fish' because 'substantive uncertainties' surrounded the effects that baitfish parasites would have on the State's unique population of wild fish, and the consequences of introducing non-native species were similarly unpredictable"; and (2) "less discriminatory means of protecting against these threats were currently unavailable" despite the "abstract possibility" of developing acceptable testing procedures in the future. The Court added:

"[A] State must make reasonable efforts to avoid restraining the free flow of commerce across its borders, but it is not required to develop new and unproven means of protection at an uncertain cost. Appellee, of course, is free to work on his own or in conjunction with other bait dealers to develop scientifically acceptable sampling and inspection procedures for golden shiners; if and when such procedures are developed, Maine no longer may be able to justify its import ban. The State need not join in those efforts, however, and it need not pretend they already have succeeded.

"[The] evidence in this case amply supports the District Court's findings that Maine's ban on the importation of live baitfish serves legitimate local purposes that could not adequately be served by available nondiscriminatory alternatives. This is not a case of arbitrary discrimination against interstate commerce; the record suggests that Maine has legitimate reasons, 'apart from their origin, to treat [out-of-state baitfish] differently,' *Philadelphia*."

Stevens, J., dissented, contending that "uncertainty" and "[a]mbiguity about dangers and alternatives should actually defeat, rather than sustain, the discriminatory measure." His summary: "There is something fishy about this case."

NOTES AND QUESTIONS

1. ***Preserving natural resources for in-state use.*** (a) Consider Norman R. Williams, *Taking Care of Ourselves: State Citizenship, the Market and the State*, 69 Ohio St.L.J. 493 (2008): "With respect to natural resources that merely happen to be found in a particular state through no effort of the state itself, such as minerals and petroleum, non-residents stand in an equal position as residents."

(b) SPORHASE v. NEBRASKA, 458 U.S. 941 (1982), per STEVENS, J., held invalid a Nebraska law requiring denial of a permit to withdraw and transport water for use in an adjoining state unless that state "grants reciprocal rights" to withdraw and transport its water for use in Nebraska. Rejecting an earlier precedent,[11] the Court ruled that ground water is an "article of commerce," requiring Commerce Clause analysis of state laws restricting its transfer to other states: "[Because] Colorado forbids the exportation of its ground water, the reciprocity provision operates as an explicit barrier to commerce between the two states. [Nebraska] therefore bears the initial burden of demonstrating a close fit between the reciprocity requirement and its asserted local purpose. [The] reciprocity requirement does not survive the 'strictest scrutiny' reserved for facially discriminatory legislation."

2. ***Wild animals.*** HUGHES v. OKLAHOMA, 441 U.S. 322 (1979), per BRENNAN, J., held invalid under the Commerce Clause an Oklahoma ban on transporting "minnows for sale outside the state which were seined or procured within the waters of this state," as applied to a Texan who transported to Texas a load of minnows taken in Oklahoma waters: "We now conclude that challenges under the Commerce Clause to state regulations of wild animals should be considered according to the same general rule applied to state regulations of other natural resources.[12]

"[The] State's interest in maintaining the ecological balance in state waters by avoiding the removal of inordinate numbers of minnows may well qualify as a legitimate local purpose. [But far] from choosing the least discriminatory alternative, Oklahoma has chosen to 'conserve' its minnows in the way that most overtly discriminates against interstate commerce. The State places no limits on the numbers of minnows that can be taken by licensed minnow dealers; nor [on] how these minnows may be disposed of within the State. Yet it forbids the transportation of any commercially significant number of natural minnows out of the State for sale. Section 4–115(B) is certainly not a 'last ditch' attempt at conservation after nondiscriminatory alternatives have

---

[11] *Hudson County Water Co. v. McCarter,* 209 U.S. 349 (1908).

[12] This holding expressly overruled *Geer v. Connecticut,* 161 U.S. 519 (1896), which had held that a state ban on exporting wild game from the state was not subject to the Commerce Clause because of a theory of state ownership of the game, later recognized as a fiction facilitating conservation.

proven unfeasible. It is rather a choice of the most discriminatory means even though nondiscriminatory alternatives would seem likely to fulfill the State's purported legitimate local purpose more effectively.

"[States] may promote [their legitimate interest in conservation] only in ways consistent with the basic principle that 'our economic unit is the Nation,' and that when a wild animal 'becomes an article of commerce [its] use cannot be limited to the citizens of one State to the exclusion of citizens of another State.' *Geer* (Field, J., dissenting)."

Rehnquist, J., joined by Burger, C.J., dissented, concluding that Oklahoma's "substantial interest in conserving and regulating exploitation of its natural minnow population" "outweighed" the "minimal burden" on commerce of requiring all who export minnows from the state, residents as well as nonresidents, to secure them from hatcheries.

II. CONGRESSIONAL AUTHORIZATION OF STATE REGULATION

Cooley v. Board of Wardens, Sec. 1, supra, assumed that "Congress cannot regrant" regulatory power to the states once the power of regulation has been given to Congress under the Commerce Clause. But *Cooley* was not the Court's last word.

PRUDENTIAL INS. CO. v. BENJAMIN, 328 U.S. 408 (1946), per RUTLEDGE, J., upheld Congress's power to authorize state taxes that discriminate against interstate commerce and thereby insulate such taxes from challenge under the dormant Commerce Clause:[13] "Prudential chiefly relies [on] cases which have outlawed state taxes found to discriminate against interstate commerce. [Those cases] presented no question of the validity of such a tax where Congress had taken affirmative action consenting to it or purporting to give it validity.

"[In] all the variations of Commerce Clause theory it has never been the law that what the states may do in the regulation of commerce, Congress being silent, is the full measure of its power. Much less has this boundary been thought to confine what Congress and the states acting together may [accomplish].

"[The] cases most important for the decision in this cause [are] the ones involving situations where the silence of Congress or the dormancy of its power has been taken judicially, [as] forbidding state action, only to have Congress later disclaim the prohibition or undertake to nullify it. Not yet has this Court held such a disclaimer invalid or that state action supported

---

[13] *Prudential* upheld a South Carolina statute that imposed a tax on gross insurance premiums from South Carolina businesses but exempted South Carolina insurance companies. The Court ruled that Congress had authorized such taxes by the McCarran Act, which made insurance companies subject to state taxes and regulations after *United States v. South-Eastern Underwriters Ass'n*, 322 U.S. 533 (1944), had given rise to doubts about state power over interstate insurance business.

by it could not stand. On the contrary, in each instance it has given effect to the congressional judgment contradicting its own previous one.

"[The McCarran Act] was a determination by Congress that state taxes, which in its silence might be held invalid as discriminatory, do not place on interstate insurance business a burden which it is unable generally to bear or should not bear in the competition with local business. Such taxes were not uncommon among the states, and the statute clearly included South Carolina's tax now in issue.

"That judgment was one of policy and reflected long and clear experience. For, notwithstanding the long incidence of the tax and its payment by Prudential without question prior to the *South-Eastern* decision, the record of Prudential's continuous success in South Carolina over decades refutes any idea that payment of the tax handicapped it in any way tending to exclude it from competition with local business or with domestic insurance companies.

"[This] broad authority [over commerce] Congress may exercise alone [or] in conjunction with coordinated action by the states, in which case limitations imposed for the preservation of their powers become inoperative and only those designed to forbid action altogether by any power or combination of powers in our governmental system remain effective. Here both Congress and South Carolina have acted, and in complete coordination, to sustain the tax. It is therefore reinforced by the exercise of all the power of government residing in our scheme. [Congress and the states] were not forbidden to cooperate or by doing so to achieve legislative consequences, particularly in the great fields of regulating commerce and taxation, which, to some extent at least, neither could accomplish in isolated exertion."

NOTES AND QUESTIONS

1. *Congressionally authorized discrimination.* The Court's decision in *Prudential* has been controversial. Consider Norman R. Williams, *Why Congress May Not "Overrule" The Dormant Commerce Clause*, 53 U.C.L.A. L.Rev. 153 (2005): "Congress's power over interstate commerce is plenary; it may promote, prohibit, or discriminate as it chooses. But the Constitution's commitment to economic union and democratic accountability precludes Congress from validating state laws that would otherwise violate the dormant Commerce Clause. If Congress wishes to foster state protectionism, it must do so directly. In only that way can we rest assured that the responsibility will be laid at Congress's door. Such accountability is important in its own right, but it also has the practical benefit of discouraging such protectionism. Likely, few Congressmen will wish to stand publicly in favor of state protectionism."[14]

---

[14] See also Donald H. Regan, *The Supreme Court and State Protectionism: Making Sense of the Dormant Commerce Clause*, 84 Mich.L.Rev. 1091 (1986).

2. *Other restraints on state discrimination.* Although Congress can waive impediments to state discrimination under the Commerce Clause, Congress cannot waive individual rights to be free from discrimination under the Privileges and Immunities Clause of Art. IV, see Sec. 4 of this chapter, or the Equal Protection Clause of the Fourteenth Amendment, see Ch. 9. The leading equal protection case on state protectionism, METROPOLITAN LIFE INS. CO. v. WARD, 470 U.S. 869 (1985), per POWELL, J., struck down a discriminatory state tax on out-of-state insurance companies under the Equal Protection Clause, notwithstanding the statute's immunity from attack on dormant Commerce Clause grounds under the McCarran Act and *Prudential Ins. Co.*

Although *Metropolitan Life Ins.* makes clear that Congress cannot authorize equal protection violations, a leading commentator describes the case as an "aberration" in finding that state legislation discriminating against out-of-state businesses violates the Equal Protection Clause. Tribe 2d ed., at 526 n. 34. Compare *Northeast Bancorp, Inc. v. Board of Governors*, 472 U.S. 159, 172–73 (1985) (holding that Congress had authorized Massachusetts and Connecticut laws imposing reciprocity requirements on out-of-state banks that seek to acquire in-state banks and that the laws were not violations of the Equal Protection Clause).

3. *Consistency with Marbury.* Is recognition of a congressional power to override the Court's Commerce Clause decisions consistent with *Marbury v. Madison?*

(a) Henry P. Monaghan, *Constitutional Common Law*, 89 Harv.L.Rev. 1 (1975), suggests that "the most satisfactory explanation of the [dormant or negative] Commerce Clause cases is that the Supreme Court is fashioning federal common law on the authority of the Commerce Clause. That clause embodies a national, free-trade philosophy" and is the "source of judicial lawmaking authority." But the Commerce Clause, although it authorizes judicial lawmaking to implement free trade values, does not uniquely require particular rules; and because Commerce Clause doctrine is judge-made common law, not "*Marbury*-like" constitutional interpretation, "the negative-impact cases are wholly subject to congressional revision."

Although this theory may rationalize congressional overruling of Supreme Court decisions under the Commerce Clause, does it adequately explain why the Commerce Clause—a grant of power to *Congress*—should be construed to authorize constitutional common law making by the *courts*?[15]

(b) An alternative theory would portray dormant Commerce Clause doctrine as embodying constitutional "default" rules—rules mandated by

---

[15] Cf. Martin H. Redish & Shane V. Nugent, *The Dormant Commerce Clause and the Constitutional Balance of Federalism*, 1987 Duke L.J. 569 (1987) (arguing that dormant Commerce Clause review is a constitutionally illegitimate judicial usurpation) with Jim Chen, *A Vision Softly Creeping: Congressional Acquiescence and the Dormant Commerce Clause*, 88 Minn.L.Rev. 1764 (2004) (arguing that Congress' failure to "repeal the dormant Commerce Clause" renders the Court's dormant Commerce Clause review constitutionally permissible).

considerations of constitutional text, history, and structure, but distinctly subject to override or displacement by express congressional action. See Laurence H. Tribe, *Constitutional Choices* 29–44 (1985). Are there principled grounds for determining which constitutional rules are merely default rules and which are "*Marbury*-like"?

III. DISCRIMINATORY STATUTES THAT FAVOR GOVERNMENTAL RATHER THAN PRIVATE ENTITIES

C & A CARBONE, INC. v. CLARKSTOWN, 511 U.S. 383 (1994): Clarkstown, New York arranged for the construction of a "waste transfer station" to collect waste, separate recyclable from nonrecyclable items, and ship the solid waste to the appropriate disposal facility. The transfer station was built and operated by a private company, but under a contract contemplating that it would be sold to the town for $1 at the end of five years. In order to ensure the transfer station's economic viability, the town adopted a "flow control ordinance" (local law no. 9) requiring that all nonrecyclable solid waste generated within the town be processed at the transfer station, which charged a fee in excess of the prevailing private market rate. Ruling on a challenge by a private recycler doing business in Clarkstown, the Court, per KENNEDY, J., held that the ordinance violated the Commerce Clause:

"[A]s the town itself points out, what makes garbage a profitable business is not its own worth but the fact that its possessor must pay to get rid of it. In other words, the article of commerce is not so much the solid waste itself, but rather the service of processing and disposing of it. With respect to this stream of commerce, the flow control ordinance discriminates, for it allows only the favored operator to process waste that is within the limits of the town. The ordinance is no less discriminatory because in-state or in-town processors are also covered by the prohibition. [*Dean Milk*.] [The] flow control ordinance is just one more instance of local processing requirements that we long have held invalid. [It] hoards solid waste, and the demand to get rid of it, for the benefit of the preferred processing facility. The only conceivable distinction from the cases cited above is that the flow control ordinance favors a single local proprietor. But this difference just makes the protectionist effect of the ordinance more acute. In *Dean Milk*, the local processing requirement at least permitted pasteurizers within five miles of the city to compete. An out-of-state pasteurizer who wanted access to that market might have built a pasteurizing facility within the radius. The flow control ordinance at issue here squelches competition in the waste-processing service altogether, leaving no room for investment from outside. * * *

"Clarkstown maintains that special financing is necessary to ensure the long-term survival of the designated facility. If so, the town may subsidize the facility through general taxes or municipal bonds. *New*

Energy Co. v. Limbach [Sec. 2, VI, infra]. But having elected to use the open market to earn revenues for its project, the town may not employ discriminatory regulation to give that project an advantage over rival businesses from out of State."

O'Connor, J., concurred in the judgment: "In my view, [the] town's ordinance is unconstitutional not because of facial or effective discrimination against interstate commerce, but rather because it imposes an excessive burden on interstate commerce. [Unlike] the regulations we have previously struck down, Local Law 9 does not give more favorable treatment to local interests as a group as compared to out-of-state or out-of-town economic interests. Rather, the garbage sorting monopoly is achieved at the expense of all competitors, be they local or nonlocal.

"[I] believe this distinction has more doctrinal significance than the majority acknowledges. In considering state health and safety regulations such as Local Law 9, we have consistently recognized that the fact that interests within the regulating jurisdiction are equally affected by the challenged enactment counsels against a finding of discrimination. And for good reason. The existence of substantial in-state interests harmed by a regulation is 'a powerful safeguard' against legislative discrimination.

"[Even] a nondiscriminatory regulation may nonetheless impose an excessive burden on interstate trade when considered in relation to the local benefits conferred. '[The] local interest in proper disposal of waste is obviously significant. But this interest could be achieved by simply requiring that all waste disposed of in the town be properly processed *somewhere.*' For example, the town could ensure proper processing by setting specific standards with which all town processors must comply.'

Souter, J., joined by Rehnquist, C.J., and Blackmun, J., dissented: "[T]he exclusion worked by Clarkstown's Local Law 9 bestows no benefit on a class of local private actors, but instead directly aids the government in satisfying a traditional governmental responsibility. The law does not differentiate between all local and all out-of-town providers of a service, but instead between the one entity responsible for ensuring that the job gets done and all other enterprises, regardless of their location. The ordinance thus falls outside that class of tariff or protectionist measures that the Commerce Clause has traditionally been thought to bar States from enacting against each other.

"[To] the degree Local Law 9 affects the market for trash processing services, it does so only by subjecting Clarkstown residents and businesses to burdens far different from the burdens of local favoritism that dormant Commerce Clause jurisprudence seeks to root out. The town has found a way to finance a public improvement, not by transferring its cost to out-of-state economic interests, but by spreading it among the local generators of trash, an equitable result with tendencies that should not disturb the Commerce Clause and should not be disturbed by us.

"[Clarkstown's] transfer station is essentially a municipal facility, built and operated under a contract with the municipality and soon to revert entirely to municipal ownership. [A] law that favors that single facility over all others is a law that favors the public sector over all private-sector processors, whether local or out of State. Because the favor does not go to local private competitors of out-of-state firms, out-of-state governments will at the least lack a motive to favor their own firms in order to equalize the positions of private competitors.

"[There] is, to be sure, an incidental local economic benefit, for the need to process Clarkstown's trash in Clarkstown will create local jobs. But this local boon is mitigated by another feature of the ordinance, in that it finances whatever benefits it confers on the town from the pockets of the very citizens who passed it into law. On the reasonable assumption that no one can avoid producing some trash, every resident of Clarkstown must bear a portion of the burden Local Law 9 imposes to support the municipal monopoly, an uncharacteristic feature of statutes claimed to violate the Commerce Clause.

"[The] Commerce Clause was not passed to save the citizens of Clarkstown from themselves. It should not be wielded to prevent them from attacking their local garbage problems with an ordinance that does not discriminate between local and out-of-town participants in the private market for trash disposal services and that is not protectionist in its purpose or effect."

UNITED TRASH HAULERS ASS'N V. ONEIDA-HERKIMER SOLID WASTE MANAGEMENT AUTH.
550 U.S. 330, 127 S.Ct. 1786, 167 L.Ed.2d 655 (2007).

CHIEF JUSTICE ROBERTS delivered the opinion of the Court, except as to Part II–D.[16]

[In the 1980's, Oneida and Herkimer Counties in New York faced a "solid waste crisis." The counties had uneasy relationships with local waste processors, who were infiltrated by organized crime elements that chronically fixed prices and drastically overcharged. Further, local landfills were operating without permits and violating state regulations, thereby causing environmental damage and costing the public tens of millions of dollars. In response, the State of New York created the Oneida-Herkimer Solid Waste Management Authority and authorized the Counties to impose "appropriate and reasonable limitations on competition." In 1989, the Counties enacted "flow control" ordinances requiring that all solid waste

---

[16] Souter, Ginsburg, and Breyer, JJ., joined in Part II–D.

collected within the counties be delivered to the Authority for processing. A trade association of solid waste management companies sued, alleging that the flow control ordinance violated the dormant Commerce Clause by discriminating against interstate commerce.]

"Flow control" ordinances require trash haulers to deliver solid waste to a particular waste processing facility. [In] this case, we face flow control ordinances quite similar to the one invalidated in *Carbone*. The only salient difference is that the laws at issue here require haulers to bring waste to facilities owned and operated by a state-created public benefit corporation. We find this difference constitutionally significant. Disposing of trash has been a traditional government activity for years, and laws that favor the government in such areas [do not] discriminate against interstate commerce for purposes of the Commerce Clause.

[II–C.] The flow control ordinances in this case benefit a clearly public facility, while treating all private companies exactly the same. Because the question is now squarely presented on the facts of the case before us, we decide that such flow control ordinances do not discriminate against interstate commerce for purposes of the dormant Commerce Clause.

Compelling reasons justify treating these laws differently from laws favoring particular private businesses over their competitors. Conceptually, of course, any notion of discrimination assumes a comparison of substantially similar entities. But States and municipalities are not private businesses—far from it. Unlike private enterprise, government is vested with the responsibility of protecting the health, safety, and welfare of its citizens. These important responsibilities set state and local government apart from a typical private business.

[As] our local processing cases demonstrate, when a law favors in-state business over out-of-state competition, rigorous scrutiny is appropriate because the law is often the product of "simple economic protectionism." Laws favoring local government, by contrast, may be directed toward any number of legitimate goals unrelated to protectionism. Here the flow control ordinances enable the Counties to pursue particular policies with respect to the handling and treatment of waste generated in the Counties, while allocating the costs of those policies on citizens and businesses according to the volume of waste they generate.

[The] dormant Commerce Clause is not a roving license for federal courts to decide what activities are appropriate for state and local government to undertake, and what activities must be the province of private market competition. [It] is not the office of the Commerce Clause to control the decision of the voters on whether government or the private sector should provide waste management services. "The Commerce Clause significantly limits the ability of States and localities to regulate or otherwise burden the flow of interstate commerce, but it does not elevate free trade above all other values." *Maine v. Taylor.*

We should be particularly hesitant to interfere with the Counties' efforts under the guise of the Commerce Clause because [w]aste disposal is both typically and traditionally a local government function. [The policy] of the State of New York favors "displac[ing] competition with regulation or monopoly public control" in this area. We may or may not agree with that approach, but nothing in the Commerce Clause vests the responsibility for that policy judgment with the Federal Judiciary.

Finally, it bears mentioning that the most palpable harm imposed by the ordinances—more expensive trash removal—is likely to fall upon the very people who voted for the laws. Our dormant Commerce Clause cases often find discrimination when a State shifts the costs of regulation to other States. [Here,] the citizens and businesses of the Counties bear the costs of the ordinances. There is no reason to step in and hand local businesses a victory they could not obtain through the political process.

We hold that the Counties' flow control ordinances, which treat in-state private business interests exactly the same as out-of-state ones, do not discriminate against interstate commerce for purposes of the dormant Commerce Clause.

[II–D] [In a section joined only by Souter, Ginsburg, and Breyer, JJ., Chief Justice Roberts proceeded to analyze the Counties' flow-control ordinance under the *Pike* balancing test, quoted in the Introduction to this Section. The trial court] could not detect any disparate impact on out-of-state as opposed to in-state businesses. [Yet the ordinances deliver public benefits by increasing] recycling in at least two ways. [First,] they create enhanced incentives for recycling and proper disposal of other kinds of waste. [Second,] by requiring all waste to be deposited at Authority facilities, the Counties have markedly increased their ability to enforce recycling laws. If the haulers could take waste to any disposal site, achieving an equal level of enforcement would be much more costly, if not impossible. For these reasons, any arguable burden the ordinances impose on interstate commerce does not exceed their public benefits.

JUSTICE SCALIA, concurring in part.

I join Part I and Parts II–A through II–C of the Court's opinion. I write separately to reaffirm my view that the so-called "negative" Commerce Clause is an unjustified judicial invention, not to be expanded beyond its existing domain. The historical record provides no grounds for reading the Commerce Clause to be other than what it says—an authorization for Congress to regulate commerce. I have been willing to enforce on *stare decisis* grounds a "negative" self-executing Commerce Clause in two situations: (1) against a state law that facially discriminates against interstate commerce, and (2) against a state law that is indistinguishable from a type of law previously held unconstitutional by this Court. As today's opinion makes clear, the flow-control law at issue in this case meets neither condition.

[I] am unable to join Part II–D of the principal opinion, in which the plurality performs so-called *"Pike* balancing." Generally speaking, the balancing of various values is left to Congress—which is precisely what the Commerce Clause (the real Commerce Clause) envisions.

JUSTICE THOMAS, concurring in the judgment.

I concur in the judgment. Although I joined [*Carbone*], I no longer believe it was correctly decided. The negative Commerce Clause has no basis in the Constitution and has proved unworkable in practice. As the debate between the majority and dissent shows, application of the negative Commerce Clause turns solely on policy considerations, not on the Constitution. Because this Court has no policy role in regulating interstate commerce, I would discard the Court's negative Commerce Clause jurisprudence.

JUSTICE ALITO, with whom JUSTICE STEVENS and JUSTICE KENNEDY join, dissenting.

This case cannot be meaningfully distinguished from *Carbone*. As the Court itself acknowledges, "[t]he only salient difference" between the cases is that the ordinance invalidated in *Carbone* discriminated in favor of a privately owned facility, whereas the laws at issue here discriminate in favor of facilities owned and operated by a state-created public benefit corporation. The Court relies on the distinction between public and private ownership to uphold the flow-control laws, even though a straightforward application of *Carbone* would lead to the opposite result. The public-private distinction drawn by the Court is both illusory and without precedent.

[The] only real difference between the facility at issue in *Carbone* and its counterpart in this case is that title to the former had not yet formally passed to the municipality. The Court exalts form over substance in adopting a test that turns on this technical distinction[.]

[I] see no basis for the Court's assumption that discrimination in favor of an in-state facility owned by the government is likely to serve legitimate goals unrelated to protectionism. Discrimination in favor of an in-state government facility serves local economic interests, inuring to the benefit of local residents who are employed at the facility, local businesses that supply the facility with goods and services, and local workers employed by such businesses. It is therefore surprising to read in the opinion of the Court that state discrimination in favor of a state-owned business is not likely to be motivated by economic protectionism.

[Proper] analysis under the dormant Commerce Clause involves more than an inquiry into whether the challenged Act is in some sense directed toward [legitimate] goals unrelated to protectionism; equally important are the means by which those goals are realized. If the chosen means take the form of a statute that discriminates against interstate commerce—either on its face or in practical effect—then "the burden falls on [the enacting government] to demonstrate both that the statute 'serves a legitimate local purpose,' and that this purpose could not be served as well by available nondiscriminatory means." *Maine v. Taylor*.

[T]hese laws discriminate against interstate commerce (generally favoring local interests over nonlocal interests), but are defended on the ground that they serve legitimate goals unrelated to protectionism (e.g., health, safety, and protection of the environment). And while I do not question that the laws at issue in this case serve legitimate goals, the laws offend the dormant Commerce Clause because those goals could be attained effectively through nondiscriminatory means.

The Court next suggests that deference to legislation discriminating in favor of a municipal landfill is especially appropriate considering that [w]aste disposal is both typically and traditionally a local government function. I disagree on two grounds.

First, this Court has previously recognized that any standard "that turns on a judicial appraisal of whether a particular governmental function is 'integral' or 'traditional' " is "unsound in principle and unworkable in practice." *Garcia v. San Antonio Metropolitan Transit Authority*, Ch. 2, Sec. 5, IV supra. [Second,] most of the garbage in this country is still managed by the private sector. In that respect, the Court is simply mistaken in concluding that waste disposal is "typically" a local government function.

Equally unpersuasive is the Court's suggestion that the flow-control laws do not discriminate against interstate commerce because they treat in-state private business interests exactly the same as out-of-state ones. [T]his Court has long recognized that a burden imposed by a State upon interstate commerce is not to be sustained simply because the statute imposing it applies alike to the people of all the States, including the people of the State enacting such statute.

NOTES AND QUESTIONS

1. **The novelty of United Haulers.** Consider Norman R. Williams & Brannon P. Denning, *The "New Protectionism" and the American Common Market*, 85 Notre Dame L.Rev. 247 (2009): "Prior to its decision in *United Haulers*, the Court had never before drawn a distinction between measures intended to protect private enterprises from outside competition versus those intended to protect public operations. [In] holding the contrary, *United Haulers* was, literally, unprecedented."

2. **The rationale.** (a) Bradford Mank, *The Supreme Court's New Public-Private Distinction Under the Dormant Commerce Clause*, 37 Hast.Const.L.Q.

1 (2009), opines: "Chief Justice Roberts [demonstrated] that public facilities are more likely to be concerned with protecting the public health and welfare than typical private facilities, which are primarily motivated by profits. In theory, local governments could enact regulations attempting to force private firms to match the environmental record of public facilities, but the *United Haulers* decision concluded it is more difficult for local governments to enforce regulations against private firms than to address public health and welfare concerns directly through a public facility. [*United Haulers*] and [*Dep't of Revenue v.*] *Davis* [infra] appropriately emphasize that the dormant Commerce Clause's purpose is to prevent local private favoritism, but not to force governments to turn over public functions to private markets."

For a competing perspective, see Norman R. Williams, *The Foundations of the American Common Market*, 84 Notre Dame L.Rev. 409 (2008): "[T]here is no obvious reason to treat 'public' or 'sovereign' protectionism as less opprobrious than 'private' protectionism. The same concerns that animate the Constitution's hostility to protectionism directed against private entities for the benefit of local companies apply equally to protectionism directed against out-of-state governments for the benefit of in-state governments. Such public protectionism undermines political union, invites retaliatory conduct from adversely affected states, and inhibits the efficient allocation of resources in ways that are unlikely to be corrected by normal state political processes."

(b) Williams & Denning, supra, find other elements of the Court's reasoning unconvincing: "[T]here is no merit to the Court's alternative argument that judicial review of governmental favoritism of its own operations is unnecessary because other in-state interests, such as businesses that must pay higher prices for waste disposal services[, are] also harmed[. Presumably,] the implication is that in-state interests burdened by the measure serve as virtual representatives of out-of-state interests, and, therefore, the domestic political process can be trusted to take account of the measure's full costs and benefits. [Yet] almost all regulations and taxes impose some local burdens[. Tariffs] on out-of-state-goods impose burdens on local consumers, yet they are clearly unconstitutional despite that fact. [If the Court meant] only that judicial review of state and local taxes and regulations is not necessary when there are a sufficient number of in-state interests harmed[, the] devil is in determining exactly what is a sufficient number[. Resolving] that question involves highly complex and contested issues of political science regarding interest group vitality and voting behavior."

———

DEPARTMENT OF REV. v. DAVIS, 553 U.S. 328 (2008), per SOUTER, J., upheld a Kentucky income tax statute that exempted interest on bonds issued by Kentucky and its political subdivisions, but not on bonds issued by other states or their local governments: "Municipal bonds currently finance roughly two-thirds of capital expenditures by state and local governments [and] by the turn of the millennium, over '$1.5 trillion in municipal bonds were outstanding.' Differential tax schemes like Kentucky's have a long pedigree, too. [Today], 41 states have laws like the one before us.

"It follows a fortiori from *United Haulers* that Kentucky must prevail. In *United Haulers,* we explained that a government function is not susceptible to standard dormant Commerce Clause scrutiny owing to its likely motivation by legitimate objectives distinct from the simple economic protectionism the Clause abhors. [In] fact, this emphasis on the public character of the enterprise supported by the tax preference is just a step in addressing a fundamental element of dormant Commerce Clause jurisprudence, the principle that 'any notion of discrimination assumes a comparison of substantially similar entities.' [Viewed] through this lens, the Kentucky tax scheme parallels the ordinance upheld in *United Haulers:* it 'benefit[s] a clearly public [issuer, that is, Kentucky and its municipalities], while treating all private [issuers] exactly the same.' There is no forbidden discrimination because Kentucky, as a public entity, does not have to treat itself as being 'substantially similar' to the other bond issuers in the market."

Having found no forbidden discrimination, Souter, J., also concluded that the balancing test of *Pike v. Bruce Church, Inc.,* did not apply because "the current record and scholarly material convince us that the Judicial Branch is not institutionally suited to draw reliable conclusions of the kind that would be necessary." For example, the Court was not well situated to predict whether national capital markets would accommodate the bonds issued by smaller municipalities in the absence of tax benefits for in-state purchasers or whether "capital [would] to some degree simply dry up, eliminating a class of municipal improvements. [What] is most significant about these cost-benefit questions is not even the difficulty of answering them or the inevitable uncertainty of the predictions that might be made in trying to come up with answers, but the unsuitability of the judicial process and judicial forums for making whatever predictions and reaching whatever answers are possible at all."

Stevens, J., filed a concurring opinion. Roberts, C.J., and Scalia, J., also declined to join parts of the majority opinion. Thomas, J., concurred in the judgment only, on the ground that the Court's dormant Commerce Clause jurisprudence lacked constitutional foundations and should be abandoned altogether.

Kennedy, J., joined by Alito, J., dissented: "The Court holds the Kentucky law is valid because bond issuance fulfills a public function [but] the premise is wrong. The law in question operates on those who hold the bonds and trade them, not those who issue them." Moreover, even if the case were about bond issuance rather than taxation, "the discrimination against interstate commerce would be too plain and prejudicial to be sustained. [A] state has no authority to use its taxing power to erect local barriers to out-of-state goods or commodities. Nothing in our cases even begins to suggest this rule is inapplicable simply because the State uses a discriminatory tax to favor its own enterprise."

Kennedy, J., thought that the Court's reliance on *United Haulers* was misplaced, for the ordinance upheld there "applied equally to interstate and in-state commerce. [Nondiscrimination], not just state involvement, was central to the rationale."

NOTES AND QUESTIONS

1.   ***Fear of consequences.*** Consider Williams & Denning, supra: "[Even if the Court were correct] that a contrary ruling would decimate public financing by small municipalities[, that] would at most suggest carving a minimal exception to the dormant Commerce Clause exclusively for municipal bonds issued by local governments with limited access to national capital markets, not all public bonds."

Does this criticism involve the sort of policy analysis for which Souter, J., concluded the courts "are not institutionally suited"? If so, is *Davis*'s blanket exemption of public bonds from dormant Commerce Clause scrutiny an appropriate response to line-drawing difficulties?

2.   ***Absence of balancing.*** A striking feature of the Court's reasoning in *Davis* involved its failure to apply the *Pike* balancing test that it normally employs in cases not triggering stricter judicial scrutiny. The Court's applications of *Pike* balancing are considered in the next Section. Is it clear when the Court will and will not apply a balancing test to protectionist legislation favoring public rather than private entities?

3.   ***Doctrinal implications.*** (a) Consider Edward A. Zelinsky, *The False Modesty of* Department of Revenue v. Davis*: Disrupting the Dormant Commerce Clause Through the Traditional Public Function Doctrine*, 29 Va. Tax Rev. 407 (2010): "*Davis*'s holding is narrow[, but its] underlying reasoning [has] far-reaching and disruptive consequences. Per *Davis*, any 'traditional public function' is immune from dormant Commerce Clause scrutiny. This [category] lacks principled limits. [Moreover, a]mong the most venerable of state and local activities is subsidizing local economies and firms. Consequently, the 'traditional public function' doctrine, as confirmed in *Davis*, disrupts the prior understanding of the dormant Commerce Clause. That doctrine implicitly overturns [cases] invalidating tax subsidies for local firms and industries."

(b)   Compare Dan T. Coenen, *Where* United Haulers *Might Take Us: The Future of the State-Self-Promotion Exception to the Dormant Commerce Clause Rule,* 95 Iowa L.Rev. 541 (2010): "*United Haulers* and *Davis* reflect a doctrinal ambitiousness that the opinions [tend] to understate. Some might argue that the innovative nature of the state-self-promotion doctrine, and the Court's unlabored endorsement of it, support a broad application of the doctrine going into the future. [However, g]iven the deep roots of the [traditional] dormant Commerce Clause rule [that forbids state discrimination] and the vital service it has rendered to the nation, courts should hesitate to apply the new *United Haulers-Davis* principle to validate starkly discriminatory state programs absent a strong indication that the principle controls the case at hand."

IV. STATUTES THAT DO NOT DISCRIMINATE ON THEIR FACES BUT NEVERTHELESS BURDEN INTERSTATE COMMERCE

As noted above, at least since the 1945 decision in *Southern Pacific Co. v. Arizona*, Part V infra, the Court has said that it will apply some form of balancing test to gauge the permissibility under the Commerce Clause of state legislation that does not discriminate on its face and has a legitimate local purpose but "incidentally" burdens interstate commerce. An example, suggested above in the Notes and Questions following *Baldwin v. Seelig*, would be a state law that forbade the in-state sale of milk produced by cattle that had been fed a hormone deemed dangerous to human health by the state legislature. If the statute were challenged by milk producers in other states, a balancing test would apply. But why? In nearly all dormant Commerce Clause cases that do not involve a facial discrimination against interstate commerce, the challenged statute has had a "discriminatory effect": It has imposed greater burdens on out-of-state than on in-state interests or enterprises—as the imagined statute regulating the sale of milk from hormone-fed cattle would have if most or all dairy farmers in the state did not feed their cows the allegedly suspect hormone but if many farmers in other states did.

In cases of this kind, a loosely connected family of "process-based" theories attempts to build on the insight of Stone, J.'s famous footnote four in *United States v. Carolene Products*, Ch. 5, Sec. 3 infra: although courts should generally not reweigh policy judgments made by legislatures, the presumption that legislatures should be trusted to make such judgments dissolves when affected interests are not fairly represented in a state's political process—making them analogous to members of "discrete and insular minorities."[17] This concern with the fairness of the states' political

---

[17] Despite significant differences as to details and applications, important examples of this general approach include Robert A. Sedler, *The Negative Commerce Clause as a Restriction on State Regulation and Taxation: An Analysis in Terms of Constitutional Structure*, 31 Wayne L.Rev. 885 (1985), and Mark Tushnet, *Rethinking the Dormant Commerce Clause*, 1979 Wis.L.Rev. 125 (1979) ("[J]udicial displacement of legislative judgment is appropriate when it seems that the legislative process operated in a distorted way—for example, by excluding some affected interest from influence on the legislative process. This theory makes sense of many cases where the Court has considered the validity of state law said to discriminate against interstate commerce."). But see Richard B. Collins, *Economic Union as a Constitutional Value*, 63 N.Y.U. L.Rev. 43 (1988): Those "who would inject personal rights jurisprudence into dormant commerce power analysis are misguided. The doctrine aims at protecting economic union, not personal rights. Given this purpose, political process and legislative motive theories [including 'the political process theory of Chief Justice Stone'] do not present compelling cases for doctrinal change."

processes also echoes through much of the case law. See Tribe 3d ed., at 1052, citing *Southern Pacific*: "Because regulation unduly burdening or discriminating against interstate or foreign commerce or out-of-state enterprise has been thought to result from the inherently limited constituency to which each state or local legislature is accountable, the [Court] has viewed with suspicion any state action which imposes special or distinct burdens on out-of-state interests unrepresented in the state's political process."

As you study the cases in this Part, consider whether the Court's balancing methodology is consistent and principled—or whether, as Scalia, J., has argued,[18] the Court should, and typically has, invalidated state legislation only when it believes that the legislature had an impermissibly protectionist purpose of aiding local economic actors at the expense of their out-of-state competitors.

———

BREARD v. ALEXANDRIA, 341 U.S. 622 (1951), per REED, J., upheld, over a Commerce Clause claim, an ordinance forbidding door-to-door soliciting of orders for the sale of merchandise other than food, as applied to Breard and his crew of sales persons seeking subscriptions to out-of-state magazines.[19] The Court viewed the ordinance as protecting an important social interest in residential privacy: "Unwanted knocks on the door by day or night are a nuisance, or worse, to peace and quiet. [As] the exigencies of trade are not ordinarily expected to have a higher rating constitutionally than the tranquillity of the fireside, responsible municipal officers have sought a way to curb the annoyances while preserving complete freedom for desirable visitors to the homes." No less restrictive alternative was available. "The idea of barring classified salesmen from homes by means of notices posted by individual householders was rejected early as less practical than an ordinance regulating solicitors."

Although acknowledging that "the local retail merchant [has] not been unmindful of the effective competition furnished by house-to-house selling" and recognizing "the importance to publishers of our many periodicals" of house-to-house solicitation, the Court found it constitutionally adequate that the "usual methods of seeking business are left open by the ordinance." "That such methods do not produce as much business as house-to-house canvassing is, constitutionally, [immaterial.] Taxation that threatens interstate commerce with prohibition or discrimination is bad, but regulation that leaves out-of-state sellers on the same basis as local sellers cannot be invalid for that reason."

---

[18] See *Bendix Autolite Corp. v. Midwesco Enterprises, Inc.*, infra.

[19] The Court also denied a freedom of the press claim.

The Court was "not willing even to appraise the suggestion, unsupported in the record, that [widespread use of comparable ordinances] springs predominantly from the selfish influence of local merchants. [When] there is a reasonable basis for legislation to protect the social, as distinguished from the economic, welfare of a community, it is not for this Court because of the Commerce Clause to deny the exercise locally of the sovereign power of Louisiana."

Vinson, C.J., joined by Douglas, J., dissented: "I think it plain that a 'blanket prohibition' upon appellant's solicitation discriminates against and unduly burdens interstate commerce in favoring local retail merchants. 'Whether or not it was so intended, those are its necessary effects.' The fact that this ordinance exempts solicitation by the essentially local purveyors of farm products [by exempting food vendors] shows that local economic interests are relieved of the burdensome effects of the ordinance."

———

HUNT v. WASHINGTON STATE APPLE ADVERTISING COMM'N, 432 U.S. 333 (1977), per BURGER, C.J., ruled unanimously that North Carolina violated the Commerce Clause when it barred sale in the state of closed apple containers bearing any grade marks except those of the U.S. Department of Agriculture ("U.S.D.A.") or a "not graded" mark. The regulation was challenged on behalf of Washington apple growers, who routinely packed their apples in containers bearing Washington grades. On account of a 60-year-old state system of inspection, grading, and advertising for Washington apples, these grades were viewed in the trade as equivalent or superior to the U.S.D.A. grades.

In ruling against North Carolina, the Chief Justice held that, once a state regulation has been found to have a disproportionately adverse effect on interstate commerce, the burden shifts onto the state to justify its regulation. Though noting "some indications" of an "economic protection motive," the Court did not question the "declared purpose of protecting consumers from deception and fraud in the market place," in which apples bearing divergent grading standards from seven states competed with North Carolina apples. But the mere fact that "state legislation furthers matters of legitimate local concern, even in the health and consumer protection areas, does not end the inquiry. [Rather], when such state legislation comes into conflict with the Commerce Clause's overriding requirement of a national 'common market,' we are confronted with the task of effecting an accommodation of the competing national and local interests. *Pike*.

"[T]he challenged statute has the practical effect of not only burdening interstate sales of Washington apples, but also discriminating against them. This discrimination takes various forms. [The statute raised] the costs of doing business in the North Carolina market for Washington apple growers and dealers, while leaving those of their North Carolina counterparts unaffected.[20] [The] statute [stripped] away from the Washington apple industry the competitive and economic advantages it has earned for itself through its expensive inspection and grading system. [By] prohibiting Washington growers and dealers from marketing apples under their State's grades, the statute has a leveling effect which insidiously operates to the advantage of local apple producers."

The Court further reasoned that, "[w]hen discrimination against commerce of the type we have found is demonstrated, the burden falls on the state to justify it in terms of the local benefit flowing from the statute and the unavailability of nondiscriminatory alternatives adequate to preserve the local interests at stake. *Dean Milk*; *Baldwin*." The state did not meet this burden. By permitting no grades at all, the statute "can hardly be thought to eliminate the problems of deception and confusion created by the multiplicity of different state grades." And a nondiscriminatory alternative was available by permitting state grades to be used on the same containers as USDA grades.

NOTES AND QUESTIONS

1. *A different standard for social interests?* *Breard* calls for heightened judicial deference to legislative judgments that protect "social, as distinguished from economic," interests. Is this distinction justified in light of the underlying purposes of the dormant Commerce Clause (whatever they are)?

2. *Discriminatory impact vs. discriminatory intent.* Why did the Court not decide *Hunt* on the basis of an "economic protection" motive? Should there have been any serious doubt that the purpose of the North Carolina legislature was to protect local apple growers against competition from Washington apple growers?

3. *Shifting the burden of proof.* How much of the weight of analysis in *Hunt* was borne by the shift of the burden of proof once a discriminatory impact on Washington apple growers was established? Who bore the burden of proof in *Baldwin*? In *Breard*?

———

MINNESOTA v. CLOVER LEAF CREAMERY CO., 449 U.S. 456 (1981), considered a statute held to be even-handed on its face. The Court, per BRENNAN, J., upheld a state law that banned nonreturnable milk containers made of plastic but permitted other nonreturnable milk containers, largely cartons made of pulpwood. The legislature had found

---

[20] To sell apples in the North Carolina market, Washington growers had to obliterate Washington grades imprinted on their standard containers, repack all shipments to North Carolina, or pack and store specially marked containers of apples.

that use of nonreturnable plastic containers "presents a solid waste management problem for the state, promotes energy waste, and depletes natural resources" in violation of a legislative policy to encourage "the reduction of the amount and type of material entering the solid waste stream." The Court upheld the statute, even though most of the plastic containers originated out of state and most of the pulpwood containers originated in state:

"[Minnesota's statute] does not effect 'simple protectionism,' but 'regulates even-handedly' by prohibiting all milk retailers from selling their products in plastic, nonreturnable milk containers, without regard to whether the milk, the containers, or the sellers are from outside the State. [Since] the statute does not discriminate between interstate and intrastate commerce, the controlling question is whether the incidental burden imposed on interstate commerce [is] 'clearly excessive in relation to the putative local benefits.' *Pike*. We conclude that it is not. [Within] Minnesota, business will presumably shift from manufacturers of plastic nonreturnable containers to producers of paperboard cartons, refillable bottles, and plastic pouches, but there is no reason to suspect that the gainers will be Minnesota firms, or the losers out-of-state firms. Indeed, two of the three dairies, the sole milk retailer, and the sole milk container producer challenging the statute in this litigation are Minnesota firms.[17]

"Pulpwood producers are the only Minnesota industry likely to benefit significantly from the Act at the expense of out-of-state firms. Respondents point out that plastic resin, the raw material used for making plastic nonreturnable milk jugs, is produced entirely by non-Minnesota firms, while pulpwood, used for making paperboard, is a major Minnesota product. Nevertheless, it is clear that respondents exaggerate the degree of burden on out-of-state interests, both because plastics will continue to be used in the production of plastic pouches, plastic returnable bottles, and paperboard itself, and because out-of-state pulpwood producers will presumably absorb some of the business generated by the Act.

"Even granting that the out-of-state plastics industry is burdened relatively more heavily than the Minnesota pulpwood industry, we find that this burden is not 'clearly excessive' in light of the substantial state interest in promoting conservation of energy and other natural resources and easing solid waste disposal problems. [We] find these local benefits ample to support Minnesota's decision under the Commerce Clause. Moreover, we find that no approach with 'a lesser impact on interstate activities,' *Pike*, is [available].

"In *Exxon* [*Corp. v. Maryland*, 437 U.S. 117 (1978), we] stressed that the Commerce Clause 'protects the interstate market, not particular

---

[17] **[Ct's Note]** The existence of major in-state interests adversely affected by the Act is a powerful safeguard against legislative abuse.

interstate firms, from prohibitive or burdensome regulations.' A nondiscriminatory regulation serving substantial state purposes is not invalid simply because it causes some business to shift from a predominantly out-of-state industry to a predominantly in-state industry. Only if the burden on interstate commerce clearly outweighs the State's legitimate purposes does such a regulation violate the Commerce Clause."[21]

BENDIX AUTOLITE CORP. v. MIDWESCO ENTERPRISES, INC., 486 U.S. 888 (1988), is noteworthy largely because of the argument presented in a much-noticed concurring opinion by Scalia, J. The Court, per KENNEDY, J., applied *Pike* balancing to invalidate an Ohio statute that tolled the statute of limitations when foreign corporations did not appoint an agent to accept process for the exercise of general judicial jurisdiction: "Where the burden of a state regulation falls on interstate commerce, restricting its flow in a manner not applicable to local business or trade, there may be either a discrimination that renders the regulation invalid without more, or cause to weigh and assess the State's putative interests against the interstate burden to determine if the burden imposed is a reasonable one. [We] find that the burden imposed on interstate commerce by the tolling statute exceeds any local interest that the state might advance.

"[The] Ohio statutory scheme [forces] a foreign corporation to choose between exposure to the general jurisdiction of Ohio courts or forfeiture of the limitations defense, remaining subject to suit in Ohio in perpetuity. Requiring a foreign corporation to appoint an agent for service in all cases and to defend itself with reference to all transactions, including those in which it did not have the minimum contacts necessary for supporting personal jurisdiction, is a significant [burden].

"The ability to execute service of process on foreign corporations and entities is an important factor to consider in assessing the local interest. [However,] Ohio cannot justify its statute as a means of protecting its residents from corporations who become liable for acts done within the State but later withdraw from the jurisdiction, for it is conceded by all parties that the Ohio long-arm statute would have permitted service on Midwesco throughout the period of limitations."

Scalia, J., concurred in the judgment: "I cannot confidently assess whether the Court's evaluation and balancing of interests in this case is right or wrong. [He pointed out uncertainties regarding both the burden on a foreign corporation and the benefits to local interests.]

---

[21] Powell, J., and Stevens, J., each dissenting separately, would have referred the Commerce Clause issue back to the Minnesota Supreme Court.

"Having [roughly] evaluated the interests on both sides, [the] Court then proceeds to judge which is more important. This process is ordinarily called 'balancing,' *Pike,* but the scale analogy is not really appropriate, since the interests on both sides are incommensurate. It is more like judging whether a particular line is longer than a particular rock is heavy. All I am really persuaded of by the Court's opinion is that the burdens the Court labels 'significant' are more determinative of its decision than the benefits it labels 'important.' Were it not for the brief implication that there is here a discrimination unjustified by *any* state interest, I suggest an opinion could as persuasively have been written coming out the opposite way. We sometimes make similar 'balancing' judgments in determining how far the needs of the State can intrude upon the liberties of the individual, but that is of the essence of the courts' function as the nonpolitical branch. Weighing the governmental interests of a State against the needs of interstate commerce is, by contrast, a task squarely within the responsibility of Congress, and 'ill suited to the judicial function.' *CTS Corp.* [infra] (Scalia, J., concurring in part and concurring in the judgment).

"I would therefore abandon the 'balancing' approach to these negative Commerce Clause cases, first explicitly adopted [in] *Pike,* and leave essentially legislative judgments to the Congress. Issues already decided I would leave untouched, but would adopt for the future an analysis more appropriate to our role and our abilities. [In] my view, a state statute is invalid under the Commerce Clause if, and only if, it accords discriminatory treatment to interstate commerce in a respect not required to achieve a lawful state purpose. When such a validating purpose exists, it is for Congress and not us to determine it is not significant enough to justify the burden on [commerce].

"Because the present statute discriminates against interstate commerce by applying a disadvantageous rule against nonresidents for no valid state purpose that requires such a rule, I concur in the judgment that the Ohio statute violates the Commerce Clause."

NOTES AND QUESTIONS

1. ***Balancing and the judicial role.*** Is Scalia, J., correct that the values to be balanced under the *Pike* test—the significance of burdens and the importance of benefits—are "incommensurate"? That the balancing function is inherently legislative and not judicial? Is there a workable alternative? Would it suffice for the Court to limit itself to identifying and invalidating tariff-like restrictions that are enacted for the "protectionist" purpose of shielding local economic actors from competition with out-of-staters? See Regan, discussed in the Notes and Questions following *Baldwin,* supra, which so argues.

2. ***Purpose and effect.*** Recall *Hunt,* supra, in which the Court struck down North Carolina apple labeling requirements. Consider once more

whether the Court "really" balanced competing interests in *Hunt* (as it purported to do) or, having found indicia of a protectionist purpose, thrust the burden onto the state to prove otherwise. Could the rationales and results in other cases be similarly explained as involving the form or pretext of balancing, but as having the real purpose of "smoking out" protectionist motivation? See Regan, supra.

CTS CORP. v. DYNAMICS CORP.
481 U.S. 69, 107 S.Ct. 1637, 95 L.Ed.2d 67 (1987).

JUSTICE POWELL delivered the opinion of the Court.

[An] Indiana takeover law provided that a purchaser who acquired "control shares"[22] in an Indiana corporation would acquire voting rights only to the extent approved by a majority vote of the pre-existing disinterested stockholders.

[The] Indiana Act [has] the same effects on tender offers whether or not the offeror is a domiciliary or resident of Indiana. [Because] nothing in the Indiana Act imposes a greater burden on out-of-state offerors than it does on similarly situated Indiana offerors, we reject the contention that the Act discriminates against interstate commerce.

[This] Court's recent Commerce Clause cases also have invalidated statutes that adversely may affect interstate commerce by subjecting activities to inconsistent regulations. [The] Indiana Act poses no such problem. So long as each State regulates voting rights only in the corporations it has created, each corporation will be subject to the law of only one State. No principle of corporation law and practice is more firmly established than a State's authority to regulate domestic corporations, including the authority to define the voting rights of [shareholders.]

[The] Court of Appeals [decision] rested on its view of the Act's potential to hinder tender offers. We think the Court of Appeals failed to appreciate the significance for Commerce Clause analysis of the fact that state regulation of corporate governance is regulation of entities whose very existence and attributes are a product of state [law.] By prohibiting certain transactions, and regulating others, such laws necessarily affect certain aspects of interstate [commerce.] Mergers are a typical example. In view of the substantial effect that a merger may have on the shareholders' interests in a corporation, many States require supermajority votes to approve [mergers.] By requiring a greater vote for mergers than is required for other transactions, these laws make it more difficult for corporations to merge. State laws also may provide for "dissenters' rights" under which minority shareholders who disagree with corporate decisions to take

---

[22] "Control shares" are reached when the acquired shares would bring the purchaser's voting power to 20, 33 and 1/3, or 50% but for the operation of the Act.

particular actions are entitled to sell their shares to the corporation at fair market value.

[A] State has an interest in promoting stable relationships among parties involved in the corporations it charters, as well as in ensuring that investors in such corporations have an effective voice in corporate affairs. There can be no doubt that the Act reflects these concerns. The primary purpose of the Act is to protect the shareholders of Indiana corporations. It does this by affording shareholders, when a takeover offer is made, an opportunity to decide collectively whether the resulting change in voting control of the corporation, as they perceive it, would be desirable. A change of management may have important effects on the shareholders' interests; it is well within the State's role as overseer of corporate governance to offer this opportunity. The autonomy provided by allowing shareholders collectively to determine whether the takeover is advantageous to their interests may be especially beneficial where a hostile tender offer may coerce shareholders into tendering their shares.

Appellee Dynamics responds to this concern by arguing that the prospect of coercive tender offers is illusory, and that tender offers generally should be favored because they reallocate corporate assets into the hands of management who can use them most effectively.[13] [But] the potentially coercive aspects of tender offers have been recognized by the Securities and Exchange Commission, and by a number of scholarly commentators. The Constitution does not require the States to subscribe to any particular economic theory. We are not inclined "to second-guess the empirical judgments of lawmakers concerning the utility of legislation." In our view, the possibility of coercion in some takeover bids offers additional justification for Indiana's decision to promote the autonomy of independent shareholders.

Dynamics argues in any event that the State has "no legitimate interest in protecting the nonresident shareholders." *MITE Corp.* [note 2 infra]. Dynamics relies heavily on the statement by the *MITE* Court that, "[i]nsofar as [the] law burdens out-of-state transactions, there is nothing to be weighed in the balance to sustain the law." But that comment was made in reference to an Illinois law that applied as well to out-of-state corporations as to in-state corporations. We agree that Indiana has no interest in protecting nonresident shareholders *of nonresident corporations.* But this Act applies only to corporations incorporated in Indiana. We reject the contention that Indiana has no interest in providing for the shareholders of its corporations the voting autonomy granted by the

---

[13] **[Ct's Note]** [No] one doubts that some successful tender offers will provide more effective management or other benefits such as needed diversification. But there is no reason to *assume* that the type of conglomerate corporation that may result from repetitive takeovers necessarily will result in more effective management or otherwise be beneficial to shareholders. The divergent views in the literature—and even now being debated in the Congress—reflect the reality that the type and utility of tender offers vary widely. * * *

Act. Indiana has a substantial interest in preventing the corporate form from becoming a shield for unfair business dealing. Moreover, unlike the Illinois statute invalidated in *MITE,* the Indiana Act applies only to corporations that have a substantial number of shareholders in Indiana. Thus, every application of the Indiana Act will affect a substantial number of Indiana residents, whom Indiana indisputably has an interest in protecting.

Dynamics' argument that the Act is unconstitutional ultimately rests on its contention that the Act will limit the number of successful tender offers. There is little evidence that this will occur. But even if true, this result would not substantially affect our Commerce Clause analysis. We reiterate that this Act does not prohibit any entity—resident or nonresident—from offering to purchase, or from purchasing, shares in Indiana corporations, or from attempting thereby to gain control. It only provides regulatory procedures designed for the better protection of the corporations' shareholders. We have rejected the "notion that the Commerce Clause protects the particular structure or methods of operation in [a] market." The very commodity that is traded in the securities market is one whose characteristics are defined by state law. Similarly, the very commodity that is traded in the "market for corporate control"—the corporation—is one that owes its existence and attributes to state law. Indiana need not define these commodities as other States do; it need only provide that residents and nonresidents have equal access to them. This Indiana has done. * * *[23]

JUSTICE SCALIA, concurring in part and [in] the judgment.

[Whether] the control shares statute "protects shareholders of Indiana corporations," or protects incumbent management seems to me a highly debatable question, but it is extraordinary to think that the constitutionality of the Act should depend on the answer. Nothing in the Constitution says that the protection of entrenched management is any less important a "putative local benefit" than the protection of entrenched shareholders, and I do not know what qualifies us to make that judgment—or the related judgment as to how effective the present statute is in achieving one or the other objective—or the ultimate (and most ineffable) judgment as to whether, given importance-level x, and effectiveness-level y, the worth of the statute is 'outweighed' by impact-on-commerce z.

[One] commentator has suggested that, at least much of the time, we do not in fact mean what we say when we declare that statutes which neither discriminate against commerce nor present a threat of multiple and inconsistent burdens might nonetheless be unconstitutional under a "balancing" test. See Regan, [discussed after *Baldwin,* supra]. If he is not

---

[23] The Court also ruled that the federal Williams Act, which regulates takeovers, did not preempt the Indiana law.

correct, he ought to be. As long as a State's corporation law governs only its own corporations and does not discriminate against out-of-state interests, it should survive this Court's scrutiny under the Commerce Clause, whether it promotes shareholder welfare or industrial stagnation. Beyond that, it is for Congress to prescribe its invalidity.

JUSTICE WHITE, with whom JUSTICE BLACKMUN and JUSTICE STEVENS join, dissenting.

[CTS's] stock is traded on the New York Stock Exchange, and people from all over the country buy and sell CTS's shares daily. Yet, under Indiana's scheme, any prospective purchaser will be effectively precluded from purchasing CTS's shares if the purchaser crosses one of the Chapter's threshold ownership levels and a majority of CTS's shareholders refuse to give the purchaser voting rights. This Court should not countenance such a restraint on interstate trade.

[Indiana] admits that at least one of the [statute's] goals is to protect Indiana corporations. The state notes that "[the] Statute permits shareholders (who may also be community residents or employees or suppliers of the corporation) to determine the intentions of any offeror concerning the liquidation of the company or its possible removal from the State."

[A] state law which permits a majority of an Indiana corporation's stockholders to prevent individual investors, including out-of-state stockholders, from selling their stock to an out-of-state tender offeror and thereby frustrate [any] transfer of corporate control, is the archetype of the kind of state law that the Commerce Clause forbids. * * *

NOTES AND QUESTIONS

1. *State interests.* (a) The state's purported interest is protecting shareholders in Indiana corporations, but the challenged statute applies only to corporations that are both chartered in Indiana and located there. "If the legislature was genuinely concerned with protecting *shareholders* [why] would it deny its 'protection' to the shareholders of Indiana corporations just because the principal activities and assets of the firm happen to be in Ohio or New York?" asks Donald C. Langevoort, *The Supreme Court and the Politics of Corporate Takeovers: A Comment on* CTS Corp. v. Dynamics Corp. of America, 101 Harv.L.Rev. 96 (1987). Moreover, if corporate shareholders *want* protection against coercive takeover bids, why do they not provide for such protection by amending the corporation's charter?

(b) What if Indiana had attempted to defend the law challenged in *CTS* by citing a state interest in protecting Indiana-based management? What if the state had avowed an interest in protecting entrenched management as a means of preserving Indiana-based jobs? Consider Donald H. Regan, *Siamese Essays: (I)* CTS Corp. v. Dynamics Corp. of America *and Dormant Commerce*

Clause Doctrine; (II) Extraterritorial State Legislation, 85 Mich.L.Rev. 1865 (1987): "A purpose to protect Indiana workers and suppliers *at the expense of non-Indianans* is impermissible, but a statute which was motivated by a *general* belief that takeovers leading to corporate removals are unacceptably disruptive of established economic relations, and which was limited to Indiana corporations simply because those were the only corporations the Indiana legislature had power to regulate, would be perfectly permissible so far as the dormant Commerce Clause is concerned."

Compare Lucien A. Bebchuk & Allen Ferrell, *Federalism and Corporate Law: The Race to Protect Managers from Takeovers,* 99 Colum.L.Rev. 1168 (1999), arguing that state anti-takeover statutes frequently are anti-competitive and inefficient and are designed to protect corporate management: "Because managers play a key role in incorporation decisions, states (especially ones with a large number of already incorporated companies such as Delaware) will give substantial weight to satisfying managers' preferences."

2. *A contrasting perspective.* In EDGAR v. MITE CORP., 457 U.S. 624 (1982), Illinois authorized its Secretary of State to adjudicate the substantive fairness of tender offers and to deny the required registration if the Secretary concluded an offer was inequitable or would tend to work a fraud or deceit on the offerees. The statute applied to all corporations 10% of whose shares were owned by Illinois residents, or that had their principal offices in Illinois. The Court, per WHITE, J., ruled that the law violated the Commerce Clause:

"It is a direct restraint on interstate commerce and [has] an extraterritorial effect" by controlling "conduct beyond the boundary of the state." Applying the *Pike* test, the opinion found harmful effects on interstate commerce by preventing shareholders from selling their shares at a premium, "hindering the reallocation of economic resources to their highest-valued use," and by reducing the incentive that "the tender offer mechanism provides [to] incumbent management to perform well." The Court saw "nothing to be weighed in the balance to sustain the law," at least "insofar as the Illinois law burden[ed] out-of-state transactions" of nonresident shareholders.

3. *Extraterritorial reach.* Is it helpful to conceive of anti-takeover statutes as impermissibly restricting transactions—i.e., sales of shares—that physically occur out of state? Is corporate law "necessarily extraterritorial in impact" in its regulation of such matters as "the duties of directors, the ease of derivative actions, and the voting rights of shareholders"? See Langevoort, supra. For further discussion of issues of "extraterritoriality" under the dormant Commerce Clause, see the materials that follow immediately.

———

BROWN-FORMAN DISTILLERS CORP. v. NEW YORK STATE LIQUOR AUTH., 476 U.S. 573 (1986), decided one year before *CTS,* expressly identified extraterritorial regulation as violating the Commerce Clause and is perhaps the leading case on extraterritorial regulation under that provision. New York had required liquor distillers selling wholesale in the state to sell at the lowest prices the distiller charged in any other state for the same month and to file a binding schedule of its prices monthly. The Court, per MARSHALL, J., held that this "lowest-price" provision violated the Commerce Clause: "[While] a State may seek lower prices for its consumers, it may not insist that producers or consumers in other States surrender whatever competitive advantages they may possess. *Baldwin.* Economic protectionism is not limited to attempts to convey advantages to local merchants; it may include attempts to give local consumers an advantage over consumers in other States.

"[A] 'prospective' statute such as [New York's liquor statute] regulates out-of-state transactions in violation of the Commerce Clause. Once a distiller has posted prices in New York, it is not free to change its price elsewhere in the United States during the relevant month. [While] New York may regulate the sale of liquor within its borders, [it] may not 'project its legislation into [other States] by regulating the price to be paid' for liquor in those States. *Baldwin.*"

NOTES AND QUESTIONS

1. ***Meaning of "extraterritorial" regulation.*** Suppose that New York forbids the sale within its borders of distilled liquors with more than a specified alcohol content. If it is not economically feasible to undertake separate distillation and bottling for New York and surrounding states, New York's legislation may have the practical effect of determining the alcohol content of liquor marketed in Vermont, too. Does the hypothetical statute have a forbidden extraterritorial effect? Is the crucial problem in *Brown-Forman* that the effect of the New York statute was to make it unlawful under New York law for liquor wholesalers to sell their products in other states at prices that would be lawful under the law of those states?

2. ***Constitutional basis for extraterritorial limit on state legislative power.*** Is the principle that states may not regulate extraterritorially (however the scope of that principle is defined) properly attributable to the Commerce Clause? Wouldn't some such principle limit state legislative power to deal with matters that have little to do with production of goods or their movement in interstate commerce—for instance, in the context of criminal law or family law? (Note, though, that the law of one state will sometimes have extraterritorial effect under choice-of-law or conflict-of-laws principles. For example, if one New York party sues another New York party in New Hampshire, for breach in New Hampshire of a contract executed in New York, New York law may govern the dispute.)[24]

---

[24] For discussion of the disparities between the due process doctrines governing when a court's choice-of-law analysis may result in the application of forum law to events occurring out of state and the dormant Commerce Clause doctrine applicable to extraterritorial legislation, see Katherine Florey, *State Courts, State Territory, State Power: Reflections on the Extraterritoriality*

3. ***Decline of suspicion of extraterritorial legislation?*** There have been few cases involving, and no expansion of, the Commerce Clause principle barring states from extraterritorial exertion of legislative powers since the 1980s. Consider Brannon P. Denning, *Extraterritoriality and the Dormant Commerce Clause: a Doctrinal Post-Mortem,* 73 La.L.Rev. 979 (2013): Dormant Commerce Clause extraterritoriality doctrine "stalled once the Justices realized (1) that the doctrine was a poor fit with the larger [dormant Commerce Clause doctrine], which focused on discrimination and protectionism rather than whether a state law 'directly' regulated interstate commerce; and [absorbed] (2) the implications of taking the new rule seriously, as illustrated by lower courts using it to thwart state regulation of the Internet and litigants claiming that common tort remedies [e.g., for negligent manufacture or design] were subject to its strictures."

V. REGULATION OF TRANSPORTATION

Cases reviewing state transportation safety measures raise many of the same issues, and are frequently addressed within the same analytical frameworks, as other dormant Commerce Clause cases. They can usefully be studied separately, however, because they sometimes involve distinctive state regulatory interests in safety, as well as distinctive national interests in permitting the free flow of commerce across state lines.

KASSEL V. CONSOLIDATED FREIGHTWAYS CORP.
450 U.S. 662, 101 S.Ct. 1309, 67 L.Ed.2d 580 (1981).

JUSTICE POWELL announced the judgment of the Court and delivered an opinion in which JUSTICE WHITE, JUSTICE BLACKMUN, and JUSTICE STEVENS joined.

The question is whether an Iowa statute that prohibits the use of certain large trucks within the State unconstitutionally burdens interstate commerce.

I.   Appellee Consolidated Freightways Corporation of Delaware (Consolidated) is one of the largest common carriers in the country. [Among] other routes, Consolidated carries commodities through Iowa on Interstate 80, the principal east-west route linking New York, Chicago, and the west coast, and on Interstate 35, a major north-south route.

Consolidated mainly uses two kinds of trucks. One consists of a three-axle tractor pulling a 40-foot two-axle trailer. This unit, commonly called a single, or "semi," is 55 feet in length overall. Such trucks have long been used on the Nation's highways. Consolidated also uses a two-axle tractor pulling a single-axle trailer which, in turn, pulls a single-axle dolly and a second single-axle trailer. This combination, known as a double, or twin, is

---

Principle in Choice of Law and Legislation, 84 Notre Dame L.Rev. 1057 (2009); Mark D. Rosen, *State Extraterritorial Powers Reconsidered,* 85 Notre Dame L.Rev. 1133 (2010).

65 feet long overall. Many trucking companies, including Consolidated, increasingly prefer to use doubles to ship certain kinds of commodities. Doubles have larger capacities, and the trailers can be detached and routed separately if necessary. Consolidated would like to use 65-foot doubles on many of its trips through Iowa.

[Unlike] all other States in the West and Midwest, Iowa generally prohibits the use of 65-foot doubles within its borders. Instead, most truck combinations are restricted to 55 feet in length. Doubles, mobile homes, trucks carrying vehicles such as tractors and other farm equipment, and singles hauling livestock, are permitted to be as long as 60 feet. [T]he District Court found that the "evidence clearly establishes that the twin is as safe as the semi. * * * Twins are more maneuverable, are less sensitive to wind, and create less splash and spray. However, they are more likely than semis to jackknife or upset. They can be backed only for a short distance. The negative characteristics are not such that they render the twin less safe than semis overall. Semis are more stable but are more likely to 'rear end' another vehicle."

In light of these findings, the District Court applied the standard we enunciated in *Raymond Motor Transportation, Inc. v. Rice*, 434 U.S. 429 (1978), and concluded that the state law impermissibly burdened interstate commerce: "[The] total effect of the law as a safety measure in reducing accidents and casualties is so slight and problematical that it does not outweigh the national interest in keeping interstate commerce free from interferences that seriously impede it." The Court of Appeals for the Eighth Circuit affirmed. * * *

II. [R]egulations that touch upon safety—especially highway safety—are those that "the Court has been most reluctant to invalidate." [Indeed], "if safety justifications are not illusory, the Court will not second-guess legislative judgment about their importance in comparison with related burdens on interstate commerce." [But] the incantation of a purpose to promote the public health or safety does not insulate a state law from Commerce Clause attack. Regulations designed for that salutary purpose nevertheless may further the purpose so marginally, and interfere with commerce so substantially, as to be invalid under the Commerce Clause. * * *

III. The State failed to present any persuasive evidence that 65-foot doubles are less safe than 55-foot singles. Moreover, Iowa's law is now out of step with the laws of all other Midwestern and Western States. Iowa thus substantially burdens the interstate flow of goods by truck. [Trucking] companies that wish to continue to use 65-foot doubles must route them around Iowa or detach the trailers of the doubles and ship them through separately. Alternatively, trucking companies must use the smaller 55-foot singles or 60-foot doubles permitted under Iowa law. Each of these options engenders inefficiency and added expense. The record shows that Iowa's law added about $12.6 million each year to the costs of trucking companies. Consolidated alone incurred about $2 million per year in increased costs.

In addition to increasing the costs of the trucking companies (and, indirectly, of the service to consumers), Iowa's law may aggravate, rather than ameliorate, the problem of highway accidents. Fifty-five foot singles carry less freight than 65-foot doubles. Either more small trucks must be used to carry the same quantity of goods through Iowa, or the same number of larger trucks must drive longer distances to bypass Iowa. In either case, as the District Court noted, the restriction requires more highway miles to be driven to transport the same quantity of goods. Other things being equal, accidents are proportional to distance traveled. Thus, if 65-foot doubles are as safe as 55-foot singles, Iowa's law tends to *increase* the number of accidents, and to shift the incidence of them from Iowa to other States.

IV. [The] Court normally does accord "special deference" to state highway safety regulations. [Less] deference to the legislative judgment is due, however, where the local regulation bears disproportionately on out-of-state residents and businesses. Such a disproportionate burden is apparent here. Iowa's scheme, although generally banning large doubles from the State, nevertheless has several exemptions that secure to Iowans many of the benefits of large trucks while shunting to neighboring States many of the costs associated with their use.

At the time of trial there were two particularly significant exemptions. First, singles hauling livestock or farm vehicles were permitted to be as long as 60 feet. [Second,] cities abutting other States were permitted to enact local ordinances adopting the larger length limitation of the neighboring State. This exemption offered the benefits of longer trucks to individuals and businesses in important border cities without burdening Iowa's highways with interstate through traffic.

The origin of the "border cities exemption" also suggests that Iowa's statute may not have been designed to ban dangerous trucks, but rather to discourage interstate truck traffic. In 1974, the legislature passed a bill that would have permitted 65-foot doubles in the State. Governor Ray vetoed the bill. He said: "I find sympathy with those who are doing business in our state and whose enterprises could gain from increased cargo carrying ability by trucks. However, with this bill, the Legislature has pursued a course that would benefit only a few Iowa-based companies while providing a great advantage for out-of-state trucking firms and competitors at the expense of our Iowa citizens." After the veto, the "border cities exemption" was immediately enacted and signed by the Governor.

[In] the District Court and Court of Appeals, the State explicitly attempted to justify the law by its claimed interest in keeping trucks out of

Iowa. The Court of Appeals correctly concluded that a State cannot constitutionally promote its own parochial interests by requiring safe vehicles to detour around [it].

V. Because Iowa has imposed [a] burden [on interstate commerce] without any significant countervailing safety interest, its statute violates the Commerce Clause.

JUSTICE BRENNAN, with whom JUSTICE MARSHALL joins, concurring in the judgment.

For me, analysis of Commerce Clause challenges to state regulations must take into account three principles: (1) The courts are not empowered to second-guess the empirical judgments of lawmakers concerning the utility of legislation. (2) The burdens imposed on commerce must be balanced against the local benefits actually sought to be achieved by the State lawmakers, and not against those suggested after the fact by counsel. (3) Protectionist legislation is unconstitutional under the Commerce Clause, even if the burdens and benefits are related to safety rather than economics.

Both the opinion of my Brother Powell and the opinion of my Brother Rehnquist are predicated upon the supposition that the constitutionality of a state regulation is determined by the factual record created by the State's lawyers in trial court. But that supposition cannot be correct, for it would make the constitutionality of state laws and regulations depend on the vagaries of litigation rather than on the judgments made by the State's lawmakers.

[A]lthough Iowa's lawyers in this litigation have defended the truck-length regulation on the basis of the safety advantages of 55-foot singles and 60-foot doubles over 65-foot doubles, Iowa's actual rationale for maintaining the regulation had nothing to do with these purported differences. Rather, Iowa sought to discourage interstate truck traffic on Iowa's highways. Thus, the safety advantages and disadvantages of the types and lengths of trucks involved in this case are irrelevant to the decision.

[Though] my Brother Powell recognizes that the State's actual purpose in maintaining the truck-length regulation was "to limit the use of its highways by deflecting some through traffic," he fails to recognize that this purpose, being *protectionist* in nature, is *impermissible* under the Commerce Clause.

[Iowa] may not shunt off its fair share of the burden of maintaining interstate truck routes, nor may it create increased hazards on the highways of neighboring States in order to decrease the hazards on Iowa highways. Such an attempt has all the hallmarks of the "simple * * * protectionism" this Court has condemned in the economic area. *Philadelphia v. New Jersey*.

JUSTICE REHNQUIST, with whom CHIEF JUSTICE BURGER and JUSTICE STEWART join, dissenting.

A determination that a state law is a rational safety measure does not end the Commerce Clause inquiry. A "sensitive consideration" of the safety purpose in relation to the burden on commerce is required. *Raymond*. When engaging in such a consideration the Court does not directly compare safety benefits to commerce costs and strike down the legislation if the latter can be said in some vague sense to "outweigh" the former. Such an approach would make an empty gesture of the strong presumption of validity accorded state safety measures, particularly those governing highways. It would also arrogate to this Court functions of forming public policy, functions which, in the absence of congressional action, were left by the Framers of the Constitution to state legislatures. [For a court to make such policy judgments would be especially inappropriate] when, as here, the question involves the difficult comparison of financial losses and "the loss of lives and limbs of workers and people using the highways."

The purpose of the "sensitive consideration" referred to above is rather to determine if the asserted safety justification, although rational, is merely a pretext for discrimination against interstate commerce. We will conclude that it is if the safety benefits from the regulation are demonstrably trivial while the burden on commerce is great.

[There] can be no doubt that the challenged statute is a valid highway safety regulation and thus entitled to the strongest presumption of validity against Commerce Clause challenges. As noted, all 50 States regulate the length of trucks which may use their highways. [There] can also be no question that the particular limit chosen by Iowa—60 feet—is rationally related to Iowa's safety objective. Most truck limits are between 55 and 65 feet, and Iowa's choice is thus well within the widely accepted range.

[The] District Court approached the case as if the question were whether Consolidated's 65-foot trucks were as safe as others permitted on Iowa highways, and the Court of Appeals as if its task were to determine if the District Court's factual findings in this regard were "clearly erroneous." The question, however, is whether the Iowa Legislature has acted rationally in regulating vehicle lengths and whether the safety benefits from this regulation are more than slight or problematical.

[The] answering of the relevant question is not appreciably advanced by comparing trucks slightly over the length limit with those at the length limit. It is emphatically not our task to balance any incremental safety benefits from prohibiting 65-foot doubles as opposed to 60-foot doubles against the burden on interstate commerce. Lines drawn for safety purposes will rarely pass muster if the question is whether a slight increment can be permitted without sacrificing safety. [The] particular line chosen by Iowa—60 feet—is relevant only to the question whether the limit is a rational one. Once a court determines that it is, it considers the overall safety benefits *from the regulation* against burdens on interstate commerce, and not any marginal benefits from the scheme the State established as opposed to that the plaintiffs desire.

[The] difficulties with the contrary approach are patent. While it may be clear that there are substantial safety benefits from a 55-foot truck as compared to a 105-foot truck, these benefits may not be discernible in 5-foot jumps. Appellee's approach would permit what could not be accomplished in one lawsuit to be done in 10 separate suits, each challenging an additional five feet.

NOTES AND QUESTIONS

1. ***Nonillusory highway safety regulations.*** After *Kassel*, what appears to be "the law" on whether the Court will balance the anticipated, "nonillusory" benefits of state highway safety regulations against their burden on interstate commerce? What *should* be the law on this matter? What meanings do the different opinions give to "nonillusory"?

2. ***Balancing, protectionism, and highway safety regulations.*** (a) Suppose the evidence would have permitted a reasonable person to conclude that the prohibition of double-trailers in Iowa would save, on average, one highway fatality per year in the state of Iowa. By what measure might a court weigh this saving against harm to the national interest in the free flow of interstate commerce?

(b) Suppose the evidence suggested that a ban on double-trailers would prevent one or more traffic fatalities in Iowa each year, but that there would be a corresponding *increase* in traffic fatalities in other states as a result of double-trailers detouring around Iowa. Would legislation aimed at protecting Iowa lives, enacted in full awareness of a likely shift of fatalities out of state, be objectionably discriminatory or protectionist?

(c) Does it matter to the analysis of (b) whether, if all states prohibited double-trailers, there would be a net decrease in traffic fatalities? Should it matter?

3. ***Relevance of protectionist purposes.*** Is Brennan, J., persuasive that, in the area of safety legislation (at least), the Commerce Clause prohibits *only* regulations that have a protectionist or discriminatory purpose? Are courts any less competent at balancing interests in safety than they are, for example, at balancing interests in privacy or the natural environment against a competing interest in the free movement of goods? Compare Regan, note 1 after *Baldwin*, supra, arguing that while there is *not* a general national interest in economic laissez-faire, there *is* a national interest "in the existence of an effective transportation network linking the states," and that judicial

balancing may be peculiarly necessary in cases in which state regulations collide with that national interest.

4. ***Inconsistency with other states.*** BIBB v. NAVAJO FREIGHT LINES, 359 U.S. 520 (1959), per DOUGLAS, J., held invalid an Illinois law that required contour rear fender mudguards on all trucks and trailers on Illinois highways in place of the straight mudflaps that were legal in "at least" 45 states: "[Arkansas requires] that trailers operating in that State be equipped with straight or conventional mud flaps. Vehicles equipped to meet the standards of the Illinois statute would not comply with Arkansas standards, and vice versa. Thus if a trailer is to be operated in both States, mudguards would have to be interchanged, causing a significant delay [of two to four hours] in an operation where prompt movement may be of the [essence].

"This is one of those cases—few in number—where local safety measures that are nondiscriminatory place an unconstitutional burden on interstate commerce. [A] State which insists on a design out of line with the requirements of almost all the other States may sometimes place a great burden of delay and inconvenience on those interstate motor carriers entering or crossing its territory. Such a new safety device—out of line with the requirements of the other States—may be so compelling that the innovating State need not be the one to give way. But the present showing—balanced against the clear burden on commerce—is far too inconclusive to make this mudguard [law] meet that test.[25] [The] heavy burden which the Illinois mudguard law places on the interstate movement of trucks and trailers seems to us to pass the permissible limits even for safety regulations."

VI.   SUBSIDIES AND LINKAGES

NEW ENERGY CO. OF IND. v. LIMBACH, 486 U.S. 269 (1988), per SCALIA, J., invalidated an Ohio statute that provided a tax credit to users of a gasoline substitute, ethanol, that was produced in Ohio or in a state that gave a reciprocal tax credit for Ohio-produced ethanol. The Court ruled unanimously that Ohio discriminated in violation of the Commerce Clause when it denied the tax credit for ethanol produced in Indiana, which granted a direct subsidy to Indiana ethanol producers, but furnished no reciprocal tax credit: "The Ohio provision at issue here explicitly deprives certain products of generally available beneficial tax treatment because they are made in certain other states, and thus on its face appears to violate the cardinal requirement of nondiscrimination.

"[It] has not escaped our notice that the appellant here, which is eligible to receive a cash subsidy under Indiana's program for in-state ethanol producers, is the potential beneficiary of a scheme no less discriminatory than the one that it attacks, and no less effective in

---

[25] The opinion mentioned the District Court's finding that contour mud flaps possessed "no advantages over [straight] mud flaps," caused heated brake drums that decreased brake effectiveness, and were "susceptible of being hit [when] the trucks backed up and of falling off on the highway."

conferring a commercial advantage over out-of-state competitors. To believe the Indiana scheme is valid, however, is not to believe that the Ohio scheme must be valid as well. The Commerce Clause does not prohibit all state action designed to give its residents an advantage in the marketplace, but only action of that description *in connection with the State's regulation of interstate commerce.* Direct subsidization of domestic industry does not ordinarily run afoul of that prohibition; discriminatory taxation of out-of-state manufacturers does."

NOTES AND QUESTIONS

1. ***Subsidies and regulations.*** Does the disparate treatment of "regulation," on the one hand, and "subsidization," on the other, make sense? Both confer economic advantages on local industry and undermine the competitive advantages of out-of-state competitors. And the expense, in both cases, is borne by in-state groups—taxpayers, who pay higher taxes (in the case of a subsidy), or consumers, who pay higher prices (in the case of a price regulation).

2. ***Possible distinctions.*** Does it matter that a subsidy imposes transparent economic costs on the subsidizing state's taxpayers, and may thus be less likely to result from a stark, discriminatory motivation to help in-staters at the expense of out-of-staters? That subsidies may be less likely to trigger retaliation? That subsidies were not one of the historic evils that the Commerce Clause was intended to remedy? See generally Regan, note 1 after *Baldwin,* supra.

WEST LYNN CREAMERY, INC. V. HEALY
512 U.S. 186, 114 S.Ct. 2205, 129 L.Ed.2d 157 (1994).

JUSTICE STEVENS delivered the opinion of the Court.

[Massachusetts taxed all sales of milk by wholesalers to Massachusetts retailers, regardless of whether the milk was produced in or out of state. The proceeds of the tax went to a fund used to make subsidy payments to Massachusetts milk producers.]

The paradigmatic example of a law discriminating against interstate commerce is the protective tariff or customs duty, which taxes goods imported from other states, but does not tax similar products produced in state. A tariff is an attractive measure because it simultaneously raises revenue and benefits local producers by burdening their out-of-state competitors. Nevertheless, it violates the principle of the unitary national market by handicapping out-of-state competitors, thus artificially encouraging in-state production even when the same goods could be produced at lower cost in other states.

[In] fact, tariffs against the products of other states are so patently unconstitutional that our cases reveal not a single attempt by any state to enact one. Instead, the cases are filled with state laws that aspire to reap some of the benefits of tariffs by other means.

[Massachusetts' combination of a facially nondiscriminatory tax with a subsidy to in-state farmers] is clearly unconstitutional. Its avowed purpose and its undisputed effect are to enable higher cost Massachusetts dairy farmers to compete with lower cost dairy farmers in other States. [The net result is to make] milk produced out of State more expensive. Although the tax also applies to milk produced in Massachusetts, its effect on Massachusetts producers is entirely (indeed more than) offset by the subsidy provided exclusively to Massachusetts dairy farmers. Like an ordinary tariff, the tax is thus effectively imposed only on out-of-state products.

[Respondent] argues that the payments to Massachusetts dairy farmers from the Dairy Equalization Fund are valid, because subsidies are constitutional exercises of state power, and that the order premium which provides money for the Fund is valid, because it is a nondiscriminatory tax. [Even] granting respondent's assertion that both components of the pricing order would be constitutional standing alone,[15] the pricing order nevertheless must fall. [R]espondent errs in assuming that the constitutionality of the pricing order follows logically from the constitutionality of its component parts. By conjoining a tax and a subsidy, Massachusetts has created a program more dangerous to interstate commerce than either part alone. Nondiscriminatory measures, like the evenhanded tax at issue here, are generally upheld, in spite of any adverse effects on interstate commerce, in part because "[t]he existence of major in-state interests adversely affected [is] a powerful safeguard against legislative abuse." However, when a nondiscriminatory tax is coupled with a subsidy to one of the groups hurt by the tax, a state's political processes can no longer be relied upon to prevent legislative abuse, because one of the in-state interests which would otherwise lobby against the tax has been mollified by the subsidy. So, in this case, one would ordinarily have expected at least three groups to lobby against the order premium, which, as a tax, raises the price (and hence lowers demand) for milk: dairy farmers, milk dealers, and consumers. But because the tax was coupled with a subsidy, one of the most powerful of these groups, Massachusetts dairy farmers, instead of exerting their influence against the tax, were in fact its primary supporters.

[Respondent] also argues that "the operation of the [scheme] disproves any claim of protectionism," because "*only* in-state consumers feel the effect of any retail price increase [and] [t]he dealers themselves [have] a substantial in-state presence." This argument, if accepted, would

---

[15] **[Ct's Note]** We have never squarely confronted the constitutionality of subsidies, and we need not do so now. We have, however, noted that "[d]irect subsidization of domestic industry does not ordinarily run afoul" of the negative Commerce Clause. *New Energy.*

undermine almost every discriminatory tax case. State taxes are ordinarily paid by in-state businesses and consumers, yet if they discriminate against out-of-state products, they are unconstitutional. [The] cost of a tariff is also borne primarily by local consumers, yet a tariff is the paradigmatic Commerce Clause violation.

SCALIA, J., joined by THOMAS, J., concurred in the judgment.

[The] Court notes that, in funding this subsidy, Massachusetts has taxed milk produced in other States, and thus "not only assists local farmers, but burdens interstate commerce." But the same could be said of almost all subsidies funded from general state revenues, which almost invariably include monies from use taxes on out-of-state products. And even where the funding does not come in any part from taxes on out-of-state goods, "merely assist[ing]" in-state businesses unquestionably neutralizes advantages possessed by out-of-state enterprises. Such subsidies, particularly where they are in the form of cash or (what comes to the same thing) tax forgiveness, are often admitted to have as their purpose—*indeed, are nationally advertised as having as their purpose*—making it more profitable to conduct business in-state than elsewhere, i.e., distorting normal market incentives.

[There] are at least four possible devices that would enable a State to produce the economic effect that Massachusetts has produced here: (1) a discriminatory tax upon the industry, imposing a higher liability on out-of-state members than on their in-state competitors; (2) a tax upon the industry that is nondiscriminatory in its assessment, but that has an "exemption" or "credit" for in-state members; (3) a nondiscriminatory tax upon the industry, the revenues from which are placed into a segregated fund, which fund is disbursed as "rebates" or "subsidies" to in-state members of the industry (the situation at issue in this case); and (4) with or without nondiscriminatory taxation of the industry, a subsidy for the in-state members of the industry, funded from the State's general revenues. It is long settled that the first of these methodologies is unconstitutional under the negative Commerce Clause. The second of them, "exemption" from or "credit" against a "neutral" tax, is no different in principle from the first, and has likewise been held invalid. The fourth methodology, application of a state subsidy from general revenues, is so far removed from what we have hitherto held to be unconstitutional, that prohibiting it must be regarded as an extension of our negative-Commerce-Clause jurisprudence and therefore, to me, unacceptable. See *Limbach*. Indeed, in my view our negative-Commerce-Clause cases have already approved the use of such subsidies. See *Hughes*.

[The] issue before us in the present case is whether the third of these methodologies must fall. Although the question is close, I conclude it would not be a principled point at which to disembark from the negative-

Commerce-Clause train. The only difference between methodology (2) (discriminatory "exemption" from nondiscriminatory tax) and methodology (3) (discriminatory refund of nondiscriminatory tax) is that the money is taken and returned rather than simply left with the favored in-state taxpayer in the first place. The difference between (3) and (4), on the other hand, is the difference between assisting in-state industry through discriminatory taxation, and assisting in-state industry by other means.

I would therefore allow a State to subsidize its domestic industry so long as it does so from nondiscriminatory taxes that go into the State's general revenue fund. Perhaps, as some commentators contend, that line comports with an important economic reality: a State is less likely to maintain a subsidy when its citizens perceive that the money (in the general fund) is available for any number of competing, non-protectionist purposes. That is not, however, the basis for my position, for as the Chief Justice explains, "[a]nalysis of interest group participation in the political process may serve many useful purposes, but serving as a basis for interpreting the dormant Commerce Clause is not one of them." [I] draw the line where I do because it is a clear, rational line.

REHNQUIST, C.J., joined by BLACKMUN, J., dissenting.

The Court is less than just in its description of the reasons which lay behind the Massachusetts law which it strikes down. The law undoubtedly sought to aid struggling Massachusetts dairy farmers, beset by steady or declining prices and escalating costs. [Massachusetts] has dealt with this problem by providing a subsidy to aid its beleaguered dairy farmers. In case after case, we have approved the validity under the Commerce Clause of such enactments. ["Direct] subsidization of domestic industry does not ordinarily run afoul of [the dormant Commerce Clause]; discriminatory taxation of out-of-state manufacturers does." *Limbach.*

["Denial] of the right to experiment may be fraught with serious consequences to the Nation. It is one of the happy incidents of the federal system that a single courageous State may, if its citizens choose, serve as a laboratory; and try novel social and economic experiments without risk to the rest of the country." [*New State Ice Co. v. Liebmann*, 285 U.S. 262, 311 (1932) (Brandeis, J., dissenting). The] wisdom of a messianic insistence on a grim sink-or-swim policy of laissez-faire economics would be debatable had Congress chosen to enact it; but Congress has done nothing of the kind. It is the Court which has imposed the policy under the dormant Commerce Clause, a policy which bodes ill for the values of federalism which have long animated our constitutional jurisprudence.

———

CAMPS NEWFOUND/OWATONNA, INC. v. HARRISON, 520 U.S. 564 (1997), held that a Maine statute providing a general property tax exemption for charitable institutions, but withholding the exemption from charitable institutions operated principally for the benefit of non-residents, violates the Commerce Clause. The tax was challenged by the operators of a summer camp for children of the Christian Science faith, about 95% of whose campers are not Maine residents. The Court, per STEVENS, J., viewed the tax as facially discriminatory against interstate commerce: "Even though petitioner's camp does not make a profit, it is unquestionably engaged in commerce," selling a product that includes "in part the natural beauty of Maine itself." With the camp viewed as a commercial enterprise, the statute created a financial incentive for it and other charitable institutions to prefer state residents over out-of-staters. Reasoning that the statute would be virtually per se illegal as applied to for-profit activities, Stevens, J., saw no reason to make an exception for not-for-profit organizations.

The Court rejected the argument that the "discriminatory tax exemption [at issue] is, in economic reality, no different from a discriminatory subsidy of those charities that cater principally to local needs" and should therefore be upheld. "Assuming, arguendo, that [a] direct subsidy benefiting only those nonprofits serving principally Maine residents would be permissible, our cases do not sanction a tax exemption serving similar ends. [E.g., *Limbach*.]"

Scalia, J., joined by Rehnquist, C.J., and Thomas and Ginsburg, JJ., dissented. "[T]he provision at issue here is [narrowly] designed [to] compensate or subsidize those organizations that contribute to the public fisc by dispensing public benefits the State might otherwise provide." So understood, the statute did not facially discriminate against interstate commerce; any effect on interstate commerce was "indirect." In any event, the selective exemption was "supported by such traditional and important state interests that it survives scrutiny [even] under the 'virtually per se rule of invalidity.' " Alternatively, the state interests would support recognition of a " 'domestic charity' exception [to] the negative Commerce Clause."[26]

---

[26] Thomas, J., joined by Scalia, J., and in part by Rehnquist, C.J., argued in a separate dissent that the Court should "abandon" its negative Commerce Clause jurisprudence. Rather than continuing with "policy-laden decisionmaking" that is unsupported by the constitutional text, the Court should consider whether there is not a textual prohibition against certain forms of discriminatory taxation in the Import-Export Clause, Art. I, § 10, cl. 2, which provides that "[n]o state shall, without the Consent of Congress, lay any Imposts or Duties on Imports or Exports." Because the Import-Export Clause would not plausibly forbid the property tax at issue, however, Thomas, J., agreed that the constitutional challenge should be rejected.

NOTES AND QUESTIONS

1. **Themes.** Two themes dominate Stevens, J.'s opinion in *West Lynn Creamery*: (i) "the principle of the unitary national market" and (ii) the notion that discriminatory legislation is suspect because the states' political processes cannot be trusted to balance the interests of in-state against out-of-state interests. How do these themes relate to each other?

2. **Subsidies.** Do nearly all subsidies, as Scalia, J., suggests, aim to "mak[e] it more profitable to conduct business in-state than elsewhere, i.e., distort[ ] normal market incentives"? *West Lynn Creamery* pointedly noted that it had never directly confronted the constitutionality of subsidies—a disclaimer repeated in *Camps Newfound/Owatonna*. But the Court did recognize in the latter case that, "although tax exemptions and subsidies serve similar ends, they differ in important respects, and our cases have recognized these distinctions." See also Walter Hellerstein & Dan T. Coenen, *Commerce Clause Restraints on State Business Development Incentives*, 81 Corn.L.Rev. 789 (1996): "On the one hand, the Court has sustained (or implicitly approved) programs adopted by states—particularly in the form of subsidies—intended to encourage business activities inside their borders. On the other hand, the Court has invalidated [state] programs—particularly in the form of tax incentives—intended to accomplish precisely the same result."

(a) Consider Note, *Functional Analysis, Subsidies, and the Dormant Commerce Clause*, 110 Harv.L.Rev. 1537 (1997): "[S]ubsidies can be a socially beneficial means of encouraging an optimal level of production. When [the production of] a good confers a positive externality on society [for example, by developing a production technique that can subsequently be used by others, or maintaining land in a use that preserves the beauty and integrity of the natural environment, a] firm will not reap all the social benefits of [the] good [that it produces]. By compensating firms for the positive externalities they confer on society, subsidies can function as efficient tools for states to encourage the optimal level of production. Indeed, all states may collectively gain from one state's subsidy if the good confers a positive externality." Consider also Robert M. Stern, *Conflict and Cooperation in International Economic Policy and Law*, 17 U.Pa.J.Int'l Econ.L. 539 (1996): "[When a good confers positive externalities,] a production subsidy would be the best policy [since] it leads firms to increase their [output] while leaving consumers free to consume at undistorted market prices. [A] tariff thus [is less good than] a subsidy."

(b) Apart from issues of economic effects, consider Dan T. Coenen, *Business Subsidies and the Dormant Commerce Clause*, 107 Yale L.J. 965 (1998): "First, considerations of constitutional history provide a firm 'formal' basis for distinguishing cash grants [which were not one of the historic concerns of the Commerce Clause] from discriminatory taxation [which was]. Second, a broad state power to subsidize rests on the fairness-based notion that state residents should be able to reap where they have sown. Third, the traditional distinction [between permissible subsidies and impermissible tax discrimination] vindicates values of federalism, by granting heightened authority to state governments to direct to the benefit of the state's citizenry those tangible assets that the state itself owns."

(c) Compare Edward A. Zelinsky, *Are Tax "Benefits" Constitutionally Equivalent to Direct Expenditures?*, 112 Harv.L.Rev. 379 (1998): "[T]ax benefits and direct expenditures are economically identical. If that identity has not been recognized in the past, such unawareness should not be celebrated as historical tradition, but rather corrected for the future. [Given] the relative ease with which some tax benefits can be transformed into similar direct spending programs and vice versa, the direct spending/tax border is too porous to be a useful boundary for Commerce Clause purposes."

3. *The political process.* (a) Won't there always be in-state interests—typically including consumers—who are adversely affected by a state regulation that restricts the flow of commerce and thus reduces price competition? If so, are consumers always adequate surrogates for out-of-staters in the state's legislative debates?

Does the majority's suggestion that Commerce Clause doctrine should correct "legislative abuse" occurring when "a state's political process can[not] be relied upon" presuppose a theory of interest group politics that distinguishes among the relative capacities of different kinds of groups to affect legislative outcomes? So-called "public choice" theories often postulate that "consumers," as a group, are likely to be diffuse and disorganized; by contrast, the dairy industry, whose relatively few members have much more at stake, may be well situated to organize successfully, to mount lobbying campaigns, and to provide or withhold financial or electoral support based on legislators' votes with respect to a single issue.[27] Can courts identify and correct abuses resulting from failures of the political process without making implicit assumptions about the *substantive* outcomes that a properly functioning political process would reach?

(b) Can state political processes be trusted or expected to balance the costs and benefits of subsidies more fairly than those of discriminatory tariffs and taxes? Consider Peter D. Enrich, *Saving the States from Themselves: Commerce Clause Constraints on State Tax Incentives for Business*, 110 Harv.L.Rev. 377 (1996): "[Discriminatory tax] incentives, unlike cash subsidies, are typically independent of the annual appropriation process and are authorized as a standing part of the tax code. As a result, they are less politically visible—indeed, their actual costs are often unknown. [This suggests] the need for stricter external constraints on tax incentives than on direct subsidy programs."

4. *Linkages.* (a) Consider Dan T. Coenen & Walter Hellerstein, *Suspect Linkage: The Interplay of State Taxing and Spending Measures in the Application of Constitutional Antidiscrimination Rules*, 95 Mich.L.Rev. 2167

---

[27] For an accessible introduction to the relevant concepts and literature, see Daniel A. Farber & Philip P. Frickey, *Law and Public Choice: A Critical Introduction* 12–37 (1991).

(1997): "A fundamental difficulty with the majority's logic [in *West Lynn Creamery*] lies in its [assumption that] what renders [the] local-business-favoring tax break constitutionally odious is its contemporaneous enactment with an otherwise 'neutral' tax that burdens interstate as well as intrastate commerce. [It] is the *fact* of the discrimination—rather than its *timing*—that renders resident-favoring tax relief provisions unconstitutional."

(b)   Scalia, J., argued in his concurring opinion that the Massachusetts scheme should have passed constitutional muster if the subsidy had come from general revenues, not a fund specifically created by a tax on the sale of milk. Consider Zelinksy, supra: "[I]t is difficult to see a constitutional difference between the actual Massachusetts program and an entitlement-type alternative placed in the state's general fund budget; in both cases, the program would be permanent, would not be subject to the annual appropriations process, and would have the same rules regarding eligibility and quantitative limits."

5.   ***The unitary market and laissez faire.*** Does *West Lynn Creamery* signal the ascendancy of laissez-faire economic policies in dormant Commerce Clause doctrine? Should it? Consider Tribe 3d ed., at 1150: "The majority in *West Lynn Creamery* did not purport to apply its prohibitions to all subsidies, and instead indicated that its rule applied only to subsidies coupled with non-discriminatory taxes. [Absent] a clearer definition of coupling, the scope of *West Lynn Creamery* is impossible to ascertain. But that uncertainty is new, and significant. After *West Lynn Creamery*, no state action (other than direct state participation in a market in a purely proprietary capacity)[28] that has the effect of benefiting in-state interests at the expense of out-of-state interests is clearly immune from scrutiny under the dormant Commerce Clause."

See also Richard Schragger, *Cities, Economic Development, and the Free Trade Constitution*, 94 Va.L.Rev. 1091 (2008): "Since *Healy*, the status of [the] tax/subsidy distinction and the distinction between discriminatory and non-discriminatory taxes are both unclear." The Court had an opportunity to clarify the doctrine in *DaimlerChrysler Corp. v. Cuno*, 547 U.S. 332 (2006), in which the Sixth Circuit had struck down a package of tax incentives offered by the city of Toledo and the state of Ohio to keep a Jeep assembly plant in Toledo. The Court upheld the property tax abatement provided by Toledo but declined to address the constitutionality of a state investment tax credit on the ground that the plaintiffs, who sued as taxpayers, lacked standing to challenge it. Consider Schragger: "Though limited to the investment tax credit, the Sixth Circuit's decision seemed to call into question numerous tax incentives that states and localities had presumed to be constitutional, but which some commentators had argued were vulnerable if the Court took its own doctrine seriously."

---

[28]   See Sec. 3 infra.

3. THE STATE AS A MARKET PARTICIPANT

REEVES, INC. v. STAKE
447 U.S. 429, 100 S.Ct. 2271, 65 L.Ed.2d 244 (1980).

JUSTICE BLACKMUN delivered the opinion of the Court.

[Responding to a 1919 cement shortage, South Dakota built and operated a cement plant, which sold to both in-state and out-of-state buyers. The latter bought 40% of the plant's production in the mid-70's. When booming construction caused a cement shortage in 1978, the state "reaffirmed its policy of supplying all South Dakota customers" before offering cement to buyers from out of state. Reeves, an out-of-state buyer for 20 years, challenged South Dakota's preferential sales policy as a violation of the Commerce Clause.]

The issue in this case is whether, consistent with the Commerce Clause, the State of South Dakota, in a time of shortage, may confine the sale of cement that it produces solely to its residents. [The court of appeals upheld the law]. It concluded that the state had "simply acted in a proprietary capacity," as permitted by *Hughes v. Alexandria Scrap Corp.*, 426 U.S. 794 (1976).

Alexandria Scrap concerned a Maryland program designed to remove abandoned automobiles from the State's roadways and junkyards. To encourage recycling, a "bounty" was offered for every Maryland-title junk car converted into scrap. [The law] imposed more exacting documentation requirements on out-of-state than in-state processors. [*Alexandria Scrap*] did not involve "the kind of action with which the Commerce Clause is concerned." Unlike prior cases voiding state laws inhibiting interstate trade, "Maryland has not sought to prohibit the flow of [junk cars], or to regulate the conditions under which it may occur. Instead, it has entered into the market itself to bid up their price as a purchaser, in effect, of a potential article of interstate commerce," and has restricted "its trade to its own citizens or businesses within the State."

Having characterized Maryland as a market participant, rather than as a market regulator, the Court found no reason to "believe the Commerce Clause was intended to require independent justification for [the State's] action." The Court couched its holding in unmistakably broad terms. "Nothing in the purposes animating the Commerce Clause prohibits a State, in the absence of congressional action, from participating in the market and exercising the right to favor its own citizens over others."

The basic distinction drawn in *Alexandria Scrap* between States as market participants and States as market regulators makes good sense and sound law. As that case explains, the Commerce Clause responds principally to state taxes and regulatory measures impeding free private trade in the national marketplace. [There] is no indication of a constitutional plan to limit the ability of the States themselves to operate freely in the free market. See Laurence H. Tribe, *American Constitutional Law* 336 (1978) ("the Commerce Clause was directed, as an historical matter, only at regulatory and taxing actions taken by states in their sovereign capacity"). The precedents comport with this distinction.[9]

Restraint in this area is also counseled by considerations of state sovereignty, the role of each State "as guardian and trustee for its people," and "the long recognized right of trader or manufacturer, engaged in an entirely private business, freely to exercise his own independent discretion as to parties with whom he will deal." *United States v. Colgate & Co.*, 250 U.S. 300, 307 (1919). Moreover, state proprietary activities may be, and often are, burdened with the same restrictions imposed on private market participants. Evenhandedness suggests that, when acting as proprietors, States should similarly share existing freedoms from federal constraints, including the inherent limits of the Commerce Clause. Finally, as this case illustrates, the competing considerations in cases involving state proprietary action often will be subtle, complex, politically charged, and difficult to assess under traditional Commerce Clause analysis. Given these factors, *Alexandria Scrap* wisely recognizes that, as a rule, the adjustment of interests in this context is a task better suited for Congress than this Court.

[We] find the label "protectionism" of little help in this context. The State's refusal to sell to buyers other than South Dakotans is "protectionist" only in the sense that it limits benefits generated by a state program to those who fund the state treasury and whom the State was created to serve. Petitioner's argument apparently also would characterize as "protectionist" rules restricting to state residents the enjoyment of state educational institutions, energy generated by a state-run plant, police and fire protection, and agricultural improvement and business development programs. Such policies, while perhaps "protectionist" in a loose sense, reflect the essential and patently unobjectionable purpose of state government—to serve the citizens of the State.

[Cement] is not a natural resource, like coal, timber, wild game, or minerals. Cf. *Hughes v. Oklahoma* (minnows); *Philadelphia v. New Jersey* (landfill sites). It is the end-product of a complex process whereby a costly physical plant and human labor act on raw materials. South Dakota has not sought to limit access to the State's limestone or other materials used

---

[9]   **[Ct's Note]** *Alexandria Scrap* does not stand alone. In *American Yearbook Co. v. Askew*, 339 F.Supp. 719 (M.D.Fla.1972), a three-judge District Court upheld a Florida statute requiring the State to obtain needed printing services from in-state shops. It reasoned that "state proprietary functions" are exempt from Commerce Clause scrutiny. This Court affirmed summarily. 409 U.S. 904 (1972). Numerous courts have rebuffed Commerce Clause challenges directed at similar preferences that exist in "a substantial majority of the states." Note, 58 Iowa L.Rev. 576 (1973). [The opinion cites state court decisions from eight states.]

to make cement. Nor has it restricted the ability of private firms or sister States to set up plants within its borders.

JUSTICE POWELL, with whom JUSTICE BRENNAN, JUSTICE WHITE, and JUSTICE STEVENS join, dissenting.

The application of the Commerce Clause to this case should turn on the nature of the governmental activity involved. [In] procuring goods and services for the operation of government, a State may act without regard to the private marketplace and remove itself from the reach of the Commerce Clause. See *American Yearbook Co.* [footnote 9 of the majority opinion, supra]. But when a State itself becomes a participant in the private market for other purposes, the Constitution forbids actions that would impede the flow of interstate commerce. These categories recognize no more than the "constitutional line between the State as Government and the State as trader." *New York v. United States,* [Ch. 2, Sec. 5, II supra].

The Court holds that South Dakota, like a private business, should not be governed by the Commerce Clause when it enters the private market. But precisely because South Dakota is a State, it cannot be presumed to behave like an enterprise "engaged in an entirely private business." A State frequently will respond to market conditions on the basis of political rather than economic concerns. To use the Court's terms, a State may attempt to act as a "market regulator" rather than a "market participant." In that situation, it is a pretense to equate the State with a private economic actor. State action burdening interstate trade is no less state action because it is accomplished by a public agency authorized to participate in the private market.

[Unlike] the market subsidies at issue in *Alexandria Scrap,* the marketing policy of the South Dakota Cement Commission has cut off interstate trade.[3] The State can raise such a bar when it enters the market to supply its own needs. In order to ensure an adequate supply of cement for public uses, the State can withhold from interstate commerce the cement needed for public projects.

The State, however, has no parallel justification for favoring private, in-state customers over out-of-state customers.[4] In response to political concerns that likely would be inconsequential to a private cement producer, South Dakota has shut off its cement sales to customers beyond its borders.

---

[3]   [Ct's Note] One distinction between a private and a governmental function is whether the activity is supported with general tax funds, as was the case for the reprocessing program in *Alexandria Scrap,* or whether it is financed by the revenues it generates. In this case, South Dakota's cement plant has supported itself for many years. There is thus no need to consider the question whether a state-subsidized business could confine its sales to local residents.

[4]   [Ct's Note] The consequences of South Dakota's "residents-first" policy were devastating to petitioner Reeves, Inc., a Wyoming firm. For 20 years, Reeves had purchased about 95% of its cement from the South Dakota plant. When the State imposed its preference for South Dakota residents in 1978, Reeves had to reduce its production by over 75%. As a result, its South Dakota competitors were in a vastly superior position to compete for work in the region.

That discrimination constitutes a direct barrier to trade "of the type forbidden by the Commerce Clause, and involved in previous cases." *Alexandria Scrap*. The effect on interstate trade is the same as if the state legislature had imposed the policy on private cement producers. The Commerce Clause prohibits this severe restraint on commerce.

NOTES AND QUESTIONS

1. ***Rationale.*** Does *Reeves* rest, as the dissent suggests, on the "pretense" that a state entering the marketplace should be equated with "a private economic actor"? Or does it rest instead on the view that a state, as a *political* unit, may legitimately take at least some actions with the distinctive aim of benefiting its citizens and its citizens alone? Consider Jonathan D. Varat, *State "Citizenship" and Interstate Equality,* 48 U.Chi.L.Rev. 487 (1981) ("[F]ulfillment of the fundamental obligation of state government—to care for the state's own residents—depends, to some ill-defined degree, on the ability to withhold from others what a state chooses to provide to its own."). Compare *United Haulers Ass'n v. Oneida-Herkimer Solid Waste Management Auth.* and *Dep't of Revenue v. Davis*, Section 2, III, supra, in which the Court upheld state statutes that discriminated in favor of state governmental entities.

2. ***Discriminatory regulations and permissible preferences.*** (a) Consider again the dicta of the unanimous opinion in *Limbach*, supra, suggesting that it is permissible under the Commerce Clause for states to provide subsidies to in-state producers or distributors that are designed to enable them to compete more favorably against out-of-staters. Are the reasons for not applying Commerce Clause restraints to the state-as-subsidizer applicable to the state-as-trader?

Consider Donald H. Regan, *The Supreme Court and State Protectionism: Making Sense of the Dormant Commerce Clause,* 84 Mich.L.Rev. 1091 (1986): "Many spending programs are [b]eneficial from the point of view of the nation as a whole—agricultural extension services, advertising (to the extent it has information content), certainly welfare programs. But many of these programs would not exist if the state could not channel the primary benefits to locals. Even the [city] construction [project] involved in *White v. Massachusetts Council of Construction Employers* [infra], to the extent it was a public works program, created an unquestioned benefit and probably would not have existed if the local preference aspect had been forbidden. [Moreover, the] very fact that spending programs involve spending and are therefore relatively expensive as a way of securing local benefit makes them less likely to proliferate than measures like tariffs. They are therefore less likely to damage the economy seriously in the aggregate, if they damage it at all."

See also Norman R. Williams, *Taking Care of Ourselves: State Citizenship, the Market, and the State,* 69 Ohio St.L.J. 469 (2008): "Although the Court has not offered a normatively attractive justification for the market participant doctrine, there is one available: the investment capture theory. According to this defense, it is permissible for states to reserve to their citizens those goods and services created by the state because the citizens are merely receiving the benefits of their investment in the state government—that they are, in a sense, recapturing their taxes through cash or in-kind distributions from the [state.]

"Allowing states to discriminate against non-residents so as to ensure that residents receive the benefit of their taxes is justified for two reasons. First, excluding non-residents from the benefits of state-created goods and services accords with basic notions of political fairness. States are, after all, political communities in which citizens decide what services they expect of the state (e.g., police, schools, medical care for the needy, etc.) and agree to pay for those services through taxes. [It] is fair for the citizens to decide to restrict the benefits of state-created resources to state residents because they are the ones who paid for such benefits.

"Second, reserving the benefits of state-funded programs to in-state residents also fosters an optimal degree of public investment. Out-of-state individuals who receive the benefits of such state-created programs are, in economic and moral terms, 'free riders;' they receive the benefits of programs for which they have not paid. Aside from its inherent unfairness, free riding discourages investment both by private businesses and governments."

Compare Michael J. Polelle, *A Critique of the Market Participant Exception*, 15 Whittier L.Rev. 647 (1994): The market participant exception "admits by the back door of the Commerce Clause the kind of invidious state economic protectionism that would never be allowed in through the front door. The proper relationship of local and national concerns has become muddled by allowing states to do indirectly through the market participant exception what they could never do directly through regulation or taxation of interstate commerce."

(b)   Should a state university be able to provide preferential admissions and tuition to state residents? See *Starns v. Malkerson*, 401 U.S. 985 (1971), summarily aff'g 326 F.Supp. 234 (D.Minn.1970) (upholding one-year residency requirement for lower, in-state tuition); *cf. Vlandis v. Kline*, 412 U.S. 441 (1973) (assuming the validity of a preference for residents but invalidating a conclusive presumption that a student who applied from out of state remained a nonresident throughout college).

———

SOUTH-CENTRAL TIMBER DEVELOPMENT, INC. v. WUNNICKE, 467 U.S. 82 (1984), held that the market participant concept did not free Alaska from Commerce Clause invalidation of the state's contractual requirement that purchasers of state-owned standing timber must generally saw it into "cants" less than nine inches wide before shipping it out of state. WHITE, J.'s plurality opinion, joined by Brennan, Blackmun, and Stevens, JJ., stressed that the requirement reached beyond the market transaction in which the state participated: "[The] market-participant doctrine permits a state to influence 'a discrete, identifiable class of economic activity in which [it] is a major participant.' Contrary to the state's contention, the doctrine is not carte blanche to impose any conditions that the state has the economic power to dictate, and does not validate any requirement merely because the state imposes it upon someone with whom it is in contractual privity.

"The limit of the market-participant doctrine must be that it allows a State to impose burdens on commerce within the market in which it is a participant, but allows it to go no further. The State may not impose conditions, whether by statute, regulation, or contract, that have a substantial regulatory effect outside of that particular market. Unless the 'market' is relatively narrowly defined, the doctrine has the potential of swallowing up the rule that States may not impose substantial burdens on interstate commerce even if they act with the permissible state purpose of fostering local industry.

"At the heart of the dispute in this case is a disagreement about the definition of the market. Alaska contends that it is participating in the processed timber market, although it acknowledges that it participates in no way in the actual processing. South-Central argues, on the other hand, that although the State may be a participant in the timber market, it is using its leverage in that market to exert a regulatory effect in the processing market, in which it is not a participant. We agree with the latter position.

"[We] reject the contention that a State's action as a market regulator may be upheld against Commerce Clause challenge on the ground that the State could achieve the same end as a market participant. We therefore find it unimportant for present purposes that the State could support its processing industry by selling only to Alaska processors, by vertical integration, or by direct subsidy."

Having found the Commerce Clause applicable, the opinion concluded that Alaska's log processing requirement fell within the *Pike* and *Philadelphia* "rule of virtual per se invalidity" because of its "protectionist nature."[29]

Rehnquist, J., joined by O'Connor, J., dissented: "Alaska is merely paying the buyer of the timber indirectly, by means of a reduced price, to hire Alaska residents to process the timber. Under existing precedent, the State could accomplish that same result in any number of ways. [T]he State could choose to sell its timber only to those companies that maintain active

---

[29] Powell, J., joined by Burger, C.J., would have remanded the foregoing issues for consideration by the court of appeals. But they joined Part II of White, J.'s opinion, which considered the relevance of a longstanding federal policy forbidding shipment from Alaska of unprocessed timber from federal lands. This federal policy did not negate the implied invalidity, under the Commerce Clause, of a similar state policy for timber harvested from state lands: for "a state regulation to be removed from the reach of the dormant Commerce Clause, congressional intent must be unmistakably clear."

primary-processing plants in Alaska. *Reeves.* Or the State could directly subsidize the primary-processing industry within the State. *Alexandria Scrap.* The State could even pay to have the logs processed and then enter the market only to sell processed logs. It seems to me unduly formalistic to conclude that the one path chosen by the State as best suited to promote its concerns is the path forbidden it by the Commerce Clause."

NOTES AND QUESTIONS

1. *The distinction of Reeves.* Was the distinction of *Reeves* persuasive? Is a case-by-case, pragmatic analysis necessary or appropriate to determine whether conditions on state contracts favoring in-state interests have more in common with forbidden regulatory discrimination or with permissible preferences by a market participant?

2. *Construction projects.* Suppose that a city raises tax revenues to support a public building project and requires contractors on the project to give an employment preference to city residents. Under the market participant doctrine, the city could prefer local contractors, but does it reach beyond the market in which it is a direct participant in dictating discrimination by its contractors? See *White v. Massachusetts Council of Constr. Employers*, 460 U.S. 204 (1983) (rejecting a Commerce Clause challenge to a mandate from the Mayor of Boston that had instituted employment preferences for Boston residents on city-funded construction projects).

Is *White* persuasively distinguishable from *South-Central Timber*? Should it matter that the state, in *South-Central Timber*, entered the market to sell a natural resource that it had not created, whereas the city in *White* had raised money from taxpayers to create public benefits? Having raised money from its citizens to benefit the political community, did the city in *White* have an especially strong claim to insist that its expenditures benefit the community and its members as broadly as possible?

Consider Williams, supra: "State citizens have no legitimate claim of entitlement to natural resources whose creation they have not funded. [At] the same time, however, state citizens do have a legitimate claim of entitlement to those natural resources that they have expended funds to create or augment, such as agricultural products grown on state-owned farms. [Courts] must engage in a fact-sensitive inquiry into the state's relationship to the natural resource to determine whether the resource's location in the state is merely a windfall or is the product of state investments."

4. INTERSTATE PRIVILEGES AND IMMUNITIES CLAUSE

Art. IV, § 2, cl. 1 provides that "The Citizens of each State shall be entitled to all Privileges and Immunities of Citizens in the several States." In most cases, the relationship between the dormant Commerce Clause and the Privileges and Immunities Clause is "mutually reinforcing." *Hicklin v.*

Orbeck, 437 U.S. 518, 531 (1978). As a result, many of the claims brought under the dormant Commerce Clause could equally well be brought under the Privileges and Immunities Clause and vice versa. Nonetheless, the overlap between the dormant Commerce and the Privileges and Immunities Clauses is not complete. One clear and important difference is that corporations cannot sue under the Privileges and Immunities Clause because they are not "citizens." *Paul v. Virginia*, 75 U.S. 168 (1868). Claims on behalf of corporations must thus be brought under the dormant Commerce Clause if they are to be brought at all. Other differences are more subtle. As you read the following materials on the Privileges and Immunities Clause, you should keep the following questions in mind. First, what exactly are the "Privileges and Immunities of Citizens" that Art. IV, § 2, cl. 1 protects? Only if a state regulation impairs a privilege or immunity of citizenship will it trigger an inquiry into whether it can nevertheless be justified under applicable standards. Second, is the applicable test for the permissibility of state infringements on the "Privileges and Immunities of Citizens" more or less stringent than the test for state violations of the Commerce Clause? Third, and perhaps most important, to what extent, if any, does the Privileges and Immunities Clause undermine the significance of "the market participant exception" to dormant Commerce Clause doctrine?

UNITED BUILDING & CONSTRUCTION TRADES COUNCIL v. MAYOR OF CAMDEN
465 U.S. 208, 104 S.Ct. 1020, 79 L.Ed.2d 249 (1984).

JUSTICE REHNQUIST delivered the opinion of the Court.

A municipal ordinance of the city of Camden, New Jersey, requires that at least 40% of the employees of contractors and subcontractors working on city construction projects be Camden residents. Appellant, the United Building and Construction Trades Council of Camden County and Vicinity (Council), challenges that ordinance as a violation of the Privileges and Immunities Clause, Art. IV, § 2, cl. 1, of the United States Constitution [and] as unconstitutional under the Commerce Clause.

Citing *Reeves* and *Alexandria Scrap*, the [New Jersey Supreme Court] held that the resident quota was not subject to challenge under the Commerce Clause because the State was acting as a market participant rather than as a market regulator. [Since] the Council filed its appeal, [this Court] decided *White*, which held that an executive order of the Mayor of Boston, requiring that at least 50% of all jobs on construction projects funded in whole or in part by city funds be filled with bona fide city residents, was immune from scrutiny under the Commerce Clause because Boston was acting as a market participant rather than as a market regulator. In light of the decision in *White*, appellant has abandoned its

Commerce Clause challenge. [The] only question left [is] whether the [ordinance] violates the Privileges and Immunities Clause.

[The City argues] that the Clause only applies to laws passed by a *State*. [But the] fact that the ordinance [is] municipal [does] not somehow place it outside the scope of the Privileges and Immunities Clause. [What] would be unconstitutional if done directly by the State can no more readily be accomplished by a city deriving its authority from the State. [Nor can we accept] that the Privileges and Immunities Clause does not apply to an ordinance that discriminates solely on the basis of *municipal* residency. The Clause is phrased in terms of *state* citizenship and was designed "to place the citizens of each State upon the same footing with citizens of other States, as far as the advantages resulting from citizenship in those States are concerned." [But we] have never read the Clause so literally as to apply it only to distinctions based on state citizenship. [A] person who is not residing in a given State is ipso facto not residing in a city within that State. Thus, whether the exercise of a privilege is conditioned on state residency or on municipal residency he will just as surely be excluded.

[It] is true that New Jersey citizens not residing in Camden will be affected by the ordinance as well as out-of-state citizens. And it is true that the disadvantaged New Jersey residents have no claim under the Privileges and Immunities Clause. *Slaughter-House Cases.* But New Jersey residents at least have a chance to remedy at the polls any discrimination against them. Out-of-state citizens have no similar opportunity.

[Application] of the Privileges and Immunities Clause to a particular instance of discrimination against out-of-state residents entails a two-step inquiry. As an initial matter, the Court must decide whether the ordinance burdens one of those privileges and immunities protected by the Clause. *Baldwin v. Montana Fish and Game Comm'n.*, 436 U.S. 371 (1978).[30] Not all forms of discrimination against citizens of other States are constitutionally suspect: "Some distinctions between residents and nonresidents merely reflect the fact that this is a Nation composed of individual States, and are permitted; other distinctions are prohibited because they hinder the formation, the purpose, or the development of a single Union of those States. Only with respect to those 'privileges' and 'immunities' bearing upon the vitality of the Nation as a single entity must the State treat all citizens, resident and nonresident, equally." Ibid.

As a threshold matter, then, we must determine whether an out-of-state resident's interest in employment on public works contracts in another State is sufficiently "fundamental" to the promotion of interstate

---

[30]   *Baldwin* upheld Montana's license fee for hunting elk—which was $225 for non-residents, compared with $30 for residents—on the ground that hunting for sport was not a protected "fundamental" right under the Privileges and Immunities Clause.

harmony so as to "fall within the purview of the Privileges and Immunities Clause." Id.

Certainly, the pursuit of a common calling [(that is, a job)] is one of the most fundamental of those privileges protected by the Clause. Many, if not most, of our cases expounding the Privileges and Immunities Clause have dealt with this basic and essential activity. See, e.g., *Hicklin v. Orbeck*, 437 U.S. 518 (1978); *Toomer v. Witsell*, 334 U.S. 385 (1948). Public employment, however, is qualitatively different from employment in the private sector; it is a subspecies of the broader opportunity to pursue a common calling. We have held that there is no fundamental right to government employment for purposes of the Equal Protection Clause. *Massachusetts Bd. of Retirement v. Murgia*, [Ch. 9, Sec. 4, V supra]. Cf. *McCarthy v. Philadelphia Civil Service Comm'n*, [Ch. 9, Sec. 5, II supra] (rejecting equal protection challenge to municipal residency requirement for municipal workers). And in *White*, we held that for purposes of the Commerce Clause everyone employed on a city public works project is, "in a substantial if informal sense, 'working for the city.'"

It can certainly be argued that for purposes of the Privileges and Immunities Clause everyone affected by the Camden ordinance is also "working for the city" and, therefore, has no grounds for complaint when the city favors its own residents. But we decline to transfer mechanically into this context an analysis fashioned to fit the Commerce Clause. Our decision in *White* turned on a distinction between the city acting as a market participant and the city acting as a market regulator. [But] the distinction between market participant and market regulator relied upon in *White* to dispose of the Commerce Clause challenge is not dispositive in this context. The two Clauses have different aims and set different standards for state conduct.

The Commerce Clause acts as an implied restraint upon state regulatory powers. Such powers must give way before the superior authority of Congress to legislate on (or leave unregulated) matters involving interstate commerce. When the State acts solely as a market participant, no conflict between state regulation and federal regulatory authority can arise. *White; Reeves; Alexandria Scrap*. The Privileges and Immunities Clause, on the other hand, imposes a direct restraint on state action in the interests of interstate harmony.

[In] *Hicklin,* we struck down as a violation of the Privileges and Immunities Clause an "Alaska Hire" statute containing a resident-hiring preference for all employment related to the development of the State's oil and gas resources. Alaska argued in that case that "because the oil and gas that are the subject of Alaska Hire are *owned* by the State, this ownership, of itself, is sufficient justification for the Act's discrimination against nonresidents, and takes the Act totally without the scope of the Privileges and Immunities Clause." We concluded, however, that the State's interest in controlling those things it claims to own is not absolute. "Rather than placing a statute completely beyond the Clause, the State's ownership of the property with which the statute is concerned is a factor—although often the crucial factor—to be considered in evaluating whether the statute's discrimination against noncitizens violates the Clause." Much the same analysis, we think, is appropriate to a city's efforts to bias private employment decisions in favor of its residents on construction projects funded with public moneys. The fact that Camden is expending its own funds or funds it administers in accordance with the terms of a grant is certainly a factor—perhaps the crucial factor—to be considered in evaluating whether the statute's discrimination violates the Privileges and Immunities Clause. But it does not remove the Camden ordinance completely from the purview of the Clause.

[The] conclusion that Camden's ordinance discriminates against a protected privilege does not, of course, end the inquiry. We have stressed in prior cases that "[l]ike many other constitutional provisions, the privileges and immunities clause is not an absolute." *Toomer*. It does not preclude discrimination against citizens of other States where there is a "substantial reason" for the difference in treatment. "[T]he inquiry in each case must be concerned with whether such reasons do exist and whether the degree of discrimination bears a close relation to them."

[Every] inquiry under the Privileges and Immunities Clause "must [be] conducted with due regard for the principle that the States should have considerable leeway in analyzing local evils and in prescribing appropriate cures." This caution is particularly appropriate when a government body is merely setting conditions on the expenditure of funds it controls. The Alaska Hire statute at issue in *Hicklin* swept within its strictures not only contractors and subcontractors dealing directly with the State's oil and gas; it also covered suppliers who provided goods and services to those contractors and subcontractors. We invalidated the Act as "an attempt to force virtually all businesses that benefit in some way from the economic ripple effect of Alaska's decision to develop its oil and gas resources to bias their employment practices in favor of the State's residents." No similar "ripple effect" appears to infect the Camden ordinance. It is limited in scope to employees working directly on city public works projects.

Nonetheless, we find it impossible to evaluate Camden's justification on the record as it now stands. No trial has ever been held in the case. No findings of fact have been made. [We], therefore, [remand for] proceedings not inconsistent with this opinion.

JUSTICE BLACKMUN, dissenting.

[The] Framers had every reason to believe that interstate discrimination based on municipal residence would be dealt with by the

States themselves. [Nor] is this mechanism for relief merely a theoretical one; in the past decade several States, including California and Georgia, have repealed or forbidden protectionist ordinances like the one at issue here. [Because] I believe that the [Privileges and Immunities Clause] does not apply to discrimination based on municipal residence, I dissent.

NOTES AND QUESTIONS

1. ***Restriction to fundamental rights.*** Is the restriction of the Privileges and Immunities Clause to fundamental rights manageable and defensible? In imposing this limitation in *Baldwin*, the Court relied heavily on the opinion of Justice Bushrod Washington in *Corfield v. Coryell*, 6 F.Cas. 546, 552 (No. 3,230) (C.C.E.D.Pa. 1825): "The inquiry is, what are the privileges and immunities of citizens in the several states? We feel no hesitation in confining these expressions to those privileges and immunities which are, in their nature, fundamental; which belong, of right, to the citizens of all free governments; and which have, at all times, been enjoyed by the citizens of the several states, [from] the time of their becoming free, independent, and sovereign. What these fundamental principles are, it would perhaps be more tedious than difficult to enumerate. They may, however, be all comprehended under the following general heads: Protection by the government; the enjoyment of life and liberty, with the right to acquire and possess property of every kind, and to pursue and obtain happiness and safety; subject nevertheless to such restraints as the government may justly prescribe for the general good of the whole."

Stewart Jay, *Origins of the Privileges and Immunities of State Citizenship Under Article IV*, 45 Loy.U.Chi.L.J. 1 (2013), argues that Justice Washington and other early judges misapprehended the original constitutional understanding: "Alexander Hamilton wrote in *Federalist No. 80* that the Privileges and Immunities Clause of Article IV was 'the basis of the union.' [Although early judges, including Justice Bushrod Washington in *Corfield v. Coryell*,] could not believe that it literally encompassed every one of the rights of citizens, [a study] made possible by searchable databases unknown to prior generations [and reviewing] thousands of published works in English from the eighteenth century and earlier [to establish the historical understanding of the Clause, shows that the early judges erred.] There is compelling reason to conclude that the Privileges and Immunities Clause was intended to do precisely what Justice Washington denied—guarantee to Americans traveling or temporarily residing in another state, or doing business or owning property outside their home states, that they would be treated exactly like the local people, without exception, and regardless of whether the right was recognized by other states, including their own." If Professor Jay were correct, what conclusions ought to follow? Should citizens be eligible for welfare while visiting in other states? Should they be able to vote?

With current doctrine clearly restricting the scope of the Privileges and Immunities Clause to "fundamental" rights, it becomes important to determine which rights count as fundamental. Although that determination will sometimes be contestable, it seems clear that the rights deemed fundamental under the Privileges and Immunities Clause are defined differently from the fundamental rights entitled to heightened judicial protection under the Due Process and Equal Protection Clauses, as considered in Ch. 6 and Ch. 9 respectively. See, e.g., Jonathan D. Varat, *State "Citizenship" and Interstate Equality*, 48 U.Chi.L.Rev. 487 (1981): "If it took a fundamental equal protection interest to activate the protection of the Privileges and Immunities Clause, the Clause would be rendered superfluous. As *Baldwin* itself indicates, nonresidents as a class are protected by the Equal Protection Clause when they are within another state's jurisdiction, and given the presence of a fundamental equal protection interest, strict scrutiny would apply without any help from the [Privileges and Immunities Clause]."

2. *Applicable test.* In cases in which the Privileges and Immunities Clause applies, what test will the Court employ to assess the permissibility of discrimination against out-of-staters? The Court's formulations have not been wholly consistent.

(a) In *United Building*, the Court relied on a much-quoted formulation from *Toomer*, which invalidated a discriminatory state tax on non-residents' access to migratory shrimp: "The Privileges and Immunities Clause is not an absolute. It does bar discrimination against citizens of other States where there is no substantial reason for the discrimination beyond the mere fact that they are citizens of other States. But it does not preclude disparity of treatment in the many situations where there are perfectly valid independent reasons for it. Thus the inquiry in each case must be concerned with whether such reasons do exist and whether the degree of discrimination bears a close relation to [them. The] purpose [is] to outlaw classifications based on the fact of non-citizenship unless there is something to indicate that non-citizens constitute a peculiar source of the evil at which the statute is aimed."

(b) LUNDING v. NEW YORK STATE TAX APPEALS TRIBUNAL, 522 U.S. 287 (1998), invalidated a New York statute that effectively denied non-resident taxpayers a state income tax deduction for alimony payments that was available to resident taxpayers. The 6–3 majority, per O'CONNOR, J., found that the state had advanced no justification for the disparate treatment adequate to satisfy the applicable standard, which it stated as follows: "[W]hen confronted with a challenge under the Privileges and Immunities Clause to a law distinguishing between residents and nonresidents, a State may defend its position by demonstrating that (i) there is a substantial reason for the difference in treatment; and (ii) the discrimination practiced against nonresidents bears a substantial relationship to the State's objective." Ginsburg, J., joined by Rehnquist, C.J., and Kennedy, J., dissented.

(c) McBURNEY v. YOUNG, 133 S.Ct. 1709 (2013), per ALITO, J., unanimously rejected an argument that Virginia's Freedom of Information Act (FOIA) violated the Privileges and Immunities Clause by granting Virginia citizens, but not out-of-staters, access to all public records: "Petitioners allege that Virginia's citizens-only FOIA provision violates four different 'fundamental' privileges or immunities: the opportunity to pursue a common calling, the ability to own and transfer property, access to the Virginia courts, and access to public information. [Although the challenged provision] has the incidental effect of preventing citizens of other States from making a profit by trading on information contained in state records[, the] Court has struck laws down as violating the privilege of pursuing a common calling only when those laws were enacted for the protectionist purpose of burdening out-of-state citizens. [Here,] the distinction that the statute makes between citizens and noncitizens has a distinctly nonprotectionist aim. The state FOIA essentially represents a mechanism by which those who ultimately hold sovereign power (*i.e.*, the citizens of the Commonwealth) may obtain an accounting from the public officials to whom they delegate the exercise of that power.

"[If] a State prevented out-of-state citizens from accessing records—like title documents and mortgage records—that are necessary to the transfer of property, the State might well run afoul of the Privileges and Immunities Clause. Virginia, however, does not prevent citizens of other States from obtaining such documents. [Requiring] noncitizens to conduct a few minutes of Internet research in lieu of using a relatively cumbersome state FOIA process cannot be said to impose any significant burden on noncitizens' ability to own or transfer property in Virginia.

"[Although] the Privileges and Immunities Clause 'secures citizens of one State the right to resort to the courts of another, equally with the citizens of the latter State,' [the] Court has made clear that 'the constitutional requirement is satisfied if the non-resident is given access [upon] terms which in themselves are reasonable and adequate. [Virginia's] rules of civil procedure provide for both discovery and subpoenas duces tecum. There is no reason to think that those mechanisms are insufficient to provide noncitizens with any relevant, nonprivileged documents needed in litigation.

"Finally, we [cannot] agree that the Privileges and Immunities Clause covers [a] broad right [of access to public information]. No such right was recognized at common law. [Nor] is such a sweeping right 'basic to the maintenance or well-being of the Union.'

"[Petitioners' dormant Commerce Clause challenge also fails because] Virginia's FOIA law neither 'regulates' nor 'burdens' interstate commerce; rather, it merely provides a service to local citizens that would not otherwise be available at all."

3. ***Distinguishing Hicklin?*** Consider whether, on remand, *United Building* is distinguishable from *Hicklin* on the ground that the city of Camden raised the money that it then spent on jobs, whereas the state of Alaska had not comparably generated the oil creating the jobs at issue. Should Camden be entitled to allocate preferentially to its residents under a theory that it should be able to "reap what it had sown"? Cf. Saul Levmore, *Interstate Exploitation and Judicial Intervention*, 69 Va.L.Rev. 563 (1983) ("[T]he distinction between 'interferences' and 'exploitations' has descriptive and normative value in

understanding the judicial response to interstate trade barriers.").[31] Does allowing states to prefer their own citizens in distributing what they "reap" encourage them to "sow" more in the first place? Should states be so encouraged? Reconsider at this point the question whether states should be able to subsidize industries by the provision of direct cash subsidies, even though they would be barred by the Commerce Clause from protecting those same industries by the enactment of discriminatory regulations. See Sec. 2, VI supra.

4. ***Discriminatory effects.*** A statute that does not facially discriminate against out-of-staters, but nonetheless has discriminatory effects, can violate the Privileges and Immunities Clause in at least some circumstances, the Court held unanimously in HILLSIDE DAIRY INC. v. LYONS, 539 U.S. 59 (2003). A complex California scheme of milk price supports required in-state processors purchasing milk from in-state producers to pay minimum prices and to make payments into an "equalization fund." The proceeds of this fund were then distributed back to the processors, depending on the nature of their ultimate products (for example, cheese, cottage cheese, and butter) and the prices those products commanded. In 1997, California amended its plan to require purchasers of milk from out-of-state producers also to make payments to this fund. Out-of-state farmers filed suit, alleging violations of the dormant Commerce Clause and the Privileges and Immunities Clause. The lower court dismissed the privileges and immunities challenge on the ground that the California scheme did not facially discriminate against out-of-state producers. The Court, per STEVENS, J., reversed, relying principally on *Chalker v. Birmingham & Northwestern Ry. Co.*, 249 U.S. 522 (1919), which had invalidated a tax that did not facially discriminate on the basis of citizenship, but imposed a higher rate on persons with their principal offices out of state: "Whether *Chalker* should be interpreted as merely applying the [Privileges and Immunities] Clause to classifications that are but proxies for differential treatment against out-of-state residents, or as prohibiting any classification with the practical effect of discriminating against such residents, is a matter we need not decide at this stage of the case. Under either interpretation, [the] absence of an express statement in the California laws identifying out-of-state citizenship as a basis for disparate treatment is not a sufficient basis for rejecting this claim."[32]

5. ***An adequate substitute for the dormant Commerce Clause?*** Some commentators have suggested that the Court should renounce dormant Commerce Clause review and trust state legislatures to balance state and federal interests (subject to congressional legislation) unless they expressly discriminate against out-of-staters and run afoul of the Privileges and

---

[31] For an exploration of when state preference laws concerning the expenditure of state funds do and do not yield net economic benefits to the nation as a whole, and a suggestion that courts should weigh this factor in Privileges and Immunities Clause cases, see Werner Z. Hirsch, *An Economic Analysis of the Constitutionality of State Preference Laws*, 14 Int'l Rev.L. & Econ. 299 (1994).

[32] The Court remanded, without expressing any opinion on the merits of the petitioners' Privileges and Immunities Clause claim.

Immunities Clause. These commentators have contrasted the firm textual anchor for Privileges and Immunities Clause doctrine with the uncertain textual foundations of dormant Commerce Clause jurisprudence.

Consider Julian N. Eule, *Laying the Dormant Commerce Clause to Rest*, 91 Yale L.J. 425 (1982): "[Our] needs today differ significantly from those of the 1940s when the Court embraced [the] suggestion that its proper role, in the absence of congressional action, was to balance national and local interests in scrutinizing state commercial enactments. Congress, the implied beneficiary of the Court's protection under that standard, no longer needs such assistance. [The] contemporary dangers of state parochialism lie in its evisceration of the democratic process, not in its impairment of free trade."

Compare Brannon P. Denning, *Why the Privileges and Immunities Clause of Article IV Cannot Replace the Dormant Commerce Clause Doctrine*, 88 Minn.L.Rev. 384 (2003): "Wholesale substitution of the Privileges and Immunities Clause for the [dormant Commerce Clause doctrine or 'DCCD'] involves some unintended consequences. [The Privileges and Immunities] Clause, as currently interpreted by the Court, does not apply to corporations [and] may not reach conduct that the DCCD strictly scrutinizes. Moreover, [relying on] the Privileges and Immunities Clause [would] also mean that Congress and the states would have less authority to regulate commerce than is now possible under the DCCD. Specifically, the Court has declined to read into the [Privileges and Immunities] Clause a 'market participant' exception, like that created for the DCCD. In addition, the text of the Clause seems to foreclose the ability of Congress to permit discrimination, as it can under the DCCD, by clearly delegating that power to the states."

Is there any persuasive reason why the market participant doctrine should apply to the Commerce Clause but not the Privileges and Immunities Clause? Is the perceived need for the exception under the Commerce Clause, but not the Privileges and Immunities Clause, indicative of broader difficulties with dormant Commerce Clause doctrine?

5. STATE POWER TO TAX

Besides imposing restrictions on state regulatory enactments, the dormant Commerce Clause constrains state taxation of interstate commerce. In some respects—in particular, in its general prohibition against taxation of out-of-staters (subject to the exception for government bonds recognized in *Dep't of Revenue v. Davis*, Sec. 2, III supra)—the doctrine applicable to state taxation parallels the doctrine for testing the validity of state regulatory measures.[33] Some dormant Commerce Clause cases involving tax statutes have, accordingly, appeared already in the preceding materials. But apart from the condemnation of discrimination, the Court has developed distinctive tests to assess the validity of state

---

[33] See, e.g., *New Energy Co. of Ind. v. Limbach*, Sec. 2, VI supra.

taxation (especially of multi-state businesses) under the dormant Commerce Clause.

This section provides a brief overview of the current doctrine for assessing state taxation of firms engaged in interstate commerce under the dormant Commerce Clause. Among the issues of foremost concern are how and why the Court's stated tests for assessing taxes that allegedly burden interstate commerce differ from its stated tests for assessing burdensome regulations.

COMPLETE AUTO TRANSIT, INC. V. BRADY
430 U.S. 274, 97 S.Ct. 1076, 51 L.Ed.2d 326 (1977).

JUSTICE BLACKMUN delivered the opinion of the Court.

[Mississippi imposed "privilege taxes" for the privilege of doing business within the state, measured by a percent of gross income. General Motors shipped vehicles by rail from other states to Jackson, Miss., destined for Mississippi dealers. Complete Auto, a contract motor carrier, hauled the cars from Jackson to the dealers. The Court unanimously upheld the application of the tax to Complete Auto's Mississippi gross income.]

Appellant claimed that its transportation was but one part of an interstate movement, and that the taxes assessed were unconstitutional as applied to operations in interstate commerce. [Appellant] did *not* allege that its activity which Mississippi taxes does not have a sufficient nexus with the State; or that the tax discriminates against interstate commerce; or that the tax is unfairly apportioned; or that it is unrelated to services provided by the State. [Rather, its] attack is based solely on decisions of this Court holding that a tax on the "privilege" of engaging in an activity in the State may not be applied to an activity that is part of interstate commerce. See, e.g., *Spector Motor Service v. O'Connor*, 340 U.S. 602 (1951). This rule looks only to the fact that the incidence of the tax is the "privilege of doing business"; it deems irrelevant any consideration of the practical effect of the tax. The rule reflects an underlying philosophy that interstate commerce should enjoy a sort of "free trade" immunity from state taxation.

Appellee, in its turn, relies on decisions of this Court stating that "[i]t was not the purpose of the Commerce Clause to relieve those engaged in interstate commerce from their just share of state tax burden even though it increases the cost of doing the business." These decisions have considered not the formal language of the tax statute, but rather its practical effect, and have sustained a tax against Commerce Clause challenge when [1] the tax is applied to an activity with a substantial nexus with the taxing state, [2] is fairly apportioned, [3] does not discriminate against interstate commerce, and [4] is fairly related to the services provided by the State.

Over the years, the Court has applied this practical analysis in approving many types of tax that avoided running afoul of the prohibition against taxing the "privilege of doing business," but in each instance it has refused to overrule the prohibition. Under the present state of the law, the *Spector* rule [has] no relationship to economic realities. Rather it stands only as a trap for the unwary draftsman.

[Not] only has the philosophy underlying the rule been rejected, but the rule itself has been stripped of any practical significance. If Mississippi had called its tax one on "net income" or on the "going concern value" of appellant's business, the *Spector* rule could not invalidate it. There is no economic consequence that follows necessarily from the use of the particular words, "privilege of doing business," and a focus on that formalism merely obscures the question whether the tax produces a forbidden effect. Simply put, the *Spector* rule does not address the problems with which the Commerce Clause is concerned. Accordingly, we now reject the rule of *Spector* * * * .

NOTES AND QUESTIONS

1. ***Break with the past.*** *Complete Auto* marked a sharp break with the "formalist" approach that had "initially gripped and later greatly influenced the Court for about three decades." Jesse H. Choper & Tung Yin, *State Taxation and the Dormant Commerce Clause: The Object-Measure Approach*, 1998 Sup.Ct.Rev. 193. See also Kirk J. Stark & Daniel J. Wilson, *What Do We Know About the Interstate Economic Effects of State Tax Incentives?*, 4 Geo. J. L. & Pub. Pol'y 133 (2006).

2. ***Modern test.*** In assessing the validity of state taxes under the Commerce Clause, subsequent cases have almost invariably applied the four-part test prescribed in *Complete Auto*, which inquires whether "[1] the tax is applied to an activity with a substantial nexus with the taxing state, [2] is fairly apportioned, [3] does not discriminate against interstate commerce, and [4] is fairly related to the services provided by the State." If these conditions are satisfied, "interstate commerce may be required to pay its own way."

COMMONWEALTH EDISON CO. v. MONTANA, 453 U.S. 609 (1981), per MARSHALL, J., upheld a Montana severance tax on coal [extracted within the state] even though 90% of the coal was shipped to other states. The tax produced "almost 20%" of the state revenue, but 50% went to a trust fund to alleviate environmental impact from strip mining and economic problems anticipated upon exhaustion of the coal resources: "Appellants assert that the Montana tax discriminate[s] against interstate commerce because 90% of Montana coal is shipped to other states under contracts that shift the tax burden primarily to non-Montana utility companies and thus to citizens of other states. But the Montana tax is

352   STATE POWER TO REGULATE   CH. 4

computed at the same rate regardless of the final destination of the coal, and there is no suggestion that the tax is administered in a manner that departs from this even-handed formula. We are not, therefore, confronted here with the type of differential tax treatment that the court has found in other 'discrimination' cases.

"[Appellants] assume that the Commerce Clause gives residents of one State a right of access at reasonable prices to resources located in another State that is richly endowed with such resources, without regard to whether and on what terms residents of the resource-rich State have access to the resources. We are not convinced that the Commerce Clause, of its own force, gives the residents of one State the right to control in this fashion the terms of resource development and depletion in a sister State. Cf. *Philadelphia v. New Jersey*.

"[The] only remaining foundation for their discrimination theory is a claim that the tax burden borne by the out-of-state consumers of Montana coal is excessive. This is, of course, merely a variant of appellants' assertion that the Montana tax does not satisfy the 'fairly related' prong of the *Complete Auto* test, and it is to this contention that we now turn.

"Appellants argue that they are entitled to an opportunity to prove that the amount collected under the Montana tax is not fairly related to the additional costs the State incurs because of coal mining. Thus, appellants' objection is to the *rate* of the Montana tax, and even then, their only complaint is that the *amount* the State receives in taxes far exceeds the *value* of the services provided to the coal mining industry. [To] accept appellants' apparent suggestion that the Commerce Clause prohibits the States from requiring an activity connected to interstate commerce to contribute to the general cost of providing governmental services, as distinct from those costs attributable to the taxed activity, would place such commerce in a privileged position. [It] was not the purpose of the Commerce Clause to relieve those engaged in interstate commerce from their just share of state tax [burden.]

"The relevant inquiry under the fourth prong of the *Complete Auto* test is not, as appellants suggest, the *amount* of the tax or the *value* of the benefits allegedly bestowed as measured by the costs the State incurs on account of the taxpayer's activities. Rather, the test is closely connected to the first prong of the *Complete Auto* test. Under this threshold test, the interstate business must have a substantial nexus with the State before *any* tax may be levied on it. Beyond that threshold requirement, the fourth prong of the *Complete Auto* test imposes the additional limitation that the *measure* of the tax must be reasonably related to the extent of the contact, since it is the activities or presence of the taxpayer in the State that may properly be made to bear a just share of state tax burden.

"[Because the tax] is measured as a percentage of the value of the coal taken, the Montana tax is in proper proportion to appellants' activities within the State and, therefore, to their consequent enjoyment of the opportunities and protections which the State has afforded in connection to those activities. When a tax is assessed in proportion to a taxpayer's activities or presence in a State, the taxpayer is shouldering its fair share of supporting the State's provision of police and fire protection, the benefit of a trained work force, and the advantages of a civilized society.

"[W]hen the measure of a tax is reasonably related to the taxpayer's activities or presence in the State—from which it derives some benefit such as the substantial privilege of mining coal—the taxpayer will realize, in proper proportion to the taxes it pays, [t]he only benefit to which it is constitutionally entitled[:] that derived from his enjoyment of the privileges of living in an organized society, established and safeguarded by the devotion of taxes to public purposes."[34]

Blackmun, J., joined by Powell and Stevens, JJ., dissented: "[The Court concludes] that the relevant inquiry under the fourth prong of the *Complete Auto* test is simply whether the *measure* of the tax is fixed as a percentage of the value of the coal taken. This interpretation emasculates the fourth prong. No trial will ever be necessary on the issue of fair relationship so long as a State is careful to impose a proportional rather than a flat tax rate. [Under] the Court's reasoning any ad valorem tax will satisfy the fourth prong; indeed, the Court implicitly ratifies Montana's contention that it is free to tax this coal at 100% or even 1000% of value should it choose to do so.

"[The Commerce] Clause is violated when, as appellants allege is the case here, the State effectively selects a class of out-of-state taxpayers to shoulder a tax burden grossly in excess of any costs imposed directly or indirectly by such taxpayers on the State. [It] is true that a trial in this case would require complex factual inquiries into whether economic conditions are such that Montana is in fact able to export the burden of its severance tax. I do not believe, however, that this threshold inquiry is beyond judicial competence. If the trial court were to determine that the tax is exported, it would then have to determine whether the tax is 'fairly related,' within the meaning of *Complete Auto*. The Court to the contrary, this would not require the trial court to second-guess legislative decisions about the amount or disposition of tax revenues. If the tax is in fact a legitimate general revenue measure identical or roughly comparable to taxes imposed upon similar industries, a court's inquiry is at an end; on the other hand, if the tax singles out this particular interstate activity and charges it with a grossly disproportionate share of the general costs of government, the court must determine whether there is some reasonable

---

[34] "With considerable doubt," White, J., joined the Court's opinion, stressing in a short concurrence the power of Congress to protect interstate commerce through legislation.

basis for the legislative judgment that the tax is necessary to compensate the State for the particular costs imposed by the activity."

NOTES AND QUESTIONS

1. *"Fairly related."* Consider Choper & Yin, supra: "The fourth requirement [of *Complete Auto Transit*]—that the tax be fairly related to the services provided by the state—[has become 'insignificant']. The Court has yet to invalidate a tax under it, as 'services' has been defined so broadly—'receipt of police and fire protection, the use of public roads and mass transit, and other advantages of civilized society'—that this condition is virtually meaningless. [Any] taxpayer with a substantial nexus to the taxing state (the first prong) would appear necessarily to benefit from police and fire protection. [The] fourth prong [has] become wholly subordinate to the first." Would a more stringent approach be desirable? Judicially manageable?

2. *Discrimination.* (a) "The third prong of the *Complete Auto Transit* test [forbidding discrimination against interstate commerce] has emerged as the dominant one," according to Tribe, 3d ed. at 1107–08: "Among other things, the [Court] has found invalid [those] state taxes that explicitly exempt local activities [such as the tax scheme in *Bacchus Imports, Ltd. v. Dias*, 468 U.S. 263 (1984), which exempted locally produced wines from a Hawaii sales tax. The Court] has also found unconstitutionally discriminatory those state taxes which, though nondiscriminatory on their face, impose economic burdens on interstate enterprises" that are "not in fact imposed on local competitors" (citing cases invalidating fixed fees on solicitation of business, including *Robbins v. Shelby County Taxing Dist.*, 120 U.S. 489 (1887), and *Nippert v. Richmond*, 327 U.S. 416 (1946)).

Is the Montana tax in *Commonwealth Edison Co.* persuasively distinguishable?

(b) In AMERICAN TRUCKING ASSN'S, INC. v. MICHIGAN PUBLIC SERV. COMM'N, 545 U.S. 429 (2005), the Court, per BREYER, J., held unanimously that a Michigan provision charging a flat fee of $100 on all trucks engaging in in-state commercial hauling did not violate the dormant Commerce Clause. The Court emphasized that states commonly tax intra-state service providers. It then distinguished *American Trucking Ass'ns v. Scheiner*, 483 U.S. 266 (1987), which invalidated a flat tax of $36 per vehicle axle that Pennsylvania levied on all trucks that used its roads (even if for purely interstate traffic): "The present fee [taxes] purely local activity; it does not tax an interstate truck's entry into the state. [Consequently,] we lack any reason to infer that Michigan's lump-sum levy erects [an] impermissible discriminatory roadblock" despite unsupported assertions that the fee would discourage interstate trucks from also engaging in intra-state hauling and thus protect in-state service providers.

CONTAINER CORP. v. FRANCHISE TAX BD., 463 U.S. 159 (1983), per BRENNAN, J., upheld California's "doing business" tax as applied to an Illinois corporation operating in California but also owning all or part of 20 foreign subsidiaries. California calculated the tax by considering the income of the entire integrated business and then using a formula to determine the amount of income attributable to business activity in California. Each subsidiary was relatively autonomous with respect to matters of personnel and day-to-day management, though officers of the parent established standards of professionalism, profitability, and ethical practices and dealt with major problems and long-term decisions. Neither parent nor subsidiaries depended on each other for a flow of goods used in the business. Only 1% of the subsidiaries' purchases were from the parent.

"Under both the Due Process and the Commerce Clauses [a] State may not, when imposing an income-based tax, tax value earned outside its borders. In the case of a more-or-less integrated business enterprise operating in more than one State, however, arriving at precise territorial allocations of value is often an elusive goal. [For] this reason [the Court has upheld income taxation pursuant to a] unitary business/formula apportionment method. [This method] calculates the local tax base by first determining the scope of the unitary business [and] then apportioning the total income of that unitary business between the taxing jurisdiction and the rest of the world on the basis of a formula taking into account objective measures of the corporation's activities within and without the jurisdiction. [Two] aspects of the unitary business/formula apportionment method have traditionally attracted judicial attention. These are [the] notions of unitary business and formula apportionment, respectively.

"[The] Due Process and Commerce Clauses [do] not allow a State to tax income arising out of interstate activities—even on a proportional basis—unless there is a minimum connection or nexus between the interstate activities and the taxing State [as per the first prong of the *Complete Auto* test. The] principles we have quoted require that the out-of-state activities of the purported 'unitary business' be related in some way to the in-state activities.

"[We] address the unitary business issue first. [The] taxpayer always has the distinct burden of showing by clear and cogent evidence that [the state tax] results in extraterritorial values being taxed.

"The state Court of Appeals relied on a large number of factors in reaching its judgment that appellant and its foreign subsidiaries constituted a unitary business. These included appellant's assistance to its subsidiaries in obtaining used and new equipment and in filling personnel needs that could not be met locally, the substantial role played by appellant in loaning funds to the subsidiaries and guaranteeing loans provided by others, the considerable interplay between appellant and its foreign subsidiaries in the area of corporate expansion, the substantial technical assistance provided by appellant to the subsidiaries, and the supervisory role played by appellant's officers in providing general guidance to the subsidiaries. [We] need not decide whether any one of these factors would be sufficient as a constitutional matter to prove the existence of a unitary business. Taken in combination, at least, they clearly demonstrate that the state court reached a conclusion within the realm of permissible judgment.

"Having determined that a certain set of activities constitute a unitary business, a state must then apply a formula apportioning the income of that business within and without the state. Such an apportionment formula must, under both the Due Process and Commerce Clauses, be fair. See *Hans Rees' Sons v. North Carolina*, 283 U.S. 123 (1931). The first [component] of fairness in an apportionment formula is what might be called internal consistency—that is, the formula must be such that, if applied by every jurisdiction, it would result in no more than all of the unitary business's income being taxed. The second and more difficult requirement is what might be called external consistency—the factor or factors used in the apportionment formula must actually reflect a reasonable sense of how income is generated. The Constitution does not 'invalidat[e] an apportionment formula whenever it *may* result in taxation of some income that did not have its source in the taxing [State].' Nevertheless, we will strike down the application of an apportionment formula if the taxpayer can prove by clear and cogent evidence that the income attributed to the State is in fact out of all appropriate proportion to the business transacted in that State, or has led to a grossly distorted result.

"California and the other States that have adopted the Uniform [Division of Income for Tax Purposes] Act use a formula—commonly called the 'three-factor' formula—which is based, in equal parts, on the proportion of a unitary business's total payroll, property, and sales which are located in the taxing State. We approved the three-factor formula in *Butler Bros. v. McColgan*, 315 U.S. 501 (1942) [and] it has become [a] benchmark against which other apportionment formulas are judged. * * *

"Appellant challenges the application of California's three-factor formula to its business on two related grounds, both arising as a practical (although not a theoretical) matter out of the international character of the enterprise. First, appellant argues that its foreign subsidiaries are significantly more profitable than it is, and that the three-factor formula, by ignoring that fact and relying instead on indirect measures of income such as payroll, property, and sales, systematically distorts the true allocation of income between appellant and the subsidiaries. The problem with this argument is obvious: the profit figures relied on by appellant are based on precisely the sort of formal geographical accounting whose basic theoretical weaknesses justify resort to formula apportionment in the first place. [W]henever a unitary business exists, 'separate [geographical] accounting, while it purports to isolate portions of income received in various States, may fail to account for contributions to income resulting from functional integration, centralization of management, and economies of scale. Because these factors of profitability arise from the operation of the business as a whole, it becomes misleading to characterize the income of the business as having a single identifiable 'source.' * * *

"Appellant's second argument [is that the payroll factor in the formula inflated the income attributed to United States operations because of the lower wages and hence lower production costs in the foreign countries.] The problem with all this evidence, however, is that it does not by itself come close to impeaching the basic rationale behind the three-factor formula. Appellant and its foreign subsidiaries have been determined to be a unitary business. It therefore may well be that in addition to the foreign payroll going into the production of any given corrugated container by a foreign subsidiary, there is also California payroll, as well as other California factors, contributing—albeit more indirectly—to the same production. The mere fact that this possibility is not reflected in appellant's accounting does not disturb the underlying premises of the formula apportionment method.

"Both geographical accounting and formula apportionment are imperfect proxies for an ideal which is not only difficult to achieve in practice, but also difficult to describe in theory. Some methods of formula apportionment are particularly problematic because they focus on only a small part of the spectrum of activities by which value is generated. [In] *Hans Rees' Sons,* for example, an apportionment method based entirely on ownership of tangible property resulted in an attribution to North Carolina of between 66 and 85% of the taxpayer's income over the course of a number of years, while a separate accounting analysis purposely skewed to resolve all doubts in favor of the State resulted in an attribution of no more than 21.7%. We struck down the application of the one-factor formula to that particular business, holding that the method, 'albeit fair on its face, operates so as to reach profits which are in no just sense attributable to transactions within its jurisdiction.'[35]

"The three-factor formula used by California has gained wide approval precisely because payroll, property, and sales appear in combination to reflect a very large share of the activities by which value is generated. It is therefore able to avoid the sorts of distortions that were present in *Hans Rees' Sons.*

"Of course, even the three-factor formula is necessarily imperfect. But we have seen no evidence demonstrating that the margin of error (systematic or not) inherent in the three-factor formula is greater than the

---

[35] Compare *Moorman Mfg. Co. v. Bair*, 437 U.S. 267 (1978) (upholding single factor (sales) apportionment formula).

margin of error (systematic or not) inherent in the sort of separate accounting urged upon us by appellant."

NOTES AND QUESTIONS

1.   *Nexus.* (a) *Unrelated business activity.* ASARCO v. IDAHO STATE TAX COMM'N, 458 U.S. 307 (1982), per POWELL, J., ruled that ASARCO—which engaged in mining, smelting, refining, and selling of non-ferrous metals—could exclude from its apportioned net income, for Idaho's income tax, dividends from partially-owned foreign subsidiaries engaged in similar business abroad over which ASARCO exercised no voting control and for which it made no operational or management decisions: "We cannot accept, consistent with recognized due process standards, a definition of 'unitary business' that would permit nondomiciliary States to apportion and tax dividends '[w]here the business activities of the dividend payor have nothing to do with the activities of the recipient in the taxing State.'

"[In] this case, it is plain that the five dividend-paying subsidiaries 'add to the riches' of ASARCO. But it is also true that they are 'discrete business enterprises' that—in 'any business or economic sense'—have 'nothing to do with the activities' of ASARCO in Idaho. Therefore there is no 'rational relationship between the [ASARCO dividend] income attributed to the State and the intrastate values of the enterprise.' "

See also *MeadWestvaco Corp. v. Illinois Dep't of Rev.*, 553 U.S. 16 (2008) (holding that a state may not impose an apportioned tax on the out-of-state income of an out-of-state subsidiary of a domestic corporation if the businesses are not "unitary"; it did not suffice that the out-of-state subsidiary served an "operational function" in the business of the in-state corporation).

(b)   *Commerce and Due Process Clauses.* In *ASARCO* as in a number of other cases, the Court did not carefully distinguish the "nexus" inquiries mandated by the Commerce and Due Process Clauses. Compare QUILL CORP. v. NORTH DAKOTA, 504 U.S. 298 (1992), which invalidated North Dakota's requirement that out-of-state mail order sellers collect North Dakota's use tax from North Dakota mail order buyers. Although North Dakota had the "minimum contacts" necessary for jurisdiction to tax under the Due Process Clause, the Court, per STEVENS, J., ruled the tax invalid under the Commerce Clause: "[T]he nexus requirements of the Due Process and Commerce Clauses are not identical. [The] 'substantial-nexus' requirement is not, like due process' 'minimum-contacts' requirement, a proxy for notice, but rather a means for limiting state burdens on interstate commerce. [A] corporation may have the 'minimum contacts' with a taxing State as required by the Due Process Clause, and yet lack the 'substantial nexus' with that State as required by the Commerce Clause."[36]

---

[36] Scalia, J., joined by Kennedy and Thomas, JJ., concurred in the due process ruling but withheld judgment on the majority's Commerce Clause reasoning. White, J., accepted the due process ruling but dissented from the Commerce Clause ruling.

The *ASARCO* dissent also recognized that the Court may sometimes choose between ruling under the Due Process and Commerce Clauses and identified an implication of that choice: "Unlike a Commerce Clause ruling, which is susceptible to repair by Congress, today's due process decision may be beyond the power of Congress to correct." *Quill* may have distinguished the clauses in response to this insight. While striking down the North Dakota tax, the Court noted: "[T]he underlying issue is not only one that Congress may be better qualified to resolve, but also one that Congress has the ultimate power to resolve."

2. ***Fair apportionment: internal and external consistency.*** According to OKLAHOMA STATE TAX COMM'N v. JEFFERSON LINES, INC., 514 U.S. 175 (1995), the *internal* consistency requirement is met "when the imposition of a tax identical to the one in question by every other State would add no burden to interstate commerce that intrastate commerce would not also bear.[37] [*External*] consistency, on the other hand, looks not to the logical consequences of cloning [of the state tax in other states], but to the economic justification for the State's claim upon the value taxed, to discover whether a State's tax reaches beyond that portion of value that is fairly attributable to economic activity within the taxing State." On its facts, the case upheld a state tax on the sale of bus tickets, including interstate bus tickets, that was not apportioned to miles traveled within the state—even though a tax levied by the same state on the gross receipts of an interstate bus company would admittedly have had to apply an apportionment formula. Should this difference in form make a difference as to result? Is it consistent with the anti-formalist aspirations of *Complete Auto*?

3. ***Review of taxes compared with regulations.*** (a) Consider Tribe 3d ed., at 1140: "The fair apportionment requirements are [analogous] to the prohibition on extraterritorial regulation discussed in [Sec. 2, IV supra]. By preventing states from effectively imposing their regulations on persons or transactions in other states, the prohibition on extraterritorial regulation prevents states from regulating more than their fair 'share' of national activity."

(b) Compare Choper & Yin, supra: "[T]he theoretical underpinnings of the test announced in *Complete Auto* [can] be seen as securing two precepts that further the dormant Commerce Clause's core prohibition of discrimination against interstate commerce: avoidance of (a) multiple taxation on interstate commerce and (b) direct commercial advantage of local businesses at the expense of multistate enterprises. This principle—that 'the Commerce Clause prohibits taxes that bear more heavily on the interstate than the intrastate enterprise merely because the former does business across state lines'— articulated a specially directed, yet expansive conception of nondiscrimination, one that seemingly differs somewhat in both purpose and effect from that

---

[37] For an application, see *American Trucking Ass'ns v. Scheiner*, 483 U.S. 266, 274 (1987), invalidating a state tax of $36 per vehicle axle per year for the privilege of using the state's highways, on the ground that if all states imposed similar taxes, interstate commerce would be disadvantaged relative to intrastate commerce.

concerning judicial review of state *regulation* of interstate commerce. Thus, when a state rule 'regulates evenhandedly to effectuate a legitimate local public interest,' it may still be rejected by the Court if 'the burden imposed on commerce is clearly excessive in relation to the local benefits,' even though neither its purpose nor effect is to treat interstate business any more onerously than local enterprises. This is not the Court's focus, however, when it reviews state taxes. Even though a particular state's system or rates of taxation may impose exceedingly heavy burdens on business enterprises, thus significantly deterring entry of interstate commerce, the decisions show that the Court will not ordinarily invalidate the tax as long as in-state businesses are subject to the same financial disadvantage.

"The bar of discrimination against interstate commerce contributes important clarification of the concept of 'multiple taxation.' The mere fact that a taxpayer is subjected to a number of different taxes does not violate the prohibition against multiple taxation if those taxes are imposed on unrelated activities, such as a sales tax, a property tax, an income tax, and a gasoline tax. On the other hand, if two states both imposed their respective income taxes on all the earnings of a taxpayer who produced income in both states, that taxpayer *would* be subjected to multiple taxation. A business earning $50,000 all in one state would pay income tax to one state on that amount, but a multistate enterprise earning $50,000, half in one state and half in another, would pay income tax on the full amount twice. The obvious effect is discrimination against interstate commerce."[38]

(c)   Besides being subject to scrutiny under the Commerce Clause, the Due Process Clause, and the Import-Export Clause, state taxes on ships and shipping can trigger constitutional scrutiny under Article I, § 10, cl. 3, which forbids a "State . . . without the consent of Congress, [to] lay any Duty of Tonnage." See *Polar Tankers, Inc. v. Valdez*, 129 S.Ct. 2277 (2009) (invalidating an Alaska port city's personal property tax on boats and vessels, which in effect applied almost exclusively to large oil tankers, under the Tonnage Clause).

---

[38]   For additional commentary on state taxation under the dormant Commerce Clause, see Samantha K. Graff, *State Taxation of Online Tobacco Sales: Circumventing the Archaic Bright Line Penned by Quill*, 58 Fla.L.Rev. 375 (2006); Walter Hellerstein et al., *Commerce Clause Restraints on State Taxation After* Jefferson Lines, 51 Tax L.Rev. 47 (1995); Daniel A. Shaviro, *An Economic and Political Look at Federalism in Taxation*, 90 Mich.L.Rev. 895 (1992).

CHAPTER 5

SUBSTANTIVE PROTECTION OF ECONOMIC INTERESTS

■ ■ ■

Introduction

Most of the remaining chapters concern constitutional limits on government power, independent of limits arising out of the horizontal and vertical distribution of powers among the branches and levels of government. Sometimes called "negative" limits, they are identical, or nearly so, whether applied to the state or federal governments, but are based on different sources. Art. I, § 9 and the Bill of Rights (comprising the first nine amendments) give rise to the major limits on the federal government, while Art. I, § 10 and the Reconstruction Amendments (i.e., the Thirteenth, Fourteenth, and Fifteenth Amendments) give rise to most of the limits on state and local government. Although outside the scope of these materials, state constitutions include additional limits on state government, some similar to federal limits, though occasionally interpreted differently, and some quite dissimilar in terms and purposes.

1. ORIGINS OF SUBSTANTIVE DUE PROCESS

A first-time reader of the Constitution might think that the Ninth Amendment and the Privileges or Immunities Clause of the Fourteenth Amendment serve as important textual grounds for rights that are not expressly enumerated in the text. However, for reasons that will be discussed at length below, historically the Due Process Clauses of the Fifth and Fourteenth Amendments have played a larger role. Yet the terms of those provisions refer only to "process," and thus appear to limit only the *procedures* by which government affects "life, liberty and property." How, then, can the Due Process Clauses be invoked to impose limits on the *substance* of governmental regulations and other activities? That these clauses embody *any* limits on the substance of legislation requires some initial explanation.

Professor Edward S. Corwin traced the origin and evolution of due process as a substantive limit on governmental power in a series of articles, later revised in his *Liberty Against Government* (1948). Although the book was concerned primarily with judicial evolution of concepts designed to limit government regulation of property and economic interests, it also provides valuable background for understanding some of the underpinnings for the later use of the Due Process Clauses and First Amendment to limit government interference with basic personal liberties.

I. EARLY EXPRESSIONS OF THE NOTION THAT GOVERNMENTAL AUTHORITY HAS IMPLIED LIMITS

An early expression of the view that there are implied or inherent limits on governmental power did not rely on the Due Process Clause of the Fifth Amendment or any other specific constitutional provision. In CALDER v. BULL, 3 Dall. (3 U.S.) 386 (1798), the Supreme Court rejected the claim of potential heirs that a Connecticut statute amounted to an ex post facto law (because the ex post facto clause only applies to criminal laws). Two Justices engaged in a notable exchange over whether it would ever be appropriate to strike down legislation without regard to explicit constitutional limitations.

CHASE, J., said yes: "I cannot subscribe to the omnipotence of a State Legislature, or that it is absolute and without control; although its authority should not be expressly restrained by the Constitution, or fundamental law of the State. The people of the United States erected their constitutions, or forms of government, to establish justice, to promote the general welfare, to secure the blessings of liberty, and to protect their persons and property from violence. The purposes for which men enter into society will determine the nature and terms of the social compact; and as they are the foundation of the legislative power, they will decide what are the proper objects of it. The nature and ends of legislative power will limit the exercise of it. This fundamental principle flows from the very nature of our free Republican governments, that no man should be compelled to do what the laws do not require; nor to refrain from acts which the laws permit. There are acts which the Federal, or State, Legislature cannot do, without exceeding their authority. There are certain vital principles in our free Republican governments, which will determine and overrule an apparent and flagrant abuse of legislative power; as to authorize manifest injustice by positive law; to take away that security for personal liberty, or private property, for the protection whereof the government was established. An ACT of the legislature (for I cannot call it a law), contrary to the great first principles of the social compact, cannot be considered a rightful exercise of legislative authority. The obligation of a law in governments established on express compact, and on republican principles, must be determined by the nature of the power on which it is founded. A few instances will suffice to explain what I mean. A law that punished a citizen for an innocent action or, in other words, for an act, which, when done, was in violation of no existing law; a law that destroys, or impairs, the lawful private contracts of citizens; a law that makes a man a Judge in his own cause; or a law that takes property from A and gives it to B: It is against all reason and justice, for a people to intrust a Legislature with SUCH powers; and therefore, it cannot be presumed that they have done it. The genius, the nature, and the spirit, of our State Governments, amount to a prohibition of such acts of legislation; and the general principles of law and reason forbid them. [To] maintain that our Federal, or State Legislature possesses such powers, if they had not been expressly restrained, would, in my opinion, be a political heresy, altogether inadmissible in our free republican governments."[1]

IREDELL, J., disagreed: "[If] a government, composed of Legislative, Executive and Judicial departments, were established, by a constitution which imposed no limits on the legislative power, the consequence would inevitably be, that whatever the legislative power chose to enact, would be lawfully enacted, and the judicial power could never interpose to pronounce it void. It is true, that some speculative jurists have held, that a legislative act against natural justice must, in itself, be void; but I cannot think that, under such a government any Court of Justice would possess a power to declare it so. [I]t has been the policy of all the American states, which have, individually, framed their state constitutions, since the revolution, and of the people of the United States, when they framed the Federal Constitution, to define with precision the objects of the legislative power, and to restrain its exercise within marked and settled boundaries. If any act of Congress, or of the Legislature of a state, violates those constitutional provisions, it is unquestionably void. [If], on the other hand, the Legislature of the Union, or the Legislature of any member of the Union, shall pass a law, within the general scope of their constitutional power, the Court cannot pronounce it to be void, merely because it is, in their judgment, contrary to the principles of natural justice. The ideas of natural justice are regulated by no fixed standard: the ablest and the purest men have differed upon the subject; and all that the Court could properly say, in such an event, would be that the Legislature (possessed of an equal right of opinion) had passed an act which, in the opinion of the judges, was inconsistent with the abstract principles of natural justice."

NOTES AND QUESTIONS

1.   *Lord Coke in Dr. Bonham's Case,* 8 Co. 113b, 118a, 77 Eng.Rep. 646, 652 (1610): "And it appears in our books, that in many cases, the common law will controul Acts of Parliament, and sometimes adjudge them to be utterly void: for when an Act of Parliament is against common right and reason, or repugnant, or impossible to be performed, the common law will controul it, and adjudge such Act to be void." For commentary on the influence of the Coke dictum, see Corwin, *Liberty Against Government* 34–40. For philosophical origins of the Chase viewpoint, see Corwin, *The "Higher Law" Background of*

---

[1]   For the view that Chase, J.'s opinion is a philosophical, not a constitutional, argument, see John H. Ely, *On Discovering Fundamental Values,* 92 Harv.L.Rev. 5 (1978).

American Constitutional Law, 42 Harv.L.Rev. 149 (1928–1929). For the extent to which similar viewpoints crept into judicial opinions and decisions between the revolution and 1830, see Corwin, *Liberty Against Government* 58–67: "The truth is that Iredell's tenet that courts were not to appeal to natural rights and the social compact as furnishing a basis for constitutional decisions was disregarded at one time or another by all of the leading judges and advocates of the initial period of our constitutional history, an era which closes about 1830."

2.   *Why not express provisions?* Look closely at Chase, J.'s examples of supposedly impermissible government actions. Can you find in the Constitution's text one or more express provisions that would forbid each? If so, why did he think it necessary to invoke general principles? *Calder* presented a challenge to a *state* law. Did the pre-Civil War Constitution contain express limits on state government covering each of Chase, J.'s examples?

In BARRON v. MAYOR AND CITY COUNCIL OF BALTIMORE, 32 U.S. (7 Pet.) 243 (1833), in the course of rejecting appellant's argument that by ruining the use of his wharf the city had violated the Fifth Amendment guarantee that private property shall not be "taken for public use, without just compensation," the Court, per MARSHALL, C.J., held that the Bill of Rights applied only to the federal government: "[The] great revolution which established the constitution of the United States was not effected without immense opposition. Serious fears were extensively entertained that [the new national powers] might be exercised in a manner dangerous to liberty. In almost every convention by which the constitution was adopted, amendments to guard against the abuse of power were recommended. These amendments demanded security against the apprehended encroachments of the general government. [They] contain no expression indicating an intention to apply them to the state governments. This court cannot so apply them."

3.   *Justice Souter calls attention to "two centuries of American constitutional practice in recognizing unenumerated, substantive limits on governmental action."* Concurring in the judgment in *Washington v. Glucksberg,* (1997) (Ch. 6, Sec. 2), which rejected the argument that there is a constitutional right to physician-assisted suicide, SOUTER, J., noted that the physicians who asserted this right "also invoke two centuries of American constitutional practice in recognizing unenumerated substantive limits on governmental action." "Although this practice has neither rested on any single textual basis nor expressed a consistent theory, [the] persistence of substantive due process in our cases points to the legitimacy of the modern justification for such judicial review.

"[Before] the ratification of the Fourteenth Amendment, substantive constitutional review resting on a theory of unenumerated rights occurred largely in the state courts applying state constitutions that commonly contained either due process clauses like that of the Fifth Amendment (and later the Fourteenth) or the textual antecedents of such clauses, repeating Magna Carta's guarantee of 'the law of the land.' On the basis of such clauses, or of general principles untethered to specific constitutional language, state courts evaluated the constitutionality of a wide range of statutes.

"Even in this early period, however, this Court anticipated the developments that would presage both the Civil War and the ratification of the Fourteenth Amendment, by making it clear on several occasions that it too had no doubt of the judiciary's power to strike down legislation that conflicted with important but unenumerated principles of American government. [In] FLETCHER v. PECK, 6 Cranch 87 (1810), [the Court] struck down an Act of the Georgia Legislature that purported to rescind a sale of public land ab initio and reclaim title for the State, and so deprive subsequent, good-faith purchasers of property conveyed by the original grantees. The Court rested the invalidation on alternative sources of authority: the specific prohibitions against bill of attainder, ex post facto laws, laws impairing contracts in Article 1, § 10, of the Constitution; and 'general principles which are common to our free institutions,' by which Chief Justice Marshall meant that a simple deprivation of property by the State could not be an authentically 'legislative' Act.

"*Fletcher* was not, though, the most telling early example of such review. For its most salient instance in the Court before the adoption of the Fourteenth Amendment was, of course, the case that the Amendment would in due course overturn, DRED SCOTT v. SANDFORD, 19 How. 393 (1857). Unlike *Fletcher*, *Dred Scott* was textually based on a due process clause (in the Fifth Amendment, applicable to the National Government), and it was in reliance on that Clauses's protection of property that the Court invalidated the Missouri Compromise. This substantive protection of an owner's property in a slave taken to the territories was traced to the absence of any enumerated power to affect that property granted to the Congress by Article 1 of the Constitution, the implication being that the Government had no legitimate interest that could support the earlier congressional compromise. The ensuing judgment of history needs no recounting here."

II. THE SEARCH FOR A CONSTITUTIONAL BASIS

The philosophical grounds asserted in the early cases for protecting economic (and other) interests from legislative power could not long prevail in the face of the growing acceptance of the federal and state constitutions as the only sources of judicially enforceable limitations on legislative power. See Corwin, *Liberty Against Government* 173: "[T]he *doctrine of vested rights* [erected] as the primary test of legislation its effect on existing property rights. [It] attained its meridian in the early thirties, when it came under attack from two sources. The first [was] the notion that the written constitution, being an expression of popular will, was the supreme law of the State and that judicial review could validly operate only on that basis; the second was the related idea, which is connoted by the term 'police power'—that legislation which was not specifically forbidden by the written constitution must be presumed to have been enacted in the *public interest*.

Confronted with these doctrines, the champions of the doctrine of vested rights were compelled to find some clause of the written constitution which could be thrown about the doctrine or else to abandon it."

Before the adoption of the Fourteenth Amendment in 1868, the federal constitution provided little basis for challenging state regulation of economic interests. Moreover, the Court narrowed the scope of the constitutional provision (Act 1, § 10) prohibiting the states from passing any laws "impairing the obligation of contracts." In *Proprietors of Charles River Bridge v. Proprietors of Warren Bridge,* 36 U.S. (11 Pet.) 420 (1837), the Court rejected the claim that the state grant of a right to operate a toll bridge implied an obligation not to authorize a nearby competing bridge.[2] Indeed, the decision seemed designed to discourage resort to the federal constitution to escape regulation of economic interests: "It is well settled by the decisions of this court, that a state law may be retrospective in its character, and may divest vested rights; and yet not violate the constitution of the United States, unless it also impairs the obligation of a contract." *Id.* at 421. "Thus it *became more and more evident that the doctrine of vested rights must, to survive, find anchorage in some clause or other of the various State constitutions."* Corwin 89.

With federal constitutional grounds not available to protect against most encroachments on economic interests, state judges resorted to the "due process" and "law of the land" clauses of state constitutions. Consider Corwin, *Liberty Against Government* 90–91: "The 'law of the land' clause of the early State constitutions was usually a nearly literal translation of the famous chapter 29 of the Magna Carta of 1225. [The] phrase 'due process of law' comes from chapter 3 of the statute of 28 Edward III (1355) which [reads]: 'No man of what state or condition he be, shall be put out of his lands or tenements, nor taken, nor imprisoned, nor disinherited, nor put to death, without he be brought to answer by due process of law.' "

The state courts began to find in these clauses a substantive limitation on legislative power, aimed first at special legislation designed to affect the rights of specific individuals, and then applied to general legislation interfering with vested rights. See Corwin, *Liberty Against Government* 89–115, 173–74: "Again the ingenuity of Bench and Bar were equal to the exigency. Most State constitutions contained from the outset a paraphrase of chapter 29 of Magna Carta, which declared that no person should be deprived of his 'estate' 'except by the law of the land or a judgment of his peers'; and following the usage of the Fifth Amendment of the United States Constitution, more and more State constitutions came after 1791 to contain a clause which, paraphrasing a statute of Plantagenet times,

---

[2]   *See also West River Bridge Co. v. Dix,* 47 U.S. (6 How.) 507 (1848) (state grant of exclusive right to operate toll bridge does not bar state from acquiring it by eminent domain); *Stone v. Mississippi,* 101 U.S. (11 Otto) 814, 25 L.Ed. 1079 (1880) (vital public interest permits state to ban lottery business three years after it granted 25-year charter).

declared that 'no person shall be deprived of life, liberty or property without due process of law.' By the outbreak of the Civil War a more or less complete transference of the doctrine of vested rights [had] been effected in the vast majority of the State jurisdictions."

III. FOURTEENTH AMENDMENT

Historical background. The history of the Civil War Amendments, particularly the Fourteenth, is thoroughly treated elsewhere. See, e.g., Charles Fairman, *Does the Fourteenth Amendment Incorporate the Bill of Rights? The Original Understanding,* 2 Stan.L.Rev. 5 (1949); Alexander M. Bickel, *The Original Understanding and the Segregation Decision,* 69 Harv.L.Rev. 1 (1955); John P. Frank & Robert F. Munro, *The Original Understanding of "Equal Protection of the Laws"* 1972 Wash.U.L.Q. 421 (citing other historical studies).

The Thirteenth Amendment forbidding slavery and involuntary servitude was ratified in 1865, but freeing the slaves did not produce the fruits of freedom, due to "Black Codes" and other repressive measures adopted in the states of the former Confederacy. The plight of African Americans and their need at the time was reflected in the Civil Rights Act of 1866, which recognized "all persons born in United States" as United States citizens, and gave to "such citizens, of every race or color, without regard to any previous condition of slavery [the] same right, in every State and Territory in the United States, to make and enforce contracts, to sue, be parties, and give evidence, to inherit, purchase, lease, sell, hold, and convey real and personal property, and to full and equal benefit of all laws and proceedings for the security of person and property, as is enjoyed by white citizens."

Even while that 1866 Civil Rights Act was awaiting enactment, action was under way designed, in part at least, to remove existing doubts as to the power of Congress to enact such legislation. One week after the Senate passed the Civil Rights Act, the Congressional Joint Committee on Reconstruction submitted to both houses of Congress its early version of a Fourteenth Amendment authorizing Congress to enact laws to protect equal rights. After Congress passed the Civil Rights Act in April over a presidential veto based in part on the view that Congress lacked power to enact the law, the Joint Commission on Reconstruction hammered out a revised proposal that added privileges and immunities, due process, and equal protection provisions as limitations on the states, and authorized Congress to enact legislation to "enforce this article." After further modifications, Congress approved the Fourteenth Amendment in June, 1866 and sent it to the states for ratification.

————

Laurence H. Tribe, *American Constitutional Law* 1299–1302 (3d ed. 2000): "A natural reading of [the Fourteenth Amendment's] Privileges or Immunities Clause ['No State shall make or enforce any law which shall abridge the privileges or immunities of citizens of the United States'] would appear to suggest essentially unqualified federal constitutional protection for at least some personal rights. [There] is no evidence that those who framed [the clause] sought a goal narrower than that suggested by the language they chose. On the contrary, the Privileges or Immunities Clause, it appears from various floor statements by the amendment's drafters and sponsors, was intended essentially to overrule *Barron v. Baltimore* and to secure basic civil rights—most significantly, those enumerated in the federal Bill of Rights—against state as well as federal governments.[3] [But] within a matter of years of the Fourteenth Amendment's adoption, the Supreme Court would squelch its framers' quite unmistakable intentions while twisting the evident import of the text itself and all but remove the Privileges or Immunities Clause from the landscape of American constitutional law."

SLAUGHTER-HOUSE CASES, 16 Wall. (83 U.S.) 36 (1873), per MILLER, J., upheld a Louisiana law granting a monopoly to operate slaughterhouses in the New Orleans area, regarding this an "appropriate," "stringent, and effectual" means to "remove from the more densely populated part of the city, the noxious slaughter-houses and large and offensive collections of animals." Excluded butchers claimed that the law violated their right "to exercise their trade" and invoked the 13th and 14th Amendments: "This court is thus called upon for the first time to give construction to [these Amendments].

"[The Civil War] being over, those who had succeeded in re-establishing the authority of the Federal government were not content to permit [the] great act of emancipation to rest on the actual results of the contest or the proclamation of the Executive, both of which might have been questioned in after times, and they determined to place this main and most valuable result in the Constitution of the restored Union as one of its fundamental articles. Hence the [13th Amendment]. To withdraw the mind from the contemplation of this grand yet simple declaration of the personal freedom of all the human race within the jurisdiction of this government [and] with a microscopic search endeavor to find in it a reference to servitudes, which may have been attached to property in certain localities, requires an effort, to say the least of it.

---

[3]   Professor Tribe recognizes that Charles Fairman, *Does the Fourteenth Amendment Incorporate the Bill of Rights?*, 2 Stan.L.Rev. 5 (1949), takes a different view of the circumstances surrounding the adoption of the Fourteenth Amendment, but maintains that although Professor Fairman's view "was long accepted as authoritative, more recent scholarship, [cited throughout Tribe's discussion of the subject] has powerfully challenged Fairman's conclusions."

"[The] process of restoring to their proper relations with the Federal government and with the other States those which had sided with the [rebellion] developed the fact that, notwithstanding the formal recognition by those States of the abolition of slavery, the condition of the slave race would, without further protection of the Federal government, be almost as bad as it was before. Among the first acts of legislation adopted by several of the States [were] laws which imposed upon the colored race onerous disabilities and burdens, and curtailed their rights [to] such an extent that their freedom was of little value. [These] circumstances [forced] upon the statesmen who had conducted the Federal government in safety through [the war], and who supposed that by [the 13th Amendment] they had secured the result of their labors, the conviction that something more was necessary in the way of constitutional protection to the unfortunate race who had suffered so much. They accordingly [proposed the 14th Amendment]. A few years' experience satisfied [those] who had been the authors of the other two amendments that [these] were inadequate for the protection of life, liberty, and property, without which freedom to the slave was no boon. [It] was urged that a race of men distinctively marked as was the negro, living in the midst of another and dominant race, could never be fully secured in their person and their property without the right of suffrage. Hence [the 15th Amendment].

"[In] the light of this recapitulation of events, almost too recent to be called history, [and] on the most casual examination of the language of these amendments, no one can fail to be impressed with the one pervading purpose found in them all, [and] without which none of them would have been even suggested; we mean the freedom of the slave race [and] the protection of the newly-made freeman and citizen from the oppressions of those who had formerly exercised unlimited dominion over him. It is true that only the fifteenth amendment, in terms, mentions the negro, [but] it is just as true that each of the other articles was addressed to the grievances of that race, and designed to remedy them as the fifteenth. We do not say that no one else but the negro can share in this protection. [But] what we do say [is] that in any fair and just construction of any section or phrase of these amendments, it is necessary to look to the purpose which [was] the pervading spirit of them all, the evil which they were designed to remedy.

"[The] first section of the [14th Amendment], to which our attention is more specially invited, opens with a definition of citizenship—not only citizenship of the United States, but citizenship of the States. * * * 'All persons born or naturalized in the United States, and subject to the jurisdiction thereof, are citizens of the United States and of the State wherein they reside.' [The section] overturns the *Dred Scott* decision by making *all persons* born within the United States [citizens] of the United States. [The] next observation is more important in view of the arguments of counsel in the present case. [T]he distinction between citizenship of the United States and citizenship of a State is clearly recognized and established. Not only may a man be a citizen of the United States without being a citizen of a State, but an important element is necessary to convert the former into the latter. He must reside within the State to make him a citizen of it, but it is only necessary that he should be born or naturalized in the United States to be a citizen of the Union.

"[We] think [the distinction between citizenship of the United States and citizenship of a State] of great weight in this argument, because the next paragraph of this same section, which is the one mainly relied on by plaintiffs in error, speaks only of privileges and immunities of citizens of the United States, and does not speak of those of citizens of the several States. The argument, however, in favor of the plaintiffs rests wholly on the assumption that the citizenship is the same, and the privileges and immunities guaranteed by the clause are the same. The language is, 'No state shall make or enforce any law which shall abridge the privileges or immunities of citizens of *the United States*.' It is a little remarkable, if this clause was intended as a protection to the citizen of a State against the legislative power of his own State, that the word citizen of the State should be left out when it is so carefully used, and used in contradistinction to citizens of the United States, in the very sentence which precedes it. It is too clear for argument that the change in phraseology was adopted understandingly and with a purpose.

"Of the privileges and immunities of the citizen of the United States, and of the privileges and immunities of the citizen of the State, and what they respectively are, we will presently consider; but we wish to state here that it is only the former which are placed by this clause under the protection of the federal Constitution, and that the latter, whatever they may be, are not intended to have any additional protection by this paragraph of the amendment.

"The first occurrence of the words 'privileges and immunities' in our constitutional history, is to be found in [the] articles of the old Confederation. [Art. IV, § 2 of the Constitution states:] 'The citizens of each State shall be entitled to all the privileges and immunities of citizens of the several States.'⁴ [It] did not create those rights, which it called privileges and immunities of citizens of the States. It threw around them in that

---

⁴   As pointed out in Tribe 3d ed., at 1306, "Justice Miller's state-citizenship construction of Article IV, § 2 [rested] entirely upon a *mis*quotation of [that section], inserting the made-up phrase 'privileges and immunities of citizens *of* the several States' in place of the Constitution's *actual text*—'Privileges and Immunities of Citizens *in* the several States.' Whereas the actual language thus spoke of citizens generally and was thought, at least by John Bingham [the Congressman who framed the Privileges or Immunities Clause of the Fourteenth Amendment], to denote citizens of the United States, Justice Miller's paraphrase undoubtedly suggests that the rights protected by the clause are those belonging to citizens of *states as such*, by virtue of *state law*. Although Justice Bradley, writing in dissent, explicitly noted Justice Miller's elementary mistake, the misquotation remained in the published opinion."

clause no security for the citizen of the State in which they were claimed or exercised. Nor did it profess to control the power of the State governments over the rights of its own citizens. Its sole purpose was to declare to the several States, that whatever those rights, as you grant or establish them to your own citizens, or as you limit or qualify [them], the same, neither more nor less, shall be the measure of the rights of citizens of other States within your jurisdiction.

"[Up] to the adoption of the recent amendments, no claim or pretense was set up that those rights depended on the Federal government for their existence or protection, beyond the very few express limitations which the Federal Constitution imposed upon the States—such, for instance, as the prohibition against ex post facto laws, bills of attainder, and laws impairing the obligation of contracts. But with the exception of these and a few other restrictions, the entire domain of the privileges and immunities of citizens of the States [lay] within the constitutional and legislative power of the States, and without that of the Federal government. Was it the purpose of the fourteenth amendment, by the simple declaration that no State should make or enforce any law which shall abridge the privileges and immunities of *citizens of the United States,* to transfer the security and protection of all the civil rights [from] the States to the Federal government? And where it is declared that Congress shall have the power to enforce that article, was it intended to bring within the power of Congress the entire domain of civil rights heretofore belonging exclusively to the States?

"[Such] a construction [would] constitute this court a perpetual censor upon all legislation of the States, on the civil rights of their own citizens, with authority to nullify such as it did not approve as consistent with those rights, as they existed at the time of the adoption of this amendment. [Such a construction] radically changes the whole theory of the relations of the State and Federal governments to each other and of both these governments to the people. [We] are convinced that no such results were intended by the Congress which proposed these amendments, nor by the legislatures of the States which ratified them.

"[The] argument has not been much pressed in these cases that the defendant's charter deprives the plaintiffs of their property without due process of law, or that it denies to them the equal protection of the law. The first of these paragraphs has been in the Constitution since the adoption of the Fifth Amendment, as a restraint upon the Federal power. It is also to be found in some form of expression in the constitutions of nearly all the States, as a restraint upon the power of the States. [U]nder no construction of that provision that we have ever seen, or any that we deem admissible, can the restraint imposed [by] Louisiana upon the exercise of their trade by the butchers of New Orleans be held to be a deprivation of property within the meaning of that provision.

"[In] the light of the history of these amendments, and the pervading purpose of them, [it] is not difficult to give a meaning to [the equal protection] clause. [Laws discriminating against] the newly emancipated negroes [were] the evil to be remedied by this clause, and by it such laws are forbidden. [We] doubt very much whether any action of a State not directed by way of discrimination against the negroes as a class, or on account of their race, will ever be held to come within the purview of this provision. It is so clearly a provision for that race and that emergency, that a strong case would be necessary for its application to any other. [Unquestionably the recent war] added largely to the number of those who believe in the necessity of a strong National government. But, however pervading this sentiment, and however it may have contributed to the adoption of the amendments we have been considering, we do not see in those amendments any purpose to destroy the main features of the general system."

FIELD, J., joined by Chase, C.J., and Swayne and Bradley, JJ., dissented: "[The] question presented [is] whether the recent [amendments] protect the citizens of the United States against the deprivation of their common rights by State legislation. In my judgment, the fourteenth amendment does afford such [protection]. The amendment does not attempt to confer any new privileges or immunities upon citizens, or to enumerate or define those already existing. It assumes that there are such privileges and immunities which belong of right to citizens as such, and ordains that they shall not be abridged by State legislation. If this inhibition [only] refers, as held by the [majority], [to] such privileges and immunities as were before its adoption specially designated in the Constitution or necessarily implied as belonging to citizens of the United States, it was a vain and idle enactment, which accomplished nothing, and most unnecessarily excited Congress and the people on its passage. With privileges and immunities thus designated or implied no State could ever have interfered by its laws, and no new constitutional provision was required to inhibit such interference. [But] if the amendment refers to the natural and inalienable rights which belong to all citizens, the inhibition has a profound significance and consequence.

"[The] terms, privileges and immunities, are not new in the amendment; they were in the Constitution before the amendment was adopted. They are found in [Art. IV, § 2.] In *Corfield v. Coryell*, Mr. Justice Washington said he had 'no hesitation in confining these expressions to those privileges and immunities which were, in their nature, fundamental; which belong of right to the citizens of all free governments.' [Field, J., continued with the *Corfield* quotation, note 1, p. 345 supra.] This appears to me to be a sound construction of the clause in question. [Clearly] among [these rights] must be placed the right to pursue a lawful employment in a lawful manner, without other restraint than such as equally affects all persons. In the discussions in Congress upon the passage of the Civil Rights Act repeated reference was made to this language of Mr. Justice Washington. It was cited by Senator Trumbull with the observation that it enumerated the very rights belonging to a citizen of the United States set forth in the first section of the act.

"[The] privileges and immunities designated in [Art. IV, § 2] are, then, according to the decision cited, those which of right belong to the citizens of all free governments. [What] the clause in question did for the protection of the citizens of one State against hostile and discriminating legislation of other States, the fourteenth amendment does for the protection of every citizen of the United States against hostile and discriminating legislation against him in favor of others, whether they reside in the same or in different [States].

"This equality of right, with exemption from all disparaging and partial enactments, in the lawful pursuits of life, throughout the whole country, is the distinguishing privilege of citizens of the United States. To them, everywhere, all pursuits, all professions, all avocations are open without other restrictions than such as are imposed equally upon all others of the same age, sex, and condition. The State may prescribe such regulations for every pursuit and calling of life as will promote the public health, secure the good order and advance the general prosperity of society, but when once prescribed, the pursuit or calling must be free to be followed by every citizen who is within the conditions designated, and will conform to the regulations. This is the fundamental idea upon which our institutions rest, and unless adhered to in the legislation of the country our government will be a republic only in name. The fourteenth amendment, in my judgment, makes it essential to the validity of the legislation of every State that this equality of right should be respected."

BRADLEY, J., also dissented: "[In] my judgment, it was the intention of the people of this country in adopting [the 14th] amendment to provide National security against violation by the States of the fundamental rights of the citizen. [A] law which prohibits a large class of citizens from adopting a lawful employment, or from following a lawful employment previously adopted, does deprive them of liberty as well as property, without due process of law. [Such] a law also deprives those citizens of the equal protection of the laws. [It] is futile to argue that none but persons of the African race are intended to be benefitted by this amendment. They may have been the primary cause of the amendment, but its language is general, embracing all citizens, and I think it was purposely so expressed. The mischief to be remedied was not merely slavery and its incidents and consequences; but that spirit of insubordination and disloyalty to the National government which had troubled the country for so many years in some of the States, and that intolerance of free speech and free discussion which often rendered life and property insecure, and led to much unequal legislation.

"[But] great fears are expressed that this construction of the amendment will lead to enactments by Congress interfering with the internal affairs of the States. [In] my judgment no such practical inconveniences would arise. Very little, if any, legislation on the part of Congress would be required to carry the amendment into effect. Like the prohibition against passing a law impairing the obligation of a contract, it would execute itself. [Even] if the business of the National courts should be increased, Congress could easily supply the remedy by increasing their number and efficiency. The great question is: What is the true construction of the amendment? [The] argument from inconvenience ought not to have a very controlling influence in questions of this sort. The National will and National interest are of far greater importance."

NOTES AND QUESTIONS

1. *Objectives of privileges and immunities and citizenship provisions.* An historical study protests that the *Slaughter-House* opinion flies in the face of the congressional purpose for inserting the citizenship sentence. Howard J. Graham, *Our "Declaratory" Fourteenth Amendment,* 7 Stan.L.Rev. 3 (1954). "[O]pponents of slavery had regarded all important 'natural' and constitutional rights as being privileges and immunities of *citizens of the United States.* This had been the cardinal premise of antislavery theory from the beginning, and this had been the underlying theory and purpose of Section One from the beginning. The real purpose of adding this citizenship definition was to remove any possible or lingering doubt about the freedman's citizenship."

2. *Resulting scope of privileges and immunities.* Professor McGovney paraphrased the clause as interpreted: "No State shall make or enforce any law which shall abridge any privilege or immunity conferred *by this Constitution, the statutes or treaties of the United States* upon any person who is a citizen of the United States." He then commented, "This narrower construction [renders] it an idle provision, in that it only declares a principle already more amply and more simply expressed in the constitution." Dudley O. McGovney, *Privileges or Immunities Clause, Fourteenth Amendment,* 4 Iowa Law Bull. (now Iowa L.Rev.) 219 (1918).

3. *The heavy blow Slaughter-House struck the Privileges or Immunities Clause—And the switch to the Due Process Clause.* As pointed out in Tribe 3d ed., at 1316, "[w]ith the Court's announcement of its exceedingly narrow interpretation of the Privileges or Immunities Clause—essentially denying the provision any significant content—responsibility for naturalizing civil rights shifted to the Due Process Clause: 'By strangling the privileges or immunities clause in its crib, *Slaughter-House* forced [litigants] to argue that the original Bill [of Rights] applied against the states either directly of its own force, or via the Fourteenth Amendment's due process

clause.'[5] And despite the semantic difficulties that the process-based language of that provision poses for incorporation of the substantive guarantees of the Bill of Rights, the Supreme Court, beginning in the late nineteenth century, has indeed interpreted the Due Process Clause expansively, so that it essentially performs many of the functions for which the Privileges or Immunities Clause was designed."

4. ***Revival of the Privileges or Immunities Clause in the Supreme Court?*** As Professor Tribe points out at 1312–14, until 1999, the Privileges or Immunities Clause "had been the basis of a majority opinion of the Supreme Court only once, [in] *Colgate v. Harvey*, 296 U.S. 404 (1935) [invalidating a state tax against residents exclusively upon dividends and interest earned outside the state]." However, in *Saenz v. Roe*, Ch. 9, Sec. 5, II, a case Tribe calls a "seminal 1999 decision," "a Court majority for the first time protected the right to travel as a privilege or immunity of United States citizenship, treating that right as encompassing the right to enter and leave another state; the right to be treated as a welcome visitor while there [and] the right, upon electing to become a permanent resident of another state, to be treated no less well than residents who have lived there longer."

More recently, the clause was offered as the basis for making the right to bear arms and, by implication, other provisions of the Bill of Rights, applicable to the states, in *McDonald v. City of Chicago*, Ch. 6, Sec. 4. Although the Court ultimately rested incorporation of that right on the Due Process Clause, according to Note, 124 Harv.L.Rev. 229 (2010), in *McDonald*, "[the] Justices provided substantial evidence that they at least doubted *Slaughter-House*'s central holding. Justice Alito['s majority opinion] engaged in careful analysis of the *Slaughter-House* decision itself, which included both the reasoning of the four *Slaughter-House* dissenters and the broad consensus that the case was wrongly decided."

5. ***Would shifting from the Due Process Clause to the Privileges or Immunities Clause have practical consequences?*** During the Supreme Court oral argument in *McDonald*, SCALIA, J., asked McDonald's attorney why he was relying on the Privileges or Immunities Clause: "what you argue is the darling of the professoriate, [but] it's also contrary to 140 years of our jurisprudence. Why do you want to undertake that burden instead of just arguing substantive due process, [which], as much as I think [is] wrong, [even] I have acquiesced in?" Presumably the Supreme Court could announce that some or all of its decisions that hitherto relied upon the Due Process Clause should henceforth be understood as resting on the Privileges or Immunities Clause, but would that wholesale shift be textually sound? Note that whereas the Due Process Clause protects *persons*, the Privileges or Immunities Clause protects *citizens*. Might that difference in wording suggest a narrower scope for rights recognized under the latter?

---

[5] The internal quotation marks contain language from Akhil R. Amar, *The Bill of Rights and the Fourteenth Amendment*, 101 Yale L.J. 1193 (1992).

2. THE *LOCHNER* ERA

I. THE ROAD TO *LOCHNER*

As the foregoing materials indicate, notwithstanding the *Slaughter-House* majority's suggestion that the Fourteenth Amendment was relevant only to cases involving the equal rights of formerly enslaved African Americans and their descendants, within a relatively short time, the Court began to give the amendment a broader interpretation, especially in cases involving economic rights. The shift was presaged in *Munn v. Illinois*, 94 U.S. (4 Otto) 113 (1876). Although the Court, per WAITE, C.J., upheld a state law regulating the rates of grain elevators, pointing out that private property may be regulated when it is "affected with a public interest," the Court made a comment that was to be relied upon years later to justify judicial control of state regulation: "Undoubtedly, in mere private contracts, relating to matters in which the public has no interest, what is reasonable must be ascertained judicially." *Mugler v. Kansas*, 123 U.S. 623 (1887), upheld a state law prohibiting intoxicating beverages, but the Court, per Harlan, J., made clear that not every statute said to be enacted for the promotion of "the public morals, the public health, or the public safety" would be sustained. If a law supposedly enacted pursuant to the police powers of the state "has no real or substantial relation to these objects, or is a palpable invasion of rights secured by the fundamental law, it is the duty of the courts to so adjudge."

ALLGEYER v. LOUISIANA, 165 U.S. 578 (1897), was the first reasoned Supreme Court decision actually to hold that the substance of economic legislation violated Fourteenth Amendment Due Process. A unanimous Court, per PECKHAM, J., struck down a Louisiana law prohibiting any act in the state that directly or indirectly facilitates a contract for marine insurance on state property with a company not licensed to do business in the state. Although the opinion hinted that Louisiana might have impermissibly extended the reach of its laws beyond its territorial limits, the ruling was ultimately based on individual liberty rather than horizontal federalism. According to the Court, the statute exceeded the police power of the state and deprived the defendants of their Fourteenth Amendment liberty to contract for insurance: "The 'liberty' mentioned in that amendment means, not only the right of the citizen to be free from the mere physical restraint of his person, but [embraces] the right of the citizen to be free in the enjoyment of all his faculties, to be free to use them in all lawful ways; to live and work where he will; [to] pursue any livelihood or avocation; and for that purpose to enter into all contracts which may be proper, necessary, and essential to his carrying out to a successful conclusion the purposes above mentioned."

"Ironically," observes Tribe 3d ed., at 1311–12, "the *Slaughter-House Cases'* reaffirmation of the [separate state and federal spheres of power] helped pave the way for the substantive due process doctrine of the post-1890s era. [Miller, J.,] affirmed the duty of the Supreme Court to safeguard the autonomy of the federal and state governments within their respective spheres of power over the same geographical territory. But the Justices of the 1890–1937 era, likewise imbued with Miller's sense of the state and federal spheres and persuaded of the need to protect their sanctity, discerned yet a third sphere—that of the citizen, whose autonomy both required federal protection and could be defended without federal suffocation of the states. [The] Court thus came to perceive [that] any state action that *invaded* the liberty or property of its citizens was, by definition, *beyond* the state's sphere."

LOCHNER V. NEW YORK
198 U.S. 45, 25 S.Ct. 539, 49 L.Ed. 937 (1905).

JUSTICE PECKHAM delivered the opinion of the Court.

[The Court held invalid a New York statute forbidding employment in a bakery for more than 60 hours per week or 10 hours per day.]

The statute necessarily interferes with the right of contract between the employer and employees. [The] general right to make a contract in relation to his business is part of the liberty of the individual protected by the 14th Amendment. [*Allgeyer*.] The right to purchase or to sell labor is part of the liberty protected by this amendment, unless there are circumstances which exclude the right. There are, however, certain powers, existing in the sovereignty of each state in the Union, somewhat vaguely termed police powers, the exact description and limitation of which have not been attempted by the courts. [This court has] upheld the exercise of the police powers of the states in many cases, [among them] *Holden v. Hardy*, 169 U.S. 366 (1898), [where it] was held that the kind of employment, mining, smelting, etc., and the character of the employees in such kinds of labor, were such as to make it reasonable and proper for the State to interfere to prevent the employees from being constrained by the rules laid down by the proprietors in regard to labor. [There] is nothing in *Holden v. Hardy* which covers the case now before us.

It must, of course, be conceded that there is a limit to the valid exercise of the police power by the state. [Otherwise] the 14th Amendment would have no efficacy and the legislatures of the states would have unbounded power. [In] every case that comes before this court, therefore, where legislation of this character is concerned, and where the protection of the Federal Constitution is sought, the question necessarily arises: Is this a fair, reasonable, and appropriate exercise of the police power of the state, or is it an unreasonable, unnecessary, and arbitrary interference with the right of the individual to his personal liberty, or to enter into those contracts in relation to labor which may seem to him appropriate or necessary for the support of himself and his family? Of course the liberty of contract relating to labor includes both parties to it. The one has as much right to purchase as the other to sell labor. This is not a question of substituting the judgment of the court for that of the legislature. If the act be within the power of the state it is valid, although the judgment of the court might be totally opposed to the enactment of such a law. But the question would still remain: Is it within the police power of the State? and that question must be answered by the court.

The question whether this act is valid as a labor law, pure and simple, may be dismissed in a few words. There is no reasonable ground for interfering with the liberty of person or the right of free contract, by determining the hours of labor, in the occupation of a baker. There is no contention that bakers as a class are not equal in intelligence and capacity to men in other trades or manual occupations, or that they are not able to assert their rights and care for themselves without the protecting arm of the state. [They] are in no sense wards of the state. Viewed in the light of a purely labor law, with no reference whatever to the question of health, we think that a law like the one before us involves neither the safety, the morals, nor the welfare, of the public, and that the interest of the public is not in the slightest degree affected by such an act. The law must be upheld, if at all, as a law pertaining to the health of the individual engaged in the occupation of a baker. It does not affect any other portion of the public than those who are engaged in that occupation. Clean and wholesome bread does not depend upon whether the baker works but ten hours per day or only sixty hours a week. [There] is, in our judgment, no reasonable foundation for holding this to be necessary or appropriate as a health law to safeguard the public health, or the health of the individuals who are following the trade of a baker.

[We] think that there can be no fair doubt that the trade of a baker, in and of itself, is not an unhealthy one to that degree which would authorize the legislature to interfere with the right to labor, and with the right of free contract on the part of the individual, either as employer or employee. [Some] occupations are more healthy than others, but we think there are none which might not come under the power of the legislature to supervise and control the hours of working therein, if the mere fact that the occupation is not absolutely and perfectly healthy is to confer that right upon the legislative department of the government. [It] is unfortunately true that labor, even in any department, may possibly carry with it the seeds of unhealthiness. But are we all, on that account, at the mercy of legislative majorities? A printer, a tinsmith, a locksmith, a carpenter, a cabinet maker, a dry goods clerk, a bank's, a lawyer's, or a physician's clerk, or a clerk in almost any kind of business, would all come under the power of the legislature, on this assumption. No trade, no occupation, no mode of earning one's living, could escape this all-pervading power, and the acts of the legislature in limiting the hours of labor in all employments would be valid, although such limitation might seriously cripple the ability of the laborer to support himself and his family.

[It] is also urged [that] it is to the interest of the state that its population should be strong and robust, and therefore any legislation which may be said to tend to make people healthy must be valid as health laws, enacted under the police power. If this be a valid argument and a justification for this kind of legislation, it follows that the protection of the Federal Constitution from undue interference with liberty of person and freedom of contract is visionary, wherever the law is sought to be justified as a valid exercise of the police power. Scarcely any law but might find shelter under such assumptions. [Not] only the hours of employees, but the hours of employers, could be regulated, and doctors, lawyers, scientists, all professional men, as well as athletes and artisans, could be forbidden to fatigue their brains and bodies by prolonged hours of exercise, lest the fighting strength of the state be impaired. We mention these extreme cases because the contention is extreme. We do not believe in the soundness of the views which uphold this law. [The] act is not, within any fair meaning of the term, a health law, but is an illegal interference with the rights of individuals, both employers and employees, to make contracts regarding labor upon such terms as they may think best, or which they may agree upon with the other parties to such contracts. Statutes of the nature of that under review, limiting the hours in which grown and intelligent men may labor to earn their living, are mere meddlesome interferences with the rights of the individual, and they are not saved from condemnation by the claim that they are passed in the exercise of the police power and upon the subject of the health of the individual whose rights are interfered with, unless there be some fair ground, reasonable in and of itself, to say that there is material danger to the public health, or to the health of the employees, if the hours of labor are not curtailed.

[This] interference on the part of the legislatures of the several states with the ordinary trades and occupations of the people seems to be on the increase. [It] is impossible for us to shut our eyes to the fact that many of the laws of this character, while passed under what is claimed to be the police power for the purpose of protecting the public health or welfare, are, in reality, passed from other motives. We are justified in saying so when, from the character of the law and the subject upon which it legislates, it is apparent that the public health or welfare bears but the most remote relation to the law. * * *

JUSTICE HARLAN (with whom JUSTICE WHITE and JUSTICE DAY concurred) dissenting: * * *

I take it to be firmly established that what is called the liberty of contract may, within certain limits, be subjected to regulations designed and calculated to promote the general welfare, or to guard the public health, the public morals, or the public safety. [It] is plain that this statute was enacted in order to protect the physical well-being of those who work in bakery and confectionery establishments. [The] statute must be taken as expressing the belief of the people of New York that, as a general rule, and in the case of the average man, labor in excess of sixty hours during a week in such establishments may endanger the health of those who thus labor. Whether or not this be wise legislation it is not the province of the court to inquire. Under our systems of government the courts are not concerned with the wisdom or policy of legislation. So that in determining the question of power to interfere with liberty or contract, the court may inquire whether the means devised by the state are germane to an end which may be lawfully accomplished and have a real or substantial relation to the protection of health, as involved in the daily work of the persons, male and female, engaged in bakery and confectionery establishments. But when this inquiry is entered upon I find it impossible, in view of common experience, to say that there is here no real or substantial relation between the means employed by the state and the end sought to be accomplished by its legislation. Nor can I say that the statute has no appropriate or direct connection with that protection to health which each state owes to her citizens or that it is not promotive of the health of the employees in question or that the regulation prescribed by the state is utterly unreasonable and extravagant or wholly arbitrary. Still less can I say that the statute is, beyond question, a plain, palpable invasion of rights secured by the fundamental law.

[The dissenting opinion cited statistics on the health problems of workers, pointing out that long hours, night hours, and difficult working conditions, such as excessive heat and exposure to flour dust, were injurious to the health of bakers, who] seldom live over their fiftieth year. [We] judicially know that the question of the number of hours during which a workman should continuously labor has been, for a long period, and is yet, a subject of serious consideration among civilized peoples, and by those having special knowledge of the laws of health. [We] also judicially know that the number of hours that should constitute a day's labor in particular occupations involving the physical strength and safety of workmen has been the subject of enactments by Congress and by nearly all of the states. Many, if not most, of those enactments fix eight hours as the proper basis of a day's labor.

I do not stop to consider whether any particular view of this economic question presents the sounder theory. [It] is enough for the determination of this case [that] the question is one about which there is room for debate and for an honest difference of opinion. There are many reasons of a weighty, substantial character, based upon the experience of mankind, in support of the theory that, all things considered, more than ten hours' steady work each day, from week to week, in a bakery or confectionery establishment, may endanger the health and shorten the lives of the workmen, thereby diminishing their physical and mental capacity to serve the State and to provide for those dependent upon them.

If such reasons exist that ought to be the end of this case, for the state is not amenable to the judiciary, in respect of its legislative enactments, unless such enactments are plainly, palpably, beyond all question, inconsistent with the Constitution of the United States. * * *

JUSTICE HOLMES dissenting: * * *

This case is decided upon an economic theory which a large part of the country does not entertain. If it were a question whether I agree with that theory, I should desire to study it further and long before making up my mind. But I do not conceive that to be my duty, because I strongly believe that my agreement or disagreement has nothing to do with the right of a majority to embody their opinions in law. It is settled by various decisions of this court that state constitutions and state laws may regulate life in many ways which we as legislators might think as injudicious, or if you like as tyrannical, as this, and which, equally with this, interfere with the liberty to contract. Sunday laws and usury laws are ancient examples. A more modern one is the prohibition of lotteries. The liberty of the citizen to do as he likes so long as he does not interfere with the liberty of others to do the same, which has been a shibboleth for some well-known writers, is interfered with by school laws, by the Post Office, by every state or municipal institution which takes his money for purposes thought desirable, whether he likes it or not. The 14th Amendment does not enact Mr. Herbert Spencer's *Social Statics*. [A] Constitution is not intended to embody a particular economic theory, whether of paternalism and the organic relation of the citizen to the state or of laissez faire. It is made for people of fundamentally differing views, and the accident of our finding certain opinions natural and familiar, or novel, and even shocking, ought not to conclude our judgment upon the question whether statutes embodying them conflict with the Constitution of the United States.

General propositions do not decide concrete cases. [But] I think that the proposition just stated, if it is accepted, will carry us far toward the end. [I] think that the word "liberty," in the 14th Amendment, is perverted when it is held to prevent the natural outcome of a dominant opinion, unless it can be said that a rational and fair man necessarily would admit that the statute proposed would infringe fundamental principles as they have been understood by the traditions of our people and our law. It does not need research to show that no such sweeping condemnation can be passed upon the statute before us. * * *

NOTES AND QUESTIONS

1. ***Lochner now, and then.*** As explored below, Sec. 3, infra, robust judicial protection of the liberty of contract under the rubric of substantive due process was repudiated in the late 1930s, and since that time, no Supreme Court Justice has advocated a return to *Lochner*, even though the American political climate became more favorable towards libertarianism beginning in the 1980s. Indeed, in the modern period, citations of *Lochner* seem most likely to occur in dissenting opinions in which a Justice accuses colleagues in the majority of judicial activism. See *United States v. Lopez*, (Ch. 2, Sec. 2, IV) (Souter, J., dissenting); *Griswold v. Connecticut*, (Ch. 6, Sec. 2) (Black, J., joined by Stewart, J., dissenting). But how was *Lochner* received in its own day?

Consider Jack M. Balkin, *"Wrong the Day It Was Decided": Lochner and Constitutional Historicism*, 85 B.U.L Rev. 677 (2005): "The true outlier in *Lochner* is Justice Holmes, who does not join Harlan's dissent. Holmes rejects the premise of limited government and police power jurisprudence and offers what is essentially a parliamentary model of democracy: the legislature can do whatever it likes. [Put] in today's terms, Holmes' dissent in *Lochner* is a bit like Clarence Thomas' concurrence [in] *Lopez,* in which Thomas argued for a drastic reduction in the federal government's constitutional powers to regulate interstate commerce; his arguments, if accepted, would call into question the constitutionality of much of the modern regulating state.

"[Legal] culture has an important place for such 'off-the-wall' arguments. They are a form of prophecy. They dare others to think differently about settled questions in a constitutional regime. [W]hat makes Holmes' dissent in *Lochner* no longer 'off-the-wall,' but rather an example of constitutional orthodoxy, is not the quality of the argument at the time, but rather what happened later [on.] Holmes became plausible, indeed orthodox, not because his reasoning was flawless—for it was not—but because of the political success of the Democratic Party during the New Deal."

Does Professor Balkin's focus on legal elites overstate the consensus in support of the approach to judicial review taken by the *Lochner* majority? Consider Barry Friedman, *The Will of the People* 176 (2009): "The mainstream press of the day, which was heavily pro-business [expressed] delight [at the outcome of *Lochner*]. As the courts assaulted popular legislation, figures from politics, social movements, the legal academy, and even the bench struck back. The central complaint in this era of direct democracy, naturally, was that judges were interfering impermissibly with the will of the people. The criticism found widespread popular support, emitting a full-throated roar against judicial power."

2. ***Did the strong rhetoric of the* Holmes *dissent reflect a wide substantive gulf between him and his colleagues?*** Gerald Leonard,

Holmes on the Lochner Court, 85 B.U.L.Rev. 1001 (2005), says it did not: "[Although] Holmes had made a big deal of his own commitment to restraint, he also acknowledged that that restraint must bow before the more general principle that judges had to recognize when fundamental principles had been violated, just as the *Lochner* majority had. In the end, he disagreed with the majority only on the question whether the New York statute really was a plausible health regulation, and with Harlan only on the question whether discussion of available empirical research was called for in deflating the majority's assumptions. Although Holmes wielded a terribly sharp rhetorical knife, he used it to defend a traditional and conventional theory of constitutional review. If he didn't mind turning that knife even on his allies, that was less because there was a deep jurisprudential gulf between him and Harlan than because, as a matter of aesthetics as much as anything else, he preferred to dismiss a mistaken majority in a handful of paragraphs that would offer no respect or quarter to the purveyors of judicial pretense."

3. ***Lochner revisited.*** Consider Richard A. Epstein, *The Classical Liberal Constitution* 338–39 (2014): "The Old Court was right and the modern critics are wrong. Doctrinally, two moves drove the *Lochner* invalidation of the New York maximum hours law. The first was a broad reading of liberty under the Due Process Clause of the Fourteenth Amendment. [The] second stage of the *Lochner* argument treated the New York law as a 'labor' statute intended to disrupt competition outside the legitimate police power interest in safety and health. That conclusion has been strongly attacked, but Justice Peckham surely had the better argument. The hour restrictions in question were limited only to those types of bakers who were directly competing with union bakers, not those in other lines that might be subject to the same health and safety risks. In *Lochner*, the union bakers worked a night and a morning shift, both of which could meet the ten-hour restrictions. Lochner's bakers worked longer hours, but slept in separate quarters on the premises between their evening and morning shifts, which accounted for their long hours. None of the bakers complained about the arrangement."

II. THREE DECADES OF CONTROL OVER LEGISLATIVE POLICY

Although the *Lochner*-era Court professed that reasonable exercises of the police power would be upheld, regardless of the underlying policy, the received wisdom holds that from *Lochner* in 1905 to *Nebbia* in 1934, infra, the Court frequently substituted its judgment for that of Congress and state legislatures on the wisdom of economic regulation said to interfere with contract and property interests.[6] The Court relied mainly upon the Due Process Clauses of the Fifth and Fourteenth Amendments, with occasional resort to the Equal Protection Clause. Between 1899 and 1937, after excluding the civil rights cases, 159 Supreme Court decisions held

---

[6] See Roscoe Pound, *Liberty of Contract*, 18 Yale L.J. 454 (1909); Ray A. Brown, *Due Process of Law, Police Power, and the Supreme Court*, 40 Harv.L.Rev. 943 (1927).

state statutes unconstitutional under the Due Process and Equal Protection Clauses, and 25 more statutes were struck down under the Due Process Clause coupled with some other provision of the Constitution. Benjamin F. Wright, *The Growth of American Constitutional Law* 154 (1942).

The Court most freely substituted its judgment for that of the legislature in cases involving labor legislation, regulation of prices, and limitations on entry into business. A few examples will suffice to show the extent to which the Court interfered with legislative policymaking in economic regulation. With regularity Holmes, J., dissented from this use of the Due Process Clause, joined later by Brandeis and Stone, JJ., and Hughes, C.J.

1. ***Hours of labor.*** Notwithstanding the holding of *Lochner*, in 1908 the Court sustained regulation of work hours for women in MULLER v. OREGON, 208 U.S. 412 (1908), basing the decision on special considerations relating to women. The Court, per BREWER, J., thought it plain that "woman's physical structure" put her at a disadvantage in the struggle for subsistence and that since "healthy mothers are essential to vigorous offspring, the physical well-being of woman becomes an object of public interest." The "inherent difference[s] between the two sexes," continued the Court, "justify special legislation restricting or qualifying the conditions under which [women] should be permitted to toil." In 1917 a 5–3 Court appeared to overrule *Lochner* (but not its philosophy) in sustaining a regulation of work hours for men in manufacturing establishments. *Bunting v. Oregon*, 243 U.S. 426. In *Muller*, the majority was influenced by the so-called "Brandeis brief," which furnished the Court with empirical evidence in support of regulation of hours of labor for women. Felix Frankfurter successfully followed the same technique as counsel in *Bunting*. See 208 U.S. at 419–20, and 243 U.S. at 433; Henry W. Biklé, *Judicial Determination of Questions of Fact Affecting the Constitutional Validity of Legislative Action*, 38 Harv.L.Rev. 6 (1924).

2. ***Anti-union discrimination.*** The Court struck down both federal and state labor legislation forbidding discrimination by employers for union activity and prohibiting employers from requiring employees to sign "yellow dog" contracts, i.e., agreements not to remain or become union members.

ADAIR v. UNITED STATES, 208 U.S. 161 (1908) (5th Amendment); COPPAGE v. KANSAS, 236 U.S. 1 (1915) (14th Amendment). The opinion in *Adair* was written by HARLAN, J., one of the dissenters in *Lochner*. He deemed the "right of a person to sell his labor upon such terms as he deems proper [to be] the same as the right of the purchaser to prescribe the conditions." An employer and his employees "have equality of right, and any legislation that disturbs that equality is an arbitrary interference with the liberty of contract." PITNEY, J.'s majority opinion in *Coppage* has been called "[p]erhaps the clearest and fullest statement of the era's dominant philosophy." Tribe, 3d ed. at 1350. The Court proclaimed that the 14th Amendment protects "the right to make contracts" and an "interference with this liberty so serious as that now under consideration, and so disturbing of equality of right, must be deemed to be arbitrary, unless it be supportable as a reasonable exercise of the police power of the state." The Court was not impressed by the argument that "employees, as a rule, are not financially able to be as independent in making contracts for the sale of their labor as are employers in making a contract of purchase thereof." It is "from the nature of things impossible," responded the Court, "to uphold freedom of contract and the right of private property without at the same time recognizing as legitimate those inequalities of fortune that are the necessary result of the exercise of those rights." HOLMES, J., dissented: "[A] workman not unnaturally may believe that only by belonging to a union can he secure a contract that shall be fair to him. [If] that belief, whether right or wrong, may be held by a reasonable man, it seems to me that it may be enforced by law in order to establish the equality of position between the parties in which liberty of contract begins."

These restrictive decisions were distinguished away in *Texas & N.O.R.R. v. Brotherhood of Ry. & S.S. Clerks,* 281 U.S. 548 (1930) and *NLRB v. Jones & Laughlin Steel Corp.*, 301 U.S. 1 (1937). They were finally expressly overruled in *Phelps Dodge Corp. v. NLRB,* 313 U.S. 177 (1941) and *Lincoln Fed. Labor Union v. Northwestern Iron & Met. Co.* (1949), Sec. 3 infra.

3. ***Regulation of wages.*** Six years after it had upheld regulation of *hours* of labor in *Bunting*, the Court, per SUTHERLAND, J., ruled that a federal statute prescribing minimum *wages* for women in the District of Columbia violated due process.

ADKINS v. CHILDREN'S HOSPITAL, 261 U.S. 525 (1923): The Court emphasized that, although "freedom of contract" is subject to a great variety of restraints, it "is, nevertheless, the general rule and restraint the exception, and the exercise of legislative authority to abridge it can be justified only by the existence of exceptional circumstances." "[This] is not a law dealing with any business charged with a public interest or with public work," continued the Court, nor is it "for the protection of persons under legal disability or for the prevention of fraud. It is simply and exclusively a price-fixing law, confined to adult women, [who] are legally as capable of contracting for themselves as men." The Court noted that the 19th Amendment had recently been adopted, thus reducing the civil inferiority of women almost to the "vanishing point." Therefore, "liberty of contract" could not be subjected to greater infringement in the case of women than of men.

HOLMES, J., dissenting, expressed his inability to "understand the principle on which the power to fix a minimum for the wages of women can be denied by those who admit the power to fix a maximum for their hours of work." As he saw it, the bargain is "equally affected whichever half you regulate." As for the recent adoption of the 19th Amendment, it "will need more than [that] to convince me that there are no differences between men and women, or that legislation cannot take those differences into account."[7]

4. ***Regulation of prices.*** The Court also held that regulation of prices for commodities and services violated due process except for a limited class labeled "business affected with a public interest."[8] *Tyson & Bro.-United Theatre Ticket Offices v. Banton,* 273 U.S. 418 (1927) (theatre tickets); *Ribnik v. McBride,* 277 U.S. 350 (1928) (fees of employment agency); *Williams v. Standard Oil Co.,* 278 U.S. 235 (1929) (gasoline prices); cf. *Chas. Wolff Packing Co. v. Court of Industrial Relations,* 262 U.S. 522 (1923) (compulsory arbitration of wages). *Nebbia v. New York* (1934) severely limited these rulings and they were expressly overruled in *Olsen v. Nebraska ex rel. Western Ref. & Bond Ass'n* (1941), both in Sec. 3 infra.

5. ***Limitations on entry into business.*** The Court also relied on the "liberty of contract" concept to strike down legislation limiting entry into a business, despite strong demonstrations of need for such limitations. *New State Ice Co. v. Liebmann,* 285 U.S. 262 (1932) (invalid to deny entry into ice business without a finding of "necessity" and that existing facilities are not "sufficient to meet the public needs"); *Liggett Co. v. Baldridge,* 278 U.S. 105 (1928) (invalid to limit new entrants into pharmacy business to pharmacists); *Adams v. Tanner,* 244 U.S. 590 (1917) (invalid to ban private employment agencies that charge fees paid by employees). Might these decisions be defended on the policy grounds that support antitrust laws? Epstein 340–41 defends the *Lochner*-era Court's anti-union decisions, supra note 2, by decrying labor monopoly power but he does not discuss *New State Ice, Liggett,* or *Adams* in this context.[9] Is it significant that Brandeis, J., who had been a leading "trust buster" in his pre-judicial career, dissented in each of these cases?

North Dakota State Board v. Snyder's Drug Stores, 414 U.S. 156 (1973) overruled *Liggett.* While no cases precisely like *Adams* or *New State Ice* have arisen, the Court in 1963 asserted in effect that *Adams* had been

---

[7]   Not until 1937 were *Adkins* and other cases to the same effect overruled in *West Coast Hotel Co. v. Parrish,* Sec. 3 infra.

[8]   See Breck P. McAllister, *Lord Hale and Business Affected with a Public Interest,* 43 Harv.L.Rev. 759 (1930); Walton H. Hamilton, *Affectation with Public Interest,* 39 Yale L.J. 1089 (1930); Maurice Finkelstein, *From Munn v. Illinois to Tyson v. Banton: A Study in the Judicial Process,* 27 Colum.L.Rev. 769 (1927).

[9]   Epstein cites *New State Ice* but the citation appears in his discussion of federalism. See Epstein 200.

overruled when it unanimously sustained a state prohibition on engaging in the debt adjusting business. See *Ferguson v. Skrupa,* Sec. 3 infra.

3. THE ABANDONMENT OF *LOCHNER*

NEBBIA V. NEW YORK
291 U.S. 502, 54 S.Ct. 505, 78 L.Ed. 940 (1934).

JUSTICE ROBERTS delivered the opinion of the Court.

[In 1933, after a year's legislative study of the state's dairy industry, New York enacted a law establishing a Milk Control Board with power to fix maximum and minimum retail prices. The Board fixed nine cents per quart as the price to be charged by a store. Nebbia, the proprietor of a grocery store, was convicted of selling milk below the minimum price.]

[Under] our form of government the use of property and the making of contracts are normally matters of private and not of public concern. The general rule is that both shall be free of governmental interference. But neither property rights nor contract rights are absolute; for government cannot exist if the citizen may at will use his property to the detriment of his fellows, or exercise his freedom of contract to work them harm. Equally fundamental with the private right is that of the public to regulate it in the common interest. [T]he guaranty of due process [demands] only that the law shall not be unreasonable, arbitrary, or capricious, and that the means selected shall have a real and substantial relation to the object sought to be attained. [A] regulation valid for one sort of business, or in given circumstances, may be invalid for another sort, or for the same business under other circumstances, because the reasonableness of each regulation depends upon the relevant facts.

[The opinion then summarized many different kinds of business and property regulations and controls previously sustained against due process attacks.]

The legislative investigation of 1932 was persuasive of the fact [that] unrestricted competition aggravated existing evils and the normal law of supply and demand was insufficient to correct maladjustments detrimental to the community. The inquiry disclosed destructive and demoralizing competitive conditions and unfair trade practices which resulted in retail price cutting and reduced the income of the farmer below the cost of production. [The Legislature] believed conditions could be improved by preventing destructive price-cutting by stores which, due to the flood of surplus milk, were able to buy at much lower prices than the larger distributors and to sell without incurring the delivery costs of the latter. [In] the light of the facts the [Milk Control Board's] order appears not to be unreasonable or arbitrary, or without relation to the purpose to prevent ruthless competition from destroying the wholesale price structure on which the farmer depends for his livelihood, and the community for an assured supply of milk. But we are told that because the law essays to control prices it denies due process. Notwithstanding the admitted power to correct existing economic ills by appropriate regulation of business, [the] appellant urges that direct fixation of prices is a type of regulation absolutely forbidden. [The] argument runs that the public control of rates or prices is per se unreasonable and unconstitutional, save as applied to businesses affected with a public interest; that a business so affected is [one] such as is commonly called a public utility; or a business in its nature a monopoly. [But] if, as must be conceded, the industry is subject to regulation in the public interest, what constitutional principle bars the state from correcting existing maladjustments by legislation touching prices? We think there is no such principle. The due process clause makes no mention of sales or of prices any more than it speaks of business or contracts or buildings or other incidents of property. The thought seems nevertheless to have persisted that there is something peculiarly sacrosanct about the price one may charge for what he makes or sells, and that, however able to regulate other elements of manufacture or trade, with incidental effect upon price, the state is incapable of directly controlling the price itself. This view was negatived many years ago. *Munn v. Illinois.*

"[Affected] with a public interest" is the equivalent of "subject to the exercise of the police power" and it is plain that nothing more was intended by the expression. [It] is clear that there is no closed class or category of businesses affected with a public interest, and the function of courts in the application of the Fifth and Fourteenth Amendments is to determine in each case whether circumstances vindicate the challenged regulation as a reasonable exertion of governmental authority or condemn it as arbitrary or discriminatory. The phrase "affected with a public interest" can, in the nature of things, mean no more than that an industry, for adequate reason, is subject to control for the public good. [There] can be no doubt that upon proper occasion and by appropriate measures the state may regulate a business in any of its aspects, including the prices to be charged for the products or commodities it sells.

So far as the requirement of due process is concerned, [a] state is free to adopt whatever economic policy may reasonably be deemed to promote public welfare, and to enforce that policy by legislation adapted to its purpose. The courts are without authority either to declare such policy, or, when it is declared by the legislature, to override it. If the laws passed are seen to have a reasonable relation to a proper legislative purpose, and are neither arbitrary nor discriminatory, the requirements of due process are satisfied. [With] the wisdom of the policy adopted, with the adequacy or practicability of the law enacted to forward it, the courts are both incompetent and unauthorized to deal. * * *

JUSTICE MCREYNOLDS, joined by JUSTICE VAN DEVANTER, JUSTICE SUTHERLAND, and JUSTICE BUTLER, dissenting:

[P]lainly, I think, this Court must have regard to the wisdom of the enactment. At least, we must inquire concerning its purpose and decide whether the means proposed have reasonable relation to something within legislative power—whether the end is legitimate, and the means appropriate. [Here,] we find direct interference with guaranteed rights defended upon the ground that the purpose was to promote the public welfare by increasing milk prices at the farm. [The] court below [has] not attempted to indicate how higher charges at stores to impoverished customers when the output is excessive and sale prices by producers are unrestrained, can possibly increase receipts at the farm. [It] appears to me wholly unreasonable to expect this legislation to accomplish the proposed end—increase of prices at the farm. [Not] only does the statute interfere arbitrarily with the rights of the little grocer to conduct his business according to standards long accepted—complete destruction may follow; but it takes away the liberty of 12,000,000 consumers. [Grave] concern for embarrassed farmers is everywhere; but this should neither obscure the rights of others nor obstruct judicial appraisement of measures proposed for relief. The ultimate welfare of the producer, like that of every other class, requires dominance of the Constitution.

NOTES AND QUESTIONS

1. **Impact.** The *Nebbia* Court retained the language and formal structure of *Lochner*-era precedents but applied them in a way that was much more deferential to government regulation. Consequently, in the immediate aftermath of the case, observers were still uncertain whether the case signaled a new approach to economic regulation.

2. WEST COAST HOTEL CO. v. PARRISH, 300 U.S. 379 (1937), dealt the decisive blow. The decision overruled *Adkins v. Children's Hospital* and sustained a state minimum wage law for women. A 5–4 majority, per HUGHES, C.J., devoted substantial space to the reasons for regulation of women's wages: "What can be closer to the public interest than the health of women and their protection from unscrupulous and overreaching employers? [The] Legislature of the state was clearly entitled to consider [the] fact that [women] are in the class receiving the least pay, that their bargaining power is relatively weak, and that they are the ready victims of those who would take advantage of their necessitous circumstances. The Legislature was entitled to adopt measures to reduce the evils of the 'sweating system,' the exploiting of workers at wages so low as to be insufficient to meet the bare cost of living, thus making their very helplessness the occasion of a most injurious competition. [What] these workers lose in wages the taxpayers are called upon to pay. [We] may take judicial notice of the unparalleled demands for relief which arose during the recent period of depression. [The] community is not bound to provide, what is in effect a subsidy for unconscionable employers. [Even] if the wisdom of the

policy be regarded as debatable and its effects uncertain, still the Legislature is entitled to its judgment."

As for the contention that the law violated "freedom of contract": "What is this freedom? The Constitution does not speak of freedom of contract. It [prohibits] the deprivation of liberty without due process of law [and in so doing] the Constitution does not recognize an absolute and uncontrollable liberty. [Liberty] under the Constitution [is] necessarily subject to the restraints of due process, and regulation which is reasonable in relation to its subject and is adopted in the interests of the community is due process. [We] think [*Adkins*] was a departure from the true application of the principles governing the regulation by the state of the relation of employer and employed."[10]

3. ***Did President Roosevelt's "Court-packing plan" have an impact on the West Coast Hotel decision?*** *West Coast Hotel* was decided in the midst of the controversy over Roosevelt's "Court-packing plan," leading some to call Roberts, J.'s vote in the case "the switch in time that saved nine." However, a memorandum left by Roberts, J., indicates that the conference vote in *West Coast Hotel* took place some weeks before the Court-packing plan was announced. See Felix Frankfurter, *Mr. Justice Roberts*, 104 U.Pa.L.Rev. 311 (1955). Controversy nonetheless persists. Michael Ariens, *A Thrice-Told Tale, or Felix the Cat*, 107 Harv.L.Rev. 620 (1994), contends that Frankfurter, J., shaded the truth so that the Court would appear above politics. Another account concludes that Hughes, C.J., certainly would have voted to abandon *Lochner* without political pressure and reaches the same conclusion, but with less confidence, about Roberts, J. See Richard D. Friedman, *Switching Time and Other Thought Experiments: The Hughes Court and Constitutional Transformation*, 142 U.Pa.L.Rev. 1891 (1994). (See also the beginning of Ch. 2, Sec. 2, II, B.)

4. ***Impact of the Great Depression.*** By the mid-1930s the composition and philosophy of the Supreme Court had changed significantly since *Lochner*, but "in large measure," observes Tribe 3d ed. 1358–59, "it was the economic realities of the Depression that graphically undermined *Lochner*'s premises. No longer could it be argued with great conviction that the invisible hand of economics was functioning simultaneously to protect individual rights and to produce a social optimum. The legal 'freedom' of contract and property came increasingly to be seen as an illusion, subject as it was to impersonal economic forces. [Thus,] the basic justification for judicial intervention under *Lochner*— that the courts were restoring the natural order which had been upset by the legislature—was increasingly perceived as fundamentally flawed. There *was* no 'natural' economic order to upset or restore, and legislative or judicial

---

[10] Sutherland, J., joined by Van Devanter, McReynolds, and Butler, JJ., dissented, emphasizing that "the meaning of the Constitution does not change with the ebb and flow of economic events." As the dissenters saw it, the minimum wage law had no relation to the capacity or earning power of the employee and, to the extent that the law exceeded the fair value of the services rendered, it constituted "a compulsory exaction from the employer for the support of a partially indigent person," thereby unfairly shifting to the employer's shoulders "a burden which, if it belongs to anyone, belongs to society as a whole."

decision in any direction could neither be restrained nor justified on any such basis. [The] suffering of the underprivileged, including the misery of underpaid, overburdened, or unemployed workers, came to be seen by many not as an inescapable corollary of personal freedom or an inevitable result of forces beyond human control, but instead as a product of conscious governmental decisions to take *some* steps affecting the [economy] while *not* taking other steps that might rescue people from conditions of intolerable deprivation."

What Was Wrong with *Lochner*?

West Coast Hotel not only overruled *Adkins* but the entire approach of the *Lochner* era. In so doing, it relegated *Lochner* to what Professor Primus calls the "anti-canon" of constitutional law, one of a very small number of cases that "are paradigmatic examples of what is not the law." Richard Primus, *Canon, Anti-Canon, and Judicial Dissent*, 48 Duke L.J. 243 (1998). It follows that the repudiation of *Lochner* is the law. But what exactly did the Supreme Court repudiate when it overruled *Lochner*?

1.   ***The ambiguity in Holmes, J.'s dissent.*** Perhaps *West Coast Hotel* vindicated Holmes, J.'s *Lochner* dissent. If so, the crucial—and crucially ambiguous—passage would appear to be the claim that the Constitution does not "embody a particular economic theory." Viewed in a broader context, that appears to be a statement of the philosophy of judicial restraint. With the exception of his later votes in free speech cases (see Ch. 7, Sec. 1, I, A), Holmes, J. frequently argued for the power of majorities to choose unwise policies. Accordingly, the *Lochner* dissent, and thus the overruling of *Lochner*, could be taken as an endorsement of the view that absent clear constitutional text, courts should defer to *all* policy judgments. For the classic statement of that view, see James B. Thayer, *The Origin and Scope of the American Doctrine of Constitutional Law*, 7 Harv.L.Rev. 129 (1893). However, in the *Lochner* dissent itself, Holmes, J. only disavows a constitutional commitment to any particular *economic* theory. Accordingly, one might read the overruling of *Lochner* as merely repudiating robust judicial protection for *economic* liberty.

2.   ***Lochner and civil liberties.*** "Often overlooked in histories" of the *Lochner* era, observes David E. Bernstein, *The Story of Lochner v. New York: Impediment to the Growth of the Regulatory State*, in Constitutional Law Stories 299 (Michael C. Dorf ed. 2d ed. 2009), "is that the Court not only revived *Lochner*'s protection of liberty of contract, but also began to protect what today we call civil liberties. [The] expansion of *Lochner*ian due process jurisprudence to civil liberties began with *Meyer v. Nebraska*[, 262 U.S. 390 (1923)], in which the Court invalidated a Nebraska law that banned the teaching of German in private schools or by private tutors. [Later, the] Court was willing to preserve the *Lochner*ian civil liberties decisions of the 1920 and 1930s by reinterpreting them as decisions protecting 'discrete and insular minorities.'

"[In addition, some] contemporary liberal scholars [have come to] reassess their understanding of *Lochner*. The *Lochner* era Court, they argue, chose an appropriate role for the Court—defender of last resort of fundamental rights—but simply chose the wrong rights to emphasize; the Court focused on liberty of contract, a right that had become anachronistic in a modern industrial economy. Instead, the Court should have focused on the civil liberties necessary for a properly-functioning modern liberal democracy.[11] These liberal scholars argue that the Court eventually got it right, and *Lochner*, perhaps, should be recognized as a misstep on an otherwise sound path, not an irredeemable mistake."

3. ***Did the Lochner-era Court mistakenly assume that the common law was a neutral baseline?*** Consider Cass R. Sunstein, *Lochner's Legacy*, 87 Colum.L.Rev. 873 (1987): "The received wisdom is that *Lochner* was wrong because it involved 'judicial activism': an illegitimate intrusion by the courts into a realm properly reserved to the political branches of government. [But we may] understand *Lochner* from a different point of view. For the *Lochner* Court, neutrality [was] a constitutional requirement. [Governmental] intervention was constitutionally troublesome, whereas inaction was not; and both neutrality and inaction were defined as respect for the behavior of private actors pursuant to the common law, in light of the existing distribution of wealth and entitlements. [Market] ordering under the common law was understood to be a part of nature rather than a legal construct, and it formed the baseline from which to measure the constitutionally critical lines that distinguished action from inaction and neutrality from impermissible partisanship. [To] some degree, *Lochner*-like themes are so deeply ingrained in the constitutional order [that] it would be hopeless to attempt to abandon them even if it were desirable to do so. But [the] baselines selected by the Court and the use of the key concepts— "neutrality" and "inaction"—are often a mistake, for the same reasons that originally led to the rejection of *Lochner* and the common law system of regulation generally. [The] case should be taken to symbolize not merely an aggressive judicial role, but an approach that imposes a constitutional requirement of neutrality, and understands the term to refer to preservation of the existing distribution of wealth and entitlements under the baseline of the common law. Thus understood, *Lochner* has hardly been overruled."

"The Most Celebrated Footnote in Constitutional Law": Footnote 4 of the *Carolene Products* Case

UNITED STATES v. CAROLENE PRODUCTS CO., 304 U.S. 144 (1938), upheld the constitutionality of a federal statute that prohibited the

---

[11] At this point, Professor Bernstein refers to Bruce Ackerman, *We the People: Transformations* 255–78 (1998) and Owen M. Fiss, *History of the Supreme Court of the United States: Troubled Beginnings of the Modern State* 9–21 (1993).

shipment in interstate commerce of "filled milk," a product compounded with fat or oil so as to resemble milk or cream. Appellee argued that the legislation violated both the commerce and due process clauses. The government countered that appellee's product posed a danger to the public. Writing for the Court, STONE, J., took the position that economic regulatory legislation, such as the statute at issue, was entitled to a presumption of constitutionality and should be upheld if supported by any rational basis. "Where the existence of a rational basis for legislation whose constitutionality is attacked depends upon facts beyond the sphere of judicial notice," continued Stone, "such facts may properly be made the subject of judicial inquiry, and the constitutionality of a statute predicated upon the existence of a particular state of facts may be challenged by showing to the court that those facts have ceased to exist. [But] by their very nature such inquiries, where the legislative judgment is drawn in question, must be restricted to the issue whether any state of facts either known or which could reasonably be assumed affords support for it." Under this approach, the challenged legislation easily passed constitutional muster.[12] In the course of writing his opinion, Stone, J., dropped a footnote (fn. 4) that has been called "the most celebrated footnote in constitutional law"[13] and "the great and modern charter for ordering the relations between judges and other agencies of government."[14] That footnote reads as follows:

"There may be narrower scope for operation of the presumption of constitutionality when legislation appears on its face to be within a specific prohibition of the Constitution, such as those of the first ten Amendments, which are deemed equally specific when held to be embraced within the Fourteenth.

"It is unnecessary to consider now whether legislation which restricts those political processes which can ordinarily be expected to bring about repeal of undesirable legislation, is to be subjected to more exacting judicial scrutiny under the general prohibitions of the Fourteenth than are most other types of legislation [referring to cases dealing with restrictions on voting rights and freedom of expression and political association].

---

[12] "The plaudits accorded [footnote 4] are matched by the disregard of the case itself." Geoffrey Miller, *The True Story of Carolene Products,* 1987 Sup.Ct.Rev. 397. This is unfortunate, contends Professor Miller, "because [the] statute upheld in the case was an utterly unprincipled example of special interest legislation. The purported 'public interest' justifications so credulously reported by Justice Stone were patently bogus." See also, Neil Komesar, *Taking Institutions Seriously,* 51 U.Chi.L.Rev. 366 (1984): "It does not take much scrutiny to see the dairy lobby at work behind the passage [of] the 'filled milk' act. Indeed, [it] is not too uncharitable [to] suggest that concern for the dairies' pocketbooks rather than for the consumer's health best explains the dairy lobby's efforts."

[13] Lewis F. Powell, Jr., [J.], *Carolene Products Revisited,* 82 Colum.L.Rev. 1087 (1982).

[14] Owen Fiss, *Supreme Court 1978 Term Foreword: The Forms of Justice,* 93 Harv.L.Rev. 1 (1979).

"Nor need we enquire whether similar considerations enter into the review of statutes directed at particular religious, or national, or racial minorities[:] whether prejudice against discrete and insular minorities may be a special condition, which tends seriously to curtail the operation of those political processes ordinarily to be relied upon to protect minorities, and which may call for a correspondingly more searching judicial inquiry."

1. *A roadmap for the representation-reinforcing Warren Court?* *Carolene Products* was decided at a historical moment when the Supreme Court was retreating from the field of policy contention. Footnote 4 signaled that this was to be only a partial retreat, reserving for the Court an important role in the controversies that would embroil it in the coming decades. John H. Ely, *Democracy and Distrust* (1980), builds a theory of judicial review on the footnote, arguing that by contrast with counter-majoritarian *Lochner*-era decisions invalidating economic legislation, the ensuing work of the Warren Court in the 1950s and 1960s was "representation-reinforcing" in the sense that it chiefly removed obstacles to participation and remedied breakdowns in the democratic process. According to Michael C. Dorf & Samuel Issacharoff, *Can Process Theory Save Courts?*, 72 U.Colo.L.Rev. 923 (2001), because of "Ely's extraordinarily influential book, [in] retrospect, we can see that the Warren Court was driving by the *Carolene Products* roadmap, but at the time, the Court's direction was less than perfectly clear." For example, the first paragraph of footnote 4 indicates that the Court will play an active role in enforcing non-economic substantive rights, regardless of whether they reinforce representation as later envisaged by Ely. See Peter Linzer, *The Carolene Products Footnote and the Preferred Position of Individual Rights: Louis Lusky and John Hart Ely vs. Harlan Fiske Stone,* 12 Const.Comm. 277 (1995): "Early on, [footnote 4] was interpreted to mean that 'personal' rights were to be preferred to economic rights, but in recent years, largely through the efforts of Louis Lusky [who was Stone's law clerk when the famous footnote was written and who wrote the first draft of the footnote] and John Hart Ely, it has been interpreted more narrowly, justifying judicial activism only when the majoritarian democracy does not work."

2. *"Revers[ing] the spin of the countermajoritarian difficulty."* Bruce Ackerman, *Beyond Carolene Products,* 98 Harv.L.Rev. 713 (1985), sees the case and footnote 4 as a "brilliant" effort "to turn the Old Court's recent defeat into a judicial victory": "*Carolene* promises relief from the problem of legitimacy raised whenever nine elderly lawyers invalidate the legislative decisions of our elected representatives. [By] demonstrating that the legislative decision itself resulted from an undemocratic procedure, a *Carolene* court hopes to reverse the spin of the countermajoritarian difficulty. For it now may seem that the original legislative decision, not the judicial invalidation, suffers the greater legitimacy deficit."

3. *Did footnote 4 replace one kind of "judicial activism" with another?* Consider the remarks of Powell, J., fn. 13 supra: "Unlike Holmes, Stone lived to see—and indeed helped to preside over—the passing of the *Lochner* era. [But] Footnote 4, as interpreted by many commentators, represented a radical departure of its own. Far from initiating a jurisprudence of judicial deference to political judgments by the legislature, Footnote 4—on this view—undertook to substitute one activist judicial mission for another. Where once the Court had championed rights of property, now—according to some—it should view its special function as the identification and protection of 'discrete and insular minorities.' Where the Court before had used the substantive due process clause to protect property rights, now it should use the equal protection clause—a generally forgotten provision that Holmes once dismissed as 'the usual last resort of constitutional arguments'—as a sword with which to promote the liberty interests of groups disadvantaged by political decisions. [If] I am correct [that there is an] implicit link between a substantive judgment and a malfunction of process, then one may inquire whether we have not returned in some cases to a kind of substantive due process. And one also may wonder what Stone—who had fought so vigorously against substantive due process—would have had to say about this."

See also Laurence H. Tribe, *The Puzzling Persistence of Process-Based Constitutional Theories*, 89 Yale.L.J. 1063 (1980): "[The] constitutional theme of perfecting the processes of governmental decision is radically indeterminate and fundamentally incomplete. The process theme by itself determines almost nothing unless its presuppositions are specified, and its content supplemented, by a full theory of substantive rights and values— the very sort of theory the process-perfecters are at such pains to avoid."

The 1940s, 50s and 60s: A Far Cry from *Lochner*

West Coast Hotel was followed quickly by a number of cases upholding New Deal legislation as falling within congressional power to regulate interstate commerce. See, e.g., *NLRB v. Jones & Laughlin Steel Co.*, 301 U.S. 1 (1937) (the National Labor Relations Act); *United States v. Darby*, 312 U.S. 100 (1941) (the Fair Labor Standards Act); *Wickard v. Filburn*, 317 U.S. 111 (1942) (the Agricultural Adjustment Act). A great deal of state economic legislation was also sustained against challenges asserting economic rights. Some representative cases follow:

OLSEN v. NEBRASKA, 313 U.S. 236 (1941), upheld a Nebraska statute fixing maximum fees for employment agencies. DOUGLAS, J.'s, unanimous opinion bluntly rejected the state court's reliance on *Ribnik v. McBride,* 277 U.S. 350 (1928), which had held a similar statute violative of due process: "[Respondents] insist that special circumstances must be shown to support the validity of such drastic legislation as price-fixing,

[that] legislative limitation of maximum fees for employment agencies is certain to react unfavorably upon those members of the community for whom it is most difficult to obtain jobs, [and that] there are no conditions which the legislature might reasonably believe would redound to the public injury unless corrected by such legislation. [We] are not concerned, however, with the wisdom, need, or appropriateness of the legislation. Differences of opinion on that score suggest a choice which 'should be left where [it] was left by the Constitution—to the states and to Congress.' *Ribnik,* dissenting opinion. [In] final analysis, the only constitutional prohibitions or restraints which respondents have suggested for the invalidation of this legislation are those notions of public policy embedded in earlier decisions of this Court but which, as Mr. Justice Holmes long ago admonished, should not be read into the Constitution."

In LINCOLN FEDERAL LABOR UNION v. NORTHWESTERN IRON & METAL CO., 335 U.S. 525 (1949), a unanimous Court, per BLACK, J., sustained a state "right-to-work" law that barred a preference for union membership in employment decisions. The Court noted that at least since *Nebbia,* it had "steadily rejected the due process philosophy enunciated in the [*Lochner-Coppage*] line of cases" and returned closer to the earlier constitutional principle that states may legislate "against what are found to be injurious practices in their internal commercial and business affairs, so long as their laws do not run afoul of some specific federal constitutional prohibition [or] some valid federal law."

WILLIAMSON v. LEE OPTICAL OF OKLAHOMA, 348 U.S. 483 (1955), where a unanimous Court, per DOUGLAS, J., upheld an Oklahoma law regulating opticians and optometrists, nicely illustrates the great distance the Court had moved away from *Lochner* by the 1950s.

The law prohibited opticians from fitting or duplicating lenses without a prescription from an ophthalmologist or optometrist. "In practical effect, it means that no optician can fit old glasses into new frames or supply a lens, whether it be a new lens or one to duplicate a lost or broken lens, without a prescription." The lower court invalidated the law because an optician of ordinary skill could read a prescription from a broken lens fragment. The Supreme Court reversed despite its acknowledgment that the "law may exact a needless, wasteful requirement in many cases. But it is for the legislature, not the courts, to balance the advantages and disadvantages of [the] requirement. [The] legislature might have concluded that the frequency of occasions when a prescription is necessary was sufficient to justify this regulation of the fitting of eyeglasses. [Or] the legislature may have concluded that eye examinations were so critical [that] every change in frames and every duplication of a lens should be accompanied by a prescription from a medical expert. To be sure, the present law does not require a new examination of the eyes every time the frames are changed or the lenses duplicated. [But] the law need not be in every respect logically consistent with its aims to be constitutional. [The] day is gone when this Court uses the Due Process Clause [to] strike down state laws, regulatory of business and industrial conditions, because they may be unwise, improvident, or out of harmony with a particular school of thought."

A provision of the law that prohibited soliciting the sale of eyeglass frames was challenged on the ground that it regulated in a commercial area "only casually related to the visual care of the public." The Court responded: "[The] legislature might conclude that to regulate [lenses] effectively, it would have to regulate [eyeglass frames]. The advertiser of frames may be using his ads to bring in customers who will buy lenses."

Yet another provision of the law prohibited retail stores from renting space to optometrists. The Court rejected the challenge to this measure as well, viewing it as "an attempt to free the profession, to as great an extent as possible, from all taints of commercialism. It certainly might be easy for an optometrist with space in a retail store to be merely a front for the retail establishment. [We] cannot say that the regulation has no rational relation [to the setting of professional standards] and therefore is beyond constitutional bounds."

In FERGUSON v. SKRUPA, 372 U.S. 726 (1963), the Court, per BLACK, J., without a dissent, rejected a due process challenge to a state law barring all but lawyers from the business of debt adjusting. And it did so in the strongest terms: "Under the system of government created by our Constitution, it is up to legislatures, not courts, to decide on the wisdom and utility of legislation. [The] doctrine that prevailed in *Lochner*, *Coppage*, *Adkins*, [and] like cases [has] long since been discarded. We have returned to the original constitutional proposition that courts do not substitute their social and economic beliefs for the judgment of legislative bodies, who are elected to pass laws. [Whether] the legislature takes for its textbook Adam Smith, Herbert Spencer, Lord Keynes or some other is no concern of ours." Harlan, J., concurred in the judgment on the ground that "[this] measure bears a rational relation to a constitutionally permissible objective."

A NOTE ON SUBSTANTIVE DUE PROCESS AND PUNITIVE DAMAGE CONSTRAINTS

Do more recent decisions placing some limits on punitive damage awards constitute a partial return of robust judicial review of economic regulation under the rubric of substantive due process?

BMW OF NORTH AMERICA, INC. v. GORE, 517 U.S. 559 (1996), marked the first time that the Court found that a punitive damages award violated due process on the ground that it was "grossly excessive," considering such factors as the degree of reprehensibility of the defendant's conduct and the disparity between the harm suffered by the plaintiff and his punitive damage award.

The defendant had been assessed $2 million in punitive damages for having knowingly failed to tell an automobile buyer that, at a cost of $600, it had repainted portions of his new $40,000 car, thereby lowering its potential resale value by about 10 percent. A 5–4 majority, per STEVENS, J., recognized that prior cases had "consistently rejected the notion that the constitutional line is marked by a simple mathematical formula, even one that compares actual *and potential* damages to the punitive award." The Court added: "When the ratio is a breathtaking 500 to 1, however, the award must surely 'raise a suspicious judicial eyebrow.'"

SCALIA, J., joined by Thomas, J., dissented: "[What] the Fourteenth Amendment's procedural guarantee assures is an opportunity to contest the reasonableness of a damages judgment in state court; but there is no federal guarantee a damages award actually *be* reasonable." In a separate dissent, GINSBURG, J., joined by REHNQUIST, C.J., maintained that "[the] Court is not well equipped for this mission. [It] has only a vague concept of substantive due process, a 'raised eyebrow' test, as its ultimate guide."

––––––––

STATE FARM MUT. AUTO INS. CO. v. CAMPBELL, 538 U.S. 408 (2003), struck down another punitive damages award. The case involved a $145 million punitive damages award where full compensatory damages were only $1 million. A 6–3 majority, per KENNEDY, J., observed: "[Due process] prohibits the imposition of grossly excessive or arbitrary punishments on a tortfeasor. [We] decline again to impose a bright-line ratio which a punitive damages award cannot exceed. Our jurisprudence and the principles it has now established demonstrate, however, that, in practice, few awards exceeding a single-digit ratio between punitive and compensatory damages, to a significant degree, will satisfy due process." Scalia, Thomas, and Ginsburg, JJ., each filed separate dissents.

––––––––

PHILIP MORRIS v. WILLIAMS, 549 U.S. 346 (2007), addressed a question about the purpose of punitive damages. A jury ordered the defendant tobacco company to pay $821,000 in compensatory damages to the widow of a smoker for negligence and deceit. A punitive damages award of $79.5 million followed the trial judge's refusal to instruct the jury "not to punish the defendant for the impact of its alleged misconduct on other persons, who may bring lawsuits of their own in which other juries can resolve their claims," after the plaintiff's attorney had urged jurors to "think about how many other Jesse Williams in the last 40 years in the State of Oregon there have been." A 5–4 majority, per BREYER, J., vacated the Oregon Supreme Court's judgment, holding that a punitive damages award based upon a jury's "desire to *punish* the defendant for harming persons who are not before the court" would violate the defendant's right to due process."

STEVENS, J., dissented: "[I] see no reason why an interest in punishing a wrongdoer 'for harming persons who are not before the court' should not be taken into consideration when assessing the appropriate sanction for reprehensible conduct."[15] GINSBURG, J., joined by Scalia and Thomas, JJ., wrote a separate dissent, contending that the punitive damages award was not in fact aimed at punishing the defendant for harm to third parties but for the reprehensibility of the conduct. THOMAS, J., also dissented separately, reiterating his "view that 'the Constitution does not constrain the size of punitive damage awards.'"

Would the decisions imposing constitutional limits on punitive damages pose less of a risk of reviving *Lochner*-style review of economic regulation if, instead of resting simply on substantive due process, they were reconceived as implementing the Eighth Amendment's prohibition on "excessive fines"? Even if so, that option was ruled out in BROWNING-FERRIS INDUSTRIES OF VERMONT v. KELCO DISPOSAL, INC., 492 U.S. 257 (1989). The Court, per BLACKMUN, J., acknowledged that "[the] Eighth Amendment received little debate in the First Congress," and that "the Excessive Fines Clause received even less attention." Nonetheless, on the basis of the "undisputed purpose and history of the Amendment generally," the majority concluded that it does not apply in private civil litigation. In an opinion concurring in part and dissenting in part, O'CONNOR, J., joined by Stevens, J., relied on historical studies of the same period to reach the opposite conclusion.

4. OTHER LIMITS ON ECONOMIC LEGISLATION: THE PROHIBITION AGAINST "TAKING" "PRIVATE PROPERTY" WITHOUT JUST COMPENSATION

The Fifth Amendment limits the federal government's power of eminent domain: "nor shall private property be taken for a public use without just compensation." This specific provision of the Bill of Rights was one of the first to be deemed binding on the states via Fourteenth Amendment due process. See *Chicago, B. & Q. R. Co. v. Chicago*, 166 U.S. 226 (1897); *Missouri Pac. Ry. Co. v. Nebraska*, 164 U.S. 403 (1896). Perhaps because the "Takings Clause" is a specifically enumerated limit, the post-

----

[15] Consider Benjamin C. Zipursky, *Palsgraf, Punitive Damages, and Preemption*, 125 Harv.L.Rev. 1757 (2012): "Our legal system judges the entitlement to some form of action against the defendant in light of what the defendant did to the plaintiff. [The] scope of the [plaintiff's] entitlement may reach beyond the self-restorative to the injury-inflicting [on the defendant] where the underlying wrong was itself a willful or wanton infliction of injury." Nevertheless, Professor Zipursky argues, traditional common law principles did not conceptualize the plaintiff seeking punitive damages as a "private attorney general." To the extent that punitive damages are now justified based on "harm to a person who is neither the plaintiff nor someone represented by the plaintiff," he contends that the defendant at least should be entitled to special procedural protection.

West Coast Hotel retreat from robust protection of economic liberty under the general rubric of substantive due process did not eliminate robust judicial scrutiny of takings.

Courses in property law typically include detailed study of the Takings Clause. The materials in this section, by contrast, are abbreviated. As you read them, consider whether the questions in play and the resources available to judges seeking to answer them differ significantly from the respective questions and resources at issue in freestanding substantive due process review of economic regulation. Even if not, might robust scrutiny of takings nonetheless be justified?

What Constitutes a Taking for a "Public Purpose"?

As illustrated by *Kelo v. New London* (set forth infra), the Court's role in determining whether a taking is for a "public purpose" is extremely limited. A use is considered "public" if it furthers moral, economic, political, or even aesthetic objectives. A use may be deemed "public" so long as there is public advantage or benefit—even though the property may not be directly *used by* the general public.

What Government Action Should Be Regarded as a "Taking," Requiring Just Compensation?

In *Pennsylvania Coal Co. v. Mahon*, 260 U.S. 393 (1922), the Court, per HOLMES, J., observed that "the general rule at least is that while property may be regulated to a certain extent, if regulation goes too far it will be recognized as a taking." Such a "rule" may strike many as at best an uninformative tautology. But is the "general rule" represented by the modern cases any more helpful?

The question presented in PENN CENTRAL TRANSP. CO. v. NEW YORK CITY, 438 U.S. 104 (1978) was whether a preservation commission's denial of approval for Penn Central to construct a 55-story office building on the roof of its property—Grand Central Terminal, which had been designated as a "landmark"—constituted a "taking." In holding that it did not, the Court, per BRENNAN, J., emphasized that the denial of approval to build the structure "does not interfere in any way" with the present and past uses of the Terminal. "More importantly, on this record, we must regard the [restriction] as permitting Penn Central not only to profit from the Terminal but also to obtain a 'reasonable return' on its investment."

The *Penn Central* Court recognized that "what constitutes a 'taking' [has] proved to be a problem of considerable difficulty. [T]his Court, quite simply, has been unable to develop any 'set formula' for determining when 'justice and fairness' require that economic injuries caused by public action be compensated by the government, rather than remain disproportionately concentrated on a few persons. [A] 'taking' may more readily be found," noted the Court, "when the interference with property can be characterized as a physical invasion by government [than] when interference arises from some public program adjusting the benefits and burdens of economic life to promote the common good."

A good illustration of the doctrinal significance of a "physical invasion" is *Loretto v. Teleprompter Manhattan CATV Corp.*, 458 U.S. 419 (1982), which held that a state law requiring landlords to allow television cable companies to install cable facilities in their apartment buildings amounted to a "taking," despite the fact that the facilities occupied at most only one and one-half cubic feet of the landlord's property.

The Court has also considered categorical treatment appropriate where the regulation denies *all* economically beneficial or productive use of land. A good illustration is LUCAS v. SOUTH CAROLINA COASTAL COUNCIL, 505 U.S. 1003 (1992), where the enactment of an anti-erosion law prevented the owner from erecting any permanent habitable structure on his land. The Court, per SCALIA, J., observed: "[R]egulations that leave the owner of land without economically beneficial or productive options for its use—typically, as here, by requiring land to be left substantially in its natural state—carry with them a heightened risk that private property is being pressed into some form of public service under the guise of mitigating serious public harm. [When] the owner of real property has been called upon to sacrifice *all* economically beneficial uses in the name of the common good, that is, to leave the property economically idle, he has suffered a taking."

———

In STOP THE BEACH RENOURISHMENT v. FLORIDA DEPT. OF ENVIRONMENTAL PROTECTION, 560 U.S. 702 (2010), all eight participating justices agreed that a Florida Supreme Court ruling did not constitute a "judicial taking," but four (SCALIA, J., joined by Roberts, C.J., and Thomas and Alito, JJ.) would have used the case to establish the proposition that a *judicial decision* can constitute an unlawful taking: "The Takings Clause bars *the State* from taking private property without paying for it, no matter which branch is the instrument of the taking. [If] a legislature *or a court* declares that what was once an established right of private property no longer exists, it has taken that property, no less than if the State had physically appropriated it or destroyed its value by regulation." The other four participating justices did not reach the qeustion of whether judicial actions can ever effect a taking.

Does a Temporary Moratorium on a New Economic Development Constitute a "Taking"?

Consider TAHOE-SIERRA PRESERVATION COUNCIL, INC. v. TAHOE REGIONAL PLANNING AGENCY, 535 U.S. 302 (2002): A regional planning compact imposed two moratoria, totaling 32 months, on land development in the Lake Tahoe Basin while formulating a comprehensive land-use plan for the area. A 6–3 majority, per STEVENS, J., held that *Lucas* did not apply and that *Penn Central*'s balancing test was the appropriate framework for analyzing whether a "taking" had occurred:

"[The] categorical rule that we applied in *Lucas* states that compensation is required when a regulation deprives an owner of '*all* economically beneficial uses' of his land. Under that rule, a statute that 'wholly eliminated the value' of Lucas' fee simple clearly qualified as a taking. But our holding was limited to the extraordinary circumstance when *no* productive or economically beneficial use of land is permitted.

"[The] duration of the restriction is one of the important factors that a court must consider in the appraisal of a regulatory takings claim, but with respect to that factor as with respect to [others], the 'temptation to adopt what amount to per se rules in either direction must be resisted.' *Palazzolo v. Rhode Island*, infra (O'Connor, J., concurring). [The] interest in 'fairness and justice' will be best served by relying on the familiar *Penn Central* approach when deciding cases like this, rather than by attempting to craft a new categorical rule."

Rehnquist, C.J., joined by Scalia and Thomas, JJ., dissented. In a separate dissent, SCALIA, J., joined by Thomas, J., said that while the "questionable rule" that a failure to take an entire parcel of land fails to qualify as a taking had "been applied to various alleged regulatory takings," that rule had been "rejected in the context of *temporal* deprivations of property by *First English Evangelical Lutheran Church of Glendale v. County of Los Angeles*, 482 U.S. 304 (1987), which held that temporary and permanent takings 'are not different in kind' when a landowner is deprived of all beneficial use of his land."

May One Claim that a Restriction Imposed on Her Property Before She Acquired It Constitutes a "Taking"?

PALAZZOLO v. RHODE ISLAND, 533 U.S. 606 (2001), established that the right to claim a "taking" is *not* limited to persons who held title to the property at the time the challenged regulation was imposed. To accept a contrary rule, observed the *Palazzolo* Court, per KENNEDY, J., would mean that "the post-enactment transfer of title would absolve the State of its obligation to defend any action restricting land use, no matter how extreme or unreasonable. A State would be allowed, in effect, to put an expiration date on the Takings Clause."

What Constitutes "Property" for Purposes of the Takings Clause?

The Takings Clause applies where a *specific* interest in physical or intellectual property is involved. But no opinion of the Court has held that the Takings Clause applies when a *general obligation* to pay money to the government or to a third party is at issue. Extension of Takings Clause doctrine to such general obligations might threaten to revive *Lochner*-style review.

In EASTERN ENTERPRISES v. APFEL, 524 U.S. 498 (1998), the Court struck down a federal statute that imposed a monetary assessment on the prior owner of a coal mine that would have been used to fund benefits for now-retired miners who had once worked for the coal mine. However, there was no opinion of the Court. Speaking for four Justices, O'CONNOR, J., concluded that as the statute affected Eastern Enterprises, it violated the Takings Clause. Concurring in the judgment, but rejecting the plurality's Takings Clause analysis, KENNEDY, J., concluded that the statute "must be invalidated as contrary to essential due process principles" because it went "far outside the bounds of retroactivity permissible under our law." It is noteworthy that (a) the O'Connor plurality seemed to avoid reliance upon the Due Process Clause at least in part out of fear of resurrecting *Lochner*, but (b) KENNEDY, J., argued forcefully that the plurality's adoption of a "novel and expansive concept of a taking" did not avoid the "normative judgment" that would otherwise need to be made under the due process rubric. Likewise, STEVENS, J., dissenting, joined by Souter, Ginsburg and Breyer, JJ., concluded that whether the statute "is analyzed under the Takings Clause or the Due Process Clause" the company "has not carried its burden of overcoming the presumption of constitutionality accorded to an Act of Congress."

Thus, a four-Justice plurality had maintained that a general obligation could be the subject of a taking, but five Justices (in concurring and dissenting opinions) had disagreed.

KELO V. NEW LONDON
545 U.S. 469, 125 S.Ct. 2655, 162 L.Ed.2d 439 (2005).

JUSTICE STEVENS delivered the opinion of the Court.

[Decades of economic decline prompted state and local officials to target New London, Conn. (hereinafter City), and especially its Fort Trumbell area, for economic revitalization. The task was assigned chiefly to the New London Development Corp. (NLDC), a private entity. Shortly thereafter, the pharmaceutical company Pfizer announced that it would build a $300 million facility on a site immediately adjacent to Fort Trumbell. Local planners hoped that the new facility would catalyze the area's rejuvenation.

[The city council approved the NLDC plan and authorized the entity to purchase property or to acquire it by exercising eminent domain in the City's name. When petitioners in the case, nine persons who owned 15 properties in Fort Trumbell, refused to sell, the City initiated condemnation proceedings. Their properties were not blighted or otherwise in poor condition. Rather, they were condemned only because they happened to be in the development area. Petitioner brought this action in state court, maintaining that the City's taking of their properties would violate the "public use" restriction in the Takings Clause. The state supreme court disagreed.]

[The] disposition of this [case] turns on the question whether the City's development plan serves a "public purpose." Without exception, our cases have defined that concept broadly, reflecting our longstanding policy of deference to legislative judgments in this field. [For] more than a century, our public use jurisprudence has wisely eschewed rigid formulas and intrusive scrutiny in favor of affording legislatures broad latitude in determining what public needs justify the use of the takings power.

Those who govern the City were not confronted with the need to remove blight in the Fort Trumbull area, but their determination that the area was sufficiently distressed to justify a program of economic rejuvenation is entitled to our deference. The City has carefully formulated an economic development plan that it believes will provide appreciable benefits to the community, including—but by no means limited to—new jobs and increased tax revenue. [Because] that plan unquestionably serves a public purpose, the takings challenged here satisfy the public use requirement of the Fifth Amendment.

[Petitioners] contend that using eminent domain for economic development impermissibly blurs the boundary between public and private takings. Again, our cases foreclose this objection. Quite simply, the government's pursuit of a public purpose will often benefit individual private parties.

[It] is further argued that without a bright-line rule nothing would stop a city from transferring citizen A's property to citizen B for the sole reason that citizen B will put the property to a more productive use and thus pay more taxes. Such a one-to-one transfer of property, executed outside the confines of an integrated development plan, is not presented in this case. While such an unusual exercise of government power would certainly raise a suspicion that a private purpose was afoot, the hypothetical cases posited by petitioners can be confronted if and when they arise. They do not warrant the crafting of an artificial restriction on the concept of public use.

[We] emphasize that nothing in our opinion precludes any State from placing further restrictions on its exercise of the takings power. Indeed, many States already impose "public use" requirements that are stricter than the federal baseline. [This] Court's authority, however, extends only to determining whether the City's proposed condemnations are for a "public use" within the meaning of the Fifth Amendment to the Federal Constitution. Because over a century of our case law interpreting that provision dictates an affirmative answer to that question, we may not grant petitioners the relief that they seek. * * *

JUSTICE KENNEDY, concurring.

[A] court confronted with a plausible accusation of impermissible favoritism to private parties should treat the objection as a serious one and review the record to see if it has merit, though with the presumption that the government's actions were reasonable and intended to serve a public purpose. Here, the trial court [did so and] concluded [that] benefitting Pfizer was not "the primary motivation or effect of this development plan." [This] case, then, survives the meaningful rational-basis review that in my view is required under the Public Use Clause. [While] there may be categories of cases in which the transfers are so suspicious, or the procedures employed so prone to abuse, or the purported benefits are so trivial or implausible, that courts should presume an impermissible private purpose, no such circumstances are present in this case. * * *

JUSTICE O'CONNOR, with whom THE CHIEF JUSTICE, JUSTICE SCALIA, and JUSTICE THOMAS join, dissenting.

[To] reason, as the Court does, that the incidental public benefits resulting from the subsequent ordinary use of private property render economic development takings "for public use" is to wash out any distinction between private and public use of property—and thereby effectively to delete the words "for public use" from the Takings Clause of the Fifth Amendment.

[Where] is the line between "public" and "private" property use? [Were] the political branches the sole arbiters of the public-private distinction, the Public Use Clause would amount to little more than hortatory fluff. An external, judicial check on how the public use requirement is interpreted, however limited, is necessary if this constraint on government power is to retain any meaning.

[This case] presents an issue of first impression: Are economic development takings constitutional? I would hold that they are not.

[The] Court protests that it does not sanction the bare transfer from A to B for B's benefit. It suggests two limitations on what can be taken after today's decision. First, it maintains a role for courts in ferreting out takings whose sole purpose is to bestow a benefit on the private transferee—without detailing how courts are to conduct that complicated inquiry. [The] trouble with economic development takings is that private benefit and incidental public benefit are, by definition, merged and mutually reinforcing. In this case, for example, any boon for Pfizer or the plan's developer is difficult to disaggregate from the promised public gains in taxes and jobs.

Even if there were a practical way to isolate the motives behind a given taking, the gesture toward a purpose test is theoretically flawed. If it is true that incidental public benefits from new private use are enough to ensure the "public purpose" in a taking, why should it matter, as far as the Fifth Amendment is concerned, what inspired the taking in the first place?

[A] second proposed limitation is implicit in the Court's opinion. The logic of today's decision is that eminent domain may only be used to upgrade—not downgrade—property. At best this makes the Public Use Clause redundant with the Due Process Clause, which already prohibits irrational government action. [In] any event, this constraint has no realistic import. For who among us can say she already makes the most productive or attractive possible use of her property? The specter of condemnation hangs over all property. Nothing is to prevent the State from replacing any Motel 6 with a Ritz-Carlton, any home with a shopping mall, or any farm with a factory.

[Any] property may now be taken for the benefit of another private party, but the fallout from this decision will not be random. The beneficiaries are likely to be those citizens with disproportionate influence and power in the political process, including large corporations and development firms. As for the victims, the government now has license to transfer property from those with fewer resources to those with more. The Founders cannot have intended this perverse result. * * *

JUSTICE THOMAS, dissenting.

[There] is no justification [for] affording almost insurmountable deference to legislative conclusions that a use serves a "public use." [W]e would not defer to a legislature's determination of the various circumstances that establish, for example, when a search of a home would be reasonable, or when a convicted double-murderer may be shackled during a sentencing proceeding without on-the-record findings, or when state law creates a property interest protected by the Due Process Clause. [I] would revisit our Public Use Clause cases and consider returning to the original meaning of the Public Use Clause: that the government may take property only if it actually uses or gives the public a legal right to use the property. * * *

———

A NOTE ON THE PROHIBITION AGAINST "IMPAIRING THE OBLIGATION OF CONTRACTS"

Art. 1, § 10, prohibits the states from enacting any "Law impairing the Obligation of Contracts." (Unlike some provisions in § 10, no parallel provision of Art. 1, § 9, restricts the federal government.) According to Thomas W. Merrill, *Public Contracts, Private Contracts, and the Transformation of the*

Constitutional Order, 37 Case.W.Res.L.Rev. 597 (1987): "Few provisions of the Constitution have experienced more dramatic ups and downs than the contract clause. The clause attracted little attention at the Constitutional Convention of 1787 or in the process of ratification. But under the guiding hand of Chief Justice John Marshall, the early Supreme Court construed the contract clause as affording broad protection against state interference with both private and public obligations. Indeed, in the days before the enactment of the fourteenth amendment, the contract clause was the second most frequently litigated provision of the Constitution (after the commerce clause), and was the principal vehicle by which the Supreme Court asserted federal constitutional control over the state governments. Today, the contract clause is but a pale shadow of its former self."

In HOME BUILDING & LOAN ASS'N v. BLAISDELL, 290 U.S. 398 (1934)—decided the same year the *Nebbia* case struck the economic due process doctrine a heavy blow—the Court upheld what might be called a "debtor relief law" despite its retrospective impact. *Blaisdell* arose as follows: During the Great Depression, Minnesota enacted a Mortgage Moratorium Law—a law that was to remain in effect "only during the continuance of the emergency and in no event beyond May 1, 1935"—which gave the state courts the authority to extend the redemption period after real estate foreclosure sales provided the mortgagor paid a reasonable part of the rental value of the property. Thus mortgagees could not obtain possession of the real estate and convey title to new purchasers as they would have been able to do if a mortgage moratorium law had not been adopted.

A 5–4 majority, per HUGHES, C.J., upheld the challenged law. Recalling the origins of the clause, the Court first stated: "The widespread distress following the revolutionary period, and the plight of debtors, had called forth in the States an ignoble array of legislative schemes for the defeat of creditors and the invasion of contractual obligations. Legislative interferences had been so numerous and extreme that the confidence essential to prosperous trade had been undermined and the utter destruction of credit was threatened. [It] was necessary to interpose the restraining power of a central authority in order to secure the foundations even of 'private faith.' "

The Court nonetheless distinguished what it called "broad expresions" in earlier opinions and found that Minnesota's law "does not impair the integrity of the mortgage indebtedness. The obligation for interest remains. [Aside] from the extension of time, the other conditions of redemption are unaltered. [While] the mortgagee-purchaser is debarred from actual possession, he has, so far as rental value is concerned, the equivalent of possession during the extended period. [Not] only is the constitutional provision qualified by the measure of control which the state retains over remedial processes, but the state also continues to possess authority to safeguard the vital interests of its people. [Not] only are existing laws read into contracts in order to fix obligations as between the parties, but the reservation of existing attributes of sovereign power is also read into contracts as a postulate of the legal order. [The Constitution would not] permit the state to adopt as its policy the repudiation of debts or the destruction of contracts or the denial of means to enforce them. But it does not follow that conditions may not arise in which a temporary restraint of enforcement may be consistent with the spirit and purpose of the constitutional provision and thus found to be within the range of the reserved power of the state to protect the vital interests of the community."

UNITED STATES TRUST CO. v. NEW JERSEY, 431 U.S. 1 (1977), was a rare post-*Lochner*-era case to find a violation of the Contract Clause. To assure bondholders of the Port Authority of New York and New Jersey that the Authority would not in the future take over mass transit deficit operations beyond its financial reserves in 1962, the two states entered into a covenant limiting the numbers of such operations the Authority would absorb. In 1974, however, in order to subsidize more mass transportation, both states repealed the legislation implementing the covenant. A 4–3 majority, per Blackmun, J., agreed with the bondholders that the retroactive repeal of the covenant, which reduced the financial security of their bonds, violated the Contract Clause.

The following year the Court found another violation of the Contract Clause:

ALLIED STRUCTURAL STEEL v. SPANNAUS, 438 U.S. 234 (1978). Allied Steel adopted a pension plan that vested pension rights only when an employee had worked to age 65, or 15 years to age 60 or 20 years to age 55. However, Minnesota then enacted a law requiring employers of 100 workers or more who had established employee pension plans and who then went out of business in the state to pay full pensions to all its Minnesota employees who had worked ten years or more. A 6–3 majority, per STEWART, J., held that the law could not survive challenge under the contract clause: The law had "change[d] the company's obligations in an area where the element of reliance was vital—the funding of a pension plan" and "impose[d] a completely unexpected liability in potentially disabling amounts." Moreover, the law did not "deal with a situation remotely approaching the broad and desperate emergency economic conditions of the early 1930s—conditions of which the Court in *Blaisdell* took official notice."

BRENNAN, J., wrote forceful dissenting opinions in both the *U.S. Trust* and *Allied Steel* cases. Noting that *U.S. Trust* was "the first case in some 40 years in which this Court has seen fit to invalidate purely economic and social legislation on the strength of the Contract Clause," Brennan, J., voiced fear that the case might signal "a return to substantive constitutional review of States' policies and a new resolve to protect property owners whose interest or circumstances may happen to appeal to Members of this Court." Dissenting in *Allied Steel*, Brennan, J., maintained that the majority's "conversion of the Contract Clause into a limitation on the power of states to enact laws that impose duties additional to obligations assumed under private contracts must inevitably produce results difficult to square with any rational conception of a constitutional order." The "necessary consequence" of the majority's approach "is to vest judges with broad subjective discretion to protect property interests that happen to appeal to them."

Although the Court appeared to have revitalized the Contract Clause, it retreated sharply in two unanimous 1983 rulings: *Energy Reserves Group v. Kansas Power & Light Co.*, 459 U.S. 400 (upholding a Kansas law that imposed price controls on intrastate gas and prohibited natural gas producers from raising the purchase price despite provisions in contracts with consumers for raising the purchase price in the event of changes in the law); *Exxon Corp. v. Eagerton*, 462 U.S. 176 (upholding an Alabama law prohibiting oil producers from passing increases in a severance tax on to consumers despite pre-existing contracts requiring purchasers to reimburse producers for such taxes).

CHAPTER 6

PROTECTION OF INDIVIDUAL RIGHTS: DUE PROCESS, THE BILL OF RIGHTS, AND UNENUMERATED RIGHTS

■ ■ ■

1. APPLICABILITY OF THE BILL OF RIGHTS TO THE STATES; NATURE AND SCOPE OF FOURTEENTH AMENDMENT DUE PROCESS

I. INCORPORATION THEORIES

Barron v. Mayor and City Council of Baltimore, (Ch. 5, Sec. 1, I) held that the individual rights protected by the Bill of Rights impose limits on the federal government but not on state or local government. Did the adoption of the Fourteenth Amendment reverse *Barron*? For many years, the Supreme Court said that it did not. *Twining v. New Jersey,* 211 U.S. 78 (1908); *Palko v. Connecticut,* 302 U.S. 319 (1937); and *Adamson v. California,* 332 U.S. 46 (1947), rejected the view that the Fourteenth Amendment made all of the provisions of the Bill of Rights fully applicable to the states.[317] But the Court recognized that "it is possible that some of the personal rights safeguarded by the first eight Amendments against National action may also be safeguarded against state action, because a denial of them would be a denial of due process" (*Twining*) or because "the specific pledges of particular amendments have been found to be implicit in the concept of ordered liberty, and thus, through the Fourteenth Amendment, become valid as against the states" (*Palko*). And the Court in this period found among the procedural requirements of due process certain rules paralleling provisions of the first eight amendments. For example, *Powell v. Alabama,* 287 U.S. 45 (1932), held that defendants in a capital case were denied due process when a state refused them the aid of counsel. "The logically critical thing, however," explained Harlan, J., years

---

[317] *Palko,* which held that the Fourteenth Amendment did not encompass at least certain aspects of the double jeopardy prohibition of the Fifth Amendment, was overruled in *Benton v. Maryland* (1969), discussed below. The *Twining-Adamson* view that the Fifth Amendment privilege against self-incrimination is not incorporated in the fourteenth was rejected in *Malloy v. Hogan* (1964), also discussed below. *Griffin v. California,* 380 U.S. 609 (1965), subsequently applied *Malloy* to overrule the specific holdings of *Twining* and *Adamson,* which had permitted comment on a defendant's failure to take the stand at his criminal trial. These later decisions, however, were still consistent with the rejection of the "total incorporation" interpretation.

later, "was not that the rights had been found in the Bill of Rights, but that they were deemed * * * fundamental."[318]

Under the "ordered liberty"/"fundamental fairness" test, which procedural safeguards included in the Bill of Rights were applicable to the states and which were not? Consider CARDOZO, J., speaking for the *Palko* Court: "[There] emerges the perception of a rationalizing principle which gives to discrete instances a proper order and coherence. The right to trial by jury and the immunity from prosecution except as the result of an indictment [are] not of the very essence of a scheme of ordered liberty. To abolish them is not to violate a 'principle of justice so rooted in the traditions and conscience of our people as to be ranked as fundamental.' Few would be so narrow or provincial as to maintain that a fair and enlightened system of justice would be impossible without them. What is true of jury trials and indictments is true also, as the cases show, of the immunity from compulsory self-incrimination. This too might be lost, and justice still be done.

"[We] reach a different plane of social and moral values when we pass [to those provisions of the Bill of Rights] brought within the Fourteenth Amendment by a process of absorption. These in their origin were effective against the federal government alone. If the Fourteenth Amendment has absorbed them, the process of absorption has had its source in the belief that neither liberty nor justice would exist if they were sacrificed. This is true, for illustration, of freedom of thought and speech. Of that freedom one may say that it is the matrix, the indispensable condition, of nearly every other form of freedom. [Fundamental] too in the concept of due process, and so in that of liberty, is the thought that condemnation shall be rendered only after trial. The hearing, moreover, must be a real one, not a sham or pretense. [The] decision [in *Powell*] did not turn upon the fact that the benefit of counsel would have been guaranteed to the defendants by [the] Sixth Amendment if they had been prosecuted in a federal court [but on] the fact that in the particular situation laid before us [the aid] of counsel was essential to the substance of a hearing."

The "total incorporation" position received its strongest support in the *Adamson* dissents. In the principal dissent, BLACK, J., joined by Douglas, J., observed: "I cannot consider the Bill of Rights to be an outworn 18th Century 'strait jacket' as the *Twining* opinion did. Its provisions may be thought outdated abstractions by some. And it is true that they were designed to meet ancient evils. But they are the same kind of human evils that have emerged from century to century wherever excessive power is sought by the few at the expense of the many. In my judgment the people of no nation can lose their liberty so long as a Bill of Rights like ours survives and its basic purposes are conscientiously interpreted, enforced

---

[318] *Duncan v. Louisiana* (dissent joined by Stewart, J.), discussed below.

and respected so as to afford continuous protection against old, as well as new, devices and practices which might thwart those purposes. I fear to see the consequences of the Court's practice of substituting its own concepts of decency and fundamental justice for the language of the Bill of Rights as its point of departure in interpreting and enforcing that Bill of Rights. If the choice must be between the selective process of the *Palko* decision applying some of the Bill of Rights to the States, or the *Twining* rule applying none of them, I would choose the *Palko* selective process. But rather than accept either of these choices, I would follow what I believe was the original purpose of the Fourteenth Amendment—to extend to all the people of the nation the complete protection of the Bill of Rights.

"[T]o pass upon the constitutionality of statutes by looking to the particular standards enumerated in the Bill of Rights and other parts of the Constitution is one thing; to invalidate statutes because of application of 'natural law' deemed to be above and undefined by the Constitution is another. 'In the one instance, courts proceeding within clearly marked constitutional boundaries seek to execute policies written into the Constitution; in the other they roam at will in the limitless area of their own beliefs as to reasonableness and actually select policies, a responsibility which the Constitution entrusts to the legislative representatives of the people.' "[319]

Responding, FRANKFURTER, J.'s concurrence in *Adamson* stressed the "independent potency" of the Fourteenth Amendment Due Process Clause, maintaining that it "neither comprehends the specific provisions by which the founders deemed it appropriate to restrict the federal government nor is it confined to them":[320] "Between the incorporation of the Fourteenth Amendment into the Constitution and the beginning of the present membership of the Court—a period of 70 years—the scope of that Amendment was passed upon by 43 judges. Of all these judges only one, who may respectfully be called an eccentric exception, ever indicated the belief that the Fourteenth Amendment was a shorthand summary of the first eight Amendments theretofore limiting only the Federal Government, and that due process incorporated those eight Amendments as restrictions upon the powers of the States. [To] suggest that it is inconsistent with a truly free society to begin prosecutions without an indictment, to try petty

[319] Dissenting separately in *Adamson,* Murphy, J., joined by Rutledge, J., expressed a view sometimes called *total incorporation plus.* He "agree[d] that the specific guarantees of the Bill of Rights should be carried over intact into [the Fourteenth Amendment but was] not prepared to say that the latter is entirely and necessarily limited by the Bill of Rights. Occasions may arise where a proceeding falls so far short of conforming to fundamental standards of procedure as to warrant constitutional condemnation in terms of a lack of due process despite the absence of a specific provision of the Bill of Rights."

[320] See also Henry Friendly, *The Bill of Rights as a Code of Criminal Procedure,* 53 Calif.L.Rev. 929 (1965): "[N]o facile formula will enable the Court to escape its assigned task of deciding just what the Constitution protects from state action, as *Estes v. Texas,* 381 U.S. 532 (1965), where no 'specific' could be invoked, showed [for] procedural due process, and *Griswold v. Connecticut* [Sec. 2 infra] demonstrated for substantive due process."

civil cases without the paraphernalia of a common law jury, to take into consideration that one who has full opportunity to make a defense remains silent is, in de Tocqueville's phrase, to confound the familiar with the necessary.

"[Those] reading the English language with the meaning which it ordinarily conveys, those conversant with the political and legal history of the concept of due process, those sensitive to the relations of the States to the central government as well as the relation of some of the provisions of the Bill of Rights to the process of justice, would hardly recognize the Fourteenth Amendment as a cover for the various explicit provisions of the first eight Amendments. Some of these are enduring reflections of experience with human nature, while some express the restricted views of Eighteenth-Century England regarding the best methods for the ascertainment of facts. The notion that the Fourteenth Amendment was a covert way of imposing upon the States all the rules which it seemed important to Eighteenth Century statesmen to write into the Federal Amendments, was rejected by judges who were themselves witnesses of the process by which the Fourteenth Amendment became part of the Constitution. * * *

"Indeed, the suggestion that the Fourteenth Amendment incorporates the first eight Amendments as such is not unambiguously urged. [There] is suggested merely a selective incorporation of the first eight Amendments into the Fourteenth Amendment. Some are in and some are out, but we are left in the dark as to which are in and which are out. [If] the basis of selection is merely that those provisions of the first eight Amendments are incorporated which commend themselves to individual justices as indispensable to the dignity and happiness of a free man, we are thrown back to a merely subjective test. [In] the history of thought 'natural law' has a much longer and much better founded meaning and justification than such subjective selection of the first eight Amendments for incorporation into the Fourteenth. If all that is meant is that due process contains within itself certain minimal standards which are 'of the very essence of a scheme of ordered liberty,' *Palko,* putting upon this Court the duty of applying these standards from time to time, then we have merely arrived at the insight which our predecessors long ago expressed.

"[A] construction which gives to due process no independent function but turns it into a summary of the specific provisions of the Bill of Rights [would] assume that no other abuses would reveal themselves in the course of time than those which had become manifest in 1791. Such a view not only disregards the historic meaning of 'due process.' It leads inevitably to a warped construction of specific provisions of the Bill of Rights to bring within their scope conduct clearly condemned by due process but not easily fitting into the pigeon-holes of the specific provisions.

" * * * Judicial review [under the Due Process Clause] inescapably imposes upon this Court an exercise of judgment upon the whole course of the proceedings in order to ascertain whether they offend those canons of decency and fairness which express the notions of justice of English-speaking peoples even toward those charged with the most heinous offenses. These standards of justice are not authoritatively formulated anywhere as though they were prescriptions in a pharmacopoeia. But neither does the application of the Due Process Clause imply that judges are wholly at large. The judicial judgment in applying the Due Process Clause must move within the limits of accepted notions of justice and is not to be based upon the idiosyncracies of a merely personal judgment."

NOTES AND QUESTIONS

1. **Rationale.** Are Frankfurter and Black, JJ., each more persuasive in elucidating the defects of the other's test than the virtues of his own?

2. **Escape from the "idiosyncrasy of a personal judgment."** If, as Frankfurter, J., insists, the *Palko-Adamson* test is not based upon "the idiosyncrasies of a merely personal judgment," *whose* moral judgments furnish the answer? Those of the framers and ratifiers? The policy-making organs of state governments? Of state courts? Perhaps, regardless of the test employed, the answer will inevitably be found in "the actual practices of ordinary Americans in their daily lives." Akhil Reed Amar, *America's Lived Constitution*, 120 Yale.L.J. 1734 (2011). Is a focus on Americans too narrow? Should courts consider the opinions of people in other countries? All other countries or only those in the Anglo-Saxon tradition? See Sanford Kadish, *Methodology and Criteria in Due Process Adjudication—A Survey and Criticism,* 66 Yale L.J. 319 (1957).

3. **History.** Historical research has produced ample support for—and ample skepticism of—incorporation of the Bill of Rights. Is further historical research likely to do more than "further obscure the judicial value-choosing inherent in due process adjudication which can proceed with greater expectation of success if pursued openly and deliberately rather than under disguise"? Kadish, supra.

———

Although the Court continued the process of selective incorporation, DUNCAN v. LOUISIANA, 391 U.S. 145 (1968) (holding the Sixth Amendment right to jury trial applicable to the states via the Fourteenth Amendment), no longer employed the Cardozo-Frankfurter terminology (i.e., whether a particular guarantee was "implicit in the concept of ordered liberty" or required by "the 'immutable principles of justice' as conceived by a civilized society") but instead inquired whether the procedural safeguard included in the Bill of Rights was "fundamental to the *American scheme of justice*" (emphasis added) or "fundamental *in the context of the criminal processes maintained by the American States*" (emphasis added).

WHITE, J., speaking for the *Duncan* majority, noted:

"Earlier the Court can be seen as having asked, when inquiring into whether some particular procedural safeguard was required of a State, if a civilized system could be imagined that would not accord the particular protection. [The] recent cases, on the other hand, have proceeded upon the valid assumption that state criminal processes are not imaginary and theoretical schemes but actual systems bearing virtually every characteristic of the common-law system that has been developing contemporaneously in England and in this country. The question thus is whether given this kind of system a particular procedure is fundamental— whether, that is, a procedure is necessary to an Anglo-American regime of ordered liberty. [It] might be said that the limitation in question is not necessarily fundamental to fairness in every criminal system that might be imagined but is fundamental in the context of the criminal processes maintained by the American States.

"[A] criminal process which was fair and equitable but used no juries is easy to imagine. It would make use of alternative guarantees and protections which would serve the purposes that the jury serves in the English and American systems. Yet no American State has undertaken to construct such a system. Instead, every American State, including Louisiana, uses the jury extensively, and imposes very serious punishments only after a trial at which the defendant has a right to a jury's verdict. In every State, including Louisiana, the structure and style of the criminal process—the supporting framework and the subsidiary procedures—are of the sort that naturally complement jury trial, and have developed in connection with and in reliance upon jury trial."

Because the *Duncan* Court believed that "trial by jury in criminal cases is fundamental to the American scheme of justice," it held that it was guaranteed by the Fourteenth Amendment: "The guarantees of jury trial in the Federal and State Constitutions reflect a profound judgment about the way in which law should be enforced and justice administered. A right to jury trial is granted to criminal defendants in order to prevent oppression by the Government. Those who wrote our constitutions knew from history and experience that it was necessary to protect against unfounded criminal charges brought to eliminate enemies and against judges too responsive to the voice of higher authority. [P]roviding an accused with the right to be tried by a jury of his peers gave him an inestimable safeguard against the corrupt or overzealous prosecutor and against the compliant, biased, or eccentric judge. [F]ear of unchecked power, so typical of our State and Federal Governments in other respects, found expression in the criminal law in this insistence upon community participation in the determination of guilt or innocence. The deep commitment of the Nation to the right of jury trial in serious criminal cases as a defense against arbitrary law enforcement qualifies for protection under the Due Process Clause of the Fourteenth Amendment, and must therefore be respected by the States."

HARLAN, J., joined by Stewart, J., dissented: "Even if I could agree that the question before us is whether Sixth Amendment jury trial is totally 'in' or totally 'out' [see Part II infra], I can find in the Court's opinion no real reasons for concluding that it should be 'in'. The basis for differentiating among clauses in the Bill of Rights cannot be that [only] some are old and much praised, or that only some have played an important role in the development of federal law. These things are true of all. The Court says that some clauses are more 'fundamental' than others, but [uses] this word in a sense that would have astonished Mr. Justice Cardozo and which, in addition, is of no help. The word does not mean 'analytically critical to procedural fairness' for no real analysis of the role of the jury in making procedures fair is even attempted. Instead, the word turns out to mean 'old,' 'much praised,' and 'found in the Bill of Rights.' The definition of 'fundamental' thus turns out to be circular.

"[Jury trial] is of course not without virtues [but its] principal original virtue—[the limitations it] imposes on a tyrannous judiciary—has largely disappeared. [The] jury system [is] a cumbersome process, not only imposing great cost in time and money on both the State and the jurors themselves, but also contributing to delay in the machinery of justice. [That] trial by jury is not the only fair way of adjudicating criminal guilt is well attested by the fact that it is not the prevailing way, either in England or in this country. [In] sum, there is a wide range of views on the desirability of trial by jury, and on the ways to make it most effective when it is used; there is also considerable variation from State to State in local conditions such as the size of the criminal caseload, the ease or difficulty of summoning jurors, and other trial conditions bearing on fairness. We have before us, therefore, an almost perfect example of a situation in which [the states should serve as laboratories. Instead,] the Court has chosen to impose upon every State one means of trying criminal cases; it is a good means, but it is not the only fair means, and it is not demonstrably better than the alternatives States might devise."

———

Although the Court has remained unwilling to accept the total incorporationists' reading of the Fourteenth Amendment, in the 1960s it "selectively" "incorporated" or "absorbed" more and more of the specifics of the Bill of Rights into the Fourteenth Amendment. As WHITE, J., observed in *Duncan*: "In resolving conflicting claims concerning the meaning of this spacious [Fourteenth Amendment] language, the Court has looked increasingly to the Bill of Rights for guidance; many of the rights guaranteed by the first eight Amendments to the Constitution have been held to be protected against state action by the Due Process Clause of the Fourteenth Amendment.[321] That clause now protects the right to compensation for property taken by the State; the rights of speech, press, and religion covered by the First Amendment; the Fourth Amendment rights to be free from unreasonable searches and seizures and to have excluded from criminal trials any evidence illegally seized; the right guaranteed by the Fifth Amendment to be free of compelled self-incrimination; and the Sixth Amendment rights to counsel, to a speedy and public trial; to confrontation of opposing witnesses; and to compulsory process for obtaining witnesses."

Most of the incorporation cases that divided the Warren Court involved rights of suspects in criminal investigations and prosecutions.[322] Such rights can be understood as part of the "process" that is "due" to a person before he or she is deprived of life or liberty. However, the foregoing catalogue also includes non-procedural rights, such as speech, press, and religion. Can these rights be incorporated via the Fourteenth Amendment's Due Process Clause without reliance on the concept of *substantive* due process? Is it notable that the Court did not distinguish between procedural and substantive rights in this context?

II. IS THE BILL OF RIGHTS INCORPORATED "JOT-FOR-JOT"?

In the 1960s, the Court seemed to be incorporating not only the general concept of federal rights, but applying each incorporated provision to the states *to the exact same extent* it applied to the federal government. Thus, BRENNAN, J., observed for a majority in *Malloy v. Hogan,* 378 U.S. 1 (1964): "We have held that the guarantees of the First Amendment, the prohibition of unreasonable searches and seizures of the Fourth Amendment, and the right to counsel guaranteed by the Sixth Amendment, are all to be enforced against the States under the Fourteenth Amendment *according to the same standards that protect those personal rights against federal encroachment.*

---

[321] See also Black, J., joined by Douglas, J., concurring in *Duncan*: "[I] believe as strongly as ever that the Fourteenth Amendment was intended to make the Bill of Rights applicable to the States. I have been willing to support the selective incorporation doctrine, however, as an alternative, although perhaps less historically supportable than complete incorporation [because it] keeps judges from roaming at will in their own notions of what policies outside the Bill of Rights are desirable and what are not. And, most importantly for me, the selective incorporation process has the virtue of having already worked to make most of the Bill of Rights' protections applicable to the States."

[322] In the area of criminal procedure, the Court has come very close to incorporating all of the relevant Bill of Rights guarantees. But one exception remains on the books. *Hurtado v. California,* 110 U.S. 516 (1884), refused to apply to the states the Fifth Amendment requirement that prosecution be initiated by grand jury indictment. For an overview of the development and application of the selective incorporation doctrine see Jerold H. Israel, *Selective Incorporation: Revisited,* 71 Geo.L.J. 253 (1982).

[The] Court thus has rejected the notion that the Fourteenth Amendment applies to the States only a 'watered-down, subjective version of the individual guarantees of the Bill of Rights.' " (Emphasis added.) And WHITE, J., put it for a majority in *Duncan:* "Because we believe that trial by jury in criminal cases is fundamental to the American scheme of justice, we hold that the Fourteenth Amendment guarantees a right of jury trial in all criminal cases which—*were they to be tried in a federal court*—would come within the Sixth Amendment's guarantee." (Emphasis added.)[323]

HARLAN, J., was the most persistent and powerful critic of the *Malloy-Duncan* approach to Fourteenth Amendment Due Process. "The consequence," he protested in his *Malloy* dissent, "is inevitably disregard of all relevant differences which may exist between state and federal criminal law and its enforcement. The ultimate result is compelled uniformity, which is inconsistent with the purpose of our federal system and which is achieved either by encroachment on the State's sovereign powers or by dilution in federal law enforcement of the specific protections found in the Bill of Rights." See also Harlan, J.'s concurring opinion in *Pointer v. Texas,* 380 U.S. 400 (1965) (holding that an accused's Sixth Amendment right to confront the witnesses against him applies in its entirety to the states via the Fourteenth Amendment) and his dissenting opinions in *Duncan* and *Benton v. Maryland* (fn. 7 supra).

———

In the 1970s matters were brought to a head by the "right to jury trial" cases: *Baldwin v. New York,* 399 U.S. 66 (1970) (no offense can be deemed "petty," thus dispensing with the Fourteenth and Sixth Amendment rights to jury trial, where more than six months incarceration is authorized); *Williams v. Florida,* 399 U.S. 78 (1970) ("the fact that the jury at common law was composed of precisely 12 is a historical accident, unnecessary to effect the purposes of the jury system" and thus 6-person jury in criminal cases does not violate Sixth Amendment, as applied to the states via Fourteenth);[324] and the 1972 *Apodaca* and *Johnson* cases, discussed below, dealing with whether unanimous jury verdicts are required in criminal cases.

Dissenting in *Baldwin* and concurring in *Williams,* HARLAN, J., maintained: "[*Williams*] evinces [a] recognition that the 'incorporationist' view of the Due Process Clause of the Fourteenth Amendment, which underlay *Duncan* and is now carried forward into *Baldwin,* must be

---

[323] See also Justice Marshall's opinion for the Court in *Benton v. Maryland,* 395 U.S. 784 (1969) (the validity of the state conviction "must be judged not by the watered-down standard enumerated in *Palko,* but *under this Court's interpretations of the Fifth Amendment double jeopardy provision*"). (Emphasis added.)

[324] But *Ballew v. Georgia,* 435 U.S. 223 (1978), subsequently held that a state trial in a non-petty criminal case to a jury of only five persons did deprive a defendant of the right to trial by jury guaranteed by the Sixth and Fourteenth Amendments.

tempered to allow the States more elbow room in ordering their own criminal systems. With that much I agree. But to accomplish this by diluting constitutional protections within the federal system itself is something to which I cannot possibly subscribe. Tempering the rigor of *Duncan* should be done forthrightly, by facing up to the fact that at least in this area the 'incorporation' doctrine does not fit well with our federal structure, and by the same token that *Duncan* was wrongly decided.

"[Rather] than bind the States by the hitherto undeviating and unquestioned federal practice of 12-member juries, the Court holds, based on a poll of state practice, that a six-man jury satisfies the guarantee of a trial by jury in a federal criminal system and consequently carries over to the States. This is a constitutional renvoi. With all respect, I consider that before today it would have been unthinkable to suggest that the Sixth Amendment's right to a trial by jury is satisfied by a jury of six, or less, as is left open by the Court's opinion in *Williams,* or by less than a unanimous verdict, a question also reserved in today's decision.[325]

"[These] decisions demonstrate that the difference between a 'due process' approach, that considers each particular case on its own bottom to see whether the right alleged is one 'implicit in the concept of ordered liberty,' and 'selective incorporation' is not an abstract one whereby different verbal formulae achieve the same results. The internal logic of the selective incorporation doctrine cannot be respected if the Court is both committed to interpreting faithfully the meaning of the federal Bill of Rights and recognizing the governmental diversity that exists in this country. The 'backlash' in *Williams* exposes the malaise, for there the Court dilutes a federal guarantee in order to reconcile the logic of 'incorporation,' the 'jot-for-jot and case-for-case' application of the federal right to the States, with the reality of federalism. Can one doubt that had Congress tried to undermine the common law right to trial by jury before *Duncan* came on the books the history today recited would have barred such action? Can we expect repeat performances when this Court is called upon to give definition and meaning to other federal guarantees that have been 'incorporated'?

"[I]t is time [for] this Court to face up to the reality implicit in today's holdings and reconsider the 'incorporation' doctrine before its leveling tendencies further retard development in the field of criminal procedure by stifling flexibility in the States and by discarding the possibility of federal leadership by example."

---

[325] Cf. Frankfurter, J., for the Court in *Rochin v. California* (1952) (discussed in Part IV infra): "Words being symbols do not speak without a gloss. [T]he gloss may be the deposit of history, whereby a term gains technical content. Thus the requirements of the Sixth and Seventh Amendments for trial by jury in the federal courts have a rigid meaning. No changes or chances can alter the content of the verbal symbol of 'jury'—a body of twelve men who must reach a unanimous conclusion if the verdict is to go against the defendant."

In the companion cases of *Apodaca v. Oregon,* 406 U.S. 404 (1972) and *Johnson v. Louisiana,* 406 U.S. 356 (1972), upholding the constitutionality of less-than-unanimous jury verdicts in state criminal cases, eight justices adhered to the *Duncan* position that each element of the Sixth Amendment right to jury trial applies to the states to the same extent it applies to the federal government, but split 4–4 over whether the federal guarantee *did require* jury unanimity in criminal cases. State convictions by less than unanimous votes were sustained only because of the views of the newly appointed ninth member of the Court.

POWELL, J., read the Sixth Amendment as requiring jury unanimity, but—taking a Harlan-type approach—concluded that *this feature* of the federal right is not "so fundamental to the essentials of jury trial" as to require unanimity in state criminal cases as a matter of Fourteenth Amendment Due Process:[326] "[I]n holding that the Fourteenth Amendment has incorporated 'jot-for-jot and case-for-case' every element of the Sixth Amendment, the Court derogates principles of federalism that are basic to our system. In the name of uniform application of high standards of due process, the Court has embarked upon a course of constitutional interpretation that deprives the States of freedom to experiment with adjudicatory processes different from the federal model. At the same time, the Court's understandable unwillingness to impose requirements that it finds unnecessarily rigid has culminated in the dilution of federal rights that were, until these decisions, never seriously questioned. The doubly undesirable consequence of this reasoning process, labeled by Mr. Justice Harlan as 'constitutional schizophrenia,' may well be detrimental both to the state and federal criminal justice systems."[327]

BRENNAN, J., joined by Marshall, J., dissented: "Readers of today's opinions may be understandably puzzled why convictions by 11–1 and 10–2 jury votes are affirmed [when] a majority of the Court agrees that the Sixth Amendment requires a unanimous verdict in federal criminal jury trials, and a majority also agrees that the right to jury trial guaranteed by the Sixth Amendment is to be enforced against the States according to the same standards that protect that right against federal encroachment. The reason is that while my Brother Powell agrees that a unanimous verdict is required in federal criminal trials, he does not agree that the Sixth

---

[326] But *Burch v. Louisiana,* 441 U.S. 130 (1979), subsequently held, without a dissent on this issue, that conviction by a nonunanimous *six-person* jury in a state criminal trial for a nonpetty offense did violate the Sixth and Fourteenth Amendment rights to trial by jury.

[327] See also Powell, J., joined by Burger, C.J., and Rehnquist, J., dissenting in *Crist v. Bretz,* 437 U.S. 28 (1978) (holding that federal rule as to when jeopardy "attaches" in jury trials applies to state cases). Consider, too, Burger, C.J.'s separate opinion in *Crist v. Bretz* (contending that constitutional guarantees are trivialized by the insistence on mechanical uniformity between state and federal practice") and Rehnquist, J.'s separate opinion in *Buckley v. Valeo,* p. 1174 infra, maintaining that "not all of the strictures which the First Amendment imposes upon Congress are carried over against the States by the Fourteenth Amendment, [but] only the 'general principle' of free speech."

Amendment right to a jury trial is to be applied in the same way to State and Federal Governments. In that circumstance, it is arguable that the affirmance of the convictions [is] not inconsistent with a view that today's decision is a holding that only a unanimous verdict will afford the accused in a state criminal prosecution the jury trial guaranteed him by the Sixth Amendment. In any event, the affirmance must not obscure that the majority of the Court remains of the view that, as in the case of every specific of the Bill of Rights that extends to the States, the Sixth Amendment's jury trial guarantee, however it is to be construed, has identical application against both State and Federal Governments."

III. IN *MCDONALD V. CITY OF CHICAGO*, THE COURT LOOKS BACK ON ITS "INCORPORATION" OF BILL OF RIGHTS GUARANTEES

McDonald v. Chicago (set forth at p. 583 infra) presented the question whether the Second Amendment right to keep and bear arms is incorporated as an individual right against state and local governments. In Part II.D of his majority opinion, ALITO, J., looked back on various cases dealing with the relationship between the Bill of Rights and Fourteenth Amendment Due Process: Although "the Court never has embraced Justice Black's 'total incorporation' theory, [it] eventually incorporated almost all of the provisions of the Bill of Rights." During the 1960s, the Court "abandoned three of [the] characteristics of the earlier period. The Court made it clear that the governing standard is not whether *any* 'civilized system [can] be imagined that would not accord the particular protection.' *Duncan*. Instead, the Court inquired whether a particular Bill of Rights guarantee is fundamental to *our* scheme of ordered liberty and system of justice.

"[The] Court also shed any reluctance to hold that rights guaranteed by the Bill of Rights met the requirements for protection under the Due Process Clause. [Only] a handful of the Bill of Rights protections remain unincorporated.

"Finally, the Court abandoned 'the notion that the Fourteenth Amendment applies to the States only a watered-down, subjective version of the individual guarantees of the Bill of Rights.' [Instead,] the Court decisively held that incorporated Bill of Rights protections 'are all to be enforced against the States under the Fourteenth Amendment according to the same standards that protect those personal rights against federal encroachment. * * * 14' "

---

14 **[Ct's Note]** There is one exception to this general rule. The Court has held that although the Sixth Amendment right to trial by jury requires a unanimous jury verdict in federal criminal trials, it does not require a unanimous jury verdict in state criminal trials. See *Apodaca*. [But] that ruling was the result of an unusual division among the Justices, not an endorsement of the two-track approach to incorporation. In *Apodaca*, eight Justices agreed that the Sixth Amendment

IV. HOW MUCH MORE SPECIFIC ARE PROVISIONS OF THE BILL OF RIGHTS THAN DUE PROCESS GENERALLY? THE CASE OF BODILY EXTRACTIONS

Black, J.'s argument for total incorporation leaned heavily on the idea that the specific provisions of the Bill of Rights provide much greater guidance to judges than the generalities of due process. Yet most language in the Bill of Rights is itself general, at least when specific problems arise under a particular phrase. In such cases, does dwelling on the language simply shift the focus of broad judicial inquiry from "due process" to e.g., "freedom of speech," "establishment of religion," "unreasonable searches and seizures," "excessive bail," "cruel and unusual punishments," and "the assistance of counsel"? See Yale Kamisar, *How Much Does It Really Matter Whether Courts Work Within the "Clearly Marked" Provisions of the Bill of Rights or with the Generalities of the Fourteenth Amendment?*, 18 J. Contemp. Legal Issues 513 (2009).

In considering whether the right to counsel attaches at the time of arrest, preliminary hearing, arraignment, or not until the trial itself, or includes probation and parole revocation hearings, or applies to juvenile delinquency proceedings, deportation hearings, or civil commitments, or, where the defendant is indigent, includes the right to *assigned* counsel or an assigned psychiatrist at state expense, how helpful is the Sixth Amendment language entitling an accused to "the assistance of counsel for his defense"? Is the specificity or direction of this language significantly greater than that of the Due Process Clause standing alone? Put differently, do cases construing "enumerated" rights employ a different methodology from those involving "unenumerated" rights?

To turn to another cluster of problems—which form the basis for this part—in considering whether, and under what conditions, the police may direct the pumping of a person's stomach to uncover incriminating evidence, or the taking of a blood sample from him, without his consent, do the specific guarantees in the Bill of Rights against "unreasonable searches and seizures" and against compelling a person to be "a witness against himself" free the Court from the demands of appraising and judging involved in answering these questions by interpreting the Due Process Clause?

———

ROCHIN v. CALIFORNIA, 342 U.S. 165 (1952): "Having 'some information' that [Rochin] was selling narcotics, three deputy sheriffs [forced] open the door to [his] room" and found him "sitting partly dressed

---

applies identically to both the Federal Government and the States. [*Apodaca*], therefore, does not undermine the well-established rule that incorporated Bill of Rights protections apply identically to the States and the Federal Government. * * *

on the side of the bed, upon which his wife was lying. On a 'night stand' beside the bed the deputies spied two capsules. When asked 'Whose stuff is this?' Rochin seized the capsules and put them in his mouth. A struggle ensued, in the course of which the three officers 'jumped upon him' and [unsuccessfully] attempted to extract the capsules. [Rochin] was handcuffed and taken to a hospital. At the direction of one of the officers a doctor forced an emetic solution through a tube into Rochin's stomach against his will. This 'stomach pumping' produced vomiting. In the vomited matter were found two capsules which proved to contain morphine. [Rochin] was convicted [of possessing morphine] and sentenced to sixty days' imprisonment. The chief evidence against him was the two capsules."

The Court, per FRANKFURTER, J., concluded that the officers' conduct violated Fourteenth Amendment due process: "This is conduct that shocks the conscience. Illegally breaking into the privacy of the petitioner, the struggle to open his mouth and remove what was there, the forcible extraction of his stomach's contents—this course of proceeding by agents of government to obtain evidence is bound to offend even hardened sensibilities. They are methods too close to the rack and the screw to permit of constitutional differentiation. [Due] process of law, as a historic and generative principle, precludes defining, and thereby confining, [civilized] standards of conduct more precisely than to say that convictions cannot be brought about by methods that offend 'a sense of justice.' It would be a stultification of the responsibility which the course of constitutional history has cast upon this Court to hold that in order to convict a man the police cannot extract by force what is in his mind but can extract what is in his stomach. [E]ven though statements contained in them may be independently established as true[,] [c]oerced confessions offend the community's sense of fair play and decency. So here, to sanction the brutal conduct which naturally enough was condemned by the court whose judgment is before us, would be to afford brutality the cloak of law. Nothing would be more calculated to discredit law and thereby to brutalize the temper of a society."

BLACK, J., concurring, maintained that the Fifth Amendment's protection against compelled self-incrimination applied to the states and that "a person is compelled to be a witness against himself not only when he is compelled to testify, but also when as here, incriminating evidence is forcibly taken from him by a contrivance of modern science." In his view, "faithful adherence to the specific guarantees in the Bill of Rights insures a more permanent protection of individual liberty than that which can be afforded by the nebulous [Fourteenth Amendment due process] standards stated by the majority."

DOUGLAS, J., concurring, also would have rested the decision on the privilege against self-incrimination.

BREITHAUPT v. ABRAM, 352 U.S. 432 (1957), set a high threshold for finding a *Rochin* violation. In *Breithaupt,* the police took a blood sample from an unconscious person who had been involved in a fatal automobile collision. A majority, per CLARK, J., affirmed a manslaughter conviction based on the blood sample (which showed intoxication). The Court distinguished the stomach-pumping in *Rochin* as "brutal" and "offensive." By contrast, in *Breithaupt* the Court emphasized that the sample was taken "under the protective eye of a physician" and that "the blood test procedure has become routine in our everyday life." The "interests of society in the scientific determination of intoxication, one of the great causes of the mortal hazards of the road," outweighed "so slight an intrusion" of a person's body.

WARREN, C.J., joined by Black and Douglas, JJ., dissenting, deemed *Rochin* controlling, and argued that police efforts to curb the narcotics traffic, involved in *Rochin,* "is surely a state interest of at least as great magnitude as the interest in highway law enforcement. [Only] personal reaction to the stomach pump and the blood test can distinguish the [two cases]."

DOUGLAS, J., joined by Black, J., dissented, maintaining that "if the decencies of a civilized state are the test, it is repulsive to me for the police to insert needles into an unconscious person in order to get the evidence necessary to convict him, whether they find the person unconscious, give him a pill which puts him to sleep, or use force to subdue him."

Nine years later, the Court upheld the taking by a physician, at police direction, of a blood sample from an injured person, over his objection.

SCHMERBER v. CALIFORNIA, 384 U.S. 757 (1966). In affirming the conviction for operating a vehicle while under the influence of intoxicating liquor, a 5–4 majority, per BRENNAN, J., ruled: (1) that the extraction of blood from petitioner under the aforementioned circumstances "did not offend" that "sense of justice" "of which we spoke in *Rochin,*" thus reaffirming *Breithaupt*; (2) that the Fifth Amendment privilege against self-incrimination, now binding on the states, "protects an accused only from being compelled to testify against himself, or otherwise provide the State with evidence of a testimonial or communicative nature, and that the withdrawal of blood and use of the analysis in question [did] not involve compulsion to these ends"; and (3) that the Fourth Amendment protection against unreasonable searches and seizures, now binding on the states, was satisfied because: (a) "there was plainly probable cause" to arrest and charge petitioner and to suggest "the required relevance and likely success of a test of petitioner's blood for alcohol"; (b) the officer "might reasonably have believed that he was confronted with an emergency, in which the delay necessary to obtain a warrant, under the circumstances, threatened 'the destruction of evidence' "; and (c) "the test chosen to measure petitioner's blood-alcohol level was a reasonable one" that "was performed in a reasonable manner."

BLACK, J., joined by Douglas, J., dissenting, expressed incredulity at the majority's "conclusion that compelling a person to give his blood to help the State convict him is not equivalent to compelling him to be a witness against himself. [It] is a strange hierarchy of values that allows the State to extract a human being's blood to convict him of a crime because of the blood's content but proscribes compelled production of his lifeless papers."[328]

WINSTON v. LEE, 470 U.S. 753 (1985), per BRENNAN, J., held that the surgical removal of a bullet from the body of an objecting suspect required more than ordinary probable cause to believe that the bullet would provide evidence of crime. "A compelled surgical intrusion into an individual's body for evidence," the Court explained in distinguishing *Schmerber*, "implicates expectations of privacy and security of such magnitude that the intrusion may be 'unreasonable' even if likely to produce evidence of a crime." The decision relied only on the Fourth Amendment (as incorporated), and did not directly address the question whether the intrusion could also be said to violate the Due Process Clause under the theory of *Rochin*.[329]

NOTES AND QUESTIONS

1.   In light of *Rochin, Breithaupt, Schmerber,* and *Winston*, when courts decide constitutional questions by "looking to" the Bill of Rights, to what extent do they proceed, as Black, J., said in *Adamson,* "within clearly marked constitutional boundaries"? To what extent does resort to these "particular standards" enable courts to avoid substituting their "own concepts of decency and fundamental justice" for the language of the Constitution?

2.   *The "shocks-the-conscience" test and substantive due process claims.* SACRAMENTO v. LEWIS, 523 U.S. 833 (1998), held, per SOUTER, J., that a police officer did not violate substantive due process by causing death through "reckless indifference" to, or "reckless disregard" for, a person's life in a high-speed automobile chase of a speeding motorcyclist. (The chase resulted

---

[328] Warren, C.J., and Douglas, J., dissented in separate opinions, each adhering to his dissenting views in *Breithaupt*. In a third dissent, Fortas, J., maintained that "petitioner's privilege against self-incrimination applies" and, moreover, that "under the Due Process Clause, the State, in its role as prosecutor, has no right to extract blood from [anyone] over his protest."

[329] Burger, C.J., concurred on the understanding that the holding would permit detaining a suspect "if there are reasonable grounds to believe that natural bodily functions will disclose the presence of contraband materials secreted internally." Blackmun and Rehnquist, JJ., concurred only in the judgment, without explaining the nature of their disagreement with the rationale of the lead opinion.

in the death of the motorcyclist's passenger when the police car skidded into the passenger after the cycle had tipped over). In such circumstances, concluded the Court, "only a purpose to cause harm unrelated to the legitimate object of arrest will satisfy the element of arbitrary conduct shocking to the conscience, necessary for a due process violation." From the early Nineteenth Century, observed the Court, "we have understood the core of the concept to be protection against arbitrary action. [Since *Rochin*] we have spoken of the cognizable level of executive abuse of power as that which shocks the conscience. [In] the intervening years we have repeatedly adhered to *Rochin*'s benchmark. [Regardless] whether [the officer's] behavior offended the reasonableness held up by tort law or the balance struck in law enforcement's own codes of sound practice, it does not shock the conscience."[330]

2. THE RIGHT OF "PRIVACY" (OR "AUTONOMY")

Introductory Note

The cases in this section concern the so-called right of "privacy" or "autonomy." They involve some of the most controversial constitutional issues of the post-*Lochner* era, especially abortion. These materials raise a variety of distinct questions that the Court and commentators sometimes treat as intersecting or overlapping: (1) does the Constitution authorize judges to recognize rights not expressly set forth in the text?; (2) if so, what method or methods should be used to discern the content of those rights?; (3) applying the proper method or methods, what rights should be recognized?; and (4) under what circumstances may government infringe such rights?

None of the foregoing questions arises *only* in the context of the right to privacy. Consider that: (1) before the Bill of Rights was even a decade old, the general question of unenumerated rights was mooted in the Supreme Court in *Calder v. Bull* (Ch. 5, Sec. 1, I), a case that involved inheritance, not privacy as used in the modern cases; (2) the Court in *Calder* also considered questions of methodology and so did the affirmative power decisions of the Marshall Court, most famously *McCulloch v. Maryland* (Ch. 2, Sec. 1); (3) The debate over incorporation of the Bill of Rights, (Sec. 1 supra) reveals that enumeration hardly eliminates controversy over what rights courts should recognize; and (4) questions about when rights may be overridden are ubiquitous, and the Court has

---

[330] Concurring in the judgment, Scalia, J., joined by Thomas, J., would not have decided the case by applying the "shocks-the-conscience" test but "on the ground that respondents offer no textual or historical support for their alleged due process right."

Kennedy, J., joined by O'Connor, J. joined the opinion of the Court, but also wrote separately. They "share[d] Justice Scalia's concerns about using the phrase 'shocks the conscience' in a manner suggesting that it is a self-defining test." The phrase, they observed, "has the unfortunate connotation of a standard laden with subjective assessments. In that respect, it must be viewed with considerable skepticism."

utilized the same basic framework for weighing government interests against rights in the privacy context that it uses with respect to freedom of speech (Ch. 7) and equal protection (Ch. 9).

What then accounts for the unusually heated debate about the right of privacy in the current era? As you read the materials in this section, consider whether the issues of constitutional interpretation posed are especially difficult or whether, instead, the underlying issues are especially divisive.

———

Two *Lochner*-era cases are often cited as antecedents of the modern right to privacy. In *Meyer v. Nebraska*, (p. 1073 infra) (1923) the Court reversed the conviction of a parochial teacher who taught an elementary student in German, in violation of a state law forbidding instruction in any language but English. *Pierce v. Society of Sisters*, (p. 1070 infra) (1925), invalidated a law that required parents to send their children to public school through the eighth grade, insofar as it forbade sending them to private school. Although *Meyer* and *Pierce* can be understood as protecting freedom of speech, they were decided long before the cases incorporating the Bill of Rights, and relied in substantial part on principles of economic liberty. In addition, the Court in *Pierce* described both cases as protecting "the liberty of parents and guardians to direct the upbringing and education of children under their control." Does the association with *Lochner*-era economic liberty render *Pierce* and *Meyer* inappropriate as precedents for modern substantive due process? Or does their recognition of parental rights represent a rare instance of the old Court affording constitutional protection to the "correct" values?

———

SKINNER v. OKLAHOMA, 316 U.S. 535 (1942), per DOUGLAS, J., invalidated Oklahoma's Habitual Criminal Sterilization Act, which authorized the sterilization of persons previously convicted and imprisoned two or more times of crimes "amounting to felonies involving moral turpitude" and thereafter convicted of such a felony and sentenced to prison. (Petitioner, previously convicted of "stealing chickens" and robbery with firearms, had again been convicted of robbery with firearms.) The Act expressly exempted embezzlement, political offenses, and revenue act violations from the category of moral turpitude felonies. Thus, one convicted three times of larceny could be subjected to sterilization, but the embezzler could not—although "the nature of the two crimes is intrinsically the same" and they are otherwise punishable in the same manner. The Oklahoma law "runs afoul of the equal protection clause" because—

"We are dealing here with legislation which involves one of the basic civil rights of man. Marriage and procreation are fundamental to the very existence and survival of the race. [In] evil or reckless hands [the power to sterilize] can cause races or types which are inimical to the dominant group to wither and disappear. There is no redemption for the individual whom the law touches. [He] is forever deprived of a basic liberty. We mention these matters [in] emphasis of our view that strict scrutiny of the classification which a State makes in a sterilization law is essential, lest unwittingly, or otherwise, invidious discriminations are made against groups or types of individuals in violation of the constitutional guaranty of just and equal laws."

The Court distinguished *Buck v. Bell*, 274 U.S. 200 (1927), which had upheld a sterilization law applicable only to "mental defectives" in state institutions: "[It] was pointed out [in that case] that 'so far as the operations enable those who otherwise must be kept confined to be returned to the world, and thus open the asylum to others, the equality aimed at will be more nearly reached.' Here there is no such saving feature."

STONE, C.J., concurring in the result in *Skinner*, thought that "the real question [is] not one of equal protection, but whether the wholesale condemnation of a class to such an invasion of personal liberty, without opportunity to any individual to show that his is not the type of case which would justify resort to it, satisfies the demands of due process. [A] law which condemns, without hearing, all the individuals of a class to so harsh a measure as the present because some or even many merit condemnation, is lacking in the first principles of due process."

JACKSON, J., concurred in both the majority and the separate opinion of Stone, C.J., arguing that equal protection and due process provided alternative grounds for the holding.

NOTES AND QUESTIONS

1. **What kind of equal protection?** Legislatures routinely provide different punishment ranges for different crimes, even when those crimes may be considered equally serious. Moreover, judges frequently have discretion to select a sentence from a wide statutory range. Yet these differences do not typically raise serious equal protection concerns except in two circumstances. Laws or other government policies trigger what the *Skinner* Court and later cases call "strict scrutiny" when they utilize invidious classifications such as race (Ch. 9, Sec. 2) or draw distinctions concerning fundamental rights (Ch. 9, Sec. 5).

In a case like *Skinner*, to what extent is the equal protection rationale *really* a liberty rationale? Do liberty and equality overlap? "The tangling" of liberty and equality, says Ira Lupu, *Untangling the Strands of the Fourteenth Amendment*, 77 Mich.L.Rev. 981 (1979), "is most apparent and most serious when viewed in its relationship to the so-called 'fundamental rights' developments in both equal protection and due process clause interpretation. In the sense used here, fundamental rights include all the claims of individual rights, drawn from sources outside of the first eight amendments, that the Supreme Court has elevated to preferred status (that is, rights which the government may infringe only when it demonstrates extraordinary justification)."

2.   ***What kind of due process?*** Stone, C.J., contends that due process provides a better justification for the result in *Skinner*, but he would still allow sterilization as punishment for crime. In modern doctrinal terms, we might term his rationale one of "procedural due process" (discussed in Sec. 5 and Sec. 6 infra). The problem with Oklahoma's law, in this view, is that it allowed the state to sterilize the wrong people. But should the state have the substantive power to limit a person's reproductive freedom as punishment for crime? Kristyn M. Walker, *Judicial Control of Reproductive Freedom: The Use of Norplant as a Condition of Probation,* 78 Iowa.L.Rev. 779 (1993), argues that conditioning probation on the surgical implantation of a contraceptive should have to satisfy strict scrutiny, a test more commonly associated with *substantive* due process than with procedural due process.

Would the Eighth Amendment's prohibition on "cruel and unusual punishments" provide a better basis for restricting the state's power to limit reproductive capacity as punishment for crime? Such a shift has at least two difficulties. First, the Eighth Amendment only applies to the states via the Fourteenth Amendment's Due Process Clause, so due process remains part of the analysis. Second, shifting from a due process to an Eighth Amendment rationale could lead to the anomalous result that the state would have greater latitude to restrict reproduction if a person has committed no crime at all, because the Eighth Amendment has been held inapplicable to persons who have not been convicted of a crime. For them, due process provides the measure of constitutional rights. See *Bell v. Wolfish*, 441 U.S. 520 (1979).

GRISWOLD V. CONNECTICUT
381 U.S. 479, 85 S.Ct. 1678, 14 L.Ed.2d 510 (1965).

JUSTICE DOUGLAS delivered the opinion of the Court.

Appellant Griswold is Executive Director of the Planned Parenthood League of Connecticut. Appellant Buxton [is] Medical Director for the League at its Center in New Haven—a center open [when] appellants were arrested. They gave information, instruction, and medical advice to *married persons* as to the means of preventing conception. [Fees] were usually charged, although some couples were serviced free.

[The constitutionality of two Connecticut statutes is involved.] [One] provides: "Any person who uses any drug, medicinal article or instrument for the purpose of preventing conception shall be fined not less than fifty dollars or imprisoned not less than sixty days nor more than one year or be both fined and imprisoned." [The other] provides: "Any person who assists, abets, counsels, causes, hires or commands another to commit any offense may be prosecuted and punished as if he were the principal offender." The appellants were found guilty as accessories and fined $100 each.

[We] are met with a wide range of questions that implicate the Due Process Clause. [Overtones] of some arguments suggest that *Lochner* should be our guide. But we decline that invitation. [We] do not sit as a super-legislature to determine the wisdom, need, and propriety of laws that touch economic problems, business affairs, or social conditions. This law, however, operates directly on an intimate relation of husband and wife and their physician's role in one aspect of that relation.

The association of people is not mentioned in the Constitution nor in the Bill of Rights. The right to educate a child in a school of the parents' choice—whether public or private or parochial—is also not mentioned. Nor is the right to study any particular subject or any foreign language. Yet the First Amendment has been construed to include certain of those rights. [See] *Pierce* [and] *Meyer*. [T]he State may not, consistently with the spirit of the First Amendment, contract the spectrum of available knowledge. The right of freedom of speech and press includes not only the right to utter or to print, but the right to distribute, the right to receive, the right to read and freedom of inquiry, freedom of thought, and freedom to teach—indeed the freedom of the entire university community. Without those peripheral rights the specific rights would be less secure. And so we reaffirm the principle [of] *Pierce* [and] *Meyer*.

In *NAACP v. Alabama* [p. 1142 infra], we protected the "freedom to associate and privacy in one's associations," noting that freedom of association was a peripheral First Amendment right. [In] other words, the First Amendment has a penumbra where privacy is protected from governmental intrusion. In like context, we have protected forms of "association" that are not political in the customary sense but pertain to the social, legal, and economic benefit of the members. *NAACP v. Button*, 371 U.S. 415 (1963). [W]hile [association] is not expressly included in the First Amendment its existence is necessary in making the express guarantees fully meaningful.

The foregoing cases suggest that specific guarantees in the Bill of Rights have penumbras, formed by emanations from those guarantees that help give them life and substance. Various guarantees create zones of privacy. The right of association contained in the penumbra of the First Amendment is one, as we have seen. The Third Amendment in its prohibition against the quartering of soldiers "in any house" [is] another facet of that privacy. The Fourth Amendment [is another]. The Fifth Amendment in its Self-Incrimination Clause enables the citizen to create a zone of privacy which government may not force him to surrender to his detriment. The Ninth Amendment provides: "The enumeration in the

Constitution, of certain rights, shall not be construed to deny or disparage others retained by the people." * * *

We have had many controversies over these penumbral rights of "privacy and repose." [*Skinner* and other] cases bear witness that the right of privacy which presses for recognition here is a legitimate one.

The present case, then, concerns a relationship lying within the zone of privacy created by several fundamental constitutional guarantees. And it concerns a law which, in forbidding the *use* of contraceptives rather than regulating their manufacture or sale, seeks to achieve its goals by means having a maximum destructive impact upon that relationship. Such a law cannot stand in light of the familiar principle [that] a "governmental purpose to control or prevent activities constitutionally subject to state regulation may not be achieved by means which sweep unnecessarily broadly and thereby invade the area of protected freedoms." *NAACP v. Alabama.* Would we allow the police to search the sacred precincts of marital bedrooms for telltale signs of the use of contraceptives? The very idea is repulsive to the notions of privacy surrounding the marriage relationship.

We deal with a right of privacy older than the Bill of Rights * * * . Marriage is a coming together for better or for worse, hopefully enduring, and intimate to the degree of being sacred. It is an association that promotes a way of life, not causes; a harmony in living, not political faiths; a bilateral loyalty, not commercial or social projects. Yet it is an association for as noble a purpose as any involved in our prior decisions.

Reversed.

JUSTICE GOLDBERG, whom THE CHIEF JUSTICE and JUSTICE BRENNAN join, concurring.

I [join the Court's opinion]. Although I have not accepted the view that "due process" as used in the Fourteenth Amendment includes all of the first eight Amendments, I do agree that the concept of liberty protects those personal rights that are fundamental, and is not confined to the specific terms of the Bill of Rights. My conclusion that [liberty] embraces the right of marital privacy though that right is not mentioned explicitly in the Constitution is supported both by numerous decisions [and] by the language and history of the Ninth Amendment [which] reveal that the Framers of the Constitution believed that there are additional fundamental rights, protected from governmental infringement. [The] Ninth Amendment [was] proffered to quiet expressed fears that a bill of specifically enumerated rights could not be sufficiently broad to cover all essential rights and that the specific mention of certain rights would be interpreted as a denial that others were protected.

[While] this Court has had little occasion to interpret the Ninth Amendment, "[i]t cannot be presumed that any clause in the constitution is intended to be without effect." *Marbury v. Madison* [p. 1 supra. To] hold that a right so basic and fundamental and so deep-rooted in our society as the right of privacy in marriage may be infringed because that right is not guaranteed in so many words by the first eight amendments to the Constitution is to ignore the Ninth Amendment and to give it no effect whatsoever. [The] Ninth Amendment shows a belief of the Constitution's authors that fundamental rights exist that are not expressly enumerated in the first eight amendments and an intent that the list of rights included there not be deemed exhaustive.

[Surely] the Government, absent a showing of a compelling subordinating state interest, could not decree that all husbands and wives must be sterilized after two children have been born to them. Yet by [the dissenters'] reasoning such an invasion of marital privacy would not be subject to constitutional challenge because, while it might be "silly," no provision of the Constitution specifically prevents the Government from curtailing the marital right to bear children and raise a family. [I]f upon a showing of a slender basis of rationality, a law outlawing voluntary birth control by married persons is valid, then, by the same reasoning, a law requiring compulsory birth control also would seem to be valid. In my view, however, both types of law would unjustifiably intrude upon rights of marital privacy which are constitutionally protected.

In a long series of cases this Court has held that where fundamental personal liberties are involved, they may not be abridged by the States simply on a showing that a regulatory statute has some rational relationship to the effectuation of a proper state purpose. [The] State, at most, argues that there is some rational relation between this statute and what is admittedly a legitimate subject of state concern—the discouraging of extra-marital relations. It says that preventing the use of birth-control devices by married persons helps prevent the indulgence by some in such extra-marital relations. The rationality of this justification is dubious, particularly in light of the admitted widespread availability to all persons [in] Connecticut, unmarried as well as married, of birth-control devices for the prevention of disease, as distinguished from the prevention of conception. But in any event, it is clear that the state interest in safeguarding marital fidelity can be served by a more discriminately tailored statute, which does not, like the present one, sweep unnecessarily broadly, reaching far beyond the evil sought to be dealt with and intruding upon the privacy of all married couples. * * *

JUSTICE HARLAN, concurring in the judgment.

I fully agree with the judgment [but cannot] join the Court's opinion [as] it seems to me to evince an approach [in which] the Due Process Clause of the Fourteenth Amendment does not touch this Connecticut statute unless the enactment is found to violate some right assured by the letter or penumbra of the Bill of Rights. [W]hat I find implicit in the Court's opinion is that the "incorporation" doctrine may be used to *restrict* the reach of Fourteenth Amendment Due Process. For me this is just as unacceptable constitutional doctrine as is the use of the "incorporation" approach to *impose* upon the States all the requirements of the Bill of Rights. * * *

[T]he proper constitutional inquiry in this case is whether this Connecticut statute infringes the Due Process Clause of the Fourteenth Amendment because the enactment violates basic values "implicit in the concept of ordered liberty." For reasons stated at length in my dissenting opinion in *Poe v. Ullman* [discussed below], I believe that it does. While the relevant inquiry may be aided by resort to one or more of the provisions of the Bill of Rights, it is not dependent on them or any of their radiations. The Due Process Clause of the Fourteenth Amendment stands, in my opinion, on its own bottom.

[While] I could not more heartily agree that judicial "self restraint" is an indispensable ingredient of sound constitutional adjudication, I do submit that the formula suggested [by the dissenters] for achieving it is more hollow than real. "Specific" provisions of the Constitution, no less than "due process," lend themselves as readily to "personal" interpretations by judges whose constitutional outlook is simply to keep the Constitution in supposed "tune with the times".

[Judicial self-restraint] will be achieved in this area, as in other[s], only by continual insistence upon respect for the teachings of history, solid recognition of the basic values that underlie our society, and wise appreciation of the great roles that the doctrines of federalism and separation of powers have played in establishing and preserving American freedoms. Adherence to these principles will not, of course, obviate all constitutional differences of opinion among judges, nor should it. Their continued recognition will, however, go farther toward keeping most judges from roaming at large in the constitutional field than will the interpolation into the Constitution of an artificial and largely illusory restriction on the content of the Due Process Clause.

[Dissenting from the jurisdictional ruling in POE v. ULLMAN, 367 U.S. 497 (1961), which failed to reach the merits of an earlier constitutional challenge to the Connecticut anti-birth control statute, Harlan, J., had maintained that the statute, "as construed to apply to these appellants, violates the Fourteenth Amendment" because "a statute making it a criminal offense for *married couples* to use contraceptives is an intolerable and unjustifiable invasion of privacy in the conduct of the most intimate concerns of an individual's personal life." Harlan, J., "would not suggest that adultery, homosexuality, fornication and incest are immune from criminal enquiry, however privately practiced," but "the intimacy of husband and wife is necessarily an essential and accepted feature of the institution of marriage, an institution which the State not only must allow, but which always and in every age it has fostered and protected. It is one thing when the State exerts its power either to forbid extra-marital sexuality altogether, or to say who may marry, but it is quite another when, having acknowledged a marriage and the intimacies inherent in it, it undertakes to regulate by means of the criminal law the details of that intimacy."

[Although the state had "argued the constitutional permissibility of the moral judgment underlying" the challenged statute, Harlan, J., could not find anything that "even remotely suggests a justification for the obnoxiously intrusive means it has chosen to effectuate that policy." He deemed "the utter novelty" of the statute "conclusive." "Although the Federal Government and many States have at one time or another [prohibited or regulated] the distribution of contraceptives, none [has] made the *use* of contraceptives a crime. Indeed, a diligent search has revealed that no nation, including several which quite evidently share Connecticut's moral policy, had seen fit to effectuate that policy by the means presented here."

[Because the constitutional challenges to the Connecticut statute "draw their basis from no explicit language of the Constitution, and have yet to find expression in any decision of this Court," Harlan, J., deemed it "desirable at the outset to state the framework of Constitutional principles in which I think the issue must be judged":

["Were due process merely a procedural safeguard it would fail to reach those situations where the deprivation of life, liberty or property was accomplished by legislation which by operating in the future could, given even the fairest possible procedure in application to individuals, nevertheless destroy the enjoyment of all three. [I]t is not the particular enumeration of rights in the first eight Amendments which spells out the reach of Fourteenth Amendment due process, but rather [those concepts embracing] rights 'which [are] *fundamental;* which belong [to] the citizens of all free governments.'

["[T]hrough the course of this Court's decisions [due process] has represented the balance which our Nation, built upon postulates of respect for the liberty of the individual, has struck between that liberty and the demands of organized society. [The] balance of which I speak is the balance struck by this country, having regard to what history teaches are the traditions from which it developed as well as the traditions from which it broke. That tradition is a living thing. A decision of this Court which radically departs from it could not long survive, while a decision which builds on what has survived is likely to be sound. No formula could serve as a substitute, in this area, for judgment and restraint.

["[The] full scope of the liberty guaranteed by the Due Process Clause cannot be found in or limited by the precise terms of the specific guarantees elsewhere provided in the Constitution. This 'liberty' is not a series of isolated points pricked out in terms of the taking of property; the freedom of speech, press, and religion; the right to keep and bear arms; the freedom from unreasonable searches and seizures; and so on. It is a rational continuum which, broadly speaking, includes a freedom from all substantial arbitrary impositions and purposeless restraints and which also recognizes, what a reasonable and sensitive judgment must, that certain interests require particularly careful scrutiny of the state needs asserted to justify their abridgment. Cf. *Skinner.*"]

JUSTICE WHITE, concurring in the judgment.

In my view this Connecticut law as applied to married couples deprives them of "liberty" without [the due process] guaranteed by the Fourteenth Amendment against arbitrary or capricious [denials]. Surely the right [to] be free of regulation of the intimacies of the marriage relationship, "come[s] to this Court with a momentum for respect lacking when appeal is made to liberties which derive merely from shifting economic arrangements." *Kovacs v. Cooper,* 336 U.S. 77 (1949) (opinion of Frankfurter, J.).

The Connecticut anti-contraceptive statute deals rather substantially with this relationship. [And] the clear effect of these statutes, as enforced, is to deny disadvantaged citizens of Connecticut, those without either adequate knowledge or resources to obtain private counseling, access to medical assistance and up-to-date information in respect to proper methods of birth control. In my view, a statute with these effects bears a substantial burden of justification when attacked under the Fourteenth Amendment.

An examination of the justification offered, however, cannot be avoided by saying that the Connecticut anti-use statute invades a protected area of privacy and association or that it demeans the marriage relationship. The nature of the right invaded is pertinent, to be sure, for statutes regulating sensitive areas of liberty do, under the cases of this Court, require "strict scrutiny," *Skinner,* and "must be viewed in the light of less drastic means for achieving the same basic purpose." [But] such statutes, if reasonably necessary for the effectuation of a legitimate and substantial state interest, and not arbitrary or capricious in application, are not invalid under the Due Process Clause. [There] is no serious contention that Connecticut thinks the use of artificial or external methods of contraception immoral or unwise in itself, or that the anti-use statute is founded upon any policy of promoting population expansion. Rather, the statute is said to serve the State's policy against all forms of promiscuous or illicit sexual relationships, be they premarital or extramarital, concededly a permissible and legitimate legislative goal.

[But] I wholly fail to see how the ban on the use of contraceptives by married couples in any way reinforces the State's ban on illicit sexual relationships. [Perhaps] the theory is that the flat ban on use prevents married people from possessing contraceptives and without the ready availability of such devices for use in the marital relationship, there will be no or less temptation to use them in extramarital ones. This reasoning rests on the premise that married people will comply with the ban in regard to their marital relationship, notwithstanding total nonenforcement in this context and apparent nonenforcibility, but will not comply with criminal statutes prohibiting extramarital affairs and the anti-use statute in respect to illicit sexual relationships, a premise whose validity has not been demonstrated and whose intrinsic validity is not very evident. At most the broad ban is of marginal utility to the declared objective. A statute limiting its prohibition on use to persons engaging in the prohibited relationship would serve the end posited by Connecticut in the same way, and with the same effectiveness, or ineffectiveness, as the broad anti-use statute under attack in this case. I find nothing in this record justifying the sweeping scope of this statute. * * *

JUSTICE BLACK, with whom JUSTICE STEWART joins, dissenting.

[The] Court talks about a constitutional "right of privacy" as though there is some constitutional provision or provisions forbidding any law ever to be passed which might abridge the "privacy" of individuals. But there is not. There are, of course, guarantees in certain specific constitutional provisions [such as the Fourth Amendment] which are designed in part to protect privacy at certain times and places with respect to certain activities. [But] I think it belittles [the Fourth] Amendment to talk about it as though it protects nothing but "privacy." * * *

One of the most effective ways of diluting or expanding a constitutionally guaranteed right is to substitute for the crucial word or words of a constitutional guarantee another word or words, more or less flexible and more or less restricted in meaning. This fact is well illustrated by the use of the term "right of privacy" as a comprehensive substitute for the Fourth Amendment's guarantee against "unreasonable searches and seizures." * * * [1] I like my privacy as well as the next one, but I am

---

[1]   [Ct's Note] The phrase "right to privacy" appears first to have gained currency from an article written by Messrs. Warren and (later Mr. Justice) Brandeis in 1890 which urged that States should give some form of tort relief to persons whose private affairs were exploited by others. *The Right to Privacy,* 4 Harv.L.Rev. 193. * * * Observing that "the right of privacy presses for recognition here," today this Court, which I did not understand to have power to sit as a court of common law, now appears to be exalting a phrase which Warren and Brandeis use in discussing grounds for tort relief, to the level of a constitutional [rule].

nevertheless compelled to admit that government has a right to invade it unless prohibited by some specific constitutional provision.

[This] brings me to the arguments made by [the concurring justices]. I discuss the due process and Ninth Amendment arguments together because on analysis they turn out to be the same thing—merely using different words to claim for this Court and the federal judiciary power to invalidate any legislative act [that] it considers to be arbitrary, capricious, unreasonable, or oppressive, or this Court's belief that a particular state law under scrutiny has no "rational or justifying" purpose, or is offensive to a "sense of fairness and justice." If these formulas based on "natural justice" [are] to prevail, they require judges to determine what is or is not constitutional on the basis of their own appraisal of what laws are unwise or unnecessary. [I] do not believe that we are granted power by the Due Process Clause or any [other] provisions [to do so].

Of the cases on which my [Brothers] rely so heavily, undoubtedly the reasoning of two of them supports their result here—[*Meyer* and *Pierce*]. *Meyer* [relying on *Lochner*,] held unconstitutional, as an "arbitrary" and unreasonable interference with the right of a teacher to carry on his occupation and of parents to hire him, a state law forbidding the teaching of modern foreign languages to young children in the schools.[7] [*Pierce*, per McReynolds, J.] said that a state law requiring that all children attend public schools interfered unconstitutionally with the property rights of private school corporations because it was an "arbitrary, unreasonable, and unlawful interference" which threatened "destruction of their business and property." Without expressing an opinion as to whether either of those cases reached a correct result in light of our later decisions applying the First Amendment to the States through the Fourteenth, I merely point out that the reasoning stated in *Meyer* and *Pierce* was the same natural law due process philosophy which many later opinions repudiated, and which I cannot accept.

[My] Brother Goldberg has adopted the recent discovery[12] that the Ninth Amendment as well as the Due Process Clause can be used by this Court as authority to strike down all state legislation which this Court thinks violates "fundamental principles of liberty and justice," or is contrary to the "traditions and collective conscience of our people." [One] would certainly have to look far beyond the language of the Ninth Amendment to find that the Framers vested in this Court any such

---

[7] **[Ct's Note]** In *Meyer*, in the very same sentence quoted in part by my Brethren in which he asserted that the Due Process Clause gave an abstract and inviolable right "to marry, establish a home and bring up children," Justice McReynolds asserted also that the Due Process Clause prevented States from interfering with "the right of the individual to contract."

[12] **[Ct's Note]** See Bennett B. Patterson, *The Forgotten Ninth Amendment* (1955) [which] urges that the Ninth Amendment be used to protect unspecified "natural and inalienable rights." The Introduction by Roscoe Pound states that "there is a marked revival of natural law ideas throughout the world. Interest in the Ninth Amendment is a symptom of that revival." * * *

awesome veto powers over lawmaking. [The Ninth] Amendment was passed [to] limit the Federal Government to the powers granted expressly or by necessary implication. [This] fact is perhaps responsible for the peculiar phenomenon that for a period of a century and a half no serious suggestion was ever made that [that] Amendment, enacted to protect state powers against federal invasion, could be used as a weapon of federal power to prevent state legislatures from passing laws they consider appropriate to govern local affairs. * * *

JUSTICE STEWART, whom JUSTICE BLACK joins, dissenting.

[T]his is an uncommonly silly law. As a practical matter, the law is obviously unenforceable, except in the oblique context of the present case. As a philosophical matter, I believe the use of contraceptives in the relationship of marriage should be left to personal and private [choice]. As a matter of social policy, I think professional counsel about methods of birth control should be available to all, so that each individual's choice can be meaningfully made. But we are not [asked] whether we think this law is unwise, or even asinine. We are asked to hold that it violates the United States Constitution. And that I cannot do.

In the course of its opinion the Court refers to no less than six Amendments [but] does not say which of these Amendments, if any, it thinks is infringed by this Connecticut law. [As] to the First, Third, Fourth, and Fifth Amendments, I can find nothing in any of them to invalidate this Connecticut law, even assuming that all those amendments are fully applicable against the States. [The] Ninth Amendment, like its companion the Tenth [was adopted] simply to make clear that the adoption of the Bill of Rights did not alter the plan that the *Federal* Government was to be a government of express and limited powers, and that all rights and powers not delegated to it were retained by the people and the individual States. Until today no member of this Court has ever suggested that the Ninth Amendment meant anything [else].

NOTES AND QUESTIONS

1.   *Did Griswold successfully avoid "renewing the romance" with "substantive due process"?* According to Robert Dixon, *The "New" Substantive Due Process and the Democratic Ethic: A Prolegomenon,* 1976 B.Y.U.L.Rev. 43, in *Griswold,* Douglas, J., "skipped through the Bill of Rights like a cheerleader—'Give me a P . . . give me an R . . . an I . . . ,' and so on, and found P-R-I-V-A-C-Y as a derivative or penumbral right."

Why did the *Griswold* majority attempt to ground the holding in specific provisions of the Bill of Rights? Lupu observes that the case "provided the severest test for a Court determined to advance chosen values [without] renewing the romance with the dreaded demon of substantive due process. [Douglas, J.,] drew upon the incorporation legacy, rather than a doctrine of 'naked' substantive due process, and tortured the Bill of Rights into yielding a protected zone of privacy that would not tolerate a law banning contraceptive use by married couples. Justice Goldberg's reliance upon the ninth amendment [was] equally disingenuous in its attempt to avoid the jaws of substantive due process. Only Justices White and Harlan were willing to grapple directly with the fearful creature, and concluded that a law invading marital choice about contraception violated the due process clause itself, independent of links with the Bill of Rights. Shocking though that analysis may have been at the time, subsequent developments seem to have confirmed the White-Harlan view, and not the magical mystery tour of the zones of privacy, as the prevailing doctrine of *Griswold*."

2. *Are the courts authorized to plug glaring gaps in the Constitution?* Consider Richard A. Posner, *Sex and Reason* 328 (1992), who disclaims any interest in "joining the snipe hunt for a convincing legal-doctrinal ground for the *Griswold* decision" and "doubt[s] that one exists." "But," he asks, "should that be the end of the legal analysis? * * *

"A constitution that did not invalidate so offensive, oppressive, probably undemocratic, and sectarian a law would stand revealed as containing major gaps. Maybe that is the nature of our, as perhaps of any, written Constitution; but yet, perhaps the courts are authorized to plug at least the more glaring gaps. Does anyone really believe, in his heart of hearts, that the Constitution should be interpreted so literally as to authorize every conceivable law that would not violate a specific constitutional clause? This would mean that a state could require everyone to marry, or to have sexual intercourse at least once a month, or that it could take away every couple's second child and place it in a foster home. Of course, no state is likely to do such things; and if it were likely, that would argue such a change of moral outlook in this nation as to make our present institutions a poor guide. Yet we do find it reassuring to think that the courts stand between us and legislative tyranny even if a particular form of tyranny was not foreseen and expressly forbidden by the framers of the Constitution."

3. *Search and Seizure.* Was Douglas, J., *wholly* unjustified in relying on specific provisions of the Bill of Rights? Consider the Fourth Amendment's protection against "unreasonable searches and seizures." Sherry F. Colb, *The Qualitative Dimension of Fourth Amendment Reasonableness*, 98 Colum.L.Rev. 1642 (1998) acknowledges that "the logic appears flawed[.] Certainly, if there were probable cause to believe that a murder, a rape, or a robbery were committed in the bedroom of a married couple," there would be probable cause to support a search. Colb goes on to argue, however, that the appearance is deceptive. She writes:

"Marital privacy (including the substantive right to marry, to have children, and to educate those children) requires as a prerequisite a physical privacy from governmental personal knowledge of the married couple's home. If the government lacks a more compelling justification for searching a marital home than the interest in stamping out the crime of contraceptive use, then the search is accordingly an unreasonable one, because it exposes the sacred precincts of the marital quarters for an insufficiently important reason. It is this link that begins to provide a response to critics of the 'privacy' nomenclature in defining substantive due process rights."

————

Griswold invalidated a ban on the *use* of contraceptives by *married* couples. EISENSTADT v. BAIRD, 405 U.S. 438 (1972), overturned a conviction for violating a Massachusetts law making it a felony to *distribute* contraceptive materials, *except* in the case of registered physicians and pharmacists furnishing the materials to *married* persons. The Court, per BRENNAN, J., concluded that, because the statute was riddled with exceptions making contraceptives freely available and because, if protection of health were the rationale, the statute would be both discriminatory and overbroad, "the goals of deterring premarital sex and regulating the distribution of potentially harmful articles cannot reasonably be regarded as legislative aims." "[V]iewed as a prohibition on contraception per se" the statute "violates the rights of single persons under the Equal Protection Clause." For, "whatever the rights of the individual to access to contraceptives may be, the rights must be the same for the unmarried and the married alike.

"If under *Griswold* the distribution of contraceptives to married persons cannot be prohibited, a ban on distribution to unmarried persons would be equally impermissible. It is true that in *Griswold* the right of privacy in question inhered in the marital relationship. Yet the marital couple is not an independent entity with a mind and heart of its own, but an association of two individuals each with a separate intellectual and emotional makeup. If the right of privacy means anything, it is the right of the *individual,* married or single, to be free from unwarranted governmental intrusion into matters so fundamentally affecting a person as the decision whether to bear or beget a child. On the other hand, if *Griswold* is no bar to a prohibition on the distribution of contraceptives, the State could not, consistently with the Equal Protection Clause, outlaw distribution to unmarried but not to married persons. In each case the evil, as perceived by the State, would be identical, and the underinclusion would be invidious."[331]

Burger, C.J., dissented, "see[ing] nothing in the Fourteenth Amendment or any other part of the Constitution that even vaguely suggests that these medicinal forms of contraceptives must be available in the open market. [By] relying on *Griswold* in the present context, the Court

———

[331] Douglas, J., who joined the Court's opinion, also concurred on free speech grounds. White, J., joined by Blackmun, J., concurred in the judgment on the ground that the record did not establish either that the particular contraceptive at issue was dangerous or that the defendant was unmarried. Powell and Rehnquist, JJ., did not participate.

has passed beyond the penumbras of the specific guarantees into the uncircumscribed area of personal predilections."

NOTES AND QUESTIONS

1.   ***Does Eisenstadt offer a new rationale for Griswold?*** Did *Eisenstadt* decide one of *Griswold*'s open issues—the constitutionality of a ban on the use or distribution of contraceptive devices that excluded from its reach the married couple—"by assertion, without a pretext of reasoning"? Harry Wellington, *Common Law Rules and Constitutional Double Standards*, 83 Yale L.J. 221 (1973), so charges: "[W]hether the 'different classes' (married, not married) are [as *Eisenstadt* states] 'wholly unrelated to the objective of the statute,' depends on whether, as *Griswold* insists, the marriage relationship is important to that aspect of liberty that the Court calls privacy. How, then, without offering a new rationale for *Griswold,* [can the Court conclude that *Griswold* protects the rights of individuals regardless of the marriage relationship?]"

2.   ***A right to premarital sex?*** "The real objection to the" law in *Eisenstadt*, observes Posner, at 330, "is not that it cannot deter fornication. It will deter some. Indeed, it will deter a good deal more than a statute, unenforceable as a practical matter, making fornication a misdemeanor—the statute whose constitutionality was not questioned. * * *

"The real objection to the statute is that there is no good reason to deter premarital sex, a generally harmless source of pleasure and for some people an important stage of marital search. (Yet this is an equal objection to a statute forbidding fornication, and the Court has never questioned the constitutionality of such statutes.) There are good reasons for wanting to deter unwanted pregnancies, but that aim is more likely to be achieved by encouraging than by discouraging the use of contraceptives. [The Court implies] that notwithstanding the unchallenged misdemeanor fornication law (easily overlooked because totally unenforced), unmarried persons have a constitutional right to engage in sexual intercourse. For if they do not, it is an illegal activity; and how can the Constitution be violated by a state's prohibiting the sale of an input (contraception) into that activity?"

In light of Judge Posner's observations, if a state *were* to attempt to enforce a fornication prohibition, would the effort be unconstitutional?

3.   ***From Griswold to Eisenstadt to Carey.*** The effect of *Eisenstadt*, notes Tribe, 2d ed., at 1339, "was to single out as decisive in *Griswold* the element of reproductive autonomy, something the Court made clear in 1977, when it extended *Griswold* and" *Eisenstadt* in CAREY v. POPULATION SERVICES, INT'L, 431 U.S. 678 (1977), to invalidate a New York law that allowed only pharmacists to sell non-medical contraceptive devices to persons over 16 and prohibited the sale of such items to those under 16. In striking down the restriction on sales to adults, BRENNAN, J., spoke for six justices; in invalidating the ban on sales to those under 16, he spoke for a four-justice plurality.

As for the restriction on distribution to adults, "where a decision as fundamental as that whether to bear or beget a child is involved, regulations imposing a burden on it may be justified only by compelling state interests, and must be narrowly drawn to express only those interests"—and the Court found none of the state interests advanced (e.g., protecting health, facilitating enforcement of other laws) to be "compelling."[332] The state argued that *Griswold* dealt only with the *use* of contraceptives, not their manufacture or sale, but read "in light of its progeny, the teaching of *Griswold* is that the Constitution protects individual decisions in matters of childbearing from unjustified intrusion by the State."

As for the ban on sales to those under 16, Brennan, J., joined by Stewart, Marshall, and Blackmun, JJ., applied a test "apparently less rigorous than the 'compelling state interest' test applied to restrictions on the privacy rights of adults"—on the dual grounds that the state generally has greater latitude to regulate minors and that minors lack the same capacity for decision making as adults. Even under this more relaxed standard of review, however, the plurality rejected what it called "the argument [that] minors' sexual activity may be deterred by increasing the hazards attendant on it," pointing out that that argument had already been rejected by the Court in related areas.

POWELL, J., concurred in the judgment, observing that by restricting not only the kinds of retail outlets that may distribute contraceptives, "but even prohibit[ing] distribution by mail to adults"—thus "requiring individuals to buy contraceptives over the counter"—the New York provision "heavily burdens constitutionally protected freedom." He saw "no justification for subjecting restrictions on the sexual activity of the young to heightened judicial review"—but concurred in the invalidation of the "distribution to minors" restriction on narrow grounds.[333]

4. ***The seed from which Roe v. Wade grew.*** According to Charles Fried, *Order and Law: Arguing the Reagan Revolution—A Firsthand Account* 77 (1991), when Brennan, J., made the "passing remark" in *Eisenstadt* about the right of the individual to be free from unwarranted governmental intrusion into such matters "as the decision whether to bear or beget a child" he "planted" the "seed [from] which *Roe* grew, so that later [he] could say that what *Griswold* stood for all along was the proposition that there is a 'constitutional protection of individual autonomy in matters of childbearing.' [When] Justice Brennan, in [*Eisenstadt*], a contraception case, slipped in the irrelevant term 'childbearing,' he was digging a kind of surreptitious doctrinal tunnel to get from *Poe* to *Roe,* a tunnel that a year later would allow Justice Blackmun to

---

[332] The Court recognized, however, that "other restrictions may well be reasonably related to the objective of quality control," and thus "express[ed] no opinion on, for example, restrictions on the distribution of contraceptives through vending machines."

[333] White and Stevens, JJ., concurred only in the judgment with respect to the restriction on minors. Rehnquist, J., dissented, observing that if those responsible for the Bill of Rights and Civil War Amendments could have lived to know what their efforts had wrought "it is not difficult to imagine their reaction." Burger, C.J., dissented without opinion.

get past the critical barrier between contraception and abortion, between what undoubtedly is a matter of privacy and what to some is murder."

ROE V. WADE

410 U.S. 113, 93 S.Ct. 705, 35 L.Ed.2d 147 (1973).

JUSTICE BLACKMUN delivered the opinion of the Court.

This Texas federal appeal and its Georgia companion, *Doe v. Bolton,* [infra,] present constitutional challenges to state criminal abortion legislation. The Texas statutes [are] typical of those that have been in effect in many States for approximately a century. The Georgia statutes, in contrast, have a modern cast and are a legislative product that, to an extent at least, obviously reflects the influences of recent attitudinal change, of advancing medical knowledge and techniques, and of new [thinking]. The Texas statutes [make procuring an abortion a crime except] "by medical advice for the purpose of saving the life of the mother."

[Jane] Roe alleged that she was unmarried and pregnant [and] that she was unable to get a "legal" abortion in Texas because her life did not appear to be threatened by the continuation of her pregnancy.[334] [The district court held the Texas abortion statutes unconstitutional, but denied the injunctive relief requested on procedural grounds. Roe appealed.]

[R]estrictive criminal abortion laws [like Texas'] in effect in a majority of States [today] derive from statutory changes effected, for the most part, in the latter half of the 19th century. [The Court then reviewed, in some detail, "ancient attitudes," "the Hippocratic Oath" which forbids abortion,

-----

[334] Who was "Jane Roe"? Her real name was Norma McCorvey. Shortly after *Roe* was decided, she revealed who she really was. She explained then that she was an unmarried woman who had become pregnant as a result of a gang rape. She had tried to get an abortion, but had been unable to pay the price demanded by a doctor she finally found who was willing to perform an abortion. Because she did not want to subject to public ridicule a young child she had from a previous marriage, Ms. McCorvey went ahead with the legal challenge but only on the condition that she remain anonymous. See Philip Bobbitt, *Constitutional Fate* 165–66 (1982); Fred Friendly & Martha J.H. Elliott, *The Constitution: That Delicate Balance* 202–04 (1984). But, as noted in Laurence H. Tribe, *Abortion: The Clash of Absolutes* 5 (1990), a decade and a half after *Roe* was decided "McCorvey explained, with embarrassment, that she had not been raped after all; she had made up the story to hide the fact that she had gotten 'in trouble' in the more usual way. Many reacted with dismay. How could the heroine of the most important abortion rights case have deceived the advocates of such rights?" Comments Tribe: "Few asked why [McCorvey] had felt a *need* to deceive them. In a different sort of society the life she would have faced as an unwed mother might not have been nearly so lonely. In such a society she might not have made up a story about how she became pregnant. In such a society she might not even have chosen an abortion."

Later still, McCorvey's life took further "odd turns," observes Lucinda M. Finley, *Contested Ground: The Story of Roe v. Wade and Its Impact on American Society*, in Michael C. Dorf, *Constitutional Law Stories* 333 (2d ed. 2009): In 1994 McCorvey's "ghost-written autobiography" revealed her to be "still strongly and unapologetically pro-choice," but later she came "to feel unappreciated and exploited by the pro-choice movement," eventually becoming "an anti-abortion speaker."

"the common law," "the English statutory law," and "the American law." Subsequently, it described the positions of the American Medical Association, the American Public Health Association, and the American Bar Association. Thus,] at common law, at the time of the adoption of our Constitution, and throughout the major portion of the 19th century, [a] woman enjoyed a substantially broader right to terminate a pregnancy than she does in most States today.

[Three] reasons have been advanced to explain historically the enactment of criminal abortion laws in the 19th century and to justify their continued existence.

It has been argued occasionally that these laws were the product of a Victorian social concern to discourage illicit sexual conduct. Texas, however, does not advance this justification [and] it appears that no court or commentator has taken the argument seriously.

[A] second reason is [that when] most criminal abortion laws were first enacted, the procedure was a hazardous one for the woman. [But modern] medical data indicat[e] that abortion in early pregnancy, that is, prior to the end of first trimester, although not without its risk, is now relatively safe.

[The] third reason is the State's interest—some phrase it in terms of duty—in protecting prenatal life. Some of the argument for this justification rests on the theory that a new human life is present from the moment of conception. [Only] when the life of the pregnant mother herself is at stake, balanced against the life she carries within her, should the interest of the embryo or fetus not prevail. [In] assessing the State's interest, recognition may be given to the less rigid claim that as long as at least *potential* life is involved, the State may assert interests beyond the protection of the pregnant woman alone. [It] is with these interests, and the weight to be attached to them, that this case is concerned.

The Constitution does not explicitly mention any right of privacy. [But] the Court has recognized that a right of personal privacy, or a guarantee of certain areas or zones of privacy, does exist under the Constitution. In varying contexts the Court or individual Justices have, indeed, found at least the roots of that right in the First Amendment; in the Fourth and Fifth Amendments; in the penumbras of the Bill of Rights, *Griswold;* in the Ninth Amendment, id. (Goldberg, J., concurring); or in the concept of liberty guaranteed by the first section of the Fourteenth Amendment, see *Meyer*. These decisions make it clear that only personal rights that can be deemed "fundamental" or "implicit in the concept of ordered liberty," are included in this guarantee of personal privacy. They also make it clear that the right has some extension to activities relating to marriage; procreation; contraception; family relationships; and child rearing and education.

This right of privacy, whether it be founded in the Fourteenth Amendment's concept of personal liberty [as] we feel it is, [or] in the [Ninth Amendment], is broad enough to encompass a woman's decision whether or not to terminate her pregnancy. The detriment that the State would impose upon the pregnant woman by denying this choice altogether is apparent. Specific and direct harm medically diagnosable even in early pregnancy may be [involved]. Psychological harm may be imminent. Mental and physical health may be taxed by child care. There is also the distress, for all concerned, associated with the unwanted child, and there is the problem of bringing a child into a family already unable, psychologically and otherwise, to care for it. In other cases, as in this one, the additional difficulties and continuing stigma of unwed motherhood may be involved. All these are factors the woman and her responsible physician necessarily will consider in consultation.

On the basis of elements such as these, appellants and some *amici* argue that the woman's right is absolute and that she is entitled to terminate her pregnancy at whatever time, in whatever way, and for whatever reason she alone chooses. With this we do not agree. [The] Court's decisions recognizing a right of privacy also acknowledge that some state regulation in areas protected by that right is appropriate. [A] State may properly assert important interests in safeguarding health, in maintaining medical standards, and in protecting potential life. At some point in pregnancy, these respective interests become sufficiently compelling to sustain regulation of the factors that govern the abortion decision.

[Where] certain "fundamental rights" are involved, the Court has held that regulation limiting these rights may be justified only by a "compelling state interest," and that legislative enactments must be narrowly drawn to express only the legitimate state interests at stake.

[Appellee argues] that the fetus is a "person" within the language and meaning of the Fourteenth Amendment. [If so,] appellant's case, of course, collapses, for the fetus' right to life would then be guaranteed specifically by the Amendment.

[The] Constitution does not define "person" in so many words. [The Court then listed each provision in which the word appears.] But in nearly all these instances, the use of the word is such that it has application only postnatally. None indicates, with any assurance, that it has any possible pre-natal application. All this, together with our observation that throughout the major portion of the 19th century prevailing legal abortion practices were far freer [than] today, persuades us that the word "person," as used in the Fourteenth Amendment, does not include the unborn. [Thus,] we pass on to other considerations.

The pregnant woman cannot be isolated in her privacy. She carries an embryo and, later, a fetus. [The] situation therefore is inherently different from marital intimacy, or bedroom possession of obscene material, or marriage, or procreation, or education, with which *Eisenstadt, Griswold*, [and other cases were] concerned.

[Texas] urges that, apart from the Fourteenth Amendment, life begins at conception and is present throughout pregnancy, and that, therefore, the State has a compelling interest in protecting that life from and after conception. We need not resolve the difficult question of when life begins. When those trained [in] medicine, philosophy, and theology are unable to arrive at any consensus, the judiciary, at this point in the development of man's knowledge, is not in a position to speculate as to the answer.

[W]e do not agree that, by adopting one theory of life, Texas may override the rights of the pregnant woman that are at stake. We repeat, however, that the State does have an important and legitimate interest in preserving and protecting the health of the pregnant woman [and] that it has still *another* important and legitimate interest in protecting the potentiality of human life. These interests are separate and distinct. Each grows in substantiality as the woman approaches term and, at a point during pregnancy, each becomes "compelling."

With respect to [the] interest in the health of the mother, the "compelling" point, in the light of present medical knowledge, is at approximately the end of the first trimester. This is so because of the now-established medical fact that until the end of the first trimester mortality in abortion may be less than mortality in normal childbirth. It follows that, from and after this point, a State may regulate the abortion procedure to the extent that the regulation reasonably relates to the preservation and protection of maternal health. Examples of permissible state regulation in this area are requirements as to the qualifications of the person who is to perform the abortion; as to the licensure of that person; as to the facility in which the procedure is to be performed, [and] the like. This means, on the other hand, that, for the period of pregnancy prior to this "compelling" point, the attending physician, in consultation with his patient, is free to determine, without regulation by the State, that in his medical judgment the patient's pregnancy should be terminated. If that decision is reached, the judgment may be effectuated by an abortion free of interference by the State.

With respect to [the] interest in potential life, the "compelling" point is at viability [which "is usually placed at about seven months (28 weeks) but may occur earlier, even at 24 weeks."] This is so because the fetus then presumably has the capability of meaningful life outside the mother's womb.[335] State regulation protective of fetal life after viability thus has

---

[335] Earlier in its opinion, the Court described the point "at which the fetus becomes 'viable' " as the point that the fetus is "potentially able to live outside the mother's womb, albeit with artificial aid." *Planned Parenthood v. Danforth*, 428 U.S. 52 (1976), per Blackmun, J., upheld a Missouri abortion statute defining "viability" as "that stage of fetal development when the life of

both logical and biological justifications. If the State is interested in protecting fetal life after viability, it may go as far as to proscribe abortion during that period except when it is necessary to preserve the life or health of the mother. Measured against these standards, [the Texas statute] sweeps too broadly [and] therefore, cannot survive the constitutional attack made upon it here.

[In] *Doe* [infra], procedural requirements contained in one of the modern abortion statutes are considered. That opinion and this one [are] to be read together.[67]

This holding, we feel, is consistent with the relative weights of the respective interests involved, with the lessons and examples of medical and legal history, with the lenity of the common law, and with the demands of the profound problems of the present day. The decision leaves the State free to place increasing restrictions on abortion as the period of pregnancy lengthens, so long as those restrictions are tailored to the recognized state interests. The decision vindicates the right of the physician to administer medical treatment according to his professional judgment up to the points where important state interests provide compelling justifications for intervention. Up to those points, the abortion decision in all its aspects is inherently, and primarily, a medical decision, and basic responsibility for it must rest with the physician.

JUSTICE STEWART, concurring.

In 1963, this Court, in *Ferguson v. Skrupa* [Ch. 5, Sec. 3], purported to sound the death knell for the doctrine of substantive due process, [but] [b]arely two years later, in *Griswold,* the Court held a Connecticut birth control law unconstitutional. [T]he *Griswold* decision can be rationally

---

the unborn child may be continued indefinitely outside the womb by natural or artificial life-supportive systems." In rejecting contentions that the Missouri statute unduly expanded the *Roe* Court's definition of "viability," failed to contain any reference to a gestational time period, and failed to incorporate and reflect the three stages of pregnancy, the Court observed: "[W]e recognized in *Roe* that viability was a matter of medical judgment, skill, and technical ability, and we preserved the flexibility of the term. [The Missouri statute] does the same. [I]t is not the proper function of the legislature or the courts to place viability, which essentially is a medical concept, at a specific point in the gestation period. The time when viability is achieved may vary with each pregnancy, and the determination of whether a particular fetus is viable is, and must be, a matter for the judgment of the responsible attending physician. [The statutory definition] merely reflects this fact."

Consider, too, *Colautti v. Franklin,* 439 U.S. 379 (1979), per Blackmun, J., reaffirming that the determination of "viability" is "a matter for medical judgment" and that viability is reached "when, in the judgment of the attending physician on the particular facts of the case before him, there is a reasonable likelihood of the fetus' sustained survival outside the womb, with or without artificial support. Because this point may differ with each pregnancy, neither the legislature nor the courts may proclaim one of the elements entering into the ascertainment of viability—be it weeks of gestation or fetal weight or any other single factor—as the determinant of when the State has a compelling interest in the life or health of the fetus."

[67] **[Ct's Note]** Neither in this opinion nor in *Doe* do we discuss the father's rights, if any exist in the constitutional context, in the abortion decision. No paternal right has been asserted in either of the [cases].

understood only as a holding that the Connecticut statute substantively invaded the "liberty" that is protected by the Due Process Clause of the Fourteenth Amendment. As so understood, *Griswold* stands as one in a long line of pre-*Skrupa* cases decided under the doctrine of substantive due process, and I now accept it as such.

[The] Constitution nowhere mentions a specific right of personal choice in matters of marriage and family life, but the "liberty" protected by the Due Process Clause of the Fourteenth Amendment covers more than those freedoms explicitly named in the Bill of Rights. [In] *Eisenstadt,* we recognized "the right of the *individual,* married or single, to be free from unwarranted governmental intrusion into matters so fundamentally affecting a person as the decision whether to bear or beget a child." That right necessarily includes the right of a woman to decide whether or not to terminate her pregnancy. [It] is evident that the Texas abortion statute infringes that right directly. [The] question then becomes whether the state interests advanced to justify this abridgment can survive the "particularly careful scrutiny" that the Fourteenth Amendment here requires.

The asserted state interests are protection of the health and safety of the pregnant woman, and protection of the potential future human life within her. These are legitimate objectives, amply sufficient to permit a State to regulate abortions as it does other surgical procedures, and perhaps sufficient to permit a State to regulate abortions more stringently or even to prohibit them in the late stages of pregnancy. But such legislation is not before us. * * *

JUSTICE DOUGLAS, concurring [in *Doe* as well as in *Roe*].

While I join the opinion of the Court, I add a few words.

[The] Ninth Amendment obviously does not create federally enforceable rights. [But] a catalogue of [the rights "retained by the people"] includes customary, traditional, and time-honored rights, amenities, privileges, and immunities that come within the sweep of "the Blessings of Liberty" mentioned in the preamble to the Constitution. Many of them, in my view, come within the meaning of the term "liberty" as used in the Fourteenth Amendment. * * *

JUSTICE WHITE, with whom JUSTICE REHNQUIST joins, dissenting [in *Doe* as well as in *Roe*].

[The] common claim before us is that for [various] reasons, or for no reason at all, and without asserting or claiming any threat to life or health, any woman is entitled to an abortion at her request if she is able to find a medical advisor willing to [perform it].

The Court for the most part sustains this position [and] simply fashions and announces a new constitutional right [and], with scarcely any reason or authority for its action, invests that right with sufficient substance to override most existing state abortion statutes. The upshot is that the people and the legislatures of the 50 States are constitutionally disentitled to weigh the relative importance of the continued existence and development of the fetus, on the one hand, against a spectrum of possible impacts on the mother, on the other hand. As an exercise of raw judicial power, the Court perhaps has authority [but] in my view its judgment is an improvident and extravagant exercise of the power of judicial review * * * .

JUSTICE REHNQUIST, dissenting. * * *

I have difficulty in concluding [that] the right of "privacy" is involved in this case. [Texas] bars the performance of a medical abortion by a licensed physician on a plaintiff such as Roe. A transaction resulting in an operation such as this is not "private" in the ordinary usage of that word. Nor is the "privacy" that the Court finds here even a distant relative of the freedom from searches and seizures protected by the Fourth Amendment.

[If] the Court means by the term "privacy" no more than that the claim of a person to be free from unwanted state regulation of consensual transactions may be a form of "liberty" [I] agree [with] Mr. Justice Stewart [that that "liberty"] embraces more than the rights found in the Bill of Rights. But that liberty is not guaranteed absolutely against deprivation, only against deprivation without due process of law. The test traditionally applied in the area of social and economic legislation is whether or not a law such as that challenged has a rational relation to a valid state objective. [If] the Texas statute were to prohibit an abortion even where the mother's life is in jeopardy, I have little doubt that such a statute would lack a rational relation to a valid state objective under the test stated in *Williamson v. Lee Optical Co.* [discussed at p. 396 supra]. But the Court's sweeping invalidation of any restrictions on abortion during the first trimester is impossible to justify under that standard, and the conscious weighing of competing factors that the Court's opinion apparently substitutes for the established test is far more appropriate to a legislative judgment than to a judicial one.

[While] the Court's opinion quotes from the dissent of Mr. Justice Holmes in *Lochner*, the result it reaches is more closely attuned to the majority opinion of Mr. Justice Peckham in that case. As in *Lochner* and similar cases applying substantive due process standards to economic and social welfare legislation, the adoption of the compelling state interest standard will inevitably require this Court to examine the legislative policies and pass on the wisdom of these policies in the very process of deciding whether a particular state interest put forward may or may not be "compelling." The decision here to break pregnancy into three distinct terms and to outline the permissible restrictions the State may impose in each one, for example, partakes more of judicial legislation than it does of a determination of the intent of the drafters of the Fourteenth Amendment.

The fact that a majority of the States, reflecting, after all, the majority sentiment in those States, have had restrictions on abortions for at least a century is a strong indication [that] the asserted right to an abortion is not "so rooted in the traditions and conscience of our people as to be ranked as fundamental." Even today, when society's views on abortion are changing, the very existence of the debate is evidence that the "right" to an abortion is not so universally accepted as the appellant would have us believe.

[By] the time of the adoption of the Fourteenth Amendment in 1868, there were at least 36 laws enacted by state or territorial legislatures limiting abortion. While many States have amended or updated their laws, 21 of the laws on the books in 1868 remain in effect today. [There] apparently was no question concerning the validity of [the Texas] provision or of any of the other state statutes when the Fourteenth Amendment was adopted. The only conclusion possible from this history is that the drafters did not intend to have the Fourteenth Amendment withdraw from the States the power to legislate with respect to this matter. * * *

———

DOE v. BOLTON, 410 U.S. 179 (1973), the companion case to *Roe v. Wade,* per BLACKMUN, J., invalidated several provisions of a Georgia abortion law. The Court first rejected the claim that a provision permitting a physician to perform an abortion "based upon his best clinical judgment that an abortion is necessary" was unconstitutionally vague. Although the provision on its face narrowly circumscribed the factors that could be deemed to render an abortion necessary, after construction by a three-judge district court, the Supreme Court accepted that necessity was to be defined more broadly: "[The physician's] medical judgment may be exercised in light of all factors—physical, emotional, psychological, familial, and the woman's age—relevant to the well-being of the patient. All these factors may relate to health. This allows the attending physician the room he needs to make his best medical judgment. And it is room that operates for the benefit, not the disadvantage, of the pregnant woman."

However, despite the fact that the Georgia statute was patterned after the American Law Institute's Model Penal Code (1962), which had served as the model for recent legislation in about one-fourth of the states, the Court invalidated substantial portions of the statute. Struck down were requirements: (1) that the abortion be performed in a hospital accredited by the Joint Commission on Accreditation of Hospitals (JCAH); (2) that the procedure be approved by a hospital staff abortion committee; and (3) that the performing physician's judgment be confirmed by independent examinations of the patient by two other physicians. "[T]he woman's right to receive medical care in accordance with her licensed physician's best judgment and the physician's right to administer it are substantially limited by this statutorily imposed overview."

NOTES AND QUESTIONS

1. *The linkage between the abortion decision and the privacy cases.* Consider Susan R. Estrich & Kathleen M. Sullivan, *Abortion Politics: Writing for an Audience of One,* 138 U.Pa.L.Rev. 119 (1989): "The privacy cases rest [on] 'the moral fact that a person belongs to himself [or herself] and not others nor to society as a whole.' Extending this principle to the abortion decision follows from the fact that '[f]ew decisions [are] more basic to individual dignity and autonomy' or more appropriate to the 'private sphere of individual liberty' than the uniquely personal, intimate, and self-defining decision whether or not to continue a pregnancy [quoting Blackmun, J., for the Court, in *Thornburgh v. American College of Obstetricians & Gynecologists*, 476 U.S. 747 (1986)].

"In two senses, abortion restrictions keep a woman from 'belonging to herself.' First [they] deprive her of bodily self-possession. [P]regnancy increases a woman's uterine size 500–1,000 times, her pulse rate by ten to fifteen beats a minute, and her body weight by 25 pounds or more. [Pregnancy also] can entail nausea, vomiting, more frequent urination, fatigue, back pain, labored breathing, or water retention. There are also numerous medical risks involved in carrying pregnancy to term. [In] addition, labor and delivery impose extraordinary physical demands, whether over the six to twelve hour or longer course of vaginal delivery, or during the highly invasive surgery involved in a cesarean section, which accounts for one out of four deliveries.

"By compelling pregnancy to term and delivery even where they are unwanted, abortion restrictions thus exert far more profound intrusions into bodily integrity than the stomach pumping the Court invalidated in *Rochin* [Sec. 1, IV supra] or the surgical removal of a bullet from a shoulder [invalidated] in *Winston* [Sec. 1, IV supra]."

2. *Are there two different rights to abortion?* Yes, maintains Jack M. Balkin, *Abortion and Original Meaning,* 24 Const.Comment. 294 (2007): "The first right is a woman's right not to be forced by the state to bear children at risk to her life or health. The second right is a woman's right not to be forced by the state to become a mother and thus to take on the responsibilities of parenthood, which, in our society are far more burdensome for women than for men. [Although] the first right to abortion continues throughout pregnancy, the second right need not. It only requires that women have a reasonable time to decide whether or not to become mothers and a fair and realistic opportunity to make that choice."

David B. Cruz, *The "Sexual Freedom Cases"? Contraception, Abortion, Abstinence, and the Constitution,* 35 Harv. C.R.-C.L. Rev. 299 (2000), draws the same distinction, adding that "[p]rinciples of robust gender equality, bodily integrity, [and] procreative autonomy" can complement one another, so long as they are supplemented by a "heretofore unarticulated" constitutional rule "forbidding government from using the threat either of physical harm or of the creation of new persons as a means of controlling citizens' behavior." Sherry F. Colb, *To Whom Do We Refer When we Speak of "Future Generations"?*, 77 Geo.Wash.L.Rev. 1582 (2009), argues that "once we distinguish the" interest in selecting one's offspring from the interest in bodily integrity, "we find a surprising amount of agreement, even among present-day abortion opponents, with the premise of abortion rights: that the [bodily integrity interest] is both weighty and directly implicated in the abortion decision."

3. ***Did the Court decide the question without admitting it?*** Consider Michael McConnell, *How Not to Promote Serious Deliberation About Abortion,* 58 U.Chi.L.Rev. 1181 (1991): "Society has no choice but to decide to whom it will extend protection. It is not helpful to call this decision 'private' for there is no more inherently political question than the definition of the political community. When the *Roe* Court stated, '[w]e need not resolve the difficult question of when life begins,' it was deciding the question without admitting it, and thus without having to support its decision with reasons. Worse yet, it was suggesting that the question of human life was irrelevant to the decision. *Any* conscientious determination of when the developing fetus attains a moral-legal status worthy of protection, supported by reasons, would be preferable to that."

4. ***Is personhood a biological fact or a socio-legal status?*** John Noonan, *The Root and Branch of Roe v. Wade,* 63 Neb.L.Rev. 668 (1984), complains that *Roe* "spoke of the unborn before viability as 'a theory of life,' as though there were competing views as to whether life in fact existed before viability. The implication could also be found that there was no reality there in the womb but merely theories about what was there. [To] judge from the weight the Court gave the being in the womb—found to be protectable in any degree only in the last two months of pregnancy—the Court itself must have viewed the unborn as pure potentiality or a mere theory before viability. The Court's opinion appeared to rest on the assumption that the biological reality could be subordinated or ignored by the sovereign speaking through the Court."

But consider Catharine MacKinnon, *Reflections on Sex Equality Under Law,* 100 Yale L.J. 1281 (1991): "[T]he only point of recognizing fetal personhood, or a separate fetal entity, is to assert the interests of the fetus *against* the pregnant woman. [Personhood] is a legal and social status, not a biological fact. [In] my opinion and in the experience of many pregnant women, the fetus is a human form of life. It is alive. But the existence of sex inequality in society requires that completed live birth mark the personhood line. If sex equality existed socially—if women were recognized as persons, sexual aggression were truly deviant, and childrearing were shared and consistent with a full life rather than at odds with it—the fetus still might not be considered a person but the question of its political status would be a very different one."

5. *Why was the state's moral justification for interference with individual liberty inadequate? Was it impermissibly religious?* Consider Louis Henkin, *Privacy and Autonomy*, 74 Colum.L.Rev. 1410 (1974): "Once, [the] promotion and protection of morals was clearly a proper concern of government; does the Right of Privacy imply that it is no longer? [While] the rights to use contraceptives [and] to have an abortion [were] held not offset by hypothesized, particular public goods, were they [not] essentially 'morals legislation'? And does it essentially all come down to the Court's saying [in effect] that these are not 'the law's business'?"

Compare Archibald Cox, *The Role of the Supreme Court in American Government,* 113–14 (1976): "My criticism of *Roe* is that the Court failed to establish the legitimacy of the decision by not articulating a precept of sufficient abstractness to lift the ruling above the level of a political judgment based upon the evidence currently available from the medical, physical, and social sciences. Nor can I articulate such a principle—unless it be that a State cannot interfere with the individual decisions relating to sex, procreation, and family with only a moral or philosophical State justification: a principle which I cannot accept or believe will be accepted by the American people."

"*[A]ll* normative judgments," observes Tribe 2d ed., at 1350, "are rooted in moral premises: surely the judgment that it is wrong to kill a two-week old infant is no less 'moral' in inspiration than the judgment, less frequently made but no less strongly felt by many of those who make it, that it is wrong to kill a two-day old fetus. Archibald Cox seems correct, therefore, when he concludes that *Roe* must be wrong if it rests on the premise that a state can never interfere with individual decisions relating to sex or procreation 'with only moral justification.' But it is clear that *Roe* rests on no such premise."

Do abortion restrictions impermissibly rest on religious judgments? So argues Ronald Dworkin, *Unenumerated Rights: Whether and How Roe Should be Overruled*, 59 U.Chi.L.Rev. 381 (1992): "the belief that the value of human life transcends its value for the creature whose life it is—that human life is objectively valuable from the point of view, as it were, of the universe—is plainly a religious belief, even when it is held by people who do not believe in a personal deity" and thus people's beliefs about the inherent value of human life, beliefs deployed in their opinions about abortion (and suicide and euthanasia as well) "should be deemed religious within the meaning of the First Amendment."

See also Thomas Emerson, *The Power of Congress to Change Constitutional Decisions of the Supreme Court: The Human Life Bill,* 77 Nw.U.L.Rev. 129 (1982); Sylvia Law, *Rethinking Sex and the Constitution,* 132 U.Pa.L.Rev. 955 (1984)("where moral values are in such sharp conflict, the first amendment requires respect for diversity."); David Richards, *Constitutional Privacy, Religious Disestablishment, and the Abortion Decisions,* in *Abortion: Moral and Legal Perspectives* 148, 172 (Garfield & Hennessey eds. 1984).

6. *Are abortion restrictions "totalitarian"?* According to Jed Rubenfeld, *The Right of Privacy*, 102 Harv.L.Rev. 737 (1989), "[t]he danger"

posed by the laws invalidated in the privacy cases "is a particular kind of creeping totalitarianism, an unarmed *occupation* of individuals' lives." The issue is less what such laws forbid than it is "their *productive* or *affirmative* consequences. There are perhaps no legal proscriptions with more profound, more extensive, or more persistent affirmative effects on individual lives than the laws struck down as violations of the right to privacy. Anti-abortion laws, anti-miscegenation laws, and compulsory education laws all involve the forcing of lives into well-defined and highly confined institutional layers. At the simplest, most quotidian level, such laws tend to *take over* the lives of the persons involved: they occupy and preoccupy."

7.   *A defense of Roe even assuming that the fetus is a person.* Is the *Roe* Court correct in its statement that if "the fetus is a 'person' within the language and meaning of the Fourteenth Amendment" then the case for a constitutional right to abortion "collapses"? Consider Judith Jarvis Thomson, *A Defense of Abortion,* 1 Phil. & Pub.Aff. 47 (1971): "Opponents of abortion commonly spend most of their time establishing that the fetus is a person, and hardly any time explaining the step from there to the impermissibility of abortion. [How] does the argument go? [Something] like this, I take it. Every person has a right to life. So the fetus has a right to life. No doubt the mother has a right to decide what shall happen in and to her body; everyone would grant that. But surely a person's right to life is stronger and more stringent [and] so outweighs it.

"[It] sounds plausible. But now [imagine that you] wake up in the morning and find yourself back to back in bed with [a] famous unconscious violinist. He has been found to have a fatal kidney ailment, and the Society of Music Lovers has [found] that you alone have the right blood type to help. They have therefore kidnapped you [and] the violinist's circulatory system was plugged into yours, so that your kidneys can be used to extract poisons from his blood as well as your own. [To] unplug you would be to kill him. But [it's] only for nine months. By then he will have recovered [and] can be safely unplugged. [Is] it morally incumbent on you to accede to this situation? [All] persons have a right to life, and violinists are persons. [I] imagine you would regard this as outrageous, which suggests that something really is wrong with that plausible-sounding argument I mentioned a moment ago.

"[Suppose] a woman voluntarily indulges in intercourse, knowing of the chance it will issue in pregnancy, and then she does become pregnant; is she not in part responsible for the presence, in fact the very existence, of the unborn person inside her? [This] argument would give the unborn person a right to its mother's body only if her pregnancy resulted from a voluntary act. [It] would leave out entirely the unborn persons whose existence is due to rape. [And] we should also notice that it is not at all plain that this argument really does go even as far as it purports to. [If] the room is stuffy, and I therefore open a window to air it, and a burglar climbs in, it would be absurd to say [that] he can stay [because I am] partially responsible for his presence. [It] would be still more absurd to say this if I had had bars installed outside my windows, precisely to prevent burglars from getting in, and a burglar got in only because of a defect in the bars. It remains equally absurd if we imagine it is not a burglar who climbs in, but an innocent person who blunders or falls in."[336]

Building on Thomson's argument, Donald Regan, *Rewriting Roe v. Wade*, 77 Mich.L.Rev. 1569 (1979), contends that "abortion should be viewed as presenting a problem in what we might call 'the law of samaritanism,' that is, the law concerning obligations imposed on certain individuals to give aid to others. It is a deeply rooted principle of American law that an individual is ordinarily not required to volunteer aid to another individual who is in danger or in need of assistance. [I]f we require a pregnant woman to carry the fetus to term and deliver it—if we forbid abortion, in other words—we are compelling her to be a Good Samaritan. [I]f we consider the special nature of the burdens imposed on pregnant women by laws forbidding abortion, we must eventually conclude that the equal protection clause forbids imposition of these burdens on pregnant women."

8.   ***Does the Good Samaritan argument succeed?*** Consider David A. Strauss, *Abortion, Toleration, and Moral Uncertainty*, 1992 Sup.Ct.Rev. 1: "The problem is that this argument depends on two libertarian premises: first, that obligations must be in some way commensurate with voluntary undertakings; and second, that there is a sharp distinction between bodily invasions and other impositions on individuals. These libertarian premises are not obviously true, are difficult to justify, and conflict with strongly held intuitions.

"The first premise is needed to meet an obvious and superficial objection to the Good Samaritan argument—that, cases of rape and incest aside, no one becomes pregnant involuntarily. The burdens of pregnancy (it is therefore said), unlike the impositions on a Good Samaritan, are to some extent voluntarily assumed. [The] principal answer to this argument offered by the proponents of the Good Samaritan view is that it is, in general, unrealistic and unfair to regard most pregnant women as voluntarily accepting the burdens of pregnancy in any meaningful sense.

---

[336] Consider Catharine MacKinnon, *Roe v. Wade: A Study in Male Ideology,* in *Abortion: Moral and Legal Perspectives* 45, 46–48 (Garfield & Hennessey eds. 1984): "Feminist investigations suggest [that women do not significantly control sex]. Feminism has found that women feel compelled to preserve the appearance—which, acted upon, becomes the reality—of male direction of sexual expression, as if it is male initiative itself that we want: it is that which turns us on. Men enforce this. It is much of what men want in a woman.

"[Under] these conditions, women often do not use birth control because [it] means acknowledging and planning and taking direction of intercourse, accepting one's sexual availability, and appearing nonspontaneous. [A] good user of contraception is a bad girl. She can be presumed sexually available and, among other consequences, raped with relative impunity. (If you think this isn't true, you should consider rape cases in which the fact that a woman had a diaphragm in is taken as an indication that what happened to her was intercourse, not rape. 'Why did you have your diaphragm in?') [I] wonder if a woman can be presumed to control access to her sexuality if she feels unable to interrupt intercourse to insert a diaphragm; or worse, cannot even want to, aware that she risks a pregnancy she knows she does not want. [Yet] abortion policy has never been explicitly approached in the context of how women get pregnant; that is, as a consequence of intercourse under conditions of gender inequality; that is, as an issue of forced sex."

"That answer seem correct, as far as it goes. But it assumes away the possibility that there are obligations and duties that arise without any voluntary act. They arise by virtue of status or just because one happened to find oneself in a certain position. Obligations to a political community are probably an example; efforts to ground such obligations on voluntary undertakings are difficult to sustain. Obligations *to* a parent or to a sibling are also in this category; they arise, at least in part, by virtue of status, not voluntary acts. One might, therefore, without taking any act of a kind that would ordinarily lead to such strong obligations, find oneself in the position of a parent who has obligations to her own unborn child that she would not have to a stranger.

"[No] one questions that parents have many burdensome obligations to their children, such as the obligation to provide for their economic and emotional support. Weighed just on some sort of quantitative scale (such as how much one would pay to avoid the obligation, other things equal), it is arguable that these burdens are greater than those incurred by a pregnant mother. If pregnancy is an unacceptable obligation to impose on a person, that must be because it involves a physical imposition that is qualitatively different from other parental obligations.

"[It] is true that in the current state of the law, parents are not generally required to sacrifice their bodily integrity even to save their children's lives. But that may just reflect institutional concerns about legal enforcement. It is certainly plausible that parents have a moral obligation to make such a sacrifice: a parent who did not give up a kidney to save a child's life, for example, would probably be widely reviled. [It] is difficult to see why a parent's extensive obligations to a child stop at the boundaries of the body. And if they do not—if it is not unacceptable to require a parent to give up a kidney for a child—then the Good Samaritan argument against restricting abortion loses much of its force."

9. ***"Privacy" or "sex equality"?*** "Nothing the Supreme Court has ever done," observes Sylvia Law, *Rethinking Sex and the Constitution,* 132 U.Pa.L.Rev. 955 (1984), "has been more concretely important for women [than *Roe*]. Laws restricting access to abortion have a devastating sex-specific impact." Yet, as Professor Law notes, not only was the abortion decision not grounded on the principle of sex equality, the plaintiffs in *Roe* and *Doe* did not even challenge the abortion restrictions as sex discriminatory. But many commentators,[337] including then Judge (now Justice) Ruth Bader Ginsburg,[338]

---

[337] See, e.g., Guido Calabresi, *Ideals, Beliefs, Attitudes and the Law* 99–102 (1985); Cass R. Sunstein, *The Partial Constitution* 272–85 (1993); Tribe, *Abortion* 105; Frances Olsen, *Unraveling Compromise,* 103 Harv.L.Rev. 105 (1989).

[338] In a lecture delivered shortly before her nomination to the Supreme Court, Judge Ginsburg noted that in *Planned Parenthood v. Casey* (infra), which reaffirmed "the essential holding" of *Roe,* the controlling Justices (O'Connor, Kennedy and Souter), speaking for the Court on this point, "added an important strand to the Court's opinions on abortion"—they "acknowledged the intimate connection between a woman's 'ability to control [her] reproductive li[fe]' and her 'ability [to] participate equally in the economic and social life of the Nation.' " Ruth Bader Ginsburg, *Speaking*

have maintained that the best argument for the right to abortion is based on principles of sexual equality, not "due process" or "privacy."

MacKinnon, note 4 supra, at 1319, puts it powerfully: "Because the social organization of reproduction is a major bulwark of women's social inequality, any constitutional interpretation of a sex equality principle must prohibit laws, state policies, or official practices and acts that deprive women of reproductive control or punish women for their reproductive role or capacity. [Women's] right to reproductive control is a sex equality right because it is inconsistent with an equality mandate for the state, by law, to collaborate with or mandate social inequality on the basis of sex, as [denials of abortion through criminalization or lack of public funding where needed] do. This is not so much an argument for an extension of the meaning of constitutional sex equality as a recognition that if it does not mean this, it does not mean anything at all.

"Under this sex equality analysis, criminal abortion statutes of the sort invalidated in *Roe* violate equal protection of the laws. They make women criminals for a medical procedure only women need, or make others criminals for performing a procedure on women that only women need, when much of the need for this procedure as well as barriers to access to it have been created by social conditions of sex inequality. Forced motherhood is sex inequality. Because pregnancy can be experienced only by women, and because of the unequal social predicates and consequences pregnancy has for women, any forced pregnancy will always deprive and hurt one sex only as a member of her gender."

But consider McConnell, note 3 supra: "[A] law does not violate the Equal Protection Clause merely because it burdens one race or sex more heavily than another. Such a law is subject to heightened judicial scrutiny only if the legislature had an intent to discriminate. There exists no substantial evidence that abortion laws, as a matter of historical fact, were motivated by such an intent to discriminate against women. Indeed, the history of abortion laws shows that they were principally a response by the medical profession to improvements in the technology of abortion and to newly-discovered information about embryology. [More] interestingly, the nineteenth century anti-abortion movement was strongly supported by the women's movement.

"[If the fetus is a person, the most] natural implication of the Equal Protection Clause is that it stands *against* abortion rights. The Equal Protection Clause is designed to protect members of vulnerable and politically unrepresented minorities from the oppressive measures of the dominant majority. Abortion laws are designed to protect fetuses or unborn children, surely a vulnerable and unrepresented group, from private violence. It is an odd interpretation of the Equal Protection Clause to say that it *prevents* states from extending protection to the vulnerable and unrepresented."

---

in a Judicial Voice, 67 N.Y.U.L.Rev. 1185 (1992) (quoting *Casey*). See also Ruth Bader Ginsburg, *Some Thoughts on Autonomy and Equality in Relation to Roe v. Wade,* 63 N.C.L.Rev. 375 (1985).

10. *Is Roe a physician's rights opinion?* In *Roe,* maintains Andrea Asaro, *The Judicial Portrayal of the Physician in Abortion and Sterilization Decisions,* 6 Harv. Women's L.J. 51 (1983), "[for] Blackmun, the key issue was quite simply one of medical discretion. [The] abortion decision is characterized [neither] as primarily the woman's nor as fundamentally or initially a moral or personal one. Blackmun's perspective is clinical, and the woman patient has taken a back seat to the male physician-protagonist. [Concluding *Roe,* Blackmun, J., states]: '[The] decision vindicates the right of the physician to administer medical treatment according to his professional judgment up to the points where important state interests provide compelling justifications for intervention. Up to these points, *the abortion decision in all its aspects is inherently, and primarily, a medical decision, and basic responsibility for it must rest with the physician.*' [Emphasis added by Asaro.] Blackmun has neglected even to mention the pregnant woman as party to the abortion decision! The state, the physician, and the court have displaced Ms. Roe altogether."

11. *The impact of Roe.* Although *Roe* increased women's access to safe abortions, "surprisingly," notes Cass R. Sunstein, *The Partial Constitution* 147 (1993) "it did not dramatically increase the actual number and rate of abortions. [In] fact most states were moving in the direction of liberal abortion laws well before *Roe,* resulting in 600,000 lawful abortions per year. Astonishingly, the rate of increase in *legal* abortions was higher in the three years before that decision than in the three years after. It may well have been the case that states would generally have legalized abortion without *Roe.* Perhaps more fundamentally, the decision probably contributed to the creation of the 'moral majority'; helped defeat the Equal Rights Amendment; prevented the eventual achievement of consensual solutions to the abortion problem; and severely undermined the women's movement, by defining that movement in terms of the single issue of abortion, by spurring and organizing opposition, and by demobilizing potential adherents."

Lucinda M. Finley, *Contested Ground: The Story of Roe v. Wade and its Impact on American Society*, in Michael C. Dorf, *Constitutional Law Stories* 333 (2d ed. 2009), views *Roe*'s legacy differently: "The principal practical consequence of *Roe* was to dramatically increase the safety of abortion." Responding to the argument that "if abortion regulation had been left to the deliberative political process in state legislatures [the] nation gradually would have achieved consensus around abortion," Finley cautions that "legislative reform efforts were becoming increasingly contentious well before the Supreme Court opinion. [*Roe*] has become an important symbol for both anti-abortion and pro-choice activists, but it is not the cause of activism on either side. [It] is unlikely that quiescent consensus on abortion will emerge in American society so long as it is a public topic for debate in any legal arena, whether judicial or legislative."

Roe v. Wade's Contribution to the Debate over Constitutional Decisionmaking

1. ***Is Roe "Noninterpretivist"?*** Richard H. Fallon, Jr., *A Constructivist Coherence Theory of Constitutional Interpretation,* 100 Harv.L.Rev. 1189 (1987), divides "interpretivists" into two camps: "On one side stand 'originalists.' [They] take the rigid view that only the original understanding of the framers' specific intent ought to count. On the other side, 'moderate interpretivists' allow contemporary understandings and the framers' general or abstract intent to enter the constitutional calculus."

According to Ira Lupu, *Constitutional Theory and the Search for the Workable Premise,* 8 Dayton L.Rev. 579 (1983), "*Roe* clarified, as had no other case since World War II, the Supreme Court's willingness to reach results which no defensible interpretivist position could support. Although rhetorically tied to the meaning of 'liberty' in the fourteenth amendment due process clause, and loosely aligned with the penumbral analysis developed in *Griswold, Roe* cut fundamental rights adjudication loose from the constitutional text. [Subsequent] scholarly efforts offered a variety of justifications for [this type of] noninterpretive review—natural law underpinnings of the 1787 Constitution, [the] search for enduring or traditional unwritten norms, [and] judicial manifestation of consensus morality."

Thomas Grey, *Do We Have an Unwritten Constitution?*, 27 Stan.L.Rev. 703 (1975), appears to have originated the "interpretivist/ noninterpretivist" terminology, but he has since concluded that these labels "distort[ ] the debate": "If the current interest in interpretive theory [does] nothing else, at least it shows that the concept of interpretation is broad enough to encompass any plausible mode of constitutional adjudication. We are all interpretivists; the real arguments are not over whether judges should stick to interpreting, but over what they should interpret and what interpretive attitudes they should adopt." Thomas Grey, *The Constitution as Scripture,* 37 Stan.L.Rev. 1 (1984).

2. ***Evolving Originalism?*** In the four decades since *Roe*, originalism has changed. Indeed, according to Thomas B. Colby and Peter J. Smith, *Living Originalism,* 59 Duke. L.J. 239 (2009), "[a] review of originalists' work reveals originalism to be not a single, coherent, unified theory of constitutional interpretation, but rather a smorgasbord of distinct constitutional theories that share little in common except a misleading reliance on a single label." To the extent that originalism does have a common core, it no longer appears to be a quest for the "framers' intent." Few originalist legal scholars still contend that the interpreter's task is to uncover the subjective intentions and expectations of the framers. Instead, nearly all contemporary originalist scholars argue that interpreters should

seek the original *meaning* of the Constitution, which may be inconsistent with the intentions and expectations of the framers and ratifiers.

For example, Professor Balkin argues that "we do not face a choice between living constitutionalism and fidelity to the original meaning of the text. They are two sides of the same coin." Jack Balkin, *Living Originalism* 20 (2011). In Balkin's view, a proper originalist understanding of the Equal Protection Clause and the Privileges or Immunities Clause of the Fourteenth Amendment guarantees a right to abortion. See id. at 214–19.

Is this blurring of the lines between originalism and nonoriginalism helpful? Professor Dorf worries that "widespread acceptance of Balkin's views would allow conservatives to say that even liberals now accept originalism but then turn around and define originalism narrowly," because notwithstanding the scholarly shift, "judges, elected officials, and the public" continue to understand originalism as a search for "the framers' and ratifiers' expected applications in considering concrete cases." Michael C. Dorf, *The Undead Constitution*, 125 Harv.L.Rev. 2011 (2012).

3.   ***What happened on the day Roe was decided?*** "The subject of abortion," observes Robert Bork, *The Tempting of America* 111–16 (1990), "had been fiercely debated in state legislatures for many years. [Whatever] the proper resolution of the moral debate, [few] imagined that the Constitution resolved it. [The] discovery this late in our history that the question was not one for democratic decision but one of constitutional law was so implausible that it certainly deserved a fifty-one page explanation. Unfortunately, in the entire opinion there is not one line of explanation, not one sentence that qualifies as legal argument. [It] is unlikely that [the Court] ever will [provide the explanation lacking in 1973] because the right to abort, whatever one thinks of it, is not to be found in the Constitution. * * *

"Attempts to overturn *Roe* will continue as long as the Court adheres to it. And, just so long as the decision remains, the Court will be perceived, correctly, as political and will continue to be the target of demonstrations, marches, television advertisements, mass mailings, and the like. *Roe,* as the greatest example and symbol of the judicial usurpation of democratic prerogatives in this century, should be overturned. The Court's integrity requires that."

Compare Laurence H. Tribe, *Abortion: The Clash of Absolutes* 99 (1990): "Judge Bork says that 'the right to abort, whatever one thinks of it, is not to be found in the Constitution.' In a sense this is obviously right. Indeed, not one of the words 'abortion,' 'pregnancy,' 'reproduction,' 'sex,' 'privacy,' 'bodily integrity,' and 'procreation' appears anywhere in [the] Constitution. But neither do such phrases as 'freedom of thought,' 'rights of parenthood,' 'liberty of association,' 'family self-determination,' and 'freedom of marital choice.' Yet nearly everyone supposes that at least some of these dimensions of personal autonomy and independence are aspects of the 'liberty' which the Fourteenth Amendment says no state may deny to any person 'without due process of law.' "

4. **Are the Abortion Cases "bad constitutional law" or "not constitutional law"?** Consider John H. Ely, *The Wages of Crying Wolf: A Comment on Roe v. Wade,* 82 Yale L.J. 920 (1973): "What is unusual about *Roe* is that the liberty involved is accorded [a] protection more stringent [than] that the present Court accords the freedom of the press explicitly guaranteed by the First Amendment. What is frightening about *Roe* is that this super-protected right is not inferable from the language of the Constitution, the framers' thinking respecting the specific problem in issue, any general value derivable from the provisions they included, or the nation's governmental structure. Nor is it explainable in terms of the unusual political impotence of the group judicially protected vis-á-vis the interest that legislatively prevailed over it.[339]

"[The] problem with *Roe* is not so much that it bungles the question it sets itself, but rather that it sets itself a question the Constitution has not made the Court's business. It *looks* different from *Lochner*—it has the shape if not the substance of a judgment that is very much the Court's business, one vindicating an interest the Constitution marks as special— and it is for that reason perhaps more dangerous. [*Roe* is] a very bad decision. [It] is bad because it is bad constitutional law, or rather because it is *not* constitutional law and gives almost no sense of an obligation to try to be."

5. **"Enumerated" and "unenumerated" rights.** Although many view the distinction between enumerated and unenumerated rights as presenting the important question whether and when courts have authority to enforce rights not actually enumerated in the Constitution (e.g., the right to travel and the right to privacy, from which the right to an abortion is said to derive), Dworkin, *Unenumerated Rights,* finds the question "unintelligible": "The Bill of Rights [consists] of broad and abstract principles of political morality, which together encompass, in

---

[339] Professor Ely argues that Stone, J.'s suggestion in his famous *Carolene Products* footnote (Ch. 5, Sec. 3), that the Court provide extraordinary constitutional protection for " 'discrete and insulate minorities' unable to form effective political alliances" does not apply to *Roe*: "Compared with men, very few women sit in our legislatures, [but] *no* fetuses sit [there]. [Stone's suggestion] was clearly intended and should be reserved for those interests which, *as compared with the interests to which they have been subordinated,* constitute minorities usually incapable of protecting themselves. Compared with men, women may constitute such a 'minority'; compared with the unborn, they do not."

However, Robert Bennett, *Abortion and Judicial Review,* 75 Nw.U.L.Rev. 978 (1981), maintains that Professor Ely's challenge to the appropriateness of judicial intervention in *Roe* "is misguided," "because it assumes that fetuses are political actors—indeed a political minority— whose 'powerlessness' is relevant to assessing the Court's appropriate role in the abortion controversy. Each political system must define, explicitly or implicitly, the universe of relevant political actors. [But] outside the abortion context there are no indications that fetuses are considered relevant political actors."

exceptionally abstract form, all the dimensions of political morality that in our political culture can ground an individual constitutional right. The key issue in applying these abstract principles to particular political controversies is not one of reference but of *interpretation,* which is very different. [The distinction between enumerated and unenumerated rights] cannot be sustained. [No] one thinks that it follows just from the meaning of the words 'freedom of speech' either that people are free to burn flags, or that they are not. No one thinks it follows just from the meaning of the words 'equal protection' that laws excluding women from certain jobs are unconstitutional, or that they are not. [Nor] are [these] arguments different in how they are interpretive. Each conclusion (if sound) follows, not from some historical hope or belief or intention of a 'framer,' but because the political principle that supports that conclusion best accounts for the general structure and history of constitutional law."

Abortion Funding

1.   MAHER v. ROE, 432 U.S. 464 (1977), per POWELL, J., sustained Connecticut's use of Medicaid funds to reimburse women for the costs of childbirth and "medically necessary" first trimester abortions (defined to include "psychiatric necessity"), but not for the costs of elective or nontherapeutic first trimester abortions.

On "the central question"—"whether the regulation 'impinges upon a fundamental right explicitly or implicitly protected by the Constitution' "—the Court held that *Roe* did not establish "an unqualified 'constitutional right to an abortion,' " but only a "right protect[ing] the woman from unduly burdensome interference with her freedom to decide whether to terminate her pregnancy. It implies no limitation on the authority of a State to make a value judgment favoring childbirth over abortion, and to implement that judgment by the allocation of public funds. [The] indigency that may make it difficult—and in some cases, perhaps, impossible—for some women to have abortions is neither created nor in any way affected by the [regulation.]"

BRENNAN, J., joined by Marshall and Blackmun, JJ., dissented, accusing the majority of "a distressing insensitivity to the plight of impoverished pregnant women." The "disparity in funding [clearly] operates to coerce indigent pregnant women to bear children they would not otherwise choose to have, and just as clearly, this coercion can only operate upon the poor, who are uniquely the victims of this form of financial pressure." *Roe* and its progeny held that "an area of privacy invulnerable to the State's intrusion surrounds the decision of a pregnant woman whether or not to carry her pregnancy to term. The Connecticut scheme clearly infringes upon that area of privacy."

2. ***The Hyde Amendment.*** Title XIX of the Social Security Act established the Medicaid program to provide federal financial assistance to states choosing to reimburse certain costs of medical treatment for needy persons. Since 1976, various versions of the so-called Hyde Amendment have limited federal funding of abortions under the Medicaid program to those necessary to save the life of the mother and certain other exceptional circumstances.

HARRIS v. McRAE, 448 U.S. 297 (1980), per STEWART, J., found no constitutional violation: "The present case does differ factually from *Maher* insofar as that case involved a failure to fund nontherapeutic abortions, whereas the Hyde Amendment withholds funding of certain medically necessary abortions. [But] regardless of [how] the freedom of a woman to choose to terminate her pregnancy for health reasons [is characterized], it simply does not follow that [this freedom] carries with it a constitutional entitlement to the financial resources to avail herself of the full range of protected choices. [T]he Hyde Amendment leaves an indigent woman with at least the same range of choice in deciding whether to obtain a medically necessary abortion as she would have had if Congress had chosen to subsidize no health care costs at all.

"[Acceptance of appellees' argument] would mark a drastic change in our understanding of the Constitution. It cannot be that because government may not prohibit the use of contraceptives, *Griswold,* or prevent parents from sending their child to a private school, *Pierce,* government, therefore, has an affirmative constitutional obligation to assure that all persons have the financial resources to obtain contraceptives or send their children to private [schools.]"

Four justices dissented—Brennan, Marshall and Blackmun, JJ. (the three *Maher* dissenters), and Stevens, J. who had joined the opinion of the Court in *Maher.* STEVENS, J., maintained that the instant case presented "[a] fundamentally different question" from the one decided in *Maher:* "[This case involves] the pool of benefits that Congress created by enacting [Title XIX]. Individuals who satisfy two neutral criteria—financial need and medical need—are entitled to equal access to that pool. The question is whether certain persons who satisfy those criteria may be denied access to benefits solely because they must exercise the constitutional right to have an abortion in order to obtain the medical care they need. Our prior cases plainly dictate the answer."

The other three dissenters wrote separately, each voicing agreement with Stevens, J.'s analysis. BRENNAN, J., joined by Marshall and Blackmun, JJ., maintained: "[W]hat the Court fails to appreciate is that it is not simply the woman's indigency that interferes with her freedom of choice, but the combination of her own poverty and the Government's unequal subsidization of abortion and childbirth."

The Court extended *Maher* and *McRae* in *Rust v. Sullivan*, 500 U.S. 173 (1991), upholding federal regulations prohibiting private physicians receiving federal funds for "family planning services" from providing abortion information to a woman client except when a pregnancy places her life in peril. (The free speech aspects of this case are discussed at Ch. 7, Sec. 7, I.)

NOTES AND QUESTIONS

1. ***Preventing constitutional caste.*** Where "rights [are] too important to be reserved for selected privileged groups," observes Kathleen M. Sullivan, *Unconstitutional Conditions,* 102 Harv.L.Rev. 1413 (1989), "conditions on benefits that affect their exercise can pose a similar danger of hierarchy. [Government] cannot universally criminalize abortion, nor universally burden it with heavy restrictions, at least in the first trimester. The only difference between such general bans and the selective subsidization of childbirth but not abortion for indigent women is the class affected. Dependency on government defines the class here. But what the government cannot restrict for all, it may not restrict for those over whom it has special leverage because of their dependency—especially where the displacement of private alternatives creates special responsibility. To hold otherwise would sanction a two-tier system of constitutional rights—a system of constitutional caste."

2. ***What about private insurance?*** The Patient Protection and Affordable Care Act extends the Hyde Amendment to the federal subsidies for which individuals purchasing health insurance on "exchanges" may be eligible. Although the Act itself does not forbid insurance plans offered on the exchanges from covering abortion, it does proportionately reduce subsidies for such plans and requires the segregation of funds. In addition, the Act authorizes states to "prohibit abortion coverage in [all] qualified health plans" offered on state exchanges. 42 U.S.C. § 18023. Do *Maher, McRae,* and *Rust* necessarily imply that these provisions are constitutional? Does the answer depend on whether the Act is understood to mandate health insurance coverage or merely to impose a tax on people who fail to obtain coverage? See *National Fed. of Indep. Bus. v. Sebelius*, Ch. 2, Sec. 2, IV and Ch. 2, Sec. 3.

———

In WEBSTER v. REPRODUCTIVE HEALTH SERVICES, 492 U.S. 490 (1989), the Court upheld various provisions of a Missouri statute. Speaking for a three-Justice plurality, REHNQUIST, C.J., joined by White and Kennedy, JJ., sustained a provision requiring a physician, prior to performing an abortion on a woman he has reason to believe is at least twenty weeks pregnant, to ascertain if the fetus is viable by using the degree of care normally exercised by a "prudent physician." The plurality read the provision as not requiring the tests to be made under all circumstances. For example, if the physician reasonably believed tests would be irrelevant to determining viability, he need not perform any.

As for the doubts cast on the viability-testing provision, the plurality viewed this as "reflection of the fact that the rigid trimester analysis of the course of a pregnancy enunciated in *Roe* has resulted in subsequent [cases] making constitutional law in this area a virtual Procustean bed.

"[We] have not refrained from reconsideration of a prior constriction of the Constitution that has proved 'unsound in principle and unworkable in practice.' [We] think the *Roe* trimester falls into that category. In the first place, [the] key elements of the *Roe* framework—trimesters and viability—are not found in the text of the Constitution or in any place else one would expect to find a constitutional principle. [In] the second place, we do not see why the State's interest in protecting potential human life should come into existence only at the point of viability, and that there should therefore be a rigid line allowing state regulation after viability, but prohibiting it before viability."

Relying on the abortion-funding cases, supra, a majority of the Court also sustained provisions of the Missouri law prohibiting state employees from performing abortions or using public facilities for abortions: "Missouri's [law] leaves a pregnant woman with the same choices as if the State had chosen not to operate any public hospitals at all.' "

O'CONNOR, J., concurring on this issue, agreed with the plurality that the viability-testing provision did not require a physician to perform examinations and tests when it would be careless and imprudent to do so. Unlike the plurality, however, she did not understand the viability testing provision (as so construed) to conflict with any of the Court's past abortion cases. Thus, she found no need to reexamine *Roe*.

SCALIA, J., concurring, voted to uphold the viability testing requirement, but agreed with the dissent of BLACKMUN, J. (joined by Brennan and Marshall, JJ.), that the portion of the plurality opinion sustaining the provision "effectively would overrule *Roe*." He thought "that should be done," but he would "do it more explicitly."

NOTES AND QUESTIONS

1.   *The significance of Webster.* Consider Estrich & Sullivan, *Abortion Politics*, supra: "[If] little was decided in *Webster,* a good deal was nonetheless said. The Chief Justice, writing for three members of the Court, made plain that he was ready to jettison [the] trimester approach of *Roe,* presumably finding the state's interest in potential life as compelling in the first month as the last, and leaving it to the state to balance its own interest against the woman's, subject only to some rationality review. The genius of the approach, if you can call it that, is that it effectively overrules *Roe* without ever even

suggesting that a woman lacks a privacy or autonomy interest in her own body."

2. ***An open invitation to state legislators?*** According to Tribe, *Abortion*, at 23, "*Webster* was and remains an open invitation to state legislators to see just how strictly they can regulate abortion without Justice O'Connor finding the burden on the abortion right 'undue.' " At the time Professor Tribe made this observation, O'Connor, J., had never found a restriction on the abortion right "unduly burdensome" and thus constitutionally defective. But shortly thereafter she did—in *Hodgson*, Note 3 infra.

3. ***Parental notification.*** In HODGSON v. MINNESOTA, 497 U.S. 417 (1990), a 5–4 majority (STEVENS, J., joined in principal part by Brennan, Marshall, Blackmun, and O'Connor, JJ.) struck down a state law requiring *both* parents of an unemancipated minor to be notified at least 48 hours before she underwent an abortion. But a different 5–4 majority—O'CONNOR, J., and the four justices who would have sustained the two-parent notification requirement *without* a judicial bypass alternative (Kennedy, J., joined by Rehnquist, C.J., and White and Scalia, JJ.) (the Kennedy group)—upheld the two-parent notification requirement *combined with* a judicial bypass, which the statute authorized as a fallback in case the two-parent notification were held invalid. (For discussion of such provisions more generally, see Michael C. Dorf, *Fallback Law*, 107 Colum.L.Rev. 303 (2007)).

Thus *Hodgson* produced two distinct majorities and in each instance O'Connor, J., provided the crucial vote. In addition, six justices—Stevens and O'Connor, JJ., and the Kennedy group—upheld a provision requiring that, before proceeding with an abortion, a minor must wait 48 hours after notifying a *single* parent of her intention to obtain an abortion.

Applying her "undue burden" test, O'CONNOR, J., concurring, concluded that the obstacles imposed by Minnesota's two-parent notice requirement "are not reasonably related to legitimate state interests" and that the requirement "is all the more unreasonable when one considers that only half of the minors [in the state] reside with both biological parents [and a] third live with only one parent."

KENNEDY, J., joined by Rehnquist, C.J., and White and Scalia, JJ., dissented on this issue, maintaining "that it was reasonable for the legislature to conclude that in most cases notice to both parents will work to the minor's benefit" (not only where the minor lives in the "ideal family setting," but also where she no longer lives with both parents).

Because O'Connor, J., agreed with the Kennedy group that the constitutional objection to the two-parent notification requirement is removed by the judicial bypass—"the interference with the internal operation of the family [simply] does not exist where the minor can avoid notifying one or both parents by use of the bypass procedure"—KENNEDY, J., joined by Rehnquist,

C.J., and White and Scalia, JJ., wrote the principal opinion upholding that provision.

SCALIA, J., who dissented from the Court's invalidation of the two-parent notification requirement without a bypass but concurred in the Court's other rulings, commented: "One will search in vain the document we are supposed to be construing for text that provides the basis for the argument over these distinctions; and will find in our society's tradition regarding abortion no hint that the distinctions are constitutionally relevant, much less any indication how a constitutional argument about them ought to be resolved. The random and unpredictable results of our consequently unchanneled individual views make it increasingly evident, Term after Term, that the tools for this job are not to be found in the lawyer's—and hence not in the judge's—workbox.[340] I continue to dissent from this enterprise of devising an Abortion Code, and from the illusion that we have authority to do so."

The Court Reaffirms "the Essential Holding of *Roe*"

PLANNED PARENTHOOD OF SOUTHEASTERN PENNSYLVANIA V. CASEY

505 U.S. 833, 112 S.Ct. 2791, 120 L.Ed.2d 674 (1992).

JUSTICE O'CONNOR, JUSTICE KENNEDY, and JUSTICE SOUTER announced the judgment of the Court and delivered the opinion of the Court with respect to Parts I, II, III, V–A, V–C, and VI, an opinion with respect to Part V–E, in which JUSTICE STEVENS joins, and an opinion with respect to Parts IV, V–B, and V–D.

I.   Liberty finds no refuge in a jurisprudence of doubt. Yet 19 years after our holding that the Constitution protects a woman's right to terminate her pregnancy in its early stages, *Roe v. Wade,* that definition of liberty is still questioned. Joining the respondents as amicus curiae, the United States, as it has done in five other cases in the last decade, again asks us to overrule *Roe.*

At issue in these cases are five provisions of the Pennsylvania Abortion Control Act of 1982 as amended in 1988 and 1989. [The] Act requires that a woman seeking an abortion give her informed consent prior to the abortion procedure, and specifies that she be provided with certain information at least 24 hours before the abortion is performed. For a minor to obtain an abortion, the Act requires the informed consent of one of her parents, but provides for a judicial bypass option if the minor does not wish to or cannot obtain a parent's consent. Another provision of the Act requires that, unless certain exceptions apply, a married woman seeking an

---

[340] But see Jed Rubenfeld, *On the Legal Status of the Proposition that "Life Begins at Conception"*, 43 Stan.L.Rev. 599 (1991): "The 'tools' for this job are not in anyone's workbox. But a judge is not a handyman, and he cannot call in state legislators as professionals whenever he feels out of his depth."

abortion must sign a statement indicating that she has notified her husband of her intended abortion. § 3209. The Act exempts compliance with these three requirements in the event of a "medical emergency," which is defined in [§ 3203]. In addition to the above provisions regulating the performance of abortions, the Act imposes certain reporting requirements on facilities that provide abortion services.

[After] considering the fundamental constitutional questions resolved by *Roe,* principles of institutional integrity, and the rule of stare decisis, we are led to conclude this: the essential holding of *Roe* should be retained and once again reaffirmed.

[*Roe*'s] essential holding, the holding we reaffirm, has three parts. First is a recognition of the right of the woman to choose to have an abortion before viability and to obtain it without undue interference from the State. Before viability, the State's interests are not strong enough to support a prohibition of abortion or the imposition of a substantial obstacle to the woman's effective right to elect the procedure. Second is a confirmation of the State's power to restrict abortions after fetal viability, if the law contains exceptions for pregnancies which endanger a woman's life or health. And third is the principle that the State has legitimate interests from the outset of the pregnancy in protecting the health of the woman and the life of the fetus that may become a child. These principles do not contradict one another; and we adhere to each.

II.   Constitutional protection of the woman's decision to terminate her pregnancy derives from the Due Process Clause. [The] controlling word in the case before us is "liberty." Although a literal reading of the Clause might suggest that it governs only the procedures by which a State may deprive persons of liberty, for at least 105 years [the] Clause has been understood to contain a substantive component as well, one "barring certain government actions regardless of the fairness of the procedures used to implement them."

[It] is tempting, as a means of curbing the discretion of federal judges, to suppose that liberty encompasses no more than those rights already guaranteed to the individual against federal interference by the express provisions of the first eight amendments to the Constitution. But of course this Court has never accepted that view.

[It] is a promise of the Constitution that there is a realm of personal liberty which the government may not enter. We have vindicated this principle before. Marriage is mentioned nowhere in the Bill of Rights and interracial marriage was illegal in most States in the 19th century, but the Court was no doubt correct in finding it to be an aspect of liberty protected against state interference by the substantive component of the Due Process Clause in *Loving v. Virginia* [Ch. 9, Sec. 2, II].

Neither the Bill of Rights nor the specific practices of States at the time of the adoption of the Fourteenth Amendment marks the outer limits of the substantive sphere of liberty which the Fourteenth Amendment protects. See U.S. Const., Amend. 9. As the second Justice Harlan recognized: "[T]he full scope of the liberty guaranteed by the Due Process Clause cannot be found in or limited by the precise terms of the specific guarantees elsewhere provided in the Constitution. This 'liberty' is not a series of isolated points pricked out in terms of the taking of property; the freedom of speech, press, and religion; the right to keep and bear arms; the freedom from unreasonable searches and seizures; and so on. It is a rational continuum which, broadly speaking, includes a freedom from all substantial arbitrary impositions and purposeless restraints * * * ." *Poe v. Ullman* (Harlan, J., dissenting from dismissal on jurisdictional grounds).

Justice Harlan wrote these words in addressing an issue the full Court did not reach in *Poe,* but the Court adopted his position four Terms later in *Griswold.* [It] is settled now, as it was when the Court heard arguments in *Roe,* that the Constitution places limits on a State's right to interfere with a person's most basic decisions about family and parenthood, as well as bodily integrity.

[Men] and women of good conscience can disagree [about] the profound moral and spiritual implications of terminating a pregnancy, even in its earliest stage. Some of us as individuals find abortion offensive to our most basic principles of morality, but that cannot control our decision. Our obligation is to define the liberty of all, not mandate our own moral code.

[Our] law affords constitutional protection to personal decisions relating to marriage, procreation, contraception, family relationships, child rearing, and education. [These] matters, involving the most intimate and personal choices a person may make in a lifetime, choices central to personal dignity and autonomy, are central to the liberty protected by the Fourteenth Amendment. At the heart of liberty is the right to define one's own concept of existence, of meaning, of the universe, and of the mystery of human life. Beliefs about these matters could not define the attributes of personhood were they formed under compulsion of the State.

[Abortion] is a unique act. It is an act fraught with consequences for others. [Though] abortion is conduct, it does not follow that the State is entitled to proscribe it in all instances. That is because the liberty of the woman is at stake in a sense unique to the human condition and so unique to the law. The mother who carries a child to full term is subject to anxieties, to physical constraints, to pain that only she must bear. [Her] suffering is too intimate and personal for the State to insist, without more, upon its own vision of the woman's role, however dominant that vision has been in the course of our history and our culture. The destiny of the woman must be shaped to a large extent on her own conception of her spiritual imperatives and her place in society.

[Moreover,] in some critical respects the abortion decision is of the same character as the decision to use contraception, to which [our cases] afford constitutional protection. We have no doubt as to the correctness of those decisions. They support the reasoning in *Roe* relating to the woman's liberty because they involve personal decisions concerning not only the meaning of procreation but also human responsibility and respect for it.

III. [When] this Court reexamines a prior holding, its judgment is customarily informed by a series of prudential and pragmatic considerations designed to test the consistency of overruling a prior decision with the ideal of the rule of law, and to gauge the respective costs of reaffirming and overruling a prior case. Thus, for example, we may ask whether the rule has proven to be intolerable simply in defying practical workability; whether the rule is subject to a kind of reliance that would lend a special hardship to the consequences of overruling and add inequity to the cost of repudiation; whether related principles of law have so far developed as to have left the old rule no more than a remnant of abandoned doctrine; or whether facts have so changed or come to be seen so differently, as to have robbed the old rule of significant application or justification. [Although] *Roe* has engendered opposition, it has in no sense proven "unworkable," representing as it does a simple limitation beyond which a state law is unenforceable.

[To] eliminate the issue of reliance [would] be simply to refuse to face the fact that for two decades of economic and social developments, people have organized intimate relationships and made choices that define their views of themselves and their places in society, in reliance on the availability of abortion in the event that contraception should fail. The ability of women to participate equally in the economic and social life of the Nation has been facilitated by their ability to control their reproductive lives. [While] the effect of reliance on *Roe* cannot be exactly measured, neither can the certain cost of overruling *Roe* for people who have ordered their thinking and living around that case be dismissed.

[The] *Roe* Court itself placed its holding in the succession of cases most prominently exemplified by *Griswold*. When it is so seen, *Roe* is clearly in no jeopardy, since subsequent constitutional developments have neither disturbed, nor do they threaten to diminish, the scope of recognized protection accorded to the liberty relating to intimate relationships, the family, and decisions about whether or not to beget or bear a child.

[Even] on the assumption that the central holding of *Roe* was in error, that error would go only to the strength of the state interest in fetal protection, not to the recognition afforded by the Constitution to the woman's liberty. The latter aspect of the decision fits comfortably within the framework of the Court's prior decisions including *Skinner, Griswold, Loving,* and *Eisenstadt,* the holdings of which are "not a series of isolated points," but mark a "rational continuum." *Poe v. Ullman* (Harlan, J., dissenting).

[We] have seen how time has overtaken some of *Roe*'s factual assumptions: advances in maternal health care allow for abortions safe to the mother later in pregnancy than was true in 1973, and advances in neonatal care have advanced viability to a point somewhat earlier. But these facts go only to the scheme of time limits on the realization of competing interests, and the divergences from the factual premises of 1973 have no bearing on the validity of *Roe*'s central holding, that viability marks the earliest point at which the State's interest in fetal life is constitutionally adequate to justify a legislative ban on nontherapeutic abortions. The soundness or unsoundness of that constitutional judgment in no sense turns on whether viability occurs at approximately 28 weeks, as was usual at the time of *Roe,* at 23 to 24 weeks, as it sometimes does today, or at some moment even slightly earlier in pregnancy, as it may if fetal respiratory capacity can somehow be enhanced in the future. [No] change in *Roe*'s factual underpinning has left its central holding obsolete, and none supports an argument for overruling it.

[In] a less significant case, stare decisis analysis could, and would, stop at the point we have reached. But the sustained and widespread debate *Roe* has provoked calls for some comparison between that case and others of comparable dimension that have responded to national controversies and taken on the impress of the controversies addressed. Only two such decisional lines from the past century present themselves for examination, and in each instance the result reached by the Court accorded with the principles we apply today.

The first example is that line of cases identified with *Lochner v. New York* [Ch. 5, Sec. 2, I] (1905) [and] *Adkins v. Children's Hospital* [Ch. 5, Sec. 2, II] (1923). [Fourteen] years later, *West Coast Hotel Co. v. Parrish* [Ch. 5, Sec. 2, III] (1937) signaled the demise of *Lochner* by overruling *Adkins.* In the meantime, the Depression had come and, with it, the lesson that seemed unmistakable to most people by 1937, that the interpretation of contractual freedom protected in *Adkins* rested on fundamentally false factual assumptions about the capacity of a relatively unregulated market to satisfy minimal levels of human welfare. [The] facts upon which the earlier case had premised a constitutional resolution of social controversy had proven to be untrue, and history's demonstration of their untruth not only justified but required the new choice of constitutional principle that *West Coast Hotel* announced. Of course, it was true that the Court lost something by its misperception, or its lack of prescience, and the Court-packing crisis only magnified the loss; but the clear demonstration that the facts of economic life were different from those previously assumed warranted the repudiation of the old law.

The second comparison that 20th century history invites is with the cases employing the separate-but-equal rule for applying the Fourteenth Amendment's equal protection guarantee. They began with *Plessy v. Ferguson* [Ch. 9, Sec. 2, II], holding that legislatively mandated racial segregation in public transportation works no denial of equal protection. [But this rule was] repudiated in *Brown v. Board of Education* [Ch. 9, Sec. 2, II].

[The *Brown* court observed] that whatever may have been the understanding in *Plessy*'s time of the power of segregation to stigmatize those who were segregated with a "badge of inferiority," it was clear by 1954 that legally sanctioned segregation had just such an effect, to the point that racially separate public educational facilities were deemed inherently unequal. Society's understanding of the facts upon which a constitutional ruling was sought in 1954 was thus fundamentally different from the basis claimed for the decision in 1896. While we think *Plessy* was wrong the day it was decided, we must also recognize that the *Plessy* Court's explanation for its decision was so clearly at odds with the facts apparent to the Court in 1954 that the decision to reexamine *Plessy* was on this ground alone not only justified but required.

[Because] neither the factual underpinnings of *Roe*'s central holding nor our understanding of it has changed [the] Court could not pretend to be reexamining the prior law with any justification beyond a present doctrinal disposition to come out differently from the Court of 1973. To overrule prior law for no other reason than that would run counter to the view repeated in our cases, that a decision to overrule should rest on some special reason over and above the belief that a prior case was wrongly decided.

[Overruling] *Roe*'s central holding would not only reach an unjustifiable result under principles of stare decisis, but would seriously weaken the Court's capacity to exercise the judicial power and to function as the Supreme Court of a Nation dedicated to the rule of law. [The] Court's power lies [in] its legitimacy, a product of substance and perception that shows itself in the people's acceptance of the Judiciary as fit to determine what the Nation's law means and to declare what it demands.

[Where,] in the performance of its judicial duties, the Court decides a case in such a way as to resolve the sort of intensely divisive controversy reflected in *Roe* and those rare, comparable cases, its decision has a dimension that the resolution of the normal case does not carry. [To] overrule under fire in the absence of the most compelling reason to reexamine a watershed decision would subvert the Court's legitimacy beyond any serious question.

[The] Court's duty in the present [case] is clear. In 1973, it confronted the already-divisive issue of governmental power to limit personal choice to undergo abortion, for which it provided a new resolution. [Whether] or not a new social consensus is developing on that issue, its divisiveness is no less today than in 1973, and pressure to overrule the decision, like pressure to retain it, has grown only more intense. A decision to overrule *Roe*'s essential holding under the existing circumstances would address error, if error there was, at the cost of both profound and unnecessary damage to the Court's legitimacy, and to the Nation's commitment to the rule of law. It is therefore imperative to adhere to the essence of *Roe*'s original decision, and we do so today.

IV. [We] conclude that the basic decision in *Roe* was based on a constitutional analysis which we cannot now repudiate. The woman's liberty is not so unlimited, however, that from the outset the State cannot show its concern for the life of the unborn, and at a later point in fetal development the State's interest in life has sufficient force so that the right of the woman to terminate the pregnancy can be restricted. [We] conclude the line should be drawn at viability, so that before that time the woman has a right to choose to terminate her pregnancy. We adhere to this principle for two reasons. First [is] the doctrine of stare decisis. [We] have twice reaffirmed [*Roe*] in the face of great opposition. [The] second reason is that the concept of viability, as we noted in *Roe,* is the time at which there is a realistic possibility of maintaining and nourishing a life outside the womb, so that the independent existence of the second life can in reason and all fairness be the object of state protection that now overrides the rights of the woman. [The] viability line also has, as a practical matter, an element of fairness. In some broad sense it might be said that a woman who fails to act before viability has consented to the State's intervention on behalf of the developing child. [The] woman's right to terminate her pregnancy before viability is the most central principle of *Roe*. It is a rule of law and a component of liberty we cannot renounce.

On the other side of the equation is the interest of the State in the protection of potential life. [We] do not need to say whether each of us, had we been Members of the Court when the valuation of the State interest came before it as an original matter, would have concluded, as the *Roe* Court did, that its weight is insufficient to justify a ban on abortions prior to viability even when it is subject to certain exceptions. The matter is not before us in the first instance, and coming as it does after nearly 20 years of litigation in *Roe*'s wake we are satisfied that the immediate question is not the soundness of *Roe*'s resolution of the issue, but the precedential force that must be accorded to its holding. And we have concluded that the essential holding of *Roe* should be reaffirmed.

Yet it must be remembered that *Roe* speaks with clarity in establishing not only the woman's liberty but also the State's "important and legitimate interest in potential life." That portion [of] *Roe* has been given too little acknowledgement and implementation by the Court in its subsequent cases. Those cases decided that any regulation touching upon the abortion decision must survive strict scrutiny, to be sustained only if drawn in narrow terms to further a compelling state interest. Not all of the cases decided under that formulation can be reconciled with the holding in *Roe* itself that the State has legitimate interests in the health of the woman and in protecting the potential life within her. In resolving this tension, we choose to rely upon *Roe,* as against the later cases.

[We] reject the trimester framework, which we do not consider to be part of the essential holding of *Roe.* Measures aimed at ensuring that a woman's choice contemplates the consequences for the fetus do not necessarily interfere with the right recognized in *Roe,* although those measures have been found to be inconsistent with the rigid trimester framework announced in that case. [The] trimester framework suffers from these basic flaws: in its formulation it misconceives the nature of the pregnant woman's interest; and in practice it undervalues the State's interest in potential life, as recognized in *Roe.*

[In] our view, the undue burden standard is the appropriate means of reconciling the State's interest with the woman's constitutionally protected liberty. [A] finding of an undue burden is a shorthand for the conclusion that a state regulation has the purpose or effect of placing a substantial obstacle in the path of a woman seeking an abortion of a nonviable fetus. A statute with this purpose is invalid because the means chosen by the State to further the interest in potential life must be calculated to inform the woman's free choice, not hinder it. [W]e answer the question, left open in previous opinions discussing the undue burden formulation, whether a law designed to further the State's interest in fetal life which imposes an undue burden on the woman's decision before fetal viability could be constitutional. The answer is no.

Some guiding principles should emerge. What is at stake is the woman's right to make the ultimate decision, not a right to be insulated from all others in doing so. Regulations which do no more than create a structural mechanism by which the State, or the parent or guardian of a minor, may express profound respect for the life of the unborn are permitted, if they are not a substantial obstacle to the woman's exercise of the right to choose. [Unless] it has that effect on her right of choice, a state measure designed to persuade her to choose childbirth over abortion will be upheld if reasonably related to that goal. Regulations designed to foster the health of a woman seeking an abortion are valid if they do not constitute an undue burden.

[We] give this summary:

(a) To protect the central right recognized by *Roe* while at the same time accommodating the State's profound interest in potential life, we will employ the undue burden analysis as explained in this opinion. An undue burden exists, and therefore a provision of law is invalid, if its purpose or effect is to place a substantial obstacle in the path of a woman seeking an abortion before the fetus attains viability.

(b) We reject the rigid trimester framework of *Roe*. To promote the State's profound interest in potential life, throughout pregnancy the State may take measures to ensure that the woman's choice is informed, and measures designed to advance this interest will not be invalidated as long as their purpose is to persuade the woman to choose childbirth over abortion. These measures must not be an undue burden on the right.

(c) As with any medical procedure, the State may enact regulations to further the health or safety of a woman seeking an abortion. Unnecessary health regulations that have the purpose or effect of presenting a substantial obstacle to a woman seeking an abortion impose an undue burden on the right.

(d) Our adoption of the undue burden analysis does not disturb the central holding of *Roe,* and we reaffirm that holding. [A] State may not prohibit any woman from making the ultimate decision to terminate her pregnancy before viability.

(e) We also reaffirm *Roe*'s holding that "subsequent to viability, the State in promoting its interest in the potentiality of human life may, if it chooses, regulate, and even proscribe, abortion except where it is necessary, in appropriate medical judgment, for the preservation of the life or health of the mother."

These principles control our assessment of the Pennsylvania statute, and we now turn to the issue of the validity of its challenged provisions.

V. [A.] Because it is central to the operation of various other requirements, we begin with the statute's definition of medical emergency. Under the statute, a medical emergency is "[t]hat condition which, on the basis of the physician's good faith clinical judgment, so complicates the medical condition of a pregnant woman as to necessitate the immediate abortion of her pregnancy to avert her death or for which a delay will create serious risk of substantial and irreversible impairment of a major bodily function."

[As construed by the Court of Appeals, the statute's definition of medical emergency as] "intended [to] assure that compliance with [the] abortion regulations would not in any way pose a significant threat to the life or health of a woman" [imposes] no undue burden on a woman's abortion right.

B.   [Except] in a medical emergency, the statute requires that at least 24 hours before performing an abortion a physician inform the woman of the nature of the procedure, the health risks of the abortion and of childbirth, and the "probable gestational age of the unborn child." The physician or a qualified nonphysician must inform the woman of the availability of printed materials published by the State describing the fetus and providing information about medical assistance for childbirth, information about child support from the father, and a list of agencies which provide adoption and other services as alternatives to abortion. An abortion may not be performed unless the woman certifies in writing that she has been informed of the availability of these printed materials and has been provided them if she chooses to view them. [This] requirement cannot be considered a substantial obstacle to obtaining an abortion, and, it follows, there is no undue burden.

[The] Pennsylvania statute also requires us to reconsider the holding in *Akron v. Akron Center for Reproductive Health (Akron I)*, 462 U.S. 416 (1983),[341] that the State may not require that a physician, as opposed to a qualified assistant, provide information relevant to a woman's informed consent. Since there is no evidence on this record that requiring a doctor to give the information as provided by the statute would amount in practical terms to a substantial obstacle to a woman seeking an abortion, we conclude that it is not an undue burden.

[Our] analysis of Pennsylvania's 24-hour waiting period between the provision of the information deemed necessary to informed consent and the performance of an abortion under the undue burden standard requires us to reconsider the premise behind the decision in *Akron I* invalidating a parallel requirement. [We] consider [the *Akron I*] conclusion to be wrong. The idea that important decisions will be more informed and deliberate if they follow some period of reflection does not strike us as unreasonable, particularly where the statute directs that important information become part of the background of the decision.

[Whether] the mandatory 24-hour waiting period is nonetheless invalid because in practice it is a substantial obstacle to a woman's choice to terminate her pregnancy is a closer question. The findings of fact [indicate] that for those women who have the fewest financial resources, those who must travel long distances, and those who have difficulty

---

[341] *Akron I* struck down various sections of an ordinance regulating abortion. Among the provisions invalidated were: a mandatory 24-hour waiting period, which increased the cost of obtaining an abortion by requiring the woman to make two separate trips to the abortion facility; a provision requiring that after the first trimester all abortions had to be performed in a hospital, thus preventing abortions in outpatient clinics; and an "informed consent" provision that the majority characterized as "designed not to inform the woman's consent but rather to persuade her to withhold it altogether." O'Connor, J., joined by White and Rehnquist, JJ., dissented, and would have upheld all the challenged regulations under an "undue burden" standard.

explaining their whereabouts to husbands, employers, or others, the 24-hour waiting period will be "particularly burdensome."

These findings are troubling in some respects, but they do not demonstrate that the waiting period constitutes an undue burden. [Under] the undue burden standard a State is permitted to enact persuasive measures which favor childbirth over abortion, even if those measures do not further a health interest. And while the waiting period does limit a physician's discretion, that is not, standing alone, a reason to invalidate it. In light of the construction given the statute's definition of medical emergency by the Court of Appeals, and the District Court's findings, we cannot say that the waiting period imposes a real health risk.

We also disagree with the District Court's conclusion that the "particularly burdensome" effects of the waiting period on some women require its invalidation. A particular burden is not of necessity a substantial obstacle. Whether a burden falls on a particular group is a distinct inquiry from whether it is a substantial obstacle even as to the women in that group.

[C.] Section 3209 of Pennsylvania's abortion law provides, except in cases of medical emergency, that no physician shall perform an abortion on a married woman without receiving a signed statement from the woman that she has notified her spouse that she is about to undergo an abortion. The woman has the option of providing an alternative signed statement certifying that her husband is not the man who impregnated her; that her husband could not be located; that the pregnancy is the result of spousal sexual assault which she has reported; or that the woman believes that notifying her husband will cause him or someone else to inflict bodily injury upon her. A physician who performs an abortion on a married woman without receiving the appropriate signed statement will have his or her license revoked, and is liable to the husband for damages.

[Various studies of domestic violence] and the District Court's findings reinforce what common sense would suggest. In well-functioning marriages, spouses discuss important intimate decisions such as whether to bear a child. But there are millions of women in this country who are the victims of regular physical and psychological abuse at the hands of their husbands. Should these women become pregnant, they may have very good reasons for not wishing to inform their husbands of their decision to obtain an abortion.

[The] spousal notification requirement is thus likely to prevent a significant number of women from obtaining an abortion. It does not merely make abortions a little more difficult or expensive to obtain; for many women, it will impose a substantial obstacle. We must not blind ourselves to the fact that the significant number of women who fear for their safety and the safety of their children are likely to be deterred from procuring an abortion as surely as if the Commonwealth had outlawed abortion in all cases.

[Section] 3209's real target is narrower even than the class of women seeking abortions identified by the State: it is married women seeking abortions who do not wish to notify their husbands of their intentions and who do not qualify for one of the statutory exceptions to the notice requirement. The unfortunate yet persisting conditions we document above will mean that in a large fraction of the cases in which § 3209 is relevant, it will operate as a substantial obstacle to a woman's choice to undergo an abortion. It is an undue burden, and therefore invalid.

This conclusion is in no way inconsistent with our decisions upholding parental notification or consent requirements. Those enactments, and our judgment that they are constitutional, are based on the quite reasonable assumption that minors will benefit from consultation with their parents and that children will often not realize that their parents have their best interests at heart. We cannot adopt a parallel assumption about adult women.

[Section] 3209 embodies a view of marriage consonant with the common-law status of married women but repugnant to our present understanding of marriage and of the nature of the rights secured by the Constitution. Women do not lose their constitutionally protected liberty when they marry.

D. [Except] in a medical emergency, an unemancipated young woman under 18 may not obtain an abortion unless she and one of her parents (or guardian) provides informed consent as defined above. If neither a parent nor a guardian provides consent, a court may authorize the performance of an abortion upon a determination that the young woman is mature and capable of giving informed consent and has in fact given her informed consent, or that an abortion would be in her best interests. [Our] cases establish, and we reaffirm today, that a State may require a minor seeking an abortion to obtain the consent of a parent or guardian, provided that there is an adequate judicial bypass procedure.

[E. As for the provisions imposing certain reporting requirements on facilities that provide abortion services, in] *Danforth* we held that recordkeeping and reporting provisions "that are reasonably directed to the preservation of maternal health and that properly respect a patient's confidentiality and privacy are permissible." [Under] this standard, all the provisions at issue here except that relating to spousal notice are constitutional.

[VI.] Our Constitution is a covenant running from the first generation of Americans to us and then to future generations. It is a coherent succession. Each generation must learn anew that the Constitution's written terms embody ideas and aspirations that must survive more ages than one. We accept our responsibility not to retreat from interpreting the full meaning of the covenant in light of all of our precedents. We invoke it once again to define the freedom guaranteed by the Constitution's own promise, the promise of liberty. * * *

JUSTICE STEVENS, concurring in part and dissenting in part. * * *

The Court is unquestionably correct in concluding that the doctrine of stare decisis has controlling significance in a case of this kind, notwithstanding an individual justice's concerns about the merits.[1] [*Roe*] was a natural sequel to the protection of individual liberty established in *Griswold*. [It] is an integral part of a correct understanding of both the concept of liberty and the basic equality of men and women. Stare decisis also provides a sufficient basis for my agreement with the joint opinion's reaffirmation of *Roe*'s post-viability analysis. Specifically, I accept the proposition that "[i]f the State is interested in protecting fetal life after viability, it may go so far as to proscribe abortion during that period, except when it is necessary to preserve the life or health of the mother."

I also accept what is implicit in the Court's analysis, namely, a reaffirmation of *Roe*'s explanation of *why* the State's obligation to protect the life or health of the mother must take precedence over any duty to the unborn. The Court in *Roe* carefully considered, and rejected, the State's argument "that the fetus is a 'person' within the language and meaning of the Fourteenth Amendment." [From] this holding, there was no dissent; indeed, no member of the Court has ever questioned this fundamental proposition. Thus, as a matter of federal constitutional law, a developing organism that is not yet a "person" does not have what is sometimes described as a "right to life."[2]

Weighing the State's interest in potential life and the woman's liberty interest, I agree with the joint opinion that the State may " 'expres[s] a preference for normal childbirth,' " that the State may take steps to ensure that a woman's choice "is thoughtful and informed," and that "States are free to enact laws to provide a reasonable framework for a woman to make a decision that has such profound and lasting meaning." Serious questions arise, however, when a State attempts to "persuade the woman to choose childbirth over abortion." [The] State may promote its preferences by funding childbirth, by creating and maintaining alternatives to abortion,

---

[1]   [Ct's Note] It is sometimes useful to view the issue of stare decisis from a historical perspective. In the last nineteen years, fifteen Justices have confronted the basic issue presented in *Roe*. Of those, eleven have voted as the majority does today: Chief Justice Burger, Justices Douglas, Brennan, Stewart, Marshall, and Powell, and Justices Blackmun, O'Connor, Kennedy, Souter, and myself. Only four—all of whom happen to be on the Court today—have reached the opposite conclusion.

[2]   [Ct's Note] Professor Dworkin has made this comment on the issue: "The suggestion that states are free to declare a fetus a person * * * assumes that a state can curtail some persons' constitutional rights by adding new persons to the constitutional population." Dworkin, *Unenumerated Rights* [supra].

and by espousing the virtues of family; but it must respect the individual's freedom to make such judgments.

[Under the principles established in the Court's previous cases, Justice Stevens deemed unconstitutional the 24-hour waiting period and those sections requiring a woman to be provided with a wide "range of materials clearly designed to persuade her to choose not to undergo the abortion." But he did not find constitutionally objectionable those sections requiring the physician to inform a woman of the nature and risks of the abortion procedure and the medical risks of carrying to term for these "are neutral requirements comparable to those imposed in other medical procedures."]

JUSTICE BLACKMUN, concurring in part, concurring in the judgment in part, and dissenting in part.

I join parts I, II, III, V–A, V–C, and VI of the joint opinion.

[The] joint opinion [is] an act of personal courage and constitutional principle. In contrast to previous decisions in which [O'Connor and Kennedy, JJ.] postponed reconsideration of *Roe*, the authors of the joint opinion today join Justice Stevens and me in concluding that "the essential holding of *Roe* should be retained and once again reaffirmed." In brief, five Members of this Court today recognize that "the Constitution protects a woman's right to terminate her pregnancy in its early stages."

[Yet today], no less than yesterday, the Constitution and decisions of this Court require that a State's abortion restrictions be subjected to the strictest of judicial scrutiny. Our precedents and the joint opinion's principles require us to subject all non-de-minimis abortion regulations to strict scrutiny. Under this standard, the Pennsylvania statute's provisions requiring content-based counseling, a 24-hour delay, informed parental consent, and reporting of abortion-related information must be invalidated. [R]estrictive abortion laws force women to endure physical invasions far more substantial than those this Court has held to violate the constitutional principle of bodily integrity in other contexts. See, e.g., *Winston*; *Rochin* [Sec. 1, IV supra].

Further, when the State restricts a woman's right to terminate her pregnancy, it deprives a woman of the right to make her own decision about reproduction and family planning—critical life choices that this Court long has deemed central to the right to privacy. The decision to terminate or continue a pregnancy has no less an impact on a woman's life than decisions about contraception or marriage. Because motherhood has a dramatic impact on a woman's educational prospects, employment opportunities, and self-determination, restrictive abortion laws deprive her of basic control over her life.

[A] State's restrictions on a woman's right to terminate her pregnancy also implicate constitutional guarantees of gender equality. [By] restricting the right to terminate pregnancies, the State conscripts women's bodies into its service, forcing women to continue their pregnancies, suffer the pains of childbirth, and in most instances, provide years of maternal care. The State does not compensate women for their services; instead, it assumes that they owe this duty as a matter of course. This assumption— that women can simply be forced to accept the "natural" status and incidents of motherhood—appears to rest upon a conception of women's role that has triggered the protection of the Equal Protection Clause. The joint opinion recognizes that these assumptions about women's place in society "are no longer consistent with our understanding of the family, the individual, or the Constitution."

[If] there is much reason to applaud the advances made by the joint opinion today, there is far more to fear from The Chief Justice's opinion. [His] criticism of *Roe* follows from his stunted conception of individual liberty. While recognizing that the Due Process Clause protects more than simply physical liberty, he then goes on to construe this Court's personal-liberty cases as establishing only a laundry list of particular rights, rather than a principled account of how these particular rights are grounded in a more general right of privacy. This constricted view is reinforced by The Chief Justice's exclusive reliance on tradition as a source of fundamental rights. [In his] world, a woman considering whether to terminate a pregnancy is entitled to no more protection than adulterers, murderers, and so-called "sexual deviates." Given The Chief Justice's exclusive reliance on tradition, people using contraceptives seem the next likely candidate for his list of outcasts.

Even more shocking than The Chief Justice's cramped notion of individual liberty is his complete omission of any discussion of the effects that compelled childbirth and motherhood have on women's lives. The only expression of concern with women's health is purely instrumental—for The Chief Justice, only women's *psychological* health is a concern, and only to the extent that he assumes that every woman who decides to have an abortion does so without serious consideration of the moral implications of their decision. In short, The Chief Justice's view of the State's compelling interest in maternal health has less to do with health than it does with compelling women to be maternal. * * *

CHIEF JUSTICE REHNQUIST, with whom JUSTICE WHITE, JUSTICE SCALIA, and JUSTICE THOMAS join, concurring in the judgment in part and dissenting in part.

The joint opinion, following its newly minted variation on stare decisis, retains the outer shell of *Roe* but beats a wholesale retreat from the substance of that case. We believe that *Roe* was wrongly decided, and that it can and should be overruled consistently with our traditional approach to stare decisis in constitutional cases. We would adopt the approach of the plurality in *Webster* and uphold the challenged provisions of the Pennsylvania statute in their entirety.

[Unlike] marriage, procreation and contraception, abortion "involves the purposeful termination of potential life." The abortion decision must therefore "be recognized as sui generis, different in kind from the others that the Court has protected under the rubric of personal or family privacy and autonomy." One cannot ignore the fact that a woman is not isolated in her pregnancy, and that the decision to abort necessarily involves the destruction of a fetus.

[Nor] do the historical traditions of the American people support the view that the right to terminate one's pregnancy is "fundamental." The common law which we inherited from England made abortion after "quickening" an offense. At the time of the adoption of the Fourteenth Amendment, statutory prohibitions or restrictions on abortion were commonplace; in 1868, at least 28 of the then-37 States and 8 Territories had statutes banning or limiting abortion. By the turn of the century virtually every State had a law prohibiting or restricting abortion on its books. By the middle of the present century, a liberalization trend had set in. But 21 of the restrictive abortion laws in effect in 1868 were still in effect in 1973 when *Roe* was decided, and an overwhelming majority of the States prohibited abortion unless necessary to preserve the life or health of the mother. On this record, it can scarcely be said that any deeply rooted tradition of relatively unrestricted abortion in our history supported the classification of the right to abortion as "fundamental" under the Due Process Clause of the Fourteenth Amendment.

[The joint opinion] cannot bring itself to say that *Roe* was correct as an original matter, but [instead] contains an elaborate discussion of stare decisis. [This discussion] appears to be almost entirely dicta, because the joint opinion does not apply that principle in dealing with *Roe*. *Roe* decided that a woman had a fundamental right to an abortion. The joint opinion rejects that view. *Roe* decided that abortion regulations were to be subjected to "strict scrutiny" and could be justified only in the light of "compelling state interests." The joint opinion rejects that view. *Roe* analyzed abortion regulation under a rigid trimester framework, a framework which has guided this Court's decisionmaking for 19 years. The joint opinion rejects that framework.

[Having] failed to put forth any evidence to prove any true reliance [on *Roe*], the joint opinion's argument is based solely on generalized assertions about the national psyche, on a belief that the people of this country have grown accustomed to the *Roe* decision over the last 19 years and have "ordered their thinking and living around" it. As an initial matter, one might inquire how the joint opinion can view the "central holding" of *Roe* as so deeply rooted in our constitutional culture, when it so casually uproots and disposes of that same decision's trimester framework. Furthermore, at various points in the past, the same could have been said about this Court's erroneous decisions that the Constitution allowed "separate but equal" treatment of minorities or that "liberty" under the Due Process Clause protected "freedom of contract." [The] simple fact that a generation or more had grown used to these major decisions did not prevent the Court from correcting its errors in those cases, nor should it prevent us from correctly interpreting the Constitution here.

[The joint opinion states] that when the Court "resolve[s] the sort of intensely divisive controversy reflected in *Roe* and those rare, comparable cases," its decision is exempt from reconsideration under established principles of stare decisis in constitutional cases. [Under] this principle, when the Court has ruled on a divisive issue, it is apparently prevented from overruling that decision for the sole reason that it was incorrect, *unless opposition to the original decision has died away.*

The first difficulty with this principle [is that the] question of whether a particular issue is "intensely divisive" enough to qualify for special protection is entirely subjective and dependent on the individual assumptions of the Members of this Court. In addition, because the Court's duty is to ignore public opinion and criticism on issues that come before it, its Members are in perhaps the worst position to judge whether a decision divides the Nation deeply enough to justify such uncommon protection.

[The joint opinion] agrees that the Court acted properly in rejecting the doctrine of "separate but equal" in *Brown*. In fact, the opinion lauds *Brown* in comparing it to *Roe*. This is strange, in that under the opinion's "legitimacy" principle the Court would seemingly have been forced to adhere to its erroneous decision in *Plessy* because of its "intensely divisive" character. To us, adherence to *Roe* today under the guise of "legitimacy" would seem to resemble more closely adherence to *Plessy* on the same ground. Fortunately, the Court did not choose that option in *Brown,* and instead frankly repudiated *Plessy*. [The] Court in *Brown* simply recognized, as Justice Harlan had recognized beforehand, that the Fourteenth Amendment does not permit racial segregation. The rule of *Brown* is not tied to popular opinion about the evils of segregation; it is a judgment that the Equal Protection Clause does not permit racial segregation, no matter whether the public might come to believe that it is beneficial. On that ground it stands, and on that ground alone the Court was justified in properly concluding that the *Plessy* Court had erred.

There is also a suggestion in the joint opinion that the propriety of overruling a "divisive" decision depends in part on whether "most people" would now agree that it should be overruled. [How] such agreement would be ascertained, short of a public opinion poll, the joint opinion does not say. [Even] the suggestion is totally at war with the idea of "legitimacy" in whose name it is invoked. The Judicial Branch derives its legitimacy, not from following public opinion, but from deciding by its best lights whether legislative enactments of the popular branches of Government comport with the Constitution.

[The] sum of the joint opinion's labors in the name of stare decisis and "legitimacy" is this: *Roe* stands as a sort of judicial Potemkin Village, which may be pointed out to passers-by as a monument to the importance of adhering to precedent. But behind the facade, an entirely new method of analysis, without any roots in constitutional law, is imported to decide the constitutionality of state laws regulating abortion. Neither stare decisis nor "legitimacy" are truly served by such an effort.

[The Chief Justice then discussed each of the challenged provisions and concluded that each should be upheld.]

JUSTICE SCALIA, with whom THE CHIEF JUSTICE, JUSTICE WHITE, and JUSTICE THOMAS join, concurring in the judgment in part and dissenting in part.

[The] issue in [these cases] [is] not whether the power of a woman to abort her unborn child is a "liberty" in the absolute sense; or even whether it is a liberty of great importance to many women. Of course it is both. The issue is whether it is a liberty protected by the Constitution of the United States. I am sure it is not. I reach that conclusion not because of anything so exalted as my views concerning the "concept of existence, of meaning, of the universe, and of the mystery of human life." Rather, I reach it for the same reason I reach the conclusion that bigamy is not constitutionally protected—because of two simple facts: (1) the Constitution says absolutely nothing about it, and (2) the longstanding traditions of American society have permitted it to be legally proscribed.[1]

The Court destroys the proposition, evidently meant to represent my position, that "liberty" includes "only those practices, defined at the most specific level, that were protected against government interference by other rules of law when the Fourteenth Amendment was ratified" (citing *Michael H. v. Gerald D.*, [set forth at p. 510 infra] (opinion of Scalia, J.). That is not, however, what *Michael H.* says; it merely observes that, in defining

---

[1] **[Ct's Note]** The Court's suggestion that adherence to tradition would require us to uphold laws against interracial marriage is entirely wrong. Any tradition in that case was contradicted *by a text*—an Equal Protection Clause that explicitly establishes racial equality as a constitutional value. [The] enterprise launched in *Roe,* by contrast, sought to *establish*—in the teeth of a clear, contrary tradition—a value found nowhere in the constitutional text.

There is, of course, no comparable tradition barring recognition of a "liberty interest" in carrying one's child to term free from state efforts to kill it. For that reason, it does not follow that the Constitution does not protect childbirth simply because it does not protect abortion. The Court's contention that the only way to protect childbirth is to protect abortion shows the utter bankruptcy of constitutional analysis deprived of tradition as a validating factor. It drives one to say that the only way to protect the right to eat is to acknowledge the constitutional right to starve oneself to death.

"liberty," we may not disregard a specific, "relevant tradition protecting, or denying protection to, the asserted right." But the Court does not wish to be fettered by any such limitation on its preferences.

[I must] respond to a few of the more outrageous arguments in today's opinion, which it is beyond human nature to leave unanswered. I shall discuss each of them under a quotation from the Court's opinion to which they pertain.

"The inescapable fact is that adjudication of substantive due process claims may call upon the Court in interpreting the Constitution to exercise that same capacity which by tradition courts always have exercised: reasoned judgment."

[The] whole argument of abortion opponents is that what the Court calls the fetus and what others call the unborn child *is a human life.* Thus, whatever answer *Roe* came up with after conducting its "balancing" is bound to be wrong, unless it is correct that the human fetus is in some critical sense merely potentially human. There is of course no way to determine that as a legal matter; it is in fact a value judgment. Some societies have considered newborn children not yet human, or the incompetent elderly no longer so.

[The] emptiness of the "reasoned judgment" that produced *Roe* is displayed in plain view by the fact that, after more than 19 years of effort by some of the brightest (and most determined) legal minds in the country, after more than 10 cases upholding abortion rights in this Court, and after dozens upon dozens of amicus briefs submitted in this and other cases, the best the Court can do to explain how it is that the word "liberty" *must* be thought to include the right to destroy human fetuses is to rattle off a collection of adjectives that simply decorate a value judgment and conceal a political choice. [But] it is obvious to anyone applying "reasoned judgment" that the same adjectives can be applied to many forms of conduct that this Court [has] held are *not* entitled to constitutional protection—because, like abortion, they are forms of conduct that have long been criminalized in American society. Those adjectives might be applied, for example, to homosexual sodomy, polygamy, adult incest, and suicide * * * .

"Liberty finds no refuge in a jurisprudence of doubt."

One might have feared to encounter this august and sonorous phrase in an opinion defending the real *Roe,* rather than the revised version fabricated today by the authors of the joint opinion. The shortcomings of *Roe* did not include lack of clarity: Virtually all regulation of abortion before the third trimester was invalid. But to come across this phrase in the joint opinion—which calls upon federal district judges to apply an "undue burden" standard as doubtful in application as it is unprincipled in origin— is really more than one should have to bear.

[To] the extent I can discern *any* meaningful content in the "undue burden" standard as applied in the joint opinion, it appears to be that a State may not regulate abortion in such a way as to reduce significantly its incidence. The joint opinion repeatedly emphasizes that an important factor in the "undue burden" analysis is whether the regulation "prevent[s] a significant number of women from obtaining an abortion," whether a "significant number of women [are] likely to be deterred from procuring an abortion," and whether the regulation often "deters" women from seeking abortions. We are not told, however, what forms of "deterrence" are impermissible or what degree of success in deterrence is too much to be tolerated. [As] Justice Blackmun recognizes (with evident hope), the "undue burden" standard may ultimately require the invalidation of each provision upheld today if it can be shown, on a better record, that the State is too effectively "express[ing] a preference for childbirth over abortion." Reason finds no refuge in this jurisprudence of confusion. * * *

"[T]o overrule under fire [would] subvert the Court's legitimacy * * * .

"To all those who will be * * * tested by following, the Court implicitly undertakes to remain steadfast * * * . The promise of constancy, once given, binds its maker for as long as the power to stand by the decision survives [and] the commitment [is not] obsolete * * * .

"[The American people's] belief in themselves as * * * a people [who aspire to live according to the rule of law] is not readily separable from their understanding of the Court invested with the authority to decide their constitutional cases and speak before all others for their constitutional ideals. If the Court's legitimacy should be undermined, then, so would the country be in its very ability to see itself through its constitutional ideals."

The Imperial Judiciary lives. It is instructive to compare this Nietzschean vision of us unelected, life-tenured judges—leading a Volk who will be "tested by following," and whose very "belief in themselves" is mystically bound up in their "understanding" of a Court that "speak[s] before all others for their constitutional ideals"—with the somewhat more modest role envisioned for these lawyers by the Founders.

[I] cannot agree with, indeed I am appalled by, the Court's suggestion that the decision whether to stand by an erroneous constitutional decision must be strongly influenced—*against* overruling, no less—by the substantial and continuing public opposition the decision has generated. [In] my history-book, the Court was covered with dishonor and deprived of legitimacy by *Dred Scott v. Sandford* [Ch. 9, Sec. 2, I], an erroneous (and widely opposed) opinion that it did not abandon, rather than by *West Coast Hotel,* which produced the famous "switch in time" from the Court's erroneous (and widely opposed) constitutional opposition to the social measures of the New Deal. (Both *Dred Scott* and one line of the cases resisting the New Deal rested upon the concept of "substantive due process" that the Court praises and employs today. Indeed, *Dred Scott* was "very possibly the first application of substantive due process in the Supreme Court, the original precedent for *Lochner* and *Roe*." David Currie, *The Constitution in the Supreme Court* 271 (1985).)

[There] is a poignant aspect to today's opinion. Its length, and what might be called its epic tone, suggest that its authors believe they are bringing to an end a troublesome era in the history of our Nation and of our Court. "It is the dimension" of authority, they say, to "cal[l] the contending sides of national controversy to end their national division by accepting a common mandate rooted in the Constitution."

[It] is no more realistic for us in this case, than it was for [Taney, C.J.,] in [*Dred Scott*] to think that an issue of the sort they both involved—an issue involving life and death, freedom and subjugation—can be "speedily and finally settled" by the Supreme Court. [Quite] to the contrary, by foreclosing all democratic outlet for the deep passions this issue arouses, by banishing the issue from the political forum that gives all participants, even the losers, the satisfaction of a fair hearing and an honest fight, by continuing the imposition of a rigid national rule instead of allowing for regional differences, the Court merely prolongs and intensifies the anguish.

We should get out of this area, where we have no right to be, and where we do neither ourselves nor the country any good by remaining.

NOTES AND QUESTIONS

1. **Did Casey bring the Court into line with public opinion?** Consider Barry Friedman, *The Will of the People* 382 (2009): "What history shows is assuredly not that Supreme Court decisions always are in line with popular opinion, but rather that they come into line with one another *over time*. There was a very good argument that the Supreme Court decision in *Roe v. Wade* was consistent with social trends, but still, it attracted only plurality support in polls, and there was profound disagreement with the Court's conclusion that had not received an extended public hearing. By the time the Court handed down [*Casey*], however, which watered down *Roe* in important ways and which—all polls and pundits agreed—was remarkably in line with popular opinion, a generation of vibrant public debate had occurred."

2. **Did the plurality opinion in Casey relocate the Court's jurisprudence of reproductive liberty?** Consider Laurence H. Tribe, *Lawrence v. Texas: The "Fundamental Right" that Dare Not Speak Its Name*, 117 Harv.L.Rev. 1893 (2004): "[The *Casey*] Court relocated its jurisprudence of reproductive liberty from a realm that, in *Roe*, had been cast in largely medical and technocratic terms, to a very different realm defined by the war against the insidious transmutation of anatomy into destiny. No longer could an

analysis of liberty and of power over the unborn simply ignore the driving force of gender inequity. In turn, no satisfying recognition of the driving force of gender inequity could leave out, or sanitize in abstract analyses of sexual liberty, the ways in which allocations of decisionmaking power and responsibility shape such realities as gender hierarchy, on the one hand, and the life or death of the fetus, on the other."

3. *Why should the abortion issue be decided by the individual rather than the state?* Answers Strauss supra: "This is the point at which the status of women, properly emphasized by *Casey,* becomes important. Allowing the abortion decision to be made at the political level, instead of the individual level, would create an impermissible risk of subordinating women. [Although] the Court has never made it entirely clear why discrimination against women is unconstitutional, it seems plausible to suppose that at least three aspects of the status of women in society, all relevant to the abortion issue, underlie this principle.

"First, the political process has a persistent tendency generally to undervalue the interests of women. [Second,] women's bodily integrity, in particular, is systematically undervalued. The Court's opinion in *Casey* alluded to this aspect of women's status. [Third,] women are treated as people whose principal responsibility is childbearing and child rearing. They are not seen as full participants in the labor market. [*Casey* did not] make clear the exact connection between the status of women and the abortion issue. The connection, I believe, is this: the tendency to subordinate women in these three ways disqualifies the political process from resolving the moral uncertainty that is central to the abortion debate. There is too great a danger that if the political process decides the abortion issue, that decision will be an act of subordinating women in one or more of these ways."

4. *Was Casey a political loss for the pro-choice movement?* Consider Sylvia Law, *Abortion Compromise—Inevitable and Impossible,* 1992 U.Ill.L.Rev. 921: "From a pro-choice point of view, one plausible assessment of the *Casey* decision is that it represents the worst of all possible worlds. The joint opinion affirmed a woman's 'fundamental constitutional right' to abortion, but simultaneously allowed the state to adopt measures that effectively curtail *many* women's exercise of the abortion right. This curtailment hits hardest those women who are most vulnerable, i.e., the poor, the unsophisticated, the young, and women who live in rural areas. The abstract recognition of a right to abortion could dampen political enthusiasm in support of reproductive choice."

To similar effect is Kathleen M. Sullivan, *Foreword: The Justices of Rules and Standards,* 106 Harv.L.Rev. 24 (1992): "It is much harder to mobilize pro-choice lobbying, voting and fund-raising efforts if *Roe* is nickel-and-dimed away rather than frankly overruled. [Why] didn't pro-choice activists celebrate when five Justices reaffirmed 'the essential holding of *Roe*'? Because the Court stole their thunder by adopting a moderate, difference-splitting standard."

5. ***Viability, fetal pain, and sentience.*** In *Casey* the Court offered three grounds for affirming a right to abortion pre-viability: stare decisis; the notion, expounded in *Roe*, that the ability to survive outside the womb marks a point in pregnancy when two separate lives are at stake; and (somewhat hesitantly) the assumption that by the start of the third trimester a woman who has not aborted has constructively consented to carrying the fetus to term. Whatever you make of these reasons, might there be a fourth reason for drawing the line roughly where the Court did? In early pregnancy, the fetus lacks sentience, i.e., does not have subjective experiences like pain and pleasure, but at some point in pregnancy, the fetus becomes sentient. As of 2014, thirteen states had enacted laws banning most abortions of fetuses capable of feeling pain, and similar legislation had passed the House of Representatives. See Teresa S. Collett, *Previability Abortion and the Pain of the Unborn*, 71 Wash. & Lee.L.Rev. 1211 (2014). Because fetal capacity for experiencing pain might occur before viability, however, these laws may be unconstitutional under *Roe* and *Casey*. Does sentience provide a more principled basis for drawing a line between stages of pregnancy than viability does? Peter Singer, Practical Ethics 151 (2d ed. 1999), argues that we should "accord the life of a fetus no greater value than the life of a nonhuman animal" with similar capacities. Singer's aim was to criticize the species-favoritism of "those who protest against abortion but dine regularly on the bodies of chickens, pigs and calves," but might his argument also provide support for extending rights to human fetuses that (or perhaps we should say *who*) have achieved sentience?

6. ***Spousal notification vs. parental consent.*** Consider Note, 106 Harv.L.Rev. 201 (1992): "Surface distinctions between pregnant adolescents and pregnant adults notwithstanding, the Court provided no principled basis for striking down the spousal notification clause because of the recognized potential for domestic violence while nonetheless upholding the parental consent requirement. [Tragically], in its application of the undue burden test, the Court failed to accord pregnant adolescent victims of family violence the same protection it granted similarly victimized pregnant women. [Given] that '[m]illions of children in the United States are victims of physical, sexual and emotional abuse,' [*Casey*'s] assumption that 'minors will benefit from consultation with their parents and that children will often not realize that their parents have their best interests at heart' must seem a cruel irony to pregnant adolescents trapped in violent homes."

7. ***What are the alternatives to an undue burden approach?*** "[T]he adoption of an expansively applied undue burden standard is hardly a panacea for the protection of fundamental rights," recognizes Alan Brownstein, *How Rights Are Infringed: The Role of Undue Burden Analysis in Constitutional Doctrine,* 45 Hast.L.J. 867 (1994), for the balancing of burdens against the state's interests "is far more conducive to judicial deference to the legislature than are categorical rules of review." The alternative, however, warns Professor Brownstein, "may even be more limited and restrictive": "If the only choice is between protecting the exercise of a right against all burdens under

strict scrutiny review or interpreting the interest at stake as something other than a right and providing it no constitutional protection at all, the latter option may be selected in far too many circumstances. It may be implicit in the framework offered by the critics of the 'undue burden' standard that rights are rarely recognized, although they receive aggressive protection in those few circumstances when they are found to exist. That approach may be successful if a very limited regime of rights is all that one believes the Constitution protects. If one aspires to a more open-ended and expansive vision of rights, however, it may be that the price to be paid to implement that vision is a commitment to judicial flexibility in determining what constitutes the infringement of a right."

8.   ***Tradition and textual specificity.*** Take a close look at how Scalia, J., in his footnote 1, distinguishes the *Loving* case and the majority's argument that "adherence to tradition would require" the Court "to uphold laws against interracial marriage." He relies on what he calls "*a text*—an Equal Protection Clause that explicitly establishes racial equality as a constitutional value." Does the Equal Protection Clause "explicitly" say anything about race?

"Partial-Birth Abortion"

GONZALES V. CARHART
550 U.S. 124, 127 S.Ct. 1610, 167 L.Ed.2d 480 (2007).

JUSTICE KENNEDY delivered the opinion of the Court.

These cases require us to consider the validity of the Partial-Birth Abortion Ban Act of 2003 (Act), a federal statute regulating abortion procedures. [We] conclude the Act should be sustained against the objections lodged by the broad, facial attack brought against it.

The Act proscribes a particular manner of ending fetal life, so it is necessary [to] discuss abortion procedures in some detail. Between 85 and 90 percent of the approximately 1.3 million abortions performed each year in the United States take place in the first three months of pregnancy, which is to say in the first trimester. The most common first-trimester abortion method is vacuum aspiration [in] which the physician vacuums out the embryonic tissue. Early in this trimester an alternative is to use medication, such as mifepristone (commonly known as RU–486), to terminate the pregnancy. The Act does not regulate these procedures.

Of the remaining abortions that take place each year, most occur in the second trimester. The surgical procedure referred to as "dilation and evacuation" or "D & E" is the usual abortion method in this trimester. [The doctor] inserts grasping forceps through the woman's cervix and into the uterus to grab the fetus. The doctor grips a fetal part with the forceps and pulls it back through the cervix and vagina, continuing to pull even after meeting resistance from the cervix. The friction causes the fetus to tear apart. For example, a leg might be ripped off the fetus as it is pulled through the cervix and out of the woman. The process of evacuating the fetus piece by piece continues until it has been completely removed.

[The] abortion procedure that was the impetus for the numerous bans on "partial-birth abortion,"[342] including the Act, is a variation of this standard D & E. [It] has been referred to as "intact D & E." [The] main difference between the two procedures is that in intact D & E a doctor extracts the fetus intact or largely intact with only a few passes. There are no comprehensive statistics indicating what percentage of all D & Es are performed in this manner. [In] an intact D & E procedure the doctor extracts the fetus in a way conducive to pulling out its entire body, instead of ripping it apart.

[In *Stenberg v. Carhart*, 530 U.S. 914 (2000), a 5–4 majority, per Breyer, J., struck down a Nebraska "partial-birth abortion" ban, citing two constitutional deficiencies. First, the Nebraska law did not contain an exception for circumstances in which the proscribed procedure was medically necessary. Second, the definition of the proscribed procedure was insufficiently clear to inform a doctor when she was violating the law, and thus imposed an undue burden.]

[The federal] Act responded to *Stenberg* in two ways. First, Congress made factual findings [that differed from the findings that bound the Supreme Court in *Stenberg*.] Congress found [a] "moral, medical, and ethical consensus [that] partial-birth abortion . . . is a gruesome and inhumane procedure that is never medically necessary and should be prohibited." Second, [the] Act's language [is clearer than] that of the Nebraska statute struck down in *Stenberg*.

Whatever one's views concerning the *Casey* joint opinion, it is evident a premise central to its conclusion—that the government has a legitimate and substantial interest in preserving and promoting fetal life—would be repudiated were the Court now to affirm the judgments of the Courts of Appeals.

[The Act is not] unconstitutionally vague on its face. [It] provides doctors "of ordinary intelligence a reasonable opportunity to know what is prohibited." [Doctors] performing D & E will know that if they do not deliver a living fetus to an anatomical landmark they will not face criminal liability. [Respondents] likewise have failed to show that the Act should be invalidated on its face because it encourages arbitrary or discriminatory enforcement. Just as the Act's anatomical landmarks provide doctors with objective standards, they also "establish minimal guidelines to govern law

---

[342] "The term 'partial-birth abortion,' " observed Ginsburg, J., dissenting, "is neither recognized in the medical literature nor used by physicians who perform second-trimester abortions."

enforcement." The scienter requirements narrow the scope of the Act's prohibitions and limit prosecutorial discretion.

[We reject the argument that] the Act imposes an undue burden, as a facial matter, because its restrictions on second-trimester abortions are too broad. [The] Act excludes most D & Es in which the fetus is removed in pieces, not intact. If the doctor intends to remove the fetus in parts from the outset, the doctor will not have the requisite intent to incur criminal liability. [A] comparison of the Act with the Nebraska statute struck down in *Stenberg* confirms this point. [There, the] Court concluded that [the] statute encompassed D & E because "D & E will often involve a physician pulling a 'substantial portion' of a still living fetus, say, an arm or leg, into the vagina prior to the death of the fetus." [Congress] responded to these concerns because the Act departs in material ways from the statute in *Stenberg*. It adopts the phrase "delivers a living fetus" instead of "delivering [a] living unborn child, or a substantial portion thereof," [thereby targeting] extraction of an entire fetus rather than removal of fetal pieces, [and] requir[ing] the fetus to be delivered so that it is partially "outside the body of the mother." [By] adding an overt-act requirement Congress sought further to meet the Court's objections to the state statute considered in *Stenberg*.

[Contrary] arguments by respondents are unavailing. [The contention] that any D & E has the potential to violate the Act, and that a physician will not know beforehand whether the abortion will proceed in a prohibited manner [fails to] take account of the Act's intent requirements, which preclude liability from attaching to an accidental intact D & E. [The] evidence also supports a legislative determination that an intact delivery is almost always a conscious choice rather than a happenstance, [thereby belying] any claim that a standard D & E cannot be performed without intending or foreseeing an intact D & E. [The] Act, measured by its text in this facial attack, [does not impose] a substantial obstacle to late-term, but previability, abortions.

[Congress] stated as follows: "Implicitly approving such a brutal and inhumane procedure by choosing not to prohibit it will further coarsen society to the humanity of not only newborns, but all vulnerable and innocent human life, making it increasingly difficult to protect such life." [Congress] was concerned, furthermore, with the effects on the medical community and on its reputation caused by the practice of partial-birth abortion. [There] can be no doubt the government "has an interest in protecting the integrity and ethics of the medical profession." *Washington v. Glucksberg* [infra].

[*Casey*] reaffirmed [that the] government may use its voice and its regulatory authority to show its profound respect for the life within the woman. A central premise of the opinion was that the Court's precedents after *Roe* had "undervalue[d] the State's interest in potential life."

[Congress] determined that the abortion methods it proscribed had a "disturbing similarity to the killing of a newborn infant." [The] Court [has] confirmed the validity of drawing boundaries to prevent certain practices that extinguish life and are close to actions that are condemned. *Glucksberg* found reasonable the State's "fear that permitting assisted suicide will start it down the path to voluntary and perhaps even involuntary euthanasia."

Respect for human life finds an ultimate expression in the bond of love the mother has for her child. The Act recognizes this reality as well. Whether to have an abortion requires a difficult and painful moral decision. While we find no reliable data to measure the phenomenon, it seems unexceptionable to conclude some women come to regret their choice to abort the infant life they once created and sustained. Severe depression and loss of esteem can follow.

In a decision so fraught with emotional consequence some doctors may prefer not to disclose precise details of the means that will be used. [It] is, however, precisely this lack of information concerning the way in which the fetus will be killed that is of legitimate concern to the State. The State has an interest in ensuring so grave a choice is well informed. It is self-evident that a mother who comes to regret her choice to abort must struggle with grief more anguished and sorrow more profound when she learns, only after the event, what she once did not know: that she allowed a doctor to pierce the skull and vacuum the fast-developing brain of her unborn child, a child assuming the human form.

[Partial-birth] abortion, as defined by the Act, differs from a standard D & E because the former occurs when the fetus is partially outside the mother to the point of one of the Act's anatomical landmarks. It was reasonable for Congress to think that partial-birth abortion, more than standard D & E, "undermines the public's perception of the appropriate role of a physician during the delivery process, and perverts a process during which life is brought into the world."

[The] prohibition in the Act would be unconstitutional, under precedents we here assume to be controlling, if it "subject[ed] [women] to significant health risks" [but t]here is documented medical disagreement whether the Act's prohibition would ever impose significant health risks on women. [The] question becomes whether the Act can stand when this medical uncertainty persists. The Court's precedents instruct that the Act can survive this facial attack. [If] the intact D & E procedure is truly necessary in some circumstances, it appears likely an injection that kills the fetus is an alternative under the Act that allows the doctor to perform the procedure.

[Respondents] contend that an abortion regulation must contain a health exception "if 'substantial medical authority supports the proposition that banning a particular procedure could endanger the woman's health.' " [But, a] zero tolerance policy would strike down legitimate abortion regulations, like the present one, if some part of the medical community were disinclined to follow the proscription. This is too exacting a standard to impose on the legislative power, exercised in this instance under the Commerce Clause, to regulate the medical profession. Considerations of marginal safety, including the balance of risks, are within the legislative competence when the regulation is rational and in pursuit of legitimate ends.

[The] considerations we have discussed support our further determination that these facial attacks should not have been entertained in the first instance. In these circumstances the proper means to consider exceptions is by as-applied challenge. [This] is the proper manner to protect the health of the woman if it can be shown that in discrete and well-defined instances a particular condition has or is likely to occur in which the procedure prohibited by the Act must be used. In an as-applied challenge the nature of the medical risk can be better quantified and balanced than in a facial attack. "[As-applied] challenges are the basic building blocks of constitutional adjudication." Richard H. Fallon, Jr., *As-Applied and Facial Challenges and Third-Party Standing*, 113 Harv.L.Rev. 1321 (2000).

The Act is open to a proper as-applied challenge in a discrete case. No as-applied challenge need be brought if the prohibition in the Act threatens a woman's life because the Act already contains a life exception. * * *[343]

JUSTICE GINSBURG, with whom JUSTICE STEVENS, JUSTICE SOUTER, and JUSTICE BREYER join, dissenting. * * *

Today's decision is alarming. It refuses to take *Casey* and *Stenberg* seriously. It tolerates, indeed applauds, federal intervention to ban nationwide a procedure found necessary and proper in certain cases by the American College of Obstetricians and Gynecologists (ACOG). It blurs the line, firmly drawn in *Casey*, between previability and postviability abortions. And, for the first time since *Roe*, the Court blesses a prohibition with no exception safeguarding a woman's health.

[As] *Casey* comprehended, at stake in cases challenging abortion restrictions is a woman's "control over her [own] destiny" (plurality opinion). [Thus,] legal challenges to undue restrictions on abortion procedures do not seek to vindicate some generalized notion of privacy; rather, they center on a woman's autonomy to determine her life's course, and thus to enjoy equal citizenship stature. [In] keeping with this

---

[343] Thomas, J., joined by Scalia, J., joined the Court's opinion, but wrote separately "to reiterate my view that the Court's jurisprudence, including *Casey* and *Roe*, has no basis in the Constitution."

comprehension of the right to reproductive choice, the Court has consistently required that laws regulating abortion, at any stage of pregnancy and in all cases, safeguard a woman's health. [In] *Stenberg*, we expressly held that a statute banning intact D & E was unconstitutional in part because it lacked a health exception. We noted that there existed a "division of medical opinion" about the relative safety of intact D & E, but we made clear that as long as "substantial medical authority supports the proposition that banning a particular abortion procedure could endanger women's health," a health exception is required.

[The] congressional findings on which the Partial-Birth Abortion Ban Act rests do not withstand inspection, as the lower courts have determined and this Court is obliged to concede. [Many] of the Act's recitations are incorrect. For example, Congress determined that no medical schools provide instruction on intact D & E. But in fact, numerous leading medical schools teach the procedure. [More] important, Congress claimed there was a medical consensus that the banned procedure is never necessary. But the evidence "very clearly demonstrate[d] the opposite." [Similarly], Congress found that "[t]here is no credible medical evidence that partial-birth abortions are safe or are safer than other abortion procedures." But the congressional record includes letters from numerous individual physicians stating that pregnant women's health would be jeopardized under the Act, as well as statements from nine professional [groups], attesting that intact D & E carries meaningful safety advantages over other methods. No comparable medical groups supported the ban. In fact, "all of the government's own witnesses disagreed with many of the specific congressional findings."

In contrast to Congress, the District Courts made findings after full trials at which all parties had the opportunity to present their best evidence. [According] to the expert testimony plaintiffs introduced, the safety advantages of intact D & E are marked for women with certain medical conditions. [Further,] plaintiffs' experts testified that intact D & E is significantly safer for women with certain pregnancy-related conditions.

[Based] on thoroughgoing review of the trial evidence and the congressional record, each of the District Courts to consider the issue rejected Congress' findings as unreasonable and not supported by the evidence. The trial courts concluded, in contrast to Congress' findings, that "significant medical authority supports the proposition that in some circumstances [intact D & E] is the safest procedure." [D]espite the District Court's appraisal of the weight of the evidence, and in undisguised conflict with *Stenberg*, the Court asserts that the Partial-Birth Abortion Ban Act can survive "[when] medical uncertainty persists." This assertion is bewildering. Not only does it defy the Court's longstanding precedent affirming the necessity of a health exception, with no carve-out for circumstances of medical uncertainty; it gives short shrift to the records before us, carefully canvassed by the District Courts. Those records indicate that "the majority of highly-qualified experts on the subject believe intact D & E to be the safest, most appropriate procedure under certain circumstances."

[The] Court offers flimsy and transparent justifications for upholding a nationwide ban on intact D & E sans any exception to safeguard a woman's health. Today's ruling, the Court declares, advances "a premise central to [*Casey*'s] conclusion—i.e., the Government's 'legitimate and substantial interest in preserving and promoting fetal life.' " [But] the Act scarcely furthers that interest: The law saves not a single fetus from destruction, for it targets only a *method* of performing abortion.

[As] another reason for upholding the ban, the Court emphasizes that the Act does not proscribe the nonintact D & E procedure. But why not, one might ask. Nonintact D & E could equally be characterized as "brutal," involving as it does "tear[ing] [a fetus] apart" and "ripp[ing] off" its limbs. "[T]he notion that either of these two equally gruesome procedures [is] more akin to infanticide than the other, or that the State furthers any legitimate interest by banning one but not the other, is simply irrational." *Stenberg* (Stevens, J., concurring).

[Ultimately], the Court admits that "moral concerns" are at work, concerns that could yield prohibitions on any abortion. [Revealing] in this regard, the Court invokes an antiabortion shibboleth for which it concededly has no reliable evidence: Women who have abortions come to regret their choices, and consequently suffer from "[s]evere depression and loss of esteem."[7] Because of women's fragile emotional state and because of the "bond of love the mother has for her child," the Court worries, doctors may withhold information about the nature of the intact D & E procedure. The solution the Court approves, then, is *not* to require doctors to inform women, accurately and adequately, of the different procedures and their attendant risks. [Instead,] the Court deprives women of the right to make an autonomous choice, even at the expense of their safety. This way of thinking reflects ancient notions about women's place in the family and under the Constitution—ideas that have long since been discredited.

[In] cases on a "woman's liberty to determine whether to [continue] her pregnancy," this Court has identified viability as a critical consideration. [Today,] the Court blurs that line, maintaining that "[t]he Act [legitimately] appl[ies] both previability and postviability because [a] fetus is a living organism while within the womb, whether or not it is viable

---

[7] **[Ct's Note]** The Court is surely correct that, for most women, abortion is a painfully difficult decision. But "neither the weight of the scientific evidence to date nor the observable reality of 33 years of legal abortion in the United States comports with the idea that having an abortion is any more dangerous to a woman's long-term mental health than delivering and parenting a child that she did not intend to have." Susan A. Cohen, *Abortion and Mental Health: Myths and Realities*, 9 Guttmacher Policy Rev. 8 (2006) * * * .

outside the womb." Instead of drawing the line at viability, the Court refers to Congress' purpose to differentiate "abortion and infanticide" based not on whether a fetus can survive outside the womb, but on where a fetus is anatomically located when a particular medical procedure is performed. One wonders how long a line that saves no fetus from destruction will hold in face of the Court's "moral concerns."

[The] Court further confuses our jurisprudence when it declares that "facial attacks" are not permissible in "these circumstances," i.e., where medical uncertainty exists. [This] holding is perplexing given that, in materially identical circumstances we held that a statute lacking a health exception was unconstitutional on its face. *Stenberg*. [Without] attempting to distinguish *Stenberg* and earlier decisions, the majority asserts that the Act survives review because respondents have not shown that the ban on intact D & E would be unconstitutional "in a large fraction of [relevant] cases." But *Casey* makes clear that, in determining whether any restriction poses an undue burden on a "large fraction" of women, the relevant class is *not* "all women," nor "all pregnant women," nor even all women "seeking abortions." Rather, a provision restricting access to abortion, "must be judged by reference to those [women] for whom it is an actual rather than an irrelevant restriction." Thus the absence of a health exception burdens *all* women for whom it is relevant—women who in the judgment of their doctors, require an intact D & E because other procedures would place their health at risk. [It] makes no sense to conclude that this facial challenge fails because respondents have not shown that a health exception is necessary for a large fraction of second-trimester abortions, including those for which a health exception is unnecessary: The very purpose of a health *exception* is to protect women in *exceptional* cases.

[Though] today's opinion does not go so far as to discard *Roe* or *Casey*, the Court, differently composed than it was when we last considered a restrictive abortion regulation, is hardly faithful to our earlier invocations of "the rule of law" and the "principles of stare decisis." [Although] Congress' findings could not withstand the crucible of trial, the Court defers to the legislative override of our Constitution-based rulings. A decision so at odds with our jurisprudence should not have staying power. In sum, the notion that the Partial-Birth Abortion Ban Act furthers any legitimate governmental interest is, quite simply, irrational. The Court's defense of the statute provides no saving explanation. In candor, the Act, and the Court's defense of it, cannot be understood as anything other than an effort to chip away at a right declared again and again by this Court— and with increasing comprehension of its centrality to women's lives.

NOTES AND QUESTIONS

1. ***What interest did the partial-birth abortion ban promote?*** Consider Michael C. Dorf, *Abortion Rights*, 23 Touro L.Rev. 815 (2008): "The

justification that Justice Kennedy identified [is] a condemnation of the symbolic meaning of this procedure. [In] banning a procedure that looks uncomfortably like infanticide, Congress aimed to preserve the line between infanticide and abortion. In tacitly crediting this rationale, [the] Court expanded the state's expressive interest in describing its moral opposition to abortion, which was set forth in *Casey*, to go so far as to warrant prohibitory legislation. The audience for partial-birth abortion bans, the audience for the expression of Congress's condemnation of this form of abortion, is not just individual women—in fact, it is primarily *not* women seeking abortions—but the population as a whole. For the first time since *Roe*, the Court in *Gonzales v. Carhart* upheld a regulation of pre-viability abortions not on grounds of maternal health or even fetal life, but on what are essentially symbolic grounds."

2.   ***Facial invalidity.*** The majority in *Gonzales v. Carhart* rejects the facial challenge but leaves open the possibility of an as-applied challenge. What is the difference? The answer is not entirely clear because unlike constitutional courts in many other countries, a U.S. "court has no power to remove a law from the statute books. When a court rules that a statute is invalid—whether as applied, in part, or on its face—the legal force of its decision resides in doctrines of claim and issue preclusion and of precedent. Under these doctrines, it generally makes no difference whether a court has 'held' that a statute is facially invalid or merely has so reasoned in the course of adjudicating an as-applied challenge." Fallon, *As-Applied and Facial Challenges and Third-Party Standing*, supra.

Why, then, does it matter whether a court classifies a constitutional challenge as facial or as-applied? The conventional wisdom states that the classification affects who may bring a claim. A plaintiff seeking as-applied relief argues that the challenged law violates *her own* rights, whereas one seeking facial relief attempts to vindicate the rights of third parties not before the court, which is generally forbidden. See Ch. 12, Sec. 2, I infra. The First Amendment overbreadth doctrine (discussed in Ch. 7, Sec. 1, VI infra) allows an exception to the prohibition on third-party claims, but, as the Court stated in *United States v. Salerno*, 481 U.S. 739 (1987) there is no " 'overbreadth' doctrine outside the limited context of the First Amendment."

Commentators dispute *Salerno*'s characterization of the case law. According to Richard H. Fallon, Jr., *Making Sense of Overbreadth,* 100 Yale L.J. 853 (1991), "virtually all of the abortion cases reaching the Supreme Court since *Roe* have involved facial attacks on state statutes, and the Court, whether accepting or rejecting the challenges on the merits, has typically accepted this framing of the question presented." Agreeing with Fallon's characterization of the case law, Michael C. Dorf, *Facial Challenges to State and Federal Statutes*, 46 Stan.L.Rev. 235 (1994), argues further that third-party standing *should* be available to plaintiffs challenging overbroad abortion regulations: "Due to pregnancy's temporary nature, pregnant women may find case-by-case legal relief from abortion restrictions particularly impractical. [In] addition, the fact that an abortion can only be carried out with the aid of a third party—typically a doctor—renders the right to choose an abortion particularly susceptible to a chilling effect. [Because] the right to choose abortion depends upon the cooperation of medical personnel, overbreadth doctrine offers an effective antidote to the chilling effect. [Overbreadth] doctrine works best when individuals who feel the chill of an overbroad statute can depend on an institution with greater financial and legal resources—such as a hospital or abortion clinic—to challenge the statute on its face."

Was the remedy left open by the Court in *Gonzales v. Carhart*—"a proper as-applied challenge in a discrete case"—adequately responsive to these concerns?

3. ***Did the Court's reliance on post-abortion regret signal a return to gender paternalism?*** Consider Reva B. Siegel, *Dignity and the Politics of Protection: Abortion Restrictions Under Casey/Carhart*, 117 Yale L.J. 1694 (2008): "On its face, *Carhart* seems to be a case about protecting the unborn, not women. [But] the Court also discussed an additional woman-protective justification for the ban that congressional findings never mention. *Carhart* cites an amicus brief with affidavits suggesting that women need protection from making uninformed abortion decisions they might regret. [That discussion] reflects the spread of abortion restrictions that are woman-protective, as well as fetal-protective, in form and justification. [*Casey*] bases the abortion right [on] the understanding that government cannot enforce customary or common-law understandings of women's roles. [By contrast, the] new gender paternalism [reflected in the woman-protective rationale for abortion restrictions] is in fact the old gender paternalism: laws (1) based on stereotypes about women's capacity and women's roles that (2) deny women agency (3) for the claimed purpose of protecting women from coercion and/or freeing them to be mothers. Gender paternalism of this kind violates the very forms of dignity that *Casey*—and the equal protection cases—protect."

Family Living Arrangements, Parental Rights, and the Right to Marry

As illustrated by WHALEN v. ROE, 429 U.S. 589 (1977) (sustaining a New York law requiring doctors to disclose the names of persons obtaining certain drugs for storage in a central computer file), parties attacking legislation can often cast their challenge in terms of an invasion of a constitutionally protected "zone of privacy." But the Court upheld the legislation as "a reasonable exercise of New York's broad police powers," holding that the program did not require extraordinary justification because it "does not, on its face, pose a sufficiently grievous threat" to either the "privacy" interest "in avoiding disclosure of personal matters" or the distinct "privacy" interest "in independence in making certain kinds of important decisions."

With respect to the first kind of privacy interest, it is useful to keep in mind how far computer technology has come since 1977. Aware of the greater possibility for invasions of informational privacy, modern case law under the Fourth Amendment has begun to react. For example, in *Riley v. California*, 134 S.Ct. 2473 (2014), the Supreme Court, per ROBERTS, C.J., unanimously ruled that police may not routinely search the mobile phone of an arrestee, absent a warrant, relying in substantial measure on the enormous quantity of private information that might thereby be discovered.

Cases involving informational privacy are generally studied in courses on criminal procedure. The cases discussed below deal with the second kind of "privacy" interest discussed in *Whalen v. Roe*.

Zoning; choice of household companions; "extended family" relationships. Relying on earlier decisions sustaining local zoning regulations, BELLE TERRE v. BORAAS, 416 U.S. 1 (1974), per DOUGLAS, J., upheld a village ordinance restricting land use to one-family dwellings (defining "family" to mean not more than two unrelated persons living together as a single housekeeping unit, and expressly excluding from the term lodging, boarding, fraternity or multiple-dwelling houses). Appellees, who had leased their houses to six unrelated college students, challenged the ordinance, inter alia, on the ground that it "trenches on the newcomers' rights of privacy." The Court disagreed: "We deal with economic and social legislation where legislatures have historically drawn lines which we respect [if the law] bears 'a rational relationship to a (permissible) state objective.' [Boarding] houses, fraternity houses, and the like present urban problems. [The] police power is not confined to elimination of filth, stench, and unhealthy places."

MARSHALL, J., dissented: The law burdened "fundamental rights of association and privacy," and thus required extraordinary justification, not a mere showing that the ordinance "bears a rational relationship to the accomplishment of legitimate governmental objectives." He viewed "the right to 'establish a home' " as an "essential part" of Fourteenth Amendment liberty and maintained that "the choice of household companions"—which "involves deeply personal considerations as to the kind and quality of intimate relationships within the home"—"surely falls within the ambit of the right to privacy protected by the Constitution." The state's purposes "could be as effectively achieved by means of an ordinance that did not discriminate on the basis of constitutionally protected choices of lifestyle."[344]

Distinguishing *Belle Terre* as involving an ordinance "affect[ing] only *unrelated* individuals," MOORE v. EAST CLEVELAND, 431 U.S. 494 (1977), invalidated a housing ordinance that limited occupancy to single families, but defined "family" so as to forbid appellant from having her two grandsons live with her. (It did not permit living arrangements if, as in this

---

[344] Brennan, J., also dissented, but on jurisdictional grounds.

case, the grandchildren were cousins rather than brothers.) POWELL, J., announcing the Court's judgment and joined by Brennan, Marshall, and Blackmun, JJ., struck down the ordinance on substantive due process grounds:

"[O]n its face [the ordinance] selects certain categories of relatives who may live together and declares that others may not. [When] a city undertakes such intrusive regulation of the family [the] usual judicial deference to the legislature is inappropriate. 'This Court has long recognized that freedom of personal choice in matters of marriage and family life is one of the liberties protected by [due process].' [When] the government intrudes on choices concerning family living arrangements, this Court must examine carefully the importance of the governmental interests advanced and the extent to which they are served by the challenged regulation. [T]hus examined, this ordinance cannot survive." Although the city's goals—preventing overcrowding, minimizing congestion and avoiding financial strain on its school system—were "legitimate," the ordinance served them "marginally, at best."

"[T]he history of the *Lochner* [era] counsels caution and restraint [but] it does [not] require what the city urges here: cutting off any protection of family rights at the first convenient, if arbitrary boundary—the boundary of the nuclear family. [Appropriate] limits on substantive due process come not from drawing arbitrary lines but rather from careful 'respect for the teachings of history [and] solid recognition of the basic values that underlie our society.' *Griswold* (Harlan, J., concurring). Our decisions establish that the Constitution protects the sanctity of the family precisely because the institution of the family is deeply rooted in this Nation's history and tradition. [Ours] is by no means a tradition limited to respect for [the] nuclear family. The tradition of uncles, aunts, cousins, and especially grandparents sharing a household along with parents and children has roots equally venerable and equally deserving of constitutional recognition. [*Pierce*] struck down an Oregon law requiring all children to attend the State's public schools, holding that the Constitution 'excludes any general power of the State to standardize its children by forcing them to accept instruction from public teachers only.' By the same token the Constitution prevents East Cleveland from standardizing its children and its adults by forcing all to live in certain narrowly defined family patterns.[345]

---

[345] Brennan, J., joined by Marshall, J., concurred, characterizing the ordinance as "senseless," "arbitrary" and "eccentric" and as reflecting "cultural myopia" and "a depressing insensitivity toward the economic and emotional needs of a very large part of our society." He called the "extended family" "virtually a means of survival" for many poor and minority families. "[The] 'nuclear family' is the pattern so often found in much of white suburbia," but "the Constitution cannot [tolerate] the imposition by government upon the rest of us of white suburbia's preference in patterns of family living."

Stevens, J., concurring in the result, thought this "unprecedented ordinance" unconstitutional even under the "limited standard of review of zoning decisions": "The city has failed totally to explain the need for a rule which would allow a homeowner to have two grandchildren live with

STEWART, J., joined by Rehnquist, J., dissented, rejecting the argument that "the importance of the 'extended family' in American society" renders appellant's "decision to share her residence with her grandsons, [like] the decisions involved in bearing and raising children, [an] aspect of 'family life' also entitled to substantive [constitutional] protection. [To] equate this interest with the fundamental decisions to marry and to bear and raise children is to extend the limited substantive contours of the Due Process Clause beyond recognition."

WHITE, J., also dissented, writing: "I cannot believe that the interest in residing with more than one set of grandchildren is one that calls for any kind of heightened protection under the Due Process Clause." He maintained that Powell, J.'s application of heightened scrutiny "suggests a far too expansive charter for this Court. [What] the deeply rooted traditions of the country are is arguable; which of them deserve the protection of the Due Process Clause is even more debatable."

NOTES AND QUESTIONS

1. **The problematic role of tradition.** Consider Joseph Grano, *Judicial Review and a Written Constitution in a Democratic Society*, 28 Wayne L.Rev. 1 (1981): "Justice Powell's plurality opinion concluded that 'the Constitution protects the sanctity of the family precisely because the institution of the family is deeply rooted in the Nation's history and tradition.' Societies do change, however, and cognizant of this, the Court could not have intended to become constitutionally committed to every practice rooted in our history and tradition. In particular, progress toward racial and sexual equality depends upon success in freeing ourselves from the yoke of history and tradition. Moreover, by implication, Justice Powell's opinion suggested that the result would have been different had an unrelated neighbor taken charge of Mrs. Moore's grandson, [but] did not explain [why] history and tradition would not protect a neighbor's decision to do what Mrs. Moore did. Nor did he explain why, if it would not, history and tradition should be determinative."

2. **What was the "real" purpose of the ordinance?** Is it significant that "East Cleveland is a predominantly Negro community, with a Negro City Manager and City Commissioner"? Consider Robert A. Burt, *The Constitution of the Family,* 1979 Sup.Ct.Rev. 329: "The plurality viewed the ordinance as directed against 'over-crowding, minimizing traffic and parking congestion,' [and the like, but] did not consider that the purpose of the ordinance was quite straightforward: to exclude from a middle-class, predominantly black community, that saw itself as socially and economically upwardly mobile, other black families most characteristic of lower-class ghetto

---

her if they are brothers, but not if they are cousins. Since this ordinance has not been shown to have any 'substantial relation to [East Cleveland's] public health, safety, morals or general welfare' [and] since it cuts so deeply into a fundamental right normally associated with the ownership of residential property—that of an owner to decide who may reside on his or her property—it must fall [as] a taking of property without due process and without just compensation."

life. Perhaps the Court did not see this purpose or, if it did, considered this an 'illegitimate goal,' though in other cases the Court had been exceedingly solicitous of white middle-class communities' attempts to preserve a common social identity—'zones,' as the Court had put the matter three years earlier [in *Belle Terre*]—'where family values, youth values, and the blessings of the quiet seclusion and clean air make the area a sanctuary for people.' "

3. ***The blood relationship of the parties.*** The *Moore* plurality emphasized the blood relationship of the parties. Should this factor be regarded as decisive? Consider Tribe 2d ed., at 1420: "If a city or town may require that every home be occupied by a single 'family,' consisting entirely of persons related by blood or marriage, it would be difficult to respond to the argument that the same city or town may also decide what a 'family' is: If longtime friends can be excluded by ordinance, why not second cousins? And if second cousins, why not certain grandchildren? [G]overnmental interference with *any* [enduring relationship] should be invalidated unless compellingly justified."

4. ***Cohabitants and singles.*** The laws at issue in both *Belle Terre* and *Moore* gave preferential treatment to married couples. But what about committed unmarried couples and individuals living alone? Consider Cynthia G. Bowman, *Unmarried Couples, Law, and Public Policy* 1 (2010): "The Census Bureau reported in 2006 that for the first time less than half of all households consisted of married couples. Instead, large numbers of people are choosing to live either in unmarried cohabiting unions, both heterosexual and gay or lesbian, or as single persons. [As] a result of [a similar trend abroad] many other countries have changed their laws to reflect the way people live now. In the United States, however, there is resistance to doing so." In light of *Moore*, is that resistance constitutionally suspect?

––––––––

The right to marry. In LOVING v. VIRGINIA, 388 U.S. 1 (1967) (also at Ch. 9, Sec. 2, II), the Court held, per WARREN, C.J., that a state statutory scheme designed to prevent marriages between persons of different races not only violated the Equal Protection Clause, but deprived the Lovings of liberty without due process. The Court recalled that in *Skinner*, it had described marriage as "one of the 'basic civil rights of man.' " It "surely" is a deprivation of liberty without due process, declared the Court, "[t]o deny this fundamental freedom on so unsupportable a basis as the racial classifications embodied in these statutes." Because racial discrimination played so large a role in the *Loving* case, its due process ruling was largely overlooked. A decade later, however, in the *Zablocki* case, discussed below, the Court confirmed that the right to marry is a fundamental right for due process purposes.

ZABLOCKI v. REDHAIL, 434 U.S. 374 (1978), invalidated a Wisconsin law forbidding marriage by any resident with minor children not in his custody whom he is under court order to support, unless he proves compliance with the support obligation and that the children "are not then and are not likely thereafter to become public charges." Appellee and the woman he desired to marry were expecting a child, but he was denied a marriage license because he had not satisfied his support obligations to his illegitimate child who had been a public charge since birth. In striking down the marriage prohibition under the "fundamental rights" branch of equal protection doctrine (Ch. 9, Sec. 5) the Court, per MARSHALL, J., observed:

"Since our past decisions make clear that the right to marry is of fundamental importance, and since the classification at issue here significantly interferes with the exercise of that right, we believe that 'critical examination' of the state interests advanced in support of the classification is required. [Cases] subsequent to *Griswold* and *Loving* have routinely categorized the decision to marry as among the personal decisions protected by the right of privacy. [It] is not surprising that the decision to marry has been placed on the same level of importance as decisions relating to procreation, childbirth, child rearing, and family relationships [for] it would make little sense to recognize a right of privacy with respect to other matters of family life and not with respect to the decision to enter the relationship that is the foundation of the family in our society. [If] appellee's right to procreate means anything at all, it must imply some right to enter the only relationship in which the [state] allows sexual relations legally to take place.

"By reaffirming the fundamental character of the right to marry, we do not mean to suggest that every state regulation which relates in any way to the incidents of or prerequisites for marriage must be subjected to rigorous scrutiny. [The] statutory classification at issue here, however, clearly does interfere directly and substantially with the right to marry. [Some] of those in the affected class, like appellee, will never be able to obtain the necessary court order, because they either lack the financial means to meet their support obligations or cannot prove that their children will not become public charges. These persons are absolutely prevented from getting married. Many others, able in theory to satisfy the statute's requirements, will be sufficiently burdened by having to do so that they will in effect be coerced into forgoing their right to marry. And even those who can be persuaded to meet the statute's requirements suffer a serious intrusion into their freedom of choice in an area in which we have held such freedom to be fundamental.

"When a statutory classification significantly interferes with the exercise of a fundamental right, it cannot be upheld unless it is supported by sufficiently important state interests and is closely tailored to effectuate only those interests. [The] State already has numerous other means for exacting compliance with support obligations, means that are at least as effective as the instant statute's and yet do not impinge upon the right to marry."

STEWART, J., who concurred in the judgment, rejected the view that the Wisconsin statute violated equal protection. As he saw it, "the problem in this case is not one of discriminatory classifications, but of unwarranted encroachment upon a constitutionally protected freedom." He deemed the statute unconstitutional "because it exceeds the bounds of permissible state regulation of marriage." He continued:

"I do not agree [that] there is a 'right to marry' in the constitutional sense. [Surely], for example, a State may legitimately say that no one can marry his or her sibling, that no one can marry who is not at least 14 years old, that no one can marry without first passing an examination for venereal disease, or that no one can marry who has a living husband or wife. But, just as surely, in regulating the intimate human relationship of marriage, there is a limit beyond which a State may not constitutionally go.

"[The] State's legitimate concern with the financial soundness of prospective marriages must stop short of telling people they may not marry because they are too poor or because they might persist in their financial irresponsibility. [A] legislative judgment so alien to our traditions and so offensive to our shared notions of fairness offends the Due Process Clause. [Equal] protection doctrine has become the Court's chief instrument for invalidating state laws. Yet, in a case like this one, the doctrine is no more than substantive due process by another name. [The] message of the Court's opinion is that Wisconsin may not use its control over marriage to achieve the objectives of the state statute. Such restrictions on basic governmental power are at the heart of substantive due process. The Court is understandably reluctant to rely on substantive due process. But to embrace the essence of that doctrine under the guise of equal protection serves no purpose but obfuscation.

POWELL, J., concurred in the judgment, but wrote separately "because the majority's rationale sweeps too broadly in an area which traditionally has been subject to pervasive state regulation [which] has included bans on incest, bigamy, and homosexuality, as well as various preconditions to marriage, such as blood tests. Likewise, a showing of fault on the part of one of the partners traditionally has been a prerequisite to the dissolution of an unsuccessful union. A 'compelling state purpose' inquiry would cast doubt on the network of restrictions that the States have fashioned to govern marriage and divorce.

"[But the] Wisconsin measure in this case does not pass muster under either due process or equal protection standards. [As for the state's 'collection device' justification, the] vice inheres [in] the failure to make provision for those without the means to comply with child-support obligations. [As for the state interest in preserving] the ability of marriage applicants to support their prior issue by preventing them from incurring new obligations, [the law is] so grossly underinclusive with respect to this objective, given the many ways that additional financial obligations may be incurred by the applicant quite apart from a contemplated marriage, that the classification 'does not bear a fair and substantial relation to the object of the legislation.' "

STEVENS, J., concurred: "Under this statute, a person's economic status may determine his eligibility to enter into a lawful marriage. A noncustodial parent whose children are 'public charges' may not marry even if he has met his court-ordered obligations. Thus, within the class of parents who have fulfilled their court-ordered obligations, the rich may marry and the poor may not. This type of statutory discrimination is, I believe, totally unprecedented, as well as inconsistent with our tradition of administering justice equally to the rich and to the poor."[346]

NOTES AND QUESTIONS

1.   In TURNER v. SAFLEY, 482 U.S. 78 (1987), a unanimous Court, per O'CONNOR, J., ruled that the right to marry, deemed to be "a fundamental right" in *Loving* and *Zablocki*, remained so in the prison setting. Thus it struck down a prison regulation that permitted inmates to marry only when the prison superintendent gave approval for "compelling reasons," which, in practice meant only "pregnancy or birth of a child." After recognizing that "the right to marry is subject to substantial restrictions as a result of incarceration," the Court went on: "Many important attributes of marriage remain, however, after taking into account the limitations imposed by prison life. First, inmate marriages, like others, are expressions of emotional support and public commitment. [In] addition, many religions recognize marriage as having spiritual significance. Third, most inmates eventually will be released [and] therefore most inmate marriages are formed in the expectation that they ultimately will be fully consummated. Finally, marital status often is a pre-condition to the receipt of government benefits, [property] rights, [and] other, less tangible, benefits (e.g., legitimation of children born out of wedlock). [Taken together], these remaining elements are sufficient to form a constitutionally protected marital relationship in the prison context."

2.   ***Same-sex marriage.*** In *United States v. Windsor* [Ch. 9, Sec. 4, I] the Court, per KENNEDY, J., invalidated Section 3 of the Defense of Marriage Act (DOMA), which, for federal purposes defined marriage as a union of a man and a woman even if state law recognized same-sex marriage. The decision rested on equal protection grounds, supplemented by federalism concerns: Given the historical deference the federal government had accorded "to state-law policy decisions with respect to domestic relations," Congress's departure

---

[346] Rehnquist, J., the sole dissenter, "view[ed] this legislative judgment in the light of the traditional presumption of validity." He concluded that the law, "despite its imperfections, is sufficiently rational to satisfy the demands of the Fourteenth Amendment."

from that pattern was seen as evidence of the impermissible purpose of imposing "a stigma upon all who enter into same-sex marriages made lawful by the unquestioned authority of the States." The Court did not decide whether there is a constitutional right to state recognition of same-sex marriage, either as a matter of substantive due process or equal protection, but SCALIA, J., joined by Thomas, J., predicted in dissent that such recognition was "inevitable," in light of the majority's rationale.

Following *Windsor*, state courts and lower federal courts overwhelmingly vindicated that prediction, and in October 2014, the Supreme Court declined to review several federal appeals court rulings finding a federal constitutional right to same-sex marriage. A month later, however, a divided panel of the United States Court of Appeals for the Sixth Circuit rejected a right to same-sex marriage in *DeBoer v. Snyder*, 772 F.3d 388 (2014), *cert. granted* in *Obergefell v. Hodges*, 135 S.Ct. 1039 (2015). "Why," the appeals court asked rhetorically, did the Supreme Court in *Windsor* consider "DOMA anomalous? Only federalism can supply the answer." Even following *DeBoer*, by early 2015, same-sex marriage was legal in most of the country, with seasoned Supreme Court-watchers mostly treating the Justices' unexplained decisions permitting same-sex marriages to go forward as a signal that the Court would soon find a constitutional right to same-sex marriage.

The lower court decisions that find a right to same-sex marriage mostly rely on equal protection grounds, but some decisions rest on substantive due process grounds as well. For example, in *Bostic v. Schaefer*, 760 F.3d 352 (4th Cir. 2014), the appeals court invalidated Virginia's ban on same-sex marriage as failing the strict scrutiny applicable to laws that infringe a fundamental right. Dissenting, Judge Niemeyer argued that the fundamental right to marry recognized in *Loving* and *Zablocki* did not encompass same-sex marriage. He said that the majority failed to explain why, in its view, the marriage right "does not also encompass the 'right' of a father to marry his daughter or the 'right' of any person to marry multiple partners."

Assuming the right to marry properly encompasses same-sex marriages, can state prohibitions on incestuous and polygamous marriages be distinguished? Do they survive strict scrutiny? If not, should (some) incestuous and polygamous marriages be deemed constitutionally protected? Or do these examples suggest that equal protection alone provides a better rationale for invalidating prohibitions on same-sex marriage? If so, was Stewart, J., correct to join only the equal protection portion of the holding in *Loving*?

3. ***Non-parental visitation rights vs. rights of parents to make decisions concerning the care, custody, and control of their children.*** Consider TROXEL v. GRANVILLE, 530 U.S. 57 (2000): A Washington statute permitted "[a]ny person" to petition for visitation rights "at any time" and authorized state superior courts to grant such rights whenever "visitation may serve the best interest of the child." The Troxels petitioned for the right to visit their deceased son's two daughters. Granville, the mother of the children, and a "fit custodial parent," did not oppose all visitation, but objected to the

frequency sought by the girls' grandparents (two weekends of overnight visitation per month and two weeks of visitation each summer). She asked the court to order one day of visitation per month with no overnight stay. The superior court ordered more visitation than Granville desired, and she appealed. The Washington Supreme Court struck down the statute on its face and the U.S. Supreme Court affirmed the judgment but on narrower grounds. There was no opinion of the Court. The principal opinion was written by O'CONNOR, J., joined by Rehnquist, C.J., and Ginsburg and Breyer, JJ. The plurality found the statute "as applied in this case" unconstitutional:

"The liberty interest at issue in this case—the interests of parents in the care, custody, and control of their children—is perhaps the oldest of the fundamental liberty interests recognized by this Court. [I]t cannot now be doubted that the Due Process Clause of the Fourteenth Amendment protects the fundamental right of parents to make decisions concerning the care, custody, and control of their children. [The Washington statute], as applied to Granville and her family in this case, unconstitutionally infringes on that fundamental parental right. [It] is breathtakingly broad. [Its] language effectively permits any third party seeking visitation to subject any decision by a parent concerning visitation of the parent's children to state-court review. Once [the] matter is placed before a judge, a parent's decision that visitation would not be in the child's best interest is accorded no deference. [The] statute places the best-interest determination solely in the hands of the judge. [Thus,] in practical effect, in the State of Washington, a court can disregard and overturn *any* decision by a fit custodial parent concerning visitation whenever a third party affected by the decision files a visitation petition, based solely on the judge's determination of the child's best interests.

"[The] Due Process Clause does not permit a State to infringe on the fundamental right of parents to make childrearing decisions simply because a state judge believes a 'better' decision could be made. Neither the Washington [statute] generally [nor] the Superior Court in this specific case required anything more. Accordingly, we hold that [the statute], as applied in this case, is unconstitutional."[347]

STEVENS, J., dissenting, maintained that the state supreme court "erred in its federal constitutional analysis because neither the provision granting 'any person' the right to petition the court for visitation nor the absence of a provision requiring a 'threshold [finding] of harm to the child' provides a sufficient basis for holding that the statute is invalid in all its applications. I believe that a facial challenge should fail whenever a statute has 'a plainly legitimate sweep.' Under the Washington statute, there are plainly any number of cases—indeed, one suspects, the most common to arise—in which the 'person' among 'any' seeking visitation is a once-custodial caregiver, an intimate relation, or even a genetic parent."

SCALIA, J., separately dissenting, thought it "entirely compatible with the commitment to representative democracy set forth in the founding documents

---

[347] In separate opinions, Souter and Thomas, JJ., concurred in the judgment.

to argue, in legislative chambers or in electoral campaigns, that the State has *no power* to interfere with parents' authority over the rearing of their children," but did "not believe that the power which the Constitution confers upon me *as a judge* entitles me to deny legal effect to laws that (in my view) infringe upon what is (in my view) that unenumerated right."

KENNEDY, J., wrote a third dissenting opinion. His "principal concern" was that the state court's holding "seems to proceed from the assumption that the parent or parents who resist visitation have always been the child's primary caregivers and that the third parties who seek visitation have no legitimate and established relationship with the child. That idea, in turn, appears influenced by the concept that the conventional nuclear family ought to establish the visitation standard for every domestic relations case. As we all know, this is simply not the structure or prevailing condition in many households. See, e.g., *Moore*."

MICHAEL H. V. GERALD D.
491 U.S. 110, 109 S.Ct. 2333, 105 L.Ed.2d 91 (1989).

JUSTICE SCALIA announced the judgment of the Court and delivered an opinion in which the CHIEF JUSTICE joins, and in all but footnote 6 of which JUSTICE O'CONNOR and JUSTICE KENNEDY join.

The facts of this case are, we must hope, extraordinary. [Claiming to be the father of Victoria, the child of Carole and Gerald D., a married couple, Michael H. brought an action in California to establish his paternity and visitation rights. Although Gerald was listed as the father on the birth certificate and has always claimed the child as her father, blood tests showed a 98.07% probability that Michael, with whom Carole had had an adulterous affair, was the father. During the first three years of Victoria's life, she and Carole resided at times with Michael, who held the child out as his own. During this time, mother and child also resided at times with another man, Scott K., and with Gerald. Under California law, a child born to a married woman living with her husband, who is neither impotent nor sterile, is presumed to be a child of the marriage, a presumption that may be rebutted only in very limited circumstances. Relying on this presumption, the California courts rejected Michael's claims. The U.S. Supreme Court affirmed.]

Michael contends as a matter of substantive due process that because he has established a parental relationship with Victoria, protection of Gerald's and Carole's marital union is an insufficient state interest to support termination of that relationship. This argument is, of course, predicated on the assertion that Michael has a constitutionally protected liberty interest in his relationship with Victoria. [In] an attempt to limit and guide interpretation of the [Due Process] Clause, we have insisted not merely that the interest denominated as a "liberty" be "fundamental" (a concept that, in isolation, is hard to objectify), but also that it be an interest traditionally protected by our society.[2] As we have put it, the Due Process Clause affords only those protections "so rooted in the traditions and conscience of our people as to be ranked as fundamental."

[This] insistence that the asserted liberty interest be rooted in history and tradition is evident, [in] our cases according constitutional protection to certain parental rights. [As] we view [these cases], they rest [on] the historic respect—indeed, sanctity would not be too strong a term— traditionally accorded to the relationships that develop within the unitary family.

[Thus,] the legal issue in the present case reduces to whether the relationship between persons in the situation of Michael and Victoria has been treated as a protected family unit under the historic practices of our society, or whether on any other basis it has been accorded special protection. We think it impossible to find that it has. In fact, quite to the contrary, our traditions have protected the marital family (Gerald, Carole, and the child they acknowledge to be theirs) against the sort of claim Michael asserts.[4]

[What] Michael asserts here is a right to have himself declared the natural father *and thereby to obtain parental prerogatives.* What he must establish, therefore, is not that our society has traditionally allowed a natural father in his circumstances to establish paternity, but that it has traditionally accorded such a father parental rights, or at least has not traditionally denied them. [What] counts is whether the States in fact award substantive parental rights to the natural father of a child conceived within, and born into, an extant marital union that wishes to embrace the child. We are not aware of a single case, old or new, that has done so. This

---

[2] **[Ct's Note]** We do not understand what Justice Brennan has in mind by an interest "that society traditionally has thought important [without] protecting it." The protection need not take the form of an explicit constitutional provision or statutory guarantee, but it must at least exclude (all that is necessary to decide the present case) a societal tradition of enacting laws *denying* the interest. Nor do we understand why our practice of limiting the Due Process Clause to traditionally protected interests turns the clause "into a redundancy." Its purpose is to prevent future generations from lightly casting aside important traditional values—not to enable this Court to invent new ones.

[4] **[Ct's Note]** Justice Brennan insists that in determining whether a liberty interest exists we must look at Michael's relationship with Victoria in isolation, without reference to the circumstance that Victoria's mother was married to someone else when the child was conceived, and that that woman and her husband wish to raise the child as their own. We cannot imagine what compels this strange procedure of looking at the act which is assertedly the subject of a liberty interest in isolation from its effect upon other people—rather like inquiring whether there is a liberty interest in firing a gun where the case at hand happens to involve its discharge into another person's body. The logic of Justice Brennan's position leads to the conclusion that if Michael had begotten Victoria by rape, that fact would in no way affect his possession of a liberty interest in his relationship with her.

is not the stuff of which fundamental rights qualifying as liberty interests are made.[6] * * *

JUSTICE O'CONNOR, with whom JUSTICE KENNEDY joins, concurring in part.

I concur in all but footnote 6 of Justice Scalia's opinion. This footnote sketches a mode of historical analysis to be used when identifying liberty interests protected by the Due Process Clause of the Fourteenth Amendment that may be somewhat inconsistent with our past decisions in this area. See *Griswold; Eisenstadt.* On occasion the Court has characterized relevant traditions protecting asserted rights at levels of generality that might not be "the most specific level" available [quoting from fn. 6 of Justice Scalia's opinion]. See *Loving* [and] *Turner v. Safley.* I would not foreclose the unanticipated by the prior imposition of a single mode of historical analysis. *Poe* (Harlan, J., dissenting).[348]

---

[6] **[Ct's Note]** Justice Brennan criticizes our methodology in using historical traditions specifically relating to the rights of an adulterous natural father, rather than inquiring more generally "whether parenthood is an interest that historically has received our attention and protection." There seems to us no basis for the contention that this methodology is "nove[l]." For example, in *Bowers v. Hardwick* [infra], we noted that at the time the Fourteenth Amendment was ratified all but 5 of the 37 States had criminal sodomy laws, that all 50 of the States had such laws prior to 1961, and that 24 States and the District of Columbia continued to have them; and we concluded from that record, regarding that very specific aspect of sexual conduct, that "to claim that a right to engage in such conduct is 'deeply rooted in this Nation's history and tradition' or 'implicit in the concept of ordered liberty' is, at best, facetious." In *Roe* we spent about a fifth of our opinion negating the proposition that there was a longstanding tradition of laws proscribing abortion.

We do not understand why, having rejected our focus upon the societal tradition regarding the natural father's rights vis-à-vis a child whose mother is married to another man, Justice Brennan would choose to focus instead upon "parenthood." Why should the relevant category not be even more general—perhaps "family relationships"; or "personal relationships"; or even "emotional attachments in general"? Though the dissent has no basis for the level of generality it would select, we do: We refer to the most specific level at which a relevant tradition protecting, or denying protection to, the asserted right can be identified. If, for example, there were no societal tradition, either way, regarding the rights of the natural father of a child adulterously conceived, we would have to consult, and (if possible) reason from, the traditions regarding natural fathers in general. But there is such a more specific tradition, and it unqualifiedly denies protection to such a parent.

[Because] general traditions provide such imprecise guidance, they permit judges to dictate rather than discern the society's views. The need, if arbitrary decision-making is to be avoided, to adopt the most specific tradition as the point of reference—or at least to announce, as Justice Brennan declines to do, some other criterion for selecting among the innumerable relevant traditions that could be consulted—is well enough exemplified by the fact that in the present case Justice Brennan's opinion and Justice O'Connor's opinion, which disapproves this footnote, *both* appeal to tradition, but on the basis of the tradition they select reach opposite results. Although assuredly having the virtue (if it be that) of leaving judges free to decide as they think best when the unanticipated occurs, a rule of law that binds neither by text nor by any particular, identifiable tradition is no rule of law at all. * * *

[348] Stevens, J., who concurred in the judgment, was "willing to assume for the purpose of deciding this case that Michael's relationship with Victoria is strong enough to give him a constitutional right to try to convince a trial judge that Victoria's best interest would be served by granting him visitation rights. I am satisfied, however, that the California statute, as applied in this case, gave him that opportunity."

JUSTICE BRENNAN, with whom JUSTICE MARSHALL and JUSTICE BLACKMUN join, dissenting. * * *

Once we recognized that the "liberty" protected by the Due Process Clause of the Fourteenth Amendment encompasses more than freedom from bodily restraint, today's plurality opinion emphasizes, the concept was cut loose from one natural limitation on its meaning. This innovation paved the way, so the plurality hints, for judges to substitute their own preferences for those of elected officials. Dissatisfied with this supposedly unbridled and uncertain state of affairs, the plurality casts about for another limitation on the concept of liberty.

It finds this limitation in "tradition." Apparently oblivious to the fact that this concept can be as malleable and as elusive as "liberty" itself, the plurality pretends that tradition places a discernible border around the Constitution. [Yet,] as Justice White observed in his dissent in *Moore v. East Cleveland:* "What the deeply rooted traditions of the country are is arguable." [Even] if we could agree, moreover, on the content and significance of particular traditions, we still would be forced to identify the point at which a tradition becomes firm enough to be relevant to our definition of liberty and the moment at which it becomes too obsolete to be relevant any longer. The plurality supplies no objective means by which we might make these determinations.

[The plurality] does not ask whether parenthood is an interest that historically has received our attention and protection; the answer to that question is too clear for dispute. Instead, the plurality asks whether the specific variety of parenthood under consideration—a natural father's relationship with a child whose mother is married to another man—has enjoyed such protection. If we had looked to tradition with such specificity in past cases, many a decision would have reached a different result. Surely the use of contraceptives by unmarried couples, *Eisenstadt;* or even by married couples, *Griswold;* [and] even the right to raise one's natural but illegitimate children, *Stanley v. Illinois,* 405 U.S. 645 (1972), were not "interest[s] traditionally protected by our society" at the time of their consideration by this Court.

[The] plurality's interpretive method is more than novel; it is misguided. It ignores the good reasons for limiting the role of "tradition" in interpreting the Constitution's deliberately capacious language. In the plurality's constitutional universe, we may not take notice of the fact that the original reasons for the conclusive presumption of paternity are out of place in a world in which blood tests can prove virtually beyond a shadow of a doubt who sired a particular child and in which the fact of illegitimacy no longer plays the burdensome and stigmatizing role it once did. [By] describing the decisive question as whether Michael and Victoria's interest is one that has been "traditionally *protected by* our society" (emphasis added), rather than one that society traditionally has thought important (with or without protecting it), and by suggesting that our sole function is to "*discern* the society's views," n. 6 (emphasis added), the plurality acts as if the only purpose of the Due Process Clause is to confirm the importance of interests already protected by a majority of the States. Transforming the protection afforded by the Due Process Clause into a redundancy mocks those who, with care and purpose, wrote the Fourteenth Amendment.

In construing the Fourteenth Amendment to offer shelter only to those interests specifically protected by historical practice, moreover, the plurality ignores the kind of society in which our Constitution exists. We are not an assimilative, homogeneous society, but a facilitative, pluralistic one, in which we must be willing to abide someone else's unfamiliar or even repellant practice because the same tolerant impulse protects our own idiosyncracies. Even if we can agree, therefore, that "family" and "parenthood" are part of the good life, it is absurd to assume that we can agree on the content of those terms and destructive to pretend that we do. In a community such as ours, "liberty" must include the freedom not to conform. The plurality today squashes this freedom by requiring specific approval from history before protecting anything in the name of liberty.

The document that the plurality construes today is unfamiliar to me. It is not the living charter that I have taken to be our Constitution; it is instead a stagnant, archaic, hidebound document steeped in the prejudices and superstitions of a time long past. * * *[349]

Levels of Generality and Tradition

1. *What is "tradition"? Does tradition ever speak with one voice?* Consider Jack Balkin, *Tradition, Betrayal, and the Politics of Deconstruction,* 11 Cardozo L.Rev. 1613 (1990): "If there is a tradition of protecting marital privacy, but not a more specific tradition protecting marital purchase of contraceptives, how do we know whether the latter situation is nevertheless subsumed under the former for purposes of constitutionally protected liberty? Might one not conclude instead that the *real* historical tradition was protection of marital privacy in the home, so that the purchase of contraceptives in the open marketplace could be regulated or even proscribed consistent with the tradition? Would this not be more consistent with the experiences of Margaret Sanger and her followers, who publicly advocated birth control in the early twentieth century, and were met with incredible resistance? [If] sexual harassment directed toward women in the workplace and respect for marital privacy are both traditions, but only one is worth protecting, how do we tell the difference? If back alley abortions are a tradition in response to the 'traditional' prohibition on abortion in America, does this make abortion (in

---

[349] White, J., also dissented.

or out of a back alley) a tradition worth protecting and sustaining? In short, what normative status should be assigned to a set of values given the fact that many people have held these values at one point or another in our nation's history?

"[W]hat is most troubling about Justice Scalia's call for respecting the most specific tradition available is that our most specific historical traditions may often be opposed to our more general commitments to liberty or equality. Curiously, then, different parts of the American tradition may conflict with each other. And indeed, this is one of the untidy facts of historical experience. The fourteenth amendment's abstract commitment to racial equality was accompanied by simultaneous acceptance of segregated public schools in the District of Columbia and acquiescence in antimiscegenation laws. The establishment clause and the principle of separation of church and state have coexisted with presidential proclamations of national days of prayer, official congressional chaplains, and national Christmas trees. Traditions do not exist as integrated wholes. They are a motley collection of principles and counterprinciples, standing for one thing when viewed narrowly and standing for another when viewed more generally. Tradition never speaks with one voice, although, to be sure, persons of particular predelictions may hear only one."

2. *What information does one "abstract away"?* Consider Laurence H. Tribe & Michael C. Dorf, *Levels of Generality in the Definition of Rights,* 57 U.Chi.L.Rev. 1057 (1990): "Justice Scalia's formulation of the rights at stake [in *Michael H.*] as the rights of 'the natural father of a child adulterously conceived' [is] already a considerable abstraction. He has abstracted away lots of information that virtually everybody would agree is irrelevant. But he has also abstracted away some information that many people would see as quite relevant. The natural father in *Michael H.* had a longstanding, albeit adulterous and sporadic, relationship with the mother of his child. He also had fairly extensive, if sporadic, contact with his child. [A] more specific formulation of the issue than Justice Scalia gives us would be: *what are the rights of the natural father of a child conceived in an adulterous but longstanding relationship, where the father has played a major, if sporadic, role in the child's early development?*

"It is unlikely that any tradition addresses this very question at this precise level of specificity. Thus, we are left with the problem of specifying the *next* most specific tradition. [But] we find no single dimension or direction along which to measure the degree of abstraction or generality. Do we abstract away the father's relationship with his child and her mother, as Justice Scalia does? Or do we instead abstract away the fact that the relationship with the mother was an adulterous one, as Justice Brennan does? If we do the latter, then we will find ourselves consulting traditions regarding natural fathers who play major roles in their children's development. This sounds an awful lot like 'traditions regarding natural fathers in general,' which Justice Scalia regarded as less specific than his formulation of the problem. By starting from an even *more* specific description of the case than did Justice Scalia, we have seen that he had no greater justification for abstracting away the father-child relationship than Justice Brennan had for abstracting away the adultery."

3. *Justice Scalia's footnote 4 approach: incorporating the state's interest into an asserted liberty.* Although footnote 6 to Justice Scalia's plurality opinion in *Michael H.* has generated much comment, footnote 4 also merits attention. In it, the plurality criticizes the Court's practice of first deciding whether a liberty is fundamental and then asking whether a government practice restricting that liberty can be justified. Consider the response of Tribe & Dorf, supra:

"When we automatically incorporate the factors that provide the state's possible justification for its regulation into the initial definition of a liberty, the fundamental nature of that liberty nearly vanishes. Unless the state's interest is facially absurd, when it is suitably incorporated into an asserted liberty it will render that liberty so specific as to seem insupportable, or at least radically disconnected from precedent. At a minimum, the privacy right protected in *Roe* becomes the implausible 'right' to destroy a living fetus. If one takes footnote 4 to its logical limit in the interpretation of *enumerated* rights, then the free speech right protected in *New York Times Co. v. Sullivan* [Ch. 7, Sec. 1, II, B] becomes the dubious 'right' to libel a public official and the right to an exclusionary remedy protected in *Mapp v. Ohio* [367 U.S. 643 (1961)] becomes the counter-intuitive 'right' of a criminal to suppress the truth. To state these cases this way is to decide them in the government's favor. Anyone is free to argue that each of these cases was wrongly decided. But arguments to this effect must explain why the state interest overcomes the liberty interest. Under Justice Scalia's footnote 4 approach, by contrast, the state interest obliterates, without explanation and at the outset, any trace of the individual liberty at stake."

4. *Is the purpose of a bill of rights to prevent societal rot?* In responding to Brennan, J.'s charge that defining fundamental rights in accordance with legal traditions, the *Michael H.* plurality renders those rights "redundan[t]," the plurality replies, in footnote 2, that with rights defined in this way, the Due Process Clause serves "to prevent future generations from lightly casting aside important traditional values." Speaking in a similar vein as a scholar, Scalia, J. has argued that this is the whole point of a bill of rights—the worry that "societies" do not "always 'mature,' as opposed to rot." Antonin Scalia, *Common Law Courts in a Civil Law System: The Role of United States Federal Courts in Interpreting the Constitution and Laws*, in *A Matter of Interpretation: Federal Courts and the Law* 3, 40–41 (Amy Gutmann ed. 1997).

Is the prevention of backsliding really the whole point of a bill of rights? Consider Michael C. Dorf, *The Aspirational Constitution*, 77 Geo.Wash.L.Rev. 1631 (2009): "Constitutional rights sometimes work [to prevent backsliding] but, in important respects, the American experience has been quite different. Constitutional rights are typically established as the culmination of a struggle to change the status quo, rather than to enshrine well-accepted fundamental values. For example, the Nineteenth Amendment [did] not take a preexisting shared norm of sex equality and entrench it against later backsliding. [Sometimes] the enshrinement of constitutional rights succeeds almost immediately, but rights [can] also lay dormant for decades, until a later generation discovers them. Perhaps our most cherished constitutional principles—those enshrined in the First and Fourteenth Amendments—fall into this latter category. Such constitutional provisions may be best understood, at least in retrospect, as aspirations for future change, rather than as a hedge against such change."

Is There a Right to Physician-Assisted Suicide?

WASHINGTON V. GLUCKSBERG

521 U.S. 702, 117 S.Ct. 2258, 138 L.Ed.2d 772 (1997).

CHIEF JUSTICE REHNQUIST delivered the opinion of the Court.

The question presented in this case is whether Washington's prohibition against "caus[ing]" or "aid[ing]" a suicide offends the Fourteenth Amendment to the United States Constitution. We hold that it does not.

[Respondents, four physicians who declare they would assist terminally ill, suffering patients in ending their lives if not for Washington's assisted-suicide ban, and Compassion in Dying, a nonprofit organization that counsels people considering physician-assisted suicide, sought a declaration that Washington's statute is, on its face, unconstitutional. They were originally joined by three gravely ill plaintiffs, who died before the case reached the Supreme Court. The respondents asserted "the existence of a liberty interest protected by the Fourteenth Amendment which extends to a personal choice by a mentally competent, terminally ill adult to commit physician-assisted suicide." They relied primarily on *Casey* and *Cruzan v. Director, Missouri Dep't of Health*, 497 U.S. 261 (1990). The *Cruzan* case involved a woman (Nancy Beth Cruzan) who, following a severe automobile accident, had been in a persistent vegetative state for many years and had virtually no chance of regaining her cognitive faculties. She was being kept alive by means of a feeding and hydration tube inserted into her stomach. When Nancy's parents sought to discontinue the tubal feeding, but were rebuffed by officials of the state hospital where Nancy was a patient, they turned to the courts. The state supreme court ruled that, in the absence of a "living will," they had to show "clear and convincing" evidence of Nancy's wish to be free of life support and that they had failed to do so. The U.S. Supreme Court affirmed 5–4, per Rehnquist, C.J., but assumed for purposes of the case that a *competent* person would have "a constitutionally protected right to refuse lifesaving hydration and nutrition."]

We begin, as we do in all due process cases, by examining our Nation's history, legal traditions, and practices. In almost every State—indeed, in almost every western democracy—it is a crime to assist a suicide. The States' assisted-suicide bans are not innovations. Rather, they are longstanding expressions of the States' commitment to the protection and preservation of all human life. [Indeed], opposition to and condemnation of suicide—and, therefore, of assisting suicide—are consistent and enduring themes of our philosophical, legal, and cultural heritages. More specifically, for over 700 years, the Anglo-American common-law tradition has punished or otherwise disapproved of both suicide and assisting suicide.

[For] the most part, the early American colonies adopted the common-law approach. [Over] time, however, [the] colonies abolished [the] harsh common-law penalties [such as forfeiture of the suicide's property. However,] the movement away from the common law's harsh sanctions did not represent an acceptance of suicide, [but instead] reflected the growing consensus that it was unfair to punish the suicide's family for his wrongdoing.

[That] suicide remained a grievous, though nonfelonious, wrong is confirmed by the fact that colonial and early state legislatures and courts did not retreat from prohibiting assisting suicide. [And] the prohibitions against assisted suicide never contained exceptions for those who were near death. [In] this century, the [American Law Institute's] Model Penal Code also prohibited "aiding" suicide, prompting many States to enact or revise their assisted-suicide bans. The code's drafters observed that "the interests in the sanctity of life that are represented by the criminal homicide laws are threatened by one who expresses a willingness to participate in taking the life of another, even though the act may be accomplished with the consent, or at the request, of the suicide victim."

Though deeply rooted, the States' assisted-suicide bans have in recent years been reexamined and, generally, reaffirmed. Because of advances in medicine and technology, Americans today are increasingly likely to die in institutions, from chronic illnesses. Public concern and democratic action are therefore sharply focused on how best to protect dignity and independence at the end of life, with the result that there have been many significant changes in state laws and in the attitudes these laws reflect. Many States, for example, now permit "living wills," surrogate health-care decisionmaking, and the withdrawal or refusal of life-sustaining medical treatment. At the same time, however, voters and legislators continue for the most part to reaffirm their States' prohibitions on assisting suicide.

The Washington statute at issue in this case was enacted in 1975 as part of a revision of that State's criminal code. Four years later, Washington passed its Natural Death Act, which specifically stated that the "withholding or withdrawal of life-sustaining treatment [shall] not, for any purpose, constitute a suicide" and that "[n]othing in this chapter shall be construed to condone, authorize, or approve mercy killing * * * ." In 1991, Washington voters rejected a ballot initiative which, had it passed, would have permitted a form of physician-assisted suicide. Washington then added a provision to the Natural Death Act expressly excluding physician-assisted suicide.

California voters rejected an assisted-suicide initiative similar to Washington's in 1993. On the other hand, in 1994, voters in Oregon enacted, also through ballot initiative, that State's "Death With Dignity Act," which legalized physician-assisted suicide for competent, terminally ill adults. Since the Oregon vote, many proposals to legalize assisted-suicide have been and continue to be introduced in the States' legislatures, but none has been enacted.

[Thus], the States are currently engaged in serious, thoughtful examinations of physician-assisted suicide and other similar issues. For example, New York State's Task Force on Life and the Law—an ongoing, blue-ribbon commission composed of doctors, ethicists, lawyers, religious leaders, and interested laymen—was convened in 1984 and commissioned with "a broad mandate to recommend public policy on issues raised by medical advances." [After] studying physician-assisted suicide, however, the Task Force unanimously concluded that "[l]egalizing assisted suicide and euthanasia would pose profound risks to many individuals who are ill and vulnerable. [T]he potential dangers of this dramatic change in public policy would outweigh any benefit that might be achieved."

[The] Due Process Clause guarantees more than fair process, and the "liberty" it protects includes more than the absence of physical restraint. [The] Clause also provides heightened protection against government interference with certain fundamental rights and liberty interests. [We] have also assumed, and strongly suggested, that the Due Process Clause protects the traditional right to refuse unwanted lifesaving medical treatment. *Cruzan.*

But we "ha[ve] always been reluctant to expand the concept of substantive due process because guideposts for responsible decisionmaking in this unchartered area are scarce and open-ended." By extending constitutional protection to an asserted right or liberty interest, we, to a great extent, place the matter outside the arena of public debate and legislative action. We must therefore "exercise the utmost care whenever we are asked to break new ground in this field," lest the liberty protected by the Due Process Clause be subtly transformed into the policy preferences of the Members of this Court.

Our established method of substantive-due-process analysis has two primary features: First, we have regularly observed that the Due Process Clause specially protects those fundamental rights and liberties which are, objectively, "deeply rooted in this Nation's history and tradition." [Second], we have required in substantive-due-process cases a "careful description" of the asserted fundamental liberty interest.

[Justice] Souter, relying on Justice Harlan's dissenting opinion in *Poe v. Ullman,* would largely abandon this restrained methodology, and instead ask "whether [Washington's] statute sets up one of those 'arbitrary impositions' or 'purposeless restraints' at odds with the Due Process Clause of the Fourteenth Amendment."[17] In our view, however, the development of this Court's substantive-due-process jurisprudence [has] been a process whereby the outlines of the "liberty" specially protected by the Fourteenth Amendment—never fully clarified, to be sure, and perhaps not capable of being fully clarified—have at least been carefully refined by concrete examples involving fundamental rights found to be deeply rooted in our legal tradition. This approach tends to rein in the subjective elements that are necessarily present in due-process judicial review. In addition, by establishing a threshold requirement—that a challenged state action implicate a fundamental right—before requiring more than a reasonable relation to a legitimate state interest to justify the action, it avoids the need for complex balancing of competing interests in every case.

[We] have a tradition of carefully formulating the interest at stake in substantive-due-process cases. For example, although *Cruzan* is often described as a "right to die" case, we were, in fact, more precise: We assumed that the Constitution granted competent persons a "constitutionally protected right to refuse lifesaving hydration and nutrition." The Washington statute at issue in this case prohibits "aid[ing] another person to attempt suicide" and, thus, the question before us is whether the "liberty" specially protected by the Due Process Clause includes a right to commit suicide which itself includes a right to assistance in doing so.

---

[17] [Ct's Note] In Justice Souter's opinion, Justice Harlan's *Poe* dissent supplies the "modern justification" for substantive-due-process review. But although Justice Harlan's opinion has often been cited in due process cases, we have never abandoned our fundamental-rights-based analytical method. [In] *Cruzan,* neither the Court's nor the concurring opinions relied on *Poe;* rather, we concluded that the right to refuse unwanted medical treatment was so rooted in our history, tradition, and practice as to require special protection under the Fourteenth Amendment. True, the Court relied on Justice Harlan's dissent in *Casey,* but [we] did not in so doing jettison our established approach. Indeed, to read such a radical move into the Court's opinion in *Casey* would seem to fly in the face of that opinion's emphasis on stare decisis.

We now inquire whether this asserted right has any place in our Nation's traditions. [Here,] we are confronted with a consistent and almost universal tradition that has long rejected the asserted right, and continues explicitly to reject it today, even for terminally ill, mentally competent adults. To hold for respondents, we would have to reverse centuries of legal doctrine and practice, and strike down the considered policy choice of almost every State.

[Respondents] contend that in *Cruzan* we "acknowledged that competent, dying persons have the right to direct the removal of life-sustaining medical treatment and thus hasten death" and that "the constitutional principle behind recognizing the patient's liberty to direct the withdrawal of artificial life support applies at least as strongly to the choice to hasten impending death by consuming lethal medication." [The] right assumed in *Cruzan,* however, was not simply deduced from abstract concepts of personal autonomy. Given the common-law rule that forced medication was a battery, and the long legal tradition protecting the decision to refuse unwanted medical treatment, our assumption was entirely consistent with this Nation's history and constitutional traditions. The decision to commit suicide with the assistance of another may be just as personal and profound as the decision to refuse unwanted medical treatment, but it has never enjoyed similar legal protection. Indeed, the two acts are widely and reasonably regarded as quite distinct. In *Cruzan* itself, we recognized that most States outlawed assisted suicide—and even more do today—and we certainly gave no intimation that the right to refuse unwanted medical treatment could be somehow transmuted into a right to assistance in committing suicide.

Respondents also rely on *Casey.* [The] Court of Appeals, like the District Court, found *Casey* " 'highly instructive' " and " 'almost prescriptive' " for determining " 'what liberty interest may inhere in a terminally ill person's choice to commit suicide.' " [Similarly], respondents emphasize the statement in *Casey* that: "At the heart of liberty is the right to define one's own concept of existence, of meaning, of the universe, and of the mystery of human life. Beliefs about these matters could not define the attributes of personhood were they formed under compulsion of the State."

By choosing this language, the Court's opinion in *Casey* described, in a general way and in light of our prior cases, those personal activities and decisions that this Court has identified as so deeply rooted in our history and traditions, or so fundamental to our concept of constitutionally ordered liberty, that they are protected by the Fourteenth Amendment. [That] many of the rights and liberties protected by the Due Process Clause sound in personal autonomy does not warrant the sweeping conclusion that any and all important, intimate, and personal decisions are so protected, and *Casey* did not suggest otherwise.

The history of the law's treatment of assisted suicide in this country has been and continues to be one of the rejection of nearly all efforts to permit it. That being the case, our decisions lead us to conclude that the asserted "right" to assistance in committing suicide is not a fundamental liberty interest protected by the Due Process Clause. The Constitution also requires, however, that Washington's assisted-suicide ban be rationally related to legitimate government interests. This requirement is unquestionably met here. As the court below recognized, Washington's assisted-suicide ban implicates a number of state interests.

First, Washington has an "unqualified interest in the preservation of human life." *Cruzan*. The State's prohibition on assisted suicide, like all homicide laws, both reflects and advances its commitment to this interest.

[The] Court of Appeals also recognized Washington's interest in protecting life, but held that the "weight" of this interest depends on the "medical condition and the wishes of the person whose life is at stake." Washington, however, has rejected this sliding-scale approach and, through its assisted-suicide ban, insists that all persons' lives, from beginning to end, regardless of physical or mental condition, are under the full protection of the law. [As] we have previously affirmed, the States "may properly decline to make judgments about the 'quality' of life that a particular individual may enjoy," *Cruzan*. This remains true, as *Cruzan* makes clear, even for those who are near death.

Relatedly, all admit that suicide is a serious public-health problem, especially among persons in otherwise vulnerable groups. [Those] who attempt suicide—terminally ill or not—often suffer from depression or other mental disorders. [Research] indicates, however, that many people who request physician-assisted suicide withdraw that request if their depression and pain are treated. The New York Task Force, however, expressed its concern that, because depression is difficult to diagnose, physicians and medical professionals often fail to respond adequately to seriously ill patients' needs. Thus, legal physician-assisted suicide could make it more difficult for the State to protect depressed or mentally ill persons, or those who are suffering from untreated pain, from suicidal impulses.

The State also has an interest in protecting the integrity and ethics of the medical profession. [The] American Medical Association, like many other medical and physicians' groups, has concluded that "[p]hysician-assisted suicide is fundamentally incompatible with the physician's role as healer." [And] physician-assisted suicide could, it is argued, undermine the trust that is essential to the doctor-patient relationship by blurring the time-honored line between healing and harming.

Next, the State has an interest in protecting vulnerable groups— including the poor, the elderly, and disabled persons—from abuse, neglect, and mistakes. The Court of Appeals dismissed [this] concern, [but we] have recognized [the] real risk of subtle coercion and undue influence in end-of-life situations. *Cruzan*. Similarly, the New York Task Force warned that "[l]egalizing physician-assisted suicide would pose profound risks to many individuals who are ill and vulnerable. [The] risk of harm is greatest for the many individuals in our society whose autonomy and well-being are already compromised by poverty, lack of access to good medical care, advanced age, or membership in a stigmatized social group." [If] physician-assisted suicide were permitted, many might resort to it to spare their families the substantial financial burden of end-of-life health-care costs. The State's interest here goes beyond protecting the vulnerable from coercion; it extends to protecting disabled and terminally ill people from prejudice, negative and inaccurate stereotypes, and "societal indifference."

[Finally,] the State may fear that permitting assisted suicide will start it down the path to voluntary and perhaps even involuntary euthanasia. [The] Court of Appeal's decision, and its expansive reasoning, provide ample support for the State's concerns.[23] [This] concern is further supported by evidence about the practice of euthanasia in the Netherlands. The Dutch government's own [1990 study] suggests that, despite the existence of various reporting procedures, euthanasia in the Netherlands has not been limited to competent, terminally ill adults who are enduring physical suffering, and that regulation of the practice may not have prevented abuses in cases involving vulnerable persons, including severely disabled neonates and elderly persons suffering from dementia. [Washington], like most other States, reasonably ensures against this risk by banning, rather than regulating, assisting suicide.

We need not weigh exactingly the relative strengths of these various interests. They are unquestionably important and legitimate, and Washington's ban on assisted suicide is at least reasonably related to their promotion and protection. We therefore hold that [the challenged Washington statute] does not violate the Fourteenth Amendment, either on its face or "as applied to competent, terminally ill adults who wish to hasten their deaths by obtaining medication prescribed by their doctors."[24]

---

[23] **[Ct's Note]** Justice Souter concludes that "[t]he case for the slippery slope is fairly made out here, not because recognizing one due process right would leave a court with no principled basis to avoid recognizing another, but because there is a plausible case that the right claimed would not be readily containable by reference to facts about the mind that are matters of difficult judgment, or by gatekeepers who are subject to temptation, noble or not." We agree that the case for a slippery slope has been made out, [but] we also recognize the reasonableness of the widely expressed skepticism about the lack of a principled basis for confining the right. See Brief for United States as Amicus Curiae ("Once a legislature abandons a categorical prohibition against physician-assisted suicide, there is no obvious stopping point.")

[24] **[Ct's Note]** Justice Stevens states that "the Court does conceive of respondents' claim as a facial challenge—addressing not the application of the statute to a particular set of plaintiffs before it, but the constitutionality of the statute's categorical prohibition. . . . " We emphasize that we today reject the Court of Appeals' specific holding that the statute is unconstitutional "as applied" to a particular class. Justice Stevens agrees with this holding, but would not "foreclose

[Throughout] the Nation, Americans are engaged in an earnest and profound debate about the morality, legality, and practicality of physician-assisted suicide. Our holding permits this debate to continue, as it should in a democratic society. * * *

JUSTICE O'CONNOR, concurring.*

[The] Court frames the issue [as] whether the Due Process Clause of the Constitution protects a "right to commit suicide which itself includes a right to assistance in doing so," and concludes that our Nation's history, legal traditions, and practices do not support the existence of such a right. I join the Court's opinions because I agree that there is no generalized right to "commit suicide." But respondents urge us to address the narrower question whether a mentally competent person who is experiencing great suffering has a constitutionally cognizable interest in controlling the circumstances of his or her imminent death. I see no need to reach that question in the context of the facial challenges to the New York and Washington laws at issue here. [The] parties and *amici* agree that in these States a patient who is suffering from a terminal illness and who is experiencing great pain has no legal barriers to obtaining medication, from qualified physicians, to alleviate that suffering, even to the point of causing unconsciousness and hastening death. In this light, even assuming that we would recognize such an interest, I agree that the State's interests in protecting those who are not truly competent or facing imminent death, or those whose decisions to hasten death would not truly be voluntary, are sufficiently weighty to justify a prohibition against physician-assisted suicide.

Every one of us at some point may be affected by our own or a family member's terminal illness. There is no reason to think the democratic process will not strike the proper balance between the interests of terminally ill, mentally competent individuals who would seek to end their suffering and the State's interests in protecting those who might seek to end life mistakenly or under pressure.

[In] sum, there is no need to address the question whether suffering patients have a constitutionally cognizable interest in obtaining relief from the suffering that they may experience in the last days of their lives. There is no dispute that dying patients in Washington and New York can obtain

---

the possibility that an individual plaintiff seeking to hasten her death, or a doctor whose assistance was sought, could prevail in a more particularized challenge." Our opinion does not absolutely foreclose such a claim. However, given our holding that the Due Process Clause of the Fourteenth Amendment does not provide heightened protection to the asserted liberty interest in ending one's life with a physician's assistance, such a claim would have to be quite different from the ones advanced by respondents here.

    * **[Ct's Note]** Justice Ginsburg concurs in the Court's judgments substantially for the reasons stated in this opinion. Justice Breyer joins this opinion except insofar as it joins the opinions of the Court. [O'Connor, J.'s opinion also constitutes her concurring opinion in the companion case of *Vacco v. Quill*.]

palliative care, even when doing so would hasten their deaths. The difficulty in defining terminal illness and the risk that a dying patient's request for assistance in ending his or her life might not be truly voluntary justifies the prohibitions on assisted suicide we uphold here.

JUSTICE STEVENS, concurring in the judgments.[350]

[Today,] the Court decides that Washington's statute prohibiting assisted suicide is not invalid "on its face," that is to say, in all or most cases in which it might be applied. That holding, however, does not foreclose the possibility that some applications of the statute might well be invalid.

[The *Cruzan*] Court assumed that the interest in liberty protected by the Fourteenth Amendment encompassed the right of a terminally ill patient to direct the withdrawal of life-sustaining treatment. [That] assumption [was] supported by the common-law tradition protecting the individual's general right to refuse unwanted medical treatment. [However,] [g]iven the irreversible nature of her illness and the progressive character of her suffering, Nancy Cruzan's interest in refusing medical care was incidental to her more basic interest in controlling the manner and timing of her death. [The] source of Nancy Cruzan's right to refuse treatment was not just a common-law rule. Rather, this right is an aspect of a far broader and more basic concept of freedom that is even older than the common law. This freedom embraces, not merely a person's right to refuse a particular kind of unwanted treatment, but also her interest in dignity, and in determining the character of the memories that will survive long after her death.

[Thus,] the common-law right to protection from battery, which included the right to reject medical treatment in most circumstances, did not mark "the outer limits of the substantive sphere of liberty" that supported the Cruzan family's decision to hasten Nancy's death. *Casey.* [Whatever] the outer limits of the concept may be, it definitely includes protection for matters "central to personal dignity and autonomy." *Casey.*

[The] *Cruzan* case demonstrated that some state intrusions on the right to decide how death will be encountered are also intolerable. The now-deceased plaintiffs in this action may in fact have had a liberty interest even stronger than Nancy Cruzan's because, not only were they terminally ill, they were suffering constant and severe pain. Avoiding intolerable pain and the indignity of living one's final days incapacitated and in agony is certainly "[a]t the heart of [the] liberty [to] define one's own concept of existence, of meaning, of the universe, and of the mystery of human life."

[Although] there is no absolute right to physician-assisted suicide, *Cruzan* makes it clear that some individuals who no longer have the option

---

[350] This opinion also constitutes Stevens, J.'s concurring opinion in *Vacco v. Quill*, infra.

of deciding whether to live or to die because they are already on the threshold of death have a constitutionally protected interest that may outweigh the State's interest in preserving life at all costs. The liberty interest at stake in a case like this differs from, and is stronger than, both the common-law right to refuse medical treatment and the unbridled interest in deciding whether to live or die. It is an interest in deciding how, rather than whether, a critical threshold shall be crossed.

The state interests supporting a general rule banning the practice of physician-assisted suicide do not have the same force in all [cases]. Properly viewed, [the interest in preserving human life] is not a collective interest that should always outweigh the interests of a person who because of pain, incapacity, or sedation finds her life intolerable, but rather, an aspect of individual freedom.

[Allowing] the individual, rather than the State, to make judgments " 'about the 'quality' of life that a particular individual may enjoy' " does not mean that the lives of terminally-ill, disabled people have less value than the lives of those who are healthy. Rather, it gives proper recognition to the individual's interest in choosing a final chapter that accords with her life story, rather than one that demeans her values and poisons memories of her. See Brief for Bioethicists as Amici Curiae; see also Ronald Dworkin, *Life's Dominion* 213 (1993).

[The] State's legitimate interest in preventing abuse does not apply to an individual who is not victimized by abuse, who is not suffering from depression, and who makes a rational and voluntary decision to seek assistance in dying. [Encouraging] the development and ensuring the availability of adequate pain treatment is of utmost importance; palliative care, however, cannot alleviate all pain and suffering. [An] individual adequately informed of the care alternatives thus might make a rational choice for assisted suicide. For such an individual, the State's interest in preventing potential abuse and mistake is only minimally implicated.

[Unlike] the Court of Appeals, I would not say as a categorical matter that [the] state interests are invalid as to the entire class of terminally ill, mentally competent patients. I do not, however, foreclose the possibility that an individual plaintiff seeking to hasten her death, or a doctor whose assistance was sought, could prevail in a more particularized challenge. Future cases will determine whether such a challenge may succeed.

JUSTICE SOUTER, concurring in the judgment.

[The question presented] is whether [state law] sets up one of those "arbitrary impositions" or "purposeless restraints" at odds with the Due Process Clause of the Fourteenth Amendment. *Poe v. Ullman* (Harlan, J., dissenting). I conclude that [it does not], but I write separately to give my reasons for analyzing the substantive due process claims as I do, and for rejecting this one.

[The] persistence of substantive due process in our cases points to the legitimacy of the modern justification for such judicial review found in Justice Harlan's dissent in *Poe*,[4] [while] the acknowledged failures of some of these cases point with caution to the difficulty raised by the present claim.

[The *Poe* dissent] is a reminder that the business of [substantive due process] review is not the identification of extratextual absolutes but scrutiny of a legislative resolution (perhaps unconscious) of clashing principles, each quite possibly worthy in and of itself, but each to be weighed within the history of our values as a people. It is a comparison of the relative strengths of opposing claims that informs the judicial task, not a deduction from some first premise. Thus informed, judicial review still has no warrant to substitute one reasonable resolution of the contending positions for another, but authority to supplant the balance already struck between the contenders only when it falls outside the realm of the reasonable.

[Constitutional] recognition of the right to bodily integrity underlies the assumed right, good against the State, to require physicians to terminate artificial life support, *Cruzan,* [and] the affirmative right to obtain medical intervention to cause abortion, see *Casey*. It is, indeed, in the abortion cases that the most telling recognitions of the importance of bodily integrity and the concomitant tradition of medical assistance have occurred. [The] analogies between the abortion cases and this one are several. Even though the State has a legitimate interest in discouraging abortion, the Court recognized a woman's right to a physician's counsel and care. Like the decision to commit suicide, the decision to abort potential life can be made irresponsibly and under the influence of others, and yet the Court has held in the abortion cases that physicians are fit assistants. Without physician assistance in abortion, the woman's right would have too often amounted to nothing more than a right to self-mutilation, and without a physician to assist in the suicide of the dying, the patient's right will often be confined to crude methods of causing death, most shocking and painful to the decedent's survivors.

[The] State claims interests in protecting patients from mistakenly and involuntarily deciding to end their lives, and in guarding against both voluntary and involuntary euthanasia. [The] argument is that a progression would occur, obscuring the line between the ill and the dying, and between the responsible and the unduly influenced, until ultimately doctors and perhaps others would abuse a limited freedom to aid suicides. [Respondents] propose an answer to all this, the answer of state regulation with teeth. Legislation proposed in several States, for example, would

---

[4] **[Ct's Note]** The status of the Harlan dissent in *Poe v. Ullman* is shown by the Court's adoption of its result in *Griswold* and by the Court's acknowledgment of its status and adoption of its reasoning in *Casey*. * * *

authorize physician-assisted suicide but require two qualified physicians to confirm the patient's diagnosis, prognosis, and competence; and would mandate that the patient make repeated requests witnessed by at least two others over a specified timespan; and would impose reporting requirements and criminal penalties for various acts of coercion.

But at least at this moment there are reasons for caution in predicting the effectiveness of the teeth proposed. Respondents' proposals, as it turns out, sound much like the guidelines now in place in the Netherlands, the only place where experience with physician-assisted suicide and euthanasia has yielded empirical evidence about how such regulations might affect actual practice. [There] is, however, a substantial dispute today about what the Dutch experience shows. Some commentators marshall evidence that the Dutch guidelines have in practice failed to protect patients from involuntary euthanasia and have been violated with impunity. This evidence is contested. The day may come when we can say with some assurance which side is right, but for now it is the substantiality of the factual disagreement, and the alternatives for resolving it, that matter. They are, for me, dispositive of the due process claim at this time.

I take it that the basic concept of judicial review with its possible displacement of legislative judgment bars any finding that a legislature has acted arbitrarily when the following conditions are met: there is a serious factual controversy over the feasibility of recognizing the claimed right without at the same time making it impossible for the State to engage in an undoubtedly legitimate exercise of power; facts necessary to resolve the controversy are not readily ascertainable through the judicial process; but they are more readily subject to discovery through legislative factfinding and experimentation. It is assumed in this case, and must be, that a State's interest in protecting those unable to make responsible decisions and those who make no decisions at all entitles the State to bar aid to any but a knowing and responsible person intending suicide, and to prohibit euthanasia. How, and how far, a State should act in that interest are judgments for the State, but the legitimacy of its action to deny a physician the option to aid any but the knowing and responsible is beyond question.

The capacity of the State to protect the others if respondents were to prevail is, however, subject to some genuine question, underscored by the responsible disagreement over the basic facts of the Dutch experience. This factual controversy is not open to a judicial resolution with any substantial degree of assurance at this time. [While] an extensive literature on any subject can raise the hopes for judicial understanding, the literature on this subject is only nascent. Since there is little experience directly bearing on the issue, the most that can be said is that whichever way the Court might rule today, events could overtake its assumptions, as experimentation in some jurisdictions confirmed or discredited the concerns about progression from assisted suicide to euthanasia.

Legislatures, on the other hand, have superior opportunities to obtain the facts necessary for a judgment about the present controversy. [Moreover,] their mechanisms include the power to experiment, moving forward and pulling back as facts emerge within their own jurisdictions. [While] I do not decide for all time that respondents' claim should not be recognized, I acknowledge the legislative institutional competence as the better one to deal with that claim at this time.

JUSTICE GINSBURG, concurring in the judgments.

I concur in the Court's judgments in these cases substantially for the reasons stated by Justice O'Connor in her concurring opinion.

JUSTICE BREYER, concurring in the judgments.

I believe that Justice O'Connor's views, which I share, have greater legal significance than the Court's opinion suggests. I join her separate opinion, except insofar as it joins the majority. And I concur in the judgments. I shall briefly explain how I differ from the Court.

I agree with the Court in *Vacco v. Quill,* [infra] that the articulated state interests justify the distinction drawn between physician assisted suicide and withdrawal of life-support. I also agree [that] the critical question in both of the cases before us is whether "the 'liberty' specially protected by the Due Process Clause includes a right" of the sort that the respondents assert. I do not agree, however, with the Court's formulation of that claimed "liberty" interest. The Court describes it as a "right to commit suicide with another's assistance." But I would not reject the respondents' claim without considering a different formulation, for which our legal tradition may provide greater support. That formulation would use words roughly like a "right to die with dignity." But irrespective of the exact words used, at its core would lie personal control over the manner of death, professional medical assistance, and the avoidance of unnecessary and severe physical suffering—combined.

As Justice Souter points out, Justice Harlan's dissenting opinion in *Poe* offers some support for such a claim. In that opinion, Justice Harlan [recognized] that "*certain interests* require particularly careful scrutiny of the state needs asserted to justify their abridgment." The "certain interests" to which Justice Harlan referred may well be similar (perhaps identical) to the rights, liberties, or interests that the Court today, as in the past, regards as "fundamental."

Justice Harlan concluded that marital privacy was such a "special interest." He found in the Constitution a right of "privacy of the home"—with the home, the bedroom, and "intimate details of the marital relation" at its heart—by examining the protection that the law had earlier provided for related, but not identical, interests described by such words as "privacy," "home," and "family." The respondents here essentially ask us to do the same. They argue that one can find a "right to die with dignity" by examining the protection the law has provided for related, but not identical, interests relating to personal dignity, medical treatment, and freedom from state-inflicted pain.

I do not believe, however, that this Court need or now should decide whether or a not such a right is "fundamental." That is because, in my view, the avoidance of severe physical pain (connected with death) would have to comprise an essential part of any successful claim and because, as Justice O'Connor points out, the laws before us do not *force* a dying person to undergo that kind of pain. Rather, the laws of New York and of Washington do not prohibit doctors from providing patients with drugs sufficient to control pain despite the risk that those drugs themselves will kill. And under these circumstances the laws of New York and Washington would overcome any remaining significant interests and would be justified, regardless.

[Were] the legal circumstances different—for example, were state law to prevent the provision of palliative care, including the administration of drugs as needed to avoid pain at the end of life—then the law's impact upon serious and otherwise unavoidable physical pain (accompanying death) would be more directly at issue. And as Justice O'Connor suggests, the Court might have to revisit its conclusions in these cases.

———

In a companion case to *Glucksberg*, VACCO v. QUILL, 521 U.S. 793 (1997), the Court without a dissent, rejected the argument that because New York permits competent persons to refuse lifesaving medical treatment, and the refusal of such treatment is "essentially the same thing" as physician-assisted suicide, the state's assisted suicide ban violates the Equal Protection Clause. REHNQUIST, C.J., again wrote for the Court: "[The] Equal Protection Clause [embodies] a general rule that States must treat like cases alike but may treat unlike cases accordingly. If a legislative classification or distinction 'neither burdens a fundamental right nor targets a suspect class, we will uphold [it] so long as it bears a rational relation to some legitimate end.' *Romer v. Evans* [p. 1513 infra]. [On] their faces, neither New York's ban on assisting suicide nor its statutes permitting patients to refuse medical treatment treat anyone differently from anyone else or draw any distinctions between persons. *Everyone,* regardless of physical condition, is entitled, if competent, to refuse unwanted lifesaving medical treatment; *no one* is permitted to assist a suicide.

"[The] Court of Appeals, however, concluded that some terminally ill people—those who are on life-support systems—are treated differently from those who are not, in that the former may 'hasten death' by ending treatment, but the latter may not 'hasten death' through physician-assisted suicide. This conclusion depends on the submission that ending or refusing lifesaving medical treatment 'is nothing more nor less than assisted suicide.' Unlike the Court of Appeals, we think the distinction between assisting suicide and withdrawing life-sustaining treatment, a distinction widely recognized and endorsed in the medical profession and in our legal traditions, is both important and logical; it is certainly rational.

"The distinction comports with fundamental legal principles of causation and intent. First, when a patient refuses life-sustaining medical treatment, he dies from an underlying fatal disease or pathology; but if a patient ingests lethal medication prescribed by a physician, he is killed by that medication. [Furthermore,] a physician who withdraws, or honors a patient's refusal to begin, life-sustaining medical treatment purposefully intends, or may so intend, only to respect his patient's wishes and 'to cease doing useless and futile or degrading things to the patient when [the patient] no longer stands to benefit from them.' The same is true when a doctor provides aggressive palliative care; in some cases, painkilling drugs may hasten a patient's death, but the physician's purpose and intent is, or may be, only to ease his patient's pain. A doctor who assists a suicide, however, 'must, necessarily and indubitably, intend primarily that the patient be made dead.' Similarly, a patient who commits suicide with a doctor's aid necessarily has the specific intent to end his or her own life, while a patient who refuses or discontinues treatment might not. [The] law has long used actors' intent or purpose to distinguish between two acts that may have the same result. [Put] differently, the law distinguishes actions taken 'because of' a given end from actions taken 'in spite of' their unintended but foreseen consequences.

"[Given] these general principles, it is not surprising that many courts, including New York courts, have carefully distinguished refusing life-sustaining treatment from suicide. [Similarly], the overwhelming majority of state legislatures have drawn a clear line between assisting suicide and withdrawing or permitting the refusal of unwanted lifesaving medical treatment by prohibiting the former and permitting the latter.

"[New York] is a case in point. [It] has acted several times to protect patients' common-law right to refuse treatment [but] reaffirmed the line between 'killing' and 'letting die.' [Recently], the New York State Task Force on Life and the Law studied assisted suicide and euthanasia and, in 1994, unanimously recommended against legalization.

"[This] Court has also recognized, at least implicitly, the distinction between letting a patient die and making that patient die. In *Cruzan* our assumption of a right to refuse treatment was grounded not, as the Court of Appeals supposed, on the proposition that patients have a general and abstract 'right to hasten death,' but on well established, traditional rights to bodily integrity and freedom from unwanted touching. In fact, we observed that 'the majority of States in this country have laws imposing criminal penalties on one who assists another to commit suicide.' *Cruzan* therefore provides no support for the notion that refusing life-sustaining medical treatment is 'nothing more nor less than suicide.'

"For all these reasons, we disagree with respondents' claim that the distinction between refusing lifesaving medical treatment and assisted suicide is 'arbitrary' and 'irrational.'[11] [By] permitting everyone to refuse unwanted medical treatment while prohibiting anyone from assisting a suicide, New York law follows a longstanding and rational distinction.

"New York's reasons for recognizing and acting on this distinction—including prohibiting intentional killing and preserving life; preventing suicide; maintaining physicians' role as their patients' healers; protecting vulnerable people from indifference, prejudice, and psychological and financial pressure to end their lives; and avoiding a possible slide towards euthanasia—are discussed in greater detail in our opinion in *Glucksberg*. These valid and important public interests easily satisfy the constitutional requirement that a legislative classification bear a rational relation to some legitimate end.[13]"

STEVENS, J., concurring in the judgment, "agree[d] that the distinction between permitting death to ensue from an underlying fatal disease and causing it to occur by the administration of medication or other means provides a constitutionally sufficient basis for the State's classification." However, unlike the Court, he was "not persuaded that in all cases there will in fact be a significant difference between the intent of the physicians, the patients or the families in the two situations." He continued:

"The illusory character of any differences in intent or causation is confirmed by the fact that the American Medical Association unequivocally endorses the practice of terminal sedation—the administration of sufficient dosages of pain-killing medication to terminally ill patients to protect them from excruciating pain even when it is clear that the time of death will be

---

[11] **[Ct's Note]** Respondents also argue that the State irrationally distinguishes between physician-assisted suicide and "terminal sedation," a process respondents characterize as "induc[ing] barbiturate coma and then starv[ing] the person to death." Petitioners insist, however, that " '[a]lthough proponents of physician-assisted suicide and euthanasia contend that terminal sedation is covert physician-assisted suicide or euthanasia, the concept of sedating pharmacotherapy is based on informed consent and the principle of double effect.' " Just as a State may prohibit assisting suicide while permitting patients to refuse unwanted lifesaving treatment, it may permit palliative care related to that refusal, which may have the foreseen but unintended "double effect" of hastening the patient's death.

[13] **[Ct's Note]** Justice Stevens observes that our holding today "does not foreclose the possibility that some applications of the New York statute may impose an intolerable intrusion on the patient's freedom." This is true, but, as we observe in *Glucksberg,* a particular plaintiff hoping to show that New York's assisted-suicide ban was unconstitutional in his particular case would need to present different and considerably stronger arguments than those advanced by respondents here.

advanced. [Thus,] although the differences the majority notes in causation and intent between terminating life-support and assisting in suicide support the Court's rejection of the respondents' facial challenge, these distinctions may be inapplicable to particular terminally ill patients and their doctors. Our holding today in *Quill* [just] like our holding in [*Glucksberg,*] does not foreclose the possibility that some applications of the New York statute may impose an intolerable intrusion on the patient's freedom."[351]

NOTES AND QUESTIONS

1.   *Judicial restraint in the face of novel claims of constitutional rights.* Consider Michael W. McConnell, *The Right to Die and the Jurisprudence of Tradition*, 1997 Utah L.Rev. 665: "The question of assisted suicide provides an excellent context for consideration of the institutional dimensions of judicial review of novel claims of constitutional right, precisely because of the unambiguous character of the historical record. The case for a right to assisted suicide rested entirely on philosophical, not historical, premises and the case thus highlighted the pitfalls of constitutional decision making based on such premises. Under the moral philosophic approach, courts are instructed to determine for themselves what is the best answer to the problem posed. Indeed, in *Glucksberg*, the Court had the benefit of an unusual amicus curiae brief, signed by six of America's leading political philosophers, which argued that the Court *should* recognize the right of terminally ill patients to the assistance of doctors in shortening their lives.

"But there is every reason for courts to be wary about overturning duly enacted legislation on the basis of untried and uncertain moral and philosophical arguments, where the result is bereft of support in directly relevant constitutional text or in national experience. It may well be true that attitudes about the end of life have changed, or will change, in response to technological developments and their attendant economic and emotional consequences. But no one knows what the actual consequences of various possible policies would be. It would be a grave mistake for the federal courts to leap in and attempt, prematurely, to resolve the issue or to accelerate the pace of change. Even on the heuristic assumption that laws against assisted suicide and euthanasia should be relaxed in some fashion, it is better that reform take place in decentralized and accountable institutions.

"A jurisprudence grounded in text and tradition is not hostile to social change, but it assigns the responsibility to determine the pace and direction of change to representative bodies. [The] great institutional strength of courts is their ability to provide uniform enforcement of legal principles, with

---

[351] Souter, J., who concurred in the judgment, observed that the reasons which led him to conclude that the challenged statute in *Glucksberg* was "not arbitrary under the due process standard also support the distinction between assistance to suicide, which is banned, and practices such as termination of artificial life support and death-hastening pain medication, which are permitted." The concurring opinions of O'Connor, Ginsburg and Breyer, JJ., in *Glucksberg* also constituted their concurrences in *Vacco*.

consistency across parties, regions, and time periods, treating like cases alike. Where operative principles are in flux and the consequences of new approaches are unpredictable, however, that virtue becomes a vice. Constitutional judicial review is too inflexible a process to deal sensitively and appropriately with the question of assisted suicide.

"[By] locating the right to die in the federal constitution, judicial recognition of such a right would nationalize the issue and eliminate the possibility of state variation and experimentation. [There] was no serious argument in *Glucksberg* that national uniformity is necessary or even desirable. The state of Oregon has undertaken an experiment in physician-assisted suicide [that] will cast light on the practical consequences: on the efficacy of the safeguards against abuse, on the ability of the medical profession to recognize and treat clinical depression and pain in patients requesting suicide, on the robustness of the lines drawn between permitted and forbidden forms of the right to die, and on the danger that death will come to be perceived as a duty owed to family and society. To treat this social policy question as controlled by federal constitutional law is to eliminate the possibility of a multiplicity of approaches, and of regional variation in light of differences in social and moral perceptions."

2. ***Pain relief and "double effect."*** Providing medication to terminally ill people knowing that it will have a "double effect"—reduce the patient's pain and hasten death—is widely accepted by the medical profession. The double effect principle also plays an important role in the international law of war: although armed forces may not target civilians, the law of war permits foreseen but collateral civilian casualties resulting from attacks against combatants, so long as the collateral harm is "proportionate" to the military objective. See Protocol Additional to the Geneva Conventions of 12 August 1949, and Relating to the Protection of Victims of International Armed Conflicts, art. 51, ¶ 5(b), June 8, 1977, 1125 U.N.T.S. 3. (The United States signed but never ratified this Protocol.) In addition, the doctrine of double effect has been offered as a justification for a right to abortion even assuming the fetus is a person. *See* Thomson *supra*. Relying on the principle of double effect, many physicians and bioethicists seem to believe that providing pain relief is always justifiable, regardless of how certain or probable the risk of death may be.

But does the physician's motive to relieve pain necessarily prevent criminal liability? According to Norman Cantor & George Thomas, *Pain Relief, Acceleration of Death, and Criminal Law,* 6 Kennedy Inst. of Ethics J. 107 (June, 1996), the answer is no. They argue that if no analgesic dosage could provide pain relief without also causing prompt death (or if under the circumstances it was almost certain that the required analgesic dosage would cause death) the physician who administered the analgesic would be criminally liable for the resulting death even though death was not intended. Under the law in most U.S. jurisdictions, criminal liability for homicide attaches when the actor intentionally takes actions that he knows will cause death, even if causing death is not his motive or purpose; indeed, the authors note that even if it were only *highly likely* that the administration of an analgesic would cause prompt death, the physician who used the painkillers that caused the death would also be criminally liable for having acted very recklessly. They argue further that a defense of justification would be unavailable: "The uniform judicial position in the United States that euthanasia is always unjustified homicide reflects a view that pain relief can never outweigh the harm of purposely causing a premature death."

In her concurring opinion in *Cruzan*, O'Connor, J. noted that both New York and Washington permit palliative care even if it has the double effect of killing the patient, but the analysis of Cantor and Thomas suggests that the application of ordinary principles of criminal law could render double effect unavailable in other states. If a case from one of those other states were to come before the Court, would the result be different? The Court's personnel have changed since *Cruzan*, but even at the time the case was decided, the answer is not entirely clear.

O'Connor, J., concurred in the majority opinions in *Glucksberg* and *Quill*. Ginsburg and Breyer, JJ., agreed with O'Connor, J.'s concurrence, but not with the majority, while Stevens and Souter, JJ., did not join the majority or the concurrence of O'Connor, J. Under these circumstances, is it fair to treat the opinion of O'Connor, J., rather than the majority opinions of Rehnquist, C.J., as controlling? If so, what propositions, if any, did the two cases decide?

Consider Cass R. Sunstein, *One Case at a Time: Judicial Minimalism on the Supreme Court* 89 (1999): "it is extremely difficult to produce any verbal formula that is satisfying, consistent with current law, and adequate to resolve the issue of physician-assisted suicide. For this reason, the best [route] is for the Court simply to assume that the right qualifies as fundamental and to proceed from there to the question of justification. [Although] Chief Justice Rehnquist rejected this route, five justices appeared to leave it open as a possibility." Thus, according to Robert A. Burt, *The Supreme Court Speaks: Not Assisted Suicide but a Constitutional Right to Palliative Care*, 337 New Eng. J. Med, 1234 (1997), a "Court majority effectively required all states to ensure that their laws do not obstruct the provision of adequate palliative care, especially for the alleviation of pain and other physical symptoms of people facing death." See also Lawrence O. Gostin, *Deciding Life and Death in the Courtroom*, 278 JAMA 1523 (1997); Yale Kamisar, *On the Meaning and Impact of the Physician-Assisted Suicide Cases,* 82 Minn. L. Rev. 895 (1998).

3.   ***The second-degree murder conviction of Dr. Kevorkian.*** In March 1999, after having assisted over 100 suicides, and after having been acquitted of assisted suicide in several previous cases, Dr. Jack Kevorkian was convicted of second-degree murder (and sentenced to 10 to 25 years in prison) for administering a lethal injection to Lou Gehrig's disease patient Thomas Youk. *The New York Times* editorialized, March 27, 1999, p. A26: "Most advocates of physician-assisted suicide hold as a first principle that the patient must be the one in full control. The Oregon laws that have legalized assisted suicide, for example, honor that principle. Dr. Kevorkian's mercy killing

violates it. Previous juries have let him off the hook for assisting in suicides. But this jury drew the line at direct killing."

Is this the message of the Kevorkian conviction? How significant was it that a video recording of Kevorkian injecting Youk with a lethal dose was shown on CBS's "60 Minutes" in a segment in which Kevorkian dared prosecutors to charge him? How significant was it that the trial judge ruled that the issue of whether Mr. Youk consented to his death was irrelevant and that the jury never heard Youk's wife or mother or brother tell how grateful they were that Kevorkian was available? How significant was it that in all the previous cases Dr. Kevorkian had been represented by Geoffrey Fieger, a prominent trial attorney, but in the Youk case he represented himself?

4. *State experimentation.* At the time *Glucksberg* was decided, Oregon, pursuant to a 1994 ballot initiative, was the only state that permitted physician-assisted suicide. The state of Washington legalized it by ballot initiative in 2008, and Vermont did so by legislation in 2013. In *Baxter v. State*, 224 P.3d 1211 (2009), the Supreme Court of Montana construed that state's Rights of the Terminally Ill Act to permit a doctor charged with aiding a suicide to defend on grounds of consent, thereby avoiding the question of whether there was a right to physician-assisted suicide under the state constitution. Does the fact that the practice remains illegal in the overwhelming majority of states show that the *Glucksberg* Court was correct in rejecting the claim of a "deeply rooted" fundamental right? Does the experience in the states show that opponents' concerns were unfounded? Consider Kathryn L. Tucker, *In the Laboratory of the States: The Progress of Glucksberg's Invitation to States to Address End-of-Life Choices*, 106 Mich.L.Rev. 1593 (2008): "The [Oregon] data demonstrate that the option of physician-assisted dying has not been unwillingly forced upon those who are poor, uneducated, uninsured, or otherwise disadvantaged. In fact, the studies show just the opposite." (Tucker argued *Glucksberg* for the plaintiffs before the Supreme Court.)[352]

---

[352] *Glucksberg* and *Quill* have generated a considerable volume of commentary. In addition to the material discussed above, see, e.g., *Symposium: Physician-Assisted Suicide: Facing Death after Glucksberg and Quill*, 82 Minn. L. Rev. 885–1101 (1998) (contributions by Howard Brody, Robert Burt, Ezekiel Emanual, Yale Kamisar, Patricia King, Sylvia Law, Kathryn Tucker, Leslie Wolf, and Susan Wolf); Yale Kamisar, *Are the Distinctions Drawn in the Debate about End-of-Life Decision Making "Principled"? If Not, How Much Does It Matter?*, 40 J. Law, Med. & Ethics 66 (Spring 2012); Martha Minow, *Which Question? Which Lie? Reflections on the Physician-Assisted Suicide Cases*, 1997 Sup. Ct. Rev. 1; David Orentlicher, *The Supreme Court and Physician-Assisted Suicide: Rejecting Assisted Suicide, but Embracing Euthanasia*, 337 New Eng. J. Med. 1236 (1997); Robert A. Sedler, *Abortion, Physician-Assisted Suicide and the Constitution: The View from Without and Within*, 12 Notre Dame J. L., Ethics & Pub. Policy 529 (1998); Sonia M. Suter, *Ambivalent Unanimity: An Analysis of the Supreme Court's Holding*, in Law at the End of Life 25 (Carl E. Schneider ed. 2000); Leading Case: *Physician-Assisted Suicide*, 111 Harv. L. Rev. 237 (1997).

Sexual Liberty

BOWERS V. HARDWICK

478 U.S. 186, 106 S.Ct. 2841, 92 L.Ed.2d 140 (1986).

JUSTICE WHITE delivered the opinion of the Court.

In August 1982, respondent [was] charged with violating the Georgia statute criminalizing sodomy[1] by committing that act with another adult male in the bedroom of respondent's home. After a preliminary hearing, the District Attorney decided not to present the matter to the grand jury unless further evidence developed.

Respondent then brought suit in the Federal District Court, challenging the constitutionality of the statute insofar as it criminalized consensual sodomy.[2] He asserted that he was a practicing homosexual, that the Georgia statute [placed] him in imminent danger of arrest, and that the statute [violated the] Constitution. The District Court [dismissed the suit] for failure to state a claim. [The] Court of Appeals for the Eleventh Circuit reversed, holding] that the Georgia statute violated respondent's fundamental rights because his homosexual activity is a private and intimate association that is beyond the reach of state regulation by reason of the Ninth Amendment and the Due Process Clause. [We reverse.]

This case does not require a judgment on whether laws against sodomy between consenting adults in general, or between homosexuals in particular, are wise or desirable. [T]he issue presented is whether the Federal Constitution confers a fundamental right upon homosexuals to engage in sodomy and hence invalidates the laws of the many States that still make such conduct illegal and have done so for a very long time. The case also calls for some judgment about the limits of the Court's role in carrying out its constitutional mandate.

We first register our disagreement with the Court of Appeals [that] the Court's prior cases have construed the Constitution to confer a right of

---

[1] [Ct's Note] Ga.Code Ann. § 16–6–2 (1984) provides, in pertinent part, as follows:

"(a) A person commits the offense of sodomy when he performs or submits to any sexual act involving the sex organs of one person and the mouth or anus of [another].

"(b) A person convicted of the offense of sodomy shall be punished by imprisonment for not less than one nor more than 20 [years]."

[2] [Ct's Note] John and Mary Doe were also plaintiffs in the action. They alleged that they wished to engage in sexual activity proscribed by § 16–6–2 in the privacy of their home, and that they had been "chilled and deterred" from engaging in such activity by both the existence of the statute and Hardwick's arrest. The District Court held, however, that because they had neither sustained, nor were in immediate danger of sustaining, any direct injury from the enforcement of the statute, they did not have proper standing to maintain the action. The Court of Appeals affirmed [and] the Does do not challenge that holding in this Court.

The only claim properly before the Court, therefore, is Hardwick's challenge to the Georgia statute as applied to consensual homosexual sodomy. We express no opinion on the constitutionality of the Georgia statute as applied to other acts of sodomy.

privacy that extends to homosexual sodomy and for all intents and purposes have decided this case. [We] think it evident that none of the rights announced in [such cases as *Skinner, Griswold* and *Roe*] bears any resemblance to the claimed constitutional right of homosexuals to engage in acts of sodomy that is asserted in this case. No connection between family, marriage, or procreation on the one hand and homosexual activity on the other has been [demonstrated]. Moreover, any claim that these cases nevertheless stand for the proposition that any kind of private sexual conduct between consenting adults is constitutionally insulated from state proscription is unsupportable. [Precedent] aside, however, respondent would have us announce [a] fundamental right to engage in homosexual sodomy. This we are quite unwilling to do.

[Striving] to assure itself and the public that announcing rights not readily identifiable in the Constitution's text involves much more than the imposition of the Justices' own choice of values on the States and the Federal Government, the Court has sought to identify the nature of the rights qualifying for heightened judicial protection. In *Palko* it was said that this category includes those fundamental liberties that are "implicit in the concept of ordered liberty," such that "neither liberty nor justice would exist if [they] were sacrificed." A different description of fundamental liberties appeared in *Moore v. East Cleveland* (opinion of Powell, J.) [p. 501 supra], where they are characterized as those liberties that are "deeply rooted in this Nation's history and tradition."

It is obvious to us that neither of these formulations would extend a fundamental right to homosexuals to engage in acts of consensual sodomy. Proscriptions against that conduct have ancient roots. Sodomy was a criminal offense at common law and was forbidden by the laws of the original thirteen States when they ratified the Bill of Rights. In 1868, when the Fourteenth Amendment was ratified, all but 5 of the 37 States in the Union had criminal sodomy laws. In fact, until 1961, all 50 States outlawed sodomy, and today, 24 States and the District of Columbia continue to provide criminal penalties for sodomy performed in private and between consenting adults. Against this background, to claim that a right to engage in such conduct is "deeply rooted in this Nation's history and tradition" or "implicit in the concept of ordered liberty" is, at best, facetious.

Nor are we inclined to take a more expansive view of our authority to discover new fundamental rights imbedded in the Due Process Clause. The Court is most vulnerable and comes nearest to illegitimacy when it deals with judge-made constitutional law having little or no cognizable roots in the language or design of the Constitution. [There] should be, therefore, great resistance to expand the substantive reach of [the due process clauses], particularly if it requires redefining the category of rights deemed to be fundamental. Otherwise, the Judiciary necessarily takes to itself further authority to govern the country without express constitutional authority.

[Respondent], however, asserts that the result should be different where the homosexual conduct occurs in the privacy of the home. He relies on *Stanley v. Georgia*, 384 U.S. 557 (1969), where the Court held that the First Amendment prevents conviction for possessing and reading obscene material in the privacy of one's home. [*Stanley*] did protect conduct that would not have been protected outside the home, and it partially prevented the enforcement of state obscenity laws; but the decision was firmly grounded in the First Amendment. The right pressed upon us here has no similar support in the text of the Constitution. [Its] limits are also difficult to discern. Plainly enough, otherwise illegal conduct is not always immunized whenever it occurs in the home. Victimless crimes, such as the possession and use of illegal drugs, do not escape the law where they are committed at home. [And] if respondent's submission is limited to the voluntary sexual conduct between consenting adults, it would be difficult, except by fiat, to limit the claimed right to homosexual conduct while leaving exposed to prosecution adultery, incest, and other sexual crimes even though they are committed in the home. We are unwilling to start down that road.

Even if the conduct at issue here is not a fundamental right, respondent asserts that there must be a rational basis for the law and that there is none in this case other than the presumed belief of a majority of the electorate in Georgia that homosexual sodomy is immoral and unacceptable. [The] law, however, is constantly based on notions of morality, and if all laws representing essentially moral choices are to be invalidated under the Due Process Clause, the courts will be very busy indeed. [Reversed.][8]

CHIEF JUSTICE BURGER, concurring.

I join the Court's opinion, but I write separately to underscore my view that in constitutional terms there is no such thing as a fundamental right to commit homosexual sodomy. [To] hold that the act of homosexual sodomy is somehow protected as a fundamental right would be to cast aside millennia of moral teaching. * * *

JUSTICE POWELL, concurring.

[I] agree with the Court that there is no fundamental right [such] as that claimed by respondent. [This] is not to suggest, however, that respondent may not be protected by the Eighth Amendment. [The] Georgia statute at issue in this case authorizes a court to imprison a person for up to 20 years for a single private, consensual act of sodomy. In my view, a

---

[8] **[Ct's Note]** Respondent does not defend the judgment below based on the Ninth Amendment, the Equal Protection Clause, or the Eighth Amendment.

prison sentence for such conduct—certainly a sentence of long duration—would create a serious Eighth Amendment issue. [In] this case, however, respondent has not been tried, much less convicted and sentenced.[2] * * *

JUSTICE BLACKMUN, with whom JUSTICE BRENNAN, JUSTICE MARSHALL, and JUSTICE STEVENS join, dissenting.

This case is no more about "a fundamental right to engage in homosexual sodomy," as the Court purports to declare, than *Stanley* was about a fundamental right to watch obscene movies. [Rather,] this case is about "the most comprehensive of rights and the right most valued by civilized men," namely, "the right to be let alone." *Olmstead v. United States,* 277 U.S. 438 (1928) (Brandeis, J., dissenting). [We] must analyze respondent's claim in the light of the values that underlie the constitutional right to privacy. If that right means anything, it means that, before Georgia can prosecute its citizens for making choices about the most intimate aspects of their lives, it must do more than assert that the choice they have made is an " 'abominable crime not fit to be named among Christians.' "

[The] Court's almost obsessive focus on homosexual activity is particularly hard to justify in light of the broad language Georgia has used. Unlike the Court, the Georgia Legislature has not proceeded on the assumption that homosexuals are so different from other citizens that their lives may be controlled in a way that would not be tolerated if it limited the choices of those other citizens. Rather, Georgia has provided that "[a] person commits the offense of sodomy when he performs or submits to any sexual act involving the sex organs of one person and the mouth or anus of another." The sex or status of the persons who engage in the act is irrelevant as a matter of state law.

[Only] the most willful blindness could obscure the fact that sexual intimacy is "a sensitive, key relationship of human existence, central to family life, community welfare, and the development of human personality." The fact that individuals define themselves in a significant way through their intimate sexual relationships with others suggests, in a Nation as diverse as ours, that there may be many "right" ways of conducting those relationships, and that much of the richness of a relationship will come from the freedom an individual has to *choose* the form and nature of these intensely personal bonds. See Kenneth Karst, *The Freedom of Intimate Association,* 89 Yale L.J. 624 (1980).

---

2   [Ct's Note] It was conceded at oral argument that, prior to the complaint against respondent Hardwick, there had been no reported decision involving prosecution for private homosexual sodomy under this statute for several decades. Moreover, the State has declined to present the criminal charge against Hardwick to a grand jury, and this is a suit for declaratory judgment brought by respondents challenging the validity of the statute. The history of nonenforcement suggests the moribund character today of laws criminalizing this type of private, consensual conduct. Some 26 states have repealed similar statutes. But the constitutional validity of the Georgia statute was put in issue by respondents, and for the reasons stated by the Court, I cannot say that conduct condemned for hundreds of years has now become a fundamental right.

[The] Court claims that its decision today merely refuses to recognize a fundamental right to engage in homosexual sodomy; what the Court really has refused to recognize is the fundamental interest all individuals have in controlling the nature of their intimate associations with others.

[The] Court's failure to comprehend the magnitude of the liberty interests at stake in this case leads it to slight the question whether petitioner [has] justified Georgia's infringement on these interests. I believe that neither of the two general justifications [that] petitioner has advanced warrants dismissing respondent's challenge for failure to state a claim.

First, petitioner asserts that the acts made criminal by the statute may have serious adverse consequences for "the general public health and welfare," such as spreading communicable diseases or fostering other criminal activity. [Nothing in the record] provides any justification for finding the activity forbidden [to] be physically dangerous, either to the persons engaged in it or to others.

The core of petitioner's defense of [the law], however, is that respondent and others who engage in the [prohibited conduct] interfere with Georgia's exercise of the " 'right of the Nation and of the States to maintain a decent society,' " *Paris Adult Theatre* [Ch. 7, Sec. 1, IV, A]. Essentially, petitioner argues, and the Court agrees, that the fact that the [prohibited acts] "for hundreds of years, if not thousands, have been uniformly condemned as immoral" is a sufficient reason to permit a State to ban them today. I cannot agree that either the length of time a majority has held its convictions or the passions with which it defends them can withdraw legislation from this Court's scrutiny [citing *Roe, Loving* and *Brown*].[5]

The assertion that "traditional Judeo-Christian values proscribe" the conduct involved cannot provide an adequate justification for [the law]. That certain, but by no means all, religious groups condemn the behavior at issue gives the State no license to impose their judgments on the entire citizenry. The legitimacy of secular legislation depends instead on whether the State can advance some justification for its law beyond its conformity to religious doctrine.

[Petitioner] and the Court fail to see the difference between laws that protect public sensibilities and those that enforce private morality. [The]

---

[5]   **[Ct's Note]** The parallel between *Loving* and this case is almost uncanny. There, too, the State relied on a religious justification for its law. [There], too, defenders of the challenged statute relied heavily on the fact that when the Fourteenth Amendment was ratified, most of the States had similar prohibitions. There, too, at the time the case came before the Court, many of the States still had criminal statutes concerning the conduct at issue. [Yet] the Court held, not only that the invidious racism of Virginia's law violated the Equal Protection Clause, but also that the law deprived the Lovings of due process by denying them the "freedom of choice to marry" that had "long been recognized as one of the vital personal rights essential to the orderly pursuit of happiness by free men."

mere fact that intimate behavior may be punished when it takes place in public cannot dictate how States can regulate intimate behavior that occurs in intimate places.

This case involves no real interference with the rights of others, for the mere knowledge that other individuals do not adhere to one's value system cannot be a legally cognizable interest, let alone an interest that can justify invading the houses, hearts, and minds of citizens who choose to live their lives differently. [I] can only hope that [the] Court soon will reconsider its analysis and conclude that depriving individuals of the right to choose for themselves how to conduct their intimate relationships poses a far greater threat to the values most deeply rooted in our Nation's history than tolerance of nonconformity could ever do. * * *

JUSTICE STEVENS, with whom JUSTICE BRENNAN and JUSTICE MARSHALL join, dissenting.

Like the statute that is challenged in this case, the rationale of the Court's opinion applies equally to the prohibited conduct regardless of whether the parties who engage in it are married or unmarried, or are of the same or different sexes. Sodomy was condemned as an odious and sinful type of behavior during the formative period of the common law. That condemnation was equally damning for heterosexual and homosexual sodomy. Moreover, it provided no special exemption for married couples. The license to cohabit and to produce legitimate offspring simply did not include any permission to engage in sexual conduct that was considered a "crime against nature."

[Because] the Georgia statute expresses the traditional view that sodomy is an immoral kind of conduct regardless of the identity of the persons who engage in it, I believe that a proper analysis of its constitutionality requires consideration of two questions: First, may a State totally prohibit the described conduct by means of a neutral law applying without exception to all persons subject to its jurisdiction? If not, may the State save the statute by announcing that it will only enforce the law against homosexuals? The two questions merit separate discussion.

Our prior cases make two propositions abundantly clear. First, the fact that the governing majority in a State has traditionally viewed a particular practice as immoral is not a sufficient reason for upholding a law prohibiting the practice; neither history nor tradition could save a law prohibiting miscegenation from constitutional attack.[9] Second, individual decisions by married persons, concerning the intimacies of their physical relationship, even when not intended to produce offspring, are a form of "liberty" protected by [due process]. *Griswold*. Moreover, this protection

---

[9]   [Ct's Note] See *Loving*. Interestingly, miscegenation was once treated as a crime similar to sodomy.

extends to intimate choices by unmarried as well as married persons. *Carey; Eisenstadt.*

[When] individual married couples are isolated from observation by others, the way in which they voluntarily choose to conduct their intimate relations is a matter for them—not the State—to decide.[10] The essential "liberty" that animated the development of the law in cases like *Griswold, Eisenstadt,* and *Carey* surely embraces the right to engage in nonreproductive, sexual conduct that others may consider offensive or immoral.

Paradoxical as it may seem, our prior cases thus establish that a State may not prohibit sodomy within "the sacred precincts of marital bedrooms," *Griswold,* or, indeed, between unmarried heterosexual adults. *Eisenstadt.* [If] the Georgia statute cannot be enforced as it is written—if the conduct it seeks to prohibit is a protected form of liberty for the vast majority of Georgia's citizens—the State must assume the burden of justifying a selective application of its law. Either the persons to whom Georgia seeks to apply its statute do not have the same interest in "liberty" that others have, or there must be a reason why the State may be permitted to apply a generally applicable law to certain persons that it does not apply to others.

The first possibility is plainly unacceptable. [From] the standpoint of the individual, the homosexual and the heterosexual have the same interest in deciding how he will live his own life, and, more narrowly, how he will conduct himself in his personal and voluntary associations with his companions. State intrusion into the private conduct of either is equally burdensome.

The second possibility is similarly unacceptable. A policy of selective application must be supported by a neutral and legitimate interest— something more substantial than a habitual dislike for, or ignorance about, the disfavored group. Neither the State nor the Court has identified any such interest in this case. The Court has posited as a justification for the Georgia statute "the presumed belief of a majority of the electorate in Georgia that homosexual sodomy is immoral and unacceptable." But the Georgia electorate has expressed no such belief—instead, its representatives enacted a law that presumably reflects the belief that *all sodomy* is immoral and unacceptable. Unless the Court is prepared to conclude that such a law is constitutional, it may not rely on the work product of the Georgia Legislature to support its holding. For the Georgia statute does not single out homosexuals as a separate class meriting special disfavored treatment. [Moreover, the] record of nonenforcement, in this case and in the last several decades, belies the Attorney General's

---

[10]   **[Ct's Note]** Indeed, the Georgia Attorney General concedes that Georgia's statute would be unconstitutional if applied to a married couple. * * *

representations about the importance of the State's selective application of its generally applicable law.

Both the Georgia statute and the Georgia prosecutor thus completely fail to provide the Court with any support for the conclusion that homosexual sodomy, *simpliciter,* is considered unacceptable conduct in that State, and that the burden of justifying a selective application of the generally applicable law has been met. * * *

NOTES AND QUESTIONS

1.   *"Sever[ing] the roots of the privacy doctrine."* Rubenfeld, *The Right of Privacy*: "Justice White stated that the Court's prior cases have recognized three categories of activity protected by the right to privacy: marriage, procreation, and family relationships[, but he] neither sought nor found any unifying principle underlying his three categories. It was as if the Court had said, 'We in the majority barely understand why even these three areas are constitutionally protected; we simply acknowledge them and note that they are not involved here.' [The] device of compartmentalizing precedent is an old jurisprudential strategy for limiting unruly doctrines. The effect here is that, after *Hardwick,* we know that the right to privacy protects some aspects of marriage, procreation, and child-rearing, but we do not know why. By identifying three disparate applications ungrounded by any unifying principle, the majority effectively severed the roots of the privacy doctrine, leaving only the branches * * * ."

2.   *Was sexuality "an anatomical irrelevance"?* Criticizing what he calls "Justice White's stunningly harsh and dismissive opinion [in] *Hardwick,"* Fried, *Order and Law* 82–84, observes: "Unless one takes the implausible line that people generally choose their sexual orientation, then to criminalize any enjoyment of the sexual powers by a whole category of persons is either an imposition of very great cruelty or an exercise in hypocrisy inviting arbitrary and abusive applications of the criminal law. *Poe* and *Griswold* did emphasize the sanctity of marital intimacy, so that a step beyond these cases would have had to be taken to reach the conclusion Justice Blackmun urged in a particularly moving dissent. But it is a short step, and one authorized by reason and tradition: Hardwick was threatened with prosecution for having consensual sex with another man behind a closed bedroom door in his own home. The police found out about it by an uninvited accident. Here the conduct was truly private. It concerned no one else except in the question-begging sense that some may be offended by the very knowledge that such conduct goes unpunished. What is left is an act of private association and communication. The fact that sexuality is implicated seems an anatomical irrelevance."

3.   *More on Powell's concurring opinion: Was Hardwick really a 4 ½–4 ½ decision?* Quoting the concurrence of Powell, J., Marc Spindelman, *Reorienting Bowers v. Hardwick,* 79 N.C.L.Rev. 359 (2001) contends: "The 'concession' at oral argument 'that, prior to the complaint against respondent Hardwick, there had been no reported decision involving prosecution for

private homosexual sodomy under this statute for several decades,' and the state's choice not 'to present the criminal charge against Hardwick to a grand jury' were strong indications of what 'the law' of sodomy in Georgia (and elsewhere) was at the time *Hardwick* was decided. As Frankfurter expressed the idea [in his *Poe* plurality]: 'deeply embedded traditional ways of carrying out state policy—*or not carrying it out*—are often tougher and truer law than the dead words of the written act.' (Emphasis added.) Powell captured the gestalt of Frankfurter's *Poe* plurality with his own remark that 'the history of nonenforcement [of Georgia's sodomy ban] suggests the moribund character today of laws criminalizing this type of private consensual conduct'— particularly given that 'some 26 States ha[d] repealed similar statutes.'

"[In] a letter for posterity to [Professor Laurence] Tribe [in response to a letter from Tribe],[353] Powell flatly declared, 'The Court should not have granted certiorari in *Hardwick*.' [Thus], in contrast to thinking about *Hardwick* as either a five-four decision for or against Hardwick, one might view the decision (as I am inclined to do) as something more akin to 'a vote of four and a half to four and a half,' or a vote of four to four, with Powell, on behalf of the Court, reserving judgment on the question that, at first glance, he may have seemed to resolve.

"[Powell's] opinion can be viewed as an indication that he was awaiting a case in which the state had put its sodomy law into play by breaking the 'tacit agreement' not to punish by prosecuting individuals for private gay sex. In such a case, unlike *Hardwick*, the controversy would have been 'real, [not] hypothetical.' [And] in such a case, as I think Powell may have sensed, social disapproval of punishment for gay sex could be used as a constitutional device to trump social disapproval of gay sex itself. With Donald Dripps, I would say that '[i]n such a case, [we] can be confident [Powell] would have voted to reverse a criminal conviction.'[201] [Instead] of interpreting Powell's opinion to have decided the matter once and for all, we can regard it as an effort to split the difference between the Justices who were and those who were not prepared to recognize Hardwick's due process right to engage in consensual, private same-sex sexual activity, an effort that took the form of Powell's staying his hand for another day."[354]

4. ***The level of generality.*** Did *Hardwick* define the claim of liberty at the wrong level of generality? Yes, maintains Tribe 2d ed., at 1427–28: "Obviously, the history of homosexuality has been largely a history of

---

[353] Some years after stepping down from the Court, Powell, J., told a group of law students that he "probably made a mistake" voting with the majority in *Hardwick*. Tribe, who had argued the case for Hardwick in the Supreme Court, then wrote Powell a personal letter praising Powell's "courage and candor" in acknowledging error. See John C. Jeffries, Jr., *Justice Lewis F. Powell, Jr.* 530 (1994).

[201] **[Orig. Note]** Donald A. Dripps, *Bowers v. Hardwick and the Law of Standing: Noncases Make Bad Law*, 44 Emory L.J. 1417 (1995).

[354] According to Powell's biographer, Jeffries, fn. 37 supra, at 514, in *Hardwick* Powell sought a middle course, but "did not find the means to translate his moderate impulses into legal doctrine. He failed to craft and publish a clear statement of his own views. In this sense, *Hardwick* was Powell's greatest defeat."

opprobrium; indeed, it would not be implausible to find on this basis that homosexuals constitute a discrete and insular minority entitled to heightened protection under the equal protection clause.[355] Yet when the Court uses the history of violent disapproval of the behavior that forms part of the very definition of homosexuality as the basis for denying homosexuals' claim to protection, it effectively inverts the equal protection axiom of heightened judicial solicitude for despised groups and their characteristic activities and uses that inverted principle to bootstrap antipathy toward homosexuality into a tautological rationale for continuing to criminalize homosexuality. Therefore, in asking whether an alleged right forms part of a traditional liberty, it is crucial to define the liberty at a high enough level of generality to permit unconventional variants to claim protection along with mainstream versions of protected conduct. The proper question, as the dissent in *Hardwick* recognized, is not whether oral sex as such has long enjoyed a special place in the pantheon of constitutional rights, but whether private, consensual, adult sexual acts partake of traditionally revered liberties of intimate association and individual autonomy."

But consider Robert H. Bork, *The Tempting of America*, 203–04 (1990): "Tribe [thinks that a] constitutional right to homosexual conduct within the home [is] part of a broader right to sexual intimacies between consenting adults. [The] Court [,he tells us,] must choose the level of generality at which it states 'traditional liberty' at any level that results in a constitutional right for unconventional behavior. This bypasses the question of whether the Constitution contains protection for any sexual conduct or whether that is left to the moral sense of the people. It also fails to come to grips with the central question[:] How can any individual, professor, judge, or moral philosopher tell us convincingly that, regardless of law or our own moral sense, certain forms of unconventional behavior must be allowed? There is no apparent reason why the Court should manipulate the level of generality to protect unconventional sexual behavior any more than liberty should be taken at a high enough level of abstraction to protect kleptomania. Tribe has more sympathy for one than for the other, but that hardly rises to the level of a constitutional principle."

5. ***Drawing guidance from the text itself; Hardwick and Roe.*** "The basic choice," maintain Tribe & Dorf, "—and neither the Constitution's text nor its structure nor its history can make it for us—is between emphasizing the 'conservative' functions of both the liberty and equality clauses (as well as others), and emphasizing their potential as generators of critique and change. We must justify the choice extratextually, but we may and should then implement it in ways that draw as much guidance as possible from the text itself. Justice Harlan exemplified such a program in his *Poe* dissent, in which he opted for a moderately conservative orientation toward generalization [and] sought unifying structures for specified rights in an intermediate level of generality, drawing heavily upon textual points of reference. In the *Hardwick*

---

[355] Cf. Frank Michelman, *Law's Republic*, 97 Yale L.J. 1493 (1988). Consider, too, Sylvia Law, *Homosexuality and the Social Meaning of Gender*, 1988 Wis. L.Rev. 187; David Richards, *Constitutional Legitimacy and Constitutional Privacy*, 61 NYU.L.Rev. 800 (1986).

context, if one is willing to generalize much at all, the Constitution's text—in the First Amendment's protection of peaceful assembly and in the Fourth Amendment's protection of the home—points toward generalizing in the direction of intimate personal association in the privacy of the home rather than generalizing in the direction of, let us say, freedom of choice in matters of procreation. It is for this reason that *Hardwick* seems to us so egregiously wrong [and] that *Roe* seems a closer and more difficult case."

LAWRENCE V. TEXAS
539 U.S. 558, 123 S.Ct. 2472, 156 L.Ed.2d 508 (2003).

JUSTICE KENNEDY delivered the opinion of the Court.

Liberty protects the person from unwarranted government intrusions into a dwelling or other private places. In our tradition the State is not omnipresent in the home. And there are other spheres of our lives and existence, outside the home, where the State should not be a dominant presence. Freedom extends beyond spatial bounds. Liberty presumes an autonomy of self that includes freedom of thought, belief, expression, and certain intimate conduct. The instant case involves liberty of the person both in its spatial and in its more transcendent dimensions. The question before the Court is the validity of a Texas statute making it a crime for two persons of the same sex to engage in certain intimate sexual conduct.

Houston [police officers] were dispatched to a private residence in response to a reported weapons disturbance. They entered an apartment [where] Lawrence resided. The right of the police to enter does not seem to have been questioned. The officers observed Lawrence and another man, Tyron Garner, engaging in a sexual act. The two petitioners were arrested, held in custody overnight, and charged and convicted before a Justice of the Peace.

The complaints described their crime as "deviate sexual intercourse, namely anal sex, with a member of the same sex (man)." The applicable state [law] provides: "A person commits an offense if he engages in deviate sexual intercourse with another individual of the same sex." The statute defines "[d]eviate sexual intercourse" as follows:

"(A) any contact between any part of the genitals of one person and the mouth or anus of another person; or

"(B) the penetration of the genitals or the anus of another person with an object."

[Petitioners were convicted. The Texas Court of Appeals rejected their constitutional arguments, considering *Bowers v. Hardwick* controlling. The Supreme Court granted certiorari to consider whether petitioners' convictions violated the Equal Protection or Due Process Clauses and whether *Hardwick* should be overruled.]

We conclude the case should be resolved by determining whether the petitioners were free as adults to engage in the private conduct in the exercise of their liberty under the Due Process Clause of the Fourteenth Amendment to the Constitution. For this inquiry we deem it necessary to reconsider the Court's holding in *Bowers*. [The Court then discussed *Griswold, Eisenstadt, Roe*, and *Carey*.] *Roe* recognized the right of a woman to make certain fundamental decisions affecting her destiny and confirmed once more that the protection of liberty under the Due Process Clause has a substantive dimension of fundamental significance in defining the rights of the person.

[The] facts in *Bowers* had some similarities to the instant case. [One] difference between the two cases is that the Georgia statute prohibited the conduct whether or not the participants were of the same sex, while the Texas statute, as we have seen, applies only to participants of the same sex.

[The] Court began its substantive discussion in *Bowers* as follows: "The issue presented is whether the Federal Constitution confers a fundamental right upon homosexuals to engage in sodomy and hence invalidates the laws of the many States that still make such conduct illegal and have done so for a very long time." That statement, we now conclude, discloses the Court's own failure to appreciate the extent of the liberty at stake. To say that the issue in *Bowers* was simply the right to engage in certain sexual conduct demeans the claim the individual put forward, just as it would demean a married couple were it to be said marriage is simply about the right to have sexual intercourse. The laws involved in *Bowers* and here are, to be sure, statutes that purport to do no more than prohibit a particular sexual act. Their penalties and purposes, though, have more far-reaching consequences, touching upon the most private human conduct, sexual behavior, and in the most private of places, the home. The statutes do seek to control a personal relationship that, whether or not entitled to formal recognition in the law, is within the liberty of persons to choose without being punished as criminals.

This, as a general rule, should counsel against attempts by the State, or a court, to define the meaning of the relationship or to set its boundaries absent injury to a person or abuse of an institution the law protects. It suffices for us to acknowledge that adults may choose to enter upon this relationship in the confines of their homes and their own private lives and still retain their dignity as free persons. When sexuality finds overt expression in intimate conduct with another person, the conduct can be but one element in a personal bond that is more enduring. The liberty protected by the Constitution allows homosexual persons the right to make this choice.

Having misapprehended the claim of liberty there presented to it, and thus stating the claim to be whether there is a fundamental right to engage in consensual sodomy, the *Bowers* Court said: "Proscriptions against that conduct have ancient roots." In academic writings, and in many of the scholarly amicus briefs filed to assist the Court in this case, there are fundamental criticisms of the historical premises relied upon by the majority and concurring opinions in *Bowers*. We need not enter this debate in the attempt to reach a definitive historical judgment, but the following considerations counsel against adopting the definitive conclusions upon which *Bowers* placed such reliance.

At the outset it should be noted that there is no longstanding history in this country of laws directed at homosexual conduct as a distinct matter. [The] absence of legal prohibitions focusing on homosexual conduct may be explained in part by noting that according to some scholars the concept of the homosexual as a distinct category of person did not emerge until the late 19th century. [Thus] early American sodomy laws were not directed at homosexuals as such but instead sought to prohibit nonprocreative sexual activity more generally. This does not suggest approval of homosexual conduct. It does tend to show that this particular form of conduct was not thought of as a separate category from like conduct between heterosexual persons.

Laws prohibiting sodomy do not seem to have been enforced against consenting adults acting in private. [Instead] of targeting relations between consenting adults in private, 19th-century sodomy prosecutions typically involved relations between men and minor girls or minor boys, relations between adults involving force, relations between adults implicating disparity in status, or relations between men and animals.

[The infrequency of prosecutions in consensual cases] makes it difficult to say that society approved of a rigorous and systematic punishment of the consensual acts committed in private and by adults. The longstanding criminal prohibition of homosexual sodomy upon which the *Bowers* decision placed such reliance is as consistent with a general condemnation of nonprocreative sex as it is with an established tradition of prosecuting acts because of their homosexual character.

[Far] from possessing "ancient roots," *Bowers,* American laws targeting same-sex couples did not develop until the last third of the 20th century. The reported decisions concerning the prosecution of consensual, homosexual sodomy between adults for the years 1880–1995 are not always clear in the details, but a significant number involved conduct in a public place. It was not until the 1970's that any State singled out same-sex relations for criminal prosecution, and only nine States have done so. [Over] the course of the last decades, States with same-sex prohibitions have moved toward abolishing them.

In summary, the historical grounds relied upon in *Bowers* are more complex than the majority opinion and the concurring opinion by Chief Justice Burger indicate. Their historical premises are not without doubt and, at the very least, are overstated.

It must be acknowledged, of course, that the Court in *Bowers* was making the broader point that for centuries there have been powerful voices to condemn homosexual conduct as immoral. [This does] not answer the question before us, however. The issue is whether the majority may use the power of the State to enforce these views on the whole society through operation of the criminal law. "Our obligation is to define the liberty of all, not to mandate our own moral code." *Casey.*

[Our] laws and traditions in the past half century [show] an emerging awareness that liberty gives substantial protection to adult persons in deciding how to conduct their private lives in matters pertaining to sex. "[H]istory and tradition are the starting point but not in all cases the ending point of the substantive due process inquiry." *Sacramento v. Lewis,* 523 U.S. 833 (1998) (Kennedy, J., concurring). This emerging recognition should have been apparent when *Bowers* was decided. In 1955 the American Law Institute promulgated the Model Penal Code and made clear that it did not recommend or provide for "criminal penalties for consensual sexual relations conducted in private." [In] 1961 Illinois changed its laws to conform to the Model Penal Code. Other States soon followed.

In *Bowers* the Court referred to the fact that before 1961 all 50 States had outlawed sodomy, and that at the time of the Court's decision 24 States and the District of Columbia had sodomy laws. Justice Powell pointed out that these prohibitions often were being ignored, however. Georgia, for instance, had not sought to enforce its law for decades.

[The] sweeping references by Chief Justice Burger to the history of Western civilization and to Judeo-Christian moral and ethical standards did not take account of other authorities pointing in an opposite direction. A committee advising the British Parliament recommended in 1957 repeal of laws punishing homosexual conduct. Parliament enacted the substance of those recommendations 10 years later. Of even more importance, almost five years before *Bowers* was decided the European Court of Human Rights considered a case with parallels to *Bowers* and to today's case. [The] court held that the laws proscribing [consensual homosexual conduct] were invalid under the European Convention on Human Rights. *Dudgeon v. United Kingdom,* 45 Eur. Ct. H.R. (1981).

[In] our own constitutional system the deficiencies in *Bowers* became even more apparent in the years following its announcement. The 25 States with laws prohibiting the relevant conduct referenced in the *Bowers* decision are reduced now to 13, of which 4 enforce their laws only against homosexual conduct. In those States where sodomy is still proscribed, whether for same-sex or heterosexual conduct, there is a pattern of nonenforcement with respect to consenting adults acting in private. The State of Texas admitted in 1994 that as of that date it had not prosecuted anyone under those circumstances. Two principal cases decided after *Bowers* cast its holding into even more doubt [discussing *Casey* and *Romer v. Evans,* Ch. 9, Sec. 4, I].

[As] an alternative argument in this case, counsel for the petitioners and some amici contend that *Romer* provides the basis for declaring the Texas statute invalid under the Equal Protection Clause. That is a tenable argument, but we conclude the instant case requires us to address whether *Bowers* itself has continuing validity. Were we to hold the statute invalid under the Equal Protection Clause some might question whether a prohibition would be valid if drawn differently, say, to prohibit the conduct both between same-sex and different-sex participants.

Equality of treatment and the due process right to demand respect for conduct protected by the substantive guarantee of liberty are linked in important respects, and a decision on the latter point advances both interests. If protected conduct is made criminal and the law which does so remains unexamined for its substantive validity, its stigma might remain even if it were not enforceable as drawn for equal protection reasons. When homosexual conduct is made criminal by the law of the State, that declaration in and of itself is an invitation to subject homosexual persons to discrimination both in the public and in the private spheres. The central holding of *Bowers* has been brought in question by this case, and it should be addressed. Its continuance as precedent demeans the lives of homosexual persons.

The stigma this criminal statute imposes, moreover, is not trivial. The offense, to be sure, is but [a] minor offense in the Texas legal system. Still, it remains a criminal offense with all that imports for the dignity of the persons charged. The petitioners will bear on their record the history of their criminal convictions. Just this Term we rejected various challenges to state laws requiring the registration of sex offenders. We are advised that if Texas convicted an adult for private, consensual homosexual conduct under the statute here in question the convicted person would come within the registration laws of a least four States were he or she to be subject to their jurisdiction. This underscores the consequential nature of the punishment and the state-sponsored condemnation attendant to the criminal prohibition. Furthermore, the Texas criminal conviction carries with it the other collateral consequences always following a conviction, such as notations on job application forms, to mention but one example.

The foundations of *Bowers* have sustained serious erosion from our recent decisions in *Casey* and *Romer.* When our precedent has been thus weakened, criticism from other sources is of greater significance. In the United States criticism of *Bowers* has been substantial and continuing, disapproving of its reasoning in all respects, not just as to its historical assumptions. See, e.g., Fried, *Order and Law* 81–84; Posner, *Sex and Reason* 341–50. The courts of five different States have declined to follow it in interpreting provisions in their own state constitutions parallel to the Due Process Clause of the Fourteenth Amendment.

To the extent *Bowers* relied on values we share with a wider civilization, it should be noted that the reasoning and holding in *Bowers* have been rejected elsewhere. The European Court of Human Rights has followed not *Bowers* but its own decision in *Dudgeon*. Other nations, too, have taken action consistent with an affirmation of the protected right of homosexual adults to engage in intimate, consensual conduct. The right the petitioners seek in this case has been accepted as an integral part of human freedom in many other countries. There has been no showing that in this country the governmental interest in circumscribing personal choice is somehow more legitimate or urgent.

[In] *Casey* we noted that when a court is asked to overrule a precedent recognizing a constitutional liberty interest, individual or societal reliance on the existence of that liberty cautions with particular strength against reversing course. [The] holding in *Bowers,* however, has not induced detrimental reliance comparable to some instances where recognized individual rights are involved. Indeed, there has been no individual or societal reliance on *Bowers* of the sort that could counsel against overturning its holding once there are compelling reasons to do so. *Bowers* itself causes uncertainty, for the precedents before and after its issuance contradict its central holding.

[Justice] Stevens' [dissenting] analysis, in our view, should have been controlling in *Bowers* and should control here. *Bowers* was not correct when it was decided, and it is not correct today. It ought not to remain binding precedent. *Bowers v. Hardwick* should be and now is overruled.

The present case does not involve minors. It does not involve persons who might be injured or coerced or who are situated in relationships where consent might not easily be refused. It does not involve public conduct or prostitution. It does not involve whether the government must give formal recognition to any relationship that homosexual persons seek to enter. The case does involve two adults who, with full and mutual consent from each other, engaged in sexual practices common to a homosexual lifestyle. The petitioners are entitled to respect for their private lives. The State cannot demean their existence or control their destiny by making their private sexual conduct a crime. Their right to liberty under the Due Process Clause gives them the full right to engage in their conduct without intervention of the government. "It is a promise of the Constitution that there is a realm of personal liberty which the government may not enter." *Casey*. The Texas statute furthers no legitimate state interest which can justify its intrusion into the personal and private life of the individual.

Had those who drew and ratified the Due Process Clauses of the Fifth Amendment or the Fourteenth Amendment known the components of liberty in its manifold possibilities, they might have been more specific. They did not presume to have this insight. They knew times can blind us to certain truths and later generations can see that laws once thought necessary and proper in fact serve only to oppress. As the Constitution endures, persons in every generation can invoke its principles in their own search for greater freedom. * * *

JUSTICE O'CONNOR, concurring in the judgment.

[O'Connor, J., did not join the Court in overruling *Bowers*, but agreed that the Texas statute was unconstitutional, relying on the Equal Protection Clause. See p. 1520 infra.] That this law as applied to private, consensual conduct is unconstitutional under the Equal Protection Clause does not mean that other laws distinguishing between heterosexuals and homosexuals would similarly fail under rational basis review. Texas cannot assert any legitimate state interest here, such as national security or preserving the traditional institution of marriage. * * *

JUSTICE SCALIA, with whom the CHIEF JUSTICE and JUSTICE THOMAS join, dissenting.

[N]owhere does the Court's opinion declare that homosexual sodomy is a "fundamental right" under the Due Process Clause; nor does it subject the Texas law to the standard of review that would be appropriate (strict scrutiny) if homosexual sodomy *were* a "fundamental right." Thus, while overruling the *outcome* of *Bowers,* the Court leaves strangely untouched its central legal conclusion: "[R]espondent would have us announce [a] fundamental right to engage in homosexual sodomy. This we are quite unwilling to do." Instead the Court simply describes petitioners' conduct as "an exercise of their liberty"—which it undoubtedly is—and proceeds to apply an unheard-of form of rational-basis review that will have far-reaching implications beyond this case.

[I] do not myself believe in rigid adherence to stare decisis in constitutional cases; but I do believe that we should be consistent rather than manipulative in invoking the doctrine. Today's opinions in support of reversal do not bother to distinguish—or indeed, even bother to mention— the paean to stare decisis coauthored by three Members of today's majority in *Casey*. There, when stare decisis meant preservation of judicially invented abortion rights, the widespread criticism of *Roe* was strong reason to *reaffirm* [it]. Today, however, the widespread opposition to *Bowers,* a decision resolving an issue as "intensely divisive" as the issue in *Roe,* is offered as a reason in favor of *overruling* it. Gone, too, is any "enquiry" (of the sort conducted in *Casey*) into whether the decision sought to be overruled has "proven 'unworkable.' "

Today's approach to stare decisis invites us to overrule an erroneously decided precedent (including an "intensely divisive" decision) *if:* (1) its foundations have been "eroded" by subsequent decisions; (2) it has been subject to "substantial and continuing" criticism; and (3) it has not induced "individual or societal reliance" that counsels against overturning. The problem is that *Roe* itself—which today's majority surely has no disposition to overrule—satisfies these conditions to at least the same degree as *Bowers.*

(1) A preliminary digressive observation with regard to the first factor: The Court's claim that *Casey* "casts some doubt" upon the holding in *Bowers* (or any other case, for that matter) does not withstand analysis. As far as its holding is concerned, *Casey* provided a *less* expansive right to abortion than did *Roe, which was already on the books when Bowers was decided.* And if the Court is referring not to the holding of *Casey,* but to the dictum of its famed sweet-mystery-of-life passage (" 'At the heart of liberty is the right to define one's own concept of existence, of meaning, of the universe, and of the mystery of human life' "): That "casts some doubt" upon either the totality of our jurisprudence or else (presumably the right answer) nothing at all. I have never heard of a law that attempted to restrict one's "right to define" certain concepts; and if the passage calls into question the government's power to regulate *actions based on* one's self-defined "concept of existence, etc.," it is the passage that ate the rule of law.

I do not quarrel with the Court's claim that *Romer* "eroded" the "foundations" of *Bowers'* rational-basis holding. But *Roe* and *Casey* have been equally "eroded" by *Glucksberg,* which held that *only* fundamental rights which are " 'deeply rooted in this Nation's history and tradition' " qualify for anything other than rational basis scrutiny under the doctrine of "substantive due process." *Roe* and *Casey,* of course, subjected the restriction of abortion to heightened scrutiny without even attempting to establish that the freedom to abort *was* rooted in this Nation's tradition.

(2) *Bowers,* the Court says, has been subject to "substantial and continuing [criticism], disapproving of its reasoning in all respects, not just as to its historical assumptions." Exactly what those nonhistorical criticisms are, and whether the Court even agrees with them, are left unsaid, although the Court does cite two [books].[1] Of course, *Roe* too (and by extension *Casey*) had been (and still is) subject to unrelenting criticism, including criticism from the two commentators cited by the Court today.

---

[1]   **[Ct's Note]** [One of the *Bowers* critics cited by the majority] actually writes: "[*Bowers*] is correct nevertheless that the right to engage in homosexual acts is not deeply rooted in America's history and tradition." Posner, *Sex and Reason,* at 343.

(3) That leaves, to distinguish the rock-solid, unamendable disposition of *Roe* from the readily overrulable *Bowers,* only the third factor. "[T]here has been," the Court says, "no individual or societal reliance on *Bowers* of the sort that could counsel against overturning its [holding]." It seems to me that the "societal reliance" on the principles confirmed in *Bowers* and discarded today has been overwhelming. Countless judicial decisions and legislative enactments have relied on the ancient proposition that a governing majority's belief that certain sexual behavior is "immoral and unacceptable" constitutes a rational basis for regulation. [L]aws against bigamy, same-sex marriage, adult incest, prostitution, masturbation, adultery, fornication, bestiality, and obscenity are likewise sustainable only in light of *Bowers'* validation of laws based on moral choices. Every single one of these laws is called into question by today's decision. [The] impossibility of distinguishing homosexuality from other traditional "morals" offenses is precisely why *Bowers* rejected the rational-basis challenge. "The law," it said, "is constantly based on notions of morality, and if all laws representing essentially moral choices are to be invalidated under the Due Process Clause, the courts will be very busy indeed."

What a massive disruption of the current social order, therefore, the overruling of *Bowers* entails. Not so the overruling of *Roe,* which would simply have restored the regime that existed for centuries before 1973, in which the permissibility of and restrictions upon, abortion were determined legislatively State-by-State. [To] tell the truth, it does not surprise me, and should surprise no one, that the Court has chosen today to revise the standards of stare decisis set forth in *Casey.* It has thereby exposed *Casey's* extraordinary deference to precedent for the result-oriented expedient that it is.

Having decided that it need not adhere to stare decisis, the Court still must establish that *Bowers* was wrongly decided and that the Texas statute, as applied to petitioners, is unconstitutional. [The Texas law at issue] undoubtedly imposes constraints on liberty. So do laws prohibiting prostitution, recreational use of heroin, and, for that matter, working more than 60 hours per week in a bakery. But there is no right to "liberty" under the Due Process Clause, though today's opinion repeatedly makes that claim. [The] Fourteenth Amendment *expressly allows* States to deprive their citizens of "liberty," *so long as "due process of law" is provided.*

[Our] opinions applying the doctrine known as "substantive due process" hold that the Due Process Clause prohibits States from infringing *fundamental* liberty interests, unless the infringement is narrowly tailored to serve a compelling state interest. *Glucksberg.* We have held repeatedly, in cases the Court today does not overrule, that *only* fundamental rights qualify for this so-called "heightened scrutiny" protection—that is, rights which are " 'deeply rooted in this Nation's history and tradition.' " [Scalia,

J., then discusses *Michael H. v. Gerald D.*, *Moore v. East Cleveland*, *Meyer v. Nebraska*, and other cases].[3] All other liberty interests may be abridged or abrogated pursuant to a validly enacted state law if that law is rationally related to a legitimate state interest.

Bowers held [that] a right to engage in homosexual sodomy was not "deeply rooted in this Nation's history and tradition." The Court today does not overrule this holding. Not once does it describe homosexual sodomy as a "fundamental right" or a "fundamental liberty interest," nor does it subject the Texas statute to strict scrutiny. Instead, [the] Court concludes that the application of Texas's statute to petitioners' conduct fails the rational-basis test, and overrules *Bowers*' holding to the contrary[:] "The Texas statute furthers no legitimate state interest which can justify its intrusion into the personal and private life of the individual."

[The] Court's description of "the state of the law" at the time of *Bowers* only confirms that *Bowers* was right. [*Griswold*] *expressly disclaimed* any reliance on the doctrine of "substantive due process," and grounded the so-called "right to privacy" in penumbras of constitutional provisions *other than* the Due Process Clause. *Eisenstadt*, likewise had nothing to do with "substantive due process"; it invalidated a Massachusetts law prohibiting the distribution of contraceptives to unmarried persons solely on the basis of the Equal Protection Clause.

[*Roe*] recognized that the right to abort an unborn child was a "fundamental right" protected by the Due Process Clause. The *Roe* Court, however, made no attempt to establish that this right was " 'deeply rooted in this Nation's history and tradition' "; instead, it based its conclusion that "the Fourteenth Amendment's concept of personal liberty [is] broad enough to encompass a woman's decision whether or not to terminate her pregnancy" on its own normative judgment that antiabortion laws were undesirable. We have since rejected *Roe*'s holding that regulations of abortion must be narrowly tailored to serve a compelling state interest, see *Casey*, (joint opinion of O'Connor, Kennedy, and Souter, JJ.); (Rehnquist, C.J., concurring in judgment in part and dissenting in part)—and thus, by logical implication, *Roe*'s holding that the right to abort an unborn child is a "fundamental right."

[After] discussing the history of antisodomy laws, the Court proclaims that, "it should be noted that there is no longstanding history in this country of laws directed at homosexual conduct as a distinct matter." This

---

[3] **[Ct's Note]** The Court is quite right that "history and tradition are the starting point but not in all cases the ending point of the substantive due process inquiry." An asserted "fundamental liberty interest" must not only be "deeply rooted in this Nation's history and tradition," *Glucksberg*, but it must *also* be "implicit in the concept of ordered liberty," so that "neither liberty nor justice would exist if [it] were sacrificed." Moreover, liberty interests unsupported by history and tradition, though not deserving of "heightened scrutiny," are *still* protected from state laws that are not rationally related to any legitimate state interest. As I proceed to discuss, it is this latter principle that the Court applies in the present case.

observation in no way casts into doubt the "definitive [historical] conclusion" on which *Bowers* relied: that our Nation has a longstanding history of laws prohibiting *sodomy in general*—regardless of whether it was performed by same-sex or opposite-sex couples.

[It] is (as *Bowers* recognized) entirely irrelevant whether the laws in our long national tradition criminalizing homosexual sodomy were "directed at homosexual conduct as a distinct matter." Whether homosexual sodomy was prohibited by a law targeted at same-sex sexual relations or by a more general law prohibiting both homosexual and heterosexual sodomy, the only relevant point is that it *was* criminalized— which suffices to establish that homosexual sodomy is not a right "deeply rooted in our Nation's history and tradition." The Court today agrees that homosexual sodomy was criminalized and thus does not dispute the facts on which Bowers *actually* relied.

Next the Court makes the claim, again unsupported by any citations, that "[l]aws prohibiting sodomy do not seem to have been enforced against consenting adults acting in private." The key qualifier here is "acting in private"—since the Court admits that sodomy laws *were* enforced against consenting adults (although the Court contends that prosecutions were "infrequent."). I do not know what "acting in private" means; surely consensual sodomy, like heterosexual intercourse, is rarely performed on stage. If all the Court means by "acting in private" is "on private premises, with the doors closed and windows covered," it is entirely unsurprising that evidence of enforcement would be hard to come by. [Surely] that lack of evidence would not sustain the proposition that consensual sodomy on private premises with the doors closed and windows covered was regarded as a "fundamental right," even though all other consensual sodomy was criminalized. [*Bowers'*] conclusion that homosexual sodomy is not a fundamental right "deeply rooted in this Nation's history and tradition" is utterly unassailable.

Realizing that fact, the Court instead says: "[W]e think that our laws and traditions in the past half century are of most relevance here. These references show *an emerging awareness* that liberty gives substantial protection to adult persons in deciding how to conduct their private lives *in matters pertaining to sex.*" (Emphasis added). [The] statement is factually false. States continue to prosecute all sorts of crimes by adults "in matters pertaining to sex": prostitution, adult incest, adultery, obscenity, and child pornography. Sodomy laws, too, have been enforced "in the past half century," in which there have been 134 reported cases involving prosecutions for consensual, adult, homosexual sodomy.

[In] any event, an "emerging awareness" is by definition not "deeply rooted in this Nation's history and tradition[s]," as we have said "fundamental right" status requires. Constitutional entitlements do not spring into existence because some States choose to lessen or eliminate criminal sanctions on certain behavior. Much less do they spring into existence, as the Court seems to believe, because *foreign nations* decriminalize conduct. The *Bowers* majority opinion *never* relied on "values we share with a wider civilization," but rather rejected the claimed right to sodomy on the ground that such a right was not " 'deeply rooted in *this Nation's* history and tradition' " (emphasis added).

[I] turn now to the ground on which the Court squarely rests its holding: the contention that there is no rational basis for the law here under attack. This proposition is so out of accord with our jurisprudence— indeed, with the jurisprudence of *any* society we know—that it requires little discussion.

The Texas statute undeniably seeks to further the belief of its citizens that certain forms of sexual behavior are "immoral and unacceptable," *Bowers*—the same interest furthered by criminal laws against fornication, bigamy, adultery, adult incest, bestiality, and obscenity. *Bowers* held that this *was* a legitimate state interest. The Court today reaches the opposite conclusion. [It] embraces instead Justice Stevens' declaration in his *Bowers* dissent, that "the fact that the governing majority in a State has traditionally viewed a particular practice as immoral is not a sufficient reason for upholding a law prohibiting the practice." This effectively decrees the end of all morals legislation. If, as the Court asserts, the promotion of majoritarian sexual morality is not even a *legitimate* state interest, none of the above-mentioned laws can survive rational-basis review.

[Today's] opinion is the product of a Court, which is the product of a law-profession culture, that has largely signed on to the so-called homosexual agenda, by which I mean the agenda promoted by some homosexual activists directed at eliminating the moral opprobrium that has traditionally attached to homosexual conduct. [The] Association of [American] Law Schools (to which any reputable law school *must* seek to belong) excludes from membership any school that refuses to ban from its job-interview facilities a law firm (no matter how small) that does not wish to hire as a prospective partner a person who openly engages in homosexual conduct.

One of the most revealing statements in today's opinion is the Court's grim warning that the criminalization of homosexual conduct is "an invitation to subject homosexual persons to discrimination both in the public and in the private spheres." It is clear from this that the Court has taken sides in the culture war, departing from its role of assuring, as neutral observer, that the democratic rules of engagement are observed. Many Americans do not want persons who openly engage in homosexual conduct as partners in their business, as scoutmasters for their children, as teachers in their children's schools, or as boarders in their home. They view this as protecting themselves and their families from a lifestyle that they believe to be immoral and destructive. The Court views it as "discrimination" which it is the function of our judgments to deter. So imbued is the Court with the law profession's anti-anti-homosexual culture, that it is seemingly unaware that the attitudes of that culture are not obviously "mainstream"; that in most States what the Court calls "discrimination" against those who engage in homosexual acts is perfectly legal; that proposals to ban such "discrimination" under Title VII have repeatedly been rejected by Congress; that in some cases such "discrimination" is *mandated* by federal statute, see 10 U.S.C. § 654(b)(1) (mandating discharge from the armed forces of any service member who engages in or intends to engage in homosexual acts); and that in some cases such "discrimination" is a constitutional right, see *Boy Scouts of America v. Dale*, [Ch. 7, Sec. 9, II]. Let me be clear that I have nothing against homosexuals, or any other group, promoting their agenda through normal democratic means. Social perceptions of sexual and other morality change over time, and every group has the right to persuade its fellow citizens that its view of such matters is the best. [But] persuading one's fellow citizens is one thing, and imposing one's views in absence of democratic majority will is something else. I would no more *require* a State to criminalize homosexual acts—or, for that matter, display *any* moral disapprobation of them—than I would *forbid* it to do so. What Texas has chosen to do is well within the range of traditional democratic action, and its hand should not be stayed through the invention of a brand-new "constitutional right" by a Court that is impatient of democratic change.

[One] of the benefits of leaving regulation of this matter to the people rather than to the courts is that the people, unlike judges, need not carry things to their logical conclusion. The people may feel that their disapprobation of homosexual conduct is strong enough to disallow homosexual marriage, but not strong enough to criminalize private homosexual acts—and may legislate accordingly. The Court today pretends that it possesses a similar freedom of action, so that that we need not fear judicial imposition of homosexual marriage, as has recently occurred in Canada (in a decision that the Canadian Government has chosen not to appeal). At the end of its opinion—after having laid waste the foundations of our rational-basis jurisprudence—the Court says that the present case "does not involve whether the government must give formal recognition to any relationship that homosexual persons seek to enter." Do not believe it. More illuminating than this bald, unreasoned disclaimer is the progression of thought displayed by an earlier passage in the Court's opinion, which notes the constitutional protections afforded to "personal decisions relating to *marriage,* procreation, contraception, family relationships, child rearing, and education," and then declares that "[p]ersons in a homosexual relationship may seek autonomy for these purposes, just as heterosexual persons do" (emphasis added). Today's opinion dismantles the structure of constitutional law that has permitted a distinction to be made between heterosexual and homosexual unions, insofar as formal recognition in marriage is concerned. If moral disapprobation of homosexual conduct is "no legitimate state interest" for purposes of proscribing that conduct; and if, as the Court coos (casting aside all pretense of neutrality), "[w]hen sexuality finds overt expression in intimate conduct with another person, the conduct can be but one element in a personal bond that is more enduring"; what justification could there possibly be for denying the benefits of marriage to homosexual couples exercising "[t]he liberty protected by the Constitution"? Surely not the encouragement of procreation, since the sterile and the elderly are allowed to marry. This case "does not involve" the issue of homosexual marriage only if one entertains the belief that principle and logic have nothing to do with the decisions of this Court. Many will hope that, as the Court comfortingly assures us, this is so.[356] * * *

JUSTICE THOMAS, dissenting.

I join Justice Scalia's dissenting opinion. I write separately to note that the law before the Court today "is . . . uncommonly silly." *Griswold* (Stewart, J., dissenting). If I were a member of the Texas Legislature, I would vote to repeal it. Punishing someone for expressing his sexual preference through noncommercial consensual conduct with another adult does not appear to be a worthy way to expend valuable law enforcement resources.

Notwithstanding this, I recognize that as a Member of this Court I am not empowered to help petitioners and others similarly situated. My duty, rather, is to "decide cases 'agreeably to the Constitution and laws of the United States.'" And, just like Justice Stewart, I "can find [neither in the Bill of Rights nor any other part of the Constitution a] general right of privacy" or as the Court terms it today, the "liberty of the person both in its spatial and more transcendent dimensions."

NOTES AND QUESTIONS

1. ***Does Lawrence protect sex outside of relationships?*** The *Lawrence* majority describes sexual intimacy as "but one element in a personal bond that is more enduring." Is it always? Dale Carpenter, *Flagrant Conduct* 16–17, 70–74, 280–81 (2012) observes: "The Texas law, like many such laws, codified a particular cultural assumption about homosexuals as hypersexualized and dangerous. [That view] crept into the arrests of Lawrence and Garner, leading sheriff's deputies to set aside doubts—and to use their power—against the two men at every step." Carpenter, who conducted

---

[356] For portions of Scalia, J.'s dissenting opinion responding to O'Connor, J.'s concurring argument that the Texas statute violates equal protection, see p. 1524 infra.

extensive independent research for the book, notes that the arresting officers told inconsistent stories about the sexual position in which they found Lawrence and Garner, whereas both men themselves denied that they ever had sex with one another; each was in a relationship with a different man.

"The background facts in *Lawrence v. Texas* do not make for an easily packaged story with idealized characters. Lawrence and Garner were not in a long-term committed relationship—if they were involved at all. [They] were never 'poster people,' their lawyers informed us. [The] background did not make for very good public relations, but the deputies whose flagrant conduct gave us *Lawrence* didn't oblige public relations needs by enforcing the sodomy law against model citizens in the privacy of their well-appointed homes.

"How could this jumble become the occasion for Justice Kennedy's musings about the 'transcendent dimensions' of life, 'the most intimate and personal choices a person may make,' and 'personal dignity,' together with a lamentation on the way the law 'demean[ed] their existence'? One obvious answer is that, by design, the Supreme Court knew little about the facts of the case. And none of these background facts would have made any difference to the constitutional claim made by Lawrence and Garner. Even if the Court had known everything we now know, the men nevertheless would have been entitled to the liberty to make their own choices about their private sexual conduct. American liberty includes the freedom to make choices the majority finds distasteful or even loathsome.

"The deeper answer is that *Lawrence*, in all its emotional, social, and legal complexity, is a reflection of life itself. People do indeed lead complex lives. They fall in love, cheat, lie, drink. None of this makes them any less entitled, as Justice Kennedy put it, to 'respect for their private lives.' If it were otherwise, there would be very few people—gay or straight—entitled to liberty."

2.   ***What journey did Lawrence launch?*** "[W]hen the history of our times is written," comments Laurence H. Tribe, *Lawrence v. Texas: The "Fundamental Right" that Dare Not Speak Its Name*, 117 Harv.L.Rev. 1893 (2004), "*Lawrence* may well be remembered as the *Brown v. Board* of gay and lesbian America. But one of the lessons of *Brown* is that we cannot assume that society's acceptance of such watershed decisions—decisions that mediate revolutions in the entrenched social order—will be a straightforward and predictable process. [Will] the ways in which *Roe v. Wade* unintentionally strengthened the political hand of the religious right, even as it contributed to the gradual emancipation of women from male subordination in American society, provide a better prediction of the journey *Lawrence* will launch?"

3.   ***The Supreme Court, the American people, and the "cultural elite."*** Consider Lino A. Graglia, *Lawrence v. Texas: Our Philosopher-Kings Adopt Libertarianism as Our Official National Philosophy and Reject Traditional Morality as a Basis for Law*, 65 Ohio St.L.J. 1139 (2004): "Justice Holmes famously wrote that the Constitution did not enact Herbert Spencer's *Social Statics*, and John Hart Ely added that neither did it enact John Rawls's

A Theory of Justice. In *Lawrence*, however, the Court in effect held, in agreement with and at the urging of the libertarian Cato Institute, that the Constitution does enact John Stuart Mill's *On Liberty*. The result, if consistently followed, would be to presume unconstitutional all laws limiting 'liberty,' i.e., substantially all laws, and put on the states or national government the burden of justifying them. As a corollary of this philosophic position and illustrating its potential, the Court explicitly rejected traditional standards of morality as a means of meeting the government's burden of justification.

"[Why] do constitutional law scholars overwhelmingly favor decisionmaking on basic issues of social policy—such as the legal status of homosexuality—by the Supreme Court? The answer in a word is, of course, that it has for some time operated and, as *Lawrence* illustrates, is likely to continue to operate overwhelmingly to give them the policies they prefer and cannot get in any other way. The salient fact of American political life for the past half-century has been a deep cultural divide—in effect a 'culture war'— between the great majority of the American people and a cultural elite, made up of the 'knowledge' or 'verbal' class. [The] nightmare of the cultural elite is that control of public policymaking should fall into the hands of the American people. [Because] it is only their ideological compatriots on the Supreme Court that saves professors of constitutional law from that fate, they consider it their primary function to find means of defending and justifying the Court's policymaking powers."

4. ***Did the dissenters also "take sides" in the "culture war"?*** Consider Robert C. Post, *Foreword: Fashioning the Legal Constitution: Culture, Courts and Law*, 117 Harv.L.Rev. 4 (2003): "[Dissenting in *Lawrence*, Justice Scalia criticized] the Court for taking 'sides in [a] culture war, departing from its role [as] neutral observer.' [The] plausibility of Scalia's position depends upon whether constitutional law can meaningfully proceed without making cultural judgments. If [it] cannot, then neither can constitutional law be autonomous from culture, nor can the Court be merely a 'neutral observer.' [Instead] of pursuing the chimerical objective of neutrality, the Court would do better to analyze the conditions under which courts should properly make cultural judgments.

"[The *Lawrence*] Court unabashedly engages the values it perceives to be at stake in the case. [It] articulates the Court's own understanding of what is 'of fundamental significance in defining the rights of the person.' And because it directly makes value judgments of this kind, *Lawrence* necessarily implicates itself in cultural controversy. Scalia is therefore right to accuse the Court of losing its neutrality. But this loss is an inevitable consequence of the Court's making the evaluative judgments necessary to fulfill the purpose of substantive due process doctrine, which is to identify and protect liberty interests that the Court deems constitutionally valuable."

5. ***What is "immorality"?*** Consider Randy E. Barnett, *Justice Kennedy's Libertarian Revolution: Lawrence v. Texas*, 2003 Cato Sup.Ct. Rev.

21: "All that was offered [to] justify [the statute invalidated in *Lawrence* was] the judgment of the legislature that the prohibited conduct is 'immoral,' which for the majority (including, on this issue, Justice O'Connor) [was] simply not enough to justify the restriction of liberty. Why not? [A] legislative judgment of 'immorality' means simply that a majority of the legislature disapproves of this conduct. But justifying legislation solely on grounds of morality would entirely eliminate judicial review of legislative powers. How could a court ever adjudicate between a legislature's claim that a particular exercise of liberty is 'immoral' and a defendant's contrary claim that it is not? In practice, therefore, a doctrine allowing legislation to be justified solely on the basis of morality would recognize an unlimited police power in state legislatures."

6. *What was the principal vice of the Texas statute?* Tribe, note 2 supra, observes: "The vice of the Texas prohibition of same-sex sodomy was not principally, as some have argued, the cruelty of punishing some people for the only mode of sexual gratification available to them. Nor was it principally the lack of 'fair notice' and the danger of 'arbitrary and unpredictable enforcement' in dealing with a law that either had become moribund or never was seriously enforced and that, in either case, was 'able to persist only because it [was] enforced so rarely.'[357] Rather, the prohibition's principal vice was its stigmatization of intimate personal relationships between people of the same sex: the Court concluded that these relationships deserve to be protected in the same way that nonprocreative intimate relationships between opposite-sex adult couples—whether marital or nonmarital, lifelong or ephemeral—are protected. Focusing on the centrality of the relationship in which intimate conduct occurs rather than on the nature of the intimate conduct itself, the Court emphasized its view that '[t]o say that the issue in *Bowers* was simply the right to engage in certain sexual conduct demeans the claim the individual put forward, just as it would demean a married couple were it to be said marriage is simply about the right to have sexual intercourse.' Justice Scalia dissenting, evidently thought he had scored a major point by parsing the majority opinion and concluding, triumphantly: 'Not once does it describe homosexual sodomy as a "fundamental right" or a "fundamental liberty interest." ' Of course not! How can one put it more clearly? Try this: 'It's not the *sodomy*. It's the *relationship!*' "

Tribe recognizes that Lawrence and Garner were not in fact in a lasting relationship. Nonetheless, he writes that "the Court evidently recognized an obligation to extend constitutional protection to some brief interactions that might not ripen into meaningful connections over time—even to some that might be chosen precisely for their fleeting and superficial character and their lack of emotional involvement. Had the Court done otherwise, it would have

---

[357] At this point Professor Tribe is quoting from Cass R. Sunstein, *What Did Lawrence Hold? Of Autonomy, Desuetude, Sexuality, and Marriage*, 2003 Sup.Ct.Rev. 27. See also Cass R. Sunstein, *Liberty after Lawrence*, 65 Ohio St.L.J. 1059 (2004): "[The *Lawrence* Court] suggested that it was not issuing a simple autonomy ruling, but was also pointing to a distinctive American-style version of the old idea of desuetude. According to that idea, certain laws lapse, and no longer can be invoked if they have fallen into near-complete nonenforcement. It would be possible to understand *Griswold* in just this way."

ceded to the state the power to determine what count as meaningful relationships and to decide when and how individuals might enter into such relationships."

7. *What standard of review was applied in Lawrence? Did the Court deem the right protected to be "fundamental"?* According to Barnett, note 5 supra: "*Lawrence* is potentially revolutionary not only because it abandons a right to privacy in favor of liberty, but for another closely related reason: In the majority's opinion, there is not even the pretense of a 'fundamental right' rebutting the 'presumption of constitutionality.' [Kennedy, J.,] never tries to justify the sexual liberty of same-sex couples as a fundamental right. [Although] he never acknowledges it, Justice Kennedy is employing here what I have called a 'presumption of liberty' that requires the government to justify its restriction on liberty, instead of requiring the citizen to establish that the liberty being exercised is somehow 'fundamental.' In this way, once an action is deemed to be a proper exercise of liberty (as opposed to license), the burden shifts to the government."

But consider Tribe, note 2 supra: "[T]he strictness of the Court's standard in *Lawrence*, however articulated, could hardly have been more obvious. That much follows not only from what the Court *did* but from what it *said* in declaring *Griswold* 'the most pertinent beginning point' for its analysis and then proceeding to invoke precedents such as *Roe*. To search for the magic words proclaiming the right protected in *Lawrence* to be 'fundamental,' and to assume that in the absence of those words mere rationality review applied, is to universalize what is in fact only an occasional practice. Moreover, it requires overlooking passage after passage in which the Court's opinion indeed invoked the talismanic verbal formula of substantive due process but did so by putting the key words in one unusual sequence or another—as in the Court's declaration that it was dealing with a 'protection of *liberty* under the Due Process Clause [that] has a *substantive* dimension of *fundamental* significance in defining the rights of the person' [emphasis added by Professor Tribe]."

Even if Tribe is correct that Kennedy, J., meant to treat the right in *Lawrence* as fundamental, did the Court invite confusion by failing to use the magic words in their customary sequence? Consider the contrary results reached by two federal appeals courts in two different circuits on the question of whether heightened scrutiny applies to a state law restricting adults' access to "sex toys." In *Williams v. Attorney General of Alabama*, 378 F.3d 1232 (11th.Cir.2004), the court found that neither *Lawrence* nor any other case recognized a "fundamental right to private sexual intimacy," and accordingly rejected a challenge to Alabama's prohibition on commercial distribution of sex toys. By contrast, in *Reliable Consultants, Inc. v. Earle*, 517 F.3d 738 (5th.Cir.2008), the court said that "the only way to make sense of" the reasoning and result in *Lawrence* was by acknowledging its recognition of "a constitutional right" to sexual intimacy, and accordingly invalidated a Texas law that forbade promoting or selling sex toys.

8. *The relation between liberty and equality in Lawrence.* Pamela S. Karlan, *Foreword: Loving Lawrence*, 102 Mich.L.Rev. 1447 (2004), maintains that "*Lawrence* resembles *Loving* in important ways. Like *Loving*, *Lawrence* marks a crystallization of doctrine. Nearly forty years after *Griswold* and *Loving*, the Court has clearly established the principle that 'the substantive reach of liberty' under the Due Process Clause extends to the way individuals choose to conduct their personal relationships. But just as *Loving* was a case about inequality that informed the jurisprudence of liberty, *Lawrence* is a case about liberty that has important implications for the jurisprudence of equality. In fact, liberty and equality are more intertwined in *Lawrence* than in *Loving*. The *Loving* Court could have rested its decision entirely on the unconstitutionality of racial subordination without looking at all at the importance of marriage; by contrast, the *Lawrence* Court's discussion of liberty would be incoherent without some underlying commitment to equality among groups. The Warren Court often espoused 'substantive' equal protection; the *Lawrence* Court attacked a 'suspect' deprivation of liberty."

By contrast, Catharine A. MacKinnon, *The Road Not Taken: Sex Equality in Lawrence v. Texas*, 65 Ohio State L.J. 1081 (2004), argues that the *Lawrence* Court chose a robust conception of liberty over an impoverished conception of equality. She characterizes the Court's logic as follows: "Equal protection has no standards of substantive validity. Due process has a substantive dimension; equal protection does not. Equality is procedural, so to speak; it is formal only, regulating how a law is drawn but not its content. To this Court, even concerns of 'stigma,' 'dignity,' and whether a law's existence 'demeans' people properly resonated in freedom's 'more transcendent dimensions,' not in equality."

9. *Does Lawrence, as Justice Scalia suggests, cast doubt on laws prohibiting adultery, polygamy, adult incest, bestiality, or prostitution?* Professor Karlan, note 8 supra, answers in the negative, pointing out that, unlike the other individuals mentioned, gay people "form a social group whose membership extends beyond their engaging in specific sexual acts." But Louis Michael Seidman, *Out of Bounds*, 65 Ohio State L.J. 1329 (2004) responds: "Suppose that people in incestuous relationships were able to organize themselves (or were organized by oppression) into a social group. Surely, this change alone would not cause Karlan to change her views about their constitutional rights. Some groups are subordinated because they deserve to be subordinated. Even if (especially if!) rapists and pederasts managed to form their own political action committees, the laws against their conduct would remain perfectly legitimate."

10. *Is Lawrence consistent with Glucksberg?* Nelson Lund & John O. McGinnis, *Lawrence v. Texas and Judicial Hubris*, 102 Mich.L.Rev. 1555 (2004), denounce *Lawrence* for its disregard of the *Glucksberg* approach to substantive due process, which, they contend, promised to put an end to what they call "the *Griswold-Roe* approach to substantive due process": "*Lawrence* is a paragon of the most anticonstitutional branch of constitutional law: substantive due process. The decision also reflects a breakdown of the Court's most recent attempt to put doctrinal restraints on that intoxicating doctrine.

[One] striking manifestation of *Lawrence*'s haughtiness toward the kind of legal analysis that had become conventional in the case law is its treatment of *Glucksberg*, which had articulated, just six years earlier, the governing test for expansions of substantive due process. Without so much as citing *Glucksberg*, *Lawrence* abandons both of its core requirements: that a fundamental right be carefully described and that there be objective evidence the right is deeply rooted in our nation's history and tradition."

Given the different approaches to substantive due process in *Lawrence* and *Glucksberg*, does *Lawrence* imply that the Court will overrule *Glucksberg*? Consider Yale Kamisar, *Can Glucksberg Survive Lawrence? Another Look at the End of Life and Personal Autonomy*, 106 Mich.L.Rev. 1453 (2008). The abstract summarizes the article thus: "Unlike the situation with respect to the pre-*Lawrence* era, *Glucksberg* does not stigmatize any politically vulnerable group. When there is no democratic default in the political process, there is much to be said for courts deferring to reasonable legislative judgments. Moreover, unlike the developments preceding *Lawrence*, there has been no emerging awareness of a right or liberty to enlist the assistance of a physician in committing suicide. No state supreme court has found a right to PAS in its own state constitution. Nor, in the decade since Glucksberg, has any state legislature legalized PAS. And attempts have been made to do so in some twenty states." Kamisar's article was published before the state law developments described in note 4 following *Glucksberg* supra. Nonetheless, his characterization of state laws regarding PAS remains broadly accurate, does it not?

Beyond state law developments, the abstract continues: "[A] right to PAS for the terminally ill is not easily cabined. If personal autonomy extends to the time and manner of one's death, why doesn't it also apply whenever a competent person believes that death is better than continued life? Once the right to PAS is grounded on self-determination or personal autonomy, it seems difficult to limit it to the terminally ill. Why should people who have to endure pain, suffering, or indignity for a much longer time than the terminally ill (often defined as those with six months or less to live) be denied this right? The argument made by many proponents of PAS that the right to forgo medical treatment and the right to PAS are merely subcategories of the same broad right is not convincing. Most of the two million people who die every year in this country do so in hospitals and long-term care institutions and do so after a decision to forgo life-sustaining treatment has been made. If medical treatment could not be rejected, vast numbers of patients would be at the mercy of every technological advance. [Allowing] a patient to die at some point is a practical condition upon the successful operation of medicine. The same can hardly be said of PAS."

The Use of Foreign and International Law

1.   *Objections to the use of foreign decisions as authorities.* The *Lawrence* majority's discussion of foreign and international law may be

part of a broader trend. Other prominent examples include cases involving the death penalty, see, e.g., *Roper v. Simmons*, Sec. 5, IV infra, and federalism, see *Printz v. United States* (Breyer, J., dissenting), Ch. 2, Sec. 5, IV supra. The citation of foreign and international sources in constitutional adjudication has been controversial. Why?

Consider Judge Richard A. Posner, *Foreword: A Political Court*, 119 Harv.L.Rev. 32 (2005): "[F]oreign decisions emerge from complex social, political, cultural, and historical backgrounds of which Supreme Court Justices, like other American judges and lawyers, are largely ignorant. To know how much weight to give a decision of the German Constitutional Court in an abortion case, one would want to know such things as how the judges of that court are appointed, how they conceive of their role, and, most important and most elusive, how German attitudes toward abortion have been shaped by peculiarities of German history, notably the abortion jurisprudence of the Weimar Republic, thought to have set the stage for Nazi Germany's program of involuntary euthanasia. Similarly, the European rejection of the death penalty probably is related to its past overuse by European nations and also to the less democratic cast of European politics, as a result of which elite opinion is more likely to override public opinion than it is in the United States. Public opinion in the United Kingdom, as in the United States, strongly favors the death penalty, despite which Parliament repealed it and cannot be persuaded to reconsider."

2.   *A ratchet effect?* According to Moshe Cohen-Eliya and Iddo Porat, *Proportionality and Constitutional Culture* 135–36 (2013), one effect of judges on national constitutional courts (such as the Supreme Court of the United States) joining the "global constitutional community" is to "expand[ ] the conception of rights within the legal system. A new—global—reference point is set for judges in making their decisions." In addition to citing empirical studies, Cohen-Eliya and Porat contend that "common knowledge seems to confirm" the existence of this ratchet effect: "seldom would a court pride itself on being the least protective of rights, and it would be more likely to find a court lamenting the fact that its legal system 'lags behind' or has yet to 'catch up' to other systems." See also David S. Law, *Globalization and the Future of Constitutional Rights*, 102 Nw.U.L.Rev. 1277 (2008). For an account of the mechanisms by which judges from different countries influence one another's rulings, see Anne-Marie Slaughter, *A New World Order* 65–103 (2004).

3.   *Did earlier cases "employ a crude form of comparative constitutional analysis"?* Tribe, note 2 after *Lawrence*, recognizes that "the library of sources" the *Lawrence* Court consulted "was less Americentric than usual, a departure that the dissent especially deplored," but adds: "[T]he Court's basic approach placed it squarely in the tradition of the substantive due process jurisprudence that links the surviving

Lochner-era precedents of *Meyer* and *Pierce*-decisions in which the Court employed a crude form of comparative constitutional analysis by contrasting childrearing in Sparta with childrearing in Athens—with the line of decisions leading to, and extending past, *Casey*."

4. ***The varied uses of foreign law.*** The Court has used foreign law for various purposes. Joan L. Larsen, *Importing Constitutional Norms from a "Wider Civilization": Lawrence and the Rehnquist Court's Use of Foreign and International Law in Domestic Constitutional Interpretation*, 65 Ohio State L.J. 1283 (2004), labels these uses "expository," "empirical," and "substantive" (including "moral fact-finding").

A court uses foreign law in an expository sense when it uses foreign law to contrast and thereby explain a domestic constitutional rule. A court uses foreign law in an empirical sense when it looks abroad to see what *the effect* of the proposed rule might be. *Glucksberg* is a good example. There, to determine whether there was any basis for the state's fear that permitting physician-assisted suicide (PAS) might lead to voluntary and perhaps even involuntary euthanasia, the Court looked to the Netherlands, the only place where PAS had yielded empirical evidence. Professor Larsen does not object to the expository and empirical uses of foreign law, but she balks at "moral fact-finding," using the fact that foreign or international jurisdictions have adopted a particular rule as a reason to conform the American constitutional rule to the foreign or international norm.

"[The *Lawrence*] majority thought that the fact that the European Court of Human Rights, and the governments of many nations, had 'protected [the] right of homosexual adults to engage in intimate, consensual conduct' spoke to whether the U.S. Constitution forbade states from criminalizing such conduct. [Foreign recognition] alone, quite apart from the reasons *why* those countries had recognized the right, was persuasive to the majority, at least in the absence of any 'showing that in this country the governmental interest in circumscribing personal choice is somehow more legitimate or urgent.' The previous Term [in *Atkins v. Virginia*, 536 U.S. 304 (2002), holding that the cruel and unusual punishment clause prohibits the execution of an intellectually disabled person], the Court employed much the same methodology, considering relevant to its constitutional decision the fact that 'within the world community, the imposition of the death penalty for crimes committed by [intellectually disabled] offenders is overwhelmingly disapproved.' Yet, curiously, none of the Justices have explained *why* they believe moral fact-finding to be a legitimate tool of constitutional interpretation.

"[It] is hard to justify the moral fact-finding approach [because] a true aggregation of international positions on a wide range of issues would produce results that run counter to many of our current constitutional doctrines—doctrines which many Americans believe to be good. To take seriously the notion of deference to the international community in constitutional interpretation would mean, for example, vast restrictions on the constitutional right to abortion as currently recognized in the United States. [Or] consider the First Amendment. [Many] nations restrict speech far more than is constitutionally permissible in the United States. For example, in the United States, hate speech generally is constitutionally protected unless it amounts to an 'incitement of violence.' By contrast, many nations, including those that typically recognize some measure of protection for the freedom of expression, substantially restrict hate speech. Indeed, most Western democracies prohibit such speech and subject it to criminal sanction."[358]

Other Dimensions of Privacy and Autonomy

1. *Personal appearance and lifestyle.* KELLEY v. JOHNSON, 425 U.S. 238 (1976), per REHNQUIST, J., held that regulations directed at the style and length of male police officers' hair, sideburns, and mustaches, and prohibiting beards and goatees except for medical reasons, violated no " 'liberty' interest protected by the Fourteenth Amendment": "The 'liberty' interest claimed [here] is distinguishable from [those] protected [in] *Roe, Eisenstadt* [and] *Griswold,* [which] involved a substantial claim of infringement on the individual's freedom of choice with respect to certain basic matters of procreation, marriage, and family life."

Moreover, the Court found that the employment context afforded the government additional latitude. "[T]he county has chosen a mode of organization which it undoubtedly deems the most efficient in enabling its police to carry out the duties assigned to them under state and local law. Such a choice necessarily gives weight to the overall need for discipline, esprit de corps, and uniformity."

MARSHALL, J., joined by Brennan, J., dissented: "An individual's personal appearance may reflect, sustain, and nourish his personality and may well be used as a means of expressing his attitude and lifestyle. In taking control over a citizen's personal appearance, the government forces him to sacrifice substantial elements of his integrity and identity as well. To say that the liberty guarantee of the Fourteenth Amendment does not encompass matters of personal appearance would be fundamentally inconsistent with the values of privacy, self-identity, autonomy, and personal integrity that I have always assumed the Constitution was designed to protect [citing *Roe, Griswold*, and other cases]."[359]

---

[358] See also Steven G. Calabresi, *Lawrence, the Fourteenth Amendment, and the Supreme Court's Reliance on Foreign Constitutional Law: An Originalist Reappraisal*, 65 Ohio St.L.J. 1097 (2004).

[359] See also J. Harvie Wilkinson III & G. Edward White, *Constitutional Protection for Personal Lifestyles*, 62 Cornell L.Rev. 563 (1977): "Appearance, like speech, is a chief medium of self-expression that involves important choices about how we wish to project ourselves and be perceived

2. *The substantive due process rights of involuntarily-committed intellectually disabled persons.* YOUNGBERG v. ROMEO, 457 U.S. 307 (1982), considered for the first time the substantive due process rights of involuntarily-committed intellectually disabled persons. On his mother's petition, Romeo, a 33-year-old man with the mental capacity of an average 18-month-old baby, was involuntarily committed to a Pennsylvania state institution (Pennhurst). Subsequently, concerned about injuries Romeo had suffered at Pennhurst, his mother sued institution officials claiming that her son had constitutional rights to: (1) safe conditions of confinement; (2) freedom from bodily restraint; and (3) "minimally adequate habilitation," i.e., minimal training and development of needed skills. (In light of his severe disability, however, respondent conceded that no amount of training would make his release possible.) The Court, per POWELL, J., pointed out that "Respondent's first two claims involve liberty interests recognized by prior decisions of this Court, interests that involuntary commitment proceedings do not extinguish," but found respondent's remaining claim "more troubling":

"Persons who have been involuntarily committed are entitled to more considerate treatment [than] criminals whose conditions of confinement are designed to punish. At the same time, the standard is lower than [a] 'compelling' or 'substantial' necessity [test for justifying restraints] that would place an undue burden on the administration of [state institutions] and also would restrict unnecessarily the exercise of professional judgment as to the needs of residents. [In] determining what is 'reasonable'—in this and in any case presenting a claim for training by a state—we emphasize that courts must show deference to the judgment exercised by a qualified professional. [The] decision, if made by a professional, is presumptively valid; liability may be imposed only when the decision by the professional is such a substantial departure from accepted professional judgment, practice, or standards as to demonstrate that the person responsible actually did not base the decision on such a judgment.[360] In an action for damages against a professional in his individual capacity, however, the professional will not be liable if he was unable to satisfy his normal professional standards because of budgetary constraints; in such a situation, good-faith immunity would bar liability."[361]

BLACKMUN, J., joined by Brennan and O'Connor, JJ., joined the Court's opinion, but concurred separately to clarify why, because of the uncertainty in the record, "that opinion properly leaves [open] difficult and important questions." BURGER, C.J., concurring, agreed with much of the

---

by others. To link appearance with privacy and speech values is not, of course, to require similar constitutional treatment. It does imply, however, that we deal with a substantive constitutional liberty."

[360] Does this place "a seemingly insurmountable burden" on plaintiff mental patients? See *Right to Training for the Mentally Retarded*, 96 Harv.L.Rev. 77 (1982).

[361] Consider, too, *DeShaney v. Winnebago County*, Ch. 10, Sec. 6.

Court's opinion, but "would hold flatly that respondent has no constitutional right to training, or 'habilitation,' per se."

The Court in *Youngberg* presumes that medical professionals will act in the best interest of persons who are civilly confined based on severe disabilities. Concurring in part and dissenting in part in *Washington v. Harper*, 494 U.S. 210 (1990), STEVENS, J., joined by Brennan, J., and Marshall, J., questioned whether a *prison* doctor would deliver treatment—in that case psychotropic medication—solely in the patient's interest, rather than in the interest of maintaining a docile prisoner population. Does the fact that civil confinement is not meant to be punitive alleviate this concern in a case like *Youngberg*? Does anything?

3. THE RIGHT TO TRAVEL

SHAPIRO v. THOMPSON (1969) (discussed at Ch. 9, Sec. 5, II), recognizes interstate travel as a fundamental right for equal protection purposes. As HARLAN, J., observed in dissent in that case: "Opinions of this Court and of individual Justices have suggested four provisions of the Constitution as possible sources of a right to travel enforceable against the federal or state governments: the Commerce Clause; the Privileges and Immunities Clause of Art. IV, § 2; the Privileges [or] Immunities Clause of the Fourteenth Amendment; and the Due Process Clause of the Fifth Amendment." After rejecting the other grounds, he concluded that for purposes of deciding *Shapiro*, "the right to travel interstate is a 'fundamental' right which [should] be regarded as having its source in the Due Process Clause of the Fifth Amendment." Other possible sources for the constitutional right to travel are the Equal Protection Clause, the "penumbra" of the First Amendment, the Ninth Amendment and "the nature of the federal union."[362] The materials in this Section concern the sources, content, and scope of the substantive right to travel. As you read them, consider whether they protect a single right to travel.

———

APTHEKER v. SECRETARY OF STATE, 378 U.S. 500 (1964), invalidated a federal statutory provision forbidding the issuance of passports to members of any "Communist organization" that was required to register as such. The Court, per GOLDBERG, J., held that the provision "too broadly and indiscriminately restricts the right to travel and thereby abridges the liberty guaranteed by the Fifth Amendment." Quoting *Kent v. Dulles*, 357 U.S. 116 (1958), the *Aptheker* Court observed that "that the right to travel abroad is 'an important aspect of the citizen's liberty' guaranteed in the Due Process Clause of the Fifth Amendment. '[Freedom]

———

[362] See generally Ira Lupu, *Untangling the Strands of the Fourteenth Amendment,* 77 Mich.L.Rev. 981 (1979).

of movement across frontiers in either direction, and inside frontiers as well, was a part of our heritage. Travel abroad, like travel within the country [is] basic in our scheme of values.' [Since] freedom of association is itself guaranteed in the First Amendment, restrictions imposed upon the right to travel cannot be dismissed by asserting that the right to travel could be fully exercised if the individual would first yield up his membership in a given association."[363]

DOUGLAS, J., joined the Court's opinion, adding that "the right to move freely from State to State is a privilege and immunity of national citizenship. [Absent] war, I see no way to keep a citizen from traveling within or without the country [unless] he has been convicted of a crime or unless there is probable cause for issuing a warrant of arrest. [Freedom] of movement [is] the very essence of our free society, setting us apart."

CLARK, J., joined by Harlan and White, JJ., dissented, maintaining that the Due Process Clause does not prohibit "reasonable regulation" of the right to travel abroad and that Congress had "a rational basis" for denying passports to members of the Communist Party.

———

ZEMEL v. RUSK, 381 U.S. 1 (1965), upheld the Secretary of State's refusal to issue passports to United States citizens for travel to Cuba. Appellant sought a passport "to satisfy my curiosity about the state of affairs in Cuba and to make me a better informed citizen." The Court, per WARREN, C.J., stated: "The requirements of due process are a function not only of the extent of the governmental restriction imposed, but also of the extent of the necessity for the restriction. [The] United States and other members of the Organization of American States have determined that travel between Cuba and the other countries of the Western Hemisphere is an important element in the spreading of subversion. [The] Secretary has justifiably concluded that travel to Cuba by American citizens might involve the Nation in dangerous international incidents, and that the Constitution does not require him to validate passports for such travel. [That] the restriction which is challenged in this case is supported by the weightiest considerations of national security is perhaps best pointed up by recalling that the Cuban Missile crisis of October 1962 preceded the filing of appellant's complaint by less than two months."

DOUGLAS, J., joined by Goldberg, J., dissented: "Pestilences may rage in a region making it necessary to protect not only the traveler but those he might infect on his return. A theatre of war may be too dangerous for travel. Other like situations can be put. But the only so-called danger

---

[363] *Kent* invalidated State Department regulations denying passports to Communists on the ground that they exceeded the congressional grant of authority, thus avoiding the constitutional question.

present here is the Communist regime in Cuba. The world, however, is filled with Communist thought; and Communist regimes are on more than one continent. They are part of the world spectrum; and if we are to know them and understand them, we must mingle with [them.]"

GOLDBERG, J., also dissented, on the ground that the Cuba travel ban was neither authorized by Congress nor within the inherent power of the Executive.[364]

———

HAIG v. AGEE, 453 U.S. 280 (1981), involved a former CIA employee residing in West Germany who, in violation of his contract, engaged in a campaign to expose undercover CIA agents stationed abroad and "to drive them out of the countries where they are operating." In furtherance of his plan, Agee traveled in various countries. Because of these activities, the Secretary of State invoked a regulation authorizing passport revocation upon his determination that an American citizen's activities abroad "are causing or likely to cause serious damage to the national security or the foreign policy of the United States." The Court, per BURGER, C.J., rejected Agee's contention that the revocation violated his right to travel, stressing the distinction between interstate and international travel:

"Revocation of a passport undeniably curtails travel, but the freedom to travel abroad with a 'letter of introduction' in the form of a passport issued by the sovereign is subordinate to national security and foreign policy considerations; as such, it is subject to reasonable governmental regulation. The Court has made it plain that the *freedom* to travel outside the United States must be distinguished from the *right* to travel within the United States. [Restricting] Agee's foreign travel, although perhaps not certain to prevent all of Agee's harmful activities, is the only avenue open to the Government to limit these activities."

BRENNAN, J., joined by Marshall, J., dissenting, argued that the regulation under which Agee's passport had been revoked was "invalid as an unlawful exercise of authority by the Secretary [of State] under the Passport Act of 1926."

---

[364] Compare *Zemel* with *Regan v. Wald,* 468 U.S. 222 (1984). In 1982, in order to "reduce Cuba's hard currency earnings from travel by U.S. persons to and from Cuba," a treasury regulation was amended to restrict travel-related economic transactions. Respondents, American citizens who wanted to travel to Cuba, challenged the amendment on both statutory and constitutional grounds. A 5–4 majority, per Rehnquist, J., rejected the constitutional challenge, seeing "no reason to differentiate between the travel restrictions imposed by the President in the present case and the passport restrictions imposed by the Secretary of State in *Zemel.*"

Blackmun, J., joined by Brennan, Marshall and Powell, JJ., dissented, maintaining that the restrictions on travel-related expenditures in Cuba were not authorized by Congress.

NOTES AND QUESTIONS

1. ***The shift from Kent to Agee.*** Daniel Farber, *National Security, The Right to Travel, and the Court,* 1981 Sup.Ct.Rev. 263: "[*Agee*] represents a major shift from previous travel cases such as *Kent* [which] laid heavy stress on the importance of the right to travel and took a correspondingly grudging approach to discretionary travel controls. *Agee,* on the other hand, distinguishes the *right* to travel within the United States from the mere *freedom* to travel outside the United States. It takes a correspondingly generous view of executive discretion. For three reasons, the *Kent* approach is preferable.

"[First] is the importance of the right to travel itself. [One] important aspect of international travel is its relation to freedom of speech. Without the right to travel, criticism of foreign policy is greatly impeded. [Second,] *Kent's* grudging attitude toward executive discretion is amply supported by history. [The] *Agee* Court seems to have assumed that the discretion to control travel had only been exercised on a principled basis. Too many counterexamples exist to allow reliance on this assumption. The third reason for preferring *Kent* to *Agee* is that *Kent* aligns more closely with congressional intent. [Not] only the holding but also the underlying policies of *Kent* have received congressional endorsement. This is of critical importance, because both *Kent* and *Agee* proceed from the premise that the President's power flows from Congress. Indeed, even if the President did have some inherent power in the area, that power would be greatly diminished by Congressional disapproval."

2. ***A rationale for the right to travel.*** Consider John Hart Ely, *Democracy and Distrust* 178–79 (1980): "The right at issue in the modern cases [is] not simply a right to travel to or through a state but rather a right to move there—the right, if you will, to relocate. [To] a large extent America was founded by persons escaping from environments they found oppressive. [And] of course the symbolism, and indeed the reality, of 'the frontier' took much of its sustenance from the notion that a person should have the option of pulling up stakes and starting over elsewhere. [A] dissenting member [of a community] should have the option of exiting and relocating in a community whose values he or she finds more compatible. [I]t's an old idea, dating back at least as far as Rousseau's 'droit d'emigration': it's just that the Court hasn't fixed on it. That is unfortunate, since it provides something the Court hasn't, a rationale for the right to travel it in fact has established."

See also Tribe 2d ed., at 1382–84: "[C]lose surveillance and control of travel in both its senses"—"as an aspect of expression or education and as a means of changing one's place of residence and beginning life anew"—"has always been a central technique of the totalitarian state, but centuries of experience should suffice to mark as especially suspect any governmental measure designed to prevent the emigration of those dissatisfied with the existing order, or the immigration of those who might alter the status quo. Just as government should be forbidden to expel the citizen who has become a source of unrest, so it cannot be permitted to imprison the citizen who seeks freedom in another land."

3.   *Quarantine.* Speaking for the Court in *Gibbons v. Ogden*, Ch. 2, Sec. 2, I, Marshall, C.J., took for granted that the state police power encompasses "quarantine laws," which restrict the movement of people who may have been exposed to disease. In 2014, governors in several states sought to quarantine health care workers returning from west Africa, where they had been treating people infected with the often-deadly Ebola virus, even though the federal Centers for Disease Control protocol did not call for quarantining asymptomatic individuals. Notwithstanding their pedigree, do state quarantines infringe the right to travel? Notwithstanding Douglas, J.'s seeming approval of federal measures to prevent the spread of "pestilences" in his *Zemel* dissent, do federal quarantines infringe the right to travel? In evaluating the constitutionality of quarantines, should courts defer to government officials, to scientific experts, or to neither?

4. THE RIGHT TO KEEP AND BEAR ARMS

DISTRICT OF COLUMBIA V. HELLER

554 U.S. 570, 128 S.Ct. 2783, 171 L.Ed.2d 637 (2008).

JUSTICE SCALIA delivered the opinion of the Court.

[The] District of Columbia generally prohibits the possession of handguns. It is a crime to carry an unregistered firearm, and the registration of handguns is prohibited. Wholly apart from that prohibition, no person may carry a handgun without a license, but the chief of police may issue licenses for 1-year periods. District of Columbia law also requires residents to keep their lawfully owned firearms, such as registered long guns, "unloaded and disassembled or bound by a trigger lock or similar device" unless they are located in a place of business or are being used for lawful recreational activities.

Respondent Dick Heller is a D.C. special police officer authorized to carry a handgun while on duty. [He] applied for a registration certificate for a handgun that he wished to keep at home, but the District refused. He [sued,] seeking, on Second Amendment grounds, to enjoin the city from enforcing the bar on the registration of handguns, the licensing requirement insofar as it prohibits the carrying of a firearm in the home without a license, and the trigger-lock requirement insofar as it prohibits the use of "functional firearms within the home."

[The] Second Amendment provides: "A well regulated Militia, being necessary to the security of a free State, the right of the people to keep and bear Arms, shall not be infringed." In interpreting this text, we are guided by the principle that "[t]he Constitution was written to be understood by the voters; its words and phrases were used in their normal and ordinary as distinguished from technical meaning."

[The] two sides in this case have set out very different interpretations of the Amendment. Petitioners and today's dissenting Justices believe that it protects only the right to possess and carry a firearm in connection with militia service. Respondent argues that it protects an individual right to possess a firearm unconnected with service in a militia, and to use that arm for traditionally lawful purposes, such as self-defense within the home.

The Second Amendment is naturally divided into two parts: its prefatory clause and its operative clause. The former does not limit the latter grammatically, but rather announces a purpose. [Although] this structure of the Second Amendment is unique in our Constitution, other legal documents of the founding era, particularly individual-rights provisions of state constitutions, commonly included a prefatory statement of purpose.

[Putting] all of [the Second Amendment's] textual elements together, we find that they guarantee the individual right to possess and carry weapons in case of confrontation. This meaning is strongly confirmed by the historical background of the Second Amendment. We look to this because it has always been widely understood that the Second Amendment, like the First and Fourth Amendments, codified a *pre-existing* right. The very text of the Second Amendment implicitly recognizes the pre-existence of the right and declares only that it "shall not be infringed."

[By] the time of the founding, the right to have arms had become fundamental for English subjects. Blackstone, whose works, we have said, "constituted the preeminent authority on English law for the founding generation," cited the arms provision of the Bill of Rights as one of the fundamental rights of Englishmen. His description of it cannot possibly be thought to tie it to militia or military service. It was, he said, "the natural right of resistance and self-preservation," and "the right of having and using arms for self-preservation and defence[.]" Other contemporary authorities concurred.

[There] seems to us no doubt, on the basis of both text and history, that the Second Amendment conferred an individual right to keep and bear arms. Of course the right was not unlimited, just as the First Amendment's right of free speech was not. Thus, we do not read the Second Amendment to protect the right of citizens to carry arms for *any sort* of confrontation, just as we do not read the First Amendment to protect the right of citizens to speak for *any purpose*.

[Does] the preface fit with an operative clause that creates an individual right to keep and bear arms? It fits perfectly, once one knows the history that the founding generation knew and that we have described above. That history showed that the way tyrants had eliminated a militia consisting of all the able-bodied men was not by banning the militia but simply by taking away the people's arms, enabling a select militia or standing army to suppress political opponents. This is what had occurred in England that prompted codification of the right to have arms in the English Bill of Rights.

The debate with respect to the right to keep and bear arms, as with other guarantees in the Bill of Rights, was not over whether it was desirable (all agreed that it was) but over whether it needed to be codified in the Constitution. During the 1788 ratification debates, the fear that the federal government would disarm the people in order to impose rule through a standing army or select militia was pervasive in Antifederalist rhetoric. [It] was understood across the political spectrum that the right helped to secure the ideal of a citizen militia, which might be necessary to oppose an oppressive military force if the constitutional order broke down. It is therefore entirely sensible that the Second Amendment's prefatory clause announces the purpose for which the right was codified: to prevent elimination of the militia. The prefatory clause does not suggest that preserving the militia was the only reason Americans valued the ancient right; most undoubtedly thought it even more important for self-defense and hunting. But the threat that the new Federal Government would destroy the citizens' militia by taking away their arms was the reason that right—unlike some other English rights—was codified in a written Constitution.

[Justice] Stevens places overwhelming reliance upon this Court's decision in *United States v. Miller*, 307 U.S. 174 (1939). [According to Justice Stevens, *Miller* holds that] the Second Amendment "protects the right to keep and bear arms for certain military purposes, but [it] does not curtail the legislature's power to regulate the nonmilitary use and ownership of weapons."

[But] *Miller* did not hold that and cannot possibly be read to have held that. [It] upheld against a Second Amendment challenge two men's federal convictions for transporting an unregistered short-barreled shotgun [in] violation of the National Firearms Act. It is entirely clear that the Court's basis for saying that the Second Amendment did not apply was [that] the *type of weapon at issue* was not eligible for Second Amendment protection. [We] read *Miller* to say only that the Second Amendment does not protect those weapons not typically possessed by law-abiding citizens for lawful purposes, such as short-barreled shotguns. That accords with the historical understanding of the scope of the right.

In the aftermath of the Civil War, there was an outpouring of discussion of the Second Amendment in Congress and in public discourse, as people debated whether and how to secure constitutional rights for newly free slaves. Since those discussions took place 75 years after the ratification of the Second Amendment, they do not provide as much insight into its original meaning as earlier sources. Yet those born and educated in the early 19th century faced a widespread effort to limit arms ownership by a large number of citizens; their understanding of the origins and continuing significance of the Amendment is instructive.

Blacks were routinely disarmed by Southern States after the Civil War. Those who opposed these injustices frequently stated that they infringed blacks' constitutional rights to keep and bear arms. Needless to say, the claim was not that blacks were being prohibited from carrying arms in an organized state militia. [It] was plainly the understanding in the post-Civil War Congress that the Second Amendment protected an individual right to use arms for self-defense.

[Like] most rights, the right secured by the Second Amendment is not unlimited. [For] example, the majority of the 19th-century courts to consider the question held that prohibitions on carrying concealed weapons were lawful under the Second Amendment or state analogues. Although we do not undertake an exhaustive historical analysis today of the full scope of the Second Amendment, nothing in our opinion should be taken to cast doubt on longstanding prohibitions on the possession of firearms by felons and the mentally ill, or laws forbidding the carrying of firearms in sensitive places such as schools and government buildings, or laws imposing conditions and qualifications on the commercial sale of arms.[26]

We also recognize another important limitation on the right to keep and carry arms. *Miller* said [that] the sorts of weapons protected were those "in common use at the time." We think that limitation is fairly supported by the historical tradition of prohibiting the carrying of "dangerous and unusual weapons."

[It] may be objected that if weapons that are most useful in military service—M-16 rifles and the like—may be banned, then the Second Amendment right is completely detached from the prefatory clause. But as we have said, the conception of the militia at the time of the Second Amendment's ratification was the body of all citizens capable of military service, who would bring the sorts of lawful weapons that they possessed at home to militia duty. It may well be true today that a militia, to be as effective as militias in the 18th century, would require sophisticated arms that are highly unusual in society at large. Indeed, it may be true that no amount of small arms could be useful against modern-day bombers and tanks. But the fact that modern developments have limited the degree of fit between the prefatory clause and the protected right cannot change our interpretation of the right.

---

[26] **[Ct's Note]** We identify these presumptively lawful regulatory measures only as examples; our list does not purport to be exhaustive.

We turn finally to the law at issue here. [The] inherent right of self-defense has been central to the Second Amendment right. The handgun ban amounts to a prohibition of an entire class of "arms" that is overwhelmingly chosen by American society for that lawful purpose. The prohibition extends, moreover, to the home, where the need for defense of self, family, and property is most acute. Under any of the standards of scrutiny that we have applied to enumerated constitutional rights,[27] banning from the home "the most preferred firearm in the nation to 'keep' and use for protection of one's home and family" would fail constitutional muster.

[It] is no answer to say, as petitioners do, that it is permissible to ban the possession of handguns so long as the possession of other firearms (i.e., long guns) is allowed. It is enough to note [that] the American people have considered the handgun to be the quintessential self-defense weapon. There are many reasons that a citizen may prefer a handgun for home defense: It is easier to store in a location that is readily accessible in an emergency; it cannot easily be redirected or wrestled away by an attacker; it is easier to use for those without the upper-body strength to lift and aim a long gun; it can be pointed at a burglar with one hand while the other hand dials the police. Whatever the reason, handguns are the most popular weapon chosen by Americans for self-defense in the home, and a complete prohibition of their use is invalid.

We must also address the District's requirement (as applied to respondent's handgun) that firearms in the home be rendered and kept inoperable at all times. This makes it impossible for citizens to use them for the core lawful purpose of self-defense and is hence unconstitutional.

[Justice Breyer] criticizes us for declining to establish a level of scrutiny for evaluating Second Amendment restrictions. He proposes, explicitly at least, none of the traditionally expressed levels (strict scrutiny, intermediate scrutiny, rational basis), but rather a judge-empowering "interest-balancing inquiry" that "asks whether the statute burdens a protected interest in a way or to an extent that is out of proportion to the statute's salutary effects upon other important governmental interests." [Justice] Breyer arrives at his interest-balanced answer: because handgun violence is a problem, because the law is limited to an urban area, and because there were somewhat similar restrictions in the founding period (a false proposition that we have already

---

[27] **[Ct's Note]** Justice Breyer correctly notes that this law, like almost all laws, would pass rational-basis scrutiny. But rational-basis scrutiny is a mode of analysis we have used when evaluating laws under constitutional commands that are themselves prohibitions on irrational laws. In those cases, "rational basis" is not just the standard of scrutiny, but the very substance of the constitutional guarantee. Obviously, the same test could not be used to evaluate the extent to which a legislature may regulate a specific, enumerated right, be it the freedom of speech, the guarantee against double jeopardy, the right to counsel, or the right to keep and bear arms. [If] all that was required to overcome the right to keep and bear arms was a rational basis, the Second Amendment would be redundant with the separate constitutional prohibitions on irrational laws, and would have no effect.

discussed), the interest-balancing inquiry results in the constitutionality of the handgun ban. QED.

We know of no other enumerated constitutional right whose core protection has been subjected to a freestanding "interest-balancing" approach. The very enumeration of the right takes out of the hands of government—even the Third Branch of Government—the power to decide on a case-by-case basis whether the right is *really worth* insisting upon. A constitutional guarantee subject to future judges' assessments of its usefulness is no constitutional guarantee at all. [We] would not apply an "interest-balancing" approach to the prohibition of a peaceful neo-Nazi march through Skokie. See [*Collin v. Smith*, Ch. 7, Sec. 1, VI, C]. The First Amendment contains the freedom-of-speech guarantee that the people ratified, which included exceptions for obscenity, libel, and disclosure of state secrets, but not for the expression of extremely unpopular and wrong-headed views. The Second Amendment is no different. Like the First, it is the very *product* of an interest-balancing by the people—which Justice Breyer would now conduct for them anew.

[We] are aware of the problem of handgun violence in this country, and we take seriously the concerns raised by [many] who believe that prohibition of handgun ownership is a solution. The Constitution leaves the District of Columbia a variety of tools for combating that problem, including some measures regulating handguns. But the enshrinement of constitutional rights necessarily takes certain policy choices off the table. These include the absolute prohibition of handguns held and used for self-defense in the home. Undoubtedly some think that the Second Amendment is outmoded in a society where our standing army is the pride of our Nation, where well-trained police forces provide personal security, and where gun violence is a serious problem. That is perhaps debatable, but what is not debatable is that it is not the role of this Court to pronounce the Second Amendment extinct.

JUSTICE STEVENS, with whom JUSTICE SOUTER, JUSTICE GINSBURG, and JUSTICE BREYER join, dissenting.

The question presented by this case is not whether the Second Amendment protects a "collective right" or an "individual right." Surely it protects a right that can be enforced by individuals. But a conclusion that the Second Amendment protects an individual right does not tell us anything about the scope of that right.

Guns are used to hunt, for self-defense, to commit crimes, for sporting activities, and to perform military duties. The Second Amendment plainly does not protect the right to use a gun to rob a bank; it is equally clear that it *does* encompass the right to use weapons for certain military purposes. Whether it also protects the right to possess and use guns for nonmilitary purposes like hunting and personal self-defense is the question presented by this case. The text of the Amendment, its history, and our decision in *United States* v. *Miller*, provide a clear answer to that question.

The Second Amendment was adopted to protect the right of the people of each of the several States to maintain a well-regulated militia. It was a response to concerns raised during the ratification of the Constitution that the power of Congress to disarm the state militias and create a national standing army posed an intolerable threat to the sovereignty of the several States. Neither the text of the Amendment nor the arguments advanced by its proponents evidenced the slightest interest in limiting any legislature's authority to regulate private civilian uses of firearms. Specifically, there is no indication that the Framers of the Amendment intended to enshrine the common-law right of self-defense in the Constitution. [The] view of the Amendment we took in *Miller*—that it protects the right to keep and bear arms for certain military purposes, but that it does not curtail the Legislature's power to regulate the nonmilitary use and ownership of weapons—is both the most natural reading of the Amendment's text and the interpretation most faithful to the history of its adoption.

[The] Court concludes its opinion by declaring that it is not the proper role of this Court to change the meaning of rights "enshrine[d]" in the Constitution. But the right the Court announces was not "enshrined" in the Second Amendment by the Framers; it is the product of today's law-changing decision. * * *

JUSTICE BREYER, with whom JUSTICE STEVENS, JUSTICE SOUTER, and JUSTICE GINSBURG join, dissenting.

[The] majority's conclusion is wrong for two independent reasons. The first reason is that set forth by Justice Stevens—namely, that the Second Amendment protects militia-related, not self-defense-related, interests. These two interests are sometimes intertwined. To assure 18th-century citizens that they could keep arms for militia purposes would necessarily have allowed them to keep arms that they could have used for self-defense as well. But self-defense alone, detached from any militia-related objective, is not the Amendment's concern.

The second independent reason is that the protection the Amendment provides is not absolute. [The] District's law is consistent with the Second Amendment even if that Amendment is interpreted as protecting a wholly separate interest in individual self-defense. That is so because the District's regulation, which focuses upon the presence of handguns in high-crime urban areas, represents a permissible legislative response to a serious, indeed life-threatening, problem.

[T]he law is tailored to the urban crime problem in that it is local in scope and thus affects only a geographic area both limited in size and entirely urban; the law concerns handguns, which are specially linked to urban gun deaths and injuries, and which are the overwhelmingly favorite weapon of armed criminals; and at the same time, the law imposes a burden upon gun owners that seems proportionately no greater than restrictions in existence at the time the Second Amendment was adopted. In these circumstances, the District's law falls within the zone that the Second Amendment leaves open to regulation by legislatures.

[Respondent] proposes that the Court adopt a "strict scrutiny" test, which would require reviewing with care each gun law to determine whether it is "narrowly tailored to achieve a compelling governmental interest." But the majority implicitly, and appropriately, rejects that suggestion by broadly approving a set of laws—prohibitions on concealed weapons, forfeiture by criminals of the Second Amendment right, prohibitions on firearms in certain locales, and governmental regulation of commercial firearm sales—whose constitutionality under a strict scrutiny standard would be far from clear.

[I] would simply adopt [an] interest-balancing inquiry explicitly. The fact that important interests lie on both sides of the constitutional equation suggests that review of gun-control regulation is not a context in which a court should effectively presume either constitutionality (as in rational-basis review) or unconstitutionality (as in strict scrutiny). Rather, "where a law significantly implicates competing constitutionally protected interests in complex ways," the Court generally asks whether the statute burdens a protected interest in a way or to an extent that is out of proportion to the statute's salutary effects upon other important governmental interests. Any answer would take account both of the statute's effects upon the competing interests and the existence of any clearly superior less restrictive alternative. Contrary to the majority's unsupported suggestion that this sort of "proportionality" approach is unprecedented, the Court has applied it in various constitutional contexts, including election-law cases, speech cases, and due process cases.

[A]ny self-defense interest at the time of the Framing could not have focused exclusively upon urban-crime related dangers. Two hundred years ago, most Americans, many living on the frontier, would likely have thought of self-defense primarily in terms of outbreaks of fighting with Indian tribes, rebellions, [marauders], and crime-related dangers to travelers on the roads, on footpaths, or along waterways.

[Nor,] for that matter, am I aware of any evidence that *handguns* in particular were central to the Framers' conception of the Second Amendment. The lists of militia-related weapons in the late 18th-century state statutes appear primarily to refer to other sorts of weapons, muskets in particular.

[A] contrary view, as embodied in today's decision, will have unfortunate consequences. The decision will encourage legal challenges to gun regulation throughout the Nation. Because it says little about the standards used to evaluate regulatory decisions, it will leave the Nation without clear standards for resolving those challenges. And litigation over the course of many years, or the mere specter of such litigation, threatens to leave cities without effective protection against gun violence and accidents during that time.

[I] can understand how reasonable individuals can disagree about the merits of strict gun control as a crime-control measure, even in a totally urbanized area. But I cannot understand how one can take from the elected branches of government the right to decide whether to insist upon a handgun-free urban populace in a city now facing a serious crime problem and which, in the future, could well face environmental or other emergencies that threaten the breakdown of law and order.

[The] majority says that that Amendment protects those weapons "typically possessed by law-abiding citizens for lawful purposes." This definition conveniently excludes machineguns, but permits handguns, which the majority describes as "the most popular weapon chosen by Americans for self-defense in the home." But what sense does this approach make? [On] the majority's reasoning, if tomorrow someone invents a particularly useful, highly dangerous self-defense weapon, Congress and the States had better ban it immediately, for once it becomes popular Congress will no longer possess the constitutional authority to do so. In essence, the majority determines what regulations are permissible by looking to see what existing regulations permit. There is no basis for believing that the Framers intended such circular reasoning.

[I] conclude that the District's measure is a proportionate, not a disproportionate, response to the compelling concerns that led the District to adopt it. * * *

MCDONALD V. CITY OF CHICAGO
561 U.S. 742, 130 S.Ct. 3020, 177 L.Ed.2d 894 (2010).

JUSTICE ALITO announced the judgment of the Court and delivered the opinion of the Court with respect to Parts I, II–A, II–B, II–D, III–A, and III–B, in which THE CHIEF JUSTICE, JUSTICE SCALIA, JUSTICE KENNEDY, and JUSTICE THOMAS, join, and an opinion with respect to Parts II–C, IV, and V, in which THE CHIEF JUSTICE, JUSTICE SCALIA and JUSTICE KENNEDY, join.

Two years ago, in *Heller*, we held that the Second Amendment protects the right to keep and bear arms for the purpose of self-defense, and we struck down a District of Columbia law that banned the possession of handguns in the home. The city of Chicago (City) and the village of Oak Park, a Chicago suburb, have laws that are similar to the District of Columbia's, but Chicago and Oak Park argue that their laws are constitutional because the Second Amendment has no application to the

States. We have previously held that most of the provisions of the Bill of Rights apply with full force to both the Federal Government and the States. Applying the standard that is well established in our case law, we hold that the Second Amendment right is fully applicable to the States.

[II–B.] Today, many legal scholars dispute the correctness of the narrow *Slaughter-House* interpretation.

[II–C.] For many decades, the question of the rights protected by the Fourteenth Amendment against state infringement has been analyzed under the Due Process Clause of that Amendment and not under the Privileges or Immunities Clause. We therefore decline to disturb the *Slaughter-House* holding.

[II–D. Nearly all provisions of the Bill of Rights have been "incorporated" in a way that provides the samel level of protection against the states as they provide against the federal government. See p. 422 supra. The relevant inquiry is] whether a particular Bill of Rights guarantee is fundamental to *our* scheme of ordered liberty and system of justice.

[III.] With this framework in mind, we now turn directly to the question whether the Second Amendment right to keep and bear arms is incorporated in the concept of due process. In answering that question [we] must decide whether the right to keep and bear arms is fundamental to *our* scheme of ordered liberty, *Duncan* [or] whether this right is "deeply rooted in this Nation's history and tradition." *Washington v. Glucksberg* [p. 517 supra].

A.   Our decision in *Heller* points unmistakably to the answer. Self-defense is a basic right, recognized by many legal systems from ancient times to the present day, and in *Heller*, we held that individual self defense is "the *central component*" of the Second Amendment right [and] "deeply rooted" in the Nation's history and tradition.

[B.] [After] the Civil War, many of the over 180,000 African Americans who served in the Union Army returned to the States of the old Confederacy, where systematic efforts were made to disarm them and other blacks. [Union] Army commanders took steps to secure the rights of all citizens to keep and bear arms, but the 39th Congress concluded that legislative action was necessary. Its efforts to safeguard the right to keep and bear arms demonstrate that the right was still recognized to be fundamental.

[The] Civil Rights Act of 1866, which was considered at the same time as the Freedmen's Bureau Act, [sought] to protect the right of all citizens to keep and bear arms. [The] unavoidable conclusion is that the Civil Rights Act, like the Freedmen's Bureau Act, aimed to protect "the constitutional right to bear arms" and not simply to prohibit discrimination. [Congress], however, ultimately deemed these legislative remedies insufficient. Southern resistance, Presidential vetoes, and this Court's pre-Civil-War precedent persuaded Congress that a constitutional amendment was necessary to provide full protection for the rights of blacks. Today, it is generally accepted that the Fourteenth Amendment was understood to provide a constitutional basis for protecting the rights set out in the Civil Rights Act of 1866.

[Despite] all this evidence, municipal respondents contend that Congress, in the years immediately following the Civil War, merely sought to outlaw "discriminatory measures taken against freedmen, which it addressed by adopting a non-discrimination principle" and that even an outright ban on the possession of firearms was regarded as acceptable, "so long as it was not done in a discriminatory manner." [This] argument is implausible.

[IV.] [Municipal] respondents, in effect, ask us to treat the right recognized in *Heller* as a second-class right, subject to an entirely different body of rules than the other Bill of Rights guarantees that we have held to be incorporated into the Due Process Clause.

Municipal respondents' main argument is nothing less than a plea to disregard 50 years of incorporation precedent and return (presumably for this case only) to a bygone era. [According] to municipal respondents, if it is possible to imagine *any* civilized legal system that does not recognize a particular right, then the Due Process Clause does not make that right binding on the States. Therefore, [because many countries] either ban or severely limit handgun ownership, it must follow that no right to possess such weapons is protected by the Fourteenth Amendment.

This line of argument is, of course, inconsistent with the long-established standard we apply in incorporation cases. And the present-day implications of [this] argument are stunning. For example, many of the rights that our Bill of Rights provides for persons accused of criminal offenses are virtually unique to this country. If *our* understanding of the right to a jury trial, the right against self-incrimination, and the right to counsel were necessary attributes of *any* civilized country, it would follow that the United States is the only civilized Nation in the world.

[Municipal] respondents maintain that the Second Amendment differs from all of the other provisions of the Bill of Rights because it concerns the right to possess a deadly implement and thus has implications for public safety. [But this] is not the only constitutional right that has controversial public safety implications. All of the constitutional provisions that impose restrictions on law enforcement and on the prosecution of crimes fall into the same category.

JUSTICE THOMAS, concurring in part and concurring in the judgment.

I agree with the Court that the Fourteenth Amendment makes the right to keep and bear arms set forth in the Second Amendment "fully applicable to the States." I write separately because I believe there is a more straightforward path to this conclusion, one that is more faithful to the Fourteenth Amendment's text and history.

[I] cannot agree that the [Second Amendment] is enforceable against the States through a clause that speaks only to "process." Instead, the right to keep and bear arms is a privilege of American citizenship that applies to the States through the Fourteenth Amendment's Privileges or Immunities Clause.

[The] notion that a constitutional provision that guarantees only "process" before a person is deprived of life, liberty or property could define the substance of [unenumerated] rights strains credulity for even the most casual user of words. Moreover, this fiction is a particularly dangerous one. The one theme that links the Court's substantive due process precedents together is their lack of a guiding principle to distinguish "fundamental" rights that warrant protection from nonfundamental rights that do not. Today's decision illustrates the point. Replaying a debate that has endured from the inception of the Court's substantive due process jurisprudence, the dissent lauds the "flexibility" in this Court's substantive due process doctrine, while the plurality makes yet another effort to impose principled restraints on its exercise. But neither side argues that the meaning they attribute to the Due Process Clause was consistent with public understanding at the time of its ratification.

[After a long discussion of the meaning of the terms "privileges" and "immunities," the Congressional debates on the Fourteenth Amendment, what the ratifying public understood the Privileges or Immunities Clause to mean, and the civil rights legislation adopted by the 39th Congress in 1866, Thomas, J., concluded that] the record makes plain that the Framers of the Privileges or Immunities Clause and the ratifying-era public understood—just as the Framers of the Second Amendment did—that the right to keep and bear arms was essential to the preservation of liberty. The record makes equally plain that they deemed this right necessary to include in the minimum baseline of federal rights that the Privileges or Immunities Clause established in the wake of the War over slavery. [I] agree with the Court that the Second Amendment is fully applicable to the States. I do so because the right to keep and bear arms is guaranteed by the Fourteenth Amendment as a privilege of American citizenship.

JUSTICE BREYER, with whom JUSTICE GINSBURG and JUSTICE SOTOMAYOR join, dissenting.

[We] are aware of no argument that gun-control regulations target or are passed with the purpose of targeting "discrete and insular minorities." *Carolene Products* [Ch. 5, Sec. 3]. Nor will incorporation help to assure equal respect for individuals. Unlike the First Amendment's rights of free speech, free press, assembly, and petition, the private self-defense right does not comprise a necessary part of the democratic process that the Constitution seeks to establish. Unlike the First Amendment's religious protections, the Fourth Amendment's protection against unreasonable searches and seizures, the Fifth and Sixth Amendments' insistence upon fair criminal procedure, and the Eighth Amendment's protection against cruel and unusual punishments, the private self-defense right does not significantly seek to protect individuals who might otherwise suffer unfair or inhumane treatment at the hands of a majority.

[D]etermining the constitutionality of a particular state gun law requires finding answers to complex empirically based questions of a kind that legislatures are better able than courts to make. [Does] the presence of a child in the house matter? Does the presence of a convicted felon in the house matter? [When] do registration requirements become severe to the point that they amount to an unconstitutional ban? [The] difficulty of finding answers to these questions is exceeded only by the importance of doing so. Firearms cause well over 60,000 deaths and injuries in the United States each year. Those who live in urban areas, police officers, women, and children, all may be particularly at risk. And gun regulation may save their lives. Some experts have calculated, for example, that Chicago's handgun ban has saved several hundred lives, perhaps close to 1,000, since it was enacted in 1983.

[At] the same time, the opponents of regulation cast doubt on these studies. And who is right? [Suppose] studies find more accidents and suicides where there is a handgun in the home than where there is a long gun in the home or no gun at all. To what extent do such studies justify a ban? What if opponents of the ban put forth counter studies? In answering such questions judges cannot simply refer to judicial homilies, such as Blackstone's 18th-century perception that a man's home is his castle. Nor can the plurality so simply reject, by mere assertion, the fact that "incorporation will require judges to assess the costs and benefits of firearms restrictions."

[N]othing in 18th-, 19th-, 20th-, or 21st-century history shows a consensus that the right to private armed defense, as described in *Heller*, is "deeply rooted in this Nation's history or tradition" or is otherwise "fundamental." Indeed, incorporating the right recognized in *Heller* may change the law in many of the 50 States. Read in the majority's favor, the historical evidence is at most ambiguous. And, in the absence of any other support for its conclusion, ambiguous history cannot show that the Fourteenth Amendment incorporates a private right of self-defense against the States.

JUSTICE STEVENS, dissenting.

[I] agree with the plurality that there are weighty arguments supporting petitioners' [Due Process contention]. But these arguments are less compelling than the plurality suggests; they are much less compelling when applied outside the home; and their validity does not depend on the Court's holding in *Heller*. For that holding sheds no light on the meaning of the Due Process Clause. [Our] decisions construing that Clause to render various procedural guarantees in the Bill of Rights enforceable against the States likewise tell us little about the meaning of the word "liberty" in the Clause or about the scope of its protection of nonprocedural rights. This is a substantive due process case.

[A] key constraint on substantive due process analysis is respect for the democratic process. If a particular liberty interest is already being given careful consideration in, and subjected to ongoing calibration by, the States, judicial enforcement may not be appropriate. When the Court declined to establish a general right to physician-assisted suicide, for example, it did so in part because "the States [were] currently engaged in serious, thoughtful examinations of physician-assisted suicide and other similar issues," rendering judicial intervention both less necessary and potentially more disruptive. *Glucksberg*. Conversely, we have long appreciated that more "searching" judicial review may be justified when the rights of "discrete and insular minorities"—groups that may face systematic barriers in the political system—are at stake. *Carolene Products Co.*

[Recognizing] a new liberty right is a momentous step. It takes that right, to a considerable extent, "outside the arena of public debate and legislative action." *Glucksberg*. Sometimes that momentous step must be taken; some fundamental aspects of personhood, dignity, and the like do not vary from State to State, and demand a baseline of protection. But sensitivity to the interaction between the intrinsic aspects of liberty and the practical realities of contemporary society provides an important tool for guiding judicial discretion. This sensitivity is an aspect of a deeper principle: the need to approach our work with humility and caution.

[While] I agree with the Court that our substantive due process cases offer a principled basis for holding that petitioners have a constitutional right to possess a usable firearm in the home, I am ultimately persuaded that a better reading of our case law supports the city of Chicago. I would not foreclose the possibility that a particular plaintiff—say, an elderly widow who lives in a dangerous neighborhood and does not have the strength to operate a long gun—may have a cognizable liberty interest in possessing a handgun. But I cannot accept petitioners' broader submission. A number of factors, taken together, lead me to this conclusion.

First, firearms have a fundamentally ambivalent relationship to liberty. Just as they can help homeowners defend their families and property from intruders, they can help thugs and insurrectionists murder innocent victims. [Amici] calculate that approximately one million Americans have been wounded or killed by gunfire in the last decade.

[T]he right to possess a firearm of one's choosing is different in kind from the liberty interests we have recognized under the Due Process Clause. [I] do not doubt for a moment that many Americans feel deeply passionate about firearms [but] it does not appear to be the case that the ability to own a handgun, or any particular type of firearm, is critical to leading a life of autonomy, dignity, or political equality. [The] liberty interest asserted by petitioners is also dissimilar from those we have recognized in its capacity to undermine the security of others. [The] handgun is itself a tool for crime; the handgun's bullets *are* the violence.

[A]lthough] it may be true that Americans' interest in firearm possession and state-law recognition of that interest are 'deeply rooted' in some important senses, it is equally true that the States have a long and unbroken history of regulating firearms. The idea that States may place substantial restrictions on the right to keep and bear arms short of complete disarmament is, in fact, far more entrenched than the notion that the Federal Constitution protects any such right.

Across the Nation, States and localities vary significantly in the patterns and problems of gun violence they face, as well as in the traditions and cultures of lawful gun use they claim. The city of Chicago, for example, faces a pressing challenge in combating criminal street gangs. Most rural areas do not. The city of Chicago has a high population density, which increases the potential for a gunman to inflict mass terror and casualties. Most rural areas do not. [Given] that relevant background conditions diverge so much across jurisdictions, the Court ought to pay particular heed to state and local legislatures' "right to experiment." *New State Ice Co. v. Liebmann*, 285 U.S. 262 (1932). (Brandeis, J., dissenting.)

[The] strength of a liberty claim must be assessed in connection with its status in the democratic process. And in this case, no one disputes "that opponents of [gun] control have considerable political power and do not seem to be at a systematic disadvantage in the democratic process," or that "the widespread commitment to an individual right to own guns * * * operates as a safeguard against excessive or unjustified gun control laws." Cass R. Sunstein, *Second Amendment Minimalism: Heller as Griswold*, 122 Harv.L.Rev. 246 (2008). [Neither] petitioners nor those most zealously committed to their views represent a group or a claim that is liable to receive unfair treatment at the hands of the majority. On the contrary, petitioners' views are supported by powerful participants in the legislative process.

[Justice] Scalia's method invites not only bad history, but also bad constitutional law. [In] evaluating a claimed liberty interest (or any constitutional claim for that matter), it makes perfect sense to give history significant weight. [But] it makes little sense to give history dispositive weight in every case. And it makes *especially* little sense to answer questions like whether the right to bear arms is "fundamental" by focusing only on the past, given that both the practical significance and the public understandings of such a right often change as society changes.

[The] concern runs still deeper. Not only can historical views be less than completely clear or informative, but they can also be wrong. [It] is not the role of federal judges to be amateur historians. And it is not fidelity to the Constitution to ignore its use of deliberately capacious language, in an effort to transform foundational legal commitments into narrow rules of decision. [The] net result of Justice Scalia's supposedly objective analysis is to vest federal judges—ultimately a majority of the judges on this Court—with unprecedented lawmaking powers in an area in which they have no special qualifications, and in which the give-and-take of the political process has functioned effectively for decades. * * *

JUSTICE SCALIA, concurring.

I join the Court's opinion. Despite my misgivings about Substantive Due Process as an original matter, I have acquiesced in the Court's incorporation of certain guarantees in the Bill of Rights "because it is both long established and narrowly limited." This case does not require me to reconsider that view, since straightforward application of settled doctrine suffices to decide it. I write separately only to respond to some aspects of Justice Stevens' dissent.

[Exactly] what is covered [under the view of Stevens, J.] is not clear. But whatever else is in, he *knows* that the right to keep and bear arms is out, despite its being as "deeply rooted in this Nation's history and tradition" as a right can be, see *Heller*.

Justice Stevens also argues that requiring courts to show "respect for the democratic process" should serve as a constraint. That is true, but [he] would have them show respect in an extraordinary manner. In his view, if a right "is already being given careful consideration in, and subjected to ongoing calibration by, the States, judicial enforcement may not be appropriate." In other words, a right, such as the right to keep and bear arms, that has long been recognized but on which the States are considering restrictions, apparently deserves *less* protection, while a privilege the political branches (instruments of the democratic process) have withheld entirely and continue to withhold, deserves *more*. That topsy-turvy approach conveniently accomplishes the objective of ensuring that the rights this Court held protected in *Casey*, *Lawrence*, and other such cases fit the theory—but at the cost of insulting rather than respecting the democratic process.

[Justice Stevens makes] the odd assertion that "firearms have a fundamentally ambivalent relationship to liberty," since sometimes they are used to cause (or sometimes accidentally produce) injury to others. [The] criterion, [is] inherently manipulable. Surely Justice Stevens does not mean that the Clause covers only rights that have *zero* harmful effect on *anyone*. Otherwise even the First Amendment is out.

[Justice] Stevens next suggests that the Second Amendment right is not fundamental because it is "different in kind" from other rights we have recognized. [Even] though he does "not doubt for a moment that many Americans * * * see [firearms] as critical to their way of life as well as to their security," he pronounces that owning a handgun is not "critical to leading a life of autonomy, dignity, or political equality." Who says? Deciding what is essential to an enlightened, liberty-filled life is an inherently political, moral judgment—the antithesis of an objective approach that reaches conclusions by applying neutral rules to verifiable evidence.

[Justice] Stevens' final reason for rejecting incorporation of the Second Amendment reveals, more clearly than any of the others, the game that is afoot. Assuming that there is a "plausible constitutional basis" for holding that the right to keep and bear arms is incorporated, he asserts that we ought not to do so *for prudential reasons.* Even if we had the authority to withhold rights that are within the Constitution's command (and we assuredly do not), two of the reasons Justice Stevens gives for abstention show just how much power he would hand to judges. The States' "right to experiment" with solutions to the problem of gun violence, he says, is at its apex here because "the best solution is far from clear." That is true of most serious social problems—whether, for example, "the best solution" for rampant crime is to admit confessions unless they are affirmatively shown to have been coerced, but see *Miranda v. Arizona,* 284 U.S. 436 (1966), or to permit jurors to impose the death penalty without a requirement that they be free to consider "any relevant mitigating factor."

[The] question to be decided is not whether the historically focused method is a *perfect means* of restraining aristocratic judicial Constitution-writing; but whether it is the *best means available* in an imperfect world. Or indeed, even more narrowly than that: whether it is demonstrably much better than what Justice Stevens proposes. I think it beyond all serious dispute that it is much less subjective, and intrudes much less upon the democratic process. [In] the most controversial matters brought before this Court—for example, the constitutionality of prohibiting abortion, assisted suicide, or homosexual sodomy, or the constitutionality of the death penalty—*any* historical methodology, under *any* plausible standard of proof, would lead to the same conclusion. Moreover, the methodological differences that divide historians, and the varying interpretive assumptions they bring to their work, are nothing compared to the differences among the American people (though perhaps not among graduates of prestigious law schools) with regard to the moral judgments Justice Stevens would have courts pronounce. * * *

NOTES AND QUESTIONS

1. ***Loosening the Constitution's grip on the legislative and executive branches.*** Consider Judge Richard A. Posner, *In Defense of Looseness: The Supreme Court and Gun Control*, The New Republic, Aug. 27, 2008, pp. 34–35: "Constitutional interpretations that relax rather than tighten the Constitution's grip on the legislative and executive branches of government are especially welcome when there are regional or local differences in relevant conditions or in public opinion. The failure to recognize this point (or perhaps indifference to it) was the mistake that the Supreme Court made when it nationalized abortion rights in *Roe v. Wade*. It would be the mistake the Court would be making in the unlikely event that it created a federal constitutional right of homosexual marriage. It is the mistake the Court has made in *Heller*. The differences in attitude toward private ownership of pistols across regions of the country and, outside the South, between urban and rural areas, are profound (mirroring the national diversity of views about gay marriage, and gay rights in general, as well as about abortion rights). A uniform rule is neither necessary nor appropriate. Yet that is what the *Heller* decision will produce.

"[The] range of historical references in the majority opinion [in *Heller*] is breathtaking, but it is not evidence of disinterested historical inquiry. It is evidence of the ability of well-staffed courts to produce snow jobs.

"[There] is no greater urgency about allowing people to possess guns for self-defense or defense of property today than there was thirty years ago, when the prevalence of violent crime was greater, or for that matter one hundred years ago. Only the membership of the Supreme Court has changed."

Despite his disagreement with the *Heller* ruling, in his judicial capacity, Judge Posner later applied it to invalidate an Illinois statute generally forbidding the carrying of firearms in public. Writing for the panel in *Moore v. Madigan*, 702 F.3d 933 (7th.Cir.2012), he acknowledged that "Twenty-first century Illinois has no hostile Indians. But a Chicagoan is a good deal more likely to be attacked on a sidewalk in a rough neighborhood than in his apartment on the 35th floor of the Park Tower. A woman who is being stalked or has obtained a protective order against a violent ex-husband is more vulnerable to being attacked while walking to or from her home than when inside. She has a stronger self-defense claim to be allowed to carry a gun in public than the resident of a fancy apartment building (complete with doorman) has a claim to sleep with a loaded gun under her mattress. But Illinois wants to deny the former claim, while compelled by *McDonald* to honor the latter. That creates an arbitrary difference. To confine the right to be armed to the home is to divorce the Second Amendment from the right of self-defense described in *Heller* and *McDonald*. It is not a property right—a right to kill a houseguest who in a fit of aesthetic fury tries to slash your copy of Norman Rockwell's painting *Santa with Elves*. That is not self-defense, and this case like *Heller* and *McDonald* is just about self-defense."

Meanwhile, Judge Posner changed his mind about the constitutionality of same-sex marriage prohibitions, writing for the panel to invalidate the Indiana and Wisconsin bans in *Baskin v. Bogan*, 766 F.3d 648 (7th.Cir.2014). Was that change of heart justified by the fact that by 2014 there was substantially less public opposition to same-sex marriage than in 2008? Should the public opposition have mattered in 2008? In *Baskin*, Judge Posner wrote for the court that "[m]inorities trampled on by the democratic process have recourse to the courts; the recourse is called constitutional law." Are people who wish to possess firearms for self-defense "minorities" whose rights are sometimes "trampled on by the democratic process?"

2.   *Is Heller like Roe v. Wade?* Consider Judge J. Harvie Wilkinson III, *Of Guns, Abortions, and the Unraveling Rule of Law*, 95 Va.L.Rev. 253 (2009): "It may no longer be possible to judge a Supreme Court ruling by anything other than result. [It] may all be bottom line: gun rights enthusiasts rush to hail *Heller* as pro-choice advocates hailed *Roe*. Who can blame them? Many gun regulations may be quite ill-advised; many restrictions on abortion may be most intrusive. But before popping the champagne on the Supreme Court's latest edict, maybe someone should wonder whether we purchase today's victory at the cost of tomorrow's freedom. The largest threat to liberty still lies in handing our democratic destiny to the courts.

"[Despite] a difference in the magnitude of judicial overreaching, the methodological similarities between *Roe* and *Heller* are large. Both cases interpreted ambiguous constitutional provisions and both claimed to find in them mandates that put to rest an extremely controversial issue of social policy, in the process overturning decisions by popularly elected officials. If there is a reasonable case for the majority's interpretation of the Second Amendment, there is also a reasonable case for the position taken by the dissenters. [When] a constitutional question is so close, when conventional interpretive methods do not begin to resolve the issue decisively, the tie for many reasons should go to the side of deference to democratic processes.

"[Justice] Breyer's dissent in *Heller* sounds familiar. He criticized the majority for acting like a legislature. He noted that courts typically defer to legislatures' empirical judgments, and that legislatures are better than courts at analyzing facts. He acknowledged there is a right at stake, but finds that the D.C. regulation is reasonable. This sounds all too much like Justice Rehnquist in *Roe*. [Every] one of the infirmities that Justice Rehnquist identified in *Roe*—the superior capacity of legislatures to evaluate facts, the narrow perspective that judges bring to contested social issues, and the straitjacket that a constitutional rule places on legislative compromise and changing information—is also present in *Heller*."

3.   *Original public meaning or law office history?* While "[b]racketing the question as to whether *Heller*'s analysis of the linguistic

evidence was correct," Lawrence B. Solum, *District of Columbia v. Heller and Originalism*, 103 Nw. U. L. Rev. 923 (2009), concludes that "it is hard to imagine finding a clearer example of original public meaning originalism in an actual judicial decision." Likewise, Randy E. Barnett, *Op-Ed., News Flash: The Constitution Means What It Says*, Wall St. J., June 27, 2008, at A13, contends that "Justice Scalia's opinion [in *Heller*] is the finest example of what is now called 'original public meaning' jurisprudence ever adopted by the Supreme Court." But consider Saul Cornell, *Heller, New Originalism, and Law Office History—"Meet the New Boss, Same as the Old Boss"*, 56 UCLA L.Rev. 1095 (2009): "if one looks closely at *Heller*, particularly at Scalia's methodology, it seems clear that the case is not the triumph of a new methodology, but really just the latest incarnation of the old law office history—a results oriented methodology in which evidence is selectively gathered and interpreted to produce a preordained conclusion."

4.   *Is Heller an exercise in popular constitutionalism?* Reva B. Siegel, *Dead or Alive: Originalism as Popular Constitutionalism in Heller*, 122 Harv.L.Rev. 191 (2008), argues that "*Heller*'s originalism enforces understandings of the Second Amendment that were forged in the late twentieth century through popular constitutionalism. [The] correspondence between the law-and-order Second Amendment forged in culture wars of the New Right and the original public meaning of the Second Amendment that *Heller* vindicates is striking. When Justice Scalia explains that the Second Amendment protects rights of the 'law-abiding, responsible citizens to use arms in defense of hearth and home,' he echoes [1970s National Rifle Association official] Harlon Carter, Ronald Reagan, and Charlton Heston, who all claim the Second Amendment protects rights of the 'law-abiding' and invoke the distinction between citizens and criminals to explain the Second Amendment. The coincidence is deeper, manifest not only in the rhetoric of the *Heller* opinion, but also in its account of the Second Amendment's core purposes. Justice Scalia's Second Amendment protects the law-abiding citizen's ability to defend himself and his family from criminals—and not the republican vision of a militia prepared to defend against government tyranny.

"Twentieth-century conflict helped tutor intuitions about the Second Amendment's core and periphery. For most of the twentieth century, literate lawyers read the Second Amendment in light of the republican purposes enunciated in its first clause; but decades of gun rights mobilization transformed the 'natural' meaning of the Constitution's text so that, for increasing numbers of Americans, a law-and-order Second Amendment simply appeared there as the founders' Constitution. [Decades] of mobilization inside and outside the academy forged modes of interpreting the Second Amendment that make libertarian, law-and-order concerns central to its meaning and republican concerns peripheral."

5.   *Questions left open.* *Heller* rejects rational basis scrutiny for laws restricting firearms, but in neither *Heller* nor *McDonald* did the Supreme Court say what level of scrutiny does apply. The rulings also leave open a number of important practical questions. Does the Second Amendment right

apply outside the home? May the government forbid the carrying of concealed firearms? May the government forbid the open carrying of firearms? May it forbid concealed firearms *or* openly carried firearms but not both? May the government restrict the magazine size of firearms? If so, what is the minimum number of bullets that would satisfy the Second Amendment? Can the government mandate personalized trigger locks? Do "arms" include weapons besides guns, such as knives or pepper spray? May the government *require* citizens to carry firearms?[365]

5. THE DEATH PENALTY AND RELATED PROBLEMS: CRUEL AND UNUSUAL PUNISHMENT

Introduction

The Eighth Amendment forbids "[e]xcessive bail," "excessive fines," and the infliction of "cruel and unusual punishments." Some courses in substantive and procedural criminal law explore the detailed implications of these provisions and other constitutional restrictions on how the state and federal governments may exact punishment for crime. This section briefly considers limitations on the death penalty and other severe punishments because of the family resemblance between the Supreme Court's methodology in such cases and the methodology employed in many of the other cases discussed in this chapter. As Warren, C.J., explained for a plurality in *Trop v. Dulles,* 356 U.S. 86 (1958), the Eighth "Amendment must draw its meaning from the evolving standards of decency that mark the progress of a maturing society." In that case, the Chief Justice deemed deprivation of a native-born American's citizenship because of wartime desertion from the army—leaving him "stateless"—a "fate forbidden by the principle of civilized treatment guaranteed by the Eighth Amendment," but was quick to add: "Whatever the arguments may be against capital punishment, both on moral grounds and in terms of accomplishing the purposes of punishment—and they are forceful—the death penalty has been employed throughout our history, and, in a day when it is still widely accepted, it cannot be said to violate the constitutional concept of cruelty."

Not long after *Trop* was decided, the NAACP Legal Defense and Educational Fund, Inc. (LDF), led by Professor Anthony Amsterdam,

---

[365] For a small sample of the large and growing body of scholarship addressing some of these and related questions, see James Bishop, Note, *Hidden or on the Hip: The Right(s) to Carry After Heller,* 97 Cornell L.Rev. 907 (2012); Joseph Blocher, *The Right Not to Keep or Bear Arms,* 64 Stan.L.Rev. 1 (2012); Michael C. Dorf, *Does Heller Protect a Right to Carry Guns Outside the Home?,* 59 Syr.L.Rev. 225 (2008); David B. Kopel, Clayton E. Cramer & Joseph Edward Olson, *Knives and the Second Amendment,* 47 U.Mich.J.L. Reform 167 (2013); Jonathan Meltzer, Note, *Open Carry for All: Heller and our Nineteenth-Century Second Amendment,* 123 Yale L.J. 1486 (2014); Darrell A.H. Miller, *Guns as Smut: Defending the Home-Bound Second Amendment,* 108 Colum.L.Rev. 1278 (2009); Eugene Volokh, *Implementing the Right to Keep and Bear Arms for Self-Defense: An Analytical Framework and a Research Agenda,* 56 UCLA L.Rev. 1443 (2009).

launched a major constitutional assault on the death penalty. Convinced that "each year the United States went without executions, the more hollow would ring claims that the American people could not do without them" and that "the longer death-row inmates waited, the greater their numbers, the more difficult it would be for the courts to permit the first execution," the LDF developed a "moratorium strategy," creating "a death-row logjam." Michael Meltsner, *Cruel and Unusual: The Supreme Court and Capital Punishment* 107 (1973). Largely as a result of LDF efforts in blocking all executions on every conceivable legal ground, by 1972 there had not been a single execution in five years. However, the number of executions had started to decline as early as the 1940s and dropped dramatically in the 1960s, several years before the LDF successfully developed its moratorium strategy. Executions peaked at 199 in 1935 but "there was a steady decline to [fewer] than 50 [in] the early 1960s." David C. Baldus, George G. Woodworth & Charles A. Pulaski, Jr., *Equal Justice and the Death Penalty* 9 (1990). See also Jack Greenberg, *Capital Punishment as a System,* 91 Yale L.J. 908 (1982).

I. IS THE DEATH PENALTY ALWAYS "CRUEL AND UNUSUAL"?

FURMAN v. GEORGIA, 408 U.S. 238 (1972), considered the death sentences in a Georgia murder case, a Georgia rape case, and a Texas rape case.[366] Each of the defendands was African American and had been sentenced to death after trial by jury. Under the applicable state statutes, the judge or jury had discretion to impose the death penalty. Also at stake, however, were the lives of almost 600 condemned persons who had "piled up" on death rows throughout the land. Effectively striking down the laws of 39 states[367] and various federal statutory provisions, a 5–4 majority, per curiam, held that "the imposition and execution of the death penalty" under the systems as then administered constituted "cruel and unusual punishment" in violation of the Eighth and Fourteenth Amendments. Each of the Justices wrote a separate concurring or dissenting opinion explaining his reasons for invalidating or upholding the death penalty. (The nine opinions totaled 230 pages in the official reports.) *Furman* has been called "not so much a case as a badly orchestrated opera, with nine characters taking turns to offer their own arias." Robert Weisberg, *Deregulating Death,* 1983 Sup.Ct.Rev. 305.

---

[366] In *Coker v. Georgia,* 433 U.S. 584 (1977), the Court held that the death penalty was unconstitutionally disproportionate punishment for the rape of an adult woman. Relying on *Coker*, the Court invalidated a death sentence for the aggravated rape of an eight year old girl in *Kennedy v. Louisiana* infra.

[367] Forty states authorized capital punishment for a variety of crimes, but since Rhode Island's only capital statute, murder by a life term prisoner, carried a mandatory death sentence, it was not invalidated in *Furman.*

The pivotal opinions of Stewart and White, JJ., left open the question whether *any* system of capital punishment, as opposed to the ones then in existence, would be unconstitutional. A third member of the majority, Douglas, J., also reserved for another day whether a mandatory death penalty would be constitutional. The following excerpts provide a range of the views expressed.

STEWART, J.: "If we were reviewing death sentences imposed under [laws making death the mandatory punishment for every person convicted of engaging in certain designated conduct] we would be faced with the need to decide whether capital punishment is unconstitutional for all crimes and under all circumstances. We would need to decide whether a legislature— state or federal—could constitutionally determine that certain criminal conduct is so atrocious that society's interest in deterrence and retribution wholly outweighs any considerations of reform or rehabilitation of the perpetrator, and that, despite the inconclusive empirical evidence, only the automatic penalty of death will provide maximum deterrence.

"On that score I would say only that I cannot agree that retribution is a constitutionally impermissible ingredient in the imposition of punishment. The instinct for retribution is part of the nature of man, and channeling that instinct in the administration of criminal justice serves an important purpose in promoting the stability of a society governed by law. When people begin to believe that organized society is unwilling or unable to impose upon criminal offenders the punishment they 'deserve,' then there are sown the seeds of anarchy—of self-help, vigilante justice, and lynch law.

"The constitutionality of capital punishment in the abstract is not, however, before us in these cases. For the Georgia and Texas legislatures have not provided that the death penalty shall be imposed upon all those who are found guilty of forcible rape [or] murder. In a word, neither State has made a legislative determination that forcible rape and murder can be deterred only by imposing the penalty of death upon all who perpetrate those offenses.

"[Instead], the death sentences now before us are the product of a legal system that brings them, I believe, within the very core of the Eighth Amendment's guarantee against cruel and unusual punishments, a guarantee applicable against the States through the Fourteenth Amendment. In the first place, it is clear that these sentences are 'cruel' in the sense that they excessively go beyond, not in degree but in kind, the punishments that the state legislatures have determined to be necessary. In the second place, it is equally clear that these sentences are 'unusual' in the sense that the penalty of death is infrequently imposed for murder, and that its imposition for rape is extraordinarily rare. But I do not rest my conclusion upon these two propositions alone.

"These death sentences are cruel and unusual in the same way that being struck by lightning is cruel and unusual. For, of all the people convicted of rapes and murders in 1967 and 1968, many just as reprehensible as these, the petitioners are among a capriciously selected random handful upon whom the sentence of death has in fact been imposed. My concurring Brothers have demonstrated that, if any basis can be discerned for the selection of these few to be sentenced to die, it is the constitutionally impermissible basis of race. But racial discrimination has not been proved, and I put it to one side. I simply conclude that the Eighth and Fourteenth Amendments cannot tolerate the inflicting of a sentence of death under legal systems that permit this unique penalty to be so wantonly and so freakishly imposed."

WHITE, J.: "The imposition and execution of the death penalty are obviously cruel in the dictionary sense. But the penalty has not been considered cruel and unusual punishment in the constitutional sense because it was thought justified by the social ends it was deemed to serve. At the moment that it ceases realistically to further these purposes, however, the emerging question is whether its imposition in such circumstances would violate the Eighth Amendment. It is my view that it would, for its imposition would then be the pointless and needless extinction of life with only marginal contributions to any discernible social or public purposes. A penalty with such negligible returns to the State would be patently excessive and cruel and unusual punishment violative of the Eighth Amendment.

"It is also my judgment that this point has been reached with respect to capital punishment as it is presently administered under the statutes involved in these cases. [The] penalty is so infrequently imposed that the threat of execution is too attenuated to be of substantial service to criminal justice.

"[I] must arrive at judgment; and I can do no more than state a conclusion based on 10 years of almost daily exposure to the facts and circumstances of hundreds and hundreds of federal and state criminal cases involving crimes for which death is the authorized penalty. [T]he death penalty is exacted with great infrequency even for the most atrocious crimes [and] there is no meaningful basis for distinguishing the few cases in which it is imposed from the many cases in which it is not. The short of it is that the policy of vesting sentencing authority primarily in juries—a decision largely motivated by the desire to mitigate the harshness of the law and to bring community judgment to bear on the sentence as well as guilt or innocence—has so effectively achieved its aims that capital punishment within the confines of the statutes now before us has for all practical purposes run its course.

"[P]ast and present legislative judgment with respect to the death penalty loses much of its force when viewed in light of the recurring practice of delegating sentencing authority to the jury and the fact that a jury, in its own discretion and without violating its trust or any statutory policy, may refuse to impose the death penalty no matter what the circumstances of the crime. Legislative 'policy' is thus necessarily defined not by what is legislatively authorized but by what juries and judges do in exercising the discretion so regularly conferred upon them. In my judgment what was done in these cases violated the Eighth Amendment."

DOUGLAS, J.: "The words 'cruel and unusual' certainly include penalties that are barbaric. But the words, at least when read in light of the English proscription against selective and irregular use of penalties, suggest that it is 'cruel and unusual' to apply the death penalty—or any other penalty—selectively to minorities whose numbers are few, who are outcasts of society, and who are unpopular, but whom society is willing to see suffer though it would not countenance general application of the same penalty across the board.

"[These] discretionary statutes are unconstitutional in their operation. They are pregnant with discrimination and discrimination is an ingredient not compatible with the idea of equal protection of the laws that is implicit in the ban on 'cruel and unusual' punishments."

As BRENNAN, J., perceived the question, there are four principles "recognized in our cases and inherent in" the Eighth Amendment prohibition "sufficient to permit a judicial determination whether a challenged punishment comports with human dignity" and therefore is not "cruel and unusual": (1) "a punishment must not be so severe as to be degrading to the dignity of human beings"; (2) the government "must not arbitrarily inflict a severe punishment"; (3) "a severe punishment must not be unacceptable to contemporary society"; and (4) "a severe punishment must not be excessive," i.e., "unnecessary." Applying the first and "primary" principle, he concluded that capital punishment "involves by its very nature a denial of the executed person's humanity" and, in comparison to all other punishments today, "is uniquely degrading to human dignity." He "would not hesitate to hold, on that ground alone, that death is today a 'cruel and unusual punishment,' were it not that death is a punishment of longstanding usage and acceptance in this country." He then turned to a discussion of the other three principles and, relying heavily upon the fact that the death sentence is inflicted very rarely and most arbitrarily, concluded that the death penalty is inconsistent with these other principles as well: "The function of these principles is to enable a court to determine whether a punishment comports with human dignity. Death, quite simply, does not."

MARSHALL, J.'s "historical foray" led to the question "whether American society has reached a point where abolition is not dependent on a successful grass roots movement in particular jurisdictions, but is demanded by the Eighth Amendment." He concluded that the death penalty constitutes "cruel and unusual" punishment on two independent grounds: (1) "it is excessive and serves no valid legislative purpose," i.e., it is not a more effective deterrent than life imprisonment; (2) "it is abhorrent to currently existing moral values."

As for the first ground: "punishment for the sake of retribution" is "not permissible under the Eighth Amendment. [The] Eighth Amendment is our insulation from our baser selves. The 'cruel and unusual' language limits the avenues through which vengeance can be channeled. Were this not so, the language would be empty and a return to the rack and other tortures would be possible in a given case."

As for the second independent ground: Although recent opinion polls indicate that Americans are about equally divided on the question of capital punishment, "whether or not a punishment is cruel or unusual depends, not on whether its mere mention 'shocks the conscience and sense of justice of the people,' but on whether people who were fully informed as to the purposes of the penalty and its liabilities would find the penalty shocking, unjust, and unacceptable." He then concluded that if the average citizen possessed "knowledge of all the facts presently available regarding capital punishment [he would] find it shocking to his conscience and sense of justice. For this reason alone capital punishment cannot stand."

There were four separate dissents. BURGER, C.J., warned that "it is essential to our role as a court that we not seize upon the enigmatic character of the [Eighth Amendment] guarantee as an invitation to enact our personal predilections into law." He found "no authority suggesting that the Eighth Amendment was intended to purge the law of its retributive elements" nor any basis for prohibiting "all punishments the States are unable to prove necessary to deter or control crime." Aside from "the limitations of the Eighth Amendment itself," he averred that "the preference for legislative action is justified by the inability of the courts to participate in the debate at the level where the controversy is focused. The case against capital punishment is not the product of legal dialectic, but rests primarily on factual claims, the truth of which cannot be tested by conventional judicial processes."

BLACKMUN, J., dissented, "personally rejoic[ing]" at the Court's result, but unable to accept it "as a matter of history, of law, or of constitutional pronouncement."

POWELL, J.'S, dissent called the Court's ruling "the very sort of judgment that the legislative branch is competent to make and for which the judiciary is ill-equipped." He maintained that "the sweeping judicial action undertaken today reflects a basic lack of faith and confidence in the democratic process."

In a fourth dissent, REHNQUIST, J., concluded that the majority's ruling lacked the "deepest humility and genuine deference to legislative judgment" with which the task of judging constitutional cases must be approached; indeed, "it is not an act of judgment, but rather an act of will."

NOTES AND QUESTIONS

1.   **Of *"life"* and *"limb."*** Leonard Levy, *Against the Law* 396 (1974), observes that the Eighth Amendment prohibition "appears in the same Bill of Rights that clearly sanctions the death penalty. The Fifth Amendment begins with a guarantee [that] '[n]o person shall be held to answer for a *capital,* or otherwise infamous crime, unless * * * .' The same amendment [also provides]: 'nor shall any person be subject for the same offense to be twice put in jeopardy of *life* or limb' [nor] 'be deprived of *life,* liberty, or property without due process * * * .' In 1868 the Fourteenth Amendment made an identical due-process clause applicable to the [states]. Thus, the Constitution itself in four places recognizes and permits capital punishment, a penalty that was common when the Fifth, Eighth and Fourteenth Amendments were adopted." Brennan, J., offers "a stunning retort to the dissenters who so heavily stressed the fact that the language of the Fifth Amendment authorized the death penalty. One of its clauses prohibited placing any person in double jeopardy of life 'or limb,' [but] Brennan asserted correctly that no one now contends that the reference to jeopardy of limb 'provides a perpetual constitutional sanction for such corporal punishments as branding and earcropping, which were common punishments when the Bill of Rights was adopted' Not one of the four dissenters took note of the point; it was irrefutable."

2.   **Legislative response.** Marshall, J.'s suggestion that the American people, if faced with the truth about the death penalty, would reject it, may or may not be true in some abstract philosophical sense, but as a concrete prediction it proved inaccurate. "The celebration" among death penalty abolitionists in the wake of *Furman* "would not last long. By the end of the twentieth century capital punishment would be back with a vengeance." Stuart Banner, *The Death Penalty: An American History* 266–67 (2002).

But consider Franklin Zimring & Gordon Hawkins, *Capital Punishment and the Eighth Amendment: Furman and Gregg in Retrospect,* 18 U.C.Davis L.Rev. 927 (1985): The "legislative extravaganza" of post-*Furman* death penalty statutes "is reminiscent of the 'pouring panic of capital statutes' which was a feature of the history of the criminal law in eighteenth-century England. Whatever the social psychology of that development may have been, the post-*Furman* reaction in America would probably be best characterized as a typical frustration-aggression response. Like parallel incidents in school prayer and pornography, legislative backlash was entirely to be expected by anyone familiar with the history of judicial invalidation in this country." For a useful summary of the post-*Furman* statutes, see Stephen Gillers, *Deciding Who Dies*, 129 U.Pa.L.Rev. 1 (1980).

———

GREGG v. GEORGIA, 428 U.S. 153 (1976), involved one of the state statutes enacted to mend, rather than end, the death penalty in light of *Furman*. The Court upheld Georgia's new capital-sentencing procedures, rejecting the contention that "the punishment of death always, regardless of the enormity of the offense or the procedure followed in imposing the sentence, is cruel and unusual punishment in violation of the Constitution." Stewart, Powell and Stevens, JJ., announced the judgment of the Court and filed a joint opinion concluding that "the concerns expressed in *Furman* that the penalty of death not be imposed in an arbitrary or capricious manner can be met by a carefully drafted statute that ensures that the sentencing authority is given adequate information and guidance. As a general proposition these concerns are best met by a system [such as Georgia's] that provides for a bifurcated proceeding at which the sentencing authority is apprised of the information relevant to the imposition of sentence and provided with standards to guide its use of the information.

"[The] new Georgia sentencing procedures, by contrast [with the pre-*Furman* ones,] focus the jury's attention on the particularized nature of the crime and the particularized characteristics of the individual defendant. While the jury is permitted to consider any aggravating or mitigating circumstances,[368] it must find and identify at least one [of ten statutory aggravating circumstances beyond a reasonable doubt] before it may impose a penalty of death. In this way the jury's discretion is channeled. No longer can a jury wantonly and freakishly impose the death sentence; it is always circumscribed by the legislative guidelines. In addition, the review function of the Supreme Court of Georgia [which must review every death sentence to determine, inter alia, whether it was imposed under the influence of passion or prejudice and whether it is 'excessive or disproportionate to the penalty imposed in similar cases, considering both the crime and the defendant'] affords additional assurance that the concerns that prompted our decision in *Furman* are not present to any significant degree in the Georgia procedure applied here.

"[T]he petitioners in *Furman* and its companion cases predicated their argument primarily upon the asserted proposition that standards of decency had evolved to the point where capital punishment no longer could be tolerated. [The] petitioners [before] the Court today renew the 'standards of decency' argument, but developments [since] *Furman* have

---

[368] The plurality noted that the jury is not required to find any mitigating circumstance in order to make a recommendation of mercy that is binding on the court, but that it must find at least one *statutory* aggravating circumstance in order to recommend a death sentence.

undercut substantially the assumptions upon which [this] argument rested. [It] is now evident that a large proportion of American society continues to regard [capital punishment] as an appropriate and necessary criminal sanction.

"The most marked indication of society's endorsement of the death penalty for murder is the legislative response to *Furman*. The legislatures of at least 35 States have enacted new statutes that provide for the death penalty for at least some crimes that result in the death of another person. And the Congress of the United States, in 1974, enacted a statute providing the death penalty for aircraft piracy that results in death.

"[The] jury also is a significant and reliable objective index of contemporary values because it is so directly involved. [It] may be true that evolving standards have influenced juries in recent decades to be more discriminating in imposing the sentence of death. But the relative infrequency of jury verdicts imposing the death sentence does not indicate rejection of capital punishment per se. Rather, [it] may well reflect the humane feeling that this most irrevocable of sanctions should be reserved for a small number of extreme cases.

"[The] Eighth Amendment demands more than that a challenged punishment be acceptable to contemporary society. The Court also must ask whether it comports with the basic concept of human dignity at the core of the Amendment. *Trop* (plurality opinion).

"[The] death penalty is said to serve two principal social purposes: retribution and deterrence of capital crimes by prospective offenders. In part, capital punishment is an expression of society's moral outrage at particularly offensive conduct. This function [is] essential in an ordered society that asks its citizens to rely on legal processes rather than self-help to vindicate their wrongs. [The] value of capital punishment as a deterrent of crime is a complex factual issue the resolution of which properly rests with the legislatures, which can evaluate the results of statistical studies in terms of their own local conditions and with a flexibility of approach that is not available to the courts.

"[In] sum, we cannot say that the judgment of the Georgia Legislature that capital punishment may be necessary in some cases is clearly wrong. Considerations of federalism, as well as respect for the ability of a legislature to evaluate, in terms of its particular State, the moral consensus concerning the death penalty and its social utility as a sanction, require us to conclude, in the absence of more convincing evidence, that the infliction of death as a punishment for murder is not without justification and thus is not unconstitutionally severe."

WHITE, J., joined by Burger, C.J., and Rehnquist, J., concurred in the judgment: "Petitioner's argument that there is an unconstitutional amount of discretion in the system which separates those suspects who receive the death penalty from those who receive life imprisonment, a lesser penalty, or are acquitted or never charged, seems to be in final analysis an indictment of our entire system of justice. Petitioner has argued, in effect, that no matter how effective the death penalty may be as a punishment, government, created and run as it must be by humans, is inevitably incompetent to administer it. This cannot be accepted as a proposition of constitutional law."[369]

BRENNAN, J., dissented: "In *Furman,* I read 'evolving standards of decency' as requiring focus upon the essence of the death penalty itself and not primarily or solely upon the procedures under which the determination to inflict the penalty upon a particular person was made. [That] continues to be my view."

MARSHALL, J., also dissented: "The two purposes that sustain the death penalty as nonexcessive in the Court's view are general deterrence and retribution. [The] evidence I reviewed in *Furman* remains convincing, in my view, that 'capital punishment is not necessary as a deterrent to crime in our society.' The justification for the death penalty must be found elsewhere.

"[The plurality's view of the important purpose served by 'channeling' 'the instinct for retribution' in the administration of criminal justice] is wholly inadequate to justify the death penalty. [It] simply defies belief to suggest that the death penalty is necessary to prevent the American people from taking the law into their own hands.

"[There] remains for consideration, however, what might be termed the purely retributive justification for the death penalty that the death penalty is appropriate, not because of its beneficial effect on society, but because the taking of the murderer's life is itself morally good. [That] society's judgment that the murderer 'deserves' death must be respected not simply because the preservation of order requires it, but because it is appropriate that society make the judgment and carry it out [is a notion] fundamentally at odds with the Eighth Amendment. The mere fact that the community demands the murderer's life in return for the evil he has done cannot sustain the death penalty, for as [the plurality] remind[s] us, 'the Eighth Amendment demands more than that a challenged punishment be acceptable to contemporary society.' "

NOTES AND QUESTIONS

1. ***Public endorsement of the death penalty.*** "The critical holding in *Gregg,*" observe Samuel Gross & Robert Mauro, *Death & Discrimination: Racial Disparities in Capital Sentencing* 216 (1990), "was not the endorsement of 'guided discretion' but the decision that the use of the death penalty is consistent with 'contemporary values' and 'public attitude[s]' toward crime,

---

[369] Blackmun, J., concurred in the judgment, referring to his dissent in *Furman.*

and therefore that it is not constitutionally 'cruel and unusual.' By 1976 the evidence of public endorsement of the death penalty was undeniable." Gallup began polling Americans about their attitudes towards the death penalty in 1936 (when 59 percent favored it) and from the mid-1960s polled nearly annually. Support fell as low as 42 percent in 1966, and then began a steady climb to a peak of 80 percent in 1994, before declining to the mid-to-low 60s in the second decade of the Twenty-first Century. See *Death Penalty*, www.gallup.com/poll/1606/death-penalty.aspx (last visited Mar. 1, 2015). In addition to falling crime rates, growing concern that substantial numbers of innocent defendants had been, and were being, sentenced to death, probably played an important role in the decline of public support for the death penalty. See Samuel R. Gross & Phoebe C. Ellsworth, *Second Thoughts: Americans' Views on the Death Penalty at the Turn of the Century*, in *Beyond Repair? America's Death Penalty* 7 (Stephen P. Garvey ed. 2003).

2. ***The continuing reluctance to impose the death penalty in all death-eligible cases.*** "[O]ne obstacle to eliminating excessive or discriminatory death sentences under the post-*Furman* statutes," note Baldus, Woodworth & Pulaski, supra at 413–14, "is the continuing reluctance of prosecutors and juries to favor imposition of death sentences in all death-eligible cases. Not only is this reluctance contrary to the Supreme Court's expectations when it decided *Gregg,* but there is no practical remedy for this inaction. No one involved in the criminal-justice process is going to argue that the Eighth Amendment requires the more frequent imposition of death sentences. The fact remains, however, that when only a few of the many defendants convicted of capital murder actually receive death sentences the ability of the selection process to operate rationally and consistently in each case undergoes substantial strain." Would switching from jury sentencing to jury sentencing "solve" this problem? See Sheri Lynn Johnson et al, *The Delaware Death Penalty: An Empirical Study*, 97 Iowa.L.Rev. 1925 (2012) (finding, inter alia, that other things being equal, judges are more likely to impose the death penalty than juries are).

II. MANDATORY DEATH SENTENCES

1.   Unlike Georgia, Florida and Texas, whose post-*Furman* capital-sentencing procedures were designed to guide and to channel sentencing authority, ten states responded to *Furman* by replacing discretionary jury sentencing in capital cases with *mandatory death penalties*. These mandatory death statutes were invalidated in WOODSON v. NORTH CAROLINA, 428 U.S. 280 (1976) and ROBERTS (STANISLAUS) v. LOUISIANA, 428 U.S. 325 (1976), both decided the same day as *Gregg*. As in *Gregg*, in both *Woodson* and *Roberts*, STEWART, POWELL and STEVENS, JJ., jointly announced the judgment of the Court. (In each case, for the reasons stated in their *Gregg* dissents, Brennan and Marshall, JJ., concurred in the result.) The history of mandatory death penalty laws in this country, observed the *Woodson* plurality, reveals that the practice "has

been rejected as unduly harsh and unworkably rigid." Post-*Furman* enactments were dismissed as merely "attempts by the States to retain the death penalty in a form consistent with the Constitution, rather than a renewed social acceptance of mandatory death sentencing."

"A separate deficiency" of the North Carolina statute was its failure to respond adequately to "*Furman's* rejection of unbridled jury discretion in the imposition of capital sentences." In light of the widespread and persistent jury resistance to mandatory death penalties—and the high probability that many juries, despite their oaths, would exercise discretion in deciding which murderers "shall live and which shall die" under these "mandatory" statutes—North Carolina had not remedied "the problem of unguided and unchecked jury discretion" that was "[c]entral to the limited holding in *Furman*," but "simply papered over" it. Not only does North Carolina's mandatory death penalty statute provide "no standards to guide the jury in its inevitable exercise" of discretion, but "there is no way under [state law] for the judiciary to check arbitrary and capricious exercise of that power through a review of death sentences."

Another constitutional shortcoming of the statute was "its failure to allow the particularized consideration of relevant aspects of the character and record of each convicted defendant before the imposition upon him of a sentence of death. [A] process that accords no significance to relevant facets of the character and record of the individual offender or the circumstances of the particular offense excludes from consideration in fixing the ultimate punishment of death the possibility of compassionate or mitigating factors stemming from the diverse frailties of humankind. It treats all persons convicted of a designated offense not as uniquely individual human beings, but as members of a faceless, undifferentiated mass to be subjected to the blind infliction of the penalty of death."[370]

REHNQUIST, J., dissenting, rejected the view that the ten post-*Furman* mandatory death statutes represented "a wrongheaded reading [of] *Furman*. [While] those States may be presumed to have preferred their prior systems reposing sentencing discretion in juries or judges, they indisputably preferred mandatory capital punishment to no capital punishment at all. Their willingness to enact statutes providing that penalty is utterly inconsistent with the notion that they regarded mandatory capital sentencing as beyond 'evolving standards of decency.' "[371]

---

[370] The *Woodson* Court reserved judgment on the constitutionality of a mandatory death penalty statute "limited to an extremely narrow category of homicide, such as murder by a prisoner serving a life sentence." A decade later, in *Sumner v. Shuman*, 483 U.S. 66 (1987), a 6–3 majority, per Blackmun, J., held that "a departure from the individualized capital-sentencing doctrine is not justified" even in such a case.

[371] White, J., joined by Burger, C.J., and Rehnquist, J., also dissented, rejecting the Court's analysis for the reasons stated in his dissent in *Roberts,* infra. Blackmun, J., also dissented in

Dissenting in *Roberts* (which invalidated a Louisiana mandatory death sentence statute the *Woodson* plurality deemed fatally similar to North Carolina's), WHITE, J., joined by Burger, C.J., and Blackmun and Rehnquist, JJ., maintained: "As the plurality now interprets the Eighth Amendment, the Louisiana and North Carolina statutes are infirm because the jury is deprived of all discretion once it finds the defendant guilty. Yet in the next breath it invalidates these statutes because they are said to invite or allow too much discretion: Despite their instructions, when they feel that defendants do not deserve to die, juries will so often and systematically disobey their instructions and find the defendant not guilty or guilty of a noncapital offense that the statute fails to satisfy the standards of *Furman*. If it is truly the case that Louisiana juries will exercise *too much* discretion—and I do not agree that it is—then it seems strange indeed that the statute is also invalidated because it purports to give the jury *too little* discretion by making the death penalty mandatory. Furthermore, if there is danger of freakish and too infrequent imposition of capital punishment under a mandatory system such as Louisiana's, there is very little ground for believing that juries will be any more faithful to their instructions under the Georgia and Florida systems where the opportunity is much, much greater for juries to practice their own brand of unbridled discretion."

2.   LOCKETT v. OHIO, 438 U.S. 586 (1978), struck down a post-*Furman* statute that required the trial judge, once a verdict of aggravated murder with specifications had been returned, to impose the death sentence unless he found one of three narrowly defined mitigating circumstances present. Writing for a four-justice plurality, BURGER, C.J., joined by Stewart, Powell and Stevens, JJ., concluded that "the sentencer, in all but the rarest kind of capital case, [must] not be precluded from considering *as a mitigating factor,* any aspect of a defendant's character or record and any of the circumstances of the offense that the defendant proffers as a basis for a sentence less than death." Dissenting on this issue, REHNQUIST, J., protested the plurality's rule thus: "By encouraging defendants in capital cases, and presumably sentencing judges and juries, to take into consideration anything under the sun as a 'mitigating circumstance,' it will not guide sentencing discretion but will totally unleash it."

3.   EDDINGS v. OKLAHOMA, 455 U.S. 104 (1982), made clear that the *Lockett* rule does not merely require that capital defendants be permitted to offer all mitigating evidence; the sentencer must actually consider it. Although the state statute permitted consideration of any mitigating circumstances, the trial judge refused to consider, as a matter of law, either defendant's emotional disturbance or the circumstances of

---

Woodson for the reasons stated in his *Furman* dissent. All four *Woodson* dissenters also dissented in *Roberts*.

his unhappy upbringing. The state appellate court found the excluded evidence irrelevant because it did not tend to provide a legal excuse from criminal responsibility. A 5–4 majority, per POWELL, J., vacated the death sentence: "[T]he rule in *Lockett* [reflects] the law's effort to develop a system of capital punishment at once consistent and principled but also humane and sensible to the uniqueness of the individual. [By] holding that the sentencer in capital cases must be permitted to consider any relevant mitigating factor, the rule in *Lockett* recognizes that a consistency produced by ignoring individual differences is a false consistency. [The] sentencer, and [the state appellate court] on review, may determine the weight to be given relevant mitigating evidence. But they may not give it no weight by excluding such evidence from their consideration."

4. ***Exacerbating the disparity in capital defendants' representation.*** The sentencer need only consider and, of course, *can* only consider the mitigating evidence that is *introduced*. And the quantity and quality of the mitigating evidence presented turns largely on the skill, dedication, resourcefulness and funding of the capital defendant's attorney. Thus, although the penalty trial affords an able defense lawyer "an opportunity to present an enormous amount of material on background and character" in order to personalize the capital defendant, "it also exacerbates the disparity in capital defendants' representation at trial, which, in turn may be expected to exacerbate the death penalty's uneven application." Welsh S. White, *The Death Penalty in the Eighties* 69 (1987).

5. ***Are we back where we started?*** Yes, say Carol S. Steiker & Jordan M. Steiker, *Sober Second Thoughts: Reflections on Two Decades of Constitutional Regulation of Capital Punishment*, 109 Harv.L.Rev. 355 (1995). They conclude that "the overall effect of twenty-odd years of doctrinal head-banging has been to substantially reproduce the pre-*Furman* world of capital sentencing." As you read the more recent materials, consider whether the subsequent twenty-odd more years of head-banging have made matters better.

Is the Court Faced with Two Incompatible Sets of Commands?

Several months before retiring, dissenting from the denial of certiorari in a death penalty case, CALLINS v. COLLINS, 510 U.S. 1141 (1994), BLACKMUN, J., maintained that "the death penalty experiment has failed": "Experience has taught us that the constitutional goal of eliminating arbitrariness and discrimination from the administration of death can never be achieved without compromising an equally essential component of fundamental fairness—individualized sentencing. See *Lockett*. It is tempting, when faced with conflicting constitutional commands, to sacrifice one for the other or to assume that an acceptable balance between them already has been struck. In the context of the death penalty, however, such jurisprudential maneuvers are wholly inappropriate. The death penalty must be imposed 'fairly, and with reasonable consistency, or not at all.' *Eddings.*

"[From] this day forward, I no longer shall tinker with the machinery of death. [The] basic question—does the system accurately and consistently determine which defendants 'deserve' to die?—cannot be answered in the affirmative. [The] problem is that the inevitability of factual, legal, and moral error gives us a system that we know must wrongly kill some defendants, a system that fails to deliver the fair, consistent, and reliable sentences of death required by the Constitution.

"[I] believe the *Woodson-Lockett* line of cases to be fundamentally sound and rooted in American standards of decency that have evolved over time. [Yet,] as several Members of the Court have recognized, there is real 'tension' between the need for fairness to the individual and the consistency promised in *Furman.* [The] power to consider mitigating evidence that would warrant a sentence less than death is meaningless unless the sentencer has the discretion and authority to dispense mercy based on that evidence. Thus, the Constitution, by requiring a heightened degree of fairness to the individual, and also a greater degree of equality and rationality in the administration of death, demands sentencer discretion that is at once generously expanded and severely restricted.

"[The] arbitrariness inherent in the sentencer's discretion to afford mercy is exacerbated by the problem of race. Even under the most sophisticated death penalty statutes, race continues to play a major role in determining who shall live and who shall die. [No] matter how narrowly the pool of death-eligible defendants is drawn according to objective standards, *Furman's* promise still will go unfulfilled so long as the sentencer is free to exercise unbridled discretion within the smaller group and thereby to discriminate. " 'The power to be lenient [also] is the power to discriminate.' " *McCleskey v. Kemp* [infra III, quoting Kenneth C. Davis, *Discretionary Justice* 170 (1973).]

"[The] consistency promised in *Furman* and the fairness to the individual demanded in *Lockett* are not only inversely related, but irreconcilable in the context of capital punishment. Any statute or procedure that could effectively eliminate arbitrariness from the administration of death would also restrict the sentencer's discretion to such an extent that the sentencer would be unable to give full consideration to the unique characteristics of each defendant and the circumstances of the offense. By the same token, any statute or procedure that would provide the sentencer with sufficient discretion to consider fully and act upon the unique circumstances of each defendant would 'thro[w] open the back door to arbitrary and irrational sentencing.' All efforts to strike an appropriate balance between these conflicting constitutional commands are futile because there is a heightened need for both in the administration of death. [In] my view, the proper course when faced with irreconcilable constitutional commands is not to ignore one or the other, nor to pretend that the dilemma does not exist, but to admit the futility of the effort to harmonize them. This means accepting the fact that the death penalty cannot be administered in accord with our Constitution."

Blackmun, J.'s opinion drew a sharp response from SCALIA, J., concurring: "[O]ver the years since 1972 this Court has attached to the imposition of the death penalty two quite incompatible sets of commands. [These] commands were invented without benefit of any textual or historical support; they are the products of just such 'intellectual, moral, and personal' perceptions as Justice Blackmun expresses [today]. Though Justice Blackmun joins those of us who have acknowledged the incompatibility of the Court's *Furman* and *Lockett-Eddings* lines of jurisprudence, he unfortunately draws the wrong conclusion from the acknowledgment. [Instead of concluding that the death penalty is unconstitutional, we should conclude] that at least one of these judicially announced irreconcilable commands which cause the Constitution to prohibit what its text explicitly permits must be wrong.[372]

"Convictions in opposition to the death penalty are often passionate and deeply held. That would be no excuse for reading them into a Constitution that does not contain them, even if they represented the convictions of a majority of Americans. Much less is there any excuse for using that course to thrust a minority's views upon the people."

III. RACIAL DISCRIMINATION IN THE ADMINISTRATION OF THE DEATH PENALTY

McCLESKEY V. KEMP
481 U.S. 279, 107 S.Ct. 1756, 95 L.Ed.2d 262 (1987).

JUSTICE POWELL delivered the opinion of the Court.

[Petitioner, an African American man, was convicted in a Georgia trial court of armed robbery and the murder of a white police officer in the course of the robbery, and sentenced to death. He sought federal habeas corpus relief, contending that the Georgia capital sentencing process was administered in a racially discriminatory manner in violation of the Eighth Amendment and the Equal Protection Clause of the Fourteenth Amendment.[373] In support of his claim, petitioner proffered a statistical

---

[372] Concurring in *Walton v. Arizona,* 497 U.S. 639 (1990), Scalia, J., stated that he would adhere to the *Furman* line of cases but not to the *Lockett-Eddings* line.

[373] For discussion of the portion of Powell, J.'s opinion for the Court rejecting petitioner's equal protection claim, see p. 1432 infra.

study by David Baldus, Charles Pulaski and George Woodworth (the Baldus study).

[This study examined over 2,000 murder cases that occurred in Georgia during the 1970s and concluded that, other things being equal, black defendants were more likely to receive a death sentence than other defendants, but only slightly. However, even after taking account of many nonracial variables, defendants charged with killing white victims were 4.3 times as likely to receive a death sentence as those charged with killing blacks. Thus, the study indicates that black defendants, such as petitioner, who kill whites have the greatest likelihood of being sentenced to death. Nonetheless, both the federal district court and the appeals court rejected McCleskey's claim as unproven.]

[McCleskey] argues that the Baldus study demonstrates that the Georgia capital sentencing system violates the Eighth Amendment.[374]

In light of our precedents under the Eighth Amendment, McCleskey cannot argue successfully that his sentence is "disproportionate to the crime in the traditional sense." He does not deny that he committed a murder in the course of a planned robbery, a crime for which this Court has determined that the death penalty constitutionally may be imposed. [Rather, he] argues that the sentence in his case is disproportionate to the sentences in other murder cases.

On the one hand, he cannot base a constitutional claim on an argument that his case differs from other cases in which defendants *did* receive the death penalty. On automatic appeal, the Georgia Supreme Court found that McCleskey's death sentence was not disproportionate to other death sentences imposed in the State. [Moreover,] where the statutory procedures adequately channel the sentencer's discretion, such proportionality review is not constitutionally required.

On the other hand, absent a showing that the Georgia capital punishment system operates in an arbitrary and capricious manner, McCleskey cannot prove a constitutional violation by demonstrating that other defendants who may be similarly situated did *not* receive the death penalty. In *Gregg*, the Court confronted the argument that "the opportunities for discretionary action that are inherent in the processing of any murder case under Georgia law," specifically the opportunities for discretionary leniency, rendered the capital sentences imposed arbitrary and capricious. We rejected this contention.

---

[374] The Court noted [fn. 7]: "Our assumption that the Baldus study is statistically valid does not include the assumption that the study shows that racial considerations actually enter into any sentencing decisions in Georgia. Even a sophisticated multiple regression analysis such as the Baldus study can only demonstrate a *risk* that the factor of race entered into some capital sentencing decisions and a necessarily lesser risk that race entered into any particular sentencing decision."

[Because] McCleskey's sentence was imposed under Georgia sentencing procedures that focus discretion "on the particularized nature of the crime and the particularized characteristics of the individual defendant," we lawfully may presume that McCleskey's death sentence was not "wantonly and freakishly" imposed, and thus that the sentence is not disproportionate within any recognized meaning under the Eighth Amendment.

Although our decision in *Gregg* as to the facial validity of the Georgia capital punishment statute appears to foreclose McCleskey's disproportionality argument, he further contends that the Georgia capital punishment system is arbitrary and capricious in *application,* and therefore his sentence is excessive, because racial considerations may influence capital sentencing decisions in Georgia. We now address this claim.

To evaluate McCleskey's challenge, we must examine exactly what the Baldus study may show. Even Professor Baldus does not contend that his statistics *prove* that race enters into any capital sentencing decisions or that race was a factor in McCleskey's particular case. Statistics at most may show only a likelihood that a particular factor entered into some decisions. There is, of course, some risk of racial prejudice influencing a jury's decision in a criminal case. There are similar risks that other kinds of prejudice will influence other criminal trials. The question "is at what point that risk becomes constitutionally unacceptable." McCleskey asks us to accept the likelihood allegedly shown by the Baldus study as the constitutional measure of an unacceptable risk of racial prejudice influencing capital sentencing decisions. This we decline to do.

[At] most, the Baldus study indicates a discrepancy that appears to correlate with race. Apparent disparities in sentencing are an inevitable part of our criminal justice system. The discrepancy indicated by the Baldus study is "a far cry from the major systemic defects identified in *Furman.*" [O]ur consistent rule has been that constitutional guarantees are met when "the mode [for determining guilt or punishment] itself has been surrounded with safeguards to make it as fair as possible." Where the discretion that is fundamental to our criminal process is involved, we decline to assume that what is unexplained is invidious. In light of the safeguards designed to minimize racial bias in the process, the fundamental value of jury trial in our criminal justice system, and the benefits that discretion provides to criminal defendants, we hold that the Baldus study does not demonstrate a constitutionally significant risk of racial bias affecting the Georgia capital sentencing process.

Two additional concerns inform our decision in this case. First, McCleskey's claim, taken to its logical conclusion, throws into serious question the principles that underlie our entire criminal justice system.

The Eighth Amendment is not limited in application to capital punishment, but applies to all penalties. Thus, if we accepted McCleskey's claim that racial bias has impermissibly tainted the capital sentencing decision, we could soon be faced with similar claims as to other types of penalty. Moreover, the claim that his sentence rests on the irrelevant factor of race easily could be extended to apply to claims based on unexplained discrepancies that correlate to membership in other minority groups, and even to gender. Similarly, since McCleskey's claim relates to the race of his victim, other claims could apply with equally logical force to statistical disparities that correlate with the race or sex of other actors in the criminal justice system, such as defense attorneys, or judges. Also, there is no logical reason that such a claim need be limited to racial or sexual bias. [T]here is no limiting principle to the type of challenge brought by McCleskey. The Constitution does not require that a State eliminate any demonstrable disparity that correlates with a potentially irrelevant factor in order to operate a criminal justice system that includes capital punishment.

[Second,] McCleskey's arguments are best presented to the legislative bodies. It is not the responsibility—or indeed even the right—of this Court to determine the appropriate punishment for particular crimes. [Despite] McCleskey's wide ranging arguments that basically challenge the validity of capital punishment in our multiracial society, the only question before us is whether in his case, the law of Georgia was properly applied. We agree with the [courts below] that this was carefully and correctly done in this case. * * *

JUSTICE BRENNAN, with whom JUSTICE MARSHALL joins, and with whom JUSTICE BLACKMUN and JUSTICE STEVENS join in all but Part I, dissenting. * * *

II.   At some point in this case, Warren McCleskey doubtless asked his lawyer whether a jury was likely to sentence him to die. A candid reply to this question would have been disturbing. First, counsel would have to tell McCleskey that few of the details of the crime or of McCleskey's past criminal conduct were more important than the fact that his victim was white. Furthermore, counsel would feel bound to tell McCleskey that defendants charged with killing white victims in Georgia are 4.3 times as likely to be sentenced to death as defendants charged with killing blacks. [The] story could be told in a variety of ways, but McCleskey could not fail to grasp its essential narrative line: there was a significant chance that race would play a prominent role in determining if he lived or died.

[The Court] finds no fault in a system in which lawyers must tell their clients that race casts a large shadow on the capital sentencing process. [The] Court's evaluation of the significance of petitioner's evidence is fundamentally at odds with our consistent concern for rationality in capital sentencing, and the considerations that the majority invokes to discount that evidence cannot justify ignoring its force.

III. It is important to emphasize at the outset that the Court's observation that McCleskey cannot prove the influence of race on any particular sentencing decision is irrelevant in evaluating his Eighth Amendment claim. Since *Furman,* the Court has been concerned with the *risk* of the imposition of an arbitrary sentence, rather than the proven fact of one. [This] emphasis on risk acknowledges the difficulty of divining the jury's motivation in an individual case.

[The] statistical evidence in this [case] relentlessly documents the risk that McCleskey's sentence was influenced by racial considerations. This evidence shows that there is a better than even chance in Georgia that race will influence the decision to impose the death penalty: a majority of defendants in white-victim crimes would not have been sentenced to die if their victims had been black. [In] light of the gravity of the interest at stake, petitioner's statistics on their face are a powerful demonstration of the type of risk that our Eighth Amendment jurisprudence has consistently condemned.

Evaluation of McCleskey's evidence cannot rest solely on the numbers themselves. We must also ask whether the conclusion suggested by those numbers is consonant with our understanding of history and human experience. Georgia's legacy of a race-conscious criminal justice system, as well as this Court's own recognition of the persistent danger that racial attitudes may affect criminal proceedings, indicates that McCleskey's claim is not a fanciful product of mere statistical artifice. * * *

IV. The Court cites four reasons for shrinking from the implications of McCleskey's evidence: the desirability of discretion for actors in the criminal-justice system, the existence of statutory safeguards against abuse of that discretion, the potential consequences for broader challenges to criminal sentencing, and an understanding of the contours of the judicial role. While these concerns underscore the need for sober deliberation, they do not justify rejecting evidence as convincing as McCleskey has presented.

[The] Court also declines to find McCleskey's evidence sufficient in view of "the safeguards designed to minimize racial bias in the [capital sentencing] process." [It] is clear that *Gregg* bestowed no permanent approval on the Georgia system. It simply held that the State's statutory safeguards were assumed sufficient to channel discretion without evidence otherwise.

[The] challenge to the Georgia system is not speculative or theoretical; it is empirical. As a result, the Court cannot rely on the statutory safeguards in discounting McCleskey's evidence, for it is the very effectiveness of those safeguards that such evidence calls into question.

[The] Court also maintains that accepting McCleskey's claim would pose a threat to all sentencing because of the prospect that a correlation might be demonstrated between sentencing outcomes and other personal characteristics. Again, such a view is indifferent to the considerations that enter into a determination of whether punishment is "cruel and unusual." Race is a consideration whose influence is expressly constitutionally proscribed. We have expressed a moral commitment, as embodied in our fundamental law, that this specific characteristic should not be the basis for allotting burdens and benefits.

[Finally,] the Court justifies its rejection of McCleskey's claim by cautioning against usurpation of the legislatures' role in devising and monitoring criminal punishment. [The] judiciary's role in this society counts for little if the use of governmental power to extinguish life does not elicit close scrutiny. [The Court] fulfills, rather than disrupts, the scheme of separation of powers by closely scrutinizing the imposition of the death penalty, for no decision of a society is more deserving of the "sober second thought."[375]

NOTES AND QUESTIONS

1. *The reluctance to "find" racial discrimination.* According to Randall Kennedy, *McCleskey v. Kemp: Race, Capital Punishment, and the Supreme Court,* 101 Harv.L.Rev. 1388 (1988), the *McCleskey* Court's "lack of concern for the feelings of blacks may be related to its very keen concern for the sensitivities of those—mainly whites—subject to being labeled 'racist.' " Continues Professor Kennedy:

"One of the great achievements of social reform in American history has involved the stigmatization of overt racial prejudice. But this triumph in principle has produced an unforeseen consequence in application: it is precisely the sense that racial discrimination is a terrible evil that inhibits the Justices from 'finding' it in all but the clearest circumstances. Perhaps they assume that conduct so horrible must be plainly observable. Or perhaps their sense of the shamefulness of racism is so intense that they find it difficult to burden an official or agency with the moral opprobrium that the 'racist' label connotes without absolutely positive proof of culpability."

2. *Was the problem too many executions or too few?* The Baldus study found that the race of the victim was a very powerful predictor of whether the defendant received the death penalty but that the defendant's race was only weakly correlated with the likelihood of a capital sentence. If the Court had accepted that evidence, what remedy would have been best suited to address the underlying constitutional problem? Kennedy supra, worried about this question. Consider David Cole, *The Paradox of Race and Crime: A Comment on Randall Kennedy's "Politics of Distinction",* 83 Geo.L.J. 2547

---

[375] Blackmun, J., and Stevens, J., also filed dissents, each of which was joined in whole or in part by other dissenting Justices.

(1995): "Pointing to statistics showing that in Georgia those who killed white persons were far more likely to be executed than those who killed black persons, [Professor] Kennedy suggested that this discrimination could be remedied either by increasing the number of persons executed for killing black victims or by decreasing the number of persons executed for killing white victims. The former approach would, because of the intraracial character of most murders, lead to more executions of black defendants. [Professor] Kennedy acknowledged some discomfort with such a remedy."

3. ***Statistical evidence post-McCleskey.*** Does *McCleskey* "doom" *all* efforts to prove racial discrimination in the administration of the death penalty. Properly understood, it should not, argue John H. Blume, Theodore Eisenberg, and Sheri Lynn Johnson, *Post-McCleskey Racial Discrimination Claims in Capital Cases*, 83 Cornell.L.Rev. 1771 (1998), but in practice lower court judges have often interpreted it to preclude statistical proof. Criticizing this practice, Blume, Eisenberg, and Johnson contend: "In any other equal protection context, the showings made in many post-*McCleskey* cases would have triggered, at a minimum, the opposing party's duty to rebut the prima facie case of racial discrimination. When lower courts, without examination, reject such prosecutor-specific proof of discrimination simply because a death row inmate—whose claims one might assume should receive more judicial scrutiny rather than less—proffers it, they distort *McCleskey* in a manner that cannot be squared with generally applicable equal protection doctrine."

IV. ADDITIONAL CONSTITUTIONAL LIMITS ON IMPOSING SEVERE PUNISHMENT

In ATKINS v. VIRGINIA, 536 U.S. 304 (2002), a 5–4 majority, per Stevens, J., relied on a "consensus" among "the American public, legislators, scholars, and judges" for the conclusion that the death penalty is cruel and unusual as applied to an intellectually disabled defendant: "This consensus unquestionably reflects widespread judgment about the relative culpability of [such] offenders, and the relationship between [intellectual disability] and the penological purposes served by the death penalty. Additionally, it suggests that some characteristics of [intellectual disability] undermine the strength of the procedural protections that our capital jurisprudence steadfastly guards."[376]

In ROPER v. SIMMONS, 543 U.S. 551 (2005), the same 5–4 majority that decided *Atkins*, this time per Kennedy, J., held that the Eighth and Fourteenth Amendments prohibited the execution of offenders under 18 at the time they committed the crime. "The differences between juvenile and adult offenders are too marked and well understood," observed the Court,

---

[376] In *Hall v. Florida*, 134 S.Ct. 1986 (2014), the Court ruled 5–4, per Kennedy, J., that a "rigid rule" of state law defining "intellectual disability to require an IQ test score of 70 or less [creates] an unacceptable risk that persons with intellectual disability will be executed, and thus is unconstitutional."

"to risk allowing a youthful person to receive the death penalty despite insufficient culpability."

In KENNEDY v. LOUISIANA, 554 U.S. 407 (2008), another 5–4 majority per Kennedy, J., concluded that the death sentence for a defendant who raped but did not kill a child under the age of 12 (in fact, the victim was the defendant's own 8-year-old stepdaughter), and who did not intend to assist another in killing the child, violated the Eighth and Fourteenth Amendments. According to the majority, "in terms of moral depravity and of the injury to the person and to the public," non-homicide crimes, even including child rape, cannot be compared to murder in their "severity and irrevocability." Alito, J., joined by Roberts, C.J., and Scalia and Thomas, JJ., dissented, maintaining that the Court had failed to support the principal justification for its holding—that murder is "unique" in its moral depravity and in the severity of the injury that it inflicts on the victim and the public.

In GRAHAM v. FLORIDA, 560 U.S. 48 (2010), a 5–4 majority, per KENNEDY, J., held that the Cruel and Unusual Punishment Clause prohibits a sentence of life imprisonment without the possibility of parole (LWOP) for any non-homicide crime committed by a juvenile:

"For the most part, [the] Court's precedents consider punishments challenged not as inherently barbaric but as disproportionate to the crime. The concept of proportionality is central to the Eighth Amendment. [The] Court's cases addressing the proportionality of sentences fall within two general classifications. [In] the first classification the Court considers all of the circumstances of the case to determine whether the sentence is unconstitutionally excessive. [The] second classification of cases has used categorical rules to define Eighth Amendment standards. The previous cases in this classification involved the death penalty.

["In] the cases adopting categorical rules, the Court has taken the following approach. The Court first considers 'objective indicia of society's standards, as expressed in legislative enactments and state practice' to determine whether there is a national consensus against the sentencing practice at issue. *Roper*. Next, [the] Court must determine in the exercise of its own independent judgment whether the punishment in question violates the Constitution. The present case involves an issue the Court has not considered previously: a categorical challenge to a term-of-years sentence. [Here,] in addressing the question presented, the appropriate analysis is the one used in cases that involved the categorical approach, specifically *Atkins*, *Roper,* and *Kennedy*."

After examining state laws and the "actual sentencing practices in jurisdictions where the sentence in question is permitted by statute," the Court concluded that there was "a consensus against" the use of LWOP sentences in the circumstances presented. The Court also concluded that a

LWOP sentence lacks any "legitimate penological justification" and is therefore disproportionate "for juvenile nonhomicide offenders."[377]

ROBERTS, C.J., concurring in the judgment, agreed with the Court that Graham's sentence of LWOP violated the Eighth Amendment, but, unlike the majority, saw "no need to invent a new constitutional rule of dubious provenance in reaching that conclusion. Instead, my analysis is based on an application of this Court's precedents, in particular (1) our cases requiring 'narrow proportionality' review of noncapital sentences and (2) our conclusion in *Roper* that juvenile offenders are generally less culpable than adults who commit the same crimes."

THOMAS, J., joined by Scalia, J., and Alito, J. (in pertinent part), dissented: "Although the text of the Constitution is silent regarding the permissibility of this sentencing practice, and although it would not have offended the standards that prevailed at the founding, the Court insists that the standards of American society have evolved such that the Constitution now requires its prohibition. The news of this evolution will, I think, come as a surprise to the American people. Congress, the District of Columbia, and 37 States allow judges and juries to consider this sentencing practice in juvenile nonhomicide cases, and those judges and juries have decided to use it in the very worst cases they have encountered."[378]

In MILLER v. ALABAMA, 132 S.Ct. 2455 (2012), the Court, per KAGAN, J., held that the Eighth Amendment forbids a sentencing scheme that mandates life without parole sentences for juvenile homicide offenders: "*Graham* concluded [that] life-without-parole sentences, like capital punishment, may violate the Eighth Amendment when imposed on children. To be sure, *Graham*'s flat ban on life without parole applied only to nonhomicide crimes, and the Court took care to distinguish those offenses from murder, based on both moral culpability and consequential harm. But none of what it said about children—about their distinctive (and transitory) mental traits and environmental vulnerabilities—is crime-specific. Those features are evident in the same way, and to the same degree, when (as in both cases here) a botched robbery turns into a killing. So *Graham*'s reasoning implicates any life-without-parole sentence imposed on a juvenile, even as its categorical bar relates only to nonhomicide offenses. [By] removing youth from the balance—by

---

[377] Stevens, J., joined by Ginsburg and Sotomayor, JJ., concurring, contended that "[p]unishments that did not seem cruel and unusual at one time may, in the light of reason and experience, be found cruel and unusual at a later time; unless we are to abandon the moral commitment embodied in the Eighth Amendment, proportionality review must never become effectively obsolete."

[378] In addition to joining Parts I and III of Thomas, J.'s dissent, Alito, J., dissented separately to emphasize that "[n]othing in the Court's opinion affects the imposition of a sentence to a term of years without the possibility of parole. Indeed, petitioner conceded at oral argument that [sentencing a juvenile to] as much as 40 years without the possibility of parole 'probably' would be constitutional."

subjecting a juvenile to the same life-without-parole sentence applicable to an adult—[the mandatory penalty schemes at issue here] prohibit a sentencing authority from assessing whether the law's harshest term of imprisonment proportionately punishes a juvenile offender."

ROBERTS, C.J., joined by Scalia, Thomas and Alito, JJ.,[379] dissented: "[T]he number of mandatory life without parole sentences for juvenile murderers, relative to the number of juveniles arrested for murder, is over 5,000 times higher than the corresponding number in *Graham*. There is thus nothing in this case like the evidence of national consensus in *Graham*. [Perhaps] science and policy suggest society should show greater mercy to young killers, giving them a greater chance to reform themselves at the risk that they will kill again. But that is not our decision to make. Neither the text of the Constitution nor our precedent prohibits legislatures from requiring that juvenile murderers be sentenced to life without parole."

By a vote of 7–2, the Court in BAZE v. REES, 553 U.S. 35 (2008), rejected an Eighth Amendment challenge to the three-drug protocol used by Kentucky in lethal injections administered to defendants sentenced to death. There was no majority opinion. ROBERTS, C.J., delivered the judgment of the Court in an opinion joined by Kennedy and Alito, JJ.: "This Court has never invalidated a State's chosen procedure for carrying out a sentence of death as the infliction of cruel and unusual punishment. [However,] in *In re Kemmler,* 136 U.S. 436 (1890), [we] observed: 'Punishments are cruel when they involve torture or a lingering death; but the punishment of death is not cruel, within the meaning of that word as used in the Constitution.' [Simply] because an execution method may result in pain, either by accident or as an inescapable consequence of death, does not establish the sort of 'objectively intolerable risk of harm' that qualifies as cruel and unusual.

"[It] is difficult to regard a practice as 'objectively intolerable' when it is in fact widely tolerated. Thirty-six States that sanction capital punishment have adopted lethal injection as the preferred method of execution. The Federal Government uses lethal injection as well. This broad consensus goes not just to the method of execution, but also to the specific three-drug combination used by Kentucky.

"[Reasonable] people of good faith disagree on the morality and efficacy of capital punishment, and for many who oppose it, no method of execution would ever be acceptable. But [this] Court has ruled that capital punishment is not prohibited under our Constitution, and that the States may enact laws specifying that sanction. [Kentucky] has adopted a method of execution believed to be the most humane available, one it shares with

---

[379] Breyer, J., concurred in an opinion joined by Sotomayor, J. Thomas, J., joined by Scalia, J., and Alito, J., joined by Scalia, J., also wrote separate dissents.

35 other States. Petitioners agree that, if administered as intended, that procedure will result in a painless death. The risks of maladministration they have suggested—such as improper mixing of chemicals and improper setting of IVs by trained and experienced personnel—cannot remotely be characterized as 'objectively intolerable.' Kentucky's decision to adhere to its protocol despite these asserted risks, while adopting safeguards to protect against them, cannot be viewed as probative of the wanton infliction of pain under the Eighth Amendment."

Baze produced six separate opinions in addition to the plurality.[380] The resulting uncertainty has produced some confusion in the lower courts and, in the years since *Baze*, states seeking to carry out executions by lethal injection have faced other obstacles as well. For example, according to Deborah W. Denno, *Lethal Injection Chaos Post-Baze*, 102 Geo.L.J. 1331 (2014), states encountered "a national shortage of sodium thiopental when Hospira, Inc., the sole U.S. manufacturer of the drug, ceased production due to difficulties procuring its active ingredient from another company. In late 2010, the British government announced plans to create an export restriction that would ban the export of sodium thiopental to the United States after learning that the drug would be solely used for executions. Hospira originally intended to resume production of the drug at its plant in Italy, but Italian authorities threatened legal action if Hospira could not successfully prevent the drug from [being used for executions.] Unwilling to risk potential liability, in January 2011, Hospira stopped manufacturing sodium thiopental entirely. Europe's prohibition of the death penalty had become an American problem." Furthermore, Denno explains that state efforts to develop substitute supplies and drug protocols have led to "botched executions." In January 2015, the Supreme Court granted review in *Warner v. Gross* (No. 14–7955) to decide whether a new drug protocol adopted by Oklahoma was constitutional.

6. PROCEDURAL DUE PROCESS IN NON-CRIMINAL CASES

According to Ely, supra, at 18 n.*, " 'procedural due process' is redundant." The concept of due *process*, after all, necessarily concerns the *procedures* that are *due* to persons before the government deprives them of life, liberty, or property. The term *"procedural* due process" entered the constitutional lexicon to distinguish what might otherwise simply be called due process from the doctrine of *substantive* due process. Ely himself called the latter "a contradiction in terms—sort of like 'green pastel redness.' " Whatever one makes of the arguments for and against substantive due process, the existence of procedural due process is uncontroversial.

---

[380] Alito, J., concurred. Stevens, J., concurred in the judgment. Scalia, J., joined by Thomas, J., concurred in the judgment. Thomas, J., joined by Scalia, J., concurred in the judgment. Breyer, J., concurred in the judgment. Ginsburg, J., joined by Souter, J., dissented.

Disagreements in this area generally involve the questions of what sorts of interests count as "liberty" or "property" sufficient to trigger procedural protection, as well as what procedures are required under various circumstances.

Courses in constitutional Criminal Procedure explore the implications of procedural due process in criminal cases, which are frequently drawn from various provisions of the Fourth, Fifth, and Sixth Amendments. The materials in this section provide a brief introduction to procedural due process in civil cases. Courses in Civil Procedure and Administrative Law may explore these issues in further detail. [381]

I. DEPRIVATION OF "LIBERTY" AND "PROPERTY" INTERESTS

1. According to most commentators, the "procedural due process revolution" began with GOLDBERG v. KELLY, 397 U.S. 254 (1970), holding that due process requires that welfare recipients be afforded an evidentiary hearing *prior* to the termination of benefits. As pointed out in Peter Simon, *Liberty and Property in the Supreme Court: A Defense of Roth and Perry,* 71 Calif.L.Rev. 146 (1983), *Goldberg* "did not in fact present the issue of whether welfare benefits were within the 'life, liberty or property' protected by the due process clauses, because [the Social Services Commissioner] conceded that 'the protections of the due process clause apply.' Nevertheless, [the Court] addressed the issue [suggesting] that whether the right to continue receiving a government benefit was within the protection of the due process clause turned upon the importance of the benefit to the individual." Thus, the Court, per BRENNAN, J., observed:

"[Welfare] benefits are a matter of statutory entitlement for persons qualified to receive them.[382] Their termination involves state action that adjudicates important rights. The constitutional challenge cannot be answered by an argument that public assistance benefits are 'a "privilege" and not a "right." ' Relevant constitutional restraints apply as much to the withdrawal of public assistance benefits as to disqualification for unemployment compensation, or to denial of a tax exemption, or to discharge from public employment. The extent to which procedural due process must be afforded the recipient is influenced by the extent to which

---

[381] The application of procedural process to the detention of captives in the "war on terror" is discussed above, Ch. 3, Sec. 1, III. Creditors' remedies cases are briefly considered in *Flagg Bros. v. Brooks,* Ch. 10, Sec. 5.

[382] At this point, the Court noted [fn. 8] that "[i]t may be more realistic today to regard welfare entitlements as more like 'property' than a 'gratuity,' " citing Charles Reich, *The New Property,* 73 Yale L.J. 733 (1964), and quoting extensively from Charles Reich, *Individual Rights and Social Welfare: The Emerging Social Issues,* 74 Yale L.J. 1245 (1965). In these articles Professor Reich maintained that public employment, welfare assistance, franchises, licenses, and other forms of governmental benefits and programs should be given the kind of protection afforded traditional property rights.

he may be 'condemned to suffer grievous loss,' and depends upon whether the recipient's interest in avoiding that loss outweighs the governmental interest in summary adjudication."

2.   As observed in Henry P. Monaghan, *Of "Liberty" and "Property,"* 62 Corn.L.Rev. 405 (1977), BELL v. BURSON, 402 U.S. 535 (1971), "represented the high-water mark of [an] approach [in which] determining whether an interest deserved due process clause process protection involved a simple pragmatic assessment of its 'importance' to the individual." The Court in *Bell,* per BRENNAN, J., invalidated a Georgia statute providing that the vehicle registration and driver's license of an uninsured motorist involved in an accident shall be suspended unless he posts security to cover the damages claimed by agreed parties in accident reports: Although a state could bar "the issuance of licenses to all motorists who did not carry liability insurance [or] post security, [o]nce licenses are issued, [their] continued possession may become essential in the pursuit of a livelihood. Suspension of issued licenses thus involves state action that adjudicates important interests of the licensees. In such cases the licenses are not to be taken away without that procedural due process required by the Fourteenth Amendment."

Monaghan notes that in *Bell* "[t]he Court could have said that the license was sufficient to qualify as 'property,' or that a suspension of an individual's freedom to drive was a restriction on his 'liberty.' The Court said neither; the importance of the interest alone sufficed, and 'importance' was determined as a matter of federal, not state, law."

3.   *Positive law as a source of liberty and property interests.* "*Bell*'s latitudinarian approach to 'liberty' and 'property' was soon eroded." Monaghan, supra. Stressing that before deciding what form of hearing is required by procedural due process the Court must "determine whether due process requirements apply in the first place," i.e., whether one has been deprived of "liberty" or "property"—and in doing so "we must look not to the 'weight' but to the nature of the interest at stake"—the Court in BOARD OF REGENTS v. ROTH, 408 U.S. 564 (1972), per STEWART, J., for the first time, rejected a procedural due process claim because it implicated neither "liberty" nor "property." Hired by Wisconsin State University for a fixed term of one year, and given no tenure rights to continued employment, Roth had been informed that he would not be rehired for the next academic year. The Court rejected his contention that the University's failure to give him any reason for its decision or any opportunity to challenge it at any sort of hearing violated procedural due process: "The requirements of procedural due process apply only to the deprivation of interests encompassed within the Fourteenth Amendment's protection of liberty and property. [T]he range of interests protected by procedural due process is not infinite. [The] State, in declining to rehire [Roth], did not make any charge against him that might seriously damage his standing

and associations in his community [e.g., accuse him of dishonesty or immorality, nor impose] on him a stigma or other disability that foreclosed his freedom to take advantage of other employment opportunities. [It did not, for example, bar him] from all other public employment in state universities. [O]n the record before us, all that clearly appears is that [Roth] was not rehired for one year at one university. It stretches the concept too far to suggest that [one] is deprived of 'liberty' when he simply is not rehired in one job but remains as free as before to seek another.

"[To] have a property interest in a benefit, [one] must have more than a unilateral expectation of it. He must, instead, have a legitimate claim of entitlement to [it]. Property interests, of course, are not created by the Constitution. Rather they are created and their dimensions are defined by existing rules or understandings that stem from an independent source such as state law—rules or understandings that secure certain benefits and that support claims of entitlement to those benefits. [Roth] surely had an abstract concern in being rehired, but he did not have a property interest sufficient to require the University authorities to give him a hearing when they declined to renew his contract of employment."[383]

4. ***Does the holder of a domestic violence restraining order have a "property interest" in police enforcement of that order?*** Consider CASTLE ROCK v. GONZALES, 545 U.S. 748 (2005): Respondent repeatedly called the police when she suspected that her estranged husband had taken their three daughters, in violation of a restraining order. Several hours after her last contact with the police, her husband entered the police station, opened fire with a semi-automatic weapon, and was killed by the return fire. Inside his vehicle, parked outside the stationhouse, the police found the bodies of all three daughters, whom he had murdered. Respondent brought a lawsuit against the town of Castle Rock, alleging that it had violated her Fourteenth Amendment due process rights because its police department had "an official policy or custom of failing to respond properly to complaints of restraining order violations" and "tolerate[d] the non-enforcement of restraining orders by its police officers."

A 7–2 majority, per SCALIA, J., rejected the claim: "Our cases recognize that a benefit is not a protected entitlement if government officials may grant or deny it in their discretion. [However, the relevant] provisions of

---

[383] Dissenting, Marshall, J., maintained that "every citizen who applies for a government job is entitled to it unless the government can establish some reason for denying the employment. This is the 'property' right that [is] protected by the Fourteenth Amendment and that cannot be denied 'without due process of law'. And it is also liberty—liberty to work—which is the 'very essence of the personal freedom and opportunity' secured by the Fourteenth Amendment." Dissenting, Brennan, J., joined by Douglas, J., agreed with Marshall, J., that Roth had been denied due process when his contract had not been renewed without his being informed of the reasons or given a chance to respond. Douglas, J., also dissented. Burger, C.J., concurred, arguing that a teacher's rights are a matter of state law that should be adjudicated by state courts in the first instance. Powell, J., did not participate.

Colorado law truly [did not make] enforcement of the restraining orders *mandatory*. A well established tradition of police discretion has long coexisted with apparently mandatory arrest statutes. [It] is hard to imagine that a Colorado peace officer would not have some discretion to determine that—despite probable cause to believe a restraining order has been violated—the circumstances of the violation or the competing duties of that officer or his agency counsel decisively against enforcement in a particular instance. The practical necessity for discretion is particularly apparent in a case such as this one, where the suspected violator is not actually present and his whereabouts are unknown.

"[Moreover,] it is by no means clear that an individual entitlement to enforcement of a restraining order could constitute a 'property' interest for purposes of the Due Process Clause. Such a right would not, of course, resemble any traditional conception of property. Although that alone does not disqualify it from due process protection, as *Roth* and its progeny show, the right to have a restraining order enforced does not 'have some ascertainable monetary value,' as even our '*Roth*-type property-as-entitlement' cases have implicitly required. Perhaps most radically, the alleged property interest here arises *incidentally*, not out of some new species of government benefit or service, but out of a function that government actors have always performed—to wit, arresting people who they have probable cause to believe have committed a criminal offense."

SOUTER, J., joined by Breyer, J., joined the Court's opinion, but also wrote a concurring opinion: "The Due Process Clause extends procedural protection to guard against unfair deprivation by state officials of substantive state-law property rights or entitlements; the federal process protects the property created by state law. But [respondent] claims a property interest in a state-mandated process in and of itself."

STEVENS, J., joined by Ginsburg, J., dissented: "The central question in this case is [whether,] as a matter of Colorado law, respondent had a right to police assistance comparable to the right she would have possessed to any other service the government or a private firm might have undertaken to provide. [The] Court places undue weight on the various statutes throughout the country that seemingly mandate police enforcement but are generally understood to provide police discretion. As a result, the Court gives short shrift to the unique case of 'mandatory arrest' statutes in the domestic violence context; States passed a wave of these statutes in the 1980's and 1990's with the unmistakable goal of eliminating police discretion in this area. [T]he Colorado statute at issue in this case was enacted for the benefit of the narrow class of persons who are beneficiaries of domestic restraining orders.

"[Because] respondent had a property interest in the enforcement of the restraining order, state officials could not deprive her of that interest without observing fair procedures. Her description of the police behavior in this case and the department's callous policy of failing to respond properly to reports of restraining order violations clearly alleges a due process violation. At the very least, due process requires that the relevant state decisionmaker *listen* to the claimant and then *apply the relevant criteria* in reaching this decision."

(a) ***Can a state ever create a property interest in police protection from third-party harm?*** The *Castle Rock* majority strongly suggests it could not, but consider Note, 119 Harv.L.Rev. 208 (2005): "Since *Roth*, the Court has taken a positivist approach to defending property for procedural due process purposes, an approach that allows people to rely on state laws that they have interpreted correctly. Although the *Castle Rock* Court did not so acknowledge, it significantly departed from this methodology when it claimed that a restraining order is not property because it lacks ascertainable monetary value and because it only benefits the protected person indirectly—factors that have nothing to do with the interpretation of underlying state law. As a result, *Castle Rock* threatens to subvert the reliance interests underlying *Roth*'s positivism."

(b) ***Why not substantive due process?*** Why did the plaintiff in *Castle Rock* rely on procedural due process rather than substantive due process? In *DeShaney v. Winnebago County Dep't of Social Serv.*, Ch. 10, Sec. 6, the Court rejected the claim that due process obligates the state or its subdivisions to protect people against private violence—there, as in *Castle Rock*, perpetrated by a father against his offspring.

5. ***"The bitter with the sweet."*** ARNETT v. KENNEDY, 416 U.S. 134 (1974): Kennedy, a nonprobationary federal civil service employee in a regional Office of Economic Opportunity station, was removed by the Regional Director for allegedly publicly accusing the Director of bribery "in reckless disregard" of the facts. Instead of responding to the charges against him in a proceeding that would have been conducted and decided by the very person he had allegedly defamed, Kennedy instituted a federal suit, asserting that the discharge procedures denied him procedural due process because they failed to provide for a trial-type hearing before an impartial agency official prior to removal. The Court, with no majority opinion, held that the challenged procedures satisfied due process.

The plurality opinion was by REHNQUIST, J., joined by Burger, C.J., and Stewart, J.: "[A]ppellee did have a statutory expectancy that he not be removed other than for 'such cause as will promote the efficiency of (the) service.' But the very section of the statute which granted him that [right] expressly provided also for the procedure by which 'cause' was to be determined, and expressly omitted the procedural guarantees which appellee insists are mandated by the Constitution. [W]here the grant of a substantive right is inextricably intertwined with the limitations on the procedures which are to be employed in determining that right, a litigant in the position of appellee must take the bitter with the sweet."

POWELL, J., joined by Blackmun, J., concurred in the result, but criticized the plurality's approach: "[The bitter-with-the sweet approach] would lead directly to the conclusion that whatever the nature of an individual's statutorily created property interest, deprivation of that interest could be accomplished without notice or a hearing at any time. This view misconceives the origin of the right to procedural due process. That right is conferred, not by legislative grace, but by constitutional guarantee. While the legislature may elect not to confer a property interest in federal employment, it may not constitutionally authorize the deprivation of such an interest, once conferred, without appropriate procedural safeguards."

Powell, J., nonetheless concluded that a prior evidentiary hearing was not required before removal. "The Government's interest in being able to act expeditiously to remove an unsatisfactory employee is substantial" and, because he would be reinstated and awarded back pay if he prevailed on the merits, Kennedy's "actual injury would consist [only] of a temporary interruption of his income during the interim." Thus, the challenged statutes and regulations "comport with due process by providing a reasonable accommodation of the competing interests."[384]

(a) *Circumventing Goldberg.* "The only difference" between *Arnett* and *Goldberg,* comments David Shapiro, *Mr. Justice Rehnquist: A Preliminary View,* 90 Harv.L.Rev. 293 (1976), "is that [in *Goldberg*] the statutes and regulations governing eligibility were not 'inextricably intertwined' with [those] providing for post-termination but not pre-termination hearings. Thus, under Justice Rehnquist's approach all the legislature would have to do to circumvent [*Goldberg*] would be to place the procedural limitations (which presumably could deny *any* opportunity to be heard at any time) in the same statutory section with the substantive provisions on eligibility. Surely, as six members of the Court seemed to agree, the effect would be to turn what looked like a landmark constitutional decision into the flimsiest of trivia."

(b) *Must a government employee always "take the bitter with the sweet"?* "It is clear," comments William Van Alstyne, *Cracks in "The New Property": Adjudicative Due Process in the Administrative State,* 62 Corn.L.Rev. 445 (1977), that he "need *not* [if] the bitter is a substantive restriction forbidden to government by the Constitution (which applies, of

---

[384] White, J., concurring in part and dissenting in part, rejected the Rehnquist plurality's analysis and largely agreed with Powell, J.'s constitutional analysis. He rejected the Court's judgment "due to the failure to provide an impartial hearing officer at the pretermination hearing." Dissenting, Marshall, J., joined by Douglas and Brennan, JJ., rejected the plurality's bitter-with-the-sweet analysis on grounds similar to Powell's, but as Marshall weighed the interests involved (stressing the long delay in the processing of adverse personnel actions), Kennedy was entitled to "an evidentiary hearing before an impartial decisionmaker prior to dismissal."

course, even when the government is operating as an employer), whether the bitter requires one to abstain from insisting upon one's first amendment rights or to relinquish one's rights to due process."

6. ***Reading "liberty" narrowly.*** In PAUL v. DAVIS, 424 U.S. 693 (1976), respondent Davis brought a civil rights suit in protest of police officials' decision to circulate a flyer to approximately 800 merchants in the Louisville, Kentucky area, designating him an "active shoplifter." Davis claimed that the police officials' action inhibited him from entering business establishments and impaired his employment opportunities. A 5–3 majority, per REHNQUIST, J., was unimpressed:

"[R]espondent's complaint would appear to state a classical claim for defamation actionable in the courts of virtually every State. [However, h]e asserted not a claim for defamation under the laws of Kentucky, but a claim that he had been deprived of rights secured to him by the Fourteenth Amendment of the United States Constitution. Concededly if the same allegations had been made about respondent by a private individual, he would have nothing more than a claim for defamation under state law. But, he contends, since petitioners are [government officials], his action is thereby transmuted into one for deprivation by the State of rights secured under the Fourteenth Amendment. [It] is hard to perceive any logical stopping place to such a line of reasoning. [It] would seem almost necessarily to result in every legally cognizable injury which may have been inflicted by a state official acting under 'color of law' establishing a violation of the Fourteenth Amendment. [Our cases do] not establish the proposition that reputation alone, apart from some more tangible interests such as employment, is either 'liberty' or 'property' by itself sufficient to invoke the procedural protection of the Due Process Clause."

BRENNAN, J., joined by White and Marshall, JJ., dissented: "The Court today holds that public officials, acting in their official capacities as law enforcers, may on their own initiative and without trial constitutionally condemn innocent individuals as criminals and thereby brand them with one of the most stigmatizing and debilitating labels in our society. [The] Court by mere fiat and with no analysis wholly excludes personal interest in reputation from the ambit of 'life, liberty, or property' under the Fifth and Fourteenth Amendments, thus rendering due process concerns *never* applicable to the official stigmatization, however arbitrary, of an individual. The logical and disturbing corollary of this holding is that no due process infirmities would inhere in a statute constituting a commission to conduct *ex parte* trials of individuals, so long as the only official judgment pronounced was limited to the public condemnation and branding of a person as a Communist, a traitor, an 'active murderer,' a homosexual, or any other mark that 'merely' carries social opprobrium. The potential of today's decision is frightening for a free people."[385]

7. ***In some situations, at least, a litigant need not "take the bitter with the sweet."*** A Nebraska law provided that if a designated physician finds that a prisoner "suffers from a mental disease or defect" that cannot be properly treated in prison the Director of Correctional Services may transfer the prisoner to a mental hospital. In VITEK v. JONES, 445 U.S. 480 (1980), per WHITE, J., the Court held the involuntary transfer of a state prisoner to a mental hospital implicates a constitutionally protected "liberty interest" and once a state grants prisoners such an interest "due process protections are necessary 'to insure that the state-created right is not arbitrarily abrogated' "—these protections "being a matter of federal law, they are not diminished by the fact that the State may have specified its own procedures that it may deem adequate for determining the preconditions to adverse official action. [We] have repeatedly held that state statutes may create liberty interests that are entitled to the procedural protections of the Due Process Clause of the Fourteenth Amendment. [The] 'objective expectation, firmly fixed in state law and [official] practice,' that a prisoner would not be transferred unless he suffered from a mental disease or defect that could not be adequately treated in the prison, gave Jones a liberty interest that entitled him to the benefits of appropriate procedures in connection with determining the conditions that warranted his transfer to a mental hospital." However, cases both before and after *Vitek* denied procedural protection to other kinds of prison transfers.[386]

8. ***Recognizing a protected 'liberty interest' independently of state law.*** The *Vitek* Court also held that quite apart from the statutory recognition of a liberty interest, "the transfer of a prisoner from a prison to a mental hospital must be accompanied by appropriate procedural protections": "[F]or the ordinary citizen, commitment to a mental hospital produces 'a massive curtailment of liberty' [and thus] 'requires due process

---

[385] Stevens, J., did not participate, but a year later, dissenting in *Ingraham v. Wright,* 430 U.S. 651 (1977), he suggested that *Paul* "may have been correctly decided on an incorrect rationale."

[386] The *Vitek* Court distinguished *Meachum v. Fano,* 427 U.S. 215 (1976), and *Montanye v. Haymes,* 427 U.S. 236 (1976), which, the Court said, had "held that the transfer of a prisoner from one prison to another does not infringe a protected liberty interest," on the ground that "in those cases transfers were discretionary with the prison authorities, and in neither case did the prisoner possess any right or justifiable expectation that he would not be transferred except for misbehavior or upon the occurrence of other specified events." See also *Olim v. Wakinekona,* 461 U.S. 238 (1983), per Blackmun, J., ruling that the transfer of a state prisoner from Hawaii to a maximum security facility in California "does not deprive an inmate of any liberty interest protected by the Due Process Clause in and of itself"; *Hewitt v. Helms,* 459 U.S. 460 (1983) (transfer of inmate from general prison population to administrative segregation implicates no liberty interest "independently protected by the Due Process Clause"); *Sandin v. Conner,* 515 U.S. 472 (1995) (because 30 days in administrative segregation "did not work a major disruption in" prisoner's "environment," he "lacked a protected liberty interest that would entitle him to the procedural protections" required in other cases).

protection.' [Were] an ordinary citizen to be subjected involuntarily to [confinement in a mental hospital], it is undeniable that protected liberty interests would be unconstitutionally infringed absent compliance with the procedures required by the Due Process Clause. We conclude that a convicted felon also is entitled to the benefit of procedures appropriate in the circumstances before he is found to have a mental disease and transferred to a mental hospital. [A] criminal conviction and sentence of imprisonment extinguish an individual's right to freedom from confinement for the term of his sentence, but they do not authorize the State to classify him as mentally ill and to subject him to involuntary psychiatric treatment without affording him additional due process protections."[387]

9.   *The continued vitality of Vitek.* In LOGAN v. ZIMMERMAN BRUSH CO., 455 U.S. 422 (1982), appellant filed a state administrative claim alleging that his employer terminated him because of his physical disability in violation of a state antidiscrimination law. Apparently through inadvertence, state agency officials scheduled a mandatory conference five days after the statutory deadline. The state court held that the failure to convene a timely conference deprived the agency of jurisdiction to consider appellant's claim. The Court, per BLACKMUN, J., reversed, deeming appellant's state law claim "a species of property" protected by Fourteenth Amendment due process and holding that the state scheme had deprived appellant of his property right:

"Because the entitlement arises from statute, the [state supreme] court reasoned, it was the legislature's prerogative to establish the 'procedures to be followed upon a charge.' This analysis, we believe, misunderstands the nature of the Constitution's due process guarantee. [B]ecause 'minimum [procedural] requirements [are] a matter of federal law, they are not diminished by the fact that the State may have specified its own procedures that it may deem adequate for determining the preconditions to adverse official action.' *Vitek.* Indeed, any other conclusion would allow the State to destroy at will virtually any state-created property interest. The Court has considered and rejected such an approach."

10.   *Why wasn't Logan's right to sue the Commission in tort for its negligence in forfeiting his claim sufficient to satisfy due*

---

[387] See also *Foucha v. Louisiana*, 504 U.S. 71 (1992), invalidating a state law permitting a person acquitted of a crime by reason of insanity who no longer suffers from a mental illness to be committed indefinitely to a mental institution until he is able to demonstrate that he is not dangerous to himself or others. Cf. *Washington v. Harper,* 494 U.S. 210 (1990), recognizing that a state prisoner has a "significant liberty interest," protected by due process, in avoiding the forced administration of antipsychotic drugs, but holding that a state's administrative procedures (an unconsenting prisoner was entitled to a hearing before a committee of medical professionals) satisfied procedural due process. But cf. *Kansas v. Hendricks*, 521 U.S. 346 (1997), upholding a statute establishing procedures for involuntary civil commitment, upon release from prison, of persons likely to engage in "predatory acts of sexual violence" because of a "mental abnormality" or "personality disorder."

process? In PARRATT v. TAYLOR, 451 U.S. 527 (1981), a state prisoner sued prison officials for losing hobby materials that came to the prison via mail order, arguing that their actions deprived him of property without due process. The Court, per REHNQUIST, J., held that where a loss of property results from "random and unauthorized" acts, due process does not require a pre-deprivation hearing, and that no federal constitutional violation occurs if the state provides an adequate post-deprivation remedy: "The loss of property, although attributable to the State as action under 'color of law,' is in almost all cases beyond the control of the State. Indeed, in most cases it is not only impracticable, but impossible, to provide a meaningful hearing before the deprivation.

"[The] State provides a remedy to persons who believe they have suffered a tortious loss at the hands of the State. Through this tort claims procedure the State hears and pays claims of prisoners housed in its penal institutions. [Although] the state remedies may not provide the respondent with all the relief which may have been available [in a federal civil rights suit], that does not mean that the state remedies are not adequate to satisfy the requirements of due process. The remedies provided could have fully compensated the respondent for the property loss he suffered, and we hold that they are sufficient to satisfy the requirements of due process."

The Zimmerman Brush Company invoked *Parratt* but the Court rejected the argument: "In *Parratt,* the Court emphasized that it was dealing with 'a tortious loss [of] property as a result of a random and unauthorized act by a state employee [rather than] some established procedure.' Here, in contrast, it is the state system itself that destroys a complainant's property interest, by operation of law, whenever the Commission fails to convene a timely conference—whether the Commission's action is taken through negligence, maliciousness, or otherwise. *Parratt* was not designed to reach such a situation. Unlike the complainant in *Parratt,* Logan is challenging not the Commission's error, but the 'established state procedure' that destroys his entitlement without according him proper procedural safeguards."

Although *Zimmerman Brush* has not been formally overruled, its scope was effectively limited by the Court's subsequent holding in *Daniels v. Williams*, 474 U.S. 327 (1986), per REHNQUIST, J., "that the Due Process Clause is simply not implicated by a *negligent* act of an official causing unintended loss of or injury to life, liberty, or property." *Daniels* was a federal civil rights suit by a prisoner who alleged that he suffered injuries after he slipped and fell on a pillow that had been negligently left on a staircase by a guard.

Do cases like *Parratt* and *Daniels* suggest that special principles ought to apply to prisoner lawsuits? Or would the concern about a flood of prisoner suits that underlies such cases be better addressed through statutory limits rather than as a matter of constitutional doctrine? Consider that the Prison Litigation Reform Act of 1995, 42 U.S.C. § 1997e(a), now requires prisoners to exhaust state administrative remedies before bringing a federal civil rights lawsuit.

II. WHAT KIND OF HEARING—AND WHEN?

GOLDBERG v. KELLY, 397 U.S. 254 (1970), per Brennan, J., held that due process requires an evidentiary hearing prior to termination of welfare benefits, stressing the "crucial factor [that] termination of aid pending resolution of a controversy over eligibility may deprive an *eligible* recipient of the very means by which to live while he waits. Since he lacks independent resources, his situation becomes immediately desperate. His need to concentrate upon [survival], in turn, adversely affects his ability to seek redress from the welfare bureaucracy." The hearing "need not take the form of a judicial or quasi-judicial trial," but a recipient must have "timely and adequate notice detailing the reasons for a proposed termination, and an effective opportunity to defend by confronting any adverse witnesses and by presenting his own arguments and evidence orally." The Court declined to "say that counsel must be provided" but the recipient must be allowed to retain counsel.

Black, J., dissented. After objecting that under the majority's methodology, "the Constitution would always be 'what the judges say it is' at a given moment, not what the Founders wrote into the document," he sounded a practical concern: "The Court apparently feels that this decision will benefit the poor and needy. In my judgment the eventual result will be just the opposite. [T]he government, once it decides to give welfare benefits, cannot reverse that decision until the recipient has had the benefits of full administrative and judicial review, including, of course, the opportunity to present his case to this Court. Since this process will usually entail a delay of several years, the inevitable result of such a constitutionally imposed burden will be that the government will not put a claimant on the rolls initially until it has made an exhaustive investigation to determine his eligibility. While this Court will perhaps have insured that no needy person will be taken off the rolls without a full 'due process' proceeding, it will also have insured that many will never get on the rolls, or at least that they will remain destitute during the lengthy proceedings followed to determine initial eligibility."[388]

Consider Jerry Mashaw, *Due Process in the Administrative State* 36 (1985): "[W]elfare recipients generally lack the human or material resources to make use of the hearings *Goldberg* provided. Except for an occasional flurry of political activism expressed through appeals requests, hearings have been utilized about as infrequently after *Goldberg* as before.

---

[388] Burger, C.J., joined by Black, J., also dissented, as did Stewart, J.

[T]he hearing technique—the demand for individualized and detailed attention through quasi-judicial process—simply misses the point of the welfare state. The problem has become one of mass, not individual, justice. Legal security for the class of welfare claimants lies, not in hearings, but in good management. Unless due process, therefore, comes to terms with administration, becomes systems-[oriented] rather than case-oriented, it will be irrelevant. [Due] process hearings [provide] no access to the administrative forums in which rights are being created and no opportunity to avoid the application of general rules on the basis of individual circumstances. *Goldberg*'s hearing rights thus leave untouched the contemporary concern with (1) the remoteness of administrative policy making from immediate participation by affected interests and (2) the unfairness and irrationality that seem to attend bureaucratic implementation of general rules."

———

MATHEWS v. ELDRIDGE, 424 U.S. 319 (1976), per Powell, J., held that although social security disability benefits constitute "a statutorily created 'property' interest protected by the fifth amendment," due process does not require a *Goldberg*-type hearing prior to their termination on the ground that "the worker is no longer disabled": "In recent years this Court increasingly has had occasion to consider the extent to which due process requires an evidentiary hearing prior to the deprivation of some type of property interest even if such a hearing is provided thereafter. In only one case, *Goldberg,* has the Court held that a hearing closely approximating a judicial trial is necessary. [O]ur prior decisions indicate that identification of the specific dictates of due process generally requires consideration of three distinct factors: First, the private interest that will be affected by the official action; second, the risk of an erroneous deprivation of such interest through the procedures used, and the probable value, if any, of additional or substitute procedural safeguards; and finally, the Government's interest, including the function involved and the fiscal and administrative burdens that the additional or substitute procedural requirement would entail."

First, in contrast to *Goldberg,* "eligibility for disability benefits [is] not based upon financial need." Rather, such benefits are "wholly unrelated to the worker's income or support from many other sources, such as earnings of other family members, workmen's compensation awards, tort claims awards, savings, [insurance, pensions, and public assistance.]" Thus, "there is less reason here than in *Goldberg* to depart from the ordinary principle, established by our decisions, that something less than an evidentiary hearing is sufficient prior to adverse administrative action."

Second, "the potential value of an evidentiary hearing, or even oral presentation to the decisionmaker, is substantially less in this context than in *Goldberg*." Here, "a medical assessment of the worker's physical or mental condition is required. This is a more sharply focused and easily documented decision than the typical determination of welfare entitlement [where] a wide variety of information may be deemed relevant, and issues of witness credibility and veracity often are critical to the decision-making process." Further, "the information critical [in the disability case] usually is derived from medical sources, [which] are likely to be able to communicate more effectively through written documents than are welfare recipients or the lay witnesses supporting their cause."

Third, as to the "additional cost in terms of money and administrative burden" if pretermination hearings were required, "[a]t some point the benefit of an additional safeguard to the individual affected by the administrative action and to society in terms of increased assurance that the action is just, may be outweighed by the cost. Significantly, the cost of protecting those whom the preliminary administrative process has identified as likely to be found undeserving may in the end come out of the pockets of the deserving since resources available for any particular program of social welfare are not unlimited."

Finally, "[i]n assessing what process is due in this case, substantial weight must be given to the good-faith judgments of the individuals charged by Congress with the administration of the social welfare system that the procedures they have provided assure fair consideration of the entitlement claims of individuals."[389]

NOTES AND QUESTIONS

1.   The *Eldridge* approach, observes Jerry Mashaw, *The Supreme Court's Due Process Calculus for Administrative Adjudication in Mathews v. Eldridge,* 44 U.Chi.L.Rev. 28 (1976), "is subjective and impressionistic. [The Court] assumes that disability recipients are less dependent on income support than welfare recipients. This assumption is buttressed only by the notion that welfare is for the needy and disability insurance is for prior taxpayers. [But] any number of circumstances might make a terminated welfare recipient's plight less desperate than that of his disabled SSA counterpart, or vice versa." Mashaw questions the wisdom of *Goldberg* but doubts that *Eldridge* improves matters: "The *Goldberg* decision's approach to prescribing due process— specification of the attributes of adjudicatory hearings by analogy to judicial trial—makes the Court resemble an administrative engineer with an outdated professional education. It is at once intrusive and ineffectual. Retreating from this stance, the *Eldridge* Court relies on the administrator's good faith—an

---

[389] Brennan, J., joined by Marshall, J., dissented: "[I]n the present case, it is indicated that because disability benefits were terminated there was a foreclosure upon the Eldridge home and the family's furniture was repossessed, forcing Eldridge, his wife, and their children to sleep in one bed. [I]t is also no argument that a worker, who has been placed in the untenable position of having been denied disability benefits, may still seek other forms of public assistance." Stevens, J., took no part.

equally troublesome posture in a political system that depends heavily on judicial review for the protection of countermajoritarian values."

2.   Consider, too, Tribe 2d ed., at 718: "[The *Eldridge*] Court's unwillingness to consider values beyond accuracy of result in the context of a utilitarian balancing test when deciding what process is due, and the Court's grant of a strong presumption of constitutionality to statutory procedural provisions, amount to a serious abdication of traditional notions of judicial responsibility under the due process clauses. Like many other provisions of the Constitution, the due process requirement represented a decision on the part of the Framers to safeguard certain rights and values, those considered fundamental in a free society and yet unusually vulnerable to the risk of denial by the majority. Adequate protection of such 'core' concerns cannot be afforded by 'balancing' the general interests of the majority against those of the individual. [Moreover,] there is no reason to believe that the judiciary would be better suited to that task of utilitarian comparison than the legislature even if it were called for."

3.   "Although the Supreme Court has treated [*Eldridge*] as furnishing a test for all seasons," the test, points out Richard H. Fallon, Jr., *Some Confusions about Due Process, Judicial Review, and Constitutional Remedies,* 93 Colum.L.Rev. 309 (1993), "was designed for resolving claims of entitlement to particular types of *administrative,* rather than judicial, procedures. Claims of a right to judicial review raise issues lying beyond the [*Eldridge*] framework."

III.   WHEN IS THE PROBABILITY OF BIAS ON THE PART OF THE DECISIONMAKER CONSTITUTIONALLY INTOLERABLE?

CAPERTON v. MASSEY COAL CO., 556 U.S. 868 (2009): A jury found Massey Coal Co. liable for tortious interference with existing contractual relations and other torts and awarded petitioner Caperton $50 million damages. After the verdict, West Virginia held its 2004 judicial elections. Knowing that the State Supreme Court of Appeals would consider the appeal, Massey's principal officer, Don Blankenship, supported Brent Benjamin, who was running against the incumbent justice seeking reelection. Blankenship's $3 million in contributions exceeded the total amount spent by all other Benjamin supporters. Benjamin won by fewer than 50,000 votes out of over 700,000 cast.

Before Massey filed its appeal, Caperton moved to disqualify now-Justice Benjamin, who denied the motion. The court then overturned the $50 million verdict by a 3–2 vote, Benjamin voting with the majority. During the rehearing process, Benjamin refused twice more to recuse himself. Once again, a 3–2 majority, including Justice Benjamin, reversed the jury's verdict. Four months later, Justice Benjamin filed a concurring opinion, defending the court's opinion and his own recusal decision.

KENNEDY, J., joined by Stevens, Souter, Ginsburg, and Breyer, JJ., reversed because "due process requires recusal" where, as here, "the probability of actual bias on the part of the judge or decisionmaker is too high to be constitutionally tolerable. [There] is a serious risk of actual bias—based on objective and reasonable perceptions—when a person with a personal stake in a particular case had a significant and disproportionate influence in placing the judge on the case by raising funds or directing the judge's election campaign when the case was pending or imminent. The inquiry centers on the contribution's relative size in comparison to the total amount of money contributed to the campaign, the total amount spent in the election, and the apparent effect such contribution had on the outcome of the election."

The Court was not impressed with the argument that "various adverse consequence will follow from recognizing a constitutional violation here— ranging from a flood of recusal motions to unnecessary interference with judicial elections. [The] parties point to no other instance involving judicial campaign contributions that presents a potential for bias comparable to the circumstances in this case."

The Court explained why it did not adopt a more restrictive rule: " 'The Due Process Clause demarks only the outer boundaries of judicial disqualifications. Congress and the states, of course, remain free to impose more rigorous standards for judicial disqualification than those we find mandated here today.' Because the codes of judicial conduct provide more protection than due process requires, most disputes over disqualification will be resolved without resort to the Constitution. Application of the constitutional standard implicated in this case will thus be confined to rare instances."

ROBERTS, C.J., joined by Scalia, Thomas, and Alito, JJ., dissented: "In any given case, there are a number of factors that could give rise to a 'probability' or 'appearance' of bias: friendship with a party or lawyer, prior employment experience, membership in clubs or associations, prior speeches and writings, religious affiliation, and countless other considerations. We have never held that the Due Process Clause requires recusal for any of these reasons, even though they could be viewed as presenting a 'probability of bias.'

"[To] its credit, the Court seems to recognize that the inherently boundless nature of its new rule poses a problem. But the majority's only answer is that the present case is an 'extreme' one, so there is no need to worry about other cases. [But c]laims that have little chance of success are nonetheless frequently filed. The success rate for certiorari petitions before this Court is approximately 1.1%, and yet the previous Term some 8,241 were filed. [Extreme] cases often test the bounds of established legal principles. There is a cost to yielding to the desire to correct the extreme case, rather than adhering to the legal principle. That cost has been demonstrated so often that it is captured in a legal aphorism: 'Hard cases make bad law.'"

SCALIA, J., also dissented: "What above all else is eroding public confidence in the Nation's judicial system is the perception that litigation is just a game, that the party with the most resourceful lawyer can play it to win, that our seemingly interminable legal proceedings are wonderfully self-perpetuating but incapable of delivering real-world justice. The Court's opinion will reinforce that perception, adding to the vast arsenal of lawyerly gambits what will come to be known as the *Caperton* claim. The facts relevant to adjudicating it will have to be litigated—and likewise the law governing it, which will be indeterminate for years to come, if not forever. [A] Talmudic maxim instructs with respect to the Scripture: 'Turn it over, and turn it over, for all is therein.' Divinely inspired text may contain the answers to all earthly questions, but the Due Process Clause most assuredly does not. The Court today continues its quixotic quest to right all wrongs and repair all imperfections through the Constitution."

NOTES AND QUESTIONS

1.   Is the real problem in a case like *Caperton* the fact that states hold elections for judgeships? Consider Pamela S. Karlan, *Electing Judges, Judging Elections, and the Lessons of Caperton*, 123 Harv.L.Rev. 80 (2009): "While the Court's opinion in *Caperton* focused explicitly only on the way that extraordinary infusions of money into a judicial election may threaten judicial impartiality, the Court's analysis cannot be so easily cabined. Money, after all, gains its power in elections because it is the fuel of politics and can be converted into votes. If gratitude for a past financial contribution can pose a sufficiently serious 'risk of actual bias or prejudgment' to threaten 'the guarantee of due process,' then what should we make of the more direct effect that comes from fear of future electoral retaliation? Political calculations could influence judges' decisions in a wide range of cases and might influence them in less visible, and thus more pernicious and less potentially self-correcting, ways than campaign spending does."

2.   In *Citizens United v. FEC*, p. 1190 infra (2010), the Court, per KENNEDY, J., invalidated a provision of federal campaign finance law that forbade corporations and unions from using general treasury funds on "electioneering communications" during the election period. "The appearance of influence or access," the Court declared, "will not cause the electorate to lose faith in our democracy." "*Caperton* is not to the contrary," the majority continued, because its "holding was limited to the rule that the judge must be recused, not that the litigant's political speech could be banned." Might the cases also be distinguished on the basis of the different functions served by judges and legislators? Is that distinction persuasive?

CHAPTER 7

FREEDOM OF EXPRESSION AND ASSOCIATION

■ ■ ■

1. THE SCOPE AND STRENGTH OF THE FIRST AMENDMENT

The First Amendment provides that "Congress shall make no law * * * abridging the freedom of speech, or of the press." Some have stressed that no law means NO LAW. For example, Black, J., dissenting in *Konigsberg v. State Bar,* 366 U.S. 36 (1961) argued that the "First Amendment's unequivocal command [shows] that the men who drafted our Bill of Rights did all the 'balancing' that was to be done in this field."

Yet laws forbidding or regulating speech are commonplace. Laws against perjury, blackmail, and fraud prohibit speech. So does much of the law of contracts. And a great deal of antitrust law, securities law, and the regulatory activities of the Federal Trade Commission and the Food and Drug Administration is focused on speech regulation as well. Black, J., himself conceded that speech pursued as an integral part of criminal conduct was beyond First Amendment protection. Indeed no one contends that citizens are free to say anything, anywhere, at any time. As Holmes, J., famously observed, citizens are not free to yell "fire" falsely in a theater.

But the spectre of a man crying fire falsely in the theater has plagued First Amendment theory, largely because the phrase is of almost no assistance in formulating principles that separate the protected from the unprotected. Too much of our lives involve "speech" in the literal sense to expect that the First Amendment can even be relevant to such a vast proportion of human existence. And speech interacts with too many other values in too many complicated ways to expect that a single formula will prove productive.

These broad questions recur in numerous more specific contexts. For example, are advocates of illegal conduct, child pornographers selling videos or magazines, advertisers promoting cigarettes and alcohol, or publishers of libel relevantly similar to the person in the theater, or are they instead engaged in freedom of speech? And what about publications that invade the privacy of citizens or officials? Or citizens who wish to speak on government property? And which property? Similarly, is there a right of access to the print or broadcast media, such that government might force private owners to grant access for speakers? Does the First Amendment offer protection for the wealthy, for powerful corporations, and for media conglomerates against government attempts to assure greater equality in the intellectual marketplace? Can government demand information about private political associations or reporters' confidential sources? Does the First Amendment require government to produce information it might otherwise withhold? And the list goes on.

The Court has tended to approach questions such as these without much attention to the language or history[1] of the First Amendment and with no commitment to any general theory.[2] Rather it has sought to develop principles in a more case-specific context and has produced a complex and conflicting body of constitutional precedent. Many of the principles were first developed in a line of cases involving the advocacy of illegal action, and these cases are commonly understood to mark the beginning of the modern First Amendment.

---

[1] For a more extensive but rare reliance on history, see *McIntyre v. Ohio Elections Comm'n,* Sec. 9, I (Thomas, J., concurring) (Scalia, J., dissenting). And for a variety of views on the history surrounding the adoption of the First Amendment, compare Leonard Levy, *Legacy of Suppression* (1960) with Leonard Levy, *Emergence of a Free Press* (1985). And see also Leonard Levy, *The Legacy Reexamined,* 37 Stan.L.Rev. 767 (1985); Leonard Levy, *On the Origins of the Free Press Clause,* 32 U.C.L.A.L.Rev. 177 (1984); George Anastaplo, *Book Review,* 39 N.Y.U.L.Rev. 735 (1964); David Anderson, *The Origins of the Press Clause,* 30 U.C.L.A.L.Rev. 455 (1983); Phillip Hamburger, *The Development of the Law of Seditious Libel and the Control of the Press,* 37 Stan.L.Rev. 661 (1985); William Mayton, *Seditious Libel and the Lost Guarantee of a Freedom of Expression,* 84 Colum.L.Rev. 91 (1984); William Mayton, *From a Legacy of Suppression to the 'Metaphor of the Fourth Estate,'* 39 Stan.L.Rev. 139 (1986); Lucas Powe, *The Fourth Estate and the Constitution* 22–50 (1991). David Rabban, *The Ahistorical Historian: Leonard Levy on Freedom of Expression in Early American History,* 37 Stan.L.Rev. 795 (1985).

For the contention that post-adoption history should play a larger role than philosophy or high theory in first amendment analysis, see L.A. Powe, *Situating Schauer,* 72 Notre D. L.Rev. 1519 (1997). For work focusing on various post-adoption periods, see Michael Kent Curtis, *Free Speech, "The People's Darling Privilege"* (2000); David Rabban, *Free Speech in Its Forgotten Years* (1997); Stewart Jay, *The Creation of the First Amendment Right to Free Expression: From the Eighteenth Century to the Mid-Twentieth Century,* 34 Wm. Mitch.L.Rev. 773 (2008); Michael Gibson, *The Supreme Court and Freedom of Expression from 1791 to 1917,* 55 Fordham L.Rev. 263 (1986). See also Zechariah Chafee, *Free Speech in the United States* (1941); Leon Whipple, *The Story of Civil Liberty in the United States* (1927).

[2] On the difficulties in developing a general theory, see Larry Alexander, *Is There a Right of Freedom of Expression?* (2005); Larry Alexander & Paul Horton, *The Impossibility of a Free Speech Principle,* 78 Nw.U.L.Rev. 1319 (1983); Daniel Farber & Phillip Frickey, *Practical Reason and the First Amendment,* 34 UCLA L.Rev. 1615 (1987); Steven Shiffrin, *The First Amendment and Economic Regulation: Away from a General Theory of the First Amendment,* 78 Nw.U.L.Rev. 1212 (1983); Laurence Tribe, *Toward A Metatheory of Free Speech,* 10 Sw.U.L.Rev. 237 (1978).

I. ADVOCACY OF ILLEGAL ACTION

A. Emerging Principles

SCHENCK V. UNITED STATES
249 U.S. 47, 39 S.Ct. 247, 63 L.Ed. 470 (1919).

JUSTICE HOLMES delivered the opinion of the Court.

This [indictment charges] a conspiracy to violate the Espionage Act of June 15, 1917 by causing and attempting to cause insubordination in the military and naval forces of the United States, and to obstruct the recruiting and enlistment service of the United States, when the United States was at war with the German Empire, to-wit, that the defendants wilfully conspired to have printed and circulated to men who had been called and accepted for military service a document set forth and alleged to be calculated to cause such insubordination and obstruction. [The] defendants were found guilty on all the counts. They set up the First Amendment to the Constitution forbidding Congress to make any law abridging the freedom of speech, or of the press.

[The] document in question upon its first printed side recited the first section of the Thirteenth Amendment, said that the idea embodied in it was violated by the Conscription Act and that a conscript is little better than a convict. In impassioned language it intimated that conscription was despotism in its worst form and a monstrous wrong against humanity in the interest of Wall Street's chosen few. It said "Do not submit to intimidation," but in form at least confined itself to peaceful measures such as a petition for the repeal of the act. The other and later printed side of the sheet was headed "Assert Your Rights." It stated reasons for alleging that any one violated the Constitution when he refused to recognize "your right to assert your opposition to the draft," and went on "If you do not assert and support your rights, you are helping to deny or disparage rights which it is the solemn duty of all citizens and residents of the United States to retain." It described the arguments on the other side as coming from cunning politicians and a mercenary capitalist press, and even silent consent to the conscription law as helping to support an infamous conspiracy. It denied the power to send our citizens away to foreign shores to shoot up the people of other lands, and added that words could not express the condemnation such cold-blooded ruthlessness deserves, winding up "You must do your share to maintain, support and uphold the rights of the people of this country." Of course the documents would not have been sent unless it had been intended to have some effect, and we do not see what effect it could be expected to have upon persons subject to the draft except to influence them to obstruct the carrying of it out. The defendants do not deny that the jury might find against them on this point. * * *

But it is said, suppose that that was the tendency of this circular, it is protected by the First Amendment to the Constitution. [It] well may be that the prohibition of laws abridging the freedom of speech is not confined to previous restraints, although to prevent them may have been the main purpose, as intimated in Patterson v. Colorado, 205 U.S. 454 [1907]. We admit that in many places and in ordinary times the defendants in saying all that was said in the circular would have been within their constitutional rights. But the character of every act depends upon the circumstances in which it is done. The most stringent protection of free speech would not protect a man in falsely shouting fire in a theatre and causing a panic. It does not even protect a man from an injunction against uttering words that may have all the effect of force. The question in every case is whether the words used are used in such circumstances and are of such a nature as to create a clear and present danger that they will bring about the substantive evils that Congress has a right to prevent. It is a question of proximity and degree. When a nation is at war many things that might be said in time of peace are such a hindrance to its effort that their utterance will not be endured so long as men fight and that no Court could regard them as protected by any constitutional right. It seems to be admitted that if an actual obstruction of the recruiting service were proved, liability for words that produced that effect might be enforced. The statute punishes conspiracies to obstruct [conscription] as well as actual obstruction. If the act, (speaking, or circulating a paper,) its tendency and the intent with which it is done are the same, we perceive no ground for saying that success alone warrants making the act a crime. * * *

Judgments affirmed.[3]

———————

DEBS v. UNITED STATES, 249 U.S. 211 (1919): Defendant was convicted of violating the Espionage Act for obstructing and attempting to obstruct the recruiting service and for causing and attempting to cause insubordination and disloyalty in the armed services. He was given a ten-

———————

[3] See also *Frohwerk v. United States,* 249 U.S. 204 (1919), where a unanimous Court, per Holmes, J., sustained a conviction for conspiracy to obstruct recruiting in violation of the Espionage Act, by means of a dozen newspaper articles praising the spirit and strength of the German nation, criticizing the decision to send American troops to France, maintaining that the government was giving false and hypocritical reasons for its course of action and implying that "the guilt of those who voted the unnatural sacrifice" is greater than the wrong of those who seek to escape by resistance: "[*Schenck* decided] that a person may be convicted of a conspiracy to obstruct recruiting by words of persuasion. [S]o far as the language of the articles goes there is not much to choose between expressions to be found in them and those before us in *Schenck*." "[The] First Amendment while prohibiting legislation against free speech cannot have been [intended] to give immunity for every possible use of language. [Neither] Hamilton nor Madison, nor any other competent person then or later, ever supposed that to make criminal the counselling of murder [would] be an unconstitutional interference with free speech.

year prison sentence on each count, to run concurrently. His criminal conduct consisted of giving the anti-war speech described in the opinion at the state convention of the Socialist Party of Ohio, held at a park in Canton, Ohio, on a June 16, 1918 Sunday afternoon before a general audience of 1,200 persons. At the time of the speech, defendant was a national political figure.[4] In affirming, HOLMES, J., observed for a unanimous Court:

"The main theme of the speech was socialism, its growth, and a prophecy of its ultimate success. With that we have nothing to do, but if a part or the manifest intent of the more general utterances was to encourage those present to obstruct the recruiting service and if in passages such encouragement was directly given, the immunity of the general theme may not be enough to protect the speech. [Defendant had come to the park directly from a nearby jail, where he had visited three socialists imprisoned for obstructing the recruiting service. He expressed sympathy and admiration for these persons and others convicted of similar offenses, and then] said that the master class has always declared the war and the subject class has always fought the battles—that the subject class has had nothing to gain and all to lose, including their lives; [and that] 'You have your lives to lose; you certainly ought to have the right to declare war if you consider a war necessary.' [He next said of a woman serving a ten-year sentence for obstructing the recruiting service] that she had said no more than the speaker had said that afternoon; that if she was guilty so was [he].

"There followed personal experiences and illustrations of the growth of socialism, a glorification of minorities, and a prophecy of the success of [socialism], with the interjection that 'you need to know that you are fit for something better than slavery and cannon fodder.' [Defendant's] final exhortation [was] 'Don't worry about the charge of treason to your masters; but be concerned about the treason that involves yourselves.' The defendant addressed the jury himself, and while contending that his speech did not warrant the charges said 'I have been accused of obstructing the war. I admit it. Gentlemen, I abhor war. I would oppose the war if I stood alone.' The statement was not necessary to warrant the jury in finding that one purpose of the speech, whether incidental or not does not matter, was to oppose not only war in general but this war, and that the opposition was so expressed that its natural and intended effect would be to obstruct recruiting. If that was intended and if, in all the circumstances, that would be its probable effect, it would not be protected by reason of its being part of a general program and expressions of a general and conscientious belief.

"[Defendant's constitutional objections] based upon the First Amendment [were] disposed of in *Schenck*. [T]he admission in evidence of the record of the conviction [of various persons he mentioned in his speech

---

[4]   Eugene Debs had run for the Presidency on the Socialist ticket for the fourth time in 1912. At the 1920 election, while in prison, Debs ran again and received over 900,000 votes as the Socialist candidate.

was proper] to show what he was talking about, to explain the true import of his expression of sympathy and to throw light on the intent of the address. [Properly admitted, too, was an 'Anti-war Proclamation and Program' adopted the previous year, coupled with testimony that shortly before his speech defendant had stated that he approved it]. Its first recommendation was, 'continuous, active, and public opposition to the war, through demonstrations, mass petitions, and all other means within our power.' Evidence that the defendant accepted this view and this declaration of his duties at the time that he made his speech is evidence that if in that speech he used words tending to obstruct the recruiting service he meant that they should have that effect. [T]he jury were most carefully instructed that they could not find the defendant guilty for advocacy of any of his opinions unless the words used had as their natural tendency and reasonably probable effect to obstruct the recruiting service [and] unless the defendant had the specific intent to do so in his mind."

NOTES AND QUESTIONS

1. *War criticism.* Geoffrey R. Stone, *Perilous Times* xxii–xxiii (2004): "It is often said that dissent in wartime is disloyal. This claim puzzles civil libertarians, who see a clear distinction. In their view, dissent in wartime can be the highest form of patriotism. Whether, when, for how long, and on what terms to fight a war are among the most profound decisions a nation encounters. A democratic society must debate these issues throughout the conflict. Dissent that questions the conduct and morality of a war is, on this view, the very essence of responsible and courageous citizenship.

"At the same time, however, dissent can readily be cast as disloyal. A critic who argues that troops are poorly trained or the war is unjust may make a significant contribution to public discourse. But he also gives 'aid and comfort' to the enemy. The enemy is more likely to fight fiercely if it is confident and believes its adversary to be divided and uncertain. Public disagreement during a war can strengthen the enemy's resolve. [T]he United States has had a long and unfortunate history of overreacting to the perceived dangers of wartime. Time and again, Americans have allowed fear and fury to get the better of them. Time and again, Americans have suppressed dissent, imprisoned and deported dissenters, and then—later—regretted their actions."

2. *The man in the theater.* Consider Harry Kalven, *A Worthy Tradition* 133–34 (1988): "*Schenck*—and perhaps even Holmes himself—are best remembered for the example of the man 'falsely shouting fire' in a crowded theater. Judge Hand said [in *Masses*, infra] [that] 'words are not only the keys of persuasion, but the triggers of action.' Justice Holmes makes the same point by means of the 'fire' example, an image which was to catch the fancy of the culture. But the example has long seemed to me trivial and misleading. It is as if the only conceivable controversy over speech policy were with an adversary who asserts that *all* use of words is absolutely immunized under the First Amendment. The 'fire' example then triumphantly impeaches this massive

major premise. Beyond that, it adds nothing to our understanding. If the point were that *only* speech which is a comparable 'trigger of action' could be regulated, the example might prove a stirring way of drawing the line at incitement, but it is abundantly clear that Justice Holmes is not comparing Schenck's leaflet to the shouting of 'fire.' Moreover, because the example is so wholly apolitical, it lacks the requisite complexity for dealing with any serious speech problem likely to confront the legal system. The man shouting 'fire' does not offer premises resembling those underlying radical political rhetoric— premises that constitute criticism of government."

3.   *Schenck and Debs.* Consider Harry Kalven, *Ernst Freund and the First Amendment Tradition,* 40 U.Chi.L.Rev. 235 (1973): "It has been customary to lavish care and attention on the *Schenck* case, [but *Debs,* argued well before *Schenck* was handed down and decided just one week later,] represented the first effort by Justice Holmes to apply what he had worked out about freedom of speech in *Schenck.* The start of the law of the First Amendment is not *Schenck;* it is *Schenck* and *Debs* read together. [Debs' speech] fell into the genre of bitter criticism of government and government policy, sometimes called seditious libel; freedom of such criticism from government marks, we have come to understand, 'the central meaning of the First Amendment' [*New York Times v. Sullivan,* Sec. 1, II, B infra] *Debs* raises serious questions as to what the First Amendment, and more especially, what the clear and present danger formula can possibly have meant at the time. [Holmes] does not comment on the fact difference between [*Schenck* and *Debs*]: the defendant in *Schenck* had sent his leaflets directly to men who awaited draft call whereas [Debs] was addressing a general audience at a public meeting. Holmes offers no discussion of the sense in which Debs's speech presented a clear and present danger. [In fact, *Debs*] did not move [Holmes] to discuss free speech at all; his brief opinion is occupied with two points about admissibility of [evidence]. It was for Holmes a routine criminal appeal."

4.   *Governmental legitimacy.* Consider Lawrence B. Solum, *Freedom of Communicative Action,* 83 Nw.U.L.Rev. 54 (1989): "Government claims a legitimate monopoly on the use of force. Any fundamental challenge to the legitimacy of this monopoly must include implicit justification or explicit advocacy of illegal action, either of nonviolent civil disobedience or of violent revolution. [S]uch fundamental challenges must be allowed if the government claims that the rightfulness of its monopoly on the use of force would be accepted in rational discourse. [I]f a violent revolutionary movement were actually likely to succeed in overthrowing the present government and if we had good reason to believe that the new regime would be worse than the present government, then we would have good reasons to temporarily suspend the right to question fundamental legitimacy in order to avoid this immediate and serious danger. The 'clear and present danger' test operationalizes a qualification of the right to advocate illegal conduct." A broader view of the latter idea is set out in Robert H. Bork, *Neutral Principles and Some First Amendment Problems*, 47 Ind. L.J. 1 (1971), where Judge Bork argues that advocating violent overthrow of the government and advocating violation of

law in general should be unprotected by a First Amendment committed to and premised on peaceful and lawful change. But see Seana Valentine Shiffrin, *Speech, Death, and Double Effect*, 78 N.Y.U. L. Rev. 1135 (2003): "The state is a poor and deeply biased judge about what visions for stability and change are defective. [O]ur vitality as a democratic collectivity depends on our joint engagement with and evaluation of competing visions * * * . We want speakers to have full freedom in the construction and dissemination of their intent. Our legitimacy depends on it. Protection of the bitter alongside the sweet, then, may be a necessary condition of protecting those valuable processes and outcomes provoked by insightful speech."

5. MASSES PUBLISHING CO. v. PATTEN, 244 Fed. 535 (S.D.N.Y.1917): The Postmaster of New York advised plaintiff that an issue of his monthly revolutionary journal, *The Masses,* would be denied the mails under the Espionage Act since it tended to encourage the enemies of the United States and to hamper the government in its conduct of the war. The Postmaster subsequently specified as objectionable several cartoons entitled, e.g., "Conscription," "Making the World Safe for Capitalism"; several articles admiring the "sacrifice" of conscientious objectors and a poem praising two persons imprisoned for conspiracy to resist the draft. Plaintiff sought a preliminary injunction against the postmaster from excluding its magazine from the mails. LEARNED HAND, D.J., granted relief:

"[The postmaster maintains] that to arouse discontent and disaffection among the people with the prosecution of the war and with the draft tends to promote a mutinous and insubordinate temper among the troops. This [is] true; men who become satisfied that they are engaged in an enterprise dictated by the unconscionable selfishness of the rich, and effectuated by a tyrannous disregard for the will of those who must suffer and die, will be more prone to insubordination than those who have faith in the cause and acquiesce in the means. Yet to interpret the word 'cause' [in the statutory language forbidding one to 'willfully cause' insubordination in the armed forces] so broadly would [necessarily involve] the suppression of all hostile criticism, and of all opinion except what encouraged and supported the existing policies, or which fell within the range of temperate argument. * * * Assuming that the power to repress such opinion may rest in Congress in the throes of a struggle for the very existence of the state, its exercise is so contrary to the use and wont of our people that only the clearest expression of such a power justifies the conclusion that it was intended.

"The defendant's position, therefore, in so far as it involves the suppression of the free utterance of abuse and criticism of the existing law, or of the policies of the war, is not, in my judgment, supported by the language of the statute. Yet there has always been a recognized limit to such expressions. [One] may not counsel or advise others to violate the law as it stands. Words are not only the keys of persuasion, but the triggers of action, and those which have no purport but to counsel the violation of law cannot by any latitude of interpretation be a part of that public opinion which is the final source of government in a democratic state. [If] one stops short of urging upon others that it is their duty or their interest to resist the law, it seems to me one should not be held to have attempted to cause its violation.[5] If that be not the test, I can see no escape from the conclusion that under this section every political agitation which can be shown to be apt to create a seditious temper is illegal. I am confident that by such language Congress had no such revolutionary purpose in view.

"It seems to me, however, quite plain that none of the language and none of the cartoons in this paper can be thought directly to counsel or advise insubordination or mutiny, without a violation of their meaning quite beyond any tolerable understanding. I come, therefore to the [provision of the Act forbidding] any one from willfully obstructing [recruiting or enlistment]. I am not prepared to assent to the plaintiff's position that this only refers to acts other than words, nor that the act thus defined must be shown to have been successful. One may obstruct without preventing, and the mere obstruction is an injury to the service; for it throws impediments in its way. Here again, however, since the question is of the expression of opinion, I construe the sentence, so far as it restrains public utterance, [as] limited to the direct advocacy of resistance to the recruiting and enlistment service. If so, the inquiry is narrowed to the question whether any of the challenged matter may be said to advocate resistance to the draft, taking the meaning of the words with the utmost latitude which they can bear.

"[It] is plain enough that the [magazine] has the fullest sympathy for [those who resist the draft or obstruct recruiting], that it admires their courage, and that it presumptively approves their conduct. [Moreover,] these passages, it must be remembered, occur in a magazine which attacks with the utmost violence the draft and the war. That such comments have a tendency to arouse emulation in others is clear enough, but that they counsel others to follow these examples is not so plain. Literally at least they do not, and while, as I have said, the words are to be taken, not literally, but according to their full import,[6] the literal meaning is the starting point for interpretation. One may admire and approve the course of a hero without feeling any duty to follow him. There is not the least implied intimation in these words that others are under a duty to follow. The most that can be said is that, if others do follow, they will get the same admiration and the same approval. * * *

"When the question is of a statute constituting a crime, it seems to me that there should be more definite evidence of the act. The question before me is quite the same as what would arise upon a motion to dismiss an indictment at the close of the proof: Could any reasonable man say, not that the indirect result of the language might be to arouse a seditious disposition, for that would

---

[5]   Charles Fried, *Perfect Freedom, Perfect Justice,* 78 B.U.L.Rev. 717 (1998): "Hand's test both excludes and includes too much. It denies First Amendment protection to pacifist teaching that it is a person's duty peaceably to disobey certain laws, while granting it—to use Mill's example—to the inflammatory denunciation of food speculation to a hungry mob assembled at a corn dealer's house."

[6]   On the extent to which it is feasible or desirable to require clarity of expression before the imposition of sanctions in this and other parts of free speech law, see Charlotte Taylor, *Free Expression and Expressness,* 33 N.Y.U. Rev. L. & Soc. Change 375 (2009).

not be enough, but that the language directly advocated resistance to the draft? I cannot think that upon such language any verdict would stand."[7]

6. ***Clear and present danger.*** Holmes in *Schenck* famously offers the idea of a "clear and present danger" as setting forth the standard for restriction of speech. This standard should be contrasted with the "rational basis" test (Ch. 5, Sec. 3), which sets forth the normal or baseline degree of scrutiny for the constitutionality of government regulation. Under the rational basis test, a danger need not be "clear" before regulation is permissible. Nor must it be "present." And thus the "clear and present danger" standard can be understood as an early and rudimentary form of heightened scrutiny. See Frederick Schauer, *Is It Better to Be Safe than Sorry?: Free Speech and the Precautionary Principle*, 36 Pepp.L.Rev. 301 (2009).

JUSTICE HOLMES—DISSENTING IN ABRAMS V. UNITED STATES

250 U.S. 616, 624, 40 S.Ct. 17, 20, 63 L.Ed. 1173, 1178 (1919).

[In the summer of 1918, the United States sent a small body of marines to Siberia. The defendants opposed the "capitalist" invasion of Russia, and characterized it as an attempt to crush the Russian Revolution. Shortly thereafter, they printed two leaflets and distributed several thousand copies in New York City. Many of the copies were thrown from a window where one defendant was employed; others were passed around at radical meetings. Both leaflets supported Russia against the United States; one called upon workers to unite in a general strike. There was no evidence that workers responded to the call.

[The Court upheld the defendants' convictions for conspiring to violate two provisions of the 1918 amendments to the Espionage Act. One count prohibited language intended to "incite, provoke and encourage resistance to the United States"; the other punished those who urged curtailment of war production. As the Court interpreted the statute, an intent to interfere with efforts against a *declared* war was a necessary element of both

---

[7] In reversing, 246 Fed. 24 (1917), the Second Circuit observed: "If the natural and probable effect of what is said is to encourage resistance to a law, and the words are used in an endeavor to persuade to resistance, it is immaterial that the duty to resist is not mentioned, or the interest of the person addressed in resistance is not suggested. That one may willfully obstruct the enlistment service, without advising in direct language against enlistments, and without stating that to refrain from enlistment is a duty or in one's interest, seems to us too plain for controversy." Geoffrey R. Stone, *Perilous Times* 159–160 (2004): "Attorney General Gregory charged that Hand had gutted the Espionage Act, and Hand's opinion in *Masses* was promptly and emphatically reversed by the court of appeals. Referring to his opinion in *Masses*, Hand wistfully 'bid a long farewell to my little toy ship which set out quite bravely on the shortest voyage ever made.' He was passed over for the court of appeals appointment, which went to a less distinguished jurist. Hand reflected later, 'The case cost me something, at least at the time,' but added, 'I have been very happy to do what I believe was some service to temperateness and sanity.' " On Judge Hand's opinion and its importance, see Gerald Gunther, *Learned Hand* 151–70, 603 (1994); Bernard Schwartz, *Holmes v. Hand*, 1994 S.Ct.Rev. 209; Vincent Blasi, *Learned Hand and the Self-Government Theory of the First Amendment*, 61 U.Col.L.Rev. 1 (1990).

offenses. Since the United States had not declared war upon Russia, "the main task of the government was to establish an [*intention*] *to interfere with the war with Germany.*" Chafee, supra, at 115. The Court found intent on the principle that "Men must be held to have intended, and to be accountable for, the effects which their acts were likely to produce. Even if their primary purpose and intent was to aid the cause of the Russian Revolution, the plan of action which they adopted necessarily involved, before it could be realized, defeat of the war program of the United States * * * ."

[HOLMES, J., dissented in an opinion with which Brandeis, J., concurred:][8]

[I] am aware of course that the word "intent" as vaguely used in ordinary legal discussion means no more than knowledge at the time of the act that the consequences said to be intended will ensue. [But,] when words are used exactly, a deed is not done with intent to produce a consequence unless that consequence is the aim of the deed. It may be obvious, and obvious to the actor, that the consequence will follow, and he may be liable for it even if he regrets it, but he does not do the act with intent to produce it unless the aim to produce it is the proximate motive of the specific act although there may be some deeper motive behind.

It seems to me that this statute must be taken to use its words in a strict and accurate sense. They would be absurd in any other. A patriot might think that we were wasting money on aeroplanes, or making more cannon of a certain kind than we needed, and might advocate curtailment with success, yet even if it turned out that the curtailment hindered and was thought by other minds to have been obviously likely to hinder the United States in the prosecution of the war, no one would hold such conduct a crime. * * *

I never have seen any reason to doubt that the questions of law that alone were before this Court in the cases of *Schenck, Frohwerk* and *Debs* were rightly decided. I do not doubt for a moment that by the same reasoning that would justify punishing persuasion to murder, the United States constitutionally may punish speech that produces or is intended to produce a clear and imminent danger that it will bring about forthwith certain substantive evils that the United States constitutionally may seek to prevent. The power undoubtedly is greater in time of war than in time of peace because war opens dangers that do not exist at other times.

But as against dangers peculiar to war, as against others, the principle of the right to free speech is always the same. It is only the present danger

---

[8] Consider Sheldon Novick, *Honorable Justice, The Life of Oliver Wendell Holmes* 331 (1989): "The majority did very highly disapprove of Holmes's dissent, and White tried to persuade him to be silent. When Holmes clung to what he thought his duty, three of the justices came to call on him in his library, and [his wife] Fanny joined them in trying to dissuade him from publishing his dissent."

of immediate evil or an intent to bring it about that warrants Congress in setting a limit to the expression of opinion where private rights are not concerned. Congress certainly cannot forbid all effort to change the mind of the country. Now nobody can suppose that the surreptitious publishing of a silly leaflet by an unknown man, without more, would present any immediate danger that its opinions would hinder the success of the government arms or have any appreciable tendency to do so.[9] Publishing those opinions for the very purpose of obstructing, however, might indicate a greater danger and at any rate would have the quality of an attempt.[10]
* * *

I do not see how anyone can find the intent required by the statute in any of the defendants' words. The leaflet advocating a general strike is the only one that affords even a foundation for the charge, and [its only object] is to help Russia and stop American intervention there against the popular government—not to impede the United States in the war that it was carrying on. * * *

In this case sentences of twenty years imprisonment have been imposed for the publishing of two leaflets that I believe the defendants had as much right to publish as the Government has to publish the Constitution of the United States now vainly invoked by them. [E]ven if what I think the necessary intent were shown; the most nominal punishment seems to me all that possibly could be inflicted, unless the defendants are to be made to suffer not for what the indictment alleges but for the creed that they avow—[which,] although made the subject of examination at the trial, no one has a right even to consider in dealing with the charges before the Court.

Persecution for the expression of opinions seems to me perfectly logical. If you have no doubt of your premises or your power and want a

---

[9]   But see John Wigmore, *Abrams v. U.S.: Freedom of Speech and Freedom of Thuggery in War-Time and Peace-Time*, 14 Ill.L.Rev. 539 (1920): "[The *Abrams* dissent] is dallying with the facts and the law. None know better than judges that what is lawful for one is lawful for a thousand others. If these five men could, without the law's restraint, urge munition workers to a general strike and armed violences then others could lawfully do so; and a thousand disaffected undesirables, aliens and natives alike, were ready and waiting to do so. Though this circular was 'surreptitious,' the next ones need not be so. If such urgings were lawful, every munitions factory in the country could be stopped by them. The relative amount of harm that one criminal act can effect is no measure of its criminality, and no measure of the danger of its criminality. [At a time] when the fate of the civilized world hung in the balance, how could the Minority Opinion interpret law and conduct in such a way as to let loose men who were doing their hardest to paralyze the supreme war efforts of our country?"

[10]   What if the defendant had no reasonable prospect of success? If his efforts were utterly ineffectual? Cf. Oliver Wendell Holmes, *The Common Law* 65–66, 68–69 (1881): "Intent to commit a crime is not itself criminal. [Moreover], the law does not punish every act which is done with the intent to bring about a crime. [We] have seen what amounts to an attempt to burn a haystack [lighting a match with intent to start fire to a haystack]; but it was said in the same case, that, if the defendant had gone no further than to buy a box of matches for the purpose, he would not have been liable. [Relevant considerations are] the nearness of the danger, the greatness of the harm and the degree of apprehension felt."

certain result with all your heart you naturally express your wishes in law and sweep away all opposition. To allow opposition by speech seems to indicate that you think the speech impotent, as when a man says that he has squared the circle, or that you do not care whole-heartedly for the result, or that you doubt either your power or your premises. But when men have realized that time has upset many fighting faiths, they may come to believe even more than they believe the very foundations of their own conduct that the ultimate good desired is better reached by free trade in ideas—that the best test of truth is the power of the thought to get itself accepted in the competition of the market, and that truth is the only ground upon which their wishes safely can be carried out. That at any rate is the theory of our Constitution. It is an experiment, as all life is an experiment. Every year if not every day we have to wager our salvation upon some prophecy based upon imperfect knowledge. While that experiment is part of our system I think that we should be eternally vigilant against attempts to check the expression of opinions that we loathe and believe to be fraught with death, unless they so imminently threaten immediate interference with the lawful and pressing purposes of the law that an immediate check is required to save the country. [Only] the emergency that makes it immediately dangerous to leave the correction of evil counsels to time warrants making any exception to the sweeping command, "Congress shall make no law * * * abridging the freedom of speech." Of course I am speaking only of expressions of opinion and exhortations, which were all that were uttered [here].[11]

NOTES AND QUESTIONS

1. *"Marketplace of ideas."* (a) Is the competition of the market—the marketplace of ideas, as it is now put—as the "best test of truth" ultimately an empirical and not a philosophical claim? Consider Frederick Schauer, *Facts and the First Amendment*, 57 UCLA L.Rev. 897 (2010): "Once we fathom the full scope of factors other than the truth of a proposition that might determine which propositions individuals or groups will accept and which they will reject-the charisma, authority, or persuasiveness of the speaker; the consistency between the proposition and the prior beliefs of the hearer; the consistency between the proposition and what the hearer believes that other hearers believe; the frequency with which the proposition is uttered; the extent to which the proposition is communicated with photographs and other visual or aural embellishments; the extent to which the proposition will make the reader

---

[11] Consider Vincent Blasi, *Reading Holmes Through the Lens of Schauer: The Abrams Dissent*, 72 Notre D. L. Rev. 1343 (1997): "Nothing [Holmes] says in *Abrams* by his own injunction, applies to regulations of speech predicated on misstatements of verifiable fact, such as the standard action for defamation. Likewise, disclosures of sensitive information remain outside the ambit of Holmes's argument for free speech, however much such disclosures might contribute to public debate or the checking of government power. The graphic depictions of pornographers, even the soft-core variety, also appear not to be the type of speech that Holmes insists must be tested in the competition of the market."

or listener feel good or happy for content-independent reasons; and almost countless others-we can see that placing faith in the superiority of truth over all of these other attributes of a proposition in explaining acceptance and rejection requires a substantial degree of faith in pervasive human rationality and an almost willful disregard of the masses of scientific and marketing research to the contrary."[12]

(b) Contrast Holmes, J.'s statement of the "marketplace of ideas" argument with John Milton's statement in *Areopagitica* (1644): "And though all the winds of doctrine were let loose to play upon the earth, so Truth be in the field, we do injuriously by licensing and prohibiting to misdoubt her strength. Let her and Falsehood grapple; who ever knew Truth put to the worse, in a free and open encounter?" Holmes, J., claims that the competition of the market is the best test of truth; Milton maintains that truth will emerge in a free and open encounter. How would one verify either hypothesis? Might Holmes be referring only to political or policy truth, where it is plausible that truth is *defined* by the marketplace of ideas rather than being located by it? See Vincent Blasi, *Holmes and the Marketplace of Ideas*, 2004 Sup. Ct. Rev. 1.

Is the "marketplace of ideas" a "free and open encounter"? Consider Charles Lindblom, *Politics and Markets* 207 (1977): "Early, persuasive, unconscious conditioning—[to] believe in the fundamental politico-economic institutions of one's society is ubiquitous in every society. These institutions come to be taken for granted. Many people grow up to regard them not as institutions to be tested but as standards against which the correctness of new policies and institutions can be tested. When that happens, as is common, processes of critical judgment are short-circuited." Consider also Tribe 2d ed., at 786: "Especially when the wealthy have more access to the most potent media of communication than the poor, how sure can we be that 'free trade in ideas' is likely to generate truth?" And see also Steven Shiffrin, *The First Amendment and Economic Regulation: Away from a General Theory of the First Amendment,* 78 Nw.U.L.Rev. 1212 (1983): "Living in a society in which children and adults are daily confronted with multiple communications that ask them to purchase products inevitably places emphasis on materialistic values. The authors of the individual messages may not intend that general emphasis, but the whole is greater than the sum of the parts. [Advertisers] spend some sixty billion dollars per year. [Those] who would oppose the materialist message must combat forces that have a massive economic advantage. Any confidence that we will know what is truth by seeing what emerges from such combat is ill placed."

Do the market failure considerations offered by Lindblom and Shiffrin constitute a rebuttal of the marketplace argument? Consider Melvin Nimmer, *Nimmer on Freedom of Speech* 1–12 (1984): "If acceptance of an idea in the competition of the market is not the 'best test' [what] is the alternative? It can only be acceptance of an idea by some individual or group narrower than that

---

[12] Despite the weaknesses of the rationality assumption, is it wiser to presume it as a matter of First Amendment policy? See Lyrissa Barnett Lidsky, *Nobody's Fools: The Rational Audience as First Amendment Ideal,* 2010 U.Ill. L.Rev. 799.

of the public at large. Thus, the alternative to competition in the market must be some form of elitism. It seems hardly necessary to enlarge on the dangers of that path." But is elitism the only alternative to the marketplace perspective? Is elitism always wrong? Is "elitism" the appropriate characterization of determination by an expert body, as when we rely on the Food and Drug Administration and not the marketplace of ideas to determine whether claims about the efficacy or not of pharmaceuticals are true?

(c) Evaluate the following hypothetical commentary: "Liberals have favored government intervention in the economic marketplace but pressed for laissez-faire in the intellectual marketplace. Conservatives have done the reverse. Liberals and conservatives have one thing in common: inconsistent positions." See R.H. Coase, *The Market for Goods and the Market for Ideas*, 64 Am.Econ.Rev. 384 (1974); Aaron Director, *The Parity of the Economic Market Place*, 7 J.Law & Econ. 1 (1964).

(d) Does the marketplace argument overvalue truth? Consider Frederick Schauer, *Free Speech: A Philosophical Enquiry* 23 (1982). Government may seek to suppress opinions "because their expression is thought to impair the authority of a lawful and effective government, interfere with the administration of justice (such as publication of a defendant's criminal record in advance of a jury trial), cause offence, invade someone's privacy, or cause a decrease in public order. When these are the motives for suppression, the possibility of losing some truth is relevant but hardly dispositive. [In such circumstances] the argument from truth [is] not wholly to the point." See also Robert Wolff, *The Poverty of Liberalism* 18 (1968) "[I]t is not to assist the advance of knowledge that free debate is needed. Rather, it is in order to guarantee that every legitimate interest shall make itself known and felt in the political [process]. Justice, not truth, is the ideal served by liberty of speech." The standard discussion of free speech values continues to be Thomas Emerson, *The System of Freedom of Expression* 6–9 (1970), which lists the search for truth as one among several values undergirding the First Amendment.

(e) For the argument that valuing dissent is preferable to an emphasis on the marketplace metaphor, see Steven Shiffrin, *The First Amendment, Democracy, and Romance* (1990): "[A] commitment to sponsoring dissent does not require a belief that what emerges in the 'market' is usually right or that the 'market' is the best test of truth. Quite the contrary, the commitment to sponsor dissent assumes that societal pressures to conform are strong and that incentives to keep quiet are often great. If the marketplace metaphor encourages the view that an invisible hand or voluntaristic arrangements have guided us patiently, but slowly, to Burkean harmony, the commitment to sponsoring dissent encourages us to believe that the cozy arrangements of the status quo have settled on something less than the true or the just. If the marketplace metaphor encourages the view that conventions, habits, and traditions have emerged as our best sense of the truth from the rigorous testing ground of the marketplace of ideas, the commitment to sponsoring dissent encourages the view that conventions, habits, and traditions are compromises open to challenge. If the marketplace metaphor counsels us that the market's version of truth is more worthy of trust than any that the government might dictate, a commitment to sponsoring dissent counsels us to be suspicious of both. If the marketplace metaphor encourages a sloppy form of relativism (whatever has emerged in the marketplace is right for now), the commitment to sponsoring dissent emphasizes that truth is not decided in public opinion polls."

(f)   In UNITED STATES v. ALVAREZ (2012), Sec. VI, F infra, a local office holder falsely claimed at a public meeting to have been awarded the Congressional Medal of Honor. A federal statute—the Stolen Valor Act—made such a representation a crime, but the Court, per Kennedy, J., held that the statute violated the First Amendment. Is the marketplace of ideas the best way of determining whether Mr. Alvarez had been awarded the medal? Is it the best way of determining whether the claims of astrology are true? Global warming? What is the role of the marketplace of ideas in determining factual and scientific truth?

2.   ***Pragmatism and scientific method.*** Consider Vincent Blasi, *Reading Holmes Through the Lens of Schauer: The Abrams Dissent*, 72 Notre D.L. Rev. 1343 (1997): "Once the eloquence has been savored (and the false modesty noted), the reader wonders whether Holmes can possibly mean what he seems to be saying about 'the best test of truth.' Is he really so cynical, or fatalistic? Is he asserting a Chicago-school level of faith in markets combined with a willingness both to commodify truth and to ignore the various sources of market failure that operate in the flesh-and-blood society he is supposedly discussing? And even if Holmes wishes to embrace such a mundane conception of truth, how then does truth become 'the only ground' of social organization and aspiration? [H]ow does the author of the quip 'the Fourteenth Amendment does not enact Mr. Herbert Spencer's Social Statics' justify the position that the First Amendment enacts an extreme version of epistemological skepticism and/or moral relativism?

"One possible response is to read Holmes as neither a borderline cynic nor a model-building neoclassical economist but rather a pragmatist impressed by how free speech can foster a culture of productive adaptation. In this view, the reference to 'the market'—observe that Holmes never employs the phrase 'marketplace of ideas'—is not meant to evoke anything so elegant and implausible as a fair procedure for determining society's finely calibrated, self-correcting cognitive equilibrium. Rather the claim is simply that the human understanding is eternally fluctuating and incomplete, and constantly in need of inquisitive energy much the way commercial prosperity depends on entrepreneurial energy. In addition, Holmes's allusion to Darwinian forces and his assertion that life is an experiment suggests his embrace of the scientific method, with the implication that the First Amendment represents a commitment by this society to test its truths continually and revise them regularly."[13]

B. State Sedition Laws

A second group of cases in the initial development of First Amendment doctrine involved state "sedition laws" of two basic types: criminal anarchy laws, typified by the New York statute in *Gitlow,* infra, and criminal syndicalism laws similar to the California statute in *Whitney,* infra. Most states enacted anarchy and syndicalism statutes between 1917 and 1921, in response to World War I and the fear of Bolshevism that developed in its wake, but the first modern sedition law was passed by New York in 1902, soon after the assassination of President McKinley and also at a time of substantial labor union activism. The law, which prohibited not only actual or attempted assassinations or conspiracies to assassinate, but advocacy of anarchy as well, lay idle for nearly twenty years, until the *Gitlow* prosecution.

GITLOW v. NEW YORK, 268 U.S. 652 (1925): Defendant was a member of the Left Wing Section of the Socialist Party and a member of its National Council, which adopted a "Left Wing Manifesto," condemning the dominant "moderate Socialism" for its recognition of the necessity of the democratic parliamentary state; advocating the necessity of accomplishing the "Communist Revolution" by a militant and "revolutionary Socialism" based on "the class struggle"; and urging the development of mass political strikes for the destruction of the parliamentary state. Defendant arranged for printing and distributing, through the mails and otherwise, 16,000 copies of the Manifesto in the Left Wing's official organ, The Revolutionary Age. There was no evidence of any effect from the publication and circulation of the Manifesto.

In sustaining a conviction under the New York "criminal anarchy" statutes, prohibiting the "advocacy, advising or teaching the duty, necessity or propriety of overthrowing or overturning organized government by force or violence" and the publication or distribution of such matter, the majority, per SANFORD, J., stated that for present purposes we

---

[13] The literature on Holmes, J.'s First Amendment views and their connection to his larger world view is substantial. See, e.g., Albert W. Alschuler, *Law Without Values: The Life, Work, and Legacy of Justice Holmes* (2000); Ronald K.L. Collins, *The Fundamental Holmes* (2010); Vincent Blasi, *Holmes and the Marketplace of Ideas,* 2004 Sup. Ct. Rev. 1 (2004); G. Edward White, *Justice Oliver Wendell Holmes* 412–54 (1993); Yogal Rogat & James O'Fallon, *Mr. Justice Holmes: A Dissenting Opinion—The Speech Cases,* 36 Stan.L.Rev. 1349 (1984); David Rabban, *The Emergence of Modern First Amendment Doctrine,* 50 U.Chi.L.Rev. 1205 (1983); David M. Rabban, *Free Speech in Progressive Social Thought,* 74 Texas L.Rev. 951 (1996). For further analysis of the Holmes-Hand correspondence, see Gerald Gunther, *Learned Hand and the Origins of Modern First Amendment Doctrine: Some Fragments of History,* 27 Stan.L.Rev. 719 (1975). For illuminating discussion of *Abrams* and the period of which it is a part, see Richard Polenberg, *Fighting Faiths* (1987).

may and do assume[14] that First Amendment freedoms of expression "are among the fundamental personal rights and 'liberties' protected by the due process clause of the Fourteenth Amendment from impairment by the States," but ruled:

"By enacting the present statute the State has determined, through its legislative body, that utterances advocating the overthrow of organized government by force, violence and unlawful means, are so inimical to the general welfare and involve such danger of substantive evil that they may be penalized in the exercise of its police power. That determination must be given great weight. Every presumption is to be indulged in favor of the validity of the statute. And the case is to be considered 'in the light of the principle that the State is primarily the judge of regulations required in the interest of public safety and welfare'; and that its police 'statutes may only be declared unconstitutional where they are arbitrary or unreasonable attempts to exercise authority vested in the State in the public interest.' That utterances inciting to the overthrow of organized government by unlawful means, present a sufficient danger of substantive evil to bring their punishment within the range of legislative discretion, is clear. Such utterances, by their very nature, involve danger to the public peace and to the security of the State. They threaten breaches of the peace and ultimate revolution. And the immediate danger is none the less real and substantial, because the effect of a given utterance cannot be accurately foreseen. The State cannot reasonably be required to measure the danger from every such utterance in the nice balance of a jeweler's scale. A single revolutionary spark may kindle a fire that, smoldering for a time, may burst into a sweeping and destructive conflagration. It cannot be said that the State is acting arbitrarily or unreasonably when in the exercise of its judgment as to the measures necessary to protect the public peace and safety, it seeks to extinguish the spark without waiting until it has enkindled the flame or blazed into the conflagration. It cannot reasonably be required to defer the adoption of measures for its own peace and safety until the revolutionary utterances lead to actual disturbances of the public peace or imminent and immediate danger of its own destruction; but it may, in the exercise of its judgment, suppress the threatened danger in its incipiency.

"[It] is clear that the question in [this case] is entirely different from that involved in those cases where the statute merely prohibits certain acts involving the danger of substantive evil, without any reference to language

---

[14] *Gitlow* is often cited for the proposition that First Amendment freedoms apply to restrict state conduct, but its language is dictum. Some would say the first case so holding is *Fiske v. Kansas*, 274 U.S. 380 (1927) (no evidence to support criminal syndicalism conviction) even though no reference to the First Amendment appears in the opinion. Perhaps the honor belongs to *Near v. Minnesota* (1931), Sec. 4, I, B infra. Current doctrine is that the First Amendment applies equally to states, localities, and the federal government, but the Court may generally have given more leeway to the federal government. See Adam Winkler, *Free Speech Federalism*, 108 Mich. L.Rev. 153 (2009).

itself, and it is sought to apply its provisions to language used by the defendant for the purpose of bringing about the prohibited results. There, if it be contended that the statute cannot be applied to the language used by the defendant because of its protection by the freedom of speech or press, it must necessarily be found, as an original question, without any previous determination by the legislative body, whether the specific language used involved such likelihood of bringing about the substantive evil as to deprive it of the constitutional protection. In such cases it has been held that the general provisions of the statute may be constitutionally applied to the specific utterance of the defendant if its natural tendency and probable effect was to bring about the substantive evil which the legislative body might prevent. *Schenck; Debs.* And the general statement in the *Schenck* case that the 'question in every case is whether the words are used in such circumstances and are of such a nature as to create a clear and present danger that they will bring about the substantive evils,' [was] manifestly intended, as shown by the context, to apply only in cases of this class, and has no application to those like the present, where the legislative body itself has previously determined the danger of substantive evil arising from utterances of a specified character."

HOLMES, J., joined by Brandeis, J., dissented: "The general principle of free speech, it seems to me, must be taken to be included in the Fourteenth Amendment, in view of the scope that has been given to the word 'liberty' as there used, although perhaps it may be accepted with a somewhat larger latitude of interpretation than is allowed to Congress by the sweeping language that governs or ought to govern the laws of the United States. If I am right then I think that the criterion sanctioned by the full Court in *Schenck* applies. [It] is true that in my opinion this criterion was departed from in *Abrams,* but the convictions that I expressed in that case are too deep for it to be possible for me as yet to believe that it [has] settled the law. If what I think the correct test is applied it is manifest that there was no present danger of an attempt to overthrow the government by force on the part of the admittedly small minority who shared the defendant's views. It is said that this manifesto was more than a theory, that it was an incitement. Every idea is an incitement. It offers itself for belief and if believed it is acted on unless some other belief outweighs it or some failure of energy stifles the movement at its birth. The only difference between the expression of an opinion and an incitement in the narrower sense is the speaker's enthusiasm for the result. Eloquence may set fire to reason. But whatever may be thought of the redundant discourse before us it had no chance of starting a present conflagration.[15]

---

[15] Consider Harry Kalven, *A Worthy Tradition* 156 (1988): "This famous passage points up the ironies in tradition building. The basic problem of finding an accommodation between speech too close to action and censorship too close to criticism might, we have argued, have been tolerably solved by settling on 'incitement' as the key term. It is a term which came easily to the mind of Learned Hand. But for Holmes it does not resonate as it did for Hand. It strikes his ear as a loose, expansible term. At an inopportune moment in the history of free speech the great master of the

If in the long run the beliefs expressed in proletarian dictatorship are destined to be accepted by the dominant forces of the community, the only meaning of free speech is that they should be given their chance and have their way.[16]

"If the publication of this document had been laid as an attempt to induce an uprising against government at once and not at some indefinite time in the future it would have presented a different question. The object would have been one with which the law might deal, subject to the doubt whether there was any danger that the publication could produce any result, or in other words, whether it was not futile and too remote from possible consequences. But the indictment alleges the publication and nothing more."

NOTES AND QUESTIONS

1. The statute in *Schenck* was not aimed directly at expression, but at conduct, i.e., certain actual or attempted interferences with the war effort. Thus, an analysis in terms of proximity between the words and the conduct prohibited (by a concededly valid law) seemed useful. But in *Gitlow* (and *Dennis*, Sec.1, I, C infra) the statute was directed expressly against *advocacy* of a certain doctrine. Once the legislature *designates the point at which words became unlawful,* how helpful is the clear and present danger test? Is the question still how close words come to achieving certain consequences? In *Gitlow*, did Holmes "evade" the difficulty of applying an unmodified *Schenck* test to a different kind of problem? See Yogal Rogat, *Mr. Justice Holmes: Some Modern Views—The Judge as Spectator,* 31 U.Chi.L.Rev. 213 (1964).

2. Consider Hans Linde, *"Clear and Present Danger" Reexamined,* 22 Stan.L.Rev. 1163 (1970): "Since New York's law itself defined the prohibited speech, the [*Gitlow*] Court could choose among three positions. It could (1) accept this legislative judgment of the harmful potential of the proscribed words, subject to conventional judicial review; (2) independently scrutinize the facts to see whether a 'danger,' as stated in *Schenck,* justified suppression of the particular expression; or (3) hold that by legislating directly against the words rather than the effects, the lawmaker had gone beyond the leeway left

---

common law turns poet: 'Every idea is an incitement.' There is of course a sense in which this is true and in which it is a 'scholastic subterfuge' to pretend that speech can be arrayed in firm categories. But the defendants' proposed instruction had offered a sense in which it was not true, in which incitement required advocacy of some definite and immediate acts of force. The weakness of the prosecution's case was not that the defendants' radicalism was not dangerous; it was that their manifesto was not concrete enough to be an incitement.

"Justice Holmes's dissent in *Gitlow,* like his *Abrams* peroration, is extraordinary prose to find in a judicial opinion, and I suspect it has contributed beyond measure to the charisma of the First Amendment. But it also carries the disturbing suggestion that the defendants' speech is to be protected precisely because it is harmless and unimportant. It smacks, as will the later protections of Jehovah's Witnesses, of a luxury civil liberty."

[16] But see Richard Posner, *Free Speech in an Economic Perspective,* 20 Suff.L.Rev. 1 (1986): "If those beliefs are destined to prevail, free speech is irrelevant. Holmes is not describing a competitive market in ideas but a natural monopoly."

to trial and proof by the holding in *Schenck* and had made a law forbidden by the First Amendment." Which course did the *Gitlow* majority choose? The dissenters?

WHITNEY V. CALIFORNIA
274 U.S. 357, 47 S.Ct. 641, 71 L.Ed. 1095 (1927).

JUSTICE SANFORD delivered the opinion of the Court.

[Charlotte Anita Whitney was convicted of violating the 1919 Criminal Syndicalism Act of California whose pertinent provisions were]:

"Section 1. The term 'criminal syndicalism' as used in this act is hereby defined as any doctrine or precept advocating, teaching or aiding and abetting the commission of crime, sabotage (which word is hereby defined as meaning willful and malicious physical damage or injury to physical property), or unlawful acts of force and violence or unlawful methods of terrorism as a means of accomplishing a change in industrial ownership or control, or effecting any political change.

"Sec. 2. Any person who: * * * 4. Organizes or assists in organizing, or is or knowingly becomes a member of, any organization, society, group or assemblage of persons organized or assembled to advocate, teach or aid and abet criminal syndicalism; * * * Is guilty of a felony and punishable by imprisonment."

The first count of the information, on which the conviction was had, charged that on or about November 28, 1919, in Alameda County, the defendant, in violation of the Criminal Syndicalism Act, "did then and there unlawfully, willfully, wrongfully, deliberately and feloniously organize and assist in organizing, and was, is, and knowingly became a member of [a group] organized and assembled to advocate, teach, aid and abet criminal syndicalism." * * *

1.   While it is not denied that the evidence warranted the jury in finding that the defendant became a member of and assisted in organizing the Communist Labor Party of California, and that this was organized to advocate, teach, aid or abet criminal syndicalism as defined by the Act, it is urged that the Act, as here construed and applied, deprived the defendant of her liberty without due process of law. [Defendant's] argument is, in effect, that the character of the state organization could not be forecast when she attended the convention; that she had no purpose of helping to create an instrument of terrorism and violence; that she "took part in formulating and presenting to the convention a resolution which, if adopted, would have committed the new organization to a legitimate policy of political reform by the use of the ballot"; that it was not until after the majority of the convention turned out to be "contrary minded, and other less temperate policies prevailed" that the convention could have taken on

the character of criminal syndicalism; and that as this was done over her protest, her mere presence in the convention, however violent the opinions expressed therein, could not thereby become a crime. This contention [is in effect] an effort to review the weight of the evidence for the purpose of showing that the defendant did not join and assist in organizing the Communist Labor Party of California with a knowledge of its unlawful character and purpose. This question, which is foreclosed by the verdict of the jury, [is] one of fact merely which is not open to review in this Court, involving as it does no constitutional question whatever. * * *

[That a state] may punish those who abuse [freedom of speech] by utterances inimical to the public welfare, tending to incite to crime, disturb the public peace, or endanger the foundations of organized government and threaten its overthrow by unlawful means, is not open to question. [*Gitlow*].

The essence of the offense denounced by the Act is the combining with others in an association for the accomplishment of the desired ends through the advocacy and use of criminal and unlawful methods. It partakes of the nature of a criminal conspiracy. That such united and joint action involves even greater danger to the public peace and security than the isolated utterances and acts of individuals is clear. We cannot hold that, as here applied, the Act is an unreasonable or arbitrary exercise of the police power of the State, unwarrantably infringing any right of free speech, assembly or association, or that those persons are protected from punishment by the due process clause who abuse such rights by joining and furthering an organization thus menacing the peace and welfare of the State. * * *

Affirmed.

JUSTICE BRANDEIS (concurring.) * * *

The felony which the statute created is a crime very unlike the old felony of conspiracy or the old misdemeanor of unlawful assembly. The mere act of assisting in forming a society for teaching syndicalism, of becoming a member of it, or assembling with others for that purpose is given the dynamic quality of crime. There is guilt although the society may not contemplate immediate promulgation of the doctrine. Thus the accused is to be punished, not for attempt, incitement or conspiracy, but for a step in preparation, which, if it threatens the public order at all, does so only remotely. The novelty in the prohibition introduced is that the statute aims, not at the practice of criminal syndicalism, nor even directly at the preaching of it, but at association with those who propose to preach it.

Despite arguments to the contrary which had seemed to me persuasive, it is settled that the due process clause of the Fourteenth Amendment applies to matters of substantive law as well as to matters of procedure. Thus all fundamental rights comprised within the term liberty are protected by the federal Constitution from invasion by the states. The right of free speech, the right to teach and the right of assembly are, of course, fundamental rights. These may not be denied or abridged. But, although the rights of free speech and assembly are fundamental, they are not in their nature absolute. Their exercise is subject to restriction, if the particular restriction proposed is required in order to protect the state from destruction or from serious injury, political, economic or moral. That the necessity which is essential to a valid restriction does not exist unless speech would produce, or is intended to produce, a clear and imminent danger of some substantive evil which the state constitutionally may seek to prevent has been settled. See *Schenck.*

[The] Legislature must obviously decide, in the first instance, whether a danger exists which calls for a particular protective measure. But where a statute is valid only in case certain conditions exist, the enactment of the statute cannot alone establish the facts which are essential to its validity. Prohibitory legislation has repeatedly been held invalid, because unnecessary, where the denial of liberty involved was that of engaging in a particular business. The powers of the courts to strike down an offending law are no less when the interests involved are not property rights, but the fundamental personal rights of free speech and assembly.

This Court has not yet fixed the standard by which to determine when a danger shall be deemed clear; how remote the danger may be and yet be deemed present; and what degree of evil shall be deemed sufficiently substantial to justify resort to abridgment of free speech and assembly as the means of protection. To reach sound conclusions on these matters, we must bear in mind why a state is, ordinarily, denied the power to prohibit dissemination of social, economic and political doctrine which a vast majority of its citizens believes to be false and fraught with evil consequence.

Those who won our independence believed that the final end of the state was to make men free to develop their faculties, and that in its government the deliberative forces should prevail over the arbitrary.[17] They valued liberty both as an end and as a means. They believed liberty to be the secret of happiness and courage to be the secret of liberty. They believed that freedom to think as you will and to speak as you think are means indispensable to the discovery and spread of political truth;[18] that

---

[17] On Brandeis, J.'s use of history, see Bradley C. Bobertz, *The Brandeis Gambit: The Making of America's "First Freedom," 1909–1931,* 40 Wm. & Mary L.Rev. 557 (1999); Stewart Jay, *The Creation of the First Amendment Right to Free Expression: From the Eighteenth Century to the Mid-Twentieth Century,* 34 Wm. Mitch. L. Rev. 773 (2008). On Brandeis and freedom of speech generally, see Phillipa Strum, *Brandeis: The Public Activist and Freedom of Speech,* 45 Brand. L.J. 659 (2007).

[18] Consider Vincent Blasi, *The First Amendment and the Ideal of Civic Courage,* 29 Wm. & Mary L.Rev. 653 (1988): "This is as close as Brandeis gets to the claim that unregulated discussion yields truth. Notice that, in contrast to Holmes, Brandeis never tells us what is 'the best test of truth.' He never employs the metaphor of the marketplace. He speaks only of 'political truth,' and he uses the phrase 'means indispensable' to link activities described in highly personal terms— 'think as you will,' 'speak as you think'—with the collective social goal of 'political truth.' I think his emphasis in this passage is on the attitudes and atmosphere that must prevail if the ideals of

without free speech and assembly discussion would be futile; that with them, discussion affords ordinarily adequate protection against the dissemination of noxious doctrine;[19] that the greatest menace to freedom is an inert people; that public discussion is a political duty; and that this should be a fundamental principle of the American government. They recognized the risks to which all human institutions are subject. But they knew that order cannot be secured merely through fear of punishment for its infraction; that it is hazardous to discourage thought, hope and imagination; that fear breeds repression; that repression breeds hate; that hate menaces stable government; that the path of safety lies in the opportunity to discuss freely supposed grievances and proposed remedies; and that the fitting remedy for evil counsels is good ones. Believing in the power of reason as applied through public discussion, they eschewed silence coerced by law—the argument of force in its worst form. Recognizing the occasional tyrannies of governing majorities, they amended the Constitution so that free speech and assembly should be guaranteed.

Fear of serious injury cannot alone justify suppression of free speech and assembly. Men feared witches and burnt women. It is the function of speech to free men from the bondage of irrational fears. To justify suppression of free speech there must be reasonable ground to fear that serious evil will result if free speech is practiced. There must be reasonable ground to believe that the danger apprehended is imminent. There must be reasonable ground to believe that the evil to be prevented is a serious one. Every denunciation of existing law tends in some measure to increase the probability that there will be violation of it. Condonation of a breach enhances the probability. Expressions of approval add to the probability. Propagation of the criminal state of mind by teaching syndicalism increases it. Advocacy of lawbreaking heightens it still further. But even advocacy of violation, however reprehensible morally, is not a justification for denying free speech where the advocacy falls short of incitement and there is nothing to indicate that the advocacy would be immediately acted on. The wide difference between advocacy and incitement, between preparation and attempt, between assembling and conspiracy, must be borne in mind. In order to support a finding of clear and present danger it must be shown either that immediate serious violence was to be expected

---

self-government and happiness through courage are to be realized. Brandeis is sketching a good society here, but not, I think, an all-conquering dialectic."

   [19]   Consider Blasi, supra,: "It is noteworthy that Brandeis never speaks of noxious doctrine being refuted or eliminated or defeated. He talks of societal self-protection and the fitting remedy. He warns us not to underestimate the value of discussion, education, good counsels. To me, his point is that noxious doctrine is most likely to flourish when its opponents lack the personal qualities of wisdom, creativity, and confidence. And those qualities, he suggests, are best developed by discussion and education, not by lazy and impatient reliance on the coercive authority of the state."

or was advocated, or that the past conduct furnished reason to believe that such advocacy was then contemplated.

Those who won our independence by revolution were not cowards. They did not fear political change. They did not exalt order at the cost of liberty. To courageous, self-reliant men, with confidence in the power of free and fearless reasoning applied through the processes of popular government, no danger flowing from speech can be deemed clear and present, unless the incidence of the evil apprehended is so imminent that it may befall before there is opportunity for full discussion. If there be time to expose through discussion the falsehood and fallacies, to avert the evil by the processes of education, the remedy to be applied is more speech, not enforced silence.[20] Only an emergency can justify repression. Such must be the rule if authority is to be reconciled with freedom. Such, in my opinion, is the command of the Constitution. It is therefore always open to Americans to challenge a law abridging free speech and assembly by showing that there was no emergency justifying it.

Moreover, even imminent danger cannot justify resort to prohibition of these functions essential to effective democracy, unless the evil apprehended is relatively serious. Prohibition of free speech and assembly is a measure so stringent that it would be inappropriate as the means for averting a relatively trivial harm to society. A police measure may be unconstitutional merely because the remedy, although effective as means of protection, is unduly harsh or oppressive. Thus, a state might, in the exercise of its police power, make any trespass upon the land of another a crime, regardless of the results or of the intent or purpose of the trespasser. It might, also, punish an attempt, a conspiracy, or an incitement to commit the trespass. But it is hardly conceivable that this court would hold constitutional a statute which punished as a felony the mere voluntary assembly with a society formed to teach that pedestrians had the moral right to cross uninclosed, unposted, waste lands and to advocate their doing so, even if there was imminent danger that advocacy would lead to a trespass. The fact that speech is likely to result in some violence or in destruction of property is not enough to justify its suppression. There must be the probability of serious injury to the State.[21] Among free men, the deterrents ordinarily to be applied to prevent crime are education and

---

[20] Is more speech necessarily or even generally the best corrective for false speech? See Richard Delgado & Jean Stefanic, *Images of the Outsider in American Law and Culture: Can Free Expression Remedy Systematic Social Ills?,* 77 Corn.L.Rev. 1258 (1992); Lawrence Lessig, *The Regulation of Social Meaning,* 62 U.Chi.L.Rev. 943 (1995); Frederick Schauer, *Social Epistemology, Holocaust Denial, and the Post-Millian Calculus,* in *The Content and Context of Hate Speech* 129 (Michael Herz & Peter Molnar eds. 2012).

[21] But see Robert Bork, *Neutral Principles and Some First Amendment Problems,* 47 Ind.L.J. 1 (1971): "It is difficult to see how a constitutional court could properly draw the distinction proposed. Brandeis offered no analysis to show that advocacy of law violation merited protection by the Court. Worse, the criterion he advanced is the importance, in the judge's eye, of the law whose violation is urged."

punishment for violations of the law, not abridgement of the rights of free speech and assembly.

* * * Whenever the fundamental rights of free speech and assembly are alleged to have been invaded, it must remain open to a defendant to present the issue whether there actually did exist at the time a clear danger, whether the danger, if any, was imminent, and whether the evil apprehended was one so substantial as to justify the stringent restriction interposed by the Legislature. The legislative declaration, like the fact that the statute was passed and was sustained by the highest court of the State, creates merely a rebuttable presumption that these conditions have been satisfied.

Whether in 1919, when Miss Whitney did the things complained of, there was in California such clear and present danger of serious evil, might have been made the important issue in the case. She might have required that the issue be determined either by the court or the jury. She claimed below that the statute as applied to her violated the federal Constitution; but she did not claim that it was void because there was no clear and present danger of serious evil, nor did she request that the existence of these conditions of a valid measure thus restricting the rights of free speech and assembly be passed upon by the court or a jury. On the other hand, there was evidence on which the court or jury might have found that such danger existed. I am unable to assent to the suggestion in the opinion of the court that assembling with a political party, formed to advocate the desirability of a proletarian revolution by mass action at some date necessarily far in the future, is not a right within the protection of the Fourteenth Amendment. In the present case, however, there was other testimony which tended to establish the existence of a conspiracy, on the part of members of the International Workers of the World, to commit present serious crimes, and likewise to show that such a conspiracy would be furthered by the activity of the society of which Miss Whitney was a member. Under these circumstances the judgment of the State court cannot be disturbed. * * *

JUSTICE HOLMES joins in this opinion.

NOTES AND QUESTIONS

1. *"They valued liberty both as an end and as a means."* Should recognition of the value of liberty as an end augment the marketplace perspective? Replace it?[22] Does a focus on liberty adequately distinguish speech

---

[22] Compare C. Edwin Baker, *Harm, Liberty, and Free Speech,* 70 So.Cal.L.Rev. 979 (1997) (harm does not justify invasion of liberty); Steven J. Heyman, *Righting the Balance: An Inquiry into the Foundations and Limits of Freedom of Expression,* 78 B.U.L.Rev. 1275 (1998) (endorsing natural rights theory of liberty as basis for free speech); and Martin Redish, *The Value of Free Speech,* 130 U.Pa.L.Rev. 591 (1982) (self-realization should be regarded as the first amendment's exclusive value) and Rodney Smolla, *Free Speech in an Open Society* 5 (1992) ("There is no logical reason, however, why the preferred position of freedom of speech might not be buttressed by

(or communication) from other manifestations of personal liberty? Is autonomy different from or preferable to liberty (or self-realization) as an organizing principle for First Amendment theory? And, again, does the idea of autonomy adequately distinguish autonomous speech from autonomous non-speech conduct? Does a focus on autonomy help determine the appropriate scope of liberty? C. Edwin Baker, *Human Liberty and Freedom of Speech* 47–51 (1989).[23] Even if we accept the philosophical assumption that human beings are capable of making autonomous choices, is the autonomy argument an empirical or a normative one? See Richard Fallon, *Two Senses of Autonomy,* 46 Stan.L.Rev. 875 (1994). C. Edwin Baker, *Autonomy and Informational Privacy, or Gossip: The Central Meaning of the First Amendment,* 21 Social Phil. & Pol'y 215 (2004): "The law affirms the formal conception of autonomy to the extent that the law recognizes an agent's legal right to choose what to do with herself (and her property * * *). The law recognizes her dominion over her own mind and body, given the inherent constraints of the environment and given her lack of any right to interfere directly with another's decisions about himself (and his property). This formal autonomy implies nothing about actual capacity, opportunity, or the availability of needed resources."

2.   ***Brandeis and Republicanism.*** Consider Pnina Lahav, *Holmes and Brandeis: Libertarian and Republican Justifications for Free Speech,* 4 J.L. & Pol. 451 (1987): "[I]n his *Whitney* concurrence, Brandeis tells us, that in the American polity, 'the deliberative forces should prevail over the arbitrary,' that 'public discussion is a political duty,' and that 'the occasional tyranny of governing majorities' should be thwarted. This is radically different from the notion that individuals are free to remain aloof from politics if they so choose (a notion espoused by Holmes), and from the principle of the separation of the

---

multiple rationales. Acceptance of one rationale need not bump another from the list, as if this were First Amendment musical chairs"); Steven Shiffrin, *The First Amendment and Economic Regulation: Away from a General Theory of the First Amendment,* 78 Nw.U.L.Rev. 1212 (1983) (many values including liberty and self-realization underpin the first amendment; single valued orientations are reductionist); Brian C. Murchison, *Speech and the Self-Realization Value,* 33 Harv.C.R.-C.L. L.Rev. 443 (1998) (emphasizing and illuminating the self-realization value while recognizing other values); But see Frederick Schauer, *Must Speech Be Special,* 78 Nw.U.L.Rev. 1284 (1983) (neither liberty nor self-realization can justify the special and differential protection of speech). See also Joshua Cohen, *Freedom of Expression,* 22 Phil. & Pub.Aff. 207 (1993); Joseph Raz, *Free Expression and Personal Identification,* 11 Oxford J.Legal St. 311 (1991).

[23] See also Robert Post, *Constitutional Domains* 268–331 (1995); Charles Fried, *The New First Amendment Jurisprudence: A Threat to Liberty,* 59 U.Chi.L.Rev. 225 (1992); Robert Post, *Managing Deliberation: The Quandary of Democratic Dialogue,* 103 Ethics 654 (1993); Robert Post, *Racist Speech, Democracy, and the First Amendment,* 32 Wm. & Mary L.Rev. 267 (1991); Thomas Scanlon, *A Theory of Freedom of Expression,* 1 Phil. & Pub.Aff. 204 (1972); David Strauss, *Persuasion, Autonomy, and Freedom of Expression,* 91 Colum.L.Rev. 334 (1991); Christina Wells, *Reinvigorating Autonomy,* 32 Harv. C.R.-C.L. L. Rev. 159 (1997).

For commentary on the differences between speaker and listener autonomy, see Cass Sunstein, *Democracy and the Problem of Free Speech* 139–44 (1993); C. Edwin Baker, *Turner Broadcasting: Content-Based Regulation of Persons and Presses,* 1994 Sup.Ct.Rev. 57. For the suggestion that the value of autonomy depends upon open and rich public discussion, see Sunstein, supra. For the contention that the value of autonomy should be subservient to open and rich discussion, see Owen Fiss, *State Activism and State Censorship,* 100 Yale L.J. 2087 (1991). Owen Fiss, *Why the State,* 100 Harv.L.Rev. 781 (1987); Owen Fiss, *Free Speech and Social Structure,* 71 Iowa L.Rev. 1405 (1986); but see Robert Post, *Equality and Autonomy in First Amendment Discourse,* 95 Mich. L.Rev. 1517 (1997).

state from society. Implied here is the notion of civic virtue—the duty to participate in politics, the importance of deliberation, and the notion that the end of the state is not neutrality but active assistance in providing conditions of freedom which in turn are the 'secret of happiness.' One may even speculate that Brandeis, the progressive leader, believed that the final end of the state was the happiness of mankind.

"These ingredients of the Brandeis position in *Whitney* resonate with republican theory. The theory rests on two central themes: the idea of civic virtue and the idea that the end of politics (or the state) is the common good, which in turn is more than the sum of individual wills. Thus, the state is not separated from society, but rather is committed to the public good, and to a substantive notion of public morality. The members of society are not individuals encased in their autonomous zones, but rather social beings who recognize that they are an integral part of the society. This organic sense of belonging implicitly rejects the notion of combat zones. The republic and its citizens care for the welfare of all. Correctly understood, Brandeis' concurrence in *Whitney* is more than a justification from self-fulfillment or from self-rule. It is a justification from civic virtue."

3.   *Character.* In keeping with the positions of Holmes and Brandeis, is the First Amendment best defended as proceeding from a "special kind of argument from character that builds from the claim that a culture that prizes and protects expressive liberty nurtures in its members certain character traits such as inquisitiveness, independence of judgment, distrust of authority, willingness to take initiative, perseverance, and the courage to confront evil"? Vincent Blasi, *Free Speech and Good Character,* 46 UCLA L.Rev. 1567 (1999). See also Vincent Blasi, *Free Speech and Good Character: From Milton to Brandeis to the Present*, in *Eternally Vigilant: Free Speech in the Modern Era* 77 (Lee C. Bollinger & Geoffrey R. Stone eds. 2002): "I do not think Brandeis wanted hopeful, vital, imaginative dissidents because he thought they could be mollified by civil liberties. Rather, he believed that in a political community personal qualities such as hope and imagination tend to be contagious and reciprocal. If the marginal, powerless members of the community retain some semblance of spirit, the mainstream is more likely to sustain its own vitality. And when dissidents become gripped by fear and hate, so too does the majority. The phrase 'repression breeds hate' can be read as a double entendre: it is not just the hate experienced by the dissidents that concerns Brandeis, but also the hate that is felt by those who possess the power to punish dissent. The passage is not primarily about consequences or tactics; it is about character."

4.   Ten years after *Whitney, DeJonge v. Oregon,* 299 U.S. 353 (1937) held that mere participation in a meeting called by the Communist party could not be made a crime. The right of peaceable assembly was declared to be "cognate to those of free speech and free press and is equally fundamental." See generally John D. Inazu, *Liberty's Refuge: The Forgotten Freedom of Assembly* (2012).

C. Communism and Illegal Advocacy

Kent Greenawalt, *Speech and Crime,* 1980 Am.B.Found.Res.J. 645, has well described the pattern of decisions for much of the period between *Whitney* and *Dennis* infra: "[T]he clear and present danger formula emerged as the applicable standard not only for the kinds of issues with respect to which it originated but also for a wide variety of other First Amendment problems. If the Court was not always very clear about the relevance of that formula to those different problems, its use of the test, and its employment of ancillary doctrines, did evince a growing disposition to protect expression." By 1951, however, anti-communist sentiment was a powerful theme in American politics. The Soviet Union had detonated a nuclear weapon; communists had firm control of the Chinese mainland; the Korean War had reached a stalemate; Alger Hiss had been convicted of perjury in congressional testimony concerning alleged spying activities for the Soviet Union while he was a State Department official; and Senator Joseph McCarthy of Wisconsin had created a national sensation by accusations that many "card carrying Communists" held important State Department jobs. In this context, the top leaders of the American Communist Party asked the Court to reverse their criminal conspiracy convictions.

DENNIS V. UNITED STATES

341 U.S. 494, 71 S.Ct. 857, 95 L.Ed. 1137 (1951).

CHIEF JUSTICE VINSON announced the judgment of the Court and an opinion in which JUSTICE REED, JUSTICE BURTON and JUSTICE MINTON join.

Petitioners were indicted in July, 1948, for violation of the conspiracy provisions of the Smith Act during the period of April, 1945, to July, 1948. * * * A verdict of guilty as to all the petitioners was [affirmed by the Second Circuit]. We granted certiorari, limited to the following two questions: (1) Whether either § 2 or § 3 of the Smith Act, inherently or as construed and applied in the instant case, violates the First Amendment and other provisions of the Bill of Rights; (2) whether either § 2 or § 3 of the Act, inherently or as construed and applied in the instant case, violates the First and Fifth Amendments, because of indefiniteness.

Sections 2 and 3 of the Smith Act provide as follows:

"Sec. 2.

"(a) It shall be unlawful for any person—

"(1) to knowingly or willfully advocate, abet, advise, or teach the duty, necessity, desirability, or propriety of overthrowing or destroying any government in the United States by force or violence, or by the assassination of any officer of any such government; * * *

"Sec. 3. It shall be unlawful for any person to attempt to commit, or to conspire to commit, any of the acts prohibited by the provisions [of] this title."

The indictment charged the petitioners with wilfully and knowingly conspiring (1) to organize as the Communist Party of the United States of America a society, group and assembly of persons who teach and advocate the overthrow and destruction of the Government of the United States by force and violence, and (2) knowingly and wilfully to advocate and teach the duty and necessity of overthrowing and destroying the Government of the United States by force and violence. The indictment further alleged that § 2 of the Smith Act proscribes these acts and that any conspiracy to take such action is a violation of § 3 of the Act.

The trial of the case extended over nine months, six of which were devoted to the taking of evidence, resulting in a record of 16,000 pages. Our limited grant of the writ of certiorari has removed from our consideration any question as to the sufficiency of the evidence to support the jury's determination that petitioners are guilty of the offense charged. Whether on this record petitioners did in fact advocate the overthrow of the Government by force and violence is not before us, and we must base any discussion of this point upon the conclusions stated in the opinion of the Court of Appeals, which treated the issue in great detail [and] held that the record supports the following broad conclusions: [that] the Communist Party is a highly disciplined organization, adept at infiltration into strategic positions, use of aliases, and double-meaning language; that the Party is rigidly controlled; that Communists, unlike other political parties, tolerate no dissension from the policy laid down by the guiding [forces]; that the literature of the Party and the statements and activities of its leaders, petitioners here, advocate, and the general goal of the Party was, during the period in question, to achieve a successful overthrow of the existing order by force and violence. * * *

The obvious purpose of the statute is to protect existing Government, not from change by peaceable, lawful and constitutional means, but from change by violence, revolution and terrorism. That it is within the *power* of the Congress to protect the Government of the United States from armed rebellion is a proposition which requires little discussion. Whatever theoretical merit there may be to the argument that there is a "right" to rebellion against dictatorial governments is without force where the existing structure of the government provides for peaceful and orderly change. We reject any principle of governmental helplessness in the face of preparation for revolution, which principle, carried to its logical conclusion, must lead to anarchy. No one could conceive that it is not within the power of Congress to prohibit acts intended to overthrow the Government by force and violence. The question with which we are concerned here is not whether Congress has such *power,* but whether the *means* which it has employed conflict with the First and Fifth Amendments to the Constitution.

One of the bases for the contention that the means which Congress has employed are invalid takes the form of an attack on the face of the statute on the grounds that by its terms it prohibits academic discussion of the merits of Marxism-Leninism, that it stifles ideas and is contrary to all concepts of a free speech and a free press. [This] is a federal statute which we must interpret as well as judge. Herein lies the fallacy of reliance upon the manner in which this Court has treated judgments of state courts. Where the statute as construed by the state court transgressed the First Amendment, we could not but invalidate the judgments of conviction.

The very language of the Smith Act negates the interpretation which petitioners would have us impose on that Act. It is directed at advocacy, not discussion. Thus, the trial judge properly charged the jury that they could not convict if they found that petitioners did "no more than pursue peaceful studies and discussions or teaching and advocacy in the realm of ideas." * * * Congress did not intend to eradicate the free discussion of political theories, to destroy the traditional rights of Americans to discuss and evaluate ideas without fear of governmental sanction. * * *

But although the statute is not directed at the hypothetical cases which petitioners have conjured, its application in this case has resulted in convictions for the teaching and advocacy of the overthrow of the Government by force and violence, which, even though coupled with the intent to accomplish that overthrow, contains an element of speech. For this reason, we must pay special heed to the demands of the First Amendment marking out the boundaries of speech.

[T]he basis of the First Amendment is the hypothesis that speech can rebut speech, propaganda will answer propaganda, free debate of ideas will result in the wisest governmental policies. [An] analysis of the leading cases in this Court which have involved direct limitations on speech, however, will demonstrate that both the majority of the Court and the dissenters in particular cases have recognized that this is not an unlimited, unqualified right, but that the societal value of speech must, on occasion, be subordinated to other values and considerations. * * *

Although no case subsequent to *Whitney* and *Gitlow* has expressly overruled the majority opinions in those cases, there is little doubt that subsequent opinions have inclined toward the Holmes-Brandeis rationale. * * *

In this case we are squarely presented with the application of the "clear and present danger" test, and must decide what that phrase imports.[24] We first note that many of the cases in which this Court has reversed convictions by use of this or similar tests have been based on the fact that the interest which the State was attempting to protect was itself too insubstantial to warrant restriction of speech. * * * Overthrow of the Government by force and violence is certainly a substantial enough interest for the Government to limit speech. Indeed, this is the ultimate value of any society, for if a society cannot protect its very structure from armed internal attack, it must follow that no subordinate value can be protected. If, then, this interest may be protected, the literal problem which is presented is what has been meant by the use of the phrase "clear and present danger" of the utterances bringing about the evil within the power of Congress to punish.

Obviously, the words cannot mean that before the Government may act, it must wait until the putsch is about to be executed, the plans have been laid and the signal is awaited. If Government is aware that a group aiming at its overthrow is attempting to indoctrinate its members and to commit them to a course whereby they will strike when the leaders feel the circumstances permit, action by the Government is required. The argument that there is no need for Government to concern itself, for Government is strong, it possesses ample powers to put down a rebellion, it may defeat the revolution with ease needs no answer. For that is not the question. Certainly an attempt to overthrow the Government by force, even though doomed from the outset because of inadequate numbers or power of the revolutionists, is a sufficient evil for Congress to prevent. The damage which such attempts create both physically and politically to a nation makes it impossible to measure the validity in terms of the probability of success, or the immediacy of a successful attempt. In the instant case the trial judge charged the jury that they could not convict unless they found that petitioners intended to overthrow the Government "as speedily as circumstances would permit." This does not mean, and could not properly mean, that they would not strike until there was certainty of success. What was meant was that the revolutionists would strike when they thought the time was ripe. We must therefore reject the contention that success or probability of success is the criterion.

The situation with which Justices Holmes and Brandeis were concerned in *Gitlow* was a comparatively isolated event, bearing little relation in their minds to any substantial threat to the safety of the community. [They] were not confronted with any situation comparable to the instant one—the development of an apparatus designed and dedicated

---

[24] Consider Harry Kalven, *A Worthy Tradition* 190–91 (1988): "The [Vinson opinion] acknowledges clear and present danger as the constitutional measure of free speech, but in the process, to meet the political exigencies of the case, it officially adjusts the test, giving it the kiss of death."

to the overthrow of the Government, in the context of world crisis after crisis.

Chief Judge Learned Hand, writing for the majority below, interpreted the phrase as follows: "In each case [courts] must ask whether the gravity of the 'evil,' discounted by its improbability, justifies such invasion of free speech as is necessary to avoid the danger." We adopt this statement of the rule. As articulated by Chief Judge Hand, it is as succinct and inclusive as any other we might devise at this time. * * *

Likewise, we are in accord with the court below, which affirmed the trial court's finding that the requisite danger existed. The mere fact that from the period 1945 to 1948 petitioners' activities did not result in an attempt to overthrow the Government by force and violence is of course no answer to the fact that there was a group that was ready to make the attempt. The formation by petitioners of such a highly organized conspiracy, with rigidly disciplined members subject to call when the leaders, these petitioners, felt that the time had come for action, coupled with the inflammable nature of world conditions, similar uprisings in other countries, and the touch-and-go nature of our relations with countries with whom petitioners were in the very least ideologically attuned, convince us that their convictions were justified on this score. And this analysis disposes of the contention that a conspiracy to advocate, as distinguished from the advocacy itself, cannot be constitutionally restrained, because it comprises only the preparation. It is the existence of the conspiracy which creates the danger. * * *

Although we have concluded that the finding that there was a sufficient danger to warrant the application of the statute was justified on the merits, there remains the problem of whether the trial judge's treatment of the issue was correct. He charged the jury, in relevant part, as follows: "In further construction and interpretation of the statute I charge you that it is not the abstract doctrine of overthrowing or destroying organized government by unlawful means which is denounced by this law, but the teaching and advocacy of action for the accomplishment of that purpose, by language reasonably and ordinarily calculated to incite persons to such action. Accordingly, you cannot find the defendants or any of them guilty of the crime charged unless you are satisfied beyond a reasonable doubt that they conspired to organize a society, group and assembly of persons who teach and advocate the overthrow or destruction of the Government of the United States by force and violence and to advocate and teach the duty and necessity of overthrowing or destroying the Government of the United States by force and violence, with the intent that such teaching and advocacy be of a rule or principle of action and by language reasonably and ordinarily calculated to incite persons to such action, all with the intent to cause the overthrow or destruction of the Government of the United States by force and violence as speedily as circumstances would permit. * * *

"If you are satisfied that the evidence establishes beyond a reasonable doubt that the defendants, or any of them, are guilty of a violation of the statute, as I have interpreted it to you, I find as matter of law that there is sufficient danger of a substantive evil that the Congress has a right to prevent to justify the application of the statute under the First Amendment of the Constitution. This is matter of law about which you have no concern. * * * "

It is thus clear that he reserved the question of the existence of the danger for his own determination, and the question becomes whether the issue is of such a nature that it should have been submitted to the jury.

[When] facts are found that establish the violation of a statute, the protection against conviction afforded by the First Amendment is a matter of law. The doctrine that there must be a clear and present danger of a substantive evil that Congress has a right to prevent is a judicial rule to be applied as a matter of law by the courts. The guilt is established by proof of facts. Whether the First Amendment protects the activity which constitutes the violation of the statute must depend upon a judicial determination of the scope of the First Amendment applied to the circumstances of the case.

[In] *Schenck* this Court itself examined the record to find whether the requisite danger appeared, and the issue was not submitted to a jury. And in every later case in which the Court has measured the validity of a statute by the "clear and present danger" test, that determination has been by the court, the question of the danger not being submitted to the jury. * * * Petitioners intended to overthrow the Government of the United States as speedily as the circumstances would permit. Their conspiracy to organize the Communist Party and to teach and advocate the overthrow of the Government of the United States by force and violence created a "clear and present danger" of an attempt to overthrow the Government by force and violence. They were properly and constitutionally convicted * * * .

Affirmed.

JUSTICE CLARK took no part in the consideration or decision of this case.

JUSTICE FRANKFURTER, concurring in affirmance of the judgment.

[The] demands of free speech in a democratic society as well as the interest in national security are better served by candid and informed weighing of the competing interests, within the confines of the judicial process, than by announcing dogmas too inflexible for the non-Euclidian problems to be solved.

But how are competing interests to be assessed? Since they are not subject to quantitative ascertainment, the issue necessarily resolves itself into asking, who is to make the adjustment?—who is to balance the relevant factors and ascertain which interest is in the circumstances to prevail? Full responsibility for the choice cannot be given to the courts. Courts are not representative bodies. They are not designed to be a good reflex of a democratic society. Their judgment is best informed, and therefore most dependable, within narrow limits. Their essential quality is detachment, founded on independence. History teaches that the independence of the judiciary is jeopardized when courts become embroiled in the passions of the day and assume primary responsibility in choosing between competing political, economic and social pressures.

Primary responsibility for adjusting the interests which compete in the situation before us of necessity belongs to the Congress. [We] are to set aside the judgment of those whose duty it is to legislate only if there is no reasonable basis for [it]. Free-speech cases are not an exception to the principle that we are not legislators, that direct policy-making is not our province. How best to reconcile competing interests is the business of legislatures, and the balance they strike is a judgment not to be displaced by ours, but to be respected unless outside the pale of fair judgment. [A] survey of the relevant decisions indicates that the results which we have reached are on the whole those that would ensue from careful weighing of conflicting interests. The complex issues presented by regulation of speech in public places by picketing, and by legislation prohibiting advocacy of crime have been resolved by scrutiny of many factors besides the imminence and gravity of the evil threatened. The matter has been well summarized by a reflective student of the Court's work. "The truth is that the clear-and-present-danger test is an oversimplified judgment unless it takes account also of a number of other factors: the relative seriousness of the danger in comparison with the value of the occasion for speech or political activity; the availability of more moderate controls than those which the state has imposed; and perhaps the specific intent with which the speech or activity is launched. No matter how rapidly we utter the phrase 'clear and present danger,' or how closely we hyphenate the words, they are not a substitute for the weighing of values. They tend to convey a delusion of certitude when what is most certain is the complexity of the strands in the web of freedoms which the judge must disentangle." Paul Freund, *On Understanding the Supreme Court* 27–28 [1949]. * * *

To make validity of legislation depend on judicial reading of events still in the womb of time—a forecast, that is, of the outcome of forces at best appreciated only with knowledge of the topmost secrets of nations—is to charge the judiciary with duties beyond its equipment. * * *

Even when moving strictly within the limits of constitutional adjudication, judges are concerned with issues that may be said to involve vital finalities. The too easy transition from disapproval of what is undesirable to condemnation as unconstitutional, has led some of the wisest judges to question the wisdom of our scheme in lodging such authority in courts. But it is relevant to remind that in sustaining the power of Congress in a case like this nothing irrevocable is done. The democratic process at all events is not impaired or restricted. Power and responsibility remain with the people and immediately with their representation. All the Court says is that Congress was not forbidden by the Constitution to pass this enactment and that a prosecution under it may be brought against a conspiracy such as the one before us. * * *

JUSTICE JACKSON, concurring.

[E]ither by accident or design, the Communist stratagem outwits the antianarchist pattern of statute aimed against "overthrow by force and violence" if qualified by the doctrine that only "clear and present danger" of accomplishing that result will sustain the prosecution.

The "clear and present danger" test was an innovation by Mr. Justice Holmes in the *Schenck* case, reiterated and refined by him and Mr. Justice Brandeis in later cases, all arising before the era of World War II revealed the subtlety and efficacy of modernized revolutionary techniques used by totalitarian parties. In those cases, they were faced with convictions under so-called criminal syndicalism statutes aimed at anarchists but which, loosely construed, had been applied to punish socialism, pacifism, and left-wing ideologies, the charges often resting on farfetched inferences which, if true, would establish only technical or trivial violations. They proposed "clear and present danger" as a test for the sufficiency of evidence in particular cases.

I would save it, unmodified, for application as a "rule of reason" in the kind of case for which it was devised. When the issue is criminality of a hotheaded speech on a street corner, or circulation of a few incendiary pamphlets, or parading by some zealots behind a red flag, or refusal of a handful of school children to salute our flag, it is not beyond the capacity of the judicial process to gather, comprehend, and weigh the necessary materials for decision whether it is a clear and present danger of substantive evil or a harmless letting off of steam. It is not a prophecy, for the danger in such cases has matured by the time of trial or it was never present. The test applies and has meaning where a conviction is sought to be based on a speech or writing which does not directly or explicitly advocate a crime but to which such tendency is sought to be attributed by construction or by implication from external circumstances. The formula in such cases favors freedoms that are vital to our society, and, even if sometimes applied too generously, the consequences cannot be grave. But its recent expansion has extended, in particular to Communists, unprecedented immunities. Unless we are to hold our Government captive in a judge-made verbal trap, we must approach the problem of a well-organized, nation-wide conspiracy, such as I have described, as realistically as our predecessors faced the trivialities that were being prosecuted until they were checked with a rule of reason.

I think reason is lacking for applying that test to this case.

If we must decide that this Act and its application are constitutional only if we are convinced that petitioner's conduct creates a "clear and present danger" of violent overthrow, we must appraise imponderables, including international and national phenomena which baffle the best informed foreign offices and our most experienced politicians. We would have to foresee and predict the effectiveness of Communist propaganda, opportunities for infiltration, whether, and when, a time will come that they consider propitious for action, and whether and how fast our existing government will deteriorate. And we would have to speculate as to whether an approaching Communist coup would not be anticipated by a nationalistic fascist movement. No doctrine can be sound whose application requires us to make a prophecy of that sort in the guise of a legal decision. The judicial process simply is not adequate to a trial of such far-flung issues. The answers given would reflect our own political predilections and nothing more.

The authors of the clear and present danger test never applied it to a case like this, nor would I. If applied as it is proposed here, it means that the Communist plotting is protected during its period of incubation; its preliminary stages of organization and preparation are immune from the law; the Government can move only after imminent action is manifest, when it would, of course, be too late.

The highest degree of constitutional protection is due to the individual acting without conspiracy. But even an individual cannot claim that the Constitution protects him in advocating or teaching overthrow of government by force or violence. I should suppose no one would doubt that Congress has power to make such attempted overthrow a crime. But the contention is that one has the constitutional right to work up a public desire and will to do what it is a crime to attempt. I think direct incitement by speech or writing can be made a crime, and I think there can be a conviction without also proving that the odds favored its success by 99 to 1, or some other extremely high ratio. * * *

What really is under review here is a conviction of conspiracy, after a trial for conspiracy, on an indictment charging conspiracy, brought under a statute outlawing conspiracy. With due respect to my colleagues, they seem to me to discuss anything under the sun except the law of conspiracy. * * *

The Constitution does not make conspiracy a civil right. [Although] I consider criminal conspiracy a dragnet device capable of perversion into an instrument of injustice in the hands of a partisan or complacent judiciary, it has an established place in our system of law, and no reason appears for applying it only to concerted action claimed to disturb interstate commerce and withholding it from those claimed to undermine our whole Government. * * *

I do not suggest that Congress could punish conspiracy to advocate something, the doing of which it may not punish. Advocacy or exposition of the doctrine of communal property ownership, or any political philosophy unassociated with advocacy of its imposition by force or seizure of government by unlawful means could not be reached through conspiracy prosecution. But it is not forbidden to put down force or violence, it is not forbidden to punish its teaching or advocacy, and the end being punishable, there is no doubt of the power to punish conspiracy for the purpose. * * *

JUSTICE BLACK, dissenting. * * *

So long as this Court exercises the power of judicial review of legislation, I cannot agree that the First Amendment permits us to sustain laws suppressing freedom of speech and press on the basis of Congress' or our own notions of mere "reasonableness." Such a doctrine waters down the First Amendment so that it amounts to little more than an admonition to Congress. The Amendment as so construed is not likely to protect any but those "safe" or orthodox views which rarely need its protection. I must also express my objection to the holding because, as Mr. Justice Douglas' dissent shows, it sanctions the determination of a crucial issue of fact by the judge rather than by the jury. * * *

Public opinion being what it now is, few will protest the conviction of these Communist petitioners. There is hope, however, that in calmer times, when present pressures, passions and fears subside, this or some later Court will restore the First Amendment liberties to the high preferred place where they belong in a free society.

JUSTICE DOUGLAS, dissenting.

If this were a case where those who claimed protection under the First Amendment were teaching the techniques of sabotage, the assassination of the President, the filching of documents from public files, the planting of bombs, the art of street warfare, and the like, I would have no doubts. The freedom to speak is not absolute; the teaching of methods of terror and other seditious conduct should be beyond the pale along with obscenity and immorality. This case was argued as if those were the facts. The argument imported much seditious conduct into the record. That is easy and it has popular appeal, for the activities of Communists in plotting and scheming against the free world are common knowledge. But the fact is that no such evidence was introduced at the trial. There is a statute which makes a seditious conspiracy unlawful. Petitioners, however, were not charged with a "conspiracy to overthrow" the Government. They were charged with a conspiracy to form a party and groups and assemblies of people who teach and advocate the overthrow of our Government by force or violence and with a conspiracy to advocate and teach its overthrow by force and violence. It may well be that indoctrination in the techniques of terror to destroy the Government would be indictable under either statute. But the teaching which is condemned here is of a different character.

So far as the present record is concerned, what petitioners did was to organize people to teach and themselves teach the Marxist-Leninist doctrine contained chiefly in four books: *Foundations of Leninism* by Stalin (1924); *The Communist Manifesto* by Marx and Engels (1848); *State and Revolution* by Lenin (1917); *History of the Communist Party of the Soviet Union* (B.) (1939).

Those books are to Soviet Communism what *Mein Kampf* was to Nazism. If they are understood, the ugliness of Communism is revealed, its deceit and cunning are exposed, the nature of its activities becomes apparent, and the chances of its success less likely. That is not, of course, the reason why petitioners chose these books for their classrooms. They are fervent Communists to whom these volumes are gospel. They preached the creed with the hope that some day it would be acted upon.

The opinion of the Court does not outlaw these texts nor condemn them to the fire, as the Communists do literature offensive to their creed. But if the books themselves are not outlawed, if they can lawfully remain on library shelves, by what reasoning does their use in a classroom become a crime? It would not be a crime under the Act to introduce these books to a class, though that would be teaching what the creed of violent overthrow of the Government is. The Act, as construed, requires the element of intent—that those who teach the creed believe in it. The crime then depends not on what is taught but on who the teacher is. That is to make freedom of speech turn not on *what is said,* but on the *intent* with which it is said. Once we start down that road we enter territory dangerous to the liberties of every citizen. * * *

The vice of treating speech as the equivalent of overt acts of a treasonable or seditious character is emphasized by a concurring opinion, which by invoking the law of conspiracy makes speech do service for deeds which are dangerous to society. [N]ever until today has anyone seriously thought that the ancient law of conspiracy could constitutionally be used to turn speech into seditious conduct. Yet that is precisely what is suggested. I repeat that we deal here with speech alone, not with speech *plus* acts of sabotage or unlawful conduct. Not a single seditious act is charged in the indictment. To make a lawful speech unlawful because two men conceive it is to raise the law of conspiracy to appalling proportions. * * *

There comes a time when even speech loses its constitutional immunity. Speech innocuous one year may at another time fan such destructive flames that it must be halted in the interests of the safety of the Republic. That is the meaning of the clear and present danger test. When conditions are so critical that there will be no time to avoid the evil that the speech threatens, it is time to call a halt. Otherwise, free speech which is the strength of the Nation will be the cause of its destruction.

Yet free speech is the rule, not the exception. The restraint to be constitutional must be based on more than fear, on more than passionate opposition against the speech, on more than a revolted dislike for its contents. There must be some immediate injury to society that is likely if speech is allowed. * * *

I had assumed that the question of the clear and present danger, being so critical an issue in the case, would be a matter for submission to the jury. [The] Court, I think, errs when it treats the question as one of law.

Yet, whether the question is one for the Court or the jury, there should be evidence of record on the issue. This record, however, contains no evidence whatsoever showing that the acts charged viz., the teaching of the Soviet theory of revolution with the hope that it will be realized, have created any clear and present danger to the Nation. The Court, however, rules to the contrary. [The majority] might as well say that the speech of petitioners is outlawed because Soviet Russia and her Red Army are a threat to world peace.

The nature of Communism as a force on the world scene would, of course, be relevant to the issue of clear and present danger of petitioners' advocacy within the United States. But the primary consideration is the strength and tactical position of petitioners and their converts in this country. On that there is no evidence in the record. If we are to take judicial notice of the threat of Communists within the nation, it should not be difficult to conclude that *as a political party* they are of little consequence. Communists in this country have never made a respectable or serious showing in any election. I would doubt that there is a village, let alone a city or county or state, which the Communists could carry. Communism in the world scene is no bogeyman; but Communism as a political faction or party in this country plainly is. Communism has been so thoroughly exposed in this country that it has been crippled as a political force. Free speech has destroyed it as an effective political party. It is inconceivable that those who went up and down this country preaching the doctrine of revolution which petitioners espouse would have any success. In days of trouble and confusion, when bread lines were long, when the unemployed walked the streets, when people were starving, the advocates of a short-cut by revolution might have a chance to gain adherents. But today there are no such conditions. The country is not in despair; the people know Soviet

Communism; the doctrine of Soviet revolution is exposed in all of its ugliness and the American people want none of it.

[Unless] and until extreme and necessitous circumstances are shown our aim should be to keep speech unfettered and to allow the processes of law to be invoked only when the provocateurs among us move from speech to action. * * *[25]

NOTES AND QUESTIONS

1. **The test.** Is the *Dennis* test problematic on its face, as applied, or both? Consider Wilson Huhn, *Scienter, Causation, and Harm in Freedom of Expression Analysis: The Right Hand Side of the Constitutional Calculus*, 13 Wm. & Mary Bill Rts. J. 125 (2004): "The central problem [with] *Dennis* was not that it utilized Judge Hand's balancing approach, but rather that it failed to estimate properly the remoteness of the threatened harm, and accordingly, it failed to evaluate properly the relative weight of the freedom to advocate for unpopular political positions." Does the *Dennis* test make it too easy to control advocacy of extremely dangerous outcomes whose probability of occurrence, even with the advocacy, is negligible?

2. **Suppression of "totalitarian movements."** Consider Carl Auerbach, *The Communist Control Act of 1954*, 23 U.Chi.L.Rev. 173 (1956): "[I]n suppressing totalitarian movements a democratic society is not acting to protect the status quo, but the very same interests which freedom of speech itself seeks to secure—the possibility of peaceful progress under freedom. That suppression may sometimes have to be the means of securing and enlarging freedom is a paradox which is not unknown in other areas of the law of modern democratic states. The basic 'postulate,' therefore, which should 'limit and control' the First Amendment is that it is part of the framework for a constitutional democracy and should, therefore, not be used to curb the power of Congress to exclude from the political struggle those groups which, if victorious, would crush democracy and impose totalitarianism."[26]

Is it relevant that Communist speakers might themselves not believe in free speech? See David E. Bernstein, *The Red Menace, Revisited*, 100 Nw. U.L. Rev. 1295 (2006). Is it relevant that some of the fears of Communist infiltration

---

[25] Eighteen years later, concurring in *Brandenburg*, Sec. 1, I, D infra, Douglas, J., declared: "I see no place in the regime of the First Amendment for any 'clear and present danger' test whether strict and tight as some would make it or free-wheeling as the Court in *Dennis* rephrased it. When one reads the opinions closely and sees when and how the 'clear and present danger' test has been applied, great misgivings are aroused. First, the threats were often loud but always puny and made serious only by judges so wedded to the status quo that critical analysis made them nervous. Second, the test was so twisted and perverted in *Dennis* as to make the trial of those teachers of Marxism an all-out political trial which was part and parcel of the cold war that has eroded substantial parts of the First Amendment."

[26] For different perspectives on respecting the freedom of those who would restrict it, see John Rawls, *A Theory of Justice* 216–21 (1971); Stephen Smith, *Radically Subversive Speech and the Authority of Law*, 94 Mich.L.Rev. 348 (1995). More broadly, should a free society tolerate the intolerant? Should it tolerate those who would end tolerance? On this paradox of tolerance, see 1 Karl R. Popper, *The Open Society and Its Enemies* 265–66 (5th ed. 1966).

had some basis in fact? See Martin H. Redish, *The Logic of Persecution: Free Expression and the McCarthy Era* (2005).

3. ***The Second Amendment.*** Does the Second Amendment guarantee individuals (or groups) the right to bear arms for protection including protection against government tyranny?[27] If the Second Amendment is so construed, does the Second amendment shed light on the First?

4. ***Dennis distinguished.*** In 1954, Senator Joseph McCarthy was censured by the United States Senate for acting contrary to its ethics and impairing its dignity. In 1957, when the convictions of 14 "second string" communist leaders reached the Supreme Court in YATES v. UNITED STATES, 354 U.S. 298 (1957), McCarthy had died, and so had McCarthyism. Although strong anti-communist sentiment persisted, the political atmosphere in *Yates'* 1957 was profoundly different from that of *Dennis'* 1951. HARLAN, J., distinguishing *Dennis,* construed the Smith Act narrowly: "[The] essence of the *Dennis* holding was that indoctrination of a group in preparation for future violent action, as well as exhortation to immediate action, by advocacy found to be directed to 'action for the accomplishment' of forcible overthrow, to violence as 'a rule or principle of action,' and employing 'language of incitement,' is not constitutionally protected when the group is of sufficient size and cohesiveness, is sufficiently oriented towards action, and other circumstances are such as reasonably to justify apprehension that action will occur. This is quite a different thing from the view of the District Court here that mere doctrinal justification of forcible overthrow, if engaged in with the intent to accomplish overthrow, is punishable per se under the Smith Act. [T]he trial court's statement that the proscribed advocacy must include the 'urging,' 'necessity,' and 'duty' of forcible overthrow, and not merely its 'desirability' and 'propriety,' may not be regarded as a sufficient substitute for charging that the Smith Act reaches only advocacy of action for the overthrow of government by force and violence. The essential distinction is that those to whom the advocacy is addressed must be urged to *do* something, now or in the future, rather than merely to *believe* in something." Applying this standard, Harlan J., acquitted 5 defendants and remanded to the lower court for proceedings against the remaining defendants.[28]

5. ***The membership clause of the Smith Act.*** After *Yates*, the government sought to prosecute communists for being members of an organization advocating the overthrow of the government by force and violence. The Court in *Scales v. United States,* 367 U.S. 203 (1961) and *Noto v. United States,* 367 U.S. 290 (1961) interpreted the membership clause to require that the organization engage in advocacy of the sort described in *Yates*

---

[27] Is the Second Amendment an embarrassment to liberals? See Sanford Levinson, *The Embarrassing Second Amendment,* 99 Yale L.J. 637 (1989). For comparative analysis of the methodology employed in First and Second Amendment cases, see Joseph Blocher, *Categoricalism and Balancing in First and Second Amendment Cases,* 84 N.Y.U. L.Rev. 375 (2009).

[28] Burton, J., concurred. Black, joined by Douglas, JJ., dissenting, would have acquitted all defendants. Clark, J., dissenting, would have affirmed the convictions of all defendants. Brennan and Whittaker, JJ., took no part. On remand, the government requested dismissal of the indictments, explaining that it could not meet *Yates'* evidentiary requirements.

and that the members be active with knowledge of the organization's advocacy and the group's specific intent to bring about violent overthrow as speedily as circumstances permit.

6. **Spock.** Dr. Benjamin Spock, Rev. William Sloan Coffin, and others were convicted of conspiring to counsel and abet Selective Service registrants to refuse to have their draft cards in their possession and to disobey other duties imposed by the Selective Service Act of 1967. Spock signed a document entitled "A Call to Resist Illegitimate Authority," which "had 'a double aspect: in part it was a denunciation of governmental policy [in Vietnam] and, in part, it involved a public call to resist the duties imposed by the [Selective Service] Act.' " Several weeks later, Spock attended a demonstration in Washington, D.C., where an unsuccessful attempt was made to present collected draft cards to the Attorney General.

UNITED STATES v. SPOCK, 416 F.2d 165 (1st Cir.1969), per ALDRICH, J., ruled that Spock should have been acquitted: The primary basis for the court's conclusion was that the trial court had impermissibly (in a criminal case) given the jury special questions, rather than simply requiring a general verdict. But the court also addressed the First Amendment issues: "[Spock] was one of the drafters of the Call, but this does not evidence the necessary intent to adhere to its illegal aspects. [H]is speech was limited to condemnation of the war and the draft, and lacked any words or content of counselling. The jury could not find proscribed advocacy from the mere fact [that] he hoped the frequent stating of his views might give young men 'courage to take active steps in draft resistance.' This is a natural consequence of vigorous speech. Similarly, Spock's actions lacked the clear character necessary to imply specific intent under the First Amendment standard. [H]e was at the Washington demonstration, [but took] no part in its planning. [His statements at this demonstration did not extend] beyond the general anti-war, anti-draft remarks he had made before. His attendance is as consistent with a desire to repeat this speech as it is to aid a violation of the law. The dissent would fault us for drawing such distinctions, but it forgets the teaching of [*Bond v. Floyd*[29]] that expressing one's views in broad areas is not foreclosed by knowledge of the consequences, and the important lesson of *Noto, Scales* and *Yates* that one may belong to a group, knowing of its illegal aspects, and still not be found to adhere thereto."

---

[29] *Bond*, 385 U.S. 116 (1966) found ambiguity in expressions of support for those unwilling to respond to the draft that earlier opinions would have characterized as clear advocacy of illegal action.

D. A Modern "Restatement"

BRANDENBURG V. OHIO

395 U.S. 444, 89 S.Ct. 1827, 23 L.Ed.2d 430 (1969).

PER CURIAM.[30]

The appellant, a leader of a Ku Klux Klan group, was convicted under [a 1919] Ohio Criminal Syndicalism statute of "advocat[ing] the duty, necessity, or propriety of crime, sabotage, violence, or unlawful methods of terrorism as a means of accomplishing industrial or political reform" and of "voluntarily assembl[ing] with any society, group or assemblage of persons formed to teach or advocate the doctrines of criminal syndicalism." He was fined $1,000 and sentenced to one to 10 years' imprisonment. * * *

The record shows that a man, identified at trial as the appellant, telephoned an announcer-reporter on the staff of a Cincinnati television station and invited him to come to a Ku Klux Klan "rally" to be held at a farm in Hamilton County. With the cooperation of the organizers, the reporter and a cameraman attended the meeting and filmed the events. Portions of the films were later broadcast on the local station and on a national network.

The prosecution's case rested on the films and on testimony identifying the appellant as the person who communicated with the reporter and who spoke at the rally. The State also introduced into evidence several articles appearing in the film, including a pistol, a rifle, a shotgun, ammunition, a Bible, and a red hood worn by the speaker in the films.

One film showed 12 hooded figures, some of whom carried firearms. They were gathered around a large wooden cross, which they burned. No one was present other than the participants and the newsmen who made the film. Most of the words uttered during the scene were incomprehensible when the film was projected, but scattered phrases could be understood that were derogatory of Negroes and, in one instance, of Jews. Another scene on the same film showed the appellant, in Klan regalia, making a speech. The speech, in full, was as follows:

---

[30] See Bernard Schwartz, *Holmes versus Hand: Clear and Present Danger or Advocacy of Unlawful Action?* 1995 S.Ct.Rev. 237: "*Brandenburg* was assigned to Justice Fortas. The draft opinion that he circulated stated a modified version of the Clear and Present test. [As] it turned out, *Brandenburg* did not come down as a Fortas opinion. Though the Justice had circulated his draft opinion in April 1969 and quickly secured the necessary votes, he followed Justice Harlan's suggestion to delay its announcement. Before then, the events occurred that led to Justice Fortas's forced resignation from the Court. The *Brandenburg* opinion was then redrafted by Justice Brennan, who eliminated all references to the Clear and Present Danger test and substituted the present *Brandenburg* language: 'where such advocacy is directed to inciting or producing imminent lawless action and is likely to incite or produce such action.' The Brennan redraft was issued as a per curiam opinion."

"This is an organizers' meeting. We have had quite a few members here today which are—we have hundreds, hundreds of members throughout the State of Ohio. I can quote from a newspaper clipping from the Columbus Ohio Dispatch, five weeks ago Sunday morning. The Klan has more members in the State of Ohio than does any other organization. We're not a revengent organization, but if our President, our Congress, our Supreme Court, continues to suppress the white, Caucasian race, it's possible that there might have to be some revengence taken.

"We are marching on Congress July the Fourth, four hundred thousand strong. From there we are dividing into two groups, one group to march on St. Augustine, Florida, the other group to march into Mississippi. Thank you."

The second film showed six hooded figures one of whom, later identified as the appellant, repeated a speech very similar to that recorded on the first film. The reference to the possibility of "revengence" was omitted, and one sentence was added: "Personally, I believe the nigger should be returned to Africa, the Jew returned to Israel." Though some of the figures in the films carried weapons, the speaker did not.

[*Whitney*] sustained the constitutionality of California's Criminal Syndicalism Act, the text of which is quite similar to that of the laws of Ohio. The Court upheld the statute on the ground that, without more, "advocating" violent means to effect political and economic change involves such danger to the security of the State that the State may outlaw it. But *Whitney* has been thoroughly discredited by later decisions [such as *Dennis* which] have fashioned the principle that the constitutional guarantees of free speech and free press do not permit a State to forbid or proscribe advocacy of the use of force or of law violation except where such advocacy is directed[31] to inciting or producing imminent lawless action[32] and is likely to incite or produce such action.[2] As we said in *Noto*, "the mere abstract teaching [of] the moral propriety or even moral necessity for a resort to

---

[31] Consider Eugene Volokh, *Crime-Facilitating Speech*, 57 Stan. L. Rev. 1095 (2005):"The incitement cases [have] never fully explained why an intent-imminence-likelihood test is the proper approach (as opposed to, say, a knowledge-imminence-likelihood test)."

[32] Consider Christina Wells, *Reinvigorating Autonomy,* 32 Harv. C.R.-C.L. L. Rev. 159 (1997), "The Court's requirement of imminent lawless action is easily justified as based upon concern for autonomy. Speech designed to incite immediate violence or lawless action does not appeal to our thought processes. Rather, it disrespects our rationality and is designed to elicit an unthinking, animalistic response. * * * Speech designed to persuade people to violate the law is not coercive in the same sense as speech designed to incite imminent lawlessness; the former contributes to rather than detracts from our deliberative processes." Compare David R. Dow & R. Scott Shieldes, *Rethinking the Clear and Present Danger Test,* 73 Indiana L.J. 1217 (1998).

[2] **[Ct's Note]** It was on the theory that the Smith Act embodied such a principle and that it had been applied only in conformity with it that this Court sustained the Act's constitutionality. That this was the basis for *Dennis* was emphasized in *Yates*, in which the Court overturned convictions for advocacy of the forcible overthrow of the Government under the Smith Act, because the trial judge's instructions had allowed conviction for mere advocacy, unrelated to its tendency to produce forcible action.

force and violence, is not the same as preparing a group for violent action and steeling it to such action." See also *Bond v. Floyd*. A statute which fails to draw this distinction impermissibly intrudes upon the freedoms guaranteed by the First and Fourteenth Amendments. It sweeps within its condemnation speech which our Constitution has immunized from governmental control. Cf. *Yates* * * * .

Measured by this test, Ohio's Criminal Syndicalism Act cannot be sustained. The Act punishes persons who "advocate or teach the duty, necessity, or propriety" of violence "as a means of accomplishing industrial or political reform"; or who publish or circulate or display any book or paper containing such advocacy; or who "justify" the commission of violent acts "with intent to exemplify, spread or advocate the propriety of the doctrines of criminal syndicalism"; or [who] "voluntarily assemble" with a group formed "to teach or advocate the doctrines of criminal syndicalism." Neither the indictment nor the trial judge's instructions to the jury in any way refined the statute's bald definition of the crime in terms of mere advocacy not distinguished from incitement to imminent lawless action.[3]

Accordingly, we are here confronted with a statute which, by its own words and as applied, purports to punish mere advocacy and to forbid, on pain of criminal punishment, assembly with others merely to advocate the described type of action.[4] Such a statute falls within the condemnation of the First and Fourteenth Amendments. The contrary teaching of *Whitney* cannot be supported, and that decision is therefore overruled.

Reversed.

JUSTICE BLACK, concurring.

I agree with the views expressed by Mr. Justice Douglas in his concurring opinion in this case that the "clear and present danger" doctrine should have no place in the interpretation of the First Amendment. I join the Court's opinion, which, as I understand it, simply cites *Dennis*, but does not indicate any agreement on the Court's part with the "clear and present danger" doctrine on which *Dennis* purported to rely.

JUSTICE DOUGLAS, concurring.

While I join the opinion of the Court, I desire to enter a caveat.

---

[3] **[Ct's Note]** The first count of the indictment charged that appellant "did unlawfully by word of mouth advocate the necessity, or propriety of crime, violence, or unlawful methods of terrorism as a means of accomplishing political reform * * * ." The second count charged that appellant "did unlawfully voluntarily assemble with a group or assemblage of persons formed to advocate the doctrines of criminal syndicalism * * * ." The trial judge's charge merely followed the language of the indictment. * * *

[4] **[Ct's Note]** Statutes affecting the right of assembly, like those touching on freedom of speech, must observe the established distinctions between mere advocacy and incitement to lawless action * * * .

[Whether] the war power—the greatest leveler of them all—is adequate to sustain [the "clear and present danger"] doctrine is debatable. The dissents in *Abrams* [and other cases] show how easily "clear and present danger" is manipulated to crush what Brandeis called "the fundamental right of free men to strive for better conditions through new legislation and new institutions" by argument and discourse even in time of war. Though I doubt if the "clear and present danger" test is congenial to the First Amendment in time of a declared war, I am certain it is not reconcilable with the First Amendment in days of peace. * * *

Mr. Justice Holmes, though never formally abandoning the "clear and present danger" test, moved closer to the First Amendment ideal when he said in dissent in *Gitlow* [quoting the passage beginning, "Every idea is an incitement."] We have never been faithful to the philosophy of that dissent.

"[In *Dennis,* we distorted] the 'clear and present danger' test beyond recognition. [I] see no place in the regime of the First Amendment for any 'clear and present danger' test whether strict and tight as some would make it or free-wheeling as the Court in *Dennis* rephrased it.

NOTES AND QUESTIONS

1. Why did the Court say that pre-*Brandenburg* decisions "have fashioned the principle" that advocacy may not be prohibited "except [where] directed to inciting or producing *imminent* lawless action *and * * * likely* to incite or produce such action"? (Emphasis added.) Did not *Dennis, Yates* and *Scales* deny that the unlawful action advocated need be "imminent" or that the advocacy must be "likely" to produce the forbidden action? See Hans Linde, *"Clear and Present Danger" Reexamined,* 22 Stan.L.Rev. 1163 (1970).

2. Does *Brandenburg* adopt the *Masses* incitement test as a major part of the required showing? Consider Gerald Gunther, *Learned Hand and the Origins of Modern First Amendment Doctrine: Some Fragments of History*, 27 Stan.L.Rev. 719 (1975): "An incitement-nonincitement distinction had only fragmentary and ambiguous antecedents in the pre-*Brandenburg* era; it was *Brandenburg* that really 'established' it; and, it was essentially an establishment of the legacy of Learned Hand. [Under] *Brandenburg*, probability of harm is no longer the central criterion for speech limitations. The inciting language of the speaker—the Hand focus on 'objective' words—is the major consideration. And punishment of the harmless inciter is prevented by the *Schenck*-derived requirement of a likelihood of dangerous consequences." (citing *Brandenburg*'s note 4.) Does the idea of incitement require explicit words, as suggested in Hand's *Masses* opinion, or explicit intent to produce the advocated effect, or both? But see Steven Shiffrin, *Defamatory Non-Media Speech and First Amendment Methodology*, 25 UCLA L.Rev. 915 (1978): "Several leading commentators assume that *Brandenburg* adopts an incitement requirement. [The] conclusion is apparently based on this line from *Brandenburg*: 'Neither the indictment nor the trial judge's instructions to the

jury in any way refined the statute's bald definition of the crime in terms of mere advocacy, not distinguished from incitement to imminent lawless action' [also citing fn 4]. The difficulty with attaching significance to this ambiguous statement is that the term 'incitement' is used in the alternative in the Court's statement of its test. Thus, advocacy of imminent lawless action is protected unless it is directed to inciting *or* producing imminent lawless action and is likely to incite *or* produce imminent lawless action. Thus, even assuming that the use of the word incitement refers to express use of language, as opposed to the nature of results (an interpretation which is strained in light of the Court's wording of the test), incitement is not necessary to divorce the speech from First Amendment protection. It is enough that the speech is directed to producing imminent lawless action and is likely to produce such action."

If one wants to argue that *Brandenburg* adopted *Masses*, is there anything to be made of the phrase "directed to" in the *Brandenburg* test? Alternatively, did *Yates* adopt the *Masses* test? If so, does its favorable citation in *Brandenburg* constitute an adoption of the *Masses* test?

3.   The *Brandenburg* "inciting or producing imminent lawless action" standard was the basis for reversal of a disorderly conduct conviction in HESS v. INDIANA, 414 U.S. 105 (1973) (per curiam). After antiwar demonstrators on the Indiana University campus had blocked a public street, police moved them to the curbs on either side. As an officer passed him, appellant stated loudly, "We'll take the fucking street later [or again]," which led to his disorderly conduct conviction. His statement, observed the Court, "was not addressed to any person or group in particular" and "his tone, although loud, was no louder than that of the other people in the area. [At] best, [the] statement could be taken as counsel for present moderation; at worst, it amounted to nothing more than advocacy of illegal action at some indefinite future time." This was insufficient, under *Brandenburg,* to punish appellant's words, as the State had, on the ground that they had a "tendency to produce violence." It could not be said that appellant "was advocating, in the normal sense, any action" and there was "no evidence" that "his words were intended to produce, and likely to produce, *imminent* disorder."

REHNQUIST, J., joined by Burger, C.J., and Blackmun, J., dissented: "The simple explanation for the result in this case is that the majority has interpreted the evidence differently from the courts below." The dissenters quarreled with the Court's conclusion that appellant's advocacy "was not directed towards inciting imminent action. [T]here are surely possible constructions of the statement which would encompass more or less immediate and continuing action against the police. They should not be rejected out of hand because of an unexplained preference for other acceptable alternatives."

Does the *Hess* understanding of imminence depend on context? Would urging a group to commit an act of violence at a specific time in a specific place in exactly one week's time be considered imminent after *Hess*? How much of the outcome in *Hess* turns on the vagueness of the exhortation rather than the period of time between the speech and action the speaker is urging?

4.   Does *Yates* survive *Brandenburg's* emphasis on *imminent* lawless action? Consider Harry Kalven, *A Worthy Tradition* 234 (1988): "It is [possible] that [*Brandenburg*] has preserved the group/individual distinction. Under such an approach the *Yates* incitement-to-future-action standard would apply to group speech and the *Brandenburg* incitement-to-immediate-action standard would apply to the individual speaker." Light may be shed on the question by COMMUNIST PARTY OF INDIANA v. WHITCOMB, 414 U.S. 441 (1974), which invalidated an Indiana statute denying a political party or its candidates access to the ballot unless the party files an affidavit that it "does not advocate the overthrow of local, state or national government by force or violence." The Court, per BRENNAN J., maintained that the required oath (which had been interpreted to include advocacy of abstract doctrine) violated the principle of *Brandenburg* and stated that the principle applied not only to attempted denials of public employment, bar licensing, and tax exemption, but also to ballot access denials. The flaw with the state's position was that it furnished access to the ballot "not because the Party urges others 'to *do* something now *or in the future* [but] merely to believe in something,' [*Yates*]" (second emphasis added).

What happened to the "imminent lawless action" requirement? Does the *Whitcomb* language clarify *Brandenburg*? Modify it?

5.   Does *Brandenburg* apply to the advocacy of trivial crimes, whether politically motivated or not? Suppose the advocacy of trespass across a lawn? What result under *Brandenburg*? Under *Dennis*? Is *Dennis* potentially more speech protective than *Brandenburg* in requiring greater likelihood and imminence for small dangers than for large ones? See the Brandeis opinion in Whitney, supra, referring to "substantial" and "serious" evils, and also Jonathan S. Masur, *Probability Threshholds*, 92 Iowa L.Rev. 1293 (2007).

6.   Does *Brandenburg* apply to solicitation of crime in non-public or non-ideological contexts? Consider Shiffrin, note 2 supra: "How different it might be if the factual context were to involve advocacy of murder in a non-socio-political context. One suspects that little rhetoric about the marketplace of ideas or other First Amendment values would be employed and that the serious and explicit advocacy of murder in a concrete way would suffice to divorce the speech from First Amendment protection even in the absence of a specific showing of likelihood." Would it matter if it were not explicit or not concrete? For analysis of the issues raised by the shift in context from public to private or in subject matter from ideological to non-ideological, see Kent Greenawalt, *Speech and Crime,* 1980 Am.B.Found.Res.J. 645, later expanded into Kent Greenawalt, *Speech, Crime and the Uses of Language* (1989).

7.   Should *Brandenburg* be construed to protect threats?[33] Nuremberg Files, an anti-abortion Web site included the names, addresses, photographs,

---

[33]   In *NAACP v. Claiborne Hardware Co.,* 458 U.S. 886 (1982), the Court stated that remarks of Charles Evers "might have been understood" as inviting violence, but stated that when "such appeals do not incite lawless action, they must be regarded as protected speech." If violent action had followed his remarks, a "substantial question" of liability would have been raised. The Court also observed, however, that the defendant might be held criminally liable for the acts of others if

and license plate numbers of those who provided abortions or were prominent pro-choice advocates together with their family members. Protected? See *Planned Parenthood of Columbia/Willamette Inc. v. American Coalition of Life Activists*, 290 F.3d 1058 (9th Cir. 2002); Steven G. Gey, *The Nuremberg Files and the First Amendment Value of Threats*, 78 Tex. L. Rev. 541, 592 (2000) ("It seems clear that the *Brandenburg* standard should apply unmodified in public situations. The situation is more complicated in cases where the speech does not occur in public, but is communicated surreptitiously to the target of the threat. Should *Brandenburg* also apply to these cases? What makes threats communicated privately more disturbing than publicly threatening speech is the intuitive judgment that the private communication of a threat is more likely to indicate a seriousness of purpose than the attention-grabbing public bluster that characterizes cases such as [the] Nuremberg Files litigation."). On the First Amendment and threats generally, see *Virginia v. Black* (2003), Sec. 3, IV, infra; Frederick Schauer, *Intentions, Conventions, and the First Amendment*, 2003 Sup.Ct.Rev. 197.

Does *Brandenburg* apply unmodified to the provision of crime-facilitating factual information? To tort actions against those whose words may have been a causal contributor to a crime? Consider Rodney A. Smolla, *Should the Brandenburg v. Ohio Incitement Test Apply in Media Violence Tort Cases?*, 27 N. Ky. L. Rev. 1 (2000): "What makes the abortion web page case difficult [is] the injection of an element not present in *Brandenburg,* the detailed provision of material on the doctors' names, business locations, residential addresses, social security numbers, vehicle license plates, phone numbers, and other identifying information. This evidence adds some highly perplexing aspects to the case. First, it may well take it beyond the realm of abstract advocacy, and into the realm of detailed information provided to assist in violent crime. Second, it is highly probative of an intent by the defendants either to assist in crime or to threaten abortion providers, itself a crime. In this fact pattern, the details of the record are likely to be critical. You are likely to find yourself closely examining the facts to determine whether or not a case can be made that these defendants subjectively intended this material as a threat or as a vehicle for aiding and abetting crime,[34] and whether, objectively, the material was so understood or used."

---

the speeches could be taken as evidence that the defendant gave "other specific instructions to carry out violent acts or threats." Compare *Watts v. United States*, 394 U.S. 705 (1969) (statute prohibiting knowing and wilful threat of bodily harm upon the President is constitutional on its face) (dictum); *Rankin v. McPherson*, Sec. 7, III infra (clerical employee's private expression of desire that Presidential assassination attempt be successful is insufficient justification for dismissal even in a law enforcement agency).

[34] On the application of *Brandenburg* to the provision of information likely to facilitate crime, a prominent example arose out of the publication by Paladin Press of a book entitled *Hit Man: A Technical Manual for Independent Contractors.* James Perry relied on the book's instructions to kill three people. See *Rice v. Paladin Enterprises*, 128 F.3d 233 (4th Cir. 1997); David A. Anderson, *Incitement and Tort Law*, 37 Wake Forest L. Rev. 957 (2002): "I have found no case in which a media defendant has been held liable on the ground that it incited physical harm, and only one case [*Rice*] in which liability has been approved on the ground of aiding and abetting. Media are simply not in the business of 'inciting . . . imminent lawless action' as that phrase is understood in *Brandenburg*. [This] is why media lawyers are so insistent that incitement, or something close to

If threats should be unprotected without regard to the *Brandenburg* standard, is it enough that a "reasonable person" would foresee that the recipients of the speaker's statement would see it a serious expression of intent to physically harm or is a "mere negligence standard [simply] not compatible with a constitutional guarantee as fundamental as free speech"? G. Robert Blakey and Brian J. Murray, *Threats, Free Speech, and the Jurisprudence of the Federal Criminal Law*, 2002 B.Y.U.L. Rev. 829 (2002). Should subjective intent to threaten be necessary? Does it matter if the threat reaches its target? If the speaker has no intention of carrying out the threat? If the speaker maintains that the threat will be carried out by unrelated third parties rather the speaker or co-conspirators? See Jennifer E. Rothman, *Freedom of Speech and True Threats*, 25 Harv. J.L. & Pub. Pol'y 283 (2001). For additional commentary on threats, see Justice Linde's opinion in *State v. Robertson,* 649 P.2d 569 (Ore. 1982); United States v. Jeffries, 692 F.3d 473 (6th Cir. 2012); Jennifer Elrod, *Expressive Activity, True Threats, and the First* Amendment, 36 Conn.L.Rev. 541 (2004); Kent Greenawalt, *Criminal Coercion and Freedom of Speech,* 78 Nw.U.L.Rev. 1081 (1984); Kenneth L.Karst, *Threats and Meaning: How the Facts Govern First Amendment* Doctrine, 58 Stan.L.Rev. 1337 (2006).

8.   Congress prohibits the providing of material support or resources to any organization designated by the Secretary of State to be a foreign terrorist organization. Plaintiffs sought to provide support to either of two such organizations: the Kurdistan Workers Party ("PKK") and the Liberation Tigers of Tamil Eelam ("LTTE"). Specifically, they wished to provide support in order to train members of the PKK to use law to peacefully resolve disputes; to teach PKK how to petition representative bodies such as the United Nations for relief; and/or to engage in political advocacy on behalf of Kurds who live in Turkey or on behalf of the LTTE. HOLDER v. HUMANITARIAN LAW PROJECT, 130 S.Ct. 2705 (2010), per ROBERTS, C.J., held that the congressional prohibition could constitutionally be applied to training and expert advice for peaceful speech activities even if the provision of such support was not intended to assist in the unlawful activities of the organization. Roberts, C.J., emphasized that the statute does not cover independent advocacy on behalf of such organizations or even membership in such organizations.[35] Rather it covers support including training, expert advice, or speech under the direction of or in coordination with an organization designated as terrorist in character.

---

it, is the only permissible basis for liability—it effectively forecloses liability." See generally Rodney Smolla, *Deliberate Intent* (1999); Cass Sunstein, *One Case at a Time* 191–96 (1999). Consider also *Herceg v. Hustler Magazine, Inc.*, 814 F.2d 1017 (5th Cir. 1987) (refusing, on the authority of *Brandenburg*, to find tort liability where juvenile died while attempting an act of autoerotic asphyxiation described in magazine); *Olivia N. v. National Broadcasting Co.*, 178 Cal.Rptr. 888 (Cal.Ct.App. 1981) (disallowing tort liability against television broadcaster for broadcasting a description of a sexual assault subsequently copied by juveniles in committing such an assault).

[35]   Roberts, C.J., stated that the record did not disclose whether the plaintiffs sought to engage in independent or coordinated advocacy.

Roberts, C.J., did not deny that the support offered in the case was a form of presumptively protected speech, but he deferred to the findings of the Congressional and Executive Branches that the organizations were "so tainted by their criminal conduct that any contribution to such an organization facilitates that conduct." He argued that support frees up other resources, helps to legitimize such organizations, and strains U.S. relationships with its allies. The skills taught could be used in manipulative ways and might gain further monetary gains for such organizations. Roberts, C.J., concluded that the prohibitions were necessary to further an urgent objective of the highest order.

BREYER, J., joined by Ginsburg and Sotomayor, JJ., dissenting, argued that the decision interfered with centrally important peaceful speech activities. He argued that peaceful advocacy should ordinarily be protected whether or not it was coordinated with a designated terrorist organization. Nor did he find a sufficient governmental showing to justify limiting this speech: "I believe the Court has failed to examine the Government's justification with sufficient care. It has failed to insist upon specific evidence, rather than general assertion. It has failed to require tailoring of means to fit compelling ends. And ultimately it deprives the individuals before us of the protection that the First Amendment demands."

Even assuming that *Brandenburg* applies in all cases involving advocacy of illegal action, it has little explanatory power across the broad range of First Amendment cases. Consider Rodney A. Smolla, *Should the Brandenburg v. Ohio Incitement Test Apply in Media Violence Tort Cases?*, 27 N. Ky. L. Rev. 1 (2000): "The *Brandenburg* case is an important First Amendment landmark, but it is not the only First Amendment landmark and does not restate the legal doctrine applied in all First Amendment contexts. To the contrary, modern First Amendment law is a complex maze of doctrinal formulas employing specific standards that have been tailored to particular topics of speech, modes of legal liability, and social contexts. There are innumerable other First Amendment contexts in which the *Brandenburg* standard just does not apply, contexts in which the Supreme Court has fashioned special standards suited for the balance of interests at hand. Because free speech issues arise in an extraordinarily wide range of circumstances and settings, the Supreme Court has not attempted to jam all free speech analysis into the "incitement" standard of *Brandenburg*, but rather has employed *Brandenburg*-style analysis only in cases dealing with *Brandenburg*-like settings."

II. REPUTATION AND PRIVACY

In an important article, Harry Kalven coined the phrase "two level theory," *The Metaphysics of the Law of Obscenity*, 1960 Sup.Ct.Rev. 1. As he described it, *Beauharnais, infra*, and other cases employed a First Amendment methodology that classified speech at two levels. Some speech—libel, obscenity, "fighting words"—was thought to be so bereft of social utility as to be beneath First Amendment protection. At the second level, speech of constitutional value was thought to be protected unless it presented a clear and present danger of a substantive evil. In some respects Kalven was plainly correct. No one seriously claims that the First Amendment is even applicable to ordinary contract law, which imposes liability based on spoken or written words, or to most of the law of wills, which does much the same thing, or to the law of blackmail, perjury, and much else. Indeed, albeit without quite the same degree of unanimity, the First Amendment is not understood even to be relevant to most of the regulatory activities of the Securities and Exchange Commission, the Federal Trade Commission, and the Food and Drug Administration, each of which is largely in the business of regulating the use of words. And if one corporate executive uses words to propose to an executive of a competitor company that they charge the same prices, and if the second executive uses words to agree to the arrangement, they will both be in plain violation of the price-fixing dimensions of the Sherman Antitrust Act, with nary an objection from the First Amendment. See Frederick Schauer, *The Boundaries of the First Amendment: A Case Study in Constitutional Salience*, 117 Harv.L.Rev. 1765 (2005) (distinguishing the "coverage" of the First Amendment from its "protection").

In other areas, however, the two-level account as understood by Kalven appears to be weakening, as the following materials on libel and privacy indicate. The purpose is not a detailed examination of libel and privacy law. Our interests include the initial exclusion of defamation from First Amendment coverage, the themes and methods contributing to the erosion of that exclusion, and the articulation of basic First Amendment values having implications and applications beyond defamation and the right to privacy.

A. Group Libel

BEAUHARNAIS v. ILLINOIS, 343 U.S. 250 (1952), per FRANKFURTER, J., sustained a statute prohibiting exhibition in any public place of any publication portraying "depravity, criminality, unchastity, or lack of virtue of a class of citizens, of any race, color, creed or religion [which exposes such citizens] to contempt, derision or obloquy or which is productive of breach of the peace or riots." The Court affirmed a conviction for organizing the distribution of a leaflet which petitioned the Mayor and City Council of Chicago "to halt the further encroachment, harassment and invasion of white people, their property, neighborhoods and persons by the Negro"; called for "one million self respecting white people in Chicago to unite"; and warned that if "the need to prevent the white race from becoming mongrelized by the Negro will not unite us, then the [aggressions], rapes, robberies, knives, guns, and marijuana of the Negro, surely will.":

"Today every American jurisdiction [punishes] libels directed at individuals. '[There] are certain well-defined and narrowly limited classes of speech, the prevention and punishment of which have never been thought to raise any constitutional problem. These include the lewd and obscene, the profane, the libelous, and the insulting or "fighting" words— those which by their very utterance inflict injury or tend to incite to an immediate breach of the peace. It has been well observed that such utterances are no essential part of any exposition of ideas, and are of such slight social value as a step to truth that any benefit that may be derived from them is clearly outweighed by the social interest in order and morality. "Resort to epithets or personal abuse is not in any proper sense communication of information or opinion safeguarded by the Constitution, and its punishment as a criminal act would raise no question under that instrument." *Cantwell v. Connecticut,* [Ch. 8, Sec. 2].' Such were the views of a unanimous Court in *Chaplinsky v. New Hampshire,* Sec. 1, IV, A infra.[6]

"No one will gainsay that it is libelous falsely to charge another with being a rapist, robber, carrier of knives and guns, and user of marijuana. The [question is whether the fourteenth amendment] prevents a State from punishing such lirreebels—as criminal libel has been defined, limited and constitutionally recognized time out of mind—directed at designated collectivities and flagrantly disseminated. [I]f an utterance directed at an individual may be the object of criminal sanctions, we cannot deny to a State power to punish the same utterance directed at a defined group, unless we can say that this is a wilful and purposeless restriction unrelated to the peace and well-being of the State.

"Illinois did not have to look beyond her own borders to await the tragic experience of the last three decades to conclude that wilful purveyors of falsehood concerning racial and religious groups promote strife and tend powerfully to obstruct the manifold adjustments required for free, orderly life in a metropolitan, polyglot community. From the murder of the abolitionist Lovejoy in 1837 to the Cicero riots of 1951, Illinois has been the scene of exacerbated tension between races, often flaring into violence and destruction. In many of these outbreaks, utterances of the character here in question, so the Illinois legislature could conclude, played a significant [part].

"In the face of this history and its frequent obligato of extreme racial and religious propaganda, we would deny experience to say that the Illinois legislature was without reason in seeking ways to curb false or malicious defamation of racial and religious groups, made in public places and by means calculated to have a powerful emotional impact on those to whom it was presented.

---

6   [Ct's Note] In all but five States, the constitutional guarantee of free speech to every person is explicitly qualified by holding him "responsible for the abuse of that right." * * *

"[It would] be arrant dogmatism, quite outside the scope of our authority [, for] us to deny that the Illinois Legislature may warrantably believe that a man's job and his educational opportunities and the dignity accorded him may depend as much on the reputation of the racial and religious group to which he willynilly belongs, as on his own merits. This being so, we are precluded from saying that speech concededly punishable when immediately directed at individuals cannot be outlawed if directed at groups with whose position and esteem in society the affiliated individual may be inextricably involved. * * * 18

"As to the defense of truth, Illinois in common with many States requires a showing not only that the utterance state the facts, but also that the publication be made 'with good motives and for justifiable ends'. Both elements are necessary if the defense is to prevail. [The] teaching of a century and a half of criminal libel prosecutions in this country would go by the board if we were to hold that Illinois was not within her rights in making this combined requirement. Assuming that defendant's offer of proof directed to a part of the defense was adequate, it did not satisfy the entire requirement which Illinois could exact."

The Court ruled that the trial court properly declined to require the jury to find a "clear and present danger": "Libelous utterances not being within the area of constitutionally protected speech, it is unnecessary, either for us or for the State courts, to consider the issues behind the phrase 'clear and present danger.' Certainly no one would contend that obscene speech, for example, may be punished only upon a showing of such circumstances. Libel, as we have seen, is in the same class."

BLACK, J., joined by Douglas, J., dissented: "[The Court] acts on the bland assumption that the First Amendment is wholly irrelevant. [Today's] case degrades First Amendment freedoms to the 'rational basis' level. [We] are cautioned that state legislatures must be left free to 'experiment' and to make legislative judgments. [State] experimentation in curbing freedom of expression is startling and frightening doctrine in a country dedicated to self-government by its people.

"[As] 'constitutionally recognized,' [criminal libel] has provided for punishment of false, malicious, scurrilous charges against individuals, not against huge groups. This limited scope of the law of criminal libel is of no small importance. It has confined state punishment of speech and expression to the narrowest of areas involving nothing more than private feuds. Every expansion of the law of criminal libel so as to punish

---

[18] **[Ct's Note]** [If] a statute sought to outlaw libels of political parties, quite different problems not now before us would be raised. For one thing, the whole doctrine of fair comment as indispensable to the democratic political process would come into play. Political parties, like public men, are, as it were, public property.

discussion of matters of public concern means a corresponding invasion of the area dedicated to free expression by the First Amendment.

"[If] there be minority groups who hail this holding as their victory, they might consider the possible relevancy of this ancient remark: 'Another such victory and I am undone.' "

REED, J., joined by Douglas, J., dissenting, argued that the statute was unconstitutionally vague: "These words—'virtue,' 'derision,' and 'obloquy'— have neither general nor special meanings well enough known to apprise those within their reach as to limitations on speech. Philosophers and poets, thinkers of high and low degree from every age and race have sought to expound the meaning of virtue. [Are] the tests of the Puritan or the Cavalier to be applied, those of the city or the farm, the Christian or non-Christian, the old or the young?"

DOUGLAS, J., dissented: "Hitler and his Nazis showed how evil a conspiracy could be which was aimed at destroying a race by exposing it to contempt, derision, and obloquy. I would be willing to concede that such conduct directed at a race or group in this country could be made an indictable offense. For such a project would be more than the exercise of free speech. [It] would be free speech plus.

"I would also be willing to concede that even without the element of conspiracy there might be times and occasions when the legislative or executive branch might call a halt to inflammatory talk, such as the shouting of 'fire' in a school or a theatre.

"My view is that if in any case other public interests are to override the plain command of the First Amendment, the peril of speech must be clear and present, leaving no room for argument, raising no doubts as to the necessity of curbing speech in order to prevent disaster."

JACKSON, J., dissenting, argued that the Fourteenth Amendment does not incorporate the first, as such, but permits the states more latitude than the Congress. He concluded, however, that due process required the trier of fact to evaluate the evidence as to the truth and good faith of the speaker and the clarity and presence of the danger. He was unwilling to assume danger from the tendency of the words and felt that the trial court had precluded the defendant's efforts to show truth and good motives.

NOTES AND QUESTIONS

1. ***The right to petition.*** Should it make a difference that the leaflet was in the form of a petition to the mayor and city council? Does the right of the people "to petition the Government for a redress of grievances" add anything of substance to Beauharnais' other First Amendment arguments? [36]

---

[36] See *McDonald v. Smith*, 472 U.S. 479 (1985) (denying any special First Amendment status for the Petition Clause).

2. ***Equality and freedom of speech.*** Consider the following hypothetical commentary: "Group libel statutes pose uniquely difficult issues for they involve a clash between two constitutional commitments: the principle of equality and the principle of free speech. They force us to decide what we want to express as a nation: Do we want a powerful symbol of our belief in uninhibited debate or do we want to be the kind of nation that will not tolerate the public calumny of religious, ethnic, and racial groups?"[37]

3. ***Tolerance and freedom of speech.*** Should the First Amendment be a means of institutionalizing a national commitment to the value of tolerance? By tolerating the intolerable, would we carve out one area of social interaction for extraordinary self-restraint and thereby develop[38] and demonstrate a vital social capacity? See Lee Bollinger, *The Tolerant Society: Freedom of Speech and Extremist Speech in America* (1986).

4. ***Dignity and group libel.*** Wholly apart from any message that group libel statutes signal about our polity, do group libel statutes safeguard individual rights to dignity that outweigh any expressive interests in this context? See Jeremy Waldron, *Dignity and Defamation: The Visibility of Hate*, 123 Harv. L.Rev. 1596 (2010).

5. ***Libel, group libel, and seditious libel.*** Consider Kalven, supra, at 15, 16 and 50–51: Seditious libel "is the doctrine that criticism of government officials and policy may be viewed as defamation of government and may be punished as a serious crime. [On] my view, the absence of seditious libel as a crime is the true pragmatic test of freedom of speech. This I would argue is what freedom of speech is about. [The] most revealing aspect of the opinions, and particularly that of Justice Frankfurter, is the absence of any sense of the proximity of the case before them to seditious libel. The case presents almost a perfect instance of that competition among analogies which Edward Levi has emphasized as the essential circumstance of legal reasoning. In the middle we have group libel and Justice Frankfurter's urging its many resemblances to individual libel. [If] the Court's speech theory had been more grounded, as it seems to me it should be, on the relevance of the concept of seditious libel and less on the analogy to the law of attempts found in the slogan 'clear and present danger,' it is difficult to believe that either the debate or the result in *Beauharnais* would have been the same."

---

[37] See, e.g., *The Price We Pay: The Case Against Racist Speech* (Laura J. Lederer & Richard Delgado eds. 1995); Robin West, *Progressive Constitutionalism: Reconstructing the Fourteenth Amendment* (1994); Mari J. Matsuda et al., *Words that Wound* (Itzin ed. 1993); Gary Goodpaster, *Equality and Free Speech: The Case Against Substantive Equality,* 82 Ia L.Rev. 645 (1997); Loren Beth, *Group Libel and Free Speech,* 39 Minn.L.Rev. 167 (1955) and sources cited in Sec. 1, V, C.

[38] For skepticism about the capacity of courts to achieve much impact in promoting tolerance, see Robert F. Nagel, *Constitutional Cultures* 27–59 (1989).

B. Public Officials and Seditious Libel

NEW YORK TIMES CO. V. SULLIVAN
376 U.S. 254, 84 S.Ct. 710, 11 L.Ed.2d 686 (1964).

JUSTICE BRENNAN delivered the opinion of the Court.

[Sullivan, the Montgomery, Ala. police commissioner, sued the New York Times and four black Alabama clergymen for alleged libelous statements in a paid, full-page fund-raising advertisement signed by a "Committee to defend Martin Luther King and the struggle for freedom in the South." The advertisement stated that "truckloads of police armed with shotguns and tear-gas ringed Alabama State College Campus" in Montgomery, and that "the Southern violators [have] bombed [Dr. King's] home, assaulted his person [and] arrested him seven times." In several respects the statements were untrue. Several witnesses testified that they understood the statements to refer to Sullivan because he supervised Montgomery police. Sullivan proved he did not participate in the events described. He offered no proof of pecuniary loss.[3] Pursuant to Alabama law, the trial court submitted the libel issue to the jury, giving general and punitive damages instructions. It returned a $500,000 verdict for Sullivan against all of the defendants.[39]] We hold that the rule of law applied by the Alabama courts is constitutionally deficient for failure to provide the safeguards for freedom of speech and of the press that are required by the First and Fourteenth Amendments in a libel action brought by a public official against critics of his official conduct.[4] We further hold that under the proper safeguards the evidence presented in this case is constitutionally insufficient to support the judgment for respondent.

I. [The] publication here [communicated] information, expressed opinion, recited grievances, protested claimed abuses, and sought financial support on behalf of a movement whose existence and objectives are matters of the highest public interest and concern. That the Times was paid

---

[3] [Ct's Note] Approximately 394 copies of the edition of the Times containing the advertisement were circulated in Alabama. Of these, about 35 copies were distributed in Montgomery County. The total circulation of the Times for that day was approximately 650,000 copies.

[39] This was the highest award in the history of the state. David A. Logan, *Libel Law in the Trenches: Reflections on Current Data on Libel Litigation*, 87 Va.L.Rev. 503 (2001). Unlike contemporary practice, there is no indication that any of the defendants had libel insurance

[4] [Ct's Note] [The] Times contends that the assumption of jurisdiction over its corporate person by the Alabama courts overreaches the territorial limits of the Due Process Clause. The latter claim is foreclosed from our review by the ruling of the Alabama courts that the Times entered a general appearance in the action and thus waived its jurisdictional objection. * * *

[Since *New York Times*, the Court has upheld expansive personal jurisdiction against media defendants. *Calder v. Jones*, 465 U.S. 783 (1984); *Keeton v. Hustler*, 465 U.S. 770 (1984). *Calder* rejected the suggestion that First Amendment concerns enter into jurisdictional analysis. It feared complicating the inquiry and argued that because First Amendment concerns are taken into account in limiting the substantive law of defamation, "to reintroduce those concerns at the jurisdictional stage would be a form of double counting."]

for publishing the advertisement is as immaterial in this connection as is the fact that newspapers and books are sold. *Smith v. California*, Sec. 1, III, B infra. Any other conclusion would discourage newspapers from carrying "editorial advertisements" of this type, and so might shut off an important outlet for the promulgation of information and ideas by persons who do not themselves have access to publishing facilities.

II.   Under Alabama law [once] "libel per se" has been established, the defendant has no defense as to stated facts unless he can persuade the jury that they were true in all their particulars. [His] privilege of "fair comment" for expressions of opinion depends on the truth of the facts upon which the comment is based. [Unless] he can discharge the burden of proving truth, general damages are presumed, and may be awarded without proof of pecuniary injury.

[Respondent] relies heavily, as did the Alabama courts, on statements of this Court to the effect that the Constitution does not protect libelous publications. Those statements do not foreclose our inquiry here. None of the cases sustained the use of libel laws to impose sanctions upon expression critical of the official conduct of public officials. [L]ibel can claim no talismanic immunity from constitutional limitations. It must be measured by standards that satisfy the First Amendment.

The First Amendment, said Judge Learned Hand, "presupposes that right conclusions are more likely to be gathered out of a multitude of tongues, than through any kind of authoritative selection. To many this is, and always will be, folly; but we have staked upon it our all." [Thus] we consider this case against the background of a profound national commitment to the principle that debate on public issues should be uninhibited, robust, and wide-open, and that it may well include vehement, caustic, and sometimes unpleasantly sharp attacks on government and public officials.[40] The present advertisement, as an expression of grievance and protest on one of the major public issues of our time, would seem clearly to qualify for the constitutional protection. The question is whether it forfeits that protection by the falsity of some of its factual statements and by its alleged defamation of respondent.

Authoritative interpretations of the First Amendment guarantees have consistently refused to recognize an exception for any test of truth—whether administered by judges, juries, or administrative officials—and especially not one that puts the burden of proving truth on the speaker. [E]rroneous statement is inevitable in free debate, and [it] must be

---

[40]   Consider Brian C. Murchison, *Speech and the Self-Governance Value,* 14 Wm. & Mary Bill Rts. J. 1251 (2006): "[Brennan, J.'s] adjectives suggest the risk of people speaking past each other. In this way, democratic consciousness can suffer slippage: from dialogue based on equal respect to potentially uncompromising debate among subjects who view each other warily from havens of walled off 'dignity.' "

protected if the freedoms of expression are to have the "breathing space" that they "need [to] survive."

[Injury] to official reputation affords no more warrant for repressing speech that would otherwise be free than does factual error. Where judicial officers are involved, this Court has held that concern for the dignity and reputation of the courts does not justify the punishment as criminal contempt of criticism of the judge or his decision. This is true even though the utterance contains "half-truths" and "misinformation." Such repression can be justified, if at all, only by a clear and present danger of the obstruction of justice. If judges are to be treated as "men of fortitude, able to thrive in a hardy climate,"[41] surely the same must be true of other government officials, such as elected city commissioners. Criticism of their official conduct does not lose its constitutional protection merely because it is effective criticism and hence diminishes their official reputations.

If neither factual error nor defamatory content suffices to remove the constitutional shield from criticism of official conduct, the combination of the two elements is no less inadequate. This is the lesson to be drawn from the great controversy over the Sedition Act of 1798, 1 Stat. 596, which first crystallized a national awareness of the central meaning of the First Amendment. [Although] the Sedition Act was never tested in this Court, the attack upon its validity has carried the day in the court of history. Fines levied in its prosecution were repaid by Act of Congress on the ground that it was unconstitutional. * * * Jefferson, as President, pardoned those who had been convicted and sentenced under the Act and remitted their fines. [Its] invalidity [has] also been assumed by Justices of this Court. [These] views reflect a broad consensus that the Act, because of the restraint it imposed upon criticism of government and public officials, was inconsistent with the First Amendment. * * *

What a State may not constitutionally bring about by means of a criminal statute is likewise beyond the reach of its civil law of libel. The fear of damage awards under a rule such as that invoked by the Alabama courts here may be markedly more inhibiting than the fear of prosecution under a criminal statute. [The] judgment awarded in this case—without the need for any proof of actual pecuniary loss—was one thousand times greater than the maximum fine provided by the Alabama criminal [libel law], and one hundred times greater than that provided by the Sedition Act. And since there is no double-jeopardy limitation applicable to civil lawsuits, this is not the only judgment that may be awarded against

---

[41] Ironically, in the post-*Sullivan* era, critical speech regarding judges is now punished by judges on standards far less stringent than those that apply to other public officials. Margaret Tarkington, *The Truth Be Damned: The First Amendment, Attorney Speech, and Judicial Reputation,* 97 Geo. L.J. 1567 (2009).

petitioners for the same publication.[18] Whether or not a newspaper can survive a succession of such judgments, the pall of fear and timidity imposed upon those who would give voice to public criticism is an atmosphere in which the First Amendment freedoms cannot [survive].

The state rule of law is not saved by its allowance of the defense of truth. A defense for erroneous statements honestly made is no less essential here than was the requirement of proof of guilty knowledge which, in *Smith v. California,* we held indispensable to a valid conviction of a bookseller for possessing obscene writings for [sale].

A rule compelling the critic of official conduct to guarantee the truth of all his factual assertions—and to do so on pain of libel judgments virtually unlimited in amount—leads to a comparable "self-censorship." Allowance of the defense of truth, with the burden of proving it on the defendant, does not mean that only false speech will be deterred.[19] [Under] such a rule, would-be critics of official conduct may be deterred from voicing their criticism, even though it is believed to be true and even though it is in fact true, because of doubt whether it can be proved in court or fear of the expense of having to do so. They tend to make only statements which "steer far wider of the unlawful zone." The rule thus dampens the vigor and limits the variety of public [debate].

The constitutional guarantees require, we think, a federal rule that prohibits a public official from recovering damages for a defamatory falsehood relating to his official conduct unless he proves that the statement was made with "actual malice"—that is, with knowledge that it was false or with reckless disregard of whether it was false or [not].[42]

Such a privilege for criticism of official conduct is appropriately analogous to the protection accorded a public official when *he* is sued for libel by a private citizen. In *Barr v. Matteo,* 360 U.S. 564 (1959), this Court held the utterance of a federal official to be absolutely privileged if made "within the outer perimeter" of his duties. The States accord the same immunity to statements of their highest officers, although some differentiate their lesser officials and qualify the privilege they enjoy. But

---

[18] [Ct's Note] The Times states that four other libel suits based on the advertisement have been filed against it by [others]; that another $500,000 verdict has been awarded in [one]; and that the damages sought in the other three total $2,000,000.

[19] [Ct's Note] Even a false statement may be deemed to make a valuable contribution to the public debate, since it brings about "the clearer perception and livelier impression of truth, produced by its collision with error." Mill, *On Liberty* 15 (1955).

[42] Compare *St. Amant v. Thompson,* 390 U.S. 727 (1968) (publishing while "in fact entertain[ing] serious doubts about the truth of the publication" satisfies standard) with *Garrison v. Louisiana,* 379 U.S. 64 (1964) (standard requires "high degree of awareness of probable falsity"). Under both *St. Amant* and *Garrison,* however, it is clear that "reckless disregard" requires a degree of knowledge going beyond common law recklessness or gross negligence. See also *Masson v. New Yorker Magazine, Inc.,* 501 U.S. 496 (1991) ("a deliberate alteration of the words uttered by a plaintiff does not equate with knowledge of falsity [unless] the alteration results in a material change of meaning conveyed by the statement").

all hold that all officials are protected unless actual malice can be proved. The reason for the official privilege is said to be that the threat of damage suits would otherwise "inhibit the fearless, vigorous, and effective administration of policies of government" and "dampen the ardor of all but the most resolute, or the most irresponsible, in the unflinching discharge of their duties." *Barr.* Analogous considerations support the privilege for the citizen-critic of government. It is as much his duty to criticize as it is the official's duty to administer. [It] would give public servants an unjustified preference over the public they serve, if critics of official conduct did not have a fair equivalent of the immunity granted to the officials themselves. We conclude that such a privilege is required by the First and Fourteenth Amendments.[23]

III. [W]e consider that the proof presented to show actual malice lacks the convincing clarity[43] which the constitutional standard demands, and hence that it would not constitutionally sustain the judgment for respondent under the proper rule of law. [T]here is evidence that the Times published the advertisement without checking its accuracy against the news stories in the Times' own files. The mere presence of the stories in the files does [not] establish that the Times "knew" the advertisement was false, since the state of mind required for actual malice would have to be brought home to the persons in the Times' organization having responsibility for the publication of the advertisement. With respect to the failure of those persons to make the check, the record shows that they relied upon their knowledge of the good reputation of many [whose] names were listed as sponsors of the advertisement, and upon the letter from A. Philip Randolph, known to them as a responsible individual, certifying that the use of the names was authorized. There was testimony that the persons handling the advertisement saw nothing in it that would render it unacceptable under the Times' policy of rejecting advertisements containing "attacks of a personal character"; their failure to reject it on this ground was not unreasonable. We think the evidence against the Times supports at most a finding of negligence in failing to discover the misstatements, and is constitutionally insufficient to show the recklessness that is required for a finding of actual malice.

---

[23] **[Ct's Note]** We have no occasion here to determine how far down into the lower ranks of government employees the "public official" designation would extend for purposes of this rule, or otherwise to specify categories of persons who would or would not be included. [Nor] need we here determine the boundaries of the "official conduct" concept. * * *

[43] Compare *Bose Corp. v. Consumers Union,* 466 U.S. 485 (1984) (appellate courts "must exercise independent judgment and determine whether the record establishes actual malice with convincing clarity."). Accord *Harte-Hanks Communications, Inc. v. Connaughton,* 491 U.S. 657 (1989). See also *Anderson v. Liberty Lobby, Inc.,* 477 U.S. 242 (1986) (same standard at summary judgment). Should *Bose* apply when the lower court finds a First Amendment violation or only when it does not? See Stuart Minor Benjamin, *Proactive Legislation and the First Amendment,* 99 Mich. L. Rev. 281 (2000). Should independent appellate judgment be required in all First Amendment cases? All constitutional cases? On the requirement of independent appellate review in First Amendment cases, see also *Jacobellis v. Ohio,* 378 U.S. 188 (1964).

[T]he evidence was constitutionally defective in another respect: it was incapable of supporting the jury's finding that the allegedly libelous statements were made "of and concerning" respondent. [On this point, the Supreme Court of Alabama] based its ruling on the proposition that: "[The] average person knows that municipal agents, such as police and firemen, and others, are under the control and direction of the city governing body, and more particularly under the direction and control of a single commissioner. In measuring the performance or deficiencies of such groups, praise or criticism is usually attached to the official in complete control of the body."

This proposition has disquieting implications for criticism of governmental conduct. [It would transmute] criticism of government, however impersonal it may seem on its face, into personal criticism, and hence potential libel, of the officials of whom the government is composed. [Raising] as it does the possibility that a good-faith critic of government will be penalized for his criticism, the proposition relied on by the Alabama courts strikes at the very center of the constitutionally protected area of free expression. We hold that such a proposition may not constitutionally be utilized to establish that an otherwise impersonal attack on governmental operations was a libel of an official responsible for those operations. Since it was relied on exclusively here, and there was no other evidence to connect the statements with respondent, the evidence was constitutionally insufficient to support a finding that the statements referred to respondent. * * *[44]

JUSTICE BLACK, with whom JUSTICE DOUGLAS joins (concurring).

* * * "Malice," even as defined by the Court, is an elusive, abstract concept, hard to prove and hard to disprove. The requirement that malice be proved provides at best an evanescent protection for the right critically to discuss public affairs and certainly does not measure up to the sturdy safeguard embodied in the First Amendment. Unlike the Court, therefore, I vote to reverse exclusively on the ground that the Times and the individual defendants had an absolute, unconditional constitutional right to publish in the Times advertisement their criticisms of the Montgomery agencies and [officials].

The half-million-dollar verdict [gives] dramatic proof [that] state libel laws threaten the very existence of an American press virile enough to publish unpopular views on public affairs and bold enough to criticize the conduct of public officials. [B]riefs before us show that in Alabama there are now pending eleven libel suits by local and state officials against the Times seeking $5,600,000, and five such suits against the Columbia

---

[44] For a similar ruling that impersonal criticism of a government operation cannot be the basis for defamation "of and concerning" the supervisor of the operation, see *Rosenblatt v. Baer*, 383 U.S. 75 (1966): "[T]antamount to a demand for recovery based on libel of government."

Broadcasting System seeking $1,700,000. Moreover, this technique for harassing and punishing a free press—now that it has been shown to be possible—is by no means limited to cases with racial overtones; it can be used in other fields where public feelings may make local as well as out-of-state newspapers easy prey for libel verdict seekers.

In my opinion the Federal Constitution has dealt with this deadly danger to the press in the only way possible without leaving the press open to destruction—by granting the press an absolute immunity for criticism of the way public officials do their public duty.

[This] Nation, I suspect, can live in peace without libel suits based on public discussions of public affairs and public officials. But I doubt that a country can live in freedom where its people can be made to suffer physically or financially for criticizing their government, its actions, or its officials. * * *[45]

———

NOTES AND QUESTIONS

1. *The First Amendment and democracy.* Professor Harry Kalven observed that the Court in *New York Times* was moving toward "the theory of free speech that Alexander Meiklejohn has been offering us for some fifteen years now." Harry Kalven, *The New York Times Case: A Note on "The Central Meaning of the First Amendment,"* 1964 Sup.Ct.Rev. 191. Indeed Kalven reported Alexander Meiklejohn's view that the case was " 'an occasion for dancing in the streets.' " Meiklejohn argued that "[The] principle of the freedom of speech springs from the necessities of the program of self-government. [It] is a deduction from the basic American agreement that public issues shall be decided by universal suffrage. [When] a question of policy is 'before the house,' free men choose to meet it not with their eyes shut, but with their eyes open. To be afraid of ideas, any idea, is to be unfit for self-government. [The] guarantee given by the First Amendment is not, then, assured to all speaking. It is assured only to speech which bears, directly or indirectly, upon issues with which voters have to deal—only, therefore, to the consideration of matters of public interest. Private speech, or private interest in speech, on the other hand, has no claim whatever to the protection of the First Amendment." Alexander Meiklejohn, *Free Speech and Its Relation to Self-Government* (1948).

---

[45] Goldberg, J., joined by Douglas, J., concurring, also asserted for "the citizen and [the] press an absolute unconditional privilege to criticize official conduct," but maintained that the imposition of liability for "[p]urely private defamation" did not abridge the First Amendment because it had "little to do with the political ends of a self-governing society." And see *Dun & Bradstreet, Inc. v. Greenmoss Builders, Inc.*, 472 U.S. 749 (1985). Most other common law countries have modified the strictness of the common law, but have not gone nearly as far as the U.S. For the Canadian approach, see *Hill v. Church of Scientology of Ontario* [1995], 126 D.L.R. 4th 129. In the United Kingdom, see *Reynolds v. Times Newspapers Ltd.* [2001] A.C. 127 (H.L.). And in Australia, see *Lange v. Australian Broadcasting Co.* (1997) 182 C.L.R. 104 (Aust'l).

To what extent does *New York Times* incorporate Meiklejohn's perspective?[46] Consider Burt Neuborne, *Toward a Democracy-Centered Reading of the First Amendment,* 93 Nw.U.L.Rev. 1055 (1999): "It is no coincidence that the textual rhythm of the First Amendment moves from protection of internal conscience in the religion clauses, to protection of individual expression in the speech clause, to broad community-wide discussion in the press clause, to concerted action in the assembly (and implied association) clause, and, finally, to formal political activity in the petition clause. Indeed, no rights-bearing document in the Western tradition approximates the precise organizational clarity of the First Amendment as a road map of democracy." Consider Susan H. Williams, *Truth, Autonomy, and Speech: Feminist Theory and the First Amendment* 2 (2004): "The democracy theory is really a conjoining of two different arguments about the connection between speech and democracy. The first is a programmatic argument about the practical effects of speech on democratic decision making: when we hear all the speech available, we have more of the information we need to make good decisions in the democratic process. The second argument is about the relationship between speech and full participation as a democratic citizen: speech is a primary mechanism through which we participate fully in creating and shaping the public opinion that guides a democracy."[47]

If the First Amendment is rooted in a conception of democracy, is it obvious that the idea of democracy is politically centered?[48] Consider Jack M. Balkin, *Digital Speech and Democratic Culture: A Theory of Freedom of Expression for the Information Society,* 79 N.Y.U. L. Rev. 1 (2004): "The purpose of freedom of speech [is] to promote a democratic culture. A democratic culture is more than representative institutions of democracy, and it is more than deliberation about public issues. Rather, a democratic culture is a culture in which individuals have a fair opportunity to participate in the forms of meaning-making that constitute them as individuals. Democratic culture is about individual liberty as well as collective self-governance; it is about each individual's ability to participate in the production and distribution of culture. [As] people express themselves, make music, create works of art, sing, gossip, converse, accuse, deny, complain, celebrate, enthuse, boast, and parody, they continually add something to the cultural mixture in which they live. They reshape, however imperceptibly, cultural conventions about what things mean,

---

[46] For elaboration and modification of Meiklejohn's views, see Alexander Meiklejohn, *The First Amendment Is an Absolute,* 1961 Sup.Ct.Rev. 245. For commentary, see Zechariah Chafee, Jr., *Book Review,* 62 Harv. L.Rev. 891 (1949); Lee Bollinger, *Free Speech and Intellectual Values,* 92 Yale L.J. 438 (1983).

[47] For emphasis on the participatory aspects of democracy, see Robert Post, *Constitutional Domains* (1995); James Weinstein, *Hate Speech, Pornography, and the Radical Attack on Free Speech Doctrine* (1999). For criticism of Post's position, see Martin H. Redish & Abby Marie Molen, *Understanding Post's and Meiklejohn's Mistakes,* 103 Nw. U.L. L.Rev. 1303 (2009).

[48] For work proceeding from a politically based interpretation of the First Amendment, see Robert Post, fn. 47; Robert C. Post, *Citizens Divided: Campaign Finance Reform and the Constitution* (2014); James Weinstein, fn. 47; Cass R. Sunstein, *Democracy and the Problem of Free Speech* (1993). For criticism of Sunstein's position, see J.M. Balkin, *Populism and Progressivism as Constitutional Categories,* 104 Yale L.J. 1935 (1995); William Marshall, *Free Speech and the "Problem" of Democracy,* 89 Nw.U.L.Rev. 191 (1994).

what is proper and improper, what is important and less important, how things are done and how they are not done. Through communicative interaction, through expression, through exchange, individual people become the architects of their culture, building on what others did before them and shaping the world that will shape them and those who follow them." See also Kenneth L. Karst, *Local Discourse and the Social Issues*, 12 Cardozo Stud. L. & Literature 1 (2000).

2. ***Providing leadership in a globalized setting.*** In a globalized setting with an increased need for an international free press, should the Court try to provide leadership and broaden its rationale in a way that might be appealing to countries that do not accept Madisonian self-government? Might an "emphasis on how a system of openness helps to moderate authoritarian tendencies and helps to generate capacities to deal with social conflict meet with a better reception in many societies." See Lee C. Bollinger, *Uninhibited, Robust, and Wide-Open* 118 (2010). Or should American courts take account of the fact that no country in the world restricts libel law to the extent that the United States does under *Sullivan*, and that other countries, even the most democratic and open of them, give more weight to reputation than the Court does in *Sullivan?*

3. Consider Richard A. Epstein, *Privacy, Publication, and the First Amendment: The Dangers of First Amendment Exceptionalism*, 52 Stan. L. Rev. 1003 (2000): "[T]he press in the United States and other common law countries had flourished under the general rules in force prior to the advent of *New York Times*. While the reversal of the Alabama court could easily be justified on the ground that Alabama played fast and loose with two elements of the common law account of the wrong—what it means for statements to be "of and concerning the plaintiff," and what is needed to prove hefty awards of general damages—the Supreme Court had little reason to fashion a broad 'actual malice' privilege out of whole cloth that would become applicable to all sorts of defamation cases that had none of the tragic overtones of the civil rights struggle in the South." But see Rodney A. Smolla, *Information as Contraband: The First Amendment and Liability for Trafficking in Speech*, 96 Nw. U. L. Rev. 1099 (2002): "[I]f the Supreme Court ever required genuine hard evidence that the 'chilling effect' of the negligence standard repudiated in *New York Times* actually exists, the media might well be fearful that the evidence could not be garnered. The point here is not that the *New York Times* rule is indefensible—it is better described as indispensable—but rather that its defense is more comfortably made by arguing principle than sociology." What is the principle? See Richard H. Fallon, Jr., *Implementing the Constitution* 29–30 (2001) (arguing that the defamation rules depend upon empirical judgments). And see generally Leslie Kendrick, *Speech, Intent, and the Chilling Effect*, 54 Wm. & Mary L.Rev. 1633 (2013).

4. ***New York Times, definitional balancing, and the two-level theory of the First Amendment.*** By holding that some libel was within the protection of the First Amendment, did the Court weaken its two-level approach? Or did it merely rearrange its conception of what was covered and

what was not? And see *Garrison v. Louisiana,* 379 U.S. 64 (1964): "Calculated falsehood falls into that class of utterances '[of] such slight social value as a step to truth that any benefit that may be derived from them is clearly outweighed by the social interest in order and morality.' *Chaplinsky.*"

The judicial process here has been called *definitional* classification— defining which categories of libel are to be viewed as "speech" within the First Amendment, and which are not? Melville Nimmer, *The Right to Speak from Times to Time: First Amendment Theory Applied to Libel and Misapplied to Privacy,* 56 Calif.L.Rev. 935 (1968): "[*New York Times*] points the way to the employment of the balancing process on the definitional rather than the litigation or ad hoc level, [that is,] balancing not for the purpose of determining which litigant deserves to prevail in the particular case, but only for the purpose of defining which forms of speech are to be regarded as 'speech' within the meaning of the First Amendment. [By] in effect holding that knowingly and recklessly false speech was not 'speech' within the meaning of the First Amendment, the Court must have implicitly (since no explicit explanation was offered) referred to certain competing policy considerations. This is surely a kind of balancing, but it is just as surely not ad hoc balancing." But for the Supreme Court's explicit rejection of definitional balancing as a way of determining the coverage of the First Amendment, see *United States v. Stevens,* Sec. 1, VI, D infra.

5. *Scope of New York Times.* Professor Kalven argued that the *New York Times* holding could not be confined: "the invitation to follow a dialectic progression from public official to government policy to public policy to matters in the public domain, like art, [seems] overwhelming." Kalven, supra.

(a) *Public officials. New York Times,* fn. 23 left open "how far down into the lower ranks of governmental employees" the rule would extend, and *Rosenblatt v. Baer,* 383 U.S. 75 (1966) suggested the rule might apply to the supervisor of a publicly owned ski resort, saying it applies among other things to those who "appear to the public to [have] substantial responsibility for or control over the conduct of government affairs." Should criticism of the official conduct of *very* high ranking government officials (e.g., the President, the Secretary of State, a general commanding troops in war) be given greater protection than that afforded in *New York Times*?

(b) *Private conduct of public officials and candidates. Garrison,* extended *New York Times* to "anything which might touch on an official's fitness for office," even if the defamation did not concern official conduct in office. Invoking that standard, *Monitor Patriot Co. v. Roy,* 401 U.S. 265 (1971) applied *New York Times* to a news column describing a candidate for public office as a "former small-time bootlegger."

(c) *Public figures.* In CURTIS PUB. CO. v. BUTTS and ASSOCIATED PRESS v. WALKER, 388 U.S. 130 (1967), the Court extended the *New York Times* principle to non-governmental "public officials." HARLAN, J., contended that because public figures were not subject to the restraints of the political process, any criticism of them was not akin to seditious libel and was, therefore, a step removed from the central meaning of the First Amendment. Nonetheless, he argued that public figure actions should not be left entirely to the vagaries of state defamation law and would have required that public figures show "highly unreasonable conduct constituting an extreme departure from the standards of investigation and reporting ordinarily adhered to by responsible publishers" as a prerequisite to recovery. In response, WARREN, C.J., argued that the inapplicability of the restraints of the political process to public figures underscored the importance for uninhibited debate about their activities since "public opinion may be the only instrument by which society can attempt to influence their conduct." He observed that increasingly "the distinctions between governmental and private sectors are blurred," that public figures, like public officials, "often play an influential role in ordering society," and as a class have a ready access to the mass media "both to influence policy and to counter criticism of their views and activities." He accordingly concluded that the *New York Times* rule should be extended to public figures. Four other justices in *Butts* and *Walker* were willing to go at least as far as Warren, C.J., and subsequent cases have settled on the position that public figures must meet the *New York Times* requirements in order to recover in a defamation action. The critical issues are how to define the concept of public figure and how to apply it in practice.[49] See *Gertz,* infra. Might this encourage media overreaching and irresponsibility? Would a negligence regime be better?

C. Private Individuals and Public Figures

GERTZ V. ROBERT WELCH, INC.
418 U.S. 323, 94 S.Ct. 2997, 41 L.Ed.2d 789 (1974).

JUSTICE POWELL delivered the opinion of the Court.

[Respondent published *American Opinion,* a monthly outlet for the John Birch Society. It published an article falsely stating that Gertz, a lawyer, was the "architect" in a "communist frameup" of a policeman convicted of murdering a youth whose family Gertz represented in resultant civil proceedings, and that Gertz had a "criminal record" and had been an officer in a named "Communist-fronter" organization that advocated violent seizure of our government. In Gertz' libel action there was evidence that *Opinion*'s managing editor did not know the statements were false and had relied on the reputation of the article's author and prior experience with the accuracy of his articles. After a $50,000 verdict for Gertz, the trial court entered judgment n.o.v., concluding that the *New York Times* rule applied to any discussion of a "public issue." The court of appeals affirmed, ruling that the publisher did not have the requisite "awareness of probable falsity." The Court held that *New York Times* did not apply to defamation of private individuals, but remanded for a new trial

---

    [49] For analysis of the public figure doctrine, see Catherine Hancock, *Origins of the Public Figure Doctrine in First Amendment Defamation Law*, 50 N.Y.L.Sch.L.Rev. 81 (2005–06); Frederick Schauer, *Public Figures*, 25 Wm. & Mary L.Rev. 905 (1984).

"because the jury was allowed to impose liability without fault [and] to presume damages without proof of injury."]

II. The principal issue in this case is whether a newspaper or broadcaster that publishes defamatory falsehoods about an individual who is neither a public official nor a public figure may claim a constitutional privilege against liability for the injury inflicted by those statements. * * *

In his opinion for the plurality in *Rosenbloom,* Mr. Justice Brennan took the *Times* privilege one step further [than *Butts* and *Walker*]. He concluded that its protection should extend to defamatory falsehoods relating to private persons if the statements concerned matters of general or public interest. He abjured the suggested distinction between public officials and public figures on the one hand and private individuals on the other. He focused instead on society's interest in learning about certain issues: "If a matter is a subject of public or general interest, it cannot suddenly become less so merely because a private individual is involved or because in some sense the individual did not choose to become involved." Thus, under the plurality opinion, a private citizen involuntarily associated with a matter of general interest has no recourse for injury to his reputation unless he can satisfy the demanding requirements of the *Times* [test].

III. [Under] the First Amendment there is no such thing as a false idea. However pernicious an opinion may seem, we depend for its correction not on the conscience of the judges and juries but on the competition of other ideas.[50] But there is no constitutional value in false statements of fact. Neither the intentional lie nor the careless error materially advances society's interest in "uninhibited, robust, and wide-open" debate on public issues. * * *

Although the erroneous statement of fact is not worthy of constitutional protection, it is nevertheless inevitable in free debate. [P]unishment of error runs the risk of inducing a cautious and restrictive exercise of the constitutionally guaranteed freedoms of speech and press. [The] First Amendment requires that we protect some falsehood in order to protect speech that matters.

The need to avoid self-censorship by the news media is, however, not the only societal value at issue. [The] legitimate state interest underlying the law of libel is the compensation of individuals for the harm inflicted on them by defamatory falsehoods. We would not lightly require the State to

---

[50] For many years the lower courts took this language seriously and deemed opinion to be absolutely protected (see, e.g., *Ollman v. Evans,* 750 F.2d 970 (D.C.Cir.1984)), but *Milkovich v. Lorain Journal Co.,* 497 U.S. 1 (1990), per Rehnquist, C.J., ultimately denied that there is any "wholesale defamation exception for anything that might be labeled 'opinion.' " Should opinions about non-public matters be subject to different standards than opinions about public matters? Robert D. Sack, *Protection of Opinion Under the First Amendment: Reflections on Alfred Hill, "Defamation and Privacy Under the First Amendment,"* 100 Colum.L.Rev. 294 (2000).

abandon this purpose, for, as Mr. Justice Stewart has reminded us, the individual's right to the protection of his own good name "reflects no more than our basic concept of the essential dignity and worth of every human being—a concept at the root of any decent system of ordered liberty. * * * " *Rosenblatt.*

Some tension necessarily exists between the need for a vigorous and uninhibited press and the legitimate interest in redressing wrongful injury. [In] our continuing effort to define the proper accommodation between these competing concerns, we have been especially anxious to assure to the freedoms of speech and press that "breathing space" essential to their fruitful exercise. To that end this Court has extended a measure of strategic protection to defamatory falsehood.

The *New York Times* standard defines the level of constitutional protection appropriate to the context of defamation of [public figures and those who hold governmental office]. Plainly many deserving plaintiffs, including some intentionally subjected to injury, will be unable to surmount the barrier of the *New York Times* test. [For] the reasons stated below, we conclude that the state interest in compensating injury to the reputation of private individuals requires that a different rule should obtain with respect to them.

[W]e have no difficulty in distinguishing among defamation plaintiffs. The first remedy of any victim of defamation is self-help—using available opportunities to contradict the lie or correct the error and thereby to minimize its adverse impact on reputation. Public officials and public figures usually enjoy significantly greater access to the channels of effective communication and hence have a more realistic opportunity to counteract false statements than private individuals normally enjoy.[9] Private individuals are therefore more vulnerable to injury, and the state interest in protecting them is correspondingly greater.

More important than the likelihood that private individuals will lack effective opportunities for rebuttal, there is a compelling normative consideration underlying the distinction between public and private defamation plaintiffs. An individual who decides to seek governmental office must accept certain necessary consequences of that involvement in public affairs. He runs the risk of closer public scrutiny than might

---

[9]   **[Ct's Note]** Of course, an opportunity for rebuttal seldom suffices to undo harm of defamatory falsehood. Indeed, the law of defamation is rooted in our experience that the truth rarely catches up with a lie. But the fact that the self-help remedy of rebuttal, standing alone, is inadequate to its task does not mean that it is irrelevant to our inquiry. [Consider Steven Shiffrin, *Defamatory Non-Media Speech and First Amendment Methodology,* 25 UCLA L.Rev. 915(1978): "[F]ootnote nine, has seemingly left the First Amendment in a peculiar spot. *Gertz* holds that the First Amendment offers some protection for defamatory utterances presumably so that our Constitution can continue 'to preserve an uninhibited marketplace of ideas in which truth will ultimately prevail. * * * ' And yet the Court recognizes that 'an opportunity for rebuttal seldom suffices to undo [the] harm of defamatory falsehood,' i.e., truth does not emerge in the marketplace of ideas. Is the Court trapped in an obvious contradiction?"]

otherwise be the case. [Those] classed as public figures stand in a similar [position.][51]

Even if the foregoing generalities do not obtain in every instance, the communications media are entitled to act on the assumption that public officials and public figures have voluntarily exposed themselves to increased risk of injury from defamatory falsehoods concerning them. No such assumption is justified with respect to a private individual. He has not accepted public office nor assumed an "influential role in ordering society." *Butts.* He has relinquished no part of his interest in the protection of his own good name, and consequently he has a more compelling call on the courts for redress of injury inflicted by defamatory falsehood. Thus, private individuals are not only more vulnerable to injury than public officials and public figures; they are also more deserving of recovery.

For these reasons we conclude that the States should retain substantial latitude in their efforts to enforce a legal remedy for defamatory falsehood injurious to the reputation of a private individual. The extension of the *Times* test proposed by the *Rosenbloom* [*v. Metromedia*, 403 U.S. 29 (1971)][52] plurality would abridge this legitimate state interest to a degree that we find unacceptable. And it would occasion the additional difficulty of forcing state and federal judges to decide on an ad hoc basis which publications address issues of "general or public interest" and which do not—to determine, in the words of Mr. Justice Marshall, "what information is relevant to self-government." *Rosenbloom.* We doubt the wisdom of committing this task to the conscience of judges. [The] "public or general interest" test for determining the applicability of the *Times* standard to private defamation actions inadequately serves both of the competing values at stake. On the one hand, a private individual whose reputation is injured by defamatory falsehood that does concern an issue of public or general interest has no recourse unless he can meet the rigorous requirements of *Times.* This is true despite the factors that distinguish the state interest in compensating private individuals from the analogous interest involved in the context of public persons. On the other hand, a publisher or broadcaster of a defamatory error which a court deems unrelated to an issue of public or general interest may be held liable in damages even if it took every reasonable precaution to ensure the accuracy of its assertions. And liability may far exceed compensation for any actual

---

[51] Consider Lee Bollinger, *Images of a Free Press* 25–26 (1994): "Essentially, the Court has said that, since these individuals have freely chosen a public life, what happens to them is their own doing, just as it is for a man who breaks his leg while hiking in the wilderness. Putting aside for the moment the fact that we also have an interest in encouraging people to enter public affairs, it simply is wrong to suppose that the pain inflicted by defamatory statements about public officials and figures is not our responsibility or concern. It should always be open to people to object to the way the world works under the rules we create, and not be dismissed by the claim that they have chosen to continue living in that world and, therefore, can be taken as having assented to it."

[52] The *Rosenbloom* plurality would have extended the *New York Times* rule to statements of general or public interest, without regard to the public or official status of the plaintiff.

injury to the plaintiff, for the jury may be permitted to presume damages without proof of loss and even to award punitive damages.

We hold that, so long as they do not impose liability without fault, the States may define for themselves the appropriate standard of liability for a publisher or broadcaster of defamatory falsehood injurious to a private individual. This approach provides a more equitable boundary between the competing concerns involved here. It recognizes the strength of the legitimate state interest in compensating private individuals for wrongful injury to reputation, yet shields the press and broadcast media from the rigors of strict liability for defamation. At least this conclusion obtains where, as here, the substance of the defamatory statement "makes substantial danger to reputation apparent." *Butts.* This phrase places in perspective the conclusion we announce today. Our inquiry would involve considerations somewhat different from those discussed above if a State purported to condition civil liability on a factual misstatement whose content did not warn a reasonably prudent editor or broadcaster of its defamatory potential. Cf. *Time, Inc. v. Hill* [Part D infra]. Such a case is not now before us, and we intimate no view as to its proper resolution.

IV. [T]he strong and legitimate state interest in compensating private individuals for injury to reputation [extends] no further than compensation for actual injury. For the reasons stated below, we hold that the States may not permit recovery of presumed or punitive damages, at least when liability is not based on a showing of knowledge of falsity or reckless disregard for the truth.

The common law of defamation is an oddity of tort [law]. Juries may award substantial sums as compensation for supposed damage to reputation without any proof that such harm actually occurred. [This] unnecessarily compounds the potential of any system of liability for defamatory falsehood to inhibit the vigorous exercise of First Amendment freedoms [and] invites juries to punish unpopular opinion rather than to compensate individuals for injury sustained by the publication of a false fact. More to the point, the States have no substantial interest in securing for plaintiffs such as this petitioner gratuitous awards of money damages far in excess of any actual injury.

We would not, of course, invalidate state law simply because we doubt its wisdom, but here we are attempting to reconcile state law with a competing interest grounded in the constitutional command of the First Amendment. It is therefore appropriate to require that state remedies for defamatory falsehood reach no farther than is necessary to protect the legitimate interest involved. It is necessary to restrict defamation plaintiffs who do not prove knowledge of falsity or reckless disregard for the truth to compensation for actual injury. We need not define "actual injury," as trial courts have wide experience in framing appropriate jury instructions in tort action. Suffice it to say that actual injury is not limited to out-of-pocket loss. Indeed, the more customary types of actual harm inflicted by defamatory falsehood include impairment of reputation and standing in the community, personal humiliation, and mental anguish and suffering. Of course, juries must be limited by appropriate instructions, and all awards must be supported by competent evidence concerning the injury, although there need be no evidence which assigns an actual dollar value to the injury.

We also find no justification for allowing awards of punitive damages against publishers and broadcasters held liable under state-defined standards of liability for defamation. In most jurisdictions jury discretion over the amounts awarded is limited only by the gentle rule that they not be excessive. Consequently, juries assess punitive damages in wholly unpredictable amounts bearing no necessary relation to the actual harm caused. And they remain free to use their discretion selectively to punish expressions of unpopular views. [J]ury discretion to award punitive damages unnecessarily exacerbates the danger of media self-censorship; [punitive] damages are wholly irrelevant to the state interest that justifies a negligence standard for private defamation actions. They are not compensation for injury. Instead, they are private fines levied by civil juries to punish reprehensible conduct and to deter its future occurrence. In short, the private defamation plaintiff who establishes liability under a less demanding standard than that stated by *Times* may recover only such damages as are sufficient to compensate him for actual injury.[53]

V. Notwithstanding our refusal to extend the *New York Times* privilege to defamation of private individuals, respondent contends that we should affirm the judgment below on the ground that petitioner is [a] public figure. [That] designation may rest on either of two alternative bases. In some instances an individual may achieve such pervasive fame or notoriety that he becomes a public figure for all purposes and in all contexts. More commonly, an individual voluntarily injects himself or is drawn into a particular public controversy and thereby becomes a public figure for a limited range of issues. In either case such persons assume special prominence in the resolution of public questions.

Petitioner has long been active in community and professional affairs. He has served as an officer of local civic groups and of various professional organizations, and he has published several books and articles on legal subjects. Although petitioner was consequently well known in some circles, he had achieved no general fame or notoriety in the community. None of the prospective jurors called at the trial had ever heard of petitioner prior to this litigation, and respondent offered no proof that this response was atypical of the local population. We would not lightly assume that a

---

[53] On remand, Gertz was awarded $100,000 in compensatory damages and $300,000 in punitive damages. In the prior trial, he had been awarded only $50,000 in damages.

citizen's participation in community and professional affairs rendered him a public figure for all purposes. Absent clear evidence of general fame or notoriety in the community, and pervasive involvement in the affairs of society, an individual should not be deemed a public personality for all aspects of his life. It is preferable to reduce the public-figure question to a more meaningful context by looking to the nature and extent of an individual's participation in the particular controversy giving rise to the defamation.

In this context it is plain that petitioner was not a public figure. He played a minimal role at the coroner's inquest, and his participation related solely to his representation of a private client. He took no part in the criminal prosecution of Officer Nuccio. Moreover, he never discussed either the criminal or civil litigation with the press and was never quoted as having done so. He plainly did not thrust himself into the vortex of this public issue, nor did he engage the public's attention in an attempt to influence its outcome. We are persuaded that the trial court did not err in refusing to characterize petitioner as a public figure for the purpose of this litigation.

We therefore conclude that the *New York Times* standard is inapplicable to this case and that the trial court erred in entering judgment for respondent. Because the jury was allowed to impose liability without fault and was permitted to presume damages without proof of injury, a new trial is necessary.[54]

JUSTICE BRENNAN, dissenting.

[While the Court's] arguments are forcefully and eloquently presented, I cannot accept them for the reasons I stated in *Rosenbloom:* "The *New York Times* standard was applied to libel of a public official or public figure to give effect to the Amendment's function to encourage ventilation of public issues, not because the public official has any less interest in protecting his reputation than an individual in private life. [In] the vast majority of libels involving public officials or public figures, the ability to respond through the media will depend on the same complex factor on which the ability of a

---

[54] Blackmun, J., concurred: "[Although I joined Brennan, J.'s plurality opinion in *Rosenbloom,* from which the Court's opinion in the present case departs, I join] the Court's opinion and its judgment for two reasons:

"1. By removing the spectres of presumed and punitive damages in the absence of *Times* malice, the Court eliminates significant and powerful motives for self-censorship that otherwise are present in the traditional libel action. By so doing, the Court leaves what should prove to be sufficient and adequate breathing space for a vigorous press. What the Court has done, I believe, will have little, if any, practical effect on the functioning of responsible journalism.

"2. The Court was sadly fractionated in *Rosenbloom.* A result of that kind inevitably leads to uncertainty. I feel that it is of profound importance for the Court to come to rest in the defamation area and to have a clearly defined majority position that eliminates the unsureness engendered by *Rosenbloom's* diversity. If my vote were not needed to create a majority, I would adhere to my prior view. A definitive ruling, however, is paramount."

private individual depends: the unpredictable event of the media's continuing interest in the story. Thus the unproved, and highly improbable, generalization that an as yet [not fully defined] class of 'public figures' involved in matters of public concern will be better able to respond through the media than private individuals also involved in such matters seems too insubstantial a reed on which to rest a constitutional distinction."

[Adoption], by many States, of a reasonable care standard in cases where private individuals are involved in matters of public interest—the probable result of today's decision—[will] lead to self-censorship since publishers will be required carefully to weigh a myriad of uncertain factors before publication. The reasonable care standard is "elusive," *Time, Inc. v. Hill;* it saddles the press with "the intolerable burden of guessing how a jury might assess the reasonableness of steps taken by it to verify the accuracy of every reference to a name, picture or portrait." Ibid. Under a reasonable care regime, publishers and broadcasters will have to make pre-publication judgments about juror assessment of such diverse considerations as the size, operating procedures, and financial condition of the news gathering system, as well as the relative costs and benefits of instituting less frequent and more costly reporting at a higher level of accuracy. [And] most hazardous, the flexibility which inheres in the reasonable care standard will create the danger that a jury will convert it into "an instrument for the suppression of those 'vehement, caustic, and sometimes unpleasantly sharp attacks,' [which] must be protected if the guarantees of the First and Fourteenth Amendments are to prevail." *Monitor Patriot Co.*

[A] jury's latitude to impose liability for want of due care poses a far greater threat of suppressing unpopular views than does a possible recovery of presumed or punitive damages. Moreover, the Court's broad-ranging examples of "actual injury" [allow] a jury bent on punishing expression of unpopular views a formidable weapon for doing so. [E]ven a limitation of recovery to "actual injury"—however much it reduces the size or frequency of recoveries—will not provide the necessary elbow room for First Amendment expression. "[The] very possibility of having to engage in litigation, an expensive and protracted process, is threat enough to cause discussion and debate to 'steer far wider of the unlawful zone' thereby keeping protected discussion from public cognizance. * * * " *Rosenbloom.*

[I] reject the argument that my *Rosenbloom* view improperly commits to judges the task of determining what is and what is not an issue of "general or public interest."[3] I noted in *Rosenbloom* that performance of

---

[3] **[Ct's Note]** The Court, taking a novel step, would not limit application of First Amendment protection to private libels involving issues of general or public interest, but would forbid the States from imposing liability without fault in any case where the substance of the defamatory statement made substantial danger to reputation apparent. As in *Rosenbloom,* I would leave open the question of what constitutional standard, if any, applies when defamatory

this task would not always be easy. But surely the courts, the ultimate arbiters of all disputes concerning clashes of constitutional values, would only be performing one of their traditional functions in undertaking this duty. [The] public interest is necessarily broad; any residual self-censorship that may result from the uncertain contours of the "general or public interest" concept should be of far less concern to publishers and broadcasters than that occasioned by state laws imposing liability for negligent falsehood. * * *55

JUSTICE WHITE, dissenting.

[T]he Court, in a few printed pages, has federalized major aspects of libel law by declaring unconstitutional in important respects the prevailing defamation law in all or most of the 50 States. * * *

I.   [These] radical changes in the law and severe invasions of the prerogatives of the States [should] at least be shown to be required by the First Amendment or necessitated by our present circumstances. Neither has been [demonstrated.]

The central meaning of *New York Times,* and for me the First Amendment as it relates to libel laws, is that seditious libel—criticism of government and public officials—falls beyond the police power of the State. In a democratic society such as ours, the citizen has the privilege of criticizing his government and its officials. But neither *New York Times* nor its progeny suggest that the First Amendment intended in all circumstances to deprive the private citizen of his historic recourse to redress published falsehoods damaging to reputation or that, contrary to history and precedent, the amendment should now be so interpreted.

---

falsehoods are published or broadcast concerning either a private or public person's activities not within the scope of the general or public interest.

Parenthetically, my Brother White argues that the Court's view and mine will prevent a plaintiff—unable to demonstrate some degree of fault—from vindicating his reputation by securing a judgment that the publication was false. This argument overlooks the possible enactment of statutes, not requiring proof of fault, which provide for an action for retraction or for publication of a court's determination of falsity if the plaintiff is able to demonstrate that false statements have been published concerning his activities. Although it may be that questions could be raised concerning the constitutionality of such statutes, certainly nothing I have said today (and, as I read the Court's opinion, nothing said there) should be read to imply that a private plaintiff, unable to prove fault, must inevitably be denied the opportunity to secure a judgment upon the truth or falsity of statements published about him.

55   Douglas, J., dissented, objecting to "continued recognition of the possibility of state libel suits for public discussion of public issues" as diluting First Amendment protection. He added: "Since this case involves a discussion of public affairs, I need not decide at this point whether the First Amendment prohibits all libel actions. 'An unconditional right to say what one pleases about public affairs is what I consider to be *the minimum guarantee* of the First Amendment.' *New York Times* (Black, J., concurring) (emphasis added). But 'public affairs' includes a great deal more than merely political affairs. Matters of science, economics, business, art, literature, etc., are all matters of interest to the general public. Indeed, any matter of sufficient general interest to prompt media coverage may be said to be a public affair. Certainly police killings, 'Communist conspiracies,' and the like qualify."

Simply put, the First Amendment did not confer a "license to defame the citizen." Douglas, *The Right of the People* 38 (1958).

[T]he law has heretofore put the risk of falsehood on the publisher where the victim is a private citizen and no grounds of special privilege are invoked. The Court would now shift this risk to the victim, even though he has done nothing to invite the calumny, is wholly innocent of fault, and is helpless to avoid his injury. I doubt that jurisprudential resistance to liability without fault is sufficient ground for employing the First Amendment to revolutionize the law of libel, and in my view, that body of legal rules poses no realistic threat to the press and its service to the public. The press today is vigorous and robust. To me, it is quite incredible to suggest that threats of libel suits from private citizens are causing the press to refrain from publishing the truth. I know of no hard facts to support that proposition, and the Court furnishes none.

[I]f the Court's principal concern is to protect the communications industry from large libel judgments, it would appear that its new requirements with respect to general and punitive damages would be ample protection. Why it also feels compelled to escalate the threshold standard of liability I cannot fathom, particularly when this will eliminate in many instances the plaintiff's possibility of securing a judicial determination that the damaging publication was indeed false, whether or not he is entitled to recover money damages. [I] find it unacceptable to distribute the risk in this manner and force the wholly innocent victim to bear the injury; for, as between the two, the defamer is the only culpable party. It is he who circulated a falsehood that he was not required to publish. * * *[56]

V.   [I] fail to see how the quality or quantity of public debate will be promoted by further emasculation of state libel laws for the benefit of the news media.[57] If anything, this trend may provoke a new and radical imbalance in the communications process . It is not at all inconceivable that virtually unrestrained defamatory remarks about private citizens will discourage them from speaking out and concerning themselves with social problems. This would turn the First Amendment on its head. * * *[58]

---

[56]   White, J., also argued against the Court's rulings on presumed and punitive damages.

[57]   Cf. Willard Pedrick, *Freedom of the Press and the Law of Libel: The Modern Revised Translation,* 49 Cornell L.Q. 581 (1964): "A great many forces in our society operate to determine the extent to which men are free in fact to express their ideas. Whether there is a privilege for good faith defamatory misstatements on matters of public concern or whether there is strict liability for such statements may not greatly affect the course of public discussion. How different has life been in those states which heretofore followed the majority rule imposing strict liability for misstatements of fact defaming public figures from life in the minority states where the good faith privilege held sway?"

[58]   Burger, C.J., also dissented: "I am frank to say I do not know the parameters of a 'negligence' doctrine as applied to the news media. [I] would prefer to allow this area of law to continue to evolve as it has up to now with respect to private citizens rather then embark on a new

NOTES AND QUESTIONS

1.   *Gertz and Meiklejohn.* By affording some constitutional protection to all media defamatory speech whether or not it relates to public issues, does the Court reject the Meiklejohn theory of the First Amendment? Consider Steven Shiffrin, *Defamatory Non-Media Speech and First Amendment Methodology,* 25 UCLA L.Rev. 915 (1978): "It may be that the Court has refused to adopt the Meiklejohn 'public issues' test not because it believes that private speech (i.e., speech unrelated to public issues) is as important as public speech but rather because it doubts its ability to distinguish unerringly between the two. [B]y placing all defamatory media speech within the scope of the First Amendment, the Court may believe it has protected relatively little non-public speech. On the other hand, [putting aside comments about public officials and public figures], the Court may fear that if *Gertz* were extended to non-media speech, the result would be to protect much speech having nothing to do with public issues, while safeguarding relatively little that does." For consideration of the distinction between public and private speech and of the media/non-media distinction, see *Greenmoss*, Sec. III, 3 infra. See also *Philadelphia Newspapers, Inc. v. Hepps,* 475 U.S. 767 (1986) (private figure plaintiff has burden of showing falsity at least when issue is of "public concern" and leaving open the question of what standards apply to non-media defendants).

2.   *Public figures.* TIME, INC. v. FIRESTONE, 424 U.S. 448 (1976), per REHNQUIST, J., declared that persons who have not assumed a role of especial prominence in the affairs of society are not public figures unless they have " 'thrust themselves to the forefront of particular public controversies in order to influence the resolution of the issues involved.' " It held that a divorce proceeding involving one of America's wealthiest industrial families and containing testimony concerning the extramarital sexual activities of the parties did not involve a "public controversy," "even though the marital difficulties of extremely wealthy individuals may be of interest to some portion of the reading public." Nor was the filing of a divorce suit, or the holding of press conferences ("to satisfy inquiring reporters") thought to be freely publicizing the issues in order to influence their outcome. Recall *Gertz* doubted the wisdom of forcing judges to determine on an ad hoc basis what is and is not of "general or public interest." Is there a basis for distinguishing a public figure test requiring judges to determine on an ad hoc basis what is or is not a "public controversy"?

What does it mean to assume a role of especial prominence in the affairs of society? If Elmer Gertz, a prominent Illinois attorney, does not qualify, does Wolfgang Puck? Naomi Campbell? Peyton Manning? If so, is the slide from public officials to chefs and models and quarterbacks too precipitous because the latter "have little, if any effect, on questions of politics, public policy, or the organization and determination of societal affairs"? See Frederick Schauer,

---

doctrinal theory which has no jurisprudential ancestry. [I would remand] for reinstatement of the verdict of the jury and the entry of an appropriate judgment on that verdict."

Public Figures, 25 Wm. & Mary L.Rev. 905 (1984): Consider Marie A. Failinger, *Five Modern Notions in Search of an Author: The Ideology of the Intimate Society in Constitutional Speech Law,* 30 U.Tol. L.Rev. 251 (1999): "[T]he Court merely adds fuel to the cultural fire created by [the] 'star' system—people who want to know intimate details that confirm their trust in those selected by the public to be 'stars,' and yet, they have a secret desire to know 'dirt' on those same persons to justify their beliefs that people just like themselves have been randomly enriched with fame, power, and wealth. [T]his politics of resentment, parlay[s] the shame and envy of those who find themselves in a lower-than-deserved status into a rising backlash against those who have unfairly taken 'their' place. Thus, protection of the cult of personality in the Court's speech doctrine only serves to fuel the fires of self-interested, mean-spirited public life." Does a narrow definition of public figures discriminate in favor of orthodox media and discourage attempts "to illuminate previously unexposed aspects of society"? Does the negligence concept threaten to discriminate "against media or outlets whose philosophies and methods deviate from those of the mainstream"? See generally David Anderson, *Libel and Press Self-Censorship,* 53 Tex.L.Rev. 422 (1975).

3. ***Taking reputation too seriously?*** Consider Rodney Smolla, *Suing the Press* 257 (1986): "[I]f we take the libel suit too seriously, we are in danger of raising our collective cultural sensitivity to reputation to unhealthy levels. We are in danger of surrendering a wonderful part of our national identity— our strapping, scrambling, free-wheeling individualism, in danger of becoming less American, less robust, wild-eyed, pluralistic and free, and more decorous, image-conscious, and narcissistic. The media is itself partly to blame for this direction, and it would be dangerous to release it totally from the important check and balance that the libel laws provide. But in the United States, the balance that must be struck between reputation and expression should never be tilted too far against expression, for the right to defiantly, robustly, and irreverently speak one's mind just because it is one's mind is quintessentially what it means to be an American."[59]

D. Emotional Distress

HUSTLER MAGAZINE v. FALWELL, 485 U.S. 46 (1988), per REHNQUIST, C.J., held that public figures and public officials offended by a mass media parody could not recover for the tort of intentional infliction of emotional distress without a showing of *New York Times* malice. Parodying a series of liquor advertisements in which celebrities speak about their "first time," the editors of *Hustler* chose plaintiff Jerry Falwell (a nationally famous minister, host of a nationally syndicated television show, and founder of the Moral Majority political organization) "as the featured celebrity and drafted an alleged 'interview' with him in which he states that his 'first time' was during a drunken incestuous rendezvous with his

---

[59] For discussion of factors causing few cases to go to trial against media defendants, see David A. Anderson, *Rethinking Defamation,* 48 Ariz. L.Rev. 1047 (2006).

mother in an outhouse. The *Hustler* parody portrays [Falwell] and his mother[60] 'as drunk and immoral,' and suggests that [Falwell] is a hypocrite who preaches only when he is drunk. In small print at the bottom of the page, the ad contains the disclaimer, 'ad parody—not to be taken seriously.' The magazine's table of contents also lists the ad as 'Fiction; Ad and Personality Parody.' * * *

"We must decide whether a public figure may recover damages for emotional harm caused by the publication of an ad parody offensive to him, and doubtless gross and repugnant in the eyes of most.[3] [Falwell] would have us find that a State's interest in protecting public figures from emotional distress is sufficient to deny First Amendment protection to speech that is patently offensive and is intended to inflict emotional injury, even when that speech could not reasonably have been interpreted as stating actual facts about the public figure involved. * * *

"Generally speaking the law does not regard the intent to inflict emotional distress as one which should receive much solicitude, and it is quite understandable that most if not all jurisdictions have chosen to make it civilly culpable where the conduct in question is sufficiently 'outrageous.' But in the world of debate about public affairs, many things done with motives that are less than admirable are protected by the First Amendment. '[Debate] on public issues will not be uninhibited if the speaker must run the risk that it will be proved in court that he spoke out of hatred; even if he did speak out of hatred, utterances honestly believed contribute to the free interchange of ideas and the ascertainment of truth.' *Garrison*. Thus while such a bad motive may be deemed controlling for purposes of tort liability in other areas of the law, we think the First Amendment prohibits such a result in the area of public debate about public figures.

"Were we to hold otherwise, there can be little doubt that political cartoonists and satirists would be subjected to damage awards without any showing that their work falsely defamed its subject. * * *

"There is no doubt that the caricature of [Falwell] and his mother published in Hustler is at best a distant cousin of [traditional] political cartoons [and] a rather poor relation at that. If it were possible by laying down a principled standard to separate the one from the other, public discourse would probably suffer little or no harm. But we doubt that there is any such standard, and we are quite sure that the pejorative description

---

[60]   Falwell's mother was not a plaintiff. What result if she were?

[3]   **[Ct's Note]** Under Virginia law, in an action for intentional infliction of emotional distress a plaintiff must show that the defendant's conduct (1) is intentional or reckless; (2) offends generally accepted standards of decency or morality; (3) is causally connected with the plaintiff's emotional distress; and (4) caused emotional distress that was severe. [On the conflict between the First Amendment and the tort of intentional infliction of emotional distress in a non-media context, see *Snyder v. Phelps*, infra.]

'outrageous' does not supply one. 'Outrageousness' in the area of political and social discourse has an inherent subjectiveness about it which would allow a jury to impose liability on the basis of the jurors' tastes or views, or perhaps on the basis of their dislike of a particular expression.

"We conclude that public figures and public officials may not recover for the tort of intentional infliction of emotional distress by reason of publications such as the one here at issue without showing in addition that the publication contains a false statement of fact which was made with 'actual malice,' i.e., with knowledge that the statement was false or with reckless disregard as to whether or not it was true."[61]

————

The father of a deceased Marine brought an action for intentional infliction of emotional distress, intrusion upon seclusion, and civil conspiracy against a fundamentalist church and its members for demonstrating near the Marine's funeral with signs whose content is detailed in the Court's opinion below, including "Thank God for Dead Soldiers."

SNYDER v. PHELPS, 131 S.Ct. 1207 (2011), per ROBERTS, C.J., held that the speech was protected and immune from tort liability: "A jury held members of the Westboro Baptist Church liable for millions of dollars in damages for picketing near a soldier's funeral service. The picket signs reflected the church's view that the United States is overly tolerant of sin and that God kills American soldiers as punishment. The question presented is whether the First Amendment shields the church members from tort liability for their speech in this case. [The] church had notified the authorities in advance of its intent to picket at the time of the funeral, and the picketers complied with police instructions in staging their demonstration. The picketing took place within a 10- by 25-foot plot of public land adjacent to a public street, behind a temporary fence. That plot was approximately 1,000 feet from the church where the funeral was held. Several buildings separated the picket site from the church. The Westboro picketers displayed their signs for about 30 minutes before the funeral began and sang hymns and recited Bible verses. None of the picketers entered church property or went to the cemetery. They did not yell or use profanity, and there was no violence associated with the picketing. The funeral procession passed within 200 to 300 feet of the picket site. Although Snyder testified that he could see the tops of the picket signs as he drove to the funeral, he did not see what was written on the signs until later that night, while watching a news broadcast covering the event. A few weeks after the funeral, one of the picketers posted a message on Westboro's Web site discussing the picketing and containing religiously oriented

---

[61] White, J., concurred, but stated that *New York Times* was irrelevant because of the jury's finding that the parody contained no assertion of fact. Kennedy, J., took no part.

denunciations of the Snyders, interspersed among lengthy Bible quotations. Snyder discovered the posting, referred to by the parties as the 'epic,' during an Internet search for his son's name. The epic is not properly before us and does not factor in our analysis. * * *

"A trial was held on the remaining claims. At trial, Snyder described the severity of his emotional injuries. He testified that he is unable to separate the thought of his dead son from his thoughts of Westboro's picketing, and that he often becomes tearful, angry, and physically ill when he thinks about it. Expert witnesses testified that Snyder's emotional anguish had resulted in severe depression and had exacerbated pre-existing health conditions.

"To succeed on a claim for intentional infliction of emotional distress in Maryland, a plaintiff must demonstrate that the defendant intentionally or recklessly engaged in extreme and outrageous conduct that caused the plaintiff to suffer severe emotional distress. The Free Speech Clause of the First Amendment [can] serve as a defense in state tort suits, including suits for intentional infliction of emotional distress.

"Whether the First Amendment prohibits holding Westboro liable for its speech in this case turns largely on whether that speech is of public or private concern, as determined by all the circumstances of the case. '[S]peech on matters of public concern [is] at the heart of the First Amendment's protection.' * * *

" '[N]ot all speech is of equal First Amendment importance,' however, and where matters of purely private significance are at issue, First Amendment protections are often less rigorous. That is because restricting speech on purely private matters does not implicate the same constitutional concerns as limiting speech on matters of public interest: '[T]here is no threat to the free and robust debate of public issues; there is no potential interference with a meaningful dialogue of ideas'; and the 'threat of liability' does not pose the risk of 'a reaction of self-censorship' on matters of public import.

"Speech deals with matters of public concern when it can 'be fairly considered as relating to any matter of political, social, or other concern to the community,' or when it 'is a subject of legitimate news interest; that is, a subject of general interest and of value and concern to the public,' The arguably 'inappropriate or controversial character of a statement is irrelevant to the question whether it deals with a matter of public concern.' * * *

"Deciding whether speech is of public or private concern requires us to examine the 'content, form, and context' of that speech, 'as revealed by the whole record.' [In] considering content, form, and context, no factor is dispositive, and it is necessary to evaluate all the circumstances of the speech, including what was said, where it was said, and how it was said.

"The 'content' of Westboro's signs plainly relates to broad issues of interest to society at large, rather than matters of 'purely private concern.' The placards read 'God Hates the USA/Thank God for 9/11,' 'America is Doomed,' 'Don't Pray for the USA,' 'Thank God for IEDs,' 'Fag Troops,' 'Semper Fi Fags,' 'God Hates Fags,' 'Maryland Taliban,' 'Fags Doom Nations,' 'Not Blessed Just Cursed,' 'Thank God for Dead Soldiers,' 'Pope in Hell,' 'Priests Rape Boys,' 'You're Going to Hell,' and 'God Hates You.' While these messages may fall short of refined social or political commentary, the issues they highlight—the political and moral conduct of the United States and its citizens, the fate of our Nation, homosexuality in the military, and scandals involving the Catholic clergy—are matters of public import. The signs certainly convey Westboro's position on those issues, in a manner designed [to] reach as broad a public audience as possible. And even if a few of the signs-such as 'You're Going to Hell' and 'God Hates You'—were viewed as containing messages related to Matthew Snyder or the Snyders specifically, that would not change the fact that the overall thrust and dominant theme of Westboro's demonstration spoke to broader public issues.

"Apart from the content of Westboro's signs, Snyder contends that the 'context' of the speech—its connection with his son's funeral—makes the speech a matter of private rather than public concern. The fact that Westboro spoke in connection with a funeral, however, cannot by itself transform the nature of Westboro's speech. Westboro's signs, displayed on public land next to a public street, reflect the fact that the church finds much to condemn in modem society. Its speech is 'fairly characterized as constituting speech on a matter of public concern,' and the funeral setting does not alter that conclusion. * * *

"Snyder goes on to argue that Westboro's speech should be afforded less than full First Amendment protection 'not only because of the words' but also because the church members exploited the funeral 'as a platform to bring their message to a broader audience.' * * * Westboro's choice to convey its views in conjunction with Matthew Snyder's funeral made the expression of those views particularly hurtful to many, especially to Matthew's father. The record makes clear that the applicable legal term-'emotional distress'-fails to capture fully the anguish Westboro's choice added to Mr. Snyder's already incalculable grief. But Westboro conducted its picketing peacefully on matters of public concern at a public place adjacent to a public street. * * *

"Westboro's choice of where and when to conduct its picketing is not beyond the Government's regulatory reach—it is 'subject to reasonable time, place, or manner restrictions' that are consistent with the standards announced in this Court's precedents. Maryland now has a law imposing restrictions on funeral picketing. To the extent these laws are content neutral, they raise very different questions from the tort verdict at issue in this case. Maryland's law, however, was not in effect at the time of the events at issue here, so we have no occasion to consider how it might apply to facts such as those before us, or whether it or other similar regulations are constitutional.

"The record confirms that any distress occasioned by Westboro's picketing turned on the content and viewpoint of the message conveyed, rather than any interference with the funeral itself. A group of parishioners standing at the very spot where Westboro stood, holding signs that said 'God Bless America' and 'God Loves You,' would not have been subjected to liability. It was what Westboro said that exposed it to tort damages. * * *

"Given that Westboro's speech was at a public place on a matter of public concern, that speech is entitled to 'special protection' under the First Amendment. Such speech cannot be restricted simply because it is upsetting or arouses contempt. * * *

"The jury here was instructed that it could hold Westboro liable for intentional infliction of emotional distress based on a finding that Westboro's picketing was 'outrageous.' Outrageousness, 'however, is a highly malleable standard with' an inherent subjectiveness about it which would allow a jury to impose liability on the basis of the jurors 'tastes or views, or perhaps on the basis of their dislike of a particular expression.' [What] Westboro said, in the whole context of how and where it chose to say it, is entitled to 'special protection' under the First Amendment, and that protection cannot be overcome by a jury finding that the picketing was outrageous.

"For all these reasons, the jury verdict imposing tort liability on Westboro for intentional infliction of emotional distress must be set aside. "Our holding today is narrow. We are required in First Amendment cases to carefully review the record, and the reach of our opinion here is limited by the particular facts before us. As we have noted, 'the sensitivity and significance of the interests presented in clashes between First Amendment and [state law] rights counsel relying on limited principles that sweep no more broadly than the appropriate context of the instant case."[62]

BREYER, J., concurred: "I agree with the Court and join its opinion. That opinion restricts its analysis here to the matter raised in the petition for certiorari, namely, Westboro's picketing activity. The opinion does not examine in depth the effect of television broadcasting. Nor does it say anything about Internet postings. The Court holds that the First Amendment protects the picketing that occurred here, primarily because the picketing addressed matters of 'public concern.' * * *

---

[62] The Court disposed of the other tort claims on similar grounds.

"Westboro's means of communicating its views consisted of picketing in a place where picketing was lawful and in compliance with all police directions. The picketing could not be seen or heard from the funeral ceremony itself. And Snyder testified that he saw no more than the tops of the picketers' signs as he drove to the funeral. To uphold the application of state law in these circumstances would punish Westboro for seeking to communicate its views on matters of public concern without proportionately advancing the State's interest in protecting its citizens against severe emotional harm. Consequently, the First Amendment protects Westboro. As I read the Court's opinion, it holds no more."

ALITO, J., dissented: "Our profound national commitment to free and open debate is not a license for the vicious verbal assault that occurred in this case. Petitioner Albert Snyder is not a public figure. He is simply a parent whose son, Marine Lance Corporal Matthew Snyder, was killed in Iraq. Mr. Snyder wanted what is surely the right of any parent who experiences such an incalculable loss: to bury his son in peace. But respondents, members of the Westboro Baptist Church, deprived him of that elementary right. They first issued a press release and thus turned Matthew's funeral into a tumultuous media event. They then appeared at the church, approached as closely as they could without trespassing, and launched a malevolent verbal attack on Matthew and his family at a time of acute emotional vulnerability. As a result, Albert Snyder suffered severe and lasting emotional injury. The Court now holds that the First Amendment protected respondents' right to brutalize Mr. Snyder. I cannot agree.

"Respondents and other members of their church have strong opinions on certain moral, religious, and political issues, and the First Amendment ensures that they have almost limitless opportunities to express their views. They may write and distribute books, articles, and other texts; they may create and disseminate video and audio recordings; they may circulate petitions; they may speak to individuals and groups in public forums and in any private venue that wishes to accommodate them; they may picket peacefully in countless locations; they may appear on television and speak on the radio; they may post messages on the Internet and send out e-mails. And they may express their views in terms that are 'uninhibited,' 'vehement,' and 'caustic.'

"It does not follow, however, that they may intentionally inflict severe emotional injury on private persons at a time of intense emotional sensitivity by launching vicious verbal attacks that make no contribution to public debate. To protect against such injury, 'most if not all jurisdictions' permit recovery in tort for the intentional infliction of emotional distress (or IIED). * * *

"Although the elements of the IIED tort are difficult to meet, respondents long ago abandoned any effort to show that those tough standards were not satisfied here. On appeal, they chose not to contest the sufficiency of the evidence. They did not dispute that Mr. Snyder suffered 'wounds that are truly severe and incapable of healing themselves. 'Nor did they dispute that their speech was 'so outrageous in character, and so extreme in degree, as to go beyond all possible bounds of decency, and to be regarded as atrocious, and utterly intolerable in a civilized community.' Instead, they maintained that the First Amendment gave them a license to engage in such conduct. * * *

"On the morning of Matthew Snyder's funeral, respondents could have chosen to stage their protest at countless locations. They could have picketed the United States Capitol, the White House, the Supreme Court, the Pentagon, or any of the more than 5,600 military recruiting stations in this country. They could have returned to the Maryland State House or the United States Naval Academy, where they had been the day before. They could have selected any public road where pedestrians are allowed. (There are more than 4,000,000 miles of public roads in the United States.) They could have staged their protest in a public park. (There are more than 20,000 public parks in this country) They could have chosen any Catholic church where no funeral was taking place. (There are nearly 19,000 Catholic churches in the United States.) But of course, a small group picketing at any of these locations would have probably gone unnoticed.

"The Westboro Baptist Church, however, has devised a strategy that remedies this problem. As the Court notes, church members have protested at nearly 600 military funerals. They have also picketed the funerals of police officers, firefighters, and the victims of natural disasters, accidents, and shocking crimes. And in advance of these protests, they issue press releases to ensure that their protests will attract public attention. This strategy works because it is expected that respondents' verbal assaults will wound the family and friends of the deceased and because the media is irresistibly drawn to the sight of persons who are visibly in grief. The more outrageous the funeral protest, the more publicity the Westboro Baptist Church is able to obtain. * * *

"[T]he Court finds that 'the overall thrust and dominant theme of [their] demonstration spoke to' broad public issues. [T]his portrayal is quite inaccurate; respondents' attack on Matthew was of central importance. But in any event, I fail to see why actionable speech should be immunized simply because it is interspersed with speech that is protected. The First Amendment allows recovery for defamatory statements that are interspersed with nondefamatory statements on matters of public concern, and there is no good reason why respondents' attack on Matthew Snyder and his family should be treated differently. * * *

"[T]he Court finds it significant that respondents' protest occurred on a public street, but this fact alone should not be enough to preclude IIED liability. To be sure, statements made on a public street may be less likely to satisfy the elements of the IIED tort than statements made on private property, but there is no reason why a public street in close proximity to the scene of a funeral should be regarded as a free-fire zone in which otherwise actionable verbal attacks are shielded from liability. If the First Amendment permits the States to protect their residents from the harm inflicted by such attacks—and the Court does not hold otherwise—then the location of the tort should not be dispositive. A physical assault may occur without trespassing; it is no defense that the perpetrator had 'the right to be where [he was].' And the same should be true with respect to unprotected speech. [D]efamatory statements are [not] immunized when they occur in a public place, and there is no good reason to treat a verbal assault based on the conduct or character of a private figure like Matthew Snyder any differently.

"One final comment about the opinion of the Court is in order. The Court suggests that the wounds inflicted by vicious verbal assaults at funerals will be prevented or at least mitigated in the future by new laws that restrict picketing within a specified distance of a funeral. It is apparent, however, that the enactment of these laws is no substitute for the protection provided by the established IIED tort; according to the Court, the verbal attacks that severely wounded petitioner in this case complied with the new Maryland law regulating funeral picketing. And there is absolutely nothing to suggest that Congress and the state legislatures, in enacting these laws, intended them to displace the protection provided by the well-established IIED tort.

"The real significance of these new laws is not that they obviate the need for IIED protection. Rather, their enactment dramatically illustrates the fundamental point that funerals are unique events at which special protection against emotional assaults is in [order.] Allowing family members to have a few hours of peace without harassment does not undermine public debate. I would therefore hold that, in this setting, the First Amendment permits a private figure to recover for the intentional infliction of emotional distress caused by speech on a matter of private concern."

NOTES AND QUESTIONS

1. **_False light privacy._** TIME, INC. v. HILL, 385 U.S. 374 (1967), applied the _New York Times_ knowing and reckless falsity standard to a right of privacy action for publishing an erroneous but not defamatory report about private individuals involved in an incident of public interest. The Court maintained that "[N]egligence would be a most elusive standard, especially when the content of the speech itself affords no warning of prospective harm

to another through falsity. A negligence test would place on the press the intolerable burden of guessing how a jury might assess the reasonableness of steps taken by it to verify the accuracy of every reference to a name, picture or [portrait]." Does *Hill* survive *Gertz*? Would it make a difference if the law suit were for intentional infliction of emotional distress?

Compare *Hill* with ZACCHINI v. SCRIPPS-HOWARD BROADCASTING CO., 433 U.S. 562 (1977): Zacchini performed as a "human cannonball," being shot from a cannon into a net some 200 feet away. Without Zacchini's permission to film or broadcast his act, Scripps-Howard obtained and broadcast the tape of his "shot" on the news. The Ohio Supreme Court held the telecast was protected under *Time, Inc. v. Hill* as a newsworthy event. The Court, per WHITE, J., reversed. *Hill* was distinguishable because Zacchini's claim was based not on privacy or reputation but "in protecting the proprietary interest," an interest "closely analogous to the goals of patent and copyright law." Unlike *Hill,* the issue was not whether Zacchini's act would be available to the public: "[T]he only question is who gets to do the publishing."[63]

2. ***False news.*** Should injury to any particular person be a prerequisite to state regulation of false publications? Consider *Keeton v. Hustler Magazine, Inc.*, 465 U.S. 770 (1984): "False statements of fact harm both the subject of the falsehood *and* the readers of the statement. New Hampshire may rightly employ its libel laws to discourage the deception of its citizens." Could New Hampshire make it a criminal offense to publish false statements with knowledge of their falsity without any requirement of injury to any particular person? See *United States v. Alvarez*, Sec. 1, VI, F infra.

E. Disclosure of Private Facts

FLORIDA STAR v. B.J.F.
491 U.S. 524, 109 S.Ct. 2603, 105 L.Ed.2d 443 (1989).

JUSTICE MARSHALL delivered the opinion of the Court.

Florida Stat. § 794.03 (1987) makes it unlawful to "print, publish, or broadcast [in] any instrument of mass communication" the name of the victim of a sexual offense. Pursuant to this statute, appellant The Florida Star was found civilly liable for publishing the name of a rape victim which it had obtained from a publicly released police report. [B.J.F.] testified that she had suffered emotional distress from the publication of her name. She stated that she had heard about the article from fellow workers and acquaintances; that her mother had received several threatening phone calls from a man who stated that he would rape B.J.F. again; and that these events had forced B.J.F. to change her phone number and residence, to seek

---

[63] Powell, J., joined by Brennan and Marshall, JJ., dissented, observing that there was no showing that the broadcast was a "subterfuge or cover for private or commercial exploitation." Stevens, J., dissented on procedural grounds. For commentary on the right to publicity, see J. Thomas McCarthy, *The Rights of Publicity and Privacy* (2d ed. 2000); Russell S. Jones, Jr., *The Flip Side of Privacy,* 39 Creight. L.Rev. 939 (2006).

police protection, and to obtain mental health counseling. [The jury] awarded B.J.F. $75,000 in compensatory damages and $25,000 in punitive damages. * * *

[We do not] accept appellant's invitation to hold broadly that truthful publication may never be punished consistent with the First Amendment. Our cases have carefully eschewed reaching this ultimate question, mindful that the future may bring scenarios which prudence counsels our not resolving anticipatorily. See, e.g., *Near v. Minnesota,* [Section 4, I, B] (hypothesizing "publication of the sailing dates of transports or the number and location of troops"); see also *Garrison v. Louisiana* (endorsing absolute defense of truth "where discussion of public affairs is concerned," but leaving unsettled the constitutional implications of truthfulness "in the discrete area of purely private libels"). Indeed, in [*Cox Broadcasting v. Cohn,* 420 U.S. 469 (1975)], we pointedly refused to answer even the less sweeping question "whether truthful publications may ever be subjected to civil or criminal liability" for invading "an area of privacy" defined by the State. [We] continue to believe that the sensitivity and significance of the interests presented in clashes between First Amendment and privacy rights counsel relying on limited principles that sweep no more broadly than the appropriate context of the instant case.

In our view, this case is appropriately analyzed with reference to such a limited First Amendment principle. It is the one, in fact, which we articulated in *Smith v. Daily Mail Pub. Co.,* [Sec. 5, I infra] in our synthesis of prior cases involving attempts to punish truthful publication: "[I]f a newspaper lawfully obtains truthful information about a matter of public significance then state officials may not constitutionally punish publication of the information, absent a need to further a state interest of the highest order."[64] * * *

Applied to the instant case, the *Daily Mail* principle clearly commands reversal. The first inquiry is whether the newspaper "lawfully obtain[ed] truthful information about a matter of public significance." It is undisputed that the news article describing the assault on B.J.F. was accurate. In addition, appellant lawfully obtained B.J.F.'s name. Appellee's argument to the contrary is based on the fact that under Florida law, police reports which reveal the identity of the victim of a sexual offense are not among the matters of "public record" which the public, by law, is entitled to inspect. But the fact that state officials are not required to disclose such reports does not make it unlawful for a newspaper to receive them when furnished by the government. Nor does the fact that the Department apparently failed to fulfill its obligation under § 794.03 not to "cause or

---

[64] Suppose a newspaper publishes the name of a confidential source who it believes has misled it for political reasons and suppose the source sues the newspaper for breach of contract? Should the *Daily Mail* principle apply? See *Cohen v. Cowles Media Co.,* 501 U.S. 663 (1991). Should the *Daily Mail* principle apply in copyright cases?

allow to [be] published" the name of a sexual offense victim make the newspaper's ensuing receipt of this information unlawful. Even assuming the Constitution permitted a State to proscribe *receipt* of information, Florida has not taken this step. It is, clear, furthermore, that the news article concerned "a matter of public significance[.]" That is, the article generally, as opposed to the specific identity contained within it, involved a matter of paramount public import: the commission, and investigation, of a violent crime which had been reported to authorities.

The second inquiry is whether imposing liability on appellant pursuant to § 794.03 serves "a need to further a state interest of the highest order." Appellee argues that a rule punishing publication furthers three closely related interests: the privacy of victims of sexual offenses; the physical safety of such victims, who may be targeted for retaliation if their names become known to their assailants; and the goal of encouraging victims of such crimes to report these offenses without fear of exposure.

At a time in which we are daily reminded of the tragic reality of rape, it is undeniable that these are highly significant interests. [We] accordingly do not rule out the possibility that, in a proper case, imposing civil sanctions for publication of the name of a rape victim might be so overwhelmingly necessary to advance these interests as to satisfy the *Daily Mail* standard. For three independent reasons, however, imposing liability for publication under the circumstances of this case is too precipitous a means of advancing these interests to convince us that there is a "need" within the meaning of the *Daily Mail* formulation for Florida to take this extreme step.

First is the manner in which appellant obtained the identifying information in question. [B.J.F.'s] identity would never have come to light were it not for the erroneous, if inadvertent, inclusion by the Department of her full name in an incident report made available in a press room open to the public. [Where] as here, the government has failed to police itself in disseminating information, it is clear [that] the imposition of damages against the press for its subsequent publication can hardly be said to be a narrowly tailored means of safeguarding anonymity.

That appellant gained access to the information in question through a government news release makes it especially likely that, if liability were to be imposed, self-censorship would result. Reliance on a news release is a paradigmatically "routine newspaper reporting techniqu[e]." The government's issuance of such a release, without qualification, can only convey to recipients that the government considered dissemination lawful, and indeed expected the recipients to disseminate the information further. Had appellant merely reproduced the news release prepared and released by the Department, imposing civil damages would surely violate the First Amendment. The fact that appellant converted the police report into a news story by adding the linguistic connecting tissue necessary to transform the report's facts into full sentences cannot change this result.

A second problem with Florida's imposition of liability for publication is the broad sweep of the negligence per se standard applied under the civil cause of action implied from § 794.03. Unlike claims based on the common law tort of invasion of privacy, civil actions based on § 794.03 require no case-by-case findings that the disclosure of a fact about a person's private life was one that a reasonable person would find highly offensive. On the contrary, under the per se theory of negligence adopted by the courts below, liability follows automatically from publication. This is so regardless of whether the identity of the victim is already known throughout the community; whether the victim has voluntarily called public attention to the offense; or whether the identity of the victim has otherwise become a reasonable subject of public concern—because, perhaps, questions have arisen whether the victim fabricated an assault by a particular person. Nor is there a scienter requirement of any kind under § 794.03, engendering the perverse result that truthful publications challenged pursuant to this cause of action are less protected by the First Amendment than even the least protected defamatory falsehoods: those involving purely private figures, where liability is evaluated under a standard, usually applied by a jury, of ordinary negligence. See *Gertz.* * * *

Third, and finally, the facial underinclusiveness of § 794.03 raises serious doubts about whether Florida is, in fact, serving, with this statute, the significant interests which appellee invokes in support of affirmance. Section 794.03 prohibits the publication of identifying information only if this information appears in an "instrument of mass communication," a term the statute does not define. Section 794.03 does not prohibit the spread by other means of the identities of victims of sexual offenses. An individual who maliciously spreads word of the identity of a rape victim is thus not covered, despite the fact that the communication of such information to persons who live near, or work with, the victim may have consequences equally devastating as the exposure of her name to large numbers of strangers.

When a State attempts the extraordinary measure of punishing truthful publication in the name of privacy, it must demonstrate its commitment to advancing this interest by applying its prohibition evenhandedly, to the small-time disseminator as well as the media giant. Where important First Amendment interests are at stake, the mass scope of disclosure is not an acceptable surrogate for injury. Without more careful and inclusive precautions against alternative forms of dissemination, we cannot conclude that Florida's selective ban on publication by the mass media satisfactorily accomplishes its stated purpose.

Our holding today is limited. We do not hold that truthful publication is automatically constitutionally protected, or that there is no zone of personal privacy within which the State may protect the individual from intrusion by the press, or even that a State may never punish publication of the name of a victim of a sexual offense. We hold only that where a newspaper publishes truthful information which it has lawfully obtained, punishment may lawfully be imposed, if at all, only when narrowly tailored to a state interest of the highest order, and that no such interest is satisfactorily served by imposing liability under § 794.03 to appellant under the facts of this case. * * *

JUSTICE SCALIA, concurring in part and concurring in the judgment.

I think it sufficient to decide this case to rely upon the third ground set forth in the Court's opinion: that a law cannot be regarded as protecting an interest "of the highest order" and thus as justifying a restriction upon truthful speech, when it leaves appreciable damage to that supposedly vital interest unprohibited. In the present case, I would anticipate that the rape victim's discomfort at the dissemination of news of her misfortune among friends and acquaintances would be at least as great as her discomfort at its publication by the media to people to whom she is only a name. Yet the law in question does not prohibit the former in either oral or written form. Nor is it at all clear, as I think it must be to validate this statute, that Florida's general privacy law would prohibit such gossip. Nor, finally, is it credible that the interest meant to be served by the statute is the protection of the victim against a rapist still at large—an interest that arguably would extend only to mass publication. There would be little reason to limit a statute with that objective to rape alone; or to extend it to all rapes, whether or not the felon has been apprehended and confined. In any case, the instructions here did not require the jury to find that the rapist was at large.

This law has every appearance of a prohibition that society is prepared to impose upon the press but not upon itself. Such a prohibition does not protect an interest "of the highest order." For that reason, I agree that the judgment of the court below must be reversed.

JUSTICE WHITE, with whom THE CHIEF JUSTICE and JUSTICE O'CONNOR join, dissenting.

"Short of homicide, [rape] is the 'ultimate violation of self.' " *Coker v. Georgia,* [433 U.S. 584 (1977)] (opinion of White, J.). For B.J.F., however, the violation she suffered at a rapist's knife-point marked only the beginning of her ordeal. [Yet] today, the Court holds that a jury award of $75,000 to compensate B.J.F. for the harm she suffered due to the Star's negligence is at odds with the First Amendment. I do not accept this result.

[T]he three "independent reasons" the Court cites for reversing the judgment for B.J.F. [do not] support its result. The first of these reasons

[is] the fact "appellant gained access to [B.J.F.'s name] through a government news release." [But the] "release" of information provided by the government was not, as the Court says, "without qualification." As the Star's own reporter conceded at trial, the crime incident report that inadvertently included B.J.F.'s name was posted in a room that contained signs making it clear that the names of rape victims were not matters of public record, and were not to be published. The Star's reporter indicated that she understood that she "[was not] allowed to take down that information" (i.e., B.J.F.'s name) and that she "[was] not supposed to take the information from the police department." Thus, by her own admission the posting of the incident report did not convey to the Star's reporter the idea that "the government considered dissemination lawful"; the Court's suggestion to the contrary is inapt. * * *

Unfortunately, as this case illustrates, mistakes happen: even when States take measures to "avoid" disclosure, sometimes rape victim's names are found out. As I see it, it is not too much to ask the press, in instances such as this, to respect simple standards of decency and refrain from publishing a victim's name, address, and/or phone number.

Second, the Court complains [that] a newspaper might be found liable under the Florida courts' negligence per se theory without regard to a newspaper's scienter or degree of fault. The short answer to this complaint is that whatever merit the Court's argument might have, it is wholly inapposite here, where the jury found that appellant acted with "reckless indifference towards the rights of others," a standard far higher than the *Gertz* standard the Court urges as a constitutional minimum today.

But even taking the Court's concerns in the abstract, they miss the mark. [The] Court says that negligence per se permits a plaintiff to hold a defendant liable without a showing that the disclosure was "of a fact about a person's private life [that] a reasonable person would find highly offensive." But the point here is that the legislature—reflecting popular sentiment—has determined that disclosure of the fact that a person was raped is categorically a revelation that reasonable people find offensive. And as for the Court's suggestion that the Florida courts' theory permits liability without regard for whether the victim's identity is already known, or whether she herself has made it known—these are facts that would surely enter into the calculation of damages in such a case. In any event, none of these mitigating factors was present [here].

Third, the Court faults the Florida criminal statute for being underinclusive. [But] our cases which have struck down laws that limit or burden the press due to their underinclusiveness have involved situations where a legislature has singled out one segment of the news media or press for adverse treatment. Here, the Florida law evenhandedly covers all "instrument[s] of mass communication" no matter their form, media, content, nature or purpose. It excludes neighborhood gossips because presumably the Florida Legislature has determined that neighborhood gossips do not pose the danger and intrusion to rape victims that "instrument[s] of mass communication" do. Simply put: Florida wanted to prevent the widespread distribution of rape victim's names, and therefore enacted a statute tailored almost as precisely as possible to achieving that end. * * *

At issue in this case is whether there is any information about people, which—though true—may not be published in the press. [The] Court accepts appellant's invitation to obliterate one of the most note-worthy legal inventions of the 20th-Century: the tort of the publication of private facts. William Prosser, John Wade, & Victor Schwartz, *Torts* 951–952 (8th ed. 1988). Even if the Court's opinion does not say as much today, such obliteration will follow inevitably from the Court's conclusion here. [The] Court's ruling has been foreshadowed. In *Time, Inc. v. Hill,* we observed that—after a brief period early in this century where Brandeis' view was ascendant—the trend in "modern" jurisprudence has been to eclipse an individual's right to maintain private any truthful information that the press wished to publish. More recently, in *Cox Broadcasting,* we acknowledged the possibility that the First Amendment may prevent a State from ever subjecting the publication of truthful but private information to civil liability. Today, we hit the bottom of the slippery slope.

I would find a place to draw the line higher on the hillside: a spot high enough to protect B.J.F.'s desire for privacy and peace-of-mind in the wake of a horrible personal tragedy. There is no public interest in publishing the names, addresses, and phone numbers of persons who are the victims of crime—and no public interest in immunizing the press from liability in the rare cases where a State's efforts to protect a victim's privacy have failed. Consequently, I respectfully dissent.[5]

NOTES AND QUESTIONS

1. ***First Amendment value?*** Consider Gavin Phillipson, *Trial By Media: The Betrayal of the First Amendment's Purpose,* 71 Law & Contemp. Probs. 15 (2008): "The glaring omission in this case was the complete absence of any attempt to ask just how and why public understanding of the criminal justice system was served by its being informed of the name and address of a particular rape victim—in other words, by the particular news report in question."

2. ***Privacy: interest or right?*** Consider Steven J. Heyman, *Spheres of Autonomy: Reforming the Content Neutrality Doctrine in First Amendment*

---

[5]   **[Ct's Note]** The Court does not address the distinct constitutional questions raised by the award of punitive damages in this case. Consequently, I do not do so either. That award is more troublesome than the compensatory award discussed above. Cf. Note, *Punitive Damages and Libel Law,* 98 Harv.L.Rev. 847 (1985).

Jurisprudence, 10 Wm. & Mary Bill Rts. J. 647 (2002): "The Court's refusal to protect informational privacy may be attributed to several factors: the justices' discomfort at recognizing new categories of regulable speech; the quasi-absolutist view that, under the First Amendment, the state may rarely if ever regulate speech that is true; and the modern tendency to frame First Amendment problems as conflicts between the right to free speech and 'state interests,' rather than other rights. When the issue is viewed from a rights-based perspective, however, it is clear that privacy is no less deserving of protection than is reputation. Both are essential aspects of the right to an 'inviolate personality.' * * * Individuals generally should be entitled to decide for themselves whether to communicate highly personal information to others. [When] such information is published without consent, the subject in effect is forced to be an unwilling speaker."

3. ***Sexual history.*** If a court clerk accidentally sends the press a rape shield hearing transcript revealing the prior sexual history of an alleged rape victim, should a court order precluding publication of the transcript or the information in it be upheld? See David E. Fialkow, *The Media's First Amendment Rights and the Rape Victim's Right to Privacy,* 39 Suf. L.Rev. 745 (2006).

4. ***Outing.*** Should the First Amendment preclude a privacy cause of action against those who publicly disclose that a private person is gay? What if the person is a public official, e.g., a member of a board of education?[65] Would your answer to this question have been different in 1975? 2005? Or is the question about what an individual wishes to keep private rather than one of social values or social disapproval?

5. ***Internet liability.*** Suppose "Jack posts private details about Jill's love life on his blog. Jack's blog has a small readership. Marty, a blogger from a popular blog, with hundreds of thousands of readers, thinks that the story is interesting and posts excerpts of Jack's post." Who should be liable—Jack, Marty, or both? See Daniel J. Solove, *The Future of Reputation* 181–82 (2007).

6. ***Buying habits.*** Suppose government prohibits or provides tort relief against merchants who disseminate information about the buying habits of their customers or firms that traffic in similar data. Constitutional? Consider Eugene Volokh, *Freedom of Speech and Information Privacy: The Troubling Implications of a Right to Stop People from Speaking About You,* 52 Stan. L. Rev. 1049 (2000): "The difficulty is that the right to information privacy—my right to control your communication of personally identifiable information

---

[65] For diverse perspectives, see Rodney Smolla, *Free Speech in an Open Society,* 137–39 (1992); Susan Becker, *The Immorality of Publicly Outing Private People,* 73 Ore.L.Rev. 159 (1994); Barbara Moretti, *Outing: Justifiable or Unwarranted Invasion of Privacy? The Private Facts Tort As a Remedy for Disclosures of Sexual Orientation,* 11 Cardozo Arts & Ent.L.J. 857 (1993); Comment, *Forced Out of the Closet,* 46 U.Miami L.Rev. 413 (1992); Note, *Outing, Privacy, and the First Amendment,* 102 Yale L.J. 747 (1992); Note, *"Outing" and Freedom of the Press: Sexual Orientation's Challenge to the Supreme Court's Categorical Jurisprudence,* 77 Corn.L.Rev. 103 (1992).

about me—is a right to have the government stop you from speaking about me."

7.   *Voyeurism.* Is the direction of television programming less about encouraging democratic dialogue and more about encouraging a nation of voyeurs, people who watch others, but do not engage with them, people who enjoy prying into the affairs of others? Do voyeuristic desires deserve substantial First Amendment protection? See Clay Calvert, *The Voyeurism Value in First Amendment Jurisprudence,* 17 Cardoza Arts & Ent.L.J. 273 (1999). Do they exploit a "weakness that drives out (or at least diminishes) public attention to official actions and policies when offered more prurient alternatives." Paul Gewirtz, *Privacy and Speech,* 2001 Sup.Ct.Rev. 139.[66]

During the course of a cell phone conversation, the president of a local teacher's union, Kane, told his chief labor negotiator, Bartnicki: "If they're not gonna move for three percent, we're gonna have to go to their, their homes * * * To blow off their front porches, we'll have to do some work on some of those guys. (PAUSES). Really, uh, really and truthfully because this is, you know, this is bad news." The conversation was illegally intercepted by an unknown person and was sent to the head of a local taxpayer's organization, Yocum, who in turn, shared it with school board members and a local broadcaster, Vopper. Vopper played the tape on his radio show. Bartnicki and Kane brought an action against Yocum and Vopper invoking state and federal laws prohibiting the disclosure of material known to be unlawfully intercepted.

BARTNICKI v. VOPPER, 532 U.S. 514 (2001), per STEVENS, J., held the statutes unconstitutional as applied to circumstances in which the defendants played no role in the illegal acquisition of the material, their access to the conversation was obtained lawfully, and the conversation was about a public issue: "We agree with petitioners that 18 U.S.C. § 2511(1)(c), as well as its Pennsylvania analog, is in fact a content-neutral law of general applicability. [In] this case, the basic purpose of the statute at issue is to 'protec[t] the privacy of wire[, electronic,] and oral communications.' S.Rep. No. 1097, 90th Cong., 2d Sess., 66 (1968). The statute does not distinguish based on the content of the intercepted conversations, nor is it justified by reference to the content of those conversations. Rather, the communications at issue are singled out by virtue of the fact that they were

---

[66] On the relationship between privacy and public discourse, see J.M. Balkin, *How Mass Media Simulate Political Transparency,* 3 Cultural Values 393 (1999); Lee Bollinger, *Images of a Free Press* 34–35 (1991); Lili Levi, *Challenging the Autonomous Press,* 78 Cornell L.Rev. 665, 669–700 (1993); Robert F. Nagel, *Privacy and Celebrity: An Essay on the Nationalization of Intimacy,* 33 U.Rich.L.Rev. 1121 (2000); Sean M. Scott, *The Hidden First Amendment Values of Privacy,* 71 Wash.L.Rev. 683 (1996); Neil M. Richards, *The Puzzle of Brandeis, Privacy, and Speech,* 63 Vand. L.Rev. 1295 (2010).

illegally intercepted—by virtue of the source, rather than the subject matter.

"On the other hand, the naked prohibition against disclosures is fairly characterized as a regulation of pure speech. Unlike the prohibition against the 'use' of the contents of an illegal interception in § 2511(1)(d), subsection (c) is not a regulation of conduct. It is true that the delivery of a tape recording might be regarded as conduct, but given that the purpose of such a delivery is to provide the recipient with the text of recorded statements, it is like the delivery of a handbill or a pamphlet, and as such, it is the kind of 'speech' that the First Amendment protects.

"[As] a general matter, 'state action to punish the publication of truthful information seldom can satisfy constitutional standards.' *Daily Mail.* [The] Government identifies two interests served by the statute— first, the interest in removing an incentive for parties to intercept private conversations, and second, the interest in minimizing the harm to persons whose conversations have been illegally intercepted. We assume that those interests adequately justify the prohibition in § 2511(1)(d) against the interceptor's own use of information that he or she acquired by violating § 2511(1)(a), but it by no means follows that punishing disclosures of lawfully obtained information of public interest by one not involved in the initial illegality is an acceptable means of serving those ends.

"The normal method of deterring unlawful conduct is to impose an appropriate punishment on the person who engages in it. If the sanctions that presently attach to a violation of § 2511(1)(a) do not provide sufficient deterrence, perhaps those sanctions should be made more severe. But it would be quite remarkable to hold that speech by a law-abiding possessor of information can be suppressed in order to deter conduct by a non-law-abiding third party.[67]

"[With] only a handful of exceptions, the violations of § 2511(1)(a) that have been described in litigated cases have been motivated by either financial gain or domestic disputes. In virtually all of those cases, the identity of the person or persons intercepting the communication has been known. Moreover, petitioners cite no evidence that Congress viewed the prohibition against disclosures as a response to the difficulty of identifying persons making improper use of scanners and other surveillance devices and accordingly of deterring such conduct, and there is no empirical evidence to support the assumption that the prohibition against disclosures reduces the number of illegal interceptions.

"Although this case demonstrates that there may be an occasional situation in which an anonymous scanner will risk criminal prosecution by

---

[67] The Court recognized some exceptional cases, but stated the speech implicated was of minimal value, *New York v. Ferber*, Sec. 1, VI, A, infra (child pornography), or did not involve a prohibition of speech (possession or receipt of stolen mail or other property).

passing on information without any expectation of financial reward or public praise, surely this is the exceptional case. Moreover, there is no basis for assuming that imposing sanctions upon respondents will deter the unidentified scanner from continuing to engage in surreptitious interceptions. Unusual cases fall far short of a showing that there is a 'need of the highest order' for a rule supplementing the traditional means of deterring antisocial conduct. The justification for any such novel burden on expression must be 'far stronger than mere speculation about serious harms.' Accordingly, the Government's first suggested justification for applying § 2511(1)(c) to an otherwise innocent disclosure of public information is plainly insufficient.[19]

"The Government's second argument, however, is considerably stronger. Privacy of communication is an important interest, [and] the fear of public disclosure of private conversations might well have a chilling effect on private speech. [Accordingly], it seems to us that there are important interests to be considered on both sides of the constitutional calculus. In considering that balance, we acknowledge that some intrusions on privacy are more offensive than others, and that the disclosure of the contents of a private conversation can be an even greater intrusion on privacy than the interception itself. As a result, there is a valid independent justification for prohibiting such disclosures by persons who lawfully obtained access to the contents of an illegally intercepted message, even if that prohibition does not play a significant role in preventing such interceptions from occurring in the first place.

"We need not decide whether that interest is strong enough to justify the application of § 2511(c) to disclosures of trade secrets or domestic gossip or other information of purely private concern. In other words, the outcome of the case does not turn on whether § 2511(1)(c) may be enforced with respect to most violations of the statute without offending the First Amendment. The enforcement of that provision in this case, however, implicates the core purposes of the First Amendment because it imposes sanctions on the publication of truthful information of public concern.

"In this case, privacy concerns give way when balanced against the interest in publishing matters of public importance. [The] months of negotiations over the proper level of compensation for teachers at the Wyoming Valley West High School were unquestionably a matter of public concern, and respondents were clearly engaged in debate about that concern. That debate may be more mundane than the Communist rhetoric

---

[19] [Ct's Note] Our holding, of course, does not apply to punishing parties for obtaining the relevant information unlawfully. "It would be frivolous to assert—and no one does in these cases—that the First Amendment, in the interest of securing news or otherwise, confers a license on either the reporter or his news sources to violate valid criminal laws. Although stealing documents or private wiretapping could provide newsworthy information, neither reporter nor source is immune from conviction for such conduct, whatever the impact on the flow of news." *Branzburg.*

that inspired Justice Brandeis' classic opinion in *Whitney v. California*, but it is no less worthy of constitutional protection."

BREYER, J., joined by O'Connor, J., concurred: "I write separately to explain why, in my view, the Court's holding does not imply a significantly broader constitutional immunity for the media.

"[As] a general matter, despite the statutes' direct restrictions on speech, the Federal Constitution must tolerate laws of this kind because of the importance of these privacy and speech-related objectives. [Nonetheless], looked at more specifically, the statutes, as applied in these circumstances, do not reasonably reconcile the competing constitutional objectives. Rather, they disproportionately interfere with media freedom. For one thing, the broadcasters here engaged in no unlawful activity other than the ultimate publication of the information another had previously obtained. [For] another thing, the speakers had little or no legitimate interest in maintaining the privacy of the particular conversation. That conversation involved a suggestion about 'blow[ing] off . . . front porches' and 'do[ing] some work on some of these guys,' thereby raising a significant concern for the safety of others. Where publication of private information constitutes a wrongful act, the law recognizes a privilege allowing the reporting of threats to public safety. [Even] where the danger may have passed by the time of publication, that fact cannot legitimize the speaker's earlier privacy expectation. Nor should editors, who must make a publication decision quickly, have to determine present or continued danger before publishing this kind of threat.

"Further, the speakers themselves, the president of a teacher's union and the union's chief negotiator, were 'limited public figures,' for they voluntarily engaged in a public controversy. They thereby subjected themselves to somewhat greater public scrutiny and had a lesser interest in privacy than an individual engaged in purely private affairs. [This] is not to say that the Constitution requires anyone, including public figures, to give up entirely the right to private communication, i.e., communication free from telephone taps or interceptions. But the subject matter of the conversation at issue here is far removed from that in situations where the media publicizes truly private matters.

"Thus, in finding a constitutional privilege to publish unlawfully intercepted conversations of the kind here at issue, the Court does not create a 'public interest' exception that swallows up the statutes' privacy-protecting general rule. Rather, it finds constitutional protection for publication of intercepted information of a special kind. Here, the speakers' legitimate privacy expectations are unusually low, and the public interest in defeating those expectations is unusually high."

REHNQUIST, C.J., joined by Scalia and Thomas, JJ., dissented: "Technology now permits millions of important and confidential conversations to occur through a vast system of electronic networks. These advances, however, raise significant privacy concerns. We are placed in the uncomfortable position of not knowing who might have access to our personal and business e-mails, our medical and financial records, or our cordless and cellular telephone conversations. In an attempt to prevent some of the most egregious violations of privacy, the United States, the District of Columbia, and 40 States have enacted laws prohibiting the intentional interception and knowing disclosure of electronic communications. The Court holds that all of these statutes violate the First Amendment insofar as the illegally intercepted conversation touches upon a matter of 'public concern,' an amorphous concept that the Court does not even attempt to define. But the Court's decision diminishes, rather than enhances, the purposes of the First Amendment: chilling the speech of the millions of Americans who rely upon electronic technology to communicate each day. * * *

"The Court correctly observes that these are 'content-neutral law[s] of general applicability' which serve recognized interests of the 'highest order': 'the interest in individual privacy [and] in fostering private speech.' It nonetheless subjects these laws to the strict scrutiny normally reserved for governmental attempts to censor different viewpoints or ideas. There is scant support, either in precedent or in reason, for the Court's tacit application of strict scrutiny.

"[Here], Congress and the Pennsylvania Legislature have acted 'without reference to the content of the regulated speech.' There is no intimation that these laws seek 'to suppress unpopular ideas or information or manipulate the public debate' or that they 'distinguish favored speech from disfavored speech on the basis of the ideas or views expressed.' [As] the concerns motivating strict scrutiny are absent, these content-neutral restrictions upon speech need pass only intermediate scrutiny.

"[I]t is obvious that the *Daily Mail* cases upon which the Court relies do not address the question presented here. Our decisions themselves made this clear: 'The *Daily Mail* principle does not settle the issue whether, in cases where information has been acquired unlawfully by a newspaper or by a source, the government may ever punish not only the unlawful acquisition, but the ensuing publication as well.' *Florida Star.* [Undaunted], the Court places an inordinate amount of weight upon the fact that the receipt of an illegally intercepted communication has not been criminalized. But this hardly renders those who knowingly receive and disclose such communications 'law-abiding,' and it certainly does not bring them under the *Daily Mail* principle. The transmission of the intercepted communication from the eavesdropper to the third party is itself illegal; and where, as here, the third party then knowingly discloses that communication, another illegal act has been committed. The third party in this situation cannot be likened to the reporters in the *Daily Mail* cases, who lawfully obtained their information through consensual interviews or public documents. * * *

"The 'dry up the market' theory, which posits that it is possible to deter an illegal act that is difficult to police by preventing the wrongdoer from enjoying the fruits of the crime, is neither novel nor implausible. It is a time-tested theory that undergirds numerous laws, such as the prohibition of the knowing possession of stolen goods. See 2 W. LaFave & A. Scott, *Substantive Criminal Law* § 8.10(a), p. 422 (1986) ("Without such receivers, theft ceases to be profitable. It is obvious that the receiver must be a principal target of any society anxious to stamp out theft in its various forms"). We ourselves adopted the exclusionary rule based upon similar reasoning, believing that it would 'deter unreasonable searches,' *Oregon v. Elstad*, 470 U.S. 298, 306 (1985), by removing an officer's 'incentive to disregard [the Fourth Amendment],' *Elkins v. United States*, 364 U.S. 206, 217 (1960). * * * Reliance upon the 'dry up the market' theory is both logical and eminently reasonable, and our precedents make plain that it is 'far stronger than mere speculation.'

"These statutes also protect the important interests of deterring clandestine invasions of privacy and preventing the involuntary broadcast of private communications. [These] statutes undeniably protect this venerable right of privacy. [The] Court concludes that the private conversation between Gloria Bartnicki and Anthony Kane is somehow a 'debate * * * worthy of constitutional protection.' Perhaps the Court is correct that '[i]f the statements about the labor negotiations had been made in a public arena—during a bargaining session, for example—they would have been newsworthy.' The point, however, is that Bartnicki and Kane had no intention of contributing to a public 'debate' at all, and it is perverse to hold that another's unlawful interception and knowing disclosure of their conversation is speech 'worthy of constitutional protection.' * * *

"The Constitution should not protect the involuntary broadcast of personal conversations. Even where the communications involve public figures or concern public matters, the conversations are nonetheless private and worthy of protection. Although public persons may have forgone the right to live their lives screened from public scrutiny in some areas, it does not and should not follow that they also have abandoned their right to have a private conversation without fear of it being intentionally intercepted and knowingly disclosed."

NOTES AND QUESTIONS

1. ***The free speech value of privacy.*** Consider Daniel J. Solove, *Understanding Privacy*, 143 (2008): "Although protecting against disclosure can limit free speech, disclosure protections can promote the same interests free speech furthers. * * * Privacy encourages uninhibited speech by enabling

individuals to direct frank communications to those people they trust and who will not cause them harm because of what they [say]. Without protections against disclosure, people might be more reluctant to criticize aspects of their public lives, such as their employers." Solove also argues that disclosure inhibits autonomy, self-development, freedom of association, and the reading and consumption of ideas.

2. ***The value of a narrow audience.*** Consider Paul Gewirtz, *Privacy and Speech*, 2001 Sup.Ct.Rev. 139 (2001): " 'Private speech' might be related to public issues or might be preparation for an ultimately more 'public' formulation, but its value does not depend only on that, and that is not the primary reason we protect it from disclosure. We protect its privateness. We protect the right to choose a narrow audience, or no audience except oneself—to be what William Carlos Williams called 'lonely, lonely,' and as such to be 'the happy genius of my household.' "

3. ***The right to tell the truth.*** Consider Rodney A. Smolla, *Information as Contraband: The First Amendment and Liability for Trafficking in Speech*, 96 Nw. U.L. Rev. 1099 (2002): "The truism that truth is presumptively protected under the First Amendment is, like most truisms, true only as far as it goes. The 'right to print the truth' cases presented a formidable analytic problem for those seeking to justify Title III, but they were by no means self-evidently invincible. First, the *Daily Mail* principle clearly did not apply all the time. [If] the First Amendment were understood to create a presumptive right to publish anything that might be deemed 'true,' legal recourse for a vast array of injuries effectuated through the revelation of truthful material would be eviscerated, from the revelation of trade secrets to disclosure of information that one is contractually bound to keep confidential."[68]

4. ***Public/private.*** If the Court doubted the wisdom of distinguishing between matters of public and private concern in *Gertz*, is it wiser here? Can the Court adequately distinguish between the two? If it can, "should we be happy about placing final editorial review in the hands of judges who, after all, are agents of the government." Randall Bezanson, *How Free Can the Press Be?* 208 (2003).

5. ***The right to joke in private.*** Jeffrey Rosen, *The Purposes of Privacy: A Response*, 89 Geo. L.J. 2136–2137 (2001): "Of course Kane was not serious when he talked about blowing off the front porches of his opponents; he was engaging in the kind of hyperbole that many of us use in private to shock or amuse friends with our heretical thoughts, and so forth. Instead of putting the conversation in context, however, Vopper, the host of the radio station, exacerbated the danger of misunderstanding by airing the tape repeatedly on his show for three days, spicing up the broadcast with harsh criticism of the union leaders."

6. ***Should the original illegality matter?*** Under current First Amendment doctrine, illegality—as with the wiretapping in *Bartnicki*—is

---

[68] See also Howard M. Wasserman, *Bartnicki as Lochner*, 33 N.Ky.L. Rev. 421 (2006).

largely irrelevant as long as the publisher of the information is not actively involved in the illegality. See *New York Times Co. v. United States*, infra; *Landmark Communications v. Virginia*, infra. But the First Amendment has never been considered a bar to prosecuting the original leaker, and insofar as a downstream publisher is actively involved in the original leak the lessons of the earlier cases are not so clear. See Patricia L. Bellia, *Wikileaks and the Institutional Framework for National Security Disclosures*, 121 Yale L.J. 1448 (2012).

III. OWNERSHIP OF SPEECH

Former President Ford had contracted with Harper & Row and Readers Digest to publish his memoirs and granted them the right to license prepublication excerpts concentrating on his pardon of former President Nixon. Some weeks before a licensed article in Time was to appear, an unknown person presented the editor of The Nation with an unauthorized copy of the 200,000 word Ford manuscript from which the editor wrote a 2,250 word article entitled, "The Ford Memoirs—Behind the Nixon Pardon." The article included 26 verbatim quotations totaling 300 words of Ford's copyrighted expression and was timed to scoop Time. Accordingly, Time cancelled its article and refused to pay the publishers the remaining half of its $25,000 contract price.

In defense against the publishers' copyright claim, The Nation maintained that its publication was protected by the fair use provision of the Copyright Revision Act of 1976, 17 U.S.C. § 107 and by the First Amendment.

HARPER & ROW v. NATION ENTERPRISES, 471 U.S. 539 (1985), per O'CONNOR, J., concluded that neither defense was viable and that the fair use provision properly accommodated the relevant First Amendment interests: "Article I, § 8, of the Constitution provides that: 'The Congress shall have Power * * * to Promote the Progress of Science and useful Arts, by securing for limited Times to Authors and Inventors the exclusive Right to their respective Writings and Discoveries.' '[This] limited grant is a means by which an important public purpose may be achieved. It is intended to motivate the creative activity of authors and inventors by the provision of a special reward, and to allow the public access to the products of their genius after the limited period of exclusive control has expired.' The monopoly created by copyright thus rewards the individual author in order to benefit the public. This principle applies equally to works of fiction and nonfiction. The book at issue here, for example, was two years in the making, and began with a contract giving the author's copyright to the publishers in exchange for their services in producing and marketing the work. In preparing the book, Mr. Ford drafted essays and word portraits of public figures and participated in hundreds of taped interviews that were later distilled to chronicle his personal viewpoint. It is evident that the monopoly granted by copyright actively served its intended purpose of inducing the creation of new material of potential historical value.

"Section 106 of the Copyright Act confers a bundle of exclusive rights to the owner of the copyright. [T]hese rights—to publish, copy, and distribute the author's work—vest in the author of an original work from the time of its creation. In practice, the author commonly sells his rights to publishers who offer royalties in exchange for their services in producing and marketing the author's work. The copyright owner's rights, however, are subject to certain statutory exceptions. Among these is § 107 which codifies the traditional privilege of other authors to make 'fair use' of an earlier writer's work.[1] In addition, no author may copyright facts or ideas. § 102. The copyright is limited to those aspects of the work—termed 'expression'—that display the stamp of the author's originality.

"[T]here is no dispute that the unpublished manuscript of 'A Time to Heal,' as a whole, was protected by § 106 from unauthorized reproduction. Nor do respondents dispute that verbatim copying of excerpts of the manuscript's original form of expression would constitute infringement unless excused as fair use. Yet copyright does not prevent subsequent users from copying from a prior author's work those constituent elements that are not original—for example, quotations borrowed under the rubric of fair use from other copyrighted works, facts, or materials in the public domain—as long as such use does not unfairly appropriate the author's original contributions. Perhaps the controversy between the lower courts in this case over copyrightability is more aptly styled a dispute over whether The Nation's appropriation of unoriginal and uncopyrightable elements encroached on the originality embodied in the work as a whole. Especially in the realm of factual narrative, the law is currently unsettled regarding the ways in which uncopyrightable elements combine with the author's original contributions to form protected expression.

"We need not reach these issues, however, as The Nation has admitted to lifting verbatim quotes of the author's original language [constituting] some 13% of The Nation article. [To thereby] lend authenticity to its

---

[1]   **[Ct's Note]** Section 107 states: "Notwithstanding the provisions of section 106, the fair use of a copyrighted work [for] purposes such as criticism, comment, news reporting, teaching (including multiple copies for classroom use), scholarship, or research, is not an infringement of copyright. In determining whether the use made of a work in any particular case is a fair use the factors to be considered shall include—

"(1) the purpose and character of the use, including whether such use is of a commercial nature or is for nonprofit educational purposes;

"(2) the nature of the copyrighted work;

"(3) the amount and substantiality of the portion used in relation to the copyrighted work as a whole; and

"(4) the effect of the use upon the potential market for or value of the copyrighted work."

[For discussion of fair use in the trademark context, see William McGeveran, *Rethinking Trademark Fair Use*, 94 Iowa L.Rev. 49 (2008)].

account of the forthcoming memoirs, The Nation effectively arrogated to itself the right of first publication, an important marketable subsidiary right. For the reasons set forth below, we find that this use of the copyrighted manuscript, even stripped to the verbatim quotes conceded by The Nation to be copyrightable expression, was not a fair use within the meaning of the Copyright Act.

"[The] nature of the interest at stake is highly relevant to whether a given use is fair. [The] right of first publication implicates a threshold decision by the author whether and in what form to release his work. First publication is inherently different from other § 106 rights in that only one person can be the first publisher; as the contract with Time illustrates, the commercial value of the right lies primarily in exclusivity. [Under] ordinary circumstances, the author's right to control the first public appearance of his undisseminated expression will outweigh a claim of fair use.

"Respondents, however, contend that First Amendment values require a different rule under the circumstances of this case. [Respondents] advance the substantial public import of the subject matter of the Ford memoirs as grounds for excusing a use that would ordinarily not pass muster as a fair use—the piracy of verbatim quotations for the purpose of 'scooping' the authorized first serialization. Respondents explain their copying of Mr. Ford's expression as essential to reporting the news story it claims the book itself represents. In respondents' view, not only the facts contained in Mr. Ford's memoirs, but 'the precise manner in which [he] expressed himself was as newsworthy as what he had to say.' Respondents argue that the public's interest in learning this news as fast as possible outweighs the right of the author to control its first publication.

"The Second Circuit noted, correctly, that copyright's idea/expression dichotomy 'strike[s] a definitional balance between the First Amendment and the Copyright Act by permitting free communication of facts while still protecting an author's expression.' No author may copyright his ideas or the facts he narrates.

"Respondents' theory, however, would expand fair use to effectively destroy any expectation of copyright protection in the work of a public figure. Absent such protection, there would be little incentive to create or profit in financing such memoirs and the public would be denied an important source of significant historical information. The promise of copyright would be an empty one if it could be avoided merely by dubbing the infringement a fair use 'news report' of the book. * * *

"In our haste to disseminate news, it should not be forgotten that the Framers intended copyright itself to be the engine of free expression. By establishing a marketable right to the use of one's expression, copyright supplies the economic incentive to create and disseminate ideas. * * *

"Moreover, freedom of thought and expression 'includes both the right to speak freely and the right to refrain from speaking at all.' We do not suggest this right not to speak would sanction abuse of the copyright owner's monopoly as an instrument to suppress facts. [But] 'the essential thrust of the First Amendment is to prohibit improper restraints on the *voluntary* public expression of ideas; it shields the man who wants to speak or publish when others wish him to be quiet. There is necessarily, and within suitably defined areas, a concomitant freedom *not* to speak publicly, one which serves the same ultimate end as freedom of speech in its affirmative aspect.' *Estate of Hemingway v. Random House, Inc.,* 244 N.E.2d 250, 255 (N.Y. 1968). * * *

"In view of the First Amendment protections already embodied in the Copyright Act's distinction between copyrightable expression and uncopyrightable facts and ideas, and the latitude for scholarship and comment traditionally afforded by fair use, we see no warrant for expanding the doctrine of fair use to create what amounts to a public figure exception to copyright. Whether verbatim copying from a public figure's manuscript in a given case is or is not fair must be judged according to the traditional equities of fair use."

In assessing the equities, the Court found the purpose of the article to count against fair use, noting that the publication "went beyond simply reporting uncopyrightable information" and made "a 'news event' out of its unauthorized first publication," that the publication was "commercial as opposed to non-profit," that The Nation intended to supplant the "right of first publication," and that it acted in bad faith, for it "knowingly exploited a purloined manuscript." In considering the nature of the copyrighted work, the Court found it significant not only that Ford's work was yet unpublished, but also that The Nation had focused "on the most expressive elements of the work" in a way that exceeded "that necessary to disseminate the facts" and in a "clandestine" fashion that afforded no "opportunity for creative or quality control" by the copyright holder. In evaluating the amount and substantiality of the portion used, the Court cited the district court finding that "The Nation took what was essentially the heart of the book" and pointed to the "expressive value of the excerpts and their key role in the infringing work." Finally, the Court observed that the effect of the use on the market for the copyrighted work was the most important element. It found the Time contract cancellation to be "clear cut evidence of actual damage."

BRENNAN, J., joined by White and Marshall, JJ., dissented: "When The Nation was not quoting Mr. Ford, [its] efforts to convey the historical information in the Ford manuscript did not so closely and substantially track Mr. Ford's language and structure as to constitute an appropriation of literary form.

"[The] Nation is thus liable in copyright only if the quotation of 300 words infringed any of Harper & Row's exclusive rights under § 106 of the Act. [Limiting] the inquiry to the propriety of a subsequent author's use of the copyright owner's literary form is not easy in the case of a work of history. Protection against only substantial appropriation of literary form does not ensure historians a return commensurate with the full value of their labors. The literary form contained in works like 'A Time to Heal' reflects only a part of the labor that goes into the book. It is the labor of collecting, sifting, organizing and reflecting that predominates in the creation of works of history such as this one. The value this labor produces lies primarily in the information and ideas revealed, and not in the particular collocation of words through which the information and ideas are expressed. Copyright thus does not protect that which is often of most value in a work of history and courts must resist the tendency to reject the fair use defense on the basis of their feeling that an author of history has been deprived of the full value of his or her labor. A subsequent author's taking of information and ideas is in no sense piratical because copyright law simply does not create any property interest in information and ideas.

"The urge to compensate for subsequent use of information and ideas is perhaps understandable. An inequity seems to lurk in the idea that much of the fruit of the historian's labor may be used without compensation. This, however, is not some unforeseen by-product of a statutory scheme intended primarily to ensure a return for works of the imagination. Congress made the affirmative choice that the copyright laws should apply in this way: 'Copyright does not preclude others from using the ideas or information revealed by the author's work. It pertains to the literary [form] in which the author expressed intellectual concepts.' This distinction is at the essence of copyright. The copyright laws serve as the 'engine of free expression,' only when the statutory monopoly does not choke off multifarious indirect uses and consequent broad dissemination of information and ideas. To ensure the progress of arts and sciences and the integrity of First Amendment values, ideas and information must not be freighted with claims of proprietary right.[13]

"In my judgment, the Court's fair use analysis has fallen to the temptation to find copyright violation based on a minimal use of literary form in order to provide compensation for the appropriation of information from a work of history."

Since news reporting is ordinarily conducted for profit and marked by attempts to "scoop" the opposition and by attempts to create "news events,"

---

[13] **[Ct's Note]** This congressional limitation on the scope of copyright does not threaten the production of history. That this limitation results in significant diminution of economic incentives is far from apparent. In any event noneconomic incentives motivate much historical research and writing. For example, former public officials often have great incentive to "tell their side of the story." And much history is the product of academic scholarship. Perhaps most importantly, the urge to preserve the past is as old as human kind.

Brennan, J., found the drawing of any negative implications from these factors to be inconsistent with congressional recognition in § 107 that news reporting is a prime example of fair use. He found reliance on bad faith to be equally unwarranted: "No court has found that The Nation possessed the Ford manuscript illegally or in violation of any common law interest of Harper & Row; all common law causes of action have been abandoned or dismissed in this case. Even if the manuscript had been 'purloined' by someone, nothing in this record imputes culpability to The Nation. On the basis of the record in this case, the most that can be said is that The Nation made use of the contents of the manuscript knowing the copyright owner would not sanction the use.

"[T]he Court purports to rely on [the] factual findings that The Nation had taken 'the heart of the book.' This reliance is misplaced, and would appear to be another result of the Court's failure to distinguish between information and literary form. When the District Court made this finding, it was evaluating not the quoted words at issue here but the 'totality' of the information and reflective commentary in the Ford work. The vast majority of what the District Court considered the heart of the Ford work, therefore, consisted of ideas and information The Nation was free to use. It may well be that, as a qualitative matter, most of the value of the manuscript did lie in the information and ideas the Nation used. But appropriation of the 'heart' of the manuscript in this sense is irrelevant to copyright analysis because copyright does not preclude a second author's use of information and ideas.

"At least with respect to the six particular quotes of Mr. Ford's observations and reflections about President Nixon, I agree with the Court's conclusion that The Nation appropriated some literary form of substantial quality. I do not agree, however, that the substantiality of the expression taken was clearly excessive or inappropriate to The Nation's news reporting purpose.

"Had these quotations been used in the context of a critical book review of the Ford work, there is little question that such a use would be fair use within the meaning of § 107 of the Act. The amount and substantiality of the use—in both quantitative and qualitative terms—would have certainly been appropriate to the purpose of such a use. It is difficult to see how the use of these quoted words in a news report is less appropriate.

"The Nation's publication indisputably precipitated Time's eventual cancellation. But that does not mean that The Nation's use of the 300 quoted words caused this injury to Harper & Row. Wholly apart from these quoted words, The Nation published significant information and ideas from the Ford manuscript. [If] The Nation competed with Time, the competition was not for a share of the market in excerpts of literary form but for a share of the market in the new information in the Ford work. * * *

"Because The Nation was the first to convey the information in this case, it did perhaps take from Harper & Row some of the value that publisher sought to garner for itself through the contractual arrangement with Ford and the license to Time. Harper & Row had every right to seek to monopolize revenue from that potential market through contractual arrangements but it has no right to set up copyright [as] a shield from competition in that market because copyright does not protect information. The Nation had every right to seek to be the first to publish that information. * * *

"The Court's exceedingly narrow approach to fair use permits Harper & Row to monopolize information. This holding 'effect[s]' an important extension of property rights and a corresponding curtailment in the free use of knowledge and of ideas.' The Court has perhaps advanced the ability of the historian—or at least the public official who has recently left office—to capture the full economic value of information in his or her possession. But the Court does so only by risking the robust debate of public issues that is the 'essence of self-government.' *Garrison*. The Nation was providing the grist for that robust debate. The Court imposes liability upon The Nation for no other reason than that The Nation succeeded in being the first to provide certain information to the public."

NOTES AND QUESTIONS

1. ***Copyright and content discrimination.*** Consider C. Edwin Baker, *First Amendment Limits on Copyright*, 55 Vand. L. Rev. 891 (2002): "Copyright's policy concern arises only because the audience of purported infringers see or hear—mentally assimilate—the infringing content. If they did not—if they used the infringing material to wrap fish—the receipt of the infringing content would not (negatively) affect the market for the original content. [Nevertheless], copyright differs from typical cases of content suppression. It is designed to promote the very content—but not the same speaker—that it also suppresses. It suppresses content as a means of promoting the original creation, and presumably the subsequent commercial distribution, of the *same* content. Its aim is to have *more* of the content that, in relation to some speakers, it also suppresses." Is that aim consistently realized? Consider Rebecca Tushnet, *Copy This Essay: How Fair Use Doctrine Harms Free Speech and How Copying Serves It*, 114 Yale L.J. 535 (2004): "Copyright is undoubtedly an engine of free expression, as it supports both large corporations and individual artists so that they can afford to be in the business of speaking. Unfortunately, however, there is not much evidence about the ideal scope of copyright or its ideal term."

2. ***Copyright and fair use.*** Consider Jed Rubenfeld, *The Freedom of Imagination: Copyright's Constitutionality*, 112 Yale L.J. 1 (2002): "Under the first factor of fair use doctrine (nature or purpose of the use), 'parodic' and 'critical' treatments of copyrighted material are highly favored. In other words, if you and I borrow exactly the same amount of material from a copyrighted

work, I may escape liability because my speech criticized the copyrighted work, while you may be forced to pay damages because yours did not. Commentators typically present the 'parody' and 'criticism' features of fair use doctrine as a First Amendment plus or even a First Amendment 'surrogate.' They do not seem to notice that it renders copyright law viewpoint-discriminatory, which, as noted earlier, amount almost everywhere else in free speech law to virtually a per se constitutional violation." Cf. Rebecca Tushnet, *Copyright as a Model for Free Speech Law: What Copyright Has in Common with Anti-Pornography Laws, Campaign Finance Reform, and Telecommunications Regulation*, 42 B.C. L. Rev. 1 (2000): "Even without the public interest subfactor, one might wonder whether fair use is unconstitutional because it discriminates on the basis of content. Fair use favors copying, even pure copying, for educational and news reporting purposes. The Supreme Court, evaluating an anticounterfeiting law that prohibited certain reproductions of images of currency but made exceptions for newsworthiness or educational value, found that these exceptions were impermissibly content-based. There seems to be no reason that the exceptions would lose their content-based nature when applied to copyright." See also Eugene Volokh, *Freedom of Speech and Intellectual Property: Some Thoughts After Eldred, 44 Liquormart, and Bartnicki*, 40 Hous. L. Rev. 697 (2003). But consider Christopher L. Eisgruber, *Censorship, Copyright, and Free Speech: Some Tentative Skepticism About the Campaign to Impose First Amendment Restrictions on Copyright Law*, 2 J. Telecomm. & High Tech. L. 17 (2003): "There is something odd about this argument. It asks us to believe that copyright law becomes worse from a First Amendment perspective because of a restriction that not only makes it less restrictive, but does so with regard to core First Amendment subjects. Indeed, First Amendment doctrine itself contains a discrimination like the one in the "fair use" provisions. Under *Times v. Sullivan* and its progeny, defendants in libel suits acquire special First Amendment protection if their speech deals with matters of public concern. It would be strange if copyright law became subject to heightened First Amendment scrutiny only because it afforded speakers protections comparable to those recommended by the First Amendment itself."

Gertz was reluctant to make ad hoc judgments as to whether statements are or are not of general or public interest. Should the Court be similarly reluctant to make ad hoc judgments as to the bona fide news purpose of an article,[69] as to whether expression goes to the "heart of the book," or whether

---

[69] Compare *Regan v. Time, Inc.*, 468 U.S. 641 (1984): 18 U.S.C. § 474 makes it a crime to photograph United States currency, but exceptions for articles and books for newsworthy purposes are permitted so long as certain size and color requirements are satisfied. 18 U.S.C. § 504. The Court, per White, J., invalidated the purpose requirement: "A determination concerning the newsworthiness [of] a photograph cannot help but be based on the content of the photograph and the message it delivers. [Regulations] which permit the Government to discriminate on the basis of the content of the message cannot be tolerated under the First Amendment. The purpose requirement of § 504 is therefore constitutionally infirm." Stevens, J., dissenting on this point, observed that if the Court's language were applied literally, the constitutionality of the fair use provision of the Copyright Act would be "highly suspect." See Eugene Volokh, *Freedom of Speech and Intellectual Property: Some Thoughts After Eldred, 44 Liquormart, and Bartnicki*, 40 Hous. L. Rev. 697 (2003).

quoted words are "necessary" to communicate the "facts"? Is there an alternative to the making of such judgments?[70]

3.   Melville Nimmer had argued that in most cases the idea/expression dichotomy is central to resolving the clash between copyright and the First Amendment. *Does Copyright Abridge the First Amendment Guarantees of Free Speech and Press?* 17 UCLA L.Rev. 1180 (1970). Is the distinction satisfactory? Consider *Cohen v. California,* protecting Cohen's use of the phrase "Fuck the Draft": "[W]e cannot indulge the facile assumption that one can forbid particular words without running a substantial risk of suppressing ideas in the process." Cohen's counsel was—Professor Nimmer. Does *Nimmer On Copyright* collide with *Nimmer on Freedom of Speech?* For Nimmer's answer, see id. § 2.05(c), at 72–77; § 3.04, at 28 n. 11.

———

The 1976 Copyright Act generally provided copyright protection until 50 years after an author's death. The Copyright Term Extension Act of 1998 ("CTEA") extended the term to 70 years for new and existing copyrights.

ELDRED v. ASHCROFT, 537 U.S. 186 (2003), per GINSBURG, J., upheld the Act against a claim that the extended copyright protection to already existing intellectual property was unconstitutional: "Petitioners [argue] that the CTEA is a content-neutral regulation of speech that fails heightened judicial review under the First Amendment. We reject petitioners' plea for imposition of uncommonly strict scrutiny on a copyright scheme that incorporates its own speech-protective purposes and safeguards. The Copyright Clause and First Amendment were adopted close in time. This proximity indicates that, in the Framers' view, copyright's limited monopolies are compatible with free speech principles. Indeed, copyright's purpose is to *promote* the creation and publication of free expression. * * *

"In addition to spurring the creation and publication of new expression, copyright law contains built-in First Amendment accommodations. First, it distinguishes between ideas and expression and makes only the latter eligible for copyright protection. [Due] to this distinction, every idea, theory, and fact in a copyrighted work becomes instantly available for public exploitation at the moment of publication. * * *

"Second, the 'fair use' defense allows the public to use not only facts and ideas contained in a copyrighted work, but also expression itself in certain circumstances. [The] fair use defense affords considerable 'latitude for scholarship and comment,' and even for parody. The CTEA itself

---

[70] For additional criticism of the Court's copyright jurisprudence, see Matthew D. Bunker, *Adventures in Copyright Zone,* 14 Comm. L.& Pol'y 273 (2009); Jed Rubenfield, supra; Lawrence Lessig, *Copyright's First Amendment,* 48 UCLA L.Rev. 1057 (2001).

supplements these traditional First Amendment safeguards. First, it allows libraries, archives, and similar institutions to 'reproduce' and 'distribute, display, or perform in facsimile or digital form' copies of certain published works 'during the last 20 years of any term of copyright [for] purposes of preservation, scholarship, or research' if the work is not already being exploited commercially and further copies are unavailable at a reasonable price. Second, Title II of the CTEA, known as the Fairness in Music Licensing Act of 1998, exempts small businesses, restaurants, and like entities from having to pay performance royalties on music played from licensed radio, television, and similar facilities. * * *

"The First Amendment securely protects the freedom to make—or decline to make—one's own speech; it bears less heavily when speakers assert the right to make other people's speeches. To the extent such assertions raise First Amendment concerns, copyright's built-in free speech safeguards are generally adequate to address them. [W]hen, as in this case, Congress has not altered the traditional contours of copyright protection, further First Amendment scrutiny is unnecessary."[71]

BREYER, J., dissented: "The Copyright Clause and the First Amendment seek related objectives—the creation and dissemination of information. When working in tandem, these provisions mutually reinforce each other, the first serving as an 'engine of free expression,' the second assuring that government throws up no obstacle to its dissemination. At the same time, a particular statute that exceeds proper Copyright Clause bounds may set Clause and Amendment at cross-purposes, thereby depriving the public of the speech-related benefits that the Founders, through both, have promised. [The] majority [invokes] the 'fair use' exception, and it notes that copyright law itself is restricted to protection of a work's expression, not its substantive content. Neither the exception nor the restriction, however, would necessarily help those who wish to obtain from electronic databases material that is not there—say, teachers wishing their students to see albums of Depression Era photographs, to read the recorded words of those who actually lived under slavery, or to contrast, say, Gary Cooper's heroic portrayal of Sergeant York with filmed reality from the battlefield of Verdun. Such harm, and more, will occur despite the 1998 Act's exemptions and despite the other 'First Amendment safeguards' in which the majority places its trust. The statute falls outside the scope of legislative power that the Copyright Clause, read in light of the First Amendment, grants to Congress."[72]

---

[71] For discussion of issues regarding the "traditional contours" of copyright law, see *Golan v. Gonzales*, 501 F.3d 1179 (10th Cir. 2007).

[72] Although the majority argued that the act created incentives for the copyright holders to further invest in and disseminate their property, Breyer, J., rejoined: "This claim cannot justify this statute, however, because the rationale is inconsistent with the basic purpose of the Copyright Clause—as understood by the Framers and by this Court. The Clause assumes an initial grant of monopoly, designed primarily to encourage creation, followed by termination of the monopoly

NOTES AND QUESTIONS

1.   Consider David McGowan, *Why the First Amendment Cannot Dictate Copyright Policy*, 65 U. Pitt. L. Rev. 281 (2004): "The Supreme Court in *Eldred* was right to imply that authors who do their own work advance some free speech values that copiers do not. Autonomy of speakers and diversity of expression are two such values. They are not the only First Amendment values, of course, but they are important. Giving upstream authors strong rights, which is what we do now, gives downstream users an incentive to do more of their own work than they would have to do if they could copy at will. Congress is not required to adopt laws that give people incentives to do their own work rather than copying others, but the First Amendment certainly does not prohibit it from doing so." See also Daniel A. Farber, *Conflicting Visions and Contested Baselines: Intellectual Property and Free Speech in the "Digital Millennium,"* 89 Minn. L. Rev. 1318 (2005); But compare Rebecca Tushnet, note 1 after *Harper & Row*: "First Amendment doctrine should recognize the value of copying, which can be an important part of self-definition and of participation in culture, from singing the national anthem to discussing The West Wing online in exact detail."

2.   Consider Neil Weinstock Netanel, *Copyright and a Democratic Civil Society*, 106 Yale L.J. 283 (1996): "Copyright law strikes a precarious balance. To encourage authors to create and disseminate original expression, it accords them a bundle of proprietary rights in their works. But to promote public education and creative exchange, it invites audiences and subsequent authors to use existing works in every conceivable manner that falls outside the province of the copyright owner's exclusive rights." Does *Eldred* strike an appropriate balance?

3.   Consider William W. Van Alstyne, *Reconciling What the First Amendment Forbids with What the Copyright Clause Permits: A Summary Explanation and Review*, 66 Law & Contemp. Probs. 238 (2003): "The clause, again, is meant to put an end to one more kind of federalism question, and on that front, it deserves to be generously interpreted and applied in what it may confide to the discretion of Congress to legislate as it thinks best to do, in preemption of various regimes that might otherwise riddle the field. It 'preempts' nothing within the protection of the First Amendment, however, and any feature of any portion of any act Congress has, or may in the future, provide under sanction of this clause, may always be brought into question respecting whether, on its face or as applied, it offends against the larger

---

grant in order to promote dissemination of already-created works. It assumes that it is the *disappearance* of the monopoly grant, not its *perpetuation,* that will, on balance, promote the dissemination of works already in existence. This view of the Clause does not deny the empirical possibility that grant of a copyright monopoly to the heirs or successors of a long-dead author could *on occasion* help publishers resurrect the work, say, of a long-lost Shakespeare. But it does deny Congress the Copyright Clause power to base its actions primarily upon that empirical possibility—lest copyright grants become perpetual, lest on balance they restrict dissemination, lest too often they seek to bestow benefits that are solely retroactive." Stevens, J., also dissented.

freedom of speech and of the press provided constitutional sanctuary in the First Amendment still unfolding in the United States."

IV. OBSCENITY

A. The Search for a Rationale

Roth v. United States, 354 U.S. 476 (1957) held that obscenity was "not within the area of constitutionally protected speech or press" because, drawing from *Chaplinsky,* such utterances were *"no essential part of any exposition of ideas, and are of such slight social value as a step to truth that any benefit that may be derived from them is clearly outweighed by the social interest in order and morality."* [Emphasis in original]. The Court determined that sexually explicit material was not necessarily obscene. Instead the question was "whether to the average person, applying contemporary community standards, the dominant theme of the material taken as a whole appeals to prurient interest." Such material, according to the Court, was "utterly without redeeming social importance."

Despite *Roth*'s view that obscene speech had no First Amendment value, *Stanley v. Georgia,* 394 U.S. 557 (1969) concluded that the First Amendment protected the possession of obscene material in the home. The Court argued that the constitutional right "to receive information and ideas, regardless of their social worth, is fundamental to our free society." The Court distinguished the public distribution of obscene materials on the ground that there was a greater danger that such material might fall into the hands of children or "intrude on the sensibilities or privacy of the general public."

Many commentators believed that *Roth* and *Stanley* left the law in an unstable position. *Roth* had insufficiently supported the view that obscenity was without constitutional value and, as interpreted, had offered an approach to defining obscenity that was difficult for prosecutors; *Stanley's* logic went further and seemed to suggest that public showings of obscene material might be constitutional if children were excluded and if individuals were not exposed to the material without informed consent. *Paris Adult Theatre,* infra, attempted to provide a rationale for the regulation of obscenity that would prevent the showing of obscene material in public theaters; *Miller,* infra, sought to crystallize the definition of obscenity.

PARIS ADULT THEATRE I V. SLATON
413 U.S. 49, 93 S.Ct. 2628, 37 L.Ed.2d 446 (1973).

CHIEF JUSTICE BURGER delivered the opinion of the Court.

[The entrance to Paris Adult Theatres I & II was conventional and inoffensive without any pictures. Signs read: "Adult Theatre—You must be

21 and able to prove it. If viewing the nude body offends you, Please Do Not Enter." The District Attorney, nonetheless, had brought an action to enjoin the showing of two films that the Georgia Supreme Court described as "hard core pornography" leaving "little to the imagination." The Georgia Supreme Court assumed that the adult theaters in question barred minors and gave a full warning to the general public of the nature of the films involved, but held that the showing of the films was not constitutionally protected.]

[We] categorically disapprove the theory [that] obscene, pornographic films acquire constitutional immunity from state regulation simply because they are exhibited for consenting adults only. [Although we have] recognized the high importance of the state interest in regulating the exposure of obscene materials to juveniles and unconsenting adults, this Court has never declared these to be the only legitimate state interests permitting regulation of obscene material.

[W]e hold that there are legitimate state interests at stake in stemming the tide of commercialized obscenity, even assuming it is feasible to enforce effective safeguards against exposure to juveniles and to the passerby.[7] [These] include the interest of the public in the quality of life and the total community environment, the tone of commerce in the great city centers, and, possibly, the public safety itself. The Hill-Link Minority Report of the Commission on Obscenity and Pornography indicates that there is at least an arguable correlation between obscene material and crime. Quite apart from sex crimes, however, there remains one problem of large proportions aptly described by Professor Bickel: "It concerns the tone of the society, the mode, or to use terms that have perhaps greater currency, the style and quality of life, now and in the future. A man may be entitled to read an obscene book in his room, or expose himself indecently there. [We] should protect his privacy. But if he demands a right to obtain the books and pictures he wants in the market, and to foregather in public places—discreet, if you will, but accessible to all—with others who share his tastes, *then to grant him his right is to affect the world about the rest of us, and to impinge on other privacies.* Even supposing that each of us can, if he wishes, effectively avert the eye and stop the ear (which, in truth, we cannot), what is commonly read and seen and heard and done intrudes upon us all, want it or not." 22 *The Public Interest* 25, 25–26

---

[7]   **[Ct's Note]** It is conceivable that an "adult" theatre can—if it really insists—prevent the exposure of its obscene wares to juveniles. An "adult" bookstore, dealing in obscene books, magazines, and pictures, cannot realistically make this claim. The Hill-Link Minority Report of the Commission on Obscenity and Pornography emphasizes evidence (the Abelson National Survey of Youth and Adults) that, although most pornography may be bought by elders, "the heavy users and most highly exposed people to pornography are adolescent females (among women) and adolescent and young males (among men)." *The Report of the Commission on Obscenity* 401 (1970). The legitimate interest in preventing exposure of juveniles to obscene materials cannot be fully served by simply barring juveniles from the immediate physical premises of "adult" bookstores, when there is a flourishing "outside business" in these materials.

(Winter, 1971). (Emphasis supplied.) [T]here is a "right of the Nation and of the States to maintain a decent [society]," *Jacobellis* (Warren, C.J., dissenting).

But, it is argued, there is no scientific data which conclusively demonstrates that exposure to obscene materials adversely affects men and women or their society. It is urged [that], absent such a demonstration, any kind of state regulation is "impermissible." We reject this argument. It is not for us to resolve empirical uncertainties underlying state legislation, save in the exceptional case where that legislation plainly impinges upon rights protected by the Constitution itself. [Although] there is no conclusive proof of a connection between antisocial behavior and obscene material, the legislature of Georgia could quite reasonably determine that such a connection does or might exist. In deciding *Roth*, this Court implicitly accepted that a legislature could legitimately act on such a conclusion to protect "*the social interest in order and morality.*"

From the beginning of civilized societies, legislators and judges have acted on various unprovable assumptions. Such assumptions underlie much lawful state regulation of commercial and business affairs. The same is true of the federal securities, antitrust laws and a host of other federal regulations. [Likewise], when legislatures and administrators act to protect the physical environment from pollution and to preserve our resources of forests, streams and parks, they must act on such imponderables as the impact of a new highway near or through an existing park or wilderness area. [The] fact that a congressional directive reflects unprovable assumptions about what is good for the people, including imponderable aesthetic assumptions, is not a sufficient reason to find that statute unconstitutional.

If we accept the unprovable assumption that a complete education requires certain books, and the well nigh universal belief that good books, plays, and art lift the spirit, improve the mind, enrich the human personality and develop character, can we then say that a state legislature may not act on the corollary assumption that commerce in obscene books,[73] or public exhibitions focused on obscene conduct, have a tendency to exert a corrupting and debasing impact leading to antisocial behavior? [The] sum of experience, including that of the past two decades, affords an ample basis for legislatures to conclude that a sensitive, key relationship of human

---

[73] The only case after *Roth* in which the Court upheld a conviction based upon books was in *Mishkin* [Sec. 1, III, B infra] and most, if not all, of those books were illustrated. *Kaplan v. California,* 413 U.S. 115 (1973) held that books without pictures can be legally obscene "in the sense of being unprotected by the First Amendment." It observed that books are "passed hand to hand, and we can take note of the tendency of widely circulated books of this category to reach the impressionable young and have a continuing impact. A State could reasonably regard the 'hard core' conduct described by *Suite 69* as capable of encouraging or causing antisocial behavior, especially in its impact on young people." Is *Kaplan*'s explanation in tension with *Butler v. Michigan,* Sec. 1, III, B infra? Why should the obscenity standard focus on the average adult if the underlying worry is that books will fall in the hands of children?

existence, central to family life, community welfare, and the development of human personality, can be debased and distorted by crass commercial exploitation of sex. Nothing in the Constitution prohibits a State from reaching such a conclusion and acting on it legislatively simply because there is no conclusive evidence or empirical data.

[Nothing] in this Court's decisions intimates that there is any "fundamental" privacy right "implicit in the concept of ordered liberty" to watch obscene movies in places of public accommodation. [W]e have declined to equate the privacy of the home relied on in *Stanley* with a "zone" of "privacy" that follows a distributor or a consumer of obscene materials wherever he goes.[74]

[W]e reject the claim that Georgia is here attempting to control the minds or thoughts of those who patronize theatres. Preventing unlimited display or distribution of obscene material, which by definition lacks any serious literary, artistic, political, or scientific value as communication, is distinct from a control of reason and the intellect. Cf. John Finnis, *"Reason and Passion": The Constitutional Dialectic of Free Speech and Obscenity,* 116 U.Pa.L.Rev. 222, 229–230, 241–243 (1967).

[Finally], petitioners argue that conduct which directly involves "consenting adults" only has, for that sole reason, a special claim to constitutional protection. Our Constitution establishes a broad range of conditions on the exercise of power by the States, but for us to say that our Constitution incorporates the proposition that conduct involving consenting adults only is always beyond state regulation,[14] is a step we are unable to take.[15] [The] issue in this context goes beyond whether someone, or even the majority, considers the conduct depicted as "wrong" or "sinful." The States have the power to make a morally neutral judgment that public

---

[74] In a series of cases, the Court limited *Stanley* strictly to its facts. It held that Stanley did not apply to the possession of child pornography even in the home. *Osborne v. Ohio,* 495 U.S. 103 (1990). It held that *Stanley* did not protect the mailing of obscene material to consenting adults, *United States v. Reidel,* 402 U.S. 351, 91 S.Ct. 1410, 28 L.Ed.2d 813 (1971) or the transporting or importing of obscene materials for private use, *United States v. Orito,* 413 U.S. 139 (1973) (transporting); *United States v. 12 200-Ft. Reels,* 413 U.S. 123 (1973) (importing). Dissenting in *Reels,* Douglas, J., argued that *Stanley* rights could legally be realized "only if one wrote or designed a tract in his attic and printed or processed it in his basement, so as to be able to read it in his study." Do these decisions take the First Amendment out of *Stanley*? Are they justified by the rationale in *Paris Adult Theatre*? For example, does importation for personal use intrude "upon us all"? Affect the total community environment?

For the declaration that *Stanley's* "privacy of the home" principle is "firmly grounded" in the First Amendment while resisting the principle's expansion to protect consensual adult homosexual sodomy in the home, see *Bowers v. Hardwick,* Ch. 6, Sec. 2. But see Blackmun, J., joined by Brennan, Marshall, and Stevens, JJ., dissenting in *Bowers* ("*Stanley* rested as much on the Court's understanding of the Fourth Amendment as it did on the First").

[14] **[Ct's Note]** Cf. John Stuart Mill, *On Liberty* 13 (1955).

[15] **[Ct's Note]** The state statute books are replete with constitutionally unchallenged laws against prostitution, suicide, voluntary self-mutilation, brutalizing "bare fist" prize fights, and duels, although these crimes may only directly involve "consenting adults." Statutes making bigamy a crime surely cut into an individual's freedom to associate, but few today seriously claim such statutes violate the First Amendment or any other constitutional provision.

exhibition of obscene material, or commerce in such material, has a tendency to injure the community as a whole, to endanger the public safety, or to jeopardize, in Mr. Chief Justice Warren's words, the States' "right [to] maintain a decent society." *Jacobellis* (dissenting). * * *

JUSTICE BRENNAN, with whom JUSTICE STEWART and JUSTICE MARSHALL join, dissenting.

[I] am convinced that the approach initiated 15 years ago in *Roth* and culminating in the Court's decision today, cannot bring stability to this area of the law without jeopardizing fundamental First Amendment values, and I have concluded that the time has come to make a significant departure from that [approach.]

[The] decision of the Georgia Supreme Court rested squarely on its conclusion that the State could constitutionally suppress these films even if they were displayed only to persons over the age of 21 who were aware of the nature of their contents and who had consented to viewing them. [I] am convinced of the invalidity of that conclusion [and] would therefore vacate the [judgment]. I have no occasion to consider the extent of State power to regulate the distribution of sexually oriented materials to juveniles or to unconsenting [adults.] [*Stanley*] reflected our emerging view that the state interests in protecting children and in protecting unconsenting adults may stand on a different footing from the other asserted state interests. It may well be, as one commentator has argued, that "exposure to [erotic material] is for some persons an intense emotional experience. A communication of this nature, imposed upon a person contrary to his wishes, has all the characteristics of a physical assault. [And it] constitutes an invasion of his [privacy]." [But] whatever the strength of the state interests in protecting juveniles and unconsenting adults from exposure to sexually oriented materials, those interests cannot be asserted in defense of the holding of the Georgia Supreme Court, [which] assumed for the purposes of its decision that the films in issue were exhibited only to persons over the age of 21 who viewed them willingly and with prior knowledge of the nature of their contents. [The] justification for the suppression must be found, therefore, in some independent interest in regulating the reading and viewing habits of consenting [adults].

In *Stanley* we pointed out that "[t]here appears to be little empirical basis for" the assertion that "exposure to obscene materials may lead to deviant sexual behavior or crimes of sexual violence." In any event, we added that "if the State is only concerned about printed or filmed materials inducing antisocial conduct, we believe that in the context of private consumption of ideas and information we should adhere to the view that '[a]mong free men, the deterrents ordinarily to be applied to prevent crime are education and punishment for violations of the [law].' "

Moreover, in *Stanley* we rejected as "wholly inconsistent with the philosophy of the First Amendment," the notion that there is a legitimate state concern in the "control [of] the moral content of a person's thoughts." [The] traditional description of state police power does embrace the regulation of morals as well as the health, safety, and general welfare of the citizenry. [But] the State's interest in regulating morality by suppressing obscenity, while often asserted, remains essentially unfocused and ill-defined. And, since the attempt to curtail unprotected speech necessarily spills over into the area of protected speech, the effort to serve this speculative interest through the suppression of obscene material must tread heavily on rights protected by the First Amendment. * * *

In short, while I cannot say that the interests of the State—apart from the question of juveniles and unconsenting adults—are trivial or nonexistent, I am compelled to conclude that these interests cannot justify the substantial damage to constitutional rights and to this Nation's judicial machinery that inevitably results from state efforts to bar the distribution even of unprotected material to consenting adults.[75]

JUSTICE DOUGLAS, dissenting. * * *

"Obscenity" at most is the expression of offensive ideas. There are regimes in the world where ideas "offensive" to the majority (or at least to those who control the majority) are suppressed. There life proceeds at a monotonous pace. Most of us would find that world offensive. One of the most offensive experiences in my life was a visit to a nation where bookstalls were filled only with books on mathematics and books on religion.

I am sure I would find offensive most of the books and movies charged with being obscene. But in a life that has not been short, I have yet to be trapped into seeing or reading something that would offend me. I never read or see the materials coming to the Court under charges of "obscenity," because I have thought the First Amendment made it unconstitutional for me to act as a censor. * * *

NOTES AND QUESTIONS

1. **Speech v. conduct.** Is pornography predominantly a form of sexual conduct rather than a communicative process? Frederick Schauer, *Speech and "Speech"—Obscenity and "Obscenity": An Exercise in the Interpretation of Constitutional Language,* 67 Geo.L.J. 899 (1979). Is this reflected in the Court's definition? Consider James Weinstein, *Democracy, Sex, and the First Amendment,* 31 N.Y.U. Rev. L. & Soc. Change 865 (2007): "[I]n accordance with the basic rule that any use of a medium essential to public discourse is presumptively protected, graphic depictions of sexual conduct in these media

---

[75] For the portion of Brennan, J.'s dissent addressing the difficulties of formulating an acceptable constitutional standard, see *Miller v. California,* infra.

are, despite the physical effect they produce for many viewers, deemed public discourse rather than sexual conduct; this material loses protection only if a court determines that, taken as a whole, it is merely an appeal 'to the prurient interest in sex' rather than a 'serious' attempt to engage in informal politics or some other activity having First Amendment value."[76]

Is it possible that questions about the constitutional protection of obscenity are better situated, especially after *Lawrence v. Texas*, Ch. 6, Sec. 2, within the Due Process Clause than the First Amendment? See *United States v. Extreme Associates, Inc.*, 352 F.Supp.2d 578 (W.D. Pa), rev'd, 431 F.3d 150 (3d Cir. 2005). If obscenity, as legally defined and narrowed, lies outside the coverage of the First Amendment, was it necessary for the Court to devote so much attention to the justifications for regulation? Under the rational basis standard, would a one sentence reference to history, tradition, and morality have been enough?

2. ***Ideas and the First Amendment.*** KINGSLEY INT'L PICTURES CORP. v. REGENTS, 360 U.S. 684 (1959), per STEWART, J., underlined the distinction between obscenity and non-obscene "portrayal of sex" in art and literature. *Kingsley* held invalid New York's denial of a license to exhibit the film *Lady Chatterley's Lover* pursuant to a statute requiring such denial when a film "portrays acts of sexual immorality [as] desirable, acceptable or proper patterns of behavior": "[What] New York has done, [is] to prevent the exhibition of a motion picture because that picture advocates an idea—that adultery under certain circumstances may be proper behavior. Yet the First Amendment's basic guarantee is of freedom to advocate ideas. The State, quite simply, has thus struck at the very heart of constitutionally protected liberty."

3. ***Beauty and imagination.*** Does the protection of art depend upon the advocacy of ideas? Consider Harry Kalven, *The Metaphysics of the Law of Obscenity,* 1960 Sup.Ct.Rev. 1: "The classic defense of John Stuart Mill and the modern defense of Alexander Meiklejohn do not help much when the question is why the novel, the poem, the painting, the drama, or the piece of sculpture falls within the protection of the First Amendment. Nor do the famous opinions of Hand, Holmes, and Brandeis. [The] people do not need novels or dramas or paintings or poems because they will be called upon to vote. Art and belles-lettres do not deal in such ideas—at least not good art or belles-lettres—and it makes little sense here to talk [of] whether there is still time for counter-speech.

"[B]eauty has constitutional status too, [and] the life of the imagination is as important to the human adult as the life of the intellect. I do not think that the Court would find it difficult to protect Shakespeare, even though it is hard to enumerate the important ideas in the plays and poems. I am only suggesting that Mr. Justice Brennan [in *Roth*] might not have found it so easy to dismiss

---

[76] For commentary, see Andrew Koppelman, *Free Speech and Pornography,* 31 N.Y.U. Rev. L. & Soc. Change 899 (2007).

obscene ity because it lacked socially useful ideas if he had recognized that as to this point, at least, obscenity is in the same position as all art and literature."

See also Jed Rubenfeld, *The Freedom of Imagination: Copyright's Constitutionality*, 112 Yale L.J. 1 (2002): "The freedom of imagination extends far beyond art and entertainment. Philosophy is an exercise of the imagination too. So is prayer. So is a call for political change. The freedom of imagination, in other words, protects 'core' First Amendment speech just as it protects novels or pictures. It does so not because imagination informs voting, nor because imagination is central to individual autonomy. It does so because the freedom of imagination articulates the First Amendment's core commitment: that no one may be legally punished for thinking an unauthorized thought or for expressing an unauthorized idea." On freedom of thought as constituting the principal value served by the First Amendment, see Seana V. Shiffrin, *A Thinker-Based Approach to Freedom of Speech*, 278 Const.Comm. 283 (2011).

4. ***Politics v. art.*** Consider Steven D. Smith, *Believing Persons, Personal Believings: The Neglected Center of the First Amendment*, 2002 U. Ill. L. Rev. 1233 (2002): "Whether or not it is rational or explicitly political, music, painting, and poetry is typically as self-consciously a manifestation of central beliefs and attitudes (in all of their subjective richness) as almost any kind of expression can be. Indeed, from this perspective, art would seem to be even more central to the First Amendment's purpose than political speech."[77]

5. ***The moral rationale for prohibition.*** Is the value of obscenity "outweighed by the social interest in order and morality?" Consider Andrew Koppelman, *Does Obscenity Cause Moral Harm?*, 105 Colum. L. Rev. 1635, 1651 (2005): "[P]eople are animals. Sexual need is part of what makes us human. Lust depersonalizes, but it also personalizes. When I am the object of lust, this sometimes means that I am appreciated in the full embodied particularity of my self, as I am not if you only love me for my mind. A person is dehumanized in a distinctive way if she is never the object of anyone's lust. The precise letting go, in sex, of one's sober self-control that Kant feared is what D.H. Lawrence thought particularly valuable about sex." David Richards, *Free Speech and Obscenity Law: Toward A Moral Theory of the First Amendment,* 123 U.Pa.L.Rev. 45 (1974): "[P]ornography can be seen as the unique medium of a vision of sexuality [, a] view of sensual delight in the erotic celebration of the body, a concept of easy freedom without consequences, a fantasy of timelessly repetitive indulgence. In opposition to the Victorian view that narrowly defines proper sexual function in a rigid way that is analogous to ideas of excremental regularity and moderation, pornography builds a model of plastic variety and joyful excess in sexuality. In opposition to the sorrowing Catholic dismissal of sexuality as an unfortunate and spiritually superficial

---

[77] On the relationship between art and the first amendment, see Mark Tushnet, *Art and the First Amendment*, 35 Colum.J.L.& Arts 169 (2012). See also Marci A. Hamilton, *Art Speech*, 49 Vand.L.Rev. 73 (1996); Sheldon H. Nahmod, *Artistic Expression and Aesthetic Theory: The Beautiful, The Sublime and The First Amendment*, 1987 Wis.L.Rev. 221.

concomitant of propagation, pornography affords the alternative idea of the independent status of sexuality as a profound and shattering ecstasy."[78]

Even if this perspective were rejected on moral grounds, consider John Stuart Mill's statement of the harm principle in *On Liberty:* "[T]he only purpose for which power can be rightfully exercised over any member of a civilized community, against his will is to prevent harm to others." Is this a principle of free speech or simply a principle of freedom? On the distinction between Mill's harm principle and a principle of free speech, see Frederick Schauer, *On the Relation Between Chapters One and Two of John Stuart Mill's* On Liberty, 39 Cap.U.L.Rev. 571 (2011).

Does the liberal view overestimate human rational capacity and underestimate the importance of the state in promoting a virtuous citizenry? See generally Harry Clor, *Obscenity and Public Morality* (1969). Do liberals fail to appreciate the morally corrosive effects of obscenity? Consider the following observation: "Obscenity emphasizes the base animality of our nature, reduces the spirituality of humanity to mere bodily functions, and debases civilization by transforming the private into the public." Consider Irving Kristol, *Reflections of a Neoconservative* 45 (1983): "Bearbaiting and cockfighting are prohibited only in part out of compassion for the suffering animals; the main reason they were abolished was because it was felt that they debased and brutalized the citizenry who flocked to witness such spectacles. And the question we face with regard to pornography and obscenity is whether [they] can or will brutalize and debase our citizenry. We are, after all, not dealing with one passing incident—one book, or one play, or one movie. We are dealing with a general tendency that is suffusing our entire culture. [W]hen men and women make love, as we say, they prefer to be alone—because it is only when you are alone that you can make love, as distinct from merely copulating in an animal and casual way. And that, too, is why those who are voyeurs, if they are not irredeemably sick, also feel ashamed at what they are witnessing. When sex is a public spectacle, a human relationship has been debased into a mere animal connection."

6. ***Low First Amendment value.*** Consider Geoffrey R. Stone, *Sex, Violence, and the First Amendment,* 74 U.Chi. L.Rev. 1857 (2007): "[W]hy is obscenity of only low First Amendment value? [C]ase law [suggests] that several factors are relevant to the analysis. First, categories of low-value speech [do] not primarily advance political discourse. Second, categories of low-value speech are not defined in terms of disfavored ideas or political

---

[78] For the view that pornography can best be defended as a form of anti-social dissent, consider Steven Gey, *The Apologetics of Suppression,* 86 Mich.L.Rev. 1564 (1988): "Porn exposes a rot in the framework of society, and the great popularity of porn makes the burghers uneasily suspicious that the surface rot may evidence a more deeply rooted degeneration of their moral and political primacy. Thus, the imperative to suppress pornography reveals a much deeper and more insidious insecurity than the moralists will ever acknowledge." Cf. Robin West, *The Feminist-Conservative Anti-Pornography Alliance and the 1986 Attorney General's Commission on Pornography Report,* 1987 Am.B.Found.Res.J. 681 (discussing victimizing and liberating aspects of pornography from the perspectives of women while contending that women's experience of pornography, albeit diverse, is different from that of men).

viewpoints. Third low-value speech usually has a strong noncognitive effect on its audience. Fourth, categories of low-value speech have long been regulated without undue harm to the overall system of free expression." How many of these categories apply to literature in general?

B. A Revised Standard

MILLER V. CALIFORNIA
413 U.S. 15, 93 S.Ct. 2607, 37 L.Ed.2d 419 (1973).

CHIEF JUSTICE BURGER delivered the opinion of the Court. [The Court remanded, "for proceedings not inconsistent" with the opinion's obscenity standard, Miller's conviction under California's obscenity law for mass mailing of unsolicited pictorial advertising brochures depicting men and women in a variety of group sexual activities.]

This is one of a group of "obscenity-pornography" cases being reviewed by the Court in a re-examination of standards enunciated in earlier cases involving what Mr. Justice Harlan called "the intractable obscenity problem." [I]n this context[79] [we] are called on to define the standards which must be used to identify obscene material that a State may [regulate].

[Nine years after Roth], in Memoirs v. Massachusetts, 383 U.S. 413 (1966), the Court veered sharply away from the Roth concept and, with only three Justices in the plurality opinion, articulated a new test of obscenity. The plurality held that under the Roth definition "as elaborated in subsequent cases, three elements must coalesce: it must be established that (a) the dominant theme of the material taken as a whole appeals to a prurient interest in sex; (b) the material is patently offensive because it affronts contemporary community standards relating to the description or representation of sexual matters; and (c) the material is utterly without redeeming social value." [While] Roth presumed "obscenity" to be "utterly without redeeming social importance," Memoirs required that to prove obscenity it must be affirmatively established that the material is "utterly without redeeming social value."

Thus, even as they repeated the words of Roth, the Memoirs plurality produced a drastically altered test that called on the prosecution to prove a negative, i.e., that the material was "utterly without redeeming social value"—a burden virtually impossible to discharge under our criminal standards of proof. [Apart] from the initial formulation in Roth, no majority of the Court has at any given time been able to agree on a standard to

---

[79] The "context" was that in Miller "sexually explicit materials have been thrust by aggressive sales action upon unwilling recipients." But nothing in Miller limited the revised standard to that context, and the companion case, Paris Adult Theatre, applied the same standard to dissemination limited to consenting adults.

determine what constitutes obscene, pornographic material subject to regulation under the States' police power. See, e.g., *Redrup v. New York*, 386 U.S. 767 (1967).[3] This is not remarkable, for in the area of freedom of speech and press the courts must always remain sensitive to any infringement on genuinely serious literary, artistic, political, or scientific expression. * * *

II. This much has been categorically settled by the Court, that obscene material is unprotected by the First Amendment. [We] acknowledge, however, the inherent dangers of undertaking to regulate any form of expression. State statutes designed to regulate obscene materials must be carefully limited. As a result, we now confine the permissible scope of such regulation to works which depict or describe sexual conduct. That conduct must be specifically defined by the applicable state law, as written or authoritatively construed.[6] A state offense must also be limited to works which, taken as a whole, appeal to the prurient interest in sex, which portray sexual conduct in a patently offensive way, and which, taken as a whole, do not have serious literary, artistic, political, or scientific value.

The basic guidelines for the trier of fact must be: (a) whether "the average person, applying contemporary community standards" would find that the work, taken as a whole, appeals to the prurient interest, (b) whether the work depicts or describes, in a patently offensive way, sexual conduct specifically defined by the applicable state law,[80] and (c) whether the work, taken as a whole, lacks serious literary, artistic, political, or scientific value. We do not adopt as a constitutional standard the "*utterly without redeeming social value*" test of *Memoirs;* that concept has never commanded the adherence of more than three Justices at one time.[7] If a

---

[3]   **[Ct's Note]** In the absence of a majority view, this Court was compelled to embark on the practice of summarily reversing convictions for the dissemination of materials that at least five members of the Court, applying their separate tests, found to be protected by the First Amendment. *Redrup.* [Beyond] the necessity of circumstances, however, no justification has ever been offered in support of the *Redrup* "policy." The *Redrup* procedure has cast us in the role of an unreviewable board of censorship for the 50 States, subjectively judging each piece of material brought before us.

[6]   **[Ct's Note]** See, e.g., Oregon Laws 1971, c. 743, Art. 29, §§ 255–262, and Hawaii Penal Code, Tit. 37, §§ 1210–1216, 1972 Hawaii Session Laws, pp. 126–129, Act 9, Pt. II, as examples of state laws directed at depiction of defined physical conduct, as opposed to expression. [We] do not hold, as Mr. Justice Brennan intimates, that all States other than Oregon must now enact new obscenity statutes. Other existing state statutes, as construed heretofore or hereafter, may well be adequate.

[80]   On the use of guidelines (a) and (b) against sexual minorities, see Comment, *Behind the Curtain of Privacy: How Obscenity Laws Inhibit the Expression of Ideas About Sex and Gender,* 1998 Wis. L. Rev. 625 (1998).

[7]   **[Ct's Note]** "[We] also reject, as a constitutional standard, the ambiguous concept of 'social importance'." [*Hamling v. United States*, 418 U.S. 87 (1974), upheld a conviction in which the jury had been instructed to find that the material was "utterly without redeeming social value." Defendant argued that the latter phrase was unconstitutionally vague and cited *Miller.* The Court rejected the vagueness challenge: "[O]ur opinion in *Miller* plainly indicates that we rejected the '[social] value' formulation, not because it was so vague as to deprive criminal defendants of

state law that regulates obscene material is thus limited, as written or construed, the First Amendment values applicable to the States [are] adequately protected by the ultimate power of appellate courts to conduct an independent review of constitutional claims when necessary.

We emphasize that it is not our function to propose regulatory schemes for the States. [It] is possible, however, to give a few plain examples of what a state statute could define for regulation under the second part (b) of the standard announced in this opinion, supra:

(a) Patently offensive representations or descriptions of ultimate sexual acts, normal or perverted, actual or simulated.

(b) Patently offensive representations or descriptions of masturbation, excretory functions, and lewd exhibition of the genitals.[81]

Sex and nudity may not be exploited without limit by films or pictures exhibited or sold in places of public accommodation any more than live sex and nudity can be exhibited or sold without limit in such public places.[8] At a minimum, prurient,[82] patently offensive depiction or description of sexual conduct must have serious literary, artistic, political, or scientific value to merit First Amendment protection. For example, medical books for the education of physicians and related personnel necessarily use graphic illustrations and descriptions of human anatomy. In resolving the inevitably sensitive questions of fact and law, we must continue to rely on the jury system, accompanied by the safeguards that judges, rules of evidence, presumption of innocence and other protective features [provide].

---

adequate notice, but instead because it represented a departure from [*Roth*], and because in calling on the prosecution to 'prove a negative,' it imposed a '[prosecutorial] burden virtually impossible to discharge' and which was not constitutionally required."]

[81] *Jenkins v. Georgia,* 418 U.S. 153 (1974), unanimously held the film *Carnal Knowledge* not obscene because it did not ' "depict or describe patently offensive 'hard core' sexual conduct" ' as required by *Miller:* "[While there] are scenes in which sexual conduct including 'ultimate sexual acts' is to be understood to be taking place, the camera does not focus on the bodies of the actors at such times. There is no exhibition whatever of the actors' genitals, lewd or otherwise, during these scenes. There are occasional scenes of nudity, but nudity alone is not enough to make material legally obscene under the *Miller* standards." *Ward v. Illinois,* 431 U.S. 767 (1977) held that it was not necessary for the legislature or the courts to provide an "exhaustive list of the sexual conduct [the] description of which may be held obscene." It is enough that a state adopt *Miller*'s explanatory examples. Stevens, J., joined by Brennan, Stewart and Marshall, JJ., dissented: "[I]f the statute need only describe the 'kinds' of proscribed sexual conduct, it adds no protection to what the Constitution itself creates. [The] specificity requirement as described in *Miller* held out the promise of a principled effort to respond to [the vagueness] argument. By abandoning that effort today, the Court withdraws the cornerstone of the *Miller* [structure]."

[8] **[Ct's Note]** Although we are not presented here with the problem of regulating lewd public conduct itself, the States have greater power to regulate nonverbal, physical conduct than to suppress depictions or descriptions of the same behavior. * * *

[82] *Brockett v. Spokane Arcades, Inc.,* 472 U.S. 491 (1985) held that appeals to prurient interest could not be taken to include appeals to "normal" interests in sex. Only appeals to a "shameful or morbid interest in sex" are prurient. Although the Court was resolute in its position that appeals to "good, old fashioned, healthy" interests in sex were constitutionally protected, it did not further specify how "normal" sex was to be distinguished from the "shameful" or "morbid."

Mr. Justice Brennan [has] abandoned his former positions and now maintains that no formulation of this Court, the Congress, or the States can adequately distinguish obscene material unprotected by the First Amendment from protected expression, *Paris Adult Theatre I v. Slaton* (Brennan, J., dissenting). Paradoxically, Mr. Justice Brennan indicates that suppression of unprotected obscene material is permissible to avoid exposure to unconsenting adults, as in this case, and to juveniles, although he gives no indication of how the division between protected and nonprotected materials may be drawn with greater precision for these purposes than for regulation of commercial exposure to consenting adults only. Nor does he indicate where in the Constitution he finds the authority to distinguish between a willing "adult" one month past the state law age of majority and a willing "juvenile" one month younger.[83]

Under the holdings announced today, no one will be subject to prosecution for the sale or exposure of obscene materials unless these materials depict or describe patently offensive "hard core" sexual conduct specifically defined by the regulating state law, as written or construed. We are satisfied that these specific prerequisites will provide fair notice to a dealer in such materials that his public and commercial activities may bring prosecution. If the inability to define regulated materials with ultimate, god-like precision altogether removes the power of the States or the Congress to regulate, then "hard core" pornography may be exposed without limit to the juvenile, the passerby, and the consenting adult alike, as indeed, Mr. Justice Douglas contends.

[N]o amount of "fatigue" should lead us to adopt a convenient "institutional" rationale—an absolutist, "anything goes" view of the First Amendment—because it will lighten our burdens. [Nor] should we remedy "tension between state and federal courts" by arbitrarily depriving the States of a power reserved to them under the Constitution, a power which they have enjoyed and exercised continuously from before the adoption of

---

[83] The suggestion that the same book may be obscene in some contexts but not in others has been endorsed in several different contexts. *Butler v. Michigan,* 352 U.S. 380 (1957), held that the state could not ban sales to the general public of material unsuitable for children: "The State insists that [by] quarantining the general reading public against books not too rugged for grown men and women in order to shield juvenile innocence, it is exercising its power to promote the general welfare. Surely, this is to burn the house to roast the pig. [The] incidence of this enactment is to reduce the adult population of Michigan to reading only what is fit for children." *Ginsberg v. New York,* 390 U.S. 629 (1968), however, held that the state could bar the distribution to children of books that were suitable for adults, the Court recognizing it was adopting a "variable" concept of obscenity. See also *Ginzburg v. United States,* 383 U.S. 463 (1966) ("pandering" method of marketing supports obscenity conviction even though the materials might not otherwise have been considered obscene); *Mishkin v. New York,* 383 U.S. 502 (1966) (material designed for and primarily disseminated to deviant sexual group can meet prurient appeal requirement even if the material lacks appeal to an average member of the general public; appeal is to be tested with reference to the sexual interests of the intended and probable recipient group).

The variable obscenity approach had previously been advocated and elaborated by William Lockhart & Robert McClure, *Censorship of Obscenity: The Developing Constitutional Standards,* 45 Minn.L.Rev. 5 (1960).

the First Amendment to this day. See *Roth.* "Our duty admits of no 'substitute for facing up to the tough individual problems of constitutional judgment involved in every obscenity case.' " *Jacobellis* (opinion of Brennan, J.).

III. Under a national Constitution, fundamental First Amendment limitations on the powers of the States do not vary from community to community, but this does not mean that there are, or should or can be, fixed, uniform national standards of precisely what appeals to the "prurient interest" or is "patently offensive." These are essentially questions of fact, and our nation is simply too big and too diverse for this Court to reasonably expect that such standards could be articulated for all 50 States in a single formulation, even assuming the prerequisite consensus exists. When triers of fact are asked to decide whether "the average person, applying contemporary community standards" would consider certain materials "prurient," it would be unrealistic to require that the answer be based on some abstract formulation. The adversary system, with lay jurors as the usual ultimate fact finders in criminal prosecutions, has historically permitted triers-of-fact to draw on the standards of their community, guided always by limiting instructions on the law. To require a State to structure obscenity proceedings around evidence of a *national* "community standard" would be an exercise in [futility].

We conclude that neither the State's alleged failure to offer evidence of "national standards," nor the trial court's charge that the jury consider state community standards, were constitutional errors. Nothing in the First Amendment requires that a jury must consider hypothetical and unascertainable "national standards" when attempting to determine whether certain materials are obscene as a matter of [fact].

It is neither realistic nor constitutionally sound to read the First Amendment as requiring that the people of Maine or Mississippi accept public depiction of conduct found tolerable in Las Vegas, or New York City. People in different States vary in their tastes and attitudes, and this diversity is not to be strangled by the absolutism of imposed uniformity. As the Court made clear in *Mishkin,* the primary concern with requiring a jury to apply the standard of "the average person, applying contemporary community standards" is to be certain that, so far as material is not aimed at a deviant group, it will be judged by its impact on an average person, rather than a particularly susceptible or sensitive person—or indeed a totally insensitive one.[84] [We] hold the requirement that the jury evaluate

---

[84] *Pinkus v. United States,* 436 U.S. 293 (1978), upheld a jury instruction stating "you are to judge these materials by the standard of the hypothetical average person in the community, but in determining this average standard you must include the *sensitive and the insensitive,* in other words, [everyone] in the community." On the other hand, in the absence of evidence that "children were the intended recipients" or that defendant "had reason to know children were likely to receive the materials," it was considered erroneous to instruct the jury that children were part of the relevant community. *Butler.* When the evidence would support such a charge, the Court stated

the materials with reference to "contemporary standards of the State of California" serves this protective purpose and is constitutionally adequate.[85] * * *

In sum we (a) reaffirm the *Roth* holding that obscene material is not protected by the First Amendment, (b) hold that such material can be regulated by the States, subject to the specific safeguards enunciated above, without a showing that the material is "*utterly* without redeeming social value," and (c) hold that obscenity is to be determined by applying "contemporary community standards," not "national standards." * * *

JUSTICE DOUGLAS, dissenting. * * *

My contention is that until a civil proceeding has placed a tract beyond the pale, no criminal prosecution should be sustained. For no more vivid illustration of vague and uncertain laws could be designed than those we have fashioned. [If] a specific book [or] motion picture has in a civil proceeding been condemned as obscene and review of that finding has been completed, and thereafter a person publishes [or] displays that particular book or film, then a vague law has been made specific. There would remain the underlying question whether the First Amendment allows an implied exception in the case of obscenity. I do not think it does and my views on the issue have been stated over and again. But at least a criminal prosecution brought at that juncture would not violate the time-honored void-for-vagueness test.[8]

No such protective procedure has been designed by California in this case. Obscenity—which even we cannot define with precision—is a hodge-podge. To send men to jail for violating standards they cannot understand, construe, and apply is a monstrous thing to do in a Nation dedicated to fair trials and due process. * * *

JUSTICE BRENNAN, with whom JUSTICE STEWART and JUSTICE MARSHALL join, dissenting.

In my dissent in *Paris Adult Theatre,* decided this date, I noted that I had no occasion to consider the extent of state power to regulate the

---

that prurient appeal to deviant sexual groups could be substituted for appeal to the average person; moreover, the jury was entitled to take pandering into account. *Ginzburg.*

[85] *Jenkins,* fn. 81, supra, stated that a judge may instruct a jury to apply "contemporary community standards" without any further specification. Alternatively, the state may choose "to define the standards in more precise geographic terms, as was done by California in *Miller.*" *Hamling,* fn. 7 supra, interpreted a federal obscenity statute to make the relevant community the one from which the jury was drawn. The judge's instruction to consider the "community standards of the 'nation as a whole' delineated a wider geographical area than would be warranted by [*Miller*]" or the Court's construction of the statute, but the error was regarded as harmless under the circumstances. See also *Sable Communications v. FCC,* Sec. 8, II infra ("dial-a-porn" company bears burden of complying with congressional obscenity ban despite diverse local community standards). After these decisions, what advice should lawyers give to publishers who distribute in national markets?

[8] **[Ct's Note]** The Commission on Obscenity and Pornography has advocated such a procedure. [See] *Report of the Commission on Obscenity and Pornography* 70–71 (1970).

distribution of sexually oriented material to juveniles or the offensive exposure of such material to unconsenting adults. [I] need not now decide whether a statute might be drawn to impose, within the requirements of the First Amendment, criminal penalties for the precise conduct at issue here. For it is clear that under my dissent in *Paris Adult Theatre,* the statute under which the prosecution was brought is unconstitutionally overbroad, and therefore invalid on its face. * * *

[In his *Paris Adult Theatre* dissent, Brennan, J., joined by Stewart and Marshall, JJ., argued that the state interests in regulating obscenity were not strong enough to justify the degree of vagueness. He criticized not only the Court's standard in *Miller,* but also a range of alternatives:]

II. [The] essence of our problem [is] that we have been unable to provide "sensitive tools" to separate obscenity from other sexually oriented but constitutionally protected speech, so that efforts to suppress the former do not spill over into the suppression of the latter. [The dissent traced the Court's experience with *Roth* and its progeny.]

III. Our experience with the *Roth* approach has certainly taught us that the outright suppression of obscenity cannot be reconciled with the fundamental principles of the First and Fourteenth Amendments. For we have failed to formulate a standard that sharply distinguishes protected from unprotected speech, and out of necessity, we have resorted to the *Redrup* approach, which resolves cases as between the parties, but offers only the most obscure guidance to legislation, adjudication by other courts, and primary conduct. [T]he vagueness problem would be largely of our own creation if it stemmed primarily from our failure to reach a consensus on any one standard. But after 15 years of experimentation and debate I am reluctantly forced to the conclusion that none of the available formulas, including the one announced today, can reduce the vagueness to a tolerable level while at the same time striking an acceptable balance between the protections of the First and Fourteenth Amendments, on the one hand, and on the other the asserted state interest in regulating the dissemination of certain sexually oriented materials. Any effort to draw a constitutionally acceptable boundary on state power must resort to such indefinite concepts as "prurient interest," "patent offensiveness," "serious literary value," and the like. The meaning of these concepts necessarily varies with the experience, outlook, and even idiosyncracies of the person defining them. Although we have assumed that obscenity does exist and that we "know it when [we] see it," *Jacobellis* (Stewart, J., concurring), we are manifestly unable to describe it in advance except by reference to concepts so elusive that they fail to distinguish clearly between protected and unprotected speech.

[Added to the inherent vagueness of standards] is the further complication that the obscenity of any particular item may depend upon nuances of presentation and the context of its dissemination. See *Ginzburg*. [N]o one definition, no matter how precisely or narrowly drawn, can possibly suffice for all situations, or carve out fully suppressible expression from all media without also creating a substantial risk of encroachment upon the guarantees of the Due Process Clause and the First Amendment. [The] resulting level of uncertainty is utterly intolerable, not alone because it makes "[b]ookselling [a] hazardous profession," *Ginsberg* (Fortas, J., dissenting), but as well because it invites arbitrary and erratic enforcement of the law. [We] have indicated that "stricter standards of permissible statutory vagueness may be applied to a statute having a potentially inhibiting effect on speech; a man may the less be required to act at his peril here, because the free dissemination of ideas may be the loser." * * *

The problems of fair notice and chilling protected speech are very grave standing alone. But [a] vague statute in this area creates a third [set] of problems. These [concern] the institutional stress that inevitably results where the line separating protected from unprotected speech is excessively vague. [Almost] every obscenity case presents a constitutional question of exceptional difficulty. [As] a result of our failure to define standards with predictable application to any given piece of material, there is no probability of regularity in obscenity decisions by state and lower federal courts. [O]ne cannot say with certainty that material is obscene until at least five members of this Court, applying inevitably obscure standards, have pronounced it [so].

We have managed the burden of deciding scores of obscenity cases by relying on per curiam reversals or denials of certiorari—a practice which conceals the rationale of decision and gives at least the appearance of arbitrary action by this Court. More important, [the] practice effectively censors protected expression by leaving lower court determinations of obscenity intact even though the status of the allegedly obscene material is entirely unsettled until final review here. In addition, the uncertainty of the standards creates a continuing source of tension between state and federal [courts].

The severe problems arising from the lack of fair notice, from the chill on protected expression, and from the stress imposed on the state and federal judicial machinery persuade me that a significant change in direction is urgently required. I turn, therefore, to the alternatives that are now open.

IV. 1. The approach requiring the smallest deviation from our present course would be to draw a new line between protected and unprotected speech, still permitting the States to suppress all material on the unprotected side of the line. In my view, clarity cannot be obtained pursuant to this approach except by drawing a line that resolves all doubts in favor of state power and against the guarantees of the First Amendment.

We could hold, for example, that any depiction or description of human sexual organs, irrespective of the manner or purpose of the portrayal, is outside the protection of the First Amendment and therefore open to suppression by the States. That formula would, no doubt, offer much fairer notice [and] give rise to a substantial probability of regularity in most judicial determinations under the standard. But such a standard would be appallingly overbroad, permitting the suppression of a vast range of literary, scientific, and artistic masterpieces. Neither the First Amendment nor any free community could possibly tolerate such a standard.

2.   [T]he Court today recognizes that a prohibition against any depiction or description of human sexual organs could not be reconciled with the guarantees of the First Amendment. But the Court [adopts] a restatement of the *Roth-Memoirs* definition of obscenity [that] permits suppression if the government can prove that the materials lack "*serious literary, artistic, political or scientific value.*" [In] *Roth* we held that certain expression is obscene, and thus outside the protection of the First Amendment, precisely *because* it lacks even the slightest redeeming social value. [The] Court's approach necessarily assumes that some works will be deemed obscene—even though they clearly have *some* social value— because the State was able to prove that the value, measured by some unspecified standard, was not sufficiently "serious" to warrant constitutional protection. That result [is] nothing less than a rejection of the fundamental First Amendment premises and rationale of the *Roth* opinion and an invitation to widespread suppression of sexually oriented speech. Before today, the protections of the First Amendment have never been thought limited to expressions of *serious* literary or political value. *Gooding v. Wilson; Cohen v. California; Terminiello v. Chicago* [Sec. 1, V, B infra].

[T]he Court's approach [can] have no ameliorative impact on the cluster of problems that grow out of the vagueness of our current standards. Indeed, even the Court makes no argument that the reformulation will provide fairer notice to booksellers, theatre owners, and the reading and viewing public. Nor does the Court contend that the approach will provide clearer guidance to law enforcement officials or reduce the chill on protected expression [or] mitigate [the] institutional [problems].

Of course, the Court's restated *Roth* test does limit the definition of obscenity to depictions of physical conduct and explicit sexual acts. And that limitation may seem, at first glance, a welcome and clarifying addition to the *Roth-Memoirs* formula. But just as the agreement in *Roth* on an abstract definition of obscenity gave little hint of the extreme difficulty that was to follow in attempting to apply that definition to specific material, the mere formulation of a "physical conduct" test is no assurance that it can be applied with any greater facility. [The] Court surely demonstrates little sensitivity to our own institutional problems, much less the other vagueness-related difficulties, in establishing a system that requires us to consider whether a description of human genitals is sufficiently "lewd" to deprive it of constitutional protection; whether a sexual act is "ultimate"; whether the conduct depicted in materials before us fits within one of the categories of conduct whose depiction the state or federal governments have attempted to suppress; and a host of equally pointless inquiries. * * *

If the application of the "physical conduct" test to pictorial material is fraught with difficulty, its application to textual material carries the potential for extraordinary abuse. Surely we have passed the point where the mere written description of sexual conduct is deprived of First Amendment protection. Yet the test offers no guidance to us, or anyone else, in determining which written descriptions of sexual conduct are protected, and which are not.

Ultimately, the reformulation must fail because it still leaves in this Court the responsibility of determining in each case whether the materials are protected by the First Amendment. * * *

3. I have also considered the possibility of reducing our own role, and the role of appellate courts generally, in determining whether particular matter is obscene. Thus, [we] might adopt the position that where a lower federal or state court has conscientiously applied the constitutional standard, its finding of obscenity will be no more vulnerable to reversal by this Court than any finding of fact. [E]ven if the Constitution would permit us to refrain from judging for ourselves the alleged obscenity of particular materials, that approach would solve at best only a small part of our problem. For while it would mitigate the institutional stress, [it] would neither offer nor produce any cure for the other vices of vagueness. Far from providing a clearer guide to permissible primary conduct, the approach would inevitably lead to even greater uncertainty and the consequent due process problems of fair notice. And the approach would expose much protected, sexually oriented expression to the vagaries of jury determinations. Plainly, the institutional gain would be more than offset by the unprecedented infringement of First Amendment rights.

4. Finally, I have considered the view, urged so forcefully since 1957 by our Brothers Black and Douglas, that the First Amendment bars the suppression of any sexually oriented expression. That position would effect a sharp reduction, although perhaps not a total elimination, of the uncertainty that surrounds our current approach. Nevertheless, I am convinced that it would achieve that desirable goal only by stripping the States of power to an extent that cannot be justified by the commands of the Constitution, at least so long as there is available an alternative approach that strikes a better balance between the guarantee of free expression and the States' legitimate interests.

* * * I would hold, therefore, that at least in the absence of distribution to juveniles or obtrusive exposure to unconsenting adults, the First and Fourteenth Amendments prohibit the state and federal governments from attempting wholly to suppress sexually oriented materials on the basis of their allegedly "obscene" contents.[86] Nothing in this approach precludes those governments from taking action to serve what may be strong and legitimate interests through regulation of the manner of distribution of sexually oriented material.

VI. * * * I do not pretend to have found a complete and infallible [answer]. Difficult questions must still be faced, notably in the areas of distribution to juveniles and offensive exposure to unconsenting adults. Whatever the extent of state power to regulate in those areas,[29] it should be clear that the view I espouse today would introduce a large measure of clarity to this troubled area, would reduce the institutional pressure on this Court and the rest of the State and Federal judiciary, and would guarantee fuller freedom of expression while leaving room for the protection of legitimate governmental interests. * * *

NOTES AND QUESTIONS

1. ***Serious value.*** Consider Harry Clor, *Obscenity and the First Amendment: Round Three,* 7 Loy.L.A.L.Rev. 207 (1974): "The *Miller* decision abandons the requirement that a censorable work must be '*utterly* without redeeming social value' and substitutes the rule of 'serious value'—literary, artistic, political, or scientific. This is the most important innovation in the law of obscenity introduced by these decisions. [Serious] literature is to be protected regardless of majority opinions about prurience and offensiveness. *This* is the national principle which is not subject to variation from community to community. If it is to perform this function, the rule will have to be elaborated and the meaning of 'serious value' articulated in some measure. This is the most important item on the legal agenda."

(a) ***An independent factor.*** Under *Miller,* is material found to have "serious artistic value" entitled to First Amendment protection regardless of how offensive or prurient? *Pope v. Illinois,* 481 U.S. 497 (1987), and *Smith v. United States,* 431 U.S. 291 (1977), answer this question in the affirmative.

(b) ***"Serious."*** How is it to be determined when a First Amendment value in material depicting sexual conduct is sufficiently "serious" to preclude finding it obscene? Does *Pope* assist: "The proper inquiry is not whether an ordinary member of any given community would find serious literary, artistic, political, or scientific value[,] but whether a reasonable person would find such

---

[86] For the portion of Brennan, J.'s dissent addressing the strength and legitimacy of the state interests, see *Paris Adult Theatre,* supra.

[29] **[Ct's Note]** The Court erroneously states, *Miller,* that the author of this opinion "indicates that suppression of unprotected obscene material is permissible to avoid exposure to unconsenting adults [and] to juveniles * * * ." I defer expression of my views as to the scope of state power in these areas until cases squarely presenting these questions are before the Court.

value in the material taken as a whole." Consider Amy Adler, *Post-Modern Art and the Death of Obscenity Law*, 99 Yale L.J. 1359 (1990): "What did the *Miller* Court mean by 'serious artistic value'? There are at least three plausible interpretations: (1) the artwork makes an important and original rather than a marginal and derivative contribution to art; (2) the artwork is 'serious' in that it reflects the sanctity and solemnity of high art; (3) the artist was serious and sincere in his attempt to make art (rather than obscenity), no matter how successful his ultimate achievement."

(c) *Scope of protected values.* Could the Court consistent with the First Amendment exclude serious educational value from those that preclude a finding of obscenity? Serious entertainment value? Could the guidelines be interpreted to include such values? What might explain their omission?

2. *Vagueness and scienter.* Is the *Miller* test vague? Is it excessively so? Consider William B. Lockhart, *Escape from the Chill of Uncertainty: Explicit Sex and the First Amendment,* 9 Ga.L.Rev. 533 (1975): "[E]ither legislative action, or constitutional adjudication, could establish as a defense to a criminal obscenity prosecution that the defendant *reasonably believed* that the material involved was not obscene, that is, was constitutionally protected. [Material] that would support such a court or jury finding is not the kind that requires or justifies quick action by the police and prosecutor. The public interest in preventing distribution of borderline material that can reasonably be believed not obscene is not so pressing as to require immediate criminal sanctions and can adequately be protected by a declaratory judgment or injunction action to establish the obscenity of the material."

Smith v. California, 361 U.S. 147 (1959), invalidated an ordinance that dispensed with any requirement that a seller of an obscene book have knowledge of its contents, but did not decide what sort of mental element was needed to prosecute. *Hamling v. United States,* supra, stated that it was constitutionally sufficient to show that a distributor of an advertising collage of pictures of sexual acts "had knowledge of the contents of the materials [and] that he knew the character and nature of the materials."

3. *The practical impact of Miller.* Consider Edward de Grazia, *Girls Lean Back Everywhere: The Law of Obscenity and the Assault on Genius* 561–71 (1992): Until Powell, J., switched his vote, Brennan, J., and "a Court majority were preparing to reverse [Miller's] obscenity conviction. [T]he Burger revision of the Brennan doctrine was soon revealed to be a sort of paper tiger[, however]; by and large, there in fact occurred no observable retardation of the country's move during the decade that followed toward nearly absolute freedom for sexual expression in literary and artistic modes, including graphic or pictorial pornography; no increase in lower court convictions for obscenity; and no increase in prosecutorial [activity]." Cf. Daniel Mark Cohen, *Unhappy Anniversary: Thirty Years Since Miller v. California: The Legacy of the Supreme Court's Misjudgment on Obscenity*, 15 St. Thomas L. Rev. 545, 711 (2003). See also David Cole, *Playing by Pornography's Rules: The Regulation of Sexual Expression,* 143 U.Pa.L.Rev. 111 (1994): "Because this prohibition is

so narrow, it serves in practice not so much to purge the community of explicit sexually arousing speech as to validate everything that remains as nonoffensive, 'normal,' or socially valuable. In this way, obscenity doctrine collectively assures the community that the pornography it consumes at such a high rate is acceptable. [There] are the few who are actually prosecuted; given the remarkable amount and variety of sexual expression that goes without prosecution, to be prosecuted for obscenity these days is akin to being struck by lightning."

4.   *The increasing irrelevance of obscenity law.* For a combination of reasons—the fact that after *Miller* and *Jenkins* only the most minuscule sliver of sexually explicit materials might be legally obscene; changes in society's cultural mores; the difficulties of prosecution; and, most importantly, the ready availability on the Internet of even legally obscene materials— criminal obscenity prosecution has become largely a thing of the past. There are virtually no federal criminal prosecutions, and not many more at the state level.

C. Vagueness and Overbreadth: An Overview

In *Paris Adult Theatre,* Brennan, J., dissents on the ground that the obscenity statute is unconstitutionally vague. He envisions the possibility that an obscenity statute might overcome his vagueness objection if it were tailored to combat distribution to unconsenting adults or to children. In *Miller,* the materials were in fact distributed to unconsenting adults. There Brennan, J., does not reach the vagueness question but objects on the ground that the statute is overbroad,—i.e., it is not confined to the protection of unconsenting adults and children, but also prohibits distribution of obscene materials to consenting adults. In Brennan, J.'s view, even if the particular conduct at issue in *Miller* might be constitutionally prohibited by a narrower statute, it cannot be reached under a statute that sweeps so much protected speech within its terms.

The doctrines of "vagueness" and "overbreadth" referred to in Brennan, J.'s dissents are deeply embedded in First Amendment jurisprudence. At first glance, the doctrines appear discrete. A statute that prohibits the use of the words "kill" and "President" in the same sentence may not be vague, but it is certainly overbroad even though some sentences using those words may be unprotected. Conversely, a vague statute may not be overbroad; it may not pertain to First Amendment freedoms at all, or it may clearly be intended to exclude all protected speech from its prohibition but use vague language to accomplish that purpose.

Ordinarily, however, the problems of "vagueness" and "overbreadth" are closely related. An Airport Commissioners resolution banning all "First Amendment activities" in the Los Angeles International Airport was declared overbroad in *Board of Airport Commissioners v. Jews for Jesus,* 482 U.S. 569 (1987). Literally read the statute would have prevented anyone from talking or reading in the airport. But if the language literally covers a variety of constitutionally protected activities, it *cannot be read literally*. If the statute cannot be read according to its terms, however, problems of vagueness will often emerge. To be sure, statutes may be interpreted in ways that will avoid vagueness or overbreadth difficulties. See, e.g., *Scales v. United States,* Sec. 1, I, D supra. It is established doctrine, for example, that an attack based either upon vagueness or overbreadth will be unsuccessful in federal court if the statute in question is "readily subject to a narrowing construction by the state courts." *Young v. American Mini Theatres, Inc.; Erznoznik v. Jacksonville,* Sec. 3, I infra. Moreover, "[f]or the purpose of determining whether a state statute is too vague and indefinite to constitute valid legislation [the Court takes] 'the statute as though it read precisely as the highest court of the State has interpreted it.'" *Wainwright v. Stone,* 414 U.S. 21 (1973). Under this policy, a litigant can be prosecuted successfully for violating a statute that by its terms appears vague or overbroad but is interpreted by the state court in the same prosecution to mean something clearer or narrower than its literal language would dictate. *Cox v. New Hampshire,* Sec. 6, I, A infra. The harshness of this doctrine is mitigated somewhat by the fact that "unexpected" or "unforeseeable" judicial constructions in such contexts violate due process. See *Marks v. United States,* 430 U.S. 188 (1977).[87]

Somewhat more complicated is the issue of when general attacks on a statute are permitted. Plainly litigants may argue that statutes are vague as to their own conduct or that their own speech is protected. In other words, litigants are always free to argue that a statute is invalid "as applied" to their own conduct. The dispute concerns when litigants can attack a statute without reference to their own conduct, an attack sometimes called "on its face."

A separate question is: when should such attacks result in partial or total invalidation of a statute? The terminology here has become as confused as the issues. The Court has frequently referred to facial attacks on statutes in a way that embraces attempts at either partial or total invalidation. In some opinions, however, including those quoted below, it uses the term "facial attack" or "on its face" to refer only to arguments seeking total invalidation of a statute.

Terminology aside, one of the recurrent questions has been the extent to which litigants may argue that a statute is unconstitutionally overbroad even though their own conduct would not otherwise be constitutionally protected. This is often characterized as a standing issue. Ordinarily litigants do not have standing to raise the rights of others. But it has been argued that litigants should have standing to challenge overbroad statutes

---

[87] For commentary on overbreadth with special focus on the implications of the doctrine mentioned in this paragraph, see Richard Fallon, *Making Sense of Overbreadth*, 100 Yale L.J. 853 (1991).

even if their own conduct would be otherwise unprotected in order to prevent a chilling effect on freedom of speech. Alternatively, it has been argued that no standing problem is genuinely presented because "[u]nder 'conventional' standing principles, a litigant has always had the right to be judged in accordance with a constitutionally valid rule of law." Henry Monaghan, *Overbreadth,* 1981 S.Ct.Rev. 1. On this view, if a statute is unconstitutionally overbroad, it is not a valid rule of law, and any defendant prosecuted under the statute has standing to make that claim.[88] However the issue may be characterized, White, J., contended for many years that a litigant whose own conduct is unprotected should not prevail on an overbreadth challenge without a showing that the statute's overbreadth is "real and substantial." After much litigation, White, J., finally prevailed. The "substantial" overbreadth doctrine now burdens all litigants who argue that a statute should be declared overbroad when their own conduct would otherwise be unprotected.[89] *Brockett v. Spokane Arcades, Inc.; New York v. Ferber,* Sec. 1, V, A infra.

Less clear are the circumstances in which a litigant whose conduct *is* protected can go beyond a claim that the statute is unconstitutional "as applied" because litigants are always free to argue that their own conduct is protected. Moreover, the Court has stated that "[t]here is no reason to limit challenges to case-by-case 'as applied' challenges when the statute [in] all its applications falls short of constitutional demands."[90] *Secretary of State of Maryland v. Joseph H. Munson Co.,* 467 U.S. 947 (1984). How far beyond this the Court will go is unclear. In *Brockett v. Spokane Arcades, Inc.,* Sec. 1, III, B supra, it referred to the "normal rule that partial, rather than facial invalidation" of statutes is to be preferred and observed that: "[A]n individual whose own speech or expressive conduct may validly be prohibited or sanctioned is permitted to challenge a statute on its face because it also threatens others not before the court—those who desire to engage in legally protected expression but who may refrain from doing so rather than risk prosecution or undertake to have the law declared partially invalid. If the overbreadth is 'substantial,' the law may not be enforced against anyone, including the party before the court, until it is

---

[88] See also Henry Monaghan, *Third Party Standing,* 84 Colum.L.Rev. 277 (1984); Robert A. Sedler, *The Assertion of Constitutional Jus Tertii: A Substantive Approach,* 70 Calif.L.Rev. 1308 (1982) ("It may be the potential chilling effect upon others' expression that makes the statute invalid, but the litigant has his own right not to be subject to the operation of an invalid statute."). For criticism of the Monaghan position, see Fallon, fn. 87; Alfred Hill, *The Puzzling Overbreadth Doctrine,* 25 Hofstra L.Rev. 1063 (1997); Lawrence Gene Sager, *Foreword: State Courts and the Strategic Space Between the Norms and Rules of Constitutional Law,* 63 Tex. L.Rev. 959(1985).

[89] For commentary on the concept of "substantial" overbreadth, see Fallon, fn. 87 supra; Lawrence A. Alexander, *Is There an Overbreadth Doctrine,* 22 San Diego L.Rev. 541 (1985); Martin Redish, *The Warren Court, The Burger Court and the First Amendment Overbreadth Doctrine,* 78 Nw.U.L.Rev. 1031 (1983).

[90] There is a terminological dispute here. Compare *Los Angeles City Council v. Taxpayers For Vincent,* Sec. 6, II infra (such challenges are not overbreadth challenges) with *Munson,* supra (such challenges are properly called overbreadth challenges).

narrowed to reach only unprotected activity, whether by legislative action or by judicial construction or partial invalidation.

"It is otherwise where the parties challenging the statute are those who desire to engage in protected speech that the overbroad statute purports to punish, or who seek to publish both protected and unprotected material. There is then no want of a proper party to challenge the statute, no concern that an attack on the statute will be unduly delayed or protected speech discouraged. The statute may forthwith be declared invalid to the extent that it reaches too far, but otherwise left intact."[91]

Brockett takes the view that it must give standing to the otherwise unprotected to raise an overbreadth challenge, in order to secure the rights of those whose speech should be protected. But it sees no purpose in giving standing to the protected in order to secure rights for those whose speech should not be protected. This position is not without its ironies. In some circumstances, a litigant whose speech is unprotected will be in a better position than one whose speech is protected, at least if the litigant's goal is completely to stop enforcement of a statute.

Finally, what of the cases when it is uncertain whether the litigant's speech is protected? Should courts consider as applied attacks before proceeding to overbreadth attacks? *Board of Trustees v. Fox,* Sec. 3, III infra, declared it "not the usual judicial practice" and "generally undesirable" to proceed to an overbreadth challenge without first determining whether the statute would be valid as applied.[92] Yet the Court has frequently (see, e.g., Sec. 1, IV, C infra (fighting words cases; *Jews For Jesus*)) declared statutes overbroad without an as applied determination. The Court has yet systematically to detail the considerations relevant to separating the "usual" judicial practice from the unusual.

The issues with respect to vagueness challenges are similar. White, J., maintained that vagueness challenges should be confined to "as applied" attacks unless a statute were vague in all of its applications. Accordingly, if a statute clearly proscribed the conduct of a particular defendant, to allow that defendant to challenge a statute for vagueness would in his view have been "to confound vagueness and overbreadth." *Kolender v. Lawson,* 461 U.S. 352 (1983) (White, J., dissenting). In response, the Court stated that a facial attack upon a statute need not depend upon a showing of

---

[91] After the Court has declared that the statute is invalid to the extent it reaches too far, the remaining portion of the statute will be examined to determine whether that portion is severable. That is, it could well be the intent of the legislature that the statute stands or falls as a single package. To invalidate a part, then, could be to invalidate the whole. Alternatively, the legislature may have intended to salvage whatever it might. The question of severability is regarded as one of legislative intent, but, at least with respect to federal legislation, courts will presume that severability was intended. See, e.g., *Regan v. Time, Inc.,* 468 U.S. 641 (1984). The question of whether a provision of a state statute is severable is one of state law.

[92] The case arose in the federal courts, and the Court might be less likely to remand to a state court for an as applied determination, but the Court did not address that distinction.

vagueness in all of a statute's applications: "[W]e permit a facial challenge if a law reaches 'a substantial amount of constitutionally protected conduct,'" *Kolender*. Moreover, the Court has previously allowed litigants to raise the vagueness issue "even though there is no uncertainty about the impact of the ordinances on their own rights." *Young*. But see, e.g., *Broadrick v. Oklahoma,* Sec. 1, VI, A infra, in which White, J., writing for the Court suggested that standing to raise the vagueness argument should not be permitted in this situation.

Much less clear are the circumstances in which litigants whose conduct is *not* clearly covered by a statute can go beyond an "as applied" attack.[93] One approach would be to apply the same rule to all litigants, e.g., allowing total invalidation of statutes upon a showing of a "substantial" vagueness. In *Kolender,* the Court made no determination whether the statute involved was vague as to the defendant's own conduct; arguably, the opinion implied that it made no difference. Another approach would analogize to the approach suggested in *Brockett* for overbreadth challenges. Thus, a court might refrain from total invalidation of a statute and confine itself to striking the vague part insofar as the vague part seems to cover protected speech, leaving the balance of the statute intact. *Kolender* itself recites that the Court has "traditionally regarded vagueness and overbreadth as logically related and similar doctrines," but the Court's attitudes toward vagueness remain unclear. The questions of what standards should govern challenges to statutes that go beyond the facts before the Court, who should be able to raise the challenges, and under what circumstances have not been systematically and consistently addressed.[94]

V. "FIGHTING WORDS," OFFENSIVE WORDS AND HOSTILE AUDIENCES

A. Fighting Words

CHAPLINSKY v. NEW HAMPSHIRE, 315 U.S. 568 (1942): In the course of proselytizing on the streets, appellant, a Jehovah's Witness, denounced organized religion. Despite the city marshal's warning to "go slow" because his listeners were upset with his attacks on religion, appellant continued and a disturbance occurred. At this point, a police officer led appellant toward the police station, without arresting him. While en route, appellant again encountered the city marshal who had previously admonished him. Appellant then said to the marshal (he

---

[93] Conceivably, it could make a difference whether the litigants in this class of those "not clearly covered" have engaged in protected or unprotected conduct.

[94] For commentary on vagueness and overbreadth, see, e.g., Alexander, fn. 89 supra; Anthony Amsterdam, *The Void-For-Vagueness Doctrine in the Supreme Court,* 109 U.Pa.L.Rev. 67 (1960); David Bogen, *First Amendment Ancillary Doctrines,* 37 Md.L.Rev. 679 (1978); Monaghan, supra; Redish, supra; Note, *The First Amendment Overbreadth Doctrine,* 83 Harv.L.Rev. 844 (1970).

claimed, but the marshal denied, in response to the marshal's cursing him): "You are a God damned racketeer" and "a damned Fascist and the whole government of Rochester are Fascists or agents of Fascists."[95] He was convicted of violating a state statute forbidding anyone to address "any offensive, derisive or annoying word to any other person who is lawfully in any [public place] [or] call[ing] him by any offensive or derisive name." The Court, per MURPHY, J., upheld the conviction:

"There are certain well-defined and narrowly limited classes of speech, the prevention and punishment of which have never been thought to raise any Constitutional problem.[96] These include the lewd and obscene, the profane, the libelous, and the insulting or 'fighting' words—those which by their very utterance inflict injury or tend to incite an immediate breach of the peace. [S]uch utterances are no essential part of any exposition of ideas, and are of such slight social value as a step to truth that any benefit that may be derived from them is clearly outweighed by the social interest in order and morality. * * *[97]

"On the authority of its earlier decisions, the state court declared that the statute's purpose was to preserve the public peace, no words being 'forbidden except such as have a direct tendency to cause acts of violence by the person to whom, individually, the remark is addressed'. It was further said: 'The word "offensive" is not to be defined in terms of what a particular addressee thinks. [The] test is what men of common intelligence would understand would be words likely to cause an average addressee to

---

[95] The Supreme Court's version of the facts is sanitized. Bowering, the city marshall, stood by as a companion named Bowman punched Chaplinsky and later used a flagstaff as a spear in an effort to impale him. Without intervention from Bowering, the crowd demanded that Chaplinsky salute the flag and assaulted him when he refused. When Chaplinsky asked Bowering to arrest those who had committed violence against him, Bowering called him a damned bastard and demanded that he come along. Then Chaplinsky responded with epithets. Burton Caine, *The Trouble with "Fighting Words": Chaplinsky v. New Hampshire Is a Threat to First Amendment Values and Should Be Overruled*, 88 MARQ. L. REV. 441 (2004); Vincent Blasi & Seana V. Shiffrin, The Story of West Virginia State Board of Education v. Barnette, in *Constitutional Law Stories* 432 (Michael C. Dorf ed. 2004).

[96] See Franklyn Haiman, *How Much of Our Speech is Free?*, The Civ.Lib.Rev., Winter, 1975, p. 111: "[T]his discrimination between two classes of speech made its first U.S. Supreme Court appearance in *Cantwell v. Connecticut* (1940) [Ch. 8, Sec. 2, I]." Jehovah's Witnesses had been convicted of religious solicitation without a permit and of breach of the peace. The Court set aside both convictions. It invalidated the permit system for "religious" solicitation, because it permitted the licensing official to determine what causes were "religious," thus allowing a "censorship of religion." In setting aside the breach of peace conviction, because the offense covered much protected conduct and left "too wide a discretion in its application," the Court, per Roberts, J., noted: "One may, however, be guilty of [breach of the peace] if he commits acts or makes statements likely to provoke violence and disturbance of good order. [I]n practically all [such decisions to this effect], the provocative language [held to constitute] a breach of the peace consisted of profane, indecent or abusive remarks directed to the person of the hearer. *Resort to epithets or personal abuse is not in any proper sense communication of information or opinion safeguarded by the Constitution,* and its punishment as a criminal act [under a narrowly drawn statute] would raise no question under that instrument." (Emphasis added).

[97] For commentary on this paragraph, see Rodney A. Smolla, *Words "Which by Their Very Utterance Inflict Injury": The Evolving Treatment of Inherently Dangerous Speech in Free Speech Law and Theory*, 36 Pepp. L.Rev. 317 (2009).

fight. [The] English language has a number of words and expressions which by general consent are "fighting words" when said without a disarming smile. [Such] words, as ordinary men know, are likely to cause a fight. So are threatening, profane or obscene revilings. Derisive and annoying words can be taken as coming within the purview of the statute as heretofore interpreted only when they have this characteristic of plainly tending to excite the addressee to a breach of the peace. [The] statute, as construed, does no more than prohibit the face-to-face words plainly likely to cause a breach of the peace by the addressee, words whose speaking constitute a breach of the peace by the speaker—including "classical fighting words", words in current use less "classical" but equally likely to cause violence, and other disorderly words, including profanity, obscenity and threats.'

"[A] statute punishing verbal acts, carefully drawn so as not unduly to impair liberty of expression, is not too vague for a criminal law. * * * [8]

"Nor can we say that the application of the statute to the facts disclosed by the record substantially or unreasonably impinges upon the privilege of free speech. Argument is unnecessary to demonstrate that the appellations 'damn racketeer' and 'damn Fascist' are epithets likely to provoke the average person to retaliation, and thereby cause a breach of the peace.

"The refusal of the state court to admit evidence of provocation and evidence bearing on the truth or falsity of the utterances is open to no Constitutional objection. Whether the facts sought to be proved by such evidence constitute a defense to the charge or may be shown in mitigation are questions for the state court to determine. Our function is fulfilled by a determination that the challenged statute, on its face and as applied, does not contravene the Fourteenth Amendment."

NOTES AND QUESTIONS

1. *Fighting words and free speech values.* (a) *Self realization.* Does speech have to step toward truth to be of First Amendment value? Consider Martin Redish, *The Value of Free Speech,* 130 U.Pa.L.Rev. 591 (1982): "Why not view Chaplinsky's comments as a personal catharsis, as a means to vent his frustration at a system he deemed—whether rightly or wrongly—to be oppressive? Is it not a mark of individuality to be able to cry out at a society viewed as crushing the individual? Under this analysis, so-called 'fighting words' represent a significant means of self-realization, whether or not they can be considered a means of attaining some elusive 'truth.' "

---

[8] **[Ct's Note]** [Even] if the interpretative gloss placed on the statute by the court below be disregarded, the statute had been previously construed as intended to preserve the public peace by punishing conduct, the direct tendency of which was to provoke the person against whom it was directed to acts of violence. Appellant need not therefore have been a prophet to understand what the statute condemned.

(b) *Fighting words and truth.* Are fighting words always false? Should truth be a defense? Always? Is truth even relevant?

(c) *Fighting words and self-government.* Was Chaplinsky's statement *something other than* the expression of an idea? Did he wish to inform the marshal of his opinion of him and did he do so "in a way which was not only unquestionably clear, [but] all too clear"? Arnold Loewy, *Punishing Flag Desecrators,* 49 N.C.L.Rev. 48 (1970). How significant is it that Chaplinsky's remarks were not made in the context of a public debate or discussion of political or social issues? Or were they? Taking into account the events preceding Chaplinsky's remarks, and that the addressee was complicit in the physical and verbal abuse against Chaplinsky, that the addressee was an important public official in dereliction of his duties, was Chaplinsky's remark simply sharp criticism of government. In any event, should provocation be a defense? Burton Caine, *The Trouble with "Fighting Words": Chaplinsky v. New Hampshire Is a Threat to First Amendment Values and Should Be Overruled,* 88 Marq. L. Rev. 441 (2004).

2. *The social interest in order and morality.* What was the social interest in this case? (a) *The likelihood and immediacy of violent retaliation?* Should the Court have considered whether a *law enforcement officer* so reviled would have been provoked to retaliate? Whatever is assumed about the reaction of an average citizen to offensive words, may it be assumed that police are "trained to remain calm in the face of citizen anger such as that expressed by Chaplinsky"? Mark Rutzick, *Offensive Language and the Evolution of First Amendment Protection,* 9 Harv.Civ.Rts.—Civ.Lib.L.Rev. 1 (1974). See also Powell, J., concurring in *Lewis v. New Orleans,* Sec. 1, IV, C infra. Does the breach of the peace interest invite discriminatory enforcement? Consider Wendy B. Reilly, *Fighting the Fighting Words Standard: A Call For It's Destruction,* 52 Rutgers L. Rev. 947 (2000): "[I]t is possible that almost nothing one could say to a woman would be proscribed by the fighting words doctrine because women are presumed to be unlikely to respond to any words with physical violence. On the other hand, words said to Black or Latino men may be considered fighting words based on a perception that those men of color are particularly prone to violence."

(b) *Psychic harm?* May the *Chaplinsky* statute be viewed as "a special type of assault statute"? Would this be superior to a statute based on breach of the peace? Can there be verbal assaults that may create no risk of breach of peace?

B. Hostile Audiences

TERMINIELLO v. CHICAGO, 337 U.S. 1 (1949): Petitioner "vigorously, if not viciously" criticized various political and racial groups and condemned "a surging, howling mob" gathered in protest outside the auditorium in which he spoke. He called his adversaries "slimy scum," "snakes," "bedbugs," and the like. Those inside the hall could hear those on the outside yell, "Fascists, Hitlers!" The crowd outside tried to tear the clothes off those who entered. About 28 windows were broken; stink bombs were thrown. But in charging the jury, the trial court defined "breach of the peace" to include speech which "stirs the public to anger, *invites dispute,* [or] brings about a condition of unrest (emphasis added)." A 5–4 majority, per DOUGLAS, J., struck down the breach of peace ordinance as thus construed: "[A] function of free speech under our system of government is to invite dispute. It may indeed best serve its high purpose when it induces a condition of unrest, creates dissatisfaction with conditions as they are, or even stirs people to anger. [That] is why freedom of speech, though not absolute, *Chaplinsky,* is nevertheless protected against censorship or punishment, unless shown likely to produce a clear and present danger of a serious substantive evil that rises far above public inconvenience, annoyance, or unrest."

———

FEINER v. NEW YORK, 340 U.S. 315 (1951): Petitioner made a speech on a street corner in a predominantly black residential section of Syracuse, N.Y. A crowd of 75 to 80 persons, black and white, gathered around him, and several pedestrians had to go into the highway in order to pass by. A few minutes after he started, two police officers arrived and observed the rest of the meeting. In the course of his speech, publicizing a meeting of the Young Progressives of America to be held that evening in a local hotel and protesting the revocation of a permit to hold the meeting in a public school auditorium, petitioner referred to the President as a "bum," to the American Legion as "a Nazi Gestapo," and to the Mayor of Syracuse as a "champagne-sipping bum" who "does not speak for the Negro people." He also indicated in an excited manner: "The Negroes don't have equal rights; they should rise up in arms and fight for them."

These statements "stirred up a little excitement." One man indicated that if the police did not get that "S * * * O * * * B* * * " off the stand, he would do so himself. There was not yet a disturbance, but according to police testimony "angry muttering and pushing." In the words of the arresting officer whose testimony was accepted by the trial judge, he "stepped in to prevent it from resulting in a fight." After disregarding two requests to stop speaking, petitioner was arrested and convicted for disorderly conduct. The Court, per VINSON, C.J., affirmed: "The language of *Cantwell* is appropriate here. '[Nobody would] suggest that the principle of freedom of speech sanctions incitement to riot or that religious liberty connotes the privilege to exhort others to physical attack upon those belonging to another sect. When clear and present danger of riot, disorder, interference with traffic upon the public street or other immediate threat to public safety, peace, or order, appears, the power of the State to prevent or punish is obvious.'

"[It] is one thing to say that the police cannot be used as an instrument for the suppression of unpopular views, and another to say that, when as here the speaker passes the bounds of argument or persuasion and undertakes incitement to riot, they are powerless to prevent a breach of the peace. Nor in this case can we condemn the considered judgment of three New York courts approving the means which the police, faced with a crisis, used in the exercise of their power and duty to preserve peace and order."

BLACK, J., dissented: "The Court's opinion apparently rests on this reasoning: The policeman, under the circumstances detailed, could reasonably conclude that serious fighting or even riot was imminent; therefore he could stop petitioner's speech to prevent a breach of peace; accordingly, it was 'disorderly conduct' for petitioner to continue speaking in disobedience of the officer's request. As to the existence of a dangerous situation on the street corner, it seems far-fetched to suggest that the 'facts' show any imminent threat of riot or uncontrollable disorder. It is neither unusual nor unexpected that some people at public street meetings mutter, mill about, push, shove, or disagree, even violently, with the speaker. Indeed, it is rare where controversial topics are discussed that an outdoor crowd does not do some or all of these things. Nor does one isolated threat to assault the speaker forebode disorder. Especially should the danger be discounted where, as here, the person threatening was a man whose wife and two small children accompanied him and who, so far as the record shows, was never close enough to petitioner to carry out the threat.

"Moreover, assuming that the 'facts' did indicate a critical situation, I reject the implication of the Court's opinion that the police had no obligation to protect petitioner's constitutional right to talk. The police of course have power to prevent breaches of the peace. But if, in the name of preserving order, they ever can interfere with a lawful public speaker, they first must make all reasonable efforts to protect him. Here the policemen did not even pretend to try to protect petitioner. According to the officers' testimony, the crowd was restless but there is no showing of any attempt to quiet it; pedestrians were forced to walk into the street, but there was no effort to clear a path on the sidewalk; one person threatened to assault petitioner but the officers did nothing to discourage this when even a word might have sufficed. Their duty was to protect petitioner's right to talk, even to the extent of arresting the man who threatened to interfere. Instead, they shirked that duty and acted only to suppress the right to speak.

"Finally, I cannot agree with the Court's statement that petitioner's disregard of the policeman's unexplained request amounted to such 'deliberate defiance' as would justify an arrest or conviction for disorderly conduct. On the contrary, I think that the policeman's action was a 'deliberate defiance' of ordinary official duty as well as of the constitutional right of free speech. For at least where time allows, courtesy and explanation of commands are basic elements of good official conduct in a democratic society. Here petitioner was 'asked' then 'told' then 'commanded' to stop speaking, but a man making a lawful address is certainly not required to be silent merely because an officer directs it. Petitioner was entitled to know why he should cease doing a lawful act. Not once was he told."

DOUGLAS, J., joined by Minton, J., dissented: "A speaker may not, of course, incite a riot any more than he may incite a breach of the peace by the use of 'fighting words'. But this record shows no such extremes. It shows an unsympathetic audience and the threat of one man to haul the speaker from the stage. It is against that kind of threat that speakers need police protection. If they do not receive it and instead the police throw their weight on the side of those who would break up the meetings, the police become the new censors of speech. Police censorship has all the vices of the censorship from city halls which we have repeatedly struck down."

NOTES AND QUESTIONS

1.   What was the subject of disagreement in *Feiner*? (1) The standard for police interruption of a speech when danger of violence exists and the speaker intends to create disorder rather than to communicate ideas? (2) The standard when such danger exists, but the speaker only desires to communicate ideas? (3) Whether the danger of disorder and violence *was* plain and imminent? (4) Whether the speaker *did* intend to create disorder and violence? May *Feiner* be limited to the proposition that when a speaker "incites to riot"—but only then—police may stop him without bothering to keep his audience in check? Cf. *Sellers v. Johnson,* 163 F.2d 877 (8th Cir.1947), cert. denied, 332 U.S. 851 (1948).

2.   *Edwards v. South Carolina,* 372 U.S. 229 (1963), reversed a breach of the peace conviction of civil rights demonstrators who refused to disperse within 15 minutes of a police command. The Court maintained that the 200 to 300 onlookers did not threaten violence and that the police protection was ample. It described the situation as a "far cry from [*Feiner*]." Clark, J., dissenting, pointed to the racially charged atmosphere ("200 youthful Negro demonstrators were being aroused to a 'fever pitch' before a crowd of some 300 people who undoubtedly were hostile.") and concluded that city officials in good faith believed that disorder and violence were imminent. Did *Edwards* miss a golden opportunity to clarify *Feiner*? What if the crowd had been pushing, shoving and pressing more closely around the demonstrators in *Edwards*? Would the case still be a "far cry" from *Feiner* because the demonstrators had not "passed the bounds of argument or persuasion and undertaken incitement to riot"?

3.   In the advocacy of illegal action context, the fear of violence arises from audience cooperation with the speaker. In the hostile audience context, the fear of violence arises from audience conflict with the speaker. How do the

elements set out in *Brandenburg* relate to those implied in *Feiner*? How should they relate? Should the standard for "fighting words" cases be different from the "hostile audience" cases?

4. Should police be able to prosecute or silence disruptive audiences? Heckling audiences? In what contexts? See generally *In re Kay,* 464 P.2d 142 (Cal. 1970).

C. Offensive Words

COHEN V. CALIFORNIA
403 U.S. 15, 91 S.Ct. 1780, 29 L.Ed.2d 284 (1971).

JUSTICE HARLAN delivered the opinion of the Court.

[Defendant was convicted of violating that part of a general California disturbing-the-peace statute which prohibits "maliciously and willfully disturb[ing] the peace or quiet of any neighborhood or person" by "offensive conduct." He had worn a jacket bearing the plainly visible words "Fuck the Draft" in a Los Angeles courthouse corridor, where women and children were present. He testified that he did so as a means of informing the public of the depth of his feelings against the Vietnam War and the draft. He did not engage in, nor threaten, any violence, nor was anyone who saw him violently aroused. Nor was there any evidence that he uttered any sound prior to his arrest. In affirming, the California Court of Appeal construed "offensive conduct" to mean "behavior which has a tendency to provoke *others* to acts of violence or to in turn disturb the peace" and held that the state had proved this element because it was "reasonably foreseeable" that defendant's conduct "might cause others to rise up to commit a violent act against [him] or attempt to forceably remove his jacket."]

In order to lay hands on the precise issue which this case involves, it is useful first to canvass various matters which this record does *not* present.

The conviction quite clearly rests upon the asserted offensiveness of the *words* Cohen used to convey his message to the public. The only "conduct" which the State sought to punish is the fact of communication. Thus, we deal here with a conviction resting solely upon "speech," not upon any separately identifiable conduct which allegedly was intended by Cohen to be perceived by others as expressive of particular views but which, on its face, does not necessarily convey any message and hence arguably could be regulated without effectively repressing Cohen's ability to express himself. Cf. *United States v. O'Brien* [Sec. 2 infra]. Further, the State certainly lacks power to punish Cohen for the underlying content of the message the inscription conveyed. At least so long as there is no showing of an intent to incite disobedience to or disruption of the draft, Cohen could not, consistently with the First and Fourteenth Amendments, be punished for asserting the evident position on the inutility or immorality of the draft his jacket reflected. *Yates.*

Appellant's conviction, then, rests squarely upon his exercise [of] "freedom of speech" [and] can be justified, if at all, only as a valid regulation of the manner in which he exercised that freedom, not as a permissible prohibition on the substantive message it conveys. This does not end the inquiry, of course, for the First and Fourteenth Amendments have never been thought to give absolute protection to every individual to speak whenever or wherever he pleases, or to use any form of address in any circumstances that he chooses. In this vein, too, however, we think it important to note that several issues typically associated with such problems are not presented here.

In the first place, Cohen was tried under a statute applicable throughout the entire State. Any attempt to support this conviction on the ground that the statute seeks to preserve an appropriately decorous atmosphere in the courthouse where Cohen was arrested must fail in the absence of any language in the statute that would have put appellant on notice that certain kinds of otherwise permissible speech or conduct would nevertheless, under California law, not be tolerated in certain places. No fair reading of the phrase "offensive conduct" can be said sufficiently to inform the ordinary person that distinctions between certain locations are thereby created.[3]

In the second place, as it comes to us, this case cannot be said to fall within those relatively few categories of instances where prior decisions have established the power of government to deal more comprehensively with certain forms of individual expression simply upon a showing that such a form was employed. This is not, for example, an obscenity case. Whatever else may be necessary to give rise to the States' broader power to prohibit obscene expression, such expression must be, in some significant way, erotic. *Roth.* It cannot plausibly be maintained that this vulgar allusion to the Selective Service System would conjure up such psychic stimulation in anyone likely to be confronted with Cohen's crudely defaced jacket.

This Court has also held that the States are free to ban the simple use, without a demonstration of additional justifying circumstances, of so-called "fighting words," those personally abusive epithets which, when addressed to the ordinary citizen, are, as a matter of common knowledge, inherently likely to provoke violent reaction. *Chaplinsky.* While the four-letter word displayed by Cohen in relation to the draft is not uncommonly employed in a personally provocative fashion, in this instance it was clearly not

---

[3] **[Ct's Note]** It is illuminating to note what transpired when Cohen entered a courtroom in the building. He removed his jacket and stood with it folded over his arm. Meanwhile, a policeman sent the presiding judge a note suggesting that Cohen be held in contempt of court. The judge declined to do so and Cohen was arrested by the officer only after he emerged from the courtroom.

"directed to the person of the hearer." No individual actually or likely to be present could reasonably have regarded the words on appellant's jacket as a direct personal insult. Nor do we have here an instance of the exercise of the State's police power to prevent a speaker from intentionally provoking a given group to hostile reaction. Cf. *Feiner; Terminiello.* There is, as noted above, no showing that anyone who saw Cohen was in fact violently aroused or that appellant intended such a result.

[T]he mere presumed presence of unwitting listeners or viewers does not serve automatically to justify curtailing all speech capable of giving offense. While this Court has recognized that government may properly act in many situations to prohibit intrusion into the privacy of the home of unwelcome views and ideas which cannot be totally banned from the public dialogue, we have at the same time consistently stressed that "we are often 'captives' outside the sanctuary of the home and subject to objectionable speech."[98] The ability of government, consonant with the Constitution, to shut off discourse solely to protect others from hearing it is, in other words, dependent upon a showing that substantial privacy interests are being invaded in an essentially intolerable manner. Any broader view of this authority would effectively empower a majority to silence dissidents simply as a matter of personal predilections.

[Given] the subtlety and complexity of the factors involved if Cohen's "speech" was otherwise entitled to constitutional protection, we do not think the fact that some unwilling "listeners" in a public building may have been briefly exposed to it can serve to justify this breach of the peace conviction where, as here, there was no evidence that persons powerless to avoid appellant's conduct did in fact object to it, and where [unlike another portion of the same statute barring the use of "vulgar, profane or indecent language within [the] hearing of women or children, in a loud and boisterous manner"], the [challenged statutory provision] evinces no concern [with] the special plight of the captive auditor, but, instead, indiscriminately sweeps within its prohibitions all "offensive conduct" that disturbs "any neighborhood or person."

Against this background, the issue flushed by this case stands out in bold relief. It is whether California can excise, as "offensive conduct," one particular scurrilous epithet from the public discourse, either upon the theory of the court below that its use is inherently likely to cause violent reaction or upon a more general assertion that the States, acting as guardians of public morality, may properly remove this offensive word from the public vocabulary.

The rationale of the California court is plainly untenable. At most it reflects an "undifferentiated fear or apprehension of disturbance [which] is

---

[98] For commentary on the captive audience concept, see J.M. Balkin, *Free Speech and Hostile Environments,* 99 Colum. L.Rev. 2295 (1999).

not enough to overcome the right to freedom of expression." *Tinker* [Sec. 7, II infra]. We have been shown no evidence that substantial numbers of citizens are standing ready to strike out physically at whoever may assault their sensibilities with execrations like that uttered by Cohen. There may be some persons about with such lawless and violent proclivities, but that is an insufficient base upon which to erect, consistently with constitutional values, a governmental power to force persons who wish to ventilate their dissident views into avoiding particular forms of expression. The argument amounts to little more than the self-defeating proposition that to avoid physical censorship of one who has not sought to provoke such a response by a hypothetical coterie of the violent and lawless, the States may more appropriately effectuate that censorship themselves.

Admittedly, it is not so obvious that the First and Fourteenth Amendments must be taken to disable the States from punishing public utterance of this unseemly expletive in order to maintain what they regard as a suitable level of discourse within the body politic. We think, however, that examination and reflection will reveal the shortcomings of a contrary viewpoint.

[The] constitutional right of free expression is powerful medicine in a society as diverse and populous as ours. It is designed and intended to remove governmental restraints from the arena of public discussion, putting the decision as to what views shall be voiced largely into the hands of each of us, in the hope that use of such freedom will ultimately produce a more capable citizenry and more perfect polity and in the belief that no other approach would comport with the premise of individual dignity and choice upon which our political system rests.

To many, the immediate consequence of this freedom may often appear to be only verbal tumult, discord, and even offensive utterance. These are, however, within established limits, in truth necessary side effects of the broader enduring values which the process of open debate permits us to achieve. That the air may at times seem filled with verbal cacophony is, in this sense not a sign of weakness but of strength. We cannot lose sight of the fact that, in what otherwise might seem a trifling and annoying instance of individual distasteful abuse of a privilege, these fundamental societal values are truly implicated. * * *

Against this perception of the constitutional policies involved, we discern certain more particularized considerations that peculiarly call for reversal of this conviction. First, the principle contended for by the State seems inherently boundless. How is one to distinguish this from any other offensive word? Surely the State has no right to cleanse public debate to the point where it is grammatically palatable to the most squeamish among us. Yet no readily ascertainable general principle exists for stopping short of that result were we to affirm the judgment below. For, while the particular four-letter word being litigated here is perhaps more distasteful than most others of its genre, it is nevertheless often true that one man's vulgarity is another's lyric. Indeed, we think it is largely because governmental officials cannot make principled distinctions in this area that the Constitution leaves matters of taste and style so largely to the individual.

Additionally, we cannot overlook the fact, because it is well illustrated by the episode involved here, that much linguistic expression serves a dual communicative function: it conveys not only ideas capable of relatively precise, detached explication, but otherwise inexpressible emotions as well. In fact, words are often chosen as much for their emotive as their cognitive force. We cannot sanction the view that the Constitution, while solicitous of the cognitive content of individual speech, has little or no regard for that emotive function which, practically speaking, may often be the more important element of the overall message sought to be communicated. * * *

Finally, and in the same vein, we cannot indulge the facile assumption that one can forbid particular words without also running a substantial risk of suppressing ideas in the process. Indeed, governments might soon seize upon the censorship of particular words as a convenient guise for banning the expression of unpopular views. We have been able [to] discern little social benefit that might result from running the risk of opening the door to such grave results.

It is, in sum, our judgment that, absent a more particularized and compelling reason for its actions, the State may not, consistently with the First and Fourteenth Amendments, make the simple public display here involved of this single four-letter expletive a criminal offense. * * *

[BLACKMUN, J., joined by Burger, C.J., and Black, J., dissented for two reasons: (1) "Cohen's absurd and immature antic [was] mainly conduct and little speech" and the case falls "well within the sphere of *Chaplinsky*"; (2) although it declined to review the state court of appeals' decision in *Cohen,* the California Supreme Court subsequently narrowly construed the breach-of-the-peace statute in another case and *Cohen* should be remanded to the California Court of Appeal in the light of this subsequent construction. White, J., concurred with the dissent on the latter ground.]

NOTES AND QUESTIONS

1.   For criticism of *Cohen,* see Alexander Bickel, *The Morality of Consent* 72 (1975) (Cohen's speech "constitutes an assault" and this sort of speech "may create [an] environment [in which] actions that were not possible before become possible"); Archibald Cox, *The Role of the Supreme Court in American Government* 47–48 (1976) (state has interest in "level at which public discourse is conducted"; state should not have to "allow exhibitionists and [others] trading upon our lower prurient interests to inflict themselves upon the public

consciousness and dull its sensibilities"). For a defense of what is perhaps a narrow reading of *Cohen*, see Daniel Farber, *Civilizing Public Discourse: An Essay on Professor Bickel, Justice Harlan, and the Enduring Significance of Cohen v. California,* 1980 Duke L.J. 283. See also John H. Ely, *Democracy and Distrust* 114 (1980).

2.   To what extent, if at all, and in what ways, if any, does *Cohen* restrict the "fighting words" doctrine? Consider Hadley Arkes, *Civility and the Restriction of Speech: Rediscovering the Defamation of Groups,* 1974 Sup.Ct.Rev. 281: *Cohen* turned "the presumptions in *Chaplinsky* around: instead of presuming that profane or defamatory speech was beneath constitutional protection, he presumed that the speech was protected and that the burden of proof lay with those who would restrict it." If "one man's vulgarity is another's lyric," how are discriminations to be made in the "fighting words" area?

3.   What does *Cohen* decide? Consider William Cohen, *A Look Back at Cohen v. California,* 34 UCLA L.Rev. 1595(1987): "Unless it is overruled or dishonestly distinguished, [*Cohen*] has settled [that] a criminal statute is unconstitutional if it punishes all public use of profanity without reference to details such as the nature of the location and the audience. The opinion, however, left much to be decided about government controls on the use of profanity based on considerations of time, place, and manner. To what extent can profanity be punished because of the nature of the audience, the nature of the occasion on which it is uttered or displayed, or the manner of its utterance or display." What if the word "draft" did not appear on Cohen's jacket? Protected? What if the word "you" were substituted for "draft"? Protected? See Robert M. O'Neil, *Rights in Conflict: The First Amendment's Third Century,* 65 Law & Contemp. Probs. 7 (2002). Do spectators have any free speech rights in the courtroom? See *Carey v. Musladin,* 549 U.S. 70 (2006) (Souter, J., concurring).

4.   A series of cases in the early 1970s reversed convictions involving abusive language. *Gooding v. Wilson,* 405 U.S. 518 (1972), invalidated a Georgia ordinance primarily because it had been previously applied to "utterances where there was no likelihood that the person addressed would make an immediate violent response." *Lewis v. New Orleans,* 415 U.S. 130 (1974), ruled that vulgar or offensive speech was protected under the First Amendment. Because the statute punished "opprobrious language," it was deemed by the Court to embrace words that do not " 'by their very utterance inflict injury or tend to invite an immediate breach of the peace.' "

Although *Gooding* seemed to require a danger of immediate violence, *Lewis* recited that infliction of injury was sufficient. Dissenting in both cases, BURGER, C.J., and Blackmun and Rehnquist, JJ., complained that the majority invoked vagueness and overbreadth analysis "indiscriminately without regard to the nature of the speech in question, the possible effect the statute or ordinance has upon such speech, the importance of the speech in relation to the exposition of ideas, or the purported or asserted community interest in preventing that speech." The dissenters focused upon the facts of the cases (e.g., Gooding to a police officer: "White son of a bitch, I'll kill you," "You son of a bitch, I'll choke you to death," and "You son of a bitch, if you ever put your hands on me again, I'll cut you to pieces."). They complained that the majority had relegated the facts to "footnote status, conveniently distant and in less disturbing focus." In *Gooding, Lewis,* and the other cases, POWELL, J., insisted upon the importance of context in decision making. Dissenting in *Rosenfeld v. New Jersey,* 408 U.S. 901 (1972), he suggested that *Chaplinsky* be extended to the "wilful use of scurrilous language calculated to offend the sensibilities of an unwilling audience"; concurring in *Lewis,* he maintained that allowing prosecutions for offensive language directed at police officers invited law enforcement abuse. Finally, he suggested in *Rosenfeld* that whatever the scope of the "fighting words" doctrine, overbreadth analysis was inappropriate in such cases. He doubted that such statutes deter others from exercising First Amendment rights.[99]

VI. SHOULD NEW CATEGORIES BE CREATED?

The categories just discussed are often described as "exceptions" to the First Amendment. But once we realize just how much human communication remains untouched by the First Amendment—contract law, the law of wills, prosecution for perjury and blackmail, and much else—the language of "exceptions" seems a bit misleading. Nevertheless, there is considerable pressure on the existing boundaries of First Amendment coverage. Should previously uncovered communication be subject to First Amendment scrutiny of some sort, as with libel and fighting words? Should forms of communication—violent videogames, for example—that are now inside the First Amendment be treated as lying outside? Such issues have been subject to a considerable amount of recent litigation, as the following materials indicate

A. Harm to Children and the Overbreadth Doctrine

NEW YORK v. FERBER, 458 U.S. 747 (1982), per WHITE, J., upheld conviction of a seller of films depicting young boys masturbating, under N.Y.Penal Law § 263.15, for "promoting[100] a sexual performance," defined as "any performance [which] includes sexual conduct[101] by a child" under 16. The Court addressed the "single question": " 'To prevent the abuse of children who are made to engage in sexual conduct for commercial purposes, could the New York State Legislature, consistent with the First Amendment, prohibit the dissemination of material which shows children

---

[99] For commentary on Powell, J.'s approach, see Gerald Gunther, *In Search of Judicial Quality on a Changing Court: The Case of Justice Powell,* 24 Stan.L.Rev. 1001 (1972).

[100] "Promote" was defined to include all aspects of production, distribution, exhibition and sale.

[101] Sec. 263.3 defined "sexual conduct" as "actual or simulated sexual intercourse, deviate sexual intercourse, sexual bestiality, masturbation, sado-masochistic abuse, or lewd exhibition of the genitals."

engaged in sexual conduct, regardless of whether such material is obscene?"[102] * * *

"The *Miller* standard, like its predecessors, was an accommodation between the state's interests in protecting the 'sensibilities of unwilling recipients' from exposure to pornographic material and the dangers of censorship inherent in unabashedly content-based laws. Like obscenity statutes, laws directed at the dissemination of child pornography run the risk of suppressing protected expression by allowing the hand of the censor to become unduly heavy. For the following reasons, however, we are persuaded that the States are entitled to greater leeway in the regulation of pornographic depictions of children.

"First. [The] prevention of sexual exploitation and abuse of children constitutes a government objective of surpassing importance. The legislative findings accompanying passage of the New York laws reflect this concern. * * *

"We shall not second-guess this legislative judgment. Respondent has not intimated that we do so. Suffice it to say that virtually all of the States and the United States have passed legislation proscribing the production of or otherwise combating 'child pornography.' The legislative judgment, as well as the judgment found in the relevant literature, is that the use of children as subjects of pornographic materials is harmful to the physiological, emotional, and mental health of the child. That judgment, we think, easily passes muster under the First Amendment.

"Second. The distribution of photographs and films depicting sexual activity by juveniles is intrinsically related to the sexual abuse of children in at least two ways. First, the materials produced are a permanent record of the children's participation and the harm to the child is exacerbated by their circulation. Second, the distribution network for child pornography must be closed if the production of material which requires the sexual exploitation of children is to be effectively controlled. Indeed, there is no serious contention that the legislature was unjustified in believing that it is difficult, if not impossible, to halt the exploitation of children by pursuing only those who produce the photographs and movies. While the production of pornographic materials is a low-profile, clandestine industry, the need to market the resulting products requires a visible apparatus of distribution. The most expeditious if not the only practical method of law enforcement may be to dry up the market for this material by imposing

---

[102] The opinion gave the background for such legislation: "In recent years, the exploitive use of children in the production of pornography has become a serious national problem. The federal government and forty-seven States have sought to combat the problem with statutes specifically directed at the production of child pornography. At least half of such statutes do not require that the materials produced be legally obscene. Thirty-five States and the United States Congress have also passed legislation prohibiting the distribution of such materials; twenty States prohibit the distribution of material depicting children engaged in sexual conduct without requiring that the material be legally obscene. New York is one of the twenty."

severe criminal penalties on persons selling, advertising, or otherwise promoting the product. Thirty-five States and Congress have concluded that restraints on the distribution of pornographic materials are required in order to effectively combat the problem, and there is a body of literature and testimony to support these legislative conclusions.

"[The] *Miller* standard, like all general definitions of what may be banned as obscene, does not reflect the State's particular and more compelling interest in prosecuting those who promote the sexual exploitation of children. Thus, the question under the *Miller* test of whether a work, taken as a whole, appeals to the prurient interest of the average person bears no connection to the issue of whether a child has been physically or psychologically harmed in the production of the work. Similarly, a sexual explicit depiction need not be 'patently offensive' in order to have required the sexual exploitation of a child for its production. In addition, a work which, taken on the whole, contains serious literary, artistic, political, or scientific value may nevertheless embody the hardest core of child pornography. 'It is irrelevant to the child [who has been abused] whether or not the material [has] a literary, artistic, political, or social value.' We therefore cannot conclude that the *Miller* standard is a satisfactory solution to the child pornography problem.

"Third. The advertising and selling of child pornography provides an economic motive for and is thus an integral part of the production of such materials, an activity illegal throughout the nation. 'It rarely has been suggested that the constitutional freedom for speech and press extends its immunity to speech or writing used as an integral part of conduct in violation of a valid criminal statute.' * * *

"Fourth. The value of permitting live performances and photographic reproductions of children engaged in lewd sexual conduct is exceedingly modest, if not de minimis. We consider it unlikely that visual depictions of children performing sexual acts or lewdly exhibiting their genitals would often constitute an important and necessary part of a literary performance or scientific or educational work. As the trial court in this case observed, if it were necessary for literary or artistic value, a person over the statutory age who perhaps looked younger could be utilized. * * *

"Fifth. Recognizing and classifying child pornography as a category of material outside the protection of the First Amendment is not incompatible with our earlier decisions. 'The question whether speech is, or is not protected by the First Amendment often depends on the content of the speech.' *Young v. American Mini Theatres, Inc.* [Sec. 3, I infra]. '[I]t is the content of an utterance that determines whether it is a protected epithet or [an] unprotected "fighting comment" '. Leaving aside the special considerations when public officials are the target, *New York Times Co. v. Sullivan,* a libelous publication is not protected by the Constitution.

Beauharnais. [It] is not rare that a content-based classification of speech has been accepted because it may be appropriately generalized that within the confines of the given classification, the evil to be restricted so overwhelmingly outweighs the expressive interests, if any, at stake, that no process of case-by-case adjudication is required. When a definable class of material, such as that covered by § 263.15, bears so heavily and pervasively on the welfare of children engaged in its production, we think the balance of competing interests is clearly struck and that it is permissible to consider these materials as without the protection of the First Amendment.

"There are, of course, limits on the category of child pornography which, like obscenity, is unprotected by the First Amendment. As with all legislation in this sensitive area, the conduct to be prohibited must be adequately defined by the applicable state law, as written or authoritatively construed. Here the nature of the harm to be combated requires that the state offense be limited to works that *visually* depict sexual conduct by children below a specified age. The category of 'sexual conduct' proscribed must also be suitably limited and described.

"The test for child pornography is separate from the obscenity standard enunciated in *Miller,* but may be compared to it for purpose of clarity. The *Miller* formulation is adjusted in the following respects: A trier of fact need not find that the material appeals to the prurient interest of the average person; it is not required that sexual conduct portrayed be done so in a patently offensive manner; and the material at issue need not be considered as a whole. We note that the distribution of descriptions or other depictions of sexual conduct, not otherwise obscene, which do not involve live performance or photographic or other visual reproduction of live performances, retains First Amendment protection. As with obscenity laws, criminal responsibility may not be imposed without some element of scienter on the part of the defendant. * * *

"It remains to address the claim that the New York statute is unconstitutionally overbroad because it would forbid the distribution of material with serious literary, scientific, or educational value or material which does not threaten the harms sought to be combated by the State. * * *

"The traditional rule is that a person to whom a statute may constitutionally be applied may not challenge that statute on the ground that it may conceivably be applied unconstitutionally to others in situations not before the Court. *Broadrick v. Oklahoma,* 413 U.S. 601 (1973). In *Broadrick,* we recognized that this rule reflects two cardinal principles of our constitutional order: the personal nature of constitutional rights and prudential limitations on constitutional adjudication.[20] [By] focusing on the factual situation before us, and similar cases necessary for development of a constitutional rule,[21] we face 'flesh-and-blood' legal problems with data 'relevant and adequate to an informed judgment.' This practice also fulfills a valuable institutional purpose: it allows state courts the opportunity to construe a law to avoid constitutional infirmities.

"What has come to be known as the First Amendment overbreadth doctrine is one of the few exceptions to this principle and must be justified by weighty countervailing policies. The doctrine is predicated on the sensitive nature of protected expression: persons whose expression is constitutionally protected may well refrain from exercising their rights for fear of criminal sanctions by a statute susceptible of application to protected expression. * * *

"In *Broadrick,* we explained [that]: '[T]he plain import of our cases is, at the very least, that facial overbreadth adjudication is an exception to our traditional rules of practice and that its function, a limited one at the outset, attenuates as the otherwise unprotected behavior that it forbids the State to sanction moves from "pure speech" toward conduct and that conduct—even if expressive—falls within the scope of otherwise valid criminal laws that reflect legitimate state interests in maintaining comprehensive controls over harmful, constitutionally unprotected conduct. * * * '

"[*Broadrick*] examined a regulation involving restrictions on political campaign activity, an area not considered 'pure speech,' and thus it was unnecessary to consider the proper overbreadth test when a law arguably reaches traditional forms of expression such as books and films. As we intimated in *Broadrick,* the requirement of substantial overbreadth extended 'at the very least' to cases involving conduct plus speech. This case, which poses the question squarely, convinces us that the rationale of *Broadrick* is sound and should be applied in the present context involving the harmful employment of children to make sexually explicit materials for distribution.

"The premise that a law should not be invalidated for overbreadth unless it reaches a substantial number of impermissible applications is hardly novel.[103] On most occasions involving facial invalidation, the Court

---

[20] **[Ct's Note]** In addition to prudential restraints, the traditional rule is grounded in Art. III limits on the jurisdiction of federal courts to actual cases and controversies. * * *

[21] **[Ct's Note]** Overbreadth challenges are only one type of facial attack. A person whose activity may be constitutionally regulated nevertheless may argue that the statute under which he is convicted or regulated is invalid on its face. See, e.g., *Terminiello.* See generally Henry Monaghan, *Overbreadth,* 1981 S.Ct.Rev. 1.

[103] Scalia, J., dissenting in *Chicago v. Morales,* 527 U.S. 41 (1999), argues that in order to avoid advisory opinions, federal courts should limit themselves to as applied attacks, but that if they insist on considering facial attacks, they should insist that a statute be unconstitutional in all its applications before declaring it unconstitutional. Are either of these positions acceptable?

has stressed the embracing sweep of the statute over protected expression.[26] Indeed, Justice Brennan observed in his dissenting opinion in *Broadrick*: 'We have never held that a statute should be held invalid on its face merely because it is possible to conceive of a single impermissible application, and in that sense a requirement of substantial overbreadth is already implicit in the doctrine.'

"The requirement of substantial overbreadth is directly derived from the purpose and nature of the doctrine. While a sweeping statute, or one incapable of limitation, has the potential to repeatedly chill the exercise of expressive activity by many individuals, the extent of deterrence of protected speech can be expected to decrease with the declining reach of the regulation. This observation appears equally applicable to the publication of books and films as it is to activities, such as picketing or participation in election campaigns, which have previously been categorized as involving conduct plus speech. We see no appreciable difference between the position of a publisher or bookseller in doubt as to the reach of New York's child pornography law and the situation faced by the Oklahoma state employees with respect to the State's restriction on partisan political activity.[104] * * *

"Applying these principles, we hold that § 263.15 is not substantially overbroad. We consider this the paradigmatic case of a state statute whose legitimate reach dwarfs its arguably impermissible applications. [While] the reach of the statute is directed at the hard core of child pornography, the Court of Appeals was understandably concerned that some protected expression, ranging from medical textbooks to pictorials in the National Geographic would fall prey to the statute. How often, if ever, it may be necessary to employ children to engage in conduct clearly within the reach of § 263.15 in order to produce educational, medical, or artistic works cannot be known with certainty. Yet we seriously doubt, and it has not been suggested, that these arguably impermissible applications of the statute amount to more than a tiny fraction of the materials within the statute's reach."[105]

---

[26] **[Ct's Note]** In *Gooding v. Wilson,* the Court's invalidation of a Georgia statute making it a misdemeanor to use " 'opprobrious words or abusive language, tending to cause a breach of the peace' " followed from state judicial decisions indicating that "merely to speak words offensive to some who hear them" could constitute a "breach of the peace." * * *

[104] *Brockett v. Spokane Arcades, Inc.,* Sec. 1, III, B supra, stated: "The Court of Appeals erred in holding that the *Broadrick* substantial overbreadth requirement is inapplicable where pure speech rather than conduct is at issue. *Ferber* specifically held to the contrary." For commentary on the overbreadth discussion in *Broadrick* and *Ferber,* see Martin Redish, *The Warren Court, The Burger Court and the First Amendment Overbreadth Doctrine,* 78 Nw.U.L.Rev. 1031 (1983).

[105] Brennan, J., joined by Marshall, J., agreed "with much of what is said in the Court's opinion. [This] special and compelling interest (in protecting the well-being of the State's youth), and the particular vulnerability of children, afford the State the leeway to regulate pornographic material, the promotion of which is harmful to children, even though the State does not have such leeway when it seeks only to protect consenting adults from exposure to such materials. * * * I also agree with the Court that the 'tiny fraction' of material of serious artistic, scientific or educational

NOTES AND QUESTIONS

1. Consider Frederick Schauer, *Codifying the First Amendment: New York v. Ferber,* 1982 Sup.Ct.Rev. 285: The new category created in *Ferber* "bears little resemblance to the category of obscenity delineated by *Miller.* The Court in *Ferber* explicitly held that child pornography need not appeal to the prurient interest, need not be patently offensive, and need not be based on a consideration of the material as a whole. This last aspect is most important, because it means that the presence of some serious literary, artistic, political, or scientific matter will not constitutionally redeem material containing depictions of sexual conduct by children. The Court referred to the foregoing factors in terms of having 'adjusted' the *Miller* test, but that is like saying a butterfly is an adjusted camel." What precisely is the new category created in *Ferber?*

2. What test or standard of review did the Court use to determine whether the speech should be protected? For general discussion, see Schauer, supra. Did it apply a different test or a standard of review when it formulated its rules in *Gertz?* Are tests or standards of review needed in these contexts? Desirable? Consider Steven Shiffrin, *The First Amendment and Economic Regulation: Away from a General Theory of the First Amendment,* 78 Nw.U.L.Rev. 1212 (1983): "The complex set of rules produced in *Gertz,* right or wrong, resulted from an appreciation that the protection of truth was important but that the protection of reputation also was important. The Court wisely avoided discussion of levels of scrutiny because any resort to such abstractions would have constitutionalized reductionism." Is "constitutionalized reductionism" desirable because it protects speech and provides guidance to the lower courts?

3. ***Absence of children.*** SIMON & SCHUSTER, INC. v. MEMBERS OF NEW YORK STATE CRIME VICTIMS BD., 502 U.S. 105 (1991), per O'CONNOR, J., struck down a law requiring that income derived from works in which individuals admit to crime involving victims be used to compensate the

---

value that could conceivably fall within the reach of the statute is insufficient to justify striking the statute on grounds of overbreadth." But the concurrence stated that application of the statute to such materials as "do have serious artistic, scientific or medical value would violate the First Amendment."

O'Connor, J., wrote a short concurrence: "Although I join the Court's opinion, I write separately to stress that the Court does not hold that New York must except 'material with serious literary, scientific or educational value' from its statute. The Court merely holds that, even if the First Amendment shelters such material, New York's current statute is not sufficiently overbroad to support respondent's facial attack. The compelling interests identified in today's opinion suggest that the Constitution might in fact permit New York to ban knowing distribution of works depicting minors engaged in explicit sexual conduct, regardless of the social value of the depictions. For example, a 12-year-old child photographed while masturbating surely suffers the same psychological harm whether the community labels the photograph 'edifying' or 'tasteless.' The audience's appreciation of the depiction is simply irrelevant to New York's asserted interest in protecting children from psychological, emotional, and mental harm."

Stevens, J., also concurred in the judgment in a short opinion that noted his conclusion that the films in the case were not entitled to First Amendment protection, and his view that overbreadth analysis should be avoided by waiting until the hypothetical case actually arises. Blackmun, J., concurred in the result without opinion.

victims: "[T]he State has a compelling interest in compensating victims from the fruits of the crime, but little if any interest in limiting such compensation to the proceeds of the wrongdoer's speech about the crime."[106]

4. ***Overbreadth without a chilling effect?*** Massachusetts prohibited adults from posing or exhibiting nude children for purposes of photographs, publications, or pictures, moving or otherwise. Bona fide scientific or medical purposes were excepted as were educational or cultural purposes for a bona fide school, museum, or library. Douglas Oakes was prosecuted for taking 10 color photographs of his 14-year-old stepdaughter in a state of nudity covered by the statute. The Massachusetts Supreme Judicial Court declared the statute overbroad. After certiorari was granted in MASSACHUSETTS v. OAKES, 491 U.S. 576 (1989), Massachusetts added a "lascivious intent" requirement to the statute and eliminated the exemptions. O'CONNOR, J., joined by Rehnquist, C.J., and White and Kennedy, JJ., accordingly refused to entertain the overbreadth challenge and voted to remand the case for determination of the statute's constitutionality as applied: "Because it has been repealed, the former version of [the Massachusetts law] cannot chill protected speech."

SCALIA, J., joined by Blackmun, Brennan, Marshall, and Stevens, JJ., disagreed:[107] "It seems to me strange judicial theory that a conviction initially invalid can be resuscitated by postconviction alteration of the statute under which it was obtained. [Even as a policy matter, the] overbreadth doctrine serves to protect constitutionally legitimate speech not merely *ex post,* that is, after the offending statute is enacted, but also *ex ante,* that is, when the legislature is contemplating what sort of statute to enact. If the promulgation of overbroad laws affecting speech was cost free[,] if *no* conviction of constitutionally proscribable conduct would be lost, so long as the offending statute was narrowed before the final appeal—then legislatures would have significantly reduced incentive to stay within constitutional bounds in the first place.[108] [More] fundamentally, however, [it] seems to me that we are only free to pursue policy objectives through the modes of action traditionally followed by the courts and by the law. [I] have heard of a voidable contract, but never of a voidable law. The notion is bizarre."

---

[106] Kennedy, J., concurring, would have stricken the statute without reference to the compelling state interest test which he condemned as ad hoc balancing. Blackmun, J., also concurred. Thomas, J., did not participate. For extensive criticism of the strict scrutiny test, see Eugene Volokh, *Freedom of Speech, Permissible Tailoring, and Transcending Strict Scrutiny,* 144 U.Pa.L.Rev. 2417 (1996).

[107] Although these five Justices agreed that the overbreadth challenge should be entertained, they divided on the merits of the challenge. Scalia, J., joined by Blackmun, J., found no merit in the overbreadth claim (see note 5 infra) and voted to reverse and to remand for determination of the statute's constitutionality as applied. The three remaining justices (see note 5 infra) agreed with the overbreadth challenge and voted to affirm the judgment below. O'Connor, J.'s opinion, therefore, became the plurality opinion, and the Court's judgment was to vacate the judgment below and to remand. In the end, six justices voted against the overbreadth challenge: four because it was moot; two because it did not meet the requirement of substantial overbreadth.

[108] For criticism of this point, see Alfred Hill, *The Puzzling First Amendment Overbreadth Doctrine,* 25 Hof.L.Rev. 1063 (1997).

5. *How substantial is substantial overbreadth?* Five Justices addressed the overbreadth question in *Oakes,* but the substantive issue was not resolved. BRENNAN, J., joined by Marshall and Stevens, JJ., objected that the statute would make it criminal for parents "to photograph their infant children or toddlers in the bath or romping naked on the beach." More generally, he argued that the First Amendment "blocks the prohibition of nude posing by minors in connection with the production of works of art not depicting lewd behavior. [Many] of the world's great artists—Degas, Renoir, Donatello, to name but a few—have worked from models under 18 years of age, and many acclaimed photographs have included nude or partially clad minors."

SCALIA, J., joined by Blackmun, J., disagreed: "[G]iven the known extent of the kiddie-porn industry[,] I would estimate that the legitimate scope [of the statute] vastly exceeds the illegitimate. [Even] assuming that proscribing artistic depictions of preadolescent genitals and postadolescent breasts is impermissible,[2] the body of material that would be covered is, as far as I am aware, insignificant compared with the lawful scope of the statute. That leaves the family photos. [Assuming] that it is unconstitutional (as opposed to merely foolish) to prohibit such photography, I do not think it so common as to make the statute *substantially* overbroad. [My] perception differs, for example, from Justice Brennan's belief that there is an 'abundance of baby and child photographs taken every day' depicting genitals."[109]

Consider Amy Adler, *Inverting the First Amendment*, 149 U. Pa. L. Rev. 921 (2001): "The Supreme Court and lower federal courts since *Ferber* have tolerated statutes that define this margin of child "sexual conduct" in increasingly broad and subjective terms. Each subtle reiteration of the definition of "lewd" or "lascivious exhibition of the genitals" since *Ferber* has expanded it. If we pushed the case law to the extreme, it seems to threaten all pictures of unclothed children, whether "lewd" or not, and even pictures of clothed children, if they meet the increasingly hazy definition of 'lascivious' or 'lewd.'" Does the increasing breadth make the failure to countenance a "serious value" exception more problematic?

6. *Digital child pornography.* The Child Pornography Act of 1996 (the "CPPA") in addition to outlawing child pornography involving minors, extends its coverage to prohibit images that "appear to be, of a minor engaging in sexually explicit conduct" or marketed in a way that "conveys the impression" that it depicts a "minor engaging in sexually explicit conduct."

---

[2] **[Ct's Note]** [Most] adults, I expect, would not hire themselves out as nude models, whatever the intention of the photographer or artist, and however unerotic the pose. There is no cause to think children are less sensitive. It is not unreasonable, therefore, for a State to regard parents' using (or permitting the use) of their children as nude models, or other adults' use of consenting minors, as a form of child exploitation.

[109] For the argument that the Court should balance a number of factors including the "state's substantive interest in being able to impose sanctions for a particular kind of conduct under a particular legal standard, as opposed to being forced to rely on other, less restrictive substitutes" instead of trying to determine the number of constitutional and unconstitutional applications, see Richard Fallon, *Making Sense of Overbreadth,* 100 Yale L.J. 853 (1991).

ASHCROFT v. FREE SPEECH COALITION, 535 U.S. 234 (2002), per KENNEDY, J., declared these provisions to be unconstitutional: "The CPPA [extends] to images that appear to depict a minor engaging in sexually explicit activity without regard to the *Miller* requirements. The materials need not appeal to the prurient interest. Any depiction of sexually explicit activity, no matter how it is presented, is proscribed. The CPPA applies to a picture in a psychology manual, as well as a movie depicting the horrors of sexual abuse. It is not necessary, moreover, that the image be patently offensive. Pictures of what appear to be 17-year-olds engaging in sexually explicit activity do not in every case contravene community standards.

"The CPPA prohibits speech despite its serious literary, artistic, political, or scientific value. The statute proscribes the visual depiction of [the idea] of teenagers engaging in sexual activity that is a fact of modern society and has been a theme in art and literature throughout the ages." Kennedy, J., argued that the Act could potentially apply to versions of Romeo and Juliet and films like Traffic and American Beauty.

"[The government] argues that the CPPA is necessary because pedophiles may use virtual child pornography to seduce children. There are many things innocent in themselves, however, such as cartoons, video games, and candy, that might be used for immoral purposes, yet we would not expect those to be prohibited because they can be misused. The Government, of course, may punish adults who provide unsuitable materials to children, and it may enforce criminal penalties for unlawful solicitation. The precedents establish, however, that speech within the rights of adults to hear may not be silenced completely in an attempt to shield children from it. [The Government] submits further that virtual child pornography whets the appetites of pedophiles and encourages them to engage in illegal conduct. This rationale cannot sustain the provision in question. The mere tendency of speech to encourage unlawful acts is not a sufficient reason for banning it. * * *

"Finally, the Government says that the possibility of producing images by using computer imaging makes it very difficult for it to prosecute those who produce pornography by using real children. Experts, we are told, may have difficulty in saying whether the pictures were made by using real children or by using computer imaging. The necessary solution, the argument runs, is to prohibit both kinds of images. The argument, in essence, is that protected speech may be banned as a means to ban unprotected speech. This analysis turns the First Amendment upside down. The Government may not suppress lawful speech as the means to suppress unlawful speech."[110]

THOMAS, J., concurred: "In my view, the Government's most persuasive asserted interest [is] the prosecution rationale that persons who possess and disseminate pornographic images of real children may escape conviction by

---

[110] In overthrowing the "conveys the impression provision," Kennedy, J., argued that it applied to a substantial amount of material that could not be reached by anti-pandering obscenity law and wrongfully proscribed possession of material that was distributed in a manner conveying a false impression even when the possessor knew the material was mislabeled.

claiming that the images are computer-generated, thereby raising a reasonable doubt as to their guilt. At this time, however, the Government asserts only that defendants raise such defenses, not that they have done so successfully. In fact, the Government points to no case in which a defendant has been acquitted based on a computer-generated images defense. While this speculative interest cannot support the broad reach of the CPPA, technology may evolve to the point where it becomes impossible to enforce actual child pornography laws because the Government cannot prove that certain pornographic images are of real children. * * *

"The Court suggests that the Government's interest in enforcing prohibitions against real child pornography cannot justify prohibitions on virtual child pornography, because 'this analysis turns the First Amendment upside down.' [But] if technological advances thwart prosecution of unlawful speech, the Government may well have a compelling interest in barring or otherwise regulating some narrow category of lawful speech in order to enforce effectively laws against pornography made through the abuse of real children."

O'CONNOR, J., concurring in part and dissenting in part, agreed that the act's attempt to ban sexually explicit images of adults that appear to be children was overbroad, but, in a portion of her opinion joined by Rehnquist, C.J., and Scalia, J., she argued that the prohibitions of computer generated sexually explicit images appearing to be children or conveying that impression were constitutional: "[D]efendants indicted for the production, distribution, or possession of actual-child pornography may evade liability by claiming that the images attributed to them are in fact computer-generated. Respondents may be correct that no defendant has successfully employed this tactic. But, given the rapid pace of advances in computer-graphics technology, the Governments concern is reasonable. Computer-generated images lodged with the Court bear a remarkable likeness to actual human beings. [T]his Court's cases do not require Congress to wait for harm to occur before it can legislate against it.

"The Court concludes that the CPPAs ban on virtual-child pornography is overbroad. The basis for this holding is unclear. [Respondents] provide no examples of films or other materials that are wholly computer-generated and contain images that 'appea[r] to be' of minors engaging in indecent conduct, but that have serious value or do not facilitate child abuse."

REHNQUIST, C.J., joined in part by Scalia, J.,[111] dissenting, would have construed the statute to apply to "visual depictions of youthful looking adult actors engaged in actual sexual activity; mere suggestions of sexual activity, such as youthful looking adult actors squirming under a blanket, are more akin to written descriptions than visual depictions, and thus fall outside the purview of the statute. The reference to simulated has been part of the definition of sexually explicit conduct since the statute was first passed. But the inclusion of simulated conduct, alongside actual conduct, does not change the hard core nature of the image banned. The reference to simulated conduct

---

[111] Scalia, J., did not join a portion of Rehnquist, C.J.'s opinion discussing the statute's legislative history.

simply brings within the statute's reach depictions of hard core pornography that are made to look genuine including the main target of the CPPA, computer generated images virtually indistinguishable from real children engaged in sexually explicit conduct. Neither actual conduct nor simulated conduct, however, is properly construed to reach depictions such as those in a film portrayal of Romeo and Juliet which are far removed from the hard core pornographic depictions that Congress intended to reach.

"To the extent the CPPA prohibits possession or distribution of materials that convey the impression of a child engaged in sexually explicit conduct, that prohibition can and should be limited to reach the sordid business of pandering which lies outside the bounds of First Amendment protection. [The] First Amendment may protect the video shopowner or film distributor who promotes material as 'entertaining' or 'acclaimed' regardless of whether the material contains depictions of youthful looking adult actors engaged in nonobscene but sexually suggestive conduct. The First Amendment does not, however, protect the panderer. Thus, materials promoted as conveying the impression that they depict actual minors engaged in sexually explicit conduct do not escape regulation merely because they might warrant First Amendment protection if promoted in a different manner. * * *

"In sum, while potentially impermissible applications of the CPPA may exist, I doubt that they would be substantial in relation to the statute's plainly legitimate sweep."

After *Free Speech Coalition,* UNITED STATES v. WILLIAMS, 553 U.S. 285 (2008), per SCALIA, J., held that "offers to provide or requests to obtain child pornography are categorically excluded from the First Amendment" even if the material offered is not actually child pornography. *Free Speech Coalition* was distinguished on the ground that it "went beyond pandering to prohibit possession of material that could not otherwise be proscribed."[112]

7.   *"Autopornography."* Approximately 11% of girls ages thirteen to sixteen admit to producing and distributing nude or semi-nude pictures of themselves. Prosecutors have charged such girls under child pornography statutes. Do the materials constitute child pornography under *Ferber*? Does *Free Speech Coalition* shed light on this? Would prosecutions of those who possess such photographs be appropriate? Does it matter that some 40% of teenagers (including distributors and possessors) would be sex offenders if *Ferber* applies? See John A. Humbach, *"Sexting" and the First Amendment,* 37 Hastings Con. L.Q. 433 (2010). See also Sarah Wastler, *The Harm in "Sexting"?,* 33 Harv. J.L. & Gender 687 (2010).

---

[112] Stevens, J., joined by Breyer, J., concurred. Souter, J., joined by Ginsburg, J., dissented.

B. Harm to Women: Feminism and Pornography

Catharine MacKinnon and Andrea Dworkin drafted an anti-pornography ordinance that was considered in a number of jurisdictions.[113]

Proposed Los Angeles County Anti-Pornography Civil Rights Law

Section 1.   Statement of Policy

Pornography is sex discrimination. It exists in the County of Los Angeles, posing a substantial threat to the health, safety, welfare and equality of citizens in the community. Existing state and federal laws are inadequate to solve these problems in the County of Los Angeles.

Section 2.   Findings

Pornography is a systematic practice of exploitation and subordination based on sex which differentially harms women. The harm of pornography includes dehumanization, sexual exploitation, forced sex, forced prostitution, physical injury, and social and sexual terrorism and inferiority presented as entertainment. The bigotry and contempt pornography promotes, with the acts of aggression it fosters, diminish opportunities for equality of rights in employment, education, property, public accommodations and public services; create public and private harassment, persecution and denigration; promote injury and degradation such as rape, battery, child sexual abuse, and prostitution and inhibit just enforcement of laws against these acts; contribute significantly to restricting women in particular from full exercise of citizenship and participation in public life, including in neighborhoods; damage relations between the sexes; and undermine women's equal exercise of rights to speech and action guaranteed to all citizens under the Constitutions and laws of the United States, the State of California and the County of Los Angeles.

Section 3.   Definitions

1.   *Pornography* is the graphic sexually explicit subordination of women through pictures and/or words that also includes one or more of the following: (i) women are presented dehumanized as sexual objects, things or commodities; or (ii) women are presented as sexual objects who enjoy pain or humiliation; or (iii) women are presented as sexual objects who experience sexual pleasure in being raped; or (iv) women are presented as

---

[113] The ordinance was first considered in Minneapolis. For political, rhetorical, and sociological discussion, see Paul Brest & Ann Vandenberg, *Politics, Feminism, and the Constitution: The Anti-Pornography Movement in Minneapolis,* 39 Stan.L.Rev. 607 (1987). Different versions of the ordinance were passed in Indianapolis, Indiana and Bellingham, Washington (see Margaret Baldwin, *Pornography and the Traffic in Women,* 1 Yale J.L. & Fem. 111 (1989)). Both versions were declared unconstitutional.

sexual objects tied up or cut up or mutilated or bruised or physically hurt; or (v) women are presented in postures of sexual submission, servility, or display; or (vi) women's body parts—including but not limited to vaginas, breasts, or buttocks—are exhibited such that women are reduced to those parts; or (vii) women are presented as whores by nature; or (viii) women are presented as being penetrated by objects or animals; or (ix) women are presented in scenarios of degradation, injury, torture, shown as filthy or inferior, bleeding, bruised or hurt in a context that makes these conditions sexual.

2.   The use of men,[114] children, or transsexuals in the place of women in (1) above is also pornography for purposes of this law.

Section 4.   Unlawful Practices

1.   *Coercion into pornography*: It shall be sex discrimination to coerce, intimidate, or fraudulently induce (hereafter, "coerce") any person, including transsexual, into performing for pornography, which injury may date from any appearance or sale of any product(s) of such performance(s). The maker(s), seller(s), exhibitor(s) and/or distributor(s) of said pornography may be sued, including for an injunction to eliminate the product(s) of the performance(s) from the public view.

Proof of one or more of the following facts or conditions shall not, without more, negate a finding of coercion:

(i)   that the person is a woman; or

(ii)   that the person is or has been a prostitute; or

(iii)   that the person has attained the age of majority; or

(iv)   that the person is connected by blood or marriage to anyone involved in or related to the making of the pornography; or

(v)   that the person has previously had, or been thought to have had, sexual relations with anyone, including anyone involved in or related to the making of the pornography; or

(vi)   that the person has previously posed for sexually explicit pictures with or for anyone, including anyone involved in or related to the making of the pornography at issue; or

(vii)   that anyone else, including a spouse or other relative, has given permission on the person's behalf; or

---

[114] Does this provision wrongly conflate gay pornography with stereotypical heterosexual pornography? See Leslie Green, *Pornographies,* 8 J. of Pol. Phil. 27 (2000). For criticism of the ordinance from a lesbian perspective, see Becki L. Ross, *'It's Merely Designed for Sexual Arousal,'* *Feminism & Pornography* 264–317 (Cornell ed. 1999).

(viii) that the person actually consented to a use of the performance that is changed into pornography; or

(ix) that the person knew that the purpose of the acts or events in question was to make pornography; or

(x) that the person showed no resistance or appeared to cooperate actively in the photographic sessions or in the events that produced the pornography; or

(xi) that the person signed a contract, or made statements affirming a willingness to cooperate in the production of pornography; or

(xii) that no physical force, threats, or weapons were used in the making of the pornography; or

(xiii) that the person was paid or otherwise compensated.

2. *Trafficking in pornography:* It shall be sex discrimination to produce, sell, exhibit, or distribute pornography, including through private clubs.

(i) City, state, and federally funded public libraries or private and public university and college libraries in which pornography is available for study, including on open shelves but excluding special display presentations, shall not be construed to be trafficking in pornography.

(ii) Isolated passages or isolated parts shall not be actionable under this section.

(iii) Any woman has a claim hereunder as a woman acting against the subordination of women. Any man, child, or transsexual who alleges injury by pornography in the way women are injured by it also has a claim.

3. *Forcing pornography on a person:* It shall be sex discrimination to force pornography on a person, including child or transsexual, in any place of employment, education, home, or public place. Only the perpetrator of the force and/or institution responsible for the force may be sued.

4. *Assault or physical attack due to pornography:* It shall be sex discrimination to assault, physically attack or injure any person, including child or transsexual, in a way that is directly caused by specific pornography. The perpetrator of the assault or attack may be sued. The maker(s), distributor(s), seller(s), and/or exhibitor(s) may also be sued, including for an injunction against the specific pornography's further exhibition, distribution or sale.

Section 5.   Defenses

1.   It shall not be a defense that the defendant in an action under this law did not know or intend that the materials were pornography or sex discrimination.

2.   No damages or compensation for losses shall be recoverable under Sec. 4(2) or other than against the perpetrator of the assault or attack in Sec. 4(4) unless the defendant knew or had reason to know that the materials were pornography.

3.   In actions under Sec. 4(2) or other than against the perpetrator of the assault or attack in Sec. 4(4), no damages or compensation for losses shall be recoverable against maker(s) for pornography made, against distributor(s) for pornography distributed, against seller(s) for pornography sold, or against exhibitor(s) for pornography exhibited, prior to the effective date of this law.

Section 6.   Enforcement

a.   Civil Action: Any person, or their estate, aggrieved by violations of this law may enforce its provisions by means of a civil action. No criminal penalties shall attach for any violation of the provisions of this law. Relief for violations of this law, except as expressly restricted or precluded herein, may include compensatory and punitive damages and reasonable attorney's fees, costs and disbursements.

b.   Injunction: Any person who violates this law may be enjoined except that:

(i)   In actions under Sec. 4(2), and other than against the perpetrator of the assault or attack under Sec. 4(4), no temporary or permanent injunction shall issue prior to a final judicial determination that the challenged activities constitute a violation of this law.

(ii)   No temporary or permanent injunction shall extend beyond such material(s) that, having been described with reasonable specificity by the injunction, have been determined to be validly proscribed under this law.

Section 7.   Severability

Should any part(s) of this law be found legally invalid, the remaining part(s) remain valid. A judicial declaration that any part(s) of this law cannot be applied validly in a particular manner or to a particular case or category of cases shall not affect the validity of that part(s) as otherwise applied, unless such other application would clearly frustrate the intent of the Board of Supervisors in adopting this law.

Section 8.   Limitation of Action

Actions under this law must be filed within one year of the alleged discriminatory acts.

NOTES AND QUESTIONS

1.   ***The Ferber analogy.*** Consider Cass Sunstein, *Neutrality in Constitutional Law (with Special Reference to Pornography, Abortion, and Surrogacy)*, 92 Colum.L.Rev. 1 (1992): "A successful action for rape and sexual assault is difficult enough. The difficulty becomes all the greater when the victims are young women coerced into, and abused during, the production of pornography. Often those victims will be reluctant to put themselves through the experience and possible humiliation and expense of initiating a proceeding. Often prosecutors will be reluctant to act on their behalf. Often they will have extremely little credibility even if they are willing to come forward. In this light, the only realistically effective way to eliminate the practice is to eliminate or reduce the financial benefits." If all women in pornographic films were coerced, would the analogy to *Ferber* be airtight? If not, how much coercion is acceptable? What is the relationship between prostitution and pornography? Consider Tonya R. Noldon, *Challenging First Amendment Protection of Adult Films with the Use of Prostitution Statutes*, 3 Va. Sports & Ent. L.J. 310 (2004): "The stated purposes behind criminalizing prostitution— preventing the spread of communicable diseases, precluding the denigration and sexual exploitation of women, reducing the collateral criminal misconduct that tends to cluster with prostitution (such as drug, alcohol, and physical abuse)—are uncharacteristic of the mainstream movie industry, but prevalent throughout the adult film industry. Not only is the adult film industry not illegal, however, it can barely be regulated at all because it has been labeled 'free speech' or 'free expression,' which is protected by the First Amendment of the United States Constitution. The purposes behind making prostitution illegal, however, are completely unrelated to suppressing free expression."

2.   ***Relationship between obscenity and pornography.*** Consider Catharine MacKinnon, *Pornography, Civil Rights, and Speech*, 20 Harv.Civ.Rts.—Civ.Lib.L.Rev. 1 (1985): "Under the obscenity rubric, much legal and psychological scholarship has centered on a search for the elusive link between pornography defined as obscenity and harm. They have looked high and low—in the mind of the male consumer, in society or in its 'moral fabric,' in correlations between variations in levels of anti-social acts and liberalization of obscenity laws. The only harm they have found has been one they have attributed to 'the social interests in order and morality.' Until recently, no one looked very persistently for harm to women, particularly harm to women through men. The rather obvious fact that the sexes *relate* has been overlooked in the inquiry into the male consumer and his mind. The pornography doesn't just drop out of the sky, go into his head and stop there. Specifically, men rape, batter, prostitute, molest, and sexually harass women. Under conditions of inequality, they also hire, fire, promote, and grade women, decide how much or whether or not we are worth paying and for what, define and approve and disapprove of women in ways that count, that determine our lives.

"In pornography, there it is, in one place, all of the abuses that women had to struggle so long even to begin to articulate, all the *unspeakable* abuse: the rape, the battery, the sexual harassment, the prostitution, and the sexual abuse of children. Only in the pornography it is called something else: sex, sex, sex, sex, and sex, respectively. Pornography sexualizes rape, battery, sexual harassment, prostitution, and child sexual abuse; it thereby celebrates, promotes, authorizes, and legitimizes them. More generally, it eroticizes the dominance and submission that is the dynamic common to them all. It makes hierarchy sexy and calls that 'the truth about sex' or just a mirror of reality." See also Deborah Cameron & Elizabeth Frazer, *On the Question of Pornography and Sexual Violence: Moving Beyond Cause and Effect,* in *Feminism & Pornography* 240 (Drucilla Cornell ed. 2000): "Whereas conservatives criticize almost all expressions of sexuality as immoral and recommend a return to traditional religious and family values, feminist analysis criticizes instead the oppressive and misogynistic forms such expressions typically take in male-dominated culture. Stressing the pervasiveness of misogyny through time—that is, denying that we are witnessing a moral decline—feminists identify religion and the family as part of the problem."

3.   *The trafficking section.* Is the trafficking section constitutional under *Miller?* Consider the following hypothetical commentary: "The Dworkin-MacKinnon proposal focuses on a narrower class of material than *Miller* because it excludes erotic materials that do not involve subordination. That class of material upon which it does focus appeals to prurient interest because it is graphic and sexually explicit. Moreover, the eroticization of dominance in the ways specified in the ordinance is so patently offensive to community standards that it can be said as a matter of law that this class of materials lacks *serious* literary, artistic, political, or scientific value as a matter of law." Do you agree?

Is there a good analogy to *Beauharnais?* To *Ferber?* Did more or less harm exist in *Gertz? Miller? Ferber?* Was there more or less of a threat to First Amendment values in *Gertz? Miller? Ferber?* Should this be accepted as a new category?

Consider Wendy Kaminer, *Pornography and the First Amendment: Prior Restraints and Private Action,* in *Take Back the Night: Women on Pornography* 239 (Laura Lederer ed. 1980): "The Women's Movement is a Civil Rights Movement, and we should appreciate the importance and the danger of turning popular sentiment into law in areas affecting individual privacy.

"Legislative or judicial control of pornography is simply not possible without breaking down the legal principles and procedures that are essential to our own right to speak and, ultimately, our freedom to control our own lives. We must continue to organize against pornography and the degradation and abuse of women, but we must not ask the government to take up our struggle for us. The power it will assume to do so will be far more dangerous to us all than the 'power' of pornography."[115]

4. ***Pornography and harm.*** Consider Andrew Koppelman, *Does Obscenity Cause Moral Harm?*, 105 Colum. L. Rev. 1635 (2005): "[L]aboratory studies cannot establish what happens outside the lab. Short-term attitudinal and behavioral changes are all that laboratory studies, by their nature, could possibly show. Moreover, the laboratory studies also found that the effect of even this kind of pornography was not inevitably malign. When men who had been exposed to these misogynistic materials were later given debriefing sessions that included materials dispelling rape myths and detailing the harms women suffer as a consequence of rape, the net effect was striking. After these men were exposed both to violent pornography and to pro-feminist material, they had more positive, less discriminatory, and less stereotyped attitudes toward women than they did before the experiment." But see Rae Langton, *Speech Acts and Unspeakable Acts*, 22 Phil. & Pub.Aff. 293 (1993): "What is important here is not whether the speech of pornographers is universally held in high esteem: it is not—hence the common assumption among liberals that in defending pornographers they are defending the underdog. What is important is whether it is authoritative in the domain that counts—the domain of speech about sex—and whether it is authoritative for the hearers that count: people, men, boys, who in addition to wanting 'entertainment,' want to discover

---

[115] Compare Nan Hunter & Sylvia Law, *Brief Amici Curiae of Feminist Anti-Censorship Taskforce* (on appeal in *Hudnut*, below), 21 U.Mich.J.L.Ref. 69 (1987–88). The ordinance conceivably "would require the judiciary to impose its views of correct sexuality on a diverse community. The inevitable result would be to disapprove those images that are least conventional and privilege those that are closest to majoritarian beliefs about proper sexuality. [Moreover] [b]y defining sexually explicit images of women as subordinating and degrading to them, the ordinance reinforces the stereotypical view that 'good' women do not seek and enjoy sex. [Finally], the ordinance perpetuates a stereotype of women as helpless victims, incapable of consent, and in need of protection." See generally Nadine Strossen, *Defending Pornography* (1995).

For collections of feminist perspectives, see Catharine MacKinnon & Reva Siegel, eds., *Directions in Sexual Harassment Law* (2002); Drucilla Cornell, ed., *Feminism and* Pornography (2000); *Take Back the Night,* supra; Varda Burstyn, ed., *Women Against Censorship* (1985); Ann Snitow, Christine Stansell & Sharon Thompson, etc., *Powers of Desire* 419–67 (1983). For a variety of views (including feminist views), see James Weinstein, *Hate Speech, Pornography, and the Radical Attack on Free Speech Doctrine* (1999); Richard Delgado & Jean Stefancic, *Must We Defend Nazis?* (1997); Nicholas Wolfson, *Hate Speech, Sex Speech, Free Speech* (1997); Michelle Chernikoff Anderson, *Speaking Freely About Reducing Violence Against Women,* 10 U.Fla. J.L. & Pub.Pol. 173 (1998); Joshua Cohen, *Freedom of Expression,* 21 Phil. & Pub.Aff. 207 (1993); Deborah Rhode, *Justice and Gender,* 263–73 (1989); Mark Tushnet, *Red, White, and Blue* 293–312 (1988); Donald Downs, *The Attorney General's Commission and the New Politics of Pornography,* 1987 Am.B.Found.Res.J. 641; Steven Gey, *The Apologetics of Suppression,* 86 Mich.L.Rev. 1564 (1988); Eric Hoffman, *Feminism, Pornography, and the Law,* 133 U.Pa.L.Rev. 497 (1985); Robert Post, *Cultural Heterogeneity and the Law,* 76 Calif.L.Rev. 297 (1988); David Richards, *Pornography Commissions and the First Amendment,* 39 Me.L.Rev. 275 (1987); Frederick Schauer, *Causation Theory and the Causes of Sexual Violence,* 1987 Am.B.Found.Res.J. 737; Suzanna Sherry, *An Essay Concerning Toleration,* 71 Minn.L.Rev. 963 (1987); Geoffrey Stone, *Anti-Pornography Legislation as Viewpoint-Discrimination,* 9 Harv.J.Pub.Pol'y 461 (1986); Nadine Strossen, *The Convergence of Feminist and Civil Liberties Principles in the Pornography Debate,* 62 N.Y.U.L.Rev. 201 (1987); Cass Sunstein, *Pornography and the First Amendment,* 1986 Duke L.J. 589; Robin West, *The Feminist-Conservative Anti-Pornography Alliance and the 1986 Attorney General's Commission on Pornography Report,* 1987 Am.B.Found.Res.J. 681. For the Canadian approach, see *Regina v. Butler,* [1992] 1 S.C.R. 452. For comparative commentary, see Kent Greenawalt, *Fighting Words* 99–123 (1995).

the right way to do things, want to know which moves in the sexual game are legitimate. What is important is whether it is authoritative for those hearers who—one way or another—do seem to learn that violence is sexy and coercion legitimate: the fifty percent of boys who 'think it is okay for a man to rape a woman if he is sexually aroused by her,' the fifteen percent of male college undergraduates who say they have raped a woman on a date, the eighty-six percent who say that they enjoy the conquest part of sex, the thirty percent who rank faces of women displaying pain and fear to be more sexually attractive than faces showing pleasure." See also Rae Langton, *Sexual Solipsism: Philosophical Essays on Pornography and Objectification* (2009).

5. ***Pornography and the internet.*** Does the prevalence of pornography on the internet make the case for regulation all the more pressing? Does it make regulation irrelevant or impossible? Or does it afford increased opportunities for feminist inspired sexually oriented speech that could challenge the eroticization of patriarchy? See Courtenay W. Daum, *Feminism and Pornography in the Twenty-First Century*, 30 Women's Rts.L.Rep. 543 (2009) (arguing for the latter).

6. ***Subordination.*** Is the absence of subordination an appropriate ideal? Consider Carlin Meyer, *Sex, Sin, and Women's Liberation: Against Porn-Suppression*, 72 Tex.L.Rev. 1097 (1994): "I am not suggesting that sex accompanied by intimacy, respect, and caring is not an appropriate ideal. Rather, I mean to argue that the sort of equality in which no one is ever the aggressor in fantasy or in reality is, at best, a 'utopian vision of sexual relations: sex without power, sex without persuasion, sex without pursuit.' [S]exual discourse needs to be free-wheeling and uncontrolled because of the hotly contested nature of issues concerning sexuality. Such issues as what constitutes pleasure for women and its connection to danger, to power, to men, and to aggression and inequality; of what sex is 'good' and 'bad'; and of whether women can escape inequality and coercion within Western sexual culture are debated and dissected with little agreement across boundaries of class, race, and nationality. Allies on other issues disagree about whether all violence is bad, over what constitutes violence or pleasure, and over the meaning of such terms as 'objectified,' 'degraded,' or 'demeaned.' " See also Susan Keller, *Viewing and Doing: Complicating Pornography's Meaning*, 81 Geo.L.J. 2195 (1993): "[R]obin West critiques MacKinnon and Dworkin for their failure to acknowledge the 'meaning and the value, to women, of the pleasure we take in our fantasies of eroticized submission.' Some like Jessica Benjamin and Kate Ellis have attempted to explain psychologically why pleasure can be found by women, as well as men, in submission and power. Of the various meanings pornography could have for a variety of audience members, one meaning for women could be pleasure in depictions of power." Can domination be eliminated?

7. ***The pornography definition.*** Is the proposed definition too vague? Is it more or less vague than the terminology employed in *Miller?* Is there a core of clear meaning? How would you clarify its meaning? Is the definition overbroad? What revisions, if any, would you suggest to narrow its scope?

Consider Thomas Emerson, *Pornography and the First Amendment: A Reply to Professor MacKinnon,* 3 Yale L. & Pol. Rev. 130 (1985): "The sweep of the Indianapolis Ordinance is breathtaking. It would subject to governmental ban virtually all depictions of rape, verbal or pictorial, and a substantial proportion of other presentations of sexual encounters. More specifically, it would outlaw such works of literature as the *Arabian Nights,* John Cleland's *Fanny Hill,* Henry Miller's *Tropic of Cancer,* William Faulkner's *Sanctuary,* and Norman Mailer's *Ancient Evenings,* to name but a few. The ban would extend from Greek mythology and Shakespeare to the millions of copies of 'romance novels' now being sold in the supermarkets. It would embrace much of the world's art, from ancient carvings to Picasso, well-known films too numerous to mention, and a large amount of commercial advertising.

"The scope of the Indianapolis Ordinance is not accidental. [As] MacKinnon emphasizes, male domination has deep, pervasive and ancient roots in our society, so it is not surprising that our literature, art, entertainment and commercial practices are permeated by attitudes and behavior that create and reflect the inferior status of women. If the answer to the problem, as Professor MacKinnon describes it, is government suppression of sexual expression that contributes to female subordination, then the net of restraint has to be cast on a nearly limitless scale." Would the ordinance inadvertently cover activist anti-pornographic art that uses violent sexual images to make its point. If not, does the intent of the artist excuse any unintended effects? See Amy Adler, *What's Left?: Hate Speech, Pornography, and the Problem of Artistic Expression,* 84 Calif.L.Rev. 1499 (1996).

8.   ***The assault provision.*** Should the maker of a pornographic work be responsible for assaults prompted by the work? Should the maker of non-pornographic works be responsible for imitative assaults. In *Olivia N. v. NBC,* 126 Cal.App.3d 488, 178 Cal.Rptr. 888 (1981), the victim of a sexual assault allegedly imitating a sexual assault in NBC's "Born Innocent" sued the network. Olivia N. claimed that NBC negligently exposed her to serious risk because it knew or should have known that someone would imitate the act portrayed in the movie. Suppose Olivia N. could show that NBC had been advised that such an assault was likely if the movie were shown? Should a court analogize to cases like *Gertz?* The California court ruled that Olivia N. could not prevail unless she met the *Brandenburg* standard.[116]

———

The Indianapolis version of the anti-pornography civil rights ordinance was struck down in AMERICAN BOOKSELLERS ASS'N v. HUDNUT, 771 F.2d 323 (7th Cir.1985), affirmed, 475 U.S. 1001 (1986). The Seventh Circuit, per EASTERBROOK, J., ruled that the definition of pornography infected the entire ordinance (including provisions against

———

[116] For relevant commentary, see J.M. Balkin, *The Rhetoric of Responsibility,* 76 Va.L.Rev. 197 (1990); Frederick Schauer, *Uncoupling Free Speech,* 92 Colum.L.Rev. 1321 (1992); Frederick Schauer, *Mrs. Palsgraf and the First Amendment,* 47 Wash. & Lee L.Rev. 161 (1990).

trafficking, coercion into pornography, forcing pornography on a person, and assault or physical attack due to pornography) because it impermissibly discriminated on the basis of point of view: "Indianapolis enacted an ordinance defining 'pornography' as a practice that discriminates against women. * * *

"The Indianapolis ordinance does not refer to the prurient interest, to offensiveness, or to the standards of the community. It demands attention to particular depictions, not to the work judged as a whole. It is irrelevant under the ordinance whether the work has literary, artistic, political, or scientific value. The City and many amici point to these omissions as virtues. They maintain that pornography influences attitudes, and the statute is a way to alter the socialization of men and women rather than to vindicate community standards of offensiveness. And as one of the principal drafters of the ordinance has asserted, 'if a woman is subjected, why should it matter that the work has other value?' Catharine MacKinnon, *Pornography, Civil Rights, and Speech,* 20 Harv.Civ.Rts.—Civ.Lib.L.Rev. 1 (1985).

"Civil rights groups and feminists have entered this case as amici on both sides. Those supporting the ordinance say that it will play an important role in reducing the tendency of men to view women as sexual objects, a tendency that leads to both unacceptable attitudes and discrimination in the workplace and violence away from it. Those opposing the ordinance point out that much radical feminist literature is explicit and depicts women in ways forbidden by the ordinance and that the ordinance would reopen old battles. It is unclear how Indianapolis would treat works from James Joyce's *Ulysses* to Homer's *Iliad;* both depict women as submissive objects for conquest and domination.

"We do not try to balance the arguments for and against an ordinance such as this. The ordinance discriminates on the ground of the content of the speech. Speech treating women in the approved way—in sexual encounters 'premised on equality' (MacKinnon, supra, at 22)—is lawful no matter how sexually explicit. Speech treating women in the disapproved way—as submissive in matters sexual or as enjoying humiliation—is unlawful no matter how significant the literary, artistic, or political qualities of the work taken as a whole. The state may not ordain preferred viewpoints in this way. The Constitution forbids the state to declare one perspective right and silence opponents.[117] [Under] the First Amendment the government must leave to the people the evaluation of ideas. Bald or

---

[117] But consider Alon Harel, *Bigotry, Pornography, and The First Amendment: A Theory of Unprotected Speech,* 65 S.Cal.L.Rev. 1887 (1992): "Some ideas and values cannot aid in the process of shaping our political obligations. This is not because these 'values' do not, as a matter of fact, influence the output of the political process but because any influence they do exert does not generate legitimate political obligations. Racist and sexist values cannot participate in the shaping of political obligations because the legal obligations they generate do not have morally binding force."

subtle, an idea is as powerful as the audience allows it to be. A belief may be pernicious—the beliefs of Nazis led to the death of millions, those of the Klan to the repression of millions. A pernicious belief may prevail. Totalitarian governments today rule much of the planet, practicing suppression of billions and spreading dogma that may enslave others. One of the things that separates our society from theirs is our absolute right to propagate opinions that the government finds wrong or even hateful. * * *

"Under the ordinance graphic sexually explicit speech is 'pornography' or not depending on the perspective the author adopts. Speech that 'subordinates' women and also, for example, presents women as enjoying pain, humiliation, or rape, or even simply presents women in 'positions of servility or submission or display' is forbidden, no matter how great the literary or political value of the work taken as a whole. Speech that portrays women in positions of equality is lawful, no matter how graphic the sexual content. This is thought control. It establishes an 'approved' view of women, of how they may react to sexual encounters, of how the sexes may relate to each other. Those who espouse the approved view may use sexual images; those who do not, may not.

"Indianapolis justifies the ordinance on the ground that pornography affects thoughts. Men who see women depicted as subordinate are more likely to treat them so. Pornography is an aspect of dominance.[1] It does not persuade people so much as change them. It works by socializing, by establishing the expected and the permissible. In this view pornography is not an idea; pornography is the injury.

"There is much to this perspective. Beliefs are also facts. People often act in accordance with the images and patterns they find around them. People raised in a religion tend to accept the tenets of that religion, often without independent examination. People taught from birth that black people are fit only for slavery rarely rebelled against that creed; beliefs coupled with the self-interest of the masters established a social structure that inflicted great harm while enduring for centuries. Words and images

---

[1] **[Ct's Note]** "Pornography constructs what a woman is in terms of its view of what men want sexually. * * * Pornography's world of equality is a harmonious and balanced place. Men and women are perfectly complementary and perfectly bipolar. [All] the ways men love to take and violate women, women love to be taken and violated. [What] pornography *does* goes beyond its content: It eroticizes hierarchy, it sexualizes inequality. It makes dominance and submission sex. Inequality is its central dynamic; the illusion of freedom coming together with the reality of force is central to its working. [P]ornography is neither harmless fantasy nor a corrupt and confused misrepresentation of an otherwise neutral and healthy sexual situation. It institutionalizes the sexuality of male supremacy, fusing the erotization of dominance and submission with the social construction of male and female. * * * Men treat women as who they see women as being. Pornography constructs who that is. Men's power over women means that the way men see women defines who women can be. Pornography [is] a sexual reality." MacKinnon, supra, at 17–18 (emphasis in original). See also Andrea Dworkin, *Pornography: Men Possessing Women* (1981). A national commission in Canada recently adopted a similar rationale for controlling pornography. Special Commission on Pornography and Prostitution, 1 *Pornography and Prostitution in Canada* 49–59 (1985).

act at the level of the subconscious before they persuade at the level of the conscious. Even the truth has little chance unless a statement fits within the framework of beliefs that may never have been subjected to rational study.

"Therefore we accept the premises of this legislation. Depictions of subordination tend to perpetuate subordination. The subordinate status of women in turn leads to affront and lower pay at work, insult and injury at home, battery and rape on the streets.[2] * * *

"Yet this simply demonstrates the power of pornography as speech. All of these unhappy effects depend on mental intermediation. Pornography affects how people see the world, their fellows, and social relations. If pornography is what pornography does, so is other speech. Hitler's orations affected how some Germans saw Jews. Communism is a world view, not simply a *Manifesto* by Marx and Engels or a set of speeches. Efforts to suppress communist speech in the United States were based on the belief that the public acceptability of such ideas would increase the likelihood of totalitarian government. [Many] people believe that the existence of television, apart from the content of specific programs, leads to intellectual laziness, to a penchant for violence, to many other ills. The Alien and Sedition Acts passed during the administration of John Adams rested on a sincerely held belief that disrespect for the government leads to social collapse and revolution—a belief with support in the history of many nations. Most governments of the world act on this empirical regularity, suppressing critical speech. In the United States, however, the strength of the support for this belief is irrelevant. Seditious libel is protected speech unless the danger is not only grave but also imminent. See *New York Times*; cf. *Brandenburg.*

"Racial bigotry, anti-semitism, violence on television, reporters' biases—these and many more influence the culture and shape our socialization. None is directly answerable by more speech, unless that speech too finds its place in the popular culture. Yet all is protected as speech, however insidious. Any other answer leaves the government in

---

[2] **[Ct's Note]** MacKinnon's article collects empirical work that supports this proposition. The social science studies are very difficult to interpret, however, and they conflict. Because much of the effect of speech comes through a process of socialization, it is difficult to measure incremental benefits and injuries caused by particular speech. Several psychologists have found, for example, that those who see violent, sexually explicit films tend to have more violent thoughts. But how often does this lead to actual violence? National commissions on obscenity here, in the United Kingdom, and in Canada have found that it is not possible to demonstrate a direct link between obscenity and rape or exhibitionism. The opinions in *Miller* discuss the U.S. commission. See also *Report of the Committee on Obscenity and Film Censorship* 61–95 (Home Office, Her Majesty's Stationery Office, 1979); 1 *Pornography and Prostitution in Canada* 71–103. In saying that we accept the finding that pornography as the ordinance defines it leads to unhappy consequences, we mean only that there is evidence to this effect, that this evidence is consistent with much human experience, and that as judges we must accept the legislative resolution of such disputed empirical questions.

control of all of the institutions of culture, the great censor and director of which thoughts are good for us.

"Sexual responses often are unthinking responses, and the association of sexual arousal with the subordination of women therefore may have a substantial effect. But almost all cultural stimuli provoke unconscious responses. Religious ceremonies condition their participants. Teachers convey messages by selecting what not to cover; the implicit message about what is off limits or unthinkable may be more powerful than the messages for which they present rational argument. Television scripts contain unarticulated assumptions. People may be conditioned in subtle ways. If the fact that speech plays a role in a process of conditioning were enough to permit governmental regulation, that would be the end of freedom of speech. * * *

"Much of Indianapolis's argument rests on the belief that when speech is 'unanswerable,' and the metaphor that there is a 'marketplace of ideas' does not apply, the First Amendment does not apply either. The metaphor is honored; Milton's *Aeropagitica* and John Stuart Mill's *On Liberty* defend freedom of speech on the ground that the truth will prevail, and many of the most important cases under the First Amendment recite this position. The Framers undoubtedly believed it. As a general matter it is true. But the Constitution does not make the dominance of truth a necessary condition of freedom of speech. To say that it does would be to confuse an outcome of free speech with a necessary condition for the application of the amendment.

"A power to limit speech on the ground that truth has not yet prevailed and is not likely to prevail implies the power to declare truth. At some point the government must be able to say (as Indianapolis has said): 'We know what the truth is, yet a free exchange of speech has not driven out falsity, so that we must now prohibit falsity.' If the government may declare the truth, why wait for the failure of speech? Under the First Amendment, however, there is no such thing as a false idea, *Gertz,* so the government may not restrict speech on the ground that in a free exchange truth is not yet dominant. * * *

"We come, finally, to the argument that pornography is 'low value' speech, that it is enough like obscenity that Indianapolis may prohibit it. Some cases hold that speech far removed from politics and other subjects at the core of the Framers' concerns may be subjected to special regulation. E.g., *FCC v. Pacifica Foundation* [Sec. 8, II infra]; *Young v. American Mini Theatres*; *Chaplinsky*. These cases do not sustain statutes that select among viewpoints, however. In *Pacifica* the FCC sought to keep vile language off the air during certain times. The Court held that it may; but the Court would not have sustained a regulation prohibiting scatological descriptions of Republicans but not scatological descriptions of Democrats, or any other form of selection among viewpoints.

"At all events, pornography is not low value speech within the meaning of these cases. Indianapolis seeks to prohibit certain speech because it believes this speech influences social relations and politics on a grand scale, that it controls attitudes at home and in the legislature. This precludes a characterization of the speech as low value. True, pornography and obscenity have sex in common. But Indianapolis left out of its definition any reference to literary, artistic, political, or scientific value. The ordinance applies to graphic sexually explicit subordination in works great and small.[118] The Court sometimes balances the value of speech against the costs of its restriction, but it does this by category of speech and not by the content of particular works. See John Hart Ely, *Flag Desecration: A Case Study in the Roles of Categorization and Balancing in First Amendment Analysis,* 88 Harv.L.Rev. 1482 (1975); Geoffrey Stone, *Restrictions of Speech Because of Its Content: The Peculiar Case of Subject-Matter Restrictions,* 46 U.Chi.L.Rev. 81 (1978). Indianapolis has created an approved point of view and so loses the support of these cases.

"Any rationale we could imagine in support of this ordinance could not be limited to sex discrimination. Free speech has been on balance an ally of those seeking change. Governments that want stasis start by restricting speech. Culture is a powerful force of continuity; Indianapolis paints pornography as a part of the culture of power. Change in any complex system ultimately depends on the ability of outsiders to challenge accepted views and the reigning institutions. Without a strong guarantee of freedom of speech, there is no effective right to challenge what is."[119]

NOTES AND QUESTIONS

1.   In response to the last paragraph, supra, Professor Frank Michelman observes: "[I]t is a fair and obvious question why preservation of 'effective

---

[118] **[Ct's Note]** Indianapolis briefly argues that *Beauharnais,* which allowed a state to penalize "group libel," supports the ordinance. In *Collin v. Smith,* [Sec. 1, V, C infra], we concluded that cases such as *New York Times v. Sullivan* had so washed away the foundations of *Beauharnais* that it could not be considered authoritative. If we are wrong in this, however, the case still does not support the ordinance. It is not clear that depicting women as subordinate in sexually explicit ways, even combined with a depiction of pleasure in rape, would fit within the definition of a group libel. The well received film *Swept Away* used explicit sex, plus taking pleasure in rape, to make a political statement, not to defame. Work must be an insult or slur for its own sake to come within the ambit of *Beauharnais,* and a work need not be scurrilous at all to be pornography under the ordinance.

[119] The balance of the opinion suggested ways that parts of the ordinance might be salvaged, if redrafted. It suggested, for example, that the city might forbid coerced participation in any film or in "any film containing explicit sex." If the latter were adopted, would it make a difference if the section applied to persons coerced into participation in such films without regard to whether they were forced into explicit sex scenes? Swygert, J., concurring, joined part of Easterbrook, J.'s opinion for the court, but objected both to the "questionable and broad assertions regarding how human behavior can be conditioned" and to the "advisory" opinion on how parts of the ordinance might be redrafted.

right[s] to challenge what is' does not require protection of a 'freedom of speech' more broadly conceived to protect social critics—'outsiders,' in Judge Easterbrook's phrase—against suppression by nongovernmental as well as by governmental power. It is a fair and obvious question why the assertion that '[g]overnments that want stasis start by restricting speech' does not apply equally to the nongovernmental agencies of power in society. It is a fair and obvious question why our society's openness to challenge does not need protection against repressive private as well as public action." *Conceptions of Democracy in American Constitutional Argument: The Case of Pornography Regulation,* 56 Tenn.L.Rev. 291 (1989), citing Catharine MacKinnon, *Feminism Unmodified* 155–58 (1987).

2.   *Free speech and silence.* Consider Catharine MacKinnon, *Toward a Feminist Theory of the State* 206 (1989): "That pornography chills women's expression is difficult to demonstrate empirically because silence is not eloquent. Yet on no more of the same kind of evidence, the argument that suppressing pornography might chill legitimate speech has supported its protection. [T]he law of the First Amendment comprehends that freedom of expression, in the abstract, is a system but fails to comprehend that sexism (and racism), in the concrete, are also systems."[120] But see Charles Fried, *Perfect Freedom, Perfect Justice,* 78 B.U. L.Rev. 717 (1998): "[R]acist or sexist speech, if it has the effect attributed to it, produces it through the mind: Potential speakers are persuaded that they are less worthy individuals and so they are less inclined to contribute their voices in debate; and potential listeners are persuaded that these speakers are not worth attending to. But as the argument must concede that the mechanism of the silencing is through persuasion, it must also concede that the government's countermeasures must be directed at silencing the attempt to persuade: The government stops the message because of what it says and the evil the government fears works through the channels of the mind. I do not see how we can escape the conclusion that the government is stopping the message because it is afraid that people might believe it. But that is precisely what the First Amendment has consistently identified as what government may not do * * * ."

3.   *"We do not try to balance."* Does the existence of point of view discrimination preclude balancing under existing law? Consider Marjorie Heins, *Viewpoint Discrimination,* 24 Hast.L.Q. 99 (1996) "Judge Easterbrook's point is well-taken, but it reaches beyond the MacKinnon/Dworkin type of ordinance. The First Amendment does not allow the government to dictate 'which thoughts are good for us,' whether it be in the guise of 'feminist' antipornography laws, indecency laws that turn on notions of 'patent offensiveness,' or obscenity laws of the type upheld in *Miller* and *Slaton*

---

[120] To what extent is discourse inherently empowering and silencing in its effects? To what extent is pornography unique? For rich commentary, see the essays collected in *Censorship and Silencing* (Post ed. 1998); *Speech and Harm: Conroversies over Free Speech* (Maitra & McGowan eds., 2012); Langton, Note 4 after Los Angeles Law; Jennifer Hornsby, *Disempowered Speech,* 23 Philos. Topics 127 (1997); Daniel Jacobson, *Freedom of Speech Acts?,* 24 Phil. & Pub. Aff. 64 (1995); Wojciech Sadurski, *On Seeing Speech Through an Equality Lens,* 16 Oxford J. Leg. Stud. 713 (1996).

because of the lascivious, family-undermining, personality-distorting, and generally immoral thoughts that the Court felt pornography inspires."

4. Does pornography as defined by Indianapolis (or some part of that category) implicate such little First Amendment value as to foreclose constitutional protection? How should such value be assessed? Consider Cass Sunstein, *Pornography and the First Amendment,* 1986 Duke L. J. 589: "First, the speech must be far afield from the central concern of the First Amendment, which, broadly speaking, is effective popular control of public affairs. Speech that concerns governmental processes is entitled to the highest level of protection; speech that has little or nothing to do with public affairs may be accorded less protection. Second, a distinction is drawn between cognitive and noncognitive aspects of speech. Speech that has purely noncognitive appeal will be entitled to less constitutional protection.[121] Third, the purpose of the speaker is relevant: if the speaker is seeking to communicate a message, he will be treated more favorably than if he is not. Fourth, the various classes of low-value speech reflect judgments that in certain areas, government is unlikely to be acting for constitutionally impermissible reasons or producing constitutionally troublesome harms."

How do Sunstein's factors apply to the Indianapolis ordinance? To what extent is it desirable to consider the value of speech in forging a balance?[122]

C. Racist Speech Revisited: The Nazis

> *"What do you want to sell in the marketplace? What idea? The idea of murder?"*

Erna Gans, a concentration camp survivor and active leader in the Skokie B'nai B'rith.[123]

COLLIN v. SMITH, 578 F.2d 1197 (7th Cir.), cert. denied, 439 U.S. 916 (1978), per PELL, J., struck down a Village of Skokie "Racial Slur" Ordinance, making it a misdemeanor to disseminate any material (defined to include "public display of markings and clothing of symbolic significance") promoting and inciting racial or religious hatred. The Village would apparently apply this ordinance to the display of swastikas and military uniforms by the NSPA, a "Nazi organization" which planned to peacefully demonstrate for some 20–30 minutes in front of the Skokie Village Hall.

---

[121] For debate about this factor compare Paul Chevigny, *Pornography and Cognition,* 1989 Duke L.J. 420 with Cass Sunstein, *The First Amendment and Cognition,* 1989 Duke L.J. 433. See also Kenneth Karst, *Boundaries and Reasons: Freedom of Expression and the Subordination of Groups,* 1990 U.Ill.L.Rev. 95.

[122] Compare, e.g., Martin Redish, *The Value of Free Speech,* 130 U.Pa.L.Rev. 591 (1982) and Larry Alexander, *Low Value Speech,* 83 Nw.U.L.Rev. 547 (1989) with Cass Sunstein, *Low Value Speech Revisited,* 83 Nw.U.L.Rev. 555 (1989). Reconsider the question after completing Sec. 3 infra.

[123] Quoted in Fred Friendly & Martha Elliot, *The Constitution: That Delicate Balance* 83 (1984).

Although there was some evidence that some individuals "might have difficulty restraining their reactions to the Nazi demonstration," the Village "does not rely on a fear of responsive violence to justify the ordinance, and does not even suggest that there will be any physical violence if the march is held. This confession takes the case out of the scope of *Brandenburg* and *Feiner*. [It] also eliminates any argument based on the fighting words doctrine of *Chaplinsky,* [which] applied only to words with a direct tendency to cause violence by the persons to whom, individually, the words were addressed."

The court rejected, inter alia, the argument that the Nazi march, with its display of swastikas and uniforms, "will create a substantive evil that it has a right to prohibit: the infliction of psychic trauma on resident holocaust survivors [some 5,000] and other Jewish residents. [The] problem with engrafting an exception on the First Amendment for such situations is that they are indistinguishable in principle from speech that 'invite[s] dispute [or] induces a condition of unrest [or] even stirs people to anger,' *Terminiello.* Yet these are among the 'high purposes' of the First Amendment. [Where,] as here, a crime is made of a silent march, attended only by symbols and not by extrinsic conduct offensive in itself, we think the words of *Street v. New York* [Sec. 2 infra] are very much on point: '[A]ny shock effect [must] be attributed to the content of the ideas expressed. [P]ublic expression of ideas may not be prohibited merely because the ideas are themselves offensive to some of their hearers.' "

Nor was the court impressed with the argument that the proposed march was "not speech, [but] rather an invasion, intensely menacing no matter how peacefully conducted" (most of Skokie's residents are Jewish): "There *need be* no captive audience, as Village residents may, if they wish, simply avoid the Village Hall for thirty minutes on a Sunday afternoon, which no doubt would be their normal course of conduct on a day when the Village Hall was not open in the regular course of business. Absent such intrusion or captivity, there is no justifiable substantial privacy interest to save [the ordinance], when it attempts, by fiat, to declare the entire Village, at all times, a privacy zone that may be sanitized from the offensiveness of Nazi ideology and symbols."[124]

---

[124] See also *Skokie v. National Socialist Party,* 69 Ill.2d 605, 373 N.E.2d 21 (1978). For commentary relating the Skokie issue to regulation of pornography, and of commercial speech, for the purpose of asking whether there are general principles of freedom of expression and whether freedom of expression should be category-dependent, see Thomas Scanlon, *Freedom of Expression and Categories of Expression,* 40 U.Pitt.L.Rev. 519 (1979). For assessment of the complicated connection between Skokie and equality values especially in light of the rest of First Amendment law, see Laurence Tribe, *Constitutional Choices* 219–20 (1985). Compare Donald Downs, *Skokie Revisited: Hate Group Speech and the First Amendment,* 60 Not.D.Law. 629 (1985). More generally, see David Kretzmer, *Freedom of Speech and Racism,* 8 Cardozo L.Rev. 445 (1987).

NOTES AND QUESTIONS

1.   Is *Beauharnais,* Sec. 1, II, A supra, still "good law"? Should it be?

2.   ***Abstraction and the First Amendment.*** Consider Frederick Schauer, *Harry Kalven and the Perils of Particularism,* 56 U.Chi.L.Rev. 397 (1989): "[O]ne sees in the *Skokie* litigation an available distinction between Nazis and others, an equally available distinction between speech designed to persuade and speech designed to assault, and a decision made by the people rather than a decision designed to interfere with the people's wishes. If doctrinal development under the free speech clause were merely an instance of common law decision making, one might expect to see some or all of these factors treated as relevant, and new distinctions developed in order to make relevant those factors, such as the ones just enumerated, that had been suppressed by previous formulations. Yet we know that this is not what happened. The particular events were abstracted in numerous ways. Nazis became political speakers, a suburban community populated by Holocaust survivors became a public forum, and popularly inspired restrictions became governmental censorship. The resolution of the controversy, therefore, stands not as a monument to the ever-more-sensitive development of common law doctrine, but instead as an embodiment of the way in which the First Amendment operates precisely by the entrenchment of categories whose breadth prevents the consideration of some number of relevant factors, and prevents the free speech decision maker from 'thinking small.' "

3.   ***Is racist speech high value?*** Consider David O. Brink, *Millian Principles, Freedom of Expression, and Hate Speech,* 7 Legal Theory 119 (2001): "On [one] view, if hate speech is not high-value, it must be low-value. But bivalence is not a necessary feature of First Amendment jurisprudence. An alternative approach is *scalar*; one assesses liberties of expression in terms of their *centrality* to First Amendment values and holds regulation of expression to a standard of review whose stringency is commensurate with the importance of the liberties at stake. Indeed, First Amendment doctrine is not consistently bivalent; under existing law, commercial speech such as advertising is treated as neither high-value nor low-value; it is accorded a kind of intermediate value, with the result that restrictions on commercial speech must satisfy an intermediate standard of review. Even on this scalar view, a good case can be made that hate speech is low-value speech. But perhaps this claim is more controversial on the scalar than on the bivalent view. However, even if we do not agree to treat hate speech as low-value speech, the case for doing so makes it very implausible to treat it as high-value speech. At most, it could be accorded a sort of intermediate value; if so, the regulation of hate speech should be subject, at most, to a standard of review intermediate between rational basis review and strict scrutiny—perhaps one that requires that the state have a significant or substantial interest that it pursues in a comparatively restrictive manner."

Is speech denying the holocaust clearly of low value? Or in the tradition of Holmes, J., is governmental agnosticism about truth and falsity a central First

Amendment value that can be dispensed with only upon the demonstration of harm to reputation and the like. See Steven G. Gey, *The First Amendment and the Dissemination of Socially Worthless Untruths,* 36 Fla. St. U.L. Rev. 1 (2008) Compare the various essays in Michael Herz & Peter Molnar, eds., *The Context and Content of Hate Speech Rethinking Regulation and Responses* (2012); Ivan Hare & James Weinstein, eds., *Extreme Speech and Democracy* (2010).

4. ***The Klan and the Communists.*** Are the arguments of those who would prohibit racist speech (or pornography), the same as those who would have restricted the speech of the communists (or anarchists). See Steven G. Gey, *The Case Against Postmodern Censorship Theory,* 145 U.Pa. L.Rev. 193 (1996). But consider Steven H. Shiffrin, *Dissent, Injustice, and the Meanings of America* n.184 (1999): "Racist speakers seek to persuade people that government (and others) should not treat all persons with equal concern and respect. If our legal system has even a prayer of claiming to be legitimate, however, it must start from the premise that all citizens are worthy of equal concern and respect. [In] this limited context, the best test of truth is the system's foundational premise of equality,[125] not whether racist speech can emerge in the marketplace of ideas. [To] the extent the communists argue against free speech, [they] are in the same position as the Ku Klux Klan, but the harm of that speech is not in the same league as racist speech."

5. ***European comparison.*** Consider Sionaidh Douglas-Scott, *The Hatefulness of Protected Speech: A Comparison of the American and European Approaches,* 7 Wm. & Mary Bill Rts.J. 305 (1999): "There clearly is a radical difference between the German or, more generally, the European and American approach to the regulation of speech. [First], European and, especially, German jurisprudence emphasize particular values—dignity, protection of personal identity, and equality. German judgments stress the potential of racist insults and denials of Nazi atrocities to affect the very core of the identities of members of certain groups, even if those individuals have not been specifically targeted for abuse. [European] case law rejects a conception of individuals as beings who merely should be left to their own devices to make up their own minds about the value of expression in the public domain, to be free to ignore it, or to counter it with more speech. Such an approach isolates human beings by forcing them to take the consequences of painful conduct and ignores the particular susceptibility of certain groups to injury, especially when the offense of the speech seems to be targeted at such groups because of their identity. Under the American model, the individual will be left to his or her less communal and somewhat atomistic existence.[126]

"Second, the European approach is fundamentally more sympathetic to a conception in which the state plays a role in facilitating the realization of freedom, democracy, and equality. Under the European approach, it becomes natural for the state to assume a more affirmative role in actualizing specific

---

[125] Are there many conceptions of equality in the American system which those who would regulate racist speech need to take account? See Gary Goodpaster, *Equality and Free Speech: The Case Against Substantive Equality,* 82 Iowa L. Rev 645 (1997).

[126] See also Guy E. Carmi, *Dignity—The Enemy from Within,* 9 U.Pa.J. Const.L. 957 (2007).

constitutional rights. Within the area of freedom of speech this would require the state not only to refrain from violating certain constitutional norms, but also to participate in their realization—an approach which usually is assumed only to be required of socio-economic rights, such as the right to work. Surely it is not enough for societies that claim to be committed to the ideals of social and political equality and respect for individual dignity to remain neutral and passive when threats to these values exist. Sometimes the State must take steps to protect democracy itself, which may involve repressing speech."

Consider Michel Rosenfeld, *Hate Speech in Constitutional Jurisprudence: A Comparative Analysis*, 24 Cardozo L. Rev. 1523 (2003): "In terms of assumptions, the American approach either underestimates the potential for harm of hate speech that is short of incitement to violence, or it overestimates the potential of rational deliberation as a means to neutralize calls to hate. In terms of impact, given its long history of racial tensions, it is surprising that the United States does not exhibit greater concern for the injuries to security, dignity, autonomy and well being which officially tolerated hate speech causes to its black minority. Likewise, America's hate speech approach seems to unduly discount the pernicious impact that racist hate speech may have on lingering or dormant racist sentiments still harbored by a non-negligible segment of the white population."

6.   *Face-to-face insults.* Should the First Amendment bar an action for intentional infliction of emotional distress for face-to-face racial insults?[127] Is it enough that the words in question inflict injury or must the victim show that the words were likely to promote a fight? Suppose a crowd of whites gathers to taunt a young black child on the way to a previously all white school? Suppose short of using violence, they do everything they can to harm the child? Is it the case that "no government that would call itself a decent government would fail to intervene [and] disperse the crowd" and that "the rights of the crowd [cannot] really stand on the same plane" as the child on the way to school? See Hadley Arkes, *Civility and the Restriction of Speech: Rediscovering the Defamation of Groups,* 1974 Sup.Ct.Rev. 281. Should the First Amendment bar state criminal or civil actions precisely tailored to punish racial insults? Insults directed against the handicapped? For the case in favor of a tort action against racial insults, see Richard Delgado, *Words That Wound: A Tort Action for Racial Insults, Epithets, and Name-Calling,* 17 Harv.Civ.Rts.—Civ.Lib.L.Rev. 133 (1982). For a spirited exchange, see Marjorie Heins, *Banning Words: A Comment on "Words that Wound,"* 18 Harv.Civ.Rts.—Civ.Lib.L.Rev. 585 (1983) and *Professor Richard Delgado Replies,* id. at 593.

7.   *Is one person's "racialist's plea" another person's act of intimidation?* Are these responses patterned? Consider Mari Matsuda, *Public Response to Racist Speech: Considering the Victim's Story,* 87 Mich.L.Rev. 2320 (1989): "The typical reaction of target-group members to an

---

[127] On the relationship between discriminatory speech and the tort of intentional infliction of emotional distress, see Jean Love, *Discriminatory Speech and the Tort of Intentional Infliction of Emotional Distress,* 47 Wash. & Lee L.Rev. 123 (1990).

incident of racist propaganda is alarm and immediate calls for redress. The typical reaction of non-target-group members is to consider the incidents isolated pranks, the product of sick-but-harmless minds. This is in part a defensive reaction: a refusal to believe that real people, people just like us, are racists. This disassociation leads logically to the claim that there is no institutional or state responsibility to respond to the incident.[128] It is not the kind of real and pervasive threat that requires the state's power to quell."[129]

See also Charles Lawrence, *If He Hollers Let Him Go: Regulating Racist Speech on Campus,* 1990 Duke L.J. 431: "If one asks why we always begin by asking whether we can afford to fight racism rather than asking whether we can afford not to, or if one asks why my colleagues who oppose all regulation of racist speech do not feel the burden is theirs (to justify a reading of the First Amendment that requires sacrificing rights guaranteed under the equal protection clause), then one sees an example of how unconscious racism operates in the marketplace of ideas. [O]ur unconscious racism causes us (even those of us who are the direct victims of racism) to view the First Amendment as the 'regular' amendment—an amendment that works for all people—and the equal protection clause and racial equality as a special interest-amendment important to groups that are less valued."[130]

8. ***Effects of regulation.*** Consider Steven Shiffrin, *Racist Speech, Outsider Jurisprudence, and the Meaning of America,* 80 Corn.L.Rev. 43 (1994): "From the perspective of many millions of Americans, to enact racist speech regulations would be to pass yet another law exhibiting special favoritism for people of color. What makes this kind of law so potentially counterproductive is that its transformation of public racists into public martyrs would tap into widespread political traditions and understanding in our culture. In short, the case of the martyr would be appealingly wrapped in the banner of the American flag. Millions of white Americans already resent people of color to some degree. To fuse that resentment with Americans' love for the First Amendment is risky business. [America] would still have a FIRST AMENDMENT and a strong First Amendment tradition even if it enacted general racist speech regulations. The problem is not the First Amendment; the problem is that racism is now and always has been a central part of the meaning of America." Would hate speech legislation have the "unfortunate effect of focusing on the individual perpetrator rather than on the victims or on social forces that assist and inform the perpetrator"? Would attention "more fruitfully turn to both the lives and the circumstances of the victims as well as

---

[128] For the argument that the best interpretation of *Brown v. Board of Education requires* government to respond, see Lawrence, infra. For response, see Strossen, infra.

[129] Are victims in a better position to evaluate the truth? Compare Richard Delgado & Jean Stefancic, *Must We Defend Nazis?* 86–87 (1997) with Gey, Note 3 supra.

[130] For discussion of the extent and character of the harm, see Delgado & Stefancic, fn. 129 supra, at 4–10; Matsuda, supra; Lawrence, infra; Richard Delgado, *Campus Antiracism Rules Constitutional Narratives in Collision,* 85 Nw.U.L.Rev. 343 (1991) ("The ubiquity and incessancy of harmful racial depiction are [the] source of its virulence. Like water dripping on sandstone, it is a pervasive harm which only the most hardy can resist. Yet the prevailing First Amendment paradigm predisposes us to treat racist speech as individual harm, as though we only had to evaluate the effect of a single drop of water.").

the surrounding social traditions and practices that have made and continue to make that group subject to dehumanization"? Martha Minow, *Regulating Hatred*, 47 UCLA L.Rev. 1253 (2000).

9. ***Proposals to restrict hate speech.*** Consider Stanford University's definition of harassment by personal vilification: "Speech or other expression constitutes harassment by personal vilification if it a) is intended to insult or stigmatize an individual or a small number of individuals on the basis of their sex, race, color, handicap, religion, sexual orientation, or national and ethnic origin; and b) is addressed directly to the individual or individuals whom it insults or stigmatizes; and c) makes use of insulting or 'fighting words' or non-verbal symbols." Is this appropriate? See Thomas Grey, *Civil Rights v. Civil Liberties*, Soc. Phil. & Pol'y 81 (Spring 1991). Does this go too far? See Nadine Strossen, *Regulating Racist Speech on Campus: A Modest Proposal?* 1990 Duke L.J. 484. Does it not go far enough? See Lawrence, Note 7 supra: "I supported a proposal which would have been broader in scope by prohibiting speech of this nature in all common areas, excepting organized rallies and speeches. It would have been narrower in its protection in that it would not have protected persons who were vilified on the basis of their membership in dominant majority groups." Compare Matsuda, Note 7 supra, arguing that speech with a message of racial inferiority, that is directed against a historically oppressed group, and that is persecutorial, hateful, and degrading should be outlawed.[131]

D. Animal Cruelty and the Flight from New Categories

18 U.S.C. § 48 criminalizes the knowing creation, sale, or possession of a depiction of animal cruelty, if done for commercial gain in interstate or foreign commerce. A depiction of animal cruelty is defined as one "in which a living animal is intentionally maimed, mutilated, tortured, wounded, or killed," if that conduct violates federal or state law where "the creation, sale, or possession takes place." The law exempts any depiction "that has serious religious, political, scientific, educational, journalistic, historical, or artistic value." Respondent was convicted under the statute for selling

---

[131] For other relevant literature, see, e.g., Sec. 3, IV supra; *The Content and Context of Hate Speech* (Herz & Molnar eds., 2012); James Weinstein, *Hate Speech, Pornography, and the Radical Attack on Free Speech Doctrine* (1999); Nicholas Wolfson, *Hate Speech, Sex Speech, Free Speech* (1997); Kent Greenawalt, *Fighting Words* (1995); Mari Matsuda, Charles Lawrence, Richard Delgado, & Kimberle Crenshaw, eds., *Words that Wound* (1993); Laura Lederer & Richard Delgado, eds., *The Price We Pay: The Case Against Racist Speech, Hate Propaganda and Pornography* (1995); Samuel Walker, *Hate Speech: The History of an American Controversy* (1994); Symposium, *Campus Hate Speech and the Constitution in the Aftermath of Doe v. University of Michigan*, 37 Wayne L.Rev. 1309 (1991); Symposium, *Free Speech & Religious, Racial & Sexual Harassment*, 32 Wm. & Mary L.Rev. 207 (1991); Symposium, *Frontiers of Legal Thought: The New First Amendment*, 1990 Duke L.J. 375; Symposium, *Hate Speech and the First Amendment: On A Collision Course?*, 37 Vill.L.Rev. 723 (1992); Symposium, *Hate Speech After R.A.V.: More Conflict Between Free Speech and Equality*, 18 Wm. Mitchell L.Rev. 889 (1992); See also sources cited in connection with *R.A.V. v. City of St. Paul*, Sec. 3, IV infra and sources cited in Steven Shiffrin, *Racist Speech, Outsider Jurisprudence, and the Meaning of America*, 80 Corn.L.Rev. 43, 44 n. 6 (1994). For the Canadian perspective, see *Regina v. Keegstra*, [1990] 3 S.C.R. 697. For relevant commentary, see Greenawalt, supra; Lawrence Douglas, *Policing the Past*, in *Censorship and Silencing* 67 (Robert C. Post ed. 1998); Lorraine Weinrib, *Hate Promotion in a Democratic Society*, 36 McGill L.Rev. 1416 (1991).

videos of dog fighting, but argued that the statute violated the First Amendment on its face.

UNITED STATES v. STEVENS, 559 U.S. 460 (2010) per ROBERTS, C.J., rejected this contention and held that the statute was substantially overbroad, but it left room for Congress to pass a more narrowly drawn statute: "The Government's primary submission is that [the] banned depictions of animal cruelty, as a class, are categorically unprotected by the First Amendment. We disagree.

" * * * 'From 1791 to the present,' [the] First Amendment has 'permitted restrictions upon the content of speech in a few limited areas,' and has never 'include[d] a freedom to disregard these traditional limitations.' These 'historic and traditional categories long familiar to the bar,'—including obscenity, *Roth*, defamation, *Beauharnais*, fraud, *Virginia Bd.*, incitement, *Brandenburg*, and speech integral to criminal conduct, *Giboney v. Empire Storage & Ice Co.*, 336 U.S. 490 (1949)—are 'well-defined and narrowly limited classes of speech, the prevention and punishment of which have never been thought to raise any Constitutional problem.' *Chaplinsky*.

"The Government argues that 'depictions of animal cruelty' should be added to the list. It contends that depictions of 'illegal acts of animal cruelty' that are 'made, sold, or possessed for commercial gain' necessarily 'lack expressive value,' and may accordingly 'be regulated as *unprotected* speech.' * * *

"The Government contends that 'historical evidence' about the reach of the First Amendment is not 'a necessary prerequisite for regulation today,' and that categories of speech may be exempted from the First Amendment's protection without any long-settled tradition of subjecting that speech to regulation. Instead, the Government points to Congress's 'legislative judgment that . . . depictions of animals being intentionally tortured and killed [are] of such minimal redeeming value as to render [them] unworthy of First Amendment protection,' and asks the Court to uphold the ban on the same basis. The Government thus proposes that a claim of categorical exclusion should be considered under a simple balancing test: 'Whether a given category of speech enjoys First Amendment protection depends upon a categorical balancing of the value of the speech against its societal costs.'

"As a free-floating test for First Amendment coverage, that sentence is startling and dangerous. The First Amendment's guarantee of free speech does not extend only to categories of speech that survive an ad hoc balancing of relative social costs and benefits. The First Amendment itself reflects a judgment by the American people that the benefits of its restrictions on the Government outweigh the costs. * * *

"To be fair to the Government, its view did not emerge from a vacuum. As the Government correctly notes, this Court has often *described* historically unprotected categories of speech as being 'of such slight social value as a step to truth that any benefit that may be derived from them is clearly outweighed by the social interest in order and morality.' In *Ferber,* we noted that within these categories of unprotected speech, 'the evil to be restricted so overwhelmingly outweighs the expressive interests, if any, at stake, that no process of case-by-case adjudication is required,' because 'the balance of competing interests is clearly struck,' The Government derives its proposed test from these descriptions in our precedents.

"But such descriptions are just that-descriptive. They do not set forth a test that may be applied as a general matter to permit the Government to imprison any speaker so long as his speech is deemed valueless or unnecessary, or so long as an ad hoc calculus of costs and benefits tilts in a statute's favor. When we have identified categories of speech as fully outside the protection of the First Amendment, it has not been on the basis of a simple cost-benefit analysis. In *Ferber,* for example, we classified child pornography as such a category. We noted that the State of New York had a compelling interest in protecting children from abuse, and that the value of using children in these works (as opposed to simulated conduct or adult actors) was de minimis. But our decision did not rest on this 'balance of competing interests' alone. We made clear that *Ferber* presented a special case: The market for child pornography was 'intrinsically related' to the underlying abuse, and was therefore 'an integral part of the production of such materials, an activity illegal throughout the Nation.' As we noted, '[i]t rarely has been suggested that the constitutional freedom for speech and press extends its immunity to speech or writing used as an integral part of conduct in violation of a valid criminal statute.' (quoting *Giboney*). *Ferber* thus grounded its analysis in a previously recognized, long-established category of unprotected speech * * * .

"Our decisions in *Ferber* and other cases cannot be taken as establishing a freewheeling authority to declare new categories of speech outside the scope of the First Amendment. Maybe there are some categories of speech that have been historically unprotected, but have not yet been specifically identified or discussed as such in our case law. But if so, there is no evidence that 'depictions of animal cruelty' is among them. We need not foreclose the future recognition of such additional categories to reject the Government's highly manipulable balancing test as a means of identifying them."

Roberts, C.J., thereafter argued that the statute was substantially overbroad. Depictions of maiming, mutilating, and torture convey cruelty, he said, but not depictions of wounding or killing, and he did not interpret the statute to apply exclusively to instances of animal cruelty. Nor was the illegality of the underlying activity a proxy for cruelty, he suggested, because many laws involving the proper treatment of animals are not related to cruelty. And the serious value section of the statute did not resolve the overbreadth issue because depictions of hunting might be protected even if they did not have *serious* value.

"Our construction of § 48 decides the constitutional question; the Government makes no effort to defend [its constitutionality] as applied beyond crush videos and depictions of animal fighting. It argues that those particular depictions are intrinsically related to criminal conduct or are analogous to obscenity (if not themselves obscene), and that the ban on such speech is narrowly tailored to reinforce restrictions on the underlying conduct, prevent additional crime arising from the depictions, or safeguard public mores. But the Government nowhere attempts to extend these arguments to depictions of any other activities—depictions that are presumptively protected by the First Amendment but that remain subject to the criminal sanctions of § 48.

"However 'growing' and 'lucrative' the markets for crush videos and dogfighting depictions might be, they are dwarfed by the market for other depictions, such as hunting magazines and videos. We therefore need not and do not decide whether a statute limited to crush videos or other depictions of extreme animal cruelty would be constitutional. We hold only that § 48 is not so limited but is instead substantially overbroad, and therefore invalid under the First Amendment."

ALITO, J., dissented: "The Court strikes down in its entirety a valuable statute that was enacted not to suppress speech, but to prevent horrific acts of animal cruelty-in particular, the creation and commercial exploitation of 'crush videos,' a form of depraved entertainment that has no social value. [A] sample crush video, which has been lodged with the Clerk, records the following event: '[A] kitten, secured to the ground, watches and shrieks in pain as a woman thrusts her high-heeled shoe into its body, slams her heel into the kitten's eye socket and mouth loudly fracturing its skull, and stomps repeatedly on the animal's head. The kitten hemorrhages blood, screams blindly in pain, and is ultimately left dead in a moist pile of blood-soaked hair and bone.'

"It is undisputed that the *conduct* depicted in crush videos may constitutionally be prohibited. All 50 States and the District of Columbia have enacted statutes prohibiting animal cruelty. But before the enactment of § 48 the underlying conduct depicted in crush videos was nearly impossible to prosecute. These videos, which 'often appeal to persons with a very specific sexual fetish,' were made in secret, generally without a live audience, and 'the faces of the women inflicting the torture in the material often were not shown, nor could the location of the place where the cruelty was being inflicted or the date of the activity be ascertained from the depiction.' Thus, law enforcement authorities often were not able to identify the parties responsible for the torture. * * *

"In light of the practical problems thwarting the prosecution of the creators of crush videos under state animal cruelty laws, Congress concluded that the only effective way of stopping the underlying criminal conduct was to prohibit the commercial exploitation of the videos of that conduct. And Congress' strategy appears to have been vindicated. We are told that '[b]y 2007, sponsors of § 48 declared the crush video industry dead. Even overseas Websites shut down in the wake of § 48. Now, after the Third Circuit's decision [facially invalidating the statute], crush videos are already back online." '

Alito, J., argued that the principles of *Ferber* lead easily to the conclusion that crush and dog fight videos were constitutionally unprotected though he conceded that the government interest was more significant in *Ferber*. He dissented from the Court's conclusion that the statute was overbroad: "I would hold that § 48 does not apply to depictions of hunting. First, because § 48 targets depictions of 'animal cruelty,' I would interpret that term to apply only to depictions involving acts of animal cruelty as defined by applicable state or federal law, not to depictions of acts that happen to be illegal for reasons having nothing to do with the prevention of animal cruelty. Virtually all state laws prohibiting animal cruelty either expressly define the term 'animal' to exclude wildlife or else specifically exempt lawful hunting activities, so the statutory prohibition [may] reasonably be interpreted not to reach most if not all hunting depictions. * * *

"Second, even if the hunting of wild animals were otherwise covered[,] I would hold that hunting depictions fall within the exception [for] depictions that have 'serious' (i.e., not "trifling") 'scientific,' 'educational,' or 'historical' value. [Thus,] it is widely thought that hunting has 'scientific' value in that it promotes conservation, 'historical' value in that it provides a link to past times when hunting played a critical role in daily life, and 'educational' value in that it furthers the understanding and appreciation of nature and our country's past and instills valuable character traits. And if hunting itself is widely thought to serve these values, then it takes but a small additional step to conclude that depictions of hunting make a non-trivial contribution to the exchange of ideas. Accordingly, I would hold that hunting depictions fall comfortably within the exception * * * .

"I do not have the slightest doubt that Congress, in enacting § 48, had no intention of restricting the creation, sale, or possession of depictions of hunting. Proponents of the law made this point clearly. [But] even if § 48 did impermissibly reach the sale or possession of depictions of hunting in a few unusual situations (for example, the sale in Oregon of a depiction of hunting with a crossbow in Virginia or the sale in Washington State of the hunting of a sharp-tailed grouse in Idaho, those isolated applications would hardly show that § 48 bans a substantial amount of protected speech."

After making similar arguments with other examples put forth by Roberts, C.J., Alito, J., concluded that the statute "has a substantial core of constitutionally permissible applications" and that the respondent had not met his burden of demonstrating that any impermissible applications of the statute were substantial.

E. Intentional Infliction of Emotional Distress

The father of a deceased Marine brought an action for intentional infliction of emotional distress, intrusion upon seclusion, and civil conspiracy against a fundamentalist church and its members for demonstrating near the Marine's funeral with signs whose content is detailed in the Court's opinion in SNYDER v. PHELPS, 131 S.Ct. 1207 (2011), which is set out above.

F. Violent Video Games

California prohibits the sale or rental of "violent video games" to minors. The prohibition covers games "in which the range of options available to a player includes killing, maiming, dismembering, or sexually assaulting an image of a human being, if those acts are depicted" in a manner that "[a] reasonable person, considering the game as a whole, would find appeals to a deviant or morbid interest of minors," that is "patently offensive to prevailing standards in the community as to what is suitable for minors," and that "causes the game, as a whole, to lack serious literary, artistic, political, or scientific value for minors."

BROWN v. ENTERTAINMENT MERCHANTS ASS'N, 132 S.Ct. 81 (2011), per SCALIA, J., held that the law did not meet First Amendment standards for establishing a new category of unprotected speech: "Last Term, in *Stevens,* we held that new categories of unprotected speech may not be added to the list [of unprotected categories] by a legislature that concludes certain speech is too harmful to be tolerated. [The] Government argued in *Stevens* that it could create new categories of unprotected speech by applying a 'simple balancing test' that weighs the value of a particular category of speech against its social costs and then punishes that category of speech if it fails the test. We emphatically rejected that 'startling and dangerous' proposition. [W]ithout persuasive evidence that a novel restriction on content is part of a long (if heretofore unrecognized) tradition of proscription, a legislature may not revise the 'judgment [of] the American people,' embodied in the First Amendment, 'that the benefits of its restrictions on the Government outweigh the costs.'

"That holding controls this case. As in *Stevens,* California has tried to make violent speech regulation look like obscenity regulation by appending a saving clause required for the latter. That does not suffice. Our cases have been clear that the obscenity exception to the First Amendment does not cover whatever a legislature finds shocking, but only depictions of 'sexual conduct.' Because speech about violence is not obscene, it is of no consequence that California's statute mimics the New York statute regulating obscenity-for-minors that we upheld in *Ginsberg v. New York*, [fn. 83 in *Miller v. California*, Sec. 1, IV, B]. That case approved a prohibition on the sale to minors of sexual material that would be obscene from the perspective of a child. We held that the legislature could 'adjus[t] the definition of obscenity "to social realities by permitting the appeal of this type of material to be assessed in terms of the sexual interests" of . . . minors.' And because 'obscenity is not protected expression,' the New York statute could be sustained so long as the legislature's judgment that the proscribed materials were harmful to children 'was not irrational.'

"The California Act is something else entirely. It does not adjust the boundaries of an existing category of unprotected speech to ensure that a definition designed for adults is not uncritically applied to children. [Instead,] it wishes to create a wholly new category of content-based regulation that is permissible only for speech directed at children.

"That is unprecedented and mistaken. '[M]inors are entitled to a significant measure of First Amendment protection, and only in relatively narrow and well-defined circumstances may government bar public dissemination of protected materials to them.' No doubt a State possesses legitimate power to protect children from harm, *Ginsberg*, but that does not include a free-floating power to restrict the ideas to which children may be exposed. 'Speech that is neither obscene as to youths nor subject to some other legitimate proscription cannot be suppressed solely to protect the young from ideas or images that a legislative body thinks unsuitable for them.' *Erznoznik*.[3]

"California's argument would fare better if there were a longstanding tradition in this country of specially restricting children's access to depictions of violence, but there is [none.] California claims that video games present special problems because they are 'interactive,' in that the player participates in the violent action on screen and determines its outcome. The latter feature is nothing new: Since at least the publication of The Adventures of You: Sugarcane Island in 1969, young readers of choose-your-own-adventure stories have been able to make decisions that determine the plot by following instructions about which page to turn to.

---

[3] **[Ct's Note]** Justice Thomas ignores the holding of *Erznoznik*, and denies that persons under 18 have any constitutional right to speak or be spoken to without their parents' consent. He cites no case, state or federal, supporting this view, and to our knowledge there is none. [Scalia, J., argued that Thomas, J.,'s interpretation would lead to the view that government could prevent children from attending political rallies or church without parental permission.]

As for the argument that video games enable participation in the violent action, that seems to us more a matter of degree than of kind.

"Justice Alito has done considerable independent research to identify video games in which 'the violence is astounding,' 'Victims are dismembered, decapitated, disemboweled, set on fire, and chopped into little pieces. . . . Blood gushes, splatters, and pools.' Justice Alito recounts all these disgusting video games in order to disgust us—but disgust is not a valid basis for restricting expression. And the same is true of Justice Alito's description of those video games he has discovered that have a racial or ethnic motive for their violence "ethnic cleansing" [of] African Americans, Latinos, or Jews.' To what end does he relate this? Does it somehow increase the 'aggressiveness' that California wishes to suppress? Who knows? But it does arouse the reader's ire, and the reader's desire to put an end to this horrible message. Thus, ironically, Justice Alito's argument highlights the precise danger posed by the California Act: that the *ideas* expressed by speech—whether it be violence, or gore, or racism—and not its objective effects, may be the real reason for governmental proscription.

"Because the Act imposes a restriction on the content of protected speech, it is invalid unless California can demonstrate that it passes strict scrutiny—that is, unless it is justified by a compelling government interest and is narrowly drawn to serve that interest." Scalia, J., argued that California did not meet that standard. He maintained that California could not show a causal link between violent video games and significant aggression, that courts considering the psychological evidence have found it wanting, that whatever harmful effects that do exist are indistinguishable from other unregulated media such as Saturday morning cartoon, that permitting parents to purchase violent video games for children is inconsistent with a purported concern about harmful effects, that a rating system already prevents children from purchasing many video games beyond their maturity level, and that the law is overinclusive because not all parents care about the video games their children purchase.

"California's legislation straddles the fence between (1) addressing a serious social problem and (2) helping concerned parents control their children. Both ends are legitimate, but when they affect First Amendment rights they must be pursued by means that are neither seriously underinclusive nor seriously overinclusive. As a means of protecting children from portrayals of violence, the legislation is seriously underinclusive, not only because it excludes portrayals other than video games, but also because it permits a parental or avuncular veto. And as a means of assisting concerned parents it is seriously overinclusive because it abridges the First Amendment rights of young people whose parents (and aunts and uncles) think violent video games are a harmless pastime. And the overbreadth in achieving one goal is not cured by the underbreadth in achieving the other. Legislation such as this, which is neither fish nor fowl, cannot survive strict scrutiny."

ALITO, J., joined by Roberts, C.J., concurring, argued that California's statute was unconstitutionally vague because the standards for what is inappropriate for children had been more clearly developed in the arena of sex than they have in the area of violence. He suggested that the statute would be on a stronger footing if it "targeted a narrower class of graphic depictions." At the same time, he argued that the majority was too casually dismissive of the "effect of exceptionally violent video games on impressionable minors, who often spend countless hours immersed in the alternative worlds that these games create. [When] all of the characteristics of video games are taken into account, there is certainly a reasonable basis for thinking that the experience of playing a video game may be quite different from the experience of reading a book, listening to a radio broadcast, or viewing a movie. And if this is so, then for at least some minors, the effects of playing violent video games may also be quite different. The Court acts prematurely in dismissing this possibility out of [hand.] I would hold only that the particular law at issue here fails to provide the clear notice that the Constitution requires. I would not squelch legislative efforts to deal with what is perceived by some to be a significant and developing social problem. If differently framed statutes are enacted by the States or by the Federal Government, we can consider the constitutionality of those laws when cases challenging them are presented to us."

THOMAS, J., dissenting, argued that the "Court's decision today does not comport with the original public understanding of the First Amendment. As originally understood, the First Amendment's protection against laws 'abridging the freedom of speech' did not extend to all speech. 'There are certain well-defined and narrowly limited classes of speech, the prevention and punishment of which have never been thought to raise any Constitutional problem. 'Laws regulating such speech do not 'abridg[e] the freedom of speech' because such speech is understood to fall outside 'the freedom of speech. * * *

"In my view, the 'practices and beliefs held by the Founders' reveal another category of excluded speech: speech to minor children bypassing their parents. The historical evidence shows that the founding generation believed parents had absolute authority over their minor children and expected parents to use that authority to direct the proper development of their children. It would be absurd to suggest that such a society understood 'the freedom of speech' to include a right to speak to minors (or a corresponding right of minors to access speech) without going through the minors' parents. The founding generation would not have considered it an abridgment of 'the freedom of speech' to support parental authority by restricting speech that bypasses minors' parents."

BREYER, J., dissented: "I would apply both this Court's 'vagueness' precedents and a strict form of First Amendment scrutiny. In doing so, the special First Amendment category I find relevant is not (as the Court claims) the category of 'depictions of violence,' but rather the category of 'protection of children.' This Court has held that the 'power of the state to control the conduct of children reaches beyond the scope of its authority over adults.' *Prince v. Massachusetts*, [Ch. 8, Sec. 2, I]. And the 'regulatio[n] of communication addressed to [children] need not conform to the requirements of the [F]irst [A]mendment in the same way as those applicable to adults.' "

The majority's claim that the California statute, if upheld, would create a 'new categor[y] of unprotected speech,' is overstated. No one here argues that depictions of violence, even extreme violence, *automatically* fall outside the First Amendment's protective scope as, for example, do obscenity and depictions of child pornography. We properly speak of *categories* of expression that lack protection when, like 'child pornography,' the category is broad, when it applies automatically, and when the State can prohibit everyone, including adults, from obtaining access to the material within it. But where, as here, careful analysis must precede a narrower judicial conclusion (say, denying protection to a shout of "fire" in a crowded theater, or to an effort to teach a terrorist group how to peacefully petition the United Nations), we do not normally describe the result as creating a 'new category of unprotected speech.' See *Schenck*; *Holder*.

"Thus, in *Stevens*, after rejecting the claim that *all* depictions of animal cruelty (a category) fall outside the First Amendment's protective scope, we went on to decide whether the particular statute at issue violates the First Amendment under traditional standards; and we held that, because the statute was overly broad, it was invalid. Similarly, here the issue is whether, applying traditional First Amendment standards, this statute does, or does not, pass muster.

"In my view, California's statute provides 'fair notice of what is prohibited,' and consequently it is not impermissibly vague. [Both] the *Miller* standard and the law upheld in *Ginsberg* lack perfect clarity. But that fact reflects the difficulty of the Court's long search for words capable of protecting expression without depriving the State of a legitimate constitutional power to regulate. Ultimately, [this] Court accepted the 'community standards' tests used in *Miller* and *Ginsberg*. They reflect the fact that sometimes, even when a precise standard proves elusive, it is easy enough to identify instances that fall within a legitimate regulation. And they seek to draw a line, which, while favoring free expression, will nonetheless permit a legislature to find the words necessary to accomplish a legitimate constitutional objective.

"What, then, is the difference between *Ginsberg* and *Miller* on the one hand and the California law on the other? It will often be easy to pick out cases at which California's statute directly aims, involving, say, a character who shoots out a police officer's knee, douses him with gasoline, lights him on fire, urinates on his burning body, and finally kills him with a gunshot to the head. As in *Miller* and *Ginsberg*, the California law clearly *protects* even the most violent games that possess serious literary, artistic, political, or scientific value. And it is easier here than in *Miller* or *Ginsberg* to separate the sheep from the goats at the statute's border. That is because here the industry itself has promulgated standards and created a review process, in which adults who 'typically have experience with children' assess what games are inappropriate for minors.

"There is, of course, one obvious difference: The *Ginsberg* statute concerned depictions of 'nudity,' while California's statute concerns extremely violent video games. But for purposes of vagueness, why should that matter? Justice Alito argues that the *Miller* standard sufficed because there are 'certain generally accepted norms concerning expression related to sex,' whereas there are no similarly 'accepted standards regarding the suitability of violent entertainment.' But there is no evidence that is so. The Court relied on 'community standards' in *Miller* precisely because of the difficulty of articulating 'accepted norms' about depictions of sex. I can find no difference—historical or otherwise—that is *relevant* to the vagueness question. * * *

"Like the majority, I believe that the California law must be 'narrowly tailored' to further a 'compelling interest,' without there being a 'less restrictive' alternative that would be 'at least as effective.' I would not apply this strict standard 'mechanically.' Rather, in applying it, I would evaluate the degree to which the statute injures speech-related interests, the nature of the potentially-justifying 'compelling interests,' the degree to which the statute furthers that interest, the nature and effectiveness of possible alternatives, and, in light of this evaluation, whether, overall, 'the statute works speech-related harm . . . out of proportion to the benefits that the statute seeks to provide.'

"First Amendment standards applied in this way are difficult but not impossible to satisfy. Applying 'strict scrutiny' the Court has upheld restrictions on speech that, for example, ban the teaching of peaceful dispute resolution to a group on the State Department's list of terrorist organizations, *Holder*, and limit speech near polling places, *Burson* (plurality opinion). * * *

"Moreover, although the Court did not specify the 'level of scrutiny' it applied in *Ginsberg*, we have subsequently described that case as finding a 'compelling interest' in protecting children from harm sufficient to justify limitations on speech. Since the Court in *Ginsberg* specified that the statute's prohibition applied to material that was *not* obscene, I cannot dismiss *Ginsberg* on the ground that it concerned obscenity. Nor need I depend upon the fact that the Court in *Ginsberg* insisted only that the legislature have a 'rational' basis for finding the depictions there at issue harmful to children. For in this case, California has substantiated its claim of harm with considerably stronger evidence. * * *

"There are many scientific studies that support California's views. Social scientists, for example, have found *causal* evidence that playing these games results in harm. Longitudinal studies, which measure changes over time, have found that increased exposure to violent video games causes an increase in aggression over the same period. Experimental studies in laboratories have found that subjects randomly assigned to play a violent video game subsequently displayed more characteristics of aggression than those who played nonviolent games. Surveys of 8th and 9th grade students have found a correlation between playing violent video games and aggression. Cutting-edge neuroscience has shown that 'virtual violence in video game playing results in those neural patterns that are considered characteristic for aggressive cognition and behavior.' And 'meta-analyses,' *i.e.*, studies of all the studies, have concluded that exposure to violent video games 'was positively associated with aggressive behavior, aggressive cognition, and aggressive affect,' and that 'playing violent video games is a *causal* risk factor for long-term harmful outcomes.'

"Some of these studies take care to explain in a commonsense way why video games are potentially more harmful than, say, films or books or television. In essence, they say that the closer a child's behavior comes, not to watching, but to *acting* out horrific violence, the greater the potential psychological harm. Experts debate the conclusions of all these studies. Like many, perhaps most, studies of human behavior, each study has its critics, and some of those critics have produced studies of their own in which they reach different conclusions. (I list both sets of research in the appendixes.) I, like most judges, lack the social science expertise to say definitively who is right. But associations of public health professionals who do possess that expertise have reviewed many of these studies and found a significant risk that violent video games, when compared with more passive media, are particularly likely to cause children harm. * * *

"Unlike the majority, I would find sufficient grounds in these studies and expert opinions for this Court to defer to an elected legislature's conclusion that the video games in question are particularly likely to harm children. * * * I add that the majority's different conclusion creates a serious anomaly in First Amendment law. *Ginsberg* makes clear that a State can prohibit the sale to minors of depictions of nudity; today the Court makes clear that a State cannot prohibit the sale to minors of the most violent interactive video games. But what sense does it make to forbid selling to a 13-year-old boy a magazine with an image of a nude woman, while protecting a sale to that 13-year-old of an interactive video game in which he actively, but virtually, binds and gags the woman, then tortures and kills her? What kind of First Amendment would permit the government to protect children by restricting sales of that extremely violent video game only when the woman—bound, gagged, tortured, and killed—is also topless?

"This anomaly is not compelled by the First Amendment. It disappears once one recognizes that extreme violence, where interactive, and without literary, artistic, or similar justification, can prove at least as, if not more, harmful to children as photographs of nudity. And the record here is more than adequate to support such a view. That is why I believe that *Ginsberg* controls the outcome here a fortiori. And it is why I believe California's law is constitutional on its face."

G. Stolen Valor

At his first public meeting of the Three Valley Water District Board, Board Member Xavier Alvarez introduced himself: "I'm a retired marine of 25 years. I retired in the year 2001. Back in 1987, I was awarded the Congressional Medal of Honor. I got wounded many times by the same guy." These statements were false, and Alvarez was indicted under the Stolen Valor Act, 18 U.S.C. § 704 which provides that "Whoever falsely represents himself or herself, verbally or in writing, to have been awarded any decoration or medal authorized by Congress for the Armed Forces of the United States . . . shall be fined under this title, imprisoned not more than six months, or both." The Act further provides that if the false representation relates to an award of the Congressional Medal of Honor, the possible imprisonment could rise to a year.

UNITED STATES v. ALVAREZ, 132 S.Ct. 2537 (2012), held that the Stolen Valor Act violated the First Amendment. KENNEDY, J., joined by Roberts, C.J., and Ginsburg and Sotomayor, JJ., found the Act defective using the interpretive approach employed in *Stevens* and *Brown*: "In light of the substantial and expansive threats to free expression posed by content-based restrictions, this Court has rejected as 'startling and dangerous' a 'free-floating test for First Amendment coverage [based on] an ad hoc balancing of relative social costs and benefits.' *Stevens*. Instead, content-based restrictions on speech have been permitted, as a general matter, only when confined to the few 'historic and traditional categories [of expression] long familiar to the bar.' * * *

"Absent from those few categories [is] any general exception to the First Amendment for false statements. This comports with the common understanding that some false statements are inevitable if there is to be an open and vigorous expression of views in public and private conversation, expression the First Amendment guarantee. See *Sullivan* ('Th[e] erroneous statement is inevitable in free debate')."

Kennedy, J., argued that prior statements by the Court to the effect that false statements of fact have no constitutional value (see, e.g., *Gertz)*, did not mean that false statements of fact were an unprotected category of speech. He maintained that the cases containing such language "all derive from cases discussing defamation, fraud, or some other legally cognizable harm associated with a false statement, such as an invasion of privacy or the costs of vexatious litigation. In those decisions the falsity of the speech at issue was not irrelevant to our analysis, but neither was it determinative. The Court has never endorsed the categorical rule the Government advances: that false statements receive no First Amendment protection. Our prior decisions have not confronted a measure, like the Stolen Valor Act, that targets falsity and nothing more. * * *

"The Government gives three examples of regulations on false speech that courts generally have found permissible: first, the criminal prohibition of a false statement made to a Government official, 18 U.S.C. § 1001; second, laws punishing perjury; and third, prohibitions on the false representation that one is speaking as a Government official or on behalf of the Government, see, e.g., § 912; § 709. These restrictions, however, do not establish a principle that all proscriptions of false statements are exempt from exacting First Amendment scrutiny. [§]1001's prohibition on false statements made to Government officials, in communications concerning official matters, does not lead to the broader proposition that false statements are unprotected when made to any person, at any time, in any context. The same point can be made about what the Court has confirmed is the 'unquestioned constitutionality of perjury statutes,' both the federal statute, § 1623, and its state-law equivalents. It is not simply because perjured statements are false that they lack First Amendment protection. Perjured testimony 'is at war with justice' because it can cause a court to render a 'judgment not resting on truth.' Perjury undermines the function and province of the law and threatens the integrity of judgments that are the basis of the legal system. Unlike speech in other contexts, testimony under oath has the formality and gravity necessary to remind the witness that his or her statements will be the basis for official governmental action, action that often affects the rights and liberties of others. Sworn testimony is quite distinct from lies not spoken under oath and simply intended to puff up oneself. Statutes that prohibit falsely representing that one is speaking on behalf of the Government, or that prohibit impersonating a Government officer, also protect the integrity of Government processes, quite apart from merely restricting false speech. [These] examples, to the extent that they implicate fraud or speech integral to criminal conduct, are inapplicable here. As our law and tradition show, then, there are instances in which the falsity of speech bears upon whether it is protected. Some false speech may be prohibited even if analogous true speech could not be. This opinion does not imply that any of these targeted prohibitions are somehow vulnerable. But it also rejects the notion that false speech should be in a general category that is presumptively unprotected.

"[T]he Stolen Valor Act, by its plain terms applies to a false statement made at any time, in any place, to any person. It can be assumed that it would not apply to, say, a theatrical performance. Still, the sweeping, quite unprecedented reach of the statute puts it in conflict with the First Amendment. Here the lie was made in a public meeting, but the statute would apply with equal force to personal, whispered conversations within a home. The statute seeks to control and suppress all false statements on this one subject in almost limitless times and settings. And it does so entirely without regard to whether the lie was made for the purpose of material gain. Permitting the government to decree this speech to be a criminal offense, whether shouted from the rooftops or made in a barely audible whisper, would endorse government authority to compile a list of subjects about which false statements are punishable. That governmental power has no clear limiting principle. Our constitutional tradition stands against the idea that we need Oceania's Ministry of Truth."

Kennedy, J., concluded that the Stolen Valor Act could not meet the exacting scrutiny required. He did not question that the statute attempted to further a compelling interest, but he denied that the statute was "actually necessary" to achieve it: "The Government points to no evidence to support its claim that the public's general perception of military awards is diluted by false claims such as those made by Alvarez. [Moreover,] the Government has not shown, and cannot show, why counterspeech would not suffice to achieve its interest. The facts of this case indicate that the dynamics of free speech, of counterspeech, of refutation, can overcome the lie. Respondent lied at a public meeting. Even before the FBI began investigating him for his false statements 'Alvarez was perceived as a phony,' [H]e was ridiculed online [and] his actions were reported in the press. [There] is good reason to believe that a similar fate would befall other false claimants. * * *

"The American people do not need the assistance of a government prosecution to express their high regard for the special place that military heroes hold in our tradition. Only a weak society needs government protection or intervention before it pursues its resolve to preserve the truth. Truth needs neither handcuffs nor a badge for its vindication."

BREYER, J., joined by Kagan, J., concurring in the judgment, departed from the approach taken in *Stevens*: "In determining whether a statute violates the First Amendment, this Court has often found it appropriate to examine the fit between statutory ends and means. In doing so, it has examined speech-related harms, justifications, and potential alternatives. In particular, it has taken account of the seriousness of the speech-related harm the provision will likely cause, the nature and importance of the provision's countervailing objectives, the extent to which the provision will tend to achieve those objectives, and whether there are other, less restrictive ways of doing so. Ultimately the Court has had to determine whether the statute works speech-related harm that is out of proportion to its justifications.

"Sometimes the Court has referred to this approach as 'intermediate scrutiny,' sometimes as 'proportionality' review, sometimes as an examination of 'fit,' and sometimes it has avoided the application of any label at all. Regardless of the label, some such approach is necessary if the First Amendment is to offer proper protection in the many instances in which a statute adversely affects constitutionally protected interests but warrants neither near-automatic condemnation (as 'strict scrutiny' implies) nor near-automatic approval (as is implicit in 'rational basis' review). But in this case, the Court's term 'intermediate scrutiny' describes what I think we should do.

"As the dissent points out, 'there are broad areas in which any attempt by the state to penalize purportedly false speech would present a grave and unacceptable danger of suppressing truthful speech.' Laws restricting false statements about philosophy, religion, history, the social sciences, the arts, and the like raise such concerns, and in many contexts have called for strict scrutiny. But this case does not involve such a law. The dangers of suppressing valuable ideas are lower where, as here, the regulations concern false statements about easily verifiable facts that do not concern such subject matter. Such false factual statements are less likely than are true factual statements to make a valuable contribution to the marketplace of ideas. And the government often has good reasons to prohibit such false speech. But its regulation can nonetheless threaten speech-related harms. * * *

"I must concede, as the Government points out, that this Court has frequently said or implied that false factual statements enjoy little First Amendment protection. But these judicial statements cannot be read to mean 'no protection at all.' False factual statements can serve useful human objectives, for example: in social contexts, where they may prevent embarrassment, protect privacy, shield a person from prejudice, provide the sick with comfort, or preserve a child's innocence; in public contexts, where they may stop a panic or otherwise preserve calm in the face of danger; and even in technical, philosophical, and scientific contexts, where (as Socrates' methods suggest) examination of a false statement (even if made deliberately to mislead) can promote a form of thought that ultimately helps realize the truth. Moreover, as the Court has often said, the threat of criminal prosecution for making a false statement can inhibit the speaker from making true statements, thereby 'chilling' a kind of speech that lies at the First Amendment's heart. * * *

"Further, the pervasiveness of false statements, made for better or for worse motives, made thoughtlessly or deliberately, made with or without accompanying harm, provides a weapon to a government broadly empowered to prosecute falsity without more. And those who are unpopular may fear that the government will use that weapon selectively, say by prosecuting a pacifist who supports his cause by (falsely) claiming to have been a war hero, while ignoring members of other political groups who might make similar false claims.

"I also must concede that many statutes and common law doctrines make the utterance of certain kinds of false statements unlawful. Those prohibitions, however, tend to be narrower than the statute before us, in that they limit the scope of their application, sometimes by requiring proof of specific harm to identifiable victims; sometimes by specifying that the lies be made in contexts in which a tangible harm to others is especially likely to occur; and sometimes by limiting the prohibited lies to those that are particularly likely to produce harm."

Breyer, J., proceeded to argue that this was true of fraud, defamation, the intentional infliction of emotional distress, perjury, materially false statements made to federal officials, false claims of terrorist attacks, impersonation of government officials, and trademark infringements: "While this list is not exhaustive, it is sufficient to show that few statutes, if any, simply prohibit without limitation the telling of a lie, even a lie about one particular matter. Instead, in virtually all these instances limitations of context, requirements of proof of injury, and the like, narrow the statute to a subset of lies where specific harm is more likely to occur. The limitations help to make certain that the statute does not allow its threat of liability or criminal punishment to roam at large, discouraging or forbidding the telling of the lie in contexts where harm is unlikely or the need for the prohibition is small.

"The statute before us lacks any such limiting features. It may be construed to prohibit only knowing and intentional acts of deception about readily verifiable facts within the personal knowledge of the speaker, thus reducing the risk that valuable speech is chilled. But it still ranges very broadly. And that breadth means that it creates a significant risk of First Amendment harm. As written, it applies in family, social, or other private contexts, where lies will often cause little harm. It also applies in political contexts, where although such lies are more likely to cause harm, the risk of censorious selectivity by prosecutors is also high. Further, given the potential haziness of individual memory along with the large number of military awards covered (ranging from medals for rifle marksmanship to the Congressional Medal of Honor), there remains a risk of chilling that is not completely eliminated by mens rea requirements; a speaker might still be worried about being prosecuted for a careless false statement, even if he does not have the intent required to render him liable. And so the prohibition may be applied where it should not be applied, for example, to bar stool braggadocio or, in the political arena, subtly but selectively to speakers that the Government does not like. * * *

"[I]t should be possible significantly to diminish or eliminate these remaining risks by enacting a similar but more finely tailored statute. For example, not all military awards are alike. Congress might determine that some warrant greater protection than others. And a more finely tailored statute might, as other kinds of statutes prohibiting false factual statements have done, insist upon a showing that the false statement caused specific harm or at least was material, or focus its coverage on lies most likely to be harmful or on contexts where such lies are most likely to cause harm. I recognize that in some contexts, particularly political contexts, such a narrowing will not always be easy to achieve. In the political arena a false statement is more likely to make a behavioral difference (say, by leading the listeners to vote for the speaker) but at the same time criminal prosecution is particularly dangerous (say, by radically changing a potential election result) and consequently can more easily result in censorship of speakers and their [ideas.] I would also note, like the plurality, that in this area more accurate information will normally counteract the lie. And an accurate, publicly available register of military awards, easily obtainable by political opponents, may well adequately protect the integrity of an award against those who would falsely claim to have earned it. And so it is likely that a more narrowly tailored statute combined with such information-disseminating devices will effectively serve Congress' end.

"The Government has provided no convincing explanation as to why a more finely tailored statute would not work. [That] being so, I find the statute as presently drafted works disproportionate constitutional harm. It consequently fails intermediate scrutiny, and so violates the First Amendment."

ALITO, J., joined by Scalia and Thomas, JJ., dissenting, also departed from the *Stevens* approach: "Time and again, this Court has recognized that as a general matter false factual statements possess no intrinsic First Amendment value. Consistent with this recognition, many kinds of false factual statements have long been proscribed without 'rais[ing] any Constitutional problem.' Laws prohibiting fraud, perjury, and defamation, for example, were in existence when the First Amendment was adopted, and their constitutionality is now beyond question. We have also described as falling outside the First Amendment's protective shield certain false factual statements that were neither illegal nor tortious at the time of the Amendment's adoption. The right to freedom of speech has been held to permit recovery for the intentional infliction of emotional distress by means of a false statement. And in *Hill*, the Court concluded that the free speech right allows recovery for the even more modern tort of false-light invasion of privacy.

"In line with these holdings, it has long been assumed that the First Amendment is not offended by prominent criminal statutes with no close common-law analog. The most well known of these is probably 18 U.S.C. § 1001. [Unlike] perjury, § 1001 is not limited to statements made under oath or before an official government tribunal. Nor does it require any showing of 'pecuniary or property loss to the government.' Instead, the statute is based on the need to protect 'agencies from the perversion which *might* result from the deceptive practices described.'

"Still other statutes make it a crime to falsely represent that one is speaking on behalf of, or with the approval of, the Federal Government. We have recognized that § 912, like § 1001, does not require a showing of pecuniary or property loss and that its purpose is to 'maintain the general good repute and dignity' of Government service. All told, there are more than 100 federal criminal statutes that punish false statements made in connection with areas of federal agency concern. These examples amply demonstrate that false statements of fact merit no First Amendment protection in their own right. It is true, as Justice Breyer notes, that many in our society either approve or condone certain discrete categories of false statements, including false statements made to prevent harm to innocent victims and so-called 'white lies.' But respondent's false claim to have received the Medal of Honor did not fall into any of these categories. His lie did not 'prevent embarrassment, protect privacy, shield a person from prejudice, provide the sick with comfort, or preserve a child's innocence.' Nor did his lie 'stop a panic or otherwise preserve calm in the face of danger' or further philosophical or scientific debate. Respondent's claim, like all those covered by the Stolen Valor Act, served no valid purpose. [The] lies covered by the Stolen Valor Act have no intrinsic value and thus merit no First Amendment protection unless their prohibition would chill other expression that falls within the Amendment's scope. * * *

"[T]here are broad areas in which any attempt by the state to penalize purportedly false speech would present a grave and unacceptable danger of suppressing truthful speech. Laws restricting false statements about philosophy, religion, history, the social sciences, the arts, and other matters of public concern would present such a threat. The point is not that there is no such thing as truth or falsity in these areas or that the truth is always impossible to ascertain, but rather that it is perilous to permit the state to be the arbiter of truth. * * *

"In stark contrast to hypothetical laws prohibiting false statements about history, science, and similar matters, the Stolen Valor Act presents no risk at all that valuable speech will be suppressed. The speech punished by the Act is not only verifiably false and entirely lacking in intrinsic value, but it also fails to serve any instrumental purpose that the First Amendment might protect. Tellingly, when asked at oral argument what truthful speech the Stolen Valor Act might chill, even respondent's counsel conceded that the answer is none.

"Neither of the two opinions endorsed by Justices in the majority claims that the false statements covered by the Stolen Valor Act possess either intrinsic or instrumental value. Instead, those opinions appear to be based on the distinct concern that the Act suffers from overbreadth." Alito, J., referred to the plurality's concern about "personal, whispered conversations within a home") and Breyer, J.'s argument that the Act "applies in family, social, or other private contexts" and in "political contexts." But, Alito, J., argued that "to strike down a statute on the basis that it is overbroad, it is necessary to show that the statute's 'overbreadth [is] substantial, not only in an absolute sense, but also relative to [its] plainly legitimate sweep.' The plurality and the concurrence do not even attempt to make this showing. The plurality additionally worries that a decision sustaining the Stolen Valor Act might prompt Congress and the state legislatures to enact laws criminalizing lies about 'an endless list of subjects.' The plurality apparently fears that we will see laws making it a crime to lie about civilian awards such as college degrees or certificates of achievement in the arts and sports.

"This concern is likely unfounded. With very good reason, military honors have traditionally been regarded as quite different from civilian awards. Nearly a century ago, Congress made it a crime to wear a military medal without authorization; we have no comparable tradition regarding such things as Super Bowl rings, Oscars, or Phi Beta Kappa keys. In any event, if the plurality's concern is not entirely fanciful, it falls outside the purview of the First Amendment. The problem that the plurality foresees— that legislative bodies will enact unnecessary and overly intrusive criminal laws—applies regardless of whether the laws in question involve speech or nonexpressive conduct. If there is a problem with, let us say, a law making it a criminal offense to falsely claim to have been a high school valedictorian, the problem is not the suppression of speech but the misuse of the criminal law, which should be reserved for conduct that inflicts or threatens truly serious societal harm. The objection to this hypothetical law would be the same as the objection to a law making it a crime to eat potato chips during the graduation ceremony at which the high school valedictorian is recognized. The safeguard against such laws is democracy, not the First Amendment. Not every foolish law is unconstitutional.* * *

"The Stolen Valor Act is a narrow law enacted to address an important problem, and it presents no threat to freedom of expression. I would sustain the constitutionality of the Act, and I therefore respectfully dissent."

2. DISTINGUISHING BETWEEN CONTENT REGULATION AND MANNER REGULATION: UNCONVENTIONAL FORMS OF COMMUNICATION

Special First Amendment questions are often said to arise by regulation of the time, place, and manner of speech as opposed to regulation of its content. But the two types of regulation are not mutually exclusive. It is possible to regulate time, place, manner, and content in the same regulation. For example, in *Linmark,* Sec. 3, II infra, the township outlawed signs (but not leaflets) advertising a house for sale (but not other advertisements or other messages) on front lawns (but not other places).

Further, the terms, manner and content are strongly contested concepts. Indeed, an issue recurring in this section is whether the regulations in question are of manner or content. To the extent this section is about manner regulation, it is not exhaustive—much comes later. Most of the cases in this section involve unconventional forms of expression. Speakers claim protection for burning draft cards, wearing armbands, mutilating flags, nude dancing, wearing long hair. Fact patterns such as these fix renewed attention on the question of how "speech" should be defined. It may be a nice question as to whether obscenity is not speech within the First Amendment lexicon, whether it is such speech but has been balanced into an unprotected state, or whether it is not *freedom* of speech or *the* freedom of speech. But assassinating a public figure, even to send a message, raises no First Amendment problem. Robbing a bank does not raise a free speech issue. What does? How do we decide?

The fact patterns in this section also invite scrutiny of other issues that appear in succeeding sections. Should it make a difference if the state's interest in regulating speech is unrelated to what is being said? Suppose the state's concern arises from the non-communicative impact of the speech act—from its manner. Should that distinction make a constitutional difference, and, if so, how much? These questions become more complicated because in context it is often difficult to determine what the state interest is and sometimes difficult to determine whether there is a meaningful distinction between what is said and how it is said.

Even when the distinction between the manner of the speech and the content of the speech is clear, further doctrinal complications abound. Sometimes the regulation considered by the Court is described as one regulating the "time, place, or manner" of speech, and the Court employs the "time, place, or manner test" which is itself differently phrased in different cases. On other occasions the regulation is described as having an "incidental" impact on freedom of speech, and the Court turns to a different test. These different tests are sometimes described by the Court as functional equivalents. Should there be different tests? In what circumstances? See generally Susan Williams, *Content Discrimination and the First Amendment,* 139 U.Pa.L.Rev. 201 (1991).

Finally, in this and succeeding sections the question arises of the extent to which freedom of speech should require special sensitivity to the methods and communications needs of the less powerful.

UNITED STATES V. O'BRIEN
391 U.S. 367, 88 S.Ct. 1673, 20 L.Ed.2d 672 (1968).

CHIEF JUSTICE WARREN delivered the opinion of the Court.

On the morning of March 31, 1966, David Paul O'Brien and three companions burned their Selective Service registration certificates on the steps of the South Boston Courthouse. A sizable crowd, including several [FBI agents] witnessed the event. Immediately after the burning, members of the crowd began attacking O'Brien [and he was ushered to safety by an FBI agent.] O'Brien stated to FBI agents that he had burned his registration certificate because of his beliefs, knowing that he was violating federal law.

[For this act, O'Brien was convicted in federal court.] He [told] the jury that he burned the certificate publicly to influence others to adopt his antiwar beliefs, as he put it, "so that other people would reevaluate their positions with Selective Service, with the armed forces, and reevaluate their place in the culture of today, to hopefully consider my position."

The indictment upon which he was tried charged that he "wilfully and knowingly did mutilate, destroy, and change by burning [his] Registration Certificate; in violation of [§ 462(b)(3) of the Universal Military Training and Service Act of 1948], amended by Congress in 1965 (adding the words italicized below), so that at the time O'Brien burned his certificate an offense was committed by any person, "who forges, alters, *knowingly destroys, knowingly mutilates,* or in any manner changes any such certificate * * * ." (Italics supplied.)

[On appeal, the] First Circuit held the 1965 Amendment unconstitutional as a law abridging freedom of speech. At the time the Amendment was enacted, a regulation of the Selective Service System required registrants to keep their registration certificates in their "personal possession at all times." Wilful violations of regulations promulgated pursuant to the Universal Military Training and Service Act were made criminal by statute. The Court of Appeals, therefore, was of the opinion that conduct punishable under the 1965 Amendment was already punishable under the nonpossession regulation, and consequently that the Amendment served no valid purpose; further, that in light of the prior regulation, the Amendment must have been "directed at public as distinguished from private destruction." On this basis, the Court concluded that the 1965 Amendment ran afoul of the First Amendment by singling out persons engaged in protests for special treatment. * * *

When a male reaches the age of 18, he is required by the Universal Military Training and Service Act to register with a local draft board. He is assigned a Selective Service number, and within five days he is issued a registration certificate. Subsequently, and based on a questionnaire completed by the registrant, he is assigned a classification denoting his eligibility for induction, and "[a]s soon as practicable" thereafter he is issued a Notice of Classification. * * *

Both the registration and classification certificates bear notices that the registrant must notify his local board in writing of every change in address, physical condition, and occupational, marital, family, dependency, and military status, and of any other fact which might change his classification. Both also contain a notice that the registrant's Selective Service number should appear on all communications to his local board.

[The 1965] Amendment does not distinguish between public and private destruction, and it does not punish only destruction engaged in for the purpose of expressing views.[132] A law prohibiting destruction of Selective Service certificates no more abridges free speech on its face than a motor vehicle law prohibiting the destruction of drivers' licenses, or a tax law prohibiting the destruction of books and records.

O'Brien nonetheless argues [first] that the 1965 Amendment is unconstitutional [as] applied to him because his act of burning his registration certificate was protected "symbolic speech" within the First Amendment. [He claims that] the First Amendment guarantees include all modes of "communication of ideas by conduct," and that his conduct is within this definition because he did it in "demonstration against the war and against the draft."

We cannot accept the view that an apparently limitless variety of conduct can be labeled "speech" whenever the person engaging in the conduct intends thereby to express an idea. However, even on the assumption that the alleged communicative element in O'Brien's conduct is sufficient to bring into play the First Amendment, it does not necessarily follow that the destruction of a registration certificate is constitutionally protected activity. This Court has held that when "speech" and "nonspeech" elements are combined in the same course of conduct, a sufficiently important governmental interest in regulating the nonspeech element can justify incidental limitations on First Amendment freedoms. To characterize the quality of the governmental interest which must appear,

---

[132] But compare Chief Judge Aldrich below, 376 F.2d at 541: "We would be closing our eyes in the light of the prior law if we did not see on the face of the amendment that it was precisely directed at public as distinguished from private destruction. [In] singling out persons engaging in protest for special treatment the amendment strikes at the very core of what the First Amendment protects."

the Court has employed a variety of descriptive terms: compelling; substantial; subordinating; paramount; cogent; strong. [W]e think it clear that a government regulation is sufficiently justified if it is within the constitutional power of the government; if it furthers an important or substantial governmental interest; if the governmental interest is unrelated to the suppression of free expression; and if the incidental restriction on alleged First Amendment freedom is no greater than is essential to the furtherance of that interest.[133] We find that the 1965 Amendment meets all of these requirements, and consequently that O'Brien can be constitutionally convicted for violating it. [Pursuant to its power to classify and conscript manpower for military service], Congress may establish a system of registration for individuals liable for training and service, and may require such individuals within reason to cooperate in the registration system. The issuance of certificates indicating the registration and eligibility classification of individuals is a legitimate and substantial administrative aid in the functioning of this system. And legislation to insure the continuing availability of issued certificates serves a legitimate and substantial purpose in the system's administration.

[O'Brien] essentially adopts the position that [Selective Service] certificates are so many pieces of paper designed to notify registrants of their registration or classification, to be retained or tossed in the wastebasket according to the convenience or taste of the registrant. Once the registrant has received notification, according to this view, there is no reason for him to retain the certificates. [However, the registration and classification certificates serve] purposes in addition to initial notification. Many of these purposes would be defeated by the certificates' destruction or mutilation. Among these are [simplifying verification of the registration and classification of suspected delinquents, evidence of availability for induction in the event of emergency, ease of communication between registrants and local boards, continually reminding registrants of the need to notify local boards of changes in status].

The many functions performed by Selective Service certificates establish beyond doubt that Congress has a legitimate and substantial interest in preventing their wanton and unrestrained destruction and assuring their continuing availability by punishing people who knowingly and wilfully destroy or mutilate them. And we are unpersuaded that the

---

[133] Michael C. Dorf, *Incidental Burdens on Fundamental Rights*, 109 Harv.L.Rev. 1175 (1996): "Prong one is not properly part of First Amendment law, because *all* regulation must be within the government's constitutional power. Prong three merely restates the proposition that the challenged regulation must be content-neutral—which is a precondition for the application of the test in the first instance. The *O'Brien* test thus can be distilled into a two-part requirement that formally resembles conventional intermediate scrutiny: a regulation must serve a substantial government interest and must be narrowly tailored to that end in order to pass constitutional muster."

pre-existence of the nonpossession regulations in any way negates this interest.

In the absence of a question as to multiple punishment, it has never been suggested that there is anything improper in Congress providing alternative statutory avenues of prosecution to assure the effective protection of one and the same interest. Here, the pre-existing avenue of prosecution was not even statutory. Regulations may be modified or revoked from time to time by administrative discretion. Certainly, the Congress may change or supplement a regulation.

[The] gravamen of the offense defined by the statute is the deliberate rendering of certificates unavailable for the various purposes which they may serve. Whether registrants keep their certificates in their personal possession at all times, as required by the regulations, is of no particular concern under the 1965 Amendment, as long as they do not mutilate or destroy the certificates so as to render them unavailable. [The 1965 amendment] is concerned with abuses involving *any* issued Selective Service certificates, not only with the registrant's own certificates. The knowing destruction or mutilation of someone else's certificates would therefore violate the statute but not the nonpossession regulations.

We think it apparent that the continuing availability to each registrant of his Selective Service certificates substantially furthers the smooth and proper functioning of the system that Congress has established to raise armies. * * *

It is equally clear that the 1965 Amendment specifically protects this substantial governmental interest. We perceive no alternative means that would more precisely and narrowly assure the continuing availability of issued Selective Service certificates than a law which prohibits their wilful mutilation or destruction. The 1965 Amendment prohibits such conduct and does nothing more. [The] governmental interest and the scope of the 1965 Amendment are limited to preventing a harm to the smooth and efficient functioning of the Selective Service System. When O'Brien deliberately rendered unavailable his registration certificate, he wilfully frustrated this governmental interest. For this noncommunicative impact of his conduct, and for nothing else, he was convicted.* * *

O'Brien finally argues that the 1965 Amendment is unconstitutional as enacted because what he calls the "purpose" of Congress was "to suppress freedom of speech." We reject this argument because under settled principles the purpose of Congress, as O'Brien uses that term, is not a basis for declaring this legislation unconstitutional.

It is a familiar principle of constitutional law that this Court will not strike down an otherwise constitutional statute on the basis of an alleged illicit legislative motive.

[I]f we were to examine legislative purpose in the instant case, we would be obliged to consider not only [the statements of the three members of Congress who addressed themselves to the amendment, all viewing draft-card burning as a brazen display of unpatriotism] but also the more authoritative reports of the Senate and House Armed Services Committees. [B]oth reports make clear a concern with the "defiant" destruction of so-called "draft cards" and with "open" encouragement to others to destroy their cards, [but they] also indicate that this concern stemmed from an apprehension that unrestrained destruction of cards would disrupt the smooth functioning of the Selective Service System. * * *

Reversed.[134]

JUSTICE HARLAN concurring. * * *

I wish to make explicit my understanding that [the Court's analysis] does not foreclose consideration of First Amendment claims in those rare instances when an "incidental" restriction upon expression, imposed by a regulation which furthers an "important or substantial" governmental interest and satisfies the Court's other criteria, in practice has the effect of entirely preventing a "speaker" from reaching a significant audience with whom he could not otherwise lawfully communicate. This is not such a case, since O'Brien manifestly could have conveyed his message in many ways other than by burning his draft card.

JUSTICE DOUGLAS, dissenting.

[Douglas, J., thought that "the underlying and basic problem in this case" was the constitutionality of a draft "in the absence of a declaration of war" and that the case should be put down for reargument on this question. The following Term, concurring in *Brandenburg*, he criticized *O'Brien* on the merits. After recalling that the Court had rejected O'Brien's First Amendment argument on the ground that "legislation to insure the continuing availability of issued certificates serves a legitimate and substantial purpose in the [selective service] system's administration," he commented: "But O'Brien was not prosecuted for not having his draft card available when asked for by a federal agent. He was indicted, tried, and convicted for burning the card. And this Court's affirmance [was not] consistent with the First Amendment." He observed, more generally in *Brandenburg*:

["Action is often a method of expression and within the protection of the First Amendment. Suppose one tears up his own copy of the Constitution in eloquent protest to a decision of this Court. May he be indicted? Suppose one rips his own Bible to shreds to celebrate his departure from one 'faith' and his embrace of atheism. May he be indicted? * * *

---

[134] Marshall, J., took no part.

["The act of praying often involves body posture and movement as well as utterances. It is nonetheless protected by the Free Exercise Clause. Picketing [is] 'free speech plus.' [Therefore], it can be regulated when it comes to the 'plus' or 'action' side of the protest. It can be regulated as to the number of pickets and the place and hours, because traffic and other community problems would otherwise suffer. But none of these considerations are implicated in the symbolic protest of the Vietnam war in the burning of a draft card."]

NOTES AND QUESTIONS

1.   *Expression vs. action.* What of the Court's rejection of the idea that conduct is speech "whenever the person engaging in the conduct intends thereby to express an idea." Was it right to question whether O'Brien's conduct was speech? What was it about O'Brien's conduct that made the Court doubt that it was speech? What if O'Brien had burned a copy of the Constitution? Consider Thomas Emerson, *The System of Freedom of Expression* 80 & 84 (1970): "To some extent expression and action are always mingled; most conduct includes elements of both. Even the clearest manifestations of expression involve some action, as in the case of holding a meeting, publishing a newspaper, or merely talking. At the other extreme, a political assassination includes a substantial mixture of expression. The guiding principle must be to determine which element is predominant in the conduct under consideration. Is expression the major element and the action only secondary? Or is the action the essence and the expression incidental? The answer, to a great extent, must be based on a common-sense reaction, made in light of the functions and operations of a system of freedom of expression. * * *

"The burning of a draft card is, of course, conduct that involves both communication and physical acts. Yet it seems quite clear that the predominant element in such conduct is expression (opposition to the draft) rather than action (destruction of a piece of cardboard). The registrant is not concerned with secret or inadvertent burning of his draft card, involving no communication with other persons. The main feature, for him, is the public nature of the burning, through which he expresses to the community his ideas and feelings about the war and the draft."

Compare John H. Ely, *Flag Desecration: A Case Study in the Roles of Categorization and Balancing in First Amendment Analysis,* 88 Harv.L.Rev. 1482 (1975): "[B]urning a draft card to express opposition to the draft is an undifferentiated whole, 100% action and 100% expression. It involves no conduct that is not at the same time communication, and no communication that does not result from conduct. Attempts to determine which element 'predominates' will therefore inevitably degenerate into question-begging judgments about whether the activity should be protected. The *O'Brien* Court thus quite wisely dropped the 'speech-conduct' distinction as quickly as it had picked it up."[135]

2. *Nature of the state interest and First Amendment methodology.* Melville Nimmer, *The Meaning of Symbolic Speech Under the First Amendment,* 21 UCLA L.Rev. 29 (1973), followed by Ely, Note 1 supra, and Tribe 2d ed., at 791–92, proposed that the crucial starting point for First Amendment methodology is and should be the nature of the state interest.[136] As Ely put it: "The critical question would therefore seem to be whether the harm that the state is seeking to avert is one that grows out of the fact that the defendant is communicating, and more particularly out of the way people can be expected to react to his message [Tribe calls this "track one"], or rather would arise even if the defendant's conduct had no communicative significance whatever [Tribe calls this "track two"]." In order to appreciate the difference this distinction makes, it is necessary to determine the standard or standards used on track one. The standard or standards used on track one are not obvious because some speech on track one can be prohibited or sanctioned (e.g., some forms of advocacy of illegal action and obscenity); some speech on track one is subject to a test whose stringency varies with the context and the membership of the Court (e.g., *Central Hudson*); some speech on track one is subject to little or no scrutiny (consider the application of the securities laws to corporate speech); and other speech on track one can be prohibited only if it is necessary to achieve a compelling state interest (e.g., speech on public issues that does not fall within recognized exceptions such as advocacy of illegal action under *Brandenburg*). Geoffrey Stone has argued for some years that the exceptions to stringent protection on what is ordinarily the functional equivalent to track one are based either on extraordinary circumstances or on the determination that the speech is of low or lesser value (e.g., obscenity, false statements of fact). See also Lee C. Bollinger & Geoffrey R. Stone, *Dialogue*, in *Eternally Vigilant: Free Speech in the Modern Era* 8 (Lee C. Bollinger & Geoffrey R. Stone eds. 2002). Steven Shiffrin, by contrast, has argued that different tests have been applied in different contexts on track one and that determinations of the degree of stringency are more complicated than Stone suggests. The weight placed upon the speech interest, he argues, depends upon the nature of the state interest, the extent to which the state regulation furthers the interest, the possibility of less restrictive alternatives together with an assessment of the extent to which the restriction has an impact on First Amendment values and an assessment of the importance of the values impacted. Steven H. Shiffrin, *The First Amendment, Democracy, and Romance* ch. 1 (1990).

---

[135] But, as Ely recognizes, the Court picked it up again in *Cohen,* Sec. 1, IV, C supra: "[W]e deal here with a conviction resting solely upon 'speech', cf. *Stromberg,* not upon any separately identifiable conduct which allegedly was intended by Cohen to be perceived by others as expressive of particular views but which, on its face, does not necessarily convey any message and hence arguably could be regulated without effectively repressing Cohen's ability to express himself. Cf. *O'Brien.*"

[136] The distinction is a major organizing principle in Rodney Smolla, *Smolla and Nimmer on Freedom of Speech* (1984).

(a) *Normative value of the distinction between track one and track two.* How much weight should be put on the distinction between track one and track two? Consider a regulation governing express warranties in commercial advertising. Is much of contract law on track one?[137] Consider "a nationwide ban on *all* posters (intended to conserve paper)." Isn't that on track two? Do these examples suggest that too much emphasis is being placed on a single factor? See Daniel Farber, *Content Regulation and the First Amendment: A Revisionist View*, 68 Geo.U.L.Rev. 727 (1980).[138] Does the distinction between track one and track two rest on an assumption that the First Amendment is primarily concerned with protecting against improper government motivation? For the suggestion that a concern with purpose or motive is at the heart of the First Amendment, see Larry Alexander, *Is There a Right of Freedom of Expression?* 38–81 (2005); Jed Rubenfeld, *The First Amendment's Purpose*, 53 Stan. L. Rev. 767 (2001); Elena Kagan, *Private Speech, Public Purpose: The Role of Governmental Motive in First Amendment Doctrine*, 63 U.Chi.L.Rev. 413 (1996); David Bogen, *Bulwark of Liberty: The Court and the First Amendment* (1984); David Bogen, *Balancing Freedom of Speech*, 38 Md.L.Rev. 387 (1979); David Bogen, *The Supreme Court's Interpretation of the Guarantee of Freedom of Speech*, 35 Md.L.Rev. 555 (1976). See Note 3 after *Arcara*, infra. If so, does this perspective neglect the positive values of the First Amendment? Was there an impermissible legislative purpose in *Schenck? Falwell? Cohen v. California?* See Eugene Volokh, *Speech as Conduct: Generally Applicable Laws, Illegal Courses of Conduct, "Situation-Altering Utterances," and the Uncharted Zones*, 90 Cornell L.Rev. 1277 (2005). In *Minneapolis Star?* See Stuart Minor Benjamin, *Proactive Legislation and the First Amendment*, 99 Mich. L. Rev. 281 (2000). Consider Volokh, supra: "When a law generally applies to a wide range of conduct, and sweeps in speech together with such conduct, there is little reason to think that lawmakers had any motivation with regard to speech, much less an impermissible one. Nonetheless, such a law should still be unconstitutional when applied to speech based on its content—even though the legislature's motivations may have been quite benign." For further criticism, see Richard A. Posner, *Law, Pragmatism, and Democracy* 368–83 (2003).

(b) *Application to O'Brien.* Consider Ely, Note 1 supra: "The interests upon which the government relied were interests, having mainly to do with the preservation of selective service records, that would have been equally threatened had O'Brien's destruction of his draft card totally lacked communicative significance—had he, for example, used it to start a campfire for a solitary cookout or dropped it in his garbage disposal for a lark. (The law prohibited all knowing destructions, public or private)."

---

[137] For the suggestion that virtually all laws have information effects and that track two embraces virtually all laws not covered by track one, see Larry Alexander, *Trouble on Track Two: Incidental Regulations of Speech and Free Speech*, 44 Hastings L.J. 921 (1993) (arguing that track two countenances an unconstitutional evaluation of the value of speech).

[138] See generally Martin Redish, *The Content Distinction in First Amendment Analysis*, 34 Stan.L.Rev. 113 (1981). See notes after *Chicago Police Dept. v. Mosley*, Sec. 6, I, B infra.

Compare Melville Nimmer, Note 2 supra, contending that the *O'Brien* statute was "overnarrow": "[An overnarrow statute] may be said to create a conclusive presumption that in fact the state interest which the statute serves is an anti-rather than a non-speech interest. If the state interest asserted in *O'Brien* were truly the non-speech interest of assuring availability of draft cards, why did Congress choose not to prohibit any knowing conduct which leads to unavailability, rather than limiting the scope of the statute to those instances in which the proscribed conduct carries with it a speech component hostile to governmental policy? The obvious inference to be drawn is that in fact the Congress was completely indifferent to the 'availability' objective, and was concerned only with an interest which the *O'Brien* opinion states is impermissible—an interest in the suppression of free expression."[139]

3. *Evidence of motive.* The *O'Brien* majority declines to consider evidence of actual congressional motivation, preferring an official statement of purpose or a potentially permissible motive. Does the Court's squeamishness about looking at the actual motivations of the members of Congress survive *Wallace v. Jaffree* and *Edwards v. Aguillard*, Ch. 8, Sec. 1, III? See also *Washington v. Davis*, Ch. 9, Sec. 2, III. And in *Minneapolis Star & Tribune Co. v. Minnesota Comm'r of Rev.*, 460 U.S. 575 (1983), the Court interpreted *Grosjean v. American Press Co.*, 297 U.S. 233 (1936), as having been based substantially on factual evidence of actual anti-press motivation.

4. *Dissent.* Does *O'Brien* shortchange the value of dissent? Consider Steven Shiffrin, *The First Amendment, Democracy, and Romance* 5–6, 81 (1990): "If an organizing symbol makes sense in First Amendment jurisprudence, it is not the image of a content-neutral government; it is not a town hall meeting or even a robust marketplace of ideas; still less is it liberty, equality, self-realization, respect, dignity, autonomy, or even tolerance. If the First Amendment is to have an organizing symbol, let it be an Emersonian[140] symbol, let it be the image of the dissenter. A major purpose of the First Amendment [is] to protect the romantics—those who would break out of classical forms: the dissenters, the unorthodox, the outcasts. [That] Emersonian ideal of freedom of speech has deep roots in the nation's culture, but it has been subtly denigrated in recent First Amendment theory and seriously abused in practice.

"[N]either the town hall metaphor nor the marketplace of ideas metaphor[, for example,] is quite apt as a symbol for why *O'Brien* is a First Amendment horror story. Town hall meetings can function without the burning of draft cards. And it is hard to claim that truth was kept from the marketplace of ideas. *O'Brien* is one of those not infrequent cases where government prosecutions assist the dissemination of the dissenter's message. Yet, *O'Brien* is perhaps the ultimate First Amendment insult. O'Brien is jailed because the authorities find his manner of expression unpatriotic, threatening,

---

[139] On the inadequacy of the *O'Brien* methodology to serve as a proxy for problematic motivation, see Lee Bollinger, *The Tolerant Society* 206–12 (1986). On its inadequacy as an organizing principle for First Amendment doctrine, see Shiffrin, Note 4 infra, ch. 1.

[140] See generally Joel Porte ed. (1983), *Ralph Waldo Emerson: Essays and Lectures.*

and offensive. When he complains that his freedom of speech has been abridged, the authorities deny that he has spoken."

TEXAS V. JOHNSON

491 U.S. 397, 109 S.Ct. 2533, 105 L.Ed.2d 342 (1989).

JUSTICE BRENNAN delivered the opinion of the Court.

[Gregory] Lee Johnson was convicted of desecrating a flag in violation of Texas law.[1]

I.   While the Republican National Convention was taking place in Dallas in 1984, respondent Johnson participated in a political demonstration dubbed the "Republican War Chest Tour." [The] demonstration ended in front of Dallas City Hall, where Johnson unfurled the American flag, doused it with kerosene, and set it on fire. While the flag burned, the protestors chanted, "America, the red, white, and blue, we spit on you." [No] one was physically injured or threatened with injury, though several witnesses testified that they had been seriously offended by the flag-burning. * * *

II.   Johnson was convicted of flag desecration for burning the flag rather than for uttering insulting words.[2] [We] must first determine whether Johnson's burning of the flag constituted expressive conduct, permitting him to invoke the First Amendment in challenging his conviction. If his conduct was expressive, we next decide whether the State's regulation is related to the suppression of free expression. *O'Brien.* If the State's regulation is not related to expression, then the less stringent standard we announced in *O'Brien* for regulations of noncommunicative conduct controls. If it is, then we are outside of *O'Brien*'s test, and we must ask whether this interest justifies Johnson's conviction under a more

---

[1]   **[Ct's Note]** Tex.Penal Code Ann. § 42.09 (1989) provides in full: "§ 42.09. Desecration of Venerated Object

"(a) A person commits an offense if he intentionally or knowingly desecrates:

"(1) a public monument;

"(2) a place of worship or burial; or

"(3) a state or national flag.

"(b) For purposes of this section, 'desecrate' means deface, damage, or otherwise physically mistreat in a way that the actor knows will seriously offend one or more persons likely to observe or discover his action.

"(c) An offense under this section is a Class A misdemeanor."

[2]   **[Ct's Note]** Because the prosecutor's closing argument observed that Johnson had led the protestors in chants denouncing the flag while it burned, Johnson suggests that he may have been convicted for uttering critical words rather than for burning the flag. He relies on *Street v. New York*, 394 U.S. 576 (1969), in which we reversed a conviction obtained under a New York statute that prohibited publicly defying or casting contempt on the flag "either by words or act" because we were persuaded that the defendant may have been convicted for his words alone. Unlike the law we faced in *Street,* however, the Texas flag-desecration statute does not on its face permit conviction for remarks critical of the flag, as Johnson himself admits. Nor was the jury in this case told that it could convict Johnson of flag desecration if it found only that he had uttered words critical of the flag and its referents. * * *

demanding standard.[3] A third possibility is that the State's asserted interest is simply not implicated on these facts, and in that event the interest drops out of the picture. * * *

In deciding whether particular conduct possesses sufficient communicative elements to bring the First Amendment into play, we have asked whether "[a]n intent to convey a particularized message was present, and [whether] the likelihood was great that the message would be understood by those who viewed it." [In] *Spence v. Washington,* 418 U.S. 405 (1974), for example, we emphasized that Spence's taping of a peace sign to his flag was "roughly simultaneous with and concededly triggered by the Cambodian incursion and the Kent State tragedy." The State of Washington had conceded, in fact, that Spence's conduct was a form of communication, and we stated that "the State's concession is inevitable on this record."

III. In order to decide whether *O'Brien*'s test [applies] we must decide whether Texas has asserted an interest in support of Johnson's conviction that is unrelated to the suppression of expression.

A. Texas claims that its interest in preventing breaches of the peace justifies Johnson's conviction for flag desecration.[4] However, no disturbance of the peace actually occurred or threatened to occur because of Johnson's burning of the flag. [The] only evidence offered by the State at trial to show the reaction to Johnson's actions was the testimony of several persons who had been seriously offended by the flag-burning.

The State's position, therefore, amounts to a claim that an audience that takes serious offense at particular expression is necessarily likely to disturb the peace and that the expression may be prohibited on this basis. [W]e have not permitted the Government to assume that every expression of a provocative idea will incite a riot, but have instead required careful

---

[3] **[Ct's Note]** [Johnson] has raised a facial challenge to Texas' flag-desecration [statute]. Section 42.09 regulates only physical conduct with respect to the flag, not the written or spoken word, and although one violates the statute only if one "knows" that one's physical treatment of the flag "will seriously offend one or more persons likely to observe or discover his action," this fact does not necessarily mean that the statute applies only to *expressive* conduct protected by the First Amendment. A tired person might, for example, drag a flag through the mud, knowing that this conduct is likely to offend others, and yet have no thought of expressing any idea; neither the language nor the Texas courts' interpretations of the statute precludes the possibility that such a person would be prosecuted for flag desecration. Because the prosecution of a person who had not engaged in expressive conduct would pose a different case, and because we are capable of disposing of this case on narrower grounds, we address only Johnson's claim that § 42.09 as applied to political expression like his violates the First Amendment.

[4] **[Ct's Note]** Relying on our decision in *Boos v. Barry*, Johnson argues [that] the violent reaction to flag-burning feared by Texas would be the result of the message conveyed by them, and that this fact connects the State's interest to the suppression of expression. This view has found some favor in the lower courts. Johnson's theory may overread *Boos* insofar as it suggests that a desire to prevent a violent audience reaction is "related to expression" in the same way that a desire to prevent an audience from being offended is "related to expression." Because we find that the State's interest in preventing breaches of the peace is not implicated on these facts, however, we need not venture further into this area.

consideration of the actual circumstances surrounding such expression, asking whether the expression "is directed to inciting or producing imminent lawless action and is likely to incite or produce such action." *Brandenburg.* To accept Texas' arguments that it need only demonstrate "the potential for a breach of the peace," and that every flag-burning necessarily possesses that potential, would be to eviscerate our holding in *Brandenburg.* This we decline to do.

Nor does Johnson's expressive conduct fall within that small class of "fighting words" that are "likely to provoke the average person to retaliation, and thereby cause a breach of the peace." *Chaplinsky.* No reasonable onlooker would have regarded Johnson's generalized expression of dissatisfaction with the policies of the Federal Government as a direct personal insult or an invitation to exchange fisticuffs.

We thus conclude that the State's interest in maintaining order is not implicated on these facts. * * *

B.   The State also asserts an interest in preserving the flag as a symbol of nationhood and national unity. [The] State, apparently, is concerned that such conduct will lead people to believe either that the flag does not stand for nationhood and national unity, but instead reflects other, less positive concepts, or that the concepts reflected in the flag do not in fact exist, that is, we do not enjoy unity as a Nation. These concerns blossom only when a person's treatment of the flag communicates some message, and thus are related "to the suppression of free expression" within the meaning of *O'Brien.* We are thus outside of *O'Brien*'s test altogether.

IV.   It remains to consider whether the State's interest in preserving the flag as a symbol of nationhood and national unity justifies Johnson's conviction. [If Johnson] had burned the flag as a means of disposing of it because it was dirty or torn, he would not have been convicted of flag desecration under this Texas law: federal law designates burning as the preferred means of disposing of a flag "when it is in such condition that it is no longer a fitting emblem for display," 36 U.S.C. § 176(k), and Texas has no quarrel with this means of disposal. The Texas law is thus not aimed at protecting the physical integrity of the flag in all circumstances, but is designed instead to protect it only against impairments that would cause serious offense to others.[6]

Whether Johnson's treatment of the flag violated Texas law thus depended on the likely communicative impact of his expressive conduct.

---

[6]   **[Ct's Note]** *Cf. Smith v. Goguen,* 415 U.S. 566 (1974) (Blackmun, J., dissenting) (emphasizing that lower court appeared to have construed state statute so as to protect physical integrity of the flag in all circumstances); id. (Rehnquist, J., dissenting) (same). [In *Goguen,* Blackmun, J., argued that "Goguen's punishment was constitutionally permissible for harming the physical integrity of the flag by wearing it affixed to the seat of his pants" and emphasized that such punishment would not be for "speech—a communicative element."].

Our decision in *Boos v. Barry*, 485 U.S. 312 (1988), tells us that this restriction on Johnson's expression is content-based. In *Boos,* we considered the constitutionality of a law prohibiting "the display of any sign within 50 feet of a foreign embassy if that sign tends to bring that foreign government into 'public odium' or 'public disrepute.' " Rejecting the argument that the law was content-neutral because it was justified by "our international law obligation to shield diplomats from speech that offends their dignity," we held that "[t]he emotive impact of speech on its audience is not a 'secondary effect' " unrelated to the content of the expression itself.

According to the principles announced in *Boos,* Johnson's political expression was restricted because of the content of the message he conveyed. We must therefore subject the State's asserted interest in preserving the special symbolic character of the flag to "the most exacting scrutiny." *Boos.*[8] * * *

If there is a bedrock principle underlying the First Amendment, it is that the Government may not prohibit the expression of an idea simply because society finds the idea itself offensive or disagreeable. [We] have not recognized an exception to this principle even where our flag has been involved. [We] never before have held that the Government may ensure that a symbol be used to express only one view of that symbol or its referents. Indeed, in *Schacht v. United States*, 398 U.S. 58 (1970), we invalidated a federal statute permitting an actor portraying a member of one of our armed forces to " 'wear the uniform of that armed force if the portrayal does not tend to discredit that armed force.' " This proviso, we held, "which leaves Americans free to praise the war in Vietnam but can send persons like Schacht to prison for opposing it, cannot survive in a country which has the First Amendment."

We perceive no basis on which to hold that the principle underlying our decision in *Schacht* does not apply to this case. To conclude that the Government may permit designated symbols to be used to communicate only a limited set of messages would be to enter territory having no discernible or defensible boundaries. Could the Government, on this theory, prohibit the burning of state flags? Of copies of the Presidential seal? Of the Constitution? In evaluating these choices under the First Amendment, how would we decide which symbols were sufficiently special to warrant this unique status? To do so, we would be forced to consult our own political preferences, and impose them on the citizenry, in the very way that the First Amendment forbids us to do.

---

[8]   [Ct's Note] Our inquiry is, of course, bounded by the particular facts of this case and by the statute under which Johnson was convicted. There was no evidence that Johnson himself stole the flag he burned, nor did the prosecution or the arguments urged in support of it depend on the theory that the flag was stolen. [Thus] nothing in our opinion should be taken to suggest that one is free to steal a flag so long as one later uses it to communicate an idea. We also emphasize that Johnson was prosecuted *only* for flag desecration—not for trespass, disorderly conduct, or arson.

There is, moreover, no indication—either in the text of the Constitution or in our cases interpreting it—that a separate judicial category exists for the American flag alone. Indeed, we would not be surprised to learn that the persons who framed our Constitution and wrote the Amendment that we now construe were not known for their reverence for the Union Jack. The First Amendment does not guarantee that other concepts virtually sacred to our Nation as a whole—such as the principle that discrimination on the basis of race is odious and destructive—will go unquestioned in the marketplace of ideas. See *Brandenburg*. We decline, therefore, to create for the flag an exception to the joust of principles protected by the First Amendment.

It is not the State's ends, but its means, to which we object. It cannot be gainsaid that there is a special place reserved for the flag in this Nation, and thus we do not doubt that the Government has a legitimate interest in making efforts to "preserv[e] the national flag as an unalloyed symbol of our country." We reject the suggestion, urged at oral argument by counsel for Johnson, that the Government lacks "any state interest whatsoever" in regulating the manner in which the flag may be displayed. Congress has, for example, enacted precatory regulations describing the proper treatment of the flag, see 36 U.S.C. §§ 173–177, and we cast no doubt on the legitimacy of its interest in making such recommendations. To say that the Government has an interest in encouraging proper treatment of the flag, however, is not to say that it may criminally punish a person for burning a flag as a means of political protest. "National unity as an end which officials may foster by persuasion and example is not in question. The problem is whether under our Constitution compulsion as here employed is a permissible means for its achievement."

[W]e submit that nobody can suppose that this one gesture of an unknown man will change our Nation's attitude towards its flag. See *Abrams* (Holmes, J., dissenting). Indeed, Texas' argument that the burning of an American flag " 'is an act having a high likelihood to cause a breach of the peace,' " and its statute's implicit assumption that physical mistreatment of the flag will lead to "serious offense," tend to confirm that the flag's special role is not in danger; if it were, no one would riot or take offense because a flag had been burned.

We are tempted to say, in fact, that the flag's deservedly cherished place in our community will be strengthened, not weakened, by our holding today. Our decision is a reaffirmation of the principles of freedom and inclusiveness that the flag best reflects, and of the conviction that our toleration of criticism such as Johnson's is a sign and source of our strength. Indeed, one of the proudest images of our flag, the one immortalized in our own national anthem, is of the bombardment it survived at Fort McHenry. It is the Nation's resilience, not its rigidity, that

Texas sees reflected in the flag—and it is that resilience that we reassert today.

The way to preserve the flag's special role is not to punish those who feel differently about these matters. It is to persuade them that they are wrong. [We] can imagine no more appropriate response to burning a flag than waving one's own, no better way to counter a flag-burner's message than by saluting the flag that burns, no surer means of preserving the dignity even of the flag that burned than by—as one witness here did—according its remains a respectful burial. * * *

JUSTICE KENNEDY, concurring. * * *

Our colleagues in dissent advance powerful arguments why respondent may be convicted for his expression, reminding us that among those who will be dismayed by our holding will be some who have had the singular honor of carrying the flag in battle. And I agree that the flag holds a lonely place of honor in an age when absolutes are distrusted and simple truths are burdened by unneeded apologetics.

With all respect to those views, I do not believe the Constitution gives us the right to rule as the dissenting members of the Court urge, however painful this judgment is to announce. Though symbols often are what we ourselves make of them, the flag is constant in expressing beliefs Americans share, beliefs in law and peace and that freedom which sustains the human spirit. The case here today forces recognition of the costs to which those beliefs commit us. It is poignant but fundamental that the flag protects those who hold it in contempt.

For all the record shows, this respondent was not a philosopher and perhaps did not even possess the ability to comprehend how repellent his statements must be to the Republic itself. But whether or not he could appreciate the enormity of the offense he gave, the fact remains that his acts were speech, in both the technical and the fundamental meaning of the Constitution. So I agree with the Court that he must go free.

CHIEF JUSTICE REHNQUIST, with whom JUSTICE WHITE and JUSTICE O'CONNOR join, dissenting.

In holding this Texas statute unconstitutional, the Court ignores Justice Holmes' familiar aphorism that "a page of history is worth a volume of logic." *New York Trust Co. v. Eisner,* 256 U.S. 345 (1921). * * *

The American flag [throughout] more than 200 years of our history, has come to be the visible symbol embodying our Nation.[141] It does not

---

[141] Rehnquist, C.J., invoked a legacy of prose, poetry, and law in honor of flags in general and the American flag in particular both in peace and in war, quoting from, among others, Ralph Waldo Emerson and John Greenleaf Whittier. Emerson's poem referred to the Union Jack, but he did not always speak warmly of the American flag. After passage of the Fugitive Slave Law Emerson wrote, "We sneak about with the infamy of crime in the streets, & cowardice in ourselves and

represent the views of any particular political party, and it does not represent any particular political philosophy. The flag is not simply another "idea" or "point of view" competing for recognition in the marketplace of ideas. Millions and millions of Americans regard it with an almost mystical reverence regardless of what sort of social, political, or philosophical beliefs they may have. I cannot agree that the First Amendment invalidates the Act of Congress, and the laws of 48 of the 50 States, which make criminal the public burning of the flag.

More than 80 years ago in *Halter v. Nebraska* [205 U.S. 34 (1907)], this Court upheld the constitutionality of a Nebraska statute that forbade the use of representations of the American flag for advertising purposes upon articles of merchandise. The Court there said: "For that flag every true American has not simply an appreciation but a deep affection. * * * Hence, it has often occurred that insults to a flag have been the cause of war, and indignities put upon it, in the presence of those who revere it, have often been resented and sometimes punished on the spot."

Only two Terms ago, in *San Francisco Arts & Athletics, Inc. v. United States Olympic Committee,* [483 U.S. 522 (1987)], the Court held that Congress could grant exclusive use of the word "Olympic" to the United States Olympic Committee. The Court thought that this "restrictio[n] on expressive speech properly [was] characterized as incidental to the primary congressional purpose of encouraging and rewarding the USOC's activities." As the Court stated, "when a word [or symbol] acquires value 'as the result of organization and the expenditure of labor, skill, and money' by an entity, that entity constitutionally may obtain a limited property right in the word [or symbol]."[142] Surely Congress or the States may recognize a similar interest in the flag.[143]

[T]he public burning of the American flag by Johnson was no essential part of any exposition of ideas, and at the same time it had a tendency to incite a breach of the peace. Johnson was free to make any verbal denunciation of the flag that he wished; indeed, he was free to burn the flag in private. He could publicly burn other symbols of the Government or effigies of political leaders. He did lead a march through the streets of Dallas, and conducted a rally in front of the Dallas City Hall. He engaged in a "die-in" to protest nuclear weapons. He shouted out various slogans

---

frankly once for all the Union is sunk, the flag is hateful, and shall be hissed." *Emerson in His Journals* 421 (Joel Porte ed. 1982).

[142] For criticism, see James Boyle, *Shamans, Software, and Spleens* 145–48 (1996); Yochai Benkler, *Constitutional Bounds of Database Protection,* 15 Berkeley L.J. 535 (2000); Robert Kravitz, *Trademarks, Speech, and the Gay Olympics Case,* 69 B.U.L.Rev. 131 (1989).

[143] In response, Brennan, J., observed that *Halter* was decided "nearly twenty years" before the First Amendment was applied to the states and "[m]ore important" that *Halter* involved "purely commercial rather than political speech." Similarly, he stated that the authorization "to prohibit certain commercial and promotional uses of the word 'Olympic' [does not] even begin to tell us whether the Government may criminally punish physical conduct towards the flag engaged in as a means of political protest."

during the march, including: "Reagan, Mondale which will it be? Either one means World War III"; "Ronald Reagan, killer of the hour, Perfect example of U.S. power"; and "red, white and blue, we spit on you, you stand for plunder, you will go under." For none of these acts was he arrested or prosecuted. [As] with "fighting words," so with flag burning, for purposes of the First Amendment: It is "no essential part of any exposition of ideas, and [is] of such slight social value as a step to truth that any benefit that may be derived from [it] is clearly outweighed" by the public interest in avoiding a probable breach of the peace. * * *

The result of the Texas statute is obviously to deny one in Johnson's frame of mind one of many means of "symbolic speech." Far from being a case of "one picture being worth a thousand words," flag burning is the equivalent of an inarticulate grunt or roar that, it seems fair to say, is most likely to be indulged in not to express any particular idea, but to antagonize others. [The] Texas statute [left Johnson] with a full panoply of other symbols and every conceivable form of verbal expression to express his deep disapproval of national policy. Thus, in no way can it be said that Texas is punishing him because his hearers—or any other group of people—were profoundly opposed to the message that he sought to convey. Such opposition is no proper basis for restricting speech or expression under the First Amendment. It was Johnson's use of this particular symbol, and not the idea that he sought to convey by it or by his many other expressions, for which he was punished. * * *

The Court concludes its opinion with a regrettably patronizing civics lecture, presumably addressed to the Members of both Houses of Congress, the members of the 48 state legislatures that enacted prohibitions against flag burning, and the troops fighting under that flag in Vietnam who objected to its being burned: "The way to preserve the flag's special role is not to punish those who feel differently about these matters. It is to persuade them that they are wrong." The Court's role as the final expositor of the Constitution is well established, but its role as a platonic guardian admonishing those responsible to public opinion as if they were truant school children has no similar place in our system of government. * * *

Uncritical extension of constitutional protection to the burning of the flag risks the frustration of the very purpose for which organized governments are instituted. The Court decides that the American flag is just another symbol, about which not only must opinions pro and con be tolerated, but for which the most minimal public respect may not be enjoined. The government may conscript men into the Armed Forces where they must fight and perhaps die for the flag, but the government may not prohibit the public burning of the banner under which they fight. I would uphold the Texas statute as applied in this case.[2]

JUSTICE STEVENS, dissenting. * * *

Even if flag burning could be considered just another species of symbolic speech under the logical application of the rules that the Court has developed in its interpretation of the First Amendment in other contexts, this case has an intangible dimension that makes those rules inapplicable.

A country's flag is a symbol of more than "nationhood and national unity." [T]he American flag [is] more than a proud symbol of the courage, the determination, and the gifts of nature that transformed 13 fledgling Colonies into a world power. It is a symbol of freedom, of equal opportunity, of religious tolerance, and of goodwill for other peoples who share our aspirations. The symbol carries its message to dissidents both at home and abroad who may have no interest at all in our national unity or survival.

The value of the flag as a symbol cannot be measured. Even so, I have no doubt that the interest in preserving that value for the future is both significant and legitimate. Conceivably that value will be enhanced by the Court's conclusion that our national commitment to free expression is so strong that even the United States as ultimate guarantor of that freedom is without power to prohibit the desecration of its unique symbol. But I am unpersuaded. The creation of a federal right to post bulletin boards and graffiti on the Washington Monument might enlarge the market for free expression, but at a cost I would not pay. Similarly, in my considered judgment, sanctioning the public desecration of the flag will tarnish its value—both for those who cherish the ideas for which it waves and for those who desire to don the robes of martyrdom by burning it. That tarnish is not justified by the trivial burden on free expression occasioned by requiring that an available, alternative mode of expression—including uttering words critical of the flag be employed.

It is appropriate to emphasize certain propositions that are not implicated by this case. [The] statute does not compel any conduct or any profession of respect for any idea or any symbol. [Nor] does the statute violate "the government's paramount obligation of neutrality in its regulation of protected communication." The content of respondent's message has no relevance whatsoever to the case. The concept of "desecration" does not turn on the substance of the message the actor

---

[2] **[Ct's Note]** In holding that the Texas statute as applied to Johnson violates the First Amendment, the Court does not consider Johnson's claims that the statute is unconstitutionally vague or overbroad. I think those claims are without merit. [By] defining "desecrate" as "deface," "damage" or otherwise "physically mistreat" in a manner that the actor knows will "seriously offend" others, § 42.09 only prohibits flagrant acts of physical abuse and destruction of the flag of the sort at issue here—soaking a flag with lighter fluid and igniting it in public—and not any of the examples of improper flag etiquette cited in Respondent's brief.

intends to convey, but rather on whether those who view the act will take serious offense. Accordingly, one intending to convey a message of respect for the flag by burning it in a public square might nonetheless be guilty of desecration if he knows that others—perhaps simply because they misperceive the intended message—will be seriously offended. Indeed, even if the actor knows that all possible witnesses will understand that he intends to send a message of respect, he might still be guilty of desecration if he also knows that this understanding does not lessen the offense taken by some of those witnesses. The case has nothing to do with "disagreeable ideas." It involves disagreeable conduct that, in my opinion, diminishes the value of an important national asset.

[Had respondent] chosen to spray paint—or perhaps convey with a motion picture projector—his message of dissatisfaction on the facade of the Lincoln Memorial, there would be no question about the power of the Government to prohibit his means of expression. The prohibition would be supported by the legitimate interest in preserving the quality of an important national asset. Though the asset at stake in this case is intangible, given its unique value, the same interest supports a prohibition on the desecration of the American flag.[*]

The ideas of liberty and equality have been an irresistible force in motivating leaders like Patrick Henry, Susan B. Anthony, and Abraham Lincoln, schoolteachers like Nathan Hale and Booker T. Washington, the Philippine Scouts who fought at Bataan, and the soldiers who scaled the bluff at Omaha Beach. If those ideas are worth fighting for—and our history demonstrates that they are—it cannot be true that the flag that uniquely symbolizes their power is not itself worthy of protection from unnecessary desecration.

NOTES AND QUESTIONS

1. **The meaning of "speech."** If the *O'Brien* Court had inquired whether a particularized message was present, and whether likelihood was great that the message would be understood by those who viewed it, would it have had any difficulty in classifying draft card burning as speech? Must a

---

[*]   [Ct's Note] The Court suggested that a prohibition against flag desecration is not content-neutral because this form of symbolic speech is only used by persons who are critical of the flag or the ideas it represents. In making this suggestion the Court does not pause to consider the far-reaching consequences of its introduction of disparate impact analysis into our First Amendment jurisprudence. It seems obvious that a prohibition against the desecration of a gravesite is content-neutral even if it denies some protesters the right to make a symbolic statement by extinguishing the flame in Arlington Cemetery where John F. Kennedy is buried while permitting others to salute the flame by bowing their heads. Few would doubt that a protester who extinguishes the flame has desecrated the gravesite, regardless of whether he prefaces that act with a speech explaining that his purpose is to express deep admiration or unmitigated scorn for the late President. Likewise, few would claim that the protester who bows his head has desecrated the gravesite, even if he makes clear that his purpose is to show disrespect. In such a case, as in a flag burning case, the prohibition against desecration has absolutely nothing to do with the content of the message that the symbolic speech is intended to convey.

particularized message be present for the First Amendment to be relevant? Would such a requirement wrongly fail to protect "a great deal of painting, music, dance, and sculpture"? Jed Rubenfeld, *The Freedom of Imagination: Copyright's Constitutionality*, 112 Yale L.J. 1 (2002). Is the presence of a particularized message sufficient to implicate the First Amendment? Is the First Amendment generally implicated in contract negotiations? Navigation maps? Instructions for handling machinery? See Robert Post, *Recuperating First Amendment Doctrine,* 47 Stan.L.Rev. 1249 (1995). Cf. Frederick Schauer, *Free Speech and the Demise of the Soapbox*, Book Review, 84 Colum.L.Rev. 558 (1984) ("[T]he First Amendment importance of the messages from an automatic teller to the bank's central computer completely escapes me, as does the First Amendment importance of the mutual exchange of electronic and visual symbols between me and the Pac-Man machine."). Does the process of defining speech for First Amendment purposes require an understanding of the purposes of the First Amendment rather than a focus on the communicative character of the phenomena examined? See Post, supra (speech in its ordinary language sense has no inherent constitutional value and should be defined to include only those social practices which implicate free speech values).[144] Cf. Stanley Fish, *There's No Such Thing as Free Speech: And It's a Good Thing Too* 102 (1994) (" 'Free speech' is just the name we give to verbal behavior that serves the substantive agendas we wish to advance"). What are the relevant purposes and values? For example, is begging speech for First Amendment purposes? Daniel Mark Cohen, *Begging the Court's Pardon: Justice Denied for the Poorest of the Poor*, 14 ST. Thomas L. Rev. 825 (2002) (yes); Randall P. Bezanson, *Speaking Through Others' Voices: Authorship, Originality, and Free Speech*, 38 Wake Forest L. Rev. 983 (2003)(no). For an argument that all communicative utterances be considered speech regardless of purpose, Consider Eugene Volokh, *Speech as Conduct: Generally Applicable Laws, Illegal Courses of Conduct, "Situation-Altering Utterances," and the Uncharted Zones*, 90 Cornell L. Rev. 1277 (2005): "Lying on the witness stand is not less speech than lying about the weather, [although] it may also be perjury. The shout of 'Fire!' is not less speech in the Holmes instance than the shout of 'Fire!' from the mouth of an actor on the state of the same theater, spoken as but a word in a play. It is futile to argue that an appropriately tailored law that punishes any or all of these utterances does not abridge speech. It does, it is meant to, and one should not take recourse to verbal subterfuge, e.g., that it is "speech-brigaded-with-action" or "conduct" alone that is curtailed. [They] are separately crafted rules that let the government punish speech in particular circumstances, based on arguments about the harm and value of speech that are specific to each exception."

2.   ***Patriotism.*** Consider Amy Adler, *The Art of Censorship*, 103 W. Va. L. Rev. 205 (2000): "Do people really die for the flag? Don't people actually die

---

[144] For other relevant commentary, see Kent Greenawalt, *Speech, Crime and the Uses of Language* (1989); Frederick Schauer, *Free Speech: A Philosophical Enquiry* 181–84 (1982); Frederick Schauer, *Speech and "Speech"—Obscenity and "Obscenity": An Exercise in the Interpretation of Constitutional Language,* 67 Geo.L.J. 899 (1979); Larry Alexander & Paul Horton, *The Impossibility of a Free Speech Principle,* 78 Nw.U.L.Rev. 1319 (1984).

for what it represents? There is a confusion here between the image and reality. [H]ere and at another point where Rehnquist says the flag 'embodies' our nation, I think his slippage between the image and what it stands for reveals something deeper about images. They are so strong, such a plain 'short cut' to our minds, that they tempt us to conflate representation with reality. [For] a brief moment Justice Rehnquist has given way to idolatry." But see George Fletcher, *Loyalty* 141 (1993): "The [question] is whether the Congress has a sufficiently clear interest in promoting national loyalty to interpret the crime of flag burning as a sanction aimed not at the message of protest, but at the act, regardless of its political slant. Whether Congress and the country possess this interest depends, of course, on what one thinks of loyalty and devotion to country as a value. A high regard for patriotism, for sharing a common purpose in cherishing our people and seeking to solve our problems, leads one easily to perceive the expression of our unity as a value important in itself. The flag is at least as important—to go from the sublime to the ridiculous—as protecting draft cards so that the Selective Service System can function efficiently."

3. ***Dissent.*** Consider Steven Shiffrin, *The First Amendment and the Meaning of America,* in *Identities, Politics, and Rights* 318 (Sarat & Kearnes eds. 1996): "The flag-burning prohibition is uniquely troubling not because it interferes with the metaphorical marketplace of ideas, not because it topples our image of a content neutral government (*that* has fallen many times), and not merely because it suppresses political speech. The flag-burning prohibition is a naked attempt to smother dissent. If we must have a 'central meaning' of the First Amendment, we should recognize that the dissenters—those who attack existing customs, habits, traditions and authorities—stand at the center of the First Amendment and not at its periphery. Gregory Johnson was attacking a symbol which the vast majority of Americans regard with reverence. But that is *exactly* why he deserved First Amendment protection. The First Amendment has a special regard for those who swim against the current, for those who would shake us to our foundations, for those who reject prevailing authority. In burning the flag, Gregory Johnson rejected, opposed, even blasphemed the Nation's most important political, social, and cultural icon. Clearly Gregory Johnson's alleged act of burning the flag was a quintessential act of dissent. A dissent centered conception of the First Amendment would make it clear that *Johnson* was an easy case—rightly decided."

4. ***The meaning of the flag.*** Consider Kenneth Karst, *Law's Promise, Law's Expression: Visions of Power in the Politics of Race, Gender, and Religion* 165 (1993): "According to those opinions the flag stands for our nationhood or national unity (Brennan, paraphrasing the state's lawyers); for principles of freedom or inclusiveness (Brennan); for the nation's resiliency (Brennan); for the nation itself (Rehnquist); for something men will die for in war (Rehnquist); for 'America's imagined past and present' (Rehnquist, in Sheldon Nahmod's apt paraphrase); for courage, freedom, equal opportunity, religious tolerance, and 'goodwill for other peoples who share our aspirations' (Stevens); and for

shared beliefs in law and peace and 'the freedom that sustains the human spirit' (Kennedy). So, even within the Supreme Court, the flag stands at once for freedom and for obedience to law, for war and for peace, for unity and for tolerance of difference." For perspectives on the relationship of the First Amendment to nationalism and national identity, Paul A. Passavant, *No Escape: Freedom of Speech and the Paradox of Rights* (2002); Steven H. Shiffrin, *The First Amendment, Democracy, and Romance* (1990).

5.   *The flag's "physical integrity."* Brennan, J., observes that the Texas law is "not aimed at protecting the physical integrity of the flag in all circumstances." What if it were?[145]

In response to *Johnson,* Congress passed, by an overwhelming majority, the Flag Protection Act of 1989, which attached criminal penalties to the knowing mutilation, defacement, burning, maintaining on the floor or ground, or trampling upon any flag of the United States.

UNITED STATES v. EICHMAN, 496 U.S. 310 (1990), per BRENNAN, J., invalidated the statute: "Although the Flag Protection Act contains no explicit content-based limitation on the scope of prohibited conduct, it is nevertheless clear that the Government's asserted *interest* is 'related "to the suppression of free expression" and concerned with the content of such expression. The Government's interest in protecting the 'physical integrity' of a privately owned flag rests upon a perceived need to preserve the flag's status as a symbol of our Nation and certain national ideals. But the mere destruction or disfigurement of a particular physical manifestation of the symbol, without more, does not diminish or otherwise affect the symbol itself in any way. For example, the secret destruction of a flag in one's own basement would not threaten the flag's recognized meaning. Rather, the Government's desire to preserve the flag as a symbol for certain national ideals is implicated 'only when a person's treatment of the flag communicates [a] message' to others that is inconsistent with those ideals."

STEVENS, J., joined by Rehnquist, C.J., White and O'Connor, JJ., dissenting, argued that the government's "legitimate interest in protecting the symbolic value of the American flag" outweighed the free speech interest. In describing the flag's symbolic value he stated that the flag "inspires and motivates the average citizen to make personal sacrifices in order to achieve societal goals of overriding importance; at all times, it serves as a reminder of the paramount importance of pursuing the ideals that characterize our society. * * * [T]he communicative value of a well-placed bomb in the Capital does not entitle it to the protection of the First Amendment. Burning a flag is not, of course, equivalent to burning a public building. Assuming that the protester is burning his own flag, it causes no physical harm to other persons or to their

---

[145] For commentary concerning the extent to which a focus on physical integrity can be separated from a concern with content, see Kent Greenawalt, *O'er the Land of the Free: Flag Burning as Speech,* 37 UCLA L.Rev. 925 (1990); Frank Michelman, *Saving Old Glory: On Constitutional Iconography,* 42 Stan.L.Rev. 1337 (1990); Geoffrey Stone, *Flag Burning and the Constitution,* 75 Ia.L.Rev. 111 (1989); Mark Tushnet, *The Flag-Burning Episode: An Essay on the Constitution,* 61 U.Col.L.Rev. 39 (1990).

property. The impact is purely symbolic, and it is apparent that some thoughtful persons believe that impact far from depreciating the value of the symbol, will actually enhance its meaning. I most respectfully disagree."[146]

6.   *Compromise?* Prior to adopting the Flag Protection Act, the Senate by a vote of 97–3 had passed a resolution expressing "profound disappointment with the [*Johnson*] decision." The House had approved a similar resolution by a vote of 411–5, and President Bush had proposed a constitutional amendment to overrule *Johnson.* Opponents of the amendment argued that a carefully drawn statute might (or would) be upheld by the Court. Suppose you were a member of the House or Senate at that time. Suppose you supported *Johnson* but believed that the statute might be held constitutional, even though you did not think it should be. Suppose you also believed that if a statute were not passed an amendment would.[147]

Consider this exchange during hearings of the House Subcommittee on Civil and Constitutional Rights in *Statutory and Constitutional Responses to the Supreme Court Decision in Texas v. Johnson* (1989): Former Solicitor General Charles Fried: "My good friends and colleagues, Rex Lee and Laurence Tribe, have testified that a statute might be drawn that would pass constitutional muster. [I] hope and urge and pray that we will not act—that no statute be passed and of course that the Constitution not be amended. In short, I believe that *Johnson* is right [in] principle." * * *

Representative Schroeder: "I thought your testimony was eloquent. I think in a purist world, that is where we should go. But [we] are not talking about a purist world. We are talking about a very political world." * * *

Mr. Fried: "There are times when you earn your rather inadequate salary by just doing the right thing, and where you seem to agree with me is that the right thing to do is to do neither one of these. [It] is called leadership."

Representative Schroeder: "It is called leadership. [But] I guess what I am saying is if we can't stop a stampede on an amendment without something, isn't it better to try to save the Bill of Rights and the Constitution?"

––––––

Community for Creative Non-Violence (CCNV) sought to conduct a wintertime demonstration near the White House in Lafayette Park and the Mall to dramatize the plight of the homeless. The National Park Service authorized the erection of two symbolic tent cities for purposes of the demonstration, but denied CCNV's request that demonstrators be

---

[146] But see Arnold Loewy, *The Flag-Burning Case: Freedom of Speech When We Need It Most,* 68 N.C.L.Rev. 165 (1989): "Perhaps the ultimate irony is that *Johnson* has done more to preserve the flag as a symbol of liberty than any prior decision, while the decision's detractors would allow real desecration of the flag by making it a symbol of political oppression." Compare Robin West, *Taking Freedom Seriously,* 104 Harv.L.Rev. 43 (1990) (the militaristic patriotism associated with the flag menaces dissent); see also Greenawalt, fn. 146 supra.

[147] For commentary, compare Michelman, fn. 146 supra with Steven H. Shiffrin, *Dissent, Injustice, and the Meanings of America* ch. 1 (1990).

permitted to sleep in the tents. National Park Service regulations permit camping (the "use of park land for living accommodation purposes such as sleeping activities") in National Parks only in campgrounds designated for that purpose.

CLARK v. COMMUNITY FOR CREATIVE NON-VIOLENCE, 468 U.S. 288 (1984), per WHITE, J., rejected CCNV's claim that the regulations could not be constitutionally applied against its demonstration: "We need not differ with the view of the Court of Appeals that overnight sleeping in connection with the demonstration is expressive conduct protected to some extent by the First Amendment.[5] We assume for present purposes, but do not decide, that such is the case, cf. *O'Brien,* but this assumption only begins the inquiry. Expression, whether oral or written or symbolized by conduct, is subject to reasonable time, place, or manner restrictions. We have often noted that restrictions of this kind are valid provided that they are justified without reference to the content of the regulated speech, that they are narrowly tailored to serve a significant governmental interest, and that they leave open ample alternative channels for communication of the information.

"It is also true that a message may be delivered by conduct that is intended to be communicative and that, in context, would reasonably be understood by the viewer to be communicative. Symbolic expression of this kind may be forbidden or regulated if the conduct itself may constitutionally be regulated, if the regulation is narrowly drawn to further a substantial governmental interest, and if the interest is unrelated to the suppression of free speech. *O'Brien.*

"[That] sleeping, like the symbolic tents themselves, may be expressive and part of the message delivered by the demonstration does not make the ban any less a limitation on the manner of demonstrating, for reasonable time, place, or manner regulations normally have the purpose and direct effect of limiting expression but are nevertheless valid. Neither does the fact that sleeping, arguendo, may be expressive conduct, rather than oral or written expression, render the sleeping prohibition any less a time, place, or manner regulation. To the contrary, the Park Service neither attempts to ban sleeping generally nor to ban it everywhere in the parks. It has established areas for camping and forbids it elsewhere, including Lafayette Park and the Mall. Considered as such, we have very little trouble concluding that the Park Service may prohibit overnight sleeping in the parks involved here.

---

[5]   **[Ct's Note]** We reject the suggestion of the plurality below, however, that the burden on the demonstrators is limited to "the advancement of a plausible contention" that their conduct is expressive. Although it is common to place the burden upon the Government to justify impingements on First Amendment interests, it is the obligation of the person desiring to engage in assertedly expressive conduct to demonstrate that the First Amendment even applies. To hold otherwise would be to create a rule that all conduct is presumptively expressive.

"The requirement that the regulation be content-neutral is clearly satisfied. The courts below accepted that view, and it is not disputed here that the prohibition on camping, and on sleeping specifically, is content-neutral and is not being applied because of disagreement with the message presented.[148] Neither was the regulation faulted, nor could it be, on the ground that without overnight sleeping the plight of the homeless could not be communicated in other ways. The regulation otherwise left the demonstration intact, with its symbolic city, signs, and the presence of those who were willing to take their turns in a day-and-night vigil. Respondents do not suggest that there was, or is, any barrier to delivering to the media, or to the public by other means, the intended message concerning the plight of the homeless.

"It is also apparent to us that the regulation narrowly focuses on the Government's substantial interest in maintaining the parks in the heart of our Capital in an attractive and intact condition, readily available to the millions of people who wish to see and enjoy them by their presence. To permit camping—using these areas as living accommodations—would be totally inimical to these purposes, as would be readily understood by those who have frequented the National Parks across the country and observed the unfortunate consequences of the activities of those who refuse to confine their camping to designated areas.

"It is urged by [CCNV] that if the symbolic city of tents was to be permitted and if the demonstrators did not intend to cook, dig, or engage in aspects of camping other than sleeping, the incremental benefit to the parks could not justify the ban on sleeping, which was here an expressive activity said to enhance the message concerning the plight of the poor and homeless. We cannot agree. In the first place, we seriously doubt that the First Amendment requires the Park Service to permit a demonstration in Lafayette Park and the Mall involving a 24-hour vigil and the erection of tents to accommodate 150 people. Furthermore, although we have assumed for present purposes that the sleeping banned in this case would have an expressive element, it is evident that its major value to this demonstration would be facilitative. Without a permit to sleep, it would be difficult to get the poor and homeless to participate or to be present at all.[149]

"Beyond this, however, it is evident from our cases that the validity of this regulation need not be judged solely by reference to the demonstration at hand.[150] Absent the prohibition on sleeping, there would be other groups

---

[148] Marshall, J., dissenting, observed that CCNV had held a demonstration the previous winter in which it set up nine tents and slept in Lafayette Park. The D.C. Circuit held that the regulations did not preclude such a demonstration. According to Marshall, J., "The regulations at issue in this case were passed in direct response" to that holding.

[149] What if it were the exclusive value? For discussion, see Gary Francione, *Experimentation and the Marketplace Theory of the First Amendment*, 136 U.Pa.L.Rev. 417 (1987).

[150] For debate about this point and its implications, compare Frank Easterbrook, *Foreword: The Court and the Economic System*, 98 Harv.L.Rev. 4 (1984) with Laurence Tribe, *Constitutional*

who would demand permission to deliver an asserted message by camping in Lafayette Park. Some of them would surely have as credible a claim in this regard as does CCNV, and the denial of permits to still others would present difficult problems for the Park Service. With the prohibition, however, as is evident in the case before us, at least some around-the-clock demonstrations lasting for days on end will not materialize, others will be limited in size and duration, and the purposes of the regulation will thus be materially served. Perhaps these purposes would be more effectively and not so clumsily achieved by preventing tents and 24-hour vigils entirely in the core areas. But the Park Service's decision to permit nonsleeping demonstrations does not, in our view, impugn the camping prohibition as a valuable, but perhaps imperfect, protection to the parks. If the Government has a legitimate interest in ensuring that the National Parks are adequately protected, which we think it has, and if the parks would be more exposed to harm without the sleeping prohibition than with it, the ban is safe from invalidation under the First Amendment as a reasonable regulation of the manner in which a demonstration may be carried out.[151]
* * *

"[The] foregoing analysis demonstrates that the Park Service regulation is sustainable under the four-factor standard of *O'Brien*, for validating a regulation of expressive conduct, which, in the last analysis is little, if any, different[152] from the standard applied to time, place, or manner restrictions.[8] No one contends that aside from its impact on speech a rule against camping or overnight sleeping in public parks is beyond the constitutional power of the Government to enforce. And for the reasons we

---

Calculus: Equal Justice or Economic Efficiency? 98 Harv.L.Rev. 592 (1985) and Frank Easterbrook, *Method, Result, and Authority: A Reply*, 98 Harv.L.Rev. 622 (1985).

[151] Alan E. Brownstein, *Alternative Maps for Navigating the First Amendment Maze*, 16 Const. Comm. 101 (1999): "It seems clear that a similar argument could be applied to prohibit leafleting (or all demonstrations for that matter) in Lafayette Park. * * * I do not believe that a ban on leafleting in Lafayette Park would be as cavalierly upheld by the Court as the ban on camping, however."

[152] Christopher Thomas Leahy, *The First Amendment Gone Awry: City of Erie v. Pap's A.M., Ailing Analytical Structures, and the Suppression of Protected Expression*, 150 U. Pa. L. Rev. 1021 (2002): "While the tests may appear similar at first glance, they are distinct in several ways. First, the Court created the *O'Brien* test in the face of the preexisting TPM test—signaling an intention to create a distinct standard. Second, the TPM test's tailoring requirement is substantially weaker than the parallel requirement in the *O'Brien* test—it does not require that the restriction be 'no greater than is essential to the furtherance of [the governmental] interest.' Third, the TPM test requires consideration of 'alternative avenues of speech,' a prong completely absent from the *O'Brien* analysis."

[8] **[Ct's Note]** Reasonable time, place, or manner restrictions are valid even though they directly limit oral or written expression. It would be odd to insist on a higher standard for limitations aimed at regulable conduct and having only an incidental impact on speech. Thus, if the time, place, or manner restriction on expressive sleeping, if that is what is involved in this case, sufficiently and narrowly serves a substantial enough governmental interest to escape First Amendment condemnation, it is untenable to invalidate it under *O'Brien* on the ground that the governmental interest is insufficient to warrant the intrusion on First Amendment concerns or that there is an inadequate nexus between the regulation and the interest sought to be served. We note that only recently, in a case dealing with the regulation of signs, the Court framed the issue under *O'Brien* and then based a crucial part of its analysis on the time, place, or manner cases.

have discussed above, there is a substantial Government interest in conserving park property, an interest that is plainly served by, and requires for its implementation, measures such as the proscription of sleeping that are designed to limit the wear and tear on park properties. That interest is unrelated to suppression of expression.

"We are unmoved by the Court of Appeals' view that the challenged regulation is unnecessary, and hence invalid, because there are less speech-restrictive alternatives that could have satisfied the Government interest in preserving park lands. [The] Court of Appeals' suggestions that the Park Service minimize the possible injury by reducing the size, duration, or frequency of demonstrations would still curtail the total allowable expression in which demonstrators could engage, whether by sleeping or otherwise, and these suggestions represent no more than a disagreement with the Park Service over how much protection the core parks require or how an acceptable level of preservation is to be attained. We do not believe, however, that either *United States v. O'Brien* or the time, place, or manner decisions assign to the judiciary the authority to replace the Park Service as the manager of the Nation's parks or endow the judiciary with the competence to judge how much protection of park lands is wise and how that level of conservation is to be [attained.]"

BURGER, C.J., joined in the Court's opinion, adding: "[CCNV's] attempt at camping in the park is a form of 'picketing'; it is conduct, not speech. [It] trivializes the First Amendment to seek to use it as a shield in the manner asserted here."

MARSHALL, J., joined by Brennan, J., dissented: "The majority assumes, without deciding, that the respondents' conduct is entitled to constitutional protection. The problem with this assumption is that the Court thereby avoids examining closely the reality of respondents' planned expression. The majority's approach denatures respondents' asserted right and thus makes all too easy identification of a Government interest sufficient to warrant its abridgment.

"[Missing] from the majority's description is any inkling that Lafayette Park and the Mall have served as the sites for some of the most rousing political demonstrations in the Nation's history.[2] [The] primary purpose for making *sleep* an integral part of the demonstration was 'to re-enact the central reality of homelessness' and to impress upon public consciousness,

---

[2]   [Ct's Note] At oral argument, the Government informed the Court "that on any given day there will be an average of three or so demonstrations going on" in the Mall-Lafayette Park area. Respondents accurately describe Lafayette Park "as the American analogue to 'Speaker's Corner' in Hyde Park."

[For commentary on the undeveloped conception of place in First Amendment law, see Timothy Zick, *Speech and Spatial* Tactics, 84 Tex. L.Rev. 581 (2006); Timothy Zick, *Space, Place, and Speech*, 74 Geo. Wash. L.Rev. 439 (2006); Timothy Zick, *Property, Place and Public Discourse*, 21 Wash U.J.L. & Pol'y 173 (2006). See also Elizabeth Craig, *Protecting the President from Protest*, 9 J.Gender Race & Just. 665 (2006).].

in as dramatic a way as possible, that homelessness is a widespread problem, often ignored, that confronts its victims with life-threatening deprivations. As one of the homeless men seeking to demonstrate explained: 'Sleeping in Lafayette Park or on the Mall, for me, is to show people that conditions are so poor for the homeless and poor in this city that we would actually sleep *outside* in the winter to get the point across.' * * * Here respondents clearly intended to protest the reality of homelessness by sleeping outdoors in the winter in the near vicinity of the magisterial residence of the President of the United States. In addition to accentuating the political character of their protest by their choice of location and mode of communication, respondents also intended to underline the meaning of their protest by giving their demonstration satirical names. Respondents planned to name the demonstration on the Mall 'Congressional Village,' and the demonstration in Lafayette Park, 'Reaganville II.' * * *

"Although sleep in the context of this case is symbolic speech protected by the First Amendment, it is nonetheless subject to reasonable time, place, and manner restrictions. I agree with the standard enunciated by the majority.[6] I conclude, however, that the regulations at issue in this case, as applied to respondents, fail to satisfy this [standard].

"[T]here are no substantial Government interests advanced by the Government's regulations as applied to respondents. All that the Court's decision advances are the prerogatives of a bureaucracy that over the years has shown an implacable hostility toward citizens' exercise of First Amendment [rights].

"The disposition of this case impels me to make two additional observations. First, in this case, as in some others involving time, place, and manner restrictions, the Court has dramatically lowered its scrutiny of governmental regulations once it has determined that such regulations are content-neutral.[153] The result has been the creation of a two-tiered approach to First Amendment cases: while regulations that turn on the content of the expression are subjected to a strict form of judicial review, regulations that are aimed at matters other than expression receive only a minimal level of scrutiny. [The] Court has seemingly overlooked the fact that content-neutral restrictions are also capable of unnecessarily restricting protected expressive activity.[13] [The] Court [has] transformed the ban against content distinctions from a floor that offers all persons at least equal liberty under the First Amendment into a ceiling that restricts

---

6   [Ct's Note] I also agree with the majority that no substantial difference distinguishes the test applicable to time, place, and manner restrictions and the test articulated in *O'Brien.*

153 In support of Marshall, J.'s contention, see generally William E. Lee, *Lonely Pamphleteers, Little People, and the Supreme Court,* 54 G.W.U.L.Rev. 757 (1986).

13 [Ct's Note] See Martin Redish, *The Content Distinction in First Amendment Analysis,* 34 Stan.L.Rev. 113 (1981).

persons to the protection of First Amendment equality—but nothing more.[14] The consistent imposition of silence upon all may fulfill the dictates of an evenhanded content-neutrality. But it offends our 'profound national commitment to the principle that debate on public issues should be uninhibited, robust, and wide-open'. *New York Times v. Sullivan.*

"Second, the disposition of this case reveals a mistaken assumption regarding the motives and behavior of Government officials who create and administer content-neutral regulations. The Court's salutary skepticism of governmental decisionmaking in First Amendment matters suddenly dissipates once it determines that a restriction is not content-based. The Court evidently assumes that the balance struck by officials is deserving of deference so long as it does not appear to be tainted by content discrimination. What the Court fails to recognize is that public officials have strong incentives to overregulate even in the absence of an intent to censor particular views. This incentive stems from the fact that of the two groups whose interests officials must accommodate—on the one hand, the interests of the general public and, on the other, the interests of those who seek to use a particular forum for First Amendment activity—the political power of the former is likely to be far greater than that of the latter.[16]"

NOTES AND QUESTIONS

1.   Consider Mark Tushnet, *Character as Argument,* 14 Law and Social Inquiry 539 (1989) (reviewing Harry Kalven, *A Worthy Tradition*): "To capture the attention of a public accustomed to dignified protest, and able to screen it from consciousness, dissidents may have to adopt novel forms of protest, such as sleeping in a national park overnight to draw attention to the disgrace of a national policy that deprives many people of decent shelter. Yet, precisely because their protests take a novel form, they may not be covered by the worthy tradition that Kalven honors. In this sense the dynamics of protest may make the protection of free speech what Kalven tellingly calls a 'luxury civil liberty,' a civil liberty to be enjoyed when nothing of consequence turns on protecting speech and to be abandoned when it really matters."

2.   Should the Court have decided whether sleeping in the park in these circumstances was a form of expression entitled to some degree of First Amendment protection? See *Schad v. Mount Ephraim,* Sec. 3, I infra: "[N]ude

---

[14] **[Ct's Note]** Furthermore, [a] content-neutral regulation that restricts an inexpensive mode of communication will fall most heavily upon relatively poor speakers and to points of view that such speakers typically espouse. [See Lee, fn. 153 supra.] This sort of latent inequality is very much in evidence in this case, for respondents lack the financial means necessary to buy access to more conventional modes of persuasion.

A disquieting feature about the disposition of this case is that it lends credence to the charge that judicial administration of the First Amendment, in conjunction with a social order marked by large disparities of wealth and other sources of power, tends systematically to discriminate against efforts by the relatively disadvantaged to convey their political ideas. * * *

[16] **[Ct's Note]** See David Goldberger, *Judicial Scrutiny in Public Forum Cases: Misplaced Trust in the Judgment of Public Officials,* 32 Buffalo L.Rev. 175 (1983).

dancing is not without its First Amendment protections from official regulation." Should hair styles be afforded First Amendment protection? Are hair styles distinguishable from nude dancing on the ground that the latter is a form of expressive entertainment?

3.   The "time, place, or manner" test set out in *Clark* is differently stated in different cases. For example, *U.S. Postal Service v. Council of Greenburgh,* 453 U.S. 114 (1981), speaks of "adequate" as opposed to "ample" alternative channels of communication, and *Renton v. Playtime Theatres, Inc.,* Sec. 3, I infra, transcends the difference by requiring that the restriction not "unreasonably limit" alternative channels of communication. Beyond these differences, a number of cases state that the regulation must serve a significant government interest without stating that it must be "narrowly tailored" to serve a significant government interest. See e.g., *Heffron v. International Soc. For Krishna Consciousness,* Sec. 6, I, A infra. But see *Ward v. Rock Against Racism,* Sec. 6, I, A infra (reaffirming and defining narrowly tailored requirement). Assuming sleeping in the *Clark* context implicates First Amendment values, what test should apply? For development of an argument that a form of intermediate scrutiny "has attained central importance in the overall structure of free speech law," see Ashutosh Bhagwat, *The Test that Ate Everything: Intermediate Scrutiny in First Amendment Jurisprudence,* 2007 U.Ill. L.Rev. 783.

———

New York Public Health law authorizes the forced closure of a building for one year if it has been used for the purpose of "lewdness, assignation or prostitution." A civil complaint alleged that prostitution solicitation and sexual activities by patrons were occurring at an adult bookstore within observation of the proprietor. Accordingly, the complaint called for the closure of the building for one year. There was no claim that any books in the store were obscene. The New York Court of Appeals held that the closure remedy violated the First Amendment because it was broader than necessary to achieve the restriction against illicit sexual activities. It reasoned that an injunction against the alleged sexual conduct could further the state interest without infringing on First Amendment values.

ARCARA v. CLOUD BOOKS, INC., 478 U.S. 697 (1986), per BURGER, C.J., reversed, holding that the closure remedy did not require any First Amendment scrutiny: "This Court has applied First Amendment scrutiny to a statute regulating conduct which has the incidental effect of burdening the expression of a particular political opinion. *O'Brien.* * * *

"We have also applied First Amendment scrutiny to some statutes which, although directed at activity with no expressive component, impose a disproportionate burden upon those engaged in protected First Amendment activities. In *Minneapolis Star & Tribune v. Minnesota Commissioner of Revenue,* 460 U.S. 575 (1983), we struck down a tax imposed on the sale of large quantities of newsprint and ink because the tax had the effect of singling out newspapers to shoulder its burden. [Even] while striking down the tax in *Minneapolis Star,* we emphasized: 'Clearly, the First Amendment does not prohibit all regulation of the press. It is beyond dispute that the States and the Federal Government can subject newspapers to generally applicable economic regulations without creating constitutional problems.'

"The New York Court of Appeals held that the *O'Brien* test for permissible governmental regulation was applicable to this case because the closure order sought by petitioner would also impose an incidental burden upon respondents' bookselling activities. [But] unlike the symbolic draft card burning in *O'Brien,* the sexual activity carried on in this case manifests absolutely no element of protected expression.[154] In *Paris Adult Theatre,* we underscored the fallacy of seeking to use the First Amendment as a cloak for obviously unlawful public sexual conduct by the diaphanous device of attributing protected expressive attributes to that conduct. First Amendment values may not be invoked by merely linking the words 'sex' and 'books.'

"Nor does the distinction drawn by the New York Public Health Law inevitably single out bookstores or others engaged in First Amendment protected activities for the imposition of its burden, as did the tax struck down in *Minneapolis Star.* [If] the city imposed closure penalties for demonstrated Fire Code violations or health hazards from inadequate sewage treatment, the First Amendment would not aid the owner of premises who had knowingly allowed such violations to persist. * * *

"It is true that the closure order in this case would require respondents to move their bookselling business to another location. Yet we have not traditionally subjected every criminal and civil sanction imposed through legal process to 'least restrictive means' scrutiny simply because each particular remedy will have some effect on the First Amendment activities of those subject to sanction.[4]"[155]

---

[154] In an earlier section of the opinion, Burger, C.J., stated that, "petitioners in *O'Brien* had, as respondents here do not, at least the semblance of expressive activity in their claim that the otherwise unlawful burning of a draft card was to 'carry a message' of the actor's opposition to the draft."

[4] **[Ct's Note]** [T]here is no suggestion on the record before us that the closure of respondents' bookstore was sought under the public health nuisance statute as a pretext for the suppression of First Amendment protected material. Were respondents able to establish the existence of such a speech suppressive motivation or policy on the part of the District Attorney, they might have a claim of selective prosecution. Respondents in this case made no such assertion before the trial court.

[155] On remand, the New York Court of Appeals held that, in the absence of a showing that the state had chosen a course no broader than necessary to accomplish its purpose, any forced closure of the bookstore would unduly impair the bookseller's rights of free expression under the New York State constitution. From New York's perspective, the question is not "who is aimed at but who is hit." *People ex rel. Arcara v. Cloud Books, Inc.,* 68 N.Y.2d 553, 510 N.Y.S.2d 844, 503 N.E.2d 492 (1986). New York has since retreated. Jeremy J. Bethel, *Freedom of Expression in New York State:*

O'CONNOR, J., joined by Stevens, J., concurred: "I agree that the Court of Appeals erred in applying a First Amendment standard of review where, as here, the government is regulating neither speech nor an incidental, non-expressive effect of speech. Any other conclusion would lead to the absurd result that any government action that had some conceivable speech-inhibiting consequences, such as the arrest of a newscaster for a traffic violation, would require analysis under the First Amendment."

BLACKMUN, J., joined by Brennan and Marshall, JJ., dissented: "Until today, this Court has never suggested that a State may suppress speech as much as it likes, without justification, so long as it does so through generally applicable regulations that have 'nothing to do with any expressive conduct.' * * *

"At some point, of course, the impact of state regulation on First Amendment rights become so attenuated that it is easily outweighed by the state interest. But when a State directly and substantially impairs First Amendment activities, such as by shutting down a bookstore, I believe that the State must show, at a minimum, that it has chosen the least restrictive means of pursuing its legitimate objectives. The closure of a bookstore can no more be compared to a traffic arrest of a reporter than the closure of a church could be compared to the traffic arrest of its clergyman.

"A State has a legitimate interest in forbidding sexual acts committed in public, including a bookstore. An obvious method of eliminating such acts is to arrest the patron committing them. But the statute in issue does not provide for that. Instead, it imposes absolute liability on the bookstore simply because the activity occurs on the premises. And the penalty—a mandatory 1-year closure—imposes an unnecessary burden on speech. Of course 'linking the words "sex" and "books" is not enough to extend First Amendment protection to illegal sexual activity, but neither should it suffice to remove First Amendment protection from books situated near the site of such activity. The State's purpose in stopping public lewdness cannot justify such a substantial infringement of First Amendment rights. * * *

"Petitioner has not demonstrated that a less restrictive remedy would be inadequate to abate the nuisance. The Court improperly attempts to shift to the bookseller the responsibility for finding an alternative site. But surely the Court would not uphold a city ordinance banning all public debate on the theory that the residents could move somewhere else.

What Remains of People ex rel. Arcara v. Cloud Books, Inc.?, 28 Fordham Urb. L.J. 1797 (2001). See also *Alexander v. United States,* 509 U.S. 544 (1993)(confiscation and destruction of protected materials for distribution of obscene materials does not violate First Amendment).

NOTES AND QUESTIONS

1. *A need for scrutiny?* Should the state's closing of a bookstore *always* trigger heightened judicial scrutiny? Should fire code regulations trigger First Amendment scrutiny? Consider Comment, *Padlock Orders and Nuisance Laws,* 51 Albany L.Rev. 1007 (1987): "Closure penalties for fire code violations or health hazards from inadequate sewage treatment were offered as examples of generally applicable regulations which could constitutionally be applied to bookstores where the owner 'had knowingly allowed such violations to persist.' Few would argue with this conclusion. These generally applicable regulations would be within the state's constitutional power, would further a substantial governmental interest unrelated to the suppression of free expression, and the incidental restriction on First Amendment freedoms, where the owner knowingly allowed the violations to persist, would be no greater than is essential to further the state's interest. Concluding that the *O'Brien* test is satisfied, however, does not support the conclusion that the test does not apply."

2. *Generally applicable laws.* A newspaper published the name of a confidential source who it believed had misled it for political reasons. The source sued for breach of contract and prevailed in the Minnesota Supreme Court.

COHEN v. COWLES MEDIA CO., 501 U.S. 663 (1991), per White, J., affirmed, dismissing the First Amendment claim with the observation that "generally applicable laws do not offend the First Amendment simply because their enforcement against the press has incidental effects on its ability to gather and report the news."[156] Consistent with *O'Brien*? *Daily Mail*? Consider Eugene Volokh, *Speech as Conduct: Generally Applicable Laws, Illegal Courses of Conduct, "Situation-Altering Utterances," and the Uncharted Zones,* 90 Cornell L. Rev. 1277 (2005): " 'Minnesota law simply requires those making promises to keep them. The parties themselves, as in this case, determine the scope of their legal obligations, and any restrictions which may be placed on the publication of truthful information are self-imposed.' So the Court rejected the free speech argument based on the principle that free speech rights, like most other rights, are waivable, rather than on an assertion that speech-neutral laws are per se constitutional."

3. *Negative theory.* Should the scope of the First Amendment be confined to instances in which government may have acted in a biased way? Consider Ronald Cass, *Commercial Speech, Constitutionalism, Collective Choice,* 56 U.Cin.L.Rev. 1317 (1988): "There is widespread agreement that limitation of official bias is the principal aim of the First Amendment, historically and as amplified over the past half-century by the courts." See generally Ronald Cass, *The Perils of Positive Thinking: Constitutional Interpretation and Negative First Amendment Theory,* 34 UCLA L.Rev. 1405

---

[156] Blackmun, J., joined by Marshall & Souter, JJ., dissented; Souter, J., joined by Marshall, Blackmun, & O'Connor, JJ., and dissented.

(1987) (emphasizing official self interest and, to a lesser extent, intolerance as the principal motives of concern).

Professor Schauer has also attempted a justification for freedom of speech not based on any positive aspects of speech, but based on the premise that governments are "less capable of regulating speech than they are of regulating other forms of conduct."[157] He suggests that bias, self-interest, and a general urge to suppress that with which one disagrees are significant reasons for this incapability. Frederick Schauer, *Free Speech: A Philosophical Enquiry* 80–86 (1982). See also Frederick Schauer, *Must Speech Be Special?*, 78 Nw.U.L.Rev. 1284 (1983). As he interprets the First Amendment, therefore, its "focus [is] on the motivations of the government." Frederick Schauer, *Cuban Cigars, Cuban Books, and the Problem of Incidental Restrictions on Communications*, 26 Wm. & Mary L.Rev. 779 (1985).[158]

Is negative theory consistent with what the Court has *said* about free speech? With the doctrine it has produced? Consider, e.g., *Arcara. O'Brien.* The defamation line of cases. Compare Frederick Schauer, *Cuban Cigars*, supra with Steven Shiffrin, *The First Amendment, Democracy, and Romance* (1990). Is the content-based/content-neutral distinction founded exclusively on a concern with government motive? See generally Geoffrey Stone, *Content Regulation and the First Amendment*, 25 Wm. & Mary L.Rev. 189 (1983) (arguing that the basis for the distinction is more complicated). Does an emphasis on motive or content unreasonably downplay the notion that the *effect* of government conduct on the quantity or quality of speech is of independent First Amendment value? See generally R. George Wright, *Content-Based and Content-Neutral Regulation of Speech: The Limitations of a Common Distinction*, 60 U.Miami L.Rev. 333 (2006); Martin Redish, *The Content Distinction in First Amendment Analysis*, 34 Stan.L.Rev. 113 (1981); Susan Williams, *Content Discrimination and the First Amendment*, 139 U.Pa.L.Rev. 201 (1991).

4. **Reading Arcara narrowly.** Could *Arcara's* failure to find the First Amendment implicated be justified without resort to negative theory or motive theory? Consider Tribe 2d ed., at 978–79 n. 2: "[W]hen *neither* the law, *nor* the act triggering its enforcement has any significant First Amendment dimension,[159] the fact that the law *incidentally* operates to restrict First Amendment activity, and that some alternative state measure might offer a less restrictive means of pursuing the state's legitimate objectives, should not serve to condemn what the state has done as unconstitutional." Why not? For discussion of the foundations of *Arcara*, see Seana V. Shiffrin, *Speech, Death, and Double Effect*, 78 N.Y.U. L. Rev. 1135 (2003).

---

[157] But see Larry Alexander, *Is There a Right of Freedom of Expression?* 145 (2005).

[158] See also Frederick Schauer, *The Phenomenology of Speech and Harm*, 103 Ethics 635 (1993) (disputing the hypothesis that the harmful consequences of speech are less than those associated with other forms of conduct); Frederick Schauer, *The Sociology of the Hate Speech Debate*, 37 Vill.L.Rev. 805 (1992).

[159] For relevant commentary, see Michael C. Dorf, *Incidental Burdens on Fundamental Rights*, 109 Harv. L. Rev. 1175 (1996).

5. ***Arcara extended?*** The Richmond Redevelopment and Housing Authority barred Hicks from trespassing on property where public low income housing existed in the absence of permission from the manager of the housing project. VIRGINIA v. HICKS, 539 U.S. 113 (2003), per SCALIA, J., held that the bar was not substantially overbroad since it prevented a wide range of conduct, and that even if Hicks wanted to enter the property to speak or leaflet, the bar would properly be applied: "Neither the basis for the barment sanction (the prior trespass) nor its purpose (preventing prior trespasses) has anything to do with the First Amendment."[160]

3. IS SOME PROTECTED SPEECH LESS EQUAL THAN OTHER PROTECTED SPEECH?

I. NEAR OBSCENE SPEECH

RENTON v. PLAYTIME THEATRES, INC., 475 U.S. 41 (1986), per REHNQUIST, J., upheld a zoning ordinance that prohibited adult motion picture theaters from locating within 1,000 feet of any residential zone, church, park, or school. The effect was to exclude such theaters from approximately 94% of the land in the city. Of the remaining 520 acres, a substantial part was occupied by a sewage disposal and treatment plant, a horse racing track and environs, a warehouse and manufacturing facilities, a Mobil Oil tank farm, and a fully-developed shopping center: "[T]he resolution of this case is largely dictated by our decision in *Young v. American Mini Theatres, Inc.*, 427 U.S. 50 (1976). There, although five Members of the Court did not agree on a single rationale for the decision, we held that the city of Detroit's zoning ordinance, which prohibited locating an adult theater within 1,000 feet of any two other 'regulated uses' or within 500 feet of any residential zone, did not violate the First and Fourteenth amendments. The Renton ordinance, like the one in *Young*, does not ban adult theaters altogether, but merely provides that such theaters may not be located within 1,000 feet of any residential zone, single-or multiple-family dwelling, church, park, or school. The ordinance is therefore properly analyzed as a form of time, place, and manner regulation.

"This Court has long held that regulations enacted for the purpose of restraining speech on the basis of its content presumptively violate the First Amendment. See *Chicago Police Dept. v. Mosley*, Sec. 6, I, B infra.[161] On the other hand, so-called 'content-neutral' time, place, and manner regulations are acceptable so long as they are designed to serve a

---

[160] Souter, J., joined by Breyer, J., concurred.

[161] *Mosley* involved an ordinance that banned picketing near a school building except the "peaceful picketing of any school involved in a labor dispute." The Court stated: "The regulation '[slips] from the neutrality of time, place, and circumstance into a concern about content.' This is never permitted."

substantial governmental interest and do not unreasonably limit alternative avenues of communication.[162]

"At first glance, the Renton ordinance, like the ordinance in *Young,* does not appear to fit neatly into either the 'content-based' or the 'content-neutral' category. To be sure, the ordinance treats theaters that specialize in adult films differently from other kinds of theaters. Nevertheless, [the] City Council's *'predominate* concerns' were with the secondary effects of adult theaters, and not with the content of adult films themselves. * * *

"[This] finding as to 'predominate' intent is more than adequate to establish that the city's pursuit of its zoning interests here was unrelated to the suppression of free expression.[163] The ordinance by its terms is designed to prevent crime, protect the city's retail trade, maintain property values,[164] and generally 'protec[t] and preserv[e] the quality of [the city's] neighborhoods, commercial districts, and the quality of urban life,' not to suppress the expression of unpopular views. As Justice Powell observed in *Young,* '[i]f [the city] had been concerned with restricting the message purveyed by adult theaters, it would have tried to close them or restrict their number rather than circumscribe their choice as to location.'

"In short, the [ordinance] does not contravene the fundamental principle that underlies our concern about 'content-based' speech regulations: that 'government may not grant the use of a forum to people whose views it finds acceptable, but deny use to those wishing to express less favored or more controversial views.' *Mosley.*

"It was with this understanding in mind that, in *Young,* a majority of this Court decided that at least with respect to businesses that purvey sexually explicit materials,[165] zoning ordinances designed to combat the undesirable secondary effects of such businesses are to be reviewed under

---

[162] Compare the statement of the time, place, and manner test in *Clark,* Sec. 2 supra. For commentary, see David Day, *The Hybridization of the Content-Neutral Standards for the Free Speech Clause,* 19 Ariz.St.L.J. 195 (1987).

[163] The Court interpreted the court of appeals opinion to require the invalidation of the ordinance if a "motivating factor" to restrict the exercise of First Amendment rights was present "apparently no matter how small a part this motivating factor may have played in the City Council's decision." This view of the law, the Court continued, "was rejected in *O'Brien:* 'It is a familiar principle of constitutional law that this Court will not strike down an otherwise constitutional statute on the basis of an alleged illicit legislative motive. [What] motivates one legislator to make a speech about a statute is not necessarily what motivates scores of others to enact it, and the stakes are sufficiently high for us to eschew guesswork.'"

[164] For support, see Charles Clarke, *Freedom of Speech and the Problem of the Lawful Harmful Public Reaction,* 20 Akron L.Rev. 187 (1986).

[165] The secondary effects justification was deemed to distinguish *Erznoznik v. City of Jacksonville,* 422 U.S. 205 (1975) (invalidating ordinance prohibiting drive-in theaters from showing films containing nudity) and *Schad v. Mount Ephraim,* 452 U.S. 61 (1981) (invalidating ordinance prohibiting live entertainment, as applied to nude dancing, in commercial zone).

the standards applicable to 'content-neutral' time, place, and manner regulations.[2]

"The appropriate inquiry in this case, then, is whether the Renton ordinance is designed to serve a substantial governmental interest and allows for reasonable alternative avenues of communication."

After concluding that the ordinance was designed to serve substantial government interests, the Court ruled that the Renton ordinance allowed "for reasonable alternative avenues of communication": "[W]e note that the ordinance leaves some 520 acres, or more than five percent of the entire land area of Renton, open to use as adult theater sites. [Respondents] argue, however, that some of the land in question is already occupied by existing businesses, that 'practically none' of the undeveloped land is currently for sale or lease, and that in general there are no 'commercially viable' adult theater sites within the 520 acres left open by the Renton ordinance. The Court of Appeals accepted these arguments. * * *

"We disagree. [That] respondents must fend for themselves in the real estate market, on an equal footing with other prospective purchasers and lessees, does not give rise to a First Amendment violation. And although we have cautioned against the enactment of zoning regulations that have 'the effect of suppressing, or greatly restricting access to, lawful speech,' *Young* (plurality opinion), we have never suggested that the First Amendment compels the Government to ensure that adult theaters, or any other kinds of speech-related businesses for that matter, will be able to obtain sites at bargain prices. [T]he First Amendment requires only that Renton refrain from effectively denying respondents a reasonable opportunity to open and operate an adult theater within the city, and the ordinance before us easily meets this requirement. * * * *[4]"[166]

BRENNAN, J., joined by Marshall, J., dissented: "The fact that adult movie theaters may cause harmful 'secondary' land use effects may arguably give Renton a compelling reason to regulate such establishments; it does not mean, however, that such regulations are content-neutral. * * *

---

[2]   [Ct's Note] See *Young* (plurality opinion) ("[I]t is manifest that society's interest in protecting this type of expression is of a wholly different, and lesser, magnitude than the interest in untrammeled political debate * * * ."). [The plurality opinion in *Young* stated that "[f]ew of us would march our sons and daughters off to war to see 'Specified Sexual Activities' exhibited in the theaters of our choice."].

[4]   [Ct's Note] [We] reject respondents' "vagueness" argument for the same reasons that led us to reject a similar challenge in *Young*. There, the Detroit ordinance applied to theaters "used to present material distinguished or characterized by an emphasis on [sexually explicit matter]." We held that "even if there may be some uncertainty about the effect of the ordinances on other litigants, they are unquestionably applicable to these respondents." We also held that the Detroit ordinance created no "significant deterrent effect" that might justify invocation of the First Amendment "overbreadth" doctrine.

[166] Blackmun, J., concurred in the result without opinion.

"The ordinance discriminates on its face against certain forms of speech based on content. Movie theaters specializing in 'adult motion pictures' may not be located within 1,000 feet of any residential zone, single-or multiple-family dwelling, church, park, or school. Other motion picture theaters, and other forms of 'adult entertainment,' such as bars, massage parlors, and adult bookstores, are not subject to the same restrictions. This selective treatment strongly suggests that Renton was interested not in controlling the 'secondary effects' associated with adult businesses, but in discriminating against adult theaters based on the content of the films they exhibit. [Moreover,] [a]s the Court of Appeals observed, '[b]oth the magistrate and the district court recognized that many of the stated reasons for the ordinance were no more than expressions of dislike for the subject matter.'[3] That some residents may be offended by the *content* of the films shown at adult movie theaters cannot form the basis for state regulation of speech. See *Terminiello*.

"Some of the 'findings' [do] relate to supposed 'secondary effects' associated with adult movie theaters[4] [but they were added by the City Council only after this law suit was filed and the Court should not] accept these post-hoc statements at face value. [As] the Court of Appeals concluded, '[t]he record presented by Renton to support its asserted interest in enacting the zoning ordinance is very thin.' [5] * * * 7

---

[3] **[Ct's Note]** For example, "finding" number 2 states that "[l]ocation of adult entertainment land uses on the main commercial thoroughfares of the City gives an impression of legitimacy to, and causes a loss of sensitivity to the adverse effect of pornography upon children, established family relations, respect for marital relationship and for the sanctity of marriage relations of others, and the concept of nonaggressive, consensual sexual relations."

"Finding" number 6 states that "[l]ocation of adult land uses in close proximity to residential uses, churches, parks, and other public facilities, and schools, will cause a degradation of the community standard of morality. Pornographic material has a degrading effect upon the relationship between spouses."

[4] **[Ct's Note]** For example, "finding" number 12 states that "[l]ocation of adult entertainment land uses in proximity to residential uses, churches, parks and other public facilities, and schools, may lead to increased levels of criminal activities, including prostitution, rape, incest and assaults in the vicinity of such adult entertainment land uses."

[5] **[Ct's Note]** As part of the amendment passed after this lawsuit commenced, the City Council added a statement that it had intended to rely on the Washington Supreme Court's opinion in *Northend Cinema, Inc. v. Seattle,* 90 Wash.2d 709, 585 P.2d 1153 (1978), cert. denied, 441 U.S. 946 (1979), which upheld Seattle's zoning regulations against constitutional attack. Again, despite the suspicious coincidental timing of the amendment, the Court holds that "Renton was entitled to rely [on] the 'detailed findings' summarized in [the] *Northend Cinema* opinion." In *Northend Cinema,* the court noted that "[t]he record is replete with testimony regarding the effects of adult movie theater locations on residential neighborhoods." The opinion however, does not explain the evidence it purports to summarize, and provided no basis for determining whether Seattle's experience is relevant to Renton's.

[7] **[Ct's Note]** As one commentator has noted: "[A]nyone with any knowledge of human nature should naturally assume that the decision to adopt almost any content-based restriction might have been affected by an antipathy on the part of at least some legislators to the ideas or information being suppressed. The logical assumption, in other words, is not that there is not improper motivation but, rather, because legislators are only human, that there is a substantial risk that an impermissible consideration has in fact colored the deliberative process." Geoffrey

"Even assuming that the ordinance should be treated like a content-neutral time, place, and manner restriction, I would still find it unconstitutional. [T]he ordinance is invalid because it does not provide for reasonable alternative avenues of communication.[167] [R]espondents do not ask Renton to guarantee low-price sites for their businesses, but seek, only a reasonable opportunity to operate adult theaters in the city. By denying them this opportunity, Renton can effectively ban a form of protected speech from its borders. The ordinance 'greatly restrict[s] access to, lawful speech,' *Young,* and is plainly unconstitutional."

NOTES AND QUESTIONS

1.   *Content neutral?* Was the ordinance fairly characterized as content-neutral? Erwin Chemerinsky, *Content Neutrality as a Central Problem of Freedom of Speech: Problems in the Supreme Court's Application,* 74 S. Cal. L. Rev. 49 (2000): "The *Renton* approach confuses whether a law is content based or content neutral with the question of whether a law is justified by a sufficient purpose. The law in Renton may have been properly upheld as needed to combat crime and the secondary effects of adult theaters, but it nonetheless was clearly content based. The law applied only to theaters showing films with sexually explicit content." See also Heidi Kitrosser, *From Marshall McLuhan to Anthropomorphic Cows: Communicative Manner and the First Amendment,* 96 Nw. U. L. Rev. 1339 (2002). Is the focus on "secondary effects" convincing? Consider Geoffrey Stone, *Content-Neutral Restrictions,* 54 U.Chi.L.Rev. 46 (1987): "[T]he Court had never before *Renton* suggested that the absence of a constitutionally disfavored justification is in itself a justification for treating an expressly content-based restriction as if it were content-neutral. To the contrary, with the single exception of *Renton,* the Court in such circumstances has always invoked the stringent standards of content-based review. [For example, *Ferber*] treated as content-based a law prohibiting 'child pornography,' even though the government defended the law not in terms of communicative impact, but on the ground that the law was necessary to protect children who participate in 'sexual performances.' [I]f taken seriously, and extended to other contexts, the Court's transmogrification in *Renton* of an expressly content-based restriction into one that is content-neutral threatens to undermine the very foundation of the content-based/content-neutral distinction. This would in turn erode the coherence and predictability of First Amendment doctrine. One can only hope that this aspect of *Renton* is soon forgotten." See also Kathleen M. Sullivan, *Sex, Money, and Groups: Free Speech and Association Decisions in the October 1999 Term,* 28 Pepp. L. Rev. 723 (2001): "The Court uses the rationale of content-neutral 'secondary effects' to uphold otherwise content-based statutes whose political counterparts would

---

Stone, *Restrictions on Speech Because of Its Content: The Peculiar Case of Subject-Matter Restrictions,* 46 U.Chi.L.Rev. 81 (1978).

[167] Brennan, J., argued that the ordinance also failed as an acceptable time, place, and manner restriction because it was not narrowly tailored to serve a significant governmental interest.

readily be struck down; no one, for example, would sustain a ban on political rallies because they tend to be associated with litter and fistfights."

Are subject matter restrictions as a class less problematic than other forms of content discrimination in that they often do not discriminate on the basis of point of view? Should *Renton's* secondary effects emphasis be limited to subject-matter-based restrictions? See Note, *The Content Distinction in Free Speech Analysis After Renton,* 102 Harv.L.Rev. 1904 (1989). Even if some subject matter restrictions are less problematic, is the Renton ordinance neutral as to point of view? Consider Geoffrey Stone, *Restrictions of Speech Because of Its Content: The Peculiar Case of Subject-Matter Restrictions,* 46 U.Chi.L.Rev. 81 (1978): "[T]he speech suppressed by restrictions such as those involved in [cases like *Erznoznik* and *Young*] will almost invariably carry an implicit, if not explicit, message in favor of more relaxed sexual mores. Such restrictions, in other words, have a potent viewpoint-differential impact. [I]n our society, the very presence of sexual explicitness in speech seems ideologically significant, without regard to whatever other messages might be intended. To treat such restrictions as viewpoint-neutral seems simply to ignore reality. Finally, [a] large percentage of citizens apparently feel threatened by nonobscene, sexually-explicit speech and believe it to be morally reprehensible. If it were not for the Court's relatively narrow construction of the obscenity concept, much of this speech would undoubtedly be banned outright. Thus, any restriction along these lines will carry an extraordinarily high risk that its enactment was tainted by this fundamentally illegitimate consideration. Such restrictions, although superficially viewpoint-neutral, pose a uniquely compelling case for content-based scrutiny." Are feminist or neo-conservative objections to near obscene speech both "fundamentally illegitimate." Should all content-based scrutiny be the same? Does *Renton* reconstruct the Court's "narrow construction of the obscenity concept"?

Is the concept of viewpoint neutrality itself problematic? Consider Cass Sunstein, *Pornography and the First Amendment,* 1986 Duke L.J. 589 : "One does not 'see' a viewpoint-based restriction when the harms invoked in defense of a regulation are obvious and so widely supported by social consensus that they allay any concern about impermissible government motivation. Whether a classification is viewpoint-based thus ultimately turns on the viewpoint of the decisionmaker." See generally Catharine MacKinnon, *Feminism, Marxism, Method, and the State,* 7 Signs 515 (1981).

2. ***Can Renton be squared with Brandenburg?*** Consider Seana V. Shiffrin, *Speech, Death, and Double Effect,* 78 N.Y.U. L. Rev. 1135 (2003): "If one puts the *Brandenburg* line of cases side by side with [the] *Young-Renton-Barnes-Erie* line of cases, it looks as though a speaker may be held responsible for incidental effects of her speech but not (except under special circumstances) for direct, intended effects. The negative or positive effects on an audience from its understanding and directly reacting to the contents of one's speech may not be the grounds for restriction, but the side effects of one's speech may be so used." Is this explainable because a "central reason for protecting speech is to permit a variety of ideas to be promulgated to, and evaluated and tested by,

independent agents." Id. Is interference with advocacy of illegal action, therefore, more problematic than interference on "secondary effects" grounds? Does it matter whether the speech in cases like *Renton* predisposes audience members to solicit prostitutes or seek drugs?

Can a distinction be drawn because advocacy of illegal action is political? Does *Renton*—see fn. 2—endorse a hierarchy of categories among types of protected speech? Consider Tribe 2d ed., at 939 n. 66: "[I]t is doubtful that *Renton* can fairly be read as endorsing the concept of a hierarchy of intermediate categories, because the case turned on the majority's characterization of the restriction as content-neutral, and the issue of the relative importance of the speech involved, was, strictly speaking, irrelevant." But cf. Philip Prygoski, *Low Value Speech: From Young to Fraser,* 32 St. L.U.L.J. 317 (1987) (despite the content-neutral language, "antipathy toward the kind of expression involved" swayed the case).

3. *Renton's* "secondary effects" notion was revisited by several justices in BOOS v. BARRY, Sec. 2, supra: A District of Columbia ordinance banned the display of any sign within 500 feet of a foreign embassy that would tend to bring the embassy into "public odium" or "public disrepute." O'CONNOR, J., joined by Stevens and Scalia, JJ., distinguished *Renton:* "Respondents and the United States do not point to the 'secondary effects' of picket signs in front of embassies. They do not point to congestion, to interference with ingress or egress, to visual clutter, or to the need to protect the security of embassies. Rather, they rely on the need to protect the dignity of foreign diplomatic personnel by shielding them from speech that is critical of their governments. This justification focuses *only* on the content of the speech and the direct impact that speech has on its listeners. The emotive impact of speech on its audience is not a 'secondary effect.'[168] Because the display clause regulates speech due to its potential primary impact, we conclude it must be considered content-based."[169]

BRENNAN, J., joined by Marshall, J., agreed with the conclusion that the ordinance was content-based, but objected to O'Connor, J.'s "assumption that

---

[168] See *Forsyth County v. The Nationalist Movement,* 505 U.S. 123 (1992)("Listener's reaction to speech is not a content-neutral basis for regulation,"—not secondary effects).

[169] In an earlier passage O'Connor, J., responded to the argument that the ordinance was not content-based on the theory that the government was not selecting between viewpoints. The argument was instead that "the permissible message on a picket sign is determined solely by the policies of a foreign government. We reject this contention, although we agree the provision is not viewpoint-based. The display clause determines which viewpoint is acceptable in a neutral fashion by looking to the policies of foreign governments. While this prevents the display clause from being directly viewpoint-based, a label with potential First Amendment ramifications of its own, it does not render the statute content-neutral. Rather, we have held that a regulation that 'does not favor either side of a political controversy' is nonetheless impermissible because the 'First Amendment's hostility to content-based regulation extends [to] prohibition of public discussion of an entire topic.' Here the government has determined that an entire category of speech—signs or displays critical of foreign governments—is not to be permitted.

the *Renton* analysis applies not only outside the context of businesses purveying sexually explicit materials but even to political speech."[170]

4. ***The nature of content regulation reconsidered.*** LOS ANGELES v. ALAMEDA BOOKS, 535 U.S. 425 (2002), per O'CONNOR, J., reaffirmed *Renton* and found a sufficient showing of secondary effects to permit Los Angeles not only to disperse adult businesses, but also to prohibit more than one adult entertainment business within the same building, i.e., a company could not have an adult bookstore and an adult video arcade in the same building.

SCALIA, J., concurring, would have gone further: "[I]n a case such as this our First Amendment traditions make secondary effects analysis quite unnecessary. The Constitution does not prevent those communities that wish to do so from regulating, or indeed entirely suppressing, the business of pandering sex."

Four Justices expressed doubts about the conception of "content" employed in *Renton*. KENNEDY, J., concurring, criticized *Renton's* conception of "content": "*Renton* described a similar ordinance as "content neutral," and I agree with the dissent that the designation is imprecise. [T]he ordinance in *Renton* 'treat[ed] theaters that specialize in adult films differently from other kinds of theaters.' The fiction that this sort of ordinance is content neutral—or 'content neutral'—is perhaps more confusing than helpful, as Justice Souter demonstrates. [These] ordinances are content based, and we should call them so."

Nonetheless, Kennedy, J., adhered to the "intermediate scrutiny" of *Renton* and required a city to "advance some basis to show that its regulation has the purpose and effect of suppressing secondary effects, while leaving the quantity and accessibility of speech substantially intact. The ordinance may identify the speech based on content, but only as a shorthand for identifying the secondary effects outside. A city may not assert that it will reduce secondary effects by reducing speech in the same proportion. [The] rationale of the ordinance must be that it will suppress secondary effects and not by suppressing speech." Kennedy, J., found that Los Angeles ordinance met this burden.

SOUTER, J., joined by Stevens and Ginsburg, and in part by Breyer, JJ., dissented:[171] "[W]hile it may be true that an adult business is burdened only because of its secondary effects, it is clearly burdened only if its expressive products have adult content. Thus, the Court has recognized that this kind of regulation, though called content neutral, occupies a kind of limbo between

---

[170] Rehnquist, J., joined by White and Blackmun, JJ., voted to uphold the ordinance on the basis of Bork, J.'s opinion below in *Finzer v. Barry,* 798 F.2d 1450 (D.C.Cir.1986). Bork, J., stated that the need to adhere to principles of international law might constitute a secondary effect under *Renton* but was not "entirely sure" whether *Renton* alone could dictate that result and did not resolve the issue.

[171] Breyer, J., joined this section of the opinion, but not the portion quoted here.

full-blown, content-based restrictions and regulations that apply without any reference to the substance of what is said.

"It would in fact make sense to give this kind of zoning regulation a First Amendment label of its own, and if we called it content correlated, we would not only describe it for what it is, but keep alert to a risk of content-based regulation that it poses. The risk lies in the fact that when a law applies selectively only to speech of particular content, the more precisely the content is identified, the greater is the opportunity for government censorship. Adult speech refers not merely to sexually explicit content, but to speech reflecting a favorable view of being explicit about sex and a favorable view of the practices it depicts; a restriction on adult content is thus also a restriction turning on a particular viewpoint, of which the government may disapprove.

"This risk of viewpoint discrimination is subject to a relatively simple safeguard, however. If combating secondary effects of property devaluation and crime is truly the reason for the regulation, it is possible to show by empirical evidence that the effects exist, that they are caused by the expressive activity subject to the zoning, and that the zoning can be expected either to ameliorate them or to enhance the capacity of the government to combat them (say, by concentrating them in one area), without suppressing the expressive activity itself. This capacity of zoning regulation to address the practical problems without eliminating the speech is, after all, the only possible excuse for speaking of secondary-effects zoning as akin to time, place, or manner regulations." Souter, J., argued that Los Angeles had not met this burden.

5.   *Beyond secondary effects.* Consider Barry P. McDonald, *Speech and Distrust: Rethinking the Content Approach to Protecting the Freedom of Expression*, 81 Notre D. L.Rev. 1347 (2006): "[A] review of the Court's post-*Renton* cases indicates that the decision was anything but an aberration in calling a facially content discriminatory regulation content-neutral. [T]he vast majority of speech regulations reviewed by the Court make content distinctions on their face, and [the] Court has taken quite often to designating them as content-neutral without resort to any sort of secondary effects rationale."

———————

Five years after *Renton*, the Court held that an Indiana statute prohibiting the knowing or intentional appearing in a public place in a state of nudity could constitutionally be applied to require that any female dancer at a minimum wear "pasties" and a "G-string" when she dances.

BARNES v. GLEN THEATRE, INC., 501 U.S. 560 (1991). The Justices upholding the ordinance were divided upon the rationale for doing so. Rehnquist, C.J., joined by O'Connor and Kennedy, JJ., applied the *O'Brien* test, characterized the statute as a "public indecency" statute, and concluded that the interests in order and morality justified the statute. Souter, J., concurring, also applied the *O'Brien* test, but concluded that the statute was justified by the "secondary effects" of prostitution, sexual assaults, and other criminal activity even though this justification had not been articulated by the Indiana legislature or its courts. Scalia, J., argued that the case law did not support the plurality's contention that the interest in morality was substantial enough to pass muster under *O'Brien*; nonetheless, he voted to uphold the statute by repudiating the *O'Brien* test. White, J. joined by Marshall, Blackmun and Stevens, JJ., dissented.

––––––––

The fragmented character of the *Barnes* majority created interpretive difficulties for the Pennsylvania Supreme Court in considering an Erie, Pennsylvania ordinance. Like Indiana, Erie's ordinance forbade knowingly or intentionally appearing in a public "state of nudity." Unlike Indiana, however, the preamble to the ordinance stated that the "Council specifically wishes to adopt the concept of Public Indecency prohibited by the laws of the State of Indiana, which was approved by the U.S. Supreme Court in *Barnes*, (for) the purpose of limiting a recent increase in nude live entertainment within the City," which led to prostitution and other crime.

Pap's A.M., operated "Kandyland," featuring nude erotic dancing by women. To comply with the ordinance, these dancers had to minimally wear "pasties" and a "G-string." Pap's sought an injunction against the ordinance's enforcement. The Pennsylvania Supreme Court, unable to find a lowest common denominator uniting the *Barnes* majority, felt free to reach an independent judgment, and found that the ordinance, although also directed at secondary effects, was primarily directed at expression and did not survive close scrutiny.

In ERIE v. PAP'S A.M., 529 U.S. 277 (2000), the plurality, per O'CONNOR, J., joined by Rehnquist, C.J., and Kennedy and Breyer, JJ., upheld application of the ordinance to prevent nude dancing:[172] "Being 'in a state of nudity' is not an inherently expressive condition. [N]ude dancing of the type at issue here is expressive conduct, although we think that it falls only within the outer ambit of the First Amendment's protection. [G]overnment restrictions on public nudity such as the ordinance at issue here should be evaluated under the framework set forth in *O'Brien* for content-neutral restrictions on symbolic speech. * * *

"The ordinance [bans] all public nudity, regardless of whether that nudity is accompanied by expressive activity [and] updates provisions of an 'Indecency and Immorality' ordinance that has been on the books since 1866, predating the prevalence of nude dancing establishments such as Kandyland. [T]he Pennsylvania Supreme Court [concluded] that the ordinance was nevertheless content based, relying on Justice White's

––––––––––––––––––––––––––

[172] O'Connor, J., rebuffed a contention that the case was moot. Scalia, J., joined by Thomas, J., would have sustained the mootness claim. Stevens, J., joined by Ginsburg, J., did not address the issue.

position in dissent in *Barnes* for the proposition that a ban of this type *necessarily* has the purpose of suppressing the erotic message [, and] that '[s]ince the State permits the dancers to perform if they wear pasties and G-strings but forbids nude dancing, it is precisely because of the distinctive, expressive content of the nude dancing performances at issue in this case that the State seeks to apply the statutory prohibition.' A majority of the Court rejected that view in *Barnes*, and we do so again here.

"Respondent's argument that the ordinance is 'aimed' at suppressing expression through a ban on nude dancing—an argument that respondent supports by pointing to statements by the city attorney that the public nudity ban was not intended to apply to 'legitimate' theater productions—is really an argument that the city council also had an illicit motive in enacting the ordinance. As we have said before, however, this Court will not strike down an otherwise constitutional statute on the basis of an alleged illicit motive. In light of the Pennsylvania court's determination that one purpose of the ordinance is to combat harmful secondary effects, the ban on public nudity here is no different from the ban on burning draft registration cards in *O'Brien*, where the Government sought to prevent the means of the expression and not the expression of antiwar sentiment itself.

"Justice Stevens argues that the ordinance enacts a complete ban on expression. [But] simply to define what is being banned as the 'message' is to assume the conclusion. [Although] there may be cases in which banning the means of expression so interferes with the message that it essentially bans the message, that is not the case here. * * *

"Similarly, even if Erie's public nudity ban has some minimal effect on the erotic message by muting that portion of the expression that occurs when the last stitch is dropped, [a]ny effect on the overall expression is de minimis. And as Justice Stevens eloquently stated for the plurality in *Young*, 'even though we recognize that the First Amendment will not tolerate the total suppression of erotic materials that have some arguably artistic value, it is manifest that society's interest in protecting this type of expression is of a wholly different, and lesser, magnitude than the interest in untrammeled political debate.' [If] States are to be able to regulate secondary effects, then de minimis intrusions on expression such as those at issue here cannot be sufficient to render the ordinance content based.

"This case is, in fact, similar to *O'Brien*, *Clark*, and *Ward*. The justification for the government regulation in each case prevents harmful 'secondary' effects that are unrelated to the suppression of expression. See, e.g., *Ward* (noting that '[t]he principal justification for the sound-amplification guideline is the city's desire to control noise levels at bandshell events, in order to retain the character of [the adjacent] Sheep Meadow and its more sedate activities,' and citing *Renton* for the proposition that '[a] regulation that serves purposes unrelated to the content of expression is deemed neutral, even if it has an incidental effect on some speakers or messages but not others'). While the doctrinal theories behind 'incidental burdens' and 'secondary effects' are, of course, not identical, there is nothing objectionable about a city passing a general ordinance to ban public nudity (even though such a ban may place incidental burdens on some protected speech) and at the same time recognizing that one specific occurrence of public nudity—nude erotic dancing—is particularly problematic because it produces harmful secondary effects.

"[E]rie's efforts to protect public health and safety are clearly within the city's police powers [and] are undeniably important. And [the] city need not 'conduct new studies or produce evidence independent of that already generated by other cities' to demonstrate the problem of secondary effects [*Renton*.] In fact, Erie expressly relied on *Barnes* and its discussion of secondary effects, including its reference to *Renton* and *American Mini Theatres*. * * *

"In any event, Erie also relied on its own findings. The preamble to the ordinance states that 'the Council of the City of Erie *has, at various times over more than a century, expressed its findings* that certain lewd, immoral activities carried on in public places for profit are highly detrimental to the public health, safety and welfare, and lead to the debasement of both women and men, promote violence, public intoxication, prostitution and other serious criminal activity.' The city council members, familiar with commercial downtown Erie, are the individuals who would likely have had first-hand knowledge of what took place at and around nude dancing establishments in Erie, and can make particularized, expert judgments about the resulting harmful secondary effects. * * *

"Justice Souter, however, would require Erie to develop a specific evidentiary record supporting its ordinance * * * . *O'Brien*, of course, required no evidentiary showing at all that the threatened harm was real. But that case is different, Justice Souter contends, because in *O'Brien* 'there could be no doubt' that a regulation prohibiting the destruction of draft cards would alleviate the harmful secondary effects flowing from the destruction of those cards.

"But whether the harm is evident to our 'intuition,' is not the proper inquiry. If it were, we would simply say there is no doubt that a regulation prohibiting public nudity would alleviate the harmful secondary effects associated with nude dancing. * * * Justice Souter [argues] that we cannot accept Erie's findings because the subject of nude dancing is 'fraught with some emotionalism.' Yet surely the subject of drafting our citizens into the military is 'fraught' with more emotionalism than the subject of regulating nude dancing.

"As to [whether] the regulation furthers the government interest—it is evident that, since crime and other public health and safety problems are caused by the presence of nude dancing establishments like Kandyland, a ban on such nude dancing would further Erie's interest in preventing such secondary effects. To be sure, requiring dancers to wear pasties and G-strings may not greatly reduce these secondary effects, but *O'Brien* requires only that the regulation further the interest in combating such effects. [It may] be true that a pasties and G-string requirement would not be as effective as, for example, a requirement that the dancers be fully clothed, but the city must balance its efforts to address the problem with the requirement that the restriction be no greater than necessary to further the city's interest. [The] requirement that dancers wear pasties and G-strings is a minimal restriction in furtherance of the asserted government interests, and the restriction leaves ample capacity to convey the dancer's erotic message. Justice Souter points out that zoning is an alternative means of addressing this problem. It is far from clear, however, that zoning imposes less of a burden on expression than the minimal requirement implemented here. In any event, since this is a content-neutral restriction, least restrictive means analysis is not required."

SCALIA, J., joined by Thomas., J., concurred: "In *Barnes*, I voted to uphold the challenged Indiana statute 'not because it survives some lower level of First Amendment scrutiny, but because, as a general law regulating conduct and not specifically directed at expression, it is not subject to First Amendment scrutiny at all.' Erie's ordinance, too, by its terms prohibits not merely nude dancing, but the act—irrespective of whether it is engaged in for expressive purposes—of going nude in public. The facts that a preamble to the ordinance explains that its purpose, in part, is to 'limi[t] a recent increase in nude live entertainment,' that city councilmembers in supporting the ordinance commented to that effect, and that the ordinance includes in the definition of nudity the exposure of devices simulating that condition, neither make the law any less general in its reach nor demonstrate that what the municipal authorities *really* find objectionable is expression rather than public nakedness. As far as appears (and as seems overwhelmingly likely), [these] simply reflect the fact that Erie had recently been having a public nudity problem not with streakers, sunbathers or hot-dog vendors, but with lap dancers.

"There is no basis for the contention that the ordinance does not apply to nudity in theatrical productions such as Equus or Hair. Its text contains no such limitation. It was stipulated in the trial court that no effort was made to enforce the ordinance against a production of Equus involving nudity that was being staged in Erie at the time the ordinance became effective. [But], neither in the stipulation, nor elsewhere in the record, does it appear that the city was aware of the nudity—and before this Court counsel for the city attributed nonenforcement not to a general exception for theatrical productions, but to the fact that no one had complained. * * *

"Moreover, even were I to conclude that the city of Erie had specifically singled out the activity of nude dancing, I still would not find that this regulation violated the First Amendment unless I could be persuaded (as on this record I cannot) that it was the communicative character of nude dancing that prompted the ban. When conduct other than speech itself is regulated, it is my view that the First Amendment is violated only '[w]here the government prohibits conduct precisely because of its communicative attributes.' I do not feel the need, as the Court does, to identify some 'secondary effects.' [The] traditional power of government to foster good morals (bonos mores), and the acceptability of the traditional judgment (if Erie wishes to endorse it) that nude public dancing *itself* is immoral, have not been repealed by the First Amendment."

SOUTER, J., concurred in part and dissented in part: "I [agree] with the analytical approach that the plurality employs in deciding this case. [But] intermediate scrutiny requires a regulating government to make some demonstration of an evidentiary basis for the harm it claims to flow from the expressive activity, and for the alleviation expected from the restriction imposed. [What] is clear is that the evidence of reliance must be a matter of demonstrated fact, not speculative supposition.[173]

"By these standards, the record before us today is deficient. [The] plurality does the best it can with the materials to hand, but the pickings are slim. [T]he ordinance's preamble assert[s] that over the course of more than a century the city council had expressed 'findings' of detrimental secondary effects flowing from lewd and immoral profitmaking activity in public places. But however accurate the recital may be and however honestly the councilors may have held those conclusions to be true over the years, the recitation does not get beyond conclusions on a subject usually fraught with some emotionalism. * * *

"There is one point, however, on which an evidentiary record is not quite so hard to find, but it hurts, not helps, the city. The final *O'Brien* requirement is that the incidental speech restriction be shown to be no greater than essential to achieve the government's legitimate purpose. To deal with this issue, we have to ask what basis there is to think that the

---

[173] For evidence suggesting that adult nightclubs are less likely to be the sites for crime, see Daniel Linz, Kenneth C. Land, Jay R. Williams, Bryant Paul, & Michael E. Ezell, *An Examination of the Assumption that Adult Businesses are Associated with Crime in Surrounding Areas: A Secondary Effects Study in Charlotte, North Carolina*, 38 Law & Soc'y Rev. 99 (2004): "The establishments themselves have evolved more closely into legitimate businesses—establishments with management attention to profitability and continuity of existence. To meet these objectives, it is essential that the management and/or owners of the clubs provide their customers with some assurance of safety. Accordingly, adult nightclubs [often] appear to have better lighting in their parking lots and better security surveillance than is standard for non-nightclub business establishments. These may be factors producing fewer crime opportunities and lower numbers of reported crime incidents in the surrounding areas of the clubs."

city would be unsuccessful in countering any secondary effects by the significantly lesser restriction of zoning to control the location of nude dancing, thus allowing for efficient law enforcement, restricting effects on property values, and limiting exposure of the public. The record shows that for 23 years there has been a zoning ordinance on the books to regulate the location of establishments like Kandyland, but the city has not enforced it. [T]his hurdle to the application of *O'Brien* requires an evidentiary response. * * *

"Careful readers, and not just those on the Erie City Council, will of course realize that my partial dissent rests on a demand for an evidentiary basis that I failed to make when I concurred in *Barnes*. [A]fter many subsequent occasions to think further about the needs of the First Amendment, I have come to believe that a government must toe the mark more carefully than I first insisted."

STEVENS, J., joined by Ginsburg, J., dissented: "Far more important than the question whether nude dancing is entitled to the protection of the First Amendment are the dramatic changes in legal doctrine that the Court endorses today. Until now, the 'secondary effects' of commercial enterprises featuring indecent entertainment have justified only the regulation of their location. For the first time, the Court has now held that such effects may justify the total suppression of protected speech. * * *

"As the preamble to Ordinance No. 75–1994 candidly acknowledges, the council of the city of Erie enacted the restriction at issue 'for the purpose of limiting a recent increase in nude live entertainment within the City.' Prior to the enactment of the ordinance, the dancers at Kandyland performed in the nude. As the Court recognizes, after its enactment they can perform precisely the same dances if they wear 'pasties and G-strings.' [The] plurality assumes, however, that the difference in the content of the message resulting from the mandated costume change is 'de minimis.' [The] crucial point to remember, however, is that whether one views the difference as large or small, nude dancing still receives First Amendment protection, even if that protection lies only in the 'outer ambit' of that Amendment. Erie's ordinance, therefore, burdens a message protected by the First Amendment. If one assumes that the same erotic message is conveyed by nude dancers as by those wearing miniscule costumes, one means of expressing that message is banned;[2] if one assumes that the messages are different, one of those messages is banned. In either event, the ordinance is a total ban.

---

[2] **[Ct's Note]** Although nude dancing might be described as one protected "means" of conveying an erotic message, it does not follow that a protected message has not been totally banned simply because there are other, similar ways to convey erotic messages. A State's prohibition of a particular book, for example, does not fail to be a total ban simply because other books conveying a similar message are available.

"[Never] before have we approved the use of ['the so-called "secondary effects" test'] to justify a total ban on protected First Amendment expression. On the contrary, we have been quite clear that the doctrine would not support that end.[3] [4]

"The reason we have limited our secondary effects cases to zoning and declined to extend their reasoning to total bans is clear and straightforward: A dispersal that simply limits the places where speech may occur is a minimal imposition whereas a total ban is the most exacting of restrictions. [T]he Court's holding rejects the explicit reasoning in *American Mini Theatres* and *Renton* and the express holding in *Schad* [and] compounds that error by dramatically reducing the degree to which the State's interest must be furthered by the restriction imposed on speech, and by ignoring the critical difference between secondary effects caused by speech and the incidental effects on speech that may be caused by a regulation of conduct.

"[T]he plurality concedes that 'requiring dancers to wear pasties and G-strings may not greatly reduce these secondary effects.' To believe that the mandatory addition of pasties and a G-string will have *any* kind of noticeable impact on secondary effects requires nothing short of a titanic surrender to the implausible. * * *

"The Court is also mistaken in equating our secondary effects cases with the 'incidental burdens' doctrine applied in cases such as *O'Brien*; and it aggravates the error by invoking the latter line of cases to support its assertion that Erie's ordinance is unrelated to speech. The incidental burdens doctrine applies when 'speech' and 'nonspeech' elements are combined in the same 'course of conduct,' and the government's interest in regulating the latter justifies incidental burdens on the former. *O'Brien*. Secondary effects, on the other hand, are indirect consequences of protected

---

[3]   **[Ct's Note]** The Court contends *Ward* shows that we have used the secondary effects rationale to justify more burdensome restrictions than those approved in *Renton* and *American Mini Theatres*. That argument is unpersuasive for two reasons. First, as in the two cases just mentioned, the regulation in *Ward* was as a time, place, and manner restriction. Second, [*Ward*] is not a secondary effects case.

[4]   **[Ct's Note]** We [held] in *Renton* [that] the city [was] permitted to rely on a detailed study conducted by the city of Seattle that examined the relationship between zoning controls and the secondary effects of adult theaters. (It was permitted to rely as well on "the 'detailed findings' summarized" in an opinion of the Washington Supreme Court to the same effect.) Renton, having identified the same problem in its own city as that experienced in Seattle, quite logically drew on Seattle's experience and adopted a similar solution. But if Erie is relying on the Seattle study as well, its use of that study is most peculiar. After identifying a problem in its own city similar to that in Seattle, Erie has implemented a solution (pasties and G-strings) bearing no relationship to the efficacious remedy identified by the Seattle study (dispersal through zoning).

But the city of Erie, of course, has not in fact pointed to any study by anyone suggesting that the adverse secondary effects of commercial enterprises featuring erotic dancing depends in the slightest on the precise costume worn by the performers—it merely assumes it to be so. If the city is permitted simply to assume that a slight addition to the dancers' costumes will sufficiently decrease secondary effects, then presumably the city can require more and more clothing as long as any danger of adverse effects remains.

speech and may justify regulation of the places where that speech may occur. See *American Mini Theatres*. When a State enacts a regulation, it might focus on the secondary effects of speech as its aim, or it might concentrate on nonspeech related concerns, having no thoughts at all with respect to how its regulation will affect speech—and only later, when the regulation is found to burden speech, justify the imposition as an unintended incidental consequence. But those interests are not the same, and the Court cannot ignore their differences and insist that both aims are equally unrelated to speech simply because Erie might have 'recogniz[ed]' that it could possibly have had either aim in mind. One can think of an apple and an orange at the same time; that does not turn them into the same fruit.

"[Erie] has expressly justified its ordinance with reference to secondary effects. [Thus,] the Court's argument that 'this case is similar to *O'Brien*,' is quite wrong, as are its citations to *Clark* and *Ward*, neither of which involved secondary effects. [E]ither Erie's ordinance was not aimed at speech and the Court may attempt to justify the regulation under the incidental burdens test, or Erie has aimed its law at the secondary effects of speech, and the Court can try to justify the law under that doctrine. But it cannot conflate the two with the expectation that Erie's interests aimed at secondary effects will be rendered unrelated to speech by virtue of this doctrinal polyglot. * * *

"Erie's ordinance differs from the statute in *Barnes* [because] the city permitted a production of Equus to proceed without prosecution, even after the ordinance was in effect, and despite its awareness of the nudity involved in the production. [As] presented to us, the ordinance is deliberately targeted at Kandyland's type of nude dancing (to the exclusion of plays like Equus), in terms of both its applicable scope and the city's enforcement.[14]

"This narrow aim is confirmed by the expressed views of the Erie City Councilmembers who voted for the ordinance. [E]ach stated his or her view that the ordinance was aimed specifically at nude adult entertainment, and not at more mainstream forms of entertainment that include total nudity, nor even at nudity in general. One lawmaker observed: 'We're not talking about nudity. We're not talking about the theater or art * * * We're talking about what is indecent and immoral * * * We're not prohibiting nudity, we're prohibiting nudity when it's used in a lewd and immoral fashion.' * * * [16]"

---

[14] **[Ct's Note]** Justice Scalia [opines] that here, the basis for singling out Kandyland is morality. But since the "morality" of the public nudity in Hair is left untouched by the ordinance, while the "immorality" of the public nudity in Kandyland is singled out, the distinction cannot be that 'nude public dancing *itself* is immoral.' Rather, the only arguable difference between the two is that one's message is more immoral than the other's.

[16] **[Ct's Note]** The Court dismisses this evidence, declaring that it "will not strike down an otherwise constitutional statute on the basis of an alleged illicit motive." *O'Brien* [said] only that

NOTES AND QUESTIONS

1. **Is nude dancing speech?** Consider Robert Post, *Recuperating First Amendment Doctrine*, 47 Stan.L.Rev. 1249 (1995): "[T]he outcome in *Barnes* would have been different if Indiana were to have applied its statute to accepted media for the communication of ideas, as for example by attempting to prohibit nudity in movies or in the theater. Any such prohibition would serve interests deemed highly problematic by fully elaborated principles of First Amendment jurisprudence. Crucial to the result in *Barnes,* then, is the distinction between what the Court is prepared to accept as a medium for the communication of ideas, and its implicit understanding of nude dancing in nightclubs, which at least three of the majority Justices explicitly characterized as merely 'expressive conduct.' " For defense of the view that nude dancing should be protected speech, see Kevin Case, *"Lewd and Immoral": Nude Dancing, Sexual Expression, and the First Amendment*, 81 Chi.-Kent L. Rev. 1185 (2006).

2. **A First Amendment test?** Assuming nude dancing is speech, is Scalia, J., correct in arguing that no First Amendment test should apply? Is his analysis consistent with the language of *O'Brien*? The holding in *Falwell*? The approach taken in *Schenck*? Is *Arcara*, Sec. 2 supra, (no First Amendment scrutiny; statute directed at prostitution and premises used regardless of other uses) consistent with *Barnes* and *Pap's*?

3. **Law and morals.** Consider Christopher Thomas Leahy, *The First Amendment Gone Awry: City of Erie v. Pap's A.M., Ailing Analytical Structures, and the Suppression of Protected Expression*, 150 U. Pa. L. Rev. 1021 (2002): " 'As of February 1997, Americans spend more money at strip clubs than at Broadway, off-Broadway, regional, and non-profit theaters; than at the opera, the ballet, and jazz and classical music performances—combined.' As such, the use of zoning and general laws to limit or eliminate adult entertainment establishments is a particularly thorny issue because it inextricably involves conflicts between passionate defenders and equally fervent detractors, as well as difficult questions of morality, government censorship, and legislative motive." Does this show the popularity of immorality or differences about the substance of morality? What accounts for political differences about the relationship between law and morals in the First Amendment context? Consider Vincent Blasi, *Six Conservatives in Search of the First Amendment: The Revealing Case of Nude Dancing*, 33 Wm. and Mary L.Rev. 611 (1992): "Can a principled conservative approve the enforcement of morals in the context of group vilification? Can a principled liberal argue that topless dancing is protected by the First Amendment but not the shouting of

---

we would not strike down a law "on the *assumption* that a wrongful purpose or motive has caused the power to be exerted," (emphasis added), and that statement was due to our recognition that it is a "hazardous matter" to determine the actual intent of a body as large as Congress "on the basis of what fewer than a handful of Congressmen said about [a law]." [We] need not base our inquiry on an "assumption," nor must we infer the collective intent of a large body based on the statements of a few, for we have in the record the actual statements of all the city councilmembers who voted in favor of the ordinance.

racial epithets? Important differences between the two categories of speech regulation may exist—hate speech ordinarily is not confined to settings in which every member of the audience has made a choice to receive the message, but hate speech also seems more political in character—but the response of many conservatives to the hate speech issue at least suggests that they do not invariably prefer a narrow interpretation of the First Amendment and do not always take a broad view of the state's power to enforce morality."

4.   *Freud and the Law.* Consider Amy Adler, *Girls! Girls! Girls!: The Supreme Court Confronts the G-String*, 80 N.Y.U. L. Rev. 1108 (2005): "The G-string conceals a very small part of the body, the sight of which is a very big deal. It covers [the evidence] that the woman does not have a penis. [T]he sight of the woman's 'lack' ushers in the panic of castration anxiety for the male viewer. [Freud] emphasizes the universality of castration anxiety: 'Probably no male human being is spared the fright of castration at the sight of a female genital.' [The] G-string as solution is hard to make sense of in the world of First Amendment or conscious logic. But in the drama of castration anxiety and fetishism, the function performed by the G-string could not be more urgent or necessary. By warding off the threat of castration, it restores order and function."

II. COMMERCIAL SPEECH

VIRGINIA STATE BOARD OF PHARMACY V. VIRGINIA CITIZENS CONSUMER COUNCIL
425 U.S. 748, 96 S.Ct. 1817, 48 L.Ed.2d 346 (1976).

JUSTICE BLACKMUN delivered the opinion of the Court.

[The Court held invalid a Virginia statute that made advertising the prices of prescription drugs "unprofessional conduct," subjecting pharmacists to license suspension or revocation. Prescription drug prices strikingly varied within the same locality, in Virginia and nationally, sometimes by several hundred percent. Such drugs were dispensed exclusively by licensed pharmacists but 95% were prepared by manufacturers, not compounded by the pharmacists.]

[Appellants] contend that the advertisement of prescription drug prices is outside the protection of the First Amendment because it is "commercial speech." There can be no question that in past decisions the Court has given some indication that commercial speech is unprotected.[174]

Last Term, in *Bigelow v. Virginia,* 421 U.S. 809 (1975), the notion of unprotected "commercial speech" all but passed from the scene. We

---

[174] Starting with *Valentine v. Chrestensen,* 316 U.S. 52 (1942), the opinion summarized the decisions and dicta that gave such "indication." Long after *Chrestensen,* strong arguments against a First Amendment exception for commercial speech had appeared. See Martin Redish, *The First Amendment in the Market Place,* 39 Geo.Wash.L.Rev. 420 (1971); Note, 50 Ore.L.Rev. 177 (1971); Note, 78 Harv.L.Rev. 1191 (1965).

SEC. 3

IS SOME PROTECTED SPEECH LESS EQUAL THAN
OTHER PROTECTED SPEECH?

895

reversed a conviction for violation of a Virginia statute that made the circulation of any publication to encourage or promote the processing of an abortion in Virginia a misdemeanor. The defendant had published in his newspaper the availability of abortions in New York. The advertisement in question, in addition to announcing that abortions were legal in New York, offered the services of a referral agency in that State. [We] concluded that "the Virginia courts erred in their assumptions that advertising, as such, was entitled to no First Amendment protection," and we observed that the "relationship of speech to the marketplace of products or of services does not make it valueless in the marketplace of ideas."

Some fragment of hope for the continuing validity of a "commercial speech" exception arguably might have persisted because of the subject matter of the advertisement in *Bigelow*. We noted that in announcing the availability of legal abortions in New York, the advertisement "did more than simply propose a commercial transaction. It contained factual material of clear 'public interest.' " And, of course, the advertisement related to activity with which, at least in some respects, the State could not interfere. See *Roe v. Wade* [Ch. 6, Sec. 2 supra]. Indeed, we observed: "We need not decide in this case the precise extent to which the First Amendment permits regulation of advertising that is related to activities the State may legitimately regulate or even prohibit."

Here, [the] question whether there is a First Amendment exception for "commercial speech" is squarely before us. Our pharmacist does not wish to editorialize on any subject, cultural, philosophical, or political. He does not wish to report any particularly newsworthy fact, or to make generalized observations even about commercial matters. The "idea" he wishes to communicate is simply this: "I will sell you the X prescription drug at the Y price." Our question, then, is whether this communication is wholly outside the protection of the First Amendment.

V. [Speech] does not lose its First Amendment protection because money is spent to project it, as in a paid advertisement of one form or another. *New York Times Co. v. Sullivan*. Speech likewise is protected even though it is carried in a form that is "sold" for profit. *Smith v. California*. [Our] question is whether speech which does "no more than propose a commercial transaction," is so removed from any "exposition of ideas," and from "truth, science, morality, and arts in general, in its diffusion of liberal sentiments on the administration of Government", *Roth,* that it lacks all protection. Our answer is that it is not.

Focusing first on the individual parties to the transaction that is proposed in the commercial advertisement, we may assume that the advertiser's interest is a purely economic one. That hardly disqualifies him for protection under the First Amendment. The interests of the contestants in a labor dispute are primarily economic, but it has long been settled that both the employee and the employer are protected by the First Amendment when they express themselves on the merits of the dispute in order to influence its outcome. * * * 17

As to the particular consumer's interest in the free flow of commercial information, that interest may be as keen, if not keener by far, than his interest in the day's most urgent political debate.175 Appellees' case in this respect is a convincing one. Those whom the suppression of prescription drug price information hits the hardest are the poor, the sick, and particularly the aged. A disproportionate amount of their income tends to be spent on prescription drugs; yet they are the least able to learn, by shopping from pharmacist to pharmacist, where their scarce dollars are best spent. When drug prices vary as strikingly as they do, information as to who is charging what becomes more than a convenience. It could mean the alleviation of physical pain or the enjoyment of basic necessities.

Generalizing, society also may have a strong interest in the free flow of commercial information. Even an individual advertisement, though entirely "commercial," may be of general public interest. The facts of decided cases furnish illustrations: advertisements stating that referral services for legal abortions are available, *Bigelow;* that a manufacturer of artificial furs promotes his product as an alternative to the extinction by his competitors of fur-bearing mammals, see *Fur Information & Fashion Council, Inc. v. E.F. Timme & Son,* 364 F.Supp. 16 (S.D.N.Y.1973); and that a domestic producer advertises his product as an alternative to imports that tend to deprive American residents of their jobs, cf. *Chicago Joint Board v. Chicago Tribune Co.,* 435 F.2d 470 (7th Cir. 1970). Obviously, not all commercial messages contain the same or even a very great public interest element. There are few to which such an element, however, could not be added. Our pharmacist, for example, could cast himself as a commentator on store-to-store disparities in drug prices, giving his own and those of a competitor as proof. We see little point in requiring him to do so, and little difference if he does not.

---

17   [Ct's Note] The speech of labor disputants, of course, is subject to a number of restrictions. The Court stated in *NLRB v. Gissel Packing Co.,* 395 U.S., at 618 (1969), for example, that an employer's threats of retaliation for the labor actions of his employees are "without the protection of the First Amendment." The constitutionality of restrictions upon speech in the special context of labor disputes is not before us here. We express no views on that complex subject, and advert to cases in the labor field only to note that in some circumstances speech of an entirely private and economic character enjoys the protection of the First Amendment.

[For the contention that labor speech receives less protection than commercial speech, see James Pope, *The Three-Systems Ladder of First Amendment Values: Two Rungs and a Black Hole,* 11 Hast.Con.L.Q. 189 (1984)].

175   "After all. As the National Enquirer likes to observe, 'Inquiring Minds Want to Know.' They 'want to know' about the kind of creme rinse Cindi Lauper uses as much as, perhaps even more than, they want to know whether the CIA may have helped bring down the government in South Vietnam." William Van Alstyne, *Remembering Melville Nimmer: Some Cautionary Notes on Commercial Speech,* 43 UCLA L.Rev. 1635 (1996).

Moreover, there is another consideration that suggests that no line between publicly "interesting" or "important" commercial advertising and the opposite kind could ever be drawn. Advertising, however tasteless and excessive it sometimes may seem, is nonetheless dissemination of information as to who is producing and selling what product, for what reason, and at what price. So long as we preserve a predominantly free enterprise economy, the allocation of our resources in large measure will be made through numerous private economic decisions. It is a matter of public interest that those decisions, in the aggregate, be intelligent and well informed. To this end, the free flow of commercial information is indispensable. And if it is indispensable to the proper allocation of resources in a free enterprise system, it is also indispensable to the formation of intelligent opinions as to how that system ought to be regulated or altered. Therefore, even if the First Amendment were thought to be primarily an instrument to enlighten public decision making in a democracy, we could not say that the free flow of information does not serve that goal.

Arrayed against these substantial individual and societal interests are a number of justifications for the advertising ban. These have to do principally with maintaining a high degree of professionalism on the part of licensed pharmacists. [Price] advertising, it is argued, will place in jeopardy the pharmacist's expertise and, with it, the customer's health. It is claimed that the aggressive price competition that will result from unlimited advertising will make it impossible for the pharmacist to supply professional services in the compounding, handling, and dispensing of prescription drugs. Such services are time-consuming and expensive; if competitors who economize by eliminating them are permitted to advertise their resulting lower prices, the more painstaking and conscientious pharmacist will be forced either to follow suit or to go out of business. [It] is further claimed that advertising will lead people to shop for their prescription drugs among the various pharmacists who offer the lowest prices, and the loss of stable pharmacist-customer relationships will make individual [attention] impossible. Finally, it is argued that damage will be done to the professional image of the pharmacist. This image, that of a skilled and specialized craftsman, attracts talent to the profession and reinforces the better habits of those who are in [it].

The strength of these proffered justifications is greatly undermined by the fact that high professional standards, to a substantial extent, are guaranteed by the close regulation to which pharmacists in Virginia are subject. [At] the same time, we cannot discount the Board's justifications entirely. [The Court regarded justifications of this type sufficient to sustain the advertising bans challenged on due process and equal protection grounds].[176]

The challenge now made, however, is based on the First Amendment. This casts the Board's justifications in a different light, for on close inspection it is seen that the State's protectiveness of its citizens rests in large measure on the advantages of their being kept in ignorance. The advertising ban does not directly affect professional standards one way or the other. It affects them only through the reactions it is assumed people will have to the free flow of drug price information. There is no claim that the advertising ban in any way prevents the cutting of corners by the pharmacist who is so inclined. That pharmacist is likely to cut corners in any event. The only effect the advertising ban has on him is to insulate him from price competition and to open the way for him to make a substantial, and perhaps even excessive, profit in addition to providing an inferior service. The more painstaking pharmacist is also protected but, again, it is a protection based in large part on public ignorance.

It appears to be feared that if the pharmacist who wishes to provide low cost, and assertedly low quality, services is permitted to advertise, he will be taken up on his offer by too many unwitting customers. They will choose the low-cost, low-quality service and drive the "professional" pharmacist out of business. [They] will go from one pharmacist to another, following the discount, and destroy the pharmacist-customer relationship. They will lose respect for the profession because it advertises. All this is not in their best interests, and all this can be avoided if they are not permitted to know who is charging what.

[A]n alternative to this highly paternalistic approach [is] to assume that this information is not in itself harmful, that people will perceive their own best interests if only they are well enough informed, and that the best means to that end is to open the channels of communication rather than to close them. If they are truly open, nothing prevents the "professional" pharmacist from marketing his own assertedly superior product, and contrasting it with that of the low-cost, high-volume prescription drug retailer. But the choice among these alternative approaches is not ours to make or the Virginia General Assembly's. It is precisely this kind of choice, between the dangers of suppressing information, and the dangers of its misuse if it is freely available, that the First Amendment makes for [us].

VI. In concluding that commercial speech, like other varieties, is protected, we of course do not hold that it can never be regulated in any way. Some forms of commercial speech regulation are surely permissible. We mention a few. [There] is no claim, for example, that the prohibition on prescription drug price advertising is a mere time, place, and manner

---

[176] The Court referred here to cases upholding bans on advertising prices for eyeglass frames and optometrist and dental services.

SEC. 3

IS SOME PROTECTED SPEECH LESS EQUAL THAN
OTHER PROTECTED SPEECH?

899

restriction. We have often approved restrictions of that kind provided that they are justified without reference to the content of the regulated speech, that they serve a significant governmental interest, and that in so doing they leave open ample alternative channels for communication of the information. Whatever may be the proper bounds of time, place, and manner restrictions on commercial speech, they are plainly exceeded by this Virginia statute, which singles out speech of a particular content and seeks to prevent its dissemination completely.

Nor is there any claim that prescription drug price advertisements are forbidden because they are false or misleading in any way.[177] Untruthful speech, commercial or otherwise, has never been protected for its own sake. *Gertz.* Obviously much commercial speech is not provably false, or even wholly false, but only deceptive or misleading. We foresee no obstacle to a State's dealing effectively with this problem.[24] The First Amendment, as we construe it today, does not prohibit the State from insuring that the stream of commercial information flows cleanly as well as freely.

Also, there is no claim that the transactions proposed in the forbidden advertisements are themselves illegal in any way. Finally, the special problems of the electronic broadcast media are likewise not in this case.

What is at issue is whether a State may completely suppress the dissemination of concededly truthful information about entirely lawful activity, fearful of that information's effect upon its disseminators and its recipients. Reserving other questions,[25] we conclude that the answer to this one is in the [negative].

---

[177] On the difficulties of determining whether commercial speech is false and misleading, see Rebecca Tushnet, *It Depends on What the Meaning of "False" Is,* 41 Loy. L.A.L. Rev. 227 (2007).

[24] **[Ct's Note]** [C]ommon sense differences between speech that does "no more than propose a commercial transaction," *Pittsburgh Press* and other varieties [suggest] that a different degree of protection is necessary to insure that the flow of truthful and legitimate commercial information is unimpaired. The truth of commercial speech, for example, may be more easily verifiable by its disseminator than, let us say, news reporting or political commentary, in that ordinarily the advertiser seeks to disseminate information about a specific product or service that he himself provides and presumably knows more about than anyone else. Also, commercial speech may be more durable than other kinds. Since advertising is the sine qua non of commercial profits, there is little likelihood of its being chilled by proper regulation and foregone entirely.

Attributes such as these, the greater objectivity and hardiness of commercial speech, may make it less necessary to tolerate inaccurate statements for fear of silencing the speaker. They may also make it appropriate to require that a commercial message appear in such a form, or include such additional information, warnings and disclaimers, as are necessary to prevent its being deceptive. They may also make inapplicable the prohibition on prior restraints. Compare *New York Times v. United States* [Sec. 4, III infra] with *Donaldson v. Read Magazine,* 333 U.S. 178 (1948).

[25] **[Ct's Note]** We stress that we have considered in this case the regulation of commercial advertising by pharmacists. Although we express no opinion as to other professions, the distinctions, historical and functional, between professions, may require consideration of quite different factors. Physicians and lawyers, for example, do not dispense standardized products; they render professional *services* of almost infinite variety and nature, with the consequent enhanced possibility for confusion and deception if they were to undertake certain kinds of advertising.

JUSTICE STEWART, concurring.[178]

[I] write separately to explain why I think today's decision does not preclude [governmental regulation of false or deceptive advertising]. The Court has on several occasions addressed the problems posed by false statements of fact in libel cases. [Factual] errors are inevitable in free debate, and the imposition of liability for [such errors] can "dampe[n] the vigor and limi[t] the variety of public debate" by inducing "self-censorship." [In] contrast to the press, which must often attempt to assemble the true facts from sketchy and sometimes conflicting sources under the pressure of publication deadlines, the commercial advertiser generally knows the product or service he seeks to sell and is in a position to verify the accuracy of his factual representations before he disseminates them. The advertiser's access to the truth about his product and its price substantially eliminates any danger that governmental regulation of false or misleading price or product advertising will chill accurate and nondeceptive commercial [expression].

Since the factual claims contained in commercial price or product advertisements relate to tangible goods or services, they may be tested empirically and corrected to reflect the truth without in any manner jeopardizing the free dissemination of thought. Indeed, the elimination of false and deceptive claims serves to promote the one facet of commercial price and product advertising that warrants First Amendment protection— its contribution to the flow of accurate and reliable information relevant to public and private decision making.

JUSTICE REHNQUIST, dissenting.

[Under] the Court's opinion the way will be open not only for dissemination of price information but for active promotion of prescription drugs, liquor, cigarettes and other products the use of which it has previously been thought desirable to discourage. Now, however, such promotion is protected by the First Amendment so long as it is not misleading or does not promote an illegal product or [enterprise].

The Court speaks of the consumer's interest in the free flow of commercial information. [This] should presumptively be the concern of the Virginia Legislature, which sits to balance [this] and other claims in the process of making laws such as the one here under attack. The Court speaks of the importance in a "predominantly free enterprise economy" of intelligent and well-informed decisions as to allocation of resources. While there is again much to be said for the Court's observation as a matter of desirable public policy, there is certainly nothing in the United States

---

[Should there be limits placed on the advertising of specific drugs to consumers? See David C. Vladek, *The Difficult Case of Direct-To-Consumer Drug Advertising,* 41 Loy. L.A.L. 259 (2007).]

[178] Burger, C.J., separately concurring, stressed the reservation in fn. 25 of the opinion with respect to advertising by attorneys and physicians. Stevens, J., took no part.

Constitution which requires the Virginia Legislature to hew to the teachings of Adam Smith in its legislative decisions regulating the pharmacy profession. E.g., *Nebbia v. New York; Olsen v. Nebraska* [Ch. 5, Sec. 3].

[There] are undoubted difficulties with an effort to draw a bright line between "commercial speech" on the one hand and "protected speech" on the other, and the Court does better to face up to these difficulties than to attempt to hide them under labels. In this case, however, the Court has unfortunately substituted for the wavering line previously thought to exist between commercial speech and protected speech a no more satisfactory line of its own—that between "truthful" commercial speech, on the one hand, and that which is "false and misleading" on the other. The difficulty with this line is not that it wavers, but on the contrary that it is simply too Procrustean to take into account the congeries of factors which I believe could, quite consistently with the First and Fourteenth Amendments, properly influence a legislative decision with respect to commercial advertising.

[S]uch a line simply makes no allowance whatever for what appears to have been a considered legislative judgment in most States that while prescription drugs are a necessary and vital part of medical care and treatment, there are sufficient dangers attending their widespread use that they simply may not be promoted in the same manner as hair creams, deodorants, and toothpaste. The very real dangers that general advertising for such drugs might create in terms of encouraging, even though not nasanctioning, illicit use of them by individuals for whom they have not been prescribed, or by generating patient pressure upon physicians to prescribe them are simply not dealt with in the Court's [opinion].

NOTES AND QUESTIONS

1.   ***Economic due process.*** As compared to political decision making, is commercial advertising "neither more nor less significant than a host of other market activities that legislatures concededly may regulate"? Is there an "absence of any principled distinction between commercial soliciting and other aspects of economic activity"? Have economic due process and *Lochner* been "resurrected, clothed in the ill-fitting garb of the First Amendment"? See Thomas Jackson & John Jeffries, *Commercial Speech: Economic Due Process and the First Amendment,* 65 Va.L.Rev. 1 (1979). See also Frederick Schauer, *First Amendment Opportunism,* in *Eternally Vigilant: Free Speech in the Modern Era* 175 (Lee C. Bollinger & Geoffrey R. Stone eds., 2002).

2.   ***Paternalism.*** Why may government "be paternalistic regarding the purchase of goods but may not be paternalistic regarding information about those goods"? Larry Alexander, *Speech in the Local Marketplace: Implications of Virginia State Board of Pharmacy v. Virginia Citizens Consumer Council, Inc. for Local Regulatory Power,* 14 San Diego L.Rev. 357 (1977). Should the

"strong anti-paternalism feature of free speech doctrine [apply] only when the government regulation addresses us qua citizen, not in various other capacities, such as consumer." With respect to ordinary commercial speech, should people be considered "dependent and vulnerable rather than independent and rational." Does this follow from democratic theory? See James Weinstein, *Speech Categorization and the Limits of First Amendment Formalism: Lessons From Nike v. Kasky*, 54 Case W. Res. L. Rev. 1091 (2004). Or is it a part of democratic theory that "individual citizens can be trusted to make legally valid life-affecting choices on the basis of an open marketplace of ideas of information and opinion ." Martin H. Redish, *Tobacco Advertising and the First Amendment*, 81 Ia. L.Rev. 589 (1996). Consider Steven H. Shiffrin, *Dissent, Injustice, and the Meanings of America* 143–44 n. 41 (1999): "This argument would seem to prove too much. If democratic theory assumes citizens can be trusted to make such choices in an open marketplace, one would imagine government would be foreclosed not only from fixing prices to discourage consumption, but also from regulating false and misleading advertising. In addition, it would be unclear why government should be permitted to make products illegal for paternalistic reasons—if citizens can truly be trusted. Assuming it were consistent with this version of democratic theory for government to ban products, it would be unclear why its paternalism could not extend to product advertising of legal products. It would not do, for example, to claim that products not made illegal have been certified as safe. To outlaw cigarettes, for example, might create black markets and enormous attendant enforcement problems. The failure to outlaw cigarettes need not suggest that government thinks of them as any less a public health problem than numerous other drugs that are currently outlawed. Whether individual citizens can be 'trusted,' seems to bear no relationship to the legal status of the product. In addition, one could argue that the notion of democracy makes no claims about the quality of *individual* decision making, but makes some relative claims about the quality of *public* decision making."

3. *Image advertising.* Does the rationale of *Virginia Pharmacy* extend to image or non-informational advertising? For relevant discussion, see Daniel Hays Lowenstein, *"Too Much Puff": Persuasion, Paternalism, and Commercial Speech,* 56 U.Cin.L.Rev. 1205 (1988).

4. *Deception.* Footnote 24 suggests that *deceptive* commercial speech may be regulated in ways that would be barred if the speech were political. Is the distinction sound? May regulation of deception in commercial speech be ased on no more than a rational basis?

(a) *"Commonsense" differences between commercial speech and other speech.* (1) *Verifiability.* Consider Daniel Farber, *Commercial Speech and First Amendment Theory,* 74 Nw.U.L.Rev. 372, (1979): "[C]ommercial speech is not necessarily more verifiable than other speech. There may well be uncertainty about some quality of a product, such as the health effect of eggs. On the other hand, political speech is often quite verifiable by the speaker. A political candidate knows the truth about his own past and his present intentions, yet misrepresentations on these subjects are immune from state regulation." (2) *Durability.* Consider Martin Redish, *The Value of Free Speech,* 130 U.Pa.L.Rev. 591 (1982): "[I]t is also incorrect to distinguish commercial from political expression on the ground that the former is somehow hardier because of the inherent profit motive. It could just as easily be said that we need not fear that commercial magazines and newspapers will cease publication for fear of governmental regulation, because they are in business for profit. Of course, the proper response to this contention is that our concern is not *whether* they will publish, but *what* they will publish: fear of regulation might deter them from dealing with controversial subjects." Does the case for treating commercial speech as a stepchild ultimately rest upon subjective disagreement with the message expressed, i.e., viewpoint discrimination? See Martin H. Redish, *Commercial Speech, First Amendment Intuitionism, and the Twilight Zone of Viewpoint Discrimination,* 41 Loy. L.A.L. Rev. 67 (2007). (3) *Incentives.* The Court implies that the profit motive might make commercial speech less vulnerable to the chilling effect. Is it possible that this is backwards, and that commercial enterprises might be more risk-averse than those who are ideologically motivated?

(b) ***Commercial speech and self-expression.*** Is commercial speech distinguishable from political speech because it is unrelated to self-expression? Consider C. Edwin Baker, *Commercial Speech: A Problem in the Theory of Freedom,* 62 Iowa L.Rev. 1 (1976): In commercial speech, the dissemination of the profit motive "breaks the connection between speech and any vision, or attitude, or value of the individual or group engaged in advocacy. Thus the content and form of commercial speech cannot be attributed to individual value allegiances." For criticism, see, e.g., Pierre Schlag, *An Attack on Categorical Approaches to Freedom of Speech,* 30 UCLA L.Rev. 671 (1983); Steven Shiffrin, *The First Amendment and Economic Regulation: Away from a General Theory of the First Amendment,* 78 Nw.U.L.Rev. 1212 (1983). Even if commercial speech is divorced from self expression (or dignity), should it merit substantial protection nonetheless? Under what rationales?

(c) ***Contract approach to commercial speech.*** Is commercial advertising distinguishable from other forms of speech because of the state interest in regulating contracts? Consider Farber, supra: "The unique aspect of commercial speech is that it is a prelude to, and therefore becomes integrated into, a contract, the essence of which is the presence of a promise. Because a promise is an undertaking to ensure that a certain state of affairs takes place, promises obviously have a closer connection with conduct than with self-expression. Second, [in] a fundamentally market economy, the government understandably is given particular deference in its enforcement of contractual expectations. Indeed, the Constitution itself gives special protection to contractual expectations in the contract clause. Finally, [the] technicalities of contract law, with its doctrines of privity, consideration, and the like, should not be blindly translated into First Amendment jurisprudence. The basic doctrines of contract law, however, provide a helpful guide in considering commercial speech problems." For discussion, see Larry Alexander

& Daniel Farber, *Commercial Speech and First Amendment Theory: A Critical Exchange,* 75 Nw.U.L.Rev. 307 (1980).

(d) ***Error costs.*** Are the error cost of mistaken commercial speech regulation smaller than for political or ideological speech? See Fred McChesney, *A Positive Regulatory Theory of the First Amendment,* 20 Conn.L.Rev. 335 (1988); Ronald Coase, *Advertising and Free Speech,* 6 J.Legal Stud. 1 (1977); Richard Posner, *Free Speech in an Economic Perspective,* 20 Suff.L.Rev. 1 (1986); Thomas Scanlon, *Freedom of Expression and Categories of Expression,* 40 U.Pitt.L.Rev. 519 (1979).

(e) ***Limits on regulation of deceptive advertising.*** *Bates v. State Bar,* 433 U.S. 350 (1977), struck down an Arizona Supreme Court rule against a lawyer "publicizing himself" through advertising. It rejected the claim that attorney price advertising was inherently misleading, but left open the "peculiar problems" associated with advertising claims regarding the quality of legal services.[179] Has the Court made it difficult for states and communities to deal with a "considerable range of highly debatable conduct by which some individuals seek to profit from the inattentiveness or lack of sophistication of consumers of goods and services"? Paul D. Carrington, *Our Imperial First Amendment,* 34 U. Rich. L. Rev. 1167 (2001). Should the Court have deferred to the judgment of the State Bar of Arizona? If not, should it defer to the SEC when it regulates the advertising of securities? The FTC when it regulates automobile advertising? The Virginia Board of Pharmacy (or the FDA) when it regulates quality advertising by pharmacists? For deferential treatment of a state ban on the use of trade names by optometrists, see *Friedman v. Rogers,* 440 U.S. 1 (1979).

5. ***Truth and commercial advertising.*** Should Mercedes Benz be able to truthfully advertise that Elton John drives its car without getting John's permission? See Eugene Volokh, *Freedom of Speech and the Right of Publicity,* 40 Houston L.Rev. 903 (2003); Melissa B. Jacoby & Diane Leenheer Zimmerman, *Foreclosing On Fame: Exploring The Uncharted Boundaries of the Right of Publicity,* 77 N.Y.U. L. Rev. 1322 (2002). Should the state be able to prevent homeowners from posting "for sale" signs in order to prevent panic selling in order to maintain an integrated neighborhood? See *Linmark Associates v. Willingboro,* 431 U.S. 85 (1977). May a state regulate the content of contraceptive advertising in order to minimize its offensive character? Cf.

---

[179] *Zauderer v. Office of Disciplinary Counsel,* Sec. 9, I infra, held that a state may not discipline attorneys who solicit legal business through newspaper advertisements containing "truthful and nondeceptive information and advice regarding the legal rights of potential clients" or for the advertising use of "accurate and nondeceptive" illustrations. Zauderer had placed illustrated ads in 36 Ohio newspapers publicizing his availability to represent women who had suffered injuries from use of a contraceptive device known as the Dalkon Shield Intrauterine Device. In the ad Zauderer stated that he had represented other women in Dalkon Shield litigation. The Court observed that accurate statements of fact cannot be proscribed "merely because it is possible that some readers will infer that he has some expertise in those areas." But it continued to "leave open the possibility that States may prevent attorneys from making non-verifiable claims regarding the quality of their services. *Bates.*"

SEC. 3

IS SOME PROTECTED SPEECH LESS EQUAL THAN
OTHER PROTECTED SPEECH?

905

Carey v. Population Services Int'l., Ch. 6, Sec. 2 (total ban on contraceptive advertising unconstitutional).

———

OHRALIK v. OHIO STATE BAR ASS'N, 436 U.S. 447 (1978), upheld the indefinite suspension of an attorney for violating the anti-solicitation provisions of the Ohio Code of Professional Responsibility. Those provisions generally do not allow lawyers to recommend themselves to anyone who has not sought "their advice regarding employment of a lawyer." Albert Ohralik had approached two young accident victims to solicit employment—Carol McClintock in a hospital room where she lay in traction and Wanda Lou Holbert on the day she came home from the hospital. He employed a concealed tape recorder with Holbert, apparently to insure he would have evidence of her assent to his representation. The next day, when Holbert's mother informed Ohralik that she and her daughter did not want to have appellant represent them, he insisted that the daughter had entered into a binding agreement. McClintock also discharged Ohralik, and Ohralik sued her for breach of contract. The Court ruled, per POWELL, J., that a state may forbid in-person solicitation of clients by lawyers for pecuniary gain:

"Expression concerning purely commercial transactions has come within the ambit of the Amendment's protection only recently. In rejecting the notion that such speech is wholly outside the protection of the First Amendment, *Virginia Pharmacy,* we were careful not to hold that it is wholly undifferentiable from other forms of speech.

"We have not discarded the common sense distinction between speech proposing a commercial transaction, which occurs in an area traditionally subject to government regulation, and other varieties of speech. To require a parity of constitutional protection for commercial and noncommercial speech alike could invite dilution, simply by a leveling process, of the force of the Amendment's guarantee with respect to the latter kind of speech. Rather than subject the First Amendment to such a devitalization, we instead have afforded commercial speech a limited measure of protection, commensurate with its subordinate position in the scale of First Amendment values, while allowing modes of regulation that might be impermissible in the realm of noncommercial expression.

"Moreover, 'it has never been deemed an abridgment of freedom of speech or press to make a course of conduct illegal merely because the conduct was in part initiated, evidenced, or carried out by means of language, either spoken, written, or printed.' *Giboney v. Empire Storage & Ice Co.,* 336 U.S. 490, 502 (1949). Numerous examples could be cited of communications that are regulated without offending the First Amendment, such as the exchange of information about securities, *SEC v. Texas Gulf Sulphur Co.,* 401 F.2d 833 (C.A.2 1968), cert. denied, 394 U.S.

976 (1969), corporate proxy statements, *Mills v. Electric Auto-Lite Co.,* 396 U.S. 375 (1970), the exchange of price and production information among competitors, *American Column & Lumber Co. v. United States,* 257 U.S. 377 (1921), and employers' threats of retaliation for the labor activities of employees, *NLRB v. Gissel Packing Co.,* 395 U.S. 575, 618 (1969). [These examples [illustrate] that the State does not lose its power to regulate commercial activity deemed harmful to the public whenever speech is a component of that activity. Neither *Virginia Pharmacy* nor *Bates* purported to cast doubt on the permissibility of these kinds of commercial regulation.

"In-person solicitation by a lawyer of remunerative employment is a business transaction in which speech is an essential but subordinate component. While this does not remove the speech from the protection of the First Amendment, as was held in *Bates* and *Virginia Pharmacy,* it lowers the level of appropriate judicial scrutiny. [A] lawyer's procurement of remunerative employment is a subject only marginally affected with First Amendment concerns. It falls within the State's proper sphere of economic and professional regulation. While entitled to some constitutional protection, appellant's conduct is subject to regulation in furtherance of important state [interests].

" 'The interest of the States in regulating lawyers is especially great since lawyers are essential to the primary function of administering justice and have historically been officers of the courts' [and] act 'as trusted agents of their clients and as assistants to the court in search of a just solution to disputes.'

"[The] substantive evils of solicitation have been stated over the years in sweeping terms: stirring up litigation, assertion of fraudulent claims, debasing the legal profession,[180] and potential harm to the solicited client in the form of overreaching, overcharging, underrepresentation, and misrepresentation." In providing information about the availability and terms of proposed legal services "in-person solicitation serves much the same function as the advertisement at issue in *Bates.* But there are significant differences as well. Unlike a public advertisement, which simply provides information and leaves the recipient free to act upon it or not, in-person solicitation may exert pressure and often demands an immediate response, without providing an opportunity for comparison or reflection. The aim and effect of in-person solicitation may be to provide a one-sided presentation and to encourage speedy and perhaps uninformed decision making; there is no opportunity for intervention or counter-education by agencies of the Bar, supervisory authorities, or persons close

---

[180] Is regulation of speech debasing the legal profession legitimate? Consider Rodney Smolla, *Lawyer Advertising and the Dignity of the Profession,* 59 Ark. L.Rev. 437 (2006): "The regulation of lawyer advertising on [the] ground that it is demeaning to the profession raises profound First Amendment questions. The central core of modern First Amendment jurisprudence is that the government may never stifle a message merely because it finds the content of the message disagreeable or offensive."

to the solicited individual. The admonition that 'the fitting remedy for evil counsels is good ones' is of little value when the circumstances provide no opportunity for any remedy at all. In-person solicitation is as likely as not to discourage persons needing counsel from engaging in a critical comparison of the 'availability, nature, and prices' of legal services; it actually may disserve the individual and societal interest, identified in *Bates,* in facilitating 'informed and reliable decision making.'

"[Appellant's argument that none of the evils of solicitation was found in his case] misconceives the nature of the State's interest. The rules prohibiting solicitation are prophylactic measures whose objective is the prevention of harm before it occurs.[181] The rules were applied in this case to discipline a lawyer for soliciting employment for pecuniary gain under circumstances likely to result in the adverse consequences the State seeks to avert. In such a situation, which is inherently conducive to overreaching and other forms of misconduct, the State has a strong interest in adopting and enforcing rules of conduct designed to protect the public from harmful solicitation by lawyers whom it has [licensed].

"The efficacy of the State's effort to prevent such harm to prospective clients would be substantially diminished if, having proved a solicitation in circumstances like those of this case, the State were required in addition to prove actual injury. Unlike the advertising in *Bates,* in-person solicitation is not visible or otherwise open to public scrutiny. Often there is no witness other than the lawyer and the lay person whom he has solicited, rendering it difficult or impossible to obtain reliable proof of what actually took place. This would be especially true if the lay person were so distressed at the time of the solicitation that he or she could not recall specific details at a later date. If appellant's view were sustained, in-person solicitation would be virtually immune to effective oversight and regulation by the State or by the legal profession, in contravention of the State's strong interest in regulating members of the Bar in an effective, objective, and self-enforcing manner. It therefore is not unreasonable, or violative of the Constitution, for a State to respond with what in effect is a prophylactic rule."

NOTES AND QUESTIONS

1. ***Companion case.*** IN RE PRIMUS, 436 U.S. 412 (1978), per POWELL, J., held that a state could not constitutionally discipline an ACLU "cooperating lawyer" who, after advising a gathering of allegedly illegally sterilized women of their rights, initiated further contact with one of the women by writing her a letter informing her of the ACLU's willingness to provide free legal representation for women in her situation and of the organization's desire to file a lawsuit on her behalf. "South Carolina's action in punishing appellant for

---

[181] But see Fred McChesney, *Commercial Speech in the Professions,* 134 U.Pa.L.Rev. 45 (1985) (anti-solicitation provisions may be motivated by anti-competitive considerations).

soliciting a prospective litigant by mail, on behalf of ACLU, must withstand the 'exacting scrutiny applicable to limitations on core First Amendment rights.' [Where] political expression or association is at issue, this Court has not tolerated the degree of imprecision that often characterizes government regulation of the conduct of commercial affairs. The approach we adopt today in *Ohralik* that the State may proscribe in-person solicitation for pecuniary gain under circumstances likely to result in adverse consequences, cannot be applied to appellant's activity on behalf of the ACLU. Although a showing of potential danger may suffice in the former context, appellant may not be disciplined unless her activity in fact involved the type of misconduct at which South Carolina's broad prohibition is said to be directed. The record does not support appellee's contention that undue influence, overreaching, misrepresentation, or invasion of privacy actually occurred in this case."

2. ***Related cases.*** *Edenfield v. Fane,* 507 U.S. 761 (1993) held that direct personal solicitation of prospective business clients by Certified Public Accountants is protected under the First Amendment,[182] but *Florida Bar v. Went For It, Inc.,* 515 U.S. 618 (1995) held that targeted direct-mail solicitations by personal injury attorneys to victims and their relatives for thirty days following an accident were not protected under the First Amendment. See also *Brentwood Academy v. Tennessee Secondary School Athletic Ass'n*, Ch. 10, Sec. 3 (five justices maintain that *Ohralik* does not apply to rules designed to protect children from recruitment solicitations by high school coaches).

3. ***A hierarchy of protected speech.*** Consider Steven Shiffrin, note 3 supra: In *Virginia Pharmacy,* "the Court never admitted that commercial speech was less valuable than political speech. The 'commonsense differences' had nothing to do with value. [Although] Justice Blackmun labored to defend the asserted equal relationship between commercial speech and political speech for the *Virginia Pharmacy* majority, Justice Powell in *Ohralik* was content to lead the Court to an opposite position without explanation. In so doing, Justice Powell steered the Court to accept a hierarchy of protected speech for the first time, despite his own stated opposition [in *Young*] to creating any such hierarchy." Does the concern that the protection of non-commercial speech would be subject to dilution if it were placed on a par with commercial speech presuppose an unexplained difference between the two types of speech? For discussion of the dilution argument, see William Marshall, *The Dilution of the First Amendment and the Equality of Ideas*, 38 Case W.Res.L.Rev. 566 (1988).

4. ***Muddying the hierarchy.*** Cincinnati permitted 1,500–2,000 news racks throughout the city for publications not classified as commercial speech,

---

[182] Blackmun, J., concurred; O'Connor, J., dissented. Compare Ibanez v. Florida Dep't of Business and Professional Regulation, 512 U.S. 136 (1994) (attorney's references in advertising, business cards and stationery to her credentials as a CPA and a Certified Financial Planner are not deceptive or misleading and are protected commercial speech); Accord, Peel v. Attorney Registration and Disciplinary Comm'n, 496 U.S. 91 (1990) (reference on letterhead to prestigious certification is protected speech).

SEC. 3

IS SOME PROTECTED SPEECH LESS EQUAL THAN
OTHER PROTECTED SPEECH?

909

but refused to allow an additional 62 news racks that contained two publications classified as commercial speech.

CINCINNATI v. DISCOVERY NETWORK, 507 U.S. 410 (1993), per STEVENS, J., held that this discrimination violated the First Amendment: "The major premise supporting the city's argument is the proposition that commercial speech has only a low value. Based on that premise, the city contends that the fact that assertedly more valuable publications are allowed to use news racks does not undermine its judgment that its esthetic and safety interests are stronger than the interest in allowing commercial speakers to have similar access to the reading public. [In] our view, the city's argument attaches more importance to the distinction between commercial and non-commercial speech than our cases warrant and seriously underestimates the value of commercial speech.[20]"[183]

5. *The reach of Discovery Network.* (a) In MARTIN v. STRUTHERS, 319 U.S. 141 (1943), a city forbade knocking on the door or ringing the doorbell of a resident in order to deliver handbills (in an industrial community where many worked night shifts and slept during the day). In striking down the ordinance, the Court, per BLACK, J., pointed out that the city's objectives could be achieved by means of a law making it an offense for any person to ring the doorbell of a householder who has "appropriately indicated that he is unwilling to be disturbed. This or any similar regulation leaves the decision as to whether distributors of literature may lawfully call at a home where it belongs—with the homeowner himself." By contrast, *Breard v. Alexandria,* 341 U.S. 622 (1951) upheld an ordinance forbidding the practice of going door to door to solicit orders for the sale of goods. The commercial element was said to distinguish *Martin.* Does *Breard* survive *Virginia Pharmacy?* Does (should) *Discovery Network* settle the issue? What if, as in *Breard,* the solicitor is selling subscriptions for magazines?

(b) Compare *Schneider,* Sec. 6, I, A infra (prohibition against leaflet distribution on streets unconstitutional) with *Valentine,* Sec. 3, II supra

---

[20] **[Ct's Note]** Metromedia, Inc. v. San Diego, 453 U.S. 490 (1981), upon which the city heavily relies, is not to the contrary. In that case, a plurality of the Court found as a permissible restriction on commercial speech a city ordinance that, for the most part, banned outdoor "offsite" advertising billboards, but permitted "onsite" advertising signs identifying the owner of the premises and the goods sold or manufactured on the site. Unlike this case, which involves discrimination between commercial and noncommercial speech, the "offsite-onsite" distinction involved disparate treatment of two types of commercial speech. Only the onsite signs served both the commercial and public interest in guiding potential visitors to their intended destinations; moreover, the plurality concluded that a "city may believe that offsite advertising, with its periodically changing content, presents a more acute problem than does onsite advertising." Neither of these bases has any application to the disparate treatment of news racks in this case.

The Chief Justice is correct that seven Justices in the Metromedia case were of the view that San Diego could completely ban offsite commercial billboards for reasons unrelated to the content of those billboards. Those seven Justices did not say, however, that San Diego could distinguish between commercial and noncommercial offsite billboards that cause the same esthetic and safety concerns. That question was not presented in Metromedia, for the regulation at issue in that case did not draw a distinction between commercial and noncommercial offsite billboards; with a few exceptions, it essentially banned all offsite billboards.

[183] Rehnquist, C.J., joined by White and Thomas, JJ., dissented.

(prohibition against distribution of commercial leaflets upheld). Does (should) the *holding* of *Valentine* survive *Virginia Pharmacy?* Does *Discovery Network* settle the issue?

(c)   *Linmark* held it unconstitutional for a locality to prohibit "For Sale" signs on residential property. Similarly, the Court has held it unconstitutional to permit property owners to display "For Sale" signs while prohibiting most other signs including those with political, religious or personal messages. *Ladue v. Gilleo,* 512 U.S. 43 (1994). After *Linmark, Ladue,* and *Discovery Network,* would it be unconstitutional to prohibit signs on residential property that advertise goods and services sold elsewhere?

———

In CENTRAL HUDSON GAS & ELEC. CORP. v. PUBLIC SERV. COMM'N, 447 U.S. 557 (1980), the Court, per POWELL, J., characterized the prior commercial speech cases as embracing a special test: "In commercial speech cases, then, a four-part analysis has developed. At the outset, we must determine whether the expression is protected by the First Amendment. For commercial speech to come within that provision, it at least must concern lawful activity and not be misleading. Next, we ask whether the asserted governmental interest is substantial. If both inquiries yield positive answers, we must determine whether the regulation directly advances the governmental interest asserted, and whether it is not more extensive than is necessary to serve that interest."

LORILLARD TOBACCO CO. V. REILLY
533 U.S. 525, 121 S.Ct. 2404, 150 L.Ed.2d 532 (2001).

JUSTICE O'CONNOR delivered the opinion of the Court.

In January 1999, the Attorney General of Massachusetts promulgated comprehensive regulations governing the advertising and sale of cigarettes, smokeless tobacco, and cigars. Petitioners, a group of cigarette, smokeless tobacco, and cigar manufacturers and retailers, filed suit in Federal District Court claiming that the regulations violate federal law and the United States Constitution.

I.   [The Court observed that the purpose of the restrictions was "to eliminate deception and unfairness in the way cigarettes and smokeless tobacco products are marketed, sold and distributed in Massachusetts in order to address the incidence of cigarette smoking and smokeless tobacco use by children under legal age [and] to prevent access to such products by underage consumers. The similar purpose of the cigar regulations is 'to eliminate [the] false perception that cigars are a safe alternative to cigarettes [and] to prevent access to such products by underage consumers.' " Among other things the restrictions prohibited outdoor advertising, "including advertising in enclosed stadiums and advertising from within a retail establishment that is directed toward or visible from the outside of the establishment, in any location that is within a 1,000 foot radius of any public playground, playground area in a public park, elementary school or secondary school."].[184]

II. [The Court concluded that the Federal Cigarette Labeling and Advertising Act of 1965 as amended, prevented states and localities from regulating the location of cigarette advertising.]

III. By its terms, the FCLAA's pre-emption provision only applies to cigarettes. Accordingly, we must evaluate the smokeless tobacco and cigar petitioners' First Amendment challenges to the State's outdoor and point-of-sale advertising regulations. The cigarette petitioners did not raise a pre-emption challenge to the sales practices regulations. Thus, we must analyze the cigarette as well as the smokeless tobacco and cigar petitioners' claim that certain sales practices regulations for tobacco products violate the First Amendment.

A. [Petitioners] urge us to reject the *Central Hudson* analysis and apply strict scrutiny. [S]everal Members of the Court have expressed doubts about the *Central Hudson* analysis and whether it should apply in particular cases. See, e.g., *44 Liquormart, Inc. v. Rhode Island*, 517 U.S. 484, 501 (1996) (joint opinion of Stevens, Kennedy, and Ginsburg, JJ.)(Scalia, J. concurring in part and concurring in judgment)(Thomas, J., concurring in part and concurring in judgment). [But] we see "no need to break new ground. *Central Hudson*, as applied in our more recent commercial speech cases, provides an adequate basis for decision."

Only the last two steps of *Central Hudson*'s four-part analysis are at issue here. The Attorney General has assumed for purposes of summary judgment that petitioners' speech is entitled to First Amendment protection. With respect to the second step, none of the petitioners contests the importance of the State's interest in preventing the use of tobacco products by minors.

The third step of *Central Hudson* [requires] that "the speech restriction directly and materially advanc[e] the asserted governmental interest. 'This burden is not satisfied by mere speculation or conjecture; rather, a governmental body seeking to sustain a restriction on commercial speech must demonstrate that the harms it recites are real and that its restriction will in fact alleviate them to a material degree.' " We do not,

---

[184] The regulations also banned such advertising at the point of sale if they were within five feet of the floor of the retail establishment and within a 1000 feet radius of the places identified in the outdoor advertising restrictions. O'Connor, J., found that these regulations violated the third and fourth prongs of *Central Hudson*. Stevens, J., joined by Ginsburg and Breyer, JJ., dissenting, found these restrictions to be "little more than an adjunct" to rules prohibiting the placement of the products within the reach of customers and of only slight impact on the ability of adults to purchase "a poisonous product and may save some children from taking the first step on the road to addiction."

however, require that "empirical data [come] accompanied by a surfeit of background information. [W]e have permitted litigants to justify speech restrictions by reference to studies and anecdotes pertaining to different locales altogether, or even, in a case applying strict scrutiny, to justify restrictions based solely on history, consensus, and 'simple common sense.'"

The last step of the *Central Hudson* analysis "complements" the third step, "asking whether the speech restriction is not more extensive than necessary to serve the interests that support it." We have made it clear that "the least restrictive means" is not the standard; instead, the case law requires a reasonable " 'fit between the legislature's ends and the means chosen to accomplish those ends, [a] means narrowly tailored to achieve the desired objective.'" * * *

B.   [1.] The smokeless tobacco and cigar petitioners [maintain] that although the Attorney General may have identified a problem with underage cigarette smoking, he has not identified an equally severe problem with respect to underage use of smokeless tobacco or cigars. The smokeless tobacco petitioner emphasizes the "lack of parity" between cigarettes and smokeless tobacco. The cigar petitioners catalogue a list of differences between cigars and other tobacco products, including the characteristics of the products and marketing strategies. The petitioners finally contend that the Attorney General cannot prove that advertising has a causal link to tobacco use such that limiting advertising will materially alleviate any problem of underage use of their products.

In previous cases, we have acknowledged the theory that product advertising stimulates demand for products, while suppressed advertising may have the opposite effect. *United States v. Edge Broadcasting Co.*, 509 U.S. 418, 434 (1993). The Attorney General cites numerous studies to support this theory in the case of tobacco products [, providing] ample documentation of the problem with underage use of smokeless tobacco and cigars. In addition, we disagree with petitioners' claim that there is no evidence that preventing targeted campaigns and limiting youth exposure to advertising will decrease underage use of smokeless tobacco and cigars. On this record and in the posture of summary judgment, we are unable to conclude that the Attorney General's decision to regulate advertising of smokeless tobacco and cigars in an effort to combat the use of tobacco products by minors was based on mere "speculation [and] conjecture."

2.   Whatever the strength of the Attorney General's evidence to justify the outdoor advertising regulations, however, we conclude that the regulations do not satisfy the fourth step of the *Central Hudson* analysis. * * *

The outdoor advertising regulations prohibit any smokeless tobacco or cigar advertising within 1,000 feet of schools or playgrounds. In the District

Court, petitioners maintained that this prohibition would prevent advertising in 87% to 91% of Boston, Worcester, and Springfield. The 87% to 91% figure appears to include not only the effect of the regulations, but also the limitations imposed by other generally applicable zoning restrictions. The Attorney General disputed petitioners' figures but "concede[d] that the reach of the regulations is substantial." * * *

In some geographical areas, these regulations would constitute nearly a complete ban on the communication of truthful information about smokeless tobacco and cigars to adult consumers. The breadth and scope of the regulations, and the process by which the Attorney General adopted the regulations, do not demonstrate a careful calculation of the speech interests involved. * * *

The Attorney General apparently selected the 1,000-foot distance based on the FDA's decision to impose an identical 1,000-foot restriction when it attempted to regulate cigarette and smokeless tobacco advertising. But [the] degree to which speech is suppressed—or alternative avenues for speech remain available—under a particular regulatory scheme tends to be case specific [for] although a State or locality may have common interests and concerns about underage smoking and the effects of tobacco advertisements, the impact of a restriction on speech will undoubtedly vary from place to place. The FDA's regulations would have had widely disparate effects nationwide. Even in Massachusetts, the effect of the Attorney General's speech regulations will vary based on whether a locale is rural, suburban, or urban. The uniformly broad sweep of the geographical limitation demonstrates a lack of tailoring. * * *

The State's interest in preventing underage tobacco use is substantial, and even compelling, but it is no less true that the sale and use of tobacco products by adults is a legal activity. We must consider that tobacco retailers and manufacturers have an interest in conveying truthful information about their products to adults, and adults have a corresponding interest in receiving truthful information about tobacco products. [In] some instances, Massachusetts' outdoor advertising regulations would impose particularly onerous burdens on speech. For example, we disagree with the Court of Appeals' conclusion that because cigar manufacturers and retailers conduct a limited amount of advertising in comparison to other tobacco products, "the relative lack of cigar advertising also means that the burden imposed on cigar advertisers is correspondingly small." If some retailers have relatively small advertising budgets, and use few avenues of communication, then the Attorney General's outdoor advertising regulations potentially place a greater, not lesser, burden on those retailers' speech. * * *

JUSTICE KENNEDY, with whom JUSTICE SCALIA joins, concurring in part and concurring in the judgment.

The obvious overbreadth of the outdoor advertising restrictions suffices to invalidate them under the fourth part of the test in *Central Hudson*. [My] continuing concerns that the test gives insufficient protection to truthful, nonmisleading commercial speech require me to refrain from expressing agreement with the Court's application of the third part of *Central Hudson*. With the exception of Part III–B–1, then, I join the opinion of the Court.

JUSTICE THOMAS, concurring in part and concurring in the judgment

I join the opinion of the Court (with the exception of Part III–B–1). * * *

I have observed previously that there is no "philosophical or historical basis for asserting that 'commercial' speech is of 'lower value' than 'noncommercial' speech." Indeed, I doubt whether it is even possible to draw a coherent distinction between commercial and noncommercial speech.[2]

It should be clear that if these regulations targeted anything other than advertising for commercial products—if, for example, they were directed at billboards promoting political candidates—all would agree that the restrictions should be subjected to strict scrutiny. In my view, an asserted government interest in keeping people ignorant by suppressing expression "is per se illegitimate and can no more justify regulation of 'commercial' speech than it can justify regulation of 'noncommercial' speech." That is essentially the interest asserted here. * * *

[R]espondents [argue] that the regulations target deceptive and misleading speech. Second, they argue that the regulations restrict speech that promotes an illegal transaction—i.e., the sale of tobacco to minors. Neither theory is properly before the Court. For purposes of summary judgment, respondents were willing to assume "that the tobacco advertisements at issue here are truthful, nonmisleading speech about a lawful activity." [E]ven if we were to entertain these arguments, neither is persuasive. Respondents suggest that tobacco advertising is misleading because "its youthful imagery [and] sheer ubiquity" leads children to believe "that tobacco use is desirable and pervasive." This justification is belied, however, by the sweeping overinclusivity of the regulations. Massachusetts has done nothing to target its prohibition to advertisements appealing to "excitement, glamour, and independence"; the ban applies with equal force to appeals to torpor, homeliness, and servility. It has not focused on "youthful imagery"; smokers depicted on the sides of buildings may no more play shuffleboard than they may ride skateboards. * * *

---

[2]   **[Ct's Note]** Tobacco advertising provides a good illustration. The sale of tobacco products is the subject of considerable political controversy, and not surprisingly, some tobacco advertisements both promote a product and take a stand in this political debate. A recent cigarette advertisement, for example, displayed a brand logo next to text reading, "Why do politicians smoke cigars while taxing cigarettes?"

[Viewed] as an effort to proscribe solicitation to unlawful conduct, these regulations clearly fail the *Brandenburg* test. [Even] if Massachusetts could prohibit advertisements reading, "Hey kids, buy cigarettes here," these regulations sweep much more broadly than that. They cover "[any] statement or representation [the] purpose or effect of which is to promote the use or sale" of tobacco products, whether or not the statement is directly or indirectly addressed to minors. [It] is difficult to see any stopping point to a rule that would allow a State to prohibit all speech in favor of an activity in which it is illegal for minors to engage. Presumably, the State could ban car advertisements in an effort to enforce its restrictions on underage driving. It could regulate advertisements urging people to vote, because children are not permitted to vote. * * *[185]

Underlying many of the arguments of respondents and their amici is the idea that tobacco is in some sense sui generis [so] that application of normal First Amendment principles should be suspended. [Nevertheless], it seems appropriate to point out that to uphold the Massachusetts tobacco regulations would be to accept a line of reasoning that would permit restrictions on advertising for a host of other products.

Tobacco use is, we are told, "the single leading cause of preventable death in the United States." The second largest contributor to mortality rates in the United States is obesity. [A] significant factor has been the increased availability of large quantities of high-calorie, high-fat foods. Such foods, of course, have been aggressively marketed and promoted by fast food companies. Respondents say that tobacco companies are covertly targeting children in their advertising. Fast food companies do so openly. Moreover, there is considerable evidence that they have been successful in changing children's eating behavior. * * *

To take another example, the third largest cause of preventable deaths in the United States is alcohol. [Although] every State prohibits the sale of alcohol to those under age 21, much alcohol advertising is viewed by children. Not surprisingly, there is considerable evidence that exposure to alcohol advertising is associated with underage drinking. * * *

Respondents have identified no principle of law or logic that would preclude the imposition of restrictions on fast food and alcohol advertising similar to those they seek to impose on tobacco advertising. In effect, they seek a "vice" exception to the First Amendment. No such exception exists. If it did, it would have almost no limit, for "any product that poses some threat to public health or public morals might reasonably be characterized by a state legislature as relating to 'vice activity.'"

---

[185] For the contention that junk food advertising to children should not be protected, see David G. Yosifon, *Resisting Deep Capture: The Commercial Speech Doctrine and Junk-Food Advertising to Children*, 39 Loy. L.A.L. Rev. 507 (2006).

No legislature has ever sought to restrict speech about an activity it regarded as harmless and inoffensive. [It] is therefore no answer for the State to say that the makers of cigarettes are doing harm: perhaps they are. But in that respect they are no different from the purveyors of other harmful products, or the advocates of harmful ideas. When the State seeks to silence them, they are all entitled to the protection of the First Amendment. * * *

JUSTICE SOUTER, concurring in part and dissenting in part.

I join Parts I, II–C, II–D, III–A, III–B–1, III–C, and III–D of the Court's opinion. I join Part I of the opinion of Justice Stevens concurring in the judgment in part and dissenting in part. I respectfully dissent from Part III–B–2 of the opinion of the Court, and like Justice Stevens would remand for trial on the constitutionality of the 1,000-foot limit.

JUSTICE STEVENS, with whom JUSTICE GINSBURG and JUSTICE BREYER join, and with whom JUSTICE SOUTER joins as to Part I, concurring in part, concurring in the judgment in part, and dissenting in part. * * *

I.   [Stevens, J., argued that the Federal Cigarette Labeling and Advertising Act of 1965 did not preclude state and local regulation of the location of cigarette advertising.]

II.   *The 1,000-Foot Rule.* I am in complete accord with the Court's analysis of the importance of the interests served by the advertising restrictions. As the Court lucidly explains, few interests are more "compelling," than ensuring that minors do not become addicted to a dangerous drug before they are able to make a mature and informed decision as to the health risks associated with that substance. [Nevertheless,] noble ends do not save a speech-restricting statute whose means are poorly tailored. Such statutes may be invalid for two different reasons. First, the means chosen may be insufficiently related to the ends they purportedly serve. Alternatively, the statute may be so broadly drawn that, while effectively achieving its ends, it unduly restricts communications that are unrelated to its policy aims.

To my mind, the 1,000-foot rule does not present a tailoring problem of the first type. For reasons cogently explained in our prior opinions and in the opinion of the Court, we may fairly assume that advertising stimulates consumption and, therefore, that regulations limiting advertising will facilitate efforts to stem consumption. Furthermore, if the government's intention is to limit consumption by a particular segment of the community—in this case, minors—it is appropriate, indeed necessary, to tailor advertising restrictions to the areas where that segment of the community congregates—in this case, the area surrounding schools and playgrounds.

SEC. 3

IS SOME PROTECTED SPEECH LESS EQUAL THAN
OTHER PROTECTED SPEECH?

917

However, I share the majority's concern as to whether the 1,000-foot rule unduly restricts the ability of cigarette manufacturers to convey lawful information to adult consumers. This, of course, is a question of line-drawing. [E]fforts to protect children from exposure to harmful material will undoubtedly have some spillover effect on the free speech rights of adults. [Though] many factors plausibly enter the equation when calculating whether a child-directed location restriction goes too far in regulating adult speech, one crucial question is whether the regulatory scheme leaves available sufficient "alternative avenues of communication." Because I do not think the record contains sufficient information to enable us to answer that question, I would vacate the award of summary judgment upholding the 1,000-foot rule and remand for trial on that issue.

[For example,] depending on the answers to empirical questions on which we lack data, the ubiquity of print advertisements hawking particular brands of cigarettes might suffice to inform adult consumers of the special advantages of the respective brands. Similarly, print advertisements, circulars mailed to people's homes, word of mouth, and general information may or may not be sufficient to imbue the adult population with the knowledge that particular stores, chains of stores, or types of stores sell tobacco products.

I note, moreover, that the alleged "overinclusivity" of the advertising regulations while relevant to whether the regulations are narrowly tailored, does not "beli[e]" the claim that tobacco advertising imagery misleads children into believing that smoking is healthy, glamorous, or sophisticated. For purposes of summary judgment, the State conceded that the tobacco companies' advertising concerns lawful activity and is not misleading. Under the Court's disposition of the case today, the State remains free to proffer evidence that the advertising is in fact misleading. * * *

III. Because I strongly disagree with the Court's conclusion on the preemption issue, I dissent from Parts II–A and II–B of its opinion. Though I agree with much of what the Court has to say about the First Amendment, I ultimately disagree with its disposition or its reasoning on each of the regulations before us.[12]

NOTES AND QUESTIONS

1. Consider Richard H. Fallon, Jr., *The Dynamic Constitution* 50–51 (2004): "The decision in *Lorillard* * * * demonstrates the tendency of legal doctrine to deal in abstraction. In the eyes of the law, companies engaged in the business of selling cigarettes become 'speakers' protected under the First Amendment even though the sole aim of their 'speech'—consisting mostly of

---

[12] **[Ct's Note]** Reflecting my partial agreement with the Court, I join Parts I, II–C, II–D, and III–B–1 and concur in the judgment reflected in Part III–D.

misleading images of healthy and sexy-looking people on billboards—was to promote the sale of a deadly product. [T]he same Justices who joined the *Lorillard* majority continue to hold that the states can regulate obscenity, simply to preserve state interests in morality."[186]

2.   Consider Kathleen M. Sullivan, *Cheap Spirits, Cigarettes, and Free Speech: The Implications of 44 Liquormart,* 1996 Sup.Ct. Rev. 123 (1996): "A plurality [is] willing to move commercial speech somewhat closer to the core of the First Amendment applying strict scrutiny to paternalistic interventions between speaker and listener for the listener's own good. It remains to be seen whether this group of Justices would extend that approach to all content-based commercial speech regulations, whether a fifth or more will join them, and whether such a move would prompt any change in the Court's currently exceptional treatment of false and misleading commercial speech." Will the category "commercial speech" be abandoned altogether?

3.   Federal law permits compounding of drugs for the needs of specific patients without resort to FDA approval, so long as advertising of such drugs is not involved. The government rationale is that advertising would be indicative of mass manufacture rather than tailoring to the specific needs of individual patients.

THOMPSON v. WESTERN STATES MEDICAL CENTER, 535 U.S. 357 (2002), per O'CONNOR, J., invalidated these restrictions in part by concluding that the government did not meet its burden to show that less restrictive alternatives were unavailable.[187]

BREYER, J., joined by Rehnquist, C.J., and Stevens and Ginsburg, JJ., dissenting, argued that the Court's approach to such issues should be flexible. He contended that the Court rightly applied the less demanding *Central Hudson* test because "it has concluded that, from a constitutional perspective, commercial speech does not warrant application of the Court's strictest speech-protective tests. And it has reached this conclusion in part because restrictions on commercial speech do not often repress individual self-expression; they rarely interfere with the functioning of democratic political processes; and they often reflect a democratically determined governmental decision to regulate a commercial venture in order to protect, for example, the consumer, the public health, individual safety, or the environment. [The] Court, in my view, gives insufficient weight to the Government's regulatory rationale, and too readily

---

[186] For material relevant to the prohibition of tobacco advertising, see Steven H. Shiffrin, *Dissent, Injustice, and the Meanings of America* ch. 2 (1999); Kathleen M. Sullivan, *Cheap Spirits, Cigarettes, and Free Speech: The Implications of 44 Liquormart,* 1996 Sup.Ct. Rev. 123 (1996); Martin H. Redish, *Tobacco Advertising and the First Amendment,* 81 Ia. L.Rev. 589 (1996); Sylvia Law, *Addiction, Autonomy, and Advertising,* 77 Iowa L.Rev. 909 (1992); Daniel Lowenstein, *"Too Much Puff": Persuasion, Paternalism, and Commercial Speech,* 56 U.Cin.L.Rev. 1205 (1988); Charles Fischette, *A New Architecture of Commercial Speech Law,* 31 Harv. J.L. & Pub. Pol'y 663 (2008).

[187] Elizabeth Spring, *Sales Versus Safety: The Loss of Balance in the Commercial Speech Standard in Thompson v. Western States Medical Center,* 37 U.C. Davis L. Rev. 1389 (2004): "The evolution of the commercial speech standard shows that the Court is now applying the *Central Hudson* test in a manner approaching strict scrutiny review."

assumes the existence of practical alternatives. It thereby applies the commercial speech doctrine too strictly. [A]n overly rigid commercial speech doctrine will transform what ought to be a legislative or regulatory decision about the best way to protect the health and safety of the American public into a constitutional decision prohibiting the legislature from enacting necessary protections. As history in respect to the Due Process Clause shows, any such transformation would involve a tragic constitutional misunderstanding."

4. ***Defining commercial speech.*** In 1996 Nike, Inc. was confronted with allegations that it underpaid and otherwise mistreated workers at foreign facilities. Nike attempted to answer these charges with press releases, letters to editors, university presidents and athletic directors, and with a commissioned report by Andrew Young about working conditions in its factories. Kasky, a California resident, sued as a private attorney general under a California statute prohibiting unfair and deceptive practices.[188] Kasky alleged that in order to boost sales, Nike made a number of false statements and/or material omissions of fact. Assume that some of Nike's communications went to customers and that some did not. Are any of the communications "commercial speech"? All of them? Compare *Kasky v. Nike, Inc.*, 45 P.3d 243 (Cal. 2002), with *Nike, Inc. v. Kasky*, 539 U.S. 654 (2003)(Breyer, J., joined by O'Connor, J., dissenting from dismissal of the writ as improvidently granted).[189] Consider Robert M. O'Neil, *Nike v. Kasky—What Might Have Been . . .* , 54 Case W. Res. L. Rev. 1259 (2004): "Might there be some merit in recognizing a third category of expression—one that is neither classically commercial speech, nor fully protected speech? Consider the possibility of treating messages such as the overseas labor bulletins in the *Nike* case (or the utility promotions in *Central Hudson*, the off-label drug reprints in *WLF*, and the contraceptive pamphlets in *Bolger*) as less than fully protected speech on one hand, yet on the other hand as more protected than pure advertising. One of the limitations of the current analysis is the absence of any middle ground or intermediate option between the two poles—a disjunction which artificially compels courts to choose one extreme or the other, with drastic consequences, when in fact the real-world spectrum of corporate communications is far more varied and complex."[190]

In order to create a level playing field, should Nike's speech be entitled to the same protection afforded to those who might attack it? Rodney A. Smolla, *Afterword: Free the Fortune 500! The Debate over Corporate Speech and the First Amendment*, 54 Case W. Res. L. Rev. 1277,(2004). Would such treatment

---

[188] The Solicitor General argued that the private attorneys general provision should have doomed the statute on First Amendment grounds because of the potential chilling effect wholly apart from the status of the speech as commercial or political. For resistance to this contention in support of a general defense of private attorneys general, see Trevor W. Morrison, *Private Attorneys General and the First Amendment,* 103 Mich. L.Rev. 589 (2004).

[189] For discussion, see Ronald K.L. Collins & David M. Skover, *The Landmark Case that Wasn't,* 54 Case W. Res. L. Rev. 965 (2004); Tom Bennigson, *Nike Revisited: Can Commercial Corporations Engage in Non-Commercial Speech?*, 39 Conn. L.Rev. 379 (2006).

[190] Should there be a middle ground? Is it enough to qualify as commercial speech that Nike is involved in marketing its image and nothing more? See Tamara R. Piety, *Free Advertising*, 10 Lewis & Clark L.Rev. 367 (2006).

interfere with the enforcement of the Securities laws? Do corporate representations about manufacturing processes "provide consumers with an opportunity to engage in purposeful, expressive activity through the medium of conscientious consumption." Would "government's monitoring of the accuracy of process representations * * * impinge only on the commercial speech of product manufacturers, and * * * do so only in order to enable and support fundamental First Amendment activity by consumers." Douglas A. Kysar, *Preferences for Processes: The Process/Product Distinction and the Regulation of Consumer Choice*, 118 Harv. L. Rev. 525 (2004). Would it be wise to rule that "[t]ies go to the protection of the non-commercial elements of hybrid speech"? Jonathan Varat, *Deception and the First Amendment: A Central, Complex, and Somewhat Curious Relationship,* 53 UCLA L.Rev. 1107 (2007).

5.   In the absence of the consent of physicians, Vermont prohibits pharmacists from selling information about the drugs physicians prescribe to pharmaceutical companies or to those who provide reports to such companies for marketing purposes. Pharmacists, on the other hand, are permitted to sell to private or academic researchers even without consent. Is the sale of such information to pharmaceutical companies commercial speech? If not, does it burden commercial speech in a way that should trigger heightened scrutiny? Should protection of physician privacy be sufficient to justify the statute? See *Sorrell v. IMS Health Inc.*, 131 S.Ct. 2653 (2011). See generally Hunter B. Thompson, *Whither Central Hudson? Commercial Speech in the Wake of Sorrell v. IMS Health,* 47 Colum. J.L.&Soc.Prob. 171 (2013).

Under current law, pharmaceutical companies are prohibited from "off-label" pharmaceutical promotion—that is, from promoting or advertising drugs for uses other than those approved by the Food and Drug Administration. The issue is a matter of considerable contemporary controversy, with much of the controversy surrounding the question whther such promotion qualifies as "false" or "misleading." Kate Greenwood, *The Ban on "Off-Label" Pharmaceutical Promotion: Constitutionally Permissible Prophylaxis Against False or Misleading Commercial Speech,* 37 Am.J.L.&Med. 278 (2011).

III.   PRIVATE SPEECH

Before studying Dun & Bradstreet, below, review *Gertz,* Sec. 1, II, C supra.

Dun & Bradstreet, Inc., a credit reporting agency, falsely and negligently reported to five of its subscribers that Greenmoss Builders, Inc. had filed a petition for bankruptcy and also negligently misrepresented Greenmoss' assets and liabilities. In the ensuing defamation action, Greenmoss recovered $50,000 in compensatory damages and $300,000 in punitive damages. Dun & Bradstreet argued that, under *Gertz,* its First Amendment rights had been violated because presumed and punitive damages had been imposed without instructions requiring a showing of *New York Times* malice. Greenmoss argued that the *Gertz* protections did

SEC. 3

IS SOME PROTECTED SPEECH LESS EQUAL THAN
OTHER PROTECTED SPEECH?

921

not extend to non-media defendants and, in any event, did not extend to commercial speech.

DUN & BRADSTREET, INC. v. GREENMOSS BUILDERS, INC., 472 U.S. 749 (1985), rejected Dun & Bradstreet's contention, but there was no opinion of the Court. The common theme of the five justices siding with Greenmoss was that the First Amendment places less value on "private" speech than upon "public" speech.

POWELL, J., joined by Rehnquist and O'Connor, JJ., noted that the Vermont Supreme Court below had held "as a matter of federal constitutional law" that "the media protections outlined in *Gertz* are inapplicable to nonmedia defamation actions." In affirming, Powell, J., stated that his reasons were "different from those relied upon by the Vermont Supreme Court": "Like every other case in which this Court has found constitutional limits to state defamation laws, *Gertz* involved expression on a matter of undoubted public concern. * * *

"We have never considered whether the *Gertz* balance obtains when the defamatory statements involve no issue of public concern. To make this determination, we must employ the approach approved in *Gertz* and balance the State's interest in compensating private individuals for injury to their reputation against the First Amendment interest in protecting this type of expression. This state interest is identical to the one weighed in *Gertz*. * * *

"The First Amendment interest, on the other hand, is less important than the one weighed in *Gertz*. We have long recognized that not all speech is of equal First Amendment importance.[5] It is speech on 'matters of public concern' that is 'at the heart of the First Amendment's protection.' [In] contrast, speech on matters of purely private concern is of less First Amendment concern. As a number of state courts, including the court below, have recognized, the role of the Constitution in regulating state libel

---

[5] **[Ct's Note]** This Court on many occasions has recognized that certain kinds of speech are less central to the interests of the First Amendment than others. Obscene speech and "fighting words" long have been accorded no protection. *Roth; Chaplinsky.* In the area of protected speech, the most prominent example of reduced protection for certain kinds of speech concerns commercial speech. Such speech, we have noted, occupies a "subordinate position in the scale of First Amendment values." *Ohralik.* * * *

Other areas of the law provide further examples. In *Ohralik* we noted that there are "[n]umerous examples [of] communications that are regulated without offending the First Amendment, such as the exchange of information about securities, * * * corporate proxy statements, [the] exchange of price and production information among competitors, [and] employers' threats of retaliation for the labor activities of employees." Yet similar regulation of political speech is subject to the most rigorous scrutiny. Likewise, while the power of the State to license lawyers, psychiatrists, and public school teachers—all of whom speak for a living—is unquestioned, this Court has held that a law requiring licensing of union organizers is unconstitutional under the First Amendment. *Thomas v. Collins*, [Sec. 4, I, A infra]; see also *Rosenbloom v. Metromedia* (opinion of Brennan, J.) ("the determinant whether the First Amendment applies to state libel actions is whether the utterance involved concerns an issue of public or general concern").

law is far more limited when the concerns that activated *New York Times* and *Gertz* are absent.[6] In such a case, '[t]here is no threat to the free and robust debate of public issues; there is no potential interference with a meaningful dialogue of ideas concerning self-government; and there is no threat of liability causing a reaction of self-censorship by the press. The facts of the present case are wholly without the First Amendment concerns with which the Supreme Court of the United States has been struggling.' *Harley-Davidson Motorsports, Inc. v. Markley*, 568 P.2d 1359 (Or. 1977).

"While such speech is not totally unprotected by the First Amendment, see *Connick v. Myers* [Sec. 7, III infra], its protections are less stringent. [In] light of the reduced constitutional value of speech involving no matters of public concern, we hold that the state interest adequately supports awards of presumed and punitive damages—even absent a showing of 'actual malice.'[7]

"The only remaining issue is whether petitioner's credit report involved a matter of public concern. In a related context, we have held that '[w]hether [speech] addresses a matter of public concern must be determined by [the expression's] content, form, and context [as] revealed by the whole record.' *Connick.* These factors indicate that petitioner's credit report concerns no public issue.[8] It was speech solely in the individual interest of the speaker and its specific business audience. Cf. *Central Hudson.* This particular interest warrants no special protection when—as in this case—the speech is wholly false and clearly damaging to the victim's business reputation. Moreover, since the credit report was made available to only five subscribers, who, under the terms of the subscription agreement, could not disseminate it further, it cannot be said that the report involves any 'strong interest in the free flow of commercial information.' *Virginia Pharmacy.* There is simply no credible argument

---

[6] **[Ct's Note]** As one commentator has remarked with respect to "the case of a commercial supplier of credit information that defames a person applying for credit"—the case before us today—"If the First Amendment requirements outlined in *Gertz* apply, there is something clearly wrong with the First Amendment or with *Gertz*." Steven Shiffrin, *The First Amendment and Economic Regulation: Away from a General Theory of the First Amendment*, 78 Nw.L.Rev. 1212 (1983).

[7] **[Ct's Note]** The dissent, purporting to apply the same balancing test that we do today, concludes that even speech on purely private matters is entitled to the protections of *Gertz*. * * *

The dissent's "balance" [would] lead to the protection of all libels—no matter how attenuated their constitutional interest. If the dissent were the law, a woman of impeccable character who was branded a "whore" by a jealous neighbor would have no effective recourse unless she could prove "actual malice" by clear and convincing evidence. This is not malice in the ordinary sense, but in the more demanding sense of *New York Times*. The dissent would, in effect, constitutionalize the entire common law of libel.

[8] **[Ct's Note]** The dissent suggests that our holding today leaves all credit reporting subject to reduced First Amendment protection. This is incorrect. The protection to be accorded a particular credit report depends on whether the report's "content, form, and context" indicate that it concerns a public matter. We also do not hold, as the dissent suggests we do, that the report is subject to reduced constitutional protection because it constitutes economic or commercial speech. We discuss such speech, along with advertising, only to show how many of the same concerns that argue in favor of reduced constitutional protection in those areas apply here as well.

that this type of credit reporting requires special protection to ensure that 'debate on public issues [will] be uninhibited, robust, and wide-open.' *New York Times.*

"In addition, the speech here, like advertising, is hardy and unlikely to be deterred by incidental state regulation. See *Virginia Pharmacy.* It is solely motivated by the desire for profit, which, we have noted, is a force less likely to be deterred than others. Arguably, the reporting here was also more objectively verifiable than speech deserving of greater protection. In any case, the market provides a powerful incentive to a credit reporting agency to be accurate, since false credit reporting is of no use to creditors. Thus, any incremental 'chilling' effect of libel suits would be of decreased significance.

"We conclude that permitting recovery of presumed and punitive damages in defamation cases absent a showing of 'actual malice' does not violate the First Amendment when the defamatory statements do not involve matters of public concern."

Although expressing the view that *Gertz* should be overruled and that the *New York Times* malice definition should be reconsidered, BURGER, C.J., concurring, stated that: "The single question before the Court today is whether *Gertz* applies to this case. The plurality opinion holds that *Gertz* does not apply because, unlike the challenged expression in *Gertz,* the alleged defamatory expression in this case does not relate to a matter of public concern. I agree that *Gertz* is limited to circumstances in which the alleged defamatory expression concerns a matter of general public importance, and that the expression in question here relates to a matter of essentially private concern. I therefore agree with the plurality opinion to the extent that it holds that *Gertz* is inapplicable in this case for the two reasons indicated. No more is needed to dispose of the present case."

WHITE, J., who had dissented in *Gertz,* was prepared to overrule that case or to limit it, but he disagreed with Powell, J.'s, suggestion that the plurality's resolution of the case was faithful to *Gertz:* "It is interesting that Justice Powell declines to follow the *Gertz* approach in this case. I had thought that the decision in *Gertz* was intended to reach cases that involve any false statements of fact injurious to reputation, whether the statement is made privately or publicly and whether or not it implicates a matter of public importance. Justice Powell, however, distinguishes *Gertz* as a case that involved a matter of public concern, an element absent here. Wisely, in my view, Justice Powell does not rest his application of a different rule here on a distinction drawn between media and non-media defendants. On that issue, I agree with Justice Brennan that the First Amendment gives no more protection to the press in defamation suits than it does to others exercising their freedom of speech. None of our cases affords such a distinction; to the contrary, the Court has rejected it at every turn. It should be rejected again, particularly in this context, since it makes no sense to give the most protection to those publishers who reach the most readers and therefore pollute the channels of communication with the most misinformation and do the most damage to private reputation. If *Gertz* is to be distinguished from this case, on the ground that it applies only where the allegedly false publication deals with a matter of general or public importance, then where the false publication does not deal with such a matter, the common-law rules would apply whether the defendant is a member of the media or other public disseminator or a non-media individual publishing privately. Although Justice Powell speaks only of the inapplicability of the *Gertz* rule with respect to presumed and punitive damages, it must be that the *Gertz* requirement of some kind of fault on the part of the defendant is also inapplicable in cases such as this. * * *

"The question before us is whether *Gertz* is to be applied in this case. For either of two reasons, I believe that it should not. First, I am unreconciled to the *Gertz* holding and believe that it should be overruled. Second, as Justice Powell indicates, the defamatory publication in this case does not deal with a matter of public importance."

BRENNAN, J., joined by Marshall, Blackmun and Stevens, JJ., dissented: "This case involves a difficult question of the proper application of *Gertz* to credit reporting—a type of speech at some remove from that which first gave rise to explicit First Amendment restrictions on state defamation law—and has produced a diversity of considered opinions, none of which speaks for the Court. Justice Powell's plurality opinion affirming the judgment below would not apply the *Gertz* limitations on presumed and punitive damages [because] the speech involved a subject of purely private concern and was circulated to an extremely limited audience. * * * Justice White also would affirm; he would not apply *Gertz* to this case on the ground that the subject matter of the publication does not deal with a matter of general or public importance. The Chief Justice apparently agrees with Justice White. The four who join this opinion would reverse the judgment of the Vermont Supreme Court. We believe that, although protection of the type of expression at issue is admittedly not the 'central meaning of the First Amendment,' *Gertz* makes clear that the First Amendment nonetheless requires restraints on presumed and punitive damage awards for this expression. * * *

"[Respondent urged that *Gertz* be restricted] to cases in which the defendant is a 'media' entity. Such a distinction is irreconcilable with the fundamental First Amendment principle that '[t]he inherent worth [of] speech in terms of its capacity for informing the public does not depend upon the identity of its source, whether corporation, association, union, or individual.' *First National Bank v. Bellotti* [Sec. 10 infra]. First Amendment difficulties lurk in the definitional questions such an approach would generate. And the distinction would likely be born an anachronism.[7] Perhaps most importantly, the argument that *Gertz* should be limited to the media misapprehends our cases. We protect the press to ensure the vitality of First Amendment guarantees. This solicitude implies no endorsement of the principle that speakers other than the press deserve lesser First Amendment protection. * * *

"The free speech guarantee gives each citizen an equal right to self-expression and to participation in self-government. [Accordingly,] at least six Members of this Court (the four who join this opinion and Justice White and The Chief Justice) agree today that, in the context of defamation law, the rights of the institutional media are no greater and no less than those enjoyed by other individuals or organizations engaged in the same activities.[10] * * *

"Purporting to 'employ the approach approved in *Gertz*,' Justice Powell balances the state interest in protecting private reputation against the First Amendment interest in protecting expression on matters not of public concern.[11]

"The five Members of the Court voting to affirm the damage award in this case have provided almost no guidance as to what constitutes a protected 'matter of public concern.' Justice White offers nothing at all, but his opinion does indicate that the distinction turns on solely the subject matter of the expression and not on the extent or conditions of dissemination of that expression. Justice Powell adumbrates a rationale that would appear to focus primarily on subject matter.[12] The opinion relies on the fact that the speech at issue was 'solely in the individual interest of

---

[7] **[Ct's Note]** Owing to transformations in the technological and economic structure of the communications industry, there has been an increasing convergence of what might be labeled "media" and "nonmedia."

[10] **[Ct's Note]** Justice Powell's opinion does not expressly reject the media/nonmedia distinction, but does expressly decline to apply that distinction to resolve this case.

[11] **[Ct's Note]** One searches *Gertz* in vain for a single word to support the proposition that limits on presumed and punitive damages obtained only when speech involved matters of public concern. *Gertz* could not have been grounded in such a premise. Distrust of placing in the courts the power to decide what speech was of public concern was precisely the rationale *Gertz* offered for rejecting the *Rosenbloom* plurality approach. * * *

[12] **[Ct's Note]** Justice Powell also appears to rely in part on the fact that communication was limited and confidential. Given that his analysis also relies on the subject matter of the credit report, it is difficult to decipher exactly what role the nature and extent of dissemination plays in Justice Powell's analysis. But because the subject matter of the expression at issue is properly understood as a matter of public concern, it may well be that this element of confidentiality is crucial to the outcome as far as Justice Powell's opinion is concerned. In other words, it may be that Justice Powell thinks this particular expression could not contribute to public welfare because the public generally does not receive it. This factor does not suffice to save the analysis. See n. 18 infra.

[In fn. 18, Brennan, J., indicated that, "Dun & Bradstreet doubtless provides thousands of credit reports to thousands of subscribers who receive the information pursuant to the same strictures imposed on the recipients in this case. As a systemic matter, therefore, today's decision diminishes the free flow of information because Dun & Bradstreet will generally be made more reticent in providing information to all its subscribers."]

the speaker and its *business* audience.' Analogizing explicitly to advertising, the opinion also states that credit reporting is 'hardy' and 'solely motivated by the desire for profit.' These two strains of analysis suggest that Justice Powell is excluding the subject matter of credit reports from 'matters of public concern' because the speech is predominantly in the realm of matters of economic concern."

Brennan, J., pointed to precedents (particularly labor cases) protecting speech on economic matters and argued that, "the breadth of this protection evinces recognition that freedom of expression is not only essential to check tyranny and foster self-government but also intrinsic to individual liberty and dignity and instrumental in society's search for truth."

Moreover, he emphasized the importance of credit reporting: "The credit reporting of Dun & Bradstreet falls within any reasonable definition of 'public concern' consistent with our precedents. Justice Powell's reliance on the fact that Dun & Bradstreet publishes credit reports 'for profit' is wholly unwarranted. Time and again we have made clear that speech loses none of its constitutional protection 'even though it is carried in a form that is "sold" for profit.' *Virginia Pharmacy*. More importantly, an announcement of the bankruptcy of a local company is information of potentially great concern to residents of the community where the company is [located]. And knowledge about solvency and the effect and prevalence of bankruptcy certainly would inform citizen opinions about questions of economic regulation. It is difficult to suggest that a bankruptcy is not a subject matter of public concern when federal law requires invocation of judicial mechanisms to effectuate it and makes the fact of the bankruptcy a matter of public record. * * *

"Even if the subject matter of credit reporting were properly considered—in the terms of Justice White and Justice Powell—as purely a matter of private discourse, this speech would fall well within the range of valuable expression for which the First Amendment demands protection. Much expression that does not directly involve public issues receives significant protection. Our cases do permit some diminution in the degree of protection afforded one category of speech about economic or commercial matters. 'Commercial speech'—defined as advertisements that 'do no more than propose a commercial transaction'—may be more closely regulated than other types of speech. [Credit] reporting is not 'commercial speech' as this Court has defined the term.

"[In] *every* case in which we have permitted more extensive state regulation on the basis of a commercial speech rationale—the speech being regulated was pure advertising—an offer to buy or sell goods and services or encouraging such buying and selling. Credit reports are not commercial advertisements for a good or service or a proposal to buy or sell such a product. We have been extremely chary about extending the 'commercial speech' doctrine beyond this narrowly circumscribed category of advertising because often vitally important speech will be uttered to advance economic interests and because the profit motive making such speech hardy dissipates rapidly when the speech is not advertising."[191]

Finally, Brennan, J., argued that even if credit reports were characterized as commercial speech, "unrestrained" presumed and punitive damages would violate the commercial speech requirement that "the regulatory means chosen be narrowly tailored so as to avoid any unnecessary chilling of protected expression. [Accordingly,] Greenmoss Builders should be permitted to recover for any actual damage it can show resulted from Dun & Bradstreet's negligently false credit report, but should be required to show actual malice to receive presumed or punitive damages."

NOTES AND QUESTIONS

1.   Which of the following are "private" according to the opinions of Powell, J., Burger, C.J., and White, J.? (a) a report in the *Wall Street Journal* that Greenmoss has gone bankrupt; (b) a confidential report by Dun & Bradstreet to a bank that a famous politician has poor credit. Would it be different if the subject of the report were an actor? (c) a statement in the campus newspaper or by one student to another that a law professor is an alcoholic. Would it make a difference if the law professor was being considered for a Supreme Court appointment?

Consider the relationship between the public/private focus of the *Greenmoss* decision and the "public controversy" aspect of the public figure definition. If the speech does not relate to a "public" controversy, can it be "public" within the terms of *Greenmoss*? See Rodney Smolla, *Law of Defamation* 3–15 (1986). Reconsider *Time, Inc. v. Firestone,* Sec. 1, II, C supra.[192]

Finally, does it matter why the D & B subscribers received the information about Greenmoss? Suppose, for investment or insurance purposes, the subscribers had asked for reports on all aspects of the construction industry in Vermont? Compare *Lowe v. SEC,* Sec. 4, III infra.

2.   Should the focus of the decision have been commercial speech instead of private speech? Would an expansion of the commercial speech definition

---

[191] Brennan, J., cited *Consolidated Edison Co. v. Public Service Comm'n,* 447 U.S. 530 (1980), which invalidated a regulation that prohibited a utility company from inserting its views on "controversial issues of public policy" into its monthly electrical bill mailings. The mailing that prompted the regulation advocated nuclear power.

[192] For discussion of the different meanings of public and private speech, see Nat Stern, *Private Concerns of Private Plaintiffs: Revisiting a Problematic Defamation Category,* 65 Mo. L.Rev. 597 (2000); Frederick Schauer, *"Private" Speech and the "Private" Forum: Givhan v. Western Line School District,* 1979 Sup.Ct.Rev. 217. Compare Michael Perry, *Freedom of Expression: An Essay on Theory and Doctrine,* 78 Nw.U.L.Rev. 1137 (1983) (denying any meaningful distinction between personal and political decisions).

have been preferable to the promotion of ad hoc decisionmaking about the nature of "private" speech? Consider Shiffrin, *The First Amendment and Economic Regulation: Away from a General Theory of the First Amendment*, 78 Nw.U.L.Rev. 1212 (1983): "[D]rawing lines based on underlying First Amendment values is a far cry from sending out the judiciary on a general ad hoc expedition to separate matters of general public interest from matters that are not. A commitment to segregate certain commercial speech from *Gertz* protection is not a commitment to general ad hoc determinations."

3.   According to Powell, J., in fn. 5, are the *Ohralik* examples, i.e., exchange of information about securities, corporate proxy statements and the like, examples of protected speech subject to regulation? In what sense, are those examples of communication protected? What is the significance of Powell, J.'s suggestion that they are something other than commercial speech?[193] Where do those examples fit into Brennan, J.'s view of the First Amendment?

4.   Should (does?) the public/private distinction of Greenmoss apply to newspapers and broadcasters? C. Edwin Baker, *Autonomy and Informational Privacy, or Gossip: The Central Meaning of the First Amendment*, 21 Social Phil. & Pol'y 215 (2004): "The business of credit reporting is in many respects more like professions that are regulated than like the press. Just as an accountant sells tax advice, a credit reporting agency sells specific, individualized financial information to clients who seek the information to guide their commercial transactions. These features distinguish credit reporting from both individuals' noncommercial speech and media communications."

IV. CONCEIVING AND RECONCEIVING THE STRUCTURE OF FIRST AMENDMENT DOCTRINE: HATE SPEECH REVISITED—AGAIN

R.A.V. v. ST. PAUL
505 U.S. 377, 112 S.Ct. 2538, 120 L.Ed.2d 305 (1992).

JUSTICE SCALIA delivered the opinion of the Court.

In the predawn hours of June 21, 1990, petitioner and several other teenagers allegedly assembled a crudely-made cross by taping together broken chair legs. They then allegedly burned the cross inside the fenced yard of a black family that lived across the street from the house where petitioner was staying. Although this conduct could have been punished under any of a number of laws, one of the two provisions under which respondent city of St. Paul chose to charge petitioner (then a juvenile) was the St. Paul Bias-Motivated Crime Ordinance, which provides: "Whoever places on public or private property a symbol, object, appellation,

---

[193] Consider *Board of Trustees v. Fox*, Sec. 3, II supra (dictum stating that attorneys or tutors dispensing advice for a fee is not commercial speech and strongly suggesting that regulations prohibiting such speech in college dormitories may be unconstitutional).

SEC. 3

IS SOME PROTECTED SPEECH LESS EQUAL THAN
OTHER PROTECTED SPEECH?

929

characterization or graffiti, including, but not limited to, a burning cross or Nazi swastika, which one knows or has reasonable grounds to know arouses anger, alarm or resentment in others on the basis of race, color, creed, religion or gender commits disorderly conduct and shall be guilty of a misdemeanor." * * *

I. [W]e accept the Minnesota Supreme Court's authoritative statement that the ordinance reaches only those expressions that constitute "fighting words" within the meaning of Chaplinsky. [W]e nonetheless conclude that the ordinance is facially unconstitutional in that it prohibits otherwise permitted speech solely on the basis of the subjects the speech addresses.

[From] 1791 to the present, our society, like other free but civilized societies, has permitted restrictions upon the content of speech in a few limited areas, which are "of such slight social value as a step to truth that any benefit that may be derived from them is clearly outweighed by the social interest in order and morality." *Chaplinsky.* * * *

We have sometimes said that these categories of expression are "not within the area of constitutionally protected speech," *Roth; Beauharnais; Chaplinsky;* or that the "protection of the First Amendment does not extend" to them, *Bose Corp. v. Consumers Union of United States, Inc.* [Sec. 1, II, B supra]; *Sable Communications of Cal., Inc. v. FCC* [Sec. 8, II infra]. Such statements must be taken in context, however, and are no more literally true than is the occasionally repeated shorthand characterizing obscenity "as not being speech at all," Cass Sunstein, *Pornography and the First Amendment,* 1986 Duke L.J. 589, 615, n. 146. What they mean is that these areas of speech can, consistently with the First Amendment, be regulated *because of their constitutionally proscribable content* (obscenity, defamation, etc.)—not that they are categories of speech entirely invisible to the Constitution, so that they may be made the vehicles for content discrimination unrelated to their distinctively proscribable content. Thus, the government may proscribe libel; but it may not make the further content discrimination of proscribing *only* libel critical of the government. * * *

Our cases surely do not establish the proposition that the First Amendment imposes no obstacle whatsoever to regulation of particular instances of such proscribable expression, so that the government "may regulate [them] freely," (White, J., concurring in judgment). That would mean that a city council could enact an ordinance prohibiting only those legally obscene works that contain criticism of the city government or, indeed, that do not include endorsement of the city government. Such a simplistic, all-or-nothing-at-all approach to First Amendment protection is at odds with common sense and with our jurisprudence as well.[1] It is not true that "fighting words" have at most a "de minimis" expressive content or that their content is *in all respects* "worthless and undeserving of constitutional protection"; sometimes they are quite expressive indeed. We have not said that they constitute "*no* part of the expression of ideas," but only that they constitute "no *essential* part of any exposition of ideas." *Chaplinsky.*

The proposition that a particular instance of speech can be proscribable on the basis of one feature (e.g., obscenity) but not on the basis of another (e.g., opposition to the city government) is commonplace, and has found application in many contexts. We have long held, for example, that nonverbal expressive activity can be banned because of the action it entails, but not because of the ideas it expresses—so that burning a flag in violation of an ordinance against outdoor fires could be punishable, whereas burning a flag in violation of an ordinance against dishonoring the flag is not. See *Johnson.* See also *Barnes* (Scalia, J., concurring in judgment) (Souter, J., concurring in judgment); *O'Brien.* Similarly, we have upheld reasonable "time, place, or manner" restrictions, but only if they are "justified without reference to the content of the regulated speech." *Ward;* see also *Clark* (noting that the *O'Brien* test differs little from the standard applied to time, place, or manner restrictions). And just as the power to proscribe particular speech on the basis of a noncontent element (e.g., noise) does not entail the power to proscribe the same speech on the basis of a content element; so also, the power to proscribe it on the basis of *one* content element (e.g., obscenity) does not entail the power to proscribe it on the basis of *other* content elements.

In other words, the exclusion of "fighting words" from the scope of the First Amendment simply means that, for purposes of that Amendment, the unprotected features of the words are, despite their verbal character, essentially a "non-speech" element of communication. Fighting words are thus analogous to a noisy sound truck: Each [is,] a "mode of speech,"; both can be used to convey an idea; but neither has, in and of itself, a claim upon the First Amendment. As with the sound truck, however, so also with fighting words: The government may not regulate use based on hostility—or favoritism—towards the underlying message expressed.

The concurrences describe us as setting forth a new First Amendment principle that prohibition of constitutionally proscribable speech cannot be

---

[1] **[Ct's Note]** Justice White concedes that a city council cannot prohibit only those legally obscene works that contain criticism of the city government, but asserts that to be the consequence, not of the First Amendment, but of the Equal Protection Clause. Such content-based discrimination would not, he asserts, "be rationally related to a legitimate government interest." But of course the only *reason* that government interest is not a "legitimate" one is that it violates the First Amendment. This Court itself has occasionally fused the First Amendment into the Equal Protection Clause in this fashion, but at least with the acknowledgment (which Justice White cannot afford to make) that the First Amendment underlies its analysis. * * *

"underinclusiv[e]" (White, J., concurring in judgment)—a First Amendment "absolutism" whereby "within a particular 'proscribable' category of expression, [a] government must either proscribe *all* speech or no speech at all" (Stevens, J., concurring in judgment). That easy target is of the concurrences' own invention. In our view, the First Amendment imposes not an "underinclusiveness" limitation but a "content discrimination" limitation upon a State's prohibition of proscribable speech. There is no problem whatever, for example, with a State's prohibiting obscenity (and other forms of proscribable expression) only in certain media or markets, for although that prohibition would be "underinclusive," it would not discriminate on the basis of content. See, e.g., *Sable Communications* (upholding 47 U.S.C. § 223(b)(1) (1988), which prohibits obscene *telephone* communications).

Even the prohibition against content discrimination that we assert the First Amendment requires is not absolute. It applies differently in the context of proscribable speech than in the area of fully protected speech. The rationale of the general prohibition, after all, is that content discrimination "rais[es] the specter that the Government may effectively drive certain ideas or viewpoints from the marketplace," *Simon & Schuster,* [Sec. 1, V, A infra]. But content discrimination among various instances of a class of proscribable speech often does not pose this threat.

When the basis for the content discrimination consists entirely of the very reason the entire class of speech at issue is proscribable, no significant danger of idea or viewpoint discrimination exists. Such a reason, having been adjudged neutral enough to support exclusion of the entire class of speech from First Amendment protection, is also neutral enough to form the basis of distinction within the class. To illustrate: A State might choose to prohibit only that obscenity which is the most patently offensive *in its prurience*—i.e., that which involves the most lascivious displays of sexual activity. But it may not prohibit, for example, only that obscenity which includes offensive *political* messages. And the Federal Government can criminalize only those threats of violence that are directed against the President, see 18 U.S.C. § 871—since the reasons why threats of violence are outside the First Amendment (protecting individuals from the fear of violence, from the disruption that fear engenders, and from the possibility that the threatened violence will occur) have special force when applied to the person of the President. See *Watts* [Sec. 1, I, D supra] (upholding the facial validity of § 871 because of the "overwhelmin[g] interest in protecting the safety of [the] Chief Executive and in allowing him to perform his duties without interference from threats of physical violence"). But the Federal Government may not criminalize only those threats against the President that mention his policy on aid to inner cities. And to take a final example (one mentioned by Justice Stevens), a State may choose to regulate price advertising in one industry but not in others, because the risk of fraud (one of the characteristics of commercial speech that justifies depriving it of full First Amendment protection) is in its view greater there. Cf. *Morales v. Trans World Airlines, Inc.,* 504 U.S. 374 (1992) (state regulation of airline advertising); *Ohralik* (state regulation of lawyer advertising). But a State may not prohibit only that commercial advertising that depicts men in a demeaning fashion.

Another valid basis for according differential treatment to even a content-defined subclass of proscribable speech is that the subclass happens to be associated with particular "secondary effects" of the speech, so that the regulation is "*justified* without reference to the content of [the] speech," *Renton.* A State could, for example, permit all obscene live performances except those involving minors. Moreover, since words can in some circumstances violate laws directed not against speech but against conduct (a law against treason, for example, is violated by telling the enemy the nation's defense secrets), a particular content-based subcategory of a proscribable class of speech can be swept up incidentally within the reach of a statute directed at conduct rather than speech. Thus, for example, sexually derogatory "fighting words," among other words, may produce a violation of Title VII's general prohibition against sexual discrimination in employment practices. Where the government does not target conduct on the basis of its expressive content, acts are not shielded from regulation merely because they express a discriminatory idea or philosophy.

These bases for distinction refute the proposition that the selectivity of the restriction is "even arguably 'conditioned upon the sovereign's agreement with what a speaker may intend to say.' " There may be other such bases as well. Indeed, to validate such selectivity (where totally proscribable speech is at issue) it may not even be necessary to identify any particular "neutral" basis, so long as the nature of the content discrimination is such that there is no realistic possibility that official suppression of ideas is afoot. (We cannot think of any First Amendment interest that would stand in the way of a State's prohibiting only those obscene motion pictures with blue-eyed actresses.) Save for that limitation, the regulation of "fighting words," like the regulation of noisy speech, may address some offensive instances and leave other, equally offensive, instances alone. See *Posadas.*[2]

II.   [Although] the phrase in the ordinance, "arouses anger, alarm or resentment in others," has been limited by the Minnesota Supreme Court's construction to reach only those symbols or displays that amount to "fighting words," the remaining, unmodified terms make clear that the

---

[2] **[Ct's Note]** Justice Stevens cites a string of opinions as supporting his assertion that "selective regulation of speech based on content" is not presumptively invalid. [A]ll that their contents establish is what we readily concede: that presumptive invalidity does not mean invariable invalidity, leaving room for such exceptions as reasonable and viewpoint-neutral content-based discrimination in nonpublic forums, or with respect to certain speech by government employees.

ordinance applies only to "fighting words" that insult, or provoke violence, "on the basis of race, color, creed, religion or gender." Displays containing abusive invective, no matter how vicious or severe, are permissible unless they are addressed to one of the specified disfavored topics. Those who wish to use "fighting words" in connection with other ideas—to express hostility, for example, on the basis of political affiliation, union membership, or homosexuality—are not covered. The First Amendment does not permit St. Paul to impose special prohibitions on those speakers who express views on disfavored subjects.

In its practical operation, moreover, the ordinance goes even beyond mere content discrimination, to actual viewpoint discrimination.[194] Displays containing some words—odious racial epithets, for example— would be prohibited to proponents of all views. But "fighting words" that do not themselves invoke race, color, creed, religion, or gender—aspersions upon a person's mother, for example—would seemingly be usable ad libitum in the placards of those arguing *in favor* of racial, color, etc. tolerance and equality, but could not be used by that speaker's opponents. One could hold up a sign saying, for example, that all "anti-Catholic bigots" are misbegotten; but not that all "papists" are, for that would insult and provoke violence "on the basis of religion." St. Paul has no such authority to license one side of a debate to fight freestyle, while requiring the other to follow Marquis of Queensbury Rules.

What we have here, it must be emphasized, is not a prohibition of fighting words that are directed at certain persons or groups (which would be *facially* valid if it met the requirements of the Equal Protection Clause); but rather, a prohibition of fighting words that contain (as the Minnesota Supreme Court repeatedly emphasized) messages of "bias-motivated" hatred and in particular, as applied to this case, messages "based on virulent notions of racial supremacy." One must wholeheartedly agree with the Minnesota Supreme Court that "[i]t is the responsibility, even the obligation, of diverse communities to confront such notions in whatever form they appear," but the manner of that confrontation cannot consist of selective limitations upon speech. St. Paul's brief asserts that a general "fighting words" law would not meet the city's needs because only a content-specific measure can communicate to minority groups that the "group hatred" aspect of such speech "is not condoned by the majority." The point of the First Amendment is that majority preferences must be expressed in some fashion other than silencing speech on the basis of its content. * * *

---

[194] Consider Alan E. Brownstein, *Alternative Maps for Navigating the First Amendment Maze*, 16 Const. Comm. 101 (1999): "Even an ostensibly innocuous subject matter regulation that prohibits speech about dogs, for example, may directly restrict at least one of the viewpoints that might be expressed in a debate about what constitutes the best household pet."

[T]he reason why fighting words are categorically excluded from the protection of the First Amendment is not that their content communicates any particular idea, but that their content embodies a particularly intolerable (and socially unnecessary) *mode* of expressing *whatever* idea the speaker wishes to convey. St. Paul has not singled out an especially offensive mode of expression—it has not, for example, selected for prohibition only those fighting words that communicate ideas in a threatening (as opposed to a merely obnoxious) manner. Rather, it has proscribed fighting words of whatever manner that communicate messages of racial, gender, or religious intolerance. Selectivity of this sort creates the possibility that the city is seeking to handicap the expression of particular ideas.

* * * St. Paul argues that the ordinance [is] aimed only at the "secondary effects" of the speech, see *Renton*. According to St. Paul, the ordinance is intended, "not to impact on [sic] the right of free expression of the accused," but rather to "protect against the victimization of a person or persons who are particularly vulnerable because of their membership in a group that historically has been discriminated against." Even assuming that an ordinance that completely proscribes, rather than merely regulates, a specified category of speech can ever be considered to be directed only to the secondary effects of such speech, it is clear that the St. Paul ordinance is not directed to secondary effects within the meaning of *Renton*. As we said in *Boos* "[l]isteners' reactions to speech are not the type of 'secondary effects' we referred to in *Renton*." * * * [7]

Finally, St. Paul [asserts] that the ordinance helps to ensure the basic human rights of members of groups that have historically been subjected to discrimination, including the right of such group members to live in peace where they wish. We do not doubt that these interests are compelling, and that the ordinance can be said to promote them. But the "danger of censorship" presented by a facially content-based statute requires that that weapon be employed only where it is *"necessary* to serve the asserted [compelling] interest". The existence of adequate content-neutral alternatives thus "undercut[s] significantly" any defense of such a statute, casting considerable doubt on the government's protestations that "the asserted justification is in fact an accurate description of the purpose and effect of the law." [An] ordinance not limited to the favored topics, for example, would have precisely the same beneficial effect. In fact the only interest distinctively served by the content limitation is that of displaying

---

[7]   **[Ct's Note]** St. Paul has not argued in this case that the ordinance merely regulates that subclass of fighting words which is most likely to provoke a violent response. But even if one assumes (as appears unlikely) that the categories selected may be so described, that would not justify selective regulation under a "secondary effects" theory. The only reason why such expressive conduct would be especially correlated with violence is that it conveys a particularly odious message; because the "chain of causation" thus *necessarily* "run[s] through the persuasive effect of the expressive component" of the conduct, it is clear that the St. Paul ordinance regulates on the basis of the "primary" effect of the speech—i.e., its persuasive (or repellent) force.

the city council's special hostility towards the particular biases thus singled out. That is precisely what the First Amendment forbids. The politicians of St. Paul are entitled to express that hostility—but not through the means of imposing unique limitations upon speakers who (however benightedly) disagree. * * *

Let there be no mistake about our belief that burning a cross in someone's front yard is reprehensible. But St. Paul has sufficient means at its disposal to prevent such behavior without adding the First Amendment to the fire. * * *

JUSTICE WHITE, with whom JUSTICE BLACKMUN and JUSTICE O'CONNOR join, and with whom JUSTICE STEVENS joins except as to Part I(A), concurring in the judgment. * * *

I.A. [T]he majority holds that the First Amendment protects those narrow categories of expression long held to be undeserving of First Amendment protection—at least to the extent that lawmakers may not regulate some fighting words more strictly than others because of their content. [Should] the government want to criminalize certain fighting words, the Court now requires it to criminalize all fighting words.

To borrow a phrase, "Such a simplistic, all-or-nothing-at-all approach to First Amendment protection is at odds with common sense and with our jurisprudence as well." It is inconsistent to hold that the government may proscribe an entire category of speech because the content of that speech is evil, but that the government may not treat a subset of that category differently without violating the First Amendment; the content of the subset is by definition worthless and undeserving of constitutional protection.

The majority's observation that fighting words are "quite expressive indeed," is no answer. Fighting words are not a means of exchanging views, rallying supporters, or registering a protest; they are directed against individuals to provoke violence or to inflict injury. Therefore, a ban on all fighting words or on a subset of the fighting words category would restrict only the social evil of hate speech, without creating the danger of driving viewpoints from the marketplace.

Therefore, the Court's insistence on inventing its brand of First Amendment underinclusiveness puzzles me.[3] [T]he Court's new "underbreadth" creation [invites] the continuation of expressive conduct that in this case is evil and worthless in First Amendment terms until the city of St. Paul cures the underbreadth by adding to its ordinance a catch-

---

[3]   [Ct's Note] The assortment of exceptions the Court attaches to its rule belies the majority's claim that its new theory is truly concerned with content discrimination. See Part I(C), infra (discussing the exceptions).

all phrase such as "and all other fighting words that may constitutionally be subject to this ordinance."

Any contribution of this holding to First Amendment jurisprudence is surely a negative one, since it necessarily signals that expressions of violence, such as the message of intimidation and racial hatred conveyed by burning a cross on someone's lawn, are of sufficient value to outweigh the social interest in order and morality that has traditionally placed such fighting words outside the First Amendment.[4] Indeed, by characterizing fighting words as a form of "debate" the majority legitimates hate speech as a form of public discussion. * * *

B.   [Although] the First Amendment does not apply to categories of unprotected speech, such as fighting words, the Equal Protection Clause requires that the regulation of unprotected speech be rationally related to a legitimate government interest. A defamation statute that drew distinctions on the basis of political affiliation or "an ordinance prohibiting only those legally obscene works that contain criticism of the city government" would unquestionably fail rational basis review.[9]

Turning to the St. Paul ordinance and assuming arguendo, as the majority does, that the ordinance is not constitutionally overbroad (but see Part II, infra), there is no question that it would pass equal protection review. The ordinance [reflects] the City's judgment that harms based on race, color, creed, religion, or gender are more pressing public concerns than the harms caused by other fighting words. In light of our Nation's long and painful experience with discrimination, this determination is plainly reasonable. Indeed, as the majority concedes, the interest is compelling.

C.   The Court has patched up its argument with an apparently nonexhaustive list of ad hoc exceptions, in what can be viewed either as an attempt to confine the effects of its decision to the facts of this case, or as an effort to anticipate some of the questions that will arise from its radical revision of First Amendment law. * * *

To save the statute [making it illegal to threaten the life of the President], the majority has engrafted the following exception onto its newly announced First Amendment rule: Content-based distinctions may

---

4   [Ct's Note] This does not suggest, of course, that cross burning is always unprotected. Burning a cross at a political rally would almost certainly be protected expression. Cf. *Brandenburg.* But in such a context, the cross burning could not be characterized as a "direct personal insult or an invitation to exchange fisticuffs," *Texas v. Johnson,* to which the fighting words doctrine.

9   [Ct's Note] The majority is mistaken in stating that a ban on obscene works critical of government would fail equal protection review only because the ban would violate the First Amendment. While decisions such as *Mosley* recognize that First Amendment principles may be relevant to an equal protection claim challenging distinctions that impact on protected expression, there is no basis for linking First and Fourteenth Amendment analysis in a case involving unprotected expression. Certainly, one need not resort to First Amendment principles to conclude that the sort of improbable legislation the majority hypothesizes is based on senseless distinctions.

be drawn within an unprotected category of speech if the basis for the distinctions is "the very reason the entire class of speech at issue is proscribable." * * *

The exception swallows the majority's rule. Certainly, it should apply to the St. Paul ordinance, since "the reasons why [fighting words] are outside the First Amendment [have] special force when applied to [groups that have historically been subjected to discrimination]."

To avoid the result of its own analysis, the Court suggests that fighting words are simply a mode of communication, rather than a content-based category, and that the St. Paul ordinance has not singled out a particularly objectionable mode of communication. Again, the majority confuses the issue. A prohibition on fighting words is not a time, place, or manner restriction; it is a ban on a class of speech that conveys an overriding message of personal injury and imminent violence, a message that is at its ugliest when directed against groups that have long been the targets of discrimination. Accordingly, the ordinance falls within the first exception to the majority's theory.

As its second exception, the Court posits that certain content-based regulations will survive under the new regime if the regulated subclass "happens to be associated with particular 'secondary effects' of the speech" which the majority treats as encompassing instances in which "words [can] violate laws directed not against speech but against conduct."[11] Again, there is a simple explanation for the Court's eagerness to craft an exception to its new First Amendment rule: Under the general rule the Court applies in this case, Title VII hostile work environment claims would suddenly be unconstitutional.

Title VII * * * regulations covering hostile workplace claims forbid "sexual harassment," which includes "[u]nwelcome sexual advances, requests for sexual favors, and other verbal or physical conduct of a sexual nature" which creates "an intimidating, hostile, or offensive working environment." The regulation does not prohibit workplace harassment generally; it focuses on what the majority would characterize as the "disfavored topi[c]" of sexual harassment. In this way, Title VII is similar to the St. Paul ordinance that the majority condemns because it "impose[s] special prohibitions on those speakers who express views on disfavored subjects." * * *

Hence, the majority's second exception, which the Court indicates would insulate a Title VII hostile work environment claim from an underinclusiveness challenge because "sexually derogatory 'fighting words'

---

[11] **[Ct's Note]** The consequences of the majority's conflation of the rarely-used secondary effects standard and the *O'Brien* test for conduct incorporating "speech" and "nonspeech" elements, see generally *O'Brien,* present another question that I fear will haunt us and the lower courts in the aftermath of the majority's opinion.

[may] produce a violation of Title VII's general prohibition against sexual discrimination in employment practices." But application of this exception to a hostile work environment claim does not hold up under close examination.

First, the hostile work environment regulation is not keyed to the presence or absence of an economic quid pro quo, but to the impact of the speech on the victimized worker. Consequently, the regulation would no more fall within a secondary effects exception than does the St. Paul ordinance. Second, the majority's focus on the statute's general prohibition on discrimination glosses over the language of the specific regulation governing hostile working environment, which reaches beyond any "incidental" effect on speech. If the relationship between the broader statute and specific regulation is sufficient to bring the Title VII regulation within *O'Brien,* then all St. Paul need do to bring its ordinance within this exception is to add some prefatory language concerning discrimination generally.

As the third exception to the Court's theory for deciding this case, the majority concocts a catchall exclusion to protect against unforeseen problems. [It] would apply in cases in which "there is no realistic possibility that official suppression of ideas is afoot." As I have demonstrated, this case does not concern the official suppression of ideas. The majority discards this notion out-of-hand. * * *

II.   * * * I would decide the case on overbreadth grounds. * * *

In construing the St. Paul ordinance, [I understand the Minnesota Supreme Court] to have ruled that St. Paul may constitutionally prohibit expression that "by its very utterance" causes "anger, alarm or resentment." Our fighting words cases have made clear, however, that [t]he mere fact that expressive activity causes hurt feelings, offense, or resentment does not render the expression unprotected. See *Eichman; Texas v. Johnson; Falwell.* * * * [13] The ordinance is therefore fatally overbroad and invalid on its face.

JUSTICE BLACKMUN, concurring in the judgment.

[B]y deciding that a State cannot regulate speech that causes great harm unless it also regulates speech that does not (setting law and logic on their heads), the Court seems to abandon the categorical approach, and inevitably to relax the level of scrutiny applicable to content-based laws. [The] simple reality is that the Court will never provide child pornography or cigarette advertising the level of protection customarily granted political

---

[13] **[Ct's Note]** Although the First Amendment protects offensive speech, it does not require us to be subjected to such expression at all times, in all settings. We have held that such expression may be proscribed when it intrudes upon a "captive audience." And expression may be limited when it merges into conduct. *O'Brien.* However, because of the manner in which the Minnesota Supreme Court construed the St. Paul ordinance, those issues are not before us in this case.

speech. If we are forbidden from categorizing, as the Court has done here, we shall reduce protection across the board. * * *

[There] is the possibility that this case will not significantly alter First Amendment jurisprudence, but, instead, will be regarded as an aberration—a case where the Court manipulated doctrine to strike down an ordinance whose premise it opposed, namely, that racial threats and verbal assaults are of greater harm than other fighting words. I fear that the Court has been distracted from its proper mission by the temptation to decide the issue over "politically correct speech" and "cultural diversity," neither of which is presented here. If this is the meaning of today's opinion, it is perhaps even more regrettable.

I see no First Amendment values that are compromised by a law that prohibits hoodlums from driving minorities out of their homes by burning crosses on their lawns, but I see great harm in preventing the people of Saint Paul from specifically punishing the race-based fighting words that so prejudice their community. * * *

JUSTICE STEVENS, with whom JUSTICE WHITE and JUSTICE BLACKMUN join as to Part I, concurring in the judgment. * * *

I.   [Our] First Amendment decisions have created a rough hierarchy in the constitutional protection of speech. Core political speech occupies the highest, most protected position; commercial speech and nonobscene, sexually explicit speech are regarded as a sort of second-class expression; obscenity and fighting words receive the least protection of all. Assuming that the Court is correct that this last class of speech is not wholly "unprotected," it certainly does not follow that fighting words and obscenity receive the *same* sort of protection afforded core political speech. Yet in ruling that proscribable speech cannot be regulated based on subject matter, the Court does just that. Perversely, this gives fighting words *greater* protection than is afforded commercial speech. If Congress can prohibit false advertising directed at airline passengers without also prohibiting false advertising directed at bus passengers and if a city can prohibit political advertisements in its buses while allowing other advertisements, it is ironic to hold that a city cannot regulate fighting words based on "race, color, creed, religion or gender" while leaving unregulated fighting words based on "union membership or homosexuality." * * * Perhaps because the Court recognizes these perversities, it quickly offers some ad hoc limitations on its newly extended prohibition on content-based regulations.[195]

---

[195] In an earlier passage and footnote of his opinion, Stevens, J., argued: "[W]hile the Court rejects the 'all-or-nothing-at-all' nature of the categorical approach, it promptly embraces an absolutism of its own: within a particular 'proscribable' category of expression, the Court holds, a government must either proscribe all speech or no speech at all. The Court disputes this characterization because it has crafted two exceptions, one for 'certain media or markets' and the other for content discrimination based upon 'the very reason that the entire class of speech at issue

[T]he Court recognizes that a State may regulate advertising in one industry but not another because "the risk of fraud (one of the characteristics that justifies depriving [commercial speech] of full First Amendment protection)" in the regulated industry is "greater" than in other industries. "[O]ne of the characteristics that justifies" the constitutional status of fighting words is that such words "by their very utterance inflict injury or tend to incite an immediate breach of the peace." *Chaplinsky.* Certainly a legislature that may determine that the risk of fraud is greater in the legal trade than in the medical trade may determine that the risk of injury or breach of peace created by race-based threats is greater than that created by other threats.

Similarly, it is impossible to reconcile the Court's analysis of the St. Paul ordinance with its recognition that "a prohibition of fighting words that are directed at certain persons or groups [would] be facially valid." A selective proscription of unprotected expression designed to protect "certain persons or groups" (for example, a law proscribing threats directed at the elderly) would be constitutional if it were based on a legitimate determination that the harm created by the regulated expression differs from that created by the unregulated expression (that is, if the elderly are more severely injured by threats than are the nonelderly). Such selective protection is no different from a law prohibiting minors (and only minors) from obtaining obscene publications. St. Paul has determined—reasonably in my judgment—that fighting-word injuries "based on race, color, creed, religion or gender" are qualitatively different and more severe than fighting-word injuries based on other characteristics. Whether the selective proscription of proscribable speech is defined by the protected target ("certain persons or groups") or the basis of the harm (injuries "based on race, color, creed, religion or gender") makes no constitutional difference: what matters is whether the legislature's selection is based on a legitimate, neutral, and reasonable distinction. * * *

III. [Unlike] the Court, I do not believe that all content-based regulations are equally infirm and presumptively invalid; unlike Justice White, I do not believe that fighting words are wholly unprotected by the First Amendment. To the contrary, I believe our decisions establish a more complex and subtle analysis, one that considers the content and context of the regulated speech, and the nature and scope of the restriction on speech. * * * Whatever the allure of absolute doctrines, it is just too simple to

---

is proscribable.' These exceptions are, at best, ill-defined. The Court does not tell us whether, with respect to the former, fighting words such as cross-burning could be proscribed only in certain neighborhoods where the threat of violence is particularly severe, or whether, with respect to the second category, fighting words that create a particular risk of harm (such as a race riot) would be proscribable. The hypothetical and illusory category of these two exceptions persuades me that either my description of the Court's analysis is accurate or that the Court does not in fact mean much of what it says in its opinion."

declare expression "protected" or "unprotected" or to proclaim a regulation "content-based" or "content-neutral."

In applying this analysis to the St. Paul ordinance, I assume arguendo—as the Court does—that the ordinance regulates *only* fighting words and therefore is *not* overbroad. Looking to the content and character of the regulated activity, two things are clear. First, by hypothesis the ordinance bars only low-value speech, namely, fighting words. * * * Second, the ordinance regulates "expressive conduct [rather] than [the] written or spoken word."

Looking to the context of the regulated activity, it is again significant that the statute (by hypothesis) regulates *only* fighting words. Whether words are fighting words is determined in part by their context. Fighting words are not words that merely cause offense; fighting words must be directed at individuals so as to "by their very utterance inflict injury." By hypothesis, then, the St. Paul ordinance restricts speech in confrontational and potentially violent situations. The case at hand is illustrative. The cross-burning in this case—directed as it was to a single African-American family trapped in their home—was nothing more than a crude form of physical intimidation. That this cross-burning sends a message of racial hostility does not automatically endow it with complete constitutional protection.

Significantly, the St. Paul ordinance regulates speech not on the basis of its subject matter or the viewpoint expressed, but rather on the basis of the *harm* the speech causes. * * * Contrary to the Court's suggestion, the ordinance regulates only a subcategory of expression that causes *injuries based on* "race, color, creed, religion or gender," not a subcategory that involves *discussions* that concern those characteristics.[9] * * *

Finally, it is noteworthy that the St. Paul ordinance is, as construed by the Court today, quite narrow. The St. Paul ordinance does not ban all "hate speech," nor does it ban, say, all cross-burnings or all swastika displays. Rather it only bans a subcategory of the already narrow category of fighting words. Such a limited ordinance leaves open and protected a vast range of expression on the subjects of racial, religious, and gender equality. As construed by the Court today, the ordinance certainly does not

---

[9] **[Ct's Note]** The Court contends that this distinction is "wordplay," reasoning that "[w]hat makes [the harms caused by race-based threats] distinct from [the harms] produced by other fighting words [is] the fact that [the former are] caused by a *distinctive idea*." In this way, the Court concludes that regulating speech based on the injury it causes is no different from regulating speech based on its subject matter. This analysis fundamentally miscomprehends the role of "race, color, creed, religion [and] gender" in contemporary American society. One need look no further than the recent social unrest in the Nation's cities to see that race-based threats may cause more harm to society and to individuals than other threats. Just as the statute prohibiting threats against the President is justifiable because of the place of the President in our social and political order, so a statute prohibiting race-based threats is justifiable because of the place of race in our social and political order. [S]uch a place and is so incendiary an issue, until the Nation matures beyond that condition, laws such as St. Paul's ordinance will remain reasonable and justifiable.

" 'raise the specter that the Government may effectively drive certain ideas or viewpoints from the marketplace.' " Petitioner is free to burn a cross to announce a rally or to express his views about racial supremacy, he may do so on private property or public land, at day or at night, so long as the burning is not so threatening and so directed at an individual as to "by its very [execution] inflict injury." Such a limited proscription scarcely offends the First Amendment. * * *[196]

NOTES AND QUESTIONS

1. ***The harm of insults based on race, gender, and religion.*** Consider Steven J. Heyman, *Spheres of Autonomy: Reforming the Content Neutrality Doctrine in First Amendment Jurisprudence*, 10 Wm. & Mary Bill Rts. J. 647 (2002): "How should we answer the critical question in *R.A.V.*? Do insults based on race, gender, and religion cause greater injury than insults in general? [First,] unlike insults that express merely personal dislike, group-based insults often deny the very humanity of those against whom they are directed. In this way, they inflict a deeper injury on their targets. Second, in an important sense, group-based insults are directed not only against specific individuals, but also against the group in general. For this reason, they may inflict injury on a greater number of people, and may tend to provoke violence on a broader scale. By exacerbating tensions between groups, such insults also tend to cause greater harm to the community as a whole. And all of these injuries are heightened when the insults are directed against members of groups that have historically been subjected to discrimination and oppression."

2. ***The harm of cross burning.*** Can cross burning be understood as a particularly virulent form of fighting words? Consider Michel Rosenfeld, *Hate Speech in Constitutional Jurisprudence: A Comparative Analysis*, 24 Cardozo L. Rev. 1523 (2003): [T]hough both the proposed march in *Skokie* and the cross burning in *R.A.V.* were meant to incite hatred on the basis of religion and race respectively, their effects were quite different. *Skokie* mainly produced contempt for the marchers and a reminder that there was little danger of an embrace of Nazism in the United States. *R.A.V.*, on the other hand, played on pervasive, and to a significant degree justified, fears concerning race relations in America. Undoubtedly, cross burning itself is rejected as repugnant by the vast majority of Americans. The underlying racism associated with it, and the message that blacks should remain in their own segregated neighborhoods, however, unfortunately still have adherents among a non-negligible portion of whites in America."

---

[196] For background on *R.A.V.*, see Edward Cleary, *Beyond the Burning Cross* (1994). For additional commentary, see Symposium, *Hate Speech After R.A.V.: More Conflict Between Free Speech and Equality*, 18 Wm. Mitchell L.Rev. 889 (1992); Akhil Amar, *The Case of the Missing Amendments*, 106 Harv.L.Rev. 124 (1992); Joshua Cohen, *Freedom of Expression*, 22 Phil. & Pub.Aff. 207 (1993); Elena Kagan, *The Changing Faces of First Amendment Neutrality*, 1992 Sup.Ct.Rev. 29; Elena Kagan, *Regulation of Hate Speech and Pornography After R.A.V.*, 60 U.Chi.L.Rev. 873 (1993); Charles Lawrence, *Crossburning and the Sound of Silence*, 37 Vill.L.Rev. 787 (1992).

Could the arguments applicable to cross-burning apply as well to wearing Ku Klux Klan regalia?

3.   (a) At the capital sentencing phase of a murder case, the prosecution sought to introduce evidence that the defendant was a member of the Aryan Brotherhood which was stipulated to be a "white racist gang."

DAWSON v. DELAWARE, 503 U.S. 159 (1992), per REHNQUIST, C.J., held that its admission violated the First Amendment: "Even if the Delaware group to which Dawson allegedly belongs is racist, those beliefs, so far as we can determine, had no relevance to the sentencing proceeding in this case. For example, the Aryan Brotherhood evidence was not tied in any way to the murder of Dawson's [white] victim. [Moreover], we conclude that Dawson's First Amendment rights were violated by the admission of the Aryan Brotherhood evidence in this case, because the evidence proved nothing more than Dawson's abstract beliefs. [Delaware] might have avoided this problem if it had presented evidence showing more than mere abstract beliefs on Dawson's part, but on the present record one is left with the feeling that the Aryan Brotherhood evidence was employed simply because the jury would find these beliefs morally reprehensible."

THOMAS, J., dissented: "Dawson introduced mitigating character evidence that he had acted kindly toward his family. The stipulation tended to undercut this showing by suggesting that Dawson's kindness did not extend to members of other racial groups. Although we do not sit in judgment of the morality of particular creeds, we cannot bend traditional concepts of relevance to exempt the antisocial."

(b)   WISCONSIN v. MITCHELL, 508 U.S. 476 (1993), per REHNQUIST, C.J., found no First Amendment violation when Wisconsin permitted a sentence for aggravated battery to be enhanced on the ground that the white victim had been selected because of his race. The Court observed that, unlike *R.A.V.*, the Wisconsin statute was aimed at conduct, not speech, that a chilling effect on speech was unlikely, that the focus on motive was no different from that employed in anti-discrimination statutes, and that bias-inspired conduct is more likely "to provoke retaliatory crimes, inflict distinct emotional harms on their victims, and incite community unrest." Consistent with *R.A.V.*?[197] After *Mitchell*, could the state "enact a general regulation against the use of fighting words, and then have a sentence enhancement based on racial motivation"? See Daniel A. Farber, *The First Amendment* 115 (1998): "There

---

[197] See Frederick Lawrence, *Punishing Hate: Bias Crimes Under American Law* (1999); James B. Jacobs & Kimberly Potter, *Hate Crimes, Criminal Law and Identity Politics* (1998); Alon Herel & Gideon Parchomovsky, *On Hate and Equality,* 109 Yale L.J 507 (1999); Alan E. Brownstein, *Rules of Engagement for Cultural Wars,* 29 U.C. Davis L.Rev. 553 (1996); Susan Gellman, *Sticks and Stones Can Put You in Jail, But Can Words Increase Your Sentence?,* 39 U.C.L.A.L.Rev. 333 (1991); See generally Laurence Tribe, *The Mystery of Motive, Private and Public: Some Notes Inspired by the Problems of Hate Crime and Animal Sacrifice,* 1993 Sup.Ct.Rev. 1.

seems to be a reasonable argument for distinguishing *R.A.V.* even when the enhancement is applied to a speech-based regulation."[198]

4.   Consider Elena Kagan, *Private Speech, Public Purpose: The Role of Governmental Motive in First Amendment Doctrine,* 63 U.Chi.L.Rev. 413 (1996): "[H]alf hidden beneath a swirl of doctrinal formulations, the crux of the dispute between the majority and the concurring opinions concerned the proper understanding of St. Paul's motive in enacting its hate-speech law. The majority understood this motive as purely censorial—a simple desire to blot out ideas of which the government or a majority of its citizens disapproved. The concurring Justices saw something different: an effort by the government, divorced from mere hostility toward ideas, to counter a severe and objectively ascertainable harm caused by (one form of) an idea's expression."

5.   In distinguishing Title VII law, Scalia, J., states that if government does not target discriminatory conduct on the basis of its expressive content, government may regulate, apparently without First Amendment scrutiny, even if the conduct expresses a discriminatory idea or philosophy. Is this consistent with *O'Brien?* The opinions in *Barnes* other than Scalia, J.'s? Suppose St. Paul outlawed all conduct that tended to create a racially or sexually hostile environment. Consider Richard Fallon, *Sexual Harassment, Content Neutrality, and the First Amendment Dog That Didn't Bark,* 1994 Sup.Ct.Rev. 1: "A statute of this kind, which would restrict the press, political orators, and private citizens engaged in conversation in their homes, would surely offend the First Amendment. Certainly Justice Scalia [does] not believe otherwise." Could St. Paul outlaw racial harassment under Scalia, J.'s rationale and apply it to the facts of *R.A.V.* without First Amendment scrutiny?

Are many applications of sexual harassment law problematic under the First Amendment?[199]

6.   After *R.A.V.*, what is (should be) the constitutional status of statutes imposing "penalties for filing false complaints against police officers, bans on

---

[198] California's anti-paparazzi legislation provides stiffer penalties for trespass if the purpose is to photograph or videotape someone without their permission. Constitutional?

[199] For a variety of views, see *Directions in Sexual Harassment Law* (MacKinnon & Siegel eds., 2003); Kent Greenawalt, *Fighting Words* 77–96 (1995); J.M. Balkin, *Free Speech and Hostile Environments,* 99 Colum. L.Rev. 2295 (1999); Kingsley Browne, *Title VII as Censorship: Hostile-Environment Harassment and the First Amendment,* 52 Ohio St.L.J. 481 (1991); Cynthia L. Estlund, *Freedom of Expression in the Workplace and the Problem of Discriminatory Harassment,* 75 Texas L.Rev. 687 (1997); Cynthia L. Estlund, *The Architecture of the First Amendment and the Case of Workplace Harassment,* 72 Notre D. L.Rev. 1361 (1997); Fallon, supra; Jules B. Gerard, *The First Amendment in a Hostile Environment: A Primer on Free Speech and Sexual Harassment,* 68 Notre D.L.Rev. 579 (1995); Linda S. Greene, *Sexual Harassment Law and the First Amendment,* 71 Chi.-Kent L.Rev. 729 (1995); Susanne Sangree, *Title VII Prohibitions Against Hostile Environment Sexual Harassment and the First Amendment: No Collision in Sight,* 47 Rutgers L.Rev. 461 (1995); Marcy Strauss, *Sexist Speech in the Workplace,* 25 Harv.C.R.-C.L.L.Rev. 1 (1990); Nadine Strossen, *Regulating Workplace Sexual Harassment and Upholding the First Amendment—Avoiding a Collision,* 37 Vill. L.Rev. 757 (1992); Eugene Volokh, *Freedom of Speech and Workplace Harassment,* 39 UCLA.L.Rev. 1791 (1992); Eugene Volokh, *How Harassment Law Restricts Free Speech,* 47 Rutgers L.Rev. 563 (1995); Eugene Volokh, *What Speech Does "Hostile Work Environment" Harassment Law Restrict?,* 85 Geo. L.J. 627 (1997). See also *Davis v. Monroe County Board of Educ.,* 526 U.S. 629 (1999) (Kennedy, J., dissenting).

defamatory statements about political candidates, prohibitions on falsely imputing unchastity to women, and civil liability for defamation of agricultural products." See Nat Stern, *The Doubtful Validity of Victim-Specific Libel Laws,* 52 Vill. L.Rev. 533 (2007).

————

In 1952, Virginia declared it a felony publicly to burn a cross with the intent of intimidating any person or group of persons. In 1968, Virginia added a provision that any such burning shall be prima facie evidence of an intent to intimidate. Barry Black led a Ku Klux Klan rally in which a cross was burned after a series of speeches marked by racial hostility, including one speaker saying that he "would love to take a .30/.30 and just random[ly] shoot the blacks." Forty to fifty cars passed the site during the rally, and eight to ten houses were located in its vicinity. The trial court used a Virginia Model Instruction that "the burning of a cross by itself is sufficient evidence from which you may infer the required intent."

Richard Elliot and Jonathan O'Mara attempted to burn a cross at the residence of an African-American. O'Mara pled guilty of attempted burning, reserving the right to challenge the statute; Elliot was convicted in a trial in which the jury was instructed that the Commonwealth had to show the intent to burn the cross and the intent to intimidate. The trial court did not instruct on the meaning of the prima facie provision of the statute, nor did it give the Model Instruction.

The Virginia Supreme Court declared the statute unconstitutional in light of *R.A.V.* and overturned the convictions of the three defendants.

VIRGINIA v. BLACK, 538 U.S. 343 (2003), per O'CONNOR, J., upheld the cross burning with intent to intimidate provision, struck down the prima facie evidence provision as interpreted by the jury instruction in the Black case, and, thereby, affirmed the dismissal of Black's prosecution while vacating and remanding for further proceedings with respect to Elliot and O'Mara: "[T]he First Amendment [permits] a State to ban a 'true threat.' [*Watts.*, Sec. 1, I, D, note 7 supra.] Intimidation in the constitutionally proscribable sense of the word is a type of true threat. [The] First Amendment permits Virginia to outlaw cross burnings done with the intent to intimidate because burning a cross is a particularly virulent form of intimidation. Instead of prohibiting all intimidating messages, Virginia may choose to regulate this subset of intimidating messages in light of cross burning's long and pernicious history as a signal of impending violence. Thus, just as a State may regulate only that obscenity which is the most obscene due to its prurient content, so too may a State choose to prohibit only those forms of intimidation that are most likely to inspire fear of bodily harm. A ban on cross burning carried out with the intent to intimidate is fully consistent with our holding in *R.A.V.* and is proscribable under the First Amendment."

In a section of the opinion joined by Rehnquist, C.J., Stevens and Breyer, JJ., O'Connor, J., addressed the prima facie evidence provision: "The Supreme Court of Virginia has not ruled on the meaning of the prima facie evidence provision. It has, however, stated that 'the act of burning a cross alone, with no evidence of intent to intimidate, will nonetheless suffice for arrest and prosecution and will insulate the Commonwealth from a motion to strike the evidence at the end of its case-in-chief.' The jury in the case of Richard Elliott did not receive any instruction on the prima facie evidence provision, and the provision was not an issue in the case of Jonathan O'Mara because he pleaded guilty. The court in Barry Black's case, however, instructed the jury that the provision means: 'The burning of a cross, by itself, is sufficient evidence from which you may infer the required intent.'

"The prima facie evidence provision, as interpreted by the jury instruction, renders the statute unconstitutional. Because this jury instruction is the Model Jury Instruction, and because the Supreme Court of Virginia had the opportunity to expressly disavow the jury instruction, the jury instruction's construction of the prima facie provision 'is a ruling on a question of state law that is as binding on us as though the precise words had been written into' the statute. [As] construed by the jury instruction, the prima facie provision strips away the very reason why a State may ban cross burning with the intent to intimidate. The prima facie evidence provision permits a jury to convict in every cross-burning case in which defendants exercise their constitutional right not to put on a defense. And even where a defendant like Black presents a defense, the prima facie evidence provision makes it more likely that the jury will find an intent to intimidate regardless of the particular facts of the case. The provision permits the Commonwealth to arrest, prosecute, and convict a person based solely on the fact of cross burning itself.

"The act of burning a cross may mean that a person is engaging in constitutionally proscribable intimidation. But that same act may mean only that the person is engaged in core political speech. The prima facie evidence provision in this statute blurs the line between these two meanings of a burning cross. As interpreted by the jury instruction, the provision chills constitutionally protected political speech because of the possibility that a State will prosecute—and potentially convict—somebody engaging only in lawful political speech at the core of what the First Amendment is designed to protect. * * *

"For these reasons, the prima facie evidence provision, as interpreted through the jury instruction and as applied in Barry Black's case, is unconstitutional on its face. We recognize that the Supreme Court of Virginia has not authoritatively interpreted the meaning of the prima facie evidence provision. Unlike Justice Scalia, we refuse to speculate on whether *any* interpretation of the prima facie evidence provision would satisfy the First Amendment. Rather, all we hold is that because of the interpretation of the prima facie evidence provision given by the jury instruction, the provision makes the statute facially invalid at this point. We also recognize the theoretical possibility that the court, on remand, could interpret the provision in a manner different from that so far set forth in order to avoid the constitutional objections we have described. We leave open that possibility. We also leave open the possibility that the provision is severable, and if so, whether Elliott and O'Mara could be retried * * * .

"With respect to Barry Black, we agree with the Supreme Court of Virginia that his conviction cannot stand, and we affirm the judgment of the Supreme Court of Virginia. With respect to Elliott and O'Mara, we vacate the judgment of the Supreme Court of Virginia, and remand the case for further proceedings."

SCALIA, J., joined by Thomas, J., concurring and dissenting, agreed that the cross burning/intimidation portion of the statute was constitutional, but he denied that the prima facie evidence aspect of the statute was unconstitutional on its face. In a portion of his opinion not joined by Thomas, J., Scalia J., nonetheless concurred with the plurality's view that that the jury instruction was invalid: "I believe the prima-facie-evidence provision in Virginia's cross-burning statute is constitutionally unproblematic. Nevertheless, because the Virginia Supreme Court has not yet offered an authoritative construction of [that provision], I concur in the Court's decision to vacate and remand the judgment with respect to respondents Elliott and O'Mara. I also agree that respondent Black's conviction cannot stand. As noted above, the jury in Black's case was instructed that '[t]he burning of a cross, *by itself,* is sufficient evidence from which you may infer the required intent.' Where this instruction has been given, it is impossible to determine whether the jury has rendered its verdict (as it must) in light of the entire body of facts before it—*including* evidence that might rebut the presumption that the cross burning was done with an intent to intimidate—or, instead, has chosen to ignore such rebuttal evidence and focused exclusively on the fact that the defendant burned a cross. Still, I cannot go along with the Court's decision to affirm the judgment with respect to Black. In that judgment, the Virginia Supreme Court, having erroneously concluded that § 18.2–423 is overbroad, not only vacated Black's conviction, but dismissed the indictment against him as well. Because I believe the constitutional defect in Black's conviction is rooted in a jury instruction and not in the statute itself, I would not dismiss the indictment and would permit the Commonwealth to retry Black if it wishes to do so. It is an interesting question whether the plurality's willingness to let the Virginia Supreme Court resolve the plurality's make-believe facial invalidation of the statute extends as well to the facial invalidation insofar as it supports dismissal of the indictment against Black. Logically, there is no reason why it would not."

SOUTER, J., joined by Kennedy and Ginsburg, JJ., concurring in part and dissenting in part, argued that both the cross burning/intimidation section and the prima facie evidence section were unconstitutional: "I agree with the majority that the Virginia statute makes a content-based distinction within the category of punishable intimidating or threatening expression, the very type of distinction we considered in *R.A.V.* I disagree that any exception should save Virginia's law from unconstitutionality under the holding in *R.A.V.* or any acceptable variation of it. [Because] of the burning cross's extraordinary force as a method of intimidation, the *R.A.V.* exception most likely to cover the statute is the first of the three mentioned there, which the *R.A.V.* opinion called an exception for content discrimination on a basis that 'consists entirely of the very reason the entire class of speech at issue is proscribable.' This is the exception the majority speaks of here as covering statutes prohibiting 'particularly virulent' proscribable expression. [*RAV*] explained that when the subcategory is confined to the most obviously proscribable instances, 'no significant danger of idea or viewpoint discrimination exists,' and the explanation was rounded out with some illustrative examples. None of them, however, resembles the case before us.

"[One example] of permissible distinction is for a prohibition of obscenity unusually offensive 'in its prurience,' with citation to a case in which the Seventh Circuit discussed the difference between obscene depictions of actual people and simulations. As that court noted, distinguishing obscene publications on this basis does not suggest discrimination on the basis of the message conveyed. *Kucharek v. Hanaway,* 902 F.2d 513 (7th Cir. 1990). The opposite is true, however, when a general prohibition of intimidation is rejected in favor of a distinct proscription of intimidation by cross burning. The cross may have been selected because of its special power to threaten, but it may also have been singled out because of disapproval of its message of white supremacy, either because a legislature thought white supremacy was a pernicious doctrine or because it found that dramatic, public espousal of it was a civic embarrassment. Thus, there is no kinship between the cross-burning statute and the core prurience example. * * *

"The majority's approach could be taken as recognizing an exception to *R.A.V.* when circumstances show that the statute's ostensibly valid reason for punishing particularly serious proscribable expression probably is not a ruse for message suppression, even though the statute may have a greater (but not exclusive) impact on adherents of one ideology than on others. * * *

SEC. 3

IS SOME PROTECTED SPEECH LESS EQUAL THAN
OTHER PROTECTED SPEECH?

949

"My concern here, in any event, is not with the merit of a pragmatic doctrinal move. For whether or not the Court should conceive of exceptions to *R.A.V.*'s general rule in a more practical way, no content-based statute should survive even under a pragmatic recasting of *R.A.V.* without a high probability that no 'official suppression of ideas is afoot,' I believe the prima facie evidence provision stands in the way of any finding of such a high probability here. * * *

"As I see the likely significance of the evidence provision, its primary effect is to skew jury deliberations toward conviction in cases where the evidence of intent to intimidate is relatively weak and arguably consistent with a solely ideological reason for burning. To understand how the provision may work, recall that the symbolic act of burning a cross, without more, is consistent with both intent to intimidate and intent to make an ideological statement free of any aim to threaten. One can tell the intimidating instance from the wholly ideological one only by reference to some further circumstance. In the real world, of course, and in real-world prosecutions, there will always be further circumstances, and the factfinder will always learn something more than the isolated fact of cross burning. Sometimes those circumstances will show an intent to intimidate, but sometimes they will be at least equivocal, as in cases where a white supremacist group burns a cross at an initiation ceremony or political rally visible to the public. In such a case, if the factfinder Black's case is aware of the prima facie evidence provision, as the jury was in respondent, the provision will have the practical effect of tilting the jury's thinking in favor of the prosecution. [The] provision will thus tend to draw nonthreatening ideological expression within the ambit of the prohibition of intimidating expression. * * *

"To the extent the prima facie evidence provision skews prosecutions, then, it skews the statute toward suppressing ideas. Thus, the appropriate way to consider the statute's prima facie evidence term, in my view, is not as if it were an overbroad statutory definition amenable to severance or a narrowing construction. The question here is not the permissible scope of an arguably overbroad statute, but the claim of a clearly content-based statute to an exception from the general prohibition of content-based proscriptions, an exception that is not warranted if the statute's terms show that suppression of ideas may be afoot. Accordingly, the way to look at the prima facie evidence provision is to consider it for any indication of what is afoot. And if we look at the provision for this purpose, it has a very obvious significance as a mechanism for bringing within the statute's prohibition some expression that is doubtfully threatening though certainly distasteful.

"It is difficult to conceive of an intimidation case that could be easier to prove than one with cross burning, assuming any circumstances suggesting intimidation are present. The provision, apparently so unnecessary to legitimate prosecution of intimidation, is therefore quite enough to raise the question whether Virginia's content-based statute seeks more than mere protection against a virulent form of intimidation. It consequently bars any conclusion that an exception to the general rule of *R.A.V.* is warranted on the ground 'that there is no realistic [or little realistic] possibility that official suppression of ideas is afoot.'

"I conclude that the statute under which all three of the respondents were prosecuted violates the First Amendment, since the statute's content-based distinction was invalid at the time of the charged activities, regardless of whether the prima facie evidence provision was given any effect in any respondent's individual case. In my view, severance of the prima facie evidence provision now could not eliminate the unconstitutionality of the whole statute at the time of the respondents' conduct. I would therefore affirm the judgment of the Supreme Court of Virginia vacating the respondents' convictions and dismissing the indictments. Accordingly, I concur in the Court's judgment as to respondent Black and dissent as to respondents Elliott and O'Mara."

THOMAS, J., dissenting, maintained that the statute was constitutional: "Although I agree with the majority's conclusion that it is constitutionally permissible to 'ban . . . cross burning carried out with intent to intimidate,' I believe that the majority errs in imputing an expressive component to the activity in question. In my view, whatever expressive value cross burning has, the legislature simply wrote it out by banning only intimidating conduct undertaken by a particular means. A conclusion that the statute prohibiting cross burning with intent to intimidate sweeps beyond a prohibition on certain conduct into the zone of expression overlooks not only the words of the statute but also reality.

" 'The world's oldest, most persistent terrorist organization is not European or even Middle Eastern in origin. Fifty years before the Irish Republican Army was organized, a century before Al Fatah declared its holy war on Israel, the Ku Klux Klan was actively harassing, torturing and murdering in the United States. Today [its] members remain fanatically committed to a course of violent opposition to social progress and racial equality in the United States.' M. Newton & J. Newton, *The Ku Klux Klan: An Encyclopedia* vii (1991). * * *

"As the Solicitor General points out, the association between acts of intimidating cross burning and violence is well documented in recent American history. [Virginia's] experience has been no exception. [In] February 1952, in light of [a] series of cross burnings and attendant reports that the Klan, 'long considered dead in Virginia, is being revitalized in Richmond,' Governor Battle announced that 'Virginia might well consider passing legislation to restrict the activities of the Ku Klux Klan.' [As] newspapers reported at the time, the bill was 'to ban the burning of crosses and other similar evidences of *terrorism*.' * * *

"Strengthening [my] conclusion, that the legislature sought to criminalize terrorizing *conduct* is the fact that at the time the statute was enacted, racial segregation was not only the prevailing practice, but also the law in Virginia. And, just two years after the enactment of this statute, Virginia's General Assembly embarked on a campaign of 'massive resistance' in response to *Brown v. Board of Education*. It strains credulity to suggest that a state legislature that adopted a litany of segregationist laws self-contradictorily intended to squelch the segregationist message. Even for segregationists, violent and terroristic conduct, the Siamese twin of cross burning, was intolerable. The ban on cross burning with intent to intimidate demonstrates that even segregationists understood the difference between intimidating and terroristic conduct and racist expression. It is simply beyond belief that, in passing the statute now under review, the Virginia legislature was concerned with anything but penalizing conduct it must have viewed as particularly vicious.

"Accordingly, this statute prohibits only conduct, not expression. And, just as one cannot burn down someone's house to make a political point and then seek refuge in the First Amendment, those who hate cannot terrorize and intimidate to make their point. In light of my conclusion that the statute here addresses only conduct, there is no need to analyze it under any of our First Amendment tests.

"[Even] assuming that the statute implicates the First Amendment, in my view, the fact that the statute permits a jury to draw an inference of intent to intimidate from the cross burning itself presents no constitutional problems. [The] inference is rebuttable and, as the jury instructions given in this case demonstrate, Virginia law still requires the jury to find the existence of each element, including intent to intimidate, beyond a reasonable doubt."

NOTES AND QUESTIONS

1.   *R.A.V.* struck the ordinance down on its face, but did not rely on the overbreadth doctrine. The Court interpreted the ordinance to apply only to fighting words; it, therefore, could not have been overbroad. The concurring justices in *R.A.V.* interpreted the ordinance to sweep beyond fighting words, and maintained that the ordinance should have been invalidated on overbreadth grounds. Does O'Connor, J., rely on overbreadth analysis in *Black*? If so, how would the analysis relate to *Brockett v. Spokane Arcades*? Recall that *Brockett* referred to the "normal rule that partial, rather than facial invalidation" of statutes is to be preferred and observed that: "[A]n individual whose own speech or expressive conduct may validly be prohibited or sanctioned is permitted to challenge a statute on its face because it also threatens others not before the court—those who desire to engage in legally

protected expression but who may refrain from doing so rather than risk prosecution or undertake to have the law declared partially invalid. If the overbreadth is 'substantial,' the law may not be enforced against anyone, including the party before the court, until it is narrowed to reach only unprotected activity, whether by legislative action or by judicial construction or partial invalidation.

"It is otherwise where the parties challenging the statute are those who desire to engage in protected speech that the overbroad statute purports to punish, or who seek to publish both protected and unprotected material. There is then no want of a proper party to challenge the statute, no concern that an attack on the statute will be unduly delayed or protected speech discouraged. The statute may forthwith be declared invalid to the extent that it reaches too far, but otherwise left intact."[200] How does Black's activity fit into this scheme? In any event, is the Virginia statute substantially overbroad?

2.   Consider Erwin Chemerinsky, *Striking a Balance on Hate Speech*, 39 (July) Trial 78 (2003): "The Court, with only Thomas dissenting, affirmed the Virginia Supreme Court's conclusion that Black's conviction, for burning a cross on a relatively isolated farm as part of a rally, violated the First Amendment. The cross was burned not to intimidate a person or group, but as part of a Klan rally to express that organization's views. [T]he Court struck a balance likely to be important in future cases involving hate speech. 'True threats' are not protected by the First Amendment, and hate speech, such as cross-burning, may be banned when it constitutes a true threat. But the burden is on the government to prove that an action is a true threat under the circumstances." But cf. Jeannine Bell, *O Say, Can You See: Free Expression by the Light of Fiery Crosses*, 39 Harv. C.R.-C.L. L. Rev. 335 (2004): "For minorities and enemies of the Klan there were few, if any, innocent cross burnings. The association between the burning cross and violent intimidation of racial, ethnic and religious minorities—or anyone else who might be an enemy of the Klan—was strengthened as cross burnings continued to be accompanied by acts of violence. [A] cross burning by the Klan at one of its gatherings, especially a gathering staged in a way that others will see it, is intended to serve two goals at the same time: promoting group solidarity and causing intimidation."[201]

---

[200] After the Court has declared that the statute is invalid to the extent it reaches too far, the remaining portion of the statute will be examined to determine whether that portion is severable. That is, it could well be the intent of the legislature that the statute stands or falls as a single package. To invalidate a part, then, could be to invalidate the whole. Alternatively, the legislature may have intended to salvage whatever it might. The question of severability is regarded as one of legislative intent, but, at least with respect to federal legislation, courts will presume that severability was intended. See, e.g., *Regan v. Time, Inc.*, 468 U.S. 641 (1984). The question of whether a provision of a state statute is severable is one of state law.

[201] For discussion of the violence and discrimination associated with hate speech, see Alexander Tsesis, *Dignity and Speech: The Regulation of Hate Speech in a Democracy*, 44 Wake For. L. Rev. 497 (2009); On the importance of context regarding threats, see Kenneth Karst, *Threats and Meanings: How the Facts Govern First Amendment Doctrine*, 58 Stan.L.Rev. 1337 (2006).

4. PRIOR RESTRAINTS

Prior restraint is a technical term in First Amendment law, referring largely to requirements that speech be licensed in advance of its delivery, or to injunctions against speeches (or publications) yet to be delivered. Of course a criminal statute prohibiting all advocacy of violent action would *restrain* speech and would have been enacted *prior* to any restrained communication. The statute would be overbroad, but it would not in this technical sense be a prior restraint. A prior restraint refers only to closely related, distinctive methods of regulating expression that are said to have in common their own peculiar set of evils and problems, in addition to those that accompany most any governmental interference with free expression. "The issue is not whether the government may impose a particular restriction of substance in an area of public expression, such as forbidding obscenity in newspapers, but whether it may do so by a particular method, such as advance screening of newspaper copy. In other words, restrictions which could be validly imposed when enforced by subsequent punishment are, nevertheless, forbidden if attempted by prior restraint." Thomas Emerson, *The Doctrine of Prior Restraint*, 20 Law and Contemp.Prob. 648 (1955).

The classic prior restraints were the English licensing laws which required a license in advance to print any material or to import or to sell any book.[202] One of the questions raised in this chapter concerns the types of government conduct beyond the classic licensing laws that should be characterized as prior restraints. Another concerns the question of when government licensing of speech, press, or assembly should be countenanced. Perhaps, most important, the Section explores the circumstances in which otherwise protected speech may be restrained on an ad hoc basis.

I. FOUNDATION CASES

A. Licensing

LOVELL v. GRIFFIN, 303 U.S. 444 (1938), per HUGHES, C.J., invalidated an ordinance prohibiting the distribution of handbooks, advertising or literature within the city of Griffin, Georgia without obtaining written permission of the City Manager: "[T]he ordinance is invalid on its face. Whatever the motive which induced its adoption, its character is such that it strikes at the very foundation of the freedom of the press by subjecting it to license and censorship. The struggle for the freedom of the press was primarily directed against the power of the licensor. It was against that power that John Milton directed his assault

---

[202] For a chronicling of the abuses in a modern licensing system, see generally Lucas Powe, *American Broadcasting and the First Amendment* (1987).

by his 'Appeal for the Liberty of Unlicensed Printing.' And the liberty of the press became initially a right to publish '*without* a license what formerly could be published only *with* one.' While this freedom from previous restraint upon publication cannot be regarded as exhausting the guaranty of liberty, the prevention of that restraint was a leading purpose in the adoption of the constitutional provision. Legislation of the type of the ordinance in question would restore the system of license and censorship in its baldest form.

"The liberty of the press is not confined to newspapers and periodicals. It necessarily embraces pamphlets and leaflets. These indeed have been historic weapons in the defense of liberty, as the pamphlets of Thomas Paine and others in our own history abundantly attest. The press in its historic connotation comprehends every sort of publication which affords a vehicle of information and opinion. * * *

"The ordinance cannot be saved because it relates to distribution and not to publication. 'Liberty of circulating is as essential to that freedom as liberty of publishing; indeed, without the circulation, the publication would be of little value.' *Ex parte Jackson,* 96 U.S. (6 Otto) 727, 733 (1877).

"[As] the ordinance is void on its face, it was not necessary for appellant to seek a permit under it. She was entitled to contest its validity in answer to the charge against her."[203]

NOTES AND QUESTIONS

1. *First Amendment procedure.* Notice that Lovell would get the benefit of the prior restraint doctrine even if the material she distributed was obscene or otherwise unprotected. In that respect, the prior restraint doctrine is similar to the doctrines of overbreadth and vagueness. For particular concerns that underlie the prior restraint doctrine, consider Thomas Emerson, *The System of Freedom of Expression* 506 (1970): "A system of prior restraint is in many ways more inhibiting than a system of subsequent punishment: It is likely to bring under government scrutiny a far wider range of expression; it shuts off communication before it takes place; suppression by a stroke of the pen is more likely to be applied than suppression through a criminal process; the procedures do not require attention to the safeguards of the criminal process; the system allows less opportunity for public appraisal and criticism; the dynamics of the system drive toward excesses, as the history of all censorship shows."[204]

2. *Scope and character of the doctrine.* What is the vice of the licensing scheme in *Lovell*? Is the concern that like vague statutes it affords

---

[203] Cardozo, J., took no part.

[204] But see Richard Posner, *Free Speech in an Economic Perspective,* 20 Suff.L.Rev. 1 (1986): "The conventional arguments for why censorship is worse than criminal punishment are little better than plausible (though I think there is at least one good argument)" [observing that speech ordinarily does not produce sufficient damage to justify sifting through massive materials].

undue discretion and potential for abuse? Is the real concern the uncontrolled power of the licensor to deny licenses? Suppose licenses were automatically issued to anyone who applied?

To what extent should the prior restraint doctrine apply to non-press activities? To a licensing ordinance that otherwise forbids soliciting membership in organizations that exact fees of their members? See *Staub v. Baxley,* 355 U.S. 313 (1958) (yes). To a licensing ordinance that otherwise prohibits attempts to secure contributions for charitable or religious causes? See *Cantwell v. Connecticut,* 310 U.S. 296 (1940) (yes).

Should the prior restraint doctrine apply to all aspects of newspaper circulation? See *Lakewood v. Plain Dealer Publishing Co.,* 486 U.S. 750 (1988) (invalidating ordinance granting Mayor power to grant or deny annual permits to place newsracks on public property).[205]

Suppose, in the above cases, that the authority of the licensor were confined by narrow, objective, and definite standards or that licenses were automatically issued to anyone who applied. *Hynes v. Mayor,* 425 U.S. 610 (1976), per Burger, C.J., stated in dictum that a municipality could regulate house to house soliciting by requiring advance notice to the police department in order to protect its citizens from crime and undue annoyance: "A narrowly drawn ordinance, that does not vest in municipal officials the undefined power to determine what messages residents will hear, may serve these important interests without running afoul of the First Amendment." But cf. *Thomas v. Collins,* 323 U.S. 516 (1945) (registration requirement for paid union organizers invalid prior restraint); *Talley v. California,* 362 U.S. 60 (1960) (ban on anonymous handbills "void on its face," noting that the "obnoxious press licensing law of England, which was also enforced on the Colonies was due in part to the knowledge that exposure of the names of printers, writers and distributors would lessen the circulation of literature critical of the government").

————

WATCHTOWER BIBLE & TRACT SOCIETY v. STRATTON, 536 U.S. 150 (2002), per STEVENS, J., struck down a village ordinance requiring door to door advocates or distributors of literature to register with the mayor: "It is offensive—not only to the values protected by the First Amendment, but to the very notion of a free society—that in the context of everyday public discourse a citizen must first inform the government of her desire to speak to her neighbors and then obtain a permit to do so. Even if the issuance of permits by the mayor's office is a ministerial task that is performed promptly and at no cost to the applicant, a law requiring a

---

[205] White, J., joined by Stevens and O'Connor, JJ., dissenting, contended that *Lovell* should apply only if the newspaper had a constitutional right to place newsracks on public sidewalks. Otherwise, the newspaper should be required to show that a denial was based on improper reasons.

permit to engage in such speech constitutes a dramatic departure from our national heritage and constitutional tradition."

Stevens, J., argued that required licensing impinged on the speaker's interest in anonymity. In addition, "requiring a permit as a prior condition on the exercise of the right to speak imposes an objective burden on some speech of citizens holding religious or patriotic views. As our World War II-era cases dramatically demonstrate, there are a significant number of persons whose religious scruples will prevent them from applying for such a license. There are no doubt other patriotic citizens, who have such firm convictions about their constitutional right to engage in uninhibited debate in the context of door-to-door advocacy, that they would prefer silence to speech licensed by a petty official.

"[Moreover,] there is a significant amount of spontaneous speech that is effectively banned by the ordinance. A person who made a decision on a holiday or a weekend to take an active part in a political campaign could not begin to pass out handbills until after he or she obtained the required permit. Even a spontaneous decision to go across the street and urge a neighbor to vote against the mayor could not lawfully be implemented without first obtaining the mayor's permission. * * *

"Also central to our conclusion that the ordinance does not pass First Amendment scrutiny is that it is not tailored to the Village's stated interests. Even if the interest in preventing fraud could adequately support the ordinance insofar as it applies to commercial transactions and the solicitation of funds, that interest provides no support for its application to petitioners, to political campaigns, or to enlisting support for unpopular causes. The Village, however, argues that the ordinance is nonetheless valid because it serves the two additional interests of protecting the privacy of the resident and the prevention of crime.

"With respect to the former, it seems clear that § 107 of the ordinance, which provides for the posting of 'No Solicitation' signs and which is not challenged in this case, coupled with the resident's unquestioned right to refuse to engage in conversation with unwelcome visitors, provides ample protection for the unwilling listener. [The] annoyance caused by an uninvited knock on the front door is the same whether or not the visitor is armed with a permit.

"With respect to the latter, it seems unlikely that the absence of a permit would preclude criminals from knocking on doors and engaging in conversations not covered by the ordinance. They might, for example, ask for directions or permission to use the telephone, or pose as surveyers or census takers. Or they might register under a false name with impunity because the ordinance contains no provision for verifying an applicant's identity or organizational credentials. Moreover, the Village did not assert an interest in crime prevention below, and there is an absence of any evidence of a special crime problem related to door-to-door solicitation in the record before us.

"The rhetoric used in the World War II-era opinions that repeatedly saved petitioners' coreligionists from petty prosecutions reflected the Court's evaluation of the First Amendment freedoms that are implicated in this case. The value judgment that then motivated a united democratic people fighting to defend those very freedoms from totalitarian attack is unchanged. It motivates our decision today."

BREYER, J., joined by Souter and Ginsburg, JJ., concurred: "While joining the Court's opinion, I write separately to note that the dissent's 'crime prevention' justification for this ordinance is not a strong one. For one thing, there is no indication that the legislative body that passed the ordinance considered this justification. In the intermediate scrutiny context, the Court ordinarily does not supply reasons the legislative body has not given. That does not mean, as the Chief Justice suggests, that only a government with a 'battery of constitutional lawyers,' could satisfy this burden. It does mean that we expect a government to give its real reasons for passing an ordinance.

"Because Stratton did not rely on the crime prevention justification, because Stratton has not now 'present[ed] more than anecdote and supposition,' and because the relationship between the interest and the ordinance is doubtful, I am unwilling to assume that these conjectured benefits outweigh the cost of abridging the speech covered by the ordinance."

SCALIA, J., joined by Thomas, J., concurring in the judgment, agreed with some of the Court's opinion, but did not "agree, for example, that one of the causes of the invalidity of Stratton's ordinance is that some people have a religious objection to applying for a permit, and others (posited by the Court) 'have such firm convictions about their constitutional right to engage in uninhibited debate in the context of door-to-door advocacy, that they would prefer silence to speech licensed by a petty official.'

"If a licensing requirement is otherwise lawful, it is in my view not invalidated by the fact that some people will choose, for religious reasons, to forgo speech rather than observe it. That would convert an invalid free-exercise claim into a valid free-speech claim—and a more destructive one at that. Whereas the free-exercise claim, if acknowledged, would merely exempt Jehovah's Witnesses from the licensing requirement, the free-speech claim exempts everybody, thanks to Jehovah's Witnesses.

"As for the Court's fairy-tale category of 'patriotic citizens,' who would rather be silenced than licensed in a manner that the Constitution (but for their 'patriotic' objection) would permit: If our free-speech jurisprudence is to be determined by the predicted behavior of such crackpots, we are in a sorry state indeed."

REHNQUIST, C.J., dissented: "The town had little reason to suspect that the negligible burden of having to obtain a permit runs afoul of the First Amendment . For over 60 years, we have categorically stated that a permit requirement for door-to-door canvassers, which gives no discretion to the issuing authority, is constitutional. The District Court and Court of Appeals, relying on our cases, upheld the ordinance. The Court today, however, abruptly changes course and invalidates the ordinance. [With] respect to the interest in protecting privacy, the Court concludes that '[t]he annoyance caused by an uninvited knock on the front door is the same whether or not the visitor is armed with a permit.' True, but that misses the key point: the permit requirement results in fewer uninvited knocks. Those who have complied with the permit requirement are less likely to visit residences with no trespassing signs, as it is much easier for the authorities to track them down.

"The Court also fails to grasp how the permit requirement serves Stratton's interest in preventing crime. We have approved of permit requirements for those engaging in protected First Amendment activity because of a common-sense recognition that their existence both deters and helps detect wrongdoing. And while some people, intent on committing burglaries or violent crimes, are not likely to be deterred by the prospect of a misdemeanor for violating the permit ordinance, the ordinance's effectiveness does not depend on criminals registering. The ordinance prevents and detects serious crime by making it a crime not to register."

Rehnquist, C.J., referred to a double murder that had taken place in Hanover, New Jersey: "The murderers did not achieve their objective until they visited their fifth home over a period of seven months. If Hanover had a permit requirement, the teens may have been stopped before they achieved their objective. One of the residents they visited may have informed the police that there were two canvassers who lacked a permit. Such neighborly vigilance, though perhaps foreign to those residing in modern day cities, is not uncommon in small towns. Or the police on their own may have discovered that two canvassers were violating the ordinance. Apprehension for violating the permit requirement may well have frustrated the teenagers' objectives; it certainly would have assisted in solving the murders had the teenagers gone ahead with their plan.

"Of course, the Stratton ordinance does not guarantee that no canvasser will ever commit a burglary or violent crime. The Court seems to think this dooms the ordinance, erecting an insurmountable hurdle that a law must provide a fool-proof method of preventing crime. In order to survive intermediate scrutiny, however, a law need not solve the crime problem, it need only further the interest in preventing crime. Some deterrence of serious criminal activity is more than enough to survive intermediate scrutiny."

B. Injunctions

NEAR V. MINNESOTA
283 U.S. 697, 51 S.Ct. 625, 75 L.Ed. 1357 (1931).

CHIEF JUSTICE HUGHES delivered the opinion of the Court.

[The *Saturday Press* published articles charging that through graft and incompetence named public officials failed to expose and punish gangsters responsible for gambling, bootlegging, and racketeering in Minneapolis. It demanded a special grand jury and special prosecutor to deal with the situation and to investigate an alleged attempt to assassinate one of its publishers. Under a statute that authorized abatement of a "malicious, scandalous and defamatory newspaper" the state secured, and its supreme court affirmed, a court order that "abated" the Press and perpetually enjoined the defendants from publishing or circulating "any publication whatsoever which is a malicious, scandalous or defamatory newspaper." The order did not restrain the defendants from operating a newspaper "in harmony with the general welfare."]

The object of the statute is not punishment, in the ordinary sense, but suppression of the offending newspaper. [In] the case of public officers, it is the reiteration of charges of official misconduct, and the fact that the newspaper [is] principally devoted to that purpose, that exposes it to suppression. [T]he operation and effect of the statute [is] that public authorities may bring the owner or publisher of a newspaper or periodical before a judge upon a charge of conducting a business of publishing scandalous and defamatory matter—in particular that the matter consists of charges against public officers of official dereliction—and, unless the owner or publisher is able and disposed to bring competent evidence to satisfy the judge that the charges are true and are published with good motives and for justifiable ends, his newspaper or periodical is suppressed and further publication is made punishable as a contempt. This is of the essence of censorship.

The question is whether a statute authorizing such proceedings [is] consistent with the conception of the liberty of the press as historically conceived and guaranteed. [I]t has been generally, if not universally, considered that it is the chief purpose of the guaranty to prevent previous restraints upon publication. The struggle in England, directed against the legislative power of the licenser, resulted in renunciation of the censorship of the press. The liberty deemed to be established was thus described by Blackstone: "The liberty of the press is indeed essential to the nature of a free state; but this consists in laying no *previous* restraints upon publications, and not in freedom from censure for criminal matter when published. Every freeman has an undoubted right to lay what sentiments he pleases before the public; to forbid this, is to destroy the freedom of the press; but if he publishes what is improper, mischievous or illegal, he must take the consequence of his own temerity." [The] criticism upon Blackstone's statement has not been because immunity from previous restraint upon publication has not been regarded as deserving of special emphasis, but chiefly because that immunity cannot be deemed to exhaust the conception of the liberty guaranteed by State and Federal Constitutions.

[T]he protection even as to previous restraint is not absolutely unlimited. But the limitation has been recognized only in exceptional cases. [N]o one would question but that a government might prevent actual obstruction to its recruiting service or the publication of the sailing dates of transports or the number and location of troops. On similar grounds, the primary requirements of decency may be enforced against obscene publications. The security of the community life may be protected against incitements to acts of violence and the overthrow by force of orderly [government].[206] * * *

The fact that for approximately one hundred and fifty years there has been almost an entire absence of attempts to impose previous restraints upon publications relating to the malfeasance of public officers is significant of the deep-seated conviction that such restraints would violate constitutional right. Public officers, whose character and conduct remain open to debate and free discussion in the press, find their remedies for false accusations in actions under libel laws providing for redress and punishment, and not in proceedings to restrain the publication of newspapers and periodicals. [The] fact that the liberty of the press may be abused by miscreant purveyors of scandal does not make any the less necessary the immunity of the press from previous restraint in dealing with official misconduct. Subsequent punishment for such abuses as may exist is the appropriate remedy, consistent with constitutional [privilege].

The statute in question cannot be justified by reason of the fact that the publisher is permitted to show, before injunction issues, that the matter published is true and is published with good motives and for justifiable ends. If such a statute, authorizing suppression and injunction on such a basis, is constitutionally valid, it would be equally permissible for the Legislature to provide that at any time the publisher of any newspaper could be brought before a court, or even an administrative

---

[206] For critical commentary on the concessions in *Near,* see Hans Linde, *Courts and Censorship,* 66 Minn.L.Rev. 171 (1981); Jeffery Smith, *Prior Restraint: Original Intentions and Modern Interpretations,* 28 Wm. & Mary L.Rev. 439 (1987). For criticism of the overuse of preliminary injunctions in a variety of intellectual property contexts, see Mark A. Lemley & Eugene Volokh, *Freedom of Speech and Injunctions in Intellectual Property Cases,* 48 Duke L.J. 147 (1998). For the contention that some of the "exceptions" to the prior restraint doctrine are not properly classified as prior restraints, see Michael I. Meyerson, *The Neglected History of the Prior Restraint Doctrine: Rediscovering the Link Between the First Amendment and the Separation of Powers,* 34 Ind. L. Rev. 295 (2001).

officer (as the constitutional protection may not be regarded as resting on mere procedural details), and required to produce proof of the truth of his publication, or of what he intended to publish and of his motives, or stand enjoined. If this can be done, the Legislature may provide machinery for determining in the complete exercise of its discretion what are justifiable ends and restrain publication accordingly. And it would be but a step to a complete system of censorship.

[For] these reasons we hold the statute, so far as it authorized the proceedings in this action, [to] be an infringement of the liberty of the press guaranteed by the Fourteenth Amendment. * * *

JUSTICE BUTLER (dissenting).

[T]he *previous restraints* referred to by [Blackstone] subjected the press to the arbitrary will of an administrative officer. [The] Minnesota statute does not operate as a *previous* restraint on publication within the proper meaning of that phrase. It does not authorize administrative control in advance such as was formerly exercised by the licensers and censors, but prescribes a remedy to be enforced by a suit in equity. In this case [t]he business and publications unquestionably constitute an abuse of the right of free press. [A]s stated by the state Supreme Court [they] threaten morals, peace, and good order. [The] restraint authorized is only in respect of continuing to do what has been duly adjudged to constitute a nuisance. [It] is fanciful to suggest similarity between the granting or enforcement of the decree authorized by this statute to prevent *further* publication of malicious, scandalous, and defamatory articles and the *previous restraint* upon the press by licensers as referred to by Blackstone and described in the history of the times to which he alludes. * * *

It is well known, as found by the state supreme court, that existing libel laws are inadequate effectively to suppress evils resulting from the kind of business and publications that are shown in this case. The doctrine [of this decision] exposes the peace and good order of every community and the business and private affairs of every individual to the constant and protracted false and malicious assaults of any insolvent publisher who may have purpose and sufficient capacity to contrive and put into effect a scheme or program for oppression, blackmail or extortion. * * *

JUSTICE VAN DEVANTER, JUSTICE MCREYNOLDS, and JUSTICE SUTHERLAND concur in this opinion.[207]

NOTES AND QUESTIONS

1. ***Near and seditious libel: a misuse of prior restraint?*** *Near* was decided three decades before *New York Times v. Sullivan.* Should the Court

---

[207] For background, see Fred Friendly, *Minnesota Rag* (1981); Paul Murphy, *Near v. Minnesota in the Context of Historical Developments,* 66 Minn.L.Rev. 95 (1981).

have looked to the substance of the regulation rather than its form? Consider John Jeffries, *Rethinking Prior Restraint,* 92 Yale L.J. 409 (1983): "In truth, *Near* involved nothing more or less than a repackaged version of the law of seditious libel, and this the majority rightly refused to countenance. Hence, there was pressure, so typical of this doctrine, to cram the law into the disfavored category of prior restraint, even though it in fact functioned very differently from a scheme of official licensing. Here there was no license and no censor, no ex parte determination of what was prohibited, and no suppression of publication based on speculation about what somebody might say. Here the decision to suppress was made by a judge (not a bureaucrat), after adversarial (not ex parte) proceedings, to determine the legal character of what had been (and not what might be) published. The only aspect of prior restraint was the incidental fact that the defendants were commanded not to repeat that which they were proved to have done.

"[I]f *Near* reached the right result, does it really matter that it gave the wrong reason? The answer [is that] *Near* has become a prominent feature of the First Amendment landscape—a landmark, as the case is so often called, from which we chart our course to future decisions. [T]he Court has yet to explain (at least in terms that I understand) what it is about an injunction that justifies this independent rule of constitutional disfavor."

Should a court be able to enjoin the continued distribution of material it has finally adjudicated to be unprotected defamation under existing law? Suppose it enjoins the publication of any material that does not comply with the mandates of *New York Times* and *Gertz*?

2. ***The collateral bar rule.*** Consider the collateral bar rule, which may shed light on the relationship between prior restraints and injunctions. That rule insists "that a court order must be obeyed until it is set aside, and that persons subject to the order who disobey it may not defend against the ensuing charge of criminal contempt on the ground that the order was erroneous or even unconstitutional." Stephen Barnett, *The Puzzle of Prior Restraint,* 29 Stan.L.Rev. 539 (1977). Is this rule defensible to protect the integrity of the judiciary and important state interests that could be thwarted by the speech restrained? Richard Favata, *Filling the Void in First Amendment Jurisprudence: Is There a Solution for Replacing the Impotent System of Prior Restraints?,* 72 Fordham L.Rev. 169 (2003).

WALKER v. BIRMINGHAM, 388 U.S. 307 (1967) upheld the rule against a First Amendment challenge in affirming the contempt conviction of defendants for violating an ex parte injunction issued by an Alabama court enjoining them from engaging in street parades without a municipal permit issued pursuant to the city's parade ordinance. The Court, per STEWART, J., (Warren, C.J., Brennan, Douglas, and Fortas, JJ., dissenting) held that because the petitioners neither moved to dissolve the injunction nor sought to comply with the city's parade ordinance, their claim that the injunction and ordinance were unconstitutional[208] did not need to be considered: "This Court cannot hold that the petitioners were constitutionally free to ignore all the procedures of the law and carry their battle to the streets. [R]espect for judicial process is a small price to pay for the civilizing hand of law, which alone can give abiding meaning to constitutional freedom." Although *Walker* suggested that its holding might be different if the court issuing the injunction lacked jurisdiction or if the injunction were "transparently invalid or had only a frivolous pretense to validity," it held that Alabama's invocation of the collateral bar rule was not itself unconstitutional.

Cf. *Poulos v. New Hampshire,* 345 U.S. 395 (1953) (claim of arbitrary refusal to issue license for open air meeting need not be entertained when a licensing statute is considered to be valid on its face in circumstance where speaker fails to seek direct judicial relief and proceeds without a license).[209] Does *Poulos* pose considerable danger to First Amendment interests because the low visibility of the administrative decision permits easy abridgement of free expression? See Henry Monaghan, *First Amendment "Due Process,"* 83 Harv.L.Rev. 518 (1970). Do *Lovell, Walker,* and *Poulos* fit easily together? Consider Vincent Blasi, *Prior Restraints on Demonstrations,* 68 Mich.L.Rev. 1482 (1970): "A refuses to apply for a permit; he undertakes a march that could have been prohibited in the first place; he is prosecuted for parading without a permit under a statute that is defective for overbreadth. B applies for a permit; he is rudely rebuffed by a city official in clear violation of the state permit statute (which is not invalid on its face); he marches anyway in a manner that would be protected by the First Amendment, he is prosecuted for parading without a permit. C applies for a permit; he is rudely rebuffed; he notifies city officials that he will march anyway; the officials obtain an injunction against the march; the injunction is overbroad and is also based on a state statute that is overbroad; C marches in a manner ordinarily within his constitutional rights; he is prosecuted for contempt. Under the law as it now stands, A wins, but B and C lose!"

3. ***Time, place, and manner regulations.*** Should injunctions that impose time, place, or manner regulations in response to proven wrongdoing be subjected to more stringent examination than that ordinarily applied to general regulations imposed by legislative or executive action? See *Madsen v. Women's Health Center,* 512 U.S. 753 (1994).

4. ***The commentators, injunctions, and prior restraint.*** Should the link between prior restraint doctrine and injunctions depend upon the collateral bar rule? Does the analogy between licensing systems and injunctions hold only in that event? See Owen Fiss, *The Civil Rights Injunction* 30, 69–74 (1978). Should the prior restraint doctrine be wholly inapplicable to injunctions so long as "expedited appellate review allows an immediate

---

[208] Indeed, the ordinance in question was declared unconstitutional two years later. *Shuttlesworth v. Birmingham,* 394 U.S. 147 (1969) (ordinance conferring unbridled discretion to prohibit any parade or demonstration is unconstitutional prior restraint).

[209] For consideration of when licensing statutes for assemblies are valid, see *Cox v. New Hampshire,* Sec. 6, I, A infra.

opportunity to test the validity of an injunction against speech and only so long as that opportunity is genuinely effective to allow timely publication should the injunction ultimately be adjudged invalid"? Jeffries, note 1 supra.[210] Indeed should the whole concept of prior restraint be abandoned? Consider id.: "In the context of administrative preclearance, talking of prior restraint is unhelpful, though not inapt. A more informative frame of reference would be overbreadth, the doctrine that explicitly identifies why preclearance is specially objectionable. In the context of injunctions, however, the traditional doctrine of prior restraint is not merely unhelpful, but positively misleading. It focuses on a constitutionally inconsequential consideration of form and diverts attention away from the critical substantive issues of First Amendment coverage. The result is a two-pronged danger. On the one hand, vindication of First Amendment freedoms in the name of prior restraint may exaggerate the legitimate reach of official competence to suppress by subsequent punishment. On the other hand, insistence on special disfavor for prior restraints outside the realm of substantive protection under the First Amendment may deny to the government an appropriate choice of means to vindicate legitimate interests. In my view, neither risk is justified by any compelling reason to continue prior restraint as a doctrinally independent category of contemporary First Amendment analysis."[211]

For a nuanced argument that the prior restraint doctrine should apply to injunctions even in those jurisdictions that reject the applicability of the collateral bar rule to First Amendment arguments, see Vincent Blasi, *Toward a Theory of Prior Restraint: The Central Linkage,* 66 Minn.L.Rev. 11 (1981). Except in particular contexts, Professor Blasi does not claim that the chilling effect of injunctions on speech is more severe than those associated with criminal laws and civil liability rules. He does argue that unlike criminal laws and civil liability rules, regulation of speech by licensing and injunctions requires abstract and unduly speculative adjudication, stimulates overuse by regulatory agents, can to some extent distort the way in which audiences perceive the message at issue, and unreasonably implies that the activity of disseminating controversial communications is "a threat to, rather than an integral feature of, the social order." Id. He argues that many of these factors are aggravated if the collateral bar rule applies and that other undesirable features are added. For example, speakers are forced to reveal planned details about their communication. He concludes that the "concept of prior restraint is coherent at the core." Id.[212] Michael I. Meyerson, *Rewriting Near v. Minnesota:*

---

[210] For the argument that regulation by injunction is generally more speech protective than regulation via subsequent punishment, see William Mayton, *Toward A Theory of First Amendment Process: Injunctions of Speech, Subsequent Punishment, and the Costs of the Prior Restraint Doctrine,* 67 Corn.L.Rev. 245 (1982). For the contention that this should count in favor of subsequent punishment in many contexts, see Martin Redish, *The Proper Role of the Prior Restraint Doctrine in First Amendment Theory,* 70 Va.L.Rev. 53 (1984).

[211] See also Marin Scordato, *Distinction Without a Difference,* 68 N.C.L.Rev. 1 (1989) (generally agreeing with Jeffries but arguing that a small part of prior restraint doctrine should be salvaged).

[212] See also Daniel A. Farber, *The First Amendment* 48–49 (1998). For detailed criticism of Blasi's position, all in defense of a different core, see Redish, fn. 210 supra.

Creating a Complete Definition of Prior Restraint, 52 Mercer L. Rev. 1087 (2001) (prior restraints more susceptible to discriminatory treatment).

II. PRIOR RESTRAINTS, OBSCENITY, AND COMMERCIAL SPEECH

KINGSLEY BOOKS, INC. v. BROWN, 354 U.S. 436 (1957), per FRANKFURTER, J., upheld a state court decree, issued pursuant to a New York statute, enjoining the publisher from further distribution of 14 booklets the state court found obscene. On appeal to the Supreme Court the publisher challenged only the prior restraint, not the obscenity finding: "The phrase 'prior restraint' is not a self-wielding sword. Nor can it serve as a talismatic test. The duty of closer analysis and critical judgment in applying the thought behind the phrase has thus been authoritatively put by one who brings weighty learning to his support of constitutionally protected liberties: 'What is needed,' writes Professor Paul A. Freund, 'is a pragmatic assessment of its operation in the particular circumstances. The generalization that prior restraint is particularly obnoxious in civil liberties cases must yield to more particularistic analysis.' *The Supreme Court and Civil Liberties,* 4 Vand.L.Rev. 533.

"Wherein does § 22–a differ in its effective operation from the type of statute upheld in *Alberts v. California,* [354 U.S. 476 (1957)]. One would be bold to assert that the in terrorem effect of [criminal] statutes less restrains booksellers in the period before the law strikes than does § 22–a. Instead of requiring the bookseller to dread that the offer for sale of a book may, without prior warning, subject him to a criminal prosecution with the hazard of imprisonment, the civil procedure assures him that such consequences cannot follow unless he ignores a court order specifically directed to him for a prompt and carefully circumscribed determination of the issue of obscenity. Until then, he may keep the book for sale and sell it on his own judgment rather than steer 'nervously among the treacherous shoals.'[213]

"Criminal enforcement and the proceeding under § 22–a interfere with a book's solicitation of the public precisely at the same stage. In each situation the law moves after publication; the book need not in either case have yet passed into the hands of the public. [H]ere as a matter of fact copies of the booklets whose distribution was enjoined had been on sale for several weeks when process was served. In each case the bookseller is put on notice by the complaint that sale of the publication charged with obscenity in the period before trial may subject him to penal consequences. In the one case he may suffer fine and imprisonment for violation of the criminal statute, in the other, for disobedience of the temporary injunction.

---

[213] In fact, § 22–a did not require a civil adjudication before criminal prosecution, as intimated by the opinion. The feasibility of such a requirement is considered in William Lockhart, *Escape from the Chill of Uncertainty,* 9 Ga.L.Rev. 533 (1975).

The bookseller may of course stand his ground and confidently believe that in any judicial proceeding the book could not be condemned as obscene, but both modes of procedure provide an effective deterrent against distribution prior to adjudication of the book's content—the threat of subsequent penalization.²"

The Court pointed out that in both criminal misdemeanor prosecutions and injunction proceedings a jury could be called as a matter of discretion, but that defendant did not request a jury trial and did not attack the statute for its failure to require a jury.

"Nor are the consequences of a judicial condemnation for obscenity under § 22–a more restrictive of freedom of expression than the result of conviction for a misdemeanor. In *Alberts,* the defendant was fined $500, sentenced to sixty days in prison, and put on probation for two years on condition that he not violate the obscenity statute. Not only was he completely separated from society for two months but he was also seriously restrained from trafficking in all obscene publications for a considerable time. Appellants, on the other hand, were enjoined from displaying for sale or distributing only the particular booklets theretofore published and adjudged to be obscene. Thus, the restraint upon appellants as merchants in obscenity was narrower than that imposed on *Alberts.*

"Section 22–a's provision for the seizure and destruction of the instruments of ascertained wrongdoing expresses resort to a legal remedy sanctioned by the long history of Anglo-American law. See Oliver Holmes, *The Common Law,* 24–26.

"[It] only remains to say that the difference between *Near* and this case is glaring in fact. The two cases are no less glaringly different when judged by the appropriate criteria of constitutional law. Minnesota empowered its courts to enjoin the dissemination of future issues of a publication because its past issues had been found offensive. In the language of Mr. Chief Justice Hughes, 'This is of the essence of censorship.' As such, it was enough to condemn the statute wholly apart from the fact that the proceeding in *Near* involved not obscenity but matters deemed to be derogatory to a public officer. Unlike *Near,* § 22–a is concerned solely with obscenity and, as authoritatively construed, it studiously withholds restraint upon matters not already published and not yet found to be offensive."[214]

---

2   [Ct's Note] This comparison of remedies takes note of the fact that we do not have before us a case where, although the issue of obscenity is ultimately decided in favor of the bookseller, the State nevertheless attempts to punish him for disobedience of the interim injunction. For all we know, New York may impliedly condition the temporary injunction so as not to subject the bookseller to a charge of contempt if he prevails on the issue of obscenity.

214 Warren, C.J., dissented, objecting that the New York law "places the book on trial" without any consideration of its "manner of use." Black and Douglas, JJ., dissented, objecting to a state-wide decree depriving the publisher of separate trials in different communities, and to substituting

TIMES FILM CORP. V. CHICAGO
365 U.S. 43, 81 S.Ct. 391, 5 L.Ed.2d 403 (1961).

JUSTICE CLARK delivered the opinion of the Court.

Petitioner challenges on constitutional grounds the validity on its face of that portion of § 155–4[1] of the Municipal Code of the City of Chicago which requires submission of all motion pictures for examination prior to their public exhibition. Petitioner is a New York corporation owning the exclusive right to publicly exhibit in Chicago the film known as "Don Juan." It applied for a permit, as Chicago's ordinance required, and tendered the license fee but refused to submit the film for examination. The appropriate city official refused to issue the permit and his order was made final on appeal to the Mayor. The sole ground for denial was petitioner's refusal to submit the film for examination as required. Petitioner then brought this suit seeking injunctive relief ordering the issuance of the permit without submission of the [film]. Its sole ground is that the provision of the ordinance requiring submission of the film constitutes, on its face, a prior restraint.[2] [Admittedly,] the challenged section of the ordinance imposes a previous restraint, and the broad justiciable issue is therefore present as to whether the ambit of constitutional protection includes complete and absolute freedom to exhibit, at least once, any and every kind of motion picture. It is that question alone which we decide.

[T]here is not a word in the record as to the nature and content of "Don Juan." We are left entirely in the dark in this regard, as were the city officials and the other reviewing courts. Petitioner claims that the nature of the film is irrelevant, and that even if this film contains the basest type of pornography, or incitement to riot, or forceful overthrow of orderly government, it may nonetheless be shown without prior submission for examination. The challenge here is to the censor's basic authority; it does not go to any statutory standards employed by the censor or procedural requirements as to the submission of the film. * * *

Petitioner would have us hold that the public exhibition of motion pictures must be allowed under any circumstances. The State's sole remedy, it says, is the invocation of criminal process under the Illinois

---

"punishment by contempt for punishment by jury trial." Brennan, J., dissenting, contended that a jury trial is required to apply properly the *Roth* standard for obscenity.

[1]   **[Ct's Note]** The portion of the section here under attack is as follows: "Such permit shall be granted only after the motion picture film for which said permit is requested has been produced at the office of the commissioner of police for examination or [censorship]."

[2]   **[Ct's Note]** That portion of § 155–4 of the Code providing standards is as follows: "If a picture or series of pictures, for the showing or exhibition of which an application for a permit is made, is immoral or obscene, or portrays, depravity, criminality, or lack of virtue of a class of citizens of any race, color, creed, or religion and exposes them to contempt, derision, or obloquy, or tends to produce a breach of the peace or riots, or purports to represent any hanging, lynching, or burning of a human being, it shall be the duty of the commissioner of police to refuse such permit; otherwise it shall be his duty to grant such permit.* * *

pornography statute and then only after a transgression. But this position [is] founded upon the claim of absolute privilege against prior restraint under the First Amendment—a claim without sanction in our cases. To illustrate its fallacy, we need only point to one of the "exceptional cases" which Chief Justice Hughes enumerated in *Near,* namely, "the primary requirements of decency [that] may be enforced against obscene publications." * * *

Affirmed.

CHIEF JUSTICE WARREN, with whom JUSTICE BLACK, JUSTICE DOUGLAS and JUSTICE BRENNAN join, dissenting. * * *

I hesitate to disagree with the Court's formulation of the issue before us, but, with all deference, I must insist that the question presented in this case is *not* whether a motion picture exhibitor has a constitutionally protected, "complete and absolute freedom to exhibit, at least once, any and every kind of motion picture." [The] question here presented is whether the City of Chicago—or, for that matter, any city, any State or the Federal Government—may require all motion picture exhibitors to submit all films to a police chief, mayor or other administrative official, for licensing and censorship prior to public exhibition within the jurisdiction. * * *

The booklets enjoined from distribution in *Kingsley* were concededly obscene. There is no indication that this is true of the moving picture here. This was treated as a particularly crucial distinction. Thus, the Court has suggested that, in times of national emergency, the Government might impose a prior restraint upon "the publication of the sailing dates of transports or the number and location of troops." *Near.* But, surely this is not to suggest that the Government might require that all newspapers be submitted to a censor in order to assist it in preventing such information from reaching print. Yet in this case the Court gives its blessing to the censorship of all motion pictures in order to prevent the exhibition of those it feels to be constitutionally unprotected.

[E]ven if the impact of the motion picture is greater than that of some other media, that fact constitutes no basis for the argument that motion pictures should be subject to greater suppression. This is the traditional argument made in the censor's behalf; this is the argument advanced against newspapers at the time of the invention of the printing press. The argument was ultimately rejected in England, and has consistently been held to be contrary to our Constitution. No compelling reason has been predicated for accepting the contention now. * * *

NOTES AND QUESTIONS

1. *Procedural safeguards.* FREEDMAN v. MARYLAND, 380 U.S. 51 (1965), per BRENNAN, J., set out procedural safeguards designed to reduce the dangers associated with prior restraints of films. It required that the procedure

must "assure a prompt final judicial decision, to minimize the deterrent effect of an interim and possibly erroneous denial of a license," that the censor must promptly institute the proceedings, that the burden of proof to show that the speech in question is unprotected must rest on the censor, and that the proceedings be adversarial. The *Freedman* standards have been applied in other contexts. *Blount v. Rizzi,* 400 U.S. 410 (1971) (postal stop orders of obscene materials); *United States v. Thirty-Seven Photographs,* 402 U.S. 363 (1971) (customs seizure of obscene materials); *Southeastern Promotions Ltd. v. Conrad,* 420 U.S. 546 (1975) (denial of permit to use municipal theater for the musical, Hair); *Carroll v. President and Commissioners,* 393 U.S. 175 (1968) (10 day restraining order against particular rallies or meetings invalid because *ex parte*); *City of Littleton v. Z.J. Gifts D–4,* 541 U.S. 774 (2004) (adult business licensing ordinances including the assurance of speedy court decisions); But see *Thomas v. Chicago Park Dist.,* 534 U.S. 316 (2002) (*Freedman* does not apply to content neutral licensing requirement granting authorities for assemblies involving more than fifty persons in public park even when ordinance as a matter of course grants authorities fourteen days to decide whether permit should be issued). Cf. *FW/PBS v. Dallas,* 493 U.S. 215 (1990) (suggesting that partial application of *Freedman* standards (dispensing with burden of going to court and burden of proof, but retaining assurance of timely decision making by licensor and prompt judicial review) to ordinance licensing sexually oriented businesses ostensibly without regard to content of films or books would be appropriate).

2. ***Informal prior restraints.*** BANTAM BOOKS, INC. v. SULLIVAN, 372 U.S. 58 (1963), per BRENNAN, J., (Harlan, J. dissenting) held unconstitutional the activities of a government commission that would identify "objectionable" books (some admittedly not obscene), notify the distributor in writing, inform the distributor of the Commission's duty to recommend obscenity prosecutions to the Attorney General and that the Commission's list of objectionable books was distributed to local police departments. The Commission thanked distributors in advance for their "cooperation," and a police officer usually visited the distributor to learn what action had been taken. In characterizing these practices as a system of prior administrative restraints, rather than mere legal advice, the Court observed that it did not mean to foreclose private consultation between law enforcement officers and distributors so long as such consultations were "genuinely undertaken with the purpose of aiding the distributor to comply" with the laws and avoid prosecution. What if the Commission circulated its list to distributors, police and prosecutors without mentioning prosecution? What if the prosecutor circulates a list of sixty books he or she regards as obscene and subject to prosecution?

3. ***Comparing obscenity and commercial speech.*** To combat deception, could commercial advertising be constitutionally subjected to a *Times Film* regime? Would such a scheme be permissible for advertising via some media, but not others? Reconsider fn. 24 in *Virginia Pharmacy,* Sec. 3, II supra. Should the prohibition on prior restraints be inapplicable to injunctions

against commercial advertising? Should *Freedman* standards be required? Should injunctions be permitted against a newspaper that carries unprotected advertising in addition to the advertiser?

PITTSBURGH PRESS CO. v. PITTSBURGH COMM'N ON HUMAN RELATIONS, 413 U.S. 376 (1973), per POWELL, J., upheld an order forbidding Pittsburgh Press to carry sex-designated "help wanted" ads, except for exempt jobs: "As described by Blackstone, the protection against prior restraint at common law barred only a system of administrative censorship. [While] the Court boldly stepped beyond this narrow doctrine in *Near* [it] has never held that all injunctions are impermissible. See *Lorain Journal Co. v. United States,* 342 U.S. 143 (1951).[215] The special vice of a prior restraint is that communication will be suppressed, either directly or by inducing excessive caution in the speaker, before an adequate determination that it is unprotected by the First Amendment.

"The present order does not endanger arguably protected speech. Because the order is based on a continuing course of repetitive conduct, this is not a case in which the Court is asked to speculate as to the effect of publication. Moreover, the order is clear and sweeps no more broadly than necessary. And because no interim relief was granted, the order will not have gone into effect until it was finally determined that the actions of Pittsburgh Press were unprotected."

STEWART, J., joined by Douglas, J., dissented: Putting to one side "the question of governmental power to prevent publication of information that would clearly imperil the military defense of our Nation," "no government agency can tell a newspaper in advance what it can print and what it cannot."[216]

III. LICENSING "PROFESSIONALS": A DICHOTOMY BETWEEN SPEECH AND PRESS?

LOWE v. SEC, 472 U.S. 181 (1985): The Investment Advisors Act of 1940 provides for injunctions and criminal penalties against anyone using the mails in conjunction with the advisory business who is not registered with the SEC or otherwise exempt from registration. The SEC sought an injunction against Lowe and his affiliated businesses primarily alleging that Lowe's registration with the SEC had been properly revoked because of various fraudulent activities,[217] and that by publishing investment newsletters, Lowe was using the mails as an investment advisor. The SEC

---

[215] *Lorain* upheld a Sherman Act injunction restraining a newspaper from seeking to monopolize commerce by refusing to carry advertising from merchants who advertised through a competing radio station.

[216] Blackmun, J., dissented "for substantially the reasons stated by" Stewart, J. Burger, C.J., dissenting, argued that the majority had mischaracterized the character and interim effect of the Commission's order.

[217] For example, during the period that he was giving personal investment advice, Lowe had been convicted of misappropriating funds of a client, tampering with evidence to cover up fraud of a client, and stealing from a bank.

did not claim that any information in the newsletters had been false or materially misleading or that Lowe had yet profited from the advice tendered. The SEC did contend that Lowe's prior criminal conduct showed his "total lack of fitness" to remain in an occupation with "numerous opportunities for dishonesty and self-dealing." Lowe denied that his newsletters were covered by the act and argued that, in any event, they were protected against registration and restraint under the First Amendment.

The Court, per STEVENS, J., denied that Lowe's publication of financial newsletters made him an investment advisor under the act. The Court's interpretation was strongly influenced by First Amendment considerations. The doctrine against prior restraints and the notion that freedom of the press includes everything from distributing leaflets to mass circulation of magazines was said to support a "broad reading" of the exclusion "that encompasses any newspaper, business publication, or financial publication provided that two conditions are met. The publication must be 'bona fide,' and it must be 'of regular and general circulation.' Neither of these conditions is defined, but the two qualifications precisely differentiate 'hit and run tipsters' and 'touts' from genuine publishers. Presumably a 'bona fide' publication would be genuine in the sense that it would contain disinterested commentary and analysis as opposed to promotional material disseminated by a 'tout.' Moreover, publications with a 'general and regular' circulation would not include 'people who send out bulletins from time to time on the advisability of buying and selling stocks' or 'hit and run tipsters.' Because the content of petitioners' newsletters was completely disinterested, and because they were offered[218] to the general public on a regular schedule, they are described by the plain language of the [exclusion].

"The dangers of fraud, deception, or overreaching that motivated the enactment of the statute are present in personalized communications but are not replicated in publications that are advertised and sold in an open market.[57] To the extent that the chart service contains factual information about past transactions and market trends, and the newsletters contain commentary on general market conditions, there can be no doubt about the protected character of the communications,[58] a matter that concerned

---

[218] Lowe's newsletters in fact did not appear according to schedule. White, J., concurring, remarked: "As is evident from the Court's conclusion that petitioner's publications meet the regularity requirement, the Court's construction of the requirement adopts the view of our major law reviews on the issue of regular publication: good intentions are enough."

[57] [Ct's Note] Cf. *Ohralik.* It is significant that the Commission has not established that petitioners have had authority over the funds of subscribers; that petitioners have been delegated decisionmaking authority to handle subscribers' portfolios or accounts; or that there have been individualized, investment-related interactions between petitioners and subscribers.

[58] [Ct's Note] Moreover, because we have squarely held that the expression of opinion about a commercial product such as a loudspeaker is protected by the First Amendment, *Bose Corp.,* Sec.

Congress when the exclusion was drafted. The content of the publications and the audience to which they are directed in this case reveal the specific limits of the exclusion. As long as the communications between petitioners and their subscribers remain entirely impersonal and do not develop into the kind of fiduciary, person-to-person relationships that were discussed at length in the legislative history of the Act and that are characteristic of investment adviser-client relationships, we believe the publications are, at least presumptively, within the exclusion."[219]

WHITE, J., joined by Burger, C.J., and Rehnquist, J., concurring, argued that the Court's statutory interpretation was "improvident" and "based on a thinly disguised conviction" that the Act was unconstitutional as applied to prohibit publication by unregistered advisors. "[While] purporting not to decide the question, the Court bases its statutory holding in large measure on the assumption that Congress already knew the answer to it when the statute was enacted. The Court thus attributes to the 76th Congress a clairvoyance the Solicitor General and the Second Circuit apparently lack—that is, the ability to predict our constitutional holdings 45 years in advance of our declining to reach them." Finding it necessary to reach the constitutional question, White, J., argued that an injunction against Lowe's publications would violate the First Amendment: "The power of government to regulate the professions is not lost whenever the practice of a profession entails speech. The underlying principle was expressed by the Court in *Giboney v. Empire Storage & Ice Co.,* 336 U.S. 490 (1949): 'it has never been deemed an abridgment of freedom of speech or press to make a course of conduct illegal merely because the conduct was in part initiated, evidenced, or carried out by means of language, either spoken, written, or printed.'

"Perhaps the most obvious example of a 'speaking profession' that is subject to governmental licensing is the legal profession. Although a lawyer's work is almost entirely devoted to the sort of communicative acts that, viewed in isolation, fall within the First Amendment's protection, we have never doubted that '[a] State can require high standards of qualification, such as good moral character or proficiency in its law, before it admits an applicant to the [bar].' [To] protect investors, the Government insists, it may require that investment advisers, like lawyers, evince the qualities of truth-speaking, honor, discretion, and fiduciary responsibility.

"But the principle that the government may restrict entry into professions and vocations through licensing schemes has never been extended to encompass the licensing of speech per se or of the press. At some point, a measure is no longer a regulation of a profession but a regulation of speech or of the press; beyond that point, the statute must

---

1, II, B supra, it is difficult to see why the expression of an opinion about a marketable security should not also be protected.

[219] Powell, J., took no part.

survive the level of scrutiny demanded by the First Amendment." [It] is for us, then, to find some principle by which to answer the question whether the Investment Advisers Act as applied to petitioner operates as a regulation of speech or of professional conduct.

"This is a problem Justice Jackson wrestled with in his concurring opinion in *Thomas v. Collins*. His words are instructive: '[A] rough distinction always exists, I think, which is more shortly illustrated than explained. A state may forbid one without its license to practice law as a vocation, but I think it could not stop an unlicensed person from making a speech about the rights of man or the rights of labor, or any other kind of right, including recommending that his hearers organize to support his views. Likewise, the state may prohibit the pursuit of medicine as an occupation without its license, but I do not think it could make it a crime publicly or privately to speak urging persons to follow or reject any school of medical thought. So the state to an extent not necessary now to determine may regulate one who makes a business or a livelihood of soliciting funds or memberships for unions. But I do not think it can prohibit one, even if he is a salaried labor leader, from making an address to a public meeting of workmen, telling them their rights as he sees them and urging them to unite in general or to join a specific union.'

"Justice Jackson concluded that the distinguishing factor was whether the speech in any particular case was 'associat[ed] [with] some other factor which the state may regulate so as to bring the whole within its official control.' If 'in a particular case the association or characterization is a proven and valid one,' he concluded, the regulation may stand.

"These ideas help to locate the point where regulation of a profession leaves off and prohibitions on speech begin. One who takes the affairs of a client personally in hand and purports to exercise judgment on behalf of the client in the light of the client's individual needs and circumstances is properly viewed as engaging in the practice of a profession. Just as offer and acceptance are communications incidental to the regulable transaction called a contract, the professional's speech is incidental to the conduct of the profession. [Where] the personal nexus between professional and client does not exist, and a speaker does not purport to be exercising judgment on behalf of any particular individual with whose circumstances he is directly acquainted, government regulation ceases to function as legitimate regulation of professional practice with only incidental impact on speech; it becomes regulation of speaking or publishing as such, subject to the First Amendment's [command].

"[E]ven where mere 'commercial speech' is concerned, the First Amendment permits restraints on speech only when they are narrowly tailored to advance a legitimate governmental interest. The interest here is certainly legitimate: the Government wants to prevent investors from falling into the hands of scoundrels and swindlers. The means chosen, however, is extreme. [Our] commercial speech cases have consistently rejected the proposition that such drastic prohibitions on speech may be justified by a mere possibility that the prohibited speech will be fraudulent. See *Zauderer; Bates.* * * *

"I emphasize the narrowness of the constitutional basis on which I would decide this case. [I] would by no means foreclose the application of, for example, the Act's antifraud or reporting provisions to investment advisers (registered or unregistered) who offer their advice through publications. Nor do I intend to suggest that it is unconstitutional to invoke the Act's provisions for injunctive relief and criminal penalties against unregistered persons who, for compensation, offer personal investment advice to individual clients. I would hold only that the Act may not constitutionally be applied to prevent persons who are unregistered (including persons whose registration has been denied or revoked) from offering impersonal investment advice through publications such as the newsletters published by petitioner."

NOTES AND QUESTIONS

1. **Professions.** Is White, J.'s speech/profession dichotomy persuasive? Should the existence of a "profession" justify prior restraints? If so, are there free speech limits on the conditions that can be employed for admitting lawyers? Can a candidate who has persistently been engaged in racist speech be excluded on that ground? See W. Bradley Wendel, *Free Speech for Lawyers*, 28 Hast. Con. L.Q. 305 (2001).

2. **Free legal advice.** Consider C. Edwin Baker, *First Amendment Limits on Copyright*, 55 Vand. L. Rev. 902 (2002): "Although doctrinally less clear, a nonlawyer or nondoctor should have a free speech right to give away her amateur legal or medical advice or views, at least if her manner of doing so would not cause the recipient to confuse her for a licensed lawyer or doctor, but no free speech right to charge for individualized provision of these views."

3. **Content control of legal advice.** Consider Eugene Volokh, *Speech as Conduct: Generally Applicable Laws, Illegal Courses of Conduct, "Situation-Altering Utterances," and the Uncharted Zones*, 90 Cornell L. Rev. 1277 (2005): "[I]t's far from clear that the government should be completely free to regulate professionals' speech to their clients. For instance, I doubt that the government may simply ban doctors from informing patients that marijuana is the best solution to their problems. Perhaps doctors could be prevented from writing recommendations that, by operation of state law, free patients from state liability for marijuana possession, though even that is not clear. But I'm fairly certain that doctors at least have the constitutional right to inform their patients of the medical benefits of marijuana, and to urge the patients to lobby their legislators to enact a medical marijuana exception."

4. ***Press privilege?*** Does White, J., suggest an element of special privilege for the press? Consider Steven Shiffrin, *The First Amendment and Economic Regulation: Away from a General Theory of the First Amendment,* 78 Nw.U.L.Rev. 1212 (1983): "The doctrine of prior restraint may have been designed to put the press on an equal footing. People could speak or write without a license and that ought not to change merely because they used a printing press. Yet we now license a good deal of speech (for example, of lawyers), and those licenses are clearly prior restraints. So we have turned the law upside down. To speak you sometimes need a license; to use the press you almost never do. A doctrine designed to create equality for the press has evolved into one that gives it a special place."

5. ***Licensing limits?*** If lawyers, psychiatrists, and investment advisors can be licensed, what about fortune tellers? Union organizers? Journalists?

———

RILEY v. NATIONAL FEDERATION OF THE BLIND, 487 U.S. 781 (1988), per BRENNAN, J., invalidated a scheme for licensing professional fundraisers who were soliciting on behalf of charitable organizations: "[North Carolina's] provision requires professional fundraisers to await a determination regarding their license application before engaging in solicitation, while volunteer fundraisers, or those employed by the charity, may solicit immediately upon submitting an application. [It] is well settled that a speaker's rights are not lost merely because compensation is received; a speaker is no less a speaker because he or she is paid to speak. [Generally,] speakers need not obtain a license to speak. However, that rule is not absolute. For example, states may impose valid time, place, or manner restrictions. North Carolina seeks to come within the exception by alleging a heightened interest in regulating those who solicit money. Even assuming that the State's interest does justify requiring fundraisers to obtain a license before soliciting, such a regulation must provide that the licensor 'will, within a specified brief period, either issue a license or go to court.' *Freedman.* [The] statute on its face does not purport to require when a determination must be made, nor is there an administrative regulation or interpretation doing so."

REHNQUIST, C.J., joined by O'Connor, J., dissented: "It simply is not true that [fundraisers] are prevented from engaging in any protected speech on their own behalf by the State's licensing requirements; the requirements only restrict their ability to engage in the profession of 'solicitation' without a license. We do not view bar admission requirements as invalid because they restrict a prospective lawyer's 'right' to be hired as an advocate by a client. So in this case we should not subject to strict scrutiny the State's attempt to license a business—professional fundraising—some of whose members might reasonably be thought to pose a risk of fraudulent activity."[220]

IV. PRIOR RESTRAINTS AND NATIONAL SECURITY

NEW YORK TIMES CO. V. UNITED STATES
[THE PENTAGON PAPERS CASE]
403 U.S. 713, 91 S.Ct. 2140, 29 L.Ed.2d 822 (1971).

PER CURIAM.

We granted certiorari in these cases in which the United States seeks to enjoin the *New York Times* and the *Washington Post* from publishing the contents of a classified study entitled "History of U.S. Decision-Making Process on Viet Nam Policy."[221]

"Any system of prior restraints of expression comes to this Court bearing a heavy presumption against its constitutional validity." *Bantam Books;* see also *Near.* The Government "thus carries a heavy burden of showing justification for the enforcement of such a restraint." [The district court in the *Times* case and both lower federal courts] in the *Post* case held that the Government had not met that burden. We agree. [T]he stays entered [by this Court five days previously] are vacated. * * *

JUSTICE BLACK, with whom JUSTICE DOUGLAS joins, concurring.

I adhere to the view that the Government's case against the *Post* should have been dismissed and that the injunction against the *Times* should have been vacated without oral argument when the cases were first presented to this Court. I believe that every moment's continuance of the injunctions against these newspapers amounts to a flagrant, indefensible, and continuing violation of the First Amendment. Furthermore, after oral arguments, I agree [with] the reasons stated by my Brothers Douglas and Brennan. In my view it is unfortunate that some of my Brethren are apparently willing to hold that the publication of news may sometimes be enjoined. Such a holding would make a shambles of the First Amendment.

[F]or the first time in the 182 years since the founding of the Republic, the federal courts are asked to hold that the First Amendment does not mean what it says, but rather means that the Government can halt the

---

[220] Stevens, J., also dissented from the Court's treatment of the licensing issue. Under what circumstances should restrictions on charitable solicitation be permitted? See John D. Inazu, *Making Sense of Schaumberg: Seeking Coherence in First Amendment Charitable Solicitation Law,* 92 Marq. L.Rev. 551 (2009). Should begging be treated differently?

[221] On June 12–14, 1971 the *New York Times* and on June 18 the *Washington Post* published portions of this "top secret" Pentagon study. Government actions seeking temporary restraining orders and injunctions progressed through two district courts and two courts of appeals between June 15–23. After a June 26 argument, ten Supreme Court opinions were issued on June 30, 1971. For discussion, see Randall Bezanson, *How Free Can the Press Be?,* 7–57 (2003).

publication of current news of vital importance to the people of this country.
* * *

The Government does not even attempt to rely on any act of Congress. Instead it makes the bold and dangerously far-reaching contention that the courts should take it upon themselves to "make" a law abridging freedom of the press in the name of equity, presidential power and national security, even when the representatives of the people in Congress have adhered to the command of the First Amendment and refused to make such a law. To find that the President has "inherent power" to halt the publication of news by resort to the courts would wipe out the First Amendment and destroy the fundamental liberty and security of the very people the Government hopes to make "secure." [The] word "security" is a broad, vague generality whose contours should not be invoked to abrogate the fundamental law embodied in the First Amendment. * * *

JUSTICE DOUGLAS, with whom JUSTICE BLACK joins, concurring.

While I join the opinion of the Court I believe it necessary to express my views more fully.

[The First Amendment leaves] no room for governmental[222] restraint on the press. There is, moreover, no statute barring the publication by the press of the material which the *Times* and *Post* seek to use. [These] disclosures may have a serious impact. But that is no basis for sanctioning a previous restraint on the press * * * .

The dominant purpose of the First Amendment was to prohibit the widespread practice of governmental suppression of embarrassing information. [A] debate of large proportions goes on in the Nation over our posture in Vietnam. That debate antedated the disclosure of the contents of the present documents. The latter are highly relevant to the debate in progress.

Secrecy in government is fundamentally anti-democratic, perpetuating bureaucratic errors. Open debate and discussion of public issues are vital to our national health. [The] stays in these cases that have been in effect for more than a week constitute a flouting of the principles of the First Amendment as interpreted in *Near*.

JUSTICE BRENNAN, concurring.

I write separately [to] emphasize what should be apparent: that our judgment in the present cases may not be taken to indicate the propriety, in the future, of issuing temporary stays and restraining orders to block the publication of material sought to be suppressed by the Government. So

---

[222] But see Mark Denbeaux, *The First Word of the First Amendment,* 80 Nw.U.L.Rev. 1156 (1986).

far as I can determine, never before has the United States sought to enjoin a newspaper from publishing information in its possession. * * *

The entire thrust of the Government's claim throughout these cases has been that publication of the material sought to be enjoined "could," or "might," or "may" prejudice the national interest in various ways. But the First Amendment tolerates absolutely no prior judicial restraints of the press predicated upon surmise or conjecture that untoward consequences may result.* Our cases, it is true, have indicated that there is a single, extremely narrow class of cases in which the First Amendment's ban on prior judicial restraint may be overridden. Our cases have thus far indicated that such cases may arise only when the Nation "is at war," [*Schenck*]. Even if the present world situation were assumed to be tantamount to a time of war, or if the power of presently available armaments would justify even in peacetime the suppression of information that would set in motion a nuclear holocaust, in neither of these actions has the Government presented or even alleged that publication of items from or based upon the material at issue would cause the happening of an event of that nature. [Thus,] only governmental allegation and proof that publication must inevitably, directly and immediately cause the occurrence of an event kindred to imperiling the safety of a transport already at sea can support even the issuance of an interim restraining order. In no event may mere conclusions be sufficient: for if the Executive Branch seeks judicial aid in preventing publication, it must inevitably submit the basis upon which that aid is sought to scrutiny by the judiciary. And therefore, every restraint issued in this case, whatever its form, has violated the First Amendment—and not less so because that restraint was justified as necessary to afford the courts an opportunity to examine the claim more thoroughly. Unless and until the Government has clearly made out its case, the First Amendment commands that no injunction may issue.

JUSTICE STEWART, with whom JUSTICE WHITE joins, concurring.

[I]n the cases before us we are asked neither to construe specific regulations nor to apply specific laws. [We] are asked, quite simply, to prevent the publication by two newspapers of material that the Executive Branch insists should not, in the national interest, be published. I am convinced that the Executive is correct with respect to some of the documents involved. But I cannot say that disclosure of any of them will surely result in direct, immediate, and irreparable damage to our Nation

---

* **[Ct's Note]** *Freedman* and similar cases regarding temporary restraints of allegedly obscene materials are not in point. For those cases rest upon the proposition that "obscenity is not protected by the freedoms of speech and press." *Roth*. Here there is no question but that the material sought to be suppressed is within the protection of the First Amendment; the only question is whether, notwithstanding that fact, its publication may be enjoined for a time because of the presence of an overwhelming national interest. * * *

or its people. That being so, there can under the First Amendment be but one judicial resolution of the issues before us. I join the judgments * * * .

JUSTICE WHITE, with whom JUSTICE STEWART joins, concurring.

I concur in today's judgments, but only because of the concededly extraordinary protection against prior restraints enjoyed by the press under our constitutional system. I do not say that in no circumstances would the First Amendment permit an injunction against publishing information about government plans or operations. Nor, after examining the materials the Government characterizes as the most sensitive and destructive, can I deny that revelation of these documents will do substantial damage to public interests. Indeed, I am confident that their disclosure will have that result. But I nevertheless agree that the United States has not satisfied the very heavy burden which it must meet to warrant an injunction against publication in these cases, at least in the absence of express and appropriately limited congressional authorization for prior restraints in circumstances such as these.

The Government's position is simply stated: The responsibility of the Executive for the conduct of the foreign affairs and for the security of the Nation is so basic that the President is entitled to an injunction against publication of a newspaper story whenever he can convince a court that the information to be revealed threatens "grave and irreparable" injury to the public interest; and the injunction should issue whether or not the material to be published is classified, whether or not publication would be lawful under relevant criminal statutes enacted by Congress and regardless of the circumstances by which the newspaper came into possession of the information.

At least in the absence of legislation by Congress, based on its own investigations and findings, I am quite unable to agree that the inherent powers of the Executive and the courts reach so far as to authorize remedies having such sweeping potential for inhibiting publications by the press. [To] sustain the Government in these cases would start the courts down a long and hazardous road that I am not willing to travel at least without congressional guidance and direction.

* * * Prior restraints require an unusually heavy justification under the First Amendment; but failure by the Government to justify prior restraints does not measure its constitutional entitlement to a conviction for criminal publication. That the Government mistakenly chose to proceed by injunction does not mean that it could not successfully proceed in another way.

* * * Congress has addressed itself to the problems of protecting the security of the country and the national defense from unauthorized disclosure of potentially damaging information. It has not, however, authorized the injunctive remedy against threatened publication. It has

apparently been satisfied to rely on criminal sanctions and their deterrent effect on the responsible as well as the irresponsible press. * * *

JUSTICE HARLAN, with whom THE CHIEF JUSTICE and JUSTICE BLACKMUN join, dissenting. * * *

With all respect, I consider that the Court has been almost irresponsibly feverish in dealing with these cases. Both [the] Second Circuit and [the] District of Columbia Circuit rendered judgment on June 23. [This] Court's order setting a hearing before us on June 26 at 11 a.m., a course which I joined only to avoid the possibility of even more peremptory action by the Court, was issued less than 24 hours before. The record in the *Post* case was filed with the Clerk shortly before 1 p.m. on June 25; the record in the *Times* case did not arrive until 7 or 8 o'clock that same night. The briefs of the parties were received less than two hours before argument on June 26.

This frenzied train of events took place in the name of the presumption against prior restraints created by the First Amendment. Due regard for the extraordinarily important and difficult questions involved in these litigations should have led the Court to shun such a precipitate timetable. In order to decide the merits of these cases properly, some or all of the following questions should have been faced: * * *

2.   Whether the First Amendment permits the federal courts to enjoin publication of stories which would present a serious threat to national security. See *Near* (dictum). * * *

4.   Whether the unauthorized disclosure of any of these particular documents would seriously impair the national security.

5.   What weight should be given to the opinion of high officers in the Executive Branch of the Government with respect to [question 4]. * * *

7.   Whether the threatened harm to the national security or the Government's possessory interest in the documents justifies the issuance of an injunction against publication in light of—

a.   The strong First Amendment policy against prior restraints on publication; b. The doctrine against enjoining conduct in violation of criminal statutes; and c. The extent to which the materials at issue have apparently already been otherwise disseminated.

These are difficult questions of fact, of law, and of judgment; the potential consequences of erroneous decision are enormous. The time which has been available to us, to the lower courts, and to the parties has been wholly inadequate for giving these cases the kind of consideration they deserve. It is a reflection on the stability of the judicial process that these great issues—as important as any that have arisen during my time on the

Court—should have been decided under the pressures engendered by the torrent of publicity that has attended these litigations from their inception.

Forced as I am to reach the merits of these cases, I dissent from the opinion and judgments of the Court. Within the severe limitations imposed by the time constraints under which I have been required to operate, I can only state my reasons in telescoped form, even though in different circumstances I would have felt constrained to deal with the cases in the fuller sweep indicated above.

[It] is plain to me that the scope of the judicial function in passing upon the activities of the Executive Branch of the Government in the field of foreign affairs is very narrowly restricted. This view is, I think, dictated by the concept of separation of powers upon which our constitutional system [rests.] I agree that, in performance of its duty to protect the values of the First Amendment against political pressures, the judiciary must review the initial Executive determination to the point of satisfying itself that the subject matter of the dispute does lie within the proper compass of the President's foreign relations power. Constitutional considerations forbid "a complete abandonment of judicial control." Moreover, the judiciary may properly insist that the determination that disclosure of the subject matter would irreparably impair the national security be made by the head of the Executive Department concerned—here the Secretary of State or the Secretary of Defense—after actual personal consideration by that officer.[223] This safeguard is required in the analogous area of executive claims of privilege for secrets of state.

But in my judgment the judiciary may not properly go beyond these two inquiries and redetermine for itself the probable impact of disclosure on the national security. "[T]he very nature of executive decisions as to foreign policy is political, not judicial. Such decisions are wholly confided by our Constitution to the political departments of the government, Executive and Legislative. They are delicate, complex, and involve large elements of prophecy. They are and should be undertaken only by those directly responsible to the people whose welfare they advance or imperil. They are decisions of a kind for which the judiciary has neither aptitude, facilities nor responsibility and which has long been held to belong in the domain of political power not subject to judicial intrusion or inquiry."

---

[223] Consider Stanley Godofsky & Howard Rogatnick, *Prior Restraints: The Pentagon Papers Case Revisited,* 18 Cum.L.Rev. 527 (1988): "Ironically, Justice Harlan's view of the Constitution might, ultimately, have presented more problems for the Government than those of most of the other Justices. Realistically, how often can the Secretary of State or Secretary of Defense devote 'actual personal consideration' to the question of whether material about to be published should be suppressed? And of what does 'actual personal consideration' consist? Must the Secretary himself read the documents? Is it sufficient 'consideration' by a Cabinet officer to act on the advice of his subordinates? If so, is not the 'actual personal consideration' test substantially meaningless? Could a Cabinet officer be required to testify as to the basis for his decision in order to test his 'bona fides'?"

Chicago & S. Air Lines v. Waterman S.S. Corp. (Jackson, J.), 333 U.S. 103 (1948).

Even if there is some room for the judiciary to override the executive determination, it is plain that the scope of review must be exceedingly narrow. I can see no indication in the opinions of either the District Court or the Court of Appeals in the *Post* litigation that the conclusions of the Executive were given even the deference owing to an administrative agency, much less that owing to a co-equal branch of the Government operating within the field of its constitutional prerogative. * * *

Pending further hearings in each case conducted under the appropriate ground rules, I would continue the restraints on publication. I cannot believe that the doctrine prohibiting prior restraints reaches to the point of preventing courts from maintaining the status quo long enough to act responsibly in matters of such national importance as those involved here.

JUSTICE BLACKMUN, dissenting.

[The First Amendment] is only one part of an entire Constitution. Article II of the great document vests in the Executive Branch primary power over the conduct of foreign affairs and places in that branch the responsibility for the Nation's safety. Each provision of the Constitution is important, and I cannot subscribe to a doctrine of unlimited absolutism for the First Amendment at the cost of downgrading other provisions. First Amendment absolutism has never commanded a majority of this Court. What is needed here is a weighing, upon properly developed standards, of the broad right of the press to print and of the very narrow right of the Government to prevent. Such standards are not yet developed. The parties here are in disagreement as to what those standards should be. But even the newspapers concede that there are situations where restraint is in order and is constitutional. Mr. Justice Holmes gave us a suggestion when he said in *Schenck,* "It is a question of proximity and degree. When a nation is at war many things that might be said in time of peace are such a hindrance to its effort that their utterance will not be endured so long as men fight and that no Court could regard them as protected by any constitutional right."

I therefore would remand these cases to be developed expeditiously, of course, but on a schedule permitting the orderly presentation of evidence from both sides [and] with the preparation of briefs, oral argument and court opinions of a quality better than has been seen to this point. [T]hese cases and the issues involved and the courts, including this one, deserve better than has been produced thus far. * * *[224]

---

[224] Marshall, J., concurring, did not deal with First Amendment issues but only with separation of powers—the government's attempt to secure through the Court injunctive relief that Congress had refused to authorize.

NOTES AND QUESTIONS

1. ***What did the case decide?*** Do you agree that "the case [did] not make any law at all, good or bad"? That on the question "whether injunctions against the press are permissible, it is clear that [the case] can supply no precedent?" See Peter Junger, *Down Memory Lane: The Case of the Pentagon Papers,* 23 Case W.Res.L.Rev. 3 (1971). Or do the several concurring opinions yield a discernible standard that must be satisfied before an injunction against the press can be issued on national security grounds? Cf. 85 Harv.L.Rev. 199 (1971). What if Congress were explicitly to authorize an injunction in narrow terms to protect national security? Might this be a separation of powers decision, like the *Steel Seizure* case, as well as a First Amendment decision? See Junger, supra.

2. ***"De facto" prior restraint.*** One difficulty with viewing the prior restraint doctrine as "simply creat[ing] a 'presumption' against the validity of the restraint" (Emerson's characterization of the current approach) rather than as "a prohibition on all restraints subject to certain categorical exceptions," observes Thomas Emerson, *First Amendment Doctrine and the Burger Court,* 68 Calif.L.Rev. 422 (1980), is that "the requirement of ad hoc scrutiny of prior restraints is itself likely to result in a 'de facto' prior restraint." Pointing to Brennan, J.'s comment in *Pentagon Papers* that "every restraint issued in this case [has] violated the First Amendment—and not less so because that restraint was justified as necessary to afford the courts an opportunity to examine the claim more thoroughly," Emerson notes that "[t]his is exactly what happened when the government sought to enjoin *The Progressive* magazine from publishing an article on the manufacture of the hydrogen bomb. The Supreme Court refused to order an expedited appeal from the [federal district court] injunction against publication [and, although the case was ultimately dismissed by the Seventh Circuit,] *The Progressive* remained under effective prior restraint for nearly seven months."

Compare *Near* and *Pentagon Papers* with UNITED STATES v. PROGRESSIVE, INC., 467 F.Supp. 990 (W.D.Wis.) (preliminary injunction issued Mar. 28, 1979), request for writ of mandamus den. sub nom. *Morland v. Sprecher,* 443 U.S. 709 (1979), case dismissed, 610 F.2d 819 (7th Cir.1979).[225] *The Progressive* planned to publish an article. "The H-Bomb Secret—How We Got It, Why We're Telling It," maintaining that the article would contribute to

---

Burger, C.J., dissenting, complained that because of "unseemly haste," "we do not know the facts of this case. [W]e literally do not know what we are acting on." He expressed no views on the merits, apart from his joinder in Harlan, J.'s opinion, and a statement that he would have continued the temporary restraints in effect while returning the cases to the lower courts for more thorough exploration of the facts and issues.

[225] The government's action against *The Progressive* was abandoned after information similar to that it sought to enjoin was published elsewhere. For discussion see David Rudenstine, *Transcript of Weapons of Mass Destruction, National Security, and a Free Press: Seminal Issues as Viewed Through the Lens of the Progressive Case,* 26 Cardozo L. Rev. 1337 (2005); Ray E. Kidder, *Weapons of Mass Destruction, National Security, and a Free Press,* 26 Cardozo L. Rev. 1389 (2005). Under what circumstances should the government be able to prosecute a nongovernmental actor for disseminating national security information? See generally Mary-Rose Papandrea, *Lapdogs, Watchdogs, and Scapegoats: The Press and National Security Information,* 83 Ind. L.J. 233 (2008).

informed opinion about nuclear weapons and demonstrate the inadequacies of a system of secrecy and classification. Although the government conceded that at least some of the information contained in the article was "in the public domain" or had been "declassified," it argued that "national security" permitted it to censor information originating in the public domain "if when drawn together, synthesized and collated, such information acquires the character of presenting immediate, direct and irreparable harm to the interests of the United States." The Secretary of State stated that publication would increase thermonuclear proliferation and that this would "irreparably impair the national security of the United States." The Secretary of Defense maintained that dissemination of the Morland article would lead to a substantial increase in the risk of thermonuclear proliferation and to use or threats that would "adversely affect the national security of the United States."

Although recognizing that this constituted "the first instance of prior restraint against a publication in this fashion in the [nation's history]," the district court enjoined defendants, pending final resolution of the litigation, from publishing or otherwise disclosing any information designated by the government as "restricted data" within the meaning of The Atomic Energy Act of 1954: "What is involved here is information dealing with the most destructive weapon in the history of mankind, information of sufficient destructive potential to nullify the right to free speech and to endanger the right to life itself. [Faced] with a stark choice between upholding the right to continued life and the right to freedom of the press, most jurists would have no difficulty in opting for the chance to continue to breathe and function as they work to achieve perfect freedom of expression.

"[A] mistake in ruling against *The Progressive* will seriously infringe cherished First Amendment rights. [A] mistake in ruling against the United States could pave the way for thermonuclear annihilation for us all. In that event, our right to life is extinguished and the right to publish becomes moot.

"[W]ar by foot soldiers has been replaced in large part by machines and bombs. No longer need there be any advance warning or any preparation time before a nuclear war could be commenced. [In light of these factors] publication of the technical information on the hydrogen bomb contained in the article is analogous to publication of troop movements or locations in time of war and falls within the extremely narrow exception to the rule against prior restraint [recognized in *Near*].[226]

"The government has met its burden under § 2274 of The Atomic Energy Act [, which authorizes injunctive relief against one who would communicate or disclose restricted data 'with reason to believe such data will be utilized to. injure the United States or to secure an advantage to any foreign nation.']. [I]t

---

[226] One of the reasons the court gave for finding that the objected-to technical portions of the article fell within the *Near* exception was that it was "unconvinced that suppression of [these portions] would in any plausible fashion impede the defendants in their laudable crusade to stimulate public knowledge of nuclear armament and bring about enlightened debate on national policy questions." Should this have been a factor in the decision to issue the preliminary injunction?

has also met the test enunciated by two Justices in *Pentagon Papers,* namely grave, direct, immediate and irreparable harm to the United States."

The court distinguished *Pentagon Papers*: "[T]he study involved [there] contained historical data relating to events some three to twenty years previously. Secondly, the Supreme Court agreed with the lower court that no cogent reasons were advanced by the government as to why the article affected national security except that publication might cause some embarrassment to the United States. A final and most vital difference between these two cases is the fact that a specific statute is involved here [§ 2274 of The Atomic Energy Act]."

3.　*CIA secrecy agreement.* The Central Intelligence Agency requires employees to sign a "secrecy agreement" as a condition of employment, an agreement committing the employee not to reveal classified information nor to publish any information obtained during the course of employment without prior approval of the Agency. In SNEPP v. UNITED STATES, 444 U.S. 507 (1980), Snepp had published a book called *Decent Interval* about certain CIA activities in South Vietnam based on his experiences as an agency employee without seeking prepublication review. At least for purposes of the litigation, the government conceded that Snepp's book divulged no confidential information. The Court, per curiam (Stevens, J., joined by Brennan and Marshall, JJ., dissenting) held that Snepp's failure to submit the book was a breach of trust and the government was entitled to a constructive trust on the proceeds of the book: "[E]ven in the absence of an express agreement, the CIA could have acted to protect substantial government interests by imposing reasonable restrictions on employee activities that in other contexts might be protected by the First Amendment. The Government has a compelling interest in protecting both the secrecy of information important to our national security and the appearance of confidentiality so essential to the effective operation of our foreign intelligence service."[227] When employees or past employees do submit publications for clearance, should *Freedman* standards apply? Can former CIA employees be required to submit all public speeches relating to their former employment for clearance? Are extemporaneous remarks permitted? To what extent can secrecy agreements be required of public employees outside the national security area?[228]

---

[227] Compare *Haig v. Agee,* 453 U.S. 280 (1981), stating that "repeated disclosures of intelligence operations and names of intelligence personnel" for the "purpose of obstructing intelligence operations and the recruiting of intelligence personnel" are "clearly not protected by the Constitution." What if the publisher of the information merely has "reason to believe that such activities would impair or impede the foreign intelligence activities of the United States"? See 50 U.S.C. § 421.

[228] For discussion of *Snepp,* see Mary Cheh, *Judicial Supervision of Executive Secrecy,* 69 Corn.L.Rev. 690 (1984); Frank Easterbrook, *Insider Trading, Secret Agents, Evidentiary Privileges, and the Production of Information,* 1981 Sup.Ct.Rev. 309; Stanley Godofsky & Howard Rogatnick, *Prior Restraints: The Pentagon Papers Case Revisited,* fn. 223 supra (1988); Judith Koffler & Bennett Gershman, *The New Seditious Libel,* 69 Corn.L.Rev. 816 (1984); Jonathan Medow, *The First Amendment and the Secrecy State: Snepp v. United States,* 130 U.Pa.L.Rev. 775 (1982). For a thorough exploration of the occasions in which secrecy has been preferred over public knowledge, see Benjamin DuVal, *The Occasions of Secrecy,* 47 U.Pitt.L.Rev. 579 (1986).

5. JUSTICE AND NEWSGATHERING

This section explores three problems connected with the fair administration of justice or with newsgathering or with both. The first problem involves pre-trial publicity. The government seeks to deter or punish speech by the press that it fears will threaten the fair administration of justice, but speech of that character falls into no recognized category of unprotected speech. Thus, the courts must consider whether absolute protection is called for, or, alternatively, whether new categories or ad hoc determinations are appropriate, and whether prior restraints are permissible. Alternatively, if the press cannot be prevented from speaking about trials, can prosecutors, defense attorneys, litigants and potential witnesses be prevented from speaking to the press?

In the second problem the government seeks to fairly administer the justice system by forcing reporters to reveal their confidential sources. The press maintains that any such authorized compulsion would have a chilling effect on its ability to gather the news.

In the final problem, government seeks not to punish speech, but to administer justice in private. It refuses to let the public or press witness its handling of prisoners, or its conduct of trial or pre-trial proceedings. The question is whether the First Amendment can serve as a sword allowing the press or citizen-critics to gather information. Assuming it can, what are its limits within the justice system? Does any right of access reach beyond the justice system? Does the First Amendment require that the press be granted access not afforded the public? Does the First Amendment permit differential access? If so, what are the limits on how government defines the press?

I. PUBLICITY ABOUT TRIALS

In a number of cases, defendants have asserted that their rights to a fair trial have been abridged by newspaper publicity.

SHEPPARD v. MAXWELL, 384 U.S. 333 (1966), is probably the most notorious "trial by newspaper" case. The Court, per CLARK, J., (Black, J. dissenting) agreed with the "finding" of the Ohio Supreme Court that the atmosphere of defendant's murder trial was that of a " 'Roman holiday' for the news media." The courtroom was jammed with reporters. And in the corridors outside the courtroom, "a host of photographers and television personnel" photographed witnesses, counsel and jurors as they entered and left the courtroom. Throughout the trial, there was a deluge of publicity, much of which contained information never presented at trial, yet the jurors were not sequestered until the trial was over and they had begun their deliberations.

The Court placed the primary blame on the trial judge. He could "easily" have prevented "the carnival atmosphere of the trial" since "the courtroom and courthouse premises" were subject to his control. For example, he should have provided privacy for the jury, insulated witnesses from the media, instead of allowing them to be interviewed at will, and "made some effort to control the release of leads, information, and gossip to the press by police officers, witnesses, and the counsel for both sides." No one "coming under the jurisdiction of the court should be permitted to frustrate its function."

The Court recognized that "there is nothing that proscribes the press from reporting events that transpire in the courtroom. But where there is a reasonable likelihood that prejudicial news prior to trial will prevent a fair trial, the judge should continue the case until the threat abates, or transfer it to another county not so permeated with publicity. In addition, sequestration of the jury was something the judge should have raised sua sponte with counsel. If publicity during the proceedings threatens the fairness of the trial, a new trial should be ordered. But we must remember that reversals are but palliatives; the cure lies in those remedial measures that will prevent the prejudice at its inception."

The Court, however, reiterated its extreme reluctance "to place any direct limitations on the freedom traditionally exercised by the news media for '[w]hat transpires in the courtroom is public property.'" The press "does not simply publish information about trials but guards against the miscarriage of justice by subjecting the police, prosecutors, and judicial processes to extensive public scrutiny and criticism."

———

In anticipation of the trial of Simants for a mass murder which had attracted widespread news coverage, the county court prohibited everyone in attendance from, inter alia, releasing or authorizing for publication "any testimony given or evidence adduced." Simants' preliminary hearing (open to the public) was held the same day, subject to the restrictive order. Simants was bound over for trial. Respondent Nebraska state trial judge then entered an order which, as modified by the state supreme court, restrained the press and broadcasting media from reporting any confessions or incriminating statements made by Simants to law enforcement officers or third parties, except members of the press, and from reporting other facts "strongly implicative" of the defendant. The order expired when the jury was impaneled.

In NEBRASKA PRESS ASS'N v. STUART, 427 U.S. 539 (1976), the Court granted review while Simants' conviction was pending on appeal in the state supreme court. The Court, per BURGER, C.J., struck down the state court order: "To the extent that the order prohibited the reporting of evidence adduced at the open preliminary hearing, it plainly violated settled principles: 'There is nothing that proscribes the press from reporting events that transpire in the courtroom.' *Sheppard.*"[229] To the extent that the order prohibited publication "based on information gained from other sources, [the] heavy burden imposed as a condition to securing a prior restraint was not met." The portion of the order regarding "implicative" information was also "too vague and too broad" to survive scrutiny of restraints on First Amendment rights.

"[P]retrial publicity—even pervasive, adverse publicity—does not inevitably lead to an unfair trial. The capacity of the jury eventually impaneled to decide the case fairly is influenced by the tone and extent of the publicity, which is in part, and often in large part, shaped by what attorneys, police and other officials do to precipitate news coverage. [T]he measures a judge takes or fails to take to mitigate the effects of pretrial publicity—the measures described in *Sheppard*—may well determine whether the defendant receives a trial consistent [with] due process.

"[The] Court has interpreted [First Amendment] guarantees to afford special protection against orders that prohibit the publication or broadcast of particular information or commentary—orders that impose [a] 'prior' restraint on speech. None of our decided cases on prior restraint involved restrictive orders entered to protect a defendant's right to a fair and impartial jury, but [they] have a common thread relevant to this case. * * *

"The thread running through [*Near* and *Pentagon Papers*], is that prior restraints on speech and publication are the most serious and the least tolerable infringement on First Amendment rights. A criminal penalty or a judgment in a defamation case is subject to the whole panoply of protections afforded by deferring the impact of the judgment until all avenues of appellate review have been exhausted. [But] a prior restraint [has] an immediate and irreversible sanction. If it can be said that a threat of criminal or civil sanctions after publication 'chills' speech, prior restraint 'freezes' it at least for the time.

"[I]f the authors of [the first and sixth amendments], fully aware of the potential conflicts between them, were unwilling or unable to resolve the issue by assigning to one priority over the other, it is not for us to rewrite the Constitution by undertaking what they declined. [Yet] it is nonetheless clear that the barriers to prior restraint remain high unless we are to abandon what the Court has said for nearly a quarter of our national existence and implied throughout all of [it.]

"We turn now to the record in this case to determine whether, as Learned Hand put it, 'the gravity of the 'evil,' discounted by its improbability, justifies such invasion of free speech as is necessary to avoid

---

[229] The Court added, however, that the county court "could not know that closure of the preliminary hearing was an alternative open to it until the Nebraska Supreme Court so construed state law.

the danger,' *Dennis* [2d Cir.], aff'd. To do so, we must examine the evidence before the trial judge when the order was entered to determine (a) the nature and extent of pretrial news coverage; (b) whether other measures would be likely to mitigate the effects of unrestrained pretrial publicity; (c) how effectively a restraining order would operate to prevent the threatened danger. The precise terms of the restraining order are also important. We must then consider whether the record supports the entry of a prior restraint on publication, one of the most extraordinary remedies known to our jurisprudence."

As to (a), although the trial judge was justified in concluding there would be extensive pretrial publicity concerning this case, he "found only 'a clear and present danger that pretrial publicity *could* impinge upon the defendant's right to a fair trial.' [Emphasis added by the Court]. His conclusion as to the impact of such publicity on prospective jurors was of necessity speculative, dealing as he was with factors unknown and unknowable."

As to (b), "there is no finding that alternative means [e.g., change of venue, postponement of trial to allow public attention to subside, searching questions of prospective jurors] would not have protected Simants' rights, and the Nebraska Supreme Court did no more than imply that such measures might not be adequate. Moreover, the record is lacking in evidence to support such a finding."

As to (c), in view of such practical problems as the limited territorial jurisdiction of the trial court issuing the order, the difficulties of predicting what information "will in fact undermine the impartiality of jurors," the problem of drafting an order that will "effectively keep prejudicial information from prospective jurors," and that the events "took place in a community of only 850 people"—throughout which, "it is reasonable to assume," rumors that "could well be more damaging than reasonably accurate news accounts" would "travel swiftly by word of mouth"—"it is far from clear that prior restraint on publication would have protected Simants' rights."

"[It] is significant that when this Court has reversed a state conviction because of prejudicial publicity, it has carefully noted that some course of action short of prior restraint would have made a critical difference. However difficult it may be, we need not rule out the possibility of showing the kind of threat to fair trial rights that would possess the requisite degree of certainty to justify restraint. [We] reaffirm that the guarantees of freedom of expression are not an absolute prohibition under all circumstances, but the barriers to prior restraint remain high and the presumption against its use continues intact. We hold that, with respect to the order entered in this case [the] heavy burden imposed as a condition to securing a prior restraint was not [met]."

BRENNAN, J., joined by Stewart and Marshall, JJ., concurring, would hold that "resort to prior restraints on the freedom of the press is a constitutionally impermissible method for enforcing [the right to a fair trial by a jury]; judges have at their disposal a broad spectrum of devices for ensuring that fundamental fairness is accorded the accused without necessitating so drastic an incursion on the equally fundamental and salutary constitutional mandate that discussion of public affairs in a free society cannot depend on the preliminary grace of judicial censors": " * * * Settled case law concerning the impropriety and constitutional invalidity of prior restraints on the press compels the conclusion that there can be no prohibition on the publication by the press of any information pertaining to pending judicial proceedings or the operation of the criminal justice system, no matter how shabby the means by which the information is obtained.[15] This does not imply, however, any subordination of Sixth Amendment rights, for an accused's right to a fair trial may be adequately assured through methods that do not infringe First Amendment values.

"[The narrow national security exception mentioned in *Near* and *Pentagon Papers*] does not mean [that] prior restraints can be justified on an ad hoc balancing approach that concludes that the 'presumption' must be overcome in light of some perceived 'justification.' Rather, this language refers to the fact that, as a matter of procedural safeguards and burden of proof, prior restraints even within a recognized exception to the rule against prior restraints will be extremely difficult to justify; but as an initial matter, the purpose for which a prior restraint is sought to be imposed 'must fit within one of the narrowly defined exceptions to the prohibition against prior restraints.' Indeed, two Justices in [*Pentagon Papers*] apparently controverted the existence of even a limited 'military security' exception to the rule against prior restraints on the publication of otherwise protected material. (Black, J., concurring); (Douglas, J., concurring). And a majority of the other Justices who expressed their views on the merits made it clear that they would take cognizance only of a 'single, extremely narrow class of cases in which the First Amendment's ban on prior judicial restraint may be overridden.' (Brennan, J., concurring). * * *

"The only exception that has thus far been recognized even in dictum to the blanket prohibition against prior restraints against publication of material which would otherwise be constitutionally shielded was the 'military security' situation addressed in [*Pentagon Papers*]. But unlike the virtually certain, direct, and immediate harm required for such a restraint [the] harm to a fair trial that might otherwise eventuate from publications

---

[15] **[Ct's Note]** Of course, even if the press cannot be enjoined from reporting certain information, that does not necessarily immunize it from civil liability for libel or invasion of privacy or from criminal liability for transgressions of general criminal laws during the course of obtaining that information.

which are suppressed pursuant to orders such as that under review must inherently remain speculative."

Although they joined the Court's opinion, White and Powell, JJ., also filed brief concurrences. WHITE, J., expressed "grave doubts" that these types of restrictive orders "would ever be justifiable." POWELL, J., "emphasize[d] the unique burden" resting upon one who "undertakes to show the necessity for prior restraint on pretrial publicity." In his judgment, a prior restraint "requires a showing that (i) there is a clear threat to the fairness of trial, (ii) such a threat is posed by the actual publicity to be restrained, and (iii) no less restrictive alternatives are available. Notwithstanding such a showing, a restraint may not issue unless it also is shown that previous publicity or publicity from unrestrained sources will not render the restraint inefficacious. [A]ny restraint must comply with the standards of specificity always required in the First Amendment context."

STEVENS, J., concurred in the judgment. He agreed with Brennan, J., that the "judiciary is capable of protecting the defendant's right to a fair trial without enjoining the press from publishing information in the public domain, and that it may not do so." But he reserved judgment, until further argument, on "[w]hether the same absolute protection would apply no matter how shabby or illegal the means by which the information is obtained, no matter how serious an intrusion on privacy might be involved, no matter how demonstrably false the information might be, no matter how prejudicial it might be to the interests of innocent persons, and no matter how perverse the motivation for publishing it." He indicated that "if ever required to face the issue squarely" he "may well accept [Brennan, J.'s] ultimate conclusion."[230]

NOTES AND QUESTIONS

1. *Why the prior restraint reliance?* Does "the reasoning used by all of the justices premised solely on the traditional aversion to prior restraints, insufficiently" protect the press? Robert Sack, *Principle and Nebraska Press Association v. Stuart,* 29 Stan.L.Rev. 411 (1977). Would the *Nebraska Press* order have been "equally objectionable" if "framed as a statutory sanction punishing publication after it had occurred"?[231] Is it objectionable at all? Gavin Phillipson, *Trial By Media: The Betrayal of the First Amendment's Purpose,* 71 Law & Contemp. Probs. 15 (2008): "The spectacle of the persistent refusal of U.S. courts to protect individuals from the prejudicial effect of media coverage of their arrest and trials by restraining the media looks from the outside the United States like the very opposite of American respect for the individual and

---

[230] For background on *Nebraska Press,* see Fred Friendly & Martha Elliot, *The Constitution: That Delicate Balance* 148–58 (1984).

[231] Id. at 415. See also Stephen Barnett, *The Puzzle of Prior Restraint,* 29 Stan.L.Rev. 539 (1977). But see Note, *Punishing the Press: Using Contempt of Court to Secure the Right to a Free Trial,* 76 B.U.L. Rev. 537 (1996).

reverence for individual liberty. Rather, it appears that the rights and freedoms of individuals are being sacrificed to the commercial interests of the mass media and the idle curiosity of the majority." See also Kathryn Webb Bradley, *The Court of Public Opinion,* 71 Law & Contemp. Probs. 15 (2008): "[T]he uses the media makes of its freedom can often directly undermine the values underlying the right to free speech itself—human dignity, the state's duty to secure equal rights for the basic rights of all, and the foundations of a democratic society, among which must be the rule of law, a vital aspect of which is the right to a fair trial."

2.   *Why the Dennis citation?* Consider Benno Schmidt, *Nebraska Press Association: An Expansion of Freedom and Contraction of Theory,* 29 Stan.L.Rev. 431 (1977): Burger, C.J.'s reliance on *Dennis* "is remarkable, almost unbelievable, because that test is both an exceedingly odd means of determining the validity of a prior restraint and a controversial and recently neglected technique of First Amendment adjudication. [If] the [*Dennis*] test is the right one for prior restraints, what tests should govern a subsequent punishment case resting on legislation?" Burger, C.J.'s citation to *Dennis* should be read in conjunction with dictum in his majority opinion in *Landmark Communications, Inc. v. Virginia,* Note 5 infra. There he questioned reliance upon the clear and present danger standard but observed: "Properly applied, the test requires a court to make its own inquiry into the imminence and magnitude of the danger said to flow from the particular utterance and then to balance the character of the evil, as well as its likelihood, against the need for free and unfettered expression. The possibility that other measures will serve the State's interests should also be weighed."

3.   *Application to non-press defendants.* Should *Nebraska Press* standards apply to court orders—commonly called "gag orders"—preventing prosecutors, witnesses, potential witnesses, jurors,[232] defendants, or defense attorneys from talking to the press about the case? Would limits on law enforcement personnel alone drastically limit the threat to fair trial? Joanne Armstrong Brandwood, *You Say "Fair Trial" and I Say "Free Press": British and American Approaches to Protecting Defendants' Rights in High Profile Trials,* 75 N.Y.U. L. Rev. 1412 (2000).

Should different standards apply to different categories of those potentially subject to court orders—e.g., do defense attorneys deserve as much protection as the press? See *Gentile v. State Bar,* 501 U.S. 1030 (1991) (less stringent standard ("substantial likelihood of material prejudice") applies to defense attorneys not clear and present danger).[233]

---

[232] Marcy Strauss, *Juror Journalism,* 12 Yale L. & Pol'y Rev. 389 (1994); Comment, *Checkbook Journalism, Free Speech, and Fair Trials,* 143 U.Pa.L.Rev. 1739 (1995).

[233] For relevant commentary, see W. Bradley Wendel, *Free Speech for Lawyers,* 28 Hastings Const. L.Q. 305 (2001); Erwin Chemerinsky, *Silence is Not Golden,* 47 Emory L.Rev. 859 (1998); David A. Strauss, *Why It's Not Free Speech versus Fair Trial,* 1998 U.Chi.Legal F. 109; Lloyd Weinreb, *Speaking Out Outside the Courtroom,* 47 Emory L.J. 889 (1998); Monroe Freedman & Janet Starwood, *Prior Restraints on Freedom of Expression by Defendants and Defense Attorneys: Ratio Decidendi v. Obiter Dictum,* 29 Stan.L.Rev. 607 (1977); Comment, *First Amendment*

4. ***Obstructing justice.*** A series of cases have held that the First Amendment greatly restricts contempt sanctions against persons whose comments on pending cases were alleged to have created a danger of obstruction of the judicial process. "Such repression can be justified, if at all, only by a clear and present danger of the obstruction of justice." *New York Times.* In *Bridges v. California,* 314 U.S. 252 (1941), union leader Bridges had caused publication or acquiesced in publication of a telegram threatening a strike if an "outrageous" California state decision involving Bridges' dock workers were enforced. The Court reversed Bridges' contempt citation. Consider Tribe 1st ed., at 624: "If Bridges' threat to cripple the economy of the entire West Coast did not present danger enough, the lesson of the case must be that almost nothing said outside the courtroom is punishable as contempt."[234]

Would it make a difference if a petit jury were impaneled? Suppose Bridges published an open letter to petit jurors? What if copies were sent by Bridges to each juror? Cf. *Wood v. Georgia,* 370 U.S. 375 (1962) (open letter to press and grand jury—contempt citation reversed). But cf. *Cox v. Louisiana,* 379 U.S. 559 (1965) (statute forbidding parades near courthouse with intent to interfere with administration of justice upheld): ("[W]e deal not with the contempt power [but] a statute narrowly drawn to punish" not a pure form of speech but expression mixed with conduct "that infringes a substantial state interest in protecting the judicial process.").

5. ***Confidentiality and privacy.*** A series of cases has rebuffed state efforts to protect confidentiality or privacy by prohibiting publication. *Cox Broadcasting Corp. v. Cohn,* Sec. 1, II, F supra (state could not impose liability for public dissemination of the name of rape victim derived from public court documents); *Oklahoma Pub. Co. v. District Court,* 430 U.S. 308 (1977) (pretrial order enjoining press from publishing name or picture of 11-year-old boy accused of murder invalid when reporters had been lawfully present at a prior public hearing and had photographed him en route from the courthouse); *Landmark Communications, Inc. v. Virginia,* 435 U.S. 829 (1978) (statute making it a crime to publish information about particular confidential proceedings invalid as applied to non-participant in the proceedings, at least when the information had been lawfully acquired); *Smith v. Daily Mail Pub. Co.,* 443 U.S. 97 (1979) (statute making it a crime for newspapers (but not broadcasters) to publish the name of any youth charged as a juvenile offender invalid as applied to information lawfully acquired from private sources). But cf. *Seattle Times Co. v. Rhinehart,* 467 U.S. 20 (1984) (order enjoining newspaper from disseminating information acquired as a litigant in pretrial discovery valid so long as order is entered on a showing of good cause and does not restrict the dissemination of the information if gained from other sources).

Protection of Criminal Defense Attorneys' Extrajudicial [Statements], 8 Whittier L.Rev. 1021 (1987).

[234] Compare Carol Rieger, *Lawyers' Criticism of Judges: Is Freedom of Speech A Figure of Speech?,* 2 Const.Comm. 69 (1985).

II. NEWSGATHERING

A. Protection of Confidential Sources

BRANZBURG V. HAYES
408 U.S. 665, 92 S.Ct. 2646, 33 L.Ed.2d 626 (1972).

JUSTICE WHITE delivered the opinion of the Court.

[Branzburg, a Kentucky reporter, wrote articles describing his observations of local hashish-making and other drug violations. He refused to testify before a grand jury regarding his information. The state courts rejected his claim of a First Amendment privilege.

[Pappas, a Massachusetts TV newsman-photographer, was allowed to enter and remain inside a Black Panther headquarters on condition he disclose nothing. When an anticipated police raid did not occur, he wrote no story. Summoned before a local grand jury, he refused to answer any questions about what had occurred inside the Panther headquarters or to identify those he had observed. The state courts denied his claim of a First Amendment privilege.

[Caldwell, a N.Y. Times reporter covering the Black Panthers, was summoned to appear before a federal grand jury investigating Panther activities. A federal court issued a protective order providing that although he had to divulge information given him "for publication," he could withhold "confidential" information "developed or maintained by him as a professional journalist." Maintaining that absent a specific need for his testimony he should be excused from attending the grand jury altogether, Caldwell disregarded the order and was held in contempt. The Ninth Circuit reversed, holding that absent "compelling reasons" Caldwell could refuse even to attend the grand jury, because of the potential impact of such an appearance on the flow of news to the public.]

[Petitioners' First Amendment claims] may be simply put: that to gather news it is often necessary to agree either not to identify [sources] or to publish only part of the facts revealed, or both; that if the reporter is nevertheless forced to reveal these confidences to a grand jury, the source so identified and other confidential sources of other reporters will be measurably deterred from furnishing publishable information, all to the detriment of the free flow of information protected by the First Amendment. Although petitioners do not claim an absolute privilege [they] assert that the reporter should not be forced either to appear or to testify before a grand jury or at trial until and unless sufficient grounds are shown for believing that the reporter possesses information relevant to a crime the grand jury is investigating, that the information the reporter has is unavailable from other sources, and that the need for the information is sufficiently compelling to override the claimed invasion of First

Amendment interests occasioned by the disclosure. [The] heart of the claim is that the burden on news gathering resulting from compelling reporters to disclose confidential information outweighs any public interest in obtaining the information.

[We agree] that news gathering [qualifies] for First Amendment protection; without some protection for seeking out the news, freedom of the press could be eviscerated. But this case involves no intrusions upon speech [and no] command that the press publish what it prefers to withhold. [N]o penalty, civil or criminal, related to the content of published material is at issue here. The use of confidential sources by the press is not forbidden or restricted; reporters remain free to seek news from any source by means within the law. No attempt is made to require the press to publish its sources of information or indiscriminately to disclose them on request.

The sole issue before us is the obligation of reporters to respond to grand jury subpoenas as other citizens do and to answer questions relevant to an investigation into the commission of crime.

[T]he First Amendment does not guarantee the press a constitutional right of special access to information not available to the public generally. [Although] news gathering may be hampered, the press is regularly excluded from grand jury proceedings, our own conferences, the meetings of other official bodies gathered in executive session, and the meetings of private organizations. Newsmen have no constitutional right of access to the scenes of crime or disaster when the general public is excluded, and they may be prohibited from attending or publishing information about trials if such restrictions are necessary to assure a defendant a fair trial before an impartial tribunal. [It] is thus not surprising that the great weight of authority is that newsmen are not exempt from the normal duty of appearing before a grand jury and answering questions relevant to a criminal investigation.

[Because] its task is to inquire into the existence of possible criminal conduct and to return only well-founded indictments, [the grand jury's] investigative powers are necessarily broad. [T]he long standing principle that "the public has a right to every man's evidence," except for those persons protected by a constitutional, common law, or statutory privilege, is particularly applicable to grand jury proceedings.

A [number] of States have provided newsmen a statutory privilege of varying breadth, [but] none has been provided by federal statute. [We decline to create one] by interpreting the First Amendment to grant newsmen a testimonial privilege that other citizens do not enjoy. [On] the records now before us, we perceive no basis for holding that the public interest in law enforcement and in ensuring effective grand jury proceedings is insufficient to override the consequential, but uncertain, burden on news gathering which is said to result from insisting that reporters, like other citizens, respond to relevant questions put to them in the course of a valid grand jury investigation or criminal trial.

This conclusion [does not] threaten the vast bulk of confidential relationships between reporters and their sources. Grand juries address themselves to the issues of whether crimes have been committed and who committed them. Only where news sources themselves are implicated in crime or possess information relevant to the grand jury's task need they or the reporter be concerned about grand jury subpoenas. Nothing before us indicates that a large number or percentage of *all* confidential news sources fall into either category and would in any way be deterred by [our holding]. * * * [33]

Accepting the fact, however, that an undetermined number of informants not themselves implicated in crime will nevertheless, for whatever reason, refuse to talk to newsmen if they fear identification by a reporter in an official investigation, we cannot accept the argument that the public interest in possible future news about crime from undisclosed, unverified sources must take precedence over the public interest in pursuing and prosecuting those crimes reported to the press by informants and in thus deterring the commission of such crimes in the future. * * *

[The] privilege claimed here is conditional, not absolute; given the suggested preliminary showings and compelling need, the reporter would be required to testify. [If] newsmen's confidential sources are as sensitive as they are claimed to be, the prospect of being unmasked whenever a judge determines the situation justifies it is hardly a satisfactory solution to the problem. For them, it would appear that only an absolute privilege would suffice.

We are unwilling to embark the judiciary on a long and difficult journey to such an uncertain destination. The administration of a constitutional newsman's privilege would present practical and conceptual difficulties of a high order. Sooner or later, it would be necessary to define those categories of newsmen who qualified for the privilege, a questionable procedure in light of the traditional doctrine that liberty of the press is the right of the lonely pamphleteer who uses carbon paper or a mimeograph just as much as of the large metropolitan publisher who utilizes the latest photocomposition methods. [The] informative function asserted by representatives of the organized press in the present cases is also performed by lecturers, political pollsters, novelists, academic researchers,

---

[33] **[Ct's Note]** In his *Press Subpoenas: An Empirical and Legal Analysis* 6–12 (1971), Prof. Blasi found that slightly more than half of the 975 reporters questioned said that they relied on regular confidential sources for at least 10% of their stories. Of this group of reporters, only 8% were able to say with some certainty that their professional functioning had been adversely affected by the threat of subpoena; another 11% were not certain whether or not they had been adversely affected. [See also Vincent Blasi, *The Newsman's Privilege: An Empirical Study,* 70 Mich.L.Rev. 229 (1971).]

and dramatists. Almost any author may quite accurately assert that he is contributing to the flow of information to the public, that he relies on confidential sources of information, and that these sources will be silenced if he is forced to make disclosures before a grand jury.

In each instance where a reporter is subpoenaed to testify, the courts would also be embroiled in preliminary factual and legal determinations with respect to whether the proper predicate had been laid for the reporters' appearance. [I]n the end, by considering whether enforcement of a particular law served a "compelling" governmental interest, the courts would be inextricably involved in distinguishing between the value of enforcing different criminal laws. By requiring testimony from a reporter in investigations involving some crimes but not in others, they would be making a value judgment which a legislature had declined to [make.]

At the federal level, Congress has freedom to determine whether a statutory newsman's privilege is necessary and desirable and to fashion standards and rules as narrow or broad as deemed necessary [and], equally important, to re-fashion those rules as experience from time to time may dictate. There is also merit in leaving state legislatures free, within First Amendment limits, to fashion their own standards in light of the conditions and problems with respect to the relations between law enforcement officials and press in their own [areas]. * * *

[G]rand jury investigations if instituted or conducted other than in good faith, would pose wholly different issues for resolution under the First Amendment. Official harassment of the press undertaken not for purposes of law enforcement but to disrupt a reporter's relationship with his news sources would have no justification. Grand juries are subject to judicial control and subpoenas to motions to quash. We do not expect courts will forget that grand juries must operate within the limits of the First Amendment as well as the Fifth.

We turn, therefore, to the disposition of the cases before us. [*Caldwell*] must be reversed. If there is no First Amendment privilege to refuse to answer the relevant and material questions asked during a good-faith grand jury investigation, then it is a fortiori true that there is no privilege to refuse to appear before such a grand jury until the Government demonstrates some "compelling need" for a newsman's testimony. [*Branzburg*] must be affirmed. [P]etitioner refused to answer questions that directly related to criminal conduct which he had observed and written about. [If] what petitioner wrote was true, he had direct information to provide the grand jury concerning the commission of serious crimes. [In *Pappas,* we] affirm [and] hold that petitioner must appear before the grand jury to answer the questions put to him, subject, of course, to the supervision of the presiding judge as to "the propriety, purposes, and scope of the grand jury inquiry and the pertinence of the probable testimony."

JUSTICE POWELL, concurring in the opinion of the Court.

I add this brief statement to emphasize what seems to me to be the limited nature of the Court's holding. The Court does not hold that newsmen, subpoenaed to testify before a grand jury, are without constitutional rights with respect to the gathering of news or in safeguarding their sources. [As] indicated in the concluding portion of the opinion, the Court states that no harassment of newsmen will be tolerated. If a newsman believes that the grand jury investigation is not being conducted in good faith he is not without remedy. Indeed, if the newsman is called upon to give information bearing only a remote and tenuous relationship to the subject of the investigation, or if he has some other reason to believe that his testimony implicates confidential source relationships without a legitimate need of law enforcement, he will have access to the Court on a motion to quash and an appropriate protective order may be entered. The asserted claim to privilege should be judged on its facts by the striking of a proper balance between freedom of the press and the obligation of all citizens to give relevant testimony with respect to criminal conduct. The balance of these vital constitutional and societal interests on a case-by-case basis accords with the tried and traditional way of adjudicating such questions.*

In short, the courts will be available to newsmen under circumstances where legitimate First Amendment interests require protection.

JUSTICE DOUGLAS, dissenting.

[T]here is no "compelling need" that can be shown [by the Government] which qualifies the reporter's immunity from appearing or testifying before a grand jury, unless the reporter himself is implicated in a crime. His immunity in my view is therefore quite complete, for absent his involvement in a crime, the First Amendment protects him against an appearance before a grand jury and if he is involved in a crime, the Fifth Amendment stands as a barrier. Since in my view there is no area of inquiry not protected by a privilege, the reporter need not appear for the futile purpose of invoking one to each [question.]

---

* **[Ct's Note]** It is to be remembered that Caldwell asserts a constitutional privilege not even to appear before the grand jury unless a court decides that the government has made a showing that meets the three preconditions specified in [Stewart, J.'s dissent]. To be sure, this would require a "balancing" of interests by the Court, but under circumstances and constraints significantly different from the balancing that will be appropriate under the Court's decision. The newsman witness, like all other witnesses, will have to appear; he will not be in a position to litigate at the threshold the State's very authority to subpoena him. Moreover, absent the constitutional preconditions that [the dissent] would impose as heavy burdens of proof to be carried by the State, the court—when called upon to protect a newsman from improper or prejudicial questioning—would be free to balance the competing interests on their merits in the particular case. The new constitutional rule endorsed by [the dissent] would, as a practical matter, defeat such a fair balancing and the essential societal interest in the detection and prosecution of crime would be heavily subordinated.

Two principles which follow from [Alexander Meiklejohn's] understanding of the First Amendment are at stake here. One is that the people, the ultimate governors, must have absolute freedom of and therefore privacy of their individual opinions and beliefs regardless of how suspect or strange they may appear to others. Ancillary to that principle is the conclusion that an individual must also have absolute privacy over whatever information he may generate in the course of testing his opinions and beliefs. In this regard, Caldwell's status as a reporter is less relevant than is his status as a student who affirmatively pursued empirical research to enlarge his own intellectual viewpoint. The second principle is that effective self-government cannot succeed unless the people are immersed in a steady, robust, unimpeded, and uncensored flow of opinion and reporting which are continuously subjected to critique, rebuttal, and re-examination. In this respect, Caldwell's status as a newsgatherer and an integral part of that process becomes critical. * * *

Sooner or later any test which provides less than blanket protection to beliefs and associations will be twisted and relaxed so as to provide virtually no protection at [all]. Perceptions of the worth of state objectives will change with the composition of the Court and with the intensity of the politics of the [times.]

JUSTICE STEWART, with whom JUSTICE BRENNAN and JUSTICE MARSHALL join, dissenting.

The Court's crabbed view of the First Amendment reflects a disturbing insensitivity to the critical role of an independent press in our society. [While] Mr. Justice Powell's enigmatic concurring opinion gives some hope of a more flexible view in the future, the Court in these cases holds that a newsman has no First Amendment right to protect his sources when called before a grand jury. The Court thus invites state and federal authorities to undermine the historic independence of the press by attempting to annex the journalistic profession as an investigative arm of government. Not only will this decision impair performance of the press' constitutionally protected functions, but it will, I am convinced, in the long run, harm rather than help the administration of justice.

[As] private and public aggregations of power burgeon in size and the pressures for conformity necessarily mount, there is obviously a continuing need for an independent press to disseminate a robust variety of information and opinion through reportage, investigation and criticism, if we are to preserve our constitutional tradition of maximizing freedom of choice by encouraging diversity of expression. * * *

A corollary of the right to publish must be the right to gather news. [This right] implies, in turn, a right to a confidential relationship between a reporter and his source. This proposition follows as a matter of simple logic once three factual predicates are recognized: (1) newsmen require informants to gather news; (2) confidentiality—the promise or understanding that names or certain aspects of communications will be kept off-the-record—is essential to the creation and maintenance of a news-gathering relationship with informants; and (3) the existence of an unbridled subpoena power—the absence of a constitutional right protecting, in *any* way, a confidential relationship from compulsory process—will either deter sources from divulging information or deter reporters from gathering and publishing information. * * *

After today's decision, the potential informant can never be sure that his identity or off-the-record communications will not subsequently be revealed through the compelled testimony of a newsman. A public spirited person inside government, who is not implicated in any crime, will now be fearful of revealing corruption or other governmental wrong-doing, because he will now know he can subsequently be identified by use of compulsory process. The potential source must, therefore, choose between risking exposure by giving information or avoiding the risk by remaining silent.

The reporter must speculate about whether contact with a controversial source or publication of controversial material will lead to a subpoena. In the event of a subpoena, under today's decision, the newsman will know that he must choose between being punished for contempt if he refuses to testify, or violating his profession's ethics[10] and impairing his resourcefulness as a reporter if he discloses confidential information. * * *

The impairment of the flow of news cannot, of course, be proven with scientific precision, as the Court seems to demand. [But] we have never before demanded that First Amendment rights rest on elaborate empirical studies demonstrating beyond any conceivable doubt that deterrent effects exist; we have never before required proof of the exact number of people potentially affected by governmental action, who would actually ·be dissuaded from engaging in First Amendment activity. * * *

We cannot await an unequivocal—and therefore unattainable—imprimatur from empirical studies. We can and must accept the evidence developed in the record, and elsewhere, that overwhelmingly supports the premise that deterrence will occur with regularity in important types of newsgathering relationships. Thus, we cannot escape the conclusion that when neither the reporter nor his source can rely on the shield of confidentiality against unrestrained use of the grand jury's subpoena power, valuable information will not be published and the public dialogue will inevitably be impoverished.

[W]hen a reporter is asked to appear before a grand jury and reveal confidences, I would hold that the government must (1) show that there is

---

[10] **[Ct's Note]** The American Newspaper Guild has adopted the following rule as part of the newsman's code of ethics: "Newspaper men shall refuse to reveal confidences or disclose sources of confidential information in court or before other judicial or investigative bodies."

probable cause to believe that the newsman has information which is clearly relevant to a specific probable violation of law; (2) demonstrate that the information sought cannot be obtained by alternative means less destructive of First Amendment rights; and (3) demonstrate a compelling and overriding interest in the information. * * *

Both the "probable cause" and "alternative means" requirements [would] serve the vital function of mediating between the public interest in the administration of justice and the constitutional protection of the full flow of information. These requirements would avoid a direct conflict between these competing concerns, and they would generally provide adequate protection for newsmen. No doubt the courts would be required to make some delicate judgments in working out this accommodation. But that, after all, is the function of courts of law. Better such judgments, however difficult, than the simplistic and stultifying absolutism adopted by the Court in denying any force to the First Amendment in these cases.[36]
* * *

[In Stewart, J.'s view, the Ninth Circuit correctly ruled that in the circumstances of the case, Caldwell need not divulge confidential information and, moreover, that in this case Caldwell had established that "his very appearance [before] the grand jury would jeopardize his relationship with his sources, leading to a severance of the news gathering relationship and impairment of the flow of news to the public." But because "only in very rare circumstances would a confidential relationship between a reporter and his source be so sensitive [as to preclude] his mere appearance before the grand jury," Stewart, J., would confine "*this* aspect of the *Caldwell* judgment [to] its own facts." Thus, he would affirm in *Caldwell* and remand the other cases for further proceedings not inconsistent with his views.]

NOTES AND QUESTIONS.

1.   *Evaluating Powell, J.'s concurrence.* Did five Justices—or only four—hold that grand juries may pursue their goals by any means short of bad faith? May one conclude that the information sought bears "only a remote and tenuous relationship to the subject of investigation" on grounds falling short of demonstrating "bad faith"? Does Powell, J.'s suggested test—the privilege claim "should be judged on its facts by [balancing the] vital constitutional and societal interests on a case-by-case basis"—resemble Stewart, J.'s dissenting approach more than White, J.'s? Extrajudicially, Stewart, J., has referred to *Branzburg* as a case which rejected claims for a journalist's privilege "by a vote

---

[36] [Ct's Note] The disclaimers in Mr. Justice Powell's concurring opinion leave room for the hope that in some future case the Court may take a less absolute position in this area. [For the claim that a legislative solution is better than waiting, see William E. Lee, *The Priestly Class: Reflections on a Journalist's Privilege*, 23 Card. Arts & Ent. L.J. 635 (2006). For defense of a qualified privilege extended to everyone who disseminates information to the public, see Mary-Rose Papandrea, *Citizen Journalism and the Reporter's Privilege*, 91 Minn. L.Rev. 515 (2007)].

of 5–4, or, considering Mr. Justice Powell's concurring opinion, perhaps by a vote of 4½–4½." Potter Stewart, *"Or of the Press,"* 26 Hast.L.J. 631 (1975). Indeed, some courts had earlier concluded that Powell, J.'s opinion read together with the dissents affords the basis for a qualified privilege. See Jennifer Elrod, *Protecting Journalists From Compelled Disclosure: A Proposal For a Federal Statute,* 7 N.Y.U. J. Legis. & Pub. Pol'y 115(2004). But the now prevailing view is that because Powell, J. had joined the majority opinion (unlike his opinion in *Bakke,* Ch. 9, Sec. 2, IV), the majority opinion in *Branzburg* rejecting the privilege is controlling and the concurrence has no operative effect. See *In re Grand Jury Subpoena, Judith Miller,* 438 F.3d 1141 (D.C. Cir. 2005); *McKevitt v. Pallasch,* 339 F.3d 530 (7th Cir. 2003) (Posner, J.).

The Court's most recent expression unanimously refuses, at least in the absence of bad faith, to extend a qualified First Amendment privilege to "confidential" tenure files and, in dictum, confines *Branzburg* to the recognition that the " 'bad faith' exercise of grand jury powers might raise First Amendment concerns." *University of Pennsylvania v. EEOC,* 493 U.S. 182 (1990) (gender discrimination claim).

2.   ***Role of the press.*** Consider Vincent Blasi, *The Checking Value in First Amendment Theory,* 1977 Am.B.Found.Res.J. 521: The White, J., opinion "characterized the press as a private-interest group rather than an institution with a central function to perform in the constitutional system of checks and balances [and] labeled the source relationships that the reporters sought to maintain 'a private system of informers operated by the press to report on criminal conduct' [cautioning] that this system would be 'unaccountable to the public' were a reporter's privilege to be recognized." In contrast to White, J.'s perspective, consider the remarks of Stewart, J., in a much-discussed address, *"Or of the Press,"* 26 Hast.L.J. 631 (1975): "In setting up the three branches of the Federal Government, the Founders deliberately created an internally competitive[235] system. [The] primary purpose[236] of [the Free Press Clause] was a similar one: to create a fourth institution outside the Government as an additional check on the three official branches."[237] Proceeding from variations of this fourth estate view of the press, many commentators endorse a reporter's privilege. See, e.g., C. Edwin Baker, *Press Rights and Government Power to Structure the Press,* 34 U.Miami L.Rev. 819 (1980) (absolute protection). But see Randall Bezanson, *The New Free Press Guarantee,* 63 Va.L.Rev. 731 (1977). For an argument that the press clause should have independent effect, see Sonja R. West, *Awakening the Press Clause,* 58 UCLA L.Rev. 1025 (2011). See also Sonja R. West, *The Stealth Press Clause,* 48 Ga.L.Rev. 729 (2014); Sonja

---

[235] For commentary on how the "cozy connections" between press and government demonstrate that the relationship is often more cooperative than adversarial, see Aviam Soifer, *Freedom of the Press in the United States,* in *Press Law in Modern Democracies* 79–110 (Lahav, ed., 1985).

[236] For spirited debate about the historical evidence, compare David Anderson, *The Origins of the Press Clause,* 30 UCLA L.Rev. 455 (1983) with Leonard Levy, *On the Origins of the Free Press Clause,* 32 UCLA L.Rev. 177 (1984). See generally Leonard Levy, *Emergence of a Free Press* (1985).

[237] For Brennan, J.'s views, see *Address,* 32 Rutg.L.Rev. 173 (1979).

R. West, *Press Exceptionalism*, 127 Harv.L.Rev. 2434 (2014). Compare David Lange, *The Speech and Press Clauses*, 23 UCLA L.Rev. 77 (1975); William W. Van Alstyne, *The Hazards to the Press of Claiming a "Preferred Position,"* 28 Hast.L.J. 761 (1977). A comprehensive overview of the issues surrounding claims of special press status under the First Amendment is Eugene Volokh, *Freedom for the Press as an Industry, or for the Press as Technology? From the Framing to Today,* 160 U.Pa.L.Rev. 59 (2012).

3.   ***Other contexts.*** Does *Branzburg's* emphasis on the grand jury's special role in the American criminal justice system warrant different treatment of the journalist's privilege when a prosecutor seeks disclosure? See Donna Murasky, *The Journalist's Privilege: Branzburg and Its Aftermath,* 52 Tex.L.Rev. 829 (1974). Are the interests of civil litigants in compelling disclosure of a journalist's confidences significantly weaker than those of criminal litigants? Should there be an absolute journalist's privilege in civil discovery proceedings? See id. What if the journalist is a party to the litigation? Should journalists have greater protection for non-confidential information than other potential witnesses? See *Gonzales v. National Broadcasting Co.,* 155 F.3d 618 (2d Cir.1998).

4.   ***Beyond confidentiality.*** Should the press receive a measure of protection from government attempts to secure information gathered on a non-confidential basis? Consider Jaynie Randall, *Freeing Newsgathering from the Reporter's Privilege,* 114 Yale L.J. 1827 (2005): "A number of recent high-profile cases have forced courts to reexamine whether reporters must respond to subpoenas seeking disclosure of confidential sources or whether they are protected from doing so by the doctrine of reporter's privilege. While these confidential-source cases have garnered the most public attention, the vast majority of subpoenas issued to reporters seek to compel disclosure of nonconfidential information. [P]reserving the checking value of the press demands protections mirroring those for attorney work products. Disclosure of the interim steps in newsgathering may result in self-censorship. * * * To the extent that resource materials, drafts, and outtakes reveal the editorial choices made by the press, they should be protected."

5.   ***Defining the press.*** Consider David McGowan, *Approximately Speech,* 89 Minn. L. Rev. 1416 (2005): "[T]he transaction cost savings that distinguish firms from bloggers are not directly relevant to free speech interests, so they do not justify differential treatment. In terms of function, bloggers have shown they can nail down stories of national importance as quickly and accurately as traditional media firms. In some cases, they do better." For some years, and especially in the wake of the issues arising out of the Judith Miller incident (In re *Grand Jury Subpoena*, Note 1 above) and out if federal efforts to subpoena New York Times reporter James Risen, attempts have been made to create a reporter's privilege by federal statute. Although a number of bills have been introduced in both houses of Congress, none has yet come to a floor vote. The reasons for the failure thus far of such attempts is partly political, partly substantive disagreement, and partly an inability to agree on who would qualify for the privilege in the Internet era. See Rachel

Harris, Note, *Conceptualizing and Reconceptualizing the Reporter's Privilege in the Age of Wikipedia,* 82 Ford.L.Rev. 1811 (2014).

6. ***Reverse* Branzburg.** Suppose a reporter reveals a confidential source who sues for redress. Any First Amendment protection? See *Cohen v. Cowles Media Co.,* note 2 after *Arcara,* Sec. 2 supra.[238]

7. ***State "shield laws" and a criminal defendant's right to compulsory process.*** Most states and the District of Columbia have enacted "shield" laws.[239] Some protect only journalists' sources; some (including New Jersey) protect undisclosed information obtained in the course of a journalist's professional activities as well as sources.

———

IN RE FARBER, 78 N.J. 259, 394 A.2d 330 (1978), cert. denied, 439 U.S. 997 (1978): New York Times investigative reporter Myron Farber wrote a series of articles claiming that an unidentified "Doctor X" had caused the death of several patients by poisoning. This led to the indictment and eventual prosecution of Dr. Jascalevich for murder. (He was ultimately acquitted.) In response to the defendant's request, the trial court demanded the disclosure of Farber's sources and the production of his interview notes and other information for his in camera inspection. Relying on the First Amendment and the state shield law, Farber refused to comply with the subpoenas. After White, J., and then Marshall, J., had denied stays, each deeming it unlikely that four justices would grant certiorari at this stage of the case, Farber was jailed for civil contempt and the *Times* heavily fined.

The state supreme court (5–2) upheld civil and criminal convictions of the *Times* and Farber. Under the circumstances, it ruled, the First Amendment did not protect Farber against disclosure. Nor did the New Jersey shield law, for Farber's statutory rights had to yield to Dr.

---

[238] For commentary on *Cohen,* see Anthony L. Fargo, *Testing the Boundaries of the First Amendment Press Clause,* 32 Harv. J.L. & Pub. Pol'y 1093 (2009); Dan Cohen, *Anonymous Source: At War Against the Media, A True Story* (2005); Kyu Ho Youm, *"Burning the Source": Cohen v. Cowles Media,* 23-SPG Comm. Law. 19 (2005); Alan E. Garfield, *The Mischief of Cohen v. Cowles Media,* 35 Georgia L.Rev. 1087 (2001); Jerome A. Barron, *Cohen v. Cowles Media and Its Significance for First Amendment Law and Journalism,* 3 Wm. & Mary Bill Rts. J. 419 (1994); Eric B. Easton, *Two Wrongs Mock a Right: Overcoming the Cohen Maledicta that Bar First Amendment Protection for Newsgathering,* 58 Ohio St. L.J. 1135 (1997); Lili Levi, *Dangerous Liasons: Seduction and Betrayal in Confidential Press-Source Relations,* 43 Rutgers L.Rev. 609 (1991).

[239] Consider Gerald F. Uelmen, *Leaks, Gags and Shields: Taking Responsibility,* 37 Santa Clara L.Rev. 943 (1997): "Current 'shield laws' encourage the leaking of information by protecting the leaker from any consequences for his breach of confidentiality, and place no responsibility on reporters for lack of restraint in promising confidentiality to their sources. Somehow the irony has escaped us, that we encourage irresponsible breaches of confidentiality by guaranteeing to violators that we will protect the confidentiality of their breach! Those who have no respect for confidentiality that protects others are rewarded by our guarantee of absolute confidentiality for their treachery."

Jascalevich's sixth amendment right "to have compulsory process for obtaining witnesses in his favor."[240]

———

ZURCHER v. STANFORD DAILY, 436 U.S. 547 (1978), again declined to afford the press special protection—dividing very much as in *Branzburg*.[241] A student newspaper that had published articles and photographs of a clash between demonstrators and police brought this federal action, claiming that a search of its offices for film and pictures showing events at the scene of the police-demonstrators clash (the newspaper was not involved in the unlawful acts) had violated its first and fourth amendment rights. A 5–3 majority, per WHITE, J., held that the fourth amendment does not prevent the government from issuing a search warrant (based on reasonable cause to believe that the "things" to be searched for are located on the property) simply because the owner or possessor of the place to be searched is not reasonably suspected of criminal involvement. The Court also rejected the argument that "whatever may be true of third-party searches generally, where the third party is a newspaper, there are additional [First Amendment factors justifying] a nearly per se rule forbidding the search warrant and permitting only the subpoena duces tecum. The general submission is that searches of newspaper offices for evidence of crime reasonably believed to be on the premises will seriously threaten the ability of the press to gather, analyze, and disseminate news.

"[Although] [a]ware of the long struggle between Crown and press and desiring to curb unjustified official intrusions, [the Framers] did not forbid warrants where the press was involved, did not require special showing that subpoenas would be impractical, and did not insist that the owner of the place to be searched, if connected with the press, must be shown to be implicated in the offense being investigated. Further, the prior cases do no more than insist that the courts apply the warrant requirements with particular exactitude when First Amendment interests would be endangered by the search. [N]o more than this is required where the warrant requested is for the seizure of criminal evidence reasonably believed to be on the premises occupied by a newspaper. Properly administered, the preconditions for a warrant—probable cause, specificity

———

[240] For analysis of the case, see Note, 32 Rutg.L.Rev. 545 (1979). The case is also discussed at length by New York Times columnist Anthony Lewis, *A Preferred Position for Journalism?*, 7 Hof.L.Rev. 595 (1979).

[241] In both cases, White, J., joined by Burger, C.J., Blackmun, Powell and Rehnquist, JJ., delivered the opinion of the Court and in both cases the "fifth vote"—Powell, J.,—also wrote a separate opinion which seemed to meet the concerns of the dissent part way. In both cases Stewart, J., dissented, maintaining that the Court's holding would seriously impair "newsgathering." Stevens, J., who had replaced Douglas, J., also dissented in Zurcher, as had Douglas in *Branzburg*. Brennan, J., who had joined Stewart, J.'s dissent in *Branzburg,* did not participate in *Zurcher*.

[as to] place [and] things to be seized and overall reasonableness—should afford [the press] sufficient protection * * * .

"[R]espondents and amici have pointed to only a very few instances [since] 1971 involving [newspaper office searches]. This reality hardly suggests abuse, and if abuse occurs, there will be time enough to deal with it. Furthermore, the press [is] not easily intimidated—nor should it be."

POWELL, J., concurring, rejected Stewart, J.'s dissenting view that the press is entitled to "a special procedure, not available to others," when the government requires evidence in its possession, but added: "This is not to say [that a warrant] sufficient to support the search of an apartment or an automobile would be reasonable in supporting the search of a newspaper office. [While] there is no justification for the establishment of a separate Fourth Amendment procedure for the press, a magistrate asked to issue a warrant for the search of press offices can and should take cognizance of the independent values protected by the First Amendment—such as those highlighted by [Stewart, J., dissenting]—when he weighs such factors."[242]

STEWART, joined by Marshall, J., dissented: "A search warrant allows police officers to ransack the files of a newspaper, reading each and every document until they have found the one named in the warrant, while a subpoena would permit the newspaper itself to produce only the specific documents requested. A search, unlike a subpoena, will therefore lead to the needless exposure of confidential information completely unrelated to the purpose of the investigation. The knowledge that police officers can make an unannounced raid on a newsroom is thus bound to have a deterrent effect on the availability of confidential news sources. [The result] will be a diminishing flow of potentially important information to the public.

"[Here, unlike *Branzburg,* the newspaper does] not claim that any of the evidence sought was privileged[, but] only that a subpoena would have served equally well to produce that evidence. Thus, we are not concerned with the principle, central to *Branzburg,* that ' "the public [has] a right to everyman's evidence," ' but only with whether any significant social interest would be impaired if the police were generally required to obtain evidence from the press by means of a subpoena rather than a search. * * *

"Perhaps as a matter of abstract policy a newspaper office should receive no more protection from unannounced police searches than, say, the office of a doctor or the office of a bank. But we are here to uphold a Constitution. And our Constitution does not explicitly protect the practice

---

[242] Powell, J., noted that his *Branzburg* concurrence may "properly be read as supporting the view expressed in the text above, and in the Court's [*Zurcher*] opinion," that under the warrant requirement "the magistrate should consider the values of a free press as well as the societal interest in enforcing the criminal laws."

of medicine or the business of banking from all abridgement by government. It does explicitly protect the freedom of the press."[243]

NOTES AND QUESTIONS

The distinctions between search and subpoena are underscored in Tribe 2d ed., at 973: "When a subpoena is served on a newspaper, it has the opportunity to assert constitutional and statutory rights [such as 'shield laws,' enacted in many states, protecting reporters from divulging information given them in confidence] to keep certain materials confidential. Such protection is circumvented when officials can proceed *ex parte,* by search warrant. And the risk of abuse may be greatest exactly when the press plays its most vital and creative role in our political system, the role of watchdog on official corruption and abuse. Officials who find themselves the targets [of] media investigations may well be tempted to conduct searches to find out precisely what various journalists have discovered, and to retaliate against reporters who have unearthed and reported official wrongdoing."

B. Access to Trials and Other Governmentally Controlled Information and Institutions

By 1978, no Supreme Court holding contradicted Burger, C.J.'s contention for the plurality in *Houchins v. KQED,* 438 U.S. 1 (1978) that, "neither the First Amendment nor the Fourteenth Amendment mandates a right of access to government information or sources of information within the government's control." Or as Stewart, J., put it in an often-quoted statement, "The Constitution itself is neither a Freedom of Information Act nor an Official Secrets Act." "*Or of the Press,*" 26 Hast.L.J. 631, 636 (1975). *Richmond Newspapers,* infra, constitutes the Court's first break with its past denials of First Amendment rights to information within governmental control.

RICHMOND NEWSPAPERS, INC. V. VIRGINIA
448 U.S. 555, 100 S.Ct. 2814, 65 L.Ed.2d 973 (1980).

[At the commencement of his fourth trial on a murder charge (his first conviction having been reversed and two subsequent retrials having ended in mistrials), defendant moved, without objection by the prosecutor or two reporters present, that the trial be closed to the public—defense counsel stating that he did not "want any information being shuffled back and forth when we have a recess as [to] who testified to what." The trial judge granted the motion, stating that "the statute gives me that power specifically." He presumably referred to Virginia Code § 19.2–266, providing that in all criminal trials "the court may, in its discretion, exclude [any] persons whose presence would impair the conduct of a fair trial,

---

[243] Stevens, J., dissented on the general Fourth Amendment issue.

provided that the [defendant's right] to a public trial shall not be violated." Later the same day the trial court granted appellants' request for a hearing on a motion to vacate the closure order. At the closed hearing, appellants observed that prior to the entry of its closure order the court had failed to make any evidentiary findings or to consider any other, less drastic measures to ensure a fair trial. Defendant stated that he "didn't want information to leak out," be published by the media, perhaps inaccurately, and then be seen by the jurors. Noting inter alia that "having people in the Courtroom is distracting to the jury" and that if "the rights of the defendant are infringed in any way [and if his closure motion] doesn't completely override all rights of everyone else, then I'm inclined to go along with" the defendant, the court denied the motion to vacate the closure order. Defendant was subsequently found not guilty.]

CHIEF JUSTICE BURGER announced the judgment of the Court and delivered an opinion in which JUSTICE WHITE and JUSTICE STEVENS joined.

[T]he precise issue presented here has not previously been before this Court for decision. [*Gannett Co. v. DePasquale,* 443 U.S. 368 (1979)] was not required to decide whether a right of access to *trials,* as distinguished from hearings on *pre*trial motions, was constitutionally guaranteed. The Court held that the Sixth Amendment's guarantee to the accused of a public trial gave neither the public nor the press an enforceable right of access to a *pre*trial suppression hearing. One concurring opinion specifically emphasized that "a hearing on a motion before trial to suppress evidence is not a *trial.*" (Burger, C.J., concurring). Moreover, the Court did not decide whether the First and Fourteenth Amendments guarantee a right of the public to attend trials; nor did the dissenting opinion reach this issue. [H]ere for the first time the Court is asked to decide whether a criminal trial itself may be closed to the public upon the unopposed request of a defendant, without any demonstration that closure is required to protect the defendant's superior right to a fair trial, or that some other overriding consideration requires closure.

[T]he historical evidence demonstrates conclusively that at the time when our organic laws were adopted, criminal trials both here and in England had long been presumptively open[, thus giving] assurance that the proceedings were conducted fairly to all concerned, [and] discourag[ing] perjury, the misconduct of participants, and decisions based on secret bias or partiality. [Moreover, the] early history of open trials in part reflects the widespread acknowledgment [that] public trials had significant therapeutic value. [When] a shocking crime occurs, a community reaction of outrage and public protest often follows. Thereafter the open processes of justice serve an important prophylactic purpose, providing an outlet for community concern, hostility, and emotion.

[The] crucial prophylactic aspects of the administration of justice cannot function in the dark; no community catharsis can occur if justice is "done in a corner [or] in any covert manner." [To] work effectively, it is important that society's criminal process "satisfy the appearance of justice," and the appearance of justice can best be provided by allowing people to observe it.

[From] this unbroken, uncontradicted history, supported by reasons as valid today as in centuries past, we are bound to conclude that a presumption of openness inheres in the very nature of a criminal trial under our system of criminal justice. [Nevertheless,] the State presses its contention that neither the Constitution nor the Bill of Rights contains any provision which by its terms guarantees to the public the right to attend criminal trials. Standing alone, this is correct, but there remains the question whether, absent an explicit provision, the Constitution affords protection against exclusion of the public from criminal trials.

[The] expressly guaranteed [First Amendment] freedoms share a common core purpose of assuring freedom of communication on matters relating to the functioning of government. Plainly it would be difficult to single out any aspect of government of higher concern and importance to the people than the manner in which criminal trials are conducted * * * .

The Bill of Rights was enacted against the backdrop of the long history of trials being presumptively open. [In] guaranteeing freedoms such as those of speech and press, the First Amendment can be read as protecting the right of everyone to attend trials so as to give meaning to those explicit guarantees. * * * Free speech carries with it some freedom to listen. "In a variety of contexts this Court has referred to a First Amendment right to 'receive information and ideas.' " *Kleindienst v. Mandel,* 408 U.S. 753 (1972).[244] What this means in the context of trials is that the First Amendment guarantees of speech and press, standing alone, prohibit government from summarily closing courtroom doors which had long been open to the public at the time that amendment was adopted.

[It] is not crucial whether we describe this right to attend criminal trials to hear, see, and communicate observations concerning them as a "right of access," cf. *Gannett* (Powell, J., concurring); *Saxbe v. Washington Post Co.,* 417 U.S. 843 (1974); *Pell v. Procunier,* 417 U.S. 817 (1974),[11] or a

---

[244] *Mandel* held that the Executive had plenary power to exclude a Belgium journalist from the country, at least so long as it operated on the basis of a facially legitimate and bona fide reason for exclusion. Although the Court decided ultimately not to balance the government's particular justification against the First Amendment interest, it recognized that those who sought personal communication with the excluded alien did have a First Amendment interest at stake. The Court apparently assumed that the excluded speaker had no rights at stake, and none were asserted on his behalf.

[11] **[Ct's Note]** *Procunier* and *Saxbe* are distinguishable in the sense that they were concerned with penal institutions which, by definition, are not "open" or public places. [See] also *Greer v. Spock* (military bases) [Sec. 6, II infra].

"right to gather information," for we have recognized that "without some protection for seeking out the news, freedom of the press could be eviscerated." *Branzburg v. Hayes.* The explicit, guaranteed rights to speak and to publish concerning what takes place at a trial would lose much meaning if access to observe the trial could, as it was here, be foreclosed arbitrarily.

The right of access to places traditionally open to the public, as criminal trials have long been, may be seen as assured by the amalgam of the First Amendment guarantees of speech and press; and their affinity to the right of assembly is not without relevance. From the outset, the right of assembly was regarded not only as an independent right but also as a catalyst to augment the free exercise of the other First Amendment rights with which it was deliberately linked by the draftsmen. [Subject] to the traditional time, place, and manner restrictions, streets, sidewalks, and parks are places traditionally open, where First Amendment rights may be exercised [see generally Sec. 6 infra]; a trial courtroom also is a public place where the people generally—and representatives of the media—have a right to be present, and where their presence historically has been thought to enhance the integrity and quality of what takes place.

* * * Notwithstanding the appropriate caution against reading into the Constitution rights not explicitly defined, the Court has acknowledged that certain unarticulated rights are implicit in enumerated guarantees [referring, inter alia, to the rights of association and of privacy and the right to travel. See generally Ch. 6, Secs. 2 & 3]. [T]hese important but unarticulated rights [have] been found to share constitutional protection in common with explicit guarantees. The concerns expressed by Madison and others have thus been [resolved].[245]

We hold that the right to attend criminal trials[17] is implicit in the guarantees of the First Amendment; without the freedom to attend such trials, which people have exercised for centuries, important aspects of freedom of speech and "of the press could be eviscerated." *Branzburg.*

[In the present case,] the trial court made no findings to support closure; no inquiry was made as to whether alternative solutions would have met the need to ensure fairness; there was no recognition of any right under the Constitution for the public or press to attend the trial. In contrast to the pretrial proceeding dealt with in *Gannett,* there exist in the context of the trial itself various tested alternatives to satisfy the constitutional

---

[245] The Chief Justice noted "the perceived need" of the Constitution's draftsmen "for some sort of constitutional 'saving clause' [which] would serve to foreclose application to the Bill of Rights of the maxim that the affirmation of particular rights implies a negation of those not expressly defined. Madison's efforts, culminating in the Ninth Amendment, served to allay the fears of those who were concerned that expressing certain guarantees could be read as excluding others."

[17] **[Ct's Note]** Whether the public has a right to attend [civil trials is] not raised by this case, but we note that historically both civil and criminal trials have been presumptively open.

demands of fairness. [For example, there was nothing] to indicate that sequestration of the jurors would not have guarded against their being subjected to any improper information.[246] [Absent] an overriding interest articulated in findings, the trial of a criminal case must be open to the public. * * *

Reversed.[247]

JUSTICE BRENNAN, with whom JUSTICE MARSHALL joins, concurring in the judgment.

[*Gannett*] held that the Sixth Amendment right to a public trial was personal to the accused, conferring no right of access to pretrial proceedings that is separately enforceable by the public or the press. [This case] raises the question whether the First Amendment, of its own force and as applied to the States through the Fourteenth Amendment, secures the public an independent right of access to trial proceedings. Because I believe that [it does secure] such a public right of access, I agree [that], without more, agreement of the trial judge and the parties cannot constitutionally close a trial to the public.[1]

While freedom of expression is made inviolate by the First Amendment, and with only rare and stringent exceptions, may not be suppressed, the First Amendment has not been viewed by the Court in all settings as providing an equally categorical assurance of the correlative freedom of access to information.[2] Yet the Court has not ruled out a public access component to the First Amendment in every circumstance. Read with care and in context, our decisions must therefore be understood as holding only that any privilege of access to governmental information is subject to a degree of restraint dictated by the nature of the information and countervailing interests in security or confidentiality. [Cases such as *Houchins*, *Saxbe* and *Pell*] neither comprehensively nor absolutely deny

---

[246] Once the jurors are selected, when, if ever, will their sequestration *not* be a satisfactory alternative to closure?

[247] Powell, J., took no part. In *Gannett,* he took the position that a First Amendment right of access applied to courtroom proceedings, albeit subject to overriding when justice so demanded or when confidentiality was necessary.

[1]   **[Ct's Note]** Of course, the Sixth Amendment remains the source of the *accused's* own right to insist upon public judicial proceedings. *Gannett.*

That the Sixth Amendment explicitly establishes a public trial right does not impliedly foreclose the derivation of such a right from other provisions of the Constitution. The Constitution was not framed as a work of carpentry, in which all joints must fit snugly without overlapping. * * *

[2]   **[Ct's Note]** A conceptually separate, yet related, question is whether the media should enjoy greater access rights than the general public. But no such contention is at stake here. Since the media's right of access is at least equal to that of the general public, this case is resolved by a decision that the state statute unconstitutionally restricts public access to trials. As a practical matter, however, the institutional press is the likely, and fitting, chief beneficiary of a right of access because it serves as the "agent" of interested citizens, and funnels information about trials to a large number of individuals.

that public access to information may at times be implied by the First Amendment and the principles which animate it.

The Court's approach in right of access cases simply reflects the special nature of a claim of First Amendment right to gather information. Customarily, First Amendment guarantees are interposed to protect communication between speaker and listener. When so employed against prior restraints, free speech protections are almost insurmountable. See generally Brennan, *Address,* 32 Rutg.L.Rev. 173 (1979). But the First Amendment embodies more than a commitment to free expression and communicative interchange for their own sakes; it has a *structural* role to play in securing and fostering our republican system of self-government. Implicit in this structural role is not only "the principle that debate on public issues should be uninhibited, robust, and wide-open," but the antecedent assumption that valuable public debate—as well as other civic behavior—must be informed. The structural model links the First Amendment to that process of communication necessary for a democracy to survive, and thus entails solicitude not only for communication itself, but for the indispensable conditions of meaningful communication.

[A]n assertion of the prerogative to gather information must [be] assayed by considering the information sought and the opposing interests invaded. This judicial task is as much a matter of sensitivity to practical necessities as it is of abstract reasoning. But at least two helpful principles may be sketched. First, the case for a right of access has special force when drawn from an enduring and vital tradition of public entree to particular proceedings or information. Such a tradition commands respect in part because the Constitution carries the gloss of history. More importantly, a tradition of accessibility implies the favorable judgment of experience. Second, the value of access must be measured in specifics. Analysis is not advanced by rhetorical statements that all information bears upon public issues; what is crucial in individual cases is whether access to a particular government process is important in terms of that very process.

[This Court has] persistently defended the public character of the trial process. *In re Oliver,* 333 U.S. 257 (1948), established that [fourteenth amendment due process] forbids closed criminal trials [and] acknowledged that open trials are indispensable to First Amendment political and religious freedoms.

By the same token, a special solicitude for the public character of judicial proceedings is evident in the Court's rulings upholding the right to report about the administration of justice. While these decisions are impelled by the classic protections afforded by the First Amendment to pure communication, they are also bottomed upon a keen appreciation of the structural interest served in opening the judicial system to public inspection. So, in upholding a privilege for reporting truthful information about judicial misconduct proceedings, *Landmark* emphasized that public scrutiny of the operation of a judicial disciplinary body implicates a major purpose of the First Amendment—"discussion of governmental affairs." Again, *Nebraska Press* noted that the traditional guarantee against prior restraint "should have particular force as applied to reporting of criminal proceedings." And *Cox Broadcasting* instructed that "[w]ith respect to judicial proceedings in particular, the function of the press serves to guarantee the fairness of trials and to bring to bear the beneficial effects of public scrutiny upon the administration of justice."

[Open] trials play a fundamental role in furthering the efforts of our judicial system to assure the criminal defendant a fair and accurate adjudication of guilt or innocence. But, as a feature of our governing system of justice, the trial process serves other, broadly political, interests, and public access advances these objectives as well. To that extent, trial access possesses specific structural significance.

[For] a civilization founded upon principles of ordered liberty to survive and flourish, its members must share the conviction that they are governed equitably. That necessity * * * mandates a system of justice that demonstrates the fairness of the law to our citizens. One major function of the trial is to make that demonstration.

Secrecy is profoundly inimical to this demonstrative [purpose]. Public access is essential, therefore, if trial adjudication is to achieve the objective of maintaining public confidence in the administration of justice. But the trial [also] plays a pivotal role in the entire judicial process, and, by extension, in our form of government. Under our system, judges are not mere umpires, but, in their own sphere, lawmakers—a coordinate branch of *government*. [Thus], so far as the trial is the mechanism for judicial factfinding, as well as the initial forum for legal decisionmaking, it is a genuine governmental proceeding.

[More] importantly, public access to trials acts as an important check, akin in purpose to the other checks and balances that infuse our system of government. "The knowledge that every criminal trial is subject to contemporaneous review in the forum of public opinion is an effective restraint on possible abuse of judicial power," *Oliver*—an abuse that, in many cases, would have ramifications beyond the impact upon the parties before the court. * * *

Popular attendance at trials, in sum, substantially furthers the particular public purposes of that critical judicial proceeding. In that sense, public access is an indispensable element of the trial process itself. Trial access, therefore, assumes structural importance in our "government of laws."

As previously noted, resolution of First Amendment public access claims in individual cases must be strongly influenced by the weight of historical practice and by an assessment of the specific structural value of public access in the circumstances. With regard to the case at hand, our ingrained tradition of public trials and the importance of public access to the broader purposes of the trial process, tip the balance strongly toward the rule that trials be open.[23] What countervailing interests might be sufficiently compelling to reverse this presumption of openness need not concern us now,[24] for the statute at stake here authorizes trial closures at the unfettered discretion of the judge and parties.[25] [Thus it] violates the First and Fourteenth Amendments * * * .

JUSTICE STEWART, concurring in the judgment.

Whatever the ultimate answer [may] be with respect to pretrial suppression hearings in criminal cases, the First and Fourteenth Amendments clearly give the press and the public a right of access to trials themselves, civil as well as criminal. * * *

In conspicuous contrast to a military base, *Greer*; a jail, *Adderley v. Florida,* 385 U.S. 39 (1966); or a prison, *Pell,* a trial courtroom is a public place. Even more than city streets, sidewalks, and parks as areas of traditional First Amendment activity, a trial courtroom is a place where representatives of the press and of the public are not only free to be, but where their presence serves to assure the integrity of what goes on.

But this does not mean that the First Amendment right of members of the public and representatives of the press to attend civil and criminal trials is absolute. Just as a legislature may impose reasonable time, place and manner restrictions upon the exercise of First Amendment freedoms, so may a trial judge impose reasonable limitations upon the unrestricted occupation of a courtroom by representatives of the press and members of the public. Moreover, [there] may be occasions when not all who wish to attend a trial may do so.[3] And while there exist many alternative ways to satisfy the constitutional demands of a fair trial, those demands may also

---

[23] **[Ct's Note]** The presumption of public trials is, of course, not at all incompatible with reasonable restrictions imposed upon courtroom behavior in the interests of decorum. Thus, when engaging in interchanges at the bench, the trial judge is not required to allow public or press intrusion upon the huddle. Nor does this opinion intimate that judges are restricted in their ability to conduct conferences in chambers, inasmuch as such conferences are distinct from trial proceedings.

[24] **[Ct's Note]** For example, national security concerns about confidentiality may sometimes warrant closures during sensitive portions of trial proceedings, such as testimony about state secrets.

[25] **[Ct's Note]** Significantly, closing a trial lacks even the justification for barring the door to pretrial hearings: the necessity of preventing dissemination of suppressible prejudicial evidence to the public before the jury pool has become, in a practical sense, finite and subject to sequestration.

[3] **[Ct's Note]** In such situations, representatives of the press must be assured access, *Houchins* (concurring opinion).

sometimes justify limitations upon the unrestricted presence of spectators in the courtroom.[5]

Since in the present case the trial judge appears to have given no recognition to the right [of] the press and [the] public to be present at [the] murder trial over which he was presiding, the judgment under review must be [reversed.]

JUSTICE WHITE, concurring.

This case would have been unnecessary had *Gannett* construed the Sixth Amendment to forbid excluding the public from criminal proceedings except in narrowly defined circumstances. But the Court there rejected the submission of four of us to this effect, thus requiring that the First Amendment issue involved here be addressed. On this issue, I concur in the opinion of the Chief Justice.

JUSTICE BLACKMUN, concurring in the judgment.

My opinion and vote in partial dissent [in] *Gannett* compels my vote to reverse the judgment. [It] is gratifying [to] see the Court now looking to and relying upon legal history in determining the fundamental public character of the criminal trial. * * *

The Court's ultimate ruling in *Gannett,* with such clarification as is provided by the opinions in this case today, apparently is now to the effect that there is no *Sixth* Amendment right on the part of the public—or the press—to an open hearing on a motion to suppress. I, of course, continue to believe that *Gannett* was in error, both in its interpretation of the Sixth Amendment generally, and in its application to the suppression hearing, for I remain convinced that the right to a public trial is to be found where the Constitution explicitly placed it—in the Sixth Amendment.

[But] with the Sixth Amendment set to one side in this case, I am driven to conclude, as a secondary position, that the First Amendment must provide some measure of protection for public access to the trial. The opinion in partial dissent in *Gannett* explained that the public has an intense need and a deserved right to know about the administration of justice in general; about the prosecution of local crimes in particular; about the conduct of the judge, the prosecutor, defense counsel, police officers, other public servants, and all the actors in the judicial arena; and about the trial itself. It is clear and obvious to me, on the approach the Court has chosen to take, that, by closing this criminal trial, the trial judge abridged these First Amendment interests of the public. * * *

---

[5]   **[Ct's Note]** This is not to say that only constitutional considerations can justify such restrictions. The preservation of trade secrets, for example, might justify the exclusion of the public from at least some segments of a civil trial. And the sensibilities of a youthful prosecution witness, for example, might justify similar exclusion in a criminal trial for rape, so long as the defendant's Sixth Amendment right to a public trial were not impaired.

JUSTICE STEVENS, concurring.

This is a watershed case. Until today the Court has accorded virtually absolute protection to the dissemination of information or ideas, but never before has it squarely held that the acquisition of newsworthy matter is entitled to any constitutional protection whatsoever. An additional word of emphasis is therefore appropriate.

Twice before, the Court has implied that any governmental restriction on access to information, no matter how severe and no matter how unjustified, would be constitutionally acceptable so long as it did not single out the press for special disabilities not applicable to the public at large. In a dissent joined by [Brennan and Marshall, JJ.] in *Saxbe,* Justice Powell unequivocally rejected [that conclusion.] And in *Houchins,* I explained at length why [Brennan, Powell, JJ.] and I were convinced that "[a]n official prison policy of concealing * * * knowledge from the public by arbitrarily cutting off the flow of information at its source abridges [First Amendment freedoms]." Since [Marshall and Blackmun, JJ.] were unable to participate in that case, a majority of the Court neither accepted nor rejected that conclusion or the contrary conclusion expressed in the prevailing opinions. Today, however, for the first time, the Court unequivocally holds that an arbitrary interference with access to important information is an abridgment of the freedoms of speech and of the press protected by the First Amendment.

It is somewhat ironic that the Court should find more reason to recognize a right of access today than it did in *Houchins.* For *Houchins* involved the plight of a segment of society least able to protect itself, an attack on a longstanding policy of concealment, and an absence of any legitimate justification for abridging public access to information about how government operates. In this case we are protecting the interests of the most powerful voices in the community, we are concerned with an almost unique exception to an established tradition of openness in the conduct of criminal trials, and it is likely that the closure order was motivated by the judge's desire to protect the individual defendant from the burden of a fourth criminal trial.[2]

In any event, for the reasons stated [in] my *Houchins* opinion, as well as those stated by the Chief Justice today, I agree that the First Amendment protects the public and the press from abridgment of their rights of access to information about the operation of their government, including the Judicial Branch; given the total absence of any record

---

[2] **[Ct's Note]** Neither that likely motivation nor facts showing the risk that a fifth trial would have been necessary without closure of the fourth are disclosed in this record, however. The absence of any articulated reason for the closure order is a sufficient basis for distinguishing this case from *Gannett.* The decision today is in no way inconsistent with the perfectly unambiguous holding in *Gannett* that the rights guaranteed by the Sixth Amendment are rights that may be asserted by the accused rather than members of the general public. * * *

justification for the closure order entered in this case, that order violated the First Amendment * * * .

JUSTICE REHNQUIST, dissenting.

[I] do not believe that [anything in the Constitution] require[s] that a State's reasons for denying public access to a trial, where both [the prosecution and defense] have consented to [a court-approved closure order], are subject to any additional constitutional review at our hands.

[The] issue here is not whether the "right" to freedom of the press * * * overrides the defendant's "right" to a fair trial, [but] whether any provision in the Constitution may fairly be read to prohibit what the [trial court] did in this case. Being unable to find any such prohibition in the First, Sixth, Ninth, or any other Amendments [or] in the Constitution itself, I dissent.

NOTES AND QUESTIONS

1.   **Whose right?** Consider David A. Anderson, *Freedom of the Press*, 80 Tex. L. Rev. 429 (2002): "The Court acknowledges that courtroom access for the general public may be restricted in order to provide 'preferential seating for media representatives.' The press probably enjoys no greater freedom than the public to disclose prejudicial information about pending trials, but those members of the public most likely to publish such information (such as attorneys and defendants) may be restricted in ways that the press may not be. [But] the Court's determination to avoid recognizing rights under the Press Clause is especially evident in the courtroom access cases. The Court granted the First Amendment right of access that the media demanded, but granted it to the public rather than to the press. Of course, as any nonpress citizen who tries to attend a highly publicized trial will quickly discover, it is the press that gains access under these decisions. But the Court adheres to the fiction, in obvious resistance to Justice Stevens's suggestion that the controlling principle is a First Amendment right to gather news.

2.   **Beyond the justice system.** May (should) "public access to information about how government operates" (to use Stevens, J.'s phrase) be denied, as the Chief Justice suggests, simply on the ground that the place at issue has not been *traditionally* open to the public (recall how the Chief Justice distinguishes penal institutions from criminal trials) or should the government also have to advance, as Stevens, J., suggests, "legitimate justification" for "abridging" public access? Is it relevant that the constitutional convention was closed to the press, that the delegates were forbidden from talking with reporters, and that only the House debates about the Bill of Rights were open to the public? Amy Jordan, *The Right of Access: Is There a Better Fit Than the First Amendment?*, 57 Vand. L. Rev. 1349 (2004). Compare the controversy over whether "the right to a public forum" should turn on whether the place at issue has *historically* been dedicated to the exercise of First Amendment rights or on whether the manner of expression is *basically incompatible* with the normal activity of the place at a particular time. See generally the materials on the

Public Forum: New Forums, Sec. 6, II infra. See also Note, *The First Amendment Right to Gather State-Held Information,* 89 Yale L.J. 923 (1979). Consider, too, Vincent Blasi, *The Checking Value in First Amendment Theory,* 1977 Am.B.Found.Res.J. 521: "[U]nder the checking value, the interest of the press (and ultimately the public) in learning certain information relevant to the abuse of official power would sometimes take precedence over perfectly legitimate and substantial government interests such as efficiency and confidentiality. Thus, the First Amendment may require that journalists have access as a general matter to some records, such as certain financial documents, which anyone investigating common abuses of the public trust would routinely want to inspect, even though the granting of such access would undoubtedly entail some costs and risks. Also, the balance might be tilted even more in the direction of access if a journalist could demonstrate that there are reasonable grounds to believe that certain records contain evidence of misconduct by public officials."

3. **Within the justice system.** How far does (should) *Richmond Newspapers* extend within the justice system? To criminal pre-trial proceedings?[248] How is a trial defined? Should it extend to conferences in chambers or at the bench? To grand jury hearings? To civil trials? To depositions? To records of any or all of the above? Should it apply outside judicial proceedings? Should wardens be permitted to completely preclude access by the public and press to prisons? To executions? What if the prisoner wants to close the execution? For wide-ranging discussion of these and related questions, see Jesse Choper, Yale Kamisar, and Laurence Tribe, *The Supreme Court: Trends and Developments, 1979–80* 145 (1981) (Professor Tribe was winning counsel in *Richmond Newspapers*). See also G. Michael Fenner & James Koley, *Access to Judicial Proceedings: To Richmond Newspapers and Beyond,* 16 Harv.Civ.Rts—Civ.Lib.L.Rev. 415 (1981).

4. **Closing trials.** After *Richmond Newspapers,* what showing should suffice to justify closure of a criminal trial? See *Globe Newspaper Co. v. Superior Court,* 457 U.S. 596 (1982) (routine exclusion of press and public during testimony of minor victim of sex offense unconstitutional); *Press-Enterprise Co. v. Superior Court,* 464 U.S. 501 (1984) (extending *Richmond Newspapers* to voir dire examination of jurors). To overcome either the First Amendment or the Sixth Amendment right to a public trial, the Court has required that the party seeking to close the proceedings "must advance an overriding interest that is likely to be prejudiced, the closure must be no broader than necessary to protect that interest, the trial court must consider reasonable alternatives to closing the proceeding, and it must make findings adequate to support the closure." *Waller v. Georgia,* 467 U.S. 39 (1984).

5. **Special access rights for the press.** Is a press section in public trials required when the seating capacity would be exhausted by the public? Is

---

[248] See *Press-Enterprise Co. v. Superior Court,* 478 U.S. 1 (1986) ("California preliminary hearings are sufficiently like a trial" to implicate *Richmond Newspapers'* "qualified First Amendment right of access"), in addition, see *El Vocero de Puerto Rico v. Puerto Rico,* 508 U.S. 147 (1993) (reaching same conclusion as to Puerto Rican preliminary hearings).

a press section permitted? What limits attach to government determinations of who shall get press passes? See, e.g., *Sherrill v. Knight,* 569 F.2d 124 (D.C.Cir.1977) (denial of White House press pass infringes upon First Amendment guarantees in the absence of adequate process); *Borreca v. Fasi,* 369 F.Supp. 906 (D.Haw.1974) (preliminary injunction against denial of access of a reporter to Mayor's press conferences justified when basis for exclusion is allegedly "inaccurate" and "irresponsible" reporting); *Los Angeles Free Press, Inc. v. Los Angeles,* 9 Cal.App.3d 448, 88 Cal.Rptr. 605 (1970) (exclusion of weekly newspaper from scenes of disaster and police press conferences upheld when newspaper did not report police and fire events "with some regularity"). Cf. *Los Angeles Police Dep't v. United Reporting Pub. Corp.*, 528 U.S. 32 (1999) (law mandating release of arrest records for a scholarly, journalistic, political, or governmental purpose, but not to sell a product or service, may not be challenged on its face; remanded for as applied attack).

When access is required, may the press be prevented from taking notes? Is the right to bring recording devices into public trials protected under *Richmond Newspapers?* What about "unobtrusive" television cameras? Cf. *Chandler v. Florida,* 449 U.S. 560 (1981) (subject to certain safeguards a state may *permit* electronic media and still photography coverage of public criminal proceedings over the objection of the accused).

6. GOVERNMENT PROPERTY AND THE PUBLIC FORUM

The case law treating the question of when persons can speak on public property has come to be known as public forum doctrine. But "[t]he public forum saga began, and very nearly ended," Geoffrey Stone, *Fora Americana: Speech in Public Places,* 1974 Sup.Ct.Rev. 233,with an effort by Holmes, J., then on the Supreme Judicial Court of Massachusetts, "to solve a difficult First Amendment problem by simplistic resort to a common-law concept," Vincent Blasi, *Prior Restraints on Demonstrations,* 68 Mich.L.Rev. 1482 (1970). For holding religious meetings on the Boston Common, a preacher was convicted under an ordinance prohibiting "any public address" upon publicly-owned property without a permit from the mayor. In upholding the permit ordinance Holmes, J., observed: "For the legislature absolutely or conditionally to forbid public speaking in a highway or public park is no more an infringement of rights of a member of the public than for the owner of a private house to forbid it in the house." *Massachusetts v. Davis,* 39 N.E. 113 (Mass 1895). On appeal, a unanimous Supreme Court adopted the Holmes position, 167 U.S. 43 (1897): "[T]he right to absolutely exclude all right to use [public property], necessarily includes the authority to determine under what circumstances such use may be availed of, as the greater power contains the lesser."

This view survived until HAGUE v. C.I.O., 307 U.S. 496 (1939), which rejected Jersey City's claim that its ordinance requiring a permit for an open air meeting was justified by the "plenary power" rationale of *Davis*. In rejecting the implications of the *Davis* dictum, ROBERTS, J., in a plurality opinion, uttered a famous "counter dictum," which has played a central role in the evolution of public forum theory: "Wherever the title of streets and parks may rest, they have immemorially been held in trust for the use of the public and, time out of mind, have been used for purposes of assembly, communicating thoughts between citizens, and discussing public questions. Such use of the streets and public places has, from ancient times, been a part of the privileges, immunities, rights, and liberties of citizens. [This privilege of a citizen] is not absolute, but relative, and must be exercised in subordination to the general comfort and convenience, and in consonance with peace and good order; but it must not, in the guise of regulation, be abridged or denied." Eight months later, the *Hague* dictum was given impressive content by Roberts, J., for the Court, in *Schneider* infra.

I.   FOUNDATION CASES

A.   Mandatory Access

SCHNEIDER v. IRVINGTON, 308 U.S. 147 (1939), per ROBERTS, J., invalidated several ordinances prohibiting leafleting on public streets or other public places: "Municipal authorities, as trustees for the public, have the duty to keep their communities' streets open and available for movement of people and property, the primary purpose to which the streets are dedicated. So long as legislation to this end does not abridge the constitutional liberty of one rightfully upon the street to impart information through speech or the distribution of literature, it may lawfully regulate the conduct of those using the streets. For example, a person could not exercise this liberty by taking his stand in the middle of a crowded street, contrary to traffic regulations, and maintain his position to the stoppage of all traffic; a group of distributors could not insist upon a constitutional right to form a cordon across the street and to allow no pedestrian to pass who did not accept a tendered leaflet; nor does the guarantee of freedom of speech or of the press deprive a municipality of power to enact regulations against throwing literature broadcast in the streets. Prohibition of such conduct would not abridge the constitutional liberty since such activity bears no necessary relationship to the freedom to speak, write, print or distribute information or opinion. * * *

"In *Lovell* [Sec. 4, I, A supra] this court held void an ordinance which forbade the distribution by hand or otherwise of literature of any kind without written permission from the city manager. [Similarly] in *Hague v. C.I.O.*, an ordinance was held void on its face because it provided for previous administrative censorship of the exercise of the right of speech and assembly in appropriate public places." The [ordinances] under review do not purport to license distribution but all of them absolutely prohibit it in the streets and, one of them, in other public places as well.

"The motive of the legislation under attack in Numbers 13, 18 and 29 is held by the courts below to be the prevention of littering of the streets and, although the alleged offenders were not charged with themselves scattering paper in the streets, their convictions were sustained upon the theory that distribution by them encouraged or resulted in such littering. We are of opinion that the purpose to keep the streets clean and of good appearance is insufficient to justify an ordinance which prohibits a person rightfully on a public street from handing literature to one willing to receive it. Any burden imposed upon the city authorities in cleaning and caring for the streets as an indirect consequence of such distribution results from the constitutional protection of the freedom of speech and press. This constitutional protection does not deprive a city of all power to prevent street littering. There are obvious methods of preventing littering. Amongst these is the punishment of those who actually throw papers on the streets.

"It is suggested that [the] ordinances are valid because their operation is limited to streets and alleys and leaves persons free to distribute printed matter in other public places. But, as we have said, the streets are natural and proper places for the dissemination of information and opinion; and one is not to have the exercise of his liberty of expression in appropriate places abridged on the plea that it may be exercised in some other place."

McREYNOLDS, J., "is of opinion that the judgment in each case should be affirmed."

NOTES AND QUESTIONS

1.   ***Leaflets and the streets as public forum.*** Consider Harry Kalven, *The Concept of the Public Forum: Cox v. Louisiana,* 1965 Sup.Ct.Rev. 1: "Leaflet distribution in public places in a city is a method of communication that carries as an inextricable and expected consequence substantial littering of the streets, which the city has an obligation to keep clean. It is also a method of communication of some annoyance to a majority of people so addressed; that its impact on its audience is very high is doubtful. Yet the constitutional balance in *Schneider* was struck emphatically in favor of keeping the public forum open for this mode of communication. [The] operative theory of the Court, at least for the leaflet situation, is that, although it is a method of communication that interferes with the public use of the streets, the right to the streets as a public forum is such that leaflet distribution cannot be prohibited and can be regulated only for weighty reasons.

2.   ***Litter prevention as a substantial interest.*** Does the interest in distributing leaflets always outweigh the interest in preventing littering? Suppose helicopters regularly dropped tons of leaflets on the town of Irvington?

3. *Beyond leaflets.* COX v. NEW HAMPSHIRE, 312 U.S. 569 (1941), per HUGHES, C.J., upheld convictions of sixty-eight Jehovah's Witnesses for parading without a permit. They had marched in four or five groups (with perhaps twenty others) along the sidewalk in single file carrying signs and handing out leaflets: "[T]he state court considered and defined the duty of the licensing authority and the rights of the appellants to a license for their parade, with regard only to consideration of time, place and manner so as to conserve the public convenience." The licensing procedure was said to "afford opportunity for proper policing" and " 'to prevent confusion by overlapping parades, [to] secure convenient use of the streets by other travelers, and to minimize the risk of disorder.' " A municipality "undoubtedly" has "authority to control the use of its public streets for parades or processions." But see C. Edwin Baker, *Unreasoned Reasonableness: Mandatory Parade Permits and Time, Place, and Manner Regulations,* 78 Nw.U.L.Rev. 937 (1984): Approximately 26,000 people walked on the same sidewalks during the same hour the defendants in *Cox* "marched." "This single difference in what [the defendants] did—'marching in formation,' which they did for expressive purposes and which presumably is an 'assembly' that the First Amendment protects—turned out to have crucial significance. This sole difference, engaging in First Amendment protected conduct, made them guilty of a criminal offense. [Surely] something is wrong with this result."

4. *Charging for use of public forum.* *Cox* said there was nothing "contrary to the Constitution" in the exaction of a fee " 'incident to the administration of the [licensing] Act and to the maintenance of public order in the matter licensed.' " But see *Forsyth County v. The Nationalist Movement,* 505 U.S. 123 (1992)(speech cannot be financially burdened for expenses associated with hostile audience in a licensing context).

5. *Reasonable time, place, and manner regulations.* (a) As *Cox* reveals, a right of access to a public forum does not guarantee immunity from reasonable time, place, and manner regulations. In HEFFRON v. INTERNATIONAL SOC. FOR KRISHNA CONSCIOUSNESS, 452 U.S. 640 (1981), for example, the Court, per WHITE, J., upheld a state fair rule prohibiting the distribution of printed material or the solicitation of funds except from a duly licensed booth on the fairgrounds. The Court noted that consideration of a forum's special attributes is relevant to the determination of reasonableness, and the test of reasonableness is whether the restrictions "are justified without reference to the content of the regulated speech, that they serve a significant governmental interest, and that in doing so they leave open ample alternative channels for communication of the information."[249]

WARD v. ROCK AGAINST RACISM, 491 U.S. 781 (1989), per KENNEDY, J., observes that "[E]ven in a public forum the government may impose reasonable restrictions on the time, place, or manner of protected speech, provided the restrictions 'are justified without reference to the content of the

---

[249] Brennan, J., joined by Marshall and Stevens, JJ., dissented in part as did Blackmun, J., in a separate opinion. Their dispute was not with the Court's test, but its application.

regulated speech, that they are narrowly tailored to serve a significant governmental interest, and that they leave open ample alternative channels for communication of the information.' " The case reasserts that the *O'Brien* test is little different from the time, place, and manner test, and then states: "[A] regulation of the time, place, or manner of protected speech must be narrowly tailored to serve the government's legitimate content-neutral interests but [it] need not be the least-restrictive or least-intrusive means of doing so. Rather, the requirement of narrow tailoring is satisfied 'so long as [the] regulation promotes a substantial government interest that would be achieved less effectively absent the regulation.' To be sure, this standard does not mean that a time, place, or manner regulation may burden substantially more speech than is necessary to further the government's legitimate interests. Government may not regulate expression in such a manner that a substantial portion of the burden on speech does not serve to advance its goals.[7]"

MARSHALL, J., dissenting, joined by Brennan and Stevens, JJ., complains of the Court's "serious distortion of the narrowly tailoring requirement" and states that the Court's rejection of the less restrictive alternative test relies on "language in a few opinions [taken] out of context." Should the time, place, and manner test be different from the *O'Brien* test? Is there any difference between those tests and the approach employed in *Schneider*?

(b) Should public universities be able to designate "free speech zones" where protest can take place (but not elsewhere) while permitting other speech elsewhere? Can it limit all public speech to such designated zones? What standards should govern? Should the standards differ if the zone is off campus? For a public library? For a place where candidates for office appear? See Joseph D. Herrold, *Capturing the Dialogue: Free Speech Zones and the "Caging" of First Amendment Rights,* 54 Drake L.Rev. 949 (2006).

B. Equal Access

CHICAGO POLICE DEPT. v. MOSLEY, 408 U.S. 92 (1972), invalidated an ordinance banning all picketing within 150 feet of a school building while the school is in session and one half-hour before and afterwards, except "the peaceful picketing of any school involved in a labor dispute." The suit was brought by a federal postal employee who, for seven months prior to enactment of the ordinance, had frequently picketed a high school in Chicago. "During school hours and usually by himself, Mosley would walk the public sidewalk adjoining the school, carrying a sign that read: 'Jones High School practices black discrimination. Jones High School has a black quota.' His lonely crusade was always peaceful, orderly, and [quiet]." The Court, per MARSHALL, J., viewed the ordinance as drawing "an impermissible distinction between labor picketing and other peaceful

---

[7] [Ct's Note] A ban on handbilling, of course, would suppress a great quantity of speech that does not cause the evils that it seeks to eliminate, whether they be fraud, crime, litter, traffic congestion, or noise. For that reason, a complete ban on handbilling would be substantially broader than necessary to achieve the interests justifying it.

picketing": "The central problem with Chicago's ordinance is that it describes permissible picketing in terms of its subject matter. Peaceful picketing on the subject of a school's labor-management dispute is permitted, but all other peaceful picketing is prohibited. The operative distinction is the message on a picket sign. But, above all else, the First Amendment means that government has no power to restrict expression because of its message, its ideas, its subject matter, or its content.

"[U]nder the Equal Protection Clause, not to mention the First Amendment itself,[250] government may not grant the use of a forum to people whose views it finds acceptable, but deny use to those wishing to express less favored or more controversial views. And it may not select which issues are worth discussing or debating in public facilities. There is an 'equality of status in the field of ideas,' and government must afford all points of view an equal opportunity to be heard. Once a forum is opened up to assembly or speaking by some groups, government may not prohibit others from assembling or speaking on the basis of what they intend to say. Selective exclusions from a public forum may not be based on content alone, and may not be justified by reference to content alone.

"[Not] all picketing must always be allowed. We have continually recognized that reasonable 'time, place and manner' regulations of picketing may be necessary to further significant governmental interests. Similarly, under an equal protection analysis, there may be sufficient regulatory interests justifying selective exclusions or distinctions among picketers. [But] [b]ecause picketing plainly involves expressive conduct within the protection of the First Amendment, discriminations among picketers must be tailored to serve a substantial governmental interest. In this case, the ordinance itself describes impermissible picketing not in terms of time, place and manner, but in terms of subject matter. The regulation 'thus slip[s] from the neutrality of time, place and circumstance into a concern about content.' This is never permitted.[251] * * *

"Although preventing school disruption is a city's legitimate concern, Chicago itself has determined that peaceful labor picketing during school hours is not an undue interference with school. Therefore, under the Equal Protection clause, Chicago may not maintain that other picketing disrupts the school unless that picketing is clearly more disruptive than the picketing Chicago already permits. If peaceful labor picketing is permitted,

---

[250] *Consolidated Edison Co. v. Public Service Comm'n,* abandoned equal protection and cited *Mosley* as a First Amendment case: "The First Amendment's hostility to content-based regulation extends not only to restrictions on particular viewpoints, but also to prohibition of public discussion of an entire topic." But see, e.g., *Minnesota State Board v. Knight,* 465 U.S. 271 (1984) (stating that *Mosley* is an equal protection case).

[251] Consider Daniel A. Farber, *The First Amendment* 23 (1998): "[T]he Court never really explained the basis for its rule. On the face of things, it is not clear that distinctions based on subject matter should always be considered particularly troublesome. For instance, there seems to be nothing suspicious about the decisions of the drafters of the National Labor Relations Act and the Taft-Hartley Act to regulate labor picketing but not antiwar picketing."

there is no justification for prohibiting all nonlabor picketing, both peaceful and nonpeaceful. 'Peaceful' labor picketing, however the term 'peaceful' is defined, is obviously no less disruptive than 'peaceful' nonlabor picketing. But Chicago's ordinance permits the former and prohibits the latter.

"[We also] reject the city's argument that, although it permits peaceful labor picketing, it may prohibit all nonlabor picketing because, as a class, nonlabor picketing is more prone to produce violence than labor picketing. Predictions about imminent disruption from picketing involve judgments appropriately made on an individualized basis, not by means of broad classifications, especially those based on subject matter. Freedom of expression, and its intersection with the guarantee of equal protection, would rest on a soft foundation indeed if government could distinguish among picketers on such a wholesale and categorical basis. '[I]n our system, undifferentiated fear or apprehension of disturbance is not enough to overcome the right to freedom of expression.' *Tinker.* Some labor picketing is peaceful, some disorderly; the same is true for picketing on other themes. No labor picketing could be more peaceful or less prone to violence than Mosley's solitary vigil. In seeking to restrict nonlabor picketing which is clearly more disruptive than peaceful labor picketing, Chicago may not prohibit all nonlabor picketing at the school forum."[252]

NOTES AND QUESTIONS

1.   Consider Kenneth Karst, *Equality as a Central Principle in the First Amendment,* 43 U.Chi.L.Rev. 20 (1975): "*Mosley* is a landmark First Amendment decision. It makes two principal points: (1) the essence of the First Amendment is its denial to government of the power to determine which messages shall be heard and which suppressed * * * . (2) Any 'time, place and manner' restriction that selectively excludes speakers from a public forum must survive careful judicial scrutiny to ensure that the exclusion is the minimum necessary to further a significant government interest. Taken together, these statements declare a principle of major importance. The Court has explicitly adopted the principle of equal liberty of expression. [The] principle requires courts to start from the assumption that all speakers and all points of view are entitled to a hearing, and permits deviation from this basic assumption only upon a showing of substantial necessity."

2.   What if the *Mosley* ordinance had not excepted labor picketing, but had banned *all* picketing within 150 feet of a school during school hours? Consider Karst, supra: "The burden of this restriction would fall most heavily on those who have something to communicate to the school [population]. Student picketers presenting a grievance against a principal, or striking custodians with a message growing out of a labor dispute, would be affected more seriously by this ostensibly content-neutral ordinance than would, say

---

[252] Burger, C.J., joined the Court's opinion, but also concurred. Blackmun and Rehnquist, JJ., concurred in the result.

the proponents of a candidate for Governor [who could just as effectively carry their message elsewhere]. This differential impact amounts to de facto content discrimination, presumptively invalid under the First Amendment equality principle. "[The city faces] an apparent dilemma. [If it] bars all picketing within a certain area, it will effectively discriminate against those groups that can communicate to their audience only by picketing within that area. But if the city adjusts its ordinance to this differential impact, as by providing a student-picketing or labor-picketing exemption, [it runs] afoul of *Mosley* itself. The city can avoid the dilemma by amending the ordinance to ban not all picketing but only noisy picketing."

3.   Does equality fully explain the special concern with content regulation? Consider Geoffrey Stone, *Content Regulation and the First Amendment,* 25 Wm. & Mary L.Rev. 189 (1983): "The problem, quite simply, is that restrictions on expression are rife with 'inequalities,' many of which have nothing whatever to do with content. The ordinance at issue in *Mosley,* for example, restricted picketing near schools, but left unrestricted picketing near hospitals, libraries, courthouses, and private homes. The ordinance at issue in *Erznoznik* restricted drive-in theaters that are visible from a public street, but did not restrict billboards. [Whatever] the effect of these content-neutral inequalities on First Amendment analysis, they are not scrutinized in the same way as content-based inequalities. Not all inequalities, in other words, are equal. And although the concern with equality may support the content-based/content-neutral distinction, it does not in itself have much explanatory power."

Is the concern with content discrimination explainable because of concerns about communicative impact, distortion of public debate, or government motivation? See generally Stone, supra. See also sources cited in notes 1 & 2 after *O'Brien,* Sec. 2 supra and Ronald Cass, *First Amendment Access to Government Facilities,* 65 Va.L.Rev. 1287 (1979); Paul Stephan, *The First Amendment and Content Discrimination,* 68 Va.L.Rev. 203 (1982); Geoffrey Stone, *Restrictions of Speech Because of Its Content: The Peculiar Case of Subject-Matter Restrictions,* 46 U.Chi.L.Rev. 81 (1978).

4.   An Illinois statute prohibited picketing residences or dwellings—except when the dwelling is "used as a place of business," or is "a place of employment involved in a labor dispute or the place of holding a meeting [on] premises commonly used to discuss subjects of general public interest," or when a "person is picketing his own [dwelling]." Can a conviction for picketing the Mayor of Chicago's home be upheld? Is *Mosley* distinguishable? See *Carey v. Brown,* 447 U.S. 455 (1980)

5.   *Discriminatory effect on the basis of viewpoint.* Protesters maintained that Secret Service agents engaged in viewpoint discrimination when they moved the protesters of President Bush two blocks away from the open-air patio where he was dining, while permitting supporters of the President to remain in their original location. *Wood v. Moss,* 134 S.Ct. 2056 (2014), per Ginsburg, J., unanimously rejected this contention explaining that

the protesters were within weapons range, and had a largely unobstructed view, of the President's location, while where the supporters stood, a large, two-story building blocked sight of and weapons access to the patio.

II. NEW FORUMS

Are First Amendment rights on government property confined to streets and parks? "[W]hat about other publicly owned property, ranging from the grounds surrounding a public building, to the inside of a welfare office, publicly run bus, or library, to a legislative gallery?" Stone, *Fora Americana,* supra, at 245.

INTERNATIONAL SOCIETY FOR KRISHNA CONSCIOUSNESS, INC. V. LEE
505 U.S. 672, 112 S.Ct. 2701, 120 L.Ed.2d 541 (1992).

CHIEF JUSTICE REHNQUIST delivered the opinion of the Court.

* * * Petitioner International Society for Krishna Consciousness, Inc. (ISKCON) is a not-for-profit religious corporation whose members perform a ritual known as sankirtan. The ritual consists of " 'going into public places, disseminating religious literature and soliciting funds to support the religion.' " The primary purpose of this ritual is raising funds for the movement.

Respondent [was] the police superintendent of the Port Authority of New York and New Jersey and was charged with enforcing the regulation at issue. The Port Authority owns and operates three major airports in the greater New York City area [which] collectively form one of the world's busiest metropolitan airport complexes. By decade's end they are expected to serve at least 110 million passengers annually. * * *

The Port Authority has adopted a regulation forbidding within the terminals the repetitive solicitation of money or distribution of literature [but permitting] solicitation and distribution on the sidewalks outside the terminal buildings. The regulation effectively prohibits petitioner from performing sankirtan in the terminals. * * *

It is uncontested that the solicitation at issue in this case is a form of speech protected under the First Amendment.[3] But it is also well settled that the government need not permit all forms of speech on property that it owns and controls. *United States Postal Service v. Council of Greenburgh Civic Assns.,* 453 U.S. 114, 129 (1981);[253] *Greer v. Spock,* 424 U.S. 828

---

³ **[Ct's Note]** We deal here only with [ISKCON's] claim raising the permissibility of solicitation. Respondent's cross-petition concerning the leafletting ban is disposed of in the companion case, *Lee v. International Society for Krishna Consciousness, Inc.*, infra.

²⁵³ *Greenburgh* held that the post office could prevent individuals from placing unstamped material in residential mail boxes.

(1976).[254] Where the government is acting as a proprietor, managing its internal operations, rather than acting as lawmaker with the power to regulate or license, its action will not be subjected to the heightened review to which its actions as a lawmaker may be subject. Thus, we have upheld a ban on political advertisements in city-operated transit vehicles, *Lehman v. City of Shaker Heights,* 418 U.S. 298 (1974), even though the city permitted other types of advertising on those vehicles. Similarly, we have permitted a school district to limit access to an internal mail system used to communicate with teachers employed by the district. *Perry Education Assn. v. Perry Local Educators' Ass'n,* 460 U.S. 37 (1983).[255]

These cases reflect, either implicitly or explicitly, a "forum-based" approach for assessing restrictions that the government seeks to place on the use of its property. *Cornelius v. NAACP Legal Defense and Educational Fund, Inc.,* 473 U.S. 788 (1985).[256] Under this approach, regulation of speech on government property that has traditionally been available for public expression is subject to the highest scrutiny. Such regulations survive only if they are narrowly drawn to achieve a compelling state interest. *Perry.* The second category of public property is the designated public forum, whether of a limited or unlimited character—property that

---

[254] *Greer* held that the military could bar a presidential candidate from speaking on a military base even though members of the public were free to visit the base, the President had spoken on the base, and other speakers (e.g., entertainers and anti-drug speakers) had spoken by invitation on the base.

[255] *Perry* held it permissible to deny access to the mailboxes for a competing union despite permitting access for the duly elected union and access for various community groups such as the cub scouts, the YMCA, and other civic and church organizations. *Mosley* and *Carey* were distinguished: "[The] key to those decisions [was] the presence of a public forum." Compare *Lamb's Chapel v. Center Moriches Union Free School Dist.,* 508 U.S. 384 (1993) (school could not exclude religious groups from access to school property for after school meetings so long as it held the property generally open for meetings by social, civic, and recreation groups). *Good News Club v. Milford Central School,* 533 U.S. 98 (2001)(viewpoint discrimination to refuse access to elementary school classrooms after school for group engaging in religious instruction and prayer to discuss morals and character while permitting access to groups who would discuss the development of character and morals in other ways).

[256] *Cornelius* upheld an executive order that included organizations providing direct health and welfare services to individuals or their families in a charity drive in the federal workplace while excluding legal defense and political advocacy organizations. A 4–3 majority, per O'Connor, J., determined that "government does not create a public forum by inaction or by permitting limited discourse, but only by intentionally opening a non-traditional forum for public discourse." Observing that the Court will look to the policy and practice of the government, the nature of the property and its compatibility with expressive activity in discerning intent, O'Connor, J., insisted that "we will not find that a public forum has been created in the face of clear evidence of a contrary intent, nor will we infer that the Government intended to create a public forum when the nature of the property is inconsistent with expressive activity."

Blackmun, J., dissented: "If the Government does not create a limited public forum unless it intends to provide an 'open forum' for expressive activity, and if the exclusion of some speakers is evidence that the Government did not intend to create such a forum, no speaker challenging denial of access will ever be able to prove that the forum is a limited public forum. The very fact that the Government denied access to the speaker indicates that the Government did not intend to provide an open forum for expressive activity, and [that] fact alone would demonstrate that the forum is not a limited public forum."

the state has opened for expressive activity by part or all of the public. Id.[257] Regulation of such property is subject to the same limitations as that governing a traditional public forum. Finally, there is all remaining public property. Limitations on expressive activity conducted on this last category of property must survive only a much more limited review. The challenged regulation need only be reasonable, as long as the regulation is not an effort to suppress the speaker's activity due to disagreement with the speaker's view.[258]

[Our] precedents foreclose the conclusion that airport terminals are public fora. Reflecting the general growth of the air travel industry, airport terminals have only recently achieved their contemporary size and character. [Moreover,] even within the rather short history of air transport, it is only "[i]n recent years [that] it has become a common practice for various religious and non-profit organizations to use commercial airports as a forum for the distribution of literature, the solicitation of funds, the proselytizing of new members, and other similar activities." 45 Fed.Reg. 35314 (1980). Thus, the tradition of airport activity does not demonstrate that airports have historically been made available for speech activity. Nor can we say that these particular terminals, or airport terminals generally, have been intentionally opened by their operators to such activity; the frequent and continuing litigation evidencing the operators' objections belies any such claim. * * *

Petitioner attempts to circumvent the history and practice governing airport activity by pointing our attention to the variety of speech activity that it claims historically occurred at various "transportation nodes" such as rail stations, bus stations, wharves, and Ellis Island. Even if we were inclined to accept petitioner's historical account[,] we think that such evidence is of little import for two reasons. First, much of the evidence is irrelevant to *public* fora analysis, because sites such as bus and rail terminals traditionally have had *private* ownership. The development of privately owned parks that ban speech activity would not change the public fora status of publicly held parks. But the reverse is also true. The practices of privately held transportation centers do not bear on the government's regulatory authority over a publicly owned airport.

Second, the relevant unit for our inquiry is an airport, not "transportation nodes" generally. When new methods of transportation

---

[257] In interpreting this approach, *Perry* also stated in Footnote 7 that: "a public forum may be created for a limited purpose such as use by certain groups, e.g., *Widmar v. Vincent* [Ch. 8, Sec. 1, III] (student groups), or for discussion of certain subjects, e.g., *Madison Joint School District v. Wisconsin Employ. Relat. Comm'n,* 429 U.S. 167 (1976) (school board business)." Can a school board preclude public discussion of one of the subjects on its agenda while permitting discussion of the other subjects?

[258] Could the President not use point of view discrimination in determining who can get access to speak in the Oval Office? See Alan Brownstein, *The Nonforum as a First Amendment Category,* 42 U.C. Davis L.Rev. 717 (2009).

develop, new methods for accommodating that transportation are also likely to be needed. And with each new step, it therefore will be a new inquiry whether the transportation necessities are compatible with various kinds of expressive activity. [The] "security magnet," for example, is an airport commonplace that lacks a counterpart in bus terminals and train stations. And public access to air terminals is also not infrequently restricted—just last year the Federal Aviation Administration required airports for a 4-month period to limit access to areas normally publicly accessible. To blithely equate airports with other transportation centers, therefore, would be a mistake. [T]he record demonstrates that Port Authority management considers the purpose of the terminals to be the facilitation of passenger air travel, not the promotion of expression. Even if we look beyond the intent of the Port Authority to the manner in which the terminals have been operated, the terminals have never been dedicated (except under the threat of court order) to expression in the form sought to be exercised [here]. Thus, we think that neither by tradition nor purpose can the terminals be described as satisfying the standards we have previously set out for identifying a public forum.

The restrictions here challenged, therefore, need only satisfy a requirement of reasonableness. * * *

We have on many prior occasions noted the disruptive effect that solicitation may have on business. "Solicitation requires action by those who would respond: The individual solicited must decide whether or not to contribute (which itself might involve reading the solicitor's literature or hearing his pitch), and then, having decided to do so, reach for a wallet, search it for money, write a check, or produce a credit card." *United States v. Kokinda*, 497 U.S. 720 (1990). Passengers who wish to avoid the solicitor may have to alter their path, slowing both themselves and those around them. The result is that the normal flow of traffic is impeded. This is especially so in an airport, where "air travelers, who are often weighted down by cumbersome baggage [may] be hurrying to catch a plane or to arrange ground transportation." Delays may be particularly costly in this setting, as a flight missed by only a few minutes can result in hours worth of subsequent inconvenience.

In addition, face to face solicitation presents risks of duress that are an appropriate target of regulation. The skillful, and unprincipled, solicitor can target the most vulnerable, including those accompanying children or those suffering physical impairment and who cannot easily avoid the solicitation. The unsavory solicitor can also commit fraud through concealment of his affiliation or through deliberate efforts to shortchange those who agree to purchase. Compounding this problem is the fact that, in an airport, the targets of such activity frequently are on tight schedules. This in turn makes such visitors unlikely to stop and formally complain to airport authorities. As a result, the airport faces considerable difficulty in achieving its legitimate interest in monitoring solicitation activity to assure that travelers are not interfered with unduly.

[T]he sidewalk areas outside the terminals [are] frequented by an overwhelming percentage of airport users. [W]e think it would be odd to conclude that the Port Authority's terminal regulation is unreasonable despite the Port Authority having otherwise assured access to an area universally traveled. * * *

Moreover, "[if] petitioner is given access, so too must other groups. "Obviously, there would be a much larger threat to the State's interest in crowd control if all other religious, nonreligious, and noncommercial organizations could likewise move freely." As a result, we conclude that the solicitation ban is reasonable. * * *

JUSTICE O'CONNOR, concurring in 91–155 [on the solicitation issue] and concurring in the judgment in 91–339 [on the distribution of literature issue]. * * *

I concur in the Court's opinion in No. 91–155 and agree that publicly owned airports are not public fora. [This], however, does not mean that the government can restrict speech in whatever way it likes. * * *

"The reasonableness of the Government's restriction [on speech in a nonpublic forum] must be assessed in light of the purpose of the forum and all the surrounding circumstances." *Cornelius.* " '[C]onsideration of a forum's special attributes is relevant to the constitutionality of a regulation since the significance of the governmental interest must be assessed in light of the characteristic nature and function of the particular forum involved.' " *Kokinda.* In this case, the "special attributes" and "surrounding circumstances" of the airports operated by the Port Authority are determinative. Not only has the Port Authority chosen *not* to limit access to the airports under its control, it has created a huge complex open to travelers and nontravelers alike. The airports house restaurants, cafeterias, snack bars, coffee shops, cocktail lounges, post offices, banks, telegraph offices, clothing shops, drug stores, food stores, nurseries, barber shops, currency exchanges, art exhibits, commercial advertising displays, bookstores, newsstands, dental offices and private clubs. The International Arrivals Building at JFK Airport even has two branches of BloomingFirst Amendment's.

We have said that a restriction on speech in a nonpublic forum is "reasonable" when it is "consistent with the [government's] legitimate interest in 'preserv[ing] the property [for] the use to which it is lawfully dedicated.' " *Perry.* [The] reasonableness inquiry, therefore, is not whether the restrictions on speech are "consistent [with] preserving the property" for air travel, but whether they are reasonably related to maintaining the multipurpose environment that the Port Authority has deliberately created.

Applying that standard, I agree with the Court in No. 91–155 that the ban on solicitation is reasonable. [In] my view, however, the regulation banning leafletting [cannot] be upheld as reasonable on this record. I therefore concur in the judgment in No. 91–339 striking down that prohibition. [W]e have expressly noted that leafletting does not entail the same kinds of problems presented by face-to-face solicitation. Specifically, "[o]ne need not ponder the contents of a leaflet or pamphlet in order mechanically to take it out of someone's [hand]. 'The distribution of literature does not require that the recipient stop in order to receive the message the speaker wishes to convey; instead the recipient is free to read the message at a later time.'" With the possible exception of avoiding litter, it is difficult to point to any problems intrinsic to the act of leafletting that would make it naturally incompatible with a large, multipurpose forum such as those at issue here. * * *

Of course, it is still open for the Port Authority to promulgate regulations of the time, place, and manner of leafletting which are "content-neutral, narrowly tailored to serve a significant government interest, and leave open ample alternative channels of communication." For example, during the many years that this litigation has been in progress, the Port Authority has not banned sankirtan completely from JFK International Airport, but has restricted it to a relatively uncongested part of the airport terminals, the same part that houses the airport chapel. In my view, that regulation meets the standards we have applied * * * .

JUSTICE KENNEDY, with whom JUSTICE BLACKMUN, JUSTICE STEVENS, and JUSTICE SOUTER join as to Part I, concurring in the judgment.

I.   [The Court] leaves the government with almost unlimited authority to restrict speech on its property by doing nothing more than articulating a non-speech-related purpose for the area, and it leaves almost no scope for the development of new public forums absent the rare approval of the government. The Court's error [in] analysis is a classification of the property that turns on the government's own definition or decision, unconstrained by an independent duty to respect the speech its citizens can voice there. The Court acknowledges as much, by reintroducing today into our First Amendment law a strict doctrinal line between the proprietary and regulatory functions of government which I thought had been abandoned long ago. *Schneider; Grayned v. Rockford,* 408 U.S. 104 (1972).[259]

[Public] places are of necessity the locus for discussion of public issues, as well as protest against arbitrary government action. At the heart of our jurisprudence lies the principle that in a free nation citizens must have the

---

[259] *Grayned* stated that: "The crucial question is whether the manner of expression is basically incompatible with the normal activity of a particular place at a particular time." Applying that test, the Court held constitutional an ordinance forbidding the making of noise which disturbs or tends to disturb the peace or good order of a school session.

right to gather and speak with other persons in public places. The recognition that certain government-owned property is a public forum provides open notice to citizens that their freedoms may be exercised there without fear of a censorial government, adding tangible reinforcement to the idea that we are a free people. * * *

The Court's analysis rests on an inaccurate view of history. The notion that traditional public forums are property which have public discourse as their principal purpose is a most doubtful fiction. The types of property that we have recognized as the quintessential public forums are streets, parks, and sidewalks. It would seem apparent that the principal purpose of streets and sidewalks, like airports, is to facilitate transportation, not public discourse. [Similarly,] the purpose for the creation of public parks may be as much for beauty and open space as for discourse. Thus under the Court's analysis, even the quintessential public forums would appear to lack the necessary elements of what the Court defines as a public forum. * * *

One of the places left in our mobile society that is suitable for discourse is a metropolitan airport [because] in these days an airport is one of the few government-owned spaces where many persons have extensive contact with other members of the public. Given that private spaces of similar character are not subject to the dictates of the First Amendment, it is critical that we preserve these areas for protected speech. [If] the objective, physical characteristics of the property at issue and the actual public access and uses which have been permitted by the government indicate that expressive activity would be appropriate and compatible with those uses, the property is a public forum. [The] possibility of some theoretical inconsistency between expressive activities and the property's uses should not bar a finding of a public forum, if those inconsistencies can be avoided through simple and permitted regulations.

The second category of the Court's jurisprudence, the so-called designated forum, provides little, if any, additional protection for speech. [I] do not quarrel with the fact that speech must often be restricted on property of this kind to retain the purpose for which it has been designated. And I recognize that when property has been designated for a particular expressive use, the government may choose to eliminate that designation. But this increases the need to protect speech in other places, where discourse may occur free of such restrictions. In some sense the government always retains authority to close a public forum, by selling the property, changing its physical character, or changing its principal use. Otherwise the State would be prohibited from closing a park, or eliminating a street or sidewalk, which no one has understood the public forum doctrine to require. The difference is that when property is a protected public forum the State may not by fiat assert broad control over speech or expressive activities; it must alter the objective physical character or uses of the property, and bear the attendant costs, to change the property's forum status.

Under this analysis, it is evident that the public spaces of the Port Authority's airports are public forums. First, the District Court made detailed findings [that] show that the public spaces in the airports are broad, public thoroughfares full of people and lined with stores and other commercial activities. An airport corridor is of course not a street, but that is not the proper inquiry. The question is one of physical similarities, sufficient to suggest that the airport corridor should be a public forum for the same reasons that streets and sidewalks have been treated as public forums by the people who use them.

Second, the airport areas involved here are open to the public without restriction. Plaintiffs do not seek access to the secured areas of the airports, nor do I suggest that these areas would be public forums. And while most people who come to the Port Authority's airports do so for a reason related to air travel, [this] does not distinguish an airport from streets or sidewalks, which most people use for travel. * * *

Third, and perhaps most important, it is apparent from the record, and from the recent history of airports, that when adequate time, place, and manner regulations are in place, expressive activity is quite compatible with the uses of major airports. The Port Authority [argues] that the problem of congestion in its airports' corridors makes expressive activity inconsistent with the airports' primary purpose, which is to facilitate air travel. The First Amendment is often inconvenient. But that is besides the point. Inconvenience does not absolve the government of its obligation to tolerate speech. * * *

[A] grant of plenary power allows the government to tilt the dialogue heard by the public, to exclude many, more marginal voices. [We] have long recognized that the right to distribute flyers and literature lies at the heart of the liberties guaranteed by the Speech and Press Clauses of the First Amendment. The Port Authority's rule, which prohibits almost all such activity, is among the most restrictive possible of those liberties. The regulation is in fact so broad and restrictive of speech, Justice O'Connor finds it void even under the standards applicable to government regulations in nonpublic forums. I have no difficulty deciding the regulation cannot survive the far more stringent rules applicable to regulations in public forums. The regulation is not drawn in narrow terms and it does not leave open ample alternative channels for communication. * * *

II. It is my view, however, that the Port Authority's ban on the "solicitation and receipt of funds" [may] be upheld as either a reasonable time, place, and manner restriction, or as a regulation directed at the nonspeech element of expressive conduct. The two standards have considerable overlap in a case like this one. * * *

I am in full agreement with the statement of the Court that solicitation is a form of protected speech. If the Port Authority's solicitation regulation prohibited all speech which requested the contribution of funds, I would conclude that it was a direct, content-based restriction of speech in clear violation of the First Amendment. The Authority's regulation does not prohibit all solicitation, however; it prohibits the "solicitation and receipt of funds." [It] reaches only personal solicitations for immediate payment of money. [The] regulation does not cover, for example, the distribution of preaddressed envelopes along with a plea to contribute money to the distributor or his organization. As I understand the restriction it is directed only at the physical exchange of money, which is an element of conduct interwoven with otherwise expressive solicitation.

[T]he government interest in regulating the sales of literature[, however,] is not as powerful as in the case of solicitation. The danger of a fraud arising from such sales is much more limited than from pure solicitation, because in the case of a sale the nature of the exchange tends to be clearer to both parties. Also, the Port Authority's sale regulation is not as narrowly drawn as the solicitation rule, since it does not specify the receipt of money as a critical element of a violation. And perhaps most important, the flat ban on sales of literature leaves open fewer alternative channels of communication than the Port Authority's more limited prohibition on the solicitation and receipt of funds. Given the practicalities and ad hoc nature of much expressive activity in the public forum, sales of literature must be completed in one transaction to be workable. Attempting to collect money at another time or place is a far less plausible option in the context of a sale than when soliciting donations, because the literature sought to be sold will under normal circumstances be distributed within the forum. * * *

Against all of this must be balanced the great need, recognized by our precedents, to give the sale of literature full First Amendment protection. We have long recognized that to prohibit distribution of literature for the mere reason that it is sold would leave organizations seeking to spread their message without funds to operate. "It should be remembered that the pamphlets of Thomas Paine were not distributed free of charge." *Murdock v. Pennsylvania,* 319 U.S. 105 (1943). The effect of a rule of law distinguishing between sales and distribution would be to close the marketplace of ideas to less affluent organizations and speakers, leaving speech as the preserve of those who are able to fund themselves. One of the primary purposes of the public forum is to provide persons who lack access to more sophisticated media the opportunity to speak. [And] while the same arguments might be made regarding solicitation of funds, the answer is that the Port Authority has not prohibited all solicitation, but only a

narrow class of conduct associated with a particular manner of solicitation.
* * *

JUSTICE SOUTER, with whom JUSTICE BLACKMUN and JUSTICE STEVENS join, concurring in the judgment in No. 91–339 [on the distribution of literature issue] and dissenting in No. 91–155 [on the solicitation issue].

[R]espondent comes closest to justifying the [total ban on solicitation of money for immediate payment] as one furthering the government's interest in preventing coercion and fraud.[1] [While] a solicitor can be insistent, a pedestrian on the street or airport concourse can simply walk [away]. Since there is here no evidence of any type of coercive conduct, over and above the merely importunate character of the open and public solicitation, that might justify a ban, the regulation cannot be sustained to avoid coercion.

As for fraud, our cases do not provide government with plenary authority to ban solicitation just because it could be [fraudulent.] The evidence of fraudulent conduct here is virtually nonexistent. It consists of one affidavit describing eight complaints, none of them substantiated, "involving some form of fraud, deception, or larceny" over an entire 11-year period between 1975 and 1986, during which the regulation at issue here was, by agreement, not enforced. [B]y the Port Authority's own calculation, there has not been a single claim of fraud or misrepresentation since 1981.
* * *

Even assuming a governmental interest adequate to justify some regulation, the present ban would fall when subjected to the requirement of narrow tailoring. Thus, in *Schaumburg v. Citizens for a Better Environment,* 444 U.S. 620 (1980), we said: "The Village's legitimate interest in preventing fraud can be better served by measures less intrusive than a direct prohibition on solicitation. Fraudulent misrepresentations can be prohibited and the penal laws used to punish such conduct directly."

[Finally,] I do not think the Port Authority's solicitation ban leaves open the "ample" channels of communication required of a valid content-

---

[1] [Ct's Note] Respondent also attempts to justify its regulation on the alternative basis of "interference with air travelers," referring in particular to problems of "annoyance," and "congestion." The First Amendment inevitably requires people to put up with annoyance and uninvited persuasion. Indeed, in such cases we need to scrutinize restrictions on speech with special care. In their degree of congestion, most of the public spaces of these airports are probably more comparable to public streets than to the fairground as we described it in *Heffron.* Consequently, the congestion argument, which was held there to justify a regulation confining solicitation to a fixed location, should have less force here. Be that as it may, the conclusion of a majority of the Court today that the Constitution forbids the ban on the sale [Ed. Does the majority of the Court conclude that the Constitution forbids the ban on the *sale* of literature?] as well as the distribution, of leaflets puts to rest respondent's argument that congestion justifies a total ban on solicitation. While there may, of course, be congested locations where solicitation could severely compromise the efficient flow of pedestrians, the proper response would be to tailor the restrictions to those choke points.

neutral time, place and manner restriction. A distribution of preaddressed envelopes is unlikely to be much of an alternative. The practical reality of the regulation, which this Court can never ignore, is that it shuts off a uniquely powerful avenue of communication for organizations like the International Society for Krishna Consciousness, and may, in effect, completely prohibit unpopular and poorly funded groups from receiving funds in response to protected solicitation. * * *

LEE V. INTERNATIONAL SOCIETY FOR KRISHNA CONSCIOUSNESS, INC.

505 U.S. 830, 112 S.Ct. 2709, 120 L.Ed.2d 669 (1992).

PER CURIAM.

For the reasons expressed in the opinions of Justice O'Connor, Justice Kennedy, and Justice Souter in *ISKCON v. Lee,* the judgment of the Court of Appeals holding that the ban on distribution of literature in the Port Authority airport terminals is invalid under the First Amendment is affirmed.

CHIEF JUSTICE REHNQUIST, with whom JUSTICE WHITE, JUSTICE SCALIA and JUSTICE THOMAS join, dissenting.

Leafletting [must] be evaluated against a backdrop of the substantial congestion problem facing the Port Authority and with an eye to the cumulative impact that will result if all groups are permitted terminal access. Viewed in this light, I conclude that the distribution ban, no less than the solicitation ban, is reasonable.

[The] weary, harried, or hurried traveler may have no less desire and need to avoid the delays generated by having literature foisted upon him than he does to avoid delays from a financial solicitation. And while a busy passenger perhaps may succeed in fending off a leafletter with minimal disruption to himself by agreeing simply to take the proffered material, this does not completely ameliorate the dangers of congestion flowing from such leafletting. Others may choose not simply to accept the material but also to stop and engage the leafletter in debate, obstructing those who follow. Moreover, those who accept material may often simply drop it on the floor once out of the leafletter's range, creating an eyesore, a safety hazard, and additional cleanup work for airport staff. See *Los Angeles City Council v. Taxpayers for Vincent,* 466 U.S. 789 (1984) (aesthetic interests may provide basis for restricting speech).

[Under] the regime that is today sustained, the Port Authority is obliged to permit leafletting. But monitoring leafletting activity in order to ensure that it is *only* leafletting that occurs, and not also soliciting, may prove little less burdensome than the monitoring that would be required if solicitation were permitted. At a minimum, therefore, I think it remains open whether at some future date the Port Authority may be able to reimpose a complete ban, having developed evidence that enforcement of a differential ban is overly burdensome. * * *

NOTES AND QUESTIONS

1. **Dissent.** Do the public forum line of cases underestimate the importance of affording opportunities for dissent? Cass R. Sunstein, *Why Societies Need Dissent* 102–06 (2003); Steven H. Shiffrin, *Dissent, Injustice, and the Meanings of America* 111 (1999).

2. **The First Amendment and geography.** Consider Daniel Farber & John Nowak, *The Misleading Nature of Public Forum Analysis: Content and Context in First Amendment Adjudication,* 70 Va.L.Rev. 1219 (1984): "Classification of public places as various types of forums has only confused judicial opinions by diverting attention from the real First Amendment issues involved in the cases. Like the fourth amendment, the First Amendment protects people, not places. Constitutional protection should depend not on labeling the speaker's physical location but on the First Amendment values and governmental interests involved in the case. Of course, governmental interests are often tied to the nature of the place. [To] this extent, the public forum doctrine is a useful heuristic [device]. But when the heuristic device becomes the exclusive method of analysis, only confusion and mistakes can result." Compare Robert Post, *Between Governance and Management: The History and Theory of the Public Forum,* 34 UCLAL.Rev. 1713 (1987): "*Grayned's* 'incompatibility' test takes into account only the specific harm incident to a plaintiff's proposed speech; it does not recognize the generic damage to managerial authority flowing from the very process of independent judicial review of institutional decisionmaking. [The Court's] present focus 'on the character of the property at issue' is a theoretical dead end, because there is no satisfactory theory connecting the classification of government property with the exercise of First Amendment rights. But there is great potential for a rich and principled jurisprudence if the Court were to focus instead on the relationship between judicial review and the functioning of institutional authority."

3. Would the Arlington National Cemetery be open to solicitation and the distribution of literature under Kennedy, J.'s approach? Consider Comment, *"Objective" Approaches to the Public Forum Doctrine,* 90 Nw. U.L.Rev. 1185 (1996): "The only differences between the Cemetery and the typical park might be concrete tombstones instead of bird baths and the increased likelihood of solemn expressions on the faces of Cemetery visitors."

4. **Footnote 7 forums.** What is the relationship between the Court's second category of property in *Perry* and its fn. 7 (see fn. 257 supra)? Is the discretion to create forums limited? Is it necessary to show that restrictions on such forums are necessary to achieve a compelling state interest? If a restriction (to certain speakers or subjects) is challenged, can the restrictions be used to show that that the property is not a public forum of the second

category? Is this inadmissible circularity? See Laurence Tribe, *Equality as a First Amendment Theme: The "Government-as-Private Actor" Exception* in Jesse Choper, Yale Kamisar & Laurence Tribe, *The Supreme Court: Trends and Developments 1982–1983*, at 221 (1984); Post, supra. In any event, does fn. 7 create a fourth category of property without setting guiding standards? Matthew D. McGill, *Unleashing the Limited Public Forum: A Modest Revision to a Dysfunctional Doctrine*, 52 Stan. L. Rev. 929 (2000): "Briefly stated, within a limited public forum it is impossible for one to differentiate between a presumptively invalid content-based restriction on speech and a legitimate adjustment of the content parameters that define the forum." Are content limitations acceptable so long as they are not viewpoint based? See Mary Jean Dolan, *The Special Public Purpose Forum and Endorsement Relationships: New Extensions of Government Speech*, 31 Hastings Const. L.Q. 71 (2004). What if there is a serious risk that a private group's message may be attributed to the government? May the government exclude the speech from the forum? See Dolan; Helen Norton, *Not for Attribution: Government's Interest in Protecting the Integrity of Its Own Expression*, 37 U.C. Davis L. Rev. 1317 (2004). Could government exclude the Klan from an Adopt-a-Highway-program? From a city website listing restaurants exclude Hooters because it did not want to be associated with a business that demeaned women? See Dolan, supra.

LEHMAN v. SHAKER HEIGHTS, 418 U.S. 298 (1974), held that a public transit system could sell commercial advertising space for cards on its vehicles while refusing to sell space for "political" or "public issue" advertising. BLACKMUN, J., joined by Burger, C.J., and White and Rehnquist, JJ., ruled that the card space is not a public forum and found the city's decision reasonable because it minimized "chances of abuse, the appearance of favoritism, and the risk of imposing upon a captive audience." DOUGLAS, J., concurring, maintained that political messages and commercial messages were both offensive and intrusive to captive audiences, noted that the commercial advertising policy was not before the Court, and voted to deny a right to spread a political message to a captive audience. BRENNAN, J., joined by Stewart, Marshall, and Powell, JJ., dissenting, observed that the "city's solicitous regard for 'captive riders' [has] a hollow ring in the present case where [it] has opened its rapid transit system as a forum for communication."

Is *Lehman* a fn. 7 forum?

5. ***The relationship between the public forum tests and other tests.*** In *Vincent*, a political candidate had placed signs on publicly owned utility poles, and the Court assessed the constitutionality of an ordinance that prohibited the placing of signs on public property. What test applies? A public forum test? A time, place, and manner test? The *O'Brien* test?[260]

---

[260] For additional commentary on public forum issues, see Curtis Berger, *Pruneyard Revisited: Political Activity on Private Lands,* 66 N.Y.U.L.Rev. 650 (1991); G. Sidney Buchanan, *The Case of the Vanishing Public Forum,* 1991 U.Ill.L.Rev. 949 (1991); David Day, *The End of the Public Forum Doctrine,* 78 Iowa L.Rev. 143 (1992); Steven G. Gey, *Reopening the Public Forum—From Public Sidewalks to Cyberspace,* 58 Ohio St.L.J. 1535 (1998); David Goldstone, *The Public Forum Doctrine*

6.   In order to prevent voter intimidation and election fraud, Tennessee prohibits the soliciting of votes and the display or distribution of campaign materials within 100 feet of the entrance to a polling place. Is the campaign-free zone, a public forum? Is the permitting of charitable or religious speech (including solicitation) or commercial speech while banning election speech (but not exit polling) impermissible content discrimination?

BURSON v. FREEMAN, 504 U.S. 191 (1992), upheld the statute. BLACKMUN, J., joined by Rehnquist, C.J., and White and Kennedy, JJ., argued that the 100 foot zone was a public forum, that the regulation was based on the content of the speech, that the state was required to show that its statute was necessary to achieve a compelling state interest and narrowly drawn to achieve that end, and determined that this was the "rare case" in which strict scrutiny against content regulation could be satisfied: "There is [ample evidence] that political candidates have used campaign workers to commit voter intimidation or electoral fraud. In contrast, there is simply no evidence that political candidates have used other forms of solicitation or exit polling to commit such electoral abuses. [The] First Amendment does not require states to regulate for problems that do not exist. * * *

"Here, the State, as recognized administrator of elections, has asserted that the exercise of free speech rights conflicts with another fundamental right, the right to cast a ballot in an election free from the taint of intimidation and fraud. A long history, a substantial consensus, and simple common sense shows that some restricted zone around polling places is necessary to protect that fundamental right. Given the conflict between those two rights, we hold that requiring solicitors to stand 100 feet[261] from the entrances to polling places does not constitute an unconstitutional compromise."[262]

SCALIA, J., agreed with Blackmun, J., that the regulation was justified, but maintained that the area around a polling place is not a public forum: "If the category of 'traditional public forum' is to be a tool of analysis rather than a conclusory label, it must remain faithful to its name and derive its content from *tradition.* Because restrictions on speech around polling places are as venerable a part of the American tradition as the secret ballot, [Tennessee's statute] does not restrict speech in a traditional public forum. [I] believe that the [statute] though content-based, is constitutional because it is a reasonable, viewpoint-neutral regulation of a non-public forum."

---

in the Age of the Information Superhighway (Where Are the Public Forums on the Information Superhighway?), 46 Hastings L.J. 335 (1995); Ronald Krotoszynski, Jr., *Celebrating Selma: The Importance of Context in Public Forum Analysis,* 104 Yale L.J. 1411 (1995); Edward Naughton, *Is Cyberspace A Public Forum? Computer Bulletin Boards, Free Speech, and State Action,* 81 Geo.L.J. 409 (1992); Note, 46 Okla.L.Rev. 155 (1993). For commentary on speaker-based restrictions, see Geoffrey Stone, *Content Regulation and the First Amendment,* 25 Wm. & Mary L.Rev. 189 (1983).

[261] Blackmun, J., argued that the question of whether the state should be required to set a smaller zone, perhaps 25 feet, would put the state to an unreasonable burden of proof, and that the difference between such zones was not of constitutional moment.

[262] Kennedy, J., concurring, reaffirmed the views he had put forward in *Simon and Schuster,* but noted that the First Amendment must appropriately give way in some cases where other constitutional rights are at stake. Thomas, J., took no part.

STEVENS, J., joined by O'Connor and Souter, JJ., did not address the question of whether the area around a polling place was a public forum, but agreed with Blackmun, J., that the regulation could not be upheld without showing that it was necessary to serve a compelling state interest by means narrowly tailored to that end. He contended that the existence of the secret ballot was a sufficient safeguard against intimidation[263] and that the fear of fraud from last minute campaigning could not be reconciled with *Mills v. Alabama,* 384 U.S. 214 (1966)(prohibition on election day editorials unconstitutional). In addition, Stevens, J., argued that the prohibition disproportionately affects candidates with "fewer resources, candidates from lesser visibility offices, and 'grassroots' candidates" who specially profit from "last-minute campaigning near the polling place. [The] hubbub of campaign workers outside a polling place may be a nuisance, but it is also the sound of a vibrant democracy."

III. PRIVACY AND THE PUBLIC FORUM

HILL V. COLORADO
530 U.S. 703, 120 S.Ct. 2480, 147 L.Ed.2d 597 (2000).

JUSTICE STEVENS delivered the opinion of the Court.

[A Colorado statute makes it unlawful, within 100 feet of the entrance to any health care facility, for any person to "knowingly approach" within eight feet of another person, without that person's consent, "for the purpose of passing a leaflet or handbill to, displaying a sign to, or engaging in oral protest, education, or counseling with such other person * * * ." The statute] does not require a standing speaker to move away from anyone passing by. Nor does it place any restriction on the content of any message that anyone may wish to communicate to anyone else, either inside or outside the regulated areas. It does, however, make it more difficult to give unwanted advice, particularly in the form of a handbill or leaflet, to persons entering or leaving medical facilities.

[P]etitioners emphasize three propositions. First, they accurately explain that the areas protected by the statute encompass all the public ways within 100 feet of every entrance to every health care facility everywhere in the State of Colorado [even] though the legislative history makes it clear that its enactment was primarily motivated by activities in the vicinity of abortion clinics. Second, they correctly state that their leafletting, sign displays, and oral communications are protected by the First Amendment. The fact that the messages conveyed by those communications may be offensive to their recipients does not deprive them

---

[263] Stevens, J., argued that the record showed no evidence of intimidation or abuse, nor did it offer a basis for denying election advocacy, while permitting other forms of political advocacy, e.g., environmental advocacy. He maintained that the plurality had shifted the strict scrutiny standard from the state to the candidate who wished to speak.

of constitutional protection. Third, the public sidewalks, streets, and ways affected by the statute are 'quintessential' public forums for free speech. * * *

On the other hand, it is a traditional exercise of the States' "police powers to protect the health and safety of their citizens." That interest may justify a special focus on unimpeded access to health care facilities and the avoidance of potential trauma to patients associated with confrontational protests. See *Madsen* [Sec. 5, I, B supra. Moreover,] rules that provide specific guidance to enforcement authorities serve the interest in even-handed application of the law. * * *

It is also important when conducting this interest analysis to recognize the significant difference between state restrictions on a speaker's right to address a willing audience and those that protect listeners from unwanted communication. This statute deals only with the latter. [The] right to avoid unwelcome speech has special force in the privacy of the home, *Rowan v. Post Office Dept.*, 397 U.S. 728 (1970), and its immediate surroundings, *Frisby v. Schultz*, 487 U.S. 474 (1988)[264] but can also be protected in confrontational settings. * * *

The dissenters argue that we depart from precedent by recognizing a "right to avoid unpopular speech in a public forum," We, of course, are not addressing whether there is such a "right." Rather, we are merely noting that our cases have repeatedly recognized the interests of unwilling listeners in situations where "the degree of captivity makes it impractical for the unwilling viewer or auditor to avoid exposure." * * *[25]

Theoretically, of course, cases may arise in which it is necessary to review the content of the statements made by a person approaching within eight feet of an unwilling listener to determine whether the approach is covered by the statute. But that review need be no more extensive than a determination of whether a general prohibition of "picketing" or

---

[264] Anti-abortion demonstrators picketed on a number of occasions outside a doctor's home. In response, the Town Board passed an ordinance prohibiting picketing taking place solely in front of, and directed at, a residence. *Frisby*, per O'Connor, J., upheld the ordinance: "The state's interest in protecting the well-being, tranquility, and privacy of the home is certainly of the highest order in a free and civilized society." Brennan, J., joined by Marshall, J., dissenting, would have permitted the town to regulate the number of residential picketers, the hours, and the noise level of the pickets. Stevens, J., dissenting, would have limited the ban to conduct that "unreasonably interferes with the privacy of the home and does not serve a reasonable communicative purpose." He worried that a sign such as "GET WELL CHARLIE—OUR TEAM NEEDS YOU," would fall within the sweep of the ordinance.

[25] [Ct's Note] Furthermore, whether there is a "right" to avoid unwelcome expression is not before us in this case. The purpose of the Colorado statute is not to protect a potential listener from hearing a particular message. It is to protect those who seek medical treatment from the potential physical and emotional harm suffered when an unwelcome individual delivers a message (whatever its content) by physically approaching an individual at close range, i.e., within eight feet. In offering protection from that harm, while maintaining free access to health clinics, the State pursues interests constitutionally distinct from the freedom from unpopular speech to which Justice Kennedy refers.

"demonstrating" applies to innocuous speech. The regulation of such expressive activities, by definition, does not cover social, random, or other everyday communications. See Webster's Third New International Dictionary 600, 1710 (1993) (defining "demonstrate" as "to make a public display of sentiment for or against a person or cause" and "picket" as an effort "to persuade or otherwise influence"). Nevertheless, we have never suggested that the kind of cursory examination that might be required to exclude casual conversation from the coverage of a regulation of picketing would be problematic. * * *

The Colorado statute's regulation [places] no restrictions on—and clearly does not prohibit—either a particular viewpoint or any subject matter that may be discussed by a speaker. Rather, it simply establishes a minor place restriction on an extremely broad category of communications with unwilling listeners. Instead of drawing distinctions based on the subject that the approaching speaker may wish to address, the statute applies equally to used car salesmen, animal rights activists, fundraisers, environmentalists, and missionaries.

Here, the statute's restriction seeks to protect those who enter a health care facility from the harassment, the nuisance, the persistent importuning, the following, the dogging, and the implied threat of physical touching that can accompany an unwelcome approach within eight feet of a patient by a person wishing to argue vociferously face-to-face and perhaps thrust an undesired handbill upon her. The statutory phrases, "oral protest, education, or counseling," distinguish speech activities likely to have those consequences from speech activities (such as Justice Scalia's "happy speech" that are most unlikely to have those consequences. The statute does not distinguish among speech instances that are similarly likely to raise the legitimate concerns to which it responds. Hence, the statute cannot be struck down for failure to maintain "content neutrality," or for "underbreadth."

Also flawed is Justice Kennedy's theory that a statute restricting speech becomes unconstitutionally content based because of its application "to the specific locations where that discourse occurs." A statute prohibiting solicitation in airports that was motivated by the aggressive approaches of Hari-Krishnas does not become content based solely because its application is confined to airports. [A] statute making it a misdemeanor to sit at a lunch counter for an hour without ordering any food would also not be 'content based' even if it were enacted by a racist legislature that hated civil rights protesters (although it might raise separate questions about the State's legitimate interest at issue).

Similarly, the contention that a statute is 'viewpoint based' simply because its enactment was motivated by the conduct of the partisans on one side of a debate is without support. The antipicketing ordinance upheld in *Frisby*, a decision in which both of today's dissenters joined, was obviously enacted in response to the activities of antiabortion protesters * * * . We nonetheless summarily concluded that the statute was content neutral.

[The statute is a reasonable place regulation.] The 8-foot separation between the speaker and the audience should not have any adverse impact on the readers' ability to read signs displayed by demonstrators. In fact, the separation might actually aid the pedestrians' ability to see the signs by preventing others from surrounding them and impeding their view. Furthermore, the statute places no limitations on the number, size, text, or images of the placards. And, as with all of the restrictions, the 8-foot zone does not affect demonstrators with signs who remain in place.

With respect to oral statements, the distance certainly can make it more difficult for a speaker to be heard, particularly if the level of background noise is high and other speakers are competing for the pedestrian's attention. Notably, the statute places no limitation on the number of speakers or the noise level, including the use of amplification equipment, although we have upheld such restrictions in past [cases]. Finally, here there is a "knowing" requirement that protects speakers "who thought they were keeping pace with the targeted individual" at the proscribed distance from inadvertently violating the statute.

It is also not clear that the statute's restrictions will necessarily impede, rather than assist, the speakers' efforts to communicate their messages. The statute might encourage the most aggressive and vociferous protesters to moderate their confrontational and harassing conduct, and thereby make it easier for thoughtful and law-abiding sidewalk counselors like petitioners to make themselves heard. But whether or not the 8-foot interval is the best possible accommodation of the competing interests at stake, we must accord a measure of deference to the judgment of the Colorado Legislature. * * *

The burden on the ability to distribute handbills is more serious because it seems possible that an 8-foot interval could hinder the ability of a leafletter to deliver handbills to some unwilling recipients. The statute does not, however, prevent a leafletter from simply standing near the path of oncoming pedestrians and proffering his or her material, which the pedestrians can easily accept.

[The statute] will sometimes inhibit a demonstrator whose approach in fact would have proved harmless. But the statute's prophylactic aspect is justified by the great difficulty of protecting, say, a pregnant woman from physical harassment with legal rules that focus exclusively on the individual impact of each instance of behavior. [Such] individualized characterization of each individual movement is often difficult to make accurately. [A] bright-line prophylactic rule may be the best way to provide protection, and, at the same time, by offering clear guidance and avoiding subjectivity, to protect speech itself. * * *

[There] are two parts to petitioners' "overbreadth" argument. On the one hand, they argue that the statute is too broad because it protects too many people in too many places, rather than just the patients at the facilities where confrontational speech had occurred. Similarly, it burdens all speakers, rather than just persons with a history of bad conduct. On the other hand, petitioners also contend that the statute is overbroad because it "bans virtually the universe of protected expression, including displays of signs, distribution of literature, and mere verbal statements."

[T]hat the coverage of a statute is broader than the specific concern that led to its enactment is of no constitutional significance. What is important is that all persons entering or leaving health care facilities share the interests served by the statute. It is precisely because the Colorado Legislature made a general policy choice that the statute is assessed under the constitutional standard set forth in *Ward*, rather than a more strict standard. In this case, it is not disputed that the regulation affects protected speech activity, the question is thus whether it is a "reasonable restrictio[n] on the time, place, or manner of protected speech." * * *

The second part of the argument is based on a misreading of the statute [, which] does not "ban" any messages, [nor] any signs, literature, or oral statements. It merely regulates the places where communications may occur. [Petitioners] have not persuaded us that the impact of the statute on the conduct of other speakers will differ from its impact on their own sidewalk counseling. Like petitioners' own activities, the conduct of other protesters and counselors at all health care facilities are encompassed within the statute's "legitimate sweep." Therefore, the statute is not overly broad.

Petitioners also claim that [the statute] is unconstitutionally vague. [This] concern is ameliorated by the fact that [it] contains a scienter requirement. The statute only applies to a person who "knowingly" approaches within eight feet of another, without that person's consent, for the purpose of engaging in oral protest, education, or counseling. The likelihood that anyone would not understand any of those common words seems quite remote.* * *

JUSTICE SOUTER, with whom JUSTICE O'CONNOR, JUSTICE GINSBURG, and JUSTICE BREYER, join concurring. * * *

It is important to recognize that the validity of punishing some expressive conduct, and the permissibility of a time, place, or manner restriction, does not depend on showing that the particular behavior or mode of delivery has no association with a particular subject or opinion. Draft card burners disapprove of the draft, see *O'Brien*, and abortion protesters believe abortion is morally wrong, *Madsen*.[265] There is always a correlation with subject and viewpoint when the law regulates conduct that has become the signature of one side of a controversy. But that does not mean that every regulation of such distinctive behavior is content based as First Amendment doctrine employs that term. The correct rule, rather, is captured in the formulation that a restriction is content based only if it is imposed because of the content of the speech. * * *

No one disputes the substantiality of the government's interest in protecting people already tense or distressed in anticipation of medical attention (whether an abortion or some other procedure) from the unwanted intrusion of close personal importunity by strangers. The issues dividing the Court, then, go to the content neutrality of the regulation, its fit with the interest to be served by it, and the availability of other means of expressing the desired message (however offensive it may be even without physically close communication).

Each of these issues is addressed principally by the fact that [the statute does] not declare any view as unfit for expression within the 100-foot zone or beyond it. [A]ll it forbids is approaching another person closer than eight feet (absent permission) to deliver the message. * * *

This is not to say that enforcement of the approach restriction will have no effect on speech; of course it will make some difference. The effect of speech is a product of ideas and circumstances, and time, place, and manner are circumstances. The question is simply whether the ostensible reason for regulating the circumstances is really something about the ideas. Here, the evidence indicates that the ostensible reason is the true reason.* * *

JUSTICE SCALIA, with whom JUSTICE THOMAS joins, dissenting.

[What] is before us [is] a speech regulation directed against the opponents of abortion, and it therefore enjoys the benefit of the "ad hoc nullification machine" that the Court has set in motion to push aside whatever doctrines of constitutional law stand in the way of that highly favored practice. [T]he regulation as it applies to oral communications is obviously and undeniably content-based. A speaker wishing to approach another for the purpose of communicating any message except one of

---

[265] *Madsen*, per Rehnquist, C.J., struck down an injunction creating a 300-foot buffer zone around the homes of those who worked in abortion clinics: "The 300-foot zone around the residence is much larger than the zone approved in *Frisby*. [It] would ban '[g]eneral marching through residential neighborhoods, or even walking a route in front of an entire block of houses.' The record before us does not contain sufficient justification for this broad a ban on picketing; it appears that a limitation on the time, duration of picketing, and number of pickets outside a smaller zone could have accomplished the desired result." In separate opinions Stevens, J., Souter, J., and Scalia, J., joined by Kennedy and Thomas, JJ., joined in the judgment of the Court on this issue. For commentary, see Christina Wells, *Of Communists and Anti-Abortion Protestors: The Consequences of Falling into the Theoretical Abyss,* 33 Ga. L. Rev. 1 (1998); Alan E. Brownstein, *Rules of Engagement for Cultural Wars: Regulating Conduct, Unprotected Speech, and Protected Expression in Anti-Abortion Protests Section II,* 29 U.C.Davis L.Rev. 1163 (1996).

protest, education, or counseling may do so without first securing the other's consent. Whether a speaker must obtain permission before approaching within eight [feet] depends entirely on *what he intends to say* when he gets there. I have no doubt that this regulation would be deemed content-based *in an instant* if the case before us involved antiwar protesters, or union members seeking to 'educate' the public about the reasons for their strike. * * *

The Court asserts that this statute is not content-based for purposes of our First Amendment analysis because it neither (1) discriminates among viewpoints nor (2) places restrictions on "any subject matter that may be discussed by a speaker." But we have never held that the universe of content-based regulations is limited to those two categories, and such a holding would be absurd. Imagine, for instance, special place-and-manner restrictions on all speech except that which "conveys a sense of contentment or happiness." This "happy speech" limitation would not be "viewpoint-based"—citizens would be able to express their joy in equal measure at either the rise or fall of the NASDAQ, at either the success or the failure of the Republican Party—and would not discriminate on the basis of subject matter, since gratification could be expressed about anything at all. Or consider a law restricting the writing or recitation of poetry—neither viewpoint-based nor limited to any particular subject matter. Surely this Court would consider such regulations to be "content-based" and deserving of the most exacting scrutiny.

[The] Court's confident assurance that the statute poses no special threat to First Amendment freedoms because it applies alike to "used car salesmen, animal rights activists, fundraisers, environmentalists, and missionaries," is a wonderful replication (except for its lack of sarcasm) of Anatole France's observation that "[t]he law, in its majestic equality, forbids the rich as well as the poor to sleep under bridges." [We] know what the Colorado legislators, by their careful selection of content ('protest, education, and counseling'), were taking aim at, for they set it forth in the statute itself: the 'right to protest or counsel against certain medical procedures' on the sidewalks and streets surrounding health care facilities.

The Court is unpersuasive in its attempt to equate the present restriction with content-neutral regulation of demonstrations and picketing—as one may immediately suspect from the opinion's wildly expansive definitions of demonstrations as "public display[s] of sentiment for or against a person or cause," and of picketing as an effort "to persuade or otherwise influence." (On these terms, Nathan Hale was a demonstrator and Patrick Henry a picket.) When the government regulates "picketing," or "demonstrating," it restricts a particular manner of expression that is, as the author of today's opinion has several times explained, "a mixture of conduct and communication." [Today], Justice Stevens gives us an opinion restricting not only handbilling but even one-on-one conversation of a particular content.

[The] Court makes too much of the statement in *Ward* that "[t]he principal inquiry in determining content neutrality . . . is whether the government has adopted a regulation of speech because of disagreement with the message it conveys." That is indeed "the *principal* inquiry"—but it is not the *only* inquiry. Even a law that has as its purpose something unrelated to the suppression of particular content cannot irrationally single out that content for its prohibition. An ordinance directed at the suppression of noise (and therefore "justified without reference to the content of regulated speech") cannot be applied only to sound trucks delivering messages of "protest."[2]

[The statute is invalid even if it were content neutral.] Just three Terms ago, in upholding an injunction against antiabortion activities, the Court refused to rely on any supposed "right of the people approaching and entering the facilities to be left alone." *Schenck v. Pro-Choice Network*, 519 U.S. 357 (1997)[266] Finding itself in something of a jam (the State here has passed a regulation that is obviously not narrowly tailored to advance any other interest) the Court today neatly re-packages the repudiated "right" as an "interest" the State may decide to protect and then places it onto the scales opposite the right to free speech in a traditional public forum.

[T]he "right to be let alone" [is] not an interest that may be legitimately weighed against the speakers' First Amendment rights (which the Court demotes to the status of First Amendment 'interests'). We have consistently held that "the Constitution does not permit the government to decide which types of otherwise protected speech are sufficiently offensive to require protection *for the unwilling listener or viewer*." *Erznoznik*. [We] have upheld limitations on a speaker's exercise of his right to speak on the public

---

2   **[Ct's Note]** The Court's contention that the statute is content-neutral because it is not a "regulation of speech" but a "regulation of the places where some speech may occur," is simply baffling. First, because the proposition that a restriction upon the places where speech may occur is not a restriction upon speech is both absurd and contradicted by innumerable cases. And second, because the fact that a restriction is framed as a "regulation of the places where some speech may occur" has nothing whatever to do with whether the restriction is content-neutral—which is why *Boos* held to be content-based the ban on displaying, within 500 feet of foreign embassies, banners designed to "bring into public odium any foreign government."

266   *Schenck*, per Rehnquist, C.J., maintained that an injunction ordering abortion protesters to cease and desist from "counseling" women entering abortion clinics, who indicate they do not wish to be counseled, could not be sustained in order to protect privacy: "As [a] general matter, we have indicated that in public debate our own citizens must tolerate insulting, and often outrageous, speech in order to provide adequate breathing space to the freedoms protected by the First Amendment." This portion of the injunction was sustained on other grounds. Demonstrators had previously engaged in physical intimidation against women and their escorts. The lower court ordered demonstrators to stay 15 feet away from doorways, driveways, and driveway entrances except for two sidewalk counselors in order to accommodate free speech rights. The Court observed that the counselors, if ordered to desist, and other demonstrators could present their messages outside the 15-foot buffer zone and that their consignment to that area was a result of their own previous intimidation.

streets *when that speech intrudes into the privacy of the home. Frisby.* [But] "Outside the home, the burden is generally on the observer or listener to avert his eyes or plug his ears against the verbal assaults, lurid advertisements, tawdry books and magazines, and other 'offensive' intrusions which increasingly attend urban life." ' Tribe, 948 (2d ed.).

[The] Court displays a willful ignorance of the type and nature of communication affected by the statute's restrictions. It seriously asserts, for example, that the 8-foot zone allows a speaker to communicate at a "normal conversational distance," [but] I have never walked along the public sidewalk—and have not seen others do so—"conversing" at an 8-foot remove. The suggestion is absurd. So is the suggestion that the opponents of abortion can take comfort in the fact that the statute "places no limitation on the number of speakers or the noise level, including the use of amplification equipment." That is good enough, I suppose, for "protesting"; but the Court must know that [t]he availability of a powerful amplification system will be of little help to the woman who hopes to forge, in the last moments before another of her sex is to have an abortion, a bond of concern and intimacy that might enable her to persuade the woman to change her mind and heart. * * *

The Court [reasons] that a leafletter may, without violating the statute, stand "near the path" of oncoming pedestrians and make his "proffe[r] which the pedestrians can easily accept." [But] leafletting will be rendered utterly ineffectual by a requirement that the leafletter obtain from each subject permission to approach, or else man a stationary post (one that does not obstruct access to the facility, lest he violate subsection (2) of statute) and wait for passersby voluntarily to approach an outstretched hand. [A] leafletter, whether he is working on behalf of Operation Rescue, Local 109, or Bubba's Bar-B-Que, stakes out the best piece of real estate he can, and then walks a few steps toward individuals passing in his vicinity, extending his arm and making it *as easy as possible* for the passerby, whose natural inclination is generally not to seek out such distributions, to simply accept the offering. * * *

"The fact," the Court says, "that the coverage of a statute is broader than the specific concern that led to its enactment is of no constitutional significance." That is true enough ordinarily, but it is not true with respect to restraints upon speech, which is what the doctrine of overbreadth is all [about.] I know of no precedent for the proposition that time, place, and manner restrictions are not subject to the doctrine of overbreadth. * * *

[T]he public forum involved here—the public spaces outside of health care facilities—has become, by necessity and by virtue of this Court's decisions, a forum of last resort for those who oppose abortion. [Those] whose concern is for the physical safety and security of clinic patients, workers, and doctors should take no comfort from today's decision.

Individuals or groups intent on bullying or frightening women out of an abortion, or doctors out of performing that procedure, will not be deterred by Colorado's statute; bullhorns and screaming from eight feet away will serve their purposes well. But those who would accomplish their moral and religious objectives by peaceful and civil means, by trying to persuade individual women of the rightness of their cause, will be deterred; and that is not a good thing in a democracy. * * *

JUSTICE KENNEDY, dissenting.

[For] the first time, the Court approves a law which bars a private citizen from passing a message, in a peaceful manner and on a profound moral issue, to a fellow citizen on a public sidewalk. [The] prohibitions against "picketing" and/or "leafleting" upheld in *Frisby*, *Grace*, and *Mosley*, the Court says are no different from the restrictions on "protest, education, or counseling" imposed by the Colorado statute. [But no] examination of the content of a speaker's message is required to determine whether an individual is picketing, or distributing a leaflet, or impeding free access to a building. Under the Colorado enactment, however, [w]hen a citizen approaches another on the sidewalk in a disfavored-speech zone, an officer of the State must listen to what the speaker says. If, in the officer's judgment, the speaker's words stray too far toward "protest, education, or counseling"—the boundaries of which are far from clear—the officer may decide the speech has moved from the permissible to the criminal. The First Amendment does not give the government such power.

The statute is content based for an additional reason: [We] would close our eyes to reality were we to deny that 'oral protest, education, or counseling' outside the entrances to medical facilities concern a narrow range of topics—indeed, one topic in particular. [If], just a few decades ago, a State with a history of enforcing racial discrimination had enacted a statute like this one, regulating "oral protest, education, or counseling" within 100 feet of the entrance to any lunch counter, our predecessors would not have hesitated to hold it was content based or viewpoint based. [To] say that one citizen can approach another to ask the time or the weather forecast or the directions to Main Street but not to initiate discussion on one of the most basic moral and political issues in all of contemporary discourse, a question touching profound ideas in philosophy and theology, is an astonishing view of the First Amendment. * * *

[The] statute's vagueness [in] the terms "protest," "counseling," "education," and "consent" [becomes] as well one source of its overbreadth. The only sure way to avoid violating the law is to refrain from picketing, leafleting, or oral advocacy altogether. Scienter cannot save so vague a statute as this. [T]he State and the Court attempt to sidestep the enactment's obvious content-based restriction by praising the statute's breadth, by telling us all topics of conversation, not just discourse on abortion, are banned within the statutory proscription. [Our] precedents do not permit content censoring to be cured by taking even more protected speech within a statute's reach. [The] happenstance of a dental office being located in a building brings the restricted-speech zone into play. If the same building also houses an organization dedicated, say, to environmental issues, a protest against the group's policies would be barred. Yet if, on the next block there were a public interest enterprise in a building with no health care facility, the speech would be unrestricted. The statute is a classic example of a proscription not narrowly tailored and resulting in restrictions of far more speech than necessary to achieve the legislature's object. * * *

The majority insists the statute aims to protect distraught women who are embarrassed, vexed, or harassed as they attempt to enter abortion clinics. If these are punishable acts, they should be prohibited in those [terms.] Citizens desiring to impart messages to women considering abortions likely do not have resources to use the mainstream media for their message, much less resources to locate women contemplating the option of abortion. [Nowhere] is the speech more important than at the time and place where the act is about to occur. As the named plaintiff, Leila Jeanne Hill, explained, "In my many years of sidewalk counseling I have seen a number of [these] women change their minds about aborting their unborn children as a result of my sidewalk counseling, and God's grace." * * *

The Court now strikes at the heart of the reasoned, careful balance I had believed was the basis for the joint opinion in *Casey*. The vital principle of the opinion was that in defined instances the woman's decision whether to abort her child was in its essence a moral one, a choice the State could not dictate. Foreclosed from using the machinery of government to ban abortions in early term, those who oppose it are remitted to debate the issue in its moral dimensions. In a cruel way, the Court today turns its back on that balance.* * *

NOTES AND QUESTIONS

1. **Overbreadth?** Consider Alan K. Chen, *Statutory Speech Bubbles, First Amendment Overbreadth, and Improper Legislative Purpose*, 38 Harv. C.R.-C.L. L. Rev. 31 (2003): "[T]he Court rejected the plaintiffs' overbreadth claim because it believed that the bubble law's comprehensiveness (treating all speech equally) suggested that the state's purposes were legitimate. But this was simply another way of stating that the law was viewpoint and content neutral. Overbreadth law's precision requirement, however, requires that laws discriminate by ensuring that lawmakers address the state's legitimate interests and no (or little) more, without sweeping in protected speech." Does the state's privacy interest address the overbreadth claim?

2. **Privacy?** Consider Robert D. Nauman, *The Captive Audience Doctrine and Floating Buffer Zones: An Analysis of Hill v. Colorado*, 30 Cap. U. L. Rev. 769 (2002): "Nowhere in the Court's discussion are there facts showing how the petitioners invaded the privacy rights of pedestrians, let alone how they did this in an 'intolerable manner.' Rather, the Court, after finding the substantial privacy interest, placed it 'in the scales with the right of others to communicate.' This suggests that the *Cohen* standard has been rejected in favor of a balancing approach, in which the unwilling listener will no longer be presumed to have the opportunity to avoid the unwanted speech in public. This gives much greater recognition to the interests of unwilling listeners in public fora than was present previously. It also runs the concurrent risk of establishing a 'heckler's veto,' in which the audience possesses the power to prohibit speech that it does not wish to hear simply by being present."

3. *Is manner distinguishable from content?* Consider Heidi Kitrosser, *From Marshall McLuhan to Anthropomorphic Cows: Communicative Manner and the First Amendment*, 96 Nw. U. L. Rev. 1339 (2002): "Although the Court's statements in *Hill* echo assumptions evinced in other cases, to the effect that content is synonymous with viewpoint and subject matter, these statements contradict broader definitions provided by the Court in other cases to the effect that content-based regulations target the 'communicative impact' of expression. Because the manner in which speech is delivered can have significant communicative impact upon listeners and viewers, the Court, applying the 'communicative impact' approach to defining content, has occasionally found restrictions on 'manner of speech' to be content-based, including restrictions on speech delivered in an indecent or offensive manner. Communicative manner includes expressive choices ranging from word choice (e.g., the use of profane language), to choice of visual displays to convey a message (e.g., the burning of a flag or the use of nudity), to place-and-manner choices affecting the communicative impact of a message (e.g., the decision to engage in face-to-face communication, or to picket in front of a particular location of symbolic or emotional significance)."

4. *Discriminatory impact.* Consider Kathleen M. Sullivan, *Sex, Money, and Groups: Free Speech and Association Decisions in the October 1999 Term*, 28 Pepp. L. Rev. 723 (2001): "The law in *Hill* arguably has a viewpoint-discriminatory effect: requiring listeners affirmatively to consent to speech will inevitably have the effect of discriminating in favor of popular or widely accepted messages and against those that are unorthodox or unpopular."

5. *Severe slippery slope?* Consider Jamin B. Raskin, *Disfavored Speech About Favored Rights: Hill v. Colorado, The Vanishing Public Forum and the Need for an Objective Speech Discrimination Test*, 51 Am. U. L. Rev. 179 (2001): "Thus, if a state is vexed by protests outside lunch counters that refuse to serve racial minorities, it can enact a regulation limiting unconsented approaches for speech purposes by any person (not just opponents of segregation) within 100 feet of the entrance of food service establishments. [Similarly,] if a state is opposed to gay rights activists leafleting on Sundays

near the churches of conservative religious congregations that oppose homosexuality, it can enact a criminal law banning unconsented approaches by any person within 100 feet of the entrance of all houses of worship. [A] legislature in a right-to-work state perturbed by union picketing outside paper mills can pass a law that prohibits unconsented approaches by any person within 100 feet of the entrance of all industrial facilities for the stated purpose of ensuring the free flow of commerce, securing the right to contract, and protecting employees from stresses that diminish worker safety and productivity."

6. ***Legislative dilemma.*** Consider Chen, Note 1 supra: "Such laws may be inextricably caught between the doctrine of substantial overbreadth and the doctrine of content neutrality. If such laws are to be truly viewpoint-and content-neutral, they must apply to a broad range of expression that is clearly protected by the First Amendment, but is unrelated to the government's interest. On the other hand, if such laws are read more narrowly to encompass only the state's primary interest in protecting women's access to abortion clinics, they may be invalidated because they are discriminatory."

7. Discriminatory effect on the basis of viewpoint. Protesters maintained that Secret Service agents engaged in viewpoint discrimination when they moved the protesters of President Bush two blocks away from the open-air patio where he was dining, while permitting supporters of the President to remain in their original location.

WOOD v. MOSS, 134 S.Ct. 2056 (2014), per GINSBURG, J., unanimously rejected this contention explaining that the protesters were within weapons range, and had a largely unobstructed view, of the President's location, while where the supporters stood, a large, two-story building blocked sight of and weapons access to the patio.

8. Compare McCULLEN v. COAKLEY, 134 S.Ct. 2518 (2014): With the exception of patients, employees, police and the like, Massachusetts prohibits anyone from standing on a public highway or street within 35 feet of a hospital where abortions are performed. McCullen and others challenged the law because they wished to counsel patients about abortion especially about access to alternatives. Without calling *Hill, Schenck,* or *Madsen* into question, the Court, per ROBERTS, C.J., held that strict scrutiny did not apply, but that the 35 feet buffer zone was not sufficiently tailored to meet the demands of a place restriction. The fact that the restriction applied only to abortion facilities did not make the restriction content based. Harms like obstruction and threats to public safety were not caused by the content of the communication. Although exceptions for employees were not designed to promote pro-abortion speech, such speech by employees in the zones would be impermissible. Roberts, C.J. suggested alternatives in meeting the state objectives such as statutes designed to prevent obstruction and harassment as well as other statutes designed to protect public safety. He also suggested that injunctions could be employed against those who had engaged in prior bad conduct.

SCALIA, J., joined by Kennedy and Thomas, JJ., concurring, argued that strict scrutiny should apply because the statute was plainly directed at anti-abortion protesters and also because employees of abortion facilities would clearly speak in favor of abortion. He did not reach the narrow tailoring issue because he did not want to create a false image of unanimity.

ALITO, J., concurring, essentially agreed with Scalia, J., on the content discrimination issue, but explicitly agreed with the majority on the narrow tailoring issue.

7. GOVERNMENT SPEECH

Public forum doctrine recognizes that government is obligated to permit some of its property to be used for communicative purposes without content discrimination, but public forum doctrine also allows other government property to be restricted to some speakers or for talk about selected subjects. In short, in some circumstances government can provide resources for some speech while denying support for other speech. Indeed, government is a significant actor in the marketplace of ideas. Sometimes the government speaks as government; sometimes it subsidizes speech without purporting to claim that the resulting message is its own. It supports speech in many ways: official government messages; statements of public officials at publicly subsidized press conferences; artistic, scientific, or political subsidies; even the classroom communications of public school teachers.

If content distinctions are suspect when government acts as censor, they are the norm when government speaks or otherwise subsidizes speech. Government makes editorial judgments; it decides that some content is appropriate for the occasion and other content is not. The public museum curator makes content decisions in selecting exhibits; the librarian in selecting books; the public board in selecting recipients for research grants; the public official in composing press releases.

The line between support for speech and censorship of speech is not always bright, however. In any event, the Constitution limits the choices government may make in supporting speech. For example, government support of religious speech is limited under the Establishment Clause. See Ch. 8. This section explores the extent to which the speech clause or constitutional conceptions of equality should limit government discretion in supporting speech.

I.   SUBSIDIES OF SPEECH

Pleasant Grove, Utah permitted private groups to place a number of permanent monuments in its Pioneer Park including a Ten Commandments monument provided by the Fraternal Order of Eagles. Summum, a religious organization, requested permission to erect a monument containing Seven Aphorisms which it believes were presented by God to Moses. The city refused and Summum challenged the refusal on the ground that the city was engaging in unacceptable content discrimination in a public forum.

PLEASANT GROVE CITY v. SUMMUM, 555 U.S. 460 (2009), per ALITO, J., upheld the city's action: "[A]lthough a park is a traditional public forum for speeches and other transitory expressive acts, the display of a permanent monument in a public park is not a form of expression to which forum analysis applies. Instead, the placement of a permanent monument in a public park is best viewed as a form of government speech and is therefore not subject to scrutiny under the Free Speech Clause. [If] government entities must maintain viewpoint neutrality in their selection of donated monuments, they must either 'brace themselves for an influx of clutter' or face the pressure to remove longstanding and cherished monuments. Every jurisdiction that has accepted a donated war memorial may be asked to provide equal treatment for a donated monument questioning the cause for which the veterans fought. New York City, having accepted a donated statue of one heroic dog (Balto, the sled dog who brought medicine to Nome, Alaska, during a diphtheria epidemic) may be pressed to accept monuments for other dogs who are claimed to be equally worthy of commemoration. The obvious truth of the matter is that if public parks were considered to be traditional public forums for the purpose of erecting privately donated monuments, most parks would have little choice but to refuse all such donations." Earlier in the opinion, the Court recited limits on government speech: "This does not mean that there are no restraints on government speech. For example, government speech must comport with the Establishment Clause. The involvement of public officials in advocacy may be limited by law, regulation, or practice. And of course, a government entity is ultimately 'accountable to the electorate and the political process for its advocacy.' 'If the citizenry objects, newly elected officials later could espouse some different or contrary position.' "267

---

267 The Court recognized that there might be situations where it is difficult to tell whether government is speaking or providing a forum for private speech. Stevens, J., joined by Ginsburg, J., concurring, doubted that it made a difference whether the city's acceptance of the Ten Commandment's monument was deemed to be government speech or implicit endorsement of the donor's message. Scalia, J., joined by Thomas J., concurring, expressed the view that the city's action did not violate the Establishment Clause (although the issue was not presented). Breyer, J., concurring, expressed the view that the phrase, "government speech" needed to be applied not as a label, but with an eye toward the category's purpose. He did not think the government action disproportionately burdened Summum's speech. Souter, J., concurring, applied a reasonable observer test to determine that the Ten Commandment's monument was government speech. He thought it premature to be deciding Establishment Clause issues.

RUST V. SULLIVAN

500 U.S. 173, 111 S.Ct. 1759, 114 L.Ed.2d 233 (1991).

CHIEF JUSTICE REHNQUIST delivered the opinion of the Court.

These cases concern a facial challenge to Department of Health and Human Services (HHS) regulations which limit the ability of Title X fund recipients to engage in abortion-related activities. * * *

A.   In 1970, Congress enacted Title X of the Public Health Service Act (Act), 84 Stat. 1506, as amended, 42 U.S.C. §§ 300–300a–41, which provides federal funding for family-planning services. The Act authorizes the Secretary to "make grants to and enter into contracts with public or nonprofit private entities to assist in the establishment and operation of voluntary family planning projects which shall offer a broad range of acceptable and effective family planning methods and services." 42 U.S.C. § 300(a). Grants and contracts under Title X must "be made in accordance with such regulations as the Secretary may promulgate." 42 U.S.C. § 300a–4. Section 1008 of the Act, however, provides that "[n]one of the funds appropriated under this subchapter shall be used in programs where abortion is a method of family planning." 42 U.S.C. § 300a–6. * * *

In 1988, the Secretary promulgated new regulations designed to provide " 'clear and operational guidance' to grantees about how to preserve the distinction between Title X programs and abortion as a method of family planning." 53 Fed.Reg. 2923–2924 (1988). * * *

The regulations attach three principal conditions on the grant of federal funds for Title X projects. First, the regulations specify that a "Title X project may not provide counseling concerning the use of abortion as a method of family planning or provide referral for abortion as a method of family planning." 42 CFR § 59.8(a)(1) (1989). Because Title X is limited to preconceptional services, the program does not furnish services related to childbirth. Only in the context of a referral out of the Title X program is a pregnant woman given transitional information. § 59.8(a)(2). Title X projects must refer every pregnant client "for appropriate prenatal and/or social services by furnishing a list of available providers that promote the welfare of the mother and the unborn child." Id. The list may not be used indirectly to encourage or promote abortion, "such as by weighing the list of referrals in favor of health care providers which perform abortions, by including on the list of referral providers health care providers whose principal business is the provision of abortions, by excluding available providers who do not provide abortions, or by 'steering' clients to providers who offer abortion as a method of family planning." § 59.8(a)(3). The Title X project is expressly prohibited from referring a pregnant woman to an abortion provider, even upon specific request. One permissible response to such an inquiry is that "the project does not consider abortion an appropriate method of family planning and therefore does not counsel or refer for abortion." § 59.8(b)(5).

Second, the regulations broadly prohibit a Title X project from engaging in activities that "encourage, promote or advocate abortion as a method of family planning." § 59.10(a). Forbidden activities include lobbying for legislation that would increase the availability of abortion as a method of family planning, developing or disseminating materials advocating abortion as a method of family planning, providing speakers to promote abortion as a method of family planning, using legal action to make abortion available in any way as a method of family planning, and paying dues to any group that advocates abortion as a method of family planning as a substantial part of its activities. Id.

Third, the regulations require that Title X projects be organized so that they are "physically and financially separate" from prohibited abortion activities. § 59.9. To be deemed physically and financially separate, "a Title X project must have an objective integrity and independence from prohibited activities. Mere bookkeeping separation of Title X funds from other monies is not sufficient." Id. The regulations provide a list of nonexclusive factors for the Secretary to consider in conducting a case-by-case determination of objective integrity and independence, such as the existence of separate accounting records and separate personnel, and the degree of physical separation of the project from facilities for prohibited activities. Id.

[Petitioners] are Title X grantees and doctors who supervise Title X funds suing on behalf of themselves and their patients. Respondent is the Secretary of the Department of Health and Human Services. [Petitioners] contend that the regulations violate the First Amendment by impermissibly discriminating based on viewpoint because they prohibit "all discussion about abortion as a lawful option—including counseling, referral, and the provision of neutral and accurate information about ending a pregnancy—while compelling the clinic or counselor to provide information that promotes continuing a pregnancy to term." They assert that the regulations violate the "free speech rights of private health care organizations that receive Title X funds, of their staff, and of their patients" by impermissibly imposing "viewpoint-discriminatory conditions on government subsidies" and thus "penaliz[e] speech funded with non-Title X monies." Because "Title X continues to fund speech ancillary to pregnancy testing in a manner that is not even-handed with respect to views and information about abortion, it invidiously discriminates on the basis of viewpoint." Relying on *Regan v. Taxation with Representation of Washington,* 461 U.S. 540 (1983)[268] and *Arkansas Writers' Project, Inc. v.*

---

[268] *Regan* upheld tax code provisions that permitted contributions to veteran's organizations to be deductible even if they engaged in substantial lobbying while denying deductions for

Ragland, 481 U.S. 221 (1987),[269] petitioners also assert that while the Government may place certain conditions on the receipt of federal subsidies, it may not "discriminate invidiously in its subsidies in such a way as to 'ai[m] at the suppression of dangerous ideas.' " *Regan.*

There is no question but that the statutory prohibition contained in § 1008 is constitutional. [The] Government can, without violating the Constitution, selectively fund a program to encourage certain activities it believes to be in the public interest, without at the same time funding an alternate program which seeks to deal with the problem in another way.[270] In so doing, the Government has not discriminated on the basis of viewpoint; it has merely chosen to fund one activity to the exclusion of the other. "[A] legislature's decision not to subsidize the exercise of a fundamental right does not infringe the right." *Regan.* * * *

The challenged regulations implement the statutory prohibition by prohibiting counseling, referral, and the provision of information regarding abortion as a method of family planning. They are designed to ensure that the limits of the federal program are observed. The Title X program is designed not for prenatal care, but to encourage family planning. A doctor who wished to offer prenatal care to a project patient who became pregnant could properly be prohibited from doing so because such service is outside the scope of the federally funded program. The regulations prohibiting abortion counseling and referral are of the same ilk; "no funds appropriated for the project may be used in programs where abortion is a method of family planning," and a doctor employed by the project may be prohibited in the course of his project duties from counseling abortion or referring for abortion. This is not a case of the Government "suppressing a dangerous idea," but of a prohibition on a project grantee or its employees from engaging in activities outside of its scope.

To hold that the Government unconstitutionally discriminates on the basis of viewpoint when it chooses to fund a program dedicated to advance certain permissible goals, because the program in advancing those goals necessarily discourages alternate goals, would render numerous government programs constitutionally suspect. When Congress

---

contributions to other religious, charitable, scientific, or educational organizations if they engaged in substantial lobbying.

[269] *Arkansas Writers' Project* held it unconstitutional to impose a sales tax on general interest magazines while exempting newspapers, religious, professional, trade, and sports journals. Discriminatory taxation against the press or segments of it has generally been invalidated. *Minneapolis Star & Tribune v. Minnesota Comm. of Rev.,* 460 U.S. 575 (1983) (some press treated more favorably and press treated differently from other enterprises); *Grosjean v. American Press Co.,* 297 U.S. 233 (1936) (same). But see *Leathers v. Medlock,* 499 U.S. 439 (1991) (upholding general sales tax extension to cable that was not applicable to the print media on the grounds that it did not suppress ideas and that the tax did not target a small group of speakers).

[270] The Court cited *Maher v. Roe,* 432 U.S. 464 (1977) (constitutional for government to subsidize childbirth without subsidizing abortions) and *Harris v. McRae,* 448 U.S. 297 (1980) (accord).

established a National Endowment for Democracy to encourage other countries to adopt democratic principles, 22 U.S.C. § 4411(b), it was not constitutionally required to fund a program to encourage competing lines of political philosophy such as Communism and Fascism. Petitioners' assertions ultimately boil down to the position that if the government chooses to subsidize one protected right, it must subsidize analogous counterpart rights. But the Court has soundly rejected that proposition. Within far broader limits than petitioners are willing to concede, when the government appropriates public funds to establish a program it is entitled to define the limits of that program.

We believe that petitioners' reliance upon our decision in *Arkansas Writers' Project* is misplaced. That case involved a state sales tax which discriminated between magazines on the basis of their content. Relying on this fact, and on the fact that the tax "targets a small group within the press," contrary to our decision in *Minneapolis Star,* the Court held the tax invalid. But we have here not the case of a general law singling out a disfavored group on the basis of speech content, but a case of the Government refusing to fund activities, including speech, which are specifically excluded from the scope of the project funded.

Petitioners rely heavily on their claim that the regulations would not, in the circumstance of a medical emergency, permit a Title X project to refer a woman whose pregnancy places her life in imminent peril to a provider of abortions or abortion-related services. This case, of course, involves only a facial challenge to the regulations, and we do not have before us any application by the Secretary to a specific fact situation. On their face, we do not read the regulations to bar abortion referral or counseling in such circumstances. * * *

Petitioners also contend that the restrictions on the subsidization of abortion-related speech contained in the regulations are impermissible because they condition the receipt of a benefit, in this case Title X funding, on the relinquishment of a constitutional right, the right to engage in abortion advocacy and counseling.

[H]ere the government is not denying a benefit to anyone, but is instead simply insisting that public funds be spent for the purposes for which they were authorized. The Secretary's regulations do not force the Title X grantee to give up abortion-related speech; they merely require that the grantee keep such activities separate and distinct from Title X activities. Title X expressly distinguishes between a Title X *grantee* and a Title X *project.* The grantee, which normally is a health care organization, may receive funds from a variety of sources for a variety of purposes. The grantee receives Title X funds, however, for the specific and limited purpose of establishing and operating a Title X project. 42 U.S.C. § 300(a). The regulations govern the scope of the Title X *project's* activities, and leave the grantee unfettered in its other activities. The Title X *grantee* can continue to perform abortions, provide abortion-related services, and engage in abortion advocacy; it simply is required to conduct those activities through programs that are separate and independent from the project that receives Title X funds.

In contrast, our "unconstitutional conditions" cases involve situations in which the government has placed a condition on the *recipient* of the subsidy rather than on a particular program or service, thus effectively prohibiting the recipient from engaging in the protected conduct outside the scope of the federally funded program. [By] requiring that the Title X grantee engage in abortion-related activity separately from activity receiving federal funding, Congress has, consistent with our teachings in *League of Women Voters*, [Sec. 8, II infra], and *Regan,* not denied it the right to engage in abortion-related activities. Congress has merely refused to fund such activities out of the public fisc, and the Secretary has simply required a certain degree of separation from the Title X project in order to ensure the integrity of the federally funded program.[271]

The same principles apply to petitioners' claim that the regulations abridge the free speech rights of the grantee's staff. Individuals who are voluntarily employed for a Title X project must perform their duties in accordance with the regulation's restrictions on abortion counseling and referral. The employees remain free, however, to pursue abortion-related activities when they are not acting under the auspices of the Title X project. The regulations, which govern solely the scope of the Title X project's activities, do not in any way restrict the activities of those persons acting as private individuals. The employees' freedom of expression is limited during the time that they actually work for the project; but this limitation is a consequence of their decision to accept employment in a project, the scope of which is permissibly restricted by the funding authority.

This is not to suggest that funding by the Government, even when coupled with the freedom of the fund recipients to speak outside the scope of the Government-funded project, is invariably sufficient to justify government control over the content of expression. For example, this Court has recognized that the existence of a Government "subsidy," in the form of Government-owned property, does not justify the restriction of speech in areas that have "been traditionally open to the public for expressive activity," or have been "expressly dedicated to speech activity." Similarly, we have recognized that the university is a traditional sphere of free expression so fundamental to the functioning of our society that the

---

[271] Accordingly, the Court, per Roberts, C.J., ruled that a program funding nongovernmental organizations to combat HIV/AIDS worldwide could not require recipients to adopt or maintain a policy explicitly opposing prostitution. Because the condition applied to speech that was not within the scope of the federal program, it unconstitutionally burdened the First Amendment rights of the recipients. *Agency for Intern. Dev. v. Alliance for Open Society Intern., Inc.,* 133 S.Ct. 2321 (2013). Scalia and Thomas, JJ., dissented. Kagan, J., did not participate.

Government's ability to control speech within that sphere by means of conditions attached to the expenditure of Government funds is restricted by the vagueness and overbreadth doctrines of the First Amendment, *Keyishian v. Board of Regents*. It could be argued by analogy that traditional relationships such as that between doctor and patient should enjoy protection under the First Amendment from government regulation, even when subsidized by the Government. We need not resolve that question here, however, because the Title X program regulations do not significantly impinge upon the doctor-patient relationship. Nothing in them requires a doctor to represent as his own any opinion that he does not in fact hold. Nor is the doctor-patient relationship established by the Title X program sufficiently all-encompassing so as to justify an expectation on the part of the patient of comprehensive medical advice. The program does not provide post-conception medical care, and therefore a doctor's silence with regard to abortion cannot reasonably be thought to mislead a client into thinking that the doctor does not consider abortion an appropriate option for her. The doctor is always free to make clear that advice regarding abortion is simply beyond the scope of the program. In these circumstances, the general rule that the Government may choose not to subsidize speech applies with full force. * * *

JUSTICE BLACKMUN, with whom JUSTICE MARSHALL joins, with whom JUSTICE STEVENS joins as to Parts II[272] and III,[273] and with whom JUSTICE O'CONNOR joins as to Part I,[274] dissenting. * * *

II. A. Until today, the Court never has upheld viewpoint-based suppression of speech simply because that suppression was a condition upon the acceptance of public funds. Whatever may be the Government's power to condition the receipt of its largess upon the relinquishment of constitutional rights, it surely does not extend to a condition that suppresses the recipient's cherished freedom of speech based solely upon the content or viewpoint of that speech. * * *

It cannot seriously be disputed that the counseling and referral provisions at issue in the present cases constitute content-based regulation of speech. Title X grantees may provide counseling and referral regarding any of a wide range of family planning and other topics, save abortion.

The Regulations are also clearly viewpoint-based. While suppressing speech favorable to abortion with one hand, the Secretary compels anti-abortion speech with the other. For example, the Department of Health and Human Services' own description of the Regulations makes plain that "Title X projects are *required* to facilitate access to prenatal care and social

---

[272] Part II discussed freedom of speech and portions of it are set out below.

[273] Part III argued that the regulations violated the Fifth Amendment Due Process Clause.

[274] Part I contended that the regulations were not authorized by the statute. O'Connor, and Stevens, JJ., each filed separate dissents advancing the same contention.

services, including adoption services, that might be needed by the pregnant client to promote her well-being and that of her child, while making it abundantly clear that the project is not permitted to promote abortion by facilitating access to abortion through the referral process." 53 Fed.Reg. 2927 (1988) (emphasis added).

Moreover, the Regulations command that a project refer for prenatal care each woman diagnosed as pregnant, irrespective of the woman's expressed desire to continue or terminate her pregnancy. 42 CFR § 59.8(a)(2) (1990). If a client asks directly about abortion, a Title X physician or counselor is required to say, in essence, that the project does not consider abortion to be an appropriate method of family planning. § 59.8(b)(4). Both requirements are antithetical to the First Amendment. See *Wooley v. Maynard*.

The Regulations pertaining to "advocacy" are even more explicitly viewpoint-based. These provide: "A Title X project may not *encourage, promote or advocate* abortion as a method of family planning." § 59.10 (emphasis added). They explain: "This requirement prohibits actions to *assist* women to obtain abortions or *increase* the availability or accessibility of abortion for family planning purposes." § 59.10(a) (emphasis added). The Regulations do not, however, proscribe or even regulate anti-abortion advocacy. These are clearly restrictions aimed at the suppression of "dangerous ideas."

Remarkably, the majority concludes that "the Government has not discriminated on the basis of viewpoint; it has merely chosen to fund one activity to the exclusion of another." But the majority's claim that the Regulations merely limit a Title X project's speech to preventive or preconceptional services rings hollow in light of the broad range of nonpreventive services that the Regulations authorize Title X projects to provide.[2] By refusing to fund those family-planning projects that advocate abortion *because* they advocate abortion, the Government plainly has targeted a particular viewpoint. The majority's reliance on the fact that the Regulations pertain solely to funding decisions simply begs the question. Clearly, there are some bases upon which government may not rest its decision to fund or not to fund. For example, the Members of the majority surely would agree that government may not base its decision to support an activity upon considerations of race. As demonstrated above, our cases make clear that ideological viewpoint is a similarly repugnant ground upon which to base funding decisions.

The majority's reliance upon *Regan* in this connection is [misplaced]. That case stands for the proposition that government has no obligation to

---

[2]   [Ct's Note] In addition to requiring referral for prenatal care and adoption services, the Regulations permit general health services such as physical examinations, screening for breast cancer, treatment of gynecological problems, and treatment for sexually transmitted diseases. 53 Fed.Reg. 2927 (1988). None of the latter are strictly preventive, preconceptional services.

subsidize a private party's efforts to petition the legislature regarding its views. Thus, if the challenged Regulations were confined to non-ideological limitations upon the use of Title X funds for lobbying activities, there would exist no violation of the First Amendment. The advocacy Regulations at issue here, however, are not limited to lobbying but extend to all speech having the effect of encouraging, promoting, or advocating abortion as a method of family planning. § 59.10(a). Thus, in addition to their impermissible focus upon the viewpoint of regulated speech, the provisions intrude upon a wide range of communicative conduct, including the very words spoken to a woman by her physician. By manipulating the content of the doctor/patient dialogue, the Regulations upheld today force each of the petitioners "to be an instrument for fostering public adherence to an ideological point of view [he or she] finds unacceptable." *Wooley v. Maynard.* This type of intrusive, ideologically based regulation of speech goes far beyond the narrow lobbying limitations approved in *Regan,* and cannot be justified simply because it is a condition upon the receipt of a governmental benefit.[3]

B. The Court concludes that the challenged Regulations do not violate the First Amendment rights of Title X staff members because any limitation of the employees' freedom of expression is simply a consequence of their decision to accept employment at a federally funded project. Ante, at 22. But it has never been sufficient to justify an otherwise unconstitutional condition upon public employment that the employee may escape the condition by relinquishing his or her job.

The majority attempts to circumvent this principle by emphasizing that Title X physicians and counselors "remain free [to] pursue abortion-related activities when they are not acting under the auspices of the Title X project." "The regulations," the majority explains, "do not in any way restrict the activities of those persons acting as private individuals." Under the majority's reasoning, the First Amendment could be read to tolerate *any* governmental restriction upon an employee's speech so long as that restriction is limited to the funded workplace. This is a dangerous proposition, and one the Court has rightly rejected in the past.

---

[3] **[Ct's Note]** The majority attempts to obscure the breadth of its decision through its curious contention that "the Title X program regulations do not significantly impinge upon the doctor-patient relationship." That the doctor-patient relationship is substantially burdened by a rule prohibiting the dissemination by the physician of pertinent medical information is beyond serious dispute. This burden is undiminished by the fact that the relationship at issue here is not an "all-encompassing" one. A woman seeking the services of a Title X clinic has every reason to expect, as do we all, that her physician will not withhold relevant information regarding the very purpose of her visit. To suggest otherwise is to engage in uninformed fantasy. Further, to hold that the doctor-patient relationship is somehow incomplete where a patient lacks the resources to seek comprehensive healthcare from a single provider is to ignore the situation of a vast number of Americans. As Justice Marshall has noted in a different context: "It is perfectly proper for judges to disagree about what the Constitution requires. But it is disgraceful for an interpretation of the Constitution to be premised upon unfounded assumptions about how people live." *United States v. Kras,* 409 U.S. 434 (1973) (dissenting opinion).

In *Abood,* it was no answer to the petitioners' claim of compelled speech as a condition upon public employment that their speech outside the workplace remained unregulated by the State.[275] Nor was the public employee's First Amendment claim in *Rankin v. McPherson,* 483 U.S. 378 (1987), derogated because the communication that her employer sought to punish occurred during business hours.[276] At the least, such conditions require courts to balance the speaker's interest in the message against those of government in preventing its dissemination.

In the cases at bar, the speaker's interest in the communication is both clear and vital. In addressing the family-planning needs of their clients, the physicians and counselors who staff Title X projects seek to provide them with the full range of information and options regarding their health and reproductive freedom. Indeed, the legitimate expectations of the patient and the ethical responsibilities of the medical profession demand no less. "The patient's right of self-decision can be effectively exercised only if the patient possesses enough information to enable an intelligent choice. [The] physician has an ethical obligation to help the patient make choices from among the therapeutic alternatives consistent with good medical practice." Current Opinions, the Council on Ethical and Judicial Affairs of the American Medical Association ¶ 8.08 (1989). * * *

The Government's articulated interest in distorting the doctor/patient dialogue—ensuring that federal funds are not spent for a purpose outside the scope of the program—falls far short of that necessary to justify the suppression of truthful information and professional medical opinion regarding constitutionally protected conduct.[4] Moreover, the offending Regulation is not narrowly tailored to serve this interest. For example, the governmental interest at stake could be served by imposing rigorous bookkeeping standards to ensure financial separation or adopting content-neutral rules for the balanced dissemination of family-planning and health information. By failing to balance or even to consider the free speech interests claimed by Title X physicians against the Government's asserted interest in suppressing the speech, the Court falters in its duty to implement the protection that the First Amendment clearly provides for this important message.

C.   Finally, it is of no small significance that the speech the Secretary would suppress is truthful information regarding constitutionally protected conduct of vital importance to the listener. One can imagine no

---

[275] *Abood v. Detroit Board of Education,* Sec. 9, II infra (compelled funding of ideological activities of union violates freedom of speech).

[276] *Rankin* (expressed hope that assassination attempt of president be successful is protected speech when uttered in private to fellow employee during working hours).

[4]   **[Ct's Note]** It is to be noted that the Secretary has made no claim that the Regulations at issue reflect any concern for the health or welfare of Title X clients.

legitimate governmental interest that might be served by suppressing such information. * * *

NOTES AND QUESTIONS

1.　***Free speech?*** Is the problem in *Rust* one of free speech or of the right to secure an abortion? Consider Abner S. Greene, *Government of the Good,* 53 Vand. L.Rev. 1 (2000): "Should it be improper as a matter of political theory, or unconstitutional, for government to condition the funding of health clinics on their advocating condom use by teens?"

2.　***Political speech.*** Are there First Amendment limits on the extent to which government can subsidize political speech. Suppose government itself enters the political fray. Should a city government be able to buy media time to speak on behalf of candidates? To influence the outcome of initiative campaigns?[277] What about refusals to subsidize political speech? See *Ysursa v. Pacatello Education Ass'n,* 555 U.S. 353 (2009) (constitutional for state to permit payroll deductions for union dues while barring deductions for political purposes).

3.　***Managerial domains.*** Consider Robert C. Post, *Subsidized Speech,* 106 Yale L.J. 151 (1996): "Public discourse must be distinguished from ['managerial'] domains. [Within] managerial domains, the state organizes its resources so as to achieve specified ends. The constitutional value of managerial domains is that of instrumental rationality, a value that conceptualizes persons as means to an end rather than as autonomous agents. [T]herefore, ends may be imposed upon persons.

"Managerial domains are necessary so that a democratic state can actually achieve objectives that have been democratically agreed upon. [Thus] the state can regulate speech within public educational institutions so as to achieve the purposes of education; it can regulate speech within the judicial system so as to attain the ends of justice; it can regulate speech within the military so as to preserve the national defense; it can regulate the speech of government employees so as to promote 'the efficiency of the public services [the government] performs through its employees'; and so forth.

"As a result of this instrumental orientation, viewpoint discrimination occurs frequently within managerial domains. To give but a few obvious examples: the president may fire cabinet officials who publicly challenge rather

---

[277] For relevant commentary, see Mark Yudof, *When Government Speaks: Politics, Law, and Government Expression in America* (1983); David Cole, *Beyond Unconstitutional Conditions: Charting Spheres of Neutrality in Government-Funded Speech,* 67 N.Y.U.L.Rev. 675 (1992). Richard Delgado, *The Language of the Arms Race,* 64 B.U.L.Rev. 961 (1984); Thomas Emerson, *The Affirmative Side of the First Amendment,* 15 Ga.L.Rev. 795 (1981); Robert Kamenshine, *The First Amendment's Implied Political Establishment Clause,* 67 Calif.L.Rev. 1104 (1979); Steven Shiffrin, *Government Speech,* 27 UCLA L.Rev. 565 (1980); Martin H. Redish & Daryl I. Kessler, *Government Subsidies and Free Expression,* 80 Minn.L.Rev. 543 (1996); Frederick Schauer, *Book Review,* 35 Stan.L.Rev. 373 (1983); Mark Yudof, *When Governments Speak: Toward A Theory of Government Expression and the First Amendment,* 57 Tex.L.Rev. 863 (1979); Edward Ziegler, *Government Speech and the Constitution: The Limits of Official Partisanship,* 21 B.C.L.Rev. 578 (1980).

than support Administration policies; the military may discipline officers who publicly attack rather than uphold the principle of civilian control over the armed forces; public defenders who prosecute instead of defend their clients may be sanctioned; prison guards who encourage instead of condemn drug use may be chastised. Viewpoint discrimination occurs within managerial domains whenever the attainment of legitimate managerial objectives requires it.

"[Clearly], First Amendment doctrine within managerial domains differs fundamentally from First Amendment doctrine within public discourse."[278]

Is the *Rust* situation an appropriate instance to invoke the managerial domain perspective? Or does it matter that the speakers whose speech is limited are not bureaucrats, but professionals who "must always qualify their loyalty and commitment to the vertical hierarchy of an organization by their horizontal commitment to general professional norms and standards." See id. at 172.

And consider Susan H. Williams, *Truth, Autonomy, and Speech: Feminist Theory and the First Amendment* 192–93 (2004): "[Post] is clearly right that certain government institutions must be seen as engaged in an activity distinct from governance; such institutions are intended to serve a particular purpose and speech within them often can be regulated in the interest of that purpose. [But] those holding power in such institutions must make themselves vulnerable to claims of injustice by other members and even by outsiders affected by the institution. Such institutions, in other words, are never only in the domain of management; they are always subject to claims of justice and not just to claims of instrumental rationality." Williams observes that this is particularly important because "It is in the nature of power hierarchies to overestimate the need for their own control and underestimate the harms done to those subject to that control. For that reason, deference toward the people holding power in such institutions is generally less appropriate as the institutions are more hierarchical."

4.   ***Deception.*** Consider Dorothy E. Roberts, *Rust v. Sullivan and the Control of Knowledge,* 61 Geo.Wash.L.Rev. 587 (1993): "[P]regnancy may accelerate the progression of certain serious medical conditions, such as heart disease, hypertension, diabetes, sickle cell anemia, cancer and AIDS. For example, a woman with diabetic retinopathy who becomes pregnant may go blind. The regulations prohibited doctors from advising women suffering from these conditions that abortion may reduce the long-term risks to their health. Moreover, the recommendation of prenatal care may give the false impression that pregnancy does not jeopardize these women's health." See also Gia B. Lee, *Persuasion, Transparency, and Government Speech,* 56 Hast. L.J. 983 (2005): "While the *Rust* majority noted that, '[n]othing in [the regulations] requires a doctor to represent as his own any opinion that he does not hold,' and that '[t]he

---

[278] For similar First Amendment perspectives, see C. Edwin Baker, *Campaign Expenditures and Free Speech,* 33 Harv. C.R.-C.L.Rev. 1 (1998) (referring to bounded contexts); Daniel Halberstam, *Commercial Speech, Professional Speech, and the Constitutional Status of Social Institutions,* 147 U.Pa.L.Rev. 771 (1991) (referring to bounded speech institutions).

doctor is always free to make clear that advice regarding abortion is simply beyond the scope of the program,' it was also true that nothing in the regulations required the doctors to disclose the government's role in restricting the scope of their counseling."

5. ***Rust distinguished.*** The University of Virginia subsidized the printing costs of a wide variety of student organizations, but refused to fund religious activities (those that "primarily promote or manifest a particular belief in or about a deity or an ultimate reality").

ROSENBERGER v. UNIVERSITY OF VIRGINIA, 515 U.S. 819 (1995), per KENNEDY, J., also set forth Ch. 8, Sec. I infra held that the refusal to fund religious speech violated the free speech clause: "[In *Rust*] the government did not create a program to encourage private speech but instead used private speakers to transmit specific information pertaining to its own program. We recognized that when the government appropriates public funds to promote a particular policy of its own it is entitled to say what it wishes.

"It does not follow [that] viewpoint-based restrictions are proper when the University does not itself speak or subsidize transmittal of a message it favors but instead expends funds to encourage a diversity of views from private speakers."[279]

SOUTER, J., joined by Stevens, Ginsburg and Breyer, JJ., dissented: "If the Guidelines were written or applied so as to limit only such Christian advocacy and no other evangelical efforts that might compete with it, the discrimination would be based on viewpoint. But that is not what the regulation authorizes; it applies to Muslim and Jewish and Buddhist advocacy as well as to Christian. And since it limits funding to activities promoting or manifesting a particular belief not only 'in' but 'about' a deity or ultimate reality, it applies to agnostics and atheists as well as it does to deists and theists. The Guidelines [thus] do not skew debate by funding one position but not its competitors. [T]hey simply deny funding for hortatory speech that 'primarily promotes or manifests' any view on the merits of religion; they deny funding for the entire subject matter of religious apologetics."[280]

Consider Randall P. Bezanson and William G. Buss, *The Many Faces of Government Speech*, 86 Iowa L. Rev. 1377 (2001): "*Rosenberger* has now become the standard bearer for one of two poles in the Court's government speech jurisprudence. At one pole, the Court says, when the government makes a decision to create a forum for individual speech, the government is stuck with it. The government may not pick and choose among speakers because it prefers some messages over others. At the opposite pole, represented by *Rust v.*

---

[279] O'Connor, J., and Thomas, J., filed concurring opinions. *Rust* was also distinguished in *Legal Services Corp. v. Velazquez,* 531 U.S. 533 (2001). The Court struck down a restriction preventing the The Legal Services Corporation from distributing federal funds to challenge the constitutionality or the statutory validity of existing welfare laws. It concluded that the speech of lawyers on behalf of indigent clients was not government speech. Scalia, J., joined by Rehnquist, C.J., and O'Connor and Thomas, JJ., dissented.

[280] For commentary on whether the Virginia practice constitutes viewpoint discrimination, see Kent Greenawalt, *Viewpoints From Olympus,* 96 Colum. L.Rev. 697 (1996).

Sullivan, [the] Court says that the government may favor one message over another because the favored message is the government's own message, and because the government has not created any forum for the expression of individual views. Between these poles is sometimes a third one; the government may create a forum for the expression of individual views, but a forum that is not open to everyone. * * *[281]

"In deciding between the poles, the Court purports to hold the government to its own decision. The Court determines either that the government was speaking its own message or that it opened an avenue for individual speech opportunities and, if the latter, whether it was opening the door wide or opening only a limited forum. It seems clear that in deciding what the government has undertaken to do, the Court will be influenced by its own broad view of First Amendment tradeoffs."

6. ***Funding Arts and Sciences.*** The government has long funded scientific projects on the basis of their perceived merit. Could Congress constitutionally prohibit the funding of "indecent" art? Would this be an example of content discrimination or viewpoint discrimination? Does it matter? The extent to which the government may make such judgments and the role that political actors may play in the process was debated in *National Endowment for the Arts v. Finley,* 524 U.S. 569 (1998) but not resolved. Consider Abner S. Greene, *Government Speech on Unsettled Issues,* 69 Ford. L. Rev. 1667 (2001): "[V]iewpoint discrimination is a term that we should leave for government regulation of a particular viewpoint. We should not use it to describe government speech favoring a given viewpoint. Such speech, absent monopoly, coercion, or [similar] concerns, should be considered a healthy part of the market and of democratic debate and as no intrusion on the liberty or autonomy of citizens to express contrary viewpoints." Consider also Steven J. Heyman, *State-Supported Speech,* 1999 Wis. L.Rev. 1119: "Suppose [a] state legislature becomes concerned about violence in popular culture and the impact it may have on young people. Instead of attempting to regulate violent entertainment, the legislature decides to create a program to support art and culture, with the proviso that no funds should be awarded to works that glorify violence. There can be little doubt that this would constitute viewpoint discrimination. Yet it seems highly implausible to suggest that if the government chooses to support non-violent art, it must support violent art as well. Instead, the proviso should be upheld on the same ground that Souter offers in defending criteria of artistic merit—that it serves a 'perfectly legitimate' governmental goal." [282]

---

[281] Can government constitutionally permit pro choice specialty license plates while refusing to issue pro life specialty life license plates? See Amy Riley Lucas, *Speciality License Plates,* 55 UCLA L.Rev. 1971 (2008); Steven G. Gey, *Why Should the First Amendment Protect Government Speech When the Government Has Nothing to Say,* 95 Iowa L.Rev. 1259 (2010).

[282] For additional commentary, see Steven H. Shiffrin, *Dissent, Injustice, and the Meanings of America* ch. 1 (1999); Owen M. Fiss, *State Activism and State Censorship,* 100 Yale L.J. 2087, 2101 (1991); Amy Sabrin, *Thinking About Contents; Can It Play An Appropriate Role in Government Funding of the Arts?* 102 Yale L.J. 1209 (1993).

7.   If government consistently with the First Amendment can impose a point of view on bureaucrats or on doctors when they are subsidized with government funds (*Rust*), is it nonetheless barred from telling giernnmentally-employed academics the point of view they can advance in the classroom? If so, should artists on panels be considered more like bureaucrats and doctors or more like academics. How does one decide which actors favor some speech over other speech? Is there a problem with giving special protection for some institutions or professionals and not others? See generally Frederick Schauer, *Principles, Institutions, and the First Amendment*, 112 Harv. L. Rev. 84 (1998).

II. GOVERNMENT AS EDUCATOR AND EDITOR

Many problems involved with government speech have arisen in the school setting. Government can compel children to attend schools, but it may not compel children to attend public schools. *Pierce v. Society of Sisters*, 268 U.S. 510 (1925), infra, held that compulsory public education violated parental substantive due process rights though government may require that basic educational requirements be met even in private schools. (For further detail, see Ch. 6, Sec. 2.) In public schools there are limits to which the institution may be an exclusive enclave for government messages. *Tinker v. Des Moines School Dist.*, 393 U.S. 503 (1969), infra, upheld the rights of school children to wear black armbands in a classroom protest of the Vietnam War. Moreover, there are constitutional limits on the government's power to shield students from ideas by removing books from a school library. *Board of Educ. v. Pico*, 457 U.S. 853 (1982).[283] On the other hand, school authorities have been granted broad editorial control over the school curriculum including school-sponsored publications, theatrical productions, and other expressive activities.

———

Oregon's Compulsory Education Act of 1922 required all students to attend public schools through the eighth grade.[284] Two operators of private

---

[283] But see *United States v. American Library Associations*, Inc., 539 U.S. 194 (2003) (constitutional to condition federal funding on the adoption of "a policy of Internet safety for minors that includes the operations of a technology protection measure [that] protects against access" by all persons to "visual depictions" that constitute "obscenity" or "child pornography," and that protects against access by minors to "visual depictions" that are "harmful to minors.").

[284] The statute provided exemptions for children with disabilities, or who had completed the eighth grade, or who lived considerable distances from a public school, or who held a special permit from the county superintendent. The Court did not believe these exemptions were especially important. For a thorough historical and perceptive analytical treatment, see Barbara B. Woodhouse, *"Who Owns the Child?": Meyer and Pierce and the Child as Property*, 33 Wm. & Mary L. Rev. 995 (1992). In the end, despite cogent criticism, Woodhouse believes that *Pierce* reached the right result. Barbara B. Woodhouse, *Child Abuse, the Constitution, and the Legacy of Pierce v. Society of Sisters*, 78 U. Det. Mercy L. Rev. 479 (2001). Others take the criticism further. See, e.g., Meira Levinson, *The Demands of Liberal Education* 158, 161–63 (1999) (arguing for education within common schools and requiring heavy regulation of private schools to reach liberal public school ideals, including the prohibition of religious private schools); Abner S. Greene, *Civil Society and Multiple Repositories of Power*, 75 Chi.-Kent. L. Rev. 477 (2000); Abner S. Greene, *Why Vouchers Are Unconstitutional and Why They Are Not*, 13 Notre D. J.L. Ethics & Pub. Pol'y 397

schools, the Society of the Sisters of the Holy Names of Jesus and Mary and the Hill Military Academy, secured an injunction against the act's enforcement.

PIERCE v. SOCIETY OF SISTERS, 268 U.S. 510 (1925), per McREYNOLDS, J., held that the law violated the substantive due process rights of the parents and the schools: "The manifest purpose is to compel general attendance at public schools by normal children, between 8 and 16, who have not completed the eighth grade. [No] question is raised concerning the power of the state reasonably to regulate all schools, to inspect, supervise and examine them, their teachers and pupils; to require that all children of proper age attend some school, that teachers shall be of good moral character and patriotic disposition, that certain studies plainly essential to good citizenship must be taught, and that nothing be taught which is manifestly inimical to the public welfare.

"The inevitable practical result of enforcing the act under consideration would be destruction of appellees' primary schools, and perhaps all other private primary schools for normal children within the state of Oregon. Appellees are engaged in a kind of undertaking not inherently harmful, but long regarded as useful and meritorious. Certainly there is nothing in the present records to indicate that they have failed to discharge their obligations to patrons, students, or the state. And there are no peculiar circumstances or present emergencies which demand extraordinary measures relative to primary education.

"Under the doctrine of *Meyer v. Nebraska*, 262 U.S. 390 (1923), we think it entirely plain that the Act of 1922 unreasonably interferes with the liberty of parents and guardians to direct the upbringing and education of children under their control. [The] fundamental theory of liberty upon which all governments in this Union repose excludes any general power of the state to standardize its children by forcing them to accept instruction from public teachers only. The child is not the mere creature of the state; those who nurture him and direct his destiny have the right, coupled with the high duty, to recognize and prepare him for additional obligations.

"Appellees are corporations, and therefore, it is said, they cannot claim for themselves the liberty which the Fourteenth Amendment guarantees. [But] they have business and property for which they claim protection. These are threatened with destruction through the unwarranted compulsion which appellants are exercising over present and prospective patrons of their schools. * * * Generally, it is entirely true, as urged by counsel, that no person in any business has such an interest in possible

---

(1999). For defenses, see, e.g., Martha Minow, *Before and After Pierce*, 78 U. Det. Mercy L. Rev. 407, 415 (2001); William G. Ross, Pierce *After Seventy-Five Years: Reasons to Celebrate*, 78 U. Det. Mercy L. Rev. 443 (2001). For the argument that *Pierce* was rightly decided for young children, but more problematic for older children, see Steven H. Shiffrin, *The First Amendment and the Socialization of Children,* 11 Cornell J.L. & Pub. Pol. 503 (2005).

customers as to enable him to restrain exercise of proper power of the state upon the ground that he will be deprived of patronage. But the injunctions here sought are not against the exercise of any proper power. Appellees asked protection against arbitrary, unreasonable, and unlawful interference with their patrons and the consequent destruction of their business and property. Their interest is clear and immediate * * * ."

NOTES AND QUESTIONS

1.　Apart from due process, did the Oregon law violate the free speech rights of the affected parents? The schools? The children?

2.　Can a law like that in *Pierce* be defended on the ground that private schools siphon off the wealthy and the academically talented from the public schools while undermining a strong base of political support for generous financing of the schools?[285] On the ground that democratic education depends on schools that are integrated in terms of race, class, and religion?

3.　If parents have a right to send their children to private schools, do they also have a right to have their children excused from instruction they find objectionable? If so, what limits, if any, accompany that right?[286] Do captive audiences of government speech have a First Amendment right not to be the recipients of what they might perceive as propaganda? Do children educated in public schools particularly have such a right? See Stephen Gottlieb, *In the Name of Patriotism: The Constitutionality of "Bending" History in Public Secondary Schools,* 62 N.Y.U.L.Rev. 497 (1987). If ad hoc methods of separating education from propaganda are unreliable, are any institutional structures or processes required? Should this be a constitutional right without a remedy?[287]

4.　Is public education itself objectionable? Consider John Stuart Mill, *On Liberty* 98 (D. Spitz ed. 1975): "A general State education is a mere contrivance for moulding people to be exactly like one another. An education established and controlled by the State should only exist, if it exists at all, as one of many competing experiments carried on for the purpose of example and stimulus, to keep the others up to a certain standard of excellence." Is point of view discrimination in public schools unacceptable? Can public schools teach that tobacco consumption is unwise? That racial discrimination is wrong? The following the law is desirable? For a skeptical view, see Martin H. Redish & Kevin Finnerty, *What Did You Learn in School Today? Free Speech, Values*

---

[285] Is the empirical assumption correct? See Amy Gutmann, *Democratic Education* 117 (1987).

[286] See generally Nomi M. Stolzenberg, *"He Drew a Circle that Shut Me Out": Assimilation, Indoctrination, and the Paradox of a Liberal Education,* 106 Harv. L. Rev. 581 (1993). On parents' free speech rights, see generally, Stephen G. Gilles, *On Educating Children: A Parentalist Manifesto,* 63 U.Chi.L.Rev. 937 (1996).

[287] Consider also captive audiences of prisoners, soldiers, workers in public institutions, or citizens called for jury duty. Do "informed consent" provisions concerning abortion raise First Amendment captive audience issues? Cf. *Public Utilities Comm'n v. Pollak,* 343 U.S. 451 (1952) (city transit company's playing of radio programs does not violate Constitution).

Inculcation, and the Democratic-Educational Paradox, 88 Cornell L. Rev. 62 (2002).

5.   Consider Mark G. Yudof, *When Government Speaks: Politics, Law, and Government Expression in America* 229–230 (1983): "*Pierce* may be construed (whatever the original motivations of the justices) as telling governments that they are free to establish their own public schools and to make education compulsory for certain age groups, but not free to eliminate competing, private-sector educational institutions that may serve to create heterogeneity and to counter the state's dominance over the education of the young. * * * *Pierce* represents a reasonable, if imperfect, accommodation of conflicting pressures. The state may promulgate its messages in the public school, while parents are free to choose private schools with different orientations. The state must tolerate private education, but need not fund it. The state may make some demands of private schools to satisfy compulsory schooling laws, but those demands may not be so excessive as to turn private schools into public schools managed and funded by the public sector. The integrity of the communications and socialization processes in private schools and families remains intact, while the state's interest in producing informed, educated, and productive citizens is not sacrificed."

Compare Abner S. Greene, *Why Vouchers are Constitutional and Why They are Not,* 13 Notre D. J. of L.Ethics & Pub. Pol. 397 (1999): "[T]he *Pierce* assumption—although, in one view, assuring multiple repositories of power by counteracting the state's school monopoly—in fact assures that children will get their basic education not from multiple sources, but rather from their parents or their parent's agents alone. [Overruling] *Pierce* would free up funds used for private schooling and would direct parental energies at improving the public schools. Different public schools would, of course, focus on different values, and parents would still therefore have significant input into the curriculum of their local public schools. But we would remove some children from the monopoly of their parents and substitute a plural system of education."

6.   A Nebraska law outlawed the teaching of languages other than English[288] in any school to students who had yet to pass the eighth grade. The Nebraska Supreme Court upheld the conviction of an instructor who taught reading in the German language in a private elementary school during recess. The Nebraska Supreme Court thought the law had a defensible purpose: "The Legislature had seen the baneful effects of permitting foreigners, who had taken residence in this country, to rear and educate their children in the language of their native land. The result of that condition was found to be inimical to our own safety. To allow the children of foreigners, who had emigrated here, to be taught from early childhood the language of the country of their parents was to rear them with that language as their mother tongue. It was to educate them so that they must always think in that language, and, as a consequence, naturally inculcate in them the ideas and sentiments foreign

---

[288] The teaching of Latin, Greek, and Hebrew was permitted.

to the best interests of this country. The statute, therefore, was intended not only to require that the education of all children be conducted in the English language, but that, until they had grown into that language and until it had become a part of them, they should not in the schools be taught any other language. [The] hours which a child is able to devote to study in the confinement of school are limited. It must have ample time for exercise or play. Its daily capacity for learning is comparatively small."

MEYER v. NEBRASKA, 262 U.S. 390 (1923), per MCREYNOLDS, J., held that the statute violated due process: "While this court has not attempted to define with exactness the liberty [guaranteed under the fourteenth amendment], the term has received much consideration and some of the included things have been definitely stated. Without doubt, it denotes not merely freedom from bodily restraint but also the right of the individual to contract, to engage in any of the common occupations of life, to acquire useful knowledge, to marry, establish a home and bring up children, to worship God according to the dictates of his own conscience, and generally to enjoy those privileges long recognized at common law as essential to the orderly pursuit of happiness by free men. [Corresponding] to the right of control, it is the natural duty of the parent to give his children education suitable to their station in life; and nearly all the states, including Nebraska, enforce this obligation by compulsory laws. Practically, education of the young is only possible in schools conducted by especially qualified persons who devote themselves thereto. The calling always has been regarded as useful and honorable, essential, indeed, to the public welfare. Mere knowledge of the German language cannot reasonably be regarded as harmful. Heretofore it has been commonly looked upon as helpful and desirable. Plaintiff in error taught this language in school as part of his occupation. His right thus to teach and the right of parents to engage him so to instruct their children, we think, are within the liberty of the amendment. * * *

"It is said the purpose of the legislation was to promote civic development by inhibiting training and education of the immature in foreign tongues and ideals before they could learn English and acquire American ideals, and 'that the English language should be and become the mother tongue of all children reared in this state.' It is also affirmed that the foreign born population is very large, that certain communities commonly use foreign words, follow foreign leaders, move in a foreign atmosphere, and that the children are thereby hindered from becoming citizens of the most useful type and the public safety is imperiled. * * *

"For the welfare of his Ideal Commonwealth, Plato suggested a law which should provide: 'That the wives of our guardians are to be common, and their children are to be common, and no parent is to know his own child, nor any child his parent. [The] proper officers will take the offspring of the good parents to the pen or fold, and there they will deposit them with certain nurses who dwell in a separate quarter; but the offspring of the inferior, or of the better when they chance to be deformed, will be put away in some mysterious, unknown place, as they should be.' In order to submerge the individual and develop ideal citizens, Sparta assembled the males at seven into barracks and intrusted their subsequent education and training to official guardians. Although such measures have been deliberately approved by men of great genius their ideas touching the relation between individual and state were wholly different from those upon which our institutions rest; and it hardly will be affirmed that any Legislature could impose such restrictions upon the people of a state without doing violence to both letter and spirit of the Constitution.

"The desire of the Legislature to foster a homogeneous people with American ideals prepared readily to understand current discussions of civic matters is easy to appreciate. Unfortunate experiences during the late war and aversion toward every character of truculent adversaries were certainly enough to quicken that aspiration. But the means adopted, we think, exceed the limitations upon the power of the state and conflict with rights assured to plaintiff in error.[289] The interference is plain enough and no adequate reason therefor in time of peace and domestic tranquility has been shown.

"As the statute undertakes to interfere only with teaching which involves a modern language, leaving complete freedom as to other matters, there seems no adequate foundation for the suggestion that the purpose was to protect the child's health by limiting his mental activities. It is well known that proficiency in a foreign language seldom comes to one not instructed at an early age, and experience shows that this is not injurious to the health, morals or understanding of the ordinary child."[290]

TINKER V. DES MOINES SCHOOL DISTRICT

393 U.S. 503, 89 S.Ct. 733, 21 L.Ed.2d 731 (1969).

JUSTICE FORTAS delivered the opinion of the Court.

[Petitioners, two high school students and one junior high student,[291] wore black armbands to school to publicize their objections to the Vietnam conflict and their advocacy of a truce. They refused to remove the armbands when asked to do so. In accordance with a ban on armbands which the city's school principals had adopted two days before in anticipation of such a protest, petitioners were sent home and suspended from school until they

---

[289] Are statutes mandating English as the only language of government constitutional? See Drucilla Cornell & William W. Bratton, *Deadweight Costs and Intrinsic Wrongs of Nativism*, 84 Corn.L.Rev. 595 (1999).

[290] Holmes and Sutherland, JJ., dissented, arguing, that the Court should defer to the state's interest. In addition, to studying *Pierce* and *Meyer* in connection with due process, the student may wish to reconsider them in the course of studying freedom of religion. In that connection, consider the argument that the law in *Pierce* was substantially motivated by anti-Catholic sentiment, that the law in *Meyer* was substantially motivated by anti-German sentiment and that the purpose of teaching German in *Meyer* was to help children participate in Lutheran services which were taught in German. For rich discussion of the other purposes present in *Pierce* and *Meyer*, see Barbara B. Woodhouse, *"Who Owns the Child?"* fn b in *Pierce*. See generally William J. Ross, *Nativism, Education, and the Constitution, 1917–1927* (1994).

[291] See Mary Beth Tinker, *Reflections on Tinker*, 58 Am. U.L.Rev. 1119 (2009).

would return without the armbands. They sought a federal injunction restraining school officials from disciplining them, but the lower federal courts upheld the constitutionality of the school authorities' action on the ground that it was reasonable in order to prevent a disturbance which might result from the wearing of the armbands.]

[T]he wearing of armbands in the circumstances of this case was entirely divorced from actually or potentially disruptive conduct by those participating in it. It was closely akin to "pure speech" which, we have repeatedly held, is entitled to comprehensive protection under the First Amendment. * * *

First Amendment rights, applied in light of the special characteristics of the school environment, are available to teachers and students. It can hardly be argued that either students or teachers shed their constitutional rights to freedom of speech or expression at the schoolhouse gate. This has been the unmistakable holding of this Court for almost 50 years. In *Meyer*, this Court [held that fourteenth amendment due process] prevents States from forbidding the teaching of a foreign language to young students. Statutes to this effect, the Court held, unconstitutionally interfere with the liberty of teacher, student, and parent. * * *

The problem presented by the present case does not relate to regulation of the length of skirts or the type of clothing, to hair style or deportment. [It] does not concern aggressive, disruptive action or even group demonstrations. Our problem involves direct, primary First Amendment rights akin to "pure speech."

The school officials banned and sought to punish petitioners for a silent, passive, expression of opinion, unaccompanied by any disorder or disturbance on the part of petitioners. There is here no evidence whatever of petitioners' interference, actual or nascent, with the school's work or of collision with the rights of other students to be secure and to be let alone. Accordingly, this case does not concern speech or action that intrudes upon the work of the school or the rights of other students.

Only a few of the 18,000 students in the school system wore the black armbands. Only five students were suspended for wearing them. There is no indication that the work of the school or any class was disrupted. Outside the classrooms, a few students made hostile remarks to the children wearing armbands, but there were no threats or acts of violence on school premises.

[I]n our system, undifferentiated fear or apprehension of disturbance [the District Court's basis for sustaining the school authorities' action] is not enough to overcome the right to freedom of expression. Any departure from absolute regimentation may cause trouble. Any variation from the majority's opinion may inspire fear. Any words spoken, in class, in the lunchroom or on the campus, that deviates from the views of another person, may start an argument or cause a disturbance. But our Constitution says we must take this risk [and] our history says that it is this sort of hazardous freedom—this kind of openness—that is the basis of our national strength and of the independence and vigor of Americans who grow up and live in this relatively permissive, often disputatious society.

In order for the State in the person of school officials to justify prohibition of a particular expression of opinion, it must be able to show that its action was caused by something more than a mere desire to avoid the discomfort and unpleasantness that always accompany an unpopular viewpoint. Certainly where there is no finding and no showing that the exercise of the forbidden right would "materially and substantially interfere with the requirements of appropriate discipline in the operation of the school," the prohibition cannot be sustained.

In the present case, the District Court made no such finding, and our independent examination of the record fails to yield evidence that the school authorities had reason to anticipate that the wearing of the armbands would substantially interfere with the work of the school or impinge upon the rights of other students.[292] Even an official memorandum prepared after the suspension that listed the reasons for the ban on wearing the armbands made no reference to the anticipation of such disruption.[3]

On the contrary, the action of the school authorities appears to have been based upon an urgent wish to avoid the controversy which might result from the expression, even by the silent symbol of armbands, of opposition to this Nation's part in the conflagration in Vietnam. * * *

It is also relevant that the school authorities did not purport to prohibit the wearing of all symbols of political or controversial significance. The record shows that students in some of the schools wore buttons relating to national political campaigns, and some even wore the Iron Cross, traditionally a symbol of Nazism. The order prohibiting the wearing of

---

[292] Would a racist t-shirt interfere with the rights of others? A t-shirt condemning homosexuality? See *Harper v. Poway Unified School Dist.,* 445 F.3d 1166 (9th Cir. 2006). For discussion, see Bonnie A. Kellman, 85 Notre D. L.Rev. 367 (2009); Jay Alan Sekulow & Erik M. Zimmerman, *Tinker at Forty,* 58 Am. U.L. Rev. 1243 (2009); Francisco M. Negron, *A Foot in the Door?, The Unwitting Move toward a "New" Student Wlefar Standar in Student Speech after Morse v. Frederick,* 58 Am. U.L. Rev. 1221 (2009).

[3] **[Ct's Note]** The only suggestions of fear of disorder in the report are these: "A former student of one of our high schools was killed in Viet Nam. Some of his friends are still in school and it was felt that if any kind of a demonstration existed, it might evolve into something which would be difficult to control.

"Students at one of the high schools were heard to say they would wear arm bands of other colors if the black bands prevailed."

Moreover, the testimony of school authorities at trial indicates that it was not fear of disruption that motivated the regulation prohibiting the armbands; the regulation was directed against "the principle of the demonstration" itself. School authorities simply felt that "the schools are no place for demonstrations," and if the students "didn't like the way our elected officials were handling things, it should be handled with the ballot box and not in the halls of our public schools."

armbands did not extend to these. Instead, a particular symbol—black armbands worn to exhibit opposition to this Nation's involvement in Vietnam—was singled out for prohibition. Clearly, the prohibition of expression of one particular opinion, at least without evidence that it is necessary to avoid material and substantial interference with school work or discipline, is not constitutionally permissible.

In our system, state-operated schools may not be enclaves of totalitarianism. School officials do not possess absolute authority over their students. Students in school as well as out of school are "persons" under our Constitution. They are possessed of fundamental rights which the State must respect, just as they themselves must respect their obligations to the State. In our system, students may not be regarded as closed-circuit recipients of only that which the State chooses to communicate. They may not be confined to the expression of those sentiments that are officially approved. In the absence of a specific showing of constitutionally valid reasons to regulate their speech, students are entitled to freedom of expression of their views.

[The principle of prior cases underscoring the importance of diversity and exchange of ideas in the schools,] is not confined to the supervised and ordained discussion which takes place in the classroom. The principal use to which the schools are dedicated is to accommodate students during prescribed hours for the purpose of certain types of activities. Among those activities is personal intercommunication among the students. This is not only an inevitable part of the process of attending school. It is also an important part of the educational process.

A student's rights therefore, do not embrace merely the classroom hours. When he is in the cafeteria, or on the playing field, or on the campus during the authorized hours, he may express his opinions, even on controversial subjects like the conflict in Vietnam, if he does so "[without] materially and substantially interfering [with] appropriate discipline in the operation of the school" and without colliding with the rights of others. *Burnside.* But conduct by the student, in class or out of it, which for any reason—whether it stems from time, place, or type of behavior—materially disrupts classwork or involves substantial disorder or invasion of the rights of others is, of course, not immunized by the [First Amendment].

We properly read [the First Amendment] to permit reasonable regulation of speech-connected activities in carefully restricted circumstances. But we do not confine the permissible exercise of First Amendment rights to a telephone booth or the four corners of a pamphlet, or to supervised and ordained discussion in a school classroom.[293] * * *

---

[293] See also Akhil Reed Amar, *A Tale of Three Wars: Tinker in Constitutional Context,* 48 Drake L.Rev. 507 (2000); Erwin Chemerinsky, *Students Do Leave Their First Amendment Rights at the Schoolhouse Door: What's Left of Tinker?,* 48 Drake L.Rev. 527 (2000); Nadine Strossen,

Reversed and remanded.

JUSTICE STEWART, concurring.[294]

Although I agree with much of what is said in the Court's opinion, and with its judgment in this case, I cannot share the Court's uncritical assumption that, school discipline aside, the First Amendment rights of children are co-extensive with those of adults. Indeed, I had thought the Court decided otherwise just last Term in *Ginsberg v. New York* [Sec. 1, III, B supra.] I continue to hold the view I expressed in that case: "[A] State may permissibly determine that, at least in some precisely delineated areas, a child—like someone in a captive audience—is not possessed of that full capacity for individual choice which is the presupposition of First Amendment guarantees." (concurring opinion). * * *

JUSTICE BLACK, dissenting. * * *

Assuming that the Court is correct in holding that the conduct of wearing armbands for the purpose of conveying political ideas is protected by the First Amendment [, the] crucial remaining questions are whether students and teachers may use the schools at their whim as a platform for the exercise of free speech—"symbolic" or "pure"—and whether the Courts will allocate to themselves the function of deciding how the pupils' school day will be spent. * * *

While the record does not show that any of these armband students shouted, used profane language, or were violent in any manner, detailed testimony by some of them shows their armbands caused comments, warnings by other students, the poking of fun at them, and a warning by an older football player that other, nonprotesting students had better let them alone. There is also evidence that the professor of mathematics had his lesson period practically "wrecked" chiefly by disputes with Beth Tinker, who wore her armband for her "demonstration." Even a casual reading of the record shows that this armband did divert students' minds from their regular lessons, and that talk, comments, etc., made John Tinker "self-conscious" in attending school with his armband. While the absence of obscene or boisterous and loud disorder perhaps justifies the Court's statement that the few armband students did not actually "disrupt" the classwork, I think the record overwhelmingly shows that the armbands did exactly what the elected school officials and principals foresaw it would, that is, took the students' minds off their classwork and diverted them to thoughts about the highly emotional subject of the Vietnam war.

[E]ven if the record were silent as to protests against the Vietnam war distracting students from their assigned class work, members of this Court,

---

Keeping the Constitution Inside the Schoolhouse Gate, 48 Drake L.Rev. 445 (2000); Mark Yudof, *When Governments Speak: Toward a Theory of Government Expression and the First Amendment*, 57 Tex.L.Rev. 863 (1979).

[294] White, J., also briefly concurred.

like all other citizens, know, without being told, that the disputes over the wisdom of the Vietnam war have disrupted and divided this country as few other issues ever have. Of course students, like other people, cannot concentrate on lesser issues when black armbands are being ostentatiously displayed in their presence to call attention to the wounded and dead of the war, some of the wounded and the dead being their friends and neighbors. It was, of course, to distract the attention of other students that some students insisted up to the very point of their own suspension from school that they were determined to sit in school with their symbolic armbands. * * *

JUSTICE HARLAN, dissenting.

I certainly agree that state public school authorities in the discharge of their responsibilities are not wholly exempt from the requirements of the Fourteenth Amendment respecting the freedoms of expression and association. At the same time I am reluctant to believe that there is any disagreement between the majority and myself on the proposition that school officials should be accorded the widest authority in maintaining discipline and good order in their institutions. To translate that proposition into a workable constitutional rule, I would, in cases like this, cast upon those complaining the burden of showing that a particular school measure was motivated by other than legitimate school concerns—for example, a desire to prohibit the expression of an unpopular point of view, while permitting expression of the dominant opinion.

Finding nothing in this record which impugns the good faith of respondents in promulgating the arm band regulation, I would affirm the judgment below.

NOTES AND QUESTIONS

1.   Should the government's interest in education trump the school child's interest in speaking in the classroom? Are the two interests compatible in this case? May students be prohibited from voicing their opinions of the Vietnam War in the middle of a math class? If so, why can't they be prevented from expressing their views on the same issue in the same class by means of "symbolic speech"? Cf. Sheldon H. Nahmod, *Beyond Tinker: The High School as an Educational Public Forum,* 5 Harv.Civ.Rts. & Civ.Lib.L.Rev. 278 (1970).

2.   Could school authorities adopt a regulation forbidding *teachers* to wear black armbands in the classroom? Or prohibiting teachers from wearing *all* symbols of political or controversial significance in the classroom or anywhere on school property? Are students a "captive" group? Do the views of a teacher occupying a position of authority carry much more influence with a student than would those of students inter sese? Consider *James v. Board of Educ.,* 461 F.2d 566 (2d Cir.1972), holding that school officials violated a high school teacher's constitutional rights by discharging him because he had worn a black armband in class in symbolic protest of the Vietnam War. But the court

stressed that "the armband did not disrupt classroom activities [nor] have any influence on any students and did not engender protest from any student, teacher or parent." What if it had? By implication, did the court confirm the potency of the "heckler's veto"? Same result if appellant had been a 3rd grade teacher rather than an 11th grade teacher? See Steven Shiffrin, *Government Speech*, 27 UCLA L.Rev. 565 (1980).

3.   *Viewpoint-discriminatory restrictions on student speech.* Can a school district prohibit the expression of racist views or anti-gay views on the ground that they threaten substantial disruption and interfere with the promotion of multicultural views with respect to race and sexual orientation? Can s school prohibit students from wearing Nazi or Klan symbols? Gang regalia? From advocating violence? See John E. Taylor, *Tinker and Viewpoint Discrimination*, 77 UMKC L.Rev. 569 (2009); Kristi L. Bowman, *Public School Student's Religious Speech and Viewpoint Discrimination*, 110 W.Va. L. Rev. 187 (2007).

4.   MORSE v. FREDERICK, 551 U.S. 393 (2007), per ROBERTS, C.J., upheld the suspension of a high school student for refusing to take down a banner at a school sponsored event that read "BONG HiTS 4 JESUS": "The concern is not that Frederick's speech is offensive, but that it was reasonably viewed as promoting illegal drug use."

ALITO, J., joined by Kennedy, J., concurring, joined the Court's opinion on the understanding that it "goes no further than to hold that a public school may restrict speech that a reasonable observer would interpret as advocating illegal drug use" and provides no support for restricting comments on political or social issues including "the wisdom of the war on drugs or legalizing marijuana for medicinal use."[295]

THOMAS, J., concurring, would overrule *Tinker*: "In light of the history of American public education, it cannot be seriously suggested that the First Amendment 'freedom of speech' encompasses a student's right to speak in public schools. Early public schools gave total control to teachers, who expected obedience and respect from students."[296]

STEVENS, J., joined by Souter and Ginsburg, JJ., dissenting, thought it was not reasonable to conclude that the message on the banner advocated drug use or that it would persuade students to use drugs.

5.   *Guidance to lower courts.* The lower courts are struggling with cases involving apprehension of or threats of student violence. And teachers and school administrators deal with these issues on a daily basis. Some of the issues involve, as noted above, Nazi or Klan symbols, some involve other forms

---

[295] Breyer, J., concurring in part and dissenting in part would not have reached the First Amendment issue except to maintain that it was close enough that the high school principal could not be held liable for monetary damages. For commentary on *Morse,* see Stephen M. Feldman, *Free Expression and Education: Between Two Democracies,* 16 Wm. & Mary Bill Rts.J. 999 (2008); Negron, fn. 293 supra.

[296] For criticism of Thomas, J.'s methodology, see Vikram D. Amar, *Morse, School Speech, and Originalism,* 42 U.C. Davis L.Rev. 637 (2009).

of offense based on race, religion, and sexual orientation. And other frequently arising controversies involve student criticism of teachers and administrators. Does *Morse* provide guidance? Consider Frederick Schauer, *Abandoning the Guidance Function: Morse v. Frederick,* 2007 Sup. Ct. Rev. 205: "Faced with an opportunity to say something helpful to and for those in the trenches, the Court not only selected a highly unrepresentative case for its first foray into the area in nineteen years, but it also decided the case on narrow grounds, and in doing so focused on those dimensions of the case least likely to be found in the conflicts that bedevil school administrators and lower courts on an almost daily basis."

     6.   Consider Jamin B. Raskin, *No Enclaves of Totalitarianism,* 58 Am. U.L. Rev. 1193 (2009): *Tinker* has been eroded "by the sharp undertow of sympathy for authoritarian structure on the Burger, Rehnquist, and Roberts Courts. The conservative court has carved out major exceptions to *Tinker* in the interests of social conformity, sexual prudishness, protection of sexual adults' feelings, and promotion of ideological unity for drug prohibition." Consider also Chemerinsky, fn. 293 supra: "[I]n the three decades since *Tinker,* the courts have made it clear that students leave most of their constitutional rights at the schoolhouse gate. The judiciary's unquestioning acceptance of the need for deference to school authority leaves relatively little room for protecting student's constitutional rights. The decisions over the past thirty years are far closer to Justice Black's dissent in *Tinker* than they are to Justice Fortas's majority opinion."[297]

HAZELWOOD SCHOOL DISTRICT V. KUHLMEIER

484 U.S. 260, 108 S.Ct. 562, 98 L.Ed.2d 592 (1988).

JUSTICE WHITE delivered the opinion of the Court. * * *

Petitioners are the Hazelwood School District in St. Louis County, Missouri; various school officials; Robert Eugene Reynolds, the principal of Hazelwood East High School, and Howard Emerson, a teacher in the school district. Respondents are three former Hazelwood East students who were staff members of Spectrum, the school newspaper. * * *

The practice at Hazelwood East during the spring 1983 semester was for the journalism teacher to submit page proofs of each Spectrum issue to Principal Reynolds for his review prior to publication. On May 10, Emerson

---

[297] For a review of the cases together with opposition to the extension of *Tinker* to off campus, student or teacher speech, see Mary-Rose Papandreu, *Student Speech Rights in the Digital Age,* 60 Fla. L.Rev. 1027 (2008). For an argument that the appropriate test should depend whether the speaker acts in the role of a student or in the role of a citizen, Benjamin F. Heidlage, *A Relational Approach to School's Regulation of Youth Online Speech,* 84 N.Y.U.L.Rev. 572 (2009). See also Clay Calvert, *Tinker Turns 40,* 58 Am. U.L. Rev. 1167 (2009); Fiona Ruthven, *Is the True Threat the Student or the School Board? Punishing Threatening Student Expression,* 88 Iowa L. Rev. 931 (2003); Robert D. Richards & Clay Calvert, *Columbine Fallout: The Long-Term Effects on Free Expression Take Hold in Public Schools,* 83 B.U. L. Rev. 1089 (2003); Lisa M. Pisciotta, *Beyond Sticks & Stones: A First Amendment Framework for Educators Who Seek to Punish Student Threats,* 30 Seton Hall L. Rev. 635 (2000).

delivered the proofs of the May 13 edition to Reynolds, who objected to two of the articles scheduled to appear in that edition. One of the stories described three Hazelwood East students' experiences with pregnancy; the other discussed the impact of divorce on students at the school.

Reynolds was concerned that, although the pregnancy story used false names "to keep the identity of these girls a secret," the pregnant students still might be identifiable from the text. He also believed that the article's references to sexual activity and birth control were inappropriate for some of the younger students at the school. In addition, Reynolds was concerned that a student identified by name in the divorce story had complained [about] her father * * * . Reynolds believed that the student's parents should have been given an opportunity to respond to these remarks or to consent to their publication. He was unaware that Emerson had deleted the student's name from the final version of the article.

Reynolds believed that there was no time to make the necessary changes in the stories before the scheduled press run and that the newspaper would not appear before the end of the school year if printing were delayed to any significant extent. He concluded that his only options under the circumstances were to publish a four-page newspaper instead of the planned six-page newspaper, eliminating the two pages on which the offending stories appeared, or to publish no newspaper at all. Accordingly, he directed Emerson to withhold from publication the two pages containing the stories on pregnancy and divorce.[1] He informed his superiors of the decision, and they concurred. * * *

[T]he First Amendment rights of students in the public schools "are not automatically coextensive with the rights of adults in other settings," *Bethel School District No. 403 v. Fraser,* 478 U.S. 675 (1986), and must be "applied in light of the special characteristics of the school environment." *Tinker.* A school need not tolerate student speech that is inconsistent with its "basic educational mission," *Fraser,* even though the government could not censor similar speech outside the school. Accordingly, we held in *Fraser* that a student could be disciplined for having delivered a speech that was "sexually explicit" but not legally obscene at an official school [assembly]. We thus recognized that "[t]he determination of what manner of speech in the classroom or in school assembly is inappropriate properly rests with the school board," rather than with the federal courts. * * *

We deal first with the question whether Spectrum may appropriately be characterized as a forum for public expression. [T]he evidence relied upon by the Court of Appeals fails to demonstrate the "clear intent to create a public forum," *Cornelius,* that existed in cases in which we found public

---

[1]   **[Ct's Note]** The two pages deleted from the newspaper also contained articles on teenage marriage, runaways, and juvenile delinquents, as well as a general article on teenage pregnancy. Reynolds testified that he had no objection to these articles and that they were deleted only because they appeared on the same pages as the two objectionable articles.

forums to have been created. School [officials] "reserve[d] the forum for its intended purpos[e]," *Perry,* as a supervised learning experience for journalism students. Accordingly, school officials were entitled to regulate the contents of Spectrum in any reasonable manner. * * *

The question whether the First Amendment requires a school to tolerate particular student speech—the question that we addressed in *Tinker*—is different from the question whether the First Amendment requires a school affirmatively to promote particular student speech. The former question addresses educators' ability to silence a student's personal expression that happens to occur on the school premises. The latter question concerns educators' authority over school-sponsored publications, theatrical productions, and other expressive activities that students, parents, and members of the public might reasonably perceive to bear the imprimatur of the school. These activities may fairly be characterized as part of the school curriculum, whether or not they occur in a traditional classroom setting, so long as they are supervised by faculty members and designed to impart particular knowledge or skills to student participants and audiences.

[A] school may in its capacity as publisher of a school newspaper or producer of a school play "disassociate itself," *Fraser,* not only from speech that would "substantially interfere with [its] work [or] impinge upon the rights of other students," *Tinker,* but also from speech that is, for example, ungrammatical, poorly written, inadequately researched, biased or prejudiced, vulgar or profane, or unsuitable for immature audiences.[4] A school must be able to set high standards for the student speech that is disseminated under its auspices—standards that may be higher than those demanded by some newspaper publishers or theatrical producers in the "real" world—and may refuse to disseminate student speech that does not meet those standards. [Otherwise,] the schools would be unduly constrained from fulfilling their role as "a principal instrument in awakening the child to cultural values, in preparing him for later professional training, and in helping him to adjust normally to his environment." *Brown v. Board of Education.*

Accordingly, we conclude that the standard articulated in *Tinker* for determining when a school may punish student expression need not also be the standard for determining when a school may refuse to lend its name and resources to the dissemination of student expression. Instead, we hold

---

[4]   **[Ct's Note]** [The] decision in *Fraser* rested on the "vulgar," "lewd," and "plainly offensive" character of a speech delivered at an official school assembly in thee context of a student election rather than on any propensity of the speech to "materially disrupt[ ] classwork or involve[ ] substantial disorder or invasion of the rights of others." Indeed, the *Fraser* Court cited as "especially relevant" a portion of Justice Black's dissenting opinion in *Tinker* "disclaim[ing] any purpose [to] hold that the Federal Constitution compels the teachers, parents and elected school officials to surrender control of the American public school system to public school students." Of course, Justice Black's observations are equally relevant to the instant case.

that educators do not offend the First Amendment by exercising editorial control over the style and content of student speech in school-sponsored expressive activities so long as their actions are reasonably related to legitimate pedagogical concerns.[7] * * *298

JUSTICE BRENNAN, with whom JUSTICE MARSHALL and JUSTICE BLACKMUN join, dissenting.

[Under] *Tinker,* school officials may censor only such student speech as would "materially disrup[t]" a legitimate curricular function. Manifestly, student speech is more likely to disrupt a curricular function when it arises in the context of a curricular activity—one that "is designed to teach" something—than when it arises in the context of a noncurricular activity. Thus, under *Tinker,* the school may constitutionally punish the budding political orator if he disrupts calculus class but not if he holds his tongue for the cafeteria. That is not because some more stringent standard applies in the curricular context. (After all, this Court applied the same standard whether the Tinkers wore their armbands to the "classroom" or the "cafeteria.") It is because student speech in the noncurricular context is less likely to disrupt materially any legitimate pedagogical purpose.

I fully agree with the Court that the First Amendment should afford an educator the prerogative not to sponsor the publication of a newspaper article that is "ungrammatical, poorly written, inadequately researched, biased or prejudiced," or that falls short of the "high standards [for] student speech that is disseminated under [the school's] auspices." But we need not abandon *Tinker* to reach that conclusion; we need only apply it. The enumerated criteria reflect the skills that the curricular newspaper "is designed to teach." The educator may, under *Tinker,* constitutionally "censor" poor grammar, writing, or research because to reward such expression would "materially disrup[t]" the newspaper's curricular purpose. * * *

The Court relies on bits of testimony to portray the principal's conduct as a pedagogical lesson to Journalism II students who "had not sufficiently mastered those portions of [the] curriculum that pertained to the treatment of controversial issues and personal attacks, the need to protect the privacy

---

7   [Ct's Note] A number of lower federal courts have similarly recognized that educators' decisions with regard to the content of school sponsored newspapers, dramatic productions, and other expressive activities are entitled to substantial deference. We need not now decide whether the same degree of deference is appropriate with respect to school-sponsored expressive activities at the college and university level.

298 White, J., concluded that Principal Reynolds acted reasonably in requiring deletion of the pages from the newspaper. In addition to concerns about privacy and failure to contact persons discussed in the stories, it was "not unreasonable for the principal to have concluded that [frank talk about sexual histories, albeit not graphic, with comments about use or nonuse of birth control] was inappropriate in a school-sponsored publication distributed to 14-year-old freshmen and presumably taken home to be read by students' even younger brothers and sisters."

of individuals [and] 'the legal, moral, and ethical restrictions imposed upon journalists * * * .' "

But the principal never consulted the students before censoring their work. [T]hey learned of the deletions when the paper was released. [Further,] he explained the deletions only in the broadest of generalities. In one meeting called at the behest of seven protesting Spectrum staff members (presumably a fraction of the full class), he characterized the articles as " 'too sensitive' for 'our immature audience of readers,' " and in a later meeting he deemed them simply "inappropriate, personal, sensitive and unsuitable for the newspaper." The Court's supposition that the principal intended (or the protesters understood) those generalities as a lesson on the nuances of journalistic responsibility is utterly incredible. If he did, a fact that neither the District Court nor the Court of Appeals found, the lesson was lost on all but the psychic Spectrum staffer.

The Court's second excuse for deviating from precedent is the school's interest in shielding an impressionable high school audience from material whose substance is "unsuitable for immature audiences." [*Tinker*] teaches us that the state educator's undeniable, and undeniably vital, mandate to inculcate moral and political values is not a general warrant to act as "thought police" stifling discussion of all but state-approved topics and advocacy of all but the official position. [The] mere fact of school sponsorship does not, as the Court suggests, license such thought control in the high school, whether through school suppression of disfavored viewpoints or through official assessment of topic sensitivity. [Moreover, the] State's prerogative to dissolve the student newspaper entirely (or to limit its subject matter) no more entitles it to dictate which viewpoints students may express on its pages, than the State's prerogative to close down the schoolhouse entitles it to prohibit the nondisruptive expression of antiwar sentiment within its gates.

Official censorship of student speech on the ground that it addresses "potentially sensitive topics" is, for related reasons, equally impermissible. I would not begrudge an educator the authority to limit the substantive scope of a school-sponsored publication to a certain, objectively definable topic, such as literary criticism, school sports, or an overview of the school year. Unlike those determinate limitations, "potential topic sensitivity" is a vaporous nonstandard [that] invites manipulation to achieve ends that cannot permissibly be achieved through blatant viewpoint discrimination and chills student speech to which school officials might not object. * * *299

---

299 Brennan, J., further argued that the material deleted was not conceivably tortious and that less restrictive alternatives, such as more precise deletions, were readily available.

NOTES AND QUESTIONS

1. Consider Bruce Hafen, *Hazelwood School District and the Role of First Amendment Institutions,* 1988 Duke L.J. 685: "[T]he question whether authoritarian or anti-authoritarian approaches will best develop the minds and expressive powers of children is more a matter of educational philosophy and practice than of constitutional law. For that reason alone, First Amendment theories applied by courts largely on the basis of anti-authoritarian assumptions are at best a clumsy and limited means of ensuring optimal educational development, whether the goal is an understanding of democratic values or a mastery of basic intellectual skills. Thus, one of *Hazelwood's* major contributions is its reaffirmation of schools' institutional role—and their accountability to the public for fulfilling it responsibly—in nurturing the underlying values of the First Amendment. * * *

"The First Amendment must [protect] not only individual writers, but newspapers; not only religious persons, but churches; not only individual students and teachers, but schools. These 'intellectual and moral associations' form a crucial part of the constitutional structure, for they help teach the peculiar and sometimes paradoxical blend of liberty and duty that sustains both individual freedom and the entire culture from one generation to the next."

2. Consider Martha Minow & Elizabeth Spelman, *Passion for Justice,* 10 Cardozo L.Rev. 37 (1988): "The majority does not acknowledge the power it is exercising in the act of deferring to the 'reasonable' judgments of the [principal:] the power to signal to school officials all around the country, that it is all right to err on the side of eliminating student speech, it is all right to indulge your paternalistic attitudes toward the students; you do not need to guard against your own discomfort with what students want to discuss, for the 'rights' really lie within your own judgment about what they need. [The] dissent is acutely sensitive to the impact of censorship on students, but less attentive to the impact of judicial review on the school officials. Although equal attention to competing sides may make a decision more difficult, refraining from seeing the power of competing arguments itself may lead to tragic blindness."

3. ***Extending Hazelwood.*** Consider Karyl R. Martin, *Demoted to High School: Are College Students' Free Speech Rights the Same as Those of High School Students?,* 45 B.C. L. Rev. 173 (2003): "Since [*Hazelwood*], lower courts have consistently applied the 'legitimate pedagogical concerns' test to allow elementary and secondary schools to restrict students' and teachers' expression in a variety of 'school-sponsored' contexts. The circuit courts have disagreed, however, on the extent to which schools can regulate speech based on the particular viewpoint expressed."[300] See *Boring v. Buncombe County*

---

[300] See Jessica B. Lyons, *Defining Freedom of the College Press After Hosty v. Carter,* 59 Vand. L.Rev. 1771 (2006); Gail Sorenson & Andrew S. LaManque, *The Application of Hazelwood v. Kuhlmeier in College Litigation,* 22 J. of College & Univ. Law 971 (1996). For a range of views on academic freedom, consider Ronald Dworkin, *Freedom's Law* ch. 11 (1996); Amy Gutmann, Democratic Education (rev. ed. 1999); William G. Buss, *Academic Freedom and Freedom of Speech:*

Board of Education, 136 F.3d 364 (4th Cir.1998)(drama teacher selects play involving a dysfunctional divorced single parent family including a lesbian daughter and an unmarried pregnant daughter); *Ward v. Hickey,* 996 F.2d 448 (1st Cir. 1993) (teacher discusses abortion of Down's Syndrome fetus in ninth grade biology class). Should *Hazelwood* have any application at the college level?[301]

Is the "legitimate pedagogical concerns" test one for which judges have no expertise? When government manages and directs speech as its primary activity in a particular sphere, should the First Amendment be inapplicable? If making content decisions in supervising a newspaper or grading student efforts is a regular part of a teacher's job is the potential for judicial intervention an unnecessarily "stifling burden"? See Alan Brownstein, *The NonForum as a First Amendment Category,* 42 UC Davis L.Rev. 717 (2009).

4. **The vitality of Tinker.** After *Bethel School District v. Fraser* (described in *Hazelwood*), *Hazelwood,* and *Morse v. Frederick,* is *Tinker* still good law? In what contexts?

III. GOVERNMENT AS EMPLOYER

Ceballos, a supervising district attorney, wrote a disposition memorandum in which he recommended dismissal of a case on the ground that the affidavit in support of a search warrant contained false representations. As a result of the memorandum, which he characterized as protected speech, Ceballos maintained he was unconstitutionally transferred to a less desirable work location and denied a promotion in retaliation.

GARCETTI v. CEBALLOS, 547 U.S. 410 (2006), per KENNEDY, J., held that the memorandum was pursuant to his official duties as a supervising district attorney and, therefore, not protected by the First Amendment: "*Pickering v. Bd. of Educ.,* 391 U.S. 563 (1968)[302] and the cases decided in its wake identify two inquiries to guide interpretation of the constitutional protections accorded to public employee speech. The first requires

---

Communicating the Curriculum, 2 J. of Gender, Race & Justice 213 (1999); J. Peter Byrne, *Academic Freedom: A "Special Concern of the First Amendment,"* 99 Yale L.J. 251 (1989); Merle H. Weiner, *Dirty Words in the Classroom: Teaching the Limits of the First Amendment,* 66 Tenn.L.Rev. 597 (1999); William W. Van Alstyne, *Academic Freedom and the First Amendment in the Supreme Court of the United States: An Unhurried Historical Review,* 53 Law & Contemp. Probs. 79 (1990).

[301] Walter E. Kuhn, *First Amendment Protection of Teacher Instructional Speech,* 55 Duke L.J. 995 (2006).

[302] *Pickering* held that the First Amendment protected a teacher who published a letter in a newspaper criticizing the Board of Education. *Givhan v. Western Line Cons. School Dist.,* 439 U.S. 410 (1979), held that a private communication of an employee with an employer concerning racially discriminatory policies was similarly protected. *Bureau of Duryea v. Guarnieri,* 131 S.Ct. 2488 (2011) held that retaliation against a public employee for seeking redress in the courts would be subject to *Pickering* standards whether the law suit was framed as a violation of freedom of speech or as a right to petition the government for redress of grievances. If the matter relates to private speech, no redress is available. If the matter relates to public speech, *Pickering* is applicable.

determining whether the employee spoke as a citizen on a matter of public concern. If the answer is no, the employee has no First Amendment cause of action based on his or her employer's reaction to the speech. If the answer is yes, then the possibility of a First Amendment claim arises. The question becomes whether the relevant government entity had an adequate justification for treating the employee differently from any other member of the general public. This consideration reflects the importance of the relationship between the speaker's expressions and employment. A government entity has broader discretion to restrict speech when it acts in its role as employer, but the restrictions it imposes must be directed at speech that has some potential to affect the entity's operations. * * *

"When a citizen enters government service, the citizen by necessity must accept certain limitations on his or her freedom. Government employers, like private employers, need a significant degree of control over their employees 'words and actions; without it, there would be little chance for the efficient provision of public services. Public employees, moreover, often occupy trusted positions in society. When they speak out, they can express views that contravene governmental policies or impair the proper performance of governmental functions.

"At the same time, the Court has recognized that a citizen who works for the government is nonetheless a citizen. The First Amendment limits the ability of a public employer to leverage the employment relationship to restrict, incidentally or intentionally, the liberties employees enjoy in their capacities as private citizens.[303] So long as employees are speaking as citizens about matters of public concern, they must face only those speech restrictions that are necessary for their employers to operate efficiently and effectively. * * *

"The controlling factor in Ceballos' case is that his expressions were made pursuant to his duties as a calendar deputy. That consideration—the fact that Ceballos spoke as a prosecutor fulfilling a responsibility to advise his supervisor about how best to proceed with a pending case— distinguishes Ceballos' case from those in which the First Amendment provides protection against discipline. We hold that when public employees make statements pursuant to their official duties, the employees are not speaking as citizens for First Amendment purposes, and the Constitution does not insulate their communications from employer discipline. * * *

"This result is consistent with our precedents' attention to the potential societal value of employee speech. Refusing to recognize First

---

[303] *Elrod v. Burns*, 427 U.S. 347 (1976), held that nonpolicymaking and nonconfidential employees could not be dismissed simply because they were not affiliated with a particular political party, and *Rutan v. Republican Party of Illinois*, 497 U.S. 62 (1990), extended *Elrod* to hiring decisions. But *United Public Workers v. Mitchell*, 330 U.S. 75 (1947), and *U.S. Civil Service Comm'n v. Letter Carriers*, 413 U.S. 548 (1973), upheld Hatch Act restrictions on participation by government employees in political campaigns.

Amendment claims based on government employees' work product does not prevent them from participating in public debate. The employees retain the prospect of constitutional protection for their contributions to the civic discourse. This prospect of protection, however, does not invest them with a right to perform their jobs however they see fit. * * *

"Ceballos' proposed contrary rule [would] commit state and federal courts to a new, permanent, and intrusive role, mandating judicial oversight of communications between and among government employees and their superiors in the course of official business. This displacement of managerial discretion by judicial supervision finds no support in our precedents. When an employee speaks as a citizen addressing a matter of public concern, the First Amendment requires a delicate balancing of the competing interests surrounding the speech and its consequences. When, however, the employee is simply performing his or her job duties, there is no warrant for a similar degree of scrutiny. To hold otherwise would be to demand permanent judicial intervention in the conduct of governmental operations to a degree inconsistent with sound principles of federalism and the separation of powers.

"The Court of Appeals based its holding in part on what it perceived as a doctrinal anomaly. The court suggested it would be inconsistent to compel public employers to tolerate certain employee speech made publicly but not speech made pursuant to an employee's assigned duties. This objection misconceives the theoretical underpinnings of our decisions. Employees who make public statements outside the course of performing their official duties retain some possibility of First Amendment protection because that is the kind of activity engaged in by citizens who do not work for the government. The same goes for writing a letter to a local newspaper, see *Pickering*, or discussing politics with a co-worker, see *Rankin v. McPherson*, 483 U.S. 378 (1987).[304] When a public employee speaks pursuant to employment responsibilities, however, there is no relevant analogue to speech by citizens who are not government employees.

"The Court of Appeals' concern also is unfounded as a practical matter. The perceived anomaly, it should be noted, is limited in scope: It relates only to the expressions an employee makes pursuant to his or her official responsibilities, not to statements or complaints (such as those at issue in cases like *Pickering* and *Connick v. Myers*, 461 U.S 138 (1983)[305] that are made outside the duties of employment. If, moreover, a government employer is troubled by the perceived anomaly, it has the means at hand

---

[304] *Rankin* held that a secretary in a law enforcement agency was protected in saying at work in private to a co-worker that next time she hoped an assassination attempt on President Reagan would be successful.

[305] *Connick* upheld the dismissal of an Assistant D.A. for distributing a questionnaire to other assistants calling into question office transfer policy, the need for a grievance committee, office morale, the level of confidence in various supervisors, and whether employees felt pressure to participate in political campaigns.

to avoid it. A public employer that wishes to encourage its employees to voice concerns privately retains the option of instituting internal policies and procedures that are receptive to employee criticism. Giving employees an internal forum for their speech will discourage them from concluding that the safest avenue of expression is to state their views in public. * * *

"Two final points warrant mentioning. First, as indicated above, the parties in this case do not dispute that Ceballos wrote his disposition memo pursuant to his employment duties. We thus have no occasion to articulate a comprehensive framework for defining the scope of an employee's duties in cases where there is room for serious debate. We reject, however, the suggestion that employers can restrict employees' rights by creating excessively broad job descriptions. The proper inquiry is a practical one. Formal job descriptions often bear little resemblance to the duties an employee actually is expected to perform, and the listing of a given task in an employee's written job description is neither necessary nor sufficient to demonstrate that conducting the task is within the scope of the employee's professional duties for First Amendment purposes.

"Second, Justice Souter suggests today's decision may have important ramifications for academic freedom, at least as a constitutional value. There is some argument that expression related to academic scholarship or classroom instruction implicates additional constitutional interests that are not fully accounted for by this Court's customary employee-speech jurisprudence. We need not, and for that reason do not, decide whether the analysis we conduct today would apply in the same manner to a case involving speech related to scholarship or teaching."[306]

SOUTER, J., joined by Stevens and Ginsburg, JJ., dissented: "In *Givhan*, we followed *Pickering* when a teacher was fired for complaining to a superior about the racial composition of the school's administrative, cafeteria, and library [staffs]. The difference between a case like *Givhan* and this one is that the subject of Cembalos' speech fell within the scope of his job responsibilities, whereas choosing personnel was not what the teacher was hired to do. The effect of the majority's constitutional line between these two cases, then, is that a *Givhan* schoolteacher is protected when complaining to the principal about hiring policy, but a school personnel officer would not be if he protested that the principal disapproved of hiring minority job applicants. This is an odd place to draw

---

[306] The case was remanded because Ceballos had made other statements that were arguably outside the scope of his official duties that may have given rise to retaliation. In another case with implications for discussion of government operations, an acquittee in a federal fraud prosecution brought an action against criminal investigators for inducing prosecution in retaliation for political speech concerning the postal department. Despite a showing of animus by the investigators and a statement by the prosecutor that he was not galvanized to prosecute by the merits of the case, *Hartman v. Moore*, 547 U.S. 250 (2006), required that the plaintiff also show a lack of probable cause as an element of the offence. For a case showing that prisoners have more limited rights than government employees, see *Beard v. Banks*, 126 S.Ct. 2572 (2006). Does the diversity of standards in special contexts have implications for First Amendment theory?

a distinction, and while necessary judicial line-drawing sometimes looks arbitrary, any distinction obliges a court to justify its choice. Here, there is no adequate justification for the majority's line categorically denying *Pickering* protection to any speech uttered 'pursuant [to] official duties.'

"As all agree, the qualified speech protection embodied in *Pickering* balancing resolves the tension between individual and public interests in the speech, on the one hand, and the government's interest in operating efficiently without distraction or embarrassment by talkative or headline-grabbing employees. The need for a balance hardly disappears when an employee speaks on matters his job requires him to address; rather, it seems obvious that the individual and public value of such speech is no less, and may well be greater, when the employee speaks pursuant to his duties in addressing a subject he knows intimately for the very reason that it falls within his duties. * * *

"Nothing [accountable] on the individual and public side of the *Pickering* balance changes when an employee speaks 'pursuant' to public duties.[307] On the side of the government employer, however, something is different, and to this extent, I agree with the majority of the Court. The majority is rightly concerned that the employee who speaks out on matters subject to comment in doing his own work has the greater leverage to create office uproars and fracture the government's authority to set policy to be carried out coherently through the ranks. [Up] to a point, then, the majority makes good points: government needs civility in the workplace, consistency in policy, and honesty and competence in public service.

"But why do the majority's concerns, which we all share, require categorical exclusion of First Amendment protection against any official retaliation for things said on the job? Is it not possible to respect the unchallenged individual and public interests in the speech through a *Pickering* balance without drawing the strange line I mentioned before? This is, to be sure, a matter of judgment, but the judgment has to account for the undoubted value of speech to those, and by those, whose specific public job responsibilities bring them face to face with wrongdoing and incompetence in government, who refuse to avert their eyes and shut their mouths. And it has to account for the need actually to disrupt government if its officials are corrupt or dangerously incompetent. It is thus no adequate justification for the suppression of potentially valuable information simply to recognize that the government has a huge interest in managing its employees and preventing the occasionally irresponsible one from turning his job into a bully pulpit. Even there, the lesson of

---

[307] Later in his opinion, Souter, J., observed: "This ostensible domain beyond the pale of the First Amendment is spacious enough to include even the teaching of a public university professor, and I have to hope that today's majority does not mean to imperil First Amendment protection of academic freedom in public colleges and universities, whose teachers necessarily speak and write 'pursuant to official duties.' "

Pickering (and the object of most constitutional adjudication) is still to the point: when constitutionally significant interests clash, resist the demand for winner-take-all; try to make adjustments that serve all of the values at stake.

"[T]he basic *Pickering* balancing scheme is perfectly feasible here. First, the extent of the government's legitimate authority over subjects of speech required by a public job can be recognized in advance by setting in effect a minimum heft for comments with any claim to outweigh it. Thus, the risks to the government are great enough for us to hold from the outset that an employee commenting on subjects in the course of duties should not prevail on balance unless he speaks on a matter of unusual importance and satisfies high standards of responsibility in the way he does it. The examples I have already given indicate the eligible subject matter, and it is fair to say that only comment on official dishonesty, deliberately unconstitutional action, other serious wrongdoing, or threats to health and safety can weigh out in an employee's favor. If promulgation of this standard should fail to discourage meritless actions [before] they get filed, the standard itself would sift them out at the summary-judgment stage."

BREYER, J., dissented: "The majority [holds] that 'when public employees make statements pursuant to their official duties, the employees are not speaking as citizens for First Amendment purposes, and the Constitution does not insulate their communications from employer discipline.' In a word, the majority says, 'never.' That word, in my view, is too absolute.

"Like the majority, I understand the need to 'affor[d] government employers sufficient discretion to manage their operations.' And I agree that the Constitution does not seek to 'displac[e] managerial discretion by judicial supervision.' Nonetheless, there may well be circumstances with special demand for constitutional protection of the speech at issue, where governmental justifications may be limited, and where administrable standards seem readily available—to the point where the majority's fears of department management by lawsuit are misplaced. [This] is such a case. * * *

"First, the speech at issue is professional speech—the speech of a lawyer. Such speech is subject to independent regulation by canons of the profession. Those canons provide an obligation to speak in certain instances. And where that is so, the government's own interest in forbidding that speech is diminished. The objective specificity and public availability of the profession's canons also help to diminish the risk that the courts will improperly interfere with the government's necessary authority to manage its work.

"Second, the Constitution itself here imposes speech obligations upon the government's professional employee. A prosecutor has a constitutional obligation to learn of, to preserve, and to communicate with the defense about exculpatory and impeachment evidence in the government's possession. So, for example, might a prison doctor have a similar constitutionally related professional obligation to communicate with superiors about seriously unsafe or unsanitary conditions in the cellblock. There may well be other examples.

"Where professional and special constitutional obligations are both present, the need to protect the employee's speech is augmented, the need for broad government authority to control that speech is likely diminished, and administrable standards are quite likely available. Hence, I would find that the Constitution mandates special protection of employee speech in such circumstances. Thus I would apply the *Pickering* balancing test here.

"While I agree with much of Justice Souter's analysis, I believe that the constitutional standard he enunciates fails to give sufficient weight to the serious managerial and administrative concerns that the majority describes. The standard would instruct courts to apply *Pickering* balancing in all cases, but says that the government should prevail unless the employee (1) 'speaks on a matter of unusual importance,' and (2) 'satisfies high standards of responsibility in the way he does it.' Justice Souter adds that 'only comment on official dishonesty, deliberately unconstitutional action, other serious wrongdoing, or threats to health and safety can weigh out in an employee's favor.'

"There are, however, far too many issues of public concern, even if defined as 'matters of unusual importance,' for the screen to screen out very much. Government administration typically involves matters of public concern. Why else would government be involved? And 'public issues,' indeed, matters of 'unusual importance,' are often daily bread-and-butter concerns for the police, the intelligence agencies, the military, and many whose jobs involve protecting the public's health, safety, and the environment. This aspect of Justice Souter's 'adjustment' of 'the basic *Pickering* balancing scheme' is similar to the Court's present insistence that speech be of 'legitimate news interest', when the employee speaks only as a private citizen. It gives no extra weight to the government's augmented need to direct speech that is an ordinary part of the employee's job-related duties.

"Moreover, the speech of vast numbers of public employees deals with wrongdoing, health, safety, and honesty: for example, police officers, firefighters, environmental protection agents, building inspectors, hospital workers, bank regulators, and so on. Indeed, this categorization could encompass speech by an employee performing almost any public function, except perhaps setting electricity rates. Nor do these categories bear any obvious relation to the constitutional importance of protecting the job-related speech at issue.

"The underlying problem with this breadth of coverage is that the standard (despite predictions that the government is likely to *prevail* in the balance unless the speech concerns 'official dishonesty, deliberately unconstitutional action, other serious wrongdoing, or threats to health and safety,') does not avoid the judicial need to *undertake the balance* in the first place. * * *

"I conclude that the First Amendment sometimes does authorize judicial actions based upon a government employee's speech that both (1) involves a matter of public concern and also (2) takes place in the course of ordinary job-related duties. But it does so only in the presence of augmented need for constitutional protection and diminished risk of undue judicial interference with governmental management of the public's affairs."[308]

NOTES AND QUESTIONS

1. ***Speech within government institutions.*** The doctrine affords diminished free speech protection within government institutions such as schools and workplaces. Is this consistent with the First Amendment goal of checking potential misconduct by government. Is it consistent with *Tinker*? Consider Jamin B. Raskin, *No Enclaves of Totalitarianism*, 58 Am. U.L. Rev. 1193 (2009): "The basic meaning of *Tinker* [was] that a student at a school is still a citizen clothed with constitutional rights that she does not surrender simply because she is in a learning relationship with teachers paid by the government. Yet, Justice Kennedy essentially finds that a public employee does shed his First Amendment rights entering the gates of the government workplace."

2. ***Political accountability.*** Is government control over the speech of employees needed if government is to be politically accountable? See Lawrence Rosenthal, *The Emerging First Amendment of Managerial Prerogative,* 77 Ford. L.Rev. 33 (2008).

3. ***Sexual harassment.*** Does *Garcetti* facilitate government's attempts to limit what it regards as sexually harassing speech? Consider Rosenthal, id: "*Garcetti* ultimately rests on a notion that management has a right to control how public employees perform their jobs; and surely that includes how they treat each other. Just as a public employer can 'prohibit its employees from being rude to its customers,' it can insist that they not be rude to each other."

4. ***Dissent.*** Does *Garcetti* allow adequate protection for dissent in the public workplace? Would balancing of the relevant values be preferable to a per se rules? See Julie A Wenell, *Garcetti v. Ceballos: Stifling the First Amendment in the Public Workplace*, 16 Wm. & Mary Bill Rights J. 621 (2007); Sheldon H. Nahmod, *Public Employee Speech, Categorical Balancing, and § 1983*, 42 U. Rich. L. Rev. 561 (2008).

---

[308] Stevens, J., also dissented.

5. ***Academic freedom.*** Should *Garcetti* be extended to teaching in elementary and secondary classrooms? Would a balancing test be preferable? See Neal H. Hutchens, *Silence at the Schoolhouse Gate,* 97 Ky. L.Rev. 37 (2008). Should *Garcetti* be extended to teaching in college classrooms? To academic research and publication? See Robert C. Post, *Democracy, Expertise, and Academic Freedom: A First Amendment Jurisprudence for the Modern State* (2012); Darryn C. Beckstrom, *Reconciling the Public Employee Speech Doctrine and Academic Speech After Garcetti v.* Ceballos, 94 Minn. L.Rev. 1202 (2010). Should universities be regarded as different for First Amendment purposes? See Paul Horwitz, *Universities as First Amendment Institutions*, 54 UCLA L.Rev. 1497 (2007); Oren R. Griffin, *Academic Freedom and Professorial Speech in the Post-Garcetti World,* 37 Seattle U.L.Rev. 1 (2013).

Consider Alexander Wohl, *Oiling the Schoolhouse Gate*, 58 Am. U.L.Rev. 1285 (2009): "Though *Garcetti* may indeed leave some room for the speech of college instructors, the likelihood that any protections will fall to K–12 teachers is extremely small." Does the existence of tenure mitigate this damage?

6. ***Off the job speech.*** (a) A long line of cases has established that employees may not be dismissed because of their affiliation with a political party. *Elrod v.* Burns, 427 U.S. 347 (1976). If employees engage in off the job speech, their protection depends upon the principles developed in *Pickering*. Will *Garcetti* provide excessive incentive for employees to go public with criticisms of their employer? See Patrick Morvan, *A Comparison of the Freedom of Speech of Workers in French and American Law*, 84 Ind. L.J. 1015 (2009). By encouraging employees to inform the public instead of their supervisors of wrongdoing, does the decision encourage twenty-two million public employees "to break the chain of command and adopt an attitude otherwise more subversive and detrimental to their employer's interests?" But see Helen Norton, *Constraining Public Employee Speech*, 59 Duke L.J. 1 (2009): "[C]ourts too readily permit government to punish public employees for their speech away from work, deferring to government claims that even off-duty expression sufficiently reflects upon the government to justify government's control of that speech as well."

It is not always obvious what speech is on the job for purposes of *Garcetti*. *Lane v. Franks*, 134 S.Ct. 2369 (2014), determined that subpoenaed testimony was not "on the job" within the meaning of *Garcetti* even though the information communicated was learned on the job. The Court did not reach the question whether *Garcetti* applied in circumstances where, for example, police officers testify as a regular part of job performance. *Lane* also used the phrase "ordinary job responsibilities" instead of *Garcetti*'s :job responsibilities." Is this significant?

(b) May government employees constitutionally be dismissed if they publicly identify as gay? Should different rules regarding this be applied to the military? To teachers? See Fadi Hanna, *Gay Self-Identification and the Right to Political Legibility,* 2006 Wis. L.Rev. 75 (2006).

8. THE ELECTRONIC MEDIA

The mass media are not invariably the most effective means of communication. For example, the right to place messages on utility poles concerning a lost dog may be more important than access to a radio or a television station. In some circumstances, picketing outside a school or placing leaflets in teachers' mailboxes may be the most effective communications medium. "Moreover, the rise of the internet and various computer applications has contributed to newspaper closings, declines in audiences for broadcasters, and layoffs in the print and broadcast media. [Nonetheless,] newspaper readership in the U.S. reaches about 100 million people daily. Network newscasts alone reach 20 to 30 million people every day." Lee C. Bollinger, *Uninhibited, Robust, and Wide-Open* 85–86 (2010). This section considers first, cases in which government seeks to force newspapers and broadcasters to grant access and cases in which the First Amendment is claimed to demand access. Second, this section considers cases involving content regulation of the electronic media, particularly those where government seeks otherwise to regulate content in broadcasting, cable, and on the internet particularly with respect to sexually oriented material.

I. ACCESS TO THE MASS MEDIA

MIAMI HERALD PUB. CO. v. TORNILLO, 418 U.S. 241 (1974), per BURGER, C.J., unanimously struck down a Florida "right of reply" statute, which required any newspaper that "assails" the personal character or official record of a candidate in any election to print, on demand, free of cost, any reply the candidate may make to the charges, in as conspicuous a place and the same kind of type, provided the reply takes up no more space than the charges. The opinion carefully explained the aim of the statute to "ensure that a wide variety of views reach the public" even though "chains of newspapers, national newspapers, national wire and news services, and one-newspaper towns, are the dominant features of a press that has become noncompetitive and enormously powerful and influential in its capacity to manipulate popular opinion and change the course of events," placing "in a few hands the power to inform the American people and shape public opinion."[309] Nonetheless, the Court concluded that to require the printing of a reply violated the First Amendment: "Compelling editors or publishers to publish that which ' "reason" tells them should not be published' is what is at issue in this case. The Florida statute operates as a command in the same sense as a statute or regulation forbidding

---

[309] The opinion developed these views at greater length, citing "generally" Jerome Barron, *Access to the Press—A New First Amendment Right,* 80 Harv.L.Rev. 1641 (1967); David Lange, *The Role of the Access Doctrine in the Regulation of the Mass Media: A Critical Review and Assessment,* 52 N.C.L.Rev. 1 (1973). For historical background and a spirited criticism of the statute, see Lucas Powe, *Tornillo,* 1987 Sup.Ct.Rev. 345. For background and criticism of the opinion, see Randall Bezanson, *How Free Can the Press Be?,* 58–82 (2003).

appellant from publishing specified matter. [The] Florida statute exacts a penalty on the basis of the content of a newspaper. The first phase of the penalty resulting from the compelled printing of a reply is exacted in terms of the cost in printing and composing time and materials and in taking up space that could be devoted to other material the newspaper may have preferred to print. It is correct, as appellee contends, that a newspaper is not subject to the finite technological limitations of time that confront a broadcaster but it is not correct to say that, as an economic reality, a newspaper can proceed to infinite expansion of its column space to accommodate the replies that a government agency determines or a statute commands the readers should have available.

"Faced with the penalties that would accrue to any newspaper that published news or commentary arguably within the reach of the right of access statute, editors might well conclude that the safe course is to avoid controversy and that, under the operation of the Florida statute, political and electoral coverage would be blunted or reduced. Government enforced right of access inescapably 'dampens the vigor and limits the variety of public debate,' *New York Times*.

"Even if a newspaper would face no additional costs to comply with a compulsory access law and would not be forced to forego publication of news or opinion by the inclusion of a reply, the Florida statute fails to clear the barriers of the First Amendment because of its intrusion into the function of editors. A newspaper is more than a passive receptacle or conduit for news, comment, and advertising. The choice of material to go into a newspaper, and the decisions made as to limitations on the size of the paper, and content, and treatment of public issues and public officials— whether fair or unfair—constitutes the exercise of editorial control and judgment. It has yet to be demonstrated how governmental regulation of this crucial process can be exercised consistent with First Amendment guarantees of a free press as they have evolved to this time."[310]

---

[310] Brennan, J., joined by Rehnquist, J., joined the Court's opinion in a short statement to express the understanding that it "implies no view upon the constitutionality of 'retraction' statutes affording plaintiffs able to prove defamatory falsehoods a statutory action to require publication of a retraction."

White, J., concurred. After agreeing that "prior compulsion by government in matters going to the very nerve center of a newspaper—the decision as to what copy will or will not be included in any given edition—collides with the First Amendment," he returned to his attack on *Gertz*, decided the same day: "Reaffirming the rule that the press cannot be forced to print an answer to a personal attack made by it [throws] into stark relief the consequences of the new balance forged by the Court in the companion case also announced today. *Gertz* goes far toward eviscerating the effectiveness of the ordinary libel action, which has long been the only potent response available to the private citizen libeled by the press. [To] me it is a near absurdity to so deprecate individual dignity, as the Court does in *Gertz*, and to leave the people at the complete mercy of the press, at least in this stage of our history when the press, as the majority in this case so well documents, is steadily becoming more powerful and much less likely to be deterred by threats of libel suits."

The Federal Communications Commission for many years imposed on radio and television broadcasters the "fairness doctrine"—requiring that stations (1) devote a reasonable percentage of broadcast time to discussion of public issues and (2) assure fair coverage for each side.[311] At issue in RED LION BROADCASTING CO. v. FCC, 395 U.S. 367 (1969), were the application of the fairness doctrine to a particular broadcast[312] and two specific access regulations promulgated under the doctrine: (1) the "political editorial" rule, requiring that when a broadcaster, in an editorial, "endorses or opposes" a political candidate, it must notify the candidate opposed, or the rivals of the candidate supported, and afford them a "reasonable opportunity" to respond; (2) the "personal attack" rule, requiring that "when, during the presentation of views on a controversial issue of public importance, an attack is made on the honesty, character [or] integrity [of] an identified person or group," the person or group attacked must be given notice, a transcript of the attack, and an opportunity to respond.[313] "[I]n view of [the] scarcity of broadcast frequencies, the Government's role in allocating those frequencies, and the legitimate claims of those unable without government assistance to gain access to those frequencies for expression of their views," a 7–0 majority, per WHITE, J., upheld both access regulations:[314]

"[The broadcasters] contention is that the First Amendment protects their desire to use their allotted frequencies continuously to broadcast whatever they choose, and to exclude whomever they choose from ever using that frequency. No man may be prevented from saying or publishing what he thinks, or from refusing in his speech or other utterances to give equal weight to the views of his opponents. This right, they say, applies equally to broadcasters.

"Although broadcasting is clearly a medium affected by a First Amendment interest, differences in the characteristics of new media justify differences in the First Amendment standards applied to [them]. Just as the Government may limit the use of sound-amplifying equipment

---

[311] For helpful background on the origins, justification and administration of the fairness doctrine, see Roscoe Barrow, *The Fairness Doctrine: A Double Standard for Electronic and Print Media,* 26 Hast.L.J. 659 (1975); Benno Schmidt, *Freedom of the Press vs. Public Access* 157–98 (1976).

[312] *Red Lion* grew out of a series of radio broadcasts by fundamentalist preacher Billy James Hargis, who had attacked Fred J. Cook, author of an article attacking Hargis and "hate clubs of the air." When Cook heard about the broadcast, he demanded that the station give him an opportunity to reply. Cook refused to pay for his "reply time" and the FCC ordered the station to give Cook the opportunity to reply whether or not he would pay for it. The Supreme Court upheld the order of free reply time. See Schmidt, fn. 311 supra, at 161–63.

[313] Excepted were "personal attacks [by] legally qualified candidates [on] other such candidates" and "bona fide newscasts, bona fide news interviews, and on-the-spot coverage of a bona fide news event."

[314] Surprisingly, none of the justices joining White, J.'s opinion felt the need to make additional remarks, but Douglas, J., who did not participate in *Red Lion,* expressed his disagreement with it in the *CBS* case, infra.

potentially so noisy that it drowns out civilized private speech, so may the Government limit the use of broadcast equipment. The right of free speech of a broadcaster, the user of a sound truck, or any other individual does not embrace a right to snuff out the free speech of [others].

"Where there are substantially more individuals who want to broadcast than there are frequencies to allocate, it is idle to posit an unabridgeable First Amendment right to broadcast comparable to the right of every individual to speak, write, or publish. [It] would be strange if the First Amendment, aimed at protecting and furthering communications, prevented the Government from making radio communication possible by requiring licenses to broadcast and by limiting the number of licenses so as not to overcrowd the spectrum. * * *

"By the same token, as far as the First Amendment is concerned those who are licensed stand no better than those to whom licenses are refused. A license permits broadcasting, but the licensee has no constitutional right [to] monopolize a radio frequency to the exclusion of his fellow citizens. There is nothing in the First Amendment which prevents the Government from requiring a licensee to share his frequency with others and to conduct himself as a proxy or fiduciary with obligations to present those views and voices which are representative of his community and which would otherwise, by necessity, be barred from the airwaves.

"[The] people as a whole retain their interest in free speech by radio and their collective right to have the medium function consistently with the ends and purposes of the First Amendment. It is the right of the viewers and listeners, not the right of the broadcasters, which is paramount. [It] is the purpose of the First Amendment to preserve an uninhibited marketplace of ideas in which truth will ultimately prevail, rather than to countenance monopolization of that market, whether it be by the Government itself or a private licensee. [It] is the right of the public to receive suitable access to social, political, esthetic, moral, and other ideas and experiences which is crucial [here.]

"In terms of constitutional principle, and as enforced sharing of a scarce resource, the personal attack and political editorial rules are indistinguishable from the equal-time provision of § 315 [of the Communications Act], a specific enactment of Congress requiring [that stations allot equal time to qualified candidates for public office] and to which the fairness doctrine and these constituent regulations are important complements. [Nor] can we say that it is inconsistent with the First Amendment goal of producing an informed public capable of conducting its own affairs to require a broadcaster to permit answers to personal attacks occurring in the course of discussing controversial issues, or to require that the political opponents of those endorsed by the station be given a chance to communicate with the public. Otherwise, station owners and a few networks would have unfettered power to make time available only to the highest bidders, to communicate only their own views on public issues, people and candidates, and to permit on the air only those with whom they agreed. There is no sanctuary in the First Amendment for unlimited private censorship operating in a medium not open to all.

"[It is contended] that if political editorials or personal attacks will trigger an obligation in broadcasters to afford the opportunity for expression to speakers who need not pay for time and whose views are unpalatable to the licensees, then broadcasters will be irresistibly forced to self-censorship and their coverage of controversial public issues will be eliminated or at least rendered wholly ineffective. Such a result would indeed be a serious matter, [but] that possibility is at best speculative. [If these doctrines turn out to have this effect], there will be time enough to reconsider the constitutional implications. The fairness doctrine in the past has had no such overall effect. That this will occur now seems unlikely, however, since if present licensees should suddenly prove timorous, the Commission is not powerless to insist that they give adequate and fair attention to public issues. It does not violate the First Amendment to treat licensees given the privilege of using scarce radio frequencies as proxies for the entire community, obligated to give suitable time and attention to matters of great public concern. To condition the granting or renewal of licenses on a willingness to present representative community views on controversial issues is consistent with the ends and purposes of those constitutional provisions forbidding the abridgment of freedom of speech and freedom of the press."[315]

NOTES AND QUESTIONS

1. ***Tension between Miami Herald and Red Lion.*** Consider Lee Bollinger, *Freedom of the Press and Public Access: Toward a Theory of Partial Regulation of the Mass Media,* 75 Mich.L.Rev. 1 (1976): "What seems so remarkable about the unanimous *Miami Herald* opinion is the complete absence of any reference to the Court's unanimous decision five years earlier in *Red Lion*[, upholding] the so-called personal attack rule, [which] is almost identical in substance to the Florida statute declared unconstitutional in *Miami Herald.* That omission, however, is no more surprising than the absence

---

[315] The Court noted that it "need not deal with the argument that even if there is no longer a technological scarcity of frequencies limiting the number of broadcasters, there nevertheless is an economic scarcity in the sense that the Commission could or does limit entry to the broadcasting market on economic grounds and license no more stations than the market will support. Hence, it is said, the fairness doctrine or its equivalent is essential to satisfy the claims of those excluded and of the public generally. A related argument, which we also put side, is that quite apart from scarcity of frequencies, technological or economic, Congress does not abridge freedom of speech or press by legislation directly or indirectly multiplying the voices and views presented to the public through time sharing, fairness doctrines, or other devices which limit or dissipate the power of those who sit astride the channels of communication with the general public." For background and discussion of *Red Lion,* see Fred Friendly, *The Good Guys, The Bad Guys and the First Amendment* (1975).

of any discussion in *Red Lion* of the cases in which the Court expressed great concern about the risks attending government regulation of the print media.

"[The] scarcity rationale [articulated in *Red Lion* does not] explain why what appears to be a similar phenomenon of natural monopolization within the newspaper industry does not constitute an equally appropriate occasion for access regulation. A difference in the cause of concentration—the exhaustion of a physical element necessary for communication in broadcasting as contrasted with the economic constraints on the number of possible competitors in the print media—would seem far less relevant from a First Amendment standpoint than the fact of concentration itself. [Instead] of exploring the relevance for the print media of the new principle developed in broadcasting, the Court merely reiterated the opposing, more traditional, principle that the government cannot tell editors what to publish. It thus created a paradox, leaving the new principle unscathed while preserving tradition."

2. ***Absence of balancing in Miami Herald.*** Did *Miami Herald* present a confrontation between the rights of speech and press? "Nowhere does [*Miami Herald*] explicitly acknowledge [such a confrontation], but implicit recognition of the speech interest," observes Melville Nimmer, *Is Freedom of the Press a Redundancy? What Does It Add to Freedom of Speech?*, 26 Hast.L.J. 639 (1975), "may be found in the Court's reference to the access advocates' argument that, given the present semimonopolistic posture of the press, speech can be effective and therefore free only if enhanced by devices such as a right of reply statute. The Court in accepting the press clause argument in effect necessarily found it to be superior to any competing speech clause claims. [But] the issue cannot be resolved merely by noting, as did [*Miami Herald*], that a right of reply statute 'constitutes the [state] exercise of editorial control and judgment.' This is but one half of the equation. [*Miami Herald*] ignored the strong conflicting claims of 'speech.' Perhaps on balance the press should still prevail, but those who doubt the efficacy of such a result are hardly persuaded by an approach that apparently fails to recognize that any balancing of speech and press rights is required."[316] Consider Gregory P. Magarian, *The Jurisprudence of Colliding First Amendment Interests,* 83 Notre D. L.Rev. 185 (2007): "Single minded emphasis on autonomy tends to favor the expressive haves over the have nots [and] tends to yield a bias toward established viewpoints."

3. ***Scope of Miami Herald.*** Consider Schmidt, fn. 311 supra: "From the perspective of First Amendment law generally, *Miami Herald* would be a stark and unexplained deviation if one were to read the decision as creating

---

[316] Does *Miami Herald* demonstrate that free speech and press can be distinct, even conflicting interests? Anthony Lewis, *A Preferred Position for Journalism?*, 7 Hof.L.Rev. 595 (1979), thinks not: "[T]he vice of the [Florida right of reply] law lay in the compulsion to publish; and I think the result would be no different if the case involved a compulsion to speak. If a state statute required any candidate who spoke falsely about another to make a corrective speech, would it survive challenge under the First Amendment?"

absolute prohibitions on access obligations.[317] [The] fact the Court offers no discussion as to why First Amendment rules respecting access should be absolute, while all other rules emanating from that Amendment are relative, suggests that the principle of *Miami Herald* probably is destined for uncharted qualifications and exceptions." But see Lucas Powe, *Tornillo,* 1987 Sup.Ct.Rev. 345: "I do not believe that a twenty page Supreme Court opinion meeting all the standards of craft (all considerations are ventilated fully and the opinion be of publishable quality for a good legal journal) can as effectively protect the right of press autonomy as the blunt rejection in *Miami Herald.* Chief Justice Burger's failure to engage, so annoying to Schmidt and other commentators, is in fact a great strength of the opinion."

Would a statute requiring nondiscriminatory access to the classified ads section of a newspaper pass muster under *Miami Herald?* A requirement that legal notices be published?

4.   ***Absolute editorial autonomy—Some of the time.*** Is it ironic that *Gertz* was decided the same day as *Miami Herald?* Which poses a greater threat to editorial autonomy—a negligence standard in defamation cases or the guaranteed access contemplated by the Florida statute? Whose autonomy is important—the editors or the owners? May government protect editors from ad hoc intervention by corporate owners? See generally C. Edwin Baker, *Human Liberty and Freedom of Speech* 225–71 (1989). May government protect reporters from ad hoc intervention by editors?

5.   ***The threat to editorial autonomy in Red Lion.*** Consider Schmidt, fn. 311 supra: *Red Lion* "left broadcaster autonomy almost entirely at the mercy of the FCC." See also William Van Alstyne, *The Möbius Strip of the First Amendment: Perspectives on Red Lion,* 29 S.C.L.Rev. 539 (1978): "Indeed, if one continues to be troubled by *Red Lion,* I think it is not because one takes lightly the difficulty of forum allocation in a society of scarce resources. Rather, it is because one believes that the technique of the fairness doctrine in particular may represent a very trivial egalitarian gain and a major First Amendment loss; that a twist has been given to the equal protection idea by a device the principal effect of which is merely to level down the most vivid and versatile forum we have, to flatten it out and to render it a mere commercial mirror of each community. What may have been lost is a willingness to risk the partisanship of licensees as catalysts and as active advocates with a freedom to exhort, a freedom that dares to exclaim 'Fuck the draft,' and not be made to yield by government at once to add, 'but on the other hand there is also the view, held by many.'"

6.   ***The best of both worlds.*** "[T]he critical difference between what the Court was asked to do in *Red Lion* and what it was asked to do in *Miami Herald,*" maintains Professor Bollinger Note 1 supra, "involved choosing between a partial regulatory system and a universal one. Viewed from that

---

[317] "Even in the area of 'the central freedom of the First Amendment,' which is criticism of the governmental acts of public officials," recalls Schmidt, fn. 311 supra, at 232, "there is no absolute protection for expression."

perspective, the Court reached the correct result in both cases": "[T]here are good First Amendment reasons for being both receptive to and wary of access regulation. This dual nature of access legislation suggests the need to limit carefully the intrusiveness of the regulation in order safely to enjoy its remedial benefits. Thus, a proper judicial response is one that will permit the legislature to provide the public with access *somewhere* within the mass media, but not throughout the press. The Court should not, and need not, be forced into an all-or-nothing position on this matter; there is nothing in the First Amendment that forbids having the best of both worlds."[318]

For a powerful critique of the regulated world, see Lucas Powe, *American Broadcasting and the First Amendment* (1987). For a powerful critique of the unregulated world, see C. Edwin Baker, *The First Amendment in Modern Garb,* 58 Ohio St.L.J. 311 (1997).

"Like many equal protection issues," observes Karst, Sec. 6, I, B supra, "the media-access problem should be approached from two separate constitutional directions. First, what does the Constitution *compel* government to do in the way of equalizing? Second, what does the Constitution *permit* government to do in equalizing by statute?" *Red Lion* and *Miami Herald* presented the second question; the first is raised by COLUMBIA BROADCASTING SYSTEM, INC. v. DEMOCRATIC NAT'L COMMITTEE, 412 U.S. 94 (1973) (*CBS*): The FCC rejected the claims of Business Executives' Move for Vietnam Peace (BEM) and the Democratic National Committee (DNC) that "responsible" individuals and groups are entitled to purchase advertising time to comment on public issues, even though the broadcaster has complied with the fairness doctrine. The D.C. Circuit held that "a flat ban on paid public issue announcements" violates the First Amendment "at least when other sorts of paid announcements are accepted," and remanded to the FCC to develop "reasonable procedures and regulations determining which and how many 'editorial advertisements' will be put on the air." The Court, per BURGER, C.J., reversed, holding that neither the "public interest" standard of the Communications Act (which draws heavily from the First Amendment) nor the First Amendment itself—assuming that refusal to accept such advertising constituted "governmental action" for First Amendment purposes[319]—requires broadcasters to accept paid editorial

----

[318] Does the existence of the threat of regulation or the Court's rhetoric about the press have a substantial impact on press decisions? Compare Lee C. Bollinger, *Images of a Free Press* (1991) with Lili Levi, *Challenging the Autonomous Press,* 78 Cornell L.Rev. 665 (1993).

[319] Burger, C.J., joined by Stewart and Rehnquist, JJ., concluded that a broadcast licensee's refusal to accept an advertisement was not "governmental action" for First Amendment purposes. Although White, Blackmun and Powell, JJ., concurred in parts of the Court's opinion, they did not decide this question for, *assuming* governmental action, they found that the challenged ban did not violate the First Amendment. Douglas, J., who concurred in the result, assumed *no* governmental action. Dissenting, Brennan, J., joined by Marshall, J., found that the challenged ban did constitute "governmental action." See Ch. 10, Sec. 2.

announcements. As pointed out in Vincent Blasi, *The Checking Value in First Amendment Theory*, 1977 Am.B.Found.Res.J. 521, although Burger, C.J. "built to some extent" on *Red Lion,* his opinion "evinced a most important change of emphasis. For whereas White, J., based his argument in *Red Lion* on the premise that broadcasters are mere 'proxies' or 'fiduciaries' for the general public, the Chief Justice's opinion [in *CBS*] invoked a concept of 'journalistic independence' or 'journalistic discretion,' the essence of which is that broadcasters do indeed have special First Amendment interests which have to be considered in the constitutional calculus."

Burger, C.J. continued: "[From various provisions of the Communications Act of 1934] it seems clear that Congress intended to permit private broadcasting to develop with the widest journalistic freedom consistent with its public obligations. Only when the interests of the public are found to outweigh the private journalistic interests of the broadcasters will government power be asserted within the framework of the Act. License renewal proceedings, in which the listening public can be heard, are a principal means of such regulation.

"[W]ith the advent of radio a half century ago, Congress was faced with a fundamental choice between total Government ownership and control of the new medium—the choice of most other countries—or some other alternative. Long before the impact and potential of the medium was realized, Congress opted for a system of private broadcasters licensed and regulated by Government. The legislative history suggests that this choice was influenced not only by traditional attitudes toward private enterprise, but by a desire to maintain for licensees, so far as consistent with necessary regulation, a traditional journalistic [role.]

"The regulatory scheme evolved slowly, but very early the licensee's role developed in terms of a 'public trustee' charged with the duty of fairly and impartially informing the public audience. In this structure the Commission acts in essence as an 'overseer,' but the initial and primary responsibility for fairness, balance, and objectivity rests with the licensee. This role of the Government as an overseer and ultimate arbiter and guardian of the public interest and the role of the licensee as a journalistic 'free agent' call for a delicate balancing of competing interests. The maintenance of this balance for more than 40 years has called on both the regulators and the licensees to walk a 'tightrope' to preserve the First Amendment values written into the Radio Act and its successor, the Communications Act.

"The tensions inherent in such a regulatory structure emerge more clearly when we compare a private newspaper with a broadcast licensee. The power of a privately owned newspaper to advance its own political, social, and economic views is bounded by only two factors: first, the acceptance of a sufficient number of readers—and hence advertisers—to assure financial success; and, second, the journalistic integrity of its editors and publishers. A broadcast licensee has a large measure of journalistic freedom but not as large as that exercised by a newspaper. A licensee must balance what it might prefer to do as a private entrepreneur with what it is required to do as a 'public trustee.' To perform its statutory duties, the Commission must oversee without censoring. This suggests something of the difficulty and delicacy of administering the Communications Act—a function calling for flexibility and the capacity to adjust and readjust the regulatory mechanism to meet changing problems and needs.

"The licensee policy challenged in this case is intimately related to the journalistic role of a licensee for which it has been given initial and primary responsibility by Congress. The licensee's policy against accepting editorial advertising cannot be examined as an abstract proposition, but must be viewed in the context of its journalistic role. It does not help to press on us the idea that editorial ads are 'like' commercial ads, for the licensee's policy against editorial spot ads is expressly based on a journalistic judgment that 10- to 60-second spot announcements are ill-suited to intelligible and intelligent treatment of public issues; the broadcaster has chosen to provide a balanced treatment of controversial questions in a more comprehensive form. Obviously, the licensee's evaluation is based on its own journalistic judgment of priorities and newsworthiness.

"Moreover, the Commission has not fostered the licensee policy challenged here; it has simply declined to command particular action because it fell within the area of journalistic discretion. [The] Commission's reasoning, consistent with nearly 40 years of precedent, is that so long as a licensee meets its 'public trustee' obligation to provide balanced coverage of issues and events, it has broad discretion to decide how that obligation will be met. We do not reach the question whether the First Amendment or the Act can be read to preclude the Commission from determining that in some situations the public interest requires licensees to re-examine their policies with respect to editorial advertisements.[320] The Commission has not yet made such a determination; it has, for the present at least, found the policy to be within the sphere of journalistic discretion which Congress has left with the licensee.

"[I]t must constantly be kept in mind that the interest of the public is our foremost concern. With broadcasting, where the available means of

---

[320] *Columbia Broadcasting System, Inc. v. FCC*, 453 U.S. 367 (1981), upheld FCC administration of a statutory provision guaranteeing "reasonable" access to the airwaves for federal election candidates. The Court, per Burger, C.J., observed that "the Court has never approved a *general* right of access to the media. *Miami Herald*; *CBS v. DNC*. Nor do we do so today." But it found that the limited right of access "properly balances the First Amendment rights of federal candidates, the public, and broadcasters." White, J., joined by Rehnquist and Stevens, JJ., dissented on statutory grounds. For criticism, see Daniel Polsby, *Candidate Access to the Air: The Uncertain Future of Broadcaster Discretion*, 1981 Sup.Ct.Rev. 223.

communication are limited in both space and time, [Meiklejohn's admonition] that '[w]hat is essential is not that everyone shall speak, but that everything worth saying shall be said' is peculiarly appropriate.

"[Congress] has time and again rejected various legislative attempts that would have mandated a variety of forms of individual access. [It] has chosen to leave such questions with the Commission, to which it has given the flexibility to experiment with new ideas as changing conditions require. In this case, the Commission has decided that on balance the undesirable effects of the right of access urged by respondents would outweigh the asserted [benefits.]

"The Commission was justified in concluding that the public interest in providing access to the marketplace of 'ideas and experiences' would scarcely be served by a system so heavily weighted in favor of the financially affluent, or those with access to wealth. Even under a first-come-first-served system [the] views of the affluent could well prevail over those of others, since they would have it within their power to purchase time more frequently. Moreover, there is the substantial danger [that] the time allotted for editorial advertising could be monopolized by those of one political persuasion.

"These problems would not necessarily be solved by applying the Fairness Doctrine, including the *Cullman* doctrine [requiring broadcasters to provide free time for the presentation of opposing views if a paid sponsor is unavailable], to editorial advertising. If broadcasters were required to provide time, free when necessary, for the discussion of the various shades of opinion on the issue discussed in the advertisement, the affluent could still determine in large part the issues to be discussed. Thus, the very premise of the Court of Appeals' holding—that a right of access is necessary to allow individuals and groups the opportunity for self-initiated speech—would have little meaning to those who could not afford to purchase time in the first instance.

"If the Fairness Doctrine were applied to editorial advertising, there is also the substantial danger that the effective operation of that doctrine would be jeopardized. To minimize financial hardship and to comply fully with its public responsibilities a broadcaster might well be forced to make regular programming time available to those holding a view different from that expressed in an editorial advertisement. [The] result would be a further erosion of the journalistic discretion of broadcasters in the coverage of public issues, and a transfer of control over the treatment of public issues from the licensees who are accountable for broadcast performance to private individuals who are not. The public interest would no longer be 'paramount' but rather subordinate to private whim especially since, under the Court of Appeals' decision, a broadcaster would be largely precluded from rejecting editorial advertisements that dealt with matters trivial or insignificant or already fairly covered by the broadcaster. If the Fairness Doctrine and the *Cullman* doctrine were suspended to alleviate these problems, as respondents suggest might be appropriate, the question arises whether we would have abandoned more than we have gained. Under such a regime the congressional objective of balanced coverage of public issues would be seriously threatened.

"Nor can we accept the Court of Appeals' view that every potential speaker is 'he best judge' of what the listening public ought to hear or indeed the best judge of the merits of his or her views. All journalistic tradition and experience is to the contrary. For better or worse, editing is what editors are for; and editing is selection and choice of material. That editors—newspaper or broadcast—can and do abuse this power is beyond doubt, but that is not reason to deny the discretion Congress provided. Calculated risks of abuse are taken in order to preserve higher values. The presence of these risks is nothing new; the authors of the Bill of Rights accepted the reality that these risks were evils for which there was no acceptable remedy other than a spirit of moderation and a sense of responsibility—and civility—on the part of those who exercise the guaranteed freedoms of expression.

"It was reasonable for Congress to conclude that the public interest in being informed requires periodic accountability on the part of those who are entrusted with the use of broadcast frequencies, scarce as they are. In the delicate balancing historically followed in the regulation of broadcasting Congress and the Commission could appropriately conclude that the allocation of journalistic priorities should be concentrated in the licensee rather than diffused among many. This policy gives the public some assurance that the broadcaster will be answerable if he fails to meet their legitimate needs. No such accountability attaches to the private individual, whose only qualifications for using the broadcast facility may be abundant funds and a point of view. To agree that debate on public issues should be 'robust, and wide-open' does not mean that we should exchange 'public trustee' broadcasting, with all its limitations, for a system of self-appointed editorial commentators.

"[T]he risk of an enlargement of Government control over the content of broadcast discussion of public issues [is] inherent in the Court of Appeals' remand requiring regulations and procedures to sort out requests to be heard—a process involving the very editing that licensees now perform as to regular programming. [Under] a constitutionally commanded and government supervised right-of-access system urged by respondents and mandated by the Court of Appeals, the Commission would be required to oversee far more of the day-to-day operations of broadcasters' conduct, deciding such questions as whether a particular individual or group has had sufficient opportunity to present its viewpoint and whether a particular viewpoint has already been sufficiently aired. Regimenting broadcasters is too radical a therapy for the ailment respondents complain of. * * *

"The Commission is also entitled to take into account the reality that in a very real sense listeners and viewers constitute a 'captive audience.' [It] is no answer to say that because we tolerate pervasive commercial advertisement [we] can also live with its political counterparts.

"The rationale for the Court of Appeals' decision imposing a constitutional right of access on the broadcast media was that the licensee impermissibly discriminates by accepting commercial advertisements while refusing editorial advertisements. The court relied on [lower court cases] holding that state-supported school newspapers and public transit companies were forbidden by the First Amendment from excluding controversial editorial advertisements in favor of commercial advertisements.[321] The court also attempted to analogize this case to some of our decisions holding that States may not constitutionally ban certain protected speech while at the same time permitting other speech in public areas [citing e.g., *Grayned* and *Mosley,* Sec. 6 supra].

"These decisions provide little guidance, however, in resolving the question whether the First Amendment required the Commission to mandate a private right of access to the broadcast media. In none of those cases did the forum sought for expression have an affirmative and independent statutory obligation to provide full and fair coverage of public issues, such as Congress has imposed on all broadcast licensees. In short, there is no 'discrimination' against controversial speech present in this case. The question here is not whether there is to be discussion of controversial issues of public importance on the broadcast media, but rather who shall determine what issues are to be discussed by whom, and when."

DOUGLAS, J., concurred in the result, but "for quite different reasons." Because the Court did not decide whether a broadcast licensee is "a federal agency within the context of this case," he assumed that it was not. He "fail[ed] to see," then "how constitutionally we can treat TV and the radio differently than we treat newspapers": "I did not participate in [*Red Lion* and] would not support it. The Fairness Doctrine has no place in our First Amendment regime. It puts the head of the camel inside the tent and enables administration after administration to toy with TV or radio in order to serve its sordid or its benevolent ends. [The uniqueness of radio and TV] is due to engineering and technical problems. But the press in a realistic sense is likewise not available to all. [T]he daily newspapers now established are unique in the sense that it would be virtually impossible for a competitor to enter the field due to the financial exigencies of this era. The result is that in practical terms the newspapers and magazines, like

---

[321] But see *Lehman v. Shaker Heights*, Sec. 6, II supra.

the TV and radio, are available only to a select few. [That] may argue for a redefinition of the responsibilities of the press in First Amendment terms. But I do not think it gives us carte blanche to design systems of supervision and control nor empower [the government to] make 'some' laws 'abridging' freedom of the press. * * *

"Licenses are, of course, restricted in time and while, in my view, Congress has the power to make each license limited to a fixed term and nonreviewable, there is no power to deny renewals for editorial or ideological reasons [for] the First Amendment gives no preference to one school of thought over the others.

"The Court in today's decision by endorsing the Fairness Doctrine sanctions a federal saddle on broadcast licensees that is agreeable to the traditions of nations that never have known freedom of press and that is tolerable in countries that do not have a written constitution containing prohibitions as absolute as those in the First Amendment."[322]

BRENNAN, J., joined by Marshall, J., dissented, viewing "the *absolute* ban on the sale of air time for the discussion of controversial issues" as "governmental action"[323] violating the First Amendment: "As a practical matter, the Court's reliance on the Fairness Doctrine as an 'adequate' alternative to editorial advertising seriously overestimates the ability—or willingness—of broadcasters to expose the public to the 'widest possible dissemination of information from diverse and antagonistic sources.' [Indeed,] in light of the strong interest of broadcasters in maximizing their audience, and therefore their profits, it seems almost naive to expect the majority of broadcasters to produce the variety and controversiality of material necessary to reflect a full spectrum of viewpoints. Stated simply, angry customers are not good customers and, in the commercial world of mass communications, it is simply 'bad business' to espouse—or even to allow others to espouse—the heterodox or the controversial. As a result, even under the Fairness Doctrine, broadcasters generally tend to permit only established—or at least moderated—views to enter the broadcast world's 'marketplace of ideas.'[24]

"Moreover, the Court's reliance on the Fairness Doctrine as the *sole* means of informing the public seriously misconceives and underestimates the public's interest in receiving ideas and information directly from the advocates of those ideas without the interposition of journalistic middlemen. Under the Fairness Doctrine, broadcasters decide what issues are 'important,' how 'fully' to cover them, and what format, time and style of coverage are 'appropriate.' The retention of such *absolute* control in the

---

[322] Noting that his views "closely approach those expressed by Mr. Justice Douglas," Stewart, J., also concurred.

[323] See Ch. 10, Sec. 2 infra.

[24] **[Ct's Note]** [Citing many secondary sources to support this statement.]

hands of a few government licensees is inimical to the First Amendment, for vigorous, free debate can be attained only when members of the public have at least *some* opportunity to take the initiative and editorial control into their own hands.

"[S]tanding alone, [the Fairness Doctrine] simply cannot eliminate the need for a further, complementary airing of controversial views through the limited availability of editorial advertising. Indeed, the availability of at least *some* opportunity for editorial advertising is imperative if we are ever to attain the 'free and general discussion of public matters [that] seems absolutely essential to prepare the people for an intelligent exercise of their rights as citizens.'

"Moreover, a proper balancing of the competing First Amendment interests at stake in this controversy must consider, not only the interests of broadcasters and of the listening and viewing public, but also the independent First Amendment interest of groups and individuals in effective self-expression. [I]n a time of apparently growing anonymity of the individual in our society, it is imperative that we take special care to preserve the vital First Amendment interest in assuring 'self-fulfillment [of expression] for each individual.' For our citizens may now find greater than ever the need to express their own views directly to the public, rather than through a governmentally appointed surrogate, if they are to feel that they can achieve at least some measure of control over their own destinies.

"[F]reedom of speech does not exist in the abstract. [It] can flourish only if it is allowed to operate in an effective forum—whether it be a public park, a schoolroom, a town meeting hall, a soapbox, or a radio and television frequency. For in the absence of an effective means of communication, the right to speak would ring hollow indeed. And, in recognition of these principles, we have consistently held that the First Amendment embodies not only the abstract right to be free from censorship, but also the right of an individual to utilize an appropriate and effective medium for the expression of his views.

"[W]ith the assistance of the Federal Government, the broadcast industry has become what is potentially the most efficient and effective 'marketplace of ideas' ever devised. [Thus], although 'full and free discussion' of ideas may have been a reality in the heyday of political pamphleteering, modern technological developments in the field of communications have made the soapbox orator and the leafleteer virtually obsolete. And, in light of the current dominance of the electronic media as the most effective means of reaching the public, any policy that *absolutely* denies citizens access to the airwaves necessarily renders even the concept of 'full and free discussion' practically meaningless.

"[T]he challenged ban can be upheld only if it is determined that such editorial advertising would unjustifiably impair the broadcaster's assertedly overriding interest in exercising *absolute* control over 'his' frequency. Such an analysis, however, hardly reflects the delicate balancing of interests that this sensitive question demands. Indeed, this 'absolutist' approach wholly disregards the competing First Amendment rights of all 'nonbroadcaster' citizens, ignores the teachings of our recent decision in *Red Lion,* and is not supported by the historical purposes underlying broadcast regulation in this Nation. [T]here is simply no overriding First Amendment interest of broadcasters that can justify the *absolute* exclusion of virtually all of our citizens from the most effective 'marketplace of ideas' ever devised.

"[T]his case deals *only* with the allocation of *advertising* time—airtime that broadcasters regularly relinquish to others without the retention of significant editorial control. Thus, we are concerned here not with the speech of broadcasters themselves but, rather, with their 'right' to decide which *other* individuals will be given an opportunity to speak in a forum that has already been opened to the public.

"Viewed in this context, the *absolute* ban on editorial advertising seems particularly offensive because, although broadcasters refuse to sell any airtime whatever to groups or individuals wishing to speak out on controversial issues of public importance, they make such airtime readily available to those 'commercial' advertisers who seek to peddle their goods and services to the public. [Yet an] individual seeking to discuss war, peace, pollution, or the suffering of the poor is denied this right to speak. Instead, he is compelled to rely on the beneficence of a corporate 'trustee' appointed by the Government to argue his case for him.

"It has been long recognized, however, that although access to public forums may be subjected to reasonable 'time, place, and manner' regulations, '[s]elective exclusions from a public forum, may not be based on *content* alone.' *Mosley* (emphasis added). Here, of course, the differential treatment accorded 'commercial' and 'controversial' speech clearly violates that principle. Moreover, and not without some irony, the favored treatment given 'commercial' speech under the existing scheme clearly reverses traditional First Amendment priorities. For it has generally been understood that 'commercial' speech enjoys *less* First Amendment protection than speech directed at the discussion of controversial issues of public importance."

NOTES AND QUESTIONS

1. *Confronting scarcity.* Consider Tribe 2d ed., at 1005: "CBS took a step away from *Red Lion* by its treatment of broadcasters as part of the 'press' with an important editorial function to perform rather than as analogous to the postal or telephone systems, but *CBS* was firmly in the *Red Lion* tradition when it refused to consider the possibility that either the technologically scarce radio and television channels, or the finite time available on such channels,

might be allocated much as economically scarce newspaper opportunities are allocated: by a combination of market mechanisms and chance rather than by government design coupled with broadcaster autonomy."

Suppose the government sold the airwaves to the highest bidder and allowed subsequent exchange according to property and contract law. Consider Note, *Reconciling Red Lion and Tornillo: A Consistent Theory of Media Regulation,* 28 Stan.L.Rev. 563 (1976): "This regulatory strategy would remove the government from direct determination of the particular individuals who are allowed to broadcast, leaving this decision to market forces, and would avoid the need for specific behavioral commands and sanctions now necessary to secure compliance by broadcasters with the various obligations imposed by the public interest standard. [Under] strict scrutiny, then, the existence of this clearly identifiable less restrictive alternative indicates that the Communications Act is unconstitutional."

But see Van Alstyne, supra: "Congress may indeed be free to 'sell off' the airwaves, and it may be wholly feasible to allocate most currently established broadcast signals by competitive bidding that, when done, may well produce private licensees operating truly without subsidy. But only a singularly insensitive observer would believe that this choice is not implicitly also a highly speech-restrictive choice by Congress. It is fully as speech-restrictive as though, in the case of land, government were to withdraw from *all* ownership and all subsidized maintenance of all land, including parks, auditoriums, and streets and to remain in the field exclusively as a policeman to enforce the proprietary decisions of all private landowners."[324]

Should it be constitutional for the government to exercise "ownership" over the entire broadcast spectrum?[325]

2. *The "fairness" doctrine criticized.* The Court's assumption that the fairness doctrine worked tolerably well was often harshly criticized by the commentators. See, e.g., Ford Rowan, *Broadcast Fairness: Doctrine, Practice, Prospects* (1984); Steven Simmons, *The Fairness Doctrine and the Media* (1978); Johnson & Dystel, *A Day in the Life: The Federal Communications Commission,* 82 Yale L.J. 1575 (1973). Consider Thomas Krattenmaker & Lucas Powe, *The Fairness Doctrine Today: A Constitutional Curiosity and an Impossible Dream,* 1985 Duke L.J. 151: "If the doctrine is to be taken seriously then suspected violations lurk everywhere and the FCC should undertake continuous oversight of the industry. If the FCC will not—or cannot—do that, then the doctrine must be toothless except for the randomly-selected few who

---

[324] For detailed, but traditional, criticism of the scarcity argument, see Matthew Spitzer, *Controlling the Content of Print and Broadcast,* 58 S.Cal.L.Rev. 1349 (1985). But see *Metro Broadcasting, Inc. v. FCC,* 497 U.S. 547 (1990) (reaffirming the government's power to regulate the "limited number" of broadcast licensees in the context of upholding minority ownership policies designed to effectuate more diverse programming and to safeguard the "rights of the viewing and listening audiences"). For criticism of the scarcity argument in light of new technology, see Lawrence Lessig, *Code* 182–85 (1999).

[325] See Glen O. Robinson, *The Electronic First Amendment: An Essay for the New Age,* 47 Duke L.J. 899 (1998); Matthew Spitzer, *The Constitutionality of Licensing Broadcasters,* 64 N.Y.U.L.Rev. 990 (1989); Steven Shiffrin, *Government Speech,* 27 UCLA L.Rev. 565 (1980).

are surprised to feel its bite after the fact." For a vigorous defense of the fairness doctrine, see Charles Ferris & James Kirkland, *Fairness—The Broadcaster's Hippocratic Oath*, 34 Cath.U.L.Rev. 605 (1985).

3. ***The fairness doctrine repealed.*** The FCC concluded a 15 month administrative proceeding with an official denunciation of the fairness doctrine, pointing in particular to the marked increase in the information services marketplace since *Red Lion* and the effects of the doctrine in application. FCC, [*General*] *Fairness Doctrine Obligations of Broadcast Licensees,* 102 F.C.C.2d 143 (1985). *Syracuse Peace Council,* 2 FCC Rcd 5043 (1987) held that "under the constitutional standard established by *Red Lion* and its progeny, the fairness doctrine contravenes the First Amendment and its enforcement is no longer in the public interest."[326]

4. ***The worst of both worlds.*** Evaluate the following hypothetical commentary: "*CBS v. DNC* allows government to grant virtually exclusive control over American's most valuable communication medium to corporations who regard it as their mission to 'deliver' audiences to advertisers. The system gives us the worst of both worlds: the world of profit-seeking—without a free market; the world of regulation—without planning." Consider Richard Moon, *The Constitutional Protection of Freedom of Expression* 81 (2000): "The domination of public discourse by advertising also means that the unnatural images or absurd associations of a particular ad seem unexceptional. Because the principal channels of public discourse are controlled by commercial interests and carry only ads and advertising-funded programming, the underlying message of advertising, that self-realization is achieved through consumption, is an almost unchallengeable cultural assumption." For the contention that advertising control undermines the quality, quantity, and diversity of programming, see Christopher S. Yoo, *Architectural Censorship and the FCC*, 78 S. Cal. L. Rev. 669 (2005).

5. ***Candidate debates on public television.*** A third party candidate was excluded from a debate sponsored by a public television station on the ground that he had little popular support. He claimed a right of access.

ARKANSAS EDUCATIONAL TELEVISION COMM'N v. FORBES, 523 U.S. 666 (1998), concluded that a candidate debate sponsored by a state-owned public television broadcaster was a nonpublic forum subject to constitutional restraints (because the views expressed were those of the candidates, not the broadcaster and because of the importance of such debates to the political process), but that the broadcaster's decision to exclude a candidate was reasonable: "We conclude that, unlike most other public television programs,

---

[326] *Syracuse Peace Council v. FCC,* 867 F.2d 654 (D.C.Cir.1989), affirmed the FCC's determination that the fairness doctrine no longer serves the public interest without reaching constitutional issues. On June 20, 1987, President had vetoed congressional legislation designed to preserve the fairness doctrine on the ground that the legislation was unconstitutional. *Radio-Television News Directors Assoc. v. FCC,* 229 F.3d 269 (D.C.Cir.2000), ordered the FCC to vacate the personal attack rules with the understanding that the rules might be reinstituted if the Commission conducted a new rule-making proceeding to determine whether the public interest, consistent with the First Amendment, required them.

the candidate debate was subject to constitutional constraints applicable to nonpublic fora under our forum precedents. Even so, the broadcaster's decision to exclude the candidate was a reasonable, viewpoint-neutral exercise of journalistic discretion."

Consider Frederick Schauer, *Principles, Institutions, and the First Amendment*, 112 Harv. L. Rev. 84 (1998): "Beyond designated public forums, [it] is hard to see the point of forum analysis in government enterprise cases. In the typical case, the complaint is not about access, but about discriminatory treatment. And at the heart of this issue is the seemingly banal but quite important point that content-based discriminatory treatment is appropriate in some contexts, but not in others. Yet once we recognize this idea, the point of combining the determination of which contexts permit content discrimination and which do not with public forum analysis is elusive. If access is mandatory, then the focus on content discrimination is redundant. But if access is not mandatory, then the existence (or not) of a public forum is superfluous. What is not superfluous is the question whether this is one of the government enterprises which may control for content or viewpoint, and as to this question public forum doctrine offers no assistance.[327] [That] forum analysis plays no role at all in *Finley*, and that the conclusory distinction between a nonpublic forum and a non-forum does all of the work in *Forbes*, serves only to underscore the point."

Should the exclusion of Forbes have been invalidated on the ground that the exclusion skews public debate? Should the state's purpose matter? Consider Jamin B. Raskin, *Disfavored Speech About Favored Rights: Hill v. Colorado, The Vanishing Public Forum and the Need For an Objective Speech Discrimination Test*, 51 Am. U. L. Rev. 179 (2001): "[T]he Court found that the exclusion of the Independent candidate from a televised, government-run election debate was not viewpoint discriminatory because it was not based on officially expressed animosity towards his views. But the whole purpose and function of excluding an Independent is to block off a political viewpoint based on its perceived unpopularity." See also Owen Fiss, *The Censorship of Television*, 93 Nw.U.L.Rev. 1215 (1999). Consider the test proposed in Tim Cramm, *The Designated Nonpublic Forum: Remedying the Forbes Mistake*, 67 Alb. L. Rev. 89 (2003): "Where the public has a separate and independent interest in the forum being accessible to the broadest possible class of potential speakers, and that interest is at least as strong as the governmental interest in regulating the forum by excluding speakers, the forum is a designated nonpublic forum. Conversely, where the public's interest is less than the government's interest, the forum is a nonpublic forum akin to those discussed in *Cornelius* and *Perry*."

Suppose Congress required state owned broadcast stations to admit all official candidates to televised debates. Constitutional?

---

[327] But see Anthony E. Varona, *Out of Thin Air: Using First Amendment Public Forum Analysis to Redeem American Public Broadcasting Regulation*, 39 U. Mich. J.L. Reform 149 (2006).

Did the public broadcast station have First Amendment rights? Consider Randall P. Bezanson & William G. Buss, *The Many Faces of Government Speech*, 86 Iowa L. Rev. 1377 (2001): "*Forbes* may be the first decision in which the government's role as a speaker with a claim to First Amendment freedom has been expressly acknowledged other than by dicta. [V]irtually every regulatory act of government could be transformed into an act of government expression, and then sheltered from attack under the shield of the First Amendment. For example, one might argue that government's decisions about candidate access to the ballot are, in reality, editorial judgments protected under the First Amendment, for they result in specific content being included or excluded from a printed ballot, a communicative artifact of the government's making. Is it clear that deciding which names will appear on a ballot is any different, for analytical purposes, from deciding which candidates will appear on the program of a government-sponsored debate?"

6.　　Consider Henry Geller, *The Transformation of Television News: Articles and Comments: Fairness and the Public Trustee Concept: Time to Move On,* 47 Fed.Com.L.J. 79 (1994): "It makes no sense to try to impose effective, behavioral regulation [when] conventional television faces such fierce and increasing competition, and viewership is declining rather than growing. It would be much sounder to truly deregulate broadcasting by eliminating the public trustee requirement and in its place substituting a reasonable spectrum fee imposed on existing stations (and an auction for all new frequency assignments), with the sums so obtained dedicated to public telecommunications. [For] the first time, we would have a structure that works to accomplish explicit policy goals. The commercial system would continue to do what it already does—deliver a great variety of entertainment and news-type programs. The noncommercial system would have the funds to accomplish its goals—to supply needed public service such as educational programming for children, cultural fare, minority presentations, and in-depth informational programs."

7.　　***Cable television.*** Can government require cable operators to grant an access channel for the public, for the government, and for educational institutions? Which is the better analogy: *Red Lion* or *Miami Herald?* Need government lease space or otherwise afford access to utility poles under its control (and grant rights of way) to all competing cable companies? Is the appropriate analogy to *Schneider? Perry? Vincent? Red Lion? Miami Herald?*

LOS ANGELES v. PREFERRED COMMUNICATIONS, INC., 476 U.S. 488 (1986), per REHNQUIST, J., upheld the refusal to dismiss a complaint brought by a cable company demanding access to a city's utility poles and asserting a right to be free of government-mandated channels: "Cable television partakes of some of the aspects of speech and the communication of ideas as do the traditional enterprises of newspapers and [book publishers]. Respondent's proposed activities would seem to implicate First Amendment interests as do the activities of wireless broadcasters, which were found to fall within the ambit of the First Amendment in [*Red Lion*]. Of course, ['Even] protected speech is not equally permissible in all places and at all times.'

Cornelius. Moreover, where speech and conduct are joined in a single course of action, the First Amendment values must be balanced against competing societal interests. See, e.g., *Los Angeles City Council v. Taxpayers for Vincent; O'Brien.*" The Court postponed fuller discussion of any cable rights until a factual record had been developed.[328]

The Cable Television and Consumer Protection and Competition Act of 1992 required cable television systems to devote a portion of their channels to local broadcasters including commercial stations and public broadcast stations.[329] Congress was concerned about the monopolistic character of cable operations in most localities and the economic incentives for cable operators to favor their own programming. It also pointed to the importance of maintaining local broadcasting.

TURNER BROADCASTING SYSTEM, INC. v. FCC, 512 U.S. 622 (1994) (TURNER I), per KENNEDY, J., joined by Rehnquist, C.J., and Blackmun and Souter, JJ., upheld the requirement so long as the Government could demonstrate on remand that in the absence of legislation, a large number of broadcast stations would not be carried or would be adversely repositioned, that such stations would be at serious risk of financial difficulty, that the cable operators' programming selections (as opposed to using unused channel capacity) would not be excessively affected, and that no less restrictive alternative means existed. The plurality, joined by Stevens, J., argued that the antitrust interests of government were content neutral, but concluded that "some measure of heightened First Amendment scrutiny" was appropriate because the act was not a generally applicable law but directed at cable operators: "The scope and operation of the challenged provisions make clear [that] Congress designed the must-carry provisions not to promote speech of a particular content, but to prevent cable operators from exploiting their economic power to the detriment of broadcasters, and thereby to ensure that all Americans, especially those unable to subscribe to cable, have access to free television programming—whatever its content."[330]

---

[328] For discussion, see Daniel Brenner, *Cable Television and the Freedom of Expression*, 1988 Duke L.J. 329. See also Powe, supra, at 216–47; David Saylor, *Municipal Ripoff: The Unconstitutionality of Cable Television Franchise Fees and Access Support Payments*, 35 Cath.U.L.Rev. 671 (1986); Ithiel de Sola Pool, *Technologies of Freedom* 151–88 (1983); Monroe Price, *Taming Red Lion: The First Amendment and Structural Approaches to Media Regulation*, 31 Fed.Comm.L.J. 215 (1979); Comment, *Access to Cable Television: A Critique of the Affirmative Duty Theory of the First Amendment*, 70 Calif.L.Rev. 1393 (1982). For discussion of other technologies, see Special Issue, *Videotex*, 36 Fed.Comm.L.J. 119 (1984). Monroe Price, *Free Expression and Digital Dreams: The Open and Closed Terrain of Speech*, 22 Critical Inquiry 64 (1995).

[329] It also required that they be placed in the same numerical position as when broadcast over the air.

[330] Blackmun, J., concurring, emphasized the importance of deferring to Congress during the new proceedings. Stevens, J., concurring, reluctantly joined the order to remand; he would have

O'CONNOR, J., joined by Scalia, Thomas and Ginsburg, JJ., concurring and dissenting in part, would have held the requirements unconstitutional without a remand. They argued that strict scrutiny was appropriate because the preference for broadcasters over cable programmers on many channels was based on content (referring to findings about local public affairs programming and public television).[331] Although the interest in public affairs programming was said to be weighty, O'Connor, J., observed that public affairs cable-programming could be displaced: "In the rare circumstances where the government may draw content-based distinctions to serve its goals, the restrictions must serve the goals a good deal more precisely than this." O'Connor, J., also argued that the requirements should fail content neutral scrutiny as well because the act disadvantaged cable operators with no anti-competitive motives and favored broadcasters who could financially survive even if dropped from a cable system.[332]

NOTES AND QUESTIONS

1. *Permissible content regulation.* Has the United States "consistently and properly engaged in content-motivated structuring of the communications realm" in ways that have usually "benefited the nation"? See C. Edwin Baker, *Turner Broadcasting: Content-Based Regulation of Persons and Presses,* 1994 Sup.Ct.Rev. 57. See also Marvin Ammori, *Beyond Content Neutrality,* 61 Fed. Comm. L.J. 273 (2009). Does the dissent's emphasis on content discrimination slight the government's interest in assuring a robust communications system? Would such an emphasis lead to the conclusion that commercial broadcasters deserved no preference but public broadcasters did? Consider Donald Hawthorne & Monroe Price, *Rewiring the First Amendment: Meaning, Content and Public Broadcasting,* 12 Cardozo Arts & Ent.L.J. 499 (1994): "If the absence of a meaningful content basis for preferring commercial broadcasters should impair their entitlement to 'must-carry' treatment, precisely the converse is true for noncommercial broadcasters. These entities have been mandated to carry on government's historic responsibility to educate the citizenry and more recent undertaking to subsidize the arts."[333]

---

preferred to affirm the must-carry legislation without further proceedings. Ginsburg, J., concurred in parts of the Court's opinion (including the section arguing for intermediate First Amendment scrutiny regarding the antitrust interest), filed a separate concurring opinion, and joined O'Connor, J's opinion.

[331] Kennedy, J., argued that such findings showed "nothing more than the recognition that the services provided by broadcast television have some intrinsic value and, thus, are worth preserving against the threats posed by cable."

[332] Thomas, J., did not join this section of the opinion.

[333] For additional commentary, see Cass R. Sunstein, *One Case at a Time* 172–82 (1999); Glen O. Robinson, *The Electronic First Amendment: An Essay for the New Age,* 47 Duke L.J. 899 (1998); Jerome Barron, *Reading Turner through a Tornillo Lens,* 13 Comm. Lawyer (1995); Monroe Price & Donald Hawthorne, *Saving Public Television,* Hast.Comm./Ent.L.J. 65 (1994); Cass Sunstein, *The First Amendment in Cyberspace,* 104 Yale L.J. 1757 (1995); Mark Tushnet, *Weak Form Judicial Review and "Core" Civil Liberties,* 41 Harv. C.R.-C.L. L.Rev. 1 (2006); R. George Wright, *Content-Based and Content-Neutral Regulation of Speech: The Limitations of a Common Distinction,* 60 U. Miami L.Rev. 333 (2006).

Given the steep decline in international news coverage and the need for more international news in an increasingly interdependent globalized setting, could government require that broadcasters set a particular amount of time for international and global issues? Lee C. Bollinger, *Uninhibited, Robust, and Wide-Open* 129 (2010). Cable operators?

2. ***Compelled speech?*** Consider C. Edwin Baker, *First Amendment Limits on Copyright*, 55 Vand. L. Rev. 938 (2002): "[T]he Court's apparent contradictory holdings in *Barnette*, Sec. 9, 1 infra, and *Turner I* got it right in both cases. Compulsion (or prohibition) is impermissible as to the individual's freedom of speech (*Barnette*) but sometimes permissible as a means to improve the overall communications environment in relation to a free press (*Turner I*). Since the cases involved no censorship, the Court could approve compelled speech in the press context that would improperly impinge on individual liberty in the speech context."

3. ***The digital revolution.*** Consider Neil Weinstock Netanel, *New Media in Old Bottles?*, 76 Geo. Wash. L.Rev. 952 (2008): "The bulk of scholarly and activist attention among those who sympathize with Barron's [fn. 310 in *Miami Herald*] egalitarian vision of the First Amendment has moved from how to regulate mass media to promote expressive diversity to how to assure that individual speakers and new media have access to the conduits of digital communication." Consider Jack M. Balkin, *Digital Speech and Democratic Culture: A Theory of Freedom of Expression for the Information Society*, 79 N.Y.U. L. REV. 20 (2004): "The digital revolution has undermined one of the traditional justifications for structural regulation of the mass media—scarcity of bandwidth. Cable can accommodate hundreds of channels, as can satellite broadcasting. The number of speakers on the Internet seems limitless. Broadcast media now compete with cable, satellite, and the Internet for viewer attention. In theory, at least, digital technologies offer everyone the potential to become broadcasters." See also Yoo, Note 4 after *CBS*; Michael J. Burstein, *Towards a New Standard for First Amendment Review of Structural Media Regulation*, 79 N.Y.U. L. Rev. 1030 (2004). And consider Randall P. Bezanson and William G. Buss, *The Many Faces of Government Speech*, 86 Iowa L. Rev. 1377 (2001): "With the scarcity rationale no longer available, and with the shelter of *FCC v. Pacifica Foundation* unavailing because the scope of government editorial discretion extended beyond the obscene and beyond material considered indecent for children, the Court rested its decision explicitly on the cable medium and its influence. 'Cable television systems, including access channels, "have established a uniquely pervasive presence in the lives of all Americans." ' [T]he logic of the Court's attitude toward cable strongly suggests the conclusion that pervasiveness and intrusiveness mask concerns about the power of the medium in shaping personal and cultural values, the persuasiveness of its multi-sensory and real-time character, and the added dimensions of force and immediacy that unrestricted access to multi-sensory stimuli provides."

4. After remand, TURNER BROADCASTING SYSTEM, INC. v. FCC, 520 U.S. 180 (1997) (TURNER II), per KENNEDY, J., joined by Rehnquist, C.J.,

Stevens, and Souter, JJ., upheld the must-carry provisions. Applying the *O'Brien* test, he emphasized the importance of deferring to Congress so long as it had "drawn reasonable inferences based upon substantial evidence." He found that the legislation was narrowly tailored to preserve the benefits of local broadcast television, to promote widespread dissemination of information from a multiplicity of sources, and to promote fair competition.

BREYER, J., concurring, joined Kennedy, J.'s opinion except for his discussion and conclusion regarding the fair competition rationale:[334] "Whether or not the statute does or does not sensibly compensate for some significant market defect, it undoubtedly seeks to provide over-the-air viewers who *lack* cable with a rich mix of over-the-air programming by guaranteeing the over-the-air stations that provide such programming with the extra dollars that an additional cable audience will generate. I believe that this purpose-to assure the over-the-air public 'access to a multiplicity of information sources,' provides sufficient basis for rejecting appellants' First Amendment claim.

"I do not deny that the compulsory carriage that creates the 'guarantee' extracts a serious First Amendment price. It interferes with the protected interests of the cable operators to choose their own programming; it prevents displaced cable program providers from obtaining an audience; and it will sometimes prevent some cable viewers from watching what, in its absence, would have been their preferred set of programs. This 'price' amounts to a 'suppression of speech.' "

Breyer, J., observed that a cable system, physically dependent upon the availability of space along city streets, at present (perhaps less in the future) typically faces little competition, that it therefore constitutes a kind of bottleneck that controls the range of viewer choice (whether or not it uses any consequent economic power for economically predatory purposes), and that *some* degree-at least a limited degree of governmental intervention and control through regulation can prove appropriate when justified under *O'Brien* (at least when not 'content based'). Cf. *Red Lion*. Breyer, J., concluded that the statute survived " 'intermediate scrutiny,' whether or not the statute [was] properly tailored to Congress' purely economic objectives."

O'CONNOR, J., joined by Scalia, Thomas, and Ginsburg, JJ., dissenting, argued again that strict scrutiny should apply, agreed that deference was owed to Congress "in its predictive judgments and its evaluation of complex economic questions," but maintained that even under intermediate scrutiny, the Court had an independent duty to examine with care the Congressional interests, the findings, and the fit between the goals and consequences. She criticized the Court for being too deferential even on the assumption that the legislation was content neutral. On her analysis, the record did not support either the

---

[334] Stevens, J., also filed a concurring opinion.

conclusion that cable posed a significant threat to local broadcast markets or that the act was narrowly tailored to deal with anti-competitive conduct.[335]

Consider Owen M. Fiss, *The Censorship of Television,* in *Eternally Vigilant: Free Speech in the Modern Era* 275 (Lee C. Bollinger & Geoffrey R. Stone eds., 2002): "Breyer's entire approach represents a revitalization of *Red Lion,* and his discussion of the economic power of cable operators allows the principle of that case to transcend the specific technological context in which it was born."

———

II. THE ELECTRONIC MEDIA AND CONTENT REGULATION

FCC v. PACIFICA FOUNDATION
438 U.S. 726, 98 S.Ct. 3026, 57 L.Ed.2d 1073 (1978).

JUSTICE STEVENS delivered the opinion of the Court (Parts I, II, III, and IV–C) and an opinion in which CHIEF JUSTICE BURGER and JUSTICE REHNQUIST joined (Parts IV–A and IV–B).

[In an early afternoon weekday broadcast which was devoted that day to contemporary attitudes toward the use of language, respondent's New York radio station aired a 12-minute selection called "Filthy Words," from a comedy album by a satiric humorist, George Carlin. The monologue, which had evoked frequent laughter from a live theater audience, began by referring to Carlin's thought about the seven words you can't say on the public airwaves, "the ones you definitely wouldn't say ever." He then listed the words ("shit," "piss," "fuck," "motherfucker," "cocksucker," "cunt," and "tits"), "the ones that will curve your spine, grow hair on your hands and (laughter) maybe, even bring us, God help us, peace without honor (laughter) um, and a bourbon (laughter)," and repeated them over and over in a variety of colloquialisms. Immediately prior to the monologue, listeners were advised that it included sensitive language which some might regard as offensive. Those who might be offended were advised to change the station and return in fifteen minutes.

[The FCC received a complaint from a man stating that while driving in his car with his young son he had heard the broadcast of the Carlin monologue. The FCC issued an order to be "associated with the station's license file, and in the event that subsequent complaints are received, the

---

[335] Would *Turner* justify the application of "must carry" rules to segments of the Internet? See also Cass Sunstein, *republic.com* (2001); Andrew Chin, *Making the World Wide Web Safe for Democracy: A Medium-Specific First Amendment Analysis,* 19 Hast. Comm/Ent L.J. 309 (1997).

Commission will then decide whether it should utilize any of the available sanctions it has been granted by Congress."]336

The Commission characterized the language used in the Carlin monologue as "patently offensive," though not necessarily obscene, and expressed the opinion that it should be regulated by principles analogous to those found in the law of nuisance where the "law generally speaks to *channeling* behavior more than actually prohibiting [it]."5

Applying these considerations to the language used in the monologue as broadcast by respondent, the Commission concluded that certain words depicted sexual and excretory activities in a patently offensive manner, noted that they "were broadcast at a time when children were undoubtedly in the audience (i.e., in the early afternoon)," and that the prerecorded language, with these offensive words "repeated over and over," was "deliberately broadcast." In summary, the Commission stated: "We therefore hold that the language as broadcast was indecent [under 18 U.S.C. 1464]."

IV. Pacifica [argues] that the Commission's construction of the statutory language broadly encompasses so much constitutionally protected speech that reversal is required even if Pacifica's broadcast of the "Filthy Words" monologue is not itself protected by the First Amendment. * * *

A. The first argument fails because our review is limited to the question whether the Commission has the authority to proscribe this particular broadcast. As the Commission itself emphasized, its order was "issued in a specific factual context." That approach is appropriate for courts as well as the Commission when regulation of indecency is at stake, for indecency is largely a function of context—it cannot be adequately judged in the abstract. * * *

It is true that the Commission's order may lead some broadcasters to censor themselves. At most, however, the Commission's definition of indecency will deter only the broadcasting of patently offensive references to excretory and sexual organs and activities.18 While some of these references may be protected, they surely lie at the periphery of First Amendment concern. * * * Invalidating any rule on the basis of its

---

336 The FCC's action is placed in the context of other similar actions in Lucas Powe, Note 6 after *Red Lion* 162–90. See Christine A. Corcos, *George Carlin, Constitutional Law Scholar,* 39 Stet. L.Rev. 899 (2008).

5 **[Ct's Note]** Thus, the Commission suggested, if an offensive broadcast had literary, artistic, political or scientific value, and were preceded by warnings, it might not be indecent in the late evening, but would be so during the day, when children are in the audience.

18 **[Ct's Note]** A requirement that indecent language be avoided will have its primary effect on the form, rather than the content, of serious communication. There are few, if any, thoughts that cannot be expressed by the use of less offensive language. [*FCC v. Fox Television Stations, Inc.*, 129 S.Ct. 1800 (2009), per Scalia, J., observed that "any chilled references to excretory and sexual material surely lie at the periphery of First Amendment concern.' "].

hypothetical application to situations not before the Court is "strong medicine" to be applied "sparingly and only as a last resort." *Broadrick* [Sec. I, 5 supra]. We decline to administer that medicine to preserve the vigor of patently offensive sexual and excretory speech.

B.   [The] words of the Carlin monologue are unquestionably "speech" within the meaning of the First Amendment. [The] question in this case is whether a broadcast of patently offensive words dealing with sex and excretion may be regulated because of its content.[20] Obscene materials have been denied the protection of the First Amendment because their content is so offensive to contemporary moral standards. *Roth*. But the fact that society may find speech offensive is not a sufficient reason for suppressing it. Indeed, if it is the speaker's opinion that gives offense, that consequence is a reason for according it constitutional protection. For it is a central tenet of the First Amendment that the government must remain neutral in the marketplace of ideas. If there were any reason to believe that the Commission's characterization of the Carlin monologue as offensive could be traced to its political content—or even to the fact that it satirized contemporary attitudes about four letter words[22]—First Amendment protection might be required. But that is simply not this case. These words offend for the same reasons that obscenity offends. Their place in the hierarchy of First Amendment values was aptly sketched by Justice Murphy when he said, "such utterances are no essential part of any exposition of ideas, and are of such slight social value as a step to truth that any benefit that may be derived from them is clearly outweighed by the social interest in order and morality." *Chaplinsky.*

Although these words ordinarily lack literary, political, or scientific value, they are not entirely outside the protection of the First Amendment. Some uses of even the most offensive words are unquestionably protected. Indeed, we may assume, arguendo, that this monologue would be protected in other contexts. [It] is a characteristic of speech such as this that both its capacity to offend and its "social value," to use Justice Murphy's term, vary with the circumstances. Words that are commonplace in one setting are shocking in another. To paraphrase Justice Harlan, one occasion's lyric is another's vulgarity. Cf. *Cohen v. California.*[25]

---

[20] **[Ct's Note]** Although neither Justice Powell nor Justice Brennan directly confronts this question, both have answered it affirmatively, the latter explicitly, at fn. 3, infra, and the former implicitly by concurring in a judgment that could not otherwise stand.

[22] **[Ct's Note]** The monologue does present a point of view; it attempts to show that the words it uses are "harmless" and that our attitudes toward them are "essentially silly." The Commission objects, not to this point of view, but to the way in which it is expressed. The belief that these words are harmless does not necessarily confer a First Amendment privilege to use them while proselytizing just as the conviction that obscenity is harmless does not license one to communicate that conviction by the indiscriminate distribution of an obscene leaflet.

[25] **[Ct's Note]** The importance of context is illustrated by the *Cohen* case. [So] far as the evidence showed no one in the courthouse was offended by [Cohen's jacket.]

In this case it is undisputed that the content of Pacifica's broadcast was "vulgar," "offensive," and "shocking." Because content of that character is not entitled to absolute constitutional protection under all circumstances, we must consider its context in order to determine whether the Commission's action was constitutionally permissible.

C. We have long recognized that each medium of expression presents special First Amendment problems. And of all forms of communication, it is broadcasting that has received the most limited First Amendment [protection.]

The reasons for these distinctions are complex, but two have relevance to the present case. First, the broadcast media have established a uniquely pervasive presence in the lives of all Americans. Patently offensive, indecent material presented over the airwaves confronts the citizen, not only in public, but also in the privacy of the home, where the individual's right to be let alone plainly outweighs the First Amendment rights of an intruder. *Rowan v. Post Office Dept.*, 397 U.S. 728. Because the broadcast audience is constantly tuning in and out, prior warnings cannot completely protect the listener or viewer from unexpected program content. To say that one may avoid further offense by turning off the radio when he hears indecent language is like saying that the remedy for an assault is to run away after the first blow.[27] * * *

Second, broadcasting is uniquely accessible to children, even those too young to read. Although Cohen's written message might have been incomprehensible to a first grader, Pacifica's broadcast could have enlarged a child's vocabulary in an instant. Other forms of offensive expression may be withheld from the young without restricting the expression at its source. Bookstores and motion picture theaters, for example, may be prohibited from making indecent material available to children. We held in *Ginsberg* [Sec. 1, III, B supra] that the government's interest in the "well being of its youth" and in supporting "parents' claim to authority in their own household" justified the regulation of otherwise protected expression.[28] * * *

In holding that criminal sanctions could not be imposed on Cohen for his political statement in a public place, the Court rejected the argument that his speech would offend unwilling viewers; it noted that "there was no evidence that persons powerless to avoid [his] conduct did in fact object to it." In contrast, in this case the Commission was responding to a listener's strenuous complaint, and Pacifica does not question its determination that this afternoon broadcast was likely to offend listeners. It should be noted that the Commission imposed a far more moderate penalty on Pacifica than the state court imposed on Cohen. Even the strongest civil penalty at the Commission's command does not include criminal prosecution.

[27] **[Ct's Note]** Outside the home, the balance between the offensive speaker and the unwilling audience may sometimes tip in favor of the speaker, requiring the offended listener to turn away. See *Erznoznik.* * * *

[28] **[Ct's Note]** The Commission's action does not by any means reduce adults to hearing only what is fit for children. Cf. *Butler v. Michigan* [Sec. 1, III, B supra]. Adults who feel the need may purchase tapes and records or go to theatres and nightclubs to hear these words. In fact, the Commission has not unequivocally closed even broadcasting to speech of this sort; whether

It is appropriate, in conclusion, to emphasize the narrowness of our holding. This case does not involve a two-way radio conversation between a cab driver and a dispatcher, or a telecast of an Elizabethan comedy. We have not decided that an occasional expletive in either setting would justify any sanction or, indeed, that this broadcast would justify a criminal prosecution. The Commission's decision rested entirely on a nuisance rationale under which context is all-important.

[R]eversed.

JUSTICE POWELL, with whom JUSTICE BLACKMUN joins, concurring.

[T]he language employed is, to most people, vulgar and offensive. It was chosen specifically for this quality, and it was repeated over and over as a sort of verbal shock treatment. [In] essence, the Commission sought to "channel" the monologue to hours when the fewest unsupervised children would be exposed to it. In my view, this consideration provides strong support for the Commission's holding.

[The] Commission properly held that the speech from which society may attempt to shield its children is not limited to that which appeals to the youthful prurient interest. The language involved in this case is as potentially degrading and harmful to children as representations of many erotic acts.

In most instances, the dissemination of this kind of speech to children may be limited without also limiting willing adults' access to it. Sellers of printed and recorded matter and exhibitors of motion pictures and live performances may be required to shut their doors to children, but such a requirement has no effect on adults' access. See *Ginsberg*. The difficulty is that [d]uring most of the broadcast hours, both adults and unsupervised children are likely to be in the broadcast audience, and the broadcaster cannot reach willing adults without also reaching children. This, as the Court emphasizes, is one of the distinctions between the broadcast and other media to which we often have adverted as justifying a different treatment of the broadcast media for First Amendment purposes. In my view, the Commission was entitled to give substantial weight to this difference in reaching its decision in this case.

[Another difference] is that broadcasting—unlike most other forms of communication—comes directly into the home, the one place where people ordinarily have the right not to be assaulted by uninvited and offensive sights and sounds. *Erznoznik; Cohen; Rowan.* * * * "That we are often 'captives' outside the sanctuary of the home and subject to objectionable

___

broadcast audiences in the late evening contain so few children that playing this monologue would be permissible is an issue neither the Commission nor this Court has decided. [Would the rationale based on supporting parental authority rule out banning Carlin's monologue in the early evening? See Baker, *The Evening Hours During Pacifica Standard Time,* 3 Vill. Sports & Ent. L.J. 45 (1996)].

speech and other sound does not mean we must be captives everywhere." *Rowan.* The Commission also was entitled to give this factor appropriate weight in the circumstances of the instant case. This is not to say, however, that the Commission has an unrestricted license to decide what speech, protected in other media, may be banned from the airwaves in order to protect unwilling adults from momentary exposure to it in their homes.[2] * * *

[M]y views are generally in accord with what is said in Part IV(C) of opinion. I therefore join that portion of his opinion. I do not join Part IV(B), however, because I do not subscribe to the theory that the Justices of this Court are free generally to decide on the basis of its content which speech protected by the First Amendment is most "valuable" and hence deserving of the most protection, and which is less "valuable" and hence deserving of less protection.[3] In my view, the result in this case does not turn on whether Carlin's monologue, viewed as a whole, or the words that comprise it, have more or less "value" than a candidate's campaign speech. This is a judgment for each person to make, not one for the judges to impose upon him.[4]

The result turns instead on the unique characteristics of the broadcast media, combined with society's right to protect its children from speech generally agreed to be inappropriate for their years, and with the interest of unwilling adults in not being assaulted by such offensive speech in their homes. Moreover, I doubt whether today's decision will prevent any adult who wishes to receive Carlin's message in Carlin's own words from doing so, and from making for himself a value judgment as to the merit of the message and words. These are the grounds upon which I join the judgment of the Court as to Part IV.

JUSTICE BRENNAN, with whom JUSTICE MARSHALL joins, dissenting.

---

[2] **[Ct's Note]** It is true that the radio listener quickly may tune out speech that is offensive to him. In addition, broadcasters may preface potentially offensive programs with warnings. But such warnings do not help the unsuspecting listener who tunes in at the middle of a program. In this respect, too, broadcasting appears to differ from books and records, which may carry warnings on their faces, and from motion pictures and live performances, which may carry warnings on their marquees.

[3] **[Ct's Note]** The Court has, however, created a limited exception to this rule in order to bring commercial speech within the protection of the First Amendment. See *Ohralik* [Sec. 3, II supra].

[4] **[Ct's Note]** For much the same reason, I also do not join Part IV(A). I had not thought that the application vel non of overbreadth analysis should depend on the Court's judgment as to the value of the protected speech that might be deterred. Except in the context of commercial speech, see *Bates* [Sec. 3, II supra], it has not in the past. See, e.g., *Lewis v. New Orleans; Gooding.*

As Justice Stevens points out, however, the Commission's order was limited to the facts of this case; "it did not purport to engage in formal rulemaking or in the promulgation of any regulations." In addition, since the Commission may be expected to proceed cautiously, as it has in the past, I do not foresee an undue "chilling" effect on broadcasters' exercise of their rights. I agree, therefore, that respondent's overbreadth challenge is meritless.

[T]he Court refuses to embrace the notion, completely antithetical to basic First Amendment values, that the degree of protection the First Amendment affords protected speech varies with the social value ascribed to that speech by five Members of this Court. See opinion of Justice Powell. Moreover, [all] Members of the Court agree that [the monologue] does not fall within one of the categories of speech, such as "fighting words," or obscenity, that is totally without First Amendment protection. [Yet] a majority of the Court[1] nevertheless finds that, on the facts of this case, the FCC is not constitutionally barred from imposing sanctions on Pacifica for its airing of the Carlin monologue. * * *

[A]n individual's actions in switching on and listening to communications transmitted over the public airways and directed to the public at-large do not implicate fundamental privacy interests, even when engaged in within the home. Instead, because the radio is undeniably a public medium, these actions are more properly viewed as a decision to take part, if only as a listener, in an ongoing public discourse. Although an individual's decision to allow public radio communications into his home undoubtedly does not abrogate all of his privacy interests, the residual privacy interests he retains vis-à-vis the communication he voluntarily admits into his home are surely no greater than those of the people present in the corridor of the Los Angeles courthouse in [Cohen].

Even if an individual who voluntarily opens his home to radio communications retains privacy interests of sufficient moment to justify a ban on protected speech if those interests are "invaded in an essentially intolerable manner," Cohen, the very fact that those interests are threatened only by a radio broadcast precludes any intolerable invasion of privacy; for unlike other intrusive modes of communication, such as sound trucks, "[t]he radio can be turned off"—and with a minimum of effort. [Whatever] the minimal discomfort suffered by a listener who inadvertently tunes into a program he finds offensive during the brief interval before he can simply extend his arm and switch stations or flick the "off" button, it is surely worth the candle to preserve the broadcaster's right to send, and the right of those interested to receive, a message entitled to full First Amendment protection. * * *

The Court's balance, of necessity, fails to accord proper weight to the interests of listeners who wish to hear broadcasts the FCC deems offensive. It permits majoritarian tastes completely to preclude a protected message from entering the homes of a receptive, unoffended minority. No decision of this Court supports such a result. Where the individuals comprising the offended majority may freely choose to reject the material being offered, we have never found their privacy interests of such moment to warrant the

---

[1] **[Ct's Note]** Where I refer without differentiation to the actions of "the Court," my reference is to this majority, which consists of my Brothers Powell and Stevens and those Members of the Court joining their separate opinions.

suppression of speech on privacy grounds. [In] *Rowan,* the Court upheld a statute, permitting householders to require that mail advertisers stop sending them lewd or offensive materials and remove their names from mailing lists. Unlike the situation here, householders who wished to receive the sender's communications were not prevented from doing so. Equally important, the determination of offensiveness vel non under the statute involved in *Rowan* was completely within the hands of the individual householder; no governmental evaluation of the worth of the mail's content stood between the mailer and the householder. In contrast, the visage of the censor is all too discernable here. * * *

Because the Carlin monologue is obviously not an erotic appeal to the prurient interests of children, the Court, for the first time, allows the government to prevent minors from gaining access to materials that are not obscene, and are therefore protected, as to them.[2] It thus ignores our recent admonition that "[s]peech that is neither obscene as to youths nor subject to some other legitimate proscription cannot be suppressed solely to protect the young from ideas or images that a legislative body thinks unsuitable for them." *Erznoznik.*[3] The Court's refusal to follow its own pronouncements is especially lamentable since it has the anomalous subsidiary effect, at least in the radio context at issue here, of making completely unavailable to adults material which may not constitutionally be kept even from children. * * * *Yoder* and *Pierce,* hold that parents, *not* the government, have the right to make certain decisions regarding the upbringing of their children. As surprising as it may be to individual Members of this Court, some parents may actually find Mr. Carlin's unabashed attitude towards the seven "dirty words" healthy, and deem it desirable to expose their children to the manner in which Mr. Carlin defuses the taboo surrounding the words. Such parents may constitute a minority of the American public, but the absence of great numbers willing to exercise the right to raise their children in this fashion does not alter the right's nature or its existence. Only the Court's regrettable decision does that.

---

[2]   **[Ct's Note]** Even if the monologue appealed to the prurient interest of minors, it would not be obscene as to them unless, as to them, "the work, taken as a whole, lacks serious literary, artistic, political, or scientific value." *Miller.*

[3]   **[Ct's Note]** It may be that a narrowly drawn regulation prohibiting the use of offensive language on broadcasts directed specifically at younger children constitutes one of the "other legitimate proscription[s]" alluded to in *Erznoznik.* This is so both because of the difficulties inherent in adapting the *Miller* formulation to communications received by young children, and because such children are "not possessed of that full capacity for individual choice which is the presupposition of the First Amendment guarantees." *Ginsberg.* (Stewart, J., concurring). I doubt, as my Brother Stevens suggests, that such a limited regulation amounts to a regulation of speech based on its content, since, by hypothesis, the only persons at whom the regulated communication is directed are incapable of evaluating its content. To the extent that such a regulation is viewed as a regulation based on content, it marks the outermost limits to which content regulation is permissible.

As demonstrated above, neither of the factors relied on by both [Powell and Stevens, JJ.]—the intrusive nature of radio and the presence of children in the listening audience—can, when taken on its own terms, support the FCC's disapproval of the Carlin monologue. [N]either of the opinions comprising the Court serve to clarify the extent to which the FCC may assert the privacy and children-in-the-audience rationales as justification for expunging from the airways protected communications the Commission finds offensive. Taken to their logical extreme, these rationales would support the cleansing of public radio of any "four-letter words" whatsoever, regardless of their context. The rationales could justify the banning from radio of a myriad of literary works, novels, poems, and plays by the likes of Shakespeare, Joyce, Hemingway, Ben Jonson, Henry Fielding, Robert Burns, and Chaucer; they could support the suppression of a good deal of political speech, such as the Nixon tapes; and they could even provide the basis for imposing sanctions for the broadcast of certain portions of the Bible.

In order to dispel the spectre of the possibility of so unpalatable a degree of censorship, and to defuse Pacifica's overbreadth challenge, the FCC insists that it desires only the authority to reprimand a broadcaster on facts analogous to those present in this case. [Powell and Stevens, JJ.] take the FCC at its word, and consequently do no more than permit the Commission to censor the afternoon broadcast of the "sort of verbal shock treatment" involved [here]. I would place the responsibility and the right to weed worthless and offensive communications from the public airways where it belongs and where, until today, it resided: in a public free to choose those communications worthy of its attention from a marketplace unsullied by the censor's hand. * * *

My Brother Stevens [finds] solace in his conviction that "[t]here are few, if any, thoughts that cannot be expressed by the use of less offensive language." The idea that the content of a message and its potential impact on any who might receive it can be divorced from the words that are the vehicle for its expression is transparently fallacious. A given word may have a unique capacity to capsule an idea, evoke an emotion, or conjure up an image. Indeed, for those of us who place an appropriately high value on our cherished First Amendment rights, the word "censor" is such a word. Justice Harlan, speaking for the Court, recognized the truism that a speaker's choice of words cannot surgically be separated from the ideas he desires to express when he warned that "we cannot indulge the facile assumption that one can forbid particular words without also running a substantial risk of suppressing ideas in the process."

[Stevens, J.] also finds relevant to his First Amendment analysis the fact that "[a]dults who feel the need may purchase tapes and records or go to theatres and nightclubs to hear [the tabooed] words." [Powell, J.,] agrees. [The] opinions of my Brethren display both a sad insensitivity to the fact that these alternatives involve the expenditure of money, time, and effort that many of those wishing to hear Mr. Carlin's message may not be able to afford, and a naive innocence of the reality that in many cases, the medium may well be the message.

The Court apparently believes that the FCC's actions here can be analogized to the zoning ordinances upheld in *American Mini Theatres*. For two reasons, it is wrong. First, the zoning ordinances found to pass constitutional muster [had] valid goals other than the channeling of protected speech. No such goals are present here. Second, [the] ordinances did not restrict the access of distributors or exhibitors to the market or impair the viewing public's access to the regulated material. Again, this is not the situation here.

[T]here runs throughout the opinions of my Brothers Powell and Stevens [a] depressing inability to appreciate that in our land of cultural pluralism, there are many who think, act, and talk differently from the Members of this Court, and who do not share their fragile sensibilities. It is only an acute ethnocentric myopia that enables the Court [to blink at] persons who do not share the Court's view as to which words or expressions are acceptable and who, for a variety of reasons, including a conscious desire to flout majoritarian conventions, express themselves using words that may be regarded as offensive by those from different socio-economic backgrounds.[8] In this context, the Court's decision may be seen for what, in the broader perspective, it really is: another of the dominant culture's inevitable efforts to force those groups who do not share its mores to conform to its way of thinking, acting, and speaking. * * *[337]

NOTES AND QUESTIONS

1.   Consider Steven H. Shiffrin, *The First Amendment, Democracy, and Romance* 80 (1990): "Most people with any First Amendment bones in their bodies are troubled by [*Pacifica*]. But the nub of the First Amendment insult has little to do with self-government or with the marketplace of ideas. The concern does not flow from a worry that voters will be deprived of valuable information. Concern that the truth about vulgar language might not emerge in the marketplace of ideas may be well placed, but is not a sufficient concern to explain the widespread outrage against the decision. Again, the decision is an affront to a notion of content neutrality, but there are many of those. The *Pacifica* case produces heat precisely because Carlin's speech is considered by

---

[8]   [Ct's Note] Under the approach taken by my Brother Powell, the availability of broadcasts *about* groups whose members comprise such audiences might also be affected. Both news broadcasts about activities involving these groups and public affairs broadcasts about their concerns are apt to contain interviews, statements, or remarks by group leaders and members which may contain offensive language to an extent my Brother Powell finds unacceptable.

[337] Stewart, J., joined by Brennan, White, and Marshall, JJ., dissenting maintained that the Commission lacked statutory authority to issue its order and did not reach the constitutional question.

many to be precisely what the First Amendment is *supposed* to protect. Carlin is attacking conventions; assaulting the prescribed orthodoxy; mocking the stuffed shirts; Carlin *is* the prototypical dissenter.

"It matters not at all whether the target of his invective is society at large or a public official. The outrage is that the stuffed shirts are in a position to silence Carlin, or at least in a position to keep him from 'offending' the mass audience."[338]

2. *Market failure and communitarian vision.* Does the market encourage programming that is inherently harmful to children? Does it lead broadcasters to pursue adult-driven ratings pushing the "boundaries of the existing indecency rules?" Does a communitarian vision of the public airwaves help to salvage the weaknesses of the scarcity argument for broadcast regulation? See Joshua B. Gordon, *Pacifica is Long Dead. Long Live Pacifica,* 79 S.Cal. L.Rev. 1451 (2006).

3. *Cohen distinguished?* Consider R. George Wright, *An Emotion-Based Approach to Freedom of Speech,* 34 Loy. U. Chi. L.J. 429 (2003): "*Cohen* emphasized that even slight changes in wording may change the emotive, if not the cognitive, message conveyed, and that there might be no fully adequate substitute available, in some contexts, for particular words. *Pacifica Foundation*, however, concluded that in an indecent radio broadcast case, requiring more decorous language tended chiefly to affect the form, as opposed to the content of the message, and that few indecently expressed thoughts were not expressible in more decorous language."

In distinguishing the facts of *Cohen,* for many years the FCC had interpreted *Pacifica* to require the dwelling upon or repeating at length descriptions of sexual or excretory organs or activities. In 2004 and 2006, however, the agency determined that fleeting expletives or partial nudity could meet the offensiveness requirement for an indecency finding. *FCC v. Fox Television Stations, Inc.* avoided confronting the question whether the fleeting expletives policy violated the First Amendment by holding that Fox, which had aired award shows in 2002 and 2003 in which Cher and Nicole Richie had used swear words and ABC, which had aired an NYPD Blue episode with 7 seconds of partial nudity, had not been afforded proper notice of the FCC policy. The Court, per Kennedy, J., concluded that the policy was unconstitutionally vague under the Due Process Clause with regard to these incidents and left its assessment of the policy as applied to those with adequate notice for another day.

4. *Implications for broadcasting.* Consider Thomas Krattenmaker & Lucas Powe, *Televised Violence: First Amendment Principles and Social Science Theory,* 64 Va.L.Rev. 1123 (1978): *Pacifica* "marks the first time any theory other than scarcity has received the official imprimatur of the Court. [S]carcity could not have authorized the result in *Pacifica* because regardless

---

[338] For an account of the censorship battles surrounding the colorful comic and critic Lenny Bruce, see Ronald K.L. Collins & David M. Skover, *The Trials of Lenny Bruce: The Fall and Rise of an American Icon* (2003).

of whether one thinks the incredible abundance of radio stations in the United States (and especially in New York City) is insufficient, scarcity supports adding voices not banning them." What is the significance of the Court's comment that "the broadcast media have established a uniquely pervasive presence in the lives of all Americans"? Consider Daniel Brenner, *Censoring the Airwaves: The Supreme Court's Pacifica Decision,* in Free But Regulated: Conflicting Traditions in Media Law 175 (1982): "[N]ewspapers, drive-in movies, direct mail advertisements and imprinted T-shirts are media that have also 'established a uniquely pervasive presence' in our lives, in and out of [home]. Offhand comments about broadcasting enjoying 'the most limited' First Amendment protection—What of comic books? Playing cards? Chinese cookie fortunes?—are not simply harmless baffle; they constitute Delphic pronouncements made at a watershed period in the development of electronic media." See also Powe, note 6 after *Miami Herald,* supra, at 210–11.

Is the Court suggesting that the broadcast media are uniquely powerful? If so, should that factor cut for or against government regulation?[339] Does *Pacifica* support regulation of sex and violence on television, of "offensive" commercials, of advertising directed toward children? See generally Matthew Spitzer, *Seven Dirty Words and Six Other Stories* (1986) (criticizing *Pacifica*'s distinctions between print and broadcast).

5.   FCC v. LEAGUE OF WOMEN VOTERS, 468 U.S. 364 (1984), per BRENNAN, J., invalidated a federal law prohibiting editorializing on public broadcast stations: "As our cases attest, [broadcast restrictions] have been upheld only when we were satisfied that the restriction is narrowly tailored to further a substantial governmental interest, such as ensuring adequate and balanced coverage of public issues.[13]"

6.   ***Public/Private.*** David Cole, *Playing by Pornography's Rules: The Regulation of Sexual Expression,* 143 U.Pa.L.Rev. 111 (1994); "The Court's sexual expression decisions can be organized along a similar public/private axis. The Court's zoning decisions allow communities to demand that when sexually explicit speech appears in public, it must be relegated to dark and distant parts of town. The Court's affirmation of the FCC's 'indecency' regulation permits the zoning of sexual speech to less 'public' times of day. And

---

[339] See Powe, supra, at 211–15; Lucas Powe, *"Or of the [Broadcast] Press,"* 55 Tex.L.Rev. 39 (1976). On the various justifications for broadcast regulation, see J.M. Balkin, *Media Filters, the V-Chip, and the Foundations of Broadcast Regulation,* 45 Duke L.J. 1131 (1996).

[13]   **[Ct's Note]** [*Pacifica*] is consistent with the approach taken in our other broadcast cases. There, the Court focused on certain physical characteristics of broadcasting—specifically, that the medium's uniquely pervasive presence renders impossible any prior warning for those listeners who may be offended by indecent language, and, second, that the case with which children may gain access to the medium, especially during daytime hours, creates a substantial risk that they may be exposed to such offensive expression without parental supervision. The governmental interest in reduction of those risks through Commission regulation of the timing and character of such "indecent broadcasting" was thought sufficiently substantial to outweigh the broadcaster's First Amendment interest in controlling the presentation of its programming. In this case, by contrast, we are faced not with indecent expression, but rather with expression that is at the core of First Amendment protections, and no claim is made by the Government that the expression of editorial opinion by noncommercial stations will create a substantial "nuisance" of the kind addressed in *Pacifica.*

while private possession of obscenity cannot be regulated, the state is free to regulate obscenity in a public place even if it is enjoyed only by consenting adults, and even where it is only being transported through public channels for private home use. What is immune from regulation in private becomes suppressible in public, even if the very same speakers, listeners, and speech are involved."

7. ***Anti-abortion advertising.*** Is graphic anti-abortion advertising indecent? Should it be channeled to the late evening hours? From the perspective of Stevens, J.? Powell, J.? See Lili Levi, *The FCC, Indecency, and Anti-Abortion Political Advertising,* 3 Vill.Spts. & Ent.L.J. 85 (1996).

8. ***Other media.*** (a) ***Telephonic "indecency" compared.*** SABLE COMMUNICATIONS v. FCC, 492 U.S. 115 (1989), per WHITE, J., unanimously invalidated a congressional ban on "indecent" interstate commercial telephone messages, i.e., "dial-a-porn."[340] The Court thought *Pacifica* was "readily distinguishable from this case, most obviously because it did not involve a total ban on broadcasting indecent material. [Second,] there is no 'captive audience' problem here; callers will generally not be unwilling listeners. [Third,] the congressional record contains no legislative findings that would justify us in concluding that there is no constitutionally acceptable less restrictive means, short of a total ban, to achieve the Government's interest in protecting minors."

(b) ***Internet "indecency" compared.*** Two provisions of the Communications Decency Act ("CDA") sought to protect minors from indecent or patently offensive material on the Internet. 47 U.S.C. § 223(a) prohibited the knowing transmission of indecent messages to any recipient under 18 years of age. 47 U.S.C. § 223(d) prohibited the knowing sending or displaying of patently offensive messages in a manner that is available to a person under 18 years of age. Patently offensive was defined as any "image or other communication that in context, depicts or describes, in terms patently offensive as measured by contemporary community standards, sexual or excretory activities or organs."

RENO v. AMERICAN CIVIL LIBERTIES UNION, 521 U.S. 844 (1997), per STEVENS, J., invalidated both provisions: "The breadth of the CDA's coverage is wholly unprecedented. Unlike the regulations upheld in *Ginsberg* and *Pacifica,* the scope of the CDA is not limited to commercial speech or commercial entities. [The] general, undefined terms 'indecent' and 'patently offensive' cover large amounts of nonpornographic material with serious educational or other value. Moreover, the 'community standards' criterion as applied to the Internet means that any communication available to a nation-wide audience will be judged by the standards of the community most likely to

---

[340] The Court upheld a ban on "obscene" interstate commercial telephonic messages. Scalia, J., concurring, noted: "[W]hile we hold the Constitution prevents Congress from banning indecent speech in this fashion, we do not hold that the Constitution requires public utilities to carry it." Brennan, J., joined by Marshall and Stevens, JJ., concurred on the indecency issue and dissented on the obscenity issue.

be offended by the message.[341] The regulated subject matter includes any of the seven 'dirty words' used in the *Pacifica* monologue, the use of which the Government's expert acknowledged could constitute a felony. It may also extend to discussions about prison rape or safe sexual practices, artistic images that include nude subjects, and arguably the card catalogue of the Carnegie Library."[342] Compare *Ashcroft v. American Civil Liberties Union* (II), 542 U.S. 656 (2004), per Kennedy, J., which struck down the Child Online Protection Act prohibiting the placement of material obscene for children on the web unless proof of age for access was required. The Court concluded that Congress could encourage the use of software that would block pornography as a less restrictive alternative. Scalia, J., dissenting, argued that strict scrutiny was inappropriate and Breyer, J., argued that encouragement of filtering software had been tried and found wanting.[343]

(c) Consider Robert Corn-Revere, *Can Indecency Broadcast Regulations Be Extended to Cable Television and Satellite Radio?*, 30 S. Ill.U.L.J. 243 (2006): "[I]ndecency regulations restrict what may be transmitted on over-the-air broadcasting but have been struck down for other media, including print, film, the mails, cable television, and the internet. As a result of this technology-specific approach, one click on the TV remote can mean the difference between full constitutional protection for a program and heavy fines."

Cable operators are required under federal law to reserve channels for commercial lease ("leased access channels"). For some years federal law prevented cable operators from employing any editorial control over the content of leased access. The Cable Television Consumer Protection and Competition of 1992, however, permitted cable operators to prohibit the

---

[341] Nonetheless, *Ashcroft v. American Civil Liberties Union*, 535 U.S. 564 (2002), per Thomas, J., held that the Child Online Protection Act's requirement in defining obscenity that prurient interest to children and patent offensiveness for children be determined by reference to "community standards" did not by itself render the statute substantially overbroad.

[342] Consider Marjorie Heins, *Indecency: The Ongoing American Debate Over Sex, Children, Free Speech, and Dirty Words* (1997): "It remains to be seen whether *Reno v. ACLU* will prove an idiosyncratically broad response to a broadly drafted law, or whether its recognition of the positive value of some speech about some speech, even for minors, will mark the beginning of a long-overdue process of actually examining the presumption that sexual explicitness or crude language is intrinsically harmful to the young." The Court suggested that regulations of speech on the internet should be subject to stricter scrutiny than broadcast regulations, prompting Stuart Minor Benjamin, *Proactive Legislation and the First Amendment*, 99 Mich. L. Rev. 281, 320 (2000) to observe: [T]he Supreme Court stated, as one of its reasons for subjecting Internet regulation to stricter scrutiny than broadcast regulation, that broadcast has a history of government regulation and has been regulated since its inception, whereas the Internet has no comparable history of regulation. This creates a somewhat perverse incentive for legislatures—regulate a medium in its infancy or lose your chance to regulate at all."

[343] The Court used strict scrutiny because content discrimination was present. Given that the speech is non-political and that no viewpoint discrimination was present, would it be better advised to employ middle level scrutiny? Should it assess the degree of burden as a part of its determination as to which level of scrutiny to employ? See generally Patrick M. Garry, *A New First Amendment Model for Evaluating Content-Based Regulation of Internet Pornography*, 2007 B.Y.U.L. Rev. 1595 (2007).

broadcast of material that the cable operator "reasonably believes describes or depicts sexual or excretory activities or organs in a patently offensive manner" on leased access channels (47 U.S.C. § 10(a)).

DENVER AREA EDUCATIONAL TELECOMMUNICATIONS CONSORTIUM, INC. v. FCC, 518 U.S. 727 (1996), upheld the constitutionality of § 10(a).[344] BREYER, J., joined by Stevens, O'Connor, and Souter, JJ., argued that the statute was sufficiently tailored to address a significant problem: "Justices Kennedy and Thomas would have us decide this case simply by transferring and applying literally categorical standards this Court has developed in other contexts. For Justice Kennedy, leased access channels are like a common carrier, cablecast is a protected medium, strict scrutiny applies, § 10(a) fails this test, and, therefore, § 10(a) is invalid. For Justice Thomas, the case is simple because the cable operator who owns the system over which access channels are broadcast, like a bookstore owner with respect to what it displays on the shelves, has a predominant First Amendment interest. Both categorical approaches suffer from the same flaws: they import law developed in very different contexts into a new and changing environment, and they lack the flexibility necessary to allow government to respond to very serious practical problems without sacrificing the free exchange of ideas the First Amendment is designed to protect. * * *

"Over the years, this Court has restated and refined [basic] First Amendment principles, adopting them more particularly to the balance of competing interests and the special circumstances of each field of application. [This] tradition teaches that the First Amendment embodies an overarching commitment to protect speech from Government regulation through close judicial scrutiny, thereby enforcing the Constitution's constraints, but without imposing judicial formulae so rigid that they become a straightjacket that disables Government from responding to serious problems. This Court, in different contexts, has consistently held that the Government may directly regulate speech to address extraordinary problems, where its regulations are appropriately tailored to resolve those problems without imposing an unnecessarily great restriction on speech. Justices Kennedy and Thomas would have us further declare which, among the many applications of the general approach that this Court has developed over the years, we are applying here. But no definitive choice among competing analogies (broadcast, common carrier, bookstore)

---

[344] O'Connor, J's concurring opinion is omitted. The Court also struck down (1) a provision permitting a cable operator to prohibit indecent speech on public access channels, distinguishing leased access channels in part because the presence of other supervisory mechanisms for public access channels made the provision seem less needed; (2) a provision requiring that a cable operator scramble or otherwise block any indecent speech permitted on leased access channels allowing for unscrambling on written request; and (3) a similar provision blocking provision for channels primarily dedicated to sexual programming. With respect to the blocking requirements, the Court was troubled by the inconsistent treatment between channels and the breadth of the restrictions.

allows us to declare a rigid single standard, good for now and for all future media and purposes. That is not to say that we reject all the more specific formulations of the standard—they appropriately cover the vast majority of cases involving Government regulation of speech. Rather, aware as we are of the changes taking place in the law, the technology, and the industrial structure, related to telecommunications, we believe it unwise and unnecessary definitively to pick one analogy or one specific set of words now.

"[W]e can decide this case more narrowly, by closely scrutinizing § 10(a) to assure that it properly addresses an extremely important problem, without imposing, in light of the relevant interests, an unnecessarily great restriction on speech. The importance of the interest at stake here—protecting children from exposure to patently offensive depictions of sex; the accommodation of the interests of programmers in maintaining access channels and of cable operators in editing the contents of their channels; the similarity of the problem and its solution to those at issue in *Pacifica*, and the flexibility inherent in an approach that permits private cable operators to make editorial decisions, lead us to conclude that § 10(a) is a sufficiently tailored response to an extraordinarily important problem. * * *

"[W]e part company with Justice Kennedy on two issues. First, Justice Kennedy's focus on categorical analysis forces him to disregard the cable system operators' interests. We, on the other hand, recognize that in the context of cable broadcast that involves an access requirement (here, its partial removal), and unlike in most cases where we have explicitly required 'narrow tailoring,' the expressive interests of cable operators do play a legitimate role. Cf. *Turner*. While we cannot agree with Justice Thomas that everything turns on the rights of the cable owner, we also cannot agree with Justice Kennedy that we must ignore the expressive interests of cable operators altogether. Second, Justice Kennedy's application of a very strict 'narrow tailoring' test depends upon an analogy with a category ('the public forum cases'), which has been distilled over time from the similarities of many cases. Rather than seeking an analogy to a category of cases, however, we have looked to the cases themselves. And, [we find] that *Pacifica* provides the closest analogy. * * *

"The Court's distinction in *Turner*, [between] cable and broadcast television, relied on the inapplicability of the spectrum scarcity problem to cable. While that distinction was relevant in *Turner* to the justification for structural regulations at issue there (the 'must carry' rules), it has little to do with a case that involves the effects of television viewing on children. Those effects are the result of how parents and children view television programming, and how pervasive and intrusive that programming is. In that respect, cable and broadcast television differ little, if at all.

"[I]f one wishes to view the permissive provisions before us through a 'public forum' lens, one should view those provisions as limiting the otherwise totally open nature of the forum that leased access channels provide for communication of other than patently offensive sexual material—taking account of the fact that the limitation was imposed in light of experience gained from maintaining a totally open 'forum.' One must still ask whether the First Amendment forbids the limitation. But unless a label alone were to make a critical First Amendment difference (and we think here it does not), the features of this case that we have already discussed—the government's interest in protecting children, the 'permissive' aspect of the statute, and the nature of the medium— sufficiently justify the 'limitation' on the availability of this forum."

STEVENS, J., concurring, agreed with Breyer, J., that it was unwise to characterize leased channels as public fora: "When the Federal Government opens cable channels that would otherwise be left entirely in private hands, it deserves more deference than a rigid application of the public forum doctrine would allow. At this early stage in the regulation of this developing industry, Congress should not be put to an all or nothing-at-all choice in deciding whether to open certain cable channels to programmers who would otherwise lack the resources to participate in the marketplace of ideas."

SOUTER, J., concurred: "All of the relevant characteristics of cable are presently in a state of technological and regulatory flux. Recent and far-reaching legislation not only affects the technical feasibility of parental control over children's access to undesirable material but portends fundamental changes in the competitive structure of the industry and, therefore, the ability of individual entities to act as bottlenecks to the free flow of information. As cable and telephone companies begin their competition for control over the single wire that will carry both their services, we can hardly settle rules for review of regulation on the assumption that cable will remain a separable and useful category of First Amendment scrutiny. And as broadcast, cable, and the cyber-technology of the Internet and the World Wide Web approach the day of using a common receiver, we can hardly assume that standards for judging the regulation of one of them will not have immense, but now unknown and unknowable, effects on the others. * * *

"The upshot of appreciating the fluidity of the subject that Congress must regulate is simply to accept the fact that not every nuance of our old standards will necessarily do for the new technology, and that a proper choice among existing doctrinal categories is not obvious. Rather than definitively settling the issue now, Justice Breyer wisely reasons by direct analogy rather than by rule, concluding that the speech and the restriction at issue in this case may usefully be measured against the ones at issue in *Pacifica*. If that means it will take some time before reaching a final method of review for cases like this one, there may be consolation in recalling that 16 years passed, from *Roth* to *Miller*, before the modern obscenity rule jelled; that it took over 40 years, from *Hague v. CIO* to *Perry*, for the public forum category to settle out; and that a round half-century passed before the clear and present danger of *Schenck* evolved into the modern incitement rule of *Brandenburg*.

"I cannot guess how much time will go by until the technologies of communication before us today have matured and their relationships become known. But until a category of indecency can be defined both with reference to the new technology and with a prospect of durability, the job of the courts will be just what Justice Breyer does today: recognizing established First Amendment interests through a close analysis that constrains the Congress, without wholly incapacitating it in all matters of the significance apparent here, maintaining the high value of open communication, measuring the costs of regulation by exact attention to fact, and compiling a pedigree of experience with the changing subject. These are familiar judicial responsibilities in times when we know too little to risk the finality of precision, and attention to them will probably take us through the communications revolution. Maybe the judicial obligation to shoulder these responsibilities can itself be captured by a much older rule, familiar to every doctor of medicine: 'First, do no harm.' "

KENNEDY, J., joined by Ginsburg, J., concurring in part and dissenting in part, faulted the plurality opinion for upholding § 10(a): "The plurality opinion, insofar as it upholds § 10(a) [is] adrift. The opinion treats concepts such as public forum, broadcaster, and common carrier as mere labels rather than as categories with settled legal significance; it applies no standard, and by this omission loses sight of existing First Amendment doctrine. When confronted with a threat to free speech in the context of an emerging technology, we ought to have the discipline to analyze the case by reference to existing elaborations of constant First Amendment principles. This is the essence of the case-by-case approach to ensuring protection of speech under the First Amendment, even in novel settings. * * *

"The plurality begins its flight from standards with a number of assertions nobody disputes. I agree, of course, that it would be unwise 'to declare a rigid single standard, good for now and for all future media and purposes.' I do think it necessary, however, to decide what standard applies to discrimination against indecent programming on cable access channels in the present state of the industry. We owe at least that much to public and leased access programmers whose speech is put at risk nationwide by these laws. * * *

"The plurality claims its resistance to standards is in keeping with our case law, where we have shown a willingness to be flexible in confronting novel First Amendment problems. [W]e have developed specialized or more or less stringent standards when certain contexts demanded them; we did not avoid the use of standards altogether. Indeed, the creation of standards and adherence to them, even when it means affording protection to speech unpopular or distasteful, is the central achievement of our First Amendment jurisprudence. Standards are the means by which we state in advance how to test a law's validity, rather than letting the height of the bar be determined by the apparent exigencies of the day. They also provide notice and fair warning to those who must predict how the courts will respond to attempts to suppress their speech. Yet formulations like strict scrutiny, used in a number of constitutional settings to ensure that the inequities of the moment are subordinated to commitments made for the long run mean little if they can be watered down whenever they seem too strong. They mean still less if they can be ignored altogether when considering a case not on all fours with what we have seen before.

"The plurality seems distracted by the many changes in technology and competition in the cable industry. The laws challenged here, however, do not retool the structure of the cable industry. [The] straightforward issue here is whether the Government can deprive certain speakers, on the basis of the content of their speech, of protections afforded all others. There is no reason to discard our existing First Amendment jurisprudence in answering this question.

"While it protests against standards, the plurality does seem to favor one formulation of the question in this case: namely, whether the Act 'properly addresses an extremely important problem, without imposing, in light of the relevant interests, an unnecessarily great restriction on speech.' [This] description of the question accomplishes little, save to clutter our First Amendment case law by adding an untested rule with an uncertain relationship to the others we use to evaluate laws restricting speech. * * *

"Justice Souter recommends to the Court the precept 'First, do no harm.' The question, though, is whether the harm is in sustaining the law or striking it down. If the plurality is concerned about technology's direction, it ought to begin by allowing speech, not suppressing it. We have before us an urgent claim for relief against content-based discrimination, not a dry run.

"The constitutionality under *Turner Broadcasting* of requiring a cable operator to set aside leased access channels is not before us. For purposes of this case, we should treat the cable operator's rights in these channels as extinguished, and address the issue these petitioners present: namely, whether the Government can discriminate on the basis of content in affording protection to certain programmers. I cannot agree with Justice Thomas that the cable operator's rights inform this analysis.

"Laws requiring cable operators to provide leased access are the practical equivalent of making them common carriers, analogous in this respect to telephone companies: They are obliged to provide a conduit for the speech of others. [Laws] removing common-carriage protection from a single form of speech based on its content should be reviewed under the same standard as content-based restrictions on speech in a public forum. Making a cable operator a common carrier does not create a public forum in the sense of taking property from private control and dedicating it to public use; rather, regulations of a common carrier dictate the manner in which private control is exercised. A common-carriage mandate, nonetheless, serves the same function as a public forum. It ensures open, nondiscriminatory access to the means of communication.

"*Pacifica* did not purport, however, to apply a special standard for indecent broadcasting. Emphasizing the narrowness of its holding, the Court in *Pacifica* conducted a context-specific analysis of the FCC's restriction on indecent programming during daytime hours. It relied on the general rule that 'broadcasting [has] received the most limited First Amendment protection.' We already have rejected the application of this lower broadcast standard of review to infringements on the liberties of cable operators, even though they control an important communications medium. *Turner.* * * *

"[Indecency] often is inseparable from the ideas and viewpoints conveyed, or separable only with loss of truth or expressive power. Under our traditional First Amendment jurisprudence, factors perhaps justifying some restriction on indecent cable programming may all be taken into account without derogating this category of protected speech as marginal.

"Congress does have, however, a compelling interest in protecting children from indecent speech. So long as society gives proper respect to parental choices, it may, under an appropriate standard, intervene to spare children exposure to material not suitable for minors. This interest is substantial enough to justify some regulation of indecent speech even under, I will assume, the [strict scrutiny standard].

"[Section 10(a) nonetheless is] not narrowly tailored to protect children from indecent programs on access channels. First, to the extent some operators may allow indecent programming, children in localities those operators serve will be left unprotected. Partial service of a compelling interest is not narrow tailoring. Put another way, the interest in protecting children from indecency only at the caprice of the cable operator is not compelling. Perhaps Congress drafted the law this way to avoid the clear constitutional difficulties of banning indecent speech * * *, but the First Amendment does not permit this sort of ill fit between a law restricting speech and the interest it is said to serve.

"Second, to the extent cable operators prohibit indecent programming on access channels, not only children but adults will be deprived of it."

THOMAS, J., joined by Rehnquist, C.J., and Scalia, J., concurring in part and dissenting in part, argued that § 10(a) validly protected the constitutional rights of cable operators: "It is one thing to compel an operator to carry leased [access] speech, in apparent violation of *Tornillo*, but it is another thing altogether to say that the First Amendment forbids Congress to give back part of the operators' editorial discretion, which all recognize as fundamentally protected, in favor of a broader access right. It is no answer to say that leased [is] content neutral and that [§ 10(a) is] not, for that does not change the fundamental fact, which petitioners never address, that it is the operators' journalistic freedom that is infringed, whether the challenged restrictions be content neutral or content based.

"Because the access provisions are part of a scheme that restricts the free speech rights of cable operators, and expands the speaking opportunities of access programmers, who have no underlying constitutional right to speak through the cable medium, I do not believe that access programmers can challenge the scheme, or a particular part of it, as an abridgment of their 'freedom of speech.' Outside the public forum doctrine, government intervention that grants access programmers an opportunity to speak that they would not otherwise enjoy—and which does not directly limit programmers' underlying speech rights—cannot be an abridgement of the same programmers' First Amendment rights, even if the new speaking opportunity is content-based.

"The permissive nature of [§]10(a) is important in this regard. If Congress had forbidden cable operators to carry indecent programming on leased * * * channels, that law would have burdened the programmer's right, recognized in *Turner* to compete for space on an operator's system. The Court would undoubtedly strictly scrutinize such a law."

NOTES AND QUESTIONS

1. Consider Yochai Benkler, *Free as the Air to Common Use: First Amendment Constraints on Enclosure of the Public Domain*, 74 N.Y.U. L. Rev. 354 (1999): "Beneath the veneer of an indecency case, *Denver Area* was a case about access rights. [A] majority of the justices acknowledged that access rights to the cable medium served the First Amendment by permitting many and diverse sources to reach viewers over this concentrated medium. These justices treated decisions by cable operators not to carry programming as 'censorial,' and acknowledged that the availability of access to the medium was a question of constitutional moment. Only the partial dissent by Justice Thomas thought that government intervention by requiring access rights was the relevant constitutional concern." Compare Jerome A. Barron, *The Electronic Media and the Flight from First Amendment Doctrine: Justice Breyer's New Balancing Approach*, 31 U. Mich. J.L. Ref. 817 (1998): "[Breyer, J.'s balancing approach

provided] specific consideration to the access for expression dimension of the cable regulations under review in *Denver Area*. Access rights must be weighed against the free speech rights of the cable operator. For Justice Thomas, no First Amendment rights conflicted in *Denver Area* because the only rights asserted that merit First Amendment status were those of the cable operator. [Thomas, J.,] noted that the rationale behind the plurality was not 'intuitively obvious' as to why programmers and viewers have any First Amendment rights. In reality, however, it is not intuitively obvious that cable operators enjoy the whole panoply of First Amendment rights either. [T]o say that mandatory public access and leased access channels violate *Tornillo* would be an extravagant statement. If the rights of the communications entity's owners were intended to trump all other claims to First Amendment protection for all media, *Tornillo* would have been the ideal occasion to make that statement. The *Tornillo* Court instead directed itself to the print media alone and did not so much as cite *Red Lion*, the most obvious contrary electronic media precedent then extant."

2.   Consider Jonathan Weinberg, *Cable TV, Indecency and the Court*, 21 Colum.-VLA J.L. & Arts 95 (1997): "[*Pacifica's*] reasoning and jurisprudential approach are back. This is disturbing. The history of First Amendment decision making in this century suggests that rules are more effective than ad hoc analysis in protecting speech from the fears and repression of the moment. Justice Breyer, in the *Denver Area* plurality opinion, attributed his contextual approach to 'the changes taking place in the law, the technology, and the industrial structure,' which, he said, made any attempt to enunciate abstract doctrine premature. The deeper message of the plurality opinion, though, is that no matter how technology evolves, *Pacifica's* contextual approach—not the law of rules—will continue to guide content-based regulation of media that feel like television." But cf. Suzanna Sherry, *Hard Cases Make Good Judges*, 99 Nw. U. L. Rev. 3 (2004): "Echoing Justice Scalia's distaste for anything other than the brightest of lines, Kennedy suggests that the plurality's approach 'end[s] up being a legalistic cover for an ad hoc balancing of interests.' Yet Justice Kennedy was perfectly content to apply highly manipulable intermediate scrutiny to the regulation of commercial speech, voted to uphold the zoning ordinance in *Alameda Books* in an opinion that carefully recognized that characterizing the ordinance as 'content neutral' was 'imprecise,' and has shown a refreshing sensitivity to fact-specific context in other areas of the law. Why not here?"

3.   § 505 of the Telecommunications Act of 1996 requires that cable television operators who provide channels "primarily dedicated to sexually-oriented programming" either "fully scramble or otherwise fully block" the channels so that non-subscribers to the programming would not be able to hear or see it. The art of scrambling has not been perfected, however. "Signal bleed" occurs on many channels, allowing some of the visual and audio aspects of the programming to be heard or seen. In the case of signal bleed, the act requires that the programming be blocked except during hours when children are unlikely to be viewing. The F.C.C.'s regulations provide that those hours are

between 10 p.m. and 6 a.m ("the safe harbor provision"). § 504 of the same act required operators to block other programming upon a subscriber's request. A cable television programmer challenged § 505.

United States v. Playboy Entertainment Group, 529 U.S. 803 (2000), applied strict scrutiny to the restriction and struck it down because the cable systems had the capacity to block unwanted channels. The dissenters argued that this alternative was impractical.[345]

9.   THE RIGHT NOT TO SPEAK, THE RIGHT TO ASSOCIATE, AND THE RIGHT NOT TO ASSOCIATE

NAACP v. Alabama ex rel. Patterson, 357 U.S. 449 (1958), per Harlan, J., held that the Constitution barred Alabama from compelling production of NAACP membership lists. The opinion used the phrase freedom of association repeatedly, "elevat[ing] freedom of association to an independent right, possessing an equal status with the other rights specifically enumerated in the First Amendment." Thomas Emerson, *Freedom of Association and Freedom of Expression,* 74 Yale L.J. 1 (1964).[346]

From the materials on advocacy of illegal action (Sec. 1, I supra) onward, it has been evident that individuals have rights to join with others for expressive purposes. This section explores other aspects of the freedom to associate and its corollary, the freedom not to associate. First, we explore cases which the Court bases on a right not to speak, but might better be understood as establishing a right not to be associated with particular ideas. Second, instead of persons resisting forced membership in a group, we confront groups resisting members. Finally, we explore aspects of free association in the employment context.

I.   THE RIGHT NOT TO BE ASSOCIATED WITH PARTICULAR IDEAS

WEST VIRGINIA STATE BD. OF EDUC. v. BARNETTE, 319 U.S. 624 (1943), per JACKSON, J., upheld the right of public school students to refuse to salute the flag:[347] "To sustain the compulsory flag salute we are required to say that a Bill of Rights which guards the individual's right to speak his own mind, left it open to public authorities to compel him to utter what is not in his mind. * * * Struggles to coerce uniformity of sentiment in support

---

[345] For commentary, see Ashutosh Bhagwat, *What if I Want My Kids to Watch Pornography?: Protecting Children from "Indecent" Speech,* 11 Wm. & Mary Bill Rts. J. 671 (2003).

[346] For discussion of the evolution of the right of association, see John Inazu, *The Strange Origins of the Constitutional Rights of Association,* 77 Tenn. L.Rev. 485 (2010).

[347] The Court observed that it was constitutional to otherwise involve students in the recitation of the pledge (which at that time did not include "Under God") during a school day. When a teacher leads a class in the pledge of allegiance, is psychological coercion involved even in the absence of a legal requirement? Should psychological coercion be sufficient to trigger a free speech violation? See Abner Greene, *The Pledge of Allegiance Problem,* 64 Ford.L.Rev. 451 (1995).

of some end thought essential to their time and country have been waged by many good as well as by evil men. [Ultimate] futility of such attempts to compel coherence is the lesson of every such effort from the Roman drive to stamp out Christianity as a disturber of its pagan unity, the Inquisition, as a means to religious and dynastic unity, the Siberian exiles as a means to Russian unity, down to the fast failing efforts of our present totalitarian enemies. Those who begin coercive elimination of dissent soon find themselves exterminating dissenters. Compulsory unification of opinion achieves only the unanimity of the graveyard. * * *

"If there is any fixed star in our constitutional constellation, it is that no official, high or petty, can prescribe what shall be orthodox in politics, nationalism, religion, or other matters of opinion or force citizens to confess by word or act their faith therein. If there are any circumstances which permit an exception, they do not now occur to us. We think the action of the local authorities in compelling the flag salute and pledge transcends constitutional limitations on their power and invades the sphere of intellect and spirit which it is the purpose of the First Amendment to our Constitution to reserve from all official control."[348]

NOTES AND QUESTIONS

1.   Is it a sufficient answer to *Barnette* that the audience need not be misled into believing that the speaker believes what he is forced to say?

2.   ***Mind control.*** Consider Seana V. Shiffrin, *What Is Really Wrong with Compelled Association?*, 99 Nw. U. L. Rev. 839 (2005): "One may worry that compulsory, frequent repetition of the Pledge will have an influence on what and how one thinks, independent of one's direct deliberations on its subject matter. Routine recitation may make its message familiar. Through regularity, it may become a comfort and an internal source of authority for consultation. At a later point, one might instinctively, without further thought and without awareness of the origin of the thought, characterize the polity as a republic, or as a place where there is freedom and justice, or perhaps more plausibly, be more likely assent to another's assertion to that effect." And on freedom of thought as a more general justification for freedom of speech, see Seana Valentine Shiffrin, *A Thinker-Based Approach to Freedom of Speech*, 27 Const. Comm. 283 (2011).

3.   ***Sincerity.*** Consider Shiffrin, Note 2 supra: "[C]ompelled speech requirements of the sort at issue in *Barnette* conflict with recognition of and respect for the value of sincerity, a virtue that is integrally related to the well-functioning of a robust First Amendment culture. [In] the case of the Pledge, students are compelled to pledge to something that they may not believe is

---

[348] Black and Douglas, JJ., concurred, abandoning their position taken in a recent flag salute case *Minersville School Dist. v. Gobitis*, 310 U.S. 586 (1940), which the Court reconsidered in *Barnette*; Roberts and Reed, JJ., citing their position in *Gobitis*, and Frankfurter, J., taking a position on the judicial role similar to that which he had expressed in *Dennis*, dissented.

worth pledging to, or that they may believe is unworthy of or an inappropriate object for such commitment. [The rote recitation and sincerity arguments] appeal not to the comprehension by the compelled speaker's audience but rather to the conditions of respect for the character, the autonomous cognitive life, and the mental contents of the compelled party."

4.   ***Dignity.*** Consider Laurence H. Tribe, *Disentangling Symmetries: Speech, Association, Parenthood*, 28 Pepp. L. Rev. 641 (2001): "The right that all of these cases affirm is better understood as a right not to be used or commandeered to do the state's ideological bidding by having to mouth, convey, embody, or sponsor a message, especially the state's message, with one's voice or body or resources, on one's personal possessions, through the composition of the associations one joins or forms, or in their selection of teachers, exemplars, and leaders." See also Vincent Blasi & Seana V. Shiffrin, *The Story of West Virginia State Board of Education v. Barnette*, in Constitutional Law Stories 432 (Michael C. Dorf ed. 2004); James P. Madigan, *Questioning the Coercive Effect of Self-Identifying Speech*, 87 Iowa L. Rev. 75 (2001); Greene, fn. 347 supra.

———

New Hampshire required that noncommercial vehicles bear license plates embossed with the state motto, "Live Free or Die." "Refus[ing] to be coerced by the State into advertising a slogan which I find morally, ethically, religiously and politically abhorrent," appellee, a Jehovah's Witness, covered up the motto on his license plate, a misdemeanor under state law. After being convicted several times of violating the misdemeanor statute, appellee sought federal injunctive and declaratory relief.

WOOLEY v. MAYNARD, 430 U.S. 705 (1977), per BURGER, C.J., held that requiring appellee to display the motto on his license plates violated his First Amendment right to "refrain from speaking": "[T]he freedom of thought protected by the First Amendment [includes] both the right to speak freely and the right to refrain from speaking at all. See *Barnette*. The right to speak and the right to refrain from speaking are complementary components of the broader concept of 'individual freedom of mind.' This is illustrated [by] *Miami Herald* [infra], where we held unconstitutional a Florida statute placing an affirmative duty upon newspapers to publish the replies of political candidates whom they had criticized.

" * * * Compelling the affirmative act of a flag salute [the situation in *Barnette*] involved a more serious infringement upon personal liberties than the passive act of carrying the state motto on a license plate, but the difference is essentially one of degree. Here, as in *Barnette,* we are faced with a state measure which forces an individual as part of his daily life— indeed constantly while his automobile is in public view—to be an instrument for fostering public adherence to an ideological point of view he finds unacceptable. In doing so, the State 'invades the sphere of intellect and spirit which it is the purpose of the First Amendment [to] reserve from all official control.' *Barnette.*

"New Hampshire's statute in effect requires that appellees use their private property as a 'mobile billboard' for the State's ideological message— or suffer a penalty, as Maynard already has. [The] fact that most individuals agree with the thrust of [the] motto is not the test; most Americans also find the flag salute acceptable. The First Amendment protects the right of individuals to hold a point of view different from the majority and to refuse to foster, in the way New Hampshire commands, an idea they find morally objectionable."

The Court next considered whether "the State's countervailing interest" was "sufficiently compelling" to justify appellees to display the motto on their license plates. The two interests claimed by the state were (1) facilitating the identification of state license plates from those of similar colors of other states and (2) promoting "appreciation of history, state pride, [and] individualism." As to (1), the record revealed that these state license plates were readily distinguishable from others without reference to the state motto and, in any event, the state's purpose could be achieved by "less drastic means," i.e., by alternative methods less restrictive of First Amendment freedoms. As to (2), where the State's interest is to communicate an "official view" as to history and state pride or to disseminate any other "ideology," "such interest cannot outweigh an individual's First Amendment right to avoid becoming the courier for such message."

REHNQUIST, J., joined by Blackmun, J., dissented, not only agreeing with what he called "the Court's implicit recognition that there is no protected 'symbolic speech' in this case," but maintaining that "that conclusion goes far to undermine the Court's ultimate holding that there is an element of protected expression here. The State has not forced appellees to 'say' anything; and it has not forced them to communicate ideas with nonverbal actions reasonably likened to 'speech,' such as wearing a lapel button promoting a political candidate or waving a flag as a symbolic gesture. The State has simply required that *all* noncommercial automobiles bear license tags with the state motto. [Appellees] have not been forced to affirm or reject that motto; they are simply required by the State [to] carry a state auto license tag for identification and registration purposes. [The] issue, unconfronted by the Court, is whether appellees, in displaying, as they are required to do, state license tags, the format of which is known to all as having been prescribed by the State, would be considered to be advocating political or ideological views.

"[H]aving recognized the rather obvious differences between [*Barnette* and this case], the Court does not explain why the same result should obtain. The Court suggests that the test is whether the individual is forced

1146 FREEDOM OF EXPRESSION AND ASSOCIATION CH. 7

'to be an instrument for fostering public adherence to an ideological point of view he finds unacceptable,' [but] these are merely conclusory words. [For] example, were New Hampshire to erect a multitude of billboards, each proclaiming 'Live Free or Die,' and tax all citizens for the cost of erection and maintenance, clearly the message would be 'fostered' by the individual citizen-taxpayers and just as clearly those individuals would be 'instruments' in that communication. Certainly, however, that case would not fall within the ambit of *Barnette.* In that case, as in this case, there is no *affirmation* of belief. For First Amendment principles to be implicated, the State must place the citizen in the position of either appearing to, or actually, 'asserting as true' the message. This was the focus of *Barnette,* and clearly distinguishes this case from that one."[349]

NOTES AND QUESTIONS

1. **Speech?** Consider Randall P. Bezanson, *Speaking Through Others' Voices: Authorship, Originality, and Free Speech*, 38 Wake Forest L. Rev. 983 (2003): "Maynard's act was an exercise of his liberty, but the question is whether it is an exercise of his liberty to speak, which is a liberty to communicate his ideas or beliefs or information to [others]. Maynard's private conceit that he was speaking when driving with the license plate was divorced from the communicative interaction with others that the First Amendment speech guarantee presumes. Since there was no evidence that anyone understood the carrying of the motto on a car to be an act of speech, much less an act of Maynard's speech, Maynard was simply speaking into the air. He was exercising his own conscience, but he was not, without more, speaking, a status that at least requires communication to others."

2. **Coercive inculcation of values.** Consider Larry Alexander, *Compelled Speech,* 23 Const. Comm. 147 (2006): "*Wooley* seems particularly difficult to explain as a case of coercive inculation of beliefs/values. Whether or not the motto was visible or taped over, it would be largely invisible to the vehicle's driver and passengers. Other vehicles' license plates would be much more effective for that purpose than the plates of Maynard's own vehicle, in which case the demand should have been to eliminate the motto from all license plates."

3. **Double irony.** Consider Laurence H. Tribe, *Disentangling Symmetries: Speech, Association, Parenthood,* 28 Pepp. L. Rev. 641 (2001): "Apparently suffering from an 'irony deficiency,' the 'Granite State' of New Hampshire had threatened to imprison those of its citizens who refused to adorn their cars with that 'Live Free or Die' motto. But, there is actually a double irony here: By holding that individuals have a right to refuse this state slogan on their plates while letting the state keep distributing plates bearing the slogan, the Court was forcing those who are most offended by the slogan to come out of the closet. No longer able to just blend in as law abiding citizens

---

[349] White, J., joined by Blackmun and Rehnquist, JJ., dissented on procedural grounds.

whose views nobody could guess from their license plates, now those keeping the "Live Free or Die" slogan would be marked as having no objection to the sentiment it expressed, while those replacing it would be marked as having affirmatively rejected the slogan." Do the same considerations apply to the District of Columbia's "Taxation Without Representation" license plates? To New Jersey's "Garden State" plates?

4. ***Use of private property as a forum for the speech of others.*** (a) Appellees sought to enjoin a shopping center from denying them access to the center's central courtyard in order to solicit signatures from passersby for petitions opposing a U.N. resolution. The California Supreme Court held they were entitled to conduct their activity at the center, construing the state constitution to protect "speech and petitioning, reasonably exercised, in shopping centers, even [when] privately owned." The shopping center appealed, arguing that its First Amendment rights had been violated.

PRUNEYARD SHOPPING CENTER v. ROBINS, 447 U.S. 74 (1980), per REHNQUIST, J., disagreed with the shopping center: "[In *Wooley,*] the government itself prescribed the message, required it to be displayed openly on appellee's personal property that was used 'as part of his daily life,' and refused to permit him [to] cover up the motto even though the Court found that the display of the motto served no important state interest. Here, by contrast, [the center] is not limited to the personal use of appellants, [but is] a business establishment that is open to the public to come and go as they please. The views expressed by members of the public in passing out pamphlets or seeking signatures for a petition thus will not likely be identified with those of the owner. Second, no specific message is dictated by the State to be displayed on appellants' property. There consequently is no danger of government discrimination for or against a particular message. Finally, [it appears] appellants can expressly disavow any connection with the message by simply posting signs in the area where the speakers or handbillers stand."

Unlike *Barnette,* appellants "are not [being] compelled to affirm their belief in any governmentally prescribed position or view, and they are free to publicly dissociate themselves from the views of the speakers or handbillers. [*Miami Herald*] rests on the principle that the State cannot tell a newspaper what it must print. [There was also a danger that the statute requiring a newspaper to publish a political candidate's reply to previously published criticism would deter] editors from publishing controversial political [statements]. Thus, the statute was found to be an 'intrusion into the function of editors.' These concerns obviously are not present here."[350]

---

[350] Could *PruneYard* be extended to parts of the Internet? To America Online? To Netscape? Are parts of the Internet already public fora. For various views, see Laurence H. Tribe, *The Constitution in Cyberspace,* The Humanist, Sept.–Oct. 1991, at 15; Edward V. Di Lello, *Functional Equivalency and Its Application to Freedom of Speech on Computer Bulletin Boards,* 26 Colum. J.L. & Soc. Probs. 199 (1993); Note, *Sidewalks in Cyberspace: Making Space for Public Forums in the Electronic Environment,* 12 Harv. J.L. & Tech. 149 (1998); Note, *Is Cyberspace a Public Forum? Computer Bulletin Boards, Free Speech, and State Action,* 81 Geo.L.J. 409 (1992).

POWELL, J., joined by White, J., concurring in the judgment, maintained that "state action that transforms privately owned property into a forum for the expression of the public's views could raise serious First Amendment questions": "I do not believe that the result in *Wooley* would have changed had [the state] directed its citizens to place the slogan 'Live Free or Die' in their shop windows rather than on their automobiles. [*Wooley*] protects a person who refuses to allow use of his property as a market place for the ideas of others. [One] who has merely invited the public onto his property for commercial purposes cannot fairly be said to have relinquished his right 'to decline to be an instrument for fostering public adherence to an ideological point of view he finds unacceptable.' *Wooley*.

"[E]ven when [as here] no particular message is mandated by the State, First Amendment interests are affected by state action that forces a property owner to admit third-party speakers. [A] right of access [may be] no less intrusive than speech compelled by the State itself. [A] law requiring that a newspaper permit others to use its columns imposes an unacceptable burden upon the newspaper's First Amendment right to select material for publication. *Miami Herald*.

"[If] a state law mandated public access to the bulletin board of a freestanding store [or] small shopping center [or allowed soliciting or pamphleteering in the entrance area of a store,] customers might well conclude that the messages reflect the view of the proprietor. [He] either could permit his customers to receive a mistaken impression [or] disavow the messages. Should he take the first course, he effectively has been compelled to affirm someone else's belief. Should he choose the second, he has been forced to speak when he would prefer to remain silent. In short, he has lost control over his freedom to speak or not to speak on certain issues. The mere fact that he is free to dissociate himself from the views expressed on his property cannot restore his 'right to refrain from speaking at all.' *Wooley*.

"A property owner may also be faced with speakers who wish to use his premises as a platform for views that he finds morally repugnant[, for example, a] minority-owned business confronted with leafleteers from the American Nazi Party or the Ku Klux Klan, [or] a church-operated enterprise asked to host demonstrations in favor of abortion. [The] pressure to respond is particularly apparent [in the above cases, but] an owner who strongly objects to some of the causes to which the state-imposed right of access would extend may oppose ideological activities 'of *any* sort' that are not related to the purposes for which he has invited the public onto his property. See *Abood*. To require the owner to specify the particular ideas he finds objectionable enough to compel a response would force him to relinquish his 'freedom to maintain his own beliefs without public disclosure.' *Abood*. * * *

"[On this record] I cannot say that customers of this vast center [occupying several city blocks and containing more than 65 shops] would be likely to assume that appellees' limited speech activity expressed the views of [the center]. [Moreover, appellants] have not alleged that they object to [appellees' views, nor asserted] that some groups who reasonably might be expected to speak at [the center] will express views that are so objectionable as to require a response even when listeners will not mistake their source. [Thus,] I join the judgment of the Court, [but] I do not interpret our decision today as a blanket approval for state efforts to transform privately owned commercial property into public forums."

(b) *Pacific Gas & Electric Co. v. Public Utilities Comm'n*, 475 U.S. 1 (1986), per Powell, J., joined by Burger, C.J., and Brennan and O'Connor, JJ., (together with Marshall, J., concurring), struck down a commission requirement that a private utility company include in its billing envelope materials supplied by a public interest group that were critical of some of the company's positions.[351] Was the result required by *Miami Herald*? Consistent with *PruneYard*?[352]

(c) The Solomon Amendment provides that if any part of an institution of higher education denies military recruiters access equal to that afforded to other recruiters, the entire institution would be deprived of federal funds. A consortium of law schools filed suit, alleging that this violated the First Amendment.

RUMSFELD v. FORUM FOR ACADEMIC AND INSTITUTIONAL RIGHTS, INC., 547 U.S. 47 (2006), per ROBERTS, C.J., held that it did not: "The Solomon Amendment neither limits what law schools may say nor requires them to say anything. Law schools remain free under the statute to express whatever views they may have on the military's congressionally mandated employment policy, all the while retaining eligibility for federal funds. See Tr. of Oral Arg. 25 (Solicitor General acknowledging that law schools "could put signs on the bulletin board next to the door, they could engage in speech, they could help organize student protests"). As a general matter, the Solomon Amendment regulates conduct, not speech. It affects what law schools must *do*—afford equal access to military recruiters—not what they may or may not *say*. * * *

"Compelling a law school that sends scheduling e-mails for other recruiters to send one for a military recruiter is simply not the same as forcing a student to pledge allegiance, or forcing a Jehovah's Witness to display the motto 'Live Free or Die,' and it trivializes the freedom protected in *Barnette* and *Wooley* to suggest that it is."[353]

---

[351] Burger, C.J., filed a concurring opinion; Rehnquist, J., joined by White and Stevens, JJ., dissented; Stevens, J., filed a separate dissent; Blackmun, J., took no part.

[352] Consider Alan Hirsch, *"The Corporate Conscience" and Other First Amendment Follies in Pacific Gas & Electric*, 41 San Diego L. Rev. 483 (2004): "The Court's treatment of *Tornillo* and *Prune Yard*, taken together, suggests the bankruptcy of its opinion. The utility company bears a far greater resemblance to a shopping center owner than to a newspaper, but the Court distinguished it from the latter and likened it to the former."

[353] For criticism of FAIR, see Paul Horwitz, *Three Faces of Deference*, 83 Notre D. L.Rev. 1061 (2008); Chai R. Feldblum, *Moral Conflict and Liberty: Gay Rights and Religion*, 72 Brook. L.Rev. 61 (2006). See generally Paul Horwitz, *Universities as First Amendment Institutions*, 54 UCLA L.Rev. 1497 (2007).

5. ***Paraders' rights.*** Boston authorized the South Boston Allied War Veterans Council to conduct the St. Patrick's Day-Evacuation parade (commemorating the evacuation of British troops from the city in 1776). The Veterans Council refused to let the Irish-American Gay, Lesbian and Bisexual Group of Boston march in the parade, but the Massachusetts courts ruled that the Council's refusal violated a public accommodations law in that the parade was an "open recreational event."

HURLEY v. IRISH-AMERICAN GAY, LESBIAN AND BISEXUAL GROUP OF BOSTON, 515 U.S. 557 (1995), per SOUTER, J., held that "[t]his use of the State's power violates the fundamental rule of protection under the First Amendment, that a speaker has the autonomy to choose the content of his own message. * * *

"[The Council's] claim to the benefit of this principle of autonomy to control one's own speech is as sound as the South Boston parade is expressive. Rather like a composer, the Council selects the expressive units of the parade from potential participants, and though the score may not produce a particularized message, each contingent's expression in the Council's eyes comports with what merits celebration on that day. Even if this view gives the Council credit for a more considered judgment than it actively made, the Council clearly decided to exclude a message it did not like from the communication it chose to make, and that is enough to invoke its right as a private speaker to shape its expression by speaking on one subject while remaining silent on another. * * *

"Unlike the programming offered on various channels by a cable network, the parade does not consist of individual, unrelated segments that happen to be transmitted together for individual selection by members of the audience. Although each parade unit generally identifies itself, each is understood to contribute something to a common theme, and accordingly there is no customary practice whereby private sponsors disavow any 'identity of viewpoint' between themselves and the selected participants. Practice follows practicability here, for such disclaimers would be quite curious in a moving parade. [*PruneYard* found] that the proprietors were running 'a business establishment that is open to the public to come and go as they please,' that the solicitations would 'not likely be identified with those of the owner,' and that the proprietors could 'expressly disavow any connection with the message by simply posting signs in the area where the speakers or handbillers stand.' "[354]

6. ***Economic pressure to engage in political activity.*** NAACP v. CLAIBORNE HARDWARE CO., 458 U.S. 886 (1982): The NAACP had organized a consumer boycott whose principal objective was, according to the lower court, "to force the white merchants [to] bring pressure upon [the

---

[354] For incisive pre-*Hurley* commentary, see Larry W. Yackle, *Parading Ourselves: Freedom of Speech at the Feast of St. Patrick,* 73 B.U.L.Rev. 791 (1993). Is *Hurley* consistent with the particularized message requirement of *Spence?* If not, how is expressive conduct defined? For commentary, see Angelica M. Sinopole, *"No Saggy Pants,"* 113 Penn. St.L.Rev. 328 (2008).

government] to grant defendants' demands or, in the alternative, to suffer economic ruin." Mississippi characterized the boycott as a tortious and malicious interference with the plaintiffs' businesses. The Court, per STEVENS, J., held for the NAACP: Although labor boycotts organized for economic ends had long been subject to prohibition, "speech to protest racial discrimination" was "essential political speech lying at the core of the First Amendment" and was therefore distinguishable. Is the boycott protected association? Are there association rights on the other side? Does the state have a legitimate interest in protecting merchants from being forced to support political change they would otherwise oppose? Cf. *NLRB v. Retail Store Employees Union,* 447 U.S. 607 (1980) (ban on labor picketing encouraging consumer boycott of neutral employer upheld). Are the white merchants neutral?[355] For commentary, compare Michael Harper, *The Consumer's Emerging Right to Boycott: NAACP v. Claiborne Hardware and Its Implications for American Labor Law,* 93 Yale L.J. 409 (1984) with Maimon Schwarzschild & Larry Alexander, *Consumer Boycotts and Freedom of Association: Comment on a Recently Proposed Theory,* 22 San Diego L.Rev. 555 (1985).

7.   *Orthodoxy and commercial advertising.* ZAUDERER v. OFFICE OF DISCIPLINARY COUNSEL, 471 U.S. 626 (1985), per WHITE, J., upheld an Ohio requirement that an attorney advertising availability on a contingency basis must disclose in the ad whether the clients would have to pay costs if their lawsuits should prove unsuccessful: "[T]he interests at stake in this case are not of the same order as those discussed in *Wooley, Miami Herald,* and *Barnette.* Ohio has not attempted to 'prescribe what shall be orthodox in politics, nationalism, religion, or other matters of opinion or force citizens to confess by word or act their faith therein.' The State has attempted only to prescribe what shall be orthodox in commercial advertising [regarding] purely factual and uncontroversial[356] information about the terms under which his services will be available. Because the extension of First Amendment

---

[355] Stevens, J., also argued in *Claiborne* that the boycott was protected as a right to petition the government. Are the white merchants the government?

[356] What if the requested disclosures are controverted? Do cigarette companies have First Amendment grounds to resist forced disclosures?

Do doctors have a First Amendment right to resist state mandated disclosures to patients regarding abortion? Consider joint opinion of O'Connor, Kennedy, and Souter, JJ., in *Planned Parenthood v. Casey,* 505 U.S. 833 (1992): "[This] is, for constitutional purposes, no different from a requirement that a doctor give certain specific information about any medical procedure. [To] be sure, the physician's First Amendment rights not to speak are implicated, see *Wooley,* but only as part of the practice of medicine, subject to reasonable licensing and regulation by the State." See Robert Post, *Informed Consent to Abortion,* 2007 U.Ill.L.Rev. 939. Is there a First Amendment right against compelled listening in some circumstances? Should it apply in the abortion context? See Caroline M. Corbin, *The First Amendment Right Against Compelled Listening,* 89 B.U. L. Rev. 939 (2009).

Can professional fundraisers be required to disclose their professional status before soliciting funds? The percent of charitable contributions that have been turned over to charity in the past 12 months? See *Riley v. National Federation of the Blind,* Sec. 4, III supra (the former can be required, not the latter). But cf. *Illinois ex rel. Madigan v. Telemarketing Associates, Inc.,* 538 U.S. 600 (2003)(fraud action cognizable when solicitor represents that a significant amount will go to charity when only 15 cents per dollar would be distributed for such purpose). On compelled commercial speech, see generally Note, *Can the Budweiser Frogs Be Forced to Sing A New Tune?,* 84 Va. L.Rev. 1195 (1998).

protection to commercial speech is justified principally by the value to consumers of the information such speech provides, *Virginia Pharmacy*, appellant's constitutionally protected interest in *not* providing any particular factual information in his advertising is minimal. [We] recognize that unjustified or unduly burdensome disclosure requirements might offend the First Amendment by chilling protected commercial speech. But we hold that an advertiser's rights are adequately protected as long as disclosure requirements are reasonably related to the State's interest in preventing deception of consumers."

The Court stated that the First Amendment interests "implicated by disclosure requirements are substantially weaker than those at stake when speech is actually suppressed." Accordingly it rejected any requirement that the advertisement in question be shown to be deceptive absent the disclosure or that the state meet a "least restrictive means" analysis.

BRENNAN, J., joined by Marshall, J., dissenting on this issue, conceded that the distinction between disclosure and suppression "supports some differences in analysis," but thought the Court had exaggerated the importance of the distinction: "[A]n affirmative publication requirement 'operates as a command in the same sense as a statute or regulation forbidding [someone] to publish specified matter,' and that [a] compulsion to publish that which 'reason tells [one] should not be published' therefore raises substantial First Amendment concerns. *Miami Herald*." Accordingly, he would have required a demonstration that the advertising was inherently likely to deceive or record evidence that the advertising was in fact deceptive, or a showing that another substantial interest was directly [advanced]. Applying this standard, Brennan, J., agreed with the Court that a state may require an advertising attorney to include a costs disclaimer, but concluded that the state had provided Zauderer with inadequate notice of what he was required to include in the advertisement.

Milavetz, Gallop & Milavetz, P.A., et al., v. United States, 559 U.S. 29 (2010), reaffirmed *Zauderer*, holding that "an advertiser's rights are adequately protected as long as disclosure requirements are reasonably related to the State's interest in preventing deception of consumers."

8. ***Compelled monetary subsidies.*** (a) A series of cases have invalidated government forced monetary contributions for support of speech opposed by the contributors. *Abood v. Detroit Bd. of Educ.*, 431 U.S. 209 (1977), held that members of a public employee bargaining unit who are not members of the union can be compelled to pay a service fee to the union for its collective bargaining expenses (because they would otherwise be free riders and that would endanger labor peace and because of the importance of stable unions), but they may not be charged for political expenses if they object to the use of union funds supporting political candidates or political views. Similarly, *Keller v. State Bar of California*, 496 U.S. 1 (1990), held that the use of compulsory dues to finance political and ideological activities with which members disagreed violated their First Amendment right of free speech when such

expenditures were not necessarily or reasonably incurred for purpose of regulating the legal profession or the improving quality of legal services.[357] *International Ass'n of Machinists v. Street*, 367 U.S. 740 (1961), held that "dissent is not to be presumed" and that only employees who have affirmatively made known to the union their opposition to political uses of their funds are entitled to relief for political expenditures. *Chicago Teachers v. Hudson*, 475 U.S. 292 (1986), spoke to the process for determining which part of the fees was germane to collective bargaining and which was political, holding that "constitutional requirements for the Union's collection of agency fees include an adequate explanation of the basis for the fee, a reasonably prompt opportunity to challenge the amount of the fee before an impartial decisionmaker, and an escrow for the amounts reasonably in dispute while such challenges are pending."

KNOX v. SERVICE EMPLOYEES INT'L UNION, 132 S.Ct. 2277 (2012), per ALITO, J., held that unions that have a special assessment for political purposes must issue a *Hudson* notice and may not exact funds from non-union members of a bargaining unit without their affirmative consent. In lengthy dicta, Alito, J., suggested that the practice of requiring non-members to opt out of supporting political expenditures authorized by *Hudson*, may not only be statutorily changed to an opt in requirement as was held in *Davenport v. Washington Educ. Ass'n*, 551 U.S. 177 (2007), but may be required under the First Amendment even when the dues assessment is not special. In further dicta, Alito, J., argued that the free rider argument for requiring non-members to pay a service fee to the unions who are required to represent them is an "anomaly." He did not discuss the merits of the argument that the service fee requirement is necessary to assure labor stability and peace.

SOTOMAYOR, J., joined by Ginsburg, J., concurred in the judgment. She agreed that non-members should not be compelled to provide financial support for political expenditures they oppose, but argued that the opt-in remedy was not argued by either party, and was outside the briefs and the scope of the questions presented.[358]

HARRIS v. QUINN, 134 S.Ct. 2618 (2014), per ALITO, J, ruled that an Illinois rule, requiring some home health workers who objected to their union to pay for bargaining expenses, violated the First Amendment right to freedom of association. These "personal assistants" were hired and fired by home-care

---

[357] But *Board of Regents v. Southworth*, 529 U.S. 217 (2000), also held that despite ideological objections, compulsory exactions might be justified by the strength of the governmental interest. It decreed that no refund of student fees was appropriate so long as allocation of funding was viewpoint neutral on the ground that the interest in stimulating diverse ideas on campus outweighed the interests of objecting students. Is the First Amendment objection mistaken because "the mere act of paying a mandatory assessment does not identify the payer with the same message her payments help fund"? Gregory Klass, *The Very Idea of a First Amendment Right Against Compelled Subsidization*, 38 U.C.Davis L. Rev. 1087 (2005).

[358] Breyer, J., joined by Kagan, J., dissenting, agreed with Sotomayor, J., but argued that nonmembers would not in fact over the course of the year be forced to support political expenditures they opposed because the percentage of their dues would not exceed the percentage used for collective bargaining purposes and even if it did the system authorized by *Hudson* would assure that they would eventually be protected.

recipients and subject to their control, but the working relationship albeit broad in scope was controlled by some government regulations and the assistants were paid by government. Alito, J., declined to extend *Abood* to this situation because of its "questionable" foundations and because the personal assistants were not like the "full-fledged" public employees present in *Abood*.

KAGAN, J., joined by Ginsburg, Breyer and Sotomayor, JJ., dissenting, argued that the differences between personal assistants and "full-fledged" public employees were irrelevant, that the foundations of Abood were not questionable, and found some satisfaction in the fact that the majority criticized but did not overrule the 40 year old *Abood* decision which was the basis of thousands of contracts between governments and unions across the country.

(b)   *United States v. United Foods, Inc.,* 533 U.S. 405 (2001) held that objecting mushroom handlers cannot be compelled to fund generic advertisements supporting mushroom sales.[359] Nonetheless, taxpayers routinely fund speech activities to which they are opposed without First Amendment rights being violated.

This paradox was addressed in a case involving beef subsidies. Pursuant to the Beef Promotion and Research Act, the Secretary of Agriculture established a beef promotion and research board funded by government compelled contributions from the sales and importation of cattle. More than 1 billion dollars have been collected, much of it used to promote the sale of beef employing the slogan, "Beef: It's What's for Dinner." Many of the promotional messages state that they are funded by America's beef producers. Plaintiffs brought suit maintaining that compelled financial support of generic advertisements for beef impeded their efforts to promote the superiority of American beef, grain-fed beef, or certified Angus or Hereford beef, and violated the First Amendment.

JOHANNS v. LIVESTOCK MARKETING ASSOCIATION, 544 U.S. 550 (2005), per SCALIA, J., concluded that compelled support of private speech raised First Amendment issues, that such compelled support of government speech did not raise First Amendment issues, and that the beef promotional messages were government speech: "We have sustained First Amendment challenges to allegedly compelled expression in two categories of cases: true 'compelled speech' cases, in which an individual is obliged personally to express a message he disagrees with, imposed by the government; and 'compelled subsidy' cases, in which an individual is required by the government to subsidize a message he disagrees with, expressed by a private entity. We have not heretofore considered the First Amendment consequences of government-compelled subsidy of the government's own speech.

---

[359] But see *Glickman v. Wileman Bros. & Elliott, Inc.,* 521 U.S. 457 (1997) (tree fruit producers can be compelled to pay assessments for advertising). Can *United Foods* be reconciled with *Zauderer?* For doubts, see Robert Post, *Transparent and Efficient Markets,* 40 Val.U.L.Rev. 555 (2006).

"Our compelled-subsidy cases have consistently respected the principle that '[c]ompelled support of a private association is fundamentally different from compelled support of government.' ['The] government, as a general rule, may support valid programs and policies by taxes or other exactions binding on protesting parties. Within this broader principle it seems inevitable that funds raised by the government will be spent for speech and other expression to advocate and defend its own policies.' We have generally assumed, though not yet squarely held, that compelled funding of government speech does not alone raise First Amendment concerns. * * *

"Respondents [assert] that the challenged promotional campaigns differ dispositively from the type of government speech that, our cases suggest, is not susceptible to First Amendment challenge. They point to the role of the Beef Board and its Operating Committee in designing the promotional campaigns, and to the use of a mandatory assessment on beef producers to fund the advertising. * * *

'The Secretary of Agriculture does not write ad copy himself. Rather, the Beef Board's promotional campaigns are designed by the Beef Board's Operating Committee. [Nonetheless, the] message set out in the beef promotions is from beginning to end the message established by the Federal Government.[5]

"Congress has directed the implementation of a 'coordinated program' of promotion, 'including paid advertising, to advance the image and desirability of beef and beef products.' * * * Congress and the Secretary have set out the overarching message and some of its elements, and they have left the development of the remaining details to an entity whose members are answerable to the Secretary (and in some cases appointed by him as well).

"Moreover, the record demonstrates that the Secretary exercises final approval authority over every word used in every promotional campaign. All proposed promotional messages are reviewed by Department officials both for substance and for wording, and some proposals are rejected or rewritten by the Department. * * *

"The compelled-*subsidy* analysis is altogether unaffected by whether the funds for the promotions are raised by general taxes or through a targeted assessment. Citizens may challenge compelled support of private speech, but have no First Amendment right not to fund government speech. And that is no less true when the funding is achieved through targeted assessments devoted exclusively to the program to which the assessed citizens object.

---

[5]   [Ct's Note] The principal dissent suggests that if this is so, then the Government has adopted at best a mixed message, because it also promulgates dietary guidelines that, if followed, would discourage excessive consumption of beef. Even if we agreed that the protection of the government-speech doctrine must be forfeited whenever there is inconsistency in the message, we would nonetheless accord the protection here. The beef promotions are perfectly compatible with the guidelines' message of moderate consumption—the ads do not insist that beef is also What's for Breakfast, Lunch, and Midnight Snack.

"[R]espondents' contend that crediting the advertising to 'America's Beef Producers' impermissibly uses not only their money but also their seeming endorsement to promote a message with which they do not agree. Communications cannot be 'government speech,' they argue, if they are attributed to someone other than the government; and the person to whom they are attributed, when he is, by compulsory funding, made the unwilling instrument of communication, may raise a First Amendment objection.

"We need not determine the validity of this argument—which relates to compelled *speech* rather than compelled *subsidy*—with regard to respondents' facial challenge. Since neither the Beef Act nor the Beef Order requires attribution, neither can be the cause of any possible First Amendment harm. The District Court's order enjoining the enforcement of the Act and the Order thus cannot be sustained on this theory.

"[This theory might form] the basis for an as-applied challenge—if it were established, that is, that individual beef advertisements were attributed to respondents. [Whether] the *individual* respondents who are beef producers would be associated with speech labeled as coming from 'America's Beef Producers' is a question on which the trial record is altogether silent. We have only the funding tagline itself, a trademarked term that, standing alone, is not sufficiently specific to convince a reasonable factfinder that any particular beef producer, or all beef producers, would be tarred with the content of each trademarked ad."[360]

BREYER, J., concurred: "The beef checkoff program in these cases is virtually identical to the mushroom checkoff program in which the Court struck down on First Amendment grounds. The 'government speech' theory the Court adopts today was not before us in *United Foods* [where I dissented] based on my view that the challenged assessments involved a form of economic regulation, not speech. * * *

"I remain of the view that the assessments in these cases are best described as a form of economic regulation. However, I recognize that a majority of the Court does not share that view. Now that we have had an opportunity to consider the 'government speech' theory, I accept it as a solution to the problem presented by these cases."

GINSBURG, J., concurred in the judgment: "I resist ranking the promotional messages funded under the Beef Promotion and Research Act of 1985 as government speech, given the message the Government conveys in its own name [discouraging the consumption of trans fatty acids found in cattle and sheep]. I remain persuaded, however, that the assessments in these cases qualify as permissible economic regulation."

SOUTER, J., joined by Stevens and Kennedy, JJ., dissented: "I take the view that if government relies on the government-speech doctrine to compel

---

[360] Thomas, J. concurred. Kennedy, J., dissented. For discussion of the food cases, see Kathleen Sullivan & Robert C. Post, *It's What's For Lunch: Nectarines, Mushrooms, and Beef— The First Amendment and Compelled Commercial Speech*, 41 Loy.L.A.L.Rev. 359 (2007).

specific groups to fund speech with targeted taxes, it must make itself politically accountable by indicating that the content actually is a government message, not just the statement of one self-interested group the government is currently willing to invest with power. Sometimes, as in these very cases, government can make an effective disclosure only by explicitly labeling the speech as its own.

"[T]he requirement of effective public accountability means the ranchers ought to prevail, it being clear that the Beef Act does not establish an advertising scheme subject to effective democratic checks. The reason for this is simple: the ads are not required to show any sign of being speech by the Government, and experience under the Act demonstrates how effectively the Government has masked its role in producing the ads. Most obviously, many of them include the tag line, '[f]unded by America's Beef Producers,' which all but ensures that no one reading them will suspect that the message comes from the National Government. But the tag line just underscores the point that would be true without it, that readers would most naturally think that ads urging people to have beef for dinner were placed and paid for by the beef producers who stand to profit when beef is on the table. No one hearing a commercial for Pepsi or Levi's thinks Uncle Sam is the man talking behind the curtain. Why would a person reading a beef ad think Uncle Sam was trying to make him eat more steak? Given the circumstances, it is hard to see why anyone would suspect the Government was behind the message unless the message came out and said so."

(c)   Consider Note, 119 Harv. L. Rev. 169 (2005): "The ranchers argued that the attribution of many of the advertisements to 'America's Beef Producers' wrongly associated them with the government's message. The Court sidestepped this argument by noting that the respondents had brought a facial challenge to the statute and that while the program as applied might appear to attribute the speech to the plaintiffs—contrary to *Wooley*—the text of the statute did not mandate this result." On the problem of concealing the government's involvement in a private message, see Brian P. Morrisey, *Speech and Taxes*, 81 Notre Dame L.Rev. 2059 (2006); Abner S. Greene, *Government of the Good,* 53 Vand. L.Rev. 1 (2000); Gia B. Lee, *Persuasion, Transparency, and Government Speech*, 56 Hast. L.J. 983 (2005).

Leaving aside the government speech question, is the claim of the ranchers unappealing because it is little more than "economic interest dressed up as constitutional principle"? Suppose the objectors instead were small organic farmers opposing undifferentiated product descriptions on moral and political grounds relating to the environment, consumer health, or humane treatment of animals? See Seana V. Shiffrin, *Compelled Association, Morality, and Market Dynamics*, 41 Loy. U.L. Law. Rev. 317 (2007). On compelled commercial speech generally, see Leslie Gielow Jacobs, *Compelled Commercial Speech as Compelled Consent Speech*, 29 J.L.&Pol. 517 (2014); Jennifer M. Keighley, *Can You Handle the Truth? Compelled Commercial Speech and the First Amendment,* 15 U.Pa.J.Const.L. 539 (2012); Nat Stern, *Graphic Labels,*

Dire Warnings, and the Facile Assumption of Factual Content in Compelled Commercial Speech, 29 J.L.&Pol, 577 (2014).

9.   **A right not to speak?** *Wooley* and succeeding cases establish a right not to be associated with ideas to which one is ideologically opposed. Yet individuals are forced to speak in a wide variety of situations. Does it violate the First Amendment to compel witnesses to speak in court or legislative proceedings? Should such compulsion have limits? Consider *Barenblatt v. United States,* 360 U.S. 109 (1959)(witness can be compelled before Congress to testify about his political connections with the Communist Party if he does not invoke the fifth amendment). Other cases are more sympathetic to those who choose to remain silent.

(a)   **Anonymous political speech.** McINTYRE v. OHIO ELECTIONS COMM'N, 514 U.S. 334 (1995), per STEVENS, J., held that Ohio's prohibition against the distribution of anonymous campaign literature was unconstitutional: "Under our Constitution, anonymous pamphleteering is not a pernicious, fraudulent practice, but an honorable tradition of advocacy and of dissent. [The] State may and does punish fraud directly. But it cannot seek to punish fraud indirectly by indiscriminately outlawing a category of speech, based on its content, with no necessary relationship to the danger sought to be prevented."[361]

THOMAS, J., concurred, but argued that instead of asking whether " 'an honorable tradition' of free speech has existed throughout American history, [we] should seek the original understanding when we interpret the Speech and Press clauses, just as we do when we read the Religion Clauses of the First Amendment." According to Thomas, J., the original understanding approach also protected anonymous speech.

SCALIA, joined by Rehnquist, C.J., dissenting, asserted that it was the "Court's (and society's) traditional view that the Constitution bears its original meaning and is unchanging." Applying that approach, he concluded that anonymous political speech is not protected under the First Amendment.

(b)   Compelled election disclosures. BROWN v. SOCIALIST WORKERS, 459 U.S. 87 (1982), per MARSHALL, J., held that an Ohio statute requiring every political party to report the names and addresses of campaign contributors and recipients of campaign disbursements could not be applied to the Socialist Workers Party. Citing *Buckley v. Valeo,* Sec. 10 infra, the Court held that the " 'evidence offered [by a minor party] need show only a reasonable probability that the compelled disclosure [of] names will subject them to threats, harassment, or reprisals from either Government officials or private parties.' " Consider Geoffrey Stone & William Marshall, *Brown v. Socialist Workers: Inequality as a Command of the First Amendment,* 1983 Sup.Ct.Rev. 583: "[I]n

---

[361] Ginsburg, J., concurred. Consider Randall P. Bezanson, *Speech Stories: How Free Can Speech Be?* 50 (1998): "The Court's decision appears to have rested on the fact that McIntyre's leaflet was an expression of *opinion*, not just of fact, and that its quality as opinion subordinated any claims about authorship that might be based on its factual content, thus avoiding any need to discuss its factual elements." What if the leaflet did not contain opinion?

Brown the Court expressly exempted particular political parties from an otherwise content-neutral regulation for reasons directly related to the content of their expression. [The] constitutionally compelled exemption substitutes a content-based law for one that is content neutral. It stands the presumption in favor of 'content neutrality' on its head." Is the decision, nonetheless, consistent with First Amendment values? See Stone & Marshall, supra.

(c) *Compelled disclosure of desire to receive Communist mail.* LAMONT v. POSTMASTER GENERAL, 381 U.S. 301 (1965), per DOUGLAS, J., invalidated a federal statute permitting delivery of "communist political propaganda" only if the addressee specifically requested in writing that it be delivered: "We rest on the narrow ground that the addressee in order to receive his mail must request in writing that it be delivered. [The] addressee carries an affirmative obligation which we do not think the government may impose on him. This requirement is almost certain to have a deterrent effect, especially as respects those who have sensitive positions. [Public] officials, like school teachers who have no tenure, might think they would invite disaster if they read what the Federal Government says contains the seeds of treason. Apart from them, any addressee is likely to feel some inhibition in sending for literature which federal officials have condemned as 'communist political propaganda.' "[362]

II. INTIMATE ASSOCIATION AND EXPRESSIVE ASSOCIATION

ROBERTS v. UNITED STATES JAYCEES, 468 U.S. 609 (1984): Appellee U.S. Jaycees, a nonprofit national membership corporation whose objective is to pursue educational and charitable purposes that promote the growth and development of young men's civic organizations, limits regular membership to young men between the ages of 18 and 35. Associate membership is available to women and older men. An associate member may not vote or hold local or national office. Two local chapters in Minnesota violated appellee's bylaws by admitting women as regular members. When they learned that revocation of their charters was to be considered, members of both chapters filed discrimination charges with the Minnesota Department of Human Rights, alleging that the exclusion of women from full membership violated the Minnesota Human Rights Act (Act), which makes it an "unfair discriminatory practice" to deny anyone "the full and equal enjoyment of goods, services, facilities, privileges, advantages, and accommodations of a place of public accommodation" because, inter alia, of sex.

Before a hearing on the state charge took place, appellee brought federal suit, alleging that requiring it to accept women as regular members would violate the male members' constitutional "freedom of association." A

---

[362] Compare *Meese v. Keene*, 481 U.S. 465 (1987)(government may label and require registration of films involving "political propaganda," so long as it permits distribution).

state hearing officer decided against appellee and the federal district court certified to the Minnesota Supreme Court the question whether appellee is "a place of public accommodation" within the meaning of the Act. With the record of the administrative hearing before it, the state Supreme Court answered that question in the affirmative. The U.S. Court of Appeals held that application of the Act to appellee's membership policies would violate its freedom of association.[363]

In rejecting appellee's claims,[364] the Court, per BRENNAN, J., pointed out that the Constitution protects " 'freedom of association' in two distinct senses," what might be called "freedom of intimate association" and "freedom of expressive association": "In one line of decisions, the Court has concluded that choices to enter into and maintain certain intimate human relationships must be secured against undue intrusion by the State because of the role of such relationships in safeguarding the individual freedom that is central to our constitutional scheme. In this respect, freedom of association receives protection as a fundamental element of personal liberty. In another set of decisions, the Court has recognized a right to associate for the purpose of engaging in those activities protected by the First Amendment—speech, assembly, petition for the redress of grievances, [and] religion. The Constitution guarantees freedom of association of this kind as an indispensable means of preserving other individual liberties."

The freedom of intimate association was deemed important because, "certain kinds of personal bonds have played a critical role in the culture and traditions of the Nation by cultivating and transmitting shared ideals and beliefs; they thereby foster diversity and act as critical buffers between the individual and the power of the State. Moreover, the constitutional shelter afforded such relationships reflects the realization that individuals draw much of their emotional enrichment from close ties with others. Protecting these relationships from unwarranted state interference therefore safeguards the ability independently to define one's identity that is central to any concept of liberty.

"The personal affiliations that exemplify these considerations [are] distinguished by such attributes as relative smallness, a high degree of selectivity in decisions to begin and maintain the affiliation, and seclusion from others in critical aspects of the relationship. [A]n association lacking

---

[363] When the state supreme court held that appellee was "a place of public accommodation" within the meaning of the Act, it suggested that, unlike appellee, the Kiwanis Club might be sufficiently "private" to be outside the scope of the Act. Appellee then amended its complaint to allege that the state court's interpretation of the Act rendered it unconstitutionally vague. The Eighth Circuit so held, but the Court reversed.

[364] There was no dissent. Rehnquist, J., concurred in the judgment. O'Connor, J., joined part of the Court's opinion and concurred in the judgment. See infra. Burger, C.J., and Blackmun, J., took no part.

these qualities—such as a large business enterprise—seems remote from the concerns giving rise to this constitutional protection. * * *

"Between these poles, of course, lies a broad range of human relationships that may make greater or lesser claims to constitutional protection from particular incursions by the State. [We] need not mark the potentially significant points on this terrain with any precision. We note only that factors that may be relevant include size, purpose, policies, selectivity, congeniality, and other characteristics that in a particular case may be pertinent. In this case, however, several features of the Jaycees clearly place the organization outside of the category of relationships worthy of this kind of constitutional protection.

"[T]he local chapters of the Jaycees are large and basically unselective groups. [Apart] from age and sex, neither the national organization nor the local chapters employs any criteria for judging applicants for membership, and new members are routinely recruited and admitted with no inquiry into their backgrounds. In fact, a local officer testified that he could recall no instance in which an applicant had been denied membership on any basis other than age or sex. [Furthermore], numerous non-members of both genders regularly participate in a substantial portion of activities central to the decision of many members to associate with one another, including many of the organization's various community programs, awards ceremonies, and recruitment meetings.

"[We] turn therefore to consider the extent to which application of the Minnesota statute to compel the Jaycees to accept women infringes the group's freedom of expressive association. * * *

"Government actions that may unconstitutionally infringe upon [freedom of expressive association] can take a number of forms. Among other things, government may seek to impose penalties or withhold benefits from individuals because of their membership in a disfavored group; it may attempt to require disclosure of the fact of membership in a group seeking anonymity; and it may try to interfere with the internal organization or affairs of the group. [There] can be no clearer example of an intrusion into the internal structure or affairs of an association than a regulation that forces the group to accept members it does not desire. Such a regulation may impair the ability of the original members to express only those views that brought them together. Freedom of association therefore plainly presupposes a freedom not to associate. See *Abood*.

"The right to associate for expressive purposes is not, however, absolute. Infringements on that right may be justified by regulations adopted to serve compelling state interests, unrelated to the suppression of ideas, that cannot be achieved through means significantly less restrictive of associational freedoms.

"[I]n upholding Title II of the Civil Rights Act of 1964, which forbids race discrimination in public accommodations, we emphasized that its 'fundamental object [was] to vindicate "the deprivation of personal dignity that surely accompanies denials of equal access to public establishments."' *Heart of Atlanta Motel,* [Ch. 2, Sec. 2, III]. That stigmatizing injury, and the denial of equal opportunities that accompanies it, is surely felt as strongly by persons suffering discrimination on the basis of their sex as by those treated differently because of their race.

"Nor is the state interest in assuring equal access limited to the provision of purely tangible goods and services. A State enjoys broad authority to create rights of public access on behalf of its citizens. *PruneYard.* Like many States and municipalities, Minnesota has adopted a functional definition of public accommodations that reaches various forms of public, quasi-commercial conduct. This expansive definition reflects a recognition of the changing nature of the American economy and of the importance, both to the individual and to society, of removing the barriers to economic advancement and political and social integration that have historically plagued certain disadvantaged groups, including women. * * *

"In applying the Act to the Jaycees, the State has advanced those interests through the least restrictive means of achieving its ends. Indeed, the Jaycees have failed to demonstrate that the Act imposes any serious burdens on the male members' freedom of expressive association. See *Hishon v. King & Spalding,* 467 U.S. 69 (1984) (law firm 'has not shown how its ability to fulfill [protected] function[s] would be inhibited by a requirement that it consider [a woman lawyer] for partnership on her merits'). To be sure, a 'not insubstantial part' of the Jaycees' activities constitutes protected expression on political, economic, cultural, and social affairs. [There] is, however, no basis in the record for concluding that admission of women as full voting members will impede the organization's ability to engage in these protected activities or to disseminate its preferred views. The Act requires no change in the Jaycees' creed of promoting the interests of young men, and it imposes no restrictions on the organization's ability to exclude individuals with ideologies or philosophies different from those of its existing members. Moreover, the Jaycees already invite women to share the group's views and philosophy and to participate in much of [its] activities. Accordingly, any claim that admission of women as full voting members will impair a symbolic message conveyed by the very fact that women are not permitted to vote is attenuated at best.

"[In] claiming that women might have a different attitude about such issues as the federal budget, school prayer, voting rights, and foreign relations, or that the organization's public positions would have a different effect if the group were not 'a purely young men's association,' the Jaycees rely solely on unsupported generalizations about the relative interests and perspectives of men and women. Although such generalizations may or may not have a statistical basis in fact with respect to particular positions adopted by the Jaycees, we have repeatedly condemned legal decisionmaking that relies uncritically on such assumptions. In the absence of a showing far more substantial than that attempted by the Jaycees, we decline to indulge in the sexual stereotyping [of appellees].

"In any event, even if enforcement of the Act causes some incidental abridgement of the Jaycees' protected speech, that effect is no greater than is necessary to accomplish the State's legitimate purposes. [A]cts of invidious discrimination in the distribution of publicly available goods, services, and other advantages cause unique evils that government has a compelling interest to prevent—wholly apart from the point of view such conduct may transmit. Accordingly, like violence or other types of potentially expressive activities that produce special harms distinct from their communicative impact, such practices are entitled to no constitutional protection."[365]

O'CONNOR, J., concurring, joined the Court's opinion except for its analysis of freedom of expressive association: "[T]he Court has adopted a test that unadvisedly casts doubt on the power of States to pursue the profoundly important goal of ensuring nondiscriminatory access to commercial opportunities" yet "accords insufficient protection to expressive associations and places inappropriate burdens on groups claiming the protection of the First Amendment":

"[The] Court declares that the Jaycees' right of association depends on the organization's making a 'substantial' showing that the admission of unwelcome members 'will change the message communicated by the group's speech.' [S]uch a requirement, especially in the context of the balancing-of-interests test articulated by the Court, raises the possibility that certain commercial associations, by engaging occasionally in certain kinds of expressive activities, might improperly gain protection for discrimination. The Court's focus raises other problems as well. [W]ould the Court's analysis of this case be different if, for example, the Jaycees membership had a steady history of opposing public issues thought (by the Court) to be favored by women? It might seem easy to conclude, in the latter case, that the admission of women to the Jaycees' ranks would affect the content of the organization's message, but I do not believe that should change the outcome of this case. Whether an association is or is not

---

[365] For cases following or extending *Roberts*, see *Board of Directors of Rotary International v. Rotary Club of Duarte*, 481 U.S. 537 (1987); *New York State Club Ass'n v. New York*, 487 U.S. 1 (1988) (upholding city ordinance against facial challenge that prohibits discrimination based on race, creed, or sex by institutions (except benevolent orders or religious corporations) with more than 400 members that provide regular meal service and receive payment from nonmembers for the furtherance of trade or business); *Dallas v. Stanglin*, 490 U.S. 19 (1989) (upholding ordinance restricting admission to certain dance halls to persons between the ages of 14 and 18).

constitutionally protected in the selection of its membership should not depend on what the association says or why its members say it.

"The Court's readiness to inquire into the connection between membership and message reveals a more fundamental flaw in its analysis. The Court pursues this inquiry as part of its mechanical application of a 'compelling interest' test, [and] entirely neglects to establish at the threshold that the Jaycees is an association whose activities or purposes should engage the strong protections that the First Amendment extends to expressive associations.

"On the one hand, an association engaged exclusively in protected expression enjoys First Amendment protection of both the content of its message and the choice of its members. * * * Protection of the association's right to define its membership derives from the recognition that the formation of an expressive association is the creation of a voice, and the selection of members is the definition of that voice. [A] ban on specific group voices on public affairs violates the most basic guarantee of the First Amendment—that citizens, not the government, control the content of public discussion.

"On the other hand, there is only minimal constitutional protection of the freedom of *commercial* association. There are, of course, some constitutional protections of commercial speech—speech intended and used to promote a commercial transaction with the speaker. But the State is free to impose any rational regulation on the commercial transaction itself. The Constitution does not guarantee a right to choose employees, customers, suppliers, or those with whom one engages in simple commercial transactions, without restraint from the State.

"[A]n association should be characterized as commercial, and therefore subject to rationally related state regulation of its membership and other associational activities, when, and only when, the association's activities are not predominantly of the type protected by the First Amendment. It is only when the association is predominantly engaged in protected expression that state regulation of its membership will necessarily affect, change, dilute, or silence one collective voice that would otherwise be heard. An association must choose its market. Once it enters the marketplace of commerce in any substantial degree it loses the complete control over its membership that it would otherwise enjoy if it confined its affairs to the marketplace of ideas.

"[N]otwithstanding its protected expressive activities, [appellee] is, first and foremost, an organization that, at both the national and local levels, promotes and practices the art of solicitation and management. The organization claims that the training it offers its members gives them an advantage in business, and business firms do indeed sometimes pay the dues of individual memberships for their employees. Jaycees members hone their solicitation and management skills, under the direction and supervision of the organization, primarily through their active recruitment of new members. [The] 'not insubstantial' volume of protected Jaycees activity found by the Court of Appeals is simply not enough to preclude state regulation of the Jaycees' commercial activities. The State of Minnesota has a legitimate interest in ensuring nondiscriminatory access to the commercial opportunity presented by membership in the Jaycees."

NOTES AND QUESTIONS

1. *Freedom of intimate association.* The reference to the freedom of intimate association is the first in the Court's history, but the notion that the concept should serve as an organizing principle is found in Kenneth Karst, *Freedom of Intimate Association,* 89 Yale L.J. 624 (1980). To what extent should freedom of intimate association itself be regarded as a First Amendment right? Compare Karst with C. Edwin Baker, *Scope of the First Amendment Freedom of Speech,* 25 UCLA L.Rev. 964 (1978) and Reena Raggi, *An Independent Right to Freedom of Association,* 12 Harv.Civ.Rts.-Civ.Lib.L.Rev. 1 (1977).

2. *Freedom of expressive association.* Should freedom of association be confined to groups that are intimate or have a message to propound? Consider Shiffrin, Note 1 after *Barnette,* Sec. 9, I supra: "An association may have no message at all and nonetheless serve important First Amendment values. To wit, an important function of private associations is that they provide sites in which the thoughts and ideas of members are formed and in which the content of their expressions is generated and germinated (although not necessarily in harmony with other members), not merely concentrated and exported. That is, associations are important from a freedom of speech perspective because of what happens inside of them, not solely or even necessarily by virtue of their relationships to the outside world or even by virtue of any internal shared beliefs." Is Brennan, J.'s conception of association's value too narrowly conceived? See also George Kateb, *The Value of Association* in *Freedom of Association* 35 (Amy Gutmann ed. 1998).[366]

3. *Commercial associations.* Is O'Connor, J.'s distinction of commercial associations defensible? Consider Shiffrin, supra: "Regulation to promote inclusive membership practices is justified when applied to associations whose primary purpose is participation in the commercial milieu because of the central importance of fair access to material resources and mechanisms of power. Second, because such associations operate within a highly competitive marketplace and have a fairly focused singular purpose whose pursuit is largely guided by this competitive context and aim of profitable operation, these associations do not function in a context that is likely to be conducive to the free, sincere, uninhibited, and undirected social

---

[366] On the value of discriminatory associations, see generally Nancy L. Rosenblum, *Membership and Morals* (1998).

interaction and consideration of ideas and ways of life."[367] To what extent should government be able to limit the discriminatory policies of groups that are commercial and expressive? What about private schools? Should they be able to discriminate in the selection of teachers but not with respect to construction workers or secretaries? See Dale Carpenter, *Expressive Association and Anti-Discrimination Law After Dale: A Tripartite Approach*, 85 Minn. L. Rev. 1515 (2001). Should hate speech codes on private college campuses be protected against government prohibition on associational grounds? See David E. Bernstein, *The Right of Expressive Association and Private Universities' Racial Preferences and Speech Codes*, 9 Wm. & Mary Bill Rts. J. 619 (2001).

What about newspapers? Should a similar analysis apply to them? Should the freedom of association concept apply to the press, or should the press clause apply? Christopher R. Edgar, *The Right to Freedom of Expressive Association and the Press*, 55 Stan. L. Rev. 191 (2002). Does the concept of freedom of association support or engulf the academic freedom enjoyed by universities? See Paul Horwitz, *Grutter's First Amendment*, 46 B.C. L. REV. 461 (2005), and also Paul Horwitz, *First Amendment Institutions* (2013).

———

James Dale's position as an assistant scoutmaster of a New Jersey troop of the Boy Scouts of America was revoked. The Scouts learned that he was gay and the co-President of the Rutgers University Lesbian/Gay Alliance. Dale had been publicly quoted on the importance in his own life on the need for gay role models. Dale sued, and the New Jersey Supreme Court ultimately held that New Jersey's anti-discrimination public accommodation law required that the Scouts readmit him.

BOY SCOUTS OF AMERICA v. DALE, 530 U.S. 640 (2000), per REHNQUIST, C.J., held that the New Jersey law violated the expressive association rights of the Boy Scouts: "The First Amendment's protection of expressive association is not reserved for advocacy groups. But to come within its ambit, a group must engage in some form of expression, whether it be public or private."

Rehnquist, C.J., cited portions of the Scout Oath requiring Scouts to be "morally straight" and to be "Clean": "The Boy Scouts [says] that it 'teach[es] that homosexual conduct is not morally straight' * * * . We need not inquire further to determine the nature of the Boy Scouts' expression with respect to homosexuality. But because the record before us contains written evidence of the Boy Scouts' viewpoint, we look to it as instructive, if only on the question of the sincerity of the professed beliefs. * * *

"We must [also] give deference to an association's view of what would impair its expression. [That] is not to say that an expressive association

---

[367] See generally Michael Burns, *The Exclusion of Women From Influential Men's Clubs: The Inner Sanctum and the Myth of Full Equality,* 18 Harv.Civ.Rts.-Civ.Lib.L.Rev. 321 (1983).

can erect a shield against antidiscrimination laws simply by asserting that mere acceptance of a member from a particular group would impair its message. But here Dale, by his own admission, is one of a group of gay Scouts who have 'become leaders in their community and are open and honest about their sexual orientation.' [His] presence in the Boy Scouts would, at the very least, force the organization to send a message, both to the youth members and the world, that the Boy Scouts accepts homosexual conduct as a legitimate form of behavior.[368] * * *

"We recognized in cases such as *Roberts* and *Duarte* that States have a compelling interest in eliminating discrimination against women in public accommodations. But in each of these cases we went on to conclude that the enforcement of these statutes would not materially interfere with the ideas that the organization sought to express. * * * New Jersey's public accommodations law directly and immediately affects associational rights, in this case associational rights that enjoy First Amendment protection. Thus, *O'Brien*['s] intermediate standard of review [is] inapplicable."

STEVENS, J., joined by Souter, Ginsburg, and Breyer, JJ., dissenting, contended that: "at a minimum, a group seeking to prevail over an antidiscrimination law must adhere to a clear and unequivocal view" and that the Scouts had not done so. Nor did precedent favor the Scouts claim: "Several principles are made perfectly clear by *Jaycees* and *Rotary Club*. First, to prevail on a claim of expressive association in the face of a State's antidiscrimination law, it is not enough simply to engage in *some kind* of expressive activity. Both the Jaycees and the Rotary Club engaged in expressive activity protected by the First Amendment, yet that fact was not dispositive. Second, it is not enough to adopt an openly avowed exclusionary membership policy. Both the Jaycees and the Rotary Club did that as well. Third, it is not sufficient merely to articulate *some* connection between the group's expressive activities and its exclusionary policy." Stevens, J., argued that it was necessary to show a serious burden on the association's expression: "The evidence before this Court makes it exceptionally clear that BSA has, at most, simply adopted an exclusionary membership policy and has no shared goal of disapproving of homosexuality [or] collective effort to foster a belief about homosexuality at all—let alone one that is significantly burdened by admitting

---

[368] Stevens, J., dissenting, responded: "Dale's inclusion in the Boy Scouts [sends] no cognizable message to the Scouts or to the world. Unlike GLIB, Dale did not carry a banner or a sign; he did not distribute any fact sheet; and he expressed no intent to send any message. If there is any kind of message being sent, then, it is by the mere act of joining the Boy Scouts. [S]ome acts are so imbued with symbolic meaning that they qualify as 'speech' under the First Amendment. At the same time, however, '[w]e cannot accept the view that an apparently limitless variety of conduct can be labeled 'speech' whenever the person engaging in the conduct intends thereby to express an idea.' *O'Brien*. [Indeed], if merely joining a group did constitute symbolic speech; and such speech were attributable to the group being joined; and that group has the right to exclude that speech (and hence, the right to exclude that person from joining), then the right of free speech effectively becomes a limitless right to exclude for every organization, whether or not it engages in any expressive activities. That cannot be, and never has been, the law."

homosexuals." Stevens argued that the majority's deferential posture toward the allegations of the Scouts reflected "an astounding view of the law. I am unaware of any previous instance in which our analysis of the scope of a constitutional right was determined by looking at what a litigant asserts in his or her brief and inquiring no further."

NOTES AND QUESTIONS

1. ***What speech?*** Consider Randall P. Bezanson, *Speaking Through Others' Voices: Authorship, Originality, and Free Speech*, 38 Wake Forest L. Rev. 983 (2003): "*Dale* represents an instance of speakerless speech since the speaker (the Scouts) never physically articulated a message. Yet the *Dale* case involved an identifiable message that was likely understood by an audience. To complicate matters further, the speaker in *Dale* (the Scouts) had no intention to communicate the message, or indeed to communicate any message whatever, by the act of employing or firing Dale." Are the Scouts entitled to exclude Dale because his coming out in a context other than scouting imputes a message to it? If so, what is Dale's message? See James P. Madigan, *Questioning the Coercive Effect of Self-Identifying Speech*, 87 Iowa L. Rev. 75 (2001); Nancy J. Knauer, *"Simply So Different": The Uniquely Expressive Character of the Openly Gay Individual After Boy Scouts of America v. Dale*, 89 Ky. L.J. 997 (2001). Consider Laurence H. Tribe, *Disentangling Symmetries: Speech, Association, Parenthood*, 28 Pepp. L. Rev. 641 (2001): "[T]he right not to have government force on you an unwanted associate cannot be overcome by the fact that it might be as clear as day to the whole world that the unwanted associate is not your idea, and that your agreement to let him or her into your group reflects nothing more than your obedience to the law. Thus, the fact that the Chief Justice overplayed his hand when he said that forcing the Boy Scouts to accept an openly gay scout leader would compel them to send a pro-gay signal to the world at large should not lead anyone to conclude that the majority's result in that case was necessarily wrong."

2. ***Standard of review.*** Does the Court apply a more demanding standard of review to the application of the statute than it did in *O'Brien*? Adam M. Samaha, *Litigant Sensitivity in First Amendment Law*, 98 Nw. U. L. Rev. 1291 (2004). Is this a particular problem for Scalia, J.? See Stephen Clark, *Judicially Straight? Boy Scouts v. Dale and the Missing Scalia Dissent*, 76 S. Cal. L. Rev. 521 (2003).

Consider Tribe, Note 1 supra: "The state's objection to the exclusion of openly gay men by groups like the Boy Scouts cannot be simply that such groups must be acting on ignorant stereotypes, using sexual orientation as a statistical proxy or as shorthand for something else that really matters to them—the sort of objection conventionally made to the use of race, and sometimes to the use of gender, as proxies for something else. That kind of objection would not carry the day against the Boy Scouts, who are, for better or for worse, using heterosexual status as a defining component of their ideal. As a result, it becomes difficult to regard the application of the antidiscrimination laws in this setting as a 'neutral' instance of mere error-correction. Rather, it becomes a direct clash of competing images of 'the good life.' And, in such a clash, the teaching of the First Amendment has long been that the state loses."

What accounts for the Court's deferential review of the Scout's ideology? Is it to be explained by hostility to civil rights for gays? See Neal Troum, *Expressive Association and the Right to Exclude: Reading Between the Lines in Boy Scouts of America v. Dale*, 35 Creighton L. Rev. 641 (2002); Darren L. Hutchinson, *"Closet Case": Boy Scouts of America v. Dale and the Reinforcement of Gay, Lesbian, Bisexual, and Transgender Invisibility*, 76 Tul. L. Rev. 81 (2001). Would a contrary result mean that the Scouts could be required to be sexually integrated? For discussion, see Evelyn Brody, *Entrance, Voice, and Exit: The Constitutional Bounds of the Right of Association*, 35 U.C. Davis L. Rev. 821 (2002).

3. ***Children.*** Does it matter that unlike *Roberts* the Scouts are children? See Seana V. Shiffrin, *What Is Really Wrong With Compelled Association?*, 99 Nw. U. L. Rev. 839 (2005) (contending that it makes it more difficult to defend the result).

4. ***The joy of ambiguity.*** Consider Andrew Koppelman, *Should Noncommercial Associations Have an Absolute Right to Discriminate?*, 67 Law & Contemp. Probs. 27 (2004): "In the end, we have a choice of pathologies. We can either live with the little pathologies created by the message-based rule, or with the big pathologies that would be created by either of the large and clear rules—absolute protection for discrimination, or no freedom of association at all—between which it uneasily perches. Ambiguity has its virtues. There is this much to be said for the Court's confused opinion in *Dale*: it has thickened the fog where clarity would be deadly." Does O'Connor, J.'s approach in *Roberts* avoid the "big" pathologies?

5. ***Restrictions on freedom of association and limited public forums.*** (a) CHRISTIAN LEGAL SOCIETY v. MARTINEZ, 561 U.S. 661 (2010), per GINSBURG, J., held that Hastings Law School could condition official recognition of a student group—and the resulting eligibility for financial resources and access to certain facilities—on its agreement to open its membership and eligibility for access to leadership positions to all students ("all-comers" policy).[369] The Christian Legal Society restricted membership to Christians and denied access to those who "engage in unrepentant homosexual conduct." Ginsburg, J., concluded that the policy, denying the Society access to a limited public forum, was viewpoint neutral; indeed it drew no distinction between groups based on their message or perspective; it regulated conduct, not speech.

---

[369] The Hastings brief observed that recognized student organizations can require students to pay dues, maintain good attendance, refrain from gross misconduct, or to pass a skill-based test, such as the writing competitions administered by the law journals. The dissent stated that this admission transformed the all-comers policy into a some-comers policy.

She also maintained that the policy was "reasonable." It ensured that students were afforded leadership, educational, and social opportunities, that Hastings students are not forced through student fees to fund a group that would reject them as members, helped Hastings enforce its anti-discrimination policy (and state anti-discrimination laws) without the necessity of determining the basis for membership restrictions, and by bringing together people of diverse backgrounds encouraged toleration, cooperation, and learning. Any claim that hostile students would take over an organization was contrary to the experience of the school and unduly speculative.

The reasonableness of the policy was also indicated by its measured character. The school offered the Society access to school facilities to conduct meetings and the use of chalkboards and some bulletin boards, and it could take advantage of electronic media and social networking sites. "It is beyond dissenter's license * * * constantly to maintain that nonrecognition of a group is equivalent to prohibiting its members from speaking."

Nor did the policy impinge on the Society's freedom of association right to choose its members. Although the Society had a right to be selective in its membership, it had no right for the state to subsidize its selectivity. Finally, the Court rejected claims that the policy had been applied in a discriminatory way and that it was a pretext to single out the Christian Legal Society for special treatment. Ginsburg, J., maintained that such claims were not before the Court because the parties stipulated that Hastings current policy was an all-comers policy and that it applied equally to religious and political groups. The Court remanded to permit the lower court to explore claims of pretext if they were still open to the plaintiffs.

STEVENS, J., concurring, argued that Hastings' exclusion of the Society from its limited public forum would have been justified even under a policy that only excluded groups discriminating on the basis of race, gender, religion, and sexual orientation: Hastings "excludes students who will not sign its Statement of Faith or who engage in 'unrepentant homosexual conduct.' [Other] groups may exclude or mistreat Jews, blacks and women—or those who do not share their contempt for Jews, blacks and women. A free society may tolerate such groups. It need not subsidize them, give them its official imprimatur, or grant them equal access to law school facilities."[370]

ALITO, J., joined by Roberts, C.J., Scalia and Thomas, JJ., dissented, mostly disagreeing with the majority's reading of the record. Alito, J., argued that the Hastings policy shifted over the years, that it had been applied in a discriminatory way (including the denial of access to facilities), that it was ultimately pretextual, and that such issues were rightly before the Court, and that the decision was a "serious setback for freedom of expression in this country."

---

[370] Kennedy, J., concurring, argued that Hastings could reasonably believe that the process of learning how to create arguments in a "convincing, rational, and respectful manner and to express doubt and disagreement in a professional way" is best enhanced when dialogue is "vibrant" which cannot occur if "students wall themselves off from opposing points of view."

As to the all-comers policy, even applied in a non-discriminatory way, he argued that it was unreasonable in large part because it impinged on freedom of association by denying access to needed facilities, and that subsidies were a minor part of the case. Respecting freedom of association also promoted leadership, educational, and social opportunities. He denied that the difficulty of enforcing a nondiscrimination policy was greater than other policies it sought to enforce and denied that California law called into question that right of religious groups to discriminate on the basis of religion. He maintained that furthering toleration, cooperation, and learning skills was consistent with pluralism. Alito, J., also denied that the all-comers policy was viewpoint neutral in that it opened the door for hostile groups to take over organizations and because of his view of discriminatory purpose and treatment.

(b) If Hastings had a policy prohibiting discrimination on the basis of race, gender, sexual orientation, and religion instead of an all-comers policy, would it be constitutional? See generally Eugene Volokh, *Freedom of Expressive Association and Government Subsidies,* 58 Stan. L.Rev. 1919 (2006) (subject to limited exceptions, government need not subsidize such discrimination).

(c) Conservative Justices have tended to deny equality claims in subsidy cases and liberal Justices have tended to support them except in *Rosenberger* and in *Hastings*. Why the departure in those cases? For discussion, see Kathleen M. Sullivan, *Two Concepts of Freedom of Speech,* 124 Harv. L.Rev.143 (2010).

———

In the *Rumsfeld* case, Note 4(c), Sec. 9, I supra, the law schools, citing *Dale,* argued that the Solomon Amendment violated law schools' freedom of expressive association. The Court disagreed: "To comply with the statute, law schools must allow military recruiters on campus and assist them in whatever way the school chooses to assist other employers. Law schools therefore 'associate' with military recruiters in the sense that they interact with them. But recruiters are not part of the law school. Recruiters are, by definition, outsiders who come onto campus for the limited purpose of trying to hire students—not to become members of the school's expressive association. This distinction is critical. Unlike the public accommodations law in *Dale,* the Solomon Amendment does not force a law school 'to accept members it does not desire.' "

10. WEALTH AND THE POLITICAL PROCESS: CONCERNS FOR EQUALITY

The idea of equality has loomed large throughout this chapter. Some feel it should be a central concern of the First Amendment. See Laurence Tribe, *Constitutional Choices* 188–220 (1985); Kenneth Karst, *Equality as a Central Principle in the First Amendment,* 43 U.Chi.L.Rev. 20 (1975). Equality has been championed by those who seek access to government property and to media facilities. It has been invoked in support of content regulation and against it. This section considers government efforts to prevent the domination of the political process by wealthy individuals and business corporations. In the end, it would be appropriate to reconsider the arguments for and against a marketplace conception of the First Amendment, to ask whether the Court's interpretations overall (e.g., taking the public forum materials, the media materials, and the election materials together) have adequately considered the interest in equality, and to inquire generally about the relationship between liberty and equality in the constitutional scheme.

BUCKLEY V. VALEO
424 U.S. 1, 96 S.Ct. 612, 46 L.Ed.2d 659 (1976).

PER CURIAM.

[In this portion of a lengthy opinion dealing with the validity of the Federal Election Campaign Act of 1971, as amended in 1974, the Court considers those parts of the Act limiting *contributions* to a candidate for federal office (all sustained), and those parts limiting *expenditures* in support of such candidacy (all held invalid).]

A. *General Principles.* The Act's contribution and expenditure limitations operate in an area of the most fundamental First Amendment activities. Discussion of public issues and debate on the qualifications of candidates are integral to the operation of the system of government established by our Constitution.

[Appellees] contend that what the Act regulates is conduct, and that its effect on speech and association is incidental at most. Appellants respond that contributions and expenditures are at the very core of political speech, and that the Act's limitations thus constitute restraints on First Amendment liberty that are both gross and [direct.]

We cannot share the view [that] the present Act's contribution and expenditure limitations are comparable to the restrictions on conduct upheld in *O'Brien* [Sec. 2 supra]. The expenditure of money simply cannot be equated with such conduct as destruction of a draft card. Some forms of communication made possible by the giving and spending of money involve speech alone, some involve conduct primarily, and some involve a combination of the two. Yet this Court has never suggested that the dependence of a communication on the expenditure of money operates itself to introduce a non-speech element or to reduce the exacting scrutiny required by the First Amendment. * * *

Even if the categorization of the expenditure of money as conduct were accepted, the limitations challenged here would not meet the *O'Brien* test because the governmental interests advanced in support of the Act involve "suppressing communication." The interests served by the Act include restricting the voices of people and interest groups who have money to spend and reducing the overall scope of federal election campaigns. [Unlike] *O'Brien,* where [the] interest in the preservation of draft cards was wholly unrelated to their use as a means of communication, it is beyond dispute that the interest in regulating the alleged "conduct" of giving or spending money "arises in some measure because the communication allegedly integral to the conduct is itself thought to be harmful."

Nor can the Act's contribution and expenditure limitations be sustained, as some of the parties suggest, by reference to the constitutional principles reflected in such decisions as *Adderley* [Ch. 5, Sec. 1] and *Kovacs v. Cooper,* 336 U.S. 77 (1949). [The] critical difference between this case and those time, place and manner cases is that the present Act's contribution and expenditure limitations impose direct quantity restrictions on political communication and association by persons, groups, candidates and political parties in addition to any reasonable time, place, and manner regulations otherwise imposed.

A restriction on the amount of money a person or group can spend on political communication during a campaign necessarily reduces the quantity of expression by restricting the number of issues discussed, the depth of their exploration, and the size of the audience reached. This is because virtually every means of communicating ideas in today's mass society requires the expenditure of [money].

The expenditure limitations contained in the Act represent substantial rather than merely theoretical restraints on the quantity and diversity of political speech. The $1,000 ceiling on spending "relative to a clearly identified candidate," 18 U.S.C. § 608(e)(1), would appear to exclude all citizens and groups except candidates, political parties and the institutional press from any significant use of the most effective modes of communication.[20] * * *

By contrast with a limitation upon expenditures for political expression, a limitation [on] the amount of money a person may give to a candidate or campaign organization [involves] little direct restraint on his political communication, for it permits the symbolic expression of support evidenced by a contribution but does not in any way infringe the contributor's freedom to discuss candidates and issues. While contributions may result in political expression if spent by a candidate or an association to present views to the voters, the transformation of contributions into political debate involves speech by someone other than the contributor.

---

[20] **[Ct's Note]** The record indicates that, as of January 1, 1975, one full-page advertisement in a daily edition of a certain metropolitan newspaper costs $6,971.04—almost seven times the annual limit on expenditures "relative to" a particular candidate imposed on the vast majority of individual citizens and associations by § 608(e)(1).

[There] is no indication [that] the contribution limitations imposed by the Act would have any dramatic adverse effect on the funding of campaigns and political associations.[23] The overall effect of the Act's contribution ceilings is merely to require candidates and political committees to raise funds from a greater number of persons and to compel people who would otherwise contribute amounts greater than the statutory limits to expend such funds on direct political expression, rather than to reduce the total amount of money potentially available to promote political expression. * * *

In sum, although the Act's contribution and expenditure limitations both implicate fundamental First Amendment interests, its expenditure ceilings impose significantly more severe restrictions on protected freedoms of political expression and association than do its limitations on financial contributions.

B. *Contribution Limitations.* [Section] 608(b) provides, with certain limited exceptions, that "no person shall make contributions to any candidate with respect to any election for Federal office which, in the aggregate, exceeds $1,000."[371]* * *

Appellants contend that the $1,000 contribution ceiling unjustifiably burdens First Amendment freedoms, employs overbroad dollar limits, and discriminates against candidates opposing incumbent officeholders and against minor-party candidates in violation of the Fifth Amendment.

[In] view of the fundamental nature of the right to associate, governmental "action which may have the effect of curtailing the freedom to associate is subject to the closest scrutiny." Yet, it is clear that "[n]either the right to associate nor the right to participate in political activities is absolute." *Letter Carriers* [fn. 303, Sec. 7, III supra]. Even a " 'significant interference' with protected rights of political association" may be sustained if the State demonstrates a sufficiently important interest and employs means closely drawn to avoid unnecessary abridgment of associational freedoms. * * *

It is unnecessary to look beyond the Act's primary purpose—to limit the actuality and appearance of corruption resulting from large individual financial contributions—in order to find a constitutionally sufficient

---

[23] **[Ct's Note]** Statistical findings agreed to by the parties reveal that approximately 5.1% of the $73,483,613 raised by the 1161 candidates for Congress in 1974 was obtained in amounts in excess of $1,000. In 1974, two major-party senatorial candidates, Ramsey Clark and Senator Charles Mathias, Jr., operated large-scale campaigns on contributions raised under a voluntarily imposed $100 contribution limitation.

[371] As defined, "person" includes "an individual, partnership, committee, association, corporation or any other organization or group." The limitation applies to: (1) anything of value, such as gifts, loans, advances, and promises to give, (2) contributions made direct to the candidate or to an intermediary, or a committee authorized by the candidate, (3) the aggregate amounts contributed to the candidate for each election, treating primaries, run-off elections and general elections separately and all Presidential primaries within a single calendar year as one election.

justification for the $1,000 contribution limitation. [The] increasing importance of the communications media and sophisticated mass mailing and polling operations to effective campaigning make the raising of large sums of money an ever more essential ingredient of an effective candidacy. To the extent that large contributions are given to secure political quid pro quos from current and potential office holders, the integrity of our system of representative democracy is undermined. Although the scope of such pernicious practices can never be reliably ascertained, the deeply disturbing examples surfacing after the 1972 election demonstrate that the problem is not an illusory one.

Of almost equal concern as the danger of actual quid pro quo arrangements is the impact of the appearance of corruption stemming from public awareness of the opportunities for abuse inherent in a regime of large individual financial contributions. In *Letter Carriers,* the Court found that the danger to "fair and effective government" posed by partisan political conduct on the part of federal employees charged with administering the law was a sufficiently important concern to justify broad restrictions on the employees' right of partisan political association. Here, as there, Congress could legitimately conclude that the avoidance of the appearance of improper influence "is also critical [if] confidence in the system of representative Government is not to be eroded to a disastrous extent."[29]

Appellants contend that the contribution limitations must be invalidated because bribery laws and narrowly-drawn disclosure requirements constitute a less restrictive means of dealing with "proven and suspected quid pro quo arrangements." But laws [against] bribes deal with only the most blatant and specific attempts of those with money to influence governmental action. [And] Congress was surely entitled to conclude that disclosure was only a partial measure, and that contribution ceilings were a necessary legislative concomitant to deal with the reality or appearance of corruption inherent in a system permitting unlimited financial contributions, even when the identities of the contributors and the amounts of their contributions are fully disclosed.

The Act's $1,000 contribution limitation focuses precisely on the problem of large campaign contributions—the narrow aspect of political association where the actuality and potential for corruption have been identified—while leaving persons free to engage in independent political expression, to associate actively through volunteering their services. [The] Act's contribution limitations [do] not undermine to any material degree

---

[29] **[Ct's Note]** Although the Court in *Letter Carriers* found that this interest was constitutionally sufficient to justify legislation prohibiting federal employees from engaging in certain partisan political activities, it was careful to emphasize that the limitations did not restrict an employee's right to express his views on political issues and candidates.

the potential for robust and effective discussion of candidates and campaign [issues].

We find that, under the rigorous standard of review established by our prior decisions, the weighty interests served by restricting the size of financial contributions to political candidates are sufficient to justify the limited effect upon First Amendment freedoms caused by the $1,000 contribution ceiling.[372]

C. *Expenditure Limitations.* [1.] Section 608(e)(1) provides that "[n]o person may make any expenditure [relative] to a clearly identified candidate during a calendar year which, when added to all other expenditures made by such person during the year advocating the election or defeat of such candidate, exceeds $1,000." [Its] plain effect [is] to prohibit all individuals, who are neither candidates nor owners of institutional press facilities, and all groups, except political parties and campaign organizations, from voicing their views "relative to a clearly identified candidate" through means that entail aggregate expenditures of more than $1,000 during a calendar year. The provision, for example, would make it a federal criminal offense for a person or association to place a single one-quarter page advertisement "relative to a clearly identified candidate" in a major metropolitan newspaper.

[Although] "expenditure," "clearly identified," and "candidate" are defined in the Act, there is no definition clarifying what expenditures are "relative to" a candidate. [But the "when" clause in § 608(e)(1)] clearly permits, if indeed it does not require, the phrase "relative to" a candidate to be read to mean "advocating the election or defeat of" a candidate.

But while such a construction of § 608(e)(1) refocuses the vagueness question, [it hardly] eliminates the problem of unconstitutional vagueness altogether. For the distinction between discussion of issues and candidates and advocacy of election or defeat of candidates may often dissolve in practical application. Candidates, especially incumbents, are intimately

---

[372] The Court rejected the challenges that the $1,000 limit was overbroad because (1) most large contributors do not seek improper influence over a candidate, and (2) much more than $1,000 would still not be enough to influence improperly a candidate or office holder. With respect to (1), "Congress was justified in concluding that the interest in safeguarding against the appearance of impropriety requires that the opportunity for abuse inherent in the process of raising large monetary contributions be eliminated." With respect to (2), "As the Court of Appeals observed, '[a] court has no scalpel to probe, whether, say, a $2,000 ceiling might not serve as well as $1,000.' Such distinctions in degree become significant only when they can be said to amount to differences in kind."

The Court also rejected as without support in the record the claims that the contribution limitations worked invidious discrimination between incumbents and challengers to whom the same limitations applied.

The Court then upheld (1) exclusion from the $1,000 limit of the value of unpaid volunteer services and of certain expenses paid by the volunteer up to a maximum of $500; (2) the higher limit of $5,000 for contributions to a candidate by established, registered political committees with at least 50 contributing supporters and fielding at least five candidates for federal office; and (3) the $25,000 limit on total contributions to all candidates by one person in one calendar year.

tied to public issues involving legislative proposals and governmental actions. Not only do candidates campaign on the basis of their positions on various public issues, but campaigns themselves generate issues of public interest.

[Constitutionally deficient uncertainty which "compels the speaker to hedge and trim"] can be avoided only by reading § 608(e)(1) as limited to communications that include explicit words of advocacy of election or defeat of a candidate, much as the definition of "clearly identified" in § 608(e)(2) requires that an explicit and unambiguous reference to the candidate appear as part of the communication. This is the reading of the provision suggested by the non-governmental appellees in arguing that "[f]unds spent to propagate one's views on issues without expressly calling for a candidate's election or defeat are thus not covered." We agree that in order to preserve the provision against invalidation on vagueness grounds, § 608(e)(1) must be construed to apply only to expenditures for communications that in express terms advocate the election or defeat of a clearly identified candidate for federal office.[373]

We turn then to the basic First Amendment question—whether § 608(e)(1), even as thus narrowly and explicitly construed, impermissibly burdens the constitutional right of free expression. * * *

We find that the governmental interest in preventing corruption and the appearance of corruption is inadequate to justify § 608(e)(1)'s ceiling on independent expenditures. First, assuming arguendo that large independent expenditures pose the same dangers of actual or apparent quid pro quo arrangements as do large contributions, § 608(e)(1) does not provide an answer that sufficiently relates to the elimination of those dangers. Unlike the contribution limitations' total ban on the giving of large amounts of money to candidates, § 608(e)(1) prevents only some large expenditures. So long as persons and groups eschew expenditures that in express terms advocate the election or defeat of a clearly identified candidate, they are free to spend as much as they want to promote the candidate and his views. The exacting interpretation of the statutory language necessary to avoid unconstitutional vagueness thus undermines the limitation's effectiveness as a loophole-closing provision by facilitating circumvention by those seeking to exert improper influence upon a candidate or office-holder. It would naively underestimate the ingenuity and resourcefulness of persons and groups desiring to buy influence to believe that they would have much difficulty devising expenditures that

---

[373] On the issues raised by this interpretation, see Richard Briffault, *Issue Advocacy: Redrawing the Elections/Politics Line,* 77 Texas L.Rev. 1751 (1999); Allison R. Hayward, *When Does an Advertisement about Issues Become an "Issues" Ad,* 49 Cath. U.L.Rev. 63 (1999); Glenn J. Moramarco, *Beyond "Magic Words": Using Self-Disclosure to Regulate Electioneering,* 49 Cath. U.L.Rev. 107 (1999).

skirted the restriction on express advocacy of election or defeat but nevertheless benefitted the candidate's campaign. * * *

Second, [the] independent advocacy restricted by the provision does not presently appear to pose dangers of real or apparent corruption comparable to those identified with large campaign contributions. The parties defending § 608(e)(1) contend that it is necessary to prevent would-be contributors from avoiding the contribution limitations by the simple expedient of paying directly for media advertisements or for other portions of the candidate's campaign activities. [Section] 608(b)'s contribution ceilings rather than § 608(e)(1)'s independent expenditure limitation prevent attempts to circumvent the Act through prearranged or coordinated expenditures amounting to disguised contributions.[53] By contrast, § 608(e)(1) limits expenditures for express advocacy of candidates made totally independently of the candidate and his campaign. [The] absence of prearrangement and coordination of an expenditure with the candidate or his agent not only undermines the value of the expenditure to the candidate, but also alleviates the danger that expenditures will be given as a quid pro quo for improper commitments from the candidate. Rather than preventing circumvention of the contribution limitations, § 608(e)(1) severely restricts all independent advocacy despite its substantially diminished potential for abuse.

While the independent expenditure ceiling thus fails to serve any substantial governmental interest in stemming the reality or appearance of corruption in the electoral process, it heavily burdens core First Amendment expression. [Advocacy] of the election or defeat of candidates for federal office is no less entitled to protection under the First Amendment than the discussion of political policy generally or advocacy of the passage or defeat of legislation.[374]

It is argued, however, that the ancillary governmental interest in equalizing the relative ability of individuals and groups to influence the outcome of elections serves to justify the limitation on express advocacy of

---

[53] **[Ct's Note]** Section 608(e)(1) does not apply to expenditures "on behalf of a candidate within the meaning of" § 608(2)(B). That section provides that expenditures "authorized or requested by the candidate, an authorized committee of the candidate, or an agent of the candidate" are to be treated as expenditures of the candidate and contributions by the person or group making the expenditure. [In] view of [the] legislative history and the purposes of the Act, we find that the "authorized or requested" standard of the Act operates to treat all expenditures placed in cooperation with or with the consent of a candidate, his agents, or an authorized committee of the candidate as contributions subject to the limitations set forth in § 608(b). [Eds. Subsequent cases have held that group expenditures on behalf of a candidate that are not coordinated with the candidate may not constitutionally be restricted. FEC v. National Conservative Political Action Comm., 470 U.S. 480 (1985)].

[374] Although restrictions on political speech are subject to First Amendment scrutiny, *Nevada Commission on Ethics v. Corrigan*, 131 S.Ct. 2343 (2011), held that legislative recusal rules did not impermissibly restrict the First Amendment rights of legislators. Indeed, the Court maintained generally that restrictions on legislators' voting are not restrictions upon legislators' protected speech.

the election or defeat of candidates imposed by § 608(e)(1)'s expenditure ceiling. But the concept that government may restrict the speech of some elements of our society in order to enhance the relative voice of others[375] is wholly foreign to the First Amendment, which was designed "to secure 'the widest possible dissemination of information from diverse and antagonistic sources,' " and " 'to assure unfettered interchange of ideas for the bringing about of political and social changes desired by the people.' " *New York Times Co. v. Sullivan.* The First Amendment's protection against governmental abridgement of free expression cannot properly be made to depend on a person's financial ability to engage in public discussion.[55]

* * * *Mills v. Alabama,* 384 U.S. 214 (1966), held that legislative restrictions on advocacy of the election or defeat of political candidates are wholly at odds with the guarantees of the First Amendment. [Yet] the prohibition on election day editorials invalidated in *Mills* is clearly a lesser intrusion on constitutional freedom than a $1,000 limitation on the amount of money any person or association can spend *during an entire election year* in advocating the election or defeat of a candidate for public office.

For the reasons stated, we conclude that § 608(e)(1)'s independent expenditure limitation is unconstitutional under the First Amendment. * * * [376]

2.   [The] Act also sets limits on expenditures by a candidate "from his personal funds, or the personal funds of his immediate family, in connection with his campaigns during any calendar year." § 608(a)(1).[377]

---

[375] For sustained defense of this aspect of *Buckley*, see Martin H. Redish & Kirk J. Kaludis, *The Right of Expressive Access in First Amendment Theory: Redistributive Values and the Democratic Dilemma,* 93 Nw.U.L.Rev. 1083 (1999). For reaffirmation, see *Davis v. Federal Election Commission,* 554 U.S. 724 (2008). On the other hand, the lower court characterized the issue somewhat differently: Can "the wealthy few [claim] a constitutional guarantee to a stronger political voice than the unwealthy many because they are able to give and spend more money, and because the amounts they give and spend cannot be limited"? 519 F.2d 821 (D.C.Cir.1975).

[55] **[Ct's Note]** Neither the voting rights cases [Ch. 10, Sec. 4, I, A] nor the Court's decision upholding the FCC's fairness doctrine [*Red Lion,* Sec. 8, I supra] lends support to appellees' position that the First Amendment permits Congress to abridge the rights of some persons to engage in political expression in order to enhance the relative voice of other segments of our [society].

[376] The Court invalidated restrictions on the amount of personal funds candidates could spend on their own behalf and on the amount of overall campaign expenditures by federal candidates. The anti-corruption rationale did not apply in the former instance and was already served by the act's contribution and disclosure provisions. On the other hand, the Court also stated that, "[A]cceptance of federal funding entails voluntary acceptance of an expenditure ceiling." *Arizona Free Enterprise Club's Freedom Club PAC v. Bennett,* 131 S.Ct. 2806 (2011) extended Davis, invalidating an Arizona scheme in which candidates who accepted public financing in exchange for foregoing private contributions were receiving matching funds virtually dollar for dollar when their opponents in conjunction with their independent supporters spent beyond the public financing cap.

[377] $50,000 for Presidential or Vice Presidential candidates; $35,000 for Senate candidates; $25,000 for most candidates for the House of Representatives. *Davis v. FEC,* fn. 376 supra, held that Congress could not increase the contribution limits for a candidate whose opponent had achieved a specified spending advantage by virtue of his or her personal funds. The Court maintained that the anti-corruption rationale did not apply and that equalizing electoral

The ceiling on personal expenditures by candidates on their own behalf [imposes] a substantial restraint on the ability of persons to engage in protected First Amendment expression. The candidate, no less than any other person, has a First Amendment right to engage in the discussion of public issues and vigorously and tirelessly to advocate his own election and the election of other candidates. Indeed, it is of particular importance that candidates have the unfettered opportunity to make their views known so that the electorate may intelligently evaluate the candidates' personal qualities and their positions on vital public issues before choosing among them on election day. [Section] 608(a)'s ceiling on personal expenditures by a candidate in furtherance of his own candidacy thus clearly and directly interferes with constitutionally protected freedoms.

The primary governmental interest served by the Act—the prevention of actual and apparent corruption of the political process—does not support the limitation on the candidate's expenditure of his own personal funds. [Indeed], the use of personal funds reduces the candidate's dependence on outside contributions and thereby counteracts the coercive pressures and attendant risks of abuse to which the Act's contribution limitations are directed.

The ancillary interest in equalizing the relative financial resources of candidates competing for elective office, therefore, provides the sole relevant rationale for Section 608(a)'s expenditure ceiling. That interest is clearly not sufficient to justify the provision's infringement of fundamental First Amendment rights. First, the limitation may fail to promote financial equality among candidates. [Indeed], a candidate's personal wealth may impede his [fundraising efforts]. Second, and more fundamentally, the First Amendment simply cannot tolerate § 608(a)'s restriction upon the freedom of a candidate to speak without legislative limit on behalf of his own candidacy. We therefore hold that § 608(a)'s restrictions on a candidate's personal expenditures is unconstitutional.

3.   [Section] 608(c) of the Act places limitations on overall campaign expenditures by candidates [seeking] election to federal office. [For Presidential candidates the ceiling is $10,000,000 in seeking nomination and $20,000,000 in the general election campaign; for House of Representatives candidates it is $70,000 for each campaign—primary and general; for candidates for Senator the ceiling depends on the size of the voting age population.]

No governmental interest that has been suggested is sufficient to justify [these restrictions] on the quantity of political expression. [The] interest in alleviating the corrupting influence of large contributions is served by the Act's contribution limitations and disclosure provisions

opportunities is not a sufficient interest to override First Amendment rights, but it indicated that Congress could raise contribution limits for *both* candidates.

rather than by § 608(c)'s campaign expenditure ceilings. [There] is no indication that the substantial criminal penalties for violating the contribution ceilings combined with the political repercussion of such violations will be insufficient to police the contribution provisions. Extensive reporting, auditing, and disclosure requirements applicable to both contributions and expenditures by political campaigns are designed to facilitate the detection of illegal contributions. * * *

The interest in equalizing the financial resources of candidates competing for federal office is no more convincing a justification for restricting the scope of federal election campaigns. Given the limitation on the size of outside contributions, the financial resources available to a candidate's campaign, like the number of volunteers recruited, will normally vary with the size and intensity of the candidate's support. There is nothing invidious, improper, or unhealthy in permitting such funds to be spent to carry the candidate's message to the electorate. Moreover, the equalization of permissible campaign expenditures might serve not to equalize the opportunities of all candidates but to handicap a candidate who lacked substantial name recognition or exposure of his views before the start of the campaign.

The campaign expenditure ceilings appear to be designed primarily to serve the governmental interests in reducing the allegedly skyrocketing costs of political campaigns. [But the] First Amendment denies government the power to determine that spending to promote one's political views is wasteful, excessive, or unwise. In the free society ordained by our Constitution it is not the government but the people individually as citizens and candidates and collectively as associations and political committees who must retain control over the quantity and range of debate on public issues in a political campaign.[65]

For these reasons we hold that § 608(c) is constitutionally invalid. * * *

CHIEF JUSTICE BURGER, concurring in part and dissenting in part.

[I] agree fully with that part of the Court's opinion that holds unconstitutional the limitations the Act puts on campaign expenditures. [Yet] when it approves similarly stringent limitations on contributions, the Court ignores the reasons it finds so persuasive in the context of expenditures. For me contributions and expenditures are two sides of the same First Amendment coin.

---

[65] **[Ct's Note]** [Congress] may engage in public financing of election campaigns and may condition acceptance of public funds on an agreement by the candidate to abide by specified expenditure limitations. Just as a candidate may voluntarily limit the size of the contributions he chooses to accept he may decide to forgo private fundraising and accept public funding. [On the merits and demerits of public financing, compare Richard Briffault, *Public Funding and Democratic Elections*, 148 U.Pa.L.Rev. 563 (1999) with Bradley A. Smith, *Some Problems with Taxpayer-funded Political Campaigns*, id. at 591].

[Limiting] contributions, as a practical matter, will limit expenditures and will put an effective ceiling on the amount of political activity and debate that the Government will permit to take place.[5]

The Court attempts to separate the two communicative aspects of political contributions—the "moral" support that the gift itself conveys, which the Court suggests is the same whether the gift is of $10 or $10,000,[6] and the fact that money translates into communication. The Court dismisses the effect of the limitations on the second aspect of contributions: "[T]he transformation of contributions into political debate involves speech by someone other than the contributor." On this premise—that contribution limitations restrict only the speech of "someone other than the contributor"—rests the Court's justification for treating contributions differently from expenditures. The premise is demonstrably flawed; the contribution limitations will, in specific instances, limit exactly the same political activity that the expenditure ceilings limit, and at least one of the "expenditure" limitations the Court finds objectionable operates precisely like the "contribution" limitations.[8]

The Court's attempt to distinguish the communication inherent in political *contributions* from the speech aspects of political *expenditures* simply will not wash. We do little but engage in word games unless we recognize that people—candidates and contributors—spend money on political activity because they wish to communicate ideas, and their constitutional interest in doing so is precisely the same whether they or someone else utter the words.

[T]he restrictions are hardly incidental in their effect upon particular campaigns. Judges are ill-equipped to gauge the precise impact of legislation, but a law that impinges upon First Amendment rights requires us to make the attempt. It is not simply speculation to think that the

---

[5]   [Ct's Note] The Court notes that 94.9% of the funds raised by congressional candidates in 1974 came in contributions of less than $1,000, n. 27, and suggests that the effect of the contribution limitations will be minimal. This logic ignores the disproportionate influence large contributions may have when they are made early in a campaign; "seed money" can be essential, and the inability to obtain it may effectively end some candidacies before they begin. Appellants have excerpted from the record data on nine campaigns to which large, initial contributions were critical. Campaigns such as these will be much harder, and perhaps impossible, to mount under the Act.

[6]   [Ct's Note] Whatever the effect of the limitation, it is clearly arbitrary—Congress has imposed the same ceiling on contributions to a New York or California senatorial campaign that it has put on House races in Alaska or Wyoming. Both the strength of support conveyed by the gift of $1,000 *and* the gift's potential for corruptly influencing the recipient will vary enormously from place to place. * * *

[8]   [Ct's Note] The Court treats the Act's provisions limiting a candidate's spending from his *personal resources* as *expenditure* limits, as indeed the Act characterizes them, and holds them unconstitutional. As Mr. Justice Marshall points out, infra, by the Court's logic these provisions could as easily be treated as limits on *contributions,* since they limit what the candidate can give to his own campaign.

limitations on contributions will foreclose some candidacies.[9] The limitations will also alter the nature of some electoral contests drastically.[10]

[In] striking down the limitations on campaign expenditures, the Court relies in part on its conclusion that other means—namely, disclosure and contribution ceilings—will adequately serve the statute's aim. It is not clear why the same analysis is not also appropriate in weighing the need for contribution ceilings in addition to disclosure requirements. Congress may well be entitled to conclude that disclosure was a "partial measure," but I had not thought until today that Congress could enact its conclusions in the First Amendment area into laws immune from the most searching review by this Court. * * *[378]

JUSTICE WHITE, concurring in part and dissenting in part. * * *

I [agree] with the Court's judgment upholding the limitations on contributions. I dissent [from] the Court's view that the expenditure limitations [violate] the First Amendment. [This] case depends on whether the nonspeech interests of the Federal Government in regulating the use of money in political campaigns are sufficiently urgent to justify the incidental effects that the limitations visit upon the First Amendment interests of candidates and their supporters.

[The Court] accepts the congressional judgment that the evils of unlimited contributions are sufficiently threatening to warrant restriction regardless of the impact of the limits on the contributor's opportunity for effective speech and in turn on the total volume of the candidate's political communications by reason of his inability to accept large sums from those willing to give.

The congressional judgment, which I would also accept, was that other steps must be taken to counter the corrosive effects of money in federal election campaigns. One of these steps is § 608(e), which [limits] what a contributor may independently spend in support or denigration of one running for federal office. Congress was plainly of the view that these expenditures also have corruptive potential; but the Court strikes down the provision, strangely enough claiming more insight as to what may

---

[9]   **[Ct's Note]** Candidates who must raise large initial contributions in order to appeal for more funds to a broader audience will be handicapped. See n. 5, supra. It is not enough to say that the contribution ceilings "merely require candidates [to] raise funds from a greater number of persons," where the limitations will effectively prevent candidates without substantial personal resources from doing just that.

[10]   **[Ct's Note]** Under the Court's holding, candidates with personal fortunes will be free to contribute to their own campaigns as much as they like, since the Court chooses to view the Act's provisions in this regard as unconstitutional "expenditure" limitations rather than "contribution" limitations. See n. 8, supra.

[378] Blackmun, J., also dissented separately from that part of the Court's opinion upholding the Act's restrictions on campaign contributions, unpersuaded that "a principled constitutional distinction" could be made between the contribution and expenditure limitations involved.

improperly influence candidates than is possessed by the majority of Congress that passed this Bill and the President who signed it. Those supporting the Bill undeniably included many seasoned professionals who have been deeply involved in elective processes and who have viewed them at close range over many years.

It would make little sense to me, and apparently made none to Congress, to limit the amounts an individual may give to a candidate or spend with his approval but fail to limit the amounts that could be spent on his behalf. Yet the Court permits the former while striking down the latter limitation. [I] would take the word of those who know—that limiting independent expenditures is essential to prevent transparent and widespread evasion of the contribution limits. * * *

The Court also rejects Congress' judgment manifested in § 608(c) that the federal interest in limiting total campaign expenditures by individual candidates justifies the incidental effect on their opportunity for effective political speech. I disagree both with the Court's assessment of the impact on speech and with its narrow view of the values the limitations will serve.

[M]oney is not always equivalent to or used for speech, even in the context of political campaigns. [There are] many expensive campaign activities that are not themselves communicative or remotely related to speech. Furthermore, campaigns differ among themselves. Some seem to spend much less money than others and yet communicate as much or more than those supported by enormous bureaucracies with unlimited financing. The record before us no more supports the conclusion that the communicative efforts of congressional and Presidential candidates will be crippled by the expenditure limitations than it supports the contrary. The judgment of Congress was that reasonably effective campaigns could be conducted within the limits established by the Act and that the communicative efforts of these campaigns would not seriously suffer. In this posture of the case, there is no sound basis for invalidating the expenditure limitations, so long as the purposes they serve are legitimate and sufficiently substantial, which in my view they are.

[E]xpenditure ceilings reinforce the contribution limits and help eradicate the hazard of corruption. [Without] limits on total expenditures, campaign costs will inevitably and endlessly escalate. Pressure to raise funds will constantly build and with it the temptation to resort in "emergencies" to those sources of large sums, who, history shows, are sufficiently confident of not being caught to risk flouting contribution [limits.]

The ceiling on candidate expenditures represents the considered judgment of Congress that elections are to be decided among candidates none of whom has overpowering advantage by reason of a huge campaign war chest. At least so long as the ceiling placed upon the candidates is not plainly too low, elections are not to turn on the difference in the amounts of money that candidates have to spend. This seems an acceptable purpose and the means chosen a common sense way to achieve [it.]

I also disagree with the Court's judgment that § 608(a), which limits the amount of money that a candidate or his family may spend on his campaign, violates the Constitution. Although it is true that this provision does not promote any interest in preventing the corruption of candidates, the provision does, nevertheless, serve salutary purposes related to the integrity of federal campaigns. By limiting the importance of personal wealth, § 608(a) helps to assure that only individuals with a modicum of support from others will be viable candidates. This in turn would tend to discourage any notion that the outcome of elections is primarily a function of money. Similarly, § 608(a) tends to equalize access to the political arena, encouraging the less wealthy, unable to bankroll their own campaigns, to run for political office.[379]

NOTES AND QUESTIONS

1.   *Equality and democracy.* Is it "foreign" to the First Amendment to curb the spending of the wealthy in an effort to preserve the integrity of the elections process? Does copyright law curb the speech of some in order to enhance the speech of others? Rebecca Tushnet, *Copyright as a Model for Free Speech Law: What Copyright Has in Common with Anti-Pornography Laws, Campaign Finance Reform, and Telecommunications Regulation*, 42 B.C. L. Rev. 1 (2000). Would it have been "foreign" to First Amendment doctrine to engage in some type of balancing? Does the Court's expenditure ruling undervalue the interests in equality and democracy?[380] See Stephen Breyer, *Our Democratic Constitution*, 77 N.Y.U. L. Rev. 245 (2002).

2.   *The nature of democracy.* Lori Ringhand, *Defining Democracy: The Supreme Court's Campaign Finance Dilemma*, 56 Hast. L.J. 77 (2004–2005):

---

[379] Marshall, J., dissented from that part of the Court's opinion invalidating the limitation on the amount a candidate or his family may spend on his campaign. He considered "the interest in promoting the reality and appearance of equal access to the political arena" sufficient to justify the limitation: "[T]he wealthy candidate's immediate access to a substantial personal fortune may give him an initial advantage that his less wealthy opponent can never overcome. [With the option of large contributions removed by § 608(b)], the less wealthy candidate is without the means to match, the large initial expenditures of money of which the wealthy candidate is capable. In short, the limitations on contributions put a premium on a candidate's personal wealth. [Section 608(a) then] emerges not simply as a device to reduce the natural advantage of the wealthy candidate, but as a provision providing some symmetry to a regulatory scheme that otherwise enhances the natural advantage of the wealthy."

For background on the *Buckley* case, see Fred Friendly & Martha Elliot, *The Constitution: That Delicate Balance* 91–107 (1984).

[380] See, e.g., Laurence Tribe, *Constitutional Choices* 193–94 (1985); Owen Fiss, *Money and Politics,* 97 Colum. L.Rev. 2470 (1997); Burt Neuborne, *Toward a Democracy-Centered Reading of the First Amendment,* 93 Nw.U.L.Rev. 1055 (1999); Marlene Nicholson, *Buckley v. Valeo: The Constitutionality of the Federal Election Campaign Act Amendments of 1974,* 1977 Wis.L.Rev. 323; J. Skelly Wright, *Money and the Pollution of Politics: Is the First Amendment an Obstacle to Political Equality?,* 82 Colum.L.Rev. 609 (1982).

"In *Buckley*, the Court found that prohibiting the appearance or actuality of quid pro quo-type corruption was a sufficiently compelling governmental interest to justify restrictions on political speech. Equalizing the ability of groups or individuals to participate in the public debate by limiting campaign expenditures, however, was not. By accepting the government's corruption rationale while denying the government's equalization rationale, *Buckley* implicitly endorsed a pluralist-inspired view of democracy. To the Court, protecting a pluralistic political process by regulating things like quid pro quo bribery, which potentially interfere with an elected official's duty to vote in accordance with pluralist preferences, is constitutionally acceptable. But regulating overall political expenditures in order to promote the civic republican ideals of political equality and public deliberation is constitutionally unacceptable."

3. *Advancing equality values?* To what extent are campaign finance laws likely to advance equality values?[381] Are they most likely to benefit incumbents, whose incumbency provides an intangible electoral advantage? See Richard Epstein, *Modern Republicanism—Or the Flight From Substance,* 97 Yale L.J. 1633 (1988); Jon Macey, *The Missing Element in the Republican Revival,* 97 Yale L.J. 1673 (1988). Would campaign finance legislation free incumbents from the need to rely on interest group funding and improve the quality of representation? Vincent Blasi, *Free Speech and the Widening Gyre of Fund-Raising,* 94 Colum.L.Rev. 1281 (1994). Is increased legislative autonomy desirable?[382]

4. *Mitigating corruption.* Will campaign finance laws mitigate public perception of corruption? Or is the cynicism of the American people too deep to allow that? Kelli Lammie, *Perceptions of Corruption and Campaign Finance: When Public Opinion Determines Constitutional Law,* 153 U. Pa. L. Rev. 119 (2004). Would such laws affect actual corruption? Consider Jamin B. Raskin, *The Campaign-Finance Crucible: Is Laissez Fair?,* 101 Mich. L. Rev. 1532 (2003): "[I]f corruption simply means compromising the moral purity or 'true beliefs' of the politician, then the claim that money corrupts legislatures seems highly doubtful. The kinds of politicians that receive huge sums from agribusiness interests are the kinds of politicians that would robotically serve these interests anyway. Corporate power does not have to buy politicians in American elections; it spawns them. [W]e need a definition [of corruption] that does not focus on the impressionable soul of the politician but rather on

---

[381] Consider Paul Brest, *Further Beyond the Republican Revival,* 97 Yale L.J. 1623 (1988): 'Those who are better off participate more, and by participating more they exercise more influence on government officials.' Unequal resources produce unequal influence in determining which issues get on the political [agenda]. Campaign finance regulations barely begin to remedy the systematic ways in which inequalities of wealth distort the political process." But see Edward B. Foley, *Equal-Dollars-Per Voter: A Constitutional Principle of Campaign Finance,* 94 Colum.L.Rev. 1204 (1994); Jamin Raskin & John Bonifaz, *Equal Protection and the Wealth Primary,* 11 Yale L. & Pol'y Rev. 273 (1993). For a variety of views, see *Symposium on Campaign Finance Reform,* 94 Colum.L.Rev. 1125 (1994).

[382] Compare Cass Sunstein, *Beyond the Republican Revival,* 97 Yale L.J. 1539 (1988) with Michael Fitts, *Look Before You Leap,* 97 Yale L.J. 1651 (1988); Michael Fitts, *The Vices of Virtue,* 136 U.Pa.L.Rev. 1567 (1988).

keeping the channels of popular democracy safe from capture by predatory elite factions, which are always made up of both politicians and the broader interests they serve." Should the concern be about the perception or appearance of corruption or about corruption itself?

5. ***Bet-hedging.*** Should contributors who give to both opposing candidates be protected under the First Amendment? See Jason Cohen, *The Same Side of Two Coins: The Peculiar Phenomenon of Bet-Hedging in Campaign Finance,* 26 N. Ill. U.L. Rev. 271 (2006).

6. ***Varying scrutiny.*** (a) Did *Buckley* apply less exacting scrutiny to impairment of associational freedoms by contribution limits than to impairment of free expression by expenditure limits? See Daniel Polsby, *Buckley v. Valeo: The Special Nature of Political Speech,* 1976 Sup.Ct.Rev. 1. Can a lesser scrutiny be justified for contributions? Or were the differing results based on the Court's perceiving a greater threat to First Amendment interests in expenditure limits and less risk of corruption and undue influence in unlimited independent expenditures? For a defense of strict scrutiny across the board, see Lillian BeVier, *Money and Politics: A Perspective on the First Amendment and Campaign Finance Reform*, 73 Calif.L.Rev. 1045 (1985). For the argument that strict scrutiny is inappropriate in institutionally bounded contexts and that elections are such contexts, see C. Edwin Baker, *Campaign Expenditures and Free Speech,* 33 Harv. C.R.-C.L.Rev. 1 (1998).[383]

(b) ***The O'Brien analogy.*** May the Court's rejection of the less-exacting *O'Brien* standard on the ground that the expenditure of money did not introduce a non-speech element fairly be criticized for asking the wrong question: whether "*pure speech* can be regulated where there is some incidental effect on *money*," rather than whether "the use of *money* can be regulated, by analogy to such conduct as draft-card burning, where there is an undoubted incidental effect on *speech*"? See J. Skelly Wright, *Politics and the Constitution: Is Money Speech?,* 85 Yale L.J. 1001 (1976). But compare J.M. Balkin, *Some Realism About Pluralism: Legal Realist Approaches to the First Amendment,* 1990 Duke L.J. 375: "I suspect that the slogan 'money is not speech' is attractive because it appeals to a certain humanistic vision—that there is something quite different between the situation of a lone individual expressing her views and the purchase of hired mouths using hired expressions created by hired minds to saturate the airwaves with ideological drivel. Yet in one sense, this humanistic vision really turns upon a set of unstated egalitarian

---

[383] For similar views, see Richard Briffault, *Issue Advocacy: Redrawing the Elections/Politics Line,* 77 Texas L.Rev. 1751 (1999); Frederick Schauer & Richard H. Pildes, *Electoral Exceptionalism and the First Amendment,* 77 Texas L. Rev. 1803 (1999); and Burt Neuborne, *The Supreme Court and Free Speech: Love and A Question,* 42 St. Louis U.L.J. 789 (1998): "If we can conceive of an election campaign as a great deliberative assembly of the people, why shouldn't we allow ourselves to establish a content-neutral, meta-Roberts' Rules of Order to help assure that our elections are preceded by debate calculated to permit our democratic institutions to perform at an acceptable level, an electoral debate where political discourse is not completely dominated by the wealthy?" See also Robert C. Post, Citizens Divided: Campaign Finance Reform and the Constitution (2014). But see Kathleen M. Sullivan, *Against Campaign Finance Reform,* 1998 Utah L.Rev. 311 (1998); Robert Post, *Commentary: Regulating Election Speech Under the First Amendment,* 77 Texas L.Rev 1837 (1999).

assumptions about economic and social power. Certainly we would have no objection to a person with a speech impediment hiring someone to do her talking for her; that is because we think that, under these circumstances, it is fair for such a person to boost her communicative powers. Modern political campaigns seem a far cry from this example because of the massive amounts of economic power expended to get the message across. I think we should isolate the egalitarian assumptions implicit in the 'money is not speech' position and put them to their best use—the justification of campaign finance reforms on the ground that gross inequalities of economic power destroy the integrity of the political process. [G]overnment is responsible for inequalities in access to the means of communication because it has created the system of property rights that makes such inequalities possible. Therefore, it is not only wrong but also incoherent for opponents of campaign finance reform to contend that the government should not regulate access to the political process. Government already regulates access to the political process—the First Amendment simply demands that it do so fairly."

7. *Judicial elections.* Are judicial elections different? Should strict scrutiny be applied to contribution limits in judicial elections? Is *Republican Party v. White*, 536 U.S. 765 (2002) (applying strict scrutiny and invalidating a canon of judicial conduct that prohibited candidates for judicial election in that State from announcing their views on disputed legal and political issues) relevant to this? Should a state be permitted to prohibit a candidate from promising to decide cases in a particular way?[384]

8. *Vitality of Buckley.* Vermont's 1997 campaign finance statute limited the amount that state candidates could spend on their campaigns and that individuals, organizations, and parties could contribute to those campaigns.

RANDALL v. SORRELL, 548 U.S. 230 (2006), struck down both the expenditure limitations and the contribution limitations with a diversity of views concerning the authority of *Buckley*. BREYER, J., announced the judgment of the Court in an opinion joined by Roberts, C.J., and, in part, by Alito, J. He determined that the expenditure provision was unconstitutional on the strength of *Buckley*. On the basis of stare decisis, he declined what he perceived to be an invitation to overrule *Buckley's* ruling on candidate expenditure limits,[385] and he rejected the view that *Buckley* could be distinguished on the ground that it failed to consider the argument that such limitations are justified because they help to prevent candidates from spending

---

[384] For discussion of *White*, see e.g., Richard Briffault, *Judicial Campaign Codes After Republican Party of Minnesota v. White*, 153 U. Pa. L. Rev. 181 (2004); Matthew J. Medina, *The Constitutionality of the 2003 Revisions to Canon 3(E) of the Model Code of Judicial Conduct*, 104 Colum. L. Rev. 1072 (2004); Ronald D. Rotunda, *Judicial Elections, Campaign Financing, and Free Speech*, 2 Election L.J. 79 (2003); Erwin Chemerinsky, *Judicial Elections and the First Amendment*, 38 (Nov) Trial 78 (2002); Robert M. O'Neil, *The Canons in the Courts: Recent First Amendment Rulings*, 35 Ind. L. Rev. 701 (2002).

[385] Alito, J., concurring in part and in the judgment, argued that the question whether to overrule *Buckley's* standard for contributions and expenditures was not properly presented to the Court and should not have been reached.

too much time raising money. With respect to the contribution limits, Breyer, J., maintained that they were too restrictive, noting, for example, that the limit on contributions for governor (adjusted for inflation) was slightly more than one-twentieth of the limit on contributions to federal office before the Court in *Buckley*. He also determined that Vermont's per election contribution limit was the lowest in the nation. Breyer, J., concluded that such limits would impair the ability of some candidates running against incumbent officeholder to mount an effective challenge.

THOMAS, J., joined by Scalia, J., concurred in the judgment, demanding strict scrutiny in examining both expenditure and contributions limitations,[386] and arguing that the plurality's attempt to distinguish permissible from impermissible contribution limits could not be administered in a principled way: "[T]he plurality's determination that this statute clearly lies on the *impermissible* side of the constitutional line gives no assistance in drawing this line, and it is clear that no such line can be drawn rationally. There is simply no way to calculate just how much money a person would need to receive before he would be corrupt or perceived to be corrupt (and such a calculation would undoubtedly vary by person). Likewise, there is no meaningful way of discerning just how many resources must be lost before speech is 'disproportionately burden[ed].' '

STEVENS, J., dissenting, would depart from *Buckley's* strict scrutiny of candidate expenditure limits. He would uphold such limits "so long as the purposes they serve are legitimate and sufficiently substantial:" "The interest in freeing candidates from the fundraising straitjacket [is] compelling. Without expenditure limits, fundraising devours the time and attention of political leaders, leaving them too busy to handle their public responsibilities effectively. That fact was well recognized by backers of the legislation reviewed in *Buckley,* by the Court of Appeals judges who voted to uphold the expenditure limitations in that statute, and by Justice White—who not incidentally had personal experience as an active participant in a Presidential campaign. The validity of their judgment has surely been confirmed by the mountains of evidence that has been accumulated in recent years concerning the time that elected officials spend raising money for future campaigns and the adverse effect of fundraising on the performance of their official duties."

SOUTER, J., joined by Ginsburg, J., and, on the contributions issue, by Stevens, J., dissented, arguing that the question whether to relax *Buckley's* standard on expenditure requirements was not properly before the Court. He voted to affirm the Court of Appeals decision to remand on the expenditures issue to determine if the record met the requirements of *Buckley,* and to uphold the contribution limits: "I believe the Court of Appeals correctly rejected the challenge to the contribution limits. Low though they are, one cannot say that 'the contribution limitation[s are] so radical in effect as to render political association ineffective, drive the sound of a candidate's voice below the level of

---

[386] Kennedy, J., who has also maintained that *Buckley's* standard regarding contributions is too relaxed, concurred in the judgment.

notice, and render contributions pointless.' *Nixon* v. *Shrink Missouri Government PAC,* 528 U.S. 377 (2000). The limits set by Vermont are not remarkable departures either from those previously upheld by this Court or from those lately adopted by other States. The plurality concedes that on a per-citizen measurement Vermont's limit for statewide elections 'is slightly more generous,' than the one set by the Missouri statute approved by this Court in *Shrink.*"[387]

9. ***Aggregate contribution limits.*** Federal election law set limits to the amount contributors could give to candidates, to national party committees, to state or local party committees, and to political action committees. In addition to these "base" limits, the law sets aggregate limits. A contributor can give $5,200 to a particular federal election candidate ($2,600 in the primary and $2,600 in the general election), but can fully support no more than nine candidates because the aggregate limit for candidates is $48,600. The maximum amount that could be given in the aggregate to all of a contributor's potential beneficiaries is $123,200.

McCUTCHEON v. FEC, 134 S.Ct. 1434 (2014), per ROBERTS, C.J., joined by Scalia, Kennedy, and Alito, JJ., announced the judgment that the aggregate contribution limits as applied to candidates and committees violated the First Amendment and argued that the limits did little to combat corruption because the base limits would still apply to any additional candidates or committees supported, and the interest in stopping circumvention of the base limits was based on speculation and was already served by other loophole closing devices. On the other hand, the aggregate limits seriously restricted participation in the democratic process.[388]

BREYER, J., joined by Ginsburg, Sotomayor, and Kagan, JJ., dissenting, primarily argued that the plurality's conception of corruption was too narrow in that it excluded influence over or access to elected officials and political parties, and that the loophole closing devices mentioned by the plurality are more complicated and ineffective than it understands.

CITIZENS UNITED v. FEC

588 U.S. 310, 130 S.Ct. 876, 175 L.Ed.2d 753 (2010).

JUSTICE KENNEDY delivered the opinion of the Court.

[In January 2008, Citizens United, a nonprofit corporation that accepts a small portion of its funds from for-profit companies, released a film entitled *Hillary: The Movie.* The film was a documentary arguing that

---

[387] In response, Breyer, J., argued: "[T]his does not necessarily mean that Vermont's limits are less objectionable than the limit upheld in *Shrink.* A campaign for state auditor is likely to be less costly than a campaign for governor; campaign costs do not automatically increase or decrease in precise proportion to the size of an electoral district."

[388] Thomas, J., concurring in the judgment, again argued that *Buckley's* restrictions on contributions, including base limits, should be subject to strict scrutiny.

Senator Hilary Clinton was an unsuitable candidate for President. Citizens United had released its film in theaters and on DVD, but it also wished to make the film available through video-on-demand on cable and to promote the film with ads on broadcast and cable television.]

Federal law prohibits corporations and unions from using their general treasury funds to make independent expenditures for speech defined as an "electioneering communication" or for speech expressly advocating the election or defeat of a candidate. Federal Election Campaign Act of 1971, 2 U.S.C. § 441b. Limits on electioneering communications were upheld in *McConnell v. Federal Election Comm'n*, (2003). The holding of *McConnell* rested to a large extent on an earlier case, *Austin v. Michigan Chamber of Commerce*, 494 U.S. 652 (1990). *Austin* had held that political speech may be banned based on the speaker's corporate identity.

In this case we are asked to reconsider *Austin* and, in effect, *McConnell*. * * * We [hold] that stare decisis does not compel the continued acceptance of *Austin*. The Government may regulate corporate political speech through disclaimer and disclosure requirements, but it may not suppress that speech altogether.

Before the Bipartisan Campaign Reform Act of 2002 (BCRA), federal law prohibited-and still does prohibit—corporations and unions from using general treasury funds to make direct contributions to candidates or independent expenditures that expressly advocate the election or defeat of a candidate, through any form of media, in connection with certain qualified federal elections. BCRA § 203 amended § 441b to prohibit any "electioneering communication" as [well,] defined as "any broadcast, cable, or satellite communication" that "refers to a clearly identified candidate for a Federal office" and is made [well] within 30 days of a primary or 60 days of a general [election.][389] Corporations and unions [may] establish, however, a "separate segregated fund" (known as a political action committee, or PAC) for these purposes. The moneys received by the segregated fund are limited to donations from stockholders and employees of the corporation or, in the case of unions, members of the union. * * *

[T]he following acts would all be felonies under § 441b: The Sierra Club runs an ad, within the crucial phase of 60 days before the general election, that exhorts the public to disapprove of a Congressman who favors logging in national forests; the National Rifle Association publishes a book urging the public to vote for the challenger because the incumbent U.S. Senator supports a handgun ban; and the American Civil Liberties Union creates a Web site telling the public to vote for a Presidential candidate in light of

---

[389] The law exempted any news story, commentary, or editorial distributed through the facilities of any broadcasting station, newspaper, magazine, or other periodical publication, unless such facilities are owned or controlled by any political party, political committee, or candidate.

that candidate's defense of free speech. These prohibitions are classic examples of censorship.

[A] PAC is a separate association from the corporation. So the PAC exemption from § 441b's expenditure ban does not allow corporations to speak. Even if a PAC could somehow allow a corporation to speak—and it does not—the option to form PACs does not alleviate the First Amendment problems with § 441b. PACs are burdensome alternatives; they are expensive to administer and subject to extensive regulations. For example, every PAC must appoint a treasurer, forward donations to the treasurer promptly, keep detailed records of the identities of the persons making donations, preserve receipts for three years, and file an organization statement and report changes to this information within 10 days. * * *

By taking the right to speak from some and giving it to others, the Government deprives the disadvantaged person or class of the right to use speech to strive to establish worth, standing, and respect for the speaker's voice. The Government may not by these means deprive the public of the right and privilege to determine for itself what speech and speakers are worthy of consideration. The First Amendment protects speech and speaker, and the ideas that flow from each.

The Court has upheld a narrow class of speech restrictions that operate to the disadvantage of certain persons, but these rulings were based on an interest in allowing governmental entities to perform their functions. See, e.g., *Bethel School Dist. No. v. Fraser,* 478 U.S. 675 (1986) (protecting the "function of public school education"); *Jones v. North Carolina Prisoners' Labor Union, Inc.,* 433 U.S. 119 (furthering "the legitimate penological objectives of the corrections system"); *Parker v. Levy,* 417 U.S. 733 (1974) (ensuring "the capacity of the Government to discharge its [military] responsibilities"); *Civil Service Comm'n v. Letter Carriers,* 413 U.S. 548 (1973) ("[F]ederal service should depend upon meritorious performance rather than political service"). The corporate independent expenditures at issue in this case, however, would not interfere with governmental functions, so these cases are inapposite. These precedents stand only for the proposition that there are certain governmental functions that cannot operate without some restrictions on particular kinds of speech. By contrast, it is inherent in the nature of the political process that voters must be free to obtain information from diverse sources in order to determine how to cast their votes. At least before *Austin,* the Court had not allowed the exclusion of a class of speakers from the general public dialogue.

[Laws] that burden political speech are "subject to strict scrutiny," which requires the Government to prove that the restriction "furthers a compelling interest and is narrowly tailored to achieve that interest." *Austin* identified a new governmental interest in limiting political speech:

an antidistortion interest. *Austin* found a compelling governmental interest in preventing "the corrosive and distorting effects of immense aggregations of wealth that are accumulated with the help of the corporate form and that have little or no correlation to the public's support for the corporation's political ideas." [As] for *Austin's* antidistortion rationale, the Government does little to defend it. * * *

If the First Amendment has any force, it prohibits Congress from fining or jailing citizens, or associations of citizens, for simply engaging in political speech. If the antidistortion rationale were to be accepted, however, it would permit Government to ban political speech simply because the speaker is an association that has taken on the corporate form. The Government contends that *Austin* permits it to ban corporate expenditures for almost all forms of communication stemming from a corporation. If *Austin* were correct, the Government could prohibit a corporation from expressing political views in media beyond those presented here, such as by printing books. The Government responds "that the FEC has never applied this statute to a book," and if it did, "there would be quite [a] good as-applied challenge." This troubling assertion of brooding governmental power cannot be reconciled with the confidence and stability in civic discourse that the First Amendment must secure. * * *

Austin sought to defend the antidistortion rationale as a means to prevent corporations from obtaining "an unfair advantage in the political marketplace" by using "resources amassed in the economic marketplace." But *Buckley* rejected the premise that the Government has an interest "in equalizing the relative ability of individuals and groups to influence the outcome of elections." *Buckley* was specific in stating that "the skyrocketing cost of political campaigns" could not sustain the governmental prohibition. The First Amendment's protections do not depend on the speaker's "financial ability to engage in public discussion."

[*Austin*] undertook to distinguish wealthy individuals from corporations on the ground that "[s]tate law grants corporations special advantages—such as limited liability, perpetual life, and favorable treatment of the accumulation and distribution of assets." This does not suffice, however, to allow laws prohibiting speech. "It is rudimentary that the State cannot exact as the price of those special advantages the forfeiture of First Amendment rights."

It is irrelevant for purposes of the First Amendment that corporate funds may "have little or no correlation to the public's support for the corporation's political ideas." All speakers, including individuals and the media, use money amassed from the economic marketplace to fund their speech. The First Amendment protects the resulting speech, even if it was enabled by economic transactions with persons or entities who disagree with the speaker's ideas.

Austin's antidistortion rationale would produce the dangerous, and unacceptable, consequence that Congress could ban political speech of media corporations [now] exempt from § 441b's ban on corporate expenditures. Yet media corporations accumulate wealth with the help of the corporate form, the largest media corporations have "immense aggregations of wealth," and the views expressed by media corporations often "have little or no correlation to the public's support" for those views. Thus, under the Government's reasoning, wealthy media corporations could have their voices diminished to put them on par with other media entities. There is no precedent for permitting this [nor any] precedent supporting laws that attempt to distinguish between corporations which are deemed to be exempt as media corporations and those which are not. "We have consistently rejected the proposition that the institutional press has any constitutional privilege beyond that of other speakers." * * *

[T]he Government falls back on the argument that corporate political speech can be banned in order to prevent corruption or its appearance. In *Buckley,* the Court found this interest "sufficiently important" to allow limits on contributions but did not extend that reasoning to expenditure limits. * * *

With regard to large direct contributions, *Buckley* reasoned that they could be given "to secure a political quid pro quo," and that "the scope of such pernicious practices can never be reliably ascertained." The practices *Buckley* noted would be covered by bribery laws if a quid pro quo arrangement were proved. The Court, in consequence, has noted that restrictions on direct contributions are preventative, because few if any contributions to candidates will involve quid pro quo arrangements. The *Buckley* Court, nevertheless, sustained limits on direct contributions in order to ensure against the reality or appearance of corruption. That case did not extend this rationale to independent expenditures, and the Court does not do so here. * * *

When *Buckley* identified a sufficiently important governmental interest in preventing corruption or the appearance of corruption, that interest was limited to quid pro quo corruption. The fact that speakers may have influence over or access to elected officials does not mean that these officials are corrupt: "[It] is in the nature of an elected representative to favor certain policies, and, by necessary corollary, to favor the voters and contributors who support those policies. It is well understood that a substantial and legitimate reason, if not the only reason, to cast a vote for, or to make a contribution to, one candidate over another is that the candidate will respond by producing those political outcomes the supporter favors. Democracy is premised on responsiveness." Reliance on a "generic favoritism or influence theory . . . is at odds with standard First Amendment analyses because it is unbounded and susceptible to no limiting principle."

The appearance of influence or access, furthermore, will not cause the electorate to lose faith in our democracy. By definition, an independent expenditure is political speech presented to the electorate that is not coordinated with a candidate. The fact that a corporation, or any other speaker, is willing to spend money to try to persuade voters presupposes that the people have the ultimate influence over elected officials. This is inconsistent with any suggestion that the electorate will refuse "to take part in democratic governance" because of additional political speech made by a corporation or any other speaker.

The *McConnell* record was "over 100,000 pages" long, yet it "does not have any direct examples of votes being exchanged for . . . expenditures," This confirms *Buckley*'s reasoning that independent expenditures do not lead to, or create the appearance of, quid pro quo corruption. In fact, there is only scant evidence that independent expenditures even ingratiate. Ingratiation and access, in any event, are not corruption. The BCRA record establishes that certain donations to political parties, called "soft money," were made to gain access to elected officials. This case, however, is about independent expenditures, not soft money. [If] elected officials succumb to improper influences from independent expenditures; if they surrender their best judgment; and if they put expediency before principle, then surely there is cause for concern. We must give weight to attempts by Congress to seek to dispel either the appearance or the reality of these influences. The remedies enacted by law, however, must comply with the First Amendment; and, it is our law and our tradition that more speech, not less, is the governing rule.

The Government contends further that corporate independent expenditures can be limited because of its interest in protecting dissenting shareholders from being compelled to fund corporate political speech. This asserted interest, like *Austin*'s antidistortion rationale, would allow the Government to ban the political speech even of media corporations. Assume, for example, that a shareholder of a corporation that owns a newspaper disagrees with the political views the newspaper expresses. Under the Government's view, that potential disagreement could give the Government the authority to restrict the media corporation's political speech. The First Amendment does not allow that power. There is, furthermore, little evidence of abuse that cannot be corrected by shareholders "through the procedures of corporate democracy."

Those reasons are sufficient to reject this shareholder-protection interest; and, moreover, the statute is both underinclusive and overinclusive. As to the first, if Congress had been seeking to protect dissenting shareholders, it would not have banned corporate speech in only certain media within 30 or 60 days before an election. A dissenting shareholder's interests would be implicated by speech in any media at any time. As to the second, the statute is overinclusive because it covers all corporations, including nonprofit corporations and for-profit corporations with only single shareholders. As to other corporations, the remedy is not to restrict speech but to consider and explore other regulatory mechanisms. The regulatory mechanism here, based on speech, contravenes the First Amendment.

[441b] is not limited to corporations or associations that were created in foreign countries or funded predominately by foreign shareholders. Section 441b therefore would be overbroad even if we assumed, arguendo, that the Government has a compelling interest in limiting foreign influence over our political process.

Austin is overruled, [thus] "effectively invalidat[ing] not only BCRA Section 203, but also 441b's prohibition on the use of corporate treasury funds for express advocacy." Section 441b's restrictions on corporate independent expenditures are therefore invalid and cannot be applied to *Hillary*.

Given our conclusion we are further required to overrule the part of *McConnell* that upheld BCRA § 203's extension of § 441b's restrictions on corporate independent expenditures. * * *[390]

JUSTICE STEVENS, with whom JUSTICE GINSBURG, JUSTICE BREYER, and JUSTICE SOTOMAYOR join, concurring in part [391] and dissenting in part.

Pervading the Court's analysis is the ominous image of a "categorical ba[n]" on corporate speech. [But our] cases have repeatedly pointed out that, "[c]ontrary to the [majority's] critical assumptions," the statutes upheld in *Austin* and *McConnell* do "not impose an *absolute* ban on all forms of corporate political spending." For starters, both statutes provide exemptions for PACs, separate segregated funds established by a corporation for political purposes. "The ability to form and administer separate segregated funds," we observed in *McConnell,* "has provided corporations and unions with a constitutionally sufficient opportunity to engage in express advocacy. That has been this Court's unanimous view."

A significant and growing number of corporations avail themselves of this option; during the most recent election cycle, corporate and union PACs raised nearly a billion dollars. Administering a PAC entails some administrative burden, but so does complying with the disclaimer, disclosure, and reporting requirements that the Court today upholds, and

---

[390] Thomas, J., joined the opinion of Kennedy, J., except for a section upholding disclosure requirements. Roberts, C.J., joined by Alito, J., concurring argued that the principle of stare decisis did not apply. Scalia, J., joined by Alito, J., and Thomas, J., in part, concurring, argued that the Stevens, J., dissent did not properly assess the original understanding of the First Amendment.

American Tradition Partnership, Inc. v. Bullock, 132 S.Ct. 1307 (2012), summarily reaffirmed *Citizens United* and rejected the argument that a long history of corruption in Montana served to distinguish that precedent.

[391] Stevens, J., joined by Ginsburg, Breyer, and Sotomayor, JJ., joined that part of the Court's opinion upholding disclosure requirements.

no one has suggested that the burden is severe for a sophisticated for-profit corporation. To the extent the majority is worried about this issue, it is important to keep in mind that we have no record to show how substantial the burden really is, just the majority's own unsupported factfinding.

The laws upheld in *Austin* and *McConnell* leave open many additional avenues for corporations' political speech. Consider the statutory provision we are ostensibly evaluating in this case, BCRA § 203. It has no application to genuine issue advertising—a category of corporate speech Congress found to be far more substantial than election-related advertising or to Internet, telephone, and print advocacy. [It] also allows corporations to spend unlimited sums on political communications with their executives and shareholders, to fund additional PAC activity through trade associations, to distribute voting guides and voting records, to underwrite voter registration and voter turnout activities, to host fundraising events for candidates within certain limits, and to publicly endorse candidates through a press release and press conference. * * *

In many ways, then, § 203 functions as a source restriction or a time, place, and manner restriction. It applies in a viewpoint-neutral fashion to a narrow subset of advocacy messages about clearly identified candidates for federal office, made during discrete time periods through discrete channels. In the case at hand, all Citizens United needed to do to broadcast *Hillary* right before the primary was to abjure business contributions or use the funds in its PAC, which by its own account is "one of the most active conservative PACs in America."

[Laws] such as § 203 target a class of communications that is especially likely to corrupt the political process, that is at least one degree removed from the views of individual citizens, and that may not even reflect the views of those who pay for it. Such laws burden political speech, and that is always a serious matter, demanding careful scrutiny. But the majority's incessant talk of a "ban" aims at a straw man. * * *

The second pillar of the Court's opinion is its assertion that "the Government cannot restrict political speech based on the speaker's . . . identity." [Yet] in a variety of contexts, we have held that speech can be regulated differentially on account of the speaker's identity, when identity is understood in categorical or institutional terms. The Government routinely places special restrictions on the speech rights of students, prisoners, members of the Armed Forces, foreigners, and its own employees. When such restrictions are justified by a legitimate governmental interest, they do not necessarily raise constitutional problems. [T]he Court, of course, is right that the First Amendment closely guards political speech. But in [the election] context, too, the authority of legislatures to enact viewpoint-neutral regulations based on content and identity is well settled. We have, for example, allowed state-run broadcasters to exclude independent candidates from televised debates. We have upheld statutes that prohibit the distribution or display of campaign materials near a polling place. Although we have not reviewed them directly, we have never cast doubt on laws that place special restrictions on campaign spending by foreign nationals. And we have consistently approved laws that bar Government employees, but not others, from contributing to or participating in political [activities].

* * * Undergirding the majority's approach to the merits is the claim that the only "sufficiently important governmental interest in preventing corruption or the appearance of corruption" is one that is "limited to quid pro quo corruption." [On] numerous occasions we have recognized Congress' legitimate interest in preventing the money that is spent on elections from exerting an "undue influence on an officeholder's judgment" and from creating "the appearance of such influence," beyond the sphere of quid pro quo relationships. Corruption can take many forms. Bribery may be the paradigm case. But the difference between selling a vote and selling access is a matter of degree, not kind. And selling access is not qualitatively different from giving special preference to those who spent money on one's behalf. Corruption operates along a spectrum, and the majority's apparent belief that quid pro quo arrangements can be neatly demarcated from other improper influences does not accord with the theory or reality of politics. It certainly does not accord with the record Congress developed in passing BCRA, a record that stands as a remarkable testament to the energy and ingenuity with which corporations, unions, lobbyists, and politicians may go about scratching each other's backs-and which amply supported Congress' determination to target a limited set of especially destructive practices.

Stevens, J., then quoted the district court: "The factual findings of the Court illustrate that corporations and labor unions routinely notify Members of Congress as soon as they air electioneering communications relevant to the Members' elections. The record also indicates that Members express appreciation to organizations for the airing of these election-related advertisements. Indeed, Members of Congress are particularly grateful when negative issue advertisements are run by these organizations, leaving the candidates free to run positive advertisements and be seen as 'above the fray.' Political consultants testify that campaigns are quite aware of who is running advertisements on the candidate's behalf, when they are being run, and where they are being run. Likewise, a prominent lobbyist testifies that these organizations use issue advocacy as a means to influence various Members of Congress. [Finally], a large majority of Americans (80%) are of the view that corporations and other organizations that engage in electioneering communications, which benefit specific elected officials, receive special consideration from those officials when matters arise that affect these corporations and organizations."

[When] private interests are seen to exert outsized control over officeholders solely on account of the money spent on (or withheld from) their campaigns, the result can depart so thoroughly "from what is pure or correct" in the conduct of Government that it amounts to a "subversion [of] the electoral process." [Starting] today, corporations with large war chests to deploy on electioneering may find democratically elected bodies becoming much more attuned to their interests. * * *

The fact that corporations are different from human beings might seem to need no elaboration, except that the majority opinion almost completely elides it. *Austin* set forth some of the basic differences. Unlike natural persons, corporations have "limited liability" for their owners and managers, "perpetual life," separation of ownership and control, "and favorable treatment of the accumulation and distribution of assets [that] enhance their ability to attract capital and to deploy their resources in ways that maximize the return on their shareholders' investments." [It] might also be added that corporations have no consciences, no beliefs, no feelings, no thoughts, no desires. Corporations help structure and facilitate the activities of human beings, to be sure, and their "personhood" often serves as a useful legal fiction. But they are not themselves members of "We the People" by whom and for whom our Constitution was established. * * *

It is an interesting question "who" is even speaking when a business corporation places an advertisement that endorses or attacks a particular candidate. Presumably it is not the customers or employees, who typically have no say in such matters. It cannot realistically be said to be the shareholders, who tend to be far removed from the day-to-day decisions of the firm and whose political preferences may be opaque to management. Perhaps the officers or directors of the corporation have the best claim to be the ones speaking, except their fiduciary duties generally prohibit them from using corporate funds for personal ends. * * *

In critiquing *Austin's* antidistortion rationale and campaign finance regulation more generally, our colleagues place tremendous weight on the example of media corporations. Yet it is not at all clear that *Austin* would permit § 203 to be applied to them. The press plays a unique role not only in the text, history, and structure of the First Amendment but also in facilitating public discourse * * * . Our colleagues have raised some interesting and difficult questions about Congress' authority to regulate electioneering by the press, and about how to define what constitutes the press. *But that is not the case before us.* Section 203 does not apply to media corporations, and even if it did, Citizens United is not a media corporation. * * *

Interwoven with *Austin's* concern to protect the integrity of the electoral process is a concern to protect the rights of shareholders from a kind of coerced speech: electioneering expenditures that do not "reflec[t] [their] support." When corporations use general treasury funds to praise or attack a particular candidate for office, it is the shareholders, as the residual claimants, who are effectively footing the bill. Those shareholders who disagree with the corporation's electoral message may find their financial investments being used to undermine their political convictions.

The PAC mechanism, by contrast, helps assure that those who pay for an electioneering communication actually support its content and that managers do not use general treasuries to advance personal agendas. [The] shareholder protection rationale has been criticized as underinclusive, in that corporations also spend money on lobbying and charitable contributions in ways that any particular shareholder might disapprove. But those expenditures do not implicate the selection of public officials, an area in which "the interests of unwilling . . . corporate shareholders [in not being] forced to subsidize that speech" "are at their zenith." And in any event, the question is whether shareholder protection provides a basis for regulating expenditures in the weeks before an election, not whether additional types of corporate communications might similarly be conditioned on voluntariness.

Recognizing the limits of the shareholder protection rationale, the *Austin* Court did not hold it out as an adequate and independent ground for sustaining the statute in question. Rather, the Court applied it to reinforce the antidistortion rationale, in two main ways. First, the problem of dissenting shareholders shows that even if electioneering expenditures can advance the political views of some members of a corporation, they will often compromise the views of others. Second, it provides an additional reason, beyond the distinctive legal attributes of the corporate form, for doubting that these "expenditures reflect actual public support for the political ideas espoused." * * *

While American democracy is imperfect, few outside the majority of this Court would have thought its flaws included a dearth of corporate money in politics.

NOTES AND QUESTIONS

1.   *Court's opinion.* Should the Court have reached the question regarding the First Amendment rights of business corporations? (a) *Documentary films.* Should the Court have ruled that the Act applied to advertising, but not to documentary films? Was there a history of corruption or its appearance arising from documentary films? If the Act did apply to documentary films, might it be argued that the difference between advertising and films is of constitutional dimension? (b) *Video on demand.* Might it be argued that the Act did not apply to video on demand because viewers decide to see such videos in ways they do not do with ads? (c) *Advocacy corporations.* The Court had already held that non-profit corporations not involved in

business and formed for the purpose of advocacy were as free as individuals to engage in campaign spending so long as they had no shareholders with claims on its assets and earnings and did not receive contributions from business corporations or unions. *FEC v. Massachusetts Citizens for Life,* 479 U.S. 238 (1986). Should the Court have ruled that Citizens United should be treated like MCFL because the amount of business funds it received was small enough that it could not be considered as a surrogate for business corporations?

2. ***First Amendment values.*** The Court had previously granted First Amendment protection to corporations in a variety of contexts. It routinely granted protection to press corporations, and, as discussed in note 1, it granted protection to advocacy corporations. But it also granted protection to business corporations in the context of commercial speech cases (see, e.g., *Central Hudson*; *Linmark Associates*). And it afforded protection for the political speech of business corporations in the context of opposing a referendum proposal. *First National Bank of Boston v. Bellotti,* 435 U.S. 765 (1978). But, as the opinion makes clear, prior to *Citizens United,* protection was not granted in candidate elections. Leaving press corporations and advocacy corporations aside, does it make sense to afford protection to non-media business corporations in commercial [392] or political contexts? What values are furthered by protection for business corporations? Is the speech of business corporations dictated by their competitive needs in the market? How is that different from the speech of individuals or associations? Do corporations have a liberty interest? If not, do they serve First Amendment values in other ways? Are corporations participants as corporations in a democracy? Do they have right to participate in discussions about the policies that will affect them? Is speech that is not necessarily connected to the genuine views of those who finance it likely to make a contribution to the marketplace of ideas? Should the lack of citizenship of corporations disqualify them from participation in the elections process (other than through PACs)?

Is the question of corporate free speech rights different from the question of the constitutionality of limitations on campaign expenditures? Might comprehensive limitations on campaign expenditures, absent *Buckley* and *Citizens United,* apply across the board without relying on a distinction between individuals and corporations? See Frederick Schauer, *Constitutions of Hope and Fear,* 124 Yale L.J. 528 (2014).

3. ***Corruption interest and contributions.*** Does the reasoning of the Court apply to corporate contributions as well as corporate independent expenditures? See Kathleen M. Sullivan, *Two Concepts of Freedom of Speech,* 124 Harv. L.Rev. 143 (2010). Although corporations may use their treasuries to solicit funds donated to a segregated independent political fund, they are not permitted to make direct contributions from their treasuries in federal election campaigns. Constitutional? Consider also Floyd Abrams, *Speaking*

---

[392] Does the refusal to create a hierarchy among speakers in *Citizens United* suggest that the Court will refuse to create hierarchies of speech and abandon the lower place of commercial speech in the free speech hierarchy? See Darrel C. Menthe, *The Market Place Metaphor and Commercial Speech Doctrine,* 38 Hast. Con. L.Q. 131 (2010).

Freely 268 (2005): "If the purpose of McCain-Feingold was truly to prevent corruption, real or apparent, why were PACs permitted? Such a statute, the NRA argued, 'makes no more sense than a bribery statute requiring corporations to pay for their bribes using funds from PACs.'"

4.   ***Contracting Corporations.*** Could Congress prohibit those who contract with government to give contributions or make political expenditures after *Citizens United?* See Samuel Issacharoff, *On Political Corruption*, 124 Harv. L. Rev. 118 (2010).

5.   ***Media corporations.*** Do most of the concerns of the last note also apply to media corporations? Can media corporations be easily distinguished from business corporations? Consider David A. Anderson, *Freedom of the Press*, 80 Tex. L. Rev. 429 (2002): "As recently as 1990, the Supreme Court assured us that 'media corporations differ significantly from other corporations in that their resources are devoted to the collection of information and its dissemination to the public.' The Court held that this 'valid distinction' constituted a compelling reason for the state to exempt media corporations from campaign finance laws that restricted other corporations' ability to influence politics. This argument may or may not have been persuasive in 1990, but it is extremely dubious today. NBC is owned by General Electric, ABC by Walt Disney Co., and CBS by Viacom, Inc.; each of these conglomerate parents owns many other businesses, media and nonmedia. Today's major media owners seem indistinguishable in most respects from other conglomerates. They devote their resources to a vast array of activities, only a fraction of which involve the gathering and dissemination of information to the public, and it is difficult to believe that they are any less eager to influence politics than their nonmedia counterparts. Through their media subsidiaries they are allowed to influence political campaigns in ways that are forbidden to other corporations, and the resulting difficulty of justifying this disparate treatment has become a significant obstacle to regulation of campaign finance."

Is a campaign finance regulation that distinguishes media from non-media corporations constitutionally permissible? Why might it not be? Is such a distinction constitutionally required? If so, would that demand rethinking the doctrine refusing to grant special privileges to the press or a preferred position n First Amendment doctrine?

6.   ***Soft money.*** *Citizens United* reopens a loophole that the Bipartisan Campaign Reform Act [BRCA] sought to close. But the same Act sought to close another loophole as well. As interpreted, the Federal Election Campaign Act of 1971 ("FECA") distinguishes between hard and soft money. Hard money is contributed money that falls under the specified contribution limits and complies with certain source limitations. Soft money encompasses contributions not subject to those restrictions which are for the most part ostensibly designed to encourage party-building activities benefitting the political parties in general, but not specific candidates. Under FECA, as interpreted, however, wealthy donors were able to use soft money directly or indirectly in ways that benefited federal candidates.

BRCA sought to close the soft money loophole. It forbids national party committees from soliciting, receiving, or directing the use of soft-money; prohibits state and local party committees from using soft money (although it permits their use of hard money and some additional funding) for activities affecting federal elections, including voter registration activity during the 120 days before a federal election, and get-out-the-vote drives conducted in connection with an election in which a federal candidate appears on the ballot; forbids the use of soft money by state and local party committees or state and local candidates and officeholders for any public communication that supports or attacks a federal candidate, whether or not the communication specifically asks for a vote for or against a particular candidate.

McCONNELL v. FEC, 540 U.S. 93 (2003), per STEVENS and O'CONNOR, JJ., joined by Souter, Ginsburg and Breyer, JJ. (the "Joint Opinion"), upheld the soft money provisions of the Act against a facial constitutional challenge: "Of the two major parties' total spending, soft money accounted for 5% ($21.6 million) in 1984, 11% ($45 million) in 1988, 16% ($80 million) in 1992, 30% ($272 million) in 1996, and 42% ($498 million) in 2000. The national parties transferred large amounts of their soft money to the state parties, which were allowed to use a larger percentage of soft money to finance mixed-purpose activities under FEC rules. In the year 2000, for example, the national parties diverted $280 million—more than half of their soft money—to state parties.

"Many contributions of soft money were dramatically larger than the contributions of hard money permitted by FECA. For example, in 1996 the top five corporate soft-money donors gave, in total, more than $9 million in nonfederal funds to the two national party committees. In the most recent election cycle the political parties raised almost $300 million—60% of their total soft-money fundraising—from just 800 donors, each of which contributed a minimum of $120,000. Moreover, the largest corporate donors often made substantial contributions to both parties. Such practices corroborate evidence indicating that many corporate contributions were motivated by a desire for access to candidates and a fear of being placed at a disadvantage in the legislative process relative to other contributors, rather than by ideological support for the candidates and parties."

Despite the fact that many of the soft money restrictions regulated spending, the Joint Opinion concluded that the less than strict scrutiny applied to the contribution limits in *Buckley* and *Nixon v. Shrink Missouri Government PAC,* 528 U.S. 377 (2000), was appropriately applied to the soft money restrictions: "The relevant inquiry is whether the mechanism adopted to implement the contribution limit, or to prevent circumvention of that limit, burdens speech in a way that a direct restriction on the contribution itself would not. That is not the case here." Applying the *Buckley* contribution limits standard, it concluded that the soft money restrictions were "closely drawn to match the important governmental interests of preventing corruption and the appearance of corruption"[393]

The dissents employed themes about incumbent protection, the failure to show quid pro quo corruption, lack of precision, and deep invasion of treasured First Amendment rights.[394]

Do the limitations approved by *McConnell* taken together with the denial in *Elrod* v. *Burns*, 427 U.S. 347 (1976), of the parties ability to use patronage as a system of reward, cripple the power of parties in the political system?[395] To the extent that the campaign finance restrictions enhance the power of advocacy groups at the expense of parties. Is this a good thing?[396] Is this aspect of *McConnell* likely to survive *Citizens United.*

     7.   ***Impact on campaigns.*** It is not clear that *United Citizens* will have a substantial impact on election campaigns. The Court had already narrowed the limitation on electioneering ads in ways that provided substantial leeway

---

[393] The Joint Opinion argued that the application of soft money restrictions to minor parties was permissible because the corruption and appearance of corruption interests were not a function of the number of legislators elected and that an as-applied challenge could be brought if the act prevented the massing of sufficient resources for effective advocacy. The Court had previously held that limitations on independent expenditures of the major parties were unconstitutional, *Colorado Republican Fed. Campaign Comm. v. FEC,* 518 U.S. 604 (1996), but prohibitions of expenditures coordinated with a candidate were constitutional. *FEC v. Colorado Republican Fed. Campaign Comm.,* 533 U.S. 431 (2001).

[394] Scalia, J., dissented. Thomas, J., joined in part by Scalia, J., dissented. Kennedy, joined Rehnquist, C.J., and in part by Scalia and Thomas, JJ., dissented. Rehnquist, C.J., joined by Scalia and Kennedy, JJ., dissented.

[395] The Court has generally upheld the association rights of the major parties. *California Democratic Party v. Jones,* 530 U.S. 567 (2000), invalidated California's "blanket primary" which required parties to permit citizens to vote in the primary of any party for any office regardless of their party membership. *Eu v. San Francisco County Democratic Central Comm.,* 489 U.S. 214 (1989) struck down California election provisions prohibiting political parties from endorsing candidates in party primaries. *Tashjian v. Republican Party of Conn.,* 479 U.S. 208 (1986) denounced Connecticut's closed-primary statute requiring voters in a party primary to be registered party members. At the same time, the Court has decided a number of cases that favor the interests of a two party system or the candidates of the two parties. *Timmons v. Twin Cities Area New Party,* 520 U.S. 351 (1997) upheld Minnesota legislation prohibiting political candidates from appearing on the ballot as candidates for more than one party. *Storer v. Brown,* 415 U.S. 724 (1974) approved a California statute denying ballot positions to independent candidates who had recently been registered with a political party. *Burdick v. Takushi,* 504 U.S. 428 (1992) validated Hawaii's ban on write-in voting. On the other hand, burdens on minor parties have occasionally been struck down particularly when they have been regarded as severe. For example, *Anderson v. Celebrezze,* 460 U.S. 780 (1983) held that unreasonably early filing deadlines for independent candidates violated the association rights of their supporters. *Williams v. Rhodes,* 393 U.S. 23 (1968) invalidated unduly stringent ballot access requirements on equal protection grounds. But *Crawford v. Marion County Elec. Bd.,* 553 U.S. 181 (2008), upheld Indiana's government issued photo identification voting requirement against an equal protection challenge.

    In other developments, *New York State Bd. of Elec. v. Torres,* 552 U.S. 196 (2008), upheld New York's party convention scheme for nominating judges against a First Amendment claim that democratic primaries would give aspiring party nominees a more realistic chance than a convention process responsive to the wishes of party leaders. And *Washington State Grange v. Washington Republican Party,* 552 U.S. 442 (2008), upheld a blanket party scheme, that narrowed the candidate field to two regardless of party affiliation, against a claim that the system infringed upon the associational rights of political parties.

[396] For discussion, see Nathaniel Persily, *Soft Parties and Strong Money,* 3 Election L.J. 315 (2004).

for business corporations. Wisconsin Right to Life, Inc., a non profit advocacy corporation, ran three broadcast ads from its treasury funds, which included contributions of $50,000 from business corporations, for the ads. Wisconsin Right to Life had previously campaigned against Senator Feingold, and one of its concerns was his support of filibustering of judicial nominees. The ads spoke out against filibustering and asked citizens to contact Senators Feingold and McCain without referring to Feingold's position on the issue (though his position was well known in Wisconsin). The ads appeared to violate BCRA § 203.

FEC v. WISCONSIN RIGHT TO LIFE, INC., 551 U.S. 449 (2007), per ROBERTS, C.J., joined only by Alito, J., concluded that § 203 was constitutional only as applied to ads that are "susceptible of no reasonable interpretation other than as an appeal to vote for or against a specific candidate." Because of the importance of political speech, any doubt on the matter was to be resolved in favor of the ads. Neither the intent nor the effect of the ads counted in the determination. Roberts, C.J., found Wisconsin Right to Life's ads to be protected under the First Amendment.[397]

SOUTER, J., joined by Stevens, Ginsburg, and Breyer, JJ., dissenting, found it hard to imagine that the majority would ever find an ad unprotected unless it contained words of express advocacy.

---

[397] Alito, J., concurring, observed that the Court would presumably be asked to reconsider its holding that § 203 is facially constitutional. Scalia, J., joined by Kennedy and Thomas, JJ., concurring in the judgment, would have overruled *McConnell's* upholding of § 203.

CHAPTER 8

FREEDOM OF RELIGION

∎ ∎ ∎

This chapter concerns the "Religion Clauses" of the First Amendment, commonly known as the "Establishment Clause" (forbidding laws "respecting an establishment of religion") and the "Free Exercise Clause" (forbidding laws "prohibiting the free exercise thereof"). It is difficult to explore either clause in isolation from the other. The extent to which the clauses interact may be illustrated by the matter of public financial aid to parochial schools, Sec. 1, II. On one hand, does such aid violate the Establishment Clause? On the other, does a state's failure to provide such aid violate the Free Exercise Clause? Another example of the potential conflict between the clauses—also considered in the materials below—is whether, on one hand, a state's exemption of church buildings from property taxes contravenes the Establishment Clause or whether, on the other, a state's taxing these buildings contravenes the Free Exercise Clause.

Despite this interrelationship of the two clauses, Sec. 1 deals almost exclusively with the Establishment Clause. Sec. 2, I then considers conventional problems under the Free Exercise Clause. Sec. 2, II examines the complex issues of defining "religion" for purposes of the First Amendment and determining the bona fides of an asserted "religious" belief—both matters usually presumed in the cases decided by the Supreme Court and the former never specifically addressed by a majority of the Justices. Sec. 3 presents the subject of preference among religions that has both establishment and free exercise ramifications, and, finally, Sec. 4 discusses problems presented by government action that attempts to accommodate the seemingly opposing demands of the two religion clauses.[1]

1. ESTABLISHMENT CLAUSE

I. INTRODUCTION

Many authorities view the Establishment Clause as seeking to assure some form of separation of church and state in a nation that has become

---

[1] For a helpful categorization and evaluation of a range of alternative judicial perspectives on both Religion Clauses, see Kathleen M. Sullivan, *Justice Scalia and the Religion Clauses*, 22 U. of Haw. L.Rev. 449 (2000). For an earlier discussion of the various "articulated justifications for the special constitutional place of religion" by the Justices, see Michael E. Smith, *The Special Place of Religion in the Constitution,* 1983 Sup.Ct.Rev. 83.

characterized by religious pluralism. Prior to 1947, only two decisions concerning the Establishment Clause produced any significant consideration by the Court. *Bradfield v. Roberts,* 175 U.S. 291 (1899), upheld federal appropriations to a hospital in the District of Columbia, operated by the Catholic Church, for ward construction and care of indigent patients. *Quick Bear v. Leupp,* 210 U.S. 50 (1908), upheld federal disbursement of funds, held in trust for the Sioux Indians, to Catholic schools designated by the Sioux for payment of tuition costs.

In the Court's first modern decision, *Everson v. Board of Educ.* (1947), Part II infra, Rutledge, J., observed that "no provision of the Constitution is more closely tied to or given content by its generating history than the religious clause of the First Amendment." Black, J., writing for the majority, recounted that the Religion Clauses "reflected in the minds of early Americans a vivid mental picture of conditions and practices which they fervently wished to stamp out in order to preserve liberty for themselves and for their posterity." Black, J., detailed the history of religious persecution in Europe "before and contemporaneous with the colonization of America" and the "repetition of many of the old world practices" in the colonies. For example, in Massachusetts, Quakers, Baptists, and other religious minorities suffered harshly and were taxed for the state's established Congregational Church. In 1776, the Maryland "Declaration of Rights" stated that "only persons professing the Christian religion" were entitled to religious freedom, and not until 1826 were Jews permitted to hold public office. The South Carolina Constitution of 1778 stated that "the Christian Protestant religion shall be [the] established religion of this state." Black, J., explained that "abhorrence" of these practices "reached its dramatic climax in Virginia in 1785–86" when "Madison wrote his great Memorial and Remonstrance" against renewal of "Virginia's tax levy for support of the established church" and the Virginia Assembly "enacted the famous 'Virginia Bill for Religious Liberty' originally written by Thomas Jefferson. [T]he provisions of the First Amendment, in the drafting and adoption of which Madison and Jefferson played such leading roles, had the same objective and were intended to provide the same protection against governmental intrusion on religious liberty as the Virginia statute."

Still, the specific historical record suggests that rather than disclosing a coherent "intent of the Framers," those who influenced the framing of the First Amendment were animated by several distinct and sometimes conflicting goals. Thus, Jefferson once wrote that the integrity of government could be preserved only by erecting "a wall of separation" between church and state. A sharp division of authority was essential, in his view, to insulate the democratic process from ecclesiastical depradations and excursions. Madison shared this view, but also perceived church-state separation as benefiting religious institutions. Even more strongly, Roger Williams, one of the earliest colonial proponents of religious freedom, posited an evangelical theory of separation, believing it vital to protect the sanctity of the church's "garden" from the "wilderness" of the state. [2] Finally, there is evidence that one purpose of the Establishment Clause was to protect the existing state-established churches from the newly ordained national government.[3] (Indeed, although disestablishment was then well under way, it did not end until 1833 with Massachusetts.

The varied ideologies that prompted the founders do, however, disclose a dominant theme: constitutional status for the integrity of individual conscience.[4] Moreover, in Virginia's Bill for Religious Liberty, a practice seen by many as anathema to religious freedom was forcing the people to support religion through compulsory taxation, although there was a division of opinion as to whether non-preferential aid to religion violated liberty of conscience.[5]

A final matter involving the history of the Establishment Clause concerns *Everson's* unanimous ruling that it was "made applicable to the states" by the Fourteenth Amendment.[6]

---

[2]   For the view that "the Constitution was written on the assumption [that] government is a threat to human liberty [and] not the other way around [i.e.,] the First Amendment constrains Congress, not churches," see Douglas Laycock, *Continuity and Change in the Threat to Religious Liberty: The Reformation Era and the Late Twentieth Century*, 80 Minn.L.Rev. 1047 (1996).

[3]   In *Elk Grove Unified School Dist. v. Newdow*, Part IV infra, Thomas, J., stated that "text and history * * * strongly suggest" that the Establishment Clause is only "a federalism provision intended to prevent Congress from interfering with state establishments." Contra according to "the members of the First Congress, who drafted and debated the Establishment Clause," see Carl H. Esbeck, *Uses and Abuses of Textualism and Originalism in Establishment Clause Interpretation*, 2011 Utah L Rev. 489 (2011). For the broader view that both "religion clauses amounted to a decision by the national government not to address substantive questions concerning the proper relationship between religion and government," but rather "did no more and no less than confirm the constitutional allocation of jurisdiction over religion to the states," see Steven D. Smith, *Foreordained Failure: The Quest for a Constitutional Principle of Religious Freedom* (1995). Compare Kurt T. Lash, *The Second Adoption of the Establishment Clause: The Rise of the Nonestablishment Principle*, 27 Ariz.St.L.J. 1085 (1995) (this understanding had changed by the time of the Fourteenth Amendment). For a different perspective, see Richard C. Schragger, *The Role of the Local in the Doctrine and Discourse of Religious Liberty*, 117 Harv.L.Rev. 1810, 1815, 1852, 1892 (2004) ("Decentralization should be incorporated as a substantive Religion Clause value" because the exercise of national and state power is "the chief threat to religious liberty," and "dispersal of political authority over religious [issues] and benefits enhances local public authority, enabling it to serve as a counterweight to private religious power.").

[4]   See Noah Feldman, *The Intellectual Origins of the Establishment Clause*, 77 N.Y.U.L.Rev. 346 (2002).

[5]   The view that it did not was endorsed by Rehnquist, J., in *Wallace v. Jaffree*, Part III, and Thomas, J., found "much to commend" this position in *Rosenberger v. University of Virginia*, Part II infra.

[6]   *Application of the Establishment Clause to the states.* Is nonestablishment as "implicit in the concept of ordered liberty" as the freedoms of speech, press, religious exercise, and assembly? See *Palko v. Connecticut*, Ch. 6, Sec. 1, I. Is it "fundamental to the American scheme"? See *Duncan v. Louisiana*, Ch. 6, Sec. 1, I.

II. AID TO RELIGION

EVERSON v. BOARD OF EDUC., 330 U.S. 1 (1947), involved one of
the major areas of controversy under the Establishment Clause: public
financial assistance to church-related institutions (mainly parochial
schools). A New Jersey township reimbursed parents for the cost of sending
their children "on regular buses operated by the public transportation
system," to and from schools, including nonprofit private and parochial
schools. The Court, per BLACK, J., rejected a municipal taxpayer's
contention that payment for Catholic parochial school students violated the
Establishment Clause:

"The 'establishment of religion' clause of the First Amendment means
at least this: Neither a state nor the Federal Government can set up a
church. Neither can pass laws which aid one religion, aid all religions, or
prefer one religion over another. Neither can force nor influence a person
to go to or to remain away from church against his will or force him to
profess a belief or disbelief in any religion. No person can be punished for
entertaining or professing religious beliefs or disbeliefs, for church
attendance or non-attendance. No tax in any amount, large or small can be
levied to support any religious activities or institutions, whatever they may
be called, or whatever form they may adopt to teach or practice religion.
Neither a state nor the Federal Government can, openly or secretly,
participate in the affairs of any religious organizations or groups and vice
versa. In the words of Jefferson, the clause against establishment of
religion by law was intended to erect 'a wall of separation between Church
and State.'

"We must [not invalidate the New Jersey statute] if it is within the
state's constitutional power even though it approaches the verge of that
power. New Jersey [cannot] contribute tax-raised funds to the support of
an institution which teaches the tenets and faith of any church. On the
other hand, other language of the amendment commands that New Jersey
cannot hamper its citizens in the free exercise of their own religion.
Consequently, it cannot exclude individual Catholics, Lutherans,
Mohammedans, Baptists, Jews, Methodists, Non-believers, Presbyterians,
or the members of any other faith, *because of their faith, or lack of it,* from
receiving the benefits of public welfare legislation. While we do not mean
to intimate that a state could not provide transportation only to children
attending public schools, we must be careful, in protecting the citizens of
New Jersey against state-established churches, to be sure that we do not
inadvertently prohibit New Jersey from extending its general State law
benefits to all its citizens without regard to their religious belief."

Noting that "the New Jersey legislature has decided that a public
purpose will be served" by having children "ride in public buses to and from
schools rather than run the risk of traffic and other hazards incident to

walking or 'hitchhiking,' " the Court conceded "that children are helped to get to church schools. There is even a possibility that some of the children might not be sent to the church schools if the parents were compelled to pay their children's bus fares out of their own pockets when transportation to a public school would have been paid for by the State. [But] state-paid policemen, detailed to protect children going to and from church schools from the very real hazards of traffic, would serve much the same [purpose]. Similarly, parents might be reluctant to permit their children to attend schools which the state had cut off from such general government services as ordinary police and fire protection, connections for sewage disposal, public highways and sidewalks. Of course, cutting off church schools from these services, so separate and so indisputably marked off from the religious function, would make it far more difficult for the schools to operate. But such is obviously not the purpose of the First Amendment. That Amendment requires the state to be a neutral in its relations with groups of religious believers and non-believers; it does not require the state to be their adversary. * * *

"This Court has said that parents may, in the discharge of their duty under state compulsory education laws, send their children to a religious rather than a public school if the school meets the secular educational requirements which the state has power to impose. See *Pierce v. Society of Sisters,* [Ch. 7, Sec. 7, II]. It appears that these parochial schools meet New Jersey's requirements. The State contributes no money to the schools. [Its] legislation, as applied, does no more than provide a general program to help parents get their children, regardless of their religion, safely and expeditiously to and from accredited schools.

"The First Amendment has erected a wall between church and state. That wall must be kept high and impregnable. We could not approve the slightest breach. New Jersey has not breached it here."

RUTLEDGE, J., joined by Frankfurter, Jackson and Burton, JJ., filed the principal dissent, arguing that the statute aided children "in a substantial way to get the very thing which they are sent to the particular school to secure, namely, religious training and [teaching.] Commingling the religious with the secular teaching does not divest the whole of its religious permeation and emphasis or make them of minor part, if proportion were material. Indeed, on any other view, the constitutional prohibition always could be brought to naught by adding a modicum of the secular. [T]ransportation is [no] less essential to education, whether religious or secular, than payment for tuitions, for teachers' salaries, for buildings, equipment and necessary materials. [Now], as in Madison's time, not the amount but the principle of assessment is wrong.

" * * * Public money devoted to payment of religious costs, educational or other, brings the quest for more. It brings too the struggle of sect against sect for the larger share or for any. Here one by numbers alone will benefit most, there another. That is precisely the history of societies which have had an established religion and dissident groups. It is the very thing Jefferson and Madison experienced and sought to guard [against]. The dominating group will achieve the dominant benefit; or all will embroil the state in their dissensions. [Nor] is the case comparable to one of furnishing fire or police protection, or access to public highways. These things are matters of common right, part of the general need for safety. Certainly the fire department must not stand idly by while the church burns." [Jackson, J., joined by Frankfurter, J., also filed a dissent.]

The Court did not again confront the subject of aid to parochial schools for more than two decades.[7] During the intervening years, however, the Court continued to develop its Establishment Clause rationale in cases involving other issues, emphasizing the "purpose and primary effect" of the challenged government action (see Part III infra).

WALZ v. TAX COMM'N, 397 U.S. 664 (1970), per BURGER, C.J., upheld state tax exemption for "property used exclusively for religious, educational or charitable purposes": The purpose "is neither the advancement nor the inhibition of religion; it is neither sponsorship nor hostility. [We] must also be sure that the end result—the effect—is not an excessive government entanglement with religion. The test is inescapably one of degree. * * * Elimination of exemption would tend to expand the involvement of government by giving rise to tax valuation of church property, tax liens, tax foreclosures, and the direct confrontations and conflicts that follow in the train of those legal processes.

"Granting tax exemptions to churches necessarily operates to afford an indirect economic benefit and also gives rise to some, but yet a lesser, involvement than taxing them.[8] [Finally,] no one acquires a vested or protected right in violation of the Constitution by long use * * * . Yet an unbroken practice of according the exemption to churches [is] not something to be lightly cast aside."

Only DOUGLAS, J., dissented: "The financial support rendered here is to the church, the place of worship. A tax exemption is a subsidy."

---

[7]   See *Board of Educ. v. Allen* (1968), discussed by Souter, J., in *Zelman*, infra.

[8]   What of the fact that exemption for churches augments the tax bills of others? For the view that there is a constitutional distinction between tax exemptions ("a standing arrangement open to a wide array of organizations") and annual appropriations, see Edward A. Zelinsky, *Are Tax "Benefits" Constitutionally Equivalent to Direct Expenditures*, 112 Harv.L.Rev. 379 (1998). Does an income tax exemption for religious organizations that engage in "religiously impelled partisan political speech" violate the Establishment Clause? See Johnny R. Buckles, *Does the Constitutional Norm of Separation of Church and State Justify the Denial of Tax Exemption to Churches that Engage in Partisan Political Speech?*, 84 Ind.L.J. 447 (2009).

NOTES AND QUESTIONS

1. ***Size of government.*** Consider William W. Van Alstyne, *Constitutional Separation of Church and State: The Quest for a Coherent Position,* 57 Am.Pol.Sci.Rev. 865 (1963): "To finance expanding government services, [taxes] may gradually divert an increasing fraction of total personal income, necessarily leaving proportionately less money in the private sector to each person to spend according to his individual choice, in support of religion or other undertakings. To the extent that the tax revenues thus collected may not be spent by government to support religious enterprises, but must be used exclusively for secular purposes, the net effect, arguably, is to reduce the relative supply of funds available to religion." Does this warrant tax exemption for "religion"? Does it "warrant the judicial junking of the Establishment Clause"? Id. Is it "equally arguable that government fiscal activity, far from reducing disposable personal income, actually increases it"? Id. See also Alan Schwarz, *The Nonestablishment Principle: A Reply to Professor Giannella,* 81 Harv.L.Rev. 1465 (1968).

2. ***"Neutrality" and "endorsement."*** TEXAS MONTHLY, INC. v. BULLOCK, 489 U.S. 1 (1989), held violative of the Establishment Clause a Texas sales tax exemption for books and "periodicals that are published or distributed by a religious faith and that consist wholly of writings promulgating the teaching of the faith." BRENNAN, J., joined by Marshall and Stevens, JJ., referred to several important themes in the Court's developing Establishment Clause doctrine:[9] "[*Walz*] emphasized that the benefits derived by religious organizations flowed to a large number of nonreligious groups as [well]. However, when government directs a subsidy exclusively to religious organizations [that] either burdens nonbeneficiaries markedly or cannot reasonably be seen as removing a significant state-imposed deterrent to the free exercise of religion, as Texas has done, it 'provide[s] unjustifiable awards of assistance to religious organizations' and cannot but 'conve[y] a message of endorsement' to slighted members of the community. This is particularly true where, as here, the subsidy is targeted at writings that *promulgate* the teachings of religious faiths. [This] lacks a secular objective." White, J., concurred on freedom of press grounds. Scalia, J., joined by Rehnquist, C.J., and Kennedy, J., dissented from Brennan, J.'s distinction of *Walz*.

––––––––

LEMON v. KURTZMAN, 403 U.S. 602 (1971), per BURGER C.J., which invalidated state salary supplements to teachers of secular subjects in nonpublic schools, articulated a three-part test for judging Establishment Clause issues. This test is frequently invoked by the lower courts and—as the materials that follow indicate—has not been overruled: "First, the statute must have a secular legislative purpose; second, its principal or

––––––––

[9] "Neutrality" and "endorsement" are discussed further in the materials in this Part. A third theme—"coercion"—is considered more fully in Part IV infra.

primary effect must be one that neither advances nor inhibits religion;"[10] third, the statute must not foster "an excessive government entanglement with religion." During the next fifteen years, the Court, using the *Lemon* test, invalidated a large number of aid programs for elementary and secondary schools, even though it found that virtually all had a "secular" purpose.[11] The Court began with a critical premise: the mission of church related elementary and secondary schools is to teach religion, and all subjects are, or carry the potential of being, permeated with religion. Thus, states would have to engage in a "comprehensive, discriminating, and continuing state surveillance" to prevent misuse of tax funds for religious purposes, which would be impermissibly entangling, and "pregnant with dangers of excessive government direction of church schools and hence of churches."[12] Furthermore, state assistance risked another sort of entanglement: "divisive political potential" along religious lines.[13]

---

[10] Compare Douglas Laycock, *Towards a General Theory of the Religion Clauses: The Case of Church Labor Relations and the Right to Church Autonomy*, 81 Colum.L.Rev. 1373 (1981): "The 'inhibits' language is at odds with the constitutional text and with the Court's own statements of the origins and purposes of [the] clause. Government support for religion is an element of every establishment claim, just as a burden or restriction on religion is an element of every free exercise claim. Regulation that burdens religion, enacted because of the government's general interest in regulation, is simply not establishment."

[11] "This reflects, at least in part, our reluctance to attribute unconstitutional motives to the states, particularly when a plausible secular purpose for the state's program may be discerned from the face of the statute." *Mueller v. Allen*, discussed infra. *Mueller* added: "A state's decision to defray the cost of educational expenses incurred by parents—regardless of the type of schools their children attend—evidences a purpose that is both secular and understandable. An educated populace is essential to the political and economic health of any community, and a state's efforts to assist parents in meeting the rising cost of educational expenses plainly serves this secular purpose. [Similarly, states] could conclude that there is a strong public interest in assuring the continued financial health of private schools, both sectarian and non-sectarian. By educating a substantial number of students such schools relieve public schools of a correspondingly great burden—to the benefit of all taxpayers. In addition, private schools may serve as a benchmark for public schools."

[12] White, J., dissenting in *Lemon*, accused the Court of "creat[ing] an insoluble paradox for the State and the parochial schools. The State cannot finance secular instruction if it permits religion to be taught in the same classroom; but if it exacts a promise that religion not be so taught—a promise the school and its teachers are quite willing and on this record able to give—and enforces it, it is then entangled in the 'no entanglement' aspect of the Court's Establishment Clause jurisprudence."

[13] *Lemon* reasoned: "In a community [where] pupils are served by church-related schools, it can be assumed that state assistance will entail considerable political activity [by partisans and opponents]. Candidates will be forced to declare and voters to choose. It would be unrealistic to ignore the fact that many people confronted with issues of this kind will find their votes aligned with their faith. Ordinarily political debate and division, however vigorous or even partisan, are normal and healthy manifestations of our democratic system of government, but political division along religious lines was one of the principal evils against which the First Amendment was intended to protect. Paul A. Freund, *Public Aid to Parochial Schools*, 82 Harv.L.Rev. 1680 (1969)."

Compare Alan Schwarz, *No Imposition of Religion: The Establishment Clause Value*, 77 Yale L.J. 692 (1968): "If avoidance of strife were an independent [Establishment Clause] value, no legislation could be adopted on any subject which aroused strong and divided [religious] feelings." See Choper, fn. 6 supra: "Nor would a denial of aid to parochial schools largely diminish the extent of religious political activity. In fact, it 'might lead to greater political ruptures caused by the alienation of segments of the religious community.' Those who send their children to parochial schools might intensify opposition to increased governmental aid to public education." For the view that the historical evidence contradicts the significance of political division along religious lines,

Zelman v. Simmons-Harris, infra, is the most recent case on the subject. It is preceded by *Mitchell v. Helms* because of its strong emphasis of the "neutrality" theme. Both review the important decisions since *Lemon*.

MITCHELL v. HELMS, 530 U.S. 793 (2000), involved a federal program that lends "secular, neutral and nonideological" educational materials (mainly for libraries and computers)—which may not "supplant funds from non-Federal sources"—to elementary and secondary schools, both public and private. THOMAS, J., joined by Rehnquist, C.J., and Scalia and Kennedy, JJ., upheld the program, overruling *Meek v. Pittenger*, 421 U.S. 349 (1975) and *Wolman v. Walter*, 433 U.S. 229 (1977), "in which we held unconstitutional programs that provided many of the same sorts of materials and equipment," and noting that *Agostini v. Felton*, 521 U.S. 203 (1997), "in which we approved a program [that] provided public employees to teach remedial classes at private schools, including religious schools, [had] overruled *Aguilar v. Felton*, 473 U.S. 402 (1985), and partially overruled *School Dist. of Grand Rapids v. Ball*, 473 U.S. 373 (1985), both of which had involved such a program": "[W]e have consistently turned to the principle of neutrality. [I]f the government, seeking to further some legitimate secular purpose, offers aid on the same terms, without regard to religion, to all who adequately further that purpose, then it is fair to say that any aid going to a religious recipient only has the effect of furthering that secular purpose.[14]

"[T]here was a period [when] whether a school that receives aid [was] pervasively sectarian [mattered, particularly if it] was a primary or secondary school. But that period [is] thankfully long past. [The] religious nature of a recipient should not matter to the constitutional analysis, so long as the recipient adequately furthers the government's secular purpose. [T]he inquiry into the recipient's religious views required by a focus on whether a school is pervasively sectarian is not only unnecessary but also offensive. It is well established [that] courts should refrain from trolling through a person's or institution's religious beliefs * * * .

"Finally, hostility to aid to pervasively sectarian schools has a shameful pedigree. [It] acquired prominence in the 1870's with Congress's consideration (and near passage) of the Blaine Amendment, which would have amended the Constitution to bar any aid to sectarian institutions [at]

---

see Peter M. Schotten, *The Establishment Clause and Excessive Governmental-Religious Entanglement*, 15 Wake For.L.Rev. 207 (1979). For the view that the doctrine is "misguided and quixotic," see Richard W. Garnett, *Religion, Division, and the First Amendment*, 94 Geo. L. J. 1667 (2006).

[14] See also Carl H. Esbeck, *When Accommodations for Religion Violate the Establishment Clause: Regularizing the Supreme Court's Analysis,* 110 W. Va. L. Rev. 359 (2007) (excluding religious organizations from aid programs for educational and social services "puts pressure on individuals, as well as the faith-based organizations they have created, to adapt their religious choices to the government's favored behaviors").

a time of pervasive hostility to the Catholic Church and to Catholics in general, and it was an open secret that 'sectarian' was code for 'Catholic.' [The term 'pervasively sectarian,'] could be applied almost exclusively to Catholic parochial schools [and] even today's dissent exemplifies chiefly by reference to such schools."

O'CONNOR, J., joined by Breyer, J., concurred only in the result: "[W]e have never held that a government-aid program passes constitutional muster solely because of the neutral criteria it employs as a basis for distributing aid." Rather, under *Agostini*, "we [ask] whether the program results in governmental indoctrination or defines its recipients by reference to religion," and plaintiffs in this case have failed to "prove that the aid in question actually is, or has been, used for religious purposes."[15]

SOUTER, J., joined by Stevens and Ginsburg, JJ., dissented: "[I]f we looked no further than evenhandedness, and failed to ask what activities the aid might support, or in fact did support, religious schools could be blessed with government funding as massive as expenditures made for the benefit of their public school counterparts, and religious missions would thrive on public money. This is [why] neutrality has never been recognized as dispositive and has always been teamed with attention to other facts bearing on the substantive prohibition of support for a school's religious objective. * * * [19]"

ZELMAN V. SIMMONS-HARRIS

536 U.S. 639, 122 S.Ct. 2460, 153 L.Ed.2d 604 (2002).

CHIEF JUSTICE REHNQUIST delivered the opinion of the Court.

* * * In 1995, a Federal District Court declared a "crisis of magnitude" and placed the entire Cleveland school district under state control. Shortly thereafter, the state auditor found that Cleveland's public schools [had] failed to meet any of the 18 state standards for minimal acceptable performance. [More] than two-thirds of high school students either dropped or failed out before graduation. [Of] those students who did graduate, few

---

[15] The plurality responded that "whether governmental aid to religious schools results in governmental indoctrination is ultimately a question whether any religious indoctrination that occurs in those schools could reasonably be attributed to governmental action. We have also indicated that the answer to the question of indoctrination will resolve the question whether a program of educational aid 'subsidizes' religion, as our religion cases use that term. In distinguishing between indoctrination that is attributable to the State and indoctrination that is not, we have consistently turned to the principle of neutrality."

[19] [Ct's Note] Adopting the plurality's rule would permit practically any government aid to religion so long as it could be supplied on terms ostensibly comparable to the terms under which aid was provided to nonreligious recipients. [T]he manipulability of this rule is breathtaking. A legislature would merely need to state a secular objective in order to legalize massive aid to all religions, one religion, or even one sect, to which its largess could be directed through the easy exercise of crafting facially neutral terms under which to offer aid favoring that religious group. Short of formally replacing the Establishment Clause, a more dependable key to the public fisc or a cleaner break with prior law would be difficult to imagine.

could read, write, or compute at levels comparable to their counterparts in other cities.

It is against this backdrop that Ohio enacted, among other initiatives, its Pilot Project Scholarship Program [which] provides financial assistance to families in any Ohio school district that is or has been "under federal court order requiring supervision" [and] Cleveland is the only Ohio school district to fall within that category.

[First,] the program provides tuition aid for students [to] attend a participating public or private school of their parent's choosing. Second, the program provides tutorial aid for students who choose to remain enrolled in public school. [Any] private school, whether religious or nonreligious, may participate in the tuition aid portion [so] long as the school is located within the boundaries of a covered district and meets statewide educational standards. Participating private schools must agree not to discriminate on the basis of race, religion, or ethnic background, or to "advocate or foster unlawful behavior or teach hatred of any person or group on the basis of race, ethnicity, national origin, or religion." Any public school located in a school district adjacent to the covered district may also participate [and is] eligible to receive a $2,250 tuition grant for each program student accepted in addition to the full amount of per-pupil state funding attributable to each additional student.

Tuition aid is distributed to parents according to financial need. Families with incomes below 200% of the poverty line are given priority [and] receive 90% of private school tuition up to $2,250. For these lowest-income families, participating private schools may not charge a parental co-payment greater than $250. For all other families, the program pays 75% of tuition costs, up to $1,875, with no co-payment cap. [If] parents choose a private school, checks are made payable to the parents who then endorse the checks over to the chosen school.

[In] the 1999–2000 school year, 56 private schools participated in the program, 46 (or 82%) of which had a religious affiliation. None of the public schools in districts adjacent to Cleveland have elected to participate. More than 3,700 students participated [most] of whom (96%) enrolled in religiously affiliated schools. Sixty percent of these students were from families at or below the poverty line. * * *

The program is part of a broader undertaking by the State to enhance the educational options of Cleveland's schoolchildren in response to the 1995 takeover. That undertaking includes programs governing community and magnet schools. Community schools are funded under state law but are run by their own school boards, not by local school districts. These schools enjoy academic independence to hire their own teachers and to determine their own curriculum. They can have no religious affiliation and are required to accept students by lottery. During the 1999–2000 school year, there were 10 start-up community schools in the Cleveland City School District with more than 1,900 students enrolled. For each child enrolled in a community school, the school receives state funding of $4,518, twice the funding a participating program school may receive.

Magnet schools are public schools operated by a local school board that emphasize a particular subject area, teaching method, or service to students. For each student enrolled in a magnet school, the school district receives $7,746, including state funding of $4,167, the same amount received per student enrolled at a traditional public school. As of 1999, parents in Cleveland were able to choose from among 23 magnet schools, which together enrolled more than 13,000 students in kindergarten through eighth grade. These schools provide specialized teaching methods, such as Montessori, or a particularized curriculum focus, such as foreign language, computers, or the arts.

[There] is no dispute that the program challenged here was enacted for the valid secular purpose of providing educational assistance to poor children in a demonstrably failing public school system. Thus, the question presented is whether the Ohio program nonetheless has the forbidden "effect" of advancing or inhibiting religion.

To answer that question, our decisions have drawn a consistent distinction between government programs that provide aid directly to religious schools, *Mitchell*; *Rosenberger v. University of Virginia*, 515 U.S. 819, 842 (1995),[16] and programs of true private choice, in which government aid reaches religious schools only as a result of the genuine and independent choices of private individuals. While our jurisprudence with respect to the constitutionality of direct aid programs has "changed significantly" over the past two decades, our jurisprudence with respect to

---

[16] The *Rosenberger* majority, Ch. 7, Sec. 7, I, which consisted of the *Mitchell* plurality and O'Connor, J., held that the Establishment Clause permits a public university to fund a student newspaper that proselytized a Christian perspective as part of a program that generally funded student publications. Although recognizing "special Establishment Clause dangers" in direct aid to religious entities, the Court noted that its decision "cannot be read as addressing an expenditure from a general tax fund." Rather, the money came from a "special student activities fund from which any group of students with [recognized] status can draw for purposes consistent with the University's educational mission." As in *Lamb's Chapel v. Center Moriches Union Free School Dist.*, 508 U.S. 384 (1993), holding that a school district did not violate the Establishment Clause in permitting a church's after-hours use of school facilities to show a religiously oriented film series on family values when the school district also permitted presentation of views on the subject by nonreligious groups, "a public university may maintain its own computer facility and give student groups access to that facility, including the use of the printers, on a religion neutral, say first-come-first-served, basis." Since the University made payments for publication costs directly to the printing companies, "we do not confront a case where, even under a neutral program that includes nonsectarian recipients, the government is making direct money payments to an institution or group that is engaged in religious activity."

The dissenters, who were the same as in *Zelman*, distinguished cases like *Lamb's Chapel* as based "on the recognition that all speakers are entitled to use the street corner (even though the State paves the roads and provides police protection to everyone on the street) and on the analogy between the public street corner and open classroom space. [Here,] new economic benefits are being extended directly to religion in clear violation of the principle barring direct aid."

true private choice programs has remained consistent and unbroken. Three times we have confronted Establishment Clause challenges to neutral government programs that provide aid directly to a broad class of individuals, who, in turn, direct the aid to religious schools or institutions of their own choosing. Three times we have rejected such challenges.

In *Mueller v. Allen,* 463 U.S. 388 (1983), we rejected an Establishment Clause challenge to a Minnesota program authorizing tax deductions for various educational expenses, including private school tuition costs, even though the great majority of the program's beneficiaries (96%) were parents of children in religious schools. [In] *Witters v. Washington Dept. of Servs. for Blind,* 474 U.S. 481 (1986), we used identical reasoning to reject an Establishment Clause challenge to a vocational scholarship program that provided tuition aid to a student studying at a religious institution to become a pastor. [Finally,] in *Zobrest v. Catalina Foothills School Dist.,* 509 U.S. 1 (1993), we applied *Mueller* and *Witters* to reject an Establishment Clause challenge to a federal program that permitted sign-language interpreters to assist deaf children enrolled in religious schools. * * *

Mueller, Witters, and *Zobrest* thus make clear that where a government aid program is neutral with respect to religion, and provides assistance directly to a broad class of citizens who, in turn, direct government aid to religious schools wholly as a result of their own genuine and independent private choice, the program is not readily subject to challenge under the Establishment Clause. [The] incidental advancement of a religious mission, or the perceived endorsement of a religious message, is reasonably attributable to the individual recipient, not to the government, whose role ends with the disbursement of benefits [citing the opinions of the plurality and O'Connor, J., in *Mitchell*].[17] [It] is precisely for these reasons that we have never found a program of true private choice to offend the Establishment Clause.

We believe that the program challenged here is a program of true private choice. [It] is neutral in all respects toward religion. It is part of a general and multifaceted undertaking by the State of Ohio to provide educational opportunities to the children of a failed school district. It confers educational assistance directly to a broad class of individuals defined without reference to religion. [The] program permits the

---

[17] O'Connor, J. reasoned: "In terms of public perception, a government program of direct aid to religious schools based on the number of students attending each school differs meaningfully from the government distributing aid directly to individual students who, in turn, decide to use the aid at the same religious schools. In the former example, if the religious school uses the aid to inculcate religion [, the] reasonable observer would naturally perceive the aid program as *government* support for the advancement of religion. [In] contrast, when government aid supports a school's religious mission only because of independent decisions made by numerous individuals to guide their secular aid to that [school,] endorsement of the religious message is reasonably attributed to the individuals who select the path of the aid."

The "endorsement" theme is considered in further detail in Part III, and particularly Part IV infra.

participation of *all* schools within the district, religious or nonreligious. Adjacent public schools also may participate and have a financial incentive to do so. [The] only preference stated anywhere in the program is a preference for low-income families* * * .

There are no "financial incentive[s]" that "ske[w]" the program toward religious schools. *Witters*. [The] program here in fact creates financial *dis*incentives for religious schools, with private schools receiving only half the government assistance given to community schools and one-third the assistance given to magnet schools. Adjacent public schools, should any choose to accept program students, are also eligible to receive two to three times the state funding of a private religious [school]. Parents that choose to participate in the scholarship program [in] a private school (religious or nonreligious) must copay a portion of the school's tuition. Families that choose a community school, magnet school, or traditional public school pay [nothing.]²² [Any] objective observer familiar with the full history and context of the Ohio program would reasonably view it as one aspect of a broader undertaking to assist poor children in failed schools, not as an endorsement of religious schooling in general.

There also is no evidence that the program fails to provide genuine opportunities for Cleveland parents to select secular educational options for their school-age children. Cleveland schoolchildren [may] remain in public school as before, remain in public school with publicly funded tutoring aid, obtain a scholarship and choose a religious school, obtain a scholarship and choose a nonreligious private school, enroll in a community school, or enroll in a magnet school. That 46 of the 56 private schools now participating in the program are religious schools does not condemn it as [t]he Establishment Clause question is whether Ohio is coercing parents into sending their children to religious schools, and that question must be answered by evaluating *all* options * * * .

Justice Souter speculates that because more private religious schools currently participate in the program, the program itself must somehow discourage the participation of private nonreligious schools.²³ But

---

²² **[Ct's Note]** Justice Souter suggests the program is not "neutral" because program students cannot spend scholarship vouchers at traditional public schools. This objection is mistaken: Public schools in Cleveland already receive $7,097 in public funding per pupil—$4,167 of which is attributable to the State. Program students who receive tutoring aid and remain enrolled in traditional public schools therefore direct almost twice as much state funding to their chosen school as do program students who receive a scholarship and attend a private school.* * *

²³ **[Ct's Note]** [But 10] secular private schools operated within the Cleveland City School District when the program was adopted. All 10 chose to participate in the program and have continued to participate to this day. And while no religious schools have been created in response to the program, several *nonreligious* schools have been created in spite of the fact that a principal barrier to entry of new private schools is the uncertainty caused by protracted litigation which has plagued the program since its inception. [Also] mistaken is Justice Souter's reliance on the low enrollment of scholarship students in nonreligious schools during the 1999–2000 school year. [In] fact the number of program students enrolled in nonreligious schools has widely varied from year

Cleveland's preponderance of religiously affiliated private schools [is] a phenomenon common to many American cities. Indeed, by all accounts the program has captured a remarkable cross-section of private schools, religious and nonreligious. It is true that 82% of Cleveland's participating private schools are religious schools, but it is also true that 81% of private schools in Ohio are religious schools. To attribute constitutional significance to this figure, moreover, would lead to the absurd result that a neutral school-choice program might [be] constitutional in some States, such as Maine or Utah, where less than 45% of private schools are religious schools, but not in other States, such as Nebraska or Kansas, where over 90% of private schools are religious schools.

Respondents and Justice Souter claim [that] the fact that 96% of scholarship recipients have enrolled in religious schools [alone] proves parents lack genuine choice, even if no parent has ever said so. [This] was flatly rejected in *Mueller*. [The] constitutionality of a neutral educational aid program simply does not turn on whether and why, in a particular area, at a particular time, most private schools are run by religious organizations, or most recipients choose to use the aid at a religious school. As we said in *Mueller*, "[s]uch an approach would scarcely provide the certainty that this field stands in need of, nor can we perceive principled standards by which such statistical evidence might be evaluated." This point is aptly illustrated here. The 96% figure upon which respondents and Justice Souter rely discounts entirely (1) the more than 1,900 Cleveland children enrolled in alternative community schools, (2) the more than 13,000 children enrolled in alternative magnet schools, and (3) the more than 1,400 children enrolled in traditional public schools with tutorial assistance. Including some or all of these children in the denominator of children enrolled in nontraditional schools during the 1999–2000 school year drops the percentage enrolled in religious schools from 96% to under 20%. The 96% figure also represents but a snapshot of one particular school year. In the 1997–1998 school year, by contrast, only 78% of scholarship recipients attended religious schools. The difference was attributable to two private nonreligious schools that had accepted 15% of all scholarship students electing instead to register as community schools, in light of larger per-pupil funding for community schools and the uncertain future of the scholarship program generated by this litigation.[24] * * *

---

to year, underscoring why the constitutionality of a neutral choice program does not turn on annual tallies of private decisions made in any given year by thousands of individual aid recipients.

[24] **[Ct's Note]** The fluctuations seen in the Cleveland program are hardly atypical. Experience in Milwaukee, which since 1991 has operated an educational choice program similar to the Ohio program, demonstrates that the mix of participating schools fluctuates significantly from year to year based on a number of factors, one of which is the uncertainty caused by persistent litigation. Since the Wisconsin Supreme Court declared the Milwaukee program constitutional in 1998, several nonreligious private schools have entered the Milwaukee market, and now represent 32% of all participating schools. [There] are currently 34 nonreligious private schools participating

Respondents finally claim that we should look to *Committee for Public Ed. & Religious Liberty v. Nyquist*, 413 U.S. 756 (1973) [involving a state partial tuition tax credit to parents who sent their children to nonpublic schools; for parents too poor to be liable for income taxes and therefore unable to benefit from a tax credit, the state gave an outright grant of up to fifty percent of tuition] to decide these cases. We disagree for two reasons. First, the program in *Nyquist* [was] "unmistakably to provide desired financial support for nonpublic, sectarian institutions." Its genesis, we said, was that private religious schools faced "increasingly grave fiscal problems." [It] provided tuition reimbursements designed explicitly to "offe[r] an incentive to parents to send their children to sectarian schools." Indeed, the program flatly prohibited the participation of any public school, or parent of any public school enrollee. Ohio's program shares none of these features. Second, [we] expressly reserved judgment with respect to "a case involving some form of public assistance (e.g., scholarships) made available generally without regard to the sectarian-nonsectarian, or public-nonpublic nature of the institution benefited." That, of course, is the very question now before us, and it has since been answered [in *Mueller*, *Witters*, and *Zobrest*].[26]

The judgment of the Court of Appeals is reversed.

JUSTICE O'CONNOR, concurring. * * *

These cases are different from prior indirect aid cases in part because a significant portion of the funds appropriated for the voucher program reach religious schools without restrictions on the use of these funds.[18] The share of public resources that reach religious schools is not, however, as significant as respondents suggest. [Even if] all voucher students came from low-income families and that each voucher student used up the entire $2,250 voucher, at most $8.2 million of public funds flowed to religious schools under the voucher program in 1999–2000. [This] is minor compared to the $114.8 million the State spent on students in the Cleveland magnet schools [alone, and] pales in comparison to the amount of funds that federal, state, and local governments already provide religious institutions. Religious organizations may qualify for exemptions from the federal corporate income tax, the corporate income tax in many States, and property taxes in all 50 States, and clergy qualify for a federal tax break on

---

in the Milwaukee program, a nearly a five-fold increase from the 7 nonreligious schools that participated when the program began in 1990. * * *

[26] **[Ct's Note]** Justice Breyer would raise the invisible specters of "divisiveness" and "religious strife" to find the program unconstitutional [but] the program has ignited no "divisiveness" or "strife" other than this litigation. * * * We quite rightly have rejected the claim that some speculative potential for divisiveness bears on the constitutionality of educational aid programs. *Mitchell.* [The plurality in *Mitchell* argued that the Court had "recast *Lemon's* entanglement inquiry as simply one criterion relevant to determining a statute's effect."]

[18] If at least *some* voucher funds might be used to support "religious indoctrination," would the program fail O'Connor, J.'s burden of proof standard in *Mitchell.* If so, what of *Witters* (and the GI Bill)?

income used for housing expenses. In addition, the Federal Government provides [a] tax deduction for charitable contributions to qualified religious groups. Finally, the Federal Government and certain state governments provide tax credits for educational expenses, many of which are spent on education at religious schools [reducing] federal tax revenues by nearly $25 billion annually * * * .[19]

JUSTICE SOUTER, with whom JUSTICE STEVENS, JUSTICE GINSBURG, and JUSTICE BREYER join, dissenting.

[In] Cleveland the overwhelming proportion of large appropriations for voucher money must be spent on religious schools if it is to be spent at all, and will be spent in amounts that cover almost all of tuition. The money will thus pay for eligible students' instruction not only in secular subjects but in religion as well, in schools that can fairly be characterized as founded to teach religious doctrine and to imbue teaching in all subjects with a religious dimension.[2] * * *

The majority's statements of Establishment Clause doctrine cannot be appreciated without some historical perspective on the Court's announced limitations on government aid to religious education. [My] object here [is] to set out the broad doctrinal stages covered in the modern era, and to show that doctrinal bankruptcy has been reached today. [F]rom 1947 to 1968, the basic principle of no aid to religion through school benefits was unquestioned. Thereafter for some 15 years, the Court termed its efforts as attempts to draw a line against aid that would be divertible to support the religious, as distinct from the secular, activity of an institutional beneficiary. Then, starting in 1983, concern with divertibility was gradually lost in favor of approving aid in amounts unlikely to afford substantial benefits to religious schools, when offered evenhandedly without regard to a recipient's religious character, and when channeled to a religious institution only by the genuinely free choice of some private

---

[19] What result for a tax credit for making a contribution to a non-profit organization that then grants scholarships to eligible children? See Stephen D. Sugarman, *Tax Credit School Scholarship Plans*, 43 J.L. & Educ. 1 (Winter 2014).

The concurring opinion of Thomas, J.—questioning whether the Establishment Clause should be applied to the states (see his opinion in *Van Orden v. Perry*, Sec. IV infra), and rejecting use of the Fourteenth Amendment "to oppose neutral programs of school choice through the incorporation of the Establishment Clause"—is omitted.

[2] **[Ct's Note]** See, e.g., App. (Saint Jerome School Parent and Student Handbook 1999–2000, p. 1) ("FAITH must dominate the entire educational process so that the child can make decisions according to Catholic values and choose to lead a Christian life"); id., (Westside Baptist Christian School Parent-Student Handbook, p. 7) ("Christ is the basis of all learning. All subjects will be taught from the Biblical perspective that all truth is God's truth").

[Compare Eugene Volokh, *Equal Treatment Is Not Establishment*, 13 Not.D.J.L.Eth. & Pub.Pol. 341, 346 (1999): "The religious schools do teach a religious value system—just as secular schools teach a secular value system. There's [no] reason why the government is obligated to discriminate against one or the other system, and thus against the parents who choose to teach their children one or the other system. Just as we wouldn't tolerate discrimination against atheistic schools, or discrimination against secular schools, so we shouldn't assume that the Constitution requires discrimination against religious schools."]

individual. Now, the three stages are succeeded by a fourth, in which the substantial character of government aid is held to have no constitutional significance, and the espoused criteria of neutrality in offering aid, and private choice in directing it, are shown to be nothing but examples of verbal formalism.

[Souter, J., began with *Everson* and continued with *Board of Educ. v. Allen*, 392 U.S. 236 (1968), upholding a program for lending state approved secular textbooks to all schoolchildren, including those attending church-related schools.] The Court relied [on] the theory that the in-kind aid could only be used for secular educational purposes, and found it relevant that "no funds or books are furnished [directly] to parochial schools, and the financial benefit is to parents and children, not to schools.⁴" * * *

Allen recognized the reality that "religious schools pursue two goals, religious instruction and secular education;" if state aid could be restricted to serve the second, it might be permissible under the Establishment Clause. But in the retrenchment that followed, the Court saw that the two educational functions were so intertwined in religious primary and secondary schools that aid to secular education could not readily be segregated, and the intrusive monitoring required to enforce the line itself raised Establishment Clause concerns about the entanglement of church and state. See *Lemon*. To avoid the entanglement, the Court's focus in the post-*Allen* cases was on the principle of divertibility. [The] greater the risk of diversion to religion (and the monitoring necessary to avoid it), the less legitimate the aid scheme was under the no-aid principle. On the one hand, the Court tried to be practical, and when the aid recipients were not so "pervasively sectarian" that their secular and religious functions were inextricably intertwined, the Court generally upheld aid earmarked for secular use. See, e.g., *Roemer v. Board of Public Works*, 426 U.S. 736 (1976); *Hunt v. McNair*, 413 U.S. 734 (1973); *Tilton v. Richardson*, 403 U.S. 672 (1971).²⁰ But otherwise the principle of nondivertibility was enforced

---

⁴ [Ct's Note] [*Allen*] noted that "the record contains no evidence that any of the private schools . . . previously provided textbooks for their students," and "[t]here is some evidence that at least some of the schools did not." This was a significant distinction: if the parochial schools provided secular textbooks to their students, then the State's provision of the same in their stead might have freed up church resources for allocation to other uses, including, potentially, religious indoctrination.

²⁰ These cases all involved higher education. *Tilton* and *Roemer* upheld direct government grants to church-related colleges and universities as part of general programs for construction of buildings and other activities not involving sectarian activities. *Tilton* noted: "The 'affirmative, if not dominant, policy' of the instruction in pre-college church-schools is 'to assure future adherents to a particular faith by having control of their total education at an early age.' There is substance to the contention that college students are less impressionable and less susceptible to religious indoctrination. [Further], by their very nature, college and postgraduate courses tend to limit the opportunities for sectarian influence by virtue of their own internal disciplines. Many church-related colleges and universities are characterized by a high degree of academic freedom and seek to evoke free and critical responses from their students." For detailed criticism of the Court's distinction of higher education from elementary and secondary schools, see Mark Strasser, *Death by a Thousand Cuts: The Illusory Safeguards Against Funding Pervasively Sectarian Institutions of Higher Learning*, 56 Buff. L. Rev. 353 (2008).

strictly, with its violation being presumed in most cases, even when state aid seemed secular on its face. Compare, e.g., *Levitt v. Committee for Public Ed. & Religious Liberty*, 413 U.S. 472 (1973) (striking down state program reimbursing private schools' administrative costs for teacher-prepared tests in compulsory secular subjects), with *Wolman* (upholding similar program using standardized tests [and] permitting state aid for diagnostic speech, hearing, and psychological testing).

The fact that the Court's suspicion of divertibility reflected a concern with the substance of the no-aid principle is apparent in its rejection of stratagems invented to dodge it. [The] *Nyquist* Court dismissed warranties of a "statistical guarantee," that the scheme provided at most 15% of the total cost of an education at a religious school which could presumably be matched to a secular 15% of a child's education at the school. And it rejected the idea that the path of state aid to religious schools might be dispositive: "[that] aid is disbursed to parents rather than to the schools is only one among many factors to be considered." The point was that "the effect of the aid is unmistakably to provide desired financial support for nonpublic, sectarian institutions." [The Court's object] had always been a realistic assessment of facts aimed at respecting the principle of no aid. [But] *Mueller* started down the road from realism to formalism. [If] public expenditure is still predominantly on public schools, then the majority's reasoning would find neutrality in a scheme of vouchers available for private tuition in districts with no secular private schools at all. "Neutrality" as the majority employs the term is, literally, verbal and nothing more. * * *

The majority addresses the issue of choice the same way [which] ignores the whole point of the choice test: it is a criterion for deciding whether indirect aid to a religious school is legitimate because it passes through private hands that can spend or use the aid in a secular school. [The] majority now has transformed this question about private choice in channeling aid into a question about selecting from examples of state spending (on education) including direct spending on magnet and community public schools that goes through no private hands and could never reach a religious school under any circumstance. [And] because it is unlikely that any participating private religious school will enroll more pupils than the generally available public system, it will be easy to generate numbers suggesting that aid to religion is not the significant intent or effect of the voucher scheme.* * *

If, contrary to the majority, we ask the right question about genuine choice to use the vouchers, the answer shows that something is influencing choices in a way that aims the money in a religious direction: * * * 96.6% of all voucher recipients go to religious schools, only 3.4% to nonreligious [ones.] One answer to these statistics, for example, which would be consistent with the genuine choice claimed to be operating, might be that

96.6% of families [choose] to educate their children in schools of their own religion. This would not, in my view, render the scheme constitutional, but it would speak to the majority's choice criterion. Evidence shows, however, that almost two out of three families [made] it clear they had not chosen the schools because they wished their children to be proselytized in a religion not their own, or in any religion, but because of educational opportunity.

Even so, [that] some 2,270 students chose to apply their vouchers to schools of other religions might be consistent with true choice if the students "chose" their religious schools over a wide array of private nonreligious options, or if it could be shown [that] Ohio's program had no effect on educational choices and thus no impermissible effect of advancing religious education. But both possibilities are contrary to fact. First, even if all existing nonreligious private schools in Cleveland were willing to accept large numbers of voucher students, [the] total enrollment at all nonreligious private schools in Cleveland for kindergarten through eighth grade is only 510 children, and there is no indication that these schools have many open seats. Second, the $2,500 cap that the program places on tuition for participating low-income pupils has the effect of curtailing the participation of nonreligious schools: "nonreligious schools with higher tuition (about $4,000) stated that they could afford to accommodate just a few voucher students." By comparison, the average tuition at participating Catholic schools in Cleveland in 1999–2000 was $1,592, almost $1,000 below the cap.

Of course, the obvious fix would be to increase the value of vouchers so that existing nonreligious private and non-Catholic religious schools would be able to enroll more voucher students, and to provide incentives for educators to create new such schools given that few presently exist. [But] it is simply unrealistic to [even approach] the statewide program for vocational and higher education in *Witters*. And to get to that hypothetical point would require that such massive financial support be made available to religion as to disserve every objective of the Establishment Clause even more than the present scheme does.

[P]ublic schools in adjacent districts hardly have a financial incentive to participate in the Ohio voucher program, and none has.[17] [It] is entirely irrelevant that the State did not deliberately design the network of private schools for the sake of channeling money into religious institutions. The criterion is one of genuinely free choice on the part of the private individuals who choose, and a Hobson's choice is not a choice, whatever the reason for being Hobsonian. * * *

---

[17] **[Ct's Note]** [The] basic state funding [of $2,250] is a drop in the bucket as compared to the cost of educating that student, as much of the cost (at least in relatively affluent areas with presumptively better academic standards) is paid by local income and property taxes. * * *

The scale of the aid to religious schools approved today is unprecedented. [In] paying for practically the full amount of tuition for thousands of qualifying students, the scholarships purchase everything that tuition purchases, be it instruction in math or indoctrination in faith. [T]he majority makes no pretense that substantial amounts of tax money are not systematically underwriting religious practice and indoctrination. [E]very objective underlying the prohibition of religious establishment is betrayed by this scheme. [The first objective is] respect for freedom of conscience. Jefferson described it as the idea that no one "shall be compelled [to] support any religious worship, place, or ministry whatsoever."

As for the second objective, to save religion from its own corruption, [a] condition of receiving government money under the program is that [the] school may not give admission preferences to children who are members of the patron faith. [In addition], a participating religious school may well be forbidden to choose a member of its own clergy to serve as teacher or principal over a layperson of a different religion claiming equal qualification for the job. Indeed, a separate condition that "[t]he school [not] teach hatred of any person or group on the basis [of] religion," could be understood (or subsequently broadened) to prohibit religions from teaching traditionally legitimate articles of faith as to the error, sinfulness, or ignorance of [others].

[T]here is no question that religious schools in Ohio are on the way to becoming bigger businesses with budgets enhanced to fit their new stream of tax-raised income. See, e.g., People for the American Way Foundation, A Painful Price 5, 9, 11 (Feb. 14, 2002) (of 91 schools participating in the Milwaukee program, 75 received voucher payments in excess of tuition, 61 of those were religious and averaged $185,000 worth of overpayment per school, justified in part to "raise low salaries"). [A] move in the Ohio State Senate [would] raise the current maximum value of a school voucher from $2,250 to the base amount of current state spending on each public school student ($4,814 for the 2001 fiscal year). Ohio, in fact, is merely replicating the experience in Wisconsin. [T]he odds are that increases in government aid will bring the threshold voucher amount closer to the tuition at even more expensive religious schools. * * *[21]

JUSTICE BREYER, with whom JUSTICE STEVENS and JUSTICE SOUTER join, dissenting.

[T]he Court's 20th century Establishment Clause cases—both those limiting the practice of religion in public schools and those limiting the public funding of private religious education—focused directly upon social

---

[21] For brief discussion of dangers to religious liberty from "creeping regulation" and "responsiveness to financial incentives," see Kent Greenawalt, 2 *Religion and the Constitution* 418–19 (2008) (hereinafter 1 Greenawalt or 2 Greenawalt).

conflict, potentially created when government becomes involved in religious education. [The] Court appreciated the religious diversity of contemporary American society. [It] understood the Establishment Clause to prohibit (among other things) [favoring some religions at the expense of others]. Yet *how* did the Clause achieve that objective? Did it simply require the government to give each religion an equal chance to introduce religion into the primary schools? [T]he Court concluded that the Establishment Clause required "separation," in part because an "equal opportunity" approach was not workable. [D]id not history show that efforts to obtain equivalent funding for the private education of children whose parents did not hold popular religious beliefs only exacerbated religious strife? * * * America boasts more than 55 different religious groups and subgroups with a significant number of members. [I]f widely adopted, ["voucher programs"] may well provide billions of dollars. [Why] will different religions not become concerned about, and seek to influence, the criteria used to channel this money to religious schools? Why will they not want to examine the implementation of the programs that provide this money—to determine, for example, whether implementation has biased a program toward or against particular sects, or whether recipient religious schools are adequately fulfilling a program's criteria? If so, just how is the State to resolve the resulting controversies without provoking legitimate fears of the kinds of religious favoritism that, in so religiously diverse a Nation, threaten social dissension? * * *

I concede that the Establishment Clause currently permits States to channel various forms of assistance to religious schools, for example, transportation costs for students, computers, and secular texts. [V]oucher programs differ, however, in both *kind* and *degree* [because] they direct financing to a core function of the church: the teaching of religious truths to young [children]. History suggests, not that such private school teaching of religion is undesirable, but that *government funding* of this kind of religious endeavor is far more contentious than providing funding for secular textbooks, computers, vocational training, or even funding for adults who wish to obtain a college education at a religious university. [H]istory also shows that government involvement in religious primary education is far more divisive than state property tax exemptions for religious institutions or tax deductions for charitable contributions, both of which come far closer to exemplifying the neutrality that distinguishes, for example, fire protection on the one hand from direct monetary assistance on the other. [T]he "parental choice" aspect of the voucher [program] cannot help the taxpayer who does not want to finance the religious education of children. It will not always help the parent who may see little real choice between inadequate nonsectarian public education and adequate education at a school whose religious teachings are contrary to his own. It will not satisfy religious minorities unable to participate because they are too few in number to support the creation of their own private schools. It will not satisfy groups whose religious beliefs preclude them from participating in a government-sponsored program, and who may well feel ignored as government funds primarily support the education of children in the doctrines of the dominant religions. And it does little to ameliorate the entanglement problems or the related problems of social division * * * .[22]

NOTES AND QUESTIONS

1. *"Endorsement" and "private choice."* The *Mitchell* plurality explained the "voucher" in *Witter* as "no different from a government issuing a paycheck to one of its employees knowing that the employee would direct the funds to a religious institution." Compare Ira C. Lupu, *The Increasingly Anachronistic Case Against School Vouchers*, 13 Not.D.J.L.Eth. & Pub.Pol. 375 (1999): "When the state pays its employees a wage, [it] cannot be held responsible for any religious benefit arising from the unfettered spending choices of its employees. By contrast, when the state constrains the benefit in certain ways—for example, a state income tax deduction for all charitable contributions—the probability and forseeability of a boost to religion are markedly increased. Contemporary voucher programs tend to constrain yet further, limiting parents to the mix of participating schools, in which sectarian institutions will be heavily represented, at least in the short run." Does *Zelman* place any limits on a "neutral" voucher plan? On a program of public funding charter schools that includes religious groups whose school "accommodates religious observance without promoting it, and grounds its teaching in [religious] values and culture without indoctrinating religion"? See Benjamin S. Hillman, Note, *Is There a Place for Religious Charter Schools?*, 118 Yale L. J. 554 (2008).

2. *"Charitable choice."* After *Zelman*, what result if a state provides vouchers for an important social service that may be used in privately operated programs. What difference does it make if (a) the program is a legal requirement (education), (b) it is an economic necessity (childcare for a single parent who must work in order to obtain welfare), (c) its purpose is to instill personal attitudes and values (drug abuse treatment), (d) there are a large (or small) number of nonreligious providers, (e) government policies affect the mix of religious/nonreligious providers (because of voucher amount), (f) a provider's religious component may be separated from its delivery of the service (schools), (g) recipients can opt out of any religious component (prayer at meals), (h) religious providers have visible symbols of their faith on the premises (summer camp)? See generally Ira C. Lupu & Robert Tuttle, *Sites of Redemption: A Wide-Angle Look at Government Vouchers and Sectarian Service Providers*, 18 J.L. & Pol. 539 (2002). See also David Cole, *Faith and Funding: Toward an Expressivist Model of the Establishment Clause*, 75 So.Cal.L.Rev. 559 (2002).[23]

---

[22] Stevens, J.'s brief separate dissent is omitted.

[23] For the view that the "original public meaning" of the Equal Protection Clause's "antidiscrimination command" against "class and caste" "protects religion in the same way that [it] protects against discrimination on the basis of race or gender," see Steven G. Calabresi & Abe

If a voucher program results in the fact that, although there are many elementary schools in the community, the only "good" one is church-related, what constitutional issues arise and how may they be remedied? See Ch. 10, Secs. 2 and 3.

3. *Other approaches.* Commentators have proposed various "tests" to measure the validity of public aid to church-related schools. In evaluating those that follow, what results would they produce in the decided cases?

(a) Choper, fn. 6 supra: "[G]overnment financial aid may be extended directly or indirectly to support parochial schools [so] long as such aid does not exceed the value of the secular educational service rendered by the school."[24] Would such aid have "a secular legislative purpose and a primary effect that neither advances nor inhibits religion"? Compare Stephen D. Sugarman, *New Perspectives on "Aid" to Private School Users,* in Nonpublic School Aid 64 (West ed. 1976): "Even if the [effect] principle were limited to cases in which there was (or the legislature knew there would be) a *large* beneficial impact on religion, it would intolerably inhibit secular government action. For example, perhaps building roads and running public transportation on Sunday may be shown to have large beneficial impacts on religion. [For] me the concerns underlying the Establishment Clause could be satisfied with an affirmative answer to this hypothetical question: Would the legislature have acted as it did were there no interdependency with religion involved? If so, then I think it would be fair to say that [the] religious benefits are constitutionally permitted side effects."[25]

(b) Ira C. Lupu, *To Control Faction and Protect Liberty: A General Theory of the Religion Clauses*, 7 J.Contemp.Leg.Issues 357 (1996): "The worry [about] coercive taxation to support religious teaching is a holdover relic from the Virginia story of coercive assessments earmarked for the support of Christian ministers and teachers. Such an exaction, taking from all to support a few on religious grounds and for religious ends, of course violates the Establishment Clause. [When] the state, however, makes funds available in a religion-neutral way for secular ends ["such as educational attainment, health care, or social services", those] programs should survive, unless the challenger can persuasively demonstrate that the program (despite facially neutral criteria) is in essence a cover for sectarian discrimination."

Salander, *Religion and the Equal Protection Clause: Why the Constitution Requires School Vouchers*, 65 Fla.L.Rev. 909 (2013).

[24] For further analysis, see Michael W. McConnell & Richard Posner, *An Economic Approach to Issues of Religious Freedom,* 56 U.Chi.L.Rev. 1 (1989); Note, *The Supreme Court, Effect Inquiry, and Aid to Parochial Education,* 37 Stan.L.Rev. 219 (1984).

[25] Problems under the Free Exercise Clause raised by the exclusion of parochial schools from public aid programs are considered in Note 2(c)which contains fn. 110.

III. RELIGION AND PUBLIC SCHOOLS

WALLACE V. JAFFREE

472 U.S. 38, 105 S.Ct. 2479, 86 L.Ed.2d 29 (1985).

JUSTICE STEVENS delivered the opinion of the Court.

[In 1978, Alabama enacted § 16–1–20 authorizing a one-minute period of silence in all public schools "for meditation"; in 1981, it enacted § 16–1–20.1 authorizing a period of silence "for meditation or voluntary prayer." Appellees] have not questioned the holding that § 16–1–20 is valid. Thus, the narrow question for decision [concerns § 16–1–20.1].

[T]he Court has [recognized] that the political interest in forestalling intolerance extends beyond intolerance among Christian sects—or even intolerance among "religions"—to encompass intolerance of the disbeliever and the uncertain. [Under *Lemon*,] even though a statute that is motivated in part by a religious purpose may satisfy the first criterion, [a] statute must be invalidated if it is entirely motivated by a purpose to advance religion. In applying the purpose test, it is appropriate to ask "whether government's actual purpose is to endorse or disapprove of religion." In this case, the answer to that question is dispositive. * * *

The sponsor of the bill that became § 16–1–20.1, Senator Donald Holmes, inserted into the legislative record—apparently without dissent—a statement indicating that the legislation was an "effort to return voluntary prayer" to the public schools. Later [in] District Court [,] he stated: "No, I did not have no other purpose in mind."[44] The State did not present evidence of *any* secular purpose. * * *

The legislative intent to return prayer to the public schools is, of course, quite different from merely protecting every student's right to engage in voluntary prayer during an appropriate moment of silence during the school day. The 1978 statute already protected that right, containing nothing that prevented any student from engaging in voluntary prayer during a silent minute of meditation. [The] legislature enacted § 16–1–20.1, despite the existence of § 16–1–20 for the sole purpose of expressing the State's endorsement of prayer activities for one minute at the beginning of each schoolday [as] a favored practice. Such an endorsement is not consistent with the established principle that the government must pursue a course of complete neutrality toward religion.

The importance of that principle does not permit us to treat this as an inconsequential case involving nothing more than a few words of symbolic

---

[44] **[Ct's Note]** [The] evidence presented to the District Court elaborated on the express admission of the Governor of Alabama (then Fob James) that the enactment of § 16–1–20.1 was intended to "clarify [the State's] intent to have prayer as part of the daily classroom activity," and that the "expressed legislative purpose in enacting Section 16–1–20.1 (1981) was to 'return voluntary prayer to public schools.'"

speech on behalf of the political majority.[51] For whenever the State itself speaks on a religious subject, one of the questions [is] "whether the government intends to convey a message of endorsement or disapproval of religion." * * *

JUSTICE O'CONNOR concurring in the judgment.

* * * Although a distinct jurisprudence has enveloped each of [the Religion] Clauses, their common purpose is to secure religious liberty. [O]ur goal should be "to frame a principle for constitutional adjudication that is not only grounded in the history and language of the first amendment, but one that is also capable of consistent application to the relevant problems." Jesse H. Choper, *Religion in the Public Schools: A Proposed Constitutional Standard*, 47 Minn.L.Rev. 329, 332–333 (1963). Last Term, I proposed a refinement of the *Lemon* test with this goal in mind. *Lynch v. Donnelly* (concurring opinion).

The *Lynch* concurrence suggested that the religious liberty protected by the Establishment Clause is infringed when the government makes adherence to religion relevant to a person's standing in the political community. Direct government action endorsing religion or a particular religious practice is invalid under this approach because it "sends a message to nonadherents that they are outsiders, not full members of the political community, and an accompanying message to adherents that they are insiders, favored members of the political community." [In] this country, church and state must necessarily operate within the same community. [Thus], it is inevitable that the secular interests of government and the religious interests of various sects and their adherents will frequently intersect, conflict, and combine. A statute that ostensibly promotes a secular interest often has an incidental or even a primary effect of helping or hindering a sectarian belief. Chaos would ensue if every such statute were invalid under the Establishment Clause. For example, the State could not criminalize murder for fear that it would thereby promote the Biblical command against killing.[26] The task for the Court is to sort out

---

[51] [Ct's Note] As this Court stated in *Engel v. Vitale,* [infra]: "The Establishment Clause, unlike the Free Exercise Clause, does not depend upon any showing of direct governmental compulsion and is violated by the enactment of laws which establish an official religion whether those laws operate directly to coerce nonobserving individuals or not." Moreover, this Court has noted that "[w]hen the power, prestige and financial support of government is placed behind a particular religious belief, the indirect coercive pressure upon religious minorities to conform to the prevailing officially approved religion is plain." Id. This comment has special force in the public-school context where attendance is mandatory. Justice Frankfurter acknowledged this reality in *McCollum v. Board of Education,* [note 1(a) infra] (concurring opinion): "That a child is offered an alternative may reduce the constraint; it does not eliminate the operation of influence by the school in matters sacred to conscience and outside the school's domain. The law of imitation operates, and non-conformity is not an outstanding characteristic of children." * * *

[26] On this analysis, *McGowan v. Maryland,* 366 U.S. 420 (1961), per Warren, C.J., upheld Maryland's Sunday Closing Laws. Although "the original laws which dealt with Sunday labor were motivated by religious forces," the Court showed that secular emphases in language and interpretation had come about, that recent "legislation was supported by labor groups and trade associations," and that "secular justifications have been advanced for making Sunday a day of rest,

those statutes and government practices whose purpose and effect go against the grain of religious liberty protected by the First Amendment.

The endorsement test [precludes] government from conveying or attempting to convey a message that religion or a particular religious belief is favored or preferred. Such an endorsement infringes the religious liberty of the nonadherent * * * .

Twenty-five states permit or require public school teachers to have students observe [a] moment of silence at the beginning of the schoolday during which students may meditate, pray, or reflect on the activities of the day. * * * Relying on this Court's decisions disapproving vocal prayer and Bible reading in the public schools, see *School Dist. v. Schempp,* 374 U.S. 203 (1963); *Engel v. Vitale,* 370 U.S. 421 (1962), the courts that have struck down the moment of silence statutes generally conclude that their purpose and effect are to encourage prayer in public schools.

The *Engel* and *Schempp* decisions are not dispositive. [In] *Engel,* a New York statute required teachers to lead their classes in a vocal prayer.[27] The Court concluded that "it is no part of the business of government to compose official prayers for any group of the American people to recite as part of a religious program carried on by the government." In *Schempp,* the Court addressed Pennsylvania and Maryland statutes that authorized morning Bible readings in public schools.[28] The Court reviewed the purpose and effect of the statutes, concluded that they required religious exercises, and therefore found them to violate the Establishment Clause. Under all of these statutes, a student who did not share the religious beliefs expressed in the course of the exercise was left with the choice of participating, thereby compromising the nonadherent's beliefs, or withdrawing, thereby calling attention to his or her nonconformity. The decisions acknowledged the coercion implicit under the statutory schemes,

---

a day when people may recover from the labors of the week just passed and may physically and mentally prepare for the week's work to come. [It] would seem unrealistic for enforcement purposes and perhaps detrimental to the general welfare to require a State to choose a common day of rest other than that which most persons would select of their own accord." Douglas, J., dissented.

[27] The prayer, composed by the N.Y. Board of Regents, provided: "Almighty God, we acknowledge our dependence upon Thee, and we beg Thy blessings upon us, our parents, our teachers and our country."

[28] The reading of the Bible, without comment, was followed by recitation of the Lord's Prayer. In Pennsylvania, various students read passages they selected from any version of the Bible. Plaintiff father testified that "specific religious doctrines purveyed by a literal reading of the Bible" were contrary to the family's Unitarian religious beliefs; one expert testified that "portions of the New Testament were offensive to Jewish tradition" and, if "read without explanation, they could [be] psychologically harmful to the child and had caused a divisive force within the social media of the school"; a defense expert testified "that the Bible [was] non-sectarian within the Christian faiths."

see *Engel*,[29] but they expressly turned only on the fact that the government was sponsoring a manifestly religious exercise.[30]

A state-sponsored moment of silence in the public schools is different from state-sponsored vocal prayer or Bible reading. First, a moment of silence [unlike] prayer or Bible reading, need not be associated with a religious exercise. Second, [d]uring a moment of silence, a student who objects to prayer is left to his or her own thoughts, and is not compelled to listen to the prayers or thoughts of others. [It] is difficult to discern a serious threat to religious liberty from a room of silent, thoughtful schoolchildren.

[E]ven if a statute specifies that a student may choose to pray silently during a quiet moment, [it] is also possible that a moment of silence statute, either as drafted or as actually implemented, could effectively favor the child who prays over the child who does not. For example, the message of endorsement would seem inescapable if the teacher exhorts children to use the designated time to pray. Similarly, the fact of the statute or its legislative history may clearly establish that it seeks to encourage or promote voluntary prayer over other alternatives. [The] crucial question is whether the State has conveyed or attempted to convey the message that children should use the moment of silence for prayer.[2] This question [requires] courts to examine the history, language, and administration of a particular statute to determine whether it operates as an endorsement of religion.

[T]he inquiry into the purpose of the legislature in enacting a moment of silence law should be deferential and limited. [If] a legislature expresses a plausible secular purpose for a moment of silence statute in either the text or the legislative history, or if the statute disclaims an intent to encourage prayer over alternatives during a moment of silence, then courts should generally defer to that stated intent. It is particularly troublesome to denigrate an expressed secular purpose due to postenactment testimony

---

[29] See fn. 51 in the Court's opinion, supra.

[30] *Engel* distinguished "the fact that school children and others are officially encouraged to express love for our country by reciting historical documents such as the Declaration of Independence which contain references to the Deity or by singing officially espoused anthems which include the composer's professions of faith in a Supreme Being, or with the fact that there are many manifestations in our public life of belief in God. Such patriotic or ceremonial occasions bear no true resemblance to the unquestioned religious exercise that the State of New York has sponsored in this instance."

[2] **[Ct's Note]** Appellants argue that *Zorach v. Clauson,* [note 1(b) infra], suggests there is no constitutional infirmity in a State's encouraging a child to pray during a moment of silence. [There] the Court stated that "[w]hen the state encourages religious instruction—[by] *adjusting the schedule of public events to sectarian needs,* it follows the best of our traditions." When the State provides a moment of silence during which prayer may occur at the election of the student, it can be said to be adjusting the schedule of public events to sectarian needs. But when the State also encourages the student to pray during a moment of silence, it converts an otherwise inoffensive moment of silence into an effort by the majority to use the machinery of the State to encourage the minority to participate in a religious exercise.

by particular legislators or by interested persons who witnessed the drafting of the statute.[31] Even if the text and official history of a statute express no secular purpose, the statute should be held to have an improper purpose only if it is beyond purview that endorsement of religion or a religious belief "was and is the law's reason for existence." *Epperson v. Arkansas,* [note 3(b) infra. * * *

[It is] possible that a legislature will enunciate a sham secular purpose for a statute. I have little doubt that our courts are capable of distinguishing a sham secular purpose from a sincere one, or that the *Lemon* inquiry into the effect of an enactment would help decide those close cases where the validity of an expressed secular purpose is in doubt. [The] issue is whether an objective observer, acquainted with the text, legislative history, and implementation of the statute, would perceive it as a state endorsement of prayer in public schools. [However] deferentially one examines its text and legislative history, [the] conclusion is unavoidable that the purpose of [§ 16–1–20.1] is to endorse prayer in public schools.* * *

CHIEF JUSTICE BURGER dissenting.

* * * Today's decision recalls the observations of Justice Goldberg: "[U]ntutored devotion to the concept of neutrality can lead [to] results which partake not simply of that noninterference and noninvolvement with the religious which the Constitution commands, but of a brooding and pervasive dedication to the secular and a passive, or even active, hostility to the religious. Such results are not only not compelled by the Constitution, but, it seems to me, are prohibited by it." *Schempp* (concurring opinion). * * *

Curiously, the opinions do not mention that *all* of the sponsor's statements relied upon—including the statement "inserted" into the Senate Journal—were made *after* the legislature had passed the statute; [there] is not a shred of evidence that the legislature as a whole shared the sponsor's motive or that a majority in either house was even aware of the sponsor's view of the bill when it was passed. [T]he sponsor also testified that one of his purposes in drafting [the] moment-of-silence bill was to clear up a widespread misunderstanding that a schoolchild is legally *prohibited* from engaging in silent, individual prayer once he steps inside a public school building. That testimony is at least as important as the statements the Court relies upon, and surely that testimony manifests a permissible purpose. * * *

The several preceding opinions conclude that [the] sole purpose behind the inclusion of the phrase "or voluntary prayer" in § 16–1–20.1 was to endorse and promote prayer. This reasoning is simply a subtle way of focusing exclusively on the religious component of the statute rather than

---

[31] For further discussion of this point, see Burger, C.J.'s opinion infra.

examining the statute as a whole. [It] would lead the Court to hold, for example, that a state may enact a statute that provides reimbursement for bus transportation to the parents of all schoolchildren, but may not *add* parents of parochial school students to an existing program providing reimbursement for parents of public school students.

* * * Without pressuring those who do not wish to pray, the statute simply creates an opportunity to think, to plan, or to pray if one wishes—as Congress does by providing chaplains and chapels. [If] the government may not accommodate religious needs when it does so in a wholly neutral and noncoercive manner, the "benevolent neutrality" that we have long considered the correct constitutional standard will quickly translate into the "callous indifference" that the Court has consistently held the Establishment Clause does not require. * * *

JUSTICE REHNQUIST, dissenting.

[There] is simply no historical foundation for the proposition that the Framers intended to build the "wall of separation" that was constitutionalized in *Everson*.[32] [And the "purpose and effect" tests] are in no way based on either the language or intent of the drafters. [If] the purpose prong is intended to void those aids to sectarian institutions accompanied by a stated legislative purpose to aid religion, the prong will condemn nothing so long as the legislature utters a secular purpose and says nothing about aiding religion. [I]f the purpose prong is aimed to void all statutes enacted with the intent to aid sectarian institutions, whether stated or not, then most statutes providing any aid, such as textbooks or bus rides for sectarian school children, will fail because one of the purposes behind every statute, whether stated or not, is to aid the target of its largesse. * * *

If a constitutional theory has no basis in the history of the amendment it seeks to interpret, is difficult to apply and yields unprincipled results, I see little use in it. [It] would come as much of a shock to those who drafted the Bill of Rights as it will to a large number of thoughtful Americans today to learn that the Constitution [prohibits] the Alabama Legislature from "endorsing" prayer. George Washington himself, at the request of the very Congress which passed the Bill of Rights, proclaimed a day of "public thanksgiving and prayer, to be observed by acknowledging with grateful hearts the many and signal favors of Almighty God." History must judge whether it was the Father of his Country in 1789, [or] the Court today, which has strayed from the meaning of the Establishment Clause. * * *

---

[32] See also Philip Hamburger, *Separation and Interpretation*, 18 J.L. & Pol. 7 (2002) ("after two centuries, it now is time for an express rejection of this non-constitutional phrase that has distorted and diminished the Constitution's religious liberty").

NOTES AND QUESTIONS

1. ***Released time.*** (a) McCOLLUM v. BOARD OF EDUC., 333 U.S. 203 (1948), per BLACK, J., held that a public school released time program violated the Establishment Clause. Privately employed religious teachers held weekly classes, on public school premises, in their respective religions, for students whose parents signed request cards, while non-attending students pursued secular studies in other parts of the building: "[N]ot only are the state's tax-supported public school buildings used for the dissemination of religious doctrines. The State also affords sectarian groups an invaluable aid in that it helps to provide pupils for their religious classes through use of the state's compulsory public school machinery."[33]

(b) ZORACH v. CLAUSON, 343 U.S. 306 (1952), per DOUGLAS, J., upheld a released time program when the religious classes were held in church buildings: Unlike *McCollum*, "[t]his involves neither religious instruction in public school classrooms nor the expenditure of public funds. All costs, including the application blanks, are paid by the religious organizations. [N]ullification of this law would have wide and profound effects. A Catholic student applies to his teacher for permission to leave the school during hours on a Holy Day of Obligation to attend a mass. A Jewish student asks his teacher for permission to be excused for Yom Kippur. A Protestant wants the afternoon off for a family baptismal ceremony. In each case the teacher requires parental consent in writing [and] to make sure the student is not a truant, goes further and requires a report from the priest, the rabbi, or the minister. The teacher in other words cooperates in a religious program to the extent of making it possible for her students to participate in it. Whether she does it occasionally for a few students, regularly for one, or pursuant to a systematized program designed to further the religious needs of all the students does not alter the character of the act.

"We are a religious people whose institutions presuppose a Supreme Being. [When] the state encourages religious instruction or cooperates [by] adjusting the schedule of public events to sectarian needs, [it] respects the religious nature of our people and accommodates the public service to their spiritual needs. To hold that it may not would [be] preferring those who believe in no religion over those who do believe. [The] problem, like many problems in constitutional law, is one of degree."

JACKSON, J., dissented: "If public education were taking so much of the pupils' time as to [encroach] upon their religious opportunity, simply shortening everyone's school day would facilitate voluntary and optional attendance at Church classes. But that suggestion is rejected upon the ground that if they are made free many students will not go to the Church. [Here,] schooling is more or less suspended during the 'released time' so the nonreligious attendants will not forge ahead of the churchgoing absentees. But it serves as a temporary jail for a pupil who will not go to Church. It takes more

---

[33] White, J., also dissenting, basically agreeing with Burger, C.J. and Rehnquist, J.Frankfurter and Jackson, JJ., each filed concurrences. Reed, J., dissented.

subtlety of mind than I possess to deny that this is governmental constraint in support of religion."[34]

(c) **Cost.** Brennan, J., has distinguished the cases "not [because] of the difference in public expenditures involved. True, the *McCollum* program involved the regular use of school facilities, classrooms, heat and light and time from the regular school day—even though the actual incremental cost may have been negligible. [But the] deeper difference was that the *McCollum* program placed the religious instructor in the public school classroom in precisely the position of authority held by the regular teachers of secular subjects, while the *Zorach* program did not. [*McCollum*] brought government and religion into that proximity which the Establishment Clause forbids." *Schempp* (concurring opinion).

(d) **Coercion.** *Zorach* found "no evidence [that] any one or more teachers were using their office to persuade or force students to take the religious instruction.[7]" Would the *Zorach* plan be inherently coercive, and therefore unconstitutional, if it were shown that many children found religious instruction more appealing than remaining in the public schools? Even if the alternative for those remaining was secular instruction with academic credit? If so, would it be permissible to excuse children from classes to enable them to attend special religious services of their faith? Would the First Amendment forbid attendance at parochial schools, as an alternative to public schools, on the ground that this was simply one hundred per cent released time?

Under this analysis, would a program of "dismissed time" as described by Jackson, J., in *Zorach* (all children released early permitting those who so wish to attend religious schools) be unconstitutional? Would "dismissed time" be nonetheless invalid if it could be shown that the *purpose* for the early school closing was to facilitate religious education? Or is this merely an accommodation "adjusting the schedule of public events to sectarian needs"?

What of the argument that the *Zorach* program is inherently coercive, and therefore unconstitutional, because, as Frankfurter, J., contended in *McCollum,* "the law of imitation operates" placing "an obvious pressure upon children to attend" religious classes? If so, what result for excusing students to attend a religious service? For parochial schools? For "dismissed time"? What of Jackson, J.'s assertion in *McCollum* that "it may be doubted whether the Constitution [protects] one from the embarrassment that always attends nonconformity, whether in religion, politics, behavior or dress"?

(e) **Use of public property.** Is the use of public school classrooms for religious education during *non*school hours distinguishable from *McCollum?*

---

[34] Black and Frankfurter, JJ., also filed separate dissents.

For a description of the interaction of the justices in fashioning the *Everson, McCollum* and *Zorach* opinions, see Note, *The "Released Time" Cases Revisited: A Study of Group Decisionmaking by the Supreme Court,* 83 Yale L.J. 1202 (1974).

[7] **[Ct's Note]** [The] only allegation in the complaint that bears on the issue is that the operation of the program "has resulted and inevitably results in the exercise of pressure and coercion upon parents and children to secure attendance by the children for religious instruction." But this charge does not even implicate the school authorities. * * *

Consider Tribe 2d ed., at 1175: "Religious instructors will no longer stand in 'the position of authority held by the regular teachers,' because the activities lie outside the mandatory school day. Although coercion is conceivable, it is not inherent, as it probably is with official school prayer; students who do not want to take part in the religious activities may take part in other activities or leave. [Thus,] the state neither lends power to religion, nor borrows legitimacy from religion. Permitting a religious group to use school facilities during non-school hours, accordingly, conveys no message of endorsement."

2. ***School prayer and coercion.*** (a) Should *Engel* and *Schempp* (and *McCollum*) have been explicitly based on "the coercion implicit under the statutory schemes"? Consider Stewart, J., dissenting in *Schempp:* "[T]he duty laid upon government in connection with religious exercises in the public schools is that of refraining from so structuring the school environment as to put any kind of pressure on a child to participate in those exercises; it is not that of providing an atmosphere in which children are kept scrupulously insulated from any awareness that some of their fellows may want to open the school day with prayer, or of the fact that there exist in our pluralistic society differences of religious belief. [A] law which provided for religious exercises during the school day and which contained no excusal provision would obviously be unconstitutionally coercive. [Even with] an excusal provision, if the exercises were held during the school day, and no equally desirable alternative were provided by the school authorities, the likelihood that children might be under at least some psychological compulsion to participate would be great. [Here,] the record shows no more than a subjective prophecy by a parent of what he thought would happen if a request were made to be [excused]. I think we must not assume that school boards so lack the qualities of inventiveness and good will as to make impossible the achievement of that goal."

What evidence of coercion does Stewart, J. require? That the objectors first ask to be excused from participation and then show that social pressures were brought to bear on them? Would this force an objector to surrender his rights in order to vindicate them? Or would Stewart, J., accept the testimony of social scientists that the program was coercive? Could this be judicially noticed? Or would he require a showing that these particular objectors were coerced? Were likely to be coerced? If so, is this a desirable approach?

(b) ***Establishment vs. Free Exercise.*** If the decisions *should* turn on the element of coercion, would it have been preferable to base them on freedom of religion or conscience? Would this permit prayer in an elementary school where every child was willing to participate? In *any* high school? Consider Louis Pollak, *Public Prayers in Public Schools,* 77 Harv.L.Rev. 62 (1963): "[T]o have pitched the decision [on the Free Exercise Clause] would presumably have meant that the prayer programs were constitutionally unobjectionable unless and until challenged, [and] school boards would have been under no discernible legal obligation [to] suspend ongoing prayer programs on their own initiative. [Indeed,] the hypothetical schoolchild plaintiff, whose free exercise rights would thus be enforced, would have to be a child with the gumption not only to disassociate himself from the prayer program but to prefer litigation to the relatively expeditious exit procedure contemplated by the excusal proviso."

3. *Secular purpose.* Several decisions, in addition to *Jaffree,* have invalidated public school practices because their "purpose" has been found to be "religious":

(a) STONE v. GRAHAM, 449 U.S. 39 (1980), per curiam, held that a Kentucky statute—requiring "the posting of a copy of the Ten Commandments, purchased with private contributions, on the wall of each public classroom in the State," with the notation at the bottom that "The secular application of the Ten Commandments is clearly seen in its adoption as the fundamental legal code of Western Civilization and the Common Law of the United States"—had "no secular legislative purpose": "The Ten Commandments is undeniably a sacred text in the Jewish and Christian faiths, and no legislative recitation of a supposed secular purpose can blind us to that [fact]. Posting of religious texts on the wall serves [no] educational function. If [they] are to have any effect at all, it will be to induce the school children to read, meditate upon, perhaps to venerate and obey, the Commandments. However desirable this might be as a matter of private devotion, it is not a permissible state objective under the Establishment Clause."[35]

(b) EPPERSON v. ARKANSAS, 393 U.S. 97 (1968), per FORTAS, J., held that an "anti-evolution" statute, forbidding public school teachers "to teach the theory or doctrine that mankind ascended or descended from a lower order of animals," violated both religion clauses: "Arkansas' law selects from the body of knowledge a particular segment which it proscribes for the sole reason that it is deemed to conflict with a particular religious doctrine." Citing newspaper advertisements and letters supporting adoption of the statute in 1928, the Court found it "clear that fundamentalist sectarian conviction was and is the law's reason for existence.* * * Arkansas did not seek to excise from the curricula [all] discussion of the origin of man."[36]

(c) EDWARDS v. AGUILLARD, 482 U.S. 578 (1987), per BRENNAN, J., held that a Louisiana statute, barring "teaching of the theory of evolution in public schools unless accompanied by instruction in 'creation science,'" had "no clear secular purpose": "True, the Act's stated purpose is to protect academic freedom. [While] the Court is normally deferential to a State's articulation of a secular purpose, it is required that the statement of such purpose be sincere and not a sham. See *Jaffree; Stone; Schempp.* [It] is clear from the legislative history [that] requiring schools to teach creation science with evolution does

---

[35] Rehnquist, J., dissented from "the Court's summary rejection of a secular purpose articulated by the legislature and confirmed by the state court." Stewart, J., also dissented. Burger, C.J., and Blackmun, J., dissented from not giving the case plenary consideration. For recent decisions on the Ten Commandments in public places, see Part IV infra.

[36] Black, J., concurring, observed that "it would be difficult to make a First Amendment case out of a state law eliminating the subject of higher mathematics, or astronomy, or biology from its curriculum. [T]here is no reason I can imagine why a State is without power to withdraw from its curriculum any subject deemed too emotional and controversial for its public schools." Harlan and Stewart, JJ., also concurred on separate grounds.

not advance academic freedom. The Act does not grant teachers a flexibility that they did not already possess to supplement the present science curriculum with the presentation of theories, besides evolution, about the origin of life. [While] requiring that curriculum guides be developed for creation science, the Act says nothing of comparable guides for evolution. [The] Act forbids school boards to discriminate against anyone who 'chooses to be a creation-scientist' or to teach 'creationism,' but fails to protect those who choose to teach evolution or any other non-creation science theory, or who refuse to teach creation science.

"If the Louisiana legislature's purpose was solely to maximize the comprehensiveness and effectiveness of science instruction, it would have encouraged the teaching of all scientific theories about the origins of humankind. But [the] legislative history documents that the Act's primary purpose was to change the science curriculum of public schools in order to provide persuasive advantage to a particular religious doctrine that rejects the factual basis of evolution in its entirety [and that] embodies the religious belief that a supernatural creator was responsible for the creation of humankind. [T]eaching a variety of scientific theories about the origins of humankind to school children might be validly done with the clear secular intent of enhancing the effectiveness of science instruction. But because the primary purpose of the Creationism Act is to endorse a particular religious doctrine, the Act furthers religion in violation of the Establishment Clause."[37]

SCALIA, J., joined by Rehnquist, C.J., dissented: "Even if I agreed with the questionable premise that legislation can be invalidated under the Establishment Clause on the basis of its motivation alone, without regard to its effects, I would still find no justification for today's decision. [The] Legislature explicitly set forth its secular purpose ('protecting academic freedom') [which] meant: *students'* freedom from *indoctrination.* The legislature wanted to ensure that students would be free to decide for themselves how life began, based upon a fair and balanced presentation of the scientific evidence. [The] legislature did not care *whether* the topic of origins was taught; it simply wished to ensure that *when* the topic was taught, [it] be 'taught as a theory, rather than as proven scientific fact' and that scientific evidence inconsistent with the theory of evolution (viz., 'creation science') be taught as well. [The law] treats the teaching of creation the same way. It does *not* mandate instruction in creation science [and] *forbids* teachers to present creation science 'as proven scientific fact'. [The] Louisiana legislators had been told repeatedly that creation scientists were scorned by most educators and scientists, who themselves had an almost religious faith in evolution. It is hardly surprising, then, that in seeking to achieve a balanced, 'nonindoctrinating' curriculum, the legislators protected from discrimination only those teachers whom they thought were *suffering* from discrimination.

---

[37] Powell, J., joined by O'Connor, J., joined the Court's opinion but wrote separately "to emphasize that nothing in the Court's opinion diminishes the traditionally broad discretion accorded state and local school officials in the selection of the public school curriculum." White, J., concurred only in the judgment.

[In] light of the unavailability of works on creation science suitable for classroom use (a fact appellees concede) and the existence of ample materials on evolution, it was entirely reasonable for the Legislature to conclude that science teachers attempting to implement the Act would need a curriculum guide on creation science, but not on evolution. * * *

"It is undoubtedly true that what prompted the Legislature [was] its awareness of the tension between evolution and the religious beliefs of many children. But [a] valid secular purpose is not rendered impermissible simply because its pursuit is prompted by concern for religious sensitivities.[38] [I] am astonished by the Court's unprecedented readiness to [disbelieve] the secular purpose set forth in the Act [and] can only attribute [this] to an intellectual predisposition [and] an instinctive reaction that any governmentally imposed requirements bearing upon the teaching of evolution must be a manifestation of Christian fundamentalist repression. In this case, however, it seems to me the Court's position is the repressive one. [Perhaps] what the Louisiana Legislature has done is unconstitutional because there *is* no [scientific] evidence, and the scheme they have established will amount to no more than a presentation of the Book of Genesis. But we cannot say that on the evidence before us in this summary judgment context, which includes ample uncontradicted testimony that 'creation science' is a body of scientific knowledge rather than revealed belief.[39] *Infinitely less* can we say (or should we say) that the scientific evidence for evolution is so conclusive that no one could be gullible enough to believe that there is any real scientific evidence to the contrary, so that the legislation's stated purpose must be a lie. Yet that illiberal judgment, that *Scopes*-in-reverse, is ultimately the basis on which the Court's facile rejection of the Louisiana Legislature's purpose must rest. * * *

"[W]hile it is possible to discern the objective 'purpose' of a statute (i.e., the public good at which its provisions appear to be directed),[40] or even the

---

[38] See also Scalia, J., joined by Rehnquist, C.J., and Thomas, J., dissenting from denial of certiorari in *Tangipahoa Parish Board of Educ. v. Freiler*, 530 U.S. 1251 (2000), which invalidated, as "not sufficiently neutral," a policy that when "the scientific theory of evolution" is taught, a statement of "disclaimer from endorsement of such theory" shall be made "to inform students of the scientific concept and not intended to influence or dissuade the Biblical version of Creation," and urging students "to exercise critical thinking and gather all information possible and closely examine each alternative." For further discussion, compare Jay D. Wexler, *Darwin, Design, and Disestablishment: Teaching the Evolution Controversy in Public Schools*, 56 Vand.L.Rev. 751 (2003) with David K. DeWolf, Stephen C. Meyer, and Mark Edward DeForest, *Teaching the Origins Controversy: Science, or Religion, or Speech*, 39 Utah. L. Rev. 29 (2000).

[39] "The only evidence in the record [defining] 'creation science' is found in five affidavits [by] two scientists, a philosopher, a theologian, and an educator, all of whom claim extensive knowledge of creation science, swear that it is essentially a collection of scientific data supporting the theory that the physical universe and life within it appeared suddenly and have not changed substantially since appearing." See generally Johnny Rex Buckles, *The Constitutionality of the Monkey Wrench: Exploring the Case for Intelligent Design*, 59 Okla. L. Rev. 527 (2006).

[40] See generally Andrew Koppelman, *Secular Purpose*, 88 Va.L.Rev. 87 (2002). Compare Suzanna Dokupil, *"Thou Shalt Not Bear False Witness": "Sham" Secular Purposes in Ten Commandments Displays*, 28 Harv.J.L. & Pub.Pol. 609 (2005) ("secular purpose analysis rarely changes ultimate conclusion"; "focusing solely on observer's perception of overall effect would improve clarity"). Contrast Josh Blackman, *This Lemon Comes as a Lemon: The Lemon Test and the Pursuit of a Statute's Secular Purpose*, 20 Geo. Mason Civ. Rts. L. J. 351 (2010).

formal motivation for a statute where that is explicitly set forth (as it was, to no avail, here), discerning the subjective motivation of those enacting the statute [is] almost always an impossible task. The number of possible motivations [is] not binary, or indeed even finite. In the present case, for example, a particular legislator need not have voted for the Act either because he wanted to foster religion or because he wanted to improve education. He may have thought the bill would provide jobs for his district, or may have wanted to make amends with a faction of his party he had alienated on another vote, or he may have been a close friend of the bill's sponsor, or he may have been repaying a favor he owed the Majority Leader, or he may have hoped the Governor would appreciate his vote and make a fundraising appearance for him, or he may have been pressured to vote for a bill he disliked by a wealthy contributor or by a flood of constituent mail, or he may have been seeking favorable publicity, or he may have been reluctant to hurt the feelings of a loyal staff member who worked on the bill, or he may have been settling an old score with a legislator who opposed the bill, or he may have been mad at his wife who opposed the bill, or he may have been intoxicated and utterly *un*motivated when the vote was called, or he may have accidentally voted 'yes' instead of 'no,' or, of course, he may have had (and very likely did have) a combination of some of the above and many other motivations. To look for *the sole purpose* of even a single legislator is probably to look for something that does not exist."

(d) Is it meaningful to distinguish between *secular* vs. *religious* purposes? Consider Phillip E. Johnson, *Concepts and Compromise in First Amendment Religious Doctrine,* 72 Calif.L.Rev. 817, 827 (1984): "Governments usually act out of secular motives, even when they are directly aiding a particular religious sect. [E]lected officials have an excellent secular reason to accommodate (or at least to avoid offending) groups and individuals who are religious, as well as groups and individuals who are not. They wish to be re-elected, and they do not want important groups to feel that the community does not honor their values." Do any (all) of these "purposes" implicate Madison's concern with "employing religion as an engine of civil policy"?

(e) If the "purpose" of government action is found to be "religious," *should* that alone be enough to invalidate it under the Establishment Clause? If so, what result in *Zorach?* For a public school "dismissed time" program implemented to facilitate religious education?[41] Consider Tribe 2d ed., at 1211: "The secular purpose requirement [might] be used to strike down laws whose effects are utterly secular. A legislature might, for example, vote to increase welfare benefits because individual legislators feel religiously compelled to do so. [A] visible religious purpose may independently convey a message of

---

[41] For use of this test to invalidate the "religiously motivated" Utah firing squad, see Martin R. Gardner, *Illicit Legislative Motivation as a Sufficient Condition for Unconstitutionality Under the Establishment Clause,* 1979 Wash.U.L.Q. 435. What about same-sex marriage? See Gary J. Simson, *Religion by Any Other Name? Prohibitions on Same-Sex Marriage and the Limits of the Establishment Clause,* 23 Colum. J. Gen. & Law 132 (2012). For discussion of whether laws whose historical or current basis is a "function of religious morality" violate the Establishment Clause, see Scott C. Idleman, *Religious Premises, Legislative Judgments, and the Establishment Clause,* 12 Corn.J.L. & Pub.Pol. 1 (2002).

endorsement or exclusion, but such a message, standing alone, should rarely if ever suffice to transform a secular action into an establishment clause violation." Compare Arnold H. Loewy, *Morals Legislation and the Establishment Clause*, 55 Ala.L.Rev. 159 (2003): "[If] the legislature simply condemns the activity because it is immoral"—i.e., "forces all citizens to act in accordance with the religious dictates of some [under] pain of criminal penalty"—"the law should be held to violate the Establishment Clause.[42] [But] if the legislation is predicated [on] morality that serves a secular function, the law should be sustained." Why should the former type law be confined to *criminal* penalties and not to other disadvantages, e.g., government benefits?

See also Jesse H. Choper, *The Religion Clauses of the First Amendment: Reconciling the Conflict*, 41 U.Pitt.L.Rev. 673 (1980): "[I]t is only when religious purpose is coupled with threatened impairment of religious freedom that government action should be held to violate the Establishment Clause. [Conceding] that the [*Epperson*] statute had a solely religious purpose, [there] was no evidence that religious beliefs were either coerced, compromised or influenced. That is, it was not shown, nor do I believe that it could be persuasively argued, that the anti-evolution law either (1) induced children of fundamentalist religions to accept the biblical theory of creation, or (2) conditioned other children for conversion to fundamentalism." Similarly, "the creation science law had a religious purpose [to] placate those religious fundamentalists whose beliefs rejected the Darwinian theory of evolution. But [so] long as the theory of creation science is taught in an objective rather than a proselytizing fashion, it does not seem to me to pose a danger to religious liberty [and] should not be held to violate the Establishment Clause." Jesse H. Choper, *Church, State and the Supreme Court: Current Controversy*, 29 Ariz.L.Rev. 551 (1987).

4. ***Purpose, primary effect, and "neutrality."*** (a) BOARD OF EDUC. v. MERGENS, 496 U.S. 226 (1990), interpreted the federal Equal Access Act to apply to public secondary schools that (a) receive federal financial aid and (b) give official recognition to noncurriculum related student groups (e.g., chess club and scuba diving club in contrast to Latin club and math club) in such ways as allowing them to meet on school premises during noninstructional time. The Act prohibited these schools from discriminating against student groups "on the basis of the religious, political, philosophical, or other content of the speech at [their] meetings." O'CONNOR, J., joined by Rehnquist, C.J., and White and Blackmun, JJ., held that the Establishment Clause did not forbid Westside High School from including within its thirty recognized student groups a Christian club "to read and discuss the Bible, to have fellowship and to pray together": "In *Widmar v. Vincent*, 454 U.S. 263 (1981), we applied the three-part *Lemon* test to hold that an 'equal access' policy, at the university level, does not violate the Establishment Clause. We concluded that 'an open-forum policy, including nondiscrimination against religious speech, would have a secular purpose,' and would in fact *avoid* entanglement with religion. We also

---

[42] How about denial of government benefits?

found that although incidental benefits accrued to religious groups who used university facilities, [a] university's forum does not 'confer any imprimatur of state approval on religious sects or practices.' Indeed, [if] a State refused to let religious groups use facilities open to others, then it would demonstrate not neutrality but hostility toward religion. Second, we noted that '[t]he [University's] provision of benefits to [a] broad spectrum of groups'—both nonreligious and religious speakers—was 'an important index of secular effect.'[43]

"We think the logic of *Widmar* applies [here. Even] if some legislators were motivated by a conviction that religious speech in particular was valuable and worthy of protection, that alone would not invalidate the Act, because what is relevant is the legislative *purpose* of the statute, not the possibly religious *motives* of the legislators who enacted [it].

"Petitioners' principal contention is that the Act has the primary effect of advancing religion. [We] disagree. First, [there] is a crucial difference between *government* speech endorsing religion, which the Establishment Clause forbids, and *private* speech endorsing religion, which the Free Speech and Free Exercise Clauses protect. We think that secondary school students are mature enough and are likely to understand that a school does not endorse or support student speech that it merely permits on a nondiscriminatory basis. * * *

"Second, we note that the Act expressly limits participation by school officials at meetings of student religious groups, and that any such meetings must be held during 'noninstructional time.' The Act therefore avoids the problems of 'the students' emulation of teachers as role models' and 'mandatory attendance requirements,' *Aguillard;* see also *McCollum.* To be sure, the possibility of *student* peer pressure remains, but there is little if any risk of official state endorsement or coercion where no formal classroom activities are involved and no school officials actively participate."

KENNEDY, J., joined by Scalia, J., concurred, emphasizing his disagreement with the plurality's "endorsement test" developed further in *Allegheny County v. ACLU,* Part IV infra: "I should think it inevitable that a public high school 'endorses' a religious club, in a common-sense use of the term, if the club happens to be one of many activities that the school permits students to choose [in] an extracurricular setting. But no constitutional violation occurs if the school's action is based upon a recognition of the fact that membership in a religious club is one of many permissible ways for a student to further his or her own personal enrichment. The inquiry with respect to coercion must be whether the government imposes pressure upon a student to participate in a religious activity. This inquiry, of course, must be undertaken with sensitivity to the special circumstances that exist in a secondary school where the line between voluntary and coerced participation may be difficult to

---

[43] For the view that "the American religious liberty regime [does] not aim to be neutral [regarding] the good of *religious freedom*," see Richard W. Garnett, *Neutrality and the Good of Religious Freedom: An Appreciative Response to Professor Koppelman,* 39 Pepp. L. Rev. 1149 (2013).

draw. No such coercion, however, has been shown to exist as a necessary result of this statute, either on its face [or] on the facts of this case."[44]

(b)   GOOD NEWS CLUB v. MILFORD CENTRAL SCHOOL, 533 U.S. 98 (2001), per THOMAS, J., used similar analysis to find no Establishment Clause violation for a public school's permitting a Christian organization to use schoolrooms for weekly after school meetings, which involved religious instruction and worship, when the school allowed such use by other groups for "the moral and character development of children": "Milford attempts to distinguish *Lamb's Chapel* and *Widmar* by emphasizing that Milford's policy involves elementary school children. [This] is unpersuasive.

"First, we have held that 'a significant factor in upholding governmental programs [is] their *neutrality* towards religion.' [Second,] to the extent we consider whether the community would feel coercive pressure to engage in the Club's activities, [b]ecause the children cannot attend without their parents' permission, they cannot be coerced into engaging in the Good News Club's religious activities. [Third, here], where the school facilities are being used for a nonschool function and there is no government sponsorship of the Club's activities, *Lee v. Weisman*, [Part IV infra, involving prayer at graduation exercises,] is inapposite. [Fourth,] even if we were to consider the possible misperceptions by schoolchildren [, the] facts of this case simply do not support Milford's conclusion. [The] meetings were held in a combined high school resource room and middle school special education room, not in an elementary school classroom. The instructors are not schoolteachers. And the children in the group are not all the same age as in the normal classroom setting; their ages range from 6 to 12. In sum, these circumstances simply do not support the theory that small children would perceive endorsement here."

SCALIA, J., concurred to underline his view, expressed in *Lamb's Chapel*, fn. 16, that "perceptions of endorsement [do] not count [when] giving [a private religious group] nondiscriminatory access to school facilities." In contrast, BREYER, J., concurred to emphasize his view that "government's 'neutrality' [is] only one of the considerations relevant to deciding whether a public school's policy violates the Establishment Clause. See, e.g., *Mitchell* (O'Connor, J., concurring). [A] child's perception that the school has endorsed a particular religion or religion in general may also prove critically important. [Today's opinion holds only] that the school was not entitled to summary judgment [and]

---

[44]   Marshall, J., joined by Brennan, J., concurred "to emphasize the steps Westside must take to avoid appearing to endorse the Christian Club's goals." Stevens, J., dissented, believing that the Act comes perilously close to an outright command to allow organized prayer [on] school premises." For the view that "so long as religious believers retain the right to express their own beliefs," persons/groups may be denied use of public forums for religious purposes, see Brian Lieter, *Why Tolerate Religion?* (2012).

May elementary or secondary schools permit their facilities to be used for instruction by religious groups if they also permit instruction by outside teachers of art, music, crafts, dance, etc. (cf. *McCollum*)? May they post the Ten Commandments if they also post the symbols of other civic or charitable groups (cf. *Stone*)? See Douglas Laycock, *Equal Access and Moments of Silence: The Equal Status of Religious Speech by Private Speakers*, 81 Nw.U.L.Rev. 1 (1986).

The most recent decisions on Religion and Public Schools are considered in Part IV infra.

both parties, if they so desire, should have a fair opportunity to fill the evidentiary gap."[45]

5. ***Military chaplains.*** In rejecting the argument that prayer exercises in public schools furthered "the majority's right to free exercise of religion," *Schempp* did "not pass upon a situation such as military service, where the Government regulates the temporal and geographic environment of individuals to a point that, unless it permits voluntary religious services to be conducted with the use of government facilities, military personnel would be unable to engage in the practice of their faiths." Might it be that, while Free Exercise may justify government provision for opportunity to worship, the Establishment Clause bars a government subsidized ministry? See M. Albert Figinski, *Military Chaplains—A Constitutionally Permissible Accommodation Between Church and State,* 24 Md.L.Rev. 377 (1964). Or might it be "that the Government need not necessarily provide chapels and chaplains to those of its armed personnel who are *not* cut off from civilian church facilities"? Klaus J. Herrmann, *Some Considerations on the Constitutionality of the United States Military Chaplaincy,* 14 Am.U.L.Rev. 24, 34 (1964). For an alternate treatment of the problem, see Antony B. Kolenc, *Not "For God and Country": Atheist Military Chaplains and the Free Exercise Clause,* 48 U.S.F. L. Rev. (2014). For the view that "the military chaplaincy system should represent the 'poster child' of an Establishment Clause violation," see Steven K. Green, *Reconciling the Irreconcilable: Military Chaplains and the First Amendment,* 110 W. Va. L. Rev. 167 (2007). For fuller consideration of the "conflict" between the Religion Clauses, see Sec. 4 infra.

6. ***Public school secularism.*** *Schempp* emphasized that "it might well be said that one's education is not complete without a study of comparative religion or the history of religion and its relationship to the advancement of civilization. It certainly may be said that the Bible is worthy of study for its literary and historic qualities. Nothing we have said here indicates that such study of the Bible or of religion, when presented objectively as part of a secular program of education, may not be [effected]." Compare Stewart, J., dissenting in *Schempp:* "[A] compulsory state educational system so structures a child's life that if religious exercises are held to be an impermissible activity in schools, [this] is seen, not as the realization of state neutrality, but rather as the establishment of a religion of secularism, or at the least, as government support of the beliefs of those who think that religious exercises should be conducted only in private." Contrast Kent Greenawalt, *Teaching About Religion in the Public Schools*, 18 J.L. & Pol. 329 (2002): "[S]ecular humanism is generally consistent with many (liberal) religious tenets. [The] crucial educational and constitutional question is not whether the schools explicitly teach a religion of secular humanism, but whether they convey messages that [are] antithetical to *many* religious believers and go to the core of their religious faith." May public schools inculcate "fundamental civic and democratic" values? Consider William H. Clune, *The Constitution and*

---

[45] Souter, J., also dissented on this ground.

Vouchers for Religious Schools: The Demise of Separatism and the Rise of Non-discrimination as Measures of State Neutrality, Unpublished Working Paper (1999): "The idea of brainwashing in religious schools only makes sense if it is contrasted with a supposed condition of free choice in secular public education. [S]ecularism and secular humanism, that the child should be able to choose among ultimate values on the basis of individual rational choice (as that faculty gradually matures), now seems just as much a value position and a value choice by parents and society as the opposite view that certain values have absolute priority and should be strongly socialized into the child's value system. Indeed the idea that individuals should choose values according to 'rational' criteria operates conceptually as the ultimate value position of secular humanism, just as the idea that individuals should choose values on the basis of religious criteria operates as the ultimate value in religious education."[46] If government requires that public employees be of "good moral character," is this a "religious test" for public office?

IV. OFFICIAL ACKNOWLEDGMENT OF RELIGION

ALLEGHENY COUNTY V. ACLU
492 U.S. 573, 109 S.Ct. 3086, 106 L.Ed.2d 472 (1989).

JUSTICE BLACKMUN announced the judgment of the Court and delivered the opinion of the Court with respect to Parts III–A, IV, and V, an opinion with respect to Parts I and II, in which JUSTICE O'CONNOR and JUSTICE STEVENS join, an opinion with respect to Part III–B, in which JUSTICE STEVENS joins, and an opinion with respect to Part VI.

This litigation concerns the constitutionality of two recurring holiday displays located on public property in downtown Pittsburgh. The first is a crèche placed on the Grand Staircase of the Allegheny County Courthouse. The second is a Chanukah menorah placed just outside the City-County Building, next to a Christmas tree and a sign saluting liberty. * * *

I.A. [The] crèche [is] a visual representation of the scene in the manger in Bethlehem shortly after the birth of Jesus. [The] crèche includes [an] angel bearing a banner that proclaims "Gloria in Excelsis Deo!" A plaque stated it had been donated by the Holy Name Society.

[III.A.] Although "the myriad, subtle ways in which Establishment Clause values can be eroded," are not susceptible to a single verbal formulation, this Court has attempted to encapsulate the essential precepts. [Thus,] in *Everson,* the Court gave this often-repeated summary [stating the second ¶ on p. 1208 supra]. In *Lemon,* the Court sought to refine these principles by focusing on three "tests." [In] recent years, we have paid particularly close attention to whether the challenged

---

[46] For a discerning discussion of how teachers might (must) deal with these matters in various courses, see Greenawalt, supra.

governmental practice either has the purpose or effect of "endorsing" religion. [See] *Lynch* (O'Connor, J., concurring).

B. [In *Lynch,*] we considered whether the city of Pawtucket, R.I., had violated the Establishment Clause by including a crèche in its annual Christmas display, located in a private [park].[47] By a 5–4 decision[,] the Court [held] that the inclusion of the crèche did [not]. Justice O'Connor['s] concurrence [provides] a sound analytical framework for evaluating governmental use of religious symbols. First and foremost, [it recognizes] any endorsement of religion as "invalid," because it "sends a message to nonadherents that they are outsiders, not full members of the political community, and an accompanying message to adherents that they are insiders, favored members of the political community." Second, [it] articulates a method for determining whether the government's use of an object with religious meaning has the effect of endorsing religion[:] the question is "what viewers may fairly understand to be the purpose of the display." That inquiry, of necessity, turns upon the context in which the contested object appears: "a typical museum setting, though not neutralizing the religious content of a religious painting, negates any message of endorsement of that content." * * *

The concurrence applied this mode of analysis to the Pawtucket crèche, seen in the context of that city's holiday celebration as a whole. In addition to the crèche the city's display contained: a Santa Claus House with a live Santa distributing candy, reindeer pulling Santa's sleigh; a live 40-foot Christmas tree strung with lights; statues of carolers in old-fashioned dress; candy-striped poles; a "talking" wishing well; a large banner proclaiming "SEASONS GREETINGS"; a miniature "village" with several houses and a church, and various "cut-out" figures, including those of a clown, a dancing elephant, a robot, and a teddy bear. The concurrence concluded that both because the crèche is "a traditional symbol" of Christmas, a holiday with strong secular elements, and because the crèche was "displayed along with purely secular symbols," the crèche's setting "changes what viewers may fairly understand to be the purpose of the display" and "negates any message of endorsement" of "the Christian beliefs represented by the crèche."

[D]espite divergence at the bottom line, the five Justices in concurrence and dissent in *Lynch* agreed upon the relevant constitutional principles [which] have been adopted by the Court in subsequent cases. [*Grand Rapids.*][48]

---

[47] "[Ten years ago], when [the] crèche was acquired, it cost the City $1365; it now is valued at $200. The erection and dismantling of the crèche costs the City about $20 per year; nominal expenses are incurred in lighting the crèche. No money has been expended on its maintenance for the past 10 years."

[48] For the view that the endorsement theory changed the Establishment Clause, which had been "designed and understood to protect religious liberty," into "a guarantor of equality," and that "equality is being used not to justify the separation of church and state, but to subvert it," see Noah

IV. We turn first to the county's crèche display. [U]nlike *Lynch*, nothing in the context of the display detracts from the crèche's religious message. [T]he crèche sits on the Grand Staircase, the "main" and "most beautiful part" of the building that is the seat of county government. No viewer could reasonably think that it occupies this location without the support and approval of the government [which] has chosen to celebrate Christmas in a way that has the effect of endorsing a patently Christian message: Glory to God for the birth of Jesus Christ. * * *

V.   Justice Kennedy and the three Justices who join [him] require a response in some depth:

A.   In *Marsh v. Chambers*, 463 U.S. 783 (1983) [upholding the practice of legislative prayer], the Court relied specifically on the fact that Congress authorized legislative prayer at the same time that it produced the Bill of Rights.[49] Justice Kennedy, however, argues that *Marsh* legitimates all "practices with no greater potential for an establishment of religion" than those "accepted traditions dating back to the Founding." Otherwise, the Justice asserts, such practices as our national motto ("In God We Trust") and our Pledge of Allegiance (with the phrase "under God," added in 1954) are in danger of invalidity.

Our previous opinions have considered in dicta the motto and the pledge, characterizing them as consistent with the proposition that government may not communicate an endorsement of religious belief. We need not return to the subject of "ceremonial deism,"[50] because there is an

---

Feldman, *From Liberty to Equality: The Transformation of the Establishment Clause*, 90 Calif.L.Rev. 673 (2002).

[49] *Marsh* also pointed, inter alia, to the practice in the colonies (including Virginia after adopting its Declaration of Rights which has been "considered the precursor of both the Free Exercise and Establishment Clauses"), to the opening invocations in federal courts (including the Supreme Court), and in the Continental Congress and First Congress: "[T]he practice of opening sessions with prayer has continued without interruption ever since that early session of Congress. It has also been followed consistently in most of the states." Brennan, Marshall and Stevens, JJ., dissented.

Is it relevant that, subsequently, "Madison acknowledged that he had been quite mistaken in approving—as a member of the House, in 1789—bills for the payment of congressional chaplains"? William W. Van Alstyne, *Trends in the Supreme Court: Mr. Jefferson's Crumbling Wall*, 1984 Duke L.J. 770, 776. See also Christopher C. Lund, *The Congressional Chaplaincies*, 17 Wm. & Mary Bill Rts. J. 1171, 1173–74 (2009): "[T]he history [is] more checkered than *Marsh* seemed to believe. [C]haplaincies have sometimes been the locus of significant religious and political conflict."

[50] Brennan, J., joined by Marshall, Blackmun and Stevens, JJ., dissenting in *Lynch* "suggest[ed] that such practices as the designation of 'In God We Trust' as our national motto, or the references to God contained in the Pledge of Allegiance can best be understood [as] a form of 'ceremonial deism,' protected from Establishment Clause scrutiny chiefly because they have lost through rote repetition any significant religious content."

For the view that "secularizing religious [practices] conveniently preserves the inclusion of symbols and practices threatens the purity and integrity of both government and religion [and] jeopardizes the historically neutral relationship between religion and the state," see Alexandra D. Furth, *Secular Idolatry and Sacred Traditions: A Critique of the Supreme Court's Secularization Analysis*. 146 U.Pa.L.Rev. 579 (1998). See also Steven B. Epstein, *Rethinking the Constitutionality of Ceremonial Deism*, 96 Colum.L.Rev. 2083 (1996) (extensive review concluding that most forms "violate a core purpose of the Establishment Clause").

obvious distinction between crèche displays and references to God in the motto and the pledge. However history may affect the constitutionality of nonsectarian references to religion by the government,[52] history cannot legitimate practices that demonstrate the government's allegiance to a particular sect or creed. [The] history of this Nation, it is perhaps sad to say, contains numerous examples of official acts that endorsed Christianity specifically [but] this heritage of official discrimination against non-Christians has no place in the jurisprudence of the Establishment Clause. * * *

C. Although Justice Kennedy repeatedly accuses the Court of harboring a "latent hostility" or "callous indifference" toward religion, nothing could be further from the truth. [The] government does not discriminate against any citizen on the basis of the citizen's religious faith if the government is secular in its functions and operations. On the contrary, the Constitution mandates that the government remain secular [in] order to avoid discriminating among citizens on the basis of their religious faiths. [A] secular state establishes neither atheism nor religion as its official creed. * * *[59]

VI. The display of the Chanukah menorah. [The] question for Establishment Clause purposes is whether the combined display of the tree, the sign, and the menorah has the effect of endorsing both Christian and Jewish faiths, or rather simply recognizes that both Christmas and Chanukah are part of the same winter-holiday season, which has attained a secular status in our society. Of the two interpretations of this particular display, the latter seems far more plausible * * *.[64]

The Christmas tree, unlike the menorah, is not itself a religious symbol. [The] widely accepted view of the Christmas tree as the preeminent secular symbol of the Christmas holiday season serves to emphasize the secular component of the message communicated by other elements of an

---

[52] **[Ct's Note]** It is worth noting that just because *Marsh* sustained the validity of legislative prayer, it does not necessarily follow that practices like proclaiming a National Day of Prayer are constitutional. Legislative prayer does not urge citizens to engage in religious practices, and on that basis could well be distinguishable from an exhortation from government to the people that they engage in religious conduct. But, as this practice is not before us, we express no judgment about its constitutionality.

[59] **[Ct's Note]** In his attempt to legitimate the display of the crèche on the Grand Staircase, Justice Kennedy repeatedly characterizes it as an "accommodation" of religion. But an accommodation of religion, in order to be permitted under the Establishment Clause, must lift "an identifiable burden *on the exercise of religion." Corporation of Presiding Bishop v. Amos,* [Sec. 4 infra]. Prohibiting the display of a crèche at this location [does] not impose a burden on the practice of Christianity [and] is not an "accommodation" of religion in the conventional sense. ["Accommodation" of religion and the relationship between the Establishment and Free Exercise Clauses is considered in Sec. 3 infra.]

[64] **[Ct's Note]** [The] conclusion that Pittsburgh's combined Christmas-Chanukah display cannot be interpreted as endorsing Judaism alone does not mean, however, that it is implausible, as a general matter, for a city like Pittsburgh to endorse a minority faith. The display of a menorah alone might well have that effect.

accompanying holiday display, including the Chanukah menorah.[66] The tree, moreover, is clearly the predominant element in the city's display. The 45-foot tree occupies the central position [in] the City-County Building; the 18-foot menorah is positioned to one side. Given this configuration, it is much more sensible to interpret the meaning of the menorah in light of the tree, rather than vice versa. * * *

Although the city has used a symbol with religious meaning as its representation of Chanukah, this is not a case in which the city has reasonable alternatives that are less religious in nature. [Where] the government's secular message can be conveyed by two symbols, only one of which carries religious meaning, an observer reasonably might infer from the fact that the government has chosen to use the religious symbol that the government means to promote religious faith. See *Schempp* (Brennan, J., concurring) (Establishment Clause forbids use of religious means to serve secular ends when secular means suffice). But where, as here, no such choice has been made, this inference of endorsement is not present.[68]

The Mayor's sign further diminishes the possibility that the tree and the menorah will be interpreted as a dual endorsement of Christianity and Judaism. The sign states that during the holiday season the city salutes liberty. Moreover, the sign draws upon the theme of light, common to both Chanukah and Christmas as winter festivals, and links that theme with this Nation's legacy of freedom, which allows an American to celebrate the holiday season in whatever way he wishes, religiously or otherwise. [While] an adjudication of the display's effect must take into account the perspective of one who is neither Christian nor Jewish, as well as of those who adhere to either of these religions, the constitutionality of its effect must also be judged according to the standard of a "reasonable observer." When measured against this standard, the menorah need not be excluded from this particular display.

The conclusion [here] does not foreclose the possibility that the display of the menorah might violate either the "purpose" or "entanglement" prong of the *Lemon* analysis. These issues [may] be considered [on] remand. * * *

---

[66]   **[Ct's Note]** Although the Christmas tree represents the secular celebration of Christmas, its very association with Christmas (a holiday with religious dimensions) makes it conceivable that the tree might be seen as representing Christian religion when displayed next to an object associated with Jewish religion. For this reason, I agree with Justice Brennan and Justice Stevens that one must ask whether the tree and the menorah together endorse the *religious* beliefs of Christians and Jews. For the reasons stated in the text, however, I conclude the city's overall display does not have this impermissible effect.

[68]   **[Ct's Note]** In *Lynch,* in contrast, there was no need for Pawtucket to include a crèche in order to convey a secular message about Christmas. (Blackmun, J., dissenting). [In] displaying the menorah next to the tree, the city has demonstrated no preference for the *religious* celebration of the holiday season. This conclusion, however, would be untenable had the city substituted a crèche for its Christmas tree or if the city had failed to substitute for the menorah [a] more secular, representation of Chanukah.

JUSTICE KENNEDY, with whom THE CHIEF JUSTICE, JUSTICE WHITE, and JUSTICE SCALIA join, concurring in the judgment in part and dissenting in part. * * *

I.   In keeping with the usual fashion of recent years, the majority applies the *Lemon* [test]. Persuasive criticism of *Lemon* has emerged. Our cases often question its utility in providing concrete answers to Establishment Clause questions, calling it but a "helpful signpos[t]" or "guidelin[e]," to assist our deliberations rather than a comprehensive test. *Mueller;* see *Lynch* ("we have repeatedly emphasized our unwillingness to be confined to any single test or criterion in this sensitive area").[51] Substantial revision of our Establishment Clause doctrine may be in order;[52] but it is unnecessary [for] even the *Lemon* test, when applied with proper sensitivity to our traditions and our caselaw, supports the conclusion that both the crèche and the menorah are permissible displays in the context of the holiday season.

[T]he Establishment Clause permits government some latitude in recognizing and accommodating the central role religion plays in our society. *Lynch; Walz.* Any approach less sensitive to our heritage would border on latent hostility toward religion, as it would require government in all its multifaceted roles to acknowledge only the secular. [A]s the modern administrative state expands to touch the lives of its citizens in such diverse ways and redirects their financial choices through programs of its own, it is difficult to maintain the fiction that requiring government to avoid all assistance to religion can in fairness be viewed as serving the goal of neutrality. [Our] cases disclose two limiting principles: government may not coerce anyone to support or participate in any religion or its exercise; and it may not [give] direct benefits to religion in such a degree that it in fact "establishes a [state] religion or religious faith, or tends to do so." *Lynch.* These two principles, while distinct, are not unrelated, for it

---

[51]   In *Marsh,* Brennan, J., joined by Marshall, J. dissenting, noted that "the Court makes no pretense of subjecting Nebraska's practice of legislative prayer to any of the formal 'tests' that have traditionally structured our inquiry under the Establishment Clause": "[I]f any group of law students were asked to apply the principles of *Lemon* to the question of legislative prayer, they would nearly unanimously find the practice to be unconstitutional. [W]e are faced here with the regularized practice of conducting official prayers, on behalf of the entire legislature, as part of the order of business constituting the formal opening of every single session of the legislative term."

[52]   Four years later, concurring in *Lamb's Chapel,* Scalia, J., joined by Thomas, J., noted that six "of the currently sitting Justices" have disagreed with *Lemon*—Rehnquist, C.J., and White, O'Connor, and Kennedy, JJ., in addition to themselves: "For my part, I agree with the long list of constitutional scholars who have criticized *Lemon* and bemoaned the strange Establishment Clause geometry of crooked lines and wavering shapes its intermittent use has produced. See, e.g., Jesse H. Choper, *The Establishment Clause and Aid to Parochial Schools—An Update,* 75 Cal.L.Rev. 5 (1987); William P. Marshall, *"We Know It When We See It": The Supreme Court and Establishment,* 59 S.Cal.L.Rev. 495 (1986); Michael W. McConnell, *Accommodation of Religion,* 1985 S.Ct.Rev. 1; Philip B. Kurland, *The Religion Clauses and the Burger Court,* 34 Cath.U.L.Rev. 1 (1984); Robert Cord, *Separation of Church and State* (1982); Jesse H. Choper, *The Religion Clauses of the First Amendment: Reconciling the Conflict,* 41 U.Pitt.L.Rev. 673 (1980). I will decline to apply *Lemon*—whether it validates or invalidates the government action in question—and therefore cannot join the opinion of the Court today."

would be difficult indeed to establish a religion without some measure of more or less subtle coercion, be it in the form of taxation to supply the substantial benefits that would sustain a state-established faith, direct compulsion to observance, or governmental exhortation to religiosity that amounts in fact to proselytizing.

[S]ome of our recent cases reject the view that coercion is the sole touchstone of an Establishment Clause violation. See *Engel* (dictum) [see fn. 53 in *Jaffree*]; *Schempp; Nyquist.* That may be true if by "coercion" is meant *direct* coercion in the classic sense of an establishment of religion that the Framers knew. But coercion need not be a direct tax in aid of religion or a test oath. Symbolic recognition or accommodation of religious faith may violate the Clause in an extreme case.[53] I doubt not, for example, that the Clause forbids a city to permit the permanent erection of a large Latin cross on the roof of city hall. This is not because government speech about religion is per se suspect, as the majority would have it, but because such an obtrusive year-round religious display would place the government's weight behind an obvious effort to proselytize on behalf of a particular religion. Speech may coerce in some circumstances, but this does not justify a ban on all government recognition of religion. [Absent] coercion, the risk of infringement of religious liberty by passive or symbolic accommodation is minimal. [In] determining whether there exists an establishment, or a tendency toward one, we refer to the other types of church-state contacts that have existed unchallenged throughout our history, or that have been found permissible in our caselaw [discussing *Lynch* and *Marsh*].

II.   These principles are not difficult to apply to the facts of the case before us. [If] government is to participate in its citizens' celebration of a holiday that contains both a secular and a religious component, enforced recognition of only the secular aspect would signify the callous indifference toward religious faith[; the] government would be refusing to acknowledge [the] historical reality, that many of its citizens celebrate its religious aspects as well. * * *

There is no suggestion here that the government's power to coerce has been used to further the interests of Christianity or Judaism in any way. No one was compelled to observe or participate in any religious ceremony or activity. Neither the city nor the county contributed significant amounts of tax money to serve the cause of one religious faith. The crèche and the menorah are purely passive symbols of religious holidays. Passersby who disagree with the message conveyed by these displays are free to ignore

---

[53] **[Ct's Note]** [The] prayer invalidated in *Engel* was unquestionably coercive in an indirect manner, as the *Engel* Court itself recognized * * * .

[*Marsh* noted that "here, the individual claiming injury by the practice is an adult, presumably not readily susceptible to 'religious indoctrination,' see *Tilton,* or peer pressure, compare *Schempp* (Brennan, J., concurring)."]

them, or even to turn their [backs]. Whether the crèche be surrounded by poinsettias, talking wishing wells, or carolers, the conclusion remains the same, for the relevant context is not the items in the display itself but the season as a whole. * * *

[III. [The endorsement test is a] most unwelcome, addition to our tangled Establishment Clause jurisprudence. [*Marsh*] stands for the proposition, not that specific practices common in 1791 are an exception to the otherwise broad sweep of the Establishment Clause, but rather that the meaning of the Clause is to be determined by reference to historical practices and understandings.[7] Whatever test we choose to apply must permit not only legitimate practices two centuries old but also any other practices with no greater potential for an establishment of religion. [Few] can withstand scrutiny under a faithful application [the endorsement test].

Some examples suffice. [Since] the Founding of our Republic, American Presidents have issued Thanksgiving Proclamations establishing a national day of celebration and prayer [and] the forthrightly religious nature of these proclamations has not waned with the years. [It] requires little imagination to conclude that these proclamations would cause non-adherents to feel excluded.* * * .[9]

The Executive has not been the only Branch of our Government to recognize the central role of religion in our society. [T]his Court opens its sessions with the request that "God save the United States and this honorable Court." [The] Legislature has gone much further, not only employing legislative chaplains, but also setting aside a special prayer room in the Capitol for use by Members of the House and Senate. The [room] depicts President Washington kneeling in prayer; around him is etched the first verse of the 16th Psalm: "Preserve me, O God, for in Thee do I put my trust." * * * Congress has directed the President to "set aside and proclaim a suitable day each year [as] a National Day of Prayer, on which the people of the United States may turn to God in prayer and meditation at churches, in groups, and as individuals." [Also] by statute, the Pledge of Allegiance to the Flag describes the United States as "one Nation under God." To be sure, no one is obligated to recite this phrase, see *West Virginia State Bd. of Educ. v. Barnette,* [Sec. 2, I infra] but it borders on sophistry to suggest that the " 'reasonable' " atheist would not feel less than a " 'full membe[r] of the political community' " every time his fellow Americans recited, as part of their expression of patriotism and love for country, a phrase he believed to be false. Likewise, our national motto, "In God we trust," which is prominently engraved in the wall above the

---

[7] **[Ct's Note]** [Acts] of "official discrimination against non-Christians" perpetrated in the eighteenth and nineteenth centuries by States and municipalities are of course irrelevant to this inquiry, but the practices of past Congresses and Presidents are highly informative.

[9] **[Ct's Note]** Similarly, our presidential inaugurations have traditionally opened with a request for divine blessing. * * *

Speaker's dias in the Chamber of the House of Representatives and is reproduced on every coin minted and every dollar printed by the Federal Government, must have the same effect.

If the intent of the Establishment Clause is to protect individuals from mere feelings of exclusion, then legislative prayer cannot escape invalidation. It has been argued that "[it serves] the legitimate secular purposes of solemnizing public occasions [in] society." *Lynch* (O'Connor, J., concurring). I fail to see why prayer is the only way to convey these messages; appeals to patriotism. [No] doubt prayer is "worthy of appreciation," but that is most assuredly not because it is secular. Even accepting the secular-solemnization explanation at face value, moreover, it seems incredible to suggest that the average observer of legislative prayer who either believes in no religion or whose faith rejects the concept of God would not receive the clear message that his faith is out of step with the political norm.[10] * * *

[IV.]   The case before us is admittedly a troubling one. It must be conceded that, however neutral the purpose of the city and county, the eager proselytizer may seek to use these symbols for his own ends [and] that some devout adherents of Judaism or Christianity may be as offended by the holiday display as are nonbelievers, if not more so. [For] these reasons, I might have voted against installation [were] I a local legislative official. But [the] principles of the Establishment Clause and our Nation's historic traditions of diversity and pluralism allow communities to make reasonable judgments respecting the accommodation or acknowledgment of holidays with both cultural and religious aspects. * * *

JUSTICE O'CONNOR with whom JUSTICE BRENNAN and JUSTICE STEVENS join as to Part II, concurring in part and concurring in the judgment. * * *

II.   * * * Justice Kennedy asserts that the endorsement test "is flawed in its fundamentals and unworkable in practice." * * *

An Establishment Clause standard that prohibits only "coercive" practices or overt efforts at government proselytization, but fails to take account of the numerous more subtle ways that government can show favoritism to particular beliefs or convey a message of disapproval to others, would [not] adequately protect the religious liberty or respect the religious diversity of the members of our pluralistic political community.

---

10   [Ct's Note] If the majority's test were to be applied logically, it would lead to the elimination of all nonsecular Christmas caroling in public buildings or, presumably, anywhere on public property. It is difficult to argue that lyrics like "Good Christian men, rejoice," "Joy to the world! the Savior reigns," "This, this is Christ the King," "Christ, by highest heav'n adored," and "Come and behold Him, Born the King of angels," have acquired such a secular nature that nonadherents would not feel "left out" by a government-sponsored or approved program that included these carols. [Like] Thanksgiving Proclamations, the reference to God in the Pledge of Allegiance, and invocations to God in sessions of Congress and of this Court, they constitute practices that the Court will not proscribe, but that the Court's reasoning today does not explain.

Thus, this Court has never relied on coercion alone as the touchstone of Establishment Clause analysis. To require a showing of coercion, even indirect coercion, as an essential element of an Establishment Clause violation would make the Free Exercise Clause a redundancy. [Moreover,] as even Justice Kennedy recognizes, any Establishment Clause test limited to "*direct* coercion" clearly would fail to account for forms of "[s]ymbolic recognition or accommodation of religious faith" that may violate the Establishment Clause.

[To] be sure, the endorsement test depends on a sensitivity to the unique circumstances and context of a particular challenged practice and, like any test that is sensitive to context, it may not always yield results with unanimous agreement at the margins. But that is true of many standards in constitutional law, and even the modified coercion test offered by Justice Kennedy involves judgment and hard choices at the margin. He admits as much by acknowledging that the permanent display of a Latin cross at city hall would violate the Establishment Clause, as would the display of symbols of Christian holidays alone. Would the display of a Latin cross for six months have such an unconstitutional effect, or the display of the symbols of most Christian holidays and one Jewish holiday? Would the Christmas-time display of a crèche inside a courtroom be "coercive" if subpoenaed witnesses had no opportunity to "turn their backs" and walk away? Would displaying a crèche in front of a public school violate the Establishment Clause under Justice Kennedy's test? * * *

Justice Kennedy submits that the endorsement test [would] invalidate many traditional practices. [But] historical acceptance of a practice does not in itself validate that practice under the Establishment Clause if the practice violates the values protected by that Clause, just as historical acceptance of racial or gender based discrimination does not immunize such practices from scrutiny under the 14th Amendment.[54] [The "history and ubiquity" of a practice is relevant because it provides part of the context in which a reasonable observer evaluates whether a challenged governmental practice conveys a message of endorsement of religion.

---

[54] In contending that "specific historical practice should [not] override [the] clear constitutional imperative," Brennan, J., joined by Marshall, J., dissenting in *Marsh,* noted that "the sort of historical argument made by the Court should be advanced with some hesitation in light of certain other skeletons in the congressional closet. See, e.g., An Act for the Punishment of certain Crimes against the United States (1790) (enacted by the First Congress and requiring that persons convicted of certain theft offenses 'be publicly whipped, not exceeding thirty-nine stripes'); Act of July 23, 1866 (reaffirming the racial segregation of the public schools in the District of Columbia; enacted exactly one week after Congress proposed Fourteenth Amendment to the States)."

Brennan, J., concurring in *Schempp,* further observed that "today the Nation is far more heterogeneous religiously, including as it does substantial minorities not only of Catholics and Jews but as well of those who worship according to no version of the Bible and those who worship no God at all. In the face of such profound changes, practices which may have been objectionable to no one in the time of Jefferson and Madison may today be highly offensive to many persons, the deeply devout and the non-believers alike. [Thus], our use of the history of their time must limit itself to broad purposes, not specific practices."

[Thus,] the celebration of Thanksgiving as a public holiday, despite its religious origins, is now generally understood as a celebration of patriotic values rather than particular religious beliefs. * * *

III. [I]n Part VI * * * Justice Blackmun's new rule that an inference of endorsement arises every time government uses a symbol with religious meaning if a "more secular alternative" is available, is too blunt an instrument for Establishment Clause analysis, which depends on sensitivity to the context and circumstances presented by each [case.]

JUSTICE BRENNAN, with whom JUSTICE MARSHALL and JUSTICE STEVENS join, concurring in part and dissenting in part.

* * * I continue to believe that the display of an object that "retains a specifically Christian [or other] religious meaning," is incompatible with the separation of church and state demanded by our Constitution. I therefore agree with the Court that Allegheny County's display of a crèche at the county courthouse signals an endorsement of the Christian faith in violation of the Establishment Clause, and join Parts III–A, IV, and V of the Court's opinion. I cannot agree, however, [with] the decision as to the menorah [which] rests on three premises: the Christmas tree is a secular symbol; Chanukah is a holiday with secular dimensions, symbolized by the menorah; and the government may promote pluralism by sponsoring or condoning displays having strong religious associations on its property.

[I.] Even though the tree alone may be deemed predominantly secular, it can hardly be so characterized when placed next to such a forthrightly religious symbol. Consider a poster featuring a star of David, a statue of Buddha, a Christmas tree, a mosque, and a drawing of Krishna. [W]hen found in such company, the tree serves as an unabashedly religious symbol. * * *

[II.] The menorah is indisputably a religious symbol, used ritually in a celebration that has deep religious significance. * * * Pittsburgh's secularization of an inherently religious symbol [recalls] the effort in *Lynch* to render the crèche a secular symbol. As I said then: "To suggest [that] such a symbol is merely 'traditional' and therefore no different from Santa's house or reindeer is not only offensive to those for whom the crèche has profound significance, but insulting to those who insist for religious or personal reasons that the story of Christ is in no sense a part of 'history' nor an unavoidable element of our national 'heritage.' " * * *

III. * * * I know of no principle under the Establishment Clause [that] governmental promotion of religion is acceptable so long as one religion is not favored. We have, on the contrary, interpreted that Clause to require neutrality, not just among religions, but between religion and nonreligion. [The] uncritical acceptance of a message of religious pluralism also ignores [that many] religious faiths are hostile to each other, and indeed, refuse even to participate in ecumenical services designed to demonstrate the very pluralism Justices Blackmun and O'Connor extol. * * *

JUSTICE STEVENS, with whom JUSTICE BRENNAN and JUSTICE MARSHALL join, concurring in part and dissenting in part. * * *

In my opinion the Establishment Clause should be construed to create a strong presumption against the display of religious symbols on public property. [Even] though "[p]assersby who disagree with the message conveyed by these displays are free to ignore them, or even turn their backs," displays of this kind inevitably have a greater tendency to emphasize sincere and deeply felt differences among individuals than to achieve an ecumenical goal. The Establishment Clause does not allow public bodies to foment such disagreement.

Application of a strong presumption [will not] "require a relentless extirpation of all contact between government and religion," (Kennedy, J., concurring and dissenting), for it will prohibit a display only when its message, evaluated in the context in which it is presented, is nonsecular. For example, a carving of Moses holding the Ten Commandments, if that is the only adornment on a courtroom wall, conveys an equivocal message, perhaps of respect for Judaism, for religion in general, or for law. The addition of carvings depicting Confucius and Mohammed may honor religion, or particular religions, to an extent that the First Amendment does not tolerate any more than it does "the permanent erection of a large Latin cross on the roof of city hall." Placement of secular figures such as Caesar Augustus, William Blackstone, Napoleon Bonaparte, and John Marshall alongside these three religious leaders, however, signals respect not for great proselytizers but for great lawgivers. It would be absurd to exclude such a fitting message from a courtroom,[13] as it would to exclude religious paintings by Italian Renaissance masters from a public museum.[55] Far from "border[ing] on latent hostility toward religion," this careful consideration of context gives due regard to religious and nonreligious members of our society. * * *

NOTES AND QUESTIONS

1. **Secular purpose.** (a) *Lynch* found that "Pawtucket has *a* secular purpose for its display": "The City [has] principally taken note of a significant historical religious event long celebrated in the Western World. [Were] the test that the government must have 'exclusively secular' objectives, much of the

---

[13] [Ct's Note] All these leaders, of course, appear in friezes on the walls of our courtroom.

[55] As an example of government "reference to our religious heritage," *Lynch* noted that "the National Gallery in Washington, maintained with Government support [has] long exhibited masterpieces with religious messages, notably the Last Supper, and paintings depicting the Birth of Christ, the Crucifixion, and the Resurrection, among many others with explicit Christian themes and messages."

conduct and legislation this Court has approved in the past would have been invalidated."

Brennan, J.'s dissent in *Lynch,* reasoned: "When government decides to recognize Christmas day as a public holiday, it does no more than accommodate the calendar of public activities to the plain fact that many Americans [spend] time visiting with their families, attending religious services, and perhaps enjoying some respite from preholiday activities. [If] public officials go further and participate in the *secular* celebration of Christmas—by, for example, decorating public places with such secular images as wreaths, garlands or Santa Claus figures—they move closer to the limits of their constitutional power but nevertheless remain within [the] Establishment Clause. But when those officials participate in or appear to endorse the distinctively religious elements of this otherwise secular event, they encroach upon First Amendment freedoms. [The] Court seems to assume that forbidding Pawtucket from displaying a crèche would be tantamount to forbidding a state college from including the Bible or Milton's *Paradise Lost* in a course on English literature. But in those cases the religiously-inspired materials are being considered solely as literature. [In] this case, by contrast, the crèche plays no comparable secular role. [It] would be another matter if the crèche were displayed in a museum setting, in the company of other religiously-inspired artifacts, as an example, among many, of the symbolic representation of religious myths. In that setting, we would have objective guarantees that the crèche could not suggest that a particular faith had been singled out for public favor and recognition."

Does the dissent's approach require that government have "exclusively secular" objectives? If so, is this inconsistent with the Court's subsequent opinion in *Jaffree* that "a statute that is motivated in part by a religious purpose may satisfy the first [*Lemon*] criterion."

(b) Two cases in 2005 involving the Ten Commandments further considered the issue of secular purpose. *McCreary*, below, was the first since *Allegheny County* to invalidate a public acknowledgment of religion outside the context of the public schools.

McCREARY COUNTY v. ACLU, 545 U.S. 844 (2005), per SOUTER, J. held that posting copies of the Ten Commandments in two Kentucky county courthouses violated the Establishment Clause because of a "predominantly religious purpose": "When government acts with the ostensible and predominant purpose of advancing religion, it violates that central Establishment Clause value of official religious neutrality * * * .

"Examination of purpose is a staple of statutory interpretation [and] is a key element of a good deal of constitutional doctrine, e.g., *Washington v. Davis*, [Ch. 9, Sec. 2, III] (discriminatory purpose required for Equal Protection violation); *Hunt v. Washington State Apple Advertising Comm'n*, [Ch. 4, Sec. 2, I] (discriminatory purpose relevant to dormant Commerce Clause claim); *Church of Lukumi Babalu Aye, Inc. v. Hialeah*, [Sec. 2, I infra] (discriminatory purpose raises level of scrutiny required by free exercise claim). [S]crutinizing purpose does make practical sense, [where] an understanding of official objective emerges from readily discoverable fact, without any judicial psychoanalysis of a drafter's heart of hearts [, and when "openly available data supported a commonsense conclusion that a religious objective permeated the government's action."] The eyes that look to purpose belong to an 'objective observer,' one who takes account of the traditional external signs that show up in the 'text, legislative history, and implementation of the statute,' or comparable official act. *Santa Fe Ind. School Dist.* [note 3 infra].[56] [A]lthough a legislature's stated reasons will generally get deference, the secular purpose required has to be genuine, not a sham, and not merely secondary to a religious objective.[13]"

The Court's detailed examination of the record showed that the counties first posted only the Ten Commandments. When suit was filed, the counties adopted "resolutions reciting that the Ten Commandments are 'the precedent legal code upon which the civil and criminal codes [of] Kentucky are founded,' and stating several grounds for taking that position," most of which were related to religion. The displays were expanded to include "eight other documents in smaller frames, each either having a religious theme or excerpted to highlight a religious element," including the Preamble to the Constitution, the Mayflower Compact, and Presidential Proclamations. After a preliminary injunction was issued, the counties installed another display, "the third within a year," entitled "The Foundations of American Law and Government Display," made up "of nine framed documents of equal size" including the Bill of Rights and a picture of Lady Justice, all with statements about their historical and legal significance.

"[T]he Commandments 'are undeniably a sacred text in the Jewish and Christian faiths' [*Stone v. Graham*]. This is not to deny that the Commandments have had influence on civil or secular law; [but where] the text is set out, the insistence of the religious message is hard to avoid in the absence of a context plausibly suggesting a message going beyond an excuse to promote the religious point of view.[57] [W]e do not decide that the Counties' past actions forever taint any effort on their part to deal with the subject matter. [But] a conclusion that centuries-old purposes may no longer be operative says nothing about the relevance of recent evidence of purpose.[58] [Nor] do we have occasion

[56] For the view favoring "a search for actual purpose" because the "form and function" of the "reasonable observer" are "unprecedently malleable and thus dangerously uncertain," see Kristi L. Bowman, *Seeing Government Purpose Through the Objective Observer's Eyes: The Evolution-Intelligent Design Debates,* 29 Harv. J. L. & Pub. Policy 419 (2006).

[13] **[Ct's Note]** The dissent nonetheless maintains that the purpose test is satisfied so long as any secular purpose for the government action is apparent. [While] heightened deference to legislatures is appropriate for the review of economic legislation, an approach that credits any valid purpose, no matter how trivial, has not been the way the Court has approached government action that implicates establishment.

[57] As for *Marsh* and *Lynch*, "créches placed with holiday symbols and prayers by legislators do not insistently call for religious action on the part of citizens; the history of posting the Commandments expressed a purpose to urge citizens to act in prescribed ways as a personal response to divine authority."

[58] Does the Court's analysis "penalize government actors for good-faith efforts to conform their actions to the Establishment Clause while litigation is in progress"? See Edith B. Clement,

here to hold that a sacred text can never be integrated constitutionally into a governmental display on the subject of law, or American history. * * *

"The dissent, however, puts forward a limitation on the application of the neutrality principle [to] show that the Framers understood [that] government may espouse a tenet of traditional monotheism. [This] means that government should be free to approve the core beliefs of a favored religion over the tenets of others, a view that should trouble anyone who prizes religious liberty. [But] there is also evidence supporting the proposition that the Framers intended the Establishment Clause to require governmental neutrality [in] statements acknowledging religion."

SCALIA, joined by Rehnquist, C.J., and Thomas, J., and by Kennedy, J., in the final two ¶s below, dissented: "[B]oth historical fact [pointing to actions beginning with President Washington and the First Congress to Congress's unanimous action in 2002 approving "under God" in the Pledge of Allegiance] and current practice ["federal, state and local governments across the Nation" have displayed the Ten Commandments] [contradict] the demonstrably false principle that the government cannot favor religion over irreligion. [T]he principle that the government cannot favor one religion over another [is valid] where public aid or assistance to religion [or] where the free exercise of religion is at issue, but it necessarily applies in a more limited sense to public acknowledgment of the Creator. [Nothing] stands behind the Court's assertion that governmental affirmation of the society's belief in God is unconstitutional except the Court's own say-so, [going] back no farther than the mid–20th [century. In] the context of public acknowledgments of God there are legitimate *competing* interests: On the one hand, the interest of that minority in not feeling 'excluded'; but on the other, the interest of the overwhelming majority of religious believers in being able to give God thanks and supplication *as a people,* and with respect to our national endeavors.[59]

"[The] constitutional problem, the Court says, is with the Counties' *purpose* in erecting the Foundations Displays, not the displays themselves. The Court [adds]: 'One consequence of taking account of the purpose underlying past actions is that the same government action may be constitutional if taken in the first instance and unconstitutional if it has a sectarian heritage.' This inconsistency may be explicable in theory, but I suspect that the 'objective observer' with whom the Court is so concerned will recognize its absurdity in [practice.] Displays erected in silence (and under the direction of good legal advice) are permissible, while those hung after discussion and debate are deemed unconstitutional. Reduction of the Establishment Clause to such minutiae trivializes the Clause's protection against religious establishment;

Public Displays of Affection . . . For God: Religious Monuments After McCreary and Van Orden, 32 Harv. J. L. & Pub. Pol'y 231 (2009).

[59] For strong criticism of Scalia, J.'s opinion, see Thomas B. Colby, *A Constitutional Hierarchy of Religions? Justice Scalia, the Ten Commandments, and the Future of the Establishment Clause,* 100 Nw. U. L. Rev. 1097 (2006).

indeed, it may inflame religious passions by making the passing comments of every government official the subject of endless litigation.

"In any event, the Court's conclusion that the Counties exhibited the Foundations Displays with the purpose of promoting religion is doubtful. [If,] as discussed above, the Commandments have a proper place in our civic history, even placing them by themselves can be civically motivated— especially when they are placed [in] a courthouse. [What] Justice Kennedy said of the crèche in *Allegheny County* is equally true of the Counties' original Ten Commandments displays [quoting last paragraph on p. 1254]. [They] are assuredly a religious symbol, but they are not so closely associated with a single religious belief that their display can reasonably be understood as preferring one religious sect over another. The Ten Commandments are recognized by Judaism, Christianity, and Islam alike as divinely given."[60]

———

VAN ORDEN v. PERRY, 545 U.S. 677 (2005), upheld the display of a monument, donated by the Eagles, inscribed with the Ten Commandments on the Texas State Capitol grounds "between the Capitol and the Supreme Court building. [The] 22 acres contain 17 monuments and 21 historical markers commemorating the 'people, ideals, and events that compose Texan identity.'[1] [A]n eagle grasping the American flag, an eye inside of a pyramid, and two small tablets with what appears to be an ancient script are carved above the text of the Ten Commandments. Below the text are two Stars of David and the superimposed Greek letters Chi and Rho, which represent Christ. The bottom of the monument bears the inscription 'PRESENTED TO THE PEOPLE AND YOUTH OF TEXAS BY THE FRATERNAL ORDER OF EAGLES OF TEXAS 1961.'" REHNQUIST, C.J., joined by Scalia, Kennedy, and Thomas, JJ. wrote the plurality opinion: "Our institutions presuppose a Supreme Being, yet these institutions must not press religious observances upon their citizens. Reconciling [these] requires that we neither abdicate our responsibility to maintain a division

---

[60] For development of the thesis that "government is not forbidden to act on religious beliefs or to make religious expressions [but] should avoid acting on religion in ways that are unnecessarily or gratuitously narrow or exclusionary," see Steven D. Smith, *Nonestablishment "Under God"? The Nonsectarian Principle*, 50 Vill.L.Rev. 1 (2005). Contrast Frederick M. Gedicks & Roger Hendrix, *Uncivil Religion: Judeo-Christianity and the Ten Commandments,* 110 W. Va. L. Rev. 275 (2007): "Judeo-Christianity excludes too many Americans for it to function as a unifying civil religion" for two reasons: (1) "dramatic increases in unbelievers, practitioners of non-Western religions, and adherents to postmodern spirituality now leave large numbers of Americans outside the boundaries of Judeo-Christianity" and (2) "the sectarianization of Judeo-Christianity by conservative Christians makes it difficult even for some monotheistic believers to see their beliefs reflected in its symbols and practices."

[1] **[Ct's Note]** The monuments are: Heroes of the Alamo, Hood's Brigade, Confederate Soldiers, Volunteer Fireman, Terry's Texas Rangers, Texas Cowboy, Spanish-American War, Texas National Guard, Ten Commandments, Tribute to Texas School Children, Texas Pioneer Woman, The Boy Scouts' Statue of Liberty Replica, Pearl Harbor Veterans, Korean War Veterans, Soldiers of World War I, Disabled Veterans, and Texas Peace Officers.

between church and state nor evince a hostility to religion by disabling the government from in some ways recognizing our religious heritage. * * *

"Whatever may be the fate of the *Lemon* test in the larger scheme of Establishment Clause jurisprudence, we think it not useful in dealing with the sort of passive monument that Texas has erected on its Capitol grounds. Instead, our analysis is driven both by the nature of the monument and by our Nation's history. As we explained in *Lynch,* 'There is an unbroken history of official acknowledgment by all three branches of government of the role of religion in American life from at least 1789.' [Recognition] of the role of God in our Nation's heritage has also been reflected in our decisions. We have acknowledged, for example, that 'religion has been closely identified with our history and government,' *Schempp,* and that '[t]he history of man is inseparable from the history of religion,' *Engel.* This recognition has led us to hold that the Establishment Clause permits a state legislature to open its daily sessions with a prayer by a chaplain paid by the State. *Marsh.*[8] Such a practice, we thought, was 'deeply embedded in the history and tradition of this country.' [In] this case we are faced with a display of the Ten Commandments on government property outside the Texas State Capitol. [Such] acknowledgments [are] common throughout America [and] can be seen throughout a visitor's tour of our Nation's Capital. * * *

"Of course, the Ten Commandments are religious. [According] to Judeo-Christian belief, the Ten Commandments were given to Moses by God on Mt. Sinai. But Moses was a lawgiver as well as a religious leader. And the Ten Commandments have an undeniable historical meaning, as the foregoing examples demonstrate. Simply having religious content or promoting a message consistent with a religious doctrine does not run afoul of the Establishment Clause. There are, of course, limits to the display of religious messages or symbols. [*Stone*] stands as an example of the fact that we have 'been particularly vigilant in monitoring compliance with the Establishment Clause in elementary and secondary schools.' [The] placement of the Ten Commandments monument on the Texas State Capitol grounds is a far more passive use of those texts than was the case in *Stone,* where the text confronted elementary school students every day."[61]

BREYER, J. concurred only in the judgment: "[T]he Establishment Clause does not compel the government to purge from the public sphere all that in any way partakes of the religious. Such absolutism is not only inconsistent with our national traditions, but would also tend to promote the kind of social conflict the Establishment Clause seeks to avoid. Thus, [the] Court has found no single mechanical formula that can accurately draw the constitutional line in every case. [T]ests designed to measure 'neutrality' alone are insufficient,

---

[8] **[Ct's Note]** Indeed, [i]n *Marsh,* the prayers were often explicitly Christian, but the chaplain removed all references to Christ the year after the suit was filed.

[61] Scalia, J., concurred based on his rationale in *McCreary.* Thomas, J., concurred, urging that the Court should "return to the views of the Framers" and hold that the Establishment Clause does not apply to the states, or even if it does, the Court should "adopt coercion as the touchstone for our Establishment Clause inquiry."

both because it is sometimes difficult to determine when a legal rule is 'neutral,' and because 'untutored devotion to the concept of neutrality can lead to invocation or approval of results which partake not simply of that noninterference and noninvolvement with the religious which the Constitution commands, but of a brooding and pervasive devotion to the secular and a passive, or even active, hostility to the religious.'

"[O]ne will inevitably find difficult borderline cases. And in such cases, I see no test-related substitute for the exercise of legal judgment. That judgment is not a personal judgment. Rather, as in all constitutional cases, it must reflect and remain faithful to the underlying purposes of the Clauses, and it must take account of context and consequences measured in light of those purposes. While the Court's prior tests provide useful guideposts—and might well lead to the same result the Court reaches today—no exact formula can dictate a resolution to such fact-intensive cases. [In] certain contexts, a display of the tablets of the Ten Commandments can convey not simply a religious message but also a secular moral message (about proper standards of social conduct). And in certain contexts, a display of the tablets can also convey a historical message (about a historic relation between those standards and the law)—a fact that helps to explain the display of those tablets in dozens of courthouses throughout the Nation, including the Supreme Court of the United States.

"Here [the] Fraternal Order of Eagles, a private civic (and primarily secular) organization, while interested in the religious aspect of the Ten Commandments, sought to highlight the Commandments' role in shaping civic morality as part of that organization's efforts to combat juvenile delinquency. [The] monument sits in a large park containing 17 monuments and 21 historical markers, all designed to illustrate the 'ideals' of those who settled in Texas and of those who have lived there since that time. The setting does not readily lend itself to meditation or any other religious activity. [T]he context suggests that the State intended the display's moral message—an illustrative message reflecting the historical 'ideals' of Texans—to predominate. [The] 40 years [that] passed in which the presence of this monument, legally speaking, went unchallenged suggest [that] the public visiting the capitol grounds has considered the religious aspect of the tablets' message as part of what is a broader moral and historical message reflective of a cultural heritage. [This] case also differs from *McCreary County*, where the short (and stormy) history of the courthouse Commandments' displays demonstrates the substantially religious objectives of those who mounted them, and the effect of this readily apparent objective upon those who view them. [This] display has stood apparently uncontested for nearly two generations. That experience helps us understand that as a practical matter of *degree* this display is unlikely to prove divisive. And this matter of degree is, I believe, critical in a borderline case such as this one. At the same time, to reach a contrary conclusion [would], I fear, lead the law to exhibit a hostility toward religion [that] might well encourage disputes concerning the removal of longstanding depictions of the Ten Commandments from public buildings across the Nation. And it could thereby create the very kind of religiously based divisiveness that the Establishment Clause seeks to avoid."[62]

STEVENS, J., joined by Ginsburg, J., dissented: "Viewed on its face, Texas' display has no purported connection to God's role in the formation of Texas or the founding of our Nation; nor does it provide the reasonable observer with any basis to guess that it was erected to honor any individual or organization. The message [is:] This State endorses the divine code of the 'Judeo-Christian' God. [In] my judgment [the] Establishment Clause has created a strong presumption against the display of religious symbols on public property. [This] Court has often recognized 'an unbroken history of official acknowledgment [of] the role of religion in American life.' [This] case, however, is not about historic preservation or the mere recognition of religion. [This] Nation's resolute commitment to neutrality with respect to religion is flatly inconsistent with the plurality's wholehearted validation of an official state endorsement of the message that there is one, and only one, God.

"[B]y disseminating the 'law of God'—directing fidelity to God and proscribing murder, theft, and adultery—the Eagles hope that this divine guidance will help wayward youths conform their behavior and improve their lives. In my judgment, the significant secular by-products that are intended consequences of religious instruction—indeed, of the establishment of most religions—are not the type of 'secular' purposes that justify government promulgation of sacred religious messages. [The] State may admonish its citizens not to lie, cheat or steal, to honor their parents and to respect their neighbors' property; and it [may] provide its schoolchildren and adult citizens with educational materials that explain the important role that our forebears' faith in God played. [The] message at issue in this case, however, is fundamentally different from either a bland admonition to observe generally accepted rules of behavior or a general history lesson. [It] cannot be analogized to an appendage to a common article of commerce ('In God we Trust') or an incidental part of a familiar recital ('God save the United States and this honorable Court'). * * *

"Even if [the] message of the monument, despite the inscribed text, fairly could be said to represent the belief system of all Judeo-Christians,[63] it would still run afoul of the Establishment Clause by prescribing a compelled code of conduct from one God, namely a Judeo-Christian God, that is rejected by prominent polytheistic sects, such as Hinduism, as well as nontheistic religions, such as Buddhism. [E]xamination of the Decalogue's prominent display at the seat of Texas government, rather than generic citation to the role of religion in American life, unmistakably reveals on which side of the

---

[62] For the view that legislative prayers (upheld in *Marsh*) present a more "divisive political issue" than other public acknowledgements of religion (such as Ten Commandments) where "government has virtually no discretion over the religious content," see Christopher C. Lund, *Legislative Prayer and the Secret Costs of Religious Endorsements,* 94 Minn. L. Rev. 972 (2010).

[63] "There are many distinctive versions of the Decalogue, ascribed to by different religions and even different denominations within a particular faith; to a pious and learned observer, these differences may be of enormous religious significance." See Lubet, *The Ten Commandments in Alabama,* 15 Constitutional Commentary 471 (1998).

'slippery slope,' (Breyer, J., concurring in judgment), this display must fall. * * *

"The speeches and rhetoric characteristic of the founding era [do] not answer the question before us. [W]hen public officials deliver public speeches, we recognize that their words are not exclusively a transmission from *the* government because those oratories have embedded within them the inherently personal views of the speaker as an individual member of the polity. The permanent placement of a textual religious display on state property is different in kind; it amalgamates otherwise discordant individual views into a collective statement of government approval. [M]any of the Founders who are often cited as authoritative expositors of the Constitution's original meaning understood the Establishment Clause to stand for a *narrower* proposition than the plurality [is] willing to accept. Namely, many of the Framers understood the word 'religion' in the Establishment Clause to encompass only the various sects of Christianity. [Scalia, J.'s] inclusion of Judaism and Islam [in his *McCreary* dissent] is a laudable act of religious tolerance, but it is one that is unmoored from the Constitution's history and text, and moreover one that is patently arbitrary in its inclusion of some, but exclusion of other (e.g., Buddhism), widely practiced non-Christian religions. * * *

"A reading of the First Amendment dependent on [the] purported original meanings [would] permit States to construct walls of their own choosing— Baptists inside, Mormons out; Jewish Orthodox inside, Jewish Reform out. [As] we have said in the context of statutory interpretation, legislation 'often [goes] beyond the principal evil [at which the statute was aimed] to cover reasonably comparable evils, and it is ultimately the provisions of our laws rather than the principal concerns of our legislators by which we are governed.' In similar fashion, we have construed the Equal Protection Clause [to] prohibit segregated schools, even though those who drafted [the Fourteenth] Amendment evidently thought that separate was not unequal. We have held that the same Amendment prohibits discrimination against individuals on account of their gender, despite the fact that the contemporaries of the Amendment 'doubt[ed] very much whether any action of a State not directed by way of discrimination against the negroes as a class, or on account of their race, will ever be held to come within the purview of this provision,' And we have construed 'evolving standards of decency' to make impermissible practices that were not considered 'cruel and unusual' at the founding. * * *

"The principle that guides my analysis is neutrality.[35] [As] religious pluralism has expanded, so has our acceptance of what constitutes valid belief systems. The evil of discriminating today against atheists, "polytheists[,] and

---

[35] **[Ct's Note]** [Thomas, J.'s] "coercion view," [would] not prohibit explicit state endorsements of religious orthodoxies of particular sects, actions that lie at the heart of what the Clause was meant to regulate. The government could, for example, take out television advertisements lauding Catholicism as the only pure religion. [T]hose programs would not be coercive because the viewer could simply turn off the television or ignore the ad. [*Query*: Would this involve using compulsorily raised tax funds for religious purposes? See Choper, p. 1283, at 16–19 infra.]

Further, [e]nshrining coercion as the Establishment Clause touchstone fails to eliminate the difficult judgment calls regarding "the form that coercion must take." * * *

believers in unconcerned deities," *McCreary County,* (Scalia, J., dissenting), is in my view a direct descendent of the evil of discriminating among Christian sects. The Establishment Clause thus forbids it and, in turn, forbids Texas from displaying the Ten Commandments monument the plurality so casually affirms."

SOUTER, J., joined by Stevens and Ginsburg, JJ., also dissented: "A governmental display of an obviously religious text cannot be squared with neutrality, except in a setting that plausibly indicates that the statement is not placed in view with a predominant purpose on the part of government either to adopt the religious message or to urge its acceptance by others.[1] "[A] pedestrian happening upon the monument at issue here needs no training in religious doctrine to realize that the statement of the Commandments, quoting God himself, proclaims that the will of the divine being is the source of obligation to obey the rules, including the facially secular ones. [The] word 'Lord' appears in all capital letters (as does the word 'am'), so that the most eye-catching segment of the quotation is the declaration 'I AM the LORD thy God.' [T]he government of Texas is telling everyone who sees the monument to live up to a moral code because God requires it, [as] the inheritances specifically of Jews and Christians. [It] stands in contrast to any number of perfectly constitutional depictions of [the Commandments], the frieze of our own Courtroom providing a good example, where the figure of Moses stands among history's great lawgivers. [N]o one looking at the lines of figures in marble relief is likely to see a religious purpose. [T]he viewers may just as naturally see the tablets of the Commandments (showing the later ones, forbidding things like killing and theft, but without the divine preface) as background from which the concept of law emerged. [But] 17 monuments with no common appearance, history, or esthetic role scattered over 22 acres is not a museum, and anyone strolling around the lawn would surely take each memorial on its own terms.[6]

"To be sure, Kentucky's compulsory-education law [in *Stone*] meant that the schoolchildren were forced to see the display every day, whereas many see the monument by choice, and those who customarily walk the Capitol grounds can presumably avoid it if they choose. But [this] distinction should make no difference. The monument in this case sits on the grounds [of] the civic home of every one of the State's citizens. [A]ny citizen should be able to visit that civic home without having to confront religious expressions clearly meant to convey an official religious position that may be at odds with his own religion, or with rejection of religion.

"Finally, [I] do not see a persuasive argument [that] Van Orden's lawsuit comes '[f]orty years after the monument's erection.' [We] have approved

---

¹ **[Ct's Note]** [In this] case, [it] was not just the terms of the moral code, but the proclamation that the terms of the code were enjoined by God, that the Eagles put forward in the monuments they donated.

⁶ **[Ct's Note]** [A]lthough the nativity scene in *Allegheny County* was donated by the Holy Name Society, we concluded that "[n]o viewer could reasonably think that [the scene] occupies [its] location [at the seat of county government] without the support and approval of the government."

framing-era practices because they must originally have been understood as constitutionally permissible, e.g., *Marsh*, and we have recognized that Sunday laws have grown recognizably secular over time, *McGowan*. There is also an analogous argument, not yet evaluated, that ritualistic religious expression can become so numbing over time that its initial Establishment Clause violation becomes at some point too diminished for notice. [But] other explanations may do better in accounting for the late resort to the courts. Suing a State over religion puts nothing in a plaintiff's pocket and can take a great deal out, and even with volunteer litigators to supply time and energy, the risk of social ostracism can be powerfully deterrent."[64]

2. ***Differing interpretations of the "coercion" test.*** (a) LEE v. WEISMAN, 505 U.S. 577 (1992), per KENNEDY, J., held violative of the Establishment Clause the practice of public school officials inviting members of the clergy to offer invocation and benediction prayers at graduation ceremonies: "[The] school district's supervision and control of a high school graduation ceremony places public pressure, as well as peer pressure, on attending students to stand as a group or, at least, maintain respectful silence during the Invocation and Benediction. [Finding] no violation [would] place objectors in the dilemma of participating, with all that implies, or protesting. * * * Research in psychology supports the common assumption that adolescents are often susceptible to pressure from their peers towards conformity, and that the influence is strongest in matters of social convention.[65] [That] the intrusion was in the course of promulgating religion that sought to be civic or nonsectarian rather than pertaining to one sect does not lessen the offense or isolation to the objectors. At best it narrows their number, at worst increases their sense of isolation and affront.

"[I]n our society and in our culture high school graduation is one of life's most significant occasions. * * * Attendance may not be required by official decree, yet it is apparent that a student is not free to absent herself from the graduation exercise in any real sense of the term 'voluntary,' for absence would require forfeiture of these intangible benefits which have motivated the student through youth and all her high school years.[66] [To] say that a student

---

[64] O'Connor, J., dissented, "for essentially the reasons given by Justice Souter." See also Alan Brownstein, *A Decent Respect for Religious Liberty and Religious Equality: Justice O'Connor's Interpretation of the Religion Clause of the First Amendment*, 32 McG.L.Rev. 837, 854–55 (2001): "Often minority groups tolerate what they cannot change because they realize it is futile to express opposition or are intimidated from doing so. Majorities, on the other hand, will all too often choose to misinterpret resigned acceptance to unequal treatment as an indication that no real harm is being done and that the system is operating fairly." For the view that the majorities' "desacralization" of "religious symbols of deep spiritual significance into cultural artifacts," in *Lynch*, *Allegheny* and *Van Orden*, means that "any more such victories for religion, and it will be truly undone," see generally Frederick M. Gedicks, *The Rhetoric of Church and State* (Duke 1995).

[65] For criticism of the psychological evidence relied on by the Court, see Donald N. Bersoff & David J. Glass, *The Not-So Weisman: The Supreme Court's Continuing Misuse of Social Science Research*, 2 U.Chi.L.S.Roundtable 279 (1995).

[66] Consider Steven G. Gey, *Religious Coercion and the Establishment Clause*, 1994 U.Ill.L.Rev. 463: "But a citizen of Allegheny County may also be compelled to transact business in the county courthouse, which would inevitably require that person to pass by the prominent display of the birth of the Christian savior. If the Allegheny County citizen is not coerced by being

must remain apart from the ceremony at the opening invocation and closing benediction is to risk compelling conformity in an environment analogous to the classroom setting, where we have said the risk of compulsion is especially high. See *Engel* and *Schempp*. [The] atmosphere at the opening of a session of a state legislature [as in *Marsh*] where adults are free to enter and leave with little comment and for any number of reasons cannot compare with the constraining potential of the one school event most important for the student to attend. * * * People may take offense at all manner of religious as well as nonreligious messages, but offense alone does not in every case show a violation. We know too that sometimes to endure social isolation or even anger may be the price of conscience or nonconformity. But, by any reading of our cases, the conformity required of the student in this case was too high an exaction to withstand the test of the Establishment Clause."

BLACKMUN, J., joined by Stevens and O'Connor, JJ., who joined the Court's opinion, concurred: "[I]t is not enough that the government restrain from compelling religious practices: it must not engage in them either. [To] that end, our cases have prohibited government endorsement of religion, its sponsorship, and active involvement in religion, whether or not citizens were coerced to conform." Souter, J., who also joined the Court's opinion also concurred on similar grounds

SCALIA, J., joined by Rehnquist, C.J., and White and Thomas, JJ., dissented: "Three terms ago, I joined an opinion recognizing that 'the meaning of the [Establishment] Clause is to be determined by reference to historical practices and understandings.' * * * *Allegheny County* (Kennedy, J., concurring in judgment in part and dissenting in part). These views of course prevent me from joining today's opinion, [which] lays waste a tradition that is as old as public-school graduation ceremonies themselves. [Since] the Court does not dispute that students exposed to prayer at graduation ceremonies retain (despite 'subtle coercive pressures,') the free will to sit, there is absolutely no basis for the Court's decision. It is fanciful enough to say that 'a reasonable dissenter,' standing head erect in a class of bowed heads, 'could believe that the group exercise signified her own participation or approval of it.' It is beyond the absurd to say that she could entertain such a belief while pointedly declining to rise. But let us assume the very worst, that the nonparticipating graduate is 'subtly coerced' [to] stand! Even that half of the disjunctive does not remotely establish a 'participation' (or an 'appearance of participation') in a religious exercise. * * *

---

required to respectfully pass by the religious display, why is [the] student coerced by respectfully remaining silent during a one-minute prayer? Conversely, if 'the act of standing or remaining silent' during a graduation prayer is 'an expression of participation' in the prayer, why is walking by an overtly Christian display in respectful silence not also 'an expression of participation' in the display?"

To what extent does *Lee* apply to similar practices at public universities? See *Bunting v. Mellen*, 541 U.S. 1019 (2004) (opinions respecting denial of certiorari).

For an intensive dissection of the "coercion" approach, see Mark Strasser, *The Coercion Test: On Prayer, Offense, and Doctrinal Inculcation*, 53 St. Louis U. L. J. 417 (2009).

"The deeper flaw in the Court's opinion does not lie in its wrong answer to the question whether there was state-induced 'peer-pressure' coercion; it lies, rather, in the Court's making violation of the Establishment Clause hinge on such a precious question. The coercion that was a hallmark of historical establishments of religion was coercion of religious orthodoxy and of financial support by force of *law and threat of penalty*. [I] concede that our constitutional tradition [has] ruled out of order government-sponsored endorsement of religion—even when no legal coercion is present, and indeed even when no ersatz, 'peer-pressure' psycho-coercion is present—where the endorsement is sectarian, in the sense of specifying details upon which men and women who believe in a benevolent, omnipotent Creator and Ruler of the world, are known to differ (for example, the divinity of Christ). But there is simply no support for the proposition that the officially sponsored nondenominational invocation and benediction read by Rabbi Gutterman—with no one legally coerced to recite them—violated the Constitution of the United States.[67] To the contrary, they are so characteristically American they could have come from the pen of George Washington or Abraham Lincoln himself.

"The Court relies on our 'school prayer' cases, *Engel* and *Schempp*. But whatever the merit of those cases, they [do] not constitute an exception to the rule, distilled from historical practice, that public ceremonies may include prayer; rather, they simply do not fall within the scope of the rule (for the obvious reason that school instruction is not a public ceremony). Second, we have made clear our understanding that school prayer occurs within a framework [of] legal coercion to attend [school]. Voluntary prayer at graduation—a one-time ceremony at which parents, friends and relatives are present—can hardly be thought to raise the same concerns."

(b) GREECE v. GALLOWAY, 134 S.Ct. 1811 (2014): A town invited or permitted "ministers or laypersons ["within its borders"] of any persuasion, including [in 2008] an atheist, [a] Jewish layman and the chairman of the local Baha'i temple [and] a Wiccan priestess" to give an opening prayer at monthly town board meetings. The invocations, however, reflecting "the predominantly Christian identity of the town's congregations," often invoked Jesus Christ and similar "Christian themes" and said "let us pray" and asked the "audience members to stand and bow their heads."

The Court, per KENNEDY, J., held "that the Establishment Clause must be interpreted 'by reference to historical practices and understandings,' " and noted that "since the framing of the Constitution," Congress "and the majority of the other States had the same, consistent practice": [An] insistence on nonsectarian or ecumenical prayer as a single, fixed standard is not consistent with our tradition," and that "Congress continues to permit [its] chaplains to

---

[67] Compare Gey, supra, at 507: "If dissenting audience members at a state-sponsored public event may walk away from the affair without subjecting themselves to legal penalties, it should not matter whether a prayer given at that function incorporates the tenets of a particular sect, or comments unfavorably on the tenets of another sect. It should not matter even if the government sponsors a prayer overtly hostile to one or more faiths, so long as the dissenters are allowed to ignore the government's advice and practice their own beliefs freely."

express themselves in a religious idiom." The "contention that legislative prayer must be generic or nonsectarian derives from dictum in *County of Allegheny* that was disputed when written and has been repudiated in later cases. [To] hold that invocations must be nonsectarian would force the legislatures that sponsor prayers and the courts that are asked to decide these cases to act as supervisors and censors of religious speech, a rule that would involve government in religious matters" and produce "the difficulty, indeed the futility, of sifting sectarian from nonsectarian speech, [a] form of government entanglement with religion that is far more troublesome than the current approach.

"[T]he Court does not imply that no constraints remain. [If the] practice over time shows that the invocations denigrate nonbelievers or religious minorities, threaten damnation, or preach conversion, many present may consider the prayer to fall short of the desire to elevate the purpose of the occasion and to unite lawmakers in their common effort. [But] our tradition assumes that adult citizens, firm in their own beliefs, can tolerate and perhaps appreciate a ceremonial prayer delivered by a person of a different faith. [That] a prayer is given in the name of Jesus, Allah, or Jehovah, or that it makes passing reference to religious doctrines, does not remove it from that tradition."

KENNEDY, J., joined by Roberts, C.J., and Alito, J., distinguished *Lee*: "The inquiry [regarding coercion] remains a fact-sensitive one that considers both the setting in which the prayer arises and the audience to whom it is directed. [T]he reasonable observer is acquainted with [and] understands that its purposes are to lend gravity to public proceedings and to acknowledge the place religion holds in the lives of many private citizens, not to afford government an opportunity to proselytize.[68] [Although] board members themselves stood, bowed their heads, or made the sign of the cross during the prayer, they at no point solicited similar gestures by the public. [T]he circumstances [in *Lee*] are not present in this case, [which involves] mature adults, who 'presumably' are 'not readily susceptible to religious indoctrination or peer pressure.' "[69]

KAGAN, J., joined by Ginsburg, Breyer, and Sotomayor, JJ., dissented: "[U]nder *Marsh*, legislative prayer has a distinctive constitutional warrant by virtue of tradition," but the Greece "Board's meetings are also occasions for ordinary citizens to engage with and petition their government." The prayers were "addressed directly to the Town's citizenry [with "10 or so citizens in attendance"], and the speaker [might ask the audience] to recite a common prayer with him. [Thus, they] were *more* sectarian, and *less* inclusive, than [in] *Marsh*. [I]n this citizen-centered venue, government officials must take steps to ensure—as none of Greece's Board members ever did—that opening prayers are inclusive of different faiths, rather than always identified with a single

---

[68] Should prayers at public meetings in which "speakers pray in their own name" be treated differently than "praying in the name of the meeting's participants"? See Alan Brownstein, *Town of Greece v. Galloway: Constitutional Challenges to State-Sponsored Prayers at Local Government Meetings*, 47 UC Davis L. Rev. 1521 (2014).

[69] Thomas, J., joined by Scalia, J., added a concurrence on what constitutes "coercion," as stated in his *Elk Grove* opinion, infra.

religion." In *Marsh* some of the Presbyterian minister's "earlier prayers explicitly invoked Christian beliefs, but he 'removed all references to Christ' after a single legislator complained," whereas in Greece, "[a]bout two-thirds of the prayers given over this decade or so invoked 'Jesus,' 'Christ,' 'Your Son,' or 'the Holy Spirit.' "[70] * * *

"Let's say that a Muslim citizen of Greece goes before the Board to share her views on policy or request some permit. [She] must think—it is hardly paranoia, but only the truth—that Christian worship has become entwined with local governance," and she is put "to the unenviable choice of either pretending to pray like the majority or declining to join its communal activity, at the very moment of petitioning their elected leaders. [When] a person goes to court, a polling place, or an immigration proceeding, [etc.], government officials do not engage in sectarian worship, nor do they ask her to do likewise. [Why] not, then, at a town meeting?

" * * * Greece had multiple ways of incorporating prayer into its town meetings [so as to] forge common bonds, rather than divide. [It] might have invited clergy of many faiths to serve as chaplains [as] Congress does. [T]he Board 'maintains [that] it would welcome a prayer by any minister or layman who wishe[s] to give one,' [but that] representation has never been publicized; nor has the Board (except for a few months surrounding this suit's filing) offered the chaplain's role to any non-Christian clergy or layman."[71]

(c)　ELK GROVE UNIFIED SCHOOL DIST. v. NEWDOW, 542 U.S. 1 (2004), reversed the Ninth Circuit's decision that daily classroom recitation by the teacher of the Pledge of Allegiance, with the words "Under God" added in 1954 by Congress, violates the Establishment Clause.[72] The Court held that the father of the schoolgirl had no standing, see Ch. 12, Sec. 2, I. Three Justices reached the merits and would reverse. REHNQUIST, C.J., joined by O'Connor, J., noted that the sponsor of the 1954 amendment "said its purpose was to contrast this country's belief in God with the Soviet Union's embrace of atheism. We do not know what other Members of Congress [thought]. Following the decision of the Court of Appeals in this case, Congress [made] extensive findings about the historic role of religion in the political development of the Nation and reaffirmed the text of the Pledge. To the

---

[70] Alito, J., joined by Scalia, J., concurring "to respond to the principal dissent": "[W]hat is important is not so much what happened in Nebraska in the years prior to *Marsh*, but what happened before congressional sessions during the period leading up to the adoption of the First Amendment."

[71] Alito, J.'s concurrence commented that under a "best practices standard, "this advice has much to recommend it," but as a constitutional requirement, it "runs headlong into a long history of contrary congressional practice." In any event, "as our country has become more diverse, composing a prayer that is acceptable to all members of the community who hold religious beliefs has [become] daunting, if not impossible." If the "clerical employees" who compiled the list of invitees from the town directory had "realized that the town's Jewish residents attended synagogues on the Rochester side of the border [she] would have added one or more synagogues to the list. But the mistake was at worst careless, [not] with a discriminatory intent."

[72] For the view that "the Court's precedents provide abundant support" for the Ninth Circuit's decision, see Steven G. Gey, *"Under God," The Pledge of Allegiance, and Other Constitutional Trivia*, 81 N.C.L.Rev. 1865 (2003).

millions of people who regularly recite the Pledge, and who have no access to, or concern with, such legislation or legislative history, 'under God' might mean several different [things]. Examples of patriotic invocations of God and official acknowledgments of religion's role in our Nation's history abound. * * *

"I do not believe that the phrase 'under God' in the Pledge converts its recital into a 'religious exercise' of the sort described in *Lee*. [It is] in no sense a prayer, nor an endorsement of any religion. [It] is a patriotic exercise, not a religious one; participants promise fidelity to our flag and our Nation, not to any particular God, faith, or church."

O'CONNOR, J., added: "For centuries, we have marked important occasions or pronouncements with references to God and invocations of divine assistance. [These] can serve to solemnize an occasion instead of to invoke divine provenance. The reasonable observer [,] fully aware of our national history and the origins of such practices, would not perceive these [as] signifying a government endorsement of any specific religion, or even of religion over non-religion.[73]

"There are no de minimis violations of the Constitution. [But] government can, in a discrete category of cases, acknowledge or refer to the divine without offending the Constitution. This category of 'ceremonial deism' most clearly encompasses such things as the national motto ("In God We Trust"), religious references in traditional patriotic songs such as the Star-Spangled Banner, and the words with which the Marshal of this Court opens each of its sessions. See *Allegheny County* (opinion of O'Connor, J.). [Although] it is a close question, I conclude that [the Pledge is "an instance of ceremonial deism." It] complies with [the] requirement [that "no religious acknowledgment could claim to be an instance of ceremonial deism if it explicitly favored one particular religious belief system over another"]. It does not refer to a nation 'under Jesus' or 'under Vishnu,' but instead acknowledges religion in [a] simple reference to a generic 'God.' Of course, some religions—Buddhism, for instance—are not based upon a belief in a separate Supreme Being. But one would be hard pressed to imagine a brief solemnizing reference to religion that would adequately encompass every religious belief expressed by any citizen of this Nation."[74]

THOMAS, J., also concurred: "Adherence to *Lee* would require us to strike down the Pledge [but] *Lee* was wrongly decided. [The] kind of coercion implicated by the Religion Clauses is that accomplished *by force of law and threat of penalty*. *Lee* (Scalia, J., dissenting). Peer pressure, unpleasant as it may be, is not coercion."

---

[73] Compare Steven H. Shiffrin, *The Pluralistic Foundations of the Religion Clauses*, 90 Corn.L.Rev. 9 (2004): "[C]hildren of atheists, agnostics, and Buddhists to name a few, are quite unlikely to be aware of this history. [If] their views match their parents, they are overwhelmingly likely to think that they are 'outsiders, not full members of the political community.'"

[74] For the view that "under God" emphasizes "that the state is limited by human dignity and rights of transcendent status [, and therefore this is] a powerful reason that the Establishment Clause must permit the state to recognize this religious rationale," see Thomas C. Berg, *The Pledge of Allegiance and the Limited State*, Tex.Rev.L. & Pol. 41 (2003).

3. ***Prayer at other school activities—Issues of government purpose and involvement.*** SANTA FE IND. SCHOOL DIST. v. DOE, 530 U.S. 290 (2000), per STEVENS, J., relied on *Lee* to hold invalid the school district's policy authorizing a student election (1) to determine whether to have a student "deliver a brief invocation and/or message [at] varsity football games to solemnize the event, to promote good sportsmanship and student safety, and to establish the appropriate environment for the competition," and (2) to select "a student volunteer [to] decide what statement or invocation [which] must be nonsectarian and nonproselytizing." The Court found "the evolution of the current policy [to be] most striking," pointing to the earlier practice of having an elected "Student Chaplain [deliver] a prayer over the public address system[,] to the title—"Prayer at Football Games"—of the most recent preceding policy, which was similar to the school's policy for prayer at graduations [and to the]' stipulation that "students voted to determine whether a student would deliver prayer at varsity football games," all of which led the Court "to infer that the specific purpose of the policy was to preserve a popular 'state-sponsored religious practice.' "[75]

"[T]he District first argues that [the] messages are private student speech, not public speech. [But] these invocations are authorized by a government policy and take place on government property at government-sponsored school-related events. [Unlike *Rosenberger* and similar cases, here,] the school allows only [the] same student for the entire season to give the invocation. [T]he majoritarian process implemented by the District guarantees, by definition, that minority candidates [will] be effectively silenced. [This] encourages divisiveness along religious lines in a public school setting, a result at odds with the Establishment Clause. [And] the members of the listening audience must perceive the pregame message as a public expression of the views of the majority of the student body delivered with the approval of the school administration." As for "coercion," "we may assume [that] the informal pressure to attend an athletic event is not as strong as a senior's desire to attend her own graduation ceremony. [But] to assert that [many] high school students do not feel immense social pressure, or have a truly genuine desire, to be involved in the extracurricular event that is American high school football is 'formalistic in the extreme.' "

REHNQUIST, C.J., joined by Scalia and Thomas, JJ., dissented: "[The] policy should not be invalidated on its face. [T]he students might vote not to have a pregame speaker, in which case there would be no threat of a constitutional violation. It is also possible that the election would not focus on prayer, but on public speaking ability or social popularity. And if student

[75] "[Further], the policy, by its terms, invites and encourages religious messages [which] is the most obvious method of solemnizing an event. Moreover, the requirements that the message 'promote good citizenship' and 'establish the appropriate environment for competition' further narrow the types of message deemed appropriate, suggesting that a solemn, yet nonreligious, message, such as commentary on United States foreign policy, would be prohibited. Indeed, the only type of message that is expressly endorsed in the text is an 'invocation', [which], as used in the past at Santa Fe High School, has always entailed a focused religious message."

campaigning did begin to focus on prayer, the school might decide to implement reasonable campaign restrictions.[76]

"[A]ny speech that may occur as a result of the election process here would be private, not government, speech. [Unlike *Lee*, the] elected student, not the government, would choose what to [say.] Under the Court's view, the mere grant of power to the students to vote for such offices, in light of the fear that those elected might publicly pray, violates the Establishment Clause.[77]

"[T]he Court dismisses the [policy's "plausible secular purpose"] of solemnization.[78] [But] it is easy to think of solemn messages that are not religious in nature, for example urging that a game be fought fairly. And sporting events often begin with a solemn rendition of our national anthem, with its concluding verse 'And this be our motto: "In God is our trust."' Under the Court's logic, a public school that sponsors the singing of the national anthem before football games violates the Establishment Clause."

4. ***Differing interpretations of the "endorsement" test.*** (a) CAPITOL SQUARE REVIEW & ADVISORY BOARD v. PINETTE, 515 U.S. 753 (1995), per SCALIA, J., relying on *Widmar* and *Lamb's Chapel,* held that petitioner's permitting the Ku Klux Klan to place a Latin cross in Capitol Square—"A 10-acre, state-owned plaza surrounding the Statehouse in Columbus, Ohio"—when it had also permitted such other unattended displays as "a State-sponsored lighted tree during the Christmas season, a privately-sponsored menorah during Chanukah, a display showing the progress of a United Way fundraising campaign, and booths and exhibits during an arts festival," did not violate the Establishment Clause: "The State did not sponsor respondents' expression, the expression was made on government property

---

[76] The Court responded: "Under the *Lemon* standard, a court must invalidate a statute if it lacks 'a secular legislative purpose.' [E]ven if no Santa Fe High School student were ever to offer a religious message, [G]overnment efforts to endorse religion cannot evade constitutional reproach based solely on the remote possibility that those attempts may fail."

[77] The Court responded: "If instead of a choice between an invocation and no pregame message, the first election determined whether a political speech should be made, and the second election determined whether the speaker should be a Democrat or a Republican, it would be rather clear that the public address system was being used to deliver a partisan message reflecting the viewpoint of the majority rather than a random statement by a private individual.

"The fact that the District's policy provides for the election of the speaker only after the majority has voted on her message identifies an obvious distinction between this case and the typical election of a 'student body president, or even a newly elected prom king or queen.'"

After *Lee,* what result if the class valedictorian begins her speech with a prayer? If students are selected to give "brief inspirational messages" that are broadcast each day over the school's public address system and some messages contain religious content? For comprehensive treatment, see Kathleen A. Brady, *The Push to Private Religious Expression: Are We Missing Something?*, 70 Ford.L.Rev. 1147 (2002) ("Where student-initiated speech takes place at a school-sponsored event in a captive audience situation, the context changes the purely private character of the speech, but it does not convert the speech into government expression.").

[78] The Court responded: "When a governmental entity professes a secular purpose for an arguably religious policy, the government's characterization is, of course, entitled to some deference. But it is nonetheless the duty of the courts to 'distinguis[h] a sham secular purpose from a sincere one.' *Wallace v. Jaffree* (O'Connor, J., concurring in judgment)."

that had been opened to the public for speech, and permission was requested through the same application process [for] other private groups."

The seven-justice majority divided, however, on the scope of the "endorsement" test. SCALIA, J., joined by Rehnquist, C.J., and Kennedy and Thomas, JJ., rejected petitioners' claim based on "the forum's proximity to the seat of government, which, they contend, may produce the perception that the cross bears the State's approval": "[W]e have consistently held that it is no violation for government to enact neutral policies that happen to benefit religion. Where we have tested for endorsement of religion, the subject [was] either expression by the government itself, *Lynch,* or else government action alleged to discriminate in favor of private religious expression or activity, *Allegheny County.* [O]ne can conceive of a case in which a governmental entity manipulates its administration of a public forum close to the seat of government (or within a government building) in such a manner that only certain religious groups take advantage of it, creating an impression of endorsement that is in fact accurate. But those situations, which involve governmental favoritism, do not exist here. * * *

"The contrary view [by] Justice Stevens [infra], but endorsed by Justice Souter and Justice O'Connor [and Breyer, J.] as well, [infra], exiles private religious speech to a realm of less-protected expression. [It] is no answer to say that the Establishment Clause tempers religious speech. [T]hat Clause applies only to the words and acts of government. It [has] never been read by this Court to serve as an impediment to purely private religious speech connected to the State only through its occurrence in a public forum."[79]

O'CONNOR, J., joined by Souter and Breyer, JJ., concurred in part: "Where the government's operation of a public forum has the effect of endorsing religion, even if the governmental actor neither intends nor actively encourages that result, [the] State's own actions (operating the forum in a particular manner and permitting the religious expression to take place therein), and their relationship to the private speech at issue, actually convey a message of endorsement."[80]

STEVENS, J., dissented: "[A] paramount purpose of the Establishment Clause is to protect "[a reasonable observer"] from being made to feel like an

---

[79] Thomas, J., filed a brief concurrence, emphasizing "a cross erected by the Ku Klux Klan [is] a political act, not a Christian one."

[80] Souter, J., joined by O'Connor and Breyer, JJ., concurred "in large part because of the possibility of affixing a sign to the cross adequately disclaiming any government sponsorship or endorsement of it.

"[T]he plurality's opinion would seem to [invite] government encouragement [of religion], even when the result will be the domination of the forum by religious displays and religious speakers. [Something] of the sort, in fact, may have happened here. Immediately after the District Court issued the injunction ordering petitioners to grant the Klan's permit, a local church council [invited] all local churches to erect crosses, and the Board granted 'blanket permission' for 'all churches friendly to or affiliated with' the council to do so. [A] part of the square was strewn with crosses, and while the effect in this case may have provided more embarrassment than suspicion of endorsement, the opportunity for the latter is clear."

outsider in matters of faith. [If] a reasonable person [does so], then the State may not allow its property to be used as a forum for that [display.][81],[5]

"[The] very fact that a sign is installed on public property implies official recognition and reinforcement of its message. That implication is especially strong when the sign stands in front of the seat of the government itself. [Even] if the disclaimer at the foot of the cross (which stated that the cross was placed there by a private organization) were legible, that inference would remain, because a property owner's decision to allow a third party to place a sign on her property conveys the same message of endorsement as if she had erected it herself. * * *

"The battle over the Klan cross underscores the power of such symbolism. The menorah prompted the Klan to seek permission to erect an anti-semitic symbol, [which] not only prompted vandalism but also motivated other sects to seek permission to place their own symbols in the Square. These facts illustrate the potential for insidious entanglement that flows from state-endorsed proselytizing."

GINSBURG, J., also dissented, reserving the question of whether an unequivocal disclaimer, "legible from a distance," "that Ohio did not endorse the display's message" would suffice: "Near the stationary cross were the government's flags and the government's statues. [No] other private display was in sight. No plainly visible sign informed the public that the cross belonged to the Klan and that Ohio's government did not endorse the display's message."[82]

(b)   SALAZAR v. BUONO, 130 S.Ct. 1803 (2010): In 1934, members of the Veterans of Foreign Wars placed a Latin cross on federal land to honor American soldiers who died in World War I. Easter services have been regularly held there over the years. After a federal court held this violative of

---

[81] O'Connor, J., responded: "Under such an approach, a religious display is necessarily precluded so long as some passersby would perceive a governmental endorsement thereof. [But the] reasonable observer in the endorsement inquiry must be deemed aware of the history and context of the community and forum in which the religious display appears. [An] informed member of the community will know how the public space in question has been used in the past—and it is that fact, not that the space may meet the legal definition of a public forum, which is relevant to the endorsement inquiry. [The] reasonable observer would recognize the distinction between speech the government supports and speech that it merely allows in a place that traditionally has been open to a range of private speakers accompanied, if necessary, by an appropriate disclaimer."

[5]   [Ct's Note] [O'Connor, J.'s] 'reasonable person' comes off as a well-schooled jurist. [T]his enhanced tort-law standard is singularly out of place in the Establishment Clause context. It strips of constitutional protection every reasonable person whose knowledge happens to fall below some 'ideal' standard. [O'Connor, J.'s] argument that 'there is always someone' who will feel excluded by any particular governmental action, ignores the requirement that such an apprehension be objectively reasonable. A person who views an exotic cow at the zoo as a symbol of the Government's approval of the Hindu religion cannot survive this test.

[Query: Should the Court "develop a national standard, rather than leaving final assessments about endorsement to local juries and courts, [which is] better able to reflect perceptions about displays in different communities"? 2 Greenawalt 89.]

[82] See Mary Jean Dolan, *Government Identity Speech and Religion: Establishment Clause Limits after Summum*, 19 Wm. & Mary Bill Rts.J. 1 (2010) (only a "clear disclaimer explaining government's intended secular message" will "satisfy Establishment Clause principles").

the Establishment Clause, Congress directed the Secretary of the Interior to transfer the cross and land to VFW in exchange for privately owned land elsewhere in the Preserve. The statute provided that the property would revert to the Government if not maintained "as a memorial commemorating United States participation in World War I and honoring the American veterans of that war." A splintered 5–4 majority reversed on grounds of (1) rules pertaining to the law of injunctions or (2) standing. Four Justices reached the constitutional issue but their discussion was somewhat influenced by their view of injunction doctrine.

ALITO, J., who was part of the majority, would uphold the statute: "Assuming that it is appropriate to apply the so-called 'endorsement test,' [the "reasonable observer"] would be familiar with the origin and history of the monument and would also know both that the land on which the monument is located is privately owned. [A] well-informed observer would appreciate that the transfer represents an effort by Congress to address a unique situation and to find a solution that best accommodates conflicting concerns [to] commemorate our Nation's war dead and to avoid the disturbing symbolism that would have been created by the destruction of the monument."[83]

STEVENS, J., joined by Ginsburg and Sotomayor, JJ., dissented: "[I]t is undisputed that the Latin cross is the preeminent symbol of Christianity. It is exclusively a Christian symbol, [I] certainly agree that the Nation should memorialize the service of those who fought and died in World War I, but it cannot lawfully do so by continued endorsement of a starkly sectarian message.

"[T]he transfer [statute] would not end government endorsement. [First,] after the transfer it would continue to appear to any reasonable observer that the Government has endorsed the cross, notwithstanding that the name has changed on the title to a small patch of underlying land. [T]he Government has designated the cross as a national memorial, [and] endorsement continues regardless of whether the cross sits on public or private land. [Second,] Congress' intent to preserve the display of the cross maintains the Government's endorsement of the cross."[84]

(c) ***"Reasonable observer."*** Consider William P. Marshall, *"We Know It When We See It," The Supreme Court and Establishment,* 59 So.Cal.L.Rev. 495 (1986): "Is the objective observer (or average person) a religious person, an agnostic, a separationist, a person sharing the predominate religious sensibility of the community, or one holding a minority view?" Compare Note, *Religion and the State,* 100 Harv.L.Rev. 1606 (1987): "[If the test] is governed

---

[83] Alito, J.'s analysis generally conforms to the discussion in the plurality opinion by Kennedy, J., joined by Roberts, C.J., and Alito, J., which based its conclusion on the law of injunctions. Scalia, J., joined by Thomas, J., concurred in the judgment on the ground that respondent had no standing. Breyer, J., also relied on the law of injunctions, but dissented. Note, *Leading Cases,* 124 Harv. L.Rev. 219 (2010), found that "five Justices [in *Buono,* Roberts, C.J., Kennedy, Scalia, Thomas and Alito, JJ.] clearly suggested that the endorsement test does not apply to objects on private lands."

[84] For the view that selling government land "to preserve the religious objects" on it violates the Establishment Clause, see Eang L. Ngov, *Selling Land and Religion,* 61 U. of Kan.L.Rev. 1 (2012).

by the perspective of the majority, it will be inadequately sensitive. [If] the Establishment Clause is to prohibit government from sending the message to religious minorities or nonadherents that the state favors certain beliefs and that as nonadherents they are not fully members of the political community, its application must turn on the message received *by the minority or nonadherent.*" Concurring in *Van Orden*, THOMAS, J., argued: "['Reasonable observer'] analysis is not fully satisfying to either nonadherents or adherents. For the nonadherent, who may well be more sensitive than the hypothetical 'reasonable observer,' or who may not know all the facts, this test fails to capture completely the honest and deeply felt offense he takes from the government conduct. For the adherent, this analysis takes no account of the message sent by removal of the sign or display, which may well appear to him to be an act hostile to his religious faith."

(d) *Ambiguities.* (i) Consider Steven D. Smith, *Symbols, Perceptions, and Doctrinal Illusions: Establishment Neutrality and the "No Endorsement" Test,* 86 Mich.L.Rev. 266 (1987): "[E]vidence of the test's indeterminate character appears in [Arnold H. Loewy, *Rethinking Government Neutrality Towards Religion Under the Establishment Clause: The Untapped Potential of Justice O'Connor's Insight,* 64 N.C.L.Rev. 1049 (1986), who] concludes that Pawtucket's sponsorship of a nativity scene violated the Establishment Clause, that Alabama's 'moment of silence' law probably did *not* violate the clause, and that ceremonial invocations of deity, such as those occurring in the Pledge of Allegiance or the opening of a Supreme Court session, *do* violate the 'no endorsement' test. In each instance, Justice O'Connor would disagree. [From] the Continental Congress[139] through the framing of the Bill of Rights[140] and on down to the present day, government and government officials—including Presidents [not] to mention the Supreme Court itself[141]—have frequently expressed approval of religion and religious ideas. Such history [at] least demonstrates that many Americans, including some of our early eminent statesmen, have *believed* such approval was proper. That fact alone is sufficient to show that the 'no endorsement' principle is controversial, not easily self-evident. [If] public institutions employ religious symbols, persons who do not adhere to the predominant religion may feel like 'outsiders.'[85] But if religious symbols are banned from such contexts, some religious people will feel that their most central values [have] been excluded from a public culture devoted purely to secular concerns. [We] might conclude, however, that any alienation felt by [the latter] groups, although perfectly sincere, should be disregarded because their dissatisfaction actually results [from] the very

---

[139] **[Orig. Note]** [The] Continental Congress "sprinkled its proceedings liberally with the mention of God, Jesus Christ, the Christian religion, and many other religious references."

[140] **[Orig. Note]** Shortly after approving the Bill of Rights, [including] the Establishment Clause, the first Congress resolved to observe a day of thanksgiving and prayer in appreciation of "the many signal favors of Almighty God."

[141] **[Orig. Note]** See, e.g., *Zorach* ("We are a religious people whose institutions presuppose a Supreme Being."); *Church of the Holy Trinity v. United States,* 143 U.S. 457, 471 (1892) (asserting that "this is a Christian nation").

[85] For support of O'Connor, J.'s approach in this setting, see Steven G. Gey, *When Is Religious Speech Not "Free Speech"?* 2000 U.Ill.L.Rev. 379.

meaning of the Establishment Clause." Contrast Jesse H. Choper, *Securing Religious Liberty: Principles for Judicial Interpretation of the Religion Clauses* 28–29 (1995): "[T]his would grant [a] self-interested veto for the minority. [Although] Justices of the Supreme Court 'cannot become someone else,' they should, with their own solicitude for the values of religious liberty, either assume the view of a reasonable member of the political community who is faithful to the Constitution's protection of individual rights or ask whether a *reasonable minority observer,* who would be 'acquainted with the text, legislative history, and implementation of the [challenged state action],' *should feel* less than a full member of the political community.[112]" For the "inherent difficulties" of the endorsement test, see Mark Strasser, *The Protection and Alienation of Religious Minorities: On the Evolution of the Endorsement Test,* 2008 Mich. St. L. Rev. 667 (the test "is invoked to rationalize a result that has been reached some other way"). Compare B. Jessie Hill, *Anatomy of the Reasonable Observer*, 79 Brook. L. Rev. 1407 (2014): "The reasonable observer" does not mean "to capture the way real people [including judges] actually view a religious display." Rather it "is an accurate model [for] understanding the process of discerning social meaning." This model "considers [all] information available: the context, the background, and the relevant social facts [to] reconstruct the intent, or purpose, behind the symbolic representation."

(ii)   Do government accommodations for religion (such as exempting the sacramental use of wine during Prohibition) violate the endorsement test? Consider Mark Tushnet, *"Of Church and State and the Supreme Court": Kurland Revisited*, 1989 Sup.Ct.Rev. 373: "They use religion as a basis for government classification, and they do [so] precisely in order to confer a benefit on some religions that does not flow either to nonbelievers or to all religions." Compare Michael W. McConnell, *Religious Freedom at a Crossroads,* 59 U.Chi.L.Rev. 115 (1992): "Any action the government takes on issues of this sort inevitably sends out messages, and it is not surprising that reasonable observers from different legal and religious perspectives respond to these messages in different ways. These examples raise some of the most important and most often litigated issues under the Establishment Clause, and the concept of endorsement does not help to resolve them." Contrast Jesse H. Choper, *The Endorsement Test: Its Status and Desirability*, 18 J.L. & Pol. 499 (2002): "[A]ttempts by government to accommodate *either minority or mainstream* religions are often (indeed, usually) benign, genuine, and sometimes even important to the larger society. These efforts should be upheld even though they may fairly be seen as endorsing or approving religion [and] may cause reasonable people to feel offended or alienated. It is regrettable when state policies that address issues of faith produce a sense of subordination or resentment in a segment of the populace. But this alone should not suffice for a judicial holding of unconstitutionality. [That] makes a decision to protect the distressed sensibilities of the religious minority (or

---

[112] **[Orig. Note]** Although this process is basically normative rather than empirical, the Court's judgment should obviously be influenced by the perception (if fairly discernible) of 'average' members of minority religious faiths and should be more strongly affected if their response is very widely shared.

nonbelievers) and to ignore those of the religious majority. [Absent] any tangible threat to religious liberty, it is not at all apparent that the minorities' feelings ought to prevail. Indeed, where equal perceptions of subordination exist, a strong case can be made to favor majority preference." For the view that *either* result in *all* of the Establishment Clause cases will cause large segments of the population to feel "a similar sense of alienation," see Steven D. Smith, *Constitutional Divide: The Transformative Significance of the School Prayer Decisions*, 38 Pepp. L. Rev. 945 (2011).[86]

5. ***Proposal to reconcile Establishment Clause problems.*** Consider Michael W. McConnell, *State Action and the Supreme Court's Emerging Consensus on the Line Between Establishment and Private Religious Expression*, 28 Pepp.L.Rev. 681 (2001): The Establishment Clause "is a limitation on the power of government [not] on the activities of private citizens." The "decisive question" is: "Was the religious activity that took place properly attributable to the government or to private parties?" If "religious activity"—even when undertaken by private parties—"is instigated, encouraged, or—in the strongest case—coerced by the government, the government's acts are unconstitutional. But if religious activity is the product of private judgment, it is permissible—even welcome—within the public sphere. [Thus], to the extent that religious teaching is to be a part of the education of young Americans, this must be the product of decisions made by individual families and religious societies and not of government direction." In respect to individual choice of schools, "the Establishment Clause does not limit the right of private institutions to engage in religious teaching, even with the benefit of neutrally available public resources."

2. FREE EXERCISE CLAUSE AND RELATED PROBLEMS

I. CONFLICT WITH STATE REGULATION

The most common problem respecting Free Exercise of religion has involved a generally applicable government regulation, whose purpose is nonreligious, that either makes illegal (or otherwise burdens) conduct that is dictated by some religious belief, or requires (or otherwise encourages) conduct that is forbidden by some religious belief.

REYNOLDS v. UNITED STATES, 98 U.S. 145 (1878), the first major Free Exercise Clause decision, upheld a federal law making polygamy illegal as applied to a Mormon whose religious duty was to practice polygamy: "Congress was deprived of all legislative power over mere

---

[86] See also Richard F. Duncan, *Just Another Brick in the Wall: The Establishment Clause as a Heckler's Veto*, 18 Tex.Rev.L. & Pol. 255 (2014) ("those offended by the display [may] avert their eyes if they wish to avoid viewing it, [thus not to] deprive a willing audience of the right to receive speech").

opinion, but was left free to reach actions which were in violation of social duties or subversive of good order."

CANTWELL v. CONNECTICUT, 310 U.S. 296 (1940), reemphasized this distinction between religious opinion or belief and action taken because of religion, although the Court this time spoke more solicitously about the latter: "Freedom of conscience and freedom to adhere to such religious organization or form of worship as the individual may choose cannot be restricted by law. [Free exercise] embraces two concepts,— freedom to believe and freedom to act. The first is absolute but, in the nature of things, the second cannot be. [The] freedom to act must have appropriate definition to preserve the enforcement of that protection [although] the power to regulate must be so exercised as not, in attaining a permissible end, unduly to infringe the protected freedom."

Beginning with *Cantwell*—which first held that the Fourteenth Amendment made the free exercise guarantee applicable to the states—a number of cases invalidated application of state laws to conduct undertaken pursuant to religious beliefs. Like *Cantwell*, these decisions, a number of which are set forth in Ch. 7,[87] rested in whole or in part on the freedom of expression protections of the First and Fourteenth Amendments. Similarly, WEST VIRGINIA STATE BD. OF EDUC. v. BARNETTE, 319 U.S. 624 (1943),[88] held that compelling a flag salute by public school children whose religious scruples forbade it violated the First Amendment: "[The] freedoms of speech and of press, of assembly, and of worship [are] susceptible of restriction only to prevent grave and immediate danger to interests which the state may lawfully protect. [The] freedom asserted by these appellees does not bring them into collision with rights asserted by any other individual. It is such conflicts which most frequently require intervention of the State to determine where the rights of one end and those of another begin. [T]he compulsory flag salute and pledge requires *affirmation of a belief* and an *attitude of mind.* [If] there is any fixed star in our constitutional constellation, it is that no official, high or petty, can prescribe what shall be orthodox in politics, nationalism or other matters of opinion or force citizens to confess by word or act their faith therein."

It was not until 1963, in *Sherbert v. Verner* (discussed in *Hobbie* below), that the Court held conduct protected by the Free Exercise Clause alone.

---

[87] E.g., *Schneider v. Irvington,* Ch.7, Sec.6, I, A; *Lovell v. Griffin,* Ch. 7, Sec. 4, I, A (involving distribution of religious literature). See also *Marsh v. Alabama,* Ch. 10, Sec. 2.

[88] Overruling *Minersville School Dist. v. Gobitis,* 310 U.S. 586 (1940).

HOBBIE V. UNEMPLOYMENT APPEALS COMM'N

480 U.S. 136, 107 S.Ct. 1046, 94 L.Ed.2d 190 (1987).

JUSTICE BRENNAN delivered the opinion of the Court.

Appellant's employer discharged her when she refused to work certain scheduled hours because of sincerely-held religious convictions adopted after beginning employment. [Under] our precedents, the [Florida] Appeals Commission's disqualification of appellant from receipt of [unemployment compensation] benefits violates the Free Exercise [Clause]. *Sherbert v. Verner,* 374 U.S. 398 (1963); *Thomas v. Review Board,* 450 U.S. 707 (1981). In *Sherbert* we considered South Carolina's denial of unemployment compensation benefits to a Sabbatarian who, like Hobbie, refused to work on Saturdays. The Court held that the State's disqualification of Sherbert "force[d] her to choose between following the precepts of her religion and forfeiting benefits, on the one hand, and abandoning one of the precepts of her religion in order to accept work, on the other hand. Governmental imposition of such a choice puts the same kind of burden upon the free exercise of religion as would a fine imposed against [her] for her Saturday worship." * * *

In *Thomas,* [a] Jehovah's Witness, held religious beliefs that forbade his participation in the production of armaments. He was forced to leave his job when the employer closed his department and transferred him to a division that fabricated turrets for tanks. Indiana then denied Thomas unemployment compensation benefits. [We] see no meaningful distinction among the situations [and] again affirm, as stated in *Thomas:* "Where the state conditions receipt of an important benefit upon conduct proscribed by a religious faith, *or where it denies such a benefit because of conduct mandated by religious belief, thereby putting substantial pressure on an adherent to modify his behavior and to violate his beliefs,* a burden upon religion exists. While the compulsion may be indirect, the infringement upon free exercise is nonetheless substantial" (emphasis added).

Both *Sherbert* and *Thomas* held that such infringements must be subjected to strict scrutiny and could be justified only by proof by the State of a compelling interest. The Appeals Commission does not seriously contend that its denial of benefits can withstand strict scrutiny;[89] rather it urges that we hold that its justification should be determined under the less rigorous standard articulated in Chief Justice Burger's opinion in *Bowen v. Roy:* "the Government meets its burden when it demonstrates

---

[89] In *Sherbert,* the state "suggest[ed] no more than a possibility that the filing of fraudulent claims by unscrupulous claimants feigning religious objections to Saturday work [might] dilute the unemployment compensation fund [but] there is no proof whatever to warrant such fears [and] it is highly doubtful whether such evidence would be sufficient to warrant a substantial infringement of religious liberties. For [it] would plainly be incumbent upon the [state] to demonstrate that no alternative forms of regulation would combat such abuses without infringing First Amendment rights."

that a challenged requirement for governmental benefits, neutral and uniform in its application, is a reasonable means of promoting a legitimate public interest."[90] 476 U.S. 693 (1986). Five Justices expressly rejected this argument in *Roy*. [See] also *Wisconsin v. Yoder,* 406 U.S. 205 (1972)[91] ("[O]nly those interests of the highest order and those not otherwise served can overbalance legitimate claims to the free exercise of religion").[92] * * *

The Appeals Commission also attempts to distinguish this case by arguing that [in] *Sherbert* and *Thomas,* the employees held their respective religious beliefs at the time of hire; subsequent changes in the conditions of employment made *by the employer* caused the conflict between work and belief. In this case, Hobbie's beliefs changed during the course of her employment. [We] decline [to] single out the religious convert for different, less favorable treatment. * * *

Finally, we reject the Appeals Commission's argument that the awarding of benefits to Hobbie would violate the Establishment Clause. This Court has long recognized that the government may (and sometimes must) accommodate religious practices and that it may do so without violating the Establishment Clause.[10] See e.g., *Yoder*; *Walz*. * * *

---

[90] Burger, C.J., joined by Powell and Rehnquist, JJ., prefaced this statement in *Roy*: "[G]overnment regulation that indirectly and incidentally calls for a choice between securing a governmental benefit and adherence to religious beliefs is wholly different from [action] that criminalizes religiously inspired activity or inescapably compels conduct. [T]hese two very different forms of government action are not governed by the same constitutional [standard.] Absent proof of an intent to discriminate against particular religious beliefs or against religion in general, the Government meets its burden [etc.]"

[91] *Yoder* invalidated a law compelling school attendance to age 16 as applied to Amish parents who refused on religious grounds to send their children to high school, noting no "showing that upon leaving the Amish community Amish children, with their practical agricultural training and habits of industry and self-reliance, would become burdens on society because of educational shortcomings. [The] independence and successful social functioning of the Amish community for a period approaching almost three centuries [is] strong evidence that there is at best a speculative gain, [in] meeting the duties of citizenship from an additional one or two years of compulsory formal education." Douglas, J., dissented. On the question of "whether children should be afforded rights of religious exercise independent of their parents," see Emily Buss, *What Does Frieda Yoder Believe?*, 2 U.Pa.J.Con.L. 53 (1999). See also Gage Raly, Note, *Yoder Revisited: Why the Landmark Amish Schooling Case Could—and Should—Be Overturned*, 97 Va. L. Rev. 681 (2011) (the "real world factual assumptions that underpin *Yoder* are no longer accurate" and have "stifled the dreams of countless young people and caused them to struggle as adults"); William A. Fischel, *Do Amish One-Room Schools Make the Grade? The Dubious Data of Yoder*, 79 U.Chi. L. Rev. 107 (2012) (the study on which *Yoder* based its factual findings "is basically flawed" and "21st century Amish are having to adapt to an economy in which they must deal with technologically sophisticated" persons).

[92] For the view that "the increasing impact of secularization" in the United States "may seriously threaten [our] societal commitment to religious liberty as a fundamental value," see Daniel O. Conkle, *Religious Truth, Pluralism, and Secularism: The Shaking Foundations of American Religious Liberty*, 32 Card. L.Rev. 1755 (2011). See also Douglas Laycock, *Sex, Atheism, and the Free Exercise of Religion*, 88 U.Det.Mercy L. Rev. 407 (2011) ("disagreements about sexual morality, and about the truth and significance of any and all religions, are reopening the debate over first principles").

[10] **[Ct's Note]** In the unemployment benefits context, the majorities *and* those dissenting have concluded that, were a state voluntarily to provide benefits to individuals in Hobbie's situation, [it] would not violate the Establishment Clause. See *Thomas* (Rehnquist, J., dissenting);

Reversed.[93]

CHIEF JUSTICE REHNQUIST, dissenting.

I adhere to the views I stated in dissent in *Thomas* [where Rehnquist, J., stated: "As to the proper interpretation of the Free Exercise Clause, I would accept the decision of *Braunfeld v. Brown,* 366 U.S. 599 (1961), and the dissent in *Sherbert.* In *Braunfeld,* we held that Sunday closing laws do not violate the First Amendment rights of Sabbatarians. Chief Justice Warren explained that the statute did not make unlawful any religious practices of appellants; it simply made the practice of their religious beliefs more expensive. We concluded that '[t]o strike down, without the most critical scrutiny, legislation which imposes only an indirect burden on the exercise of religion, i.e., legislation which does not make unlawful the religious practice itself, would radically restrict the operating latitude of the legislature.'[94] Likewise in this case, it cannot be said that the State discriminated against Thomas on the basis of his religious beliefs or that he was denied benefits *because* he was a Jehovah's Witness.[1] Where, as here, a State has enacted a general statute, the purpose and effect of which is to advance the State's secular goals, the Free Exercise Clause does not in my view require the State to conform that statute to the dictates of religious conscience of any group."]

NOTES AND QUESTIONS

1. *Scope of decisions.* After *Sherbert, Thomas* and *Hobbie,* may a state deny unemployment benefits (a) to a member of a pacifist religion who agreed to produce tanks as a condition of employment and who was fired for subsequently refusing to do so because of religious beliefs, see *Employment Division v. Smith,* 485 U.S. 660 (1988); (b) to a Sabbatarian who is dismissed from a post office job for refusal to work on Saturday because to grant an exemption would require paying overtime to another employee?[95] May (c) a

---

Sherbert (Harlan, J., dissenting). [The conflict between the Establishment and Free Exercise Clauses is considered in Sec. 4 infra.]

[93] The opinions of Powell and Stevens, JJ., concurring in the judgment, are omitted.

[94] *Braunfeld* continued: "Statutes which tax income and limit the amount which may be deducted for religious contributions impose an indirect economic burden on the observance of the religion of the citizen whose religion requires him to donate a greater amount to his church; statutes which require the courts to be closed on Saturday and Sunday impose a similar indirect burden on the observance of the religion of the trial lawyer whose religion requires him to rest on a weekday. The list of legislation of this nature is nearly limitless."

Query: If a statute makes a religious practice unlawful but maximum penalty is a fine, is this a "direct" or "indirect" burden? Is there a distinction between a large and small fine?

[1] **[Ct's Note]** [T]he Indiana Supreme Court *has* construed the State's unemployment statute to make every personal subjective reason for leaving a job a basis for disqualification. [Because] Thomas left his job for a personal reason, the State of Indiana should not be prohibited from disqualifying him from receiving benefits.

[95] See also *TWA v. Hardison,* 432 U.S. 63 (1977), interpreting the Civil Rights Act ban on religious discrimination in employment as permitting dismissal of a Sabbatarian if accommodating his work schedule would require "more than a de minimis cost" by the employer. Brennan and Marshall, JJ., dissented.

state deny worker's compensation to the widow of an employee who, after being injured at work, died because of his refusal on religious grounds to accept a blood transfusion?

2.   *Rejections of Free Exercise claims.* (a) *Taxation.* (i) JIMMY SWAGGART MINISTRIES v. BOARD OF EQUAL., 493 U.S. 378 (1990), per O'CONNOR, J., unanimously held that the Free Exercise Clause does not prohibit imposing a sales and use tax on sale of religious materials by a religious organization: "[T]o the extent that imposition of a generally applicable tax merely decreases the amount of money appellant has to spend on its religious activities, any such burden is not constitutionally significant. [B]ecause appellant's religious beliefs do not forbid payment of the sales and use tax, appellant's reliance on *Sherbert* and its progeny is misplaced. [Although] it is of course possible to imagine that a more onerous tax, even if generally applicable, might effectively choke off an adherent's religious practices, we face no such situation in this case."

(ii)   UNITED STATES v. LEE, 455 U.S. 252 (1982), per BURGER, C.J., held that the Free Exercise Clause does not require an exemption for members of the Old Order Amish from payment of social security taxes even though "both payment and receipt of social security benefits is forbidden by the Amish faith": "The state may justify a limitation on religious liberty by showing that it is essential to accomplish an overriding governmental interest [and] mandatory participation is indispensable to the fiscal vitality of the social security system. [To] maintain an organized society that guarantees religious freedom to a great variety of faiths requires that some religious practices yield to the common good. [The] tax system could not function if denominations were allowed to challenge the tax system because tax payments were spent in a manner that violates their religious belief."

STEVENS, J., concurred in the judgment: "As a matter of fiscal policy, an enlarged exemption probably would benefit the social security system because the nonpayment of these taxes by the Amish would be more than offset by the elimination of their right to collect benefits.[96] [Nonetheless,] the difficulties associated with processing other claims to tax exemption on religious grounds justify a rejection of this claim."

(b)   *Conscription.* (i) GILLETTE v. UNITED STATES, 401 U.S. 437 (1971), per MARSHALL, J., held that the Free Exercise Clause does not forbid Congress from "conscripting persons who oppose a particular war on grounds of conscience and religion. * * * [23]": "The conscription laws [are] not designed to interfere with any religious ritual or practice, and do not work a penalty

---

[96]   Stevens, J., found the distinction between this case and *Yoder* "unconvincing [because] Wisconsin's interest in requiring its children to attend school until they reach the age of 16 is surely not inferior to the federal interest in collecting these social security taxes."

[23]   **[Ct's Note]** We are not faced with the question whether the Free Exercise Clause itself would require exemption of any class other than objectors to particular wars. [T]he Court has previously suggested that relief for conscientious objectors is not mandated by the Constitution. See *Hamilton v. Regents*, 293 U.S. 245 (1934); *United States v. Macintosh,* 283 U.S. at 623–24 (1931).

against any theological position. The incidental burdens felt by [petitioners] are strictly justified by substantial governmental interests [in] procuring the manpower necessary for military purposes."

DOUGLAS, J., dissented: "[M]y choice is the dicta of Chief Justice Hughes who, dissenting in *Macintosh,* spoke for Holmes, Brandeis, and Stone: '[Among] the most eminent statesmen here and abroad have been those who condemned the action of their country in entering into wars they thought to be unjustified."[97]

(ii) In JOHNSON v. ROBISON, 415 U.S. 361 (1974), a federal statute granted educational benefits for veterans who served on active duty but disqualified conscientious objectors who performed alternate civilian service. The Court, per BRENNAN, J., found a "rational basis" for the classification and thus no violation of equal protection, because the "disruption caused by military service is quantitatively greater [and] qualitatively different." Further, the statute "involves only an incidental burden upon appellee's free exercise of religion—if, indeed, any burden exists at [all.]"[19] Douglas, J., dissented.

(c) *Tax exemption.* BOB JONES UNIV. v. UNITED STATES, 461 U.S. 574 (1983), per BURGER, C.J., held that IRS denial of tax exempt status to private schools that practice racial discrimination on the basis of sincerely held religious beliefs does not violate the Free Exercise Clause: "[T]he Government has a fundamental, overriding interest in eradicating racial discrimination in education [which] substantially outweighs [petitioners'] exercise of their religious beliefs. The interests asserted by petitioners cannot be accommodated with that compelling governmental interest, see *Lee;* and no 'less restrictive means' are available to achieve the governmental interest."[98]

(d) *Internal government affairs.* LYNG v. NORTHWEST INDIAN CEMETERY PROTECTIVE ASS'N, 485 U.S. 439 (1988), per O'CONNOR, J., held the federal government's building a road in a national forest did not violate the Free Exercise rights of American Indian tribes even though this would "virtually destroy the Indians' ability to practice their religion" because it would irreparably damage "sacred areas which are an integral and necessary

---

[97] See also Tribe 2d ed., at 1266: "In light of the relative ease with which the conscientious-objector exemption has been administered throughout our history without placing a noticeable burden on the country's military manpower needs, a court might well require a concrete showing of threat to such needs in order to justify abolition of the exemption. The use of conscientious objectors [in] paramedical or other non-military roles could meet both the personnel argument and the morale argument well enough to constitute a required alternative [means] under *Sherbert.*"

[19] [Ct's Note] * * * Congress has bestowed relative benefits upon conscientious objectors by permitting them to perform their alternate service obligation as civilians. Thus, [to] grant educational benefits to military servicemen might arguably be viewed as an attempt to equalize the burdens of military service and civilian alternate service." [See also Kent Greenawalt, 1 *Religion and the Constitution* 53 (2006): "The government can grant everyone an option between a term of military service and *a longer term* of civilian service, or an option between a certainty of civilian service and a chance of military service."]

[98] Contra, Douglas Laycock, *Tax Exemptions for Racially Discriminatory Religious Schools,* 60 Tex.L.Rev. 259 (1982); Mayer G. Freed & Daniel D. Polsby, *Race, Religion, and Public Policy: Bob Jones University v. United States,* 1983 Sup.Ct.Rev. 1.

part of [their] belief systems": "In *Bowen v. Roy,* we considered a challenge to a federal statute that required the States to use Social Security numbers in administering certain welfare programs. Two applicants [contended] that their religious beliefs prevented them from acceding to the use of a Social Security number [that had been assigned to] their two-year-old daughter because the use of a numerical identifier would ' "rob the spirit" of [their] daughter and prevent her from attaining greater spiritual power.' [The] Court rejected [this]: 'The Free Exercise Clause simply cannot be understood to require the Government to conduct its own internal affairs in ways that comport with the religious beliefs of particular citizens. Just as the Government may not insist that [the Roys] engage in any set form of religious observance, so [they] may not demand that the Government join in their chosen religious practices by refraining from using a number to identify their daughter. [The] Free Exercise Clause affords an individual protection from certain forms of governmental compulsion; it does not afford an individual a right to dictate the conduct of the Government's internal procedures.'

"The building of a road [on] publicly owned land cannot meaningfully be distinguished from the use of a Social Security number in *Roy.* In both cases, the challenged government action would interfere significantly with private persons' ability to pursue spiritual fulfillment according to their own religious beliefs. In neither case, however, would the affected individuals be coerced by the Government's action into violating their religious beliefs; nor would either governmental action penalize religious activity by denying any person an equal share of [benefits]. [G]overnment simply could not operate if it were required to satisfy every citizen's religious needs and desires. [The] First Amendment must apply to all citizens alike, and it can give to none of them a veto over public programs that do not prohibit the free exercise of religion.

"[The] dissent now offers to distinguish [*Roy*] by saying that the Government was acting there 'in a purely internal manner,' whereas land-use decisions 'are likely to have substantial external effects.' [But robbing] the spirit of a child, and preventing her from attaining greater spiritual power, is both a 'substantial external effect' and one that is remarkably similar to the injury claimed [today]."[99]

BRENNAN, J., joined by Marshall and Blackmun, JJ., dissented: "[T]oday's ruling sacrifices a religion at least as old as the Nation itself, along with the spiritual well-being of its approximately 5,000 adherents, so that the Forest Service can build a six-mile segment of road that two lower courts found had only the most marginal and speculative utility, both to the Government itself and to the private lumber interests that might conceivably use it." Kennedy, J., did not participate.

---

[99] *Nature of remedy.* Is there a difference between the remedy needed to satisfy the Free Exercise claim in *Roy* and that in *Lyng?* If so, what about the required remedy in the other instances in which the Court has sustained the Free Exercise claim?

EMPLOYMENT DIVISION V. SMITH

494 U.S. 872, 110 S.Ct. 1595, 108 L.Ed.2d 876 (1990).

JUSTICE SCALIA delivered the opinion of the Court. * * *

Respondents [were] fired from their jobs with a private drug rehabilitation organization because they ingested peyote for sacramental purposes at a ceremony of the Native American Church, of which both are members. When respondents applied to petitioner [for] unemployment compensation, they were determined to be ineligible for benefits because they had been discharged for work-related "misconduct." [We believe] that "if a State has prohibited through its criminal laws certain kinds of religiously motivated conduct without violating the First Amendment, it certainly follows that it may impose the lesser burden of denying unemployment compensation benefits to persons who engage in that conduct."

[The] free exercise of religion means [the] right to believe and profess whatever religious doctrine one desires. [But] the "exercise of religion" often involves not only belief and profession but the performance of (or abstention from) physical acts: assembling with others for a worship service, participating in sacramental use of bread and wine, proselytizing, abstaining from certain foods or certain modes of transportation. It would be true, we think (though no case of ours has involved the point), that a state would be "prohibiting the free exercise [of religion]" if it sought to ban such acts or abstentions only when they are engaged in for religious reasons. [But respondents] contend that their religious motivation for using peyote places them beyond the reach of a criminal law that is not specifically directed at their religious practice, and that is concededly constitutional as applied to those who use the drug for other reasons. [As] a textual matter, we do not think the words must be given that meaning. It is no more necessary to regard the collection of a general tax, for example, as "prohibiting the free exercise [of religion]" by those citizens who believe support of organized government to be sinful, than it is to regard the same tax as "abridging the freedom [of] the press" of those publishing companies that must pay the tax as a condition of staying in business. It is a permissible reading of the text [to] say that if prohibiting the exercise of religion (or burdening the activity of printing) is not the object of the tax but merely the incidental effect of a generally applicable and otherwise valid provision, the First Amendment has not been offended. Compare *Citizen Publishing Co. v. United States,* 394 U.S. 131 (1969) (upholding application of antitrust laws to press), with *Grosjean v. American Press Co.,* [Ch. 7, fn. 269] (striking down license tax applied only to newspapers with weekly circulation above a specified level); see generally *Minneapolis Star & Tribune Co. v. Minnesota Commissioner of Revenue* [id].

Our decisions reveal that the latter reading is the correct one. We have never held that an individual's religious beliefs excuse him from compliance with an otherwise valid law prohibiting conduct that the State is free to regulate. [In] *Prince v. Massachusetts,* 321 U.S. 158 (1944), we held that a mother could be prosecuted under the child labor laws for using her children to dispense literature in the streets, her religious motivation notwithstanding. [The opinion also discusses *Braunfeld, Gillette,* and *Lee.*]

The only decisions in which we have held that the First Amendment bars application of a neutral, generally applicable law to religiously motivated action have involved [the] Free Exercise Clause in conjunction with other constitutional protections, such as freedom of speech and of the press, see *Cantwell* (invalidating a licensing system for religious and charitable solicitations under which the administrator had discretion to deny a license to any cause he deemed nonreligious); *Murdock*; *Follett*, or the right of parents, acknowledged in *Pierce v. Society of Sisters* [Sec. 2 supra] to direct the education of their children, see *Yoder*.[1] Some of our cases prohibiting compelled expression, decided exclusively upon free speech grounds, have also involved freedom of religion, cf. *Wooley v. Maynard* [Ch. 7, Sec. 9, I] (invalidating compelled display of a license plate slogan that offended individual religious beliefs); *Barnette*. And it is easy to envision a case in which a challenge on freedom of association grounds would likewise be reinforced by Free Exercise Clause concerns. Cf. *Roberts v. United States Jaycees* [Ch. 7, Sec. 9, III] ("An individual's freedom to speak, to worship [could] not be vigorously protected from interference by the State [if] a correlative freedom to engage in group effort toward those ends were not also guaranteed."). * * *

Respondents argue that [the] claim for a religious exemption must be evaluated under the balancing test set forth in *Sherbert*[:] governmental actions that substantially burden a religious practice must be justified by a compelling governmental interest. [We] have never invalidated any governmental action on the basis of the *Sherbert* test except the denial of unemployment compensation. Although we have sometimes purported to apply the *Sherbert* test in contexts other than that, we have always found the test satisfied, see *Lee, Gillette*. In recent years we have abstained from

---

[1] **[Ct's Note]** [*Yoder*] said that "[*Pierce*] stands as a charter of the rights of parents to direct the religious upbringing of their children. And, when the interests of parenthood are combined with a free exercise claim of the nature revealed by this record, more than merely a 'reasonable relation to some purpose within the competency of the State' is required to sustain the validity of the State's requirement under the First Amendment." [Compare Mark V. Tushnet, *Questioning the Value of Accommodating Religion*, in Law & Religion 245 (Stephen M. Feldman ed. 2000): "In virtually every case a careful litigant can identify another constitutional claim that rides along with the free exercise one: most obviously, free speech claims, but occasionally substantive due process claims as well." For a review of post-*Smith* decisions in the lower courts, concluding that "hybrid rights claims have overwhelmingly failed to succeed," see Steven H. Aden & Lee J. Strang, *When a "Rule" Doesn't Rule: The Failure of the Oregon Employment Division v. Smith "Hybrid Rights Exception,"* 108 Penn St.L.Rev. 573 (2003). See further, Note, *The Best of a Bad Lot: Compromise and Hybrid Religious Exemptions*, 123 Harv. L. Rev. 1494 (2010).]

applying the *Sherbert* test (outside the unemployment compensation field) at all [discussing *Roy* and *Lyng*]. In *Goldman v. Weinberger,* 475 U.S. 503 (1986), we rejected application of the *Sherbert* test to military dress regulations that forbade the wearing of yarmulkes. In *O'Lone v. Shabazz,* 482 U.S. 342 (1987), we sustained, without mentioning the *Sherbert* test, a prison's refusal to excuse inmates from work requirements to attend worship services.[100]

[The] *Sherbert* test [was] developed in a context that lent itself to individualized governmental assessment of the reasons for the relevant conduct. [O]ur decisions in the unemployment cases stand for the proposition that where the State has in place a system of individual exemptions, it may not refuse to extend that system to cases of "religious hardship" without compelling reason.[101]

Whether or not the decisions are that limited, they at least have nothing to do with an across-the-board criminal prohibition on a particular form of conduct. [T]he sounder approach [is] to hold the test inapplicable to such challenges. [To] make an individual's obligation to obey such a law contingent upon the law's coincidence with his religious beliefs, except where the State's interest is "compelling"—permitting him, by virtue of his beliefs, "to become a law unto himself," *Reynolds*—contradicts both constitutional tradition and common sense.[2]

---

[100] For a careful review of the cases, both in the Supreme Court and in the U.S. courts of appeals for ten years preceding *Smith,* concluding that "despite the apparent protection afforded claimants by the language of the compelling interest test, courts overwhelmingly sided with the government when applying that test," see James E. Ryan, *Smith and the Religious Freedom Restoration Act: An Iconoclastic Assessment,* 78 Va.L.Rev. 1407 (1992). See also Jesse H. Choper, *The Rise and Decline of the Constitutional Protection of Religious Liberty,* 70 Neb.L.Rev. 651 (1991).

[101] For the view that the system of discretionary hearings involved in the unemployment cases presents "a fertile ground for the undervaluation of minority religious interests" and is therefore "vulnerable to a distinct constitutional objection," see Christopher L. Eisgruber & Lawrence G. Sager, *The Vulnerability of Conscience: The Constitutional Basis for Protecting Religious Conduct,* 61 U.Chi.L.Rev. 1245 (1994). For an empirical study reaching an opposite conclusion, see Prabha S. Bhandari, *The Failure of Equal Regard to Explain the Sherbert Quartet,* 72 N.Y.U.L.Rev. 97 (1997). See also Ira C. Lupu, *The Case Against Legislative Codification of Religious Liberty,* 21 Card.L.Rev. 565 (1999): "Long prior to *Smith,* our civil liberties tradition had recognized the dangers of permitting local officials to exercise licensing authority over expressive activity without the benefit of determinate criteria. The absence of such criteria invites discriminatory treatment of groups disfavored by local decision makers." For review of lower court decisions that have attempted to "evade" *Smith* through the "individual exemptions" analysis and the "hybrid rights exemption," see Carol M. Kaplan, *The Devil is in the Details: Neutral, Generally Applicable Laws and Exceptions from Smith,* 75 N.Y.U.L.Rev. 1045 (2000). See also Nelson Tebbe, *Smith in Theory and Practice,* 32 Card.L.Rev. 2055 (2011) ("lower courts now find that they have significant flexibility to relieve religious actors from laws or policies that appear to be neutral and generally applicable").

[2] **[Ct's Note]** Justice O'Connor seeks to distinguish *Lyng* and *Roy* on the ground that those cases involved the government's conduct of "its own internal affairs." [But] it is hard to see any reason in principle or practicality why the government should have to tailor its health and safety laws to conform to the diversity of religious belief, but should not have to tailor its management of public lands, *Lyng,* or its administration of welfare programs, *Roy.*

The "compelling government interest" requirement [as] the standard that must be met before the government may accord different treatment on the basis of race, see [Ch. 9, Sec. 2, I], or before the government may regulate the content of speech, is not remotely comparable to using it for the purpose asserted here. What it produces in those other fields—equality of treatment, and an unrestricted flow of contending speech—are constitutional norms; what it would produce here—a private right to ignore generally applicable laws—is a constitutional anomaly.[3]

Nor is it possible to [require] a "compelling state interest" only when the conduct prohibited is "central" to the individual's religion. It is no more appropriate for judges to determine the "centrality" of religious beliefs [than] it would be for them to determine the "importance" of ideas before applying the "compelling interest" test in the free speech field. [I]n many different contexts, we have warned that courts must not presume to determine the place of a particular belief in a religion or the plausibility of a religious claim. See, e.g., *Thomas* [Part II infra]; *Jones v. Wolf,* [Sec. 3 infra]; *United States v. Ballard* [Part II infra].[4]

[I]f "compelling interest" really means what it says (and watering it down here would subvert its rigor in the other fields where it is applied), many laws will not meet the test. Any society adopting such a system would be courting anarchy, but that danger increases in direct proportion to the society's diversity of religious [beliefs].[102] Precisely because "we are a cosmopolitan nation made up of people of almost every conceivable religious preference," and precisely because we value and protect that religious divergence, we cannot afford the luxury of deeming *presumptively invalid,* as applied to the religious objector, every regulation of conduct that

---

[3] **[Ct's Note]** [Just] as we subject to the most exacting scrutiny laws that make classifications based on race or on the content of speech, so too we strictly scrutinize governmental classifications based on religion, see *McDaniel;* see also *Torcaso.* But we have held that race-neutral laws that have the *effect* of disproportionately disadvantaging a particular racial group do not thereby become subject to compelling-interest analysis under the Equal Protection Clause, see *Washington v. Davis* [Ch. 9, Sec. 2, III] (police employment examination); and we have held that generally applicable laws unconcerned with regulating speech that have the *effect* of interfering with speech do not thereby become subject to compelling-interest analysis under the First Amendment, see *Citizen Publishing Co. v. United States* (antitrust laws). Our conclusion [today] is the only approach compatible with these precedents.

[4] **[Ct's Note]** [In] any case, dispensing with a "centrality" inquiry is utterly unworkable. It would require, for example, the same degree of "compelling state interest" to impede the practice of throwing rice at church weddings as to impede the practice of getting married in church. [I]f general laws are to be subjected to a "religious practice" exception, *both* the importance of the law at issue *and* the centrality of the practice at issue must reasonably be considered. [For the conclusion that "the Court has never required that the claimant establish either centrality or compulsion to receive protection under the First Amendment," see Steven C. Seeger, *Restoring Rights to Rites: The Religious Motivation Test and the Religious Freedom Restoration Act,* 95 Mich.L.Rev. 1472 (1997).]

[102] Contra, Gary Simson, *Endangering Religious Liberty,* 84 Calif.L.Rev. 441, 461 (1996): "[S]ince the legislative process generally makes allowance for the needs of adherents of mainstream religions, court-ordered exemptions typically would be limited in scope to affected members of relatively small groups."

does not protect an interest of the highest order. [It] would open the prospect of constitutionally required religious exemptions from civic obligations of almost every conceivable kind—ranging from compulsory military service, see, e.g., *Gillette,* to the payment of taxes, see, e.g., *Lee,* to health and safety regulation such as manslaughter and child neglect laws, compulsory vaccination laws, drug laws, and traffic laws, to social welfare legislation such as minimum wage laws, see *Tony and Susan Alamo Foundation v. Secretary of Labor,* 471 U.S. 290 (1985), child labor laws, see *Prince;* animal cruelty laws, environmental protection laws, and laws providing for equality of opportunity for the races, see e.g., *Bob Jones University.* The First Amendment's protection of religious liberty does not require this.[5]

[A] number of States have made an exception to their drug laws for sacramental peyote use. But to say that a nondiscriminatory religious-practice exemption is permitted, or even that it is desirable, is not to say that it is constitutionally required, and that the appropriate occasions for its creation can be discerned by the courts.[103] It may fairly be said that leaving accommodation to the political process will place at a relative disadvantage those religious practices that are not widely engaged in;[104] but that unavoidable consequence of democratic government must be preferred to a system in which each conscience is a law unto itself or in

---

[5] **[Ct's Note]** Justice O'Connor contends that the "parade of horribles" in the text only "demonstrates [that] courts have been quite capable of strik[ing] sensible balances between religious liberty and competing state interests." But the cases we cite have struck "sensible balances" only because they have all applied the general laws, despite the claims for religious exemption. In any event, Justice O'Connor mistakes the purpose of our parade: [to] suggest that courts would constantly be in the business of determining whether the "severe impact" of various laws on religious practice (to use Justice Blackmun's terminology) or the "constitutiona[l] significan[ce]" of the "burden on the particular plaintiffs" (to use Justice O'Connor's terminology) suffices to permit us to confer an exemption. It [is] horrible to contemplate that federal judges will regularly balance against the importance of general laws the significance of religious practice. [Compare Douglas Laycock & Oliver S. Thomas, *Interpreting the Religious Freedom Restoration Act,* 73 Tex. L. Rev. 209 (1994): "[T]he reality of the legislative process is totally unsuited to principled decisions about whether one faction's desire to suppress an annoying religious practice is really the least restrictive means of serving a compelling government interest."]

[103] Does a "religious-practice exemption" violate the Religion Clauses principle of "neutrality"? Consider Phillip Kurland, *Religion and the Law* 112 (1962): "The [Free Exercise and Establishment] clauses should be read as stating a single precept: that government cannot utilize religion as a standard for action or inaction because these clauses, read together as they should be, prohibit classification in terms of religion either to confer a benefit or to impose a burden." For thoughtful comment, see Paul Kauper, *Book Review,* 41 Texas L.Rev. 467 (1963); Leo Pfeffer, *Religion-Blind Government,* 15 Stan.L.Rev. 389 (1963); John Mansfield, *Book Review,* 52 Calif.L.Rev. 212 (1964). For consideration of "the extent to which equality, as a constitutional value, constrains our understanding of religious guarantees," see Laura S. Underkuffler-Freund, *Yoder and the Question of Equality,* 25 Cap.U.L.Rev. 789 (1996).

[104] Since *Smith,* "more than half the states appear to have adopted some version of the *Sherbert-Yoder* test." Douglas Laycock, *Comment: Theology Scholarships, the Pledge of Allegiance, and Religious Liberty: Avoiding the Extremes but Missing the Liberty,* 118 Harv.L.Rev. 155 (2004).

which judges weigh the social importance of all laws against the centrality of all religious beliefs. * * *[105]

JUSTICE O'CONNOR, with whom JUSTICE BRENNAN, JUSTICE MARSHALL, and JUSTICE BLACKMUN join as to [Part II], concurring in the judgment. * * *

II. "[T]o agree that religiously grounded conduct must often be subject to the broad police power of the State is not to deny that [a] regulation neutral on its face may, in its application, nonetheless offend the constitutional requirement for government neutrality if it unduly burdens the free exercise of religion," [*Yoder*, and in] each of the other cases cited by the Court to support its categorical rule, we rejected the particular constitutional claims before us only after carefully weighing the competing interests. [A] neutral criminal law prohibiting conduct that a State may legitimately regulate is, if anything, *more* burdensome than a neutral civil statute placing legitimate conditions on the award of a state benefit.

[Even] if, as an empirical matter, a government's criminal laws might usually serve a compelling interest in health, safety, or public order, the First Amendment at least requires a case-by-case determination of the question, sensitive to the facts of each particular claim. Given the range of conduct that a State might legitimately make criminal, we cannot assume, merely because a law carries criminal sanctions and is generally applicable, that the First Amendment *never* requires the State to grant a limited exemption for religiously motivated conduct.

Moreover, we have not "rejected" or "declined to apply" the compelling interest test in our recent cases. [In] both *Roy* and *Lyng,* for example, we expressly distinguished *Sherbert* on the ground that the First Amendment does not "require the Government *itself* to behave in ways that the individual believes will further his or her spiritual development. * * *" This distinction makes sense because "the Free Exercise Clause is written in terms of what the government cannot do to the individual, not in terms of what the individual can exact from the government." *Sherbert* (Douglas, J., concurring).[106] Because [this case] plainly falls into the former category, I would apply those established precedents to the facts of this case.

Similarly, the other cases cited by the Court for the proposition that we have rejected application of the *Sherbert* test outside the unemployment compensation field are distinguishable because they arose in the narrow,

---

[105] For a comprehensive and sensitive discussion of the role of judges in reviewing the nature of the burden on religious exercise and the strength of the state interest in not granting an exemption, see 1 Greenawalt ch. 13.

[106] For the view that *Lyng's* approach attracts the Court because it functions to "reduce the number of claims that must be afforded the searching inquiry demanded by the free exercise clause" and to permit the Court to avoid resolving the difficult issues of "cognizability of the asserted burden, the sincerity of the claimant, and religiosity of the claim," see Ira C. Lupu, *Where Rights Begin: The Problem of Burdens on the Free Exercise of Religion,* 102 Harv.L.Rev. 933 (1989).

specialized contexts in which we have not traditionally required the government to justify a burden on religious conduct by articulating a compelling interest. *Goldman v. Weinberger* and *O'Lone v. Shabazz* [military and prison regulations] say nothing about whether the test should continue to apply in paradigm free exercise cases such as the one presented here. [Our] free speech cases similarly recognize that neutral regulations that affect free speech values are subject to a balancing, rather than categorical, approach. See, e.g., *United States v. O'Brien,* [Ch. 7, Sec. 2]; *Renton v. Playtime Theatres, Inc.,* [Ch. 7, Sec. 3, I]; cf. *Anderson v. Celebrezze,* 460 U.S. 780 (1983) (generally applicable laws may impinge on free association concerns). * * *

Finally, the Court today suggests that [accommodating] minority religions [must] be left to the political process. In my view, however, the First Amendment was enacted precisely to protect the rights of those whose religious practices are not shared by the majority and may be viewed with hostility. The history of our free exercise doctrine amply demonstrates the harsh impact majoritarian rule has had on unpopular or emerging religious groups such as the Jehovah's Witnesses and the Amish.[107] * * *

III. The Court's holding today [is] unnecessary to this [case.] Oregon has a significant interest in enforcing laws that control the possession and use of controlled substances by its citizens [and] a compelling interest in prohibiting the possession of peyote. [Although] the question is close, I would conclude that uniform application of Oregon's criminal prohibition is "essential to accomplish," *Lee,* its overriding interest in preventing the physical harm caused by the use of a [federal] Schedule I controlled substance. [R]egardless of the motivation of the user, [use] for religious purposes, violates the very purpose of the laws that prohibit them. [T]hat the Federal Government and several States provide exemptions for the religious use of peyote [does not result in] Oregon, with its specific asserted

---

[107] See also Douglas Laycock, *Formal, Substantive, and Disaggregated Neutrality Toward Religion,* 39 De Paul L.Rev. 993 (1990): "Of course, inadvertence can interact with hostility, or with an insensitivity that borders on hostility. Consider what might happen when [a person, whose sincerely held religious beliefs forbid her to be photographed, was denied a driver's license,] writes her legislator [who] may find it so impossible to empathize with her belief that he never seriously considers whether an exemption would be workable. Even if he empathizes, the legislative calendar is crowded, and the original statute having been enacted, all the burdens of legislative inertia now work against an exemption."

Compare Eisengruber & Sager, fn. 101: "[After *Lyng,*] the political process responded to interests the judiciary had not protected, and the Bureau of Land Management relocated the road. [After *Lee,*] Congress accommodated churches that had religious objections to participating in the social security system. [After *Goldman,*] Congress granted relief. And [after *Smith,*] Oregon legislated an exemption to its law," and Congress protected religious use of peyote in all states. But contrast Dhananjai Shivakumar, *Neutrality and the Religion Clauses,* 33 Harv. Civ. Rts.— Civ. Lib. L. Rev. 505 (1998): "[R]ejection of meaningful judicial review will deprive free exercise claimants of one historically effective way of eliciting attention and public support[:] litigation. Many well-known examples of political accommodation were preceded by lengthy, well-publicized free exercise litigation."

FREE EXERCISE CLAUSE AND

interest in uniform application of its drug laws, being *required* to do so by the First Amendment * * *[108]

JUSTICE BLACKMUN, with whom JUSTICE BRENNAN and JUSTICE MARSHALL join, dissenting.

This Court over the years painstakingly has [held that] a state statute that burdens the free exercise of religion [and] may stand only if the law in general, and the State's refusal to allow a religious exemption in particular, are justified by a compelling interest that cannot be served by less restrictive means.

[T]he state interest involved [here is the] State's narrow interest in refusing to make an exception for the religious, ceremonial use of peyote. [The] State cannot plausibly assert that [is] essential to fulfill any compelling interest [as it] has never sought to prosecute respondents, and does not claim that it has made significant enforcement efforts against other religious users of peyote. The State's asserted interest thus amounts only to the symbolic preservation of an unenforced prohibition. * * *

Similarly, this Court's prior decisions [have] demanded evidentiary support for a refusal to allow a religious exception. [In] this case, the State [offers] no evidence that the religious use of peyote has ever harmed anyone. The factual findings of other courts cast doubt on the State's assumption that religious use of peyote is harmful. See *State v. Whittingham,* 504 P.2d 950 (Ariz.App. 1973) ("the State failed to prove that the quantities of peyote used in the sacraments of the Native American Church are sufficiently harmful to the health and welfare of the participants * * * "); *People v. Woody,* 40 Cal.Rptr. 69, 394 P.2d 813 (1964) ("as the Attorney General [admits,] the opinion of scientists and other experts is 'that peyote [works] no permanent deleterious injury to the Indian' "). [The] Federal Government [does] not find peyote so dangerous as to preclude an exemption for religious use.[5] Moreover, other Schedule I

---

[108] In *Boerne v. Flores,* Ch. 11, Sec. 3, O'Connor, J., joined by Breyer, J., argued that "the historical evidence [bears] out the conclusion that, at the time the Bill of Rights was ratified, it was accepted that government should, when possible, accommodate religious practice." Scalia, J., joined by Stevens, J., disagreed: "The historical evidence put forward by the dissent does nothing to undermine the conclusion we reached in *Smith.*" For an extensive review, see Michael W. McConnell, *Freedom From Persecution or Protection of the Rights of Conscience?: A Critique of Justice Scalia's Historical Arguments,* 39 Wm. & M. L. Rev. 819 (1998). See also Wesley J. Campbell, *A New Approach to 19th Century Religious Exemption Cases,* 63 Stan. L. Rev. 973 (2011) (disputing Scalia, J.'s "claim that the dearth of successfully litigated nineteenth century exemption claims reveals a lack of historical support for religious accommodations"). For support at the time of the Fourteenth Amendment for O'Connor, J.'s position, see Kurt T. Lash, *The Second Adoption of the Free Exercise Clause: Religious Exemptions Under the Fourteenth Amendment,* 88 Nw.U.L.Rev. 1106 (1994). For the view that the original understanding of the Free Exercise Clause was an "unqualified" right to be free from "penalty" or "discrimination" on the basis of religion, see Phillip Hamburger, *More Is Less,* 90 Va.L.Rev. 835 (2004).

[5] **[Ct's Note]** [Moreover,] 23 States, including many that have significant Native American populations, have statutory or judicially crafted exemptions in their drug laws for religious [use].

drugs have lawful uses. See *Olsen v. Drug Enforcement Administration,* 878 F.2d 1458 (D.C.Cir.1989) (medical and research uses of marijuana).

The carefully circumscribed ritual context in which respondents used peyote is far removed from the irresponsible and unrestricted recreational use of unlawful drugs.[6] * * * [7] [J]ust as in *Yoder,* the values and interests of those seeking a religious exemption in this case are congruent, to a great degree, with those the State seeks to promote through its drug laws. See *Yoder* (since the Amish accept formal schooling up to 8th grade, and then provide "ideal" vocational education, State's interest in enforcing its law against the Amish is "less substantial than [for] children generally"). Not only does the Church's doctrine forbid nonreligious use of peyote; it also generally advocates self-reliance, familial responsibility, and abstinence from alcohol. There is considerable evidence that the spiritual and social support provided by the Church has been effective in combatting the tragic effects of alcoholism on the Native American population. * * *

The State also seeks to support its refusal to make an exception [by] invoking its interest in abolishing drug trafficking. There is, however, practically no illegal traffic in peyote. Also, the availability of peyote for religious use [would] still be strictly controlled by federal regulations, see 21 U.S.C. §§ 821–823 (registration requirements for distribution of controlled substances); and by the State of Texas, the only State in which peyote grows in significant quantities. * * *

Finally, the State argues that, [if] it grants an exemption for religious peyote use, a flood of other claims to religious exemptions will follow. [But almost] half the States, and the Federal Government, have maintained an exemption for religious peyote use for many years, and apparently have not found themselves overwhelmed by claims to other religious exemptions.[8] [The] unusual circumstances that make the religious use of peyote compatible with the State's interests in health and safety and in preventing drug trafficking would not apply to other religious claims. Some religions, for example, might not restrict drug use to a limited ceremonial context, as does the Native American Church. See, e.g., *Olsen* ("the Ethiopian Zion Coptic Church [teaches] that marijuana is properly smoked 'continually all day'"). Some religious claims involve drugs such as marijuana and heroin, in which there is significant illegal traffic, [so] that it would be difficult to

---

[6] **[Ct's Note]** In this respect, respondents' use of peyote seems closely analogous to the sacramental use of wine by the Roman Catholic Church. During Prohibition, the Federal Government exempted such use of wine from its general [ban]. However compelling the Government's then general interest in prohibiting the use of alcohol may have been, it could not plausibly have asserted an interest sufficiently compelling to outweigh Catholics' right to take communion.

[7] **[Ct's Note]** The use of peyote is, to some degree, self-limiting. [It] is extremely bitter, and eating it is an unpleasant experience, which would tend to discourage casual or recreational use.

[8] **[Ct's Note]** [V]arious sects have raised free exercise claims regarding drug use. In no reported case, except those involving claims of religious peyote use, has the claimant prevailed.

grant a religious exemption without seriously compromising law enforcement efforts.[9] [Though] the State must treat all religions equally, and not favor one over another, this obligation is fulfilled by the uniform application of the "compelling interest" *test* to all free exercise claims, not by reaching uniform *results* as to all claims. * * *

Respondents believe, and their sincerity has *never* been at issue, that the peyote plant embodies their deity, and eating it is an act of worship and communion[,] the essential ritual of their religion. * * *[109]

NOTES AND QUESTIONS

1.   ***Significance of other constitutional provisions.*** What result under *Smith* if a state law barring religious discrimination in employment is applied to churches' selection of their clergy? If a church is sued for "negligent supervision of employees" because its clergy have been found guilty of sexual abuse? Of what relevance is the freedom of expressive association (*Boy Scouts of America v. Dale*, Ch. 7, Sec. 9, III)? See Mark Tushnet, *The Redundant Free Exercise Clause?*, 33 Loy.U.Chi.L.J. 71 (2001); Kathleen A. Brady, *Religious Organizations and Free Exercise: The Surprising Lessons of Smith*, 2004 B.Y.U.L.Rev. 1633 ("*Smith* supports a broad right of church autonomy" because of its emphasis that "religious *beliefs* as such" are absolutely protected and the fact that religious groups "play an important role in the formation of religious beliefs"); Ira C. Lupu & Robert W. Tuttle, *Sexual Misconduct and*

---

[9]   **[Ct's Note]** Thus, this case is distinguishable from *Lee,* in which the Court concluded that there was "no principled way" to distinguish other exemption claims, and the "tax system could not function if denominations were allowed to challenge the tax system because tax payments were spent in a manner that violates their religious belief."

[109] In 1993, Congress passed the Religious Freedom Restoration Act which effectively reinstated the *Sherbert-Yoder* test for generally applicable laws that burden religious practices. RFRA was held unconstitutional in *Boerne v. Flores*, Ch. 11, Sec. 3, but only as applied to state (and not to federal) legislation, and the *Sherbert-Yoder* test thus continues to apply to the national government as a result of RFRA's mandate. *Burwell v. Hobby Lobby Stores, Inc.*, per Alito, J., held that RFRA exempted two closely held for-profit corporations from the obligation to provide employees with contraception coverage under the Affordable Care Act (see Ch. 2, Sec. 2, IV) because their owners' religious beliefs were opposed to after-conception contraceptives. The Court assumed that a guarantee of cost-free contraceptives is a "compelling government interest," but found that there are "less restrictive alternatives" available to the government to satisfy it, e.g., the government might pay for the insurance itself or require insurers to pay. Ginsburg, J., joined by Breyer, Sotomayor and Kagan, JJ., dissented in a lengthy opinion, contending that complying with the statute did not "substantially" burden the corporations, and that "none of the preferred alternatives would serve the compelling interests to which Congress responded." In a part of her opinion joined only by Sotomayor, J., Ginsburg, J., also concluded that for-profit corporations were not "persons" entitled to religious exemptions under RFRA.

For the view that the *Hobby Lobby* exception violates the Establishment Clause "by shifting the material costs of accommodating contraception beliefs from employers to their employees," see Frederick M. Gedicks & Rebecca G. Van Tassell, *Exceptions from the Contraception Mandate: An Unconstitutional Accommodation of Religion,* 49 Harv.Civ.Rts.-Civ.Lib.L.Rev. 343 (2014).

For the view that the "core meaning of the Establishment Clause" prevents congressional efforts to "tell states what relation their laws must have to the fostering of one or all religions," which "means that Congress may not try to dictate church-state relations even to vindicate religious toleration or free exercise," see Jed Rubenfeld, *Antidisestablishmentarianism: Why RFRA Really Was Unconstitutional*, 95 Mich.L.Rev. 2347 (1997).

Ecclesiastical Immunity, 2004 B.Y.U.L.Rev. 1789 (*Smith's* recognition of "ecclesiastical immunities," which are rooted in the Establishment Clause, forbids the state to "adjudicate or regulate the ways in which communities of faith are organized"). See further *Jones v. Wolf*, Sec. 3 infra. Compare Paul Horwitz, *Churches as First Amendment Institutions: Of Sovereignty and Spheres*, 44 Harv. Civ. Rts.—Civ. Libs. L. Rev. 79 (2009) (under "sphere sovereignty" approach, "churches are entitled to a substantial degree of decision-making autonomy with respect to membership and employment matters, regardless of the nature of the employee or the grounds of discrimination") with Ira C. Lupu & Robert W. Tuttle, *Courts, Clergy, and Congregations: Disputes Between Religious Institutions and Their Leaders*, 7 Geo. J. L. & Pub. Pol'y, 119 (2009) (permitting "adjudication between clergy and their employers" when "limited to secular and temporal concerns"). Contrast Laura S. Underkuffler, *Thoughts on Smith and Religious-Group Autonomy*, 2004 B.Y.U.L.Rev. 1773 ("there is no convincing basis for distinguishing individual religious exemptions, struck down in *Smith*, from aggressive forms of religious-group autonomy" which "pose far more dangers of individual oppression, governmental interference, and undermining of societal norms than autonomously acting individuals"). For the view that Free Exercise claims should be treated "no differently than free expression claims," see Marshall, *Solving the Free Exercise Dilemma: Free Exercise as Expression*, 67 Minn.L.Rev. 545 (1983). For a discussion of the comparative advantages of the Free Speech and Free Exercise Clauses in protecting religious liberty, see Alan Brownstein, *Protecting Religious Liberty: The False Messiahs of Free Speech Doctrine and Formal Neutrality*, 18 J.L. & Pol. 119 (2002).

2. **Discrimination.** (a) CHURCH OF THE LUKUMI BABALU AYE, INC. v. HIALEAH, 508 U.S. 520 (1993), per KENNEDY, J., held that city ordinances barring ritual animal sacrifice violated the Free Exercise Clause: "[I]f the object of a law is to infringe upon or restrict practices because of their religious motivation, the law is not neutral, see *Smith;* and it is invalid unless it is justified by a compelling interest and is narrowly tailored to advance that interest. [The] ordinances had as their object the suppression of [the Santeria] religion. The [record] discloses animosity to Santeria adherents and their religious practices; the ordinances by their own terms target this religious exercise; the texts of the ordinances were gerrymandered with care to proscribe religious killings of animals but to exclude almost all secular killings; and the ordinances suppress much more religious conduct than is necessary in order to achieve the legitimate ends asserted in their defense. [A] law that targets religious conduct for distinctive treatment or advances legitimate governmental interests only against conduct with a religious motivation will survive strict scrutiny only in rare cases."

SOUTER, J., concurred specially, noting that "the Court should re-examine the rule *Smith* declared." BLACKMUN, J., joined by O'Connor, J., concurred only in the judgment, contending that "when a law discriminates against religion as such, as do the ordinances in this case, it automatically will fail strict scrutiny [because] a law that targets religious practice for disfavored treatment both burdens the free exercise of religion and, by definition, is not precisely tailored to a compelling governmental interest." Finally, "this case does not [decide] whether the Free Exercise Clause would require a religious exemption from a law that sincerely pursued the goal of protecting animals from cruel treatment. [That] is not a concern to be treated lightly."

(b) *Scope.* Does the *Smith-Lukumi* rule bar only those laws whose "object is suppression" of a religious practice? For the view that "empirical data show [a] "persistent judicial bias and religious insensitivity" in applying strict scrutiny under *Sherbert,* and that a rule requiring the government to "bear the burden of establishing the actual reason for the law" would "provide a powerful tool for rooting out more subtle forms of discrimination against unpopular minority religions," see Ronald J. Krotoszynski, Jr., *If Judges Were Angels: Religious Equality, Free Exercise, and the (Underappreciated) Merits of Smith,* 102 Nw. U. L. Rev. 1189 (2008). After *Lukumi,* what result in *Smith* if Oregon had permitted the medicinal use of peyote (or marijuana) in designated circumstances to relieve pain? Would the law barring other uses of peyote (including sacramental use) be "generally applicable"? Or would it "target religious conduct"? Of what relevance is *Smith's* reaffirmation of *Sherbert's* "individualized governmental assessment" context? Consider Richard F. Duncan, *Free Exercise Is Dead, Long Live Free Exercise: Smith, Lukumi and the General Applicability Requirement,* 3 U.Pa.J.Con.L. 850 (2001): "[W]henever you are dealing with burdensome regulations [there] will often be some process for requesting an exemption, waiver, or variance. Even if the regulation [is] generally applicable on its face, if a state agency grants ad hoc exemptions [in] even a few cases involving secular claims, it may not refuse to grant similar exemptions [for] 'religious hardship' without satisfying strict scrutiny." See also Frederick M. Gedicks, *The Normalized Free Exercise Clause: Three Abnormalities,* 75 Ind. L.J. 77 (2000): "[F]ree exercise of religion is a fundamental right, the protection of which is specified by the constitutional text [but] the Court is not treating free exercise rights like privacy, speech, travel, and other fundamental [rights.] Fundamental rights/equal protection analysis [Ch. 9, Sec. 5] makes clear that any law or government action that excuses—by administrative exemption, legislative exemption, or otherwise— one or more secular activities but not *comparable* religious practices creates a classification that impermissibly burdens the fundamental right of free exercise of religion, and thus should normally be subject to strict scrutiny."

If a state bars ingestion of all alcoholic beverages but exempts sacramental use, may it bar ingestion of all hallucinogenic substances without exempting sacramental use? See Michael J. Perry, *Freedom of Religion in the United States: Fin de Siècle Sketches,* 75 Ind.L.J. 295 (2000). If "a school committed to the Montessori philosophy of education, or to a pacifist or multiculturalist approach, is legally free to require that its staff adhere to that ideology," may a religious school be forbidden to discriminate in employment on the basis of religion? Suppose it receives vouchers as part of a general program? See Thomas C. Berg, *Vouchers and Religious Schools: The New Constitutional Questions,* 72 U.Cinc.L.Rev. 151 (2003). What result if Hialeah's ordinance barred "all other exhibitionistic killings, like those that are sometimes performed by entertainers or as part of college fraternity or other initiation ceremonies." See Lino A. Graglia, *Church of the Lukumi Babalu Aye: Of Animal Sacrifice and Religious Persecution,* 85 Geo. L. J. 1 (1996). What result under the *Smith-Lukumi* rule if a state prohibits *all* polygamous marriages after a religious group that engages in the practice becomes active in the state? See Garrett Epps, *What We Talk About When We Talk About Free Exercise,* 30 Ariz.St.L.J. 563 (1998).

(c) **Aid to religious schools.** Is the Court's statement, that denial of financial benefits to religious schools does not infringe the Free Exercise rights of attending children,[110] consistent with *Smith* and *Lukumi*? Could a student bus transportation program include all nonprofit private schools except religious schools? See *Luetkemeyer v. Kaufmann,* 419 U.S. 888 (1974). Would affording aid to *all* schools (public and nonpublic) *except* those that are church-related "target religious conduct" (*Lukumi*)? Consider Jesse H. Choper, *Federal Constitutional Issues,* in *School Choice and Social Controversy* 235 (Sugarman & Kemerer eds. 1999): "First, such a program would plainly discriminate on its face against 'some or all religious beliefs,' violating the basic protections of the Free Exercise Clause, unless justified after strict scrutiny. Second, since all schools teach values, the state could be fairly seen as discriminating against religious viewpoints, much as the University of Virginia had done in *Rosenberger,* and would also be subject to strict scrutiny under the Free Speech Clause [see Ch. 7, Sec. 1]. *Lukumi* and *Rosenberger* would appear to compel inclusion of religious schools in any voucher program or other aid to education that included nonreligious private schools."

Would *Sherbert* require aid for parochial schools even though public support was given only to public schools? If some religions impose a duty on parents to send children to religious schools, may the parents argue that, since they must pay school taxes, the state's failure to support parochial schools as well "conditions the availability of benefits upon their willingness to violate a cardinal principle of their religious faith [and] effectively penalizes the free exercise of their constitutional liberties" (*Sherbert*); that there is no "compelling state interest to justify the substantial infringement of their First Amendment rights"? May these parents further argue that their position is stronger than *Sherbert* because the purpose of granting an exemption in that case was *solely* to aid religion whereas there is a nonreligious purpose in giving aid to all nonpublic schools—improving the quality of the secular education? What result after *Smith*? See Choper, supra.

(d) LOCKE v. DAVEY, 540 U.S. 712 (2004), per REHNQUIST, C.J., held that the exclusion (as required by the state constitution) from Washington's Promise Scholarship Program to assist academically gifted postsecondary students, of pursuit of a devotional theology degree (i.e., one "designed to induce religious faith"), did not violate the Free Exercise Clause: "[W]e have

---

[110] See the dictum in *Sloan v. Lemon,* 413 U.S. 825 (1973): "[V]alid aid to nonpublic, nonsectarian schools would provide no lever for aid to their sectarian counterparts."

long said that 'there is room for play in the points' between [the religion clauses]. *Walz* [i.e.,] there are some state actions permitted by the Establishment Clause but not required by the Free Exercise Clause. [And] there is no doubt that the State could, consistent with the Federal Constitution, permit Promise Scholars to pursue a degree in devotional theology, see *Witters* * * * .

"[Respondent] contends that [under] *Lukumi*, the program is presumptively unconstitutional because it is not facially neutral with respect to religion. [But here], the State's disfavor of religion (if it can be called that) is of a far milder kind [than in *Lukumi*]. It imposes neither criminal nor civil sanctions on any type of religious service or rite. It does not deny to ministers the right to participate in the political affairs of the community. See *McDaniel*. And it does not require students to choose between their religious beliefs and receiving a government benefit.[4] *Sherbert*. The State has merely chosen not to fund a distinct category of instruction.[111]

"[M]ajoring in devotional theology is akin to a religious calling as well as an academic pursuit. [T]he interest that [the Washington constitution] seeks to further is scarcely novel. [Since] the founding of our country, there have been popular uprisings against procuring taxpayer funds to support church leaders, which was one of the hallmarks of an 'established' religion. [Most] States that sought to avoid such an establishment around the time of the founding placed in their constitutions formal prohibitions against using tax funds to support the ministry. [T]hat early state constitutions saw no problem in explicitly excluding *only* the ministry from receiving state dollars reinforces the conclusion that religious instruction is of a different ilk. Far from evincing the hostility toward religion which was manifest in *Lukumi,* we believe that the entirety of the Promise Scholarship Program goes a long way toward including religion in its benefits.[8] The program permits students to attend pervasively religious schools, so long as they are accredited [and] students are still eligible to take devotional theology courses."

SCALIA, J., joined by Thomas, J., dissented, finding *Lukumi* "irreconcilable with today's decision": "When the State makes a public benefit generally available, that benefit becomes part of the baseline against which burdens on religion are measured; and when the State withholds that benefit from some individuals solely on the basis of religion, it violates the Free Exercise Clause no less than if it had imposed a special tax.

---

⁴ **[Ct's Note]** Promise Scholars may still use their scholarship to pursue a secular degree at a different institution from where they are studying devotional theology.

¹¹¹ For the view that *Davey*'s "goal was to extend the *Lukumi* rules from regulation to funding. That effort failed; *Lukumi* does not apply to funding. But neither was *Lukumi* rolled back as applied to regulation," see Laycock, fn. 104 (criticizing *Locke*). For a rationale that permits government to "single out many religious actors and entities for exclusion from its support programs," see Nelson Tebbe, *Excluding Religion,* 156 U. Pa. L. Rev. 1263 (2008). See also "Abortion Funding," Ch. 6, Sec. 2.

⁸ **[Ct's Note]** Washington has also been solicitous in ensuring that its constitution is not hostile towards religion, and at least in some respects, its constitution provides greater protection of religious liberties than the Free Exercise Clause (rejecting standard in *Smith*) * * * .

"[The history relied on by the Court] involved not the inclusion of religious ministers in public benefits programs like the one at issue here, but laws that singled them out for financial aid. [No] one would seriously contend, for example, that the Framers would have barred ministers from using public roads on their way to church.[1]

"[T]he State already has all the play in the joints it needs. [It] could make the scholarships redeemable only at public universities (where it sets the curriculum), or only for select courses of study. Either option would replace a program that facially discriminates against religion with one that just happens not to subsidize it.

"[T]he interest to which the Court defers is not fear of a conceivable Establishment Clause violation, budget constraints, avoidance of endorsement, or substantive neutrality[, but] a pure philosophical preference: the State's opinion that it would violate taxpayers' freedom of conscience *not* to discriminate against candidates for the ministry. This sort of protection of 'freedom of conscience' has no logical limit and can justify the singling out of religion for exclusion from public programs in virtually any context.[112] The Court never says whether it deems this interest compelling (the opinion is devoid of any mention of standard of review) but, self-evidently, it is not.[2]

"The Court [identifies] two features thought to render its discrimination less offensive. The first is the lightness of Davey's burden. The Court offers no authority for approving facial discrimination against religion simply because its material consequences are not severe. I might understand such a test if we were still in the business of reviewing facially neutral laws that merely happen to burden some individual's religious exercise, but we are not. See *Smith.* Discrimination *on the face of a statute* is something else. The indignity of being singled out for special burdens on the basis of one's religious calling is so profound that the concrete harm produced can never be dismissed as insubstantial[,] see e.g., *Brown v. Board of Education,* and it should not do so here. * * *

"The other reason the Court thinks this particular facial discrimination less offensive is that the scholarship program was not motivated by animus

---

[1] **[Ct's Note]** No State [with] a constitutional provision [that] prohibited the use of tax funds to support the ministry [has,] so far as I know, ever prohibited the hiring of public employees who use their salary to conduct ministries, or excluded ministers from generally available disability or unemployment benefits. * * * [For the view that the rule barring preferences among religions (Sec. 3 infra) "applies with particular force in cases in which religious lines are drawn by funding laws in which the benefit 'if applied uniformly to all religions' would comply with the Establishment Clause," see Richard F. Duncan, *The "Clearest Command" of the Establishment Clause: Denominational Preferences, Religious Liberty, and Public Scholarships that Classify Religions*, 55 S. D. L. Rev. 390 (2010).]

[112] The Court responded that "the only interest at issue here is the State's interest in not funding the religious training of clergy."

[2] **[Ct's Note]** [If] religious discrimination required only a rational basis, the Free Exercise Clause would impose no constraints other than those the Constitution already imposes on all government action. The question is not whether theology majors are different, but whether the differences are substantial enough to justify a discriminatory financial penalty that the State inflicts on no other major. Plainly they are not. * * *

toward religion. [We] do sometimes look to legislative intent to smoke out more subtle instances of discrimination, but we do so as a *supplement* to the core guarantee of facially equal treatment, not as a replacement for it.

"[Most] citizens of this country identify themselves as professing some religious belief, but [t]hose the statutory exclusion actually affects—those whose belief in their religion is so strong that they dedicate their study and their lives to its ministry—are a far narrower set. One need not delve too far into modern popular culture to perceive a trendy disdain for deep religious conviction."

(e) Does *Locke* permit a state to exclude religious elementary and secondary schools (or colleges and universities)—at least those that are "pervasively religious"—from a generally available program of state aid to education? See fn. 112. May a state choose not to fund religious aspects of the education provided by recipient schools? See Laycock, fn. 104; Ira C. Lupu & Robert W. Tuttle, *The Faith-Based Initiative and the Constitution,* 55 De Paul L. Rev. 1 (2005).

3. ***Action vs. inaction.*** Of what significance is it that all decisions sustaining Free Exercise claims against government regulations of conduct (*Sherbert—Thomas—Hobbie,* and *Yoder*) involved *inaction,* i.e., religious refusal to engage in conduct required by government rather than religiously dictated action forbidden by the state? In the case of *action* due to religious beliefs, should a distinction be drawn between action that is requested by the people affected and action that is imposed on others? Should the conviction of a religious Spiritualist for fortune telling be sustained despite the fact that fortunes were told only upon request?[113]

4. ***Choosing a "minister."*** In HOSANNA-TABOR EVANGELICAL LUTHERAN CHURCH AND SCHOOL v. EQUAL EMPLOYMENT OPPORTUNITY COMM'N, 132 S.Ct. 694 (2012), after the church school terminated Perich, a teacher who had completed the church's academic requirements to become a "minister," she filed a claim with the EEOC that her termination violated the Americans with Disabilities Act. Although "the Courts of Appeals have uniformly recognized [a] ministerial exception barring certain employment discrimination claims against religious institutions—an exception 'rooted in the First Amendment's guarantees of religious freedom,'" the Sixth Circuit concluded that Perich "did not qualify as a 'minister' under the exception." A unanimous Court, per ROBERTS, C.J., reversed: "The Establishment Clause prevents the Government from appointing ministers,

---

[113] For several recent approaches that evaluate a wide range of factors in considering religious exemptions from generally applicable laws, see Eugene Volokh, *A Common-Law Model for Religious Exemptions,* 46 UCLA L.Rev. 1465 (1999); Eugene Volokh, *Intermediate Questions of Religious Exemptions—A Research Agenda with Test Suites,* 21 Card.L.Rev. 595 (1999); Jesse H. Choper, *Securing Religious Liberty* ch. 3 (1995).

and the Free Exercise Clause prevents it from interfering with the freedom of religious groups to select [those] who will personify its beliefs."[114]

The Court was "reluctant [to] adopt a rigid formula for deciding when an employee qualifies as a minister," but noted that the church "held Perich out as a minister," and that she "held herself out as a minister of the church" in various ways. "Perich's title as a minister reflected a significant degree of religious training followed by a formal process of commissioning. [S]he had to pass an oral examination by a faculty committee at a Lutheran college. It took Perich six years to fulfill these requirements. [She] taught her students religion four days a week, and led them in prayer three times a day. Once a week, she took her students to a school-wide chapel service, and—about twice a year—she took her turn leading [it.]" Finally, in regarding "the relative amount of time Perich spent performing religious functions as largely determinative" (this "consumed only 45 minutes of each workday") rather than just "relevant," the Sixth Circuit "gave too much weight to the fact that lay teachers at the school performed the same religious duties. [The] heads of congregations themselves often have a mix of duties, including secular ones such as helping to manage the congregations' finances, supervising purely secular personnel, and overseeing the upkeep of facilities."

Alito, J., joined by Kagan, J., concurred, urging that "courts should focus on the function performed by persons who work for religious bodies. [The] 'ministerial' exception [should] apply to any 'employee' who leads a religious organization, conducts worship services or important religious ceremonies or rituals, or serves as a messenger or teacher of its faith."[115]

II. UNUSUAL RELIGIOUS BELIEFS AND PRACTICES

1. *Validity and sincerity.* In UNITED STATES v. BALLARD, 322 U.S. 78 (1944), defendant was indicted for mail fraud. He had solicited funds for the "I Am" movement, asserting, inter alia, that he had been selected as a divine messenger, had divine power of healing incurable diseases, and had talked with Jesus and would transmit these conversations to mankind. The Court, per DOUGLAS, J., held that the First Amendment barred submitting to the jury the question whether these religious beliefs were true: "Men may believe what they cannot [prove.] Religious experiences real as life to some may be incomprehensible to others. [The] miracles of the New Testament, the Divinity of Christ, life after death, the power of prayer are deep in the religious convictions of many. If one could be sent to jail because a jury in a hostile environment found those teachings false, little indeed would be left of religious freedom."

---

[114] For the point that ministers have "precisely the same right" as churches, e.g., "a minister who leaves one church for another cannot be sued for breach of fiduciary duty," see Christopher C. Lund, *In Defense of the Ministerial Exception*, 90 N.C.L. Rev. 1 (2011).

[115] Thomas, J., concurred, adding that the fact that the church "sincerely considered Perich a minister" was sufficient for him to apply the ministerial exception.

(a) *Ballard* permits the prosecution to prove that, whether or not the incidents described by defendant happened, he did not honestly believe that they had. If so, may the prosecution introduce evidence that the incidents did not in fact happen and thus defendant could not honestly believe that they did? Should this line of proof be permitted in the prosecution of a Catholic church official for soliciting funds to construct a shrine commemorating the Miracle of Fatima in 1930?

(b) Is it relevant that in *Ballard* the alleged divine revelation was made only to Ballard and that the experiences had allegedly occurred at a definite time and place? Many Biblical happenings are so identified. Could the prosecution introduce evidence that Ballard was not physically present at the alleged place and time? If Protestant, Catholic or Jewish clergy were prosecuted and there was overwhelming scientific evidence disputing the Biblical doctrine, what would the jury be likely to find as to the sincerity of the beliefs? Should the First Amendment permit people to obtain money in the name of religion by knowingly making false statements? See Ronald J. Krotoszynski, Jr., *The Apostle, Mr. Justice Jackson, and the "Pathological Perpsective" of the Free Exercise Clause,* 65 Wash. & Lee L. Rev. 1071 ("inquiries into subjective good faith are virtually certain to devolve into questions about the cultural acceptability—indeed plausibility—of a particular sect"). Compare Tribe 2d ed., at 1243–47.

(c) Should the prosecution be able to prove that defendant had stated on many occasions that he believed none of his representations but by saying that he did he was amassing great wealth? Suppose it can be shown that a priest or rabbi is *somewhat* skeptical as to the truth of certain Biblical occurrences? See John T. Noonan, Jr., *How Sincere Do You Have to Be to Be Religious,* 1988 U.Ill.L.Rev. 713. After *Smith,* could Ballard be convicted on the ground that fraudulent procurement of money is a generally applicable regulation of conduct which may be constitutionally prohibited even if done in the name of religion?

2. *What is "religion"?* May the Court determine that asserted religious beliefs and practices do not constitute a valid religion? Consider Jonathan Weiss, *Privilege, Posture and Protection—"Religion" in the Law,* 73 Yale L.J. 593 (1964): "[A]ny definition of religion would seem to violate religious freedom in that it would dictate to religions, present and future, what they must [be]. Furthermore, an attempt to define religion, even for purposes of increasing freedom for religions, would run afoul of the Establishment Clause as excluding some religions, or even as establishing a notion respecting religion."

Is it relevant that the beliefs of a group do not include the existence of God?

TORCASO v. WATKINS, per BLACK, J., 367 U.S. 488 (1961), invalidated a Maryland provision requiring a declaration of belief in God as a test for public office: "[Government cannot] impose requirements which aid all religions as against nonbelievers, and neither can aid those religions based on a belief in the existence of God as against those religions founded on different beliefs." The Court noted that "among religions [that] do not teach what would generally be considered a belief in the existence of God are Buddhism, Taoism, Ethical Culture, Secular Humanism and others."[116]

Are atheism and agnosticism "religions"? Contrast Douglas Laycock, *Religious Liberty as Liberty,* 7 J. Contemp. Leg. Issues 313 (1996) ("for constitutional purposes, any answer to religious questions is religion") and 1 Greenawalt at 149–150 ("atheists have free exercise rights [that do] not necessarily parallel rights of traditional believers"). Consider Paul G. Kauper, *Religion and the Constitution* 31 (1964): "What makes secular humanism a religion? Is it because it is an ideology or system of belief that attempts to furnish a rationale of life? [If so], must not democracy, fascism, and communism also qualify as religions? [S]ome find in these systems an adequate explanation of the meaning and purpose of life and the source of values that command faith and devotion." Compare Nelson Tebbe, *Nonbelievers,* 97 Va. L. Rev. 1111 (2011): Courts "should handle nonbelievers [including "atheists, agnostics, secular humanists, and freethinkers"] differently according to [a] range of considerations, including not only constitutional principles but also history, precedent, popular opinion, and practicality."

May a single person establish his or her own religion? Consider Milton Konvitz, *Religious Liberty and Conscience* 84 (1968): "[Many religions] had their origin in a 'private and personal' religious experience. Mohammed did not take over an on-going, established religion; the history of Islam records the names of his first three converts. John Wesley is given credit as the founder of Methodism. Mary Baker Eddy was the founder of the Christian Science church. Menno Simons organized a division of Anabaptists that in due course became the sect known as the Mennonites. Jacob Ammon broke away from the Mennonites and founded the sect known as the Amish."

How important is it that the group has regular weekly services? Designated leaders who conduct the services? Ceremonies for naming, marrying and burying members? Does the First Amendment extend only to those groups that conform to the "conventional" concept of religion? Consider Harvey Cox (Harvard Divinity School), N.Y. Times 25 (Feb. 16, 1977): "[C]ourts [often] turn to some vague 'man-in-the-street' idea of what 'religion' should be. [But that] approach would surely have ruled out early

---

[116] Contra, Abner S. Greene, *Religion and Theistic Faith: On Koppelman, Leiter, Secular Purpose, and Accommodations,* 49 Tulsa L. Rev. 441 (2013) ("for most Americans, from the founding through today, religion includes theistic belief of some sort"). For a review of Ronald Dworkin's position "that believers and nonbelievers should stand as political equals," see Micah Schwartzman, *Religion, Equality, and Public, Reason,* 94 B. U. L. Rev. 1321 (2014).

Christianity, which seemed both subversive and atheistic to the religious Romans of the day. The truth is that one man's 'bizarre cult' is another's true path to salvation, and the Bill of Rights was designed to safeguard minorities from the man-on-the-street's uncertain capacity for tolerance." To what extent should a group's "brainwashing," mental coercion techniques affect its constitutional status as a "religion"? Compare Richard Delgado, *Religious Totalism: Gentle and Ungentle Persuasion Under the First Amendment,* 51 So.Cal.L.Rev. 1 (1977) with 1 Greenawalt 310–15.

Suppose that a group has certain characteristics of "traditional" religions, such as a holy book, ministers, houses of worship, prescribed prayers, a strict moral code, a belief in the hereafter and an appeal to faith, but also has announced social and economic tenets? (Methodism developed originally out of social concerns.) Consider Note, *Toward a Constitutional Definition of Religion,* 91 Harv.L.Rev. 1056 (1978): "[A] spokesman for the new 'liberation theology' within Catholicism argues that true religion is to be found in ['the] creation of a new social consciousness and as a social appropriation not only of the means of production, but also of the political processes.' The church, he says, seeks 'the abolition of the exploitation of man by man.' The views [of] significant Christian theologians coalesce around one important theme: the Christian church will find itself only by discarding what until now has been perceived to be religious and by immersing itself in the secular world." Does the First Amendment encompass any political, philosophical, moral or social doctrine that some group sincerely espouses as its "religion"?

UNITED STATES v. SEEGER, 380 U.S. 163 (1965): § 6(j) of the Universal Military Training and Service Act exempted from combat any person "who, by reason of religious training and belief, is conscientiously opposed to participation in war in any form. Religious training and belief in this [means] an individual's belief in a relation to a Supreme Being involving duties superior to those arising from any human relation, but does not include essentially political, sociological or philosophical views or a merely personal moral code."[117] The Court, per CLARK, J., avoided constitutional questions and upheld claims for exemption of three conscientious objectors. One declared "that he preferred to leave the question as to his belief in a Supreme Being open, [and] that his was a 'belief in and devotion to goodness and virtue for their own sakes, and a religious faith in a purely ethical creed.' " Another said "that he felt it a violation of his moral code to take human life and that he considered this belief superior to his obligation to the state. [He quoted] Reverend John

---

[117] The statute was subsequently amended to omit the "belief in a Supreme Being" element. For the view that "religion" under the First Amendment "involves some conception of God," see Michael S. Paulsen, *God is Great, Garvey is Good: Making Sense of Religious Freedom,* 72 Not.D.L.Rev. 1597 (1997): "Text and historical evidence of original meaning should settle the matter. If this seems illiberal today, [it is] unfortunate, but irrelevant to the task of textual interpretation of the constitutional provision the framers wrote."

Haynes Holmes' definition of religion as 'the consciousness of some power manifest in nature which helps man in the ordering of his life in harmony with its demands * * *; it is man thinking his highest, feeling his deepest, and living his best.' The source of his conviction he attributed to reading and meditation 'in our democratic American culture, with its values derived from the western religious and philosophical tradition.' As to his belief in a Supreme Being, Peter stated that he supposed 'you could call that a belief in the Supreme Being or God. These just do not happen to be the words I use.' "

The Court "concluded that Congress, in using the expression 'Supreme Being' [was] merely clarifying the meaning of religious training and belief so as to embrace all religions and to exclude essentially political, sociological, or philosophical views [and that] the test [is] whether a given belief that is sincere and meaningful occupies a place in the life of its possessor parallel to that filled by the orthodox belief in God of one who clearly qualifies for the exemption. [No] party claims to be an atheist. [We] do not deal with [that. The] use by Congress of the words 'merely personal' seems to us to restrict the exception to a moral code which [is] in no way related to a Supreme Being. [Congress did] not distinguish between externally and internally derived beliefs. Such a determination [would] prove impossible as a practical matter."

In WELSH v. UNITED STATES, 398 U.S. 333 (1970), petitioner's application for exemption, "struck the word 'religious' entirely and later characterized his beliefs as having been formed 'by reading in the fields of history and sociology.' " BLACK, J., joined by Douglas, Brennan and Marshall, JJ., held that, under *Seeger,* "if an individual deeply and sincerely holds beliefs which are purely ethical or moral in source and content but that nevertheless impose upon him a duty of conscience to refrain from participating in any war at any time, those beliefs certainly occupy in the life of that individual 'a place parallel to that filled [by] God' in traditionally religious persons." "Although [Welsh] originally characterized his beliefs as nonreligious, he later upon reflection wrote a long and thoughtful letter to his Appeal Board in which he declared that his beliefs were 'certainly religious in the ethical sense of that word.' [§ 6(j)'s] exclusion [of] 'essentially political, sociological, or philosophical views or a merely personal moral code' should [not] be read to exclude those who hold strong beliefs about our domestic and foreign affairs or even those whose conscientious objection to participation in all wars is founded to a substantial extent [on] public policy. The two groups of registrants which obviously do fall within these exclusions from the exemption are those whose beliefs are not deeply held and those whose objection to war does not rest at all upon moral, ethical, or religious principle [but] solely upon considerations of policy, pragmatism, or expediency."[118]

3. *What is "religious belief"?* (a) Of what significance is that the practice is an "age-old form" of religious conduct (*Murdock*)? A "cardinal principle" of the asserted religious faith (*Sherbert*)? Consider Laycock, fn. 10: "Many activities that obviously are exercises of religion are not required by conscience or doctrine. Singing in the church choir and saying the Roman Catholic rosary are [two] examples. Any activity engaged in by a church as a body is an exercise of religion. [Indeed,] many would say that an emphasis on rules and obligations misconceives the essential nature of some religions." Compare Donald Giannella, *Religious Liberty Nonestablishment and Doctrinal Development*, 80 Harv.L.Rev. 1381 (1967): "Personal alienation from one's Maker, frustration of one's ultimate mission in life, and violation of the religious person's integrity are all at stake when the right to worship is threatened. Although the seeker of new psychological worlds [through use of hallucinogens] may feel equally frustrated when deprived of his gropings for a higher reality, there is not the same sense [of] loss of the Be-all and End-all of life. [A] different problem presents itself when an individual who does not believe in a supernatural or personal God asserts conscientious objection to certain conduct because of its injurious effects on his fellow man. [T]his ethical belief may be held with such a degree of intensity that its violation occasions the same interior revulsion and anguish as does violation of the law of God to the pious." On what evidence should these factual questions be determined?

For the view that "belief [in] 'extratemporal consequences'—whether the effects of actions taken pursuant or contrary to the dictates of a person's beliefs extend in some meaningful way beyond his lifetime—is a sensible and desirable criterion (albeit plainly far short of ideal) for determining when the Free Exercise Clause should trigger judicial consideration of whether exemption from general government regulations of conduct is constitutionally required," see Jesse H. Choper, *Defining "Religion" in the First Amendment*, 1982 U.Ill.L.Rev. 579:[119] "It may be persuasively argued that *all* beliefs that invoke a transcendent reality—and especially those that provide their adherents with glimpses of meaning and truth that make them so important and so uncompromisable—should be encompassed by the special constitutional protection granted 'religion' by the Free Exercise clause. [In] many ways, however, there is at bedrock only a gossamer line

---

[118] In separate opinions, Harlan, J., and White, J., (joined by Burger, C.J., and Stewart, J.) dissented on the issue of statutory construction. For their views on the constitutional issue, see Sec. 4 infra. Blackmun, J., took no part.

[119] For criticism, see Stanley Ingber, *Religion or Ideology: A Needed Clarification of the Religion Clauses*, 41 Stan.L.Rev. 233 (1989); Note, *Religion and Morality Legislation: A Reexamination of Establishment Clause Analysis*, 59 N.Y.U.L.Rev. 301 (1984); Note, *Defining "Religion" in the First Amendment: A Functional Approach*, 74 Corn.L.Rev. 532 (1989).

between 'rational' and 'supernatural' causation—the former based on such 'rational' disciplines as economics, political science, sociology, or psychology, or even such 'hard' sciences [as] physics really being little more capable of 'scientific proof' than the latter."[120] Compare Kent Greenawalt, *Religion as a Concept in Constitutional Law,* 72 Calif.L.Rev. 753 (1984): "No specification of essential conditions will capture all and only the beliefs, practices, and organizations that are regarded as religious in modern culture and should be treated as such under the Constitution. [Rather, determining] whether questionable beliefs, practices, and organizations are religious by seeing how closely they resemble what is undeniably religious is a method that has been implicitly used by courts [and] is consonant with Supreme Court decisions."[121]

(b) *Judicial role.* In THOMAS v. REVIEW BD., Part I supra, petitioner testified that, although his religious convictions forbade him to manufacture weapons, "he could, in good conscience, engage indirectly in the production, [for] example, as an employee of a raw material supplier." The state court, viewing petitioner's positions as inconsistent, ruled that he had made a "personal philosophical rather than a religious choice." The Court, per BURGER, C.J. reversed: "[D]etermination of what is a 'religious' belief or practice is [a] difficult and delicate task, [but] resolution of that question is not to turn upon a judicial perception of the particular belief or practice[;] religious beliefs need not be acceptable, logical, consistent, or comprehensible to others in order to merit First Amendment protection. [It is] not for us to say that the line Thomas drew was an unreasonable one. Courts should not undertake to dissect religious beliefs because the believer admits that he is 'struggling' with his position or because his beliefs are not articulated with the clarity and precision that a more sophisticated person might employ.

"The Indiana court also appears to have given significant weight to the fact that [for] another Jehovah's Witness [such] work was 'scripturally' acceptable. Intra-faith differences of that kind are not uncommon [and] the judicial process is singularly ill equipped to resolve such differences in

---

[120] For the view that religion should be defined as dealing with "quintessentially religious questions," "addressing the profound questions of human existence," "such as God's existence or the proper definition of life and death," see Tom Stacy, *Death, Privacy, and the Free Exercise of Religion,* 77 Corn.L.Rev. 490 (1992). Compare Donald L. Beschle, *Does a Broad Free Exercise Right Require a Narrow Definition of "Religion"?* 39 Hast. Con. L. Q. 357 (2012): "Courts should respond to the expansion of the scope of religion in recent decades by substituting the concept of conscience for a traditional or social science-based definition of religion" and use a test of "intermediate scrutiny."

[121] Accord, George C. Freeman, III, *The Misguided Search for the Constitutional Definition of "Religion,"* 71 Geo.L.J. 1519 (1983). See also Eduardo Peñalver, *The Concept of Religion,* 107 Yale L.J. 791 (1997) (supporting approach that "takes into account the evolutionary nature of language" and "tries to minimize [western] judicial bias"). For the view that "the original meaning of religion is a monotheistic belief system, such as Christianity, that holds true to a future state of rewards and punishments and thus imposes duties on believers in this world," see Lee J. Strang, *The Meaning of "Religion" in the First Amendment,* 40 Duq.L.Rev. 181 (2002).

relation to the Religion Clauses. [The] narrow function of a reviewing court in this context is to determine [whether] petitioner terminated his work because of an honest conviction that such work was forbidden by his religion."

4. *Variable definition.* May "religion" be defined differently for purposes of the Establishment Clause than the Free Exercise Clause? Consider Marc S. Galanter, *Religious Freedom in the United States: A Turning Point?* 1966 Wis.L.Rev. 217: "[For purposes of the Establishment Clause, the] effect and purpose of government action are not to be assessed by the religious sensibilities of the person who is complaining [but] in some widely shared public understanding. [For the Free Exercise Clause, the] claimants' view of religion controls the characterization of their objection as a religious one." Does this analysis solve the dilemma of Leonard F. Manning, *The Douglas Concept of God in Government,* 39 Wash.L.Rev. 47 (1964): "If religion need not be predicated on a belief in God or even in a god and if it may not be tested by the common consensus of what reasonable men would reasonably call religion, [might] not a group of gymnasts proclaiming on their trampolines that physical culture is their religion be engaged in a religious exercise? And if Congress, in a particular Olympic year, appropriated funds to subsidize their calisthenics would this not [be] an establishment of religion?" See generally Note, *Transcendental Meditation and the Meaning of Religion Under the Establishment Clause,* 62 Minn.L.Rev. 887 (1978); 1 Greenawalt at 141–42.

3. PREFERENCE AMONG RELIGIONS

In BOARD OF EDUC. OF KIRYAS JOEL v. GRUMET, 512 U.S. 687 (1994), a New York statute constituted the Village of Kiryas Joel—"a religious enclave of Satmar Hasidim, practitioners of a strict form of Judaism"—as a separate school district. Most of the children attend pervasively religious private schools. The newly created district "currently runs only a special education program for handicapped [Satmar] children" who reside both inside and outside the village. The statute was passed "to enable the village's handicapped children to receive a secular, public-school education" because when they previously attended public schools in the larger school district outside the village, they suffered "panic, fear and trauma [in] leaving their own community and being with people whose ways were so different." The Court, per SOUTER, J., invoked "a principle at the heart of the Establishment Clause, that government should not prefer one religion to another. [As] Kiryas Joel did not receive [its] new authority simply as one of many communities eligible for equal treatment under a general law, we have no assurance that the next similarly situated group seeking a school district of its own will receive one; [and] a legislature's failure to enact a special law is itself unreviewable.[122] [Here] the benefit flows only to a single sect,[123] [and] therefore crosses the line from permissible accommodation to impermissible establishment."[124]

KENNEDY, J., concurred in the judgment: "Whether or not the purpose is accommodation and whether or not the government provides similar gerrymanders to people of all religious faiths, the Establishment Clause forbids the government to use religion [as] a criterion to draw political or electoral lines."[125]

SCALIA, J., joined by Rehnquist, C.J., and Thomas, J., dissented: "[A]ll the residents of the Kiryas Joel Village School District are Satmars. But all its residents also wear unusual dress, have unusual civic customs, and have not much to do with people who are culturally different from them. [I]t was not theology but dress, language, and cultural alienation that posed the educational problem for the children [and caused the Legislature to] provide a public education for these students, in the same way it addressed, by a similar law, the unique needs of children institutionalized in a hospital. [T]he creation of a special, one-culture school district for the benefit of [children whose] parents were nonreligious commune dwellers, or American Indians, or gypsies [would] pose no problem. The neutrality demanded by the Religion Clauses requires the same indulgence towards cultural characteristics that are accompanied by religious belief."[126]

---

[122] Kennedy, J., disagreed: if another religious community were denied legislative help, it "could sue the State of New York, contending that New York's discriminatory treatment of the two religious communities violated the Establishment Clause. [T]he court would have only to determine whether the community does indeed bear the same burden on its religious practice as [did] Kiryas Joel. While a finding of discrimination would then raise a difficult question of relief, [but see] *Califano v. Westcott*, 443 U.S. 76 (1979) (curing gender discrimination in the AFDC program by extending benefits to children of unemployed mothers instead of denying benefits to children of unemployed fathers), the discrimination itself would not be beyond judicial remedy."

[123] Compare Thomas C. Berg, *Slouching Towards Secularism*, 44 Emory L.J. 433 (1995): "[T]he legislature specifically accommodated the Satmars [because] their plight was unique: no other group of children was being denied effective special education because they were traumatized by the atmosphere of the mainstream public schools. [Even] if the children of other groups had been harmed by the public school ethos, few if any such groups live together communally [like] the Satmars." But see Ira C. Lupu, *The Lingering Death of Separationism*, 62 Geo.Wash.L.Rev. 230 (1994): "Is it imaginable that New York State would create a new public school district at the behest of an insular group of Branch Davidians or the Unification Church, whose children [may] suffer panic, fear, and trauma at encountering those outside their own community?"

[124] Within ten days of *Kiryas Joel,* the New York legislature passed a new law allowing "any municipality situated wholly within a single school district" to form its own district if it meets designated criteria regarding population, enrollment and property wealth. Constitutional when used by the Village of Kiryas Joel?

[125] For similarities and differences between the use of religion and race [Ch. 9, Sec. 5, B] in drawing political districts, see Abner S. Greene, *Kiryas Joel and Two Mistakes About Equality*, 96 Colum.L.Rev. 1 (1996).

[126] Is this persuasive when there is total congruence between a religion and distinctive cultural needs *and* the cultural distinctiveness is defined by the religion?

NOTES AND QUESTIONS

1. ***Delegation of government power.*** In *Kiryas Joel,* SOUTER, J., joined by Blackmun, Stevens and Ginsburg, JJ., found an additional ground for invalidating the statute: "delegating the State's discretionary authority over public schools to a group defined by its character as a religious community, in a legal and historical context that gives no assurance that governmental power has been or will be exercised neutrally." They relied on LARKIN v. GRENDEL'S DEN, INC., 459 U.S. 116 (1982), per BURGER, C.J., which held that a Massachusetts law (§ 16C), giving churches and schools the power "to veto applications for liquor licenses within a five hundred foot radius of the church or school, violates the Establishment Clause": "§ 16C [delegates] discretionary governmental powers [to] religious bodies.

"[The] valid secular objectives [of protecting] from the 'hurly-burly' associated with liquor outlets [can] be readily accomplished by [an] absolute legislative ban on liquor outlets within reasonable prescribed distances from churches, schools, hospitals and like institutions, or by ensuring a hearing for the views of affected institutions at licensing proceedings. [But the] churches' power under the statute is standardless [and] may therefore be used [for] example, favoring liquor licenses for members of that congregation. [And] the mere appearance of a joint exercise of legislative authority by Church and State provides a significant symbolic benefit to religion in the minds of some. [T]he statute can be seen as having a 'primary' and 'principal' effect of advancing religion. [Finally, § 16C] enmeshes churches in the processes of government and creates the danger of 'political fragmentation and divisiveness along religious lines.' "

REHNQUIST, J., dissented: A "flat ban [on] the grant of an alcoholic beverages license to any establishment located within 500 feet of a church or a [school], which the majority concedes is valid, is more protective of churches and more restrictive of liquor sales than the present § 16C [which] does not sponsor or subsidize any religious group or activity. It does not encourage, much less compel, anyone to participate in religious activities or to support religious institutions. [If] a church were to [favor] its members [for licenses], there would be an occasion to determine whether it had violated any right of an unsuccessful applicant for a liquor license."

SCALIA, J., joined by Rehnquist, C.J., and Thomas, J., dissenting in *Kiryas Joel,* argued that *Grendel's Den* had ruled that "a state may not delegate its civil authority *to a church,"* not to "groups of people sharing a common religious and cultural heritage": "If the conferral of governmental power upon a religious institution *as such* (rather than upon American citizens who belong to the religious institution) is not the test of *Grendel's Den* invalidity, [it] might have made the entire States of Utah and New Mexico unconstitutional at the time of their admission to the Union."

2. ***"Excessive government entanglement" in ecclesiastical disputes.*** (a) In JONES v. WOLF, 443 U.S. 595 (1979), a majority of the Vineville Presbyterian Church voted to separate from the Presbyterian Church

in the United States (PCUS). A commission of PCUS, acting pursuant to the PCUS constitution (called the Book of Church Order), declared the Vineville minority to be "the true congregation." The minority sued for the local church property. The state court applied "the 'neutral principles of law' method for resolving church property disputes. The court examined the deeds to the properties, the state statutes dealing with implied trusts, and the Book of Church Order, to determine whether there was any basis for a trust in favor of the general church. Finding [none], the court awarded the property on the basis of legal title, which was in the local church."

The Court, per BLACKMUN, J., stated the established principle that "the First Amendment prohibits civil courts from resolving church property disputes on the basis of religious doctrine and practice. *Presbyterian Church v. Hull Church,* 393 U.S. 440 (1969). [The] Amendment requires that civil courts defer to the resolution of issues of religious doctrine [by] the highest court of a hierarchical church organization. *Serbian Eastern Orthodox Diocese v. Milivojevich,* 426 U.S. 696 (1976).[127] Subject to these limitations, [however,] 'a State may adopt *any* of various approaches for settling church property [disputes].'

"[W]e think the 'neutral principles of law' approach is consistent with the foregoing constitutional principles. [It] relies extensively on objective, well-established concepts of trust and property law [to] free civil courts completely from entanglement in questions of religious doctrine, polity, and practice. Furthermore, [it affords] flexibility [to] reflect the intentions of the parties. [R]eligious societies can specify what is to happen to church property in the event of a particular contingency. [The] neutral principles method [does require] a civil court to examine certain religious documents, such as a church constitution, for language of trust in favor of the general church. [A] civil court must take special care to scrutinize the document in purely secular terms [in] determining whether the document indicates that the parties have intended to create a trust. [If] the interpretation of the instruments of ownership would require the civil court to resolve a religious controversy, then the court must defer to [the] authoritative ecclesiastical body. *Serbian.*"

POWELL, J., joined by Burger, C.J., and Stewart and White, JJ., dissented, finding that the neutral principles "approach inevitably will increase the involvement of civil courts in church controversies[rather than relying on whether] the rules of polity, accepted by its members[, had] placed ultimate authority over the use of the church property. The courts, in answering this question have recognized two broad categories of church government. One is

---

[127] *Serbian,* per Brennan, J., reversed a state court decision that the Mother Church's removal of respondent as bishop was "procedurally and substantively defective under the internal regulations of the Mother Church and were therefore arbitrary and invalid": "[W]hether or not there is room for 'marginal civil court review' [when] church tribunals act in bad faith for secular purposes, no 'arbitrariness' exception—in the sense of an inquiry whether the decisions of the highest ecclesiastical tribunal of a hierarchical church complied with church laws and regulations—is consistent with the constitutional mandate. [E]cclesiastical decisions are reached and are to be accepted as matters of faith whether or not rational or measurable by objective criteria." Rehnquist and Stevens, JJ., dissented.

congregational, in which authority over questions of church doctrine, practice, and administration rests entirely in the local congregation or some body within [it]. The second is hierarchical [and] this Court has held that the civil courts must give effect to the duly made decisions of the highest body within the hierarchy that has considered the dispute." See generally 1 Greenawalt ch. 16.

(b) **Scope of the decision.** After *Jones*, what results for the following: (i) A donor who made a bequest "to the First Methodist Church" seeks return of the money because subsequently a majority of the church's members decided to affiliate with another denomination.[128] Suppose the bequest had been "to the First Methodist Church so long as it does not substantially deviate from existing doctrine"? (ii) A statute makes it a crime for sellers to falsely represent food to be "kosher." See Kent Greenawalt, *Religious Law and Civil Law: Using Secular Law to Assure Observance of Practices with Religious Significance*, 71 So.Cal.L.Rev. 781 (1998). (iii) An adult sues a member of the clergy for "malpractice" based on consensual sexual acts with plaintiff. See Scott C. Idleman, *Tort Liability, Religious Entities, and the Decline of Constitutional Protection*, 75 Ind. L.J., 219 (2000).

LARSON v. VALENTE, 456 U.S. 228 (1982): The Unification Church ("Moonies") challenged "a Minnesota statute, imposing certain registration and reporting requirements upon only those religious organizations that solicit more than fifty per cent of their funds from nonmembers." The Court, per BRENNAN, J., noting that "the clearest command of the Establishment Clause is that one religious denomination cannot be officially preferred over another, [*Everson*]," and that this "is inextricably connected with the continuing vitality of the Free Exercise Clause," held that the statute violated the Establishment Clause because it did not survive "strict scrutiny."[129] Assuming that the state's "valid secular purpose [in] protecting its citizens from abusive practices in the solicitation of funds for charity" is "compelling,"[130] the state "failed to demonstrate that the fifty per cent rule [is] 'closely fitted' " to furthering that interest. Moreover, the statute failed the third *Lemon* "test": "The [rule] effects the *selective* legislative imposition of burdens and advantages upon particular denominations. The 'risk of politicizing religion' that inheres in such legislation [is] confirmed by the provision's legislative history [which]

---

[128] For discussion of the complexities in the conflict between the "religious liberty of religious institutions" and church members who "feel that the decisions of the national leadership are burdening their religious liberty rather than affirming or protecting it," see Alan Brownstein, *Protecting the Religious Liberty of Religious Institutions*, 21 J. Contemp. Leg. Issues 201 (2013).

[129] The Court reasoned that this "effectively distinguishes between 'well-established churches' that have 'achieved strong but not total financial support from their members,' on the one hand, and 'churches which are new [or,] which, as a matter of policy, may favor public solicitation over general reliance on financial support from members,' on the other hand."

[130] *Gillette* held that there was no religious "gerrymander" if there was "a neutral, secular basis for the lines government has drawn."

demonstrates that the provision was drafted with the explicit intention of including particular religious denominations and excluding others."

WHITE, J., joined by Rehnquist, J., dissented:[131] "The rule [names] no churches or denominations. [Some] religions will qualify and some will not, but this depends on the source of their contributions, not on their brand of religion."

NOTES AND QUESTIONS

1. ***The Gillette rationale.*** (a) Should a "neutral and secular basis" (*Gillette* opinion) justify government preference—de jure or de facto—among religions? Consider Kent Greenawalt, *All or Nothing at All: The Defeat of Selective Conscientious Objection,* 1971 Sup.Ct.Rev. 31: "If a sociological survey indicated that Protestants generally work harder than Catholics, the government might simplify its hiring problems by interviewing only Protestants. If the doctors of Catholic hospitals were determined to be on the average more qualified than those at Lutheran hospitals, aid might be limited to the Catholic hospitals." How significant was the Court's observation that the *Gillette* law "attempts to accommodate free exercise values"?

(b) Was the Draft Act of 1917, which exempted only conscientious objectors affiliated with some "well-recognized religious sect" whose principles forbade participation in war, valid under *Gillette* and *Larson?* See Jeremy Patrick-Justice, *Strict Scrutiny for Denominational Preferences: Larson in Retrospect,* 8 N. Y. City L. Rev. 53 (2005). Consider 48 Minn.L.Rev. 776 (1964): "[S]ince membership in an organized pacifist sect may be better evidence of sincerity than the mere assertion of pacificist beliefs, a requirement to that effect should be permissible." May (should) an exemption for peyote be limited to religious groups like the Native American Church that consider its use essential? (The federal exemption is limited to that church.) See Greenawalt, 1 *Religion and the* Constitution at 71–74. See also id. at 98–100.

For a comprehensive analysis concluding that "the Court's accommodation decisions represent a surprisingly coherent model [that] religious accommodations must satisfy four" norms, see Ira C. Lupu & Robert W. Tuttle, *Instruments of Accommodation: The Military Chaplaincy and the Constitution,* 110 W. Va. L. Rev. 89 (2007): (1) "a reasonable effort to relieve a government-imposed burden on religious practice"; (2) beneficiaries must "participate voluntarily"; (3) the accommodation must be "available on a denominationally-neutral basis"; and (4) must not "impose significant burdens on third parties."

2. ***The Larson rationale.*** (a) Consider Jesse H. Choper, *The Free Exercise Clause: A Structural Overview and an Appraisal of Recent Developments,* 27 Wm. & M.L.Rev. 943 (1986): "The major thrust of the Court's opinion [used] classic Free Exercise Clause analysis[:] strict scrutiny. [Even if] the Minnesota statute did not specifically give preference to some religions

---

[131] Rehnquist, J., joined by Burger, C.J. and White and O'Connor, JJ., also dissented on the ground that the church had no standing.

over others, [it] resulted in favoring some and disfavoring others [and] should have [been] subject to the same level of scrutiny as a general, neutral law that says nothing about religion but [has] an adverse impact on some faiths, [as] in *Yoder*. [In] reality, I believe that the Selective Service Act survived strict scrutiny in *Gillette* [because of the] powerful government interest in raising an army and the difficulties in administering a draft exemption based on 'just war' beliefs. [In] sum, the doctrine in *Gillette,* [plainly] supports Justice White's dissent in *Larson.* The *Gillette* doctrine, however, effectively has been abandoned, and rightly so."

(b) HERNANDEZ v. COMMISSIONER, 490 U.S. 680 (1989), per MARSHALL, J., found no violation of the Establishment Clause in not permitting federal taxpayers to deduct as "charitable contributions" required "donations" to the Church of Scientology for "training" sessions to study the faith's tenets and to increase spiritual awareness. The proceeds are the Church's primary source of income. *Larson* was distinguished on the ground that IRS disallowance for payments made "with some expectation of a quid pro quo in terms of goods or services [makes] no 'explicit and deliberate distinctions between different religious organizations.' "

O'CONNOR, J., joined by Scalia, J., dissented: "[S]ome of the fixed payments which the IRS has treated as charitable deductions [are as much a 'quid pro quo exchange'] as the payments [here]": "In exchange for their payment of pew rents, Christians receive particular seats during worship services. Similarly, in some synagogues attendance at the worship services for Jewish High Holy Days is often predicated upon the purchase of a [ticket.] Mormons must tithe ten percent of their income as a necessary but not sufficient condition [for] the right to be admitted into the temple. A Mass stipend—a fixed payment given to a Catholic priest, in consideration of which he is obliged to apply the fruits of the Mass for the intention of the donor—has similar overtones of exchange." Brennan and Kennedy, JJ., did not participate.

3. ***Preference for "religious" objectors.*** Is Congress' limitation of draft exemption to "religious" conscientious objectors valid? Consider John H. Mansfield, *Conscientious Objection—1964 Term,* 1965 Relig. & Pub.Or. 3: "[Compared to a] non-religious conscientious objector [t]he religious objector's opposition rests on somewhat more fundamental grounds [and] makes reference to realities that can more easily be described as spiritual. But the non-religious conscientious objector's opposition does rest on basic propositions about the nature of reality and the significance of human existence; this is what distinguishes it from objection that is not even conscientious." Does the "religious" exemption result in more or less government "entanglement" with religion than an exemption for *all* conscientious objectors?

4. CONFLICT BETWEEN THE CLAUSES

The decision in *Employment Division v. Smith* appeared to have relieved some of the tension that had existed between the doctrines that the Court had developed under the Establishment and Free Exercise

Clauses. But substantial questions remained, e.g., do (a) the decisions in *Sherbert (Thomas, Hobbie), Yoder* and *Roy,* and (b) statutes granting religious exemptions from laws of general applicability violate the Establishment Clause because they impermissibly aid religion?

CORPORATION OF THE PRESIDING BISHOP OF THE CHURCH OF JESUS CHRIST OF LATTER-DAY SAINTS V. AMOS

483 U.S. 327, 107 S.Ct. 2862, 97 L.Ed.2d 273 (1987).

JUSTICE WHITE delivered the opinion of the Court.

Section 702 of the Civil Rights Act of 1964 exempts religious organizations from Title VII's prohibition against discrimination in employment on the basis of religion. [The] Deseret Gymnasium (Gymnasium) in Salt Lake City, Utah, is a nonprofit facility, open to the public, run by [the] Mormon or LDS Church. Appellee Mayson worked at the Gymnasium [as a] building engineer. He was discharged because he failed to qualify for [a] certificate that he is a member of the Church and eligible to attend its temples. Mayson [contended that] § 702 violates the Establishment Clause. * * *

"This Court has long recognized that the government may (and sometimes must) accommodate religious practices [without] violating the Establishment Clause." It is well established, too, that "[t]he limits of permissible state accommodation to religion are by no means co-extensive with the noninterference mandated by the Free Exercise Clause." *Walz.*[132] [At] some point, accommodation may devolve into "an unlawful fostering of religion," but [this is not such a case].

Lemon [does] not mean that the law's purpose must be unrelated to religion [but] aims at preventing the relevant governmental decisionmaker—in this case, Congress—from abandoning neutrality and acting with the intent of promoting a particular point of view in religious matters.

Under the *Lemon* analysis, it is a permissible legislative purpose to alleviate significant governmental interference with the ability of religious organizations to define and carry out their religious missions.[133] [§ 702

---

[132] Consider Michael W. McConnell, *Accommodation of Religion,* 1985 Sup.Ct.Rev. 1: "[S]ome government employees may view attendance at religious services on a holy day a sacred duty; they could make out a plausible free exercise case if the government refused them leave. Others may view attendance at services as no more than a spiritually wholesome activity; their free exercise claim would be much weaker. It is not unreasonable for the government to disregard these distinctions—to implement a general policy permitting leave for employees on the holy days of their faith. * * * Religious liberty is not enhanced by a rule confining government accommodations to the minimum compelled under the Constitution."

[133] See also Wilbur Katz, *Note on the Constitutionality of Shared Time,* 1964 Relig. & Pub.Or. 85: "It is no violation of neutrality for the government to express its concern for religious freedom by measures which merely neutralize what would otherwise be restrictive effects of government action. Provision for voluntary worship in the armed forces is constitutional, not because

originally] exempted only the religious activities of such employers from the statutory ban on religious discrimination. [Nonetheless,] it is a significant burden on a religious organization to require it [to] predict which of its activities a secular court will consider religious. The line is hardly a bright one, and an organization might understandably be concerned that a judge would not understand its religious tenets [and] affect the way an organization carried out what it understood to be its religious mission. * * *

The second requirement under *Lemon* is that the law in question have "a principal or primary effect [that] neither advances nor inhibits religion." Undoubtedly, religious organizations are better able now to advance their purposes than they were prior to [the] amendment to § 702. But religious groups have been better able to advance their purposes on account of many laws that have passed constitutional muster: for example, the property tax exemption at issue in *Walz,* or the loans of school books to school children, including parochial school students, upheld in *Allen.* A law is not unconstitutional simply because it *allows* churches to advance religion, which is their very purpose. For a law to have forbidden "effects" under *Lemon,* it must be fair to say that the *government itself* has advanced religion through its own activities and influence. [Moreover,] we find no persuasive evidence in the record before us that the Church's ability to propagate its religious doctrine through the Gymnasium is any greater now than it was prior to the passage of the Civil Rights Act in 1964. In such circumstances, we do not see how any advancement of religion achieved by the Gymnasium can be fairly attributed to the Government, as opposed to the Church.[15]

We find unpersuasive [that] § 702 singles out religious entities for a benefit. [The Court] has never indicated that statutes that give special consideration to religious groups are per se invalid. [Our cases provide] ample room for accommodation of religion under the Establishment Clause. Where, as here, government acts with the proper purpose of lifting a regulation that burdens the exercise of religion, we see no reason to require that the exemption come packaged with benefits to secular [entities.] *Larson* indicates that laws discriminating *among* religions are subject to strict scrutiny, and that laws "affording a uniform benefit to all religions" should be analyzed under *Lemon.* In a case such as this, where a statute is neutral on its face and motivated by a permissible purpose of limiting governmental interference with the exercise of religion, [it] passes

---

government policy may properly favor religion, but because the government is not required to exercise its military powers in a manner restrictive of religious freedom. Affirmative government action to maintain religious freedom in these instances serves the secular purpose of promoting a constitutional right, the free exercise of religion."

[15] **[Ct's Note]** Undoubtedly, Mayson's freedom of choice in religious matters was impinged upon, but it was the Church [and] not the Government, who put him to the choice of changing his religious practices or losing his job. * * *

the *Lemon* [test.] § 702 is rationally related to the legitimate purpose of alleviating significant governmental interference with the ability of religious organizations to define and carry out their religious missions. * * *

JUSTICE BRENNAN, with whom JUSTICE MARSHALL joins, concurring in the judgment.

[E]xemption from Title VII's proscription on religious discrimination [says] that a person may be put to the choice of either conforming to certain religious tenets or losing a job opportunity. [The] potential for coercion created by such a provision [is] in serious tension with our commitment to individual freedom of conscience in matters of religious belief. [But] religious organizations have an interest in [d]etermining that certain activities are in furtherance of an organization's religious mission, and that only those committed to that mission should conduct [them]. Solicitude for a church's ability to do so reflects the idea that furtherance of the autonomy of religious organizations often furthers individual religious freedom as well.[134]

[I]deally, religious organizations should be able to discriminate on the basis of religion *only* with respect to religious activities [because] the infringement on religious liberty that results from conditioning performance of *secular* activity upon religious belief cannot be defended as necessary for the community's self-definition. Furthermore, the authorization of discrimination in such circumstances is not an accommodation that simply enables a church to gain members by the normal means of prescribing the terms of membership. [Rather,] it puts at the disposal of religion the added advantages of economic leverage in the secular realm.

[A] religious-secular distinction [as] the character of an activity is not self-evident [and] requires a searching case-by-case analysis. This results in considerable ongoing government entanglement in religious affairs [and] raises concern that a religious organization may be chilled in its Free Exercise activity. [The] risk [is] most likely to arise with respect to *nonprofit* activities. The fact that an operation is not organized as a profit-making commercial enterprise makes colorable a claim that it is not purely secular in orientation. * * *

Sensitivity to individual religious freedom dictates that religious discrimination be permitted only with respect to employment in religious

---

[134] For the view that the Establishment Clause requires an exemption from a neutral, generally applicable law that "interferes with the relationship between clergy and church" or "intrudes on religious organizations' sphere of autonomy," see Carl H. Esbeck, *The Establishment Clause as a Structural Restraint on Governmental Power*, 84 Ia.L.Rev. 1 (1998). Should the constitutional rights of religious institutions "not be reducible to the rights and interests of their members," but for "a web of independent, thriving, distinctive institutions" needed to "check secular power"? See Richard W. Garnett, *Do Churches Matter? Towards an Institutional Understanding of the Religion Clauses*, 53 Vill.L.Rev. 273 (2008).

activities.[135] Concern for the autonomy of religious organizations demands that we avoid the entanglement and the chill on religious expression that a case-by-case determination would produce. We cannot escape the fact that these aims are in tension. Because of the nature of nonprofit activities, I believe that a categorical exemption for such enterprises appropriately balances these competing concerns. * * *

JUSTICE O'CONNOR, concurring in the judgment.[136] * * *

In *Jaffree,* I noted [that, "on] the one hand, a rigid application of the *Lemon* test would invalidate legislation exempting religious observers from generally applicable government obligations. By definition, such legislation has a religious purpose and effect in promoting the free exercise of religion.[137] On the other hand, [a]lmost any government benefit to religion could be recharacterized as simply "allowing" a religion to better advance itself,"[138] unless perhaps it involved actual proselytization by government agents. In nearly every case of a government benefit to religion, the religious mission would not be advanced if the religion did not take advantage of the benefit * * * .

The necessary first step in evaluating an Establishment Clause challenge to a government action lifting from religious organizations a generally applicable regulatory burden is to recognize that such government action *does* have the effect of advancing religion. The necessary second step is to separate those benefits to religion that constitutionally accommodate the free exercise of religion from those that provide unjustifiable awards of assistance to religious organizations. [T]he inquiry framed by the *Lemon* test should be "whether government's purpose is to endorse religion and whether the statute actually conveys a message of endorsement" [and] how it would be perceived by an objective

---

[135] If the employee engaging in "religious activities" is paid with public funds, does this "result in religious favoritism" (Sec. 1, II) and thus violate the Establishment Clause? Does this mean that the *most* protected activities may *not* be funded, but the least protected may? See Steven K. Green, *Religious Discrimination, Public Funding, and Constitutional Values*, 30 Hast.Con.L.Q. 1 (2002).

[136] Blackmun, J., concurred in the judgment, "essentially for the reasons set forth in Justice O'Connor's opinion."

[137] In her *Jaffree* concurrence, O'Connor, J., added: "Indeed, the statute at issue in *Lemon* [can] be viewed as an accommodation of the religious beliefs of parents who choose to send their children to religious schools."

[138] In *Jaffree,* O'Connor, J. added: "[The] solution [lies] in identifying workable limits to the Government's license to promote the free exercise of religion. [O]ne can plausibly assert that government pursues free exercise clause values when it lifts a government-imposed burden on the free exercise of religion. [T]hen the standard Establishment Clause test should be modified accordingly. [T]he Court should simply acknowledge that the religious purpose of such a statute is legitimated by the Free Exercise Clause."

Compare Suzanna Sherry, *Lee v. Weisman: Paradox Redux*, 1992 Sup.Ct.Rev. 123: "This formulation can also be reversed: protecting the values of the Establishment Clause should constitute a compelling government interest sufficient to justify the impact of neutral laws on religious exercise. Whichever clause serves as the compelling interest trumps the other. Which formulation one prefers depends solely on whether one places a higher priority on the values of the Establishment Clause or on those of the Free Exercise Clause."

observer, acquainted with the text, legislative history, and implementation of the statute.[139] [Because] there is a probability that a nonprofit activity of a religious organization will itself be involved in the organization's religious mission, in [this case] the objective observer should perceive the government action as an accommodation of the exercise of religion rather than as a government endorsement of religion. * * *

NOTES AND QUESTIONS

1. ***Draft exemption.*** Did the statute in *Gillette,* exempting only "religious" conscientious objectors, impermissibly prefer religion over nonreligion? In WELSH v. UNITED STATES, Sec. 2, II supra, WHITE, J., joined by Burger, C.J., and Stewart, J., found it valid: "First, § 6(j) may represent a purely practical judgment that religious objectors, however admirable, would be of no more use in combat than many others unqualified for military service. [T]he exemption has neither the primary purpose nor the effect of furthering religion. [Second], Congress may have [believed that] to deny the exemption would violate the Free Exercise Clause or at least raise grave problems in this respect. [It] cannot be ignored that the First Amendment itself contains a religious classification [and the Free Exercise Clause] protects conduct as well as religious belief and speech. [It] was not suggested [in *Braunfeld*] that the Sunday closing laws in 21 States exempting Sabbatarians and others violated the Establishment Clause because no provision was made for others who claimed nonreligious reasons for not working on some particular day of the week. Nor was it intimated in *Zorach* that the no-establishment holding might be infirm because only those pursuing religious studies for designated periods were released from the public school routine; neither was it hinted that a public school's refusal to institute a released time program would violate the Free Exercise Clause. The Court in *Sherbert* construed the Free Exercise Clause to require special treatment for Sabbatarians under the State's unemployment compensation law. But the State could deal specially with Sabbatarians whether the Free Exercise Clause required it or [not]."

---

[139] In *Jaffree,* O'Connor, J., added: "[C]ourts should assume that the 'objective observer,' is acquainted with the Free Exercise Clause and the values it promotes. Thus individual perceptions, or resentment that a religious observer is exempted from a particular government requirement, would be entitled to little weight if the Free Exercise Clause strongly supported the exemption."

Compare William P. Marshall, *The Religious Freedom Restoration Act: Establishment, Equal Protection and Free Speech Concerns,* 56 Mont.L.Rev. 227 (1995): "Prior to *Smith,* one could argue that the Constitution demanded some accommodation from general laws of neutral applicability for free exercise interests. [The] denial of the Free Exercise right in *Smith,* however, suggests that exempting religion from neutral laws is no longer based upon a constitutional requirement. Accordingly, after *Smith,* the strength of the state interest supporting the legislative exemption is necessarily diminished." For the view that both clauses "support and reinforce each other in critical ways" and that "interpretations of the clauses that subordinate one clause to the [other] risk rendering both clauses dysfunctional," see Alan Brownstein, *The Religion Clauses as Mutually Reinforcing Mandates: Why the Arguments for Rigorously Enforcing [both Clauses] are Stronger When Both Clauses are Taken Seriously,* 32 Card. L. Rev. 1701 (2011).

HARLAN, J., disagreed, believing that "having chosen to exempt, [Congress] cannot draw the line between theistic or nontheistic religious beliefs on the one hand and secular beliefs on the other. [I]t must encompass the class of individuals it purports to exclude, those whose beliefs emanate from a purely moral, ethical, or philosophical source.[140] The common denominator must be the intensity of moral [conviction]. *Everson, McGowan* and *Allen,* all sustained legislation on the premise that it was neutral [notwithstanding] that it may have assisted religious groups by giving them the same benefits accorded to nonreligious groups.[12] To the extent that *Zorach* and *Sherbert* stand for the proposition that the Government may (*Zorach*), or must (*Sherbert*), shape its secular programs to accommodate the beliefs and tenets of religious groups, I think these cases unsound.[13]"

2. ***Unemployment compensation.*** (a) Did the Court's decisions in *Sherbert, Thomas* and *Hobbie* impermissibly prefer religion? In THOMAS v. REVIEW BD., Sec. 2 supra, REHNQUIST, J., dissented, finding the result "inconsistent with many of our prior Establishment Clause cases"[2]: "If Indiana were to legislate [an] unemployment compensation law which permitted benefits to be granted to those persons who quit their jobs for religious reasons—the statute would 'plainly' violate the Establishment Clause as interpreted in such cases as [*Lemon*]. First, [the] proviso would clearly serve only a religious purpose. It would grant financial benefits for the sole purpose of accommodating religious beliefs. Second, [the] primary effect of the proviso would be to 'advance' religion by facilitating the exercise of religious belief. Third, [it] would surely 'entangle' the State in religion. [By] granting financial benefits to persons solely on the basis of their religious beliefs, the State must necessarily inquire whether the claimant's belief is 'religious' and whether it is sincerely [held.] Conversely, governmental assistance which does not have the effect of 'inducing' religious belief, but instead merely 'accommodates' or implements an independent religious choice does not impermissibly involve the

---

[140] Accord, Lisa S. Bressman, *Accommodations and Equal Liberty,* 42 Wm. & M.L.Rev. 1007 (2001). *Query*: If a religious accommodation is granted for peyote, must a medical accommodation also be granted? See id.

[12] **[Ct's Note]** [I] fail to see how [§ 6(j)] has "any substantial legislative purpose" apart from honoring the conscience of individuals who oppose war on only religious grounds. * * *

[13] **[Ct's Note]** [At] the very least the Constitution requires that the State not excuse students early for the purpose of receiving religious instruction when it does not offer to nonreligious students the opportunity to use school hours for spiritual or ethical instruction of a nonreligious nature. Moreover, whether a released-time program cast in terms of improving "conscience" to the exclusion of artistic or cultural pursuits, would be "neutral" and consistent with the requirement of "voluntarism," is by no means an easy question. * * *

[2] **[Ct's Note]** To the extent *Sherbert* was correctly decided, it might be argued that cases such as *McCollum, Engel, Schempp, Lemon,* and *Nyquist* were wrongly decided. The "aid" rendered to religion in these latter cases may not be significantly different, in kind or degree, than the "aid" afforded Mrs. Sherbert or Thomas. For example, if the State in *Sherbert* could not deny compensation to one refusing work for religious reasons, it might be argued that a State may not deny reimbursement to students who choose for religious reasons to attend parochial schools. The argument would be that although a State need not allocate any funds to education, once it has done so, it may not require any person to sacrifice his religious beliefs in order to obtain an equal education. There can be little doubt that to the extent secular education provides answers to important moral questions without reference to religion or teaches that there are no answers, a person in one sense sacrifices his religious belief by attending secular schools. * * *

government in religious choices and therefore does not violate the Establishment Clause. * * * "

(b) *Accommodation/inducement/imposition/coercion.* Consider Alan Schwarz, *No Imposition of Religion: The Establishment Clause Value,* 77 Yale L.J. 692 (1968): "[T]he Establishment Clause [should] be read to prohibit only aid which has as its motive or substantial effect the imposition of religious belief or [practice]. Exemption of Mrs. Sherbert [represents] a judgment that the exercise of Seventh-day Adventism is more worthy than bowling on Saturdays, but the exemption has no significant effect [on] whether someone becomes a Seventh-day Adventist. Similarly, the Sabbatarian exemption from Sunday closing laws does not induce one to become a Jew; draft exemption to conscientious objectors does not normally induce one to become a Quaker; closing the public schools on all religious holidays or on every Wednesday at 2 P.M. does not induce the adoption of religion; and compulsory Sunday closing, while implementing an independent desire to attend church services, has no substantial effect upon the creation of such desire. The availability of preferential aid to religious exercise [may] induce false claims of religious belief, but the Establishment Clause is not concerned with false claims of belief, only with induced belief." Does this distinguish *McCollum, Engel* and *Schempp* from *Sherbert?* Do you agree with all of the *factual* assumptions made? Under this analysis, what result in *Epperson?* What of a small government payment to all who would lose salary because they have to be absent from their jobs in order to attend religious services? Would the state's failure to provide Sherbert with unemployment compensation be the same as its not having on-premises released time and school prayer in that all of these actions simply "make the practice of religious beliefs more expensive"?

Compare Jesse H. Choper, *The Religion Clauses of the First Amendment: Reconciling the Conflict,* 41 U.Pitt.L.Rev. 673 (1980): "My proposal for resolving the conflict between the two Religion Clauses seeks to implement their historically and contemporarily acknowledged common goal: to safeguard religious liberty [that] it would fail. [For example, in *Yoder,* unless] it could be shown that relieving the Amish [would] tend to coerce, compromise, or influence religious choice—and it is extremely doubtful that it could—the exemption was permissible under the Establishment Clause. In contrast, in *Sherbert,* [the] exemption results in impairment of religious liberty because compulsorily raised tax funds must be used to subsidize Mrs. Sherbert's exercise of religion.[141] [In the draft exemption cases], draftees seeking exemption had to formulate a statement of personal doctrine that would pass muster. This would involve deep and careful thought, and perhaps reading in philosophy and religion. Some undoubtedly would be persuaded by what they read. Moreover, the theory of 'cognitive dissonance'—which posits that to avoid

---

[141] See also Jesse H. Choper, *The Free Exercise Clause,* 27 Wm. & M.L.Rev. 943 (1986): "Under Justice Rehnquist's [and Professor Schwarz's] rationale, if a municipally-owned bus company wanted to waive the fare to take people to churches, it could do so. According to Justice Rehnquist, the waiver would not 'induce' religion, but would simply 'accommodate' a religious choice that already had been made. [B]ut the waiver also would result in what the religion clauses protect against—the use of tax funds for exclusively religious purposes."

madness we tend to become what we hold ourselves to be and what others believe us to be—also suggests that some initially fraudulent claims of belief in a personal religion would develop into true belief. Thus, a draft exemption for religious objectors threatens values of religious freedom by encouraging the adoption of religious beliefs."

(c) ***Breadth of exemption.*** In TEXAS MONTHLY, INC. v. BULLOCK, Sec. 1, II supra, SCALIA, J., joined by Rehnquist, C.J., and Kennedy, J., charged that according to Brennan, J.'s plurality opinion, "no law is constitutional whose 'benefits [are] confined to religious organizations,' except [those] that are unconstitutional *unless* they contain benefits confined to religious organizations. [But] 'the limits of permissible state accommodation to religion are by no means co-extensive with the noninterference mandated by the Free Exercise Clause.' Breadth of coverage is essential to constitutionality whenever a law's benefiting of religious activity [is] defended [as] merely the incidental consequence of seeking to benefit *all* activity that achieves a particular secular goal. But [w]here accommodation of religion is the justification, by definition religion is being singled out. [And] if the exemption comes so close to being a constitutionally required accommodation, there is no doubt that it is at least a permissible one."[142]

BRENNAN, J., joined by Marshall and Stevens, JJ., responded: "[W]e in no way suggest that *all* benefits conferred exclusively upon religious groups or upon individuals on account of their religious beliefs are forbidden by the Establishment Clause unless they are mandated by the Free Exercise Clause. [Permissible benefits] however, involve legislative exemptions that did not or would not impose substantial burdens on nonbeneficiaries while allowing others to act according to their religious beliefs. [Thus,] the application of Title VII's exemption for religious organizations that we approved in *Amos* though it had some adverse effect on those holding or seeking employment with those organizations (if not on taxpayers generally), prevented potentially serious encroachments on protected religious freedoms. Texas' tax exemption, by contrast, does not remove a demonstrated and possible grave imposition on religious activity sheltered by the Free Exercise Clause. Moreover, it burdens nonbeneficiaries by increasing their tax bills by whatever amount is needed to offset the benefit bestowed on subscribers to religious publications."

3. ***Sabbath observance.*** THORNTON v. CALDOR, INC., 472 U.S. 703 (1985), per BURGER, C.J., held that a Connecticut law—"that those who observe a Sabbath any day of the week as a matter of religious conviction must be relieved of the duty to work on that day, no matter what burden or inconvenience this imposes on the employer or fellow workers"—"has a primary effect that impermissibly advances a particular religious practice" and thus violates the Establishment Clause: "The statute arms Sabbath observers with an absolute and unqualified right not to work on whatever day they

---

[142] Why didn't Texas' exemption violate the Establishment Clause test articulated by Kennedy, J. (joined by Rehnquist, C.J., and White and Scalia, JJ.) in *Allegheny County v. ACLU*, Sec. 1, IV supra, because it gave "direct benefits to religion" and involved "subtle coercion [in] the form of taxation"?

designate as their Sabbath [and thus] goes beyond having an incidental or remote effect of advancing religion."

O'CONNOR, J., joined by Marshall, J., concurred, distinguishing "the religious accommodation provisions of Title VII of the Civil Rights Act [which] require private employers to reasonably accommodate the religious practices of employees unless to do so would cause undue hardship to the employer's business": "Since Title VII calls for reasonable rather than absolute accommodation and extends [to] all religious beliefs and practices rather than protecting only the Sabbath observance, I believe an objective observer would perceive it as an anti-discrimination law rather than an endorsement of religion or a particular religious practice."[143]

Was the purpose or effect of the *Caldor* statute any different than that of the *Amos* statute or the Court's decisions in *Sherbert, Thomas, Hobbie, Roy* and *Yoder? Amos* distinguished *Caldor* on the ground that in *Amos,* "appellee was not legally obligated to take the steps necessary to qualify for a temple recommend, and his discharge was not required by statute." Should it make a difference that, unlike the other cases, the *Caldor* statute sought to alleviate burdens on religion posed by private parties rather than the state?

Does the *Caldor* statute "promote"/"endorse" a particular "religion" or "religious belief" or "religious practice" any more than the Court's decisions in *Sherbert, Thomas, Hobbie, Yoder* and *Roy,* or than the statutory exemptions from the draft or Sunday Closing laws? *Hobbie* distinguished *Caldor:* "Florida's provision of unemployment benefits to religious observers does not single out a particular class of such persons for favorable treatment with the effect of implicitly endorsing a particular religious belief. Rather, the provision of unemployment benefits generally available within the State to religious observers who must leave their employment due to an irreconcilable conflict between the demands of work and conscience neutrally accommodates religious beliefs and practices, without endorsement."

In *Kiryas Joel,* Sec. 3 supra, SCALIA, J., joined by Rehnquist, C.J., and Thomas, J., disagreed with the Court's conclusion that New York had impermissibly preferred one religion: "[M]ost efforts at accommodation seek to solve a problem that applies [to] only one or a few religions. Not every religion uses wine in its sacraments, but that does not make an exemption from Prohibition for sacramental wine-use impermissible, nor does it require the State granting such an exemption to explain [how] it will treat every other

---

[143] Rehnquist, J., dissented without opinion. Consider Richard A. Epstein, *Religious Liberty in the Welfare State,* 31 Wm. & M.L.Rev. 375 (1990): "[It would plainly be unconstitutional] if the state offered to pay a small sum [to] the employer to defray the additional costs it had to bear to keep the religious worker on its payroll. [If] a public subsidy of religious workers is not acceptable under the Establishment Clause, then a public mandate of a private subsidy is unacceptable as well." For the view that since "securing individual constitutional rights often (or almost always) imposes impediments to the smooth functioning of our system, if accommodations for religion impose only imprecise social/economic costs, then these prices of religious tolerance are permitted to be paid," see Jesse H. Choper, *Securing Religious Liberty* 123–26 (1995).

claim for dispensation from its controlled-substances laws." Kennedy, J., expressed a similar view.

Is a *general* rule for Free Exercise exemptions—as under *Sherbert-Yoder*, or the Religious Freedom Restoration Act (fn. 109)—preferable to a specific exemption for religion (as the statutes in *Texas Monthly* and *Caldor*)? Consider Thomas C. Berg, *The New Attacks on Religious Freedom Legislation, and Why They are Wrong*, 21 Card.L.Rev. 415 (1999): "Requiring the same standard for all religious freedom claims, in the less political forum of the courts, serves the goal of religious equality by minimizing the chance that only politically powerful groups will get accommodations.[89]" What result if a state grants an exemption from compulsory education for religions with beliefs like the Amish but not for farmers who badly need their children for farming, or an exemption for sacramental, but not medical, use of peyote? See William K. Kelley, *The Primacy of Political Actors in Accommodation of Religion*, 22 U. of Haw. L. Rev. 403 (2000).

4. ***Unanimous approval.*** CUTTER v. WILKINSON, 544 U.S. 709 (2005), per GINSBURG, J., relying on *Amos* held that the Religious Land Use and Institutionalized Persons Act of 2000—"No government shall impose a substantial burden on the religious exercise of a person residing [in] an institution," unless it survives strict scrutiny—does not violate the Establishment Clause: RLUIPA "does not, on its face, exceed the limits of permissible government accommodation [because] it alleviates exceptional government-created burdens on private religious exercise [and] does not founder on shoals the Court's prior decisions. [C]ourts must take adequate account of the burdens a requested accommodation may impose on nonbeneficiaries, see *Caldor*, and they must be satisfied that the Act's prescriptions [are] administered neutrally among different faiths, see *Kiryas Joel*.[8] [It] covers state-run institutions—mental hospitals, prisons, and the like—in which the government exerts a degree of control unparalleled in civilian society and severely disabling to private religious exercise.[9] * * * [10] [RLUIPA's sponsors] anticipated that courts would apply the Act's standard with 'due deference to the experience and expertise of prison and jail [administrators']."

---

[89] **[Orig. Note]** See Ira C. Lupu, *Reconstructing the Establishment Clause: The Case Against Discretionary Accommodation of Religion*, 140 U.Pa.L.Rev. 555 (1991) (claiming that statute-by-statute legislative accommodations are unconstitutional because they reflect the varying political power of different religious groups).

[8] **[Ct's Note]** Directed at obstructions institutional arrangements place on religious observances, RLUIPA does not require a State to pay for an inmate's devotional accessories.

[9] **[Ct's Note]** See, e.g., *Charles v. Verhagen*, 348 F.3d 601 (C.A.7 2003) (prison's regulation prohibited Muslim prisoner from possessing ritual cleansing oil); *Young v. Lane*, 922 F.2d 370 (C.A.7 1991) (restricted wearing of yarmulkes); *Hunafa v. Murphy*, 907 F.2d 46 (C.A.7 1990) (Jewish and Muslim prisoners were served pork, with no substitute available).

[10] **[Ct's Note]** [While] some accommodations of religious observance, notably the opportunity to assemble in worship services, might attract joiners seeking a break in their closely guarded day, we doubt that all accommodations would be perceived as "benefits." For example, congressional hearings on RLUIPA revealed that one state corrections system served as its kosher diet "a fruit, a vegetable, a granola bar, and a liquid nutritional supplement—each and every meal." * * * .

5. *School prayer.* In *Jaffree,* O'CONNOR, J., applied her "solution"[144] to Alabama's moment of silence law: "No law prevents a student who is so inclined from praying silently in public schools. [Of] course, the State might argue that § 16–1–20.1 protects not silent prayer, but rather group silent prayer under State sponsorship. Phrased in these terms, the burden lifted by the statute is not one imposed by the State of Alabama, but by the Establishment Clause."

6. *Reconciling the conflict.* Assuming the validity of the distinction between *McCollum, Engel, Schempp* and *Jaffree* on one hand, and programs such as that in *Amos* and draft exemption etc. on the other, are *all* exemptions undesirable because they often result not merely in protection of Free Exercise (or neutrality or accommodation) but in relieving persons with certain religious beliefs of significant burdens from which many others strongly desire to be exempted? That, in this sense, there is "preference" for minority religions?[145]

Might religious exemptions be seen as "restorative or equalizing" (Galanter, note 4, Sec. 2, II supra)? Consider James D. Gordon III, *The New Free Exercise Clause,* 26 Cap.U. L.Rev. 65 (1997): "In a democracy, laws inevitably will reflect the majority's values, and [consequently] majority religions generally have a kind of inherent exemption from the force of law. In addition, politically powerful minority religions often are able to obtain express exemptions. [The] accommodation principle provides powerless minority religions with some measure of the same protection that other religions already enjoy in the democratic process." What about exemptions (accommodations) for majority (mainstream) religions? Consider Greene, fn. 125 in *Kiryas Joel:* "When a majority pushes for governmentally organized prayer in public schools or for the placement of its favored religious symbols in the halls of government, it is wrong to call such actions 'accommodation.' [But] when the effect of the majority's actions is to make life easier for a minority, there is no concern about an 'Establishment' of religion. It also seems wrong to say that accommodation of minority religions constitutes a symbolic endorsement of those religions; rather, accommodation in this context suggests that the majority is coming to the aid of a burdened minority, not that the majority agrees with the minority on any matter of religious truth." Compare Ira C. Lupu, *Uncovering the Village of Kiryas Joel,* 96 Colum.L.Rev. 104 (1996): "If Jews are a relatively small minority in New York State but a sizable minority or a majority in some New York City area suburbs, may the state close public schools on Yom Kippur while the suburb is forbidden from doing likewise? May Pennsylvania accommodate Mormon traditions, while Utah may not?"

---

[144] See fn. 138.

[145] Should the Court "either suggest or require that an alternative burden be imposed on individuals who would otherwise qualify for religious exemptions"? Choper, fn. 43, at 92. See generally Alan Brownstein, *Taking "Free Exercise Rights Seriously,* 57 Case W. Res. L. Rev. 55 (2006).

CHAPTER 9

EQUAL PROTECTION

■ ■ ■

Laws frequently classify (or "discriminate") by imposing special burdens (or granting exemptions from such burdens) or by conferring benefits on some people and not others. To take uncontroversial examples, only those who can pass an examination and possess good eyesight qualify for driver's licenses. Those with expensive homes frequently must pay higher taxes than those with less expensive homes. People who are not high school graduates typically are denied admission to state universities. Against this background of accepted practice, under what circumstances do legislative classifications violate the Fourteenth Amendment's command that no state shall "deny to any person within its jurisdiction the equal protection of the laws"?

Although the language of the Equal Protection Clause is not confined to racial discrimination, the *Slaughter-House Cases,* Ch. 5, Sec. 1, III supra (one of the first decisions interpreting the Civil War amendments), "doubt[ed] very much whether any action of a State not directed by way of discrimination against the negroes as a class, or on account of their race, will ever be held to come within the purview of this provision." At least as early as 1897, however, the Court invoked the Equal Protection Clause to invalidate a commonplace economic regulation that obligated railroad defendants (but not others) to pay the attorneys' fees of successful plaintiffs. The Court acknowledged that "as a general proposition, [it] is undeniably true" that "it is not within the scope of the Fourteenth Amendment to withhold from States the power of classification." But, the Court continued, "it must appear" that a classification is "based upon some reasonable ground—some difference which bears a just and proper relation to the attempted classification—and is not a mere arbitrary selection." *Gulf, Colo. & Santa Fé Ry. Co. v. Ellis,* 165 U.S. 150 (1897).[1]

Sec. 1 of this Chapter considers this "traditional approach" under the Equal Protection Clause to general economic and social welfare regulations. Sec. 2 then deals with the "strict scrutiny" given to explicit racial and ethnic classifications, which the Court has deemed "suspect," as well as with related issues involving race. Sec. 3 reviews the Court's treatment of gender-based classifications. Sec. 4 addresses the use of a

---

[1] For an even earlier invocation of the Equal Protection Clause to invalidate a classification of transportation rates, see *Reagan v. Farmers' Loan & Trust Co.,* 154 U.S. 362 (1894).

nondeferential standard of review for governmental action that disadvantages several other groups. Finally, Sec. 5 examines standards for equal protection review of classifications affecting what the Court classifies as "fundamental" rights.

One potential source of confusion should be kept in mind throughout. By its terms, the Equal Protection Clause—the relevant language of which provides that "[n]o *State* shall . . ."—does not apply to the federal government. Nonetheless, at least since its 1954 decision in *Bolling v. Sharpe,* Sec. 2, II infra, the Court has held that the Due Process Clause of the Fifth Amendment incorporates equal protection norms binding on the federal government. The *Bolling* Court explained: "The Fifth Amendment, which is applicable in the District of Columbia, does not contain an equal protection clause as does the Fourteenth Amendment which applies only to the states. But the concepts of equal protection and due process, both stemming from our American ideal of fairness, are not mutually exclusive. [D]iscrimination may be so unjustifiable as to be violative of due process."

In applying equal protection norms to the federal government, the Court's pattern of decisions has not been perfectly consistent, as will be explained in the materials that follow. For the most part, however, the Court has insisted that the "approach to Fifth Amendment equal protection claims [is] precisely the same as to equal protection claims under the Fourteenth Amendment." *Weinberger v. Wiesenfeld,* Sec. 3, III infra; see also *Adarand Constructors, Inc. v. Pena,* Sec. 2, V infra.[2] Accordingly, in many parts of this Chapter, challenges to federal legislation under the Due Process Clause will be treated as offering de facto interpretations of the Equal Protection Clause.

1. TRADITIONAL APPROACH

As seen in Ch. 5, the Due Process Clause was the usual provision invoked by the Court in the first third of the twentieth century to overturn a great many economic and social welfare regulations. But despite Justice Holmes's dismissive reference to the Equal Protection Clause as "the usual last resort of constitutional arguments,"[3] the Court held during this period that approximately twenty state and local laws violated equal protection. For the most part, the Court at least purported to take a deferential approach that granted the states "a broad discretion in classification in the exercise of [their] power of regulation" and interposed the "constitutional guaranty of equal protection" only "against discriminations that are entirely arbitrary."[4] But compare the formulation used in *F.S. Royster*

---

[2] The principal exception to this general rule of "congruence" involves the treatment of aliens. Current doctrine subjects state discriminations against aliens to more searching judicial scrutiny than federal discriminations against aliens—a disparity considered in Sec. 4, II infra.

[3] *Buck v. Bell,* 274 U.S. 200 (1927).

[4] *Smith v. Cahoon,* 283 U.S. 553 (1931).

Guano Co. v. Virginia, 253 U.S. 412 (1920): "[T]he classification must be reasonable, not arbitrary, and must rest upon some ground of difference having a fair and substantial relation to the object of the legislation, so that all persons similarly circumstanced shall be treated alike."

The materials that follow concern the Court's equal protection scrutiny of economic and social welfare regulations since the late 1930s, when it abandoned searching substantive due process review of such legislation.

RAILWAY EXPRESS AGENCY V. NEW YORK
336 U.S. 106, 69 S.Ct. 463, 93 L.Ed. 533 (1949).

JUSTICE DOUGLAS delivered the opinion of the Court.

[T]he Traffic Regulations of the City of New York [provide]: "No person shall operate [on] any street an advertising vehicle; [except for] business notices upon business delivery vehicles, so long as such vehicles are engaged in the usual business [of] the owner and not used merely or mainly for advertising."

Appellant [operates] about 1,900 trucks in New York City and sells the space on the exterior sides of these trucks for advertising [for] the most part unconnected with its own business. It was convicted * * * .

The court [below] concluded that advertising on [vehicles] constitutes a distraction to vehicle drivers and to pedestrians alike and therefore affects the safety of the public in the use of the streets. We do not sit to weigh evidence on the due process issue in order to determine whether the regulation is sound or appropriate; nor is it our function to pass judgment on its wisdom. See *Olsen v. Nebraska* [Ch. 5, Sec. 3]. We would be trespassing on one of the most intensely local and specialized of all municipal problems if we held that this regulation had no relation to the traffic problem of New York City. It is the judgment of the local authorities that it does have such a relation.

[The] question of equal protection of the laws is pressed more strenuously on us. [It] is said, for example, that one of appellant's trucks carrying the advertisement of a commercial house would not cause any greater distraction of pedestrians and vehicle drivers than if the commercial house carried the same advertisement on its own truck. Yet the regulation allows the latter to do what the former is forbidden from doing. It is therefore contended that the classification which the regulation makes has no relation to the traffic problem since a violation turns not on what kind of advertisements are carried on trucks but on whose trucks they are carried.

That, however, is a superficial way of analyzing the [problem]. The local authorities may well have concluded that those who advertised their own wares on their trucks do not present the same traffic problem in view of the nature or extent of the advertising which they use. * * *

We cannot say that that judgment is not an allowable one. Yet if it is, the classification has relation to the purpose for which it is made and does not contain the kind of discrimination against which the Equal Protection Clause affords protection. It is by such practical considerations based on experience rather than by theoretical inconsistencies that the question of equal protection is to be answered. And the fact that New York City sees fit to eliminate from traffic this kind of distraction but does not touch what may be even greater ones in a different category, such as the vivid displays on Times Square, is immaterial. It is no requirement of equal protection that all evils of the same genus be eradicated or none at all. * * *

Affirmed.

JUSTICE RUTLEDGE acquiesces in the Court's opinion and judgment, dubitante on the question of equal protection of the laws.

JUSTICE JACKSON, concurring. * * *

The burden should rest heavily upon one who would persuade us to use the Due Process Clause to strike down a substantive [law]. Even its provident use against municipal regulations frequently disables all government—state, municipal and federal—from dealing with the conduct in question because the requirement of due process is also applicable to State and Federal Governments. * * *

Invocation of the Equal Protection Clause, on the other hand, does not disable any governmental body from dealing with the subject at hand. It merely means that the prohibition or regulation must have a broader impact. I regard it as a salutary doctrine that cities, states and the Federal Government must exercise their powers so as not to discriminate between their inhabitants except upon some reasonable differentiation fairly related to the object of regulation. [T]here is no more effective practical guaranty against arbitrary and unreasonable government than to require that the principles of law which officials would impose upon a minority must be imposed generally. Conversely, nothing opens the door to arbitrary action so effectively as to allow those officials to pick and choose only a few to whom they will apply legislation and thus to escape the political retribution that might be visited upon them if larger numbers were affected. Courts can take no better measure to assure that laws will be just than to require that laws be equal in operation. * * *

In this case, if the City of New York should assume that display of any advertising on vehicles tends and intends to distract the attention of persons using the highways and to increase the dangers of its traffic, I should think it fully within its constitutional powers to forbid it all. [Instead], however, the City seeks to reduce the hazard only by saying that while some may, others may not exhibit such appeals. The same display, for example, advertising cigarettes, which this appellant is forbidden to carry on its trucks, may be carried on the trucks of a cigarette dealer. [The] courts of New York have declared that the sole nature and purpose of the regulation before us is to reduce traffic hazards. There is not even a pretense here that the traffic hazard created by the advertising which is forbidden is in any manner or degree more hazardous than that which is permitted. * * *

* * * I do not think differences of treatment under law should be approved on classification because of differences unrelated to the legislative purpose. The Equal Protection Clause ceases to assure either equality or protection if it is avoided by any conceivable difference that can be pointed out between those bound and those left free. This Court has often announced the principle that the differentiation must have an appropriate relation to the object of the [legislation].

The question in my mind comes to this. Where individuals contribute to an evil or danger in the same way and to the same degree, may those who do so for hire be prohibited, while those who do so for their own commercial ends but not for hire be allowed to continue? I think the answer has to be that the hireling may be put in a class by himself and may be dealt with differently than those who act on their own. But this is not merely because such a discrimination will enable the lawmaker to diminish the evil. That might be done by many classifications, which I should think wholly unsustainable. It is rather because there is a real difference between doing in self-interest and doing for hire, so that it is one thing to tolerate action from those who act on their own and it is another thing to permit the same action to be promoted for a price. * * *

NEW ORLEANS V. DUKES
427 U.S. 297, 96 S.Ct. 2513, 49 L.Ed.2d 511 (1976).

PER CURIAM.

[A 1972 New Orleans ordinance banned all pushcart food vendors in the French Quarter ("Vieux Carre") except those who had continuously operated there for eight or more years. Two vendors had done so for twenty or more years and qualified under the "grandfather clause." Appellee, who had operated a pushcart for only two years, attacked the ordinance.]

When local economic regulation is challenged solely as violating the Equal Protection Clause, this Court consistently defers to legislative determinations as to the desirability of particular statutory discriminations. Unless a classification trammels fundamental personal rights or is drawn upon inherently suspect distinctions such as race, religion, or alienage, our decisions presume the constitutionality of the statutory discriminations and require only that the classification challenged be rationally related to a legitimate state interest. States are accorded wide latitude in the regulation of their local economies under their police powers, and rational distinctions may be made with substantially less than mathematical exactitude. Legislatures may implement their program step by step in such economic areas, adopting regulations that only partially ameliorate a perceived evil and deferring complete elimination of the evil to future regulations. See, e.g., *Williamson v. Lee Optical Co.*[5] In short, the judiciary may not sit as a superlegislature to judge the wisdom or desirability of legislative policy determinations made in areas that neither affect fundamental rights nor proceed along suspect lines; in the local economic sphere, it is only the invidious discrimination, the wholly arbitrary act, which cannot stand consistently with the Fourteenth Amendment. See, e.g., *Ferguson v. Skrupa.*[5]

[New Orleans'] classification rationally furthers the purpose which [the] city had identified as its objective in enacting the provision, that is, as a means "to preserve the appearance and custom valued by the Quarter's residents and attractive to tourists." The legitimacy of that objective is obvious. The City Council plainly could further that objective by making the reasoned judgment that street peddlers and hawkers tend to interfere with the charm and beauty of an historic area [and] that to ensure the economic vitality of that area, such businesses should be substantially curtailed in the Vieux Carre, if not totally banned.

It is suggested that the "grandfather provision" [was] a totally arbitrary and irrational method of achieving the city's purpose. But rather than proceeding by the immediate and absolute abolition of all pushcart food vendors, the city could rationally [decide] that newer businesses were less likely to have built up substantial reliance interests in continued operation in the Vieux Carre and that the two vendors who qualified under the "grandfather clause" [had] themselves become part of the distinctive character and charm that distinguishes the Vieux Carre. We cannot say that these judgments so lack rationality that they constitute a constitutionally impermissible denial of equal protection. * * *

Reversed.

---

[5] In *Lee Optical,* Ch. 5, Sec. 3, a statute that otherwise prohibited the fitting of eyeglasses without a prescription exempted businesses that sold ready-to-wear glasses. The Court found no violation of equal protection: "Evils in the same field may be of different dimensions and proportions, requiring different remedies. Or so the legislature may think. Or the reform may take one step at a time, addressing itself to the phase of the problem which seems most acute to the legislative mind. The legislature may select one phase of one field and apply a remedy there, neglecting the others. [For] all this record shows, the ready-to-wear branch of this business may not loom large in Oklahoma or may present problems of regulation distinct from the other branch."

[5] [Ct's Note] *Ferguson* [Ch. 5, Sec. 3] presented an analogous situation. There, a Kansas statute excepted lawyers from the prohibition of a statute making it a misdemeanor for any person to engage in the business of debt adjusting. We held that the exception of lawyers was not a denial of equal protection * * * .

JUSTICE MARSHALL concurs in the judgment.

JUSTICE STEVENS took no part in [the] case.

NOTES AND QUESTIONS

1.   *The theory of equal protection.* In what sense were the challengers in *Railway Express* and *Dukes* afforded the equal protection of the laws when they were forced to bear burdens that others were not forced to bear? According to a classic and highly influential article by Joseph Tussman & Jacobus tenBroek, *The Equal Protection of the Laws*, 37 Calif.L.Rev. 341 (1949), the Court effectively reads the "equal protection" guarantee as establishing a requirement of "reasonable classification," under which individuals cannot claim that they personally have been treated "unequally" so long as it is reasonable to treat the general class of which they are members differently from other classes. This approach makes the permissibility of legislation turn on means-ends rationality, with the Court asking whether the classificatory scheme adopted by the legislature is a rational means of achieving a legitimate governmental goal.

Is this the only way in which the Equal Protection Clause could sensibly be interpreted? Compare the view of Ronald Dworkin, *Freedom's Law* 10 (1996), that the Equal Protection Clause embodies a moral principle that "government must treat everyone as of equal status and with equal concern." Is the Court's approach in *Railway Express* and *Dukes* consistent with this principle? Should it be? Note that the Court's decisions in these "modern" cases occurred under the long shadow of the judicial judgments of fairness and reasonableness reflected in cases such as *Lochner v. New York*—and the nearly unanimous view that the Court's performance in those cases was disastrous. What lessons has the Court learned from the *Lochner* era? Has it carried those lessons too far?

2.   *Underinclusive legislation.* Does the "one step at a time" approach to legislation that the Court permits in *Railway Express* and *New Orleans v. Dukes* allow officials to give preferential treatment to favored groups and thereby promote unfairness? Consider Note, *Equal Protection,* 82 Harv.L.Rev. 1076 (1969): "To require that the state remedy all aspects of a particular mischief or none at all might preclude a state from undertaking any program of correction until its resources were adequate to deal with the entire problem. [In] some instances, the state may not be convinced that a particular policy is a wise one, or it may prove impossible to marshal a legislative majority in favor of extending the policy's coverage any further. Thus, to demand application of the policy to all whom it might logically encompass would severely restrict the state's opportunities to experiment." But what are (and should be) the limits on state "experiments"? According to Michael Klarman, *An Interpretive History of Modern Equal Protection*, 90 Mich.L.Rev. 213 (1991), the legislation in *Railway Express* tested the limits: "[The] facially bizarre classification probably was attributable primarily to the powerful lobbying arm of the city's newspapers [which successfully demanded an exemption applicable to the

advertisements on their trucks]. Several Justices were troubled by a classification difficult to justify in terms other than raw interest group power. While *Railway Express* came down unanimous as to result, the Court initially was divided five to four, with Justice Reed arguing (correctly) in his draft dissent that to sustain a law based on such a 'whimsical' distinction was essentially to render the Equal Protection Clause 'useless in state regulation of business practices.' "

3.   *Legislative purpose.* Of what relevance was it in *Railway Express* that the state courts "declared that the sole purpose" of the law "is to reduce traffic hazards"? Would it be more accurate (and realistic) to describe the purpose as being "to promote public safety slightly by reducing the number of distractions on the sides of moving vehicles to the extent this is feasible without jeopardizing the economic well-being of those merchants who advertise on their own trucks"—a purpose to which the classification unquestionably was "rationally related"? See Note, *Legislative Purpose, Rationality and Equal Protection*, 82 Yale L.J. 123 (1972).

It is not uncommon for legislation to have mixed or multiple purposes—or for the Court to uphold legislation as long as it is rationally related to any governmental purpose (even if it might appear to conflict with others). For example, *Fitzgerald v. Racing Ass'n*, 539 U.S. 103 (2003), unanimously rejected an equal protection attack on a state statute imposing a higher tax on revenues from slot machines at racetracks than on revenues from slot machines at riverboat casinos. Although the state had permitted slot machines at racetracks in order to save the tracks from economic distress, it was not irrational, the Court reasoned, to tax the racetrack machines at a higher rate than the riverboat machines, because the legislature may have had independent reasons to promote the financial viability of riverboats: "[T]he Iowa law, like most laws, might predominantly serve one general objective, say, helping the racetracks, while containing subsidiary provisions that seek to achieve other desirable (perhaps even contrary) ends as well, thereby producing a law that balances objectives but still serves the general objective when seen as a whole."

Consider Tussman & tenBroek, supra: "[T]he requirement that laws be equal rests upon a theory of legislation quite distinct from that of pressure groups—a theory which puts forward some conception of a 'general good' as the 'legitimate public purpose' at which legislation must aim, and according to which the triumph of private or group pressure marks the corruption of the legislative process." Compare Richard A. Posner, *The* DeFunis *Case and the Constitutionality of Preferential Treatment of Racial Minorities,* 1974 Sup.Ct.Rev. 1: "[A] vast part of the output of the governmental process would be seen to consist of discrimination, in the sense of an effort to redistribute wealth (in one form or another) from one group in the community to another, founded on the superior ability of one group to manipulate the political process rather than on any principle of justice or efficiency. Yet it would be odd, indeed, to condemn as unconstitutional the most characteristic product of a democratic (perhaps of any) political system."

4. ***Protecting disadvantaged minorities?*** When "politically disadvantaged minorities are affected," should "the legislative judgment [be] more critically regarded"? Note, *Equal Protection*, 82 Harv.L.Rev. 1076 (1969). Were the excluded vendors in *Railway Express* and *Dukes* disadvantaged minorities? Consider Jesse H. Choper, *Judicial Review and the National Political Process* 75–77 (1980): "[A]lmost all, if not all, groups [in] the American political process are 'minorities.' Thus, each time any group loses any political battle in which it has an interest—and some group always does—it may lay claim to the label of 'political weakness' or 'submerged and beaten minority.' [It] is true that some minorities, because of their sophistication and combined arithmetical and financial strength, are more influential than others on most political issues; and that some groups with modest numbers may win powerful surrogates who give them forceful representation. Similarly, there are some minorities who are less effective than others on most legislative matters because of their geographic isolation, the general inexcitability or unpopularity of their ideas, their relative inarticulateness, their lack of numbers and resources, or because they are viewed with such resentment, distaste, or hatred that they can neither join working coalitions nor prevent hostile action. But there are many disparate groups who may legitimately claim to meet some or all of these varied criteria for judicial solicitude."

5. ***Deference and the "underenforcement" thesis.*** Consider the possibility—first advanced in Lawrence G. Sager, *Fair Measure: The Legal Status of Underenforced Constitutional Norms,* 91 Harv.L.Rev. 1212 (1978)— that the deferential test applied in cases such as *Railway Express* and *Dukes* does not reflect the "meaning" of the Equal Protection Clause, but instead embodies a judgment about the limits of effective judicial enforcement. "According to Professor Sager, the Equal Protection Clause of the Fourteenth Amendment expresses the principle that '[a] state may treat persons differently only when it is fair to do so.' If this is the norm, then the most familiar equal protection test, under which courts uphold classifications that are rationally related to any actual or hypothesized state interest, is an instance of constitutional 'underenforcement.' The Court has determined that allowing judges to make independent, case-by-case assessments of the fairness of statutory classifications would invite excessive litigation and generate unpredictable and conflicting results. This judgment about undesirable consequences, rather than a decision about constitutional 'meaning,' has led the Court to develop a doctrine that prescribes broad judicial deference to legislative decisions." Richard H. Fallon, Jr., *Implementing the Constitution*, 111 Harv.L.Rev. 54 (1997). Would adoption of a deferential standard on this basis reflect judicial abdication? A defensible recognition that the Court must sometimes share the function of constitutional "implementation" with other governmental institutions? See id.

———

In the *Railway Express* and *Dukes* cases, there was no doubt that the parties challenging legislation on equal protection grounds contributed to the problem that the legislature sought to solve. The question—often denominated as one of "underinclusiveness"—involved the permissibility of imposing the burden of ameliorating (but not wholly eliminating) that problem on some but not on others. In contrast, the legislation involved in NEW YORK CITY TRANSIT AUTH. v. BEAZER, 440 U.S. 568 (1979), which upheld the exclusion of all methadone users from any Transit Authority (TA) employment, arguably posed a problem of "overinclusiveness." According to the Court, an estimated 75% of "patients who have been on methadone maintenance for at least a year are free from illicit drug use" and, if they could be properly identified, would pose no special safety risk. In addition, the exclusion applied to non-safety-sensitive as well as to safety-sensitive jobs. Nevertheless, the Court, per STEVENS, J., rejected the finding of the lower court that the methadone exclusion had "no rational relation to the demands of the job to be performed": "[T]he District Court [concluded] that employment in nonsensitive jobs could not be denied to methadone users who had progressed satisfactorily with their treatment for one year, and who, when examined individually, satisfied the TA's employment criteria. [But] any special rule short of total exclusion that TA might adopt is likely to be less precise—and will assuredly be more costly—than the one that it currently enforces. If eligibility is marked at any intermediate point—whether after one year of treatment or later—the classification will inevitably discriminate between employees or applicants equally or almost equally apt to achieve full recovery. [By] contrast, the 'no drugs' policy now enforced by TA is supported by the legitimate inference that as long as a treatment program (or other drug use) continues, a degree of uncertainty persists.* * *

"[T]he District Court's conclusion was that TA's rule is broader than necessary to exclude those methadone users who are not actually qualified to work for TA. We may assume [that] it is probably unwise for a large employer like TA to rely on a general rule instead of individualized consideration of every job applicant. But these assumptions concern matters of personnel policy that do not implicate the principle safeguarded by the Equal Protection Clause. As the District Court recognized, the special classification created by TA's rule serves the general objectives of safety and efficiency. Moreover, the exclusionary line challenged by respondents [does] not circumscribe a class of persons characterized by some unpopular trait or affiliation, it does not create or reflect any special likelihood of bias on the part of the ruling majority. Under these circumstances, it is of no constitutional significance that the degree of rationality is not as great with respect to certain ill-defined subparts of the classification as it is with respect to the classification as a whole."[6]

---

[6] See also *Vance v. Bradley*, 440 U.S. 93 (1979), per White, J., (sustaining mandatory retirement at age 60 for federal Foreign Service personnel), conceding that the classification was "to some extent both under- and over-inclusive" but holding that "perfection is by no means required. [In] an equal protection case of this type, [those] challenging the legislative judgment

WHITE, J., joined by Marshall, J., dissented: Both courts below "found that those who have been maintained on methadone for at least a year and who are free from the use of illicit drugs and alcohol can easily be identified through normal personnel procedures and, for a great many jobs, are as employable as and present no more risk than applicants from the general population. [On] the facts as found [one] can reach the Court's result only if [equal protection] imposes no real constraint at all in this situation. * * *

"Of course, the District Court's order permitting total exclusion of all methadone users maintained for less than one year, whether successfully or not, would still exclude some employables and would to this extent be overinclusive. [But although] many of those who have not been successfully maintained for a year are employable, as a class they, unlike the protected group, are not as employable as the general population. Thus, even assuming the bad risks could be identified, serving the end of employability would require unusual efforts to determine those more likely to revert. But that legitimate secondary goal is not fulfilled by excluding the protected [class]. Accordingly, the rule's classification of successfully maintained persons as dispositively different from the general population is left without any justification and, with its irrationality and invidiousness thus uncovered, must fall before the Equal Protection Clause."

Justice White added in a footnote: "I have difficulty also with the Court's easy conclusion that the challenged rule was '[q]uite plainly' not motivated 'by any special animus against a specific group of persons.' Heroin addiction is a special problem of the poor, and the addict population is composed largely of racial minorities that the Court has previously recognized as politically powerless and historical subjects of majoritarian neglect. Persons on methadone maintenance have few interests in common with members of the majority, and thus are unlikely to have their interests protected, or even considered, in governmental decisionmaking. Indeed, petitioners stipulated that '[o]ne of the reasons for [the] drug policy is the fact that [petitioners] feel[ ] an adverse public reaction would result if it were generally known that [petitioners] employed persons with a prior history of drug abuse, including persons participating in methadone maintenance programs.' It is hard for me to reconcile that stipulation of animus against former addicts with our past holdings that 'a bare [desire] to harm a politically unpopular group cannot constitute a *legitimate* governmental interest.' *U.S. Dept. of Agriculture v. Moreno*, [infra]. On the other hand, the afflictions to which petitioners are more sympathetic, such as alcoholism and mental illness, are shared by both white and black, rich and poor.

"Some weight should also be given to the history of the rule. Petitioners admit that it was not the result of a reasoned policy decision and stipulated

---

must convince the court that the legislative facts on which the classification is apparently based could not reasonably be conceived to be true by the governmental decisionmaker."

that they had never studied the ability of those on methadone maintenance to perform petitioners' jobs. Petitioners are not directly accountable to the public, are not the type of official body that normally makes legislative judgments of fact such as those relied upon by the majority today, and are by nature more concerned with business efficiency than with other public policies for which they have no direct responsibility. Both the State and City of New York, which do exhibit those democratic characteristics, hire persons in methadone programs for similar jobs.

"These factors together strongly point to a conclusion of invidious discrimination. * * * "

NOTES AND QUESTIONS

1. ***Standard applicable to overinclusive legislation.*** Should the Court apply the same rational basis standard to overinclusive legislation— such as that barring the employment even of those methadone users who would have presented none of the risks associated with illegal drug use—as to underinclusive legislation?

2. ***Contrasting perspectives.*** Should the Court be more deferential to overinclusiveness because it "poses less danger than underinclusiveness, at least from the viewpoint of political accountability, for overinclusiveness does not ordinarily exempt potentially powerful opponents from a law's reach"? Tribe 2d ed., at 1049. Or is overinclusion "less tolerable than underinclusion, for while the latter fails to impose the burden on some who should logically bear it, the former actually does impose the burden on some who do not belong in the class"? Note, *Equal Protection*, 82 Harv.L.Rev. 1076 (1969).

ARMOUR v. INDIANAPOLIS, 132 S.Ct. 2073 (2012), per BREYER, J., rejected an equal protection challenge to a city's policy for apportioning the costs of sewer construction. Under its initial financing scheme, Indianapolis billed property owners who wished to be hooked up to a sewer line $9,278 each, payable either in one lump sum or in installments spread over as many as 30 years. Very shortly thereafter, but after some property owners had paid in full, the city switched to a new financing system and decided to forgive the debts of those paying on the installment plan. It refused, however, to provide refunds to those who had paid upfront. As a result, some property owners paid as little as $309 while others paid $9,278. The Court ruled that considerations of administrative convenience provided a rational basis for the city's policy of forgiving unpaid assessments but not refunding any money already paid. After switching financing schemes, to continue "unpaid-debt collection could have proved complex and expensive," and "[t]o have added refunds to forgiveness" would have produced the "administrative costs [of] processing refunds" for a multitude of projects. The Court declined to find that the city had another rational basis in avoiding the "fiscal challenge" of paying refunds. Nevertheless, it noted that the city could not just issue checks to every complaining party "without taking funding from other programs or finding additional revenue." It also added that if "the City had tried to keep the amount of revenue it lost constant (a rational goal) but spread it evenly among the apparently thousands of homeowners involved in any of the [projects for which assessments had initially been made under the old system, with some property owners paying upfront and others in installments], the result would have been yet smaller individual payments, even more likely to have been too small to justify the administrative expense."

ROBERTS, C.J., joined by Scalia and Alito, JJ., dissented, emphasizing that the Indiana law that authorized the apportionment of sewer costs among property owners required at least roughly equal apportionment: "We have never before held that administrative burdens justify grossly disparate tax treatment of those the State has provided should be treated alike." Because "[t]he Equal Protection Clause is concerned [only] with 'gross' disparity in taxing," the Chief Justice would not have required refunds to owners who had paid upfront for hook-ups to other lines if other owners' installment payments over a period of years had produced less egregious inequalities. He added: "The Court is willing to concede that 'administrative considerations could not justify [an] unfair system' in which 'a city arbitrarily allocate[s] taxes among a few citizens while forgiving many others on the ground that it is cheaper and easier to collect taxes from a few people than from many.' [If] the quoted language does not accurately describe this case, I am not sure what it would reach."

With rational basis review requiring a judgment about the fit between the purpose of legislation and the means by which it seeks to achieve that purpose, prior cases have necessarily touched upon the question of how legislative purpose is to be identified. The next case poses that question even more starkly.

UNITED STATES R.R. RETIREMENT BD. V. FRITZ
449 U.S. 166, 101 S.Ct. 453, 66 L.Ed.2d 368 (1980).

JUSTICE REHNQUIST delivered the opinion of the Court.

The United States District Court [held violative of the "equal protection component of the Fifth Amendment" § 231b(h)] of the Railroad Retirement Act of 1974. [Under the] Act's predecessor statute, a person who worked for both railroad and nonrailroad employers and who qualified for railroad retirement benefits and social security benefits received retirement benefits under both systems and an accompanying "windfall" benefit. [Congress] determined to place the system on a "sound financial basis" by eliminating future accruals of those benefits. Congress also enacted various transitional provisions [which] expressly preserved windfall benefits for some classes of employees.

* * * First, those employees who lacked the requisite 10 years of railroad employment to qualify for railroad retirement benefits as of January 1, 1975, the changeover date, would have their retirement benefits computed under the new system and would not receive any windfall benefit. Second, those individuals already retired and already receiving dual benefits [would] continue to receive a windfall benefit. Third, those employees who had qualified for both railroad and social security benefits as of the changeover date, but who had not yet retired as of that date (and thus were not yet receiving dual benefits), were entitled to windfall benefits if they had (1) performed some railroad service in 1974 or (2) had a "current connection" with the railroad industry as of December 31, 1974,[6] or (3) completed 25 years of railroad service as of December 31, 1974. * * *

Thus, an individual who, as of the changeover date, was unretired and had 11 years of railroad employment and sufficient nonrailroad employment to qualify for social security benefits is eligible for the full windfall amount if he worked for the railroad in 1974 or had a current connection with the railroad as of December 31, 1974, or his later retirement date. But an unretired individual with 24 years of railroad service and sufficient nonrailroad service to qualify for social security benefits is not eligible for a full windfall amount unless he worked for the railroad in 1974, or had a current connection with the railroad as of December 31, 1974 or his later retirement date. * * *

The District Court agreed with appellees that a differentiation based solely on whether an employee was "active" in the railroad business as of 1974 was not "rationally related" to the congressional purposes of insuring the solvency of the railroad retirement system and protecting vested benefits. We disagree and reverse.

[The] plain language of § 231b(h) marks the beginning and end of our inquiry. There Congress determined that some of those who in the past received full windfall benefits would not continue to do so. Because Congress could have eliminated windfall benefits for all classes of employees, it is not constitutionally impermissible for Congress to have drawn lines between groups of employees for the purpose of phasing out those benefits. *Dukes.*

The only remaining question is whether Congress achieved its purpose in a patently arbitrary or irrational way. [Congress] could properly conclude that persons who had actually acquired statutory entitlement to windfall benefits while still employed in the railroad industry had a greater

---

[6]   **[Ct's Note]** The term "current connection" is defined [to] mean, in general, employment in the railroad industry in 12 of the preceding 30 calendar months.

equitable claim to those benefits than the members of appellees' class who were no longer in railroad employment when they became eligible for dual benefits. [Furthermore,] Congress could assume that those who had a current connection with the railroad industry when the Act was passed in 1974, or who returned to the industry before their retirement, were more likely than those who had left the industry prior to 1974 and who never returned, to be among the class of persons who pursue careers in the railroad industry, the class for whom the Railroad Retirement Act was designed.

Where, as here, there are plausible reasons for Congress' action, our inquiry is at an end. It is, of course, "constitutionally irrelevant whether this reasoning in fact underlay the legislative decision," because this Court has never insisted that a legislative body articulate its reasons for enacting a statute. This is particularly true where the legislature must necessarily engage in a process of line drawing. The "task of classifying persons for [benefits] inevitably requires that some persons who have an almost equally strong claim to favorite treatment be placed on different sides of the line," *Mathews v. Diaz*, [Sec. 4, II infra], and the fact the line might have been drawn differently at some points is a matter for legislative, rather than judicial, consideration.

Finally, we disagree with the District Court's conclusion that Congress was unaware of what it accomplished or that it was misled by the groups that appeared before it. If this test were applied literally to every member of any legislature that ever voted on a law, there would be very few laws which would survive it. The language of the statute is clear, and we have historically assumed that Congress intended what it enacted. To be sure, appellees lost a political battle in which they had a strong interest, but this is neither the first nor the last time that such a result will occur in the legislative forum. * * *[7]

JUSTICE BRENNAN, with whom JUSTICE MARSHALL joins, dissenting.

[When] faced with a challenge to a legislative classification under the rational basis test, the court should ask, first, what the purposes of the statute are, and second, whether the classification is rationally related to achievement of those purposes. The purposes of the Railroad Retirement Act of 1974 are clear, because Congress has commendably stated them in the House and Senate reports accompanying the Act. A section of the reports is entitled "Principal Purpose of the Bill." It notes generally that "[t]he bill provides for a complete restructuring of the Railroad Retirement Act of 1937, and will place it on a sound financial basis," and then states: "Persons who already have vested rights under both the Railroad Retirement and the Social Security systems will in the future be permitted to receive benefits computed under both systems just as is true under

---

[7]   Stevens, J., concurred in the judgment.

existing law."[3] Moreover, Congress explained that this purpose was based on considerations of fairness and the legitimate expectations of the retirees. [The] classification at issue here, which deprives some retirees of vested dual benefits that they had earned prior to 1974, directly conflicts with Congress' stated purpose. As such, the classification is not only rationally unrelated to the congressional purpose; it is inimical to it. * * *

A.   The Court states that "the plain language of § 231b(h) marks the beginning and end of our inquiry." [Since] the Act deprives appellees of their vested earned dual benefits, the Court apparently assumes that Congress must have *intended* that result. But by presuming purpose from result, the Court reduces analysis to tautology. It may always be said that Congress intended to do what it in fact did. If that were the extent of our analysis, we would find every statute, no matter how arbitrary or irrational, perfectly tailored to achieve its purpose. But equal protection scrutiny under the rational basis test requires the courts first to deduce the independent objectives of the statute, usually from statements of purpose and other evidence in the statute and legislative history, and second to analyze whether the challenged classification rationally furthers achievement of those objectives. The Court's tautological approach will not suffice.

B.   The Court analyzes the rationality of § 231b(h) in terms of a justification suggested by Government attorneys, but never adopted by Congress. [But] this Court has frequently recognized that the actual purposes of Congress, rather than the post hoc justifications offered by Government attorneys, must be the primary basis for analysis under the rational basis test. * * *

The Court argues that Congress chose to discriminate against appellees for reasons of equity, [but, as] I have shown, Congress expressed the view that it would be inequitable to deprive any retirees of any portion of the benefits they had been promised and that they had earned under prior law. The Court is unable to cite even one statement in the legislative history by a Representative or Senator that makes the equitable judgment it imputes to Congress. * * *

[L]abor representatives demanded that benefits be increased for their current members, the cost to be offset by divesting the appellee class of a portion of the benefits they had earned under prior law. [In] fact, the [management and labor representatives] and Railroad Retirement Board members who testified at congressional hearings perpetuated the

---

[3]   **[Ct's Note]** Several pages later, the reports again make clear that persons with vested rights to earned dual benefits would retain them[.] . . . Only in technical discussions and in the section-by-section analyses do the reports reflect the actual consequences of the Act on the appellee class. * * *

inaccurate impression that all retirees with earned vested dual benefits under prior law would retain their benefits unchanged. * * *

Of course, a misstatement or several misstatements by witnesses before Congress would not ordinarily lead us to conclude that Congress misapprehended what it was doing. In this instance, however, where complex legislation was drafted by outside parties and Congress relied on them to explain it, where the misstatements are frequent and unrebutted, and where no Member of Congress can be found to have stated the effect of the classification correctly, we are entitled to suspect that Congress may have been misled. As the District Court found: "At no time during the hearings did Congress even give a hint that it understood that the bill by its language eliminated an earned benefit of plaintiff's class."

Therefore, I do not think that this classification was rationally related to an *actual* governmental purpose.

[Because] the Court is willing to accept a tautological analysis of congressional purpose, an assertion of "equitable" considerations contrary to the expressed judgment of Congress, and a classification patently unrelated to achievement of the identified purpose, it succeeds in effectuating neither equity nor congressional intent. * * *

NOTES AND QUESTIONS

1. **Legislative purpose.** Do *Fritz* and similar cases signal that *actual* legislative purpose is never relevant to equal protection analysis? Is this a sensible and workable position? For the view that if "rationality is to be a meaningful standard of review, the court must conceive of its task as identifying the legislature's *probable* goals based on the available evidence," see Scott H. Bice, *Rationality Analysis in Constitutional Law*, 65 Minn.L.Rev. 1 (1980).

2. **Reality and reform.** Is the Court's approach justified or explained by the likelihood, discussed supra, that the legislative arena is frequently, possibly even typically, one in which interest groups compete for self-interested advantages?

Consider the suggestion of Cass R. Sunstein, *Interest Groups in American Public Law*, 38 Stan.L.Rev. 29 (1985), that "[t]he rationality requirement may [be] understood precisely as a requirement that regulatory measures be something other than a response to political pressure." See also Gerald Gunther, *Foreword: In Search of Evolving Doctrine on a Changing Court: A Model for a Newer Equal Protection*, 86 Harv.L.Rev. 1 (1972): "If the Court were to require an articulation of purpose from an authoritative state source"— "a state court's or attorney general office's description of purpose should be acceptable"—"rather than hypothesizing one on its own, there would at least be indirect pressure on the legislature to state its own reasons for selecting particular means and classifications [and thus] improve the quality of the political process [by] encouraging a fuller airing in the political arena of the grounds for legislative action." Is improving the political process a proper function of the judiciary? See generally John H. Ely, *Democracy and Distrust* 125–31 (1980).

———

Despite its frequent protestations that rational basis review "is a paradigm of judicial restraint," *FCC v. Beach Communications, Inc.*, 508 U.S. 307, 314 (1993), the Court occasionally holds that legislation fails to satisfy it. As you read the following cases, consider what factors explain the Court's occasional deviations from its usual pattern of extreme deference.

UNITED STATES DEPT. OF AGRICULTURE v. MORENO, 413 U.S. 528 (1973), per BRENNAN, J., applying " 'traditional' equal protection analysis," held that a provision of the Food Stamp Act—excluding "any household containing an individual who is unrelated to any other member of the household"—was "wholly without any rational basis": The exclusion "is clearly irrelevant to the stated purposes of the Act [to] raise levels of nutrition among low-income households. [Thus], the challenged classification must rationally further some legitimate governmental interest other than those specifically stated in the Congressional 'Declaration of Policy.'

"[The] little legislative history [that] does exist" indicates that the provision "was intended to [prevent] 'hippie communes' from participating in the food stamp program. [But equal protection] at the very least mean[s] that a bare congressional desire to harm a politically unpopular group cannot constitute a *legitimate* governmental interest." Nor does the classification "operate so as rationally to further the prevention of fraud" because, under the Act, "two *unrelated* persons living together" may "avoid the 'unrelated person' exclusion simply by altering their living arrangements so as [to] create two separate 'households,' both of which are eligible for assistance. [Thus], in practical operation, the [provision] excludes from participation [not] those persons who are 'likely to abuse the program' but, rather, only those persons who are so desperately in need of aid that they cannot even afford to alter their living arrangements so as to retain their eligibility."

DOUGLAS, J., concurred: "I could not say that [this] provision has no 'rational' relation to control of fraud. We deal here, however, with the right of association, protected by the First Amendment." Thus, the classification "can be sustained only on a showing of a 'compelling' governmental interest."

REHNQUIST, J., joined by Burger, C.J., dissented: "Congress attacked the problem with a rather blunt instrument, [b]ut I do not think it is unreasonable for Congress to conclude that the basic unit which it was willing to support [with] food stamps is some variation on the family as we know it—a household consisting of related individuals. This unit provides a guarantee which is not provided by households containing unrelated individuals that the household exists for some purpose other than to collect federal food stamps.

"Admittedly, [the] limitation will make ineligible many households which have not been formed for the purpose of collecting federal food stamps, and will [not] wholly deny food stamps to those households which may have been formed in large part to take advantage of the program. But, as the Court concedes, 'traditional' equal protection analysis does not require that every classification be drawn with precise mathematical nicety."

Moreno is one of a small number of cases in which the Court has identified equal protection violations, purportedly pursuant to a rational basis test, based on judicial findings that the state acted for impermissible purposes. See *Romer v. Evans*, Sec. 4, I infra (involving "animus" against gays); *Cleburne v. Cleburne Living Center, Inc.*, Sec. 4, IV infra (invalidating action predicated on "irrational prejudice against the mentally retarded").[8] Even apart from cases involving impermissible purposes, however, there are at least a few modern cases in which the Court, although employing the traditional "rational basis" standard, has held laws violative of equal protection.

In LOGAN v. ZIMMERMAN BRUSH CO. (1982), Ch. 6, Sec. 6, I, a majority of the justices, without questioning the legitimacy of the state's purpose, employed "the lowest level of permissible equal protection scrutiny" and found a violation of equal protection. Appellant filed an employment discrimination complaint before an Illinois Commission, but the Commission inadvertently scheduled the hearing at a date after the statutory time period expired. The state court held that the time lapse, though it was not the fault of the claimant, deprived the Commission of jurisdiction and terminated the appellant's claim. BLACKMUN, J., joined by Brennan, Marshall, and O'Connor, JJ., found the statutory discrimination against claimants who did not get a timely hearing through no fault of their own to be "patently irrational in light of [the law's] stated purpose": "I cannot agree that terminating a claim that the State itself has misscheduled is a rational way of expediting the resolution of disputes. [The] state's rationale must be something more than the exercise of a strained imagination; while the connection between means and ends need not be precise, it, at the least, must have some objective basis. That is not

---

8   Additional cases in which the Court has found that a state's articulated justifications for a statute are constitutionally impermissible under the Equal Protection Clause include *Zobel v. Williams*, Sec. 5, II infra, and *Metropolitan Life Ins. Co. v. Ward*, 470 U.S. 869 (1985) (state tax that discriminated against out-of-state insurance companies for the purpose of "promoting local industry" "constitutes the very sort of parochial discrimination that the Equal Protection Clause was intended to prevent").

so here." POWELL, J., joined by Rehnquist, J., concurred as to "this unusual classification": "As appellants possessed no power to convene hearings, it is unfair and irrational to punish them for the Commission's failure to do so."

———

VILLAGE OF WILLOWBROOK v. OLECH, 528 U.S. 562 (2000), found that a homeowner who alleged that her village had imposed unusual easement requirements on her as a condition of connecting her to the public water supply had an actionable equal protection complaint alleging that she constituted a "class of one" and had "been intentionally treated differently from others similarly situated." In so holding, the Court, per curiam, declined to consider an alternative theory of "subjective ill will."

Compare ENGQUIST v. OREGON DEPT. OF AGRICULTURE, 553 U.S. 591 (2008), per ROBERTS, C.J., holding that "the class-of-one theory of equal protection does not apply in the public employment context" because it would be untenable if "any personnel action in which a wronged employee [could] conjure up a claim of differential treatment" provided the basis for a constitutional case: "There are some forms of state action [which] by their nature involve discretionary decisionmaking based on a vast array of subjective, individualized assessments. In such cases the rule that people should be 'treated alike, under like circumstances and conditions' is not violated when one person is treated differently from others, because treating like individuals differently is an accepted consequence of the discretion granted. In such situations, allowing a challenge based on the arbitrary singling out of a particular person would undermine the very discretion that such state officials are entrusted to exercise.

"Suppose, for example, that a traffic officer is stationed on a busy highway where people often drive above the speed limit, and there is no basis upon which to distinguish them. [Allowing] an equal protection claim on the ground that a ticket was given to one person and not others, even if for no discernible or articulable reason, would be incompatible with the discretion inherent in the challenged action. It is no proper challenge to what in its nature is a subjective, individualized decision that it was subjective and individualized.

"This principle applies most clearly in the employment context, for employment decisions are quite often subjective and individualized, resting on a wide array of factors that are difficult to articulate and quantify."

STEVENS, J., joined by Souter and Ginsburg, JJ., dissented, reasoning that the Equal Protection Clause proscribes only "arbitrary" decisions unsupported by any rational basis and that "[t]here is therefore no need to create an exception [to the class-of-one theory] in order to prevent [all] discretionary [employment] decisions from giving rise to equal protection claims."

Consider Robert C. Farrell, *The Equal Protection Class of One Claim: Olech, Engquist, and the Supreme Court Misadventure*, 61 S.C.L.Rev. 107 (2009): "*Engquist* [went] too far and not far enough. By excepting all discretionary government action from the class of one claim, *Engquist* seems to eliminate any cause of action for a plaintiff harmed by the vindictive act of a government official when that act is part of an exercise of discretion. By failing to impose a bad faith requirement on the class of one claim, *Engquist* seems to endorse a federal equal protection claim every time a rule is not enforced in an absolutely uniform way."

————

According to Robert C. Farrell, *Successful Rational Basis Claims in the Supreme Court from the 1971 Term Through* Romer v. Evans, 32 Ind.L.Rev. 357 (1999), during the period from 1971–96, the Court upheld rational basis claims in ten cases, while rejecting such claims in one hundred other decisions: "The Court never explains why it has selected a particular case for heightened rationality. [None] of these cases [upholding rational basis claims] has had a significant precedential impact on subsequent cases." Would it be fair to say that the dominant thread of the Court's "rational basis" jurisprudence is extremely deferential, but that there is a recessive strain of cases in which the Court conducts a more searching review of legislative classifications? Should the dominant strain wholly replace the recessive one? Should the recessive replace the dominant?

2. RACE AND ETHNIC ANCESTRY

I. HISTORICAL BACKGROUND

Racism and practices of race discrimination are deeply embedded in American constitutional history. According to David O. Stewart, *The Summer of 1787*, at 70–71 (2007), in 1787, Massachusetts was the only state that wholly "banned slavery, and that state's prohibition came from a court ruling, not from a legislative act."[9] At least six of the thirteen original colonies—Maryland, Delaware, Virginia, the Carolinas, and Georgia—gave express legal support to slavery. At the Constitutional Convention, the existence of slavery was accepted as a political fact. There was no serious discussion of the Constitution forbidding slavery altogether.

---

[9] "Four other states (New Hampshire, Connecticut, Rhode Island, and Pennsylvania) had 'gradual emancipation' laws that freed children of slave parents. New York adopted gradual emancipation in 1799, and New Jersey followed in 1804. [In] 1802, Virginia enacted a manumission law allowing masters to set slaves free, but not many took the opportunity to do so." *Id.*

On the contrary, at least three provisions of the original Constitution recognized and arguably promoted slavery: Art. I, § 2, which based a state's representation in the House of Representatives on its free population and three-fifths of "all other Persons" within its territory; Art. I, § 9, which barred Congress from abolishing the slave trade before 1808; and Art. IV, § 2, which provided that "no Person held to Service or Labor" under the laws of one state could escape that status upon flight to another state but, on the contrary, "shall be delivered up on the Claim of the Party to whom such Service or Labour may be due." Even in many "free" states, at the time of the Constitutional Convention and thereafter African Americans were denied the vote, excluded from jury service, and separated from whites in public conveyances.

In the antebellum years, the Supreme Court decided major cases involving the African slave trade,[10] the return of fugitive slaves,[11] slavery in the federal territories, and the rights of slaves in transit through free states—virtually all in a manner accepting slavery's basic lawfulness. The most notorious of the antebellum decisions involving slavery came in the *Dred Scott* case.

The plaintiff-appellant in DRED SCOTT v. SANDFORD, 60 U.S. (19 How.) 393 (1857), was born in slavery in Virginia but, in the company of his master, later traveled in the free state of Illinois and the territory of Wisconsin, where slavery was prohibited by federal statute under the Missouri Compromise. Following his return to Missouri, a slave state, Dred Scott brought suit against his owner, John Sandford, in federal court, arguing that he had attained his freedom under Illinois and federal law. Scott predicated his claim of federal jurisdiction on diversity of citizenship, alleging that he was a citizen of Missouri and Sandford a citizen of New York. The Court, per TANEY, C.J., dismissed the suit by a vote of 7–2. It held (1) that Scott was incapable of becoming a "citizen" of Missouri eligible to invoke federal diversity jurisdiction; (2) that Congress's effort in the Missouri Compromise to abolish slavery in federal territories was unconstitutional; and (3) that whatever Scott's status in Illinois, after he had returned to Missouri his status was governed by the law of Missouri, which treated him as a slave:

"The question before us is, whether the class of persons described in the plea in abatement [are 'citizens' capable of invoking federal jurisdiction based on diversity of citizenship]. We think they are not, and that they are

---

[10] See, e.g., *The Antelope*, 23 U.S. (10 Wheat.) 66 (1825) (recognizing the right of foreigners to engage in the slave trade, if the laws of their nation permitted them to do so, but upholding prosecutions against American slave traders).

[11] See *Prigg v. Pennsylvania*, 41 U.S. (16 Pet.) 539 (1842) (upholding the federal Fugitive Slave Act of 1793, which established federal procedures for the capture and return of runaway slaves, and invalidating a Pennsylvania law creating impediments to the recapture of slaves).

not included, and were not intended to be included, under the word 'citizens' in the Constitution, and can therefore claim none of the rights and privileges which that instrument provides for and secures to citizens of the United States. On the contrary, they were at that time considered as a subordinate and inferior class of beings, who had been subjugated by the dominant race, and, whether emancipated or not, yet remained subject to their authority, and had no rights or privileges but such as those who held the power and the Government might choose to grant them. [It] is difficult at this day to realize the state of public opinion in relation to that unfortunate race, which prevailed in the civilized and enlightened portions of the world at the time of the Declaration of Independence, and when the Constitution of the United States was framed and adopted. But the public history of every European nation displays it in a manner too plain to be mistaken. [Negroes] had for more than a century before been regarded as beings of inferior order, and altogether unfit to associate with the white race, either in social or political relations; and so far inferior, that they had no rights which the white man was bound to respect; and that the negro might justly and lawfully be reduced to slavery for his benefit. He was bought and sold, and treated as an ordinary article of merchandise and traffic, whenever a profit could be made by it. This opinion was at that time fixed and universal in the civilized portion of the white race. It was regarded as an axiom in morals as well as in politics, which no one thought of disputing, or supposed to be open to dispute; and men in every grade and position in society daily and habitually acted upon it in their private pursuits, as well as in matters of public concern, without doubting for a moment the correctness of this opinion.

"But it is too clear for dispute, that the enslaved African race were not intended to be included, and formed no part of the people who framed and adopted this declaration; for if the language, as understood in that day, would embrace them, the conduct of the distinguished men who framed the Declaration of Independence would have been utterly and flagrantly inconsistent with the principles they asserted; and instead of the sympathy of mankind, to which they so confidently appealed, they would have deserved and received universal rebuke and reprobation.

"Yet the men who framed this declaration were great men—high in literary acquirements—high in their sense of honor, and incapable of asserting principles inconsistent with those on which they were acting. They perfectly understood the meaning of the language they used, and how it would be understood by others; and they knew that it would not in any part of the civilized world be supposed to embrace the negro race, which, by common consent, had been excluded from civilized Governments and the family of nations, and doomed to slavery. They spoke and acted according to the then established doctrines and principles, and in the ordinary language of the day, no one misunderstood them. The unhappy black race were separated from the white by indelible marks, and laws long before established, and were never thought of or spoken of except as property, and when the claims of the owner or the profit of the trader were supposed to need protection. * * *

"No one, we presume, supposes that any change in public opinion or feeling, in relation to this unfortunate race, in the civilized nations of Europe or in this country, should induce the court to give to the words of the Constitution a more liberal construction in their favor than they were intended to bear when the instrument was framed and adopted. Such an argument would be altogether inadmissible in any tribunal called on to interpret it. If any of its provisions are deemed unjust, there is a mode prescribed in the instrument itself by which it may be amended; but while it remains unaltered, it must be construed now as it was understood at the time of its adoption. [Any] other rule of construction would abrogate the judicial character of this court, and make it the mere reflex of the popular opinion or passion of the day. This court was not created by the Constitution for such purposes. Higher and graver trusts have been confided to it, and it must not falter in the path of duty. * * *

"[Nor does Article IV, § 3, cl. 2, which empowers Congress to 'make all needful Rules and Regulations respecting the Territory and other Property of the United States,' authorize Congress to prohibit slavery in the territories. As the language indicates, this grant of power applies only to those territories that were already a part of one of the States in 1789, the cession of which to the United States was therefore contemplated. Moreover, general regulatory powers] in relation to rights of person, which it is not necessary here to enumerate, are, in express and positive terms, denied to the General Government; and the rights of private property have been guarded with equal care. Thus the rights of property are united with the rights of persons, and placed on the same ground by the fifth amendment to the Constitution, which provides that no person shall be deprived of life, liberty, and property, without due process of law. And an act of Congress which deprives a citizen of the United States of his liberty or property merely because he came himself or brought his property into a particular Territory of the United States, and who had committed no offence against the laws, could hardly be dignified with the name of due process of law.

"[The] powers of the Government, and the rights of the citizen under it, are positive and practical regulations plainly written down. [It] has no power over the person or property of a citizen but what the citizens of the United States have granted. And no laws or usages of other nations, or reasoning of statesmen or jurists upon the relations of master and slave, can enlarge the powers of the Government, or take from the citizens the rights they have reserved. And if the Constitution recognizes the right of property of the master in a slave, and makes no distinction between that description of property and other property owned by a citizen, no tribunal, acting under the authority of the United States, whether it be legislative, executive, or judicial, has a right to draw such a distinction, or deny to it the benefit of the provisions and guarantees which have been provided for the protection of private property against the encroachments of the Government.

"Now, as we have already said in an earlier part of this opinion, upon a different point, the right of property in a slave is distinctly and expressly affirmed in the Constitution. The right to traffic in it, like an ordinary article of merchandise and property, was guarantied to the citizens of the United States, in every State that might desire it, for twenty years. And the Government in express terms is pledged to protect it in all future time, if the slave escapes from his owner. This is done in plain words—too plain to be misunderstood. And no word can be found in the Constitution which gives Congress a greater power over slave property, or which entitles property of that kind to less protection than property of any other description. The only power conferred is the power coupled with the duty of guarding and protecting the owner in his rights.

"Upon these considerations, it is the opinion of the court that the act of Congress which prohibited a citizen from holding and owning property of this kind in the territory of the United States north of the line therein mentioned, is not warranted by the Constitution, and is therefore void; and that neither Dred Scott himself, nor any of his family, were made free by being carried into this territory; even if they had been carried there by the owner, with the intention of becoming a permanent resident."

CURTIS, J., dissented: "The first section of the second article of the Constitution uses the language, 'a citizen of the United States at the time of the adoption of the Constitution.' One mode of approaching this question is, to inquire who were citizens of the United States at the time of the adoption of the Constitution. * * * At the time of the ratification of the Articles of Confederation, all free native-born inhabitants of the States of New Hampshire, Massachusetts, New York, New Jersey, and North Carolina, though descended from African slaves, were not only citizens of those States, but such of them as had the other necessary qualifications possessed the franchise of electors, on equal terms with other citizens. * * * I can find nothing in the Constitution which, proprio vigore, deprives of their citizenship any class of persons who were citizens of the United States at the time of its adoption, or who should be native-born citizens of any State after its adoption; nor any power enabling Congress to disfranchise persons born on the soil of any State, and entitled to citizenship of such State by its Constitution and laws. And my opinion is, that, under the Constitution of the United States, every free person born on the soil of a State, who is a citizen of that State by force of its Constitution or laws, is also a citizen of the United States. * * *

"[A]s, in my opinion, the Circuit Court had jurisdiction, I am obliged to consider the question [whether] the plaintiff's status, as a slave, was so changed by his residence within [free territory] that he was not a slave in the State of Missouri, at the time this action was brought. * * *

"First. The rules of international law respecting the emancipation of slaves, by the rightful operation of the laws of another State or country upon the status of the slave, while resident in such foreign State or country, are part of the common law of Missouri, and have not been abrogated by any statute law of that State. Second. The laws of the United States, constitutionally enacted, which operated directly on and changed the status of a slave coming into the Territory of Wisconsin with his master, who went thither to reside for an indefinite length of time, in the performance of his duties as an officer of the United States, had a rightful operation on the status of the slave, and it is in conformity with the rules of international law that this change of status should be recognised everywhere. * * *

"I have thus far assumed, merely for the purpose of the argument, that the laws of the United States, respecting slavery in this Territory, were constitutionally enacted by Congress. It remains to inquire whether they are constitutional and binding laws. [When] the Federal Constitution was framed, and presented to the people of the several States for their consideration, the unsettled territory was viewed as justly applicable to the common benefit, so far as it then had or might attain thereafter a pecuniary value; and so far as it might become the seat of new States, to be admitted into the Union upon an equal footing with the original States. * * * The importance of conferring on the new Government regular powers commensurate with the objects to be attained, and thus avoiding the alternative of a failure to execute the trust assumed by the acceptance of the cessions made and expected, or its execution by usurpation, could scarcely fail to be perceived. That it was in fact perceived, is clearly shown by the Federalist, (No. 38,) where this very argument is made use of in commendation of the Constitution. * * * Keeping these facts in view, it may confidently be asserted that there is very strong reason to believe, before we examine the Constitution itself, that the necessity for a competent grant of power to hold, dispose of, and govern territory, ceded and expected to be ceded, could not have escaped the attention of those who framed or adopted the Constitution; and that if it did not escape their attention, it could not fail to be adequately provided for.

"[Article IV thus provides:] 'The Congress shall have power to dispose of and make all needful rules and regulations respecting the territory or other property belonging to the United States; and nothing in this Constitution shall be so construed as to prejudice any claims of the United States or any particular State.' * * * No reason has been suggested why any reluctance should have been felt, by the framers of the Constitution, to apply this provision to all the territory which might belong to the United States, or why any distinction should have been made, founded on the accidental circumstance of the dates of the cessions; a circumstance in no way material as respects the necessity for rules and regulations, or the propriety of conferring on the Congress power to make them. And if we look at the course of the debates in the Convention on this article, we shall find that the then unceded lands, so far from having been left out of view in adopting this article, constituted, in the minds of members, a subject of even paramount importance.

"[With Congress's power to prohibit slavery in the territories otherwise being clear, the] the position, that a prohibition to bring slaves into a Territory deprives any one of his property without due process of law, [will not] bear examination. It must be remembered that this restriction on the legislative power is not peculiar to the Constitution of the United States; it was borrowed from Magna Charta; was brought to America by our ancestors, as part of their inherited liberties, and has existed in all the States, usually in the very words of the great charter. It existed in every political community in America in 1787, when the [Northwest] ordinance prohibiting slavery north and west of the Ohio was passed. * * *

"It was certainly understood by the Convention which framed the Constitution, and has been so understood ever since, that, under the power to regulate commerce, Congress could prohibit the importation of slaves; and the exercise of the power was restrained till 1808. A citizen of the United States owns slaves in Cuba, and brings them to the United States, where they are set free by the legislation of Congress. Does this legislation deprive him of his property without due process of law? If so, what becomes of the laws prohibiting the slave trade? If not, how can a similar regulation respecting a Territory violate the fifth amendment of the Constitution? * * *

"In my opinion, the judgment of the Circuit Court should be reversed."[12]

NOTES AND QUESTIONS

1.   *Law and politics.* (a) Consider Barry Friedman, *The Will of the People: How Public Opinion has Influenced the Supreme Court and the Supreme Court has Shaped the Meaning of the Constitution* 110–12 (2009): "With the country so deeply divided over slavery in the territories [that the national political process appeared on the edge of breakdown,] politicians of various stripes had begun to look to the Supreme Court to resolve the issue. * * * Although the justices had initially intended to dispose of the case on narrow grounds, they were driven by forces internal and external to render the decision that subsequently caused so much controversy. Incoming President James Buchanan wrote his friend Justice John Catron to inquire whether the

---

[12]   Other concurring and dissenting opinions in the case are omitted.

Court would decide the case by the time of his inauguration in March 1857. Buchanan had been elected as a peacemaker and undoubtedly hoped the Court could solve the slavery issue for him. [Catron] wrote back [to inform Buchanan of the Court's internal deliberations] and enlisted Buchanan's help in persuading fellow justice Robert Grier, a Democrat from Pennsylvania, to join the five southern justices in holding that Congress lacked power over slavery in the territories. (Buchanan did as asked.) At his inauguration, [Buchanan] was able to instruct the country that '[this] is a judicial question which legitimately belongs to the Supreme Court of the United States before whom it [will] be speedily and finally settled.' "

Keith Whittington, *The Political Foundations of Judicial Supremacy* 254 (2007), reports that President Buchanan in his Annual Message of December 19, 1858, again " 'congratulat[ed]' the American people 'upon the final settlement by the Supreme Court of the United States of the question of slavery in the Territories' which 'irrevocably fixed' the issue and put an end to the 'dangerous excitement.' "

(b)   Consider Stephen G. Breyer, *A Look Back at the* Dred Scott *Decision*, 35 J.Sup.Ct.Hist. 110 (2010): "A [lesson of the *Dred Scott* case] concerns the relation between Court decisions and politics. [Judges] are not necessarily good politicians. Their view about what is politically expedient could well turn out to be [wrong.] *Dred Scott* [also] tells us something about morality's relation to law. [When] discussing *Dred Scott* at a law school conference, I asked the audience to consider a hypothetical question. Suppose you were Benjamin Curtis [and] that Chief Justice Taney comes to your Chambers and proposes a narrow ground for deciding the case. He asks if you will agree to a single paragraph unsigned opinion for the entire Court, in which the Court upholds the lower court on the ground that the matter is one of Missouri law in respect to which the Missouri supreme court must have the last word. He will agree to this approach provided that there is no dissent.

"Should you agree? If you do, the majority will say nothing about citizenship, nothing about the Missouri Compromise, nothing about slavery in the territories and the Due Process Clause. As a result the Court will create no significant new law; it will not diminish its own position in the eyes of the Nation. [Not] a bad bargain. The audience was uncertain. Then a small voice came from the back of the room. 'Say no.' And the audience broke into applause. That applause made clear the moral nature of the judge's legal obligation in that case." Do you agree?

2.   ***Subsequent developments.*** "*Dred Scott* was ultimately reversed [by] a constitutional amendment. Before that could happen, however, the country was forced to fight its bloodiest war ever." Friedman, supra, at 119. For illuminating commentary on the *Dred Scott* case and its historical context, see Don E. Fehrenbacher, *The Dred Scott Case* (1979); Paul Finkelman, Dred Scott v. Sandford: *A Brief History with Documents* (1997); Mark Graber, *Dred Scott and the Problem of Constitutional Evil* (2006). According to Professor

Graber, *Dred Scott* was entirely defensible within the prevailing constitutional assumptions of its times.

II. DISCRIMINATION AGAINST RACIAL AND ETHNIC MINORITIES

The "evil to be remedied" by the Equal Protection Clause, declared the *Slaughter-House Cases*, was "the existence of laws in the States where the newly emancipated negroes resided, which discriminated with gross injustice and hardship against them as a class."

STRAUDER v. WEST VIRGINIA, 100 U.S. (10 Otto) 303 (1880)—the first post-Civil War race discrimination case to reach the Court—per STRONG, J., invalidated the state murder conviction of an African American on the ground that state law forbade blacks from serving on grand or petit juries. In the course of its opinion, the Court observed that "the true spirit and meaning" of the Civil War amendments was "securing to a race recently emancipated [the] enjoyment of all the civil rights that under the law are enjoyed by [whites]. What is [equal protection but] that all persons, whether colored or white, shall stand equal before the laws of the States, and, in regard to the colored race, for whose protection the amendment was primarily designed, that no discrimination shall be made against them by law because of their color? The words of the amendment [contain] a positive immunity or right, most valuable to the colored race,—the right to exemption from unfriendly legislation against them distinctively as colored,—exemption from legal discriminations, implying inferiority in civil society, lessening the security of their enjoyment of the rights which others enjoy, and discriminations which are steps towards reducing them to the condition of a subject race.

"That the West Virginia statute respecting juries [is] such a discrimination ought not to be doubted. [And if] in those States where the colored people constitute a majority of the entire population a law should be enacted excluding all white men from jury service, [we] apprehend no one would be heard to claim that it would not be a denial to white men of the equal protection of the laws. Nor if a law should be passed excluding all naturalized Celtic Irishmen, would there be any doubt of its inconsistency with the spirit of the amendment. * * *

"We do not say that within the limits from which it is not excluded by the amendment a State may not prescribe the qualifications of its jurors, and in so doing make discriminations. It may confine the selection to males, to freeholders, to citizens, to persons within certain ages, or to persons having educational qualifications. We do not believe the Fourteenth Amendment was ever intended to prohibit this. Looking at its history, it is clear it had no such purpose. Its aim was against discrimination because of race or color."

PLESSY V. FERGUSON
163 U.S. 537, 16 S.Ct. 1138, 41 L.Ed. 256 (1896).

JUSTICE BROWN delivered the opinion of the Court.

[An 1890 Louisiana law required that railway passenger cars have "equal but separate accommodations for the white, and colored races." Plessy, alleging that he "was seven-eighths Caucasian and one-eighth African blood; that the mixture of colored blood was not discernible in him; and that he was entitled to every right [of] the white race," was arrested for refusing to vacate a seat in a coach for whites.]

That [the challenged statute] does not conflict with the Thirteenth Amendment [is] too clear for argument. Slavery implies involuntary servitude,—a state of bondage * * * . This amendment [was] regarded by the statesmen of that day as insufficient to protect the colored race from certain laws [imposing] onerous disabilities and burdens, and curtailing their rights in the pursuit of life, liberty, and property to such an extent that their freedom was of little value; [and] the Fourteenth Amendment was devised to meet this exigency. * * *

The object of the amendment was undoubtedly to enforce the absolute equality of the two races before the law, but, in the nature of things, it could not have been intended to abolish distinctions based upon color, or to enforce social, as distinguished from political equality, or a commingling of the two races upon terms unsatisfactory to either. Laws permitting, and even requiring, their separation, in places where they are liable to be brought into contact do not necessarily imply the inferiority of either race to the other, and have been generally, if not universally, recognized as within the competency of the state legislatures in the exercise of their police power. The most common instance of this is connected with the establishment of separate schools for white and colored children, which have been [upheld] even by courts of states where the political rights of the colored race have been longest and most earnestly enforced [citing cases from Mass., Ohio, Mo., Cal., La., N.Y., Ind., and Ky.].

Laws forbidding the intermarriage of the two races may be said in a technical sense to interfere with the freedom of contract, and yet have been universally recognized as within the police power of the state. The distinction between laws interfering with the political equality of the negro and those requiring the separation of the two races in schools, theatres and railway carriages have been frequently drawn by this court. Thus in *Strauder v. West Virginia* it was held that a law of West Virginia [forbidding blacks to serve on juries] was a discrimination which implied a legal inferiority in civil society, which lessened the security of the colored race, and was a step toward reducing them to a condition of servility.

[S]tatutes for the separation of the two races upon public conveyances were held to be constitutional in [federal decisions and cases from Pa., Mich., Ill., Tenn. and N.Y. Almost] directly on point is [a Mississippi case] wherein the railway company was indicted for a violation of a statute of Mississippi, enacting that all railroads carrying passengers should provide equal, but separate, accommodations for the white and colored races. [It is suggested] that the same argument that will justify the state legislature in requiring railways to provide separate accommodations for the two races will also authorize them to require separate cars to be provided for people whose hair is of a certain color, or who are aliens, or who belong to certain nationalities, or to enact laws requiring colored people to walk upon one side of the street, and white people upon the other, or requiring white men's houses to be painted white, and colored men's black, or their vehicles or business signs to be of different colors, upon the theory that one side of the street is as good as the other, or that a house or vehicle of one color is as good as one of another color. The reply to all this is that every exercise of the police power must be reasonable, and extend only to such laws as are enacted in good faith for the promotion of the public good, and not for the annoyance or oppression of a particular class. [In] determining the question of reasonableness, [the state] is at liberty to act with reference to the established usages, customs, and traditions of the people, and with a view to the promotion of their comfort, and the preservation of the public peace and good order. Gauged by this standard, we cannot say [this law] is unreasonable, or more obnoxious to the Fourteenth Amendment than the [acts] requiring separate schools for colored children in the District of Columbia, the constitutionality of which does not seem to have been questioned, or the corresponding acts of state legislatures.

We consider the underlying fallacy of the plaintiff's argument to consist in the assumption that the enforced separation of the two races stamps the colored race with a badge of inferiority. If this be so, it is not by reason of anything found in the act, but solely because the colored race chooses to put that construction upon it. [The] argument also assumes that social prejudices may be overcome by legislation, and that equal rights cannot be secured to the negro except by an enforced commingling of the two races. We cannot accept this proposition. If the two races are to meet upon terms of social equality, it must be the result [of] voluntary consent of individuals. * * * Legislation is powerless to eradicate racial instincts, or to abolish distinctions based upon physical differences, and the attempt to do so can only result in accentuating the difficulties of the present situation. If the civil and political rights of both races be equal, one cannot be inferior to the other civilly or politically. If one race be inferior to the other socially, the Constitution of the United States cannot put them on the same plane. * * *

JUSTICE BREWER did [not] participate in the decision of this case.

JUSTICE HARLAN, dissenting.

[No] legislative body or judicial tribunal may have regard to the race of citizens when the civil rights of those citizens are involved. * * *

It was said in argument that the statute of Louisiana does not discriminate against either race, but prescribes a rule applicable alike to white and colored citizens. But [e]very one knows that [it] had its origin in the purpose, not so much to exclude white persons from railroad cars occupied by blacks, as to exclude colored people from coaches occupied by or assigned to white persons. [The] fundamental objection, therefore, to the statute is that it interferes with the personal freedom of citizens. * * *

The white race deems itself to be the dominant race in this country. And so it is, in prestige, in achievements, in education, in wealth, and in power. So, I doubt not, it will continue to be for all time, if it remains true to its great heritage, and holds fast to the principles of constitutional liberty. But in view of the constitution, in the eye of the law, there is in this country no superior, dominant, ruling class of citizens. There is no caste here. Our constitution is color-blind * * * .

In my opinion, the judgment this day rendered will, in time, prove to be quite as pernicious as the decision made by this tribunal in the *Dred Scott Case*. [What] can more certainly arouse race hate, what more certainly create and perpetuate a feeling of distrust between these races, than state enactments which, in fact, proceed on the ground that colored citizens are so inferior and degraded that they cannot be allowed to sit in public coaches occupied by white citizens? [The] thin disguise of "equal" accommodations for passengers in railroad coaches will not mislead any one, nor atone for the wrong this day done. * * *

I do not deem it necessary to review the decisions of state courts to which reference was made in argument. Some [are] inapplicable, because rendered prior to the adoption of the last amendments of the [Constitution]. Others were made at a time [when] race prejudice was, practically, the supreme law of the land. Those decisions cannot be guides in the era introduced by the recent amendments of the supreme law, which established universal civil freedom * * * .

NOTES AND QUESTIONS

1. ***Strauder, Plessy, and the original understanding of the Fourteenth Amendment.*** Although no one doubts that the Fourteenth Amendment was drafted to address state discrimination against African-Americans, it is less than wholly clear which specific kinds of discrimination the Fourteenth Amendment was originally intended and understood to protect against. (It may be one measure of the gap between common understandings of "equal protection" in the Reconstruction era and prevailing understandings today that the Congress that proposed the Fourteenth Amendment maintained

segregated galleries.) *Strauder* is most naturally read as offering one account, while *Plessy*, by maintaining that the Fourteenth Amendment does not guarantee equality with respect to "social rights," appears to assume another. But complications lurk beneath the surface, as has been brought out by historians' efforts to explicate the sometimes baffling categories of nineteenth century legal thought.

In the quest for historical understanding, several reference points stand out, though their significance is disputed. The first involves the limited scope of the Thirteenth Amendment and the former Confederate states' efforts to exploit the leeway that that Amendment arguably left them. The Thirteenth Amendment, which was proposed in 1864 and ratified in 1865, outlawed slavery and authorized Congress to enact implementing legislation, but it did not expressly confer any further guarantee of equal protection. Virtually all the former Confederate states took advantage of this gap by passing widely publicized "Black Codes." According to Daniel A. Farber & John E. Muench, *The Ideological Origins of the Fourteenth Amendment*, 1 Const.Comment. 235 (1994): "These codes prohibited blacks from renting land, provided for the seizure of those who breached labor contracts, prohibited servants from leaving their masters' premises, and authorized the hiring out of black children and of blacks unable to pay vagrancy fines. They also made certain conduct criminal only when done by blacks."

Despite doubts about its constitutional authority to do so, Congress responded to the Black Codes and to the absence of general equality guarantees in the Thirteenth Amendment by enacting (over the veto of President Andrew Johnson) the Civil Rights Act of 1866 (CRA). Section 1 of the CRA, which furnishes a second reference point for understanding the Fourteenth Amendment, provided that "there shall be no discrimination in civil rights or immunities, among the inhabitants of any State or Territory of the United States on account of race, color, or previous condition of slavery; but the inhabitants of every race and color . . . shall have the same right, in every State and Territory in the United States, to make and enforce contracts, to sue, to be parties and give evidence, to inherit, purchase, lease, sell, hold and convey real and personal property and proceedings for the security of person and property, as is enjoyed by white citizens." In debates about the CRA, it is clear that many members of Congress regarded the limitation on the statute's reach to "civil rights" as having great significance within a then-common but loosely delineated conceptual framework that distinguished among "social," "political," and "civil" or "fundamental" rights. By all accounts, the CRA protected only civil rights—some and possibly all of which Section 1 listed—and did not protect social rights or political rights. The category of social rights apparently embraced the rights of one citizen against another and, according to *Plessy*, some additional rights against the government that were less important or fundamental than civil rights. The right to vote was the paradigmatic political right. See, e.g., Cong. Globe, 39th Cong., 1st Sess. 1117 (1866) (statement of Rep. James F. Wilson).

The third reference point is of course the language of the Fourteenth Amendment itself, which, on nearly all historical accounts, had a complicated relationship to the 1866 CRA. An important part of the motivation for Section 1 of the Fourteenth Amendment—which includes the Privileges or Immunities, Equal Protection, and Due Process Clauses—was to resolve questions about whether Congress had the necessary authority to enact the CRA. Members of Congress seem to have broadly assumed that the privileges or immunities of citizenship protected by the Fourteenth Amendment's Privileges or Immunities Clause corresponded to the "civil rights" protected by the 1866 Civil Rights Act. See Alexander M. Bickel, *The Original Understanding and the Segregation Decision*, 69 Harv.L.Rev. 1 (1955); Farber & Muench, supra. At the very least, it seems to have been broadly understood in the halls of Congress that Section 5 of the Fourteenth Amendment, which provides that Congress may "enforce . . . this article," vested Congress with ample power to enact the CRA.

Of more direct pertinence to the issues in *Strauder* and *Plessy* is that, insofar as the Privileges or Immunities Clause was intended and understood to protect "civil rights," it would have categorically prohibited race-based discrimination with respect to the distribution of such rights. The originally understood relation of the Equal Protection Clause to the CRA is more obscure, but if the Privileges or Immunities Clause guaranteed racial equality with respect to fundamental or civil rights, the equal protection guarantee might both have ratified this understanding—thus making it arguably appropriate for *Strauder* to be resolved on equal protection grounds—and further mandated that the law, as written, must be enforced even-handedly. It would not, however, necessarily have prohibited race-based discrimination in the distribution of "social rights," as the *Plessy* Court assumed the right at issue to be. This account would also explain how, as the Court noted in *Plessy*, state statutes providing for racially segregated public schools could have been widely thought to be consistent with the equal protection guarantee.

From a modern perspective, however, it is remarkable how little discussion on the floor of Congress directly addressed the meaning of the now vitally important Section 1 of the Fourteenth Amendment. Another feature of the political context of the 1866 congressional debates may explain why. As historian Eric Foner has observed: "What [one representative] called a 'somewhat startling result' of emancipation was the first constitutional issue to confront the Joint Committee on Reconstruction. Before the war, three fifths of the South's slaves had been included in calculating Congressional representation. Now, as free persons, all would be counted, significantly enhancing Southern power in the House of Representatives and the Electoral College." Eric Foner, *Reconstruction* 252 (2002). Under these circumstances, the lion's share of debate over the Fourteenth Amendment concerned Sections 2 through 4, which tied each state's representation in Congress to the ability of free males in the state to vote; limited the political power of former Confederates; and ensured that no future Congress would assume the debt of the former Confederacy.

It therefore deserves emphasis that despite the speculations offered above concerning the possible linkage between the expected meanings of Section 1's Privileges or Immunities and Equal Protection Clauses and nineteenth-century distinctions among civil, political, and social rights, the evidence is far short of conclusive on many points. Consider Foner, *supra*, at 257–58: "On the precise definition of equality before the law, Republicans differed among themselves. Even moderates in Congress understood Reconstruction as a dynamic process, in which phrases like 'privileges and immunities' were subject to changing interpretation. They preferred to allow both Congress and the federal courts maximum flexibility in implementing the Amendment's provisions and combating the multitude of injustices that confronted blacks in many parts of the South. [As a result of the phrasing of Section 1 as a limitation on states' power,] discriminatory state laws could be overturned by the federal courts regardless of which party dominated Congress. (Indeed, as in the Civil Rights Act, Congress placed great reliance on an activist federal judiciary for civil rights enforcement—a mechanism that appeared preferable to maintaining indefinitely a standing army in the South, or establishing a permanent national bureaucracy to oversee Reconstruction.)"

Further confounding efforts to ascribe a single, clear originally understood meaning to Section 1 of the Fourteenth Amendment is that the Supreme Court implicitly rejected any equation of the Privileges or Immunities Clause with the civil rights protected by the 1866 Civil Rights Act in the *Slaughter-House Cases* (1873), Chap. 5, Sec. 1, III supra. Nevertheless, it is wholly understandable that some nineteenth century jurists considering issues involving race discrimination would have done so within a conceptual framework—which drew distinctions among the protections offered to diverse categories of rights—that is foreign to twenty-first century thinking and difficult even to reconstruct with confident precision.[13]

2. ***Surrounding attitudes.*** (a) C. Vann Woodward, *The Strange Career of Jim Crow* 64 (1955), argues that race relations in the United States, but especially in the South, had worsened dramatically during the last two decades of the nineteenth century, which provided the social and political context for the *Plessy* decision: "Economic, political, and social frustrations had pyramided to a climax of social tensions. No real relief was in sight from the long cyclical depression of the nineties, an acute period of suffering that only intensified the distress of the much longer agricultural depression. Hopes for [a variety of

---

[13] The story of the ratification of the Fourteenth Amendment is equally complex and fascinating. Consider Thomas B. Colby, *Originalism and the Ratification of the Fourteenth Amendment,* 107 Northwestern U.L.Rev. 1627 (2013): "The Fourteenth Amendment was [drafted] and enacted entirely by Republicans in a rump Reconstruction Congress in which the Southern states were denied representation; it would never have made it through Congress had all of the elected Senators and Representatives been permitted to vote. And it was not ratified by the collective assent of the American people, but rather at gunpoint. The Southern states had been placed under military rule, and they were forced to ratify the Amendment [as] a condition of ending military occupation and rejoining the Union. The Amendment [was] added to the Constitution despite its open failure to obtain the support of the necessary supermajority of the American people." For a response to the resulting constitutional objections, see, e.g., John Harrison, *The Lawfulness of the Reconstruction Amendments,* 68 U.Chi.L.Rev. 375 (2001).

political reforms] had likewise met with cruel disappointments and frustration. There had to be a scapegoat. And all along the line signals were going up to indicate that the Negro was an approved object of aggression. These 'permissions-to-hate' came from sources that had formerly denied such permission. They came from the federal courts in numerous opinions, from Northern liberals eager to conciliate the South, from Southern conservatives who had abandoned their race policy of moderation in their struggle against the Populists, from the Populists in their mood of disillusionment with their former Negro allies, and from a national temper suddenly expressed by imperialistic adventures and aggressions against colored peoples in distant lands."

(b)   Could the Court have resisted the mounting tide of racism in the late nineteenth century, even if it had wanted to do so? Consider Michael Klarman, *The Plessy Era*, 1998 Sup.Ct.Rev. 303: "[Given] the background of race relations at the turn of the century and the limited capacity of the Supreme Court generally to frustrate public opinion, it may be implausible to think that the Justices realistically could have reached different results [in cases such as *Plessy*]" since, among other things, political officials especially in southern states might simply have ignored a Court ruling that mandated equal treatment of the races. According to Professor Klarman, *Strauder* was a case in which it was relatively easy for the Court to ensure compliance by signaling that it would simply reverse convictions in cases where its ruling was ignored.[14]

Compare Paul Finkelman, *Civil Rights in Historical Context: In Defense of* Brown, 118 Harv.L.Rev. 973 (2005): A different decision in *Plessy* "would not necessarily have required any kind of enforcement other than the Court making sure that Louisiana [did] not prosecute the railroads [or] their passengers [for] ignoring the [unconstitutional] segregation statutes." (According to Finkelman, "[t]he railroads [did] not like having to provide separate cars for blacks; it was expensive and inefficient.")

See Richard L. Aynes, *An Examination of* Brown *in Light of* Plessy *and* Croson: *Lessons for the 1990s*, 7 Harv. Blackletter L.J. 149 (1990): "As long as John Harlan's dissent remains in volume 163 of the United States Reports, no one can say with accuracy that the *Plessy* decision was merely a product of its times. Justice Harlan bears witness to the fact that there were other possibilities open to the Court and that there were people who lived in those times who were not as inhibited by racist views as the majority of the Court was in Plessy." See also *Planned Parenthood v. Casey*, Ch. 6, Sec. 2 supra: "[W]e think *Plessy* was wrong the day it was decided."

(c)   Within the social climate of the times, could the Court in *Plessy* truly have believed that if the forced separation of the races "stamps the colored race with a badge of inferiority," it is "solely because the colored race chooses to put

---

[14]   For discussion of *Plessy* and its background, see Charles A. Lofgren, *The* Plessy *Case: A Legal Historical Interpretation* (1987); Paul Oberst, *The Strange Career of* Plessy v. Ferguson, 15 Ariz.L.Rev. 389 (1973).

that construction upon it"? Consider Charles Black, *The Lawfulness of the Segregation Decisions*, 69 Yale L.J. 421 (1960): At this point in the Court's opinion, "[t]he curves of callousness and stupidity intersect at their respective maxima."

(d)   According to Lofgren, supra, at 5, "the nation's press met the [*Plessy*] decision mainly with apathy."

3.   *Justice Harlan and the "colorblind" Constitution.* In *Cumming v. Richmond County Board of Education*, 175 U.S. 528 (1899), Harlan, J., after noting that the question of the constitutionality of racial segregation in public schooling had not been raised, wrote for a unanimous Court in upholding a county school board's decision to close an all-black high school while continuing to maintain an all-white high school. In his view, the board had permissibly chosen to use its limited resources to provide primary schooling to a larger number of black elementary school children, rather than to maintain an all-black high school for a smaller number of students: "The substantial relief asked is an injunction that would either impair the efficiency of the high school provided for white children or compel the Board to close it. [The] colored school children of the county would not be advanced [by] a decree compelling the defendant Board to cease giving support to a high school for white children. The Board had before it the question whether it should maintain, under its control, a high school for about sixty colored children or withhold the benefits of education in primary schools from three hundred children of the same race. It was impossible, the Board believed, to give educational facilities to the three hundred colored children who were unprovided for, if it maintained a separate school for the sixty children who wished to have a high school education. Its decision was in the interest of the greater number of colored children, leaving the smaller number to obtain a high school education in existing private institutions at an expense not beyond that incurred in the high school discontinued by the Board. We are not permitted by the evidence in the record to regard that decision as having been made with any desire or purpose on the part of the Board to discriminate against any of the colored school children of the county on account of their race."

In *United States v. Wong Kim Ark*, 169 U.S. 649 (1898), Harlan, J., dissented from a Court decision holding that a Chinese person born in the United States to non-citizen parents was entitled to citizenship by birth. He joined Fuller, C.J., in concluding that Congress could permissibly "prescribe that all persons of a particular race, or their children, cannot become citizens." For further discussion, see Earl M. Maltz, *Only Partially Color-Blind: John Marshall Harlan's View of Race and the Constitution*, 12 Ga.St.U.L.Rev. 973 (1996).

4.   *"Separate but equal."* Although the phrase itself is not emphasized in *Plessy*, the decision came to be recognized as having established a "separate but equal" test for the permissibility of racially segregated public accommodations. See Michael Klarman, *An Interpretive History of Modern Equal Protection*, 90 Mich.L.Rev. 213 (1991): "*Plessy,* the case first introducing

separate-but-equal to the Supreme Court, apparently contemplated that unequal segregated facilities would be subject to justification just like any other sort of inequality. [E]quality was required in *Plessy* [only] because the Court could conceive of no rational explanation for a state's refusal to provide equal railway facilities for blacks. Racial classifications, in other words, were subjected to the same general rationality test which had come to govern equal protection review of economic regulation."[15]

5. *Insensitivity to black rights and doctrinal inconsistency?* Consider Finkelman, supra: "[T]he Court's insensitivity to black rights led to enormous inconsistencies in the Court's jurisprudence. [In] *Berea College v. Kentucky*, [211 U.S. 45 (1908),] for example, the Court upheld a Kentucky statute that prohibited integration at private colleges. [As] the attorneys for Berea College [pointed out], this result denied the college its due process rights of property and contract under [the doctrine of *Lochner v. New York*]. In *Hall v. DeCuir,* [95 U.S. 485 (1878),] the Court struck down mandatory integration in transportation on Commerce Clause grounds, but it failed to apply the same logic when looking at state law requiring segregation in transportation [in *Plessy*]."

KOREMATSU V. UNITED STATES
323 U.S. 214, 65 S.Ct. 193, 89 L.Ed. 194 (1944).

JUSTICE BLACK delivered the opinion of the Court.

[Following the Japanese attack on Pearl Harbor, President Franklin Roosevelt signed Executive Order 9066, which gave military officials the legal authority to exclude any or all persons from designated areas on the west coast in order to insure against sabotage and espionage. Congress implicitly ratified the Executive Order by providing that the violation of an implementing order by a military commander constituted a misdemeanor punishable by fine or imprisonment. Under the authority of the Executive Order, the War Relocation Authority subjected all persons of Japanese ancestry on the west coast to a curfew, excluded them from their homes, detained them in assembly centers, and then evacuated them to "relocation centers" in California, Idaho, Utah, Arizona, Wyoming, Colorado, and Arkansas. By the end of 1942, roughly 112,000 persons—over 65,000 of whom were U.S. citizens—had been involuntarily removed to relocation centers.]

The petitioner, an American citizen of Japanese descent, was convicted in a federal district court for remaining in San Leandro, California, a "Military Area," contrary to Civilian Exclusion Order No. 34 of the Commanding General of the Western Command, U.S. Army, which directed that after May 9, 1942, all persons of Japanese ancestry should be

---

[15] Compare Lofgren, supra (arguing that the separate-but-equal doctrine emerged from common law cases involving the obligations of common carriers, gained hold in a number of state statutes, and achieved constitutional status in *Plessy*).

excluded from that area. No question was raised as to petitioner's loyalty to the United States. * * *

[A]ll legal restrictions which curtail the civil rights of a single racial group are immediately suspect. That is not to say that all such restrictions are unconstitutional. It is to say that courts must subject them to the most rigid scrutiny. Pressing public necessity may sometimes justify the existence of such restrictions; racial antagonism never can. * * *

Exclusion Order No. 34 [was] one of a number of military orders. [In] *Hirabayashi v. United States,* 320 U.S. 81 (1943), we sustained a conviction [for] violation of [a] curfew order [applicable only to persons of Japanese ancestry as] an exercise of the power [to] take steps necessary to prevent espionage and sabotage in an area threatened by Japanese attack.

In the light of the principles we announced in the *Hirabayashi* case, we are unable to conclude that it was beyond the war power of Congress and the Executive to exclude those of Japanese ancestry from the West Coast war area at the time they did. [Nothing] short of apprehension by the proper military authorities of the gravest imminent danger to the public safety can constitutionally justify either [the *Hirabayashi* curfew order or Exclusion Order No. 34]. But exclusion from a threatened area, no less than curfew, has a definite and close relationship to the prevention of espionage and sabotage. * * *

Here, as in *Hirabayashi,* "we cannot reject as unfounded the judgment of the military authorities and of Congress that there were disloyal members of that population, whose number and strength could not be precisely and quickly ascertained. We cannot say that the war-making branches of the Government did not have ground for believing that in a critical hour such persons could not readily be isolated and separately dealt with, and constituted a menace to the national defense and safety, which demanded that prompt and adequate measures be taken to guard against it."

[This] answers the contention that the exclusion was in the nature of group punishment based on antagonism to those of Japanese origin. That there were members of the group who retained loyalties to Japan has been confirmed by investigations made subsequent to the exclusion. Approximately five thousand American citizens of Japanese ancestry refused to swear unqualified allegiance to the United States [and] several thousand evacuees requested repatriation to Japan.

[H]ardships are part of war, and war is an aggregation of hardships. [E]xclusion of large groups of citizens from their homes, except under circumstances of direst emergency and peril, is inconsistent with our basic governmental institutions. But when under conditions of modern warfare our shores are threatened by hostile forces, the power to protect must be commensurate with the threatened danger. * * *

It is said that we are dealing here with the case of imprisonment of a citizen in a concentration camp solely because of his ancestry, without evidence or inquiry concerning his loyalty and good disposition towards the United States. [But] we are dealing specifically with nothing but an exclusion order. To cast this case into outlines of racial prejudice, without reference to the real military dangers which were presented, merely confuses the issue. Korematsu was not excluded from the Military Area because of hostility to him or his race. He was excluded because we are at war with the Japanese Empire, because the properly constituted military authorities feared an invasion of our West Coast and felt constrained to take proper security measures, because they decided that the military urgency of the situation demanded that all citizens of Japanese ancestry be segregated from the West Coast temporarily, and finally, because Congress, reposing its confidence in this time of war in our military leaders—as inevitably it must—determined that they should have the power to do just this. There was evidence of disloyalty on the part of some, the military authorities considered the need for action was great, and time was short. We cannot—by availing ourselves of the calm perspective of hindsight—now say that at that time these actions were unjustified.

Affirmed.

JUSTICE FRANKFURTER, concurring.

[To] find that the Constitution does not forbid the military measures now complained of does not carry with it approval of that which Congress and the Executive did. That is their business, not ours.

JUSTICE MURPHY, dissenting.

[T]he exclusion, either temporarily or permanently, of all persons with Japanese blood in their veins [must] rely for its reasonableness upon the assumption that *all* persons of Japanese ancestry may have a dangerous tendency to commit sabotage and espionage and [it] is difficult to believe that reason, logic or experience could be marshalled in support of such an assumption. [The] reasons appear, instead, to be largely an accumulation of much of the misinformation, half-truths and insinuations that for years have been directed against Japanese Americans by people with racial and economic prejudices—the same people who have been among the foremost advocates of the evacuation. A military judgment based upon such racial and sociological considerations is not entitled to the great weight ordinarily given the judgments based upon strictly military considerations. Especially is this so when every charge relative to race, religion, culture, geographical location, and legal and economic status has been substantially discredited by independent studies made by experts in these matters. * * *

Moreover, there was no adequate proof that the FBI and the military and naval intelligence services did not have the espionage and sabotage situation well in hand during this long period. Nor is there any denial of the fact that not one person of Japanese ancestry was accused or convicted of espionage or sabotage after Pearl Harbor while they were still free, a fact which is some evidence of the loyalty of the vast majority of these individuals and of the effectiveness of the established methods of combatting these evils. It seems incredible that under these circumstances it would have been impossible to hold loyalty hearings for the mere 112,000 persons involved—or at least for the 70,000 American citizens—especially when a large part of this number represented children and elderly men and women. Any inconvenience that may have accompanied an attempt to conform to procedural due process cannot be said to justify violations of constitutional [rights].

JUSTICE JACKSON, dissenting.

Korematsu was born on our soil, of parents born in Japan. [Had] Korematsu been one of four—the others being, say, a German alien enemy, an Italian alien enemy, and a citizen of American-born ancestors, convicted of treason but out on parole—only Korematsu's presence would have violated the order. The difference between their innocence and his crime would result, not from anything he did, said, or thought, different than they, but only in that he was born of different racial stock.

Now, if any fundamental assumption underlies our system, it is that guilt is personal and not inheritable. [If] Congress in peace-time legislation should enact such a criminal law, I should suppose this Court would refuse to enforce it.

But [it] would be impracticable and dangerous idealism to expect or insist that each specific military command in an area of probable operations will conform to conventional tests of constitutionality. When an area is so beset that it must be put under military control at all, the paramount consideration is that its measures be successful, rather than legal. * * * I cannot say, from any evidence before me, that the orders of General DeWitt were not reasonably expedient military precautions, nor could I say that they were. But even if they were permissible military procedures, I deny that it follows that they are constitutional. If, as the Court holds, it does follow, then we may as well say that any military order will be constitutional and have done with it.

The limitation under which courts always will labor in examining the necessity for a military order are illustrated by this case. How does the Court know that these orders have a reasonable basis in necessity? No evidence whatever on that subject has been taken by this or any other court. There is sharp controversy as to the credibility of the DeWitt report. So the Court, having no real evidence before it, has no choice but to accept General DeWitt's own unsworn, self-serving statement, untested by any cross-examination, that what he did was reasonable. And thus it will always be when courts try to look into the reasonableness of a military order. * * *

[A] judicial construction of the Due Process Clause that will sustain this order is a far more subtle blow to liberty than the promulgation of the order itself. A military order, however unconstitutional, is not apt to last longer than the military emergency. [But] once a judicial opinion rationalizes [the] Constitution to show that the Constitution sanctions such an order, the Court for all time has validated the principle of racial discrimination in criminal procedure and of transplanting American citizens. The principle then lies about like a loaded weapon ready for the hand of any authority that can bring forward a plausible claim of an urgent need. * * *

My duties as a justice as I see them do not require me to make a military judgment as to whether General DeWitt's evacuation and detention program was a reasonable military necessity. I do not suggest that the courts should have attempted to interfere with the Army in carrying out its task. But I do not think they may be asked to execute a military expedient that has no place in law under the Constitution. I would reverse the judgment and discharge the prisoner.[16]

————

EX PARTE ENDO, 323 U.S. 283 (1944), which came down the same day as *Korematsu*, involved the lawfulness of the detention in a relocation center of a person of Japanese ancestry who was conceded by the government to be "loyal" to the United States. The Court, per DOUGLAS, J., determined that neither the Executive Order authorizing the exclusion of Japanese from the West Coast nor the statute that ratified it empowered the War Relocation Authority to detain in a relocation center a person of conceded loyalty. The Court therefore ordered Endo's release. Its opinion did not rest on constitutional grounds, however, nor did it hold forced, race-based confinement in relocation centers to be categorically impermissible, as explained by JACKSON, J., in a draft concurrence that he ultimately decided not to publish: "This decision and that in Korematsu's case are separated by a wide chasm, and the real question in this case seems to have fallen therein. In Korematsu's case the Court [formally approves only an exclusion order commanding persons of Japanese ancestry to leave designated West Coast areas and] stops short of the question whether an American citizen may be detained in camps without conviction of crime. In Endo's case the Court is careful to start beyond it and to hold no more than that such a citizen may not be held after the government confesses that it has no security reason for holding her. [The] difference in grounds is substantial. No one may as a right obtain a certification of loyalty. [Anyone]

_____

[16] The dissenting opinion of Roberts, J., is omitted.

bent on keeping another in custody may say [that] it cannot be known that his prisoner would not commit a crime if he were at large. So the grounds taken by the Court is one available to but few and favored ones." Quoted in Patrick O. Gudridge, Essay, *Remember Endo?*, 116 Harv.L.Rev. 1933 (2003).

MURPHY, J., concurred in the judgment but not the Court's opinion, noting that Endo wished to return to Sacramento, California, from which she continued to be excluded by the military orders upheld in *Korematsu*.

NOTES AND QUESTIONS

1. **Standard of review.** The Court's invocation of "the most rigid scrutiny" appears to have been a doctrinal innovation. According to Klarman, note 4, after *Plessy*, no previous opinion had suggested that race-based classifications were categorically "suspect." Yet the Court articulated this new standard not under the Equal Protection Clause, which refers only to states (and not the federal government), but under the Due Process Clause that had been a part of the Constitution since 1791 and was not motivated by any suspicion of race-based classifications. Was the Court justified in formulating such a standard to test the validity of federal action under the Due Process Clause?

With respect to whether the Court actually applied "rigid scrutiny" in *Korematsu*, consider Klarman's argument that "[n]otwithstanding its grandiose rhetoric, the Court actually applied its most deferential brand of rationality review."

2. **Justice Jackson's dissent.** Jackson, J., dissented in *Korematsu*, even though he pointedly did "not suggest that the courts should have attempted to interfere with the Army in carrying out its task." The process that Jackson, J., contemplated is not wholly self-evident, but if the Court had reversed Korematsu's criminal conviction, as Jackson, J., believed that it should, the Army might possibly have continued to detain Korematsu on the basis of asserted military authority or necessity. If events had unfolded in this way, Korematsu (or his lawyer) would then presumably have returned to federal court to file a petition for a writ of habeas corpus—the traditional mechanism for challenging detentions that have not been authorized by a state or federal court. In doing so, he could have demanded a judicial decision under the Suspension Clause of Art. I, § 9, cl. 2, which provides that "[t]he privilege of the writ of habeas corpus shall not be suspended, unless when in cases of rebellion or invasion the public safety may require it." At that point, the federal courts would have been in roughly the same situation of needing to adjudicate the lawfulness of Korematsu's detention that they were in in the actual *Korematsu* case—unless, of course, Congress exercised its authority to suspend the privilege of the writ. If Congress had chosen to do so, the Japanese attack on Pearl Harbor would likely have counted as an "invasion" making the suspension constitutionally permissible. How would you evaluate this possible outcome in comparison with the actual outcome in *Korematsu*?

3. ***The scope of the threat.*** (a) Relatively little effort at fact-finding appears to have supported the military exclusion orders. Consider David M. Kennedy, *Freedom from Fear: The American People in Depression and War, 1929–1945,* at 750–51 (1999): "As war rumors took wing in the weeks following Pearl Harbor, sobriety gave way to anxiety, then to a rising cry for draconian action against the Japanese on the West Coast. Inflammatory and invariably false reports of Japanese attacks on the American mainland flashed through coastal communities. [The] release at the end of January [1942] of a governmental investigation of Pearl Harbor proved the decisive blow. The report, prepared by Supreme Court Justice Owen Roberts, alleged without documentation that Hawaii-based espionage agents, including Japanese-American citizens, had abetted [Japan's] strike force. [Within days, General John DeWitt—the official responsible for the assessment of military necessity—] reported 'a tremendous volume of public opinion developing against the Japanese of all classes' [and he] soon succumbed to Rumor's siren himself [in the absence of any hard evidence of traitorous activity].

"While Korematsu's case began its slow journey through the legal system, DeWitt's deputy [was] drafting [DeWitt's] official explanation for [the Japanese exclusion. To] buttress the argument that forced evacuation was a matter of military necessity, [the deputy] laced the *Final Report* with hundreds of examples of subversive activities on the West Coast in the winter and spring of 1942. [But] Justice Department lawyers quickly saw that he had cooked his facts [and, in fact, had little or no evidence of actual attempted subversion.] Armed with [findings as to the unreliability of the *Final Report*,] Justice Department attorneys determined to disavow [it] in their presentation of the *Korematsu* case [but were overruled by top officials in the War and Justice Departments]. Ignorant of this [background], the Supreme Court justices proceeded to deliberate on the *Korematsu* case deprived of a basis on which to challenge the factual assertions of the *Final Report*. [When] the Court pronounced on the *Korematsu* case on December 18, 1944, safely after the November presidential election, the camps had already begun to empty."[17]

(b) Consider William H. Rehnquist, *All the Laws But One* 205–06, 210–11 (1998): "[In response to the criticism that the Court's review was too deferential,] one can only echo Justice Jackson's observation [that] 'in the very nature of things, military decisions are not susceptible of intelligent judicial appraisal.' [It is also sometimes suggested] that [citizens of Japanese descent] were relocated simply because the Caucasian majority [disliked] them. [The] Court's answer to this broad attack seems satisfactory—those of Japanese descent were displaced because of fear that disloyal elements among them would aid Japan in the war. [But] a narrower criticism has more force to it: [The Court should have distinguished between American *citizens* of Japanese descent and non-citizens of Japanese descent.] Even in wartime, citizens may not be rounded up and required to prove their loyalty. They may be excluded from sensitive military areas in the absence of a security clearance and may

---

[17] For vehement, relatively contemporary criticism of *Korematsu*, see Eugene V. Rostow, *The Japanese American Cases—A Disaster*, 54 Yale L.J. 489 (1945).

otherwise be denied access to any classified information. But it pushes these propositions to an extreme to say that a sizable geographic area may be declared off-limits and the residents required to move.

"The most frequently made charge on behalf of [non-U.S. citizen Japanese affected by the relocation orders] is that the government treated Japanese enemy aliens differently from enemy aliens of German or Italian citizenship. [But] there do not appear to have been the same concentrations of German or Italian nationals along the west coast in areas near major defense plants. [While] there were areas of German or Italian concentration on the eastern seaboard, [there was no live fear of] attacks from German bombers or the invasion of German troops. [And] aircraft production was highly concentrated on the west coast. [These] distinctions seem insufficient to justify such a sharp difference of treatment between Japanese and German and Italian aliens in peacetime. But they do seem legally adequate to support the difference [in] time of war."

(c) Compare Earl Warren, *The Bill of Rights and the Military,* 37 N.Y.U.L.Rev. 181 (1962): "[*Hirabayashi* and *Korematsu*] demonstrate dramatically that there are some circumstances in which the Court will, in effect, conclude that it is simply not in a position to reject descriptions by the Executive of the degree of military necessity. Thus, in a case like *Hirabayashi,* only the Executive is qualified to determine whether, for example, an invasion is imminent."[18]

As the Attorney General of California, Warren—the Chief Justice of the United States at the time of the Court's decision in *Brown v. Board of Education*, infra—played a "leading role" in enforcing the Japanese exclusion from his state. Consider David Halberstam, *The Fifties* 417–18 (1993): "The one serious blot on [Warren's] record was [his role in the Japanese relocation]. He was playing to the growing fear of sabotage and the country's anger against the Japanese, particularly in California. Later he expressed considerable regret for his actions, although he was somewhat defensive in his memoirs: In 1972, when he was interviewed on the subject, he broke down in tears as he spoke of little children being taken from their homes and schools. [That] a record otherwise so admirable had a blot so serious was a reminder [that] even in the very best politicians there is always some fatal imperfection."

4. ***Subsequent developments.*** A 1980 Act of Congress established a Commission on Wartime Relocation and Internment of Civilians to study the Japanese relocation during World War II. The Commission concluded that: "The promulgation of Executive Order 9066 was not justified by military necessity, and the decisions which followed from it [were] not driven by analysis of military conditions. The broad historical causes which shaped [the

---

[18] See also Craig Green, *Ending the Korematsu Era: An Early View from the War on Terror Cases*, 105 Northwestern U.L Rev. 983 (2011): "[T]he originally dominant feature of *Korematsu*-era case law was not racism but a permissive approach to asserted military necessity and unsupervised presidential activity. *Korematsu*'s sixty-five-year-old bigotry, which so deeply offends modern morals, was secondary to the Court's judgments about war powers and executive deference."

exclusion decisions] were race prejudice, war hysteria, and the failure of political leadership. [A] grave injustice was done."[19] In 1988, President Ronald Reagan signed legislation formally acknowledging injustices imposed by the internment and providing for the payment of reparations.[20] In 1984, a federal district court relied on the Commission's findings in granting the writ of *coram nobis* and vacating the conviction of Fred Korematsu, the original defendant in *Korematsu*. See *Korematsu v. United States*, 584 F.Supp. 1406 (N.D.Cal.1984).[21]

Speaking in 2014 to students at the University of Hawaii Law School, Justice Antonin Scalia reportedly said this: "[O]f course, *Korematsu* was wrong. [And] I think we have repudiated it in a later case.[22] But [there was] panic about the war. [That's] what happens. It was wrong, but I would not be surprised to see it happen again, in time of war. It's no justification but it is the reality." Debra Cassens Weiss, *Scalia:* Korematsu *Was Wrong, but "You Are Kidding Yourself" If You Think It Won't Happen Again*, A.B.A.J. (Feb. 4, 2014).

BROWN V. BOARD OF EDUCATION
347 U.S. 483, 74 S.Ct. 686, 98 L.Ed. 873 (1954).

CHIEF JUSTICE WARREN delivered the opinion of the Court.

These cases come to us from the States of Kansas, South Carolina, Virginia, and Delaware. * * *

In each of the cases, minors of the Negro race [seek] the aid of the courts in obtaining admission to the public schools of their community on a nonsegregated basis. [In] each of the cases other than the Delaware case, a three-judge federal district court denied relief to the plaintiffs on the so-called "separate but equal" doctrine announced by this Court in [*Plessy*]. In the Delaware case, the Supreme Court of Delaware adhered to that doctrine, but ordered that the plaintiffs be admitted to the white schools because of their superiority to the Negro schools.

* * * Argument was heard in the 1952 Term, and reargument was heard this Term on certain questions propounded by the Court.

Reargument was largely devoted to the circumstances surrounding the adoption of the Fourteenth Amendment in 1868. It covered exhaustively consideration of the Amendment in Congress, ratification by the states, then existing practices in racial segregation, and the views of proponents

---

[19] Report of the Commission on Wartime Relocation and Internment of Civilians, *Personal Justice Denied* 18 (1982).

[20] Civil Liberties Act of 1988, Pub.L.No. 100–383, 102 Stat. 903 (codified at 50 U.S.C. app. § 1989).

[21] For further historical discussion, see Peter Irons, *Justice at War: The Story of the Japanese American Internment* (1983). For biting criticism of the role played by the Supreme Court, see Jerry Kang, *Denying Prejudice: Internment, Redress, and Denial*, 51 U.C.L.A. L.Rev. 933 (2004).

[22] The Court has not done so formally.

and opponents of the Amendment. This discussion and our own investigation convince us that, although these sources cast some light, it is not enough to resolve the problem with which we are faced. At best, they are inconclusive. The most avid proponents of the post-War Amendments undoubtedly intended them to remove all legal distinctions among "all persons born or naturalized in the United States." Their opponents, just as certainly, were antagonistic to both the letter and the spirit of the Amendments and wished them to have the most limited effect. What others in Congress and the state legislatures had in mind cannot be determined with any degree of certainty.

An additional reason for the inconclusive nature of the Amendment's history, with respect to segregated schools, is the status of public education at that time. In the South, the movement toward free common schools, supported by general taxation, had not yet taken hold. Education of white children was largely in the hands of private groups. Education of Negroes was almost nonexistent, and practically all of the race were illiterate. In fact, any education of Negroes was forbidden by law in some states. Today, in contrast, many Negroes have achieved outstanding success in the arts and sciences as well as in the business and professional world. It is true that public school education at the time of the Amendment had advanced further in the North, but the effect of the Amendment on Northern States was generally ignored in the congressional debates. Even in the North, the conditions of public education did not approximate those existing today. The curriculum was usually rudimentary; ungraded schools were common in rural areas; the school term was but three months a year in many states; and compulsory school attendance was virtually unknown. As a consequence, it is not surprising that there should be so little in the history of the Fourteenth Amendment relating to its intended effect on public education.

In the first cases in this Court construing the Fourteenth Amendment, decided shortly after its adoption, the Court interpreted it as proscribing all state-imposed discriminations against the Negro race.[5] The doctrine of "separate but equal" did not make its appearance in this Court until 1896 in *Plessy,* involving not education but transportation. [In] this Court, there have been six cases involving the "separate but equal" doctrine in the field of public education. In *Cumming v. Board of Education,* 175 U.S. 528, and *Gong Lum v. Rice,* 275 U.S. 78, the validity of the doctrine itself was not challenged.[8] In more recent cases, all on the graduate school level,

---

[5]　**[Ct's Note]** *Slaughter-House Cases; Strauder * * * .* See also *Virginia v. Rives,* 1879, 100 U.S. 313, 318; *Ex parte Virginia,* 1879, 100 U.S. 339, 344–345. [See generally Brief for the Committee of Law Teachers Against Segregation in Legal Education, *Segregation and the Equal Protection Clause,* 34 Minn.L.Rev. 289 (1950).]

[8]　**[Ct's Note]** In the *Cumming* case, Negro taxpayers sought an injunction requiring the defendant school board to discontinue the operation of a high school for white children until the board resumed operation of a high school for Negro children. Similarly, in the *Gong Lum* case, the

inequality was found in that specific benefits enjoyed by white students were denied to Negro students of the same educational qualifications. *Missouri ex rel. Gaines v. Canada,* 305 U.S. 337;[23] *Sipuel v. Oklahoma,* 332 U.S. 631; *Sweatt v. Painter,* 339 U.S. 629;[24] *McLaurin v. Oklahoma State Regents,* 339 U.S. 637.[25] In none of these cases was it necessary to re-examine the doctrine to grant relief to the Negro plaintiff. And in *Sweatt,* the Court expressly reserved decision on the question whether *Plessy* should be held inapplicable to public education.

In the instant cases, that question is directly presented. [T]here are findings below that the Negro and white schools involved have been equalized, or are being equalized, with respect to buildings, curricula, qualifications and salaries of teachers, and other "tangible" factors. Our decision, therefore, cannot turn on merely a comparison of these tangible factors in the Negro and white schools involved in each of the cases. We must look instead to the effect of segregation itself on public education.

In approaching this problem, we cannot turn the clock back to 1868 when the Amendment was adopted, or even to 1896 when *Plessy* was written. We must consider public education in the light of its full development and its present place in American life throughout the Nation. Only in this way can it be determined if segregation in public schools deprives these plaintiffs of the equal protection of the laws.

Today, education is perhaps the most important function of state and local governments. Compulsory school attendance laws and the great expenditures for education both demonstrate our recognition of the importance of education to our democratic society. It is required in the performance of our most basic public responsibilities, even service in the armed forces. It is the very foundation of good citizenship. Today it is a principal instrument in awakening the child to cultural values, in preparing him for later professional training, and in helping him to adjust normally to his environment. In these days, it is doubtful that any child

---

plaintiff, a child of Chinese descent, contended only that state authorities had misapplied the doctrine by classifying him with Negro children and requiring him to attend a Negro school.

[23] *Gaines,* in 1938, invalidated the refusal to admit blacks to the University of Missouri School of Law, despite the state's offer to pay petitioner's tuition at an out-of-state law school pending establishment of a state law school for African-Americans.

[24] *Sweatt,* in 1950, required admission of African Americans to the University of Texas Law School, despite the recent establishment of a state law school for blacks: "In terms of number of the faculty, variety of courses and opportunity for specialization, size of the student body, scope of the library, availability of law review and similar activities, the University of Texas Law School is superior. [Equally troubling is that the] law school to which Texas is willing to admit petitioner excludes from its student body members of the racial groups which number 85% of the population of the State and include most of the lawyers, witnesses, jurors, judges and other officials with whom petitioner will inevitably be dealing when he becomes a member of the Texas Bar."

[25] *McLaurin,* in 1950, held violative of equal protection requirements that African-American graduate students at the University of Oklahoma sit at separate desks adjoining the classrooms and separate tables outside the library reading room, and eat at separate times in the school cafeteria.

may reasonably be expected to succeed in life if he is denied the opportunity of an education. Such an opportunity, where the state has undertaken to provide it, is a right which must be made available to all on equal terms.

We come then to the question presented: Does segregation of children in public schools solely on the basis of race, even though the physical facilities and other "tangible" factors may be equal, deprive the children of the minority group of equal educational opportunities? We believe that it does.

In *Sweatt*, in finding that a segregated law school for Negroes could not provide them equal educational opportunities, this Court relied in large part on "those qualities which are incapable of objective measurement but which make for greatness in a law school." In *McLaurin*, the Court, in requiring that a Negro admitted to a white graduate school be treated like all other students, again resorted to intangible considerations: "[his] ability to study, to engage in discussions and exchange views with other students, and in general, to learn his profession." Such considerations apply with added force to children in grade and high schools. To separate them from others of similar age and qualifications solely because of their race generates a feeling of inferiority as to their status in the community that may affect their hearts and minds in a way unlikely ever to be undone. The effect of this separation on their educational opportunities was well stated by a finding in the Kansas case by a court which nevertheless felt compelled to rule against the Negro plaintiffs: "Segregation of white and colored children in public schools has a detrimental effect upon the colored children. The impact is greater when it has the sanction of the law; for the policy of separating the races is usually interpreted as denoting the inferiority of the Negro group. A sense of inferiority affects the motivation of a child to learn. Segregation with the sanction of law, therefore, has a tendency to [retard] the educational and mental development of Negro children and to deprive them of some of the benefits they would receive in a racial[ly] integrated school system."[10] Whatever may have been the extent of psychological knowledge at the time of *Plessy*, this finding is amply supported by modern authority.[11] Any language in *Plessy* contrary to this finding is rejected.

---

[10] **[Ct's Note]** A similar finding was made in the Delaware case: "I conclude from the testimony that in our Delaware society, State-imposed segregation in education itself results in the Negro children, as a class, receiving educational opportunities which are substantially inferior to those available to white children otherwise similarly situated."

[11] **[Ct's Note]** K. B. Clark, *Effect of Prejudice and Discrimination on Personality Development* (Midcentury White House Conference on Children and Youth, 1950); Witmer and Kotinsky, *Personality in the Making* (1952), c. VI; Deutscher and Chein, *The Psychological Effects of Enforced Segregation: A Survey of Social Science Opinion,* 26 J.Psychol. 259 (1948); Chein, *What are the Psychological Effects of Segregation Under Conditions of Equal Facilities?,* 3 Int.J. Opinion and Attitude Res. 229 (1949); Brameld, *Educational Costs in Discrimination and National Welfare* (MacIver, ed., 1949), 44–48; Frazier, *The Negro in the United States* (1949), 674–681. And, see generally Gunnar Myrdal, *An American Dilemma* (1944).

We conclude that in the field of public education the doctrine of "separate but equal" has no place. Separate educational facilities are inherently unequal. Therefore, we hold that the plaintiffs and others similarly situated for whom the actions have been brought are, by reason of the segregation complained of, deprived of [equal protection].

Because these are class actions, because of the wide applicability of this decision, and because of the great variety of local conditions, the formulation of decrees in these cases presents problems of considerable complexity. On reargument, the consideration of appropriate relief was necessarily subordinated to the primary question—the constitutionality of segregation in public education. We have now announced that such segregation is a denial of the equal protection of the laws. In order that we may have the full assistance of the parties in formulating decrees, the cases will be restored to the docket, and the parties are requested to present further argument on Questions 4 and 5 previously propounded by the Court for the reargument this Term.[13] * * *

BOLLING v. SHARPE, 347 U.S. 497 (1954), per WARREN, C.J., held— on the same day as *Brown*—that public school segregation in the District of Columbia "constitutes an arbitrary deprivation [of] liberty in violation of the Due Process Clause" of the Fifth Amendment: "The Fifth Amendment [does] not contain an Equal Protection Clause as does the Fourteenth Amendment which applies only to the states. But the concepts of equal protection and due process, both stemming from our American ideal of fairness, are not mutually exclusive. The 'equal protection of the laws' is a more explicit safeguard of prohibited unfairness than 'due process of law,' and, therefore, we do not imply that the two are always interchangeable

---

[13] **[Ct's Note]** "4. Assuming it is decided that segregation in public schools violates the Fourteenth Amendment

"(a) would a decree necessarily follow providing that, within the limits set by normal geographic school districting, Negro children should forthwith be admitted to schools of their choice, or

"(b) may this Court, in the exercise of its equity powers, permit an effective gradual adjustment to be brought about from existing segregated systems to a system not based on color distinctions?

"5. On the assumption on which questions 4(a) and (b) are based, and assuming further that this Court will exercise its equity powers to the end described in question 4(b),

"(a) should this Court formulate detailed decrees in these cases;

"(b) if so, what specific issues should the decrees reach;

"(c) should this Court appoint a special master to hear evidence with a view to recommending specific terms for such decrees;

"(d) should this Court remand to the courts of first instance with directions to frame decrees in these cases, and if so what general directions should the decrees of this Court include and what procedures should the courts of first instance follow in arriving at the specific terms of more detailed decrees?"

phrases. But, as this Court has recognized, discrimination may be so unjustifiable as to be violative of due process.

"Classifications based solely upon race must be scrutinized with particular care, since they are contrary to our traditions and hence constitutionally suspect. *Korematsu.* ['Liberty'] extends to the full range of conduct which the individual is free to pursue, and it cannot be restricted except for a proper governmental objective. Segregation in public education is not reasonably related to any proper governmental objective * * * .

"In view of our decision that the Constitution prohibits the states from maintaining racially segregated public schools, it would be unthinkable that the same Constitution would impose a lesser duty on the Federal Government."

NOTES AND QUESTIONS

1. ***Historical context.*** Consider Klarman, Note 4 after *Plessy*: "[I]t is far too easy to regard *Brown v. Board of Education* as an inevitable decision. Yet quite plainly it was not. Justice Frankfurter probably spoke for a majority of the Justices when he [recounted] that had the school segregation challenge been forced upon him in the 1940s he would have felt compelled to reject it. Indeed, the NAACP's choice prior to 1950 to refrain from direct attacks on school segregation, instead pursuing an equalization strategy, was largely owing to the organization's perception that the sociopolitical environment was not yet conducive to a segregation challenge. Nor did *Brown* ineluctably follow from [the] 1950 decision in *Sweatt v. Painter*. Justice Clark, for example, [wrote] in a *Sweatt* memorandum that he was not then prepared to invalidate primary and secondary school segregation. Southern resistance to grade school desegregation, Clark warned, would be of a different order than to graduate school desegregation. [When] *Brown* was first argued in 1952, the Justices were closely divided; their own subsequent tabulations indicated a vote somewhere between five to four for sustaining school segregation and six to three for striking it down."

After the Supreme Court had heard the initial arguments in *Brown*, and had decided to set a reargument, Chief Justice Fred M. Vinson—who was generally unsympathetic to the plaintiffs' case—died, to be replaced by Earl Warren. Upon learning of Vinson's death, Justice Frankfurter is said to have remarked, "This is the first indication I have ever had that there is a God."[26]

2. ***"Original understanding."*** (a) In setting *Brown* for re-argument, the Court specifically asked the parties to brief whether the Fourteenth Amendment was originally understood to bar segregation in the public schools. In its final opinion, however, the Court largely evaded discussion of the history, which in the view of most historians did not support the Court's result. According to a memorandum by one of Justice Frankfurter's law clerks (the future Professor Alexander Bickel), which the Justice circulated to the Court,

---

[26] Quoted in Richard Kluger, *Simple Justice* 656 (1975).

the immediate aim of the Fourteenth Amendment was to guarantee equality with respect to a set of what were then understood to be fundamental rights of citizenship—such as rights to own property and sue and be sued—that did not necessarily encompass rights involving public education.[27] See Alexander M. Bickel, *The Original Understanding and the Segregation Decision*, 69 Harv.L.Rev. 1 (1955). See also Note 1 after *Plessy*, supra; Klarman, supra (reviewing historiographical debates and embracing the view that most of the Fourteenth Amendment's drafters viewed it as protecting only fundamental rights). Even if that specific claim were questioned, it is undisputed—as *Plessy* affirmed—that in the aftermath of ratification of the Fourteenth Amendment, state and local governments continued to maintain segregated schools and to enforce racial separation in a number of other domains, and courts widely approved their practices in doing so. See, e.g., Kluger, supra, at 633–34 (noting that following the ratification of the Fourteenth Amendment, a number of northern states continued either to tolerate or require segregation in their public schools). Indeed, the Congress that proposed the Fourteenth Amendment maintained segregated schools in the District of Columbia.

If the framers and ratifiers of the Fourteenth Amendment did not specifically understand or intend it to abolish segregation in public education,[28] would it follow that the *Brown* Court should not have reached its decision?

Consider Bickel, supra: "If the Fourteenth Amendment were a statute, a court might very well hold [that] it was foreclosed from applying it to segregation in public schools. [But] we are dealing with a constitutional amendment, not a statute. The tradition of a broadly worded organic law not frequently or lightly amended was well-established by 1866, and [it] cannot be assumed that [anyone] expected or wished the future role of the Constitution in the scheme of American government to differ from the past. Should not the search for congressional purpose, therefore, properly be twofold? One inquiry should be directed at the congressional understanding of the immediate effect of the enactment on conditions then present. Another should aim to discover what if any thought was given to the long-range effect, under future circumstances, of provisions necessarily intended for permanence. [With respect to the latter inquiry, the Fourteenth Amendment may have reflected] a compromise permitting [moderates and radicals] to go to the country with language which they could, where necessary, defend against damaging alarms raised [by opponents of broad racial equality rights], but which at the same time was sufficiently elastic to permit reasonable future advances [toward

---

[27] For accounts of the Court's internal decisionmaking process, see Dennis Hutchinson, *Unanimity and Desegregation: Decisionmaking in the Supreme Court, 1948–1958*, 68 Geo.L.J. 1 (1979); Mark Tushnet, *What Really Happened in* Brown v. Board of Education, 91 Colum.L.Rev. 1867 (1991).

[28] For a rare originalist argument that the Fourteenth Amendment was understood from the beginning as barring school segregation (based largely on unsuccessful Republican efforts in a *subsequent* Congress to forbid school segregation under the 1875 Civil Rights Act), see Michael W. McConnell, *Originalism and the Desegregation Decisions*, 81 Va.L.Rev. 947 (1995). For a critical response, see Michael J. Klarman, Brown, *Originalism, and Constitutional Theory*, 81 Va.L.Rev. 1881 (1995).

racial equality]." See also Foner, Note 1 after *Plessy*, at 257–58 (noting that congressional Republicans disagreed among themselves about the implications of Section 1 of the Fourteenth Amendment and that many moderates sought to preserve judicial "flexibility" in its implementation).

Based on his conclusion that "most of the Fourteenth Amendment's drafters [intended] racial discrimination [to be] impermissible with regard to certain fundamental rights, rather than across the board," Professor Klarman argues that "rather than stating a racial classification rule, *Brown* elevated education to the level of other fundamental rights with regard to which the Equal Protection Clause forbade racial discrimination." See Klarman, note 4 after *Plessy*. If the premise about the drafters' understanding is granted, should it be permissible for the Court to recognize that education had become a "fundamental right" in the intervening years as a matter of fact or common perception?

(b)   Consider also Ronald Dworkin, *Freedom's Law* 7–11 (1996), arguing that courts should give a "moral reading" to provisions, such as the Equal Protection Clause, that "are drafted in exceedingly abstract language [and embody] abstract moral principles." According to Dworkin, "the Equal Protection Clause [has] a moral principle as its content," and the function of the courts is not to discover what the framers and ratifiers understood that "principle" to mean, but what it *really* means: "Most of [the framers and ratifiers] plainly did not expect [the Equal Protection Clause] to outlaw official racial discrimination in school. [But] they did not *say* anything about [school] segregation[,] one way or the other. They said that 'equal protection of the laws' is required, which plainly describes a very general principle, not any concrete application of it." The job of judges, says Dworkin, is "to find the best conception of constitutional moral principles—the best understanding of what equal moral status for men and women really requires, for example—that fits the broad story of America's historical record," including evolving social and moral understandings and relevant judicial precedents.

Does this approach give too much power to judges? See Dworkin, supra, at 14: "Constitutional scholars often say that we must avoid the mistakes of both the moral reading, which gives too much power to judges, and of originalism, which makes the contemporary Constitution too much the dead hand of the past. The right method, they say, is something in between. [But] they do not indicate what the right balance is. [Though] the call for an intermediate constitutional strategy is often heard, it has not been answered."

(c)   Whatever might be the case with the Equal Protection Clause, nearly all agree that it is hard to find support in original constitutional understandings for the Court's holding in *Bolling v. Sharpe*—sometimes described as "reverse incorporation"—that the Fifth Amendment's Due Process Clause, ratified in 1791, incorporates the equal protection norms of the Fourteenth Amendment, which was ratified in 1868. But consider Jack M. Balkin, *Living Originalism* 251–54 (2012): "*Bolling* is not a particularly difficult case and [Chief] Justice Warren's [conclusion] is actually quite reasonable" if the Due Process Clause is read in light of an "originalism" of "text and principle" that focuses not on the Framers' "expectations" of how constitutional language would be applied, but on the meanings that their language will bear. "History shows us that the Fifth Amendment's language can easily bear [a] construction [under which it forbids race-based discrimination], for [this construction] was widely held throughout the nineteenth century. [By] the time the Fourteenth Amendment was ratified, the concept of due process embodied in the Fifth Amendment required equality before the law and banned special, partial, or class legislation. Although this construction developed a few decades after the ratification of the Fifth Amendment, antebellum lawyers [saw] equality as simply an elaboration of the basic principles of procedural due process."[29]

Can the Court's decision be defended as offering a "moral reading" of the "extremely abstract language" of the Due Process Clause? On the basis of felt normative necessity? Consider Richard H. Fallon, Jr., *Legitimacy and the Constitution*, 118 Harv.L.Rev. 1787 (2005): "[T]he Supreme Court acted morally legitimately in deciding *Bolling v. Sharpe* as it did, even if the Court's constitutional holding was erroneous or possibly even illegitimate as a strictly legal matter. [The] moral importance of the situation would have justified the Court in appealing less to the letter of positive law than to principles of moral right and what Lincoln termed 'the better angels of our nature' in calling upon the parties and the nation to accept its decision as deserving of lawful status."

3.   *Social science and the Court's rationale.* Did the result in *Brown* turn on social scientific data of the kind cited in fn. 11? Consider Edmund Cahn, *Jurisprudence,* 30 N.Y.U.L.Rev. 150 (1955): "It is one thing to use the current scientific findings, however ephemeral they may be, in order to ascertain whether the legislature has acted reasonably in adopting some scheme of social or economic regulation; deference here is shown not so much to the findings as to the legislature. It would be quite another thing to have our fundamental rights rise, fall, or change along with the latest fashions of psychological literature." Does *Brown* rest on a finding that "in terms of the most familiar and universally accepted standards of right and wrong [racial] segregation under government auspices inevitably inflicts humiliation, [and] official humiliation of innocent, law-abiding citizens is psychologically injurious and morally evil"? Id.

---

[29] See also Ryan C. Williams, *Originalism and the Other Desegregation Decision*, 99 Va.L.Rev. 493 (2013): "[A] surprisingly strong originalist argument supporting both *Bolling's* specific holding and the broader unconstitutionality of most forms of invidious federal discrimination can be made by looking to the original public meaning of the Fourteenth Amendment's Citizenship Clause, which provides that '[a]ll persons born or naturalized in the United States and subject to the jurisdiction thereof, are citizens of the United States and of the State wherein they reside.' [There] is [a] strong textual and historical argument for recognizing an equality component in the Fourteenth Amendment's Citizenship Clause. [This] 'equal citizenship' interpretation of the Citizenship Clause would require the federal government to extend to all citizens equality rights that are at least as broad as those that states are required to extend to all 'persons' under the Equal Protection Clause. [Those] originalists who support *Brown* as correctly decided should thus feel little hesitancy in concluding that *Bolling* was correctly decided as well."

4. ***Contemporary criticisms.*** *Brown* was highly controversial at the time of its decision and for a number of years thereafter. Some of the criticisms rested on the decision's reliance on social science, but probably the most celebrated critique protested that the *Brown* Court had failed to ground its decision in "neutral principles." Consider Herbert Wechsler, *Toward Neutral Principles of Constitutional Law,* 73 Harv.L.Rev. 1 (1959): "[A]ssuming equal facilities, the question posed by state-enforced segregation is not one of discrimination at all. Its human and its constitutional dimensions lie [in] the denial by the state of freedom to associate, a denial that impinges in the same way on any groups or races that may be involved. [But] if the freedom of association is denied by segregation, integration forces an association upon those for whom it is unpleasant or repugnant. [W]here the state must practically choose between denying the association to those individuals who wish it or imposing it on those who would avoid it, is there a basis in neutral principles for holding that the Constitution demands that the claims for association should prevail?"

Consider the reply of Charles Black, *The Lawfulness of the Segregation Decisions,* 69 Yale L.J. 421 (1960): "The Fourteenth Amendment [forbids] disadvantaging the Negro race by law. It was surely anticipated that the following of this directive would entail some disagreeableness for some white southerners. [When] the directive of equality cannot be followed without displeasing the white, then something that can be called a 'freedom' of the white must be impaired. If the Fourteenth Amendment commands equality, and if segregation violates equality, then the status of the reciprocal 'freedom' is automatically settled."

Compare Cass R. Sunstein, *Black on* Brown, 90 Va.L.Rev. 1649 (2004): "Black assumes far too readily that the Equal Protection Clause forbids any intentional disadvantaging of African-Americans. The Clause does not unambiguously do any such thing. It would be possible to understand the Clause far more narrowly, in a way that does not touch the practice of 'separate but equal.' All by itself, *Plessy v. Ferguson* provides some evidence of the plausibility of this reading. [In] any case, a great deal of historical research supports the view that the Fourteenth Amendment was not meant to eliminate racial segregation—and indeed, that it was not meant to prohibit all intentional disadvantaging of African-Americans. * * *

"In the end, Black's reading of the Equal Protection Clause can only be understood as 'interpretive' in Ronald Dworkin's sense of the word. Black is attempting not to track the unambiguous meaning of the Clause, but to make the best constructive sense of it in a way that inevitably involves his own judgments. [If] we were to be harsh, we might even say that Black's confidence about his view of the Clause emerges as a form of self-delusion, a claim of necessity that masks normative judgments of Black's own."

5. ***Extent of the decision.*** (a) Did *Brown* bar all forms of state-imposed racial segregation? Or did it apply only to public schools? For comment immediately after *Brown,* consider Paul G. Kauper, *Segregation in Public*

Education, 52 Mich.L.Rev. 1137 (1954): "[*Brown*] placed emphasis upon the intangible factors that make the *Plessy* doctrine inapplicable to public schools. Education is an experience and not simply an enjoyment of physical facilities. But with respect to common carrier and public recreational facilities, the emphasis is upon the enjoyment of the physical facilities and services so that it is more nearly possible to speak of equality of enjoyment within the pattern of segregation." Compare Robert McKay, *Segregation and Public Recreation,* 40 Va.L.Rev. 697 (1954): "[T]here appears to be no reason to believe that the sense of inferiority engendered by segregation in recreation is any less than in education."

(b) After *Brown,* the Court, in summary per curiam decisions citing *Brown,* consistently held invalid state-imposed racial segregation in other public facilities—e.g., golf courses, parks, playgrounds. The one notable exception is *Naim v. Naim,* 350 U.S. 891 (1955), a case that came to the Court by way of appeal and involved the constitutionality of a Virginia statute forbidding interracial marriage. Apparently persuaded by Frankfurter, J., that the miscegenation issue aroused such "deep feeling" that a Court pronouncement would "have the effect of 'thwarting or seriously handicapping the enforcement of [our] decision in the segregation cases[,]' the Court remanded *Naim* to the Virginia Supreme Court on the pretext that the parties' domicile stood in need of clarification. After the state court belligerently refused to cooperate, the Justices narrowly voted to deny review, apparently preferring to permit an insolent state court to flout its authority than to stir up another hornets' nest in the immediate wake of *Brown.*" Klarman, supra. As a result, the Court did not confront the miscegenation issue until 1967 in *Loving v. Virginia,* infra. Was the Court's course of action in *Naim* an exercise of wise, prudent, and legitimate judicial statesmanship? A supine abnegation of constitutional responsibility? Compare Alexander M. Bickel, *The Passive Virtues,* 75 Harv.L.Rev. 40 (1961) with Gerald Gunther, *The Subtle Vices of the "Passive Virtues"—A Comment on Principle and Expediency in Judicial Review,* 64 Colum.L.Rev. 1 (1964).

BROWN V. BOARD OF EDUCATION (II)
349 U.S. 294, 75 S.Ct. 753, 99 L.Ed. 1083 (1955).

CHIEF JUSTICE WARREN delivered the opinion of the Court.

These cases were decided on May 17, 1954. [There] remains for consideration the manner in which relief is to be accorded. * * *

Full implementation of these constitutional principles may require solution of varied local school problems. School authorities have the primary responsibility for elucidating, assessing, and solving [them]; courts will have to consider whether the action of school authorities constitutes good faith implementation of the governing constitutional principles. Because of their proximity to local conditions and the possible need for further hearings, the courts which originally heard these cases can best perform this judicial appraisal. Accordingly, we believe it appropriate to remand the cases to those courts.

In fashioning and effectuating the decrees, the courts will be guided by equitable principles. Traditionally, equity has been characterized by a practical flexibility in shaping its remedies and by a facility for adjusting and reconciling public and private needs. [A]t stake is the personal interest of the plaintiffs in admission to public schools as soon as practicable on a nondiscriminatory basis. To effectuate this interest may call for elimination of a variety of obstacles in making the transition to school systems operated in accordance with the constitutional principles set forth in our May 17, 1954, decision. Courts of equity may properly take into account the public interest in the elimination of such obstacles in a systematic and effective manner. But it should go without saying that the vitality of these constitutional principles cannot be allowed to yield simply because of disagreement with them.

While giving weight to these public and private considerations, the courts will require that the defendants make a prompt and reasonable start toward full compliance with our May 17, 1954, ruling. Once such a start has been made, the courts may find that additional time is necessary to carry out the ruling in an effective manner. The burden rests upon the defendants to establish that such time is necessary in the public interest and is consistent with good faith compliance at the earliest practicable date. To that end, the courts may consider problems related to administration, arising from the physical condition of the school plant, the school transportation system, personnel, revision of school districts and attendance areas into compact units to achieve a system of determining admission to the public schools on a nonracial basis, and revision of local laws and regulations which may be necessary in solving the foregoing problems. They will also consider the adequacy of any plans the defendants may propose to meet these problems and to effectuate a transition to a racially nondiscriminatory school system. During this period of transition, the courts will retain jurisdiction of these cases.

The [cases are remanded] to take such proceedings and enter such orders and decrees consistent with this opinion as are necessary and proper to admit to public schools on a racially nondiscriminatory basis with all deliberate speed the parties to these cases. * * *

NOTES AND QUESTIONS

1. *"Individual" vs. "race" rights.* Was the decree consistent with *Brown I*? Since plaintiffs had only a limited number of years of school remaining, did postponement of relief partially or totally destroy the very rights the decree was intended to enforce? Does the "deliberate speed" formula assume that "Negroes (unlike whites) possess rights as a race rather than as individuals, so that a particular Negro can rightly be delayed in the enjoyment

of his established rights if progress is being made in improving the legal status of Negroes generally"? Louis Lusky, *The Stereotype: Hard Core of Racism,* 13 Buf.L.Rev. 450 (1963).

Consider the complaint of Thurgood Marshall that "the argument [to postpone enforcement of a constitutional right] is never made until Negroes are involved."[30] Compare Richard H. Fallon, Jr., *Implementing the Constitution* (2001), asserting that "Marshall's claim bears the sting of truth, but it is not the whole truth," as there sometimes are other gaps between constitutional rights and constitutional remedies.

2. *"Deliberate speed."* Consider Richard A. Wasserstrom, *Racism, Sexism, and Preferential Treatment: An Approach to the Topics*, 24 U.C.L.A. L.Rev. 581 (1977): "The Supreme Court's solution assumed that [only black children should go to black schools] until the black schools were brought up to par or eliminated. That is a kind of conceptual racism [that] accepts the dominant racist ideology [that] the claims of black children are worth less than the claims of white children." Compare Lino A. Graglia, *The Brown Cases Revisited: Where Are They Now?,* 1 Benchmark 23 (Mar.–Apr. 1984): "There can be little doubt that if the Court had ordered the end of segregation in 1954 or 1955 the result would have been the closing of public schools in much of the South, about which the Court could have done nothing. The principal impact would have been on poor blacks, and *Brown* could have come to be seen as a blunder and symbol of judicial impotence."

3. *History of school desegregation.* The history of school desegragation in the aftermath of *Brown II* is discussed in Sec. 2, III below.

LOVING V. VIRGINIA
388 U.S. 1, 87 S.Ct. 1817, 18 L.Ed.2d 1010 (1967).

CHIEF JUSTICE WARREN delivered the opinion of the Court.

This case presents a constitutional question never addressed by this Court: whether a statutory scheme adopted by Virginia to prevent marriages between persons solely on the basis of racial classifications violates [the] Fourteenth Amendment. [Appellants, a black woman and white man, were married in the District of Columbia, returned to reside in Virginia, and were convicted under the state antimiscegenation statute.]

Virginia is now one of 16 States which prohibit and punish marriages on the basis of racial classifications.[5] [The] state court concluded that the State's legitimate purposes were "to preserve the racial integrity of its citizens," and to prevent "the corruption of blood," "a mongrel breed of citizens," and "the obliteration of racial pride," obviously an endorsement of the doctrine of White Supremacy. [T]he State [argues] that the meaning

---

[30] Quoted in Paul Gewirtz, *Remedies and Resistance,* 92 Yale L.J. 585 (1983).

[5] **[Ct's Note]** [Over] the past 15 years, 14 States have repealed laws outlawing interracial marriages * * * .

of the Equal Protection Clause, as illuminated by the statements of the Framers, is only that state penal laws containing an interracial element as part of the definition of the offense must apply equally to whites and Negroes in the sense that members of each race are punished to the same degree. * * *

Because we reject the notion that the mere "equal application" of a statute containing racial classifications is enough to remove the classifications from the Fourteenth Amendment's proscription of all invidious racial discriminations, we do not accept the State's contention that these statutes should be upheld if there is any possible basis for concluding that they serve a rational purpose. [Here], we deal with statutes containing racial classifications, and the fact of equal application does not immunize the statute from the very heavy burden of justification which the Fourteenth Amendment has traditionally required of state statutes drawn according to race.

The State argues that statements in the Thirty-ninth Congress about the time of the passage of the Fourteenth Amendment indicate that the Framers did not intend the Amendment to make unconstitutional state miscegenation laws. Many of the statements [have] some relevance to the intention of Congress in submitting the Fourteenth Amendment, [but] it must be understood that they pertained to the passage of specific statutes and not to the broader, organic purpose of a constitutional amendment. As for the various statements directly concerning the Fourteenth Amendment, we have said in connection with a related problem, that although these historical sources "cast some light" they are not sufficient to resolve the problem; "[a]t best, they are inconclusive." *Brown.* We have rejected the proposition that the debates in the Thirty-ninth Congress or in the state legislatures which ratified the Fourteenth Amendment supported the theory [that equal protection] is satisfied by penal laws defining offenses based on racial classifications so long as white and Negro participants in the offense were similarly punished. *McLaughlin v. Florida,* 379 U.S. 184 (1964).[31]

The State finds support for its "equal application" theory [in] *Pace v. Alabama,* 106 U.S. 583 (1883). In that case, the Court upheld a conviction under an Alabama statute forbidding adultery or fornication between a white person and a Negro which imposed a greater penalty than that of a statute proscribing similar conduct by members of the same race. The Court reasoned that the statute could not be said to discriminate against Negroes because the punishment for each participant in the offense was the same. However, as recently as the 1964 Term, in rejecting the reasoning of that case, we stated "*Pace* represents a limited view of the Equal Protection Clause which has not withstood analysis in the

---

[31] *McLaughlin* invalidated a statute making interracial cohabitation a crime.

subsequent decisions of this Court." *McLaughlin.* [The] clear and central purpose of the Fourteenth Amendment was to eliminate all official state sources of invidious racial discrimination in the States. [At] the very least, the Equal Protection Clause demands that racial classifications, especially suspect in criminal statutes, be subjected to the "most rigid scrutiny," and, if they are ever to be upheld, they must be shown to be necessary to the accomplishment of some permissible state objective, independent of the racial discrimination which it was the object of the Fourteenth Amendment to eliminate.[32] Indeed, two [justices] have already stated that they "cannot conceive of a valid legislative purpose [which] makes the color of a person's skin the test of whether his conduct is a criminal offense." *McLaughlin* (Stewart, J., joined by Douglas, J., concurring).

There is patently no legitimate overriding purpose independent of invidious racial discrimination which justifies this classification. The fact that Virginia only prohibits interracial marriages involving white persons demonstrates that the racial classifications must stand on their own justification, as measures designed to maintain White Supremacy.[11] We have consistently denied the constitutionality of measures which restrict the rights of citizens on account of race. There can be no doubt that restricting the freedom to marry solely because of racial classifications violates the central meaning of the Equal Protection Clause.

These statutes also deprive the Lovings of liberty without [due process].

Marriage is one of the "basic civil rights of man," fundamental to our very existence and survival. *Skinner v. Oklahoma* [Ch. 6, Sec. 2]. To deny this fundamental freedom on so unsupportable a basis as the racial classifications embodied in these statutes [surely denies due process].

Reversed.

JUSTICE STEWART, concurring.

I have previously expressed the belief that "it is simply not possible for a state law to be valid under our Constitution which makes the criminality of an act depend upon the race of the actor." *McLaughlin* (concurring

---

[32] *McLaughlin* also stated that racial classifications were " 'in most circumstances irrelevant' to any constitutionally acceptable legislative purpose." Harlan, J., concurring, added that "necessity, not mere reasonable relationship, is the proper test"; this "test which developed to protect free speech against state infringement should be equally applicable in a case involving state racial discrimination—prohibition of which lies at the very heart of the Fourteenth Amendment."

[11] **[Ct's Note]** [While] Virginia prohibits whites from marrying any nonwhite (subject to the exception for the descendants of Pocahontas), Negroes, Orientals and any other racial class may intermarry without statutory interference. Appellants contend that this distinction renders Virginia's miscegenation statutes arbitrary and unreasonable even assuming the constitutional validity of an official purpose to preserve "racial integrity." We need not reach this contention because we find the racial classifications in these statutes repugnant to the Fourteenth Amendment, even assuming an evenhanded state purpose to protect the "integrity" of all races.

opinion). Because I adhere to that belief, I concur in the judgment of the Court.

NOTES AND QUESTIONS

1. ***Standard of review.*** (a) Is the constitutional test for laws that *classify* by race or ethnicity different from the test for laws that *discriminate* against racial or ethnic minorities? How crucial was it to the Court's ruling that the challenged statute had no legitimate purpose whatsoever?

(b) Consider Deborah Hellman, *Two Types of Discrimination: The Familiar and the Forgotten*, 86 Calif.L.Rev. 315 (1998), arguing that equal protection doctrine has developed to assess the legitimacy of "proxy discrimination"—involving the use of classificatory schemes to promote a racially non-discriminatory objective—and deals awkwardly with "non-proxy" discrimination, in which a law's actual purpose is to advance or harm a particular group.

Although the Court refers to a "heavy burden of justification," it does not, in *Loving*, invoke a formula that would become prominent in later cases involving overt racial classifications—that of "strict judicial scrutiny," under which suspect classifications must be "necessary" or "narrowly tailored" to a compelling governmental interest. Consider Richard H. Fallon, Jr., *Strict Judicial Scrutiny,* 54 UCLA L.Rev. 1267 (2007): "In the evolution of constitutional doctrine, perhaps the biggest step toward the modern test in race discrimination cases came in *McLaughlin*, [which] involved a challenge under the Equal Protection Clause to a Florida statute that forbade the habitual occupation of a room at night by '[a]ny Negro man and white woman, or any white man and Negro woman, who [were] not married to each other.' *McLaughlin* pronounced all race-based classifications 'constitutionally suspect,' quoting *Bolling*, and 'subject to the most rigid scrutiny,' quoting *Korematsu*. Laws embodying race-based classifications could be upheld, the Court said, 'only if . . . necessary, and not merely rationally related, to the accomplishment of a permissible state policy.' From the modern formulation, only the demand for a compelling state interest was missing—a requirement that a Supreme Court majority first formally articulated in a race discrimination case in 1984 in *Palmore v. Sidoti*, [infra].

"Intervening between *McLaughlin* and *Palmore*, however, was *Regents of the University of California v. Bakke,* [Sec. 2, V infra] in which Justice Powell's controlling opinion, much of which was joined by no other Justice, expressly applied what he called 'strict' or 'the most exacting scrutiny' to gauge the permissibility of an affirmative action program. A case could thus be made that the first application of strict scrutiny in a race case involved affirmative action."

2. ***Racial information.*** ANDERSON v. MARTIN, 375 U.S. 399 (1964), held violative of equal protection a statute requiring that the race of candidates for elective office be on the ballot: "The vice lies [in] the placing of the power of

the State behind a racial classification that induces racial prejudice at the polls."

3. ***Family issues.*** PALMORE v. SIDOTI, 466 U.S. 429 (1984), per BURGER, C.J., held that Florida's denial of child custody to a white mother because her new husband was black violated equal protection: "There is a risk that a child living with a step-parent of a different race may be subject to a variety of pressures and stresses not present if the child were living with parents of the same racial or ethnic origin. [But the] effects of racial prejudice, however real, cannot justify a racial classification removing an infant child from the custody of its natural mother found to be an appropriate person to have such custody."

May a state take race into account in assigning children to foster homes and in choosing adoptive parents?[33] Consider Katie Eyer, *Constitutional Colorblindness and the Family,* 162 U.Pa.L.Rev. 537 (2014): "*Palmore* did not eradicate the continuing use of race in adoption and foster care, nor in custody disputes between interracial parents. [C]ourts addressing post-*Palmore*, race-based family law practices typically held them to be categorically constitutional [before a congressional statutory intervention precluding the use of race as a basis for denying or delaying adoption and foster care placements] where race was not the exclusive factor considered as part of the best interest of the child assessment. [Family] law has been conceived of as simply too 'different' [to] warrant the type of intervention typically demanded in the affirmative action context. [And] the Court has self-consciously—but sub silentio [through denials of certiorari]—endorsed the lower courts' loose and permissive approach."

4. ***Law enforcement issues.*** JOHNSON v. CALIFORNIA, 543 U.S. 499 (2005), held that the "strict scrutiny" test developed in prior race discrimination cases (under which racial classifications will be upheld only if proven to be "narrowly tailored" to further "compelling governmental interests") applied to a policy of the California Department of Corrections (CDC) to assign newly arrived prisoners to temporary cells "based on a number of factors, [but] predominantly race." The Court, per O'CONNOR, J., rejected arguments for applying "the deferential standard of review articulated in *Turner v. Safley*, 482 U.S. 78 (1987)," under which courts will ordinarily uphold any prison regulation that is "reasonably related" to "legitimate penological interests." Unlike burdens on prisoners' rights to privacy, speech, and religion, "[t]he right not to be discriminated against based on one's race is not susceptible to the logic of *Turner*. It is not a right that need necessarily be compromised for the sake of proper prison administration."

Although STEVENS, J., agreed with the majority about the applicable standard of review, he dissented from the Court's decision to remand the case to the district court to apply the compelling interest test and would have held squarely that the challenged policy violated the Equal Protection Clause.

---

[33] For discussion, see, e.g., Richard Banks, *The Color of Desire: Fulfilling Adoptive Parents' Racial Preferences Through Discriminatory State Action*, 107 Yale L.J. 875 (1998).

THOMAS, J., joined by Scalia, J., dissented. In light of the threats of race-based prison violence and the general needs of prison administration, he would have upheld the CDC's policy on the basis of *Turner*.

May a police department use race as part of a "profile" of those who are most likely to engage in certain kinds of criminal activities and, therefore, should be watched especially closely or pulled over for minor traffic infractions?[34] Cf. *United States v. Brignoni-Ponce*, 422 U.S. 873, 885–86 (1975) (ruling that the use of a "single factor" of Mexican ancestry is impermissible in Border Patrol stops, but that immigration officers may base stops on the "characteristic appearance of persons who live in Mexico [including such] factors as the mode of dress and haircut").

When, if ever, would reliance on Middle Eastern origin as part of a "terrorist" profile survive strict judicial scrutiny? Kevin R. Johnson, *Racial Profiling After September 11: The Department of Justice's 2003 Guidelines*, 50 Loy.L.Rev. 67 (2004), argues that there is a contradiction between the federal government's condemnation of racial profiling for purposes of ordinary law enforcement and its suggestion that the use of racial profiling as part of a war on terrorism may survive strict scrutiny on national security grounds. Do especially "compelling" government interests justify racial profiling in some instances but not in others?

III. HISTORY OF SCHOOL DESEGREGATION

1. ***Massive resistance.*** Although there was prompt compliance with *Brown* in the District of Columbia and some border states, the initial response in the Deep South was "massive resistance." See generally Robert McKay, *"With All Deliberate Speed": Legislative Reaction and Judicial Development 1956–1957,* 43 Va.L.Rev. 1205 (1957). Reports Michael J. Klarman, *From Jim Crow to Civil Rights: The Supreme Court and the Struggle for Racial Equality* 350–51 (2004): "For personal and political reasons, school board members resisted prompt and effective action toward desegregation. [Board] members were elected officials, who could ill afford to ignore public opinion. [Such] officials also had personal incentives to delay and evade compliance with *Brown*, as they had to live in communities that were staunchly opposed to desegregation. [School] board members had [particularly] strong reasons not to be the first in a state or region to desegregate, which would make them the focal point of segregationist pressure."

2. ***Reaffirmation of Brown.*** In the late 1950s, some states sought to comply with *Brown* by simply permitting students to apply for transfer from one previously all-black or all-white school to another school. Procedures were complex and time-consuming; standards were vague, making it difficult to

---

[34] See Randall Kennedy, *Race, Crime, and the Law* 137–38, 141–45 (1997); Bernard Harcourt, *Rethinking Racial Profiling: A Critique of the Economics, Civil Liberties, and Constitutional Literature and of Criminal Profiling More Generally*, 71 U.Chi.L.Rev. 1275 (2004); cf. Ligon v. City of New York, 959 F. Supp. 2d 540, 660–67 (S.D.N.Y. 2013) (finding that the New York City Police Department was in violation of the Equal Protection Clause because the City's "stop and frisk" policy had been applied in a racially discriminatory manner).

show that denials were due to race. But the Court generally took a hands-off stance, leaving the burden of grappling with the "massive resistance" campaign largely to the lower federal courts. The justices' most notable intervention in the immediate post-*Brown* decade came in COOPER v. AARON, 358 U.S. 1 (1958), also discussed in Ch. 1, Sec. 1 supra. At issue in *Cooper* was a request by the Little Rock, Arkansas, School Board to stay an integration plan that had been in operation at Central High School during the 1957–58 school year. During that year, implementation of the plan became possible only after President Eisenhower sent federal troops to protect black students from "extreme public hostility" fueled by inflammatory opposition by the governor and state legislature. The opinion, unprecedented in that it was signed by all nine Justices (including those appointed since *Brown*), "unanimously reaffirmed" *Brown* and further asserted that the decision "can neither be nullified openly and directly by state legislators or state executive or judicial officers, nor nullified indirectly by them through evasive schemes."

3. ***The 1964 Civil Rights Act.*** Despite these firm-sounding words, little school desegregation ensued in *Cooper*'s immediate aftermath. Relevant developments occurred on other fronts, however. A growing civil rights movement galvanized attention, much of it sympathetic. Largely in response, and with firm leadership by President Lyndon Johnson, Congress in 1964 enacted a sweeping civil rights act, two titles of which specifically dealt with schools. Title IV authorized the attorney general to assist in the development and implementation of school desegregation plans and, where such plans were not adopted voluntarily, empowered the attorney general to initiate lawsuits to remedy racial discrimination. Title VI barred federal financial assistance for any program, including school programs, administered in a racially discriminatory manner.

In the years following enactment of the Civil Rights Act, the pace of integration accelerated dramatically. According to Erwin Chemerinsky, *Can Courts Make a Difference?*, *in* Redefining Equality 191, 198–99 (Neal Devins & Davison M. Douglas, 1998), "[i]n the South, just 1.2 percent of black schoolchildren were attending school with whites a decade after *Brown*. [By] 1968, the integration rate in the South rose to 32 percent, and by 1972–73, 91.3 percent of southern schools were desegregated." The relationship between the Supreme Court's decision in *Brown I* and *II* and the school desegregation that occurred after 1964 has emerged as a source of controversy among legal historians. The traditional view gave *Brown* great credit; a revisionist view represented by Gerald N. Rosenberg, *The Hollow Hope: Can Courts Bring About Social Change?* (1991), deprecated *Brown*'s impact. Michael Klarman, *Brown v. Board of Education and the Civil Rights Movement* 124 (2007), concludes: "The 1964 Civil Rights Act, not *Brown*, was plainly the proximate cause of most school desegregation in the South." Although Professor Klarman believes that *Brown* had little direct role in ending segregation in the South, because it was little enforced for over a decade, he thinks it nonetheless played a large *indirect* role in advancing civil rights: "*Brown* created a massive backlash among southern whites, radicalized politics, and fomented violence.

[Although *Brown* failed to achieve immediate school desegregation,] that violence, especially when directed at protestors and broadcast on television, produced a counter-backlash" in the form of the Civil Rights Movement, and then the 1964 Civil Rights Act, which ultimately led to vast strides for the cause of racial equality. Klarman, *From Jim Crow to Civil Rights*, supra, at 466–68.[35]

4. ***Court demands for desegregation.*** Whatever the cause, 1964 marked a turning point in the Court's demands for actual desegregation.

(a)　GRIFFIN v. COUNTY SCHOOL BD., 377 U.S. 218 (1964), addressed the situation in Prince Edward County, Virginia, which in 1959 closed its public schools rather than comply with a desegregation order. Private schools, supported by state and local tuition grants and tax credits, were operated for whites. The Court, per BLACK, J., held that the closing denied African Americans equal protection: "[Whatever] nonracial grounds might support a state's allowing a county to abandon public schools, the object must be a constitutional one, and grounds of race and opposition to desegregation do not qualify."

(b)　In GREEN v. COUNTY SCHOOL BD., 391 U.S. 430 (1968), the Court, per BRENNAN, J., invalidated a "freedom-of-choice" plan that a rural Virginia county had grudgingly adopted to remain eligible for federal financial aid. Under the plan, enrolled students could annually choose between the county's previously all-white and all-black high schools, with pupils who did not register an alternative preference being automatically reassigned to the school they had attended the year before. When, after three years, no white child chose to go to the black school that 85% of the black children continued to attend, the Court held that: "[It] is incumbent upon the school board to establish that its proposed plan promises meaningful and immediate progress toward disestablishing state-imposed segregation. [The School] Board must be required [to] fashion steps which promise realistically to convert promptly to a system without a 'white' school and a 'Negro' school, but just schools."

Consider John Jeffries, *The Right-Remedy Gap in Constitutional Law*, 109 Yale L.J. 87 (1999): *Green* "transformed the constitutional obligation [recognized in *Brown*]. Most courts had thought it a sufficient response to *Brown* that the government stop requiring separation by race. [In] *Green* [the] Court charged formerly de jure school districts with the 'affirmative duty' to undo the effects of prior practice and achieve a 'unitary' school system without racially identifiable schools."

(c)　SWANN v. CHARLOTTE-MECKLENBURG BD. OF EDUC., 402 U.S. 1 (1971), per BURGER, C.J., affirmed a lower court order establishing

---

[35] For criticisms of Klarman's thesis, see, e.g., David E. Bernstein & Ilya Somin, *Judicial Power and Civil Rights Reconsidered: From Jim Crow to Civil Rights*, 117 Yale L.J. 591 (2004) (arguing that *Brown*'s triggering of massive resistance is evidence that the decision itself had bite); David J. Garrow, *"Happy" Birthday, Brown v. Board of Education? Brown's Fiftieth Anniversary and the New Critics of Supreme Court Muscularity*, 90 Va.L.Rev. 693 (2004) (associating Klarman's claim about *Brown*'s relative lack of direct importance with growing liberal skepticism about the power of judicial review to protect minorities and promote change).

flexible mathematical targets for permissible racial balance in individual schools and requiring school busing as a tool for achieving those goals in an urban district that had previously practiced de jure segregation. The Court opinion invited voluntary efforts to achieve broad racial integration: "School authorities are traditionally charged with broad power to formulate and implement educational policy and might well conclude, for example, that in order to prepare students to live in a pluralistic society each school should have a prescribed ratio of Negro to white students reflecting the proportion for the district as a whole."

At a minimum, however, previously segregated districts were obliged to "to eliminate from the public schools all vestiges of state-imposed segregation." If they failed to do so, "judicial authority may be invoked. [When] school authorities present a district court with a 'loaded game board,' affirmative action in the form of remedial altering of attendance zones is proper to achieve truly non-discriminatory assignments. [The] importance of bus transportation as a normal and accepted tool of educational policy is readily discernible. [The lower court's] decree provided that [trips] for elementary school pupils average about seven miles and the District Court found that they would take 'not over 35 minutes at the most.' This system compares favorably with the transportation plan previously operated in Charlotte under which each day 23,600 students on all grade levels were transported an average of 15 miles one way for an average trip requiring over an hour. In these circumstances, we find no basis for holding that the local school authorities may not be required to employ bus transportation as one tool of school desegregation. Desegregation plans cannot be limited to the walk-in school."

Following *Swann*, the permissibility, wisdom, and fairness of court-ordered busing became a heated source of legal and political controversy. See, e.g., James T. Patterson, Brown v. Board of Education: *A Civil Rights Milestone and Its Troubled Legacy* 173–77 (2001).

(d) KEYES v. SCHOOL DIST., 413 U.S. 189 (1973), was the Court's first case involving a northern school district (Denver, Colorado) in which segregation had never been statutorily mandated. Per BRENNAN, J., it held that where school officials had previously taken actions such as teacher placement, the location of schools, and the drawing of district lines with the "*purpose* or *intent*" to maintain substantially all-white or all-black schools, they had violated the Constitution and incurred remedial obligations. Moreover, "a finding of intentionally segregative school board actions in a meaningful portion of a school system [creates] a prima facie case of unlawful segregative design [with respect to the school system as a whole], and shifts to [school] authorities the burden of proving that other segregated schools within the system are not also the result of intentionally segregative actions. [In] discharging that burden, it is not enough, of course, that the school authorities rely upon some allegedly logical, racially neutral explanation [such as a 'neighborhood school policy'] for their actions. Their burden is to adduce proof sufficient to support a finding that segregative intent was not among the factors that motivated their actions."

POWELL, J., filed a lengthy separate opinion: "I would hold [that] where [racial imbalance exists within the some or all of the schools in] a school district to a substantial degree, there is a prima facie case that the duly constituted public authorities [are] sufficiently responsible to impose upon them a nationally applicable burden to demonstrate they nevertheless are operating a genuinely integrated school system." But Powell, J., argued for "special caution" concerning "any proposal as disruptive of family life and interests— and ultimately of education itself—as extensive transportation of elementary age children solely for desegregation purposes. As a minimum, this Court should not require school boards to engage in the unnecessary transportation away from their neighborhoods of elementary age children."

REHNQUIST, J., dissented: "[I]t would be a quite unprecedented application of principles of equitable relief to determine that if the gerrymandering of one attendance zone were proven, particular racial mixtures could be required by a federal district court for every school in the district."[36]

5. *Limits of the remedial obligation.* The Court's demand that previously unconstitutionally segregated school districts root out the vestiges of past segregation raised the question of how long remedial policies— including court-ordered busing—must continue.

(a) In OKLAHOMA CITY BD. OF EDUC. v. DOWELL, 498 U.S. 237 (1991), a school district that previously had been under a desegregation order that included forced busing satisfied the district court that "unitariness had been achieved." Eight years later, the school board adopted a new neighborhood assignment plan that resulted in about half the schools becoming primarily uniracial. Successors to the parties in the initial action then challenged the school board's actions as incompatible with prior judicial orders, which they maintained continued in effect. The Court, per REHNQUIST, C.J., held that the previously entered desegregation decree should be dissolved, even if a substantial reduction in actual integration would occur, if the board has "complied in good faith [since the injunction] was entered" and "the vestiges of past discrimination have been eliminated to the extent practicable. [The] District Court should then evaluate the Board's decision to implement

---

[36] Even at the high tide of the era of judicially enforced busing during the 1970s, the Court insisted that the scope of judicial remedies must be limited to the scope of judicially identified constitutional violations—even when the Court, as in *Columbus*, relied heavily on presumptions to identify the scope of the remediable violation. A significant implication of this principle was a prohibition against so-called "interdistrict remedies," which would have permitted courts to order desegregation of suburban schools in order to remedy past de jure segregation of urban schools. See *Millikin v. Bradley*, 418 U.S. 717 (1974): "[Before] imposing a cross-district remedy, it must first be shown that there has been a constitutional violation within one district that produces a significant segregative effect in [another]. The constitutional right of the Negro respondents residing in Detroit is to attend a unitary school system in that district."

Marshall, J., joined by Douglas, Brennan, and White, JJ., dissented: "The State's creation, through de jure acts of segregation, of a growing core of all-Negro schools inevitably acted as a magnet to attract Negroes to the areas served by such schools [and] helped drive whites to other areas of the city or to the suburbs. [Having] created a system where whites and Negroes were intentionally kept apart so that they could not become accustomed to learning together, the State is responsible for the fact that many whites will react to the dismantling of that segregated system by attempting to flee to the suburbs."

the [new assignment plan] under appropriate equal protection principles [that tolerate government decisions that are not explicitly race-based unless they are made with a racially discriminatory intent]. See *Washington v. Davis,* [Sec. 2, III, infra]."

MARSHALL, J., joined by Blackmun and Stevens, JJ., dissented: "I believe a desegregation decree cannot be lifted so long as conditions likely to inflict the stigmatic injury condemned in *Brown I* persist and there remain feasible methods of eliminating such conditions." SOUTER, J., did not participate.

(b)   In FREEMAN v. PITTS, 503 U.S. 467 (1992), the district court had found that the De Kalb County, Georgia, School System had "achieved unitary status [with] regard to student assignments, transportation, physical facilities, and extracurricular activities," but not in respect to "teacher and principal assignments, resource allocation, and quality of education." The Court, per KENNEDY, J., remanded the case for more specific findings, but, in doing so, emphasized that "returning schools to the control of local authorities at the earliest practicable date is essential to restore their true accountability in our government system": "[W]hile retaining jurisdiction over the case, the court [may] withdraw judicial supervision with respect to discrete categories in which the school district has achieved compliance with a court-ordered desegregation plan [and] need not retain active control over every aspect of school administration until a school district has demonstrated unitary status in all facets of its system. [As] the de jure violation becomes more remote in time and these demographic changes intervene, it becomes less likely that a current racial imbalance in a school district is a vestige of the prior de jure system. [It] is true that the school district was not in compliance [with the judicial desegregation plan] with respect to faculty assignments, but the record does not show that student reassignments would be a feasible or practicable way to remedy this defect."

SCALIA, J., concurred: "[Our] post-*Green* cases provide that, once state-enforced school segregation is shown to have existed in a jurisdiction in 1954, there arises a presumption, effectively irrebuttable (because the school district cannot prove the negative), that any current racial imbalance is the product of that violation, at least if the imbalance has continuously existed. [Granting] the merits of this approach at the time of *Green,* it is now 25 years later. [Since] a multitude of private factors has shaped school systems in the years after abandonment of de jure segregation—normal migration, population growth (as in this case), 'white flight' from the inner cities, increases in the costs of new facilities—the percentage of the current makeup of school systems attributable to the prior, government-enforced discrimination has diminished with each passing year, to the point where it cannot realistically be assumed to be a significant factor. [We] must soon revert to the ordinary principles [that] plaintiffs alleging Equal Protection violations must prove intent and causation and not merely the existence of racial disparity, see *Washington v. Davis.* [infra, Sec. 2, III.]"

BLACKMUN, J., joined by Stevens and O'Connor, JJ., concurred only in the judgment of remand, stressing that "the District Court's jurisdiction should continue until the school board demonstrates full compliance with the Constitution." SOUTER, J., also concurred. THOMAS, J., did not participate.

———

PARENTS INVOLVED IN COMMUNITY SCHOOLS V. SEATTLE SCHOOL DIST.

551 U.S. 701, 127 S.Ct. 2738, 168 L.Ed.2d 508 (2007).

ROBERTS, C.J., announced the judgment of the Court, and delivered the opinion of the Court with respect to Parts I, II, III–A, and III–C, and an opinion with respect to Parts III–B and IV, in which JUSTICES SCALIA, THOMAS, and ALITO join.

The school districts in these cases [in Seattle, Washington, and Jefferson County, Kentucky] voluntarily adopted student assignment plans that rely upon race to determine which public schools certain children may attend. * * *

I.   Both cases present the same underlying legal question—whether a public school that had not operated legally segregated schools or has been found to be unitary may choose to classify students by race and rely upon that classification in making school assignments.

[The Seattle School District was never officially segregated by law, but racial imbalances led to threatened and actual lawsuits in the 1960s and 1970s and to a series of steps to settle those lawsuits that once included mandatory busing, despite the fact that official discrimination was never proved nor admitted. In 1998, the district] adopted the plan at issue in this case for assigning students to [its ten high] schools. The plan allows incoming ninth graders to choose from among any of the district's high schools, ranking however many schools they wish in order of preference. [If] too many students list the same school as their first choice, the district employs a series of "tiebreakers" to determine who will fill the open slots at the oversubscribed school. The first tiebreaker selects for admission students who have a sibling currently enrolled in the chosen school. The next tiebreaker depends upon the racial composition of the particular school and the race of the individual student. [This second tiebreaker comes into play if a school's enrollment deviates by more than 10% from the district's overall balance of approximately 41% white and 59% nonwhite students.]

Jefferson County Public Schools operates the public school system in metropolitan Louisville, Kentucky. [In] 2001, after [a judicially mandated school desegregation] decree had been dissolved, Jefferson County adopted the voluntary student assignment plan at issue in this case. [That plan, which covers 97,000 students—roughly 34% of whom are black and the remaining 66% of whom are mostly white—] requires all nonmagnet schools to maintain a minimum black enrollment of 15 percent, and a maximum black enrollment of 50 percent. [The requirements can sometimes block initial assignments and transfers, including assignments and transfers to neighborhood schools, that would otherwise occur.]

III. A. It is well established that when the government distributes burdens or benefits on the basis of individual racial classifications, that action is reviewed under strict scrutiny. *Johnson* v. *California*; *Grutter v. Bollinger,* [Sec. 2, V infra].

As the Court recently reaffirmed, " 'racial classifications are simply too pernicious to permit any but the most exact connection between justification and classification.' " *Gratz v. Bollinger*, [Sec. 2, V]. In order to satisfy this searching standard of review, the school districts must demonstrate that the use of individual racial classifications in the assignment plans here under review is "narrowly tailored" to achieve a "compelling" government interest.

[O]ur prior cases, in evaluating the use of racial classifications in the school context have recognized two interests that qualify as compelling. The first is [remedying] the effects of past intentional discrimination. See *Freeman* v. *Pitts*. Yet the Seattle public schools have not shown that they were ever segregated by law, and were not subject to court-ordered desegregation decrees. The Jefferson County public schools [have been found to have] "eliminated the vestiges associated with [their] former policy of segregation and its pernicious effects" and thus [to have] achieved "unitary" status. Jefferson County accordingly does not rely upon an interest in remedying the effects of past intentional discrimination in defending its present use of race in assigning students. Nor could it. We have emphasized [that] "the Constitution is not violated by racial imbalance in the schools, without more." *Milliken v. Bradley*.

[The] second government interest we have recognized as compelling for purposes of strict scrutiny is the interest in diversity in higher education upheld in *Grutter* [which sustained an affirmative plan that took race into account in law school admissions]. [The] diversity interest was not focused on race alone but encompassed "all factors that may contribute to student body diversity." [The] entire gist of the analysis in *Grutter* was that the admissions program at issue there focused on each applicant as an individual, and not simply as a member of a particular racial group.

[In] the present cases, by contrast, race is not considered as part of a broader effort to achieve "exposure to widely diverse people, cultures, ideas, and viewpoints"; race, for some students, is determinative standing alone. [Even] when it comes to race, the plans here employ only a limited notion of diversity, viewing race exclusively in white/nonwhite terms in Seattle and black/"other" terms in Jefferson County. [Under] the Seattle plan, a school with 50 percent Asian-American students and 50 percent white students but no African-American, Native-American, or Latino students would qualify as balanced, while a school with 30 percent Asian-American, 25 percent African-American, 25 percent Latino, and 20 percent white students would not. [The] present cases are not governed by *Grutter*.

B.   Each school district argues that educational and broader socialization benefits flow from a racially diverse learning environment, and each contends that because the diversity they seek is racial diversity—not the broader diversity at issue in *Grutter*—it makes sense to promote that interest directly by relying on race alone. The parties and their amici dispute whether racial diversity in schools in fact has a marked impact on test scores and other objective yardsticks or achieves intangible socialization benefits. The debate is not one we need to resolve, however, because it is clear that the racial classifications employed by the districts are not narrowly tailored to the goal of achieving the educational and social benefits asserted to flow from racial diversity. In design and operation, the plans are directed only to racial balance, pure and simple, an objective this Court has repeatedly condemned as illegitimate. [The] districts offer no evidence that the level of racial diversity necessary to achieve the asserted educational benefits happens to coincide with the racial demographics of the respective school districts—or rather the white/nonwhite or black/"other" balance of the districts, since that is the only diversity addressed by the plans. * * *

[It is a further constitutional defect that] in each case the extreme measure of relying on race in assignments is unnecessary to achieve the stated goals, even as defined by the districts. For example, at Franklin High School in Seattle, the racial tiebreaker was applied because nonwhite enrollment exceeded 69 percent, and resulted in an incoming ninth-grade class in 2000–2001 that was 30.3 percent Asian-American, 21.9 percent African-American, 6.8 percent Latino, 0.5 percent Native-American, and 40.5 percent Caucasian. Without the racial tiebreaker, the class would have been 39.6 percent Asian-American, 30.2 percent African-American, 8.3 percent Latino, 1.1 percent Native-American, and 20.8 percent Caucasian. When the actual racial breakdown is considered, enrolling students without regard to their race yields a substantially diverse student body under any definition of diversity.

C.   The districts assert, as they must, that the way in which they have employed individual racial classifications is necessary to achieve their stated ends. The minimal effect these classifications have on student assignments, however, suggests that other means would be effective. Seattle's racial tiebreaker results, in the end, only in shifting a small number of students between schools. [T]he district could identify only 52 students who were ultimately affected adversely by the racial tiebreaker in that it resulted in assignment to a school they had not listed as a preference and to which they would not otherwise have been assigned.

[Similarly,] Jefferson County's use of racial classifications has only a minimal effect on the assignment of [students.] Jefferson County estimates that the racial guidelines account for only 3 percent of assignments. While we do not suggest that *greater* use of race would be preferable, the minimal impact of the districts' racial classifications on school enrollment casts doubt on the necessity of using racial classifications. In *Grutter*, the consideration of race was viewed as indispensable in more than tripling minority representation at the law school-from 4 to 14.5 percent.

[The] districts have also failed to show that they considered methods other than explicit racial classifications to achieve their stated goals. Narrow tailoring requires "serious, good faith consideration of workable race-neutral alternatives." *Grutter*.

IV. Justice Breyer's dissent [fails] to ground the result it would reach in law. [It] seeks to justify the plans at issue under our precedents recognizing the compelling interest in remedying past intentional discrimination. [But the] distinction between segregation by state action and racial imbalance caused by other factors has been central to our jurisprudence in this area for generations. [*Swann* and the other cases relied on by the dissent to establish once-prevailing legal assumptions were decided "before this Court definitively determined that 'all racial classifications [must] be analyzed by a reviewing court under strict scrutiny.'" *Adarand Constructors, Inc. v. Pena*, [Sec. 2, V infra].

In *Brown* v. *Board of Education*, we held that segregation deprived black children of equal educational opportunities regardless of whether school facilities and other tangible factors were equal, because government classification and separation on grounds of race themselves denoted inferiority. [The] parties and their amici debate which side is more faithful to the heritage of *Brown*, but the position of the plaintiffs in *Brown* was spelled out in their brief and could not have been clearer: "[T]he Fourteenth Amendment prevents states from according differential treatment to American children on the basis of their color or race." Before *Brown*, schoolchildren were told where they could and could not go to school based on the color of their skin. The school districts in these cases have not carried the heavy burden of demonstrating that we should allow this once again—even for very different reasons. For schools that never segregated on the basis of race, such as Seattle, or that have removed the vestiges of past segregation, such as Jefferson County, the way "to achieve a system of determining admission to the public schools on a nonracial basis," is to stop assigning students on a racial basis. The way to stop discrimination on the basis of race is to stop discriminating on the basis of race.

JUSTICE THOMAS, concurring.

* * * I wholly concur in The Chief Justice's opinion. I write separately to address several of the contentions in Justice Breyer's dissent. * * *

Disfavoring a color-blind interpretation of the Constitution, the dissent would give school boards a free hand to make decisions on the basis of race—an approach reminiscent of that advocated by the segregationists in *Brown.* This approach is just as wrong today as it was a half-century ago. [The] dissent repeatedly claims that the school districts are threatened with resegregation and that they will succumb to that threat if these plans are declared unconstitutional. [But racial] imbalance is not segregation, and the mere incantation of terms like resegregation and remediation cannot make up the difference. * * *

The dissent points to data that indicate that "black and white students in desegregated schools are less racially prejudiced than those in segregated schools." [But] it is unclear whether increased interracial contact improves racial attitudes and relations. [Some] studies have even found that a deterioration in racial attitudes seems to result from racial mixing in schools.* * *

Most of the dissent's criticisms of today's result can be traced to its rejection of the color-blind Constitution. [The] dissent appears to pin its interpretation of the Equal Protection Clause to current societal practice and expectations, deference to local officials, likely practical consequences, and reliance on previous statements from this and other courts. Such a view was ascendant [in] *Plessy,* where the Court asked whether a state law providing for segregated railway cars was "a reasonable regulation." [In] place of the color-blind Constitution, the dissent would permit measures to keep the races together and proscribe measures to keep the races apart. Although no such distinction is apparent in the Fourteenth Amendment, the dissent would constitutionalize today's faddish social theories that embrace that distinction. The Constitution is not that malleable. [Can] we really be sure that the racial theories that motivated *Dred Scott* and *Plessy* are a relic of the past or that future theories will be nothing but beneficent and progressive? That is a gamble I am unwilling to take, and it is one the Constitution does not allow.

JUSTICE KENNEDY, concurring in part and concurring in the judgment.

I.   * * * Diversity, depending on its meaning and definition, is a compelling educational goal a school district may pursue. [But the] government bears the burden of justifying its use of individual racial classifications. As part of that burden it must establish, in detail, how decisions based on an individual student's race are made in a challenged governmental program. The Jefferson County Board of Education fails to meet this threshold mandate. * * *

II.   [Parts] of the opinion by The Chief Justice imply an all-too-unyielding insistence that race cannot be a factor in instances when, in my view, it may be taken into account. The plurality opinion is too dismissive of the legitimate interest government has in ensuring all people have equal opportunity regardless of their race. [To] the extent the plurality opinion suggests the Constitution mandates that state and local school authorities must accept the status quo of racial isolation in schools, it is, in my view, profoundly mistaken.

[In] the administration of public schools by the state and local authorities it is permissible to consider the racial makeup of schools and to adopt general policies to encourage a diverse student body, one aspect of which is its racial composition. Cf. *Grutter* (Kennedy, J., dissenting). If school authorities are concerned that the student-body compositions of certain schools interfere with the objective of offering an equal educational opportunity to all of their students, they are free to devise race-conscious measures to address the problem in a general way and without treating each student in different fashion solely on the basis of a systematic, individual typing by race.

School boards may pursue the goal of bringing together students of diverse backgrounds and races through other means, including strategic site selection of new schools; drawing attendance zones with general recognition of the demographics of neighborhoods; allocating resources for special programs; recruiting students and faculty in a targeted fashion; and tracking enrollments, performance, and other statistics by race. These mechanisms are race conscious but do not lead to different treatment based on a classification that tells each student he or she is to be defined by race, so it is unlikely any of them would demand strict scrutiny to be found permissible. See *Bush* v. *Vera*, [Sec. 5, I, D infra] (plurality opinion). Executive and legislative branches, which for generations now have considered these types of policies and procedures, should be permitted to employ them with candor and with confidence that a constitutional violation does not occur whenever a decisionmaker considers the impact a given approach might have on students of different races. Assigning to each student a personal designation according to a crude system of individual racial classifications is quite a different matter; and the legal analysis changes accordingly.

[I] join Part III–C of the Court's opinion because I agree that in the context of these plans, the small number of assignments affected suggests that the schools could have achieved their stated ends through different means. These include the facially race-neutral means set forth above or, if necessary, a more nuanced, individual evaluation of school needs and student characteristics that might include race as a component. The latter approach would be informed by *Grutter*, though of course the criteria relevant to student placement would differ based on the age of the students, the needs of the parents, and the role of the schools.

III. [In relying on lower court opinions that have upheld explicitly race-conscious student-assignment plans, the dissent] ignores the dangers presented by individual classifications, dangers that are not as pressing when the same ends are achieved by more indirect means. When the government classifies an individual by race, it must first define what it means to be of a race. Who exactly is white and who is nonwhite? To be forced to live under a state-mandated racial label is inconsistent with the dignity of individuals in our society. And it is a label that an individual is powerless to change. Governmental classifications that command people to march in different directions based on racial typologies can cause a new divisiveness. The practice can lead to corrosive discourse, where race serves not as an element of our diverse heritage but instead as a bargaining chip in the political process. On the other hand, race-conscious measures that do not rely on differential treatment based on individual classifications present these problems to a lesser degree. * * *

JUSTICE STEVENS, dissenting.

While I join Justice Breyer's eloquent and unanswerable dissent in its entirety, it is appropriate to add these words. [If] we look at cases decided during the interim between *Brown* and *Adarand,* we can see how [the Court's] rigid adherence to tiers of scrutiny obscures *Brown*'s clear message. Perhaps the best example is provided by our approval of the decision of the Supreme Judicial Court of Massachusetts in 1967 upholding a state statute mandating racial integration in that State's school system. See *School Comm. of Boston* v. *Board of Education,* 352 Mass. 693, 227 N. E. 2d 729. [Our] ruling on the merits simply stated that the appeal was "dismissed for want of a substantial federal question." *School Comm. of Boston* v. *Board of Education*, 389 U.S. 572 (1968) (per curiam). The Court has changed significantly since it decided *School Comm. of Boston* in 1968. It was then more faithful to *Brown* and more respectful of our precedent than it is today. It is my firm conviction that no Member of the Court that I joined in 1975 would have agreed with today's decision.

JUSTICE BREYER, with whom JUSTICE STEVENS, JUSTICE SOUTER, and JUSTICE GINSBURG, join, dissenting. * * *

I.   The historical and factual context in which these cases arise is critical. In *Brown*, this Court held that the government's segregation of schoolchildren by race violates the Constitution's promise of equal protection. [In] dozens of subsequent cases, this Court told school districts previously segregated by law what they must do at a minimum to comply with *Brown*'s constitutional holding. The measures required by those cases often included race-conscious practices, such as mandatory busing and race-based restrictions on voluntary transfers. Beyond those minimum requirements, the Court left much of the determination of how to achieve integration to the judgment of local communities. Thus, in respect to race-conscious desegregation measures that the Constitution *permitted,* but did not *require* (measures similar to those at issue here), this Court unanimously stated: "School authorities are traditionally charged with broad power to formulate and implement educational policy and might well conclude, for example, that in order to prepare students to live in a pluralistic society each school should have a prescribed ratio of Negro to white students reflecting the proportion for the district as a whole. *To do this as an educational policy is within the broad discretionary powers of school authorities.*" *Swann* (emphasis added).

As a result [of this and similar signals from the Court], different districts—some acting under court decree, some acting in order to avoid threatened lawsuits, some seeking to comply with federal administrative orders, some acting purely voluntarily—adopted, modified, and experimented with hosts of different kinds of plans, including race-conscious plans, all with a similar objective: greater racial integration of public schools. [Overall] these efforts brought about considerable racial integration. More recently, however, progress has stalled [and then reversed direction]. [In] light of the evident risk of a return to school systems that are in fact (though not in law) resegregated, many school districts have felt a need to maintain or to extend their integration efforts.

[Breyer, J., here offered a lengthy recitation of the historical context in Seattle and Louisville as "typical" of "school integration stories" throughout the country. His account of events in Seattle emphasized that although there was never a formal finding of school segregation, a 1956 school board memo spoke of discriminatory policies making it difficult for blacks to transfer from one city school to another, and many of the school district's desegregation efforts in the 1960s and 1970s occurred in response to threatened and actual litigation. More generally, his account emphasized ongoing, adaptive efforts by the Seattle and Louisville school districts to achieve meaningful integration through politically acceptable mechanisms.]

Is Seattle free on remand to say that its schools were de jure segregated, just as in 1956 a memo for the School Board admitted? The plurality does not seem confident as to the answer. * * *

Moreover, Louisville's history makes clear that a community under a court order to desegregate might submit a race-conscious remedial plan *before* the court dissolved the order, but with every intention of following that plan even *after* dissolution. How could such a plan be lawful the day before dissolution but then become unlawful the very next day? On what legal ground can the majority rest its contrary view? * * *

II. A longstanding and unbroken line of legal authority tells us that the Equal Protection Clause permits local school boards to use race-conscious criteria to achieve positive race-related goals, even when the

Constitution does not compel it. [The plain dicta of *Swann, supra*, established] a basic principle of constitutional law—a principle of law that has found "wide acceptance in the legal culture." [In] fact, without being exhaustive, I have counted 51 federal statutes that use racial classifications. I have counted well over 100 state statutes that similarly employ racial classifications. Presidential administrations for the past half-century have used and supported various race-conscious measures. And during the same time, hundreds of local school districts have adopted student assignment plans that use race-conscious criteria.

That *Swann*'s legal statement should find such broad acceptance is not surprising. [There] is reason to believe that those who drafted [the Fourteenth Amendment] would have understood the legal and practical difference between the use of race-conscious criteria [to] keep the races apart, and the use of race-conscious criteria to [bring] the races together.

[No] case—not *Adarand, Gratz, Grutter*, or any other—has ever held that the test of "strict scrutiny" means that all racial classifications—no matter whether they seek to include or exclude—must in practice be treated the same. [Nonetheless,] in light of *Grutter* and other precedents, I shall [apply] the version of strict scrutiny that those cases embody. * * *

III. The principal interest advanced in these cases to justify the use of race-based criteria goes by various names. Sometimes a court refers to it as an interest in achieving racial "diversity." Other times a court, like the plurality here, refers to it as an interest in racial "balancing." [Regardless] of its name, however, the interest at stake possesses three essential elements. First, there is a historical and remedial element: an interest in setting right the consequences of prior conditions of segregation. This refers back to a time when public schools were highly segregated, often as a result of legal or administrative policies that facilitated racial segregation in public schools. It is an interest in continuing to combat the remnants of segregation caused in whole or in part by these school-related policies, which have often affected not only schools, but also housing patterns, employment practices, economic conditions, and social attitudes. It is an interest in maintaining hard-won gains. And it has its roots in preventing what gradually may become the de facto resegregation of America's public schools.

Second, there is an educational element: an interest in overcoming the adverse educational effects produced by and associated with highly segregated schools. Studies suggest that children taken from those schools and placed in integrated settings often show positive academic gains. Other studies reach different conclusions. But the evidence supporting an educational interest in racially integrated schools is well established and strong enough to permit a democratically elected school board reasonably to determine that this interest is a compelling one.

Third, there is a democratic element: an interest in producing an educational environment that reflects the "pluralistic society" in which our children will live. It is an interest in helping our children learn to work and play together with children of different racial backgrounds. It is an interest in teaching children to engage in the kind of cooperation among Americans of all races that is necessary to make a land of three hundred million people one Nation. [This] Court from *Swann* to *Grutter* has treated these civic effects as an important virtue of racially diverse education.

[In] light of this Court's conclusions in *Grutter,* the "compelling" nature of these interests in the context of primary and secondary public education follows here a fortiori. [If] an educational interest that combines these three elements is not "compelling," what is?

[Several] factors, taken together, [similarly lead] me to conclude that the boards' use of race-conscious criteria in these plans passes even the strictest "tailoring" test. First, the race-conscious criteria at issue only help set the outer bounds of *broad* ranges. They constitute but one part of plans that depend primarily upon other, nonracial elements. To use race in this way is not to set a forbidden "quota." * * *

Second, broad-range limits on voluntary school choice plans are less burdensome, and hence more narrowly tailored, than other race-conscious restrictions this Court has previously approved. Here, race becomes a factor only in a fraction of students' non-merit-based assignments—not in large numbers of students' merit-based applications. Moreover, the effect of applying race-conscious criteria here affects potentially disadvantaged students *less severely,* not more severely, than the criteria at issue in *Grutter.* Disappointed students are not rejected from a State's flagship graduate program; they simply attend a different one of the district's many public schools, which in aspiration and in fact are substantially equal. * * *

Third, the manner in which the school boards developed these plans itself reflects "narrow tailoring." [Each] plan embodies the results of local experience and community consultation. Each plan is the product of a process that has sought to enhance student choice, while diminishing the need for mandatory busing. And each plan's use of race-conscious elements is *diminished* compared to the use of race in preceding integration plans. * * *

Justice Kennedy suggests that school boards "may pursue the goal of bringing together students of diverse backgrounds and races through other means * * * ." But, as to "strategic site selection," Seattle has built one new high school in the last 44 years (and that specialized school serves only 300 students). [As] to "drawing" neighborhood "attendance zones" on a racial basis, Louisville tried it, and it worked only when forced busing was also part of the plan. As to "allocating resources for special programs," Seattle and Louisville have both experimented with this; indeed, these programs are often referred to as "magnet schools," but the limited desegregation effect of these efforts extends at most to those few schools to which additional resources are granted. In addition, there is no evidence from the experience of these school districts that it will make any meaningful impact. * * *

V.　The Founders meant the Constitution as a practical document that would transmit its basic values to future generations through principles that remained workable over time. [As] I have pointed out, de facto resegregation is on the rise. It is reasonable to conclude that such resegregation can create serious educational, social, and civic problems. Given the conditions in which school boards work to set policy, they may need all of the means presently at their disposal to combat those problems.* * * I use the words "may need" here deliberately. The plurality, or at least those who follow Justice Thomas' "color-blind" approach, may feel confident that, to end invidious discrimination, one must end *all* governmental use of race-conscious criteria including those with inclusive objectives. By way of contrast, I do not claim to know how best to stop harmful discrimination; how best to create a society that includes all Americans; how best to overcome our serious problems of increasing de facto segregation, troubled inner city schooling, and poverty correlated with race. [But] I do know that the Constitution does not authorize judges to dictate solutions to these problems.

VI.　[To] invalidate the plans under review is to threaten the promise of *Brown*. The plurality's position, I fear, would break that promise. This is a decision that the Court and the Nation will come to regret.

NOTES AND QUESTIONS

1.　***From Brown to Parents Involved.*** Consider Martha Minow, *After Brown: What Would Martin Luther King Say?*, 12 Lewis & Clark L.Rev. 599 (2008): "Using race and ethnicity to redress effects of past discrimination, to overcome poor educational outcomes associated with schools with majority non-white enrollments, and to promote work, play, and democratic cooperation across racial lines simply are not the same kind of invidious discrimination that *Brown* struck down. Somehow, colorblindness replaced equality as the measure of the law."

See also Goodwin Liu, *"History Will Be Heard": An Appraisal of the Seattle/Louisville Decision*, 2 Harv.L. & Pol'y Rev. 53 (2008): "Tellingly, the forty-one-page plurality opinion in *Seattle/Louisville* contains only one quotation from *Brown*: a paltry sentence fragment: 'The impact [of segregation] is greater when it has the sanction of law'—that omits the crucial adjacent words locating the illegality of segregation in the detrimental effects on black children. [The *Brown*] Court nowhere used the term 'colorblind' or availed itself of the familiar quotation from Harlan's dissent in *Plessy*. Instead, *Brown*'s most memorable utterance was its recognition that segregation harms black children by 'generat[ing] a feeling of inferiority as to their status in the community that may affect their hearts and minds in a way unlikely ever to be undone.' The plurality's interpretation reduces this plain statement of why segregation is wrong to mere dictum."

Compare Mark Graber, *The Price of Fame:* Brown *as Celebrity*, 69 Ohio St.L.J. 939 (2008): "*Brown* contributed to the [current debate about its meaning]. Warren set out to write a ['nonaccusatory'] opinion that would not antagonize opponents of racial equality. Chief Justice Warren, in private, made clear that his commitment was to [an] anti-subordination [conception of equal protection that forbade uses of racial classifications to disadvantage minorities] rather than [an] anti-classification [conception that forbade uses of race under any circumstances]. The same is true for the lawyers from the NAACP Legal Defense Fund who litigated *Brown*. [Chief] Justice Warren declared that children of color developed 'feeling[s] of inferiority' from segregation, not that segregation and racial classifications diminished persons of all races. Still, that is a rather weak reed to hang the strong antisubordination theory necessary to sustain the dissents in *Parents Involved*."

Is the dispute about *Brown* and its legacy just one about history, or do views about the moral values appropriately ascribed to *Brown* inevitably come into play? As James E. Ryan, *The Supreme Court and Voluntary Integration*, 121 Harv.L.Rev. 131 (2007), points out: "Whatever else one might say about the Court's opinion, it is not originalist. Nor does Justice Thomas's concurring opinion rely, more than fleetingly and vaguely, on originalism." Why not?

None of the Justices in the majority contradicted the estimation of Stevens, J., that "no Member of the Court that I joined in 1975 would have agreed with today's decision." Was *Parents Involved*, which invalidated decisions made by locally elected political officials, a case of "conservative judicial activism"? See Kermit Roosevelt III, *Judicial Supremacy, Judicial Activism:* Cooper v. Aaron *and* Parents Involved, 52 St.Louis U.L.J. 1191 (2008), arguing that *Parents Involved* "shows us Justices both largely ignoring what they have previously asserted is determinative with respect to constitutional meaning and voting in line with what they have previously announced as policy preferences."

2. ***Practical effects.*** Ryan, supra, reports that of the roughly 16,000 school districts in the country, only about 1,000 made any use of race in making school assignments at the time of *Parents Involved,* and that "[r]oughly 300 school districts remain under desegregation decrees" not affected by the Court's holding.

Professor Ryan also notes that, apart from the Court's decision in *Parents Involved*, enthusiasm for aggressive desegregation efforts has been on the wane: "From the birth of the common school movement through the early desegregation cases, schools were seen not simply as places where students learned how to read and write, but also places where they learned to become better citizens. [But over] the last several decades, education reforms have focused primarily on academic achievement, pure and simple. [In] this context, it is not altogether surprising that integration has been left aside [for it] has always been hard to defend on purely academic grounds. The consensus among social scientists seems to be that integration leads to some moderate achievement gains for black students and does not harm white students, which is hardly a ringing endorsement for integration as a method to boost test scores."

   3.   ***Desegregation and de facto partial resegregation.*** According to Gary Orfield & John T. Yun, *Resegregation in American Schools* (1999), "[t]he percentage of black students in majority white schools in the South fell from a peak of 43.5% in 1988 to 34.7% in 1996"—roughly where it was in 1970. Nationwide, in 2010 the typical black student attended a school that was only 29.2% white—a decline from 32.0% in 1970. Whites, on average, attended schools where three-quarters of their peers were white. *See* Gary Orfield et al., *E Pluribus . . . Separation* (2012).

   Experts appear divided on whether efforts to promote school desegregation should be counted a success, a failure, or a mixture of both. Compare Erica Frankenburg, *School Integration: The Time is Now*, in *Lessons in Integration* 7 (Erica Frankenburg & Gary Orfield eds., 2007) (reaching the relatively optimistic conclusion that desegregation increased the welfare of African-American students and warning that resegregation threatens to take away educational and social benefits that minority students have achieved) and Rucker C. Johnson, *Long-Run Impacts of School Desegregation & School Quality on Adult Attainments* (2011) (concluding that the long-term effect of a black student's five-year exposure to a desegregated school between 1950 and 1975 yielded an estimated 25 percent increase in annual earnings and resulted in the equivalent health benefits of being seven years younger), with Abigail Thernstrom & Stephan Thernstrom, *No Excuses: Closing the Racial Gap in Learning* 170–82 (2004) (arguing that "it is seriously misleading [to] confuse racial imbalance with legally enforced separation of the races" and questioning whether busing and other integration efforts had any appreciable effect on minority educational achievement) and Sarah Garland, *Divided We Fail* (2013) (suggesting that many black community members opposed desegregation because it led to mass firings of black teachers and widespread closings of traditionally black schools).[37]

IV. DE JURE VS. DE FACTO DISCRIMINATION

   Part II of this Section involved laws that explicitly discriminate against racial and ethnic minorities by drawing facially race-based lines. But intentional (or "de jure") discrimination may exist even though the law in question is racially "neutral" on its face: the law may be deliberately

---

   [37] For a comprehensive and lucid survey of the first half-century of *Brown*'s aftermath, see Patterson, supra. See also Jack M. Balkin (ed.), *What* Brown v. Board of Education *Should Have Said* (2001) (presenting judicial-style "opinions" by nine prominent scholars, reflecting their views about how *Brown* should have been written in light of developments over the subsequent half-century, but relying only on legal materials available in 1954).

administered in a discriminatory way; or the law, although neutral in its language and applied in accordance with its terms, may have been enacted with a purpose (or motive) of disadvantaging a "suspect" class. This section begins by considering these additional types of "de jure" discrimination. It then examines the Court's response to government action that is racially neutral in its terms, administration, and purpose but has a discriminatory effect or impact.

YICK WO V. HOPKINS

118 U.S. 356, 6 S.Ct. 1064, 30 L.Ed. 220 (1886).

JUSTICE MATTHEWS delivered the opinion of the Court.

[A San Francisco ordinance made it unlawful to operate a laundry in a wood building without the consent of the board of supervisors. Yick Wo, a Chinese alien who had operated a laundry for 22 years, had certificates from the health and fire authorities, but was refused consent by the board. It was admitted that "there were about 320 laundries in the city [and] about 240 were owned [by] subjects of China, and of the whole number, viz., 320, about 310 were constructed of wood"; that "petitioner, and more than 150 of his countrymen, have been arrested" for violating the ordinance "while those who are not subjects of China, and who are conducting 80 odd laundries under similar conditions, are left unmolested."]

[T]he facts shown establish an administration directed so exclusively against a particular class of persons as to warrant and require the conclusion that, whatever may have been the intent of the ordinances as adopted, they are applied [with] a mind so unequal and oppressive as to amount to a practical denial by the State of [equal protection]. Though the law itself be fair on its face and impartial in appearance, yet, if it is applied and administered by public authority with an evil eye and an unequal hand, so as practically to make unjust and illegal discriminations between persons in similar circumstances, material to their rights, the denial of equal justice is still within the prohibition of the Constitution. [The] fact of this discrimination is admitted. No reason for it is shown, and the conclusion cannot be resisted that no reason for it exists except hostility to [Yick Wo's] race and nationality * * * .

WASHINGTON V. DAVIS

426 U.S. 229, 96 S.Ct. 2040, 48 L.Ed.2d 597 (1976).

JUSTICE WHITE delivered the opinion of the Court.

This case involves the validity of a qualifying test administered to applicants for positions as police officers in the District of Columbia. [T]he police recruit was required to satisfy certain physical and character standards, to be a high school graduate or its equivalent and to receive a grade of at least 40 out of 80 on "Test 21," which is "an examination that is used generally throughout the federal service," which "was developed by the Civil Service Commission, not the Police Department," and which was "designed to test verbal ability, vocabulary, reading and comprehension."

[The evidence showed that roughly four times as many blacks as whites failed Test 21. Apart from the test, however, the Police Department had systematically and affirmatively sought to enroll black officers. As a result, 44% of new police force recruits had been black in the years immediately preceding the litigation. There was, accordingly, no allegation that the Department had acted with discriminatory intent—only that a test with a substantially discriminatory impact could not be used, at least in the absence of a showing that performance on Test 21 bore a substantial and demonstrated relationship to performance on the job.]

[The] District Court rejected the assertion that Test 21 was culturally slanted to favor whites and was "satisfied that the undisputable facts prove the test to be reasonably and directly related to the requirements of the police recruit training program and that it is neither so designed nor operates to discriminate against otherwise qualified blacks." [The Court of Appeals held] that lack of discriminatory intent in designing and administering Test 21 was irrelevant; the critical fact was rather [that] four times as many [blacks] failed the test than did whites. This disproportionate impact [was] held sufficient to establish a constitutional violation, absent proof by petitioners that the test was an adequate measure of job performance in addition to being an indicator of probable success in the training program, a burden which the court ruled petitioners had failed to discharge. * * *

The central purpose of the Equal Protection Clause [is] the prevention of official conduct discriminating on the basis of race. It is also true that the Due Process Clause of the Fifth Amendment contains an equal protection component prohibiting the United States from invidiously discriminating between individuals or groups. But our cases have not embraced the proposition that a law or other official act, without regard to whether it reflects a racially discriminatory purpose, is unconstitutional *solely* because it has a racially disproportionate impact.

Almost 100 years ago, *Strauder* established that the exclusion of Negroes from grand and petit juries in criminal proceedings violated the Equal Protection Clause, but the fact that a particular jury or a series of juries does not statistically reflect the racial composition of the community does not in itself make out an invidious discrimination forbidden by the Clause. "A purpose to discriminate must be present which may be proven by systematic exclusion of eligible jurymen of the prescribed race or by an unequal application of the law to such an extent as to show intentional discrimination." * * *

The school desegregation cases have also adhered to the basic equal protection principle that the invidious quality of a law claimed to be racially discriminatory must ultimately be traced to a racially discriminatory purpose. That there are both predominantly black and predominantly white schools in a community is not alone violative of the Equal Protection Clause. The essential element ["differentiating] between de jure segregation and so-called de facto segregation [is] *purpose* or *intent* to segregate." *Keyes v. School Dist.,* [Sec. 2, III supra].

This is not to say that the necessary discriminatory racial purpose must be express or appear on the face of the statute, or that a law's disproportionate impact is irrelevant. [A] statute, otherwise neutral on its face, must not be applied so as invidiously to discriminate on the basis of race. *Yick Wo.* It is also clear from the cases dealing with racial discrimination in the selection of juries that [a] prima facie case of discriminatory purpose may be proved [by] the absence of Negroes on a particular jury combined with the failure of the jury commissioners to be informed of eligible Negro jurors in a community, or with racially non-neutral selection procedures. With a prima facie case made out, "the burden of proof shifts to the State to rebut the presumption of unconstitutional action by showing that permissible racially neutral selection criteria and procedures have produced the monochromatic result."

Necessarily, an invidious discriminatory purpose may often be inferred from the totality of the relevant facts, including [that] the law bears more heavily on one race than another. It is also not infrequently true that the discriminatory impact—in the jury cases for example, the total or seriously disproportionate exclusion of Negroes from jury venires—may for all practical purposes demonstrate unconstitutionality because in various circumstances the discrimination is very difficult to explain on nonracial grounds. Nevertheless, we have not held that a law, neutral on its face and serving ends otherwise within the power of government to pursue, is invalid under the Equal Protection Clause simply because it may affect a greater proportion of one race than of another. Disproportionate impact is not irrelevant, but it is not the sole touchstone of an invidious racial discrimination forbidden by the Constitution. Standing alone, it does not trigger the rule that racial classifications are to be subjected to the strictest scrutiny and are justifiable only by the weightiest of considerations.

[Test 21] seeks to ascertain whether those who take it have acquired a particular level of verbal skill; and it is untenable that the Constitution prevents the government from seeking modestly to upgrade the communicative abilities of its employees rather than to be satisfied with some lower level of competence, particularly where the job requires special ability to communicate orally and in writing. * * *Nor on the facts of the case before us would the disproportionate impact of Test 21 warrant the conclusion that it is a purposeful device to discriminate against Negroes. [T]he test is neutral on its face and rationally may be said to serve a purpose the government is constitutionally empowered to pursue. Even agreeing with the District Court that the differential racial effect of Test 21 called for further inquiry, we think the District Court correctly held that the affirmative efforts of the Metropolitan Police Department to recruit black officers, the changing racial composition of the recruit classes and of the force in general, and the relationship of the test to the training program negated any inference that the Department discriminated on the basis of race * * * .

Under Title VII [of the Civil Rights Act of 1964], Congress provided that when hiring and promotion practices disqualifying substantially disproportionate numbers of blacks are challenged, discriminatory purpose need not be proved, and that it is an insufficient response to demonstrate some rational basis for the challenged practices. It is necessary, in addition, that they be "validated" in terms of job performance * * * . However this process proceeds, it involves a more probing judicial review of, and less deference to, the seemingly reasonable acts of administrators and executives than is appropriate under the Constitution where special racial impact, without discriminatory purpose, is claimed. We are not disposed to adopt this more rigorous standard for the purposes of applying the Fifth and the Fourteenth Amendments in cases such as this.

A rule that a statute designed to serve neutral ends is nevertheless invalid, absent compelling justification, if in practice it benefits or burdens one race more than another would be far-reaching and would raise serious questions about, and perhaps invalidate, a whole range of tax, welfare, public service, regulatory, and licensing statutes that may be more burdensome to the poor and to the average black than to the more affluent white.[14]

Given that rule, such consequences would perhaps be likely to follow. However, in our view, extension of the rule beyond those areas where it is already applicable by reason of statute, such as in the field of public employment, should await legislative prescription. * * *[38]

---

[14] **[Ct's Note]** Goodman, *De Facto School Segregation: A Constitutional and Empirical Analysis,* 60 Calif.L.Rev. 275, 300 (1972), suggests that disproportionate-impact analysis might invalidate "tests and qualifications for voting, draft deferment, public employment, jury service, and other government-conferred [benefits]; [s]ales taxes, bail schedules, utility rates, bridge tolls, license fees, and other state-imposed charges." It has also been argued that minimum wage and usury laws as well as professional licensing requirements would require major modifications in light of the unequal-impact rule. William Silverman, *Equal Protection, Economic Legislation, and Racial Discrimination,* 25 Vand.L.Rev. 1183 (1972). * * *

[38] The Court also found no violation of the relevant statutory provisions. Stewart, J., joined only the constitutional aspects of the Court's opinion. Brennan, J., joined by Marshall, J., did not address the constitutional questions but dissented on statutory grounds.

JUSTICE STEVENS, concurring. * * *

The requirement of purposeful discrimination is a common thread running through the cases summarized [by the Court. But] in each of these contexts, the burden of proving a prima facie case may well involve differing evidentiary considerations. The extent of deference that one pays to the trial court's determination of the factual issue, and indeed, the extent to which one characterizes the intent issue as a question of fact or a question of law, will vary in different contexts.

Frequently the most probative evidence of intent will be objective evidence of what actually happened rather than evidence describing the subjective state of mind of the actor. For normally the actor is presumed to have intended the natural consequences of his deeds. This is particularly true in the case of governmental action which is frequently the product of compromise, of collective decisionmaking, and of mixed motivation. It is unrealistic, on the one hand, to require the victim of alleged discrimination to uncover the actual subjective intent of the decisionmaker or conversely, to invalidate otherwise legitimate action simply because an improper motive affected the deliberation of a participant in the decisional process. A law conscripting clerics should not be invalidated because an atheist voted for it.

My point [is] to suggest that the line between discriminatory purpose and discriminatory impact is not nearly as bright, and perhaps not quite as critical, as the reader of the Court's opinion might assume. I agree [that] a constitutional issue does not arise every time some disproportionate impact is shown. On the other hand, when the disproportion is as dramatic as in *Gomillion v. Lightfoot,* 364 U.S. 339 (1960),[39] or *Yick Wo,* it really does not matter whether the standard is phrased in terms of purpose or effect. * * *

There are two reasons why I am convinced that the challenge to Test 21 is insufficient. First, the test serves the neutral and legitimate purpose of requiring all applicants to meet a uniform minimum standard of literacy. Reading ability is manifestly relevant to the police function, there is no evidence that the required passing grade was set at an arbitrarily high level, and there is sufficient disparity among high schools and high school graduates to justify the use of a separate uniform test. Second, the same test is used throughout the federal service. The applicants for employment in the District of Columbia Police Department represent such a small

---

[39] In *Gomillion,* an Alabama statute changed the Tuskegee city boundaries from a square to a 28-sided figure, allegedly removing "all save only four or five of its 400 Negro voters while not removing a single white voter or resident." The Court held that the complaint "amply alleges a claim of racial discrimination" in violation of the Fifteenth Amendment: "If these allegations upon a trial remained uncontradicted or unqualified, the conclusion would be irresistible, tantamount for all practical purposes to a mathematical demonstration, that the legislation is solely concerned with segregating white and colored voters by fencing Negro citizens out of town so as to deprive them of their pre-existing municipal vote."

fraction of the total number of persons who have taken the test that their experience is of minimal probative value [to] overcome the presumption that a test which is this widely used by the Federal Government is in fact neutral in its effect as well as its "purpose" as that term is used in constitutional adjudication. * * *

NOTES AND QUESTIONS

1. **Background.** Consider Michael Klarman, *An Interpretive History of Modern Equal Protection*, 90 Mich.L.Rev. 213 (1991): "Scattered dicta in Warren Court decisions [suggested] that facially neutral legislation producing disparate racial impacts possibly violated the Equal Protection Clause regardless of legislative motivation. [But the Warren Court never definitively resolved] the constitutionality of de facto racial classifications. [The] first case [squarely raising the question whether a facially neutral statute with an underlying discriminatory intent violated equal protection] was *Palmer v. Thompson*, [403 U.S. 217 (1971), involving a city's closure of its] public swimming pools to avoid court-ordered integration. The city's action unquestionably had a constitutionally objectionable purpose, but its impact seemed nondiscriminatory: neither blacks nor whites could any longer enjoy public swimming pools. [*Palmer*] produced chaos in the courts, [including the Supreme Court, which divided 5–4 in finding no constitutional violation]. [By] emphasizing the difficulty of discerning legislative purpose, [*Palmer*] seemed to [signal that legislative purpose was irrelevant to equal protection].

"Lower courts [plausibly inferred that the Court, by rejecting an intent-based inquiry in *Palmer*,] had opted instead for the [disparate] impact theory of equal protection [under which legislation is impermissibly discriminatory, regardless of intent, if it tends to disadvantage racial minorities. They were bolstered in this conclusion] by the Court's contemporaneous interpretation of Title VII [of the 1964 Civil Rights Act in *Griggs v. Duke Power Co.*, 401 U.S. 424 (1971), as establishing] a disparate impact test" under which employment tests with discriminatory impacts were invalid unless the employer could make a showing of "business necessity."

Compare *Griffin v. County School Bd.*, discussed in Sec. 2, III, supra, which held that a municipality in Virginia could not close its schools to avoid complying with a desegregation order. Why did the Court find a constitutional violation in *Griffin* but not in *Palmer*?

2. **The discriminatory purpose requirement.** Should "racially disproportionate impact" alone suffice to trigger special judicial scrutiny under the Equal Protection Clause? Consider Tribe 2d ed., at 1516–20: "The goal of the Equal Protection Clause is not to stamp out impure thoughts, but to guarantee a full measure of human dignity for all. [Beyond] the purposeful, affirmative adoption or use of rules that disadvantage [them,] minorities can also be injured when the government is 'only' indifferent to their suffering or 'merely' blind to how prior official discrimination contributed to it and how current official acts will perpetuate it. [S]trict judicial scrutiny [should be used]

for those government acts that, given their history, context, source, and effect, seem most likely not only to perpetuate subordination but also to reflect a tradition of hostility toward an historically subjugated group, or a pattern of blindness or indifference to the interests of that group."

Compare Michael J. Perry, *The Disproportionate Impact Theory of Racial Discrimination,* 125 U.Pa.L.Rev. 540 (1977): "Laws employing a racial criterion of selection are inherently more dangerous than laws involving no racial criterion. The former, unlike the latter, directly encourage racism [and] are usually difficult if not impossible to justify on legitimate grounds. [Laws] having a disproportionate racial impact [should therefore not trigger strict scrutiny, but] the standard of review [should be] more rigorous than that required by the rational relationship test. [In] determining whether a disproportionate disadvantage is justified, a court would weigh several factors: (1) the degree of disproportion in the impact; (2) the private interest disadvantaged; (3) the efficiency of the challenged law in achieving its objective and the availability of alternative means having a less disproportionate impact; and (4) the government objective sought to be advanced."

Consider Richard H. Fallon, Jr., *Implementing the Constitution,* 111 Harv.L.Rev. 54 (1997): The Court disfavors "effects" tests that trigger elevated scrutiny based on a statute's disproportionate impact on minority groups because "the Justices believe that for courts [strictly to scrutinize] every governmental act that [disadvantages] minorities would infringe too far on [governmental decision-making]. And for courts to engage in open-ended balancing of all acts [with racially disproportionate impacts] would invite too many inquiries that are too little determined by legal rules. [The] Court believes [that] the judicial role must be cabined to protect reasonable choices by politically accountable decisionmakers against too many costly and unpredictable assessments by courts."

But compare the balancing approach that the Court prescribed in *Pike v. Bruce Church, Inc.,* Ch. 4, Sec. 2, for assessing facially neutral regulations that incidentally burden interstate commerce: "Where the statute regulates evenhandedly to effectuate a legitimate local public interest, and its effects on interstate commerce are only incidental, it will be upheld unless the burden imposed on commerce is clearly excessive in relation to the putative local benefits. If a legitimate local purpose is found, then the question becomes one of degree. And the extent of the burden that will be tolerated will of course depend on the nature of the local interest involved, and on whether it could be promoted as well with a lesser impact on interstate activities." Could a similar approach be applied to statutes that "incidentally" burden racial minorities?

3. ***Context and perspective.*** Consider David Crump, *Evidence, Race, Intent, and Evil: The Paradox of Purposelessness in the Constitutional Racial Discrimination Cases,* 27 Hofstra L.Rev. 285 (1998): "On the question of whether racial discrimination is tied to intent, [or] whether it can be unconscious and accidental, blacks and whites are sharply divided. African-Americans, in polls, tend to see racism as an ongoing and pervasive condition

of American life, while whites tend to think of it as individual actions or attitudes of bigotry that are the exception rather than the rule. Thus, whites tend to use the word 'racism' to refer to explicit and conscious belief in racial superiority. African-Americans mean something different by racism: a set of practices and institutions that result in the oppression of black people."[40] If this assertion is correct, does *Washington v. Davis* adopt a characteristically white outlook—that there can be no discrimination in the absence of personally invidious intent—and reject the perspective of minorities who regard themselves as victims of pervasive discrimination?[41]

4. ***Judicial role.*** (a) Is the Court's approach in *Davis* consistent with the theory, often traced to footnote 4 of the *Carolene Products* case, Ch. 5, Sec. 3 supra, that the courts have a special role in protecting "discrete and insular" minorities? Consider Fallon, supra: "Traditional minorities may suffer at least two types of disadvantage in the political and legislative processes. One is hostility. The other is a relative dearth of sympathy, empathy, or concern.[42] [The Court's approach gives no protection against the latter disadvantage and, in its indifference,] reflect[s] at most a thin, minimalist conception of the democratic processes to which courts are [asked] to defer."

Compare Robert W. Bennett, *"Mere" Rationality in Constitutional Law: Judicial Review and Democratic Theory,* 67 Calif.L.Rev. 1049 (1979): "If members of racial minorities statistically obtain benefits and suffer detriments as one or another piece of legislation is passed without attention to its racial impact, they are obtaining, not being deprived of, equal protection of the laws. To forbid all legislation that disadvantages them would give them the gains from political bargaining without the losses. This would be so regardless of the degree of the racially disproportionate impact or the importance of the interest affected."

(b) Is *Davis's* mandate of judicial inquiries into legislative purposes a sensible and manageable one?[43] Consider Fallon, supra: Within a doctrinal regime in which the Court frequently defers to legislative judgments, such as under the "rational basis" test, "purpose tests single out a class of cases in which" political officials "forfeit any reasonable claim to judicial deference. [In

---

[40] For an ambitious effort to develop a "New Institutional" theory of racism, which explains how entrenched assumptions and routinized patterns can produce outcomes that are unfairly skewed along racial lines even in the absence of conscious discriminatory intent, see Ian F. Haney López, *Institutional Racism: Judicial Conduct and a New Theory of Racial Discrimination,* 109 Yale L.J. 1717 (2000).

[41] See also Alan D. Freeman, *Legitimizing Racial Discrimination Through Antidiscrimination Law: A Critical Review of Supreme Court Doctrine,* 62 Minn.L.Rev. 1049 (1978) (arguing that *Davis* adopts a "perpetrator" rather than a "victim" perspective on the relevance of past race discrimination).

[42] See, e.g., Charles R. Lawrence, *The Id, the Ego, and Equal Protection: Reckoning with Unconscious Racism,* 39 Stan.L.Rev. 317 (1987).

[43] For a range of views, see, e.g., Paul Brest, Palmer v. Thompson: *An Approach to The Problem of Unconstitutional Motive,* 1971 Sup.Ct. Rev. 95; John H. Ely, *Legislative and Administrative Motivation in Constitutional Law,* 79 Yale L.J. 1205 (1970); Kenneth L. Karst, *The Costs of Motive-Centered Inquiry,* 15 San Diego L.Rev. 1163 (1978); Ashutosh Bhagwat, *Purpose Scrutiny in Constitutional Analysis,* 85 Calif.L.Rev. 297 (1997).

this sense, purpose tests are] a lowest common denominator. The [Court] can often agree that action [taken] for forbidden purposes should be invalidated, even when no majority believes that relevant constitutional norms merit the further protections that other constitutional tests [would] afford."

5. ***Intent and impact under other amendments.*** The Court strongly suggested that discriminatory impact alone (in the absence of a showing of discriminatory intent) will not establish a Fifteenth Amendment violation in *Mobile v. Bolden*, Sec. 5, I, D infra.

The Court considered the requisites for establishing a Thirteenth Amendment violation in MEMPHIS v. GREENE, 451 U.S. 100 (1981). At the behest of citizens of Hein Park, a white residential district, the city closed West Drive, a street that traversed Hein Park and was used mainly by African Americans living nearby, in part to reduce "traffic pollution," described as "noise, litter, [and] interruption of community living." The Court, per STEVENS, J., agreeing that "the adverse impact on blacks was greater than on whites," found no violation of 42 U.S.C. § 1982 [quoted in Ch. 11, Sec. 1 infra] or the Thirteenth Amendment: "[T]he critical facts established by the record are these: The city's decision to close West Drive was motivated by its interest in protecting the safety and tranquility of a residential neighborhood. The procedures followed in making the decision were fair and were not affected by any racial or other impermissible factors. The city has conferred a benefit on certain white property owners but there is no reason to believe that it would refuse to confer a comparable benefit on black property owners. The closing has not affected the value of property owned by black citizens, but it has caused some slight inconvenience to black motorists.

"[T]he record discloses no racially discriminatory motive on the part of the City Council [and] a review of the justification for the official action challenged in this case demonstrates that its disparate impact on black citizens could not [be] fairly characterized as a badge or incident of slavery.

"[To] decide the narrow constitutional question presented by this record we need not speculate about the sort of impact on a racial group that might be prohibited by the Amendment itself. We merely hold that the impact of the closing of West Drive on nonresidents of Hein Park [does] not reflect a violation of the Thirteenth Amendment."

MARSHALL, J., joined by Brennan and Blackmun, JJ., dissented: "The majority treats this case as involving nothing more than a dispute over a city's race-neutral decision to place a barrier across a road. My own examination of the record suggests [a] white community disgruntled over sharing its streets with Negroes, taking legal measures to keep out the 'undesirable traffic,' and of a city, heedless to the harm to its Negro citizens, acquiescing in the plan.

"I [do] not mean to imply that all municipal decisions that affect Negroes adversely and benefit whites are prohibited by the Thirteenth Amendment. I would, however, insist that the government carry a heavy burden of justification before I would sustain against Thirteenth Amendment challenge conduct as egregious as erection of a barrier to prevent predominantly-Negro traffic from entering a historically all-white neighborhood. [I] do not believe that the city has discharged that burden in this case, and for that reason I would hold that the erection of the barrier at the end of West Drive amounts to a badge or incident of slavery forbidden by the Thirteenth Amendment."

Although *Washington v. Davis* rejected the "disparate impact" theory and held that a facially neutral statute violates the Equal Protection Clause only if motivated by a discriminatory purpose, the Court did not address in detail what counts as a discriminatory purpose. The leading case addressing that issue involved gender, not race, but the Court's approach to identifying forbidden intent or purposes appears to be the same in both contexts.

PERSONNEL ADMINISTRATOR v. FEENEY, 442 U.S. 256 (1979), per STEWART, J., upheld Massachusetts' "absolute lifetime preference to veterans" for state civil service positions, even though "the preference operates overwhelmingly to the advantage of males": "When a statute gender-neutral on its face is challenged on the ground that its effects upon women are disproportionately adverse, a two-fold inquiry [is] appropriate. The first question is whether the statutory classification is indeed neutral * * * . If the classification itself, covert or overt, is not based upon gender, the second question is whether the adverse effect reflects invidious gender-based discrimination. In this second inquiry, impact provides an 'important starting point,' but purposeful discrimination is 'the condition that offends the Constitution.' "

As to the first question, "The District Court [found] first, that ch. 31 serves legitimate and worthy purposes; second, that the absolute preference was not established for the purpose of discriminating against women. [Thus,] the distinction between veterans and nonveterans drawn by ch. 31 is not a pretext for gender discrimination. * * *

"If the impact of this statute could not be plausibly explained on a neutral ground, impact itself would signal that the real classification made by the law was in fact not neutral. But there can be but one answer to the question whether this veteran preference excludes significant numbers of women from preferred state jobs because they are women or because they are nonveterans. [Although] few women benefit from the preference, * * * significant numbers of nonveterans are men, and all nonveterans—male as well as female—are placed at a disadvantage. Too many men are affected by ch. 31 to permit the inference that the statute is but a pretext for preferring men over women. * * *

"The dispositive question, then, is whether the appellee has shown that a gender-based discriminatory purpose has, at least in some measure, shaped [ch. 31. Her] contention that this veterans' preference is 'inherently non-neutral' or 'gender-biased' presumes that the State, by favoring veterans, intentionally incorporated into its public employment policies the panoply of sex-based and assertedly discriminatory federal laws that have prevented all but a handful of women from becoming veterans. There are two serious difficulties with this argument. First, it is wholly at odds with the District Court's central finding that Massachusetts has not offered a preference to veterans for the purpose of discriminating against women. Second, [t]o the extent that the status of veteran is one that few women have been enabled to achieve, every hiring preference for veterans, however modest or extreme, is inherently gender-biased. If Massachusetts by offering such a preference can be said intentionally to have incorporated into its state employment policies the historical gender-based federal military personnel practices, the degree of the preference would or should make no constitutional difference. Invidious discrimination does not become less so because the discrimination accomplished is of a lesser magnitude.[23] Discriminatory intent is simply not amenable to calibration. It either is a factor that has influenced the legislative choice or it is not. The District Court's conclusion that the absolute veterans' preference was not originally enacted or subsequently reaffirmed for the purpose of giving an advantage to males as such necessarily compels the conclusion that the State intended nothing more than to prefer 'veterans.' * * *

"To be sure, this case is unusual in that it involves a law that by design is not neutral. [As] opposed to the written test at issue in *Davis,* it does not purport to define a job related characteristic. To the contrary, it confers upon a specifically described group—perceived to be particularly deserving—a competitive head start. But the District Court found, and the appellee has not disputed, that this legislative choice was legitimate. [Thus, it] must be analyzed as is any other neutral law that casts a greater burden upon women as a group than upon men as a group. The enlistment policies of the armed services may well have discriminated on the basis of sex. But the history of discrimination against women in the military is not on trial in this case.

"The appellee's ultimate argument rests upon the presumption, common to the criminal and civil law, that a person intends the natural and foreseeable consequences of his voluntary actions. * * *

" 'Discriminatory purpose,' however, implies more than intent as volition or intent as awareness of consequences. It implies that the decisionmaker, in this case a state legislature, selected or reaffirmed a particular course of action at least in part 'because of,' not merely 'in spite

---

[23] **[Ct's Note]** This is not to say that the degree of impact is irrelevant to the question of intent. But it is to say that a more modest preference, while it might well lessen impact and, as the State argues, might lessen the effectiveness of the statute in helping veterans, would not be any more or less "neutral" in the constitutional sense.

of,' its adverse effects upon an identifiable group.[25] Yet nothing in the record demonstrates that this preference for veterans was originally devised or subsequently re-enacted because it would accomplish the collateral goal of keeping women in a stereotypic and predefined place in the Massachusetts Civil Service."

STEVENS, J., joined by White, J., concurred in the Court's opinion, adding: "[F]or me the answer is largely provided by the fact that the number of males disadvantaged by Massachusetts' Veterans Preference (1,867,000) is sufficiently large—and sufficiently close to the number of disadvantaged females (2,954,000)—to refute the claim that the rule was intended to benefit males as a class over females as a class."

MARSHALL, J., joined by Brennan, J., dissented: "In my judgment, [ch. 31] evinces purposeful gender-based discrimination. [That] a legislature seeks to advantage one group does not, as a matter of logic or of common sense, exclude the possibility that it also intends to disadvantage another. Individuals in general and lawmakers in particular frequently act for a variety of reasons. [S]ince reliable evidence of subjective intentions is seldom obtainable, resort to inference based on objective factors is generally unavoidable. To discern the purposes underlying facially neutral policies, this Court has therefore considered the degree, inevitability, and foreseeability of any disproportionate impact as well as the alternatives reasonably available.

"[T]he impact of the Massachusetts statute on women is undisputed. Any veteran with a passing grade on the civil service exam must be placed ahead of a nonveteran, regardless of their respective scores. [Because] less than 2% of the women in Massachusetts are veterans, the absolute preference formula has rendered desirable state civil service employment an almost exclusively male prerogative. [Where] the foreseeable impact of a facially neutral policy is so disproportionate, the burden should rest on the State to establish that sex-based considerations played no part in the choice of the particular legislative scheme.

"Clearly, that burden was not sustained here. The legislative history of the statute reflects the Commonwealth's patent appreciation of the impact the preference system would have on women, and an equally evident desire to mitigate that impact only with respect to certain traditionally female occupations. Until 1971, the statute [and] regulations

---

[25] **[Ct's Note]** This is not to say that the inevitability or foreseeability of consequences of a neutral rule has no bearing upon the existence of discriminatory intent. Certainly, when the adverse consequences of a law upon an identifiable group are as inevitable as the gender-based consequences of ch. 31, a strong inference that the adverse effects were desired can reasonably be drawn. But in this inquiry—made as it is under the Constitution—an inference is a working tool, not a synonym for proof. When as here, the impact is essentially an unavoidable consequence of a legislative policy that has in itself always been deemed to be legitimate, and when, as here, the statutory history and all of the available evidence affirmatively demonstrate the opposite, the inference simply fails to ripen into proof.

exempted from operation of the preference any job requisitions 'especially calling for women.' In practice, this exemption, coupled with the absolute preference for veterans, has created a gender-based civil service hierarchy, with women occupying low grade clerical and secretarial jobs and men holding more responsible and remunerative positions. [Particularly] when viewed against the range of less discriminatory alternatives available to assist veterans,[2] Massachusetts's choice of a formula that so severely restricts public employment opportunities for women cannot reasonably be thought gender-neutral. The Court's conclusion to the contrary—that 'nothing in the record' evinces a 'collateral goal of keeping women in a stereotypic and predefined place in the Massachusetts Civil Service'— displays a singularly myopic view of the facts established below.[3]"

NOTES AND QUESTIONS

1. ***The Court's definition of discriminatory purpose.*** Consider the argument of Ian Haney-Lopez, *Intentional Blindness,* 87 NYU L.Rev. 1779 (2012), that although the modern doctrine requiring proof of invidious mental states to establish racially discriminatory intent is often traced to *Washington v. Davis, Davis* actually assumed the continuing validity of a "contextual approach" that drew inferences of racially discriminatory purpose from surrounding contexts and "focused on motives only in the loosest sense (and sometimes not at all)." According to Professor Haney-Lopez, the requirement "that plaintiffs prove a state of mind akin to malice on the part of an identified state action"—which "is so exacting that [the Court has never found it to be] met"—originated in *Personnel Administrator v. Feeney* and is part of an overall doctrinal structure "that might best be termed [one of] 'intentional blindness'" to continuing racial discrimination against non-whites.

See also Reva Siegel, *Why Equal Protection No Longer Protects: The Evolving Forms of Status-Enforcing State Action,* 49 Stan.L.Rev. 1111 (1997), arguing that "discriminatory purpose, as discussed in [*Feeney* and other cases], is a juridical concept that does not reflect prevailing understandings of the ways in which racial or gender bias operates, but instead functions to protect the prerogatives of coordinate branches of government." Should decision-making affected by race- or gender-based assumptions be counted as reflecting discriminatory intent even when taken merely "in spite of," not "because of" its adverse effects upon an identifiable group"? Stated another way, should courts consider unconscious or implicit biases when determining whether government action violates the Equal Protection Clause?

---

[2] **[Ct's Note]** Only four States afford a preference comparable in scope. . . . Other States and the Federal Government grant point or tie-breaking preferences that do not foreclose opportunities for women.

[3] **[Ct's Note]** Although it is relevant that the preference statute also disadvantages a substantial group of men, it is equally pertinent that 47% of Massachusetts men over 18 are veterans, as compared to 0.8% of Massachusetts women. Given this disparity, and the indicia of intent noted supra, the absolute number of men denied preference cannot be dispositive, especially since they have not faced the barriers to achieving veteran status confronted by women.

2. ***Reversed roles.*** Should and would the Court find a "discriminatory purpose" if the challenged law would not have been passed "if its racial impact had been reversed—if the disparate impact had been on whites rather than on blacks"? Eric Schnapper, *Two Categories of Discriminatory Intent,* 17 Harv.C.R.-C.L.L.Rev. 31 (1982). Is this an inquiry that a court is competent to conduct? Consider id.: "The central issue [in *Feeney*] is whether Massachusetts would have adopted in 1896 a veterans' preference [that would have excluded 98% of all male applicants] or would have amended its statutes successively in 1919, 1943, 1949, and 1968 to assure such preferential treatment for new generations of predominantly female veterans. The all too familiar history of discrimination on the basis of sex in this country renders implausible the suggestion."[44]

Since *Washington v. Davis* and in light of *Feeney*, the Court has struggled recurrently with problems of proof in cases alleging discriminatory motives or purposes. As you read the next case and the notes that follow, consider what general principles, if any, govern the requisite inquiry.

ARLINGTON HEIGHTS v. METROPOLITAN HOUSING DEV. CORP., 429 U.S. 252 (1977), per POWELL, J., held that petitioner Village's refusal to rezone land from single-family (R–3) to multiple-family (R–5), thereby blocking respondent's proposed construction of racially integrated housing, did not violate equal protection:

"*Davis* does not require a plaintiff to prove that the challenged action rested solely on racially discriminatory purposes. Rarely can it be said that a legislature or administrative body operating under a broad mandate made a decision motivated solely by a single concern, or even that a particular purpose was the 'dominant' or 'primary' one. In fact, it is because legislators and administrators are properly concerned with balancing numerous competing considerations that courts refrain from reviewing the merits of their decisions, absent a showing of arbitrariness or irrationality. But racial discrimination is not just another competing consideration. When there is proof that a discriminatory purpose has been a motivating factor in the decision, this judicial deference is no longer justified.

"Determining whether invidious discriminatory purpose was a motivating factor demands a sensitive inquiry into such circumstantial and direct evidence of intent as may be available. The impact of the official action [may] provide an important starting point. Sometimes a clear pattern, unexplainable on grounds other than race, emerges from the effect of the state action even when the governing legislation appears neutral on its face. *Yick Wo*; *Guinn v. United States,* 238 U.S. 347 (1915); *Lane v.*

----

[44] For detailed development of this approach, see also David A. Strauss, *Discriminatory Intent and the Taming of* Brown, 56 U.Chi.L.Rev. 935 (1989).

Wilson, 307 U.S. 268 (1939);[45] *Gomillion.* The evidentiary inquiry is then relatively easy. But such cases are rare. Absent a pattern as stark as that in *Gomillion* or *Yick Wo,* impact alone is not determinative,[14] and the Court must look to other evidence.

"The historical background of the decision is one evidentiary source, particularly if it reveals a series of official actions taken for invidious purposes. See *Lane.* The specific sequence of events leading up to the challenged decision also may shed some light on the decision-maker's purposes. *Reitman v. Mulkey,* [Ch. 10, Sec. 3]. For example, if the property involved here always had been zoned R–5 but suddenly was changed to R–3 when the town learned of MHDC's plans to erect integrated housing, we would have a far different case. Departures from the normal procedural sequence also might afford evidence that improper purposes are playing a role. Substantive departures too may be relevant, particularly if the factors usually considered important by the decisionmaker strongly favor a decision contrary to the one reached.

"The legislative or administrative history may be highly relevant, especially where there are contemporary statements by members of the decisionmaking body, minutes of its meetings, or reports. In some extraordinary instances the members might be called to the stand at trial to testify concerning the purpose of the official action, although even then such testimony frequently will be barred by privilege. See *Tenney v. Brandhove,* 341 U.S. 367 (1951); *United States v. Nixon,* [Ch. 3, Sec. 3].[18]

Both courts below found that the rezoning denial was not racially motivated. "We also have reviewed the evidence. The impact of the Village's decision does arguably bear more heavily on racial minorities. [But] there is little about the sequence of events leading up to the decision that would spark suspicion. The area [has] been zoned R–3 since 1959, the year when Arlington Heights first adopted a zoning map. Single-family homes surround the 80-acre site, and the Village is undeniably committed to single-family homes as its dominant residential land use. The rezoning request progressed according to the usual procedures. * * *

---

[45] *Guinn* held that Oklahoma's literacy test for voting violated the Fifteenth Amendment because its "grandfather clause" effectively exempted whites. Oklahoma then immediately enacted a new law providing that all persons who previously voted were qualified for life but that all others must register within a twelve day period or be permanently disenfranchised. *Lane* held that this new law violated the Fifteenth Amendment.

[14] **[Ct's Note]** This is not to say that a consistent pattern of official racial discrimination is a necessary predicate to a violation of [equal protection]. A single invidiously discriminatory governmental act—in the exercise of the zoning power as elsewhere—would not necessarily be immunized by the absence of such discrimination in the making of other comparable decisions.

[18] **[Ct's Note]** This Court has recognized, ever since *Fletcher v. Peck* [Ch. 5, Sec. 1, I], that judicial inquiries into legislative or executive motivation represent a substantial intrusion into the workings of other branches of government. Placing a decisionmaker on the stand is therefore "usually to be avoided."

"The statements by the Plan Commission and Village Board members, as reflected in the official minutes, focused almost exclusively on the zoning aspects of the MHDC petition, and the zoning factors on which they relied are not novel criteria in the Village's rezoning decisions. * * * MHDC called one member of the Village Board to the stand at trial. Nothing in her testimony supports an inference of invidious purpose.

"In sum, [r]espondents simply failed to carry their burden of proving that discriminatory purpose was a motivating factor in the Village's decision.[21] This conclusion ends the constitutional inquiry."

NOTES AND QUESTIONS

1. *Consequences of "discriminatory purpose."* If it is found that a law "was motivated by a racially discriminatory purpose," should the state be permitted to prove "that the same decision would have resulted had the impermissible purpose not been considered"? *Arlington Heights,* fn. 21. Or should the Court invalidate a racially motivated law and "remand to the legislature for a reconsideration [on] the basis of purely legitimate factors"? Robert G. Schwemm, *From* Washington *to* Arlington Heights *and Beyond: Discriminatory Purpose in Equal Protection Litigation*, 1977 U.Ill.L.F. 961.

2. *Proving intentional discrimination in administration of a law.*

(a) *Jury selection.* In CASTANEDA v. PARTIDA, 430 U.S. 482 (1977), respondent, a criminal defendant, challenged the grand jury that indicted him in 1972. He showed that, though 79% of the county's population had Spanish surnames, the average percentage of Spanish-surnamed grand jurors between 1962–72 was 39%. In 1972, 52.5% of persons on the county's grand jury list had Spanish surnames, as did 50% of those on the list of grand jurors that indicted the respondent. The Court, per BLACKMUN, J., held that respondent had made a prima facie case of discrimination against Mexican-Americans: "While the earlier cases involved absolute exclusion of an identifiable group, later cases established the principle that substantial underrepresentation of the group constitutes a constitutional violation as well, if it results from purposeful discrimination. [T]he degree of underrepresentation must be proved, by comparing the proportion of the group in the total population to the proportion called to serve as grand jurors, over a significant period of time. [If] a disparity is sufficiently large, then it is unlikely that it is due solely to chance or accident, and, in the absence of evidence to the contrary, one must conclude that racial or other class-related factors entered into the selection process. [A] selection procedure that is susceptible of abuse [such as the Texas procedure under

---

[21] **[Ct's Note]** Proof that the decision by the Village was motivated in part by a racially discriminatory purpose would not necessarily have required invalidation of the challenged decision. Such proof would, however, have shifted to the Village the burden of establishing that the same decision would have resulted even had the impermissible purpose not been considered. If this were established, the complaining party in a case of this kind no longer fairly could attribute the injury complained of to improper consideration of a discriminatory purpose.

which jury commissioners had broad discretion in compiling grand jury lists] or is not racially neutral [also] supports the presumption of discrimination raised by the statistical showing. Once the defendant has shown substantial underrepresentation of his group, he has made out a prima facie case of discriminatory purpose, and the burden then shifts to the State to rebut that case."

Should the state's proof that a majority of the jury commissioners were Mexican-American rebut the prima facie case? See *Castaneda* (answering in the negative).[46]

(b) ***Selective prosecution.*** According to David Cole, *No Equal Justice* 159 (1999), there are "no reported federal or state cases since 1886 that [have] dismissed a criminal prosecution on the ground that the prosecutor acted for racial reasons."[47]

UNITED STATES v. ARMSTRONG, 517 U.S. 456 (1996), per REHNQUIST, C.J., held that the defendants had failed to make out a prima facie case of racially selective prosecution in cases involving the sale and possession of cocaine and thus were not entitled to discovery on the issue of prosecutorial intent to discriminate. The evidence showed that all 24 defendants in "crack" cocaine cases closed by a Public Defender's office in the Central District of California during the previous year were black. In addition, the defendants submitted "an affidavit alleging that an intake coordinator at a drug treatment center had told her that there are 'an equal number of caucasian users and dealers to minority users and dealers,' [an] affidavit from a criminal defense attorney alleging that in his experience many nonblacks are prosecuted in state court for crack offenses, and a newspaper article reporting that Federal 'crack criminals [are] being punished far more severely than if they had been caught with powder cocaine, and almost every single one of them is black.' " But this was not enough: "the claimant must show that similarly situated individuals of a different race were not prosecuted."[48] STEVENS, J., dissented: "I am persuaded that the District Judge did not abuse her discretion when she

---

[46] For a detailed study of the Los Angeles superior court's grand juror selection process, and the conclusion that although the judges "exhibit no purposeful embrace of racial discrimination, they nevertheless" act repeatedly in ways that reflect and enforce the significance of racial status, see Ian F. Haney-Lopez, *Institutional Racism: Judicial Conduct and a New Theory of Racial Discrimination*, 109 Yale L.J. 1717 (2000).

[47] According to Gabriel J. Chin, *Unexplainable on Grounds of Race: Doubts About* Yick Wo, 2008 U.Ill.L.Rev. 1359, *Yick Wo* was really a due process case, predicated on the existence of a constitutionally protected property right in operating a laundry, and the case's lengthy equal protection discussion occurs only because, within the jurisprudence of the time, every due process violation was also an equal protection violation.

[48] For the suggestion that the *Armstrong* standard is virtually impossible to meet, and indeed establishes a nearly insurmountable bar to "obtaining discovery of information that would help to prove discriminatory intent when it does exist," see Angela J. Davis, *Prosecution and Race: The Power and Privilege of Discretion*, 67 Fordham L.Rev. 13 (1998).

concluded that the factual showing was sufficiently disturbing to require some response from the United States Attorney's Office."[49]

If users of crack cocaine are disproportionately black, whereas users of powder cocaine are disproportionately white, is it prima facie evidence of race discrimination if legislatures enact higher penalties for possession of crack cocaine than for possession of powder cocaine? If police and prosecutors devote far more resources to crack cocaine than to powder cocaine cases? See Note, 19 Cardozo L.Rev. 1149 (1997). Compare Kate Stith, *The Government Interest in Criminal Law: Whose Interest Is It, Anyway?*, in *Public Values in Constitutional Law* 158 (Stephen E. Gottlieb ed. 1993): "While it appears true that the enhanced penalties for crack cocaine more often fall upon black defendants, the legislature's action might also have been a laudatory attempt to provide enhanced protection to those communities—largely black * * *—who are ravaged by abuse of this potent drug." See also Randall Kennedy, *Race, Crime, and the Law* 369–75 (1997) (arguing that inadequate protection from law enforcement has harmed black communities as much if not more than selective prosecution and mistreatment of black criminal defendants).

(c) *Executive appointments.* In MAYOR OF PHILA. v. EDUCATIONAL EQUALITY LEAGUE, 415 U.S. 605 (1974), respondents contended that in 1971 the mayor had racially discriminated in appointments to the city's Nominating Panel for school board members. Approximately "34% of the population of Philadelphia and approximately 60% of the students attending the city's various schools were Negroes" but "the 1971 Panel had 11 whites and two Negroes." The Court, per POWELL, J., held the proof "too fragmentary and speculative" to establish "a prima facie case of racial discrimination." The statistics were "simplistic percentage comparisons [in] the context of this case"; because of the designated qualifications for Panel members, it could not "be assumed that all citizens are fungible for purposes of determining whether members of a particular class have been unlawfully excluded."[50]

3. *Peremptory challenges.* BATSON v. KENTUCKY, 476 U.S. 79 (1986), per POWELL, J.—declining to follow *Swain v. Alabama,* 380 U.S. 202 (1965)—held that, using the same "combination of factors" as in cases such as *Castaneda,* "a defendant may establish a prima facie case of purposeful discrimination in selection of the petit jury solely on evidence concerning the prosecutor's exercise of peremptory challenges at the defendant's trial. [Then], the burden shifts to the State to come forward with a neutral explanation for challenging black jurors. [T]he prosecution's explanation need not rise to the level justifying exercise of a challenge for cause. [B]ut the prosecutor may not rebut the defendant's prima facie case of discrimination by stating merely that he challenged jurors of the defendant's race on the assumption—or his intuitive judgment—that they would be partial to the defendant because of

---

[49] The Court has held in other cases that the trial court's decision on the ultimate question of discriminatory intent represents a finding of fact of the sort accorded great deference on appeal, particularly on issues of credibility. See, e.g., *Hernandez v. New York,* 500 U.S. 352 (1991).

[50] White, J., joined by Douglas, Brennan, and Marshall, JJ., dissented.

their shared race, [because the] core guarantee of equal protection, ensuring citizens that their State will not discriminate on account of race, would be meaningless" if this were permitted.

REHNQUIST, J., joined by Burger, C.J., dissented: "[T]here is simply nothing 'unequal' about the State using its peremptory challenges to strike blacks from the jury in cases involving black defendants, so long as such challenges are also used to exclude whites in cases involving white defendants, Hispanics in cases involving Hispanic defendants, Asians in cases involving Asian defendants, and so on."[51]

4. ***Capital sentencing.*** McCLESKEY v. KEMP, the facts of which are set forth in detail in Ch. 6, Sec. 5, III, per POWELL, J., rejected the claim of a black petitioner subject to a sentence of death "that the Baldus study [finding that black defendants who, like the petitioner, were charged with killing white victims were far more likely to be sentenced to death than other accused killers] compels an inference that his sentence rests on purposeful discrimination." Unlike the jury selection cases, where "the factors that may be considered are limited, usually by state [statute], each particular decision to impose the death penalty is made by a [jury] unique in its composition, and the Constitution requires that its decision rest on consideration of innumerable factors that vary according to the characteristics of the individual defendant and the facts of the particular capital offense." Further, unlike the jury selection context, "here, the State has no practical opportunity to rebut the Baldus study" because "policy considerations" (1) "dictate that jurors [not] be called [to] testify to the motives and influences that led to their verdict" and (2) "suggest the impropriety of our requiring prosecutors to defend their decisions to seek death penalties, often years after they were made." Furthermore, "[r]equiring a prosecutor to rebut a study that analyzes the past conduct of scores of prosecutors is quite different from requiring a prosecutor to rebut a contemporaneous challenge to his own acts. See *Batson*." Finally, implementation of laws against murder, which are "at the heart of the State's criminal justice system, [requires] discretionary judgments. [W]e would

---

[51] *Georgia v. McCollum*, 505 U.S. 42 (1992), per Blackmun, J., extended *Batson* and *Edmonson v. Leesville Concrete Co.*, 500 U.S. 614 (1991) (holding *Batson* applicable to civil litigants), to peremptory challenges by a criminal defendant: "Just as public confidence in criminal justice is undermined by a conviction in a trial where racial discrimination has occurred in jury selection, so is public confidence undermined where a defendant, assisted by racially discriminatory peremptory strikes, obtains an acquittal."

O'Connor and Scalia, JJ., dissented on the ground that there was no "state action" (as discussed in her dissent in *Edmonson*). Rehnquist, C.J. and Thomas, J., agreed, but concurred in the judgment because "*Edmonson* governs this case." On the merits, Thomas, J., added: "In *Strauder*, we put the rights of defendants foremost. Today's decision, while protecting jurors, leaves defendants with less means of protecting themselves. [B]lack criminal defendants will rue the day that this court ventured down this road that inexorably will lead to the elimination of peremptory strikes."

Subsequent cases make clear that *Batson* challenges are very difficult but not impossible to establish. *See, e.g., Snyder v. Louisiana*, 552 U.S. 472 (2008) (upholding a *Batson* challenge on the ground that a prosecutor's explanation for the exercise of a peremptory challenge was clearly pretextual).

demand exceptionally clear proof before we would infer that the discretion has been abused."

BLACKMUN, J., joined by Brennan, Marshall, and Stevens, JJ., dissented, reviewing parts of the Baldus study in detail: "I concentrate on the decisions within the prosecutor's office through which the State decided to seek the death penalty and, in particular, the point at which the State proceeded to the penalty phase after conviction. This is a step at which the evidence of the effect of the racial factors was especially strong" and not adequately rebutted by the state.

"I agree [as] to the difficulty of examining the jury's decisionmaking process [but not with the] Court's refusal to require that the prosecutor provide an explanation for his actions * * * . Prosecutors undoubtedly need adequate discretion to allocate the resources of their offices and to fulfill their responsibilities to the public in deciding how best to enforce the law, but this does not place them beyond the constraints imposed on state action under the Fourteenth Amendment."

Does *McCleskey* absolutely foreclose selective prosecution claims involving the death penalty, or only establish that the Baldus study is not enough by itself to make out a prima facie case?[52] If the latter, what kind of showing would a challenger need to make? See John H. Blume, Theodore Eisenberg & Sheri Lynn Johnson, *Post-McCleskey Racial Discrimination Claims in Capital Cases*, 83 Cornell L.Rev. 1771 (1998) (arguing that *McCleskey* has led lower courts to wrongly reject selective prosecution challenges to capital sentences even where the challenge would, in "any other equal protection context," establish a prima facie case for unconstitutional race discrimination).

Consider Cass R. Sunstein & Adrian Vermeule, *Is Capital Punishment Morally Required? Acts, Omissions, and Life-Life Tradeoffs,* 58 Stan.L.Rev. 703 (2005): "[M]ost murder is intraracial, not interracial. African-Americans are disproportionately victims of homicide, and their murderers are disproportionately African-American. For this reason, they have a great deal to gain from capital punishment if it does have a deterrent effect—very plausibly more, on balance, than white people do."

5.   *The "myth of intent"?* Is it fair to say that the Court requires individualized showings of discriminatory intent by relevant officials in *Armstrong* and *McCleskey*, but that it accepts general statistical evidence as

---

[52]   The Baldus study's strongest evidence of race-based disparities did not involve the race of the criminal defendant, but rather the race of the victim. If a criminal defendant (whether black or white) is targeted for the death penalty for having killed a white (rather than a black) victim, is the criminal defendant the victim of a racially discriminatory intent? Does this depend on what counts as a racially discriminatory intent? See Evan Tsen Lee & Ashutosh Bhagwat, *The* McCleskey *Puzzle: Remedying Prosecutorial Discrimination Against Black Victims in Capital Sentencing,* 1998 Sup.Ct.Rev. 145.

highly probative in *Castaneda* and *Batson*?[53] Consider the suggestion of David Crump, *Evidence, Race, Intent, and Evil: The Paradox of Purposelessness in Constitutional Racial Discrimination Cases*, 27 Hofstra L.Rev. 285 (1998), that the Court's willingness to find discriminatory intent may depend partly on whether a finding of discriminatory intent would have remedial implications that the Court would find difficult or unacceptable: "In *McCleskey*, if one were to find a violation, it would be difficult to conceive a complete judicial remedy unless the State were either to abolish jury determinations of death sentences or to abolish capital punishment. In the driving while black situation [involving accusations that police tend to stop disproportionately large numbers of minority motorists], systematic judicial responses [requiring a racially proportionate number of stops] might interfere unacceptably with the government's responsibility to enforce traffic laws that benefit members of all races."

See also Richard H. McAdams, *Race and Selective Prosecution: Discovering the Pitfalls of* Armstrong, 73 Chi.-Kent L.Rev. 605 (1998): *Armstrong* creates a situation in which "the defendant 'cannot obtain discovery unless she first makes a threshold showing [of] selective prosecution. [Yet] making a sufficient preliminary showing of discriminatory intent may be impossible without some discovery.' [As a result,] many meritorious claims will never be proven. [The] tradeoff implicit in *Armstrong* [can] be justified only by great hostility to the selective prosecution doctrine itself. [The Court appears to believe] that there are no 'meritorious' selective prosecution claims, either because there is no selective prosecution or because selectively prosecuted defendants should not be entitled to the relief they seek—dismissal of the charge."

In the view of Daniel R. Ortiz, *The Myth of Intent in Equal Protection*, 41 Stan.L.Rev. 1105 (1989), the Court has used the allocation of burdens of proof of discriminatory purpose to obscure its own "balancing of competing individual and public interests" and its making "many of the ultimate value choices implicit in equal protection."[54]

V. AFFIRMATIVE ACTION

Prior to *Brown v. Board of Education*, public policies that drew race-based distinctions almost invariably did so for the purpose of advantaging whites by disadvantaging racial minorities. In the decades that followed, however, some state universities and other public institutions began to implement "affirmative action" programs that expressly took race into account not to exclude racial minorities but to increase their representation

---

[53] See generally Sheila Foster, *Intent and Incoherence*, 72 Tul.L.Rev. 1065 (1998) (reviewing leading cases and arguing that the Court effectively accepts different concepts of intent, and transparently applies different burdens of proof, in different contexts).

[54] See also Michael Selmi, *Proving Discrimination: The Reality of Supreme Court Rhetoric*, 86 Geo.L.J. 279 (1997) (arguing that "the Court never fully embraced its own rhetoric" and that the Justices have "acted like the political branches by treating the issue of race as a subject for compromise and continually subjugating concerns of racial equality to other purported interests").

in higher education, employment, and government contracts. Affirmative action programs raise a variety of issues under the Equal Protection Clause. One involves the appropriate standard of judicial review: Should strict judicial scrutiny be triggered whenever the government classifies on the basis of race, or only when racial classifications disadvantage "discrete and insular minorities," see *United States v. Carolene Products*, as opposed to the white majority? Are all race-based classifications inherently objectionable, or only those that subordinate or stigmatize on the basis of race? A second issue involves government purposes in implementing affirmative action programs. Are some, such as remedying past discrimination or promoting diversity, more weighty or acceptable than others (such as achieving racial proportionality, for example)? If affirmative action is ever acceptable, a third question is which groups are constitutionally acceptable beneficiaries. A fourth involves the demands that the Constitution places on the structure of programs designed to serve constitutionally acceptable ends (if there are any). For example, are targets or goals that allow for exceptions more acceptable than rigid quotas, and if so, why? In examining these and other questions, this subsection begins with cases involving affirmative action programs in public higher education. It then considers the slightly different issues presented by affirmative action programs in the context of public employment and government contracts.

A. Affirmative Action in Higher Education

The first major affirmative action case to be decided by the Supreme Court on the merits, REGENTS OF UNIV. OF CALIFORNIA v. BAKKE, 438 U.S. 265 (1978), presented a challenge to the affirmative action program of the Medical School of the University of California at Davis, which reserved 16 out of 100 places in its entering class for members of minority groups, which the University defined as "Blacks," "Chicanos," "Asians," and "American Indians." The constitutionality of the program was challenged by Allan Bakke, a white male applicant who was rejected, even though some applicants were admitted under the affirmative action program who had "significantly lower" grade point averages and test scores. The issues presented by the case divided the Court almost literally down the middle. Four Justices—Burger, C.J., and Stewart, Rehnquist, and Stevens, JJ.—believed that a federal statute, Title VI of the 1964 Civil Rights Act, forbade schools receiving federal funds from taking any account of race in their admissions processes. Four other Justices—Brennan, White, Marshall, and Blackmun—concluded that all aspects of the Medical School's policy passed muster under a level of judicial scrutiny less searching than "strict scrutiny." With the Court thus divided, the determining vote lay with Justice Lewis Powell, who sought to stake out an intermediate position in an opinion that was not joined in some critical sections by even a single other Justice.

In a part of his opinion joined by Brennan, White, Marshall, and Blackmun, JJ., POWELL, J., first found that Title VI of the Civil Rights Act of 1964—which provides that "No person in the United States shall, on the ground of race, color, or national origin, be excluded from participation in, be denied the benefits of, or be subjected to discrimination under any program or activity receiving Federal financial assistance"—proscribes "only those racial classifications that would violate the Equal Protection Clause or the Fifth Amendment." Then, writing mostly only for himself, he turned to the equal protection arguments: "[P]etitioner argues that the court below erred in applying strict scrutiny to the special admissions program because white males, such as respondent, are not a 'discrete and insular minority' requiring extraordinary protection from the majoritarian political process. *Carolene Products Co.,* n. 4 [Ch. 5, Sec. 3, supra. These] characteristics may be relevant in deciding whether or not to add new types of classifications to the list of 'suspect' categories or whether a particular classification survives close examination. Racial and ethnic classifications, however, are subject to stringent examination without regard to these additional characteristics.

"[This] perception of racial and ethnic distinctions is rooted in our Nation's constitutional and demographic history. [T]he white 'majority' itself is composed of various minority groups, most of which can lay claim to a history of prior discrimination at the hands of the State and private individuals. [It] is the individual who is entitled to judicial protection against classifications based upon his racial or ethnic background. [When legal classifications] touch upon an individual's race or ethnic background, he is entitled to a judicial determination that the burden he is asked to bear on that basis is precisely tailored to serve a compelling governmental interest.

"[The] special admissions program purports to serve the purposes of: (i) 'reducing the historic deficit of traditionally disfavored minorities in medical schools and the medical profession,' (ii) countering the effects of societal discrimination; (iii) increasing the number of physicians who will practice in communities currently underdeserved; and (iv) obtaining the educational benefits that flow from an ethnically diverse student body.

"[If] petitioner's purpose is to assure within its student body some specified percentage of a particular group merely because of its race or ethnic origin, such a preferential purpose must be rejected not as insubstantial but as facially invalid. Preferring members of any one group for no reason other than race or ethnic origin is discrimination for its own sake. This the Constitution forbids. E.g., *Loving; Brown.*

"The State certainly has a legitimate and substantial interest in ameliorating, or eliminating where feasible, the disabling effects of identified discrimination. [That] goal [is] far more focused than the remedying of the effects of 'societal discrimination,' an amorphous concept of injury that [would *not* provide a compelling justification for affirmative action]. We have never approved a classification that aids persons perceived as members of relatively victimized groups at the expense of other innocent individuals in the absence of judicial, legislative, or administrative findings of constitutional or statutory violations. [Without] such findings of constitutional or statutory violations, [which have not been made in this case,] it cannot be said that the government has any greater interest in helping one individual than in refraining from harming another. [To] hold otherwise would be to convert a remedy heretofore reserved for violations of legal rights into a privilege that all institutions throughout the Nation could grant at their pleasure to whatever groups are perceived as victims of societal discrimination.

"Petitioner identifies, as another purpose of its program, improving the delivery of health-care services to communities currently underserved. It may be assumed that in some situations a State's interest in facilitating the health care of its citizens is sufficiently compelling to support the use of a suspect classification. But there is virtually no evidence in the record indicating that petitioner's special admissions program is either needed or geared to promote that goal. The court below addressed this failure of proof: 'The University concedes it cannot assure that minority doctors who entered under the program, all of whom express an 'interest' in participating in a disadvantaged community, will actually do so.'

"[The] fourth goal asserted by petitioner is the attainment of a diverse student body. This is clearly a permissible goal for an institution of higher education. Academic freedom, though not a specifically enumerated constitutional right, long has been viewed as a special concern of the First Amendment. [Thus,] in arguing that its universities must be accorded the right to select those students who will contribute the most to the 'robust exchange of ideas', petitioner invokes a countervailing constitutional interest, [and] must be viewed as seeking to achieve a goal that is of paramount importance in the fulfillment of its mission. * * *

"Ethnic diversity, however, is only one element in a range of factors a university properly may consider in attaining the goal of a heterogeneous student body. Although a university must have wide discretion in making the sensitive judgments as to who should be admitted, constitutional limitations protecting individual rights may not be disregarded. [As] the interest of diversity is compelling in the context of a university's admissions program, the question remains whether the program's racial classification is necessary to promote this interest.

"[P]etitioner's argument that this is the only effective means of serving the interest of diversity is seriously flawed. [The] diversity that furthers a compelling state interest encompasses a far broader array of qualifications and characteristics of which racial or ethnic origin is but a single though important element. Petitioner's special admissions program, focused *solely* on ethnic diversity, would hinder rather than further attainment of genuine diversity. * * * "

Powell, J., then referred favorably to the Harvard College admissions program, under which, "when the Committee on Admissions reviews the large middle group of applicants who are 'admissible' and deemed capable of doing good work in their courses, the race of an applicant may tip the balance in his favor just as geographic origin or a life spent on a farm may tip the balance in other candidates' cases. [This] kind of program treats each applicant as an individual in the admissions process. The applicant who loses out [to] another candidate receiving a 'plus' on the basis of ethnic background will not have been foreclosed from all consideration simply because he was not the right color or had the wrong surname. It would mean only that his combined qualifications, which may have included similar nonobjective factors, did not outweigh those of the other applicant. His qualifications would have been weighed fairly and competitively and he would have no basis to complain of unequal treatment under the Fourteenth Amendment."

Because the Medical School had applied a quota system, Powell, J., found it invalid, despite his recognition that a properly tailored affirmative action program designed to promote diversity could survive strict judicial scrutiny.

In a joint opinion, BRENNAN, WHITE, MARSHALL, AND BLACKMUN, JJ., concurred in part and dissented in part: "[C]laims that law must be 'color-blind' or that the datum of race is no longer relevant to public policy must be seen as aspiration rather than as description of reality. [We] cannot [let] color blindness become myopia which masks the reality that many 'created equal' have been treated within our lifetimes as inferior both by the law and by their fellow citizens.

"[A] government practice or statute which [contains] 'suspect classifications' is to be subjected to 'strict scrutiny.' [But] whites as a class [do not] have any of the traditional indicia of suspectness: the class is not saddled with such disabilities, or subjected to such a history of purposeful unequal treatment, or relegated to such a position of political powerlessness as to command extraordinary protection from the majoritarian political process.

"[On] the other hand, the fact that this case does not fit neatly into our prior analytic framework for race cases does not mean that it should be analyzed by applying the very loose rational-basis [standard]. Instead, a number of considerations—developed in gender discrimination cases but which carry even more force when applied to racial classifications—lead us to conclude that racial classifications designed to further remedial purposes 'must serve important governmental objectives and must be substantially related to achievement of those objectives.' *Craig v. Boren,* [Sec. 3, I infra].

"[Davis'] articulated purpose of remedying the effects of past societal discrimination is, under our cases, sufficiently important to justify the use of race-conscious admissions programs where there is a sound basis for concluding that minority underrepresentation is substantial and chronic, and that the handicap of past discrimination is impeding access of minorities to the medical school.

"[Davis] had a sound basis for believing that the problem of underrepresentation of minorities was substantial and chronic and that the problem was attributable to handicaps imposed on minority applicants by past and present racial discrimination. [For] example, the entering classes in 1968 and 1969 [included] only 1 Chicano and 2 Negroes out of the 50 admittees for each year. [A]s petitioner argues, there are no practical means by which it could achieve its ends in the foreseeable future without the use of race-conscious measures. With respect to any factor (such as poverty or family educational background) that may be used as a substitute for race as an indicator of past discrimination, whites greatly outnumber racial minorities simply because whites make up a far larger percentage of the total population and therefore far outnumber minorities in absolute terms at every socio-economic level. * * *

"Finally, Davis' special admissions program cannot be said to violate the Constitution simply because it has set aside a predetermined number of places for qualified minority applicants rather than using minority status as a positive factor to be considered in evaluating the applications of disadvantaged minority applicants. For purposes of constitutional adjudication, there is no difference between the two approaches. In any admissions program which accords special consideration to disadvantaged racial minorities, a determination of the degree of preference to be given is unavoidable, and any given preference that results in the exclusion of a white candidate is no more or less constitutionally acceptable than a program such as that at Davis."

MARSHALL, J., also wrote a separate opinion: "[I]t must be remembered that, during most of the past 200 years, the Constitution as interpreted by this Court did not prohibit the most ingenious and pervasive forms of discrimination against the Negro. Now, when a State acts to remedy the effects of that legacy of discrimination, I cannot believe that this same Constitution stands as a barrier. [In] light of the sorry history of discrimination and its devastating impact on the lives of Negroes, bringing the Negro into the mainstream of American life should be a state interest of the highest order. To fail to do so is to ensure that America will forever remain a divided society. * * *

"Since the Congress that considered and rejected the objections to the 1866 Freedmen's Bureau Act concerning special relief to Negroes also proposed the Fourteenth Amendment, it is inconceivable that the Fourteenth Amendment was intended to prohibit all race-conscious relief measures. [T]o hold that it barred state action to remedy the effects [of] discrimination [would] pervert the intent of the framers by substituting abstract equality for the genuine equality the amendment was intended to achieve."

In an additional separate opinion, BLACKMUN, J., wrote: "I yield to no one in my earnest hope that the time will come when an 'affirmative action' program is unnecessary. [In the meantime, however, it] is somewhat ironic to have us so deeply disturbed over a program where race is an element of consciousness, and yet be aware of the fact [that] institutions of higher learning [have] given conceded preferences [to] those possessed of athletic skills, to the children of alumni, to the affluent who may bestow largesse on the institutions, and to those having connections with celebrities, the famous, and the powerful.

"I suspect that it would be impossible to arrange an affirmative action program in a racially neutral way and have it successful. To ask this is to demand the impossible. In order to get beyond racism, we must first take account of race. There is no other way. And in order to treat some persons equally, we must treat them differently. We cannot—we dare not—let the Equal Protection Clause perpetuate racial supremacy."

STEVENS, J, with whom Burger, C.J. and Stewart and Rehnquist, JJ., joined, did not reach any constitutional issue. He thought that the specific admissions program challenged in the case was illegal under Title VI and that "the question whether race can ever be used as a factor in an admissions decision" was "not an issue in this case" nor one appropriate for the Court to consider under the circumstances.

———

After *Bakke*, the Supreme Court did not revisit the issues raised by affirmative action in the context of admissions to educational institutions for another twenty-five years. In the meantime, however, it invalidated affirmative action programs involving teacher lay-offs in 1986, see *Wygant v. Jackson Bd. of Educ.*, infra, and municipal preferences for minority-owned businesses in 1989, see *Richmond v. J.A. Croson Co.*, infra, and made clear more generally that all affirmative action programs would trigger strict judicial scrutiny. By 2003, many regarded the continuing constitutionality of educational affirmative action as very much in doubt, even though a number of state schools continued to practice affirmative action in reliance on Powell, J.'s, *Bakke* opinion.

GRUTTER V. BOLLINGER

539 U.S. 306, 123 S.Ct. 2325, 156 L.Ed.2d 304 (2003).

JUSTICE O'CONNOR delivered the opinion of the Court.

This case requires us to decide whether the use of race as a factor in student admissions by the University of Michigan Law School (Law School) is unlawful.

I A. The Law School ranks among the Nation's top law schools. It receives more than 3,500 applications each year for a class of around 350 students. The hallmark of [the Law School's admission] policy is its focus on academic ability coupled with a flexible assessment of applicants' talents, experiences, and potential "to contribute to the learning of those around them." [In] reviewing an applicant's file, admissions officials must consider the applicant's undergraduate grade point average (GPA) and Law School Admissions Test (LSAT) score because they are important (if imperfect) predictors of academic success in law school. [But] so-called "soft variables" such as "the enthusiasm of recommenders, the quality of the undergraduate institution, the quality of the applicant's essay, and the areas and difficulty of undergraduate course selection" are all brought to bear in assessing an "applicant's likely contributions to the intellectual and social life of the institution."

[The] policy aspires to "achieve that diversity which has the potential to enrich everyone's education and thus make a law school class stronger than the sum of its parts." [By] enrolling a "critical mass of [underrepresented] minority students," the Law School seeks to "ensur[e] their ability to make unique contributions to the character of the Law School."

B. Petitioner Barbara Grutter is a white Michigan resident who applied to the Law School in 1996 with a 3.8 grade point average and 161 LSAT score. The Law School initially placed petitioner on a waiting list, but subsequently rejected her application. [She then filed suit alleging that University officials] discriminated against her on the basis of race in violation of the Fourteenth Amendment [and civil rights statutes including the 1964 Civil Rights Act].

[During] the 15-day bench trial, the parties introduced extensive evidence concerning the Law School's use of race in the admissions process. [A former admissions director] testified that at the height of the admissions season, he would frequently consult the so-called "daily reports" that kept track of the racial and ethnic composition of the class (along with other information such as residency status and gender). This was done, [he] testified, to ensure that a critical mass of underrepresented minority students would be reached so as to realize the educational benefits of a diverse student body. [The current admissions director Erica Munzel] testified that "critical mass" means "meaningful numbers" or "meaningful representation," which she understood to mean a number that encourages underrepresented minority students to participate in the classroom and not feel isolated. Munzel stated there is no number, percentage, or range of numbers or percentages that constitute critical mass. [An expert witness testified] that in 2000, [underrepresented] minority students would have comprised 4 percent of the entering class in 2000 instead of the actual figure of 14.5 percent. * * *

II.   We last addressed the use of race in public higher education over 25 years ago [in] the landmark *Bakke* case. [Justice] Powell approved the university's use of race to further only one interest: "the attainment of a diverse student body." * * * [We] apply strict scrutiny to all racial classifications to " 'smoke out' illegitimate uses of race by assuring that [government] is pursuing a goal important enough to warrant use of a highly suspect tool." *Richmond v. J.A. Croson Co.* Strict scrutiny is not "strict in theory, but fatal in fact." *Adarand Constructors, Inc. v. Pena*, 515 U.S. 200 (1995) [infra]. [When] race-based action is necessary to further a compelling governmental interest, such action does not violate the constitutional guarantee of equal protection so long as the narrow-tailoring requirement is also satisfied.

III A.   [R]espondents assert only one justification for their use of race in the admissions process: obtaining "the educational benefits that flow from a diverse student body." [We] first wish to dispel the notion that the Law School's argument has been foreclosed, either expressly or implicitly, by our affirmative-action cases decided since *Bakke*. It is true that some language in those opinions might be read to suggest that remedying past discrimination is the only permissible justification for race-based governmental action. But we have never held that the only governmental use of race that can survive strict scrutiny is remedying past discrimination.

[Today], we hold that the Law School has a compelling interest in attaining a diverse student body. The Law School's educational judgment that such diversity is essential to its educational mission is one to which we defer. * * *

As part of its goal of "assembling a class that is both exceptionally academically qualified and broadly diverse," the Law School seeks to "enroll a 'critical mass' of minority students." The Law School's interest is not simply "to assure within its student body some specified percentage of a particular group merely because of its race or ethnic origin." That would amount to outright racial balancing, which is patently unconstitutional. Rather, the Law School's concept of critical mass is defined by reference to the educational benefits that diversity is designed to produce. These benefits are substantial. As the District Court emphasized, the Law

School's admissions policy promotes "cross-racial understanding," helps to break down racial stereotypes, and "enables [students] to better understand persons of different races." These benefits are "important and laudable," because "classroom discussion is livelier, more spirited, and simply more enlightening and interesting" when the students have "the greatest possible variety of backgrounds." [Numerous] studies show that student body diversity promotes learning outcomes, and "better prepares students for an increasingly diverse workforce and society, and better prepares them as professionals."

These benefits are not theoretical but real, as major American businesses have made clear that the skills needed in today's increasingly global marketplace can only be developed through exposure to widely diverse people, cultures, ideas, and viewpoints. What is more, high-ranking retired officers and civilian leaders of the United States military assert that, "[b]ased on [their] decades of experience," a "highly qualified, racially diverse officer corps is essential to the military's ability to fulfill its principle mission to provide national security." The primary sources for the Nation's officer corps are the service academies and the Reserve Officers Training Corps (ROTC), the latter comprising students already admitted to participating colleges and universities. At present, "the military cannot achieve an officer corps that is *both* highly qualified *and* racially diverse unless the service academies and the ROTC used limited race-conscious recruiting and admissions policies." To fulfill its mission, the military "must be selective in admissions for training and education for the officer corps, and it must train and educate a highly qualified, racially diverse officer corps in a racially diverse setting." Ibid. We agree that "[i]t requires only a small step from this analysis to conclude that our country's other most selective institutions must remain both diverse and selective."

[U]niversities, and in particular, law schools, represent the training ground for a large number of our Nation's leaders. *Sweatt v. Painter.* [In] order to cultivate a set of leaders with legitimacy in the eyes of the citizenry, it is necessary that the path to leadership be visibly open to talented and qualified individuals of every race and ethnicity. All members of our heterogeneous society must have confidence in the openness and integrity of the educational institutions that provide this training. As we have recognized, law schools "cannot be effective in isolation from the individuals and institutions with which the law interacts." See *Sweatt.* Access to legal education (and thus the legal profession) must be inclusive of talented and qualified individuals of every race and ethnicity, so that all members of our heterogeneous society may participate in the educational institutions that provide the training and education necessary to succeed in America.

The Law School does not premise its need for critical mass on "any belief that minority students always (or even consistently) express some characteristic minority viewpoint on any issue." To the contrary, diminishing the force of such stereotypes is both a crucial part of the Law School's mission, and one that it cannot accomplish with only token numbers of minority students. Just as growing up in a particular region or having particular professional experiences is likely to affect an individual's views, so too is one's own, unique experience of being a racial minority in a society, like our own, in which race unfortunately still matters. The Law School has determined, based on its experience and expertise, that a "critical mass" of underrepresented minorities is necessary to further its compelling interest in securing the educational benefits of a diverse student body.

B. Even in the limited circumstance when drawing racial distinctions is permissible to further a compelling state interest, government is still "constrained in how it may pursue that end." [A] university may consider race or ethnicity only as a " 'plus' in a particular applicant's file," without "insulat[ing] the individual from comparison with all other candidates for the available seats." [We] find that the Law School's admissions program bears the hallmarks of a narrowly tailored plan. [The] Law School's goal of attaining a critical mass of underrepresented minority students does not transform its program into a quota. [Nor] does the Law School's consultation of the "daily reports," which keep track of the racial and ethnic composition of the class (as well as of residency and gender), "sugges[t] there was no further attempt at individual review save for race itself" during the final stages of the admissions process. To the contrary, the Law School's admissions officers testified without contradiction that they never gave race any more or less weight based on the information contained in these reports. Moreover, [between] 1993 and 1998, the number of African-American, Latino, and Native-American students in each class at the Law School varied from 13.5 to 20.1 percent, a range inconsistent with a quota.

[Petitioner] and the United States argue that the Law School's plan is not narrowly tailored because race-neutral means exist to obtain the educational benefits of student body diversity that the Law School seeks. We disagree. Narrow tailoring does not require exhaustion of every conceivable race-neutral alternative. Nor does it require a university to choose between maintaining a reputation for excellence or fulfilling a commitment to provide educational opportunities to members of all racial groups. [The] District Court took the Law School to task for failing to consider race-neutral alternatives such as "using a lottery system" or "decreasing the emphasis for all applicants on undergraduate GPA and LSAT scores." But these alternatives would require a dramatic sacrifice of diversity, the academic quality of all admitted students, or both. [The] United States advocates "percentage plans," recently adopted by public undergraduate institutions in Texas, Florida, and California to guarantee admission to all students above a certain class-rank threshold in every high school in the State. [In part because some high schools have disproportionately large minority enrollments, these programs help to increase minority admissions, though often less so than explicitly race-based affirmative action programs.] The United States does not, however, explain how such plans could work for graduate and professional schools.

[We] acknowledge that "there are serious problems of justice connected with the idea of preference itself." [We] are mindful, [too], that "[a] core purpose of the Fourteenth Amendment was to do away with all governmentally imposed discrimination based on race." Accordingly, race-conscious admissions policies must be limited in time. This requirement reflects that racial classifications, however compelling their goals, are potentially so dangerous that they may be employed no more broadly than the interest demands. In the context of higher education, the durational requirement can be met by sunset provisions in race-conscious admissions policies and periodic reviews to determine whether racial preferences are still necessary to achieve student body diversity. [We] take the Law School at its word that it would "like nothing better than to find a race-neutral admissions formula" and will terminate its race-conscious admissions program as soon as practicable. It has been 25 years since Justice Powell first approved the use of race to further an interest in student body diversity in the context of public higher education. Since that time, the number of minority applicants with high grades and test scores has indeed increased. We expect that 25 years from now, the use of racial preferences will no longer be necessary to further the interest approved today.

JUSTICE GINSBURG, with whom JUSTICE BREYER joins, concurring.

[It] was only 25 years before *Bakke* that this Court declared public school segregation unconstitutional, a declaration that, after prolonged resistance, yielded an end to a law-enforced racial caste system, itself the legacy of centuries of slavery. [Today, it] is well documented that conscious and unconscious race bias, even rank discrimination based on race, remain alive in our land, impeding realization of our highest values and ideals. As to public education, data for the years 2000–2001 show that 71.6% of African-American children and 76.3% of Hispanic children attended a school in which minorities made up a majority of the student body. And schools in predominantly minority communities lag far behind others measured by the educational resources available to them. [Despite] these inequalities, some minority students are able to meet the high threshold requirements set for admission to the country's finest undergraduate and graduate educational institutions. As lower school education in minority communities improves, an increase in the number of such students may be anticipated. From today's vantage point, one may hope, but not firmly forecast, that over the next generation's span, progress toward nondiscrimination and genuinely equal opportunity will make it safe to sunset affirmative action.

CHIEF JUSTICE REHNQUIST, with whom JUSTICE SCALIA, JUSTICE KENNEDY, and JUSTICE THOMAS join, dissenting.

I agree with the Court that, "in the limited circumstance when drawing racial distinctions is permissible," the government must ensure that its means are narrowly tailored to achieve a compelling state interest. I do not believe, however, that the University of Michigan Law School's (Law School) means are narrowly tailored to the interest it asserts. [Stripped] of its "critical mass" veil, the Law School's program is revealed as a naked effort to achieve racial balancing.

[From] 1995 through 2000, the Law School admitted between 1,130 and 1,310 students. Of those, between 13 and 19 were Native American, between 91 and 108 were African-Americans, and between 47 and 56 were Hispanic. If the Law School is admitting between 91 and 108 African-Americans in order to achieve "critical mass," thereby preventing African-American students from feeling "isolated or like spokespersons for their race," one would think that a number of the same order of magnitude would be necessary to accomplish the same purpose for Hispanics and Native Americans. Similarly, even if all of the Native American applicants admitted in a given year matriculate, which the record demonstrates is not at all the case,* how can this possibly constitute a "critical mass" of Native Americans in a class of over 350 students? * * *

These different numbers, moreover, come only as a result of substantially different treatment among the three underrepresented minority groups. [For] example, in 2000, 12 Hispanics who scored between a 159–160 on the LSAT and earned a GPA of 3.00 or higher applied for admission and only 2 were admitted. Meanwhile, 12 African-Americans in the same range of qualifications applied for admission and all 12 were admitted. Likewise, that same year, 16 Hispanics who scored between a 151–153 on the LSAT and earned a 3.00 or higher applied for admission and only 1 of those applicants was admitted. Twenty-three similarly qualified African-Americans applied for admission and 14 were admitted.

Only when the "critical mass" label is discarded does a likely explanation for these numbers emerge. [The] correlation between the percentage of the Law School's pool of applicants who are members of the three minority groups and the percentage of the admitted applicants who are members of these same groups is far too precise to be dismissed as merely the result of the school paying "some attention to [the] numbers." As the tables below show, from 1995 through 2000 the percentage of

---

* **[Ct's Note]** Indeed, during this 5-year time period, enrollment of Native American students dropped to as low as three such students. Any assertion that such a small group constituted a "critical mass" of Native Americans is simply absurd.

admitted applicants who were members of these minority groups closely tracked the percentage of individuals in the school's applicant pool who were from the same groups.

For example, in 1995, when 9.7% of the applicant pool was African-American, 9.4% of the admitted class was African-American. By 2000, only 7.5% of the applicant pool was African-American, and 7.3% of the admitted class was African-American. [The] tight correlation between the percentage of applicants and admittees of a given race, therefore, must result from careful race based planning by the Law School. It suggests a formula for admission based on the aspirational assumption that all applicants are equally qualified academically, and therefore that the proportion of each group admitted should be the same as the proportion of that group in the applicant pool. [This] is precisely the type of racial balancing that the Court itself calls "patently unconstitutional."

JUSTICE KENNEDY, dissenting.

The opinion by Justice Powell in *Bakke*, in my view, states the correct rule for resolving this case. The Court, however, does not apply strict scrutiny. By trying to say otherwise, it undermines both the test and its own controlling precedents. [At] the very least, the constancy of admitted minority students and the close correlation between the racial breakdown of admitted minorities and the composition of the applicant pool, [require] the Law School either to produce a convincing explanation or to show it has taken adequate steps to ensure individual assessment. The Law School does neither. * * *

JUSTICE SCALIA, with whom JUSTICE THOMAS joins, concurring in part and dissenting in part.

The "educational benefit" that the University of Michigan seeks to achieve by racial discrimination consists, according to the Court, of "cross-racial understanding," and "better prepar[ation of] students for an increasingly diverse workforce and society," all of which is necessary not only for work, but also for good "citizenship." This is not, of course, an "educational benefit" on which students will be graded on their Law School transcript (Works and Plays Well with Others: B+) or tested by the bar examiners (Q: Describe in 500 words or less your cross-racial understanding). For it is a lesson of life rather than law—essentially the same lesson taught to (or rather learned by, for it cannot be "taught" in the usual sense) people three feet shorter and twenty years younger than the full-grown adults at the University of Michigan Law School, in institutions ranging from Boy Scout troops to public-school kindergartens. If properly considered an "educational benefit" at all, it is surely not one that is either uniquely relevant to law school or uniquely "teachable" in a formal educational setting. *And therefore*: If it is appropriate for the University of Michigan Law School to use racial discrimination for the purpose of putting together a "critical mass" that will convey generic lessons in socialization and good citizenship, surely it is no less appropriate—indeed, *particularly* appropriate—for the civil service system of the State of Michigan to do so. There, also, those exposed to "critical masses" of certain races will presumably become better Americans, better Michiganders, better civil servants. And surely private employers cannot be criticized—indeed, should be praised—if they also "teach" good citizenship to their adult employees through a patriotic, all-American system of racial discrimination in hiring. The nonminority individuals who are deprived of a legal education, a civil service job, or any job at all by reason of their skin color will surely understand.

Unlike a clear constitutional holding that racial preferences in state educational institutions are impermissible, or even a clear anticonstitutional holding that racial preferences in state educational institutions are OK, today's [decision in *Grutter*, when coupled with the Court's decision in *Gratz*, which follows immediately,] seems perversely designed to prolong the controversy and the litigation. Some future lawsuits will presumably focus on whether the discriminatory scheme in question contains enough evaluation of the applicant "as an individual," and sufficiently avoids "separate admissions tracks" [to be constitutionally permissible]. Some will focus on whether a university has gone beyond the bounds of a " 'good faith effort' " and has so zealously pursued its "critical mass" as to make it an unconstitutional de facto quota system, rather than merely " 'a permissible goal.' " Other lawsuits may focus on whether, in the particular setting at issue, any educational benefits flow from racial diversity. (That issue was not contested in *Grutter*; and while the opinion accords "a degree of deference to a university's academic decisions," "deference does not imply abandonment or abdication of judicial review.") Still other suits may challenge the bona fides of the institution's expressed commitment to the educational benefits of diversity that immunize the discriminatory scheme in *Grutter*. (Tempting targets, one would suppose, will be those universities that talk the talk of multiculturalism and racial diversity in the courts but walk the walk of tribalism and racial segregation on their campuses—through minority-only student organizations, separate minority housing opportunities, separate minority student centers, even separate minority-only graduation ceremonies.) And still other suits may claim that the institution's racial preferences have gone below or above the mystical *Grutter*-approved "critical mass." Finally, litigation can be expected on behalf of minority groups intentionally short changed in the institution's composition of its generic minority "critical mass." I do not look forward to any of these cases. The Constitution proscribes government discrimination on the basis of race, and state-provided education is no exception.

JUSTICE THOMAS, with whom JUSTICE SCALIA joins as to Parts I–VII, concurring in part and dissenting in part.

Frederick Douglass, speaking to a group of abolitionists almost 140 years ago, delivered a message lost on today's majority: "[I]n regard to the colored people, there is always more that is benevolent, I perceive, than just, manifested towards us. What I ask for the negro is not benevolence, not pity, not sympathy, but simply *justice*. . . . And if the negro cannot stand on his own legs, let him fall. . . . All I ask is, give him a chance to stand on his own legs! Let him alone! [Y]our interference is doing him positive injury." [Like] Douglass, I believe blacks can achieve in every avenue of American life without the meddling of university administrators. Because I wish to see all students succeed whatever their color, I share, in some respect, the sympathies of those who sponsor the type of discrimination advanced by the University of Michigan Law School. [The] Constitution does not, however, tolerate institutional devotion to the status quo in admissions policies when such devotion ripens into racial discrimination. Nor does the Constitution countenance the unprecedented deference the Court gives to the Law School, an approach inconsistent with the very concept of "strict scrutiny."

II.   Unlike the majority, I seek to define with precision the interest being asserted by the Law School before determining whether that interest is so compelling as to justify racial discrimination. The Law School maintains that it wishes to obtain "educational benefits that flow from student body diversity." This statement must be evaluated carefully, because it implies that both "diversity" and "educational benefits" are components of the Law School's compelling state interest. [The] Law School [apparently] believes that only a racially mixed student body can lead to the educational benefits it seeks. How, then, is the Law School's interest in these allegedly unique educational "benefits" *not* simply the forbidden interest in "racial balancing" that the majority expressly rejects? A distinction between these two ideas (unique educational benefits based on racial aesthetics and race for its own sake) is purely sophistic—so much so that the majority uses them interchangeably.

III.   [Justice] Powell's opinion in *Bakke* and the Court's decision today rest on the fundamentally flawed proposition that racial discrimination can be contextualized so that a goal, such as classroom aesthetics, can be compelling in one context but not in another. [Under] the proper standard, there is no pressing public necessity in maintaining a public law school at all and, it follows, certainly not an elite law school. Likewise, marginal improvements in legal education do not qualify as a compelling state interest. * * *

IV. [With] the adoption of different admissions methods, such as accepting all students who meet minimum qualifications, the Law School could achieve its vision of the racially aesthetic student body without the use of racial discrimination. The Law School concedes this, but the Court holds, implicitly and under the guise of narrow tailoring, that the Law School has a compelling state interest in doing what it wants to do. I cannot agree. First, under strict scrutiny, the Law School's assessment of the benefits of racial discrimination and devotion to the admissions status quo are not entitled to any sort of deference, grounded in the First Amendment or anywhere else. Second, even if its "academic selectivity" must be maintained at all costs along with racial discrimination, the Court ignores the fact that other top law schools have succeeded in meeting their aesthetic demands without racial discrimination.

[The] Court relies heavily on social science evidence to justify its deference. The Court never acknowledges, however, the growing evidence that racial (and other sorts) of heterogeneity actually impairs learning among black students. See, e.g., Flowers & Pascarella, *Cognitive Effects of College Racial Composition on African American Students After 3 Years of College*, 40 J. of College Student Development 669 (1999) (concluding that black students experience superior cognitive development at Historically Black Colleges (HBCs) and that, even among blacks, "a substantial diversity moderates the cognitive effects of attending an HBC"); Allen, *The Color of Success: African-American College Student Outcomes at Predominantly White and Historically Black Public Colleges and Universities*, 62 Harv. Educ. Rev. 26, 35 (1992) (finding that black students attending HBCs report higher academic achievement than those attending predominantly white colleges). * * *

VI. [I] believe what lies beneath the Court's decision today are the benighted notions that one can tell when racial discrimination benefits (rather than hurts) minority groups, and that racial discrimination is necessary to remedy general societal ills. [I] must contest the notion that the Law School's discrimination benefits those admitted as a result of it. The Court spends considerable time discussing the impressive display of amicus support for the Law School in this case from all corners of society. But nowhere in any of the filings in this Court is any evidence that the purported "beneficiaries" of this racial discrimination prove themselves by performing at (or even near) the same level as those students who receive no preferences. Cf. Thernstrom & Thernstrom, *Reflections on the Shape of the River*, 46 U.C.L.A. L.Rev. 1583, 1605–1608 (1999) (discussing the failure of defenders of racial discrimination in admissions to consider the fact that its "beneficiaries" are underperforming in the classroom).

[The] Law School tantalizes unprepared students with the promise of a University of Michigan degree and all of the opportunities that it offers. These overmatched students take the bait, only to find that they cannot succeed in the cauldron of competition. And this mismatch crisis is not restricted to elite institutions. See T. Sowell, *Race and Culture* 176–177

(1994) ("Even if most minority students are able to meet the normal standards at the 'average' range of colleges and universities, the systematic mismatching of minority students begun at the top can mean that such students are generally overmatched throughout all levels of higher education"). [While] these students may graduate with law degrees, there is no evidence that they have received a qualitatively better legal education (or become better lawyers) than if they had gone to a less "elite" law school for which they were better prepared.

[It] is uncontested that each year, the Law School admits a handful of blacks who would be admitted in the absence of racial discrimination. Who can differentiate between those who belong and those who do not? The majority of blacks are admitted to the Law School because of discrimination, and because of this policy all are tarred as undeserving. This problem of stigma does not depend on determinacy as to whether those stigmatized are actually the "beneficiaries" of racial discrimination. When blacks take positions in the highest places of government, industry, or academia, it is an open question today whether their skin color played a part in their advancement. The question itself is the stigma—because either racial discrimination did play a role, in which case the person may be deemed "otherwise unqualified," or it did not, in which case asking the question itself unfairly marks those blacks who would succeed without discrimination.[55]

GRATZ V. BOLLINGER

539 U.S. 244, 123 S.Ct. 2411, 156 L.Ed.2d 257 (2003).

CHIEF JUSTICE REHNQUIST delivered the opinion of the Court.

[Petitioner Gratz was a Caucasian resident of Michigan who was denied admission to the University of Michigan's (University) College of Literature, Science, and the Arts ("LSA"). She subsequently filed suit challenging the constitutionality of the University's undergraduate affirmative action policies.]

The University changed its admissions guidelines a number of times during the period relevant to this litigation, [but the version in place at the time of the Court's decision, introduced during the 1998 academic year, employed] a "selection index," on which an applicant could score a maximum of 150 points. This index was divided linearly into ranges

---

[55] Compare Randall Kennedy, *For Discrimination: Race, Affirmative Action, and the Law* 124–25 (2013): "[A]ffirmative action imposes a stigmatic cost on anyone perceived to be a beneficiary. [But t]he proper response to the stigma objection is to (1) acknowledge its strength, (2) diminish avoidable harms through careful design of affirmative action programs, (3) argue against exaggerations of stigmatic harms, and (4) insist that [affirmative action's] benefits must be weighted against its drawbacks. [There] are reasons to believe that affirmative action is not so stigmatically burdensome as certain anti-affirmative action detractors suggest. Especially among racial minorities, relatively few complain about this cost, against the concomitant benefit."

generally calling for admissions dispositions as follows: 100–150 (admit); 95–99 (admit or postpone); 90–94 (postpone or admit); 75–89 (delay or postpone); 74 and below (delay or reject). Each application received points based on high school grade point average, standardized test scores, academic quality of an applicant's high school, strength or weakness of high school curriculum, in-state residency, alumni relationship, personal essay, and personal achievement or leadership. Of particular significance here, under a "miscellaneous" category, an applicant was entitled to 20 points based upon his or her membership in an underrepresented racial or ethnic minority group. [Under the same category, 20 points could also be awarded based upon socioeconomic status, upon status as a recruited athlete, or upon a designation by the provost.]

[Starting] in 1999, [the] University established an Admissions Review Committee (ARC), to provide an additional level of consideration for some applications. Under the new system, counselors may, in their discretion, "flag" an application for the ARC to review after determining that the applicant (1) is academically prepared to succeed at the University, (2) has achieved a minimum selection index score, and (3) possesses a quality or characteristic important to the University's composition of its freshman class, such as high class rank, unique life experiences, challenges, circumstances, interests or talents, socioeconomic disadvantage, and underrepresented race, ethnicity, or geography. After reviewing "flagged" applications, the ARC determines whether to admit, defer, or deny each applicant.

II. [Petitioners' argument that the Fourteenth Amendment categorically prohibits the use of racial preferences to promote educational diversity fails under the holding of *Grutter*. But] the University's policy, which automatically distributes 20 points, or one-fifth of the points needed to guarantee admission, to every single "underrepresented minority" applicant solely because of race, is not narrowly tailored to achieve the interest in educational diversity that respondents claim justifies their program.

In *Bakke*, Justice Powell reiterated that "[p]referring members of any one group for no reason other than race or ethnic origin is discrimination for its own sake." [His opinion] emphasized the importance of considering each particular applicant as an individual, assessing all of the qualities that individual possesses, and in turn, evaluating that individual's ability to contribute to the unique setting of higher education. [The] current LSA policy does not provide such individualized consideration. The LSA's policy automatically distributes 20 points to every single applicant from an "underrepresented minority" group, as defined by the University. The only consideration that accompanies this distribution of points is a factual review of an application to determine whether an individual is a member of one of these minority groups. Moreover, unlike Justice Powell's example, where the race of a "particular black applicant" could be considered without being decisive, the LSA's automatic distribution of 20 points has the effect of making "the factor of race * * * decisive" for virtually every minimally qualified underrepresented minority applicant.

[Respondents] contend that "[t]he volume of applications and the presentation of applicant information make it impractical for [LSA] to use [the] admissions system" upheld by the Court today in *Grutter*. But the fact that the implementation of a program capable of providing individualized consideration might present administrative challenges does not render constitutional an otherwise problematic system. Nothing in Justice Powell's opinion in *Bakke* signaled that a university may employ whatever means it desires to achieve the stated goal of diversity without regard to the limits imposed by our strict scrutiny analysis.

JUSTICE O'CONNOR, with whom JUSTICE BREYER joins except as to the last sentence, concurring.

Unlike the law school admissions policy the Court upholds today in *Grutter v. Bollinger*, the procedures employed by the University of Michigan's Office of Undergraduate Admissions do not provide for a meaningful individualized review of applicants. [Although] the Office of Undergraduate Admissions does assign 20 points to some "soft" variables other than race, the points available for other diversity contributions, such as leadership and service, personal achievement, and geographic diversity, are capped at much lower levels. [The] only potential source of individualized consideration appears to be the Admissions Review Committee. The evidence in the record, however, reveals very little about how the review committee actually functions. And what evidence there is indicates that the committee is a kind of afterthought, rather than an integral component of a system of individualized review. [As] a result, I join the Court's opinion reversing the decision of the District Court.

JUSTICE THOMAS, concurring.

I join the Court's opinion because I believe it correctly applies our precedents, including today's decision in *Grutter*. For similar reasons to those given in my separate opinion in that case, however, I would hold that a State's use of racial discrimination in higher education admissions is categorically prohibited by the Equal Protection Clause.

JUSTICE BREYER, concurring in the judgment.

[I] join Justice O'Connor's opinion except insofar as it joins that of the Court. [I] agree with Justice Ginsburg that, in implementing the Constitution's equality instruction, government decisionmakers may properly distinguish between policies of inclusion and exclusion, for the former are more likely to prove consistent with the basic constitutional obligation that the law respect each individual equally.

JUSTICE STEVENS, with whom JUSTICE SOUTER joins, dissenting.

[Because the case should be dismissed for lack of standing,] I respectfully dissent.

JUSTICE SOUTER, with whom JUSTICE GINSBURG joins as to Part II, dissenting.

[The] very nature of a college's permissible practice of awarding value to racial diversity means that race must be considered in a way that increases some applicants' chances for admission. [It] suffices for me that there are no *Bakke*-like set-asides and that consideration of an applicant's whole spectrum of ability is no more ruled out by giving 20 points for race than by giving the same points for athletic ability or socioeconomic disadvantage.

JUSTICE GINSBURG, with whom JUSTICE SOUTER joins, dissenting.

I.   [A]s I see it, government decisionmakers may properly distinguish between policies of exclusion and inclusion. [Our] jurisprudence ranks race a "suspect" category, "not because [race] is inevitably an impermissible classification, but because it is one which usually, to our national shame, has been drawn for the purpose of maintaining racial inequality." But where race is considered "for the purpose of achieving equality," no automatic proscription is in order. * * *

II.   [The] racial and ethnic groups to which the College accords special consideration (African-Americans, Hispanics, and Native-Americans) historically have been relegated to inferior status by law and social practice; their members continue to experience class-based discrimination to this day. There is no suggestion that the College adopted its current policy in order to limit or decrease enrollment by any particular racial or ethnic group, and no seats are reserved on the basis of race. Nor has there been any demonstration that the College's program unduly constricts admissions opportunities for students who do not receive special consideration based on race.

The stain of generations of racial oppression is still visible in our society, and the determination to hasten its removal remains vital. One can reasonably anticipate, therefore, that colleges and universities will seek to maintain their minority enrollment—and the networks and opportunities thereby opened to minority graduates—whether or not they can do so in full candor through adoption of affirmative action plans of the kind here at issue. Without recourse to such plans, institutions of higher education may resort to camouflage. For example, schools may encourage applicants to write of their cultural traditions in the essays they submit, or to indicate whether English is their second language. Seeking to improve their chances for admission, applicants may highlight the minority group associations to which they belong, or the Hispanic surnames of their mothers or grandparents. In turn, teachers' recommendations may emphasize who a student is as much as what he or she has accomplished. If honesty is the best policy, surely Michigan's accurately described, fully disclosed College affirmative action program is preferable to achieving similar numbers through winks, nods, and disguises.

NOTES AND QUESTIONS

1. ***Standard of review.*** Should race-based classificatory schemes that aim to advantage previously disadvantaged minorities be evaluated under the same strict judicial scrutiny as other racial classifications? If so, on what basis is strict scrutiny justified?

(a) ***History.*** Consider Jed Rubenfeld, *Affirmative Action*, 107 Yale L.J. 427 (1997): "In July 1866, the Thirty-Ninth Congress [that] had just framed the Fourteenth Amendment [passed] a statute appropriating money [for] 'the relief of destitute colored women and children.' In 1867, the Fortieth Congress—the same body that was driving the Fourteenth Amendment down the throat of the bloody South—passed a statute providing money for [the] destitute 'colored' persons in the [the District of Columbia]. Year after year in the Civil War period [Congress] made special appropriations for [the] 'colored' soldiers and sailors of the Union Army. [What] do [these statutes] prove? Only that those who profess fealty to the 'original understanding' [cannot] categorically condemn color-based distribution of governmental benefits."[56] Compare the view of Lino Graglia, *Racially Discriminatory Admission to Public Institutions of Higher Education,* in *Constitutional Government in America* 255, 263 (Ronald K.L. Collins ed., 1980), that arguments such as this risk proving "too much": "It is equally clear that the Fourteenth Amendment was not intended to prohibit school segregation either."

(b) ***Moral relevance and permissibility.*** Is the relevant constitutional principle that government should not classify by race (a principle sometimes labeled the "colorblindness" or "antidiscrimination" principle)? Or is it that government should not use race as a basis to demean, suppress, or stigmatize (a principle sometimes called the "antisubordination" principle)? Reva B. Siegel, *Equality Talk: Antisubordination and Anticlassification Values in Constitutional Struggles over* Brown, 117 Harv.L.Rev. 1470 (2004), argues that *Brown v. Board of Education* was initially understood as predicated on the harmfulness of segregation to subordinated blacks and that it was not viewed as creating a general prohibition against race-based classifications. It was for this reason, she says, that "throughout the 1960s, courts repeatedly held that state and local governments could use race-specific measures to break down de

---

[56] See also Eric Schnapper, *Affirmative Action and the Legislative History of the Fourteenth Amendment*, 71 Va.L.Rev. 753 (1985). But see Michael B. Rappaport, *Originalism and the Colorblind Constitution*, 89 Notre Dame L.Rev. 71 (2013) (arguing that because the Fourteenth Amendment does not apply to the federal government, federal statutes from the Reconstruction era do not reliably indicate the Amendment's original understanding, and further arguing that federal statutes that appear to discriminate on the basis of race "do not upon examination necessarily turn out to do so").

facto segregation or 'racial imbalance' in the nation's public schools, even when there was no finding of a constitutional violation." But courts "began to respond differently when plaintiffs challenged new race-conscious measures designed to help integrate the nation's universities."

Compare the views of Thomas, J., concurring in *Adarand*: "So-called 'benign' discrimination teaches many that because of chronic and apparently immutable handicaps, minorities cannot compete with them without their patronizing indulgence. Inevitably, such programs engender attitudes of superiority or, alternatively, provoke resentment among those who believe that they have been wronged by the government's use of race. These programs stamp minorities with a badge of inferiority and may cause them to develop dependencies or to adopt an attitude that they are 'entitled' to preferences."

(c) *The (variable) strictness of strict scrutiny?* A number of commentators have questioned whether *Grutter* applies the same "strict scrutiny" to affirmative action that it applies to classifications that burden racial minorities. Writes Joel Goldstein, *Beyond* Bakke: Grutter—Gratz *and the Promise of* Brown, 48 St. Louis U.L.J. 899 (2004): "The Court seemed [to] be placing a lower hurdle for racial classifications benefiting minorities [than] on those burdening them. [Imagine] that a particular law school determined that student diversity would be served by admitting fewer Jewish [or] Asian-American [students] and [designed] a narrowly tailored [program] to serve that end. For Justice O'Connor to perform her strict scrutiny test consistently she would need to [ask] whether campus diversity was a compelling interest and whether the minority restriction was narrowly tailored. Yet it is possible that such a program would be invalidated as a per se violation of the Equal Protection Clause. [If] this prediction is correct, it suggests that in fact the *Grutter* majority would treat differently preferences that benefit minorities from those that burden them." Recall that in *Bakke,* Brennan, White, Marshall, and Blackmun, JJ., argued for less searching judicial scrutiny of affirmative action than for racial classifications applied to disadvantage minorities. Did their view prevail in *Grutter*?[57]

2. *Diversity.* What is the nature of the "diversity" in which educational institutions have a compelling interest?

(a) *Changing conceptions?* Consider Siegel, note 1(b) supra: "*Grutter* does not simply incorporate Justice Powell's diversity rationale, [but rather] transforms the diversity rationale in the course of adopting it. [In] *Grutter,* diversity is no longer merely the state's interest in ensuring that the learning environment in institutions of higher education is populated by persons of divergent life experience; the opinion also explains the value of diversity as the value of an educated citizenry in a democratic society. As it does so, the opinion defines the state interest in achieving 'diversity' as an interest in ensuring that

---

[57] According to Adam Winkler, *Fatal in Theory and Strict in Fact: An Empirical Analysis of Strict Scrutiny in the Federal Courts*, 59 Vand.L.Rev. 793 (2006), an empirical study of strict scrutiny in both the Supreme Court and in the lower federal courts from 1990 through 2003 reveals a survival rate of slightly more than 30% in the lower federal courts and of 25% in the Supreme Court.

no group is excluded from participating in public life and thus relegated to an outsider, or second-class status, as well as an interest in cultivating the confidence of all citizens that they have the opportunity to serve in positions of national leadership."

See also Lani Guinier, *Admissions Rituals as Political Acts: Guardians at the Gates of our Democratic Ideals*, 117 Harv.L.Rev. 113 (2003): "[D]iversity has three important elements, which together justify the Court's deference to [a] law school's deployment of sponsored mobility to admit a critical mass of underrepresented students of color: diversity is pedagogical and dialogic; it helps challenge stereotypes; and it helps legitimate the democratic mission of higher education. Justice Powell's opinion in *Bakke* endorsed only the first of these three benefits as a compelling interest[.] Justice O'Connor's opinion in *Grutter*, by contrast, included encomiums to them all."

(b) ***Diversity as distraction?*** Consider Derrick Bell, *Diversity's Distractions*, 103 Colum.L.Rev. 1622 (2003): "For at least four reasons, the concept of diversity, far from a viable means of ensuring affirmative action in the admissions processes of colleges and graduate schools, is a serious distraction in the ongoing efforts to achieve racial justice: 1) Diversity enables courts and policymakers to avoid addressing directly the barriers of race and class that adversely affect so many applicants; 2) Diversity invites further litigation by offering a distinction without a real difference between those uses of race approved in college admissions programs, and those in other far more important affirmative action programs that the Court has rejected; 3) Diversity serves to give undeserved legitimacy to the heavy reliance on grades and test scores that privilege well-to-do, mainly white applicants; and 4) The tremendous attention directed at diversity programs diverts concern and resources from the serious barriers of poverty that exclude far more students from entering college than are likely to gain admission under an affirmative action program." Are these matters that should appropriately concern courts that are called upon to review challenges to affirmative action programs?

See also Meera E. Deo, *Empirically Derived Compelling State Interests in Affirmative Action Jurisprudence,* 65 Hastings L.J. 661 (2014): "Relying exclusively on educational diversity as a rationale for affirmative action is somewhat ironic: though most assume that students of color admitted through race-conscious policies are the (only) beneficiaries of affirmative action, the diversity rationale actually suggests that whites may be the primary beneficiaries. If the purpose of affirmative action is educational diversity, then applicants of color are given a 'plus' not because of their promise or potential or the assumption that they have overcome adversity or discrimination; rather, that 'plus' is for the purpose of improving the learning experience for all of the other admitted students. [Instead,] courts and university officials should add the compelling state interest of avoiding racial isolation to the existing goal of educational diversity."

3. ***Individualized judgments and quotas.*** Is there any practical distinction between (a) a separate, identified program for minority admissions,

(b) a program in which racial background gets an applicant a certain number of points that contribute to an overall admissions score, and (c) a program in which racial background can be counted as a "plus," and those administering the program—in order to get the desired "diversity"—monitor the number of admittees who fall within relevant categories?

Consider Reva Siegel, *From Colorblindness to Antibalkanization: An Emerging Ground of Decision in Race Equality Cases,* 120 Yale L.J. 1278 (2011): "[T]he Justices at the center of the Court who have cast the deciding votes to uphold and limit race-conscious civil rights initiatives often explain their position in opinions concerned with threats to social cohesion. Justices reasoning from this antibalkanization perspective enforce the Equal Protection Clause with attention to the forms of estrangement that both racial stratification and practices of racial remediation may engender. [Because] Justices reasoning from an antibalkanization perspective understand that interventions promoting racial integration can become a locus of racial conflict, they insist that race-conscious interventions undertaken for compelling public-regarding purposes must nonetheless anticipate and endeavor to ameliorate race-conscious resentments[, for example by requiring individualized judgment and forbidding quotas]. Race-conscious resentments among the racially privileged matter because, if ignored, they may inhibit the amelioration of racial stratification and because these resentments may reflect displaced expressions of other forms of inequality."

Compare Cristina M. Rodriguez, *Against Individualized Consideration,* 83 Indiana L.J. 1405 (2008): "Contrary to [conventional] wisdom, it is crude, mechanical decision making that [best] restrains the state in its race consciousness [in implementing affirmative action. [By] giving state actors the power to consider how race relates to particular individuals and their potential contributions, we encourage the development of semi-official definitions of the category—the very sorts of definitions that produce stereotypical thinking and deny that the experiences of race or ethnicity differ from individual to individual. [A] second danger posed by the individualized model is [the] personal essay problem: individualized consideration demands that people perform their ethnicity for admissions officers, either through their personal statements or in entrance interviews. [T]hese tensions [demonstrate] how the rise of the diversity interest as the justification for affirmative action has moved [us] away from an honest approach to what should be the animating purposes of a civil rights agenda: combating discrimination and eliminating its effects."

Jim Chen, *Diversity in a Different Dimension: Evolutionary Theory and Affirmative Action's Destiny,* 59 Ohio St.L.J. 811 (1998), argues that the "diversity" sought by affirmative action, which exalts the significance of race and levels differences among racial minorities, "is in many ways the polar opposite of [genuine] diversity."

4. ***Educational affirmative action in practice.*** William G. Bowen & Derek Bok, *The Shape of the River: Long-Term Consequences of Considering*

Race in College and University Admissions (1998), presents the results of the first comprehensive, long-term study of affirmative action in 28 academically selective colleges and universities (based on data involving more than 80,000 undergraduates who matriculated in 1951, 1976, and 1989). The authors' assessments are generally enthusiastic. Among their conclusions: (i) In 1989, blacks made up about 7% of the classes in the colleges that they sampled; without affirmative action, the number of black entrants would have been between 2.1% and 3.6%. (ii) Although the black drop-out rate was 11% higher than that for whites, 75% of the blacks in the 1989 cohort graduated from their original institution, and 79% graduated from some college, within six years. (iii) Black graduates of the elite schools earned considerably more on average than black graduates of non-elite schools. (iv) Almost twice as many blacks as whites from the 1976 cohort participate in community service organizations.

For a sustained critique of the methodology and argumentation of *The Shape of the River*, see Abigail Thernstrom & Stephen Thernstrom, *Reflections on The Shape of the River*, 46 U.C.L.A. L.Rev. 1583 (1999). Among the Thernstroms' major arguments are that black students admitted under what they call "racial double standards" tend not to do as well academically as students admitted without regard to race; that admissions policies at elite institutions have little impact on the socio-economic fabric of African-American life; and that racial categorization perpetuates habits of mind antithetical to egalitarian ideals. Richard H. Sander, *A Systemic Analysis of Affirmative Action in American Law Schools*, 57 Stan.L.Rev. 367 (2004), similarly finds that black law students who are admitted on the basis of affirmative action "preferences" (as distinguished from black students admitted without such "preferences") tend to receive lower grades than their white classmates, to be more likely to drop out of law school, and to be less likely to pass the bar exam. Sander further contends that African-American students are widely "mismatched" with law schools for which they lack proper credentials; that they therefore tend to drop out and to fail the bar exam at disproportionately high rates; and that, if racial preferences did not exist, "the production of black lawyers would rise significantly [and] blacks as a whole would be significantly better off." Sander's analysis has triggered a number of critical replies, largely focused on his methodology, to which he has in turn replied. See, for example, the exchange in 57 Stan.L.Rev. 1807 et seq. (2005).

5. *The alternative of class-based affirmative action.* Would affirmative action based on class or economic background be fairer or more constitutionally acceptable than affirmative action based on race?[58]

(a) *Class-based affirmative action and minorities.* There are varying estimates of the extent to which class-based affirmative action would succeed in promoting racial diversity in higher education, for example, and many observers are quite pessimistic. See, e.g., Matthew N. Gaertner & Melissa

---

[58] For affirmative arguments, see, e.g., Richard H. Sander, *Class in American Legal Education*, 88 Denv. U.L.Rev. 631 (2011); Richard D. Kahlenberg, *Class-Based Affirmative Action*, 84 Calif. L.Rev. 1037 (1996); see also Deborah C. Malamud, *Class-Based Affirmative Action: Lessons and Caveats*, 74 Tex. L. Rev. 1847 (1996).

Hart, *Considering Class: College Access and Diversity*, 7 Harv. L. & Pol'y Rev. 367 (2013) ("Even if universities [in providing class-based preferences] were to grant low-income students 'minority-size' boosts, racial diversity would plummet because minority status and poverty are not sufficiently correlated. These simulations have been reproduced in subsequent research, and their results are consistently confirmed."). An additional consideration is that the African-American students currently attending elite institutions tend not to come from the poorest black families. See Bowen & Bok, supra, at 50.

(b) ***Level of judicial scrutiny.*** If a class-based affirmative action program is racially neutral on its face, but is implemented for the *purpose* of achieving a racially defined effect (i.e., heightened minority representation), should it be subjected to rational basis review or to strict judicial scrutiny? Under *Washington v. Davis*, a facially neutral statute adopted for the purpose of advantaging whites and disadvantaging racial minorities would trigger strict scrutiny. Does the converse also hold? Kathleen M. Sullivan, *After Affirmative Action*, 59 Ohio St.L.J. 1039 (1998), argues that where the aim is diversity, "the government action is taken despite, rather than because of, the effect on white interests." Compare Brian T. Fitzpatrick, *Strict Scrutiny of Facially Race-Neutral State Action and the Texas Ten Percent Plan*, 53 Baylor L.Rev. 289 (2001), objecting to Texas's so-called "10-percent plan," under which all students in the top 10 percent of the graduating class in every Texas high school are eligible for admission to the University of Texas's flagship campus: "When confronted with the inability to continue the use of explicit racial classifications [as the result of a lower court decision], the Texas Legislature did what so many legislators have done before it in different contexts: it manipulated race-neutral criteria to achieve the same racial results that it had achieved under its old, illegal regime. [When] it comes to the Fourteenth Amendment, the Constitution is more concerned with substance than form. Manipulating race neutral admissions criteria to achieve the same results that had been illegally obtained by explicit racial classifications is an attempt to flout the Constitution. The Ten Percent Plan should be struck down as quickly as the racial preference scheme it replaced."

―――――

FISHER V. UNIVERSITY OF TEXAS
___ U.S. ___, 133 S.Ct. 2411, 186 L.Ed.2d 474 (2013).

JUSTICE KENNEDY delivered the opinion of the Court.

[Abigail Fisher, a Caucasian who was denied admission to the University of Texas, brought suit, challenging the University's use of race in its admissions process. The University's admissions policy had a complex history. Before 1997, the University "considered two factors: a numerical score reflecting an applicant's" test scores and high school grades (Academic Index or AI) and the applicant's race. After a lower court held that any consideration of race was unconstitutional, the University replaced the race-based component of its process with a Personal Achievement Index (PAI), reflecting such considerations as leadership, work experience, extra-curricular activities, and "special circumstances" including "growing up in a single-parent home, speaking a language other than English at home, [and] the socioeconomic condition of the student's family." At about the same time, the Texas Legislature adopted a Top Ten Percent Law that "grants automatic admission to [all] students in the top 10% of their class at high schools in Texas that comply with certain standards." Roughly three-quarters of the University's students gain admission under the Top Ten Percent formula. In the last year that the University admitted part of its class based on a formula that combined AI and race-blind PAI scores, while admitting its other students under the Top Ten Percent Plan, the entering class was 4.5% African-American and 16.9 percent Hispanic, in comparison with 4.1% and 14.5% in the last year in which the University took race into account.

[Following the 2003 decision in *Grutter v. Bollinger*, the University resumed making race a consideration in its admissions process, this time as an express factor in computing the PAI that it continued to use for applicants who were not admitted pursuant to the Top Ten Percent Plan. "Race [was] not assigned an explicit numerical value, but it is undisputed that race [was] a meaningful factor." The internal document expressing the University's decision to inquire into race as part of its admission process "relied in substantial part on a study of a subset of undergraduate classes containing between 5 and 24 students," few of which "had substantial enrollment" by racial minorities. [In] challenging the University's reliance on race in computing applicants' PAI, Fisher did not attack any other element of the admissions process, including the Top Ten Percent Plan. Nor did she ask the Court to overrule *Grutter*, which she argued that the lower courts had misapplied when they ruled against her.]

Grutter made clear that racial "classifications are constitutional only if they are narrowly tailored to further compelling governmental interests." And *Grutter* endorsed Justice Powell's conclusion in *Bakke* that "the attainment of a diverse student body . . . is a constitutionally permissible goal for an institution of higher education." [According] to *Grutter*, a university's "educational judgment that such diversity is essential to its educational mission is one to which we defer." [The] District Court and Court of Appeals were thus correct in finding that *Grutter* calls for deference to the University's conclusion that a diverse student body would serve its educational goals. There is disagreement about whether *Grutter* was consistent with the principles of equal protection in approving this compelling interest in diversity. See [opinions in this case] (Scalia, J., concurring); (Thomas, J., concurring); (Ginsburg, J., dissenting). But the parties here do not ask the Court to revisit that aspect of *Grutter*'s holding.

[Once] the University has established that its goal of diversity is consistent with strict scrutiny, [the] University must prove that [its] means are narrowly tailored to that goal. On this point, the University receives no deference. [I]t remains at all times the University's obligation to demonstrate, and the Judiciary's obligation to determine, that admissions processes "ensure that each applicant is evaluated as an individual and not in a way that makes an applicant's race or ethnicity the defining feature of his or her application." Narrow tailoring also requires that the reviewing court verify that it is "necessary" for a university to use race to achieve the educational benefits of diversity. Although "[n]arrow tailoring does not require exhaustion of every *conceivable* race-neutral alternative," [strict] scrutiny imposes on the university the ultimate burden of demonstrating [that] available, workable race-neutral alternatives do not suffice.

Rather than perform this searching examination, [the] Court of Appeals held petitioner could challenge only "whether [the University's] decision to reintroduce race as a factor in admissions was made in good faith." [It further] ruled that to "second-guess the merits" of this aspect of the University's decision was a task it was "ill-equipped to perform" and that it would attempt only to "ensure that [the University's] decision to adopt a race-conscious admissions policy followed from [a process of] good faith consideration." The Court of Appeals thus concluded that "the narrow-tailoring inquiry—like the compelling-interest inquiry—is undertaken with a degree of deference to the Universit[y]." These expressions of the controlling standard are at odds with *Grutter*'s command that "all racial classifications imposed by government 'must be analyzed by a reviewing court under strict scrutiny.' " [Strict] scrutiny does not permit a court to accept a school's assertion that its admissions process uses race in a permissible way without a court giving close analysis to the evidence of how the process works in practice.

[Strict] scrutiny must not be "strict in theory, but fatal in fact." But the opposite is also true. Strict scrutiny must not be strict in theory but feeble in fact. [The] judgment of the Court of Appeals is vacated, and the case is remanded for further proceedings consistent with this opinion.

JUSTICE SCALIA, concurring.

I adhere to the view I expressed in *Grutter* that "The Constitution proscribes government discrimination on the basis of race, and state-provided education is no exception." [But because t]he petitioner in this case did not ask us to overrule *Grutter,* [I] join the Court's opinion in full.

JUSTICE THOMAS, concurring.

[Our] desegregation cases establish that the Constitution prohibits public schools from discriminating based on race, even if discrimination is necessary to the schools' survival. [It] follows, a fortiori, that the putative educational benefits of student body diversity cannot justify racial discrimination: If a State does not have a compelling interest in the *existence* of a university, it certainly cannot have a compelling interest in the supposed benefits that might accrue to that university from racial discrimination.

My view of the Constitution is the one advanced by the plaintiffs in *Brown*: "[N]o State has any authority under the equal-protection clause of the Fourteenth Amendment to use race as a factor in affording educational opportunities among its citizens." [This] principle is neither new nor difficult to understand. In 1868, decades before *Plessy*, the Iowa Supreme Court held that schools may not discriminate against applicants based on their skin color. In *Clark v. Board of Directors*, 24 Iowa 266 (1868), a school denied admission to a student because she was black, and "public sentiment [was] opposed to the intermingling of white and colored children in the same schools." The Iowa Supreme Court rejected that flimsy justification, holding that "all the youths are equal before the law, and there is no discretion vested in the board . . . or elsewhere, to interfere with or disturb that equality."[59]

[The] worst forms of racial discrimination in this Nation have always been accompanied by straight-faced representations that discrimination helped minorities. Slaveholders argued that slavery was a "positive good" that civilized blacks and elevated them in every dimension of life. [A] century later, segregationists similarly asserted [that] separate schools protected black children from racist white students and teachers. [The] University's discrimination "stamp[s] [blacks and Hispanics] with a badge of inferiority." [Although] most blacks and Hispanics attending the University were admitted without discrimination under the Top Ten Percent plan [no] one can distinguish those students from the ones whose race played a role in their admission.

JUSTICE GINSBURG, dissenting.

[Because] the University's admissions policy [satisfies the standards set out in] Justice Powell's opinion in *Bakke* and the Court's decision in *Grutter*, [I] would affirm the judgment of the Court of Appeals.[60]

NOTES AND QUESTIONS

1. *Narrow tailoring. Fisher* rendered a narrow holding that states' decisions with respect to narrow tailoring do not command judicial deference. But a narrow tailoring inquiry necessarily subsumes the question: narrowly tailored to what? Although a narrow majority of the Justices appears to recognize a compelling interest in "diversity," note that Kennedy, J., who appears to be the "swing" Justice in *Fisher*, may not hold as capacious a view

---

[59] The decision was based on Iowa law, not the Fourteenth Amendment.

[60] Kagan, J., did not participate.

as that of O'Connor, J., who was the "swing" Justice and wrote the majority opinion in *Grutter*.

　2.　***Pertinence of Parents Involved.*** In thinking about what "narrow tailoring" requires, consider the pertinence of the Court's 2007 decision in *Parents Involved in Community Schools v. Seattle School Dist. No. 1*, supra.

―――――

B.　Employment and Government Contracts

　WYGANT v. JACKSON BD. OF EDUC., 476 U.S. 267 (1986), involved a minority preference in teacher lay-offs. When a budget crisis required cutting teaching positions, the school board, pursuant to a contract with the local teachers union, laid off white teachers in order to retain minority teachers. The court of appeals upheld the school board's action as justified by its interest in "providing role models for its minority students, as an attempt to alleviate the effects of societal discrimination." Although there was no majority opinion, five Justices agreed that the school board had violated the Constitution.

　Writing for a plurality,[61] POWELL, J., found that race-based preferences must be subjected to strict scrutiny. The plurality concluded that the school board had no compelling interest in remedying "societal discrimination," and suggested that "prior [institutional] discrimination" supplied the only permissible justification for "race-based remedies." But even if the school board had discriminated in the past, "the burden that a preferential-layoffs scheme imposes on innocent parties" would be too great to be constitutionally acceptable. "While hiring goals impose a diffuse burden, often foreclosing only one of several opportunities, layoffs impose the entire burden of achieving racial equality on particular individuals, often resulting in serious disruption of their lives. That burden is too intrusive" and therefore fails the requirement that a race-based remedy be "narrowly tailored" to achieve its ends.

　O'CONNOR, J., concurring, subscribed to the view that "racial classifications of any sort must be subjected to 'strict scrutiny.'" Under this standard, she "agree[d] with the plurality that a governmental agency's interest in remedying 'societal' discrimination [cannot] be deemed sufficiently compelling to pass constitutional muster." Even if the school board had discriminated in the past, it had attempted to justify its layoff program by reference to discrimination with respect to student assignments, not faculty hiring, and the remedy was not closely tailored to the violation. With respect to other possible compelling government interests: "[A]lthough its precise contours are uncertain, a state interest in the promotion of racial diversity has been found sufficiently 'compelling,'

―――――

[61]　Burger, C.J., and Rehnquist, J., joined in all, and O'Connor, J., in parts, of the opinion.

at least in the context of higher education, to support the use of racial considerations in furthering that interest. And certainly nothing the Court has said today necessarily forecloses the possibility that the Court will find other governmental interests which have been relied upon in the lower courts but which have not been passed on here to be sufficiently 'important' or 'compelling' to sustain the use of affirmative action policies."[62]

Dissenting, MARSHALL, J., joined by Brennan and Blackmun, JJ., found the school board's actions adequately justified by its interest in "preserv[ing] the levels of faculty integration" achieved during the 1970s by an affirmative action program of unchallenged validity. It was a mistake to regard laid-off whites as singled out to bear a unique and disproportionate burden. The aim of the contract between the school board and the union was to apportion the burden of layoffs that were not deserved by anyone, and there was no basis for thinking that "the tradition of basing layoff decisions on seniority is so fundamental that its modification can never be permitted."

In a separate dissent, STEVENS, J., argued that the Equal Protection Clause permits "inclusionary" but not "exclusionary" use of racial classifications to promote legitimate government purposes. He would not have asked whether the race-based preference was justified "as a remedy for sins that were committed in the past," but whether by maintaining "an integrated faculty" it provided educational benefits that "could not be provided by an all-white" faculty.

NOTES AND QUESTIONS

1. ***Diversity.*** If the government in *Bakke* had a compelling interest in achieving a diverse student body, why did the school board in *Wygant* not have a compelling interest in retaining a diverse faculty?[63] If layoff decisions had been based on individualized assessments, rather than seniority, could a faculty member's contribution to faculty diversity have been treated as a "plus"? Compare *Wittmer v. Peters*, 87 F.3d 916, 920 (7th Cir. 1996), cert. denied, 519 U.S. 1111 (1997), which upheld a hiring plan for a prison boot camp—nearly 70% of the inmates at which were racial minorities—that used race as a hiring criterion for camp lieutenants. In an opinion by Judge Posner, the court explicitly rejected an argument attempting to justify racial hiring preferences on a general "role-model" theory, "because of lack of substantiation and [its] well-nigh unlimited reach." The court held, however, that the

---

[62] White, J., wrote a brief opinion concurring in the judgment, but did not specifically endorse any standard of review.

[63] Compare Robert A. Sedler, *Racial Preference and the Constitution: The Societal Interest in the Equal Participation Objective,* 26 Wayne L.Rev. 1227 (1980), arguing that, under the logic of Powell, J.'s opinion in *Bakke*, "there is strong societal interest in [the] equal participation of blacks * * * whenever a 'black [can] bring something that a white person cannot offer,' " and that this extends to *all* "institutions of government, the 'power professions,' such as law and medicine, [and] the economic system."

argument for black lieutenants was "backed up by expert evidence the plaintiffs did not rebut" to the effect that "the boot camp [would] not succeed in its mission of pacification and reformation with as white a staff as it would have had if a black male had not been appointed to one of the lieutenant slots."

2. ***Remedial justifications.*** Apart from any possible interest in diversity, the lower courts have accepted that affirmative action hiring can be justified where necessary to remedy past discrimination by the institution implementing the remedy (but not to remedy "societal" discrimination), provided that the requirement of narrow tailoring is met. *See* John C. Day, *Retelling the Story of Affirmative Action: Reflections on a Decade of Federal Jurisprudence in the Public Workplace*, 89 Calif.L.Rev. 59 (2001).

3. ***Weight of burden.*** Should it matter that *Wygant* involved a lay-off, not a hiring, decision and that the dislocations attending a job loss are likely to be significantly greater than the hardships of not getting a job in the first place? See Richard H. Fallon, Jr. & Paul C. Weiler, Firefighters v. Stotts*: Conflicting Models of Racial Justice*, 1984 Sup.Ct.Rev. 1 (yes).

4. ***Title VII of the 1964 Civil Rights Act.*** RICCI v. DeSTEFANO, 557 U.S. 557 (2009), per KENNEDY, J., avoided questions involving the constitutionality of New Haven, Connecticut's decision to discard an employment test after minority candidates scored less well than whites by finding that the decision violated Title VII of the 1964 Civil Rights Act. City officials decided not to certify the test results, which would have determined promotions of firefighters to lieutenant and captain, in order to avoid a suit by minority applicants under one provision of Title VII, which bars employment tests that have a "disparate impact" on or disproportionately exclude minority applicants unless such tests are justified by "business necessity." But the City's action to avoid a lawsuit by minority applicants triggered another, brought primarily by white firefighters, who claimed that the defendants violated another Title VII provision, which bars racially "disparate treatment" or intentional discrimination, as well as the Equal Protection Clause. The Court, by 5–4, found a violation of the statutory prohibition against racially disparate treatment. In doing so, it concluded that New Haven's actions were not compelled by Title VII's "disparate impact" prohibition and thereby avoided needing to decide whether Congress's mandate that employers eschew tests with adverse disparate impacts on minority groups (absent a showing of business necessity) violates the equal protection rights of whites in some or all cases. For discussion of "whether Title VII's disparate impact doctrine, which requires employers and public officials to classify the workforce into racial categories and then allocate social goods on the basis of that classification, can be consistent with equal protection after decisions [like] *Parents Involved*," see Richard Primus, *The Future of Disparate Impact*, 108 Mich.L.Rev. 1341 (2010).

RICHMOND v. J.A. CROSON CO., 488 U.S. 469 (1989), invalidated the City of Richmond, Virginia's Minority Business Utilization Plan, which required prime contractors on city construction contracts to subcontract at least 30% of the dollar amount of the contract to one or more Minority Business Enterprises (MBEs), defined as "[a] business at least fifty-one (51) percent of which is owned and controlled" by "[c]itizens of the United States who are Blacks, Spanish-speaking, Orientals, Indians, Eskimos, or Aleuts." The Plan authorized waivers of the minority subcontracting requirement in some cases. At the time of its adoption, the City of Richmond was about 50% black, and blacks controlled five of nine seats on the city council, but less than 1% of the city's prime construction contracts had been awarded to minority businesses in the 5-year period from 1978 to 1983.

O'CONNOR, J., announced the judgment of the Court and delivered the opinion of the Court only in part, with Kennedy, J., and Scalia, J., both declining to join some parts of her opinion (which was joined in full by Rehnquist, C.J., and White, J). Writing for a plurality only, O'Connor, J., distinguished an earlier case, *Fullilove v. Klutznick,* 448 U.S. 448 (1980), in which the Court had upheld a federal government preference for minority contractors, largely on the basis that "Congress, unlike any State or political subdivision, has a specific constitutional mandate to enforce the dictates of the Fourteenth Amendment. The power to 'enforce' may at times also include the power to define situations which *Congress* determines threaten principles of equality and to adopt prophylactic rules to deal with those situations. See *Katzenbach v. Morgan*, [Ch. 11, Sec. 3]." In this section of the opinion, O'Connor, J., also affirmed the permissibility of race-based preferences by state and local governments under some circumstances: "[A] state or local subdivision (if delegated the authority from the State) has the authority to eradicate the effects of private discrimination within its own legislative jurisdiction." Moreover, "if the city could show that it had essentially become a 'passive participant' in a system of racial exclusion practiced by elements of the local construction industry, we think it clear that the city could take affirmative steps to dismantle such a system."

Still speaking only for a plurality, O'Connor, J., affirmed "the view expressed by the plurality in *Wygant* that the standard of review under the Equal Protection Clause is not dependent on the race of those burdened or benefitted by a particular classification" and held that "heightened scrutiny" applied. The Richmond plan failed that standard, she wrote, in parts of her opinion that commanded a majority: "Appellant argues that it is attempting to remedy various forms of past discrimination that are alleged to be responsible for the small number of minority businesses in the local contracting industry. [While] there is no doubt that the sorry history of both private and public discrimination in this country has contributed to a lack of opportunities for black entrepreneurs, this observation, standing alone, cannot justify a rigid racial quota in the awarding of public contracts in Richmond, Virginia. [There] is nothing approaching a prima facie case of a constitutional or statutory violation by *anyone* in the Richmond construction industry. [And the] foregoing analysis applies only to the inclusion of blacks within the Richmond set-aside program. There is *absolutely no evidence* of past discrimination against Spanish-speaking, Oriental, Indian, Eskimo, or Aleut persons in any aspect of the Richmond construction industry. * * *

"[It] is almost impossible to assess whether the Richmond Plan is narrowly tailored to remedy prior discrimination since it is not linked to identified discrimination in any way."

STEVENS, J., concurred in part and in the judgment: "[T]he city makes no claim that the public interest in the efficient performance of its construction contracts will be served by granting a preference to minority-business enterprises. This case is therefore completely unlike *Wygant,* in which I thought it quite obvious that the School Board had reasonably concluded that an integrated faculty could provide educational benefits to the entire student body that could not be provided by an all-white, or nearly all-white faculty."

KENNEDY, J., also concurred in part and in the judgment: "[The] moral imperative of racial neutrality is the driving force of the Equal Protection Clause. Justice Scalia's opinion underscores that proposition, quite properly in my view. The rule suggested in his opinion, which would strike down all preferences which are not necessary remedies to victims of unlawful discrimination, would serve important structural goals, as it would eliminate the necessity for courts to pass upon each racial preference that is enacted.

"Nevertheless, given that a rule of automatic invalidity for racial preferences in almost every case would be a significant break with our precedents that require a case-by-case test, I am not convinced we need adopt it at this point."

SCALIA, J., concurred in the judgment: "I agree with much of the Court's opinion, and, in particular, with its conclusion that strict scrutiny must be applied to all governmental classification by race, whether or not its asserted purpose is 'remedial' or 'benign.' I do not agree, however, with the Court's dicta suggesting that, despite the Fourteenth Amendment, state and local governments may in some circumstances discriminate on the basis of race in order (in a broad sense) 'to ameliorate the effects of past discrimination.' The benign purpose of compensating for social disadvantages, whether they have been acquired by reason of prior discrimination or otherwise, can no more be pursued by the illegitimate means of racial discrimination than can other assertedly benign purposes we have repeatedly rejected. See, e.g., [*Wygant*]. At least where state or local action is at issue, only a social emergency rising to the level of imminent danger to life and limb—for example, a prison race riot, requiring temporary segregation of inmates, cf. *Lee v. Washington,* 390 U.S. 333 (1968)—can justify an exception to the principle embodied in the Fourteenth Amendment that '[o]ur Constitution is color-blind, and neither knows nor tolerates classes among citizens,' *Plessy* (Harlan, J., dissenting) * * * .

"I agree with the Court's dictum that a fundamental distinction must be drawn between the effects of 'societal' discrimination and the effects of 'identified' discrimination, and that the situation would be different if Richmond's plan were 'tailored' to identify those particular bidders who 'suffered from the effects of past discrimination by the city or prime contractors.' In my view, however, the reason that would make a difference is not, as the Court states, that it would justify race-conscious action but rather that it would enable race-neutral remediation. Nothing prevents Richmond from according a contracting preference to identified victims of discrimination. While most of the beneficiaries might be black, neither the beneficiaries nor those disadvantaged by the preference would be identified *on the basis of their race.* In other words, far from justifying racial classification, identification of actual victims of discrimination makes it less supportable than ever, because more obviously unneeded."

MARSHALL, J., joined by Brennan and Blackmun, JJ., dissented: "My view has long been that race-conscious classifications designed to further remedial goals 'must serve important governmental objectives and must be substantially related to achievement of those objectives' in order to withstand constitutional scrutiny. Analyzed in terms of this two-prong standard, Richmond's set-aside, like the federal program on which it was modeled, is 'plainly constitutional.'

"Richmond has two powerful interests in setting aside a portion of public contracting funds for minority-owned enterprises. The first is the city's interest in eradicating the effects of past racial discrimination. * * * Richmond has a second compelling interest in setting aside, where possible, a portion of its contracting dollars. [In] my view, the interest in ensuring that the government does not reflect and reinforce prior private discrimination in dispensing public contracts is every bit as strong as the interest in eliminating private discrimination—an interest which this Court has repeatedly deemed compelling. See, e.g., *Roberts v. United States Jaycees,* [Ch. 7, Sec. 9, II].

"[In] my judgment, Richmond's set-aside plan also comports with the second prong of the equal protection inquiry, for it is substantially related to the interests it seeks to serve in remedying past discrimination and in ensuring that municipal contract procurement does not perpetuate that discrimination. [The] majority overlooks the fact that since 1975, Richmond has barred both discrimination by the city in awarding public contracts and discrimination by public contractors. The virtual absence of minority businesses from the city's contracting rolls, indicated by the fact that such businesses have received less than 1% of public contracting dollars, strongly suggests that this ban has not succeeded in redressing the impact of past discrimination or in preventing city contract procurement from reinforcing racial homogeneity. * * *

"As for Richmond's 30% target, the majority [ignores] two important facts. First, the set-aside measure affects only 3% of overall city contracting; thus, any imprecision in tailoring has far less impact than the majority suggests. But more important, the majority ignores the fact that Richmond's 30% figure was patterned directly on the *Fullilove* precedent. Congress' 10% figure fell "roughly halfway between the present percentage of minority contractors and the percentage of minority group members in the Nation." The Richmond City Council's 30% figure similarly falls roughly halfway between the present percentage of Richmond-based minority contractors (almost zero) and the percentage of minorities in Richmond (50%)."

NOTES AND QUESTIONS

1. **Standard.** A clear majority in *Croson* agreed that affirmative action programs should be upheld only if closely tailored to serve a compelling government interest. But did a majority also agree on what this standard means in practice?

Suppose that the City of Richmond could have established past discrimination that it had a compelling interest in remedying. Could it immediately have implemented race-based preferences, or would it need to have attempted other, race-neutral measures—or at least demonstrated their futility—first?[64]

2. **"Individual" and "group" justice.** (a) Consider the position of Charles Fried, Metro Broadcasting, Inc. v. FCC: *Two Concepts of Equality*, 104 Harv.L.Rev. 107 (1990), that O'Connor, J., for the *Croson* plurality, reads the Equal Protection Clause as embodying an "individualistic" conception of fairness, whereas the position of the dissenters rests on a conception of "group" justice. On the individualistic conception, Fried says, race-based remedies are permissible only to compensate for past wrongs by an individual wrongdoer; this is why remedies for "societal" discrimination are inappropriate. But how "individualistic" is a position that requires identified wrongdoing as a predicate for race-based remedies, but then allows the benefit of those remedies to flow to persons not proven to be the victims of the identified wrongdoing? In other words, the position identified (and defended) as individualistic requires individually identified wrongdoing, but then—once the wrongdoing is

---

[64] Consider Ian Ayres, *Narrow Tailoring*, 43 U.C.L.A. L.Rev. 1781 (1996), arguing that the Court's preference for race-neutral remedies is inconsistent with its demand for narrow tailoring, since a remedy for discrimination against racial minorities can be more narrowly tailored if only minorities benefit.

identified—allows group-based remedies in at least some circumstances. Does this asymmetry make sense?

(b) Does the dissenting position of Marshall, J., necessarily reflect the "collectivist" assumption that racial groups "hav[e] a status independent of and even superior to that of individual group members"? Fried, supra.

3. ***Preferences for majorities.*** Should it have mattered to the analysis in *Croson* that blacks held more than half the seats on the Richmond city council? That the set-aside program benefitted a range of groups with diverse histories and current economic statuses? Did the facts illustrate a serious risk of race-based division and resentment engendered by "a form of racial politics"?

———

In ADARAND CONSTRUCTORS, INC. v. PENA, 515 U.S. 200 (1995), the Court, per O'CONNOR, J., overruled its earlier decision in *Metro Broadcasting, Inc. v. FCC*, 497 U.S. 547 (1990),[65] which had held that affirmative action programs implemented by the federal government, need only satisfy intermediate scrutiny. In doing so, the Court relied on *Croson*, which had said that "[a]bsent searching judicial inquiry into the justification for such race-based measures, there is simply no way of determining what classifications are 'benign' or 'remedial' and what classifications are in fact motivated by illegitimate notions of racial inferiority or simple racial politics": "We adhere to that view. Accordingly, we hold today that all racial classifications, imposed by whatever federal, state, or local governmental actor, must be analyzed by a reviewing court under strict scrutiny [and] are constitutional only if they are narrowly tailored measures that further compelling governmental interests. * * *

"It is true that various Members of this Court have taken different views of the authority § 5 of the Fourteenth Amendment confers upon Congress to deal with the problem of racial discrimination, and the extent to which courts should defer to Congress' exercise of that authority. We need not, and do not, address these differences today. * * *

"[Finally,] we wish to dispel the notion that strict scrutiny is 'strict in theory, but fatal in fact.' The unhappy persistence of both the practice and the lingering effects of racial discrimination against minority groups in this country is an unfortunate reality, and government is not disqualified from acting in response to it. As recently as 1987, for example, every Justice of this Court agreed that the Alabama Department of Public Safety's 'pervasive, systematic, and obstinate discriminatory conduct' justified a

---

[65] *Metro Broadcasting*, per Brennan, J., upheld FCC policies granting preferences to minority ownerships in the acquisition and transfer of broadcast licenses on the basis of the governmental interest "in enhancing broadcast diversity." The opinion was joined by Justice White, who had joined the plurality opinion in *Croson*; it distinguished *Croson* as having established the level of scrutiny applicable to affirmative action programs initiated by state and local governments, not to federal affirmative action. O'Connor, J., joined by Rehnquist, C.J., and Scalia and Kennedy, JJ., dissented.

narrowly tailored race-based remedy. See *United States v. Paradise*, 480 U.S. 149 (1987).[66] When race-based action is necessary to further a compelling interest, such action is within constitutional constraints if it satisfies the 'narrow tailoring' test this Court has set out in previous cases."

SCALIA, J., concurred in part and in the judgment: "In my view, government can never have a 'compelling interest' in discriminating on the basis of race in order to 'make up' for past racial discrimination in the opposite direction."

THOMAS, J., concurred in part and in the judgment: "I agree with the majority's conclusion that strict scrutiny applies to *all* government classifications based on race. I write separately, however, to express my disagreement with the premise underlying Justice Stevens' and Justice Ginsburg's dissents: that there is a racial paternalism exception to the principle of equal protection. I believe that there is a 'moral [and] constitutional equivalence,' (Stevens, J., dissenting), between laws designed to subjugate a race and those that distribute benefits on the basis of race in order to foster some current notion of equality. Government cannot make us equal; it can only recognize, respect, and protect us as equal before the law."

STEVENS, J., joined by Ginsburg, J., dissented. In his view, there was "no moral or constitutional equivalence between a policy that is designed to perpetuate a caste system and one that seeks to eradicate racial subordination." Stevens, J., also criticized the majority for overruling *Metro Broadcasting* and holding that federal and state affirmative action programs were equally constitutionally suspect: "The majority in *Metro Broadcasting* [was] not alone in relying upon a critical distinction between federal and state programs. In his separate opinion in [*Croson*], Justice Scalia discussed the basis for this distinction. He observed that 'it is one thing to permit racially based conduct by the Federal Government—whose legislative powers concerning matters of race were explicitly enhanced by the Fourteenth Amendment—and quite another to permit it by the precise entities against whose conduct in matters of race that Amendment was specifically directed.' [In] her plurality opinion in *Croson*, Justice O'Connor also emphasized the importance of this distinction when she responded to the City's argument that *Fullilove* was controlling. [It] is one thing to say (as no one seems to dispute) that the Fifth Amendment encompasses a general guarantee of equal protection as broad as that contained within the Fourteenth Amendment. It is another thing entirely to say that Congress' institutional competence and constitutional authority entitles it to no

---

[66] *Paradise* upheld a *judicially* ordered race-conscious remedy. The Court was unanimous that the federal government has a compelling interest in remedying proven race discrimination. Per Brennan, J., it found the particular order at issue to be "narrowly tailored," and thus upheld it, by a closely divided vote of 5–4.

greater deference when it enacts a program designed to foster equality than the deference due a State legislature."[67]

NOTES AND QUESTIONS

1. ***Shifting standards?*** (a) Consider Stephen A. Siegel, *The Federal Government's Power to Enact Color-Conscious Laws: An Originalist Inquiry*, 92 Nw.U.L.Rev. 477 (1998): "[T]here is no plausible originalist argument that the Constitution proscribes the federal government's power to enact benign color-conscious laws, such as affirmative action [under the Fifth Amendment's Due Process Clause]. The color-blind Constitution is an evolutionary, not an originalist, Constitution."

(b) O'Connor, J.'s plurality opinion in *Croson* had defended a divergence between the judicial scrutiny applicable to congressionally mandated affirmative action, on the one hand, and affirmative action by state and local governments, on the other hand. Why did she change her mind—or did she?

2. ***Applying strict scrutiny to federal affirmative action.*** While holding that federal affirmative action triggers the same strict judicial scrutiny as state affirmative action, *Adarand* alluded to, but did not resolve, the possible relevance of Section 5 of the Fourteenth Amendment—which provides that "[t]he Congress shall have the power to enforce, by appropriate legislation, the provisions of this article"—in determining whether congressional action might satisfy that standard. How might Section 5 matter? Since *Adarand*, the Court has held that the Section 5 power is exclusively a power to prevent or remedy *state action* that violates the Constitution and that federal statutes enacted under Section 5 must be "congruent" and "proportional" to the pattern of unconstitutional action to which they are addressed. See *City of Boerne v. Flores*, Ch. 11, Sec. 3.

––––––––

C. "The Political Process Doctrine"

SCHUETTE v. COALITION TO DEFEND AFFIRMATIVE ACTION, INTEGRATION, AND IMMIGRATION RIGHTS BY ANY MEANS NECESSARY (BAMN), 134 S.Ct. 1623 (2014), arose after Michigan voters approved a ballot proposition, which became Article I, § 26, of the Michigan Constitution, that effectively barred race-based affirmative action preferences by the state government, including by public colleges and universities. In mounting an equal protection attack, the challengers relied on what the court of appeals called "the political process doctrine"—the precise definition of which was a subject of dispute among the Justices, as will be explained below—that it traced principally to *Hunter v. Erickson*, 393 U.S. 385 (1969), and *Washington v. Seattle School Dist. No. 1*, 458 U.S.

––––––––––––––––

[67] The dissenting opinions of Souter, J., joined by Ginsburg and Breyer, JJ., and of Ginsburg, J., joined by Breyer, J., are omitted.

457 (1982). By a vote of 6–2, the Court rejected the challenge, with a plurality of the Justices finding that § 26 did not run afoul of the political-process doctrine and with two Justices repudiating that doctrine altogether.[68]

KENNEDY, J., joined by the Chief Justice and Justice Alito, explicated the political process doctrine by summarizing *Hunter* and *Seattle*: In *Hunter,* after the Akron City Council found racial discrimination in the private housing market, it "enacted a fair housing ordinance. [In] response, voters amended the city charter to overturn the ordinance and to require that any additional antidiscrimination housing ordinance be approved by referendum. [The] Court found that the city charter amendment, by singling out antidiscrimination ordinances, 'places special burden on racial minorities within the governmental process,' thus becoming as impermissible as any other government action taken with the invidious intent to injure a racial minority."

In *Seattle,* after "the school board adopted a mandatory busing program to alleviate racial isolation of minority students in local schools[, v]oters who opposed the school board's busing plan passed a state initiative that barred [voluntary] busing." The Court found the state initiative invalid because " 'the practical effect' [was] to 'remov[e] the authority to address a racial problem—and only a racial problem—from the existing decisionmaking body, in such a way as to burden minority interests' because advocates of busing 'now must seek relief from the state legislature, or from the statewide electorate.' "

The plurality understood both cases, and the political-process doctrine generally, as only applicable to state action that has "the serious risk, if not purpose, of causing specific injuries on account of race."[69] As Kennedy, J., acknowledged, "*Seattle* [also] stated that where a government policy 'inures primarily to the benefit of the minority and minorities [consider] the policy to be in their interest, then any state action that place[s] effective decisionmaking authority over that policy at a different level of government must be reviewed under strict scrutiny.' " But that "broad language [went] well beyond the analysis needed to resolve" *Seattle* and "must be rejected. The court of appeals'] expansive reading of *Seattle* has no principled limitation and [would] contradict central equal protection principles" by requiring courts to reason based on " 'impermissible racial

---

[68] Kagan, J., did not participate.

[69] Kennedy, J. characterized "the State's disapproval of the [busing] remedy [in *Seattle* as] an aggravation of [a] racial injury in which the State itself was complicit." In doing so, he acknowledged that, "[a]s the Court held in *Parents Involved*, the school board's purported remedial action would not be permissible today absent a showing of de jure segregation. That holding prompted Justice Breyer to observe in dissent [that] one permissible reading of the record was that the school board had maintained policies to perpetuate segregation in the schools. In all events, [the] legitimacy and constitutionality of the remedy in question (busing for desegregation) was assumed, and *Seattle* must be understood on that basis."

stereotypes' [that] 'members of the same racial group [think] alike, share the same political interests, and will prefer the same candidates.' [And] if it were deemed necessary to probe how some races define their own interest in political matters, still another beginning point would be to define individuals according to race. [That approach would] risk [the] creation of incentives for those who support or oppose certain policies to cast the debate in terms of racial advantage or disadvantage."

Properly defined, the political-process doctrine did not apply to § 26, which involved "no infliction of a specific injury. [The] question is not how to address or prevent injury caused on account of race but whether voters may determine whether a policy of race-based preferences should be continued. [Our] constitutional system embraces [the] right of citizens to [use] the political process [to] shape the course of [public policy.]

"[This] case is not about how the debate about racial preferences should be resolved. It is about who may resolve it. There is no authority [for] the Judiciary to set aside Michigan laws that commit this policy determination to the voters."

ROBERTS, C.J., concurred: "To disagree with the dissent's views on the costs and benefits of racial preferences is not to 'wish away, rather than confront' racial inequality. People can disagree in good faith on this issue, but it [does] more harm than good to question the openness and candor of those on either side of the debate."

SCALIA, J., joined by Thomas, J., concurring, began by reiterating his view that " '[t]he Constitution proscribes government discrimination on the basis of race, and state-provided education is no exception.' *Grutter* (Scalia, J, concurring in part and dissenting in part). It is [the] correct understanding [of] the federal Equal Protection Clause that the people of the State of Michigan have adopted for their own fundamental law. By adopting it, they did not simultaneously *offend* it."

In so concluding, Scalia, J., thought that the plurality erred in failing flatly to repudiate "the political-process doctrine." In his view, "[*Hunter*] and *Seattle* should be overruled," because "the logic" of both cases wrongly called for a finding of constitutional invalidity whenever "a higher level of government" withdrew the capacity of a lower level to "exercise[ ] [authority] over an apparently 'racial issue' [regardless] of whether it facially classified according to race or reflected an invidious purpose to discriminate. [The] problems with the political-process doctrine begin with its triggering prong, which assigns to a court the [judicially unmanageable] task of determining whether a law that reallocates policymaking authority concerns a 'racial issue.' [M]aybe judges need only ask this question: Is it possible 'that minorities may consider' the policy in question to be 'in their interest'?[4] [No] good can come of such random judicial musing, [which] involves judges in the dirty business of dividing the Nation 'into racial blocs.'"

Scalia, J., also thought that the political process doctrine should be rejected as incompatible with "the near-limitless sovereignty of each State to design its governing structure as it sees fit." He additionally "part[ed] ways with *Hunter, Seattle,* and (I think) the plurality [because e]ach endorses a version of the proposition that a facially neutral law may deny equal protection solely because it has a disparate racial impact."

BREYER, J., concurred in the judgment: "This case [does] not involve a reordering of the *political* process. [Michigan] delegated broad policymaking authority to elected university boards, but those boards delegated admissions-related decisionmaking authority to unelected university faculty members and administrators. Although the boards unquestionably retained the *power* to set policy regarding race-conscious admissions, in *fact* faculty members and administrators set the race-conscious admissions policies in question. [One] cannot [easily] characterize the movement of the decisionmaking mechanism at issue here—from an administrative process to an electoral process—as diminishing the minority's ability to participate meaningfully in the *political* process. There is no prior electoral process in which the minority participated."

SOTOMAYOR, J., joined by Ginsburg, J., dissented: "[To] know the history of our Nation is to understand its long and lamentable record of stymieing the right of racial minorities to participate in the political process. [This] case involves [the] last chapter of discrimination: A majority of the Michigan electorate changed the basic rules of the political process [in] a manner that uniquely disadvantaged racial minorities.[1]

"Under [the political process] doctrine, governmental action deprives minority groups of equal protection when it (1) has a racial focus, targeting a policy or program that 'inures primarily to the benefit of the minority,' and (2) alters the political process in a manner that uniquely burdens racial minorities' ability to achieve their goals through that process. [Section] 26 has a 'racial focus.' [Like] desegregation of public schools, race-sensitive admissions policies 'inur[e] primarily to the benefit of the minority,' as they are designed to increase minorities' access to institutions of higher

---

[4] **[Ct's Note]** "[According to the dissent] an issue is 'racial' if the policy benefits *primarily* a racial minority and '[is] designed for that purpose.' [But] under that standard, § 26 does not affect a 'racial issue,' because under *Grutter,* race-based admissions policies may not constitutionally be 'designed for [the] purpose' of benefitting primarily racial minorities, but must be designed for the purpose of achieving educational benefits for students of all races."

[1] **[Ct's Note]** I of course do not mean to suggest that Michigan's voters acted with anything like the invidious intent of those who historically stymied the rights of racial minorities. But like earlier chapters of political restructuring, the Michigan amendment at issue in this case changed the rules of the political process to the disadvantage of minority members of our society.

education. [Section 26 also] restructures the political process [in] a manner that places unique burdens on racial minorities. [Before] the enactment of § 26, [Michigan's] political structure permitted both supporters and opponents of race-sensitive admissions policies to vote [in statewide general elections] for their candidates of choice [to serve on public universities' governing boards. As] a result of § 26, [the] one and only policy a Michigan citizen may not seek [to achieve] through this long-established process is a race-sensitive admissions policy."

Sotomayor, J., rejected the plurality's characterization of *Hunter* and *Seattle* as involving "nothing more than the intentional and invidious infliction of a racial injury. *Seattle* "unmistakably rested" on the state's " 'us[ing] the racial nature of an issue to define the governmental decisionmaking structure, [thus] impos[ing] substantial and unique burdens on racial minorities.' [The] political-process doctrine not only resolves this case as a matter of *stare decisis*; it is correct as a matter of first principles. [The] values identified in *Carolene Products* lie at the heart of the political-process doctrine.

"[Scalia, J.] argues that the political-process doctrine 'misreads the Equal Protection Clause to protect particular group[s], running counter to a line of cases that treat equal protection as a personal right.' [This] criticism ignores the obvious: Discrimination against an individual occurs because of that individual's membership in a particular group.

"[My] colleagues also attack the [political process] doctrine as ['unadministrable.' Yet] *Hunter* and *Seattle* provide a standard: Does the public policy at issue 'inur[e] primarily to the benefit of the minority, and [was it] designed for that purpose'? ['No] good can come' from these inquiries, Justice Scalia responds, because they divide the Nation along racial lines and perpetuate racial stereotypes. [My] colleagues [believe] that we should leave race out of the picture entirely and let the voters sort it out. [But r]ace matters. Race matters in part because of the long history of racial minorities' being denied access to the political process. [Race] also matters because of persistent racial inequality in society—inequality that cannot be ignored and that has produced stark socioeconomic disparities. [And] race matters for reasons that [cannot] be discussed any other way, and that cannot be wished away. Race matters to a young man's view of society when he spends his teenage years watching others tense up as he passes, no matter the neighborhood where he grew up. Race matters to a young woman's sense of self when she states her hometown, and then is pressed, 'No, where are you really from? [Race] matters because of the slights, the snickers, the silent judgments that reinforce that most crippling of thoughts: 'I do not belong here.' [As] members of the judiciary tasked with intervening to carry out the guarantee of equal protection, we ought not sit back and wish away, rather than confront, the racial inequality that exists in our society. It is this view that works harm, by perpetuating the facile notion that what makes race matter is acknowledging the simple truth that race does matter."

3. DISCRIMINATIONS BASED ON GENDER

I. DEFINING THE LEVEL OF SCRUTINY

Prior to 1971, the Court used the deferential "traditional approach" (see Sec. 1 supra) to test the constitutionality of classifications based on gender. *Muller v. Oregon,* 208 U.S. 412 (1908), per Brewer, J., upheld a law barring factory work by women for more than ten hours a day, reasoning that "as healthy mothers are essential to vigorous offspring, the physical well-being of a woman becomes an object of public interest and care."[70] *Goesaert v. Cleary,* 335 U.S. 464 (1948), per Frankfurter, J., upheld a law denying bartender's licenses to most women, reasoning that "the fact that women may now have achieved the virtues that men have long claimed as their prerogatives and now indulge in vices that men have long practiced, does not preclude the States from drawing a sharp line between the sexes, certainly in such matters as the regulation of the liquor traffic."[71] As recently as 1961, *Hoyt v. Florida,* 368 U.S. 57, per Harlan, J., sustained a law placing women on the jury list only if they made special request, stating that a "woman is still regarded as the center of home and family life."[72]

Consider Barry Friedman, *The Will of the People: How Public Opinion Has Influenced the Supreme Court and Shaped the Meaning of the Constitution* 290–91 (2009): "By the 1960s, though, the Court's decisions were running up against reality. Women flooded into the workplace, only to encounter great discrimination once there. Between 1940 and 1960, the number of women working outside the home doubled. As of 1970, 43 percent of women held jobs. [Yet] women worked for about 60 percent of what men were paid and constituted a tiny portion of the professions.

"Discrimination continued as the women's movement coalesced in the 1960s. Betty Friedan's *The Feminine Mystique* [1963] provided the spark. [It] described the deep unease of '[m]illions of women . . . kissing their husbands goodbye [and] depositing their stationwagonsful of children at

---

[70] But see *Adkins v. Children's Hospital,* 261 U.S. 525 (1923) (minimum wage for women violates due process), overruled, *West Coast Hotel Co. v. Parrish,* Ch. 5, Sec. 3 supra.

[71] See also the concurring opinion of Bradley, J., joined by Swayne and Field, JJ., in *Bradwell v. Illinois,* 83 U.S. (16 Wall.) 130 (1873), which upheld a statute denying women the right to practice law against challenge based on the Privileges or Immunities Clause: "[T]he natural and proper timidity and delicacy which belongs to the female sex evidently unfits it for many of the occupations of civil life. [The] paramount destiny and mission of woman are to fulfill the noble and benign offices of wife and mother. This is the law of the Creator."

[72] *Hoyt* was effectively overruled in *Taylor v. Louisiana,* 419 U.S. 522 (1975), holding that a similar statute, operating largely to exclude women from jury service, deprived a criminal defendant of the Sixth and Fourteenth Amendment right to an impartial jury drawn from a fair cross section of the community.

school and smiling as they ran the new electric waxer over the spotless kitchen floor.' Friedan urged women to 'do the work you are capable of doing.' [The National Organization for Women was organized] in 1966. By 1974, NOW had grown to forty thousand members under Friedan's leadership. [Even] Madison Avenue reached out to the new woman with a new cigarette, Virginia Slims, whose slogan was 'You've Come a Long Way, Baby.'"

———

The first decision holding sex discrimination violative of equal protection, REED v. REED, 404 U.S. 71 (1971), per BURGER, C.J., involved a law preferring males to females when two persons were otherwise equally entitled to be the administrator of an estate: "A classification 'must be reasonable, not arbitrary, and must rest upon some ground of difference having a fair and substantial relation to the object of the [law].' The question" is whether the classification "bears a rational relationship to a state objective that is sought to be advanced by the [law]." It was contended that the law had the reasonable "objective of reducing the workload on probate courts by eliminating one class of contests" and that the legislature might reasonably have "concluded that in general men are better qualified to act as an administrator than are women." But "to give a mandatory preference to members of either sex over members of the other, merely to accomplish the elimination of hearings on the merits, is to make the very kind of arbitrary legislative choice forbidden by [equal protection]."

Did *Reed* really involve "rational basis" review, or did the Court in fact apply elevated scrutiny? Consider Catharine A. MacKinnon, *Sexual Harassment of Working Women* 108 (1979): "It would have been considerably more rational, factually based, not arbitrary, and substantially related to the statutory purpose to presume that men would be the better administrators if most women were illiterate and wholly excluded from business affairs. Yet this reasoning would reveal a society in severe need of prohibitions on sex discrimination."

———

Reed was followed by FRONTIERO v. RICHARDSON, 411 U.S. 677 (1973), which invalidated a federal statute permitting males in the armed services an automatic dependency allowance for their wives but requiring servicewomen to prove that their husbands were dependent. BRENNAN, J., joined by Douglas, White, and Marshall, JJ., argued that "classifications based upon sex [are] inherently suspect and must therefore be subjected to close judicial scrutiny." The plurality found "at least implicit support for such an approach in [*Reed's*] departure from 'traditional' rational basis analysis": "[O]ur Nation has had a long and unfortunate history of sex discrimination. Traditionally, such discrimination was rationalized by an attitude of 'romantic paternalism' which, in practical effect, put women not on a pedestal, but in a cage. * * *

"As a result of notions such as these, [statutes] became laden with gross, stereotypical distinctions between the sexes and, indeed, throughout much of the 19th century the position of women in our society was, in many respects, comparable to that of blacks under the pre-Civil War slave codes. Neither slaves nor women could hold office, serve on juries, or bring suit in their own names, and married women traditionally were denied the legal capacity to hold or convey property or to serve as legal guardians of their own children. And although blacks were guaranteed the right to vote in 1870, women were denied even [that] until adoption of the Nineteenth Amendment half a century later.

"It is true, of course, that the position of women in America has improved markedly in recent decades. [But] in part because of the high visibility of the sex characteristic, women still face pervasive, although at times more subtle, discrimination in our educational institutions, on the job market and, perhaps most conspicuously, in the political arena.[17]

"Moreover, since sex, like race and national origin, is an immutable characteristic [the] imposition of special disabilities [would] seem to violate 'the basic concept of our system that legal burdens should bear some relationship to individual responsibility.' And what differentiates sex from such non-suspect statuses as intelligence or physical disability [is] that the sex characteristic frequently bears no relation to ability to perform or contribute to society.

"[The] Government [maintains] that, as an empirical matter, wives in our society frequently are dependent upon their husbands, while husbands rarely are dependent upon their wives. Thus, the Government argues that Congress might reasonably have concluded that it would be both cheaper and easier simply conclusively to presume that wives of male members are financially dependent upon their husbands, while burdening female members with the task of establishing dependency in fact.

"The Government offers no concrete evidence, however, tending to support its view that such differential treatment in fact saves the Government any money. [And any] statutory scheme which draws a sharp line between the sexes, *solely* [for] administrative convenience [violates equal protection]."

POWELL, J., joined by Burger, C.J., and Blackmun, J., concurring, would rely "on the authority of *Reed* and reserve for the future any expansion of its rationale" because of the "Equal Rights Amendment, which if adopted will resolve [the] question." Stewart, J., concurred, "agreeing

---

[17] **[Ct's Note]** It is true . . . that when viewed in the abstract, women do not constitute a small and powerless minority. Nevertheless, in part because of past discrimination, women are vastly underrepresented in this Nation's decisionmaking councils. * * *

that the [statutes] work an invidious discrimination." Rehnquist, J., dissented.

NOTES AND QUESTIONS

1. ***Basis for heightened scrutiny.*** Should sex-based classifications be treated as "suspect"? If so, on what basis?

(a) ***Economic disadvantage.*** Women, on average, earn lower incomes than men;[73] own less property; and are more likely to be below the poverty line.[74]

(b) ***Historical discrimination and prejudice.*** How persuasive is the analogy of historical gender-based discrimination to discrimination based on race? In her brief in *Reed*, Ruth Bader Ginsburg—now a Justice, but then arguing as a lawyer—wrote that being a woman, like being of a minority race, is "an unalterable identifying trait which the dominant culture views as a badge of inferiority justifying disadvantaged treatment in social, legal, economic and political contexts." The brief also quoted Note, *Sex Discrimination and Equal Protection: Do We Need a Constitutional Amendment?*, 84 Harv.L.Rev. 1499 (1971): "The similarities between race and sex discrimination are indeed striking. Both classifications create large, natural classes, membership in which is beyond the individual's control; both are highly visible characteristics on which legislators have found it easy to draw gross, stereotypical distinctions. Historically, the legal position of black slaves was justified by analogy to the legal status of women. Both slaves and wives were once subject to the all-encompassing paternalistic power of the male head of the house. Arguments justifying different treatment for the sexes on the grounds of female inferiority, need for male protection, and happiness in their assigned roles bear a striking resemblance to the half-truths surrounding the myth of the 'happy slave.' The historical patterns of race and sex discrimination have, in many instances, produced similar present day results."[75]

Compare Richard A. Wasserstrom, *Racism, Sexism, and Preferential Treatment: An Approach to the Topics*, 24 U.C.L.A. L.Rev. 581 (1977): "[T]o be

---

[73] Median weekly earnings for women who were full-time wage and salary workers were 81% of men's median earnings in 2012. "In 1979, the first year of comparable earnings data, women earned 63% as much as men." Bureau of Labor Statistics, U.S. Dep't of Labor, Rep. 1045, *Highlights of Women's Earnings in 2012*, at 1 (2013). That number rose gradually throughout the 1980s and 1990s, but it has remained at 80–82% since 2003. *See, e.g.*, Bureau of Labor Statistics, U.S. Dep't of Labor, Rep. 1025, *Highlights of Women's Earnings in 2009*, at 1 (2010).

[74] In 2012, 25.8 million females were below the poverty line, compared with 20.7 million males. Bureau of the Census, U.S. Dep't of Com., POV01, *Current Population Survey, 2012 Annual Social and Economic Supplement* (2013).

[75] But cf. Ruth Bader Ginsburg, *Speaking in a Judicial Voice*, 67 N.Y.U.L.Rev. 1185 (1992), noting "a reason that distances race discrimination from discrimination based on sex": "Most women are life partners of men; women bear and raise both sons and daughters. Once women's own consciousness was awakened to the unfairness of allocating opportunity and responsibility on the basis of sex, education of others—of fathers, husbands, sons as well as daughters—could begin, or be reinforced, at home. When blacks were confined by law to a separate sector, there was no similar prospect for educating the white majority."

female, as opposed to being black, is not to be conceived of as simply a creature of less worth. That is one important thing that differentiates sexism from racism: The ideology of sex, as opposed to the ideology of race, is a good deal more complex and confusing. Women are both put on a pedestal and deemed not fully developed persons. They are idealized; their approval and admiration is sought; and they are at the same time regarded as less competent than men and less able to live fully developed, fully human lives—for that is what men do."

Consider Jill Elaine Hasday, *Women's Exclusion from the Constitutional Canon*, 2013 U.Ill.L.Rev. 1715 (2013): "The *Frontiero* plurality emphasized commonalities between sex discrimination and race discrimination [and thus] left the impression that sex dicrimination should be the concern of the Equal Protection Clause only to the extent that it resembles race discrimination and that any differences between sex and race discrimination undercut the case for focusing constitutional attention on sex discrimination. Another consequence of how the *Frontiero* plurality analogized sex to race is that the plurality left little room for women of color. [Sex] discrimination directed at white women may have purported to place them on a pedestal, but no one pretended that women of color were up there as well."

See also Catharine A. MacKinnon, *Reflections on Sex Equality Under Law*, 100 Yale L.J. 1281 (1991): "The African American struggle for social equality has been the crucible for equality law in America. [The] inequality of women to men deserves a theory of its own."

(c) ***Lack of political power.*** Historical discrimination against women might be taken to suggest that, within the terms of the *Carolene Products* footnote, Ch. 5, Sec. 3 supra, gender-based prejudice and stereotypes of women constitute "a special condition, which tends seriously to curtail the operation of those political processes ordinarily to be relied upon to protect minorities, and which may call for a correspondingly more searching judicial inquiry." On the other hand, women are a not a minority, but a majority, of the national population.

Consider John H. Ely, *Democracy and Distrust* 166–69 (1980): "The very stereotypes that gave rise to laws 'protecting' women by barring them from various activities are under daily and publicized attack. [Given] such open discussion [the] claim that the numerical majority is being 'dominated' [is] one it has become impossible to maintain except at the most inflated rhetorical level. It also renders the broader argument self-contradictory, since to make such a claim in the context of the current debate one must at least implicitly grant the validity of the stereotype, that women are in effect mental infants who will believe anything men tell them to believe. [But] most laws classifying by sex [probably pre-date women's suffrage]: they should be invalidated. [To] put on the group affected the burden of using its recently unblocked access to get the offending laws repealed would be to place in their path an additional hurdle that the rest of us do not have to contend with in order to protect ourselves—hardly an appropriate response to the realization that they have been unfairly blocked in the past. [If, however] women don't protect themselves from sex discrimination in the future, [it] will be because for one reason or another—substantive disagreement or more likely the assignment of a low priority to the issue—they don't choose to."

Compare Tracy E. Higgins, *Democracy and Feminism*, 110 Harv.L.Rev. 1657 (1997): "By invoking women's political authority as a justification [for modern laws discriminating on the basis of gender, defenders of such laws] simply assume[ ] that, given preexisting preferences, women (like any other interest group within the polity) are free to exercise their power unproblematically through the democratic process. Yet, the preferences of [women] are not independent of [existing distributions of power and opportunities]. The existing power structure contributes to the entrenchment of particular preferences, which in turn influence the democratic process."

(d) *Moral irrelevance.* In considering the appropriate level of scrutiny for gender-based discrimination, note that, for many people, gender would be relevant for many purposes even in an ideal, gender-egalitarian world. Should it matter if, for example, separate men's and women's restrooms convey no inherent message of superiority or inferiority? For a subtle discussion, see Wasserstrom, supra.

2. *Original intent or understanding.* No one suggests that the Fourteenth Amendment was originally intended or understood to bar gender discrimination. Is this relevant? Dispositive?[76]

Was Powell, J., right in thinking that the Court should hesitate to move too quickly while it appeared that the proposed Equal Rights Amendment might resolve the question? This proposed amendment—that "equality of rights under the law shall not be denied or abridged by the United States or by a State on account of sex"—was approved by 35 states (three less than the 38 required for ratification) at the expiration date set by Congress in 1982.[77]

Consider Friedman, supra, at 293: "Justice Brennan's decision to apply strict scrutiny despite the brawl over the ERA was no accident: he could count.

---

[76] Some originalists who focus attention on "the original public meaning" of constitutional provisions regard prohibitions against some forms of gender discrimination as consistent with constitutional originalism. See, e.g., Steven G. Calabresi & Julia T. Rickert, *Originalism and Sex Discrimination,* 90 Tex.L.Rev. 1 (2011): "Our thesis starts from the premise that originalists ought to begin and end all analysis with the original public meaning of constitutional texts. . . . [T]he text of the Fourteenth Amendment was meant, as an original matter, to forbid class-based legislation and any law that creates a system of caste [such as the] Black Codes enacted by southern states in 1865 in an attempt to relegate the freed slaves to second-class citizenship. [Did] the Framers and ratifiers of the Fourteenth Amendment understand sex discrimination to be a form of caste or of special-interest class legislation? Certainly not. But [sometimes] legislators misapply or misunderstand their own rules. For this reason, although the Framers' original expected applications of the constitutional text are worth knowing, they are not the last word on the Fourteenth Amendment's reach. [In this case, the Framers were] mistaken in their belief that laws discriminating on the basis of sex are not relevantly similar to laws that discriminate on the basis of race."

[77] For arguments in favor of the amendment, see generally Barbara A. Brown, Thomas I. Emerson, Gail Falk, & Ann E. Freedman, *The Equal Rights Amendment: A Constitutional Basis for Equal Rights for Women,* 80 Yale L.J. 871 (1971).

His early draft avoided the more demanding standard, but once Justices White, Douglas, and Marshall indicated they wanted to go all the way, he happily obliged. When Justices Powell and Blackmun wrote to complain about leapfrogging the national debate, Brennan wrote back, saying: 'Since rejection in 13 states is sufficient to kill the Amendment it looks like a lost cause. . . . I therefore don't see that we gain anything by awaiting what is at best an uncertain outcome." See also Lucas A. Powe, Jr., *The Supreme Court and the American Elite, 1789–2008* at 277 (2009): The four Justices in the *Frontiero* plurality "demonstrated a belief that the amendment process was a waste of time. A reform Court could do it faster." Do you agree?

What are the implications, if any, of the failure of the proposed Equal Rights Amendment to win adoption by the requisite number of states?

Consider Reva Siegel, *Constitutional Culture, Social Movement Conflict and Constitutional Change: The Case of the De Facto ERA*, 94 Cal.L.Rev. 1323 (2006): "The ERA was not ratified, but the amendment's proposal and defeat played a crucial role in enabling and shaping the modern law of sex discrimination. [An] extended and highly structured national conversation about questions of equal citizenship and the family focused public debate on how the abstract principles of the constitutional tradition applied to concrete practices, and provided material on which different members of the Court would draw as they argued over the meaning of the Constitution's equal protection guarantee. [Long] running dispute about whether to amend the Constitution's text changed public understandings of the Constitution's text, and so imbued the Court with authority to enforce the Constitution in new and unprecedented ways."

CRAIG V. BOREN

429 U.S. 190, 97 S.Ct. 451, 50 L.Ed.2d 397 (1976).

JUSTICE BRENNAN delivered the opinion of the Court.

The interaction of two sections of an Oklahoma statute prohibits the sale of "nonintoxicating" 3.2% beer to males under the age of 21 and to females under the age of 18. The question to be decided is whether such a gender-based differential constitutes a denial to males 18–20 years of age of the equal protection of the laws in violation of the Fourteenth Amendment.

[To] withstand constitutional challenge, previous cases establish that classifications by gender must serve important governmental objectives and must be substantially related to achievement of those objectives. * * * Decisions following *Reed* [have] rejected administrative ease and convenience as sufficiently important objectives to justify gender-based classifications. * * *[6]

---

[6] **[Ct's Note]** *Kahn v. Shevin,* [Part III infra], and *Schlesinger v. Ballard,* [Part III infra], upholding the use of gender-based classifications, rested upon the Court's perception of the

Reed has also provided the underpinning for decisions that have invalidated statutes employing gender as an inaccurate proxy for other, more germane bases of classification. Hence, "archaic and overbroad" generalizations concerning the financial position of servicewomen, *Frontiero,* and working women, *Wiesenfeld* [Part III infra], could not justify use of a gender line in determining eligibility for certain governmental entitlements. Similarly, increasingly outdated misconceptions concerning the role of females in the home rather than in the 'marketplace and world of ideas' were rejected as loose-fitting characterizations incapable of supporting state statutory schemes that were premised upon their accuracy. *Stanton v. Stanton*, 421 U.S. 7 (1975). In light of the weak congruence between gender and the characteristic or trait that gender purported to represent, it was necessary that the legislatures choose either to realign their substantive laws in a gender-neutral fashion, or to adopt procedures for identifying those instances where the sex-centered generalization actually comported with fact.

[We] turn then to the question whether, under *Reed,* the difference between males and females with respect to the purchase of 3.2% beer warrants the differential in age drawn by the Oklahoma statute. We conclude it does not.

[We] accept for purposes of discussion the District Court's identification of the objective underlying [the challenged statute] as the enhancement of traffic safety. Clearly, the protection of public health and safety represents an important function of state and local governments. However, appellees' statistics in our view cannot support the conclusion that the gender-based distinction closely serves to achieve that objective and therefore the distinction cannot under *Reed* withstand equal protection challenge. The appellees introduced a variety of statistical surveys [to support the statute, but the] most focused and relevant of the statistical surveys, arrests of 18–20-year-olds for alcohol-related driving offenses, exemplifies the ultimate unpersuasiveness of this evidentiary record. Viewed in terms of the correlation between sex and the actual activity that Oklahoma seeks to regulate—driving while under the influence of alcohol—the statistics broadly establish that .18% of females and 2% of males in that age group were arrested for that offense. While such a disparity is not trivial in a statistical sense, it hardly can form the basis for employment of a gender line as a classifying device. Certainly if maleness is to serve as a proxy for drinking and driving, a correlation of 2% must be considered an unduly tenuous "fit." [Indeed,] prior cases have consistently rejected the use of sex as a decisionmaking factor even though the statutes

---

laudatory purposes of those laws as remedying disadvantageous conditions suffered by women in economic and military life. Needless to say, Oklahoma does not suggest that the age-sex differential was enacted to ensure the availability of 3.2% beer for women as compensation for previous deprivations.

in question certainly rested on far more predictive empirical relationships than this.

Moreover, the statistics exhibit a variety of other shortcomings that seriously impugn their value to equal protection analysis. Setting aside the obvious methodological problems,[14] the surveys do not adequately justify the salient features of Oklahoma's gender-based traffic-safety law. None purports to measure the use and dangerousness of 3.2% beer as opposed to alcohol generally, a detail that is of particular importance since, in light of its low alcohol level, Oklahoma apparently considers the 3.2% beverage to be "nonintoxicating."

[W]hen it is further recognized that Oklahoma's statute prohibits only the selling of 3.2% beer to young males and not their drinking the beverage once acquired (even after purchase by their 18–20-year-old female companions), the relationship between gender and traffic safety becomes far too tenuous to satisfy *Reed*'s requirement that the gender-based difference be substantially related to achievement of the statutory objective. We hold, therefore, that [Oklahoma's] 3.2% beer statute invidiously discriminates against males 18–20 years of age. * * *

JUSTICE POWELL concurring.

I join the opinion of the Court as I am in general agreement with it. I do have reservations as to some of the discussion concerning the appropriate standard for equal protection analysis and the relevance of the statistical evidence. * * *

With respect to the equal protection standard, I agree that *Reed* is the most relevant precedent. But I find it unnecessary, in deciding this case, to read that decision as broadly as some of the Court's language may imply. *Reed* and subsequent cases involving gender-based classifications make clear that the Court subjects such classifications to a more critical examination than is normally applied when "fundamental" constitutional rights and "suspect classes" are not present.

I view this as a relatively easy case. [T]his gender-based classification does not bear a fair and substantial relation to the object of the legislation. * * *

JUSTICE STEVENS concurring.

I am inclined to believe that what has become known as the two-tiered analysis of equal protection claims does not describe a completely logical method of deciding cases, but rather is a method the Court has employed

---

[14] **[Ct's Note]** The very social stereotypes that find reflection in age-differential laws are likely substantially to distort the accuracy of these comparative statistics. Hence, "reckless" young men who drink and drive are transformed into arrest statistics, whereas their female counterparts are chivalrously escorted home. * * *

to explain decisions that actually apply a single standard in a reasonably consistent fashion. * * *

In this case, the classification is not as obnoxious as some the Court has condemned, nor as inoffensive as some the Court has accepted. It is objectionable because it is based on an accident of birth, because it is a mere remnant of the now almost universally rejected tradition of discriminating against males in this age bracket, and because, to the extent it reflects any physical difference between males and females, it is actually perverse.[4] * * *

The classification is not totally irrational. For the evidence does indicate that there are more males than females in this age bracket who drive and also more who drink. Nevertheless, [i]t is difficult to believe that the statute was actually intended to cope with the problem of traffic safety, since it has only a minimal effect on access to a not very intoxicating beverage and does not prohibit its consumption. [But] even assuming some such slight benefit, it does not seem to me that an insult to all of the young men of the State can be justified by visiting the sins of the 2% on the 98%.

JUSTICE REHNQUIST, [with whom CHIEF JUSTICE BURGER was "in general agreement"] dissenting.

The Court's disposition of this case is objectionable on two grounds. First is its conclusion that *men* challenging a gender-based statute which treats them less favorably than women may invoke a more stringent standard of judicial review than pertains to most other types of classifications. Second is the Court's enunciation of this standard, without citation to any source, as being that "classifications by gender must serve *important* governmental objectives and must be *substantially* related to achievement of those objectives." The only redeeming feature of the Court's opinion, to my mind, is that it apparently signals a retreat by those who joined the plurality opinion in *Frontiero* from their view that sex is a "suspect" classification for purposes of equal protection analysis. I think the Oklahoma statute challenged here need pass only the "rational basis" equal protection analysis expounded in [prior cases].

[T]here being no plausible argument that this is a discrimination against females, the Court's reliance on our previous sex-discrimination cases is ill-founded. It treats gender classification as a talisman which— without regard to the rights involved or the persons affected—calls into effect a heavier burden of judicial review.

The Court's [standard of review] apparently comes out of thin air. The Equal Protection Clause contains no such language, and none of our previous cases adopt that standard. I would think we have had enough

---

[4] **[Ct's Note]** Because males are generally heavier than females, they have a greater capacity to consume alcohol without impairing their driving ability than do females.

difficulty with the two standards of review which our cases have recognized—the norm of "rational basis," and the "compelling state interest" required where a "suspect classification" is involved—so as to counsel weightily against the insertion of still another "standard" between those two. How is this Court to divine what objectives are important? How is it to determine whether a particular law is "substantially" related to the achievement of such objective, rather than related in some other way to its achievement?

[Under the] applicable rational-basis test [the] evidence suggests clear differences between the drinking and driving habits of young men and women. Those differences are grounds enough for the State reasonably to conclude that young males pose by far the greater drunk-driving hazard, both in terms of sheer numbers and in terms of hazard on a per-driver basis. The gender-based difference in treatment in this case is therefore not irrational.

NOTES AND QUESTIONS

1. ***Level of scrutiny.*** Is the intermediate level of scrutiny applied in *Craig* soundly justified? If so, on what basis? Consider Jill Elaine Hasday, *Women's Exclusion from the Constitutional Canon,* 2013 U.Ill.L.Rev. 1715 (2013): "*Craig* never explained why it would be inappropriate to require strict scrutiny[. The] implication in *Craig* was that the Court did not fully accept the analogy between sex discrimination and race discrimination and that race discrimination was the core case."

2. ***Protection of men.*** Is there any reason why statutes discriminating against *men* should be subject to heightened equal protection scrutiny? Did "[t]he Court's selection of a male plaintiff's suit deemphasize[ ] women's long historical experience of legalized subordination as a central narrative in American law and American life"? Hasday, supra.

Alternatively, do laws that distinguish between men and women inherently promote discrimination against women? In a footnote to his dissenting opinion in *Craig,* Justice Rehnquist notes: "I am not unaware of the argument from time to time advanced, that all discriminations between the sexes ultimately redound to the detriment of females, because they tend to reinforce 'old notions' restricting the roles and opportunities of women. As a general proposition applying equally to all sex categorizations, I believe that this argument was implicitly found to carry little weight in [several decisions upholding classifications designed to compensate women for actual or presumed employment and economic disadvantages]. Seeing no assertion that it has special applicability to the situation at hand, I believe it can be dismissed as an insubstantial consideration."

Is it plausible to think that *both* men and women are semi-suspect classes? Consider Tribe 2d ed., at 1564–65: "It is no surprise that many of [the leading] sex discrimination cases were brought by male plaintiffs, since legislative assumptions about traditional sex roles often impinge on the rights of both men and women [by impliedly derogating the capacity of women to function effectively outside the home]. [In defending gender-based classifications,] the government's almost uniform argument [has] emphasized the [benefits achieved by reliance on] the accurate and therefore 'rational' assumption of traditional male and female inclinations and capacities. The Supreme Court's thoughtful response [has] recognized the argument's essence as self-fulfilling prophecy: The 'accuracy' of the government's assumption is derived in some significant degree from the chill on sex-role experimentation and change generated by the classifications themselves."

3. ***Application in Craig.*** Did *Craig* rest on the conclusion that the challenged law was unlikely to save any lives through a reduction in traffic accidents attributable to drinking by 18–21-year-old males? That it was unlikely to save enough lives to be constitutionally tolerable? Or was the point that the state, in order to be able to restrict the sale of 3.2% beer to young men, must also prohibit sales to women of the same age? Should the state, in order to achieve important ends (such as saving lives by improving highway safety), be required to impose restrictions that it regards as unnecessary (as well as those it thinks vital)?

UNITED STATES v. VIRGINIA
518 U.S. 515, 116 S.Ct. 2264, 135 L.Ed.2d 735 (1996).

JUSTICE GINSBURG delivered the opinion of the Court.

Virginia's public institutions of higher learning include an incomparable military college, Virginia Military Institute (VMI). The United States maintains that the Constitution's equal protection guarantee precludes Virginia from reserving exclusively to men the unique educational opportunities VMI affords. We agree.

Founded in 1839, VMI is today the sole single-sex school among Virginia's 15 public institutions of higher learning. VMI's distinctive mission is to produce "citizen-soldiers." [Assigning] prime place to character development, VMI uses an "adversative method" modeled on English public schools and once characteristic of military instruction. [This model] features "physical rigor, mental stress, absolute equality of treatment, absence of privacy, minute regulation of behavior, and indoctrination in desirable values." [VMI] cadets live in spartan barracks where surveillance is constant and privacy nonexistent. [Entering] students are incessantly exposed to the rat line, "an extreme form of the adversative model," [which] bonds new cadets to their fellow sufferers and, when they have completed the 7-month experience, to their former tormentors.

In 1990, prompted by a complaint filed with the Attorney General by a female high-school student seeking admission to VMI, the United States sued the Commonwealth of Virginia and VMI, alleging that VMI's exclusively male admission policy violated the Equal Protection Clause of the Fourteenth Amendment. [The district court upheld the policy, but the court of appeals reversed, finding an equal protection violation. Following the remand, the state of Virginia proposed a remedial plan, under which the state would adopt] a parallel program for women: Virginia Women's Institute for Leadership (VWIL). The 4-year, state-sponsored undergraduate program would be located at Mary Baldwin College, a private liberal arts school for women, and would be open, initially, to about 25 to 30 students. Although VWIL would share VMI's mission—to produce "citizen-soldiers"—the VWIL program would differ, as does Mary Baldwin College, from VMI in academic offerings, methods of education, and financial resources.

The average combined SAT score of entrants at Mary Baldwin is about 100 points lower than the score for VMI freshmen. [While] VMI offers degrees in liberal arts, the sciences, and engineering, Mary Baldwin, at the time of trial, offered only bachelor of arts degrees. [Under the proposed remedial plan,] VWIL students would participate in ROTC programs [but in] lieu of VMI's adversative method, [VWIL would offer] "a cooperative method which reinforces self-esteem."

Virginia represented that it will provide equal financial support for in-state VWIL students and VMI cadets, and the VMI Foundation agreed to supply a $5.4625 million endowment for the VWIL program. Mary Baldwin's own endowment is about $19 million; VMI's is $131 million. Mary Baldwin will add $35 million to its endowment based on future commitments; VMI will add $220 million. [Both the district court and the court of appeals held that the proposed remedial plan satisfied the Equal Protection Clause.]

The cross-petitions in this case present two ultimate issues. First, does Virginia's exclusion of women from the educational opportunities provided by VMI—extraordinary opportunities for military training and civilian leadership development—deny to women "capable of all of the individual activities required of VMI cadets," the equal protection of the laws guaranteed by the Fourteenth Amendment? Second, if VMI's "unique" situation—as Virginia's sole single-sex public institution of higher education—offends the Constitution's equal protection principle, what is the remedial requirement?

We note, once again, the core instruction of this Court's pathmarking decisions in *J.E.B. v. Alabama ex rel. T.B.*, [511 U.S. 127 (1994) (finding gender-based peremptory challenges in a criminal case to be based on stereotypes and not substantially related to an important state interest), and *Mississippi Univ. for Women*, [Part II infra}]: Parties who seek to defend gender-based government action must demonstrate an "exceedingly persuasive justification" for that action. [The] burden of justification is demanding and it rests entirely on the State. The State must show "at least that the [challenged] classification serves 'important governmental objectives and that the discriminatory means employed' are 'substantially related to the achievement of those objectives.' " The justification must be genuine, not hypothesized or invented post hoc in response to litigation. And it must not rely on overbroad generalizations about the different talents, capacities, or preferences of males and females.

The heightened review standard our precedent establishes does not make sex a proscribed classification. Supposed "inherent differences" are no longer accepted as a ground for race or national origin classifications. See *Loving v. Virginia*. Physical differences between men and women, however, are enduring. Inherent differences between men and women, we have come to appreciate, remain cause for celebration, but not for denigration of the members of either sex or for artificial constraints on an individual's opportunity. Sex classifications may be used to compensate women "for particular economic disabilities [they have] suffered," *Califano v. Webster,* [Part III infra], to "promote equal employment opportunity," see *California Federal Sav. & Loan Assn. v. Guerra,* [Part III infra], [and] to advance full development of the talent and capacities of our Nation's people.[7] But such classifications may not be used, as they once were, to create or perpetuate the legal, social, and economic inferiority of women. [Measuring] the record in this case against the review standard just described, we conclude that Virginia has shown no "exceedingly persuasive justification" for excluding all women from the citizen-soldier training afforded by VMI.

[Single-sex] education affords pedagogical benefits to at least some students, Virginia emphasizes, and that reality is uncontested in this litigation. Similarly, it is not disputed that diversity among public educational institutions can serve the public good. But Virginia has not shown that VMI was established, or has been maintained, with a view to diversifying, by its categorical exclusion of women, educational opportunities within the State. In cases of this genre, our precedent instructs that "benign" justifications proffered in defense of categorical exclusions will not be accepted automatically; a tenable justification must describe actual state purposes, not rationalizations for actions in fact differently grounded.

---

[7] **[Ct's Note]** Several amici have urged that diversity in educational opportunities is an altogether appropriate governmental pursuit and that single-sex schools can contribute importantly to such diversity. Indeed, it is the mission of some single-sex schools "to dissipate, rather than perpetuate, traditional gender classifications." We do not question the State's prerogative evenhandedly to support diverse educational opportunities. We address specifically and only an educational opportunity recognized by the District Court and the Court of Appeals as "unique," an opportunity available only at Virginia's premier military institute, the State's sole single-sex public university or college.

[Neither] recent nor distant history bears out Virginia's alleged pursuit of diversity through single-sex educational options. In 1839, when the State established VMI, a range of educational opportunities for men and women was scarcely contemplated. [In] admitting no women, VMI followed the lead of [the] University of Virginia, founded in 1819. [Beginning in 1884,] Virginia eventually provided for several women's seminaries and colleges. [By] the mid-1970's, [however,] all [had] become coeducational. [The] University of Virginia introduced coeducation [in 1970] and, in 1972, began to admit women on an equal basis with men.

[Virginia] describes the current absence of public single-sex higher education for women as "an historical anomaly." But the historical record indicates action more deliberate than anomalous: First, protection of women against higher education; next, schools for women far from equal in resources and stature to schools for men; finally, conversion of the separate schools to coeducation. [In] sum, we find no persuasive evidence in this record that VMI's male-only admission policy "is in furtherance of a state policy of 'diversity.' "

[Virginia] next argues that VMI's adversative method of training provides educational benefits that cannot be made available, unmodified, to women. Alterations to accommodate women would necessarily be "radical," so "drastic," Virginia asserts, as to transform, indeed "destroy," VMI's program. [The] District Court [found] that coeducation would materially affect "at least these three aspects of VMI's program—physical training, the absence of privacy, and the adversative approach." And it is uncontested that women's admission would require accommodations, primarily in arranging housing assignments and physical training programs for female cadets. It is also undisputed, however, that "the VMI methodology could be used to educate women."

[The] notion that admission of women would downgrade VMI's stature, destroy the adversative system and, with it, even the school, is a judgment hardly proved, a prediction hardly different from other "self-fulfilling prophecies" once routinely used to deny rights or opportunities. [Women's] successful entry into the federal military academies, and their participation in the Nation's military forces, indicate that Virginia's fears for the future of VMI may not be solidly grounded. [Virginia], in sum, "has fallen far short of establishing the 'exceedingly persuasive justification' " that must be the solid base for any gender-defined classification.

In the second phase of the litigation, Virginia presented its remedial plan—maintain VMI as a male-only college and create VWIL as a separate program for women. [Having] violated the Constitution's equal protection requirement, Virginia was obliged to show that its remedial proposal "directly addressed and related to" the violation, i.e., the equal protection denied to women ready, willing, and able to benefit from educational opportunities of the kind VMI offers. Virginia described VWIL as a "parallel program," and asserted that VWIL shares VMI's mission of producing "citizen-soldiers" and VMI's goals of providing "education, military training, mental and physical discipline, character [and] leadership development." [But] VWIL affords women no opportunity to experience the rigorous military training for which VMI is famed. Instead, the VWIL program "deemphasizes" military education, and uses a "cooperative method" of education "which reinforces self-esteem."

[Virginia] maintains that these methodological differences are "justified pedagogically," based on "important differences between men and women in learning and developmental needs," "psychological and sociological differences" Virginia describes as "real" and "not stereotypes." [As] earlier stated, [however], generalizations about "the way women are," estimates of what is appropriate for most women, no longer justify denying opportunity to women whose talent and capacity place them outside the average description. "[S]ome women, at least, would want to attend [VMI] if they had the opportunity"; "some women are capable of all of the individual activities required of VMI cadets" and "can meet the physical standards [VMI] now imposes on men". It is on behalf of these women that the United States has instituted this suit, and it is for them that a remedy must be crafted.[19]

[In] myriad respects other than military training, VWIL does not qualify as VMI's equal. VWIL's student body, faculty, course offerings, and facilities hardly match VMI's. Nor can the VWIL graduate anticipate the benefits associated with VMI's 157-year history, the school's prestige, and its influential alumni network.

[Virginia's] VWIL solution is reminiscent of the remedy Texas proposed 50 years ago, in response to a state trial court's 1946 ruling that, given the equal protection guarantee, African-Americans could not be denied a legal education at a state facility. See *Sweatt v. Painter,* [Sec. 2, II supra]. Reluctant to admit African-Americans to its flagship University of Texas Law School, the State set up a separate school for Heman Sweatt and other black law students. [This] Court contrasted resources at the new school with those at the school from which Sweatt had been excluded. Accordingly, the Court held, the Equal Protection Clause required Texas to admit African-Americans to the University of Texas Law School. In line with *Sweatt,* we rule here that Virginia has not shown substantial equality in the separate educational opportunities the State supports at VWIL and VMI. * * *

---

[19] **[Ct's Note]** Admitting women to VMI would undoubtedly require alterations necessary to afford members of each sex privacy from the other sex in living arrangements, and to adjust aspects of the physical training programs. Experience [at the United States military academies] shows such adjustments are manageable.

JUSTICE THOMAS took no part in the consideration or decision of this case.

CHIEF JUSTICE REHNQUIST, concurring in the judgement.

Two decades ago in *Craig v. Boren,* we announced that "to withstand constitutional challenge, * * * classifications by gender must serve important governmental objectives and must be substantially related to achievement of those objectives." [While] the majority adheres to this test today, it also says that the State must demonstrate an " 'exceedingly persuasive justification' " to support a gender-based classification. [To] avoid introducing potential confusion, I would have adhered more closely to our traditional [standard].

[I] agree with the Court that there is scant evidence in the record that [diversity] was the real reason that Virginia decided to maintain VMI as men only. [Even] if diversity in educational opportunity were the Commonwealth's actual objective, the Commonwealth's position would still be problematic. The difficulty is that the diversity benefited only one sex.

[Virginia] offers a second justification for the single-sex admissions policy: maintenance of the adversative method. [But a] State does not have substantial interest in the adversative methodology unless it is pedagogically beneficial. While considerable evidence shows that a single-sex education is pedagogically beneficial for some students, and hence a State may have a valid interest in promoting that methodology, there is no similar evidence in the record that an adversative method is pedagogically beneficial or is any more likely to produce character traits than other methodologies.

The Court defines the constitutional violation in this case as "the categorical exclusion of women from an extraordinary educational opportunity afforded to men." By defining the violation in this way, [the] Court necessarily implies that the only adequate remedy would be the admission of women to the all-male institution. [I] would not define the violation in this way; it is not the "exclusion of women" that violates the Equal Protection Clause, but the maintenance of an all-men school without providing any—much less a comparable—institution for women. * * *

JUSTICE SCALIA, dissenting.

* * * Much of the Court's opinion is devoted to deprecating the closed-mindedness of our forebears with regard to women's education, and even with regard to the treatment of women in areas that have nothing to do with education. Closed-minded they were—as every age is, including our own, with regard to matters it cannot guess, because it simply does not consider them debatable. The virtue of a democratic system with a First Amendment is that it readily enables the people, over time, to be persuaded that what they took for granted is not so, and to change their laws

accordingly. That system is destroyed if the smug assurances of each age are removed from the democratic process and written into the Constitution. So to counterbalance the Court's criticism of our ancestors, let me say a word in their praise: they left us free to change. The same cannot be said of this most illiberal Court, which has embarked on a course of inscribing one after another of the current preferences of the society (and in some cases only the counter-majoritarian preferences of the society's law-trained elite) into our Basic Law. Today it enshrines the notion that no substantial educational value is to be served by an all-men's military academy—so that the decision by the people of Virginia to maintain such an institution denies equal protection to women who cannot attend that institution but can attend others.

[In] my view the function of this Court is to preserve our society's values regarding (among other things) equal protection, not to revise them. [Whatever] abstract tests we may choose to devise, they cannot supersede—and indeed ought to be crafted so as to reflect—those constant and unbroken national traditions that embody the people's understanding of ambiguous constitutional texts. More specifically, it is my view that "when a practice not expressly prohibited by the text of the Bill of Rights bears the endorsement of a long tradition of open, widespread, and unchallenged use that dates back to the beginning of the Republic, we have no proper basis for striking it down."

The all-male constitution of VMI comes squarely within such a governing tradition. For almost all of VMI's more than a century and a half of existence, its single-sex status reflected the uniform practice for government-supported military colleges.

[To] reject the Court's disposition today, however, it is [only] necessary to apply honestly the test the Court has been applying to sex-based classifications for the past two decades. [Only] the amorphous "exceedingly persuasive justification" phrase, and not the standard elaboration of intermediate scrutiny, can be made to yield [the] conclusion that VMI's single-sex composition is unconstitutional because there exist several women (or, one would have to conclude under the Court's reasoning, a single woman) willing and able to undertake VMI's program. Intermediate scrutiny has never required a least-restrictive-means analysis, but only a "substantial relation" between the classification and the state interests that it serves.

[It] is beyond question that Virginia has an important state interest in providing effective college education for its citizens. That single-sex instruction is an approach substantially related to that interest should be evident enough from the long and continuing history in this country of men's and women's colleges. But beyond that, [there was] "virtually uncontradicted" [expert evidence introduced in this case tending to show the benefits of single-sex education].

[Besides] its single-sex constitution, VMI [employs] a "distinctive educational method," sometimes referred to as the "adversative, or doubting, model of education." [It] was uncontested that "if the state were to establish a women's VMI-type [i.e., adversative] program, the program would attract an insufficient number of participants to make the program work"; and it was found by the District Court that if Virginia were to include women in VMI, the school "would eventually find it necessary to drop the adversative system altogether." Thus, Virginia's options were an adversative method that excludes women or no adversative method at all.

There can be no serious dispute that single-sex education and a distinctive educational method "represent legitimate contributions to diversity in the Virginia higher education system." As a theoretical matter, Virginia's educational interest would have been best served (insofar as the two factors we have mentioned are concerned) by six different types of public colleges—an all-men's, an all-women's, and a coeducational college run in the "adversative method," and an all-men's, an all-women's, and a coeducational college run in the "traditional method." But as a practical matter, of course, Virginia's financial resources, like any State's, are not limitless, and the Commonwealth must select among the available options. [In] these circumstances, Virginia's election to fund one public all-male institution and one on the adversative model—and to concentrate its resources in a single entity that serves both these interests in diversity— is substantially related to the State's important educational interests.

[The] Court argues that VMI would not have to change very much if it were to admit women. The principal response to that argument is that it is irrelevant: If VMI's single-sex status is substantially related to the government's important educational objectives, as I have demonstrated above and as the Court refuses to discuss, that concludes the inquiry. [But] if such a debate were relevant, the Court would certainly be on the losing side.

[Finally], the absence of a precise "all-women's analogue" to VMI is irrelevant. [VWIL] was carefully designed by professional educators who have long experience in educating young women. [None] of the United States' own experts in the remedial phase of this case was willing to testify that VMI's adversative method was an appropriate methodology for educating women.

[The] Court's decision today will have consequences that extend far beyond the parties to the case. [Under] the constitutional principles announced and applied today, single-sex public education is unconstitutional. [Although] the Court [purports] to have said nothing of relevance to other public schools [and to have considered] only an educational opportunity recognized [as] "unique," [footnote 7, supra], I suggest that the single-sex program that will not be capable of being characterized as "unique" is not only unique but nonexistent.

[A broader] potential of today's decision for widespread disruption of existing institutions lies in its application to private single-sex education. Government support is immensely important to private educational institutions. [When government funding is challenged, the] issue will be not whether government assistance turns private colleges into state actors, but whether the government itself would be violating the Constitution by providing state support to single-sex colleges. For example, in *Norwood v. Harrison*, [Ch. 10, Sec. 3], we saw no room to distinguish between state operation of racially segregated schools and state support of privately run segregated schools. [The] only hope for state-assisted single-sex private schools is that the Court will not apply in the future the principles of law it has applied today. * * *

NOTES AND QUESTIONS

1.   *Requirement of an "exceedingly persuasive justification."* Consider the suggestion of Cass R. Sunstein, *Leaving Things Undecided*, 110 Harv.L.Rev. 4 (1996), that Ginsburg, J.'s, opinion "did not merely restate the intermediate scrutiny test but pressed it closer to strict scrutiny." Do you agree? Is Scalia, J., correct that single-sex education cannot survive this test? See Section III, infra.

2.   *Means and ends.* Did the Court invalidate the scheme involved in *VMI* because the state's articulated ends were not "important" enough or because its means—gender classification—were not related closely enough to those ends? For both reasons? Deborah Hellman, *Two Types of Discrimination: The Familiar and the Forgotten*, 86 Calif.L.Rev. 315 (1998), distinguishes between "proxy" discrimination, in which a classifying trait is used as a means to achieve some other end, and "non-proxy" discrimination, in which the state views the advantaging (or disadvantaging) of one group as an end in itself. According to Professor Hellman, *VMI* involved "non-proxy" discrimination—a simple determination to provide a richer menu of educational opportunities to men than to women—for which the Court's analytical framework is ill-suited. Compare Mary Anne Case, *Two Cheers for Cheerleading: The Noisy Integration of VMI and the Quiet Success of Virginia Women in Leadership*, 1999 U.Chi.L. Forum 347: "What really mattered to VMI was [its] cult of masculinity. [This] makes *United States v. Virginia* [like] the many race cases from *Plessy v. Ferguson* through *Brown* and *Loving*." Do you agree?

II. DIFFERENCES—REAL AND IMAGINED

Whatever standard of scrutiny applies, the Court has consistently assumed that differences between men and women sometimes justify different treatment. But a recurrent problem has been to distinguish "real" differences and permissible distinctions based upon them from impermissible reliance on and reinforcement of gender-based stereotypes. As you read the cases in this section, consider how consistent and successful the Court's efforts have been, and how much the Court has been aided—if at all—by the doctrinal tests that it has purported to apply.

———

GEDULDIG v. AIELLO, 417 U.S. 484 (1974), per STEWART, J., held that exclusion of "disability that accompanies normal pregnancy and childbirth" from California's disability insurance system "does not exclude [anyone] because of gender * * * . While it is true that only women can become pregnant, it does not follow that every legislative classification concerning pregnancy is [sex-based]. Absent a showing that distinctions involving pregnancy are mere pretexts designed to effect an invidious discrimination against the members of one sex or the other, lawmakers are constitutionally free to include or exclude pregnancy from the coverage of legislation such as this on any reasonable basis, just as with respect to any other physical condition. [The] program divides potential recipients into two groups—pregnant women and nonpregnant persons. While the first group is exclusively female, the second includes members of both sexes. The fiscal and actuarial benefits of the program thus accrue to members of both sexes. [There] is no risk from which men are protected and women are not. Likewise, there is no risk from which women are protected and men are not.[21]"

BRENNAN, J., joined by Douglas and Marshall, JJ., dissented, finding "sex discrimination" in the state's "singling out for less favorable treatment a gender-linked disability peculiar to women [while] men receive full compensation for all disabilities suffered, including those that affect only or primarily their sex, such as prostatectomies, circumcision, hemophilia and gout."[78]

———

DOTHARD v. RAWLINSON, 433 U.S. 321 (1977), per STEWART, J., upheld the exclusion of women prison guards from duty in "contact positions" in all-male prisons: "In this environment of violence and disorganization, it would be an oversimplification to characterize [the exclusion of women] as an exercise in 'romantic paternalism.' [A] woman's relative ability to maintain order in a male, maximum-security, unclassified penitentiary could [be] directly reduced by her womanhood.

---

[21] [Ct's Note] Indeed, the [data indicated] that both the annual claim rate and the annual claim cost are greater for women than for [men.]

[78] Cf. *Cleveland Bd. of Educ. v. LaFleur*, 414 U.S. 632 (1974) (invalidating a requirement that pregnant teachers go on leave on the ground that an "irrebuttable presumption" of inability to teach during pregnancy violated due process).

There is a basis in fact for expecting that sex offenders who have criminally assaulted women in the past would be moved to do so again if access to women were established within the prison. There would also be a real risk that other inmates, deprived of a normal heterosexual environment, would assault women guards because they were women."[79]

———

MICHAEL M. v. SUPERIOR COURT, 450 U.S. 464 (1981), upheld a "statutory rape" law that punished the male, but not the female, party to intercourse when the female was under 18 and not the male's wife. REHNQUIST, J., joined by Burger, C.J., and Stewart and Powell, JJ., observed that "the traditional minimum rationality test takes on a somewhat 'sharper focus' when gender-based classifications are challenged. See *Craig* (Powell, J., concurring). [But] this Court has consistently upheld statutes where the gender classification is not invidious, but rather realistically reflects the fact that the sexes are not similarly situated in certain circumstances. * * *

"We are satisfied not only that the prevention of illegitimate [teenage] pregnancy is at least one of the 'purposes' of the statute, but that the State has a strong interest in preventing such pregnancy.[7]

"Because virtually all of the significant harmful and inescapably identifiable consequences of teenage pregnancy fall on the young female, a legislature acts well within its authority when it elects to punish only the participant who, by nature, suffers few of the consequences of his conduct. It is hardly unreasonable for a legislature acting to protect minor females to exclude them from punishment. Moreover, the risk of pregnancy itself constitutes a substantial deterrence to young females. [A] criminal sanction imposed solely on males thus serves to roughly 'equalize' the deterrents on the sexes.

"[The] State persuasively contends that a gender-neutral statute would frustrate its interest in effective enforcement. Its view is that a female is surely less likely to report violations of the statute if she herself would be subject to criminal prosecution. In an area already fraught with prosecutorial difficulties, we decline to hold that the Equal Protection

---

[79] For criticism, see Christine A. Littleton, *Equality and Feminist Legal Theory*, 48 U.Pitt.L.Rev. 1043 (1987) (arguing that the Court's finding of "real difference" was irrational, since men are also raped in prisons).

[7] **[Ct's Note]** Although petitioner concedes that the State has a "compelling" interest in preventing teenage pregnancy, he contends that the "true" purpose [is] to protect the virtue and chastity of young women. As such, the statute is unjustifiable because it rests on archaic stereotypes. [Even] if the preservation of female chastity were one of the motives of the statute, and even if that motive be impermissible, petitioner's argument must fail because "[this] court will not strike down an otherwise constitutional statute on the basis of an alleged illicit legislative motive." *United States v. O'Brien*, [Ch. 7, Sec. 2].

Clause requires a legislature to enact a statute so broad that it may well be incapable of enforcement."

BLACKMUN, J., concurred: "I [cannot] vote to strike down the California statutory rape law, for I think it is a sufficiently reasoned and constitutional effort to control the problem at its inception. [I] am persuaded that, although a minor has substantial privacy rights in intimate affairs connected with procreation, California's [efforts] to prevent teenage pregnancy are to be viewed differently from efforts to inhibit a woman from dealing with pregnancy once it has become an inevitability. * * *

"I think [it] is only fair, with respect to this particular petitioner, to point out that his partner, Sharon, appears not to have been an unwilling participant in at least the initial stages of the intimacies that took place the night of June 3, 1978.* Petitioner's and Sharon's nonacquaintance with each other before the incident; their drinking; their withdrawal from the others of the group; their foreplay, in which she willingly participated and seems to have encouraged; and the closeness of their ages (a difference of only one year and 18 days) are factors that should make this case an unattractive one to prosecute at all, and especially to prosecute as a felony, rather than as a misdemeanor. But the State has chosen to prosecute in that manner, and the facts, I reluctantly conclude, may fit the crime."[80]

---

* **[Ct's Note]** Sharon at the preliminary hearing testified as follows: * * *

"We were drinking at the railroad tracks and we walked over to this bush and he started kissing me and stuff, and I was kissing him back, too, at first. Then, I was telling him to stop * * * .

"[T]hen he asked me if I wanted to walk him over to the park; so we walked over to the park and we sat down on a bench and then he started kissing me again and we were laying on the bench. And he told me to take my pants off.

"I said, 'No,' and I was trying to get up and he hit me back down on the bench and then I just said to myself, 'Forget it,' and I let him do what he wanted to do. * * *

"Q. Did you have sexual intercourse with the defendant?

"A. Yeah. * * *

"Q. You said that he hit you?

"A. Yeah.

"Q. How did he hit you?

"A. He slugged me in the face.

"[The Court]: Did he hit you one time or did he hit you more than once?

"The Witness: He hit me about two or three times. * * *"

[80] Stewart, J., also concurred, noting "that the statutory discrimination, when viewed as part of the wider scheme of California law, is not as clearcut as might at first appear. Females are not freed from criminal liability in California for engaging in sexual activity that may be harmful. It is unlawful, for example, for any person, of either sex, [to] contribute to the delinquency of anyone under 18 years of age. All persons are prohibited [from] consensual intercourse with a child under 14. [Finally,] females may be brought within the proscription of § 261.5 itself, since a female may be charged with aiding and abetting its violation. [A]pproximately 14% of the juveniles arrested for participation in acts made unlawful by § 261.5 between 1975 and 1979 were females. Moreover, an underage female who is as culpable as her male partner, or more culpable, may be prosecuted as a juvenile delinquent."

BRENNAN, J., joined by White and Marshall, JJ., dissented: "None of the three opinions upholding the California statute fairly applies the equal protection analysis this Court has so carefully developed since *Craig*. [The] plurality assumes that a gender-neutral statute would be less effective [in] deterring sexual activity because a gender-neutral statute would create significant enforcement problems. [But] a State's bare assertion [is] not enough to meet its burden of proof under *Craig*. Rather, the State must produce evidence that will persuade the Court that its assertion is true [and the] State has [not].

"The second flaw in the State's assertion is that even assuming that a gender-neutral statute would be more difficult to enforce, the State has still not shown that those enforcement problems would make such a statute less effective than a gender-based statute in deterring minor females from engaging in sexual intercourse. Common sense, however, suggests that a gender-neutral statutory rape law is potentially a *greater* deterrent of sexual activity than a gender-based law, for the simple reason that a gender-neutral law subjects both men and women to criminal sanctions and thus arguably has a deterrent effect on twice as many potential violators. Even if fewer persons were prosecuted under the gender-neutral law, as the State suggests, it would still be true that twice as many persons would be *subject* to arrest."

STEVENS, J., also dissented: "[T]hat a female confronts a greater risk of harm than a male is a reason for applying the prohibition to her—not a reason for granting her a license to use her own judgment on whether or not to assume the risk. Surely, if we examine the problem from the point of view of society's interest in preventing the risk-creating conduct from occurring at all, it is irrational to exempt 50% of the potential violators. * * *

"Finally, even if my logic is faulty and there actually is some speculative basis for treating equally guilty males and females differently, I still believe that any such speculative justification would be outweighed by the paramount interest in even-handed enforcement of the law. A rule that authorizes punishment of only one of two equally guilty wrongdoers violates the essence of the constitutional requirement that the sovereign must govern impartially."

NOTES AND QUESTIONS

1. ***Discrimination and the dissenting opinions.*** On what basis did the dissenting Justices object to the statute in *Michael M.*? Consider Frances Olsen, *Statutory Rape: A Feminist Critique of Rights Analysis*, 63 Tex.L.Rev. 387 (1984): "[T]he statute discriminates in two different ways: it outlaws sexual intercourse by minor females, but not by minor males, and it protects minor females from exploitative intercourse with anyone, but does not protect minor males from exploitative intercourse with females who are above the age

of consent. The dissenters ignored the first discrimination altogether and appeared confused about the second."

According to Professor Olsen, the dissenters would have regarded the law as "gender-neutral" as long as it punished underage women and their sexual partners equally for engaging in the same sexual acts—even if it allowed minor males (but not minor females) to engage in intercourse with partners above the age of consent. Id. Should the latter discrimination be regarded as constitutionally objectionable?

In Professor Olsen's view, the "revision" that the dissenting Justices would have found acceptable "would be the worst alternative for women, because it would increase the coercive aspects of the California law and diminish any protective elements it now might have. A woman would find it more difficult to use statutory rape laws as a shield against male aggression [because] the woman would have to admit that she had violated the law in order to prosecute the male."

2. ***Feminist criticisms of statutory rape laws.*** Consider Olsen, supra: "Feminists charge that [statutory rape laws] are harmful to women on both a practical and an ideological level. First, as an effort to control the sexual activities of young women, statutory rape [laws] interfere[ ] with the sexual freedom of the underage female. [They] violate the female's right [to] be as free sexually as her male counterpart. [Second, g]ender-based statutory rape laws reinforce the sexual stereotype of men as aggressors and women as passive victims. The laws perpetuate the double standard of sexual morality [in which] sex is an accomplishment [for men but a debasing activity for women].

"Unfortunately, [however,] invalidating statutory rape laws altogether [might] undermine the right of young women to be free of unwanted sexual conduct. [Since the stereotypes that statutory rape laws reinforce may have a basis in current social reality, underage] females might discover that although the abolition of [such] laws would protect their rights against the state, it would remove some of their already-minimal protection against individual men. [Among other needed protections,] statutory rape laws may prohibit certain instances of sexual assault that should be considered illegal, but cannot be prosecuted as forcible rape."

3. ***The focus on "difference."*** Should the constitutionality of gender-based classifications be based on an assessment of whether males and females are relevantly "different"?

(a) Consider Laurence H. Tribe, *Constitutional Choices* 241 (1985): "That 'the sexes are not similarly situated' in such cases as *Michael M.* and *Dothard* would not, to anyone less mesmerized [than the Court] by the ideal of law as a mirror of nature, be thought to *justify* a gender discrimination as noninvidious; it would instead raise the question whether such discrimination formed part of the law's systemic support for male supremacy." See also Reva B. Siegel, *She the People: The Nineteenth Amendment, Sex Equality, Federalism, and the Family*, 115 Harv.L.Rev. 947 (2002), arguing that "the manner in which the

Court derived sex discrimination doctrine from the race discrimination paradigm produced foundational weaknesses in this body of law that continue to haunt it."

Viewing sex discrimination issues through what he terms a different "lens," Professor Tribe concludes that "[t]he law must be prepared to act [by] affirmatively combating the inequities that result when we all too casually allow biological differences to justify the imposition of legal disabilities on women." Tribe, 2d ed. at 1577. Do you agree? How might this approach be applied to *Dothard*? To *Michael M.*? What would be the costs?

May women employees, because women live longer, be required to make larger contributions than men to a state pension fund? See *Los Angeles Dep't of Water & Power v. Manhart,* 435 U.S. 702 (1978) (violation of Title VII).

(b)   Consider Deborah Rhode, *Gender and Justice* 2–3 (1989): "The law's conventional approach to gender issues has focused on gender difference. [Within] this framework, sex-based discrimination remains justifiable if the sexes are different in some sense that is related to valid regulatory objectives. [But] this difference-oriented approach has proved inadequate in both theory and practice. As a theoretical matter, it tends toward tautology. It permits different treatment for those who differ with respect to legitimate purposes but provides no standards for determining what differences are relevant and what counts as legitimate. As a practical matter, this approach has both over-and undervalued gender differences. In some instances, biology has determined destiny, while in other contexts, women's particular needs have gone unacknowledged or unaddressed. [Reliance] on 'real difference' [has] often done more to reflect sex-based inequalities than to challenge them."

(c)   Consider the suggestion of Martha Minow, *Introduction: Finding Our Paradoxes, Affirming Our Beyond,* 24 Harv.C.R.C.L.L.Rev. 1 (1989), that feminist scholarship addressing issues of "difference" has included at least three stages: "[T]he first stage articulated women's claims to be granted the same rights and privileges as men [including] rights to vote and to hold the same jobs as men. The second stage advocated respect and accommodation for women's historical and contemporary differences. For those writing in this second stage, the problem needing redress was the undervaluation or disregard for women's historic and persistent interests, traits, and needs. Examples of second-stage goals include obtaining pregnancy and maternity leaves from paid employment, pursuing comparable worth to revalue traditional women's work, and elaborating special rights for women to respond to rape, battery of women by men, and self-determination about whether to conceive or bear a child.

"The third stage rejects the preoccupation with similarities and differences between men and women. As third-stage representatives see it, this preoccupation has itself helped perpetuate the degradation and subordination of women. Focusing on the similarities and differences between men and women threatens to preserve men as the starting point for analysis. For example, an unstated male norm makes pregnancy and maternity leaves 'special treatment,' contrasted to the 'normal treatment' given to employees. But these programs are special only in comparison with background rules that treat as the norm the person—a man—who never gets pregnant."

(d) Would it be better to declare that a "rule or practice is discriminatory [if] it participates in the systemic social deprivation of one sex because of sex"? Should the "only question for litigation [be] whether the policy or practice in question integrally contributes to the maintenance of an underclass [because] of gender"? For a discussion of this "anti-subordination" or "dominance" approach, see Catharine A. MacKinnon, *Sexual Harassment of Working Women* 117 (1979).

According to Catharine MacKinnon, *Women's Lives, Men's Law* 132–33 (2005): "[The dominance approach to issues of gender equality] is neither to affirm women's sameness to men, nor to affirm women as 'different,' a currently fashionable strategy in some circles. [It] is to point out the collision between the existing equality paradigm and the social definition of women and men as such. How sex equality can be produced if sex is a difference is problematic. Sex equality becomes something of an oxymoron, a contradiction in terms. * * * Sexual violation symbolizes and actualizes women's subordinate status to men. [What] it comes down to is that the most extreme instances of sex inequality in society are considered sex differences, hence reasons equality law does not apply, as in *Michael M.*, or reasons discrimination can be openly justified, as in *Dothard*."

———

ROSTKER v. GOLDBERG, 453 U.S. 57 (1981), per REHNQUIST, J., upheld a Military Selective Service Act (MSSA) provision "authorizing the President to require the registration of males and not females": "The case arises in the context of Congress'" authority over national defense and military affairs, and perhaps in no other area has the Court accorded Congress greater deference. * * *

"Congress determined that any future draft, which would be facilitated by the registration scheme, would be characterized by a need for combat troops. [Since] women are [statutorily] excluded from combat, Congress concluded that they would not be needed in the event of a draft, and therefore decided not to register them. [The] exemption of women from registration is not only sufficiently but closely related to Congress' purpose in authorizing registration. See *Michael M.; Craig; Reed.* [It] realistically reflects the fact that the sexes are not 'similarly situated' in this case. *Michael M.*

"In holding the MSSA constitutionally invalid the District Court relied heavily on the President's decision to seek authority to register women and the testimony of members of the Executive Branch and the military in support of that decision. As stated by the Administration's witnesses before Congress, however, the President's 'decision to ask for authority to register women is based on equity.' * * * Congress was certainly entitled, in the exercise of its constitutional powers to raise and regulate armies and navies, to focus on the question of military need rather than 'equity.' * * *

"Although the military experts who testified in favor of registering women uniformly opposed the actual drafting of women, there was testimony that in the event of a draft of 650,000 the military could absorb some 80,000 female inductees [to] fill noncombat positions, freeing men to go to the front. [Even] assuming that a small number of women could be drafted for noncombat roles, Congress simply did not consider it worth the added burdens of including women in draft and registration [plans.] Congress also concluded that whatever the need for women for noncombat roles during mobilization, [it] could be met by volunteers.

"Most significantly, Congress determined that staffing noncombat positions with women during a mobilization would be positively detrimental to the important goal of military flexibility."

MARSHALL, J., joined by Brennan, J., dissented:[81] "[The] Government makes no claim that preparing for a draft of combat troops cannot be accomplished just as effectively by *registering* both men and women but *drafting* only men if only men turn out to be needed.[11] Nor can the Government argue that this alternative entails the additional cost and administrative inconvenience of registering women. This Court has repeatedly stated that [administrative convenience] is not an adequate constitutional justification under the *Craig* test."

NOTES AND QUESTIONS

1.   *Agreement and disagreement.* All the justices in *Rostker* appear to agree that it is constitutionally permissible for the armed services (a) to exclude women from combat positions and (b) in the event of a draft, to conscript males only. Why? Would it be fair to say that the majority and dissenting justices differ mostly if not exclusively about the implications of their shared assumptions?[82]

---

[81]   White, J., joined by Brennan, J., dissented separately.

[11]   **[Ct's Note]** Alternatively, the Government could employ a classification that is related to the statutory objective but is not based on gender, for example, combat eligibility. Under the current scheme, large subgroups of the male population who are ineligible for combat because of physical handicaps or conscientious objector status are nonetheless required to register.

[82]   In 1994, the Department of Defense issued a rule that restricted women members of the armed forces from serving in artillery, armor, infantry, and other similar combat roles. This rule lasted through the conflicts in Iraq and Afghanistan, in which more than 280,000 women were deployed, over 800 were wounded, and more than 130 died. In January of 2013, the military eliminated its categorical exclusion of women from combat, but reserved to commanders a continuing discretion to exclude women from particular combat roles (such as, possibly, participation in the infantry). For a skeptical appraisal of how far and fast change will occur, and an argument that equal protection norms should forbid continuing exclusions of women, see Tim Bakken, *A Woman Soldier's Right to Combat: Equal Protection in the Military,* 20 Wm. & Mary L.Rev. 271 (2014).

2. ***Feminist divisions.*** Consider Wendy W. Williams, *The Equality Crisis: Some Reflections on Culture, Courts, and Feminism,* 7 Women's Rts.L.Rep. 175 (1982): "As for *Rostker,* the conflicts among feminists were overtly expressed. Some of us felt it essential that we support the notion that a single-sex draft was unconstitutional; others felt that feminists should not take such a position. These latter groups explicitly contrasted the female ethic of nurturance and life-giving with a male ethic of aggression and militarism and asserted that if we argued to the Court that single-sex registration is unconstitutional we would be betraying ourselves and supporting what we find least acceptable about the male world.[83]

"To me, this latter argument quite overtly taps qualities that the culture has ascribed to woman-as-childrearer and converts them to a normative value statement, one with which it is easy for us to sympathize. This is one of the circumstances in which the feeling that 'I want what he's got but I don't want to be what he's had to be in order to get it' comes quickly to the surface. But I also believe that the reflexive response based on these deeper cultural senses leads us to untenable positions. [To] me, *Rostker* never posed the question of whether women should be forced as men now are to fight wars, but whether we, like them, must take the responsibility for deciding whether or not to fight, whether or not to bear the cost of risking our lives, on the one hand, or resisting in the name of peace, on the other. And do we not, by insisting upon our differences at these crucial junctures, promote and reinforce the us-them dichotomy that permits the Rehnquists and the Stewarts to resolve matters of great importance and complexity by the simplistic, reflexive assertion that men and women 'are simply not similarly situated?' "[84]

––––––––

NGUYEN v. INS, 533 U.S. 53 (2001), upheld a provision of the Immigration and Naturalization Act that distinguishes between American citizen mothers and American citizen fathers who are the parents of out-of-wedlock children born abroad: Whereas the mothers pass their American citizenship automatically to their out-of-wedlock offspring, the statute establishes various procedural barriers before the nonmarital child of a citizen father can become a citizen. Writing for the Court, KENNEDY, J.,

––––––––––––––––––––

[83] Compare Carol Gilligan, *In a Different Voice* (1982), suggesting that women tend to have a different moral framework—more concerned with issues of relationships and of caring—from the characteristically rights-based outlook of men. Questions raised about Gilligan's theory include (i) whether the characteristic difference that she identifies in fact exists; (ii) whether, even if it does, it is the result of social conditioning rather than reflective of a "natural" difference between men and women; and (iii) whether governmental action predicated on the notion that women have a distinctive moral perspective helps to perpetuate a stereotype that works to women's overall disadvantage. For a sustained effort to apply ideas derived from Gilligan to legal contexts, see Robin West, *Caring for Justice* (1997). For feminist commentary on and criticism of Gilligan's work, see Mary Joe Frug, *Progressive Feminist Legal Scholarship: Can We Claim "A Different Voice"?*, 15 Harv. Women's L.J. 37 (1992); MacKinnon, supra, at 32–45.

[84] For further commentary, see Diane H. Mazur, *A Call to Arms,* 22 Harv. Women's L.J. 39 (1999) (arguing that a consistent application of most feminist approaches should "not only permit, but would demand, greater feminist support for military service by women").

recognized that heightened scrutiny applied, but he found the different treatment of mothers and fathers of out-of-wedlock children to be substantially related to two important governmental interests: "assuring that a biological parent-child relationship exists" and "ensur[ing] that the child and the citizen parent have some demonstrated opportunity or potential to develop [a] relationship [that] consists of the real, everyday ties that provide a connection between child and citizen parent and, in turn, the United States. In the case of a citizen mother and a child born overseas, the opportunity for a meaningful relationship between citizen parent and child inheres in the very event of birth, an event so critical to our constitutional and statutory understandings of citizenship. The mother knows that the child is in being and is hers and has an initial point of contact with him. * * *

"To fail to acknowledge even our most basic biological differences—such as the fact that a mother must be present at birth but the father need not be—risks making the guarantee of equal protection superficial, and so disserving it."

O'CONNOR, J., joined by Souter, Ginsburg, and Breyer, JJ., dissented: "While the Court invokes heightened scrutiny, the manner in which it [applies] this standard is a stranger to our precedents." According to O'Connor, J., no real differences justified the differential treatment. As a result of "[m]odern DNA testing," it was not substantially more difficult to determine biological fatherhood than motherhood in most cases. And if Congress cared about parent-child relationships, it "could require some degree of regular contact between the child and the citizen parent over a period of time" in order for either a mother or a father to be able to pass on American citizenship to an illegitimate child born abroad: "[The statute] finds support not in biological differences but instead in a stereotype—i.e., 'the generalization that mothers are significantly more likely than fathers [to] develop caring relationships with their children.' [No] one should mistake the majority's analysis for a careful application of this Court's equal protection jurisprudence concerning sex-based classifications. Today's decision instead represents a deviation from a line of cases in which we have vigilantly applied heightened scrutiny."[85]

---

[85] The Court's previous cases involving discrimination against unmarried fathers in comparison with unmarried mothers, both decided by 5–4, are hard to reconcile. Compare *Caban v. Mohammed*, 441 U.S. 380 (1979) (holding violative of equal protection a New York statute granting the mother—but not the father—of an out-of-wedlock child the right to veto the child's adoption), with *Parham v. Hughes*, 441 U.S. 347 (1979) (upholding a law denying the father—but not the mother—of an out-of-wedlock child the right to sue for the child's wrongful death unless he had legitimated the child). In *Miller v. Albright*, 523 U.S. 420 (1998), a sharply divided Court had upheld the same provision involved in *Nguyen v. INS*, but had done so without a majority opinion, with two Justices concurring in the result only because they thought that the nonmarital child seeking to establish citizenship in that case lacked standing to assert the rights of the biological father to be free from gender-based discrimination.

Do you agree? Does the Court's decision at least indicate—contrary to the conclusion that some had drawn from *United States v. Virginia*, supra—that the Justices remain far more tolerant of gender-based than of race-based discriminations? Consider William N. Eskridge, Jr., *Some Effects of Identity-Based Social Movements on Constitutional Law in the Twentieth Century*, 100 Mich.L.Rev. 2062 (2002): "The Court's disposition[ ] reflects the continued difference between race and sex distinctions in equality jurisprudence. Is there much doubt that the Court would have overturned a law making one's citizenship turn in any way on the race of one's American (or non-American) parent?"

III. "BENIGN" OR 'REMEDIAL" DISCRIMINATION

The most paradigmatic forms of historic gender discrimination, as of race discrimination, have involved classifications predicated on the assumption that one sex is less competent, trustworthy, or deserving than the other. Some gender-based classifications explicitly reject this assumption; they may have as their aim compensating women for past discrimination, public or private, or expanding opportunities for women. In cases of purportedly "benign" discrimination, one question involves the standard of judicial review that ought to apply. The cases also reflect—albeit to varying degrees—a concern that gender-based classifications, even when their ostensible aim is to help women, may reflect and possibly reinforce stereotypes that redound to women's overall disadvantage. As you read the cases in this section, consider how consistent a theme this has been, and ought to be, in the Court's decisions. Is concern about harmful stereotypes an aspect of the level of scrutiny that the Court applies or a factor independent of the standard of review?

CALIFANO v. WEBSTER
430 U.S. 313, 97 S.Ct. 1192, 51 L.Ed.2d 360 (1977).

PER CURIAM.

[Social Security Act § 215(b)(3)'s formula—which has since been amended—afforded the chance of higher old-age benefits to female wage earners than to similarly situated males.]

To withstand scrutiny under [equal protection], "classifications by gender must serve important governmental objectives and must be substantially related to achievement of those objectives." *Craig*. Reduction of the disparity in economic condition between men and women caused by the long history of discrimination against women has been recognized as such an important governmental objective. *Schlesinger v. Ballard*, 419 U.S.

498 (1975);[86] *Kahn v. Shevin*, 416 U.S. 351 (1974).[87] But "the mere recitation of a benign, compensatory purpose is not an automatic shield which protects against any inquiry into the actual purposes underlying a statutory scheme." *Weinberger v. Wiesenfeld*, 420 U.S. 636 (1975).[88] Accordingly, we have rejected attempts to justify gender classifications as compensation for past discrimination against women when the classifications in fact penalized women wage earners, *Califano v. Goldfarb*, 430 U.S. 199 (1977);[89] *Wiesenfeld*, or when the statutory structure and its legislative history revealed that the classification was not enacted as compensation for past discrimination. *Goldfarb; Wiesenfeld*.

[The] more favorable treatment of the female wage earner enacted here was not a result of "archaic and overbroad generalizations" about women, or of "the role-typing society has long imposed" upon women such as casual assumptions that women are "the weaker sex" or are more likely to be child-rearers or dependents. Rather, "the only discernible purpose of [§ 215's more favorable treatment is] the permissible one of redressing our society's longstanding disparate treatment of women." *Goldfarb*.

The challenged statute operated directly to compensate women for past economic discrimination. Retirement benefits [are] based on past earnings. But as we have recognized: "Whether from overt discrimination or from the socialization process of a male-dominated culture, the job market is inhospitable to the woman seeking any but the lowest paid jobs." *Kahn*. Thus, allowing women, who as such have been unfairly hindered from earning as much as men, to eliminate additional low-earning years

---

[86] *Schlesinger*, per Stewart, J., upheld a federal statute providing for the discharge of naval "line" officers who had not been promoted for nine years (males) or thirteen years (females): Because of Navy restrictions on combat and sea duty for women, "Congress [may] quite rationally have believed that women line officers had less opportunity for promotion than did their male counterparts, and that a longer period of tenure for women officers would, therefore, be consistent with the goal to provide women officers with 'fair and equitable career advancement programs.' "

[87] *Kahn*, per Douglas, J., upheld a property tax exemption for widows (but not widowers) on the ground that the law was "reasonably designed to further the state policy of cushioning the financial impact of spousal loss upon the sex for whom that loss imposes a disproportionately heavy burden."

[88] *Weinberger*, per Brennan, J., held that Social Security Act § 402(g)'s payment of benefits to the wife—but not to the husband—of a deceased wage earner with minor children violated equal protection because it "unjustifiably discriminated against women wage-earners": as in *Frontiero*, an " 'archaic and overbroad' generalization [underlies] the distinction drawn by § 402(g), namely, that male [but not female] workers' earnings are vital to the support of their families." Unlike in *Kahn*, "[i]t is apparent both from the statutory scheme itself and from the legislative history of § 402(g) that Congress' purpose [was] not to provide an income to women who were, because of economic discrimination, unable to provide for themselves."

[89] *Goldfarb* held that Social Security Act § 402(f)'s payment of benefits to a widow of a covered employee, but not to a widower unless he proves dependency on his deceased wife-employee, violated equal protection.

from the calculation of their retirement benefits works directly to remedy some part of the effect of past discrimination.[5]

[T]he legislative history is clear that the differing treatment of men and women in former § 215(b)(3) was not "the accidental byproduct of a traditional way of thinking about females," *Goldfarb* (Stevens, J., concurring in the result), but rather was deliberately enacted to compensate for particular economic disabilities suffered by women. * * *

Reversed.

CHIEF JUSTICE BURGER, with whom JUSTICE STEWART, JUSTICE BLACKMUN, and JUSTICE REHNQUIST join, concurring in the judgment.

* * * I question whether certainty in the law is promoted by hinging the validity of important statutory schemes on whether five Justices view them to be more akin to the "offensive" provisions struck down in *Wiesenfeld* and *Frontiero,* or more like the "benign" provisions upheld in *Ballard* and *Kahn.* I therefore concur in the judgment [for] reasons stated by Mr. Justice Rehnquist in his dissenting opinion in *Goldfarb*: ["Favoring aged widows is scarcely an invidious discrimination. [It] in no way perpetuates the economic discrimination which has been the basis for heightened scrutiny of gender-based classifications, and is, in fact, explainable as a measure to ameliorate the characteristically depressed condition of aged widows."]

———

ORR v. ORR, 440 U.S. 268 (1979), considered "two legislative objectives" for an Alabama statute providing that only husbands may be required to pay alimony—(1) to "provide help for needy spouses, using sex as a proxy for need," and (2) to "compensat[e] women for past discrimination during marriage, which assertedly has left them unprepared to fend for themselves." The Court, per BRENNAN, J., held that the statute failed the *Craig* standard: "Under the statute, individualized hearings at which the parties' relative financial circumstances are considered *already* occur. There is no reason, therefore, to use sex as a proxy for need. Needy males could be helped along with needy females with little if any additional burden on the [state]. Similarly, since individualized hearings can determine which women were in fact discriminated against vis-à-vis their husbands, as well as which family units defied the stereotype and left the husband dependent on the wife, Alabama's alleged

---

[5]   **[Ct's Note]** Even with the advantage[,] women on the average received lower retirement benefits than men. "As of December 1972, the average monthly retirement insurance benefit for males was $179.60 and for females, $140.50."

compensatory purpose may be effectuated without placing burdens solely on husbands."[90]

MISSISSIPPI UNIV. FOR WOMEN V. HOGAN
458 U.S. 718, 102 S.Ct. 3331, 73 L.Ed.2d 1090 (1982).

JUSTICE O'CONNOR delivered the opinion of the Court.

[Mississippi University for Women ("MUW"), "the oldest state-supported all-female college in the United States," denied Hogan admission to its School of Nursing solely because of his sex.[91]] Our decisions [establish] that the party seeking to uphold a statute that classifies individuals on the basis of their gender must carry the burden of showing an "exceedingly persuasive justification" for the classification. The burden is met only by showing at least that the classification serves "important governmental objectives and that the discriminatory means employed" are "substantially related to the achievement of those objectives."[9] * * *

The State's primary justification for maintaining the single-sex admissions policy of MUW's School of Nursing is that it compensates for discrimination against women and, therefore, constitutes educational affirmative action. [A] state can evoke a compensatory purpose to justify an otherwise discriminatory classification only if members of the gender benefited by the classification actually suffer a disadvantage related to the classification. We considered such a situation in *Webster* [and *Ballard*].

In sharp contrast, Mississippi has made no showing that women lacked opportunities to obtain training in the field of nursing or to attain positions of leadership in that field when the MUW School of Nursing opened its door or that women currently are deprived of such opportunities. In fact, in 1970, the year before the School of Nursing's first class enrolled, women earned 94 percent of the nursing baccalaureate degrees conferred in Mississippi and 98.6 percent of the degrees earned nationwide.

Rather than compensate for discriminatory barriers faced by women, MUW's [policy] tends to perpetuate the stereotyped view of nursing as an exclusively woman's job.[15] By assuring that Mississippi allots more openings in its state-supported nursing schools to women than it does to

---

[90] Blackmun, J., concurred. Burger, C.J., and Powell and Rehnquist, JJ., dissented on procedural grounds to which Stevens, J.'s concurrence responded.

[91] The Court declined "to address the question of whether MUW's admissions policy, as applied to males seeking admission to schools other than the School of Nursing, violates the Fourteenth Amendment."

[9] [Ct's Note] [Because] we conclude that the challenged statutory classification is not substantially related to an important objective, we need not decide whether classifications based upon gender are inherently suspect.

[15] [Ct's Note] Officials of the American Nurses Association have suggested that excluding men from the field has depressed nurses' wages. To the extent the exclusion of men has that effect, MUW's admissions policy actually penalizes the very class the State purports to benefit. Cf. *Wiesenfeld*.

men, MUW's admissions policy lends credibility to the old view that women, not men, should become nurses, and makes the assumption that nursing is a field for women a self-fulfilling prophecy. Thus, we conclude that, although the State recited a "benign, compensatory purpose," it failed to establish that the alleged objective is the actual purpose underlying the discriminatory classification.

The policy is invalid also because [the] State has made no showing that the gender-based classification is substantially and directly related to its proposed compensatory objective. To the contrary, MUW's policy of permitting men to attend classes as auditors fatally undermines its claim that women, at least those in the School of Nursing, are adversely affected by the presence of men.

Affirmed.

CHIEF JUSTICE BURGER, dissenting.

I agree generally with Justice Powell's dissenting opinion. I write separately, however, to emphasize that [s]ince the Court's opinion relies heavily on its finding that women have traditionally dominated the nursing profession, it suggests that a State might well be justified in maintaining, for example, the option of an all-women's business school or liberal arts program.

JUSTICE POWELL, with whom JUSTICE REHNQUIST joins, dissenting.[92]

[T]he Court errs seriously by assuming [that] the equal protection standard generally applicable to sex discrimination is appropriate here. That standard was designed to free women from "archaic and overbroad generalizations." *Ballard.* In no previous case have we applied it to invalidate state efforts to *expand* women's choices. * * *

By applying heightened equal protection analysis to this case, the Court frustrates the liberating spirit of the Equal Protection Clause. It forbids the States from providing women with an opportunity to choose the type of university they prefer. And yet it is these women whom the Court regards as the *victims* of an illegal, stereotyped perception of the role of women in our society. The Court reasons this way in a case in which no woman has complained, and the only complainant is a man who advances no claims on behalf of anyone else. His claim [is] not that he is being denied a substantive educational opportunity, or even the right to attend an all-male or a coeducational college. It is *only* that the colleges open to him are located at inconvenient distances.

* * * I would sustain Mississippi's right to continue MUW on a rational basis analysis. But I need not apply this "lowest tier" of scrutiny. [More] than 2,000 women presently evidence their preference for MUW by having

---

[92] Blackmun, J.'s brief dissent—agreeing essentially with Powell, J.—is omitted.

enrolled [there.] Generations of our finest minds, both among educators and students, have believed that single-sex, college-level institutions afford distinctive benefits. There are many persons, of course, who have different views. But simply because there are these differences is no reason— certainly none of constitutional dimension—to conclude that no substantial state interest is served when such a choice is made available.

NOTES AND QUESTIONS

1. *"Affirmative action" preferences for women.* Does *Webster* suggest that classifications enacted to remedy past discrimination against women will be tested under "intermediate" scrutiny, rather than the strict scrutiny applicable to race-based affirmative action? Should it be? Does *Hogan* alter or supplement the framework for analysis?

Consider, too, the possible relevance of *United States v. Virginia*, in which the Court said: "Sex classifications may be used to compensate women 'for particular economic disabilities [they have] suffered,' *Califano v. Webster,* to 'promote equal employment opportunity, see *California Federal Sav. & Loan Assn. v. Guerra,* [infra], [and] to advance full development of the talent and capacities of our Nation's people. But such classifications may not be used, as they once were, to create or perpetuate the legal, social, and economic inferiority of women."

What government interests, if any, should be sufficiently "substantial" to support gender-based affirmative action? Remedying past "societal" discrimination? "Diversity" in education? In employment?[93] In government contracting?

2. *Single-gender schools.* In *Hogan,* the Court stated that it was "not faced with the question of whether States can provide 'separate but equal' undergraduate institutions for males and females." Compare Jill Hasday, *The Principle and Practice of Women's 'Full Citizenship': A Case Study of Sex-Segregated Public Education,* 101 Mich.L.Rev. 755 (2002): "[In] rejecting Mississippi's argument [that a history of past discrimination justified excluding men in the present], the *Hogan* Court at least implied that even asymmetrical sex segregation in public schooling might be permissible if it responded to current (rather than past) inequities, a position that would place the law of sex-segregated public education in even starker contrast to the constitutional jurisprudence on racially segregated public schools." Does *United States v. Virginia*, supra, establish that single-gender education is never permissible? Compare footnote 7 of the majority opinion in that case with the assertions of Scalia, J., dissenting.

Consider Kimberly J. Jenkins, *Constitutional Lessons for the Next Generation of Public Single-Sex Elementary and Secondary Schools,* 47 Wm. &

---

[93] Does the validity of this interest depend on the controversial claim, often associated with Carol Gilligan's *In a Different Voice* (1982), discussed in fn. 83 after *Rostker*, that women's characteristic moral framework tends to differ from that of men?

Mary L.Rev. 1953 (2009): "[P]ublic single-sex elementary and secondary schools are experiencing a renaissance that appears likely to continue in coming years. [Two] factors determine the nature of the potential harm presented by single-sex public schools: (1) voluntary attendance at the schools and (2) the provision of substantially equal single-sex schools for each sex. [Voluntary] attendance and the provision of substantially equal benefits should modify the substantial relationship component of intermediate scrutiny." For a contrary perspective, debunking purported support for single-sex education in brain science and emphasizing the dangers of stereotyping, see David S. Cohen & Nancy Levit, *Still Unconstitutional: Our Nation's Experiment with State-Sponsored Sex Segregation in Education*, 44 Seton Hall L.Rev. 339 (2014).

    3.   ***Single-sex athletic programs.*** May public schools have separate athletic programs for boys and girls? May boys be excluded from "girls' teams"? Girls from "boys' teams"? According to Note, *Boys Muscling in on Girls' Sports*, 53 Ohio St.L.J. 891 (1992), most lower courts have held that " 'separate but equal' teams remain a constitutionally permissible alternative to gender-integrated teams. [The] important governmental objective in denying boys access to girls' athletic teams has been articulated as: 'maintaining, fostering, and promoting athletic opportunities for girls' and 'redressing past discrimination against women in athletics and promoting equality of athletic opportunity between the sexes'; in short, 'redressing the disparate opportunities available to males and females.' Most courts addressing the issue have found a substantial relationship between excluding boys from girls' teams and providing equal opportunities for females. Hence, exclusion is considered a permissible means of achieving this objective."

    Do you agree with this analysis? Is it consistent with the Court's frequent admonition in cases involving race-based affirmative action that equal protection rights attach to individuals, not groups?

    4.   ***Pregnancy and maternity leaves.*** *General Electric Co. v. Gilbert*, 429 U.S. 125 (1976), held that Title VII's prohibition of sex discrimination did not prevent companies from excluding pregnancy from their disability plans. In response, Congress enacted the Pregnancy Discrimination Act, 42 U.S.C.A. § 2000e(k) (1978), which defined sex discrimination to include pregnancy discrimination. Some states have given maternity leave rights that go beyond that afforded to non-pregnant employees who are unable to work. Is this sex discrimination? See *California Federal Savings & Loan Ass'n v. Guerra*, 479 U.S. 272 (1987) (protection for physical disabilities associated with pregnancy with no similar protection for disabilities unrelated to pregnancy is neither inconsistent with nor preempted by federal antidiscrimination statutes).

    In order to pass muster under the Equal Protection Clause, should a state statute providing post-natal maternity leaves also have to make identical provision for paternity leaves? Is an approach based upon "special treatment" for women a "double-edged sword"? See Wendy W. Williams, *The Equality Crisis: Some Reflections on Culture, Courts, and Feminism*, 7 Women's

Rts.L.Rep. 175 (1982) ("[I]f we can't have it both ways, we need to think carefully about which way we want to have it."). Does the phrase "special treatment" presuppose a male perspective?

4. SPECIAL SCRUTINY FOR OTHER CLASSIFICATIONS: DOCTRINE AND DEBATES

Are there are other classifications besides those based on race and gender that should be subject to special scrutiny? If so, by what criteria should those classifications be identified?

I.   SEXUAL ORIENTATION

ROMER V. EVANS
517 U.S. 620, 116 S.Ct. 1620, 134 L.Ed.2d 855 (1996).

JUSTICE KENNEDY delivered the opinion of the Court.

One century ago, the first Justice Harlan admonished this Court that the Constitution "neither knows nor tolerates classes among citizens." *Plessy v. Ferguson* (dissenting opinion). [T]his principle [requires] us to hold invalid a provision of Colorado's Constitution.

[The] enactment challenged in this case is an amendment to the Constitution of the State of Colorado, adopted in a 1992 statewide referendum [and referred to] as "Amendment 2." [It] reads: "No Protected Status Based on Homosexual, Lesbian, or Bisexual Orientation. Neither the State of Colorado, through any of its branches or departments, nor any of its agencies, political subdivisions, municipalities or school districts, shall enact, adopt or enforce any statute, regulation, ordinance or policy whereby homosexual, lesbian or bisexual orientation, conduct, practices or relationships shall constitute or otherwise be the basis of or entitle any person or class of persons to have or claim any minority status, quota preferences, protected status or claim of discrimination. This Section of the Constitution shall be in all respects self-executing."

[The] State's principal argument in defense of Amendment 2 is that it puts gays and lesbians in the same position as all other persons. So, the State says, the measure does no more than deny homosexuals special rights. This reading of the amendment's language is implausible. We rely not upon our own interpretation of the amendment but upon the authoritative construction of Colorado's Supreme Court, [which held that] "The immediate objective of Amendment 2 is, at a minimum, to repeal existing statutes, regulations, ordinances, and policies of state and local entities that barred discrimination based on sexual orientation." [Under Amendment 2 as thus construed, homosexuals], by state decree, are put in a solitary class with respect to transactions and relations in both the private and governmental spheres. The amendment withdraws from homosexuals, but no others, specific legal protection from the injuries caused by discrimination, and it forbids reinstatement of these laws and policies.

The change that Amendment 2 works in the legal status of gays and lesbians in the private sphere is far-reaching, both on its own terms and when considered in light of the structure and operation of modern antidiscrimination laws. "[At] common law, innkeepers, smiths, and others who 'made profession of a public employment,' were prohibited from refusing, without good reason, to serve a customer." The duty was a general one and did not specify protection for particular groups. The common law rules, however, proved insufficient in many instances, and [most] States have chosen to counter discrimination by enacting detailed statutory schemes.

Colorado's state and municipal laws typify this emerging tradition of statutory protection and follow a consistent pattern. The laws first enumerate the persons or entities subject to a duty not to discriminate. [The] Boulder ordinance, for example, include[s] "any place of business engaged in any sales to the general public and any place that offers services, facilities, privileges, or advantages to the general public or that receives financial support through solicitation of the general public or through governmental subsidy of any kind."

[These] statutes and ordinances also depart from the common law by enumerating the groups or persons within their ambit of protection. [In] following this approach, Colorado's state and local governments have not limited anti-discrimination laws to groups that have so far been given the protection of heightened equal protection scrutiny under our cases. [They] [include] age, military status, marital status, pregnancy, parenthood, custody of a minor child, political affiliation, physical or mental disability of an individual or of his or her associates—and, in recent times, sexual orientation.

Amendment 2 bars homosexuals from securing protection against the injuries that these public-accommodations laws address. That in itself is a severe consequence, but there is more. Amendment 2, in addition, nullifies specific legal protections for this targeted class in all transactions in housing, sale of real estate, insurance, health and welfare services, private education, and employment.

[Not] confined to the private sphere, Amendment 2 also operates to repeal and forbid all laws or policies providing specific protection for gays or lesbians from discrimination by every level of Colorado government. The State Supreme Court cited two examples of protections in the governmental sphere that are now rescinded and may not be reintroduced. The first is [an] Executive Order which forbids employment discrimination against " 'all state employees, classified and exempt' on the basis of sexual orientation." Also repealed, and now forbidden, are "various provisions prohibiting discrimination based on sexual orientation at state colleges."

Amendment 2's reach may not be limited to specific laws passed for the benefit of gays and lesbians. It is a fair, if not necessary, inference from the broad language of the amendment that it deprives gays and lesbians even of the protection of general laws and policies that prohibit arbitrary discrimination [such as statutes subjecting agency action to judicial review under the arbitrary and capricious standard and making it a criminal offense for a public servant knowingly, arbitrarily, or capriciously to refrain from performing a duty imposed by law]. At some point in the systematic administration of these laws, an official must determine whether homosexuality is an arbitrary and thus forbidden basis for decision. Yet a decision to that effect would itself amount to a policy prohibiting discrimination on the basis of homosexuality, and so would appear to be no more valid under Amendment 2 than the specific prohibitions against discrimination the state court held invalid.

[The] state court did not decide whether the amendment has this effect, however, and neither need we. [Even] if, as we doubt, homosexuals could find some safe harbor in laws of general application, we cannot accept the view that Amendment 2's prohibition on specific legal protections does no more than deprive homosexuals of special rights. To the contrary, the amendment imposes a special disability upon those persons alone. Homosexuals are forbidden the safeguards that others enjoy or may seek without constraint. They can obtain specific protection against discrimination only by enlisting the citizenry of Colorado to amend the state constitution or perhaps, on the State's view, by trying to pass helpful laws of general applicability. This is so no matter how local or discrete the harm, no matter how public and widespread the injury. We find nothing special in the protections Amendment 2 withholds. These are protections taken for granted by most people either because they already have them or do not need them; these are protections against exclusion from an almost limitless number of transactions and endeavors that constitute ordinary civic life in a free society.

[If] a law neither burdens a fundamental right nor targets a suspect class, we will uphold the legislative classification so long as it bears a rational relation to some legitimate end. Amendment 2 fails, indeed defies, even this conventional inquiry.

[It] is at once too narrow and too broad. It identifies persons by a single trait and then denies them protection across the board. [It] is not within our constitutional tradition to enact laws of this sort. Central both to the idea of the rule of law and to our own Constitution's guarantee of equal protection is the principle that government and each of its parts remain open on impartial terms to all who seek its assistance. [Respect] for this principle explains why laws singling out a certain class of citizens for disfavored legal status or general hardships are rare. A law declaring that in general it shall be more difficult for one group of citizens than for all others to seek aid from the government is itself a denial of equal protection of the laws in the most literal sense. * * *

[A] second and related point is that laws of the kind now before us raise the inevitable inference that the disadvantage imposed is born of animosity toward the class of persons affected. "[I]f the constitutional conception of 'equal protection of the laws' means anything, it must at the very least mean that a bare * * * desire to harm a politically unpopular group cannot constitute a *legitimate* governmental interest." *Moreno*, [Sec. 1 supra]. Even laws enacted for broad and ambitious purposes often can be explained by reference to legitimate public policies which justify the incidental disadvantages they impose on certain persons. Amendment 2, however, in making a general announcement that gays and lesbians shall not have any particular protections from the law, inflicts on them immediate, continuing, and real injuries that outrun and belie any legitimate justifications that may be claimed for it.

[The] primary rationale the State offers for Amendment 2 is respect for other citizens' freedom of association, and in particular the liberties of landlords or employers who have personal or religious objections to homosexuality. Colorado also cites its interest in conserving resources to fight discrimination against other groups. The breadth of the Amendment is so far removed from these particular justifications that we find it impossible to credit them. [It] is a status-based enactment divorced from any factual context from which we could discern a relationship to legitimate state interests; it is a classification of persons undertaken for its own sake, something the Equal Protection Clause does not permit. * * *

JUSTICE SCALIA, with whom THE CHIEF JUSTICE and JUSTICE THOMAS join, dissenting.

[In] rejecting the State's arguments that Amendment 2 "puts gays and lesbians in the same position as all other persons," and "does no more than deny homosexuals special rights," [the] Court considers it unnecessary to decide the validity of the State's argument that Amendment 2 does not deprive homosexuals of the "protection [afforded by] general laws and policies that prohibit arbitrary discrimination in governmental and private settings." I agree that we need not resolve that dispute, because the Supreme Court of Colorado has resolved it for us. [The] Colorado court stated: "[I]t is significant to note that Colorado law currently proscribes discrimination against persons who are not suspect classes, including discrimination based on age, marital or family status, veterans' status, and for any legal, off-duty conduct such as smoking tobacco. *Of course*

Amendment 2 is not intended to have any effect on this legislation, but seeks only to prevent the adoption of antidiscrimination laws intended to protect gays, lesbians, and bisexuals." (emphasis added). [This] analysis, which is fully in accord with (indeed, follows inescapably from) the text of the constitutional provision, lays to rest such horribles [as] the prospect that assaults upon homosexuals could not be prosecuted. The amendment prohibits *special treatment* of homosexuals, and nothing more. It would not affect, for example, a requirement of state law that pensions be paid to all retiring state employees with a certain length of service; homosexual employees, as well as others, would be entitled to that benefit. But it would prevent the State or any municipality from making death-benefit payments to the "life partner" of a homosexual when it does not make such payments to the long-time roommate of a nonhomosexual employee.

[Despite] all of its hand-wringing about the potential effect of Amendment 2 on general antidiscrimination laws, the Court's opinion ultimately does not dispute all this, but assumes it to be true. The only denial of equal treatment it contends homosexuals have suffered is this: They may not obtain *preferential* treatment without amending the state constitution. That is to say, the principle underlying the Court's opinion is that one who is accorded equal treatment under the laws, but cannot as readily as others obtain *preferential* treatment under the laws, has been denied equal protection of the laws. If merely stating this alleged "equal protection" violation does not suffice to refute it, our constitutional jurisprudence has achieved terminal silliness.

The central thesis of the Court's reasoning is that any group is denied equal protection when, to obtain advantage (or, presumably, to avoid disadvantage), it must have recourse to a more general and hence more difficult level of political decisionmaking than others. The world has never heard of such a principle, which is why the Court's opinion is so long on emotive utterance and so short on relevant legal citation. And it seems to me most unlikely that any multilevel democracy can function under such a principle. For *whenever* a disadvantage is imposed, or conferral of a benefit is prohibited, at one of the higher levels of democratic decisionmaking (i.e., by the state legislature rather than local government, or by the people at large in the state constitution rather than the legislature), the affected group has (under this theory) been denied equal protection. To take the simplest of examples, consider a state law prohibiting the award of municipal contracts to relatives of mayors or city councilmen. Once such a law is passed, the group composed of such relatives must, in order to get the benefit of city contracts, persuade the state legislature—unlike all other citizens, who need only persuade the municipality. It is ridiculous to consider this a denial of equal protection, which is why the Court's theory is unheard of. * * *

I turn next to whether there was a legitimate rational basis for the substance of the constitutional amendment—for the prohibition of special protection for homosexuals.[1] It is unsurprising that the Court avoids discussion of this question, since the answer is so obviously yes. The case most relevant to the issue before us today is not even mentioned in the Court's opinion: In *Bowers v. Hardwick*, [Ch. 6, Sec. 2], we held that the Constitution does not prohibit what virtually all States had done from the founding of the Republic until very recent years—making homosexual conduct a crime. [If] it is constitutionally permissible for a State to make homosexual conduct criminal, surely it is constitutionally permissible for a State to enact other laws merely *disfavoring* homosexual conduct. [And] a fortiori it is constitutionally permissible for a State to adopt a provision *not even* disfavoring homosexual conduct, but merely prohibiting all levels of state government from bestowing *special protections* upon homosexual conduct. Respondents (who, unlike the Court, cannot afford the luxury of ignoring inconvenient precedent) counter *Bowers* with the argument that a greater-includes-the-lesser rationale cannot justify Amendment 2's application to individuals who do not engage in homosexual acts, but are merely of homosexual "orientation."

[Assuming] that, in Amendment 2, a person of homosexual "orientation" is someone who does not engage in homosexual conduct but merely has a tendency or desire to do so, *Bowers* still suffices to establish a rational basis for the provision. If it is rational to criminalize the conduct, surely it is rational to deny special favor and protection to those with a self-avowed tendency or desire to engage in the conduct.

[The] Court's opinion contains grim, disapproving hints that Coloradans have been guilty of "animus" or "animosity" toward homosexuality, as though that has been established as Unamerican. Of course it is our moral heritage that one should not hate any human being or class of human beings. But I had thought that one could consider certain conduct reprehensible—murder, for example, or polygamy, or cruelty to animals—and could exhibit even "animus" toward such conduct. Surely that is the only sort of "animus" at issue here: moral disapproval of homosexual conduct, the same sort of moral disapproval that produced the centuries-old criminal laws that we held constitutional in *Bowers*.

[But] though Coloradans are, as I say, *entitled* to be hostile toward homosexual conduct, the fact is that the degree of hostility reflected by Amendment 2 is the smallest conceivable.

---

[1]   [Ct's Note] The Court evidently agrees that "rational basis"—the normal test for compliance with the Equal Protection Clause—is the governing standard. The trial court rejected respondents' argument that homosexuals constitute a "suspect" or "quasi-suspect" class, and respondents elected not to appeal that ruling to the Supreme Court of Colorado. And the Court implicitly rejects the Supreme Court of Colorado's holding that Amendment 2 infringes upon a "fundamental right" of "independently identifiable class[es]" to "participate equally in the political process."

[The] constitutions of the States of Arizona, Idaho, New Mexico, Oklahoma, and Utah *to this day* contain provisions stating that polygamy is "forever prohibited." Polygamists, and those who have a polygamous "orientation," have been "singled out" by these provisions for much more severe treatment than merely denial of favored status; and that treatment can only be changed by achieving amendment of the state constitutions. The Court's disposition today suggests that these provisions are unconstitutional, and that polygamy must be permitted in these States on a state-legislated, or perhaps even local-option, basis—unless, of course, polygamists for some reason have fewer constitutional rights than homosexuals.

[To] suggest [that] this constitutional amendment springs from nothing more than " 'a bare * * * desire to harm a politically unpopular group,' " is nothing short of insulting. (It is also nothing short of preposterous to call "politically unpopular" a group which enjoys enormous influence in American media and politics, and which, as the trial court here noted, though composing no more than 4% of the population had the support of 46% of the voters on Amendment 2.) [When] the Court takes sides in the culture wars, it tends to be with the knights rather than the villeins—and more specifically with the Templars, reflecting the views and values of the lawyer class from which the Court's Members are drawn. How that class feels about homosexuality will be evident to anyone who wishes to interview job applicants at virtually any of the Nation's law schools. The interviewer may refuse to offer a job because the applicant is a Republican; because he is an adulterer; [or] because he went to the wrong prep school or belongs to the wrong country club. But if the interviewer should wish not to be an associate or partner of an applicant because he disapproves of the applicant's homosexuality, *then* he will have violated the pledge which the Association of American Law Schools requires all its member-schools to exact from job interviewers: "assurance of the employer's willingness" to hire homosexuals. This law-school view of what "prejudices" must be stamped out may be contrasted with the more plebeian attitudes that apparently still prevail in the United States Congress, which has been unresponsive to repeated attempts to extend to homosexuals the protections of federal civil rights laws. * * *

NOTES AND QUESTIONS

1. ***Rationale of decision and standard of review.*** What standard of review did the Court apply in *Romer*? Was it "ordinary" rational basis review?[94]

If so, the crucial move is to distinguish the expression of moral disapprobation, which is a legitimate governmental purpose, from the

---

[94] See Larry Alexander, *Sometimes Better Boring and Correct*: Romer v. Evans *as an Exercise of Ordinary Equal Protection Analysis*, 68 U.Colo.L.Rev. 335 (1997).

expression of animus, which is not. Does the Court provide a tenable basis for its distinction?

Why did the majority make no reference to *Bowers v. Hardwick*? If *Romer* implicitly rejected *Bowers,* would it follow that it is *never* permissible for the government to discriminate against those who commit homosexual acts of the kind involved in *Bowers* or who have a proclivity to engage in such acts? If not, does *Romer* assume (or at least leave open the possibility) that some discrimination against gays and lesbians can be rational?

(a) As is pointed out by William N. Eskridge, *Multivocal Prejudices and Homo Equality*, 74 Ind.L.J. 1085 (1999), so-called gay rights litigation is likely to involve challenges to at least three analytically different kinds of statutes: (i) those involving explicit discrimination against gays and lesbians, (ii) those that only apply to same-sex behavior (such as bans on gay marriage and same-sex sodomy), and (iii) those that have a discriminatory effect, such as general sodomy laws. How much does and should the analysis change with the kind of statute in issue?

How would, and should, the Court have assessed the constitutionality of the "don't ask, don't tell" policy, codified in 10 U.S.C.A. § 654(b), under which gays and lesbians were subject to exclusion from the United States military, but the military would not—at least in theory—seek to discover evidence of homosexual acts or orientation when it was not openly disclosed?[95] Congress authorized abandonment of the policy in 2010, nearly fifteen years after *Romer*.

(b) A number of commentators have argued that "status-based" (even if not conduct-based) discriminations against gays target a paradigmatic discrete and insular minority who have been the victims of historic "prejudice" and should, therefore, be subject to heightened judicial scrutiny. See, e.g., John H. Ely, *Democracy and Distrust* 162–63 (1980); U.S. Dep't of Justice, Letter from the Attorney General to Congress on Litigation Involving the Defense of Marriage Act (Feb. 23, 2011). Did *Romer* implicitly reject this position?

Should it matter to the question whether discriminations against gays should be strictly scrutinized whether homosexual oreintation is an "immutable" characteristic? Kenji Yoshino, *Assimilationist Bias in Equal Protection: The Visibility Presumption and the Case of "Don't Ask, Don't Tell,"* 108 Yale L.J. 485 (1998), argues that equal protection doctrine treats visible

---

[95] The courts of appeals were unanimous in upholding the policy in the aftermath of *Romer*. In *Able v. United States*, 155 F.3d 628 (2d Cir.1998), for instance, the Second Circuit reasoned that it was constitutionally obliged to give deference to military judgments and credited as rational the government's stated purposes of maintaining unit cohesion, reducing sexual tension, and promoting "esprit de corps." The courts of appeals also rejected free speech and substantive due process challenges to the "don't ask, don't tell" policy. However, a district court in California reached a contrary conclusion shortly before Congress repealed the policy. See *Log Cabin Republicans v. United States*, 716 F. Supp. 2d 884 (C.D. Cal. 2010). For discussion, see Aaron Belkin, *How We Won: Progressive Lessons from the Repeal of 'Don't Ask, Don't Tell'* (2011); Janet Halley, *Don't: A Reader's Guide to the Military Anti-Gay Policy* (1998); Tobias Barrington Wolff, *Compelled Affirmations, Free Speech, and the U.S. Military's Don't Ask, Don't Tell Policy*, 63 Brooklyn L.Rev. 1141 (1997).

and immutable characteristics (such as race or gender) as more suspect than invisible characteristics (such as sexual orientation), but that it is wrong to do so. Support for that view comes from Bruce Ackerman, *Beyond* Carolene Products, 98 Harv.L.Rev. 713 (1985), which argues that diffuse and anonymous minority groups such as homosexuals are especially needful of strict scrutiny to protect them against prejudice in the political process because they face significant barriers to organizing politically.

(c) Commentators have described *Romer* as "narrowly" written and shallowly theorized;[96] as opaque; and as notable for its "unwritten pages."[97] Do you agree?

2. ***The relevance of Lawrence.*** LAWRENCE v. TEXAS, Ch. 6, Sec. 2 supra, per KENNEDY, J., overruled *Bowers* and held that a Texas statute prohibiting homosexual but not heterosexual sodomy lacked a legitimate purpose and violated a liberty right protected under the Due Process Clause. The Court passed quickly by an equal protection argument: "[P]etitioners [contend] that *Romer* provides the basis for declaring the Texas statute invalid under the Equal Protection Clause. That is a tenable argument, but we conclude the instant case requires us to address whether *Bowers* [has] continuing validity." In characterizing the equal protection argument as "tenable," did the majority endorse it?

O'CONNOR, J., concurring, would have put the decision wholly on equal protection grounds: "When a law exhibits [a bare] desire to harm a politically unpopular group, we have applied a more searching form of rational basis review to strike down such laws under the Equal Protection Clause. [And we] have been most likely to apply rational basis review to hold a law unconstitutional under the Equal Protection Clause where, as here, the challenged legislation inhibits personal relationships. [O'Connor, J., here cited, inter alia, *Moreno, Eisenstadt v. Baird*, and *Romer*.] The statute at issue here [treats] the same conduct differently based solely on the participants. Those harmed by this law are people who have a same-sex sexual orientation. [The] Texas statute makes homosexuals unequal in the eyes of the law by making particular conduct—and only that conduct—subject to criminal sanction. [Texas] attempts to justify its law [by] arguing that the statute satisfies rational basis review because it furthers the legitimate governmental interest of the promotion of morality. In *Bowers*, we [rejected] the argument that no rational basis existed to justify [a prohibition against sodomy], pointing to the government's interest in promoting morality. [But] *Bowers* did not hold that moral disapproval of a group is a rational basis under the Equal Protection Clause to criminalize homosexual sodomy when heterosexual sodomy is not punished. [Moral] disapproval of a group cannot be a legitimate governmental interest under the Equal Protection Clause because legal classifications must

---

[96] Cass R. Sunstein, *One Case at a Time: Judicial Minimalism in the Supreme Court* 138–62 (1999).

[97] Lynn A. Baker, *The Missing Pages of the Majority Opinion in* Romer v. Evans, 68 U.Colo.L.Rev. 387 (1997); see also Janet E. Halley, Romer *v.* Hardwick, 68 U.Colo.L.Rev. 429 (1997) (emphasizing the importance of *Romer*'s silences).

not be 'drawn for the purpose of disadvantaging the group burdened by the law.' Texas' invocation of moral disapproval as a legitimate state interest proves nothing more than Texas' desire to criminalize homosexual sodomy. But the Equal Protection Clause prevents a State from creating 'a classification of persons undertaken for its own sake.'

"Texas argues [that] the law discriminates only against homosexual conduct. While it is true that the law applies only to conduct, the conduct targeted by this law is conduct that is closely correlated with being homosexual. Under such circumstances, Texas' sodomy law is targeted at more than conduct. It is instead directed toward gay persons as a class."

SCALIA, J., joined by Rehnquist, C.J., and Thomas, J., dissenting, rejected the equal protection as well as the due process argument: "On its face [the challenged statute] applies equally to all persons. [To] be sure, § 21.06 does distinguish between the sexes insofar as concerns the partner with whom the sexual acts are performed: men can violate the law only with other men, and women only with other women. But this cannot itself be a denial of equal protection, since it is precisely the same distinction regarding partner that is drawn in state laws prohibiting marriage with someone of the same sex while permitting marriage with someone of the opposite sex.

"Justice O'Connor argues that [this law discriminates] with regard to the sexual proclivity of the principal actor. [But a similar claim could be made about] any law. A law against public nudity targets 'the conduct that is closely correlated with being a nudist,' and hence 'is targeted at more than conduct'; it is 'directed toward nudists as a class.' But be that as it may. Even if the Texas law does deny equal protection to 'homosexuals as a class,' that denial still does not need to be justified by anything more than a rational basis, which our cases show is satisfied by the enforcement of traditional notions of sexual morality."

3.   *Is sexual orientation discrimination gender discrimination?* Is discrimination against gays a form of sex discrimination appropriately subject to intermediate scrutiny? Consider Andrew Koppelman, *Why Discrimination Against Lesbians and Gay Men is Sex Discrimination*, 69 N.Y.U.L.Rev. 197 (1994): "If a business fires Ricky, or if the state prosecutes him, because of his sexual activities with Fred, while these actions would not be taken against Lucy if she did exactly the same things with Fred, then Ricky is being discriminated against because of his sex."[98]

---

[98]   See also Sylvia A. Law, *Homosexuality and the Social Meaning of Gender*, 1988 Wisc.L.Rev. 187; Cass R. Sunstein, *Homosexuality and the Constitution*, 70 Ind.L.J. 1 (1994) (arguing that discrimination against homosexuals reinforces traditional assumptions concerning the general superiority of heterosexual males and devalues the sexual "passivity" traditionally associated with women). Compare Craig M. Bradley, *The Right Not to Endorse Gay Rights: A Reply to Sunstein*, 70 Ind.L.J. 29 (1994). Courts have almost uniformly rejected this theory. See, e.g., *Dawson v. Bumble & Bumble*, 398 F.3d 211, 218 (2d Cir. 2005) (rejecting efforts to "bootstrap protection for sexual orientation" into a statute that prohibits discrimination based on sex). But see *Baehr v. Lewin*, 74 Haw. 530 (1993) (holding that a state law prohibition on same-sex marriage established a sex-based classification, triggering heightened scrutiny under the state constitution)

UNITED STATES V. WINDSOR

___ U.S. ___, 133 S.Ct. 2675, 186 L.Ed.2d 808 (2013).

JUSTICE KENNEDY delivered the opinion of the Court.

In 1996, as some States were beginning to consider the concept of same-sex marriage, and before any State had acted to permit it, Congress enacted the Defense of Marriage Act (DOMA). [Section] 2, which has not been challenged here, allows States to refuse to recognize same-sex marriages performed under the laws of other States. Section 3 [provides that in] "determining the meaning of any Act of Congress [or other provision of federal law], the word 'marriage' means only a legal union between one man and one woman as husband and wife, and the word 'spouse' refers only to a person of the opposite sex who is a husband or a wife." The definitional provision does not [forbid] States from enacting laws permitting same-sex marriages [but it] does control over 1,000 federal laws in which marital or spousal status is addressed as a matter of federal law.

Edith Windsor and Thea Spyer [were a single-sex New York couple who got married in Canada and whose marriage the] State of New York deems to be a valid one. Spyer died in February 2009, and left her entire estate to Windsor. Because DOMA denies federal recognition to same-sex spouses, Windsor did not qualify for the marital exemption from the federal estate tax. [She] paid $363,053 in estate taxes and [brought suit arguing that DOMA violated her equal protection rights by denying her treatment as] a "surviving spouse."

[Until] recent years, many citizens had not even considered the possibility that two persons of the same sex might aspire to occupy the same status and dignity as that of a man and woman in lawful marriage. [But the] limitation of lawful marriage to heterosexual couples, which for centuries had been deemed both necessary and fundamental, came to be seen in New York and certain other States as an unjust exclusion. [By] history and tradition the definition and regulation of marriage [has] been treated as being within the authority and realm of the separate States. Yet it is further established that Congress, in enacting discrete statutes, can make determinations that bear on marital rights and privileges. [For example,] in establishing income-based criteria for Social Security benefits, Congress decided that although state law would determine in general who qualifies as an applicant's spouse, common-law marriages also should be recognized, regardless of any particular State's view on these relationships.

Though th[is and other] examples establish the constitutionality of limited federal laws that regulate the meaning of marriage in order to further federal policy, DOMA has a far greater reach. And its operation is directed to a class of persons that the laws of New York, and of 11 other States, have sought to protect. [DOMA] rejects the long established precept that the incidents, benefits, and obligations of marriage are uniform for all married couples within each State, though they may vary, subject to constitutional guarantees, from one State to the next. Despite these considerations, it is unnecessary to decide whether this federal intrusion on state power is a violation of the Constitution because it disrupts the federal balance. The State's power in defining the marital relation is of central relevance in this case quite apart from principles of federalism. Here the State's decision to give this class of persons the right to marry conferred upon them a dignity and status of immense import. When the State used its historic and essential authority to define the marital relation in this way, its role and its power in making the decision enhanced the recognition, dignity, and protection of the class in their own community. DOMA, because of its reach and extent, departs from this history and tradition of reliance on state law to define marriage.

[DOMA] seeks to injure the very class New York seeks to protect. By doing so it violates basic due process and equal protection principles applicable to the Federal Government. See U.S. Const., Amdt. 5; *Bolling* v. *Sharpe*. The Constitution's guarantee of equality "must at the very least mean that a bare congressional desire to harm a politically unpopular group cannot" justify disparate treatment of that group. In determining whether a law is motivated by an improper animus or purpose, "[d]iscriminations of an unusual character" especially require careful consideration. DOMA cannot survive under these principles. DOMA's unusual deviation from the usual tradition of recognizing and accepting state definitions of marriage here operates to deprive same-sex couples of the benefits and responsibilities that come with the federal recognition of their marriages. This is strong evidence of a law having the purpose and effect of disapproval of that class. The avowed purpose and practical effect of the law here in question are to impose a disadvantage, a separate status, and so a stigma upon all who enter into same-sex marriages made lawful by the unquestioned authority of the States.

The history of DOMA's enactment and its own text demonstrate that interference with the equal dignity of same-sex marriages [was] more than an incidental effect of the federal statute. It was its essence. The House [Report] concluded that DOMA expresses "both moral disapproval of homosexuality, and a moral conviction that heterosexuality better comports with traditional (especially Judeo-Christian) morality." The stated purpose of the law was to promote an "interest in protecting the traditional moral teachings reflected in heterosexual-only marriage laws." *Ibid.*

[DOMA's] principal effect is to identify a subset of state sanctioned marriages and make them unequal. The principal purpose is to impose inequality, not for other reasons like governmental efficiency. [DOMA] undermines both the public and private significance of state sanctioned same-sex marriages; for it tells those couples, and all the world, that their otherwise valid marriages are unworthy of federal recognition. This places same-sex couples in an unstable position of being in a second-tier marriage. The differentiation demeans the couple, whose moral and sexual choices the Constitution protects, see *Lawrence*, and whose relationship the State has sought to dignify. And it humiliates tens of thousands of children now being raised by same-sex couples.

[The Court therefore holds that] DOMA is unconstitutional as a deprivation of the liberty of the person protected by the Fifth Amendment of the Constitution. [The] federal statute is invalid, for no legitimate purpose overcomes the purpose and effect to disparage and to injure those whom the State, by its marriage laws, sought to protect in personhood and dignity. By seeking to displace this protection and treating those persons as living in marriages less respected than others, the federal statute is in violation of the Fifth Amendment. This opinion and its holding are confined to those lawful marriages. * * *

CHIEF JUSTICE ROBERTS, dissenting.

Interests in uniformity and stability amply justified Congress's decision to retain the definition of marriage that, at that point, had been adopted by every State in our Nation, and every nation in the world. [That] the Federal Government treated this fundamental question differently than it treated variations over consanguinity or minimum age is hardly surprising—and hardly enough to support a conclusion that the "principal purpose" [of those] who voted for it, and the President who signed it, was a bare desire to harm. Nor do the snippets of legislative history and the banal title of the Act to which the majority points suffice to make such a showing. At least without some more convincing evidence that the Act's principal purpose was to codify malice, and that it furthered *no* legitimate government interests, I would not tar the political branches with the brush of bigotry.

But while I disagree with the result to which the majority's analysis leads it in this case, I think it more important to point out that its analysis leads no further. The Court does not have before it, and the logic of its opinion does not decide, the distinct question whether the States, in the exercise of their "historic and essential authority to define the marital relation," may continue to utilize the traditional definition of marriage. [I] think the majority goes off course, as I have said, but it is undeniable that its judgment is based on federalism. * * *

JUSTICE SCALIA, with whom JUSTICE THOMAS joins, dissenting.

There are many remarkable things about the majority's merits holding. The first is how rootless and shifting its justifications are. For example, the opinion starts with seven full pages about the traditional power of States to define domestic relations[, but] we are eventually told that "it is unnecessary to decide whether this federal intrusion on state power is a violation of the Constitution." [Near] the end of the opinion, we are told that although the "equal protection guarantee of the Fourteenth Amendment makes [the] Fifth Amendment [due process] right all the more specific and all the better understood and preserved"—what can *that* mean?—"the Fifth Amendment itself withdraws from Government the power to degrade or demean in the way this law does." The only possible interpretation of this statement is that the Equal Protection Clause, even the Equal Protection Clause as incorporated in the Due Process Clause, is not the basis for today's holding.

[Moreover], if this is meant to be an equal-protection opinion, it is a confusing one. The opinion does not resolve and indeed does not even mention what had been the central question in this litigation: whether, under the Equal Protection Clause, laws restricting marriage to a man and a woman are reviewed for more than mere rationality. [As] nearly as I can tell, the Court [does] not apply strict scrutiny, and its central propositions are taken from rational-basis cases like *Moreno*. But the Court certainly does not *apply* anything that resembles that deferential framework.

The majority opinion need not get into the strict-vs. rational-basis scrutiny question, and need not justify its holding under either, because it says that DOMA is unconstitutional as "a deprivation of the liberty of the person protected by the Fifth Amendment of the Constitution"; that it violates "basic due process" principles; and that it inflicts an "injury and indignity" of a kind that denies "an essential part of the liberty protected by the Fifth Amendment. The majority never utters the dread words "substantive due process," perhaps sensing the disrepute into which that doctrine has fallen, but that is what those statements mean.

[The] sum of all the Court's nonspecific hand-waving is that this law is invalid because it is motivated by a "bare . . . desire to harm" couples in same-sex marriages. [But] the Constitution does not forbid the government to enforce traditional moral and sexual norms. [Even] setting aside traditional moral disapproval of same-sex marriage (or indeed same-sex sex), there are many perfectly valid—indeed, downright boring—justifying rationales for this legislation. [To] choose just one[,] DOMA avoids difficult choice-of-law issues that will now arise absent a uniform federal definition of marriage. Imagine a pair of women who marry in Albany and then move to Alabama, which does not "recognize as valid any marriage of parties of the same sex." When the couple files their next federal tax return, may it be a joint one? Which State's law controls, for federal-law purposes: their State of celebration (which recognizes the marriage) or their State of domicile (which does not)? [Further,] DOMA preserves the intended effects of prior legislation against then-unforeseen changes in circumstance. When

Congress provided (for example) that a special estate-tax exemption would exist for spouses, this exemption reached only *opposite-sex* spouses—those being the only sort that were recognized in *any* State at the time of DOMA's passage.

[The] Court mentions none of this. Instead, it accuses the Congress that enacted this law and the President who signed it of [having] acted with *malice*—with *the "purpose"* "to disparage and to injure" same-sex couples. * * * I am sure these accusations are quite untrue.

The penultimate sentence of the majority's opinion is a naked declaration that [t]his opinion and its holding are confined" to those couples "joined in same-sex marriages made lawful by the State." [In] my opinion, however, the view that *this* Court will take of state prohibition of same-sex marriage is indicated beyond mistaking by today's opinion.

JUSTICE ALITO, with whom JUSTICE THOMAS joins in relevant part, dissenting.

[By] asking the Court to strike down DOMA as not satisfying some form of heightened scrutiny, Windsor and the United States are really seeking to have the Court resolve a debate between two competing views of marriage. The first and older view, which I will call the "traditional" or "conjugal" view, sees marriage as an intrinsically opposite-sex institution. [The] other, newer view is what I will call the "consent based" vision of marriage, a vision that primarily defines marriage as the solemnization of mutual commitment—marked by strong emotional attachment and sexual attraction—between two persons. [Proponents] of same-sex marriage argue that because gender differentiation is not relevant to this vision, the exclusion of same-sex couples from the institution of marriage is rank discrimination. The Constitution does not codify either of these views of marriage (although I suspect it would have been hard at the time of the adoption of the Constitution or the Fifth Amendment to find Americans who did not take the traditional view for granted). The silence of the Constitution on this question should be enough to end the matter as far as the judiciary is concerned. [Because] our constitutional order assigns the resolution of questions of this nature to the people, I would not presume to enshrine either vision of marriage in our constitutional jurisprudence. * * *

NOTES AND QUESTIONS

1. ***Basis for the decision.*** Do you agree with Reva Siegel, *Equality Divided,* 127 Harv.L.Rev. 1 (2013), that the Court's opinion in *Windsor* abounds with "deliberately constructed ambiguities"—which "[t]he dissenting opinions discuss [at] length"—"that were plainly designed to shape the debate over [whether there is a right to gay] marriage in the several states, without resolving it"? According to Professor Siegel, "*Windsor* endeavors to give voice to the perspectives of the minority, the historically disadvantaged group, in

ways the affirmative action opinions do not [and] is an equality opinion unlike any the Court has handed down in quite some time."

Consider Michael J. Klarman, Windsor *and* Brown: *Marriage Equality and Racial Equality,* 127 Harv.L.Rev. 127 (2013): "*Windsor* [is] unconvincing as a doctrinal matter. Obviously, it would be difficult to make an originalist case that the drafters and ratifiers of the Fourteenth Amendment intended to protect gay marriage, and Justice Kennedy made no overtures in that direction. Much of Justice Kennedy's opinion emphasized that the federal government has traditionally deferred to state definitions of marriage. [Yet] Justice Kennedy ultimately chose not to [invalidate DOMA on federalism grounds. The] references [to] 'liberty' protected by the Fifth Amendment [hint] at a ruling grounded in substantive due process. Yet the Court has typically required that interests protected under this doctrine be grounded in history and tradition, which gay marriage clearly is not. Conventional equal protection analysis [proceeds] by identifying the relevant tier of scrutiny. Yet the Supreme Court has never ruled that laws classifying on the basis of sexual orientation are subject to a heightened standard of review, [and] Justice Kennedy eschewed this route as well.

"In the end, Justice Kennedy's opinion relied mainly on the assertion that DOMA was motivated by a simple desire to disparage and demean gays and lesbians. He failed to say a word in response to the principal justifications proffered for the statute—most notably, honoring the choice of past Congresses to provide benefits to couples satisfying the traditional definition of marriage and preserving national uniformity in the definition of marriage for federal purposes. Nor did Justice Kennedy offer any elaboration [on] how one might distinguish a 'bare [legislative] desire to harm' from a traditional morals justification. To take one specific example, Justice Kennedy says nothing that would help a subsequent court decide whether a criminal ban on polygamy is based on an illegitimate 'desire to harm' polygamists. [C]onstitutional doctrine seems not to matter very much to the Justices—at least not in landmark cases about which they probably have strong intuitions of fairness and right."

2. ***Same-sex marriage.*** On the same day that the Court decided *Windsor,* it dismissed on standing grounds the appeal in *Hollingsworth v. Perry,* 133 S. Ct. 2652 (2013), which sought reversal of a lower federal court decision that had restored state law same-sex marriage rights in California after a citizen-initiated ballot proposition had withdrawn them. The standing ruling had the effect of permitting same-sex couples to wed in California while avoiding any Court ruling on whether state prohibitions against same-sex marriage violate the Constitution.

Do statutes limiting marriage to one man and one woman violate the equal protection rights of gay couples who want to marry?[99]

---

[99] For a sustained argument in favor of a constitutional right to same-sex marriage, see William N. Eskridge, *The Case for Same-Sex Marriage: From Sexual Liberty to Civilized Commitment* (1996). See also Steve Sanders, *The Constitutional Right to (Keep Your) Same-Sex*

(a)   One theory would be that such statutes discriminate on the basis of gender, as discussed above. Note that statutes limiting marriage to one man and one woman are not facially discriminatory against gays and lesbians (since they would not stop a gay person from marrying someone of the opposite sex), but they obviously have a discriminatory effect (in stopping gays but not straight people from marrying whom they would like to marry).

(b)   Are prohibitions against gay marriage analogous to the antimiscegenation statute invalidated in *Loving v. Virginia*? Andrew Koppelman, *Why Discrimination Against Lesbians and Gay Men is Sex Discrimination*, 69 N.Y.U.L.Rev. 197 (1994), so argues. Compare William N. Eskridge, *Multivocal Prejudices and Homo Equality*, 74 Ind.L.J. 1085 (1999), noting that whereas antimiscegenation statutes tried to support a race-based hierarchy, bans based on same-sex marriage do not attempt to inflict a harm or stigma based on sex, but one based on sexual orientation. Is this a pertinent difference?

(c)   Should laws that limit marriage to one man and one woman be deemed invalid under rational basis review, either because they reflect animus or because the limitations have no rational basis? The Massachusetts Supreme Judicial Court essentially accepted a version of this argument in its pioneering ruling in *Goodridge v. Department of Public Health*, 440 Mass. 309, 798 N.E.2d 941 (2003), which made Massachusetts the first state to authorize same-sex marriages, but it rested its conclusion on the Massachusetts state constitution, rather than the federal Constitution (with the practical effect that its decision was insulated from review by the U.S. Supreme Court). Since *Goodridge*, a number of other state supreme courts have entered similarly reasoned rulings. More recently, a number of lower federal courts have ruled that state prohibitions against same-sex marriages violate the federal Equal Protection Clause because they reflect animus or otherwise lack a rational basis.

II. ALIENAGE

Up to the late 1940s, the Supreme Court found a "special public interest"[100] that justified rejecting almost all challenges to state discriminations against aliens involving such activities as land ownership, *Terrace v. Thompson,* 263 U.S. 197 (1923); killing wild game, *Patsone v. Pennsylvania,* 232 U.S. 138 (1914); operating poolhalls, *State of Ohio ex rel. Clarke v. Deckebach,* 274 U.S. 392 (1927); and working on public construction projects, *Crane v. New York,* 239 U.S. 195 (1915). But *Takahashi v. Fish & Game Com'n,* 334 U.S. 410 (1948), relying on both Congress' "broad constitutional powers in determining what aliens shall be admitted to the United States" and the Fourteenth Amendment's "general

---

Marriage, 110 Mich.L.Rev. 1421 (2012); Laurence H. Tribe & Joshua Matz, *Essay, The Constitutional Inevitability of Same-Sex Marriage*, 71 Md.L.Rev. 471 (2012).

   [100] *Truax v. Raich,* 239 U.S. 33 (1915). *Truax,* however, invalidated Arizona's forbidding employers of five or more persons from hiring over 20% aliens.

policy" of "equality," invalidated California's denial of licenses for commercial fishing in coastal waters to aliens lawfully residing in the state.

GRAHAM v. RICHARDSON, 403 U.S. 365 (1971), took a much further step. Reasoning that "aliens as a class are a prime example of a 'discrete and insular minority,' " the Court ruled that "classifications based on alienage [are] inherently suspect and subject to close judicial scrutiny" and held that state laws denying welfare benefits to aliens violate equal protection.

SUGARMAN v. DOUGALL, 413 U.S. 634 (1973), applied the close scrutiny prescribed by *Graham* to Section 53 of New York's Civil Service Law, which required citizenship as a condition of public employment in positions subject to competitive examination. The Court, per BLACKMUN, J., held that Section 53 unconstitutionally discriminated against aliens:

"[We] recognize a State's interest in establishing its own form of government, and in limiting participation in that government to those who are within 'the basic conception of a political community.' We recognize, too, the State's broad power to define its political community. But in seeking to achieve this substantial purpose, with discrimination against aliens, the means the State employs must be precisely drawn in light of the acknowledged purpose.

"Section 53 is neither narrowly confined nor precise in its application. Its imposed ineligibility may apply to the 'sanitation man, class B,' to the typist, and to the office worker, as well as to the person who directly participates in the formulation and execution of important state policy. The citizenship restriction sweeps indiscriminately. [At the same time, other provisions] of the Civil Service Law, relating generally to persons holding elective and high appointive offices, contain no citizenship restrictions. Indeed, even § 53 permits an alien to hold a classified civil service position under certain circumstances. In view of the breadth and imprecision of § 53 in the context of the State's interest, we conclude that the statute does not withstand close judicial scrutiny."

———

IN RE GRIFFITHS, 413 U.S. 717 (1973), which was decided the same day as *Sugarman*, per POWELL, J., invalidated Connecticut's attempt to exclude resident aliens from practicing law: "[T]he status of holding a license to practice law [does not] place one so close to the core of the political process as to make him a formulator of government policy." Burger, C.J., and Rehnquist, J., dissented in *Griffiths*.

REHNQUIST, J., dissenting in *Sugarman* and *Griffiths*, stated: "The Court, by holding in these cases and in *Graham,* that a citizen-alien classification is 'suspect' in the eyes of our Constitution, fails to mention, let alone rationalize, the fact that the Constitution itself recognizes a basic difference between citizens and aliens. That distinction is constitutionally important in no less than 11 instances in a political document noted for its brevity. [Indeed,] the very Amendment which the Court reads to prohibit classifications based on citizenship establishes the very distinction which the Court now condemns as 'suspect.' [The] language of that Amendment carefully distinguishes between 'persons' who, whether by birth or naturalization, had achieved a certain status, and 'persons' in general. That a 'citizen' was considered by Congress to be a rationally distinct subclass of all 'persons' is obvious from the language of the Amendment."

NOTES AND QUESTIONS

1. ***Aliens as a suspect class.*** How persuasive is the argument that discriminations against aliens should be subject to strict scrutiny?

(a) Is it sufficient to justify strict scrutiny that aliens are a "discrete and insular" minority? Should it be relevant that the Constitution, as Rehnquist, J., pointed out in *Sugarman*, assumes the relevance of citizenship for at least some purposes—including the distribution of rights to vote and to hold some federal political offices?[101] Compare T. Alexander Aleinikoff, *Citizens, Aliens, Membership and the Constitution*, 7 Const.Comm. 9 (1990): "[T]he textual references to citizenship can be read two ways. Either the framers thought that their Constitution was really about citizens and therefore constantly reminded us of that; or they thought their document was primarily about persons, and therefore mentioned citizens in particular situations as a special case. [M]uch can be said for the latter [approach]."

Consider Tribe 2d ed., at 1545: "Because aliens are ordinarily eligible to become citizens, alienage [is] not an unalterable trait. That aliens do not vote might be seen as demonstrating their lack of political power; but, at least if it is alien disenfranchisement that is being challenged, it would seem oddly circular to rely on the very practice challenged to establish the propriety of so strictly scrutinizing it as to make very probable its invalidation."

(b) Does the history of prejudice against aliens justify strict scrutiny?

2. ***Trajectory of the doctrine.*** Although the Supreme Court has never formally withdrawn its judgment that discriminations against aliens are inherently suspect and subject to strict judicial scrutiny, it has created a number of important exceptions to that rule. The next case and the materials that come after it explore the leading exceptions. As you read the materials that follow, consider whether the exceptions can be justified as a matter of principle, whether they reveal the unsoundness of cases such as *Graham* and *Sugarman*, or whether the pattern of rule and exceptions reflects a sensible accommodation of competing interests and concerns.

---

[101] See also Earl M. Maltz, *Citizenship and the Constitution: A History and Critique of the Supreme Court's Alienage Jurisprudence*, 28 Ariz.St.L.J. 1137 (1996).

AMBACH V. NORWICK

441 U.S. 68, 99 S.Ct. 1589, 60 L.Ed.2d 49 (1979).

JUSTICE POWELL delivered the opinion of the Court.

This case presents the question whether a State, consistently with the Equal Protection Clause, may refuse to employ as elementary and secondary school teachers aliens who are eligible for United States citizenship but who refuse to seek naturalization. * * *

[*Graham* for] the first time treated classifications based on alienage as "inherently suspect and subject to close judicial scrutiny." Applying *Graham,* this Court has held invalid statutes that prevented aliens from entering a State's classified civil service, *Sugarman,* practicing law, *Griffiths,* working as an engineer, *Examining Bd. v. Flores de Otero,* 426 U.S. 572 (1976), and receiving state educational benefits, *Nyquist v. Mauclet,* 432 U.S. 1 (1977). * * *

In *Sugarman,* we recognized that a State could, "in an appropriately defined class of positions, require citizenship as a qualification for office." [*Sugarman* thus contemplated that the] exclusion of aliens from [influential] governmental positions would not invite as demanding scrutiny from this Court.

Applying the rational basis standard, we held last Term that New York could exclude aliens from the ranks of its police force. *Foley v. Connelie,* 435 U.S. 291 (1978). Because the police function fulfilled "a most fundamental obligation of government to its constituency" and by necessity cloaked policemen with substantial discretionary powers, we viewed the police force as being one of those appropriately defined classes of positions for which a citizenship requirement could be imposed.[102]

The rule for governmental functions, which is an exception to the general standard applicable to classifications based on alienage, rests on important principles inherent in the Constitution. The distinction between citizens and aliens, though ordinarily irrelevant to private activity, is fundamental to the definition and government of a State. [Citizenship] denotes an association with the polity which, in a democratic republic, exercises the powers of governance. The form of this association is important; an oath of allegiance or similar ceremony cannot substitute for the unequivocal legal bond citizenship represents. It is because of this special significance of citizenship that governmental entities, when exercising the functions of government, have wider latitude in limiting the participation of noncitizens. * * *

---

[102] *Cabell v. Chavez-Salido,* 454 U.S. 432 (1982), extended *Foley* to probation officers. Marshall, J., joined by Brennan, Blackmun, and Stevens, JJ., dissented in *Foley.* Blackmun, J., joined by Brennan, Marshall, and Stevens, JJ., dissented in *Cabell.*

Public education, like the police function, "fulfills a most fundamental obligation of government to its constituency." *Foley.* The importance of public schools in the preparation of individuals for participation as citizens, and in the preservation of the values on which our society rests, long has been recognized by our decisions [*Brown I*]. Within the public school system, teachers play a critical part in developing students' attitude toward government and understanding of the role of citizens in our society. [In] shaping the students' experience to achieve educational goals, teachers by necessity have wide discretion over the way the course material is communicated to students. [Further], a teacher serves as a role model for his students, exerting a subtle but important influence over their perceptions and values. Thus, [a] teacher has an opportunity to influence the attitudes of students toward government, the political process, and a citizen's social responsibilities. This influence is crucial to the continued good health of a democracy. * * *

As the legitimacy of the State's interest in furthering the educational goals outlined above is undoubted, it remains only to consider whether [the statute] bears a rational relationship to this interest. The restriction is carefully framed to serve its purpose, as it bars from teaching only those aliens who have demonstrated their unwillingness to obtain United States citizenship. * * *

Reversed.

JUSTICE BLACKMUN, with whom JUSTICE BRENNAN, JUSTICE MARSHALL, and JUSTICE STEVENS, join, dissenting.

[T]he New York classification is irrational. Is it better to employ a poor citizen-teacher than an excellent resident alien teacher? Is it preferable to have a citizen who has never seen Spain or a Latin American country teach Spanish to eighth graders and to deny that opportunity to a resident alien who may have lived for 20 years in the culture of Spain or Latin America? The State will know how to select its teachers responsibly, wholly apart from citizenship, and can do so selectively and intelligently. * * *

[Further], it is logically impossible to differentiate between this case [and *Griffiths*]. One may speak proudly of the role model of the teacher, of his ability to mold young minds, of his inculcating force as to national ideals, and of his profound influence in the impartation of our society's values. Are the attributes of an attorney any the less? [The attorney] is an influence in legislation, in the community, and in the role model figure that the professional person enjoys. * * *

NOTES AND QUESTIONS

1. *"Political function" exception.* (a) Is the Court's governing principle—that it is permissible for states to exclude aliens from functions related to "the process of self-government" but not to discriminate against

aliens generally—a sound one? Consider Note, *A Dual Standard for State Discrimination Against Aliens,* 92 Harv.L.Rev. 1516 (1979): "Some dual standard [appears] fundamentally consistent with general equal protection doctrine interpreted in light of distinctions the Constitution makes on the basis of citizenship. [But despite *Foley*'s] attempt to draw an analogy to exclusion of aliens from voting and holding high office, the existence of those exclusions only underscores the need for close review of other measures disadvantaging aliens. [Since] aliens are politically powerless because of their disenfranchisement and disqualification from high office, [the] political decision to bar aliens from the police should be stringently scrutinized."

(b) Are the Court's applications of the "political function exception" persuasively reasoned? With *Ambach* compare BERNAL v. FAINTER, 467 U.S. 216 (1984), per MARSHALL, J., which held that Texas could not bar an alien from becoming a notary public: "We emphasize, as we have in the past, that the political-function exception must be narrowly construed; otherwise the exception will swallow the rule and depreciate the significance that should attach to the designation of the group as a 'discrete and insular' minority for whom heightened judicial solicitude is appropriate."[103] Was the political function exception narrowly construed in *Ambach? Foley? Cabell?*

2. ***Discrimination against undocumented aliens.*** PLYLER v. DOE (1982), Sec. 5, IV infra, "reject[ed] the claim that 'illegal aliens' are a 'suspect class.' [U]ndocumented status is not irrelevant to any proper legislative goal. Nor is [it] an absolutely immutable characteristic since it is the product of conscious, indeed unlawful, action." But the Court, per BRENNAN, J., invalidated a Texas statute denying free public education to undocumented alien *children,* stressing both the special status of the children—who can " 'affect neither their parents' conduct nor their own status' "—and "the importance of education," both to the children themselves and to the nation more generally, since so many undocumented residents were almost certain to remain in the United States.[104]

Under *Plyler,* may states permissibly deny welfare to undocumented alien adults? To undocumented alien children? May states permissibly refuse to furnish undocumented aliens with emergency medical care? See Gerald L. Neuman, *Aliens as Outlaws: Government Services, Proposition 187, and the Structure of Equal Protection Doctrine,* 42 U.C.L.A. L.Rev. 1425 (1995) (arguing for "a limited extension of *Plyler* that forbids the states to exclude 'illegal' alien adults from a minimal level of government services"). Might the denial of some services to undocumented aliens be impermissible under "rational basis" scrutiny?

———

Federal statutes that discriminate against aliens do not trigger the same equal protection analysis as state statutes, largely due to the long-

---

[103] Rehnquist, J., dissented.

[104] Burger, C.J., joined by White, Rehnquist, and O'Connor, JJ., dissented.

recognized power of the national government "to exclude aliens altogether from the United States, or to prescribe the terms and conditions upon which they may come to this country." *Lem Moon Sing v. United States,* 158 U.S. 538 (1895). Relying on the traditional federal authority to regulate immigration, MATHEWS v. DIAZ, 426 U.S. 67 (1976), per STEVENS, J., upheld a federal statute denying Medicare benefits to aliens unless they have (i) been admitted for permanent residence and (ii) resided for at least five years in the United States. Although "aliens and citizens alike, are protected by the Due Process Clause, [i]n the exercise of its broad power over naturalization and immigration, Congress regularly makes rules that would be unacceptable if applied to citizens.

"[T]he responsibility for regulating the relationship between the United States and [aliens] has been committed to the political branches of the Federal Government. Since decisions in these matters may implicate our relations with foreign powers, and since a wide variety of classifications must be defined in the light of changing political and economic circumstances, such decisions are frequently of a character more appropriate to either the Legislature or the Executive than to the Judiciary. [The] reasons that preclude judicial review of political questions also dictate a narrow standard of review of decisions made by the Congress or the President in the area of immigration and naturalization.

"Since it is obvious that Congress has no constitutional duty to provide *all aliens* with the welfare benefits provided to citizens, the party challenging the constitutionality of the particular line Congress has drawn" [—allowing benefits to some aliens but not to others—] "has the burden of advancing principled reasoning that will at once invalidate that line and yet tolerate a different line separating some aliens from others. [Since neither of the two requirements] is wholly irrational, this case essentially involves nothing more than a claim that it would have been more reasonable for Congress to select somewhat different requirements of the same kind. [But] it remains true that some line is essential, that any line must produce some harsh and apparently arbitrary consequences, and, of greatest importance, that those who qualify under the test Congress has chosen may reasonably be presumed to have a greater affinity with the United States than those who do not."

NOTES AND QUESTIONS

1.   *Equal protection analysis.* Why do the arguments for treating aliens as a suspect class, if valid with respect to state legislation, not apply equally to the federal government and federal legislation?

2.   *Other constitutional rights.* Although equal protection doctrine leaves the federal government free to distinguish between citizens and non-citizens for many purposes, Congress' power to exclude aliens or impose conditions on their admission to the United States does not imply a power to

deny them all constitutional rights while they are here. E.g., *Boumediene v. Bush*, 553 U.S. 723 (2008) (habeas corpus); *Almeida-Sanchez v. United States*, 413 U.S. 266, 273 (1973) (Fourth Amendment); *Wong Wing v. United States*, 163 U.S. 228, 237 (1896) (Fifth and Sixth Amendments). To put the point differently, equal protection norms are not the only constitutional rights of which aliens can claim the benefit—even though questions involving aliens' other rights can often be complex and fraught. See, e.g., Gerald L. Neuman, *Strangers to the Constitution: Immigrants, Borders, and Fundamental Law* (1996).

But aliens, unlike citizens, are vulnerable to being deported, and the courts have consistently upheld nonpunitive detention of aliens, without a warrant requirement, as part of the deportation process. In the aftermath of the September 11, 2001 terrorist attacks, the government relied on its immigration powers to detain more than a thousand aliens while it conducted investigations, purportedly of immigration violations. For critical comment, see David Cole, *Enemy Aliens*, 54 Stan.L.Rev. 953 (2002).

Once it is recognized that Congress' power over immigration does not entitle it to strip aliens of all constitutional rights that it might otherwise be minimally "rational" for Congress to withdraw, consider whether, in the equal protection context, "courts have wrongly assumed that every federal regulation based on *alienage* [including that involved in *Mathews v. Diaz*] is necessarily sustainable as an exercise of the *immigration* power." T. Alexander Aleinikoff, *Federal Regulation of Aliens and the Constitution*, 83 Am.J.Int'l L. 862 (1989).

————

With respect to aliens' rights, Congress' power over immigration is a two-edged sword, capable not only of justifying federal discriminations against aliens, but also of conferring rights against state discrimination that otherwise would be permissible under the Equal Protection Clause. Building on earlier decisions, TOLL v. MORENO, 458 U.S. 1 (1982), per BRENNAN, J., held that a University of Maryland rule—flatly denying "in-state" tuition to nonimmigrant aliens with G–4 visas (issued to employees of certain international organizations and their immediate families)—was incompatible with Congress' manifest policy in admitting aliens to the United States and thus violated the Supremacy Clause: "To be sure, when Congress has done nothing more than permit a class of aliens to enter the country temporarily, the proper application of the principle [that state discriminations are impermissible if they impose burdens not contemplated by Congress] is likely to be a matter of some dispute. But [in] light of Congress' explicit decision not to bar G–4 aliens from acquiring domicile, [the Maryland rule] surely amounts to an ancillary 'burden not contemplated by Congress.' "[105]

REHNQUIST, J., joined by Burger, C.J., dissented: "[T]hat a state statute can be said to discriminate against aliens does not, standing alone, demonstrate that the statute is preempted. [A] state law is invalid only if there is 'such actual conflict between the two schemes of regulation that both cannot stand in the same area,' or if Congress has in some other way unambiguously declared its intention to foreclose the state law in question. [The] Court offers no evidence that Congress' intent in permitting respondents to establish 'domicile in the United States' has any bearing at all on the tuition available to them at state universities."[106]

———

ARIZONA v. UNITED STATES, 132 S.Ct. 2492 (2012), per KENNEDY, J., similarly relied on the Supremacy Clause and statutory preemption analysis to invalidate several provisions of a state statute targeted at aliens, including undocumented aliens. Frustrated with what it viewed as lax federal enforcement of the immigration laws, Arizona enacted S.B. 1070 to "deter the unlawful entry and presence" of undocumented aliens. The Court emphasized that immigration was an area of special federal concern and that congressional regulation was "pervasive." Testing state law against federal law, it held that federal law preempted provisions of S.B. 1070 (1) imposing stiffer penalties than federal law for failing to carry federal registration documents, (2) making it a crime for unauthorized aliens to work when Congress had imposed criminal prohibitions on employers but not employees, and (3) giving broader authority to Arizona law enforcement personnel than federal law gives to federal officials to make warrantless arrests of suspected deportable aliens. These provisions created "obstacles" to Congress's objectives or otherwise contravened its aims in enacting less harsh legislation. ["Arizona] may have understandable frustrations with the problems caused by illegal immigration[,] but the State may not pursue policies that undermine federal law."

Scalia, Thomas, and Alito, JJ., each filed separate opinions dissenting from some or all of the Court's rulings of statutory invalidity. Scalia, J., would have upheld S.B. 1070 in its entirety, because the authority to

---

[105] Blackmun, J., who joined the Court's opinion, concurred, vehemently denying the suggestion in Rehnquist, J.'s dissent that "decisions holding resident aliens to be a 'suspect class' no longer are good law."

[106] O'Connor, J., concurred in part and dissented in part: "I conclude that the Supremacy Clause does not prohibit the University from charging out-of-state tuition to those G–4 aliens who are exempted by federal law from federal taxes only." For further discussions of the relation between federal immigration policy and state obligations to aliens, see Stephen H. Legomsky, *Immigration, Federalism, and the Welfare State*, 42 UCLA L.Rev. 1453 (1995); Evangeline G. Abriel, *Rethinking Preemption for Purposes of Aliens and Public Benefits*, 42 UCLA L.Rev. 1597 (1995).

regulate immigration was not inherently federal. Because "the power to exclude" touched "the core of state sovereignty," Scalia, J., would not have found that Congress preempted state regulation unless it "unequivocally expres[sed]" its intent to do so. "The laws under challenge here do not extend or revise federal immigration restrictions, but merely enforce those restrictions more effectively. If securing its territory in this fashion is not within the power of Arizona, we should cease referring to it as a sovereign State."[107]

III. OUT-OF-WEDLOCK CHILDREN AND RELATED CLASSIFICATIONS

MATHEWS V. LUCAS
427 U.S. 495, 96 S.Ct. 2755, 49 L.Ed.2d 651 (1976).

MR. JUSTICE BLACKMUN delivered the opinion of the Court.

[The Social Security Act provides survivor's benefits to children who are "dependent" on the deceased parent at time of death. Legitimate children and some classes of illegitimate children [*i.e.,* children born out of wedlock] are statutorily presumed to be dependent; other illegitimate children must prove "that the deceased wage earner was the claimant child's parent and at the time of his death, was living with the child or was contributing to his support." Appellees, illegitimate children, proved that the deceased was their father but "failed to demonstrate their dependency by proof that [he] either lived with them or was contributing to their support at the time of his death, or by any of the statutory presumptions of dependency." Appellees "urged that denial of benefits in this case, where paternity was clear, violated the Fifth Amendment's Due Process Clause, as that provision comprehends the principle of equal protection of the laws, because other children, including all legitimate children, are statutorily entitled, as the Lucas children are not, to survivorship benefits regardless of actual dependency."]

[It] is true, of course, that the legal status of illegitimacy, however defined, is, like race or national origin, a characteristic determined by causes not within the control of the illegitimate individual, and it bears no relation to the individual's ability to participate in and contribute to society. The Court recognized in *Weber v. Aetna Casualty & Surety Co.,* 406 U.S. 164 (1972), that visiting condemnation upon that child in order to express society's disapproval of the parents' liaisons "is illogical and unjust. Moreover, imposing disabilities on the illegitimate child is contrary to the basic concept of our system that legal burdens should bear some

---

[107] Kagan, J., did not participate.

relationship to individual responsibility or wrongdoing. Obviously, no child is responsible for his birth and penalizing the illegitimate child is an ineffectual—as well as an unjust—way of deterring the parent." But where the law is arbitrary in such a way, we have had no difficulty in finding the discrimination impermissible on less demanding standards than those advocated here. *Levy v. Louisiana*, 391 U.S. 68 (1968).[108] And such irrationality in some classifications does not in itself demonstrate that other, possibly rational, distinctions made in part on the basis of legitimacy are inherently untenable. Moreover, [discrimination] against illegitimates has never approached the severity or pervasiveness of the historic legal and political discrimination against women and Negroes. We therefore adhere to [the] view [that] the Act's discrimination between individuals on the basis of their legitimacy does not "command extraordinary protection from the majoritarian political process," which our most exacting scrutiny would entail. * * *

Applying [rational basis review], we think that the statutory classifications challenged here are justified as reasonable empirical judgments that are consistent with a design to qualify entitlement to benefits upon a child's dependency at the time of the parent's death. [It] could not have been fairly argued, with respect to any of the statutes struck down in [prior cases such as *Weber and Levy*] that the legitimacy of the child was simply taken as an indication of dependency, or of some other valid ground of qualification. Under all but one of the statutes [struck down in prior cases], not only was the legitimate child automatically entitled to benefits, but an illegitimate child was denied benefits solely and finally on the basis of illegitimacy, and regardless of any demonstration of dependency or other legitimate factor. In *Weber*, the sole partial exception, the statutory scheme provided for a child's equal recovery under a workmen's compensation plan in the event of the death of the father, not only if the child was dependent, but *also* only if the dependent child was legitimate. [Here], the statute does not broadly discriminate between legitimates and illegitimates without more, but is carefully tuned to alternative considerations. The presumption of dependency is withheld only in the absence of any significant indication of the likelihood of actual dependency. * * *

Reversed.

MR. JUSTICE STEVENS, with whom MR. JUSTICE BRENNAN and MR. JUSTICE MARSHALL join, dissenting.

---

[108] *Levy,* per Douglas, J., invalidated a statute denying illegitimate children the right to recover for the wrongful death of their mother: "[The test] is whether the line drawn is a rational one [but] we have been extremely sensitive when it comes to basic civil rights and have not hesitated to strike down an invidious classification even though it had history and tradition on its side."

In this statute, one or another of the criteria giving rise to a "presumption of dependency" exists to make almost all children of deceased wage earners eligible, [including many] who are no more likely to be "dependent" than are the children in appellees' situation. Yet in the name of "administrative convenience" the Court allows these survivors' benefits to be allocated on grounds which have only the most tenuous connection to the supposedly controlling factor—the child's dependency on his father.

I am persuaded that the classification [is] more probably the product of a tradition of thinking of illegitimates as less deserving persons than legitimates. The sovereign should firmly reject that tradition. The fact that illegitimacy is not as apparent to the observer as sex or race does not make this governmental classification any less odious. It cannot be denied that it is a source of social opprobrium, even if wholly unmerited, or that it is a circumstance for which the individual has no responsibility whatsoever. * * *

NOTES AND QUESTIONS

1. *Origins of discrimination.* Consider Harry D. Krause, *Equal Protection for the Illegitimate,* 65 Mich.L.Rev. 477 (1967): "There has been a long history of discrimination against the illegitimate. The medieval church, in both its concern for the family and its aversion to illicit sex, reinforced the basic self-interest of the father, which self-interest may ultimately have been most directly responsible for the situation of the illegitimate. It was natural that men, as legislators, would have limited their accidental offsprings' claims against them, both economically and in terms of a family relationship, especially since the social status of the illegitimate mother often did not equal their own. Moreover, their legitimate wives had an interest in denying the illegitimate's claim on their husbands, since any such claim could be allowed only at the expense of the legitimate family. Against these forces have stood only the illegitimate mother and the helpless child, and thus it is not surprising that our laws are inconsiderate of the child's interests."

2. *The level of scrutiny.* Although the Court's decisions reveal somewhat less than perfect consistency in stating the equal protection standard applicable to illegitimacy cases, CLARK v. JETER, 486 U.S. 456 (1988), unanimously concluded that between the "extremes of rational basis review and strict scrutiny lies a level of intermediate scrutiny, which generally has been applied to discriminatory classifications based on sex or illegitimacy. To withstand intermediate scrutiny, a statutory classification must be substantially related to an important governmental objective." Applying that standard, *Clark* invalidated a statute providing that child-support actions for out-of-wedlock children must be brought before the child turns six. Although acknowledging an important state interest in avoiding litigation of stale or fraudulent claims, the Court found the six-year statute of limitations not substantially related to that interest. The six-year period was not necessarily a reasonable one, given the social pressures that might stop an unmarried

mother from filing a claim, and "increasingly sophisticated tests for genetic markers permit the exclusion of over 99% of those who might be accused of paternity" regardless of when a claim is filed.

3. ***Discrimination against parents of children born out of wedlock.*** In *Nguyen v. INS*, Sec. 3, II supra, the Court upheld a statutory provision that made it easier for women than men to pass their U.S. citizenship to out-of-wedlock children born abroad in cases in which the other parent is not a U.S. citizen. Is it constitutionally acceptable for Congress, in determining whether to grant citizenship to the children of citizen parents who are born abroad, to treat the children of unmarried parents less favorably than children whose parents were married at the time of their birth?

IV. PEOPLE WITH INTELLECTUAL DISABILITIES

CLEBURNE V. CLEBURNE LIVING CENTER, INC.
473 U.S. 432, 105 S.Ct. 3249, 87 L.Ed.2d 313 (1985).

JUSTICE WHITE delivered the opinion of the Court.

A Texas city denied a special permit for the operation of a group home for the mentally retarded. [Permits under the zoning ordinance must be renewed annually and applicants must "obtain the signatures of the property owners within 200 feet of the property to be used."] It was anticipated that the [Featherston] home would house 13 retarded men and women, who would be under the constant supervision of CLC staff members. * * *

[The] general rule [under the Equal Protection Clause] is that legislation is presumed to be valid and will be sustained if the classification drawn by the statute is rationally related to a legitimate state interest. *United States R.R. Retirement Bd. v. Fritz*, [Sec. 1 supra]; *Vance v. Bradley*, [Part V infra]. [White, J., then surveyed recognized exceptions to the general rule, involving discriminations based on race, alienage, national origin, gender, and illegitimacy.]

We have declined, however, to extend heightened review to differential treatment based on [age]. The lesson of *Murgia*, [Part V infra], is that where individuals in the group affected by a law have distinguishing characteristics relevant to interests the state has the authority to implement, the courts have been very reluctant [to] closely scrutinize legislative choices as to whether, how, and to what extent those interests should be pursued. In such cases, the Equal Protection Clause requires only a rational means to serve a legitimate end.

[The] Court of Appeals erred in holding mental retardation a quasi-suspect classification. [First, those] who are mentally retarded have a reduced ability to cope with and function in the everyday world. [T]hey range from those whose disability is not immediately evident to those who must be constantly cared for. They are thus different, immutably so, in relevant respects, and the states' interest in dealing with and providing for them is plainly a legitimate one. * * *

Second, the distinctive legislative response, both national and state, to the plight of those who are mentally retarded demonstrates [that] lawmakers have been addressing their difficulties in a manner that belies a continuing antipathy or prejudice and a corresponding need for more intrusive oversight by the judiciary. Thus, the Federal Government has not only outlawed discrimination against the mentally retarded in federally funded programs, but it has also provided the retarded with the right to receive "appropriate treatment, services, and habilitation" in a setting that is "least restrictive of [their] personal liberty." * * * Texas has similarly enacted legislation that acknowledges the special status of the mentally retarded by conferring certain rights upon them, such as "the right to live in the least restrictive setting appropriate to [their] individual needs and abilities." * * *

Third, the legislative response, which could hardly have occurred and survived without public support, negates any claim that the mentally retarded are politically powerless in the sense that they have no ability to attract the attention of the lawmakers. * * *

Fourth, if the large and amorphous class of the mentally retarded were deemed quasi-suspect, [it] would be difficult to find a principled way to distinguish a variety of other groups who have perhaps immutable disabilities setting them off from others, who cannot themselves mandate the desired legislative responses, and who can claim some degree of prejudice from at least part of the public at large. One need mention in this respect only the aging, the disabled, the mentally ill, and the infirm. We are reluctant to set out on that course, and we decline to do so.

Doubtless, there have been and there will continue to be instances of discrimination against the retarded that are in fact invidious, and that are properly subject to judicial correction under constitutional norms. * * * Our refusal to recognize the retarded as a quasi-suspect class does not leave them entirely unprotected from invidious discrimination. To withstand equal protection review, legislation that distinguishes between the mentally retarded and others must be rationally related to a legitimate governmental purpose. [The] State may not rely on a classification whose relationship to an asserted goal is so attenuated as to render the distinction arbitrary or irrational. See *Zobel v. Williams*, [Sec. 5, II infra]; *U.S. Dep't of Agriculture v. Moreno*, [Sec. 1 supra]. Furthermore, some objectives— such as "a bare * * * desire to harm a politically unpopular group," *Moreno*—are not legitimate state interests. * * *

The constitutional issue is clearly posed. The City does not require a special use permit in an R–3 zone for apartment houses, multiple dwellings, boarding and lodging houses, fraternity or sorority houses, dormitories, apartment hotels, hospitals, sanitariums, nursing homes for convalescents or the aged (other than for the insane or feebleminded or alcoholics or drug addicts), private clubs or fraternal orders, and other specified uses. [I]n our view the record does not reveal any rational basis for believing that the Featherston home would pose any special threat to the city's legitimate interests * * * .

The District Court found that the City Council's insistence on the permit rested on several factors. First, the Council was concerned with the negative attitude of the majority of property owners located within 200 feet of the Featherston facility, as well as with the fears of elderly residents of the neighborhood. But mere negative attitudes, or fear, unsubstantiated by factors which are properly cognizable in a zoning proceeding, are not permissible bases for treating a home for the mentally retarded differently from apartment houses, multiple dwellings, and the like. * * *

Second, the Council [was] concerned that the facility was across the street from a junior high school, and it feared that the students might harass the occupants of the Featherston home. But the school itself is attended by about 30 mentally retarded students, and denying a permit based on such vague, undifferentiated fears is again permitting some portion of the community to validate what would otherwise be an equal protection violation. The other objection to the home's location was that it was located on "a five hundred year flood plain." This concern with the possibility of a flood, however, can hardly be based on a distinction between the Featherston home and, for example, nursing homes, homes for convalescents or the aged, or sanitariums or hospitals, any of which could be located on the Featherston site without obtaining a special use permit. * * *

Fourth, the Council was concerned with the size of the home and the number of people that would occupy it. [But] there would be no restrictions on the number of people who could occupy this home as a boarding house, nursing home, family dwelling, fraternity house, or dormitory. [At] least this record does not clarify how, in this connection, the characteristics of the intended occupants of the Featherston home rationally justify denying to those occupants what would be permitted to groups occupying the same site for different purposes. * * *

The short of it is that requiring the permit in this case appears to us to rest on an irrational prejudice against the mentally retarded. [Thus, the] judgment of the Court of Appeals is affirmed insofar as it invalidates the zoning ordinance as applied to the Featherston home. * * *

JUSTICE STEVENS, with whom THE CHIEF JUSTICE joins, concurring.

[O]ur cases reflect a continuum of judgmental responses to differing classifications which have been explained in opinions by terms ranging from "strict scrutiny" at one extreme to "rational basis" at the other. I have never been persuaded that these so called "standards" adequately explain the decisional process. Cases involving classifications based on alienage, illegal residency, illegitimacy, gender, age, or—as in this case—mental retardation, do not fit well into sharply defined classifications.

[I] have always asked myself whether I could find a "rational basis" for the classification at issue. The term "rational," of course, includes a requirement that an impartial lawmaker could logically believe that the classification would serve a legitimate public purpose that transcends the harm to the members of the disadvantaged class. Thus, the word "rational" [includes] elements of legitimacy and neutrality that must always characterize the performance of the sovereign's duty to govern impartially. The rational basis test, properly understood, adequately explains why a law that deprives a person of the right to vote because his skin has a different pigmentation than that of other voters violates [equal protection]. We do not need to apply a special standard, or to apply "strict scrutiny," or even "heightened scrutiny," to decide such cases. * * *

[The record in this case] convinces me that this permit was required because of the irrational fears of neighboring property owners, rather than for the protection of the mentally retarded persons who would reside in respondent's [home.] I cannot believe that a rational member of this disadvantaged class could ever approve of the discriminatory application of the city's ordinance in this case. * * *

JUSTICE MARSHALL, with whom JUSTICE BRENNAN and JUSTICE BLACKMUN join, concurring in the judgment in part and dissenting in part.

The Court holds [the] ordinance invalid on rational basis grounds and disclaims that anything special, in the form of heightened scrutiny, is taking place. Yet Cleburne's ordinance surely would be valid under the traditional rational basis test applicable to economic and commercial regulation. [The] Court, for example, concludes that legitimate concerns for fire hazards or the serenity of the neighborhood do not justify singling out respondents to bear the burdens of these concerns, for analogous permitted uses appear to pose similar threats. Yet under the traditional and most minimal version of the rational basis test, "reform may take one step at a time, addressing itself to the phase of the problem which seems most acute to the legislative mind." * * *

The refusal to acknowledge that something more than minimum rationality review is at work here is, in my view, unfortunate in at least two respects.[4] The suggestion that the traditional rational basis test allows

_____

4   [Ct's Note] The two cases the Court cites in its rational basis discussion, *Zobel* and *Moreno*, expose the special nature of the rational basis test employed today. As two of only a handful of modern equal protection cases striking down legislation under what purports to be a rational basis standard, these cases must be and generally have been viewed as intermediate review decisions masquerading in rational basis language.

this sort of searching inquiry creates precedent for this Court and lower courts to subject economic and commercial classifications to similar and searching "ordinary" rational basis review—a small and regrettable step back toward the days of *Lochner*. Moreover, by failing to articulate the factors that justify today's "second order" rational basis review, the Court provides no principled foundation for determining when more searching inquiry is to be invoked. * * *

I have long believed the level of scrutiny employed in an equal protection case should vary with "the constitutional and societal importance of the interest adversely affected and the recognized invidiousness of the basis upon which the particular classification is drawn." *San Antonio Ind. Sch. Dist. v. Rodriguez* [Sec. 5, IV infra] (Marshall, J., dissenting). See also *Dandridge v. Williams* [Sec. 5, IV infra] (Marshall, J., dissenting). When a zoning ordinance works to exclude the retarded from all residential districts in a community, these two considerations require that the ordinance be convincingly justified as substantially furthering legitimate and important purposes.

First, the interest [in] establishing group homes is substantial, [for] as deinstitutionalization has progressed, group homes have become the primary means by which retarded adults can enter life in the community. * * *

Second, the mentally retarded have been subject to a "lengthy and tragic history" of segregation and discrimination that can only be called grotesque. [E]ven when judicial action *has* catalyzed legislative change, that change certainly does not eviscerate the underlying constitutional principle. The Court, for example, has never suggested that race-based classifications became any less suspect once extensive legislation had been enacted on the subject.

For the retarded, just as for Negroes and women, much has changed in recent years, but much remains the same; outdated statutes are still on the books, and irrational fears or ignorance, traceable to the prolonged social and cultural isolation of the retarded, continue to stymie recognition of the dignity and individuality of retarded people. * * *

The Court's [assumption] that the standard of review must be fixed with reference to the number of classifications to which a characteristic would validly be relevant [is] flawed. [Our] heightened scrutiny precedents belie the claim that a characteristic must virtually always be irrelevant to warrant heightened scrutiny. * * * Heightened but not strict scrutiny is considered appropriate in areas such as gender, illegitimacy, or alienage because the Court views the trait as relevant under some circumstances but not others. [An] inquiry into constitutional principle, not mathematics, determines whether heightened scrutiny is appropriate. Whenever evolving principles of equality, rooted in the Equal Protection Clause, require that certain classifications be viewed as *potentially* discriminatory, and when history reveals systemic unequal treatment, more searching judicial inquiry than minimum rationality becomes relevant. * * * 24

In light of the scrutiny that should be applied here, Cleburne's ordinance sweeps too broadly to dispel the suspicion that it rests on a bare desire to treat the retarded as outsiders, pariahs who do not belong in the community. The Court, while disclaiming that special scrutiny is necessary or warranted, reaches the same conclusion. Rather than striking the ordinance down, however, the Court invalidates it merely as applied to respondents. I must dissent from the novel proposition that "the preferred course of adjudication" is to leave standing a legislative act resting on "irrational prejudice," thereby forcing individuals in the group discriminated against to continue to run the act's gauntlet. * * *

NOTES AND QUESTIONS

1. ***Tiers of scrutiny.*** Are the Court's justifications for refusing to apply heightened scrutiny persuasive? Is the dissent persuasive that the Court *in fact* applies heightened scrutiny? That equal protection analysis both is and should be too complex to be captured in a short list of tiers or standards of review?

2. ***"Rationality" and morality.*** Do you agree with Stevens, J., that inquiry into the "rationality" of a law "includes elements of legitimacy and neutrality" and assessment of whether the sovereign has acted "impartially"? Is this approach consistent with the *Carolene Products* footnote and suggested

---

24 [Ct's Note] No single talisman can define those groups likely to be the target of classifications offensive to the Fourteenth Amendment and therefore warranting heightened or strict scrutiny; experience, not abstract logic, must be the primary guide. The "political powerlessness" of a group may be relevant, but that factor is neither necessary, as the gender cases demonstrate, nor sufficient, as the example of minors illustrates. [W]e see few statutes reflecting prejudice or indifference to minors, and I am not aware of any suggestion that legislation affecting them be viewed with the suspicion of heightened scrutiny. Similarly, immutability of the trait at issue may be relevant, but many immutable characteristics, such as height or blindness, are valid bases of governmental action and classifications under a variety of circumstances.

The political powerlessness of a group and the immutability of its defining trait are relevant insofar as they point to a social and cultural isolation that gives the majority little reason to respect or be concerned with that group's interests and needs. Statutes discriminating against the young have not been common nor need be feared because those who do vote and legislate were once themselves young, typically have children of their own, and certainly interact regularly with minors. Their social integration means that minors, unlike discrete and insular minorities, tend to be treated in legislative arenas with full concern and respect, despite their formal and complete exclusion from the electoral process.

The discreteness and insularity warranting a "more searching judicial inquiry" must therefore be viewed from a social and cultural perspective as well as a political one. To this task judges are well suited, for the lessons of history and experience are surely the best guide as to when, and with respect to what interests, society is likely to stigmatize individuals as members of an inferior caste or view them as not belonging to the community. Because prejudice spawns prejudice, and stereotypes produce limitations that confirm the stereotype on which they are based, a history of unequal treatment requires sensitivity to the prospect that its vestiges endure. In separating those groups that are discrete and insular from those that are not, as in many important legal distinctions, "a page of history is worth a volume of logic."

limitations of the judicial role in equal protection cases to the protection of discrete and insular minorities? Consider the suggestion of Bruce A. Ackerman, *Beyond* Carolene Products, 98 Harv.L.Rev. 713 (1985), that "*Carolene*'s emphasis on 'prejudice' " cannot mask the need for the courts to make substantive judgments of fairness, since "[o]ne person's 'prejudice' is, notoriously, another's 'principle.' " According to Professor Ackerman, the responsibility for substantive review of the fairness of legislative classifications cannot be limited to cases involving discrete and insular minorities. As Ackerman points out, women are not a minority at all, and children born to unmarried parents are neither discrete (readily identifiable) nor insular (geographically clustered).

Do you agree with Marshall, J., that equal protection analysis should depend on both the classification used by government and the nature of the burden or benefit being distributed?

3. ***Retreat from Cleburne?*** The Court appears to have applied a much less stringent form of "rational basis" review in its one post-*Cleburne* case involving the equal protection rights of those with intellectual disabilities. HELLER v. DOE, 509 U.S. 312 (1993), per KENNEDY, J., upheld a Kentucky scheme that allows the involuntary commitment of those with intellectual disabilities under less stringent standards than the standards employed for the involuntary commitment of the mentally ill. Treating as canonical the formulation that "a classification 'must be upheld against equal protection challenge if there is any reasonably conceivable state of facts that could provide a rational basis for the classification,' " the Court concluded that the lesser standard of proof was justified because it was "reasonably conceivable" that violent behavior by those with intellectual disabilities was easier to predict than such behavior by the mentally ill and because the treatment is less invasive.

SOUTER, J., joined by Blackmun and Stevens, JJ., dissented: "While the Court cites *Cleburne* once, and does not purport to overrule it, neither does the Court apply it, and at the end of the day *Cleburne*'s status is left uncertain. [While] difficulty of proof, and of interpretation of evidence, could legitimately counsel against setting the standard so high that the State may be unable to satisfy it (thereby effectively thwarting efforts to satisfy legitimate interests in protection, care, and treatment), that would at most justify a lower standard in the allegedly more difficult cases of illness, not in the easier cases of retardation. We do not lower burdens of proof merely because it is easy to prove the proposition at issue, nor do we raise them merely because it is difficult. * * * Kentucky is being allowed to draw a distinction that is difficult to see as resting on anything other than the stereotypical assumption that the retarded are 'perpetual children.' "[109]

---

[109] Blackmun, J., dissenting, observed that he would subject laws discriminating against individuals with mental retardation to heightened review. O'Connor, J., concurring and dissenting in part, agreed with Souter, J.'s analysis of the differential burden of proof requirements.

V. OTHER CHALLENGED BASES FOR DISCRIMINATION

1. *Age.* MASSACHUSETTS BD. OF RETIREMENT v. MURGIA, 427 U.S. 307 (1976), per curiam, upheld—"under the rational basis standard"—a law requiring uniformed state police officers to retire at age 50. After first rejecting the contention "that a right of governmental employment per se is fundamental" and thus makes the legislative classification subject to "strict scrutiny" (see Sec. 5 infra), the Court continued: "While the treatment of the aged in this Nation has not been wholly free of discrimination, such persons, unlike, say, those who have been discriminated against on the basis of race or national origin, have not experienced a 'history of purposeful unequal treatment' or been subjected to unique disabilities on the basis of stereotyped characteristics not truly indicative of their abilities. The [Massachusetts statute] cannot be said to discriminate only against the elderly. Rather, it draws the line at a certain age in middle life. But even old age does not define a 'discrete and insular' group, *Carolene Products,* n.4, in need of 'extraordinary protection from the majoritarian political process.' Instead, it marks a stage that each of us will reach if we live out our normal span. Even if the statute could be said to impose a penalty upon a class defined as the aged, it would not impose a distinction sufficiently akin to those classifications that we have found suspect to call for strict judicial scrutiny."

MARSHALL, J., dissented from "the rigid two-tier model [that] still holds sway as the Court's articulated description of the equal protection test," urging a "flexible equal protection standard" of the kind discussed in his concurring opinion in *Cleburne,* supra: "[T]he Court is quite right in suggesting that distinctions exist between the elderly and traditional suspect classes such as [blacks]. The elderly are protected not only by certain antidiscrimination legislation, but by legislation that provides them with positive benefits not enjoyed by the public at large. Moreover, the elderly are not isolated in society, and discrimination against them is not pervasive but is centered primarily in employment. The advantage of a flexible equal protection standard, however, is that it can readily accommodate such variables. The elderly are undoubtedly discriminated against, and when legislation denies them an important benefit— employment—I conclude that to sustain the legislation the Commonwealth must show a reasonably substantial interest and a scheme reasonably closely tailored to achieving that interest."

See also *Vance v. Bradley,* 440 U.S. 93 (1979) (upholding mandatory retirement at age 60 for federal Foreign Service personnel); *Gregory v. Ashcroft,* 501 U.S. 452 (1991) (upholding Missouri's mandatory retirement for judges at age 70). On discriminations against children, see generally Tribe, 2d ed. at 1588–93. An issue much litigated in the lower courts involves juvenile curfew ordinances adopted as crime prevention measures. Constitutionally permissible? (Lower courts are divided.)[110]

2. **Wealth.** Laws that explicitly distinguish on the basis of wealth or poverty, and work directly to the disadvantage of the poor, are rare. But cf. *Edwards v. California*, 314 U.S. 160 (1941) (invalidating, under the Commerce Clause, a California statute making it a misdemeanor knowingly to transport a non-resident indigent into the state). Today, laws seldom if ever prescribe that the poor cannot vote, attend public universities, utilize legal processes, or receive medical care in public hospitals. The disadvantage experienced by the poor more typically arises from the discriminatory impact of statutes that condition opportunities on the payment of money, or that draw lines—such as those separating relatively poor from relatively wealthy school districts—that strongly correlate with wealth. Equal protection issues involving discriminatory impact on the poor are discussed in Sec. 5, Parts II–V, infra.

Rare though they may be, should explicit discriminations against poor people be held "suspect"? Although the Warren Court *stated* on several occasions that "lines drawn on the basis of wealth or property" "render a classification highly suspect,"[111] the Burger Court observed in 1973 that the Court had "never held that wealth discrimination alone provides an adequate basis for invoking strict scrutiny,"[112] and, in 1980, *Harris v. McRae,* Ch. 6, Sec. 2 supra, said that "this Court has held repeatedly that poverty, standing alone, is not a suspect classification. See, e.g. *James v. Valtierra.*"

JAMES v. VALTIERRA, 402 U.S. 137 (1971), per BLACK, J., upheld Art. 34 of the California Constitution, which provided that no "low-rent housing project"—defined as any development "for persons of low income"—could be constructed unless approved by local referendum: "Provisions for referendums demonstrate devotion to democracy, not to bias, discrimination, or prejudice." A "law making procedure that 'disadvantages' a particular group does not always deny equal protection." Nor were "persons advocating low-income [housing] singled out": Mandatory referendums were "required for approval of state constitutional amendments, for the issuance of general obligation long-term bonds by local governments, and for certain municipal territorial annexations."

MARSHALL, J., joined by Brennan and Blackmun, JJ., dissented. Under California law, "publicly assisted housing developments designed to accommodate the aged, veterans, state employees, persons of moderate income, or any class of citizens other than the poor, need not be approved

---

[110] See Note, *Juvenile Curfews and the Major Confusion Over Minor Rights*, 118 Harv.L.Rev. 2400 (2005).

[111] *Harper v. Virginia Bd. of Elections,* Sec. 5, I infra, and *McDonald v. Board of Elec. Comm'rs,* 394 U.S. 802 (1969).

[112] *San Antonio Ind. School Dist. v. Rodriguez,* Sec. 5, IV infra.

by prior referenda. [Art. 34 is] an explicit classification on the basis of poverty—a suspect classification which demands exacting judicial scrutiny."[113]

Do you agree that *James* involved "an explicit classification on the basis of poverty"? What result if the state were to make it a crime for a person without visible means of support to refuse employment? If it were to discriminate against the poor in offering admissions to prestigious state universities due to the risk that those without minimum resources would drop out for financial reasons (and thus squander some of the state's investment in their education)?

Consider Frank I. Michelman, *On Protecting the Poor Through the Fourteenth Amendment,* 83 Harv.L.Rev. 7 (1969): "[I]f money is power, then a class deliberately defined so as to include everyone who has less wealth or income than any person outside it may certainly be deemed [to] be especially susceptible to abuse by majoritarian process; and classification of 'the poor' as such, may, like classification of racial minorities as such, be popularly understood as a badge of inferiority. Especially is this so in light of the extreme difficulty of imagining proper governmental objectives which require for their achievement the explicit carving out, for relatively disadvantageous treatment, of a class defined by relative paucity of wealth or income."[114]

Note that poverty often correlates with race. Writes Kimberlé Williams Crenshaw, *Race, Reform, and Retrenchment: Transformation and Legitimation in Antidiscrimination Law,* 101 Harv. L. Rev. 1331 (1988) (discussing Alan Freeman, *Antidiscrimination Law: A Critical Review,* in *The Politics of Law: A Progressive Critique* (D. Kairys ed. 1982)): "[E]conomic exploitation and poverty have been central features of racial domination—poverty is its long-term result. A legal strategy that does not include redistribution of wealth cannot remedy one of the most significant aspects of racial domination. Similarly, the myths of 'vested rights' and 'equality of opportunity' were necessary to protect the legitimacy of the dominant order and thus constituted insuperable barriers to the quest for significant redistributive reform."

Compare Ralph K. Winter, Jr., *Poverty, Economic Equality, and the Equal Protection Clause,* 1972 Sup.Ct.Rev. 41: "Race is [the] basis of a stereotype which served as a systematic vehicle of governmental discrimination. Moreover, it is not a stereotype with a pretense at being related to individual merit, even though it [is] unalterable by the individual. [But] poverty is not absolutely unalterable for all those afflicted by it. The history of this nation is a history of virtually all of its people

---

[113] Douglas, J., did not participate.

[114] See also Stephen Loffredo, *Poverty, Democracy, and Constitutional Law,* 141 U.Pa.L.Rev. 1277 (1993).

bettering themselves [economically].[115] Beyond that, [t]here simply has not been any legislation invoking a poverty classification even remotely resembling the widespread, official, racial segregation of schools and other facilities. To the contrary, there is an enormous amount of legislation [to] help the poor. [Finally], to the extent low income is related to low productivity—and it is to a large extent—poverty is not entirely unrelated to individual merit. One need not adopt productivity as the sole criterion of merit to say that poverty resulting from low productivity is far different from legal exclusion from public facilities because of one's race."

5. FUNDAMENTAL RIGHTS

In the equal protection cases studied thus far, the crucial variable has been the basis on which the government draws classificatory lines. Suspect bases for classification trigger strict judicial scrutiny, whereas statutory lines that disadvantage most other groups attract only rational basis review. For the most part, the nature of the benefit or burden being distributed, and its relative importance or unimportance, have not mattered. Beginning in the late 1950s, however, and especially in the 1960s and 1970s, the Court began to develop the notion that discriminatory classifications burdening "fundamental" rights will trigger strict judicial scrutiny even if they do not employ an otherwise suspect classification. In other words, the Court adopted a methodology pursuant to which there are two distinct ways to trigger strict scrutiny under the Equal Protection Clause (and the equal protection component of the Fifth Amendment), one involving suspect classifications and the other involving fundamental rights.

As with the Due Process Clause, fundamental rights cases under the Equal Protection Clause have often proved controversial, partly because of the difficulty of identifying fundamental rights to which the Constitution makes no explicit reference (even if they can fairly be regarded as implicit in the Constitution). Indeed, the Court's methodology in identifying fundamental rights under the Equal Protection Clause does not seem clearly different from its methodology in identifying fundamental rights under the Due Process Clause—whatever that methodology either is or ought to be. Many of the methodological controversies studied in Chapter Six thus recur in equal protection fundamental rights cases. If there is any difference, it may be this: If a right counts as fundamental under the Due Process Clause, then the government has an obligation to recognize that right and extend it to everyone. By contrast, if a right is a fundamental right under the Equal Protection Clause, then strict scrutiny may become

---

[115] See also Comment, 85 Harv.L.Rev. 129 (1971): "The poor seem to be a less cohesive and less readily identifiable group than are racial minorities. Because the class of 'poor' is constantly in flux, the reinforced sense of stigma which characterizes de jure racial classifications is probably mitigated even where explicit wealth classifications are concerned."

applicable only when the government denies the right to some, while allowing it to others (absent a compelling countervailing interest). Voting rights, the first example of an equal protection fundamental right to be studied in this section, provide an illustration. A city may not need to allow anyone to vote for candidates for mayor. If the mayor were chosen by an elected city council, no constitutional issue would arise.[116] But if a city has mayoral elections at all, then rules allowing some residents to vote, while denying the vote to others, would trigger strict judicial scrutiny.

This Section begins by examining three rights that the Court has recognized as fundamental under the Equal Protection Clause: the right to vote, the right to travel, and the right of access to the courts. It then examines cases in which the Court has refused to classify the rights to welfare and to education as fundamental for purposes of equal protection analysis.

I. VOTING

A. Denial or Qualification of the Right

HARPER v. VIRGINIA STATE BD. OF ELECS., 383 U.S. 663 (1966), built upon earlier cases—a number of which are discussed below—to overrule *Breedlove v. Suttles,* 302 U.S. 277 (1937), and hold that Virginia's $1.50 poll tax as "a prerequisite of voting" violated the Equal Protection Clause because the right to vote was a fundamental right. Writing for the Court, DOUGLAS, J., held that "the right to vote in state elections is nowhere expressly mentioned" in the Constitution, but "once the franchise is [granted] lines may not be drawn which [violate equal protection]."[3]

"Long ago in *Yick Wo,* [Sec. 2, III supra], the Court referred to 'the political franchise of voting' as a 'fundamental political right, because preservative of all rights.' * * * Wealth, like race, creed, or color, is not germane to one's ability to participate intelligently in the electoral process. Lines drawn on the basis of wealth or property, like those of race, are traditionally disfavored. See *Edwards v. California,* [Sec. 4, V supra] (Jackson, J., concurring); *Griffin v. Illinois; Douglas v. California,* [Part III infra]. To introduce wealth or payment of a fee as a measure of a voter's qualifications is to introduce a capricious or irrelevant factor. * * *

"In determining what lines are unconstitutionally discriminatory, we have never been confined to historic notions of equality" and "notions of

---

[116] Cf. *Fortson v. Morris,* 385 U.S. 231 (1966), upholding a Georgia election procedure under which, if no gubernatorial candidate received a majority of the popular vote, the state legislature elected the governor from the two candidates receiving the most votes: There is no federal constitutional provision "which either expressly or impliedly dictates the method a state must use to select its governor. A method which would be valid if initially employed is equally valid when employed as an alternative."

[3] **[Ct's Note]** [While] the "Virginia poll tax was born of a desire to disenfranchise the Negro," we do not stop to determine whether [the] Virginia tax in its modern setting serves the same end.

what constitutes equal treatment for purposes of the Equal Protection Clause *do* change [citing *Plessy* and *Brown,* Sec. 2, II supra]. * * * Our conclusion, like that in *Reynolds v. Sims*,[117] is founded not on what we think governmental policy should be, but on what the Equal Protection Clause requires.

"We have long been mindful that where fundamental rights and liberties are asserted under the Equal Protection Clause, classifications which might invade or restrain them must be closely scrutinized and carefully confined. See, e.g., *Reynolds; Carrington v. Rash.*"[118]

BLACK, J., dissented: "[P]oll tax legislation can 'reasonably,' 'rationally' and without an 'invidious' or evil purpose to injure anyone be found to rest on a number of state policies including (1) the State's desire to collect its revenue, and (2) its belief that voters who pay a poll tax will be interested in furthering the State's welfare when they vote. [H]istory is on the side of 'rationality' of the State's poll tax policy. Property qualifications existed in the Colonies and were continued by many States after the Constitution was adopted. [The Court] seems to be using the old 'natural-law-due-process formula' to justify striking down state laws as violations of [equal protection]."

HARLAN, J., joined by Stewart, J., dissented: "The [equal protection] test evolved by this Court [is whether] a classification can be deemed to be founded on some rational and otherwise constitutionally permissible state [policy].[3] *Reynolds* marked a departure from these traditional and wise principles. [I]t was probably accepted as sound political theory by a large percentage of Americans through most of our history, that people with some property have a deeper stake in community affairs, and are consequently more responsible, more educated, more knowledgeable, more worthy of [confidence. It] is all wrong, in my view, for the Court to adopt the political doctrines popularly accepted at a particular moment of our history and to declare all others to be irrational and invidious."

---

[117] *Reynolds,* Part B infra, was among the first of the Court's so-called "one-person, one-vote" decisions requiring that voting districts have roughly equal populations.

[118] *Carrington,* 380 U.S. 89 (1965), invalidated as an "invidious discrimination" a Texas provision barring members of the military who moved to Texas from voting in state elections, so long as they remained in the military: "We deal here with matters close to the core of our constitutional system." Only "where military personnel are involved has Texas been unwilling to develop more precise tests to determine the bona fides on an individual claiming to have actually made his home in the state long enough to vote. * * * 'Fencing out' from the franchise a sector of the population because of the way they may vote is constitutionally impermissible."

[3] **[Ct's Note]** I think the somewhat different application of the Equal Protection Clause to racial discrimination cases finds justification in the fact that insofar as that clause may embody a particular value in addition to rationality, the historical origins of the Civil War Amendments might attribute to racial equality this special status. * * *

EQUAL PROTECTION CH. 9

KRAMER V. UNION FREE SCHOOL DISTRICT

395 U.S. 621, 89 S.Ct. 1886, 23 L.Ed.2d 583 (1969).

CHIEF JUSTICE WARREN delivered the opinion of the Court.

[§ 2012 of the New York Education Law] provides that in certain New York school districts residents [may] vote in the school district election only if they [or their spouse] (1) own (or lease) taxable real property within the district, or (2) are parents (or have custody of) children enrolled in the local public schools. Appellant, a bachelor who neither owns nor leases taxable real property, [claimed] § 2012 denied him equal protection * * * .

[I]t is important to note what is *not* at issue in this case. The requirements of § 2012 that school district voters must (1) be citizens of the United States, (2) be bona fide residents of the school district, and (3) be at least 21 years of age are not challenged. * * *

In determining whether or not [this statute] violates the Equal Protection Clause, [we] must give the statute a close and exacting examination. [This] careful examination is necessary because statutes distributing the franchise constitute the foundation of our representative society. Any unjustified discrimination in determining who may participate in political affairs or in the selection of public officials undermines the legitimacy of representative government. [Therefore,] if a [statute] grants the right to vote to some bona fide residents of requisite age and citizenship and denies the franchise to others, the Court must determine whether the exclusions are necessary to promote a compelling state interest. See *Carrington.*

[The] presumption of constitutionality and the approval given "rational" classifications in other types of enactments are based on an assumption that the institutions of state government are structured so as to represent fairly all the people. However, when the challenge to the statute is in effect a challenge of this basic assumption, the assumption can no longer serve as the basis for presuming constitutionality. And, the assumption is no less under attack because the legislature which decides who may participate at the various levels of political choice is fairly elected. * * *

The need for exacting judicial scrutiny of statutes distributing the franchise is undiminished simply because, under a different statutory scheme, the offices subject to election might have been filled through appointment[11] [since] "once the franchise is granted to the electorate, lines may not be drawn which are inconsistent with [equal protection]." *Harper.* Nor is the need for close judicial examination affected because the district

---

[11] **[Ct's Note]** Similarly, no less a showing of a compelling justification for disenfranchising residents is required merely because the questions scheduled for the election need not have been submitted to the voters.

[and] the school board do not have "general" legislative powers. Our exacting examination is not necessitated by the subject of the election [but] because some resident citizens are permitted to participate and some are not. * * *

Besides appellant and others who similarly live in their parents' homes, the statute also disenfranchises the following persons (unless they are parents or guardians of children enrolled in the district public school): senior citizens and others living with children or relatives; clergy, military personnel and others who live on tax-exempt property; boarders and lodgers; parents who neither own nor lease qualifying property and whose children are too young to attend school [or] attend private schools.

[A]ppellees argue that the State has a legitimate interest in limiting the franchise in school district elections [to] those "primarily interested in such elections" [and] that the State may reasonably and permissibly conclude that "property taxpayers" (including lessees of taxable property who share the tax burden through rent payments) and parents of the children enrolled in the district's schools are those "primarily interested" in school affairs. * * *

[A]ssuming, arguendo, that New York legitimately might limit the franchise in these school district elections to those "primarily interested in school affairs," close scrutiny of the § 2012 classifications demonstrates that they do not accomplish this purpose with sufficient precision to justify denying appellant the franchise.

[T]he classifications must be tailored so that the exclusion of appellant and members of his class is necessary to achieve the articulated state goal.[14] Section 2012 does not meet the exacting standard of precision [because it permits] inclusion of many persons who have, at best, a remote and indirect interest in school affairs and on the other hand, exclude[s] others who have a distinct and direct interest in the school meeting decisions.[15] * * *

JUSTICE STEWART, with whom JUSTICE BLACK and JUSTICE HARLAN join, dissenting. * * *

Clearly a State may reasonably assume that its residents have a greater stake in the outcome of elections held within its boundaries than do other persons [and] that residents, being generally better informed regarding state affairs than are nonresidents, will be more likely [to] vote responsibly. And the same may be said of legislative assumptions

---

[14] **[Ct's Note]** Of course, if the exclusions are necessary to promote the articulated state interest, we must then determine whether the interest promoted by limiting the franchise constitutes a compelling state interest. We do not reach that issue in this case.

[15] **[Ct's Note]** For example, appellant resides with his parents in the school district, pays state and federal taxes and is interested in and affected by school board decisions [but cannot vote, whereas] an uninterested unemployed young man who pays no state or federal taxes, but who rents an apartment in the district, can [vote].

regarding the electoral competence of adults and literate persons on the one hand, and of minors and illiterates on the other. It is clear, of course, that lines thus drawn cannot infallibly perform their intended legislative function. Just as "[i]lliterate people may be intelligent voters," nonresidents or minors might also in some instances be interested, informed, and intelligent participants in the electoral process. Persons who commute across a state line to work may well have a great stake in the affairs of the State in which they are employed; some college students under 21 may be both better informed and more passionately interested in political affairs than many adults. But such discrepancies are the inevitable concomitant of the line-drawing that is essential to lawmaking. So long as the classification is rationally related to a permissible legislative end, therefore—as are residence, literacy, and age requirements imposed with respect to voting—there is no denial of equal protection.

Thus judged, the statutory classification involved here seems to me clearly to be valid [and] the Court does not really argue the contrary. Instead, it [asserts] that the traditional equal protection standard is [inapt]. But the asserted justification for applying [a stricter] standard cannot withstand analysis. [The] voting qualifications at issue have been promulgated not by Union Free School District, but by the New York State Legislature, and the appellant is of course fully able to participate in the election of representatives in that body. There is simply no claim whatever here that the state government is not "structured so as to represent fairly all the people," including the appellant.

[§ 2012] does not involve racial classifications [and] is not one that impinges upon a constitutionally protected right, and that consequently can be justified only by a "compelling" state interest. For "the Constitution of the United States does not confer the right of suffrage upon any one."

In any event, it seems to me that under *any* equal protection standard, short of a doctrinaire insistence that universal suffrage is somehow mandated by the Constitution, the appellant's claim must be rejected. * * *

NOTES AND QUESTIONS

1. *Classification as "fundamental."* Is the right to vote appropriately classified as fundamental? If so, on what basis?[119]

Although the right to vote in state elections is not mentioned expressly in the Constitution, could it fairly be said to be presupposed? Is that a sufficient ground? Consider John Hart Ely, *Democracy and Distrust: A Theory of Judicial Review* 117 (1980): "Freedom of association is not mentioned in the First Amendment or anywhere else, and neither speech nor association is mentioned

---

[119] See generally Pamela S. Karlan, *Ballots and Bullets: The Exceptional History of the Right to Vote*, 71 U.Cin.L.Rev. 1345 (2003); Joshua A. Douglas, *Is the Right to Vote Really Fundamental?*, 18 Cornell J.L.& Pub. Pol'y 143 (2008).

in the Fourteenth, yet those have been quite properly protected." Is strict judicial scrutiny of restrictions on voting rights similarly a functional imperative? See id.: "A more complete account of the voting cases is that they involve rights (1) that are essential to the democratic process and (2) whose dimensions cannot safely be left to our elected representatives, who have an obvious vested interest in the status quo." As Professor Ely emphasizes, strict judicial scrutiny of restrictions on voting rights accords with the theory of the *Carolene Products* fn. 4, which suggested that the normal presumption of legislative constitutionality might appropriately be relaxed, not only in cases involving burdens on "discrete and insular minorities," but also in cases involving "legislation which restricts those political processes which can [normally] be expected to bring about repeal of undesirable legislation," including voting rights cases.

2. ***Permissible discriminations.*** May a state deny the vote to smart seventeen-year-olds? Compare *Oregon v. Mitchell,* discussed in Ch. 11, Sec. 3 (upholding an age requirement for voting in state elections). To felons? See *Richardson v. Ramirez,* 418 U.S. 24 (1974) (constitutional). To members of the military? See *Carrington v. Rash*, supra (unconstitutional invidious discrimination).

————

In CRAWFORD v. MARION COUNTY ELEC. BD., 553 U.S. 181 (2008), the Court rejected a facial challenge to an Indiana law requiring each voter to present government-issued photo identification as a condition of voting. STEVENS, J., announced the judgment in a plurality opinion joined by Roberts, C.J., and Kennedy, J.: "Under the standard applied in *Harper* [*v. Virginia Bd. of Elections,*] even rational restrictions on the right to vote are invidious [and unconstitutional] if they are unrelated to voter qualifications [but] 'evenhanded restrictions that protect the integrity and reliability of the electoral process itself' are not invidious" and may be upheld based on "relevant and legitimate state interests 'sufficiently weighty to justify the limitation.' [T]he state interests [asserted by Indiana, including deterring voter fraud and safeguarding voter confidence,] are both neutral and sufficiently strong to require us to reject petitioners' facial attack." Stevens, J., left open the possibility, however, that some otherwise qualified voters might be able to establish on an individual basis that they faced such severe difficulties in obtaining government-issued photo identification that the statute would be unconstitutional as applied to them.

SCALIA, J., joined by Thomas and Alito, J., concurred in the judgment: "*Burdick v. Takushi*, 504 U.S. 428 (1992),[120] [calls] for application of a deferential [standard] for nonsevere, nondiscriminatory restrictions,

---

[120] *Burdick* held that a state prohibition against write-in ballots did not impermissibly burden the right to vote.

reserving strict scrutiny for laws that severely restrict the right to vote. [T]he Indiana photo-identification law is a generally applicable, nondiscriminatory voting regulation" that easily survives deferential review, and does not trigger the "balancing" approach apparently contemplated by Stevens, J. The law's effects on individual voters should not matter: "A voter complaining about [the] law's effect on him has no valid equal protection claim because, without proof of discriminatory intent, a generally applicable law with disparate impact is not unconstitutional."

SOUTER, J., joined by Ginsburg, J., dissented: "Indiana's 'Voter ID Law' threatens to impose nontrivial burdens on the voting rights of [an estimated 43,000 citizens, or roughly 1% of all eligible voters,] and a significant number of those individuals are likely to be deterred from voting [by the costs of time and money involved in traveling to the offices of the Bureau of Motor Vehicles where photo identification must be obtained.] Poor, old, and disabled voters who do not drive a car [may] find the trip prohibitive. [A] state may not burden the right to vote merely by invoking abstract interests, [but] must make a particular, factual showing. [T]he State has made no such justification here. [Without] a shred of evidence that in-person voter impersonation is a problem in the State, [Indiana] has adopted one of the most restrictive photo identification requirements in the country."

NOTES AND QUESTIONS

1. *Necessity of voter identification laws.* As suggested in Souter, J.'s dissent, the question of the scope of the problem to which voter identification laws respond is much disputed. See, e.g., Justin Levitt, *Election Deform: The Pursuit of Unwarranted Electoral Regulation*, 11 Election L.J. 97 (2012): "[P]reliminary evidence indicates that restrictive identification rules may have *already* prevented more individuals from voting than any incidence of fraud to justify the impact. The evidence submitted in *Crawford* cited [only] nine potentially fraudulent votes—nationwide and over seven years—that strict identification rules might have prevented." What burden of empirical justification should otherwise rational voter identification laws need to bear?

2. *Impact of voter identification laws.* Commentators have argued that voter ID requirements disproportionately disenfranchise racial minorities as well as older and lower-income segments of the population. See, e.g., Matt A. Barreto et al., *The Disproportionate Impact of Voter-ID Requirements on the Electorate: New Evidence from Indiana*, 42 Pol.Sci. & Politics 111 (2009); Christopher Watts, Note, *Road to the Poll: How the Wisconsin Voter ID Law of 2011 is Disenfranchising its Poor, Minority, and Elderly Citizens*, 3 Colum.J. Race & L. 119 (2013). Does *Washington v. Davis* bar consideration of such disparate impacts absent evidence of discriminatory purpose?

B. "Dilution" of the Right: Apportionment

Distinct from the question of who gets to cast a vote in elections are questions involving how the lines dividing electoral districts are drawn and, relatedly, whether it is constitutionally permissible for voters in some districts to have proportionally more voting power than voters in others. (If there are more voters in one district then in another, then individual voters in the larger districts will have proportionally less voting power than voters in the smaller districts.) In *Colegrove v. Green*, 328 U.S. 549 (1946), which presented a challenge to malapportioned congressional districts, the principal opinion, by Frankfurter, J., characterized apportionment issues as being "of a peculiarly political nature" and beyond the capacity of courts to resolve under the political question doctrine. A bitterly divided Court subsequently distinguished *Colegrove* (on the ground that it arose under the Guarantee Clause of Article IV rather than the Fourteenth Amendment) and held equal protection challenges to legislative apportionments justiciable in a 1962 decision in *Baker v. Carr*, Ch. 1, Sec. 2 supra. But *Baker* left unresolved the substantive question of what rights, if any, voters have under the Equal Protection Clause to be free from what is sometimes called vote dilution.

REYNOLDS V. SIMS

377 U.S. 533, 84 S.Ct. 1362, 12 L.Ed.2d 506 (1964).

CHIEF JUSTICE WARREN delivered the opinion of the Court.

[Although the Alabama constitution required the legislature to reapportion decennially on the basis of population, no such reapportionment had taken place since 1901. The federal district court held the existing malapportionment violative of equal protection. Under] 1960 census figures, only 25.1% of the State's total population resided in districts represented by a majority of the members of the Senate, and only 25.7% lived in counties which could elect a majority of the members of the House of Representatives. Population-variance ratios of up to about 41-to-1 existed in the Senate, and up to about 16-to-1 in the House. * * *

We indicated in *Baker* that the Equal Protection Clause provides discoverable and manageable standards for [determining] the constitutionality of a state legislative apportionment scheme. [In this case] we are faced with the problem [of] determining the basic standards and stating the applicable guidelines for implementing our decision in *Baker*.

Gray v. Sanders, 372 U.S. 368 (1963),[121] and *Wesberry v. Sanders*, 376 U.S. 1 (1964),[122] are of course [relevant to but] not dispositive [of] these cases involving state legislative [apportionment]. But neither are they wholly inapposite. [*Gray*] established the basic principle of equality among voters within a State, [and] *Wesberry* clearly established that the fundamental principle of representative government in this country is one of equal representation for equal numbers of people, without regard to race, sex, economic status, or place of residence within a State. Our problem, then, is to ascertain [whether] there are any constitutionally cognizable principles which would justify departures from the basic standard of equality among voters in the apportionment of seats in state legislatures.

A predominant consideration in determining whether a State's legislative apportionment scheme constitutes an invidious discrimination [is] that the rights allegedly impaired are individual and personal in nature. [Since] the right of suffrage is a fundamental matter in a free and democratic society [and] is preservative of other basic civil and political rights, any alleged infringement [must] be carefully and meticulously scrutinized. * * *

Legislators represent people, not trees or acres. Legislators are elected by voters, not farms or cities or economic interests. [It] is inconceivable that a state law to the effect that, in counting votes for legislators, the votes of citizens in one part of the State would be multiplied by two, five, or 10, while the votes of persons in another area would be counted only at face value, could be [constitutional]. Of course, the effect of state legislative districting schemes which give the same number of representatives to unequal numbers of constituents is identical. * * *

Logically, in a society ostensibly grounded on representative government, it would seem reasonable that a majority of the people of a State could elect a majority of that State's legislators. [T]o sanction minority control of state legislative bodies would appear to deny majority rights in a way that far surpasses any possible denial of minority rights that might otherwise be thought to result. [[Any] suggested criteria for the differentiation of citizens are insufficient to justify any discrimination, as to the weight of their votes, unless relevant to the permissible purposes of legislative apportionment. Since the achieving of fair and effective

---

[121] *Gray* invalidated the "county unit system" employed in Georgia primaries for statewide offices, under which the candidate receiving the highest number of votes in each county obtained "two votes for each representative to which the county is entitled in the lower House of the General Assembly," and the winner was determined on the basis of the county unit vote. Because counties were not represented in the state legislature in accordance with their population, counties comprising only a third of the state's population had "a clear majority of county units." *Gray* was not dispositive in *Reynolds* since it involved "the weighing of votes in statewide elections."

[122] *Wesberry* struck down Georgia's congressional districting statute, under which some districts had more than twice the population of others: "[T]he command of Art. I, § 2, that representatives be chosen 'by the people of the several states' means that as nearly as is practicable one man's vote in a congressional election is to be worth as much as another's."

representation for all citizens is concededly the basic aim of legislative apportionment, we conclude that the Equal Protection Clause guarantees the opportunity for equal participation by all voters in the election of state legislators. [Diluting] the weight of votes because of place of residence impairs basic constitutional rights under the Fourteenth Amendment just as much as invidious discriminations based upon factors such as race, or economic status. Our constitutional system amply provides for the protection of minorities by means other than giving them majority control of state legislatures. * * *

We are told that the matter of apportioning representation in a state legislature is a complex and many-faceted one. We are advised that States can rationally consider factors other than [population]. We are admonished not to restrict the power of the States to impose differing views as to political philosophy on their citizens. We are cautioned about the dangers of entering into political thickets and mathematical quagmires. Our answer is this: a denial of constitutionally protected rights demands judicial protection; our oath and our office require no less of us. [To] the extent that a citizen's right to vote is debased, he is that much less a citizen. * * *

We hold that, as a basic constitutional standard, the Equal Protection Clause requires that the seats in both houses of a bicameral state legislature must be apportioned on a population basis. [We] find the federal analogy inapposite and irrelevant to state legislative districting schemes. [T]he Founding Fathers clearly had no intention of establishing a pattern or model for the apportionment of seats in state legislatures when the system of representation in the Federal Congress was adopted. Demonstrative of this is the fact that the Northwest Ordinance, adopted in the same year, 1787, as the Federal Constitution, provided for the apportionment of seats in territorial legislatures solely on the basis of population.

The system of representation in the two Houses of the Federal Congress [is] based on the consideration that in establishing our type of federalism a group of formerly independent States bound themselves together under one national government. [A] compromise between the larger and smaller States on this matter averted a deadlock in the Constitutional Convention * * * .

Political subdivisions of States [never] have been considered as sovereign entities. Rather, they have been traditionally regarded as subordinate governmental instrumentalities created by the State. * * *

We do not believe that the concept of bicameralism is rendered anachronistic and meaningless when the predominant basis of representation in the two state legislative bodies is required to be the same—population. A prime reason for bicameralism, modernly considered, is to insure mature and deliberate consideration of, and to prevent precipitate action on, proposed legislative measures. [T]he Equal Protection Clause requires that a State make an honest and good faith effort to construct districts, in both houses of its legislature, as nearly of equal population as is practicable. We realize that it is a practical impossibility to arrange legislative districts so that each one has an identical number of residents, or citizens, or voters.

[So] long as the divergences from a strict population standard are based on legitimate considerations incident to the effectuation of a rational state policy, some deviations from the equal-population principle are constitutionally permissible, [b]ut neither history alone, nor economic or other sorts of group interests, are permissible factors in attempting to justify disparities from population-based representation. Citizens, not history or economic interests, cast votes.

* * * Decennial reapportionment appears to be a rational approach to readjustment of legislative representation in order to take into account population shifts and growth [and] if reapportionment were accomplished with less frequency, it would assuredly be constitutionally suspect. * * *[123]

[Clark and Stewart, JJ., concurred in the result in *Reynolds,* but STEWART, J., joined by Clark, J., dissented in two of the companion cases in an opinion sharply at odds with the *Reynolds* rationale:]

First, says the Court, it is "established that the fundamental principle of representative government in this country is one of equal representation for equal numbers of [people]." [But] this "was not the colonial system, it was not the system chosen for the national government by the Constitution, it was not the system exclusively or even predominantly practiced by the States at the time of adoption of the Fourteenth Amendment, it is not predominantly practiced by the States today." Secondly, says the Court, unless legislative districts are equal in population, voters in the more populous districts will suffer a "debasement" amounting to a constitutional injury. [I] find it impossible to understand how or why a voter in California, for instance, either feels or is less a citizen than a voter in Nevada, simply because, despite their population disparities, each of those States is represented by two United States Senators.

[My] own understanding of the various theories of representative government is that no one theory has ever commanded unanimous [assent]. But even if it were thought that the rule announced today by the Court is, as a matter of political theory, the most desirable, [I] could not join in the

---

[123] In addition to striking down Alabama's apportionment scheme in *Reynolds,* the Court invalidated apportionments in Colorado, *Lucas v. Forty-Fourth Gen. Assembly,* 377 U.S. 713; Delaware, *Roman v. Sincock,* 377 U.S. 695; Maryland, *Maryland Comm. for Fair Rep. v. Tawes,* 377 U.S. 656; New York, *WMCA, Inc. v. Lomenzo,* 377 U.S. 633; and Virginia, *Davis v. Mann,* 377 U.S. 678.

fabrication of a constitutional mandate which imports and forever freezes one theory of political thought into our Constitution, and forever denies to every State any opportunity for enlightened and progressive innovation * * *.

[The] fact of geographic districting, the constitutional validity of which the Court does not question, carries with it an acceptance of the idea of legislative representation of regional needs and interests. Yet if geographical residence is irrelevant, as the Court suggests, and the goal is solely that of equally "weighted" votes, I do not understand why the Court's constitutional rule does not require the abolition of districts and the holding of all elections at large. * * *

JUSTICE HARLAN, dissenting [in all the cases decided that day.]

The Court's constitutional discussion [is] remarkable [for] its failure to address itself at all to the Fourteenth Amendment as a whole or to the legislative history of the Amendment pertinent to the matter at hand. [I] am unable to understand the Court's utter disregard of [§ 2 of the Fourteenth Amendment], which expressly recognizes the States' power to deny "or in any way" abridge the right of their inhabitants to vote for "the members of the [State] Legislature," and its express provision of a remedy for such denial or abridgement.[124] The comprehensive scope of the second section and its particular reference to the state legislatures precludes the suggestion that the first section was intended to have the result reached by the [Court].

The history of the adoption of the Fourteenth Amendment provides conclusive evidence that neither those who proposed nor those who ratified the Amendment believed that the Equal Protection Clause limited the power of the States to apportion their legislatures as they saw fit. Moreover, the history demonstrates that the intention to leave this power undisturbed was deliberate and was widely believed to be essential to the adoption of the Amendment. [N]ote should [also] be taken of the Fifteenth and Nineteenth Amendments. [If] constitutional amendment was the only means by which all men and, later, women, could be guaranteed the right to vote at all, even for *federal* officers, how can it be that the far less obvious right to a particular kind of apportionment of *state* legislatures—a right to which is opposed a far more plausible conflicting interest of the State than the interest which opposes the general right to vote—can be conferred by judicial construction of the Fourteenth Amendment?

---

[124] Section 2 of the Fourteenth Amendment provides, in relevant part: "[W]hen the right to vote at any election for . . . the members of the Legislature [of a State], is denied to any of the male inhabitants of such State, being twenty-one years of age, and citizens of the United States, or in any way abridged, except for participation in rebellion, or other crime, the basis of representation therein shall be reduced in the proportion which the number of such male citizens shall bear to the whole number of male citizens twenty-one years of age in such State."

[The] consequence of today's decision is that in all but the handful of States which may already satisfy the new requirements the [courts] are given blanket authority and the constitutional duty to supervise apportionment of the State Legislatures. It is difficult to imagine a more intolerable and inappropriate interference by the judiciary with the independent legislatures of the States. * * *

Although the Court—necessarily, as I believe—provides only generalities in elaboration of its main thesis, its opinion nevertheless fully demonstrates how far removed these problems are from fields of judicial competence. Recognizing that "indiscriminate districting" is an invitation to "partisan gerrymandering," the Court nevertheless excludes virtually every basis for the formation of electoral districts other than "indiscriminate districting." In one or another of today's opinions, the Court declares it unconstitutional for a State to give effective consideration to any of the following in establishing legislative districts: (1) history; (2) "economic or other sorts of group interests"; (3) area; (4) geographical considerations; (5) a desire "to insure effective representation for sparsely settled areas"; (6) "availability of access of citizens to their representatives"; (7) theories of bicameralism (except those approved by the Court); (8) occupation; (9) "an attempt to balance urban and rural power"; (10) the preference of a majority of voters in the State. So far as presently appears, the *only* factor which a State may consider, apart from numbers, is political subdivisions. But even "a clearly rational state policy" recognizing this factor is unconstitutional if "population is submerged as the controlling consideration * * * ."

I know of no principle of logic or practical or theoretical politics, still less any constitutional principle, which establishes all or any of these exclusions. [The] Constitution is not a panacea for every blot upon the public welfare, nor [does] this Court [serve] its high purpose when it exceeds its authority, even to satisfy justified impatience with the slow workings of the political [process.]

NOTES AND QUESTIONS

1. ***Results.*** By mid-1968, "congressional district lines were redrawn in thirty-seven states"; "only nine states had any district with a population deviation in excess of ten per cent from the state average, while twenty-four states had no deviation as large as five per cent from the state norm"; every state legislature "had made some adjustment, and it seemed probable that more than thirty of the state legislatures satisfied any reasonable interpretation of the equal-population principle." Robert McKay, *Reapportionment: Success Story of the Warren Court,* 67 Mich.L.Rev. 223 (1968).

According to John Hart Ely, *Democracy and Distrust* 120–21 (1980), the leading contemporary concerns about *Reynolds* quickly proved misplaced:

"Justice Frankfurter used to say that reapportionment was a 'political thicket' that courts should avoid. [Sometimes this charge] meant that there can be no administrable standard for determining the legality of apportionments. [But] that is nothing short of silly. [The] 'one person, one vote' standard [is] certainly administrable. In fact administrability is its long suit, and the more troublesome question is what else it has to recommend it. On other occasions the 'thicket' criticism has signaled a 'realist's' point, that a reapportionment order is one unusually calculated to get the Court in trouble, dangerously to decrease its prestige. [But] the critics were wrong on this one: the equal weighting of everyone's vote turned out to be a notion with which most people could sympathize."

2. ***Supermajority requirements.*** GORDON v. LANCE, 403 U.S. 1 (1971), per BURGER, C.J., upheld a West Virginia rule that forbade political subdivisions from incurring bonded indebtedness or increasing tax rates beyond designated limits without 60% approval in a referendum: "The defect [in previous cases] lay in the denial or dilution of voting power because of group characteristics—geographic location and property ownership—that bore no valid relation to the interest of those groups in the subject matter of the [election]. In contrast we can discern no independently identifiable group or category that favors bonded indebtedness over other forms of financing. Consequently no sector of the population may be said to be 'fenced out' from the franchise because of the way they will vote." The Court added in a footnote that "[w]e intimate no view on the constitutionality of a provision requiring unanimity or giving a veto power to a very small group. Nor do we decide whether a State [may] require extraordinary majorities for the election of public officers."

3. ***Permissible population deviation.*** The Court has permitted considerably less deviation from the one person, one vote requirement for congressional districts than for state and local elections. Compare *Karcher v. Daggett,* 462 U.S. 725 (1983) (invalidating a percentage deviation in New Jersey's congressional districts of 0.7%)[125] with *Mahan v. Howell,* 410 U.S. 315 (1973) (upholding Virginia's state legislative apportionment, which had a maximum percentage deviation from the ideal of "16.4%—[one] district being overrepresented by 6.8% and [another] being underrepresented by 9.6%").

4. ***Calculating the population base.*** BURNS v. RICHARDSON, 384 U.S. 73 (1966), per BRENNAN, J., upheld a Hawaii plan that used *registered voters* as the population base and, "probably because of uneven distribution of military residents—largely unregistered," produced results significantly different than if total population figures had been used: States are not "required to include aliens, transients, short-term or temporary residents, or

---

[125] Emphasizing a reviewing court's obligation to afford deference to a state legislature's "reasonable exercise of its political judgment," *Tennant v. Jefferson County Comm'n,* 133 S.Ct. 3 (2012) (per curiam) unanimously upheld a variance of 0.79% between West Virginia's largest and smallest districts in light of the state's legitimate interests in "avoiding contests between incumbents, [not] splitting political subdivisions," and minimizing populations shifts from one district to another.

persons denied the vote for conviction of crime in the apportionment [base]. [But use] of a registered voter or actual voter basis [is] susceptible to improper influences by which those in political power might be able to perpetuate underrepresentation of groups constitutionally entitled to participate in the electoral [process]. [W]e hold that the present apportionment satisfies the Equal Protection Clause only because on this record it was found to have produced a distribution of legislators not substantially different from that which would have resulted from the use of [state citizen population, which is] a permissible population base."

C. "Dilution" of the Right: Partisan Gerrymanders

According to Pamela S. Karlan, *The Rights to Vote: Some Pessimism about Formalism*, 71 Tex.L.Rev. 1705 (1993), "Chief Justice Warren called *Reynolds v. Sims* his most important opinion 'because it insured that henceforth elections would reflect the collective public interest—embodied in the "one-man, one-vote" standard—rather than the machinations of special interests.' " "Measured against that ambition," Karlan writes, "*Reynolds* has been a spectacular failure. Advances in the technology of districting [which allow partisan legislatures to engage in partisan gerrymanders even while maintaining equal-sized districts] have stripped the substantive principles of one-person, one-vote of any real constraining force."

By all accounts, "gerrymandering"—a word constructed from the name of an early practitioner of the art of drawing district lines for partisan advantage, Elbridge Gerry, and the word "salamander," which a district drawn by Gerry was said to resemble—is now widespread. Where one party is able to do so, it gerrymanders to its own advantage. Where a single party lacks the dominant position to gerrymander unilaterally, so-called "bipartisan gerrymanders" often occur. See Samuel Issacharoff & Pamela S. Karlan, *Where to Draw the Line?: Judicial Review of Political Gerrymanders*, 153 U.Pa.L.Rev. 541 (2004): "Whereas a partisan gerrymander is a declaration of war, a bipartisan gerrymander is a nonaggression pact between the parties in which they agree to divide up the state in favor of incumbent sinecure. The result on the day of the general election can be that elections are simply not competitive at all. [In] the first post-reapportionment elections in 2002, only four House incumbents lost to their challengers, and only 43 incumbents received less than 60% of the vote. [In California,] not a single challenger in the general election received over 40% of the vote. In other words, every single incumbent won by landslide margins."

The question whether the Equal Protection Clause creates rights to be free from partisan gerrymanders has sharply divided the Supreme Court.

DAVIS V. BANDEMER
478 U.S. 109, 106 S.Ct. 2797, 92 L.Ed.2d 85 (1986).

JUSTICE WHITE announced the judgment of the Court and delivered [an] opinion in which JUSTICE BRENNAN, JUSTICE MARSHALL, and JUSTICE BLACKMUN joined * * * .

[Democrats challenged Indiana's 1981 state apportionment—enacted by Republican majorities in both houses of the legislature and signed by a Republican governor—on the ground that it "constituted a political gerrymander intended to disadvantage Democrats on a statewide basis."] We [agree] with the District Court that in order to succeed the Bandemer plaintiffs were required to prove both intentional discrimination against an identifiable political group and an actual discriminatory effect on that group. [As] long as redistricting is done by a legislature, it should not be very difficult to prove that the likely political consequences of the reapportionment were intended.[11]

[With respect to effects, our prior holdings] foreclose any claim that the Constitution requires proportional representation or that legislatures in reapportioning must draw district lines to come as near as possible to allocating seats to the contending parties in proportion to what their anticipated statewide vote will be.

[These] holdings rest on a conviction that the mere fact that a particular apportionment scheme makes it more difficult for a particular group in a particular district to elect the representatives of its choice does not render that scheme constitutionally infirm. This conviction, in turn, stems from a perception that the power to influence the political process is not limited to winning elections. An individual or a group of individuals who votes for a losing candidate is usually deemed to be adequately represented by the winning candidate and to have as much opportunity to influence that candidate as other voters in the district. * * *

As with individual districts, where unconstitutional vote dilution is alleged in the form of statewide political gerrymandering, the mere lack of proportional representation will not be sufficient to prove unconstitutional discrimination. [Rather], unconstitutional discrimination occurs only when the electoral system is arranged in a manner that will consistently degrade a voter's or a group of voters' influence on the political process as a [whole. S]uch a finding of unconstitutionality must be supported by evidence of continued frustration of the will of a majority of the voters or effective denial to a minority of voters of a fair chance to influence the political process.

---

[11] **[Ct's Note]** That discriminatory intent may not be difficult to prove in this context does not, of course, mean that it need not be proved at all to succeed on such a claim.

Based on these views, we would reject the District Court's apparent holding that *any* interference with an opportunity to elect a representative of one's choice would be sufficient to allege or make out an equal protection violation, unless justified by some acceptable state interest that the State would be required to demonstrate. [S]uch a low threshold for legal action would invite attack on all or almost all reapportionment statutes. [Inviting] attack on minor departures from some supposed norm would too much embroil the judiciary in second-guessing what has consistently been referred to as a political task for the legislature * * * .

[The] District Court's findings do not satisfy this threshold condition to stating and proving a cause of action. In reaching its conclusion, the District Court relied primarily on the results of the 1982 elections: Democratic candidates for the State House of Representatives had received 51.9% of the votes cast statewide and Republican candidates 48.1%; yet, out of the 100 seats to be filled, Republican candidates won 57 and Democrats 43. In the Senate, 53.1% of the votes were cast for Democratic candidates and 46.9% for Republicans; of the 25 Senate seats to be filled, Republicans won 12 and Democrats 13. The court also relied upon the use of multi-member districts in Marion and Allen counties, where Democrats or those inclined to vote Democratic in 1982 amounted to 46.6% of the population of those counties but Republicans won 86 percent—18 of 21—seats allocated to the districts in those counties. These disparities were enough to require a neutral justification by the State, which in the eyes of the District Court was not forthcoming.

Relying on a single election to prove unconstitutional discrimination is unsatisfactory. [The] appellants argue here, without a persuasive response from appellees, that had the Democratic candidates received an additional few percentage points of the votes cast statewide, they would have obtained a majority of the seats in both houses. Nor was there any finding that the 1981 reapportionment would consign the Democrats to a minority status in the Assembly throughout the 1980's or that the Democrats would have no hope of doing any better in the reapportionment that would occur after the 1990 census.

[We] recognize that our [test] may be difficult of application. Determining when an electoral system has been "arranged in a manner that will consistently degrade a voter's or a group of voters' influence on the political process as a whole" is of necessity a difficult inquiry. Nevertheless, we believe that it recognizes the delicacy of intruding on this most political of legislative functions and is at the same time consistent with our prior cases regarding individual multi-member districts, which have formulated a parallel standard. * * *

JUSTICE POWELL, with whom JUSTICE STEVENS joins, concurring [on the issue of justiciability], and dissenting.

[T]he plurality expresses the view, with which I agree, that a partisan political gerrymander violates the Equal Protection Clause only on proof of "both intentional discrimination against an identifiable political group and an actual discriminatory effect on that group." The plurality acknowledges that the record in this case supports a finding that the challenged redistricting plan was adopted for the purpose of discriminating against Democratic voters. The plurality argues, however, that appellees failed to establish that their voting strength was diluted statewide despite uncontradicted proof that certain key districts were grotesquely gerrymandered to enhance the election prospects of Republican candidates. * * *

[The] Equal Protection Clause guarantees citizens that their State will govern them impartially [and accordingly requires that] district lines should be determined in accordance with neutral and legitimate criteria.

[The] most basic flaw in the plurality's opinion is its failure to enunciate any standard that affords guidance to legislatures and courts. [This] places the plurality in the curious position of inviting further litigation even as it appears to signal the "constitutional green light" to would-be gerrymanderers. * * *

[To determine whether the state has met its obligation to govern impartially, courts must attend to several factors, the most important of which] are the shapes of voting districts and adherence to established political subdivision boundaries. Other relevant considerations include the nature of the legislative procedures [and] legislative history reflecting contemporaneous legislative goals. To make out a case of unconstitutional partisan gerrymandering, the plaintiff should be required to offer proof concerning these factors, as well as evidence concerning population disparities and statistics tending to show vote dilution. No one factor should be dispositive.

[Here], the District Court found that the procedures used in redistricting Indiana were carefully designed to exclude Democrats from participating in the legislative process [and] consisted of nothing more than the majority party's private application of computer technology to mapmaking. [T]he only data used in the computer program were precinct population, race of precinct citizens, precinct political complexion, and statewide party voting trends. [Next], the District Court found [how] the mapmakers carved up counties, cities, and even townships in their effort to draw lines beneficial to the majority party.

[Confronted with these findings,] appellants failed to justify the discriminatory impact of the plan by showing that the plan had a rational basis in permissible neutral criteria. * * *

JUSTICE O'CONNOR, with whom THE CHIEF JUSTICE and JUSTICE REHNQUIST join, concurring in the judgment.

[T]he legislative business of apportionment is fundamentally a political affair, and challenges to the manner in which an apportionment has been carried out—by the very parties that are responsible for this process—present a political question in the truest sense of the term. To turn these matters over to the federal judiciary is to inject the courts into the most heated partisan issues. It is predictable that the courts will respond by moving away from the nebulous standard a plurality of the Court fashions today and toward some form of rough proportional representation for all political groups.

[The] Equal Protection Clause does not supply judicially manageable standards for resolving purely political gerrymandering claims, and no group right to an equal share of political power was ever intended by the Framers. [Unlike racial minorities], members of the Democratic and Republican parties cannot claim that they are a discrete and insular group vulnerable to exclusion from the political process by some dominant group: these political parties *are* the dominant groups, and the Court has offered no reason to believe that they are incapable of fending for themselves through the political process. * * *

Furthermore, the Court fails to explain why a bipartisan gerrymander—which is what was approved in *Gaffney*—affects individuals any differently than a partisan gerrymander. [As] the plurality acknowledges, the scheme upheld in *Gaffney* tended to "deny safe district minorities any realistic chance to elect their own representatives." If this bipartisan arrangement between two groups of self-interested legislators is constitutionally permissible, as I believe and as the Court held in *Gaffney,* then—in terms of the rights of individuals—it should be equally permissible for a legislative majority to employ the same means to pursue its own interests over the opposition of the other party.

VIETH V. JUBELIRER

541 U.S. 267, 124 S.Ct. 1769, 158 L.Ed.2d 546 (2004).

JUSTICE SCALIA announced the judgment of the Court and delivered an opinion, in which THE CHIEF JUSTICE, JUSTICE O'CONNOR, and JUSTICE THOMAS join.

[After the 2000 census showed that Pennsylvania was entitled to only 19 Representatives in the U.S. House of Representatives, a decrease of two from its previous delegation, the Republican-controlled Pennsylvania legislature adopted and the Republican governor signed into law a redistricting plan designed to advantage Republicans. The plaintiff Democratic voters brought suit alleging that the "meandering and irregular" districts created by the plan "ignored all traditional redistricting criteria, including the preservation of local government boundaries, solely for the sake of partisan advantage," and thereby violated the Equal Protection Clause.]

Political gerrymanders are not new to the American scene. [It] is significant that the Framers provided a remedy for such practices in the Constitution. Article 1, § 4, while leaving in state legislatures the initial power to draw districts for federal elections, permitted Congress to "make or alter" those districts if it wished.

[Eighteen] years ago, [over] the dissent of three Justices, the Court held in *Bandemer* that, since it was "not persuaded that there are no judicially discernible and manageable standards by which political gerrymander cases are to be decided," such cases *were* justiciable. [But there was no majority on what the appropriate standards were. Nor] can it be said that the lower courts have, over 18 years, succeeded in shaping the standard that this Court was initially unable to enunciate. As one commentary has put it, "throughout its subsequent history, *Bandemer* has served almost exclusively as an invitation to litigation without much prospect of redress." S. Issacharoff, P. Karlan, & R. Pildes, *The Law of Democracy* 886 (rev. 2d ed. 2002). The [only lower court] case in which relief was provided (and merely preliminary relief, at that) did *not* involve the drawing of district lines [but instead involved a North Carolina system of electing all superior court judges statewide—a system that had resulted in the election of only a single Republican since 1900]; in *all* of the cases we are aware of involving that most common form of political gerrymandering, relief was denied. [Eighteen] years of judicial effort with virtually nothing to show for it [demonstrate that] no judicially discernible and manageable standards for adjudicating political gerrymandering claims have emerged. Lacking them, we must conclude that political gerrymandering claims are nonjusticiable and that *Bandemer* was wrongly decided.

We begin our review of possible standards with that proposed by Justice White's plurality opinion in *Bandemer* because, as the narrowest ground for our decision in that case, it has been the standard employed by the lower courts. The plurality concluded that a political gerrymandering claim could succeed only where plaintiffs showed "both intentional discrimination against an identifiable political group and an actual discriminatory effect on that group" [so severe that it was] "denied its chance to effectively influence the political process" as a whole, which could be achieved even without electing a candidate. [In] the lower courts, the legacy of the plurality's test is one long record of puzzlement and consternation. [We] decline to affirm it as a constitutional requirement.

Appellants take a run at enunciating their own workable standard. [Their proposal] retains the two-pronged framework of the *Bandemer* plurality—intent plus effect—but modifies the type of showing sufficient to satisfy each. [But it too is unworkable.]

For many of the same reasons, we also reject the standard suggested by Justice Powell in *Bandemer*. He agreed with the plurality that a plaintiff should show intent and effect, but believed that the ultimate inquiry ought to focus on whether district boundaries had been drawn solely for partisan ends to the exclusion of "all other neutral factors relevant to the fairness of redistricting." [This] is essentially a totality-of-the-circumstances analysis, where all conceivable factors, none of which is dispositive, are weighed with an eye to ascertaining whether the particular gerrymander has gone too far—or, in Justice Powell's terminology, whether it is not "fair." "Fairness" does not seem to us a judicially manageable standard. Fairness is compatible with noncontiguous districts, it is compatible with districts that straddle political subdivisions, and it is compatible with a party's not winning the number of seats that mirrors the proportion of its vote.

IV. We turn next to consideration of the standards proposed by today's dissenters. [The] mere fact that these four dissenters come up with three different standards—all of them different from the two proposed in *Bandemer* and the one proposed here by appellants—goes a long way to establishing that there is no constitutionally discernible standard. [Careful assessment of the proposed standards confirms that they are either not judicially manageable or not discernible in the Constitution.]

V. Justice Kennedy [who concurs in the Court's judgment dismissing the case before it but does not join this opinion holding all allegations of political gerrymanders to present nonjusticiable political questions] recognizes that we have "demonstrated the shortcomings of the other standards that have been considered to date." [Yet] he concludes that courts should continue to adjudicate such claims because a standard *may* one day be discovered.

[Reduced] to its essence, Justice Kennedy's opinion boils down to this: "As presently advised, I know of no discernible and manageable standard that can render this claim justiciable. I am unhappy about that, and hope that I will be able to change my opinion in the future." What are the lower courts to make of this pronouncement? We suggest that they must treat it as a reluctant fifth vote against justiciability at district and statewide levels—a vote that may change in some future case but that holds, for the time being, that this matter is nonjusticiable.

JUSTICE KENNEDY, concurring in the judgment.

[The] plurality demonstrates the shortcomings of the [standards] that have been considered to date. [But the fact that] no [adequate] standard has emerged in this case should not be taken to prove that none will emerge in the future. Where important rights are involved, the impossibility of full analytical satisfaction is reason to err on the side of caution.

[Because], in the case before us, we have no standard by which to measure the burden appellants claim has been imposed on their representational rights, appellants cannot establish that the alleged political classifications burden those same rights.

JUSTICE STEVENS, dissenting.

The central question presented by this case is whether political gerrymandering claims are justiciable. Although our reasons for coming to this conclusion differ, five Members of the Court are convinced that the plurality's answer to that question is erroneous.

[In] evaluating a challenge to a specific district, I would apply the standard set forth in [cases involving the deliberate creation of majority-minority districts] and ask whether the legislature allowed partisan considerations to dominate and control the lines drawn, forsaking all neutral principles. Under my analysis, if no neutral criterion can be identified to justify the lines drawn, and if the only possible explanation for a district's bizarre shape is a naked desire to increase partisan strength, then no rational basis exists to save the district from an equal protection challenge. * * *

JUSTICE SOUTER, with whom JUSTICE GINSBURG joins, dissenting.

For a claim based on a specific single-member district, I would require the plaintiff to make out a prima facie case with five elements. First, the resident plaintiff would identify a cohesive political group to which he belonged, which would normally be a major party, as in this case and in *Davis*. [Second], a plaintiff would need to show that the district of his residence paid little or no heed to those traditional districting principles whose disregard can be shown straightforwardly: contiguity, compactness, respect for political subdivisions, and conformity with geographic features like rivers and mountains. [Third], the plaintiff would need to establish specific correlations between the district's deviations from traditional districting principles and the distribution of the population of his group. [Fourth], a plaintiff would need to present the court with a hypothetical district including his residence, one in which the proportion of the plaintiff's group was lower (in a packing claim) or higher (in a cracking one) and which at the same time deviated less from traditional districting principles than the actual district. [Fifth], and finally, the plaintiff would have to show that the defendants acted intentionally to manipulate the shape of the district in order to pack or crack his group. [A] plaintiff who got this far would [then] shift the burden to the defendants to justify their decision by reference to objectives other than naked partisan advantage.

[As] for a statewide claim, I would not attempt an ambitious definition without the benefit of experience with individual district claims, and for now I would limit consideration of a statewide claim to one built upon a number of district-specific ones.

JUSTICE BREYER, dissenting.

[T]he legislature's use of political boundary drawing considerations ordinarily does *not* violate the Constitution's Equal Protection Clause. [But there is] at least one circumstance where use of purely political boundary-drawing factors can amount to a serious, and remediable, abuse, namely the *unjustified* use of political factors to entrench a minority in power. By entrenchment I mean a situation in which a party that enjoys only minority support among the populace has nonetheless contrived to take, and hold, legislative power. * * *

NOTES AND QUESTIONS

1. *Current state of the law.* (a) When confronted with a partisan gerrymandering claim, what should a lower court now do? Is Scalia, J., correct that a lower court should treat Kennedy, J., as having cast a reluctant fifth vote for the proposition that partisan gerrymandering claims are nonjusticiable? Or if the problem is that no judicially manageable standard has yet "emerged," as Kennedy, J., put it, is a lower court entitled to try to devise and apply a standard that it believes to be judicially manageable? In considering these questions, note that at least five Justices in *Vieth* had found the tests developed in *Bandemer* and by the *Vieth* dissenters specifically *not* to be judicially manageable. With all of those tests ruled out, does a challenger have any realistic hope of success?

(b) The Court again rejected a partisan gerrymandering claim for a mix of political question and substantive reasons in LEAGUE OF UNITED LATIN AMERICAN CITIZENS v. PERRY, 548 U.S. 399 (2006). The case arose after a mid-decennial partisan gerrymander of Texas congressional districts, implemented in 2003 by a newly established Republican majority in both houses of the Texas legislature.

The Court, by a 5–4 majority, upheld the plaintiffs' statutory claim of minority vote dilution with respect to one district, but by a different majority rejected the constitutional challenge to the entire redistricting plan (as well as a statutory challenge to another district). In an opinion in which he spoke sometimes for a majority, sometimes for shifting pluralities, and in part for himself alone, KENNEDY, J., wrote for a majority of five that the Court would not "revisit the justiciability holding" of *Vieth*, in which a plurality "would have held [partisan gerrymandering] standards to be nonjusticiable, but a majority declined to do so," and would instead "proceed to examine whether appellants' claims offer the Court a manageable, reliable measure" for adjudicating the constitutional challenge. (No one doubted the existence of judicially manageable standards with respect to the statutory claims of racial, rather than partisan, vote dilution.) As in *Vieth*, however, Kennedy, J., then found (for himself alone) that the plaintiffs had failed to identify any judicially manageable standard under which their partisan gerrymandering claim could prevail under the Equal Protection Clause, nor could he identify such a standard himself. He rejected the plaintiffs' proposed standard—which would outlaw "mid-decennial redistricting [that was] motivated solely by partisan objectives"—because he thought the challengers should also have to "show a burden" on their rights to fair representation, and the challengers had furnished no judicially manageable standard for measuring harms to representational rights. "Under appellants' theory, a highly effective partisan gerrymander that coincided with decennial redistricting would receive less scrutiny than a bumbling, yet solely partisan, mid-decade redistricting."[126]

2. ***Proposed antitrust approach.*** Consider Samuel Issacharoff, *Gerrymandering and Political Cartels*, 116 Harv.L.Rev. 593 (2002): "[T]he harm in gerrymandering is not really the discrimination that the Court [has] identified. [Rather], the harm is the insult to the competitiveness of the process resulting from the ability of insiders to lessen competitive pressures." In order to avoid this harm, Issacharoff maintains, the Court should forbid all purposeful districting for political advantage, "much as the antitrust laws reach not only the actual cartelization of markets but also conspiracies that set out to frustrate competition." According to Issacharoff, "the Court should forbid ex ante the participation of self-interested political insiders in the redistricting process": "Various approaches to nonpartisan districting, such as blue-ribbon commissions, panels of retired judges, and Iowa's computer-based models, recommend themselves as viable alternatives to the pro-incumbent status quo."

See also D. Theodore Rave, *Politicians as Fiduciaries*, 126 Harv. L. Rev. 671 (2013): "[C]ourts can effectively check incumbent self-dealing in gerrymandering without exceeding their institutional competence—that is, without the need to make first-order decisions about the proper allocation of political power—by taking a cue from corporate law. [As] in corporate law, when incumbent decisions are tainted by a conflict of interest (such as when a legislature draws its own districts), courts should apply a strict standard of review and invalidate laws showing any sign of self-dealing. But when the taint is cleansed through the use of a neutral process (such as an independent districting commission), courts should apply a much more deferential standard of review, focusing on the adequacy and independence of the process and deferring to the substantive outcome of a sufficiently independent process. Just as it does in corporate law, the threat of searching judicial review would likely create a powerful incentive for legislators to adopt neutral processes for redistricting, allowing reviewing courts to focus not on the substantive political outcomes, but on ensuring that the processes are free from incumbent interference—a role for which courts are institutionally well suited."

---

[126] As in *Vieth*, Scalia and Thomas, JJ., deemed the partisan gerrymandering claims to be categorically nonjusticiable. Roberts, C.J., joined by Alito, J., "agreed with the determination" of Kennedy, J., that "appellants have not provided 'a reliable standard for identifying unconstitutional political gerrymanders,'" but did not join that section of Kennedy, J.'s opinion or further explain his reasoning. The Chief Justice added: "The question whether any such standard exists [has] not been argued in these cases. I therefore take no position on that question." The remaining Justices continued to insist that judicially manageable standards existed for assessing equal protection challenges to partisan gerrymanders, but they continued to disagree about what exactly those standards were.

Compare Ronald H. Brown & Daniel Hays Lowenstein, *A Democratic Perspective on Legislative Districting*, 6 J.L. & Pol. 673 (1990): "The most common 'neutral' criterion Republicans try to impose [is] compactness. The usual way of levying a political attack on a districting plan is to show diagrams of selected oddly-shaped districts. This is supposed to prove that the plan is an outrageous gerrymander. [The] real reason the Republicans promote the compactness requirement is that it tends to work systematically to their [benefit]. Inner-city areas tend to contain Democratic voters concentrated in extraordinarily high percentages. Many surrounding affluent areas are predominantly but not nearly so overwhelmingly Republican. Accordingly, it may be relatively easy to draw compact districts separating these areas and thereby to accomplish the objective of a Republican gerrymander—a small number of overwhelmingly Democratic districts surrounded by a larger number of much closer but still safely Republican districts."

3. *The problem of judicially manageable standards.* Consider Richard H. Pildes, *The Constitutionalization of Democratic Politics*, 118 Harv.L.Rev. 28 (2004): "Problems like gerrymandering require a shift in the way manageable judicial remedies are conceived. [Academics] typically demand that legal doctrines achieve stability through clear, necessary-and-sufficient criteria of doctrinal application. [In] the gerrymandering context, these critiques translate into the view that, if the Court is going to rule excessive partisan gerrymandering unconstitutional, it must be able to specify a fair partisan distribution of districts. [But] vague constitutional constraints can produce stable political or social practices. [Given] politicians' interests in certainty and control, judicial creation of general but necessarily vague constraints, with a credible threat of application, might generate a process [in which politicians would steer clear of excessively partisan gerrymandering to avoid the threat of judicial intervention]." Do you agree?

4. *The Constitution and political democracy.* Consider Richard H. Fallon, Jr., *The Dynamic Constitution: An Introduction to American Constitutional Law* 209–10 (2004): "Many commentators believe that the Court misses a vital dimension of the problem in election law cases when it talks exclusively in the vocabulary of individual rights and fails to focus directly on issues of how best to structure political democracy under the Constitution. Perhaps for this reason, the Court's analysis in election law cases often seems shallow and unsatisfying." If so, however, is the fault that of the Court or the Constitution—or both? See id.: "If the Court thought that the Constitution embodied a general theory of democracy, it could resolve election law cases under that theory. But the Justices have been unable to discern or develop such a theory."

D. "Dilution" of the Right: Issues Involving Race

As issues involving partisan gerrymanders will have attested, voters in equally populous districts do not necessarily have equal political influence in electing representatives of their choice. Among the groups that may be advantaged or disadvantaged by the drawing of district lines are groups defined by race. What guarantees, if any, does the Equal Protection Clause give to minority groups that they will be able to cast *effective* votes (as opposed to votes that satisfy the one-person, one-vote principle but are otherwise ineffectual)? A voting scheme that was deliberately structured to disadvantage racial minorities would of course violate the Equal Protection Clause because of its discriminatory intent under the rule of *Washington v. Davis*. But does or should the *fundamental* status of the right to vote trigger heightened judicial scrutiny of voting schemes that make it hard for racial minorities to elect a representative of their choice even if those schemes do not reflect a demonstrably discriminatory purpose?

MOBILE V. BOLDEN
446 U.S. 55, 100 S.Ct. 1490, 64 L.Ed.2d 47 (1980).

JUSTICE STEWART announced the judgment of the Court and delivered an opinion in which THE CHIEF JUSTICE, JUSTICE POWELL, and JUSTICE REHNQUIST join.

The City of Mobile, Ala., has since 1911 been governed by a City Commission consisting of three members elected by the voters of the city at-large. [This] is the same basic electoral system that is followed by literally thousands of municipalities and other local governmental units throughout the Nation.

[The] constitutional objection to multimember districts is not and cannot be that, as such, they depart from apportionment on a population basis in violation of *Reynolds* and its progeny. Rather the focus in such cases has been on the lack of representation multimember districts afford various elements of the voting population in a system of representative legislative democracy. "Criticism [of multimember districts] is rooted in their winner-take-all aspects, their tendency to submerge minorities, [a] general preference for legislatures reflecting community interests as closely as possible and disenchantment with political parties and elections as devices to settle policy differences between contending interests." *Whitcomb v. Chavis*, 403 U.S. 124 (1971).

Despite repeated constitutional attacks upon multimember legislative districts, the Court has consistently held that they are not unconstitutional per se, e.g., *White v. Regester*, 412 U.S. 755 (1973); *Burns v. Richardson*, supra. We have recognized, however, that such legislative apportionments could violate the Fourteenth Amendment if their purpose were invidiously to minimize or cancel out the voting potential of racial or ethnic minorities. To prove such a purpose it is not enough to show that the group allegedly discriminated against has not elected representatives in proportion to its numbers. A plaintiff must prove that the disputed plan was "conceived or operated as [a] purposeful devic[e] to further racial discrimination."

This burden of proof is simply one aspect of the basic principle that only if there is purposeful discrimination can there be a violation of [equal protection]. See *Washington v. Davis; Arlington Heights; Personnel Adm'r v. Feeney*, [Sec. 2, III supra]. Although dicta may be drawn from a few of the Court's earlier opinions suggesting that disproportionate effects alone may establish a claim of unconstitutional racial vote dilution, the fact is that such a view is not supported by any decision of this Court. More importantly, such a view is not consistent with the meaning of the Equal Protection Clause as it has been understood in a variety of other contexts involving alleged racial discrimination. *Davis* (employment); *Arlington Heights* (zoning); *Keyes*, [(public schools); *Akins v. Texas*, 325 U.S. 398 (1945) (jury selection).

[It] is clear that the evidence in the present case fell far short of showing [purposeful] discrimination. [T]he District Court [affirmed by the Court of Appeals] based its conclusion of unconstitutionality primarily on the fact that no Negro had ever been elected to the City Commission, apparently because of the pervasiveness of racially polarized voting in Mobile. The trial court also found that city officials had not been as responsive to the interests of Negroes as to those of white persons. On the basis of these findings, the court concluded that the political processes in Mobile were not equally open to Negroes, despite its seemingly inconsistent findings that there were no inhibitions against Negroes becoming candidates, and that in fact Negroes had registered and voted without hindrance. [But] past discrimination cannot, in the manner of original sin, condemn governmental action that is not itself unlawful. The ultimate question remains whether a discriminatory intent has been proved in a given [case].

[We] turn finally [to] Justice Marshall's dissenting opinion. The theory [appears] to be that every "political group," or at least every such group that is in the minority, has a federal constitutional right to elect candidates in proportion to its numbers. Moreover, a political group's "right" to have its candidates elected is said to be a "fundamental interest," the infringement of which may be established without proof that a State has acted with the purpose of impairing anybody's access to the political process. This dissenting opinion finds the "right" infringed [because] no Negro has been elected to the Mobile City Commission.

Whatever appeal the dissenting opinion's view may have as a matter of political theory, it is not the law. The Equal Protection Clause [does] not require proportional representation as an imperative of political organization. * * *

It is of course true that a law that impinges upon a fundamental right explicitly or implicitly secured by the Constitution is presumptively unconstitutional. See *Shapiro v. Thompson*, [Part II infra]. See also *San*

Antonio Ind. School Dist. v. Rodriguez, [Part IV infra]. But plainly "[i]t is not the province of this Court to create substantive constitutional rights in the name of guaranteeing equal protection of the laws," id. [In] *Whitcomb,* the trial court had found that a multimember state legislative district had invidiously deprived Negroes and poor persons of rights guaranteed them by the Constitution, notwithstanding the absence of any evidence whatever of discrimination against them. Reversing the trial court, this Court said: "The District Court's holding, although on the facts of this case limited to guaranteeing one racial group representation, is not easily contained. It is expressive of the more general proposition that any group with distinctive interests must be represented in legislative halls if it is numerous enough to command at least one seat and represents a majority living in an area sufficiently compact to constitute a single-member district. This approach would make it difficult to reject claims of Democrats, Republicans, or members of any political [organization]. There are also union oriented workers, the university community, religious or ethnic groups occupying identifiable areas of our heterogeneous cities and urban areas. Indeed, it would be difficult for a great many, if not most, multi-member districts to survive analysis under the District Court's view unless combined with some voting arrangement such as proportional representation or cumulative voting aimed at providing representation for minority parties or interests. At the very least, affirmance [would] spawn endless litigation concerning the multi-member district systems now widely employed in this country." * * *

JUSTICE BLACKMUN, concurring in the result.

Assuming that proof of intent is a prerequisite to appellees' prevailing on their constitutional claim of vote dilution, I am inclined to agree with Justice White that, in this case, "the findings of the District Court amply support an inference of purposeful discrimination." I concur in the Court's judgment of reversal, however, because I believe that the relief afforded appellees by the District Court [ordering a new form of government "of a Mayor and a City Council with members elected from single-member districts"] was not commensurate with the sound exercise of judicial discretion. * * *

JUSTICE STEVENS, concurring in the judgment.

[The antidiscrimination command] is applicable, not merely to gerrymanders directed against racial minorities, but to those aimed at religious, ethnic, economic and political groups as well. My conclusion that the same standard should be applied to racial groups as is applied to other groups leads me also to conclude that the standard cannot condemn every adverse impact on one or more political groups without spawning more dilution litigation than the judiciary can manage. [N]othing comparable to the mathematical yardstick used in apportionment cases is available to identify the difference between permissible and impermissible adverse impacts on the voting strength of political groups. * * *

In my view, the proper standard is suggested by three characteristics of the gerrymander condemned in *Gomillion:* (1) the 28-sided configuration [was] manifestly not the product of a routine or a traditional political decision; (2) it had a significant adverse impact on a minority group; and (3) it was unsupported by any neutral justification and thus was either totally irrational or entirely motivated by a desire to curtail the political strength of the minority. These characteristics suggest that a proper test should focus on the objective effects of the political decision rather than the subjective motivation of the decisionmaker. [A] political decision that is supported by valid and articulable justifications cannot be invalid simply because some participants in the decisionmaking process were motivated by a purpose to disadvantage a minority group. [A] contrary view "would spawn endless litigation concerning the multimember districts now widely employed in this Country," and would entangle the judiciary in a voracious political thicket.

JUSTICE MARSHALL, dissenting. * * *

The Court does not dispute the proposition that multimember districting can have the effect of submerging electoral minorities. [Further], we decided a series of vote-dilution cases under the Fourteenth Amendment that were designed to protect electoral minorities from precisely the combination of electoral laws and historical and social factors found in the present cases.[4] [Although] we have held that multimember districts are not unconstitutional per se, there is simply no basis for the plurality's conclusion that under our prior cases proof of discriminatory intent is a necessary condition for the invalidation of multimember districting.

[Under] this line of cases, an electoral districting plan is invalid if it has the effect of affording an electoral minority "less opportunity [than] other residents in the district to participate in the political processes and to elect legislators of their choice," *Regester*. It is also apparent that the Court in *Regester* considered equal access to the political process as meaning more than merely allowing the minority the opportunity to vote. *Regester* stands for the proposition that an electoral system may not

---

[4] **[Ct's Note]** [T]hough municipalities must be accorded some discretion in arranging their affairs, see *Abate*, there is all the more reason to scrutinize assertions that municipal, rather than State, multi-member districting dilutes the vote of an electoral minority: "In statewide elections, it is possible that a large minority group in one multi-member district will be unable to elect any legislators, while in another multi-member district where the same group is a slight majority, they will elect the entire slate of legislators. [In] at-large elections, [t]here is no way to balance out the discrimination against a particular minority group because the entire city is one huge election district. The minority's loss is absolute." Barbara Berry & Thomas Dye, *The Discriminatory Effects of At-Large Elections*, 7 Fla.St.U.L.Rev. 85, 87 (1979). * * *

relegate an electoral minority to political impotence by diminishing the importance of its [vote].

The plurality fails to apply the discriminatory effect standard of *Regester* because that approach conflicts with what the plurality takes to be an elementary principle of law. "[O]nly if there is purposeful discrimination," announces the plurality, "can there be a violation of [equal protection]." That proposition [fails] to distinguish between two distinct lines of equal protection decisions: those involving suspect classifications, and those involving fundamental rights. * * *

Under the Equal Protection Clause, if a classification "impinges upon a fundamental right explicitly or implicitly protected by the [Constitution], strict judicial scrutiny" is required, *Rodriguez,* regardless of whether the infringement was intentional. As I will explain, our cases recognize a fundamental right to equal electoral participation that encompasses protection against vote dilution. Proof of discriminatory purpose is, therefore, not required to support a claim of vote dilution.[10] The plurality's erroneous conclusion to the contrary is the result of a failure to recognize the central distinction between *Regester* and *Davis*: the former involved an infringement of a constitutionally protected right, while the latter dealt with a claim of racially discriminatory distribution of an interest to which no citizen has a constitutional entitlement. * * *

Reynolds and its progeny focused solely on the discriminatory *effects* of malapportionment. [In] the present cases, the alleged vote dilution, though caused by the combined effects of the electoral structure and social and historical factors rather than by unequal population distribution, is analytically the same concept: the unjustified abridgement of a fundamental right. It follows, then, that a showing of discriminatory intent is just as unnecessary under the vote-dilution approach adopted in *Dorsey* and applied in *Regester,* as it is under our reapportionment cases. * * *

The plurality's response is that my approach amounts to nothing less than a constitutional requirement of proportional representation for groups. That assertion amounts to nothing more than a red herring. [Appellees] proved that no Negro had ever been elected to the Mobile City Commission, despite the fact that Negroes constitute about one-third of the electorate, and that the persistence of severe racial bloc voting made it highly unlikely that any Negro could be elected at-large in the foreseeable

---

10 **[Ct's Note]** [Although] the right to vote is indistinguishable for present purposes from the other fundamental rights our cases have recognized, surely the plurality would not require proof of discriminatory purpose in those cases. The plurality fails to articulate why the right to vote should receive such singular treatment. Furthermore, the plurality refuses to recognize the disutility of requiring proof of discriminatory purpose in fundamental rights cases. For example, it would make no sense to require such a showing when the question is whether a state statute regulating abortion violates the right of personal choice recognized in *Roe v. Wade*. The only logical inquiry is whether, regardless of the legislature's motive, the statute has the effect of infringing that right. See, e.g., *Planned Parenthood v. Danforth*, [428 U.S. 52 (1976)].

future. Contrary to the plurality's contention, however, I do not find unconstitutional vote dilution in this case simply because of that showing. The plaintiffs convinced the District Court that Mobile Negroes were unable to use alternative avenues of political influence. They showed that Mobile Negroes still suffered pervasive present effects of massive historical official and private discrimination, and that the city commission had been quite unresponsive to the needs of the minority community. Mobile has been guilty of such pervasive racial discrimination in hiring employees that extensive intervention by the Federal District Court has been required. Negroes are grossly underrepresented on city boards and committees. The city's distribution of public services is racially discriminatory. City officials and police were largely unmoved by Negro complaints about police brutality and "mock lynchings." The District Court concluded that "[t]his sluggish and timid response is another manifestation of the low priority given to the needs of the black citizens and of the [commissioners'] political fear of a white backlash vote when black citizens' needs are at stake."

[The] plurality's requirement of proof of *intentional discrimination* [may] represent an attempt to bury the legitimate concerns of the minority beneath the soil of a doctrine almost as impermeable as it is specious. If so, the superficial tranquility created by such measures can be but short-lived. If this Court refuses to honor our long-recognized principle that the Constitution "nullifies sophisticated as well as simple-minded modes of discrimination," it cannot expect the victims of discrimination to respect political channels of seeking redress. I dissent.[127]

––––––

ROGERS v. LODGE, 458 U.S. 613 (1982), per WHITE, J., affirmed a decision that the at-large election system for a Georgia County Board of Commissioners violated equal protection: "The district court [demonstrated] its understanding of the controlling standard by observing that a determination of discriminatory intent is 'a requisite to a finding of unconstitutional vote dilution' [and] concluded that the [system] 'although racially neutral when adopted, is being *maintained* for invidious purposes.' [For] the most part, the district court dealt with the evidence in terms of the factors [that had been used by the district court in *Mobile*], but as the court of appeals stated: 'Judge Alaimo [did] not treat [those factors] as absolute, but rather considered them only to the extent that they were relevant to the question of discriminatory intent.' Although a tenable argument can be made to the contrary, we are not inclined to disagree with the court of appeals' conclusion that the district court applied the proper legal standard. * * *

––––––––––––––––––––

[127] The dissenting opinions of Brennan, J., and White, J., are omitted.

"The Court of Appeals [stated that the] District Court correctly anticipated *Mobile* and required appellees to prove that the at-large voting system was maintained for a discriminatory purpose. The Court of Appeals also held that the District Court's findings not only were not clearly erroneous, but its conclusion that the at-large system was maintained for invidious purposes was 'virtually mandated by the overwhelming proof.' [This Court has] noted that issues of intent are commonly treated as factual matters [and] has frequently noted its reluctance to disturb findings of fact concurred in by two lower courts."

POWELL, J., joined by Rehnquist, J., dissented: "[T]he Court's opinion cannot be reconciled persuasively with [*Mobile*]. There are some variances in the largely sociological evidence presented in the two cases. But *Mobile* held that this *kind* of evidence was not enough. * * * I would hold that the factors cited by the Court of Appeals are too attenuated as a matter of law to support an inference of discriminatory intent."

NOTES AND QUESTIONS

1. ***The (ir)relevance of race.*** Governmental policies that intentionally burden minorities are subject to invalidation even when no fundamental right is involved. See *Washington v. Davis*. Should the fundamental character of the right to vote make no difference to the analysis? Or is the problem one of identifying what counts, and does not count, as an infringement of that right?

Should the standard of proof necessary to establish discriminatory intent be relaxed in voting rights cases?

2. ***Group rights?*** Is the right at issue in *Mobile* (if there is one) inherently a "group" rather than an individual right—that is, a right of (some) groups to be able to elect a representative of their choice?[128]

Consider Heather Gerken, *Understanding the Right to an Undiluted Vote*, 114 Harv.L.Rev. 1663 (2002): "[T]he notion of [vote] dilution [hinges] on the assumption that like-minded voters should have a fair chance to coalesce— that is, that an individual's ability to aggregate her vote with others matters in a representative democracy. [E]ven numeric minorities should have an opportunity, consistent with their voting strength, to aggregate their votes effectively."

Compare Larry Alexander, *Still Lost in the Political Thicket (or Why I Don't Understand the Concept of Vote Dilution)*, 50 Vand.L.Rev. 327 (1997), arguing that, beyond a requirement that each district have equal numbers, the concept of vote dilution makes no sense. Because literally any districting scheme will make it more difficult for members of some groups to elect a representative than would an alternative scheme, every plan "dilutes" some

---

[128] See generally Vikram Amar & Alan Brownstein, *The Hybrid Nature of Political Rights*, 50 Stan.L.Rev. 915 (1998) (arguing that political rights have an irreducibly hybrid nature, with a group as well as an individual dimension).

group's votes; and "[i]f every plan dilutes votes, we might as well say that no plan does."

3. ***Proportional representation.*** Stewart, J., asserts that the theory of Justice Marshall's dissenting opinion in *Mobile* would require "proportional representation" of groups, such that "every 'political group,' or at least every such group that is in the minority, has a federal constitutional right to elect candidates in proportion to its numbers." Is this a fair charge? Should there be a right to proportional representation?[129] Could such a right be limited to racial groups?

4. ***Identifying the relevant discriminatory purpose.*** Bertrall L. Ross II, *The Representative Equality Principle: Disaggregating the Equal Protection Intent Standard*, 81 Fordham L.Rev. 17 (2012), notes that *Rogers v. Lodge* found that a voting system was being "maintained for discriminatory purposes," but "[n]owhere in the opinion did the Court explain who the perpetrator of discrimination was; nor did it identify who maintained the at-large system for discriminatory purposes." According to Ross, this approach was at variance with *Washington v. Davis*, which requires the identification of a specific perpetrator with discriminatory intent, and accords with the theory of the one person, one vote cases that "established a representative equality principle that encompassed not only the familiar democratic principle of individual political equality and majority rule, but also the principle of effective representation of minorities. [It] is against this baseline that districting practices alleged to violate the right to vote are measured."

5. ***Legislative response.*** After the decision in *Mobile v. Bolden*, Congress amended the Voting Rights Act of 1965 ("VRA"), 42 U.S.C. § 1973c, in a manner that has been interpreted to obviate the need for proof of discriminatory purpose in cases asserting *statutory* claims of race-based vote dilution. Under *Thornburg v. Gingles*, 478 U.S. 30 (1986), plaintiffs may prove a violation of § 2 of the VRA by establishing that (i) a minority community is large and compact enough to constitute the majority in a voting district, (ii) the minority community is politically cohesive, and (iii) the majority has engaged in racially polarized voting practices.

———

Whereas *Mobile v. Bolden* involved issues of minority vote dilution, partly symmetrical issues may arise in cases in which legislatures act with the goal of *increasing* the voting power of racial minorities through the deliberate design of so-called majority-minority districts. There are a variety of reasons that legislatures might seek to create majority-minority districts, including the need to comply with the Voting Rights Act of 1965, supra. As noted immediately above, § 2 of the VRA prohibits minority vote dilution as defined by effects, without need for proof of discriminatory intent. In addition, during the period when the Court decided the cases

---

[129] For an illuminating and spirited defense, see Note, *The Constitutional Imperative of Proportional Representation*, 94 Yale L.J. 163 (1984).

that follow immediately, § 5 mandated that any proposed districting changes in covered jurisdictions should not be "retrogressive" with respect to the representation of racial minorities. To enforce this requirement, § 5 provided that covered jurisdictions must "pre-clear" proposed districting changes with either a federal court or the Department of Justice. As a result of these provisions, the VRA not only permits, but sometimes actually requires, policy-makers to be race-conscious in drawing electoral districts. See Daniel Hays Lowenstein, *You Don't Have to Be Liberal to Hate the Racial Gerrymandering Cases*, 50 Stan.L.Rev. 779 (1998).

The Court's 2013 decision in *Shelby County v. Holder,* Chap. 11, effectively rendered § 5 of the Voting Rights Act inoperative by invalidating the "coverage" provision that made it applicable to some jurisdictions, which were initially specified in 1965, but not to others. Nevertheless, in part because of the continued operation of § 2, the issues raised by the cases that follow—involving the deliberate creation of majority-minority voting districts—have not been mooted.

———

UNITED JEWISH ORGANIZATIONS v. CAREY, 430 U.S. 144 (1977), rejected an equal protection attack on a race-conscious districting plan implemented by the state of New York to comply with the VRA. In order to create a majority-minority district, the state splintered what previously had been a dominant voting majority of white residents, by deliberately dividing a Hasidic Jewish community among several state legislative districts. By a 7–1 vote, the Court rejected the challenge, but fractured badly concerning the rationale. The plurality opinion, written by WHITE J.—but joined in relevant part only by Rehnquist and Stevens, JJ.—stated that the New York plan "represented no racial slur or stigma" and that there was no discrimination against white voters (including the Hasidic Jewish petitioners) "as long as whites[,] as a group, were provided with fair representation."[130]

After largely disappearing for a decade or more, attacks such as that in *United Jewish Organizations* began to surface again in the aftermath of the 1990 Census, when the Department of Justice mounted aggressive efforts pursuant to its pre-clearance role to insist that states create as many majority-minority districts as possible.[131]

---

[130] Concurring opinions were filed by Brennan, J., and by Stewart, J., joined by Powell, J. Marshall, J., did not participate.

[131] The surrounding political motivations were complex. See Samuel Issacharoff, Pamela S. Karlan, & Richard H. Pildes, *The Law of Democracy: Legal Structure of the Political Process* 582 (1998): "Republicans were delighted to pack pro-Democratic minority voters into new majority-minority districts, thereby drawing away from the electoral strength of Democratic incumbents. By the time the Clinton administration assumed office in 1993, the battles over redistricting were waged in terms of preserving the districts of newly elected Democratic minority representatives— not a group a Democratic administration was likely to abandon."

SHAW V. RENO

509 U.S. 630, 113 S.Ct. 2816, 125 L.Ed.2d 511 (1993).

JUSTICE O'CONNOR delivered the opinion of the Court.

[As] a result of the 1990 census, North Carolina became entitled to a twelfth seat in the United States House of Representatives. The General Assembly enacted a reapportionment plan that included one majority-black congressional district. After the Attorney General of the United States objected to the plan pursuant to § 5 of the Voting Rights Act of 1965, the General Assembly passed new legislation creating a second majority-black district. Appellants allege that the revised plan, which contains district boundary lines of dramatically irregular shape, constitutes an unconstitutional racial gerrymander. * * *

The voting age population of North Carolina is approximately 78% white, 20% black, and 1% Native American; the remaining 1% is predominantly Asian. The black population is relatively dispersed; blacks constitute a majority of the general population in only 5 of the State's 100 counties. [The] largest concentrations of black citizens live in the Coastal Plain, primarily in the northern part. The General Assembly's first redistricting plan contained one majority-black district centered in that area of the State. [I]t moves southward until it tapers to a narrow band; then, with finger-like extensions, it reaches far into the southern-most part of the State near the South Carolina border. District 1 has been compared to a "Rorschach ink-blot test," and a "bug splattered on a windshield."

The second majority-black district, District 12, is even more unusually shaped. It is approximately 160 miles long and, for much of its length, no wider than the I–85 corridor. It winds in snake-like fashion through tobacco country, financial centers, and manufacturing areas "until it gobbles in enough enclaves of black neighborhoods." Northbound and southbound drivers on I–85 sometimes find themselves in separate districts in one county, only to "trade" districts when they enter the next county. Of the 10 counties through which District 12 passes, five are cut into three different districts; even towns are divided. At one point the district remains contiguous only because it intersects at a single point with two other districts before crossing over them. One state legislator has remarked that "[i]f you drove down the interstate with both car doors open, you'd kill most of the people in the district." * * *

An understanding of the nature of appellants' claim is critical to our resolution of the case. In their complaint, appellants did not claim that the General Assembly's reapportionment plan unconstitutionally "diluted" white voting strength. They did not even claim to be white. Rather, appellants' complaint alleged that the deliberate segregation of voters into separate districts on the basis of race violated their constitutional right to participate in a "color-blind" electoral process. [This] Court never has held that race-conscious state decisionmaking is impermissible in all circumstances. What appellants object to is redistricting legislation that is so extremely irregular on its face that it rationally can be viewed only as an effort to segregate the races for purposes of voting, without regard for traditional districting principles and without sufficiently compelling justification. For the reasons that follow, we conclude that appellants have stated a claim upon which relief can be granted under the Equal Protection Clause.

[R]edistricting differs from other kinds of state decisionmaking in that the legislature always is aware of race when it draws district lines, just as it is aware of age, economic status, religious and political persuasion, and a variety of other demographic factors. That sort of race consciousness does not lead inevitably to impermissible race discrimination. [W]hen members of a racial group live together in one community, a reapportionment plan that concentrates members of the group in one district and excludes them from others may reflect wholly legitimate purposes. The district lines may be drawn, for example, to provide for compact districts of contiguous territory, or to maintain the integrity of political subdivisions.

The difficulty of proof, of course, does not mean that a racial gerrymander, once established, should receive less scrutiny under the Equal Protection Clause than other state legislation classifying citizens by race. Moreover, it seems clear to us that proof sometimes will not be difficult at all. In some exceptional cases, a reapportionment plan may be so highly irregular that, on its face, it rationally cannot be understood as anything other than an effort to "segregat[e] voters" on the basis of race. *Gomillion*, in which a tortured municipal boundary line was drawn to exclude black voters, was such a case. So, too, would be a case in which a State concentrated a dispersed minority population in a single district by disregarding traditional districting principles such as compactness, contiguity, and respect for political subdivisions. We emphasize that these criteria are important not because they are constitutionally required—they are not—but because they are objective factors that may serve to defeat a claim that a district has been gerrymandered on racial lines.

[A] reapportionment plan that includes in one district individuals who belong to the same race, but who are otherwise widely separated by geographical and political boundaries, and who may have little in common with one another but the color of their skin, bears an uncomfortable resemblance to political apartheid. It reinforces the perception that members of the same racial group—regardless of their age, education, economic status, or the community in which they live—think alike, share the same political interests, and will prefer the same candidates at the polls. We have rejected such perceptions elsewhere as impermissible racial stereotypes. By perpetuating such notions, a racial gerrymander may exacerbate the very patterns of racial bloc voting that majority-minority districting is sometimes said to counteract.

The message that such districting sends to elected representatives is equally pernicious. When a district obviously is created solely to effectuate the perceived common interests of one racial group, elected officials are more likely to believe that their primary obligation is to represent only the members of that group, rather than their constituency as a whole. This is altogether antithetical to our system of representative democracy. * * *

For these reasons, we conclude that a plaintiff challenging a reapportionment statute under the Equal Protection Clause may state a claim by alleging that the legislation, though race-neutral on its face, rationally cannot be understood as anything other than an effort to separate voters into different districts on the basis of race, and that the separation lacks sufficient justification. * * *

Racial gerrymandering, even for remedial purposes, may balkanize us into competing racial factions; it threatens to carry us further from the goal of a political system in which race no longer matters—a goal that the Fourteenth and Fifteenth Amendments embody, and to which the Nation continues to aspire. It is for these reasons that race-based districting by our state legislatures demands close judicial scrutiny. * * *

JUSTICE WHITE, with whom JUSTICE BLACKMUN and JUSTICE STEVENS join, dissenting.

[The] question in gerrymandering cases is "whether a particular group has been unconstitutionally denied its chance to effectively influence the political process."

[It] strains credulity to suggest that North Carolina's purpose in creating a second majority-minority district was to discriminate against members of the majority group by "impair[ing] or burden[ing their] opportunity [to] participate in the political process." The State has made no mystery of its intent, which was to respond to the Attorney General's objections by improving the minority group's prospects of electing a candidate of its choice. I doubt that this constitutes a discriminatory purpose as defined in the Court's equal protection cases—i.e., an intent to aggravate "the unequal distribution of electoral power." But even assuming that it does, there is no question that appellants have not alleged the requisite discriminatory effects. Whites constitute roughly 76 percent of the total population and 79 percent of the voting age population in North Carolina. Yet, under the State's plan, they still constitute a voting majority in 10 (or 83 percent) of the 12 congressional districts. * * *

[In other cases] we have put the plaintiff challenging district lines to the burden of demonstrating that the plan was meant to, and did in fact, exclude an identifiable racial group from participation in the political process. Not so, apparently, when the districting "segregates" by drawing odd-shaped lines. In that case, [it] is the State that must rebut the allegation that race was taken into account, a fact that, together with the legislators' consideration of ethnic, religious, and other group characteristics, I had thought we practically took for granted.

[Although] I disagree with the holding that appellants' claim is cognizable, the Court's discussion of the level of scrutiny it requires warrants a few comments. I have no doubt that a State's compliance with the Voting Rights Act clearly constitutes a compelling interest. [The] Court, while seemingly agreeing with this position, warns that the State's redistricting effort must be "narrowly tailored" to further its interest in complying with the law. It is evident to me, however, that what North Carolina did was precisely tailored to meet the objection of the Attorney General to its prior plan. * * *

State efforts to remedy minority vote dilution are wholly unlike what typically has been labeled "affirmative action." To the extent that no other racial group is injured, remedying a Voting Rights Act violation does not involve preferential treatment. It involves, instead, an attempt to equalize treatment, and to provide minority voters with an effective voice in the political process. The Equal Protection Clause of the Constitution, surely, does not stand in the way. * * *

JUSTICE STEVENS, dissenting.

[If] it is permissible to draw boundaries to provide adequate representation for rural voters, for union members, for Hasidic Jews, for Polish Americans, or for Republicans, it necessarily follows that it is permissible to do the same thing for members of the very minority group whose history in the United States gave birth to the Equal Protection Clause. A contrary conclusion could only be described as perverse.

JUSTICE SOUTER, dissenting.

[Unlike] other contexts in which we have addressed the State's conscious use of race, see, e.g., *Croson; Wygant,* electoral districting calls for decisions that nearly always require some consideration of race for legitimate reasons where there is a racially mixed population. As long as members of racial groups have the commonality of interest implicit in our ability to talk about concepts like "minority voting strength," and "dilution of minority votes," and as long as racial bloc voting takes place, legislators will have to take race into account in order to avoid dilution of minority voting strength in the districting plans they adopt. [In] addition, the mere placement of an individual in one district instead of another denies no one a right or benefit provided to others. [Under] our cases there is in general a requirement that in order to obtain relief under the Fourteenth Amendment, the purpose and effect of the districting must be to devalue the effectiveness of a voter compared to what, as a group member, he would otherwise be able to enjoy. * * *

There is thus no theoretical inconsistency in having two distinct approaches to equal protection analysis, one for cases of electoral districting and one for most other types of state governmental decisions. Nor, because of the distinctions between the two categories, is there any risk that Fourteenth Amendment districting law as such will be taken to imply anything for purposes of general Fourteenth Amendment scrutiny about "benign" racial discrimination, or about group entitlement as distinct from individual protection, or about the appropriateness of strict or other heightened scrutiny. * * *

NOTES AND QUESTIONS

1. *Constitutional injury.* What exactly is the constitutional injury or harm to the plaintiffs in *Shaw*? Is the shape of the district itself all, or part, of the problem? Consider Richard H. Pildes & Richard G. Niemi, *Expressive Harms, "Bizarre Districts," and Voting Rights: Evaluating Election-District Appearances After* Shaw v. Reno, 92 Mich.L.Rev. 483 (1993): "[V]ote dilution is not involved in this case. [With] effective control of more than a proportionate share of seats, white voters [could] not prove [that] the redistricting plan diluted their relative voting power. [One] can only understand *Shaw* [in] terms of a view [that the injury is an] expressive harm [that] results from the ideas or attitudes expressed through a governmental action, rather than from the more tangible [consequences] the action brings [about.] *Shaw* [rests] on the principle that, when government appears to use race in the redistricting context in a way that subordinates all other relevant values, the state has impermissibly endorsed too dominant a role for race. The constitutional harm must lie in this endorsement itself: the very expression of this value reductionism becomes the constitutional violation."

Compare John Hart Ely, *Standing to Challenge Pro-Minority Gerrymanders*, 111 Harv.L.Rev. 576 (1997): "[G]iven racial block voting, the [white] filler people [who are typically included to make up roughly forty percent of a majority-minority district] are being denied the opportunity to elect one of 'their own.' [This] intentionally achieved inability on the part of filler people to elect someone of their own race can in turn be labeled harmless [by] asserting that there is no disadvantage whatsoever in being represented by someone not of one's own race. [But this] can't be true if the entire enterprise of pro-minority gerrymandering is to make any sense at all."[132]

---

[132] The question of injury is of course closely linked to questions of standing, and issues of standing in vote-dilution cases have generated both recurring judicial controversies and a large literature of their own. In *United States v. Hays*, 515 U.S. 737 (1995), the Court held unanimously that, regardless of race, "a voter who lives within a challenged district has standing, whereas a voter who lives outside the district normally does not." Samuel Issacharoff & Pamela S. Karlan, *Standing and Misunderstanding in Voting Rights Law*, 111 Harv.L.Rev. 2276 (1998). Is this holding consistent with the "expressive harms" theory of Pildes, supra? Consider Issacharoff & Karlan, supra: "[T]here is no coherent theory of injury that justifies the standing rule the Court

2. ***Minority representation.*** Are efforts to create majority-minority districts a form of affirmative action that should be subjected to the same level of scrutiny as other affirmative action initiatives? Is the deliberate creation of majority-minority districts an especially objectionable effort to rig the political process? See John Hart Ely, *Gerrymanders: The Good, the Bad, and the Ugly*, 50 Stan.L.Rev. 607 (1998). Or, given the frequent reliance on the political process to protect minority interests (as, for example, under the doctrine of *Washington v. Davis*), should efforts to ensure effective minority representation trigger less judicial skepticism than other forms of affirmative action?

How might the role of elected representatives be changed, improved, or compromised by majority-minority districting? Consider K. Anthony Appiah & Amy Gutmann, *Color Conscious: The Political Morality of Race* 154–55 (1996): "The prospect of greater descriptive and substantive representation of black voters provides good reason to recommend [majority-minority districting], not because blacks 'think alike, share the same political interests, and will prefer the same candidates at the polls' but because blacks [are] more likely [to] place the interest of overcoming racial injustice near the top of their political agenda. [The] electoral influence of black citizens would be most effectively expanded by reforms that encourage the formation of cross-racial coalitions. But there is ample evidence that majority-white districts in the South rarely form cross-racial coalitions. Quite the contrary; as the black voting population in Southern electoral districts increases from a small to a sizable minority (approaching and exceeding 40 percent), the district tends to become more racially polarized, and white voters tend to form tighter, all-white coalitions, electing white representatives whose politics do not appeal to black voters."

See also T. Alexander Aleinikoff & Samuel Issacharoff, *Race and Redistricting: Drawing Constitutional Lines After* Shaw v. Reno, 92 Mich.L.Rev. 588 (1993): "What is the evidence that race-conscious districting exacerbates racial bloc voting, or that it sends a message to an elected representative that she need only represent members of her group? There is only rudimentary evidence of the relative quality of representation and responsiveness in racially drawn districts, none of which is referred to by the Court, and none of which supports the categorical assertion that representation from such districts is fundamentally different from that afforded other constituent groups who form a majority in a congressional district. [Furthermore,] claiming that representatives should look primarily to interests beyond their district calls into question the entire edifice of geographically based districting."

3. ***Beyond territorial districting?*** Could problems of "vote dilution" and the representation of minorities be successfully alleviated through the use of voting schemes that do not rely on territorially based voting districts?

---

has established. [The] Court has made a hash of standing and injury in the *Shaw* context because of its deep ambivalence and confusion about race, the meaning of the right to vote, and the structure of the political system." Notable contributions to the standing literature include Ely, supra, and Issacharoff & Karlan, supra.

Consider Lani Guinier, *The Tyranny of the Majority* 149 (1994): "[M]odified at-large systems used in corporate governance, such as cumulative voting, should be considered. Under a modified at-large system, each voter is given the same number of votes as open seats, and the voter may plump or cumulate her votes to reflect the intensity of her preferences. Depending on the exclusion threshold, politically cohesive minority groups are assured representation if they vote strategically. Similarly, *all* voters have the potential to form voluntary constituencies based on their own assessment of their interests. As a consequence, semiproportional systems such as cumulative voting give more voters, not just racial minorities, the opportunity to vote for a winning candidate."

Would such voting schemes be desirable? A federal statute, 2 U.S.C. § 2c, requires that the states establish "a number of districts equal to the number of Representatives" with "no district to elect more than one Representative." Apart from that restriction, would modified at-large systems that are designed to enhance minority representation be subject to any degree of heightened judicial scrutiny?[133] Are there any circumstances under which such systems should, or could, be imposed by courts?

———

MILLER v. JOHNSON, 515 U.S. 900 (1995), involved Georgia's creation of three majority-minority congressional districts (out of a total of eleven) in response to the Justice Department's earlier refusals to grant preclearance under the Voting Rights Act to plans that created only two such districts. Georgia's population was about 27% black. One of the majority-minority districts created by the state—the Eleventh—cut through eight counties and five municipalities. The Court, per KENNEDY, J., held that this plan violated equal protection because "race was the predominant factor motivating the drawing of the eleventh district":

"Our observation in *Shaw* of the consequences of racial stereotyping was not meant to suggest that a district must be bizarre on its face before there is a constitutional violation. * * * Shape is relevant not because bizarreness is a necessary element of the constitutional wrong or a threshold requirement of proof, but because it may be persuasive circumstantial evidence that race for its own sake, and not other districting principles, was the legislature's dominant and controlling rationale in drawing its district lines. The logical implication, as courts applying *Shaw* have recognized, is that parties may rely on evidence other than bizarreness to establish race-based districting.

"[The] courts, in assessing the sufficiency of a challenge to a districting plan, must be sensitive to the complex interplay of forces that enter a legislature's redistricting calculus. Redistricting legislatures will, for

---

[133] See Steven J. Mulroy, *Alternative Ways Out: A Remedial Road Map for the Use of Alternative Electoral Systems as Voting Rights Act Remedies*, 77 N.C.L.Rev. 1867 (1999).

example, almost always be aware of racial demographics; but it does not follow that race predominates in the redistricting process. [The] plaintiff's burden is to show, either through circumstantial evidence of a district's shape and demographics or more direct evidence going to legislative purpose, that [the] legislature subordinated traditional race-neutral districting principles, including but not limited to compactness, contiguity, respect for political subdivisions or communities defined by actual shared interests, to racial considerations. * * *

"[Whether] or not in some cases compliance with the Voting Rights Act, standing alone, can provide a compelling interest independent of any interest in remedying past discrimination, it cannot do so here. [When] a state governmental entity seeks to justify race-based remedies to cure the effects of past discrimination, we do not accept the government's mere assertion that the remedial action is required. Rather, we insist on a strong basis in evidence of the harm being remedied. [The] State does not argue, however, that it created the Eleventh District to remedy past discrimination, and with good reason: there is little doubt that the State's true interest in designing the Eleventh District was creating a third majority-black district to satisfy the Justice Department's preclearance demands. [It] does not follow, however, that the plan was required by the substantive provisions of the Voting Rights Act. * * *

"Georgia's drawing of the Eleventh District was not required under the Act because there was no reasonable basis to believe that Georgia's earlier enacted plans violated [the non-retrogression principle of § 5]. Georgia's first and second proposed plans increased the number of majority-black districts from 1 out of 10 (10%) to 2 out of 11 (18.18%). These plans were 'ameliorative' and could not have violated § 5's non-retrogression principle.

"[T]he Justice Department's implicit command that States engage in presumptively unconstitutional race-based districting brings the Voting Rights Act, once upheld as a proper exercise of Congress' authority under § 2 of the Fifteenth Amendment, into tension with the Fourteenth Amendment. [We] need not, however, resolve these troubling and difficult constitutional questions today. There is no indication Congress intended such a far-reaching application of § 5, so we reject the Justice Department's interpretation of the statute and avoid the constitutional problems that interpretation raises."

O'CONNOR, J., concurring, added: "Application of the Court's standard does not throw into doubt the vast majority of the Nation's 435 congressional districts, where presumably the States have drawn the boundaries in accordance with their customary districting principles. That is so even though race may well have been considered in the redistricting process. But application of the Court's standard helps achieve *Shaw*'s basic objective of making extreme instances of gerrymandering subject to meaningful judicial review. I therefore join the Court's opinion."

GINSBURG, J., joined by Stevens, Souter and Breyer, JJ., dissented: "Although the Georgia General Assembly prominently considered race in shaping the Eleventh District, race did not crowd out all other factors, as the Court found it did in North Carolina's delineation of the *Shaw* district. Of the 22 counties in the District, 14 are intact and 8 are divided. That puts the Eleventh District at about the state average in divided counties. [And] notably, the Eleventh District's boundaries largely follow precinct lines. Evidence at trial similarly shows that [political considerations] went into determining the Eleventh District's boundaries. * * * Tellingly, the District that the Court's decision today unsettles is not among those on a statistically calculated list of the 28 most bizarre districts in the United States, a study prepared in the wake of our decision in *Shaw*. * * *

"To accommodate the reality of ethnic bonds, legislatures have long drawn voting districts along ethnic lines. Our Nation's cities are full of districts identified by their ethnic character—Chinese, Irish, Italian, Jewish, Polish, Russian, for example. The creation of ethnic districts reflecting felt identity is not ordinarily viewed as offensive or demeaning to those included in the delineation. [If] Chinese-Americans and Russian-Americans may seek and secure group recognition in the delineation of voting districts, then African-Americans should not be dissimilarly treated. Otherwise, in the name of equal protection, we would shut out 'the very minority group whose history in the United States gave birth to the Equal Protection Clause.'"

BUSH v. VERA, 517 U.S. 952 (1996), struck down congressional districts crafted to meet what Texas argued were the requirements of the Voting Rights Act. Although race was a factor in drawing the lines, Texas argued that the predominant factor was the protection of incumbents. O'CONNOR, J., joined by Rehnquist, C.J., and Kennedy, J., agreed that avoiding contests between incumbents was a legitimate districting consideration, and she emphasized that the "decision to create majority-minority districts was not objectionable in and of itself." O'Connor, J., noted that "[o]ur precedents have used a variety of formulations to describe the threshold for the application of strict scrutiny" and cited as possible triggering standards for strict scrutiny language from both *Shaw* ("so extremely irregular on its face that it rationally can be viewed only as an effort to segregate the races for purposes of voting, without regard for traditional districting principles") and *Miller* ("race for its own sake, and not other districting principles, was the legislature's dominant and controlling rationale"). Noting that strict scrutiny does not "apply to all cases of intentional creation of majority-minority districts," she nonetheless concluded on the facts that strict scrutiny was appropriate because race had predominated over legitimate districting considerations. Among the findings weighing in favor of the application of strict scrutiny were "that the State substantially neglected traditional districting criteria such as compactness, that it was committed from the outset to creating majority-minority districts, and that it manipulated district lines to exploit unprecedentedly detailed racial data."

"As we have done in each of our previous cases, in which [compliance with Section 2 of the Voting Rights Act] has been raised as a defense to charges of racial gerrymandering, we assume without deciding that compliance with [Section 2's] results test [can be] a compelling state interest." O'Connor, J., concluded, however, that the Texas districts were not narrowly tailored to meet the requirements of the Voting Rights Act because the act does not require a state to create districts that are not reasonably compact:[134] "If, because of the dispersion of the minority population, a reasonably compact majority-minority district cannot be created, the [Voting Rights Act] does not require a majority-minority district; if a reasonably compact district can be created, nothing in [the Voting Rights Act] requires the race-based creation of a district that is far from compact."

THOMAS, J., joined by Scalia, J., concurring, maintained that the intentional creation of majority-minority districts should be enough to invoke strict scrutiny: "In my view, application of strict scrutiny in this suit was never a close question," because "a majority-minority district is created 'because of,' and not merely 'in spite of,' racial demographics." KENNEDY, J., concurring separately, strongly suggested he would join Thomas and Scalia, JJ., on that point if the issue were presented.

STEVENS, J., joined by Ginsburg and Breyer, JJ., dissenting, denied that race was a predominant consideration in the formation of the Texas districts and maintained that the creation of districts that were not reasonably compact was consistent with the Voting Rights Act. (He conceded, however, that a state was not *compelled* by the VRA to create a majority-minority district unless it could create a majority-minority

---

[134] The Court reached the same conclusion, again over the vigorous dissents of Stevens, J., and Souter, J., both joined by Breyer and Ginsburg, JJ., in the companion case of *Shaw v. Hunt* ("*Shaw II*"), 517 U.S. 899 (1996).

In *League of Latino Citizens v. Perry*, supra, Scalia, J., joined by Roberts, C.J., and Thomas and Alito, JJ., concurring in the judgment in part and dissenting in part, said that although the Court had previously left the question undecided, "I would hold that compliance with § 5 of the Voting Rights Act" is a compelling governmental interest: "We long ago upheld the constitutionality of § 5 as a proper exercise of Congress's authority under § 2 of the Fifteenth Amendment to enforce that Amendment's prohibition on the denial or abridgment of the right to vote. See *South Carolina v. Katzenbach*, Ch. 11, Sec. 3. If compliance with § 5 were not a compelling state interest, then a State could be placed in the impossible position of having to choose between compliance with § 5 and compliance with the Equal Protection Clause. Moreover, the compelling nature of the State's interest in § 5 compliance is supported by our recognition in previous cases that race may be used where necessary to remedy identified past discrimination."

district that was reasonably compact). He also vehemently questioned the underlying premise of *Shaw*, in which the Court "struck out into a jurisprudential wilderness that lacks a definable constitutional core and threatens to create harms more significant than any suffered by the individual plaintiffs challenging these districts."[135]

O'CONNOR, J., who wrote the plurality opinion in *Bush v. Vera*, also wrote a separate concurring opinion in which she attempted to summarize "the rules governing the States' consideration of race in the districting process[:] First, so long as they do not subordinate traditional districting criteria to the use of race for its own sake or as a proxy, States may intentionally create majority-minority districts, and may otherwise take race into consideration, without coming under strict scrutiny. See [the plurality opinion and the dissenting opinions of Stevens and Souter, JJ.]. Only if traditional districting criteria are neglected and that neglect is predominantly due to the misuse of race does strict scrutiny apply.

"Second, where voting is racially polarized, § 2 [of the Voting Rights Act] prohibits States from adopting districting schemes that would have the effect that minority voters 'have less opportunity than other members of the electorate [to] elect representatives of their choice.' § 2(b). That principle may require a State to create a majority-minority district where the three *Gingles* factors are present—viz., (i) the minority group 'is sufficiently large and geographically compact to constitute a majority in a single-member district,' (ii) 'it is politically cohesive,' and (iii) 'the white majority votes sufficiently as a bloc to enable it * * * usually to defeat the minority's preferred candidate.'

"Third, the state interest in avoiding liability under [§ 2] is compelling.[136] If a State has a strong basis in evidence for concluding that the *Thornburg v. Gingles* factors [supra] are present, it may create a majority-minority district without awaiting judicial findings. Its 'strong basis in evidence' need not take any particular form, although it cannot simply rely on generalized assumptions about the prevalence of racial bloc voting.

"Fourth, if a State pursues that compelling interest by creating a district that 'substantially addresses' the potential liability, and does not deviate substantially from a hypothetical court-drawn § 2 district for predominantly racial reasons, its districting plan will be deemed narrowly tailored. Cf. (plurality opinion) (acknowledging this possibility); (Souter, J., dissenting) (same); (Stevens, J., dissenting) (contending that it is applicable here).

---

[135] Souter, J., joined by Ginsburg and Breyer, JJ., dissenting, also raised administrability, separation of powers, and federalism objections to the Court's *Shaw* jurisprudence.

[136] The four dissenters in *Vera* (who also dissented in *Hunt*), together with O'Connor, J., supported this proposition.

"Finally, however, districts that are bizarrely shaped and non-compact, and that otherwise neglect traditional districting principles and deviate substantially from the hypothetical court-drawn district, for predominantly racial reasons, are unconstitutional. (plurality opinion)."

NOTES AND QUESTIONS

1.   *Applicable test.* Is the "dominant purpose" test applied in *Miller* and *Bush* a workable one? How does it relate to the test applied in *Shaw*?

In EASLEY v. CROMARTIE, 532 U.S. 234 (2001)—the Supreme Court's third encounter with the litigation that first came to it eight years earlier in *Shaw v. Reno*—the Court, by 5–4, reversed a lower court decision to invalidate a majority-minority district on the ground that the lower court's finding of predominant racial motivation was "clearly erroneous." Emphasizing the challengers' burden to show that "a facially neutral [districting] law is unexplainable on grounds other than race," BREYER, J., found the evidence inadequate to establish that the legislature was predominantly motivated to create a majority-minority district, as opposed to a "safe Democratic seat" that would maintain the existing partisan balance among the state's congressional delegation: "[W]here racial identification correlates highly with political affiliation, the party attacking the legislatively drawn boundaries must show at the least that the legislature could have achieved its legitimate political objectives in alternative ways that are comparably consistent with traditional districting principles. That party must also show that those districting alternatives would have brought about significantly greater racial balance. Appellees failed to make any such showing here."

THOMAS, J., joined by Rehnquist, C.J., and Scalia and Kennedy, JJ., dissented: "In light of the direct evidence of racial motive and the inferences that may be drawn from the circumstantial evidence, [the] District Court's finding was permissible, even if not compelled by the record."

2.   *The future of majority-minority districts?* Richard H. Pildes, *The Decline of Legally Mandated Minority Representation*, 68 Ohio State L.J. 1139 (2007), traces the rise of majority-minority voting districts largely to the Supreme Court's interpretation of the Voting Rights Act in its 1986 decision in *Thornburg v. Gingles*, supra: "As the Court saw the consequences of its *Gingles* decision [in mandating the creation of majority-minority districts], particularly as the membership of the Court changed, it sought to pull back from [what] *Gingles* had wrought. Wittingly or not, the Court had precipitated a revolution in the design of election districts. The center of the Court has been seeking ever since to put the genie it unleashed back in a bottle." But Pildes thinks Court decisions restricting expressly race-based districting are unlikely to purge minority representatives from Congress: "With minority communities increasingly integrated into politics, [safe] minority districts will arise and be sustained by the give and take of routine (and routinely ugly) redistricting politics. [When] the Court began cutting back on legally-mandated safe districts in the 1990s with the *Shaw* decision, critics [predicted] that the

Congressional Black Caucus (CBC) would soon have to start meeting 'in the backseat of a taxicab.' Subsequent years have revealed just how exaggerated these fears were, for the CBC today is more powerful than ever."

   3.   ***Racial and political gerrymanders.*** If a state can draw voting district lines predominantly based on considerations of political affiliation, does it make sense that the state cannot equally make a decision based on racial identification? If racial minorities predominantly joined a third, race-based political party, could a state draw district lines with the predominant purpose of creating a district in which members of that party were a voting majority?[137]

   Is it peculiar (or acceptable) for the Court to treat incumbent-protection as an acceptable purpose in the drawing of voting districts, as it did in *Bush v. Vera*, but to look askance at efforts to create majority-minority districts? Does current law invest whites with "an equal protection right not to be part of [majority-minority districts] that have an odd shape," but not invest racial minorities with any corresponding right "not to be part of majority white districts that have an odd shape"? Jamin B. Raskin, *The Supreme Court's Racial Double Standard in Redistricting: Unequal Protection in Politics and the Scholarship That Defends It*, 14 J.L. & Pol. 591 (1998).

E.   Equality in the Counting and Recounting of Votes

BUSH V. GORE
531 U.S. 98, 121 S.Ct. 525, 148 L.Ed.2d 388 (2000).

PER CURIAM.

[After a machine count and recount of ballots in the 2000 Florida presidential election, Democrat Albert Gore trailed Republican George W. Bush by fewer than 1,000 votes. Returns from other states made it clear that the winner of Florida's electoral votes would have an electoral college majority. With the election thus in the balance, Gore sought further manual recounts in selected, heavily Democratic Florida counties, and a complex series of legal battles unfolded. Among the signal events was a United States Supreme Court decision, entered on December 4, vacating a decision of the Florida Supreme Court that effectively extended the deadline established by Florida's Secretary of State for the completion of recounts. When the deadline for "recounts" passed with a full manual recount having been completed in only one county, the legal battles entered a second phase in which Florida law permits legal "contests" of disputed elections. In an appeal from a lower court ruling, the Florida Supreme Court, by 4–3, ordered a manual recount of all so-called "undervotes"— ballots on which the earlier machine counts had failed to record any presidential choice—in one of the counties in which Gore had sought a

---

[137] See Terry Smith, *A Black Party? Timmons, Black Backlash and the Endangered Two-Party Paradigm*, 48 Duke L.J. 1 (1998).

recount and further directed a manual recount of "undervotes" in all counties. Many of the "undervote" ballots were punchcards on which voters using a stylus had apparently left hanging "chads" or produced "dimples" but made no full perforation. In determining when votes should be recorded, the Florida Supreme Court said only that election officials and lower court judges should follow the legislatively prescribed standard of attempting to discern "the will of the voter."]

[Bush immediately sought a Supreme Court stay of the Florida Supreme Court's ruling, alleging that the state court's decision lacked any foundation in pre-existing Florida law and thus violated both a federal statute and the command of Art. II of the federal constitution that the choice of presidential electors should occur "in such Manner as the [state] Legislature"—as distinguished, Bush argued, from the state constitution or state courts—"may direct." Bush also contended that the unelaborated "will of the voter" standard for counting or not counting ballots with hanging chads and dimples would produce unjustified disparities and violate the Due Process and Equal Protection Clauses. The Supreme Court stayed the Florida Supreme Court's order on Saturday, December 9—just three days before what a majority of the Justices understood to be a Florida statutory deadline of December 12 for the completion of proceedings bearing on the final certification of the state's electors. The Court held oral argument in the case on Monday December 11 and handed down its decision shortly after 10 p.m. on December 12.]

[When] the state legislature vests the right to vote for President in its people, the right to vote as the legislature has prescribed is fundamental; and one source of its fundamental nature lies in the equal weight accorded to each vote and the equal dignity owed to each voter. See [*McPherson v. Blacker*, 146 U.S. 1, 35 (1892)].

The right to vote is protected in more than the initial allocation of the franchise. Equal protection applies as well to the manner of its exercise. Having once granted the right to vote on equal terms, the State may not, by later arbitrary and disparate treatment, value one person's vote over that of another. See, e.g., *Harper v. Virginia Bd. of Elections,* [supra]. * * *

The question before us [is] whether the recount procedures the Florida Supreme Court has adopted are consistent with its obligation to avoid arbitrary and disparate treatment of the members of its electorate. * * *

For purposes of resolving the equal protection challenge, it is not necessary to decide whether the Florida Supreme Court had the authority under the legislative scheme for resolving election disputes to define what a legal vote is and to mandate a manual recount implementing that definition. The recount mechanisms implemented in response to the decisions of the Florida Supreme Court do not satisfy the minimum requirement for non-arbitrary treatment of voters necessary to secure the fundamental right. Florida's basic command for the count of legally cast votes is to consider the "intent of the voter." This is unobjectionable as an abstract proposition and a starting principle. The problem inheres in the absence of specific standards to ensure its equal application.

[T]he standards for accepting or rejecting contested ballots might vary not only from county to county but indeed within a single county from one recount team to another. The record provides some examples. A monitor in Miami-Dade County testified at trial that he observed that three members of the county canvassing board applied different standards in defining a legal vote. * * *

[The Court also expressed concern about the disparate treatment of so-called "overvotes," involving ballots on which a voter made a mark next to the name of more than one candidate. Under the recount scheme mandated by the Florida Supreme Court,] the citizen whose ballot was not read by a machine because he failed to vote for a candidate in a way readable by machine may still have his vote counted in a manual recount; on the other hand, the citizen who marks two candidates in a way discernable by the machine will not have the same opportunity to have his vote count, even if a manual examination of the ballot would reveal the requisite indicia of intent. * * *

In addition [the] Florida Supreme Court's [order] did not specify who would recount the ballots. The county canvassing boards were forced to pull together ad hoc teams comprised of judges from various Circuits who had no previous training in handling and interpreting ballots. Furthermore, while others were permitted to observe, they were prohibited from objecting during the recount.

The recount process, in its features here described, is inconsistent with the minimum procedures necessary to protect the fundamental right of each voter in the special instance of a statewide recount under the authority of a single state judicial officer. Our consideration is limited to the present circumstances, for the problem of equal protection in election processes generally presents many complexities.

The question before the Court is not whether local entities, in the exercise of their expertise, may develop different systems for implementing elections. Instead, we are presented with a situation where a state court with the power to assure uniformity has ordered a statewide recount with minimal procedural safeguards. When a court orders a statewide remedy, there must be at least some assurance that the rudimentary requirements of equal treatment and fundamental fairness are satisfied. * * *

Upon due consideration of the difficulties identified to this point, it is obvious that the recount cannot be conducted in compliance with the requirements of equal protection and due process without substantial additional work. * * *

The Supreme Court of Florida has said that the legislature intended the State's electors to [be chosen] by December 12. That date is upon us, and there is no recount procedure in place under the State Supreme Court's order that comports with minimal constitutional standards. Because it is evident that any recount seeking to meet the December 12 date will be unconstitutional for the reasons we have discussed, we reverse the judgment of the Supreme Court of Florida ordering a recount to proceed. * * *

[Rehnquist, C.J., joined by Scalia and Thomas, J.J., joined the per curiam opinion, but wrote separately, concluding that the Florida Supreme Court violated Art. II by applying rules of decision at odds with those mandated by the Florida legislature.]

Justice STEVENS, with whom Justices GINSBURG and BREYER, join, dissenting.

* * * [Although we have previously found equal protection violations] when individual votes within the same State were weighted unequally, [we] have never before called into question the substantive standard by which a State determines that a vote has been legally cast. And there is no reason to think that the guidance provided to the factfinders, specifically the various canvassing boards, by the "intent of the voter" standard is any less sufficient—or will lead to results any less uniform—than, for example, the "beyond a reasonable doubt" standard employed everyday by ordinary citizens in courtrooms across this country.

Admittedly, the use of differing substandards for determining voter intent in different counties employing similar voting systems may raise serious concerns. Those concerns are alleviated—if not eliminated—by the fact that a single impartial magistrate will ultimately adjudicate all objections arising from the recount process. Of course, as a general matter, "[t]he interpretation of constitutional principles must not be too literal. We must remember that the machinery of government would not work if it were not allowed a little play in its joints." *Bain Peanut Co. of Tex. v. Pinson*, 282 U.S. 499, 501 (1931) (Holmes, J.). If it were otherwise, Florida's decision to leave to each county the determination of what balloting system to employ—despite enormous differences in accuracy—might run afoul of equal protection. So, too, might the similar decisions of the vast majority of state legislatures to delegate to local authorities certain decisions with respect to voting systems and ballot design. * * *

If we assume—as I do—that the [Florida Supreme Court] and the judges who would have carried out its mandate are impartial, its decision does not even raise a colorable federal question. What must underlie petitioners' entire [case] is an unstated lack of confidence in the impartiality and capacity of the state judges who would make the critical decisions if the vote count were to proceed. [The] endorsement of that position by a majority of this Court can only lend credence to the most cynical appraisal of the work of judges throughout the land. [Although] we may never know with complete certainty the winner of this year's Presidential election, the identity of the loser is perfectly clear. It is the Nation's confidence in the judge as an impartial guardian of the rule of law.

Justice SOUTER, with whom Justice BREYER, joins, dissenting.

* * * I would [remand] the case to the courts of Florida with instructions to establish uniform standards for evaluating the several types of ballots that have prompted differing treatments, to be applied within and among counties when passing on such identical ballots in any further recounting (or successive recounting) that the courts might order. * * *

Justice GINSBURG, with whom Justice STEVENS, joins, dissenting:

* * * Ideally, perfection would be the appropriate standard for judging the recount. But we live in an imperfect world, one in which thousands of votes have not been counted. I cannot agree that the recount adopted by the Florida court, flawed as it may be, would yield a result any less fair or precise than the certification that preceded that recount. See, e.g., *McDonald v. Board of Election Comm'rs of Chicago*, 394 U.S. 802, 807 (1969) (even in the context of the right to vote, the state is permitted to reform " 'one step at a time' "). * * *

Justice BREYER, with whom Justice STEVENS, Justice SOUTER, and Justice GINSBURG, join, dissenting.

* * * By halting the manual recount, and thus ensuring that the uncounted legal votes will not be counted under any standard, this Court crafts a remedy out of proportion to the asserted harm. [I]n a system that allows counties to use different types of voting systems, voters already arrive at the polls with an unequal chance that their votes will be counted. I do not see how the fact that this results from counties' selection of different voting machines rather than a court order makes the outcome any more fair. Nor do I understand why the Florida Supreme Court's recount order, which helps to redress this inequity, must be entirely prohibited based on a deficiency that could easily be remedied. * * *

NOTES AND QUESTIONS

1. ***The holding.*** What exactly was the holding of *Bush v. Gore*? The Court described its "consideration" as "limited to the present circumstances" involving "the special instance of a statewide recount under the authority of a single state judicial officer" who has "the power to assure uniformity" but has not exercised that power. In a dissenting opinion in *Smith v. Allwright*, 321 U.S. 649 (1944), Roberts, J., analogized the Court's holding to "a restricted

railroad ticket, good for this day and train only." Could the same be said of *Bush v. Gore?*

Consider Richard L. Hasen, *The Untimely Death of* Bush v. Gore, 60 Stan.L.Rev. 1 (2007): "*Bush v. Gore* is dead. [No] Court opinion—majority, concurrence, or dissent—has cited the opinion since it was decided. [We] should abandon any hope created by the case that the judiciary would serve as an engine of election administration reform." But cf. Richard L. Hasen, *The 2012 Voting Wars, Judicial Backstops, and the Resurrection of* Bush v. Gore, 81 Geo.Wash.L.Rev. 1865 (2013) (observing that in 2012, two federal voting rights decisions by courts of appeals relied in part on *Bush v. Gore* to find that state policies violated the Equal Protection Clause).

2. ***Doctrinal support.*** Do the Court's prior voting rights cases support the result in *Bush v. Gore?* Consider Pamela S. Karlan, *Unduly Partial: The Supreme Court and the Fourteenth Amendment in* Bush v. Gore, 29 Fla.St.U.L.Rev. 587 (2001): "[T]he decision to stop the recount had virtually nothing to do with equal protection. It vindicated no identifiable voter's interests. The form of equality it created was empty: it treated all voters whose ballots had not already been tabulated the same, by denying any of them the ability to have his ballot counted. And its remedy perpetuated other forms of inequality that were far more severe: between voters whose ballots were counted by the machine count and voters whose ballots were not, and even between voters in counties that performed timely manual recounts [and] voters in other counties."

Compare Michael W. McConnell, *Two-and-a-Half Cheers for* Bush v. Gore, 68 U.Chi.L.Rev. 657 (2001), reprinted in *The Vote: Bush, Gore & the Supreme Court* (Cass R. Sunstein & Richard A. Epstein eds., 2001): "It may be true that the Equal Protection Clause typically protects against discrimination against identifiable groups, but [the Court has elsewhere] summarily affirmed the principle that it also protects against 'irrational and wholly arbitrary' state action, even where the plaintiff does not allege that the unequal treatment was on account of 'membership in a class or group.' [To] treat one voter's ballot as a legal vote, and another voter's identical ballot as spoiled, in the same jurisdiction, for no conceivable public purpose, certainly states a plausible equal protection claim."

Akhil Reed Amar, *Bush, Gore, Florida, and the Constitution*, 61 Fla.L.Rev. 945 (2009) argues: "The Equal Protection Clause was [designed] to remedy the inequalities heaped upon blacks in America. [In] Florida [black] precincts in 2000 typically had much glitchier voting machines, which generated undercounts *many times* the rate of wealthier (white) precincts with sleek voting technology. [In] fixating on the small glitches of the recount rather than on the large and systemic glitches of the machines, the Rehnquist Court majority turned a blind eye to the real inequalities staring them in the face, piously attributing the problems to 'voter error' (as opposed to outdated and seriously flawed machines)."

3.   *The non-remedy.* Although seven Justices appear to have agreed that the recount ordered by the Florida Supreme Court was constitutionally defective, only a bare majority endorsed the remedy of halting the recount altogether, rather than allowing the Florida Supreme Court to devise an adequate vote-counting standard (or even permitting it to determine whether a timely recount was feasible). Many commentators regard this aspect of *Bush v. Gore* as the most difficult to defend on doctrinal grounds, with critics describing the Court's remedial ruling as "utterly indefensible,"[138] "transparently phony,"[139] and "Kafkaesque."[140] Even Michael McConnell, who otherwise endorses the Court's decision, questions the remedy: "Having rested the decision on the standardless character of the recount ordered by the state court, the logical outcome was to remand under proper constitutional standards." McConnell, supra. Compare Charles Fried, *An Unreasonable Reaction to a Reasonable Decision,* in Bush v. Gore: *The Question of Legitimacy* 3, 16 (Bruce Ackerman ed., 2002): "[T]he Court [did] not just make it up that the Florida court had stated several times its interpretation of Florida law as requiring compliance with [the December 12] deadline. [The] Court was justified in holding [the Florida Supreme Court] to that interpretation."

4.   *Further reactions.* In addition to the positions already noted, consider the following points of view:

(a)   *Bush v. Gore was not only erroneous, but also partisan in motivation.* See Alan M. Dershowitz, *Supreme Injustice: How the High Court Hijacked Election 2000,* 174 (2001): "[The] majority justices violated their own previously declared judicial principles—principles they still believe in and will apply in other cases. In this respect, the decision in the Florida election case may be ranked as the single most corrupt decision in Supreme Court history, because it is the only one that I know of where the majority justices decided as they did because of the personal identity and political affiliation of the litigants."

(b)   *The decision was sound on its peculiar facts.* Michael McConnell, supra, emphasizes that "[e]ven Justice Stevens [acknowledged] that 'the use of differing standards for determining voter intent in different counties employing similar voting systems may raise serious concerns.' [Justice Stevens] declined to find a constitutional violation, however, on the ground that 'those concerns are alleviated—if not eliminated—by the fact that a single impartial magistrate will ultimately adjudicate all objections arising from the recount process.'" With all the pressures that would have surrounded a Florida recount, and all the ballots that would have required examination, is it doubtful that a truly impartial counting process before a truly impartial magistrate could possibly have been achieved within the time available? If so,

---

[138] Laurence H. Tribe, *eroG v. hsuB and Its Disguises: Freeing Bush v. Gore from Its Hall of Mirrors,* 115 Harv.L.Rev. 170 (2001).

[139] Larry D. Kramer, *We the Court,* 115 Harv.L.Rev. 4 (2001).

[140] Margaret Jane Radin, *Can the Rule of Law Survive* Bush v. Gore?, in Bush v. Gore: *The Question of Legitimacy* 110, 116 (Bruce Ackerman ed., 2002).

was the fairest result simply to accept the tally recorded by the voting machines?

(c) ***The decision reflected rough, pragmatic justice.*** According to Richard A. Posner, *Breaking the Deadlock: The 2000 Election, the Constitution, and the Courts* (2001), *Bush v. Gore* originated with a reckless, partisan decision by the Florida Supreme Court to order a recount not properly authorized by state law. That recount threatened to create a national constitutional crisis: If Al Gore had prevailed, the Florida legislature would have appointed an alternative set of electors pledged to Bush, and a division would have ensued between the Republican-controlled House of Representatives and the Democrat-controlled Senate about which set of electors' votes should be counted. Given the "real and disturbing potential for disorder and temporary paralysis," id. at 143, Posner concludes that the Supreme Court was justified in intervening and, in view of the misconduct of the Florida Supreme Court, that its decision achieved a kind of "rough justice," even if its legal reasoning was shaky.[141]

Compare Ward Farnsworth, *"To Do a Great Right, Do a Little Wrong": A User's Guide to Judicial Lawlessness*, 86 Minn.L.Rev. 227 (2001), arguing that although result-oriented judicial "lawlessness" might occasionally be defensible, there was no excuse in *Bush v. Gore*: "[There] were processes in place for resolving the controversy without judicial intervention. The Court itself had too large a stake in the outcome of the controversy to be a good arbiter of it, and the Court was too split by its usual ideological division to be able to offer a credible resolution that reflected judgment detached from the underlying stakes. [If] regarded as an exercise in stepping outside the conventional bounds of the law to do the country a favor, *Bush v. Gore* remains a study in temptation best resisted."

(d) ***The Court's willingness to accept the case at all revealed the Justices' inflated sense of the Court's indispensable role.*** See Kramer, supra: "Nothing jumps off the pages of the opinion quite so starkly as the majority's evident determination to call a halt to things before Congress could get its hands on the problem. [Unsought] responsibility?! Forced to confront?! Nothing kept the Justices from ruling that the Supreme Court was not the proper forum in which to decide a presidential election. Nothing in the law, that is." See also Jesse H. Choper, *Why the Supreme Court Should Not Have Decided the Presidential Election of 2000*, 18 Const.Comm. 335 (2001): "[The] Court's adjudication was both unnecessary and unwise, creating a widely-based popular perception of partisanship by the Judicial Branch that carries

---

[141] Posner finds the Court's equal protection rationale wholly unpersuasive and thinks the Court would have done better to rest on the alternative basis offered in Rehnquist, C.J.'s concurrence, in which Scalia and Thomas, JJ., joined. See Posner at 153–61. Rehnquist, C.J., pointed to Art. II, § 1, cl. 2, which provides that each state shall choose its electors "in such Manner as the Legislature thereof shall direct." He argued that the Florida Supreme Court had adopted an "absurd" construction of state election law contrary to the "clearly expressed intent of the legislature." But cf. Tribe, supra (characterizing the Art. II issue as a "red herring").

the threat of diminishing the public's trust and confidence in the Justices and endangering the Court's institutional standing and overall effectiveness."

II. TRAVEL

The Court has long held that there is a constitutionally protected right to travel. An early case is *Crandall v. Nevada*, 73 U.S. (6 Wall.) 35 (1867), which struck down a state tax of $1 on rail and stage tickets for out-of-state destinations. In ruling as it did, however, the Court pointedly declined to identify any particular provision of the Constitution as the source of the right. "The people of these United States constitute one nation," the Court emphasized, and it further suggested that implicit in the idea of nationhood was a prohibition against state interferences with the right to travel from one state to another. Since *Crandall*, the Court has consistently recognized a right to travel, but it has had far more difficulty identifying the specific bounds of that right.

As you read the materials that follow, consider whether the phrase "right to travel" refers to just one right or to a collection of quite diverse rights including (1) a right to move physically from one location to another without undue impediment, (2) a right to be treated as a welcome visitor when traveling in a state that is not one's own state of residence, and (3) a right to relocate from one state to another and to be treated as an equal citizen of the state to which one has relocated. See *Saenz v. Roe*, infra (so suggesting).

If the right to travel encompasses diverse rights, consider which of these rights might be implicit in the structure of the Constitution, such as the right upheld in *Crandall* (prior to the ratification of the Fourteenth Amendment), and which might arise from specific but distinct constitutional provisions such as: the Privileges and Immunities Clause of Article IV, previously studied in Ch. 4, Sec. 4 supra, which protects visitors to a state against certain discriminations in the distribution of "fundamental" rights as identified pursuant to a largely historical test; the Equal Protection Clause, which also calls for elevated scrutiny of distributions of "fundamental" rights, but may (confusingly) use a different, less clearly historical methodology in determining which rights count as "fundamental"; and the Privileges or Immunities Clause of the Fourteenth Amendment, which provides that "[a]ll persons born or naturalized in the United States * * * are citizens of the United States" entitled to "the privileges or immunities of citizens of the United States."

SHAPIRO V. THOMPSON

394 U.S. 618, 89 S.Ct. 1322, 22 L.Ed.2d 600 (1969).

JUSTICE BRENNAN delivered the opinion of the Court.

These three appeals [are from federal courts] holding unconstitutional [Connecticut, Pennsylvania, and D.C. statutes denying welfare] to residents [who] have not resided within their jurisdictions for at least one [year].

There is no dispute that the effect of the waiting-period requirement [is] to create two classes of needy resident families indistinguishable from each other except that one is composed of residents who have resided a year or more, and the second of residents who have resided less than a year, in the jurisdiction. [T]he second class is denied welfare aid upon which may depend the ability of the families to obtain the very means to subsist—food, shelter, and other necessities of life. [We] agree [that the statutes deny equal protection]. The interests which appellants assert are promoted by the classification either may not constitutionally be promoted by government or are not compelling governmental interests.

Primarily, appellants justify the waiting-period requirement as a protective device to preserve the fiscal integrity of state public assistance programs. It is asserted that people who require welfare assistance during their first year of residence in a State are likely to become continuing burdens on state welfare programs. Therefore, the argument runs, if such people can be deterred from entering the jurisdiction by denying them welfare benefits during the first year, state programs to assist long-time residents will not be impaired. [But] the purpose of inhibiting migration by needy persons into the State is constitutionally impermissible.

This Court long ago recognized that the nature of our Federal Union and our constitutional concepts of personal liberty unite to require that all citizens be free to travel throughout the length and breadth of our land uninhibited by statutes, rules, or regulations which unreasonably burden or restrict this movement.

Alternatively, appellants argue that even if it is impermissible for a State to attempt to deter the entry of all indigents, the challenged classification may be justified as a permissible state attempt to discourage those indigents who would enter the State solely to obtain larger benefits. [But] a State may no more try to fence out those indigents who seek higher welfare benefits than it may try to fence out indigents generally. [W]e do not perceive why a mother who is seeking to make a new life for herself and her children should be regarded as less deserving because she considers, among other factors, the level of a State's public assistance. Surely such a mother is no less deserving than a mother who moves into a particular State in order to take advantage of its better educational facilities.

Appellants argue further that the challenged classification may be sustained as an attempt to distinguish between new and old residents on the basis of the contribution they have made to the community through the payment of taxes. [But this] would logically permit the State to bar new residents from schools, parks, and libraries or deprive them of police and fire protection. Indeed it would permit the State to apportion all benefits and services according to the past tax contributions of its citizens. The Equal Protection Clause prohibits such an apportionment of state services.[10]

We recognize that a State [may] legitimately attempt to limit its expenditures, whether for public assistance, public education, or any other program. But a State may not accomplish such a purpose by invidious distinctions between classes of its citizens. It could not, for example, reduce expenditures for education by barring indigent children from its schools. [Thus], appellants must do more than show that denying welfare benefits to new residents saves [money.]

[S]ince the classification here touches on the fundamental right of interstate movement, its constitutionality must be judged by the stricter standard of whether it promotes a *compelling* state interest. Under this standard, the waiting period requirement clearly violates the Equal Protection Clause.[21]

[The Court rejected the contention that Social Security Act § 402(b) approved imposition of one-year residence requirements. But] even if it could be argued that the constitutionality of § 402(b) is [in issue,] Congress may not authorize the States to violate the Equal Protection Clause. * * *

Affirmed.

CHIEF JUSTICE WARREN with whom JUSTICE BLACK joins, dissenting.

[§ 402(b)] intended to authorize state residence requirements of up to one [year.] Congress, pursuant to its commerce power, has enacted a variety of restrictions upon interstate travel. It has taxed air and rail fares and [gasoline]. Many of the federal safety regulations of common carriers which cross state lines burden the right to travel. And Congress has prohibited by criminal statute interstate travel for certain purposes. * * *

---

[10] **[Ct's Note]** We are not dealing here with state insurance programs, which may legitimately tie the amount of benefits to the individual's contributions.

[21] **[Ct's Note]** We imply no view of the validity of waiting period *or* residence requirements determining eligibility to vote, [for] tuition-free education, to obtain a license to practice a profession, to hunt or fish, [etc. These] may promote compelling state interests on the one hand, or, on the other, may not be penalties upon the exercise of the constitutional right of interstate travel.

The Court's right-to-travel cases lend little support to the view that congressional action is invalid merely because it burdens the right to travel. Most of our cases fall into two categories: those in which *state* imposed restrictions were involved, see, e.g., *Edwards v. California,* [Sec. 4, V supra], and those concerning congressional decisions to remove impediments to interstate movement, see, e.g., [*United States v. Guest*, 383 U.S. 745 (1966)]. *Aptheker v. Secretary of State,* [Ch. 6, Sec. 3 supra] is the only case in which this Court invalidated on a constitutional basis a congressionally imposed restriction. *Aptheker* also involved [a] claim that the congressional restriction compelled a potential traveler to choose between his right to travel and his First Amendment right of freedom of association. [*Aptheker*] thus contains two characteristics distinguishing it from the [instant case]: a combined infringement of two constitutionally protected rights and a flat prohibition upon travel. [Here], travel itself is not prohibited. Any burden inheres solely in the fact that a potential welfare recipient might take into consideration the loss of welfare benefits for a limited period of time if he changes his residence. Not only is this burden of uncertain degree,[5] but appellees themselves assert there is evidence that few welfare recipients have in fact been deterred by residence requirements.

The insubstantiality of the restriction imposed by residence requirements must then be evaluated in light of the possible congressional reasons for such requirements. [Given] the apprehensions of many States that an increase in benefits without minimal residence requirements would result in an inability to provide an adequate welfare system, Congress deliberately adopted the intermediate course of a cooperative program. [Our] cases require only that Congress have a rational basis for finding that a chosen regulatory scheme is necessary to the furtherance of interstate commerce. See, e.g., *Katzenbach v. McClung,* [Ch. 2, Sec. 2, III supra]. I conclude that residence requirements can be imposed by Congress as an exercise of its power to control interstate commerce consistent with the constitutionally guaranteed right to travel. * * *

JUSTICE HARLAN, dissenting. * * *

I think that [the] "compelling interest" doctrine is sound when applied to racial classifications, for historically the Equal Protection Clause was largely a product of the desire to eradicate legal distinctions founded upon race. However, I believe that the more recent extensions have been unwise. [When] a classification is based upon the exercise of rights guaranteed against state infringement by the federal Constitution, then there is no need for any resort to the Equal Protection Clause; in such instances, this Court may properly and straightforwardly invalidate any undue burden

---

[5] **[Ct's Note]** [I]ndigents who are disqualified from categorical assistance by residence requirements are not left wholly without assistance. All of the appellees in these cases found alternative sources of assistance * * * .

upon those rights under the Fourteenth Amendment's Due Process Clause. [But] when a statute affects only matters not mentioned in the federal Constitution and is not arbitrary or irrational, I must reiterate that I know of nothing which entitles this Court to pick out particular human activities, characterize them as "fundamental," and give them added protection under an unusually stringent equal protection test. * * *

[Because] a legislature might rationally find that the imposition of a welfare residence requirement would aid in the accomplishment of [valid] governmental objectives, [I] can find no objection to these residence requirements under the Equal Protection Clause.

[The] next issue [is] whether a one-year welfare residence requirement amounts to an undue burden upon the right of interstate travel[, which I conclude] is a "fundamental" right [that] should be regarded as having its source in the Due Process Clause of the Fifth Amendment.

[In] my view, a number of considerations militate in favor of constitutionality. First, [legitimate] governmental interests are furthered by residence requirements. Second, the impact of the requirements upon the freedom of individuals to travel interstate is indirect and, according to evidence put forward by the appellees themselves, insubstantial. Third, these are [cases] in which the States have acted within the terms of a limited authorization by the National Government, and in which Congress itself has laid down a like rule for the District of Columbia. Fourth, the legislatures which enacted these statutes have been fully exposed to the arguments of the appellees as to why these residence requirements are unwise, and have rejected them.

[Fifth, the] field of welfare assistance is one in which there is a widely recognized need for fresh solutions and consequently for experimentation. [Sixth, the] statutes come to us clothed with the authority of Congress and attended by a correspondingly heavy presumption of constitutionality. * * *

Today's decision, it seems to me, reflects to an unusual degree the current notion that this Court possesses a peculiar wisdom all its own whose capacity to lead this Nation out of its present troubles is contained only by the limits of judicial ingenuity in contriving new constitutional principles to meet each problem as it arises. [This] resurgence of the expansive view of "equal protection" carries the seeds of more judicial interference with the state and federal legislative process, much more indeed than does the judicial application of "due process" according to traditional concepts, about which some members of this Court have expressed fears as to its potentialities for setting us judges "at large."

NOTES AND QUESTIONS

1.   *Theory of the decision.* (a) *Scope of the "right to travel."* If a state simply eliminated welfare, or granted lower payments than other states, would

this "touch on the fundamental right of interstate movement" just as harshly as the programs in *Shapiro?* Would state policies of this kind be invalid under *Shapiro* "unless shown to be necessary to promote a *compelling* governmental interest"?

(b) *Equal protection or due process?* Does Harlan, J.'s contention—that "when the right affected is one assured by the Constitution, any infringement can be dealt with under the Due Process Clause"—make superfluous the *Shapiro* approach of finding a fundamental right to travel under equal protection?[142] Or does *Shapiro's* equal protection analysis add another dimension to the problem by distinguishing between the state interests needed to justify reducing expenditures generally and reducing expenditures by denying benefits to recent travelers?

(c) *Relation of right to travel and equal protection.* Is the central rationale of *Shapiro* that the state must not create "invidious distinctions between classes of citizens" based on whether those in one class have exercised their right to travel? If so, which discriminations should be classed as "invidious"?

2. *Bona fide residency requirements.* In thinking about *Shapiro,* it may be helpful to distinguish between *residency* requirements, which limit some benefits to bona fide residents of a state, and *durational* requirements, such as that involved in *Shapiro* itself, which discriminate against some residents or citizens based on the length of time that they have inhabited a state. The Court has declined to invalidate bona fide residency requirements in a number of contexts.

McCARTHY v. PHILADELPHIA CIVIL SERVICE COMM'N, 424 U.S. 645 (1976), per curiam—involving a Philadelphia fireman who was terminated when he moved to New Jersey—held that "a municipal regulation requiring employees of the city [to] be residents of the city" did not impair the "right to travel interstate as defined in *Shapiro*," which questioned neither "the validity of a condition placed upon municipal employment that a person be a resident *at the time* of his application," nor "the validity of appropriately defined and uniformly applied bona fide residence requirements."

Similarly, MARTINEZ v. BYNUM, 461 U.S. 321 (1983), per POWELL, J., upheld Texas's denial of free public education to children who, apart from their parents or guardians, reside in the school district "for the sole purpose of attending" the public schools: "A bona fide residence requirement [with] respect to attendance in public free schools does not violate the Equal Protection Clause [nor does it] burden or penalize the constitutional right of interstate travel, for any person is free to move to a State and to establish residence there. [A]t the very least, a school district generally would be justified in requiring school-age children or their parents to satisfy the traditional, basic residence criteria—i.e., to live in the district with a bona fide

---

[142] For support of this view, see Arnold Loewy, *A Different and More Viable Theory of Equal Protection,* 57 N.C.L.Rev. 1 (1978); Michael Perry, *Modern Equal Protection: A Conceptualization and Appraisal,* 79 Colum.L.Rev. 1023 (1979).

intention of remaining there—before it treated them as residents." MARSHALL, J., dissented, mainly on the ground that an "intention of remaining" is not a proper criterion for a bona fide residence requirement.

By contrast, DOE v. BOLTON, Ch. 6, Sec. 2 supra, invalidated the residency requirement of the Georgia abortion law under which it was unlawful for physicians to perform an abortion on any woman who was not a resident of the state: "Just as the Privileges and Immunities Clause, Art. IV, § 2, protects persons who enter other States to ply their trade, so must it protect persons who enter Georgia seeking the medical services that are available there. A contrary holding would mean that a State could limit to its own residents the general medical care available within its borders." On Art. IV, § 2, see generally Ch. 4, Sec. 4 supra.

Is *Doe* consistent with *McCarthy* and *Martinez*? Consider Laurence H. Tribe, Saenz *Sans Prophecy: Does the Privileges or Immunities Revival Portend the Future—Or Reveal the Structure of the Present?*, 113 Harv.L.Rev. 110 (1999): "On the same day that the Court had controversially protected, in the name of the Due Process Clause, a sphere of reproductive autonomy in *Roe v. Wade*, the Court in *Doe* relied instead on the Privileges and Immunities Clause of Article IV—the provision of the pre-Bill of Rights Constitution that most clearly links the structure of federalism with the protection of individual rights. At stake, in effect, was the right not to be treated as an unwelcome alien when one ventures outside the borders of one's state of residence. This is not a right to be treated as a full citizen of each state through which one passes or in which one stays temporarily in order to go to school, find work, or take a vacation, but is only a right to be treated as a friendly rather than a hostile presence. [The distinction is] between (1) those state resources, services, or benefits, access to which our system treats as the defining characteristics of state citizenship—things a state might deny to the citizens of sister states without threatening the cohesive structure of the Union—and (2) those state resources, services, or benefits that no hospitable community of American citizens would be expected to withhold from their fellow Americans just because their home state was elsewhere."

3. *Durational residency or waiting-period requirements in contexts other than welfare.* *Shapiro* invalidated a durational residency requirement as a condition for receiving welfare. But did it suggest that states could never enforce durational residency requirements, either for reasons of administrative necessity or to test the bona fides of a newcomer's claims to have become a resident?

(a) *Voting.* DUNN v. BLUMSTEIN, 405 U.S. 330 (1972), per MARSHALL, J., held that Tennessee's voting registration requirements—of residence in the state for one year and in the county for three months—violated equal protection. Although "States have the power to require that voters be bona fide residents of the relevant political subdivision," it is the "additional *durational* residence requirement which appellee challenges. [Here], whether we look to the benefit withheld by the classification (the opportunity to vote) or the basis for the classification (recent interstate travel)," the classification must be "*necessary* to promote a *compelling* governmental interest."

First, as for the state's interest in "preventing fraud [by] keeping nonresidents from voting, [the] record is totally devoid of any evidence that durational residence requirements are in fact necessary to identify bona fide residents." Second, "the State cannot seriously maintain that it is 'necessary' to reside for a year in the State and three months in the county in order to be minimally knowledgeable about congressional, state or even purely local elections."

BURGER, C.J., dissented: "It is no more a denial of Equal Protection for a State to require newcomers to be exposed to state and local problems for a reasonable period such as one year before voting, than it is to require children to wait 18 years before [voting.] Some lines must be drawn. To challenge such lines by the 'compelling state interest' standard is to condemn them all."[143]

(b) *Medical care.* MEMORIAL HOSPITAL v. MARICOPA COUNTY, 415 U.S. 250 (1974), per MARSHALL, J., held an Arizona statute—requiring one year's residence in the county for indigents to receive nonemergency hospitalization or medical care at county expense—violative of equal protection: "Although any durational residence requirement impinges to some extent on the right to travel," *Shapiro* "did not declare such requirements to be per se unconstitutional." It is only a state classification that "operates to *penalize* [indigents] for exercising their right to migrate to and settle in that state" that "must be justified by a compelling state interest. [*Dunn*] found that the denial of the franchise, 'a fundamental political right,' was a penalty [and *Shapiro*] found denial of the basic 'necessities of life' to be a penalty. Nonetheless, the Court has declined to strike down state statutes requiring one year of residence as a condition to lower tuition at state institutions of higher education.[12] Whatever the ultimate parameters of the *Shapiro* penalty analysis, it is at least clear that medical care is as much 'a basic necessity of life' to an indigent as welfare assistance." For reasons similar to those in *Shapiro,* the state has not met its "heavy burden of justification."

REHNQUIST, J., dissented: "[F]ees for use of transportation facilities such as taxes on airport users,[12] have been upheld [against] attacks based upon the right to travel. [T]he line to be derived from our prior cases is that some financial impositions on interstate travelers have such indirect or inconsequential impact on travel that they simply do not constitute the type of direct purposeful barriers struck down" in *Shapiro*. "The solicitude which the

---

[143] *Marston v. Lewis,* 410 U.S. 679 (1973), per curiam, upheld Arizona's 50-day durational residency requirement for state and local elections as "necessary to permit preparation of accurate voter lists." *Burns v. Fortson,* 410 U.S. 686 (1973), upheld a similar Georgia provision.

[12] **[Ct's Note]** See *Vlandis v. Kline,* [412 U.S. 441 (1973) (invalidating a conclusive statutory presumption that a student who applied from out of state was, therefore, a non-resident for tuition purposes for the entire period of attendance at a public university); *Starns v. Malkerson,* 401 U.S. 985 (1971) (summarily affirming a Minnesota regulation denying a student the opportunity to show residency for tuition purposes until the student had lived in the state for one year).]

[12] **[Ct's Note]** See *Evansville-Vanderburgh Airport Auth. Dist. v. Delta Airlines,* 405 U.S. 707 (1972).

Court has shown in cases involving the right to vote, and the virtual denial of entry inherent in denial of welfare benefits—'the very means by which to live'—ought not be so casually extended to the alleged deprivation here. Rather the Court should examine, as it has done in the past, whether the challenged requirement erects a real and purposeful barrier to movement, [or] whether the effects on travel, viewed realistically, are merely incidental and remote."

(c) *Divorce.* SOSNA v. IOWA, 419 U.S. 393 (1975), per REHNQUIST, J., upheld a one-year residency requirement to file for divorce: The laws in *Shapiro* and *Maricopa* "were justified on the basis of budgetary or record-keeping considerations which were held insufficient to outweigh the constitutional claims of the individuals. But Iowa's divorce residency requirement is of a different stripe. [A] decree of divorce [will] affect [both spouses'] marital status and very likely their property rights. Where a married couple has minor children, a decree of divorce would usually include provisions for their custody and support. With consequences of such moment riding on a divorce decree issued by its courts, Iowa may insist that one seeking to initiate such a proceeding have the modicum of attachment to the State required here."

MARSHALL, J., joined by Brennan, J., dissented, relying on *Boddie v. Connecticut,* Part III infra: The right to divorce "is of such fundamental importance" that the law "penalizes interstate travel within the meaning of *Shapiro, Dunn,* and *Maricopa.*"

(d) *The decisions' rationales.* Do the cases explain how the Court determines whether a "waiting-period" requirement "operates to *penalize*" the right to travel? In both *Dunn* and *Maricopa* the Court conceded "that there is no evidence in the record before us that anyone was actually deterred from traveling by the challenged restriction" but observed that "*Shapiro* did not rest upon a finding that denial of welfare actually deterred travel." Could the cases be rationalized on the view that classifications based on duration of residency are invidious when they involve eligibility for some benefits or opportunities but not for others? Does the Court *presume* that withholding of certain benefits (but not others) deters travel? Would this explain the "basic necessity of life" emphasis in *Shapiro* and *Maricopa?* Does it account for the result in *Sosna?* Is *Dunn* explicable on other grounds? See Part I supra.

———

SAENZ V. ROE
526 U.S. 489, 119 S.Ct. 1518, 143 L.Ed.2d 689 (1999).

JUSTICE STEVENS delivered the opinion of the Court.

In 1992, California enacted a statute limiting the maximum welfare benefits available to newly arrived residents. The scheme limits the amount payable to a family that has resided in the State for less than 12 months to the amount payable by the State of the family's prior residence. The questions presented by this case are whether the 1992 statute was constitutional when it was enacted and, if not, whether an amendment to the Social Security Act enacted by Congress in 1996 affects that determination. * * *

The word "travel" is not found in the text of the Constitution. Yet the "constitutional right to travel from one State to another" is firmly embedded in our jurisprudence. [In] *Shapiro*, we reviewed the constitutionality of three statutory provisions that denied welfare to residents of [states] who had resided within those respective jurisdictions less than one year immediately preceding their applications for assistance. Without pausing to identify the specific source of the right, [we] squarely held that it was "constitutionally impermissible" for a State to enact durational residency requirements for the purpose of inhibiting the migration by needy persons into the State. We further held that a classification that had the effect of imposing a penalty on the exercise of the right to travel violated the Equal Protection Clause "unless shown to be necessary to promote a *compelling* governmental interest" and that no such showing had been made. In this case, California argues that [its statute], unlike the legislation reviewed in *Shapiro*, [does] not penalize the right to travel because new arrivals are not ineligible for benefits during their first year of residence. California submits that, instead of being subjected to the strictest scrutiny, the statute should be upheld if it is supported by a rational basis and that the State's legitimate interest in saving over $10 million a year satisfies that test.

[The] "right to travel" discussed in our cases embraces at least three different components. It protects the right of a citizen of one State to enter and to leave another State, the right to be treated as a welcome visitor rather than an unfriendly alien when temporarily present in the second State, and, for those travelers who elect to become permanent residents, the right to be treated like other citizens of that State.* * *

What is at issue in this case [is the] third aspect of the right to travel— the right of the newly arrived citizen to the same privileges and immunities enjoyed by other citizens of the same State. That right is protected not only by the new arrival's status as a state citizen, but also by her status as a citizen of the United States. That additional source of protection is plainly identified in the opening words of the Fourteenth Amendment: "All persons born or naturalized in the United States, and subject to the jurisdiction thereof, are citizens of the United States and of the State wherein they reside. No state shall make or enforce any law which shall abridge the privileges or immunities of citizens of the United States."

Despite fundamentally differing views concerning the coverage of the Privileges or Immunities Clause of the Fourteenth Amendment, most notably expressed in the majority and dissenting opinions in the *Slaughter-House Cases*, [Chap. 5. Sec. 1, III] it has always been common ground that this Clause protects the third component of the right to travel. Writing for the majority in the *Slaughter-House Cases*, Justice Miller explained that one of the privileges conferred by this Clause "is that a citizen of the United States can, of his own volition, become a citizen of any State of the Union by a *bona fide* residence therein, with the same rights as other citizens of that State." * * *

Neither mere rationality nor some intermediate standard of review should be used to judge the constitutionality of a state rule that discriminates against some of its citizens because they have been domiciled in the State for less than a year. The appropriate standard may be more categorical than that articulated in *Shapiro*, but it is surely no less strict. * * *

Because this case involves discrimination against citizens who have completed their interstate travel, the State's argument that its welfare scheme affects the right to travel only "incidentally" is beside the point. Were we concerned solely with actual deterrence of migration, we might be persuaded that a partial withholding of benefits constitutes a lesser incursion on the right to travel than an outright denial of all benefits. But since the right to travel embraces the citizen's right to be treated equally in her new State of residence, the discriminatory classification is itself a penalty.

It is undisputed that respondents and the members of the class that they represent are citizens of California and that their need for welfare benefits is unrelated to the length of time that they have resided in California. We thus have no occasion to consider what weight might be given to a citizen's length of residence if the bona fides of her claim to state citizenship were questioned. Moreover, because whatever benefits they receive will be consumed while they remain in California, there is no danger that recognition of their claim will encourage citizens of other States to establish residency for just long enough to acquire some readily portable benefit, such as a divorce or a college education, that will be enjoyed after they return to their original domicile. See, e.g., *Sosna*; *Vlandis v. Kline*. * * *

Disavowing any desire to fence out the indigent, California has instead advanced an entirely fiscal justification for its [scheme]. The enforcement of [the statute] will save the State approximately $10.9 million a year. The question is not whether such saving is a legitimate purpose but whether the State may accomplish that end by the discriminatory means it has chosen. An evenhanded, across-the-board reduction of about 72 cents per month for every beneficiary would produce the same result. But our negative answer to the question does not rest on the weakness of the State's purported fiscal justification. It rests on the fact that the Citizenship Clause of the Fourteenth Amendment expressly equates citizenship with residence: "That Clause does not provide for, and does not allow for, degrees of citizenship based on length of residence." *Zobel*. [Neither] the duration of respondents' California residence, nor the identity of their prior States of residence, has any relevance to their need for benefits. Nor do those factors bear any relationship to the State's interest in making an equitable allocation of the funds to be distributed among its needy citizens. As in *Shapiro*, we reject any contributory rationale for the denial of benefits to new residents. [S]ee also *Zobel*. In short, the State's legitimate interest in saving money provides no justification for its decision to discriminate among equally eligible citizens.

The question that remains is whether congressional approval of durational residency requirements in the 1996 amendment to the Social Security Act somehow resuscitates the constitutionality of [the statute]. That question is readily answered, for we have consistently held that Congress may not authorize the States to violate the Fourteenth Amendment.

CHIEF JUSTICE REHNQUIST, with whom JUSTICE THOMAS joins, dissenting:

The Court today breathes new life into the previously dormant Privileges or Immunities Clause of the Fourteenth Amendment—a Clause relied upon by this Court in only one other decision, *Colgate v. Harvey*, 296 U.S. 404 (1935), overruled five years later by *Madden v. Kentucky*, 309 U.S. 83 (1940). It uses this Clause to strike down what I believe is a reasonable measure falling under the head of a "good-faith residency requirement." Because I do not think any provision of the Constitution—and surely not a provision relied upon for only the second time since its enactment 130 years ago—requires this result, I dissent. * * *

I agree with the proposition that a "citizen of the United States can, of his own volition, become a citizen of any State of the Union by a *bona fide* residence therein, with the same rights as other citizens of that State." *Slaughter-House Cases*. But I cannot see how the right to become a citizen of another State is a necessary "component" of the right to travel, or why the Court tries to marry these separate and distinct rights. A person is no longer "traveling" in any sense of the word when he finishes his journey to a State which he plans to make his home. Indeed, under the Court's logic, the protections of the Privileges or Immunities Clause recognized in this case come into play only when an individual *stops* traveling with the intent to remain and become a citizen of a new State.

[No] doubt the Court has, in the past 30 years, essentially conflated the right to travel with the right to equal state citizenship in striking down durational residence requirements similar to the one challenged here. [The] Court today tries to clear much of the underbrush created by these prior right-to-travel cases, abandoning its effort to define what residence requirements deprive individuals of "important rights and benefits" or "penalize" the right to travel. Under its new analytical framework, a State, outside certain ill-defined circumstances, cannot classify its citizens by the length of their residence in the State without offending the Privileges or Immunities Clause of the Fourteenth Amendment.

[In] unearthing from its tomb the right to become a state citizen and to be treated equally in the new State of residence, however, the Court ignores a State's need to assure that only persons who establish a bona fide residence receive the benefits provided to current residents of the State. [T]he Court has consistently recognized that while new citizens must have the same opportunity to enjoy the privileges of being a citizen of a State, the States retain the ability to use bona fide residence requirements to ferret out those who intend to take the privileges and run.* * *

If States can require individuals to reside in-state for a year before exercising the right to educational benefits, the right to terminate a marriage, or the right to vote in primary elections that all other state citizens enjoy, then States may surely do the same for welfare benefits. Indeed, there is no material difference between a 1-year residence requirement applied to the level of welfare benefits given out by a State, and the same requirement applied to the level of tuition subsidies at a state university.

[The] Court today recognizes that States retain the ability to determine the bona fides of an individual's claim to residence, but then tries to avoid the issue. It asserts that because respondents' need for welfare benefits is unrelated to the length of time they have resided in California, it has "no occasion to consider what weight might be given to a citizen's length of residence if the bona fides of her claim to state citizenship were questioned." * * *

The Court tries to distinguish education and divorce benefits by contending that the welfare payment here will be consumed in California, while a college education or a divorce produces benefits that are "portable" and can be enjoyed after individuals return to their original domicile. But this "you can't take it with you" distinction is more apparent than real, and offers little guidance to lower courts who must apply this rationale in the future. Welfare payments are a form of insurance, giving impoverished individuals and their families the means to meet the demands of daily life while they receive the necessary training, education, and time to look for a job. The cash itself will no doubt be spent in California, but the benefits from receiving this income and having the opportunity to become employed or employable will stick with the welfare recipient if they stay in California or go back to their true domicile. Similarly, tuition subsidies are "consumed" in-state but the recipient takes the benefits of a college education with him wherever he goes. A welfare subsidy is thus as much an investment in human capital as is a tuition subsidy, and their attendant benefits are just as "portable." More importantly, this foray into social economics demonstrates that the line drawn by the Court borders on the metaphysical, and requires lower courts to plumb the policies animating certain benefits like welfare to define their "essence" and hence their "portability." * * *

I therefore believe that the durational residence requirement challenged here is a permissible exercise of the State's power to "assur[e] that services provided for its residents are enjoyed only by residents."

JUSTICE THOMAS, with whom THE CHIEF JUSTICE joins, dissenting.

[Because] I believe that the demise of the Privileges or Immunities Clause has contributed in no small part to the current disarray of our Fourteenth Amendment jurisprudence, I would be open to reevaluating its meaning in an appropriate case. Before invoking the Clause, however, we should endeavor to understand what the framers of the Fourteenth Amendment thought that it meant. We should also consider whether the Clause should displace, rather than augment, portions of our equal protection and substantive due process jurisprudence. The majority's failure to consider these important questions raises the specter that the Privileges or Immunities Clause will become yet another convenient tool for inventing new rights, limited solely by the "predilections of those who happen at the time to be Members of this Court." * * *

NOTES AND QUESTIONS

1. *Relationship to Shapiro.* Consider Tribe, Note 2 after *Shapiro*: "*Saenz* cannot be understood as a simple corollary of *Shapiro* and its progeny. Rather, it appears to represent a new generation of constitutional ideas altogether. [Except] in the process of recapping the decision in *Shapiro*, the majority opinion in *Saenz* did not even specifically mention [the] Equal Protection Clause that had figured so prominently in the earlier case. Instead, the Court invoked a set of constitutional provisions largely ignored in *Shapiro*—the Privileges and Immunities Clause of Article IV, the Privileges or Immunities Clause of the Fourteenth Amendment, and the Citizenship Clause of the Fourteenth Amendment—to flesh out the right to travel on which it based its decision. [The] right, upon arriving in a state and deciding to remain permanently, to be treated at once as a full citizen of that state, no less privileged than those who had been the state's citizens for years [was] the right directly at stake in *Saenz*, and the Court almost casually announced that its source was the Privileges or Immunities Clause of the Fourteenth Amendment, coupled with the Citizenship Clause of that amendment.

"[The] holding of *Saenz* reflected the Court's vision of governmental design in a federal union of equal states, and not primarily the Court's perception of a personal right ineluctably flowing from constitutional text or deeply rooted tradition. [The] component of the right to travel confirmed in *Saenz* involved the elaboration of a structural principle of equal citizenship more than the protection of an individual right. [*Saenz*] revealed a Court far more comfortable protecting rights that it can describe in architectural terms, especially in terms of federalism, than it is protecting rights that present themselves as spheres of personal autonomy or dimensions of constitutionally mandated equality."

See also Mark Tushnet, *The New Constitutional Order and the Chastening of Constitutional Aspiration*, 113 Harv.L.Rev. 29 (1999): "[T]he Court's reliance on the Privileges or Immunities Clause allowed the Court simultaneously to connect itself to the *outcome* reached by the Warren Court in *Shapiro* and distance itself from the Warren Court's *doctrine*."

2. ***Rule of decision.*** Consider Roderick M. Hills, Jr., *Poverty, Residency, and Federalism: States' Duty of Impartiality Toward Newcomers,* 1999 Sup.Ct.Rev. 277, arguing that *Saenz* reflects a nondiscrimination theory: "[O]nce a new resident demonstrates that he or she is a bona fide resident, then states are categorically barred from drawing distinctions that burden the new resident based on length of residence." Professor Hills disagrees with this approach. According to him, states may be reluctant to expend their resources creating costly public goods such as public university systems if they must share those goods on an equal basis with temporary residents who may come just to enjoy those goods—as the Court appears to recognize in its discussion of "portability." Yet, writes Hills: "*Saenz* reaches the right result for the wrong reason. California's discrimination [is] suspect because it involves discrimination in a means-tested redistributive program—welfare benefits. This sort of discrimination against indigent newcomers is suspect because, unlike restrictions on divorce decrees or college education, it is likely to be rooted in cultural animosity rather than fiscal self-defense. [The] Fourteenth Amendment prohibits all durational residence requirements designed to maintain the current demographic character of the state against what the current population regards as socially undesirable migrants."

Is the categorical approach that Professor Hills ascribes to *Saenz* a tenable one? Compare *Zobel v. Williams,* 457 U.S. 55 (1982) (Brennan, J., concurring): "[D]iscrimination on the basis of residence must be supported by a valid state interest independent of the discrimination itself. [L]ength of residence may, for example, be used to test the bona fides of citizenship—and allegiance and attachment may bear some rational relationship to a very limited number of legitimate state purposes. Cf. *Chimento v. Stark,* 353 F.Supp. 1211 (D.N.H.), affirmed, 414 U.S. 802 (1973) (seven year citizenship requirement to run for governor); U.S. Const., art. I, § 2, cl. 2, § 3, cl. 3; art. II, § 1, cl. 4. But those instances in which length of residence could provide a legitimate basis for distinguishing one citizen from another are rare."[144]

3. ***Privileges or immunities rationale.*** What is the significance of the Court's reliance on the long dormant Privileges or Immunities Clause?

---

[144] *Zobel* held that Alaska's scheme of distributing its revenue from state-owned oil reserves to its citizens "in varying amounts, based on the length of each citizen's residence, violates the equal protection rights of newer state citizens."

Consider Kevin Newsom, *Setting Incorporationism Straight: A Reinterpretation of the Slaughter-House Cases*, 109 Yale L.J. 643 (2000): "[*Saenz*] indicates that the Court might be poised to reevaluate the role of the Privileges or Immunities Clause in our constitutional system." Compare Tribe, supra: "Even as one who has long advocated overruling the *Slaughter-House Cases* and taking up the cudgels of privileges or immunities, [I] am hard-pressed to read nearly so much significance into *Saenz*. Ours is [an] era of largely unexamined preferences for [structure-based constitutional interpretation, as in a number of cases and doctrines protecting constitutional federalism]. I see *Saenz* more as a monument to that truth than as a herald of a new dawn in constitutional doctrine."

III. ACCESS TO THE COURTS

The Supreme Court has listed a "fundamental constitutional right of access to the courts," *Bounds v. Smith*, 430 U.S. 817, 828 (1977), among the fundamental rights protected by the Due Process or Equal Protection Clauses. But the scope of the right remains somewhat obscure, as does the relation between the Due Process and Equal Protection Clauses in supporting the results in leading cases.

———

GRIFFIN v. ILLINOIS, 351 U.S. 12 (1956), held that a state must furnish an indigent criminal defendant with a free trial transcript (or its equivalent) if it were necessary for "adequate and effective appellate review" of the conviction. BLACK, J., joined by Warren, C.J., and Douglas and Clark, JJ., found that "both equal protection and due process emphasize [that in] criminal trials a state can no more discriminate on account of poverty than on account of religion, race, or color. Plainly the ability to pay costs in advance bears no rational relationship to a defendant's guilt or innocence and could not be used as an excuse to deprive a defendant of a fair trial. [It] is true that a state is not required by the federal constitution to provide appellate [review]. See, e.g., *McKane v. Durston,* 153 U.S. 684, 687–88 (1894). But that is not to say that a state that does grant appellate review can do so in a way that discriminates against some convicted defendants on account of their poverty. * * *

"All of the States now provide some method of appeal from criminal convictions, recognizing the importance of appellate review to a correct adjudication of guilt or innocence. [Thus] to deny adequate review to the poor means that many of them may lose their life, liberty or property because of unjust convictions which appellate courts would set aside.

[There] can be no equal justice where the kind of trial a man gets depends on the amount of money he has."[145]

––––––––

DOUGLAS v. CALIFORNIA, 372 U.S. 353 (1963), per DOUGLAS, J., relying on *Griffin*, held that a state must appoint counsel for an indigent for "the first appeal, granted as a matter of [statutory right] from a criminal conviction." It disapproved California's system of appointing counsel only when the appellate court made "an independent investigation of the record and determine[d] it would be of advantage to the defendant or helpful to [the] Court": "[A] state can, consistently with the Fourteenth Amendment, provide for differences so long as the result does not amount to a denial of due process or an 'invidious discrimination.' Absolute equality is not [required]. But where the merits of the one and only appeal an indigent has as of right are decided without benefit of counsel, we think an unconstitutional line has been drawn between rich and poor.

"When an indigent is forced to run this gantlet of a preliminary showing of merit, the right to appeal does not comport with fair procedure. [There] is lacking that equality demanded by the Fourteenth Amendment where the rich man, who appeals as of right, enjoys the benefit of counsel's examination into the record, research of the law, and marshalling of arguments on his behalf, while the indigent, already burdened by a preliminary determination that his case is without merit, is forced to shift for himself. The indigent, where the record is unclear or the errors are hidden, has only the right to a meaningless ritual, while the rich man has a meaningful appeal."

HARLAN, J., joined by Stewart, J., dissented from the Court's reliance, as in *Griffin*, "on a blend of the Equal Protection and Due Process Clauses," believing that "this case should be judged solely under the Due Process Clause": "States, of course, are prohibited by the Equal Protection Clause from discriminating between 'rich' and 'poor' *as such* in the formulation and application of their laws. But it is a far different thing to suggest that this provision prevents the State from adopting a law of general applicability that may affect the poor more harshly than it does the rich, or, on the other hand, from making some effort to redress economic imbalances while not eliminating them entirely.

"Every financial exaction which the State imposes on a uniform basis is more easily satisfied by the well-to-do than by the indigent. Yet I take it that no one would dispute the constitutional power of the State to levy a uniform sales tax, to charge tuition at a state university, to fix rates for the purchase of water from a municipal corporation, to impose a standard fine

––––––––

[145] Frankfurter, J., concurred in the result. Burton, Minton, Reed and Harlan, JJ., dissented. For analysis of *Griffin*, see Michael Klarman, *An Interpretive History of Modern Equal Protection*, 90 Mich.L.Rev. 213 (1991).

for criminal violations, or to establish minimum bail for various categories of offenses. Nor could it be contended that the State may not classify as crimes acts which the poor are more likely to commit than are the rich. And surely, there would be no basis for attacking a state law which provided benefits for the needy simply because those benefits fell short of the goods or services that others could purchase for themselves.

"Laws such as these do not deny equal protection to the less fortunate for one essential reason: the Equal Protection Clause does not impose on the States 'an affirmative duty to lift the handicaps flowing from differences in economic circumstances.' To so construe it would be to read into the Constitution a philosophy of leveling that would be foreign to many of our basic concepts of the proper relations between government and society. [N]o matter how far the state rule might go in providing counsel for indigents, it could never be expected to satisfy an affirmative duty—if one existed—to place the poor on the same level as those who can afford the best legal talent available."

As for due process, "we have today held [that] there is an absolute right to the services of counsel at trial. *Gideon v. Wainwright,* 372 U.S. 335 (1963). But [a]ppellate review is in itself not required by the Fourteenth Amendment, [and] thus the question presented is the narrow one whether the State's rules with respect to the appointment of counsel are so arbitrary or unreasonable, *in the context of the particular appellate procedure that it has established,* as to require their invalidation." CLARK, J., also dissented.

———

ROSS v. MOFFITT, 417 U.S. 600 (1974), per REHNQUIST, J., held that *Douglas* does not require counsel for discretionary state appeals or for applications for review in the Supreme Court: "[The] duty of the State under our cases is not to duplicate the legal arsenal that may be privately retained by a criminal defendant, [but] only to assure the indigent defendant an adequate opportunity to present his claims fairly in the context of the State's appellate [process]."

DOUGLAS, J., joined by Brennan and Marshall, JJ., dissented: "The right to discretionary review is a substantial one, and one where a lawyer can be of significant assistance to an indigent defendant. It was correctly perceived below that the 'same concepts of fairness and equality, which require counsel in a first appeal of right, require counsel in other and subsequent discretionary appeals.' "

M.L.B. v. S.L.J.

519 U.S. 102, 117 S.Ct. 555, 136 L.Ed.2d 473 (1996).

JUSTICE GINSBURG delivered the opinion of the Court.

By order of a Mississippi Chancery Court, petitioner M.L.B.'s parental rights to her two minor children were forever terminated. M.L.B. sought to appeal from the termination decree, but Mississippi required that she pay in advance record preparation fees estimated at $2,352.36. Because M.L.B. lacked funds to pay the fees, her appeal was dismissed.

[Concerning] access to appeal in general, and transcripts needed to pursue appeals in particular, *Griffin* is the foundation case. [The] *Griffin* principle * * * "is a flat prohibition" against "making access to appellate processes from even [the State's] most inferior courts depend upon the [convicted] defendant's ability to pay."

[We] have also recognized a narrow category of civil cases in which the State must provide access to its judicial processes without regard to a party's ability to pay fees. In *Boddie v. Connecticut*, 401 U.S. 371 (1971), we held that the State could not deny a divorce to a married couple based on their inability to pay approximately $60 in court costs. Crucial to our decision in *Boddie* was the fundamental interest at stake. "[G]iven the basic position of the marriage relationship in this society's hierarchy of values and the concomitant monopolization of the means for legally dissolving this relationship," we said, due process "prohibit[s] a State from denying, solely because of inability to pay, access to its courts to individuals who seek judicial dissolution of their marriages." Soon after *Boddie,* [in] *United States v. Kras*, 409 U.S. 434 (1973), the Court clarified that a constitutional requirement to waive court fees in civil cases is the exception, not the general rule, [and approved] fees, totaling $50, required to secure a discharge in bankruptcy.[146] *Ortwein v. Schwab*, 410 U.S. 656 (1973), [adhered] to the line drawn in *Kras* [and rejected a challenge to] an Oregon statute requiring appellants in civil cases to pay a $25 fee. [A]s *Ortwein* underscored, this Court has not extended *Griffin* to the broad array of civil cases. But tellingly, the Court has consistently set apart from the mine run of cases those involving state controls or intrusions on family relationships. [The Court here cited and discussed what it described as the "two prior decisions most immediately in point": *Lassiter v. Department of Social Servs.*, 452 U.S. 18 (1981), which held that indigents involved in proceedings aimed at the termination of parental rights were entitled to a

---

[146] *Kras* noted the difference between proceedings involving bankruptcy and marriage: "[A] debtor, in theory, and often in actuality, may adjust his debts by negotiated agreement with his creditors. [Thus,] *Boddie*'s emphasis on judicial exclusivity finds no counterpart in the bankrupt's situation." Moreover, unlike free speech or marriage, bankruptcy is not a "fundamental right." Stewart, J., joined by Douglas, Brennan and Marshall, JJ., dissented: "[In] the unique situation of the indigent bankrupt the government provides the only effective means of his ever being free of these government imposed obligations. [The] Court today holds that Congress may say that some of the poor are too poor even to go bankrupt."

case-by-case determination of their need for appointed counsel, and *Santosky v. Kramer*, 455 U.S. 745 (1982), which held that an elevated standard of proof is constitutionally required in parental termination proceedings.]

[The] Court's decisions concerning access to judicial processes [reflect] both equal protection and due process concerns. [The] equal protection concern relates to the legitimacy of fencing out would-be appellants based solely on their inability to pay core costs. The due process concern hones in on the essential fairness of the state-ordered proceedings anterior to adverse state action. [Nevertheless], "[m]ost decisions in this area," we have recognized, "res[t] on an equal protection framework," [for due] process does not independently require that the State provide an appeal.

[Unlike *Washington v. Davis*,] the Mississippi prescription here at issue [is] not merely *disproportionate* in impact. Rather [it is] wholly contingent on one's ability to pay, and thus "visi[ts] different consequences on two categories of persons;" [it applies] to all indigents and do[es] not reach anyone outside that class. In sum, under [a broad] reading of *Washington v. Davis*, our overruling of the *Griffin* line of cases would be two decades overdue. It suffices to point out that this Court has not so conceived the meaning and effect of our 1976 "disproportionate impact precedent."

Respondents and the dissenters urge that we will open floodgates if we do not rigidly restrict *Griffin* to cases typed "criminal." But we have repeatedly noticed what sets parental status termination decrees apart from [the] mine run [of] civil actions, even from other domestic relations matters such as divorce, paternity, and child custody. To recapitulate, termination decrees "wor[k] a unique kind of deprivation." In contrast to matters modifiable at the parties' will or based on changed circumstances, termination adjudications involve the awesome authority of the State "to destroy permanently all legal recognition of the parental relationship." Our [decisions], recognizing that parental termination decrees are among the most severe forms of state action have not served as precedent in other areas. We are therefore satisfied that the label "civil" should not entice us to leave undisturbed the Mississippi courts' disposition of this case.

For the reasons stated, we hold that Mississippi may not withhold from M.L.B. "a 'record of sufficient completeness' to permit proper [appellate] consideration of [her] claims."[147]

JUSTICE THOMAS, with whom JUSTICE SCALIA joins, and with whom CHIEF JUSTICE REHNQUIST joins except as to Part II, dissenting:

---

[147] Kennedy, J., concurring, would have rested on the Due Process Clause "given the existing appellate structure in Mississippi" though he also observed that "the authorities do not hold that an appeal is required even in a criminal case."

Today the majority holds that the Fourteenth Amendment requires Mississippi to afford petitioner a free transcript because her civil case involves a "fundamental" right. The majority seeks to limit the reach of its holding to the type of case we confront here, one involving the termination of parental rights. I do not think, however, that the new-found constitutional right to free transcripts in civil appeals can be effectively restricted to this case.[148] The inevitable consequences will be greater demands on the States to provide free assistance to would-be appellants in all manner of civil cases involving interests that cannot, based on the test established by the majority, be distinguished from the admittedly important interest at issue here.

[I] do not think the equal protection theory underlying the *Griffin* line of cases remains viable. [The lesson of *Washington v. Davis*] is that the Equal Protection Clause shields only against purposeful discrimination: A disparate impact, even upon members of a racial minority, [does] not violate equal protection. The Clause is not a panacea for perceived social or economic inequity; it seeks to "guarante[e] equal laws, not equal results."

[M.L.B.] defended against the "destruction of her family bonds" in the Chancery Court hearing at which she was accorded all the process this Court has required of the States in parental termination cases. She now desires "state aid to subsidize [her] privately initiated" appeal—an appeal that neither petitioner nor the majority claims Mississippi is required to provide—to overturn the determination that resulted from that hearing. I see no principled difference between a facially neutral rule that serves in some cases to prevent persons from availing themselves of state employment, or a state-funded education, or a state-funded abortion—each of which the State may, but is not required to, provide—and a facially neutral rule that prevents a person from taking an appeal that is available only because the State chooses to provide it.[1]

The *Griffin* line of cases ascribed to—one might say announced—an equalizing notion of the Equal Protection Clause that would, I think, have startled the Fourteenth Amendment's Framers. In those cases, the Court did not find, nor did it seek, any purposeful discrimination on the part of the state defendants. That their statutes had disproportionate effect on

---

[148] At a later point in his opinion, Thomas, J., explained: "Several kinds of civil suits involving interests that seem fundamental enough leap to mind. Will the Court, for example, now extend the right to a free transcript to an indigent seeking to appeal the outcome of a paternity suit? To those who wish to appeal custody determinations? How about persons against whom divorce decrees are entered? Civil suits that arise out of challenges to zoning ordinances with an impact on families? Why not foreclosure actions—or at least foreclosure actions seeking to oust persons from their homes of many years?"

[1] **[Ct's Note]** *Harper* struck down a poll tax that directly restricted the exercise of a right found in that case to be fundamental—the right to vote in state elections. The fee that M.L.B. is unable to pay does not prevent the exercise of a fundamental right directly: The fundamental interest identified by the majority is not the right to a civil appeal, it is rather the right to maintain the parental relationship.

poor persons was sufficient for us to find a constitutional violation. In *Davis,* among other cases, we began to recognize the potential mischief of a disparate impact theory writ large, and endeavored to contain it. In this case, I would continue that enterprise. Mississippi's requirement of prepaid transcripts in civil appeals seeking to contest the sufficiency of the evidence adduced at trial is facially neutral; it creates no classification. The transcript rule reasonably obliges would-be appellants to bear the costs of availing themselves of a service that the State chooses, but is not constitutionally required, to provide. Any adverse impact that the transcript requirement has on any person seeking to appeal arises not out of the State's action, but out of factors entirely unrelated to it.[149]

NOTES AND QUESTIONS

1. ***Relation to Washington v. Davis.*** Is Thomas, J., correct that *M.L.B.* is inconsistent with the spirit and logic of *Washington v. Davis,* which holds that racially disparate impact does not violate the Equal Protection Clause in the absence of either an explicit race-based classification or a racially discriminatory intent? If a racially disparate impact does not trigger heightened judicial scrutiny, then why should an economically disparate impact? Consider Note, *Disparate Impact on Death Row:* M.L.B. *and the Indigent's Right to Counsel at Capital State Postconviction Proceedings,* 107 Yale L.J. 2211 (1998): "While the facts of *Davis* were limited to race-based disparate impact, the Court also addressed disparate impact based on wealth. [*Davis's*] discriminatory purpose requirement [was] the biggest roadblock for wealth-based disparate impact theory [prior to the decision in *M.L.B.*]. For the first time in twenty years, a majority of the Court has limited *Davis's* discriminatory purpose requirement. [The] Court should [extend its rationale] to recognize a fundamental rights exception to *Davis.*"

2. ***Rationale for decision.*** Has the Court successfully distinguished cases in which the Constitution mandates assistance to indigents seeking access to the courts from those in which it does not?

HALBERT v. MICHIGAN, 545 U.S. 605 (2005), a case involving the denial of state funding to indigents who wanted the assistance of counsel in prosecuting an appeal, arose under a Michigan appellate scheme that requires defendants who plead guilty or nolo contendere to seek leave of court before bringing a first-level appeal. Appellants claimed a right to appointed counsel under *Douglas v. California*; the state argued that because the appeal was discretionary, *Ross v. Moffitt* controlled. The Court per GINSBURG, J., framed the question before it as whether *Douglas* or *Ross* "provide[d] the controlling instruction" and ruled that *Douglas* applied: Although review by the state court of appeals was discretionary, the court sat to correct errors and did not, like the appellate court in *Ross,* base its decisions to grant review on the general importance of the questions presented. "The Court of Appeals' ruling

---

[149] In Part II of his opinion, Thomas, J., argued that he would overrule *Griffin* in a proper case, but would, in any event, confine *Griffin* to criminal cases.

on a plea-convicted defendants' claims [also] provides the first, and likely the only, direct review the defendant's conviction and sentence will receive," whereas the defendant in *Ross* had already had the assistance of counsel in a first-tier review.

THOMAS, J., joined by Rehnquist, C.J., and Scalia, J., dissented: "The majority does not say where in the Constitution [the right that it upholds] is located—the Due Process Clause, the Equal Protection Clause, or some purported confluence of the two. [It] substitutes its own policy preferences for that of Michigan voters, and it does so based on an untenable reading of *Douglas*" as applicable to discretionary appeals.

IV. WELFARE AND EDUCATION

Based on a number of Warren Court decisions that seemed to have as their practical aim ensuring that the poor would have access to opportunities that are routinely enjoyed by the economically better off, by the late 1960s a number of commentators thought that the Justices might be poised either to recognize fundamental rights to education and possibly welfare or to identify the poor as a suspect class. The Court, however, never formally confronted whether to do so during the Warren years. Subsequent decisions have rejected claims that welfare and education are fundamental rights for purposes of equal protection analysis.

———

DANDRIDGE v. WILLIAMS, 397 U.S. 471 (1970): Maryland's Aid to Families With Dependent Children Program gave most eligible families their computed "standard of need," but imposed a "maximum limitation" on the total amount any family could receive. The Court, per STEWART, J., held that the statutory ceiling did not violate equal protection: "[H]ere we deal with state regulation in the social and economic field, not affecting freedoms guaranteed by the Bill of Rights, and claimed to violate the Fourteenth Amendment only because the regulation results in some disparity in grants of welfare payments to the largest AFDC families.[16] In [this area] a state does not violate [equal protection] merely because the classifications made by its laws are imperfect." "It is enough that the state's action be rationally based and free from invidious discrimination."

"To be sure, [many cases] enunciating this [standard] have in the main involved state regulation of business or industry. The administration of public welfare assistance, by contrast, involves the most basic economic needs of impoverished human beings, [but] we can find no basis for applying a different constitutional standard. [By] combining a limit on the recipient's grant with permission to retain money earned, without reduction in the amount of the grant, Maryland provides an incentive to

---

[16] **[Ct's Note]** Cf. *Shapiro,* [Part II supra,] where, by contrast, the Court found state interference with the constitutionally protected freedom of interstate travel.

seek gainful employment. And by keeping the maximum family AFDC grants to the minimum wage a steadily employed head of a household receives, the State maintains some semblance of an equitable balance between families on welfare and those supported by an employed breadwinner.

"It is true that in some AFDC families there may be no person who is employable. It is also true that with respect to AFDC families whose determined standard of need is below the regulatory maximum, [the] employment incentive is absent. But the Equal Protection Clause does not require that a State must choose between attacking every aspect of a problem or not attacking the problem at all. [T]he intractable economic, social, and even philosophical problems presented by public welfare assistance programs are not the business of this Court."[150]

MARSHALL, J., joined by Brennan, J., dissented:[151] "[T]he only distinction between those children with respect to whom assistance is granted and those [denied] is the size of the family into which the child permits himself to be born. [This] is grossly underinclusive in terms of the class which the AFDC program was designed to assist, namely *all* needy dependent children, [and requires] a persuasive justification * * * .

"The Court never undertakes to inquire for such a justification; rather it avoids the task by focusing upon the abstract dichotomy between two different approaches to equal protection problems which have been utilized by this Court.

"[The] cases relied on by the Court, in which a 'mere rationality' test was actually used, [involve] regulation of business interests. The extremes to which the Court has gone in dreaming up rational bases for state regulation in that area may in many instances be ascribed to a healthy revulsion from the Court's earlier excesses in using the Constitution to protect interests which have more than enough power to protect themselves in the legislative halls. This case, involving the literally vital interests of a powerless minority—poor families without breadwinners—is far removed from the area of business regulation, as the Court concedes. * * *

"In my view, equal protection analysis of this case is not appreciably advanced by the a priori definition of a 'right,' fundamental [and thus invoking the 'compelling' interest test] or otherwise.[14] Rather,

---

[150] See also *Lindsey v. Normet,* 405 U.S. 56 (1972) (the assurance of adequate housing is not a fundamental right).

[151] Douglas, J., dissented on the ground (agreed to also by Marshall and Brennan, JJ.) that the Maryland law was inconsistent with the Social Security Act.

[14] **[Ct's Note]** [T]he Court's insistence that equal protection analysis turns on the basis of a closed category of "fundamental rights" involves a curious value judgment. It is certainly difficult to believe that a person whose very survival is at stake would be comforted by the knowledge that his "fundamental" rights are preserved intact. * * *

concentration must be placed upon the character of the classification in question, the relative importance to individuals in the class discriminated against of the governmental benefits which they do not receive, and the asserted state interests in support of the classification. * * *

"It is the individual interests here [that] most clearly distinguish this case from the 'business regulation' [cases]. AFDC support to needy dependent children provides the stuff which sustains those children's lives: food, clothing, shelter. And this Court has already recognized [that] when a benefit, even a 'gratuitous' benefit, is necessary to sustain life, stricter constitutional standards, both procedural[17] and substantive,[18] are applied to the deprivation of that benefit.

"Nor is the distinction upon which the deprivation is here based—the distinction between large and small families—one which readily commends [itself]. Indeed, governmental discrimination between children on the basis of a factor over which they have no control [bears] some resemblance to the classification between legitimate and illegitimate children which we condemned [in cases discussed in Sec. 4, III supra]."

On examination, the asserted state interests were either "arbitrary," impermissible, of "minimum rationality," "drastically overinclusive," or "grossly underinclusive." "The existence of [other] alternatives [to satisfy asserted state interests] does not, of course, conclusively establish the invalidity of the maximum grant regulation. It is certainly relevant, however, in appraising the overall interest of the State in the maintenance of the regulation [against] a fundamental constitutional challenge."

SAN ANTONIO IND. SCHOOL DIST. V. RODRIGUEZ
411 U.S. 1, 93 S.Ct. 1278, 36 L.Ed.2d 16 (1973).

JUSTICE POWELL delivered the opinion of the Court.

This suit attacking the Texas system of financing public education was initiated by Mexican-American parents [as] a class action on behalf of schoolchildren throughout the State who are members of minority groups or who are poor and reside in school districts having a low property tax base. * * *

Recognizing the need for increased state funding to help offset disparities in local spending [because of sizable differences in the value of assessable property between local school districts,] the state legislature [established the] Minimum Foundation School Program [which] accounts

---

[17] **[Ct's Note]** See *Goldberg v. Kelly*, Chap. 6, Sec. 6, I supra.

[18] **[Ct's Note]** [See] *Kirk v. Board of Regents,* 273 Cal.App.2d 430, 440–441 (1969), appeal dismissed, 396 U.S. 554 (1970), upholding a one-year residency requirement for tuition-free graduate education at state university, and distinguishing *Shapiro* on the ground that it "involved the immediate and pressing need for preservation of life and health of persons unable to live without public assistance, and their dependent children."

for approximately half of the total educational expenditures in Texas. [It] calls for state and local contributions to a fund earmarked specifically for teacher salaries, operating expenses, and transportation costs. The State [finances] approximately [80%]. The districts' share, known as the Local Fund Assignment, is apportioned among the school districts under a formula designed to reflect each district's relative taxpaying ability. * * *

The school district in which appellees reside, [Edgewood,] has been compared throughout this litigation with the Alamo Heights [District. Edgewood] is situated in the core-city sector of San Antonio in a residential neighborhood that has little commercial or industrial property. [A]pproximately 90% of the student population is Mexican-American and over 6% is Negro. The average assessed property value per pupil is $5,960—the lowest in the metropolitan area—and the median family income ($4,686) is also the lowest. At an equalized tax rate of $1.05 per $100 of assessed property—the highest in the metropolitan area—the district contributed $26 to the education of each child for the 1967–1968 school year above its Local Fund Assignment for the Minimum Foundation Program. The Foundation Program contributed $222 per pupil for a state-local total of $248. Federal funds added another $108 for a total of $356 per pupil.

Alamo Heights is the most affluent school district in San Antonio. [Its] school population [has] only 18% Mexican-Americans and less than 1% Negroes. The assessed property value per pupil exceeds $49,000 and the median family income is $8,001. In 1967–1968 the local tax rate of $.85 per $100 of valuation yielded $333 per pupil over and above its contribution to the Foundation Program. Coupled with the $225 provided from that Program, the district was able to supply $558 per student. Supplemented by a $36 per pupil grant from federal sources, Alamo Heights spent $594 per pupil.

[M]ore recent partial statistics indicate that [the] trend of increasing state aid has been significant. For the 1970–1971 school year, the Foundation School Program allotment for Edgewood was $356 per [pupil and] Alamo Heights [received] $491 per [pupil].[35] These recent figures also reveal the extent to which these two districts' allotments were funded from their own required contributions to the Local Fund Assignment. Alamo

---

[35] **[Ct's Note]** [I]t is apparent that Alamo Heights has enjoyed a larger gain [due] to the emphasis in the State's allocation formula on the guaranteed minimum salaries for teachers. Higher salaries are guaranteed to teachers having more years of experience and possessing more advanced degrees. Therefore, Alamo Heights, which has a greater percentage of experienced personnel with advanced degrees, receives more State support. [Because] more dollars have been given to districts that already spend more per pupil, such Foundation formulas have been described as "anti-equalizing." The formula, however, is anti-equalizing only if viewed in absolute terms. The percentage disparity between the two Texas districts is diminished substantially by State aid. Alamo Heights derived in 1967–1968 almost 13 times as much money from local taxes as Edgewood did. The State aid grants to each district in 1970–1971 lowered the ratio to approximately two to [one].

Heights, because of its relative wealth, was required to contribute out of its local property tax collections approximately $100 per pupil, or about 20% of its Foundation grant. Edgewood, on the other hand, paid only $8.46 per pupil, which is about 2.4% of its grant. [Finding] that wealth is a "suspect" classification and that education is a "fundamental" interest, the District Court held that the Texas system could be sustained only if the State could show that it was premised upon some compelling state interest. * * *

II.   [The] wealth discrimination discovered [is] quite unlike any of the forms of wealth discrimination heretofore reviewed by this Court. [The] individuals [who] constituted the class discriminated against in our prior cases shared two distinguishing characteristics: because of their impecunity they were completely unable to pay for some desired benefit, and as a consequence, they sustained an absolute deprivation of a meaningful opportunity to enjoy that benefit. [For example,] *Douglas v. California* [provides] no relief for those on whom the burdens of paying for a criminal defense are, relatively speaking, great but not insurmountable. Nor does it deal with relative differences in the quality of counsel acquired by the less wealthy.

[Neither] of the two distinguishing characteristics of wealth classifications can be found here. First, [there] is reason to believe that the poorest families are not necessarily clustered in the poorest property districts. A [recent] Connecticut study found, not surprisingly, that the poor were clustered around commercial and industrial areas—those same areas that provide the most attractive sources of property tax income for school districts. * * *

Second, [lack] of personal resources has not occasioned an absolute deprivation of the desired benefit. The argument here is not that the children [are] receiving no public education; rather, it is that they are receiving a poorer quality education [than] children in districts having more assessable wealth. [A] sufficient answer to appellees' argument is that at least where wealth is involved the Equal Protection Clause does not require absolute equality or precisely equal advantages. [Texas] asserts that the Minimum Foundation Program provides an "adequate" education for all children in the State. [No] proof was offered at trial persuasively discrediting or refuting the State's assertion. * * * [60]

This brings us [to] the third way in which the classification scheme might be defined—*district* wealth discrimination. Since the only correlation indicated by the evidence is between district property wealth and expenditures, it may be argued that discrimination might be found

---

[60] **[Ct's Note]** [If] elementary and secondary education were made available by the State only to those able to pay a tuition assessed against each pupil, there would be a clearly defined class of "poor" people—definable in terms of their inability to pay the prescribed sum—who would be absolutely precluded from receiving an education. That case would present a far more compelling set of circumstances for judicial assistance than [this one].

without regard to the individual income characteristics of district residents. * * *

However described, it is clear that appellees' suit asks this Court to extend its most exacting scrutiny to review a system that allegedly discriminates against a large, diverse, and amorphous class, unified only by the common factor of residence in districts that happen to have less taxable wealth than other districts. The system of alleged discrimination and the class it defines have none of the traditional indicia of suspectness: the class is not saddled with such disabilities, or subjected to such a history of purposeful unequal treatment, or relegated to such a position of political powerlessness as to command extraordinary protection from the majoritarian political process.

We thus conclude that the Texas system does not operate to the peculiar disadvantage of any suspect class.

[Recognizing] that this Court has never heretofore held that wealth discrimination alone provides an adequate basis for invoking strict scrutiny, appellees [also] assert that the State's system impermissibly interferes with the exercise of a "fundamental" right [requiring] the strict standard of judicial review. * * *

Nothing this Court holds today in any way detracts from our historic dedication to public education. [But] the importance of a service performed by the State does not determine whether it must be regarded as fundamental for purposes of examination under the Equal Protection Clause. [In *Shapiro,* the] right to interstate travel had long been recognized as a right of constitutional significance, and the Court's decision, therefore, did not require an ad hoc determination as to the social or economic importance of that right. [In *Dandridge*], the central importance of welfare benefits to the poor was not an adequate foundation for requiring the State to justify its law by showing some compelling state interest. * * *

The lesson of these cases [is that it] is not the province of this Court to create substantive constitutional rights in the name of guaranteeing equal protection of the laws. Thus the key to discovering whether education is "fundamental" is not to be found in comparisons of the relative societal significance of education as opposed to subsistence or housing [or] by weighing whether education is as important as the right to travel. Rather, the answer lies in assessing whether there is a right to education explicitly or implicitly guaranteed by the Constitution. *Dunn;*[74] *Skinner.*[76]

---

[74] **[Ct's Note]** *Dunn* fully canvasses this Court's voting rights cases and explains that "this Court has made clear that a citizen has a *constitutionally protected right* to participate in elections on an equal basis with other citizens in the jurisdiction." (emphasis supplied). The constitutional underpinnings of [this right] can no longer be doubted even though, as the Court noted in *Harper,* "the right to vote in state elections is nowhere expressly mentioned."

[76] **[Ct's Note]** *Skinner* applied the standard of close scrutiny to a state law permitting forced sterilization of "habitual criminals." Implicit in the Court's opinion is the recognition that the right

Education, of course, is not among the rights afforded explicit protection under [the] Constitution. Nor do we find any basis for saying it is implicitly so protected. [But] appellees [contend] that education is distinguishable from other services and benefits provided by the State because it bears a peculiarly close relationship to other rights and liberties accorded protection under the Constitution [in that] it is essential to the effective exercise of First Amendment freedoms and to intelligent utilization of the right to vote. In asserting a nexus between speech and education, appellees urge that the right to speak is meaningless unless the speaker is capable of articulating his thoughts intelligently and persuasively. [A] similar line of reasoning is pursued with respect to the right to [vote]: a voter cannot cast his ballot intelligently unless his reading skills and thought processes have been adequately developed.

We need not dispute any of these propositions. [Yet] we have never presumed to possess either the ability or the authority to guarantee to the citizenry the most *effective* speech or the most *informed* electoral choice. That these may be desirable goals [is] not to be doubted. [But] they are not values to be implemented by judicial intrusion into otherwise legitimate state activities.

[The] logical limitations on appellees' nexus theory are difficult to perceive. [Empirical] examination might well buttress an assumption that the ill-fed, ill-clothed, and ill-housed are among the most ineffective participants in the political process and that they derive the least enjoyment from the benefits of the First Amendment. * * *

[The] present case, in another basic sense, is significantly different from any of the cases in which the Court has applied strict scrutiny [to] legislation touching upon constitutionally protected rights. [These] involved legislation which "deprived," "infringed," or "interfered" with the free exercise of some such fundamental personal right or liberty. [We] think it plain that, in substance, the thrust of the Texas system is affirmative and reformatory and, therefore, should be scrutinized under judicial principles sensitive to the nature of the State's efforts and to the rights reserved to the States under the Constitution.

[A] century of Supreme Court adjudication under the Equal Protection Clause affirmatively supports the application of the traditional standard of review, which requires only that the State's system be shown to bear some rational relationship to legitimate state purposes. This case represents [a] direct attack on the way in which Texas has chosen to raise and disburse state and local tax revenues. [This] Court has often admonished against such interferences with the State's fiscal policies under the Equal Protection Clause [and] we continue to acknowledge that the Justices of

---

of procreation is among the rights of personal privacy protected under the Constitution. See *Roe v. Wade.*

this Court lack both the expertise and the familiarity with local problems so necessary to the making of wise decisions with respect to the raising and disposition of public revenues. Yet, we are urged to direct the States either to alter drastically the present system or to throw out the property tax altogether in favor of some other form of taxation. No scheme of taxation [has] yet been devised which is free of all discriminatory impact. In such a complex arena in which no perfect alternatives exist, the Court does well not to impose too rigorous a standard of scrutiny lest all local fiscal schemes become subjects of criticism under the Equal Protection Clause.

[T]his case also involves the most persistent and difficult questions of educational policy, another area in which this Court's lack of specialized knowledge and experience counsels against premature interference with the informed judgments made at the state and local levels. [I]t would be difficult to imagine a case having a greater potential impact on our federal system than the one now before us, in which we are urged to abrogate systems of financing public education presently in existence in virtually every State. * * *

Reversed.

JUSTICE BRENNAN, dissenting.

Although I agree with my Brother White that the Texas statutory scheme is devoid of any rational basis, [I] also record my disagreement with the Court's rather distressing assertion that a right may be deemed "fundamental" for the purposes of equal protection analysis only if it is "explicitly or implicitly guaranteed by the Constitution." As my Brother Marshall convincingly demonstrates our prior cases stand for the proposition that "fundamentality" is, in large measure, a function of the right's importance in terms of the effectuation of those rights which are in fact constitutionally guaranteed. * * *

JUSTICE WHITE, with whom JUSTICE DOUGLAS and JUSTICE BRENNAN join, dissenting.

[T]his case would be quite different if it were true that the Texas system, while insuring minimum educational expenditures in every district through state funding, extended a meaningful option to all local districts to increase their per-pupil [expenditures. But for] districts with a low per-pupil real estate tax base [the] Texas system utterly fails to extend a realistic choice to parents because the property tax, which is the only revenue-raising mechanism extended to school districts, is practically and legally unavailable. * * *

In order to equal the highest yield in any other Bexar County district, Alamo Heights would be required to tax at the rate of 68 cents per $100 of assessed valuation. Edgewood would be required to tax at the prohibitive rate of $5.76 per $100. But state law places a $1.50 per $100 ceiling on the maintenance tax [rate]. Requiring the State to establish only that unequal treatment is in furtherance of a permissible goal, without also requiring the State to show that the means chosen to effectuate that goal are rationally related to its achievement, makes equal protection analysis no more than an empty gesture. * * *

JUSTICE MARSHALL, with whom JUSTICE DOUGLAS, concurs, dissenting.

[T]he majority's holding can only be seen as a retreat from our historic commitment to equality of educational opportunity. [At] the very least, in view of the substantial interdistrict disparities in funding, [the] burden of proving that these disparities do not in fact affect the quality of children's education must fall upon the appellants. Yet [they] have argued no more than that the relationship is ambiguous. * * *

Nor can I accept the appellants' apparent suggestion [that equal protection] cannot be offended by substantially unequal state treatment of persons who are similarly situated so long as the State provides everyone with some unspecified amount of education which evidently is "enough." [The] Equal Protection Clause is not addressed to the minimal sufficiency but rather to the unjustifiable inequalities of state action. [In] light of the data introduced before the District Court, the conclusion that the school children of property poor districts constitute a sufficient class for our purposes seems indisputable to me. [Whether] this discrimination against [them] is violative of the Equal Protection Clause is the question to which we must now turn.

[The] Court apparently seeks to establish [that] equal protection cases fall into one of two neat categories which dictate the appropriate standard of review—strict scrutiny or mere rationality. But [a] principled reading of what this Court has done reveals that it has applied a spectrum of standards [which] clearly comprehends variations in the degree of care with which the Court will scrutinize particular classifications, depending [on] the constitutional and societal importance of the interest adversely affected and the recognized invidiousness of the basis upon which the particular classification is drawn. * * *

I therefore cannot accept the majority's labored efforts to demonstrate that fundamental interests, which call for strict scrutiny of the challenged classification, encompass only established rights which we are somehow bound to recognize from the text of the Constitution itself. * * *

I would like to know where the Constitution guarantees the right to procreate, *Skinner,* or the right to vote in state elections, e.g., *Reynolds v. Sims,* or the right to an appeal from a criminal conviction, e.g., *Griffin.* These are instances in which, due to the importance of the interests at stake, the Court has displayed a strong concern with the existence of discriminatory state treatment. But the Court has [never] indicated that these are interests which independently enjoy full-blown constitutional protection. * * *

The majority is, of course, correct when it suggests that the process of determining which interests are fundamental is a difficult one. But I do not think the problem is insurmountable. [The task] should be to determine the extent to which constitutionally guaranteed rights are dependent on interests not mentioned in the Constitution. As the nexus between the specific constitutional guarantee and the nonconstitutional interest draws closer, the nonconstitutional interest becomes more fundamental and the degree of judicial scrutiny applied when the interest is infringed on a discriminatory basis must be adjusted accordingly. * * * Procreation is now understood to be important because of its interaction with the established constitutional right of privacy. The exercise of the state franchise is closely tied to basic civil and political rights inherent in the First Amendment. And access to criminal appellate processes enhances the integrity of the range of rights implicit in the Fourteenth Amendment guarantee of due process of law. Only if we closely protect the related interests from state discrimination do we ultimately ensure the integrity of the constitutional guarantee itself. This is the real lesson that must be taken from our previous decisions involving interests deemed to be fundamental.

[It] is true that this Court has never deemed the provision of free public education to be required by the Constitution. [But] the fundamental importance of education is amply indicated by the prior decisions of this Court, by the unique status accorded public education by our society, and by the close relationship between education and some of our most basic constitutional [values].

[I] do not question that local control of public education, as an abstract matter, constitutes a very substantial state interest. [But] on this record, it is apparent that the State's purported concern with local control is offered primarily as an excuse rather than as a justification for interdistrict inequality.

In Texas statewide laws regulate [the] most minute details of local public education. For example, the State prescribes required courses. All textbooks must be submitted for state [approval]. The State has established the qualifications necessary for teaching in Texas public schools and the procedures for obtaining certification. The State has even legislated on the length of the school [day.]

Moreover, even if we accept Texas' general dedication to local control in educational matters, [i]f Texas had a system truly dedicated to local fiscal control one would expect the quality of the educational opportunity provided in each district to vary with the decision of the voters in that district as to the level of sacrifice they wish to make for public education. [But local] districts cannot choose to have the best education [by] imposing the highest tax rate. Instead, the quality of the educational opportunity offered by any particular district is largely determined by the amount of taxable property located in the district—a factor over which local voters can exercise no control.

[In] my judgment, any substantial degree of scrutiny of the operation of the Texas financing scheme reveals that the State has selected means wholly inappropriate to secure its purported interest in assuring its school districts local fiscal control.[96] At the same time, appellees have pointed out a variety of alternative financing schemes which may serve the State's purported interest in local control as well as, if not better than, the present scheme without the current impairment of the educational opportunity of vast numbers of Texas schoolchildren.[98] * * *

NOTES AND QUESTIONS

1. ***Positive and negative rights.*** Consider Richard H. Fallon, Jr., *Individual Rights and the Powers of Government*, 27 Ga.L.Rev. 343 (1993): "Perhaps the most pervasive strategy in constitutional law is for courts to distinguish between negative and positive freedoms: to insist that constitutional rights stand as barriers against government coercion and discrimination, but do not require the government affirmatively to come to anyone's aid." Is this strategy generally defensible?[152] Does it recognize exceptions—for example, in cases involving rights to appointed counsel or the waiver of litigation fees? If there are recognized exceptions, do they compromise the general rule?

According to Barry Friedman & Sara Solow, *The Federal Right to an Adequate Education*, 81 Geo.Wash.L.Rev. 92 (2013), "every state constitution contains a provision on education. In addition, some thirty-one state courts [have] held that the state constitutional provision [guarantees] a right to a minimally adequate education." The authors also note that the Supreme Court, in *Papasan v. Allain*, 478 U.S. 265, 285 (1986), observed that it had "not yet definitively settled the question[ ] whether a minimally adequate education is a fundamental right." Noting that much constitutional adjudication is not originalist, they argue that application of "traditional" interpretive methodologies yields the conclusion that a right to education exists under the Due Process Clause because it is rooted "in the 'traditions and conscience' of

---

[96] **[Ct's Note]** [Although] my Brother White purports to reach this result by application of that lenient standard of mere rationality, [it] seems to be that the care with which he scrutinizes the practical effectiveness of the present local property tax as a device for affording local fiscal control reflects the application of a more stringent standard of [review].

[98] **[Ct's Note]** [Central] financing would leave in local hands the entire gamut of local educational policy-making—teachers, curriculum, school sites, the whole process of allocating resources among alternative educational objectives. [A] second possibility is the much discussed theory of district power equalization [under which] each school district would receive a fixed amount of revenue per pupil for any particular level of tax effort regardless of the level of local property tax base. * * *

[152] For criticism, see, e.g., Susan Bandes, *The Negative Constitution: A Critique*, 88 Mich.L.Rev. 2271 (1990).

the country, reflected in our laws and practices over the 150 years from the 1830s through the 1980s."

2. ***Wealth classifications.*** If *Rodriguez* involved a wealth classification, what exactly was the group that suffered from discrimination? Did the issue involve discriminatory impact rather than de jure discrimination? If so, did *Rodriguez* anticipate the approach of *Washington v. Davis* that in the absence of proof of discriminatory intent, discriminatory impact alone does not generally establish an equal protection violation?

Does *Rodriguez* hold that de facto discriminations against poor people are subject to strict scrutiny only if they involve a right "explicitly or implicitly guaranteed by the Constitution"? May *all* the prior "wealth discrimination" cases be explained on this basis? Or does the Court's fn. 60 suggest that a state payment requirement resulting in "an absolute deprivation" of an important (albeit not "fundamental") right requires strict scrutiny?

Consider Martha Minow, *In Brown's Wake: Legacies of America's Educational Landmark* 93 (2010): "[E]qualizing expenditures would not address the potentially greater needs in schools with high levels of low-income students, with high numbers of students learning English, and with many others with special needs."

3. ***Identifying "fundamental" rights.*** The Court decided *Rodriguez* in the same Term in which it decided *Roe v. Wade*, which is cited in fn. 76 as supporting the conclusion that the Court cannot recognize fundamental rights that are not "explicitly or implicitly guaranteed by the Constitution." How does the Court determine which rights are implicitly guaranteed? Consider Richard H. Fallon, Jr., *Implementing the Constitution* 50 (2001): "Scholars have [advanced] forceful arguments for constitutional rights to education, health care, and other practical prerequisites to the enjoyment of explicit constitutional guarantees. The argument for such rights takes much the same form as the argument supporting other recognized but not precisely delineated rights, such as the right to freedom of association. Although neither a right to freedom of association nor a right to effective education is expressly enumerated in the Constitution, effective speech and political activity often require association and collaboration, and they often require education as well. If we want to know why the Court has recognized a fundamental right to free association but not to effective public education, the explanation surely involves the Court's belief that the federal judiciary can sensibly enforce the former but not the latter. Implementing a right to effective public education would require assessments of educational quality that courts are poorly equipped to make, [and] a right to effective public education could draw the courts into general oversight of the government's budget process."

4. ***Fundamental rights and basic necessities.*** *Should* the Court recognize fundamental rights to governmentally provided goods and opportunities that are of fundamental practical importance?

(a)   Consider Frank I. Michelman, *On Protecting the Poor Through the Fourteenth Amendment*, 83 Harv.L.Rev. 7 (1969), arguing that the harms alleged in cases such as *Dandridge* and *Rodriguez* involve claims of "minimum protection" more than "equal protection": "[T]he only inequality turns out to be that some persons, less than all, are suffering from inability to satisfy certain 'basic' wants which presumably are felt by all alike; [if] we define the inequality that way, [the] injury consists more essentially of deprivation than of discrimination, [and the] cure accordingly lies more in provision than in equalization." Cf. Joshua E. Weishart, *Transcending Equality Versus Adequacy*, 66 Stan.L.Rev. 477 (2014) (noting a convergence of egalitarian and "adequacy" theories and arguing that "all children are owed an adequately equal and equally adequate education").

(b)   Consider Goodwin Liu, *Rethinking Constitutional Welfare Rights*, 61 Stan.L.Rev. 203 (2008): "Once a subject of intense interest in the courts and legal academy, the idea that our Constitution guarantees affirmative rights to social and economic welfare has for some time been out of fashion [but the idea should not be regarded as defunct. J]usticiable welfare rights should take the form of rights to concrete and specific goods. In order to render welfare rights persuasive and intelligible to the citizenry, the judge's task is not to discover and pronounce them from 'an objective and universal standpoint' but instead 'to interpret to one's fellow citizens the world of meanings that we share.' [This] interpretive approach [informed] *Brown v. Board of Education* [in which the Court] emphasized the need to 'consider public education in the light of its full development and its present place in American life throughout the Nation.' [If] the policy context continues to evolve in ways that give substance and institutional form to concepts of equity and adequacy, a well-documented claim of educational inequality or deprivation may one day prompt a court to revisit and distinguish the outdated norms of school finance and organization that prevailed in *Rodriguez*."

Compare Jeremy Waldron, *Socioeconomic Rights and Theories of Justice*, 48 San Diego L.Rev. 773 (2011): "It is an unhappy feature of the language of rights that it expresses demanding moral claims in a sort of line-item way, presenting each individual's case peremptorily, as though it brooked no denial, no balancing, and no compromise. [T]his applies as well to socioeconomic rights as to other rights claims. [The right starting point is a] general theory of justice [that] purports to take into account urgent claims of all kinds. [W]hat is required in the way of, say, education will emerge from a process in which both the competition between education and other demands on resources and the relation between education and other arrangements' impact on people's life prospects have been properly considered together. [T]oo often this dimension of argument about rights is rudimentary, and sophisticated argument about conflicts of rights is nonexistent. It seems best, therefore, to postpone talking about socioeconomic rights until we have considered how various socioeconomic claims fare in a theory of justice. [I]t is better to let socioeconomic rights emerge from a theory of justice than to try to defend them, line by line, on their own merits."

(c) Consider Martha C. Nussbaum, *Foreword*: *Constitutions and Capabilities: "Perception" Against Lofty Formalism*, 121 Harv.L.Rev. 4 (2007): "For several centuries, an approach to the foundation of basic political principles that draws its key insights from Aristotle and the ancient Greek and Roman Stoics has played a role in shaping European and American conceptions of the proper role of government, the purpose of constitution-making, and the nature of basic constitutional entitlements. This normative approach, the Capabilities Approach ('CA'), holds that a key task of a nation's constitution, and the legal tradition that interprets it, is to secure for all citizens the prerequisites of a life worthy of human dignity—a core group of 'capabilities'—in areas of central importance to human life. [The] United States has had an inconstant relation to the CA, protecting some entitlements very effectively, but shying away from the protection of entitlements in the area of what are usually called social and economic rights—that is, welfare rights. This reluctance (which distinguishes the United States from most of the nations of Europe and the developing world) is made more complicated by disputes over institutional competence and the proper scope of judicial action. Sometimes, when courts refuse to protect a given entitlement (refusing, for example, to give education the status of a fundamental right), the reason may be that judges do not believe that the existing constitution is plausibly interpreted to protect a certain entitlement. At other times, judges may simply oppose the recognition of such a right."

(d) Suppose the argument were convincing that fundamental rights to education and welfare are "implicit" in the Constitution. Would it necessarily follow that rights to education and welfare should be judicially enforceable to their "full conceptual limits"? Consider Lawrence Gene Sager, *Fair Measure: The Legal Status of Underenforced Constitutional Norms*, 91 Harv.L.Rev. 1212 (1978), arguing that there are some constitutional norms—including the equal protection norm at issue in *Rodriguez*—that the Court, for practical or institutional reasons, believes it is not competent to enforce fully; it lacks relevant expertise (for example, in school finance and management) and does not wish to federalize a broad area of traditionally local decision-making. The bite of Professor Sager's view lies in the proposition that political officials other than judges have an obligation—albeit a judicially unenforceable one—to "regulate their behavior by standards more severe than those imposed by the federal judiciary" in creating statutory entitlements.

5.   ***Standards of equal protection review.*** Is Marshall, J., correct that the Court "has applied a spectrum of standards" to assess claims under the Equal Protection Clause? Should it have pursued a balancing or totality-of-the-circumstances approach in *Rodriguez*? In *Dandridge*? Why didn't the Court do so? Or did it?

———

PLYLER v. DOE, 457 U.S. 202 (1982), per BRENNAN, J., held that a Texas statute (§ 21.031) denying free public education to illegal alien children violated equal protection: "Persuasive arguments support the view that a State may withhold its beneficence from those whose very presence within the United States is the product of their own unlawful conduct. [But the children] in these cases 'can affect neither their parents' conduct nor their own status.' Even if the State found it expedient to control the conduct of adults by acting against their children, legislation directing the onus of a parent's misconduct against his children does not comport with fundamental conceptions of justice. [Citing cases involving discrimination against illegitimate children, Sec. 4, III supra].

"We reject the claim that 'illegal aliens' are a 'suspect class.' [U]ndocumented status is not irrelevant to any proper legislative goal. Nor is [it] an absolutely immutable characteristic since it is the product of conscious, indeed unlawful, action. But § 21.031 [imposes] its discriminatory burden on the basis of a legal characteristic over which children can have little control. It is thus difficult to conceive of a rational justification for penalizing these children for their presence within the United States. * * *

"Public education is not a 'right' granted to individuals by the Constitution.[153] *Rodriguez.* But neither is it merely some governmental 'benefit' indistinguishable from other forms of social welfare legislation. Both the importance of education in maintaining our basic institutions, and the lasting impact of its deprivation on the life of the child, mark the distinction. [We] cannot ignore the significant social costs borne by our Nation when select groups are denied the means to absorb the values and skills upon which our social order rests.[20] [Thus], the discrimination contained in § 21.031 can hardly be considered rational unless it furthers some substantial goal of the State.

"[First,] appellants appear to suggest that the State may seek to protect the State from an influx of illegal immigrants. While a State might have an interest in mitigating the potentially harsh economic effects of sudden shifts in population, [t]here is no evidence in the record suggesting that illegal entrants impose any significant burden on the State's economy. To the contrary, the available evidence suggests that illegal aliens underutilize public services, while contributing their labor to the local economy and tax money to the State fisc. The dominant incentive for illegal entry [into] Texas is the availability of employment; few if any illegal immigrants come to this country [to] avail themselves of a free education. * * *

---

[153] Consider Michael Klarman, *An Interpretive History of Modern Equal Protection,* 90 Mich.L.Rev. 213 (1991): "Internal documents suggest that four of the five Justices in the *Plyler* majority were prepared forthrightly to hold education a fundamental interest for equal protection purposes. * * * Justice Powell, however, who supplied the fifth [vote], balked at the idea of 'creating another heretofore unidentified right.'"

[20] **[Ct's Note]** * * * Whatever the current status of these children, the courts below concluded that many will remain here permanently and that some indeterminate number will eventually become citizens. * * *

"Second, [appellants] suggest that undocumented children are appropriately singled out for exclusion because of the special burdens they impose on the State's ability to provide high quality public education. [In] terms of educational cost and need, however, undocumented children are 'basically indistinguishable' from legally resident alien children.

"Finally, appellants suggest that undocumented children are appropriately singled out because their unlawful presence within the United States renders them less likely than other children to remain within the boundaries of the State, and to put their education to productive social or political use within the State. Even assuming that such an interest is legitimate, it is an interest that is most difficult to quantify. The State has no assurance that any child, citizen or not, will employ the education provided by the State within the confines of the State's borders. In any event, the record is clear that many of the undocumented children disabled by this classification will remain in this country indefinitely, and that some will become lawful residents or citizens of the United States. It is difficult to understand precisely what the State hopes to achieve by promoting the creation and perpetuation of a subclass of illiterates within our boundaries, surely adding to the problems and costs of unemployment, welfare, and crime. It is thus clear that whatever savings might be achieved [are] wholly insubstantial in light of the costs involved to these children, the State, and the Nation."

BLACKMUN, J., who joined the Court's opinion, concurred: "I joined [the] Court in *Rodriguez,* and I continue to believe that it provides the appropriate model for resolving most equal protection disputes. [Classifications] involving the complete denial of education are in a sense unique, for they strike at the heart of equal protection values by involving the State in the creation of permanent class distinctions."

POWELL, J., who joined the Court's opinion, concurred "to emphasize the unique character of the case": "Although the analogy is not perfect, our holding today does find support in decisions of this Court with respect to the status of illegitimates. [Thus,] review in a case such as this is properly heightened. [These children] have been singled out for a lifelong penalty and stigma. A legislative classification that threatens the creation of an underclass of future citizens and residents cannot be reconciled with one of the fundamental purposes of the Fourteenth Amendment. In these unique circumstances, the Court properly may require that the State's interests be substantial and that the means bear a 'fair and substantial relation' to these interests.[3]"

---

[3] **[Ct's Note]** [I]n *Rodriguez* no group of children was singled out by the State and then penalized because of their parents' status. [Nor] was any group of children totally deprived of all education as in this case. If the resident children of illegal aliens were denied welfare assistance, made available by government to all other children who qualify, this also—in my opinion—would be an impermissible penalizing of children because of their parents' status.

BURGER, C.J., joined by White, Rehnquist and O'Connor, JJ., dissented: "[B]y patching together bits and pieces of what might be termed quasi-suspect-class and quasi-fundamental-rights analysis, the Court spins out a theory custom-tailored to the facts [and its] opinion rests on such a unique confluence of theories and rationales that it will likely stand for little beyond the results in these particular [cases].

"[Once] it is conceded—as the Court does—that illegal aliens are not a suspect class, and that education is not a fundamental right, our inquiry should focus on and be limited to whether the legislative classification at issue bears a rational relationship to a legitimate state purpose. [I]t simply is not 'irrational' for a State to conclude that it does not have the same responsibility to provide benefits for persons whose very presence in the State and this country is illegal as it does to provide for persons lawfully present."

For discussion of the Court's internal deliberations in *Plyler*, see Linda Greenhouse, *What Would Justice Powell Do? The "Alien Children" Case and the Meaning of Equal Protection*, 25 Const.Comment. 29 (2009).

CHAPTER 10

THE CONCEPT OF STATE ACTION

∎ ∎ ∎

1. INTRODUCTION

The "state action" doctrine has long established that, because of their language or history, most provisions of the Constitution that protect individual liberty—including those set forth in Art. 1, §§ 9 and 10, the Bill of Rights, and the Fourteenth and Fifteenth Amendments—impose restrictions or obligations only on government. The subject received its first extensive treatment in the CIVIL RIGHTS CASES, 109 U.S. 3 (1883), per BRADLEY, J., which held that neither the Thirteenth nor Fourteenth Amendments empowered Congress to pass the Civil Rights Act of 1875, making racial discrimination unlawful in public accommodations (inns, public conveyances, places of public amusement, etc.)—"and no other ground of authority for its passage being suggested, it must necessarily be declared void." Although the issue presented did not simply concern the authority granted the *Court* under § 1 of the Thirteenth and Fourteenth Amendments, but rather involved the scope of *Congress'* power under the final sections of these amendments to enforce their substantive provisions "by appropriate legislation" (a topic to be considered in detail in Ch. 11), the Court's discussion of "state action" remains the classic exposition.

The Court held that, under the Fourteenth Amendment, "individual invasion of individual rights is not the subject-matter of the amendment. [It] nullifies and makes void all state legislation, and state action of every kind, which impairs the privileges and immunities of citizens of the United States, or which injures them in life, liberty, or property without due process of law, or which denies to any of them the equal protection of the laws. [T]he last section of the amendment [does] not authorize Congress to create a code of municipal law for the regulation of private rights; but to provide modes of redress against the operation of state laws, and the action of state officers, executive or judicial, when these are subversive of the fundamental rights specified in the amendment. * * *

"An inspection of the [Civil Rights Act of 1875] shows that [it] proceeds ex directo to declare that certain acts committed by individuals shall be deemed offenses. [It] does not profess to be corrective of any constitutional wrong committed by the states; [it] applies equally to cases arising in states which have the justest laws respecting the personal rights of citizens, and whose authorities are ever ready to enforce such laws as to those which arise in states that may have violated the prohibition of the amendment. In other words, it steps into the domain of local jurisprudence, and lays down rules for the conduct of individuals in society towards each other. [C]ivil rights, such as are guaranteed by the Constitution against state aggression, cannot be impaired by the wrongful acts of individuals, unsupported by state authority in the shape of laws, customs, or judicial or executive proceedings. [An] individual cannot deprive a man of his right to vote, to hold property, to buy and to sell, to sue in the courts, or to be a witness or a juror; he may, by force or fraud, interfere with the enjoyment of the right in a particular case; [but] unless protected in these wrongful acts by some shield of state law or state authority, he cannot destroy or injure the right; he will only render himself amenable [to] the laws of the state where the wrongful acts are committed. [The] abrogation and denial of rights, for which the states alone were or could be responsible, was the great seminal and fundamental wrong which was intended to be remedied."

The Court recognized that the Thirteenth Amendment "is not a mere prohibition of state laws establishing or upholding slavery, but an absolute declaration that slavery or involuntary servitude shall not exist in any part of the United States [and] that the power vested in Congress to enforce the article by appropriate legislation, clothes Congress with power to pass all laws necessary and proper for abolishing all badges and incidents of slavery, in the United States. [T]he civil rights bill of 1866, passed in view of the Thirteenth Amendment, before the fourteenth was adopted, undertook to wipe out these burdens and disabilities, [namely,] the same right to make and enforce contracts, to sue, be parties, give evidence, and to inherit, purchase, lease, sell, and convey property, as is enjoyed by white citizens. [At] that time (in 1866) Congress did not assume, under the authority given by the Thirteenth Amendment, to adjust what may be called the social rights of men and races in the community; but only to declare and vindicate those fundamental rights which appertain to the essence of citizenship, and the enjoyment or deprivation of which constitutes the essential distinction between freedom and slavery.

"[It] would be running the slavery argument into the ground to make it apply to every act of discrimination which a person may see fit to make as to the guests he will entertain, or as to the people he will take into his coach or cab or car, or admit to his concert or theater, or deal with in other matters of intercourse or business. Innkeepers and public carriers, by the laws of all the states, so far as we are aware, are bound, to the extent of their facilities, to furnish proper accommodation to all unobjectionable persons who in good faith apply for them. If the laws themselves make any unjust discrimination, amenable to the probimition of the Fourteenth

Amendment, Congress has full power to afford a remedy under that amendment and in accordance with it."[1]

HARLAN, J., dissented: "Was it the purpose of the nation [by the Thirteenth Amendment] simply to destroy the institution [of slavery], and remit the race, theretofore held in bondage, to the several states for such protection, in their civil rights, necessarily growing out of freedom, as those states [choose] to provide? [S]ince slavery [rested] wholly upon the inferiority, as a race, of those held in bondage, their freedom necessarily involved immunity from, and protection against, all discrimination against them, because of their race, in respect of such civil rights as belong to freemen of other races. Congress, therefore, [may] enact laws of a direct and primary character, operating upon states, their officers and agents, and also upon, at least, such individuals and corporations as exercise public functions and wield power and authority under the state. * * *

"It remains now to inquire what are the legal rights of colored persons in respect of the accommodations * * * .

"1. As to public conveyances on land and water. [R]ailroads [are] none the less public highways because controlled and owned by private corporations; that it is a part of the function of government to make and maintain highways for the conveyance of the public; that no matter who is the agent, and what is the agency, the function performed is *that of the state* * * * .

"Such being the relations these corporations hold to the public, it would seem that the right of a colored person to use an improved public highway, upon the terms accorded to freemen of other races, is as fundamental in the state of freedom, established in this country, as are any of the rights which my brethren concede to be so far fundamental as to be deemed the essence of civil freedom.

"2. As to inns. [A] keeper of an inn is in the exercise of a quasi public employment. The law gives him special privileges, and he is charged with certain duties and responsibilities to the public [which] forbids him from

---

[1] In *Bell v. Maryland,* 378 U.S. 226 (1964), Goldberg, J., joined by Warren, C.J., and Douglas, J., examining the "historical evidence" in detail, concluded that the *Civil Rights Cases* were based on the assumption of the framers of the Fourteenth Amendment that "under state law, when the Negro's disability as a citizen was removed, he would be assured the same public civil rights that the law had guaranteed white persons," and that "the duties of the proprietors of places of public accommodation would remain as they had long been and that the States would now be affirmatively obligated to insure that these rights ran to Negro as well as white citizens." Black, J., joined by Harlan and White, JJ., disagreed. Cf. Tribe 2d ed. n. 14. See generally John P. Frank & Robert F. Munro, *The Original Understanding of "Equal Protection of the Laws,"* 1972 Wash.U.L.Q. 421. For the view that the *Civil Rights Cases* interpreted the Fourteenth Amendment to reflect the intent of its framers that the "prohibited state action is the *failure* to protect fundamental interests," see Alan R. Madry, *Private Accountability and the Fourteenth Amendment; State Action; Federalism and Congress,* 59 Mo.L.Rev. 499 (1994).

discriminating against any person asking admission as a guest on account of [race].

"3.   As to places of public amusement. [W]ithin the meaning of the act of 1875, [they] are such as are established and maintained under direct license of the law. [The] local government granting the license represents [the colored race] as well as all other races within its jurisdiction. A license from the public to establish a place of public amusement, imports, in law, equality of right, at such [places]."[2]

Turning to the Fourteenth Amendment, "the first clause of the first section—'all persons born or naturalized in the United States, and subject to the jurisdiction thereof, are citizens of the United States, and of the state wherein they reside'—is of a distinctly affirmative character. In its application to the colored race, previously liberated, it [granted] citizenship of the state in which they respectively resided. [Further], they were brought, by this supreme act of the nation, within the direct operation of that provision of the Constitution which declares that 'the citizens of each state shall be entitled to all privileges and immunities of citizens in the several states.' Article IV, § 2.

"The citizenship thus acquired [may be protected] by congressional legislation of a primary direct character; this, because the power of Congress is not restricted to the enforcement of prohibitions upon state laws or state action. It is, in terms distinct and positive, to enforce 'the *provisions of this article*' of amendment * * * *all* of the provisions,— affirmative and prohibitive * * * .

"But what was secured to colored citizens of the United States—as between them and their respective states—by the grant to them of state citizenship? With what rights, privileges, or immunities did this grant from the nation invest them? There is one, if there be no others—exemption from race discrimination in respect of any civil right belonging to citizens of the white race in the same state [by] the state, or its officers, or by individuals, or corporations exercising public functions or authority. [It] was perfectly well known that the great danger to the equal enjoyment by citizens of their rights, as citizens, was to be apprehended, not altogether from unfriendly

---

[2]   For general support of Harlan, J.'s Thirteenth Amendment view, see Arthur Kinoy, *The Constitutional Right of Negro Freedom,* 21 Rutg.L.Rev. 387 (1967). Although the Court has since ruled that the Thirteenth Amendment grants broad enforcement power to *Congress* (see Ch. 11, Sec. 2, I), the Court has confined its use of the amendment, absent congressional legislation, to holding state peonage laws invalid. See *Memphis v. Greene,* Ch. 9, Sec. 2, III. For application of the Thirteenth Amendment to the areas of "employment discrimination and affirmative action, jury selection and peremptory challenges, and capital crimes and the death penalty," and for a review of contemporary scholarship that applies the Thirteenth Amendment to "racial hate speech legislation, reproductive rights, and federal prosecution of racially motivated violence" and to "abused children, battered women, and women coerced into prostitution," see Douglas L. Colbert, *Liberating the Thirteenth Amendment,* 30 Harv.Civ.Rts.Civ.Lib.L.Rev. 1591 (1995).

state legislation, but from the hostile action of corporations and individuals in the states. * * *[3]

"But if it were conceded that the power of Congress could not be brought into activity until the rights specified in the act of 1875 had been abridged or denied by some state law or state action, I maintain that the decision of the court is erroneous. [In] every material sense applicable to the practical enforcement of the Fourteenth Amendment, railroad corporations, keepers of inns, and managers of places of public amusement are agents of the state, because amenable, in respect of their public duties and functions, to public regulation. * * * I agree that if one citizen chooses not to hold social intercourse with another, he is not and cannot be made amenable to the law for his conduct in that regard. [The] rights which Congress, by the act of 1875, endeavored to secure and protect are legal, not social, rights. The right, for instance, of a colored citizen to use the accommodations of a public highway upon the same terms as are permitted to white citizens is no more a social right than his right, under the law, to use the public streets of a city, or a town, or a turnpike road, or a public market, or a post-office, or his right to sit in a public building with others, of whatever race, for the purpose of hearing the political questions of the day discussed."

———

The basic doctrine of the *Civil Rights Cases*—that it is "state action" that is prohibited by the Fourteenth Amendment—has remained undisturbed. But the question of what constitutes "state action" has generated significant controversy. It is settled that the term comprehends statutes enacted by national, state and local legislative bodies and the official actions of all government officers.[4] The more difficult problems arise when the conduct of private individuals or groups is challenged as being unconstitutional. Although—as will be pointed out in the materials that follow (see, e.g., note 7 after *Shelley v. Kraemer,* Sec. 3 infra)—it has often been argued that the inquiries are misperceived, the questions that the Court has asked are whether the private actor (a) is performing a "government function," or (b) is sufficiently "involved" or "entwined" with, or "encouraged by" the state so as to be held to the state's constitutional obligations.

Until the 1970's, most cases involved racial discrimination (or, occasionally, denial of free speech). But, as will be detailed in Ch. 11, the

---

[3] See Ch. 11, fn. 10.

[4] On the question of what constitutes a "government" agency, *Lebron v. National R.R. Passenger Corp.,* 513 U.S. 374 (1995), per Scalia, J., held that Amtrak—created by a special federal statute as a corporation "for the furtherance of governmental objectives," with the President having "permanent authority to appoint a majority of the directors"—"is part of the government for purposes of the First Amendment," even though the authorizing statute disclaims this fact. O'Connor, J., dissented.

enactment and strengthening of federal (and state) civil rights statutes since the 1960s has largely mooted the problem of private racial discrimination. Further, with the growth under the Equal Protection Clause of the number of "suspect" and "quasi-suspect" classifications (see Ch. 9, Secs. 3 and 4) and the expansion under the Due Process Clause of the procedural rights that the state must afford persons before depriving them of liberty or property (see Ch. 6, Sec. 5), an increasing number of cases have involved attempts to require "private" adherence to these constitutional responsibilities.

2. "GOVERNMENT FUNCTION"

SMITH v. ALLWRIGHT, 321 U.S. 649 (1944), held that the Fifteenth Amendment forebade exclusion of African-Americans from primary elections conducted by the Democratic Party of Texas, pursuant to party resolution. The Court, per REED, J., reasoned that state delegation to a party of the power to fix the qualifications of primary elections is delegation of a state function that may make the party's action the action of the state. [The] right to participate in the choice of elected officials without restriction by any state because of race [is] not to be nullified by a state through casting its electoral process in a form which permits a private organization to practice racial discrimination in the election." Frankfurter, J., concurred in the result. Roberts, J., dissented.

———

TERRY v. ADAMS, 345 U.S. 461 (1953), involved the exclusion of African-Americans from the "pre-primary" elections of the Jaybird Democratic Association, an organization of all the white voters in a Texas county that was run like a regular political party and whose candidates since 1889 had nearly always run unopposed and won in the regular Democratic primary and the general election. The record showed "complete absence of any compliance with the state law or practice, or cooperation by or with the State." The Court held the election subject to the Fifteenth Amendment.

BLACK, J., joined by Douglas and Burton, JJ., found that "the admitted party purpose" was "to escape the Fifteenth Amendment's command." The "Amendment excludes social or business clubs" but "no election machinery could be sustained if its purpose or effect was to deny Negroes on account of their race an effective voice in the governmental affairs. [The] only election that has counted in this Texas county for more than fifty years has been that held by the Jaybirds. [For] a state to permit such a duplication of its election processes is to permit a flagrant abuse [of] the Fifteenth Amendment."

CLARK, J., joined by Vinson, C.J., and Reed and Jackson, JJ., described the Jaybirds as not merely a "private club" "organized to influence public candidacies or political action," but rather a "part and parcel of the Democratic Party, an organization existing under the auspices of Texas law. [W]hen a state structures its electoral apparatus in a form which devolves upon a political organization the uncontested choice of public officials, that organization itself, in whatever disguise, takes on those attributes of government which draw the Constitution's safeguards into play."[5]

MINTON, J., dissented: The Jaybird's activity "seems to differ very little from situations common in many other places [where] a candidate must obtain the approval of a religious group. [E]lections and other public business are influenced by all sorts of pressures from carefully organized groups. [Far] from the activities of these groups being properly labeled as state action, [they] are to be considered as attempts to influence or obtain state action."[6]

———

MARSH v. ALABAMA, 326 U.S. 501 (1946): A Jehovah's Witness sought "to distribute religious literature on the premises of a company-owned town contrary to the wishes of the town's management." The town, owned by a shipbuilding company, had "all the characteristics of any other American town." Appellant was warned that she could not distribute the literature and when she refused to leave the sidewalk of the town's "business block," a deputy sheriff, who was paid by the company to serve as the town's policeman, arrested her and she was convicted of trespass.

The Court, per BLACK, J., reversed: Under *Lovell v. Griffin,* Ch.7, Sec. 4, I, A, an ordinary municipality could not have barred appellant's activities, and the fact that "a single company had legal title to all the town" may not result in impairing "channels of communication" of its inhabitants or those persons passing through. "Ownership does not always mean absolute dominion. The more an owner, for his advantage, opens up his property for use by the public in general, the more do his rights become

---

[5] Frankfurter, J., stated that the "vital requirement is State responsibility" and found it as "a matter of practical politics": "[W]e may assume [those] charged by State law with the duty of assuring all eligible voters an opportunity to participate in the selection of candidates at the primary—the county election officials who are normally leaders in their communities—participate by voting in the Jaybird primary [and] condone [a] wholly successful effort to withdraw significance from the State-prescribed primary, to subvert the operation of what is formally the law of the State for primaries in this county."

[6] Are these examples distinguishable because "the only election that has counted in this Texas county for more than fifty years has been that held by the Jaybirds"? Because the Fifteenth Amendment outlawed discrimination *on the basis of race or color* with respect to the right to vote? Would it be "state action" if one of the major political parties imposed a registration fee in order to attend its convention to nominate candidates (assuming this would be barred by the 24th Amendment if done by a state)? See *Morse v. Republican Party of Virginia,* 517 U.S. 186 (1996). Suppose the party excluded African-Americans?

circumscribed by the statutory and constitutional rights of those who use it. Thus, the owners of privately held bridges, ferries, turnpikes and railroads may not operate them as freely as a farmer does his farm. Since these facilities are built and operated primarily to benefit the public and since their operation is essentially a public function, it is subject to state regulation." In balancing property rights against freedom of press and religion, "the latter occupy a preferred position" and the former do not "justify the State's permitting a corporation to govern a community of citizens so as to restrict their fundamental liberties and the enforcement of such restraint by the application of a State statute." Frankfurter, J., concurred. Jackson, J., did not participate.[7]

———

AMALGAMATED FOOD EMPLOYEES UNION v. LOGAN VALLEY PLAZA, 391 U.S. 308 (1968), per MARSHALL, J.—reasoning that a large privately owned shopping center was the "functional equivalent of the business district [in] *Marsh*"—held that it could not enjoin peaceful union picketing on its property against a store located in the shopping center. Black and White, JJ., dissented. Harlan, J., did not reach the merits.

Four years later, LLOYD CORP. v. TANNER, 407 U.S. 551 (1972), per POWELL, J., held that a shopping center's refusal to permit antiwar handbilling on its premises was not state action. *Logan Valley* was distinguished because the picketing there had been specifically directed to a store in the shopping center and the pickets had no other reasonable opportunity to reach their audience. In *Marsh,* "the company town was performing the full spectrum of municipal powers and stood in the shoes of the State." Marshall, J., joined by Douglas, Brennan and Stewart, JJ., dissented.

Finally, HUDGENS v. NLRB, 424 U.S. 507 (1976), per STEWART, J.—involving picketing of a store in a shopping center by a union with a grievance against the store's warehouse (located elsewhere)—overruled *Logan Valley*. [8] MARSHALL, J., joined by Brennan, J., dissented: "[T]he owner of the modern shopping center complex, by dedicating his property to public use as a business district, to some extent displaces the 'State' from control of historical First Amendment forums, and may acquire a virtual monopoly of places suitable for effective communication. The roadways, parking lots, and walkways of the modern shopping center may be as

———

[7]   Reed, J., joined by Vinson, C.J., and Burton, J., dissented, noting that "there was [no] objection to appellant's use of the nearby public highway and under our decisions she could rightfully have continued her activities [thirty feet parallel] from the spot she insisted upon using."

[8]   White, J., concurred in the result, finding that *Logan Valley* "does not cover the facts of this case [which concern] a warehouse not located on the center's premises. The picketing was thus not 'directly related in its purpose to the use to which the shopping center property was being put.'" Stevens, J., did not participate.

essential for effective speech as the streets and sidewalks in the municipal or company-owned town."[9]

———

EVANS v. NEWTON, 382 U.S. 296 (1966): In 1911, Senator A.O. Bacon devised land to Macon, Ga., to be used as a park for whites only. After *Pennsylvania v. Board of City Trusts,* 353 U.S. 230 (1957)—finding "state action" when public officials act as trustees under a private will requiring racial discrimination—the city permitted African-Americans to use the park. When Bacon's heirs sued to remove the city as trustee, the Georgia courts accepted the city's resignation and appointed private individuals as trustees so that the trust's purpose would not fail.

The Court, per DOUGLAS, J., reversed, reasoning, inter alia, that "the service rendered even by a private park of this character is municipal in nature, [more] like a fire department or police department [than like] golf clubs, social centers, luncheon clubs, schools such as Tuskegee was at least in origin, and other like organizations in the private sector. * * * Mass recreation through the use of parks is plainly in the public domain and state courts that aid private parties to perform that public function on a segregated basis implicate the State in conduct proscribed by the Fourteenth Amendment. Like the streets of the company town in *Marsh,* the elective process of *Terry,* and the transit system of *Pollak,*[10] the predominant character and purpose of this park are municipal." White, J., concurred on a separate ground.

HARLAN, J., joined by Stewart, J., dissented: In *Pollak,* "state action was explicitly premised on the close legal regulation of the company by the public utilities commission and the commission's approval of the particular action under attack."[11] *Marsh* is the "only Fourteenth Amendment case finding state action in the 'public function' performed by a technically private institution."

The failing of the majority's theory "can be shown by comparing [the] 'public function' of privately established schools with that of privately

---

[9] For a decision that the free speech and petition provisions of the California constitution require that "shopping center owners permit expressive activity on their property," see *Robins v. Pruneyard Shopping Center,* 153 Cal.Rptr. 854, 592 P.2d 341 (1979). For consideration under the National Labor Relations Act of the right of unions to engage in communicative activity on the employer's premises, see *Eastex, Inc. v. NLRB,* 437 U.S. 556 (1978); *Scott Hudgens,* 230 N.L.R.B. 414 (1977).

[10] In *Public Utilities Comm'n v. Pollak,* 343 U.S. 451 (1952), a city transit company subject to public regulation was considered in "sufficiently close relation" with the government as to cause the Court to determine whether the company's playing of radio programs on buses violated the Due Process Clause.

[11] Compare Thomas P. Lewis, *The Meaning of State Action,* 60 Colum.L.Rev. 1083 (1960), who argues that "voting is a purely governmental function. No private organization can decree that a majority vote shall entitle a candidate to public office, while most of the functions involved in [other] cases are those traditionally performed by private organizations or at least within their performance capabilities."

owned parks.[12] Like parks, the purpose schools serve is important to the public. Like parks, private control exists, but there is also a very strong tradition of public control in this field. Like parks, schools may be available to almost anyone of one race or religion but to no others. Like parks, there are normally alternatives for those shut out but there may also be inconveniences and disadvantages caused by the restriction.[13] Like parks, the extent of school intimacy varies greatly depending on the size and character of the institution."[14]

NOTES AND QUESTIONS

1. **Scope of decisions.** (a) In *Marsh,* could the shipbuilding company discriminate against African-Americans in hiring production workers? In hiring peace officers or street cleaners for the town? In *Smith,* could the Democratic Party refuse to hire Jewish secretaries? In *Terry,* could the Jaybirds refuse to hire African-American secretaries? May "private organizations" that perform "government functions" be subject to some constitutional limitations but not others?

(b) **Residential communities.** Homeowners own in common a 150 acre property with 12,000 houses for over 35,000 people. The homeowners association furnishes services to the homeowners, establishes rules for common property and individual units, and assesses fees for its operations. May the association refuse to rent to African-Americans? May refuse to permit residents (or nonresidents) to distribute political pamphlets on the privately owned "sidewalks" within the community? Of what relevance is the fact that the complex contains a "business district"? See Steven Siegel, *The Constitution and Private Government: Toward the Recognition of Constitutional Rights in Private Residential Communities Fifty Years After Marsh v. Alabama*, 6 Wm. & Mary Bill of Rts. J. 461 (1998).

2. **Statutory bargaining agents.** Suppose a labor union, the exclusive bargaining agent for all employees by authority of federal law, does not bargain as strenuously for black employees? May the union, although bargaining fairly for black employees, bar them from union membership?

3. **"Private" function.** (a) If the activities of private groups may become a "government function," may certain official activities of government ever be considered a "private function"? If a privately owned amusement park contracts with a state deputy sheriff, who is regularly employed by the park during off-duty hours as sheriff, to enforce its racial segregation policy, may the state convict African-Americans, whom the deputy arrests when they

---

[12] For further consideration of "private schools," see note 3 after *Moose Lodge v. Irvis,* Sec. 3 infra.

[13] Is there a "strong tradition" of private operation of parks in cities? Is it likely that, if Senator Bacon had not provided the park in *Evans,* the city would have provided its own?

[14] Black, J., agreed with the position also stated in Harlan, J.'s opinion that "the writ of certiorari should have been dismissed as improvidently granted."

For subsequent litigation in respect to this park, see *Evans v. Abney,* Sec. 3 infra.

refuse to leave the premises, for trespass? See *Griffin v. Maryland,* 378 U.S. 130 (1964).

(b) ***Scholarships.*** May a state university constitutionally award scholarships that the donor has designated for whites only? For persons of a particular religion? If the donor personally selects the scholarship recipients each year and racially discriminates, may the university constitutionally admit them?

JACKSON V. METROPOLITAN EDISON CO.
419 U.S. 345, 95 S.Ct. 449, 42 L.Ed.2d 477 (1974).

JUSTICE REHNQUIST delivered the opinion of the Court.

Respondent, "a heavily regulated private utility" with a state certificate of public convenience to sell electricity, terminated service to petitioner for nonpayment pursuant to a provision of its general tariff that had been filed with the Pennsylvania Public Utilities Commission. Petitioner claimed that termination "without adequate notice and a hearing before an impartial body" deprived her of property without due process of law.

[The] mere fact that a business is subject to state regulation does not by itself convert its action into that of the State for purposes of the Fourteenth Amendment. [It] may well be that acts of a heavily regulated utility with at least something of a governmentally protected monopoly will more readily be found to be "state" acts than will the acts of an entity lacking these characteristics. But the inquiry must be whether there is a sufficiently close nexus between the State and the challenged action of the regulated entity so that the action of the latter may be fairly treated as that of the State itself. * * *

Petitioner first argues that "state action" is present because of the monopoly status allegedly conferred upon Metropolitan by the State of Pennsylvania. As a factual matter, it may well be doubted that the State ever granted or guaranteed Metropolitan a monopoly.[8] But assuming that it had, this fact is not determinative * * * . In *Pollak,* [we] expressly disclaimed reliance on the monopoly status of the transit authority. * * *

Petitioner next urges that state action is present because respondent provides an essential public service [and] hence performs a "public function." We have, of course, found state action present in the exercise by a private entity of powers traditionally exclusively reserved to the State.

---

[8] **[Ct's Note]** [In] fact Metropolitan does face competition within portions of its service area from another private utility company and from municipal utility companies. [As] petitioner admits, such public utility companies are natural monopolies created by the economic forces of high threshold capital requirements and virtually unlimited economy of scale. Regulation was superimposed on such natural monopolies as a substitute for competition and not to eliminate it. * * *

See, e.g., *Terry* (election); *Marsh* (company town); *Evans* (municipal park). If we were dealing with the exercise by Metropolitan of some power delegated to it by the State which is traditionally associated with sovereignty, such as eminent domain, our case would be quite a different one. But while the Pennsylvania statute imposes an obligation to furnish service on regulated utilities, it imposes no such obligation on the State. * * *15

Perhaps in recognition of the fact that the supplying of utility service is not traditionally the exclusive prerogative of the State, petitioner urges a broad principle that all businesses "affected with the public interest" are state actors in all their actions.

We decline the invitation for reasons stated long ago in *Nebbia v. New York,* [Ch. 5, Sec. 3]. "It is clear that there is no closed class or category of businesses affected with a public interest. * * * " Doctors, optometrists, lawyers, Metropolitan, and Nebbia's upstate New York grocery selling a quart of milk are all in regulated businesses, providing arguably essential goods and services, "affected with a public interest." We do not believe that such a status converts their every action, absent more, into that of the State.

We also reject the notion that Metropolitan's termination is state action because the State "has specifically authorized and approved" the termination [practice.] 11 Although the Commission did hold hearings on portions of Metropolitan's general tariff relating to a general rate increase, it never even considered the reinsertion of this provision in the newly filed general tariff. * * *

The case most heavily relied on by petitioner is *Pollak.* There the Court dealt with the contention that Capital Transit's installation of a piped music system on its buses violated the First Amendment rights of the bus riders. [The] District of Columbia Public Utilities Commission, on its own motion, commenced an investigation of the effects of the piped music, and after a full hearing concluded [that] the practice "in fact, through the creation of better will among passengers, [tends] to improve the conditions under which the public ride." Here, on the other hand, there was no such imprimatur placed on the practice of Metropolitan about which petitioner complains. The nature of governmental regulation of private utilities is such that a utility may frequently be required by the state regulatory scheme to obtain approval for practices a business regulated in less detail

---

15 Query: If a state is not *constitutionally required* to perform a function—such as conducting elections, or providing "adequate medical care to those whom it has incarcerated," *West v. Atkins,* 487 U.S. 42 (1988)—why should it not be permitted to privatize that activity for reasons of economic efficiency, even though it may traditionally have been the states' exclusive prerogative, without making the delegee a state actor?

11 **[Ct's Note]** Petitioner does not contest the fact that Metropolitan had this right at common law before the advent of regulation.

would be free to institute without any approval from a regulatory body. Approval by a state utility commission of such a request from a regulated utility, where the commission has not put its own weight on the side of the proposed practice by ordering it, does not transmute a practice initiated by the utility and approved by the commission into "state action." At most, the Commission's failure to overturn this practice amounted to no more than a determination that a Pennsylvania utility was authorized to employ such a practice if it so desired. * * *

Affirmed.

JUSTICE MARSHALL, dissenting. * * *

Our state-action cases have repeatedly relied on several factors clearly presented by this case: a state-sanctioned monopoly; an extensive pattern of cooperation between the "private" entity and the State; and a service uniquely public in nature. [Even] when the Court has not found state action based solely on the State's conferral of a monopoly, it has suggested that the monopoly factor weighs heavily in determining whether constitutional obligations can be imposed on formally private entities. See *Steele v. Louisville & Nashville R. Co.* * * *

The majority distinguishes this line of cases with a cryptic assertion that public utility companies are "natural monopolies." [I]t is far from obvious that an electric company would not be subject to competition if the market were unimpeded by governmental restrictions. [The] State has chosen to forbid the high profit margins that might invite private competition or increase pressure for state ownership and operation of electric power facilities [, thus] to ensure that the company's service will be the functional equivalent of service provided by the State. * * *

I agree with the majority that it requires more than a finding that a particular business is "affected with the public interest" before constitutional burdens can be imposed on that business. But when the activity in question is of such public importance that the State invariably either provides the service itself or permits private companies to act as state surrogates in providing it, much more is involved than just a matter of public interest. In those cases, the State has determined that if private companies wish to enter the field, they will have to surrender many of the prerogatives normally associated with private enterprise and behave in many ways like a governmental body. [The] majority's analysis would seemingly apply as well to a company that refused to extend service to Negroes, welfare recipients, or any other group that the company preferred, for its own reasons, not to serve. I cannot believe that this Court would hold that the State's involvement with the utility company was not sufficient to impose upon the company an obligation to meet the constitutional mandate of nondiscrimination. [16] * * *

NOTES AND QUESTIONS

1. ***The "power" theory.*** (a) Of what significance should it be that Metropolitan was "the only public utility furnishing electricity to the city"? Is the "power" held by certain organizations today was conceived by the framers of the Fourteenth Amendment to be only within the possession of government? That such "power" creates such a threat to individual freedom that it should fall within the purview of state action? See Note, *State Action: Theories for Applying Constitutional Restrictions to Private Activity,* 74 Colum.L.Rev. 656 (1974).

Does (should) this "power theory" approach extend to holding the only ice skating rink in town to the state's constitutional responsibilities? Or is it limited to an activity that "is of such public importance that the State invariably either provides the service itself or permits private companies to act as state surrogates in providing it"?

(b) Does (should) the "power theory" depend on (active) state participation in conferring the status?

(i) ***Corporations.*** Consider Adolf A. Berle, *Constitutional Limitations on Corporate Activity—Protection of Personal Rights from Invasion Through Economic Power,* 100 U.Pa.L.Rev. 933, 942–43 (1952): "[A corporation should be] as subject to constitutional limitations which limit action as is the state itself. [The] preconditions of application are two: the undeniable fact that the corporation was created by the state and the existence of sufficient economic power concentrated in this vehicle to invade the constitutional right of an individual to a material degree. [The] modern state has set up, and come to rely on, the corporate system to carry out functions for which in modern life by community demand the government is held ultimately responsible." See also Arthur S. Miller, *The Constitutional Law of the "Security State,"* 10 Stan.L.Rev. 620 (1958). Does this rationale apply to *all* corporations? Should it be restricted to entities "created by the state"?

(ii) ***Private schools.*** Consider Glenn Abernathy, *Expansion of the State Action Concept Under the Fourteenth Amendment,* 43 Corn.L.Q. 375 (1958): "[T]he only purely privately operated functions which properly should be considered as governmental are those which are indispensable to the maintenance of democratic government. * * * Education is desirable and useful in a democratic system but it is not indispensable [in] the sense that access to the ballot and the processes of selecting public officials is." If the state closed all of its public schools, would that make private schools "indispensable to the maintenance of democratic government"? If so, would some (all) private schools

---

[16]   Brennan, J., dissented on procedural grounds. Douglas, J.'s dissent is omitted.

    For a decision finding state action under the California constitution when a privately owned utility discriminates in hiring, see *Gay Law Students Ass'n v. Pacific Telephone & Telegraph Co.,* 24 Cal.3d 458, 156 Cal.Rptr. 14, 595 P.2d 592 (1979).

be barred from racially (sexually, religiously) discriminating? Compare Jesse H. Choper, *Thoughts on State Action: The "Government Function" and "Power Theory" Approaches,* 1979 Wash.U.L.Q. 757: "[I]t is clear that the operation of elementary and secondary schools is not an enterprise that is 'traditionally *exclusively* reserved to the State.' [But] virtually all maintained at least one public elementary and secondary school unless, because of some peculiar development, the educational needs of the community's children were historically always met by a privately funded school. Such a school[is,] in effect, serving as a substitute for the conventional public school that the school district would otherwise provide. In this sense, it is performing a function 'traditionally *exclusively* reserved to the State.' "

(c) Does the "power theory" aid in analyzing the questions in this note? Might it be argued that a particular union has sufficient "power" in respect to job opportunities in the industry as to be constitutionally forbidden from racially discriminating among its members, but insufficient power over general job opportunities as to be constitutionally barred from using a religious test for its non-union employees? See Harry H. Wellington, *The Constitution, The Labor Union, and "Governmental Action,"* 70 Yale L.J. 345(1961). That the "state's duty to take preventive action [or the "state action" issue] varies with the magnitude of the discrimination and the consequent problem it creates"? Henry Friendly, *The Dartmouth College Case and the Public-Private Penumbra* 22 (1969). See generally Choper, note (b) (ii) supra; compare Gary C. Leedes, *State Action Limitations on Courts and Congressional Power,* 60 N.C.L.Rev. 747 (1981).[17]

2. ***Constitutional rights of "power holders."*** In CBS v. DEMOCRATIC NAT'L COMM., Ch. 7, Sec. 8, I—in which the FCC had ruled that a broadcaster is not required to accept editorial advertisements—some Justices addressed the question of whether the action of the broadcast licensee was "governmental action" for purposes of the First Amendment. BURGER, C.J., joined by Stewart and Rehnquist, JJ., concluded that it was not: "[T]he Commission has not fostered the licensee policy challenged here; it has simply declined to command particular action because it fell within the area of journalistic discretion. [Were] we to read the First Amendment to spell out governmental action in the circumstances presented here, few licensee decisions on the content of broadcasts or the processes of editorial evaluation would escape constitutional scrutiny. [That] would go far in practical effect to undermine nearly a half century of unmistakable congressional purpose to

---

[17] For the view that the state action doctrine may be justified by values of pluralism, see Maimon Schwarzschild, *Value Pluralism and the Constitution: In Defense of the State Action Doctrine,* 1988 Sup.Ct.Rev. 129. See also John Fee, *The Formal State Action Doctrine and Free Speech Analysis,* 83 N.C.L.Rev. 569(2005): "[T]he state action doctrine also affects the substance of constitutional law, even as applied to the government [because] courts are likely to interpret constitutional provisions in light of their understanding as to how broadly the rules they announce will apply. [Thus, if] government-owned places are the only locations to which the First Amendment public forum doctrine applies, it is even more crucial [to] jealously guard speech in this domain so there remain adequate avenues for public expression."

maintain—no matter how difficult the task—essentially private broadcast journalism held only broadly accountable to public interest standards."

BRENNAN, J., joined by Marshall, J., disagreed: "[T]he public nature of the airwaves, the governmentally created preferred status of broadcast licensees, the pervasive federal regulation of broadcast programming, and the Commission's specific approval of the challenged broadcaster policy combine in this case to bring the promulgation and enforcement of that policy within the orbit of constitutional imperatives. [Compared to *Pollak*], this case concerns not an incidental activity of a bus company but, rather, the primary activity of the regulated entities—communication.* * * 12"

3. STATE "INVOLVEMENT" OR "ENCOURAGEMENT" OR "ENTWINEMENT"

SHELLEY V. KRAEMER
334 U.S. 1, 68 S.Ct. 836, 92 L.Ed. 1161 (1948).

CHIEF JUSTICE VINSON delivered the opinion of the Court.

[In two cases from Missouri and Michigan, petitioners were African-Americans who had purchased houses from whites despite the fact that the properties were subject to restrictive covenants, signed by most property owners in the block, providing that for a specified time (in one case fifty years from 1911) the property would be sold only to Caucasians. Respondents, owners of other property subject to the covenants, sued to enjoin the buyers from taking possession and to divest them of title. The state courts granted the relief.]

Equality in the enjoyment of property rights was regarded by the framers of [the Fourteenth] Amendment as an essential pre-condition to the realization of other basic civil rights and liberties which the Amendment was intended to guarantee.[7] Thus, [42 U.S.C. § 1982] derived from § 1 of the Civil Rights Act of 1866 which was enacted by Congress while the Fourteenth Amendment was also under consideration, provides: "All citizens of the United States shall have the same right, in every State and Territory, as is enjoyed by white citizens thereof to inherit, purchase, lease, sell, hold, and convey real and personal property." * * *

It is likewise clear that restrictions on the right of occupancy of the sort sought to be created by the private agreements in these cases could not be squared with the requirements of the Fourteenth Amendment if

---

[12] **[Ct's Note]** [W]here, as here, the Government has implicated itself in the actions of an otherwise private individual, that individual must exercise his own rights with due regard for the First Amendment rights of others. In other words, an accommodation of competing rights is required, and "balancing" [is the result.]

[7] **[Ct's Note]** *Slaughter-House Cases* [Ch. 5, Sec. 1, III]. See Horace E. Flack, *The Adoption of the Fourteenth Amendment.*

imposed by state statute or local ordinance. [But here] the particular patterns of discrimination and the areas in which the restrictions are to operate, are determined, in the first instance, by the terms of agreements among private individuals. Participation of the State consists in the enforcement of the restrictions so defined. * * *

Since [the] *Civil Rights Cases,* the principle has become firmly embedded in our constitutional law that the action inhibited by the first section of the Fourteenth Amendment is only such action as may fairly be said to be that of the States. That Amendment erects no shield against merely private conduct, however discriminatory or wrongful. We conclude, therefore, that the restrictive agreements standing alone cannot be regarded as a violation of any rights guaranteed to petitioners by the Fourteenth Amendment. So long as the purposes of those agreements are effectuated by voluntary adherence to their terms, it would appear clear that there has been no action by the State and the provisions of the Amendment have not been violated.

But here [the] purposes of the agreements were secured only by judicial enforcement by state courts of the restrictive terms of the agreements. [That] the action of state courts and of judicial officers in their official capacities is to be regarded as action of the State within the meaning of the Fourteenth Amendment, is a proposition which has long been established. [In] the *Civil Rights Cases,* this Court pointed out that the Amendment makes void "state action of every kind" which is inconsistent with the guaranties therein contained, and extends to manifestations of "state authority in the shape of laws, customs, or judicial or executive proceedings." * * *

One of the earliest applications of the prohibitions contained in the Fourteenth Amendment to action of state judicial officials occurred in cases in which Negroes had been excluded from jury service. [These] cases demonstrate, also, the early recognition by this Court that state action in violation of the Amendment's provisions is equally repugnant to the constitutional commands whether directed by state statute or taken by a judicial official in the absence of statute. * * *

The action of state courts in imposing penalties or depriving parties of other substantive rights without providing adequate notice and opportunity to defend, has, of course, long been regarded as a denial of the due process of law guaranteed by the Fourteenth Amendment. In numerous cases, this Court has reversed criminal convictions in state courts for failure of those courts to provide the essential ingredients of a fair hearing. Thus it has been held that convictions obtained in state courts under the domination of a mob are void. Convictions obtained by coerced confessions, by the use of perjured testimony known by the prosecution to be such, or without the effective assistance of counsel, have also been held to be exertions of state authority in conflict with the fundamental rights protected by the Fourteenth Amendment.

But the examples of state judicial action which have been held by this Court to violate the Amendment's commands are not restricted to situations in which the judicial proceedings were found in some manner to be procedurally unfair. It has been recognized that the action of state courts in enforcing a substantive common-law rule formulated by those courts, may result in the denial of rights guaranteed by the Fourteenth Amendment. [Thus,] in *AFL v. Swing,* 1941 U.S. 321, enforcement by state courts of the common-law policy of the State, which resulted in the restraining of peaceful picketing, was held to be state action of the sort prohibited by the Amendment's guaranties of freedom of discussion. In *Cantwell v. Connecticut,* 1940, [Ch. 8, Sec. 2, I], a conviction in a state court of the common-law crime of breach of the peace was, under the circumstances of the case, found to be a violation of the Amendment's commands relating to freedom of religion. In *Bridges v. California,* 1941 U.S. 252, enforcement of the state's common-law rule relating to contempts by publication was held to be state action inconsistent with the prohibitions of the Fourteenth Amendment. * * *

We have no doubt that there has been state action in these cases in the full and complete sense of the phrase. The undisputed facts disclose that petitioners were willing purchasers of properties upon which they desired to establish homes. The owners of the properties were willing sellers; and contracts of sale were accordingly consummated. It is clear that but for the active intervention of the state courts, supported by the full panoply of state power, petitioners would have been free to occupy the properties in question without restraint.

These are not cases, as has been suggested, in which the States have merely abstained from action, leaving private individuals free to impose such discriminations as they see fit. Rather, these are cases in which the States have made available to such individuals the full coercive power of government to deny to petitioners, on the grounds of race or color, the enjoyment of property rights in premises which petitioners are willing and financially able to acquire and which the grantors are willing to sell. * * *

The enforcement of the restrictive agreements by the state courts in these cases was directed pursuant to the common-law policy of the States as formulated by those courts in earlier decisions. [The] judicial action in each case bears the clear and unmistakable imprimatur of the State. We have noted that previous decisions of this Court have established the proposition that judicial action is not immunized from the operation of the Fourteenth Amendment simply because it is taken pursuant to the state's common-law policy. Nor is the Amendment ineffective simply because the particular pattern of discrimination, which the State has enforced, was defined initially by the terms of a private agreement. * * * We have noted that freedom from discrimination by the States in the enjoyment of property rights was among the basic objectives sought to be effectuated by the framers of the Fourteenth Amendment. That such discrimination has occurred in these cases is clear. * * *

Respondents urge, however, that since the state courts stand ready to enforce restrictive covenants excluding white persons[,] enforcement of covenants excluding colored persons may not be deemed a denial of equal protection of the laws to the colored persons who are thereby affected. [But the] rights created by the first section of the Fourteenth Amendment are, by its terms, guaranteed to the individual. The rights established are personal rights. It is, therefore, no answer to these petitioners to say that the courts may also be induced to deny white persons rights of ownership and occupancy on grounds of race or color. Equal protection of the laws is not achieved through indiscriminate imposition of inequalities. * * *

Reversed.

JUSTICE REED, JUSTICE JACKSON, and JUSTICE RUTLEDGE took no part in the consideration or decision of these cases.[18]

NOTES AND QUESTIONS

1. *Authority of prior decisions.* Do the cases holding that "judicial action is state action" call for the result in *Shelley*? Consider Comment, *The Impact of Shelley v. Kraemer on the State Action Concept*, 44 Calif.L.Rev. 718 (1956): "In the cases exemplifying 'orthodox' judicial violation the prohibited activity [e.g., barring black jurors] was practiced by the judge himself. [But in *Shelley*] the discrimination originated with private persons." What about "convictions obtained under the domination of a mob"?

As to those cases (*Swing, Cantwell, Bridges*—as well as *N.Y. Times v. Sullivan*, Ch. 7, Sec. 1, II, B) involving "the action of state courts in enforcing a substantive common-law rule," consider Comment, 45 Mich.L.Rev. 733 (1947): "The common law is simply the policy of the state in certain of its aspects, [and] that policy as seen in respect to [*Shelley*] looks no further than to the protection of property and contract rights." Did the state policy in *Cantwell* look any further than to the protection of public tranquility? Did it, in *Bridges,* look any further than to the protection of the integrity of the court? For careful analysis, see William W. Van Alstyne, *Mr. Justice Black, Constitutional Review, and the Talisman of State Action*, 1965 Duke L.J. 219; Stephen Gardbaum, *The "Horizontal Effect" of Constitutional Rights*, 102 Mich. L.Rev. 387 (2003).

---

[18] For a history of the battle against restrictive covenants, see Clement E. Vose, *NAACP Strategy in the Covenant Cases,* 6 W.Res.L.Rev. 101 (1955).

Is *Shelley* different from these cases because it involves equal protection rather than due process? Because these other cases involve free speech? Should there be a distinction between civil suits and criminal prosecutions?

2.   *Zoning ordinances.* Is *Shelley* supportable because "so long as it is unconstitutional for a state to require racial segregation by zoning statutes [it] is equally unconstitutional for the state to bring it about by any other form of state action"? Dudley O. McGovney, *Racial Residential Segregation by State Court Enforcement of Restrictive Agreements, Covenants or Conditions in Deeds is Unconstitutional,* 33 Calif.L.Rev. 5 (1945). Is the source of the discrimination the same in both instances? Consider Carol Rose, *Shelley v. Kraemer,* in Property Stories 169 (Gerald Korngold & Andrew P. Morriss, eds., 2004): "[N]orms and customs may be so widespread and so powerful that they have the practical force of law. [A] widespread pattern of covenanted segregation effectively appropriated a governmental function and [used] the courts to enforce what was in effect racial zoning." See also fn. 26.

3.   BARROWS v. JACKSON, 346 U.S. 249 (1953), held that an action by a co-covenantor to recover damages from a property owner who sold to an African-American was barred by equal protection. Would this suit, like the one in *Shelley,* involve "the full coercive power of government to deny [on] grounds of race [the] enjoyment of property rights"? Would the suit in *Barrows* have the same effect as a suit to enjoin a white property owner from breaching the covenant? See *Hurd v. Hodge,* 334 U.S. 24 (1948).

4.   *Other devices.* After *Shelley* and *Barrows,* consider the validity of:

(a)   A deed conveying property on condition that if sold to an African-American it automatically reverts to the original grantor.

(i)   Suppose the grantor sues to evict the black purchaser? Suppose the grantor retakes possession and the black purchaser sues to evict? Might a court deny relief in the latter situation on the ground that it had "merely abstained from action, leaving private individuals free to impose such discrimination as they see fit"?

(ii)   Suppose a suit for declaratory judgment as to the validity of the reverter? If it were declared invalid, could it be said "that the restrictive agreements standing alone cannot be regarded as a violation of [the] Fourteenth Amendment"? If it were declared valid, could a court deny the original grantor's suit to enjoin the black purchaser's taking possession? See generally Arthur S. Miller, *Racial Discrimination and Private Schools,* 41 Minn.L.Rev. 245 (1957).

(b)   A will devising property on condition that if the beneficiary marries a non-Jewish person, the property goes to someone else. Suppose the beneficiary marries a Catholic and the remainderman sues for the property?

(c)   A child custody decree directing the father to pay private school tuition. Suppose the father refuses to pay because the school racially discriminates and the mother sues to enforce the decree.

5. ***The limits of Shelley.*** (a) Consider Comment, 44 Calif.L.Rev. at 733: "If obtaining court aid to carry out 'private' activity 'converts' such private action into 'state' action, then there could never be any private action in any practical sense. So entwined are our lives with the law that the logical result would be that almost *all* action, to be effective, must result in state action.

(b)   Evaluate the following analyses of *Shelley:*

(i) "Professor Louis Pollak, *Racial Discrimination and Judicial Integrity,* 108 U.Pa.L.Rev. 1, 13 (1959)] would apply *Shelley* to prevent the state from enforcing a discrimination by one who does not wish to discriminate;[19] but he would allow the state to give its support to willing discrimination. [This] raises a number of possible objections. [The Equal Protection] clause seems to be designed to protect the victim against discrimination, not to protect an unwilling 'actor' against being compelled to discriminate. [Moreover,] the distinction is offered as a definition of 'state action.' But whether the judgment of a court enforces a voluntary discrimination or compels a no-longer-voluntary discrimination, the discrimination is private in origin; in both cases it requires a court judgment to make the discrimination effective." Louis Henkin, *Shelley v. Kraemer: Notes for a Revised Opinion,* 110 U.Pa.L.Rev. 473 & n. 10 (1962).

Compare Harold W. Horowitz, *The Misleading Search for "State Action" Under the Fourteenth Amendment,* 30 So.Cal.L.Rev. 208 (1957): "There is involved here a question of the degree of effect of different forms of state action on a prospective Negro buyer's opportunity to purchase and use [land]. The state does not substantially deny the Negro that opportunity by *permitting* a private person to refuse to deal with him because of his race. This would be the situation where there was 'voluntary adherence' to the restrictive covenant by the landowner. But the state does to a far greater degree deny the Negro the opportunity to acquire land, because of his race, if it *compels* a landowner not to deal with the Negro. This is the situation where the state enforces the restrictive covenant after a landowner has decided not to adhere to it."

(ii)   Since restraints on alienation of property are presumptively void, being valid generally only if the court finds the restraint a reasonable one and consistent with public policy, Restatement, *Property* § 406 (1944 1st ed.), was there state action in *Shelley* because the court placed its imprimatur on a racially discriminatory restraint? Might it be argued that, due to this, the source of discrimination was public rather than private? See Jesse H. Choper, *Thoughts on State Action,* 1979 Wash.U.L.Q. 757.

(c)   Consider Comment, 44 Calif.L.Rev.: "It is submitted that the doctrine of judicial enforcement as interpreted by *Shelley* is applicable only when the

---

[19] See *Moose Lodge v. Irvis,* infra, for this application of *Shelley*—in the only opinion of the Court (apart from *Barrows v. Jackson*) that has relied on *Shelley* to find state action. Cf. also fn. 10 in *Flagg Bros. v. Brooks,* Sec. 4 infra, and note 1 thereafter.

court action abets private discrimination which in the absence of such judicial aid would be ineffective. [Where] the private activity, admitted in *Shelley* to be valid in itself, is already effective, it is not to be said that the court, recognizing or failing to abolish the activity, is itself an arm of the discrimination; the situation has remained the same, court action or no. It is only where the proponents of discrimination, unable to further their ends privately, seek court aid is the state itself causing discrimination under *Shelley*."

(i)   Suppose plaintiff is denied relief in a breach of contract suit against a cemetery for refusing to bury an African-American because the burial lot purchase contract was restricted to Caucasians? What result under *Shelley*? Under the above theory? Would denial of plaintiff's cause of action make the discrimination "effective"? If the body had already been interred, could the cemetery obtain the court's aid in removing it?

(ii) Suppose a landlord seeks the court's aid to evict a tenant whose defense is that the eviction is solely on the grounds of race (or religion, or speech)? Suppose the tenant seeks to restrain the landlord from recovering possession of the leased premises? If the tenant refuses to give up possession and is forcibly evicted by the landlord, what result in the tenant's suit for assault? Would a sensible rule produce different results in the above situations?

6.   ***Reconsideration of prior problems in light of Shelley.*** (a) *Evans v. Newton.* (a) When the state court accepted the city's resignation and appointed private trustees to carry out the testator's discriminatory intent, was this state action that abetted otherwise private discrimination? If the city had not resigned and the state court had granted the relief sought to remove the city as trustee, would this be enforcing discrimination by one who did not wish to discriminate in violation of the *Shelley* rule?

(b) On remand, after *Evans,* the Georgia courts interpreted Senator Bacon's will and held that "because the park's segregated, whites-only character was an essential and inseparable part of the testator's plan," the "cy pres doctrine to amend the terms of the will by striking the racial restrictions" was inapplicable; that, therefore, the trust failed and the trust property "by operation of law reverted to the heirs of Senator Bacon."

EVANS v. ABNEY, 396 U.S. 435 (1970), per BLACK, J., affirmed, finding that "the Georgia court had no alternative under its relevant trust laws, which are long standing and neutral with regard to race": "[T]here is not the slightest indication that any of the Georgia judges involved were motivated by racial animus or discriminatory intent of any sort in construing and enforcing Senator Bacon's will. Nor is there any indication that Senator Bacon in drawing up his will was persuaded or induced to include racial restrictions by the fact that such restrictions were permitted by the Georgia trust statutes." *Shelley* was "easily distinguishable" because here "the termination of the park was a loss shared equally by the white and Negro citizens of Macon."

BRENNAN, J., dissented: " [When] a public facility would remain open but for the constitutional command that it be operated on a nonsegregated basis, the closing of that facility conveys an unambiguous message of community involvement in racial discrimination": "First, there is state action whenever a State enters into an arrangement which creates a private right to compel or enforce the reversion of a public facility" and, here, "in accepting title to the park," city officials agreed to that "if the city should ever incur a constitutional obligation to desegregate the park." Second, "nothing in the record suggests that after our decision in *Evans v. Newton* the City of Macon retracted its previous willingness to manage Baconsfield on a nonsegregated basis, or that the white beneficiaries of Senator Bacon's generosity were unwilling to share it with Negroes, rather than have the park revert to his heirs." Thus, contrary to *Shelley,* "this is a case of a state court's enforcement of a racial restriction to prevent willing parties from dealing with one another." Douglas, J., also dissented. Marshall, J., did not participate.

(c) Was the Georgia courts' action a judicial choice between two incompatible terms of his will—"(1) to keep African Americans out of the park; and (2) to keep the land a park forever"—thus, state action placing its imprimatur on racial discrimination (see note 5(b)(ii) supra)?

7. ***The balancing approach.*** Is the ultimate solution in *Shelley,* and other cases, a balancing of *all* of the particular interests involved? Consider William W. Van Alstyne & Kenneth L. Karst, *State Action,* 14 Stan.L.Rev. 3 (1961): There has been "an attempt to discover or invent the *kind* of state connection which will satisfy the state action requirement. It is suggested, for example, that the state acts in the sense of the amendment when it coerces private discrimination, but not when it simply lends its aid to such racial discrimination as private individuals may choose to practice. [This analysis] perpetuates the untenable distinction between the state action requirement on the one hand and the balance of 'substantive' constitutional interests on the other. This [is] even more dangerous than the suggestion's other unfortunate aspect: its assumption that every private discrimination is invalid once the right formal state connection has been found."

Compare Henkin, note 5(b)(i) supra at 496: "There is [a] small area of liberty favored by the Constitution even over claims to equality. Rights of liberty and property, of privacy and voluntary association, must be balanced, in close cases, against the right not to have the state enforce discrimination against the victim. In the few instances in which the right to discriminate is protected or preferred by the Constitution, the state may enforce it."[20] Is it the contention that the inquiry is not whether state action is present but whether the state policy preference, expressed through its laws, between conflicting claims of individuals, denies equal protection?

---

[20] See also Charles L. Black, *"State Action," Equal Protection, and California's Proposition 14,* 81 Harv.L.Rev. 69 (1967); Frank S. Sengstock & Mary C. Sengstock, *Discrimination: A Constitutional Dilemma,* 9 Wm. & Mary L.Rev. 59 (1967).

See Harold W. Horowitz, *Fourteenth Amendment Aspects of Racial Discrimination in "Private" Housing,* 52 Calif.L.Rev. 1 (1964): "[State] law permitting a private person to discriminate, on racial grounds, against another private person in a specific fact situation requires consideration of various interdependent factors: the nature and degree of injury to the person discriminated against, the interest of the discriminator in being permitted to discriminate, and the interest of the discriminatee in having opportunity of access equal to that of other persons. [If] there is extensive state participation and involvement related to the activities of the discriminator, it is more likely that those activities will be public in nature, with consequent public indignity and humiliation suffered by the person discriminated against, and more likely that denial of access to those activities will be of some significance to the discriminatee. [When] there is governmental assistance to the discriminator in carrying on his activities, and the assistance is being provided to further the purposes of a governmental program designed to provide benefits for the public or a permissible segment of the public, the effect of the discrimination is to deny to the discriminatee the opportunity to have equal opportunity of access to the benefits of the governmental program."[21]

Compare Choper, note 5(b)(ii) supra: "Although [the Fourteenth Amendment's] major purpose was to augment the authority of the national government to secure certain constitutional rights, its primary thrust was to accomplish this goal by outlawing deprivations of these rights by state governments and their legal structures rather than by the impact of private choice. By effectively obliterating the distinction between state action and private action, [the balancing approaches] eviscerate the Fourteenth Amendment's restriction on the authority of the national government vis-à-vis the states regarding the regulation of the myriad relationships that occur between one individual and another. [A]t the initiative of any litigant who is offended by another person's behavior, these theories would subject to the scrutiny of federal judges, under substantive constitutional standards customarily developed for measuring the actions of government, all sorts of private conduct that because of political constraints and collective good sense would probably never be mandated by law. Further, by permitting private actors to violate constitutional norms when they have a constitutionally protected liberty interest to do so, these theories would delegate to federal judges the power to implement the vague mandate of the Due Process Clause in speaking the final word about the validity of virtually all transactions between individuals. In doing so, the national judiciary would be required to determine whether private conduct was constitutionally immune from government control even though, because of general political sensitivity to

---

[21] For other discussions of a balancing approach, see Robert J. Glennon & John E. Nowak, *A Functional Analysis of the Fourteenth Amendment "State Action" Requirement,* 1976 Sup.Ct.Rev. 221; Thomas G. Quinn, *State Action: A Pathology and a Proposed Cure,* 64 Calif.L.Rev. 146 (1976); Anthony Thompson, *Piercing the Veil of State Action: The Revisionist Theory and a Mythical Application to Self-Help Repossession.* 1977 Wis.L.Rev. 1; Arval A. Morris & L.A. Scot Powe, Jr., *Constitutional & Statutory Rights to Open Housing,* 44 Wash.L.Rev. 1–56 (1968); David Haber, *Notes on the Limits of Shelley v. Kraemer,* 18 Rutgers L.Rev. 811 (1964).

individual autonomy, such private conduct probably would never be regulated by the state." See also Thomas P. Lewis, *The Role of Law in Regulating Discrimination in Places of Public Accommodation,* 13 Buf.L.Rev. 402 (1964).[22]

8. *"Sit-in" cases.*[23] (a) In PETERSON v. GREENVILLE, 373 U.S. 244 (1963), an ordinance forebade restaurants to seat whites and blacks together. The Court, per WARREN, C.J., reversed trespass convictions of black youths who, when denied service at a lunch counter, refused to leave: "[T]hese convictions cannot stand, even assuming [that] the manager would have acted as he did independently of the existence of the ordinance. [When] a state agency passes a law compelling persons to discriminate [such] a palpable violation of the Fourteenth Amendment cannot be saved by attempting to separate the mental urges of the discriminators."[24] Douglas, J., concurred.[25] HARLAN, J., noting "a clash of competing constitutional claims of a high order: liberty and equality," would have "the issue of state action" turn on the "question of fact" whether the restaurant "might have preferred for reasons entirely of its own not to serve meals to Negroes along with whites, [or] whether the ordinance played some part in [the] decision to segregate."[26]

(b) In BELL v. MARYLAND, 378 U.S. 226 (1964), GOLDBERG, J., joined by Warren, C.J., and Douglas, J., relying on the historical view in fn. 1 and cited *Marsh, Shelley, Terry* and *Barrows* for the point that "a State, obligated

---

[22] For a recent review and evaluation of many scholarly efforts to rationalize the result in *Shelley,* see Mark D. Rosen, *Was* Shelley v. Kraemer *Incorrectly Decided? Some New Answers,* 95 Calif. L. Rev. 451 (2007); Erwin Chemerinsky, *Rethinking State Action,* 80 Nw.U.L.Rev. 503 (1985); William P. Marshall, *Diluting Constitutional Rights: Rethinking "Rethinking State Action,"* 80 Nw.U.L.Rev. 558 (1985); Erwin Chemerinsky, *More Is Not Less: A Rejoinder to Professor Marshall,* 80 Nw.U.L.Rev. 571 (1985).

[23] In the early 1960s, the Court—employing a variety of doctrines, but never relying on *Shelley*—reversed a long series of trespass convictions of "sit-in" demonstrators who were protesting racial discrimination by restaurants and other businesses. The Civil Rights Act of 1964 (Ch. 2, Sec. 2, III) largely mooted the constitutional problem of equal rights in public accommodations.

[24] See also *Lombard v. Louisiana,* 373 U.S. 267 (1963) (statements by city officials that sit-ins "would not be permitted" had "as much coercive effect as an ordinance"); *Robinson v. Florida,* 378 U.S. 153 (1964) (state health regulations, requiring racially separate toilets in restaurants, impose "burdens bound to discourage the serving of the two races together").

Query: If a statute requires private colleges to enact regulations for maintenance of order on campus, must such a college's procedures for dismissal of students comport with procedural due process?

[25] See also Douglas, J.'s view that "state policy may be as effectively expressed in *customs* as in formal legislative, executive, or judicial action," *Garner v. Louisiana,* 368 U.S. 157 (1961) (concurring opinion). Cf. Kenneth L. Karst & William W. Van Alstyne, *Sit-Ins and State Action— Mr. Justice Douglas Concurring,* 14 Stan.L.Rev. 762 (1962); and Brennan, J.'s view that *Peterson, Lombard,* and *Robinson* "together hold that a state policy of discouraging privately chosen integration or encouraging privately chosen segregation, even though the policy is expressed in a form nondiscriminatory on its face, is unconstitutional and taints the privately chosen segregation it seeks to bring about," *Adickes v. S.H. Kress & Co.,* 398 U.S. 144 (1970) (separate opinion). See further, note 2 after *Reitman v. Mulkey,* infra.

[26] Consider Thomas P. Lewis, *The Sit-In Cases: Great Expectations,* 1963 Sup.Ct.Rev. 101: "When only the proprietor can know what his 'mental urges' are, and when even he might find difficulty in separating them, judicial review will be more effective for the mass of cases [if] the Court by the announcement of its rule makes it as certain as it can that proprietors and officials alike appreciate the precise status of segregation laws."

under the Fourteenth Amendment to maintain a system of law in which Negroes are not denied protection in their claim to be treated as equal members of the community, may not use its criminal trespass laws to frustrate it. [Nor may] a State frustrate this right by legitimating a proprietor's attempt at self-help."[27]

BLACK, J., joined by Harlan and White, JJ., dissented: Reliance on *Shelley* was "misplaced" because it established only these propositions: "(1) When an owner of property is willing to sell and a would-be purchaser is willing to buy, then the Civil Rights Act of 1866, which gives all persons the same right to 'inherit, lease, sell, hold, and convey' property, prohibits a State, whether through its legislature, executive, or judiciary, from preventing the sale on the grounds of the race or color of one of the parties. * * * (2) Once a person has become a property owner, then he [may] sell his property to whom he pleases and admit to that property whom he will; so long as *both* parties are willing parties, then the principles stated in *Buchanan v. Warley,* 245 U.S. 60 (1917) and *Shelley* protect this right. But equally, when one party is unwilling, as when the property owner chooses *not* to sell to a particular person or *not* to admit that person, [then] he is entitled to rely on the guarantee of due process of law [to] protect his free use and enjoyment of property and to know that only by valid legislation, passed pursuant to some constitutional grant of power, can anyone disturb this free use."

REITMAN V. MULKEY
387 U.S. 369, 87 S.Ct. 1627, 18 L.Ed.2d 830 (1967).

JUSTICE WHITE delivered the opinion of the Court.

[Section 26 of the California constitution], an initiated measure submitted to the people [in] a statewide ballot in 1964, provides in part as follows: "Neither the State nor any subdivision or agency thereof shall deny [the] right of any person [to] decline to sell, lease or rent such property to such person or persons as he, in his absolute discretion, chooses." [Respondents sued under California's [fair housing act] alleging that petitioners had refused to rent them an apartment solely on account of their race. [Petitioners contended that the statute violated § 26. The California Supreme Court held that § 26] was invalid as denying [equal protection].

[T]he court conceded that the State was permitted a neutral position with respect to private racial discriminations and that the State was not bound by the Federal Constitution to forbid them. But [the court reasoned] that a prohibited state involvement could be found "even where the state can be charged with only encouraging," rather than commanding

---

[27] See also Souter, J., dissenting in *Bray v. Alexandria Women's Health Clinic,* 506 U.S. 263 (1993): "[G]overnment enforcement of private segregation by use of a state trespass law, rather than 'securing to all persons [the] equal protection of the laws,' itself amounted to an unconstitutional act in violation of the Equal Protection Clause. [Cf.] *Shelley.*"

discrimination. [It] did not read [the] Fourteenth Amendment as establishing a rule that a State may never put in statutory form an existing policy of neutrality with respect to private discriminations. [It] dealt with § 26 as though it expressly authorized and constitutionalized the private right to discriminate [and] the court assessed the ultimate impact of § 26 in the California environment and concluded that the section would encourage and significantly involve the State in private racial discrimination contrary to the Fourteenth Amendment. [Here] the California court, armed as it was with the knowledge of the facts and circumstances concerning the passage and potential impact of § 26, and familiar with the milieu in which that provision would operate, has determined that the provision would involve the State in private racial discriminations to an unconstitutional degree. We accept this holding of the California court. * * * .28

JUSTICE HARLAN, whom JUSTICE BLACK, JUSTICE CLARK, and JUSTICE STEWART join, dissenting.

[A]ll that has happened is that California has effected a pro tanto repeal of its prior statutes forbidding private discrimination. This runs no more afoul of the Fourteenth Amendment than would have California's failure to pass any such antidiscrimination statutes in the first instance. The fact that such repeal was also accompanied by a constitutional prohibition against future enactment of such laws [cannot] well be thought to affect, from a federal constitutional standpoint, the validity of what California has done. [§ 26] is neutral on its face, and it is only by in effect asserting that this requirement of passive official neutrality is camouflage that the Court is able to reach its conclusion. [The] Court declares that the California court "held the purpose and intent of § 26 was to authorize private racial discriminations in the housing market," but there is no supporting fact in the record for this characterization. [But this appears] to state only a truism: people who want to discriminate but were previously forbidden to do so by state law are now left free because the State has chosen to have no law on the subject at all. Obviously whenever there is a change in the law it will have resulted from the concerted activity of those who desire the change, and its enactment will allow those supporting the legislation to pursue their private goals.

* * * . Under this theory "state action" in the form of laws that do nothing more than passively permit private discrimination could be said to tinge *all* private discrimination with the taint of unconstitutional state encouragement. * * *

---

28 Douglas, J., joined the Court's opinion, adding that "we deal here with a problem in the realm of zoning, similar to the one we had in *Shelley*. [When] the state leaves [the zoning] function to private agencies or institutions [including real estate brokers who are state licensees], it suffers a governmental function to be performed under private auspices in a way the State itself may not act. The present case is therefore kin to *Terry*."

NOTES AND QUESTIONS

1. ***Court's rationale.*** (a) What was the specific basis for § 26's invalidity? Was it that it made it much more difficult for minorities to get governmental antidiscrimination help? Would this call for the same result even if California had never enacted anti-discrimination laws? Suppose a state provides that *all* legislation requires approval by 2/3 of the voters? All legislation having *anything* to do with the sale and purchase of real and personal property? Was § 26 a less "neutral provision"? Sufficiently "nonneutral"? Was *this* the thrust of the opinion? If so, does *Reitman* hold that racial discrimination in housing by private individuals in California is "state action"? See also Ch. 9, Sec. 2, V.

(b) Or did the Court rest on the finding (whose finding?) that § 26, given "the milieu in which that provision would operate," "would involve the State in private racial discriminations to an unconstitutional degree"? If so, could "mere repeal of existing statutes" so operate? Failure to enact a proposed antidiscrimination law? The mere absence of an antidiscrimination law? See Archibald Cox, *The Warren Court* 45 (1968); Charles L. Black, *"State Action," Equal Protection, and California's Proposition 14,* 81 Harv.L.Rev. 69 (1967); Philip B. Kurland, *Egalitarianism and the Warren Court,* 68 Mich. 629 (1970); Kenneth L. Karst & Harold W. Horowitz, *Reitman v. Mulkey: A Telophase of Substantive Equal Protection,* 1967 Sup.Ct.Rev. 39.

2. ***State "encouragement" or "authorization."*** (a) To what extent does *Reitman* establish the principle that state law which *encourages* (or *authorizes*) private conduct results in "state action"? Is this the basis for Brennan, J.'s view in *Adickes*? What result if "a state passed a statute which provided that individuals shall have the legal right to engage in racial discrimination in their own homes"? Jerre Williams, *The Twilight of State Action,* 41 Texas L.Rev. 347 (1963). Consider William M. Burke & David J. Reber, *State Action, Congressional Power and Creditors' Rights: An Essay on the Fourteenth Amendment,* 46 So.Cal.L.Rev. 1003 (1973): "California statutory [or judicial] law authorizes [the] use of force in self-defense; the disposition of real and personal property; [the] creation of a contractual relationship; [the] execution of a will; the formation of a corporation [etc.]. If state authority or encouragement is a valid state action test, then all of the above forms of private conduct would present Fourteenth Amendment equal protection and due process problems. [It] is almost impossible to consider any form of activity that is not somehow authorized by state [law. As] long as the law is permissive in nature and leaves the initial decision to take the action entirely within the realm of private choice, neither the state nor the individual should be held constitutionally responsible. [Further], constitutional significance should not attach to such extraneous considerations as whether the law restates a long-standing law, clarifies an existing law, changes the law, creates entirely new law or repeals existing law." Accord, Lillian BeVier & John Harrison, *The State Action Principle and Its Critics*, 96 Va. L. Rev. 1767 (2010): The principle "rests on the thesis that private individuals are

principals, entitled to act to pursue their own interests, whereas government decisionmakers are agents, whose function is to further the interests of the citizens."

See also Harold W. Horowitz & Kenneth L. Karst, *The California Supreme Court and State Action Under the Fourteenth Amendment: The Leader Beclouds the Issue,* 21 UCLA L.Rev. 1421 (1974).

(b) The "state 'encouragement' or 'authorization' " issue is considered further in *Flagg Bros. v. Brooks,* Sec. 5 infra.

3. ***Repeal of discriminatory legislation.*** Recall *Lombard, Peterson* and *Robinson.* Suppose all official pronouncements *requiring* discrimination are repealed or retracted? Is subsequent "private" discrimination [in] matters previously covered by official pronouncements "state action"? Is the state "significantly involved" because its repeals have now made "private discriminations legally possible"? "Authorized" and "encouraged" discrimination? Or is this "mere repeal of existing statutes"? Is discrimination more "authorized and encouraged" by repeal of laws requiring discrimination or by repeal of laws forbidding it?

MOOSE LODGE V. IRVIS
407 U.S. 163, 92 S.Ct. 1965, 32 L.Ed.2d 627 (1972).

JUSTICE REHNQUIST delivered the opinion of the Court.

Appellee Irvis, a Negro, [who] was refused service [as the guest of a member] by appellant Moose Lodge, [claimed] that because the Pennsylvania liquor board had issued appellant Moose Lodge a private club license that authorized the sale of alcoholic beverages on its premises, the refusal of service to him was "state action." * * *

While the principle is easily stated, the question of whether particular discriminatory conduct is private, on the one hand, or amounts to "state action," on the other hand, frequently admits of no easy answer. "Only by sifting facts and weighing circumstances can the non-obvious involvement of the State in private conduct be attributed its true significance." *Burton v. Wilmington Parking Authority,* 365 U.S. 715 (1961).

[*Burton* held] that a private restaurant owner who refused service because of a customer's race violated the Fourteenth Amendment, where the restaurant was located in a building owned by a state-created parking authority and leased from the authority. The Court, after a comprehensive review of the relationship between the lessee and the parking authority concluded that the latter had "so far insinuated itself into a position of interdependence with Eagle [the restaurant owner] that it must be recognized as a joint participant in the challenged activity, which, on that account, cannot be considered to have been so 'purely private' as to fall without the scope of the Fourteenth Amendment." * * *

In *Burton,* the Court's full discussion of the facts in its opinion indicates the significant differences between that case and this: "The land and building were publicly owned.[29] As an entity, the building was dedicated to 'public uses' in performance of the Authority's 'essential governmental functions.'[30] The costs of land acquisition, construction, and maintenance are defrayed entirely from donations by the City of Wilmington, from loans and revenue bonds and from the proceeds of rentals and parking services out of which the loans and bonds were payable. Assuming that the distinction would be significant, the commercially leased areas were not surplus state property, but constituted a physically and financially integral and, indeed, indispensable part of the State's plan to operate its project as a self-sustaining unit.[31] Upkeep and maintenance of the building, including necessary repairs, were responsibilities of the Authority and were payable out of public funds. It cannot be doubted that the peculiar relationship of the restaurant to the parking facility in which it is located confers on each an incidental variety of mutual benefits. Guests of the restaurant are afforded a convenient place to park their automobiles, even if they cannot enter the restaurant directly from the parking area. Similarly, its convenience for diners may well provide additional demand for the Authority's parking facilities.[32] Should any improvements effected in the leasehold by Eagle become part of the realty, there is no possibility of increased taxes being passed on to it since the fee is held by a tax-exempt government agency. Neither can it be ignored, especially in view of Eagle's affirmative allegation that for it to serve Negroes would injure its business, that profits earned by discrimination not only contribute to, but also are indispensable elements in, the financial success of a governmental agency."[33]

---

[29] If the space has been leased to a law firm, could it constitutionally discriminate among its clients?

[30] If the Authority had municipal immunity from tort liability, is Eagle liable for a customer's food poisoning?

[31] "Other portions of the structure were leased to other tenants, including a bookstore, a retail jeweler, and a food store. Upon completion of the building, the Authority located at appropriate places thereon official signs indicating the public character of the building, and flew from mastheads on the roof both the state and national flags." *Burton.* Query: If Wilmington, instead of including rental space in the parking building, had relied on rental income from other of its properties located throughout the city to help finance the parking facility, could lessees of these properties refuse to do business with African-Americans?

[32] Suppose Eagle were located in a private building immediately adjacent to the public parking building?

[33] *Burton* added: "It is irony amounting to grave injustice that in one part of a single building, erected and maintained with public funds by an agency of the State to serve a public purpose, all persons have equal rights, while in another portion, also serving the public, a Negro is a second-class citizen [but] at the same time fully enjoys equal access to nearby restaurants in wholly privately owned buildings. [I]n its lease with Eagle the Authority could have affirmatively required Eagle to discharge the responsibilities under the Fourteenth Amendment imposed upon the private enterprise as a consequence of state participation. But no State may effectively abdicate its responsibilities by either ignoring them or by merely failing to discharge them whatever the motive may be." Query: If the state sells surplus property without requiring its nondiscriminatory use because such a requirement would bring the city a lower price, may the purchaser

Here there is nothing approaching the symbiotic relationship between lessor and lessee that was present in [*Burton*]. Moose Lodge quite ostentatiously proclaims the fact that it is not open to the public at large. Nor is it located and operated in such surroundings that although private in name, it discharges a function or performs a service that would otherwise in all likelihood be performed by the State. In short, while Eagle was a public restaurant in a public building, Moose Lodge is a private social club in a private building.

With the exception hereafter noted, the Pennsylvania Liquor Control Board plays absolutely no part in establishing or enforcing the membership or guest policies of the club which it licenses to serve liquor.[3] [The] only effect that the state licensing of Moose Lodge to serve liquor can be said to have [is] that for some purposes club licenses are counted in the maximum number of licenses which may be issued in a given municipality. * * *

The District Court was at pains to [note that] an applicant for a club license must make such physical alterations in its premises as the board may require, must file a list of the names and addresses of its members and employees, and must keep extensive financial records. The board is granted the right to inspect the licensed premises at any time * * * .

However detailed this type of regulation may be in some particulars, it cannot be said to in any way foster or encourage racial discrimination. Nor can it be said to make the State in any realistic sense a partner or even a joint venturer in the club's enterprise. The limited effect of the prohibition against obtaining additional club licenses when the maximum number of retail licenses allotted to a municipality has been issued, when considered together with the availability of liquor from hotel, restaurant, and retail licensees falls far short of conferring upon club licensees a monopoly in the dispensing of liquor * * * . We therefore hold that, with the exception hereafter noted, the operation of the regulatory scheme enforced by the Pennsylvania Liquor Control Board does not sufficiently implicate the State in the discriminatory guest policies of Moose Lodge * * * .

The District Court found that [Regulations § 113.09] of the Liquor Control Board adopted pursuant to statute affirmatively require that "every club licensee shall adhere to all the provisions of its constitution and by-laws." Appellant argues that the purpose of this provision "is purely and

---

constitutionally discriminate? If such a requirement were financially irrelevant but the state neglected to include it, may the buyer discriminate?

Harlan, J., joined by Whittaker, J., dissented: "The Court's opinion, by a process of first undiscriminatingly throwing together various factual bits and pieces and then undermining the resulting structure by an equally vague disclaimer, seems to me to leave completely at sea just what it is in this record that satisfies the requirement of 'state action.' " See generally Thomas P. Lewis, *Burton v. Wilmington Parking Authority—A Case Without Precedent,* 61 Colum.L.Rev. 1458 (1961).

[3]   **[Ct's Note]** Unlike the situation in *Pollak,* where the regulatory agency had affirmatively approved the practice of the regulated entity after full investigation * * * .

simply and plainly the prevention of subterfuge." [There] can be no doubt that the label "private club" can and has been used to evade both regulations of State and local liquor authorities, and statutes requiring places of public accommodation to serve all persons without regard to race, color, religion, or national origin. * * *

Even though the Liquor Control Board regulation in question is neutral in its terms, the result of its application in a case where the constitution and by-laws of a club required racial discrimination [as Moose Lodge did in respect to membership and guest privileges,] would be to invoke the sanctions of the State to enforce a concededly discriminatory private rule. * * * *Shelley v. Kraemer* makes it clear that the application of state sanctions to enforce such a rule would violate the Fourteenth Amendment. * * *

Appellee was entitled to a decree enjoining the enforcement of § 113.09 [but] no more. The judgment of the District Court is reversed * * * .

JUSTICE DOUGLAS, with whom JUSTICE MARSHALL joins, dissenting.

[The] associational rights which our system honors permits all white, all black, all brown, and all yellow clubs to be formed. [And] the fact that a private club gets some kind of permit from the State or municipality does not make it ipso facto a public enterprise or undertaking, any more than the grant to a householder of a permit to operate an incinerator puts the householder in the public domain. We must therefore examine whether there are special circumstances involved in the Pennsylvania scheme which differentiate the liquor license possessed by Moose Lodge from the incinerator permit.

[The opinion then agrees with the Court's disposition of Regulations § 113.09]. But there is another flaw in the scheme not so easily cured. Liquor licenses in Pennsylvania [are] not freely available to those who meet racially neutral qualifications. There is a complex quota system [and] the Harrisburg quota, where Moose Lodge No. 107 is located, has been full for many years. No more club licenses may be issued in that city.

This state-enforced scarcity of licenses restricts the ability of blacks to obtain liquor, for liquor is commercially available *only* at private clubs for a significant portion of each week.[3] [A] group desiring to form a nondiscriminatory club which would serve blacks must purchase a license held by an existing club, which can exact a monopoly price for the transfer [and] without a liquor license a fraternal organization would be hard-pressed to survive.

---

[3]   **[Ct's Note]** Hotels and restaurants may serve liquor between 7:00 a.m. and 2:00 a.m. the next day, Monday through Saturday. On Sunday, such licensees are restricted to sales between 12:00 a.m. and 2:00 a.m., and between 1:00 p.m. and 10:00 p.m. * * * Club licensees, however, are permitted to sell liquor to members and guests from 7:00 a.m. to 3:00 a.m. the next day, seven-days-a-week. * * *

Thus, the State of Pennsylvania is putting the weight of its liquor license, concededly a valued and important adjunct to a private club, behind racial discrimination. * * *

JUSTICE BRENNAN, with whom JUSTICE MARSHALL joins, dissenting.

When Moose Lodge obtained its liquor license, the State of Pennsylvania became an active participant in the operation of the Lodge bar. Liquor licensing laws [are] primarily pervasive regulatory schemes under which the State dictates and continually supervises virtually every detail of the operation of the licensee's business. Very few, if any, other licensed businesses experience such complete state involvement. * * * Liquor licenses have been employed in Pennsylvania to regulate a wide variety of moral conduct, such as the presence and activities of homosexuals, performance by a topless dancer, lewd dancing, swearing, being noisy or disorderly. So broad is the state's power that the courts of Pennsylvania have upheld its restriction of freedom of expression of a licensee on the ground that in doing so it merely exercises its plenary power to attach conditions to the privilege of dispensing liquor which a licensee holds at the sufferance of the state. * * * "[34]

NOTES AND QUESTIONS

1.   *Court's rationale.* Does *Moose Lodge* rest ultimately on a "balancing approach"? See Note, *State Action and the Burger Court,* 60 Va.L.Rev. 840 (1974). Consider Note, *Developing Legal Vistas for the Discouragement of Private Club Discrimination,* 58 Iowa L.Rev. 108 (1972): "[There is evidence that] large, nationwide fraternal orders which are segregated [serve] substantially economic interests. Furthermore, a glance at the membership requirement and size of these clubs indicates they are not closely knit clubs involving a high quotient of intimacy. They are certainly not primarily religious or political in nature. Hence, under the balancing approach, the associational rights asserted by these clubs would not seem strong."

2.   *Burton vs. Moose Lodge.* Consider Christopher D. Stone, *Corporate Vices and Corporate Virtues: Do Public/Private Distinctions Matter?,* 130 U.Pa.L.Rev. 1441 (1982): "There are several ways to interpret the contrasting results in *Burton* and *Moose Lodge.* One way is to contrast the symbolic elements of the situation: after all, the parking authority building flew, quite literally, the flags of government. [Second,] in *Burton,* the government stood to capture essentially all the economic benefits of the discrimination, assuming perfect competition among bidders for the lease. Hence, the Court's decision prohibiting the arrangement eliminated from public revenues essentially the full measure of the ill-gotten gains. [T]he preponderant costs of setting a

---

[34] Irvis also complained to the Pennsylvania Human Rights Commission. *Commonwealth v. Loyal Order of Moose,* 448 Pa. 451, 294 A.2d 594, appeal dismissed, 409 U.S. 1052 (1972), upheld the Commission's ruling that the Harrisburg Moose Lodge was a "public accommodation" under state law and could not bar guests on the basis of race.

morally correct example will be borne by the public, which is exactly where they ought to lie. Note that [the] apportionment of essentially all 'fairness' costs on general revenues, would not result from a plaintiff's victory when the government is insuring mortgages, or guaranteeing loans, or is a regulatory licensor, as in *Moose Lodge*."

3. *"Entwinement."* (a) BRENTWOOD ACADEMY v. TENNESSEE SECONDARY SCHOOL ATHLETIC ASS'N, 531 U.S. 288 (2001): TSSAA was a membership corporation organized (and so designated by the state board of education in 1972) to regulate interscholastic sports among the public and private high schools in Tennessee. Almost all of the state's public high schools (290) and 55 private schools belonged. Its rules (specifically approved by the state board in 1972, and subject to subsequent review) governed such matters as student eligibility and academic standards and financial aid. Its operating committees were limited to principals elected by member schools, all of whom at the time of the action challenged in this case were from public schools, and ex-officio appointees of the state board. In 1997, TSSAA penalized Brentwood Academy, a parochial school, for violating a rule against "undue influence" in recruiting. The Court, per SOUTER, J., held that this was "state action": "The nominally private character of the Association is overborne by the pervasive entwinement of public institutions and public officials in its composition and workings.

"[Although] the terms of the State Board's Rule expressly designating the Association as regulator of interscholastic athletics in public schools was deleted in 1996, the year after a Federal District Court held that the Association was a state actor because its rules were 'caused, directed and controlled by the Tennessee Board of Education' [this] affected nothing but words." Nor is it dispositive "that the State neither coerced nor encouraged the actions complained of. 'Coercion' and 'encouragement' are like 'entwinement' in referring to kinds of facts that can justify characterizing an ostensibly private action as public instead. [When] the relevant facts show pervasive entwinement to the point of largely overlapping identity, the implication of state action is not affected by pointing out that the facts might not loom large under a different test.

"[Even] facts that suffice to show public action [may] be outweighed in the name of some value at odds with finding public accountability in the circumstances. [For example], full-time public employment would be conclusive of state action for some purposes, but not when the employee is doing a defense lawyer's primary job; then, the public defender does 'not ac[t] on behalf of the State; he is the State's adversary.' *Polk County v. Dodson*."

THOMAS, J., joined by Rehnquist, C.J. and Scalia and Kennedy, JJ., dissented: "We have never found state action based upon mere 'entwinement,' [but] only when the organization performed a public function; was created, coerced, or encouraged by the government; or acted in a symbiotic relationship with the government. [Although *Evans v. Newton*] uses the word 'entwined,'

[our] analysis rested on the recognition that the subject of the dispute, a park, served a 'public function,' much like a fire department or a police department."

(b) NATIONAL COLLEGIATE ATHLETIC ASS'N v. TARKANIAN, 488 U.S. 179 (1988): The NCAA is an association of virtually all colleges with major athletic programs, and its rules governing these programs are binding on its members. After its investigation that found 38 recruitment violations by the staff of the University of Nevada, Las Vegas (including 10 by Tarkanian, who was UNLV's basketball coach), NCAA imposed sanctions. The Court, per STEVENS, J., conceded that UNLV's suspension of Tarkanian, which was clearly state action, "was influenced by the rules and recommendations of the NCAA," but held that this did not turn the NCAA's conduct into "state action," and thus the NCAA did not violate Tarkanian's right to procedural due process: Although, as a member of the NCAA, UNLV played a role in formulating its rules, "UNLV delegated no power to the NCAA to take specific action against any University employee. The commitment by UNLV to adhere to NCAA enforcement procedures was enforceable only by sanctions that the NCAA might impose on UNLV," and which UNLV could choose to ignore by withdrawing from the NCAA. And even if "the power of the NCAA is so great that the UNLV had no practical alternative to compliance with its demands, [it] does not follow that such a private party [is] acting under color of state law." Finally, "in the case before us the state and private parties' relevant interests do not coincide, as they did in *Burton;* rather, they have clashed throughout the investigation, the attempt to discipline Tarkanian, and this litigation. UNLV and the NCAA were antagonists, not joint participants, and the NCAA may not be deemed a state actor on this ground."

WHITE, J., joined by Brennan, Marshall and O'Connor, JJ., dissented: "[I]t was the NCAA's findings that Tarkanian had violated NCAA rules, made at NCAA-conducted hearings, all of which were agreed to by UNLV in its membership agreement with the NCAA, that resulted in Tarkanian's suspension by UNLV. On these facts, the NCAA was 'jointly engaged with [UNLV] officials in the challenged action,' and therefore was a state actor."

NORWOOD v. HARRISON, 413 U.S. 455 (1973), per BURGER, C.J., enjoined Mississippi's lending of textbooks to all students in public and private schools as applied to racially segregated private schools: "[T]hat the Constitution may compel toleration of private discrimination in some circumstances does not mean that it requires state support for such discrimination."

The textbook program, "enacted first in 1940, long before [there] was any occasion to have a policy or reason to foster the development of racially segregated private academies," may have been "motivated by [a] sincere interest in the educational welfare of all Mississippi children. But good intentions as to one valid objective do not serve to negate the State's involvement in violation of a constitutional duty. [A] State may not grant the type of tangible financial aid here involved if that aid has a significant tendency to facilitate, reinforce, and support private discrimination. * * * Textbooks are a basic educational tool and, like tuition grants, they are provided only in connection with schools; they are to be distinguished from generalized services government might provide to schools in common with others. Moreover, the textbooks provided to private school students by the State in this case are a form of assistance readily available from sources entirely independent of the State—unlike, for example, 'such necessities of life as electricity, water, and police and fire protection.' " Douglas and Brennan, JJ., concurred in the result.

————

In GILMORE v. MONTGOMERY, 417 U.S. 556 (1974), a federal court enjoined the city's "permitting the use of public park recreational facilities by private segregated school groups and by other non-school groups that racially discriminate in their membership." The Court, per BLACKMUN, J., modified the decree in part: It "was wholly proper for the city to be enjoined from permitting *exclusive* access to public recreational facilities by segregated private schools" (emphasis added), which had been "formed in reaction against" the federal court's school desegregation order. "[T]his assistance significantly tended to undermine the federal court order mandating [a] unitary school system in Montgomery." But, "upon this record, we are unable to draw a conclusion as to whether the use of zoos, museums, parks, and other recreational facilities by private school groups *in common with others,* and by private nonschool organizations, involves government so directly in the actions of those users as to warrant" intervention (emphasis added).

"It is possible that certain uses of city facilities will be judged to be in contravention of the parks [or school] desegregation order, [or] in some way to constitute impermissible 'state action' ascribing to the city the discriminatory actions of the groups." This concerns "whether there is significant state involvement in the private discrimination alleged. * * * Traditional state monopolies, such as electricity, water, and police and fire protection—all generalized governmental services—do not by their mere provision constitute a showing of state involvement in invidious discrimination. *Norwood.* The same is true of a broad spectrum of municipal recreational [facilities].

"If, however, the city or other governmental entity rations otherwise freely accessible recreational facilities, the case for state action will naturally be stronger than if the facilities are simply available to all comers without condition or reservation. Here, for example, petitioners allege that the city engages in scheduling softball games for an all-white church league and provides balls, equipment, fields, and lighting. The city's role in that situation would be dangerously close to what was found to exist in *Burton* * * * ."[35]

WHITE, J., joined by Douglas, J., concurred: "[T]he question is not whether there is state action, but whether the conceded action by the city [must] be deemed to have denied the equal protection of the laws. In other words, [has] the State furnished such aid to the group's segregated policies or become so involved in them that the State itself may fairly be said to have denied equal protection? [*Burton*]" Marshall, J. generally agreed with White, J.

NOTES AND QUESTIONS

1. *Significance of remedy.* In contrast to almost all previous cases, since the only remedy sought in *Norwood* and *Gilmore* was against the state or city itself, did these cases really present any "state action" issue at all? Was the issue in *Moose Lodge* whether the club's refusal to serve Irvis constituted "state action"? Or was it whether Pennsylvania could grant a liquor license to a club that practiced racial discrimination? Are these constitutional issues the same? What result in *Marsh* if the leafletter sued the shipbuilding company for violation of her constitutional rights? What results in *Norwood* and *Gilmore* if the remedy sought had been to compel the private schools to desegregate?[36] Consider Robert C. Brown, *State Action Analysis of Tax Expenditures,* 11 Harv.Civ.Rts.-Civ.Lib.L.Rev. 97 (1976): "[T]wo kinds of 'state action' cases should [be] distinguished: only in suits in which relief is sought against a private actor should the private actor's interests be taken into account. [Thus,] it is quite possible that a plaintiff proceeding under a state action theory might prevail in enjoining the government's action but fail in his efforts to enjoin the private activity." Compare Thomas R. McCoy, *Current State Action Theories, the Jackson Nexus Requirement, and Employee Discharges by Semi-Public and State-Aided Institutions,* 31 Vand.L.Rev. 785 (1978): "[E]ither kind of suit presents the private actor with precisely the same basic option—either modify the private action to conform to fourteenth amendment standards or do without the state aid." Contrast Brown, supra, at 119 n. 102: "In some cases the pressure to conform private behavior to constitutional standards generated by the loss of assistance will be as coercive as an injunction. In such a case, however, the fact that withdrawing the aid had a strong influence on private behavior would imply a high level of significance of government involvement with the private actor. In that case it would be appropriate to impose relief on the private actor as well as on the government, so the remedy distinction would not apply." See also fn. 44.

---

[35] Brennan, J., concurred in part but would enjoin *any* "school-sponsored or directed uses of the city recreational facilities that enable private segregated schools to duplicate public school operations at public expense."

[36] See *Runyon v. McCrary,* Ch. 11, Sec. 2, I, holding that a federal statute prohibits private schools from refusing to accept black students.

2. ***Significance of government purpose.*** Since the practices in *Norwood* and *Gilmore* were not shown to be "motivated" to perpetuate racial discrimination, can these decisions be squared with *Washington v. Davis,* Ch. 9, Sec. 2, III?

3. ***Public subsidy.*** If private schools receive extensive financial aid from the state, should it result in state action only in respect to a specific activity being funded? Consider Comment, *Tax Incentives as State Action,* 122 U.Pa.L.Rev. 414 (1973): "This [theory] incorrectly assumes that government involvement that bears directly upon a specific activity of an entity can be meaningfully distinguished from government involvement that serves more generally to perpetuate that entity as a whole." May a person whose sole source of income is public relief constitutionally refuse to sell his home to African-Americans?

4. ***Public regulation.*** Suppose the private schools' curriculum and admission policy are subject to state regulation? If a statute regulates election procedures of voluntary organizations, is a social club barred from racially discriminating? If the state licenses all barber schools and requires that barbers attend such schools, are the schools "state functions"? If the state provides private schools with extensive financial aid and strict regulation, are the schools "state functions"?[37]

5. ***Tax exempt organizations.*** May government give tax exemptions (or permit tax deductions for donations) to private schools, fraternal groups and charitable foundations that fail to adhere to Fourteenth Amendment requirements? See generally Boris I. Bittker & Kenneth M. Kaufman, *Taxes and Civil Rights: "Constitutionalizing" the Internal Revenue Code,* 82 Yale L.J. 51 (1972). Consider Note, *State Action and the United States Junior Chamber of Commerce,* 43 Geo.Wash.L.Rev. 1407 (1975): "[T]he Internal Revenue Code's tax exemptions for charitable organizations are based upon the theory that the Government is compensated for the loss of revenue by being relieved of the financial burden that would otherwise have to be met by appropriations of government funds. [Where] the private entity is thus acting as a surrogate for the government, any discrimination connected with the performance of public services, even if not affirmatively approved by the government, subjects the victims to discrimination that would not have occurred had the government performed the services directly. The government cannot avoid these constitutional limitations by delegating its functions to private entities, even if the delegation is well-intentioned." See also Frank R. Parker, *Evans v. Newton and the Racially Restricted Charitable Trust,* 13 How.L.J. 223 (1967). Reconsider note 3(c) supra.

6. ***Redevelopment housing.*** Are major urban redevelopment housing projects by private companies, undertaken pursuant to statutory authority

---

[37] See generally Note, *The Wall of Racial Separation: The Role of Private and Parochial Schools in Racial Integration,* 43 N.Y.U.L.Rev. 514 (1968); Note, *Segregation Academies and State Action,* 82 Yale L.J. 1436 (1973); O'Neil, Robert M., *Private Universities and Public Law,* 19 Buf.L.Rev. 155 (1970).

with benefit of public condemnation power and tax exemption, constitutionally barred from racially discriminating? How about ordinary private housing projects that receive public "aid" in the form of water and sewage disposal, police and fire protection? See Note, *Nondiscrimination Implications of Federal Involvement in Housing,* 19 Vand.L.Rev. 865 (1966); 17 J.Pub.L. 175 (1968). Is urban redevelopment distinguishable from a smaller private housing project because the former has the effect of racial zoning? Is this a restatement of the "government function" theory? Is "state action" affected if the claim is that the redevelopment housing project evicted a tenant without affording procedural due process?

4. STATE SUBSIDY AND REGULATION

RENDELL-BAKER V. KOHN
457 U.S. 830, 102 S.Ct. 2764, 73 L.Ed.2d 418 (1982).

CHIEF JUSTICE BURGER delivered the opinion of the Court.

[New Perspectives is a private school that] specializes in dealing with students who have experienced difficulty completing public high [schools]. In recent years, nearly all of the students at the school have been referred to it by the Brookline or Boston school committees, or by the Drug Rehabilitation Division of the Massachusetts Department of Mental Health. [In] recent years, public funds have accounted for at least 90%, and in one year 99%, of respondent's operating budget. [T]he school must comply with a variety [of] detailed regulations concerning matters ranging from recordkeeping to student-teacher ratios. [T]he regulations require the school to [maintain] personnel standards and procedures, but they impose few specific requirements.

[Petitioners were teachers and a vocational counselor discharged by the school for, inter alia, supporting student criticisms against various school policies. They sued under 42 U.S.C. § 1983. The] core issue presented [is] not whether petitioners were discharged because of their speech or without adequate procedural protections, but whether the school's action in discharging them can fairly be seen as state action. * * *

In *Blum v. Yaretsky,* 457 U.S. 991 (1982), [t]he Court considered whether certain nursing homes were state actors for the purpose of determining whether decisions regarding transfers of patients could [be] subjected to Fourteenth Amendment due process requirements. [Like] the New Perspectives School, the nursing homes were privately owned and operated. [T]he Court held that, "[A] State normally can be held responsible for a private decision only when it has exercised coercive power or has provided such significant encouragement, either overt or covert, that the choice must in law be deemed to be that of the State." In determining that the transfer decisions were not actions of the state, the Court considered each of the factors alleged by petitioners [here].

First, [the] State subsidized the operating and capital costs of the nursing homes, and paid the medical expenses of more than 90% of the patients. * * *

The school, like the nursing homes, is not fundamentally different from many private corporations whose business depends primarily on contracts to build roads, bridges, dams, ships, or submarines for the government. Acts of such private contractors do not become acts of the government by reason of their significant or even total engagement in performing public contracts. * * *

A second factor considered in *Blum* was the extensive regulation of the nursing homes by the State. There the State was indirectly involved in the transfer decisions challenged in that case because a primary goal of the State in regulating nursing homes was to keep costs down by transferring patients from intensive treatment centers to less expensive facilities when possible.[38] [The] nursing homes were extensively regulated in many other ways as well. The Court relied on *Jackson,* where we held that state regulation, even if "extensive and detailed," did not make a utility's actions state action.

Here the decisions to discharge the petitioners were not compelled or even influenced by any state regulation. [The] most intrusive personnel regulation promulgated by the various government agencies was the requirement that the Committee on Criminal Justice had the power to approve persons hired as vocational counselors.[6] Such a regulation is not sufficient to make a decision to discharge, made by private management, state action.

The third factor asserted to show that the school is a state actor is that it performs a "public function." However, our holdings have made clear that the relevant question [is] whether the function performed has been "traditionally the *exclusive* prerogative of the State." [U]ntil recently the State had not undertaken to provide education for students who could not be served by traditional public schools. That a private entity performs a function which serves the public does not make its acts state action.[7]

---

[38] Brennan, J., joined by Marshall, J., dissented in *Blum:* "[Not] only has the State established the system of treatment levels and utilization review in order to further its own fiscal goals, [but] the State prescribes with as much precision as is possible the standards by which individual determinations are to be made. [The] Court thus fails to perceive the decisive involvement of the State in the private conduct challenged by the respondents."

[6] **[Ct's Note]** [The] Committee did not take any part in discharging Rendell-Baker; on the contrary, it attempted to use leverage to aid her. [T]here is no evidence that the Committee had any authority to take even those steps.

[7] **[Ct's Note]** There is no evidence that the State has attempted to avoid its constitutional duties by a sham arrangement which attempts to disguise provision of public services as acts of private parties. Cf. *Evans v. Newton.*

Fourth, petitioners argue that there is a "symbiotic relationship" [as] in *Burton.* Such a claim was rejected in *Blum,* and we reject it here. In *Burton,* [i]n response to the argument that the restaurant's profits, and hence the State's financial position, would suffer if it did not discriminate, the Court concluded that this showed that the State profited from the restaurant's discriminatory conduct. [Here] the school's fiscal relationship with the State is not different from that of many contractors performing services for the government.[39] * * *

Affirmed.[40]

JUSTICE MARSHALL, with whom JUSTICE BRENNAN joins, dissenting.

[I]t is difficult to imagine a closer relationship between a government and a private enterprise. [The] school's very survival depends on the State. If the State chooses, it may exercise complete control over the school's operations simply by threatening to withdraw financial support if the school takes action that it considers objectionable. [Almost] every decision the school makes is substantially affected in some way by the State's regulations.[1]

[Under state law], the State is *required* to provide a free education to all children, including those with special needs. Clearly, if the State had decided to provide the service itself, its conduct would be measured against constitutional standards. The State should not be permitted to avoid constitutional requirements simply by delegating its statutory duty to a private entity. * * *

The majority repeatedly compares the school to a private contractor * * * . Although shipbuilders and dambuilders, like the school, may be dependent on government funds, they are not so closely supervised by the government. And unlike most private contractors, the school is performing a statutory duty of the State. * * *

———

In SAN FRANCISCO ARTS & ATHLETICS, INC. v. UNITED STATES OLYMPIC COMM., 483 U.S. 522 (1987), USOC, to which Congress granted the right to prohibit certain uses of the word "Olympic," enjoined petitioner from calling its athletic competitions the "Gay Olympic

---

[Compare Brennan, J., joined by Marshall, J., dissenting in *Blum:* "For many, the totality of their social network is the nursing home community. Within that environment, the nursing home operator is the immediate authority, the provider of food, clothing, shelter, and health care, and, in every significant respect, the functional equivalent of a State. Cf. *Marsh.*"]

[39] Does this adopt the "moral exemplar model" in note 2 after *Moose Lodge?*

[40] White, J., concurred in the judgment (and in *Blum*): "For me, the critical factor is the absence of any allegation that the employment decision was itself based upon some rule of conduct or policy put forth by the State."

[1] **[Ct's Note]** [By] analyzing the various indicia of state action separately, without considering their cumulative impact, the majority commits a fundamental error.

Games." Petitioner claimed that USOC's enforcement violated equal protection. The Court, per POWELL, J.—relying mainly on *Rendell-Baker*, *Blum* and *Jackson*—held that USOC is not a "governmental actor."

BRENNAN, J., joined by Marshall, J.—and "largely" by O'Connor and Blackmun, JJ.—dissented on the basis of "a symbiotic relationship sufficient to provide a nexus between the USOC's challenged action and the Government": "The Act gave the USOC authority and responsibilities that no private organization in this country had ever held. The Act also [authorized USOC] to seek up to $16 million annually in grants from the Secretary of Commerce, and afford[ed] it unprecedented power to control the use of the word 'Olympic' and related emblems to raise additional funds. As a result of the Act, the United States obtained, for the first time in its history, an exclusive and effective organization to coordinate and administer all amateur athletics related to international competition* * * .

"Second, in the eye of the public, both national and international, the connection between the decisions of the United States Government and those of the United States Olympic Committee is profound. The President of the United States has served as the Honorary President of the USOC. The national flag flies both literally and figuratively over the central product of the USOC, the United States Olympic Team.[41] [While] in *Burton* the restaurant was able to pursue a policy of discrimination because the State had failed to impose upon it a policy of non-discrimination, the USOC could pursue its alleged policy of selective enforcement only because Congress *affirmatively* granted it power that it would not otherwise have to control the use of the word 'Olympic.' "[42]

5. CREDITORS' REMEDIES

FLAGG BROS., INC. V. BROOKS
436 U.S. 149, 98 S.Ct. 1729, 56 L.Ed.2d 185 (1978).

JUSTICE REHNQUIST delivered the opinion of the Court.

The question presented [is] whether a warehouseman's proposed sale of goods entrusted to him for storage, as permitted by New York Uniform

---

[41] The Court responded that "all sorts of private organizations send 'national representatives' to participate in world competitions. Although many are of interest only to a select group, others, like the Davis Cup Competition, the America's Cup, and the Miss Universe Pageant, are widely viewed as involving representation of our country. The organizations that sponsor United States participation in these events all perform 'national representational,' as well as 'administrative [and] adjudicative role[s],' in selecting and presenting the national representatives."

[42] The Court responded that petitioner "has failed to demonstrate that the Federal Government can or does exert any influence over the exercise of the USOC's enforcement decisions. Absent proof of this type of 'close nexus between the [Government] and the challenged action of the [USOC],' the challenged action may not be 'fairly treated as that of the [Government] itself.' *Jackson*."

Commercial Code § 7–210, is an action properly attributable to the State * * * .

[R]espondent Shirley Brooks and her family were evicted from their apartment in Mount Vernon, N.Y., on June 13, 1973. The city marshal arranged for Brooks' possessions to be stored by petitioner Flagg Brothers, Inc., in its warehouse. [A]fter a series of disputes over the validity of the charges being claimed by petitioner Flagg Brothers, Brooks received a letter demanding that her account be brought up to date within 10 days "or your furniture will be sold." Brooks thereupon initiated this class action [and] the declaration that such a sale pursuant to § 7–210 would violate [due process].

It must be noted that respondents have named no public officials as defendants in this action. The city marshal, who supervised their evictions, was dismissed from the case by the consent of all the parties. This total absence of overt official involvement plainly distinguishes this case from earlier decisions imposing procedural restrictions on creditors' remedies such as *North Georgia Finishing, Inc. v. Di-Chem, Inc.,* 419 U.S. 601 (1975); *Fuentes v. Shevin,* 407 U.S. 67 (1972); *Sniadach v. Family Finance Corp.,* 395 U.S. 337 (1969).[43] [While] any person with sufficient physical power may deprive a person of his property, only a State or a private person whose action "may be fairly treated as that of the State itself," *Jackson,* may deprive him of "an interest encompassed within the Fourteenth Amendment's protection," *Fuentes* * * * .

Respondents' primary contention is that New York has delegated to Flagg Brothers a power "traditionally exclusively reserved to the State." *Jackson.* They argue that the resolution of private disputes is a traditional function of civil government, and that the State in § 7–210 has delegated this function to Flagg Brothers. Respondents, however, have read too much into the language of our previous cases. While many functions have been traditionally performed by governments, very few have been "exclusively reserved to the State." [8]

One such area has been elections. *[Terry v. Adams; Smith v. Allwright.* A second] originated with *Marsh.* Just as the Texas Democratic Party in *Smith* and the Jaybird Democratic Association in *Terry* effectively

---

[43] The facts and rationale of *Sniadach, Fuentes* and *North Georgia Finishing* are discussed in the Court's and dissent's opinions. For discussion of these cases, see Robert E. Scott, *Constitutional Regulation of Provisional Creditor Remedies: The Cost of Procedural Due Process,* 61 Va.L.Rev. 807 (1975); Linda J. Silberman, *Shaffer v. Heitner: The End of an Era,* 53 N.Y.U.L.Rev. 33 (1978).

[8] **[Ct's Note]** Respondents also contend that *Evans v. Newton* establishes that the operation of a park for recreational purposes is an exclusively public function. We doubt that *Newton* intended to establish any such broad doctrine in the teeth of the experience of several American entrepreneurs who amassed great fortunes by operating parks for recreational purposes. We think *Newton* rests on a finding of ordinary state action under extraordinary circumstances. The Court's opinion emphasizes that the record showed "no change in the municipal maintenance and concern over this facility" after the transfer of title to private trustees. * * *

performed the entire public function of selecting public officials, so too the Gulf Shipbuilding Corp. performed all the necessary municipal functions in the town of Chickasaw. [But] the proposed sale by Flagg Brothers under § 7–210 is not the only means of resolving this purely private dispute. Respondent Brooks has never alleged that state law barred her from seeking a waiver of Flagg Brothers' right to sell her goods at the time she authorized their storage. Presumably, [a person] who alleges that she never authorized the storage of her goods, could have sought to replevy her goods at any time under state law. The challenged statute itself provides a damages remedy against the warehouseman for violations of its provisions. This system of rights and remedies, recognizing the traditional place of private arrangements in ordering relationships in the commercial world,[9] can hardly be said to have delegated to Flagg Brothers an exclusive prerogative of the sovereign.[10]

Whatever the particular remedies available under New York law, we do not consider a more detailed description of them necessary to our conclusion that the settlement of disputes between debtors and creditors is not traditionally an exclusive public function.[11] [T]here are a number of

---

[9]   **[Ct's Note]** Unlike the parade of horribles suggested by our Brother Stevens in dissent, this case does not involve state authorization of private breach of the peace.

[10]   **[Ct's Note]** [It] would intolerably broaden [the] notion of state action [to] hold that the mere existence of a body of property law in a State, whether decisional or statutory, itself amounted to "state action" even though no state process or state officials were ever involved in enforcing that body of law.

This situation is clearly distinguishable from cases such as *North Georgia Finishing; Fuentes;* and *Sniadach.* In each of those cases a government official participated in the physical deprivation of what had concededly been the constitutional plaintiff's property under state law before the deprivation occurred. The constitutional protection attaches not because, as in *North Georgia Finishing,* a clerk issued a ministerial writ out of the court, but because as a result of that writ the property of the debtor was seized and impounded by the affirmative command of the law of Georgia. The creditor in *North Georgia Finishing* had not simply sought to pursue the collection of his debt by private means permissible under Georgia law; he had invoked the authority of the Georgia court, which in turn had ordered the garnishee not to pay over money which previously had been the property of the debtor. See *Shelley v. Kraemer.* * * *

Since *Flagg Bros.* was decided, *Connecticut v. Doehr,* 501 U.S. 1 (1991), held that a state statute authorizing prejudgment attachment of real estate upon plaintiff's ex parte showing that there is probable cause to sustain the validity of his or her claim—without a showing of extraordinary circumstances, and without a requirement that the person seeking the attachment post a bond—violated due process. Petitioner sought an attachment on respondent's home in conjunction with a civil action for assault and battery that he was seeking to institute against respondent in the same court. On the strength of statements in petitioner's affidavit, the court ordered the attachment. Only after the sheriff attached his property did respondent receive notice, which informed him of his right to a postattachment hearing. Instead, respondent filed a federal action, successfully arguing that the state statute violated Due Process.

[11]   **[Ct's Note]** It may well be, as my Brother Stevens' dissent contends, that "[t]he power to order legally binding surrenders of property and the constitutional restrictions on that power are necessary correlatives in our system." But here New York, unlike Florida in *Fuentes,* Georgia in *North Georgia Finishing,* and Wisconsin in *Sniadach,* has not ordered respondents to surrender any property whatever. It has merely enacted a statute which provides that a warehouseman conforming to the provisions of the statute may convert his traditional lien into good title. There is no reason whatever to believe that either Flagg Brothers or respondents could not, if they wished, seek resort to the New York courts in order to either compel or prevent the "surrenders of property" to which that dissent refers, and that the compliance of Flagg Brothers with applicable

state and municipal functions not covered by our election cases or governed by the reasoning of *Marsh* which have been administered with a greater degree of exclusivity by States and municipalities than has the function of so-called "dispute resolution." Among these are such functions as education, fire and police protection, and tax collection. We express no view as to the extent, if any, to which a city or State might be free to delegate to private parties the performance of such functions and thereby avoid the strictures of the Fourteenth Amendment.[44] [This] Court, however, has never held that a State's mere acquiescence in a private action converts that action into that of the State. * * *

It is quite immaterial that the State has embodied its decision not to act in statutory form. If New York had no commercial statutes at all, its courts would still be faced with the decision whether to prohibit or to permit the sort of sale threatened here the first time an aggrieved bailor came before them for relief. [If] the mere denial of judicial relief is considered sufficient encouragement to make the State responsible for those private acts, all private deprivations of property would be converted into public acts whenever the State, for whatever reason, denies relief sought by the putative property owner. * * *

Here, the State of New York has not compelled the sale of a bailor's goods, but has merely announced the circumstances under which its courts will not interfere with a private sale. Indeed, the crux of respondents' complaint is not that the State *has* acted, but that it has *refused* to act. This statutory refusal to act is no different in principle from an ordinary statute of limitations whereby the State declines to provide a remedy for private deprivations of property after the passage of a given period of time. * * *

Reversed.

JUSTICE STEVENS, with whom JUSTICE WHITE and JUSTICE MARSHALL join, dissenting.

New York property law would be reviewed after customary notice and hearing in such a proceeding.

The fact that such a judicial review of a self-help remedy is seldom encountered bears witness to the important part that such remedies have played in our system of property rights. This is particularly true of the warehouseman's lien, which [is] burdened by procedural constraints and provides for a compensatory remedy and judicial relief against abuse, [and] is not atypical of creditors' liens historically, whether created by statute or legislatively enacted. The conduct of private actors in relying on the rights established under these liens to resort to self-help remedies does not permit their conduct to be ascribed to the State.

[44] For the view that there is a "non-delegable governmental duty" in respect to "certain governmental functions involving peculiar risks of abuse," see John L. Watts, *Tyranny by Proxy: State Action and the Private Use of Deadly Force*, 89 Notre D.L.Rev. 1237 (2014). For the view that "the appropriate judicial response to [delegations] is not subjecting private entities to direct constitutional scrutiny, but instead requiring that the government create such mechanisms as the constitutionally-imposed price of delegating government power to private hands," see Gillian E. Metzger, *Privatization as Delegation*, 103 Colum.L.Rev. 1367 (2003).

[Under the Court's] approach a State could enact laws authorizing private citizens to use self-help in countless situations without any possibility of federal challenge. [It] could authorize the warehouseman to retain all proceeds of the lien sale, even if they far exceeded the amount of the alleged debt; it could authorize finance companies to enter private homes to repossess merchandise; or indeed, it could authorize "any person with sufficient physical power" to acquire and sell the property of his weaker neighbor. [The] Court's rationale would characterize action pursuant to such a statute as purely private action, which the State permits but does not compel, in an area not exclusively reserved to the State.

As these examples suggest, [t]here is no great chasm between "permission" and "compulsion" requiring particular state action to fall within one or the other definitional camp. [In] this case, the State of New York, by enacting § 7–210 of the Uniform Commercial Code, has acted in the most effective and unambiguous way a State can act. This section specifically authorizes petitioner Flagg Brothers to sell respondents' possessions; it details the procedures that petitioner must follow; and it grants petitioner the power to convey good title to goods that are now owned by respondents to a third party.

[Petitioners] argue that the nonconsensual transfer of property rights is not a traditional function of the sovereign. [T]he Court reasons that state action cannot be found because the State has not delegated to the warehouseman an *exclusive* sovereign function.[8] This distinction [is] inconsistent with the line of cases beginning with *Sniadach* [which have] scrutinized various state statutes regulating the debtor-creditor relationship for compliance with the Due Process Clause. [The] Court today seeks to explain these [on] the ground that in each case there was some element of "overt official involvement." [But] until today, this Court had never held that purely ministerial acts of "minor governmental functionaries" were sufficient to establish state action. [The] number of private actions in which a governmental functionary plays some ministerial role is legion;[12] to base due process review on the fortuity of

---

[8] **[Ct's Note]** [Even] if I were to accept the notion that sovereign functions must be "exclusive," the Court's description of exclusivity is incomprehensible. The question is whether a particular action is a uniquely sovereign function, not whether state law forecloses any possibility of recovering for damages for such activity. For instance, it is clear that the maintenance of a police force is a unique sovereign function, and the delegation of police power to a private party will entail state action. Under the Court's analysis, however, there would be no state action if the State provided a remedy, such as an action for wrongful imprisonment, for the individual injured by the "private" policeman. [Of] course, the availability of other state remedies may be relevant in determining whether the statute provides sufficient procedural protections under the Due Process Clause, but it is not relevant to the state-action issue.

[12] **[Ct's Note]** For instance, state officials often perform ministerial acts in the transferring of ownership in motor vehicles or real estate. It is difficult to believe that the Court would hold that all car sales are invested with state action.

such governmental intervention would demean the majestic purposes of the Due Process Clause.

Instead, cases such as *North Georgia Finishing* must be viewed as reflecting this Court's recognition of the significance of the State's role in defining *and controlling* the debtor-creditor relationship. [In *Fuentes*, the] statutes placed the state power to repossess property in the hands of an interested private party, just as the state statute in this case places the state power to conduct judicially binding sales in satisfaction of a lien in the hands of the warehouseman. "Private parties, serving their own private advantage, may unilaterally invoke state power to replevy goods from another. No state official participates in the decision to seek a writ; no state official reviews the basis for the claim to repossession; and no state official evaluates the need for immediate seizure. There is not even a requirement that the plaintiff provide any information to the court on these matters." Ibid. [Yet] the very defect that made the statutes in *Fuentes* and *North Georgia Finishing* unconstitutional—lack of state control—is, under today's decision, the factor that precludes constitutional review of the state statute. The Due Process Clause cannot command such incongruous results. If it is unconstitutional for a State to allow a private party to exercise a traditional state power because the state supervision of that power is purely mechanical, the State surely cannot immunize its actions from constitutional *scrutiny* by removing even the mechanical supervision. * * *

It is important to emphasize that, contrary to the Court's apparent fears, this conclusion does not even remotely suggest that "all private deprivations of property [will] be converted into public acts whenever the State, for whatever reason, denies relief sought by the putative property owner." The focus is not on the private deprivation but on the state authorization. [The] State's conduct in this case takes the concrete form of a statutory enactment, and it is that statute that may be challenged. * * *

Finally, it is obviously true that the overwhelming majority of disputes in our society are resolved in the private sphere. But it is no longer possible, if it ever was, to believe that a sharp line can be drawn between private and public actions. [In] the broadest sense, we expect government "to provide a reasonable and fair framework of rules which facilitate commercial transactions." This "framework of rules" is premised on the assumption that the State will control nonconsensual deprivations of property and that the State's control will, in turn, be subject to the restrictions of the Due Process Clause. * * *[45]

---

[45] The separate dissent of Marshall, J., is omitted. Brennan, J., did not participate.

NOTES AND QUESTIONS

1. ***Authority of prior decisions.*** (a) Does the Court's use of *Shelley v. Kraemer* (in fn. 10) refute the dissent's objection that the Court's handling of the prior debtor-creditor decisions establishes the principle that "purely ministerial acts of minor governmental functionaries" constitute state action? If so, then would the Court have found state action in *Flagg Bros.* if the state courts had to be used to enforce the warehouseman's lien? Would this read *Shelley* for all it is worth? Does fn. 10 so read *Shelley*? In any event, is the dissent correct in complaining that "the very defect that made the statutes in *Fuentes* and *North Georgia Finishing* unconstitutional—lack of state control— is, under *Flagg Bros.*, the factor that precludes constitutional review of the state statute"?

(b) LUGAR v. EDMONDSON OIL CO., 457 U.S. 922 (1982), per WHITE, J.,—involving a statute that authorized a creditor to file a petition with a court clerk and thus obtain a prejudgment attachment of a debtor's property which was executed by the sheriff—relied on all the debtor-creditor decisions as establishing the doctrine "that a private party's joint participation with state officials in the seizure of disputed property is sufficient to characterize that party as a 'state actor' for purposes of the Fourteenth Amendment." POWELL, J., joined by Rehnquist and O'Connor, JJ., dissented: "It is unclear why a private party engages in state action when filing papers seeking an attachment of property, but not [when] summoning police to investigate a suspected crime." Burger, C.J., also dissented.

2. ***"Governmental function."*** (a) ***Dispute resolution.*** Do you agree that the authority exercised by the warehouseman under the New York statute was not a "governmental function"? Consider 92 Harv.L.Rev. 128 (1978): "Regardless of the fact that there are many ways to go about resolving a private dispute, the ability to conclude unresolved disputes by making authoritative determinations of rights in property is central to our conception of government's role in society. If a state chose to assign part of its judicial function to private tribunals, giving them all the authority of trial courts, there would be little doubt that a vital attribute of sovereignty was involved." What about judicial enforcement of (i) a private arbitrator's decision made pursuant to an earlier contract between the parties, or (2) the agreement to arbitrate? Of what relevance is the fact that arbitrators "are statutorily vested with broad judicial powers to administer depositions and discovery, including subpoena and sanction powers," and "receive the same 'judicial' immunity from civil liability that is reserved exclusively for the states' own constitutionally authorized judiciary"? See Richard C. Reuben, *Public Justice: Toward a State Action Theory of ADR,* 85 Calif.L.Rev. 577 (1997).

What result in *Flagg Bros.* if the warehouseman's lien had not been "burdened by procedural constraints" and had not provided "for a compensatory remedy and judicial relief against abuse"?

(b) ***Jury selection.*** EDMONSON v. LEESVILLE CONCRETE CO., 500 U.S. 614 (1991), per KENNEDY, J., held that use by a private litigant in a civil trial of a peremptory challenge to exclude jurors on the basis of race violated "the excluded jurors' equal protection rights": "[I]n determining whether a particular action or course of conduct is governmental in character, it is relevant to examine the following: the extent to which the actor relies on governmental assistance and benefits, see *Burton;* whether the actor is performing a traditional governmental function, see *Terry*; *Marsh*; and whether the injury caused is aggravated in a unique way by the incidents of governmental authority, see *Shelley* * * * .

"Although private use of state-sanctioned private remedies or procedures does not rise, by itself, to the level of state action, our cases have found state action when private parties make extensive use of state procedures with 'the overt, significant assistance of state officials.' See *Lugar*. [The] government summons jurors, constrains their freedom of movement, and subjects them to public scrutiny and examination. The party who exercises a challenge invokes the formal authority of the court, which must discharge the prospective juror, thus effecting the 'final and practical denial' of the excluded individual's opportunity to serve on the petit jury. [By] enforcing a discriminatory peremptory challenge, the court 'has not only made itself a party to the [biased act], but has elected to place its power, property and prestige behind the [alleged] discrimination.' *Burton*.

"[Further, a] traditional function of government is evident here. The peremptory challenge is used in selecting an entity that is a quintessential governmental body, having no attributes of a private actor. [If] a government confers on a private body the power to choose the government's employees or officials, the private body will be bound by the constitutional mandate of race neutrality [*Terry*]. If peremptory challenges based on race were permitted, persons could be required by summons to be put at risk of open and public discrimination as a condition of their participation in the justice system. The injury to excluded jurors would be the direct result of governmental delegation and participation."[46]

O'CONNOR, J., joined by Rehnquist, C.J., and Scalia, J., dissented: "It is the nature of a peremptory that its exercise is left wholly within the discretion of the litigant. [The] peremptory is, by design, an enclave of private action in a government-managed proceeding. [That] these actions may be necessary to a peremptory challenge [no] more makes the challenge state action than the building of roads and provision of public transportation makes state action of riding on a bus.

"[The] government 'normally can be held responsible for a private decision only when it has exercised coercive power or has provided such significant encouragement, either overt or covert, that the choice must in law be deemed to be that of the State.' *Blum*. [A] judge does not 'significantly encourage'

---

[46] For the view that *Edmonson* (and *Tarkanian*) "heralded a halt to the Court's retreat from the *Burton* totality approach," see G. Sidney Buchanan, *A Conceptual History of the State Action Doctrine: The Search for Governmental Responsibility*, 34 Hous.L.Rev. 333, 665 (1997).

discrimination by the mere act of excusing a juror in response to an unexplained request."

3. ***The limits (or lack of limits) of the state action concept.*** Do you agree that "an ordinary statute of limitations whereby the State declines to provide a remedy for private deprivations of property after the passage of a given period of time" is *not* state action? If it *is* state action, then is New York's rule—that "its courts will not interfere with a private sale" pursuant to a warehouseman's lien—also state action? If so, is it not true that "all private deprivations of property would be converted into public acts whenever the State, for whatever reason, denies relief sought by the putative property owner"? Of what relevance is it that "the State's conduct in *Flagg Bros.* takes the concrete form of a statutory enactment"? May a "state procedure" providing a "framework of rules which facilitate commercial transactions" be promulgated by common law as well as by statute? See generally Paul Brest, *State Action and Liberal Theory: A Casenote on Flagg Brothers v. Brooks,* 130 U.Pa.L.Rev. 1296 (1982); Frank I. Goodman, *Professor Brest on State Action and Liberal Theory,* 130 U.Pa.L.Rev. 1331 (1982).

6. STATE FAILURE TO ACT

DESHANEY V. WINNEBAGO COUNTY DEP'T OF SOCIAL SERV.
489 U.S. 189, 109 S.Ct. 998, 103 L.Ed.2d 249 (1989).

CHIEF JUSTICE REHNQUIST delivered the opinion of the Court.

[I]n January 1982, [the] Department of Social Services (DSS) interviewed [Joshua DeShaney's father about alleged child abuse], but he denied the accusations, and DSS did not pursue them. [In] January 1983, Joshua was admitted to a local hospital with multiple bruises and abrasions. The examining physician suspected child abuse and notified DSS. [T]he county convened an ad hoc "Child Protection Team" [which] decided that there was insufficient evidence of child abuse to retain Joshua in the custody of the court. The Team did, however, decide to recommend several measures to protect Joshua, including enrolling him in a preschool program, providing his father with certain counselling services, and encouraging his father's girlfriend to move out of the home. [A month later] emergency room personnel called the DSS caseworker handling Joshua's case to report that he had once again been treated for suspicious injuries. The caseworker concluded that there was no basis for action. [For] six months, the caseworker made monthly visits to the DeShaney home, during which she observed a number of suspicious injuries on Joshua's head; [and] that he had not been enrolled in school and that the girlfriend had not moved out. The caseworker dutifully recorded these incidents in her files, along with her continuing suspicions that someone in the DeShaney household was physically abusing Joshua, but she did nothing more. In November 1983, the emergency room notified DSS that Joshua had been treated once again for injuries that they believed to be caused by child abuse. On the caseworker's next two visits to the DeShaney home, she was told that Joshua was too ill to see her. Still DSS took no action.

In March 1984, Randy DeShaney beat 4-year-old Joshua so severely that he fell into a life-threatening coma [and] is expected to spend the rest of his life confined to an institution for the profoundly retarded. Randy DeShaney was subsequently tried and convicted of child abuse.

Joshua and his mother brought this action under 42 U.S.C. § 1983. [But] nothing in the language of the Due Process Clause itself requires the State to protect the life, liberty, and property of its citizens against invasion by private actors. [Nor] does history support such an expansive reading of the constitutional text. [The Clause's] purpose was to protect the people from the State, not to ensure that the State protected them from each other. The Framers were content to leave the extent of governmental obligation in the latter area to the democratic political processes. * * *

Petitioners contend, however, that even if the Due Process Clause imposes no affirmative obligation on the State to provide the general public with adequate protective services, such a duty may arise out of certain "special relationships" created or assumed by the State with respect to particular individuals [and] that such a "special relationship" existed here because the State knew that Joshua faced a special danger of abuse at his father's hands, and specifically proclaimed, by word and by deed, its intention to protect him against that danger. * * *

We reject this argument. It is true that in certain limited circumstances the Constitution imposes upon the State affirmative duties of care and protection with respect to particular individuals [discussing *Youngberg v. Romeo,* Ch. 6, Sec. 2; *Estelle v. Gamble,* 429 U.S. 97 (1976); and other cases.] But these [cases] stand only for the proposition that when the State takes a person into its custody and holds him there against his will, the Constitution imposes upon it a corresponding duty to assume some responsibility for his safety and general well-being. [I]ncarceration, institutionalization, or other similar restraint of personal liberty [is] the "deprivation of liberty" triggering the protections of the Due Process Clause. [While] the State may have been aware of the dangers that Joshua faced in the free world, it played no part in their creation, nor did it do anything to render him any more vulnerable to them.[47] That the State once took temporary custody of Joshua does not alter the analysis, for when it returned him to his father's custody, it placed him in no worse position than that in which he would have been had it not acted at all. [The] most that can be said of the state functionaries in this case is that they stood by and

---

[47] For developments in the lower courts based on this language, see Laura Oren, *Safari Into the Snake Pit: The State-Created Danger Doctrine,* 13 Wm. & Mary Bill of Rts. J. 1139 (2005); Laura Oren, *Some Thoughts on the State-Created Danger Doctrine: DeShaney is Still Wrong and Castle Rock is More of the* Same, 16 Temple Pol.&Civ. R. L. Rev. 47 (2007).

did nothing when suspicious circumstances dictated a more active role for them. In defense of them it must also be said that had they moved too soon to take custody of the son away from the father, they would likely have been met with charges of improperly intruding into the parent-child relationship, charges based on the same Due Process Clause * * * .

JUSTICE BRENNAN, with whom JUSTICE MARSHALL and JUSTICE BLACKMUN join, dissenting.

* * * I [would] recognize, as the Court apparently cannot, that "the State's knowledge of [an] individual's predicament [and] its expressions of intent to help him" can amount to a "limitation of his freedom to act on his own behalf" or to obtain help from others. Thus, I would read *Youngberg* and *Estelle* to stand for the much more generous proposition that, if a State cuts off private sources of aid and then refuses aid itself, it cannot wash its hands of the harm that results from its inaction. * * *

The specific facts before us bear out this view of Wisconsin's system of protecting children. Each time someone voiced a suspicion that Joshua was being abused, that information was relayed to the Department for investigation and possible action. [If] DSS ignores or dismisses these suspicions, no one will step in to fill the gap. [Through] its child-protection program, the State actively intervened in Joshua's life and, by virtue of this intervention, acquired ever more certain knowledge that Joshua was in grave danger. * * * My disagreement with the Court arises from its failure to see that inaction can be every bit as abusive of power as action, that oppression can result when a State undertakes a vital duty and then ignores it. * * *[48]

JUSTICE BLACKMUN, dissenting. * * *

Like the antebellum judges who denied relief to fugitive slaves, the Court today claims that its decision, however harsh, is compelled by existing legal doctrine. [O]ur Fourteenth Amendment precedents may be read more broadly or narrowly depending upon how one [chooses]. I would adopt a "sympathetic" reading, one which comports with dictates of fundamental justice and recognizes that compassion need not be exiled from the province of judging. * * *

NOTES AND QUESTIONS

1. ***"State of mind" of government officials.*** Consider David A. Strauss, *Due Process, Government Inaction and Private Wrongs,* 1989 Sup.Ct.Rev. 53: "Suppose that police officers learn that a murder is about to occur that they can prevent with minimal cost. [They] decide not to [intervene] because the targeted victim is someone whom they believe is guilty of another

---

[48] See also *Castle Rock v. Gonzales,* Ch. 6, Sec. 5, I.

crime. The officers would rather see him killed by private persons than brought to trial where, they fear, he might escape with an acquittal or a light sentence.

"This must be a case of government inaction, assuming that there is such a thing. The police officers did not instigate or facilitate the murder in any way, except to refrain from intervening. They did not make the victim worse off than he would have been if the officers had never become aware of the predicament."

Is "this hypothetical case indistinguishable from *DeShaney*"? Id. Should there be a constitutional difference between government inaction that is careless or inadvertent rather than deliberate? Consider Richard S. Kay, *The State Action Doctrine, the Public-Private Distinction, and the Independence of Constitutional Law,* 10 Const.Comm. 329 (1993): "The harms that follow on a state's failure to act are, in a sense, happenstance. In the usual case no official person will have planned for those results to follow. Affirmative acts, on the other hand, are more likely to have been deliberate and, therefore, they are more likely to have been undertaken with a dangerous state of mind. [This] need not be so in every case, but it is a reasonable enough assumption to explain why the state may be thought more threatening when it acts than when it fails to act." Compare Don Herzog, *The Kerr Principle, State Action, and Legal Rights,* 105 Mich. L. Rev. 1 (2006): "[S]tate action is about responsibility, not causation. Causing an outcome is a standard way of being responsible for it, but causation is neither necessary nor sufficient."

2. ***Limited government resources and affirmative obligations.*** Consider Barbara E. Armacost, *Affirmative Duties, Systemic Harms, and the Due Process Clause,* 94 Mich.L.Rev. 982 (1996): "Because the social-work context [will] involve more cases of possible child abuse or neglect than plausibly can be addressed, the line between claims that raise resource-allocation concerns and those that do not is difficult to draw. That is exactly what makes *DeShaney* hard. It is, on the one hand, not an 'easy' case for *nonliability*, as if it had involved a single report of child abuse that went uninvestigated or a claim that more social workers should have been assigned to a particular neighborhood. [T]hese sorts of claims rarely result in liability [at common law] because they raise the most serious resource-allocation issues. But *DeShaney* is also not simply a case where social workers 'on the scene' stood by and failed to intervene. [The] social worker was 'on the scene,' so to speak, of many potentially abusive situations involving many at-risk children. In order to evaluate the reasonableness of her behavior toward one child, one would want to know more about her obligations and behavior in connection with these other cases as well."

CHAPTER 11

CONGRESSIONAL ENFORCEMENT OF CIVIL RIGHTS

■ ■ ■

The exercise of congressional authority under the Commerce Clause to protect civil rights was examined in detail in Ch. 2, Sec. 2, III. But the potentially most pervasive sources of federal legislative power to enforce personal liberty are found in the final sections of the Thirteenth, Fourteenth, and Fifteenth Amendments which grant Congress power to enforce the substantive provisions of these amendments "by appropriate legislation."

1. HISTORICAL FRAMEWORK

I. LEGISLATION

The Civil Rights Act of 1866, enacted pursuant to the Thirteenth Amendment, was the first Reconstruction Act seeking "to protect all persons in the United States in their civil rights." (See Ch. 5, Sec. 1, III) Its current provisions are:

42 U.S.C. § 1981. *"Equal rights under the law.* All persons within the jurisdiction of the United States shall have the same right in every State and Territory to make and enforce contracts, to sue, be parties, give evidence, and to the full and equal benefit of all laws and proceedings for the security of persons and property as is enjoyed by white citizens, and shall be subject to like punishment, pains, penalties, taxes, licenses, and exactions of every kind, and to no other."

42 U.S.C. § 1982. *"Property rights of citizens.* All citizens of the United States shall have the same right, in every State and Territory, as is enjoyed by white citizens thereof to inherit, purchase, lease, sell, hold, and convey real and personal property."

The 1866 Act then provided criminal penalties against any person denying such rights under color of law. With certain changes (the most important being addition of the word "willfully" in 1909, and the substantial increase of penalties in 1968), this has survived as a significant federal criminal statute enforcing civil rights:

18 U.S.C. § 242. *"Deprivation of rights under color of law.* Whoever, under color of any law, statute, ordinance, regulation, or custom, willfully subjects any inhabitant of any State, Territory, or District to the deprivation of any rights, privileges, or immunities secured or protected by the Constitution or laws of the United States, or to different punishments, pains or penalties, on account of such inhabitant being an alien, or by reason of his color, or race, than are prescribed for the punishment of citizens, shall be fined [or] imprisoned not more than one year, or both; and if bodily injury results [or] if such acts include the use, attempted use, or threatened use of a dangerous weapon, explosives, or fire, shall be fined under this title or imprisoned not more than ten years, or both; and if death results [or] if such acts include kidnapping [or] aggravated sexual abuse, [shall] be fined under this title, or imprisoned for any term of years or for life, or both, or may be sentenced to death."

———

Doubt as to the adequacy of the Thirteenth Amendment to support the 1866 Act was a significant force leading to adoption of the Fourteenth Amendment. After the Fifteenth Amendment, Congress passed the Act of May 31, 1870, principally to enforce the right to vote guaranteed by the amendment. One section, barring private conspiracies, evolved as an important existing protection:

18 U.S.C. § 241. *"Conspiracy against rights.* If two or more persons conspire to injure, oppress, threaten, or intimidate any citizen in the free exercise or enjoyment of any right or privilege secured to him by the Constitution or laws of the United States, or because of his having exercised the same; or

"If two or more persons go in disguise on the highway, or on the premises of another, with intent to prevent or hinder his free exercise or enjoyment of any right or privilege so secured—

"They shall be fined [or] imprisoned not more than ten years, or both; and if death results [or] if such acts include kidnapping [or] aggravated sexual abuse, [they] shall be fined [or] imprisoned for any term of years or for life, [or] may be sentenced to death."

———

Next came the Ku Klux Klan Act of 1871, which made criminal private conspiracies against the operations of government officials or courts, or to deprive persons of equal protection of the laws. The Act also established civil liabilities that have evolved to be important existing provisions. One is the civil counterpart of 18 U.S.C. § 242:

42 U.S.C. § 1983. *"Civil action for deprivation of rights.* Every person who, under color of any statute, ordinance, regulation, custom, or usage, of any State or Territory [subjects], any citizen of the United States or other person within the jurisdiction thereof to the deprivation of any rights, privileges or immunities secured by the Constitution and laws, shall be liable to the person injured in an action of law, suit in equity, or other proper proceedings for redress. . . ."

Another is roughly the civil counterpart of 18 U.S.C.A. § 241:

42 U.S.C. § 1985. "*Conspiracy to interfere with civil rights. * * * (3) If two or more persons in any State or Territory conspire or go in disguise on the highway or on the premises of another, for the purpose of depriving, either directly or indirectly, any person or class of persons of the equal protection of the laws, or of equal privileges and immunities under the laws; or for the purpose of preventing or hindering the constituted authorities of any State or Territory from giving or securing to all persons within such State or Territory the equal protection of the laws; [the] party so injured or deprived may have an action for the recovery of damages, occasioned by such injury or deprivation, against any one or more of the conspirators."*

————

The final Reconstruction enactment in this area was the Civil Rights Act of 1875, dealing with racial discrimination in public accommodations, held invalid in the *Civil Rights Cases,* Ch. 10, Sec. 1.[1] Thereafter, no significant congressional action to enforce civil rights took place until the Civil Rights Act of 1957. The principal thrust of the 1957 Act and of the Civil Rights Act of 1960 was against racial discrimination in voting. The Civil Rights Act of 1964, mainly concerned with matters already considered in Ch. 2, Sec. 2, III, also dealt with voting. But the most comprehensive federal legislation in aid of the franchise is the Voting Rights Act of 1965 and its later amendments, fully explored in Sec. 3 of this Ch. Finally, the Civil Rights Act of 1968 provides protection against interference with designated "federally protected activities," and against discrimination in housing, both considered at several points infra.

II. JUDICIAL DECISIONS

Necessity of "state action" for violation of constitutional rights.
(a) ***In general.*** Shortly after enactment of the Reconstruction civil rights laws, a series of decisions culminating in the *Civil Rights Cases*, Ch. 10, Sec. 1, significantly limited their impact by interpreting the Fourteenth (and Fifteenth) Amendments as barring only "state action," thus

---

[1]　For general discussion and evolution of the Reconstruction civil rights legislation, see Eugene Gressman, *The Unhappy History of Civil Rights Legislation,* 50 Mich.L.Rev. 1323 (1952); Will Maslow & Joseph B. Robison, *Civil Rights Legislation and the Fight for Equality, 1862–1952,* 20 U.Chi.L.Rev. 363 (1953); U.S. Comm'n on Civil Rights, *Enforcement* 103 (1965).

precluding congressional legislation against "private individuals" for violating rights of persons created by these amendments.[2]

Sec. 241 exceptions. But the Court has long recognized that there is a limited category of constitutional rights, protected by § 241, that, as stated in UNITED STATES v. WILLIAMS, 341 U.S. 70 (1951), "Congress can beyond doubt constitutionally secure against interference by private individuals. [T]his category includes rights which arise from the relationship of the individual and the Federal Government. The right of citizens to vote in congressional elections, for instance, may obviously be protected by Congress from individual as well as from State interference. *Ex parte Yarbrough,* 110 U.S. 651."[3] The Court has also included, as "attributes of national citizenship," "the right of the people peaceably to assemble for the purpose of petitioning Congress for a redress of grievances"[4] and the "constitutional right to travel from one State to another."[5]

2.   REGULATION OF PRIVATE PERSONS

I.   THIRTEENTH AMENDMENT

JONES v. ALFRED H. MAYER CO.
392 U.S. 409, 88 S.Ct. 2186, 20 L.Ed.2d 1189 (1968).

JUSTICE STEWART delivered the opinion of the Court.

[P]etitioners filed a complaint [that] respondents had refused to sell them a home [for] the sole reason that petitioner [is] a Negro. Relying in part upon 42 U.S.C. § 1982 [Sec. 1, I supra], the petitioners sought injunctive and other relief.[1] The [courts below] sustained the respondents' motion to dismiss [concluding] that § 1982 applies only to state action * * *

[I]t is important to make clear precisely what this case does *not* involve. Whatever else it may be, § 1982 is not a comprehensive open housing law, [but] deals only with racial discrimination [and] does not deal specifically with discrimination in the provision of services or facilities in connection with the sale or rental of a dwelling.

---

[2]   See *United States v. Cruikshank,* 92 U.S. 542, 23 L.Ed. 588 (1876); *Virginia v. Rives,* 100 U.S. 313, 25 L.Ed. 667 (1879).

[3]   *United States v. Classic,* 313 U.S. 299 (1941), included within this category the right to vote in a state congressional primary.

[4]   *Cruikshank,* fn. 2 (dictum).

[5]   Ch. 6, Sec. 3.

[1]   **[Ct's Note]** To vindicate their rights under § 1982, the petitioners invoked the jurisdiction of the District Court to award "damages [or] equitable or other relief under any Act of Congress providing for the protection of civil rights * * * ." 28 U.S.C. § 1343(4). * * *

* * *

On its [face] § 1982 appears to prohibit *all* discrimination against Negroes in the sale or rental of property—discrimination by private owners as well as discrimination by public [authorities.] Stressing what they consider to be the revolutionary implications of so literal a reading of § 1982, the respondents argue that Congress cannot possibly have intended any such result. Our examination of the relevant history, however, persuades us that Congress meant exactly what it said.

In its original form, § 1982 was part [of] the Civil Rights Act of 1866. [The Court then extensively examined antecedent statutes and studies and debate in the Congress, contemporaneous with the proposal and ratification of the Thirteenth Amendment, in support of its conclusion respecting § 1982.] It is quite true that some members of Congress supported the Fourteenth Amendment "in order to eliminate doubt as to the constitutional validity of the Civil Rights Act as applied to the States." [*Hurd v. Hodge,* 334 U.S. 24 (1948)]. But it certainly does not follow that the adoption of the Fourteenth Amendment or the subsequent readoption of the Civil Rights Act were meant somehow to *limit* its application to state action. The legislative history furnishes not the slightest factual basis for any such speculation, and the conditions prevailing in 1870 make it highly implausible. * * *

The remaining question is whether Congress has power under the Constitution to do what § 1982 purports to [do]. Our starting point is the Thirteenth Amendment, for it was pursuant to that constitutional provision that Congress originally enacted what is now § 1982. [It] has never been [doubted] "that the power vested in Congress to enforce the article by appropriate legislation," [*Civil Rights Cases,*] includes the power to enact laws "direct and primary, operating upon the acts of individuals, whether sanctioned by State legislation or not." [Id.]

"By its own unaided force and effect," the Thirteenth Amendment "abolished slavery, and established universal freedom." *Civil Rights Cases.* Whether or not the Amendment *itself* did any more than that—a question not involved in this case—it is at least clear that the Enabling Clause of that Amendment empowered Congress to do much more.[6] For that clause clothed "Congress with power to pass *all laws necessary and proper for abolishing all badges and incidents of slavery in the United States.*" Ibid. (Emphasis added.)

[The] majority leaders in Congress—who were, after all, the authors of the Thirteenth Amendment—had no doubt that its Enabling Clause contemplated the sort of positive legislation that was embodied in the 1866 Civil Rights Act. [Surely] Congress has the power under the Thirteenth

---

[6] For discussion of the use of judicial power under § 1 see Ch. 10, fn. 2.

Amendment rationally to determine what are the badges and the incidents of slavery, and the authority to translate that determination into effective legislation. Nor can we say that the determination Congress has made is an irrational one. For this Court recognized long ago that, whatever else they may have encompassed, the badges and incidents of slavery—its "burdens and disabilities"—included restraints upon "those fundamental rights which are the essence of civil freedom, namely the same right [to] inherit, purchase, lease, sell and convey property, as is enjoyed by white citizens." *Civil Rights Cases.* Just as the Black Codes, enacted after the Civil War to restrict the free exercise of those rights, were substitutes for the slave system, so the exclusion of Negroes from white communities became a substitute for the Black Codes. And when racial discrimination herds men into ghettos and makes their ability to buy property turn on the color of their skin, then it too is a relic of slavery.

[At] the very least, the freedom that Congress is empowered to secure under the Thirteenth Amendment includes the freedom to buy whatever a white man can buy, the right to live wherever a white man can live. If Congress cannot say that being a free man means at least this much, then the Thirteenth Amendment made a promise the Nation cannot keep. * * *

Reversed.

JUSTICE HARLAN, whom JUSTICE WHITE joins, dissenting.

[In a lengthy opinion, Harlan, J., relied on statements in prior Supreme Court opinions, the use of the word "right" in § 1982, the legislative history and debates of the Civil Rights Act of 1866 and of companion legislation, and on the ethics of the times to demonstrate that the Court's construction of § 1982 was "open to the most serious doubt" if not "wholly untenable."][7]

RUNYON v. McCRARY, 427 U.S. 160 (1976), per STEWART, J., relying on *Mayer's* interpretation of § 1982, held that § 1981 (Sec. 1, I supra), prohibits private schools—that were operated commercially and open to the public in that they engaged in general advertising to attract students—from refusing to accept black students. POWELL, J., joined the opinion, but added that "choices, including those involved in entering into a contract, that are 'private' in the sense that they are not part of a commercial relationship offered generally or widely, and that reflect the selectivity exercised by an individual entering into a personal relationship, certainly were never intended to be restricted by" § 1981. Stevens, J., joined the

---

[7]   The concurring opinion of Douglas, J., is omitted. For conflicting views as to § 1982's history, compare Charles Fairman, *Reconstruction and Reunion: 1864–1888, Part One* (1971) with Sanford Levinson, *Book Review,* 26 Stan.L.Rev. 461 (1974); Robert L. Kohl, *The Civil Rights Act of 1866, Its Hour Come Round at Last,* 55 Va.L.Rev. 272 (1969) with Gerhard Casper, *Jones v. Mayer: Clio, Bemused and Confused Muse,* 1968 Sup.Ct.Rev. 89.

Court's opinion, feeling bound by, but disagreeing with, the statutory interpretation in *Mayer*. White, J., joined by Rehnquist, J., dissented on grounds of statutory interpretation.

NOTES AND QUESTIONS

1.   ***Scope of §§ 1982 and 1981.*** What other discriminations against African-Americans are presently prohibited by these provisions? Consider Louis Henkin, *On Drawing Lines,* 82 Harv.L.Rev. 63 (1968): "Will no bequest stand up which includes a racial discrimination since that would deprive Negroes of 'the same right [to] inherit'? Has there been an easier answer to [Senator Bacon's] will all this time while the Court struggled with theories of state action to find escape from his discrimination [see *Newton* and *Abney,* Ch. 10, Secs. 2 and 3]? Indeed, [Title II of the Civil Rights Act of 1964] provides that certain places of public accommodations may not discriminate on the basis of race in selling goods and services; the Court's construction of § 1982, when applied to personal property, renders the title (and its limitations) superfluous. Moreover, by the Court's technique of construction, the right 'to make and enforce contracts' guaranteed by [§ 1981] should prevent a restaurant or hotel management from refusing on grounds of race to 'make a contract' for service with a Negro. Indeed, that construction should prevent any employer from refusing 'to make a contract' of employment with a Negro; and the fair employment provisions of the 1964 Act likewise become superfluous, as does the entire struggle, since the days of the New Deal, to enact adequate fair employment legislation."[8] Do you agree? Or do these instances "run the slavery argument into the ground" (*Civil Rights Cases*)?

Does the Thirteenth Amendment empower Congress to prohibit action that has a racially disproportionate impact, regardless of its purpose? Do §§ 1981–82 do so? See Note, *Section 1981: Discriminatory Purpose or Disproportionate Impact?* 80 Colum.L.Rev. 137 (1980); *Memphis v. Greene,* Ch. 9, Sec. 2, III.

2.   ***Scope of § 1985.*** GRIFFIN v. BRECKENRIDGE, 403 U.S. 88 (1971), was a damages action under § 1985. Allegedly, respondents had wilfully conspired to assault and terrorize petitioners—who "were travelling upon the federal, state and local highways"—in order to prevent petitioners "and other Negro-Americans [from] seeking the equal protection of the laws and from enjoying the equal rights, privileges and immunities of citizens under the laws"—including rights to free speech, association, petition for redress of grievances, "their rights not to be enslaved nor deprived of life, liberty or property other than by due process of law, and their rights to travel the public highways without restraint in the same terms as white citizens." The Court, per STEWART, J., held "that all indicators—text, companion provisions, and legislative history—point unwaveringly to § 1985's coverage of private conspiracies." And the "constitutional shoals that would lie in the path of

---

8   Does § 1981 also make *Moose Lodge v. Irvis,* Ch. 10, Sec. 3, incorrect? Or do other constitutional provisions (values) justify the decision?

interpreting § 1985 as a general federal tort law can be avoided" because the "language requiring intent to deprive of *equal* protection, or *equal* privileges and immunities, means that there must be some racial, or perhaps otherwise class-based, invidiously discriminatory animus behind the conspirators' action.[9]"

The Court then found *at least* two sources of "congressional power to reach the private conspiracy alleged." First, under § 2 of the Thirteenth Amendment, Congress was "wholly within its powers [in] creating a statutory cause of action for Negro citizens who have been the victims of conspiratorial, racially discriminatory private action aimed at depriving them of the basic rights that the law secures to all free men." Second, "the right of interstate travel is constitutionally protected [against] private as well as governmental interference." Since "it is open to the petitioners to prove at trial that they had been engaging in interstate travel or intended to do so, that [the] conspirators intended to drive out-of-state civil rights workers from the State, or that they meant to deter the petitioners from associating with such persons," this "could make it clear that the petitioners had suffered from conduct which Congress may [reach]."

3.   ***Beyond racial discrimination.*** (a) CARPENTERS, LOCAL 610 v. SCOTT, 463 U.S. 825 (1983), per WHITE, J., held "that an alleged conspiracy to infringe First Amendment rights is not a violation of § 1985 unless it is proved that the state is involved in the conspiracy or that the aim of the conspiracy is to influence the activity of the state": "The complaint in *Griffin* alleged, among other things, a deprivation of First Amendment rights but we did not sustain the action on the basis of that allegation and paid it scant attention. Instead, we upheld the application of § 1985 to private conspiracies aimed at interfering with rights [such as the freedom from slavery and the right to travel] constitutionally protected against private, as well as official, encroachment." Blackmun, J., joined by Brennan, Marshall and O'Connor, JJ., dissented. Does § 1985 provide a cause of action to whites who suffer injury because of their espousal of the rights of African-Americans?

In BRAY v. ALEXANDRIA WOMEN'S HEALTH CLINIC, 506 U.S. 263 (1993), an injunction was sought against anti-abortion demonstrators' trespassing on, and obstructing access to, the premises of abortion clinics. The Court per SCALIA, J., held that § 1985 does not apply to private conspiracies aimed against abortion because that involves "a right only against state interference." STEVENS, J., joined by Blackmun, J., dissented on the ground that § 1985 covers "a large-scale conspiracy that violates the victims'

---

[9]   **[Ct's Note]** We need not decide, given the facts of this case, whether conspiracy motivated by invidiously discriminatory intent other than racial bias would be actionable under the portion of § 1985(3) before us. [See *Carpenters, Local 610 v. Scott*, note 3 infra, holding that § 1985 does not "reach conspiracies motivated by economic or commercial animus."]

[See also *Bray v. Alexandria Women's Health Clinic,* note 3 infra, leaving open the question of whether "an invidiously discriminatory animus" against women comes within § 1985, but holding that opposition to abortion does not reflect such animus because it does not involve "a purpose that focuses upon women *by reason of their sex.*" Blackmun, Stevens and O'Connor, JJ., disagreed.]

constitutional rights by overwhelming the local authorities." O'Connor and Souter, JJ., agreed with Stevens, J., in separate opinions.

(b)   How broadly does *Mayer* empower Congress to define the substantive terms of the Civil War amendments? For example, pursuant to § 2 of the Thirteenth Amendment, may Congress "rationally determine" that discriminations against groups other than African-Americans are "badges and incidents of slavery"? Consider George Rutherglen, *State Action, Private Action and the Thirteenth Amendment,* 94 Va. L. Rev. 1367 (2008): "American slavery has always involved subordination of particular racial groups, from Africans (and for a short period Indians) in antebellum slavery, to Mexicans in forms of peonage, and to Asians under the 'coolie system' of forced labor." See also Note, *The "New" Thirteenth Amendment: A Preliminary Analysis,* 82 Harv. L. Rev. 1294 (1969). Compare Note, *Jones v. Mayer: The Thirteenth Amendment and the Federal Anti-Discrimination Laws,* 69 Colum.L.Rev. 1019 (1969): "[T]he Court's conclusion that housing discrimination *today* is a badge or incident of slavery is itself a recognition that the 'slavery' referred to in the Thirteenth Amendment now encompasses the second class citizenship imposed on members of disparate minority groups. [A] victim's people need not have been enslaved in order to invoke its protection. He need only be suffering today under conditions that could reasonably be called symptoms of a slave society, inability to raise a family with dignity caused by unemployment, poor schools and housing, and lack of a place in the body politic."[9] Consider Jesse H. Choper, *Congressional Power to Expand Judicial Definitions of the Substantive Terms of the Civil War Amendments,* 67 Minn.L.Rev. 299 (1982): "*Mayer* need not be interpreted as conferring any *definitional* authority on Congress. Rather, it can be persuasively argued on either of two theories that the Court upheld the Civil Rights Act of 1866 as only a *remedial* exercise of Congress's enforcement power under the thirteenth amendment. First, 'slavery' may be regarded as a status to be defined by the Court, [and] the 'badges and incidents of slavery' may be regarded, not as elements of that definition, but as stigmas and disabilities related to slavery. [Thus,] to say that Congress may rationally determine the badges and incidents of slavery is nothing more than to say that Congress may prohibit certain practices, although those practices themselves do not constitute slavery, when Congress rationally finds that their prohibition will help to *prevent* slavery.[83] Alternatively, since Congress's [remedial power] encompasses eradicating the *effects* of constitutional violations as well as preventing future ones, the congressional prohibition in *Mayer* may be readily

---

[9]   For the view that *McDonald* strongly supports this approach, see Emily Calhoun, *The Thirteenth and Fourteenth Amendments: Constitutional Authority for Federal Legislation Against Private Sex Discrimination,* 61 Minn.L.Rev. 313 (1977). For criticism of *McDonald,* see Note, *The Thirteenth Amendment and Private Affirmative Action,* 89 Yale L.J. 399 (1979).

The Court has interpreted § 1981 "to protect from discrimination identifiable classes of persons who are subjected to intentional discrimination solely because of their ancestry of ethnic characteristics." *Saint Francis College v. Al-Khazraji,* 481 U.S. 604 (1987) (Arabs); *Shaare Tefila Congregation v. Cobb,* 481 U.S. 615 (1987) (Jews).

[83]   **[Ct's Note]** David E. Engdahl, *Constitutional Power: Federal and State in a Nutshell* 247–48 (1974) (emphasis added).

sustained as an effort to eliminate the persistent legacies of the past condition of slavery."[10]

4.   ***Self-executing force of Thirteenth Amendment.*** Apart from federal legislation pursuant to § 2, are any (all) of the discriminations referred to in the preceding notes made unconstitutional by § 1 of "the Amendment *itself*"? If so, by what means should (can) the Court enforce § 1?

II. STATE "INVOLVEMENT"

UNITED STATES v. PRICE, 383 U.S. 787 (1966), involved indictments for conspiracy and substantive violations under §§ 241 and 242, Sec. 1, I supra, against three Mississippi police officials and fifteen "nonofficial persons," for having willfully killed three civil rights workers—the police officials first jailing the victims, then releasing them and intercepting them and, then, all 18 defendants "punishing" the victims by shooting them—thus depriving "the victims due process of law."

A unanimous Court, per FORTAS, J., treating the case as raising issues "of construction, not of constitutional power," held that, as to the conspiracy count against the "private persons" under § 242: "[I]t is immaterial to the conspiracy that these private individuals were not acting under color of law because the count charges that they were conspiring with persons who were so acting." As to the substantive counts against the "private persons" under § 242, the Court, stating that the statutory language "under color of law" has "consistently been treated as the same thing as the 'state action' required by the Fourteenth Amendment," held that "private persons, jointly engaged with state officials in the prohibited action, are acting 'under color' of law for purposes of the statute. To act 'under color' of law does not require that the accused be an officer of the State. It is enough that he is a wilful participant in joint activity with the State or its agents," citing *Burton v. Wilmington Parking Auth.*, Ch. 10, Sec. 3. "[A]ccording to the indictment, the brutal joint adventure was made possible by state detention and calculated release of the prisoners by an officer of the State."[1] "Those who took advantage of participation by state officers in accomplishment of the foul purpose alleged must suffer the consequences of that participation."[2]

---

[10]   For the view—drawing on Harlan, J.'s dissent in the *Civil Rights Cases*—that, like the Thirteenth Amendment, "the Citizenship Clause, designed to secure equality of citizenship for the freedmen, gives Congress the corresponding power to protect the *badges and incidents of citizenship*. Congress may therefore ban discriminatory private conduct that it reasonably believes will contribute to or produce second-class citizenship," see Jack M. Balkin, *The Reconstruction Power,* 85 N. Y. U. L. Rev. 1801 (2010).

[1]   [Ct's Note] See also *United States v. Guest*, 383 U.S. 745 (1966).

[2]   [Ct's Note] See also *Screws v. United States,* 325 U.S. 91 (1945), holding that it was no defense under § 242 that defendant's actions were in violation of state law: "Misuse of power, possessed by virtue of state law and made possible only because the wrongdoer is clothed with the authority of state law, is action taken 'under color of' state law. [It] is clear that under 'color' of law means under 'pretense' of law. Thus acts of officers in the ambit of their personal pursuits are

NOTES AND QUESTIONS

1. *"Participation" of private persons with state officers.* In *Price*, the "official" and "nonofficial" defendants all appeared to be actively and equally participating in the venture. Could private persons be constitutionally convicted under § 242 if they were "passive" participants with state officers? Suppose the private person were the "active" participant while the state officers were merely "passive"? See Thomas J. Klitgaard, *The Civil Rights Act and Mr. Monroe,* 49 Calif.L.Rev. 145 (1961). Could the private person be convicted if all the state officers are acquitted?

2. *Consider the constitutionality of the following prosecutions under § 242:*

(a) Defendant sheriff beats prisoner to death because prisoner cursed the sheriff. Suppose the sheriff encounters a personal enemy on the street and beats him to death? Suppose this personal enemy declined to resist because he feared the consequences of a victory over a police officer? Suppose the sheriff first tells the personal enemy that he is under arrest?

(b) Defendant private citizen secretly enters a jail and beats a prisoner to death, thus preventing a fair trial by the state. Suppose the citizen joined the sheriff in beating the prisoner to death in order to obtain a confession?

(c) Defendant sheriff stands by while a private citizen beats to death the sheriff's prisoner, who is the citizen's personal enemy.

(d) Defendant private citizen is part of a mob that so intimidates parents of school children as to cause them to keep the children away from the school with the result that the school is closed. Suppose the private citizen intimidates state officials in an attempt to thwart their racial integration of public schools? See Stevens, J., concurring in *Great American Fed. S. & L. Ass'n v. Novotny,* 442 U.S. 366 (1979).

(e) Defendant private citizen makes a "citizen's arrest" without probable cause. Suppose the citizen had masqueraded as a policeman? Suppose the citizen, dressed as a policeman, killed a personal enemy? Suppose the citizen making an unlawful arrest were a private detective who became a "special police officer" by local law? See *Williams v. United States,* 341 U.S. 97 (1951).

(f) Defendant attorney, an "officer of the court," makes false statements in a sanity proceeding which result in the commitment of another person. Suppose defendant is court-appointed? See *Polk County v. Dodson,* 454 U.S. 312 (1981) (public defender does not act under color of law when performing traditional adversarial functions as appointed counsel).

(g) Defendant private citizen denies another use of a state park because of the latter's race? See *Guest* (Brennan, J., joined by Warren, C.J., and

---

plainly excluded. Acts of officers who undertake to perform their official duties are included whether they hew to the line of their authority or overstep it."

Douglas, J., concurring). Suppose the denial involved a privately owned trailer camp?

3.   (a) *Civil Rights Act of 1968.* 18 U.S.C.A. § 245(b), applies to anyone "whether or not acting under color of law [who] willfully injures or threatens any person" because of race, national origin, or religion who is enrolled in any public school, or is participating in any program or activity of a state government unit, or is employed by "any private employer or any agency of any State [or] using the services [of] any labor organization [or] employment agency," or serving on a jury, or stays at any hotel or eats at any restaurant, or "any gasoline station, or of any motion picture house, theater, concert hall, sports arena, [or] stadium [which] serves the public."

(b)   Suppose a private individual murders African-Americans. It is clear that the *effect* (irrespective of the murderer's *intent*) is to prevent the victims' equal use of state facilities; that it prevents their right to be jurors, etc. These facts would be equally true if the victim were white. May the murderer be punished under the above statute? Under a more narrowly drawn federal criminal statute? Consider Archibald Cox, *Constitutional Adjudication and the Promotion of Human Rights,* 80 Harv.L.Rev. 91 (1966): "The differences between purpose, awareness that a consequence must follow, conscious indifference, and responsibility for the natural and probable consequences of an act are far too elusive to measure the scope of congressional power. [The] suggestion was once made that the power of Congress to regulate local activities under the Commerce Clause depended upon the intent with which the activities were conducted, but the idea was shortly abandoned in favor of legislative or administrative determination of the practical effects on commerce." Does congressional power fail in the above instance because "its authority is confined to instances in which there is a special relationship between the person injured and the state"? Or is "the responsibility for the federal system" left to Congress: "possession of congressional power should not be confused with its exercise"? Id.

3.   REGULATION OF STATE ACTORS

SOUTH CAROLINA v. KATZENBACH, 383 U.S. 301 (1966): South Carolina challenged the Voting Rights Act of 1965—"the heart of [which] is a complex scheme of stringent remedies aimed at areas where voting discrimination has been most flagrant." The Court, per WARREN, C.J., referred to "the voluminous legislative history" that showed, inter alia, "unremitting and ingenious defiance of the Constitution," the enactment of literacy tests in Alabama, Georgia, Louisiana, Mississippi, North Carolina, South Carolina, and Virginia, still in use, which, because of their various qualifications, "were specifically designed to prevent Negroes from voting." It pointed out that "discriminatory application of voting tests" "pursuant to a widespread 'pattern or practice' " "is now the principal method used to bar Negroes from the polls," and that "case-by-case litigation against voting discrimination" under federal statutes of 1957, 1960 and 1964 has "done little to cure the problem."

"As against the reserved powers of the States, Congress may use any rational means to effectuate the constitutional prohibition of racial discrimination in voting. [The] basic test to be applied in a case involving § 2 of the Fifteenth Amendment is the same as in all cases concerning the express powers of Congress with relation to the reserved powers of the [states.] 'Let the end be legitimate, let it be within the scope of the constitution, and all means which are appropriate, which are plainly adapted to that end, which are not prohibited, but consist with the letter and spirit of the constitution, are constitutional.' *McCulloch v. Maryland* [Ch. 2, Sec. 1]."

The "coverage formula" of the Act applied "to any State [or] political subdivision [for] which two findings have been made: (1) [on] November 1, 1964, it maintained a 'test or device,' and (2) [that] less than 50% of its voting-age residents were registered on November 1, 1964, or voted in the presidential election of November 1964. * * * § 4(b). [T]he phrase 'test or device' means any requirement that a registrant or voter must '(1) demonstrate the ability to read, write, understand, or interpret any matter, (2) demonstrate any educational achievement or his knowledge of any particular subject, (3) possess good moral character, or (4) prove his qualifications by the voucher of registered voters or members of any other class.' § 4(c)." Statutory coverage was terminated by a so-called "bail out" provision—if the area obtained a judgment from a three-judge federal court in the District of Columbia "that tests and devices have not been used during the preceding five years to abridge the franchise on racial grounds." "In acceptable legislative fashion, Congress chose to limit its attention to the geographic areas where immediate action seemed necessary."

The areas covered, "for which there was evidence of actual voting discrimination,"—Alabama, Georgia, Louisiana, Mississippi, South Carolina and much of North Carolina—shared the "two characteristics incorporated by Congress into the coverage formula." "It was therefore permissible to impose the new remedies on the few remaining States and political subdivisions covered by the formula, at least in the absence of proof that they have been free of substantial voting discrimination in recent years." That there are excluded areas "for which there is evidence of voting discrimination by other means" is irrelevant: "Legislation need not deal with all phases of a problem in the same way, so long as the distinctions drawn have some basis in political experience." "There are no States or political subdivisions exempted from coverage under § 4(b) in which the record reveals recent racial discrimination involving tests and devices. This fact confirms the rationality of the formula."

In areas covered, § 4(a) suspended "literacy tests and similar voting qualifications for a period of five years from the last occurrence of substantial voting discrimination," and § 5 suspended "all new voting regulations pending review by [the Attorney General or a three-judge court in the District of Columbia] to determine whether their use would perpetuate voting discrimination."[11] Both were upheld as a "legitimate response to the problem," the Court recounting the evidence Congress had before it of prior discriminatory administration of old tests and use of new tests to evade court decrees.[12]

KATZENBACH V. MORGAN
384 U.S. 641, 86 S.Ct. 1717, 16 L.Ed.2d 828 (1966).

JUSTICE BRENNAN delivered the opinion of the Court.

[Section] 4(e) of the Voting Rights Act of 1965 [provides] that no person who has successfully completed the sixth primary grade in a [school] accredited by the Commonwealth of Puerto Rico in which the language of instruction was other than English shall be denied the right to vote in any election because of his inability to read or write English. [Thus, it] prohibits the enforcement of the election laws of New York requiring an ability to read and write English * * * .

The Attorney General of New York argues that an exercise of congressional power under § 5 of the Fourteenth Amendment that prohibits the enforcement of a state [law] cannot be sustained as appropriate legislation to enforce the Equal Protection Clause unless the judiciary decides—even with the guidance of a congressional judgment—that the application of the English literacy requirement prohibited by § 4(e) is forbidden by the Equal Protection Clause itself. We disagree. Neither the language nor history of § 5 supports such a construction.[7] [A] judicial determination that the enforcement of the state law precluded by Congress violated the Amendment, as a condition of sustaining the congressional enactment [would] confine the legislative power in this context to the

---

[11] For examples of the Court's subsequent broad interpretation of "voting regulations" that are subject to the suspension provision of section 5, see *United Jewish Orgs. v. Carey,* Ch. 9, Sec. 5, I, D (new or revised reapportionment plan); *Rome v. United States,* infra (election of officials "at large" rather than by district; annexation of adjacent area thus increasing number of eligible voters).

[12] Black, J., agreed "with substantially all of the Court's opinion" but dissented in respect to § 5 of the Act: "[I]f all the provisions of our Constitution which limit the power of the Federal Government and reserve other power to the States are to mean anything, they mean at least that the States have power to pass laws [without] first sending their officials hundreds of miles away to beg federal authorities to approve them."

[7] For the historical evidence suggesting that the sponsors and supporters of the Amendment were primarily interested in augmenting the power of Congress, rather than the judiciary, see generally Laurent B. Frantz, *Congressional Power to Enforce the Fourteenth Amendment Against Private Acts,* 73 Yale L.J. 1353 (1964); Robert J. Harris, *The Quest for Equality,* 33–56 (1960); Jacobus tenBroek, *The Antislavery Origins of the Fourteenth Amendment* 187 (1951). [But see Robert A. Burt, *Miranda and Title II: A Morganatic Marriage,* 1969 Sup.Ct.Rev. 81.]

insignificant role of abrogating only those state laws that the judicial branch was prepared to adjudge unconstitutional, or of merely informing the judgment of the judiciary by particularizing the "majestic generalities" of [§ 1]. in [Rather,] the question before us here [is when may] the judiciary find that the Equal Protection Clause itself nullifies New York's English literacy requirement as so applied, Congress prohibit the enforcement of the state law by legislating under § 5? In answering this question, our task is limited to determining whether such legislation is, as required by § 5, appropriate legislation to enforce the Equal Protection Clause.

By including § 5 the draftsmen sought to grant to Congress [the] same broad powers expressed in the Necessary and Proper Clause.[9] The classic formulation of the reach of those powers was established by Chief Justice Marshall in *McCulloch v. Maryland*, [Ch. 2, Sec. 1]. *Ex parte Virginia*, 100 U.S. 339, 25 L.Ed. 676 (1879), decided 12 years after the adoption of the Fourteenth Amendment, held that congressional power under § 5 had this same broad [scope]. Section 2 of the Fifteenth Amendment grants Congress a similar power [and] we recently held in *South Carolina* that [the test was] the one formulated in *McCulloch*. * * * Correctly viewed, § 5 is a positive grant of legislative power authorizing Congress to exercise its discretion in determining whether and what legislation is needed to secure the guarantees of the Fourteenth Amendment. * * * [10]

There can be no doubt that § 4(e) may be regarded as an enactment to enforce the Equal Protection Clause. [The] practical effect of § 4(e) is to prohibit New York from denying the right to vote to large segments of its Puerto Rican community [—the] right that is "preservative of all rights." This enhanced political power will be helpful in gaining nondiscriminatory treatment in public services ["such as public schools, public housing, and law enforcement"] for the entire Puerto Rican community.[11] [It] was for Congress, as the branch that made this judgment, to assess and weigh the various conflicting considerations—the risk or pervasiveness of the discrimination in governmental services, the effectiveness of eliminating the state restriction on the right to vote as a means of dealing with the evil,

---

[9] [Ct's Note] In fact, earlier drafts of the proposed Amendment employed the "necessary and proper" terminology to describe the scope of congressional power under the Amendment. The substitution of the "appropriate legislation" formula was never thought to have the effect of diminishing the scope of this congressional power. See, e.g., Cong. Globe, 42d Cong., 1st Sess., App. 83. * * * [But see Note, *Theories of Federalism and Civil Rights*, 75 Yale L.J. 1007 (1966). Compare discussion in *Argument: The Oral Argument Before the Supreme Court in Brown v. Board of Education of Topeka,* 1952 (Friedman ed. 1969).]

[10] [Ct's Note] Contrary to the suggestion of the [dissent,] § 5 is limited to adopting measures to enforce the guarantees of the Amendment; § 5 grants Congress no power to restrict, abrogate, or dilute these guarantees. Thus, for example, an enactment authorizing the States to establish racially segregated systems of education would not be—as required by § 5—a measure "to enforce" the Equal Protection Clause since that clause of its own force prohibits such state laws.

[11] [Ct's Note] Cf. * * * *United States v. Darby* [Ch. 2, Sec. 2, II, B], that the power of Congress to regulate interstate commerce "extends to those activities intrastate which so affect interstate commerce or the exercise of the power of Congress over it as to make regulation of them appropriate means to the attainment of a legitimate end * * * ."

the adequacy or availability of alternative remedies, and the nature and significance of the state interests that would be affected by the nullification of the English literacy requirement. [It] is enough that we be able to perceive a basis upon which the Congress might resolve the conflict as it did. There plainly was such a [basis]. Any contrary conclusion would require us to be blind to the realities familiar to the legislators.

The result is no different if we confine our inquiry to the question whether § 4(e) was merely legislation aimed at the elimination of an invidious discrimination in establishing voter qualifications. We are told that New York's English literacy requirement originated in the desire to provide an incentive for non-English speaking immigrants to learn the English language and in order to assure the intelligent exercise of the franchise. Yet Congress might well have questioned, in light of the many exemptions provided,[13] and some evidence suggesting that prejudice played a prominent role in the enactment of the requirement,[14] whether these were actually the interests being served. Congress might have also questioned whether denial of a right deemed so precious and fundamental in our society was a necessary or appropriate means of encouraging persons to learn English, or of furthering the goal of an intelligent exercise of the franchise.[15] Finally, Congress might well have concluded that as a means of furthering the intelligent exercise of the franchise, an ability to read or understand Spanish is as effective as ability to read English for those to whom Spanish-language newspapers and Spanish-language radio and television programs are available to inform them of election issues and governmental affairs.[16] Since Congress undertook to legislate so as to preclude the enforcement of the state law, and did so in the context of a general appraisal of literacy requirements for voting, see *South Carolina,* to which it brought a specially informed legislative competence,[17] it was Congress' prerogative to weigh these competing considerations. Here again, it is enough that we perceive a basis upon which Congress might

---

[13] **[Ct's Note]** The principal exemption complained of is that for persons who had been eligible to vote before January 1, 1922.

[14] **[Ct's Note]** This evidence consists in part of statements made in the [New York State] Constitutional Convention first considering the English literacy requirement * * * . Congress was aware of this evidence. See, e.g., *Literacy Tests and Voter Requirements in Federal and State Elections,* Senate Hearings 507; *Voting Rights,* House Hearings 508.

[15] **[Ct's Note]** [O]ur cases have held that the States can be required to tailor carefully the means of satisfying a legitimate state interest when fundamental liberties and rights are threatened, see, e.g., *Carrington v. Rash*; *Harper v. Virginia Board of Elections* [Ch. 9, Sec. 5, I, A]; *United States v. Carolene Products Co.* [Ch. 5, Sec. 3]; and Congress is free to apply the same principle in the exercise of its powers.

[16] **[Ct's Note]** See, e.g., 111 Cong.Rec. 10675 (May 20, 1965), 15102 (July 6, 1965), 15666 (July 9, 1965). The record in this case includes affidavits describing the nature of New York's two major Spanish-language newspapers [and] its three full-time Spanish-language radio stations and affidavits from those who have campaigned in Spanish speaking areas.

[17] **[Ct's Note]** See, e.g., 111 Cong.Rec. 10676 (Senator Long of Louisiana and Senator Young), 10678 (Senator Holland) (May 20, 1965), drawing on their experience with voters literate in a language other than English. * * *

predicate a judgment that the application of New York's English literacy [requirement] constituted an invidious discrimination in violation of the Equal Protection Clause.

[The Court rejected the contention that the "American-flag schools" limitation itself violates "the letter and spirit of the Constitution"].

Reversed.

JUSTICE HARLAN, whom JUSTICE STEWART joins, dissenting.

[The dissent first argued that the New York law was not forbidden by the Equal Protection Clause itself.] I believe the Court has confused the issue of how much enforcement power Congress possesses under § 5 with the distinct issue of what questions are appropriate for congressional determination and what questions are essentially judicial in nature.

When recognized state violations of federal constitutional standards have occurred, Congress is of course empowered by § 5 to take appropriate remedial measures. [But the] question here is not whether the statute is appropriate remedial legislation to cure an established violation of a constitutional command, but whether [a] particular state practice or, as here, a statute is so arbitrary or irrational as to offend the command of [equal protection]. That question is one for the judicial branch ultimately to determine. [In] view of [*Lassiter v. Northampton Cty. Bd. of Elec.*, 360 U.S. 45 (1959), sustaining the North Carolina English literacy requirement as not in all circumstances prohibited by the first sections of the Fourteenth and Fifteenth Amendments,], I do not think it is open to Congress to limit the effect of that decision as it has undertaken to do by § 4(e). In effect the Court reads § 5 of the Fourteenth Amendment as giving Congress the power to define the *substantive* scope of the Amendment. If that indeed be the true reach of § 5, then I do not see why Congress should not be able as well to exercise its § 5 "discretion" by enacting statutes so as in effect to dilute equal protection and due process decisions of this Court. In all such cases there is room for reasonable men to differ as to whether or not a denial of equal protection or due process has occurred, and the final decision is one of judgment. Until today this judgment has always been one for the judiciary to resolve.

I do not mean to suggest in what has been said that a legislative judgment of the type incorporated in § 4(e) is without any force whatsoever. Decisions on questions of equal protection and due process are based not on abstract logic, but on empirical foundations. To the extent "legislative facts" are relevant to a judicial determination, Congress is well equipped to investigate them, and such determinations are of course entitled to due respect.[13] In *South Carolina,* such legislative findings were made to show

---

[13] For the view that "Congress cannot alter the *normative component* of a judicial decision" but that "the *empirical component* [is] the province of Congress," see Irving Gordon, *The Nature*

that racial discrimination in voting was actually occurring. Similarly, in *Heart of Atlanta* and *Katzenbach v. McClung,* [Ch. 2, Sec. 2, III], the congressional determination that racial discrimination in a clearly defined group of public accommodations did effectively impede interstate commerce was based on "voluminous testimony" which had been put before the Congress and in the context of which it passed remedial legislation.

But no such factual data provide a legislative record supporting § 4(e)[9] by way of showing that Spanish-speaking citizens are fully as capable of making informed decisions in a New York election as are English-speaking citizens. Nor was there any showing whatever to support the Court's alternative argument that § 4(e) should be viewed as but a remedial measure designed to cure or assure against unconstitutional discrimination of other varieties, e.g., in "public schools, public housing and law enforcement" * * * .

Thus, we have [here] what can at most be called a legislative announcement that Congress believes a state law to entail an unconstitutional deprivation of equal protection. Although this kind of declaration is of course entitled to the most respectful consideration, coming as it does from a concurrent branch and one that is knowledgeable in matters of popular political participation, I do not believe it lessens our responsibility to decide the fundamental issue of whether in fact the state enactment violates federal constitutional rights.

In assessing the deference we should give to this kind of congressional expression of policy, it is relevant that the judiciary has always given to congressional enactments a presumption of validity. However, it is also a canon of judicial review that state statutes are given a similar presumption, [and] although it has been suggested that this Court should give somewhat more deference to Congress than to a State Legislature, such a simple weighing of presumptions is hardly a satisfying way of resolving a matter that touches the distribution of state and federal power in an area so sensitive as that of the regulation of the franchise. Rather it should be recognized that while the Fourteenth Amendment is a "brooding omnipresence" over all state legislation, the substantive matters which it touches are all within the primary legislative competence of the States. Federal authority, legislative no less than judicial, does not intrude unless there has been a denial by state action of Fourteenth Amendment [limitations].

---

and Uses of Congressional Power Under Section Five of the Fourteenth Amendment to Overcome Decisions of the Supreme Court, 72 Nw.U.L.Rev. 656 (1977). See also note 1 after *Boerne* infra.

[9] **[Ct's Note]** There were no committee hearings or reports referring to this section, which was introduced from the floor during debate on the full Voting Rights Act.

NOTES AND QUESTIONS

1. ***Morgan's "substantive" branch.*** (a) ***Equal protection.*** After *Morgan,* could Congress enact legislation prohibiting *all* state discrimination on the basis of alienage, illegitimacy and gender? Cf. Ch. 9, Secs. 3–4. Forbidding state discrimination against opticians, debt adjustors and methadone users? Cf. Ch. 9, Sec. 1. Requiring that, in all instances in which state action has a racially disproportionate impact, the courts should balance the strength of the government interest against the disadvantage imposed on the racial minority? Cf. Ch. 9, Sec. 2, III.

(b) ***Procedural due process.*** After *Morgan,* could Congress impose the federal rules of civil and criminal procedure on the states on the ground that the Fourteenth Amendment requires that due process be accorded all litigants and that in "its discretion" the federal rules are "needed to secure the guarantees of the Fourteenth Amendment"?

(c) ***Substantive due process.*** After *Morgan*, could Congress enact the proposed Freedom of Choice Act (FOCA), H.R. 25, 102d Cong., 1st Sess. (1991); S. 25, 102d Cong.2d Sess. (1992), which would respond to *Planned Parenthood v. Casey,* Ch. 6, Sec. 2, by codifying the holding of *Roe v. Wade?* May Congress grant a federal right to "abortion on demand"?

(d) ***State action.*** If *Morgan* gives Congress "the power to define the *substantive* scope" of equal protection (and due process), does it similarly permit Congress to determine the question of what constitutes "state action"? For example, might Congress, in "exercise of its discretion," determine that any judicial enforcement of racial discrimination shall be prohibited? For the view that the Fourteenth Amendment's "Privileges or Immunities Clause (coupled with the § 5 Enforcement Clause)" was intended "as an authorization of Federal legislation to prohibit private racial discrimination if the states did not," see Louis Lusky, *By What Right?* 181–203 (1975).

2. ***Dilution.*** Does *Morgan* give Congress power "to dilute equal protection and due process decisions" of the Court? Consider Cox, supra: "According to the conventional theory [enunciated in fn. 10 of *Morgan*], the Court has invalidated state statutes under the Due Process and Equal Protection Clauses only when no state of facts which can reasonably be conceived would sustain them. Where that is true, a congressional effort to withdraw the protection granted by the clause would lack the foundation of a reasonably conceivable set of facts and would therefore be just as invalid as the state legislation. But while that is true in the realm of economic regulation, the Court has often substituted its own evaluation of actual conditions in reviewing legislation dealing with 'preferred rights.' It is hard to see how the Court can consistently give weight to the congressional judgment in expanding the definition of equal protection in the area of human rights but refuse to give it weight in narrowing the definition where the definition depends upon appraisal of the facts." Compare William Cohen, *Congressional Power to Interpret Due Process and Equal Protection,* 27 Stan.L.Rev. 603 (1975): "[A] theory that distinguishes between congressional competence to make 'liberty'

and 'federalism' judgments resolves the dilemma. A congressional judgment rejecting a judicial interpretation of the Due Process or Equal Protection Clauses—an interpretation that had given the individual procedural or substantive protection from state and federal government alike—is entitled to no more deference than the identical decision of a state legislature. Congress is no more immune to momentary passions of the majority than are the state legislatures. But a congressional judgment resolving at the national level an issue that could—without constitutional objection—be decided in the same way at the state level, ought normally to be binding on the courts, since Congress presumably reflects a balance between both national and state interests and hence is better able to adjust such conflicts." See also Jesse H. Choper, *Judicial Review and the National Political Process* 198 (1980). For the view that this reasoning is supported by both constitutional structure and original intent, see Douglas Laycock, *RFRA, Congress, and the Ratchet,* 56 Mont.L.Rev. 145 (1995).

BOERNE V. FLORES
521 U.S. 507, 117 S.Ct. 2157, 138 L.Ed.2d 624 (1997).

JUSTICE KENNEDY delivered the opinion of the Court.

A decision by local zoning authorities to deny a church a building permit was challenged under the Religious Freedom Restoration Act of 1993 (RFRA). * * *

Congress enacted RFRA in direct response to the Court's decision in *Employment Div. v. Smith,* [Ch. 8, Sec. 2, I]. *Smith* held that neutral, generally applicable laws may be applied to religious practices even when not supported by a compelling governmental interest. [Many] criticized the Court's reasoning, and this disagreement resulted in the passage of RFRA. * * *

RFRA prohibits "[g]overnment" from "substantially burden[ing]" a person's exercise of religion even if the burden results from a rule of general applicability unless the government can demonstrate the burden "(1) is in furtherance of a compelling governmental interest; and (2) is the least restrictive means of furthering that compelling governmental interest." * * * Legislation which deters or remedies constitutional violations can fall within the sweep of Congress' [Fourteenth Amendment] enforcement power even if in the process it prohibits conduct which is not itself unconstitutional and intrudes into "legislative spheres of autonomy previously reserved to the States." *Fitzpatrick v. Bitzer*, 427 U.S. 445 (1976). [As examples, the Court discussed the practices that Congress had made unlawful in *South Carolina, Morgan* and *Rome*, note 3(c) infra.] We agree with respondent, of course, that Congress can enact legislation under § 5 enforcing the constitutional right to the free exercise of religion. * * *

Congress' power under § 5, however, extends only to "enforc[ing]" the provisions of the Fourteenth Amendment. The Court has described this power as "remedial," *South Carolina*. The design of the Amendment and the text of § 5 are inconsistent with the suggestion that Congress has the power to decree the substance of the Fourteenth Amendment's restrictions on the States. Legislation which alters the meaning of the Free Exercise Clause cannot be said to be enforcing the Clause. [Were] it not so, what Congress would be enforcing would no longer be, in any meaningful sense, the "provisions of [the Fourteenth Amendment]."

While the line between measures that remedy or prevent unconstitutional actions and measures that make a substantive change in the governing law is not easy to discern, and Congress must have wide latitude in determining where it lies, the distinction exists and must be observed. There must be a congruence and proportionality between the injury to be prevented or remedied and the means adopted to that end. Lacking such a connection, legislation may become substantive in operation and effect. * * *

The Fourteenth Amendment's history confirms the remedial, rather than substantive, nature of the Enforcement Clause.[14] [The] objections to the [Joint] Committee's first draft of the Amendment ["The Congress shall have power to make all laws which shall be necessary and proper to secure to the citizens of each State all privileges and immunities of citizens in the several States, and to all persons in the several States equal protection in the rights of life, liberty, and property."] have a direct bearing on the central issue of defining Congress' enforcement power. * * * Members of Congress from across the political spectrum criticized the Amendment, and the criticisms had a common theme: The proposed Amendment gave Congress [a] power to intrude into traditional areas of state responsibility, a power inconsistent with the federal design central to the Constitution. [Under] the revised Amendment, Congress' power was no longer plenary but remedial [and] did not raise the concerns expressed earlier regarding

---

[14] Contra, Douglas Laycock, *Conceptual Gulfs in Boerne v. Flores*, 39 Wm. & M. L. Rev. 743 (1998): "Senators and representatives argued [that] the enforcement power would add nothing if it were confined to the judicially enforceable meaning of the Amendment"; Evan Caminker, *"Appropriate" Means-End Constraints on Section 5 Powers*, 53 Stan.L.Rev. 1127 (2001): "[A]n originalist inquiry—whether focused on the Framers' actual subjective intentions, as the Court did with respect to the interpretation of Section 5 ends, or whether focused on the most likely public understanding of the amendment's plain language, as many contemporary originalists would do—firmly supports the conclusion that Section 5 was designed [and] understood as codifying Chief Justice Marshall's especially deferential ['necessary and proper' formulation] in *McCulloch*"; Ruth Colker, *The Supreme Court's Historical Errors in City of Boerne v. Flores*, 43 B.C.L.Rev. 783 (2002). Compare J. Randy Beck, *The Heart of Federalism: Pretext Review of Means-End Relationships*, 36 U.C. Davis L.Rev. 407 (2003) ("means-end limitations such as proportionality and proximity to prevent pretextual legislation comports [with] *McCulloch*").

broad congressional power to prescribe uniform national laws with respect to life, liberty, and property.[15] * * *

The design of the Fourteenth Amendment has proved significant also in maintaining the traditional separation of powers between Congress and the Judiciary. The first eight Amendments to the Constitution set forth self-executing prohibitions on governmental action, and this Court has had primary authority to interpret those prohibitions. The [Joint Committee's first] draft, some thought, departed from that tradition by vesting in Congress primary power to interpret and elaborate on the meaning of the new Amendment through legislation. Under it, "Congress, and not the courts, was to judge whether or not any of the privileges or immunities were not secured to citizens in the several States." [But the] power to interpret the Constitution in a case or controversy remains in the Judiciary. * * *

Any suggestion that Congress has a substantive, non-remedial power under the Fourteenth Amendment is not supported by our case law. In *Oregon v. Mitchell*, [400 U.S. 112 (1970)], a majority of the Court concluded Congress had exceeded its enforcement powers by enacting legislation lowering the minimum age of voters from 21 to 18 in state and local elections.[16] The five Members of the Court who reached this conclusion explained that [the] legislation was unconstitutional because the Constitution "reserves to the States the power to set voter qualifications in state and local elections." Four of these five were explicit in rejecting the position that § 5 endowed Congress with the power to establish the meaning of constitutional provisions. See (opinion of Harlan, J.); (opinion of Stewart, J., joined by Burger, C. J., and Blackmun, J.). * * *[17]

There is language in our opinion in *Morgan* which could be interpreted as acknowledging a power in Congress to enact legislation that expands the rights contained in § 1 of the Fourteenth Amendment. This is not a

---

[15] For the view that "although the *Boerne* Court properly rejected the plenary 'substantive' interpretation of Section Five, the Court's conclusion that judicial interpretations of the provisions of the Amendment are the exclusive touchstone for congressional enforcement power finds no support in the history of the Fourteenth Amendment," see Michael W. McConnell, *Institutions and Interpretation: A Critique of Boerne v. Flores*, 111 Harv.L.Rev. 153 (1997).

[16] A different majority—Black, Douglas, Brennan, White and Marshall, JJ.—voted to uphold this provision as to federal elections. Black, J., who was in both majorities, distinguished the situations on the ground (which no other justice joined) that Congress had power under Art. I, § 4 to set qualifications for voters in federal elections. For an alternative rationale, see David E. Engdahl, *Constitutionality of the Voting Age Statute,* 39 Geo.Wash.L.Rev. 1 (1970): "Since no *state* [has] a legitimate interest in protecting the integrity of *national* elections, it is difficult to imagine any *state* interest sufficient to justify, under the equal protection clause, any *state* exclusion of a significant 'stake-holder' in *national* elections."

[17] Black, J., stated: "Congress made no legislative findings that 21-year-old vote requirements were used by the States to disenfranchise voters on account of race. I seriously doubt that such a finding, if made, could be supported by substantial evidence. Since Congress has attempted to invade an area preserved to the States by the Constitution without a foundation for enforcing the Civil War Amendments' ban on racial discrimination, I would hold that Congress has exceeded its powers in attempting to lower the voting age in state and local elections."

necessary interpretation, however, or even the best one. [As] Justice Stewart explained in *Mitchell,* interpreting *Morgan* to give Congress the power to interpret the Constitution "would require an enormous extension of that decision's rationale."[18]

If Congress could define its own powers by altering the Fourteenth Amendment's meaning, no longer would the Constitution be "superior paramount law, unchangeable by ordinary means." It would be "on a level with ordinary legislative acts, and, like other [acts,] alterable when the legislature shall please to alter it." *Marbury v. Madison.* Under this approach, it is difficult to conceive of a principle that would limit congressional power. Shifting legislative majorities could change the Constitution and effectively circumvent the difficult and detailed amendment process contained in Article V. * * *

Respondent contends that RFRA is a proper exercise of Congress' remedial or preventive power. The Act, it is [said,] prevents and remedies laws which are enacted with the unconstitutional object of targeting religious beliefs and practices. See *Church of the Lukumi Babalu Aye, Inc. v. Hialeah,* [Ch. 8, Sec. 2, I]. To avoid the difficulty of proving such violations, it is said, Congress can simply invalidate any law which imposes a substantial burden on a religious practice unless it is justified by a compelling interest and is the least restrictive means of accomplishing that interest. If Congress can prohibit laws with discriminatory effects in order to prevent racial discrimination in violation of the Equal Protection Clause, then it can do the same, respondent argues, to promote religious liberty.

While preventive rules are sometimes appropriate remedial measures, there must be a congruence between the means used and the ends to be achieved. * * * Strong measures appropriate to address one harm may be an unwarranted response to another, lesser one.

A comparison between RFRA and the Voting Rights Act is instructive. In contrast to the record which confronted Congress and the judiciary in the voting rights cases, RFRA's legislative record lacks examples of modern instances of generally applicable laws passed because of religious bigotry. [Rather,] the emphasis of the hearings was on laws of general applicability which place incidental burdens on religion. * * *

Regardless of the state of the legislative record, RFRA [is] so out of proportion to a supposed remedial or preventive object that it cannot be understood as responsive to, or designed to prevent, unconstitutional behavior. It appears, instead, to attempt a substantive change in constitutional protections. Preventive measures prohibiting certain types of laws may be appropriate when there is reason to believe that many of

---

[18] For the view that "the scope of the definitional power" granted Congress in *Morgan,* "although by no means insignificant, may nonetheless be quite limited," see Choper, note 3(b) after *Mayer.*

the laws affected by the congressional enactment have a significant likelihood of being unconstitutional. See *Rome.* * * *

The reach and scope of RFRA distinguish it from other measures passed under Congress' enforcement power, even in the area of voting rights. In *South Carolina,* the challenged provisions were confined to those regions of the country where voting discrimination had been most flagrant, and affected a discrete class of state laws, i.e., state voting laws. Furthermore, to ensure that the reach of the Voting Rights Act was limited to those cases in which constitutional violations were most likely (in order to reduce the possibility of overbreadth), the coverage under the Act would terminate "at the behest of States and political subdivisions in which the danger of substantial voting discrimination has not materialized during the preceding five years." The provisions restricting and banning literacy tests, upheld in *Morgan,* attacked a particular type of voting qualification, one with a long history as a "notorious means to deny and abridge voting rights on racial grounds." [This] is not to say, of course, that § 5 legislation requires termination dates, geographic restrictions or egregious predicates. Where, however, a congressional enactment pervasively prohibits constitutional state action in an effort to remedy or to prevent unconstitutional state action, limitations of this kind tend to ensure Congress' means are proportionate to ends legitimate under § 5. * * *

The substantial costs RFRA exacts, both in practical terms of imposing a heavy litigation burden on the States and in terms of curtailing their traditional general regulatory power, far exceed any pattern or practice of unconstitutional conduct under the Free Exercise Clause as interpreted in *Smith.*[19] [In] addition, the Act imposes in every case a least restrictive means requirement—a requirement that was not used in the pre-*Smith* jurisprudence RFRA purported to codify—which also indicates that the legislation is broader than is appropriate if the goal is to prevent and remedy constitutional violations.

When [the] political branches of the Government act against the background of a judicial interpretation of the Constitution already issued, it must be understood that in later cases and controversies the Court will treat its precedents with the respect due them under settled principles, including stare decisis, and contrary expectations must be disappointed. RFRA was designed to control cases and controversies, such as the one before us; but as the provisions of the federal statute here invoked are

---

[19] Is Title VII of the Civil Rights Act, which requires that state employers "reasonably accommodate" the religious practices of their employees when they conflict with generally applicable rules of employment, a proper exercise of Congress power under § 5? See James M. Oleske, Jr., *Federalism, Free Exercise, and Title VII, Reconsidering Reasonable Accommodation,* 6 U.Pa.J.Const.L. 525 (2004).

beyond congressional authority, it is this Court's precedent, not RFRA, which must control. * * *[20]

JUSTICE STEVENS, concurring.

In my opinion, RFRA is a "law respecting an establishment of religion" that violates the First Amendment * * * .[21]

JUSTICE O'CONNOR, with whom JUSTICE BREYER joins except as to [the first sentence below].

* * * I agree with much of the reasoning set forth in [the] Court's opinion. [But] I remain of the view that *Smith* was wrongly decided, and I would use this case to reexamine the Court's holding there. Therefore, I would direct the parties to brief the question whether *Smith* represents the correct understanding of the Free Exercise Clause and set the case for reargument. If the Court were to correct the misinterpretation of the Free Exercise Clause set forth in *Smith,* it would simultaneously put our First Amendment jurisprudence back on course and allay the legitimate concerns of a majority in Congress who believed that *Smith* improperly restricted religious liberty. We would then be in a position to review RFRA in light of a proper interpretation of the Free Exercise Clause. * * *

NOTES AND QUESTIONS

1.   *Institutional limits and judicial "underenforcement."* (a) Apart from the "history" and "design" of the Fourteenth Amendment, are there good reasons for affording Congress some role in respect to "substantive scope"? Consider Lawrence G. Sager, *Fair Measure: The Legal Status of Underenforced Constitutional Norms,* 91 Harv.L.Rev. 1212 (1978): "There are reasons which explain and to some degree justify federal judicial restraint in [applying the provisions of § 1 of the Fourteenth Amendment]. In the most general of terms, the claims for restraint typically turn on the propriety of unelected federal judges' displacing the judgments of elected state officials, or upon the competence of federal courts to prescribe workable standards of state conduct and devise measures to enforce them."[22] See also Lawrence G. Sager, *Justice in Plain Clothes: Reflections on the Thinness of Constitutional Law,* 88

---

[20] Does *Boerne* also invalidate RFRA as applied to federal laws? Compare Thomas C. Berg, *The Constitutional Future of Religious Freedom Legislation,* 20 U.Ark. Little Rock L.J. 715 (1998); Gregory P. Magarian, *How to Apply the Religious Freedom Restoration Act to Federal Law Without Violating the Constitution,* 99 Mich.L.Rev. 1903 (2001) with Marci A. Hamilton, *The Religious Freedom Restoration Act Is Unconstitutional, Period,* 1 U.Pa.J.Const.L. 1 (1998). See note 4 in Ch. 8, Sec. 4.

[21] The concurring opinion of Scalia, J., joined by Stevens, J., both of whom joined the Court's opinion, is omitted. Souter, J. would dismiss the writ of certiorari as improvidently granted.

[22] For the view that "Congress may expand the judiciary's role by identifying additional suspect classes and fundamental rights and by increasing the level of scrutiny in specified types of equal protection cases," see Stephen F. Ross, *Legislative Enforcement of Equal Protection,* 72 Minn.L.Rev. 311 (1987).

Nw.U.L.Rev. 410 (1993): "The Supreme Court superintends a sprawling establishment of state and federal courts, courts that will be called upon to review a wide range of governmental behavior, [some] of which will have been carefully disguised precisely to avoid judicial invalidation. The Court, accordingly, has good reason to adopt rules that are blunter, less nuanced, but which overall better serve its objective of securing compliance with its underlying norm."[23] See also David Cole, *The Value of Seeing Things Differently: Boerne v. Flores and Congressional Enforcement of the Bill of Rights*, 1997 Sup.Ct.Rev. 31: "When the Court interprets a constitutional provision, it creates rights that cannot be altered except by a judicial departure from stare decisis or a constitutional amendment. And when the Court interprets the Fourteenth Amendment to impose duties on the states, it does so without the benefit of state representation. When Congress interprets the Fourteenth Amendment for purposes of statutory enforcement, by contrast, its interpretations are subject to amendment at any time by majority vote, and its deliberations structurally reflect the interests of the states."[24]

See also McConnell, fn. 15: "Judicial interpretations of the Constitution are often influenced by institutional considerations, such as the principle of judicial restraint, that create 'slippage' between the Constitution as enforced and the Constitution itself. [*Smith*] was predicated on just such an institutional concern: the fear that there are no judicially manageable standards for balancing the impact of a law on religious freedom against its importance to the public interest. [But the] democratic values underlying the doctrine of judicial restraint do not apply to Congress. [Its] decision to adopt a more robust, freedom-protective interpretation of the Free Exercise Clause did not 'alter' the Constitution or create 'new' rights. Rather, RFRA merely liberated the enforcement of free exercise rights from constraints derived from judicial restraint."

(b) *"Factfinding."* In *Mitchell*, Brennan, J.'s dissent stressed that "when a state [law] comes before the courts [it is] cloaked by the presumption [of constitutionality]. But this limitation on judicial review [stems] not from the Fourteenth Amendment itself, but from the nature of [the] judicial process

---

[23] See also Caminker, fn. 14: "[J]udicial doctrine sometimes *overenforces* rather than underenforces the 'pure' scope of a right, because the requirement that courts devise workable doctrines to decide concrete cases sometimes leads the Court to deploy doctrines such as bright-line rules that proscribe more conduct than that which actually contravenes the norm in question. Perhaps the most prominent of many examples of such overenforcement is *Miranda*." May Congress respond by "reducing" the scope of such rights? See also note 4 infra.

[24] For the view that "constitutional history suggests that the Court is misguided to depict judicial control of constitutional meaning as an unalloyed systemic good and contamination of constitutional interpretation by politics as an unalloyed systemic harm," and that "both legal and political dimensions of the American Constitution [must] remain in dynamic tension if the legal Constitution enforced by courts is to retain legitimacy and authority," see Robert C. Post & Reva B. Siegel, *Legislative Constitutionalism and Section Five Power: Policentric Interpretation of the Family and Medical Leave Act*, 112 Yale L.J. 1943 (2003). Compare Roderick M. Hills, Jr., *The Individual Right to Federalism in the Rehnquist Court,* 74 Geo. Wash. L. Rev. 888 (2006): "Contrary to [Post & Siegel], the Rehnquist Court did not arrogate power to itself [but rather] delegated this power to the states [by creating] a nonfederal space for debates about rights in the state lawmaking processes."

[which] makes it an inappropriate forum for the determination of complex factual questions of the kind so often involved in constitutional adjudication. [Should Congress, however,] undertake an investigation in order to determine whether the factual basis necessary to support a state legislative discrimination actually exists, it need not stop once it determines that some reasonable men could believe the factual basis exists. Section 5 empowers Congress to make its own determination on the matter." And note Harlan, J.'s view in *Morgan* that Congress' determinations as to "legislative facts" are "entitled to due respect."[25]

Compare Neal Devins, *Congressional Factfinding and the Scope of Judicial Review: A Preliminary Analysis*, 50 Duke L.J. 1169 (2001): "[L]obbyists (as well as senior staffers) understand [that] it is useful to pad the legislative history in ways that support their objectives. Ultimately, with fundraising, constituent service, and other demands, members of Congress cannot pursue knowledge for knowledge's sake. Rather, most members simply follow the lead of agenda-setters within their party [and] while 'judges on review can ensure that factfinding be based on empirical evidence, enterprising staffers should be able to surmount any such obstacle.' * * * Congress does a better job when it has the incentive to get the facts right while the courts may do a better job when the litigants skillfully present conflicting social science data."

(c) Did *Boerne* adhere to these approaches? Consider Tribe 3d ed., at 960: "[RFRA] provided perhaps the least suitable context imaginable for making the institutional argument: Unlike most § 5 legislation, RFRA [was] aimed directly at judicial procedures and rules of decision for every federal and state court in the nation, and, as if to dare the Court to defend its turf, RFRA was written less like an ordinary statute than like an opinion reversing or overruling the Supreme Court's decision in *Smith*."

2.   ***Deference to Congress.*** Consider McConnell, supra, at 188: "Unlike enactments under the Commerce Clause or most other sources of congressional power, interpretations of the Bill of Rights under Section Five limit the powers of Congress and the federal government to precisely the same extent that they limit the powers of the states. When Congress decides that the freedom of religion warrants greater protection than has been provided by the courts, the federal government will bear no less cost and inconvenience than the states. [Rather] than aggrandizing federal power at the expense of the states, legislation like RFRA constrains the power and discretion of federal and state governments alike. This makes it exceedingly unlikely that Congress will act from anything other than a genuine interest in enforcement of constitutional freedoms."

---

[25] Does Congress' special competence to resolve complex factual issues and to "craft solutions to public problems" deny that "the Court is more competent than Congress to decide the content of constitutional norms"? Calvin Massey, *Congressional Power to Regulate Sex Discrimination: The Effect of the Supreme Court's "New Federalism,"* 55 Me.L.Rev. 64 (2002).

3. ***Congress's "remedial" power.*** (a) How much of *Morgan's* "remedial" branch survives *Boerne*? May Congress outlaw *all* age and residence requirements for voting? Consider Alexander M. Bickel, *The Voting Rights Cases,* 1966 Sup.Ct.Rev. 79: "[S]uppose Congress decided that aliens or eighteen-year-olds or residents of New Jersey are being discriminated against in New York. The decision would be as plausible as the one concerning Spanish-speaking Puerto Ricans. Could Congress give these groups the vote? If Congress may freely bestow the vote as a means of curing other discriminations, which it fears may be practiced against groups deprived of the vote, essentially because of this deprivation and on the basis of no other evidence, then there is nothing left of state autonomy in setting qualifications for voting."

(b) May Congress use its "remedial" power to forbid all racial discrimination in housing? Consider Cox, Sec. 2, II: "[T]he isolation of unpopular minorities in poverty-stricken, socially and economically isolated neighborhoods, lacking political influence, invites a lower quality of state services. [*Morgan* held that] Congress might legislate to remove an obstacle to the state's performance of its constitutional duty not to discriminate in providing public services, even though the immediate subject matter of the legislation—there the requirement of English literacy—was not itself a violation of the Fourteenth Amendment. It follows that Congress may likewise legislate to eliminate racial ghettos as obstacles to the states' performance of that same constitutional duty, even though the immediate subject matter of this legislation—the practices that result in ghettos—do not themselves involve violations of the Fourteenth Amendment. The only important difference is that in *Morgan* the obstacle was itself a state law whereas discrimination in housing has a private origin. [But] that difference in the source of the threat to performance of the state's obligation is irrelevant."

(c) ***Changed circumstances over time.*** SHELBY COUNTY v. HOLDER, 133 S.Ct. 2612 (2013): As discussed in *South Carolina v. Katzenbach*, supra, the Voting Rights Act of 1965 "covered" those "States or political subdivisions that had maintained a test or device [described in *South Carolina* as a prerequisite to voting as of November 1, 1964, and had less than 50 percent voter registration or turnout in the 1964 Presidential election.] A covered jurisdiction [described in *South Carolina*] could 'bail out' of coverage if it had not used a test or device in the preceding five years, 'for the purpose or with the effect of denying or abridging the right to vote on account of race or color.' § 4(a).

"[In] those jurisdictions, § 4 of the Act banned all such tests or devices. § 4(a). Section 5 provided that no change in voting procedures could take effect until it was approved by federal authorities in Washington, D.C.—either the Attorney General or a court of three judges. A jurisdiction could obtain such 'preclearance' only by proving that the change had neither 'the purpose [nor] the effect of denying or abridging the right to vote on account of race or color.' Sections 4 and 5 [were] set to expire after five years. [In] 1970, Congress reauthorized the Act for another five years, and extended the coverage formula in § 4(b) to jurisdictions that had a voting test and less than 50 percent voter registration or turnout as of 1968. That swept in several counties in California, New Hampshire, and New York. Congress also extended the ban in § 4(a) on tests and devices nationwide.

"In 1975, Congress reauthorized the Act for seven more years, and extended its coverage to jurisdictions that had a voting test and less than 50 percent voter registration or turnout as of 1972. Congress also amended the definition of 'test or device' to include the practice of providing English-only voting materials in places where over five percent of voting-age citizens spoke a single language other than English. As a [result] Alaska, Arizona, and Texas, as well as several counties in California, Florida, Michigan, New York, North Carolina, and South Dakota, became covered jurisdictions. Congress correspondingly amended sections 2 and 5 to forbid voting discrimination on the basis of membership in a language minority group. * * * Section 2, not at issue in [either *South Carolina* or] this case, is applicable in all states and enforceable by both the federal government and by private individuals. It forbids any 'standard, practice, or procedure' that 'results in a denial or abridgement of the right of any citizen of the United States to vote on account of race or color'. [Finally,] Congress made the nationwide ban on tests and devices permanent.

"In 1982, Congress reauthorized the Act for 25 years, but did not alter its coverage formula." The Court, per ROBERTS, C.J., held § 4 (the coverage formula required for preclearance under § 5) unconstitutional: "In *Northwest Austin Municipal Utility Dist. v. Holder*, 557 U.S. 193 (2009), which 'expressed serious doubts about the Act's continued constitutionality,' but construed the Act to avoid that issue. we stated that 'the Act imposes current burdens and must be justified by current needs.' And we concluded that 'a departure from the fundamental principle of equal sovereignty requires a showing that a statute's disparate geographic coverage is sufficiently related to the problem that it targets.' [D]espite the tradition of equal sovereignty, the Act applies to only nine States (and several additional counties). [Even] if a noncovered jurisdiction is sued [under § 2], there are important differences between those proceedings and preclearance proceedings; the preclearance proceeding 'not only switches the burden of proof to the supplicant jurisdiction, but also applies substantive standards quite different from those governing the rest of the nation.'

"[In 1966], the coverage formula [made] sense. We found that 'Congress chose to limit its attention to the geographic areas where immediate action seemed necessary, where voting discrimination ha[d] been most flagrant.' Nearly 50 years later, things have changed dramatically. [In] the covered jurisdictions, '[v]oter turnout and registration rates now approach parity. Blatantly discriminatory evasions of federal decrees are rare. * * * Census Bureau data from the most recent election indicate that African-American voter turnout exceeded white voter turnout in five of the six States originally covered by § 5, with a gap in the sixth State of less than one half of one percent. [In] the first decade after enactment of § 5, the Attorney General objected to

14.2 percent of proposed voting changes. In the last decade before reenactment, the Attorney General objected to a mere 0.16 percent. There is no doubt that these improvements are in large part because of the Voting Rights Act. [Yet] the Act has not eased the restrictions in § 5 or narrowed the scope of the coverage formula in § 4(b) along the [way]—as if nothing had changed. In fact, the Act's unusual remedies have grown even stronger [as indicated supra. Under] this theory, however, § 5 would be effectively immune from scrutiny; no matter how 'clean' the record of covered jurisdictions, the argument could always be made that it was deterrence that accounted for the good behavior.

"[The] Fifteenth Amendment [is] not designed to punish for the past; its purpose is to ensure a better future. See *Rice v. Cayetano*, 528 U. S. 495 (2000). To serve that purpose, Congress—if it is to divide the States—must identify those jurisdictions to be singled out on a basis that makes sense in light of current conditions. [If] Congress had started from scratch in 2006, it plainly could not have enacted the present coverage formula. It would have been irrational for Congress to distinguish between States in such a fundamental way based on 40-year-old data, when today's statistics tell an entirely different story [and] when such [voting] tests have been illegal since that time. But that is exactly what Congress has done.

* * * We issue no holding on § 5 itself, only on the coverage formula. Congress may draft another formula based on current conditions.[26] Such a formula is an initial prerequisite to a determination that exceptional conditions still exist justifying such an 'extraordinary departure from the traditional course of relations between the States and the Federal Government.' "[27]

GINSBURG, J., joined by Breyer, Sotomayor, and Kagan JJ., dissented in a long and detailed opinion, pointing to "volumes of evidence" Congress considered, including "large numbers of proposed changes to voting laws that the Attorney General declined to approve"; the emergence of " 'second generation barriers' to minority voting" (those that "reduce the impact of minority votes, in contrast to direct attempts to block access to the ballot," such as "racial gerrymandering," "a system of at-large voting in lieu of district-by-district voting," and "discriminatory annexation [of] majority-white areas into city limits").

In response to the Court's statistics, "between 1982 and 2006, DOJ objections blocked over 700 voting changes based on a determination that the changes were discriminatory. Congress found that the majority of DOJ

---

[26] Should this traditional point "reflect that the 'Congress' of our era is constituted by hyperpolarized political parties more ideologically unified and more politically distant from each other than throughout the 20th century"? See Richard H. Pildes, *Institutional Formalism and Realism in Constitutional and Public Law*, 2013 Sup. Ct. Rev. 1.

[27] Thomas, J., concurred on the ground that the Court's opinion "compellingly demonstrates" that § 5 is also unconstitutional. For a detailed "conceptual, empirical, and political investigation," concluding that unless "acted upon by Congress and the Court [,] minority representation in the South will be adversely affected" by the decision, see Nicholas O. Stephanopoulos, *The South After Shelby County,* 2013 Sup. Ct. Rev. 55.

objections included findings of discriminatory intent, and that the changes blocked by preclearance were 'calculated decisions to keep minority voters from fully participating in the political process.' * * * Congress received evidence that more than 800 proposed changes were altered or withdrawn since the last reauthorization in 1982. Congress also received empirical studies finding that DOJ's requests for more information had a significant effect on the degree to which covered jurisdictions 'compl[ied] with their obligatio[n]' to protect minority voting rights. Congress also received evidence that litigation under § 2 of the VRA was an inadequate substitute for preclearance in the covered jurisdictions. [This evidence] of preclearance's continuing efficacy in blocking constitutional violations in the covered jurisdictions, itself grounded Congress' conclusion that the remedy should be retained for those jurisdictions.

"[A study] of § 2 lawsuits in covered and noncovered jurisdictions indicated that racial discrimination in voting remains 'concentrated in the jurisdictions singled out for preclearance.'

[The] evidence before Congress, furthermore, indicated that voting in the covered jurisdictions was more racially polarized than elsewhere in the country. [T]he Court does not even deign to grapple with the legislative record. [In] 2008, for example, the city of Calera, located in Shelby County, requested preclearance of a redistricting plan that 'would have eliminated the city's sole majority-black district, which had been created pursuant to the consent decree.' [Although] DOJ objected to the plan, Calera forged ahead with elections based on the unprecleared voting changes, resulting in the defeat of the incumbent African-American councilman who represented the former majority-black district. The city's defiance required DOJ to bring a § 5 enforcement action that ultimately yielded appropriate redress, including restoration of the majority-black district. [These] recent episodes forcefully demonstrate that § 5's preclearance requirement is constitutional as applied to Alabama and its political subdivisions. And under our case law, that conclusion should suffice to resolve this case.

"[Under the] VRA's exceptionally broad severability provision, [even] if the VRA could not constitutionally be applied to certain States—e.g., Arizona and Alaska, it calls for those unconstitutional applications to be severed, leaving the Act in place for jurisdictions as to which its application does not transgress constitutional limits. [W]ithout considering whether application of the VRA to Shelby County is constitutional, or even addressing the VRA's severability provision, the Court's opinion can hardly be described as an exemplar of restrained and moderate decisionmaking.

"[Today's] unprecedented extension of the equal sovereignty principle outside its proper domain—the admission of new States—is capable of much mischief. Federal statutes that treat States disparately are hardly novelties [citing 7 federal statutes as examples].

"[The] situation Congress faced in 2006, when it took up reauthorization of the coverage formula, was not the same [as in 1965]. By [then,] *all* of the jurisdictions covered by it were 'familiar to Congress by name.' [There] was at that point no chance that the formula might inadvertently sweep in new areas that were not the subject of congressional findings. And Congress could determine from the record whether the jurisdictions captured by the coverage formula still belonged under the preclearance regime. If they did, there was no need to alter the formula. That is why the Court, in addressing prior reauthorizations of the VRA, did not question the continuing 'relevance' of the formula. [In] light of this record, Congress had more than a reasonable basis to conclude that the existing coverage formula was not out of sync with conditions on the ground in covered areas.

"[The] question this case presents is who decides whether, as currently operative, § 5 remains justifiable, this Court, or a Congress charged with the obligation to enforce the post-Civil War Amendments. [The] record supporting the 2006 reauthorization of the VRA [was] described by the Chairman of the House Judiciary Committee as 'one of the most extensive considerations of any piece of legislation that the United States Congress has dealt with in the 27½ years' he had served in the House. [With] overwhelming support in both Houses, Congress concluded that, for two prime reasons, § 5 should continue in force, unabated. First, continuance would facilitate completion of the impressive gains thus far made; and second, continuance would guard against backsliding. [That] determination of the body empowered to enforce the Civil War Amendments 'by appropriate legislation' merits this Court's utmost respect."

(d) ***De facto discrimination.*** (i) ROME v. UNITED STATES, 446 U.S. 156 (1980), involved the Attorney General's refusal to approve, under § 5 of the Voting Rights Act, various changes in the Rome, Ga.'s electoral system and a number of city annexations. A federal court found that the city had not employed any discriminatory barriers to black voting or black candidacy in the past 17 years and that the city had proved that the electoral changes and annexations were not discriminatorily motivated, but that they were prohibited by the Act because they had a discriminatory effect. The Court, per MARSHALL, J., affirmed: "[T]he Act's ban on electoral changes that are discriminatory in effect is an appropriate method of promoting the purposes of the Fifteenth Amendment, even if it is assumed that § 1 of the Amendment prohibits only intentional discrimination in voting. [See *Mobile v. Bolden,* Ch. 9, Sec. 5, I, B.] Congress could rationally have concluded that, because electoral changes by jurisdictions with a demonstrable history of intentional racial discrimination in voting create the risk of purposeful discrimination, it was proper to prohibit changes that have a discriminatory impact. See *South Carolina v. Katzenbach.*"

REHNQUIST, J., joined by Stewart, J., dissented: "Congress had before it evidence that various governments were enacting electoral changes and annexing territory to prevent the participation of blacks in local government by measures other than outright denial of the franchise. [G]iven the difficulties of proving that an electoral change or annexation has been undertaken for the purpose of discriminating against blacks, Congress could properly conclude that as a remedial matter it was necessary to place the burden of proving lack of discriminatory purpose on the localities. But all of this does not support the conclusion that Congress is acting remedially when it continues the presumption of purposeful discrimination even after the locality has disproved that presumption. Absent other circumstances, it would be a topsy-turvy judicial system which held that electoral changes which have been affirmatively proven to be permissible under the Constitution nonetheless violate the Constitution. [Thus,] the result of the Court's holding is that Congress effectively has the power to determine for itself that this conduct violates the Constitution." Powell, J., dissented on narrower grounds.

(ii) Do you agree that *Rome* empowers Congress "to determine for itself [what] conduct violates the Constitution" and therefore does not survive *Boerne*? Consider Choper, note 3(b) after *Mayer*: "[*Rome's*] rationale permits Congress to create a 'conclusive presumption' of racial motivation with respect to specified state or local practices that Congress finds have been widely or consistently employed for the purpose of disadvantaging racial minorities— and thus effectively authorizes a congressional conclusion that such practices violate the substance of the Fourteenth Amendment. But this is a much narrower license than empowering Congress to declare that all state or local rules with a racially disproportionate impact violate equal protection for that reason alone. [A] variety of factors make it extremely difficult for plaintiffs to prove that a state legislative or administrative body has acted with discriminatory intent and make it much more appropriate for Congress than for the judiciary to combat the problem of illicit motivation. Thus, there are powerful reasons for Congress to choose not to rely upon district judges for the highly sensitive task of ascertaining racially discriminatory intent on a case by case basis in respect to state of local schemes whose real purpose Congress has grounds to suspect. [*Rome*] did no more than recognize this reality when is [used] what is principally a remedial or prophylactic rationale." Does this rationale support the Civil Rights Act of 1964's regulation of state employment practices that disqualify a disproportionate number of African-Americans (see p. 1415 supra)?

4. *"Dilution."* To what extent do the approaches in notes 1, 2 and 3 supra relate to Congress' inability to "dilute" Fourteenth Amendment rights?

(a) *Competence as to "facts."* Does *Miranda v. Arizona,* 384 U.S. 436 (1966), rest on the *factual* assumption that there is "compulsion inherent in custodial surroundings" and thus "no statement obtained from the defendant can truly be the product of his free choice"? See Yale Kamisar, *Can (Did) Congress "Overrule" Miranda*, 85 Corn.L.Rev. 883 (2000). Does *Mapp v. Ohio,* 367 U.S. 643 (1961), rest on the *factual* assumption that the exclusionary rule is a "deterrent safeguard without insistence upon which the Fourth Amendment would have been reduced to 'a form of words' "? Does *Gideon v. Wainwright,* 372 U.S. 335 (1963), rest on the *factual* assumption that a person "who is poor to hire a lawyer, cannot be assured a fair trial unless counsel is provided for him"? Does *Brown v. Board of Education,* Ch. 9, Sec. 2, II, rest on the *factual* assumption that racially "separate educational facilities are inherently unequal"? Does *Planned Parenthood v. Casey,* Ch. 6, Sec. 2, rest on *factual* assumptions that "informed consent" requirements and 24-hour waiting periods do *not* "impose an undue burden on a woman's abortion right"? See generally Ira C. Lupu, *Statutes Revolving in Constitutional Law Orbits,* 79 Va.L.Rev. 1 (1993). If so, may Congress, pursuant to § 5, find the *facts* to be otherwise and legislate a contrary rule? What result after *Boerne?*

(b) *Line-drawing.* After *Boerne,* what deference is owed congressional action, pursuant to § 5, that precisely defines (i) how long a delay constitutes denial of the "right to a speedy trial," see *Barker v. Wingo,* 407 U.S. 514 (1972); (ii) how great a deviation from absolute population equality among legislative districts constitutes a violation of the "one person-one vote" requirement, see Ch. 9, Sec. 5, I, B.

(c) *Conflicting constitutional provisions.* If de facto racial segregation in the schools arguably violates equal protection, and if use of racial criteria to alleviate de facto segregation also arguably violates equal protection (see Ch. 9, Secs. 2, III and 2, VI), what deference is owed congressional action, pursuant to § 5, dealing with this? See opinion of White, J., in *Welsh v. United States,* Ch. 8, Sec. 2, II.

(d) *Rights vs. remedies.* May Congress, pursuant to its remedial power under § 5, withdraw the "exclusionary rule" of *Mapp v. Ohio* on the ground that this does not "dilute" any substantive constitutional right but merely modifies a remedy for its violation?[28] (How about *replacing* it with an alternative remedy?) On similar analysis, may Congress forbid busing (or substitute alternatives) to remedy school segregation? See Note, *The Nixon Busing Bills and Constitutional Power,* 81 Yale L.J. 1542 (1972); Ronald D. Rotunda, *Congressional Power to Restrict the Jurisdiction of the Lower Federal Courts and the Problem of School Busing,* 64 Geo.L.J. 839 (1976). [29]

(e) *Definition of "dilution."* If Congress believed that more wrongdoers would be convicted and crime deterred by changing the *Miranda* rule, would such legislation "dilute" the due process rights of the accused, or "secure" the rights of the public generally not to be denied life or property without due process of law? Who should *ultimately* determine these issues? See generally J. Edmond Nathanson, *Congressional Power to Contradict the Supreme Court's Constitutional Decisions. Accommodation of Rights in Conflict,* 27 Wm. & M.L.Rev. 331 (1986).

---

[28] *Dickerson v. United States*, 530 U.S. 428 (2000), per Rehnquist, C.J., invalidated a federal statute which was "intended [to] overrule *Miranda,*" which was "a constitutional decision of this Court": "Congress [may] not supersede this Court's decisions interpreting and applying the Constitution, see, *Boerne.*" Scalia and Thomas, JJ., dissented, arguing that the *Miranda* warnings were "only 'prophylactic' rules that go beyond the [constitutional] right against compelled self-incrimination."

[29] For the view that many judicial decisions implementing constitutional rights are not "true constitutional interpretations" but rather only "constitutional common law" rules that may be modified by Congress, see Henry P. Monaghan, *Constitutional Common Law,* 89 Harv.L.Rev. 1 (1975). Compare Thomas S. Schrock & Robert C. Welsh, *Reconsidering the Constitutional Common Law,* 91 Harv.L.Rev. 1117 (1978).

(f) *"Human Life Bill."* What of the constitutionality of the following proposed statute, S. 158 and H.R. 900, 97th Cong., 1st Sess. (1981):

"Sec. 1. The Congress finds that present day scientific evidence indicates a significant likelihood that actual human life exists from conception.

"The Congress further finds that the fourteenth amendment to the Constitution of the United States was intended to protect all human beings.

"Upon the basis of these findings, and in the exercise of the powers of the Congress, including its power under section 5 of the fourteenth amendment to the Constitution of the United States, the Congress hereby declares that for the purpose of enforcing the obligation of the States under the fourteenth amendment not to deprive persons of life without due process of law, human life shall be deemed to exist from conception [and] without regard to race, sex, age, health, defect, or condition of dependency; and for this purpose 'person' shall include all human life as defined herein." [30]

(i) *Questions of "fact."* Do the issues of when "human life" begins and what is a "person" involve questions of fact? Consider Laurence H. Tribe, *Prepared Statement,* Hearings on S. 158: "Such questions [call] at bottom for normative judgments no less profound than those involved in defining 'liberty' or 'equality.' [They] entail 'question[s] to which science can provide no answer,' as the National Academy of Sciences itself acknowledged * * * . Congress cannot transform an issue of religion, morality, and law into one of fact by waving the magic wand of Section 5." See also Archibald Cox, *Prepared Statement,* id.

(ii) *"Dilution" vs. "expansion."* Does the Bill dilute the right to an abortion? Consider John T. Noonan, Jr., *Prepared Statement,* id.: "In recognizing the unborn as persons, [the] Act treats no one unequally but gives equal protection to one class of humanity now unequally [treated.] Necessarily, the expression of the rights of one class of human beings has an impact on the rights of others. The elimination of literacy tests in this way 'diluted' the voting rights of the literate. It is inescapable that congressional expression of the right to life will have an impact on the abortion right; but in the eyes of Congress, [there] will be a net gain for Fourteenth Amendment rights by the expansion and the attendant diminution."

5. *"Last word."* Would a contrary analysis in *Boerne* give interpretive "control" to Congress rather than the Court? (a) Consider William G. Buss, *Federalism, Separation of Powers, and the Demise of the Religious Freedom Restoration Act,* 83 Ia.L.Rev. 391 (1998): "The fact that the particular result in the *Smith* case would ordinarily be altered by the RFRA is not tantamount to

---

[30] For argument in favor of its validity, see Stephen H. Galebach, *A Human Life Statute,* 7 Human Life Rev. 3 (1981), reprinted in Hearings on S. 158, before the Subcomm. on Separation of Powers of the Senate Comm. on the Judiciary, 97th Cong., 1st Sess. 205 (1981); Thomas Nagel, *Prepared Statement,* id. 321. For exhaustive consideration, see Samuel Estreicher, *Congressional Power and Constitutional Rights: Reflections on Proposed "Human Life" Legislation,* 68 Va.L.Rev. 333 (1982). For an "institutional" perspective, see Stephen L. Carter, *The Morgan "Power" and the Forced Reconsideration of Constitutional Decisions,* 53 U.Chi.L.Rev. 819 (1986).

recognition that Congress has a power to overrule the Supreme Court or to make authoritative decisions about constitutional rights. [It] would mean simply that Congress had *enacted a statute* within its enforcement power. [*Smith*] would continue to determine the constitutional meaning of the free exercise of religion, and would govern any situation with respect to which the RFRA did not apply—because of a statute of limitations, a pleading failure, an Eleventh Amendment bar, or any other reason. If the RFRA were repealed, the constitutional rule established by *Smith* would govern."

(b)   Consider McConnell, supra, at 184: "Acceptance of the 'interpretive' reading of Congress's Section Five authority does not imply that Congress has the final word on the Amendment's meaning. [The] question in a Section Five case should be whether the congressional interpretation is within a reasonable range of plausible interpretations—not whether it is the same as the Supreme Court's. An analogy might be drawn to the *Chevron* doctrine [see Ch. 3, Sec.2, I], which holds that courts should not overturn agency interpretations of their governing statutes as long as they are within a reasonable range of interpretations of the statutory language."

(c)   Might the *Boerne* majority be swayed by the points in notes (a) and (b)?

6.   ***Spending power.*** To what extent may Congress use the spending power to achieve the ends sought in RFRA? Consider Jesse H. Choper, *On the Difference in Importance Between Supreme Court Doctrine and Actual Consequences*, 19 Card.L.Rev. 2259 (1998): "[C]onditions on [existing] federal spending could likely reverse [*Smith*] and replicate the results in [the other pre-Smith Supreme Court decisions requiring religious exemptions from neutral, generally applicable laws]." See also Daniel O. Conkle, *Congressional Alternatives in the Wake of City of Boerne v. Flores: The (Limited) Role of Congress in Protecting Religious Freedom from State and Local Infringement*, 20 U.Ark.Little Rock L.Rev. 633 (1998); Sayers-Fay, note 1(b) after *Dole*, Ch. 2, Sec. 3, II." [31]

7.   ***Further restrictions on § 5.*** (a) ***Equal protection.*** (i) KIMEL v. FLORIDA BD. OF REGENTS, 528 U.S. 62 (2000), per O'CONNOR, J., explored *Boerne's* scope in the context of Congress' exercising its § 5 power—which may be used to abrogate the states' immunity from suits in federal court guaranteed by the Eleventh Amendment—to make states subject to federal court actions for violating the Age Discrimination in Employment Act:[32] "We have considered claims of unconstitutional age discrimination under the Equal Protection Clause three times [and held that] age is not a suspect classification [Ch. 9, Sec. 4, V]. Our Constitution permits States to draw lines on the basis of

---

[31] See the Religious Land Use and Institutionalized Persons Act of 2000, which creates a RFRA-like federal right applicable, inter alia, to land use regulations in connection with "a program or activity that receives federal financial assistance."

[32] Thomas, J., joined by Kennedy, J., concurred because the ADEA did not "reveal Congress' intention" to abro-gate state immunity from private suits for damages.

age when they have a rational basis for doing so at a class-based level, even if it 'is probably not true' that those reasons are valid in the majority of cases.

"Judged against the backdrop of our equal protection jurisprudence, it is clear that the ADEA is 'so out of proportion to a supposed remedial or preventive object that it cannot be understood as responsive to, or designed to prevent, unconstitutional behavior.' *Boerne.* The Act, through its broad restriction on the use of age as a discriminating factor, prohibits substantially more state employment decisions and practices than would likely be held unconstitutional under the applicable equal protection, rational basis standard. [Petitioners] contend that the Act's prohibition, considered together with its exceptions, applies only to arbitrary age discrimination, which in the majority of cases corresponds to conduct that violates the Equal Protection Clause. We disagree.

"Petitioners stake their claim [on] the 'bona fide occupational qualification' (BFOQ) defense. [But to] succeed under the BFOQ defense, we held that an employer must demonstrate either 'a substantial basis for believing that all or nearly all employees above an age lack the qualifications required for the position,' or that reliance on the age classification is necessary because 'it is highly impractical for the employer to insure by individual testing that its employees will have the necessary qualifications for the job.' Measured against the rational basis standard, [the] ADEA plainly imposes substantially higher burdens on state employers [at] a level akin to our heightened scrutiny cases under the Equal Protection Clause. Difficult and intractable problems often require powerful remedies, and we have never held that § 5 precludes Congress from enacting reasonably prophylactic legislation. Our task is to determine whether the ADEA is in fact just such an appropriate remedy or, instead, merely an attempt to substantively redefine the States' legal obligations with respect to age discrimination.

"Our examination of the ADEA's legislative record confirms [that] Congress never identified any pattern of age discrimination by the States, much less any discrimination whatsoever that rose to the level of constitutional violation. The evidence compiled by petitioners [consists] almost entirely of isolated sentences clipped from floor debates and legislative reports. * * *

"Our decision today does not signal the end of the line for [state employees who] are protected by state age discrimination statutes, and may recover money damages from their state employers, in almost every [State]."

STEVENS, J., joined by Souter, Ginsburg and Breyer, JJ., dissented, relying on their dissenting view in *Seminole Tribe of Florida v. Florida,* 517 U.S. 44 (1996): "Congress' power to authorize federal remedies against state agencies that violate federal statutory obligations is coextensive with its power [under the Commerce Clause] to impose those obligations on the States in the first place. Neither the Eleventh Amendment nor the doctrine of sovereign immunity places any limit on that power.[33] "Federalism concerns do make it

---

[33] *Central Va. Comm. College v. Katz,* 546 U.S. 356 (2006), per Stevens, J., held that the Art. 1, § 8, cl. 4 bankruptcy power "was intended" to subordinate "state sovereign immunity in the

appropriate for Congress to speak clearly when it regulates state action. But when it does so, as it has in these cases, we can safely presume that the burdens the statute imposes on the sovereignty of the several States were taken into account during the deliberative process leading to the enactment of the measure."

(ii) *Required congressional record.* BOARD OF TRUSTEES OF UNIV. OF ALA. v. GARRETT, 531 U.S. 356 (2001), per REHNQUIST, C.J. held that Congress had no § 5 power to abrogate state immunity and provide its employees a damages remedy under Title I of the Americans with Disabilities Act, which forbids employment discrimination because of "disability" and requires "reasonable accommodations" to achieve this end: "[*Cleburne*, Ch. 9, Sec. 4, III, held that a legislative classification based on disability] incurs only the minimum 'rational-basis' review applicable to general social and economic legislation. [Breyer, J.'s dissent suggests] that state decisionmaking reflecting 'negative attitudes' or 'fear' necessarily runs afoul of the Fourteenth Amendment. [But] States are not required by the Fourteenth Amendment to make special accommodations for the disabled, so long as their actions towards such individuals are rational. They could quite hard headedly—and perhaps hardheartedly—hold to job-qualification requirements which do not make allowance for the disabled. [Thus] we have determined the metes and bounds of the constitutional right in question, we examine whether Congress identified a history and pattern of unconstitutional employment discrimination by the States against the disabled. * * *

"Respondents contend that the inquiry as to unconstitutional discrimination should extend not only to States themselves, but to units of local governments, such as cities and counties. [B]ut the Eleventh Amendment does not extend its immunity to units of local government. [It] would make no sense to consider constitutional violations on their part, as well as by the States themselves, when only the States are the beneficiaries of the Eleventh Amendment.

"Congress made a general finding in the ADA that 'historically, society has tended to isolate and segregate individuals with disabilities, and, despite some improvements, such forms of discrimination against individuals with disabilities continue to be a serious and pervasive social problem.' The record assembled by Congress includes many instances to support such a finding. But the great majority of these incidents do not deal with the activities of States.[34]

---

bankruptcy arena" as "a uniform federal response" to the problems and injustice of the then existing "patchwork of insolvency and bankruptcy laws." Roberts, C.J., and Scalia, Kennedy and Thomas, JJ., dissented.

For the view that "historical understanding of text [and] coherent application of precedent support the conclusion" that "federal statutory rights are privileges and immunities" under the Fourteenth Amendment and can thus be enforced against states under § 5, see William J. Rich, *Taking 'Privileges or Immunities' Seriously: A Call to Expand the Constitutional Canon*, 87 Minn.L.Rev. 153 (2002). See also James W. Fox, Jr., *Re-readings and Misreadings: Slaughter-House, Privileges or Immunities, and Section Five Enforcement Powers*, 91 Ky. L.J. 67 (2002–03).

[34] Compare Robert C. Post & Reva B. Siegel, *Protecting the Constitution from the People: Juricentric Restrictions on Section Five Power*, 78 Ind.L.J. 1 (2003): "If units of local government

"Respondents in their brief cite half a dozen examples from the record that did involve States. [But] these incidents taken together fall far short of even suggesting the pattern of unconstitutional discrimination on which § 5 legislation must be based. [Further, the] host of incidents [in Appendix C to Breyer, J.'s dissent] consists not of legislative findings, but of unexamined, anecdotal accounts of 'adverse, disparate treatment by state officials.' [Of course,] 'adverse, disparate treatment' often does not amount to a constitutional violation where rational-basis scrutiny applies. These accounts, moreover, were submitted not directly to Congress but to the Task Force on the Rights and Empowerment of Americans with Disabilities, which made no findings on the subject of state discrimination in employment.[7] And, had Congress truly understood this information as reflecting a pattern of unconstitutional behavior by the States, one would expect some mention of that conclusion in the Act's legislative findings. There is none. Although Justice Breyer would infer from Congress' general conclusions regarding societal discrimination against the disabled that the States had likewise participated in such action, the House and Senate committee reports on the ADA flatly contradict this assertion. [The Senate] Committee's report reached, among others, the following conclusion: 'Discrimination still persists in such critical areas as *employment in the private sector,* public accommodations, public services, transportation, and telecommunications.' The House Committee [reached] the same conclusion * * * .

"Even were it possible to squeeze out of these examples a pattern of unconstitutional discrimination by the States, the rights and remedies created by the ADA against the States would raise the same sort of concerns as to congruence and proportionality as were found in *Boerne.* For example, whereas it would be entirely rational (and therefore constitutional) for a state employer to conserve scarce financial resources by hiring employees who are able to use existing facilities, the ADA requires employers to 'make existing facilities used by employees readily accessible to and usable by individuals with disabilities.' The ADA does except employers from the 'reasonable accommodation' requirement where the employer 'can demonstrate that the accommodation would impose an undue hardship on the operation of the business of such covered entity.' However, even with this exception, the accommodation duty far exceeds what is constitutionally required. [The] Act also makes it the employer's duty to prove that it would suffer such a burden, instead of

---

are violating Section 1 of the Fourteenth Amendment by irrationally discriminating against the disabled, Congress has power to enact Title I of the ADA under Section 5. Congress's authority under Section 5 is determined by the standards of the Fourteenth Amendment, and not by the Eleventh Amendment criteria *Garrett* employs. Congress's Section 5 power circumscribes Eleventh Amendment immunities, and not the reverse."

   [7]   **[Ct's Note]** Only a small fraction of the anecdotes Justice Breyer identifies in his Appendix C relate to state discrimination against the disabled in employment. At most, somewhere around 50 of these allegations describe conduct that could conceivably amount to constitutional violations by the States, and most of them are so general and brief that no firm conclusion can be drawn. The overwhelming majority of these accounts pertain to alleged discrimination by the States in the provision of public services and public accommodations, which areas are addressed in Titles II and III of the ADA.

requiring (as the Constitution does) that the complaining party negate reasonable bases for the employer's decision.

"The ADA also forbids 'utilizing standards, criteria, or methods of administration' that disparately impact the disabled, without regard to whether such conduct has a rational basis. Although disparate impact may be relevant evidence of racial discrimination, see *Washington v. Davis,* [Ch. 9, Sec. 2, III] such evidence alone is insufficient even where the Fourteenth Amendment subjects state action to strict scrutiny.

"The ADA's constitutional shortcomings are apparent when the Act is compared to Congress' efforts in the Voting Rights Act of 1965 [in which] Congress documented a marked pattern of unconstitutional action by the States. State officials, Congress found, routinely applied voting tests in order to exclude African-American citizens from registering to vote. Congress also determined that litigation had proved ineffective and that there persisted an otherwise inexplicable 50-percentage-point gap in the registration of white and African-American voters in some States."

KENNEDY, J., joined by O'Connor, J., who joined the Court's opinion, concurred: "For the reasons explained by the Court, an equal protection violation has not been [shown]. If the States had been transgressing the Fourteenth Amendment by their mistreatment or lack of concern for those with impairments, one would have expected to find in decisions of the [courts] extensive litigation and discussion of the constitutional violations. This confirming judicial documentation does not exist. That there is a new awareness, a new consciousness, a new commitment to better treatment of those disadvantaged by mental or physical impairments does not establish that an absence of state statutory correctives was a constitutional violation."

BREYER, J. joined by Stevens, Souter and Ginsburg, JJ., dissented: "There are roughly 300 examples of discrimination by state governments themselves in the legislative record. I fail to see how this evidence 'fall[s] far short of even suggesting the pattern of unconstitutional discrimination on which § 5 legislation must be based.'

"The congressionally appointed task force collected numerous specific examples, provided by persons with disabilities themselves, of adverse, disparate treatment by state officials. They reveal, not what the Court describes as 'half a dozen' instances of discrimination, but hundreds of instances of adverse treatment at the hands of state officials—instances in which a person with a disability found it impossible to obtain a state job, to retain state employment, to use the public transportation that was readily available to others in order to get to work, or to obtain a public education, which is often a prerequisite to obtaining employment. State-imposed barriers also frequently made it difficult or impossible for people to vote, to enter a public building, to access important government services, such as calling for emergency assistance, and to find a place to live due to a pattern of irrational zoning decisions similar to the discrimination that we held unconstitutional in *Cleburne.*

"As the Court notes, those who presented instances of discrimination rarely provided additional, independent evidence sufficient to prove in court that, in each instance, the discrimination they suffered lacked justification from a judicial standpoint. [But] Congress, unlike courts, must, and does, routinely draw general conclusions—for example, of likely motive or of likely relationship to legitimate need—from anecdotal and opinion-based evidence of this kind, particularly when the evidence lacks strong refutation. In reviewing § 5 legislation, we have never required the sort of extensive investigation of each piece of evidence that the Court appears to contemplate. Nor has the Court traditionally required Congress to make findings as to state discrimination, or to break down the record evidence, category by category. * * * Congress could have reasonably believed that these examples represented signs of a widespread problem of unconstitutional discrimination. * * *[35]

"The problem with the Court's approach is that neither the 'burden of proof' that favors States nor any other rule of restraint applicable to *judges* applies to *Congress* when it exercises its § 5 power. * * * Rational-basis review—with its presumptions favoring constitutionality—is 'a paradigm of *judicial* restraint.' *FCC v. Beach Communications,* [Ch. 9, Sec. 1]. And the Congress of the United States is not a lower court. Indeed, [*Cleburne*] made clear that the absence of a contrary congressional finding was critical to our decision to apply mere rational-basis review to disability discrimination claims—a 'congressional direction' to apply a more stringent standard would have been 'controlling.' * * *

"[Unlike] courts, Congress can readily gather facts from across the Nation, assess the magnitude of a problem, and more easily find an appropriate remedy. Cf. *Cleburne* (addressing the problems of the 'large and diversified group' of persons with disabilities 'is a difficult and often a technical matter, very much a task for legislators guided by qualified professionals and not by the perhaps ill-informed opinions of the judiciary'). Unlike courts, Congress directly reflects public attitudes and beliefs, enabling Congress better to understand where, and to what extent, refusals to accommodate a disability amount to behavior that is callous or unreasonable to the point of lacking constitutional justification. Unlike judges, Members of Congress can directly obtain information from constituents who have first-hand experience with discrimination and related issues.[36] Moreover, unlike judges, Members of Congress are elected. [To] apply a rule designed to restrict courts as if it

---

[35] "*Garrett* demanded a depth and breadth of documentation [under] a legal standard that was unknown at the time the statute was enacted." Ruth Colker & James J. Brudney, *Dissing Congress,* 100 Mich.L.Rev. 80 (2001).

[36] Accord, Robert C. Post & Reva B. Siegel, fn. 24: "We would actually regard it as both infeasible and improper for Congress to conduct the mini-trials that would be necessary to find constitutional violations in the technical sense ordinarily required in the framework of litigation. See also Philip P. Frickey & Steven S. Smith, *Judicial Review, the Congressional Process, and the Federalism Cases: An Interdisciplinary Critique,* 111 Yale L.J. 1707 (2002). See also note 1(b) after *Boerne.*

restricted Congress' legislative power is to stand the underlying principle—a principle of judicial restraint—on its head. * * *[37]

"The Court argues in alternative that the statute's damage remedy is not 'congruent' with and 'proportional' to the equal protection problem that Congress found. [But] it is just that power—the power to require more than the minimum that §§ 5 grants to Congress, as this Court has repeatedly confirmed. [Nothing in the ADA's] 'reasonable accommodation' suggests that the requirement has no 'tend[ency] to enforce' the Equal Protection Clause, *Ex parte Virginia,* that it is an irrational way to achieve the objective, *South Carolina,* that it would fall outside the scope of the Necessary and Proper Clause, *Morgan,* or that it somehow otherwise exceeds the bounds of the 'appropriate,' U.S. Const., Amdt. 14, § 5.* * *

"[The] legislation before us [does] not discriminate against anyone, nor does it pose any threat to basic liberty. And it is difficult to understand why the Court, which applies 'minimum "rational-basis" review' to statutes that *burden* persons with disabilities, subjects to far stricter scrutiny a statute that seeks to *help* those same individuals.

"I recognize nonetheless that this statute imposes a burden upon States in that it removes their Eleventh Amendment protection from suit, thereby subjecting them to potential monetary liability. Rules for interpreting §§ 5 that would provide States with special protection, however, run counter to the very object of the Fourteenth Amendment. By its terms, that Amendment prohibits *States* from denying their citizens equal protection of the laws."

(iii) ***Prophylactic legislation.*** NEVADA DEP'T OF HUMAN RESOURCES v. HIBBS, 538 U.S. 721 (2003), per REHNQUIST, C.J., upheld Congress' § 5 power to abrogate state sovereign immunity and provide state employees damages under the Family and Medical Leave Act which entitles eligible employees up to 12 work weeks of unpaid leave annually for several reasons, including onset of a 'serious health condition' in an employee's spouse, child, or parent: "The FMLA aims to protect the right to be free from gender-based discrimination in the workplace. [According] to evidence that was before Congress when it enacted the FMLA, States continue to rely on invalid gender stereotypes in the employment context, specifically in the administration of leave benefits. Reliance on such stereotypes cannot justify the States' gender discrimination in this area. *United States v. Virginia,* [Ch. 9, Sec. 3, I]. The long and extensive history of sex discrimination prompted us to hold that measures that differentiate on the basis of gender warrant heightened scrutiny; here, as in *Fitzpatrick* persistence of such unconstitutional

---

[37] See also Steven G. Calabresi & Nicholas P. Stabile, *On Section 5 of the Fourteenth Amendment,* 11 U. Pa. J. Con. L. 1431 (2009): The "Court ought to review the work product of Congress with more deference than it accords to the work product of state legislatures [because] Congress has had a much better track record on civil liberties than have the state legislatures."

discrimination by the States justifies Congress' passage of prophylactic § 5 legislation.[38]

"As the FMLA's legislative record reflects, a 1990 Bureau of Labor Statistics (BLS) survey stated that 37 percent of surveyed private-sector employees were covered by maternity leave policies, while only 18 percent were covered by paternity leave policies. [The] data show an increase in the percentage of employees eligible for such leave, [but] they also show a widening of the gender gap [from 1989]. Thus, stereotype-based beliefs about the allocation of family duties remained firmly rooted, and employers' reliance on them in establishing discriminatory leave policies remained widespread.[3]

"Congress also heard testimony that '[p]arental leave for fathers [is] rare. Even [w]here child-care leave policies do exist, men, *both in the public and private sectors,* receive notoriously, discriminatory treatment in their requests for such leave." [This] and other differential leave policies [e.g., state employers' collective bargaining agreements] were not attributable to any differential physical needs of men and women, but rather to the pervasive sex-role stereotype that caring for family members is women's work.[5]

"Finally, Congress [was also] aware of the 'serious problems with the discretionary nature of family leave,' because when 'the authority to grant leave and to arrange the length of that leave rests with individual supervisors,' it leaves 'employees open to discretionary and possibly unequal treatment.' * * *

"In spite of all of the above evidence, Justice Kennedy argues in dissent that Congress' passage of the FMLA was unnecessary because 'the States appear to have been ahead of Congress in providing gender-neutral family leave benefits,' and points to Nevada's leave policies in particular. However, it was only '[s]ince Federal family leave legislation was first introduced' that the States had even 'begun to consider similar family leave initiatives.'

"Furthermore, the dissent's statement that some States 'had adopted some form of family-care leave' before the FMLA's enactment, glosses over important shortcomings of some state policies. First, seven States had childcare leave provisions that applied to women only. [Second,] 12 States

---

[38] For the view that *Fitzpatrick v. Bitzer* (discussed in *Boerne*) was incorrectly decided because neither the "text, structure, and history of the Constitution," nor the "understandings of the people who [framed] the Reconstruction amendments," granted "Congress power to override sovereign immunity" and "create private causes of action against [nonconsenting] states," in contrast to authorizing such remedies against state officers, see John Harrison, *State Sovereign Immunity and Congress's Enforcement Powers,* 2006 Sup. Ct. Rev. 353.

[3] **[Ct's Note]** While this and other material described leave policies in the private sector, a 50-state survey also before Congress demonstrated that "[t]he proportion and construction of leave policies available to public sector employees differs little from those offered private sector employees."

[5] **[Ct's Note]** * * *Justice Kennedy's dissent ignores this common foundation that, as Congress found, has historically produced discrimination in the hiring and promotion of women. Consideration of such evidence does not, as the dissent contends, expand our §§ 5 inquiry to include "*general* gender-based stereotypes in employment." To the contrary, because parenting and family leave address very similar situations in which work and family responsibilities conflict, they implicate the same stereotypes.

provided their employees no family leave, beyond an initial childbirth or adoption, to care for a seriously ill child or family member. Third, many States provided [only] voluntary or discretionary leave programs.[39] Three States left the amount of leave time primarily in employers' hands. Congress could reasonably conclude that such discretionary family-leave programs would do little to combat the stereotypes about the roles of male and female employees that Congress sought to eliminate. [N]o matter how generous petitioner's [leave policies] may have been, Congress was justified in enacting the FMLA as remedial legislation.

"[Here, unlike *Kimel* and *Garrett*,] Congress directed its attention to state gender discrimination, which triggers a heightened level of scrutiny [that makes it] easier for Congress to show a pattern of state constitutional violations. Congress was similarly successful in *South Carolina*.[40]

"We believe that Congress' chosen remedy [is] 'congruent and proportional to the targeted violation.' [By] setting a minimum standard of family leave for *all* eligible employees, irrespective of gender, the FMLA attacks the formerly state-sanctioned stereotype that only women are responsible for family caregiving, thereby reducing employers' incentives to engage in discrimination by basing hiring and promotion decisions on stereotypes.

"[In] the dissent's view, in the face of evidence of gender-based discrimination by the States in the provision of leave benefits, Congress could do no more in exercising its § 5 power than simply proscribe such discrimination. But this position cannot be squared with our recognition that Congress 'is not confined to the enactment of legislation that merely parrots the precise wording of the Fourteenth Amendment,' but may prohibit 'a

---

[39]   Kennedy, J., responded: "The Court does not argue the States intended to enable employers to discriminate in the provision of family leave; nor [is] there evidence state employers discriminated in the administration of leave benefits."

[40]   Consider Robert C. Post, *Foreword: Fashioning the Legal Constitution: Culture, Courts, and Law*, 117 Harv.L.Rev. 4 (2003): "[*Hibbs'*] conception of the relevant constitutional violation is quite distant from narrower formulations, which the Court tends to use in Section I litigation, and which associate the constitutional prohibition of sex discrimination either with explicit classifications based upon sex or with neutral government actions taken 'because of,' not merely 'in spite of, [their] adverse effects upon' women. Although *Hibbs* refers time and again to the pervasive harms of sex stereotyping, it never demonstrates a pattern of violations that a court would find violates Section I of the Fourteenth Amendment." Do you agree? Or is *Hibbs* like *Rome*? Was Rehnquist, C.J., "concerned to write the opinion in a way that would avoid a major constitutional controversy over the constitutional status of Title VII of the Civil Rights Act of 1964, [which] prohibits certain facially neutral government regulations that have a 'disparate impact' on women, even though the Court has held that in constitutional adjudication such neutral regulations are legitimate unless they are motivated by a discriminatory purpose," and in which Congress did not "document 'a history and pattern of unconstitutional [state] transgressions' in a manner that would satisfy the *Garrett* requirement"? Id. See Evan Tsen Lee, *The Trouble with City of Boerne, and Why It Matters for the Fifteenth Amendment as Well*, 90 Denver U. L. Rev. 483 (2012): For congressional enactments to enforce the Fourteenth and Fifteenth Amendments, "if the classification or right at stake triggers strict scrutiny, then Congress should be permitted to authorize broad prophylactic measures—anything that is rationally related to eradicating or preventing: violation of the right involved. Compare Calvin Massey, *Two Zones of Prophylaxis: The Scope of the Fourteenth Amendment Enforcement Power*, 76 Geo. Wash. L. Rev. 1 (2007), for a detailed review of various possibilities concerning the consequences of "heightened scrutiny."

somewhat broader swath of conduct, including that which is not itself forbidden by the Amendment's text.' [*Kimel*.]

"Indeed, in light of the evidence before Congress, a statute mirroring Title VII, that simply mandated gender equality in the administration of leave benefits, would not have achieved Congress' remedial object. Such a law would allow States to provide for no family leave at all. Where '[t]wo-thirds of the nonprofessional caregivers for older, chronically ill, or disabled persons are working women,' and state practices continue to reinforce the stereotype of women as caregivers, such a policy would exclude far more women than men from the workplace.

"Unlike the statutes at issue in *Boerne, Kimel*, and *Garrett,* which applied broadly to every aspect of state employers' operations, the FMLA is narrowly targeted at the fault line between work and family—precisely where sex-based overgeneralization has been and remains strongest—and affects only one aspect of the employment relationship."

"We also find significant the many other limitations that Congress placed on the scope of this measure. The FMLA requires only unpaid leave, and applies only to employees who have worked for the employer for at least one year and provided 1,250 hours of service within the last 12 months. Employees in high-ranking or sensitive positions are simply ineligible for FMLA leave; of particular importance to the States, the FMLA expressly excludes from coverage state elected officials, their staffs, and appointed policymakers. [In] choosing 12 weeks as the appropriate leave floor, Congress chose a middle ground, a period long enough to serve 'the needs of families' but not so long that it would upset 'the legitimate interests of employers.' [The] damages recoverable are strictly defined and measured by actual monetary losses, and the accrual period for backpay is limited by the Act's 2-year statute of limitations (extended to three years only for willful violations)."

KENNEDY, J., joined by Scalia and Thomas, JJ., dissented on the ground that Congress had failed "to make the requisite showing. [The] Act's findings of purpose are devoid of any discussion of the relevant evidence. * * *

"The Court seeks to connect the evidence of private discrimination to an alleged pattern of unconstitutional behavior by States through inferences drawn from two sources. [Both] statements were made during the hearings on the proposed 1986 national leave legislation,[which] sought to provide parenting leave, not leave to care for another ill family member. [This] evidence concerns the Act's grant of parenting leave, and is too attenuated to justify the family leave provision.* * *

"The Court next argues [that] many States did not guarantee the right to family leave by statute, instead leaving the decision up to individual employers, who could subject employees to 'discretionary and possibly unequal treatment.' The study from which the Court derives this conclusion examined 'the parental leave policies of Federal executive branch agencies.' [A] history of discrimination on the part of the Federal Government may, in some situations, support an inference of similar conduct by the States, but the Court does not explain why the inference is justified here. * * *

"Stripped of the conduct which exhibits no [purposeful discrimination], the Court's 'exten[sive] and specifi[c] record of unconstitutional state conduct,' boils down to the fact that three States, Massachusetts, Kansas, and Tennessee, provided parenting leave only to their female employees, and had no program for granting their employees (male or female) family leave. [The] few incidents identified by the Court 'fall far short of even suggesting the pattern of unconstitutional discrimination on which § 5 legislation must be based.' *Garrett.* [T]he unfortunate fact that stereotypes about women continue to be a serious and pervasive social problem would not alone support the charge that a State has engaged in a practice designed to deny its citizens the equal protection of the laws. *Garrett.*

"[If] Congress had been concerned about different treatment of men and women with respect to family leave, a congruent remedy would have sought to ensure the benefits of any leave program enacted by a State are available to men and women on an equal basis. Instead, the Act imposes, across the board, a requirement that States grant a minimum of 12 weeks of leave per year. This requirement may represent Congress' considered judgment as to the optimal balance. [It] does not follow, however, that if the States choose to enact a different benefit scheme, they should be deemed to engage in unconstitutional conduct and forced to open their treasuries to private suits for damages."

SCALIA, J., dissenting, added: "The constitutional violation that is a prerequisite to 'prophylactic' congressional action to 'enforce' the Fourteenth Amendment is a violation *by the State against which the enforcement action is taken.* There is no guilt by association, enabling the sovereignty of one State to be abridged under §§ 5 of the Fourteenth Amendment because of violations by another State, or by most other States, or even by 49 other States. [T]he Court does not even attempt to demonstrate that each one of the 50 States covered by [the Act] was in violation of the Fourteenth Amendment. [This] will not do. Prophylaxis in the sense of extending the remedy beyond the violation is one thing; prophylaxis in the sense of extending the remedy beyond the violator is something else. See *Rome.*"

Compare: COLEMAN v. MARYLAND COURT OF APPEALS, 132 S.Ct. 1327 (2012) per KENNEDY, J.,joined by Roberts, C.J. and Thomas and Alito, JJ., held that FMLA provision for unpaid leave for "self-care" was beyond Congress's § 5 power because, unlike the "well-documented pattern of sex-based discrimination in family-leave policies [in] *Hibbs*, the self-care provision was not directed at an identified pattern of gender-based discrimination and was not congruent and proportional."[41]

GINSBURG, J., joined by Breyer, Sotomayor and Kagan, JJ., dissented.[42] "The FMLA, in its entirety, is directed at sex discrimination [and] Congress

---

[41] Scalia, J. concurred only in the judgment based on his opinion in *Tennessee v. Lane,* infra.

[42] Ginsburg, J., joined only by Breyer, J., expressed her continued disagreement with *Seminole Tribe* and *Garrett.*

has evidence of a well-documented pattern of workplace discrimination against pregnant women. [Because] discrimination against women is tightly interwoven with society's beliefs about pregnancy and motherhood, I [believe] that [*Geduldig v. Aiello*, Ch. 9, Sec. 3, II] was egregiously wrong to hold that discrimination on the basis of pregnancy is not discrimination on the basis of sex. [It] would make scant sense to provide job-protected leave for a woman to care for a newborn, but not [for] 'ongoing pregnancy, miscarriages, . . . the need for prenatal care, childbirth, and recovery from childbirth.' * * *

"If Congress had drawn a line at leave for caring for other family members, there is greater likelihood that the FMLA would have been perceived [by employers] as further reason to avoid granting employment opportunities to women.' [Further], 'the availability of self-care leave to men serves to blunt the force of stereotypes of women as primary caregivers by increasing the odds that men and women will invoke the FMLA's leave provisions in near-equal numbers.' [By] reducing an employer's perceived incentive to avoid hiring women [the self care provision] lessens the risk that the FMALA as a whole would give rise to the very sex discrimination it was enacted to thwart."

(b) *Due process.* (i) FLORIDA PREPAID POSTSECONDARY EDUCATION EXPENSE BOARD v. COLLEGE SAVINGS BANK, 527 U.S. 627 (1999), per REHNQUIST, C.J., concerned Congress' § 5 power to expressly make states subject to federal court actions for patent infringement: Although patents "have long been considered a species [of] 'property' of which no person may be deprived by a State without due process [,] Congress identified no pattern of patent infringement by the States, let alone a pattern of constitutional violations. [Further,] only where the State provides no remedy, or only inadequate remedies, to injured patent owners [could] a deprivation of property without due process result.

"Congress [did] hear a limited amount of testimony to the effect that the remedies available in some States were uncertain. The primary point made by these witnesses, however, [was] that they were less convenient than federal remedies, and might undermine the uniformity of patent law.[9] * * *

"The legislative record thus suggests that the Patent Remedy Act does not respond to a history of 'widespread and persisting deprivation of constitutional rights' of the sort Congress has faced in enacting proper prophylactic § 5 legislation. [Because] of this lack, the provisions of the Patent Remedy Act are 'so out of proportion to a supposed remedial or preventive object that [they] cannot be understood as responsive to, or designed to prevent, unconstitutional behavior.' *Boerne.* Congress did nothing to limit the coverage of the Act to cases involving arguable constitutional violations, such as where a State refuses to offer any state-court remedy for patent owners whose patents it had infringed. Nor did it make any attempt to confine the reach of the Act by limiting the

---

[9]   **[Ct's Note]** It is worth mentioning that the State of Florida provides remedies to patent owners for alleged infringement on the part of the State. Aggrieved parties may pursue a legislative remedy through a claims bill for payment in full, or a judicial remedy through a takings or conversion claim.

remedy to certain types of infringement, such as nonnegligent infringement or infringement authorized pursuant to state policy; or providing for suits only against States with questionable remedies or a high incidence of infringement."

STEVENS, J., joined by Souter, Ginsburg and Breyer, JJ., dissented: "It is true that, when considering the Patent Remedy Act, Congress did not review the remedies available in each State for patent infringements and surmise what kind of recovery a plaintiff might obtain in a tort suit in all 50 jurisdictions. But, [g]iven that Congress had long ago pre-empted state jurisdiction over patent infringement cases, it was surely reasonable for Congress to assume that such remedies simply did not exist. Furthermore, it is well known that not all States have waived their sovereign immunity from suit, and among those States that have, the contours of this waiver vary widely.

"Even if such remedies might be available in theory, it would have been 'appropriate' for Congress to conclude that they would not guarantee patentees due process in infringement actions against state defendants.

[Here, the Act] has no impact whatsoever on any substantive rule of state law, but merely effectuates settled federal policy to confine patent infringement litigation to federal judges. There is precise congruence between 'the means used' (abrogation of sovereign immunity in this narrow category of cases) and 'the ends to be achieved' (elimination of the risk that the defense of sovereign immunity will deprive some patentees of property without due process of law)."

(ii) *State "waivers."* COLLEGE SAVINGS BANK v. FLORIDA PREPAID POSTSECONDARY EDUCATION EXPENSE BOARD, 527 U.S. 666 (1999), per SCALIA, J., held that state sovereign immunity was not (a) validly abrogated by a federal law that states that use false or misleading advertising while engaging in activities regulated by the law are subject to suit in federal court, nor (b) voluntarily waived by the state's engaging in such activities. The Court observed, however, that under *Dole*, "Congress may, in the exercise of its spending power, condition its grant of funds to the States upon their taking certain actions that Congress could not require them to take, and that acceptance of the funds entails an agreement to the actions. These cases seem to us fundamentally different from the present one. Under the Compact Clause, Art. I, § 10, cl. 3, States *cannot* form an interstate compact without first obtaining the express consent of Congress; the granting of such consent is a gratuity. So also, Congress has no obligation to use its Spending Clause power to disburse funds to the States; such funds are gifts. In the present case, however, what Congress threatens if the State refuses to agree to its condition is not the denial of a gift or gratuity, but a sanction: exclusion of the State from otherwise permissible activity. [Breyer, J.,'s dissent, joined by Stevens, Souter, and Ginsburg, JJ., argues that "given the amount of money at stake, it may be harder, not easier, for a State to refuse highway funds [or "funds needed to educate its children"] than to refrain from entering [business regulated by this law]."] Perhaps so, which is why, in cases involving conditions attached to federal funding, we have acknowledged that 'the financial inducement offered by Congress might be so coercive as to pass the point at which "pressure turns into compulsion." ' *Dole.* In any event, we think where the constitutionally guaranteed protection of the States' sovereign immunity is involved, the point of coercion is automatically passed—and the voluntariness of waiver destroyed—when what is attached to the refusal to waive is the exclusion of the State from otherwise lawful activity."

Consider Jesse H. Choper & John C. Yoo, *Who's So Afraid of the Eleventh Amendment: The Limited Impact of the Court's Sovereign Immunity Rulings,* 106 Colum.L.Rev. 213 (2005): "Seemingly, this means only that there is a simpler rule for finding 'coercion' when the 'penalty' imposed on the states is a bar on engaging in desired conduct rather than just a loss of funds. While this edict would appear to be established by fiat rather than reason, it does not limit Congress's capacious ability to work its will by use of the purse. But if the Court intended instead to fashion a new definition of 'coercion' (i.e., its 'automatic existence') when the condition on the federal carrot is the stick of loss of the 'State's sovereign immunity,' then Congress's spending authority has been seriously curtailed." Compare Gibson, note 1 after *Steward Machine,* Ch. 2, Sec. 3, II.

(iii) *Fundamental rights.* TENNESSEE v. LANE, 541 U.S. 509 (2004), involved a paraplegic who alleged that he had to crawl up two flights of stairs because the courthouse where he faced criminal charges had no elevator. The Court, per STEVENS, J., upheld Congress' § 5 power to authorize private citizens to sue states for damages under Title II of the ADA, which "seeks to enforce a variety [of] basic constitutional guarantees [like] the right of access to the courts [that] are protected by the Due Process Clause": "Congress identified [hundreds] of examples of unequal treatment of persons with disabilities by States and their political subdivisions. [It] learned that many individuals, in many States across the country, were being excluded from courthouses and court proceedings by reason of their disabilities. [And various judicial decisions] also demonstrate a pattern of unconstitutional treatment in the administration of justice.

"[In] *Hibbs,* we approved the [FMLA] based primarily on evidence of disparate provision of parenting leave, little of which concerned unconstitutional state conduct. We explained that because the FMLA was targeted at sex-based classifications, which are subject to a heightened standard of judicial scrutiny, 'it was easier for Congress to show a pattern of state constitutional violations' than in *Garrett* or *Kimel,* both of which concerned legislation that targeted classifications subject to rational-basis review. Title II is aimed at the enforcement of a variety of basic rights, including the right of access to the courts at issue in this case, that call for a standard of judicial review at least as searching, and in some cases more searching, than the standard that applies to sex-based classifications.

" * * * Petitioner urges [that] the fact that Title II applies not only to public education and voting-booth access but also to seating at state-owned hockey rinks indicates that Title II is not appropriately tailored to serve its objectives. But [the] question presented in this case is not whether Congress can validly subject the States to private suits for money damages for failing to provide reasonable access to hockey rinks, or even to voting booths, but whether Congress had the power under § 5 to enforce the constitutional right of access to the courts. [See] *United States v. Raines*, 362 U.S. 17 (1960).[19]

" * * * Title II's requirement of program accessibility, is congruent and proportional to its object of enforcing the right of access to [courts.] Congress required the States to take reasonable measures to remove architectural and other barriers to accessibility. [It] requires only 'reasonable modifications.' [In] the case of facilities built or altered [before] 1992, [for] which structural change is likely to be more difficult, a public entity may comply with Title II by adopting a variety of less costly measures, including relocating services to alternative, accessible sites and assigning aides to assist persons with disabilities in accessing services. [I]n no event is the entity required to undertake measures that would impose an undue financial or administrative burden, threaten historic preservation interests, or effect a fundamental alteration in the nature of the service.

"[Under due process,] a State must afford to all individuals '[a] meaningful opportunity to be heard' in its courts. *Boddie v. Connecticut*, [Ch.9, Sec. 5, III].[20] Our cases have recognized a number of affirmative obligations that flow from this principle: the duty to waive filing fees in certain family-law and criminal cases,[21] the duty to provide transcripts to criminal defendants seeking review of their convictions,[22] and the duty to provide counsel to certain criminal defendants.[23] Each of these cases makes clear that ordinary considerations of cost and convenience alone cannot justify a State's failure to provide individuals with a meaningful right of access to the courts.[24]"[43]

---

[19] **[Ct's Note]** In *Raines*, a State subject to suit under the Civil Rights Act of 1957 contended that the law exceeded Congress' power to enforce the Fifteenth Amendment because it prohibited "any person," and not just state actors, from interfering with voting rights. We rejected that argument, concluding that "if the complaint here called for an application of the statute clearly constitutional under the Fifteenth Amendment, that should have been an end to the question of constitutionality."

[20] **[Ct's Note]** Because this case implicates the right of access to the courts, we need not consider whether Title II's duty to accommodate exceeds what the Constitution requires in the class of cases that implicate only *Cleburne's* prohibition on irrational discrimination.

[21] **[Ct's Note]** *Boddie* (divorce filing fee); *M.L.B. v. S.L.J.,* [Ch. 9, Sec. 5, III] (record fee in parental rights termination action).

[22] **[Ct's Note]** *Griffin v. Illinois*, [Ch. 9, Sec. 5, III].

[23] **[Ct's Note]** *Gideon v. Wainwright*; *Douglas v. California*, [Ch. 9, Sec. 5, III].

[24] **[Ct's Note]** The Chief Justice contends that Title II cannot be understood as remedial legislation because it "subjects a State to liability for failing to make a vast array of special accommodations, *without regard for whether the failure to accommodate results in a constitutional wrong*." (emphasis in original). But as we have often acknowledged, Congress "is not confined to the enactment of legislation that merely parrots the precise wording of the Fourteenth Amendment," and may prohibit "a somewhat broader swath of conduct, including that which is not itself forbidden by the Amendment's text." *Kimel.*

[43] The Court upheld the Sixth Circuit's affirmance of the federal district judge's denial of the state's motion to dismiss on Eleventh Amendment grounds. The Sixth Circuit "noted that the case

REHNQUIST, J., joined by Kennedy and Thomas, JJ., dissented: "[T]he majority identifies nothing in the legislative record that shows Congress was responding to widespread violations of the due process rights of disabled persons. Rather, [the] majority sets out on a wide-ranging account of societal discrimination against the disabled [through] institutionalization laws, restrictions on marriage, voting, and public education, conditions in mental hospitals, and various other forms of unequal treatment * * * .

"With respect to the due process 'access to the courts' rights on which the Court ultimately relies, [there] is nothing in the legislative record or statutory findings to indicate that disabled persons were systematically denied the right to be present at criminal trials, denied the meaningful opportunity to be heard in civil cases, unconstitutionally excluded from jury service, or denied the right to attend criminal trials.[4][9]

"Even if the anecdotal evidence and conclusory statements relied on by the majority could be properly considered, the mere existence of an architecturally 'inaccessible' courthouse—i.e., one a disabled person cannot utilize without assistance—does not state a constitutional violation. A violation of due process occurs only when a person is actually denied the constitutional right to access a given judicial proceeding. We have never held that a person has a *constitutional* right to make his way into a courtroom without any external assistance. * * *

"The majority concludes that Title II's massive overbreadth can be cured by considering the statute only 'as it applies to the class of cases implicating the accessibility of judicial services.' [In] conducting its as-applied analysis, however, the majority posits a hypothetical statute, never enacted by Congress, that applies only to courthouses. [If] we had arbitrarily constricted the scope of the statutes to match the scope of a core constitutional right, [our] § 5 precedents] might have come out differently. [It] is thus not surprising that the only authority cited by the majority is *Raines*, a case decided long before we enunciated the congruence-and-proportionality test.

---

presented difficult questions that 'cannot be clarified absent a a factual record,' and remanded for further proceedings."

Similarly, see *United States v. Georgia*, 546 U.S. 151 (2006), per Scalia, J., unanimously upholding Congress' § 5 power to authorize damages against states under Title II of the ADA for conditions of confinement for disabled prisoners that violate the Eighth Amendment's prohibition of cruel and unusual punishment, made applicable to the states through the Due Process Clause.

⁴ **[Ct's Note]** Certainly, [Lane was] not denied these constitutional rights. The majority admits that Lane was able to attend the initial hearing of his criminal trial [by crawling up two flights of stairs]. Lane was arrested for failing to appear at his second hearing only after he refused assistance from officers dispatched by the court to help him to the courtroom. The court conducted a preliminary hearing in the first-floor library to accommodate Lane's disability, and later offered to move all further proceedings in the case to a handicapped-accessible courthouse in a nearby town. * * *

⁹ **[Ct's Note]** The Court correctly explains that "it [i]s easier for Congress to show a pattern of state constitutional violations" when it targets state action that triggers a higher level of constitutional scrutiny. [But] Congress may not dispense with the required showing altogether simply because it purports to enforce due process rights. See *Florida Prepaid*; *Boerne*. * * *

"[R]eliance on *Boddie*, and other cases in which we held that due process requires the State to waive filing fees for indigent litigants, [support] the principle that the State must remove financial requirements that in fact prevent an individual from exercising his constitutional rights, [but] do not support a statute that subjects a State to liability for failing to make a vast array of special accommodations, *without regard for whether the failure to accommodate results in a constitutional wrong.*"

SCALIA, J., also dissented because "the 'congruence and proportionality' standard, like all such flabby tests, is a standing invitation to judicial arbitrariness and policy-driven decisionmaking. Worse still, it casts this Court in the role of Congress's taskmaster. Under it, the courts (and ultimately this Court) must regularly check Congress's homework to make sure that it has identified sufficient constitutional violations to make its remedy congruent and proportional. As a general matter, we are ill advised to adopt or adhere to constitutional rules that bring us into constant conflict with a coequal branch of Government. * * *

"I would replace 'congruence and proportionality' with another test—one that provides a clear, enforceable limitation supported by the text of § 5. [It would] also authorize measures that do not restrict the States' substantive scope of action but impose requirements directly related to the facilitation of 'enforcement'—for example, reporting requirements that would enable violations of the Fourteenth Amendment to be identified. But what § 5 does not authorize is so-called 'prophylactic' measures, prohibiting primary conduct that is itself not forbidden by the Fourteenth Amendment.

"[P]rincipally for reasons of stare decisis, I shall henceforth apply the permissive *McCulloch* standard [used in *South Carolina* and *Morgan*] to congressional measures designed to remedy racial discrimination by the States. I would not, however, abandon the requirement that Congress may impose prophylactic § 5 legislation only upon those particular States in which there has been an identified history of relevant constitutional violations."[44]

Query: On remand, what must Lane prove in order to win (see fn. 43 supra)? Does the Court's approval of "Title II's remedial requirement of program accessibility" confirm the validity of Title VII of the Civil Rights Act of 1964's prohibition on state employers using facially neutral regulations that have a disparate impact on the basis of race or sex (see fn. 40)? See Kevin S. Schwartz, Note, *Applying Section 5: Tennessee v. Lane and Judicial Conditions on the Congressional Enforcement Power*, 114 Yale L.J. 1133 (2005).

"On its face" vs. "as applied." May *Raines* be reconciled with the congruence and proportionality test? If not which approach *should* govern? Consider Catherine Carroll, Note, *Section Five Overbreadth: The Facial*

---

[44] In a separate concurring opinion, Ginsburg, J., joined by Souter and Breyer, JJ., responded: "Members of Congress are understandably reluctant to condemn their own States as constitutional violators, complicit in maintaining the isolated and unequal status of persons with disabilities. I would not disarm a National Legislature for resisting an adversarial approach to lawmaking better suited to the courtroom."

Approach to Adjudicating Challenges Under Section Five of the Fourteenth Amendment, 101 Mich.L.Rev. 1026 (2003): "[T]he Court's decisions since *Boerne* have introduced a form of overbreadth doctrine into the analysis of section 5 legislation akin to the approach used in the First Amendment context [where it has been justified] because of the privileged status of the individual rights at stake and because of the likelihood that persons not before the court will be deterred from exercising their expressive rights. [See Ch. 7, III, C. But no] direct analogue to this reasoning arises in the section 5 context." See also Gillian E. Metzger, *Facial Challenges and Federalism,* 105 Colum.L.Rev. 873 (2005): (The "rigor of the congruence-and-proportionality test [means] that Section 5 legislation is much more likely to appear invalid if assessed in its entirety. The question the Court faces therefore [is] whether the probability of facial invalidity should preclude the possibility of as-applied validity.") (answering no).

(c)   *State action.* (i) UNITED STATES v. MORRISON, Ch. 2, Sec. 2, IV, per REHNQUIST, C.J., held that Congress had no § 5 power to grant a civil remedy to victims of gender-motivated violence despite Congress' (1) receiving "evidence that many participants in state justice systems are perpetuating an array of erroneous stereotypes and assumptions," and (2) concluding "that these discriminatory stereotypes often result in insufficient investigation and prosecution of gender-motivated crime, inappropriate focus on the behavior and credibility of the victims, [and] unacceptably lenient punishments for those who are actually convicted": [T]he language and purpose of the Fourteenth Amendment place certain limitations on the manner in which Congress may attack [gender discrimination. Foremost] is that the Fourteenth Amendment, by its very terms, prohibits only state action. * * *

"Shortly after the Fourteenth Amendment was adopted, we [decided] *United States v. Harris,* 106 U.S. 629 (1883), [which] considered a challenge to § 2 of the Civil Rights Act of 1871. That section sought to punish 'private persons' for 'conspiring to deprive any one of the equal protection of the laws enacted by the State.' We concluded that this law exceeded Congress' § 5 power because the law was 'directed exclusively against the action of private persons, without reference to the laws of the State, or their administration by her officers.' [We] reached a similar conclusion in the *Civil Rights Cases.* * * *

Sec. 13981 "is directed not at any State or state actor, but at individuals who have committed criminal acts motivated by gender bias. [It] visits no consequence whatever on any Virginia public official involved in investigating or prosecuting [the rape involved in this case]. The section is, therefore, unlike any of the § 5 remedies that we have previously upheld"—as in *Morgan, South Carolina,* and *Ex parte Virginia,* which were directed at states or state officials.[45] Further "as we have phrased it in more recent cases, prophylactic

---

[45]   The Court noted: "There is abundant evidence [t]o show that the Congresses that enacted the [laws in the *Civil Rights Cases*] had a purpose similar to that of Congress in enacting § 13981: There were state laws on the books bespeaking equality of treatment, but in the administration of these laws there was discrimination against newly freed slaves."

legislation under § 5 must have a 'congruence and proportionality between the injury to be prevented or remedied and the means adopted to that end.'

"Section 13981 is also different from these previously upheld remedies in that it applies uniformly throughout the Nation. Congress' findings indicate that the problem of discrimination against the victims of gender-motivated crimes does not exist in all States, or even most States. By contrast, the § 5 remedy upheld in *Morgan* was directed only to the State where the evil found by Congress existed, and in *South Carolina,* the remedy was directed only to those States in which Congress found that there had been discrimination."

BREYER, J., joined by Stevens, J., dissented[46]: "The Federal Government's argument [is] that Congress used § 5 to remedy the actions of *state actors*, namely, those States which, through discriminatory design or the discriminatory conduct of their officials, failed to provide adequate (or any) state remedies for women injured by gender-motivated violence—a failure that the States, and Congress, documented in depth." The *Civil Rights Cases* did not consider "this kind of claim," because the statute "did 'not profess to be corrective of any constitutional wrong committed by the States' [but] established 'rules for the conduct of individuals in society towards each other, [without] referring in any manner to any supposed action of the State or its authorities.'

"[W]hy can Congress not provide a remedy against private actors? Those private actors, of course, did not themselves violate the Constitution. But this Court has held that Congress at least sometimes can enact remedial 'legislation [that] prohibits conduct which is not itself unconstitutional.' The statutory remedy [may] lead state actors to improve their own remedial systems, primarily through example. It restricts private actors only by imposing liability for private conduct that is, in the main, already forbidden by state law. Why is the remedy 'disproportionate'? And given the relation between remedy and violation—the creation of a federal remedy to substitute for constitutionally inadequate state remedies—where is the lack of 'congruence'?

" * * * Congress had before it the task force reports of at least 21 States documenting constitutional violations. And it made its own findings about pervasive gender-based stereotypes hampering many state legal systems, sometimes unconstitutionally so. [This] Court has not previously held that Congress must document the existence of a problem in every State prior to proposing a national solution." [47]

---

[46] Souter and Ginsburg, JJ., having found the law valid under the Commerce Clause, felt no occasion to reach the § 5 issue.

[47] Oregon v. *Mitchell* discussed in Boerne, unanimously upheld the extension *nationwide* of Voting Rights Act of 1965 § 4a's prohibition of "any test or device" (including literacy tests) "as a prerequisite for voting or registration." Black, J., reasoned that "Congress had before it a long history of the discriminatory use of literacy tests to disfranchise voters on account of their race. [A]s to the Nation as a whole, Congress had before it statistics which demonstrate that voter registration and voter participation are consistently greater in States without literacy tests." Harlan, J., added: "Despite the lack of evidence of specific instances of discriminatory application

(ii) ***Thirteenth Amendment***? Consider Ira C. Lupu, *The Failure of RFRA*, 20 U.Ark.Little Rock L. Rev. 575 (1998): "[I]t is certainly a plausible argument that violent spouses attempt to keep their mates in a form of physical and emotional bondage, and that Congress would therefore have a rational basis for finding domestic violence to be an instrument of domination analogous to enslavement." See also Lawrence G. Sager, *A Letter to the Supreme Court Regarding the Missing Argument in Brzonkala v. Morrison*, 75 N.Y.U.L.Rev. 150 (2000).

---

or effect, Congress could have determined that racial prejudice is prevalent throughout the Nation, and that literacy tests unduly lend themselves to discriminatory application, either conscious or unconscious. This danger of violation of § 1 of the Fifteenth Amendment was sufficient to authorize the exercise of congressional power under § 2. [While] a less sweeping approach in this delicate area might well have been appropriate, the choice which Congress made was within the range of the reasonable." Stewart, J., joined by Burger, C.J., and Blackmun, J., held: " Congress was not required to make state-by-state [findings]. In the interests of uniformity, Congress may paint with a much broader brush than may this Court, which must confine itself to the judicial function of deciding individual cases and controversies upon individual records. * * * Experience gained under the 1965 Act has now led Congress to conclude that it should go the whole distance. This approach to the problem is a rational one; consequently it is within [the] power of Congress under § 2 of the Fifteenth Amendment."

CHAPTER 12

LIMITATIONS ON JUDICIAL POWER AND REVIEW

∎ ∎ ∎

Judicial power is limited under Article III to the resolution of "cases or controversies." Perhaps not surprisingly, however, significant disagreement exists about what this requirement means, with some taking a narrower and some a broader view. *Marbury v. Madison*, Ch. 1, Sec. 1, supra, provides a good starting point for thinking about the two major schools of thought.

1. ***Dispute resolution or private rights model.*** According to a "dispute resolution," or "private rights," model, the function of courts is exclusively to resolve the rights of the parties before them in the context of traditionally structured lawsuits involving specifically injured plaintiffs or criminal defendants seeking relief from specific wrongdoers. In *Marbury v. Madison*, the plaintiff William Marbury thus claimed that he had a right to a commission as a justice of the peace, much as he might have had a right to a piece of property, that the defendant James Madison had violated this right, and that the Court should order Madison to remedy the specific wrong that he had done to Marbury. Henry P. Monaghan, *Constitutional Adjudication: The Who and When*, 82 Yale L.J. 1363 (1973), explains how *Marbury* supports the dispute resolution or private rights model:

"In important part, *Marbury* found the power of constitutional exposition to be an incident of the Court's obligation to decide the particular 'case or controversy' before it. [In] *Marbury*, Justice Marshall repeatedly emphasized the necessity for the judicial protection of 'vested' or 'legal' rights; and he declared that 'the province of the Court is *solely* to decide on the rights of individuals * * * .' Moreover, *Marbury*'s analogy of constitutional litigation to 'ordinary' common law litigation strongly suggested that the occasions for judicial review were limited to the protection of identifiable and concrete personal rights, similar to those protected by the common law courts. This view of the judicial function took deep roots, particularly as the nineteenth century wore on. And the Court, while quick to protect private rights from 'arbitrary' social legislation, repeatedly disclaimed any general commission to expound on the meaning of the Constitution. Professor Wechsler reflected this tradition when, writing in 1966, he denied that the Court had any 'special function' of 'policing or advising Legislatures or Executives,' and yet reasoned that where individual rights were at issue, the Court had an inescapable duty 'to decide the litigated case and to decide it in accordance with the [Constitution].' "

Proponents of the private rights or dispute resolution model argue that limiting the judicial role to deciding sharply and traditionally framed disputes between individual victims and alleged wrongdoers has a number of virtues. First, it provides concrete factual framing that both narrows the issues presented for resolution and helps to make vivid their stakes. Second, and perhaps more importantly, it keeps the judicial role within historically accepted bounds and preserves the separation of powers by preventing the judiciary from broadly interfering with the actions of the legislative and executive branches.

2.   *Special functions or public rights model.* There is, however, an alternative conception of the judicial role, which Professor Monaghan calls a "special functions" model and others have called a "public rights" or "law declaration" model.[1] According to this model, it is the special function of the Court to make sure that other branches of government adhere to constitutional limitations on their power or, in slightly different language, to enforce the frequently shared rights of the public as a whole. In the view of Monaghan, supra, a public rights model, fully as much as its private rights rival, traces its roots to *Marbury v. Madison* and its famous declaration that "[i]t is emphatically the province and duty of the judicial department to say what the law is":

"Once the Court's 'special function' and the 'unique' character of constitutional adjudications are stressed, 'the old notion that the power to decide constitutional questions is simply incident to the power to dispose of a concrete case loses much of its substance.' * * * *Marbury* welded judicial review to the political axiom of limited government."[2]

As you read the remainder of this Chapter, consider how far a "special function" or "public rights" model of constitutional adjudication has displaced and should displace the kind of limitations on the judicial function called for by a more traditional, private rights conception.

---

[1]   See Richard H. Fallon, Jr., John Manning, Daniel J. Meltzer & David L. Shapiro, *Hart & Wechsler's The Federal Courts and the Federal System* 73–75 (6th ed. 2009).

[2]   Among the most influential articles exemplifying a "public rights" or "special function" approach are Abram Chayes, *The Role of the Judge in Public Law Litigation,* 89 Harv.L.Rev. 1281 (1976); Owen M. Fiss, *The Forms of Justice,* 93 Harv.L.Rev. 1 (1979); and Cass R. Sunstein, *Standing and the Privatization of Public Law,* 88 Colum.L.Rev. 1432 (1988).

1. ADVISORY OPINIONS AND EXECUTIVE REVISION

Correspondence of the Justices (1793)[3]

Letter from Thomas Jefferson, Secretary of State, to Chief Justice Jay and Associate Justices:

Philadelphia, July 18, 1793.

Gentlemen:

The war which has taken place among the powers of Europe produces frequent transactions within our ports and limits, on which questions arise of considerable difficulty, and of greater importance to the peace of the United States. These questions depend for their solution on the construction of our treaties, on the laws of nature and nations, and on the laws of the land, and are often presented under circumstances *which do not give a cognizance of them to the tribunals of the country.* Yet their decision is so little analogous to the ordinary functions of the executive, as to occasion much embarrassment and difficulty to them. The President therefore would be much relieved if he found himself free to refer questions of this description to the opinions of the judges of the Supreme Court of the United States, whose knowledge of the subject would secure us against errors dangerous to the peace of the United States, and their authority insure the respect of all parties. He has therefore asked the attendance of such of the judges as could be collected in time for the occasion, to know, in the first place, their opinion, whether the public may, with propriety, be availed of their *advice on these questions?* And if they may, to present, for their advice, the abstract questions which have already occurred, or may soon occur, from which they will themselves strike out such as any circumstances might, in their opinion, forbid them to pronounce on. I have the honour to be with sentiments of the most perfect respect, gentlemen,

Your most obedient and humble servant,

Thos. Jefferson.

———

The following are some of the questions submitted by the President to the Justices:

1. Do the treaties between the United States and France give to France or her citizens a *right,* when at war with a power with whom the

---

[3] The letters are taken from 3 *Correspondence and Public Papers of John Jay* 486–89 (Henry P. Johnston ed. 1891), and the questions from 10 Jared Sparks, *Writings of George Washington* 542–45 (1836).

United States are at peace, to fit out originally in and from the ports of the United States vessels armed for war, with or without commission?

17. Do the laws of neutrality, considered as aforesaid, authorize the United States to permit France, her subjects, or citizens, the sale within their ports of prizes made of the subjects or property of a power at war with France, before they have been carried into some port of France and there condemned, refusing the like privilege to her enemy?

18. Do those laws authorize the United States to permit to France the erection of courts within their territory and jurisdiction for the trial and condemnation of prizes, refusing that privilege to a power at war with France?

20. To what distance, by the laws and usages of nations, may the United States exercise the right of prohibiting the hostilities of foreign powers at war with each other within rivers, bays, and arms of the sea, and upon the sea along the coasts of the United States?

22. What are the articles, by name, to be prohibited to both or either party?

25. May we, within our own ports, sell ships to both parties, prepared merely for merchandise? May they be pierced for guns?

29. May an armed vessel belonging to any of the belligerent powers follow *immediately* merchant vessels, enemies, departing from our ports, for the purpose of making prizes of them? If not, how long ought the former to remain, after the latter have sailed? And what shall be considered as the place of departure from which the time is to be counted? And how are the facts to be ascertained?

On August 8, 1793, the Justices wrote to the President refusing to tender the requested advice and explaining their decision as follows:

Sir:

We have considered the previous question stated in a letter written to us by your direction by the Secretary of State on the 18th of last month. The lines of separation drawn by the Constitution between the three departments of the government—their being in certain respects checks upon each other—and our being judges of a court in the last resort—are considerations which afford strong arguments against the propriety of our extrajudicially deciding the questions alluded to; especially as the power given by the Constitution to the President of calling on the heads of departments for opinions, seems to have been *purposely* as well as expressly limited to the *executive* departments.

NOTES AND QUESTIONS

1. ***Pros and cons of advisory opinions.*** According to Charles Alan Wright, *Law of Federal Courts* 65 (5th ed. 1994): "[T]he oldest and most consistent thread in the federal law of justiciability is that the federal courts will not give advisory opinions," or nonbinding statements of the law in response to executive or legislative inquiries, "though at least by 1770 the power of the English judges to give advisory opinions was well recognized. Thus, the refusal to give advisory opinions must be based on 'the implicit policies embodied in Article III, and not history alone.'" What might those policies be?

(a) Does the Opinion Clause of Article II, § 2, cl. 1—which provides that the President "may require the Opinion, in writing, of the principal Officer in each of the executive Departments, upon any Subject relating to the Duties of their respective Offices"—impliedly establish that the President may not require the judicial branch to provide such opinions? See Akhil Reed Amar, *Some Opinions on the Opinion Clause,* 82 Va.L.Rev. 647 (1996). Impliedly bar the judicial branch from furnishing such opinions voluntarily?

(b) Is the opposition to advisory opinions justified by the necessity for specific facts and the antagonistic assertion of rights by one individual against another?

(c) Does refusal to render advisory opinions help to symbolize the status of the Article III judiciary as an independent and co-equal branch of the national government, which cannot be impressed into service as a mere legal advisor to Congress or the President? Consider Russell Wheeler, *Extrajudicial Activities of the Early Supreme Court,* 1973 Sup.Ct.Rev. 123, asserting that the position taken in the Correspondence of the Justices was "part of a broader attempt by the early Supreme Court to deemphasize the obligatory extrajudicial service concept, so widely held in the early period."

(d) Is the Supreme Court's capacity to function as an organ of sober second thought enhanced by its refusal to render opinions except as an incident to the resolution of concrete cases?[4]

2. ***Practices of other courts.*** (a) The Massachusetts Constitution of 1789 (part 2, chap. 3, art. 2) provides: "Each branch of the legislature, as well as the governor and council, shall have authority to require the opinions of the justices of the supreme judicial court, upon important questions of law, and upon solemn occasions." Today, roughly 10 states besides Massachusetts retain advisory opinion practices. Consider Helen Hershkoff, *State Courts and the "Passive Virtues": Rethinking the Judicial Function,* 114 Harv.L.Rev. 1833 (2001), asserting that advisory opinions "allow state courts to articulate constitutional principles while effectively 'remanding' disputes back to the

---

[4] See also Stewart Jay, *Most Humble Servants: The Advisory Role of Early Judges* 149–70 (1997) (arguing that the position taken in the Correspondence of the Justices traced to historically peculiar considerations, including the concern of Federalist Justices to maintain foreign policy as an exclusive executive prerogative and to avoid embroilment in political controversy at a time when the Justices were eager to have Congress excuse them from the burden of "circuit-riding").

other branches [for a dialogic response. Advisory] opinions suit the conditional nature of all state constitutional decisions, which are easily amended and frequently experimental in approach."

(b)   Consider Richard H. Fallon, Jr., John F. Manning, Daniel J. Meltzer & David L. Shapiro, *Hart & Wechsler's The Federal Courts and the Federal System* 58 (6th ed. 2009): "In contrast with the United States, many European countries employ 'constitutional courts' whose primary function is to review constitutional claims, especially regarding the constitutionality of statutes; within such regimes, other courts are generally barred from holding statutes unconstitutional. In tribunals established to hear constitutional claims under this 'European model,' review is often 'initiated by political authorities.' [In] such proceedings, constitutional courts characteristically require only 'an *abstract* or *objective* question' to determine the constitutionality of a new law; 'no concrete dispute involving individual situations' is necessary."

3.   ***Identifying advisory opinions.*** What makes the judicial expression of an opinion "advisory" in the constitutional sense and thus prohibited? Judicial dicta are commonplace; indeed, it seems to be an important function of the Supreme Court to provide guidance to lower courts. But if not all dicta are forbidden advisory opinions, it may be very difficult to draw lines, at least outside of "classic" cases in which the executive or legislative branches ask the courts for nonbinding advice (as in *The Correspondence of the Justices*). According to Evan Tsen Lee, *Deconstitutionalizing Justiciability: The Example of Mootness,* 105 Harv.L.Rev. 603 (1992), the Court has used the term "advisory opinion" to embrace "[a]ny judgment subject to review by a co-equal branch of government," "[a]dvice to a co-equal branch of government prior to the other branch's contemplated action (that is, pre-enactment review)," "Supreme Court review of any state judgment for which there is or may be an adequate and independent state ground of decision," "[a]ny opinion, or portion thereof, not truly necessary to the disposition of the case at bar (that is, dicta)," and "[a]ny decision on the merits of a case that is moot or unripe or in which one of the parties lacks standing." But, Lee concludes, "only the first two of these usages denote a constitutional bar. The other three usages are a function of judicial discretion."

2.   STANDING

I.   THE STRUCTURE OF STANDING DOCTRINE

ALLEN V. WRIGHT

468 U.S. 737, 104 S.Ct. 3315, 82 L.Ed.2d 556 (1984).

JUSTICE O'CONNOR delivered the opinion of the Court.

Parents of black public school children allege in this nation-wide class action that the Internal Revenue Service (IRS) has not adopted sufficient standards and procedures to fulfill its obligation to deny tax-exempt status to racially discriminatory private schools. They assert that the IRS thereby harms them directly and interferes with the ability of their children to receive an education in desegregated public schools. The issue before us is whether plaintiffs have standing to bring this suit. We hold that they do not.

[Respondents] allege in their complaint that many racially segregated private schools were created or expanded in their communities at the time the public schools were undergoing desegregation. According to the complaint, many such private schools, including 17 schools or school systems identified by name in the complaint (perhaps some 30 schools in all), receive tax exemptions either directly or through the tax-exempt status of "umbrella" organizations that operate or support the [schools.][11] Respondents allege that the IRS grant of tax exemptions to such racially discriminatory schools is unlawful [under federal statutes and the Constitution, and they seek declaratory and injunctive relief].

[R]espondents do not allege that their children have been the victims of discriminatory exclusion from the schools whose tax exemptions they challenge as unlawful. [Rather,] respondents claim a direct injury from the mere fact of the challenged Government conduct and, as indicated by the restriction of the plaintiff class to parents of children in desegregating school districts, injury to their children's opportunity to receive a desegregated education. * * *

II. Article III of the Constitution confines the federal courts to adjudicating actual "cases" and "controversies." As the Court explained in *Valley Forge Christian College v. Americans United for Separation of Church and State, Inc.*, [Part III infra,] the "case or controversy" requirement defines with respect to the Judicial Branch the idea of separation of powers on which the Federal Government is founded. The several doctrines that have grown up to elaborate that requirement are "founded in concern about the proper—and properly limited—role of the courts in a democratic society." * * *

The Art. III doctrine that requires a litigant to have "standing" to invoke the power of a federal court is perhaps the most important of these doctrines. In essence the question of standing is whether the litigant is entitled to have the court decide the merits of the dispute or of particular issues. Standing doctrine embraces several judicially self-imposed limits on the exercise of federal jurisdiction, such as the general prohibition on a litigant's raising another person's legal rights, the rule barring adjudication of generalized grievances more appropriately addressed in the representative branches, and the requirement that a plaintiff's complaint

---

[11] **[Ct's Note]** * * * Contrary to Justice Brennan's statement, the complaint does not allege that each desegregating district in which they reside contains one or more racially discriminatory private schools unlawfully receiving a tax exemption.

fall within the zone of interests protected by the law invoked. The requirement of standing, however, has a core component derived directly from the Constitution. A plaintiff must allege personal injury fairly traceable to the defendant's allegedly unlawful conduct and likely to be redressed by the requested relief.

Like the prudential component, the constitutional component of standing doctrine incorporates concepts concededly not susceptible of precise definition. The injury alleged must be, for example, "distinct and palpable," and not "abstract" or "conjectural" or "hypothetical," *Los Angeles v. Lyons*, [infra]. The injury must be "fairly" traceable to the challenged action, and relief from the injury must be "likely" to follow from a favorable decision. See *Simon v. Eastern Kentucky Welfare Rights Org.*, [infra]. These terms cannot be defined so as to make application of the constitutional standing requirement a mechanical exercise.

The absence of precise definitions, however, [hardly] leaves courts at sea in applying the law of standing. Like most legal notions, the standing concepts have gained considerable definition from developing case law. [More] important, the law of Art. III standing is built on a single basic idea—the idea of separation of powers. It is this fact which makes possible the gradual clarification of the law through judicial application. * * *

Respondents allege two injuries in their complaint to support their standing to bring this lawsuit. First, they say that they are harmed directly by the mere fact of Government financial aid to discriminatory private schools. Second, they say that the federal tax exemptions to racially discriminatory private schools in their communities impair their ability to have their public schools desegregated. [N]either suffices to support respondents' standing.

Respondents' first claim of injury [might] be a claim simply to have the Government avoid the violation of law alleged in respondents' complaint. Alternatively, it might be a claim of stigmatic injury, or denigration, suffered by all members of a racial group when the Government discriminates on the basis of race. Under neither interpretation is this claim of injury judicially cognizable.

This Court has repeatedly held that an asserted right to have the Government act in accordance with law is not sufficient, standing alone, to confer jurisdiction on a federal court. In *Schlesinger v. Reservists Committee to Stop the War*, 418 U.S. 208 (1974), for example, the Court rejected a claim of citizen standing to challenge Armed Forces Reserve commissions held by Members of Congress as violating the Incompatibility Clause of Art. I, § 6, of the Constitution. As citizens, the Court held, plaintiffs alleged nothing but "the abstract injury in nonobservance of the Constitution." More recently, in *Valley Forge*, we rejected a claim of standing to challenge a Government conveyance of property to a religious institution. Insofar as the plaintiffs relied simply on "their shared individuated right" to a Government that made no law respecting an establishment of religion, we held that plaintiffs had not alleged a judicially cognizable injury. * * *

Neither do they have standing to litigate their claims based on the stigmatizing injury often caused by racial discrimination. There can be no doubt that this sort of noneconomic injury is one of the most serious consequences of discriminatory government action and is sufficient in some circumstances to support standing. Our cases make clear, however, that such injury accords a basis for standing only to "those persons who are personally denied equal treatment" by the challenged discriminatory conduct. [If an] abstract stigmatic injury were cognizable, standing would extend nationwide to all members of the particular racial groups against which the Government was alleged to be discriminating by its grant of a tax exemption to a racially discriminatory school, regardless of the location of that school. [A] black person in Hawaii could challenge the grant of a tax exemption to a racially discriminatory school in Maine. Recognition of standing in such circumstances would transform the federal courts into "no more than a vehicle for the vindication of the value interests of concerned bystanders." *United States v. SCRAP*, [infra]. Constitutional limits on the role of the federal courts preclude such a transformation.

It is in their complaint's second claim of injury that respondents allege harm to a concrete, personal interest that can support standing in some circumstances. The injury they identify—their children's diminished ability to receive an education in a racially integrated school—is, beyond any doubt, not only judicially cognizable but, as shown by cases [since] *Brown v. Board of Education*, [Ch. 9, Sec. 2, II] one of the most serious injuries recognized in our legal system. Despite the constitutional importance of curing the injury alleged by respondents, however, the federal judiciary may not redress it unless standing requirements are met. In this case, respondents' second claim of injury cannot support standing because the injury alleged is not fairly traceable to the Government conduct respondents challenge as unlawful.[22]

The illegal conduct challenged by respondents is the IRS's grant of tax exemptions to some racially discriminatory schools. The line of causation

---

[22] **[Ct's Note]** Respondents' stigmatic injury, though not sufficient for standing in the abstract form in which their complaint asserts it, is judicially cognizable to the extent that respondents are personally subject to discriminatory treatment. See *Heckler v. Mathews*, [infra] [involving the denial of monetary benefits on an allegedly discriminatory basis]. The stigmatic injury thus requires identification of some concrete interest with respect to which respondents are personally subject to discriminatory treatment. That interest must independently satisfy the causation requirement of standing doctrine.

[Here,] respondents identify only one interest that they allege is being discriminatorily impaired—their interest in desegregated public school education. Respondents' asserted stigmatic injury, therefore, is sufficient to support their standing in this litigation only if their school-desegregation injury independently meets the causation requirement of standing doctrine.

between that conduct and desegregation of respondents' schools is attenuated at best. From the perspective of the IRS, the injury to respondents is highly indirect and "results from the independent action of some third party not before the court." *Simon.* * * *

The diminished ability of respondents' children to receive a desegregated education would be fairly traceable to unlawful IRS grants of tax exemptions only if there were enough racially discriminatory private schools receiving tax exemptions in respondents' communities for withdrawal of those exemptions to make an appreciable difference in public school integration. Respondents have made no such allegation. It [is] entirely speculative, as respondents themselves conceded in the Court of Appeals, whether withdrawal of a tax exemption from any particular school would lead the school to change its policies. It is just as speculative whether any given parent of a child attending such a private school would decide to transfer the child to public school as a result of any changes in educational or financial policy made by the private school once it was threatened with loss of tax-exempt status. It is also pure speculation whether, in a particular community, a large enough number of the numerous relevant school officials and parents would reach decisions that collectively would have a significant impact on the racial composition of the public schools. * * *

The Court of Appeals relied for its contrary conclusion on *Gilmore v. City of Montgomery* [and] *Norwood v. Harrison*, [both discussed in Ch. 10, Sec. 3 supra. Neither], however, requires that we find standing in this lawsuit.

In *Gilmore*, the plaintiffs [alleged] that the city was violating [their] equal protection right by permitting racially discriminatory private schools and other groups to use the public parks. The Court recognized plaintiffs' standing to challenge this city policy insofar as the policy permitted the exclusive use of the parks by racially discriminatory private [schools]. Standing in *Gilmore* thus rested on an allegation of direct deprivation of a right to equal use of the parks. * * *

In *Norwood v. Harrison*, parents of public school children in Tunica County, Miss., filed a statewide class action challenging the State's provision of textbooks to students attending racially discriminatory private schools in the State. The Court held the State's practice unconstitutional because it breached "the State's acknowledged duty to establish a unitary school system." The Court did not expressly address the basis for the plaintiffs' standing.

In *Gilmore*, however, the Court identified the basis for standing in *Norwood*: "The plaintiffs in Norwood were parties to a school desegregation order and the relief they sought was directly related to the concrete injury they suffered." Through the school-desegregation decree, the plaintiffs had acquired a right to have the State "steer clear" of any perpetuation of the racially dual school system that it had once sponsored. The interest acquired was judicially cognizable because it was a personal interest, created by law, in having the State refrain from taking specific actions. * * *

III. "The necessity that the plaintiff who seeks to invoke judicial power stand to profit in some personal interest remains an Art. III requirement." *Simon*. Respondents have not met this fundamental requirement. The judgment of the Court of Appeals is accordingly reversed, and the injunction issued by that court is vacated.

JUSTICE BRENNAN, dissenting.

[In] these cases, the respondents have alleged at least one type of injury that satisfies the constitutional requirement of "distinct and palpable injury."[3] In particular, they claim that the IRS's grant of tax-exempt status to racially discriminatory private schools directly injures their children's opportunity and ability to receive a desegregated education. * * *

The Court acknowledges that this alleged injury is sufficient to satisfy constitutional standards. [Moreover,] in light of the injuries they claim, the respondents have alleged a direct causal relationship between the Government action they challenge and the injury they suffer: [Common] sense alone would recognize that the elimination of tax-exempt status for racially discriminatory private schools would serve to lessen the impact that those institutions have in defeating efforts to desegregate the public schools.

The Court admits that "[t]he diminished ability of respondents' children to receive a desegregated education would be fairly traceable to unlawful IRS grants of tax exemptions [if] there were enough racially discriminatory private schools receiving tax exemptions in respondents' communities for withdrawal of those exemptions to make an appreciable difference in public school integration," but concludes that "[r]espondents have made no such allegation." With all due respect, the Court has either misread the complaint or is improperly requiring the respondents to prove their case on the merits in order to defeat a motion to dismiss. For example, the respondents specifically refer by name to at least 32 private schools that discriminate on the basis of race and yet continue to benefit illegally from tax-exempt status. Eighteen of those schools [are] located in the city of Memphis, Tenn., which has been the subject of several court orders to desegregate. * * *

More than one commentator has noted that the causation component of the Court's standing inquiry is no more than a poor disguise for the

---

[3] **[Ct's Note]** Because I conclude that the second injury alleged by the respondents is sufficient to satisfy constitutional requirements, I do not need to reach what the Court labels the "stigmatic injury." * * *

Court's view of the merits of the underlying claims. The Court today does nothing to avoid that criticism. * * *

JUSTICE STEVENS, with whom JUSTICE BLACKMUN joins, dissenting.

[In the] final analysis, the wrong respondents allege that the Government has committed is to subsidize the exodus of white children from schools that would otherwise be racially integrated. The critical question in these cases, therefore, is whether respondents have alleged that the Government has created that kind of subsidy.

[If] the granting of preferential tax treatment would "encourage" private segregated schools to conduct their "charitable" activities, it must follow that the withdrawal of the treatment would "discourage" them, and hence promote the process of desegregation. [This] causation analysis is nothing more than a restatement of elementary economics: when something becomes more expensive, less of it will be purchased. [W]ithout tax-exempt status, private schools will either not be competitive in terms of cost, or have to change their admissions policies, hence reducing their competitiveness for parents seeking "a racially segregated alternative" to public schools, which is what respondents have alleged many white parents in desegregating school districts seek.

[Because] [c]onsiderations of tax policy, economics, and pure logic all confirm the conclusion that respondents' injury in fact is fairly traceable to the Government's allegedly wrongful conduct[,] [t]he Court [is] forced to introduce the concept of "separation of powers" into its analysis. [In doing so,] the Court could be saying that it will require a more direct causal connection when it is troubled by the separation of powers implications of the case before it. That approach confuses the standing doctrine with the justiciability of the issues that respondents seek to raise. The purpose of the standing inquiry is to measure the plaintiff's stake in the outcome, not whether a court has the authority to provide it with the outcome it seeks.

[As the Court has previously recognized,] the " 'fundamental aspect of standing' is that it focuses primarily on the *party* seeking to get his complaint before the federal court rather than 'on the issues he wishes to have adjudicated,' " *United States v. Richardson*, 418 U.S. 166 (1974). [If] a plaintiff presents a nonjusticiable issue, or seeks relief that a court may not award, then its complaint should be dismissed for those reasons, and not because the plaintiff lacks a stake in obtaining that relief and hence has no standing. Imposing an undefined but clearly more rigorous standard for redressability for reasons unrelated to the causal nexus between the injury and the challenged conduct can only encourage undisciplined, ad hoc litigation.

[Alternatively], the Court could be saying that it will not treat as legally cognizable injuries that stem from an administrative decision concerning how enforcement resources will be allocated. This surely is an important point. Respondents do seek to restructure the IRS's mechanisms for enforcing the legal requirement that discriminatory institutions not receive tax-exempt status. Such restructuring would dramatically affect the way in which the IRS exercises its prosecutorial discretion. The Executive requires latitude to decide how best to enforce the law, and in general the Court may well be correct that the exercise of that discretion, especially in the tax context, is unchallengeable.

However, as the Court also recognizes, this principle does not apply when suit is brought "to enforce specific legal obligations whose violation works a direct harm." [Here,] respondents contend that the IRS is violating a specific constitutional limitation on its enforcement discretion. There is a solid basis for that contention. In *Norwood*, we wrote: "A State's constitutional obligation requires it to steer clear, not only of operating the old dual system of racially segregated schools, but also of giving significant aid to institutions that practice racial or other invidious discrimination."

Deciding whether the Treasury has violated a specific legal limitation on its enforcement discretion does not intrude upon the prerogatives of the Executive, for in so deciding we are merely saying "what the law is." * * *

In short, I would deal with the question of the legal limitations on the IRS's enforcement discretion on its merits, rather than by making the untenable assumption that the granting of preferential tax treatment to segregated schools does not make those schools more attractive to white students and hence does not inhibit the process of desegregation.[5]

NOTES AND QUESTIONS

1. ***Origins of the doctrine.*** The Court appears to have referred to "standing" on only eight occasions prior to 1965, with the earliest reference coming in *Stark v. Wickard*, 321 U.S. 288 (1944).[6] Prior to the modern age, the typical plaintiff in federal court may have suffered injury-in-fact, but the Court seems not to have regarded injury-in-fact as an absolute requirement of a judicially cognizable case or controversy under Article III. See, e.g., Steven L. Winter, *The Metaphor of Standing and the Problem of Self-Governance*, 40 Stan.L.Rev. 1371 (1988) (arguing that, prior to the twentieth century, courts granted relief whenever a plaintiff asserted a right for which one of the forms of action afforded a remedy and that some of these forms, particularly the prerogative writs, permitted suit by persons lacking a distinctive personal stake in the dispute); Raoul Berger, *Standing to Sue in Public Actions: Is It a Constitutional Requirement?*, 78 Yale L.J. 816 (1969) (asserting that when the Constitution was adopted, "the English practice in prohibition, certiorari, quo

---

[5]   Marshall, J., did not participate in the decision.

[6]   See Cass R. Sunstein, *What's Standing After* Lujan? *Of Citizen Suits, "Injuries," and Article III,* 91 Mich.L.Rev. 163 (1992).

warranto, and informers' and relators' actions encouraged strangers to attack *unauthorized action*").[7]

Compare Anne Woolhandler & Caleb Nelson, *Does History Defeat Standing Doctrine?*, 102 Mich.L.Rev. 689 (2004), arguing that although "early American courts did not use the term 'standing' much, and modern research tools might therefore convince one that the concept did not exist," early decisions regularly insisted on "proper parties" and "designated some areas of litigation as being under public control and others as being under private control. Within the area of private control, moreover, courts paid close attention to whether the correct private parties were before them." Although the authors "do not claim that history *compels* acceptance of the modern Supreme Court's vision of standing," they "argue that history does not *defeat* standing doctrine." (emphasis added).

2. ***Nature and purposes.*** As Stevens, J., noted in *Allen*, the Court has frequently stated that standing doctrine addresses issues of parties—and focuses, in particular, on the nature and sufficiency of the litigants' asserted injury or interest in the litigation—rather than the fitness of the issues for judicial resolution or even the question whether constitutionally protected rights have been invaded. See, e.g., *Flast v. Cohen*, Part III infra. What purposes are served by this distinctive focus on appropriate parties? Consider the following views:

(a) Judicial review is an anomalous and potentially precarious function in a predominantly democratic government, which should be permitted only where strictly necessary to stop concrete harms to identified individuals. See, e.g., *Valley Forge*, Part III infra.

Consider Elizabeth Magill, *Standing for the Public: A Lost History*, 95 Va.L.Rev. 1131 (2008): As lawsuits by "public interest" litigants such as environmental organizations proliferated during the 1970s, "some of the Justices thought that entertaining these cases raised some sort of flag representing illegitimate judicial action. [The] Court should not, Justice Powell warned, abandon its historic role of protecting rights and liberties of individual citizens and minority groups in favor of 'public-interest suits' that involve 'amorphous general supervision of the operations of government.' [The] concern here is not simply 'supervision' of the executive branch by the courts, but supervision at the behest of ideological advocates who are attempting to enlist the courts in their policy-reform campaign."

(b) Concretely adverse interests sharpen the issues for judicial resolution and enhance the likelihood of illuminating argument. See, e.g., *Baker v. Carr*, Ch. 1, Sec. 2.

Compare Louis L. Jaffe, *The Citizen as Litigant in Public Actions: The Non-Hohfeldian or Ideological Plaintiff*, 116 U.Pa.L.Rev. 1033 (1968): "[T]he

---

[7] But see Bradley S. Clanton, *Standing and the English Prerogative Writs: The Original Understanding*, 63 Brook.L.Rev. 1001 (1997) (disputing that prerogative writs were available to persons without a personal stake in the relief sought).

very fact of [an 'ideological plaintiff'] investing money in a lawsuit from which the plaintiff is to acquire no further monetary profit argues, to my mind, a quite exceptional kind of interest, and one peculiarly indicative of a desire to say all that can be said in the support of one's contention. From this I would conclude that, insofar as the argument for a traditional plaintiff runs in terms of the need for effective advocacy, the argument is not persuasive."

(c) Restricting judicial review to cases brought by concretely harmed individuals reflects "three interrelated policies of Article III: the smooth allocation of power among courts over time; the unfairness of holding later litigants to an adverse judgment in which they may not have been properly represented; and the importance of placing control over political processes in the hands of the people most closely involved." Lea Brilmayer, *The Jurisprudence of Article III: Perspectives on the "Case or Controversy" Requirement*, 93 Harv.L.Rev. 297 (1979). Compare Maxwell Stearns, *Standing Back From the Forest: Justiciability and Social Choice*, 83 Cal.L.Rev. 1309 (1995) (arguing that standing doctrine is necessary to prevent ideologically motivated litigants from exerting unfair influence over the "path" of legal doctrine by suing at early or otherwise opportune moments).

3. ***Standing and the separation of powers.*** The concept of standing, and the concerns about the scope of judicial power that underlie it, have attained prominence as plaintiffs increasingly have sought to use the Constitution as a sword to establish affirmative rights against the government, rather than as a shield against invasion of traditionally recognized liberty and property interests. For an exploration of this thesis by then-Judge Scalia, which foreshadows more recent doctrinal developments, see Antonin Scalia, *The Doctrine of Standing as an Essential Element of the Separation of Powers*, 17 Suffolk U.L.Rev. 881 (1983).

As *Allen* emphasized, separation-of-powers considerations are obviously at stake when plaintiffs ask courts to grant judicial remedies against other branches of government. But is standing doctrine, as formulated in *Allen* and elsewhere to focus on the plaintiff's personal stake in the controversy, a sensible response to those considerations? Might doctrines that focus on the nature of the issue sought to be adjudicated or the character of the relief requested permit a more straightforward assessment of the extent to which separation-of-powers concerns are implicated in particular cases?

Consider the argument of Richard H. Fallon, Jr., *The Linkage Between Justiciability and Remedies—And Their Connections to Substantive Rights*, 92 Va.L.Rev. 633 (2006), that both the structure and application of standing doctrine reflect judicial concern about "unacceptable" remedies. According to Professor Fallon, the Court views injunctions directing executive officials to enforce the law against third parties—including the injunction sought by the plaintiffs in *Allen v. Wright*—as especially problematic, though not as categorically forbidden. He believes that the Court is less likely to find injury-in-fact, as well as causation and redressability, when it believes that the requested remedy would raise touchy separation-of-powers or federalism issues, and he cites *Allen* as a case in point. How analytically or predictively helpful is the idea of "unacceptable" remedies?

4. ***The doctrinal requirement of injury-in-fact.*** The Court's insistence that standing minimally requires injury-in-fact has occasioned sharp disputes about what constitutes an "injury" in the constitutional sense.

(a) ***Non-economic injuries.*** Although unwilling to find an actionable stigmatic injury in *Allen*,[8] the Court has regularly accepted the proposition that non-economic injuries can satisfy the constitutional requirement, provided that they are pleaded with sufficient specificity.

(i) UNITED STATES v. STUDENTS CHALLENGING REGULATORY AGENCY PROCEDURES (SCRAP), 412 U.S. 669 (1973), upheld the standing of a group of law students to challenge the failure of the Interstate Commerce Commission to prepare an environmental impact statement before declining to suspend a surcharge on railroad freight rates. The theory of the suit was that the surcharge on rail rates would result in damage to the outdoor environment in the Washington, D.C., metropolitan area that the students used for recreational purposes: higher rail rates would increase the cost of recycled products and thus occasion "the need to use more natural resources to produce such goods, some of which resources might be taken from the Washington area, and resulting in more refuse that might be discarded in national parks in the Washington area." If so, the result would be an injury to the plaintiffs' recreational interests.[9]

(ii) FRIENDS OF THE EARTH, INC. v. LAIDLAW ENVIRONMENTAL SERVICES (TOC), INC., 528 U.S. 167 (2000), upheld standing under the citizen suit provisions of the Clean Water Act. The defendant argued that standing was defeated because the District Court, in imposing a penalty, ruled that the defendant's illegal actions had not been proved to "result in any health risk or environmental harm." But the Court, per GINSBURG, J., held that the relevant injury "is not injury to the environment but injury to the plaintiff" and that the plaintiffs suffered injury from their "reasonable concerns" that pollution had damaged land that they otherwise would have used. Scalia, J., joined by Thomas, J., dissented.

(b) ***Injury and the Equal Protection Clause.*** In HECKLER v. MATHEWS, 465 U.S. 728 (1984), a challenged statute gave larger Social Security benefits to women than to men and further provided that if a court should find the disparity unconstitutional, then women's benefits should be reduced to the men's level. Despite the fact that the male plaintiffs could achieve no material benefit from a decision in their favor, the Court, per

---

[8] See Thomas Healy, *Stigmatic Harm and Standing*, 92 Iowa L.Rev. 417 (2007) (arguing that the Court has implicitly recognized stigmatic harm as a basis for standing in other cases and that it should do so more broadly).

[9] Even if *SCRAP* remains good law on the issue of what constitutes a constitutionally cognizable injury, it seems doubtful that the pleading would any longer suffice to satisfy the causation and redressability requirements, discussed below. See *Lujan v. National Wildlife Federation*, Part II infra (noting that *SCRAP's* "expansive expression of what would suffice" for standing "has never since been emulated by this Court").

BRENNAN, J., upheld standing: "[T]he right to equal treatment guaranteed by the Constitution is not co-extensive with any substantive rights to the benefits denied the party discriminated against. [Rather,] discrimination itself [can] cause serious non-economic injuries to those persons who are personally denied equal treatment solely because of their membership in a disfavored group. Accordingly, [the] appropriate remedy is a *mandate* of equal treatment, a result that can be accomplished by withdrawal of benefits from the favored class as well as by extension of benefits to the excluded class."

Is *Mathews* consistent with the holding of *Allen* that the stigma suffered by the plaintiffs did not constitute cognizable injury?

(c) ***Assignments.*** SPRINT COMMUNICATIONS CO. v. APCC SERVICES, INC., 554 U.S. 269 (2008), per BREYER, J., held that the assignee of a legal claim for money has standing to sue in federal court, even when the assignee is a "collection firm" that has promised to remit the proceeds to the assignor: For purposes of Art. III's injury requirement, the assignee stands in the shoes of the assignor, and an award of damages would redress the assigned injury, regardless of whether the plaintiff kept the proceeds. Roberts, C.J., joined by Scalia, Thomas, and Alito, JJ., dissented, arguing that an assignee who can retain none of the benefits of a judgment lacks the "personal stake" that Article III standing requires.

(d) ***Threatened future injuries.*** When a party cannot credibly demonstrate past injury, but seeks injunctive relief to prevent a threatened future injury, how certain or imminent does the threat of future injury need to be to ground standing? In CLAPPER v. AMNESTY INTERNATIONAL, 133 S.Ct. 1138 (2013), U.S. citizens residing in the United States challenged the constitutionality of an amendment to the Foreign Intelligence Surveillance Act under which, they alleged, their communications with non-Americans abroad were likely to be intercepted. Despite the plaintiffs' specific allegations that their professional activities (including as lawyers and journalists) required them to be in regular contact with organizations abroad that were likely targets of government surveillance, the Court, per ALITO, J., denied standing based on the plaintiffs' failure to establish that an injury-in-fact was "certainly impending" in light, inter alia, of the opacity of the Government's criteria for seeking foreign-security wiretaps. The Court also said: "[W]e have often found a lack of standing in cases in which the Judiciary has been requested to review actions of the political branches in the fields of intelligence gathering and foreign affairs. [The] assumption that if respondents have no standing to sue, no one would have standing, is not a reason to find standing."

Breyer, J., joined by Ginsburg, Sotomayor, and Kagan, JJ., dissenting, maintained that although some past Court decisions had referred to a need for "certainly impending" injury, future injury was seldom if ever "absolutely certain" and that "federal courts frequently [and appropriately] entertain actions for injunctions and for declaratory relief aimed at preventing future injures that are reasonably likely or highly likely [to] take place."[10]

Compare *Susan B. Anthony List v. Driehaus,* 134 S.Ct. 2334 (2014),upholding standing to seek an injunction against enforcement of a penal statute alleged to violate the First Amendment and affirming that "a plaintiff satisfies the injury-in-fact requirement where he alleges 'an intention to engage in [conduct] arguably affected with a constitutional interest, but proscribed by a statute, and there exists a credible threat of prosecution.' " Should a credible threat of prosecution, as in *Susan B. Anthony List,* be easier to establish than the threat of being subjected to allegedly unconstitutional surveillance involved in *Clapper?*

5.   ***Standing and the merits.*** Consider the argument of William A. Fletcher, *The Structure of Standing,* 98 Yale L.J. 221 (1988), that it is a systematic mistake to conceive the standing inquiry as focused on the concept of "injury in fact" and abstracted from the existence of underlying rights. According to then-Professor Fletcher, people should always have standing to sue for redress of violations of their rights, and the standing question should essentially be one of what rights, if any, people possess under particular constitutional and statutory provisions. Under this approach, *Heckler* was rightly decided because the plaintiffs clearly asserted a right under the Equal Protection Clause. With respect to *Allen,* the central question would become whether the plaintiffs had an enforceable right under applicable law to an injunction against the challenged conduct of officials in the Treasury Department. The answer to this question might of course depend on whether the defendants had caused the plaintiffs harm and whether relief would redress it—questions that the Court emphasized in *Allen.* Is anything gained by separating the question of standing—conceived as involving issues of injury, causation, and redressability—from the question of what judicially enforceable rights the Constitution confers on whom?

6.   ***Causation requirement.*** (a) The Court's causation analysis in *Allen* was controversial. Should it have sufficed, as Stevens, J., suggested, that the question was resolved by "elementary economics: when something becomes more expensive, less of it will be purchased"? However you think that question ought to be answered, *Allen*'s analysis was not unprecedented. In SIMON v. EASTERN KENTUCKY WELFARE RIGHTS ORG., 426 U.S. 26 (1976), a class action on behalf of all persons unable to afford hospital services, the Court, per POWELL, J., held that plaintiffs lacked standing to challenge an IRS Revenue Ruling eliminating a requirement that non-profit hospitals provide some care for indigents in order to qualify for favorable tax treatment. The Court termed it "purely speculative" that "the denial of access to hospital services [from

---

[10] The cases on the standards necessary to support "probabilistic" standing are not easily reconciled. For discussions of probabilistic standing, see, *e.g.,* Jonathan Remy Nash, *Standing's Expected Value,* 111 Mich.L.Rev. 1283 (2013); F. Andrew Hessick, *Probabilistic Standing,* 106 Nw.U.L.Rev. 55 (2012); Bradford Mank, *Standing and Statistical Persons: A Risk-Based Approach to Standing,* 36 Ecology L.Q. 665 (2009); Heather Elliott, *The Functions of Standing,* 61 Stan.L.Rev.459 (2008).

which the plaintiffs suffered] in fact results from the petitioners' new Ruling, or that a court-ordered return by petitioners to their previous policy would result in these respondents' receiving the hospital services they desire."

(b) Compare REGENTS OF THE UNIVERSITY OF CALIFORNIA v. BAKKE, Ch. 9, Sec. 2, IV, in which the Court upheld the standing of a white plaintiff to challenge a special admissions program for minority applicants to medical school. A standing question arose because it was not clear that the existence of an affirmative action program caused Bakke's rejection (he might have been turned down anyway). Rebuffing a standing challenge, Powell, J., wrote for a majority of five that Bakke suffered injury through his deprivation, on grounds of race, of the chance to compete for every place in the entering class regardless of whether the affirmative action program caused his being ultimately rejected.[11]

Does *Bakke* suggest satisfaction of the causation requirement will frequently turn on how the alleged injury is characterized? Could plaintiffs in *Warth, Simon,* and possibly *Allen* have established standing if they had alleged denial of a constitutionally guaranteed *chance* or opportunity, rather than denial of a specific benefit? Consider Cass R. Sunstein, *Standing and the Privatization of Public Law,* 88 Colum.L.Rev. 1432 (1988): "The central problem [is] how to characterize the relevant injury. [In *Simon,*] the plaintiffs might have characterized their injury as an impairment of the opportunity to obtain medical services under a regime undistorted by unlawful tax incentives. In *Allen,* the plaintiffs themselves argued that their injury should be characterized as the deprivation of an opportunity to undergo desegregation in school systems unaffected by unlawful tax deductions. Thus recharacterized, the injuries are not speculative at all. [If *Simon*] was rightly decided, it was because the tax statutes have been interpreted so as to deny standing, not because of a problem with causation; and if people now thought to be indirectly or incidentally harmed by regulatory action or inaction are to be denied standing, it is because the denial is a sensible reading of congressional purposes in enacting regulatory legislation."

7. ***Redressability.*** In perhaps the majority of cases, the requirement that an injury be redressable can be viewed as an aspect of the causation requirement: if a defendant has caused injury, relief against the defendant will ordinarily remedy the injury. Occasionally, however, the redressability requirement exercises independent bite.

---

[11] *Northeastern Florida Chapter of the Associated General Contractors of America v. Jacksonville,* 508 U.S. 656 (1993), per Thomas, J., pursued a similar analysis, holding that the challenger to an affirmative action set-aside program need not show that, but for the program, the challenger would have received a concrete benefit: "The 'injury in fact' in an equal protection case of this variety is the denial of equal treatment resulting from the imposition of [a barrier that makes it more difficult for members of a group to obtain a benefit], not the ultimate inability to obtain the benefit." Are the Court's standing holdings in *Bakke* and *Associated General Contractors* "racially suspicious"? See Girardeau Spann, *Color-Coded Standing,* 80 Corn.L.Rev. 1422 (1995) (yes). See also Christian B. Sundquist, *The First Principles of Standing: Privilege, System Justification, and the Predictable Incoherence of Article III,* 1 Colum.J.Race & L. 119 (2011).

In LOS ANGELES v. LYONS, 461 U.S. 95 (1983), for example, the plaintiff had been choked to unconsciousness by the Los Angeles police after being stopped for a traffic violation. Alleging that the department had a policy of applying life-threatening chokeholds unnecessarily, Lyons sued for injunctive relief. Standing could not be grounded on the threat of future injury, the Court held, because it was too speculative that Lyons himself would be subjected to a choke-hold again. And, although Lyons undoubtedly had suffered an injury in the past, that injury could not be redressed by an injunction against future police conduct.[12]

As *Lyons* explicitly recognized, the plaintiff undoubtedly had standing to seek *damages* relief for the injury caused him in the past. What purpose is served by treating eligibility for injunctive relief—which the redressability requirement precluded—as a component of standing or the Article III case or controversy requirement? Wouldn't Lyons's claim to an injunction have been better addressed as a question of entitlement to equitable remedies? See Richard H. Fallon, Jr., *Of Justiciability, Remedies, and Public Law Litigation: Notes on the Jurisprudence of* Lyons, 59 N.Y.U.L.Rev. 1 (1984).

8. ***Standing, manipulation, and the merits.*** As Brennan, J., noted in *Allen*, numerous commentators have complained that "the causation component of the Court's standing inquiry is no more than a poor disguise for the Court's view of the merits of the underlying claims." See, e.g., Richard Pierce, *Is Standing Law or Politics?*, 77 N.C.L.Rev. 1741 (1999) (arguing that standing doctrine is widely manipulated and that in order to predict when standing will be upheld, lawyers should "ignore doctrine" and proceed on the assumption that "judges provide access to the courts to individuals who seek to further the political and ideological agendas of judges"). Do you agree?

9. ***The prohibition against asserting third parties' rights.*** As recognized in *Allen*, the Court has established a number of "self-imposed [or 'prudential'] limits on the exercise of federal jurisdiction" that are not directly mandated by Article III. Among these is a "general prohibition on a litigant's raising another person's legal rights." A celebrated example of the traditional doctrine is *Tileston v. Ullman*, 318 U.S. 44 (1943), which denied standing to a doctor to assert his patients' rights in challenging a state law prohibiting the use of contraceptives.

In recent decades the prohibition against third-party standing has been honored more frequently in the breach than in the observance—as, for example, in *Craig v. Boren*, Ch. 9, Sec. 3, I, in which a store owner was permitted to assert the equal protection rights of would-be customers not to be discriminated against on the basis of gender. The Court has attempted to explain its practice in cases such as *Powers v. Ohio*, 499 U.S. 400 (1991), in which it upheld the standing of a criminal defendant to assert the rights of a prospective juror not to be dismissed from the panel on account of race: "We have recognized the right of litigants to bring actions on behalf of third parties, provided three important criteria are satisfied: The litigant must have suffered

---

[12] Marshall, J., joined by Brennan, Blackmun, and Stevens, JJ., dissented.

an 'injury in fact,' thus giving him or her a 'sufficiently concrete interest' in the outcome of the issue in dispute * * *; the litigant must have a close relation to the third party * * *; and there must exist some hindrance to the third party's ability to protect his or her own interests." Are these sound and stable criteria to govern the assertion of third-party rights? Were they satisfied in *Craig* and *Powers*?

Might many cases characterized by the Court as involving "discretionary" decisions to permit standing to assert third-party rights be better analyzed as involving assertions by litigants of their own derivative rights? Consider Richard H. Fallon, Jr., *As-Applied and Facial Challenges and Third-Party Standing*, 113 Harv.L.Rev. 1321 (2000): "[E]veryone has a personal constitutional right not to be subjected to governmental sanctions except pursuant to a constitutionally valid rule of law. [The] notion that an 'invalid law' is not law at all underlies *Marbury v. Madison*. [M]any, if not most, seeming departures from the prohibition against third-party standing can be understood as applications of the [valid] rule requirement. For example, [a] doctor challenging anti-abortion legislation need not rely directly on her patients' rights, but can instead invoke a personal right not to be sanctioned except pursuant to a constitutionally valid rule of law."[13] See also *Bond v. United States*, 131 S.Ct. 2355 (2011) (Ginsburg, J., concurring) (concluding that a criminal defendant was entitled to challenge the constitutionality of a federal statute on the ground that it exceeded congressional authority under Article I and the Tenth Amendment because he "has a personal right not to be convicted under a constitutionally invalid law").[14]

II. CONGRESSIONAL POWER TO CREATE STANDING

In nearly all of the cases considered so far, plaintiffs based their claim to standing directly on the Constitution. Does Congress have the power to confer standing where it would not otherwise exist? And if so, how far does Congress' power extend?

---

[13] According to Henry P. Monaghan, *Third Party Standing*, 84 Colum.L.Rev. 277, 278–79, 299 (1984), the "first party" view is preferable because it eliminates "unanalyzed and ungrounded notions of judicial 'discretion.' "

[14] In *Lexmark Int'l, Inc. v. Static Control Components, Inc.*, 134 S.Ct. 1377 (2014), the Court noted "some tension" between prudential standing doctrine and its affirmation in other cases that the federal courts have a "virtually unflagging" obligation to entertain all cases within their jurisdiction. The Court then quoted an earlier case as having recognized that "third-party standing is closely related to the question whether a person in the litigant's position will have a right of action on the claim," but also acknowledged that "most of our cases have not framed the inquiry in that way." *Id.* at 1387 n.3 (internal quotations and citations omitted). The footnote concluded: "This case does not present any issue of third-party standing, and consideration of that doctrine's proper place in the standing firmament can await another day."

LUJAN V. DEFENDERS OF WILDLIFE
504 U.S. 555, 112 S.Ct. 2130, 119 L.Ed.2d 351 (1992).

JUSTICE SCALIA delivered the opinion of the Court with respect to Parts I, II, III–A, and IV, and an opinion with respect to Part III–B in which the CHIEF JUSTICE, JUSTICE WHITE, and JUSTICE THOMAS join.

[The Endangered Species Act of 1973 (ESA) § 7(a)(2) requires federal agencies to consult with the Secretary of the Interior to "insure" that projects that they fund do not threaten endangered species. Regulations promulgated in 1978 construed the consultation requirement as extending to actions taken in foreign nations. In 1986, however, the Department of the Interior reinterpreted the ESA to require consultation only for actions taken in the United States or on the high seas. Several organizations filed suits challenging the new regulation as contrary to law.]

III–A. [The Court first held that the groups and their members had failed to present sufficient evidence of injury-in-fact. Although affidavits testified that at least two members had previously traveled abroad to observe endangered species and intended to do so again,] [t]hat the women "had visited" the areas of [identified] projects before the projects commenced proves nothing. [And] the affiants' profession of an "inten[t]" to return to the places they had visited [before]—without any description of concrete plans, or indeed even any specification of *when* the some day will be—do not support a finding of the "actual or imminent" injury that our cases require.

[No more persuasive are] a series of novel standing theories, [including] the "animal nexus" approach, whereby anyone who has an interest in studying or seeing the endangered animals anywhere on the globe has standing; and the "vocational nexus" approach, under which anyone with a professional interest in such animals can sue. Under these theories, anyone who goes to see Asian elephants in the Bronx Zoo, and anyone who is a keeper of Asian elephants in the Bronx Zoo, has standing to sue because the Director of AID did not consult with the Secretary regarding the AID-funded project in Sri Lanka. This is beyond all reason. [It is] pure speculation and fantasy, to say that anyone who observes or works with an endangered species, anywhere in the world, is appreciably harmed by a single project affecting some portion of that species with which he has no more specific connection.

B.   Besides failing to show injury, respondents failed to demonstrate redressability. [Since] the agencies funding the projects were not parties to the case, the District Court could accord relief only against the Secretary. [There was no assurance that other agencies would feel bound by the Secretary's regulation, or that the withdrawal of American funding would cause projects to be terminated and the threat to endangered species thereby eliminated.]

IV. The Court of Appeals found that respondents had standing for an additional reason: because they had suffered a "procedural injury." The so-called "citizen-suit" provision of the ESA provides, in pertinent part, that "any person may commence a civil suit on his own behalf (A) to enjoin any person, including the United States and any other governmental instrumentality or agency [who] is alleged to be in violation of any provision of this chapter." The court held that, because § 7(a)(2) requires inter-agency consultation, the citizen-suit provision creates a "procedural righ[t]" to consultation in all "persons"—so that *anyone* can file suit in federal court to challenge the Secretary's (or presumably any other official's) failure to follow the assertedly correct consultative procedure, notwithstanding their inability to allege any discrete injury flowing from that failure. To understand the remarkable nature of this holding one must be clear about what it does *not* rest upon: This is not a case where plaintiffs are seeking to enforce a procedural requirement the disregard of which could impair a separate concrete interest of theirs (*e.g.*, the procedural requirement for a hearing prior to denial of their license application, or the procedural requirement for an environmental impact statement before a federal facility is constructed next door to them).[7] Nor is it simply a case where concrete injury has been suffered by many persons, as in mass fraud or mass tort situations. Nor, finally, is it the unusual case in which Congress has created a concrete private interest in the outcome of a suit against a private party for the government's benefit, by providing a cash bounty for the victorious plaintiff. Rather, the court held that the injury-in-fact requirement had been satisfied by congressional conferral upon *all* persons of an abstract, self-contained, non-instrumental "right" to have the Executive observe the procedures required by law.

[The] question presented here is whether the public interest in proper administration of the laws (specifically, in agencies' observance of a particular, statutorily prescribed procedure) can be converted into an individual right by a statute that denominates it as such, and that permits all citizens (or, for that matter, a subclass of citizens who suffer no distinctive concrete harm) to sue. If the concrete injury requirement has the separation-of-powers significance we have always said, the answer must be obvious: To permit Congress to convert the undifferentiated public

---

7 **[Ct's Note]** There is this much truth to the assertion that "procedural rights" are special: The person who has been accorded a procedural right to protect his concrete interests can assert that right without meeting all the normal standards for redressability and immediacy. Thus, under our case-law, one living adjacent to the site for proposed construction of a federally licensed dam has standing to challenge the licensing agency's failure to prepare an Environmental Impact Statement, even though he cannot establish with any certainty that the Statement will cause the license to be withheld or altered, and even though the dam will not be completed for many years. (That is why we do not rely, in the present case, upon the Government's argument that, *even if* the other agencies were obliged to consult with the Secretary, they might not have followed his advice.) What respondents' "procedural rights" argument seeks, however, is quite different from this: standing for persons who have no concrete interests affected—persons who live (and propose to live) at the other end of the country from the dam.

interest in executive officers' compliance with the law into an "individual right" vindicable in the courts is to permit Congress to transfer from the President to the courts the Chief Executive's most important constitutional duty, to "take Care that the Laws be faithfully executed," Art. II, § 3. It would enable the courts, with the permission of Congress, "to assume a position of authority over the governmental acts of another and co-equal department," *Frothingham*, and to become "virtually continuing monitors of the wisdom and soundness of Executive action." *Allen*. We have always rejected that vision of our role * * * .

Nothing in this contradicts the principle that "[the] injury required by Art. III may exist solely by virtue of 'statutes creating legal rights, the invasion of which creates standing.'" *Warth v. Seldin*, 422 U.S. 490 (1975). [T]he cases [previously cited by the Court] as an illustration of that principle involved Congress's elevating to the status of legally cognizable injuries concrete, de facto injuries that were previously inadequate in law (namely, injury to an individual's personal interest in living in a racially integrated community, see *Trafficante v. Metropolitan Life Ins. Co.*, 409 U.S. 205 (1972), and injury to a company's interest in marketing its product free from competition, see *Hardin v. Kentucky Utilities Co.*, 390 U.S. 1 (1968)). As we said in *Sierra Club v. Morton*, 505 U.S. 727 (1972), "[Statutory] broadening [of] the categories of injury that may be alleged in support of standing is a different matter from abandoning the requirement that the party seeking review must himself have suffered an injury." Whether or not the principle set forth in *Warth* can be extended beyond that distinction, it is clear that in suits against the government, at least, the concrete injury requirement must remain.

JUSTICE KENNEDY, with whom JUSTICE SOUTER joins, concurring in part and concurring in the judgment.

[I] join Part IV of the Court's opinion with the following observations. As government programs and policies become more complex and far-reaching, we must be sensitive to the articulation of new rights of action that do not have clear analogs in our common-law tradition. Modern litigation has progressed far from the paradigm of Marbury suing Madison to get his commission. [In] my view, Congress has the power to define injuries and articulate chains of causation that will give rise to a case or controversy where none existed before, and I do not read the Court's opinion to suggest a contrary view. [In] exercising this power, however, Congress must at the very least identify the injury it seeks to vindicate and relate the injury to the class of persons entitled to bring suit. The citizen-suit provision of the Endangered Species Act does not meet these minimal requirements, because [it] does not of its own force establish that there is an injury in "any person" by virtue of any "violation."

The Court's holding that there is an outer limit to the power of Congress to confer rights of action is a direct and necessary consequence of the case and controversy limitations found in Article III. I agree that it would exceed those limitations if, at the behest of Congress and in the absence of any showing of concrete injury, we were to entertain citizen-suits to vindicate the public's nonconcrete interest in the proper administration of the laws. While it does not matter how many persons have been injured by the challenged action, the party bringing suit must show that the action injures him in a concrete and personal way. This requirement is not just an empty formality. It preserves the vitality of the adversarial process by assuring both that the parties before the court have an actual, as opposed to professed, stake in the outcome, and that "the legal questions presented [will] be resolved, not in the rarefied atmosphere of a debating society, but in a concrete factual context conducive to a realistic appreciation of the consequences of judicial action." *Valley Forge*. In addition, the requirement of concrete injury confines the Judicial Branch to its proper, limited role in the constitutional framework of government. * * *

JUSTICE STEVENS, concurring in the judgment.

Because I am not persuaded that Congress intended the consultation requirement in § 7(a)(2) [to] apply to activities in foreign countries, I concur in the judgment of reversal. I do not, however, agree with the Court's conclusion that respondents lack standing because the threatened injury to their interest in protecting the environment and studying endangered species is not "imminent." Nor do I agree with the plurality's additional conclusion that respondents' injury is not "redressable" in this [litigation.]

JUSTICE BLACKMUN, with whom JUSTICE O'CONNOR joins, dissenting.

I part company with the Court in this case in two respects. First, I believe that respondents have raised genuine issues of fact—sufficient to survive summary judgment—both as to injury and as to redressability. Second, I question the Court's breadth of language in rejecting standing for "procedural" injuries. * * *

The Court concludes that any "procedural injury" suffered by respondents is insufficient to confer standing. It rejects the view that the "injury-in-fact requirement [is] satisfied by congressional conferral upon *all* persons of an abstract, self-contained, noninstrumental 'right' to have the Executive observe the procedures required by law." Whatever the Court might mean with that very broad language, it cannot be saying that "procedural injuries" *as a class* are necessarily insufficient for purposes of Article III standing.

Most governmental conduct can be classified as "procedural." [When] the Government, for example, "procedurally" issues a pollution permit, those affected by the permittee's pollutants are not without standing to sue.

Only later cases will tell just what the Court means by its intimation that "procedural" injuries are not constitutionally cognizable injuries. In the meantime, I have the greatest of sympathy for the courts across the country that will struggle to understand the Court's standardless exposition of this concept today.

The Court expresses concern that allowing judicial enforcement of "agencies' observance of a particular, statutorily prescribed procedure" would "transfer from the President to the courts the Chief Executive's most important constitutional duty, to 'take Care that the Laws be faithfully executed,' Art. II, sec. 3." In fact, the principal effect of foreclosing judicial enforcement of such procedures is to transfer power into the hands of the Executive at the expense—not of the courts—but of Congress, from which that power originates and emanates.

Under the Court's anachronistically formal view of the separation of powers, Congress legislates pure, substantive mandates and has no business structuring the procedural manner in which the Executive implements these mandates. To be sure, in the ordinary course, Congress does legislate in black-and-white terms of affirmative commands or negative prohibitions on the conduct of officers of the Executive Branch. In complex regulatory areas, however, Congress often legislates, as it were, in procedural shades of gray. That is, it sets forth substantive policy goals and provides for their attainment by requiring Executive Branch officials to follow certain procedures, for example, in the form of reporting, consultation, and certification requirements.

[There] may be factual circumstances in which a congressionally imposed procedural requirement is so insubstantially connected to the prevention of a substantive harm that it cannot be said to work any conceivable injury to an individual litigant. But, as a general matter, the courts owe substantial deference to Congress' substantive purpose in imposing a certain procedural requirement. In all events, [t]here is no room for a per se rule or presumption excluding injuries labeled "procedural" in [nature.]

NOTES AND QUESTIONS

1. ***Statutory rights to sue and constitutional standing.*** In *Warth v. Seldin*, 422 U.S. 490 (1975), the Court had asserted, albeit in dictum, that "[t]he actual or threatened injury required by Art. III may exist solely by virtue of 'statutes creating legal rights, the invasion of which creates standing.'" *Lujan* clearly rejects the notion that Congress may confer standing wherever it chooses, but it distinguishes between two kinds of cases. (a) In cases involving "actual" injuries that have not previously been viewed as adequate to support standing—perhaps because they are too widely shared—Congress' power to confer standing remains. See, e.g., *Trafficante, supra* (involving loss

of benefits of living in a racially diverse community). (b) In cases that involve no actual injury, Congress cannot confer standing.

Will the notion of a concrete or actual injury bear the weight that *Lujan* places on it? Consider Cass R. Sunstein, *What's Standing After Lujan? Of Citizen Suits, "Injuries," and Article III*, 91 Mich.L.Rev. 163 (1992): "[T]he real question is what harms *that people perceive as such* ought to be judicially cognizable. [W]hether there is a so-called nonjusticiable ideological interest, or instead a legally cognizable 'actionable injury,' is a product of legal conventions and nothing else."

How would (and should) the Court resolve a hypothetical formulated by Sunstein, supra: "Suppose [that] Congress attempts to create a citizen suit" by first legislating that "all Americans have [a] property right—a tenancy in common—[in] clean air anywhere in the country, or pristine areas, or the continued existence of endangered species anywhere in the United States or abroad. If this seems odd, we might note that Congress could surely create property rights in unowned land within the United States. [And] surely Congress' capacity to create property rights is not limited to land. If Congress thus creates property rights," can it then further prescribe that violation of those rights constitutes injury to all right-holders, and thereby authorize standing to sue by all citizens? *Lujan* appears to signal that it could not, but compare the opinion of Kennedy, J., joined by Souter, J., concurring.

2. ***Subsequent developments.*** (a) FEC v. AKINS, 524 U.S. 11 (1998), per BREYER, J., upheld the power of Congress to confer standing on any "aggrieved" person who suffers the harm of "inability to obtain information" as a result of a decision by the FEC that reporting and disclosure requirements are not applicable to a private party. Although the interest in acquiring information was not protected at common law, and although "prudential" considerations might have precluded recognition of standing to sue based on so widespread an injury in the absence of a statute, Congress had specifically authorized suit under the Federal Election Campaign Act. Judicially imposed "prudential" limitations on standing therefore had to give way; the "failure to obtain relevant information" is a "concrete" enough injury to satisfy the requirements of Art. III.

SCALIA, J., joined by O'Connor and Thomas, JJ., dissented on the ground that the asserted injury was too generalized and undifferentiated to support standing, and a statute could not cure the constitutional defect. "If today's decision is correct, it is within the power of Congress to authorize any interested person to manage (through the courts) the Executive's enforcement of any law that includes a requirement for the filing and public availability of a piece of paper. This is not the system we have had, and it is not the system we should desire."

Consider Cass R. Sunstein, *Informational Regulation and Informational Standing:* Akins *and Beyond*, 147 U.Pa.L.Rev. 613 (1999): "If Congress creates a legal right to information and gives people the authority to vindicate that right in court, the standing question is essentially resolved."

(b)   MASSACHUSETTS v. EPA, 549 U.S. 497 (2007), per STEVENS, J., upheld the standing of a state to challenge a refusal by the EPA to issue regulations governing greenhouse gas emissions by motor vehicles: Congress had authorized "this type of challenge to EPA action," albeit in a statutory provision that otherwise made no specific reference to standing, and "a litigant to whom Congress has 'accorded a procedural right to protect his interests' * * * 'can assert that right without meeting all the normal standards for redressability and immediacy.' When a litigant is vested with a procedural right, that litigant has standing if there is some possibility that the requested relief will prompt the injury-causing party to reconsider the decision that allegedly harmed the litigant. [Moreover,] Massachusetts' stake in protecting its quasi-sovereign interests," which set it apart from ordinary litigants, entitled it to "special solicitude in our standing analysis." With the framework for standing analysis thus apparently loosened, Stevens, J., concluded that Massachusetts had alleged an injury, involving the threatened loss of state-owned coastal property as a result of global warming that was traceable to greenhouse gas emissions and a consequent rise in sea levels. Domestic greenhouse gas traceable to automobile emissions contributed causally to the threat of loss even if "predicted increases in greenhouse gas emissions from developing nations, especially China and India, are likely to offset any marginal domestic decrease." And the redressability requirement was met because the risk of catastrophic environmental damages "would be reduced to some extent if the petitioners received the relief they seek."

ROBERTS, C.J., joined by Scalia, Thomas and Alito, JJ., dissenting, argued that the state had alleged no threat of imminent or particularized injury: "Global warming is a phenomenon 'harmful to humanity at large,' and the redress petitioners seek is focused no more on them than on the public generally—it is literally to change the atmosphere of the world. [Petitioners] are never able to trace their alleged injuries [to] the fractional amount of global emissions that might have been limited with EPA standards [and] given events elsewhere in the world [the] Court never explains" why the injury resulting from Massachusetts' alleged, impending loss of land would be redressed. "The good news is that the Court's 'special solicitude' for Massachusetts limits the future applicability of the diluted standing requirements applied in this case. The bad news is that the Court's self-professed relaxation of [Article] III requirements has caused us to transgress 'the proper—and properly limited—role of the courts in a democratic society.' "

3.   *Standing and the separation of powers revisited.* (a) Recall the Court's statement in *Allen v. Wright* that "the law of Art. III standing is built on a single basic idea—the idea of separation of powers." Is it an adequate response to concerns of intrusion on presidential authority that "the Take Care Clause confers a duty [on] the President [to] enforce the law as it has been enacted" and that this duty should be as enforceable by the intended beneficiaries of legislation as by the targets of regulation (who would have

undoubted standing to challenge the President's enforcement actions as beyond the bounds of law)? Sunstein, *What's Standing After* Lujan?, *supra.*[15]

(b)   The False Claims Act authorizes private citizens—called "relators"— to bring "qui tam" actions for civil penalties and damages against "any person" who procured payment on a false claim against the United States. The Court held without dissent in VERMONT AGENCY OF NATURAL RESOURCES v. UNITED STATES EX REL. STEVENS, 529 U.S. 765 (2000), that a relator had Article III standing. The Court, per SCALIA, J., first held that standing could not be supported on the basis of the relator's interest in recovering a bounty; "an interest that is merely a 'byproduct' of the suit itself" did not satisfy the Article III requirement of injury-in-fact. Standing was sustainable, however, on the alternative ground that the relator, as the assignee of the government's claim, "has standing to assert the injury in fact suffered by the assignor." The Court was "confirmed in this conclusion by the long tradition of *qui tam* actions in England and the American Colonies." Having resolved the "standing" question, the Court dropped a footnote: "[W]e express no view on the question whether *qui tam* suits violate Article II, in particular the Appointments Clause of § 2 and the 'take Care' Clause of § 3. [See] Steel Co. v. Citizens for a Better Environment, 523 U.S. 83, 102 n.4 (1998) ('[O]ur standing jurisprudence, [though] it may sometimes have an impact on Presidential powers, derives from Article III and not Article II.')."[16]

The assignment in *Vermont Agency* involved a "proprietary" or financial interest. Could Congress assign to private individuals the government's "sovereign" interest in enforcing the criminal or general civil regulatory laws? For discussion and a negative answer, see Myriam E. Gilles, *Representational Standing:* U.S. ex rel Stevens *and the Future of Public Law Litigation*, 89 Cal.L.Rev. 315 (2001).

4.   ***Congressionally authorized standing under the Administrative Procedure Act.*** Apparently unaffected by the *Lujan* decision was Congress' most sweeping grant of statutory standing, § 10(a) of the Administrative Procedure Act (APA), which authorizes suit by "any person adversely affected or aggrieved by agency action within the meaning of a relevant statute." As consistently construed, the test for standing under the APA incorporates the constitutional requirements of injury-in-fact,[17] causation, and redressability, but suits under the APA also introduce the further complication of determining when a plaintiff is adversely affected or aggrieved within the meaning of a relevant statute. The leading case, *Association of Data Processing Serv. Orgs. v. Camp*, 397 U.S. 150 (1970), attempted to give meaning to this requirement by formulating a so-called

---

[15]   For a direct reply to Professor Sunstein, see Harold J. Krent & Ethan G. Shenkman, *Of Citizen Suits and Citizen Sunstein*, 91 Mich.L.Rev. 1793 (1993).

[16]   Stevens, J., joined by Souter, J., dissented on other grounds. Ginsburg, J., concurred in the judgment only.

[17]   Indeed, the emergence of injury as a central concept in modern standing law may be traced to the leading case on standing under the APA, *Association of Data Processing Serv. Orgs. v. Camp*, discussed in this paragraph.

"zone-of-interests" test, which turns on "whether the interest sought to be protected by the complainant is arguably within the zone of interests to be protected or regulated by the statutory * * * guarantee in question." *Lexmark Int'l, Inc. v. Static Control Components, Inc.*, 134 S.Ct. 1317 (2014), characterized the "zone of interests" question as "an issue that requires [a court] to determine, using traditional tools of statutory interpretation, whether a legislatively conferred cause of action encompasses a particular plaintiff's claim."

III. TAXPAYER STANDING AND OTHER STATUS-BASED STANDING ISSUES

In FROTHINGHAM v. MELLON, 262 U.S. 447 (1923), a federal taxpayer contended that a federal statute providing funds to states undertaking programs to reduce maternal and infant mortality exceeded Congress' power, and "that the effect of the appropriations complained of will be to increase the burden of future taxation and thereby take her property without due process of law." The Court, per SUTHERLAND, J., dismissed "for want of jurisdiction." A federal taxpayer's "interest in the moneys of the treasury [is] shared with millions of others, is comparatively minute and indeterminable, and the effect upon future taxation, of any payment out of the funds, so remote, fluctuating and uncertain, that no basis is afforded for an appeal to the preventive powers of a court of equity." To permit such suits might result in attacks on "every other appropriation act and statute whose administration requires the outlay of public money * * * . The bare suggestion of such a result, with its attendant inconveniences, goes far to sustain the conclusion which we have reached, that a suit of this character cannot be maintained." A person asking the Court to hold a federal act unconstitutional "must be able to show, not only that the statute is invalid, but that he has sustained or is immediately in danger of sustaining some direct injury as the result of its enforcement, and not merely that he suffers in some indefinite way in common with people generally." Here, the complaint "is merely that [federal officials] will execute an act of Congress asserted to be unconstitutional; and this we are asked to prevent. To do so would be, not to decide a judicial controversy, but to assume a position of authority over the governmental acts of another and coequal department, an authority which plainly we do not possess."

––––––––

FLAST v. COHEN, 392 U.S. 83 (1968), per WARREN, C.J., upheld the standing of federal taxpayers to challenge federal expenditures for parochial schools under the religion clauses of the First Amendment. The Court noted, at the outset, that standing doctrine blends "constitutional requirements and policy considerations" and implied that *Frothingham* rested largely on policy grounds. It framed the essence of the standing inquiry as distinct from the fitness of the issues presented for resolution on the merits: "[The] fundamental aspect of standing is that it focuses on the party seeking to get his complaint before a federal court and not on the issues he wishes to have adjudicated." But the Court then acknowledged that "in ruling on standing, it is both appropriate and necessary to look to the substantive issues [to] determine whether there is a logical nexus between the status asserted and the claim sought to be adjudicated [to] assure that [the litigant] is a proper and appropriate party to invoke federal judicial power [so as] to satisfy Article III requirements": "The nexus demanded of federal taxpayers has two aspects to it. First, the taxpayer must establish a logical link between that status and the type of legislative enactment attacked. [Secondly,] the taxpayer must establish a nexus between that status and the precise nature of the constitutional infringement alleged."

"The taxpayer-appellants in this case have satisfied both nexuses * * * ." With respect to the first, it sufficed that the "constitutional challenge is made to an exercise by Congress of its power under Art. I, § 8, to spend for the general welfare, and the challenged program involves a substantial expenditure of federal tax funds." With respect to the second, "appellants have alleged that the challenged expenditures violate the Establishment and Free Exercise Clauses of the First Amendment." In light of its historic purposes, the Establishment Clause "operates as a specific constitutional limitation upon the exercise by Congress of the taxing and spending power conferred by Art. I, § 8."

Frothingham was distinguishable. Although the "taxpayer in *Frothingham* attacked a federal spending program [and therefore] established the first nexus required," her general allegation that "Congress [had] exceeded the general powers delegated to it" failed to identify any specific limitation on spending that Congress had breached. The Court reserved the question whether "the Constitution contains other specific limitations" that would support standing by taxpayers to challenge federal expenditures.

HARLAN, J., dissenting, protested that the Court's dual nexus standard for taxpayer standing was "entirely unrelated" to the purportedly controlling standard of whether the plaintiff had the requisite personal stake to justify standing. "It is surely clear that a plaintiff's interest in the outcome of a suit in which he challenges the constitutionality of a federal expenditure is not made greater or smaller" by the nature of the program being attacked or the constitutional provision under which the attack is mounted. "[H]ow can it be said that Mrs. Frothingham's interests in her suit were, as a consequence of her choice of a constitutional claim, necessarily less intense than those, for example, of the present appellants?"

The plaintiffs' claim did not rest on any distinctive individual stake in the outcome, but involved an assertion of standing to represent the public interest—shared equally by all citizens—in the observance of the establishment clause. "[I]ndividual litigants have standing to represent the public interest, despite their lack of economic or other personal interests, if [but only if] Congress has appropriately authorized such suits. [Any] hazards to the proper allocation of authority among the three branches of the Government would be substantially diminished if public actions had been pertinently authorized by Congress and the President."

———

Although *Flast* has never been formally overruled, two subsequent decisions have limited it nearly to its facts.

VALLEY FORGE CHRISTIAN COLLEGE v. AMERICANS UNITED FOR SEPARATION OF CHURCH AND STATE, INC., 454 U.S. 464 (1982), per REHNQUIST, J., held that respondents lacked standing as taxpayers or citizens to challenge, as violating the Establishment Clause, the giving of surplus federal property to a church college that trained students "for Christian services as either ministers or laymen": " '[R]espondents fail the first prong of the [*Flast*] test for taxpayer standing [in] two respects. First, the source of their complaint is not a congressional action, but a decision by HEW to transfer a parcel of federal property. *Flast* limited taxpayer standing to challenges directed 'only [at] exercises of congressional power.' * * * Second, [the] property transfer [was] not an exercise of authority conferred by the Taxing and Spending Clause of Art. I, § 8. The authorizing legislation [was] an evident exercise of Congress' power under the Property Clause, Art. IV, § 3, cl. 2. * * *

"The complaint in this case shares a common deficiency with those in *Schlesinger [v. Reservists Committee to Stop the War]* and *[United States v.] Richardson* [both cited in *Allen*]. Although [they] claim that the Constitution has been violated, [they] fail to identify any personal injury suffered by the plaintiffs *as a consequence* of the alleged constitutional error, other than the psychological consequence presumably produced by observation of conduct with which one disagrees. That is not an injury sufficient to confer standing under Art. III, even though the disagreement is phrased in constitutional terms. It is evident that respondents are firmly committed to the constitutional principle of separation of church and State, but standing is not measured by the intensity of the litigant's interest or the fervor of his advocacy."

BRENNAN, J., joined by Marshall and Blackmun, JJ.,[18] dissented: "The Court makes a fundamental mistake when it determines that a plaintiff has failed to satisfy [the] 'injury-in-fact' test, or indeed any other test of 'standing,' without first determining whether the Constitution [defines] injury, and creates a cause of action for redress of that injury, in precisely

---

[18] Stevens, J., dissented separately.

the circumstance presented to the Court. * * * [5] [One] of the primary purposes of the Establishment Clause was to prevent the use of tax moneys for religious purposes. *The taxpayer was the direct and intended beneficiary of the prohibition on financial aid to religion.* [Each], and indeed every, federal taxpayer suffers precisely the injury that the Establishment Clause guards against when the Federal Government directs that funds be taken from the pocketbooks of the citizenry and placed into the coffers of the ministry."

In HEIN v. FREEDOM FROM RELIGION FOUNDATION, INC., 549 U.S. 1109 (2007), the plurality opinion read *Flast v. Cohen* so narrowly that two concurring Justices and four dissenters believed that *Flast* was indistinguishable and should therefore be either overruled or applied. The case arose when the President, by executive orders, created a White House office and several "centers" within federal agencies to ensure that faith-based community groups would be eligible to apply for federal financial support for activities that were not inherently religious. Suing as taxpayers, respondents challenged a number of executive actions that, they said, violated the Establishment Clause by expending public funds to promote religious community groups over secular ones. The plurality opinion by ALITO, J., joined by Roberts, C.J., and Kennedy, J., held *Flast* distinguishable on the ground that the expenditures at issue were not made pursuant to any specific Act of Congress, as was the case in *Flast*, but rather occurred under general appropriations to the Executive Branch to fund day-to-day activities. *Flast,* the plurality said, "gave too little weight" to separation-of-powers concerns, and to extend it "would repeat and compound this mistake": "Because almost all Executive Branch activity is ultimately funded by some congressional appropriation, extending the Flast exception to purely executive expenditures would effectively subject every federal action—be it a conference, proclamation, or speech—to Establishment Clause challenge by any taxpayer in federal court." Of the three Justices in the plurality, only Kennedy, J., in a separate concurring opinion, affirmed expressly that "[i]n my view the result reached in *Flast* is correct and should not be called into question."

Concurring in the judgment, Scalia, J., joined by Thomas, J., argued that *Flast* ultimately needed to rest on the indefensible principle that "Psychic Injury," rather than "Wallet Injury," sufficed to establish standing. Admission of that principle into the law rendered efforts to distinguish *Flast* arbitrary and unconvincing, he maintained, and it should be overruled so that its underlying rationale would be expunged: "*Flast*'s

---

[5] **[Ct's Note]** When the Constitution makes it clear that a particular person is to be protected from a particular form of government action, then that person has a "right" to be free of that action; when that right is infringed, then there is injury, and a personal stake, within the meaning of Art. III.

lack of a logical theoretical underpinning has rendered our taxpayer standing doctrine [a] jurisprudential disaster." Souter, J., joined by Stevens, Ginsburg, and Breyer, JJ., argued that "[w]hen executive agencies spend identifiable sums of tax money for religious purposes, no less than when Congress authorizes the same thing, taxpayers suffer injury."[19]

NOTES AND QUESTIONS

1. *Generalized grievances and the separation of powers.* Consider Antonin Scalia, *The Doctrine of Standing as an Essential Element of the Separation of Powers*, 17 Suffolk U.L.Rev. 881 (1983): "[T]he law of standing roughly restricts courts to their traditional undemocratic role of protecting individuals and minorities against impositions of the majority, and excludes them from the even more undemocratic role of prescribing how the other two branches should function in order to serve the interest *of the majority itself*. [U]nless the plaintiff can show some respect in which he is harmed *more* than the rest of [us] he has not established any basis for concern that the majority is suppressing or ignoring the rights of a minority that wants protection, and thus has not established the prerequisite for judicial intervention." Compare Cass R. Sunstein, *What's Standing After* Lujan? *Of Citizen Suits, Injuries, and Article III*, 91 Mich.L.Rev. 163 (1992): "[S]ome majorities are so diffuse and ill-organized that they face systematic transaction costs barriers to the exercise of ongoing political influence [and their interests may] require judicial protection."

2. *Standing and the merits revisited.* Consider again the suggestion of Fletcher, note 5 after *Allen*—which is echoed by the dissenting opinion of Brennan, J., in *Valley Forge*—that the crucial question in determining standing should not be whether a grievance is widely shared, but whether it stems from a violation of the plaintiff's constitutional rights. On this view, there might be some constitutional provisions that create no enforceable rights at all. An example might come from the Incompatibility Clause that was involved in *Schlesinger*. See U.S. Const., Art. I, § 6, cl. 2 ("[N]o Person holding any Office under the United States, shall be a Member of either House during his Continuance in Office"). But the Establishment Clause would stand on a different footing. On what principled ground can denial of standing in cases such as *Valley Forge* and *Hein* be distinguished from the recognition of standing in cases in which plaintiffs challenge the constitutionality under the

---

[19] See also *Arizona Christian School Tuition Org. v. Winn,* 131 S.Ct. 1436 (2011), holding, per Kennedy, J., that taxpayers lack standing to challenge dollar-for-dollar tax credits for contributions to organizations that provide scholarships to children attending religious schools: "A dissenter whose tax dollars are 'extracted and spent' knows that he has in some small measure been made to contribute to an establishment of religion in violation of conscience. *Flast.* [By contrast, a] tax credit is not tantamount to a religious tax and does not visit the injury identified in *Flast*." Kagan, J., joined by Ginsburg, Breyer, and Sotomayor, JJ., dissented: In five previous cases challenging tax credits that subsidize religion, "we have [always] resolved the suit without questioning the plaintiffs' standing. [The] Court's opinion [offers] a roadmap—more truly, just a one-step instruction—to any government that wishes to insulate its financing of religious activity from legal challenge. Structure the funding as a tax expenditure, and *Flast* will not stand in the way."

Establishment Clause of public displays of crèches, see, e.g., *County of Allegheny v. American Civil Liberties Union Greater Pittsburgh Chapter*, and the Ten Commandments, see, e.g., *Van Orden v. Perry*, Chap. 8, Sec. 1, IV?

3. ***Local and state taxpayer standing.*** In denying the standing of a federal taxpayer to challenge federal expenditures, *Frothingham* distinguished the case of municipal taxpayers: "The interest of a taxpayer of a municipality in the application of its moneys is direct and immediate and the remedy by injunction to prevent their misuse is not inappropriate." But ASARCO INC. v. KADISH, 490 U.S. 605 (1989), per KENNEDY, J., held that the exception from the *Frothingham* rule for municipal taxpayers does not apply to state taxpayers: "[W]e have refused to confer standing upon a state taxpayer absent a showing of 'direct injury,' pecuniary or otherwise." Brennan, J., joined by White, Marshall, and Blackmun, JJ., did not join this part of the Court's opinion.[20]

4. ***Standing of voters.*** Numerous cases have upheld the standing of individual voters to claim deprivations of constitutional voting rights of various kinds. See, e.g., *Baker v. Carr*, Ch. 1, Sec. 2 (alleging malapportionment in violation of one-person, one-vote requirement); *Rogers v. Lodge*, Ch. 9, Sec. 5, I, D (involving race-based dilution of voting power); *Davis v. Bandemer*, Ch. 9, Sec. 5, I, C (challenging political gerrymander). Why don't cases such as these involve mere "generalized grievances"?

Controversy has also surrounded the question of what injury—if any—either white or non-white voters suffer when the legislature deliberately takes race into account in creating a majority-minority voting district. In *Shaw v. Reno*, Ch. 9, Sec. 5, I, D, the Court, over the protest of Stevens, J., who denied the presence of any actionable injury at all, upheld the standing of white voters living within the challenged district: "[W]e believe that reapportionment is one area in which appearances do matter. A reapportionment plan that includes in one district individuals who belong to the same race, but who are otherwise widely separated by geographical and political boundaries, and who may have little in common with one another but the color of their skin, bears an uncomfortable resemblance to political apartheid. [We] conclude that a plaintiff challenging a reapportionment statute under the Equal Protection Clause may state a claim by alleging that the legislation, though race neutral on its face, rationally cannot be understood as anything other than an effort to separate voters into different districts on the basis of race, and that the separation lacks sufficient justification."

But UNITED STATES v. HAYS, 515 U.S. 737 (1995), per O'CONNOR, J., held that persons living outside a voting district lack standing to bring a challenge. The plaintiffs had not suffered the "representational harm" of having their representatives feel especially beholden to a racially defined

---

[20] See also *DaimlerChrysler Corp. v. Cuno*, 547 U.S. 332 (2006) (reaffirming the rule that taxpayer status does not confer standing to challenge state tax and spending programs, while continuing to contemplate that municipal taxpayer status will support standing to attack municipal programs and policies).

constituency, nor been subjected personally to racially discriminatory treatment.[21] Concurring separately, Stevens, J., analyzed the standing question as largely inseparable from the merits and concluded that the plaintiffs lacked standing because they had failed to allege a constitutional violation.

5. ***Standing of legislators.*** (a) In COLEMAN v. MILLER, Ch. 1, Sec. 2, an action was brought by 21 members of the Kansas senate and three members of the house of representatives to nullify the Kansas legislature's ratification of an amendment to the Constitution. The plaintiffs complained (1) that the lieutenant governor had broken a 20–20 tie in the senate by voting in favor and that he had no right to cast the deciding vote, and (2) that the proposed amendment "had lost its vitality," having been rejected over a thirteen-year period by 26 states and having failed to win ratification "within a reasonable time." The Court upheld standing: "[P]laintiffs include twenty senators whose votes against ratification have been overridden and virtually held for naught although if they are right in their contentions their votes would have been sufficient to defeat ratification. We think [they] have a plain, direct and adequate interest in maintaining the effectiveness of their votes."

(b) Compare RAINES v. BYRD, 521 U.S. 811 (1997), per REHNQUIST, C.J., holding that members of Congress lacked standing to challenge the constitutionality of the Line Item Veto Act ("the Act"), which authorized the President to "cancel" certain spending and tax benefit measures after signing them into law: *Coleman* "stands (at most * * *) for the proposition that legislators whose votes would have been sufficient to defeat (or enact) a specific legislative Act have standing to sue if that legislative action goes into effect (or does not go into effect), on the ground that their votes have been completely nullified." Although plaintiffs alleged that the Line Item Veto Act diluted the significance of their votes for bills that are subject to presidential cancellation, there was a "vast difference" between the "level of vote nullification" in this case and that in *Coleman*. "We attach some importance to the fact that appellees have not been authorized to represent their respective Houses of Congress, and indeed both Houses actively oppose their suit. [N]or [does the decision] foreclose[ ] the Act from constitutional challenge (by someone who suffers judicially cognizable injury as a result of the Act). Whether the case would be different if any of these circumstances were different we need not now decide."[22]

6. ***Standing to sue in state court.*** The Court has consistently held that standing to sue in state court is governed by state law, not Article III of the Constitution, with the result that a plaintiff who lacks standing to sue in federal court may sometimes be able to bring a suit in state court raising a complaint that a federal court could not hear. What happens, however, when a plaintiff who would not have standing in federal court sues in state court and

---

[21] See also *Shaw v. Hunt,* 517 U.S. 899 (1996).

[22] Souter, J., joined by Ginsburg, J., concurred that the plaintiffs lacked standing. Stevens, J., dissented, as did Breyer, J.

prevails on the merits? Does the *defendant* then have standing to seek review of the state judgment in the Supreme Court? By a vote of 6–2, *ASARCO*, note 3 supra, answered in the affirmative.

3. TIMING OF ADJUDICATION

I. MOOTNESS

DeFunis v. Odegaard

416 U.S. 312, 94 S.Ct. 1704, 40 L.Ed.2d 164 (1974).

PER CURIAM.

[Petitioner was admitted to the University of Washington Law School after a state trial court had sustained his claim that the school's special admissions policy violated equal protection. The Washington Supreme Court reversed, but its judgment was stayed. By the time the case was argued in the Supreme Court, petitioner had registered for the final term of his third year. Although the school stated that if its admissions policy were upheld, petitioner would be subject to it if he had to register for any additional terms, his present registration "would not be canceled [regardless] of the outcome of this litigation."]

The starting point for analysis is the familiar proposition that "federal courts are without power to decide questions that cannot affect the rights of litigants in the case before them." *North Carolina v. Rice*, 404 U.S. 244 (1971). The inability of the federal judiciary "to review moot cases derives from the requirement of Art. III of the Constitution under which the exercise of judicial power depends upon the existence of a case or controversy." *Liner v. Jafco, Inc.*, 375 U.S. 301 n.3 (1964).

[A]ll parties agree that DeFunis is now entitled to complete his legal studies at the University of Washington and to receive his degree from that institution. A determination by this Court of the legal issues tendered by the parties is no longer necessary to compel that result, and could not serve to prevent it. DeFunis did not cast his suit as a class action, and the only remedy he requested was an injunction commanding his admission to the Law School. He was not only accorded that remedy, but he now has also been irrevocably admitted to the final term of the final year of the Law School course. The controversy between the parties has thus clearly ceased to be "definite and concrete" and no longer "touch[es] the legal relations of parties having adverse legal interests." *Aetna Life Ins. Co. v. Haworth*, 300 U.S. 227 (1937).

[There] is a line of decisions in this Court standing for the proposition that the "voluntary cessation of allegedly illegal conduct does not deprive the tribunal of power to hear and determine the case, i.e., does not make the case moot." [E.g.,] *United States v. W.T. Grant Co.*, 345 U.S. 629 (1953).

These decisions and the doctrine they reflect would be quite relevant if the question of mootness here had arisen by reason of a unilateral change in the *admissions procedures* of the Law School. For it was the admissions procedures that were the target of this litigation, and a voluntary cessation of the admissions practices complained of could make this case moot only if it could be said with assurance "that 'there is no reasonable expectation that the wrong will be repeated.' " *W.T. Grant Co.* Otherwise, "[t]he defendant is free to return to his old ways," id., and this fact would be enough to prevent mootness because of the "public interest in having the legality of the practices settled." Ibid. But mootness in the present case depends not at all upon a "voluntary cessation" of the admissions practices that were the subject of this litigation. It depends, instead, upon the simple fact that DeFunis is now in the final quarter of the final year of his course of study, and the settled and unchallenged policy of the Law School to permit him to complete the term for which he is now enrolled.

It might also be suggested that this case presents a question that is "capable of repetition, yet evading review," *Southern Pacific Terminal Co. v. ICC*, 219 U.S. 498, 515 (1911); *Roe v. Wade*, [Ch. 6, Sec. 2], and is thus amenable to federal adjudication even though it might otherwise be considered moot. But DeFunis will never again be required to run the gauntlet of the Law School's admission process, and so the question is certainly not "capable of repetition" so far as he is concerned. Moreover, just because this particular case did not reach the Court until the eve of the petitioner's graduation from law school, it hardly follows that the issue he raises will in the future evade review. If the admissions procedures of the Law School remain unchanged, there is no reason to suppose that a subsequent case attacking those procedures will not come with relative speed to this Court, now that the Supreme Court of Washington has spoken. This case, therefore, in no way presents the exceptional situation in which the *Southern Pacific Terminal* doctrine might permit a departure from "[t]he usual rule in federal cases [that] an actual controversy must exist at stages of appellate or certiorari review, and not simply at the date the action is initiated." *Roe v. Wade.*

[W]e conclude that the Court cannot, consistently with the limitations of Art. III of the Constitution, consider the substantive constitutional issues tendered by the parties.[5]

JUSTICE BRENNAN, with whom JUSTICE DOUGLAS, JUSTICE WHITE, and JUSTICE MARSHALL concur, dissenting.[23]

---

[5] **[Ct's Note]** It is suggested in dissent that "[a]ny number of unexpected events—illness, economic necessity, even academic failure—might prevent his graduation at the end of the term." "But such speculative contingencies afford no basis for our passing on the substantive issues [the petitioner] would have us decide," *Hall v. Beals*, 396 U.S. 45 (1969), in the absence of "evidence that this is a prospect of 'immediacy and reality.' " *Golden v. Zwickler*, 394 U.S. 109 (1969).

[23] Douglas, J., also filed a separate dissent on the merits.

[Many] weeks of the school term remain, and [a]ny number of unexpected events—illness, economic necessity, even academic failure—might prevent [petitioner's] graduation at the end of the term. Were that misfortune to befall, and were petitioner required to register for yet another term, the prospect that he would again face the hurdle of the admissions policy is real, not fanciful * * * .

In these circumstances, and because the University's position implies no concession that its admissions policy is unlawful, this controversy falls squarely within the Court's long line of decisions holding that the "[m]ere voluntary cessation of allegedly illegal conduct does not moot a case." *United States v. Concentrated Phosphate Export Ass'n*, 393 U.S. 199 (1968).

[T]he Court concedes that, if petitioner has lost his stake in this controversy, he did so only when he registered for the spring term. But petitioner took that action only after the case had been fully litigated in the state courts, briefs had been filed in this Court, and oral argument had been heard. The case is thus ripe for decision on a fully developed factual record with sharply defined and fully canvassed legal issues.

Moreover, in endeavoring to dispose of this case as moot, the Court clearly disserves the public interest. The constitutional issues which are avoided today concern vast numbers of people, organizations, and colleges and universities, as evidenced by the filing of twenty-six amicus curiae briefs. Few constitutional questions in recent history have stirred as much debate, and they will not disappear. [Because] avoidance of repetitious litigation serves the public interest, that inevitability counsels against mootness determinations, as here, not compelled by the record. * * *

NOTES AND QUESTIONS

1.   ***Possible bases of mootness doctrine.*** Is the principle that "moot cases [are] beyond the judicial power" simply an application of the bar against advisory opinions? A reflection of the fact that "[t]here is no case or controversy once the matter has been resolved"? Charles Alan Wright, *Law of Federal Courts* 62–63 (5th ed. 1994). Or is the doctrine merely a judicially created rule for judicial economy? According to Evan Tsen Lee, *Deconstitutionalizing Justiciability: The Example of Mootness*, 105 Harv.L.Rev. 603 (1992): "The marriage of Article III to the mootness doctrine was remarkably casual. The Supreme Court's first mention of Article III in connection with mootness came in a 1964 case [*Liner v. Jafco, Inc.*, 375 U.S. 301 (1964)] found not to be moot at all."

In *Honig v. Doe,* 484 U.S. 305 (1988), Rehnquist, C.J., concurring, argued that early Supreme Court cases had not treated the mootness doctrine as constitutionally mandated and further contended that mootness should not categorically bar the Court from reviewing lower court decisions rendered at a time when there was a live controversy between the parties. If the Article III "case or controversy" requirement posed no barrier, what would be the costs and benefits of such an approach?[24]

2. ***Capable of repetition, yet evading review.*** When a statute directly applies to particular plaintiffs only for a short period, it may sometimes be difficult for plaintiffs to carry a legal challenge to its conclusion before the statute has ceased to apply to them. For example, by the time a court is ready to rule on the constitutionality of a statute conditioning the right to vote on residency in a district for three or six months, the election may have passed. Or a pregnancy may have run its course before an affected woman could secure a court ruling on a statute regulating abortion. In response to cases such as these, the Court has established an exception to otherwise applicable mootness doctrine for cases in which the issue presented is "capable of repetition, yet evading review." See, e.g., *Moore v. Ogilvie*, 394 U.S. 814 (1969). In applying this exception, however, the Court sometimes demands assurances that the plaintiff may again be *personally* affected by the challenged statute. E.g., *Weinstein v. Bradford*, 423 U.S. 147 (1975).[25]

Is acceptance of jurisdiction in cases capable of repetition, yet evading review incompatible with the view that moot cases are outside Article III? See *Honig v. Doe*, supra (Rehnquist, C.J., concurring).

3. ***Mootness and standing.*** Although the Court on several occasions had characterized mootness as "the doctrine of standing set in a time frame,"[26] the Court reconsidered that description in FRIENDS OF THE EARTH v. LAIDLAW ENV. SERVS. (TOC), INC., 528 U.S. 167 (2000). After Friends of the Earth sued to enjoin a violation of the environmental laws, the defendants ceased their illegal conduct, and the court of appeals ordered the case dismissed as moot. Reasoning that all elements of Article III standing must persist throughout federal litigation, the lower court found it too unlikely that a judicial remedy would effectively redress any current injury to the plaintiffs.[27] The Court, per GINSBURG, J., reversed, holding that "the Court of Appeals confused mootness with standing": "[T]here are circumstances in which the prospect that a defendant will engage in (or resume) harmful conduct may be too speculative to support standing, but not too speculative to

[24] See generally Matthew I. Hall, *The Partially Prudential Doctrine of Mootness*, 77 Geo. Wash. L. Rev. 562 (2009); Gene R. Nichol, Jr., *Moot Cases, Chief Justice Rehnquist, and the Supreme Court*, 22 U.Conn.L.Rev. 703 (1990).

[25] The Court more recently applied the capable of repetition, yet evading review doctrine in *Turner v. Rogers*, 131 S.Ct. 2507 (2011), involving whether the Due Process Clause creates a right to appointed counsel for indigents facing incarceration in civil contempt proceedings. The Court found "more than a 'reasonable' likelihood" that Turner, who had been the subject of several such proceedings based on non-payment of child support, would again be subject to them in the future. Because the 12-month maximum sentence was too brief for Turner to bring his constitutional claims before the Court during any particular period of incarceration, the dispute was capable of repetition, yet evading review.

[26] See *Arizonans for Official English v. Arizona*, 520 U.S. 43 n.22 (1997), quoting *United States Parole Comm'n v. Geraghty*, 445 U.S. 388 (1980), in turn quoting Henry P. Monaghan, *Constitutional Adjudication: The Who and When*, 82 Yale L.J. 1363 (1973).

[27] The clearly available remedy under the Clean Water Act on which the "redressability" debate focused was a civil money penalty payable to the government, not to the plaintiffs.

overcome mootness. [Standing] doctrine functions to ensure, among other things, that the scarce resources of the federal courts are devoted to those disputes in which the parties have a concrete stake. In contrast, by the time mootness is an issue, the case has been brought and litigated, often (as here) for years. To abandon the case at an advanced stage may prove more wasteful than frugal. This argument from sunk costs does not license courts to retain jurisdiction over cases in which one or both of the parties plainly lacks a continuing interest[, but it] surely highlights an important difference between the two doctrines." Scalia, J., joined by Thomas, J., dissented on the ground that the plaintiffs never possessed standing.

4. ***Mootness and class actions.*** The Supreme Court has asserted unequivocally that a plaintiff claiming standing to file a class action must have a personal stake at the time the lawsuit is filed; that other class members may have suffered injury will not suffice. See *Simon v. Eastern Kentucky Welfare Rights Org.*, 426 U.S. 26 n.20 (1976). But in cases such as *DeFunis,* in which the plaintiff has standing at the time suit is filed, the plaintiff's request for class certification may affect any subsequent mootness analysis. The leading case is UNITED STATES PAROLE COMM'N v. GERAGHTY, 445 U.S. 388 (1980), in which a federal prisoner filed a class action challenging the guidelines governing release on parole. The district court denied class certification and rejected the claim on the merits, and Geraghty himself had been released from prison before the case reached the Court. Nevertheless, the Court, per BLACKMUN, J., held the case not moot. "[A]n action brought on behalf of a class does not become moot upon expiration of the named plaintiff's substantive claim," and it made no difference that the plaintiff's substantive claim had been mooted before the class had been certified: "The proposed [class] representative retains a 'personal stake' in obtaining class certification sufficient to assure that Art. III values are not undermined. If the appeal results in a reversal of the class certification denial, and a class subsequently is properly certified, the merits of the class claim then may be adjudicated."

POWELL, J., joined by Burger, C.J., and Stewart and Rehnquist, JJ., dissented: "The Court makes no effort to identify any injury to respondent that may be redressed by, or any benefit to respondent that may accrue from, a favorable ruling on the certification question. Instead, respondent's 'personal stake' is said to derive from two factors having nothing to do with concrete injury or stake in the outcome. First, the Court finds that the Federal Rules of Civil Procedure create a 'right,' 'analogous to the private attorney general concept,' to have a class certified. Second, the Court thinks that the case retains the 'imperatives of a dispute capable of judicial resolution,' which are identified as (i) a sharply presented issue, (ii) a concrete factual setting, and (iii) a self-interested party actually contesting the case.

"The Court's reliance on some new 'right' inherent in Rule 23 is misplaced. We have held that even Congress may not confer federal court jurisdiction when Art. III does not. Far less so may a rule of procedure which 'shall not be construed to extend [the] jurisdiction of the United States district courts.' Fed. Rule Civ. Proc. 82. [Although] we have refused steadfastly to countenance the 'public action,' the Court's redefinition of the personal stake requirement leaves no principled basis for that practice."

But cf. *Genesis Healthcare Corp. v. Symczyk*, 133 S.Ct. 1523 (2013) (holding, 5–4, that mootness doctrine required dismissal of a "collective action" under the Fair Labor Standards Act when a named plaintiff's personal claim had already become moot before she moved for "provisional certification" of a class).

II. RIPENESS

UNITED PUBLIC WORKERS V. MITCHELL
330 U.S. 75, 67 S.Ct. 556, 91 L.Ed. 754 (1947).

JUSTICE REED delivered the opinion of the Court.

[Appellants, federal civil service employees, sought a federal declaratory judgment that the Hatch Act's prohibition against taking "any active part in political management or in political campaigns" violated their first amendment rights. They also requested injunctive relief. Only one appellant (Poole) had actually violated the Act. The others alleged that they desired to do so by, inter alia, serving as party officials, writing articles and circulating petitions to support candidates, acting as poll watchers, and transporting voters to the polls.[28]]

At the threshold of consideration, we are called upon to decide whether the complaint states a controversy cognizable in this Court. [Except with respect to Poole, the affidavits submitted by the plaintiffs] follow the generality of purpose expressed by the complaint. They declare a desire to act contrary to the rule against political activity but not that the rule has been violated. * * *

As is well known, the federal courts established pursuant to Article III of the Constitution do not render advisory opinions. For adjudication of constitutional issues, "concrete legal issues, presented in actual cases, not abstractions," are requisite. This is as true of declaratory judgments as any other field. These appellants seem clearly to seek advisory opinions upon broad claims of [constitutional rights]. As these appellants are classified employees, they have a right superior to the generality of citizens, [but] the facts of their personal interest in their civil rights, of the general threat of possible interference with those rights by the Civil Service Commission under its rules, if specified things are done by appellants, does not make a justiciable case or controversy. Appellants want to engage in "political management and political campaigns," to persuade others to follow

---

[28] One did allege that, at the last congressional election, he wanted to be a poll watcher but was informed by a Civil Service Commission official "that if I used my watcher's certificate, the Civil Service Commission would see that I was dismissed from my job." This matter, the Court found, "had long been moot when this complaint was filed."

appellants' views by discussion, speeches, articles and other acts reasonably designed to secure the selection of appellants' political choices. Such generality of objection is really an attack on the political expediency of the Hatch Act, not the presentation of legal issues. It is beyond the competence of courts to render such a decision.

The power of courts, and ultimately of this Court, to pass upon the constitutionality of acts of Congress arises only when the interests of litigants require the use of this judicial authority for their protection against actual interference. A hypothetical threat is not enough. We can only speculate as to the kinds of political activity the appellants desire to engage in or as to the contents of their proposed public statements or the circumstances of their publication. It would not accord with judicial responsibility to adjudge, in a matter involving constitutionality, between the freedom of the individual and the requirements of public order except when definite rights appear upon the one side and definite prejudicial interferences upon the other.

The Constitution allots the nation's judicial power to the federal courts. Unless these courts respect the limits of that unique authority, they intrude upon powers vested in the legislative or executive branches. [Should] the courts seek to expand their power so as to bring under their jurisdiction ill-defined controversies over constitutional issues, they would become the organ of political theories. Such abuse of judicial power would properly meet rebuke and restriction from other branches. [No] threat of interference by the Commission with rights of these appellants appears beyond that implied by the existence of the law and the regulations.

[Poole, however] has been charged by the Commission with political activity and a proposed order for his removal from his position adopted subject to his right under Commission procedure to [reply]. Since Poole admits that he violated the rule against political activity and that removal from office is therefore mandatory under the [act,] we see no reason why a declaratory judgment action, even though constitutional issues are involved, does not lie. [The Court then rejected Poole's challenge on the merits.]

JUSTICE DOUGLAS, dissenting in part:

[What] these appellants propose to do is plain enough. If they do what they propose to do, it is clear that they will be discharged * * * .[2] The threat against them is real not fanciful, immediate not remote. The case is therefore an actual not a hypothetical one. [T]o require these employees first to suffer the hardship of a discharge is not only to make them incur a

---

[2]   [Ct's Note] The case is, therefore, unlike those situations where the Court refused to entertain actions for declaratory judgments, the state of facts being hypothetical in the sense that the challenge was to statutes which had not as yet been construed or their specific application known.

penalty; it makes inadequate, if not wholly illusory, any legal remedy which they may have. [At] least to the average person in the lower income groups the burden of taking that course is irreparable injury* * * .[29]

NOTES AND QUESTIONS

1. ***Ripeness criteria.*** In a much quoted opinion in *Abbott Laboratories v. Gardner*, 387 U.S. 136 (1967), the Court characterized the ripeness inquiry as having two aspects: (i) "the hardship to the parties of withholding court consideration" and (ii) "the fitness of the issues for judicial decision." How would these criteria apply to *Mitchell*? Were the plaintiffs in that case subjected to a considerable hardship—a choice between foregoing possibly protected political activity and risking the loss of their jobs? If the issues were unfit for judicial resolution, in what sense were they unfit?

2. ***Ripeness and standing.*** Consider Erwin Chemerinsky, *Federal Jurisdiction* § 2.4.1 (6th ed. 2012): "Ripeness [is] a justiciability doctrine determining when review is appropriate. [Specifically], the ripeness doctrine seeks to separate matters that are premature for review because the injury is speculative and never may occur, from those cases that are appropriate for federal court action. Although the phrasing makes the questions of who may sue and when may they sue seem distinct, in practice there is an obvious overlap between the doctrines of standing and ripeness. If no injury has occurred, the plaintiff might be denied standing or the case might be dismissed as not ripe. * * *

"To the extent that the substantive requirements overlap and the result will be the same regardless of whether the issue is characterized as ripeness or standing, little turns on the choice of the label. However, for the sake of clarity, especially in those cases where the law of standing and ripeness is not identical, ripeness can be given a narrower definition that distinguishes it from standing and explains the existing case law. Ripeness properly should be understood as involving the question of *when may a party seek preenforcement review of a statute or regulation.* Customarily, a person can challenge the legality of a statute or regulation only when he or she is prosecuted for violating it. At that time, a defense can be that the law is invalid, for example, as being unconstitutional."

See also *Abbott Laboratries,* supra (asserting that the "basic rationale" of ripeness doctrine is "to prevent the courts, through avoidance of premature adjudication, from entangling themselves in abstract disagreements").

3. ***Challenges to threatened enforcement of statutes.*** Suppose plaintiffs wish to challenge the constitutionality of a state statute that the state has not enforced for a number of years. Is a challenge ripe, or is the threat

---

[29] Black, J., agreed with Douglas, J., "that all the petitioners' complaints state a case or controversy" and further that "the challenged provision is unconstitutional on its face." Rutledge, J., agreed with Black, J., as to Poole; as to the others, however, the controversy "is not yet appropriate for the discretionary exercise of declaratory judgment jurisdiction." Frankfurter, J., concurred in the Court's opinion. Murphy and Jackson, JJ., took no part.

of enforcement too remote and conjectural? Compare *Poe v. Ullman*, 367 U.S. 497 (1961), finding that a long pattern of non-enforcement rendered a challenge to a state statute prohibiting the use of contraceptive devices non-justiciable, with *Epperson v. Arkansas*, Ch. 8, Sec. 1, III, finding no ripeness difficulty with a challenge to a forty-year-old statute making the teaching of evolution unlawful, despite the absence of any record of enforcement. Is it relevant to ripeness analysis whether the issue presented on the merits is a hard one? See also *Susan B. Anthony List v. Driehaus,* 134 S.Ct. 2334 (2014), treating standing and ripeness issues as overlapping and authorizing suit to enjoin enforcement of a penal statute alleged to violate the First Amendment where "there exists a credible threat of prosecution."

Consider Gene R. Nichol, Jr., *Ripeness and the Constitution*, 54 U.Chi. L.Rev. 153 (1987): "The ripeness requirement consistently has been molded to meet the dictates of the substantive claim on the merits. [Laws] threatening sanctions for expression are said to 'chill' potential speech. Rather than force citizens to curtail the exercise of their asserted first amendment rights in order to avoid prosecution, courts have permitted facial challenges to regulations of expression even before the institution of other legal proceedings.[30]

"The law of the Takings Clause of the Fifth Amendment, however, has followed a very different path. The Supreme Court has characterized the takings inquiry as turning on 'ad hoc factual' determinations directed to 'particular estimates of [the] economic impact' on the property in question. [P]art of the concrete factual setting necessary to the demonstration of a takings claim, apparently, is a showing that the regulatory authority would deny approval for all uses that would enable the plaintiff to obtain a 'reasonable return' on its investment [citing *Penn Central Transp. Co. v. New York City*, Ch. 5, Sec. 4. [It] is obviously more difficult, therefore, to present a ripe takings claim than a ripe first amendment challenge. [The] common theme [is] the examination of what it takes to state a concrete cause of action under the substantive principles upon which the claim is based."

4. ***Challenges to threatened official conduct other than statutory enforcement.*** In O'SHEA v. LITTLETON, 414 U.S. 488 (1974), black and white residents who had protested racial discrimination in Cairo, Illinois, alleged a deliberately discriminatory pattern of law enforcement practices directed against them by the city's police commissioner, a state's attorney, and a magistrate and judge of the county court, including illegal bond-setting, sentencing, and jury-fees. They did not allege the unconstitutionality of any statute. Although some respondents "had actually been defendants in proceedings before petitioners and had suffered from the alleged unconstitutional practices," the Court, per WHITE, J., ordered the case dismissed: "Of course, past wrongs are evidence bearing on whether there is a real and immediate threat of repeated injury. [But] respondents here have not pointed to any imminent prosecutions contemplated against any of their

---

[30] For detailed consideration of the question of whether laws allegedly violative of the First Amendment should be held facially invalid, see Ch. 7, Sec. 1, IV, C.

number and they naturally do not suggest that any one of them expects to violate valid criminal laws. [Thus], the threat of injury from the alleged course of conduct they attack is simply too remote to satisfy the case-or-controversy requirement and permit adjudication by a federal court."[31]

Even if there were "an existing case or controversy," White, J., continued, "a proper balance in the concurrent operation of federal and state courts" precludes federal equitable relief. A decision awarding equitable relief "would contemplate interruption of state proceedings to adjudicate assertions of noncompliance by petitioners. This seems to us nothing less than an ongoing federal audit of state criminal proceedings [that] is antipathetic to established principles of comity.[32] [Respondents] have failed, moreover, to establish the basic requisites of the issuance of equitable relief in these circumstances—the likelihood of substantial and immediate irreparable injury, and the inadequacy of remedies at law. [I]f any of the respondents are ever prosecuted and face trial, or if they are illegally sentenced, there are available state and federal procedures which could provide relief from the wrongful conduct alleged."[33]

(a)   Consider *Hart & Wechsler,* supra, at 217: "[A] case such as *O'Shea* differs from a case such as [*United Public Workers v. Mitchell*] in several respects. [In] a case such as *O'Shea,* [in which plaintiffs complain about official misconduct not tied to any statute,] it is especially difficult to identify the individuals who are likely to be harmed [in] the future. [In addition], such cases may also involve requests for 'structural relief'—for the shaping of a decree designed to modify significantly the way in which an arm of government [conducts] its affairs. The Court's evident reluctance to become enmeshed in disputes of this kind, especially when state institutions are at the bar, has been expressed, in part, in terms of justiciability doctrines—notably ripeness and standing."

(b)   In *O'Shea,* the Court did not make wholly clear whether it meant to rest its holding on standing or on ripeness grounds. Commenting on the distinction, Richard H. Fallon, Jr., *The Linkage Between Justiciability and Remedies—And Their Connections to Substantive Rights,* 92 Va.L.Rev. 633 (2006), argues that it would be preferable if courts set the threat-of-injury barrier to standing relatively low and disposed of cases such as *O'Shea* and *City of Los Angeles v. Lyons,* Sec. 2, I, another case in which the plaintiff sought an injunction against an alleged pattern of police misconduct, under more flexible, discretionary doctrines such as those of ripeness and equitable remedies: "With the question framed in terms of ripeness or equitable discretion, judicial intrusion into the running of police departments, as of other complex governmental institutions, clearly has the potential to do harm as well as good. [It] is only realistic, not cynical, to acknowledge that no practically

---

[31]   For similar analysis, see *Rizzo v. Goode,* 423 U.S. 362 (1976).

[32]   Compare *Allee v. Medrano,* 416 U.S. 802 (1974) (upholding a federal injunction against state police disruption of unionization efforts).

[33]   Blackmun, J., concurred in the first part of the Court's opinion. Douglas, J., joined by Brennan and Marshall, JJ., dissented.

desirable, or even acceptable, injunctive fix exists for every legal and constitutional shortfall.

"[As] the examples of *O'Shea* and *Lyons* will signal, open discussion about appropriate injunctive remedies might sometimes prove painful and divisive. Remedies inherently involve a jurisprudence of second-best. Exacerbating the painful, awkward character of the discussion, the parties who are relegated to second-best may come disproportionately from the racial minorities and other disadvantaged groups that have the greatest need for judicial protection. It seems a fair guess, however, that these groups would fare no worse under an open balancing of public and private interests than under a regime in which courts manipulatively deny standing."

As to the ultimate results that the Court should have reached: "Whereas the plaintiffs in *O'Shea* sought far-reaching structural relief, Adolph Lyons's complaint was relatively narrowly targeted on police choke-holds. An injunction in *Lyons* would have posed far fewer risks to important public interests than the relief requested in *O'Shea*."

APPENDIX A

THE JUSTICES OF THE SUPREME COURT

■ ■ ■

Originally prepared by JOHN J. COUND

Professor of Law, University of Minnesota

The following data summarize the prior public careers of the justices of the Supreme Court. The first dates in parentheses are those of birth and death; these are followed by the name of the appointing President and the dates of service on the Court. The states in which the justices were residing when appointed and their political affiliations at that time are then given. In detailing prior careers, I have followed chronological order, with two exceptions: I have listed first that a justice was a signer of the Declaration of Independence or the Federal Constitution, and I have indicated state legislative experience only once for each justice. I have not distinguished between different bodies in the state legislature, and I have omitted service in the Continental Congresses. Private practice, except where deemed especially significant, and law teaching have been omitted, except where a justice was primarily engaged therein upon or shortly before appointment. The activity in which a justice was engaged upon appointment has been italicized. Figures in parentheses indicate years of service in the position. In only a few cases, a justice's extra-Court or post-Court activity has been indicated or some other note made. An asterisk designates the Chief Justices.

The accompanying Table of Justices on pages [1754] and [56] has been planned so that the composition of the Court at any time can be readily ascertained.

(This material has been compiled from a great number of sources, but special acknowledgment must be made to the *Dictionary of American Biography* (Charles Scribner's Sons), the A.N. Marquis Company works, and Ewing, *The Judges of the Supreme Court, 1789–1937* (University of Minnesota Press, 1938).)

ALITO, JR., SAMUEL A. (1950–____; G.W. Bush, 2006–___). N.J. Rep.—U.S., Assistant U.S. Attorney (4); Assistant to Solicitor General (4); Deputy Assistant Attorney General (3); U.S. Attorney (4); *Judge, Court of Appeals (16)*.

BALDWIN, HENRY (1780–1844; Jackson, 1830–1844). Pa.Dem.—U.S., House of Representatives (5). *Private practice.*

BARBOUR, PHILIP P. (1783–1841; Jackson, 1836–1841). Va.Dem.—Va., Legislature (2). U.S., House of Representatives (14). Va., Judge, General Court (2); President, State Constitutional Convention, 1829–30. *U.S., Judge, District Court (5).*

BLACK, HUGO L. (1886–1971; F.D. Roosevelt, 1937–1971). Ala.Dem.— Captain, Field Artillery, World War I. Ala., Judge, Police Court (1); County Solicitor (2). *U.S., Senate (10).*

BLACKMUN, HARRY A. (1908–1999; Nixon, 1970–1994). Minn.Rep.— Resident Counsel, Mayo Clinic, (10). *U.S., Judge, Court of Appeals (11).*

BLAIR, JOHN (1732–1800; Washington, 1789–1796). Va.Fed.—Signer, U.S. Constitution, 1787. Va., Legislature (9); Judge and Chief Justice, General Court (2), *Court of Appeals (9).* His opinion in *Commonwealth v. Caton,* 4 Call 5, 20 (Va.1782), is one of the earliest expressions of the doctrine of judicial review.

BLATCHFORD, SAMUEL (1820–1893; Arthur, 1882–1893). N.Y.Rep.— U.S., Judge, District Court (5); *Circuit Court (10).*

BRADLEY, JOSEPH P. (1803–1892; Grant, 1870–1892). N.J.Rep.— Actuary. *Private practice.*

BRANDEIS, LOUIS D. (1856–1941; Wilson, 1916–1939). Mass.Dem.— *Private practice.* Counsel, variously for the government, for industry, and "for the people," in numerous administrative and judicial proceedings, both state and federal.

BRENNAN, WILLIAM J. (1906–1997; Eisenhower, 1956–1990). N.J.Dem.—U.S. Army, World War II. N.J., Judge, Superior Court (1); Appellate Division (2); *Supreme Court (4).*

BREWER, DAVID J. (1837–1910; B. Harrison, 1889–1910). Kans.Rep.— Kans., Judge, County Criminal and Probate Court (1), District Court (4); County Attorney (1); Judge, Supreme Court (14), *U.S., Judge, Circuit Court (5).*

BREYER, STEPHEN GERALD (1937–____; Clinton, 1994–____). Mass.Dem.—U.S., Special Assistant to Assistant Attorney General for Antitrust (2); Assistant Special Prosecutor (during Watergate) (1); Special Counsel of the Senate Judiciary Committee (1); Chief Counsel, same (2); Judge, Court of Appeals (10); *Chief Judge, Court of Appeals (4).*

BROWN, HENRY, B. (1836–1913; B. Harrison, 1890–1906). Mich.Rep.— U.S., Assistant U.S. Attorney (5). Mich., Judge, Circuit Court (1). *U.S., Judge, District Court (15).*

*BURGER, WARREN E. (1907–1995; Nixon, 1969–1986). Va.Rep.—U.S., Assistant Attorney General, Civil Division (3), *Judge, Court of Appeals (13).*

BURTON, HAROLD H. (1888–1964; Truman, 1945–1958). Ohio Rep.— Capt., U.S Army, World War I. Ohio, Legislature (2). Mayor, Cleveland, OH. (5). *U.S., Senate (4).*

BUTLER, PIERCE (1866–1939; Harding, 1922–1939). Minn.Dem.— Minn., County Attorney (4). *Private practice.*

BYRNES, JAMES F. (1879–1972; F.D. Roosevelt, 1941–1942). S.C.Dem.—S.C., Solicitor, Circuit Court (2). U.S., House of Representatives

(14); *Senate (12)*. Resigned from the Court to become U.S. Director of Economic Stabilization.

CAMPBELL, JOHN A. (1811–1889; Pierce, 1853–1861). Ala.Dem.— *Private practice*. After his resignation, he became Assistant Secretary of War, C.S.A.

CARDOZO, BENJAMIN N. (1870–1938; Hoover, 1932–1938). N.Y.Dem.— N.Y., Judge, Supreme Court (6 weeks); Associate Judge and *Chief Judge, Court of Appeals (18)*.

CATRON, JOHN (1778–1865; Van Buren, 1837–1865). Tenn.Dem.— Tenn., Judge and Chief Justice, Supreme Court of Errors and Appeals (10). *Private practice.*

*CHASE, SALMON P. (1808–1873; Lincoln, 1864–1873). Ohio Rep.— U.S., Senate (6). Ohio, Governor (4). *U.S., Secretary of the Treasury (3).*

CHASE, SAMUEL (1741–1811; Washington, 1796–1811). Md.Fed.— Signer, U.S. Declaration of Independence, 1776. Md., Legislature (20); Chief Judge, Court of Oyer and Terminer (2), *General Court (5)*. Impeached and acquitted, 1804–05.

CLARK, TOM C. (1899–1977; Truman, 1949–1967). Tex.Dem.—U.S. Army, World War I. Tex., Civil District Attorney (5). U.S., Assistant Attorney General (2), *Attorney General (4)*.

CLARKE, JOHN H. (1857–1945; Wilson, 1916–1922). Ohio Dem.—*U.S. Judge, District Court (2)*.

CLIFFORD, NATHAN (1803–1881; Buchanan, 1858–1881). Me.Dem.— Me., Legislature (4); Attorney General (4). U.S., House of Representatives (4); Attorney General (2); Minister Plenipotentiary to Mexico, 1848. *Private practice.*

CURTIS, BENJAMIN R. (1809–1874; Fillmore, 1851–1857). Mass.Whig.—Mass., Legislature (1). *Private practice.*

CUSHING, WILLIAM (1732–1810; Washington, 1789–1810). Mass.Fed.—Mass., Judge, Superior Court (3); Justice and *Chief Justice, Supreme Judicial Court (14)*.

DANIEL, PETER V. (1784–1860; Van Buren, 1841–1860). Va.Dem.—Va., Legislature (3); Member, Privy Council (23). *U.S., Judge, District Court (5)*.

DAVIS, DAVID (1815–1886; Lincoln, 1862–1877). Ill.Rep.—Ill., Legislature (2); *Judge, Circuit Court (14)*. His resignation to become U.S. Senator upset the agreed-upon composition of the Hayes-Tilden Electoral Commission.

DAY, WILLIAM R. (1849–1923; T. Roosevelt, 1903–1922). Ohio Rep.— Ohio, Judge, Court of Common Pleas (4). U.S., Assistant Secretary of State (1), Secretary of State (½); Chairman, U.S. Peace Commissioners, 1898; *Judge, Circuit Court of Appeals (4)*.

DOUGLAS, WILLIAM O. (1898–1980; F.D. Roosevelt, 1939–1975). Conn.Dem.—Pvt., U.S. Army, World War I. *U.S., Chairman, Securities and Exchange Commission (3).* His was the longest tenure in the history of the Court.

DUVAL(L), GABRIEL (1752–1844; Madison, 1811–1835). Md.Rep.— Declined to serve as delegate, U.S. Constitutional Convention, 1787. Md., State Council (3). U.S., House of Representatives (2). Md., Judge, General Court (6). *U.S., Comptroller of the Treasury (9).*

*ELLSWORTH, OLIVER (1745–1807; Washington, 1796–1800). Conn.Fed.—Delegate, U.S. Constitutional Convention, 1787. Conn., Legislature (2); Member, Governor's Council (4); Judge, Superior Court (5). *U.S., Senate (7).*

FIELD, STEPHEN J. (1816–1899; Lincoln, 1863–1897). Calif.Dem.— Calif., Justice, and *Chief Justice, Supreme Court (6).*

FORTAS, ABE (1910–1982; L.B. Johnson, 1965–1969). Tenn.Dem.—U.S. Government attorney and consultant (A.A.A., S.E.C., P.W.A., Dep't of Interior) (9); Undersecretary of Interior (4). *Private practice in Washington, D.C.* Nominated as Chief Justice; nomination withdrawn, 1968. Resigned.

FRANKFURTER, FELIX (1882–1965; F.D. Roosevelt, 1939–1962). Mass. Independent.—U.S., Assistant U.S. Attorney (4); Law Officer, War Department, Bureau of Insular Affairs (3); Assistant to Secretary of War (1). *Professor of Law (25).*

*FULLER, MELVILLE W. (1833–1910; Cleveland, 1888–1910). Ill.Dem.—Ill., Legislature (2). *Private practice.*

GINSBURG, RUTH BADER (1933–___; Clinton, 1993–___); N.Y.Dem.— *U.S., Judge, Court of Appeals (13).*

GOLDBERG, ARTHUR J. (1908–1990; Kennedy, 1962–1965). Ill.Dem.— Major, U.S.A., World War II. General Counsel, USW-AFL-CIO (13). *U.S., Secretary of Labor (1).* Resigned to become Ambassador to U.N.

GRAY, HORACE (1828–1902; Arthur, 1881–1902). Mass.Rep.—*Mass., Associate Justice and *Chief Justice, Supreme Judicial Court (18).*

GRIER, ROBERT O. (1794–1870; Polk, 1846–1870). Pa.Dem.—*Pa., Presiding Judge, District Court (13).*

HARLAN, JOHN M. (1833–1911; Hayes, 1877–1911). Ky.Rep.—Ky., Judge, County Court (1). Col., Union Army, 1861–63. Ky., Attorney General (4). U.S., Member, President's Louisiana Commission, 1877. *Private practice.* Grandfather of:

HARLAN, JOHN M. (1899–1971; Eisenhower, 1955–1971). N.Y.Rep.— Col., U.S.A.A.F., World War II. N.Y. Chief Counsel, State Crime Commission (2). *U.S., Judge, Court of Appeals (1).*

HOLMES, OLIVER W., JR. (1841–1935; T. Roosevelt, 1902–1932). Mass.Rep.—Lt. Col., Mass. Volunteers, Civil War. Mass., Associate Justice, and *Chief Justice, Supreme Judicial Court (20).*

*HUGHES, CHARLES E. (1862–1948; Taft, 1910–1916, and Hoover, 1930–1941). N.Y.Rep.—N.Y., Counsel, legislative committees investigating gas and insurance industries (2); U.S., Special Assistant to Attorney General for Coal Investigation (1). *N.Y., Governor (3).* [Between appointments to the Supreme Court: Presidential Nominee, Republican Party, 1916. U.S., Secretary of State (4). *Member, Permanent Court of Arbitration, The Hague (4). Judge, Permanent Court of International Justice (2).*] Chief Justice on second appointment.

HUNT, WARD (1810–1886; Grant, 1872–1882). N.Y.Rep.—N.Y., Legislature (2). Mayor of Utica, N.Y. (1). N.Y., Associate Judge, and Chief Judge, Court of Appeals (4); *Commissioner of Appeals (4).* He did not sit from 1879 to his retirement in 1882.

IREDELL, JAMES (1750–1799; Washington, 1790–1799). N.C.Fed.— Comptroller of Customs (6), Collector of Port (2), Edenton, N.C. N.C., Judge, Superior Court (½); Attorney General (2); Member, Council of State, 1787; *Reviser of Statutes (3).*

JACKSON, HOWELL E. (1832–1895; B. Harrison, 1893–1895). Tenn.Dem.—Tenn., Judge, Court of Arbitration (4); Legislature (1). U.S. Senate (5); *Judge, Circuit Court of Appeals (7).*

JACKSON, ROBERT H. (1892–1954; F.D. Roosevelt, 1941–1954). N.Y.Dem.—U.S., General Counsel, Bureau of Internal Revenue (2); Assistant Attorney General (2); Solicitor General (2); *Attorney General (1).*

*JAY, JOHN (1745–1829; Washington, 1789–1795). N.Y.Fed.—N.Y., Chief Justice, Supreme Court (2). U.S., Envoy to Spain (2); Commissioner, Treaty of Paris, 1782–83; Secretary for Foreign Affairs (6). Co-author, The Federalist.

JOHNSON, THOMAS (1732–1819; Washington, 1791–1793). Md.Fed.— Md., Brigadier-General, Militia (1); Legislature (5); Governor (2); *Chief Judge, General Court (1).*

JOHNSON, WILLIAM (1771–1834; Jefferson, 1804–1834). S.C.Rep.— S.C., Legislature (4); *Judge, Court of Common Pleas (6).*

KAGAN, ELENA (1960–____; Obama, 2010–___). Mass.Dem.—U.S., Associate Counsel to the President (1); Deputy Assistant to the President for Domestic Policy (2). Professor and Dean (10). *U.S., Solicitor General (1).*

KENNEDY, ANTHONY M. (1936–___; Reagan, 1988–___). Calif.Rep.— Calif. Army National Guard (1). *U.S., Judge, Court of Appeals (11).*

LAMAR, JOSEPH R. (1857–1916; Taft, 1910–1916). Ga.Dem.—Ga., Legislature (3); Commissioner to Codify Laws (3); Associate Justice, Supreme Court (4). *Private practice.*

LAMAR, LUCIUS Q.C. (1825–1893; Cleveland, 1888–1893). Miss.Dem.— Ga., Legislature (2). U.S., House of Representatives (4). Draftsman, Mississippi Ordinance of Secession, 1861. C.S.A., Lt. Col. (1); Commissioner to Russia (1); Judge-Advocate, III Corps. Army of No. Va. (1). U.S., House of Representatives (4); Senate (8); *Secretary of the Interior (3).*

LIVINGSTON, (HENRY) BROCKHOLST (1757–1823; Jefferson, 1806–1823). N.Y.Rep.—Lt. Col., Continental Army. *N.Y., Judge, Supreme Court (4).*

LURTON, HORACE H. (1844–1914; Taft, 1909–1914). Tenn.Dem.—Sgt. Major, C.S.A. Tenn., Chancellor (3); Associate Justice and Chief Justice, Supreme Court (7). *U.S., Judge, Circuit Court of Appeals (16).*

McKENNA, JOSEPH (1843–1926; McKinley, 1898–1925). Calif.Rep.— Calif., District Attorney (2); Legislature (2). U.S., House of Representatives (7); Judge, Circuit Court of Appeals (5); Attorney General (1).

McKINLEY, JOHN (1780–1852; Van Buren, 1837–1852). Ala.Dem.— Legislature (4). U.S., Senate (5); House of Representatives (2); *re-elected to Senate,* but appointed to Court before taking seat.

McLEAN, JOHN (1785–1861; Jackson, 1829–1861). Ohio Dem.—U.S., House of Representatives (4). Ohio, Judge, Supreme Court (6). U.S., Commissioner, General Land Office (1); *Postmaster-General (6).*

McREYNOLDS, JAMES C. (1862–1946; Wilson, 1914–1941). Tenn.Dem.—U.S., Assistant Attorney General (4); *Attorney General (1).*

*MARSHALL, JOHN (1755–1835; J. Adams, 1801–1835). Va.Fed.—Va., Legislature (7); U.S., Envoy to France (1); House of Representatives (1); *Secretary of State (1).*

MARSHALL, THURGOOD (1908–1993; L.B. Johnson, 1967–1991). N.Y.Dem.—Counsel, Legal Defense and Educational Fund, NAACP (21). U.S., Judge, Court of Appeals (4); *Solicitor General (2).*

MATTHEWS, STANLEY (1824–1889; Garfield, 1881–1889). Ohio Rep.— Ohio, Judge, Court of Common Pleas (2); Legislature (3). U.S., District Attorney (3). Col., Ohio Volunteers. Ohio, Judge, Superior Court (2). Counsel before Hayes-Tilden Electoral Commission, 1877. U.S., Senate (2). *Private practice.* His first appointment to the Court by Hayes in 1881 was not acted upon by the Senate.

MILLER, SAMUEL F. (1816–1890; Lincoln, 1862–1890). Iowa Rep.— Physician. *Private practice.*

MINTON, SHERMAN (1890–1965; Truman, 1949–1956). Ind.Dem.— Capt., Inf., World War I. U.S., Senate (6); *Judge, Court of Appeals (8).*

MOODY, WILLIAM H. (1853–1917; T. Roosevelt, 1906–1910). Mass.Rep.—U.S., District Attorney (5), House of Representatives (7); Secretary of the Navy (2); *Attorney General (2).*

MOORE, ALFRED (1755–1810; J. Adams, 1799–1804). N.C.Fed.—N.C., Col. of Militia; Legislature (2); Attorney General (9). U.S. Commissioner, Treaty with Cherokee Nation (1); *N.C., Judge, Superior Court (1).*

MURPHY, FRANK (1893–1949; F.D. Roosevelt, 1940–1949). Mich.Dem.—Capt., Inf., World War I. U.S., Assistant U.S. Attorney (1). Mich., Judge, Recorder's Court (7). Mayor, Detroit, Mich. (3). U.S., Governor-General, and High Commissioner, P.I. (3). Mich., Governor (2). *U.S., Attorney General (1).*

NELSON, SAMUEL (1792–1873; Tyler, 1845–1872). N.Y.Dem.—N.Y., Judge, Circuit Court (8); Associate Justice, and *Chief Justice, Supreme Court (14).*

O'CONNOR, SANDRA DAY (1930–____; Reagan, 1981–2006). Ariz.Rep.—Calif., Deputy County Attorney (2); Ariz., Assistant Attorney General (4); Legislature (6); Judge, Superior Court (4); *Court of Appeals (2).*

PATERSON, WILLIAM (1745–1806; Washington, 1793–1806). N.J.Fed.—Signer, U.S. Constitution, 1787. N.J., Legislature (2); Attorney General (7). U.S., Senate (1). *N.J., Governor (3).* Reviser of English Pre-Revolutionary Statutes in Force in N.J.

PECKHAM, RUFUS W. (1838–1909; Cleveland, 1895–1909). N.Y.Dem.—N.Y., District Attorney (1); Justice, Supreme Court (3); *Associate Judge, Court of Appeals (9).*

PITNEY, MAHLON (1858–1924; Taft, 1912–1922). N.J.Rep.—U.S., House of Representatives (4). N.J., Legislature (2); Associate Justice, Supreme Court (7); Chancellor (4).

POWELL, LEWIS F. (1907–1998; Nixon, 1972–1987). Va.Dem.—Col., U.S.A.A.F., World War II. U.S., Special Assistant to the Attorney General on Selective Service (4). Va., Member, State Board of Education (8). *Private practice.*

REED, STANLEY F. (1884–1980; F.D. Roosevelt, 1938–1957). Ky.Dem.—Ky., Legislature (4). 1st Lt., U.S.A., World War I. U.S., General Counsel, Federal Farm Board (3); General Counsel, Reconstruction Finance Corporation (3); *Solicitor General (3).*

*REHNQUIST, WILLIAM H. (1924–2005; Nixon, later Reagan, 1972–2005). Ariz.Rep.—U.S.A.F., World War II. *U.S., Assistant Attorney General, Office of Legal Counsel (3).*

*ROBERTS, JOHN G. (1955–____); G.W. Bush (2005–____). D.C. Rep.—U.S., Special Assistant to Attorney General (1); Associate Counsel to the President (4); Principal Deputy Solicitor General (4). Private practice (14). *U.S., Judge, Court of Appeals (2).*

ROBERTS, OWEN J. (1875–1955; Hoover, 1930–1945). Pa.Rep.—Pa., Assistant District Attorney (3). U.S., Special Deputy Attorney General in

Espionage Act Cases, World War I; Special Prosecutor, Oil Cases, 1924. *Private practice.*

*RUTLEDGE, JOHN (1739–1800; Washington, 1789–1791, and Washington, 1795). S.C.Fed.—Signer, U.S. Constitution, 1787. S.C., Legislature (18); Attorney General (1); President and Governor (6); *Chancellor (7).* [Between appointments to the Supreme Court: *S.C., Chief Justice, Court of Common Pleas and Sessions (4).*] He did not sit under his first appointment; he sat with a recess appointment as Chief Justice, but his regular appointment was rejected by the Senate.

RUTLEDGE, WILEY B. (1894–1949; F.D. Roosevelt, 1943–1949). Iowa Dem.—Mo., then Iowa, Member, National Conference of Commissioners on Uniform State Laws (10). *U.S., Judge, Court of Appeals (4).*

SANFORD, EDWARD T. (1865–1930; Harding, 1923–1930). Tenn.Rep.— U.S., Assistant Attorney General (1); *Judge, District Court (15).*

SCALIA, ANTONIN (1936–___; Reagan, 1986–___). Va.Rep.—U.S., General Counsel, Office of Telecommunications Policy (1); Chairman, Administrative Conference of the United States (2); Assistant Attorney General, Office of Legal Counsel (3); *Judge, Court of Appeals (4).*

SHIRAS, GEORGE (1832–1924; B. Harrison, 1892–1903). Pa.Rep.— *Private practice.*

SOTOMAYOR, SONIA M. (1954–___; Obama, 2009–___). N.Y.Dem.— N.Y., Assistant District Attorney (4). U.S., Judge, District Court (6); *Court of Appeals (11).*

SOUTER, DAVID H. (1939–___; G.H.W. Bush, 1990–2009). N.H.Rep.— N.H., Assistant Attorney General (3); Deputy Attorney General (5); Attorney General (2); Associate Justice, Superior Court (5); Associate Justice, Supreme Court (7). *U.S., Judge, Court of Appeals (½).*

STEVENS, JOHN PAUL (1920–___; Ford, 1975–2010). Ill.Independent.— U.S.N.R., World War II. U.S., Associate Counsel, Subcommittee on the Study of Monopoly Power, Committee on the Judiciary, House of Representatives (1); Member, Attorney General's National Committee to Study the Antitrust Laws (2). Ill., Chief Counsel, Special Commission of the Supreme Court. *U.S., Judge, Court of Appeals (5).*

STEWART, POTTER (1915–1985; Eisenhower, 1958–1981). Ohio Rep.— Lt., U.S.N.R., World War II. *U.S., Judge, Court of Appeals (4).*

*STONE, HARLAN F. (1872–1946; Coolidge, later F.D. Roosevelt, 1925– 1946). N.Y.Rep.—*U.S., Attorney General (1).* Chief Justice, 1941–1946.

STORY, JOSEPH (1779–1845; Madison, 1811–1845). Mass.Rep.—Mass., Legislature (5). U.S., House of Representatives (2). *Private practice.*

STRONG, WILLIAM (1808–1895; Grant, 1870–1880). Pa.Rep.—U.S., House of Representatives (4). Pa., Justice, Supreme Court (11). *Private practice.*

SUTHERLAND, GEORGE (1862–1942; Harding, 1922–1938). Utah Rep.—Utah, Legislature (4). U.S., House of Representatives (2); Senate (12). *Private practice.*

SWAYNE, NOAH H. (1804–1884; Lincoln, 1862–1881). Ohio Rep.—Ohio, County Attorney (4); Legislature (2). U.S., District Attorney (9). *Private practice.*

*TAFT, WILLIAM H. (1857–1930; Harding, 1921–1930). Conn.Rep.— U.S., Collector of Internal Revenue (1). Ohio, Judge, Superior Court (3). U.S., Solicitor General (2); Judge, Circuit Court of Appeals (8); Governor-General, P.I. (3); Secretary of War (4); President (4). *Professor of Law.*

*TANEY, ROGER B. (1777–1864; Jackson, 1836–1864). Md.Dem.—Md., Legislature (7); Attorney General (2). U.S., Attorney General (2), Secretary of the Treasury (¾; rejected by the Senate). *Private practice.*

THOMAS, CLARENCE (1948–___; G.H.W. Bush, 1991–___). Ga.Rep.— Mo., Assistant Attorney General (3). U.S., Legislative Assistant (2); Assistant Secretary for Civil Rights, Department of Education (1); Chairman, Equal Employment Opportunity Commission (8); *Judge, Court of Appeals (1).*

THOMPSON, SMITH (1768–1843; Monroe, 1823–1843). N.Y.Rep.—N.Y., Legislature (2); Associate Justice, and Chief Justice, Supreme Court (16). *U.S., Secretary of the Navy (4).*

TODD, THOMAS (1765–1826; Jefferson, 1807–1826). Ky.Rep.—*Ky., Judge, and Chief Justice, Court of Appeals (6).*

TRIMBLE, ROBERT (1777–1828; J.Q. Adams, 1826–1828). Ky.Rep.— Ky., Legislature (2). Judge, Court of Appeals (2). U.S., District Attorney (4); *Judge, District Court (9).*

VAN DEVANTER, WILLIS (1859–1941; Taft, 1910–1937). Wyo.Rep.— Wyo., Legislature (2); Chief Justice, Supreme Court (1). U.S., Assistant Attorney General (Interior Department) (6); *Judge, Circuit Court of Appeals (7).*

*VINSON, FRED M. (1890–1953; Truman, 1946–1953). Ky.Dem.—Ky., Commonwealth Attorney (3). U.S., House of Representatives (14); Judge, Court of Appeals (5); Director, Office of Economic Stabilization (2); Federal Loan Administrator (1 mo.); Director, Office of War Mobilization and Reconversion (3 mo.); *Secretary of the Treasury (1).*

*WAITE, MORRISON R. (1816–1888; Grant, 1874–1888). Ohio Rep.— Ohio, Legislature (2). Counsel for United States, U.S.—Gr. Brit. Arbitration ("Alabama" Claims), 1871–72. *Private practice.*

*WARREN, EARL (1891–1974; Eisenhower, 1953–1969). Calif.Rep.—1st Lt., Inf., World War I. Deputy City Attorney (1); Deputy District Attorney (5); District Attorney (14); Attorney General (4); *Governor (10).*

WASHINGTON, BUSHROD (1762–1829; J. Adams, 1798–1829). Pa.Fed.—Va., Legislature (1). *Private practice.*

WAYNE, JAMES M. (1790–1867; Jackson, 1835–1867). Ga.Dem.—Ga., Officer, Hussars, War of 1812; Legislature (2). Mayor of Savannah, Ga. (2). Ga., Judge, Superior Court (5). *U.S., House of Representatives (6).*

WHITE, BYRON R. (1917–2002; Kennedy, 1962–1993). Colo.Dem.— U.S.N.R., World War II. *U.S., Deputy Attorney General (1).*

*WHITE, EDWARD D. (1845–1921; Cleveland, later Taft, 1894–1921). La.Dem.—La., Legislature (4); Justice, Supreme Court (2). *U.S., Senate (3).* Chief Justice, 1910–1921.

WHITTAKER, CHARLES E. (1901–1973; Eisenhower, 1957–1962). Mo.Rep.—U.S., Judge, District Court (2); *Court of Appeals (1).*

WILSON, JAMES (1724–1798; Washington, 1789–1798). Pa.Fed.— Signer, U.S. Declaration of Independence, 1776, and U.S. Constitution, 1787. Although he was strongly interested in western-land development companies for several years prior to his appointment, his primary activity in the period immediately preceding his appointment was in obtaining ratification of the Federal and Pennsylvania Constitutions.

WOODBURY, LEVI (1789–1851; Polk, 1845–1851). N.H. Dem.—N.H., Associate Justice, Superior Court (6); Governor (2); Legislature (1). U.S., Senate (6); Secretary of the Navy (3); Secretary of the Treasury (7); *Senate (4).*

WOODS, WILLIAM B. (1824–1887; Hayes, 1880–1887). Ga.Rep.—Mayor, Newark, Oh. (1). Ohio, Legislature (4). Brevet Major General, U.S. Vol., Civil War. Ala., Chancellor (1). *U.S., Judge, Circuit Court (11).*

APPENDIX B

THE CONSTITUTION OF THE UNITED STATES

∎ ∎ ∎

We the People of the United States, in Order to form a more perfect Union, establish Justice, insure domestic Tranquility, provide for the common defence, promote the general Welfare, and secure the Blessings of Liberty to ourselves and our Posterity, do ordain and establish this Constitution for the United States of America.

ARTICLE I

Section 1. All legislative Powers herein granted shall be vested in a Congress of the United States, which shall consist of a Senate and House of Representatives.

Section 2. [1] The House of Representatives shall be composed of Members chosen every second Year by the People of the several States, and the Electors in each State shall have the Qualifications requisite for Electors of the most numerous Branch of the State Legislature.

[2] No Person shall be a Representative who shall not have attained to the Age of twenty five Years, and been seven Years a Citizen of the United States, and who shall not, when elected, be an Inhabitant of that State in which he shall be chosen.

[3] Representatives and direct Taxes shall be apportioned among the several States which may be included within this Union, according to their respective Numbers, which shall be determined by adding to the whole Number of free Persons, including those bound to Service for a Term of Years, and excluding Indians not taxed, three fifths of all other Persons. The actual Enumeration shall be made within three Years after the first Meeting of the Congress of the United States, and within every subsequent Term of ten Years, in such Manner as they shall by Law direct. The Number of Representatives shall not exceed one for every thirty Thousand, but each State shall have at Least one Representative; and until such enumeration shall be made, the State of New Hampshire shall be entitled to chuse three, Massachusetts eight, Rhode Island and Providence Plantations one, Connecticut five, New York six, New Jersey four, Pennsylvania eight, Delaware one, Maryland six, Virginia ten, North Carolina five, South Carolina five, and Georgia three.

[4] When vacancies happen in the Representation from any State, the Executive Authority thereof shall issue Writs of Election to fill such Vacancies.

[5]   The House of Representatives shall chuse their Speaker and other Officers; and shall have the sole Power of Impeachment.

Section 3. [1] The Senate of the United States shall be composed of two Senators from each State, chosen by the Legislature thereof, for six Years; and each Senator shall have one Vote.

[2]   Immediately after they shall be assembled in Consequence of the first Election, they shall be divided as equally as may be into three Classes. The Seats of the Senators of the first Class shall be vacated at the Expiration of the Second Year, of the second Class at the Expiration of the fourth Year, and of the third Class at the Expiration of the sixth Year, so that one third may be chosen every second Year; and if Vacancies happen by Resignation, or otherwise, during the Recess of the Legislature of any State, the Executive thereof may make temporary Appointments until the next Meeting of the Legislature, which shall then fill such Vacancies.

[3]   No Person shall be a Senator who shall not have attained to the Age of thirty Years, and been nine Years a Citizen of the United States, and who shall not, when elected, by an Inhabitant of that State for which he shall be chosen.

[4]   The Vice President of the United States shall be President of the Senate, but shall have no Vote, unless they be equally divided.

[5]   The Senate shall chuse their other Officers, and also a President pro tempore, in the Absence of the Vice President, or when he shall exercise the Office of President of the United States.

[6]   The Senate shall have the sole Power to try all Impeachments. When sitting for that Purpose, they shall be on Oath or Affirmation. When the President of the United States is tried, the Chief Justice shall preside: And no Person shall be convicted without the Concurrence of two thirds of the Members present.

[7]   Judgment in Cases of Impeachment shall not extend further than to removal from Office, and disqualification to hold and enjoy any Office of honor, Trust, or Profit under the United States: but the Party convicted shall nevertheless be liable and subject to Indictment, Trial, Judgment, and Punishment, according to Law.

Section 4. [1] The Times, Places and Manner of holding Elections for Senators and Representatives, shall be prescribed in each State by the Legislature thereof; but the Congress may at any time by Law make or alter such Regulations, except as to the Places of chusing Senators.

[2]   The Congress shall assemble at least once in every Year, and such Meeting shall be on the first Monday in December, unless they shall by Law appoint a different Day.

Section 5. [1] Each House shall be the Judge of the Elections, Returns, and Qualifications of its own Members, and a Majority of each shall constitute a Quorum to do Business; but a smaller Number may adjourn from day to day, and may be authorized to compel the Attendance of absent Members, in such Manner, and under such Penalties as each House may provide.

[2]   Each House may determine the Rules of its Proceedings, punish its Members for disorderly Behavior, and, with the Concurrence of two thirds, expel a Member.

[3]   Each House shall keep a Journal of its Proceedings, and from time to time publish the same, excepting such Parts as may in their Judgment require Secrecy; and the Yeas and Nays of the Members of either House on any question shall, at the Desire of one fifth of those Present, be entered on the Journal.

[4]   Neither House, during the Session of Congress, shall without the Consent of the other, adjourn for more than three days, nor to any other Place than that in which the two Houses shall be sitting.

Section 6. [1] The Senators and Representatives shall receive a Compensation for their Services, to be ascertained by Law, and paid out of the Treasury of the United States. They shall in all Cases, except Treason, Felony and Breach of the Peace, be privileged from Arrest during their Attendance at the Session of their respective Houses, and in going to and returning from the same; and for any Speech or Debate in either House, they shall not be questioned in any other Place.

[2]   No Senator or Representative shall, during the Time for which he was elected, be appointed to any civil Office under the Authority of the United States, which shall have been created, or the Emoluments whereof shall have been increased during such time; and no Person holding any Office under the United States, shall be a Member of either House during his Continuance in Office.

Section 7. [1] All Bills for raising Revenue shall originate in the House of Representatives; but the Senate may propose or concur with Amendments as on other Bills.

[2]   Every Bill which shall have passed the House of Representatives and the Senate, shall, before it become a Law, be presented to the President of the United States; If he approve he shall sign it, but if not he shall return it, with his Objections to the House in which it shall have originated, who shall enter the Objections at large on their Journal, and proceed to reconsider it. If after such Reconsideration two thirds of that House shall agree to pass the Bill, it shall be sent together with the Objections, to the other House, by which it shall likewise be reconsidered, and if approved by two thirds of that House, it shall become a Law. But in all such Cases the Votes of both Houses shall be determined by yeas and Nays, and the Names of the Persons voting for and against the Bill shall be entered on the Journal of each House respectively. If any Bill shall not be returned by the President within ten Days (Sundays excepted) after it shall have been presented to him, the Same shall be a Law, in like Manner as if he had signed it, unless the Congress by their Adjournment prevent its Return in which Case it shall not be a Law.

[3] Every Order, Resolution, or Vote, to Which the Concurrence of the Senate and House of Representatives may be necessary (except on a question of Adjournment) shall be presented to the President of the United States; and before the Same shall take Effect, shall be approved by him, or being disapproved by him, shall be repassed by two thirds of the Senate and House of Representatives, according to the Rules and Limitations prescribed in the Case of a Bill.

Section 8. [1] The Congress shall have Power To lay and collect Taxes, Duties, Imposts and Excises, to pay the Debts and provide for the common Defence and general Welfare of the United States; but all Duties, Imposts and Excises shall be uniform throughout the United States;

[2] To borrow money on the credit of the United States;

[3] To regulate Commerce with foreign Nations, and among the several States, and with the Indian Tribes;

[4] To establish an uniform Rule of Naturalization, and uniform Laws on the subject of Bankruptcies throughout the United States;

[5] To coin Money, regulate the Value thereof, and of foreign Coin, and fix the Standard of Weights and Measures;

[6] To provide for the Punishment of counterfeiting the Securities and current Coin of the United States;

[7] To Establish Post Offices and Post Roads;

[8] To promote the Progress of Science and useful Arts, by securing for limited Times to Authors and Inventors the exclusive Right to their respective Writings and Discoveries;

[9] To constitute Tribunals inferior to the supreme Court;

[10] To define and punish Piracies and Felonies committed on the high Seas, and Offenses against the Law of Nations;

[11] To declare War, grant Letters of Marque and Reprisal, and make Rules concerning Captures on Land and Water;

[12] To raise and support Armies, but no Appropriation of Money to that Use shall be for a longer Term than two Years;

[13] To provide and maintain a Navy;

[14] To make Rules for the Government and Regulation of the land and naval Forces;

[15] To provide for calling forth the Militia to execute the Laws of the Union, suppress Insurrections and repel Invasions;

[16] To provide for organizing, arming, and disciplining, the Militia, and for governing such Part of them as may be employed in the Service of the United States, reserving to the States respectively, the Appointment of the

APP. B THE CONSTITUTION OF THE UNITED STATES 1817

Officers, and the Authority of training the Militia according to the discipline prescribed by Congress;

[17] To exercise exclusive Legislation in all Cases whatsoever, over such District (not exceeding ten Miles square) as may, by Cession of particular States, and the Acceptance of Congress, become the Seat of the Government of the United States, and to exercise like Authority over all Places purchased by the Consent of the Legislature of the State in which the Same shall be, for the Erection of Forts, Magazines, Arsenals, dock-Yards, and other needful Buildings;—And

[18] To make all Laws which shall be necessary and proper for carrying into Execution the foregoing Powers, and all other Powers vested by this Constitution in the Government of the United States, or in any Department or Officer thereof.

Section 9. [1] The Migration or Importation of Such Persons as any of the States now existing shall think proper to admit, shall not be prohibited by the Congress prior to the Year one thousand eight hundred and eight, but a Tax or duty may be imposed on such Importation, not exceeding ten dollars for each Person.

[2]   The privilege of the Writ of Habeas Corpus shall not be suspended, unless when in Cases of Rebellion or Invasion the public Safety may require it.

[3]   No Bill of Attainder or ex post facto Law shall be passed.

[4]   No Capitation, or other direct, Tax shall be laid, unless in Proportion to the Census or Enumeration herein before directed to be taken.

[5]   No Tax or Duty shall be laid on Articles exported from any State.

[6]   No Preference shall be given by any Regulation of Commerce or Revenue to the Ports of one State over those of another: nor shall Vessels bound to, or from, one State be obliged to enter, clear, or pay Duties in another.

[7]   No money shall be drawn from the Treasury, but in Consequence of Appropriations made by Law; and a regular Statement and Account of the Receipts and Expenditures of all public Money shall be published from time to time.

[8]   No Title of Nobility shall be granted by the United States: And no Person holding any Office of Profit or Trust under them, shall, without the Consent of the Congress, accept of any present, Emolument, Office, or Title, of any kind whatever, from any King, Prince, or foreign State.

Section 10. [1] No State shall enter into any Treaty, Alliance, or Confederation; grant Letters of Marque and Reprisal; coin Money; emit Bills of Credit; make any Thing but gold and silver Coin a Tender in Payment of Debts; pass any Bill of Attainder, ex post facto Law, or Law impairing the Obligation of Contracts, or grant any Title of Nobility.

[2]   No State shall, without the Consent of the Congress, lay any Imposts or Duties on Imports or Exports, except what may be absolutely necessary for

executing it's inspection Laws: and the net Produce of all Duties and Imposts, laid by any State on Imports or Exports, shall be for the Use of the Treasury of the United States; and all such Laws shall be subject to the Revision and Controul of the Congress.

[3]   No State shall, without the Consent of Congress, lay any Duty of Tonnage, keep Troops, or Ships of War in time of Peace, enter into any Agreement or Compact with another State, or with a foreign Power, or engage in War, unless actually invaded, or in such imminent Danger as will not admit of delay.

ARTICLE II

Section 1. [1] The executive Power shall be vested in a President of the United States of America. He shall hold his Office during the Term of four Years, and, together with the Vice President, chosen for the same Term, be elected, as follows:

[2]   Each State shall appoint, in such Manner as the Legislature thereof may direct, a Number of Electors, equal to the whole Number of Senators and Representatives to which the State may be entitled in the Congress; but no Senator or Representative, or Person holding an Office of Trust or Profit under the United States, shall be appointed an Elector.

[3]   The Electors shall meet in their respective States, and vote by Ballot for two Persons, of whom one at least shall not be an Inhabitant of the same State with themselves. And they shall make a List of all the Persons voted for, and of the Number of Votes for each; which List they shall sign and certify, and transmit sealed to the Seat of the Government of the United States, directed to the President of the Senate. The President of the Senate shall, in the Presence of the Senate and House of Representatives, open all the Certificates, and the Votes shall then be counted. The Person having the greatest Number of Votes shall be the President, if such Number be a Majority of the whole Number of Electors appointed; and if there be more than one who have such Majority, and have an equal Number of Votes, then the House of Representatives shall immediately chuse by Ballot one of them for President; and if no Person have a Majority, then from the five highest on the List the said House shall in like Manner chuse the President. But in chusing the President, the Votes shall be taken by States the Representation from each State having one Vote; A quorum for this Purpose shall consist of a Member or Members from two thirds of the States, and a Majority of all the States shall be necessary to a Choice. In every Case, after the Choice of the President, the Person having the greater Number of Votes of the Electors shall be the Vice President. But if there should remain two or more who have equal Votes, the Senate shall chuse from them by Ballot the Vice President.

[4]   The Congress may determine the Time of chusing the Electors, and the Day on which they shall give their Votes; which Day shall be the same throughout the United States.

[5]   No person except a natural born Citizen, or a Citizen of the United States, at the time of the Adoption of this Constitution, shall be eligible to the Office of President; neither shall any Person be eligible to that Office who shall not have attained to the Age of thirty five Years, and been fourteen Years a Resident within the United States.

[6]   In case of the removal of the President from Office, or of his Death, Resignation or Inability to discharge the Powers and Duties of the said Office, the Same shall devolve on the Vice President, and the Congress may by Law provide for the Case of Removal, Death, Resignation or Inability, both of the President and Vice President, declaring what Officer shall then act as President, and such Officer shall act accordingly, until the Disability be removed, or a President shall be elected.

[7]   The President shall, at stated Times, receive for his Services, a Compensation, which shall neither be increased nor diminished during the Period for which he shall have been elected, and he shall not receive within that Period any other Emolument from the United States, or any of them.

[8]   Before he enter on the Execution of his Office, he shall take the following Oath or Affirmation: "I do solemnly swear (or affirm) that I will faithfully execute the Office of President of the United States, and will to the best of my Ability, preserve, protect and defend the Constitution of the United States."

Section 2. [1] The President shall be Commander in Chief of the Army and Navy of the United States, and of the militia of the several States, when called into the actual Service of the United States; he may require the Opinion, in writing, of the principal Officer in each of the Executive Departments, upon any Subject relating to the Duties of their respective Offices, and he shall have Power to grant Reprieves and Pardons for Offenses against the United States, except in Cases of Impeachment.

[2]   He shall have Power, by and with the Advice and Consent of the Senate to make Treaties, provided two thirds of the Senators present concur; and he shall nominate, and by and with the Advice and Consent of the Senate, shall appoint Ambassadors, other public Ministers and Consuls, Judges of the supreme Court, and all other Officers of the United States, whose Appointments are not herein otherwise provided for, and which shall be established by Law; but the Congress may by Law vest the Appointment of such inferior Officers, as they think proper, in the President alone, in the Courts of Law, or in the Heads of Departments.

[3]   The President shall have Power to fill up all Vacancies that may happen during the Recess of the Senate, by granting Commissions which shall expire at the End of their next Session.

Section 3. He shall from time to time give to the Congress Information of the State of the Union, and recommend to their Consideration such Measures as he shall judge necessary and expedient; he may, on extraordinary Occasions, convene both Houses, or either of them, and in Case of Disagreement between them, with Respect to the Time of Adjournment, he may adjourn them to such Time as he shall think proper; he shall receive Ambassadors and other public Ministers; he shall take Care that the Laws be faithfully executed, and shall Commission all the Officers of the United States.

Section 4. The President, Vice President and all civil Officers of the United States, shall be removed from Office on Impeachment for, and Conviction of, Treason, Bribery, or other high Crimes and Misdemeanors.

ARTICLE III

Section 1. The judicial Power of the United States, shall be vested in one supreme Court, and in such inferior Courts as the Congress may from time to time ordain and establish. The Judges, both of the supreme and inferior Courts, shall hold their Offices during good Behaviour, and shall, at stated Times, receive for their Services a Compensation, which shall not be diminished during their Continuance in Office.

Section 2. [1] The judicial Power shall extend to all Cases, in Law and Equity, arising under this Constitution, the Laws of the United States, and Treaties made, or which shall be made, under their Authority;—to all Cases affecting Ambassadors, other public Ministers and Consuls;—to all Cases of admiralty and maritime Jurisdiction;—to Controversies to which the United States shall be a Party;—to Controversies between two or more States;—between a State and Citizens of another State;—between Citizens of different States;—between Citizens of the same State claiming Lands under the Grants of different States, and between a State, or the Citizens thereof, and foreign States, Citizens or Subjects.

[2] In all Cases affecting Ambassadors, other public Ministers and Consuls, and those in which a State shall be a Party, the supreme Court shall have original Jurisdiction. In all the other Cases before mentioned, the supreme Court shall have appellate Jurisdiction, both as to Law and Fact, with such Exceptions, and under such Regulations as the Congress shall make.

[3] The trial of all Crimes, except in Cases of Impeachment, shall be by Jury; and such Trial shall be held in the State where the said Crimes shall have been committed; but when not committed within any State, the Trial shall be at such Place or Places as the Congress may by Law have directed.

Section 3. [1] Treason against the United States, shall consist only in levying War against them, or, in adhering to their Enemies, giving them Aid and Comfort. No Person shall be convicted of Treason unless on the Testimony of two Witnesses to the same overt Act, or on Confession in open Court.

[2] The Congress shall have Power to declare the Punishment of Treason, but no Attainder of Treason shall work Corruption of Blood, or Forfeiture except during the Life of the Person attainted.

ARTICLE IV

Section 1. Full Faith and Credit shall be given in each State to the public Acts, Records, and judicial Proceedings of every other State. And the Congress may by general Laws prescribe the Manner in which such Acts, Records and Proceedings shall be proved, and the Effect thereof.

Section 2. [1] The Citizens of each State shall be entitled to all Privileges and Immunities of Citizens in the several States.

[2]   A Person charged in any State with Treason, Felony, or other Crime, who shall flee from Justice, and be found in another State, shall on demand of the executive Authority of the State from which he fled, be delivered up, to be removed to the State having Jurisdiction of the Crime.

[3]   No Person held to Service or Labour in one State, under the Laws thereof, escaping into another, shall, in Consequence of any Law or Regulation therein, be discharged from such Service or Labour, but shall be delivered up on Claim of the Party to whom such Service or Labour may be due.

Section 3. [1] New States may be admitted by the Congress into this Union; but no new State shall be formed or erected within the Jurisdiction of any other State; nor any State be formed by the Junction of two or more States, or Parts of States, without the Consent of the Legislatures of the States concerned as well as of the Congress.

[2]   The Congress shall have Power to dispose of and make all needful Rules and Regulations respecting the Territory or other Property belonging to the United States; and nothing in this Constitution shall be so construed as to Prejudice any Claims of the United States, or of any particular State.

Section 4. The United States shall guarantee to every State in this Union a Republican Form of Government, and shall protect each of them against Invasion; and on Application of the Legislature, or of the Executive (when the Legislature cannot be convened) against domestic Violence.

ARTICLE V

The Congress, whenever two thirds of both Houses shall deem it necessary, shall propose Amendments to this Constitution, or, on the Application of the Legislatures of two thirds of the several States, shall call a Convention for proposing Amendments, which, in either Case, shall be valid to all Intents and Purposes, as part of this Constitution, when ratified by the Legislatures of three fourths of the several States, or by Conventions in three fourths thereof, as the one or the other Mode of Ratification may be proposed by the Congress; Provided that no Amendment which may be made prior to the Year One thousand eight hundred and eight shall in any Manner affect the first and fourth Clauses in the Ninth Section of the first Article; and that no State, without its Consent, shall be deprived of its equal Suffrage in the Senate.

ARTICLE VI

[1]   All Debts contracted and Engagements entered into, before the Adoption of this Constitution shall be as valid against the United States under this Constitution, as under the Confederation.

[2]   This Constitution, and the Laws of the United States which shall be made in Pursuance thereof; and all Treaties made, or which shall be made, under the Authority of the United States, shall be the supreme Law of the Land; and the Judges in every State shall be bound thereby, any Thing in the Constitution or Laws of any State to the Contrary notwithstanding.

[3]   The Senators and Representatives before mentioned, and the Members of the several State Legislatures, and all executive and judicial Officers, both of the United States and of the several States, shall be bound by Oath or Affirmation, to support this Constitution; but no religious Test shall ever be required as a Qualification to any Office or public Trust under the United States.

ARTICLE VII

The Ratification of the Conventions of nine States shall be sufficient for the Establishment of this Constitution between the States so ratifying the Same.

AMENDMENTS OF THE CONSTITUTION OF THE UNITED STATES OF AMERICA, PROPOSED BY CONGRESS AND RATIFIED BY THE LEGISLATURES OF THE SEVERAL STATES PURSUANT TO THE FIFTH ARTICLE OF THE ORIGINAL CONSTITUTION.

AMENDMENT I [1791]

Congress shall make no law respecting an establishment of religion, or prohibiting the free exercise thereof; or abridging the freedom of speech, or of the press; or the right of the people peaceably to assemble, and to petition the Government for a redress of grievances.

AMENDMENT II [1791]

A well regulated Militia, being necessary to the security of a free State, the right of the people to keep and bear Arms, shall not be infringed.

AMENDMENT III [1791]

No Soldier shall, in time of peace be quartered in any house, without the consent of the Owner, nor in time of war, but in a manner to be prescribed by law.

AMENDMENT IV [1791]

The right of the people to be secure in their persons, houses, papers, and effects, against unreasonable searches and seizures, shall not be violated, and no Warrants shall issue, but upon probable cause, supported by Oath or affirmation and particularly describing the place to be searched, and the persons or things to be seized.

AMENDMENT V [1791]

No person shall be held to answer for a capital, or otherwise infamous crime, unless on a presentment or indictment of a Grand Jury, except in cases arising in the land or naval forces, or in the Militia, when in actual service in time of War or public danger; nor shall any person be subject for the same offence to be twice put in jeopardy of life or limb; nor shall be compelled in any criminal case to be a witness against himself, nor be deprived of life, liberty, or property, without due process of law; nor shall private property be taken for public use, without just compensation.

AMENDMENT VI [1791]

In all criminal prosecutions, the accused shall enjoy the right to a speedy and public trial, by an impartial jury of the State and district wherein the crime shall have been committed, which district shall have been previously ascertained by law, and to be informed of the nature and cause of the accusation; to be confronted with the witnesses against him; to have compulsory process for obtaining witnesses in his favor, and to have the Assistance of Counsel for his defence.

AMENDMENT VII [1791]

In Suits at common law, where the value in controversy shall exceed twenty dollars, the right of trial by jury shall be preserved, and no fact tried by jury, shall be otherwise re-examined in any Court of the United States, than according to the rules of the common law.

AMENDMENT VIII [1791]

Excessive bail shall not be required, nor excessive fines imposed, nor cruel and unusual punishments inflicted.

AMENDMENT IX [1791]

The enumeration in the Constitution, of certain rights, shall not be construed to deny or disparage others retained by the people.

AMENDMENT X [1791]

The powers not delegated to the United States by the Constitution, nor prohibited by it to the States, are reserved to the States respectively, or to the people.

AMENDMENT XI [1798]

The Judicial power of the United States shall not be construed to extend to any suit in law or equity, commenced or prosecuted against one of the United States by Citizens of another State, or by Citizens or Subjects of any Foreign State.

AMENDMENT XII [1804]

The Electors shall meet in their respective states and vote by ballot for President and Vice-President, one of whom, at least, shall not be an inhabitant of the same state with themselves; they shall name in their ballots the person voted for as President, and in distinct ballots the person voted for as Vice-President, and they shall make distinct lists of all persons voted for as President, and of all persons voted for as Vice-President, and of the number of votes for each, which lists they shall sign and certify, and transmit sealed to the seat of the government of the United States, directed to the President of the Senate;—The President of the Senate shall, in the presence of the Senate and House of Representatives, open all the certificates and the votes shall then be counted;—The person having the greatest number of votes for President, shall be the President, if such number be a majority of the whole number of Electors appointed; and if no person have such majority, then from the persons having the highest numbers not exceeding three on the list of those voted for as President, the House of Representatives shall choose immediately, by ballot, the President. But in choosing the President, the votes shall be taken by states, the representation from each state having one vote; a quorum for this purpose shall consist of a member or members from two-thirds of the states, and a majority of all the states shall be necessary to a choice. And if the House of Representatives shall not choose a President whenever the right of choice shall devolve upon them before the fourth day of March next following, then the Vice-President shall act as President, as in the case of the death or other constitutional disability of the President.—The person having the greatest number of votes as Vice-President, shall be the Vice-President, if such number be a majority of the whole number of Electors appointed, and if no person have a majority, then from the two highest numbers on the list, the Senate shall choose the Vice-President; a quorum for the purpose shall consist of two-thirds of the whole number of Senators, and a majority of the whole number shall be necessary to a choice. But no person constitutionally ineligible to the office of President shall be eligible to that of Vice-President of the United States.

AMENDMENT XIII [1865]

Section 1. Neither slavery nor involuntary servitude, except as a punishment for crime whereof the party shall have been duly convicted, shall exist within the United States, or any place subject to their jurisdiction.

Section 2. Congress shall have power to enforce this article by appropriate legislation.

AMENDMENT XIV [1868]

Section 1. All persons born or naturalized in the United States, and subject to the jurisdiction thereof, are citizens of the United States and of the State wherein they reside. No State shall make or enforce any law which shall abridge the privileges or immunities of citizens of the United States; nor shall any State deprive any person of life, liberty, or property, without due process of law; nor deny to any person within its jurisdiction the equal protection of the laws.

Section 2. Representatives shall be apportioned among the several States according to their respective numbers, counting the whole number of persons in each State, excluding Indians not taxed. But when the right to vote at any election for the choice of electors for President and Vice President of the United States, Representatives in Congress, the Executive and Judicial officers of a State, or the members of the Legislature thereof, is denied to any of the male inhabitants of such State, being twenty-one years of age, and citizens of the

United States, or in any way abridged, except for participation in rebellion, or other crime, the basis of representation therein shall be reduced in the proportion which the number of such male citizens shall bear to the whole number of male citizens twenty-one years of age in such State.

Section 3. No person shall be a Senator or Representative in Congress, or elector of President and Vice President, or hold any office, civil or military, under the United States, or under any State, who having previously taken an oath, as a member of Congress, or as an officer of the United States, or as a member of any State legislature, or as an executive or judicial officer of any State, to support the Constitution of the United States, shall have engaged in insurrection or rebellion against the same, or given aid or comfort to the enemies thereof. But Congress may by a vote of two-thirds of each House, remove such disability.

Section 4. The validity of the public debt of the United States, authorized by law, including debts incurred for payment of pensions and bounties for services in suppressing insurrection or rebellion, shall not be questioned. But neither the United States nor any State shall assume or pay any debt or obligation incurred in aid of insurrection or rebellion against the United States, or any claim for the loss or emancipation of any slave; but all such debts, obligations and claims shall be held illegal and void.

Section 5. The Congress shall have power to enforce, by appropriate legislation, the provisions of this article.

AMENDMENT XV [1870]

Section 1. The right of citizens of the United States to vote shall not be denied or abridged by the United States or by any State on account of race, color, or previous condition of servitude.

Section 2. The Congress shall have power to enforce this article by appropriate legislation.

AMENDMENT XVI [1913]

The Congress shall have power to lay and collect taxes on incomes, from whatever source derived, without apportionment among the several States, and without regard to any census or enumeration.

AMENDMENT XVII [1913]

[1] The Senate of the United States shall be composed of two Senators from each State, elected by the people thereof, for six years; and each Senator shall have one vote. The electors in each State shall have the qualifications requisite for electors of the most numerous branch of the State legislatures.

[2] When vacancies happen in the representation of any State in the Senate, the executive authority of such State shall issue writs of election to fill such vacancies: *Provided,* That the legislature of any State may empower the executive thereof to make temporary appointments until the people fill the vacancies by election as the legislature may direct.

[3]   This amendment shall not be so construed as to affect the election or term of any Senator chosen before it becomes valid as part of the Constitution.

AMENDMENT XVIII [1919]

Section 1. After one year from the ratification of this article the manufacture, sale, or transportation of intoxicating liquors within, the importation thereof into, or the exportation thereof from the United States and all territory subject to the jurisdiction thereof for beverage purposes is hereby prohibited.

Section 2. The Congress and the several States shall have concurrent power to enforce this article by appropriate legislation.

Section 3. This article shall be inoperative unless it shall have been ratified as an amendment to the Constitution by the legislatures of the several States, as provided in the Constitution, within seven years from the date of the submission hereof to the States by the Congress.

AMENDMENT XIX [1920]

[1]   The right of citizens of the United States to vote shall not be denied or abridged by the United States or by any State on account of sex.

[2]   Congress shall have power to enforce this article by appropriate legislation.

AMENDMENT XX [1933]

Section 1. The terms of the President and Vice President shall end at noon on the 20th day of January, and the terms of Senators and Representatives at noon on the 3d day of January, of the years in which such terms would have ended if this article had not been ratified; and the terms of their successors shall then begin.

Section 2. The Congress shall assemble at least once in every year, and such meeting shall begin at noon on the 3d day of January, unless they shall by law appoint a different day.

Section 3. If, at the time fixed for the beginning of the term of the President, the President elect shall have died, the Vice President elect shall become President. If the President shall not have been chosen before the time fixed for the beginning of his term, or if the President elect shall have failed to qualify, then the Vice President elect shall act as President until a President shall have qualified; and the Congress may by law provide for the case wherein neither a President elect nor a Vice President elect shall have qualified, declaring who shall then act as President, or the manner in which one who is to act shall be selected, and such person shall act accordingly until a President or Vice President shall have qualified.

Section 4. The Congress may by law provide for the case of the death of any of the persons from whom the House of Representatives may choose a President whenever the right of choice shall have devolved upon them, and for the case of the death of any of the persons from whom the Senate may choose a Vice President whenever the right of choice shall have devolved upon them.

Section 5. Sections 1 and 2 shall take effect on the 15th day of October following the ratification of this article.

Section 6. This article shall be inoperative unless it shall have been ratified as an amendment to the Constitution by the legislatures of three-fourths of the several States within seven years from the date of its submission.

AMENDMENT XXI [1933]

Section 1. The eighteenth article of amendment to the Constitution of the United States is hereby repealed.

Section 2. The transportation or importation into any State, Territory, or possession of the United States for delivery or use therein of intoxicating liquors, in violation of the laws thereof, is hereby prohibited.

Section 3. This article shall be inoperative unless it shall have been ratified as an amendment to the Constitution by conventions in the several States, as provided in the Constitution, within seven years from the date of the submission hereof to the States by the Congress.

AMENDMENT XXII [1951]

Section 1. No person shall be elected to the office of the President more than twice, and no person who has held the office of President, or acted as President, for more than two years of a term to which some other person was elected President shall be elected to the office of President more than once. But this Article shall not apply to any person holding the office of President when this Article was proposed by the Congress, and shall not prevent any person who may be holding the office of President, or acting as President, during the term within which this Article becomes operative from holding the office of President or acting as President during the remainder of such term.

Section 2. This article shall be inoperative unless it shall have been ratified as an amendment to the Constitution by the legislatures of three-fourths of the several States within seven years from the date of its submission to the States by the Congress.

AMENDMENT XXIII [1961]

Section 1. The District constituting the seat of Government of the United States shall appoint in such manner as the Congress may direct:

A number of electors of President and Vice President equal to the whole number of Senators and Representatives in Congress to which the District would be entitled if it were a State, but in no event more than the least populous state; they shall be in addition to those appointed by the states, but they shall be considered, for the purposes of the election of President and Vice President, to be electors appointed by a state; and they shall meet in the District and perform such duties as provided by the twelfth article of amendment.

Section 2. The Congress shall have power to enforce this article by appropriate legislation.

AMENDMENT XXIV [1964]

Section 1. The right of citizens of the United States to vote in any primary or other election for President or Vice President, for electors for President or Vice President, or for Senator or Representative in Congress, shall not be denied or abridged by the United States or any State by reason of failure to pay any poll tax or other tax.

Section 2. The Congress shall have power to enforce this article by appropriate legislation.

AMENDMENT XXV [1967]

Section 1. In case of the removal of the President from office or of his death or resignation, the Vice President shall become President.

Section 2. Whenever there is a vacancy in the office of the Vice President, the President shall nominate a Vice President who shall take office upon confirmation by a majority vote of both Houses of Congress.

Section 3. Whenever the President transmits to the President pro tempore of the Senate and the Speaker of the House of Representatives his written declaration that he is unable to discharge the powers and duties of his office, and until he transmits to them a written declaration to the contrary, such powers and duties shall be discharged by the Vice President as Acting President.

Section 4. Whenever the Vice President and a majority of either the principal officers of the executive departments or of such other body as Congress may by law provide, transmit to the President pro tempore of the Senate and the Speaker of the House of Representatives their written declaration that the President is unable to discharge the powers and duties of his office, the Vice President shall immediately assume the powers and duties of the office as Acting President.

Thereafter, when the President transmits to the President pro tempore of the Senate and the Speaker of the House of Representatives his written declaration that no inability exists, he shall resume the powers and duties of his office unless the Vice President and a majority of either the principal officers of the executive department or of such other body as Congress may by law provide, transmit within four days to the President pro tempore of the Senate and the Speaker of the House of Representatives their written declaration that the President is unable to discharge the powers and duties of his office. Thereupon Congress shall decide the issue, assembling within forty-eight hours for that purpose if not in session. If the Congress, within twenty-one days after receipt of the latter written declaration, or, if Congress is not in session, within twenty-one days after Congress is required to assemble, determines by two-thirds vote of both Houses that the President is unable to discharge the powers and duties of his office, the Vice President shall continue to discharge the same as Acting President; otherwise, the President shall resume the powers and duties of his office.

AMENDMENT XXVI [1971]

Section 1. The right of citizens of the United States, who are eighteen years of age or older, to vote shall not be denied or abridged by the United States or by any State on account of age.

Section 2. The Congress shall have power to enforce this article by appropriate legislation.

AMENDMENT XXVII [1992]*

No law, varying compensation for the services of Senators and Representatives, shall take effect, until an election of Representatives shall have intervened.

---

*   On May 7, 1992, more than 200 years after it was first proposed by James Madison, the Twenty-Seventh Amendment was ratified by a 38th State (Michigan). Although Congress set no time limit for ratification of this amendment, ten of the *other* amendments proposed at the same time (1789)—now known as the Bill of Rights—were ratified in a little more than two years. After all this time, is the ratification of the Twenty-Seventh Amendment valid? Does it matter that many of the states that ratified the amendment did not exist at the time it was first proposed?

INDEX

References are to Pages